D0852153

Canadian
Medical
Association

CANADIAN MEDICAL ASSOCIATION

COMPLETE HOME MEDICAL GUIDE

CANADIAN
MEDICAL
ASSOCIATION

CANADIAN MEDICAL ASSOCIATION

COMPLETE HOME MEDICAL GUIDE

Editor-in-Chief
CATHERINE YOUNGER-LEWIS MD MJ

SECOND EDITION

DK

CANADIAN
MEDICAL
ASSOCIATION

Second Canadian Edition 2005

Dorling Kindersley is represented in Canada by
Tourmaline Editions Inc.
662 King Street West, Suite 304
Toronto, Ontario M5V 1M7

The Canadian Medical Association Complete Home Medical Guide provides general information on a wide range of health and medical topics. The book is not a substitute for medical diagnosis, and you are advised always to consult your doctor for specific information on personal health matters. The naming of any organization, product, or alternative therapy in this book does not imply endorsement by the CMA, CMA Media Inc., or the publisher. The omission of any such name does not imply disapproval by the CMA, CMA Media Inc., or the publisher. The CMA, CMA Media Inc., and the publisher do not assume any responsibility for liability arising from any error in or omission from the book, or from the use of any information contained in it.

Library and Archives Canada Cataloguing in Publication

Canadian Medical Association complete home medical guide / Catherine Younger-Lewis, editor-in-chief, 2nd. ed.

Includes index.
ISBN 1-55363-054-8

1. Medicine, Popular. I. Younger-Lewis, Catherine
II. Canadian Medical Association. III Title: Complete home medical guide
RC81.C36 2005 616.02'4 C2005-900710-9

Color reproduction by GRB Editrice, Verona, Italy
Printed and bound in China by SNP Leefung

05 06 07 08 09 9 8 7 6 5 4 3 2 1

Discover more at
www.dk.com

FOREWORD

THE CANADIAN MEDICAL ASSOCIATION *Complete Home Medical Guide* is dedicated to the idea that accurate knowledge is essential to maintaining good health. First published in Canada in 2001, this guide has been completely revised and updated to reflect the medical advances of the past four years. As well, new diseases such as SARS and West Nile virus are included. Using clearly written text and abundant illustrations, the guide explains how the body works, provides tools for interpreting symptoms, describes how and why diseases occur, and outlines the details of modern diagnostic tests and treatments. These features allow Canadians to know what to expect if disease develops, to ask the right questions, and to actively take part in managing their health. Additional, up-to-the-minute information is available through a comprehensive selection of authoritative, reliable online medical sites.

A major theme of the *Complete Home Medical Guide* is the effect of genetic makeup and lifestyle on health throughout life. With the publication of the human genome in 2001, there has been a great advance in genetic-based treatments. The book explains how appropriate screening for disease and informed choices about aspects of lifestyle, such as diet and exercise, can modify the effects of genetic factors to optimize good health.

The *Complete Home Medical Guide* is the most extensively physician-reviewed Canadian home reference available. It is a vital and complementary component of the Canadian Medical Association's series of health books for Canadians.

We hope that the guide will serve not only as a reference during times of illness but also as a source of ongoing advice for all family members in maintaining the best of health throughout their lives.

RLCollins-Nakai

RUTH L. COLLINS-NAKAI MD
MBA FRCPC FACC
PRESIDENT
CANADIAN MEDICAL ASSOCIATION

Canadian Medical Association

President Ruth L. Collins-Nakai MD MBA FRCPC FACC

Secretary General and CEO William G. Tholl

Acting Director, Publications Lorne Ross

Editor-in-Chief, Publications John Hoey MD

Medical Editor Catherine Younger-Lewis MD MJ

Program Manager, Book Publishing Christine A. Pollock

Assistant Nunzia Parent

Information Services Elizabeth Czanyo

Dorling Kindersley

Editor, Canada Julia Roles

Project Editor, Canada Carolyn Jackson

Senior Editor (US) Jill Hamilton

Senior Art Editor Ian Spick

DTP Design Julian Dams

Picture Researcher Anna Bedewell

Production Joanna Bull

Senior Managing Editor Martyn Page

Managing Art Editor Marianne Markham

Art Director Bryn Walls

Project Director Sharon Lucas

Creative Director Tina Vaughan

First Edition

Project Managing Editor Andrea Bagg

Deputy Managing Editor Maxine Lewis

Senior Editors Paul Docherty, Nicki Lampon, Mary Lindsay, Andrew Macintyre, Janet Mohun

Deputy Senior Editor Jolyon Goddard

Senior Editor (US) Jill Hamilton

Editors Ann Baggaley, Judith Bettesworth, Edda Bohnsack, Martin Bryant, Jane de Burgh, Alan Byrne, Louise Clairmonte, Sue Cooper, Patricia Davis, Kim Dennis-Bryan, Patricia Dent, Kathy Fahey, Francesca George, Peter Harrison, Fiona Hunter, Katie John, Sarah Keer-Keer, Jo Lankester, Alyson McGaw, Ben Morgan, Sean O'Connor, Mukul Patel, Hazel Richardson, Esther Ripley, Nikki Taylor, Stephen Taylor, Gaia Vince, John Watson

Editorial Assistance Peter Frances, Angeles Gavira, Rachel Hutchinson, Robert Johnston, Heather Jones, Donna Loh, Rebecca Marsland, Ann Mummery, Andrew Pine, Teresa Pritlove, Juliet Roberts

Editorial Assistance (US) Judit Z. Bodnar, Nancy Lieberman, Irene Pavitt, Jennifer Quasha

Medical Editor-in-Chief Tony Smith MA BM BCh

Senior Medical Editor Sue Davidson MB BS MRCP MRCGP DRCOG

Medical Editors Naomi Craft BSc MB BS MRCGP, Gabrielle Murphy BA BSc MB ChB, Fiona Payne MB BS, Penny Preston MB ChB MRCGP, Amanda Rouse BSc MB BS MRCP MRCGP, Frances Williams MA MB BChir MRCP DTM&H MRCPCH

Project Managing Art Editor Louise Dick

Project Deputy Managing Art Editor Marianne Markham

Senior Designer Mark Batley

Designers Amanda Carroll, Janice English, Sara Freeman, Spencer Holbrook, Johnny Pau, Chris Walker

Design Assistance Kirsten Cashman, Nicola Hampel, Elaine Hewson, Richard Horsford, Sasha Howard, Anne Renel, Mark Wilde

DTP Design Jason Little

DTP Assistance Zirrinia Austin, Louise Waller

Anatomy Visualizer Richard Tibbitts

Illustrators Debbie Maizels, Patrick Mulrey, Richard Tibbitts, Halli Verrinder

Picture Researcher Suzanne Williams

Production Michelle Thomas

Project Researcher Claire Isaac BSc MB ChB

Senior Managing Editor Martyn Page

Senior Managing Art Editor Bryn Walls

Editorial Director Jackie Douglas

Art Director Peter Luff

Dorling Kindersley India

Manager Aparna Sharma

Editors Dipali Singh, Rohan Sinha, Aekta Jerath

DTP Designer Pankaj Sharma

Medical Editors and Contributors

Canadian Editor-in-Chief
Catherine Younger-Lewis MD MJ

US Editor-in-Chief David R. Goldmann MD FACP
US Associate Editor David A. Horowitz MD

Canada

David Atack MD FRCPC
Gail Beck MD CM FRCPC
Denise Beatty RD
Sharon C. Caughey MD FRCSC
John P. Collins MD FRCSC
Kathleen Davis MD FRCPC
Harsha V. Dehejia MD FRCPC
Susan F. Dent MD FRCPC
Catherine Dubé MD FRCPC
Melissa Forgie MD FRCPC
Dale Fyman DMD
Sargon B. Gandilo MD FRCPC
John A. Gordon MD FRCSC
Gail E. Graham MD FRCPC
M. Shirley Gross MD CM CCFP
Shirley A. Hovan MD
William James MD FRCPC
Arthur Leader MD FRCSC
Michel Le May MD FRCPC
Diane Logan MD FRCPC
Charmaine E. Lok MD FRCPC
Anne E. McCarthy MD FRCPC
Dennis Pitt MD FRCSC
Linda M. Rapson MD CAFCI
Catherine M. Ruddy MD FRCPC
Brian L. Sheridan MB BS FRCPC FRCPath
Robert W. Slinger MD FRCPC
Adam Telner MD FRCPC
M. Louise Walker MD CCFP FCFP Dip (Sport Med)
C. Peter W. Warren MB FRCPC
Brian Weitzman MD CM CCFP (EM) FRCPC
Allan Wilson MD PhD
John G. Young MD FRCSC
Canadian Red Cross
Health Canada, Minister of Public Works and Government Services, Canada
Transport Canada

Drug Glossary
Tina Papastavros BSc Phm PharmD
Health Solutions Initiatives

United States and United Kingdom

Michael Adler MD FRCP FFPHM
Robert N. Allan MD FRCP
Samir Alvi BSc MB BS PhD
Ursula Arens
Victor Aviles MD
Helen Barnett BPharm
Jeffrey L. Barron MB ChB MSc MMed FRCPath
Jack M. Becker MD
A. Graham Bird FRCP FRCPath
Robin L. Blair MB FRCS(C) FRCS(Ed.) FACS
Sue Bosanko
Patrick J. Brennan MD
C. G. D. Brook MA MD FRCP FRCPCH
Jane de Burgh RGN
Helen Byrt PhD
Peter E. Callegari MD
Pamela G. Cobb MD
Catherine J. Datto MD
Gary Diamond MD
J. Michael Dixon MD FRCS
Andrew Doble MS FRCS(Urol.)
Nancy Duin
Jemima Dunne
Martin Edwards BDS SDSRCS PhD
Mark I. Ellen MD
Stephanie Ennis BS RPH
Helen Epstein PhD
Sarah Erush PharmD BCPS
Marie Fallon MB ChB DRCOG
Mary Fogarty MSc MB BCh BAO NUI
Philip Gaut PhD
Bruce George MS FRCS
Jennifer Glasspool PhD
Stephen J. Gluckman MD
Sandra Goldbeck-Wood MB ChB
Lee R. Goldberg MD MPH
Terry Hamblin DM FRCP FRCPath
Philip M. Hanno MD
Katherine Heimann
Bruce Hendry MD PhD
Chris Higgins
Ann Honebrink MD FACOG
Kate Hope MB BS MRCS LRCP
B. David Horn MD
Abby Horowitz LPT
S. R. Iliffe MRCGP
Amanda Jackson-Russell PhD
Dina Jacobs MD
Anthony S. Jennings MD
Paresh Jobanputra DM MRCP MRCGP
Mark D. Joffe MD FAAP
Frederick L. Jones III MD
Marion Jowett
Jacqueline M. Junkins-Hopkins MD
Scott E. Kasner MD
Kevin J. Kelly MD
W. F. Kelly MD FRCP
P. Kendall-Taylor MD FRCP
Peng T. Khaw PhD MRCP FRCS FRCOphth
Helen Kingston MD FRCP DCH
Leslie Klenerman ChM FRCS
Sharon Kolasinsky MD
Ann Kramer
David A. Lenrow MD
Lawrence M. Levin DMD MD
G.T. Lewith MA DM MRCP MRCGP
Gary R. Lichtenstein MD
Lynne Low MB ChB
Alice D. Ma MD
David Mabey BM BCH DM FRCP
Theresa McCrone RGN
Ian McKee MB ChB DRCOG DFFP
Chris McLaughlin
J. Jeffrey Malatack MD
H. Manji MA MD MRCP
Joseph Melvin DO
Sheena Meredith MB BS LRCP MRCS
David Miller MD
G. Keith Morris MD FRCP
Christen Mowad MD
Katherine L. Nathanson MD
Charles W. Nichols MD
Enyi Okereke PharmD MD
Sanjida O'Connell
Noel D. L. Olsen MsC FRCP FFPHM
Beth Parish MD
A. Parshall BSc MB BS PhD MRCPsych
M. R. Partridge MD FRCP
D. A. Pearson MA MRCGP
R. C. Peveler DPhil MRCPsych
Elliot Philipp MMA FRCS FRCOG
Paulette Pratt
Punit S. Ramrakha MA BM BCh MRCP PhD
Rosalind Ramsay
Michael J. Rennie PhD FRSE
Iris M. Reyes MD
T. M. Reynolds MB ChB BSc MD
Mike Rogers BPharm MRPharmS
Eric S. Rovner MD
Michael J. Ruckenstein MD
P. J. Sanderson MB PhD FRCPath
Omar Sattaur
J. A. Savin MA MD FRCP DIH
Helena Schotland MD
Ira Schwartz MD PhD
Christine Scott-Moncrieff MB ChB MFHom
Frank E. Silvestry MD
David V. Skinner FRCS FFAEM
Anne Slavotinek MB BS FRCP PhD
Mary C. Sokoloski MD
Patricia Spallone PhD
Steven Stein MD
Jane Stirling PhD
David Sutton MD FRCP FRCR DMRD MCAR
Roy Taylor BSc MB ChB MD FRCP FRCPE
Erica R. Thaler MD
Joanna Thomas
Martin Thornhill MB BS BDS MSc PhD FDSRCS(Ed.) FFDRCSI
Gregory Tino MD
Raymond R. Townsend MD
Eileen E. Tyrala MD
Elena Umland PharmD
Lindy Van den Berghe BMedSci BM BS
James Walker MD FRCP(Glas.) FRCP(Edin.) FRCOG FRSM
Richard Walker PhD
Robert Whittle MB BS
Sam Wilde
Chris Williams DM FRCP
Jennifer A. Young MA MD FRCPath RCPI
Robert Youngson MB ChB DTM&H DO FRCOpht

CONTENTS

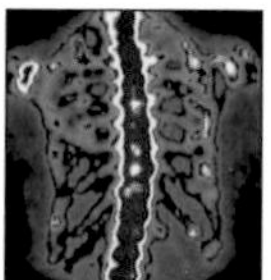

LOOKING FOR DISEASE

211–256

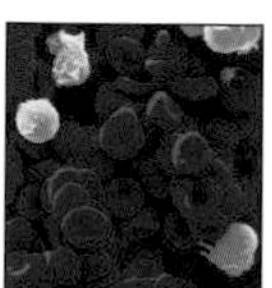

YOUR BODY AND DISEASE

257–872

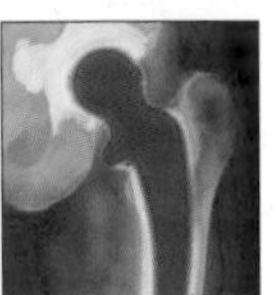

TREATING DISEASE 873–998

DRUG GLOSSARY, USEFUL ONLINE SITES AND ADDRESSES, AND INDEX 999–1104

HOW TO USE THIS BOOK

This book is arranged into thematic sections that deal with all aspects of health, disease, and medicine. The following pages explain this structure and supply detail on special features in each section. If you want to locate a specific topic, use the contents list at the beginning of the book or the comprehensive index at the end, which direct you to articles, boxes, and charts. Extensive cross-references in the text direct you to further information on related topics and to carefully selected online sites that provide further information to help you manage your health.

STRUCTURE OF THE BOOK

HOW THE BOOK IS ORGANIZED

This book contains six sections. The first five are arranged around themes of health and disease and deal with a healthy lifestyle, symptoms, diagnosis, diseases, and treatments. The sixth section contains additional information and an index.

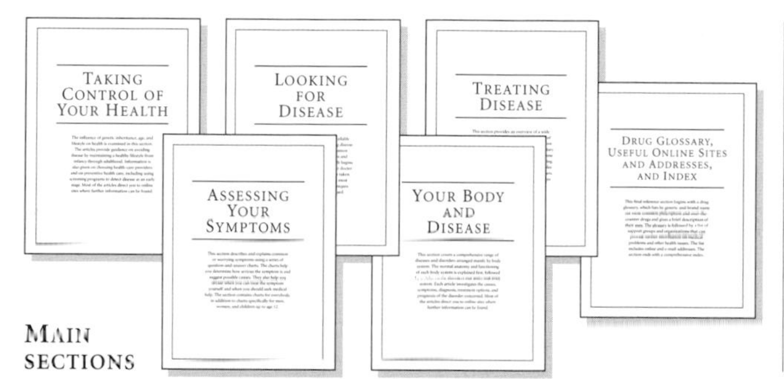

TAKING CONTROL OF YOUR HEALTH
LOOKING FOR DISEASE
TREATING DISEASE
ASSESSING YOUR SYMPTOMS
YOUR BODY AND DISEASE
DRUG GLOSSARY, USEFUL ONLINE SITES AND ADDRESSES, AND INDEX

MAIN SECTIONS

Heart and Stroke Foundation of Canada
Online:
www.heartandstroke.ca
222 Queen Street, Suite 1402
Ottawa, ON K1P 5V9
Tel: (613) 569-4361

Further information
The final section has a drug glossary, a list of useful online sites and addresses, and an index.

HOW EACH SECTION IS ORGANIZED

Each section has an introduction and contains two or more subsections with their own introductions. The subsections cover their subjects in a series of articles, which are accompanied by feature boxes that highlight and illustrate key information.

Section opener
A single page at the beginning of each section displays the section title

Section introduction
These pages provide an overview of the entire contents of the section

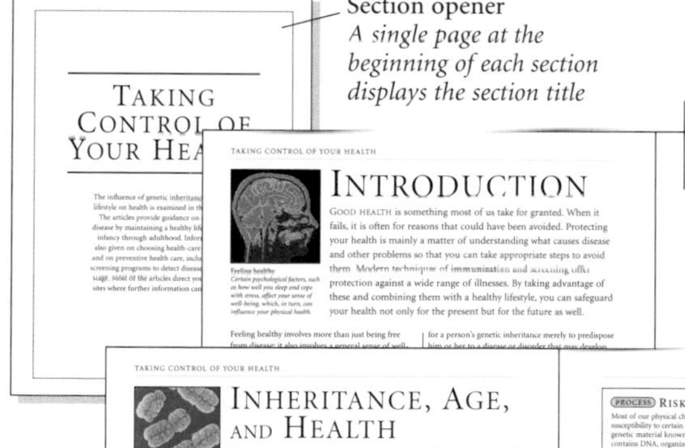

TAKING CONTROL OF YOUR HEALTH
INTRODUCTION
HEALTH ACTION LIFESTYLE CHOICES FOR HEALTH
INHERITANCE, AGE, AND HEALTH

Subsection introduction
Each subsection has its own introduction, which explains the basic principles underlying the articles that follow

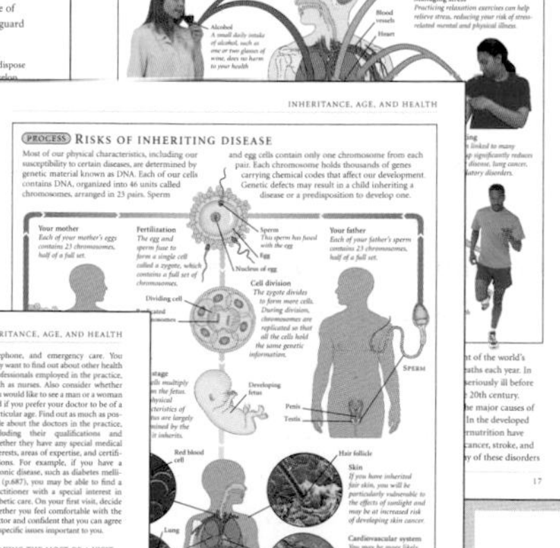

PROCESS RISKS OF INHERITING DISEASE

Articles introduction
The articles in each subsection are outlined in a brief introduction, which may provide cross-references to related subsections

Article
Each article deals with a specific subject, such as a disease, a type of drug, or another aspect of health care

Online symbol
Articles that end with this symbol direct you to useful online sites and addresses listed at the back of the book

HEALTH CARE THROUGHOUT LIFE
Universal health care
You and your doctor

Illustration box
Highly illustrated boxes throughout the book explain specific medical information clearly. The type of information in each box is indicated by a label in the top left corner

WHAT EACH SECTION CONTAINS

TAKING CONTROL OF YOUR HEALTH

Articles in this section help you assess your current and potential health status by looking at aspects of your genetic inheritance and lifestyle. The articles also examine the influence of aging and environment on health. In addition, this section provides guidance on following a healthy lifestyle and on other preventive health-care measures, such as lifelong screening programs to give early warning of disease.

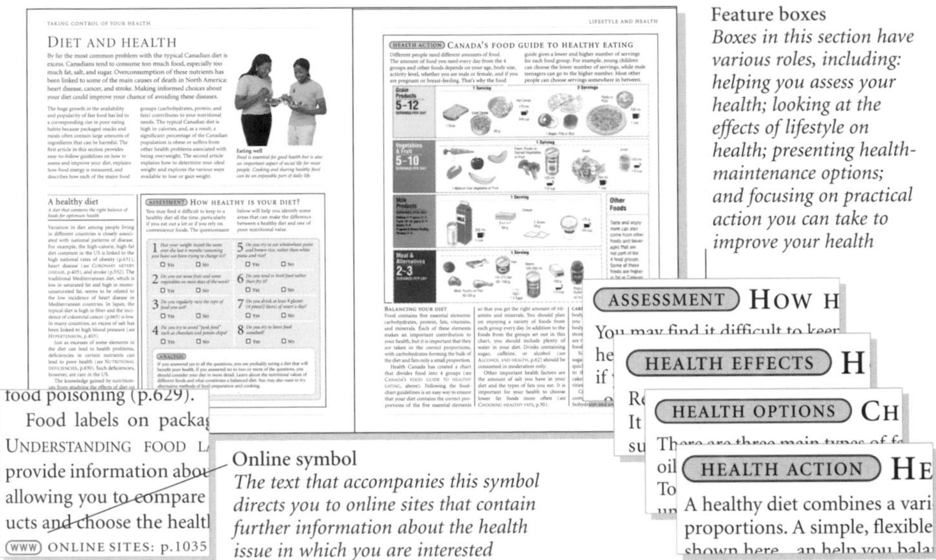

Feature boxes
Boxes in this section have various roles, including: helping you assess your health; looking at the effects of lifestyle on health; presenting health-maintenance options; and focusing on practical action you can take to improve your health

Online symbol
The text that accompanies this symbol directs you to online sites that contain further information about the health issue in which you are interested

ASSESSING YOUR SYMPTOMS

In this section, 70 charts cover the most common symptoms experienced by men, women, and children. Each chart focuses on one main symptom, explores possible causes, and advises on whether you should use self-help measures or seek medical help. For detailed instructions on how to use the charts, *see* p.90.

Color-coding
The charts are grouped in four color-coded sections, which respectively contain charts that apply to everyone, to men, to women, and to children

Questions and answers
Each chart contains a series of questions. Your answers to these lead you from a starting point to a finishing point, where you will be advised on what action to take

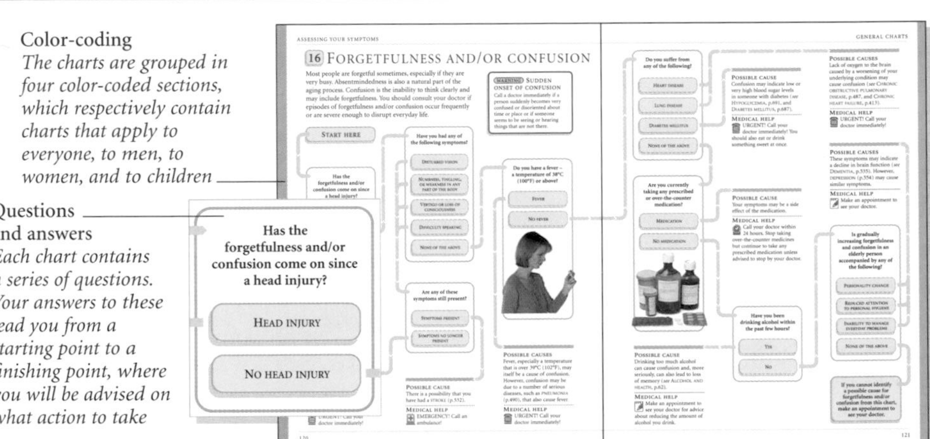
16 FORGETFULNESS AND/OR CONFUSION
Has the forgetfulness and/or confusion come on since a head injury?
HEAD INJURY
NO HEAD INJURY

LOOKING FOR DISEASE

This section explains the principles of commonly used screening and diagnostic tests and investigations, including laboratory tests and techniques for looking inside the human body, such as endoscopy and scanning. The method used in each test or investigation is explained and illustrated.

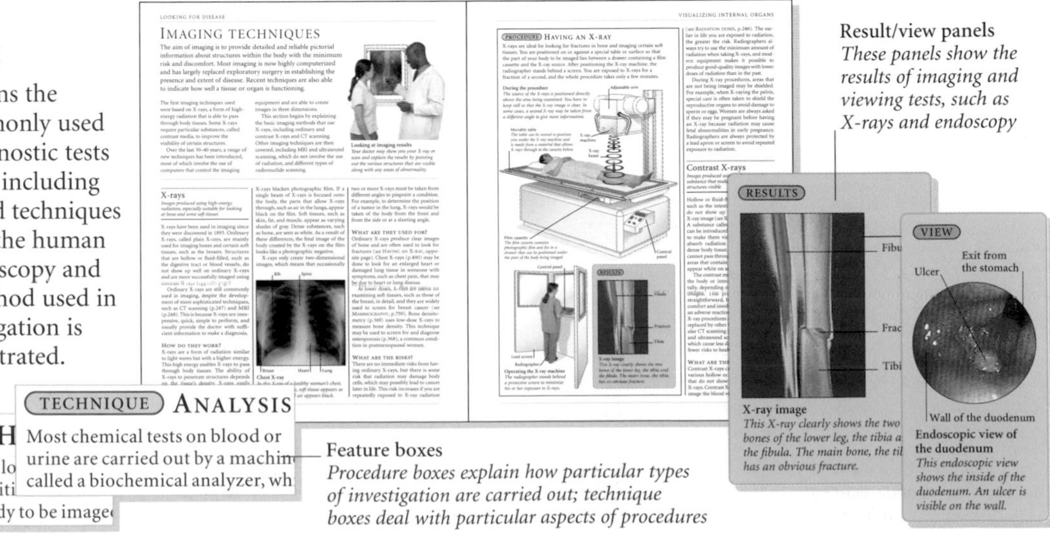

Result/view panels
These panels show the results of imaging and viewing tests, such as X-rays and endoscopy

Feature boxes
Procedure boxes explain how particular types of investigation are carried out; technique boxes deal with particular aspects of procedures

YOUR BODY AND DISEASE

This section examines more than 750 disorders, ranging from minor conditions, such as warts, to more serious diseases, such as lung cancer. The section contains 21 subsections, generally arranged by body system. There are special subsections on genetic disorders, cancer, infections and infestations, serious injuries, disorders during pregnancy and childbirth, and disorders in infants and children.

ANATOMY AND PHYSIOLOGY INTRODUCTIONS

These highly illustrated subsection introductions explain the normal anatomy (structure) and physiology (function) of a particular body system. They both stand on their own as detailed guides to the body and provide background information to the disorders considered in the articles that follow them.

Photographic detail
Magnified photographs show the detailed structure of crucial parts of the anatomy

Overview illustration
Large illustrations identify the main anatomical components of each body system

Location
Where useful, the location in the body of various parts of the anatomy is illustrated

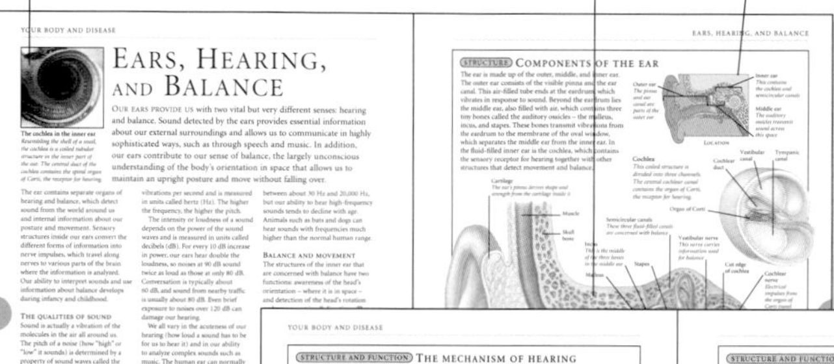

Detail illustration
The structure and function of each main anatomical component of the body system is illustrated and explained

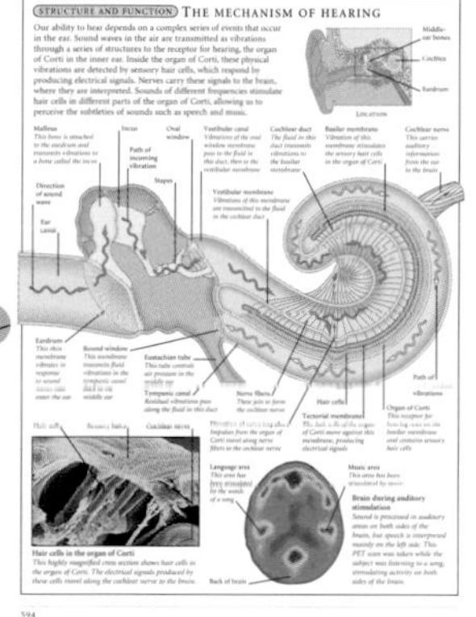

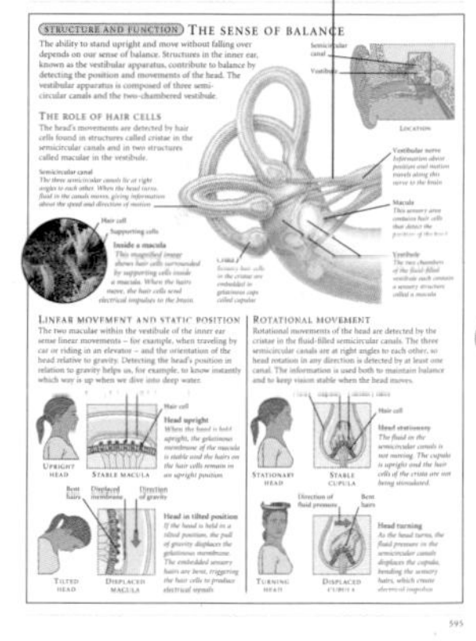

Color-coding
Throughout this section of the book, pages are color-coded according to the subsection to which they belong to help you locate subjects quickly for easy reference

DISORDER ARTICLES

Each article covers the causes and symptoms of a disorder, the methods used to diagnose it, treatment choices, and the likely prognosis. Particular factors that either increase the risk of developing the disorder or are not significant are listed for each article.

Key anatomy
The key parts of the anatomy affected by the disorders covered in each group of articles are clearly illustrated

Online symbol
Text accompanying this symbol cross-refers you to online sites that give you information and advice on the disorder you are concerned about

Risk factor information
Factors that increase the risk of developing a particular disorder are highlighted at the beginning of each article. When factors are variable or not significant, this is also indicated

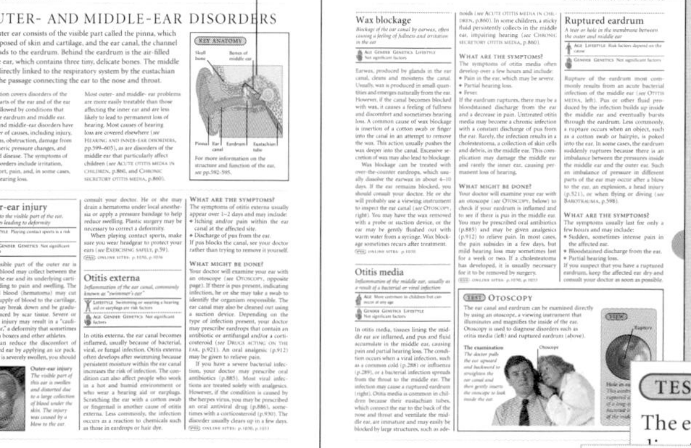

Age symbol
Any ages at which a disease or disorder is more likely to develop are listed here

Gender symbol
Text accompanying this symbol tells you if a disorder affects only or mostly males or females

Genetics symbol
Text accompanying this symbol indicates if a disease or disorder has an inherited component

Lifestyle symbol
Lifestyle factors that may increase the risk of developing a condition are listed here

Variable risk factors symbol
When a condition has various forms or causes, this symbol indicates that risk factors depend on the cause or type of disorder

Not significant symbol
If age, gender, genetics, or lifestyle are not risk factors for a condition, they are listed here

Feature boxes
Test boxes explain and illustrate particular test procedures; self-help boxes detail measures you can carry out at home; treatment boxes describe and illustrate how a treatment for a particular disorder is carried out

Treating disease

This section gives an overview of patient care and the wide range of medical treatments in current use, including drugs, surgery, and various therapies. The final part of the section covers the main first aid techniques.

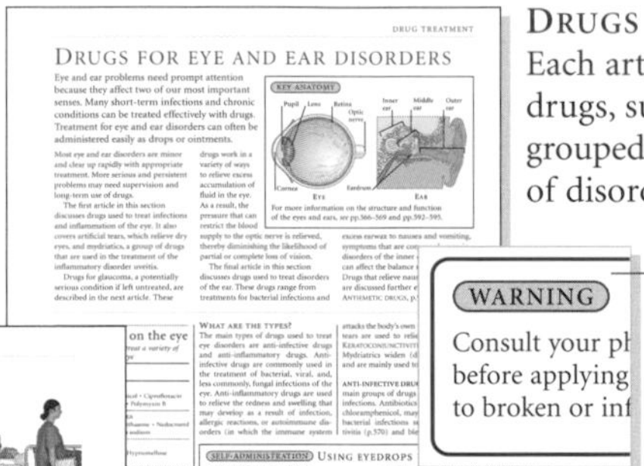

Surgery

These articles describe the experience of having an operation, including preparations for surgery and postoperative care. They also explain how types of surgery work.

Feature boxes
Procedure boxes deal with different types of operations; technique boxes focus on particular surgical techniques

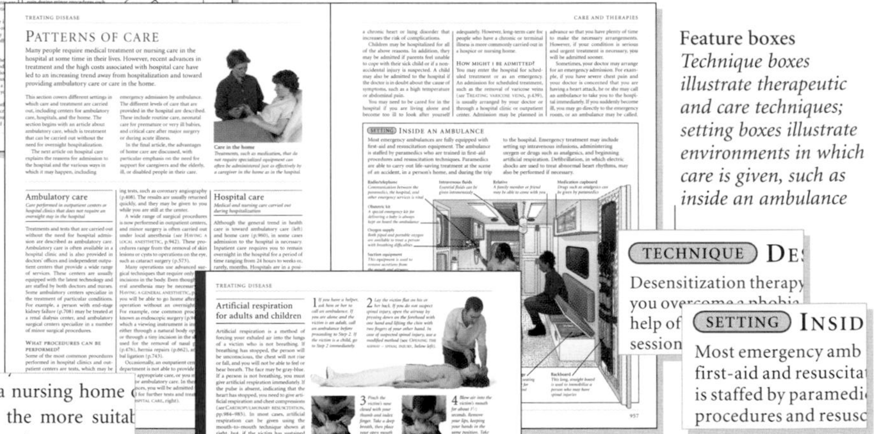

Care and therapies

This part of the treatments section covers different types of care, from critical care to home nursing. It also looks at rehabilitation, psychological, and complementary therapies.

Online symbol
Articles in the surgery and care and therapies sections that finish with this symbol direct you to online sites

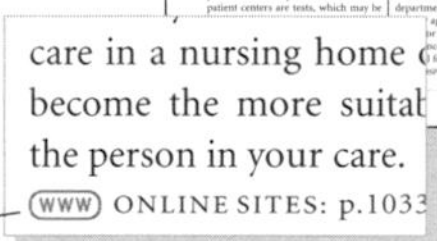

First aid

These articles tell you what to do in an emergency. They illustrate the general principles of first aid for a range of injuries and disorders and list the essential components of a first aid kit for the home.

Warning box
These boxes detail key information that should be read before using particular first aid techniques

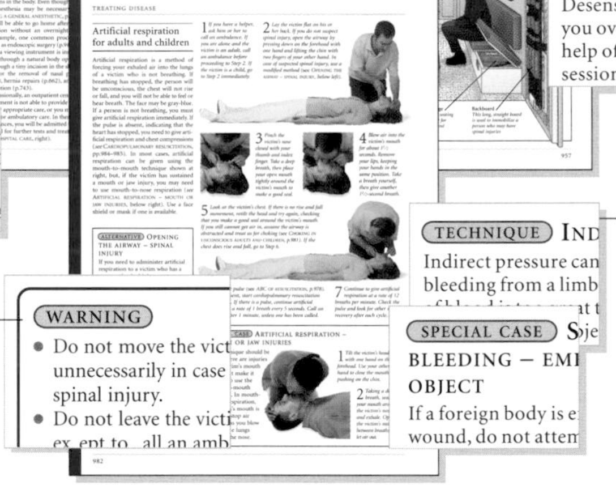

Drugs

Each article deals with a group of drugs, such as antibiotics. Articles are grouped by the body system or the type of disorder the drugs are used to treat.

Warning boxes
Precautions that apply when using certain drugs and situations in which certain drugs should not be used are detailed here

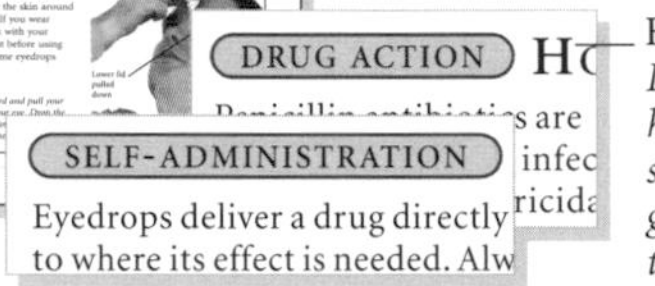

Feature boxes
Drug action boxes illustrate how particular drugs work; self-administration boxes give instructions on how to take certain drugs

Feature boxes
Technique boxes illustrate therapeutic and care techniques; setting boxes illustrate environments in which care is given, such as inside an ambulance

Feature boxes
Technique boxes look at techniques that are needed in many first aid situations; special case boxes outline variations on certain techniques that may be used when treating particular injuries

Drug glossary, online sites, and index

This final section of the book provides additional information, including a drug glossary and a list of organizations that provide information related to medical conditions. The section ends with a comprehensive index.

Drug glossary

This glossary provides a guide to many common prescription and over-the-counter drugs.

Canadian Association of Optometrists
Online: www.opto.ca
234 Argyle Avenue
Ottawa, ON K2P 1B9
Tel: (888) 263-4676
Fax: (613) 235-2025
E-mail: info@opto.ca

Online address
Mailing address
E-mail address

Index

This detailed 65-page index contains 13,000 entries and lists all the book's articles, feature boxes, and illustrations.

Useful online sites and addresses

These pages list the contact addresses of organizations that provide further information about specific medical conditions and other health issues.

Taking Control of Your Health

The influence of genetic inheritance, age, and lifestyle on health is examined in this section. The articles provide guidance on avoiding disease by maintaining a healthy lifestyle from infancy through adulthood. Information is also given on choosing health-care providers and on preventive health care, including using screening programs to detect disease at an early stage. Most of the articles direct you to online sites where further information can be found.

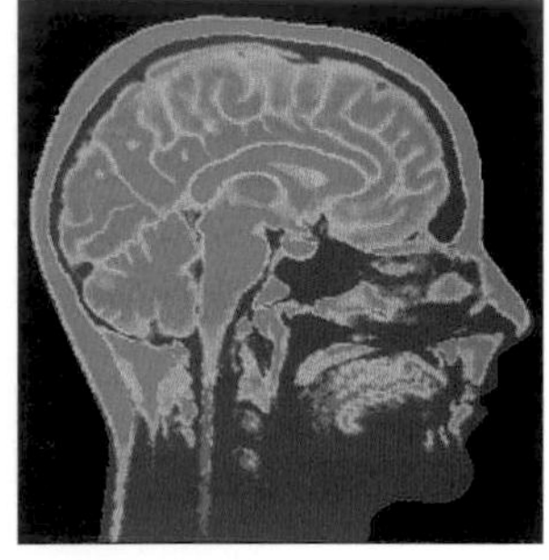

Feeling healthy
Certain psychological factors, such as how well you sleep and cope with stress, affect your sense of well-being, which, in turn, can influence your physical health.

INTRODUCTION

GOOD HEALTH is something most of us take for granted. When it fails, it is often for reasons that could have been avoided. Protecting your health is mainly a matter of understanding what causes disease and other problems so that you can take appropriate steps to avoid them. Modern techniques of immunization and screening offer protection against a wide range of illnesses. By taking advantage of these and combining them with a healthy lifestyle, you can safeguard your health not only for the present but for the future as well.

Feeling healthy involves more than just being free from disease; it also involves a general sense of well-being. Your health and well-being depend in part on factors that may be beyond your control, such as living in a pollution-free environment and having secure employment. However, there are many aspects of your lifestyle that you can change or adapt in order to improve your physical and mental health and reduce your chance of becoming ill. This part of the book explores the measures available that can enable you to take control of your health. It also explains the health-care system and screening methods that are used by doctors to identify potential health problems.

WHAT DETERMINES HEALTH?

Your health is partly determined by your genes, but it is also inextricably linked with your environment and lifestyle. Your chance of developing many diseases is determined at the moment of conception by the mix of genetic material that you have inherited from your parents. The inheritance of certain faulty genes, such as those that cause cystic fibrosis, inevitably causes the development of disease. However, it is more common for a person's genetic inheritance merely to predispose him or her to a disease or disorder that may develop later in life, such as diabetes mellitus.

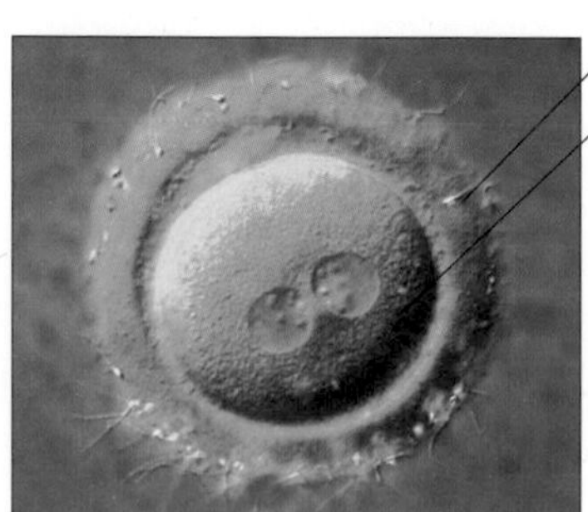
Sperm
Egg

The moment of conception
Your susceptibility to many diseases is programmed at conception when the sperm and egg cells fuse, bringing together half a set of genes from each parent.

If you are genetically susceptible to a certain disease or disorder, whether or not you develop it may also depend on a number of other factors, many of which are related to the way you live. For example, lifestyle factors such as diet, exercise, smoking, and alcohol consumption are important determinants of health. Following a healthy lifestyle and having appropriate screening tests may enable you to moderate the effects of your genetic susceptibility on your future health.

The environment in which you live also influences your health and susceptibility to certain diseases. For example, excessive exposure to the sun increases the risk of skin cancer. Living at high altitudes with a thinner atmosphere may pose problems for people who have respiratory diseases. In towns and cities, high levels of atmospheric pollution may worsen the symptoms of respiratory diseases such as asthma.

Other determinants of health include age, gender, ethnicity, and occupation. For example, the risk of heart disease increases with age and is more common in men, Asians, and people who have sedentary jobs.

ARE PEOPLE GETTING HEALTHIER?

At the turn of the 20th century, many people died before they reached age 50, and a large number of deaths occurred in childhood. Most people now survive well into adulthood, and the average life expectancy for a child born in Canada today is over

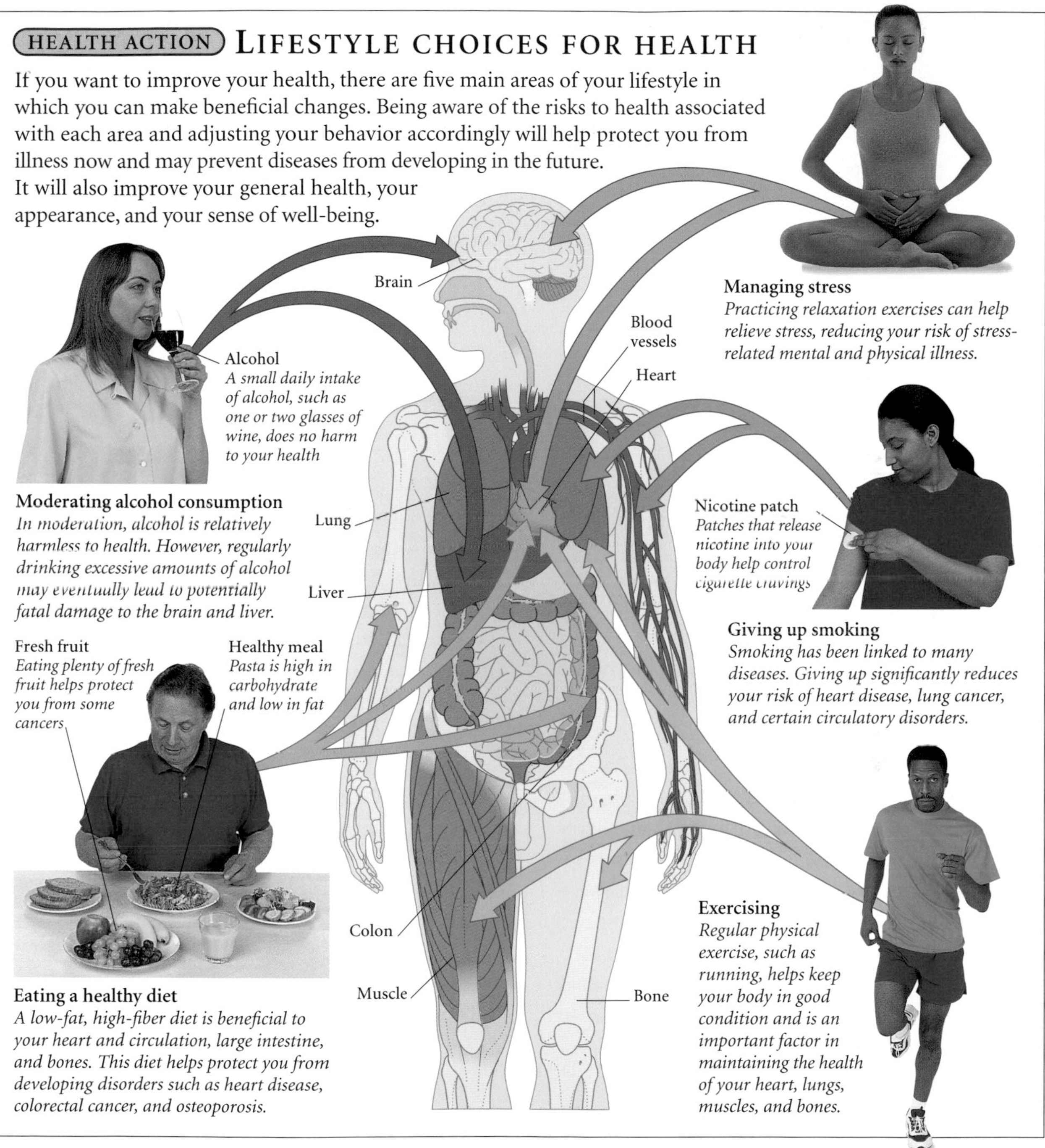
HEALTH ACTION
LIFESTYLE CHOICES FOR HEALTH
If you want to improve your health, there are five main areas of your lifestyle in which you can make beneficial changes. Being aware of the risks to health associated with each area and adjusting your behavior accordingly will help protect you from illness now and may prevent diseases from developing in the future. It will also improve your general health, your appearance, and your sense of well-being.
Brain
Blood vessels
Heart
Lung
Liver
Colon
Muscle
Bone
Alcohol
A small daily intake of alcohol, such as one or two glasses of wine, does no harm to your health
Moderating alcohol consumption
In moderation, alcohol is relatively harmless to health. However, regularly drinking excessive amounts of alcohol may eventually lead to potentially fatal damage to the brain and liver.
Fresh fruit
Eating plenty of fresh fruit helps protect you from some cancers
Healthy meal
Pasta is high in carbohydrate and low in fat
Eating a healthy diet
A low-fat, high-fiber diet is beneficial to your heart and circulation, large intestine, and bones. This diet helps protect you from developing disorders such as heart disease, colorectal cancer, and osteoporosis.
Managing stress
Practicing relaxation exercises can help relieve stress, reducing your risk of stress-related mental and physical illness.
Nicotine patch
Patches that release nicotine into your body help control cigarette cravings
Giving up smoking
Smoking has been linked to many diseases. Giving up significantly reduces your risk of heart disease, lung cancer, and certain circulatory disorders.
Exercising
Regular physical exercise, such as running, helps keep your body in good condition and is an important factor in maintaining the health of your heart, lungs, muscles, and bones.

78 years. In the US, a man who has already reached age 70 can expect to live at least to age 85, and a woman of 70 to reach at least age 89. Life expectancy began to rise toward the end of the 19th century as improvements in nutrition and public hygiene took effect. In the first half of the 20th century, the discovery of antibiotics further increased life expectancy by reducing deaths from infection. Immunization programs for a range of infectious diseases started around the middle of the century and now protect 80 percent of the world's children, preventing millions of deaths each year. In addition, far fewer adults become seriously ill before age 70 than at the beginning of the 20th century.

However, as people live longer, the major causes of ill health and death have changed. In the developed world, infectious disease and undernutrition have been superseded by heart disease, cancer, stroke, and smoking-related lung disease. Many of these disorders

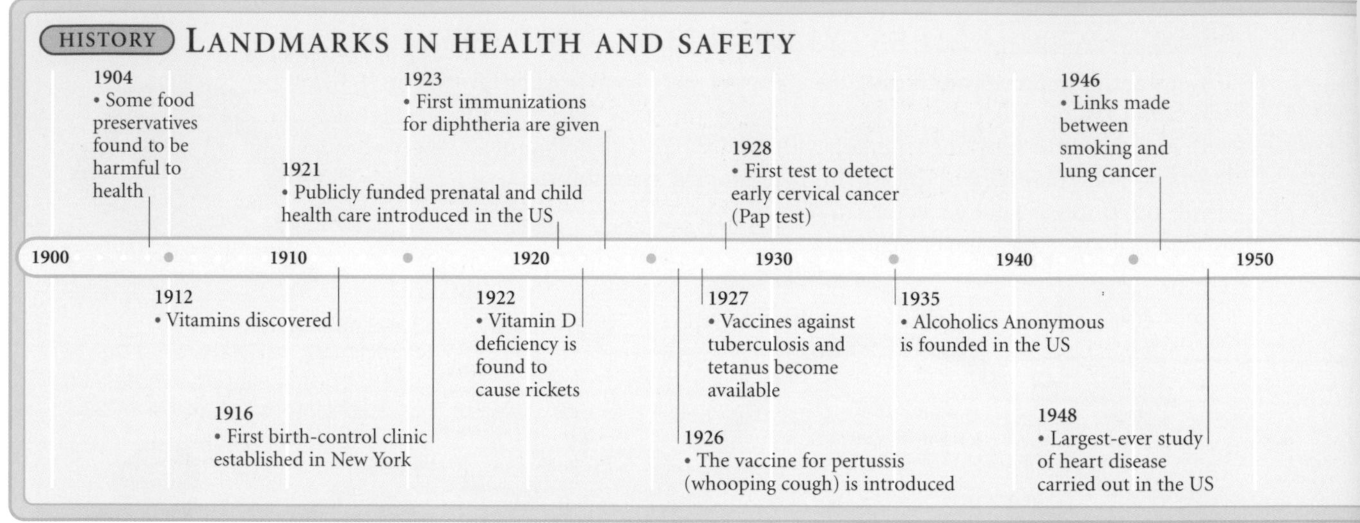
HISTORY
LANDMARKS IN HEALTH AND SAFETY
1900
1910
1920
1930
1940
1950
1904
• Some food preservatives found to be harmful to health
1912
• Vitamins discovered
1916
• First birth-control clinic established in New York
1921
• Publicly funded prenatal and child health care introduced in the US
1922
• Vitamin D deficiency is found to cause rickets
1923
• First immunizations for diphtheria are given
1926
• The vaccine for pertussis (whooping cough) is introduced
1927
• Vaccines against tuberculosis and tetanus become available
1928
• First test to detect early cervical cancer (Pap test)
1935
• Alcoholics Anonymous is founded in the US
1946
• Links made between smoking and lung cancer
1948
• Largest-ever study of heart disease carried out in the US

Advances in prevention and protection
A better understanding of the mechanisms of disease led to the discovery that lifestyle factors such as smoking and a high-fat diet contribute to major illnesses. The response was an emphasis on people living healthily to reduce their chance of disease and safety legislations and immunizations to protect the population.

are strongly associated with lifestyle factors that are typical of an affluent society, such as a high-fat diet and lack of exercise. Accidents, particularly traffic accidents, are another major cause of death and disability. Some disorders tend to develop with increasing age, including poor vision, deafness, arthritis, and loss of memory. Although people now enjoy more years of good health than previously, elderly people can still expect a period of substantial disability from mental or physical disease, lasting on average for 10 years, a figure that has not changed much over the century. As more people live past age 80, this period of impaired health is likely to lengthen.

Assessing your health

To understand your inheritance and reduce your risk of disease, you need to know as much as possible about conditions that run in your family. There may be certain patterns of disease, especially cases of cancer or heart disease, that have occurred in family members under age 50. You can create a family medical tree of disorders that run in your family and then arrange a health checkup with your doctor. He or she will check your current state of health and advise you about changes to your lifestyle, such as cutting down on high-fat foods or doing more exercise, that help reduce your risk of developing the diseases in your family history. You may be offered screening to detect these disorders at an early stage.

Regular health checkups help you monitor changes in your health and avoid complications from any existing diseases you may have. At certain times in your life, particularly as you become older, you will also be offered screening tests for early signs of diseases, such as bowel or breast cancer.

Choosing a healthy lifestyle

Evidence that we can influence our health comes from the fall in the numbers of deaths before age 65 from stroke, coronary artery disease, and certain types of cancer in the past 20 years. Much of this change has

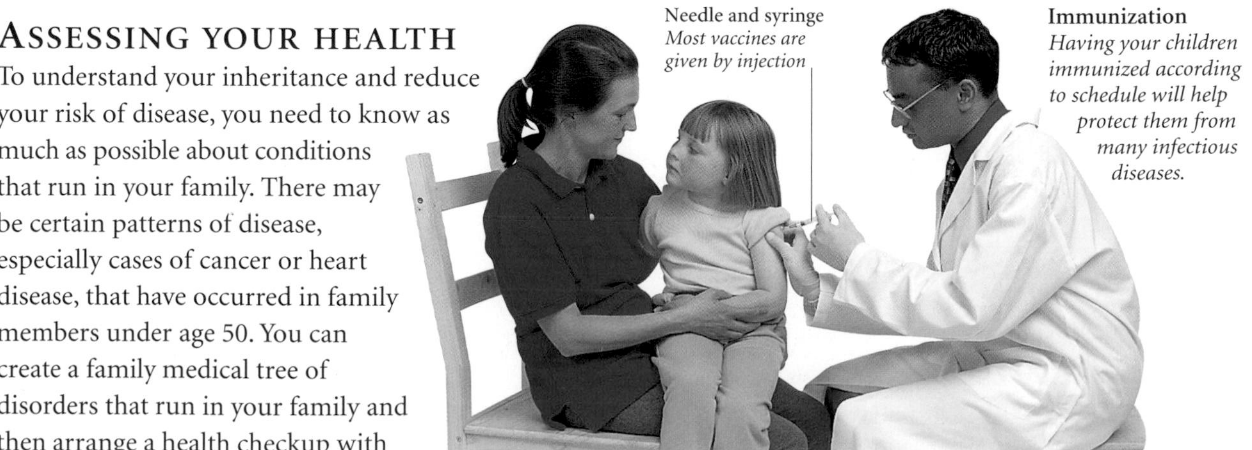

Needle and syringe
Most vaccines are given by injection

Immunization
Having your children immunized according to schedule will help protect them from many infectious diseases.

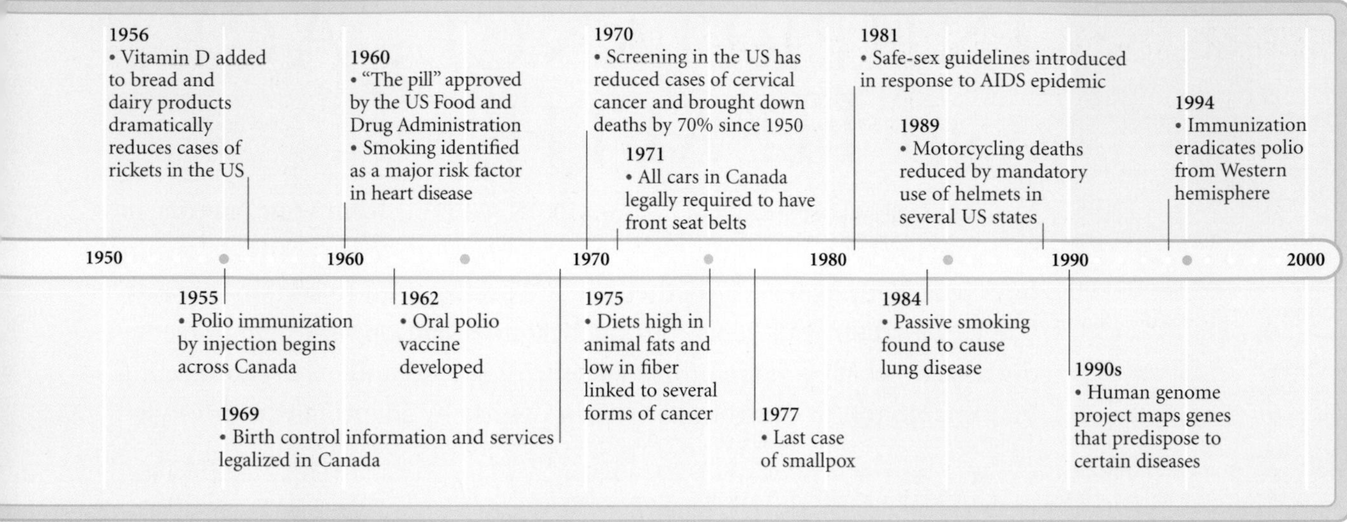

1950
1960
1970
1980
1990
2000
1956
• Vitamin D added to bread and dairy products dramatically reduces cases of rickets in the US
1960
• "The pill" approved by the US Food and Drug Administration
• Smoking identified as a major risk factor in heart disease
1970
• Screening in the US has reduced cases of cervical cancer and brought down deaths by 70% since 1950
1971
• All cars in Canada legally required to have front seat belts
1981
• Safe-sex guidelines introduced in response to AIDS epidemic
1989
• Motorcycling deaths reduced by mandatory use of helmets in several US states
1994
• Immunization eradicates polio from Western hemisphere
1955
• Polio immunization by injection begins across Canada
1962
• Oral polio vaccine developed
1969
• Birth control information and services legalized in Canada
1975
• Diets high in animal fats and low in fiber linked to several forms of cancer
1977
• Last case of smallpox
1984
• Passive smoking found to cause lung disease
1990s
• Human genome project maps genes that predispose to certain diseases

been attributed to a reduction in the number of smokers and improved dietary habits. There is also evidence that the strains and stresses of modern living, such as the breakup of close relationships, long working hours in stressful jobs, and loss of contact with family and friends, can ultimately affect our mental and physical well-being. Most people are aware of the basic features of a healthy lifestyle, but too few people act on this information. By adopting a healthy diet, exercising regularly, not smoking, and limiting your alcohol intake, you can bring about almost immediate improvements in your general health and reduce your long-term risk of disease. You will also find that you look and feel better.

Unhealthy habits can be difficult to break, especially if they seem to cause no immediate damage to your health. Making long-term changes to your lifestyle, such as giving up smoking or losing weight, require considerable willpower, and you may find it easier if you seek support from family and friends. You will benefit whatever your age because it is never too late to make lifestyle changes to improve your health.

ORGANIZATION HOW THIS PART OF THE BOOK IS ORGANIZED

This part of the book begins by looking at how your genetic inheritance influences your health and risk of disease and the way in which your health priorities change with increasing age. Whatever your genetic inheritance or age, changing certain aspects of your lifestyle can have a significant effect on your health and well-being and reduce your risk of disease. Practical guidance is given on how to make health-promoting changes to your lifestyle.

INHERITANCE, AGE, AND HEALTH p.20
How genetic makeup influences health and health priorities change with age.

Understanding inheritance p.24
How your genetic background causes or increases the risk of certain disorders.

Health at different ages p.27
How health risks and priorities change over your lifetime.

Health care throughout life p.38
Financing your health care and using preventive health care to maintain health.

LIFESTYLE AND HEALTH p.46
The influence that various lifestyle factors have on your health and well-being.

Diet and health p.48
Advice on the foods that make up a healthy diet, understanding food labeling, and controlling your weight.

Exercise and health p.55
The health benefits of exercise, choosing an exercise plan, and exercising safely.

Alcohol, tobacco, and drugs p.62
The effects on health of smoking, alcohol, and the use of recreational drugs.

Sex and health p.67
The positive health benefits of sexual relationships plus guides to safe sex and different forms of contraception.

Psychological health p.72
Lifestyle factors that affect psychological health, particularly the influence of stress on health, advice on sleeping well, and coping with loss and bereavement.

Safety and health p.77
Safety in a variety of environments: at home, at work, on the roads, around water, and on vacation, as well as guidelines for travel immunizations.

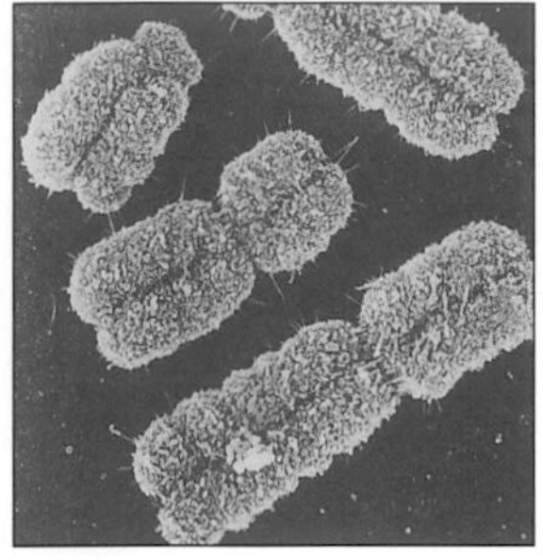

Chromosomes
Every body cell contains 23 pairs of chromosomes. These carry the genetic material that you inherit from your parents.

INHERITANCE, AGE, AND HEALTH

YOUR PHYSICAL CHARACTERISTICS ARE INHERITED from your parents and so are many genes that influence your health. Your genes partly determine how your body ages and whether you are predisposed to certain diseases. You cannot alter your genes, but medical intervention may help prevent diseases to which you are prone. Genetic diagnosis and expert counseling may enable you to control your risk of disease by adapting your lifestyle.

The genes that you inherit from your parents form the basis of your physical and mental characteristics. They determine many aspects of your appearance, such as the color of your eyes and hair. They direct the striking bodily changes brought about by growth and aging, noticeably during infancy and puberty. Genes also affect your body chemistry, which may influence your risk of disease.

YOUR INHERITANCE

At conception, the fertilized egg, or zygote, is a single cell that contains all the information necessary to make a new human being. This information is unique to each individual and is carried in genes, which are sections of tightly coiled DNA strands. As the fertilized egg divides, the information is duplicated so that a copy exists in every cell of the growing baby's body.

There are about 30,000 pairs of genes in each body cell, but only certain ones are active, depending on the cell's specialized function. Genes direct the activity of every cell by controlling the production of proteins. For example, some genes are responsible for the production of proteins that cause cells to form tissues, such as skin, hair, and muscle; others give rise to proteins that control body organs or fight infection. Faulty genes may cause an organ to develop or function abnormally. They may also be responsible for an inherited predisposition to develop certain disorders, such as heart disease.

If a disorder runs in your family, you may be able to undergo tests to find out if you have inherited the faulty genes. In addition, screening can detect many disorders at an early, treatable stage and is particularly important if your family history suggests you are at risk.

CHANGING HEALTH NEEDS

As you age and pass through distinct life stages, your body's needs and your health concerns change accordingly. For example, infants need high-energy diets to promote rapid growth, whereas elderly people require less energy and eat proportionately less, which may lead them to have a nutritionally deficient diet. While accidents present the greatest health risk for young adults, susceptibility to degenerative disease increases with age as the functioning of the body's organs and systems gradually declines. The immune system's resistance to disease decreases with age and natural healing processes become less efficient. Body systems age at different rates, which also vary among individuals, depending on genetic and lifestyle factors. Being aware of your changing health needs enables you to adapt your way of life, whatever your age. Life expectancy has increased dramatically in Canada over the past century (*see* LENGTHENING LIVES, left), but, if you are to remain in good health into old age, you will need to follow a sensible lifestyle.

DATA LENGTHENING LIVES

In Canada during the last 100 years, life expectancy has risen dramatically due to improvements in nutrition, sanitation, and health care. As a result, the proportion of older people in the population has grown. This trend has led to changing demands on the health-care system because there are now more people experiencing long-term illness and the effects of aging.

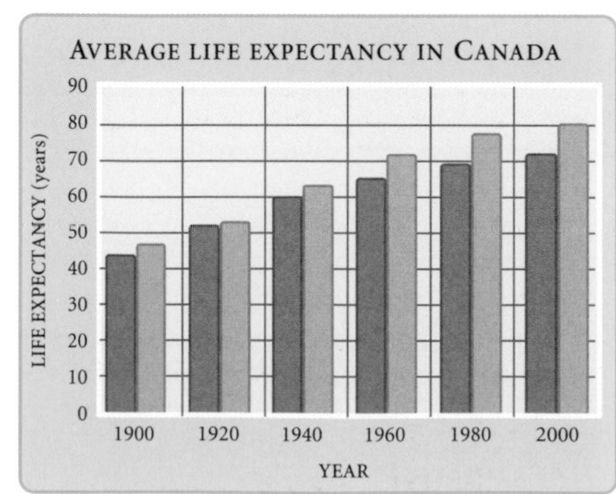
AVERAGE LIFE EXPECTANCY IN CANADA
LIFE EXPECTANCY (years)
90
80
70
60
50
40
30
20
10
0
1900
1920
1940
1960
1980
2000
YEAR

Life expectancy
At the beginning of the 20th century, average life expectancy at birth in Canada was only about 45 years. One hundred years later, it has risen by two-thirds to about 78 years. Females continue to live longer than males.

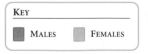

KEY
MALES
FEMALES

PROCESS RISKS OF INHERITING DISEASE

Most of our physical characteristics, including our susceptibility to certain diseases, are determined by genetic material known as DNA. Each of our cells contains DNA, organized into 46 units called chromosomes, arranged in 23 pairs. Sperm and egg cells contain only one chromosome from each pair. Each chromosome holds thousands of genes carrying chemical codes that affect our development. Genetic defects may result in a child inheriting a disease or a predisposition to develop one.

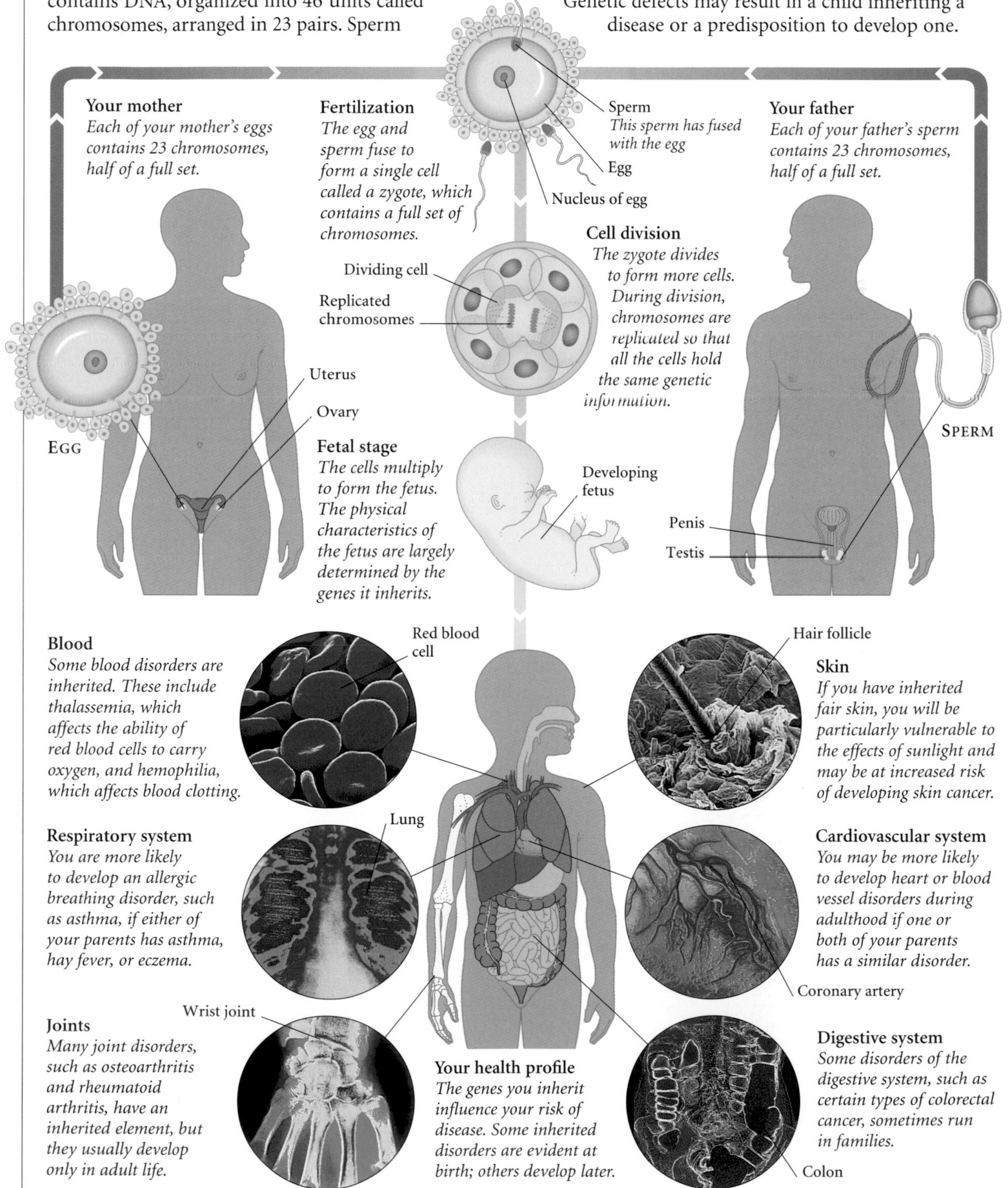

Your mother
Each of your mother's eggs contains 23 chromosomes, half of a full set.

Fertilization
The egg and sperm fuse to form a single cell called a zygote, which contains a full set of chromosomes.

Sperm
This sperm has fused with the egg

Egg

Nucleus of egg

Your father
Each of your father's sperm contains 23 chromosomes, half of a full set.

Dividing cell

Replicated chromosomes

Cell division
The zygote divides to form more cells. During division, chromosomes are replicated so that all the cells hold the same genetic information.

Uterus

Ovary

EGG

SPERM

Fetal stage
The cells multiply to form the fetus. The physical characteristics of the fetus are largely determined by the genes it inherits.

Developing fetus

Penis

Testis

Blood
Some blood disorders are inherited. These include thalassemia, which affects the ability of red blood cells to carry oxygen, and hemophilia, which affects blood clotting.

Red blood cell

Hair follicle

Skin
If you have inherited fair skin, you will be particularly vulnerable to the effects of sunlight and may be at increased risk of developing skin cancer.

Lung

Respiratory system
You are more likely to develop an allergic breathing disorder, such as asthma, if either of your parents has asthma, hay fever, or eczema.

Cardiovascular system
You may be more likely to develop heart or blood vessel disorders during adulthood if one or both of your parents has a similar disorder.

Coronary artery

Wrist joint

Joints
Many joint disorders, such as osteoarthritis and rheumatoid arthritis, have an inherited element, but they usually develop only in adult life.

Your health profile
The genes you inherit influence your risk of disease. Some inherited disorders are evident at birth; others develop later.

Digestive system
Some disorders of the digestive system, such as certain types of colorectal cancer, sometimes run in families.

Colon

PROCESS GROWTH AND AGING

The process of growth begins in the developing embryo and continues throughout childhood until early adulthood. By adulthood, the organs have fully developed, and the individual is capable of having children. After a peak at around age 30, the functioning of almost every body system gradually begins to decline. The rate of decline and its consequences for the individual are determined by a complex interaction of genetic characteristics and lifestyle factors. The chart below describes some specific changes that occur in the body's organs during each life stage.

BODY SYSTEM	BIRTH–1 YEAR	1–12 YEARS	12–18 YEARS
Bones, muscles, and joints	• Long bones are two-thirds cartilage at birth but gradually become harder. • Muscles gradually become able to support body weight.	• During childhood, bones grow larger and stronger as areas of cartilage are gradually replaced by bone, which is harder.	• Bone growth stops when all the cartilage has been replaced by bone. • By age 18, muscles have become fully developed.
Digestive organs and daily energy needs	• Breast milk or formula provide all nutrition for the first 4–6 months. • A high-energy diet is needed to provide energy for rapid growth.	• Digestive system is now mature and child can digest most foods. • Energy needs decrease because rate of growth slows after age 1.	• Adolescents need a balanced diet that is high in energy to fuel rapid growth; boys need more energy from food than girls.
Brain and nerves	• All nerve cells are present at birth; nerve connections continue to form. • Newborn baby has several basic reflexes, such as sucking.	• Connections between nerve cells develop fastest before age 6 and enable walking, talking, and bowel and bladder control by age 3.	• By age 18, the nervous system is fully developed; intellectual abilities are still developing. Puberty signals major psychological change.
Eyes and ears	• By 4 months, an infant can see a full range of colors and shades. • By 6 months, an infant can distinguish voices from other noises.	• Vision becomes sharper up to age 7 and hearing more acute as nerve connections form.	• Nearsightedness, which is often inherited, tends to become apparent in adolescence.
Heart and blood vessels	• A newborn baby has a relatively fast resting heart rate of about 120 beats per minute, but this rate gradually decreases.	• Resting heart rate continues to slow down as child grows older.	• Average resting heart rate is about 60–80 beats per minute; the rate is slowest in people who are athletic and physically fit.
Lungs and airways	• Smaller airways and lungs make infants more susceptible to respiratory problems. A baby takes 40–50 breaths a minute.	• As the lungs mature during childhood, breathing rate decreases. • In children under age 5, airways are small and easily irritated.	• As the lungs become more efficient at taking in oxygen, the average breathing rate falls to 12–15 breaths a minute by adulthood.
Reproductive organs	• Ovaries contain over one million eggs at birth, and testes contain primitive sperm, which mature at puberty.	• At puberty, hormonal changes stimulate sexual development. First signs of puberty occur in girls from about age 10 and in boys from age 12.	• Most adolescents have reached sexual maturity by age 18.
Urinary organs	• Blood flow to the kidneys is low in the first few months, creating a potential risk of a buildup of toxins normally excreted by the kidneys.	• Urine becomes more concentrated as the kidneys become more efficient at retaining water needed by the body.	• No significant changes.
Skin, hair, and teeth	• First primary teeth appear: lower central incisors erupt at age 6–10 months, upper central incisors at age 8–12 months.	• Full set of primary teeth present by age 33 months. Adult incisors and 1st molars appear at 6–9 years, canines and premolars at 9–12 years.	• Hormones stimulate oil and sweat production in skin. • 2nd molars appear at age 11–13, 3rd molars after age 17.

18–50 YEARS	50–70 YEARS	OVER 70 YEARS
• Bones are at maximum density during early adulthood. • After age 25, muscle bulk and strength start to decrease.	• Bones become weaker, particularly in postmenopausal women. • Muscle strength and bulk continue to decrease.	• Wear and tear on joints leads to increasing stiffness and pain. • Muscle strength at age 85 is about half the strength at age 25.
• After age 30, energy needs drop by 5 percent every decade. Decreasing energy needs cause many people to gain weight in middle age unless diet is adjusted.	• The volume of digestive fluids decreases and the intestines work less efficiently, leading to harder feces that may require straining to expel.	• Sense of taste becomes less acute as fewer than half the taste buds remain active. Chewing and swallowing may be more difficult due to tooth loss and gum disease.
• Ability to learn gradually declines, but life experience accumulates and intellectual abilities continue to develop.	• Short-term memory and ability to concentrate may become less efficient. • Physical reactions become slower.	• By age 90, the brain has lost up to one-tenth of its tissue, making it less efficient and leading to some loss of intellectual ability and physical coordination.
• By age 40, the lenses of the eyes may become less elastic, leading to difficulty focusing on close objects. • Loss of hearing begins in the 30s.	• After age 50, people may find it harder to see in low light or to see moving objects. • By age 70, people may find it difficult to hear faint or high-pitched sounds.	• Ability to distinguish fine visual detail continues to decline. • Deterioration in hearing may make hearing aids necessary.
• After age 40, artery walls lose elasticity, causing a rise in blood pressure. High blood pressure is one factor that may potentially lead to heart disease.	• Heart muscle becomes less elastic; the heart pumps harder but is less able to respond to increased effort.	• By age 85, the heart is unable to support long periods of strenuous activity. As stamina decreases, elderly people become fatigued more easily.
• Optimum lung function is reached at age 20–30. By age 45, the lungs may be less able to expand fully due to loss of some alveoli (air sacs) and weakening of rib muscles.	• By age 65, lung efficiency has decreased to about three-fifths of optimum level.	• By age 80, the lungs function only half as effectively as the lungs of a young adult, and moderate exertion may cause shortness of breath.
• Women usually go through menopause at age 45–55 and afterward are no longer fertile. In men, testosterone levels start to decline after age 40–50.	• In men, the prostate gland usually starts to enlarge after age 50; it may constrict the bladder outlet, making urination difficult.	• A decreasing level of testosterone in men reduces sexual desire. Fewer viable sperm are produced.
• Women who have given birth may have reduced pelvic muscle strength and tone, which may cause problems with urination.	• In women, falling estrogen levels also reduce pelvic muscle strength and tone. This may cause further difficulty in controlling urination.	• After age 75–80, kidneys become less efficient, and it takes longer for them to clear toxic chemicals from the blood.
• By the late 40s, the skin is less elastic and wrinkles appear. • Half of people over age 40 have gray hair. Some men begin to lose their hair.	• Surface of the skin becomes drier. • Hair may become considerably thinner, especially in men. • Teeth may begin to fall out.	• Skin becomes less able to regulate body temperature by retaining or losing heat, making people more susceptible to the effects of cold or hot weather.

UNDERSTANDING INHERITANCE

Only recently has evidence emerged showing the importance of inherited factors in determining our risk of developing disease. We take for granted the fact that children resemble their parents and other relatives and that families typically share physical and behavioral characteristics. It is this shared biological inheritance that also accounts for certain diseases "running in families."

Many of our physical and behavioral characteristics are determined by our genes. An explanation of the structure and function of genes and how they are inherited is given elsewhere (*see* GENES AND INHERITANCE, pp.262–267).

Genetic factors, along with lifestyle factors, play a part in causing many common diseases. The genes we inherit from our parents help explain variations between families in their susceptibility to certain diseases, although only a few rare disorders are directly caused by abnormal genes.

Gathering information on your family's medical history may help you identify unusually common diseases. Compiling such a history may give an early warning of a possible inherited genetic disorder or a genetic tendency to a particular disease. Medical geneticists are developing an ever-increasing range of tests to determine whether or not couples have inherited faulty genes (*see* GENETIC TESTS, pp.238–241). These tests enable geneticists to estimate the risk of children inheriting the faulty genes and to give advice on the likely effects on the children's health. In many cases, the symptoms of a genetic disorder can be treated or alleviated.

Family similarities
Children resemble their parents not only in appearance and personality traits but also in susceptibility to certain diseases.

You and your inheritance

Understanding how the genes you inherit may influence your health

The genes you inherit from your parents program your development from a single fertilized cell at the moment of conception to an adult. In each body cell you have about 30,000 pairs of genes arranged on 23 pairs of chromosomes. One chromosome from each pair is inherited from your mother, the other from your father. The mix of genes is slightly different in each sibling.

Each gene provides instructions for a cell to carry out a single chemical process, which in most cases involves building a protein. Genes also control the growth and reproduction of cells. They are responsible for the development of the embryo, first into a baby, then a child, and eventually an adult. Throughout your life, genes control cell functions and the repair and replacement of dead or damaged cells.

Blood relatives have many genes in common, and these genes help determine family physical characteristics and other traits. Most of these traits, such as the shape of the nose, are trivial and have no significance for your health. Other traits, such as being abnormally tall or short or having a tendency to be overweight, can be associated with an increased risk of certain diseases.

Some diseases, including hemophilia (p.452) and cystic fibrosis (p.824), are directly caused by a fault or mutation in a single gene or pair of genes. These rare diseases follow a predictable pattern of inheritance, and this means that families in which the gene is present can usually be given clear, reliable information regarding the risk of the disease affecting future generations.

More common than these genetic disorders are those in which genes, along with other factors, contribute to a family's susceptibility to certain diseases. For example, some disorders, such as coronary artery disease (p.405), tend to run in families, but lifestyle factors such as a high-fat diet, smoking, and lack of exercise also play a part in determining whether these diseases develop.

In some diseases that have a genetic component, including asthma (p.483), environmental factors, such as living in a polluted area, also play a crucial role. The complex interplay between genetic susceptibility and environment makes it difficult to predict the risks in adult life for children who are born into families affected by disorders of this kind.

(WWW) ONLINE SITES: p.1032

Your family medical history

Assessing your risk of developing a genetic disorder or passing one on to your children

You may have noticed that some diseases or disorders seem to "run in your family." These disorders may have a genetic basis, a lifestyle basis, or both. By making a medical family tree (opposite page) you can create a record of disorders that have affected your family. This record may help you calculate your own risk of disease.

GATHERING INFORMATION

Information on your parents, brothers, and sisters is the most important, but you can provide a fuller picture by finding out about as many generations as possible, including your uncles, aunts, and grandparents. It is also helpful to

ASSESSMENT MAKING A MEDICAL FAMILY TREE

To make your medical family tree, you need key pieces of information about your relatives. You should research at least as far back as your grandparents because a genetic predisposition to a certain disease may be masked in one generation but nevertheless passed on to succeeding generations. Key facts include date of birth and, if the person is deceased, cause of death and the age at which it occurred. If possible, you should find out about lifestyle factors, such as smoking, body weight, alcohol consumption, and exercise.

YOUR PATERNAL GRANDFATHER (1916–1978)

MEDICAL HISTORY *Angina*
LIFESTYLE FACTORS *Nonsmoker*
CAUSE OF DEATH *Heart attack at age 62*

YOUR PATERNAL GRANDMOTHER (1919–1975)

MEDICAL HISTORY *None*
LIFESTYLE FACTORS *Nonsmoker*
CAUSE OF DEATH *Colorectal cancer at age 56*

YOUR MATERNAL GRANDFATHER (1922–)

MEDICAL HISTORY *None*
LIFESTYLE FACTORS *Active, nonsmoker*
HEALTH STATUS *In good health*

YOUR MATERNAL GRANDMOTHER (1925–1995)

MEDICAL HISTORY *Diabetes mellitus*
LIFESTYLE FACTORS *Smoker*
CAUSE OF DEATH *Stroke at age 70*

YOUR PATERNAL UNCLE (1942–)

MEDICAL HISTORY *None*
LIFESTYLE FACTORS *Active, nonsmoker*
HEALTH STATUS *In good health*

YOUR PATERNAL UNCLE (1939–)

MEDICAL HISTORY *Coronary artery disease*
LIFESTYLE FACTORS *Sedentary, smoker*
HEALTH STATUS *In poor health*

YOUR FATHER (1938–)

MEDICAL HISTORY *Treated for polyps in the colon*
LIFESTYLE FACTORS *Active, nonsmoker*
HEALTH STATUS *In good health*

YOUR MOTHER (1946–)

MEDICAL HISTORY *Diabetes mellitus*
LIFESTYLE FACTORS *Nonsmoker*
HEALTH STATUS *Overweight*

YOUR MATERNAL UNCLE (1948–1960)

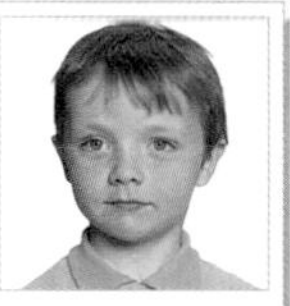

MEDICAL HISTORY *None*
LIFESTYLE FACTORS *Was active*
CAUSE OF DEATH *Meningitis at age 12*

YOUR MATERNAL UNCLE (1950–)

MEDICAL HISTORY *None*
LIFESTYLE FACTORS *Nonsmoker*
HEALTH STATUS *In good health*

SISTER (1974–)

MEDICAL HISTORY *None*
LIFESTYLE FACTORS *Active, smoker*
HEALTH STATUS *Overweight*

SISTER (1976–)

MEDICAL HISTORY *Kidney failure, age 12. Kidney transplant, age 14*
LIFESTYLE FACTORS *Smoker*
HEALTH STATUS *In good health*

BROTHER (1978–)

MEDICAL HISTORY *None*
LIFESTYLE FACTORS *Nonsmoker*
HEALTH STATUS *In good health*

YOU (FEMALE) (1980–)

MEDICAL HISTORY *None*
LIFESTYLE FACTORS *Nonsmoker*
HEALTH STATUS *In good health*

PARTNER

Example of a family tree
A family tree enables you to detect disease trends, but you will need your doctor's help to interpret your risk of disease. This example assumes that you are female and were born in 1980. From this record, the doctor would conclude that you and your siblings are at risk of polyps in the colon, which may lead to colorectal cancer, and diabetes mellitus. If you are planning to have a child, you should look at both your own and your partner's family trees to assess possible health risks for the child.

know something about your relatives' lifestyles to help you and your doctor assess whether any diseases were largely due to behavior or inheritance.

You may want to find out about your medical family tree out of curiosity, but the information might also help you answer questions that your doctor may ask. You are likely to be asked about your family medical history when you first see a new doctor; when you are expecting a baby; if you are admitted to the hospital; and if you develop symptoms of a disorder with an inherited component, such as asthma.

Assessing the information

You may be able to come to some conclusions about your risk of disease by looking at your medical family tree. If your investigation suggests that a particular disease has affected more than one member of your family, you should consult your doctor. In some cases, you may be referred for genetic counseling to assess your risk of developing a disorder or passing it on to your children.

DRAWING YOUR OWN CONCLUSIONS Longevity runs in families, and, if many of your relatives lived past age 80, you also have a good chance of doing so, especially if you maintain a healthy lifestyle. If many of your relatives died young, you should look at the causes of death. You may be susceptible to disorders that have occurred more than once in your family.

You should suspect an inherited disorder if more than one child in your family was stillborn or died in childhood; if more than one adult died from heart disease or cancer before age 60; if a chronic disorder, such as arthritis (p.374), affected more than two people in the family; or if more than one family member had the same disabling or fatal disease. Deaths before age 60 are especially relevant, unless they were caused by accidents or by infections, such as tuberculosis, that occurred before effective treatment became available.

PROFESSIONAL INTERPRETATION Genetic counselors are trained to assess your risk of disease and determine whether you are a carrier of a faulty gene that causes a genetic disorder. Carriers do not have the disorder because the faulty gene is masked by a normal gene, but children of carriers can inherit the faulty gene. The counselor will try to find out whether the high frequency of a disease in your family is due more to genetics or lifestyle. For example, if primary lung cancer (p.503) runs in your family, this could be due to the family members smoking, although there may still be an inherited component. In addition, some occupations are linked with lung cancer (*see* OCCUPATIONAL LUNG DISEASES, p.499) and may be common in a family.

CONSIDERING THE OPTIONS Your family medical history may suggest that you are at risk of an inherited disorder. In this case, the counselor will tell you whether a specific gene abnormality for the disorder has been identified and whether there is a diagnostic test to see if you have the gene (*see* GENETIC TESTS, pp.238–241). If a test is available, the counselor can provide information to help you decide whether or not to have the test. For example, you may be told whether the disease develops in everyone who inherits the faulty gene and whether preventive treatment is available. You may also be told whether prenatal testing of the embryo or fetus is possible and what the implications are for children you might have.

Some people decide against having genetic tests and there are several possible reasons for this. Prospective parents may choose to carry on with a pregnancy despite the risk that their child may be affected, or they may not want to worry about a disorder that may not necessarily affect them or their child. They may also be concerned about the stigma associated with "labeling" someone as having or being a carrier of a disorder. Other people want to know the results of a test even if they would not act on them. Bear in mind that the test results of one family member may have implications for others in the family who may not want to know the result.

Members of some ethnic groups are susceptible to particular genetic disorders, and individuals may be offered a screening test based on this fact alone. For example, 1 in 10 African–Americans carries the gene for sickle-cell anemia (p.448), a disorder of red blood cells. If you are Jewish, a genetic counselor may recommend that you be screened for the metabolic disorder Tay–Sachs disease (p.868) because 1 in 30 Ashkenazi Jews, compared with only 1 in 300 of the general population, carries the faulty gene that causes the disease.

What you can do

If tests show that you have a faulty gene, then your course of action will depend on whether you already have the symptoms of a genetic disorder or you are at high risk of developing the disorder. If you carry a faulty gene and you are planning a family, there are several options to consider.

PEOPLE WITH A GENETIC DISORDER Certain genetic disorders can be treated. For example, the high levels of cholesterol that run in some families (*see* HYPERCHOLESTEROLEMIA, p.691) may be lowered by changes in diet combined with the use of lipid-lowering drugs (p.935). If your child has hemophilia (p.452), this may be treated by regular injections of Factor VIII, a protein that helps the blood clot.

PEOPLE AT RISK If you discover that you have a gene that predisposes you to a particular disorder, such as breast cancer (p.759), you can be screened regularly to detect cancerous changes at an early stage. You may also be able to make lifestyle changes to help lower the risk of developing the disease. For example, if you are predisposed to developing diabetes mellitus (p.687), you will be advised to keep your weight within the normal range.

CARRIERS If you carry a faulty gene that could be passed on to your children, you and your partner may decide not to have children or may consider various family planning options such as adoption or artificial insemination (p.775). You may be able to take advantage of advances in assisted conception (p.776), in which fertilization is carried out in the laboratory and the embryo is tested for the faulty gene. Only an embryo that does not have the genetic fault is then implanted into the uterus. If you are already expecting a baby and are told that your baby is affected by a genetic abnormality, you may want to consider terminating the pregnancy (p.789).

(WWW) ONLINE SITES: p.1032

Health at Different Ages

Your risk of various health hazards changes over your lifetime, and you should adjust your health priorities accordingly. During childhood and early adult life, the main risks are from accidents, but after age 50 the leading causes of death are cancer and heart disease. Later on, falls, strokes, and dementia are major threats.

Healthy relationships
Involving the whole family in major life events strengthens family relationships and contributes to psychological health.

Canadians born today can expect, on average, to live for nearly 80 years, but one-quarter of them will die before they reach the age of 65. Some of these premature deaths will be the result of unavoidable accidents or of disorders present at birth, but most will be due to preventable conditions.

People of all ages can reduce their risk of illness and premature death by adopting a three-pronged strategy. The first priority is a healthy lifestyle; the second and third are immunization and early identification of disease by health checkups and screening (*see* HEALTH CARE THROUGHOUT LIFE, pp.38–45).

For many families, the most crucial determinant of health is their lifestyle. People who exercise regularly, eat a healthy selection of foods, and do not smoke substantially reduce their risk of disease. In Canada, variations from province to province in the rate of premature mortality are due mostly to variations in these well-known risk factors.

The articles in this section review normal physical and emotional development and examine the factors that promote continued good health at each of the major stages of life. These stages include infancy, the preschool years, the school years, adolescence, adulthood, older adulthood, and old age. In addition, there are separate articles that look at health issues during pregnancy and the periods following childbirth and menopause.

Health in infants

Taking care of your baby from birth until age 1 year

A baby's physical growth is rapid after birth, and, during the first year of life, your baby will triple his or her weight and double in height. Changes in the child's internal organs are less obvious but equally important. During the early years of childhood, the brain grows rapidly, reaching three-quarters of its adult weight, and, as the nervous system matures, your child will acquire a whole range of instinctive skills that start with mobility and go on to include language and physical coordination.

Thanks to improved hygiene, immunization programs, and the use of antibiotics, serious threats to health in the first year of life are relatively few in developed countries. With the exception of some problems that cannot be prevented, such as those associated with prematurity, congenital abnormalities (those present from birth), and genetic diseases, the major risks at this age are sudden infant death syndrome (p.820) and accidents.

Diet and tooth care

An average baby has doubled his or her birth weight by about 6 months of age. Babies need more calories in proportion to their body weight than adults do, more even than adults involved in heavy manual work, and therefore need to be fed frequently. Both formula and breast milk provide the correct balance of nutrients and allow you to form a close bond with your baby. However, breast milk has other additional benefits (*see* FEEDING YOUR INFANT, p.28).

By age 7 months, your baby's primary teeth may already have begun to break through the gums. As soon as they do appear, you should brush them twice a day and follow advice on fluoride supplements from your doctor or dentist.

Preventing illness

Infections are uncommon in the first few months of life, partly because babies are protected by the immunity that they obtain from maternal antibodies, and partly because they do not have much contact with the outside world. However, later in infancy, babies become vulnerable to minor illnesses caused by bacteria and viruses, including colds, coughs, and diarrhea. Although your baby gradually acquires immunity to the organisms that cause these illnesses, you can reduce the risk of infection by keeping him or her away from people who have an infectious illness, regularly cleaning toys, and maintaining hygiene.

Infections such as pertussis (p.492) and measles (p.291) can be prevented by having your baby immunized (*see* ROUTINE IMMUNIZATIONS, p.45). Most

Interacting with your baby
You can encourage healthy psychological development by interacting with your baby from the day he or she is born.

HEALTH OPTIONS FEEDING YOUR INFANT

Pediatricians advise that breast-feeding your baby should be continued for at least 2 years. Breast milk is much better for babies than formula. If you do not breast-feed, you should use baby formula prepared carefully according to the instructions. During the second half of the first year, your baby can digest increasingly complex foods, and you can gradually introduce solid foods into his or her diet. However, breast milk (or formula) is the main food for your baby's first year. Solid foods are meant to complement it.

BREAST- OR BOTTLE-FEEDING

If possible, all mothers should breast-feed. Every extra month brings more benefits. If you are breast-feeding and require medication, make sure that the doctor knows you are breast-feeding (*see* HEALTH IN PREGNANCY AND AFTER CHILDBIRTH, p.33). Give breast-fed babies vitamin D during the first year. Breast-fed babies are less susceptible to sudden infant death syndrome (p.820), Crohn's disease, and ulcerative colitis, and are less likely to become overweight as adults.

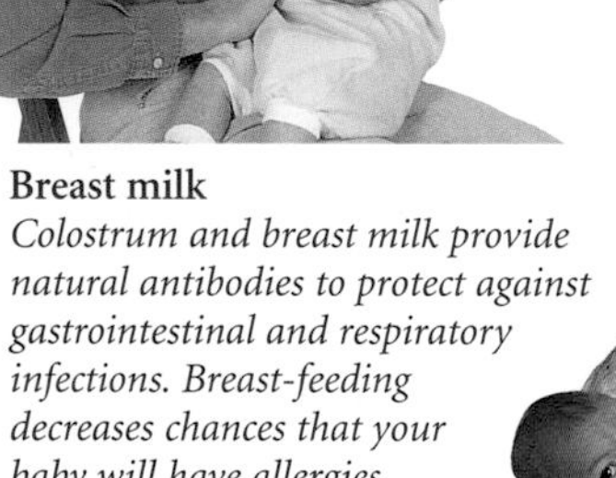

Breast milk
Colostrum and breast milk provide natural antibodies to protect against gastrointestinal and respiratory infections. Breast-feeding decreases chances that your baby will have allergies.

Formula
Formulas come in three main types: cows' milk based, soy-bean based, and hydrolyzed. Consult your doctor.

COMPLEMENTARY FOODS

At 6 months, gradually introduce your baby to solid foods, first as purees and later in mashed or minced form. Do not give your baby eggs, nuts, cows' milk, juice, or honey. Avoid sweet foods and do not add salt to food. Talk to your local public health nurse about making your own baby food. It is nutritious, easy to make, and much less expensive than commercial baby food.

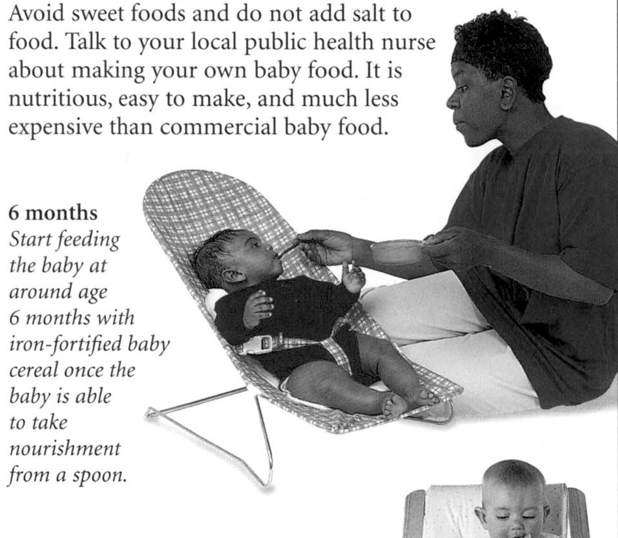

6 months
Start feeding the baby at around age 6 months with iron-fortified baby cereal once the baby is able to take nourishment from a spoon.

9 months
At around age 9 months, your baby will be able to start eating solid foods such as peeled apples and bread. The introduction of these items to the diet will encourage self-feeding and provide first chewing practice for the baby.

of the life-threatening infections, such as meningitis (p.848), can be successfully treated if diagnosed promptly.

Although sudden infant death syndrome, known as SIDS (p.820), is one of the greatest risks for babies in this age group, the number of deaths from SIDS is decreasing. To reduce the risk, babies below age 6 months should sleep on their backs on a firm mattress, with their feet near the bottom of a well-ventilated crib. Do not let your baby get too warm because babies cannot regulate their own temperature well, and overheating is known to be a risk factor in SIDS.

Babies who are regularly exposed to tobacco smoke are at increased risk of respiratory infections, asthma (p.483), ear infections, and SIDS. The risk can be minimized by restricting smoking to outside the home or to specific areas well away from the baby. Breast-feeding can also reduce the risk of SIDS.

A SAFE ENVIRONMENT

Injuries are one of the major causes of death in infants under age 1 year. Many serious injuries could be avoided by taking safety precautions (*see* HOME SAFETY AND HEALTH, p.77). It is also a good idea for you and your babysitters to take a first-aid course. Never leave a baby unattended on a raised or high surface; in the bathtub or near a pool of water (*see* SAFETY IN AND AROUND WATER, p.81); or with a dog or a cat, even if the pet is well trained (*see* PETS AND HEALTH, p.82).

From age 6–8 months, your baby may be mobile enough to get hold of objects that may present a danger. An older sibling's toys may have small parts that can be pulled off and pose a choking hazard. Plastic bags put your baby at risk of suffocation. Keep dangerous chemicals and drugs locked away, and store matches and sharp or fragile objects out of reach.

In the car, your baby should travel in an appropriate car seat (*see* CHILDREN'S CAR SEATS, opposite page).

PSYCHOLOGICAL HEALTH

The bonding process begins at birth and is important for your baby's emotional development. A regular routine and consistent emotional care from a limited number of adults is essential for your baby to develop self-confidence, trust, and a feeling of security.

Maintaining eye contact and talking to your newborn baby from the day of birth encourages communication. Your child should also spend some time with other adults and with infants of his or her own age. This interaction with different people will encourage your baby's social development.

(WWW) ONLINE SITES: p.1028, p.1036

Health in preschool children

Taking care of your child's health from age 1–5 years

Between the ages of 1 and 5 years, your child continues to grow and to develop in four important areas: movement and coordination; vision and manipulative skills; hearing and speech; and play and social skills. The most important preventable health threats during this time are accidents and infections.

Diet and tooth care

The preschool years are the time to promote healthy eating habits that should last a lifetime. A balanced diet (*see* A HEALTHY DIET, p.48) is important for healthy growth, and mealtimes can also provide a focus for social development. In particular, preschool children need plenty of fruit and vegetables in their diet. To build strong bones and teeth, children should eat calcium-rich food, such as milk, cheese, and yogurt. A pint of milk daily provides the recommended calcium level. Fats, which are present in foods such as cheese and yogurt, are important for growth and development, and these foods should not be replaced by low-fat equivalents.

Although many families eat three meals a day, your child may prefer to have several smaller meals, and there are many healthy snacks, such as fruit, bread, and cheese. Preschool children do not usually need vitamin or mineral supplements if they have a balanced diet. However, because they need about 15 mg a day of iron at a time when many are particular about their food, iron-deficiency anemia (p.447) may develop. Consult your doctor if you think your child might need supplements.

By age 3, all of your child's primary (milk) teeth should have appeared, and he or she should start making regular visits to the dentist. Dental visits are important since many children develop cavities as a result of tooth decay (*see* DENTAL CARIES, p.609). You can help prevent tooth decay by restricting sweet foods and brushing your child's teeth twice a day. If the public water supply in your area does not contain added fluoride, your dentist may apply a protective fluoride solution to your child's teeth or provide fluoride drops or tablets for you to give him or her.

Exercise

The preschool years are the right time to encourage your child to begin regular exercise. Exercise increases muscular and cardiovascular strength and respiratory capacity, strengthens bones, and develops coordination (*see* THE BENEFITS OF EXERCISE, p.55).

Preventing illness

Preschool children usually have frequent minor infections, such as coughs, colds, and diarrhea. These will become less frequent as your child acquires immunity to the bacteria and viruses to

HEALTH ACTION Children's car seats

During childhood, traffic collisions are a leading cause of injury and death. Children must be restrained properly to protect them from collisions or sudden stops. Even on a short trip, your child should be safely secured in a seat complying with current federal motor vehicle safety standards. A child's weight and age determine if the seat should be forward- or rear-facing and when a new, larger one is needed. Children age 12 and under should be placed in your vehicle's rear seat. Never place a child in a passenger seat fitted with an airbag. Airbags can cause a child serious injury or even death. Using second-hand children's car seats is not recommended. Seats sold in Canada must meet Transport Canada's safety regulations and a National Safety Mark must be visible on the seat. A child weighing over 60 lb (27 kg) can use a normal seat and belt rather than a car seat.

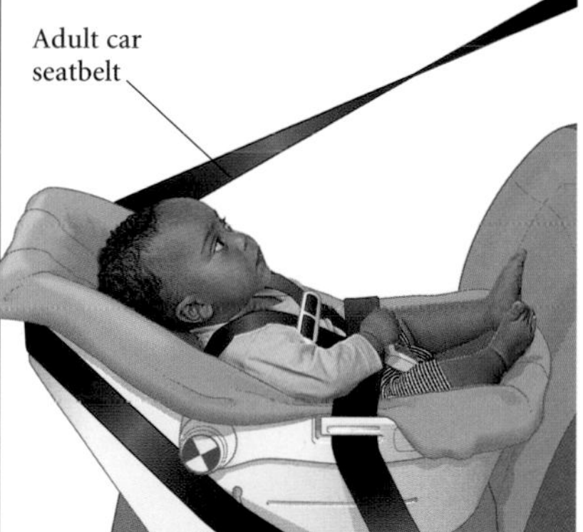
Adult car seatbelt

Rear-facing infant seat
You must use a seat that faces to the rear, secured with a car seatbelt or Universal Anchorage System, for infants who weigh less than 22 lb (10 kg). This will be until your baby is around 1 year old.

Forward-facing child seat
These child seats are for the use of a child weighing 22–40 lb (10–18 kg), about age 1 to 4 years. The seat has three important features – a built in harness which secures the child and absorbs forward motion in a collision, a base which is secured by the vehicle seat belt or Universal Anchorage System, and a tether strap which secures the top of the child seat to the vehicle.

Booster seat
A booster seat is used for a child from 40 lb (18 kg), usually about age 4 to 8. The booster seat is the safest way to correctly position a seat belt over a child's body. An incorrectly positioned seat belt can cause serious injury to a child in a collision. The lap belt should be low and snug across the child's hips and the shoulder belt positioned across the chest. Never tuck the shoulder belt behind the child or under the arm.

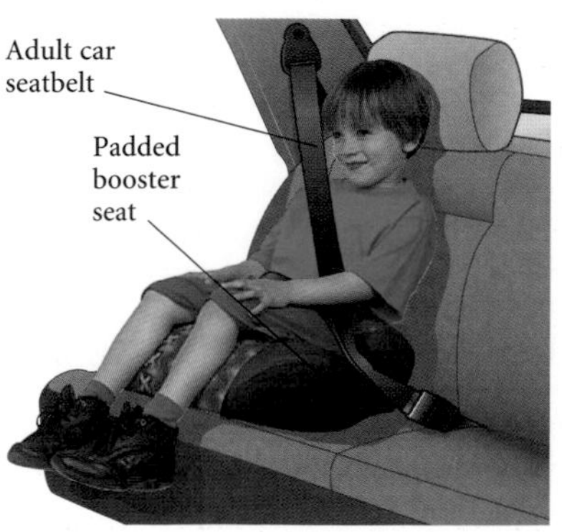
Adult car seatbelt
Padded booster seat

Using a highchair
Children who have started feeding themselves should be placed in a highchair for their meals. Make sure that the harness is fastened securely to prevent falls, and do not leave your child alone.

which he or she is exposed. Immunization can help prevent some of the more serious infections (*see* ROUTINE IMMUNIZATIONS, p.45).

A SAFE ENVIRONMENT

Injuries in the home, such as poisoning, falls, and drowning, are the major problem at this age. A child's natural curiosity makes an occasional minor injury unavoidable, but you can reduce the chance of serious injury by making your environment as safe as you can (*see* HOME SAFETY AND HEALTH, p.77). If you learn simple first aid, you may be better able to deal with injuries. Make sure that caregivers and babysitters are trained to deal with emergencies.

HOME SAFETY Hazardous items such as cleaning liquids, bleaches, alcohol, medicines, and matches should be stored in locked cabinets or out of reach. Cover all unused electrical outlets, especially those near the floor, with safety caps; install safety locks on your windows; ensure that glass doors and tables are made of shatterproof glass; and put protective corner devices on furniture.

SAFETY OUTSIDE THE HOME Parents should help their children recognize and avoid potential hazards they may encounter away from home. For example, make sure that your child always crosses the street with an adult and that he or she understands the importance of traffic safety; never leave your child unattended near water; teach him or her about the danger of eating unidentified berries or leaves; give clear advice about which types of adults are likely to be helpful and which should be avoided; allow your child to use playground apparatus only if it is on a soft surface such as grass; and help your child learn his or her address. In the car, make sure that your child travels in a car seat of the appropriate type and size (*see* CHILDREN'S CAR SEATS, p.29).

PSYCHOLOGICAL HEALTH

Playing forms an important part of your child's emotional and social development by encouraging him or her to develop new skills and learn about the world, other people, and him- or herself. You can stimulate your child by giving him or her plenty of activities to look at, think about, and do. By praising your child's achievements during play, you can boost his or her self-esteem and self-confidence. Local play groups often offer organized play and provide the opportunity to make friends with other children and adults.

(WWW) ONLINE SITES: p.1028

Health in school-age children

Good physical and emotional health for your child between the ages of 5 and 12

Physical growth and development are slow and steady during the school years, in contrast to the rapid changes that occur during the preschool years and adolescence. Your child's motor skills are refined between the ages of 5 and 12, and running, jumping, and throwing steadily improve. School significantly influences your child's intellectual and emotional development, and he or she becomes noticeably better at logic, reasoning, and problem-solving.

Just as during the preschool years, the major preventable threats to a child's health while he or she is at school are injuries and infections. During the school years, your child becomes much more independent and should continue to be taught to take responsibility for his or her own health and safety.

DIET AND TOOTH CARE

You can establish good eating habits at home by providing your child with a healthy breakfast, incorporating fruit and vegetables into the diet, and limiting the amount of food and drinks containing sugar (*see* A HEALTHY DIET, p.48). Iron-deficiency anemia (p.447) may become a problem because many children of school age are very particular about what they eat. Try to ensure an iron-rich diet by encouraging your child to eat foods that are high in iron, such as lean red meats, egg yolks, and leafy green vegetables. Dietary calcium is also essential for bones to develop normally and increase in strength and density. Seek medical advice if you feel that your child requires vitamin or mineral supplements.

You should not replace dietary fats with low-fat substitutes. Even if a child is overweight, he or she has the same nutritional needs as other children, and you should never put your child on a diet without medical advice. If your child is overweight, the doctor may suggest smaller portions of food and may encourage exercise rather than altering diet content.

Good dental hygiene is important because your child's permanent teeth emerge during the school years. Your child may still need help with toothbrushing, and you should also show him or her how to use dental floss (*see* CARING FOR YOUR TEETH AND GUMS, p.610). Minimal snacking on sweet foods will help limit tooth decay. Orthodontic problems, in which teeth grow irregularly or are overcrowded, are common in children of this age, and regular dental checkups are essential. If the fluoridation of your water supply is inadequate, your dentist may recommend fluoride supplements.

EXERCISE

In addition to making sure that your child has enough calcium in the diet, you should check that he or she does regular weight-bearing exercise, such as walking and running (*see* THE BENEFITS OF EXERCISE, p.55), in order to build strong bones. School will provide opportunities for your child to participate in sports, which can improve his or her motor skills and are a good way of socializing.

PREVENTING ILLNESS

By the time he or she is in school, your child should have received most routine immunizations (p.45). Infectious diseases, such as influenza (p.287), can spread rapidly in the school environment. Keep your child at home if he or she has an infectious disease so as not to infect other children.

A SAFE ENVIRONMENT

Your child's susceptibility to injuries increases as he or she develops physically and emotionally. About half of all deaths of children aged 5–12 are caused by injuries that can usually be prevented by teaching your child to follow a few simple, common-sense rules.

HOME SAFETY Encourage your child to put away toys that could cause an injury and teach him or her what to do in a home emergency, such as a fire (*see* HOME SAFETY AND HEALTH, p.77).

Store matches, lighters, and knives in cupboards, drawers, or other storage spaces that are inaccessible to your child. It is safest not to keep firearms in the home at all. However, if you do have firearms stored at home, make sure that they are locked away, that the ammunition is stored separately in a locked place, and that your child fully understands the potential dangers.

SAFETY OUTSIDE THE HOME Make sure that your child understands the importance of safety in traffic (*see* SAFETY ON THE ROAD, p.83) and that he or she uses safety equipment in vehicles (*see* CHILDREN'S CAR SEATS, p.29) and during sports activities. You should also make sure that your child is able to swim and knows that water can be dangerous (*see* SAFETY IN AND AROUND WATER, p.81). If your child has a medical condition, such as asthma (p.483), or a food allergy (p.467), he or she should be taught what the implications of the condition are and how to prevent problems.

Using home computers wisely
Time spent at the computer should not compromise time spent exercising, and children should also spend time taking part in more social activities.

Find out what health education your child is receiving at school so that you can reinforce messages about addictive substances such as alcohol, tobacco, and drugs (pp.62–66), and sexual issues, such as pregnancy, contraception, and sexually transmitted diseases (*see* SEX AND HEALTH, pp.67–71). A child needs knowledge in order to resist pressure from peers or older people to engage in sexual activity at too young an age.

PSYCHOLOGICAL HEALTH

School provides your child with the first chance to have independence and develop social skills. School-age children begin to rely on friends of their own age for companionship, support, and to share advice and feelings. Although you need to respect your child's increasing need for independence and privacy, firm guidance and clear boundaries are necessary for healthy growth.

Children with siblings, particularly a newborn brother or sister, may experience feelings of rivalry and jealousy. Set aside time to listen to your child and acknowledge his or her feelings. All children need to recognize their individual strengths and to feel that they are valued members of the family.

(WWW) ONLINE SITES: p.1028

Health in adolescents

Special health needs between the ages of 12 and 18

The physical changes of adolescence, known as puberty, usually begin between the ages of 10 and 14 and can continue for 3–4 years. Girls generally start puberty earlier than boys, and the first sign in most girls is breast enlargement, followed by growth of underarm and pubic hair. Menstruation starts at about age 12–13; consult your doctor if it has not started by age 15. At about 16–17, body fat has increased around the hips and thighs, and the pelvis has broadened. In boys, the first signs of puberty are pubic and underarm hair. The chest and shoulders broaden, the testes and penis enlarge, and the voice deepens. These changes are usually obvious by ages 13–15, and facial hair is usually well established by age 17.

Emotional changes during adolescence can be difficult and may strain family relationships unless communication is maintained. These emotional changes may cause insecurity, boredom, moodiness, and withdrawal, and lead to participation in high-risk activities. The serious health threats in the teenage years are injuries, suicide, sexually transmitted infections, and pregnancy.

DIET

Weight may double during adolescence due to increases in height, muscle development, and fat deposition. During puberty, teenagers require more calories in proportion to their body weight than at any other period in their lives apart from in infancy. Parents should therefore make sure that family meals are well balanced and healthy (*see* A HEALTHY DIET, p.48) and that healthy snacks are always available.

Many teenagers feel physically unattractive and are preoccupied with their appearance. This may develop into an obsession with food. About 1 in 100 teenagers, usually girls, suffers from an eating disorder such as anorexia nervosa (p.562) or bulimia (p.563).

EXERCISE

Aerobic activities, such as swimming or jogging, keep the cardiovascular, respiratory, and musculoskeletal systems in healthy condition if done regularly (*see* THE BENEFITS OF EXERCISE, p.55). Team sports also promote physical and psychological health and are a good way to make friends. Organized sports activities can teach your child the importance of dedication, discipline, and practice, and the skills required to work in a team.

PREVENTING ILLNESS

Many adolescents suffer from acne (p.340), a condition that is associated with increased hormone levels during puberty. Early treatment of the problem can prevent teenagers from losing their self-confidence and forming a negative self-image at a stage when peer relationships are paramount.

Parents should be alert to signs that show teenagers may be suffering from depression (p.554) or even feeling suicidal (*see* ATTEMPTED SUICIDE AND SUICIDE, p.556). Behavior changes in teenagers may also be a sign of drug abuse (*see* DRUGS AND HEALTH, p.65) or alcohol abuse (*see* ALCOHOL AND HEALTH, p.62). More bizarre personality changes or paranoia may be a sign of a serious psychiatric illness, such as schizophrenia (p.560).

Most schools provide education on alcohol, tobacco, and drugs, but it is vital that parents reinforce these messages at home and encourage teenagers to ask questions and discuss issues freely. Your child should be able to make safe, informed choices.

A SAFE ENVIRONMENT

Most adolescent deaths in Canada are caused by motor vehicle collisions, watersports accidents, and poisoning (including drug-related poisoning). Many of these deaths result from the participation in high-risk activities by teenagers, who often may believe that they are invulnerable to injury. Teenagers may be more likely to take precautions and steps to protect their health if they understand that seemingly harmless activities may put them, as well as others, in serious danger of death or injury.

The risk of a sports injury can be reduced by adequate physical conditioning and by using protective equipment (*see* EXERCISING SAFELY, p.59).

All teenagers need to be aware of the risks of drinking and driving (*see* SAFETY ON THE ROAD, p.83), whether as a driver or as a passenger, and should know how to use safety equipment, such as motorcycle helmets and car seatbelts.

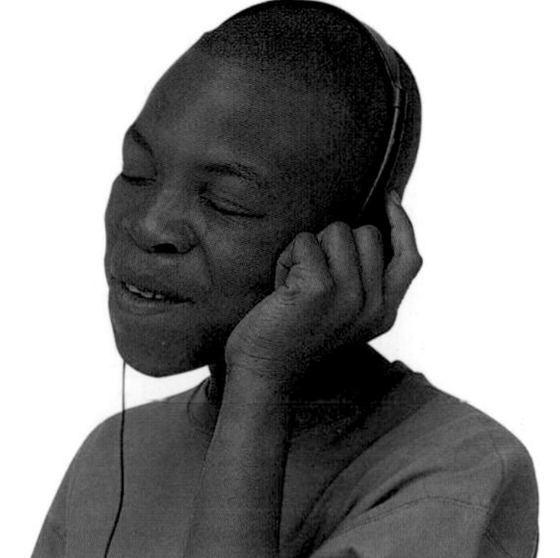

Loud music
*Teenagers should be warned that frequent listening to loud music may lead to permanent hearing loss (*see NOISE-INDUCED HEARING LOSS, p.601*).*

SEXUAL SAFETY

Canada has a high rate of teenage pregnancies. Most of these pregnancies are not planned and could be prevented by educating teenagers about safe sex and contraception (*see* SEX AND HEALTH, pp.67–71). There are many books and resources available to inform or reinforce conversations on these subjects. Books on sexual health should include information on homosexuality, sexual fantasies, and masturbation. Teenagers may also need information to explain how to use a condom in order to help prevent HIV infection (*see* HIV INFECTION AND AIDS, p.295), other sexually transmitted diseases, and pregnancy.

PSYCHOLOGICAL HEALTH

During adolescence, teenagers often experiment with friends, appearance, and behavior. Relationships between parents and teenagers change, and maintaining good communication can become difficult. Poor communication can make teenagers and their families feel powerless and frustrated. It is important to listen to each other and also to try to express your point of view without blame or judgment.

Teenagers should bear in mind that achieving independence does not mean cutting themselves off from others. It is important to know when and how to ask others for support. If it is not possible to discuss problems with parents, a grandparent, teacher, or counselor may be a source of guidance and support.

(WWW) ONLINE SITES: p.1028

Health in adults

Factors most likely to affect your health between the ages of 18 and 50

By age 25, all of your body systems have fully matured and should be in good condition. Toward the end of your 20s, the strength and bulk of your muscles start to decrease as part of the normal aging process. The strength and density of bone continue to increase steadily until your mid-30s but tend to decrease slowly after this time. However, early adulthood is usually the healthiest period of many people's lives.

Suicide and accidents are the greatest causes of death for adult men and women up to age 25. It has been found that women in their 30s and 40s are more likely to die from illness than from accidents, with breast cancer (p.759) being the leading single cause of death after age 40. The greatest risk to the health of young adult men is HIV infection (*see* HIV INFECTION AND AIDS, p.295), followed by accidents, suicide, and coronary artery disease (p.405). Before the age of 50, the most common cancer in men is cancer of the testis (p.719), but advances in treatment have led to most men with this type of cancer being cured by a combination of surgery and chemotherapy.

DIET

Try to eat a healthy diet (p.48). Eating less fat and more fiber protects against heart disease and may reduce your risk of developing colorectal cancer (p.665) in later life. Vitamins A, C, and E may help protect against cancer. To ensure an adequate intake, try to eat plenty of citrus fruits and vegetables, which contain large amounts of these vitamins.

EXERCISE

Any weight-bearing exercise, such as walking or running, slows down the deterioration of muscle and bone that is a normal part of aging (*see* THE BENEFITS OF EXERCISE, p.55). Heart disease and osteoporosis (p.368) are less likely to develop when you are older if you build up the strength of your skeleton while you are young.

It is important to maintain a regular exercise routine throughout your life (*see* DOING REGULAR EXERCISE, p.57). Research has shown that athletes who exercise vigorously when they are young but who stop completely when they are older are even less likely to stay healthy than those who have never exercised.

PREVENTING ILLNESS

In addition to modifying your diet and exercising regularly, you can reduce the chance of developing illnesses such as AIDS, cancer, and heart disease by changing other aspects of your lifestyle if they are not healthy. Safe sex (p.68) protects against HIV infection and, if you are female, may also lower your risk of cancer of the cervix (p.750).

If you are careful about exposure to the sun (*see* SAFETY IN THE SUN, p.80), you can significantly reduce the risk of developing skin cancer (p.344).

Heavy alcohol use (*see* ALCOHOL AND HEALTH, p.62) and smoking or chewing tobacco (*see* TOBACCO AND HEALTH, p.63) are risk factors for lung cancer (p.503), mouth cancer (p.634), stomach cancer (p.642), and cancer of the esophagus (p.638). Smokers are three times more likely to die of cancer than nonsmokers, and stopping smoking is the single most important preventive measure. Even if you have been a heavy smoker until your 40s, giving up significantly reduces your risk of cancer, coronary artery disease, and chronic obstructive pulmonary disease (p.487). A woman who stops smoking lowers her risk of developing Crohn's disease (p.658). You can also reduce your risk of heart disease and liver disease by reducing alcohol consumption.

A SAFE ENVIRONMENT

Men are 3–4 times more likely than women to be killed or injured in accidents, probably because men tend to take greater risks than women. For example, young men are more likely to drink and drive than are women.

Many sports and leisure activities, such as mountain climbing and skiing, carry risks. Before taking part in these activities, make sure you receive the correct training. You should avoid alcohol when driving and always take safety precautions (*see* VEHICLE SAFETY, p.84).

PSYCHOLOGICAL HEALTH

During this stage of your life, you may form a long-term relationship. Relationships are ideally loving and mutually supportive, but, if you are experiencing problems, it is important to communicate your feelings to your partner or a professional counselor (*see* YOUR PSYCHOLOGICAL HEALTH, p.72).

If you decide to have a baby, you will need to prepare mentally as well as physically (*see* HEALTH IN PREGNANCY AND AFTER CHILDBIRTH, right). If you and your partner have been trying to conceive for more than a year and have been unsuccessful, consult your doctor (*see* INFERTILITY, p.774).

Balancing family and work pressures
Maintaining the correct balance between the demands of home life and those of a job can often be difficult.

If you begin a job, you may encounter new forms of stress (p.74) in your workplace. Discussing problems with a colleague or friend may be helpful. Promotion and demotion may be stressful too, but you can reduce stress by preparing for changes in role. Allow yourself time to adjust to the new situation, and do not expect to grasp all the implications of a change immediately. If you still feel anxious, especially if you cannot establish any particular reason for having these feelings, you should consult a therapist or doctor (*see* MENTAL HEALTH DISORDERS, pp.551–565).

(WWW) ONLINE SITES: p.1034, p.1037

Health in pregnancy and after childbirth

Health during pregnancy and following the birth of your baby

Having a baby is a major life event, and you and your partner should make sure that both of you are emotionally prepared. You can influence the health of your unborn child by ensuring that you remain healthy both before and during pregnancy. Preparing for the birth and postnatal period can help you adapt more easily to rapid changes in your body and may make your pregnancy much more enjoyable (*see* PREGNANCY AND CHILDBIRTH, pp.778–809).

HEALTH BEFORE CONCEPTION

Ideally, you and your partner should see your doctor at least 3 months before you begin to try conceiving because the health of both parents affects the health of the child. For example, if either of you has a family history of genetic disease, there may be a risk of passing the disease to your child, in which case your doctor may suggest investigation and genetic counseling (p.270). Your doctor will advise you both to follow a healthy diet (p.48), not to smoke, and to avoid alcohol and drugs that could affect fertility and general health (*see* ALCOHOL, TOBACCO, AND DRUGS, pp.62–66).

Your doctor can check that you are immune to rubella (p.292) and not carrying a virus such as hepatitis B (*see* CHRONIC HEPATITIS, p.645) or HIV infection (p.295) that could affect your baby. To reduce the risk of neural tube defects (p.844), such as spina bifida, you should take at least 400 micrograms of folic acid daily, starting at least 3 months before you try to conceive. If you have a preexisting disease that could influence your pregnancy, such as asthma (p.483), it should be well controlled beforehand.

A HEALTHY PREGNANCY

Pregnant women can provide a healthy environment for their growing babies and make the pregnancy more comfortable by eating a nutritious diet and exercising regularly (*see* EXERCISE AND RELAXATION IN PREGNANCY, p.34).

DIET Pregnant women require about twice the amount of protein, iron, calcium, pantothenic acid, and folic acid from the diet as women who are not pregnant (*see* GOOD SOURCES OF VITAMINS AND MINERALS, p.52). A healthy diet that incorporates an extra 300 calories per day, plus 6–8 glasses of fluid, should provide recommended levels of most nutrients. You need to take daily supplements of folic acid until week 12 of pregnancy to reduce the risk of your child developing neural tube defects, since you are not likely to get enough folic acid in your diet. Many pregnant women also need to boost their intake of iron by taking iron supplements, but your doctor can advise you whether or not these are appropriate for you.

In order to protect your baby from the damaging effects of salmonellosis (*see* FOOD POISONING, p.629), listeriosis (p.300), or toxoplasmosis (p.307), you should avoid eating pâté, raw shellfish, foods that contain raw eggs, and unpasteurized food such as certain soft or blue-veined cheeses. Make sure that all poultry and meat are cooked until they are no longer pink inside and wash vegetables and salads thoroughly to remove soil. You can avoid contact with harmful organisms by wearing gloves when gardening and not touching cat litter boxes.

ALCOHOL, TOBACCO, AND DRUGS Fetal growth can be affected by alcohol, and, ideally, you should not consume alcoholic drinks during pregnancy. Tobacco smoking increases the risk of abnormalities, miscarriage (p.791), sudden infant death syndrome (p.820), and stillbirth (p.805), and it is therefore especially important that you and your partner do not smoke while you are pregnant. Consult with your doctor before taking any drugs, including over-the-counter preparations. If you take prescribed drugs for a disorder such as asthma (p.483) or epilepsy (p.524), in most cases the drugs are less harmful to the fetus than would be the effects of the uncontrolled disorder. Your doctor will advise you regarding your particular disorder.

RELATIONSHIPS Expectant parents may feel excited, nervous, or frightened by the prospect of having a baby. Men sometimes describe feelings of alienation because their partner's attention is focused on the baby. Sexual relationships often change too. Some couples experience an increase in libido, but, especially during the first 3 months, the nausea and fatigue a woman may experience may decrease her interest in sex. Some men find their partner's new shape disturbing or worry about hurting the baby during intercourse. It may help to experiment with different sexual positions in order to avoid putting too much pressure on the woman's uterus. Whatever your feelings about sex during pregancy, it is important to talk about them with your partner and to find mutually acceptable ways of showing your love for each other.

HEALTH ACTION EXERCISE AND RELAXATION IN PREGNANCY

Prenatal and other gentle exercises help keep you fit, prepare you for the physical demands of labor, and speed recovery after the birth. Relaxation exercises relieve stress and conserve energy to allow you to cope more effectively with labor.

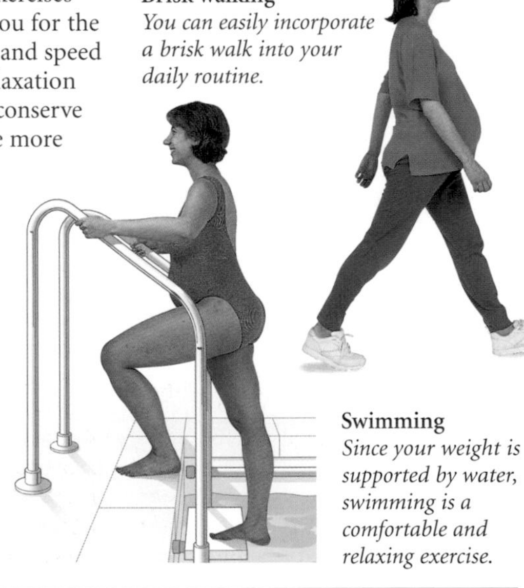

Brisk walking
You can easily incorporate a brisk walk into your daily routine.

EXERCISE

Try not to change your previous level of exercise during pregnancy. Keep exercising as usual if you feel comfortable, but be aware that you are now more vulnerable to injury. Drink lots of water and try not to push your heart rate over 140 beats per minute.

Swimming
Since your weight is supported by water, swimming is a comfortable and relaxing exercise.

PRENATAL EXERCISES

Exercises can help relieve some of the discomforts of pregnancy, such as backache, and in most cases are very beneficial for both mother and baby. For example, pelvic tilt exercises are an excellent way to improve posture. Prenatal exercise classes can teach you how to exercise safely.

Straight back

Knees slightly bent

Feet apart

Pelvic tilt exercises
Tighten your buttocks and tuck your pelvis under, then relax the buttocks and rock the pelvis back; repeat several times. Do this a number of times a day.

RELAXATION

Breathing and relaxation techniques, such as massage, can help you cope better with labor. Prenatal or yoga classes may teach you how to contract and relax muscle groups all over your body at will (*see* RELAXATION EXERCISES, p.75).

Massage
Massage can help you relax and can lessen pain during the early stages of labor.

PREPARING FOR THE BIRTH

Discuss with your doctor or midwife your concerns about the birth. Ask him or her about pain relief during labor and delivery. A birth plan may help clarify your expectations, but try to remain open-minded in case things do not go as planned during the birth.

If you plan to breast-feed, you can prepare for this during pregnancy by reading about it or attending classes. Breast milk has many advantages over formula for your baby (*see* FEEDING YOUR INFANT, p.28). The advantage for you is that the milk needs no preparation since it is already sterile and at the right temperature. In addition, the hormones your body produces during breast-feeding tighten up the uterus, helping you get back into shape after giving birth. Breast-feeding also reduces your long-term risk of breast cancer (p.759). Drawbacks include having to be available for feeding, unless you can express and store your milk, and having your sleep interrupted. Breast-feeding may be painful if you develop mastitis

Safe lifting during pregnancy
Bend your knees before lifting. Use your center of gravity to take the strain by holding heavy objects close to your body.

(p.809) or cracked nipples (p.808), but you can often prevent these problems (*see* AVOIDING CRACKED NIPPLES, p.809).

If you plan to return to work, you may choose to bottle-feed, using stored breast milk or formula for those times you are away from the baby. Bottle-feeding gives your partner an opportunity to bond closely with the baby. It is important to maintain good hygiene when preparing formula.

After the birth

Caring for a baby can be very demanding on your energy, patience, time, and finances. There is a lot to learn at a time when you may feel exhausted and uncomfortable. Most new mothers experience a few days of depression after childbirth (p.807). If your depression is severe or persistent, discuss it with your doctor or midwife. Although it may be difficult, try to take care of yourself by maintaining a healthy diet, exercising gently, and getting enough rest. Enlist the support of friends and family to help you. Be aware that the emotional upheaval a baby brings can put a strain on relationships with your partner and other children, who may feel left out.

Following the birth, the mother's vagina may be tender, especially after an episiotomy (*see* ASSISTED DELIVERY, p.805). Most doctors recommend waiting six weeks before resuming sexual intercourse. During this time, you can investigate different forms of contraception (p.69). If you were using a cap or a diaphragm before pregnancy, your doctor should check the fitting. If you want to use an intrauterine device, you should wait at least a month after the birth before having it inserted. The oral contraceptive pill can be taken while breast-feeding. Breast-feeding reduces fertility, but it is not a reliable method of contraception.

(WWW) ONLINE SITES: p.1036

Health in older adults

Taking care of your health between the ages of 50 and 70

You may notice the first signs of aging during your middle years, even if you are fit and healthy. Wrinkles and gray hair are common, and your face and extremities look thinner because fat moves to your trunk and abdomen. Your muscles lose some bulk and strength; your heart becomes less efficient; and blood vessels lose elasticity. Bones continue to decrease in size and density.

By age 50, "natural causes" begin to replace accidents as the major health threat. Cancer poses the greatest risk for women, followed by coronary artery disease (p.405) and stroke (p.532). For men, coronary artery disease is the greatest threat at this age, followed by cancer and accidents.

All cancers are more common with increasing age, but, if detected early, they may be treated successfully. Ensure that you undergo appropriate screening, such as tests for bowel or breast cancer (*see* COMMON SCREENING TESTS, p.44). Older men are more likely to develop primary lung cancer (p.503), prostate cancer (p.726), bladder tumors (p.715), colorectal cancer (p.665), stomach cancer (p.642), and mouth cancer (p.634). Older women are likely to develop lung cancer, breast cancer (p.759), cancer of the uterus (p.748), and colorectal cancer.

Aging is inevitable, but, by following a healthy lifestyle, you can maintain a good level of fitness and delay or minimize some of the associated changes. A diet low in fat, cholesterol, and salt can slow the deposition of fat on the walls of the arteries (*see* ATHEROSCLEROSIS, p.402), preventing coronary artery disease and stroke. Women may be able to prevent osteoporosis (p.368) by making sure that they get enough calcium in their diet (*see* HEALTH AT MENOPAUSE, p.36). Fiber and water should form a substantial part of everyone's diet to prevent constipation. A high intake of fruits and vegetables may also help reduce your risk of colorectal cancer.

Tooth care

Good dental hygiene can help prevent dental caries (p.609) and gingivitis (p.617). Gingivitis occurs in about 1 in 10 adults over age 45, and about half of those have inflammation of the tissues that support the teeth (*see* PERIODONTITIS, p.618). Before modern dentistry, losing teeth was considered an inevitable part of aging, but, today, many older people require only a partial denture or do not need one at all (*see* CROWNS AND REPLACEMENT TEETH, p.615).

Exercise

Regular exercise plays a major role in preventing coronary artery disease and stroke (*see* THE BENEFITS OF EXERCISE, p.55). Osteoarthritis (p.374), in which the protective cartilage at the ends of bone wears away, often begins during the middle years, but exercise can prevent stiffness and keep joints mobile. However, be aware that age-related bone and muscle loss makes you more susceptible to injury, even if you follow your usual exercise routine. If you have been inactive for a while, seek medical advice before starting to exercise (*see* EXERCISING SAFELY, p.59). Make sure that you have proper training and use appropriate protective equipment if you take part in risky leisure activities.

Preventing illness

By age 65, the efficiency of the immune system has started to decline in most people, increasing their vulnerability to infections and cancer. You will therefore be advised to have regular health checkups (p.40) during your middle years, and to review your immunization history (*see* IMMUNIZATION, p.45). You can reduce your risks of developing cancer and heart disease by not smoking and not drinking excessive amounts of alcohol. It is never too late to change bad habits and reap the health benefits (*see* HEALTH IN ADULTS, p.32).

By age 65, 9 in 10 people have difficulty focusing on nearby objects (*see* PRESBYOPIA, p.589). Many other treatable eye problems are more common

The joy of being a grandparent
As a grandparent, you can enjoy a child's company without the responsibilities associated with being a parent.

with increasing age, including glaucoma (p.575) and cataract (p.573). If such conditions are not detected, deteriorating vision could make activities such as driving dangerous. Many problems can be prevented by making sure that you have regular eye examinations.

Psychological health

Many people look forward to retiring during this time. Although this transition can be a rewarding experience, it can also generate feelings of isolation and loss. Preparing for retirement can help ease the way. Personal relationships can change significantly during these years, often because of illness or even death. Children may be reaching adulthood at the same time, possibly moving away from home and allowing more time and space in the family home. For many couples, this can also be a time to renew their own relationships and to rediscover old pastimes and shared experiences.

Sex can be more rewarding at this time of your life, although menopause may affect the lining of the vagina, making it feel dry (*see* MENOPAUSAL PROBLEMS, p.737), and men may find erections are less firm or long-lasting than in their youth. Although the frequency and prevalence of erectile dysfunction (p.770) does increase with advancing age, it is not an inevitable consequence of aging. Men who experience more than an occasional episode of erectile dysfunction should consult their doctor.

(WWW) ONLINE SITES: p.1026, p.1034, p.1037

Health at menopause

Health considerations at the time when a woman stops menstruating

Menopause is the stage in a woman's life when her menstrual periods stop because the ovaries no longer produce eggs or the hormone estrogen. Menopause usually takes place between the ages of 45 and 55 and may occur suddenly or take several years.

Some women experience unpleasant symptoms, but many have only mild problems or none at all. Common symptoms include fluid retention, aches and pains, hot flashes, night sweats, and mood swings, all of which are linked to fluctuating levels of hormones (*see* MENOPAUSAL PROBLEMS, p.737). Most of these symptoms are temporary, but others, such as vaginal dryness caused by decreased estrogen, may be permanent unless treated.

Before menopause, women have a lower risk of coronary artery disease (p.405) than men because estrogen has a protective effect. During menopause, the reduction in estrogen increases a woman's susceptibility to heart disease and speeds up the age-related process of osteoporosis (p.368), in which bones become brittle and more vulnerable to fracture.

You may also experience problems linked with the psychological impact of menopause and feelings about your changing fertility and sexuality.

Positive steps

The symptoms and risks that are associated with menopause can be greatly reduced by modifying your lifestyle. Hormone replacement therapy (p.937) or other drug treatment may be advisable for some women. Support from your friends and relatives can also help you cope better with menopause.

LIFESTYLE CHANGES Regular aerobic exercise, such as swimming and running, helps reduce the risk of heart disease. The earlier you start the better, but it is never too late. Stopping smoking (*see* TOBACCO AND HEALTH, p.63) and eating a healthy diet (p.48) also protect against heart disease.

You can delay the onset of osteoporosis by not smoking, keeping your alcohol intake within the recommended limits (*see* SAFE ALCOHOL LIMITS, p.62), and doing regular weight-bearing exercise, such as low-impact aerobics and walking. A calcium-rich diet is vital because it stimulates healthy bone growth and helps prevent the progression of osteoporosis. If your diet is not high in calcium, you may wish to take a daily supplement of 1,000–1,500 mg of calcium with added vitamin D.

DRUG TREATMENT You may consider hormone replacement therapy (HRT) to reduce symptoms such as hot flashes and vaginal dryness. HRT usually involves taking a combination of the female sex hormones estrogen and progestin. Estrogen boosts levels that have fallen during menopause, relieves symptoms, and reduces the rate of bone loss. Progestin is included in HRT because estrogen taken alone may increase your susceptibility to cancer of the uterus (p.748).

Treatment with HRT is usually continued while symptoms persist. Some women may be at an increased risk of developing breast cancer if they take HRT for 5 years or more. However, the prognosis for a woman diagnosed with breast cancer while taking HRT is better than that for someone who is not taking HRT. Talk to your doctor about the relative risks and benefits of HRT and how they apply to you.

Alternatives to HRT for bone protection are available, including drugs that imitate the action of estrogen, such as raloxifene. You may also modify your diet to include products of soybean, which contain isoflavones, chemicals (not estrogen) that have a weak estrogenic effect.

PSYCHOLOGICAL SUPPORT If you are experiencing psychological problems associated with menopause, it is important to talk about your feelings with your partner or with another woman who is also going through menopause. Relaxation (*see* RELAXATION EXERCISES, p.75) and other natural treatments may also help. If psychological problems persist, you should consult your doctor, who may prescribe antidepressant drugs (p.916).

(WWW) ONLINE SITES: p.1026, p.1037

Health in old age

Maintaining health and fitness when you are over age 70

Many people maintain good health and remain fit into old age. With fewer responsibilities and more leisure time, you can enjoy a high quality of life. However, some of the physical changes that started during your middle years continue. You may find that you are not able to move as quickly and easily as you used to. Recovery from illness and injury will take longer. Failing eyesight and hearing, urinary incontinence (p.710), an enlarged prostate gland (p.725) in men, and prolapse of the uterus and vagina (p.747) in women are common concerns among older people.

Serious health threats include accidents, heart disease, cancers of the respiratory, digestive, and genital tracts, stroke (p.532), pneumonia (p.490), and diabetes mellitus (p.687).

DIET AND EXERCISE

You should continue to follow a healthy diet (p.48) and drink plenty of water. You may find that you need more protein and fewer calories as you get older. If you have a specific disorder, such as diabetes mellitus, your nutritionist or doctor will be able to provide dietary advice. Making appropriate changes to your diet may add years to your life.

By age 75, up to 9 in 10 women have substantial bone loss (*see* OSTEOPOROSIS, p.368), making them vulnerable to fractures. To prevent bone thinning, eat plenty of calcium-rich foods, such as dairy products, and exercise regularly (*see* KEEPING PHYSICALLY ACTIVE, right).

PREVENTING ILLNESS

It is never too late to stop smoking, and doing so will prevent premature aging of many of the body's organs, in particular the skin, bones, lungs, and heart. Stopping smoking will also reduce your risk of developing heart disease and cancer. You should make sure that you have regular health checkups (p.40). It is also advisable at this stage of life to review your medicines with your doctor on a regular basis. This enables him or her to identify potential interactions between your prescribed drugs and any over-the-counter drugs you are taking.

HEALTH ACTION: KEEPING PHYSICALLY ACTIVE

It is important to stay active as you get older because it keeps you fit and delays problems associated with aging. Regular exercise improves strength, muscle tone, and coordination, increases your alertness and reaction time, and can help prevent falls. It is never too late to begin enjoying the benefits of regular exercise, as long as you do not strain yourself. You should try to exercise at least 3–4 times a week.

Gentle activity
Gardening and other gentle activities help keep you mobile and independent. Joining a club can also be a good way of meeting others with similar interests.

Walking
Even gentle exercise, such as walking at least 2 miles (3 km) each day, can significantly improve your health.

AVOIDING ACCIDENTS

Half of all people over 65 who are hospitalized after a fall never regain their independence. You can help prevent falls by getting up slowly to reduce feelings of faintness and using a cane or walker to help you keep your balance. Ask your doctor whether any of the drugs you are taking affect balance and coordination, and have your vision and hearing checked regularly because the eyes and ears help you maintain your balance. You can also make certain changes in your home to make it safer (*see* HOME SAFETY AND HEALTH, p.77).

As you age, it becomes more difficult for your body to adjust to changes in temperature. To prevent hypothermia (p.323), you should keep the room you are in at a temperature of 19°C (68°F), even if you do not feel cold.

PSYCHOLOGICAL HEALTH

As you get older, your memory may not be what it once was. Make sure that you continue to stimulate your intellect, perhaps by solving crossword puzzles, taking up a new hobby, or even learning a new language. More than 8 in 10 people over age 80 are free from dementia (p.535), a general impairment of intellect, memory, and personality. About half of all dementia cases are caused by Alzheimer's disease (p.536), a progressive disorder of the brain. You should seek medical advice if you are worried about possible memory loss.

By the time they reach age 75, more than 6 in 10 women and 3 in 10 men have lost their partners. Losing family and friends can be very difficult, sometimes leading to depression (*see* LOSS AND BEREAVEMENT, p.76). Seek medical advice if your feelings of depression continue. Losing a partner can also lead to feelings of isolation. Activities can make you feel less lonely and bored and may also provide opportunities to form a close bond or friendship with another person. The potential for fulfilling sexual relationships is no less at this age than it is at earlier stages of adulthood.

(WWW) ONLINE SITES: p.1026, p.1034, p.1037

Stimulating your mind
Learning to use a home computer can stimulate your mind and give you access to a wide range of interesting information.

HEALTH CARE THROUGHOUT LIFE

Until the mid-20th century, people consulted a doctor only when they were ill, injured, or pregnant. In the past 55 years, there has been an explosion in knowledge about the causes and prevention of disease. Today, more emphasis is placed on preventing disease and promoting health for as long as possible.

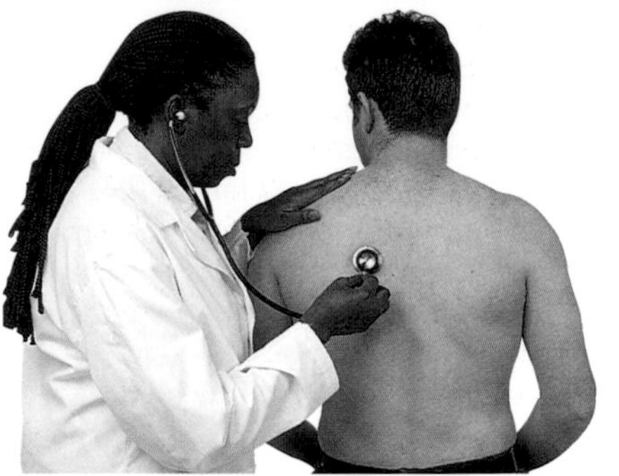

Having your health checked
Preventative health care involves seeing a doctor for checkups when in good health and having recommended screening tests.

Today's increased emphasis on preventing disease and promoting health means that people now need to develop an active partnership with their professional health-care providers. Taking charge of your health and taking part in health decisions is not only a right, it is also a responsibility. It is important for everyone to understand the available health-care options and to use them effectively. This section begins with an article on how health care is funded in Canada. The second article advises you on choosing a doctor and making the most of a visit to the doctor. This article also gives advice on assessing a potential doctor and practice. It is followed by a guide to periodic health checkups throughout life for infants, children, and adults.

The remaining articles cover two important aspects of preventive health care: screening, which helps doctors detect disorders at an early stage and identify risk factors that should be addressed, and immunization, a public health measure using vaccines that are designed to help you avoid previously common infectious diseases.

Universal health care

Comprehensive and accessible, government-funded health care is an integral part of Canadian life

For 3 decades, all Canadians have enjoyed a publicly funded health-care system, receiving care when they need it, not only when they can pay for it. The underlying philosophy of the system is that health is a public good and that the costs of treating illness should be broadly shared.

This system, called medicare, is made up of an interlocking set of 10 provincial and 3 territorial health insurance plans. Having these 13 single-payer health insurance plans, as opposed to many more privately funded plans, reduces administrative costs and provides more consistency and bargaining power in dealing with health-care providers and the health-care industry. The provincial and territorial governments are in charge of managing and delivering their health services, including providing hospital care, physician and allied health-care services, and some aspects of prescription care and public health. They help pay for medicare through tax dollars and, in the cases of British Columbia, Alberta, and Ontario, health-care premiums.

Medicare is national in that these 13 plans must all adhere to national principles set at the federal level (the *Canada Health Act*). In addition, the federal government contributes financially to the provincial and territorial health-care expenses. Through Health Canada, the federal government also strives to protect Canadians from health threats such as infectious disease, unsafe food and drugs, and environmental pollutants. In addition, it provides direct health services to certain groups including veterans, Aboriginal Canadians who live on reserves, military personnel, inmates of federal penitentiaries, and the Royal Canadian Mounted Police.

THE *CANADA HEALTH ACT*

This 1984 act of Parliament ties the whole system together by stipulating the standards the provincial and territorial health insurance plans must meet in order to qualify for federal money. These standards are mostly contained in the act's 5 principles of Canada's national health-care system.

PUBLIC ADMINISTRATION These health-care insurance plans must be operated and administrated on a nonprofit basis by a public authority, which is accountable to the provincial government.

COMPREHENSIVENESS The plan must insure all medically necessary services provided by hospitals, medical practitioners, and, where permitted, other health-care practitioners. Insured hospital services include in-patient care; all necessary drugs, supplies, and tests; and a broad range of outpatient services. Chronic-care services are also insured.

UNIVERSALITY The plan must cover 100 percent of the insured population (that is, all eligible residents).

PORTABILITY Residents who move to another province must continue to be covered for insured health services by the home province for up to three months.

ACCESSIBILITY The plan must provide reasonable access to insured hospital and physician services without barriers. Additional charges to insured patients for insured services are not allowed. No one may be discriminated against on the basis of income, age, or health status.

HOW DOES MEDICARE WORK?

When Canadians need medical care, they usually go to the doctor or clinic of choice and present their health insurance card. These primary care physicians are the gatekeepers to medicare, allowing

Canadians access to specialists, allied providers, hospital, testing, and prescription drug therapy. Canadians do not pay directly for insured hospital and physicians' services, nor pay deductibles.

Medicare is publicly funded, but doctors are not government employees. Most are private practitioners, paid a set fee by the government for each service provided. More than 95 percent of Canadian hospitals are private nonprofit entities. Canadians do pay for some health services such as drugs and dental; this varies between provinces. Many Canadians also have private plans covering some or all of these extra expenses.

How did medicare begin?

Medicare began in 1947 when Saskatchewan introduced a public insurance plan for hospital services. In 1956, the federal government offered to split the cost of hospital and diagnostic services with the provinces and territories; within 5 years, all had agreed to provide universal coverage for at least inpatient hospital care. In 1972, all the provincial and territorial plans included doctors' services. This was the birth of the national health insurance plan for hospital and medical care. For 20 years, the federal government paid about half of provincial expenditures on insured services, before switching to per capita cash transfers to provinces and territories.

Over the years, complaints of waiting lists, extra billing, and limited access have arisen. Health services reviews help address these concerns. These endeavors, and surveys and polls, confirm that medicare is considered integral to the national identity. It will surely continue to evolve to meet the needs of Canadians.

(WWW) ONLINE SITES: p.1032

You and your doctor

Finding the right doctor and maintaining good communication with him or her

Good health care should be a partnership between you and your doctor. Ideally, you should have easy access to the doctor, with no long delays. You should also feel comfortable discussing any aspect of your health and be confident that the doctor and his or her team will give you advice in an understandable way, as well as high-quality care.

Types of doctors

There are several categories of doctors. A family practitioner provides primary medical care for all members of the family. He or she organizes the ongoing maintenance of your health (*see* Health checkups, p.40; Screening, p.42; and Immunization, p.45) and will refer you to a specialist when necessary. Your doctor also provides follow-up care when you have been in the hospital. A pediatrician focuses on the care of children, a general internist diagnoses and treats the diseases of adults, and geriatricians specialize in the care of older people. Obstetrician-gynecologists are specialists in pregnancy, childbirth, and the female reproductive system.

Once referred to a specialist, you will remain under his or her care for that medical problem until the specialist refers you back to your family doctor. You can choose the specialist you wish to consult, or your family doctor will do so. A specialist may also be able to give you detailed advice on matters such as whether you need an operation.

You also need regular health checkups from other specialists, including eye examinations from an ophthalmologist and dental care from a dentist.

How to find a doctor

Choose a health-care provider who suits your particular health needs. If you have a choice, first obtain the names of possible doctors in your area. Sources of information range from the recommendations of family, friends, and colleagues at work to physician associations.

Choosing a doctor

Before you choose a doctor, it is important to find out as much as you can about potential candidates and their practices. Make a list of three or four suitable practices in your area. Find out if they are taking on new patients. Some practical considerations include the proximity of the practice to your home; whether it has suitable access for elderly or disabled people, if necessary; and whether the hospital with which it is affiliated is nearby. Inquire about practice hours, the office and appointments procedures, and whether it is possible to have same-day appointments if needed. Ask if the practice provides home visits, advice over the telephone, and emergency care. You may want to find out about other health professionals employed in the practice, such as nurses. Also consider whether you would like to see a man or a woman and if you prefer your doctor to be of a particular age. Find out as much as possible about the doctors in the practice, including their qualifications and whether they have any special medical interests, areas of expertise, and certifications. For example, if you have a chronic disease, such as diabetes mellitus (p.687), you may be able to find a practitioner with a special interest in diabetic care. On your first visit, decide whether you feel comfortable with the doctor and confident that you can agree on specific issues important to you.

Making the most of a visit

Your reason for visiting the doctor obviously influences the way a visit proceeds (*see* Visiting your doctor, p.216). For example, if you make an urgent visit with a sick baby, the focus will be on finding a cause for the problem. If you arrange a health checkup in advance, you will have more time to plan what you would like to discuss.

The key to getting the most from your doctor is good communication. Be honest with your doctor. Try to provide accurate information about your symptoms, past history, and lifestyle to help your doctor better understand your health needs. Your doctor should offer advice and health-care choices clearly so that you can be actively involved in improving your condition and maintaining good health. Do not be afraid to ask questions or raise issues.

(WWW) ONLINE SITES: p.1032

Communicating with your doctor
When you are comfortable and relaxed with your doctor, it is easier to discuss problems openly. You should always try to discuss important issues first.

ASSESSMENT GROWTH CHARTS FOR BABIES

During regular checkups in the first 2 years of life, a baby's growth is monitored by a doctor to detect problems at an early stage. Weight, length, and head circumference (measured around the largest part of the head) are plotted against the baby's age on growth charts. Your baby's growth curves can then be compared with the range of typical measurements for babies of the same age, shown as shaded bands on the charts. If a growth curve falls outside the shaded area or displays an erratic pattern, it indicates a possible problem.

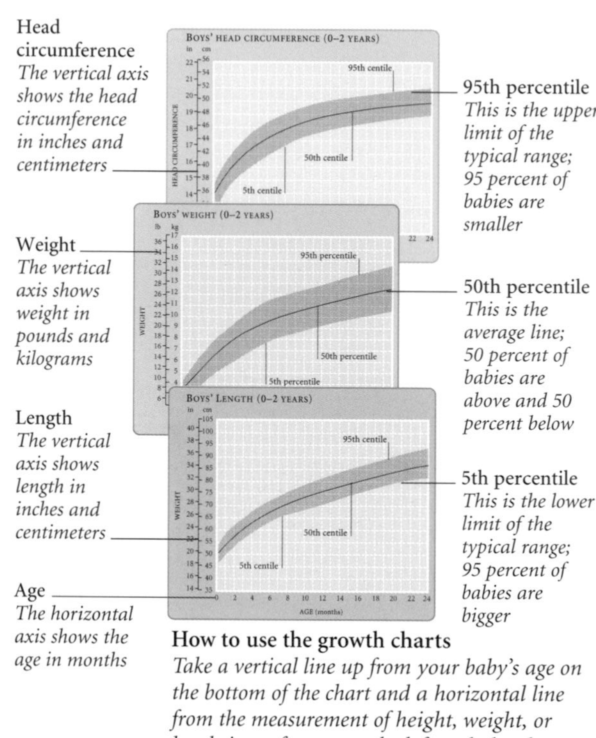
Head circumference
The vertical axis shows the head circumference in inches and centimeters
Weight
The vertical axis shows weight in pounds and kilograms
Length
The vertical axis shows length in inches and centimeters
Age
The horizontal axis shows the age in months
95th percentile
This is the upper limit of the typical range; 95 percent of babies are smaller
50th percentile
This is the average line; 50 percent of babies are above and 50 percent below
5th percentile
This is the lower limit of the typical range; 95 percent of babies are bigger

How to use the growth charts
Take a vertical line up from your baby's age on the bottom of the chart and a horizontal line from the measurement of height, weight, or head circumference on the left and plot the point at which they cross.

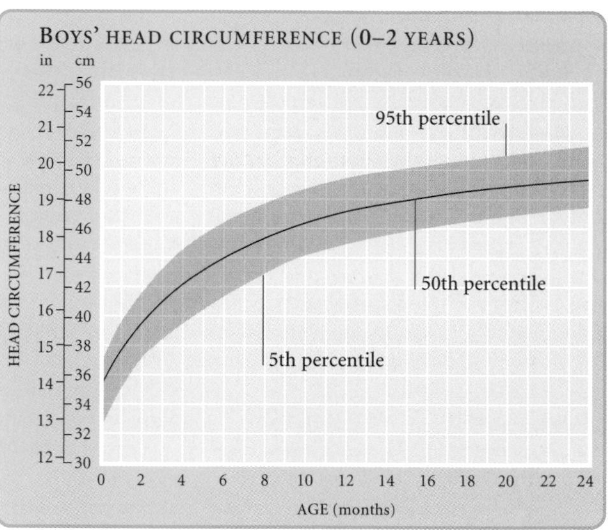
BOYS' HEAD CIRCUMFERENCE (0–2 YEARS)
in cm
HEAD CIRCUMFERENCE
95th percentile
50th percentile
5th percentile
AGE (months)

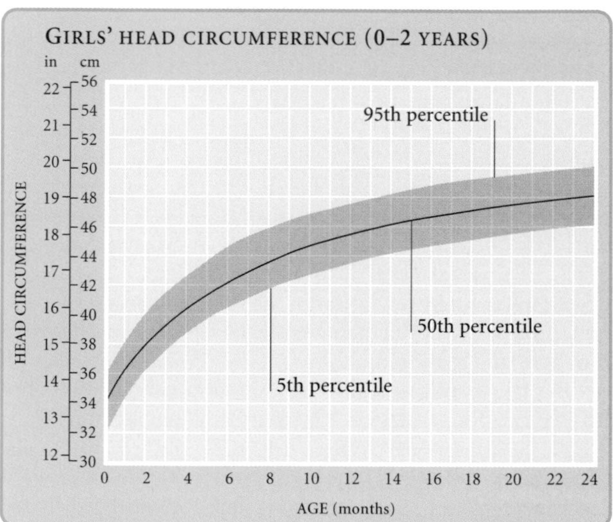
GIRLS' HEAD CIRCUMFERENCE (0–2 YEARS)
in cm
HEAD CIRCUMFERENCE
95th percentile
50th percentile
5th percentile
AGE (months)

Health checkups

Visits to your doctor to check your current state of health, identify potential problems, and find out how to improve your health

Health checkups provide you with regular opportunities to talk about your overall health with your doctor. They also give your doctor a chance to monitor factors that might increase your risk of disease and help you plan ways to modify them. They also enable the doctor to detect early signs of disease.

The kind of checkups you need and their frequency change over your lifetime. Babies and children have frequent checkups, which are used to monitor their growth and development of their physical and intellectual skills. During adulthood, checkups become less frequent, although women require regular tests during pregnancy and further checkups at menopause. In middle age and beyond, health checkups are used increasingly to detect the early stages of diseases that are known to be more common later in life, such as colorectal cancer and, in women, breast cancer (*see* COMMON SCREENING TESTS, p.44).

Checkups become more frequent in old age and tend to focus on making sure that elderly people are able to function as well as possible.

Generally, health checkups include an initial assessment, during which you are asked about lifestyle factors that influence your health; a physical examination; and finally a discussion with your doctor about the findings from the checkup. During this discussion you are given advice and have the opportunity to ask questions.

INITIAL ASSESSMENT

Before your first visit, your doctor may ask you to complete a questionnaire about your medical history and lifestyle or on that of your child if he or she is having a checkup. Your doctor may use the questionnaire as a starting point for

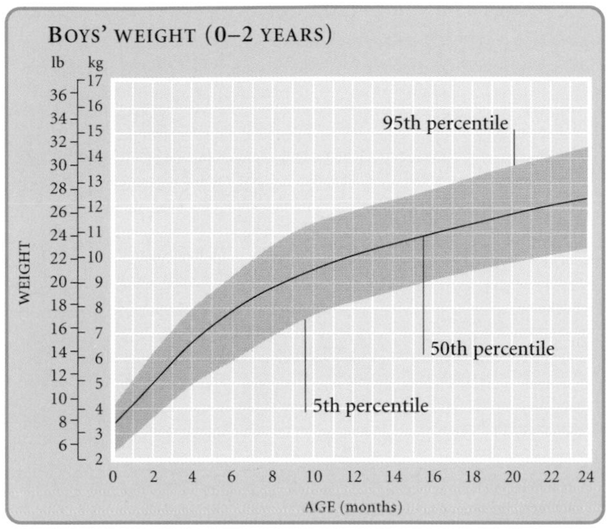
BOYS' WEIGHT (0–2 YEARS)
lb kg
WEIGHT
95th percentile
50th percentile
5th percentile
0 2 4 6 8 10 12 14 16 18 20 22 24
AGE (months)

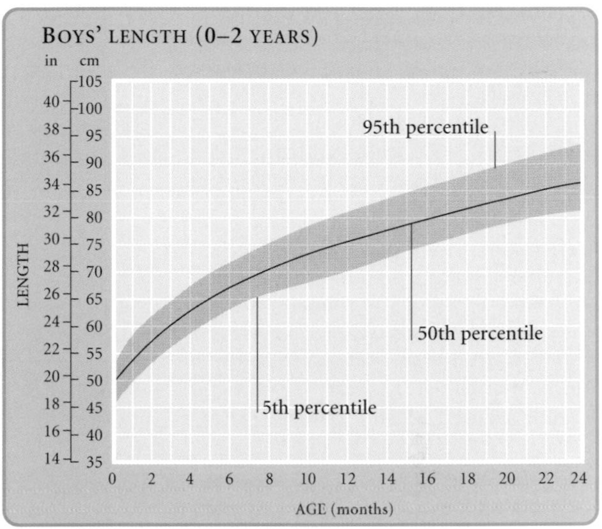
BOYS' LENGTH (0–2 YEARS)
in cm
LENGTH
95th percentile
50th percentile
5th percentile
0 2 4 6 8 10 12 14 16 18 20 22 24
AGE (months)

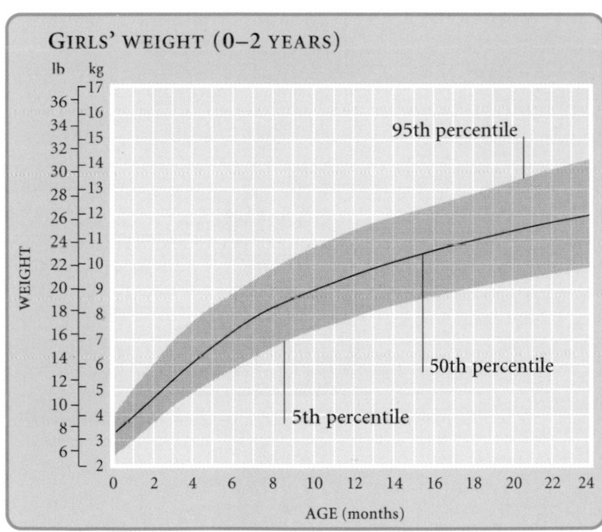
GIRLS' WEIGHT (0–2 YEARS)
lb kg
WEIGHT
95th percentile
50th percentile
5th percentile
0 2 4 6 8 10 12 14 16 18 20 22 24
AGE (months)

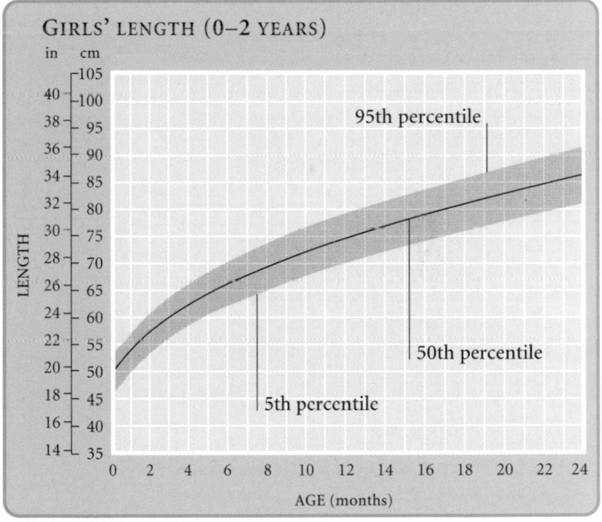
GIRLS' LENGTH (0–2 YEARS)
in cm
LENGTH
95th percentile
50th percentile
5th percentile
0 2 4 6 8 10 12 14 16 18 20 22 24
AGE (months)

asking further questions during the visit. Your doctor may ask for information about your diet, work, personal relationships, the amount of alcohol you drink, the amount of exercise you do, and whether or not you smoke. He or she will also make sure that you are up to date with immunizations (p.45) and screening tests appropriate for your age and gender (*see* SCREENING, p.42).

PHYSICAL EXAMINATION

Different physical examinations carried out over your lifetime are designed to check for healthy growth, development, and/or function and to detect problems more common at different ages.

INFANTS AND CHILDREN All newborn babies have a full, structured examination within 24 hours of birth to identify potential problems. For example, the doctor will listen to the baby's heart to detect irregularities and will check the eyes for abnormalities such as cataracts (p.573). Subsequent checkups are carried out regularly by a doctor to ensure that the child's physical, social, and intellectual development is following the predicted pattern. Although the exact age at which children reach certain developmental milestones varies, the doctor will check that the child has gained certain skills within predicted age ranges. These include gross motor skills, such as the ability to sit up; fine motor skills, such as picking up a small object; and social skills, such as talking. In addition, your doctor will test your child's hearing and vision.

Physical growth is monitored by taking measurements of a baby's weight and length as well as head circumference, which is an accurate indicator of general growth during the first 2 years. Growth charts (*see* GROWTH CHARTS FOR BABIES, above) are used to record these measurements.

Throughout childhood, the doctor will continue to monitor your child's growth, general development, and physical and social skills so that any problems in these areas can be detected promptly. Measuring height and weight is an essential part of these examinations. You may also want to keep your own record of your child's growth to show to the doctor (*see* GROWTH CHARTS FOR CHILDREN, right).

ADULTS During physical examinations in adult life, your doctor measures your height and weight to make sure that you are within a healthy range (*see* ARE YOU A HEALTHY WEIGHT?, p.53). Excess weight is a risk factor for several disorders, especially atherosclerosis (p.402), in which arteries are narrowed by fatty deposits. Women who are underweight may have reduced fertility (*see* FEMALE INFERTILITY, p.775), and, in either sex, being underweight increases the risk of osteoporosis (p.368) in later life.

In addition, the doctor will carry out a detailed assessment of various body systems and organs, such as the heart and lungs (*see* PHYSICAL EXAMINATION, p.219). He or she may also check your blood pressure and blood cholesterol level (*see* BLOOD CHOLESTEROL TESTS, p.231) and arrange for you to have blood and urine tests to look for factors that may increase your risk of disease.

As you grow older, physical examinations are used to detect the early stages of disease and assess aspects of health important to your future independence. Your doctor may test your muscle strength and coordination to check your mobility and assess your hearing, vision, and mental health.

DISCUSSION AND ADVICE

Using information from your history and physical examination, your doctor can suggest ways to improve or maintain your health. You can discuss your health concerns with your doctor and review medications that you are taking. Your doctor may suggest preventive treatments, such as taking a folic acid supplement to reduce the risk of neural tube defects (p.844) in the fetus if you are planning a pregnancy.

You may have further tests if your doctor thinks there are risk factors for a disease associated with your lifestyle, family history, or occupation, or with travel abroad. Tests may also be needed if you have a chronic health problem.

(WWW) ONLINE SITES: p.1032

(ASSESSMENT) GROWTH CHARTS FOR CHILDREN

Growth charts are used to record a child's growth from 2 to 18 years. The doctor measures your child's weight and height during regular health checkups and plots them against age on a chart. Your child's growth curve can then be compared with the typical range, represented by the shaded part of the chart, for all children of the same age. You may also want to measure and record your child's growth at more frequent intervals yourself.

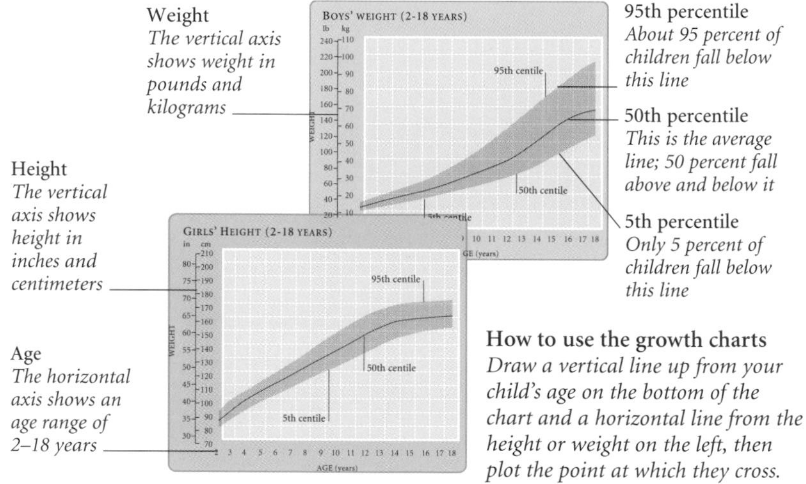
Weight
The vertical axis shows weight in pounds and kilograms
BOYS' WEIGHT (2-18 YEARS)
95th centile
50th centile
95th percentile
About 95 percent of children fall below this line
50th percentile
This is the average line; 50 percent fall above and below it
5th percentile
Only 5 percent of children fall below this line
Height
The vertical axis shows height in inches and centimeters
GIRLS' HEIGHT (2-18 YEARS)
95th centile
50th centile
5th centile
AGE (years)
Age
The horizontal axis shows an age range of 2–18 years

How to use the growth charts
Draw a vertical line up from your child's age on the bottom of the chart and a horizontal line from the height or weight on the left, then plot the point at which they cross.

MEASURING YOUR CHILD

To measure your child's height, ask the child to stand up straight, with his or her back against a wall or door. Lower a book onto your child's head and mark where the base of the book meets the wall. Measure the distance from this mark to the floor using a lockable metal tape measure. If you weigh your child on bathroom scales, make sure that they are accurate and standing on a flat, hard surface.

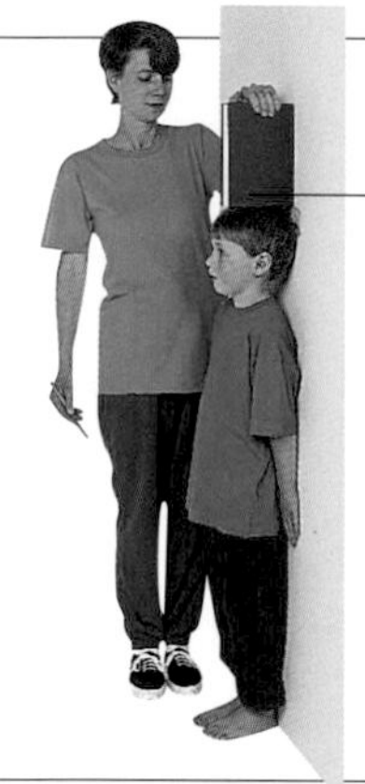

Marker guide
To get an accurate measurement, use a book or cereal box as a guide

Measuring height
Make sure your child is barefoot and is standing up straight.

Screening

Preventive health care aimed at detecting disease or risk factors for a disease before symptoms develop

Screening is an important element of preventive medicine. Screening tests are used to detect risk factors associated with disease, to make an early diagnosis of a treatable condition, or to find out if you have an abnormal gene that could cause a disorder in your children.

Throughout your life, you will be offered various screening tests. Before agreeing to a test, you should find out from your doctor what it involves, whether it carries any risks, and how reliable it is. You will also want to consider the implications of certain test results. For example, no form of test is completely accurate, and, sometimes, a screening test can miss disease or suggest disease when it may not be present. Abnormal results also frequently lead to additional investigation for which you might not be prepared.

WHAT CAN BE SCREENED FOR?

It is not possible or even worthwhile to screen for every risk factor or disease. Screening tests are useful only if the disease or risk factor they detect can be treated and if early treatment has been

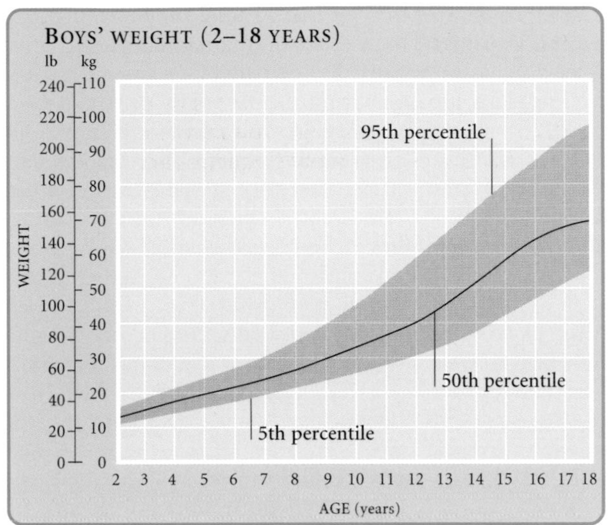
BOYS' WEIGHT (2–18 YEARS)
lb kg
WEIGHT
95th percentile
50th percentile
5th percentile
AGE (years)

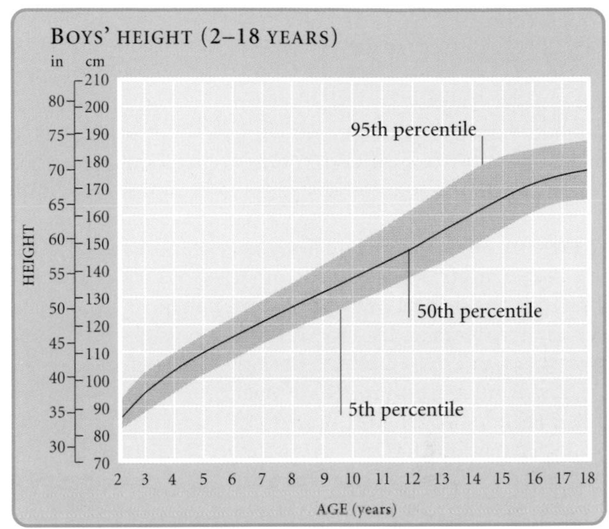
BOYS' HEIGHT (2–18 YEARS)
in cm
HEIGHT
95th percentile
50th percentile
5th percentile
AGE (years)

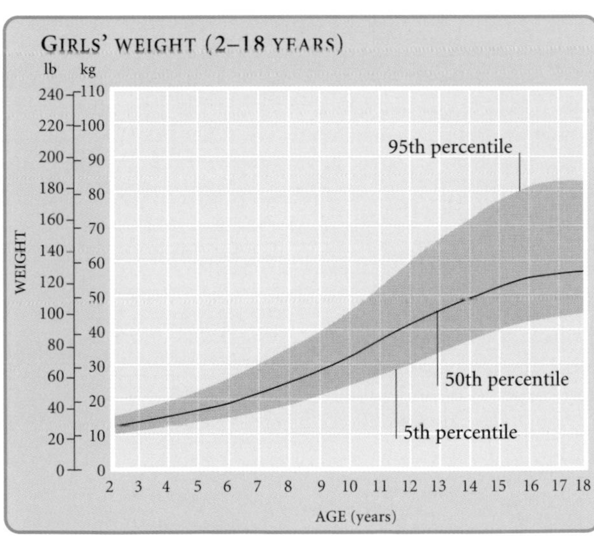
GIRLS' WEIGHT (2–18 YEARS)
lb kg
WEIGHT
95th percentile
50th percentile
5th percentile
AGE (years)

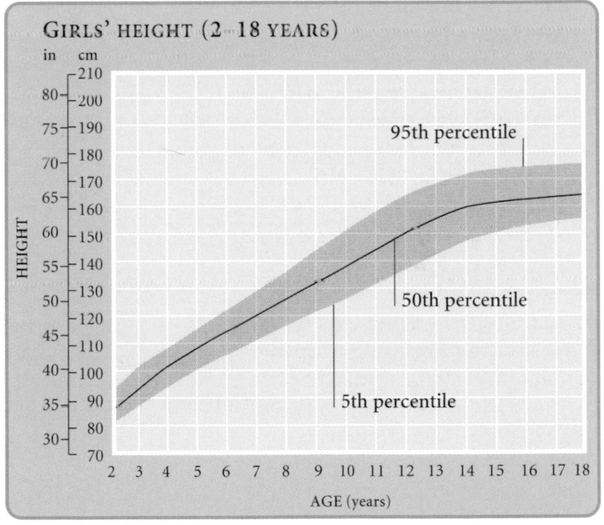
GIRLS' HEIGHT (2–18 YEARS)
in cm
HEIGHT
95th percentile
50th percentile
5th percentile
AGE (years)

shown to be beneficial. For example, it is useful to screen for high blood pressure, a risk factor for stroke and heart disease, because it can be reduced by lifestyle changes or medical treatment.

WHY PEOPLE ARE SCREENED

Only a few screening tests, such as eye examinations, are necessary for everyone, although many tests are offered to most adults (*see* COMMON SCREENING TESTS, p.44). You may be offered other tests if you have a higher than normal risk of developing a disorder due to factors such as family history of disease, age, or a pre-existing chronic disease that increases the risk of other disorders.

STAGE OF LIFE Your risk of developing certain disorders depends on what age you are. For this reason, the types and frequency of screening tests that your doctor may recommend to you will change as you grow older. Women are offered specific programs of screening during pregnancy (*see* ROUTINE PRENATAL CARE, p.786), when they are tested regularly for conditions that can be damaging to either the mother or the baby, such as diabetes mellitus (p.687) or preeclampsia (*see* PREECLAMPSIA AND ECLAMPSIA, p.794). In addition, the fetus may be screened for abnormalities that may require treatment after birth, such as heart disorders.

INHERITED DISORDERS There are several disorders, including abnormally high blood levels of cholesterol and other lipids (*see* INHERITED HYPERLIPOPROTEINEMIAS, p.692), colorectal cancer (p.665), and breast cancer (p.759), that have been demonstrated to run in families. If any members of your family have been affected by one of these disorders, your doctor may recommend that you undergo screening tests to look for early disease. In some cases, such as the occurrence of breast cancer at a young age in more than one member of your family, the doctor may suggest that you have a genetic screening test (*see* TESTS FOR ABNORMAL GENES, p.239).

CHRONIC CONDITIONS If you have a long-term medical condition, you may be offered regular screening to detect early signs of complications. For example, people who have diabetes mellitus are routinely screened to look for kidney disease, nerve damage, and problems in the blood vessels of the eye, which, if they are not treated, may eventually result in blindness.

HAZARDOUS OCCUPATIONS There are some occupations, such as those that expose workers to dust or toxic chemicals, that may increase the risk of some diseases. For example, bladder tumors (p.715) are more common in rubber workers than in the general population. If your occupation increases your susceptibility to a disease, make sure that you take appropriate safety measures (*see* SAFETY AND HEALTH AT WORK, p.82) and take part in screening programs offered by your employer.

WHO CARRIES OUT SCREENING?

Most screening is carried out by your usual health-care provider as part of routine health checkups. However, it may be necessary for your doctor to refer you to specialists for certain tests, such as sigmoidoscopy, in which a small viewing instrument is inserted into the rectum and lower colon in order to check for any abnormalities (*see* COLONOSCOPY, p.661).

You can screen yourself regularly for some health problems. Self-screening includes breast examination (p.755), examining your testes (p.720), and inspecting your skin for signs of skin cancer (p.344). If during self-screening you detect a sign of a possible abnormality, always discuss it as soon as possible with your doctor. If you are concerned about a health risk, consult your doctor, who will arrange for you to have appropriate tests. He or she will then interpret the results of the tests and will advise you about any further tests that you should have.

YOUR TEST RESULTS

Some tests, such as those for metabolic disorders in children (*see* SCREENING FOR METABOLIC DISORDERS, p.867), produce a clear positive or negative result that does not usually require further investigation. The results of other tests may not be as easy to interpret.

If your test results are negative, no further action may be needed until the next screening test is due. No screening test is 100 percent accurate, and on rare occasions a disorder may be present even though test results were negative. When this happens, the result is called a false-negative. In some cases, the disease could have developed soon after the test took place. Therefore, if symptoms of a disease become apparent, even after a test has proved negative, always consult your doctor for advice about whether further action should be taken. In most cases, regular repeated screening should pick up diseases before symptoms develop.

If your test result is positive, your doctor may want you to do the test again or may arrange for additional investigations to confirm the result and perhaps provide more information. For example, the results of a breast X-ray (*see* MAMMOGRAPHY, p.759) may reveal an abnormality. However, an additional test, in which a sample of cells is collected using a needle and syringe (*see* ASPIRATION OF A BREAST LUMP, p.756), may be necessary to find out if the abnormality represents cancer.

(WWW) ONLINE SITES: p.1032

(ASSESSMENT) COMMON SCREENING TESTS

Apart from the screening test for babies, all of the tests to detect common disorders in this table are offered routinely during health checkups for adults. You may be offered tests more frequently or at an earlier age than usual if your family history or lifestyle places you at a higher risk of developing a disease. The use of other tests depends on individual circumstances. Recommendations vary among professional organizations.

Tests at different ages
Most tests to detect early signs of disease begin in adulthood. Additional tests are introduced after age 50.

SCREENING TEST	WHEN TEST IS DONE	WHAT IT SCREENS FOR	WHAT IT INVOLVES
Heel prick blood test (*see* SCREENING FOR METABOLIC DISORDERS, p.867)	Shortly after birth	Two metabolic disorders: hypothyroidism (p.680), phenylketonuria (p.867)	Analysis of a blood sample taken from the heel
Blood pressure measurement (p.404)	After age 21	High blood pressure (*see* HYPERTENSION, p.403)	Measurement of blood pressure
Blood cholesterol tests (p.231)	Every 5 years from age 40 for males, age 50 for females	High cholesterol (*see* HYPERCHOLESTEROLEMIA, p.691)	Analysis of a blood sample
Pap test (p.749)	From first sexual activity, at regular intervals	Cancer of the cervix (p.750)	Microscopic analysis of cells scraped from the cervix
Sigmoidoscopy (*see* COLONOSCOPY, p.661)	As advised by your doctor	Colorectal cancer (p.665)	Inspection of the sigmoid colon and rectum through an endoscope
Fecal occult blood (p.233)	As advised by your doctor	Colorectal cancer	Analysis of a stool sample
Mammography (p.759)	In women, every 2 years from age 50	Breast cancer (p.759)	Breast X-rays

Immunization

A method of producing artificial immunity to infectious diseases, usually involving a course of injections

Immunization is a way of boosting the body's defenses against infectious diseases. Infectious organisms that cause disease enter the body by direct contact with another person's skin or blood or by sexual contact. They also spread from person to person in food, water, or air.

When you are immunized, a vaccine containing a small amount of a weakened or an inactivated form of the disease-causing organism is introduced into your body. This will stimulate your immune system to produce antibodies that protect against the disease (*see* VACCINES AND IMMUNOGLOBULINS, p.883) if you are exposed to the organism in the future. Most vaccines are given by injection, although a few, such as poliomyelitis, can be given orally. For most immunizations, several injections are given over a period of months or years to build up adequate protection.

Timing of immunizations

Most routine immunizations (right) are given during infancy and childhood in accordance with an accepted immunization schedule. People at particular risk, due to the nature of their work or travel, may be offered additional immunizations in adulthood. Keep records of all your immunizations and those of your children in case a doctor needs to know about your immune status.

CHILDHOOD PROGRAM Immunizations are given to babies during their first year, when infectious diseases are likely to be serious. Although a baby is naturally protected from some diseases by antibodies that pass through the placenta during pregnancy, this immunity wears off about 6 months after birth. Premature babies are always immunized because they are at high risk of serious illness if they develop an infection.

In addition, it is possible to give a rotavirus vaccine to protect babies from gastroenteritis (p.628) in their first year. It is important that bottle-fed babies are protected because they lack protective antibodies provided by breast milk (*see* FEEDING YOUR INFANT, p.28).

HEALTH ACTION Routine immunizations

Immunizations give protection against several infectious diseases and are scheduled during childhood. Rotavirus immunization to protect against gastroenteritis is being introduced but is not routine. Routine immunization schedules may vary. Always consult your doctor.

Routine schedule
Timing of immunizations can be adjusted if some doses are missed. Most immunizations are given by injection.

Disease	Doses	Timing
Hepatitis B	3 doses	Optional. May be started at birth. A routine vaccination in some provinces' school systems
Diphtheria, tetanus, pertussis (DTP)	5 doses	Doses 1, 2, and 3 at about 2, 4, and 6 months; dose 4 at about 18 months; dose 5 at 4–6 years
Poliomyelitis	5 doses	Given in combination with DTP
Tetanus, pertussis, and diphtheria (Td)	1 dose	At 14–16 years and then every 10 years
H. influenzae type b	4 doses	Doses 1, 2, and 3 at about 2, 4, and 6 months; dose 4 at about 18 months. Given with DTP
Measles, mumps, rubella (MMR)	2 doses	Dose 1 after 12 months; dose 2 at 4–6 years
Chickenpox	1 dose	After 12 months
Pneumococcal	4 doses	Doses 1, 2, and 3 at about 2, 4, and 6 months; dose 4 at 12–15 months
Meningococcal c	1, 2, or 3 doses	Infancy or adolescence

Pre-school children must complete a full schedule of immunizations. If a child has missed some or started the program late, the schedule can be adjusted. Provinces provide free immunizations for children.

SPECIAL CIRCUMSTANCES Adults who have completed their childhood schedule of immunization may occasionally need to have a booster (additional dose) in special circumstances. If your work exposes you to specific risks, you and your employer should make sure that you have the appropriate immunizations. For example, farm laborers may need to be up to date in their immunization against tetanus (p.301).

Influenza (p.287) and pneumococcal pneumonia (p.490) can be serious disorders, particularly in people over age 65 or in those with reduced immunity because of chronic conditions such as diabetes mellitus (p.687) or HIV infection and AIDS (p.295). Both children and adults in these high-risk groups are offered immunization against these diseases.

You may need extra immunizations if you are visiting a country that has a high incidence of infectious diseases, such as yellow fever, typhoid, hepatitis A or B, or tuberculosis (*see* TRAVEL IMMUNIZATIONS, p.86). Discuss your travel plans and possible immunizations with your doctor well ahead of your travel date.

Risks of immunization

Immunizations have few side effects, although there may be some inflammation around the injection site or a mild fever. If you have any reactions to initial doses, tell your doctor so that he or she can advise you about subsequent doses. Ask your doctor if there are any factors that put you or your child at a higher risk of side effects. Generally, the risks of immunization are far less dangerous than having the disease itself.

Homeopathic vaccines have been shown to be ineffective. If you rely on them, you could be putting yourself or your children at risk.

(WWW) ONLINE SITES: p.1028, p.1033, p.1037

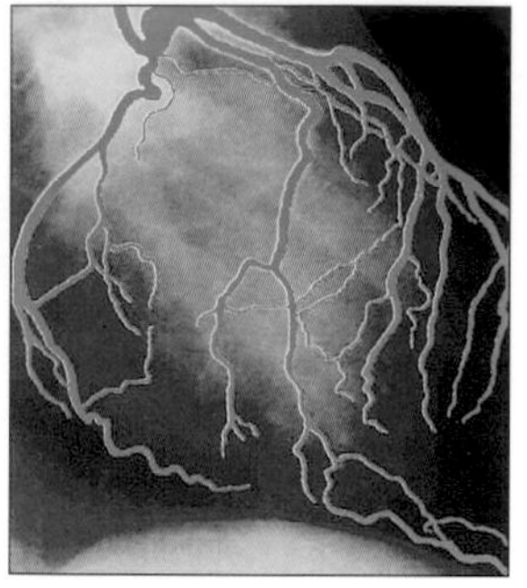

Healthy heart
Lifestyle factors such as diet can affect the coronary arteries and thus the health of your heart.

LIFESTYLE AND HEALTH

YOUR HEALTH IS INFLUENCED by two major factors: your genetic makeup, which determines your predisposition to disease, and your lifestyle. You cannot change inherited factors, but you can adapt your behavior to control your risk of disease or injury. You have some control over what you eat and drink and whether you smoke, exercise, or practice safe sex. Your lifestyle choices affect your present and future health.

Life expectancy has risen dramatically over the last century because of improvements in public health. However, one-quarter of Canadians still die before age 65, often from chronic diseases such as cancer or heart disease. You can reduce your risk of developing chronic disease by adopting a healthy lifestyle.

UNDERSTANDING THE RISKS

It is important to be aware of the lifestyle factors associated with chronic disease so that you can make informed choices. For example, tobacco smoking is a critical factor in one-third of all deaths from cancer. Several lifestyle factors, including smoking and a high-fat diet, are known to contribute to the development of heart disease.

To make informed decisions about health, you need to take into account your individual circumstances when assessing health priorities. Your doctor can help you do this. Your age is one of the most important factors to consider and greatly influences the lifestyle decisions you need to make. For example, young adults are statistically more likely to experience illness or injury associated with risk-taking behavior, such as reactions to drugs or sexually transmitted diseases, than they are to suffer ill health due to chronic disease. If you have a dangerous occupation, such as construction work, paying close attention to safety could be the most important factor in protecting your health in the short term. Nevertheless, it is important to recognize that some lifestyle choices, such as tobacco smoking, do not carry an immediate and obvious threat but can ultimately cause serious damage (*see* ASSESSING HEALTH RISKS, left).

ASSESSMENT ASSESSING HEALTH RISKS

Some activities are clearly dangerous, such as hang-gliding, and carry a significant risk every time you do them. For other types of behavior, the risks to health may not be as obvious. Eating one high-fat meal does not damage your health, but consistently including too much fat in your diet may increase your risk of developing heart disease over time.

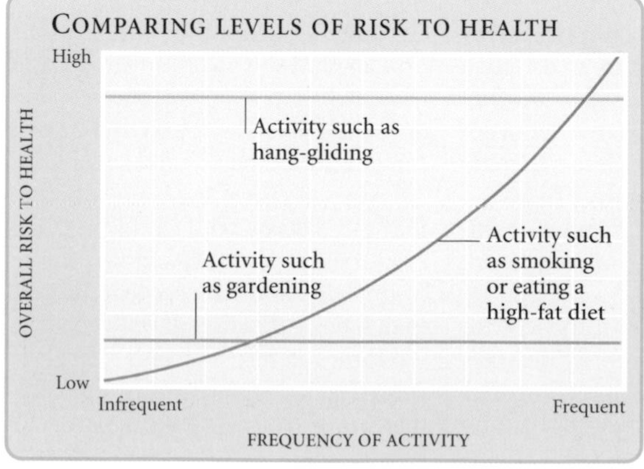
COMPARING LEVELS OF RISK TO HEALTH
High
Low
OVERALL RISK TO HEALTH
Activity such as hang-gliding
Activity such as gardening
Activity such as smoking or eating a high-fat diet
Infrequent
Frequent
FREQUENCY OF ACTIVITY

Cumulative risk
Some activities, such as gardening, carry the same risk each time you do them. With other activities, such as smoking, the risk tends to be cumulative; they are likely to damage your health only if the behavior is carried out repeatedly over a period of time.

MAKING LIFESTYLE CHANGES

Most health habits, such as food choices and doing exercise, are formed in our families when we are children. Giving children a healthy lifestyle from birth maximizes their chances of growing into healthy adults and establishes habits that they may find easier to maintain in later life. Some families may find it difficult to make healthy lifestyle choices. For example, they may not be able to afford good food or housing. However, everyone can do something to improve health.

The first step toward a healthier lifestyle is to look closely at your usual behavior to identify activities that pose significant risks to health. It is easier to change these activities if you can see immediate benefits. Long-term changes, such as giving up smoking, increasing the amount of exercise you do, or changing your diet, are often more difficult to make and maintain, especially if they involve overcoming social pressure. You may need to seek support from family, friends, and health professionals.

(HEALTH OPTIONS) MAKING LIFESTYLE CHOICES

All aspects of life, including work, travel, home, and leisure, carry risks and benefits to health. These risks differ among individuals. For example, a high-fat diet may be more harmful for a man over age 45 than for a young girl. You need to balance the risks and benefits of your lifestyle choices so that you can enjoy life while staying healthy.

Work and travel
Some occupations, such as construction work, carry a much greater risk of injury than sedentary occupations. Your method of transportation also involves specific health benefits and risks.

Home
Activities that take place in the home, such as eating, sleeping, and being with your family, have a major influence on physical and mental health. As children, we learn healthy or unhealthy habits in the home environment.

Leisure
You should consider the health benefits and risks of different activities when deciding how to spend your free time. Sports, hobbies, and socializing can all benefit your physical and mental health, but some carry risk of injury or harm.

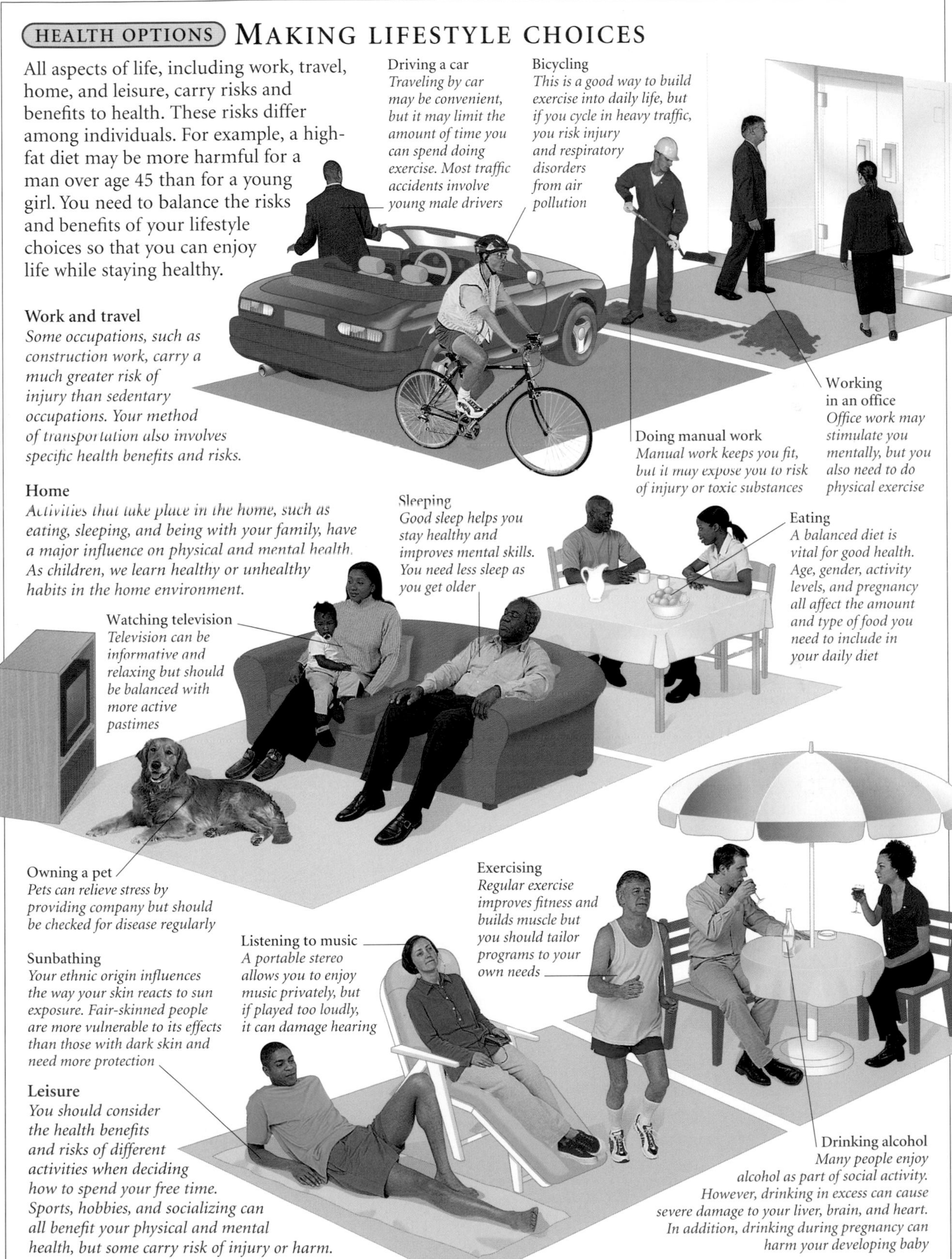
Driving a car
Traveling by car may be convenient, but it may limit the amount of time you can spend doing exercise. Most traffic accidents involve young male drivers
Bicycling
This is a good way to build exercise into daily life, but if you cycle in heavy traffic, you risk injury and respiratory disorders from air pollution
Working in an office
Office work may stimulate you mentally, but you also need to do physical exercise
Doing manual work
Manual work keeps you fit, but it may expose you to risk of injury or toxic substances
Sleeping
Good sleep helps you stay healthy and improves mental skills. You need less sleep as you get older
Eating
A balanced diet is vital for good health. Age, gender, activity levels, and pregnancy all affect the amount and type of food you need to include in your daily diet
Watching television
Television can be informative and relaxing but should be balanced with more active pastimes
Owning a pet
Pets can relieve stress by providing company but should be checked for disease regularly
Exercising
Regular exercise improves fitness and builds muscle but you should tailor programs to your own needs
Listening to music
A portable stereo allows you to enjoy music privately, but if played too loudly, it can damage hearing
Sunbathing
Your ethnic origin influences the way your skin reacts to sun exposure. Fair-skinned people are more vulnerable to its effects than those with dark skin and need more protection
Drinking alcohol
Many people enjoy alcohol as part of social activity. However, drinking in excess can cause severe damage to your liver, brain, and heart. In addition, drinking during pregnancy can harm your developing baby

DIET AND HEALTH

By far the most common problem with the typical Canadian diet is excess. Canadians tend to consume too much food, especially too much fat, salt, and sugar. Overconsumption of these nutrients has been linked to some of the main causes of death in North America: heart disease, cancer, and stroke. Making informed choices about your diet could improve your chance of avoiding these diseases.

The huge growth in the availability and popularity of fast food has led to a corresponding rise in poor eating habits because packaged snacks and meals often contain large amounts of ingredients that can be harmful. The first article in this section provides easy-to-follow guidelines on how to assess and improve your diet, explains how food energy is measured, and describes how the major food groups (grain products; vegetables and fruit; milk products; meat and alternatives) contribute to your nutritional needs. The typical Canadian diet is high in calories, and, as a result, a significant percentage of the Canadian population is obese or suffers from other health problems associated with being overweight. The second article explains how to determine your ideal weight and explores the ways available to lose or gain weight.

Eating well
Food is essential for good health but is also an important aspect of social life for most people. Cooking and sharing healthy food can be an enjoyable part of daily life.

A healthy diet

A diet that contains the right balance of foods for optimum health

Variation in diet among people living in different countries is closely associated with national patterns of disease. For example, the high-calorie, high-fat diet common in Canada is linked to the high national rates of obesity (p.631), heart disease (*see* CORONARY ARTERY DISEASE, p.405), and stroke (p.532). The traditional Mediterranean diet, which is low in saturated fat and high in monounsaturated fat, seems to be related to the low incidence of heart disease in Mediterranean countries. In Japan, the typical diet is high in fiber and the incidence of colorectal cancer (p.665) is low. In many countries, an excess of salt has been linked to high blood pressure (*see* HYPERTENSION, p.403).

Just as excesses of some elements in the diet can lead to health problems, deficiencies in certain nutrients can lead to poor health (*see* NUTRITIONAL DEFICIENCIES, p.630). Such deficiencies, however, are rare in Canada.

The knowledge gained by nutritionists from studying the effects of diet on health in countries around the world has led to the development of guidelines for healthy eating.

ASSESSMENT HOW HEALTHY IS YOUR DIET?

You may find it difficult to keep to a healthy diet all the time, particularly if you eat out a lot or if you rely on convenience foods. The questionnaire below will help you identify some areas that can make the difference between a healthy diet and one of poor nutritional value.

1 *Has your weight stayed the same over the last 6 months (assuming you have not been trying to change it)?*
☐ YES ☐ NO

2 *Do you eat 5–10 servings of fruit and vegetables every day?*
☐ YES ☐ NO

3 *Do you regularly vary the type of food you eat?*
☐ YES ☐ NO

4 *Do you try to avoid "junk food" such as chocolate and potato chips?*
☐ YES ☐ NO

5 *Do you try to eat wholewheat pasta and brown rice, rather than white pasta and rice?*
☐ YES ☐ NO

6 *Do you tend to broil food rather than fry it?*
☐ YES ☐ NO

7 *Do you drink at least 8 glasses (4 pints/2 liters) of fluid a day?*
☐ YES ☐ NO

8 *Do you try to leave food unsalted?*
☐ YES ☐ NO

ANALYSIS

If you answered yes to all the questions, you are probably eating a diet that will benefit your health. If you answered no to two or more of the questions, you should consider your diet in more detail. Learn about the nutritional values of different foods and what constitutes a balanced diet. You may also want to try alternative methods of food preparation and cooking.

HEALTH ACTION CANADA'S FOOD GUIDE TO HEALTHY EATING

Different people need different amounts of food. The amount of food you need every day from the 4 groups and other foods depends on your age, body size, activity level, whether you are male or female, and if you are pregnant or breast-feeding. That's why the food guide gives a lower and higher number of servings for each food group. For example, young children can choose the lower number of servings, while male teenagers can go to the higher number. Most other people can choose servings somewhere in between.

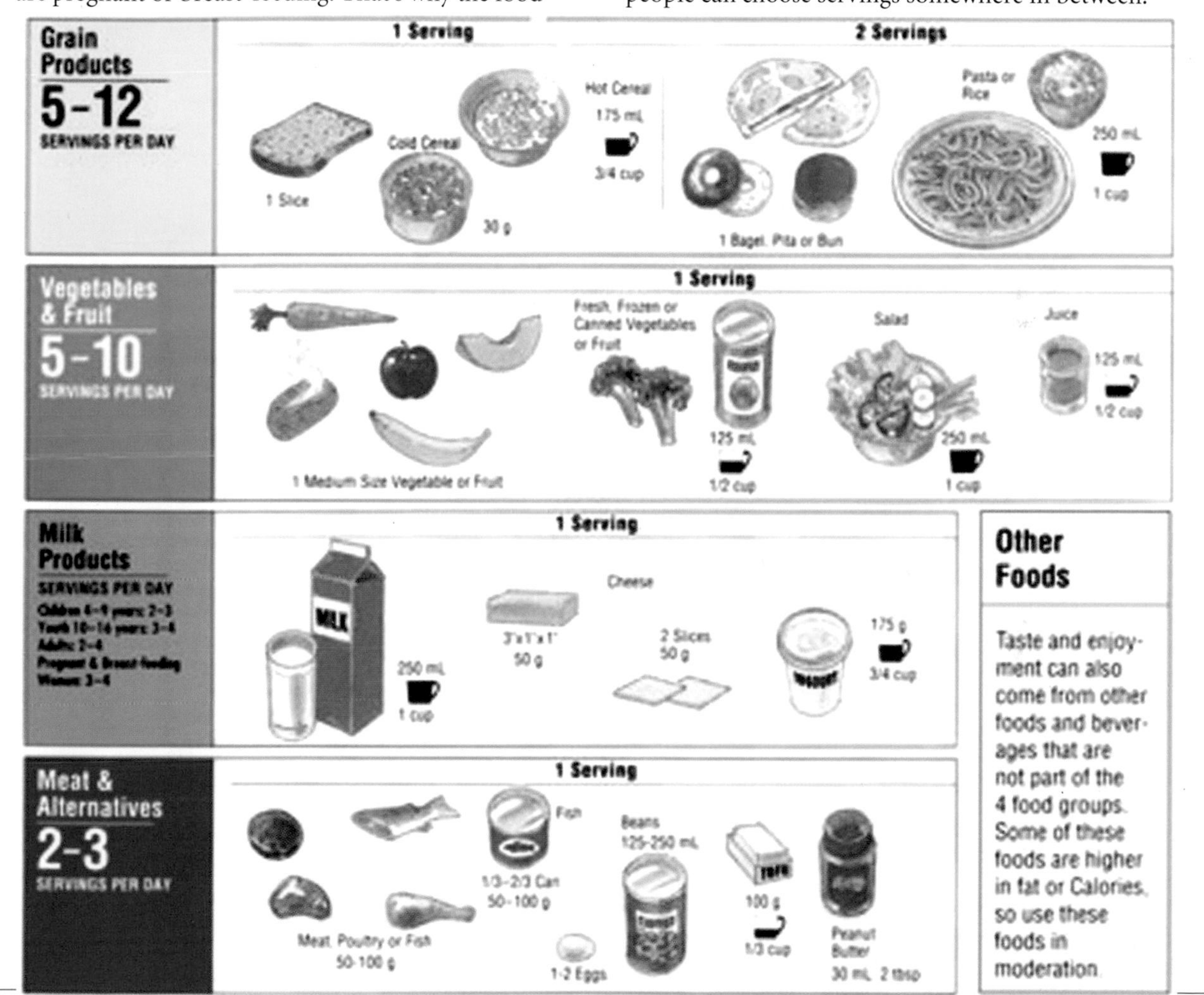
Grain Products
5-12
SERVINGS PER DAY
1 Serving
2 Servings
1 Slice
Cold Cereal
30 g
Hot Cereal
175 mL
3/4 cup
1 Bagel, Pita or Bun
Pasta or Rice
250 mL
1 cup
Vegetables & Fruit
5-10
SERVINGS PER DAY
1 Serving
1 Medium Size Vegetable or Fruit
Fresh, Frozen or Canned Vegetables or Fruit
125 mL
1/2 cup
Salad
250 mL
1 cup
Juice
125 mL
1/2 cup
Milk Products
SERVINGS PER DAY
1 Serving
MILK
250 mL
1 cup
Cheese
3"x1"x1"
50 g
2 Slices
50 g
175 g
3/4 cup
Meat & Alternatives
2-3
SERVINGS PER DAY
1 Serving
Meat, Poultry or Fish
50-100 g
Fish
1/3-2/3 Can
50-100 g
1-2 Eggs
Beans
125-250 mL
100 g
1/3 cup
Peanut Butter
30 mL 2 tbsp
Other Foods
Taste and enjoyment can also come from other foods and beverages that are not part of the 4 food groups. Some of these foods are higher in fat or Calories, so use these foods in moderation.

BALANCING YOUR DIET

Food contains five essential elements: carbohydrates, protein, fats, vitamins, and minerals. Each of these elements makes an important contribution to your health, but it is important that they are taken in the correct proportions, with carbohydrates forming the bulk of the diet and fats a smaller proportion.

Health Canada has created a chart that divides food into 4 groups (*see* CANADA'S FOOD GUIDE TO HEALTHY EATING, above). Following the food-chart guidelines is an easy way to ensure that your diet contains the correct proportions of the five essential elements so that you get the right amount of vitamins and minerals. You should plan on enjoying a variety of foods from each group every day. In addition to the foods from the groups set out in this chart, you should include plenty of water in your diet. Drinks containing sugar, caffeine, or alcohol (*see* ALCOHOL AND HEALTH, p.62) should be consumed in moderation only.

Other important health factors are the amount of salt you have in your diet and the types of fats you eat. It is important for your health to choose lower fat foods more often (*see* CHOOSING HEALTHY FATS, p.50).

CARBOHYDRATES These should be the body's main energy source. However, if you eat more carbohydrate than your body actually needs, the excess will be stored in your body tissue as fat. There are two main types of carbohydrates in food: simple and complex.

Simple carbohydrates come from sugars. They provide your body with a quick energy boost but can be harmful to the teeth. Foods such as cookies, cakes, and candies contain large quantities of simple carbohydrates.

Complex carbohydrates have a more complicated structure than simple carbohydrates and are made up of

HEALTH OPTIONS CHOOSING HEALTHY FATS

There are three main types of fats found in foods and oils: saturated, monounsaturated, and polyunsaturated. Too much fat in the diet, particularly saturated fat, is unhealthy. Your total fat consumption should contribute 30–35 percent of your daily calorie intake, with most of the fat coming from monounsaturates and polyunsaturates.

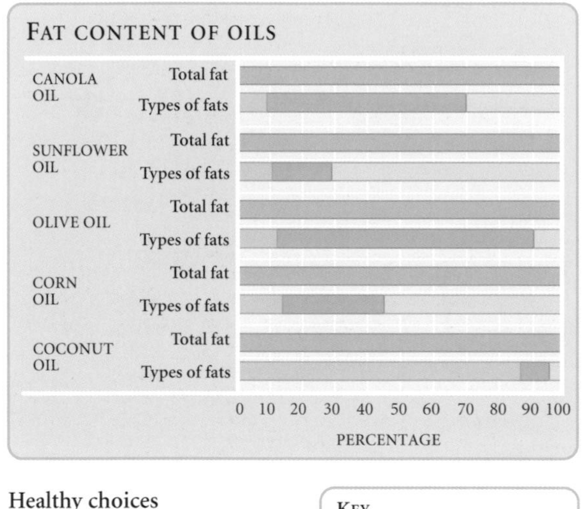
FAT CONTENT OF OILS
CANOLA OIL
SUNFLOWER OIL
OLIVE OIL
CORN OIL
COCONUT OIL
Total fat
Types of fats
0 10 20 30 40 50 60 70 80 90 100
PERCENTAGE

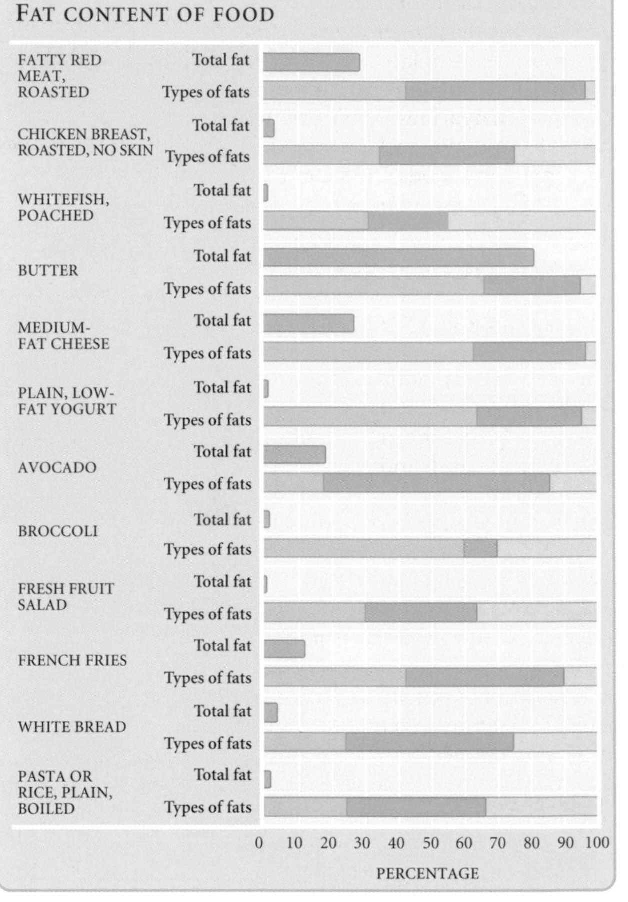
FAT CONTENT OF FOOD
FATTY RED MEAT, ROASTED
CHICKEN BREAST, ROASTED, NO SKIN
WHITEFISH, POACHED
BUTTER
MEDIUM-FAT CHEESE
PLAIN, LOW-FAT YOGURT
AVOCADO
BROCCOLI
FRESH FRUIT SALAD
FRENCH FRIES
WHITE BREAD
PASTA OR RICE, PLAIN, BOILED
Total fat
Types of fats
0 10 20 30 40 50 60 70 80 90 100
PERCENTAGE

Healthy choices
The amount and type of fats in foods vary greatly. Red meat, most dairy products, and some oils all have a fairly high saturated fat content. Lean meat, whitefish, and olive and canola oils are healthier choices.

KEY
TOTAL FAT
Fat content
TYPES OF FATS
Saturated fat
Monounsaturated fat
Polyunsaturated fat

starches and dietary fiber. Pasta, bread, vegetables such as potatoes, and rice contain high levels of starch. Dietary fiber consists of the fibrous parts of plants that are not completely broken down during digestion. Fiber can be divided into two kinds: soluble fiber and insoluble fiber.

Insoluble fiber adds bulk to feces, aiding the passage of material through the intestine. Major sources of insoluble fiber are brown rice, fruits, legumes, vegetables, wheat bran, seeds, and whole grains.

Soluble fiber may lower blood cholesterol levels, and it has also been associated with a reduced risk of heart disease and stroke. Good sources of this type of fiber include fruits, oats, legumes, pysllium, and vegetables.

Complex carbohydrates should form the major part of your daily diet. Simple carbohydrates should be a minimal part of your diet because, although they provide the body with fast energy, they are low in vitamins and minerals and contain very little fiber.

PROTEIN Protein is essential for building and repairing cells in the human body. Insufficient protein in the diet causes serious health problems, but such deficiency is most likely to occur in developing countries, where food sources may be limited. A more common problem in Canada is a diet that contains too much protein, particularly animal protein. Excess protein is converted into fat in the body. Many foods that are rich in protein are also high in calories and saturated fat, and a high-protein diet may lead to obesity. Foods that are high in protein include meat, fish, cheese, and nuts. About one-sixth of your total calorie intake should ideally be obtained from protein.

FATS Fats are a source of energy and are essential for the absorption of some vitamins. The amounts and types of fats in your diet are important in determining your general health. They also affect your risk of developing coronary artery disease or of having a stroke. The link is cholesterol, a fatlike substance that is vital for normal body functioning but can be a health risk in excess. The higher the level of cholesterol in a person's blood (*see* HYPERCHOLESTEROLEMIA, p.691), the greater his or her risk of developing atherosclerosis (p.402), the narrowing of the arteries that may eventually lead to cardiovascular disease.

An individual's level of blood cholesterol depends partly on genetic factors, but in many cases the main influence is the type of fat in the diet. Fats may be saturated or unsaturated, depending on their chemical structure; it is the saturated fats found in dairy products and meat that mainly contribute to raised cholesterol levels. It is also advisable to avoid transfats, sometimes known as hydrogenated fats, which are artificially produced and have properties similar to saturated fats. Transfats may be found in hard, brick-type margarines and manufactured food items such as cookies, cakes, and fast foods. In contrast, unsaturated fats seem to protect against cardiovascular disease, with monounsaturates having a greater protective effect than polyunsaturates.

For a healthier diet, try to keep your fat intake low and change to monounsaturated fats in your diet. If you have a high blood cholesterol level, try to avoid foods that are rich in cholesterol, such as shellfish and eggs.

VITAMINS AND MINERALS Vitamins and minerals both play vital roles in growth and metabolism (*see* GOOD SOURCES OF VITAMINS AND MINERALS, p.52). Apart from vitamin K, which is formed by intestinal bacteria, and vitamin D, which is produced in the skin by the action of sunlight, all vitamins and minerals must come from your diet.

The majority of people who live in Canada receive adequate amounts of vitamins and minerals in their normal diet. Some vitamins, including vitamins A, D, E, and K, are harmful if they are consumed in excess. However, some people may need vitamin and mineral supplements (p.927). For example, women who have heavy menstrual periods may be prescribed iron supplements.

FLUIDS Water is essential for life, and almost four-fifths of the human body is composed of it. Water is lost through sweating and urination and must be replaced. Inadequate fluid intake may lead to constipation and dehydration. You can obtain some of the water you need by eating solid foods, but you should also drink plenty of fluids. Try to drink at least 8 glasses (4 pints/2 liters) a day, but, if it is very hot or you are exercising, you may need to drink more. Other factors that will increase your need for fluids include diarrhea, vomiting, diuretics (drugs that increase urine output), and caffeine.

HEALTH OPTIONS UNDERSTANDING FOOD LABELS

Manufacturers of most packaged foods are required by law to provide nutritional information on food labels. Very small items may give only a telephone number or an address for obtaining information. Nutritional information is not required for foods with no significant nutrient content, such as coffee, for some deli and bakery products, or for raw foods.

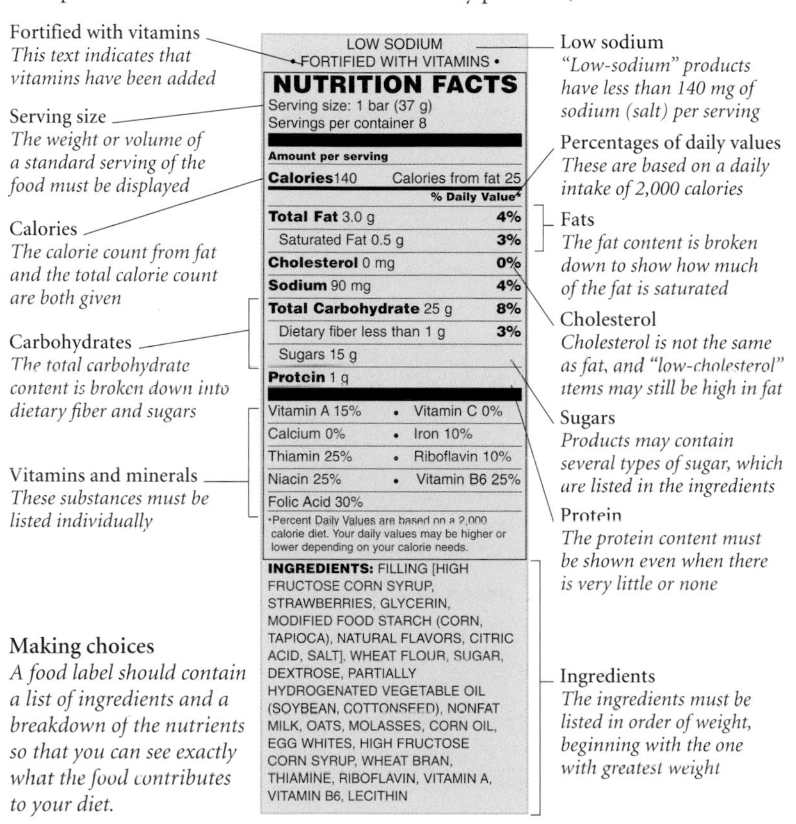
Fortified with vitamins
This text indicates that vitamins have been added
Serving size
The weight or volume of a standard serving of the food must be displayed
Calories
The calorie count from fat and the total calorie count are both given
Carbohydrates
The total carbohydrate content is broken down into dietary fiber and sugars
Vitamins and minerals
These substances must be listed individually
Making choices
A food label should contain a list of ingredients and a breakdown of the nutrients so that you can see exactly what the food contributes to your diet.
LOW SODIUM
• FORTIFIED WITH VITAMINS •
NUTRITION FACTS
Serving size: 1 bar (37 g)
Servings per container 8
Amount per serving
Calories 140 Calories from fat 25
% Daily Value*
Total Fat 3.0 g 4%
Saturated Fat 0.5 g 3%
Cholesterol 0 mg 0%
Sodium 90 mg 4%
Total Carbohydrate 25 g 8%
Dietary fiber less than 1 g 3%
Sugars 15 g
Protein 1 g
Vitamin A 15% • Vitamin C 0%
Calcium 0% • Iron 10%
Thiamin 25% • Riboflavin 10%
Niacin 25% • Vitamin B6 25%
Folic Acid 30%
*Percent Daily Values are based on a 2,000 calorie diet. Your daily values may be higher or lower depending on your calorie needs.
INGREDIENTS: FILLING [HIGH FRUCTOSE CORN SYRUP, STRAWBERRIES, GLYCERIN, MODIFIED FOOD STARCH (CORN, TAPIOCA), NATURAL FLAVORS, CITRIC ACID, SALT], WHEAT FLOUR, SUGAR, DEXTROSE, PARTIALLY HYDROGENATED VEGETABLE OIL (SOYBEAN, COTTONSEED), NONFAT MILK, OATS, MOLASSES, CORN OIL, EGG WHITES, HIGH FRUCTOSE CORN SYRUP, WHEAT BRAN, THIAMINE, RIBOFLAVIN, VITAMIN A, VITAMIN B6, LECITHIN
Low sodium
"Low-sodium" products have less than 140 mg of sodium (salt) per serving
Percentages of daily values
These are based on a daily intake of 2,000 calories
Fats
The fat content is broken down to show how much of the fat is saturated
Cholesterol
Cholesterol is not the same as fat, and "low-cholesterol" items may still be high in fat
Sugars
Products may contain several types of sugar, which are listed in the ingredients
Protein
The protein content must be shown even when there is very little or none
Ingredients
The ingredients must be listed in order of weight, beginning with the one with greatest weight

YOUR ENERGY REQUIREMENTS

The body needs a constant reserve of energy in order to function properly. Energy from food is measured in units called calories. Because one calorie is a tiny amount of energy, units known as kilocalories (one kilocalorie equals 1,000 calories) are often used for convenience. You should be aware that "calorie" is often used to mean "kilocalorie."

The number of calories you need to obtain from your diet depends on how much energy your body uses. The rate at which your body uses energy simply to maintain basic processes such as respiration, circulation, and digestion is called your basal metabolic rate (BMR). Extra calories are needed for everything you do as part of your daily life. You have to ensure that you eat enough food to match your energy output. Energetic activities, such as playing sports, increase the calorie requirement. Most of these extra calories should come from complex carbohydrates, but people who have very physically demanding jobs also require extra fat and sugar, which are rich sources of energy.

CHOOSING NUTRITIOUS FOOD

Although fresh foods tend to be generally healthy, they can have a short shelf life. Processing techniques are used to increase shelf life and to prevent the contamination of food. In particular, food preservatives prevent the growth of microorganisms, which could cause food poisoning (p.629).

Food labels on packaged food (*see* UNDERSTANDING FOOD LABELS, above) provide information about the content, allowing you to compare similar products and choose the healthiest.

WWW ONLINE SITES: p.1035

HEALTH ACTION GOOD SOURCES OF VITAMINS AND MINERALS

Vitamins and minerals are essential for growth and good health. Your need for each nutrient varies with age, sex, energy output, and in special circumstances such as pregnancy and lactation. However, the Recommended Daily Intake (RDI) below can be used as a general guideline for the daily intake of nutrients for people over age 2. The RDI was developed for use in the nutrition labeling of packaged foods.

Eating for health
RDIs represent the highest recommended intake of each nutrient, omitting supplemental needs for pregnancy and lactation.

VITAMINS	RDI	GOOD SOURCES	EFFECTS
Vitamin A	1,000 RE	Calf liver, eggs, margarine, dairy products, dark green and orange vegetables and fruit	• Important for healthy eyes, hair, skin, and bones • Can be toxic in excess
Vitamin B_1 (thiamine)	1.3 mg	Meat, whole grains, legumes, fortified cereals, breads, pasta, flour	• Helps in energy production • Essential for the proper functioning of the nervous system
Vitamin B_2 (riboflavin)	1.6 mg	Meat, eggs, milk products, leafy vegetables, fortified cereals, bread, pasta, flour	• Involved in the release of proteins from nutrients • Helps maintain the nervous system and muscles
Vitamin B_3 (niacin)	23 NE	Fish, whole grains, peanuts, legumes, fortified cereals, bread, pasta, flour, meat and milk	• Essential for the utilization of energy from food • Helps maintain healthy skin
Vitamin B_6 (pyridoxine)	1.8 mg	Meat, fish, whole grains, nuts, seeds	• Necessary for blood formation • Helps regulate the cells in the nervous system
Vitamin B_{12}	2 mcg	Dairy products, fish, meat, eggs	• Vital for the growth of blood cells in the bone marrow • Essential for a healthy nervous system
Vitamin C	60 mg	Many fruits and vegetables, all juices	• Strengthens tissues • Helps the body use iron • May help the immune system fight disease
Vitamin D	5 mcg	Milk, margarine, oily fish, also formed in the skin by sunlight	• Enhances calcium absorption for strong teeth and bones • Can be toxic in excess
Vitamin E	10 mg	Margarine, vegetable oils, wheat germ, nuts, seeds, whole grains	• Protects tissues and organs against degenerative disease • Can be toxic in excess
Folic acid	220 mcg†	Leafy green vegetables, organ meats, fortified breads and cereals, nuts, legumes, orange juice, pasta, flour	• Helps prevent neural tube defects (p.844) in fetuses • Contributes to healthy cells and blood

† Pregnant women and those planning pregnancy should take 400 mcg a day

MINERALS	RDI	GOOD SOURCES	EFFECTS
Calcium	1,100 mg	Dairy products, tofu set with calcium sulphate, peas, dry beans, edible fish bones, almonds, sesame, sunflower seeds	• Necessary for healthy bones, teeth, and muscles • Helps with conduction of nerve impulses
Chromium	120 mcg	Brewer's yeast, meat, whole grains, cheese, egg yolk	• Helps regulate sugar levels in the blood
Iodide	160 mcg	Salt, dairy products, seafood	• Synthesized into the hormone thyroxine, which helps regulate the rate at which you use energy
Iron	14 mg	Meat, enriched breakfast cereals and pasta, legumes, nuts, seeds, whole grains	• Aids formation of red blood cells and certain proteins • Maintains healthy muscles
Magnesium	250 mg	Nuts, dark green vegetables, seafood, dried fruit, dairy products, legumes, whole grains	• Essential for healthy bones, teeth, nerves, and muscles • Necessary for the production of DNA
Selenium	50 mcg	Fish, meat, wholegrain cereals, dairy products	• Maintains normal heart and liver function
Zinc	9 mg	Meat, shellfish, dry beans, nuts, wholegrain cereals, oysters	• Boosts or enhances immune system • Necessary for sperm formation • Aids proper wound healing

Controlling your weight

Maintaining your weight within a healthy range for your height and gender

An essential part of a healthy lifestyle is maintaining your body weight within the range considered normal for your gender and height. In recent decades, the number of people living in developed countries who are overweight has increased significantly. For example, in the US, the proportion of people over age 20 who are overweight increased from 1 in 4 during the early 1970s to 1 in 3 in the late 1990s. In Canadian children ages 7–13, 35% of girls and almost 40% of boys are overweight or obese.

Excess weight amounting to obesity (p.631) is now a major health issue in North America. Disorders associated with being overweight, such as coronary artery disease (p.405), high blood pressure (*see* HYPERTENSION, p.403), and stroke (p.532), rank among the leading causes of illness and death in the country. Being underweight can also cause health problems, including a higher than normal risk of infertility (pp.774–777) and osteoporosis (p.368).

ASSESSMENT ARE YOU A HEALTHY WEIGHT?

You can check whether you are a healthy weight by using the Body Mass Index height/weight graph below and by measuring the circumference of your waist. Even if the graph indicates that you are in the healthy weight range, you may still be at risk from cardiovascular disease and stroke if fat is mainly around your abdomen. Women at high risk have a waist circumference over 35 in (89 cm); men at risk have a waist of over 40 in (102 cm).

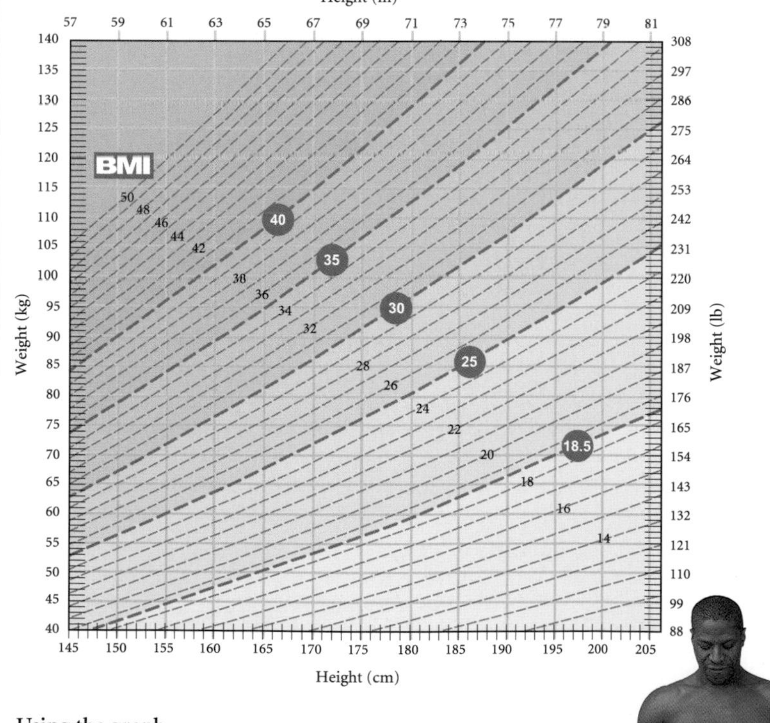
Height (in)
57 59 61 63 65 67 69 71 73 75 77 79 81
Weight (kg)
140 135 130 125 120 115 110 105 100 95 90 85 80 75 70 65 60 55 50 45 40
Weight (lb)
308 297 286 275 264 253 242 231 220 209 198 187 176 165 154 143 132 121 110 99 88
BMI
50 48 46 44 42 40 38 36 34 32 35 30 28 26 25 24 22 20 18.5 18 16 14
145 150 155 160 165 170 175 180 185 190 195 200 205
Height (cm)

Using the graph
Find your height and weight on the axes. Trace a vertical line from your height and a horizontal line from your weight, and note where they intersect – this is your BMI. A healthy BMI lies between 18.5 and 25.

Measuring your waist
The circumference of your waist indicates whether you have excess abdominal fat.

CAUSES OF WEIGHT PROBLEMS

In Canada, the main factor contributing to the general weight gain of the population is lack of exercise combined with overeating. Children's pastimes are far more sedentary than those of former generations, and many adults do not exercise at all. In addition, an increasing number of people rely on convenience foods, which tend to be high in saturated fat and simple carbohydrates, both of which are high in calories.

There are various reasons why someone may be underweight. Some people are naturally thin and find it difficult to gain weight no matter what sort of food they eat. Others start within the normal weight range but develop an eating disorder, such as anorexia nervosa (p.562) or bulimia (p.563), and lose a great deal of weight, eventually becoming abnormally thin. Weight loss can also result from loss of appetite due to illness such as depression (p.554), influenza (p.287), or serious chronic diseases.

FINDING YOUR HEALTHY WEIGHT

Height and weight charts offer a quick and easy way to discover if you are within the recommended weight range for your particular height. Your ideal weight depends on both your height and the amount of muscle you have. For example, an athlete should weigh more than a healthy but relatively sedentary person of the same height. This is because exercise increases muscle, which is heavier than other types of body tissues. Because of this, the charts give healthy ranges for height and weight, and not precise measurements.

Recent research indicates that the location of fat in the body is an important determinant of health. Excess fat around the abdomen is more closely linked to cardiovascular diseases than fat elsewhere in the body. To find out whether you are a healthy weight, you should check both if your weight falls in the recommended range for your height and measure your waist size (*see* ARE YOU A HEALTHY WEIGHT?, left).

Doctors and nutritionists use weight and height measurements in order to calculate body mass index (BMI). This is a widely accepted and more specific way of checking if you are over- or underweight by providing an indication of total body fat content. The BMI is calculated by dividing a person's weight in kilograms by the square of his or her height in meters. A BMI figure under 18.5 means that you are underweight, while a figure of 25 or more indicates that you are overweight.

LOSING WEIGHT

First check if your weight is within a healthy range. If you are overweight, there are several measures you can take to lose weight. These include diet, exercise, drugs, and surgery.

Before you begin attempting to lose weight, you should try to identify why you may be overweight. The most likely cause is a combination of overeating and lack of exercise, but you may find it helpful to look at your reasons for overeating. For example, do you tend to eat when you feel unhappy, or is overeating a habit that has become established in your family?

The best way to lose weight is to combine calorie reduction with regular exercise. Plan what you need to do to succeed. For example, if you need more exercise, arrange a time each day to take a brisk walk. If you are tempted by the wrong foods, make a list of healthy foods before going to the supermarket.

Success in dieting also depends on being realistic about how much weight you can lose. When starting a weight-loss program, set yourself a practical, short-term target, revising it as you go along. About 4–9 lb (2–4 kg) a month is sensible. If you want to lose more than this or have any health problems, talk to your doctor before you start.

You also need to look at what you hope to achieve by losing excess weight. It is important for you to accept that weight loss may not solve all your problems. It may make you feel better and more confident, will certainly improve some aspects of your health, but is unlikely, for instance, to help a failing relationship or make you more popular. However, the health benefits are worth any effort and lifestyle changes you may have to make.

REDUCING DIETS If your diet does not provide you with enough calories for all your energy needs, your body will start to use up excess fat as an energy source. Therefore, you should experience some weight loss if you change your diet to one containing fewer calories than before. Publications that list the calorie content of a variety of foods, both natural and processed, are widely available, and this information can also be found on the labels of most packaged food (*see* UNDERSTANDING FOOD LABELS, p.51). A good starting point for most people is to try to reduce their daily calorie intake by 500–1,000 calories. This can be done by cutting down on high-fat foods, such as cakes, cheese, and fried dishes, and eating healthy, low-calorie foods such as fruit, vegetables, and broiled dishes.

If your normal diet already consists mainly of low-calorie foods, you simply need to cut down on the quantity of food you eat. The best type of reducing diet is one that is low in calories but balanced so that you stay well nourished (*see* HEALTHY EATING, p.49).

Alcohol contains no healthy nutrients and is high in calories. It is therefore advisable to reduce your alcohol consumption as much as possible when you are trying to lose weight.

Rapid weight-loss plans and fasting to lose weight should be avoided. These plans can damage your health by forcing your body to function on insufficient energy supplies and depriving it of the range of nutrients it needs to function well. Such weight-loss plans do not help you adopt sensible, long-term healthy eating habits.

EXERCISE Doing exercise to lose weight need not be strenuous, but it does have to be regular. Sustained regular exercise raises your basal metabolic rate (BMR), the rate at which your body's metabolism needs to function to maintain basic body processes such as respiration and digestion. If your BMR rises, you use up more calories (*see* EXERCISE AND HEALTH, pp.55–61) and will lose weight if you have a calorie-controlled diet. Exercise tones and builds muscles, which weigh more than fat. Therefore, as you become fitter, you may find that the scales initially register a few more pounds, although you will not actually be any fatter. Exercise can also stimulate your appetite; you must resist eating more than your new diet allows. As you grow older, your metabolism slows down, and therefore your body uses up fewer calories. It is important to remain as active as possible in order to prevent the gradual weight gain that is common among older people.

DRUGS AND SURGERY Many different drug-based treatments are available for weight loss. Some are easily obtainable from the pharmacy, others are available only by prescription, and some are illegal. Taking weight-reducing drugs is not recommended and should never take the place of a balanced, low-calorie diet. All types of reducing drugs have disadvantages. Prescription drugs, such as appetite suppressants, and over-the-counter products, such as those that numb the taste buds, have side effects. Amphetamines have been found to be addictive and are no longer prescribed for weight loss. The newer drugs that act by blocking the absorption of fat should be combined with a reducing diet and should not be taken long term.

Surgical procedures, such as stomach stapling and jaw-wiring, are usually considered only as last resorts for people who are very obese.

GAINING WEIGHT

Many people think that being underweight is not a health risk. It can be just as unhealthy as being overweight and requires careful treatment. Check your weight to see if it is in the healthy range for your height. If you are excessively fatigued, are unable to keep warm, and are more than 15 percent under the lowest normal weight for your height, you need to talk to your doctor.

It is important to gain weight sensibly to build up muscle and bone and maintain a healthy level of body fat. Although high-fat and fast foods are high in calories, you should avoid eating large quantities to gain weight because of their unhealthy effects, such as causing high blood pressure and increased risk of heart disease. Put on weight slowly by eating a healthy, balanced diet. Several small, nutritious meals each day provide a better supply of energy than one or two large meals.

Doing regular exercise helps build muscles, increases strength, and may also improve your appetite. You should start slowly, especially if you tire easily, and build up the amount you do gradually.

(WWW) ONLINE SITES: p.1031, p.1035

EXERCISE AND HEALTH

Exercise is an essential part of any healthy lifestyle. This idea is not a new one; the fact that physical activity is linked to good health can be traced back to the Greeks in the fifth century BC. Since then, research has proven that exercise prolongs life, protects health, and can reduce the risk of disease. Taking part in team sports also provides the opportunity to socialize.

Developments in mechanization and computerization over the past century have meant that people in developed countries now lead a more sedentary lifestyle, and too few people exercise regularly. By making a concerted effort to incorporate physical activity into your daily life, you can become significantly healthier.

The first article in this section outlines the overwhelming physical and psychological benefits of being active.

Exercise also has an effect on other aspects of your lifestyle. For example, people who exercise tend to smoke less than those who do not. Developing a habit of regular physical activity may encourage you to give up smoking.

The second article provides practical guidelines for assessing how fit you are and improving your level of fitness.

The last article explores safe habits and routines to adopt when exercising to minimize the risk of injury.

Exercise for life
Exercising on a regular basis can improve the quality of your life by improving your strength, stamina, and psychological health and by providing you with the opportunity to socialize with other people.

The benefits of exercise

How regular exercise benefits your physical and psychological health

Most people now know that exercise is part of a healthy lifestyle. As a result, the number of people in Canada doing regular exercise has increased substantially. Despite this increase, only 1 in 5 adults does enough exercise to protect his or her health whereas 3 in 5 adults do not do any exercise at all.

The main benefit of exercise is to protect health. Exercise has a positive effect on your respiratory, cardiovascular, and musculoskeletal systems (*see* HOW EXERCISE BENEFITS HEALTH, p.56).

By exercising regularly, you reduce your risk of developing long-term disease, increase your life expectancy, and improve your quality of life in later years. When you include exercise in your daily routine, you will probably find it a lot easier to perform ordinary day-to-day tasks such as shopping, working in the garden, doing housework, and climbing stairs. In addition to the more obvious physical benefits, exercising regularly can improve your psychological well-being. Developing a habit of exercising with other people can also help you make new friends.

CARDIOVASCULAR HEALTH

Research has shown that people who lead relatively inactive lives with no exercise are at increased risk of coronary artery disease (p.405) and heart attack (*see* MYOCARDIAL INFARCTION, p.410). However, for exercise to be effective against heart disease, it has to be regular and sustained over a person's lifetime. Exercising only in your youth is no guarantee of benefits later in life.

When you exercise regularly, your heart becomes stronger and more efficient, and it can pump more blood with every heartbeat, making it better able to cope with extra demands. Exercise also influences whether or not you survive a heart attack. People who do no exercise are three times more likely to die after having a heart attack than are people who do regular exercise.

Regular exercise helps reduce blood cholesterol levels and lowers blood pressure. Both of these factors reduce your risk of developing fatty plaques in the arteries (*see* ATHEROSCLEROSIS, p.402). Research shows that people who have coronary artery disease or lower limb ischemia (p.434) may benefit from regular exercise because of the improvement it makes to blood supply. These benefits may be experienced within two months of starting regular exercise.

RESPIRATORY HEALTH

Regular exercise improves the efficiency of your respiratory muscles and increases the usable volume of the alveoli (air sacs) in the lungs. It also increases the efficiency of the exchange of oxygen and carbon dioxide in the lungs. Active people are able to extract more oxygen from a single breath and have a slower breathing rate. If you have a respiratory disease, such as chronic obstructive pulmonary disease (p.487), regular exercise may help improve the amount of activity you can do on a daily basis without feeling breathless.

MUSCULOSKELETAL HEALTH

Exercising improves the condition of your bones, joints, and muscles. Doing regular exercise helps you keep yourself flexible and mobile for longer and improves your quality of life.

MAINTAINING STRONG BONES Weight-bearing exercises, such as walking and running, help improve bone strength, density, and development. This kind of exercise is particularly important for physical development during childhood and adolescence, when the bones are still growing. It is also important for women of all ages to do weight-bearing exercises regularly because they help

HEALTH EFFECTS HOW EXERCISE BENEFITS HEALTH

Regular exercise protects your health by benefiting different body systems. It may be planned and structured, such as going for a run, or incidental, such as bicycling to work. Below is a selection of exercises, both structured and part of daily living, that benefit different parts of your body; many exercises are beneficial to more than one part. For example, tennis is aerobic and benefits your heart, lungs, and muscles; it is weight-bearing and improves bone strength; and it requires a range of movements that improves joint mobility.

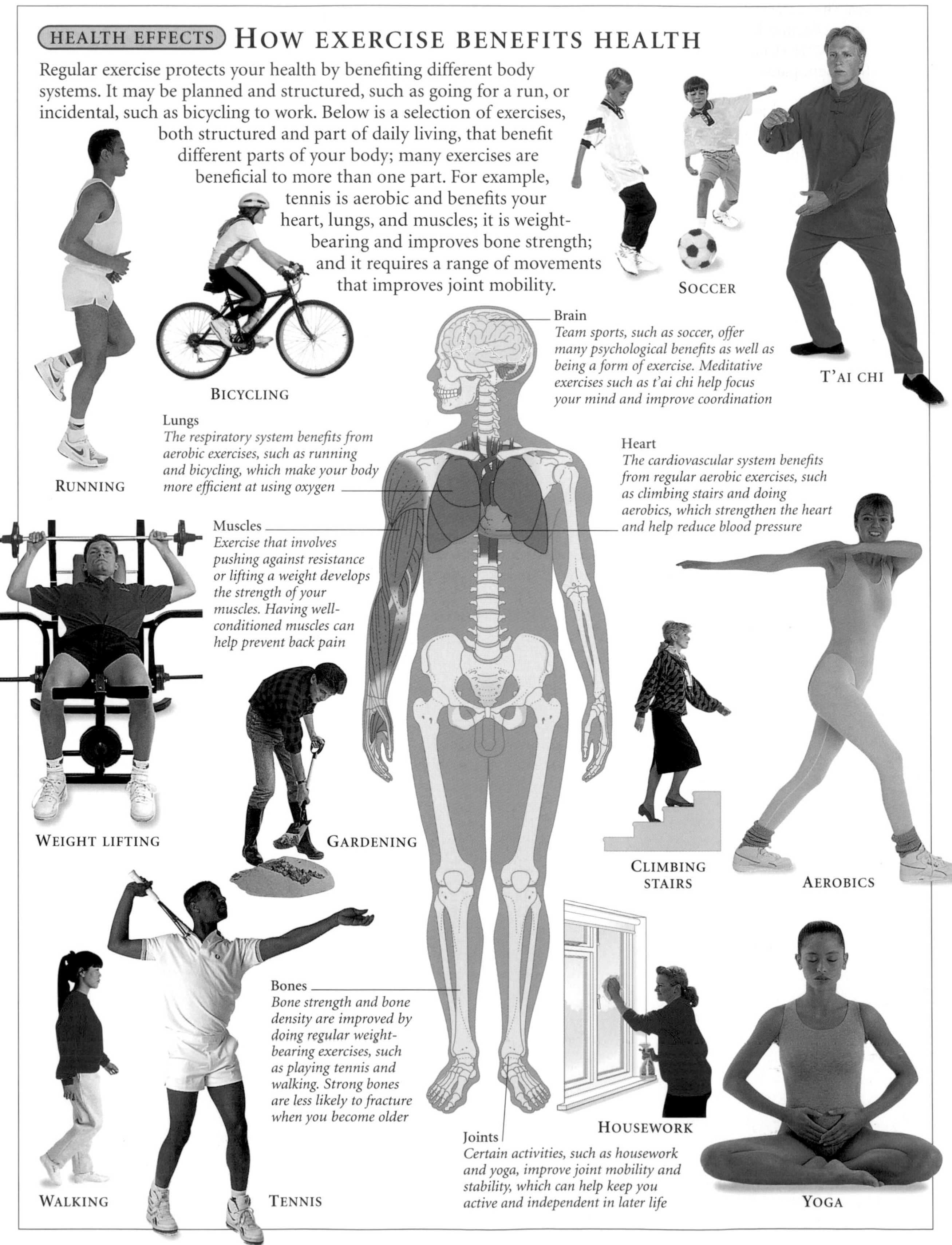

SOCCER
T'AI CHI
RUNNING
BICYCLING
Brain
Team sports, such as soccer, offer many psychological benefits as well as being a form of exercise. Meditative exercises such as t'ai chi help focus your mind and improve coordination
Lungs
The respiratory system benefits from aerobic exercises, such as running and bicycling, which make your body more efficient at using oxygen
Heart
The cardiovascular system benefits from regular aerobic exercises, such as climbing stairs and doing aerobics, which strengthen the heart and help reduce blood pressure
Muscles
Exercise that involves pushing against resistance or lifting a weight develops the strength of your muscles. Having well-conditioned muscles can help prevent back pain
WEIGHT LIFTING
GARDENING
CLIMBING STAIRS
AEROBICS
Bones
Bone strength and bone density are improved by doing regular weight-bearing exercises, such as playing tennis and walking. Strong bones are less likely to fracture when you become older
HOUSEWORK
Joints
Certain activities, such as housework and yoga, improve joint mobility and stability, which can help keep you active and independent in later life
WALKING
TENNIS
YOGA

slow down the accelerated bone loss caused by the decline in the hormone estrogen (*see* OSTEOPOROSIS, p.368) that occurs after menopause.

MOBILIZING AND STABILIZING JOINTS Regular exercise improves the flexibility of joints and minimizes stiffness. It also helps stabilize joints by strengthening the muscles and ligaments surrounding them. By maintaining the mobility of joints, exercise helps you remain independent and able to do more in later life. If you have a joint disease, such as rheumatoid arthritis (p.377), strength-building exercises may stabilize affected joints and reduce further damage.

INCREASING MUSCLE STRENGTH You should exercise your muscles regularly to keep them in good condition. Muscle size and strength can be increased with exercises that work against resistance, such as lifting moderate weights. Aerobic exercises that build stamina, such as running and bicycling, make the muscles more efficient so that they can work for longer periods of time. Stronger muscles, and the increased confidence that often comes from feeling and looking fit, also improve your posture.

After about age 25, you lose a small amount of muscle each year as part of the normal aging process. If you keep your muscles strong and healthy, this loss of muscle bulk and strength can be kept to a minimum.

Lower back pain (p.381) is often a result of poor muscle strength and lack of flexibility. Regularly doing exercises that concentrate on strengthening particular muscle groups and improving overall flexibility can help prevent back pain (*see* PREVENTING BACK PAIN, p.382) and keep you mobile.

PSYCHOLOGICAL WELL-BEING

When you begin a program of regular exercise, you may experience some psychological benefits from early on. For example, many people notice a feeling of well-being after they have been exercising, and this is commonly thought to be the result of an increase in the production by the brain of morphinelike chemical compounds known as endorphins. These chemical compounds act as natural antidepressants and they can help you feel more relaxed.

Mildly anxious or depressed people may notice a marked change in their mood after exercising regularly for some time. For this reason, exercise is increasingly being incorporated into psychological therapies (pp.968–971). You may find that exercise helps you cope with stress (p.74). It also promotes regular, deeper, and refreshing sleep (p.73).

By exercising regularly, you are more likely to look and feel healthy, which increases your confidence and self-esteem. You may also experience a sense of achievement when you meet short-term goals in your exercise routine.

Taking part in a team sport or joining a health club or gym can be a way of expanding your circle of friends. Team sports foster mutual respect, shared responsibility, and self-discipline. These benefits are widely recognized and are particularly important for children.

Research into the effects of exercise among people who work in offices has found that regular exercise generally leads to a more productive workforce.

(WWW) ONLINE SITES: p.1031

Doing regular exercise

Taking steps to increase the amount of physical activity in your daily life

For exercise to be beneficial (*see* THE BENEFITS OF EXERCISE, p.55), it has to be regular and consistent. The type and amount of activity you can incorporate into your lifestyle depends on the time you have available to exercise. The best form of exercise is one that you enjoy doing and can fit into your daily routine. Exercise should be tailored to your age, state of health, and lifestyle.

RECOMMENDED LEVEL OF EXERCISE

Recent evidence has shown that even gentle exercise has measurable positive effects on life expectancy; consequently, everyone should try to lead an active life. If your life is fairly active already, there are guidelines on the amount and the frequency of additional exercise you can do to gain the maximum benefit to your general health. Current

ASSESSMENT HOW FIT ARE YOU?

When trying to assess how much exercise you do in your everyday life, it is important to be as honest as possible. Completing the simple questionnaire below can give you an indication of whether or not you need to increase the amount of regular exercise that you do.

1 *Can you climb one or two flights of stairs without shortness of breath or heaviness or fatigue in your legs?*

☐ YES ☐ NO

2 *When you have the choice, do you take the stairs rather than the escalator or elevator?*

☐ YES ☐ NO

3 *Do you have plenty of energy to enjoy your leisure time at the end of the working day?*

☐ YES ☐ NO

4 *Would you walk for 10 minutes rather than drive?*

☐ YES ☐ NO

5 *Can you carry out a conversation during light to moderate exercise, such as brisk walking?*

☐ YES ☐ NO

6 *If you exercise regularly, do you do moderate exercise that makes you sweat and breathe harder for 15 minutes or more at least three times a week?*

☐ YES ☐ NO

ANALYSIS

If you answered yes to all of the questions above, you are reasonably fit and are exercising to a level that will benefit your health. If you answered no to any of the questions, you should consider incorporating more physical exercise into your daily routine, and, after consultation with your doctor, consider starting a regular exercise routine.

Walking is for everyone
People of all ages can enjoy walking. Walking briskly for 2 miles (3 km) a day will significantly benefit your health.

recommendations are that you should do at least 30 minutes of exercise at moderate intensity for 3 days or more per week. A brisk 30-minute walk will provide a healthy amount of exercise for the day. However, if you want to change your appearance by improving your muscle tone or losing excess body fat, or if you want to become even more fit, you will have to exercise harder and for longer periods of time.

STARTING OUT

If your life is sedentary, begin by taking simple steps to become more active in your day-to-day routine. For example, make a habit of climbing the stairs instead of taking the elevator. However, if your life already includes some physical activity, think about starting a regular exercise routine, such as swimming, brisk walking, or jogging.

Make sure that your exercise routine is realistic for you, that you slowly build up the amount of exercise you do, and that you learn safe techniques in order to protect yourself from injury (*see* EXERCISING SAFELY, opposite page). You may be encouraged to continue doing exercise on a regular basis once you begin to experience its positive physical and psychological effects. If you begin an exercise program with a friend, you can motivate each other.

CONSULT YOUR DOCTOR If you have never exercised regularly before, or if you think you may be at particular risk from exercise, you should consult your doctor before starting a regular exercise program. You should consult your doctor if you have a chronic medical condition, such as coronary artery disease (p.405), high blood pressure (*see* HYPERTENSION, p.403), diabetes mellitus (p.687), kidney failure (p.705), or asthma (p.483). You should ask your doctor for advice if you are overweight or if you are over age 35 and have not exercised regularly for several years.

Your doctor may recommend certain types of exercises that are appropriate for you. For example, if you are overweight and have not exercised for some years, your doctor may suggest gentle exercise, such as walking or bicycling, to avoid putting too much strain on your heart and to reduce the risk of injury to your knees, feet, or ankles. If you have asthma, your doctor may suggest that you start swimming. You may need to take your regular medication beforehand. He or she may also tell you to avoid exercising in a cold environment, which can trigger asthma.

ASSESS YOUR FITNESS Overall fitness is a combination of three main factors: stamina, flexibility, and strength. To improve your fitness, you need to do regular exercise that works your heart and lungs (builds stamina), improves your joint mobility (flexibility), and increases your muscle strength.

Before starting regular exercise, it is a good idea to estimate your overall fitness (*see* HOW FIT ARE YOU?, p.57). Think about the activity you do in a normal day or week. You may be surprised to find that you already do some exercise most days, such as playing with your children or walking to work.

HEALTH OPTIONS CHOICES FOR FITNESS

Different exercises benefit different aspects of fitness (stamina, flexibility, strength) to a greater or lesser extent. Some exercises, such as swimming, offer all of these benefits. You can look for the best activity to improve a particular aspect of your fitness or review the overall fitness benefits of activities that you are already doing or are considering taking up.

FITNESS BENEFITS OF DIFFERENT ACTIVITIES

ACTIVITY	FITNESS BENEFITS		
	STAMINA	FLEXIBILITY	STRENGTH
Aerobics	★★★★	★★★	★★
Basketball	★★★★	★★★	★★
Bicycling (fast)	★★★★	★★	★★★
Climbing stairs	★★★	★	★★★
Dancing (aerobic)	★★★	★★★★	★
Golf	★	★★	★
Hiking	★★★	★	★★
Jogging	★★★★	★★	★★
Swimming	★★★★	★★★★	★★★★
Tennis	★★	★★★	★★
Walking (briskly)	★★	★	★
Yoga	★	★★★★	★

Using the chart
The activities above have been graded according to their benefit to each aspect of fitness. By comparing the benefits of each activity, you can tailor an exercise program to your personal fitness needs.

KEY

★ Small effect
★★ Good effect
★★★ Very good effect
★★★★ Excellent effect

(ASSESSMENT) YOUR PULSE RECOVERY TIME

The time it takes for your pulse to return to its resting rate after exercise can be used to monitor improvements in your fitness. As you become fitter, your pulse recovery time decreases. You should be able to notice a difference in how quickly your pulse recovers within 4 weeks of starting regular exercise that makes your heart and lungs work hard.

Neck pulse
Find your pulse on the side of the neck with your first and second fingers

Watch
Use a watch to time beats per minute

Taking your neck pulse after exercise
Count the number of beats for 10 seconds and multiply the result by 6 to calculate beats per minute. Continue taking your pulse every minute until it returns to its resting rate.

Your resting pulse can be used as an indication of your general cardiovascular fitness. A slower pulse indicates that your heart is fit. If you stop exercising regularly, you will lose the level of fitness you have attained. However, you can regain your fitness by starting an appropriate exercise program.

CHOOSING THE RIGHT EXERCISE

Exercise needs vary, depending on age, lifestyle, and fitness. Individual sports and activities improve different aspects of fitness (*see* CHOICES FOR FITNESS, opposite page). You should choose exercises that help you develop a balance of stamina, suppleness, and strength and that you can do all year round. Decide what your particular goal is and choose an activity that will help you achieve it.

GETTING THE MOST FROM YOUR EXERCISE PROGRAM

If your goal from regular exercise is to achieve an optimal level of fitness, you should set yourself a target heart rate. It is a good idea to monitor and record improvements in your fitness at regular intervals, such as once a month. This should encourage you to continue your program as you see your fitness gradually improving. You can keep track of your fitness level by taking your pulse at rest and then measuring how quickly it returns to its resting rate after exercising vigorously (*see* YOUR PULSE RECOVERY TIME, above). As you become fitter, your pulse recovery time decreases.

TARGET HEART RATE To calculate this, first estimate your maximum heart rate, which is normally about 220 minus your age. Your target heart rate is the range of 60–80 percent of your maximum heart rate. You can measure your pulse to monitor your heart rate during exercise, but wearing an electronic heart-rate monitor is easier and gives a more accurate measurement. At first, it may be hard to exercise at this rate, but it will become easier as you become more fit.

PLANNING YOUR PROGRAM When you start to increase the amount of exercise you do, you must build up gradually (*see* EXERCISING SAFELY, right). Initially, you should increase the number of times each week that you exercise and not be too concerned about how long you exercise or how hard you work. When you have built up the frequency of your exercise, you can then focus on increasing the length of time for which you exercise. Finally, you should increase the intensity of your exercise so that you eventually achieve your target heart rate. For maximum benefit, aim to exercise every day for at least 30 minutes at your target heart rate.

(WWW) ONLINE SITES: p.1031

Exercising safely

Taking all sensible precautions to avoid injury from exercise

Each type of exercise has its own potential hazards and may require the use of specialized equipment. Be sure that you set yourself realistic goals in order to avoid overexertion or injury. If you are not fit or have exercised only sporadically, you should begin slowly and build up gradually. Sudden strenuous exercise could result in injury (*see* SPORTS INJURIES, p.391). You may need advice from your doctor before you start exercising (*see* DOING REGULAR EXERCISE, p.57).

SPECIALIZED EQUIPMENT AND PROTECTION

Some activities, such as walking and swimming, require little or no specialized equipment. However, for sports such as football and skiing, having the appropriate equipment is essential. Proper footwear and clothing is very important; for example, badly designed or poorly fitting shoes may result in injury to the Achilles tendon and may aggravate hip, knee, and back problems. Make sure that you always wear the right amount and type of clothing. If you are exercising outside, it is important to protect your skin and eyes from the sun (*see* SAFETY IN THE SUN, p.80). If you are using exercise equipment at home, make sure that you fully understand the instructions so that you do not harm yourself by using it incorrectly. At a gym, ask an instructor to show you how to use the equipment safely if you are unsure.

Foot restraints
Adjust the straps to secure your feet
Sliding seat
The seat position should suit your leg length

Using equipment safely
To prevent physical injury through misuse, any type of exercise equipment, such as this rowing machine, should be used according to the manufacturer's instructions.

Good exercise habits

Develop a simple routine of warming up and cooling down (right) to minimize the risk of injury while exercising, and repeat it every time you exercise.

Knowing when to stop is a vital part of exercising safely. Common sense and your body will tell you what your upper limit is and when not to push yourself above it. If you notice signs that suggest you may be overexerting yourself, stop at once. Warning symptoms include:

- Chest pain.
- Pain in the neck, jaw, or arms.
- Sensation of irregular heartbeats (palpitations).
- Nausea.
- Severe shortness of breath.
- Dizziness and light-headedness.
- Muscle or joint pain.

Resting between exercise sessions is essential to allow your body to recover. Mild muscle stiffness is common if you exercise regularly, and you may find that a gentle walk helps relieve the stiffness. However, if your muscles are very stiff and your joints are painful, rest until you feel able to exercise again.

Dangers of overexercise

Exercising too often or too hard, often called overtraining, seems to undo the benefits of moderate exercise (*see* THE BENEFITS OF EXERCISE, p.55). Common injuries due to overexercising include severe muscle stiffness, tendon inflammation, and stress fractures (p.392).

You may be overexercising and need to reduce your level of training if you develop any of the following symptoms:

- Reduced appetite.
- Difficulty sleeping.
- Feeling constantly exhausted.
- Waking up tired and listless.
- Unintentional loss of weight.
- Loss of desire to keep fit.
- Recurrent infections or injuries.

In women, overtraining may stop menstrual periods (*see* AMENORRHEA, p.735), and in girls, it can delay the start of menstruation. Too much vigorous exercise may contribute to infertility (p.774) and osteoporosis (p.368).

You may need to make small adjustments to include physical activity in your life. However, if you find that you are rearranging your life around exercise, you are doing too much.

(WWW) ONLINE SITES: p.1031

HEALTH ACTION Warming up and cooling down in your exercise routine

You should follow a routine to stretch muscles, tendons, and ligaments both before and after exercise to prevent cramping and stiffness and to minimize the risk of injury. Your warm-up should involve aerobic exercise followed by a series of stretches. After exercise, slow down the pace (cool down) so that you are still warm while you stretch out your muscles. Repeat the stretches on both sides of the body and hold each stretch for at least 10 seconds. Some suitable warm-up and cool-down exercises are shown here.

Aerobic exercises

Aerobic activity increases the flow of blood through the soft tissues of the body. This increased blood flow raises their temperature and makes them more flexible. You should aim to do gentle aerobic exercises for between 8 and 10 minutes as part of both your warm-up and your cool-down routines.

Jogging
Gentle jogging or running is a good way to warm up your muscles. You need to run fast enough to raise your heart rate and breathing rate. Moving your arms helps raise your heart rate and create momentum.

Stationary bicycling
Bicycling slowly or with little resistance is an easy aerobic exercise to include as part of your cool-down routine and allows the heart rate to decrease gradually.

Upper body stretches

Stretching your chest and neck can help relieve the type of tension that centers across the top of your back. Stretching your upper back by holding your arms in front of you, clasping your hands, and rounding your back may also help. Upper body stretches improve your shoulder mobility.

Hands clasped behind back

Chest stretch
Clasp your hands behind you, and, while keeping your shoulders down, slowly move your arms up as far as they will go.

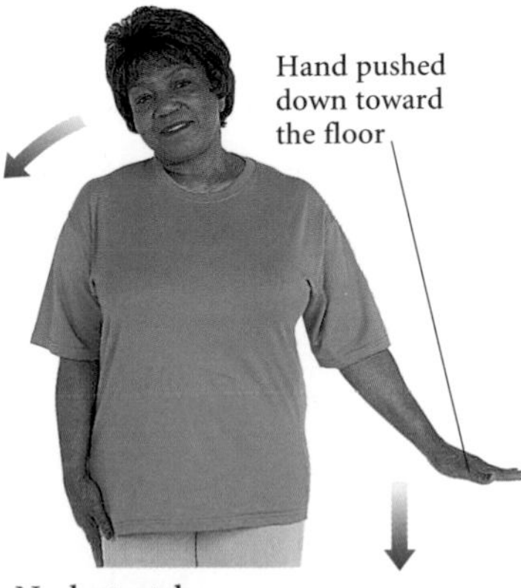

Hand pushed down toward the floor

Neck stretch
While holding your arm out to one side, push your hand downward. Then let your head fall to the opposite side.

ARM STRETCHES

Like the upper body stretches, stretching your arms can help relieve tension across the top of your back. You may find stretching easier on one side, depending on whether you are right- or left-handed. You should stretch your arms and shoulders before and after playing racket sports.

Palms of hands facing each other

Full arm stretch
Cross your arms and put your hands together. Raise your arms overhead, behind your ears, and stretch upward.

Elbow held beside head

Back of arm stretch
Put one hand between your shoulder blades and pull gently on the elbow to stretch the muscle.

LEG STRETCHES

Many sports injuries affect the legs; therefore, making sure that you stretch your leg muscles is especially important. You should always perform leg stretches before and after taking part in activities that rely heavily on using your legs, such as brisk walking, running, jogging, and bicycling.

Knee bent at about 90°

Hip and thigh stretch
Kneel with one knee directly above its ankle and stretch the other leg back so that the knee touches the floor. Place your hands on your front knee for stability.

Hands pressed against wall
Foot pointed ahead
Heel pushed to the floor

Lower leg stretch
With one leg in front of the other, put both hands on a vertical surface. Transfer your weight to your front leg and push your back heel to the floor.

Trunk of body held upright

Inner thigh muscles stretched

Knee slightly bent

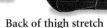

Inner thigh stretch
With your feet wide apart, bend one knee and lean your body weight to that side. Keep your back straight; avoid twisting.

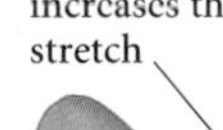

Hand increases the stretch

Back of thigh stretch
In a lying position, bend both legs and bring one knee toward your chest. Grasp your toes with one hand and gently pull on the back of the thigh with the other.

TRUNK STRETCHES

Do not forget to stretch muscles in your trunk. For example, by stretching out your back and the sides of your body before and after working in the garden, you may prevent back pain.

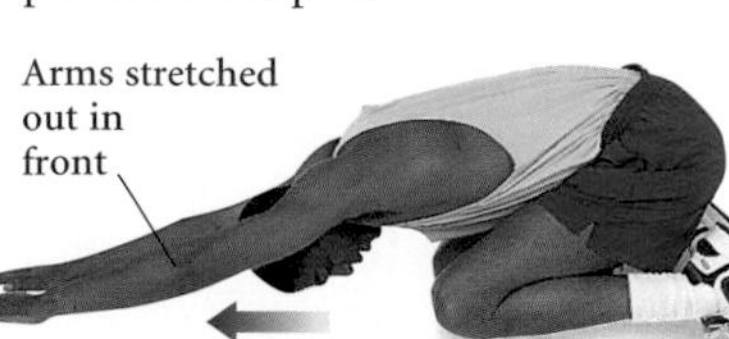
Arms stretched out in front

Lower back stretch
While kneeling, place your head on the floor in front of you and stretch your arms above your head, away from your body.

Knee pushed back by the arm

Trunk turned past bent knee

Trunk-twisting stretch
Sit with one leg straight and the other bent and crossed over it. Turn toward the knee that is bent, place your arm on the outside of it, and push against that leg while turning your body toward your other arm.

Shoulders in line with each other

Side stretch
With your feet shoulder-width apart, stand up straight. Then put one arm over your head, lean from the waist, and reach slowly to the side with your upper hand to feel the stretch.

ALCOHOL, TOBACCO, AND DRUGS

Many people use alcohol, tobacco, or recreational drugs for pleasure. However, all of these substances may cause severe health problems. Knowledge of their harmful effects can help you make informed choices about whether or not to use them.

Alcohol is safe in moderation, but having more than two or three drinks a day can pose short-term risks, from alcohol poisoning to traffic accidents. In the long term, excess alcohol causes serious health problems, such as heart, liver, and brain disease, and can lead to alcohol dependence.

Tobacco smoke contains nicotine, which is addictive, and chemicals that increase susceptibility to cancer and to narrowing of the arteries, a cause of heart disease and stroke. It may affect the health of people, particularly children, who live around a smoker. Tobacco is also harmful when it is chewed or taken as snuff.

All recreational drugs alter your state of mind; many can impair judgment and increase the risk of accidents. Drugs may be highly addictive and may cause death from overdose or side effects. Most recreational drugs are illegal.

Social drinking
Alcohol consumption can be an enjoyable part of your social life, but you should keep your consumption within safe limits.

Alcohol and health

How alcohol affects health and how to use alcohol responsibly

Alcohol has been used for centuries at celebrations and social occasions. It is a drug that alters a person's mental and physical state, reducing tension and facilitating social interaction, but it may also cause loss of control over behavior. Although moderate alcohol consumption (*see* SAFE ALCOHOL LIMITS, right) promotes a feeling of relaxation and has a beneficial effect on health, excessive use of alcohol over a long period can result in serious physical, psychological, and social problems.

Excessive long-term drinking severely reduces life expectancy and is a significant cause of preventable death. In Canada, disease caused by excessive consumption of alcohol contributes to thousands of deaths each year, and about 1 in 3 people who die in motor vehicle crashes have been found to have alcohol in their bloodstream (*see* SAFETY ON THE ROAD, p.83).

HEALTH ACTION: SAFE ALCOHOL LIMITS

Excessive alcohol can damage your health, and many health authorities have set guidelines to help you minimize risk. Alcohol intake is measured in units. Current American guidelines state that, in general, men should drink no more than 3 units a day and women no more than 2 units. Try to keep within these limits and have one or two alcohol-free days each week.

Units of alcohol
In order to calculate the number of units in a drink, you need to know the volume of the drink and the percentage of alcohol by volume (ABV). Measures served in bars or at home do not always correspond to those shown here.

1 UNIT OF ALCOHOL

BEER (ABV 4%)	WINE (ABV 11%)	FORTIFIED WINE (ABV 20%)	HARD LIQUOR (ABV 40%)
11 fl oz (330 ml)	4½ fl oz (125 ml)	2½ fl oz (75 ml)	1½ fl oz (40 ml)

EFFECTS OF ALCOHOL USE

When you drink alcohol, it is absorbed into the blood from the stomach and small intestine. It is carried to the liver, where it is broken down by enzymes to be used for energy or stored as fat. A small amount is eliminated unchanged in urine and in exhaled breath. Alcohol reaches its maximum concentration in the blood about 35–45 minutes after intake. The actual concentration depends on various factors, such as the weight of the individual and whether the alcohol has been drunk with food or on an empty stomach.

The rate at which alcohol is broken down in the liver also varies between individuals, and heavy drinkers are able to metabolize it more quickly. The average rate is about 1 unit per hour. On any occasion, your body cannot alter the rate at which it breaks down alcohol, so the more you drink, the longer it will take for your blood alcohol concentration to return to normal. If you drink heavily at night, you may still be intoxicated the next morning.

SHORT-TERM EFFECTS Alcohol depresses the action of the central nervous system. In particular, it affects the part of the brain that controls movement, impairing coordination and reaction times. Inhibitions are suppressed, and, although you may feel more confident, your judgment may be impaired for several hours after drinking. Just one drink is enough to have this effect, making it dangerous to drive or operate machinery. Alcohol causes blood vessels in the skin to dilate. Although this increased blood flow may make you feel warm and can cause excessive sweating, you are actually losing heat. Therefore, alcohol should not be given to anyone chilled from exposure to the cold.

Alcohol causes increased urine production, and you may feel dehydrated if you have several drinks in quick succession. Heavy drinking often leads to a hangover, with headache, nausea, dizziness, and a dry mouth. Hangovers are the result of adverse reactions to alcohol and to chemicals called congeners. These are found particularly in dark-colored drinks such as red wine and whisky. You can slow the absorption of alcohol by eating when you drink. Drinking very large quantities of alcohol may cause confusion and loss of memory, loss of consciousness, coma, or, in extreme cases, death.

Some, mostly Asian, people have a gene that causes an immediate adverse reaction to alcohol. Signs are reactions such as nausea and facial flushing.

LONG-TERM EFFECTS Drinking alcohol within safe limits (opposite page) may protect against coronary artery disease (p.405) and stroke (p.532). Men over age 40 and postmenopausal women are most likely to benefit. However, when safe limits are exceeded, the risks outweigh the benefits. Since alcohol has a high calorie content, regular drinkers often put on weight (*see* CONTROLLING YOUR WEIGHT, p.53). Alcohol damages most body systems and is a major cause of liver disease (*see* ALCOHOL-RELATED LIVER DISEASE, p.646). In the brain, cells that control learning and memory may be damaged (*see* WERNICKE–KORSAKOFF SYNDROME, p.538). Drinking more than the safe alcohol limit increases the risk of cardiovascular disorders such as dilated cardiomyopathy (p.427), stroke, and high blood pressure (*see* HYPERTENSION, p.403). Excessive consumption of alcohol increases the risk of several kinds of cancer, especially cancer of the nasopharynx (p.480), cancer of the larynx (p.481), mouth cancer (p.634), and cancer of the esophagus (p.638). If you also smoke, cancer risk is even greater.

Drinking too much alcohol reduces fertility and is dangerous during pregnancy. A pregnant woman who drinks any alcohol in early pregnancy or more than 1 unit a day in later pregnancy risks damaging her fetus.

Excessive drinking on a regular basis can lead to alcohol dependence (p.564) and is a major cause of social problems. In Canada, offenders and victims in homicides, serious assaults, and domestic violence are often affected by alcohol at the time, and many people who commit suicide are dependent on alcohol. Regular drinking can damage relationships and cause great stress to a drinker's family and friends.

ASSESSMENT — DO YOU DRINK TOO MUCH?

If you drink more than two alcoholic drinks a day on most days, you may be putting your health at risk. The questions below may help you judge the degree to which your drinking is affecting your lifestyle and whether you are at risk of letting drinking become an uncontrollable habit.

1 *Have you ever thought that you ought to cut down on your drinking?*
☐ YES ☐ NO

2 *Have other people ever annoyed you by criticizing your drinking?*
☐ YES ☐ NO

3 *Have you ever felt guilty about your drinking?*
☐ YES ☐ NO

4 *Have you ever had an "eye-opener" drink first thing in the morning?*
☐ YES ☐ NO

ANALYSIS

If you have answered yes to two or more of these questions, your drinking may be becoming a problem. You should think about how you can change your drinking habits and seek help from either your doctor or a support group.

ASSESSING YOUR CONSUMPTION

If you think you may be drinking too much, consult your doctor, who might ask you to keep a diary for several weeks to record each drink you have.

Some people use alcohol to relieve stressful situations or painful emotions. Stress-related consumption may lead to the development of a drinking problem. Warning signs include drinking more than you intended on any one occasion, severe hangovers, and becoming involved in accidents or arguments after drinking. Try completing a test (*see* DO YOU DRINK TOO MUCH?, above) to see whether you have a problem.

WHAT YOU CAN DO

To enjoy alcohol safely, limit your intake. At social events, eat first, alternate alcoholic and nonalcoholic drinks, and finish each drink before refilling so that you know how many units you have had. Never drive if you intend to drink; try to go with a designated driver who will not drink. Set a good example for your children. Discuss the effects of alcohol with them and reinforce the message of school awareness programs. To relieve painful emotions or worries, try approaches such as counseling.

WWW ONLINE SITES: p.1027

Tobacco and health

The effects of tobacco on health and reasons for avoiding its use

Tobacco is most commonly smoked in cigarettes but can be smoked in cigars and pipes, inhaled as snuff, or chewed. However it is used, tobacco is harmful to health. In developed countries, smoking is the main cause of death in people under age 65, leading to about 3 million deaths each year. It is known to be a major contributing factor to coronary artery disease (p.405) and primary lung cancer (p.503). Smoking also damages the health of "passive smokers," who inhale other people's smoke from the air around them. The only way to avoid the risks associated with tobacco smoking is to avoid smoking and those situations in which you come into contact with other people's smoke.

In affluent countries such as Canada, the number of smokers declined from about half of the population in the 1970s to about 1 in 3 in the 1990s. The decline is due to increasing numbers of older people who decide to stop. However, the number of young people (particularly young girls) starting to smoke rose slightly during the 1990s. Most of those people who continue to smoke are poor and disadvantaged.

Healthy lung tissue
NONSMOKER

Tar deposits
SMOKER

Effects of smoking on the lungs
Over time, the tar from cigarette smoke gradually builds up in the lungs, as these sections through the lungs of a long-term smoker and a nonsmoker show.

EFFECTS OF TOBACCO USE

Tobacco smoke contains several substances that are toxic or irritating to the body. The three substances that have been studied most closely are tar, carbon monoxide, and nicotine. Tobacco smoke also contains carcinogenic (cancer-causing) substances that have toxic effects on the lungs and other organs.

Tar in tobacco smoke irritates and inflames the tissues of the lungs. Carbon monoxide attaches itself to red blood cells, reducing their capacity to carry oxygen. Nicotine acts as a tranquilizer, beginning to take effect within 10 seconds of ingestion and producing a temporary feeling of well-being and relaxation. The substance is also known to increase the ability to concentrate. It stimulates the release of the hormone epinephrine into the bloodstream, and this causes a rise in blood pressure. Nicotine is highly addictive, which is why most tobacco users find it hard to give up the habit. There are many damaging long-term effects of tobacco use, some of which are exacerbated by other aspects of a person's lifestyle, such as drinking excessive amounts of alcohol.

DAMAGE TO THE RESPIRATORY SYSTEM Substances in cigarette smoke irritate the mucous membranes that line the air passages to the lungs, causing them to produce more mucus (sputum). These substances also paralyze the tiny hairs, called cilia, that help expel sputum from the air passages. To clear their lungs, many smokers develop the characteristic "smoker's cough." Eventually, smoking may result in chronic obstructive pulmonary disease (p.487), which leads to severe shortness of breath.

Carcinogens in cigarette smoke are the major cause of lung cancer and cause 9 in 10 of the deaths from this disorder. In some countries, lung cancer has overtaken breast cancer as the leading cause of cancer-related deaths in women, reflecting the large number of women who took up smoking during the second half of the 20th century. Regular exposure to tobacco may also cause cancer of the nasopharynx (p.480) or cancer of the larynx (p.481). The risk of developing cancer of the larynx is even higher for people who use snuff or chewing tobacco and for those who both smoke and drink alcohol.

VASCULAR DAMAGE Smoking is known to cause permanent damage to the cardiovascular system and has been linked to about 1 in 4 deaths from cardiovascular disease. This damage is thought to be caused by the nicotine and carbon monoxide present in cigarette smoke, which may encourage the development of atherosclerosis (p.402), a condition in which the arteries become narrowed. Atherosclerosis in turn is known to increase the risk of stroke (p.532) and cardiovascular disorders such as coronary artery disease (p.405). In women over age 35, tobacco smoking increases the risk of developing disorders associated with the use of oral contraceptives, in particular deep vein thrombosis (p.437) and stroke.

DAMAGE TO OTHER BODY SYSTEMS Smokers are at increased risk of developing mouth cancer (p.634) and cancer of the esophagus (p.638), particularly if they also drink alcohol. Carcinogenic chemicals from tobacco smoke that enter the bloodstream may also cause cancer in other parts of the body, such as the bladder (*see* BLADDER TUMORS, p.715) and the cervix (*see* CANCER OF THE CERVIX, p.750).

The toxic effect of tobacco smoke may aggravate conditions such as peptic ulcers (p.640). Smoking may reduce fertility in men and women. If a pregnant woman smokes, her baby's birth weight is likely to be about 7 oz (200 g) lower than the average, and the baby is at greater risk of illness or death just after birth. Menopause may occur earlier in women who smoke. Smoking also affects the skin and accelerates skin changes, such as wrinkling, caused by aging and sunlight.

People who smoke cigars or pipes suffer less harm from smoke inhalation than those who smoke cigarettes. However, together with people who use snuff or chewing tobacco, they run a higher risk of mouth cancer. Snuff and chewing tobacco may also irritate the lining of the nose, mouth, and stomach.

RISKS OF PASSIVE SMOKING

Inhaling the smoke from other people's cigarettes is known as passive smoking. Secondhand smoke, also called environmental tobacco smoke (ETS), is a mixture of smoke from burning cigarettes and that exhaled by smokers.

In the short term, ETS irritates the eyes, nose, and throat and may cause headaches and nausea. The risk of developing lung cancer is one-third higher for nonsmokers who are regularly exposed to ETS than for those who are not exposed to tobacco smoke. The partners of smokers are at slightly greater risk of developing cardiovascular diseases than the partners of nonsmokers.

The children of smokers are particularly at risk from passive smoking. ETS aggravates respiratory disorders such as asthma (*see* ASTHMA IN CHILDREN, p.839). Children whose mothers smoke more than 10 cigarettes a day are twice as likely to have asthma as those with nonsmoking mothers, and attacks may be more severe and frequent. ETS can also provoke allergies, such as hay fever (*see* ALLERGIC RHINITIS, p.466).

Exposure to ETS raises children's susceptibility to infections such as sinusitis (p.475), acute bronchitis (p.486), colds, sore throats, and ear infections. Up to 1 in 3 cases of chronic ear infections (*see* CHRONIC SECRETORY OTITIS MEDIA, p.860), the most common cause of deafness in children, is linked to parental smoking. ETS is also a factor in sudden infant death syndrome (p.820).

WHAT YOU CAN DO

You can prevent disease by not smoking or by giving up smoking before you begin to develop heart or lung disease. However, no matter how long you have been smoking, you can prevent further damage to your health by giving it up (*see* HEALTH OF EX-SMOKERS, left). As soon as you give up smoking, you begin to reduce your risk of developing lung cancer and other respiratory disorders, cardiovascular disease, and stroke. You will also be less likely to suffer from a range of conditions that are associated with smoking, such as peptic ulcer. You are never too old to benefit from this reduction in risk; even elderly people who have been smoking for most of their adult lives can improve their health and life expectancy by stopping.

If you need help giving up smoking, consult your doctor. He or she may recommend an aid, such as nicotine gum or patches, or the drug bupropion, or participation in a support group.

If you want to try on your own, plan in advance how you will stop. First, make a list of the reasons why you want to give up. Then work out the most common reasons why you smoke. You may crave cigarettes in certain situations or enjoy the ritual of smoking. Plan ways to cope with temptation and tell your family and friends so that they can offer support. Telephone helplines staffed by ex-smokers can provide help.

The next step is to choose a relatively stress-free day on which you will stop smoking completely. Dispose of all your cigarettes, lighters, and ashtrays, and distract yourself with enjoyable activities. Boost your willpower by looking at your list of reasons for giving up.

As soon as you give up, your body will start to repair the damage caused by smoking. You may feel withdrawal symptoms, such as irritability, and crave nicotine. If you relapse, work out why you felt the need to smoke, refer to your reasons for giving up, and try again.

Teach children about the health risks of smoking. Explain that people may enjoy smoking, but it makes them very ill. If your child's school runs an antismoking program, you should reinforce its messages. Most smokers take up the habit in adolescence. If young people can be prevented from starting, they are more likely never to smoke. Teenagers may regard smoking as glamorous, and girls may think it helps control weight. Deter them by stressing the immediate drawbacks, such as bad breath.

(WWW) ONLINE SITES: p.1037

(HEALTH EFFECTS) HEALTH OF EX-SMOKERS

The body starts to repair damage caused by smoking as soon as the habit is stopped. The risk of developing lung cancer and other disorders such as cardiovascular disease and stroke lessens the longer smoking has been stopped; smokers who give up for 15 years or more reduce their risk of lung cancer by more than half.

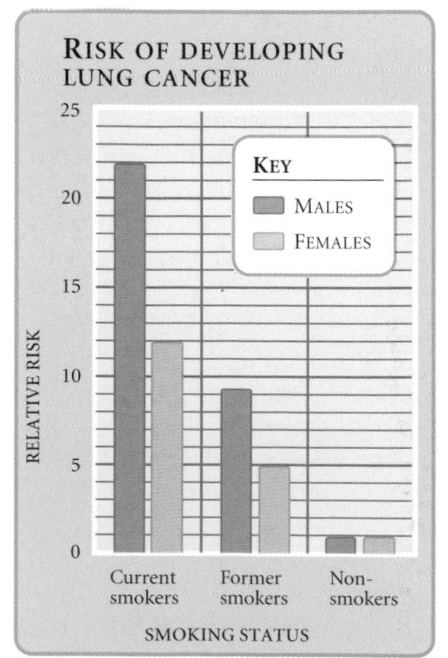
RISK OF DEVELOPING LUNG CANCER
25
20
15
10
5
0
RELATIVE RISK
KEY
MALES
FEMALES
Current smokers
Former smokers
Non-smokers
SMOKING STATUS

Smoking and lung cancer
This graph shows the relative risk of smokers and former smokers compared with that of nonsmokers, shown here as 1. Statistics appear to show that women have a lower risk than men, but this may be due to different patterns of smoking.

Drugs and health

Health hazards associated with the recreational use of drugs

A drug is any chemical that alters the function of an organ or a process in the body. Drugs that have been developed to improve body functions or treat disorders are known as medicines (*see* DRUG TREATMENTS, pp.878–939). Some drugs, such as temazepam (*see* SLEEPING DRUGS, p.915), which is prescribed for insomnia (p.554), are used as medicines and for recreation. Other drugs, such as ecstasy, have no medicinal value and are used only for recreation.

Recreational drug use can cause serious health problems, particularly if the user takes an overdose or becomes dependent on a drug (*see* DRUG DEPENDENCE, p.564). Since the sale or use of most recreational drugs is illegal, a user may be arrested and even face imprisonment. Caffeine, alcohol, and nicotine are also drugs that can be addictive and harmful (*see* ALCOHOL AND HEALTH, p.62, and TOBACCO AND HEALTH, p.63), but they are viewed differently by society because they have been used for centuries and are sold legally.

"Hard" drugs, such as heroin and cocaine, are more addictive than "soft" drugs, such as marijuana. Although hard drugs are used regularly by fewer people than are soft drugs, they have more potent effects on behavior and health. For example, in the US, there are 10 times more marijuana users than cocaine users, but 4 in 10 people entering drug treatment centers are seeking help for cocaine addiction.

EFFECTS OF DRUG USE

Recreational drugs are usually used to alter mood. They are classified according to the predominant change that they cause but often have a mixture of effects. Stimulants, such as cocaine, cause increased physical and mental activity; relaxants, such as marijuana and heroin, produce a feeling of calm; intoxicants, such as glue, make users feel giggly and dreamy; and the main effect of hallucinogens, such as LSD, is to alter perception and cause the user to see or hear things that do not exist.

In addition, recreational drugs can affect functions such as breathing and temperature control. These effects can be damaging in both the short and long term, and some are potentially fatal. Some of the potential health risks, such as those of dependence or of an extreme reaction, apply to many or all drugs. Drugs that are injected carry additional risks associated with the use of needles. Each drug also carries a range of specific risks to the health of users (*see* RISKS OF SPECIFIC DRUGS, right). The health hazards associated with certain recently developed recreational drugs are not yet fully understood, although ecstasy use has been reported to lead to brain damage in the long term.

EXTREME REACTIONS Any recreational drug can be dangerous, even if not used regularly. One risk is an extreme reaction to a drug. The effects of any drug can vary among users, and a drug that has only mild effects on one person may severely affect another. In addition, a drug may be mixed with other substances, and the amount of active drug may vary considerably from dose to dose. Since the drugs are illegal, there is no control over the standards of drug purity. Many drugs, such as cocaine and LSD, can cause delusions, leading to abnormal or hazardous behavior.

Uncertainty and recklessness about the strength of a drug may lead to overdose, which can be fatal. Alcohol and certain medicinal drugs, such as aspirin, interact with recreational drugs to produce intensified or unexpected effects.

DEPENDENCE Regular users of recreational drugs may face the problem of dependence. Physical dependence develops when a drug alters the chemistry of the body. The body begins to crave the drug, and the user feels ill if he or she does not take the drug. Physical dependence develops more rapidly if the drug is injected. Even if a drug is not physically addictive, drug users may become psychologically dependent, coming to rely on the enjoyable effects of a drug or the rituals that surround its use. They may also risk psychological disturbance and malnutrition due to self-neglect or loss of appetite. Some users may also spend a lot of time taking or obtaining drugs and withdraw from ordinary life. Since illegal drugs are expensive, many users support their habit by crime.

HEALTH EFFECTS RISKS OF SPECIFIC DRUGS

People use drugs for recreation because they enjoy some of their effects, but there are also many short- and long-term effects that are unpleasant, harmful, or potentially fatal. It is important to be aware of the risks involved.

Hazardous effects
Short-term hazards may occur soon after taking a drug, possibly after only one dose. Long-term risks result from repeated use.

DRUG	SHORT-TERM HAZARDS	LONG-TERM HAZARDS
STIMULANTS		
Ecstasy	• Nausea • Tense muscles • Panic • Loss of temperature control and/or fluid retention, which can cause coma and death	• Sleep problems • Lethargy • Possible liver and kidney problems and brain damage
Amphetamines	• Tension • Anxiety • Overdose may be fatal • Effects include fatigue and depression	• Heart disorders • Severe psychological disorders
Cocaine	• Paranoia • Overdose can cause heart attack • Effects include fatigue and depression	• Damage to nose and lungs from sniffing • Anxiety and paranoia • Heart disorders
Crack	• Loss of self-control • Violent or erratic behavior • Burned mouth and throat • Chest pain	• Heart disorders • Damage to lungs • Paranoia
RELAXANTS		
Marijuana	• Decreased coordination and concentration • Impairment of skills, such as driving vehicles	• Apathy • Increased risk of lung cancer and other respiratory disorders
Heroin	• Overdose can cause coma and death • Infection with HIV or hepatitis if needles are shared	• Tremor • Apathy • Blood-vessel damage from repeated injections
INTOXICANTS		
Glue, gasoline, aerosols	• Vomiting • Suffocation if inhaling from plastic bag • Loss of consciousness • Possibly fatal reaction upon inhalation	• Cough • Rash around nose and mouth • Damage to brain, liver, kidneys, and nervous system
HALLUCINOGENS		
Lysergic acid diethylamide (LSD)	• Extreme anxiety • Loss of self-control and increased risk of accidents	• Hallucinations that occur months or even years after use of drug
Phencyclidine, or phenocyclopiperidine (PCP)	• Confusion • Vomiting • Sharp rise or fall in pulse rate and blood pressure • Seizures • Heart failure • Overdose may be fatal	• Loss of short-term memory and coordination • Speech difficulties • Depression • Paranoia • Violent behavior

RISKS ASSOCIATED WITH INJECTION Users who inject drugs risk infection and damage to blood vessels, which can lead to tissue death (*see* GANGRENE, p.435) or septicemia (p.298). If syringes and needles are shared, users also risk infection with HIV (*see* HIV INFECTION AND AIDS, p.295) and hepatitis B or C (*see* ACUTE HEPATITIS, p.644).

WHAT YOU CAN DO

If you or someone close to you has a problem with drug use, ask your doctor about health risks, counseling, and treatment. Tell children about the hazards of drug use, act as a role model, and, if the school has a drug awareness program, reinforce its messages.

WWW ONLINE SITES: p.1030

SEX AND HEALTH

Human beings are unique among animals in having the capacity for sexual desire even when the female is not fertile and in retaining desire into old age, long after conception has ceased to be possible. The explanation may be that sex helps maintain partnerships. Regular sex also seems to improve cardiovascular fitness and prolong life. People who are involved in stable sexual relationships live longer than those without sexual partners.

Enjoying intimacy
When two partners are establishing an intimate, sexual relationship, it is important for them to trust each other.

A satisfying sexual relationship is an important part of life but not always easy to achieve, and sexual contact may be risky. In particular, casual sex and sex with multiple partners carry the risks of unwanted pregnancy and sexually transmitted diseases (STDs).

The first article in the section covers the basic elements of a healthy sexual relationship. The article on safe sex discusses ways of reducing your risk of exposure to sexually transmitted diseases. The final article provides an overview of the advantages and disadvantages of different forms of contraception. Education about sex, pregnancy, and STDs is particularly important for teenagers, who often fail to make use of contraceptives and ignore advice about safe sex. In the US, this has resulted in one of the highest rates of teenage pregnancy in the world.

Specific sexual problems and the symptoms and treatment of sexually transmitted diseases are discussed in other sections of the book (*see* SEXUAL PROBLEMS, pp.769–773, and SEXUALLY TRANSMITTED DISEASES, pp.764–768), as are possible problems in conceiving (*see* INFERTILITY, pp.774–777).

Sexual relationships

The physical and emotional elements of satisfying sexual relationships

The physical maturity necessary for a sexual relationship is signaled by the onset of puberty, when the individual's body makes the transition from childhood to adulthood. The development of emotional maturity frequently takes much longer, and early sexual encounters, although sometimes exciting, may just as often be disappointing or cause anxiety. With age and experience, most people become better able to establish and fully enjoy sexual relationships.

A HEALTHY RELATIONSHIP

What constitutes a healthy sexual relationship varies widely from person to person. Sexual fulfillment depends on a blend of physical and psychological factors, and what is right for one couple may not suit another. You and your partner should both be happy with the frequency of sexual activity, and you should be able to discuss which sexual activities you find pleasant and which you find unappealing.

Anyone in a sexual relationship should be aware of the risks posed by sexually transmitted diseases (STDs) and understand how to minimize the risk of exposure to them (*see* SAFE SEX, p.68). To avoid an unwanted pregnancy, you should be familiar with the options for contraception (p.69), including emergency contraception. It is important that children approaching puberty are given education about STDs, safe sex, and contraception. Most schools provide sex-education programs.

POTENTIAL PROBLEMS

It is normal to experience fluctuations in sex drive or occasional temporary loss of sexual desire, lack of sexual response, or inability to perform sexually. However, if sexual problems persist, they may be distressing and cause you anxiety, which further impairs your ability to enjoy sexual activity, and this creates a vicious cycle.

Sexual problems may have a number of causes. Emotional difficulties in your current relationship will affect your sex life. External stress will also affect a relationship and may lead to problems. For example, ongoing problems at work or financial difficulties may cause anxiety, irritability, or lack of sleep, all of which may decrease your desire for sex. Past upsets of an emotional nature, such as the breakup of a former relationship or sexual abuse, can affect your current situation even when the problem seems to have disappeared.

Decrease in sex drive or impaired sexual function may also be the result of complications of certain long-term physical conditions, such as diabetes mellitus (p.687); disabilities that cause pain and restrict movement; convalescence from surgery or severe illness; and the use of alcohol, recreational drugs, and certain medications.

WHAT YOU CAN DO

If there are matters that are bothering you, it is important to talk about them with your partner. If the problem is persistent, discuss it with your doctor, who can refer you for appropriate help. If you have a long-term illness or a disability that impairs your sex life, you may find it helpful to get in touch with an organization that has been established to help people with the problem.

(WWW) ONLINE SITES: p.1036

Safe sex

Sexual practices that minimize your risk of contracting sexually transmitted diseases

One of the hazards of sexual contact is exposure to certain infections. These range from uncomfortable but minor problems, such as pubic lice (p.768), to life-threatening disorders, such as HIV infection (*see* HIV INFECTION AND AIDS, p.295). Certain disorders, such as genital herpes (p.767), genital warts (p.768), and gonorrhea (p.764), are almost always transmitted only by sexual contact and are known as sexually transmitted diseases (STDs), and are also referred to as sexually transmitted infections (STIs). Others, such as hepatitis B and C (*see* ACUTE HEPATITIS, p.644) and HIV infection, may be transmitted by other means as well as through sex. For example, people who inject drugs and share needles with other people risk infection with HIV or hepatitis. Others, such as scabies (p.355), are transmitted by contact and are common among people living in overcrowded conditions and among schoolchildren. These disorders may also be transmitted during sexual intercourse.

Assessing the risks

It is important to assess your risk of exposure to STDs so that you can make informed choices about the level of risk that you find acceptable. To be able to do this, you need to understand how infection is spread and know which sexual activities carry the highest risks. If you think you are likely to be exposed to infection, or if you are not sure what your own risk might be, you should use a condom (see USING CONTRACEPTIVES, p.70) or avoid sex. It is essential that you do not have unprotected sex until your relationship has been established and is monogamous and both partners are known to be free of disease.

HIGH-RISK ACTIVITIES Diseases such as hepatitis B and C and HIV infection may spread through contact with semen, blood, or vaginal secretions. Other disorders, such as genital warts and genital herpes, transmit by contact with a wart, sore, or infected skin. The areas most vulnerable to infection are the skin of the genitals and mucous membranes such as the lining of the vagina, anus, mouth, and urethra (the tube that leads from the bladder to the outside of the body).

The sexual activities that pose the highest risks are those in which there is a chance that the mucous membranes will be damaged, allowing infectious agents from body fluids or body parts to enter the bloodstream. Vaginal, anal, and oral intercourse that involves penetration, and in which partners do not use a condom, are considered to be the activities carrying the highest risks. Anal penetration can be particularly hazardous because the lining of the anus and rectum is easily damaged.

SEXUAL HISTORY The risk of exposure to STDs increases with the more sexual partners you have and the more times that you practice unsafe sex. Having a monogamous relationship with someone whom you know has been screened and found free of disease carries the lowest risk. You may be more vulnerable if your partner has had sex with someone else and has not told you, particularly if you do not use a condom with that partner. In addition, you or your partner may already have an STD and may be infectious but have no symptoms. Examples of disorders that carry this risk include chlamydial cervicitis (p.765) in women and genital warts, which have a latent period of about 9 months during which you have no symptoms but are still infectious. Casual sex without a condom carries most risk because you are unlikely to know if your partner is infected.

Some STDs are particularly prevalent in certain groups of people. For example, HIV infection is more common among people living in some parts of Africa and Asia, prostitutes, people who inject recreational drugs and share needles, and people who have unprotected anal sex. You may run a higher than usual risk of infection if you have unsafe sex with someone from one of these high-risk groups.

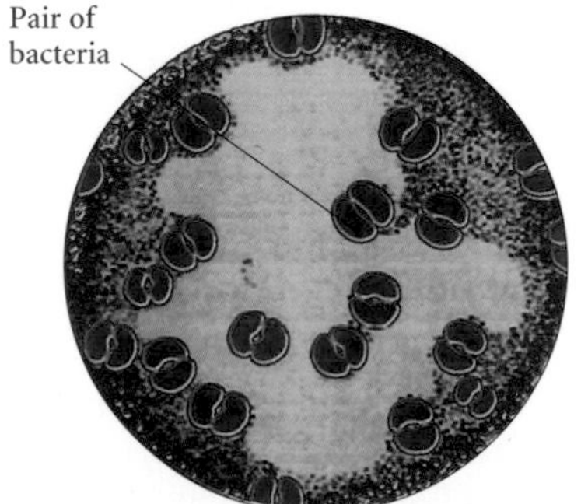
Pair of bacteria

Gonorrhea organisms
This highly magnified view shows the bacteria that cause gonorrhea, Neisseria gonorrhoeae, *which may be found in genital, rectal, and throat secretions.*

What you can do

Condoms are able to protect you from infections that are transmitted during sexual intercourse. However, they do not protect you from contact with sores or warts on areas of the body that are not covered by the condom or from pubic lice or scabies.

If you choose not to use condoms, make sure that neither you nor your partner is carrying an infection. Discuss your past sexual contacts honestly, particularly if either of you is in a high-risk group. If you suspect that you have been exposed to infection, arrange to have a screening test at a clinic that specializes in treating STDs. With HIV infection, there is a latent period of at least 2–3 months between acquiring the infection and the time when the antibody to the virus can be detected in the test. For this reason, many clinics advise using condoms for the first 3 months of a new relationship before having an HIV test.

Once you and your partner are sure that you are free from STDs, the most effective way to protect yourselves is by remaining monogamous. If you do have sexual intercourse with other partners, be sure that you use condoms. If you are not using condoms and develop an STD, use condoms until you have been treated and are free of disease or abstain from penetrative sex. Both you and your partner should be treated at the same time to avoid the risk of reinfecting each other, and you should both be free of disease before you stop using condoms. Sexual activities that carry a relatively low risk of infection include kissing your partner's mouth (or body areas other than the genitals) and mutual masturbation by hand. The activities that have little or no risk are those that do not involve contact with your partner's genitals. These include intimate activities, such as cuddling, massage, and bathing together.

(WWW) ONLINE SITES: p.1036

Contraception

Artificial and natural methods for controlling fertility

Contraception allows people to choose whether and when to have children. There are several types and each works differently (*see* USING CONTRACEPTIVES, p.70). Nearly all types, apart from the male condom and male sterilization, are designed for use by women.

Most contraceptives, with the exception of condoms, are supplied by your doctor, who considers your age, medical history, and sexual lifestyle. No contraceptive is entirely free from risk. Some types may not be suitable for you, while others have side effects that you must weigh against the benefits. You may also need to change your contraceptive as you grow older, have children, or alter your sexual lifestyle. It is important that you are happy with your choice of contraceptive. Even if your doctor has recommended a particular type, do not accept it if you have doubts about it.

BARRIER METHODS

Barrier contraceptive methods include diaphragms, condoms, and cervical caps. They act by preventing sperm from entering the uterus and reaching the egg. Male condoms cover the penis, female condoms line the vagina, and caps and diaphragms cover the cervix. Barrier contraceptives do not disrupt normal body functions or affect fertility, but they are unreliable if not used correctly and can also affect the spontaneity of sex. Some people who use condoms may be allergic to the material from which the condom is made.

When used correctly, condoms are an effective method of preventing unwanted pregnancy. Condoms are also thought to protect women from cancer of the cervix (p.750) by reducing the risk of infection with the human papilloma virus, which has been strongly linked with this type of cancer.

The male condom is the only contraceptive method that helps to protect users and their partners from STDs (*see* SAFE SEX, opposite page) and other infections. Condoms may also be used to reduce risk of infection when one partner has a chronic infection such as HIV (*see* HIV INFECTIONS AND AIDS, p.295).

HORMONAL METHODS

Hormonal contraceptives alter the hormone balance in a woman's body to prevent conception. They may be taken as oral contraceptives in the form of the combined pill or progestin-only pill. Other options are an injection into a muscle (from where the hormone is gradually released) every 2 or 3 months or inserting an implant that releases hormones under the skin. Hormonal methods are useful because they do not interrupt sexual activities, but they can cause side effects or health risks in some women. Oral contraceptives may be less reliable after vomiting or diarrhea or if you are taking some types of antibiotics (p.885). For this reason, if you are taking an oral contraceptive, you should tell your doctor in case it interacts with other prescribed medication.

COMBINED PILL The combined contraceptive pill, containing both estrogen and progestin, is highly reliable. This is the most commonly used contraceptive among women under 35, who are in their most fertile time of life and need an effective method. There may be side effects, such as changes in weight and mood, but these usually disappear after the first few months of use.

The combined hormone pill lowers the risk of cancer of the ovary (p.744) but increases the risk of some other disorders. Since the combined pill can cause a slight rise in blood pressure, you may be advised not to use it if you have a family history of high blood pressure (*see* HYPERTENSION, p.403). It also causes blood to clot more readily, slightly increasing your risk of stroke (p.532) and heart attacks (*see* MYOCARDIAL INFARCTION, p.410). The risk is substantially increased if you are over age 35 and smoke, but you should also avoid the combined pill if you are very overweight or have a family history of deep vein thrombosis (p.437).

PROGESTIN-ONLY PILL This type of contraceptive pill contains only progestin and does not carry the blood pressure or clotting risks of the combined pill. It is effective but must be taken at the same time every day to be reliable. Taking the progestin pill often causes lighter menstrual periods but may also make your cycle irregular. However, its effect on menstruation does not alter its effectiveness as a contraceptive. There may be other side effects, such as acne and breast tenderness, but these should last only a few months. There is also a small risk of ovarian cysts (p.743) or of having an ectopic pregnancy (p.790) if you conceive while taking it.

INJECTIONS AND PATCHES Injections of progestin or patches that deliver combined hormone treatment are reliable and give excellent protection. They are useful if you regularly forget to take pills. However, the injection may initially make your menstrual periods irregular or heavier and may cause weight gain of about 2–4 lb (1–2 kg). After the initial period, most women stop menstruating while they are receiving injections. Fertility may not return for several months after injections are stopped. Patches are much like combined pills, as far as side effects and return to fertility when discontinued.

MECHANICAL METHODS

The intrauterine device (IUD) and intrauterine system (IUS) are contraceptive devices inserted into the uterus by a doctor. They cause changes in the uterus that prevent fertilized eggs from being implanted there. The IUS acts on the uterus in the same way as the IUD, but it also releases progestin. The devices provide immediate protection and last for several years. They may be difficult to insert if you have never been pregnant and may be better for women who wish to defer future pregnancies or have completed their families. Both the IUD and the IUS may increase your susceptibility to certain infections (*see* PELVIC INFLAMMATORY DISEASE, p.741) and may not be suitable if you have multiple short-term sexual contacts that increase your exposure to infections. There is a small risk that the IUD or IUS may be expelled from the uterus or pierce the uterus and enter the abdomen, causing a serious inflammation of the abdominal lining called peritonitis (p.665), which may be fatal.

The IUD does not affect hormones or ovulation, but it may worsen heavy or painful menstrual periods, especially in the first few months after insertion. The progestin in the IUS usually makes periods lighter and less painful after the first 3 months of use. The IUS can be useful for women with heavy menstrual periods or women nearing menopause because it greatly reduces blood loss during menstruation. There may be temporary side effects similar to those of the progestin-only pill.

Natural methods

Natural birth control involves working out when you are fertile and avoiding intercourse at those times. It does not affect the body and has no side effects. It can be used to determine when you can conceive, if you wish to. However, natural birth control can disrupt the spontaneity of sexual activity and should not be used without training. It also requires that you have a regular menstrual cycle. This method works best if you are in a long-term relationship and feel that you could handle an unplanned pregnancy.

Surgical methods

Surgical contraception, or sterilization, is an operation that makes you infertile. This surgery can be carried out on men (*see* VASECTOMY, p.721) or women (*see* TUBAL LIGATION, p.743). Since the operation is considered permanent, it is suitable only for those who are sure that they do not want children. The operations have low failure rates of about 1 in 1,000 men and 7 in 1,000 women.

Male sterilization (vasectomy) is not immediately effective. The seminal vesicles (sacs that hold semen) still contain sperm after the operation, and a condom must be used until semen analysis (p.777) shows that no sperm are left. Female sterilization is effective immediately, but the risk of ectopic pregnancy is slightly increased.

Emergency methods

Emergency contraception is used to prevent pregnancy if you have had unprotected sex or if you think that your contraception has not worked. If you have had sex within the previous 3 days, you may be given a hormone similar to an oral contraceptive (if the treatment will not pose health risks for you). An IUD may be inserted, depending on the dates of your unprotected sex and your last menstrual period.

(WWW) ONLINE SITES: p.1031

HEALTH OPTIONS Using contraceptives

Contraception provides a high degree of protection against unwanted pregnancy, although the effectiveness of different methods varies. For each method described here, effectiveness is defined as the number of women per hundred per year who do not become pregnant while using it and is expressed as a percentage. For most methods, apart from the IUD or IUS, your doctor will need to explain how to use them so that they are effective. It may take some time to learn how to use a diaphragm, a cap, or natural methods, and they are not suitable for times when you need contraception immediately. A condom is usually the best method in this situation.

Barrier methods

Condoms, diaphragms, and caps prevent sperm from reaching the egg. They may be used with spermicide, a substance that kills sperm. These methods are 92–98 percent effective, and the male condom is the most effective. Note that the use of certain lubricants can make condoms less reliable.

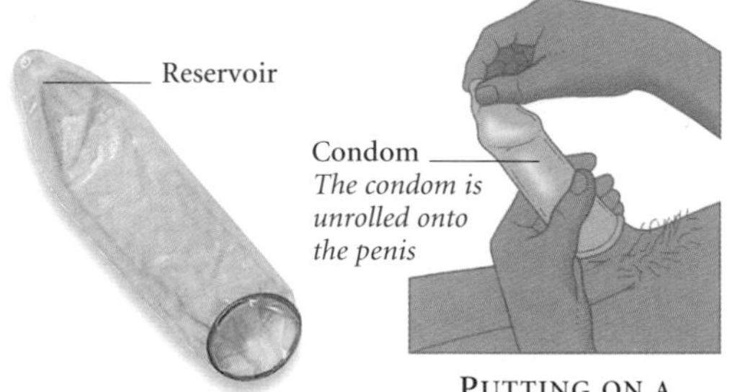
Reservoir
Condom
The condom is unrolled onto the penis

MALE CONDOM

PUTTING ON A MALE CONDOM

Male condom
Before a condom is unrolled onto the penis, the air must be squeezed out of the reservoir (end) so that the condom will not split. After intercourse, the penis must be withdrawn with the condom held on to prevent semen from leaking out.

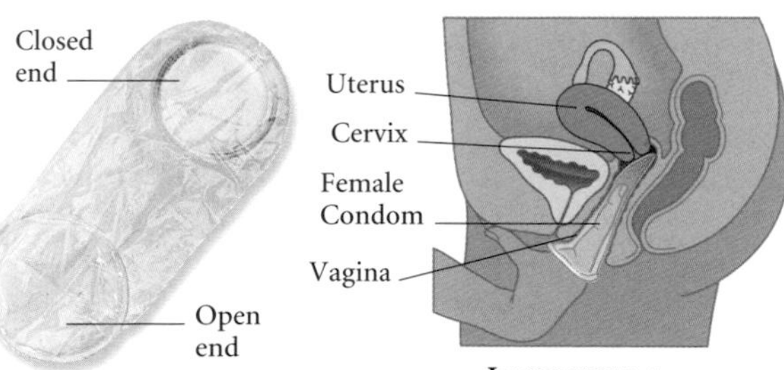
Closed end
Open end
Uterus
Cervix
Female Condom
Vagina

FEMALE CONDOM

INSERTING A FEMALE CONDOM

Female condom
The closed end of the condom is pushed up to the cervix. The open end extends just beyond the vaginal opening. During intercourse it is vital to make sure that the penis enters the condom, inside the vagina.

Cervical cap
The cap is partially filled with spermicide then pushed over the cervix. If intercourse does not occur within 3 hours of inserting it, extra spermicide must be added. To be effective, the cap must be left in place for at least 6 hours after intercourse.

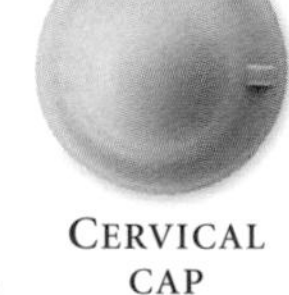

CERVICAL CAP

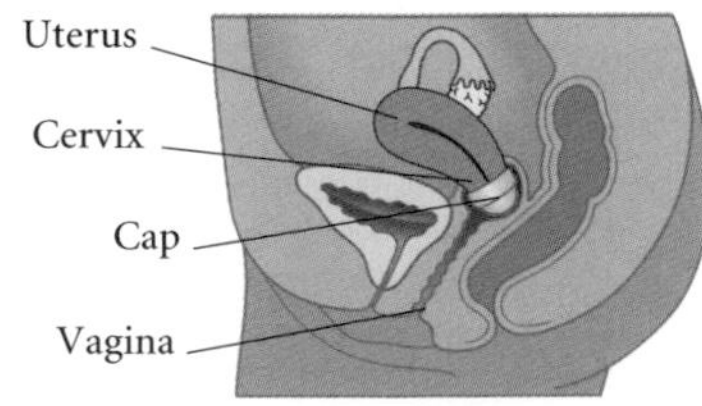
Uterus
Cervix
Cap
Vagina

IN POSITION

Diaphragm
The diaphragm is coated with spermicide on both surfaces. It is positioned so that the concave side covers the cervix. Like the cervical cap, it must be left in place for at least 6 hours after intercourse.

DIAPHRAGM

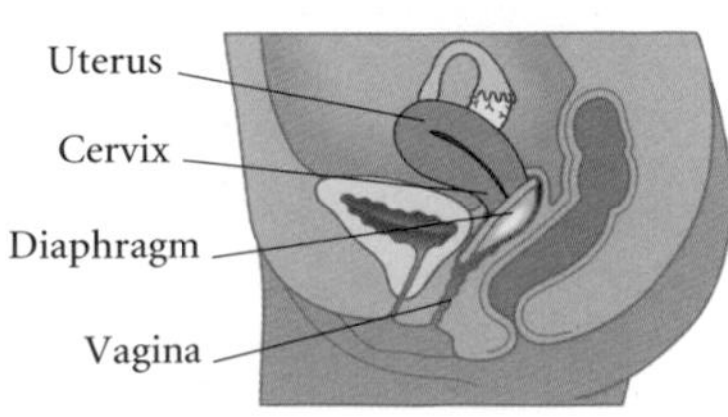
Uterus
Cervix
Diaphragm
Vagina

IN POSITION

Hormonal methods

Hormones are prescribed as pills, patches, or injections. Some hormonal contraceptives contain only progestin, which is a type of female hormone. Progestins act as a contraceptive by thickening the cervical mucus so that sperm cannot pass through; they also thin the lining of the uterus. The combined pill contains progestin and estrogen and prevents ovulation. Hormonal contraceptive methods are over 99 percent effective, but they must be taken as prescribed.

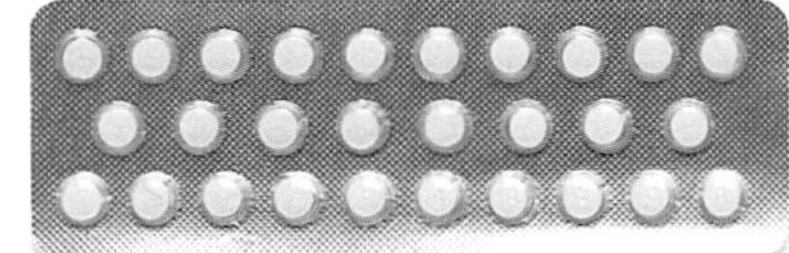

Progestin-only pill
The progestin-only pill must be taken at approximately the same time each day, even during menstrual bleeding.

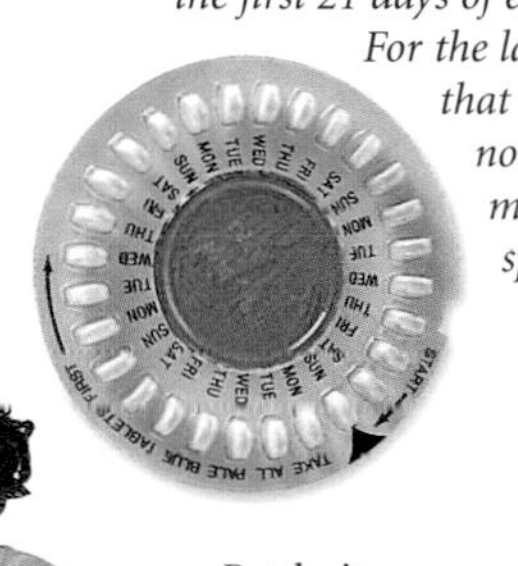

Combined oral contraceptive
The combined pill includes estrogen and progestin. The pills contain hormones for the first 21 days of each menstrual cycle. For the last 7 days, you take pills that contain no hormone or no pills at all. The pills must be taken in the specified order.

Syringe

Contraceptive injection
Your doctor or nurse injects progestin into a muscle in your arm or buttock, and it is released into your body over 12 weeks. To maintain the protective effect, you must have the next injection before the supply of hormone from the first one runs out.

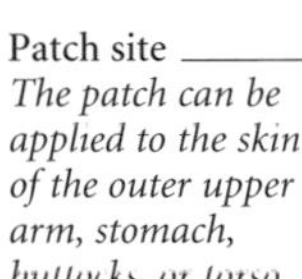

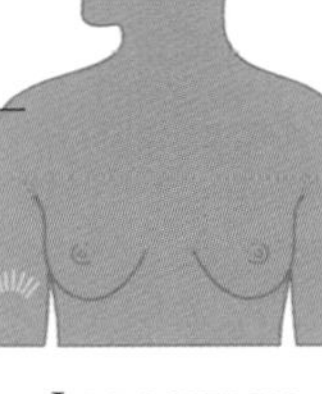
Patch site
The patch can be applied to the skin of the outer upper arm, stomach, buttocks, or torso.
IN POSITION

Patch
The patch contains estrogen and progestin that are released through the skin to prevent pregnancy. A new patch is placed on the skin once a week for three weeks; like combined oral contraceptives, no patch is needed the fourth week of each menstrual cycle.

Mechanical methods

The intrauterine device (IUD) and intrauterine system (IUS) are fitted by a doctor and can be left in place for 3–8 years. The IUD is thought to keep fertilized eggs from implanting in the uterus; some contain copper to kill sperm. The progestin in the IUS also thickens cervical mucus. Both are over 98 percent effective.

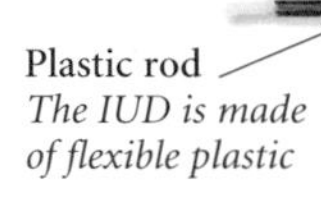
Plastic rod
The IUD is made of flexible plastic
Copper wire coating
This wire is made from copper, which is an effective spermicide
Threads
The two threads extend through the cervix into the vagina
INTRAUTERINE DEVICE

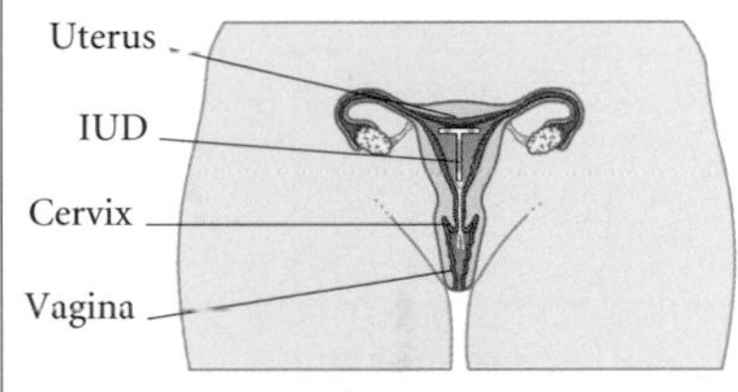
Uterus
IUD
Cervix
Vagina
IN POSITION

Intrauterine device (IUD)
An IUD has two threads that extend through the cervix. Once a month, the user should check that the threads are still there to make sure that the IUD has not been expelled during menstruation.

Natural methods

Natural methods of contraception are used to identify days in your menstrual cycle when you are fertile and times when you are less likely to conceive. Having identified these times, you can refrain from sex on your fertile days or use another form of contraception. The symptothermal method, which is only about 80 percent effective, is the most commonly used natural method. It is based on two factors: body temperature rising just after ovulation (which occurs 12–16 days before each period) and staying high for at least 3 days and increased amounts of mucus in the vagina around the time of ovulation. If you plan to use natural methods, seek advice from your doctor first.

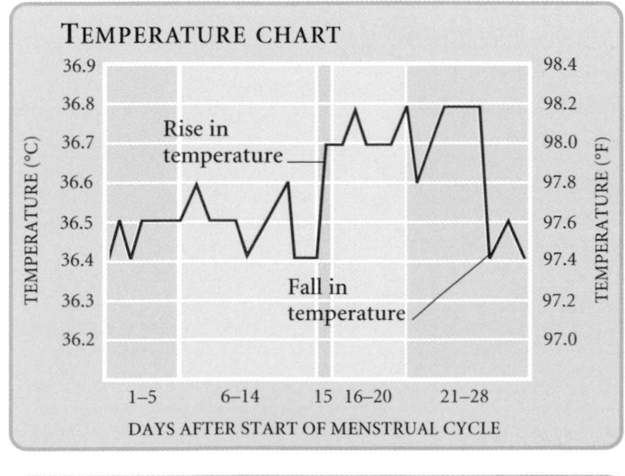
TEMPERATURE CHART
TEMPERATURE (°C)
36.9
36.8
36.7
36.6
36.5
36.4
36.3
36.2
TEMPERATURE (°F)
98.4
98.2
98.0
97.8
97.6
97.4
97.2
97.0
Rise in temperature
Fall in temperature
1–5
6–14
15
16–20
21–28
DAYS AFTER START OF MENSTRUAL CYCLE

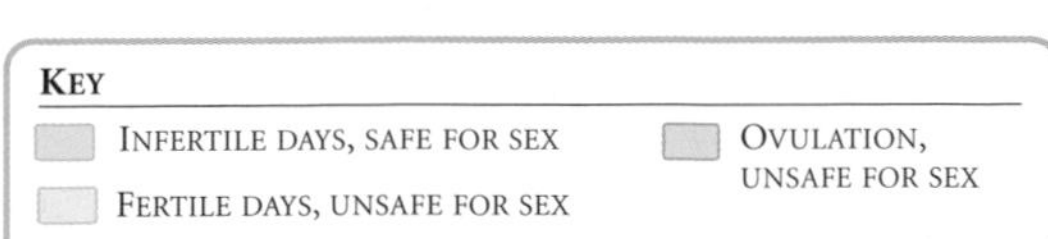
KEY
INFERTILE DAYS, SAFE FOR SEX
FERTILE DAYS, UNSAFE FOR SEX
OVULATION, UNSAFE FOR SEX

Using a temperature chart
You can monitor your fertility by recording your temperature on a chart like the one shown here. Take your temperature at the same time every day, immediately after waking and before getting up. Ovulation (on day 15 on this chart) is followed by a rise in temperature. When you have recorded higher temperatures for 3 days in a row, your fertile time is over. A period of infertility then follows and continues until the last day of your next menstrual period.

PSYCHOLOGICAL HEALTH

Your physical and psychological health are closely linked. A chronic physical illness is likely to make you feel low, while a mental health disorder such as depression may cause physical symptoms. You can make changes in your lifestyle to improve your physical and psychological state so that you are better able to deal with the stresses and strains of daily life.

Some life events, such as a death in the family, inevitably cause stress. People's reactions to such stressful events depend in part on personality and in part on other current causes of stress, such as financial problems. The more stress you have to face, the greater your risk of developing a psychiatric disorder.

To help you identify problems at an early stage, this section starts with a discussion of the difference between the normal range in personality and a mental health disorder. The next two articles provide advice on how to develop good sleep habits and on ways to identify and minimize stress. The final article explains the process of grieving and suggests ways in which you might cope with your feelings.

Specific psychiatric disorders are covered elsewhere (*see* MENTAL HEALTH DISORDERS, pp.551–565).

Maintaining psychological health
Learning how to relax by using techniques such as breathing exercises can be a key factor in maintaining psychological health.

Your psychological health

Your mental approach to dealing with everyday stress and life events

Growing up is a process of learning psychological responses to life events, both positive and negative. People vary in their ability to deal with these events, and everyone on occasion feels anger, frustration, sadness, mild depression, worry, loneliness, or uncertainty.

However, when these feelings prevent you from functioning normally for a sustained period, you may need to see your doctor. People have different personality traits and sometimes these can become sufficiently exaggerated to be classified as a disorder (*see* MENTAL HEALTH DISORDERS, pp.551–565).

Children and adults express their concerns differently. Recognizing early signs of problems enables action to be taken before they become serious.

RECOGNIZING PROBLEMS IN CHILDREN

Because children often cannot explain how they feel or what is upsetting them, they may express their feelings in unexpected ways, often as a change in behavior. As a parent, it is important to

ASSESSMENT HOW WELL DO YOU COPE?

How well you deal with the various aspects of your life depends mainly on your attitude and confidence. The eight questions below may be a useful guide to help you judge how well you cope with the stresses of everyday life. Some surroundings are more stressful than others; for example, you may react differently depending on whether you are at home or at work.

1 *Do you live in a supportive environment and have friends or relatives nearby you can call on?*
☐ YES ☐ NO

2 *Are you able to cope with everyday stresses without resorting to alcohol, tobacco, or drugs (including caffeine)?*
☐ YES ☐ NO

3 *Are you able to express your positive and negative feelings clearly?*
☐ YES ☐ NO

4 *Do you fall asleep easily when you go to bed?*
☐ YES ☐ NO

5 *Are you able to adapt when faced with a difficult change or life event?*
☐ YES ☐ NO

6 *Are you assertive about what you need and want?*
☐ YES ☐ NO

7 *Are you good at organizing your time and being effective at work?*
☐ YES ☐ NO

8 *Can you deal with stress flexibly so that you don't suffer from stress-related complaints, such as headaches and upset stomach?*
☐ YES ☐ NO

ANALYSIS

If you answered a confident yes to all of the questions above, you clearly have a positive outlook. If you considered answering no or answered no to several of the questions, you may have a less confident disposition, and it may help to discuss your feelings with your doctor.

be aware of warning signs. For example, your child may have a problem if he or she suddenly starts wetting the bed after a period of dryness or is unusually withdrawn, sad, or nervous. Children who are unhappy often complain of pain, typically stomachache. If your doctor cannot identify a physical cause, he or she may ask you about possible sources of stress at school or at home.

RECOGNIZING PROBLEMS IN ADULTS

If you notice changes in your normal behavior, such as increased moodiness, irritability, constant depression, anxiety attacks, trouble sleeping, poor concentration, or loss of appetite, you may be under some kind of emotional strain. If these feelings continue for a sustained period of time or grow more intense, they could signal a developing psychological problem. They may stem from a specific cause, such as the death of a relative (*see* LOSS AND BEREAVEMENT, p.76), but may develop for no apparent reason.

Your psychological health changes with age and may reflect your physical well-being. Physical and psychological problems often coexist in older people, and, if you become seriously ill or have a major operation, you are more likely to suffer from psychological problems (*see* MENTAL PROBLEMS DUE TO PHYSICAL ILLNESS, p.558).

If an aspect of your behavior or personality makes you or someone close to you unhappy and you want to change but cannot, seek help or advice from your doctor or a therapist (*see* PSYCHOLOGICAL THERAPIES, pp.968–971).

WWW ONLINE SITES: p.1029

Sleep

Understanding sleep and how it contributes to your health

Sleep is an important factor in maintaining good health. When you sleep well, you wake up feeling refreshed and alert; if you regularly sleep badly, every aspect of your life can suffer as a result. About 1 in 3 Canadians experience sleep problems. Many problems can be overcome by altering your lifestyle, but, if you experience persistent sleep problems, you should consult your doctor (*see* INSOMNIA, p.554).

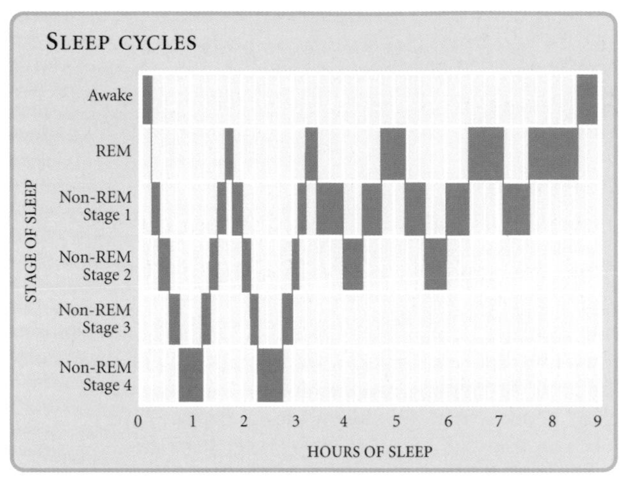
SLEEP CYCLES
STAGE OF SLEEP
Awake
REM
Non-REM Stage 1
Non-REM Stage 2
Non-REM Stage 3
Non-REM Stage 4
0 1 2 3 4 5 6 7 8 9
HOURS OF SLEEP

A typical night's sleep
The cycles in a night's sleep are made up of lengthening phases of REM sleep, when you dream, and four stages of non-REM sleep. In stages 1 and 2 you sleep lightly and wake easily; stages 3 and 4 are deep sleep, when you are difficult to wake.

WHY WE NEED TO SLEEP

Although scientists do not completely understand why people need to sleep, research shows that the body and mind require time to rest and recover from the day's activities. While you sleep, your body undergoes a series of repair processes and conserves energy.

There are two types of sleep: rapid eye movement (REM) sleep and non-REM sleep. During REM sleep, brain activity increases, dreaming occurs, and information is processed to reinforce memory and learning. Non-REM sleep consists of four stages: stage 1 is light sleep, in which you may wake spontaneously, and stage 4 is the deepest, in which you are very hard to wake. Each complete cycle of non-REM and REM sleep lasts about 90 minutes, starting with non-REM sleep. An average sleep cycle is made up of three-quarters non-REM sleep and one-quarter REM sleep.

SLEEP REQUIREMENTS

Sleep runs on a daily cycle regulated by an internal clock. Although people tend to sleep at night and are awake during the day, the cycle adapts to individual needs. The amount of sleep needed changes over a person's lifetime and depends on the individual. Newborn babies sleep up to 16 hours a day. Most people sleep an average of 7–8 hours a night, but generally the amount of sleep you need decreases as you grow older. Many people over 60 need only 6 hours sleep a night, although they may take an occasional nap during the day.

Most people can cope with a couple of nights in which they have little or no sleep, without experiencing serious harmful effects on their health. At certain times, such as when you are ill or convalescing, you may find that you need more sleep than is normal for you.

PROMOTING GOOD SLEEP

The most successful approach to getting a good night's sleep is to have a healthy lifestyle and to establish a regular routine before getting into bed.

A HEALTHY LIFESTYLE The key lifestyle factors that will help ensure good sleep patterns are getting sufficient exercise, moderating your alcohol and caffeine intake, and not smoking.

Exercise promotes a sense of calm and well-being by increasing the production of endorphins in the brain (*see* THE BENEFITS OF EXERCISE, p.55). It also helps tire you out physically.

Caffeine and nicotine are both central nervous system stimulants and may prevent you from falling asleep. Reduce your caffeine intake during the afternoon and evening. If you smoke, quitting may improve your sleep and also your general health (*see* TOBACCO AND HEALTH, p.63). Alcohol is a sedative (*see* ALCOHOL AND HEALTH, p.62), but you should not use it to help you sleep because alcohol-induced sleep is not as refreshing as normal sleep.

BEDTIME ROUTINE By adopting a consistent bedtime routine, you may find it easier to relax and sleep normally. Your routine could include listening to the radio, reading, or practicing relaxation exercises (p.75). Try soaking in a hot bath before going to bed or having a warm drink made with milk at bedtime. Try to avoid working late into the evening. Make sure your bed is comfortable and your bedroom is well ventilated, not too hot or too cold, and sheltered from outdoor light.

DEALING WITH SLEEP PROBLEMS

At some time in their lives, most people experience changes in their sleep patterns. Common problems are trouble getting to sleep, waking during the night or too early in the morning, and sleepiness during the day. Problems are often due to stress-associated behavior such as drinking more alcohol than normal or working until late at night.

If you have a sleep problem, examine your lifestyle to see if a change in activity or behavior could account for it. If you cannot sleep, get out of bed, walk around, read, or do some light household chores until you feel sleepy. Try to establish regular times for sleep and waking up. If you have a bad night, try not to sleep during the next day, but, if you feel very tired, a nap of up to 20 minutes may improve your alertness.

If you continue to have difficulty sleeping, you should see your doctor. Your problem may be a symptom of an illness, such as depression (p.554), or a side effect of medication.

(WWW) ONLINE SITES: p.1037

Stress

How to identify signs of stress and find ways to manage it effectively

Stress is a physical or mental demand that provokes responses that enable us to meet challenges or escape from danger. The demand may be sudden, such as the need to avoid a speeding car, or long-term, such as job pressures. Responses include both physical reactions, such as an increase in heart rate and sweating, and psychological reactions, such as an intense concentration on the source of stress.

A certain amount of stress can improve your performance in some sports and challenging physical activities, but excessive stress can be harmful to your health and interfere with your ability to cope with life. You can minimize harmful stress by identifying the types of situations you find stressful and developing ways to avoid or limit them.

SOURCES OF STRESS

Stress may result from external events or circumstances, your particular personality traits and how these affect your reaction to pressure, or a combination of both of these factors.

EXTERNAL EVENTS There are three main types of external circumstances that may lead to stress.

Long-term problems, such as an unhappy personal relationship, debilitating illness, or unemployment, are major sources of stress for many people.

Major life events that require a lot of readjustment, such as marriage, can be highly stressful even if you consider the change a desirable one (*see* LIFE EVENTS AND STRESS, below).

An accumulation of minor everyday occurrences, such as being late for work or getting caught in a traffic jam, can cause you to reach a breaking point if you are already under a lot of strain.

ATTITUDES AND BEHAVIOR Some patterns of behavior may result in stress. For example, if you suffer from low self-esteem you may doubt your ability to cope with challenges that arise in your life. You may also feel that you are not entitled to receive help from other people when you are under excessive stress. Highly competitive people may find it difficult to relax and may have a higher than usual risk of developing stress-associated disorders. People who do not express anxiety or anger even when they are under stress may suffer from accumulated tension.

RECOGNIZING STRESS

You may recognize that you have been stressed only when the source of the stress is removed. However, there are early warning symptoms of excessive stress that you can learn to recognize. If you experience any of the symptoms listed below, you may need to take action to reduce your stress level.

PHYSICAL SYMPTOMS Stress may affect your general health. You may feel tired, have problems such as tension headaches (p.518), mouth ulcers (p.632), or muscle pain, or be unusually susceptible to minor infections such as colds.

Excessive stress may also lead to or aggravate disorders such as high blood pressure (*see* HYPERTENSION, p.403), peptic ulcers (p.640), eczema (p.333), irritable bowel syndrome (p.656), psoriasis (p.332), menstrual disorders (*see* MENSTRUAL, MENOPAUSAL, AND HORMONAL PROBLEMS, pp.734–740), and erectile dysfunction (p.770).

PSYCHOLOGICAL SYMPTOMS If you feel very stressed, you may be anxious, tearful, or irritable. Even small problems may provoke an emotional response that is out of proportion to the cause.

(ASSESSMENT) LIFE EVENTS AND STRESS

Major life events, such as divorce or retirement, are potential sources of stress. You are most likely to suffer from excessive stress if the event is unpleasant, if you view it as out of your control, or if several major events happen at once.

Assessing stress
Stress levels associated with major and minor life events are rated from very high to low.

STRESS RATINGS OF DIFFERENT LIFE EVENTS

VERY HIGH	HIGH	MODERATE	LOW
• Death of a spouse • Divorce or marital separation • Personal injury or illness • Loss of job • Moving house	• Retirement • Serious illness of family member • Pregnancy • Change of job • Death of close friend	• Big mortgage • Legal action over debt • Trouble with in-laws • Spouse begins or stops work • Trouble with boss	• Change in work conditions • Change in schools • Small mortgage or loan • Change in eating habits • Christmas or other holidays

HEALTH ACTION RELAXATION EXERCISES

When you are under stress, your muscles tighten, your heart beats more rapidly, and your breathing becomes fast and shallow. A good way to relax both mind and body is to learn simple relaxation routines that slow down your body's stress responses. Two simple techniques are shown here. For further information, ask your doctor about relaxation classes.

BREATHING TECHNIQUES

Controlled breathing, which uses the diaphragm and the abdominal muscles, is the basis of all relaxation methods. To prepare for abdominal breathing exercises, you should wear loose clothing and try to find a quiet spot away from distractions. Sit or lie in a comfortable position.

1 *Put one hand on your chest and the other hand on your abdomen. Inhale slowly, hold your breath for a moment, then exhale slowly. Try to breathe using your abdominal muscles so that the lower hand moves more than the upper hand.*

Cushion to help you sit comfortably

2 *Once you are breathing from your abdomen, place your hands just below your ribs. Feel your hands move as your abdomen rises and falls.*

MUSCLE RELAXATION

For muscle relaxation exercises, wear comfortable clothing and lie on a bed or on the floor. Put your arms by your sides and let your feet fall open. Tense and relax each part of your body in turn. During the exercise, keep your eyes closed. Breathe slowly using your abdominal muscles.

1 *Begin by taking one or two slow, deep breaths. Focus on your breathing. Starting with your feet, tense the muscles in each part of your body, hold for a count of three, then release the tension.*

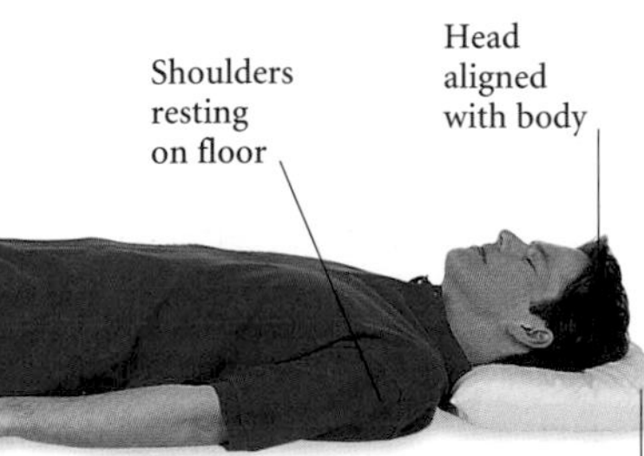
Shoulders resting on floor
Head aligned with body
Pillow supporting head and neck

2 *When you have finished, lie still for a few moments, then roll onto your side. Support your body with your arms and knees. After a few minutes, open your eyes and get up slowly.*

Eyes closed

Knees slightly bent to prevent you from rolling over

Arms supporting upper body

You may lack concentration and be unable to make decisions. Your sleep patterns may be disrupted. You may lose your appetite and find you have less energy than you used to have. Relationships may suffer, especially if you become impatient or feel anxious when dealing with people. To distract yourself, you may begin to rely on alcohol, smoking, or drugs (*see* ALCOHOL, TOBACCO, AND DRUGS, pp.62–66), which may further affect your health.

MINIMIZING HARMFUL STRESS

To avoid excessive stress and maintain good health, you should learn to identify the sources of stress and try to manage your life so that you can anticipate and prepare for problems or crises.

MAINTAINING GOOD HEALTH Attempt to improve your mental health and well-being by keeping up contact with your family, maintaining friendships, and pursuing leisure activities that give you pleasure without adding to your anxieties or stresses. Exercising regularly can help relieve physical tension (*see* HOW EXERCISE BENEFITS HEALTH, p.56), but you may also find it helpful to learn to relax your body consciously (*see* RELAXATION EXERCISES, left).

IDENTIFYING SOURCES OF STRESS A useful way of identifying sources of stress is to keep a diary and record daily events and how you have responded to them. After a few weeks, look through your diary and identify events that you found stressful. Note whether the stress made you perform better or worse and try to identify activities that may have reduced your stress level.

ANTICIPATING PROBLEMS If you know that you will soon have to face a stressful event, prepare for it thoroughly so that you feel you have a good chance of managing it successfully. Break tasks or events down into smaller parts if they seem too big to cope with all at once. If you have several tasks to do in a limited time, list them and give the most important or urgent ones the highest priority. Limit the tasks that are not important or urgent in order to conserve your time and energy. If other people regularly make heavy demands on you, try to set limits.

Dealing with a crisis

Stress is a normal response to crises, and in most cases it need not be a cause for concern. However, if it leads to unmanageable symptoms, it has itself become a crisis. Seek help from your family and friends. Ask your doctor for help with the symptoms. He or she may refer you for counseling (p.971) if needed.

(WWW) ONLINE SITES: p.1037

Loss and bereavement

Understanding and coping with the feelings, emotions, and stress that characterize the grieving process

Many types of change may result in a sense of loss. Events that may provoke this feeling include the breakup of a relationship, children leaving home, job loss, or sudden disability. The loss felt after the death of a relative, a close friend, or a pet is called bereavement.

Loss provokes overwhelming physical and emotional reactions that can have a serious effect on your health. For example, bereaved people, especially widowed men, are at increased risk of dying from disease or suicide in the first year of bereavement, and their risk of developing depression (p.554) also increases. The process of gradual adjustment to loss, known as grieving, takes time. Understanding this process should help you anticipate and handle your feelings and reduce the health risks associated with loss.

Normal reactions to loss

The grieving process has several elements, which may appear in a different order for different people and may overlap. You may not experience all of them. At any one time, you are likely to experience a mixture of emotions, some stronger than others. Throughout the grieving process, you may find that you oscillate between focusing on your loss and distracting yourself with work or plans for the future.

INITIAL REACTIONS At first, you may be overcome by shock or feel numb and detached. You may even act as though nothing has happened. These reactions are a natural psychological mechanism that shields you from the immediate impact of the loss. You are likely to experience signs of stress (p.74), such as loss of appetite, inability to sleep, and lack of energy. You may feel run down and become susceptible to minor illnesses.

PROTEST After the initial shock, you may feel overcome with intense emotions. The most common emotion is sadness. Other feelings may include anger, guilt, or fear. The emotional pain may be interrupted by periods in which feelings of emptiness predominate.

You may think about your loss constantly as your mind challenges the fact that the event has occurred. If a loved one has died, you may find yourself searching for him or her and may have hallucinations in which you believe that you have seen or heard the person.

DISORGANIZATION As your mind accepts the reality of the loss, you may feel bleakness, apathy, and confusion and have no hope in the future. You may even feel suicidal.

REORGANIZATION As time passes, you accept the loss and achieve a new normality, even though your life may have changed forever. You may feel stronger as a result of coping with the loss. You can remember happy times and hope to be happy again without forgetting the loss or minimizing its impact.

How to cope with grief

If you know that you are going to suffer a loss – for example, if someone close to you has a terminal illness – find out about the grieving process in advance. By doing so, you may be able to cope more easily with your grief. Once the loss has occurred, it is important for you to acknowledge it in some way, such as by viewing the dead body of a loved person and attending the funeral service if you feel you can.

It is also important for you to recognize the difference between normal and abnormal responses to loss. The most common abnormal reactions are very intense emotions that last for a long time; inability to stop grieving, even after several years; and the inability to grieve at all. To cope with any of these reactions, it may be helpful to contact an organization that counsels bereaved people or allows grieving people to offer each other mutual support.

When supporting other people who have suffered a loss, take time to listen to them and acknowledge their painful feelings but try to avoid giving advice about how they should overcome their emotions. People who are grieving may also appreciate practical help, perhaps with shopping or child care, especially in the days immediately after a loss.

Very young children may not realize that death is permanent, but by about the age of 5 more than half of them fully understand. Be honest but gentle with a grieving child. Explain what has happened and avoid euphemisms for death. Allow time for the child to talk about the loss. He or she might like to make a scrapbook of pictures and writings to commemorate the deceased. You and the child may also find it helpful to have professional counseling (p.971).

(WWW) ONLINE SITES: p.1029

The grieving process
Grieving is like a loop in the course of normal life. You will eventually come to terms with your feelings and achieve a new form of normality.

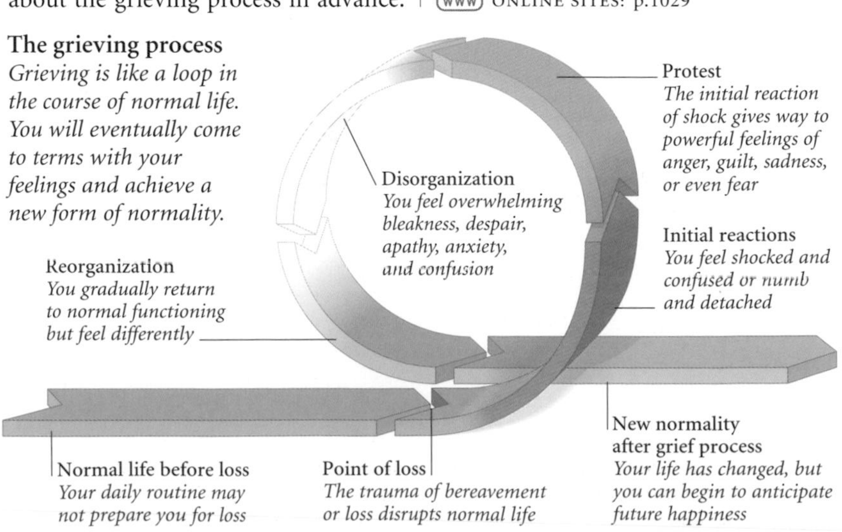
Protest
The initial reaction of shock gives way to powerful feelings of anger, guilt, sadness, or even fear
Disorganization
You feel overwhelming bleakness, despair, apathy, anxiety, and confusion
Initial reactions
You feel shocked and confused or numb and detached
Reorganization
You gradually return to normal functioning but feel differently
New normality after grief process
Your life has changed, but you can begin to anticipate future happiness
Normal life before loss
Your daily routine may not prepare you for loss
Point of loss
The trauma of bereavement or loss disrupts normal life

SAFETY AND HEALTH

Although most deaths and disabilities are caused by disease, a substantial number are the result of other causes. Unintentional injuries are the third most common cause of death in Canada. At home, at work, during recreational activities, and when traveling, accidents result in injuries to millions of people every year.

Unintentional injuries are the leading cause of death among Canadians age 1 to 44. More importantly, they are the leading cause of permanent disability. For every death in a motor vehicle collision, seven people are left with some type of disability. These injuries result in substantial social and economic costs, lead to huge amounts of litigation, and have psychological effects, such as post-traumatic stress disorder, on those involved.

The prevention of injuries has become a major concern for both medical and economic reasons. This section is designed to alert you to potentially dangerous circumstances in your everyday life, whether you are at work or at home. The first article addresses safety and health in your home and is followed by others on health and safety in the yard, in the sun, in and around water, with pets, at work, on the road, and when traveling.

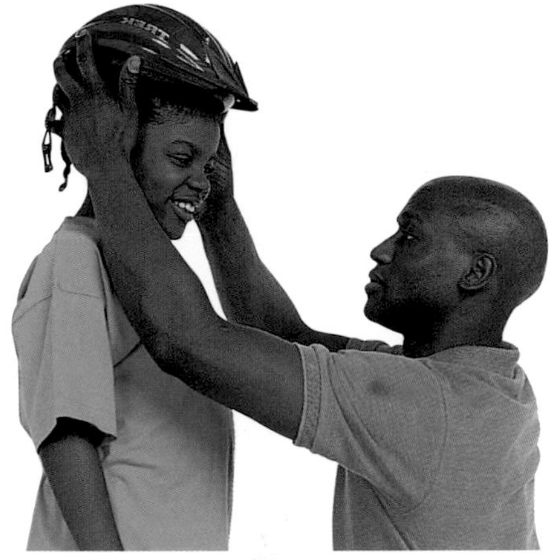

Family safety
When taking part in sports or traveling on the road, make yourself aware of potential dangers and take action to minimize the risks to you and your family.

Home safety and health

How to prevent injuries and avoid health problems in the home

Injuries in the home are a significant cause of injury in Canada. Each year, Canadians are killed and many more injured as a result of incidents that occur in their own homes. By taking a few simple precautions to make your home safer, many of these injuries can be prevented from happening (*see* MAKING YOUR HOME SAFE, p.78).

Age is the major factor influencing people's risk of injuries. People over 75 have the greatest risk of having fatal injuries at home, and children under age 5 have the highest rate of injury. This is partly a reflection of the amount of time people in these particular age groups spend at home. Falls are one of the most common causes of injuries, as is poisoning by substances such as drugs, chemicals used for household cleaning, and toxic gases. Other common causes of injuries in the home include fire, electrocution, drowning, and suffocation. A significant risk to health is posed by poor hygiene in the kitchen, which can cause digestive system upsets through food poisoning (*see* FOOD HYGIENE, p.79).

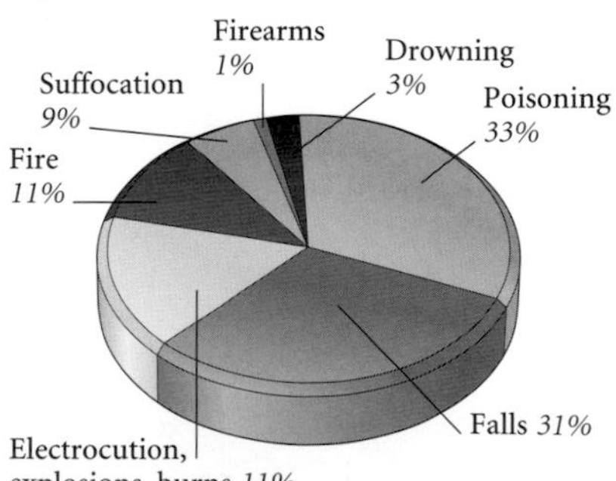

Firearms 1%
Drowning 3%
Suffocation 9%
Poisoning 33%
Fire 11%
Falls 31%
Electrocution, explosions, burns 11%

Accidental deaths in the home
US statistics show that poisoning and falls are the most common causes of accidental deaths in the home.

PREVENTING FALLS

About one-third of all injuries that occur in the home are the result of falls. Elderly people are especially vulnerable because they may often be frail and less steady on their feet than people in younger age groups, and they may have attacks of fainting or dizziness. Elderly people are also more likely to have poor vision. To prevent falls in the home, make sure that the lighting in your house is adequate, that floor coverings are secure, that no objects are left on the stairs, and that safety rails are installed in the bathroom. If you have babies or toddlers, you can control their access to stairways by installing safety gates specifically designed for stairways.

AVOIDING POISONING

Poisoning accounts for about one-third of all injuries that take place in the home. The poisons responsible are frequently prescription or over-the-counter drugs, household cleaning materials, and gases such as carbon monoxide. Since children are particularly at risk of poisoning, all drugs, cleaning materials, and other household chemicals should be locked up or kept out of children's reach.

CARBON MONOXIDE Incomplete combustion of any fuel produces carbon monoxide (CO), a colorless and odorless gas. If inhaled, this gas reduces the ability of the blood to transport oxygen, potentially leading to death. To prevent the accumulation of CO, you should have chimneys, vents, and flues checked, and heating systems and gas appliances should be inspected yearly. You should also buy a CO monitor to check levels yourself. The combustion engines used in cars, chainsaws, and some lawnmowers release CO and should never be run in a closed garage.

LEAD Children are particularly vulnerable to the effects of lead, which can cause damage to the brain, nerves, red blood cells, and the digestive system. One common source of lead is drinking water supplied through lead pipes in

HEALTH ACTION MAKING YOUR HOME SAFE

Injuries can occur in any part of your home or yard (*see* SAFETY IN THE YARD, p.80), but the living room and kitchen each account for about one-quarter of all injuries. About 1 in 6 injuries takes place on the stairs or in the bedroom, and the bathroom accounts for about 1 in 15 injuries.

Bathroom
The main hazards in the bathroom are slipping on wet surfaces, drowning, electrocution, and scalding yourself with hot water.

Shower
Always test the water temperature before getting into the shower

Safety rail
Fasten a firm handrail over the bathtub

Electrical outlet
Make sure that the outlet is specially designed for bathroom use

Nonslip mats
Use nonslip mats in the shower and bathtub

Living room
The living or family room is where people spend most of their time at home. Many injuries here involve electrical appliances, falls, or fire.

Wiring
Do not let wires trail across the floor or under the carpet

Electrical outlets
Do not overload outlets

Fire
Keep firescreens around the fire at all times

Toys
Put away children's toys after use

Furnishings
All furnishings should be flame-resistant

Rugs
Use nonslip mats under rugs

Bookcases
Secure bookcases and other items of heavy furniture to a wall to prevent them from falling over

Kitchen
Most injuries in the kitchen involve scalds from hot liquids or solids, cuts from knives or broken glass, or electrocution from electrical appliances.

Cooker hood
Replace the filter at regular intervals

Saucepan handles
Turn pan handles away from the front of the stove

Fire extinguisher
Keep an extinguisher in the kitchen and make sure that you know how to use it

Knife block
Store knives safely in a knife block

Stove
Use the back burners of stoves in preference to the front ones

Appliance cords
Fit electrical appliances with coiled cords and keep the appliances near the wall

Floor
Wipe up spilled liquid immediately and make sure that floors are dry before walking on them

older homes. If your home has lead pipes, they should be replaced with copper or plastic ones. Any lead-based paint inside your house should be removed by professional contractors. Make sure that toys and playground equipment used by your children are not coated with lead-based paint.

PREVENTING FIRES

If you have a fireplace, place a screen in front of it and make sure that both the fireplace and the chimney are swept. Teach your children not to play with matches, lighters, utility lighters, or electrical equipment, and do not overload wall outlets with adapters. Highly flammable materials, such as certain paints and paintbrush cleaners, should be locked away. Smoke detectors and fire extinguishers should be installed on every floor in case a fire does break out. Make sure that they are in good working order at all times. Consult with your local fire department regarding the proper fire extinguisher to have for each area of the house. For example, you may need an outdoor fire extinguisher for the patio area. Plan and practice your escape route out of the house in the event of a fire.

Fitting a smoke detector
Smoke detectors should be fitted on every level of your home. Keep them free of dust and cobwebs and test the batteries every month.

AVOIDING GUNSHOT INJURY

Although firearms account for few injuries in the home, the injuries resulting from them can be serious or fatal. Many injuries occur when loaded firearms are being cleaned or when children discover loaded firearms and play with them.

Storing firearms safely significantly reduces the risk of injury. Always keep firearms unloaded, uncocked, and locked away.

Ammunition for the firearm should always be stored in a separate locked cabinet well out of reach of children.

MONITORING AIR POLLUTION IN AND AROUND THE HOME

Air pollution may trigger flare-ups of asthma in susceptible people and appears to worsen symptoms in people with existing asthma (p.483).

The major sources of air pollution are industrial and power plants, which release sulfur oxides into the atmosphere. Other common sources are dry cleaning machines, air conditioners, and refrigerators, which produce chlorofluorocarbons; motor vehicle exhaust, which contains CO, nitrogen oxide, and lead; and radon. The National Air Pollution Surveillance (NAPS), a program run by the federal and provincial governments, monitors air quality in Canada. Contact Environment Canada or your provincial environment ministry for information.

Radon is an odorless, colorless gas released from granite rock. It can damage the lungs if inhaled in large amounts. It is not possible to radon-proof your home, but you can reduce the risk of exposure by keeping your home well ventilated and sealing cracks in floors and walls. If you live in a region where granite has been used in the construction of house basements, get advice from a specialist.

(WWW) ONLINE SITES: p.1036

HEALTH ACTION FOOD HYGIENE

Food poisoning is usually caused by eating food contaminated by bacteria. The risk of poisoning is increased if food is left at room temperature because any bacteria present can multiply rapidly. Food is usually safe if stored in the refrigerator because the low temperature prevents bacteria from multiplying.

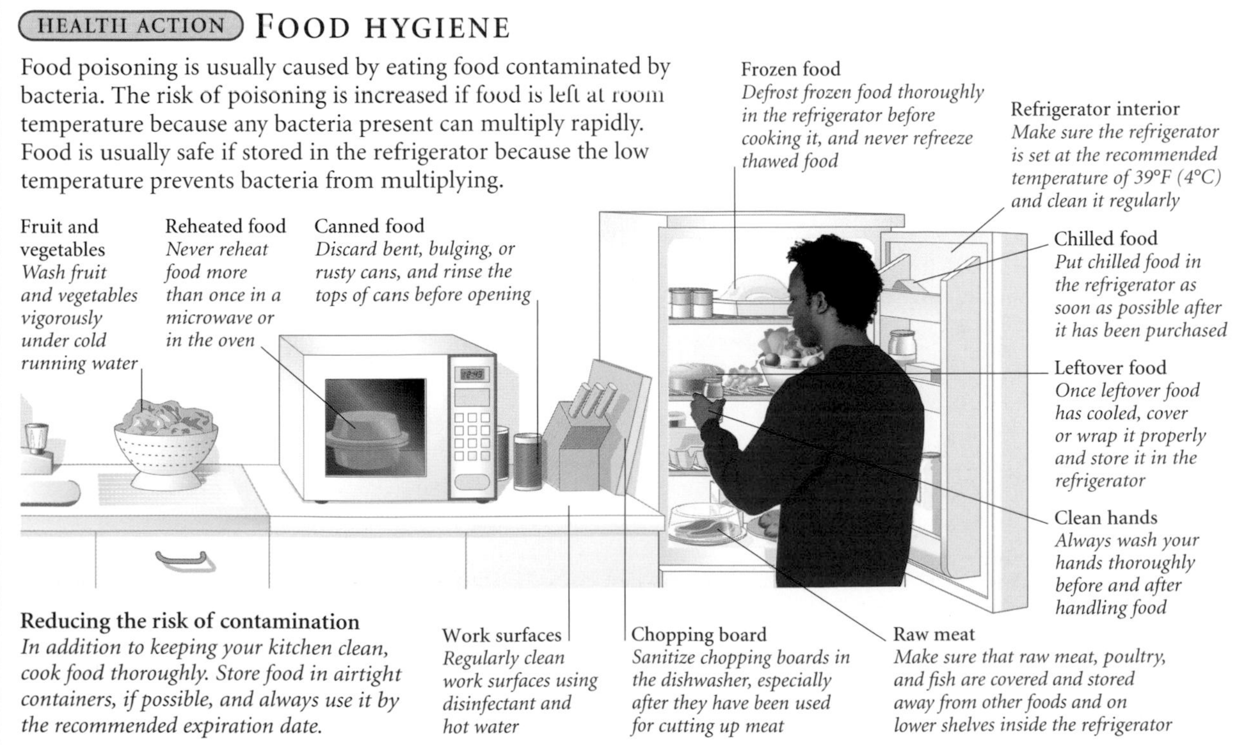

Fruit and vegetables *Wash fruit and vegetables vigorously under cold running water*

Reheated food *Never reheat food more than once in a microwave or in the oven*

Canned food *Discard bent, bulging, or rusty cans, and rinse the tops of cans before opening*

Frozen food *Defrost frozen food thoroughly in the refrigerator before cooking it, and never refreeze thawed food*

Refrigerator interior *Make sure the refrigerator is set at the recommended temperature of 39°F (4°C) and clean it regularly*

Chilled food *Put chilled food in the refrigerator as soon as possible after it has been purchased*

Leftover food *Once leftover food has cooled, cover or wrap it properly and store it in the refrigerator*

Clean hands *Always wash your hands thoroughly before and after handling food*

Reducing the risk of contamination
In addition to keeping your kitchen clean, cook food thoroughly. Store food in airtight containers, if possible, and always use it by the recommended expiration date.

Work surfaces *Regularly clean work surfaces using disinfectant and hot water*

Chopping board *Sanitize chopping boards in the dishwasher, especially after they have been used for cutting up meat*

Raw meat *Make sure that raw meat, poultry, and fish are covered and stored away from other foods and on lower shelves inside the refrigerator*

Safety in the yard

Taking precautions to keep your yard safe for all age groups

The greatest risk in the yard is from water (*see* SAFETY IN AND AROUND WATER, p.81), although poisonous plants, garden chemicals, gardening tools, barbecues, and play equipment also pose significant risks.

AVOIDING POISONOUS PLANTS

Some plants may cause irritation if they come into contact with the skin. If swallowed, other plants may produce symptoms ranging from irritation of the mouth, throat, and stomach to nausea and vomiting, and a small number of plants may be lethal if eaten. Your local poison control center can provide a list of poisonous plants common in your area, but children should be taught that touching or eating plants may be dangerous. If a child does swallow anything poisonous, take him or her to a hospital emergency room, taking a sample of the plant with you.

USING GARDEN CHEMICALS AND TOOLS SAFELY

Many products for use in the garden are poisonous. Always store products in their original containers as the safety information is displayed on the packaging. Consider safe alternatives, such as removing weeds by hand or applying chemical-free pesticides. If you do use poisonous products, store them in a locked shed or cabinet and follow the manufacturer's instructions.

Sharp tools should not be left where they can be found by children. Wear protective clothing, such as goggles, ear protectors, gloves, long pants, and boots, when using tools such as chainsaws.

USING BARBECUES SAFELY

Barbecues should always be supervised in case children wander too close to them. Avoid lighting barbecues in a high wind, and do not wear loose clothing near flames. When using a gas-fired barbecue, check for gas leaks and make sure that the flame is blue. A yellow flame indicates incomplete combustion or the production of carbon monoxide (CO). Always keep an outdoor fire extinguisher on hand.

Safety in the sun

Precautions and procedures to avoid skin damage and overexposure to heat

Overexposure to sunlight may lead to sunburn (p.357), premature aging, skin cancer (p.344), and damage to the eyes. Tanning, once fashionable, is now considered to be harmful. The link between sunlight exposure and skin cancers is strong. It was first suspected because of the high rates of skin cancer in persons with outdoor jobs, those living in southern latitudes, and among fair-skinned people. As well, too much sun can contribute to heat exhaustion and heatstroke. If you are outside in strong sun, protect yourself with suitable clothing, sunscreens, and sunglasses. It is particularly important to protect young children's skin from the sun.

DAMAGING EFFECTS OF SUN

Exposure to strong sunlight without adequate protection is likely to result in burns that require medical treatment. Damage to the skin is caused by the ultraviolet (UV) component of sunlight, of which there are two main types, UVA light and UVB light. Overexposure to UVB light is known to be a cause of skin cancer and cataract (p.573). UVA light may also play a role.

UV light is partially filtered by haze or clouds in the atmosphere, which means that the UV content of sunlight is greater at high altitude. However, you can still burn on a cloudy day at lower altitudes because some UV light penetrates clouds. Snow and ice reflect up to three-quarters of UV light, and water may reflect almost all of it.

Certain drugs may increase the sensitivity of your skin to sunlight (*see* PHOTOSENSITIVITY, p.338). You should stay out of the sun if you are taking tetracycline antibiotics (*see* ANTIBIOTICS, p.885). If you are using oral contraceptives, you may notice areas of patchy skin pigmentation after exposure to the sun, and your doctor may suggest you use alternative contraception. Some perfumes and deodorants may cause skin discoloration in strong sunlight, in which case they should be avoided.

The risk of developing skin cancer is greater if you had severe sunburn as a child and if you have red or blond hair and green or blue eyes. People with fair complexions are at higher risk because their skin contains low levels of melanin, which absorbs UVB light. Whatever their skin type, babies and small children are more vulnerable to the sun than adults.

PROTECTION FROM THE SUN

You can minimize the risk of sun damage by avoiding exposure to the sun between 11 am and 3 pm. If you must be out in direct sunlight, there are three important types of protection: clothing, sunscreens, and sunglasses.

CLOTHING Wear a wide-brimmed hat and tightly woven clothing that covers your shoulders and neck. Pale-colored clothes may become translucent when wet, offering little protection. Special protective clothing is available for children, such as a "legionnaire's hat," to protect the back of the neck. Loose-fitting clothes, with long sleeves and pants, may help you to avoid prickly heat (p.342), a rash caused by sweat trapped under the skin.

SUNSCREENS The chemicals present in sunblocks and sunscreens partially or completely absorb UV rays (*see* SUNSCREENS AND SUNBLOCKS, p.893). White

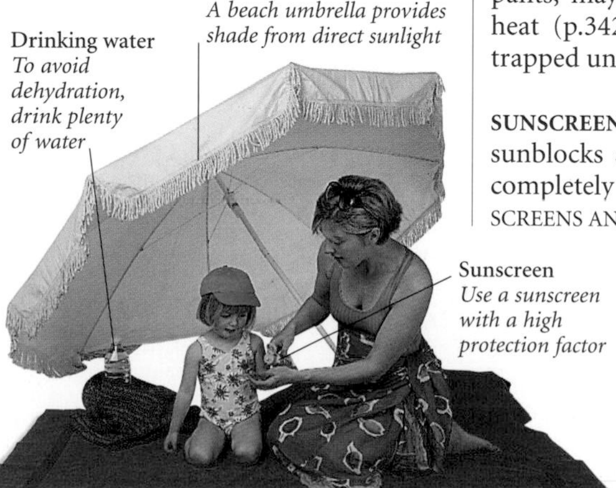
Umbrella
A beach umbrella provides shade from direct sunlight
Drinking water
To avoid dehydration, drink plenty of water
Sunscreen
Use a sunscreen with a high protection factor

Protection at the beach
Extra precautions may be necessary when you are at the beach because sunlight is reflected by water onto your skin, and sea breezes can keep you deceptively cool.

or colored sunblocks block sunlight completely and can be used to protect exposed skin, especially on vulnerable areas such as the nose. Sunscreens are less effective than sunblocks because they only partially absorb UV rays, but since they are more transparent they are more acceptable for all-over use.

The effectiveness of a sunscreen is rated by a sun protection factor (SPF). The higher the factor, the greater the protection, although the degree of protection depends on your skin type. Sunscreens should be applied liberally 15–30 minutes before you go outside and reapplied every 2 hours. They are especially important if you are near water, snow, or ice or at high altitude. Wear sunscreens even when in the shade and on cloudy days. They are not suitable for babies under 6 months old, who should be kept out of direct sun.

SUNGLASSES Sunglasses should have an American National Standards Institute label that shows how much UV light they block out. Choose ones that give maximum protection from both UVA and UVB light. Never look at the sun directly, even when wearing sunglasses, or through a camera, since it may cause temporary or permanent eye damage.

(WWW) ONLINE SITES: p.1036

Safety in and around water

Avoiding accidents and injuries in and around water

Between 1991 and 1997, drownings from boating, aquatic activities, falls into water, and bathing combined accounted for about 80 percent of all water-related deaths in Canada. Waterborne infections may also be a danger to anyone who is in or near the water.

PREVENTING DROWNING AND NEAR-DROWNING

The situations that most often result in drowning or near-drowning are swimming in a strong current, falling into very cold water, and swimming or boating after drinking alcohol. In particular, children should always be closely supervised when they are playing in or around water.

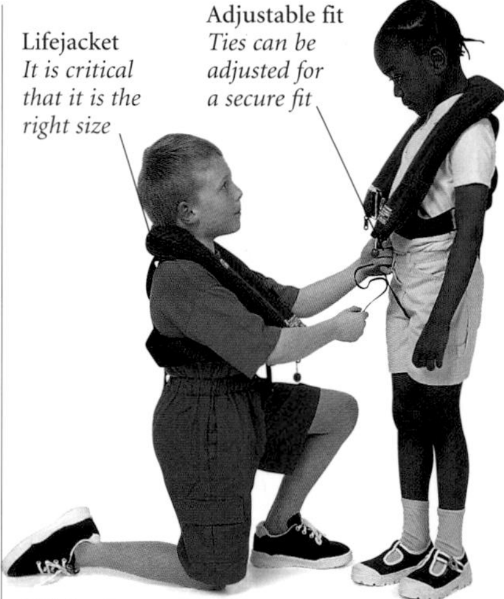
Lifejacket
It is critical that it is the right size
Adjustable fit
Ties can be adjusted for a secure fit

Lifejackets
A lifejacket should be worn for activities in which there is a risk of falling into water. It should fit comfortably, support the head, and allow the arms to move freely.

UNDERSTANDING WATER CONDITIONS Many victims of drowning are strong swimmers who have been caught in currents or undertow. Even confident swimmers should always heed advice about local swimming conditions.

Swimming in very cold water should be avoided because low water temperature may lead to drowning. A person immersed in water loses heat up to 27 times faster than a person in air at the same temperature. Water below 5°C (41°F) stiffens muscles and may cause cardiac arrest (*see* HYPOTHERMIA, p.323).

AVOIDING ALCOHOL More than one-third of victims of drowning accidents have a significant amount of alcohol in their blood (*see* ALCOHOL AND HEALTH, p.62). You should never drink alcohol before going swimming or boating since it will make you more likely to take risks. Alcohol will also make you less able to tackle difficulties that may arise and more susceptible to panic.

SUPERVISING CHILDREN Do not leave children of any age alone when they are swimming or bathing because it is possible to drown in only a few inches of water. If you have a swimming pool, pond, or well in your yard, fence it off in a self-latching or self-closing area. Develop safety rules with your family for swimming areas. Children should be taught how to swim at as early an age as possible. Many cities have legislation that limits the age at which children may swim in public pools without adult supervision. Older children are not an appropriate substitute for an adult to supervise younger children.

FIRST AID If someone has been submerged in cold water long enough to have stopped breathing, artificial respiration (p.982) or cardiopulmonary resuscitation (pp.984–985) should be administered immediately. Even if a person appears to have drowned, he or she may be resuscitated when body temperature rises (*see* DROWNING AND NEAR-DROWNING, p.325).

AVOIDING HAZARDS IN WATER

Drowning is not the only hazard associated with water. Shallow water, hidden objects, marine and freshwater animals, and infections all present dangers.

SHALLOW WATER AND HIDDEN OBJECTS Every year, thousands of people injure their spines by diving into water that is too shallow or that contains hidden objects. Many of these accidents result in permanent paralysis. Always check the depth of water before diving or jumping, and check for rocks, fallen trees, or glass below the surface.

ANIMAL LIFE AND INFECTIONS Marine and freshwater life can be a hazard in some areas. Follow warnings about local dangers, such as sharks or alligators, and swim only in areas that have been designated as safe. Look out for animals that may sting or bite if you step on or touch them, such as jellyfish, anemones, sea urchins, sea snakes, and stingrays. Coral can cause cuts and abrasions, which may become infected.

The sea near large coastal resorts and rivers downstream from cities may be polluted with sewage. Water contaminated with rat or fox urine can cause a flulike infection called Weil's disease or leptospirosis (p.301). In tropical countries, swimming or wading in rivers, lakes, or ponds is inadvisable due to the risk of contracting schistosomiasis (p.312). Also known as bilharzia, this serious disease, caused by larvae that burrow through the skin, may damage the liver and urinary system.

(WWW) ONLINE SITES: p.1036

Pets and health

Minimizing health risks associated with domestic pets

Diseases contracted from pets are uncommon. However, owners should be aware that pets can bite or cause allergies and that infections and infestations with viruses, bacteria, fungi, worms, and insects can spread to members of the family. Exotic pets, such as snakes and spiders, pose their own health hazards.

You should check pets regularly for ticks. If your pet scratches more than usual or develops bald patches, consult your veterinarian in case your pet has a fungal infection, such as ringworm (p.352), that could infect you.

Cat and dog feces contain a number of dangerous organisms, such as the eggs of the toxocara worm. If ingested, these worm eggs may cause toxocariasis (p.310), a potentially serious disease that may lead to blindness. Cat feces may also contain toxoplasma protozoa. Pregnant women in particular should avoid touching cat feces, because toxoplasmosis (p.307) may cause serious harm to the developing fetus. Deworm pets regularly, dispose of their feces hygienically, and teach children to wash their hands after touching animals. Ensure your pet has a rabies vaccination.

(WWW) ONLINE SITES: p.1036

Safety and health at work

Practical steps to promote safety and health in the workplace

There are well-established connections between conditions in the workplace and certain health problems. In particular, some occupations carry high risks of specific disorders. As a result, measures have been developed to protect employees from a wide range of occupational disorders.

Occupational health and safety programs focus on preventing injuries or illnesses and eliminating hazards. Employee assistance programs (EAP) help employees with personal problems that may affect their ability to work. If you develop symptoms of ill health or disease during employment and suspect that your symptoms are caused by certain conditions in your work environment, you should talk to your supervisor or occupational health department, or to your doctor.

Reducing risks in the office

Your office may be a surprising source of health hazards, particularly if you spend a substantial part of your day working with a computer.

If you sit at a desk, you need to give careful thought to the layout of your work area (*see* USING A WORK STATION, below). A risk for keyboard operators is repetitive strain injury (p.389), which causes approximately 2 in 3 occupational injuries in the US. This disorder is caused by repeated movement of one part of the body. By using a wrist rest or a specially designed keyboard, you may help prevent this injury.

Sick building syndrome is a group of symptoms sometimes reported by workers in modern offices. Symptoms include loss of energy, headaches, and sore throat. The cause is unknown but has been attributed to air-conditioning, exposure to tobacco smoke, lack of natural light, and dust, solvents, and ozone emitted by printers and photocopiers.

Strained relationships with your colleagues or poor job satisfaction can be causes of stress. If this is the case, seek advice on managing stress (p.74).

Reducing risks in the industrial workplace

Some occupations are inherently more dangerous than others. If your work involves contact with heavy machinery, organic solvents, loud noise, or extreme heat or cold, you should be aware of the dangers and be provided

HEALTH ACTION: Using a work station

Your work area should be designed so that everything is easy to reach and use. Make sure that you have good lighting and ventilation. If you are working at a computer, take breaks every 40 minutes from using the keyboard and monitor. Focus on a distant object occasionally to relax your eye muscles and to prevent your eyes from getting tired.

Ventilation
Your work area should be adequately ventilated or air conditioned
Monitor
The monitor should be positioned so that the screen is level with your eyes
Desk lamp
Use an adjustable desk lamp with a bulb that is not too bright
Keyboard
Adjust your posture so that your wrists and forearms form a straight line to the keyboard. Try to keep an angle of 70–90° between your upper arms and forearms
Electric cords
Make sure that electric cords are not underfoot
Adjustable chair
Position your chair so that you can sit with your back supported and your feet flat on the floor
Wrist rest
A wrist rest helps support your wrists and may provide comfort while you work

Working at a computer
Good posture and a correctly positioned chair and monitor may prevent problems such as back pain and repetitive strain injury.

with protection. Protective clothing should fit well, cover all vulnerable parts of the body, and be worn routinely. Particular jobs may require specific clothing or equipment. For instance, work involving ionizing radiation or heavy metals requires specialized protective clothing.

Many substances in the workplace cause lung diseases. The most common occupational chest disorder is asthma (p.483), which causes severe breathing problems if untreated. More than 200 substances, ranging from latex in gloves to the isocyanates used in paint spraying, are known to trigger this disorder. Your doctor can arrange for special tests to identify triggers of asthma.

A number of other lung disorders are linked with the inhalation of specific particles. Occupations that carry particular risks include mining, farming, and any work involving contact with asbestos or silica (a constituent of sand and many types of rocks).

Other substances, such as detergents, may irritate your skin and may cause problems such as eczema (p.333) or contact dermatitis (p.355). Emollient creams and protective clothing may help protect your skin, but you should seek medical advice.

If your work involves lifting heavy loads or sitting for long periods with poor back support, you are vulnerable to back pain (*see* LOWER BACK PAIN, p.381). Make sure that you are given proper training, are aware of your posture, and always try to lift safely (*see* PREVENTING BACK PAIN, p.382).

TAKING RESPONSIBILITY FOR HEALTH AT WORK

In many countries, employers are required by law to conform to safety standards, monitor employees' health, and compensate any employees who develop permanent health problems.

Employees should be aware of the health hazards associated with their particular occupation and of the legally required safety practices. If you repeatedly report a hazard to your employer and no positive action is taken by him or her, you should contact the local office of the Workers' Compensation Board to file a written complaint.

(WWW) ONLINE SITES: p.1036

Safety on the road

Safety precautions for motorists, motorcyclists, bicyclists, and pedestrians

Collisions involving motorists, motorcyclists, bicyclists, and pedestrians are among the leading causes of accidental death in the world today. Teenagers and young adults have more collisions on the roads than elderly drivers, but they also have a higher survival rate. The fatality rate for drivers over age 65 is more than three times higher than the rate for teenage drivers.

During 1998, there were close to 220,000 injured persons and almost 3,000 traffic deaths across Canada. However, this represents a one-third decrease in the death rate compared with a decade ago. This decrease is due to improved vehicle safety (p.84) and better public compliance with speed limits and with drinking and driving laws, which have compensated for the effect of increasing numbers of cars.

Alcohol is still involved in nearly half of all traffic deaths. About 1 in 4 drivers killed in single vehicle collisions were speeding. Other significant causes of vehicle collisions include poor eyesight, fatigue, illegal drugs, prescription drugs such as tranquilizers or analgesics, and over-the-counter drugs (including antihistamines and cough medicines), all of which can reduce reaction times. Even if you are a careful and defensive driver, you should be aware that other drivers may involve you in collisions.

STAYING SAFE IN CARS

The most important vehicle safety device is the seatbelt, which saved about 7,700 lives in Canada between 1990 and 1995 alone. Airbags have also saved many lives. In addition to seatbelts and airbags, modern cars and trucks have many other built-in safety features, including headrests, antilock brakes, and tires that are designed to run safely when deflated, even after a serious puncture. Bear in mind, however, that although these devices reduce the risk for the vehicle's occupants, research shows that they do not make traveling safer for other road users. You should not drive at higher speeds merely because you are reassured by the safety features on your own vehicle.

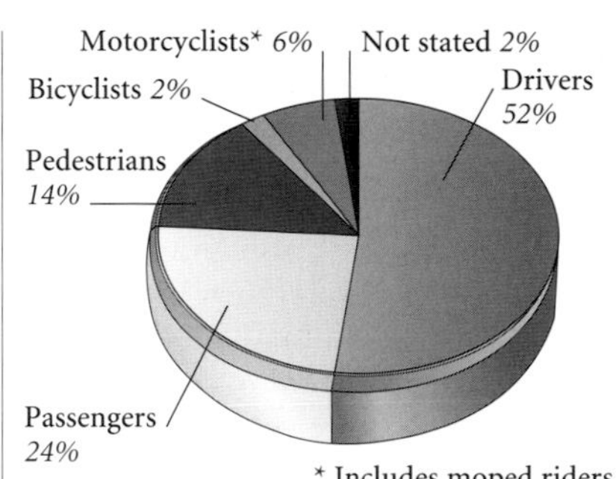
Motorcyclists* 6%
Not stated 2%
Bicyclists 2%
Drivers 52%
Pedestrians 14%
Passengers 24%
* Includes moped riders

Traffic deaths

Car occupants accounted for the largest number of traffic deaths in Canada in 2003, mainly because there were more car occupants than other travelers.

STAYING SAFE ON MOTORCYCLES AND BICYCLES

Although the occupants of cars still account for most traffic fatalities in Canada, motorcyclists are more than 60 times as likely as car occupants to die in a vehicle collision. Motorcyclists need to wear helmets and other special clothing to help protect themselves from the road surface and other vehicles, as well as from the weather.

Almost 80 bicyclists were killed and about 8,500 were injured in Canada in 1998. One-third of these deaths were among children aged 5–15. Since 3 in 4 bicyclists killed in accidents die as a result of head injuries, wearing a crash helmet is essential. It is important that a helmet fits you well. If you have a collision while wearing your helmet, you will probably need to replace it. You should also be trained in road safety and take extra care in wet or icy conditions, when braking ability is reduced.

STAYING SAFE AS A PEDESTRIAN

In 1998, about 400 pedestrians were killed in collisions in Canada, and about 14,000 were injured. Nearly one-third of all children between the ages of 5 and 9 years who were killed in collisions with vehicles were pedestrians.

Teach children to be alert and stay on the sidewalk. Where there is no sidewalk, people should walk on the same side of the road as the oncoming traffic. When crossing streets, children should use pedestrian crosswalks, tunnels, or overpasses. Everyone walking or jogging at night should wear bright clothes and reflectors so they can be seen.

(WWW) ONLINE SITES: p.1036

HEALTH ACTION

VEHICLE SAFETY

Almost 3,000 people die on Canadian roads every year, and many more are severely injured. Accidents more often result from carelessness or driving after drinking alcohol than from mechanical failure. Whether traveling by car, motorcycle, or bicycle, you should maintain your vehicle properly and take measures to make yourself less vulnerable and to protect other drivers.

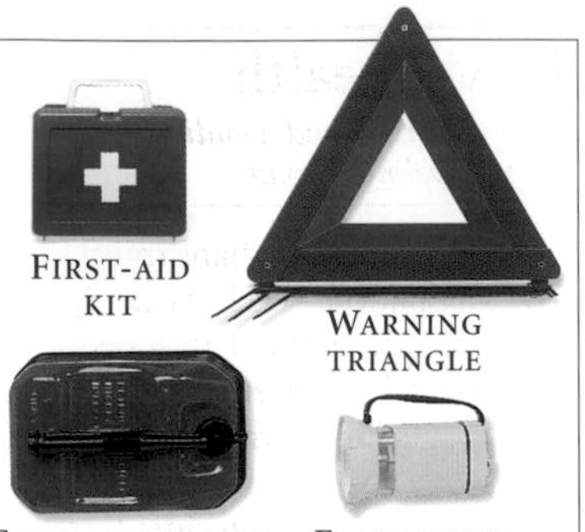

FIRST-AID KIT

WARNING TRIANGLE

EMPTY FUEL CAN

FLASHLIGHT

Essential equipment
Carry a flashlight, an empty fuel can, a first-aid kit, and a hazard triangle or flare in your car's trunk.

CAR SAFETY

Make sure that you use built-in safety features according to the manufacturer's guidelines. Children under age 12 should not travel in a seat that has been fitted with airbags, and small adults should not use side airbags.

Seatbelt
Every passenger should wear a seatbelt

Headrest
A well-positioned headrest reduces neck injuries

Side mirrors
Position your mirrors to provide a clear view of the road behind you

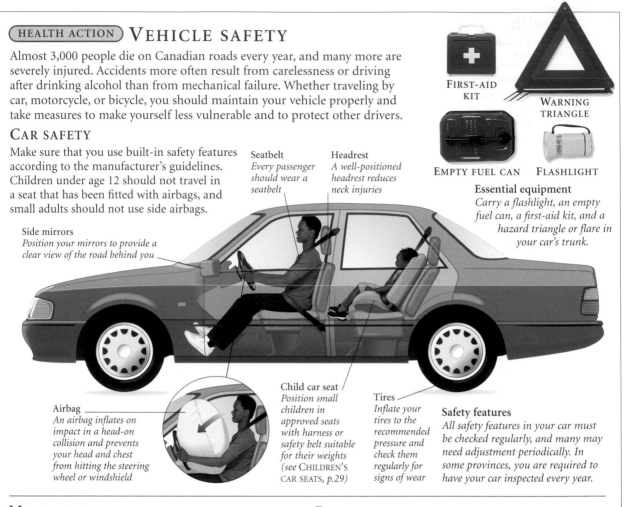

Airbag
An airbag inflates on impact in a head-on collision and prevents your head and chest from hitting the steering wheel or windshield

Child car seat
Position small children in approved seats with harness or safety belt suitable for their weights *(see* CHILDREN'S CAR SEATS, *p.29)*

Tires
Inflate your tires to the recommended pressure and check them regularly for signs of wear

Safety features
All safety features in your car must be checked regularly, and many may need adjustment periodically. In some provinces, you are required to have your car inspected every year.

MOTORCYCLE SAFETY

Specialized motorcycle clothing helps prevent or reduce injuries caused by a crash or fall and helps you stay comfortable in all weather conditions. Additionally, modern motorcycles have several built-in safety features to help you see and be seen.

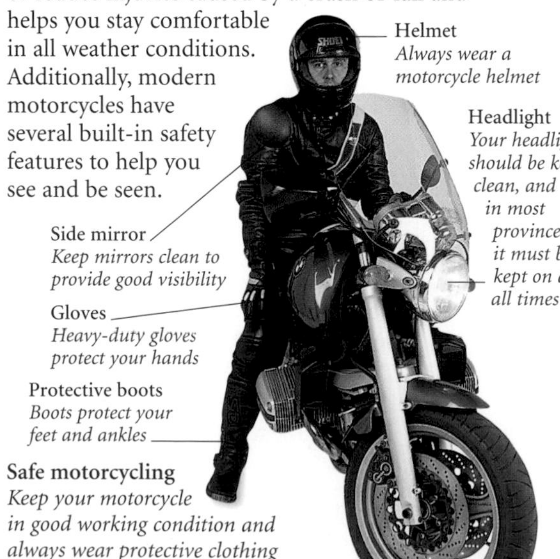
SHOEI

Helmet
Always wear a motorcycle helmet

Headlight
Your headlight should be kept clean, and in most provinces it must be kept on at all times

Side mirror
Keep mirrors clean to provide good visibility

Gloves
Heavy-duty gloves protect your hands

Protective boots
Boots protect your feet and ankles

Safe motorcycling
Keep your motorcycle in good working condition and always wear protective clothing that is designed for motorcycling.

BICYCLE SAFETY

Lights, reflectors, and light-colored or reflective clothing make bicyclists more visible to drivers and pedestrians. A bicycle helmet and protective glasses help keep you safe whether you are bicycling on or off the road.

Safe cycling
Keep your bicycle well maintained and be aware of drivers and pedestrians.

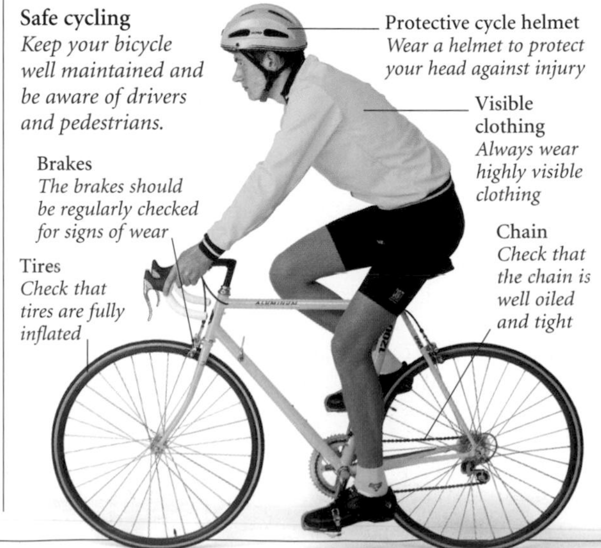

Protective cycle helmet
Wear a helmet to protect your head against injury

Visible clothing
Always wear highly visible clothing

Brakes
The brakes should be regularly checked for signs of wear

Chain
Check that the chain is well oiled and tight

Tires
Check that tires are fully inflated

Travel health

Staying healthy and avoiding accidents when traveling abroad

Over 1 million Canadians travel to tropical destinations each year. Although most are safe, about 1 in 4 people who goes abroad experiences some type of injury or illness while traveling. The most common problems are digestive system upsets, traffic accidents, and sexually transmitted diseases. Tropical diseases are rare. Risks can be minimized by seeking information about the country you are visiting, checking out hotels and facilities before you travel, and being prepared for both minor illnesses and major medical emergencies.

Preparing to travel

If you are planning to travel abroad, contact your doctor or a travel clinic, well in advance of your trip. They can provide advice on immunizations and prevention measures for your individual risk.

IMMUNIZATIONS Immunization needs depend on your destination, state of health, current immune status, the duration and type of travel, and the time available before you travel. Seek advice on recommended immunizations at least 8 weeks before traveling because some immunizations require several weeks to take effect (*see* TRAVEL IMMUNIZATIONS, p.86). Most countries do not require visitors to have specific immunizations, but a few require a certificate for yellow fever (p.294).

PREVENTING MALARIA No vaccine is available against malaria (p.305), but it can be prevented by a combination of precautions. Depending on the area you are visiting, your doctor may prescribe a drug to help prevent the disease (*see* ANTIPROTOZOAL DRUGS, p.888). However, the most effective method of preventing malaria is to avoid mosquito bites. Pack long-sleeved shirts and long pants, mosquito repellents (containing the chemical DEET), a mosquito net treated with insecticide to sleep under, and mosquito pellets or coils (*see* PREVENTING MALARIA, p.305) to burn in the evening, when mosquitoes are most active. These precautions can also prevent dengue fever (p.294), another mosquito-borne disease. Since scratching bites can lead to infection, pack insect bite treatment or antihistamine cream for relief.

MEDICATION If you are taking medication for an existing condition, take an extra supply. Keep medication in its original packaging and carry a doctor's letter describing your treatment. Carry medication in your hand luggage.

EMERGENCY MEDICAL TRAVEL KIT The recommended contents of a medical travel kit depend on your destination. If you are traveling to a developed country, you may need only a mild analgesic (such as acetaminophen), antihistamine cream to treat insect bites, and treatment for diarrhea. If you are visiting a developing country, you should take sterile needles with you, 10 ml syringes (for blood tests), and materials for stitching wounds for use by local medical personnel. Such kits can be purchased at travel clinics and pharmacies. A letter from your doctor should explain to customs officials why you are carrying needles and syringes.

Staying healthy in transit

If you are affected by motion sickness (p.604), avoid drinking alcohol and eat only a small amount of food before traveling. Choose the most stable part of the vehicle, try not to read, and stay close to a source of air. Your doctor or pharmacist can advise you on suitable drug treatment (*see* ANTIHISTAMINES, p.906, and ANTIEMETIC DRUGS, p.922).

Flying across time zones may disrupt your cycle of sleeping and waking, a condition known as jet lag. To reduce its effects when flying east, go to bed about an hour earlier each night a few days before you fly. When flying west, go to bed about an hour later each night. Avoid heavy meals and salty or fatty food during the flight, and drink plenty of nonalcoholic fluids.

Air travel should be avoided by those who have had a recent heart attack and those who have severe lung disease, sinusitis (p.475), or an ear infection (*see* OTITIS MEDIA, p.597, and ACUTE OTITIS MEDIA IN CHILDREN, p.860). Seek your doctor's advice if you have recently had surgery or if you have been ill, especially if the illness was infectious. Most airlines will not allow a woman who is more than 35 weeks pregnant to fly.

Prolonged sitting on very long flights can put you at risk for a blood clot in your leg (*see* DEEP VEIN THROMBOSIS, p.437).

Staying healthy at your destination

Upsets of the digestive system and sexually transmitted diseases are the most common problems, but hot weather and local wildlife also present hazards.

DIGESTIVE-SYSTEM PROBLEMS The most common travel illness is diarrhea, which may be due to a change in the bacteria normally present in the bowel or to water- or food-borne gastroenteritis (p.628). Although it is difficult to avoid completely, the risk of gastroenteritis can be reduced in areas where there is inadequate hygiene by washing your hands thoroughly with soap and water or alcohol-based hand sanitizers before meals; avoiding raw vegetables, salads, shellfish, and ice cream; and by peeling all fruit. When you are doubtful of water cleanliness, use bottled or purified water for drinking and brushing your teeth. You can purify water using iodine liquid or tablets or a filter. Avoid adding ice that may contain tap water to any types of drinks.

If you develop diarrhea, rest for at least a day, eat nothing, and drink lots of fluids (preferably rehydration fluids containing glucose and salt). Before you travel, ask your doctor for advice about carrying drugs with you to treat traveler's diarrhea. These include over-the-counter antidiarrheal drugs (p.924) and possibly a 3-day course of antibiotics (p.885), such as ciprofloxacin. If diarrhea persists, seek medical help.

SEXUALLY TRANSMITTED INFECTIONS Abstinence from sex with new partners is the best defense to take against sexually transmitted diseases, but the risk of infection can be reduced by practicing safe sex (p.68). Since good-quality condoms are not always available, they should be brought from home.

HOT WEATHER Hot and humid climates result in nearly constant perspiration. Moist skin is an excellent growth medium for bacteria and fungi, especially

HEALTH ACTION TRAVEL IMMUNIZATIONS

The immunizations that you need before traveling depend on the area you intend to visit, although some diseases can be contracted almost anywhere. All adults need immunization against tetanus, diphtheria, measles, mumps, and rubella. Older adults should also have pneumococcal vaccine and yearly protection against influenza. Most of these should be covered if you received a full course of immunizations during childhood (*see* ROUTINE IMMUNIZATIONS, p.45), but you may need booster doses before traveling.

Immunization advice
The immunizations you need depend on your destination, the purpose of your visit, and your immunization history. Timings of doses you receive may differ from those shown here.

DISEASE	DOSE	WHEN EFFECTIVE	PERIOD OF PROTECTION	WHO SHOULD BE IMMUNIZED
Yellow fever (p.294)	1 injection	After 10 days	10 years	People traveling to parts of South America and Africa. Caution in elderly and immune-suppressed.
Typhoid (p.300)	1 injection or 3 oral doses	After 14 days (injection), 1 week (oral)	Injection: 3 years Oral: 7 years	People traveling to areas with poor sanitation.
Hepatitis A (p.644)	1 injection	After 2–4 weeks	1 year	People traveling to developing countries. A second injection 6–12 months later gives lasting protection.
Hepatitis B (p.644)	3 injections over 6 months, at least 4 weeks apart	Immediately after 2nd dose	15 years or longer, unless exposure is high	People traveling to developing countries in which hepatits B is prevalent; those likely to have unprotected sex.
Traveler's diarrhea	2 oral doses, 1 week apart	About 1 week after second dose	3 months	People traveling in developing countries.
Meningitis A, C (p.527), W-135 and Y (quadravalent)	1 injection	After 15 days	3–5 years	People traveling to areas in which meningitis A, C, and W-135 are prevalent.
Poliomyelitis (p.293)	1 injection	Immediately	No booster needed for adults	Travelers to areas where poliomyelitis is endemic or epidemic, such as South Asia, West Africa, and Central Africa.
Rabies (p.294)	3 injections. 1 week between 1st and 2nd doses, 3 weeks between 2nd and 3rd doses	Immediately after 3rd dose	Depends on degree of exposure; blood test checks need for booster	People traveling to areas where rabies is endemic and who are at high risk (veterinarians, people working with animals, and those traveling into remote country).
Japanese B encephalitis (p.528)	3 injections over a 1-month period	10–14 days after last dose	3 years	People staying for an extended period in rural areas of countries where Japanese B encephalitis is prevalent.

in the skin folds under the breasts, the armpits, between the toes and fingers, the groin, and sometimes the scalp. However, most skin and fungal infections can be prevented by frequently showering and changing clothes, drying completely before dressing, wearing loose clothing preferably made from natural fibers, and taking precautions to avoid the harmful effects of strong sunlight (*see* SAFETY IN THE SUN, p.80).

BITES AND STINGS Mosquitoes are not the only potential biting pests. Even when you are traveling in the US, you should be aware of potential dangers. For example, in the Southwest, scorpions and rattlesnakes present dangers, and in many areas ticks carry serious diseases, such as Lyme disease (p.302).

To prevent stings and bites, take the same precautions as you would for preventing mosquito bites. In addition, keep beds away from walls and shake clothes and shoes vigorously before wearing them. Put on shoes whenever you get out of bed. Inspect your legs, groin, genitals, and belt line. Remove attached ticks using a pair of tweezers or a fingernail. Apply a dab of alcohol first, and be careful not to leave the head or mouthparts embedded.

STAYING HEALTHY AFTER RETURNING HOME

Some diseases contracted while traveling might not show up until after you are home. For example, flulike symptoms (fever, severe headaches, shivering, and aching joints) could be due to malaria. Consult a doctor immediately and report details of the trip. Seek medical advice if you have an unexplained rash or diarrhea that persists for 10 days or longer. Although symptoms are likely to clear up on their own, persistent symptoms should be reported to exclude unusual infections.

WWW ONLINE SITES: p.1037

Assessing Your Symptoms

This section describes and explains common or worrying symptoms using a series of question-and-answer charts. The charts help you determine how serious the symptom is and suggest possible causes. They also help you decide when you can treat the symptom yourself and when you should seek medical help. The section contains charts for everybody, in addition to charts specifically for men, women, and children up to age 12.

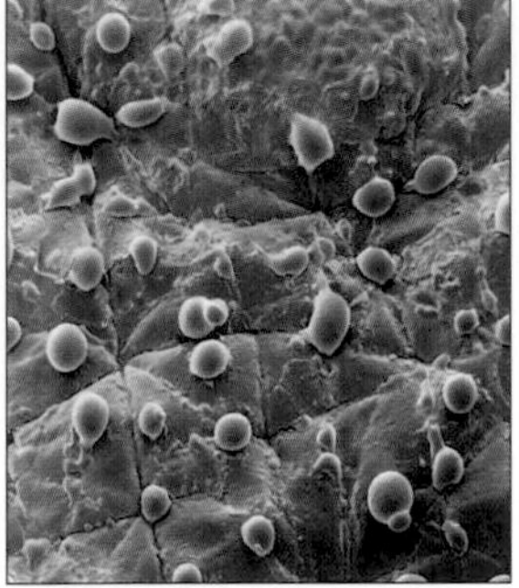

Droplets of sweat
Secretion of sweat helps control body temperature. However, excessive sweating is a common symptom of feverish illnesses.

INTRODUCTION

THE BODY FUNCTIONS RELIABLY most of the time, and we are not aware of the internal processes that keep us alive and enable us to carry out our everyday activities. However, sometimes we experience warning signals, called symptoms, that tell us something is wrong. Most of these symptoms are caused by minor illness or injury and clear up within a few days. However, it is important to be able to tell when a symptom may require medical attention, and it is the purpose of the question-and-answer symptom charts in this section to provide such guidance.

Symptoms take many forms. Some symptoms involve a new sensation, such as pain in the chest, that only you can perceive. Others involve a change in a normal body function, such as frequent urination, or a change in appearance, such as the development of a rash. Such new sensations or changes in the way we look or function alert us to the possibility of illness and may prompt us to seek medical help. However, when investigating the cause of your problem, your doctor does not rely only on a description of your symptoms. He or she will also look for signs of illness. Signs are physical evidence of a disorder or illness that the doctor can detect during a physical examination but of which you may be unaware. For example, if you have a lung condition, shortness of breath might be one of the symptoms that you experience. When the doctor listens to your chest through a stethoscope, he or she may detect abnormal sounds with each breath; these are a sign of the disorder. The combination of symptoms and signs provides the doctor with a pattern that may suggest a diagnosis.

UNDERSTANDING SYMPTOMS

Doctors learn by experience to recognize patterns of symptoms and signs, and most of us learn to do the same for a particular illness if we have had similar symptoms on several occasions. For example, a person who has recurrent attacks of migraine is usually able to recognize the symptoms at an early stage and knows the best way to bring the attacks under control. Similarly, the symptoms of many common infectious illnesses have become general knowledge. Most people recognize aching muscles, runny nose, fatigue, and fever as the usual symptoms of flu. However, dealing with unfamiliar symptoms is not as easy. In these cases, you should note the characteristics of your symptoms so that you are able to describe all of them accurately to the doctor or pharmacist. Information that may be helpful includes when the symptom started; which part of the body is affected; whether it came on suddenly or developed gradually; and whether it is

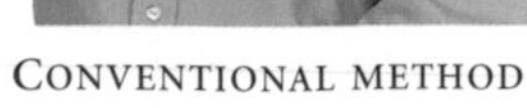

Disposable tip
The ear thermometer has a hygienic, disposable tip

Digital display
Thermometers that have a digital display are easy to read

EAR METHOD

CONVENTIONAL METHOD

Measuring body temperature
A temperature above 37°C (98.6°F) is a common symptom of infectious illness. Temperature can be measured using a thermometer placed in the mouth or armpit. For children, using an ear thermometer, the tip of which is gently inserted into the ear, is an easier alternative. Modern thermometers have easy-to-read digital displays.

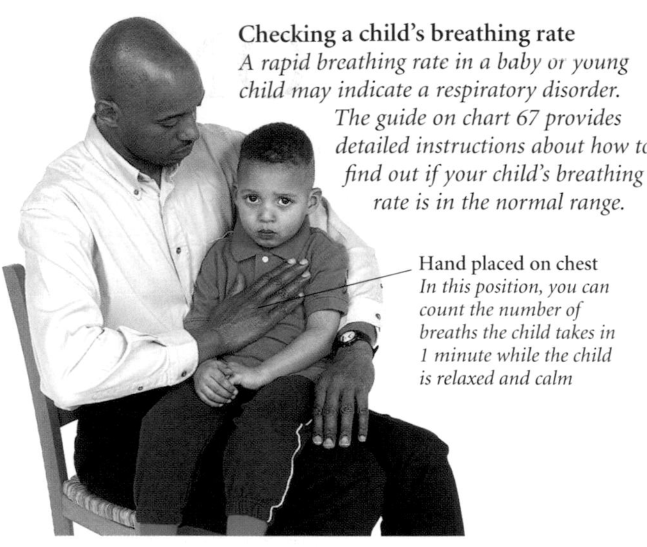
Hand placed on chest
In this position, you can count the number of breaths the child takes in 1 minute while the child is relaxed and calm

Checking a child's breathing rate
A rapid breathing rate in a baby or young child may indicate a respiratory disorder. The guide on chart 67 provides detailed instructions about how to find out if your child's breathing rate is in the normal range.

continuous or intermittent. If you have a pain, it may also be useful to consider how it feels, such as whether it is dull, sharp, burning, or throbbing.

Certain symptoms can be assessed very accurately because they can be measured. Probably the most familiar example is assessing whether or not a person has a fever and, if so, how high the fever is, by measuring body temperature using a thermometer. It is especially useful to be able to measure a symptom in young children because they may not be able to understand or tell you how they are feeling.

Most people are motivated to seek treatment for symptoms that they find troublesome, but it is not wise to assume that an apparently harmless symptom does not require treatment. For example, a rash may cause distress even though it is unlikely to have a serious cause, but a painless swelling may be the first sign of cancer and should not be ignored.

What the charts are for

The charts contained in this section guide you through a series of questions about your symptoms in order to suggest possible causes and the most appropriate course of action. The charts tell you whether you can safely treat your symptoms yourself or whether they need to receive medical attention and how urgently this should be sought if required.

Some symptoms, such as loss of consciousness or vomiting blood, are obvious emergencies. If a symptom could indicate a medical emergency in some circumstances, this is clearly highlighted on the charts. Other symptoms, such as a sore throat or runny nose, are often due to a minor infection and are likely to clear up whether or not they are treated. In these cases, the charts provide advice about self-help measures or first aid that may help relieve discomfort in the meantime. If over-the-counter remedies would be appropriate, the charts will tell you. However, you should always consult your doctor if you are unsure whether a particular remedy is suitable for you and read the manufacturer's instructions before taking medication. The charts give you guidance on how long to continue treating yourself and when you need to see your doctor.

Although the charts can help you decide on the best way to deal with your symptoms, they do not apply to all situations. For example, even apparently minor complaints should receive medical attention when they occur in people who are elderly or in those whose immune systems are suppressed, such as people having chemotherapy as part of cancer treatment.

Consulting your doctor

If you do need to see your doctor, he or she will assess your condition by asking you detailed questions about the symptoms you have. The questions on the charts should have helped you think about your symptoms so that you are able to describe them accurately to the doctor. The doctor will probably carry out a physical examination and will usually arrange for tests to confirm whatever diagnosis is suggested by your symptoms and signs.

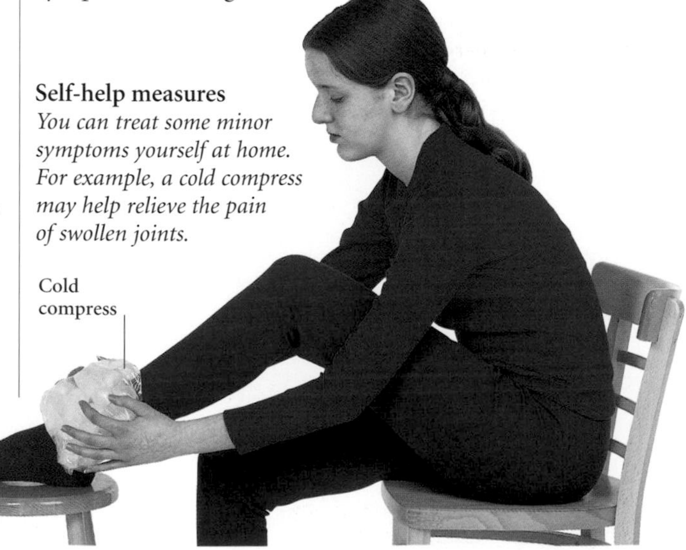
Cold compress

Self-help measures
You can treat some minor symptoms yourself at home. For example, a cold compress may help relieve the pain of swollen joints.

How to use the charts

A complete list of the 70 symptom charts in this section can be found in the contents list at the beginning of this book. If you have more than one symptom, choose the chart that describes the main one. If the chart you have selected contains a danger sign box, read that first and, if you have any of the symptoms listed, call for an ambulance or get to Emergency immediately. Similarly, any warning boxes, which highlight advice that applies only in certain circumstances, should be

Special boxes
There are three different types of boxes. Danger sign boxes alert you to situations in which emergency medical help may save a life. Warning boxes highlight specific advice that applies in particular circumstances. Symptom assessment boxes tell you how to gather the information you need to answer the questions in the chart

Introductory text
This text describes common causes of the symptom concerned and lists key information you may need to know

Starting point
The starting point is always at the top left side of the chart. From here, arrow pathways guide you around the chart through each question to the possible cause or causes of your symptom

Question box
Each question is followed by two or more possible answers. Choose the one that is most applicable and follow the arrows to another location on the chart

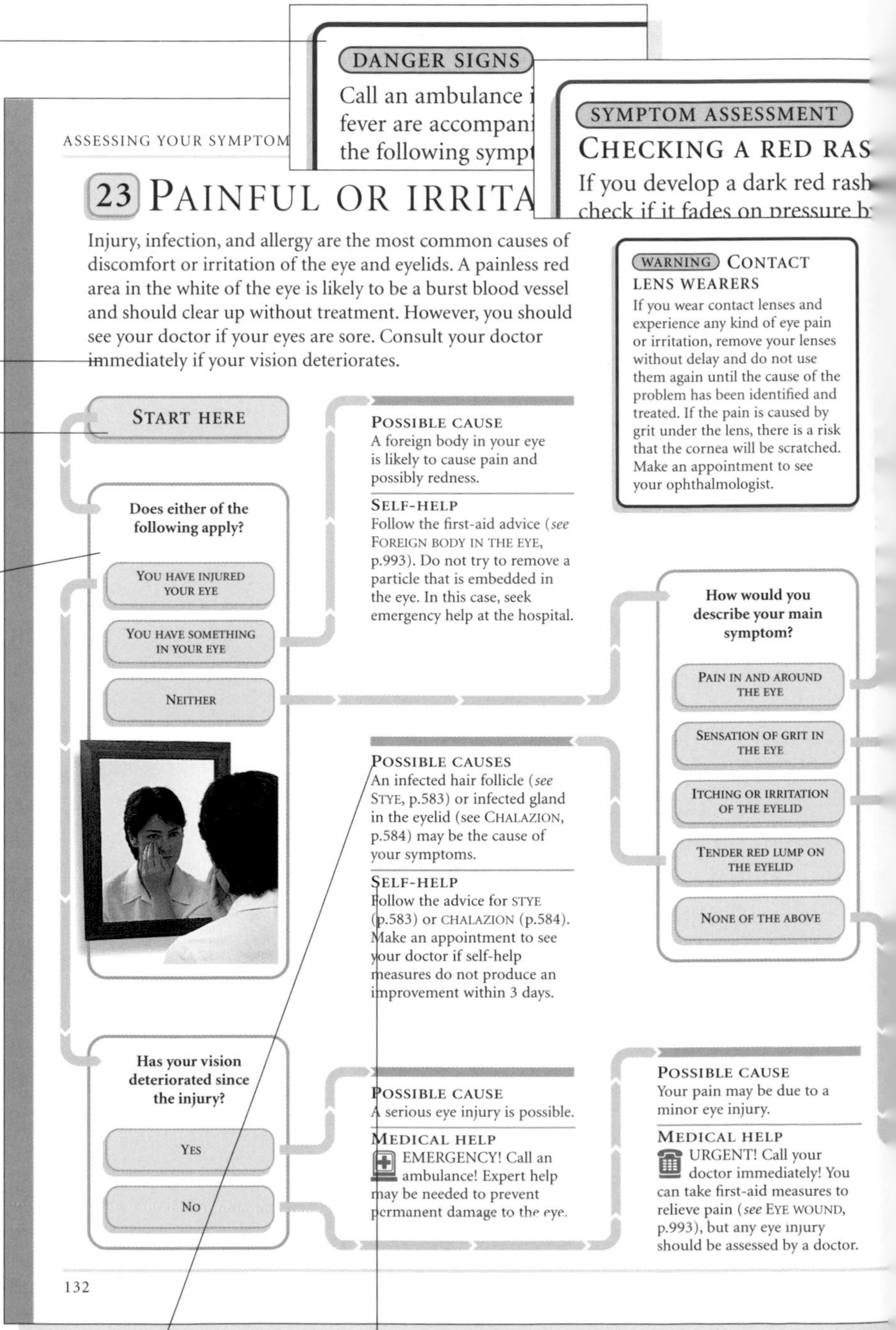

DANGER SIGNS
Call an ambulance i
fever are accompani
the following sympt

SYMPTOM ASSESSMENT
CHECKING A RED RAS
If you develop a dark red rash
check if it fades on pressure b

ASSESSING YOUR SYMPTOM

23 PAINFUL OR IRRITA

Injury, infection, and allergy are the most common causes of discomfort or irritation of the eye and eyelids. A painless red area in the white of the eye is likely to be a burst blood vessel and should clear up without treatment. However, you should see your doctor if your eyes are sore. Consult your doctor immediately if your vision deteriorates.

WARNING CONTACT LENS WEARERS
If you wear contact lenses and experience any kind of eye pain or irritation, remove your lenses without delay and do not use them again until the cause of the problem has been identified and treated. If the pain is caused by grit under the lens, there is a risk that the cornea will be scratched. Make an appointment to see your ophthalmologist.

START HERE

Does either of the following apply?
- YOU HAVE INJURED YOUR EYE
- YOU HAVE SOMETHING IN YOUR EYE
- NEITHER

POSSIBLE CAUSE
A foreign body in your eye is likely to cause pain and possibly redness.

SELF-HELP
Follow the first-aid advice (*see* FOREIGN BODY IN THE EYE, p.993). Do not try to remove a particle that is embedded in the eye. In this case, seek emergency help at the hospital.

How would you describe your main symptom?
- PAIN IN AND AROUND THE EYE
- SENSATION OF GRIT IN THE EYE
- ITCHING OR IRRITATION OF THE EYELID
- TENDER RED LUMP ON THE EYELID
- NONE OF THE ABOVE

POSSIBLE CAUSES
An infected hair follicle (*see* STYE, p.583) or infected gland in the eyelid (see CHALAZION, p.584) may be the cause of your symptoms.

SELF-HELP
Follow the advice for STYE (p.583) or CHALAZION (p.584). Make an appointment to see your doctor if self-help measures do not produce an improvement within 3 days.

Has your vision deteriorated since the injury?
- YES
- NO

POSSIBLE CAUSE
A serious eye injury is possible.

MEDICAL HELP
EMERGENCY! Call an ambulance! Expert help may be needed to prevent permanent damage to the eye.

POSSIBLE CAUSE
Your pain may be due to a minor eye injury.

MEDICAL HELP
URGENT! Call your doctor immediately! You can take first-aid measures to relieve pain (*see* EYE WOUND, p.993), but any eye injury should be assessed by a doctor.

132

Possible causes
This text suggests what may have caused the symptom. Bear in mind that these are likely diagnoses only, and not all possibilities are covered

Self-help advice
This text describes what you can do to treat the symptom yourself at home and tells you how soon you need to contact a doctor if there is no improvement in your symptom

ORGANIZATION **HOW THIS SECTION IS ORGANIZED**

There are four color-coded groups of charts for symptoms appropriate to different groups of people.

GENERAL CHARTS p.92
These symptom charts apply to people of all ages. Some symptoms in children are also covered in a separate group of children's charts.

MEN'S CHARTS p.180
Symptoms that are experienced only by men, such as erectile dysfunction, are dealt with in these charts.

WOMEN'S CHARTS p.184
This group of charts covers symptoms that are specific to women, such as menstrual problems.

CHILDREN'S CHARTS p.198
These charts feature certain important symptoms in children under age 12 for which special advice is needed.

read before other parts of the chart. Otherwise, begin at the box that reads "Start here," follow the arrow to the first question, and choose the most appropriate answer. Follow the arrows and answer further questions until you reach an endpoint. If the endpoint suggests a possible cause for your symptom, the chart advises you on whether to seek medical help or whether you can safely treat the symptom yourself. If your symptom or symptoms do not suggest a possible cause, the chart will advise you to seek the opinion of your doctor.

Cross-references
The charts feature cross-references that direct you to articles containing further information

Medical help
The icons and text indicate how urgently you should see a doctor

GENERAL CHARTS

Is your vision blurry?

BLURRY

NOT BLURRY

Is your eyelid turning inward or outward?

POSSIBLE CAUSE
ENTROPION (p.584) may be the cause of your problem.

MEDICAL HELP
Make an appointment to see your doctor.

POSSIBLE CAUSE
ACUTE GLAUCOMA (p.575) is a possible cause.

MEDICAL HELP
URGENT! Call your doctor im...

52 ERECTILE DYSFUNCTION

53 TESTES AND SCROTUM PROBLEMS

55 BREAST PROBLEMS

67 BREATHING PROBLEMS IN CHILDREN

POSSIBLE CA...
BLEPHARITIS (p...
the cause of irr...
itching of the e...
especially if the...
and inflamed.

SELF-HELP
Follow the self-...
BLEPHARITIS (p...
appointment to...
doctor if self-h...
do not help.

If you cannot identify a possible cause for your painful or irritated eye from this chart, make an appointment to see your doctor.

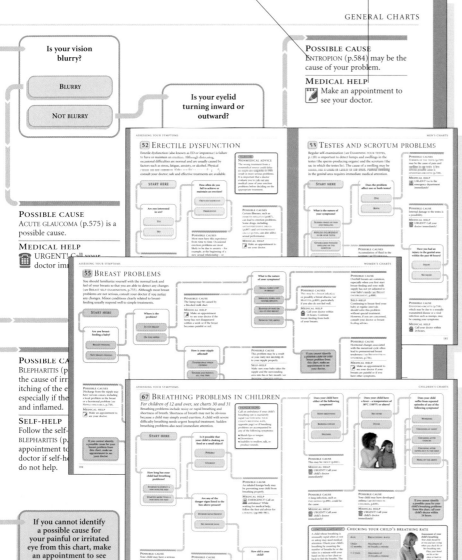

Possible cause not identified
In some cases, your symptoms do not suggest a diagnosis. The chart then recommends that you should see your doctor, who will decide if the symptom needs further investigation

Color-coding
The color-coding at the edge of each page indicates whether the chart applies to everyone or specifically to men, women, or children

ACTION MEDICAL HELP

At the end of a pathway, medical help symbols with accompanying text tell you that you need to seek medical advice and indicate how soon you should contact a doctor. Four levels of medical urgency are indicated, which range from a life-threatening emergency to a situation that can be dealt with next time you see your doctor.

EMERGENCY! Call an ambulance!

Your condition may be life-threatening unless treated quickly
Dial 911 if available or call for an ambulance because you may need trained care in transit. If there may be a delay in the arrival of assistance, going by car may be the quickest way to get to the hospital.

URGENT! Call your doctor immediately!

Your symptoms require immediate medical assessment
Contact the doctor, day or night, by telephone. Go to Emergency if you fail to make contact within one hour. Admission to a hospital may be necessary.

Call your doctor within 24 hours.

A short delay should not cause your condition to worsen
Symptoms should be assessed and, if necessary, treated by a doctor within 24 hours of their onset.

Make an appointment to see your doctor.

Your symptoms do not require urgent medical assessment
Your condition may require medical treatment, but a reasonable delay is unlikely to lead to problems.

1 NOT FEELING WELL

There may be times when you may not feel well without being able to pinpoint a precise symptom. This feeling is commonly caused by the onset of a minor viral illness, psychological pressures, or just an unhealthy lifestyle. You should always consult your doctor if the feeling persists because there may be a more serious underlying problem.

START HERE

Do you have a fever – a temperature of 38°C (100°F) or above?

FEVER

NO FEVER

Have you lost more than 10 lb (4 kg) in weight over the past 10 weeks without a deliberate change in eating habits?

LOST OVER 10 LB (4 KG)

LOST UNDER 10 LB (4 KG) OR GAINED WEIGHT

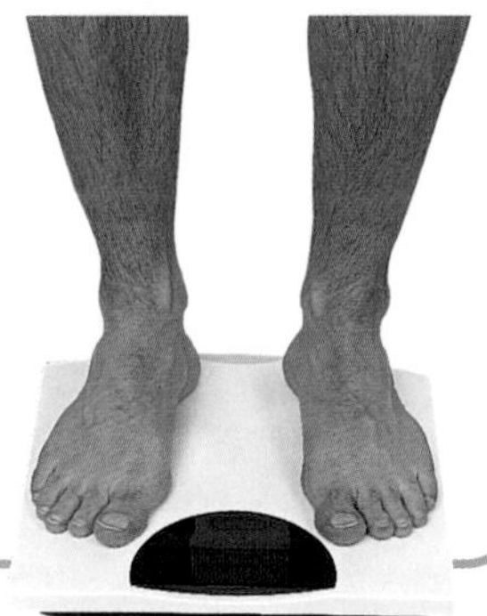

Do you have any of the following symptoms?

FEELING CONSTANTLY ON EDGE

DIFFICULTY SLEEPING

INABILITY TO CONCENTRATE OR TO MAKE DECISIONS

NONE OF THE ABOVE

Are you currently taking any prescribed or over-the-counter medication?

MEDICATION

NO MEDICATION

POSSIBLE CAUSE
A mild fever is likely to make you not feel well (*see* chart 6, FEVER if you are 12 or over or chart 66, FEVER IN CHILDREN for a child under 12).

Go to chart 3
LOSS OF WEIGHT

POSSIBLE CAUSE
Your symptoms may be a side effect of the medication.

MEDICAL HELP
Make an appointment to see your doctor. Stop taking any over-the-counter medicines but continue to take prescribed medication unless advised to stop by your doctor.

Possible causes
Your symptoms may be due to an ANXIETY DISORDER (p.551). DEPRESSION (p.554) can also cause some of these symptoms.

Medical help
Make an appointment to see your doctor.

Might you be pregnant?

- POSSIBLY PREGNANT
- NOT PREGNANT

Possible cause
Body changes that start to occur just after conception can make you not feel well (*see* COMMON COMPLAINTS OF NORMAL PREGNANCY, p.784).

Self-help
If you are not sure whether you are pregnant, try using a HOME PREGNANCY TEST (p.232) or consult your doctor.

Are you feeling more fatigued than usual?

- MORE FATIGUED
- NO CHANGE

Go to chart 2
FATIGUE

Do you regularly drink more than the recommended limit of alcohol (*see* SAFE ALCOHOL LIMITS, p.62)?

- MORE THAN THE LIMIT
- WITHIN THE LIMIT

Possible cause
Regularly drinking too much alcohol is likely to make you not feel well (*see* ALCOHOL AND HEALTH, p.62).

Medical help
Make an appointment to see your doctor for advice about reducing the amount of alcohol you drink.

Do you have any of the following symptoms?

- LOSS OF APPETITE
- NAUSEA
- DIARRHEA
- NONE OF THE ABOVE

Possible cause
You may have a mild digestive upset as a result of infection or having eaten something that disagrees with you (*see* GASTROENTERITIS, p.628).

Self-help
Avoid rich or spicy foods and drink plenty of clear fluids. Consult your doctor if you do not feel better in 2 days or if other symptoms develop.

If you cannot identify a possible cause for not feeling well from this chart, make an appointment to see your doctor.

2 FATIGUE

For fatigue caused by poor sleep, see chart 5

Fatigue, which is a feeling of tiredness, is normal if you have had difficulty sleeping or if you have been working hard or exercising. You should not feel concerned unless fatigue is persistent and severe. If you are uncertain about the cause of your fatigue, you should consult your doctor.

START HERE

Do you have any of the following symptoms?

- FEELING FAINT OR PASSING OUT
- SHORTNESS OF BREATH
- PALER SKIN THAN NORMAL
- NONE OF THE ABOVE

Have you lost more than 10 lb (4 kg) in weight over the past 10 weeks without a deliberate change in eating habits?

- LOST UNDER 10 LB (4 KG) OR GAINED WEIGHT
- LOST OVER 10 LB (4 KG)

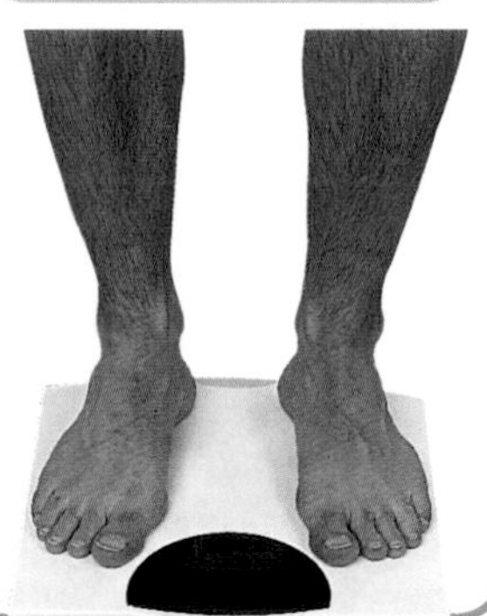

Do you have any of the following symptoms?

- INCREASED DRYNESS OR ROUGHNESS OF THE SKIN
- FEELING THE COLD MORE THAN YOU USED TO
- GENERALIZED HAIR THINNING
- NONE OF THE ABOVE

Have you been experiencing any of the following symptoms?

- INCREASED THIRST
- PASSING MORE URINE THAN NORMAL
- BLURRY VISION
- NONE OF THE ABOVE

POSSIBLE CAUSE

ANEMIA (p.446) is a possible cause of your symptoms.

MEDICAL HELP

 Call your doctor within 24 hours.

POSSIBLE CAUSE

DIABETES MELLITUS (p.687) may be a possibility.

MEDICAL HELP

 Call your doctor within 24 hours.

Possible cause
Hypothyroidism (p.680) is a possible cause.

Medical help
Make an appointment to see your doctor.

Possible cause
Regularly drinking too much alcohol can lead to fatigue (*see* Alcohol and health, p.62).

Medical help
Make an appointment to see your doctor for advice about reducing the amount of alcohol you drink.

Go to chart 17
Feeling depressed

Do you have any of the following symptoms?

- Low self-esteem
- Inability to concentrate or to make decisions
- Lack of interest in sex
- None of the above

Do you regularly drink more than the recommended limit of alcohol (*see* Safe alcohol limits, p.62)?

- More than the limit
- Within the limit

Possible causes
Certain drugs, particularly some of those used to treat high blood pressure (*see* Antihypertensive drugs, p.897) may cause fatigue.

Medical help
Make an appointment to see your doctor. Stop taking over-the-counter medicines but continue any prescribed medication unless advised to stop by your doctor.

Are you currently taking any prescribed or over-the-counter medication?

- Medication
- No medication

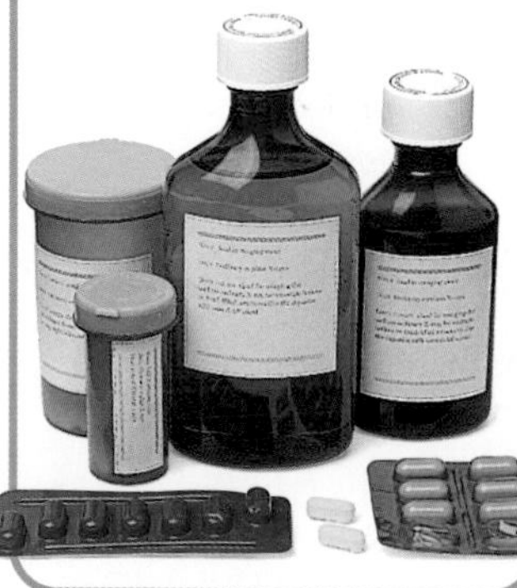

Have you recently had a viral illness such as flu?

- Recent illness
- No recent illness

Possible cause
It may take several weeks to recover from an illness, particularly from some viral infections, such as Infectious mononucleosis (p.289).

Medical help
Make an appointment to see your doctor if you are still feeling fatigued 1 month after any other symptoms you had have disappeared.

If you cannot identify a possible cause for your fatigue from this chart, make an appointment to see your doctor.

3 LOSS OF WEIGHT

For children under 12, see chart 70

Most people experience small fluctuations in their weight. However, weight loss is of concern if you lose more than 10 lb (4 kg) in 10 weeks or less without a deliberate change in diet and/or increased exercise. Consult your doctor if you have been losing weight without an obvious cause.

START HERE

How much weight have you lost in the past 10 weeks?

- 10 LB (4 KG) OR MORE
- LESS THAN 10 LB (4 KG)

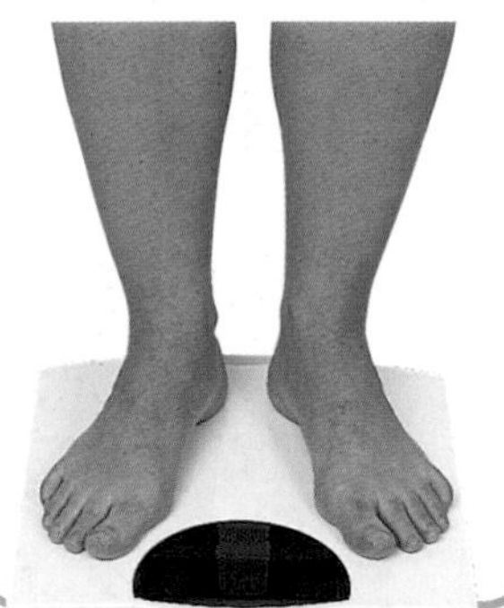

How has your appetite been lately?

- POOR
- NORMAL OR INCREASED

Have you been experiencing any of the following symptoms?

- RECURRENT FEVER
- PROFUSE SWEATING AT NIGHT
- PERSISTENT COUGH
- BLOODSTAINED SPUTUM
- NONE OF THE ABOVE

Have you been experiencing any of the following symptoms?

- INCREASED THIRST
- PASSING MORE URINE THAN USUAL
- BLURRY VISION
- NONE OF THE ABOVE

Do you have any of the following symptoms?

- FEELING CONSTANTLY ON EDGE
- INCREASED SWEATING
- BULGING EYES
- NONE OF THE ABOVE

POSSIBLE CAUSE

Your weight loss is unlikely to be a serious cause for concern unless you are below your ideal weight (*see* ARE YOU A HEALTHY WEIGHT?, p.53).

SELF-HELP

Increase the amount of food you eat (*see* CONTROLLING YOUR WEIGHT, p.53). Make an appointment to see your doctor if you continue to lose weight or have fallen below the ideal weight for your height.

POSSIBLE CAUSE

DIABETES MELLITUS (p.687) is a possible cause.

MEDICAL HELP

 Call your doctor within 24 hours.

POSSIBLE CAUSES

HYPERTHYROIDISM (p.679) is a possibility. However, ANXIETY DISORDERS (p.551) can cause some of these symptoms.

MEDICAL HELP

 Make an appointment to see your doctor.

POSSIBLE CAUSES
A chronic infection, such as TUBERCULOSIS (p.491) or an AIDS-related illness (*see* HIV INFECTION AND AIDS, p.295), could be the cause of your symptoms. An underlying CANCER (pp.272–281) is also a possible cause.

MEDICAL HELP

Call your doctor within 24 hours.

POSSIBLE CAUSE
You are probably eating less than you need to meet your energy requirements.

MEDICAL HELP
Make an appointment to see your doctor to make sure that an underlying problem is not responsible for your weight loss.

Have you recently increased the amount of exercise you do?

- NO INCREASE
- INCREASED EXERCISE

POSSIBLE CAUSES
An intestinal infection, such as GIARDIASIS (p.307), or a chronic bowel condition, such as ULCERATIVE COLITIS (p.659) or CROHN'S DISEASE (p.658), could be the cause of your symptoms. COLORECTAL CANCER (p.665) is also a possibility.

MEDICAL HELP

Call your doctor within 24 hours.

Have you noticed any of the following symptoms?

- RECURRENT DIARRHEA
- RECURRENT CONSTIPATION
- RECURRENT ABDOMINAL PAIN
- BLOOD IN FECES
- NONE OF THE ABOVE

POSSIBLE CAUSE
Your increase in energy output is the most probable cause of your weight loss.

SELF-HELP
Increase the amount of food you eat to make up for your increased energy needs (*see* CONTROLLING YOUR WEIGHT, p.53). Make an appointment to see your doctor if you continue to lose weight or are below the ideal weight for your height (*see* ARE YOU A HEALTHY WEIGHT?, p.53).

POSSIBLE CAUSES
DEPRESSION (p.554) could be the cause. However, ANXIETY DISORDERS (p.551) sometimes produce similar symptoms.

MEDICAL HELP

Make an appointment to see your doctor.

Do you have any of the following symptoms?

- DIFFICULTY SLEEPING
- LOW SELF-ESTEEM
- LACK OF INTEREST IN SEX
- INABILITY TO CONCENTRATE OR TO MAKE DECISIONS
- LACK OF ENERGY
- NONE OF THE ABOVE

If you cannot identify a possible cause for your weight loss from this chart, call your doctor within 24 hours.

4 OVERWEIGHT

For children under 12, see chart 70

You are overweight if you weigh more than is ideal for your height (*see* ARE YOU A HEALTHY WEIGHT?, p.53). Being overweight is most often due to eating more than you need and/or lack of exercise. Extreme overweight may lead to various medical problems (*see* OBESITY, p.631).

START HERE

In the past, has your weight been consistently within ideal limits?

- PREVIOUSLY IDEAL WEIGHT
- PREVIOUSLY UNDERWEIGHT
- ALWAYS OVERWEIGHT

Do you have any of the following symptoms?

- FATIGUE
- INCREASED DRYNESS OR ROUGHNESS OF THE SKIN
- FEELING THE COLD MORE THAN YOU USED TO
- GENERALIZED HAIR THINNING
- NONE OF THE ABOVE

POSSIBLE CAUSE
A hormone disorder, such as HYPOTHYROIDISM (p.680), is a possible cause.

MEDICAL HELP
 Make an appointment to see your doctor.

Are you currently taking any prescribed medication?

- MEDICATION
- NO MEDICATION

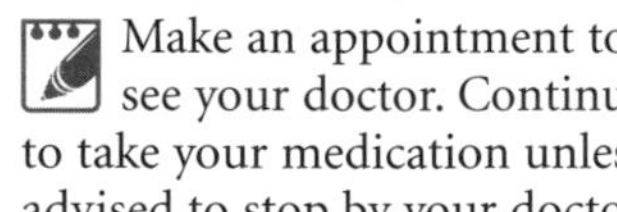

POSSIBLE CAUSE
Your weight gain may be a side effect of the medication.

MEDICAL HELP
Make an appointment to see your doctor. Continue to take your medication unless advised to stop by your doctor.

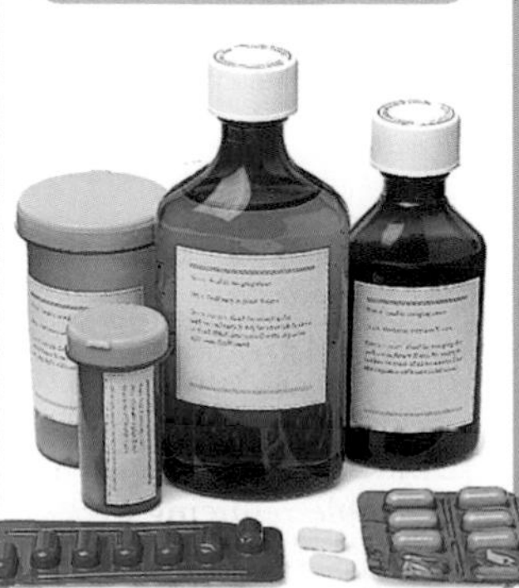

Are or were your parents overweight?

- OVERWEIGHT
- IDEAL WEIGHT OR UNDERWEIGHT

POSSIBLE CAUSE
A family tendency to being overweight may result from unhealthy family eating habits and/or a genetic predisposition to put on weight.

SELF-HELP
Adopt a sensible reducing diet (*see* CONTROLLING YOUR WEIGHT, p.53) and get more exercise. Make an appointment to see your doctor if you have not started to lose weight within 2 weeks.

Do any of the following apply?

- YOU HAVE RECENTLY HAD A BABY
- YOU HAVE RECENTLY GIVEN UP SMOKING
- YOU HAVE BEEN SUFFERING FROM DEPRESSION OR STRESS
- YOU HAVE REDUCED YOUR LEVEL OF PHYSICAL ACTIVITY
- NONE OF THE ABOVE

POSSIBLE CAUSE
During pregnancy, women often put on weight that they find hard to lose after the baby has been born.

SELF-HELP
You will probably lose excess weight gradually over the next few months or so. If you are breast-feeding, it is not a good idea to reduce your calorie intake substantially. If you are still unhappy with your weight when you have finished breast-feeding, consult your doctor.

POSSIBLE CAUSE
Giving up smoking often leads to a temporary weight gain. However, the benefits to your health from giving up smoking far outweigh the much smaller risk from any excess weight.

SELF-HELP
When you are sure that you have overcome your smoking habit, start a sensible reducing diet (*see* CONTROLLING YOUR WEIGHT, p.53).

POSSIBLE CAUSES
Both DEPRESSION (p.554) and ANXIETY DISORDERS (p.551) can cause weight gain.

MEDICAL HELP
Make an appointment to see your doctor.

POSSIBLE CAUSE
Reducing your level of physical activity without cutting down the amount of food that you eat will usually lead to weight gain (*see* CONTROLLING YOUR WEIGHT, p.53).

SELF-HELP
Be sure to maintain a healthy level of exercise (*see* DOING REGULAR EXERCISE, p.57) and follow a sensible diet (*see* A HEALTHY DIET, p.48).

How old are you?

- UNDER 40 YEARS
- 40 YEARS OR OVER

POSSIBLE CAUSE
Regularly eating more than you need is the most likely cause of your weight gain.

SELF-HELP
Adopt a sensible reducing diet (*see* CONTROLLING YOUR WEIGHT, p.53) and get more exercise. Make an appointment to see your doctor if you have not started to lose weight within 2 weeks.

POSSIBLE CAUSE
It is normal to gain a little weight as you become older.

SELF-HELP
If you are above the ideal weight for your height, adopt a sensible reducing diet (*see* CONTROLLING YOUR WEIGHT, p.53) and get more exercise. Make an appointment to see your doctor if you have not lost any weight within 2 weeks.

If you cannot identify a possible cause for your weight problem from this chart, adopt a sensible reducing diet (*see* CONTROLLING YOUR WEIGHT, p.53). Make an appointment to see your doctor if you have not started to lose weight within 2 weeks.

5 DIFFICULTY SLEEPING

Most people are affected by difficulty sleeping on occasion. The causes include worry, drinking too much caffeine, or insufficient exercise. If you wake feeling unrested but are not aware of difficulty sleeping, the cause may be interruption of breathing during sleep (*see* SLEEP APNEA, p.477). Consult your doctor if you have frequent sleeping problems.

START HERE

What kind of sleeping difficulty have you been experiencing?

- DIFFICULTY GETTING TO SLEEP
- DIFFICULTY STAYING ASLEEP

Are you awakened from sleep by attacks of shortness of breath?

- NO
- YES

Go to chart 30
SHORTNESS OF BREATH

Do you have any of the following symptoms?

- LACK OF ENERGY
- LOW SELF-ESTEEM
- INABILITY TO CONCENTRATE OR TO MAKE DECISIONS
- LACK OF INTEREST IN SEX
- NONE OF THE ABOVE

Go to chart 17
FEELING DEPRESSED

Do you take sleeping pills regularly or have you recently stopped taking them?

- TAKING SLEEPING PILLS
- RECENTLY STOPPED
- NEITHER

POSSIBLE CAUSE
The regular use of sleeping pills can lead to a gradual reduction in their effectiveness (*see* SLEEPING DRUGS, p.915).

MEDICAL HELP
 Make an appointment to see your doctor.

POSSIBLE CAUSE
Withdrawal from sleeping pills can lead to difficulty sleeping as your body adapts (*see* SLEEPING DRUGS, p.915).

MEDICAL HELP
 Make an appointment to see your doctor.

POSSIBLE CAUSES
HYPERTHYROIDISM (p.679) is a possible cause. However, ANXIETY DISORDERS (p.551) can also cause these symptoms.

MEDICAL HELP
 Make an appointment to see your doctor.

On nights that you have difficulty sleeping, have you consumed any of the following?

- LARGE AMOUNTS OF COFFEE, TEA, OR COLA
- LARGE AMOUNTS OF ALCOHOL
- A LATE, HEAVY MEAL
- NONE OF THE ABOVE

POSSIBLE CAUSE
Consumption of any of these can lead to difficulty sleeping.

SELF-HELP
Follow the advice for getting a good night's sleep (*see* SLEEP, p.73). Make an appointment to see your doctor if difficulty sleeping continues.

Do you have either of the following symptoms?

- FEELING CONSTANTLY ON EDGE
- INABILITY TO CONCENTRATE
- NEITHER

Are you currently taking any prescribed or over-the-counter medication?

- MEDICATION
- NO MEDICATION

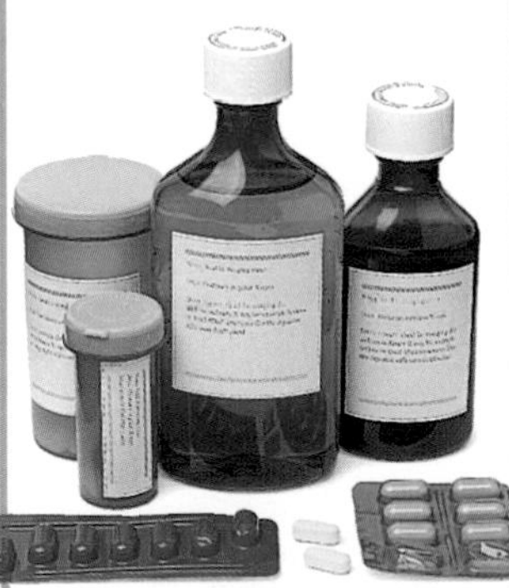

POSSIBLE CAUSE
Your symptoms may be a side effect of the medication.

MEDICAL HELP
Make an appointment to see your doctor. Stop taking over-the-counter medicines but continue any prescribed medication unless advised to stop by your doctor.

On nights that you have difficulty sleeping, have either of the following applied?

- YOU HAVE TAKEN A NAP DURING THE DAY
- YOU HAVE BEEN AWAKE FOR FEWER THAN 18 HOURS
- NEITHER

POSSIBLE CAUSE
You may need less sleep than you think. It is possible that some of the sleep that you need has been taken as naps during the day.

SELF-HELP
Follow the advice for getting a good night's sleep (*see* SLEEP, p.73). Make an appointment to see your doctor if difficulty sleeping continues.

How physically active is your usual daily routine?

- MAINLY SEDENTARY
- PHYSICALLY ACTIVE

POSSIBLE CAUSE
Insufficient physical activity in the day can lead to sleeping problems at night.

SELF-HELP
Build more exercise into your daily routine (*see* DOING REGULAR EXERCISE, p.57). Make an appointment to see your doctor if problems with sleeping persist.

If you cannot identify a possible cause for your difficulty sleeping from this chart, make an appointment to see your doctor.

6 FEVER

For children under 12, see chart 66

Normal temperature varies among people, but if your temperature is 38°C (100°F) or above, you have a fever. Most fevers are due to infection, but heat exposure or certain drugs can also raise body temperature. In all cases, follow the self-help advice for BRINGING DOWN A FEVER (p.287).

WARNING HIGH TEMPERATURE

If you are not feeling well, you should take your temperature every 4 hours. Call your doctor immediately if your temperature rises to 39°C (102°F) or above, and take steps to lower the fever without delay (*see* BRINGING DOWN A FEVER, p.287).

START HERE

Do you have a rash?

- RASH
- NO RASH

Go to chart 21
RASH WITH FEVER

Do you have a headache?

- SEVERE HEADACHE
- MILD HEADACHE
- NO HEADACHE

Do you have any of the following symptoms?

- DROWSINESS OR CONFUSION
- DISLIKE OF BRIGHT LIGHT
- NECK PAIN ON BENDING THE HEAD FORWARD
- NONE OF THE ABOVE

POSSIBLE CAUSE

There is a possibility that you have MENINGITIS (p.527).

MEDICAL HELP

EMERGENCY! Call an ambulance!

Are you having problems breathing?

- YOU ARE SHORT OF BREATH
- BREATHING IS PAINFUL
- BREATHING IS NORMAL

Do you have a cough?

- COUGH
- NO COUGH

POSSIBLE CAUSES

CYSTITIS (p.709) is the most likely cause of your symptoms, but PYELONEPHRITIS (p.698) is also possible, especially if you have back pain.

MEDICAL HELP

 Call your doctor within 24 hours.

Have you been coughing up sputum?

- SPUTUM
- NO SPUTUM

POSSIBLE CAUSE
A chest infection, such as PNEUMONIA (p.490), is a possible cause.

MEDICAL HELP
URGENT! Call your doctor immediately!

POSSIBLE CAUSE
A chest infection, such as ACUTE BRONCHITIS (p.486), may cause your symptoms.

MEDICAL HELP

Call your doctor within 24 hours.

Do you have either of the following symptoms?

- GENERALIZED ACHES AND PAINS
- RUNNY NOSE
- NEITHER

POSSIBLE CAUSES
A viral illness, such as a severe cold (*see* COMMON COLD, p.286) or INFLUENZA (p.287), is the most probable cause of your symptoms.

SELF-HELP
Follow the self-help advice for BRINGING DOWN A FEVER (p.287). Consult your doctor if your symptoms get worse, if you are no better in 2 days, or if other symptoms develop.

Have you had several bouts of fever over the past few weeks?

- RECURRENT FEVER
- NO OTHER RECENT FEVER

POSSIBLE CAUSES
A long-term infection, such as TUBERCULOSIS (p.491) or an AIDS-related illness (*see* HIV INFECTION AND AIDS, p.295), may cause recurrent fever. An underlying cancer, such as LYMPHOMA (p.459), is also a possible cause.

MEDICAL HELP

Call your doctor within 24 hours.

Do you have any urinary problems?

- PAINFUL URINATION
- FREQUENT URINATION
- NEITHER

Do you have a sore throat?

- SORE THROAT
- NO SORE THROAT

Go to chart 27
SORE THROAT

If you cannot identify a possible cause for your fever from this chart, call your doctor within 24 hours.

7 Excessive sweating

Sweating is one of the body's cooling mechanisms. It is a normal response to heat, exercise, and stress or fear. Some people naturally sweat more than others. Wearing natural fibers, such as cotton, and using antiperspirants often help reduce sweating. You should consult your doctor if you sweat excessively and are unsure of the cause.

START HERE

Do you have a fever – a temperature of 38°C (100°F) or above?

- FEVER
- NO FEVER

POSSIBLE CAUSE
A fever will generally cause increased sweating (*see* chart 6, FEVER if you are 12 or over or chart 66, FEVER IN CHILDREN for a child under 12).

When does the sweating occur?

- MAINLY AT NIGHT
- AT OTHER TIMES

Do you have any of the following symptoms?

- WEIGHT LOSS WITH INCREASED APPETITE
- FEELING CONSTANTLY ON EDGE
- BULGING EYES
- NONE OF THE ABOVE

POSSIBLE CAUSES
HYPERTHYROIDISM (p.679) is a possibility. However, ANXIETY DISORDERS (p.551) can cause some of these symptoms.

MEDICAL HELP
 Make an appointment to see your doctor.

POSSIBLE CAUSES
A chronic infection, such as TUBERCULOSIS (p.491), or an AIDS-related illness (*see* HIV INFECTION AND AIDS, p.295) may cause your symptoms. A cancer such as LYMPHOMA (p.459) is also a possibility.

MEDICAL HELP
 Call your doctor within 24 hours.

Do you feel otherwise well?

- WELL
- UNWELL

POSSIBLE CAUSES
Hormonal changes associated with the menstrual cycle or menopause (*see* HEALTH AT MENOPAUSE, p.36) may cause excessive sweating.

MEDICAL HELP
 Make an appointment to see your doctor.

Does either of the following apply?

- SWEATING OCCURS WITH MENSTRUAL PERIODS
- MENSTRUAL PERIODS HAVE BECOME IRREGULAR
- NEITHER

Is your weight within ideal limits (*see* ARE YOU A HEALTHY WEIGHT?, p.53)?

- OVERWEIGHT
- IDEAL WEIGHT
- UNDERWEIGHT

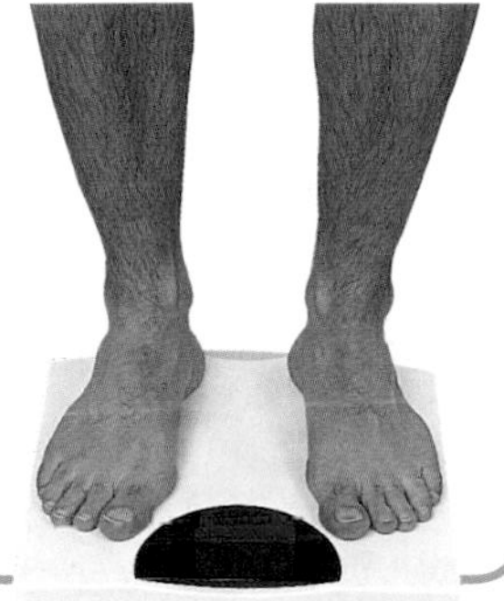

POSSIBLE CAUSE
Being overweight can lead to excessive sweating, particularly after physical exertion.

MEDICAL HELP
Make an appointment to see your doctor. Adopt a sensible reducing diet (*see* CONTROLLING YOUR WEIGHT, p.53) and follow the advice for HYPERHIDROSIS (p.342).

Do you regularly drink more than the recommended limit of alcohol (*see* SAFE ALCOHOL LIMITS, p.62)?

- MORE THAN THE LIMIT
- WITHIN THE LIMIT

POSSIBLE CAUSE
Drinking excessive amounts of alcohol can lead to increased sweating (*see* ALCOHOL AND HEALTH, p.62).

MEDICAL HELP
Make an appointment to see your doctor for advice about reducing the amount of alcohol you drink.

Are you currently taking any prescribed or over-the-counter medication?

- MEDICATION
- NO MEDICATION

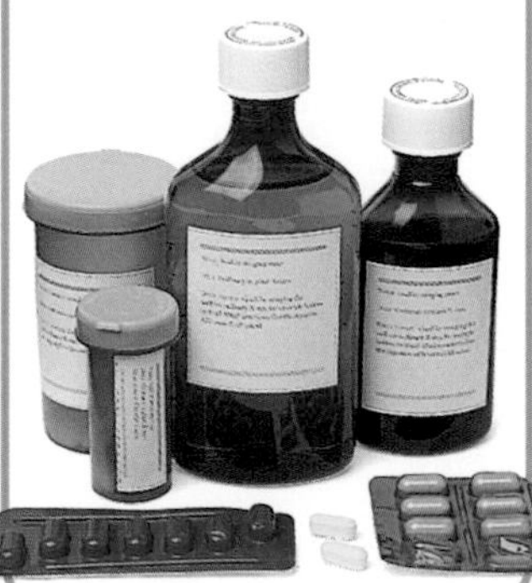

POSSIBLE CAUSE
Your symptoms may be a side effect of the medication.

MEDICAL HELP
Make an appointment to see your doctor. Stop taking any over-the-counter medicines but continue to take prescribed medication unless advised to stop by your doctor.

Is the excessive sweating limited to certain parts of the body?

- MAINLY HANDS
- MAINLY FEET
- OTHER PARTS AFFECTED

POSSIBLE CAUSE
Excessive sweating that chiefly affects the hands and feet is a fairly common problem.

SELF-HELP
Try self-help measures (*see* HYPERHIDROSIS, p.342). Make an appointment to see your doctor if your symptoms do not improve.

If you cannot identify a possible cause for your excessive sweating from this chart, call your doctor within 24 hours.

8 LUMPS AND SWELLINGS

Lumps and swellings under the skin, particularly in the neck, under the arms, or in the groin, are often enlarged lymph nodes (glands). These glands usually become swollen due to an infection. The swelling subsides shortly after the infection clears up. If the lumps are painful or if they are persistent but painless, you should consult your doctor.

START HERE

What are the characteristics of the lump or swelling?

- RED AND PAINFUL
- OTHER

POSSIBLE CAUSE

An abscess or a BOIL (p.351) may be the cause of a painful, inflamed swelling.

MEDICAL HELP

Call your doctor within 24 hours.

Are the lumps or swellings in more than one area?

- ONE AREA ONLY
- SEVERAL AREAS

POSSIBLE CAUSES

MUMPS (p.291), an infectious disease that mainly occurs in nonimmunized children and adults, can cause swelling in this area. A SALIVARY GLAND TUMOR (p.635) is another possible explanation.

MEDICAL HELP

Call your doctor within 24 hours.

Do you have a fever – a temperature of 38°C (100°F) or above?

- FEVER
- NO FEVER

POSSIBLE CAUSES

A viral infection is the most likely cause. There is also a possibility of a cancer of the lymphatic system (*see* LYMPHOMA, p.459) or an AIDS-related illness (*see* HIV INFECTION AND AIDS, p.295).

MEDICAL HELP

Make an appointment to see your doctor.

Do you have a rash?

- RASH
- NO RASH

POSSIBLE CAUSES

INFECTIOUS MONONUCLEOSIS (p.289) is a possible cause of swelling of the lymph nodes in several areas, especially if you feel generally unwell. LYME DISEASE (p.302) is another possibility, particularly if you think you may have been bitten by a tick recently.

MEDICAL HELP

Call your doctor within 24 hours.

Go to chart 53
TESTES AND SCROTUM PROBLEMS

Where is the lump or swelling?

- TESTIS
- GROIN
- BREAST
- BETWEEN THE EAR AND THE JAW
- SIDES OR BACK OF NECK
- OTHER

What happens to the swelling if you press on it or if you lie down?

- IT DISAPPEARS
- IT REDUCES IN SIZE
- NO CHANGE

POSSIBLE CAUSE
You may have an inguinal hernia (*see* HERNIAS, p.661).

MEDICAL HELP

Make an appointment to see your doctor.

POSSIBLE CAUSE
A trapped inguinal hernia (*see* HERNIAS, p.661) could be responsible for the swelling.

MEDICAL HELP

URGENT! Call your doctor immediately!

Go to chart 55
BREAST PROBLEMS

Do you have a sore throat?

- SORE THROAT
- NO SORE THROAT

Go to chart 27
SORE THROAT

POSSIBLE CAUSES
A number of viral illnesses can cause swollen glands and a rash. LYME DISEASE (p.302) is another possibility, particularly if you think you may have been bitten by a tick recently.

MEDICAL HELP

Call your doctor within 24 hours.

Do you have a recent injury near the site of the swelling?

- INJURY
- NO INJURY

POSSIBLE CAUSES
An injury is likely to cause some swelling as a result of damage to the tissues. An infected wound or a localized rash can also cause nearby lymph nodes to swell (*see* LYMPHADENOPATHY, p.458).

SELF-HELP
Make sure the wound is clean and protect it with an adhesive bandage or light dressing. Consult your doctor if there is any pain, redness, or pus around the wound, or if the swelling persists after the wound has healed.

If you cannot identify a possible cause for your lumps or swellings from this chart, make an appointment to see your doctor.

9 FEELING FAINT AND PASSING OUT

Feeling faint is a sensation of dizziness or lightheadedness. It may be followed by passing out (loss of consciousness). The cause is usually lack of food or a reduction in blood flow to the brain. A brief episode of feeling faint without other symptoms need not alarm you, but you should always consult your doctor if such episodes recur or if you have passed out.

WARNING
UNCONSCIOUSNESS
If someone remains unconscious for more than a minute or so, whatever the suspected cause, you should get emergency medical help. If you need to leave the person to call for help, first lay him or her in the recovery position (p.979). Do not move the person if you suspect spinal injury.

START HERE

Have you had any of the following symptoms?

- DISTURBED VISION
- NUMBNESS, TINGLING, OR WEAKNESS IN ANY PART OF THE BODY
- CONFUSION
- DIFFICULTY IN SPEAKING
- NONE OF THE ABOVE

Have you noticed any of the following?

- BLOODSTAINED VOMIT
- RED BLOOD IN THE FECES
- BLACK TARRY FECES
- NONE OF THE ABOVE

POSSIBLE CAUSE
Feeling faint or passing out may be caused by bleeding in the digestive tract, perhaps from a PEPTIC ULCER (p.640).

MEDICAL HELP
EMERGENCY! Call an ambulance!

Did any of the following occur when you passed out?

- UNCONTROLLABLE SHAKING
- YOU BIT YOUR TONGUE
- YOU PASSED URINE
- NONE OF THE ABOVE

POSSIBLE CAUSE
EPILEPSY (p.524) is a possible cause of your symptoms.

MEDICAL HELP
EMERGENCY! Call an ambulance!

Are any of your symptoms still present?

- SYMPTOMS PRESENT
- SYMPTOMS NO LONGER PRESENT

POSSIBLE CAUSE
It is possible that you have had a STROKE (p.532).

MEDICAL HELP
EMERGENCY! Call an ambulance!

POSSIBLE CAUSE
A TRANSIENT ISCHEMIC ATTACK (p.531) is a possibility.

MEDICAL HELP
URGENT! Call your doctor immediately!

Possible cause
Sudden psychological shock can affect the nerves that control the blood circulation to the brain, resulting in feeling faint or passing out.

Medical help

Make an appointment to see your doctor.

Did you feel faint or pass out immediately after either of the following?

- Getting up suddenly
- Emotional shock
- Neither

Possible cause
The most likely explanation is postural hypotension, in which there is a temporary drop in blood pressure; it is usually not a cause for concern (*see* Hypotension, p.414).

Medical help

Call your doctor within 24 hours if you passed out. Make an appointment to see your doctor, even if you did not pass out.

Possible causes
You may have low blood pressure (*see* Hypotension, p.414) due to worsening of a preexisting heart condition or an irregular heartbeat (*see* Arrhythmias, p.415).

Medical help

URGENT! Call your doctor immediately!

Does either of the following apply?

- You are diabetic
- You had not eaten for several hours before passing out
- Neither

Do you have any of the following symptoms?

- Shortness of breath
- Paler skin than normal
- Undue fatigue
- None of the above

Does either of the following apply?

- You have chest pain or a heart condition
- You have had palpitations
- Neither

Possible cause
Low blood sugar levels are a possible cause of feeling faint or passing out, often with sweating, anxiety, and nausea (*see* Diabetes mellitus, p.687, and Hypoglycemia, p.691).

Medical help
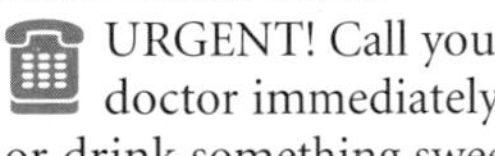
URGENT! Call your doctor immediately! Eat or drink something sweet.

Possible cause
Anemia (p.446) is a possible cause of your symptoms.

Medical help

Make an appointment to see your doctor.

Possible cause
Changes in pregnancy can lead to feeling faint.

Medical help
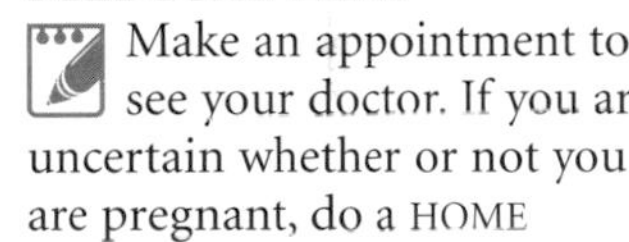
Make an appointment to see your doctor. If you are uncertain whether or not you are pregnant, do a home pregnancy test (p.232).

Might you be pregnant?

- Possibly pregnant
- Not pregnant

If you cannot identify a possible cause for passing out from this chart, phone your doctor immediately. If you cannot identify a possible cause for feeling faint, call your doctor within 24 hours.

10 HEADACHE

Tension in head and neck muscles and fever are common causes of headache. Too much alcohol, caffeine, or nicotine may also cause a headache. Most headaches do not last for more than a few hours. If your headache lasts for more than 24 hours, is not improved by over-the-counter analgesics, or recurs several times in a week, consult your doctor.

DANGER SIGNS

Call an ambulance immediately if you have a headache that is accompanied by any of the following symptoms:

- Drowsiness or confusion.
- Weakness of a limb.
- Blurry vision.
- Loss of consciousness.

START HERE

Have you hit your head within the past 24 hours?

- HEAD INJURY
- NO HEAD INJURY

Are any of the danger signs listed in the box (above right) present, or have you vomited?

- DANGER SIGNS PRESENT
- VOMITED AFTER HEAD INJURY
- NO DANGER SIGNS OR VOMITING

POSSIBLE CAUSE

There may be damage to the tissues that surround the brain (*see* HEAD INJURIES, p.521).

MEDICAL HELP

EMERGENCY! Call an ambulance!

Do you have a fever – a temperature of 38°C (100°F) or above?

- FEVER
- NO FEVER

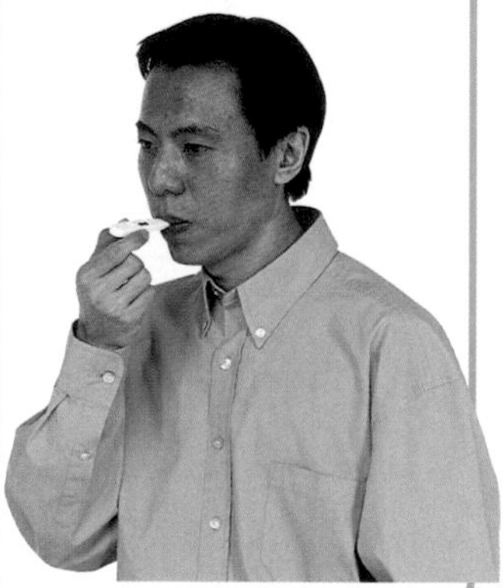

POSSIBLE CAUSE

A mild headache is common following a minor head injury (*see* HEAD INJURIES, p.521).

SELF-HELP

Take an analgesic (not aspirin). If your headache lasts for more than 2 hours, or if you develop other symptoms, call your doctor immediately.

POSSIBLE CAUSE

Many minor illnesses associated with fever are accompanied by a headache. However, a serious illness such as MENINGITIS (p.527) may also be the cause (*see* chart 6, FEVER if you are 12 or over or chart 66, FEVER IN CHILDREN for a child under 12).

Have you experienced nausea and/or vomiting with your headache?

- YES
- NO

POSSIBLE CAUSE

SINUSITIS (p.475) is the likely cause of your headache.

SELF-HELP

Try INHALING MOIST AIR (p.475). Get medical advice if you feel no better in 2 days.

How is your vision?

- BLURRY VISION
- DISTURBED IN OTHER WAYS
- UNCHANGED

POSSIBLE CAUSE
ACUTE GLAUCOMA (p.575) is a possibility, particularly if the pain is around your eye.

MEDICAL HELP
 URGENT! Call your doctor immediately!

POSSIBLE CAUSE
Your symptoms may be a side effect of the medication.

MEDICAL HELP
Make an appointment to see your doctor. Stop taking any over-the-counter medicines but continue to take prescribed medication unless advised to stop by your doctor.

POSSIBLE CAUSES
MIGRAINE (p.518) is the most likely cause of your headache, particularly if any visual problems occurred before the headache started. However, the possibility of another disorder, such as a STROKE (p.532), needs to be ruled out.

MEDICAL HELP
URGENT! Call your doctor immediately if this is your first attack. Although the condition is probably not dangerous, your doctor should confirm the diagnosis.

Are you currently taking any prescribed or over-the-counter medication?

- MEDICATION
- NO MEDICATION

Where is the pain?

- OVER ONE OR BOTH TEMPLES
- ELSEWHERE

Have you had this type of headache before?

- YES
- NO

Does either of the following apply?

SITES OF PAIN

- THE PAIN IS FELT CHIEFLY IN THE AREAS SHOWN
- YOU HAVE RECENTLY HAD A RUNNY OR STUFFY NOSE
- NEITHER

POSSIBLE CAUSE
TEMPORAL (GIANT CELL) ARTERITIS (p.464) is a possibility, particularly if you are over 50 and have not been feeling well.

MEDICAL HELP
URGENT! Call your doctor immediately!

If you cannot identify a possible cause for your headache from this chart, make an appointment to see your doctor.

POSSIBLE CAUSE
A recurrent HEADACHE (p.518) for which there is no obvious cause, such as drinking too much alcohol, should always be investigated by your doctor.

MEDICAL HELP
 Make an appointment to see your doctor.

11 VERTIGO

Vertigo is the sensation that your surroundings are spinning around you. It can be very unpleasant and is often associated with nausea and vomiting. Healthy people may experience vertigo temporarily after a ride at an amusement park or after drinking too much alcohol. You should consult your doctor if you develop vertigo for no obvious reason.

WARNING RECURRING ATTACKS OF VERTIGO

If you have been experiencing attacks of vertigo, it is very important to avoid certain potentially hazardous activities. You should not climb ladders, operate machinery or drive until the cause of your symptoms has been diagnosed and treated.

START HERE

Have you had any of the following symptoms?

- DISTURBED VISION
- NUMBNESS, TINGLING, OR WEAKNESS IN ANY PART OF THE BODY
- CONFUSION
- DIFFICULTY SPEAKING
- NONE OF THE ABOVE

Have you noticed either of the following?

- HEARING LOSS
- RINGING IN THE EAR
- NEITHER

Have you experienced either of the following?

- NAUSEA OR VOMITING
- DIFFICULTY KEEPING YOUR BALANCE
- NEITHER

Are any of these symptoms still present?

- SYMPTOMS PRESENT
- SYMPTOMS NO LONGER PRESENT

POSSIBLE CAUSE

There is a possibility that you have had a STROKE (p.532).

MEDICAL HELP

EMERGENCY! Call an ambulance!

POSSIBLE CAUSE

A TRANSIENT ISCHEMIC ATTACK (p.531) is a possible cause of your symptoms.

MEDICAL HELP

URGENT! Call your doctor immediately!

POSSIBLE CAUSES

LABYRINTHITIS (p.604) is a likely explanation. However, a more serious disorder, such as a STROKE (p.532), is also a possible cause.

MEDICAL HELP

EMERGENCY! Call an ambulance!

POSSIBLE CAUSES
MÉNIÈRE'S DISEASE (p.604) may be the cause of your symptoms. ACOUSTIC NEUROMA (p.605) is another, although less likely, possibility.

MEDICAL HELP

Call your doctor within 24 hours.

POSSIBLE CAUSE
Your symptoms may be a side effect of your medication.

MEDICAL HELP
URGENT! Call your doctor immediately! Stop taking any over-the-counter medicines but continue to take prescribed medication unless advised to stop by your doctor.

POSSIBLE CAUSE
Your symptoms are most likely to be caused by drinking more alcohol than usual or drinking on an empty stomach (*see* ALCOHOL AND HEALTH, p.62).

SELF-HELP
The effects of alcohol should wear off within a few hours. Meanwhile, drink plenty of water. Consult your doctor if the spinning sensation persists for longer than 12 hours.

Are you currently taking any prescribed or over-the-counter medication?

MEDICATION

NO MEDICATION

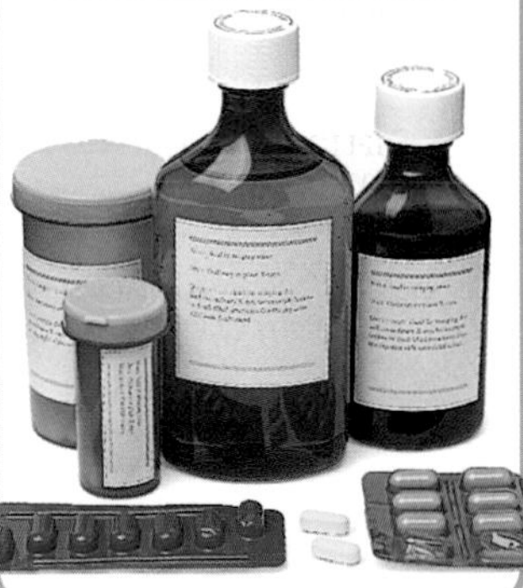

Have you been drinking alcohol?

YES

NO

How old are you?

50 OR OVER

UNDER 50

Does turning or raising your head bring on vertigo?

BRINGS ON VERTIGO

NO NOTICEABLE EFFECT

POSSIBLE CAUSES
Vertigo may be due to pressure on arteries resulting from arthritis in the neck (*see* OSTEOARTHRITIS, p.374) or to a harmless condition called benign positional vertigo (*see* VERTIGO, p.603).

MEDICAL HELP

Make an appointment to see your doctor.

If you cannot identify a possible cause for your vertigo from this chart, call your doctor within 24 hours.

12 NUMBNESS AND/OR TINGLING

Almost everyone has experienced numbness, the loss of sensation in a part of the body, after sitting or lying in an awkward position for a while. Tingling, a prickly feeling, often occurs as sensation returns to a numb area. You should consult this chart if you experience numbness and/or tingling for which there is no obvious cause.

DANGER SIGNS

Call an ambulance if the numbness and/or tingling is accompanied by any of the following:

- Feeling faint or passing out.
- Disturbed vision.
- Confusion.
- Difficulty speaking.
- Weakness in a limb.

START HERE

Did the numbness and/or tingling occur in either of the following circumstances?

- AFTER SITTING IN ONE POSITION FOR A LONG TIME
- ON WAKING FROM A DEEP SLEEP
- NEITHER

POSSIBLE CAUSE

Pressure on nerves or on the blood vessels that supply them is the most likely cause of the numbness and tingling.

SELF-HELP

Sensation should return to normal within a few minutes of changing position. Consult your doctor if numbness or tingling persists for longer than 1 hour.

Where is the numbness and/or tingling?

- HAND OR ARM
- ELSEWHERE

Have you noticed any stiffness in your neck?

- NO STIFF NECK
- STIFF NECK

Does either of the following apply?

- NUMBNESS AND/OR TINGLING IS WORSE AT NIGHT
- PAIN SHOOTS INTO PALM OF HAND
- NEITHER

POSSIBLE CAUSE

CERVICAL SPONDYLOSIS (p.376) is a possible cause of this combination of symptoms.

MEDICAL HELP

Make an appointment to see your doctor.

Possible cause
Carpal tunnel syndrome (p.547) is probably the cause of your symptoms.

Medical help

Make an appointment to see your doctor.

Have you had any of the following symptoms?

- Feeling faint or passing out
- Disturbed vision
- Confusion
- Difficulty speaking
- Weakness in a limb
- None of the above

Possible cause
There is a possibility that you have had a stroke (p.532).

Medical help
EMERGENCY! Call an ambulance!

Are any of these symptoms still present?

- Symptoms present
- Symptoms no longer present

Are the affected areas on only one side of the body?

- One side only
- Both sides

Do your fingers become numb and white or blue in either of the following circumstances?

- In cold weather
- When using vibrating machinery
- Neither

Possible cause
A transient ischemic attack (p.531) is a possible cause of your symptoms.

Medical help

URGENT! Call your doctor immediately!

Possible cause
This type of numbness is most likely to be caused by hand–arm syndrome (p.436), which is associated with long-term use of vibrating machinery.

Medical help

Make an appointment to see your doctor.

If you cannot identify a possible cause for your numbness and/or tingling from this chart, make an appointment to see your doctor.

Possible cause
Raynaud's phenomenon and Raynaud's disease (p.436) are possible causes.

Medical help

Make an appointment to see your doctor.

13 TWITCHING AND TREMOR

Twitching (intermittent, isolated movements) and tremor (persistent shaking) are movements that cannot be controlled. Involuntary movements affect most people during times of anxiety or excitement or when falling asleep. You should consult your doctor, however, if you develop twitching or tremor at any other time.

START HERE

Was the twitching and/or tremor accompanied by either of the following?

- LOSS OF CONSCIOUSNESS
- LOSS OF CONCENTRATION OR AWARENESS
- NEITHER

POSSIBLE CAUSE
You may have had an epileptic seizure (*see* EPILEPSY, p.524).

MEDICAL HELP
EMERGENCY! Call an ambulance if this is the first attack. Otherwise, make an appointment to see your doctor as soon as possible. For first-aid advice on what to do, see MAJOR SEIZURES (p.989).

What kind of involuntary movement have you been experiencing?

- TREMOR (TREMBLING) OF THE HANDS
- TWITCHING OF A SMALL PART OF THE BODY SUCH AS AN EYELID
- OTHER

POSSIBLE CAUSE
NERVOUS TICS (p.550) are very common, and they are unlikely to be a sign that you have an underlying condition.

MEDICAL HELP
Make an appointment to see your doctor if you are worried about the twitching.

Before the onset of tremor had you done any of the following?

- CONSUMED LARGE AMOUNTS OF COFFEE, TEA, OR COLA
- STOPPED DRINKING ALCOHOL AFTER A PERIOD OF HEAVY DRINKING
- STOPPED TAKING SLEEPING PILLS OR TRANQUILIZERS
- NONE OF THE ABOVE

POSSIBLE CAUSES
Tremor following alcohol withdrawal indicates that you may have become dangerously dependent (*see* ALCOHOL DEPENDENCE, p.564). Stopping sleeping pills or tranquilizers after a long period of regular use can sometimes produce similar symptoms.

MEDICAL HELP
URGENT! Call your doctor immediately!

Do you have any of the following symptoms?

- WEIGHT LOSS WITH INCREASED APPETITE
- FEELING CONSTANTLY ON EDGE
- INCREASED SWEATING
- BULGING EYES
- NONE OF THE ABOVE

How old are you?

- 55 OR OVER
- UNDER 55

POSSIBLE CAUSE
Excessive caffeine intake is most likely to be the cause of your tremor.

SELF-HELP
Abstain from all products that contain caffeine for at least 24 hours. If the tremor persists, make an appointment to see your doctor.

POSSIBLE CAUSES
HYPERTHYROIDISM (p.679) is a possibility. However, ANXIETY DISORDERS (p.551) can cause some of these symptoms.

MEDICAL HELP
 Make an appointment to see your doctor.

Do any of the following apply?

- SYMPTOMS ARE WORSE WHEN THE AFFECTED PART IS AT REST
- YOUR FACE HAS BECOME EXPRESSIONLESS
- YOU HAVE DIFFICULTY INITIATING ANY MOVEMENT
- NONE OF THE ABOVE

POSSIBLE CAUSE
PARKINSON'S DISEASE (p.539) could be the cause.

MEDICAL HELP
 Make an appointment to see your doctor.

Are you currently taking any prescribed or over-the-counter medication?

- MEDICATION
- NO MEDICATION

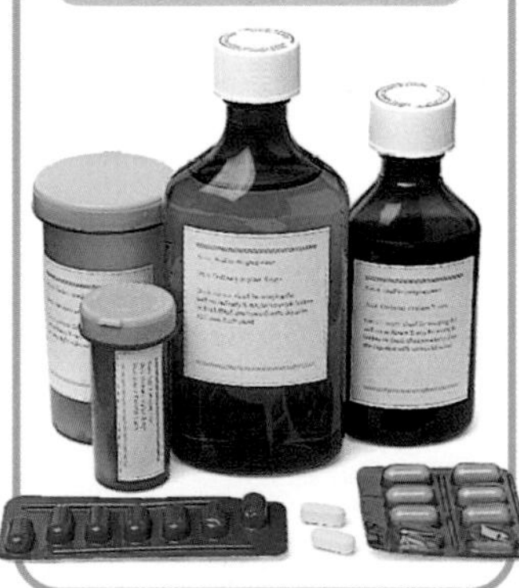

POSSIBLE CAUSE
Your symptoms may be a side effect of the medication.

MEDICAL HELP
Call your doctor within 24 hours. Stop taking over-the-counter medicines but continue to take any prescribed medication unless advised to stop by your doctor.

If you cannot identify a possible cause for your twitching or tremor from this chart, make an appointment to see your doctor.

14 FACIAL PAIN

Pain in the face may be sharp and stabbing or dull and throbbing. Inflammation of structures in the face, such as the sinuses or teeth, is the most common cause of facial pain. Facial pain is usually shortlived but some types, such as neuralgia, may persist. Consult your doctor if the pain is persistent, unexplained, or not relieved by taking analgesics.

START HERE

Where is the pain?

- OVER ONE OR BOTH TEMPLES
- IN OR AROUND THE EYE
- ELSEWHERE

Go to chart 23 PAINFUL OR IRRITATED EYE

Do any of the following apply?

- YOUR SCALP IS SENSITIVE TO TOUCH
- YOU HAVE NOT BEEN FEELING WELL
- PAIN COMES ON WHEN CHEWING
- NONE OF THE ABOVE

POSSIBLE CAUSE
TEMPORAL (GIANT CELL) ARTERITIS (p.464) is a possibility, especially if you are over 50.

MEDICAL HELP
 URGENT! Call your doctor immediately!

POSSIBLE CAUSES
SINUSITIS (p.475) is the likely cause of your symptoms, especially if you have recently had a cold. A dental problem, such as a DENTAL ABSCESS (p.611), is another possibility.

SELF-HELP
If you have pain in both of your cheekbones and think you may have sinusitis, try INHALING MOIST AIR (p.475). Get advice from your doctor or dentist if you do not feel better in 2 days.

Which of the following describes your pain?

- STABBING PAIN THAT OCCURS WHEN TOUCHING THE FACE OR CHEWING
- ACHING PAIN ON CHEWING AND/OR YAWNING
- DULL ACHING AROUND ONE OR BOTH CHEEKBONES
- NONE OF THE ABOVE

POSSIBLE CAUSE
TRIGEMINAL NEURALGIA (p.546) is a possible cause of this type of pain.

MEDICAL HELP
 Make an appointment to see your doctor.

POSSIBLE CAUSE
TEMPOROMANDIBULAR JOINT DISORDER (p.616) is a possible cause of this type of pain.

MEDICAL HELP
 Make an appointment to see your doctor or dentist.

If you cannot identify a possible cause for your facial pain from this chart, make an appointment to see your doctor.

15 DIFFICULTY SPEAKING

Difficulty speaking includes the recent development of slurred or unclear speech and the inability to find or use words. These symptoms may have an obvious cause, such as drinking too much alcohol, but a more serious condition affecting the brain's speech centers could be to blame. If your speech deteriorates suddenly, consult your doctor.

START HERE

Have you had any of the following symptoms ?

- DISTURBED VISION
- NUMBNESS, TINGLING, OR WEAKNESS IN ANY PART OF THE BODY
- FEELING FAINT OR PASSING OUT
- CONFUSION
- INABILITY TO MOVE THE MUSCLES ON ONE SIDE OF THE FACE
- NONE OF THE ABOVE

Are any of your symptoms still present?

- SYMPTOMS PRESENT
- SYMPTOMS NO LONGER PRESENT

POSSIBLE CAUSE
A STROKE (p.532) is a possible cause of your symptoms.

MEDICAL HELP
EMERGENCY! Call an ambulance!

POSSIBLE CAUSE
It is possible that you have had a TRANSIENT ISCHEMIC ATTACK (p.531).

MEDICAL HELP

URGENT! Call your doctor immediately!

POSSIBLE CAUSES
FACIAL PALSY (p.548) may be the cause of your symptoms. However, a STROKE (p.532) is also a possibility.

MEDICAL HELP
EMERGENCY! Call an ambulance!

Do any of the following apply?

- YOU HAVE A SORE MOUTH OR TONGUE
- YOU HAVE BEEN DRINKING ALCOHOL
- YOU HAVE BEEN TAKING MEDICATION OR DRUGS OF ANY KIND
- NONE OF THE ABOVE

POSSIBLE CAUSE
Pain or soreness of the mouth or tongue from a condition such as GLOSSITIS (p.633) can impair speech.

MEDICAL HELP

Make an appointment to see your doctor.

POSSIBLE CAUSE
Drinking even a moderate amount of alcohol can cause slurred speech.

MEDICAL HELP
If you regularly drink enough alcohol to cause slurred speech, you should make an appointment to see your doctor for advice about reducing your alcohol intake.

POSSIBLE CAUSE
Your symptoms may be a side effect of medication or drugs.

MEDICAL HELP
URGENT! Call your doctor immediately! He or she may advise you to stop taking a particular drug.

If you cannot identify a possible cause for your difficulty speaking from this chart, make an appointment to see your doctor.

16 FORGETFULNESS AND/OR CONFUSION

Most people are forgetful sometimes, especially if they are very busy. Absentmindedness is also a natural part of the aging process. Confusion is the inability to think clearly and may include forgetfulness. You should consult your doctor if episodes of forgetfulness and/or confusion occur frequently or are severe enough to disrupt everyday life.

WARNING SUDDEN ONSET OF CONFUSION
Call a doctor immediately if a person suddenly becomes very confused or disoriented about time or place or if someone seems to be seeing or hearing things that are not there.

START HERE

Has the forgetfulness and/or confusion come on since a head injury?

- HEAD INJURY
- NO HEAD INJURY

POSSIBLE CAUSE
Damage to the brain may cause such symptoms (*see* HEAD INJURIES, p.521).

MEDICAL HELP
 URGENT! Call your doctor immediately!

Have you had any of the following symptoms?

- DISTURBED VISION
- NUMBNESS, TINGLING, OR WEAKNESS IN ANY PART OF THE BODY
- VERTIGO OR LOSS OF CONSCIOUSNESS
- DIFFICULTY SPEAKING
- NONE OF THE ABOVE

Are any of these symptoms still present?

- SYMPTOMS PRESENT
- SYMPTOMS NO LONGER PRESENT

POSSIBLE CAUSE
A TRANSIENT ISCHEMIC ATTACK (p.531) is a possible cause of your symptoms.

MEDICAL HELP
 URGENT! Call your doctor immediately!

POSSIBLE CAUSE
There is a possibility that you have had a STROKE (p.532).

MEDICAL HELP
 EMERGENCY! Call an ambulance!

Do you have a fever – a temperature of 38°C (100°F) or above?

- FEVER
- NO FEVER

POSSIBLE CAUSES
Fever, especially a temperature that is over 39°C (102°F), may itself be a cause of confusion. However, confusion may be due to a number of serious diseases, such as PNEUMONIA (p.490), that also cause fever.

MEDICAL HELP
 URGENT! Call your doctor immediately!

Do you suffer from any of the following?

- HEART DISEASE
- LUNG DISEASE
- DIABETES MELLITUS
- NONE OF THE ABOVE

POSSIBLE CAUSES
Lack of oxygen to the brain caused by a worsening of your underlying condition may cause confusion (*see* CHRONIC OBSTRUCTIVE PULMONARY DISEASE, p.487, and CHRONIC HEART FAILURE, p.413).

MEDICAL HELP
URGENT! Call your doctor immediately!

POSSIBLE CAUSE
Confusion may indicate low or very high blood sugar levels in someone with diabetes (*see* HYPOGLYCEMIA, p.691, and DIABETES MELLITUS, p.687).

MEDICAL HELP
URGENT! Call your doctor immediately! You should also eat or drink something sweet at once.

Are you currently taking any prescribed or over-the-counter medication?

- MEDICATION
- NO MEDICATION

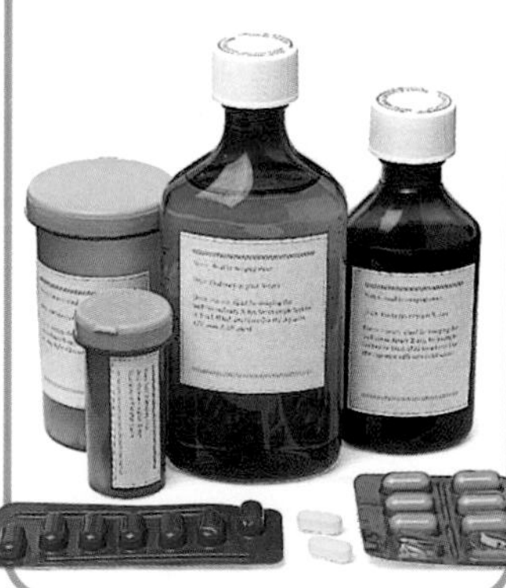

POSSIBLE CAUSE
Your symptoms may be a side effect of the medication.

MEDICAL HELP
Call your doctor within 24 hours. Stop taking over-the-counter medicines but continue to take any prescribed medication unless advised to stop by your doctor.

Have you been drinking alcohol within the past few hours?

- YES
- NO

POSSIBLE CAUSE
Drinking too much alcohol can cause confusion and, more seriously, can also lead to loss of memory (*see* ALCOHOL AND HEALTH, p.62).

MEDICAL HELP
Make an appointment to see your doctor for advice about reducing the amount of alcohol you drink.

Is gradually increasing forgetfulness and confusion in an elderly person accompanied by any of the following?

- PERSONALITY CHANGE
- REDUCED ATTENTION TO PERSONAL HYGIENE
- INABILITY TO MANAGE EVERYDAY PROBLEMS
- NONE OF THE ABOVE

POSSIBLE CAUSES
These symptoms may indicate a decline in brain function (*see* DEMENTIA, p.535). However, DEPRESSION (p.554) may cause similar symptoms.

MEDICAL HELP

Make an appointment to see your doctor.

If you cannot identify a possible cause for forgetfulness and/or confusion from this chart, make an appointment to see your doctor.

17 FEELING DEPRESSED

Feeling depressed may include a lack of energy, sadness, and low self-esteem. It is normal to feel down from time to time, especially after disappointments. More severe feelings of depression are also natural after major upsets, such as the death of someone close. However, if you feel depressed for more than 2 weeks you should consult your doctor.

WARNING HAVING SUICIDAL THOUGHTS

Anyone who considers suicide is in need of urgent medical help. If you cannot persuade the person to contact a doctor, try to encourage him or her to seek other professional advice or to call a suicide prevention hotline. Such services, which are available 24 hours a day, specialize in counseling people in despair.

START HERE

Do you have any of the following symptoms?

- LACK OF ENERGY
- DIFFICULTY SLEEPING
- LOW SELF-ESTEEM
- INABILITY TO CONCENTRATE OR TO MAKE DECISIONS
- LACK OF INTEREST IN SEX
- NONE OF THE ABOVE

POSSIBLE CAUSE

You are unlikely to be suffering from serious depression. Your low spirits are probably the result of a temporary stress or disappointment.

MEDICAL HELP

Make an appointment to see your doctor if your feelings of depression last for more than 2 weeks, if your depression gets worse, or if you develop other symptoms.

Did your depression develop after any of the following?

- BEREAVEMENT
- DIVORCE
- JOB LOSS
- OTHER DISTRESSING LIFE EVENT
- NONE OF THE ABOVE

POSSIBLE CAUSE

Grief and depression are quite normal following the loss of someone close (*see* LOSS AND BEREAVEMENT, p.76).

MEDICAL HELP

Make an appointment to see your doctor.

POSSIBLE CAUSE

Distressing life events can often be followed by a period of DEPRESSION (p.554).

MEDICAL HELP

Make an appointment to see your doctor.

Do any of the following apply?

- YOU HAVE RECENTLY HAD A BABY
- YOU HAVE RECENTLY HAD A VIRAL ILLNESS
- YOU ARE RECUPERATING FROM MAJOR SURGERY OR A SERIOUS ILLNESS
- NONE OF THE ABOVE

POSSIBLE CAUSE

Major hormonal changes after childbirth sometimes lead to depression (*see* DEPRESSION AFTER CHILDBIRTH, p.807).

MEDICAL HELP

Call your doctor within 24 hours.

POSSIBLE CAUSE

A serious accident, major surgical operation, or serious illness can be followed by DEPRESSION (p.554).

MEDICAL HELP

Make an appointment to see your doctor.

POSSIBLE CAUSE
Viral illnesses may sometimes be followed by a period of mild DEPRESSION (p.554).

SELF-HELP
Follow a healthy diet and get plenty of sleep to rebuild your strength. If your depression continues longer than 2 weeks after the viral symptoms have gone, make an appointment to see your doctor.

POSSIBLE CAUSE
Regularly drinking too much alcohol leads to depression in some people (*see* ALCOHOL DEPENDENCE, p.564).

MEDICAL HELP
Make an appointment to see your doctor for advice about cutting down your alcohol intake.

Do you regularly drink more than the recommended limit of alcohol (*see* SAFE ALCOHOL LIMITS, p.62)?

- MORE THAN THE LIMIT
- WITHIN THE LIMIT

POSSIBLE CAUSE
Your depression may be related to your monthly hormonal changes (*see* PREMENSTRUAL SYNDROME, p.736).

MEDICAL HELP
Make an appointment to see your doctor.

POSSIBLE CAUSE
STRESS (p.74) is a common cause of depression.

SELF-HELP
Try to reduce the impact of stress in your life (*see* STRESS, p.74). Make an appointment to see your doctor if you have severe depression or if it is interfering with your normal everyday activities.

Have you been suffering from particular stress at home or at work?

- YES
- NO

Are you male or female?

- MALE
- FEMALE

Do you feel depressed only in the days before your menstrual period is due?

- YES
- NO

POSSIBLE CAUSE
Your symptoms may be a side effect of the medication.

MEDICAL HELP
Make an appointment to see your doctor. Continue to take the medication unless advised to stop by your doctor.

Are you currently taking any prescribed medication or recreational drugs?

- MEDICATION
- RECREATIONAL DRUGS
- NEITHER

POSSIBLE CAUSE
Recreational drugs can cause psychological disturbances, including depression (*see* DRUGS AND HEALTH, p.65).

MEDICAL HELP
Call your doctor within 24 hours.

If you cannot identify a possible cause for your depression from this chart, make an appointment to see your doctor.

18 ANXIETY

A feeling of unease or agitation, anxiety is often a normal response to stress. It may also occur as a side effect of caffeine or certain drugs. Often, there is no obvious cause. Anxiety can cause symptoms such as palpitations and sweating and may interfere with sleep. If anxiety is disrupting your everyday activities, consult your doctor.

START HERE

Do you feel anxious in either of the following situations?

- WHEN FACED WITH CERTAIN ANIMALS, OBJECTS, OR SITUATIONS
- WHEN YOUR USUAL WAY OF DOING THINGS IS DISRUPTED
- NEITHER OR BOTH OF THE ABOVE

POSSIBLE CAUSES
Anxiety when faced with social situations such as public speaking is a normal reaction. Unfounded anxiety related to animals, objects, or situations is termed a PHOBIA (p.552).

MEDICAL HELP
Make an appointment to see your doctor if anxiety is interfering with normal everyday activities.

POSSIBLE CAUSE
You may have an OBSESSIVE–COMPULSIVE DISORDER (p.553).

MEDICAL HELP
Make an appointment to see your doctor if anxiety is interfering with normal everyday activities.

Have you been feeling anxious since stopping addictive behavior, such as smoking, drinking alcohol, taking drugs, or gambling?

- NO
- YES

POSSIBLE CAUSES
Withdrawal from any addictive substance, including some prescribed medications, or from addictive behavior, such as gambling, is likely to lead to strong feelings of anxiety.

MEDICAL HELP
Call your doctor within 24 hours.

POSSIBLE CAUSE
You may be suffering from DEPRESSION (p.554) as well as an ANXIETY DISORDER (p.551).

MEDICAL HELP
Make an appointment to see your doctor.

Do you have any of the following symptoms?

- LACK OF ENERGY
- LOW SELF-ESTEEM
- LACK OF INTEREST IN SEX
- NONE OF THE ABOVE

Do you have either of the following symptoms?

- WEIGHT LOSS DESPITE GOOD APPETITE
- BULGING EYES
- NEITHER

POSSIBLE CAUSE
HYPERTHYROIDISM (p.679) is a possible cause.

MEDICAL HELP

Make an appointment to see your doctor

If you cannot identify a possible cause for your anxiety from this chart, make an appointment to see your doctor.

19 ITCHING

Itching – irritation of the skin that leads to an intense desire to scratch – has many possible causes, including allergy and infection. Itchiness can affect the whole body or may be confined to a small area. Itching may sometimes lead to skin changes, often as result of scratching. Itching may also occur with no noticeable change in the appearance of the skin.

START HERE

Is the itching confined to any of the following areas?

- SCALP → *Go to chart 22* HAIR AND SCALP PROBLEMS
- GENITAL AREA (WOMEN) → *Go to chart 62* GENITAL IRRITATION IN WOMEN
- GENITAL AREA (MEN) → see below
- ANUS → *Go to chart 38* ANAL AND RECTAL PROBLEMS
- NONE OF THE ABOVE → Is there a rash in the itchy area?

POSSIBLE CAUSES
Itching of the genital area in men may be due to a fungal infection (*see* RINGWORM, p.352) or PUBIC LICE (p.768).

MEDICAL HELP
Make an appointment to see your doctor.

Is there a rash in the itchy area?

- RASH → Are you currently taking any prescribed or over-the-counter medication?
- NO RASH → Do you have either of the following symptoms?

Are you currently taking any prescribed or over-the-counter medication?

- MEDICATION → see below
- NO MEDICATION → *Go to chart 20* GENERAL SKIN PROBLEMS

POSSIBLE CAUSE
Your symptoms may be a side effect of the medication.

MEDICAL HELP
Make an appointment to see your doctor. Stop taking any over-the-counter medicines but continue to take prescribed medication unless advised to stop by your doctor.

Do you have either of the following symptoms?

- YELLOW SKIN AND WHITES OF EYES (JAUNDICE)
- VERY DRY, SCALY SKIN
- NEITHER

POSSIBLE CAUSE
JAUNDICE (p.643) sometimes causes itching.

MEDICAL HELP

Call your doctor within 24 hours.

POSSIBLE CAUSE
Dry skin is often itchy.

SELF-HELP
Apply moisturizing cream daily. If this does not relieve itching, make an appointment to see your doctor.

If you cannot identify a possible cause for your itching from this chart, make an appointment to see your doctor.

20 GENERAL SKIN PROBLEMS

Skin problems are often caused by localized infection, allergy, or irritation. They are not usually serious, although widespread skin problems may be distressing. You should consult your doctor if a skin problem lasts more than a month or causes severe discomfort; a new lump appears, especially if it is dark-colored; or a sore fails to heal.

START HERE

What type of skin problem do you have?

- RASH
- OTHER SKIN PROBLEM

Do you have a fever – a temperature of 38°C (100°F) or above?

- FEVER
- NO FEVER

Go to chart 21
RASH WITH FEVER

Is the affected skin itchy?

- ITCHY
- NOT ITCHY

Have you noticed any of the following?

- RED, TENDER, AND HOT AREA OF SKIN
- NEW MOLE OR A CHANGE IN AN EXISTING MOLE
- AN OPEN SORE THAT HAS NOT HEALED AFTER 3 WEEKS
- HARD, SKIN-COLORED LUMP ON HAND OR SOLE
- NONE OF THE ABOVE

POSSIBLE CAUSE
CELLULITIS (p.352) may be the cause of your symptoms.

MEDICAL HELP
URGENT! Call your doctor immediately!

POSSIBLE CAUSE
SKIN CANCER (p.344) is a possible cause.

MEDICAL HELP
Make an appointment to see your doctor.

POSSIBLE CAUSES
This is likely to be a wart or verruca (*see* WARTS, p.354), or a callus (*see* CALLUSES AND CORNS, p.349).

MEDICAL HELP
Make an appointment to see your doctor if you are uncertain about the diagnosis.

POSSIBLE CAUSE
PSORIASIS (p.332) can produce this type of rash.

MEDICAL HELP
Make an appointment to see your doctor.

Does your skin problem fit any of the following descriptions?

- A PAINFUL BLISTERY RASH IN ONLY ONE AREA ON ONE SIDE OF THE BODY
- REDDENED PATCHES COVERED WITH SILVERY SCALES
- BLISTERY, OOZING RASH ON OR AROUND THE LIPS
- A PAINFUL RED LUMP WITH A YELLOW CENTER
- NONE OF THE ABOVE

POSSIBLE CAUSE
This may be a BOIL (p.351).

SELF-HELP
Follow the self-help measures for a BOIL (p.351). Call your doctor if the condition has not improved in 24 hours.

What does the affected skin look like?

- AREAS OF INFLAMED SKIN WITH A SCALY SURFACE
- ONE OR MORE RED BUMPS WITH A CENTRAL DARK SPOT
- ONE OR MORE RED RAISED AREAS (WELTS) THAT COME AND GO
- NONE OF THE ABOVE

POSSIBLE CAUSE
URTICARIA (p.468) is possible.

SELF-HELP
Soothe the irritation with cold compresses or calamine lotion. You might find that over-the-counter antihistamine tablets help. Get medical advice at once if breathing difficulties or other symptoms develop.

POSSIBLE CAUSE
Shingles (*see* HERPES ZOSTER, p.288) is a possible cause of this type of rash.

MEDICAL HELP

Make an appointment to see your doctor.

POSSIBLE CAUSES
This is likely to be a COLD SORE (p.354). If the blisters burst to form a honey-colored crust, IMPETIGO (p.351) is more likely.

MEDICAL HELP
Call your doctor within 24 hours if you are unsure of the diagnosis.

What do the edges of the rash look like?

- MERGE INTO SURROUNDING SKIN
- CLEARLY DEFINED MARGINS

POSSIBLE CAUSE
RINGWORM (p.352) may be the cause of your rash.

MEDICAL HELP

Make an appointment to see your doctor.

POSSIBLE CAUSE
Insect bites, possibly from fleas or mosquitoes, may be the cause of such itchy bumps.

SELF-HELP
The first-aid advice for INSECT STINGS (p.995) may help relieve symptoms.

Does either of the following apply?

- YOU HAVE A RASH THAT SPREADS OUT FROM A CENTRAL RED SPOT
- YOU HAVE BEEN BITTEN BY A TICK
- NEITHER

POSSIBLE CAUSE
There is a possibility that you have LYME DISEASE (p.302).

MEDICAL HELP

Call your doctor within 24 hours.

POSSIBLE CAUSES
Either SEBORRHEIC DERMATITIS (p.335) or ECZEMA (p.333) may be causing your rash.

SELF-HELP
Avoid using harsh soaps or detergents on the skin. A mild emollient cream should help to soothe the rash. Make an appointment to see your doctor if your rash does not improve within 1 week or if other symptoms develop.

POSSIBLE CAUSE
Your symptoms may be a side effect of the medication.

MEDICAL HELP
URGENT! Call your doctor immediately! He or she may advise you to stop taking a particular medication.

Are you currently taking any prescribed or over-the-counter medication?

- MEDICATION
- NO MEDICATION

If you cannot identify a possible cause for your skin problem from this chart, make an appointment to see your doctor.

21 RASH WITH FEVER

If you have a rash without fever, see chart 20

If you or your child has a temperature of 38°C (100°F) or above, you should check whether a rash is also present. A rash with fever is usually caused by viral infections. Most of these are not serious. However, a rash may alert you to the possibility of potentially life-threatening meningitis.

DANGER SIGNS

Call an ambulance if a rash and fever are accompanied by any of the following symptoms:

- Drowsiness.
- Seizures.
- Temperature of 39°C (102°F) or above.
- Abnormally rapid breathing (*see* CHECKING YOUR CHILD'S BREATHING RATE, p.205).
- Noisy or difficult breathing.
- Severe headache.

START HERE

What are the features of the rash?

- WIDESPREAD ITCHY, BLISTERY RASH
- A RASH THAT SPREADS OUT FROM A CENTRAL RED SPOT
- FLAT, DARK RED SPOTS THAT DO NOT FADE WHEN PRESSED
- DULL RED SPOTS OR BLOTCHES THAT FADE WHEN PRESSED
- BRIGHT RED RASH, PARTICULARLY AFFECTING THE CHEEKS
- LIGHT RED OR PINK RASH MAINLY ON THE TRUNK AND/OR FACE
- NONE OF THE ABOVE

POSSIBLE CAUSE

CHICKENPOX (p.288) is a possible cause of this type of rash with fever, especially if you have not been immunized and have recently been exposed to infection.

MEDICAL HELP

Call your doctor within 24 hours. Meanwhile, follow the advice for BRINGING DOWN A FEVER (p.287).

POSSIBLE CAUSE

There is a possibility that you have LYME DISEASE (p.302).

MEDICAL HELP

Call your doctor within 24 hours. Meanwhile, follow the advice for BRINGING DOWN A FEVER (p.287).

POSSIBLE CAUSES

RUBELLA (p.292), also known as German measles, may be the cause of these symptoms. ROSEOLA INFANTUM (p.830), which mainly affects children under 4 years, is another possibility, particularly if a high fever preceded the rash.

MEDICAL HELP

Call your doctor within 24 hours. Meanwhile, follow the advice for BRINGING DOWN A FEVER (p.287).

POSSIBLE CAUSE

A PARVOVIRUS INFECTION (p.292) may be the cause of such a rash and other symptoms in a young child.

MEDICAL HELP

Call your doctor within 24 hours. Meanwhile, follow the advice for BRINGING DOWN A FEVER (p.287).

If you cannot identify a possible cause for your rash and fever from this chart, call your doctor within 24 hours.

Do you have any of the following symptoms?

- Severe headache
- Drowsiness or confusion
- Dislike of bright light
- Neck pain on bending the head forward
- Nausea or vomiting
- None of the above

Possible cause
Meningitis (p.527) could be a cause of your symptoms.

Medical help

EMERGENCY! Call an ambulance!

Possible causes
This type of rash may be due to a severe allergic reaction, such as a reaction to penicillin (*see* Drug allergy, p.467). It may also be the result of a blood disorder, such as thrombocytopenia (p.453) or, in children, Henoch–Schönlein purpura (p.838).

Medical help

URGENT! Call your doctor immediately!

Have you noticed any of the following symptoms in the past few days?

- Runny nose
- Cough
- Red eyes
- None of the above

Possible cause
Measles (p.291) is a possible cause of your symptoms.

Medical help

Call your doctor within 24 hours. Meanwhile, follow the advice for bringing down a fever (p.287).

Do you have a severe sore throat?

- Yes
- No

Possible causes
You may have a viral illness, but scarlet fever (p.299) is also a possibility.

Medical help

Call your doctor within 24 hours. Meanwhile, follow the advice for bringing down a fever (p.287).

If you cannot identify a possible cause for your rash and fever from this chart, call your doctor within 24 hours.

SYMPTOM ASSESSMENT

Checking a red rash

If you develop a dark red rash, check if it fades on pressure by pressing the side of a drinking glass onto it. If the rash is still visible through the glass, it may be a form of purpura (p.339), a rash caused by bleeding from tiny blood vessels near the surface of the skin. Purpura can be caused by one of several serious disorders, and needs immediate medical attention. You should call an ambulance if the rash occurs along with a high fever or severe headache.

Checking a rash
This test reveals whether a rash is on the skin's surface or caused by bleeding beneath the skin.

22 HAIR AND SCALP PROBLEMS

The condition and appearance of your hair can be affected by your general state of health. Hair is also susceptible to damage and usually becomes thinner with age, especially in men. The scalp may be affected by the same skin problems as other areas of the body. You should consult your doctor if you are particularly worried about a hair or scalp problem.

START HERE

Have you noticed either of the following?

- GENERALIZED HAIR THINNING
- HAIR LOSS FROM LOCALIZED AREAS
- NEITHER

Have any of the following occurred in the past 2–3 months?

- YOU HAVE HAD A PROLONGED OR SERIOUS ILLNESS
- YOU HAVE HAD A BABY
- YOU HAVE STOPPED TAKING ORAL CONTRACEPTIVES
- NONE OF THE ABOVE

POSSIBLE CAUSE
Any of these events can cause temporary hair thinning.

MEDICAL HELP
Make an appointment to see your doctor if hair growth does not start to return to normal within a few weeks.

Do you have any of the following symptoms?

- FATIGUE
- INCREASED DRYNESS OR ROUGHNESS OF THE SKIN
- FEELING THE COLD MORE THAN YOU USED TO
- UNEXPLAINED WEIGHT GAIN
- NONE OF THE ABOVE

Do you have either of the following problems affecting the scalp?

- FLAKING WITH OR WITHOUT ITCHING
- ITCHING
- NEITHER

POSSIBLE CAUSE
An itchy scalp may indicate HEAD LICE (p.831), especially in children or adults who have close contact with children.

MEDICAL HELP
Make an appointment to see your doctor if you are uncertain about the diagnosis.

POSSIBLE CAUSES
DANDRUFF (p.358) is the most common cause of a flaky scalp. However, PSORIASIS (p.332) is also a possibility.

SELF-HELP
Use an antidandruff shampoo. Make an appointment to see your doctor if this self-help measure does not bring about an improvement in your symptoms within a month.

POSSIBLE CAUSE
HYPOTHYROIDISM (p.680) may be a possibility.

MEDICAL HELP
Make an appointment to see your doctor.

POSSIBLE CAUSE
Your hair loss may be a side effect of the medication.

MEDICAL HELP
Make an appointment to see your doctor. Continue to take the medication unless advised to stop by your doctor.

POSSIBLE CAUSE
Any of these forms of styling can damage the hair, leading to overall hair thinning.

SELF-HELP
Your hair should recover if you do not use heat and harsh chemicals and avoid braiding your hair. If your hair has been severely damaged, it may help to have it cut short.

Are you currently taking any prescribed medication?

- MEDICATION
- NO MEDICATION

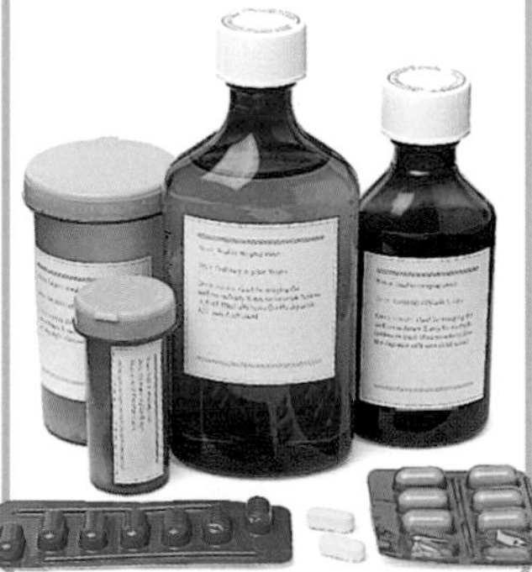

POSSIBLE CAUSE
MALE-PATTERN BALDNESS (p.359) typically causes this type of hair loss in adult men. It may also occur in women with a hormone imbalance.

MEDICAL HELP
Make an appointment to see your doctor if you are concerned about hair loss.

Have you used any of the following hair-styling methods?

- TIGHT BRAIDING
- HEATED ROLLERS OR TONGS
- BLEACHING, PERMING, OR DYEING
- NONE OF THE ABOVE

What type of hair loss have you noticed?

- THINNING HAIR FROM THE FOREHEAD OR CROWN
- BALD PATCHES SURROUNDED BY NORMAL HAIR GROWTH
- NONE OF THE ABOVE

POSSIBLE CAUSES
Patchy hair loss may be the result of RINGWORM (p.352) of the scalp or ALOPECIA (p.358).

MEDICAL HELP
Make an appointment to see your doctor.

If you cannot identify a possible cause for your hair or scalp problem from this chart, make an appointment to see your doctor.

23 PAINFUL OR IRRITATED EYE

Injury, infection, and allergy are the most common causes of discomfort or irritation of the eye and eyelids. A painless red area in the white of the eye is likely to be a burst blood vessel and should clear up without treatment. However, you should see your doctor if your eyes are sore. Consult your doctor immediately if your vision deteriorates.

WARNING CONTACT LENS WEARERS
If you wear contact lenses and experience any kind of eye pain or irritation, remove your lenses without delay and do not use them again until the cause of the problem has been identified and treated. If the pain is caused by grit under the lens, there is a risk that the cornea will be scratched. Make an appointment to see your ophthalmologist.

START HERE

Does either of the following apply?

- YOU HAVE INJURED YOUR EYE
- YOU HAVE SOMETHING IN YOUR EYE
- NEITHER

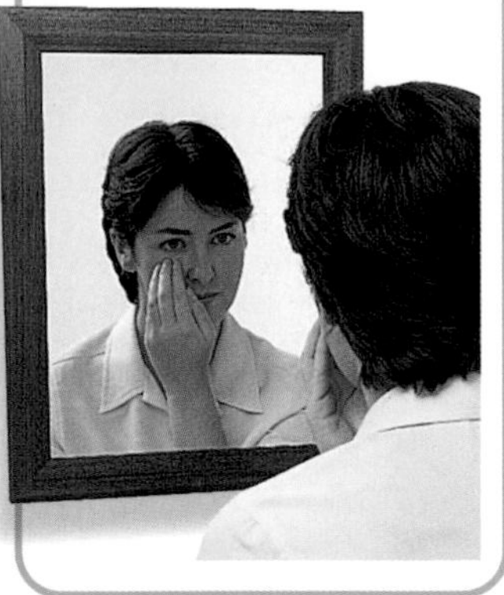

POSSIBLE CAUSE
A foreign body in your eye is likely to cause pain and possibly redness.

SELF-HELP
Follow the first-aid advice (*see* FOREIGN BODY IN THE EYE, p.993). Do not try to remove a particle that is embedded in the eye. In this case, seek emergency help at the hospital.

How would you describe your main symptom?

- PAIN IN AND AROUND THE EYE
- SENSATION OF GRIT IN THE EYE
- ITCHING OR IRRITATION OF THE EYELID
- TENDER RED LUMP ON THE EYELID
- NONE OF THE ABOVE

POSSIBLE CAUSES
An infected hair follicle (*see* STYE, p.583) or infected gland in the eyelid (see CHALAZION, p.584) may be the cause of your symptoms.

SELF-HELP
Follow the advice for STYE (p.583) or CHALAZION (p.584). Make an appointment to see your doctor if self-help measures do not produce an improvement within 3 days.

Has your vision deteriorated since the injury?

- YES
- NO

POSSIBLE CAUSE
A serious eye injury is possible.

MEDICAL HELP
EMERGENCY! Call an ambulance! Expert help may be needed to prevent permanent damage to the eye.

POSSIBLE CAUSE
Your pain may be due to a minor eye injury.

MEDICAL HELP
URGENT! Call your doctor immediately! You can take first-aid measures to relieve pain (*see* EYE WOUND, p.993), but any eye injury should be assessed by a doctor.

Is your vision blurry?

- BLURRY
- NOT BLURRY

POSSIBLE CAUSE
ACUTE GLAUCOMA (p.575) is a possible cause.

MEDICAL HELP
URGENT! Call your doctor immediately!

Is your eyelid turning inward or outward?

- EYELID TURNING INWARD
- EYELID TURNING OUTWARD
- APPEARS NORMAL

POSSIBLE CAUSE
ENTROPION (p.584) may be the cause of your problem.

MEDICAL HELP

Make an appointment to see your doctor.

POSSIBLE CAUSE
ECTROPION (p.584) may be the cause of your problem.

MEDICAL HELP

Make an appointment to see your doctor.

POSSIBLE CAUSES
CLUSTER HEADACHES (p.519) or UVEITIS (p.574) are possible causes, especially if the eye is red and/or watery.

MEDICAL HELP

Call your doctor within 24 hours.

POSSIBLE CAUSE
BLEPHARITIS (p.583) may be the cause of irritation or itching of the eyelids, especially if the skin is scaly and inflamed.

SELF-HELP
Follow the self-help advice for BLEPHARITIS (p.583). Make an appointment to see your doctor if self-help measures do not help.

Is there any discharge from the eye?

- WATERY DISCHARGE
- STICKY DISCHARGE
- NO DISCHARGE

POSSIBLE CAUSE
CONJUNCTIVITIS (p.570), which can occur as a result of allergy or infection, is the likely explanation.

MEDICAL HELP

Make an appointment to see your doctor.

POSSIBLE CAUSE
KERATOCONJUNCTIVITIS SICCA (p.585), in which the eye fails to produce enough tears, can lead to discomfort.

MEDICAL HELP

Make an appointment to see your doctor.

If you cannot identify a possible cause for your painful or irritated eye from this chart, make an appointment to see your doctor.

24 DISTURBED OR IMPAIRED VISION

Disturbed or impaired vision might include blurry vision or seeing double. You may also see flashing lights or floating spots. Visual disturbances may be caused by a problem in one or both eyes or by damage to the areas in the brain that process visual information. If your vision deteriorates suddenly, you should consult your doctor immediately.

START HERE

Do you have pain in the affected eye?

- PAIN → *Go to chart 23* PAINFUL OR IRRITATED EYE
- NO PAIN → How long has your vision been disturbed or impaired?

How long has your vision been disturbed or impaired?

- LESS THAN 24 HOURS → Have you injured your head in the past 48 hours?
- 24 HOURS OR LONGER → Do you have diabetes?

Have you injured your head in the past 48 hours?

- RECENT HEAD INJURY
- NO HEAD INJURY

POSSIBLE CAUSE
You may have damaged the part of the brain that is responsible for vision (*see* HEAD INJURIES, p.521).

MEDICAL HELP
URGENT! Call your doctor immediately!

Do you have diabetes?

- YES
- NO → How old are you?

POSSIBLE CAUSES
DIABETIC RETINOPATHY (p.579) or a high blood sugar level can lead to blurry vision.

MEDICAL HELP

Call your doctor within 24 hours.

How old are you?

- 50 OR OVER → What kind of visual disturbance or impairment have you been experiencing?
- UNDER 50

What kind of visual disturbance or impairment have you been experiencing?

- BLURRY VISION
- INCREASING DIFFICULTY FOCUSING ON NEARBY OBJECTS
- OTHER DISTURBANCE

What is the nature of your disturbed or impaired vision?

- SUDDEN LOSS OF ALL OR PART OF THE VISION IN ONE OR BOTH EYES
- BLURRY VISION
- SEEING FLASHING LIGHTS OR FLOATING SPOTS
- DOUBLE VISION
- NONE OF THE ABOVE

POSSIBLE CAUSES
Blockage of a blood vessel that supplies the brain or eye or a serious eye condition, such as RETINAL DETACHMENT (p.578), are possible causes.

MEDICAL HELP
 EMERGENCY! Call an ambulance!

POSSIBLE CAUSES
MIGRAINE (p.518) is a possible cause of recurrent headaches with visual disturbance, but urgent medical assessment is needed to rule out a more serious condition.

MEDICAL HELP
 URGENT! Call your doctor immediately!

POSSIBLE CAUSES
This may be due to bleeding inside the brain (*see* STROKE, p.532, and SUBARACHNOID HEMORRHAGE, p.534). It may also be due to an abnormality in the muscles moving the eyes (*see* DOUBLE VISION, p.589).

MEDICAL HELP
 EMERGENCY! Call an ambulance!

If you cannot identify a possible cause for your disturbed or impaired vision from this chart, call your doctor immediately.

POSSIBLE CAUSE
A CATARACT (p.573) can cause blurry vision in older people.

MEDICAL HELP
 Make an appointment to see your ophthalmologist.

POSSIBLE CAUSE
You may be developing PRESBYOPIA (p.589) as part of the normal aging process.

MEDICAL HELP
 Make an appointment to see your ophthalmologist.

Are you currently taking any prescribed or over-the-counter medication?

- MEDICATION
- NO MEDICATION

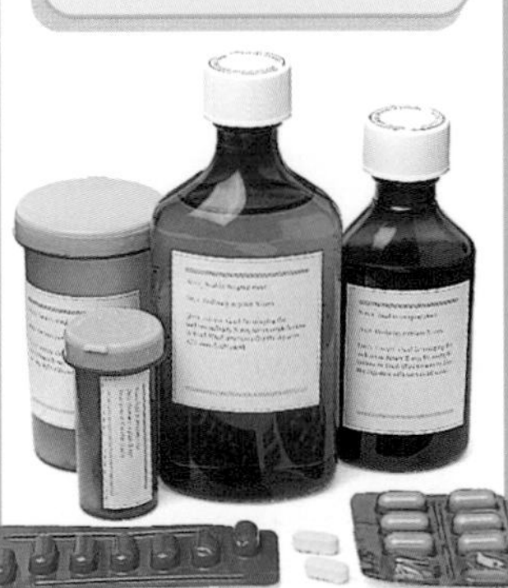

POSSIBLE CAUSE
Your symptoms may be a side effect of the medication.

MEDICAL HELP
 Call your doctor within 24 hours. Stop taking over-the-counter medicines but continue to take any prescribed medication unless advised to stop by your doctor.

If you cannot identify a possible cause for your disturbed or impaired vision from this chart, call your doctor within 24 hours.

25 HEARING LOSS

Hearing loss is a sudden or gradual reduction in the ability to hear clearly in one or both ears. Total, permanent hearing loss is rare. It is usually partial and temporary. Wax blockage or an ear infection may cause temporary hearing loss. Aging may result in partial, permanent hearing loss, which can sometimes be treated with surgery or with a hearing aid.

START HERE

Do you have an earache?

- EARACHE → *Go to chart 26* EARACHE
- NO EARACHE

Have you noticed any discharge from the ear?

- DISCHARGE
- NO DISCHARGE

Do any of the following apply?

- YOUR EAR FEELS BLOCKED
- YOU HAVE BEEN SUFFERING FROM VERTIGO
- YOU HAVE RINGING IN THE EAR
- NONE OF THE ABOVE

Do you have either of the following symptoms?

- RUNNY OR STUFFY NOSE
- SORE THROAT
- NEITHER

POSSIBLE CAUSE
An infection of the outer ear is a possible cause (*see* OTITIS EXTERNA, p.596).

MEDICAL HELP
Make an appointment to see your doctor.

POSSIBLE CAUSES
You could have MÉNIÈRE'S DISEASE (p.604). ACOUSTIC NEUROMA (p.605) or another problem of the nervous system are also possibilities.

MEDICAL HELP
Call your doctor within 24 hours.

POSSIBLE CAUSE
It is likely that the tube linking your middle ear and throat has become blocked as a result of a COMMON COLD (p.286).

SELF-HELP
INHALING MOIST AIR (p.475) can help. Make an appointment to see your doctor if your hearing has not returned to normal 1–2 days after the other cold symptoms have disappeared or if new symptoms develop.

POSSIBLE CAUSE
Your symptoms may be a side effect of the medication.

MEDICAL HELP
Make an appointment to see your doctor. Stop taking any over-the-counter medicines but continue to take prescribed medication unless advised to stop by your doctor.

Have you recently had any of the following illnesses?

- MEASLES
- MUMPS
- MENINGITIS
- ENCEPHALITIS
- NONE OF THE ABOVE

POSSIBLE CAUSE
These infections sometimes cause damage to hearing (*see* HEARING LOSS, (p.599).

MEDICAL HELP
 Make an appointment to see your doctor.

Has hearing loss developed since you started any medication?

- MEDICATION
- NO MEDICATION

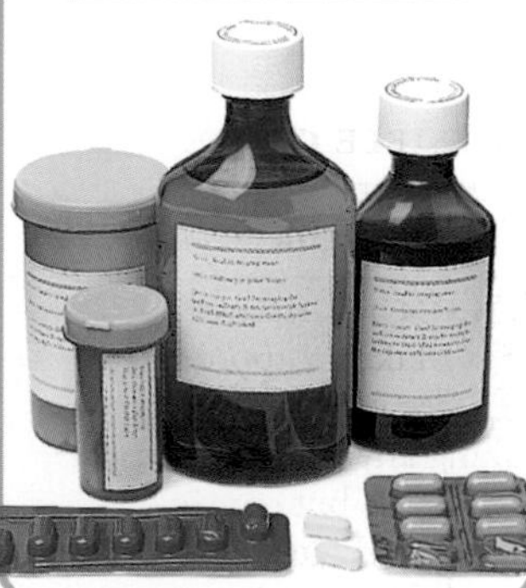

Does either of the following apply?

- YOU REGULARLY LISTEN TO LOUD MUSIC
- YOU ARE EXPOSED TO LOUD NOISE AT WORK
- NEITHER

POSSIBLE CAUSE
Exposure to loud noise can result in damage to your hearing (*see* NOISE-INDUCED HEARING LOSS, p.601).

MEDICAL HELP
 Make an appointment to see your doctor.

Have other family members suffered from increasing hearing loss that started before the age of 50?

- NO FAMILY HISTORY OF HEARING LOSS
- FAMILY HISTORY OF HEARING LOSS

POSSIBLE CAUSES
OTOSCLEROSIS (p.598) or one of a group of rare inherited disorders that affect hearing are possibilities.

MEDICAL HELP
 Make an appointment to see your doctor.

How old are you?

- 50 OR OVER
- UNDER 50

POSSIBLE CAUSES
Gradual loss of hearing that develops in later life may be due to PRESBYCUSIS (p.601). WAX BLOCKAGE (p.597) can also cause hearing loss.

MEDICAL HELP
 Make an appointment to see your doctor.

If you cannot identify a possible cause for your hearing loss from this chart, make an appointment to see your doctor.

26 EARACHE

Pain in one or both ears is a distressing symptom, especially for children. An earache is usually caused by an infection in the outer or middle ear. Mild discomfort, however, may be due to wax blockage. Consult your doctor if you have earache, particularly if it is persistent. A middle-ear infection may damage hearing permanently if left untreated.

START HERE

Does pulling the earlobe make the pain worse?

- INCREASES PAIN
- PAIN IS NO WORSE

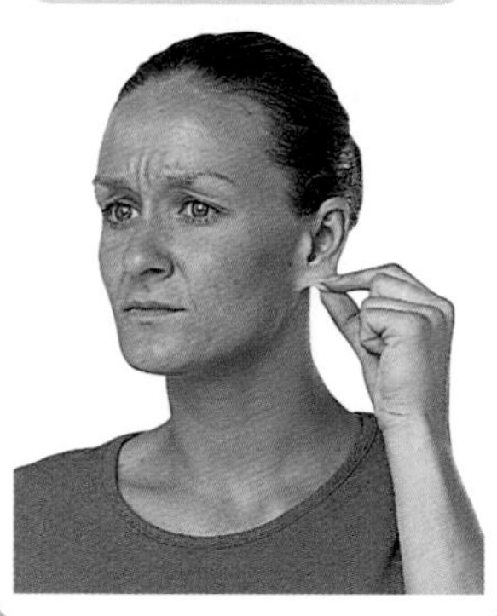

POSSIBLE CAUSES
Your earache is probably due to an infection of the outer ear (*see* OTITIS EXTERNA, p.596) or a BOIL (p.351) in the ear canal.

MEDICAL HELP
 Make an appointment to see your doctor.

Is there a discharge from the affected ear?

- DISCHARGE
- NO DISCHARGE

POSSIBLE CAUSES
Your symptoms could be due to an outer-ear infection (*see* OTITIS EXTERNA, p.596) or to a middle-ear infection (*see* OTITIS MEDIA, p.597).

MEDICAL HELP
 Call your doctor within 24 hours.

Do you have a runny or stuffy nose?

- YES
- NO

POSSIBLE CAUSES
A cold (*see* COMMON COLD, p.286) is often accompanied by mild earache. Persistent or severe earache is likely to be due to a middle-ear infection (*see* OTITIS MEDIA, p.597).

SELF-HELP
Take decongestants to relieve stuffiness and analgesics to relieve the pain. Make an appointment to see your doctor if pain is severe or persists for longer than 2 days.

Did pain start during or immediately after an airplane flight?

- DURING OR IMMEDIATELY AFTER AN AIRPLANE FLIGHT
- UNRELATED TO AIR TRAVEL

POSSIBLE CAUSE
BAROTRAUMA (p.598) may be the cause of your pain.

MEDICAL HELP
 Make an appointment to see your doctor if the discomfort persists for longer than 24 hours.

If you cannot identify a possible cause for your earache from this chart, call your doctor within 24 hours.

27 Sore Throat

A raw or rough feeling in the throat is a symptom most people have from time to time. A sore throat is often the first sign of a common cold and is also a feature of other viral infections. Sore throats can usually be safely treated at home unless you otherwise do not feel well. However, if your sore throat persists or is severe, consult your doctor.

START HERE

Do you have a fever – a temperature of 38°C (100°F) or above?

- FEVER
- NO FEVER

Do you have swelling in your groin and/or armpit ?

- YES
- NO

POSSIBLE CAUSE
INFECTIOUS MONONUCLEOSIS (p.289) can cause a sore throat and swollen lymph nodes.

MEDICAL HELP
Make an appointment to see your doctor.

Do you have any of the following symptoms?

- GENERALIZED ACHES AND PAINS
- RUNNY NOSE
- HEADACHE
- COUGH
- NONE OF THE ABOVE

POSSIBLE CAUSE
A throat infection is a possible cause (*see* PHARYNGITIS AND TONSILLITIS, p.479).

MEDICAL HELP
Make an appointment to see your doctor. Follow the advice for SOOTHING A SORE THROAT (p.479) to help relieve your symptoms.

POSSIBLE CAUSES
A viral illness, such as a severe cold (*see* COMMON COLD, p.286) or INFLUENZA (p.287), is the most probable cause.

SELF-HELP
Follow the advice for BRINGING DOWN A FEVER (p.287). If your symptoms worsen, change, or are no better after 2 days, consult your doctor.

Before the onset of your sore throat had you been doing any of the following?

- SMOKING HEAVILY OR BREATHING SMOKE
- SHOUTING OR SINGING LOUDLY
- NONE OF THE ABOVE

POSSIBLE CAUSE
These activities are likely to result in inflammation of the throat (*see* PHARYNGITIS AND TONSILLITIS, p.479).

SELF-HELP
Follow the advice for SOOTHING A SORE THROAT (p.479). If your symptoms worsen, change, or are no better in 2 days, consult your doctor.

You may be developing a cold. Follow the advice for SOOTHING A SORE THROAT (p.479). Make an appointment to see your doctor if you are no better in 2 days.

28 HOARSENESS AND/OR VOICE LOSS

The sudden onset of hoarseness or huskiness of the voice is a common symptom of upper respiratory tract infections that involve the larynx or vocal cords. Such infections are almost always due to viruses. Hoarseness and loss of voice that develop gradually are most commonly caused by overuse of the voice, smoking, or rarely cancer of the larynx.

WARNING PERSISTENT CHANGE IN THE VOICE

It is important to seek medical advice if you develop hoarseness or any other voice change that lasts for more than 4 weeks because the slight possibility of CANCER OF THE LARYNX (p.481) needs to be ruled out.

START HERE

How long ago did the hoarseness or loss of voice develop?

- OVER A WEEK AGO
- WITHIN THE PAST WEEK

Do you use your voice a lot; for example, are you a singer, actor, or teacher?

- NORMAL VOICE USE
- REGULAR LOUD VOICE USE

POSSIBLE CAUSES

Regular overuse of your voice can lead to inflammation of the vocal cords (*see* VOCAL CORD NODULES, p.480, and LARYNGITIS, p.479).

MEDICAL HELP

Make an appointment to see your doctor.

Have you had any of the following symptoms in the past week?

- RUNNY NOSE AND/OR SNEEZING
- COUGH
- SORE THROAT
- NONE OF THE ABOVE

POSSIBLE CAUSE

A viral throat infection has probably affected your vocal cords (*see* LARYNGITIS, p.479).

SELF-HELP

INHALING MOIST AIR (p.475) may help relieve symptoms. Make an appointment to see your doctor if you do not feel better in 2 days or if other symptoms develop.

Before the onset of hoarseness, had you been shouting, singing, or using your voice more than usual?

- MORE VOICE USE THAN USUAL
- NORMAL VOICE USE

Do you smoke, or have you smoked in the past?

- YES
- NO

POSSIBLE CAUSES
Smoking, particularly smoking heavily over a long period of time, can result in chronic inflammation of the vocal cords (*see* LARYNGITIS, p.479). Another possibility is CANCER OF THE LARYNX (p.481), which is more common in people who smoke regularly.

MEDICAL HELP
 Make an appointment to see your doctor.

POSSIBLE CAUSE
HYPOTHYROIDISM (p.680) can cause increasing huskiness.

MEDICAL HELP
Make an appointment to see your doctor.

Do you have any of the following symptoms?

- FATIGUE
- INCREASED SKIN DRYNESS OR ROUGHNESS
- FEELING THE COLD MORE THAN YOU USED TO
- UNEXPLAINED WEIGHT GAIN
- GENERALIZED HAIR THINNING
- NONE OF THE ABOVE

POSSIBLE CAUSE
Excessive use of the voice can inflame the vocal cords (*see* LARYNGITIS, p.479).

SELF-HELP
INHALING MOIST AIR (p.475) may help. You should also rest your voice as much as possible. Make an appointment to see your doctor if your voice is no better in 2 days or if you develop other symptoms.

POSSIBLE CAUSE
Breathing in dust, fumes, or smoke can severely inflame the respiratory tract.

MEDICAL HELP
 URGENT! Call your doctor immediately!

Did either of the following apply before the onset of hoarseness?

- YOU HAD INHALED DUST, CHEMICAL FUMES, OR SMOKE FROM A FIRE
- YOU HAD SPENT TIME IN A SMOKY ATMOSPHERE
- NEITHER

POSSIBLE CAUSE
Being in a smoky atmosphere can inflame the vocal cords (*see* LARYNGITIS, p.479).

SELF-HELP
INHALING MOIST AIR (p.475) may be helpful. Rest your voice as much as possible and avoid smoky environments. Make an appointment to see your doctor if your voice is no better in 2 days or if you develop other symptoms.

If you cannot identify a possible cause for your hoarseness or loss of voice from this chart, make an appointment to see your doctor.

29 COUGHING

For children under 12, see chart 68

Coughing is the body's defense mechanism for clearing the airways of inhaled particles or secretions. Persistent coughing may be due to infection or inflammation in the lungs or to the effects of irritants such as tobacco smoke. Persistent coughing should be investigated by your doctor.

WARNING COUGHING UP BLOOD

If you cough up sputum that contains streaks of blood on one occasion only, the most likely cause is a small tear in the lining of the windpipe; if you are feeling well, you need not be concerned. However, if you have more than one such episode, there may be a more serious cause; you should see a doctor without delay.

START HERE

How long have you had a cough?

- A WEEK OR LESS
- OVER A WEEK

Do you have a fever – a temperature of 38°C (100°F) or above?

- FEVER
- NO FEVER

Are you coughing up sputum?

- SPUTUM
- NO SPUTUM

Are you currently taking any prescribed medication?

- MEDICATION
- NO MEDICATION

Are you a smoker?

- SMOKER
- NONSMOKER

POSSIBLE CAUSE

Being in a smoky atmosphere can irritate the lungs.

SELF-HELP

Move into a well-ventilated area. Call your doctor if you become breathless or develop other symptoms.

POSSIBLE CAUSE

Your symptoms may be a side effect of the medication.

MEDICAL HELP

Make an appointment to see your doctor. Continue to take the medication unless advised to stop by your doctor.

POSSIBLE CAUSES

A persistent dry cough may be due to GASTROESOPHAGEAL REFLUX DISEASE (p.636), ASTHMA (p.483), or exposure to irritants in your workplace (*see* OCCUPATIONAL LUNG DISEASES, p.499). However, the slight possibility of PRIMARY LUNG CANCER (p.503) needs to be excluded.

MEDICAL HELP

Make an appointment to see your doctor.

If you cannot identify a possible cause for your cough from this chart, make an appointment to see your doctor.

Are you having either of the following problems with breathing?

- BREATHING IS PAINFUL
- YOU ARE SHORT OF BREATH
- NEITHER

POSSIBLE CAUSE
Coughing is the body's natural response to a foreign body that has lodged in the lungs.

MEDICAL HELP
Call your doctor if the cough has not subsided within 2 hours.

Is it possible that you may have inhaled any of the following?

- PARTICLE OF FOOD
- TOBACCO SMOKE
- DUST, FUMES, OR SMOKE FROM A FIRE
- NONE OF THE ABOVE

POSSIBLE CAUSES
A persistent smoker's cough that produces sputum may be due to CHRONIC OBSTRUCTIVE PULMONARY DISEASE (p.487) or, in rare cases, to PRIMARY LUNG CANCER (p.503).

MEDICAL HELP

Make an appointment to see your doctor.

POSSIBLE CAUSE
PNEUMONIA (p.490) may be the cause of these symptoms.

MEDICAL HELP

URGENT! Call your doctor immediately!

Have you coughed up sputum?

- SPUTUM
- NO SPUTUM

POSSIBLE CAUSE
Severe inflammation of the respiratory tract can occur as a result of breathing in any of these substances.

MEDICAL HELP

URGENT! Call your doctor immediately!

Do you have either of the following symptoms?

- RUNNY NOSE
- SORE THROAT
- NEITHER

POSSIBLE CAUSE
ACUTE BRONCHITIS (p.486) is a possibility.

MEDICAL HELP

Call your doctor within 24 hours.

POSSIBLE CAUSES
A viral illness such as a severe cold (*see* COMMON COLD, p.286) or INFLUENZA (p.287) is a likely cause of your cough.

SELF-HELP
Follow the self-help advice for BRINGING DOWN A FEVER (p.287). Consult your doctor if you are no better in 2 days, or if other symptoms develop,

POSSIBLE CAUSE
A cold (*see* COMMON COLD, p.286) is the probable cause of your cough.

SELF-HELP
INHALING MOIST AIR (p.475) may help. Consult your doctor if your breathing becomes painful or you start to wheeze, if you are no better in 2 days, or if other symptoms develop.

POSSIBLE CAUSES
A cough without any other symptoms may be caused by ASTHMA (p.483). CHRONIC HEART FAILURE (p.413) is a less likely possibility.

MEDICAL HELP

Make an appointment to see your doctor.

30 SHORTNESS OF BREATH

For children under 12, see chart 67

Shortness of breath can be expected after strenuous exercise. Breathing should return to normal after resting. If you are short of breath at rest or after normal activities, such as getting dressed, you should consult your doctor because your symptom may be due to a serious heart or lung disorder.

DANGER SIGNS

Call an ambulance if you or someone you are with has either of the following symptoms:

- Severe shortness of breath.
- Bluish lips.

While waiting for medical help, loosen tight clothing and help the person upright.

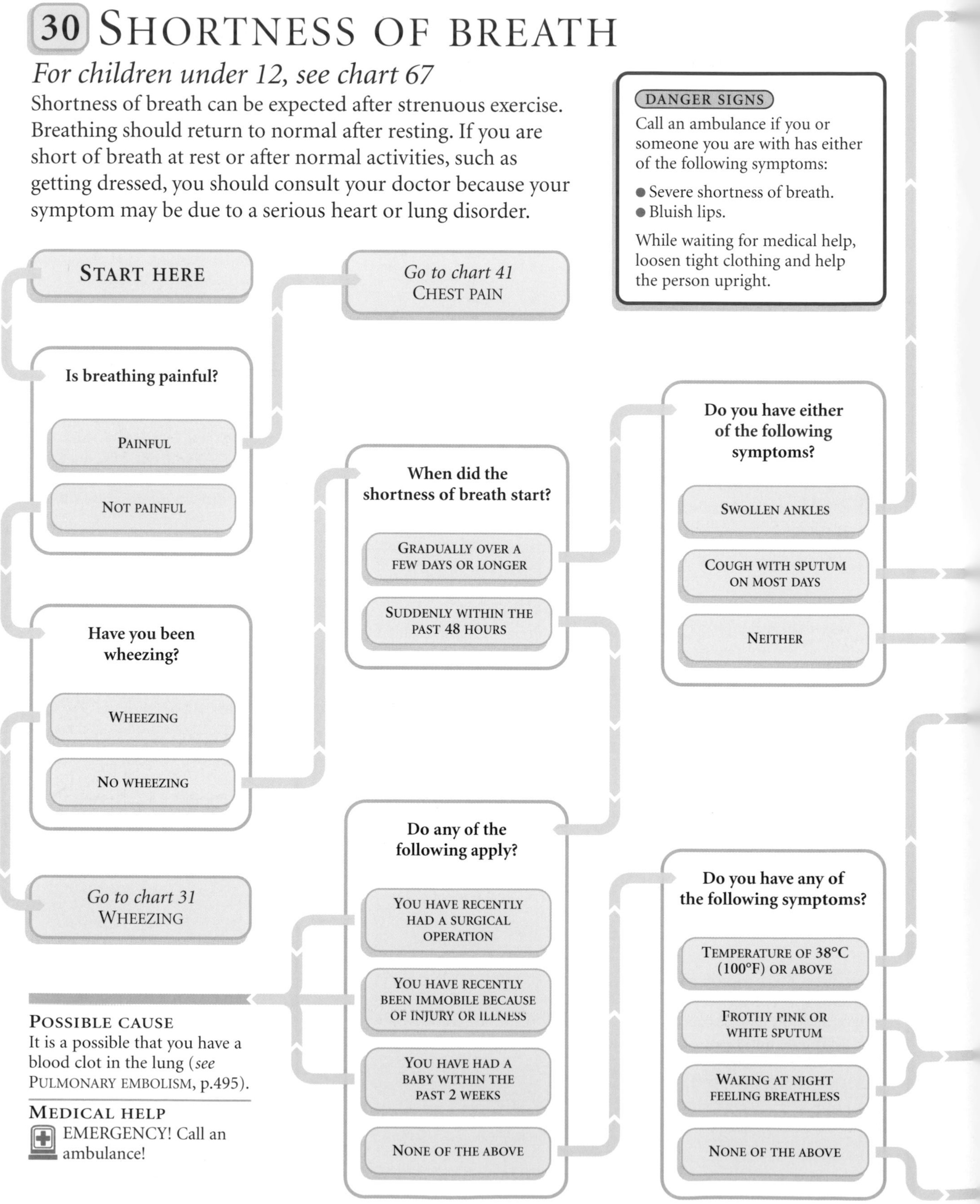

START HERE

Is breathing painful?

PAINFUL

NOT PAINFUL

Go to chart 41
CHEST PAIN

Have you been wheezing?

WHEEZING

NO WHEEZING

Go to chart 31
WHEEZING

When did the shortness of breath start?

GRADUALLY OVER A FEW DAYS OR LONGER

SUDDENLY WITHIN THE PAST 48 HOURS

Do you have either of the following symptoms?

SWOLLEN ANKLES

COUGH WITH SPUTUM ON MOST DAYS

NEITHER

Do any of the following apply?

YOU HAVE RECENTLY HAD A SURGICAL OPERATION

YOU HAVE RECENTLY BEEN IMMOBILE BECAUSE OF INJURY OR ILLNESS

YOU HAVE HAD A BABY WITHIN THE PAST 2 WEEKS

NONE OF THE ABOVE

POSSIBLE CAUSE

It is a possible that you have a blood clot in the lung (*see* PULMONARY EMBOLISM, p.495).

MEDICAL HELP

EMERGENCY! Call an ambulance!

Do you have any of the following symptoms?

TEMPERATURE OF 38°C (100°F) OR ABOVE

FROTHY PINK OR WHITE SPUTUM

WAKING AT NIGHT FEELING BREATHLESS

NONE OF THE ABOVE

POSSIBLE CAUSE
A possible cause is CHRONIC HEART FAILURE (p.413).

MEDICAL HELP

Call your doctor within 24 hours.

POSSIBLE CAUSES
One possible cause is CHRONIC OBSTRUCTIVE PULMONARY DISEASE (p.487). However, a respiratory tract infection, such as ACUTE BRONCHITIS (p.486), can also be a cause of shortness of breath that comes on gradually.

MEDICAL HELP

Call your doctor within 24 hours.

POSSIBLE CAUSE
Your symptoms may be due to PNEUMONIA (p.490); this is particularly likely if you also have a cough.

MEDICAL HELP

URGENT! Call your doctor immediately!

POSSIBLE CAUSE
Your symptoms may be caused by fluid on the lungs (*see* ACUTE HEART FAILURE, p.412).

MEDICAL HELP

URGENT! Call your doctor immediately!

POSSIBLE CAUSE
Your symptoms may be the result of an OCCUPATIONAL LUNG DISEASE (p.499).

MEDICAL HELP

Call your doctor within 24 hours.

Do you have, or have you ever had, regular exposure to, or contact with, the following?

- DUST OR FUMES
- GRAIN CROPS, CAGED BIRDS, OR ANIMALS
- NEITHER

POSSIBLE CAUSE
You may have had a panic attack brought on by stress (*see* ANXIETY DISORDERS, p.551).

MEDICAL HELP

URGENT! Call your doctor immediately if this is a first attack. Otherwise, follow the advice for COPING WITH A PANIC ATTACK (p.552).

Did the shortness of breath start immediately after a stressful event?

- YES
- NO

POSSIBLE CAUSE
Your shortness of breath may be the result of an allergic reaction (*see* HYPERSENSITIVITY PNEUMONITIS, p.502).

MEDICAL HELP

Make an appointment to see your doctor.

POSSIBLE CAUSE
You may be suffering from ANEMIA (p.446).

MEDICAL HELP

Make an appointment to see your doctor.

Do you have any of the following symptoms?

- FAINTNESS OR FAINTING
- PALER SKIN THAN NORMAL
- UNDUE FATIGUE
- NONE OF THE ABOVE

If you cannot identify a possible cause for your shortness of breath from this chart, call your doctor within 24 hours.

33 VOMITING

For children under 12, see chart 64

Vomiting is most often caused by irritation or inflammation of the digestive tract. It may also be triggered by conditions affecting the brain or by an inner-ear disorder, or it can be a side effect of medication. If you have been vomiting on more than 1 day, consult chart 34, RECURRENT VOMITING (p.150).

DANGER SIGNS

Call an ambulance if your vomit contains blood, which may appear as any of the following:

- Bright red streaks.
- Black material that resembles coffee grounds.
- Blood clots.

START HERE

Have you vomited repeatedly in the past week?

ON 2 OR MORE DAYS

ON 1 DAY ONLY

Go to chart 34
RECURRENT VOMITING

Do you have pain in the abdomen?

SEVERE PAIN

MILD PAIN

NO PAIN

POSSIBLE CAUSE
You could have a serious abdominal condition, such as APPENDICITIS (p.664).

MEDICAL HELP
URGENT! Call your doctor immediately!

Do you have pain in or around an eye?

EYE PAIN

NO EYE PAIN

POSSIBLE CAUSE
ACUTE GLAUCOMA (p.575) is a possibility, especially if your vision is also blurry.

MEDICAL HELP

URGENT! Call your doctor immediately!

Do you have a headache?

HEADACHE

NO HEADACHE

Do you have any of the following symptoms?

TEMPERATURE OF 38°C (100°F) OR ABOVE

DIARRHEA

VERTIGO

NONE OF THE ABOVE

POSSIBLE CAUSES
LABYRINTHITIS (p.604) is a possibility. However, it is important that your doctor rules out a disorder of the nervous system, such as a STROKE (p.532).

MEDICAL HELP
URGENT! Call your doctor immediately!

WARNING

VOMITING AND MEDICATIONS

If you are taking any oral medication, including oral contraceptives, an episode of vomiting may reduce the effectiveness of the drug because your body cannot absorb the active ingredients of the drug. If you are using oral contraceptives, continue taking the pills as usual, but take additional contraceptive precautions, and continue with these precautions after the vomiting has stopped. Contact your doctor for further advice. If you have not been able to continue taking your contraceptive pills because of vomiting, call your doctor for advice on how to restart them. You should also consult your doctor if you are taking any other prescribed medicine.

Go to chart 10
HEADACHE

POSSIBLE CAUSE
Your symptoms may be the result of infection (*see* GASTROENTERITIS, p.628).

SELF-HELP
Follow the self-help advice for PREVENTING DEHYDRATION (p.627). Consult your doctor if you are no better in 2 days or if other symptoms develop.

Have you eaten or drunk any of the following?

- AN UNUSUALLY LARGE OR RICH MEAL
- A LARGE AMOUNT OF ALCOHOL
- FOOD THAT COULD HAVE BEEN SPOILED
- NONE OF THE ABOVE

POSSIBLE CAUSE
You may be suffering from FOOD POISONING (p.629).

SELF-HELP
Follow the self-help advice for PREVENTING DEHYDRATION (p.627). Consult your doctor if you are no better in 2 days or if other symptoms develop.

POSSIBLE CAUSE
Your symptoms may be a side effect of the medication.

MEDICAL HELP
Call your doctor within 24 hours. Stop taking over-the-counter medicines but continue to take any prescribed medication unless advised to stop by your doctor.

POSSIBLE CAUSE
The lining of your stomach has probably become inflamed (*see* GASTRITIS, p.640).

SELF-HELP
Follow the self-help measures for GASTRITIS (p.640). Consult your doctor if you are no better in 2 days or if other symptoms develop.

Are you currently taking any prescribed or over-the-counter medication?

- MEDICATION
- NO MEDICATION

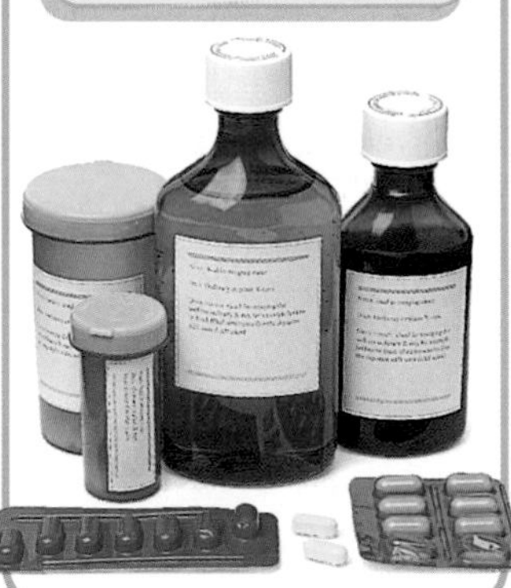

If you cannot identify a possible cause for your vomiting from this chart, call your doctor within 24 hours.

34 RECURRENT VOMITING

For children under 12, see chart 64

Consult this chart if you have been vomiting repeatedly over a number of days or weeks. Recurrent vomiting may be caused by a digestive tract disorder but is also common in early pregnancy. You should consult your doctor if you have persistent or recurrent vomiting.

START HERE

Could you be pregnant?

- POSSIBLY PREGNANT
- NOT PREGNANT

POSSIBLE CAUSE
Nausea and/or vomiting are often the first indicators of pregnancy (*see* COMMON COMPLAINTS OF NORMAL PREGNANCY, p.784).

MEDICAL HELP
Make an appointment to see your doctor if vomiting is preventing you from keeping down fluids. If you are not sure whether you are pregnant, do a HOME PREGNANCY TEST (p.232).

Have you experienced any of the following kinds of recurrent pain?

- BURNING CENTRAL CHEST PAIN IF YOU BEND OR LIE DOWN
- PAIN IN THE UPPER RIGHT ABDOMEN THAT MAY SPREAD TO THE BACK
- PAIN IN THE CENTER OF THE UPPER ABDOMEN THAT IS RELIEVED BY EATING
- NONE OF THE ABOVE

POSSIBLE CAUSES
GASTROESOPHAGEAL REFLUX DISEASE (p.636) and NONULCER DYSPEPSIA (p.626) are possible causes of your symptoms.

MEDICAL HELP

Make an appointment to see your doctor.

POSSIBLE CAUSE
GALLSTONES (p.651) could be the cause of your symptoms.

MEDICAL HELP

Call your doctor within 24 hours.

POSSIBLE CAUSE
Your symptoms may be due to a PEPTIC ULCER (p.640).

MEDICAL HELP

Make an appointment to see your doctor.

Have you noticed either of the following symptoms?

- YELLOWING OF THE SKIN
- YELLOWING OF THE WHITES OF THE EYES
- NEITHER

POSSIBLE CAUSE
Yellowing of the skin and the whites of the eyes, known as JAUNDICE (p.643), is often accompanied by vomiting. Jaundice has many causes but in most cases is due to liver disease such as hepatitis (*see* ACUTE HEPATITIS, p.644).

MEDICAL HELP

Call your doctor within 24 hours.

POSSIBLE CAUSES
Your symptoms may be the result of a PEPTIC ULCER (p.640), but there is also a possibility of STOMACH CANCER (p.642).

MEDICAL HELP

Make an appointment to see your doctor.

Have you noticed changes in your weight or appetite since you began vomiting?

- LOSS OF OVER 10 LB (4 KG) IN WEIGHT
- LOSS OF APPETITE
- NEITHER

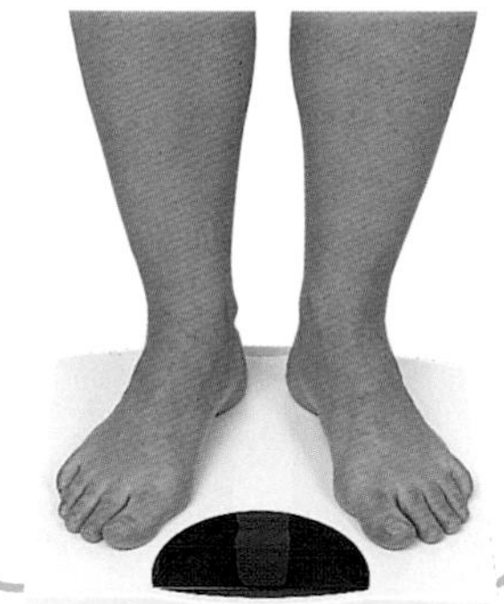

POSSIBLE CAUSES
Recurrent headaches with vomiting but no nausea may, in rare cases, indicate pressure on the brain due to bleeding or a tumor (*see* SUBDURAL HEMORRHAGE, p.535, and BRAIN TUMORS, p.530).

MEDICAL HELP

URGENT! Call your doctor immediately!

Do you regularly drink more than the recommended limit of alcohol (*see* SAFE ALCOHOL LIMITS, p.62)?

- MORE THAN THE LIMIT
- WITHIN THE LIMIT

Have you been suffering from recurrent headaches?

- HEADACHES WITH VOMITING BUT NO NAUSEA
- HEADACHES WITH VOMITING AND NAUSEA
- NO HEADACHES

POSSIBLE CAUSE
You may be suffering from MIGRAINE (p.518).

MEDICAL HELP
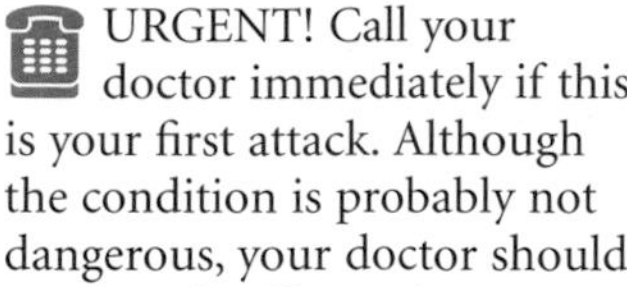
URGENT! Call your doctor immediately if this is your first attack. Although the condition is probably not dangerous, your doctor should confirm the diagnosis.

POSSIBLE CAUSE
Excessive consumption of alcohol over a prolonged period can cause long-term inflammation of the stomach lining (*see* GASTRITIS, p.640).

MEDICAL HELP

Make an appointment to see your doctor.

POSSIBLE CAUSE
Your symptoms may be a side effect of the medication.

MEDICAL HELP

Call your doctor within 24 hours. Stop taking over-the-counter medicines but continue to take any prescribed medication unless advised to stop by your doctor.

Are you currently taking any prescribed or over-the-counter medication?

- MEDICATION
- NO MEDICATION

If you cannot identify a possible cause for your recurrent vomiting from this chart, make an appointment to see your doctor.

35 ABDOMINAL PAIN

For children under 12, see chart 69

Mild abdominal pain is often due to a stomach or bowel upset that will clear up without treatment. However, severe or persistent abdominal pain, especially if it is accompanied by other symptoms, may indicate a more serious problem that your doctor should investigate.

DANGER SIGNS

Call an ambulance if you have severe abdominal pain that lasts for longer than 4 hours and is associated with any of the following additional symptoms:

- Vomiting.
- Fever.
- Swollen or tender abdomen.
- Feeling faint, drowsy, or confused.
- Blood in the urine or feces.

START HERE

Have you had more than one episode of pain?

- SINGLE CONTINUOUS EPISODE → How severe is the pain?
- RECURRENT EPISODES → *Go to chart 36* RECURRENT ABDOMINAL PAIN

How severe is the pain?

- SEVERE → Are any danger signs present?
- MILD OR MODERATE → Do you have diarrhea?

Are any danger signs present?

- DANGER SIGNS → Possible cause: serious abdominal condition
- NO DANGER SIGNS → Do you have diarrhea?

Do you have diarrhea?

- DIARRHEA → Possible cause: gastroenteritis
- NO DIARRHEA → Continued on next page

POSSIBLE CAUSE

Severe abdominal pain may be an indication of a serious abdominal condition, such as APPENDICITIS (p.664) or severe diverticulitis (*see* DIVERTICULITIS, p.663).

MEDICAL HELP

EMERGENCY! Call an ambulance!

POSSIBLE CAUSE

Your pain may be the result of GASTROENTERITIS (p.628).

SELF-HELP

Maintain fluid intake (*see* PREVENTING DEHYDRATION, p.627). Consult your doctor if you are no better in 2 days or if other symptoms develop.

POSSIBLE CAUSE

GALLSTONES (p.651) are a possibility, especially if you have vomited.

MEDICAL HELP

Make an appointment to see your doctor.

What kind of pain have you been experiencing?

- Pain that starts in the back and may move to the groin
- Pain in the center of the upper abdomen
- Pain in the upper right abdomen that may spread to the back
- Pain mainly below the waist
- None of the above

POSSIBLE CAUSE

A kidney problem is possible, especially if you have vomited (*see* PYELONEPHRITIS, p.698, and KIDNEY STONES, p.701).

MEDICAL HELP

Call your doctor within 24 hours.

Do any of the following apply?

- Pain is related to eating
- Pain is relieved by antacids
- Pain comes on when lying or bending over
- None of the above

POSSIBLE CAUSES

Your abdominal pain may be caused by GASTROESOPHAGEAL REFLUX DISEASE (p.636) or NONULCER DYSPEPSIA (p.626).

MEDICAL HELP

Make an appointment to see your doctor. In the meantime, follow the self-help measures for PREVENTING INDIGESTION (p.627).

POSSIBLE CAUSE

The pain may be caused by a heart attack, especially if you are also short of breath and are sweating (*see* MYOCARDIAL INFARCTION, p.410).

MEDICAL HELP

EMERGENCY! Call an ambulance! While waiting, chew half an aspirin unless you are allergic to it.

Do you have either of the followng symptoms?

- Painful urination
- Frequent urination
- Neither

POSSIBLE CAUSE

You may have a urinary tract infection (*see* PYELONEPHRITIS, p.698, and CYSTITIS, p.709).

MEDICAL HELP

Call your doctor within 24 hours.

Are you female or male?

- Female
- Male

Go to chart 60
LOWER ABDOMINAL PAIN IN WOMEN

If you cannot identify a possible cause for your abdominal pain from this chart, call your doctor within 24 hours

36 RECURRENT ABDOMINAL PAIN

For children under 12, see chart 69

Abdominal discomfort that has occurred on more than one day in the past month may be a symptom of a digestive tract disorder or, less commonly, of a urinary tract problem. It is important to consult your doctor if you experience recurrent attacks of abdominal pain even if they are short-lived.

START HERE

Where is the pain mainly felt?

- BELOW THE WAIST
- ABOVE THE WAIST

Is pain accompanied by bouts of diarrhea and/or constipation?

- DIARRHEA AND/OR CONSTIPATION
- NO CHANGE IN BOWEL HABIT

POSSIBLE CAUSES

It is possible that you have a chronic intestinal condition, such as CROHN'S DISEASE (p.658), ULCERATIVE COLITIS (p.659), or IRRITABLE BOWEL SYNDROME (p.656), or an intestinal infection, such as GIARDIASIS (p.307). However, the possibility of COLORECTAL CANCER (p.665) also needs to be ruled out.

MEDICAL HELP

Make an appointment to see your doctor.

POSSIBLE CAUSES

Your symptoms may be due to a PEPTIC ULCER (p.640). STOMACH CANCER (p.642) is also a remote possibility.

MEDICAL HELP

Make an appointment to see your doctor.

What kind of pain have you been experiencing?

- BURNING CENTRAL CHEST PAIN WHEN YOU BEND OR LIE DOWN
- PAIN THAT IS RELIEVED BY ANTACIDS
- PAIN IN THE UPPER RIGHT ABDOMEN THAT MAY SPREAD TO THE BACK
- NONE OF THE ABOVE

POSSIBLE CAUSES

NONULCER DYSPEPSIA (p.626) or GASTROESOPHAGEAL REFLUX DISEASE (p.636) may cause this type of upper abdominal pain.

MEDICAL HELP

Make an appointment to see your doctor.

POSSIBLE CAUSE

GALLSTONES (p.651) are a possible cause.

MEDICAL HELP

Make an appointment to see your doctor.

Does either of the following apply?

- YOUR APPETITE IS POOR
- YOU HAVE LOST OVER 10 LB (4 KG) IN WEIGHT IN THE PAST 10 WEEKS
- NEITHER

Does either of the following apply?

- YOU HAVE LOST OVER 10 LB (4 KG) IN WEIGHT IN THE PAST 10 WEEKS
- YOU HAVE NOTICED BLOOD IN YOUR FECES
- NEITHER

POSSIBLE CAUSES

Recurrent abdominal pain in association with weight loss or blood in the feces may be the result of a chronic intestinal condition, for example, DIVERTICULOSIS (p.663), CROHN'S DISEASE (p.658), or ULCERATIVE COLITIS (p.659). However, the possibility of COLORECTAL CANCER (p.665) needs to be excluded.

MEDICAL HELP

 Make an appointment to see your doctor.

Are you female or male?

- FEMALE
- MALE

Go to chart 60 LOWER ABDOMINAL PAIN IN WOMEN

Do you have either of the following symptoms?

- SWELLING IN THE GROIN
- DISCOMFORT IN THE GROIN MADE WORSE BY LIFTING OR COUGHING
- NEITHER

Do you have any of these symptoms?

- BLOOD IN THE URINE
- PAINFUL URINATION
- FREQUENT URINATION
- NONE OF THE ABOVE

Are you currently taking any prescribed or over-the-counter medication?

- MEDICATION
- NO MEDICATION

POSSIBLE CAUSE

Such symptoms suggest the possibility of a HERNIA (p.661).

MEDICAL HELP

 Make an appointment to see your doctor.

POSSIBLE CAUSES

You may have a urinary tract infection, such as CYSTITIS (p.709) or PYELONEPHRITIS (p.698). However, there is also the slight possibility of a BLADDER TUMOR (p.715) or KIDNEY CANCER (p.704).

MEDICAL HELP

 Call your doctor within 24 hours.

POSSIBLE CAUSE

Your symptoms may be a side effect of the medication.

MEDICAL HELP

 Make an appointment to see your doctor. Stop taking any over-the-counter medicines but continue to take prescribed medication unless advised to stop by your doctor.

If you cannot identify a possible cause for your recurrent abdominal pain from this chart, make an appointment to see your doctor.

37 SWOLLEN ABDOMEN

Enlargement of the abdomen is usually due to weight gain or poor muscle tone from lack of exercise. A swollen abdomen may also result from a disorder of either the digestive system or the urinary system. If you have abdominal swelling that has come on rapidly, you should consult your doctor irrespective of any other symptoms you may have.

START HERE

How long has your abdomen been swollen?

- LESS THAN 24 HOURS
- LONGER THAN 24 HOURS

Do you have abdominal pain?

- SEVERE PAIN
- MILD PAIN
- NO PAIN

Go to chart 35
ABDOMINAL PAIN

Is pain relieved by passing gas or having a bowel movement?

- RELIEVED
- UNRELIEVED

POSSIBLE CAUSES
You may be suffering from excessive intestinal gas or CONSTIPATION (p.628). Either of these symptoms may suggest you have IRRITABLE BOWEL SYNDROME (p.656).

MEDICAL HELP
 Make an appointment to see your doctor.

Do any of the following apply?

- YOUR ANKLES ARE SWOLLEN
- SOCKS OR PRESSING ON THE SKIN OF THE FOOT LEAVES AN INDENTATION
- YOU HAVE DIFFICULTY URINATING
- YOU PASS ONLY SMALL VOLUMES OF URINE
- NONE OF THE ABOVE

POSSIBLE CAUSE
The swelling could be due to an abnormally full bladder (*see* URINARY RETENTION, p.713).

MEDICAL HELP
 Call your doctor within 24 hours.

POSSIBLE CAUSES
Swelling due to fluid retention can be the result of CHRONIC HEART FAILURE (p.413). Some kidney disorders, such as NEPHROTIC SYNDROME (p.700), and liver problems, such as CIRRHOSIS (p.647), can also cause this problem.

MEDICAL HELP
 Call your doctor within 24 hours.

If you cannot identify a possible cause for your swollen abdomen from this chart, make an appointment to see your doctor.

38 ANAL AND RECTAL PROBLEMS

The anus is the opening of the lower large intestine (rectum) to the outside. Discomfort during bowel movements may be due to a disorder of the rectum, the anus, or the skin around the anus. Rectal or anal bleeding is often due to hemorrhoids but can also be an early symptom of cancer. Consult your doctor if you have any bleeding or persistent discomfort.

START HERE

Have you noticed bleeding from the anus?

- BLEEDING → Possible causes (hemorrhoids, constipation, cancer)
- NO BLEEDING → Do you have either of the following?

POSSIBLE CAUSES
HEMORRHOIDS (p.668) may be responsible for anal bleeding. Bowel movements following CONSTIPATION (p.628) may also cause this symptom. However, COLORECTAL CANCER (p.665) or ANAL CANCER (p.669) is also a possibility.

MEDICAL HELP

Call your doctor within 24 hours.

Do you have either of the following?

- PAIN IN OR AROUND THE ANUS OR RECTUM → Possible causes (hemorrhoids, constipation, cancer)
- SORE AREA IN THE CREASE ABOVE THE ANUS → Possible cause (pilonidal sinus)
- NEITHER → Do you have itching around the anus?

POSSIBLE CAUSE
You may have a PILONIDAL SINUS (p.360).

MEDICAL HELP
Call your doctor within 24 hours.

Do you have itching around the anus?

- ITCHING → Does either of the following apply?
- NO ITCHING → Do you have small irregular fleshy lumps around the anus?

Does either of the following apply?

- YOU HAVE NOTICED WHITE "THREADS" IN YOUR FECES → Possible cause (pinworm infestation)
- ITCHING IS WORSE DURING THE NIGHT → Possible cause (pinworm infestation)
- NEITHER → Possible cause (hemorrhoids or anal itching)

POSSIBLE CAUSE
A PINWORM INFESTATION (p.310) is a possibility.

MEDICAL HELP

Make an appointment to see your doctor.

POSSIBLE CAUSE
HEMORRHOIDS (p.668) are a possible cause, but ANAL ITCHING (p.669) can also occur for no obvious reason.

MEDICAL HELP
Make an appointment to see your doctor if anal itching continues for longer than 3 days.

Do you have small irregular fleshy lumps around the anus?

- YES → Possible cause (genital warts)
- NO → If you cannot identify a possible cause…

POSSIBLE CAUSE
It is possible that you have GENITAL WARTS (p.768).

MEDICAL HELP

Make an appointment to see your doctor.

If you cannot identify a possible cause for your anal problem from this chart, make an appointment to see your doctor.

39 DIARRHEA

For children under 12 years, see chart 65

Diarrhea, which is the frequent passing of abnormally loose or watery feces, is usually a result of infection or allergy. However, persistent diarrhea may be caused by a serious gastrointestinal disorder. Consult your doctor if diarrhea continues for more than 2 days or if it recurs.

WARNING

DEHYDRATION

A person with severe diarrhea can become dehydrated if fluids are not replaced quickly enough. The symptoms of dehydration include drowsiness or confusion, a dry mouth, loss of elasticity in the skin, and failure to urinate for several hours. Elderly people are particularly at risk. Get urgent medical help if there are symptoms of dehydration.

START HERE

Have you noticed blood in your feces?

- BLOOD
- NO BLOOD

POSSIBLE CAUSES

You may be suffering from an intestinal infection, such as AMEBIASIS (p.306), or an inflammatory condition of the intestines, such as ULCERATIVE COLITIS (p.659). However, there is a slight possibility of COLORECTAL CANCER (p.665).

MEDICAL HELP

Call your doctor within 24 hours.

Have you suffered from repeated bouts of diarrhea over the past few weeks?

- RECURRENT DIARRHEA
- FIRST ATTACK

Have you been experiencing constipation alternating with diarrhea?

- CONSTIPATION AND DIARRHEA
- DIARRHEA ALONE

POSSIBLE CAUSES

IRRITABLE BOWEL SYNDROME (p.656) is the most likely cause of your symptoms. In rare cases, these symptoms may be an indication of COLORECTAL CANCER (p.665).

MEDICAL HELP

Make an appointment to see your doctor.

Have you recently eaten either of the following?

- FOOD THAT COULD HAVE BEEN SPOILED
- FOOD TO WHICH YOU MAY BE ALLERGIC OR INTOLERANT
- NEITHER

POSSIBLE CAUSES

You may have FOOD POISONING (p.629), a FOOD ALLERGY (p.467), or FOOD INTOLERANCE (p.657).

SELF-HELP

Maintain fluid intake (*see* PREVENTING DEHYDRATION, p.627). Consult your doctor if you are no better in 2 days, if any other symptoms develop, or if you suspect a food allergy.

Do you have either of the following symptoms?

- NAUSEA OR VOMITING
- TEMPERATURE OF 38°C (100°F) OR ABOVE
- NEITHER

Have the attacks of diarrhea occurred since a visit abroad?

- FOREIGN TRAVEL
- NO FOREIGN TRAVEL

POSSIBLE CAUSE

You may have picked up traveller's diarrhea (see GASTROENTERITIS (p.628) or an intestinal infection, such as GIARDIASIS (p.307), during your foreign visit.

MEDICAL HELP

 Call your doctor within 24 hours.

POSSIBLE CAUSES

There is a possibility that you have a FOOD ALLERGY (p.467) or FOOD INTOLERANCE (p.657).

MEDICAL HELP

 Make an appointment to see your doctor.

Do you have recurrent pain in the lower abdomen?

- YES
- NO

Is your diarrhea associated with either of the following?

- EATING PARTICULAR FOODS
- PERIOD OF STRESS
- NEITHER

POSSIBLE CAUSE

ANXIETY DISORDERS (p.551) can be a cause of diarrhea.

MEDICAL HELP

 Make an appointment to see your doctor.

Go to chart 36 RECURRENT ABDOMINAL PAIN

Are you currently taking any prescribed or over-the-counter medication?

- MEDICATION
- NO MEDICATION

POSSIBLE CAUSE

Your symptoms may be a side effect of the medication.

MEDICAL HELP

 Make an appointment to see your doctor. Stop taking any over-the-counter medicines but continue to take prescribed medication unless advised to stop by your doctor.

POSSIBLE CAUSES

GASTROENTERITIS (p.628) or FOOD POISONING (p.629) are the most likely possibilities.

SELF-HELP

Maintain fluid intake (*see* PREVENTING DEHYDRATION, p.627). Consult your doctor if you are no better in 2 days or if other symptoms develop.

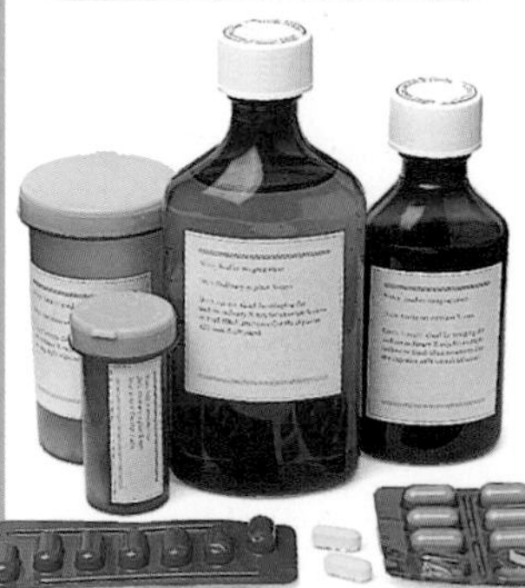

If you cannot identify a possible cause for your diarrhea from this chart, make an appointment to see your doctor.

40 CONSTIPATION

Some people have a bowel movement once or twice a day; others do so less frequently. If you have fewer bowel movements than is usual for you or feces are small and hard, you are constipated. The cause is often a lack of fluid or fiber-rich foods in the diet. If constipation occurs suddenly or persists despite a change in your diet, consult your doctor.

WARNING BLOOD IN THE FECES
Blood can appear in the feces as red streaks or in larger amounts. It can also make the stools look black. Small amounts of blood in the feces are usually caused by minor anal problems, such as HEMORRHOIDS (p.668). However, you should always consult your doctor if you notice blood in the feces because it is vital that other causes, such as COLORECTAL CANCER (p.665), are ruled out.

START HERE

How long have you suffered from constipation?

- FOR A FEW WEEKS OR LESS
- FOR SEVERAL MONTHS OR YEARS

Do you have pain in your rectum or anus when you move your bowels?

- PAIN
- NO PAIN

Do you have intermittent bouts of cramping pain in the lower abdomen?

- CRAMPING PAIN
- NO CRAMPING PAIN

POSSIBLE CAUSE
Your bowel reflexes may have become sluggish as a result of being constantly resisted.

SELF-HELP
Try following the advice for PREVENTING CONSTIPATION (p.628). Consult your doctor if your symptoms have not improved within 2 weeks.

POSSIBLE CAUSES
Pain on defecation can cause or worsen constipation. HEMORRHOIDS (p.668) may be a cause, especially if you also have anal itching.

MEDICAL HELP
Make an appointment to see your doctor.

Does either of the following apply?

- YOU REGULARLY IGNORE THE URGE TO MOVE YOUR BOWELS
- YOU REGULARLY USE STIMULANT LAXATIVES
- NEITHER

POSSIBLE CAUSE
Regular use of stimulant laxatives can seriously disrupt normal bowel function (*see* CONSTIPATION, p.628).

MEDICAL HELP

Make an appointment to see your doctor.

POSSIBLE CAUSES
Your constipation is probably due to a lack of fiber or fluid in your diet. Lack of exercise may also be a factor if you are not physically active (*see* CONSTIPATION, p.628).

SELF-HELP
Try following the advice for PREVENTING CONSTIPATION (p.628). Consult your doctor if your symptoms have not improved within 2 weeks.

POSSIBLE CAUSES

IRRITABLE BOWEL SYNDROME (p.656) is a possible cause, especially if your constipation alternates with bouts of diarrhea. However, other causes, such as COLORECTAL CANCER (p.665), may need to be ruled out.

MEDICAL HELP

Make an appointment to see your doctor.

POSSIBLE CAUSE

HYPOTHYROIDISM (p.680) is a possible cause.

MEDICAL HELP

Make an appointment to see your doctor.

Do you have any of the following symptoms?

- FATIGUE
- INCREASED DRYNESS OR ROUGHNESS OF THE SKIN
- FEELING THE COLD MORE THAN YOU USED TO
- UNEXPLAINED WEIGHT GAIN
- GENERALIZED HAIR THINNING
- NONE OF THE ABOVE

Are you currently taking any prescribed or over-the-counter medication?

- MEDICATION
- NO MEDICATION

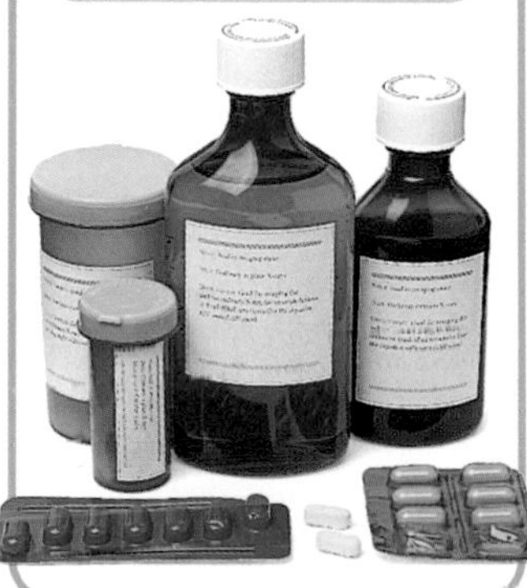

POSSIBLE CAUSE

Constipation is common in pregnancy (*see* COMMON COMPLAINTS OF NORMAL PREGNANCY, p.784).

SELF-HELP

Try following the advice for PREVENTING CONSTIPATION (p.628). Consult your doctor if your symptoms have not improved within 2 weeks.

POSSIBLE CAUSE

Lack of fluid in the bowel as a result of an inadequate fluid intake or excessive fluid loss can lead to constipation.

SELF-HELP

Be sure to drink plenty of fluids, especially if the weather is hot. Consult your doctor if your symptoms have not improved within 3 days.

POSSIBLE CAUSE

Your symptoms may be a side effect of the medication.

MEDICAL HELP

Make an appointment to see your doctor. Stop taking any over-the-counter medicines but continue to take prescribed medication unless advised to stop by your doctor.

POSSIBLE CAUSE

A change in your regular diet, especially if you are traveling, can make you constipated.

SELF-HELP

Try following the advice for PREVENTING CONSTIPATION (p.628). Consult your doctor if your symptoms have not improved within 2 weeks.

Do any of the following apply?

- YOU ARE PREGNANT
- YOU HAVE BEEN DRINKING LESS FLUID THAN USUAL
- YOU HAVE CHANGED YOUR DIET
- NONE OF THE ABOVE

If you cannot identify a possible cause for your constipation from this chart, make an appointment to see your doctor.

41 CHEST PAIN

Chest pain includes any discomfort felt in the front or back of the rib cage. Most chest pain is due to minor disorders such as muscle strain or dyspepsia. However, you should call an ambulance if you have a crushing pain in the center or left side of your chest, if you are also short of breath or feel faint, or if the pain is unlike any pain you have had before.

START HERE

What kind of pain are you experiencing?

- TIGHT, HEAVY, OR SQUEEZING ACHE
- SPREADING FROM THE CENTER OF THE CHEST TO THE NECK, ARMS, OR JAW
- NEITHER OF THE ABOVE

Does the pain subside after you rest for a few minutes?

- PAIN SUBSIDES
- PAIN PERSISTS

POSSIBLE CAUSE
You may be having a heart attack (*see* MYOCARDIAL INFARCTION, p.410).

MEDICAL HELP
EMERGENCY! Call an ambulance! While waiting, chew half an aspirin unless you are allergic to it.

Are you short of breath?

- SHORT OF BREATH
- NOT SHORT OF BREATH

POSSIBLE CAUSE
Recurrent chest pain could be an indication of ANGINA (p.407), especially if pain in the chest occurs with exertion and disappears with rest.

MEDICAL HELP
URGENT! Call your doctor immediately! Go to an emergency room if the pain is lasting longer than usual or coming on more often.

Have you had this kind of pain before?

- PREVIOUS EPISODES OF THIS KIND OF PAIN
- NEVER BEFORE

Do any of the following apply?

- YOU HAVE RECENTLY HAD A SURGICAL OPERATION
- YOU HAVE RECENTLY BEEN IMMOBILE DUE TO INJURY OR ILLNESS
- YOU HAVE HAD A BABY WITHIN THE PAST 2 WEEKS
- NONE OF THE ABOVE

Do you have a cough?

- COUGH
- NO COUGH

What are the features of the pain?

- RELATED TO EATING OR TO PARTICULAR FOODS
- RELIEVED BY ANTACIDS
- BROUGHT ON BY BENDING OR LYING DOWN
- NONE OF THE ABOVE

POSSIBLE CAUSE
You may have a blood clot in the lung (*see* PULMONARY EMBOLISM, p.495).

MEDICAL HELP
EMERGENCY! Call an ambulance!

POSSIBLE CAUSE
It is possible that you have a chest infection, such as PNEUMONIA (p.490).

MEDICAL HELP

URGENT! Call your doctor immediately!

POSSIBLE CAUSE
There is a possibility that you have a partially collapsed lung (*see* PNEUMOTHORAX, p.496).

MEDICAL HELP
URGENT! Call your doctor immediately or go to an emergency room!

Do you have a fever – a temperature of 38°C (100°F) or above?

- FEVER
- NO FEVER

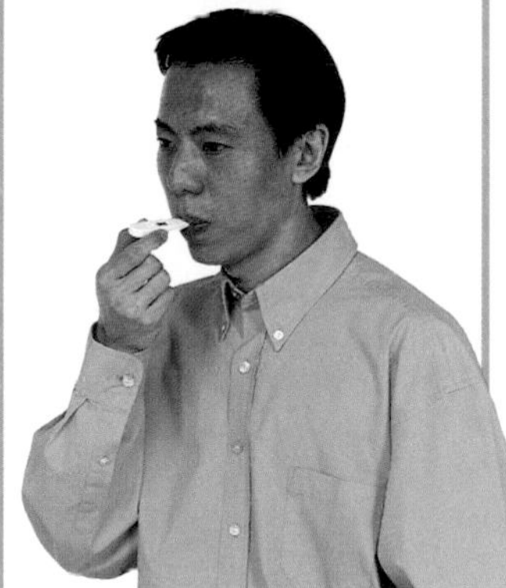

POSSIBLE CAUSE
Muscle strain and/or bruising is the most likely cause of your symptoms.

SELF-HELP
Take an analgesic and rest for 24 hours. If the pain has not improved after this time, make an appointment to see your doctor.

POSSIBLE CAUSES
You may have PLEURISY (p.493) or ACUTE BRONCHITIS (p.486), particularly if you have a fever.

MEDICAL HELP

Call your doctor within 24 hours.

Where is the pain?

- IN THE CENTER OR LEFT SIDE OF THE CHEST
- ELSEWHERE IN THE CHEST

Does either of the following apply?

- YOU HAVE HAD A CHEST INJURY
- YOU HAVE BEEN EXERCISING
- NEITHER

POSSIBLE CAUSE
This type of chest pain may be due to GASTROESOPHAGEAL REFLUX DISEASE (p.636) or NONULCER DYSPEPSIA (p.626).

MEDICAL HELP

Make an appointment to see your doctor.

POSSIBLE CAUSE
You may be having a heart attack (*see* MYOCARDIAL INFARCTION, p.410).

MEDICAL HELP

EMERGENCY! Call an ambulance! While waiting, chew half an aspirin unless you are allergic to it.

If you cannot identify a possible cause for your chest pain from this chart, call your doctor or go to an emergency room

42 PALPITATIONS

Palpitations are an awareness of abnormally fast or irregular heartbeats. They are most often caused by stimulants, such as caffeine and nicotine, or by anxiety. Palpitations may also occur as a side effect of medication or because of a heart disorder. Call your doctor immediately if you have other symptoms or if palpitations are frequent or persistent.

START HERE

Do you have any of the following symptoms?

- SHORTNESS OF BREATH
- CHEST DISCOMFORT
- FEELING FAINT OR PASSING OUT
- NONE OF THE ABOVE

POSSIBLE CAUSE
You may be suffering from a serious heart disorder, such as an ARRHYTHMIA (p.415).

MEDICAL HELP

EMERGENCY! Call an ambulance!

Do you have any of the following symptoms?

- WEIGHT LOSS WITH INCREASED APPETITE
- FEELING CONSTANTLY ON EDGE
- INCREASED SWEATING
- BULGING EYES
- NONE OF THE ABOVE

POSSIBLE CAUSES
HYPERTHYROIDISM (p.679) is a possibility. However, ANXIETY DISORDERS (p.551) can cause some of these symptoms.

MEDICAL HELP

Make an appointment to see your doctor.

Do any of the following apply?

- YOU HAVE BEEN DRINKING A LOT OF COFFEE, TEA, OR COLA
- YOU HAVE BEEN SMOKING MORE THAN USUAL FOR YOU
- YOU ARE TAKING MEDICATIONS
- NONE OF THE ABOVE

POSSIBLE CAUSE
Caffeine (in coffee, tea, and cola) and nicotine (in tobacco) are stimulants that can disturb heart rhythm.

SELF-HELP
Avoid all stimulants. Consult your doctor if your symptoms have not disappeared within 24 hours or if other symptoms also develop.

POSSIBLE CAUSE
Your symptoms may be a side effect of the medication.

MEDICAL HELP

Call your doctor within 24 hours. Stop taking over-the-counter medicines but continue to take any prescribed medication unless advised to stop by your doctor.

Have you been feeling tense or under stress?

- FEELING UNDER STRESS
- NO STRESS

Go to chart 18 ANXIETY

If you cannot identify a possible cause for your palpitations from this chart, make an appointment to see your doctor.

43 POOR BLADDER CONTROL

If urination is painful, see chart 45

Inability to control the passage of urine may result in leakage of urine or difficulty urinating. These symptoms may be due to a bladder, nerve, or muscle disorder. In men, an enlarged prostate gland is a common cause. Urinary tract infections can also cause leakage of urine, especially in elderly people.

WARNING BEING UNABLE TO URINATE

Inability to urinate, even though the bladder is full, is a serious symptom. It may be the result of an obstruction or of damage to nerves supplying the bladder, or it may be due to the action of certain drugs. You should call your doctor immediately.

START HERE

Are you female or male?

- FEMALE
- MALE

Have you been experiencing either of the following symptoms?

- A STRONG URGE TO URINATE WITH LITTLE URINE PASSED
- LEAKAGE OF URINE WHEN YOU COUGH, SNEEZE, LAUGH, OR RUN
- NEITHER

POSSIBLE CAUSE

You may be suffering from an irritable bladder (*see* URGE INCONTINENCE, p.712).

MEDICAL HELP

Make an appointment to see your doctor.

POSSIBLE CAUSE

STRESS INCONTINENCE (p.711) is the most likely cause.

SELF-HELP

Try KEGEL EXERCISES (p.712). Consult your doctor if there is no improvement in your symptoms within 1 month.

Do you have either of the following symptoms?

- DIFFICULTY STARTING TO URINATE
- WEAK URINARY STREAM
- NEITHER

POSSIBLE CAUSES

You may have an ENLARGED PROSTATE GLAND (p.725) or a URETHRAL STRICTURE (p.714), especially if you are over 55.

MEDICAL HELP

Make an appointment to see your doctor.

Are you currently taking any prescribed or over-the-counter medication?

- MEDICATION
- NO MEDICATION

POSSIBLE CAUSE

Some drugs, particularly those that act on urine production or the nervous system, can affect bladder control.

MEDICAL HELP

Make an appointment to see your doctor. Stop taking any over-the-counter medicines but continue to take prescribed medication unless advised to stop by your doctor.

If you cannot identify a possible cause for your poor bladder control from this chart, make an appointment to see your doctor.

44 FREQUENT URINATION

If urination is painful, see chart 45

How often you urinate depends largely on how much you drink and how much your bladder can hold before you feel the need to empty it. If your urine looks abnormal, the appearance may give a clue to the cause of the frequency (*see* CHECKING THE APPEARANCE OF YOUR URINE, p.169).

START HERE

How much urine do you pass each time you go to the toilet?

- LESS THAN USUAL
- AS MUCH OR MORE THAN USUAL

Are you female or male?

- FEMALE
- MALE

Have you been feeling more thirsty than usual?

- MORE THIRSTY
- NO INCREASED THIRST

Have you been experiencing either of the following?

- UNEXPLAINED WEIGHT LOSS
- BLURRY VISION
- NEITHER

POSSIBLE CAUSE

DIABETES MELLITUS (p.687) is a possible cause of your symptoms.

MEDICAL HELP

 Call your doctor within 24 hours.

Have you been drinking large amounts of the following?

- COFFEE OR TEA
- ALCOHOL
- NEITHER

POSSIBLE CAUSE

Substances in these drinks may increase urination.

SELF-HELP

Reduce your consumption of such drinks. Consult your doctor if you continue to be troubled by frequent urination after cutting down.

POSSIBLE CAUSES

A kidney disorder, such as GLOMERULONEPHRITIS (p.699), or a hormonal disorder, such as DIABETES INSIPIDUS (p.678), are possible causes.

MEDICAL HELP

 Make an appointment to see your doctor.

Could you be pregnant?

- NOT PREGNANT
- POSSIBLY PREGNANT

Have you been experiencing either of the following ?

- A STRONG URGE TO URINATE WITH LITTLE URINE PASSED
- DIFFICULTY CONTROLLING URINATION
- NEITHER

POSSIBLE CAUSES

Your symptoms may be due to an irritable bladder (*see* URGE INCONTINENCE, p.712) or to a urinary tract infection, such as CYSTITIS (p.709).

MEDICAL HELP

Make an appointment to see your doctor.

POSSIBLE CAUSE

An increase in the frequency of urination is common in early, as well as later, pregnancy (*see* COMMON COMPLAINTS OF NORMAL PREGNANCY, p.784).

SELF-HELP

Carry out a HOME PREGNANCY TEST (p.232) if you are not sure whether you are pregnant.

Are you currently taking any prescribed or over-the-counter medication?

- MEDICATION
- NO MEDICATION

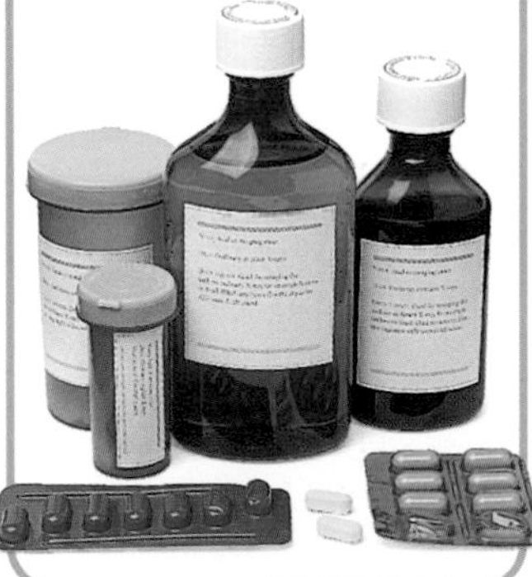

Do you feel the need to urinate frequently when you are anxious?

- RELATED TO ANXIETY
- NOT RELATED TO ANXIETY

POSSIBLE CAUSE

ANXIETY DISORDERS (p.551) commonly cause an urge to urinate frequently, even when the bladder is not full.

MEDICAL HELP

Make an appointment to see your doctor to discuss the causes of your anxiety.

Do you have either of the following symptoms?

- DIFFICULTY STARTING TO URINATE
- WEAK URINARY STREAM
- NEITHER

POSSIBLE CAUSE

You may have an ENLARGED PROSTATE GLAND (p.725), especially if you are over 55.

MEDICAL HELP

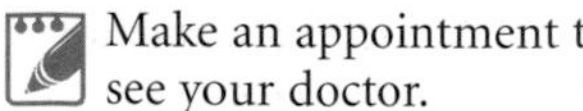

Make an appointment to see your doctor.

POSSIBLE CAUSE

Your symptoms may be a side effect of the medication.

MEDICAL HELP

Make an appointment to see your doctor. Stop taking any over-the-counter medicines but continue to take prescribed medication unless advised to stop by your doctor.

If you cannot identify a possible cause for your frequent urination from this chart, make an appointment to see your doctor.

45 PAINFUL URINATION

Pain or discomfort while urinating is usually caused by inflammation of the urinary tract, often due to infection. In women, painful urination may be associated with vaginal infection. Discolored urine sometimes accompanies painful urination but can occur in the absence of disease (*see* CHECKING THE APPEARANCE OF YOUR URINE, opposite page).

START HERE

Do you have either of the following symptoms?

- PAIN IN THE BACK JUST ABOVE THE WAIST
- A TEMPERATURE OF 38°C (100°F) OR ABOVE
- NEITHER

POSSIBLE CAUSE
A kidney infection is a possible cause of your symptoms (*see* PYELONEPHRITIS, p.698).

MEDICAL HELP
URGENT! Call your doctor immediately!

Have you felt the need to urinate more frequently than usual?

- INCREASED FREQUENCY
- NO INCREASED FREQUENCY

Do you have any of the following symptoms?

- LOWER ABDOMINAL PAIN
- BLOOD IN THE URINE
- CLOUDY URINE
- NONE OF THE ABOVE

POSSIBLE CAUSE
A urinary tract infection, such as CYSTITIS (p.709), is possible.

MEDICAL HELP
Call your doctor within 24 hours. Meanwhile, follow the self-help advice for CYSTITIS (p.709).

Are you female or male?

- FEMALE
- MALE

Do you have an unusual discharge from your penis?

- DISCHARGE
- NO DISCHARGE

Have you noticed soreness or itching in the genital area?

- SORENESS
- ITCHING
- NEITHER

POSSIBLE CAUSE
A vaginal yeast infection is the most likely possibility (*see* VULVOVAGINITIS, p.752).

SELF-HELP
Try treatment at home using an over-the-counter product recommended by your pharmacist. Consult your doctor if symptoms have not improved within 2 days or if symptoms recur.

POSSIBLE CAUSE
A urinary tract infection, such as CYSTITIS (p.709), is possible.

MEDICAL HELP
Call your doctor within 24 hours. Meanwhile follow the self-help advice for CYSTITIS (p.709).

Do you have an unusual vaginal discharge?

- THICK WHITE DISCHARGE
- YELLOWISH GREEN DISCHARGE
- NO UNUSUAL DISCHARGE

POSSIBLE CAUSE
A sexually transmitted disease, such as GONORRHEA (p.764) or NONGONOCOCCAL URETHRITIS (p.765), may be causing your symptoms.

MEDICAL HELP

Call your doctor within 24 hours.

POSSIBLE CAUSES
The most likely cause is either a vaginal infection, such as BACTERIAL VAGINOSIS (p.753) or TRICHOMONIASIS (p.767), or a sexually transmitted disease, such as GONORRHEA (p.764).

MEDICAL HELP

Call your doctor within 24 hours.

If you cannot identify a possible cause for your painful urination from this chart, make an appointment to see your doctor.

POSSIBLE CAUSE
You may have GENITAL HERPES (p.767). This infection causes sores, which are painful if urine contacts them.

MEDICAL HELP

Make an appointment to see your doctor.

SYMPTOM ASSESSMENT

CHECKING THE APPEARANCE OF YOUR URINE

The appearance of urine varies considerably. For example, urine is often darker in the morning than later in the day. Some drugs and foods may also cause a temporary color change in the urine. Beets, for example, may turn the urine red.

A change in your urine can indicate a disorder. Very dark urine may be a sign of liver disease (*see* ACUTE HEPATITIS, p.644); red or cloudy urine may be due to bleeding or infection in the kidney or bladder.

If you are not sure about the cause of a change in the appearance of your urine, consult your doctor.

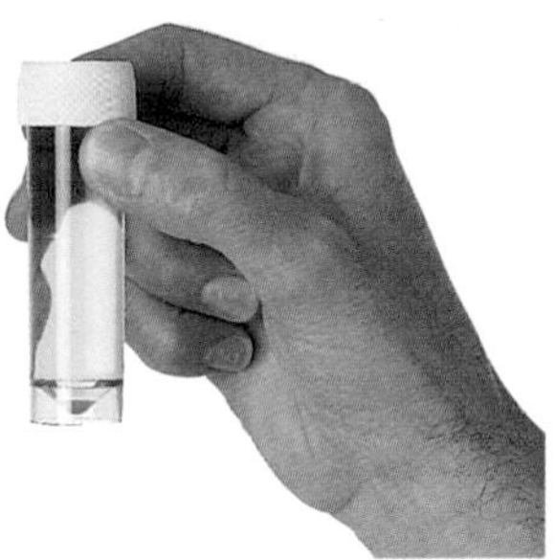

Normal appearance of urine
Unless passed first thing in the morning, urine is normally clear, pale, and straw colored.

46 BACK PAIN

Mild back pain is usually caused by poor posture, sudden movements, or lifting heavy objects, all of which may strain the back. Back pain is also common in pregnancy. Persistent or severe back pain may be the result of a more serious problem. You should consult your doctor if pain persists or is associated with other symptoms.

DANGER SIGNS

Call an ambulance if you have back pain that is associated with any of the following symptoms:

- Difficulty in controlling your bladder.
- Difficulty in controlling your bowel.
- Sudden back pain above the waist with shortness of breath.

START HERE

Did the pain in your back come on after either of the following?

- AN INJURY OR FALL
- A SUDDEN AWKWARD MOVEMENT
- NEITHER

Do you have either of the following?

- PAIN IN THE BACK JUST ABOVE THE WAIST
- A TEMPERATURE OF 38°C (100°F) OR ABOVE
- NEITHER

POSSIBLE CAUSE
PYELONEPHRITIS (p.698) is a likely cause of your symptoms.

MEDICAL HELP
URGENT! Call your doctor immediately!

Did the pain occur after any of the following?

- LIFTING A HEAVY WEIGHT
- A FIT OF COUGHING
- STRENUOUS OR UNACCUSTOMED PHYSICAL ACTIVITY
- NONE OF THE ABOVE

Have you noticed any of the following symptoms?

- DIFFICULTY MOVING A LEG
- PAIN, NUMBNESS, OR TINGLING IN A LEG
- LOSS OF BLADDER CONTROL
- NONE OF THE ABOVE

POSSIBLE CAUSE
Your symptoms indicate that there may be spinal damage (*see* SPINAL INJURIES, p.524).

MEDICAL HELP
URGENT! Call your doctor immediately!

POSSIBLE CAUSE
Your back is probably strained and/or bruised (*see* MUSCLE STRAINS AND TEARS, p.395).

SELF-HELP
Take an analgesic and rest. A covered hot-water bottle or a heating pad placed against your back may give you additional pain relief. Consult your doctor if you are no better in 24 hours.

Does either of the following apply?

- PAIN MAKES ANY MOVEMENT DIFFICULT
- PAIN SHOOTS FROM THE BACK DOWN THE BACK OF THE LEG
- NEITHER

POSSIBLE CAUSE
You have probably strained some of the muscles in your back or sprained some of the ligaments (*see* LOWER BACK PAIN, p.381).

SELF-HELP
See the advice for LOWER BACK PAIN (p.381). Consult your doctor if you do not feel any better in 2 or 3 days or if other symptoms develop.

Have you been suffering from increasing pain and stiffness over several months or longer?

- YES
- NO

POSSIBLE CAUSE
Fracture of a vertebra as a result of thinning of the bones is a possible cause (*see* OSTEOPOROSIS, p.368).

MEDICAL HELP

Call your doctor within 24 hours.

POSSIBLE CAUSES
You may have SCIATICA (p.546), caused by a PROLAPSED OR HERNIATED DISK (p.384) or by a fractured vertebra (*see* OSTEOPOROSIS, p.368).

MEDICAL HELP

Call your doctor within 24 hours.

How old are you?

- 45 OR OVER
- UNDER 45

POSSIBLE CAUSE
ANKYLOSING SPONDYLITIS (p.378) is a possible cause of your symptoms, especially if you are male.

MEDICAL HELP

Make an appointment to see your doctor.

Does either of the following apply?

- YOU HAVE RECENTLY BEEN IMMOBILE DUE TO ILLNESS OR INJURY
- YOU ARE OVER 60
- NEITHER

POSSIBLE CAUSE
OSTEOARTHRITIS (p.374) in the back is the most likely cause of your symptoms.

MEDICAL HELP

Make an appointment to see your doctor.

POSSIBLE CAUSE
A change in back pain or worsening pain may indicate the start of labor.

MEDICAL HELP
URGENT! Call your doctor or nurse/midwife immediately if you think that you may be going into labor.

Are you pregnant?

- PREGNANT
- NOT PREGNANT

If you cannot identify a possible cause for your back pain from this chart, make an appointment to see your doctor.

47 NECK PAIN OR STIFFNESS

Pain and/or stiffness in the neck is usually due to a minor problem, such as muscle strain or ligament sprain, that does not require treatment. However, if the pain occurs with fever, meningitis is a possibility. Neck pain or stiffness becomes more common as a person gets older and may then be due to a disorder of the bones and joints of the neck.

START HERE

How long have you had pain and/or stiffness in the neck?

- LESS THAN 24 HOURS
- 24 HOURS OR LONGER

Have you jolted or injured your neck, for example in a car accident or fall?

- NECK INJURY
- NO NECK INJURY

POSSIBLE CAUSE
MENINGITIS (p.527) could be the cause of these symptoms.

MEDICAL HELP
EMERGENCY! Call an ambulance!

Have you noticed any of the following symptoms?

- DIFFICULTY MOVING AN ARM OR LEG
- PAIN, NUMBNESS, OR TINGLING IN AN ARM OR LEG
- LOSS OF BLADDER CONTROL
- NONE OF THE ABOVE

POSSIBLE CAUSE
Your symptoms indicate that there may be spinal damage (*see* SPINAL INJURIES, p.524).

MEDICAL HELP
EMERGENCY! Call an ambulance!

POSSIBLE CAUSE
Your neck is probably strained and/or bruised (*see* MUSCLE STRAINS AND TEARS, p.395).

SELF-HELP
Take a NONSTEROIDAL ANTI-INFLAMMATORY DRUG (p.894) and rest lying down. A heating pad placed against your neck may give you additional pain relief. Consult your doctor if you are no better in 24 hours.

Which of the following describes your symptoms?

- GRADUALLY WORSENING PAIN AND STIFFNESS OVER MANY MONTHS
- NECK PAIN WITH NUMBNESS OR PAIN IN THE ARM AND/OR HAND
- NEITHER

Do you have any of the following symptoms?

- TEMPERATURE OF 38°C (100°F) OR ABOVE
- SEVERE HEADACHE
- ABNORMAL DROWSINESS OR CONFUSION
- DISLIKE OF BRIGHT LIGHT
- NAUSEA OR VOMITING
- NONE OF THE ABOVE

Does either of the following apply?

- PAIN IS SEVERE ENOUGH TO PREVENT MOVEMENT
- PAIN SHOOTS DOWN ONE ARM FROM THE NECK
- NEITHER

POSSIBLE CAUSES
Your neck pain may be due to pressure on a nerve as a result of a PROLAPSED OR HERNIATED DISK (p.384) or CERVICAL SPONDYLOSIS (p.376).

MEDICAL HELP
 Call your doctor within 24 hours.

POSSIBLE CAUSE
You may have neck strain (*see* MUSCLE STRAINS AND TEARS, p.395) or TORTICOLLIS (p.388).

SELF-HELP
Rest your neck as much as possible by lying down and take a NONSTEROIDAL ANTI-INFLAMMATORY DRUG (p.894) to ease the pain. Keeping it warm with a heating pad may also help. Consult your doctor if you are no better in 3 days.

Can you feel any tenderness or swelling at the sides or the back of the neck?

- YES
- NO

Go to chart 8
LUMPS AND SWELLINGS

Did either of the following apply in the 24 hours before the onset of pain?

- YOU EXERCISED UNUSUALLY STRENUOUSLY
- YOU SAT OR SLEPT IN AN AWKWARD POSITION
- NEITHER

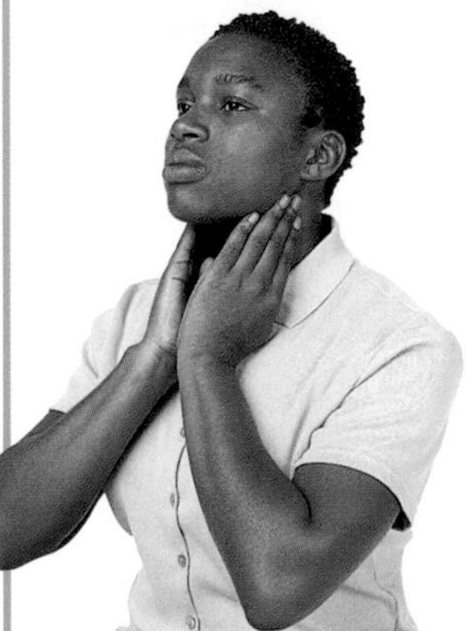

POSSIBLE CAUSE
The cause of your symptoms may be CERVICAL SPONDYLOSIS (p.376), especially if you are over age 50.

MEDICAL HELP
Make an appointment to see your doctor.

If you cannot identify a possible cause for your neck pain or stiffness from this chart, make an appointment to see your doctor.

48 PAINFUL ARM OR HAND

If you have painful joints, see chart 50

Pain in the arm or hand is often caused by injury or a problem in the neck or shoulder. Rarely, pain in the arm is due to a heart attack or a serious neck disorder. Consult your doctor if the pain is severe, recurrent, or persistent.

START HERE

Did the pain start during or soon after either of the following?

- AN INJURY OR FALL
- REPETITIVE MOVEMENTS OF THE AFFECTED ARM OR HAND
- NEITHER

POSSIBLE CAUSES
A serious injury is possible (*see* MUSCLE STRAINS AND TEARS, p.395, and FRACTURES, p.392).

MEDICAL HELP
URGENT! Call your doctor immediately if you are in severe pain. Otherwise, use first-aid measures (*see* SPRAINS AND STRAINS, p.991), but make an appointment to see your doctor if the pain is no better after 48 hours or if other symptoms develop.

POSSIBLE CAUSE
REPETITIVE STRAIN INJURY (p.389) is a possible explanation for your symptoms.

MEDICAL HELP

Make an appointment to see your doctor.

Is the pain associated with any of the following symptoms?

- CHEST TIGHTNESS
- SHORTNESS OF BREATH
- NAUSEA, SWEATING, OR FEELING FAINT
- NONE OF THE ABOVE

POSSIBLE CAUSE
You may be having a heart attack (*see* MYOCARDIAL INFARCTION, p.410).

MEDICAL HELP

EMERGENCY! Call an ambulance! While waiting, chew half an aspirin unless you are allergic to it.

What are the features of the pain?

- LOCALIZED IN UPPER ARM OR SHOULDER
- SHOOTS DOWN THE LENGTH OF THE ARM
- EXTENDS FROM THE WRIST INTO THE PALM AND LOWER ARM
- NONE OF THE ABOVE

POSSIBLE CAUSES
Inflammation around the shoulder may be the cause (*see* POLYMYALGIA RHEUMATICA, p.464, and TENDINITIS AND TENOSYNOVITIS, p.390).

MEDICAL HELP

Make an appointment to see your doctor.

POSSIBLE CAUSES
You may have a pinched nerve in your neck, particularly if you also have neck pain (*see* PROLAPSED OR HERNIATED DISK, p.384, and CERVICAL SPONDYLOSIS, p.376).

MEDICAL HELP

Call your doctor within 24 hours.

POSSIBLE CAUSE
You may have CARPAL TUNNEL SYNDROME (p.547), particularly if you also have numbness or tingling in your fingers.

MEDICAL HELP
Make an appointment to see your doctor.

If you cannot identify a possible cause for your painful arm or hand from this chart, make an appointment to see your doctor.

49 Painful leg

If you have painful joints, see chart 50

Leg pain due to a strained muscle or pulled ligament usually goes away with rest. Pain may also result from a problem in the low back or in the blood vessels in the leg. If your leg is also swollen, hot, or red, consult your doctor at once.

Start here

Did the pain start during or soon after either of the following?

- An injury or fall
- Unaccustomed exercise
- Neither

Possible causes
You may have strained a muscle (*see* Muscle strains and tears, p.395).

Self-help
Try first-aid measures (*see* Sprains and strains, p.991).

Possible causes
A serious injury is possible (*see* Muscle strains and tears, p.395, and Fractures, p.392).

Medical help
URGENT! Call your doctor immediately if you are in severe pain. Otherwise, use first-aid measures (*see* Sprains and strains, p.991), but make an appointment to see your doctor if the pain is no better after 48 hours or if other symptoms develop.

What are the features of the pain?

- Affects a small area that is also red and hot
- Sudden tightening of the muscles in the calf
- Constant pain in the calf, which may be swollen
- Shooting pain down the back of the leg
- Heavy, aching legs
- None of the above

Possible causes
Your symptoms may be caused by an infection under the skin (*see* Cellulitis, p.352) or an inflamed vein (*see* Superficial thrombophlebitis, p.439).

Medical help

Call your doctor within 24 hours.

Possible causes
You may have muscle cramps (p.388), but, if the pain occurs with exercise and disappears with rest, you may have narrowing of the blood vessels in the leg (*see* Lower limb ischemia, p.434).

Medical help

Make an appointment to see your doctor.

Possible cause
You may have a blood clot in a vein in your leg (*see* Deep vein thrombosis, p.437).

Medical help
URGENT! Call your doctor immediately!

Possible cause
Sciatica (p.546) is a likely cause of your symptoms.

Medical help
Make an appointment to see your doctor.

Does sitting down with your feet up relieve the pain?

- Yes
- No

Possible cause
Varicose veins (p.438) are a possible cause.

Medical help

Make an appointment to see your doctor.

If you cannot identify a possible cause for your painful leg from this chart, make an appointment to see your doctor.

50 PAINFUL JOINTS

If you have a painless swollen ankle, see chart 51

Pain in a joint may be caused by injury or strain and often gets better without a cause being found. Gout or a joint infection can cause a joint to become red, hot, and swollen. Widespread joint pain may be due to arthritis or infection. Consult your doctor if pain is severe or persistent.

START HERE

Have you injured the joint?

INJURY

NO INJURY

Does either of the following apply?

YOU ARE UNABLE TO MOVE THE JOINT

THE JOINT APPEARS MISSHAPEN OR SWOLLEN

NEITHER

POSSIBLE CAUSE

A ligament around the joint is probably sprained.

SELF-HELP

Try first-aid measures (*see* SPRAINS AND STRAINS, p.991). Consult your doctor if the joint is no better in 24 hours.

Do you have either of the following?

HOT JOINT(S)

RED JOINT(S)

NEITHER

POSSIBLE CAUSES

A severe injury is possible (*see* FRACTURES, p.392; MUSCLE STRAINS AND TEARS, p.395; and LIGAMENT INJURIES, p.394).

MEDICAL HELP

URGENT! Call your doctor immediately! You should also follow the first-aid advice for FRACTURES (p.992).

POSSIBLE CAUSE

OSTEOARTHRITIS (p.374) is the most likely cause of pain and stiffness in the joints.

MEDICAL HELP

Make an appointment to see your doctor.

How many joints are affected?

ONE JOINT

MORE THAN ONE

POSSIBLE CAUSES

GOUT (p.380), PSEUDOGOUT (p.381), or SEPTIC ARTHRITIS (p.381), which may occur with GONORRHEA (p.764), can all cause pain and heat or redness in a single joint.

MEDICAL HELP

URGENT! Call your doctor immediately!

Does moving the joint affect the pain?

CONSIDERABLY WORSENS IT

SLIGHTLY WORSENS IT OR NO CHANGE

Did the pain come on gradually over months or years?

YES

NO

Have you recently had either of the following?

- AN INFECTION WITH A RASH
- AN INFECTION WITHOUT A RASH
- NEITHER

POSSIBLE CAUSES
Certain bacterial infections of the intestines and genital tract may cause a reaction that leads to painful joints (*see* REACTIVE ARTHRITIS, p.379).

MEDICAL HELP

Call your doctor within 24 hours.

POSSIBLE CAUSES
Some viral illnesses, such as RUBELLA (p.292), can cause joint pain, but LYME DISEASE (p.302) is also a possibility, particularly if you have been bitten by a tick.

MEDICAL HELP

Call your doctor within 24 hours.

POSSIBLE CAUSES
RHEUMATOID ARTHRITIS (p.377) is a possible cause of your symptoms.

MEDICAL HELP

Make an appointment to see your doctor.

Which joint or joints are affected?

- HIP
- SHOULDER
- NECK
- OTHER JOINT(S)

Is the problem in a child under age 12, or in someone aged 12 or over?

- UNDER 12
- 12 OR OVER

POSSIBLE CAUSE
A FROZEN SHOULDER (p.385) could be the cause.

MEDICAL HELP

Make an appointment to see your doctor.

POSSIBLE CAUSES
Most childhood hip problems are not serious, but a SLIPPED FEMORAL EPIPHYSIS (p.834), PERTHES' DISEASE (p.833), or SEPTIC ARTHRITIS (p.381) are rare possibilities.

MEDICAL HELP
URGENT! Call your child's doctor immediately!

POSSIBLE CAUSES
Your symptoms are probably a result of overuse of a joint, for example as a result of excessive exercise. A recent minor viral illness may also be the cause of such symptoms.

MEDICAL HELP
Make an appointment to see your doctor if there is no improvement in 48 hours.

Go to chart 47
NECK PAIN OR STIFFNESS

If you cannot identify a possible cause for your painful joints from this chart, make an appointment to see your doctor.

51 SWOLLEN ANKLES

If you have painful swollen ankles, see chart 50

Slight, painless swelling of the ankles is most often caused by fluid accumulating in the tissues after long periods of sitting or standing still. It is common in pregnancy, but it may be due to heart, liver, or kidney disorders. Consult your doctor if swelling persists or if you have other symptoms.

START HERE

Are both ankles affected?

- BOTH ANKLES
- ONE ANKLE

Have you been suffering from increasing shortness of breath?

- SHORTNESS OF BREATH
- NO SHORTNESS OF BREATH

POSSIBLE CAUSES

Swelling of the ankles (due to fluid retention) and shortness of breath may be the result of CHRONIC HEART FAILURE (p.413). Other possible causes of these symptoms are liver problems (*see* CIRRHOSIS, p.647) or kidney problems (*see* NEPHROTIC SYNDROME, p.700).

MEDICAL HELP

Call your doctor within 24 hours.

Are you pregnant?

- PREGNANT
- NOT PREGNANT

Is the calf of the affected leg either of the following?

- SWOLLEN
- TENDER
- NEITHER

POSSIBLE CAUSE

You may have a blood clot in a vein in your leg (*see* DEEP VEIN THROMBOSIS, p.437).

MEDICAL HELP

URGENT! Call your doctor immediately!

Have you injured your ankle within the past few weeks?

- RECENT INJURY
- NO RECENT INJURY

POSSIBLE CAUSE

Swelling can persist or recur for several weeks following an injury. This is unlikely to be a cause for concern.

SELF-HELP

If the injury occurred within the past 48 hours, follow the first-aid advice for SPRAINS AND STRAINS (p.991). For a less recent injury, try resting the limb. Make an appointment to see your doctor if swelling persists despite rest or if the ankle is painful, tender, or inflamed.

POSSIBLE CAUSE

Several hours of inactivity can lead to accumulation of fluid in the ankles due to less efficient circulation. The decreased cabin pressure in a plane increases this tendency.

SELF-HELP

Encourage circulation by getting up and walking around at regular intervals during any long journey. When seated, keep your legs raised and take a brisk walk when you reach your destination.

Does either of the following apply?

- YOUR FACE OR FINGERS ARE SWOLLEN
- YOU HAVE GAINED OVER 4 LB (2 KG) IN THE PAST WEEK
- NEITHER

POSSIBLE CAUSE
Retaining excessive amounts of fluid may be a sign of pre-eclampsia (*see* PREECLAMPSIA AND ECLAMPSIA, p.794).

MEDICAL HELP
Call your doctor or nurse/midwife within 24 hours. Meanwhile, rest with your legs raised.

POSSIBLE CAUSE
You may have VARICOSE VEINS (p.438), which can cause fluid to accumulate in the ankles.

SELF-HELP
Avoid standing still for long periods. Walk as much as possible, and when sitting down try to keep your feet raised. Make an appointment to see your doctor if the swelling worsens or if other symptoms develop.

POSSIBLE CAUSE
Fluid retention, leading to swollen ankles, is common in pregnancy (*see* COMMON COMPLAINTS OF NORMAL PREGNANCY, p.784).

SELF-HELP
Avoid standing still for long periods and put your feet up whenever possible to reduce swelling. Consult your doctor if your face and/or fingers become swollen or if you start to put on weight rapidly.

POSSIBLE CAUSE
Your symptom may be a side effect of the drug.

MEDICAL HELP
Make an appointment to see your doctor. Stop taking any over-the-counter medicines but continue to take prescribed medication unless advised to stop by your doctor.

Do you have prominent veins in the leg or legs affected by swelling?

- PROMINENT VEINS
- NO PROMINENT VEINS

Did your ankles become swollen after either of the following?

- A LONG TRIP BY CAR OR TRAIN
- AN AIRPLANE FLIGHT
- NEITHER

Are you currently taking any prescribed or over-the-counter medication?

- MEDICATION
- NO MEDICATION

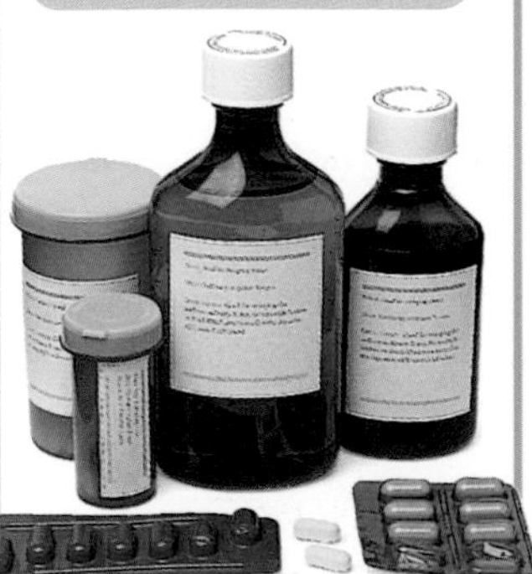

If you cannot identify a possible cause for your swollen ankles from this chart, make an appointment to see your doctor.

52 ERECTILE DYSFUNCTION

Erectile dysfunction (also known as ED or impotence) is failure to have or maintain an erection. Although distressing, occasional difficulties are normal and are usually caused by factors such as stress, fatigue, anxiety, or alcohol. Physical causes are not common. If the condition occurs frequently, consult your doctor; safe and effective treatments are available.

WARNING

NONMEDICAL ADVICE

The wrong treatment from a nonmedical source could delay an important diagnosis or even result in more serious problems. It is important that a doctor evaluate you to rule out any medical cause of your erection problems before deciding on the appropriate treatment.

START HERE

Are you interested in sex?

- YES
- NO

POSSIBLE CAUSE

Lack of interest in sex is likely to reduce your ability to achieve an erection (*see* DECREASED SEX DRIVE, p.769).

MEDICAL HELP

Make an appointment to see your doctor.

How often do you fail to achieve or maintain an erection?

- ONLY OCCASIONALLY
- FREQUENTLY

POSSIBLE CAUSES

Most men have this experience from time to time. Occasional erection problems are most likely to be due to anxiety – for example, at the beginning of a new sexual relationship – or to factors such as fatigue or having too much alcohol to drink (*see* ERECTILE DYSFUNCTION, p.770).

MEDICAL HELP

Make an appointment to see your doctor if you are concerned about problems with your sexual performance.

Do you wake with an erection?

- SOMETIMES
- NEVER

POSSIBLE CAUSE

Anxiety about your sexual performance is the most likely explanation (*see* ERECTILE DYSFUNCTION, p.770). A physical cause is unlikely.

MEDICAL HELP

Make an appointment to see your doctor.

Are you currently receiving treatment for an illness?

- TREATMENT
- NO TREATMENT

POSSIBLE CAUSES

Certain illnesses, such as DIABETES MELLITUS (p.687), can lead to erection problems. Some drugs, including ANTIHYPERTENSIVE DRUGS (p.897) and ANTIDEPRESSANT DRUGS (p.916), can also affect sexual performance.

MEDICAL HELP

Make an appointment to see your doctor.

If you cannot identify a possible cause for your erection problem from this chart, make an appointment to see your doctor.

53 TESTES AND SCROTUM PROBLEMS

Regular self-examination (*see* EXAMINING YOUR TESTES, p.720) is important to detect lumps and swellings in the testes (the sperm-producing organs) and the scrotum (the sac in which the testes lie). The cause of a swelling may be minor, but it could be cancer of the testis. Painful swelling in the genital area requires immediate medical attention.

START HERE

What is the nature of your symptoms?

- SUDDEN ONSET OF PAIN AND SWELLING
- PAINLESS ENLARGEMENT IN OR NEAR TESTIS
- GENERALIZED PAINLESS SWELLING OF THE SCROTUM
- NONE OF THE ABOVE

Does the problem affect one or both testes?

- ONE
- BOTH

POSSIBLE CAUSES

TORSION OF THE TESTIS (p.719) may be the cause of pain and swelling in one testis. A less serious possible cause is EPIDIDYMO-ORCHITIS (p.718).

MEDICAL HELP

URGENT! Go to the emergency department immediately!

Have you had an injury in the genital area within the past 48 hours?

- INJURY
- NO INJURY

POSSIBLE CAUSE

Internal damage to the testes is a possibility.

MEDICAL HELP

URGENT! Call your doctor immediately!

POSSIBLE CAUSES

Accumulation of fluid in the scrotum (*see* HYDROCELE, p.721), varicose veins in the scrotum (*see* VARICOCELE, p.720), or an inguinal hernia (*see* HERNIAS, p.661) are the most likely causes of your symptoms. However, there is a possibility that you may have CANCER OF THE TESTIS (p.719).

MEDICAL HELP

Make an appointment to see your doctor.

POSSIBLE CAUSES

An EPIDIDYMAL CYST (p.718) is the probable cause of your symptoms. However, there is a possibility that you have CANCER OF THE TESTIS (p.719).

MEDICAL HELP

Make an appointment to see your doctor.

If you cannot identify a possible cause for your testes or scrotum problem from this chart, make an appointment to see your doctor.

POSSIBLE CAUSE

EPIDIDYMO-ORCHITIS (p.718), which may be due to a sexually transmitted disease or a viral infection such as mumps, may be causing your symptoms.

MEDICAL HELP

Call your doctor within 24 hours.

54 PROBLEMS WITH THE PENIS

If you have erectile dysfunction, see chart 52

Pain or soreness of the penis that is not related to injury is often due to infection in the urinary tract or of the skin of the penis. Inflammation may be caused by friction during sexual intercourse. You should consult your doctor if there is any change in the appearance of the skin of the penis.

WARNING BLOOD IN THE SEMEN

Blood-streaked semen is usually caused by leakage from small blood vessels in the testes or epididymis. A single episode is unlikely to be a cause for concern, but, if it recurs, you should consult your doctor. It is also important to consult your doctor if you notice a blood-stained discharge that is not related to ejaculation or if you notice blood in your urine.

START HERE

What kind of problem are you experiencing?

- PAINFUL OR SORE PENIS
- DISCHARGE FROM PENIS
- FORESKIN PROBLEM
- CHANGE IN APPEARANCE OF ERECT PENIS
- NONE OF THE ABOVE

When does the pain occur?

- ONLY WITH AN ERECTION
- ONLY WITH URINATION
- AT OTHER TIMES

Go to chart 45
PAINFUL URINATION

How is the foreskin affected?

- HAS BEEN RETRACTED BUT CANNOT BE REPLACED
- AFTER CHILDHOOD, CANNOT BE FULLY RETRACTED
- BALLOONS WHEN URINATING
- NONE OF THE ABOVE

POSSIBLE CAUSE
Inability to replace a retracted foreskin is called paraphimosis (*see* PHIMOSIS, p.721).

MEDICAL HELP
EMERGENCY! Call an ambulance! While waiting for help, surround the affected area with an ice pack.

POSSIBLE CAUSE
You may have a sexually transmitted disease, such as GONORRHEA (p.764).

MEDICAL HELP
Call your doctor within 24 hours.

POSSIBLE CAUSE
Your problem may be caused by PEYRONIE'S DISEASE (p.723).

MEDICAL HELP
Make an appointment to see your doctor.

POSSIBLE CAUSE
An overly tight foreskin (*see* PHIMOSIS, p.721) is a possible cause of these problems.

MEDICAL HELP
Make an appointment to see your doctor.

Has the painful erection now subsided?

- SUBSIDED
- STILL PRESENT

POSSIBLE CAUSE
If you are not circumcised, the cause may be an overly tight foreskin (*see* PHIMOSIS, p.721).

MEDICAL HELP
Make an appointment to see your doctor.

POSSIBLE CAUSE
PRIAPISM (p.723), in which there is an obstruction to the flow of blood leaving the penis, could be the cause of your symptoms.

MEDICAL HELP

URGENT! Call your doctor immediately!

Has your penis become inflamed?

- ONLY TIP INFLAMED
- WHOLE PENIS INFLAMED
- NEITHER

POSSIBLE CAUSE
This may be BALANITIS (p.722).

MEDICAL HELP
Make an appointment to see your doctor.

POSSIBLE CAUSE
An allergic reaction, such as to the latex in condoms or to a contraceptive cream, may cause inflammation of this type (*see* ECZEMA, p.333, and CONTACT DERMATITIS, p.335).

MEDICAL HELP

Make an appointment to see your doctor.

Do you have any of the following on the skin of your penis?

- ULCERS
- SORE AREAS
- BLISTERS
- NONE OF THE ABOVE

POSSIBLE CAUSES
This may be a chancre (*see* SYPHILIS, p.766) or CANCER OF THE PENIS (p.723).

MEDICAL HELP

Make an appointment to see your doctor.

POSSIBLE CAUSE
Any of these skin symptoms may be the result of a sexually transmitted disease, such as GENITAL HERPES (p.767).

MEDICAL HELP

Make an appointment to see your doctor.

Have you noticed either of the following on your penis?

- FLAT, PAINLESS SORE
- SMALL, FLESHY LUMPS
- NEITHER

POSSIBLE CAUSE
You probably have GENITAL WARTS (p.768).

MEDICAL HELP

Make an appointment to see your doctor.

If you cannot identify a possible cause for your problem from this chart, make an appointment to see your doctor.

55 BREAST PROBLEMS

You should familiarize yourself with the normal look and feel of your breasts so that you are able to detect any changes (*see* BREAST SELF-EXAMINATION, p.755). Although most breast problems are not serious, consult your doctor if you notice any changes. Minor conditions clearly related to breast-feeding usually respond well to simple treatments.

START HERE

Are you breast-feeding a baby?

- BREAST-FEEDING
- NOT BREAST-FEEDING

Where is the problem?

- IN THE BREAST
- ON THE NIPPLE

POSSIBLE CAUSE
The lump may be caused by a blocked milk duct.

MEDICAL HELP
Make an appointment to see your doctor if the lump has not disappeared within 2 days or if the breast becomes painful or red.

How is your nipple affected?

- TENDER ONLY WHEN FEEDING
- TENDER AND PAINFUL ALL THE TIME

What is the nature of your breast problem?

- SINGLE LUMP IN THE BREAST
- A NIPPLE HAS CHANGED IN APPEARANCE
- DISCHARGE FROM THE NIPPLE
- BREASTS FEEL TENDER
- BREASTS FEEL LUMPY AND HARD
- NONE OF THE ABOVE

POSSIBLE CAUSES
Discharge from the nipple may have various causes, including a local problem in the breast or a hormonal problem (*see* NIPPLE DISCHARGE, p.758).

MEDICAL HELP
Make an appointment to see your doctor.

POSSIBLE CAUSES
These symptoms may not have a serious cause (*see* BREAST LUMPS, p.754, and ABNORMAL NIPPLES, p.757). However, such changes must be investigated promptly to rule out the possibility of BREAST CANCER (p.759).

MEDICAL HELP

Make an appointment to see your doctor.

If you cannot identify a possible cause for your breast problem from this chart, make an appointment to see your doctor.

What is the nature of your symptoms?

- SMALL, HARD LUMP IN BREAST
- SWOLLEN, HARD, AND TENDER BREASTS
- REDNESS OF PART OR ALL OF ONE BREAST
- NONE OF THE ABOVE

POSSIBLE CAUSE
Overfull breasts are common, especially when you first start breast-feeding and your milk supply has not yet adjusted to your baby's needs (*see* BREAST ENGORGEMENT, p.808).

SELF-HELP
Continuing to breast-feed your baby at regular intervals should solve this problem without special treatment. However, if you are concerned, consult your doctor or breast-feeding adviser.

POSSIBLE CAUSES
This may be a breast infection or possibly a breast abscess (*see* MASTITIS, p.809), particularly if you also do not feel well.

MEDICAL HELP
Call your doctor within 24 hours. Continue breast-feeding from both of your breasts.

POSSIBLE CAUSE
This problem may be a result of your baby not latching on to your nipple properly.

SELF-HELP
Make sure your baby takes the nipple and the surrounding area into his or her mouth (*see* AVOIDING CRACKED NIPPLES, p.809). If you are still having problems when you use the correct feeding technique, consult your doctor or breast-feeding adviser.

If you cannot identify a possible cause for your breast problem from this chart, make an appointment to see your doctor.

POSSIBLE CAUSE
Hormonal changes associated with the menstrual cycle often lead to premenstrual breast tenderness (*see* PREMENSTRUAL SYNDROME, p.736).

MEDICAL HELP
Make an appointment to see your doctor if your breasts are painful or if you have other symptoms.

Does either of the following apply?

- MENSTRUATION IS DUE TO START WITHIN 10 DAYS
- YOU MIGHT BE PREGNANT
- NEITHER

POSSIBLE CAUSE
Breast tenderness is common in pregnancy (*see* COMMON COMPLAINTS OF NORMAL PREGNANCY, p.784).

SELF-HELP
If you are not sure whether you are pregnant, do a HOME PREGNANCY TEST (p.232).

POSSIBLE CAUSE
Your symptoms may be due to CRACKED NIPPLES (p.808).

SELF-HELP
Continue to breastfeed. Consult your doctor or breast-feeding adviser as soon as possible.

If you cannot identify a possible cause for your breast problem from this chart, make an appointment to see your doctor.

56 ABSENT MENSTRUAL PERIODS

The time between menstrual periods varies between women but, once established, periods usually occur regularly every 3 to 5 weeks. Pregnancy or menopause are the most common causes of absent menstruation. Stress or loss of weight may also cause menstruation to stop or occur less often. Consult your doctor if your menstrual periods stop unexpectedly.

WARNING **POSSIBLE PREGNANCY**

Any sexually active woman who misses a menstrual period should consider the possibility that she might be pregnant, even if contraceptive measures have been taken during sexual intercourse.

In the years leading up to menopause, menstrual periods become erratic. Ovulation may still occur until menstruation has stopped completely for at least 6 months. It is, therefore, possible for a woman to become pregnant while going through perimenopause. If you think you might be pregnant, check using a HOME PREGNANCY TEST (p.232).

START HERE

Have you ever had a menstrual period?

- PREVIOUS PERIODS
- NEVER HAD A PERIOD

Could you be pregnant?

- NOT PREGNANT
- POSSIBLY PREGNANT

POSSIBLE CAUSE
A missed menstrual period is a key indicator of pregnancy.

SELF-HELP
If you are not sure whether you are pregnant, do a HOME PREGNANCY TEST (p.232). If the result of the test is positive, make an appointment to see your doctor.

Have you had a baby within the past 6 months?

- NO
- YES

How old are you?

- UNDER 14
- 14 OR OVER

POSSIBLE CAUSE
Some girls, especially those who are small and slim, may develop late but, provided there are no other symptoms of ill health, there is unlikely to be a cause for concern.

MEDICAL HELP
Make an appointment to see your doctor if you are underweight (*see* ARE YOU A HEALTHY WEIGHT?, p.53) or if you have other symptoms.

POSSIBLE CAUSES
Late puberty may be the result of hormonal imbalance, low weight, or regular strenuous exercise (*see* ABNORMAL PUBERTY IN FEMALES, p.739).

MEDICAL HELP
Make an appointment to see your doctor.

Do any of the following apply?

- You have recently lost over 10 lb (4 kg) in weight
- You have recently begun a program of strenuous exercise
- You have recently stopped taking oral contraceptives
- None of the above

Possible causes

Sudden weight loss, whatever the cause, and/or rigorous physical training can cause menstruation to stop (*see* AMENORRHEA, p.735).

Medical help

Make an appointment to see your doctor.

Possible cause

It may take several weeks for normal menstruation to begin again after stopping oral contraceptives.

Medical help

Make an appointment to see your doctor if you have not had a period within 3 months of stopping.

Are you under particular stress at home, school, or work?

- Yes
- No

Possible cause

Emotional stress can disrupt the menstrual cycle (*see* AMENORRHEA, p.735).

Medical help

Make an appointment to see your doctor.

How old are you?

- Over 40
- 40 or under

Possible cause

A reduction in the frequency of menstruation is normal during the years preceding menopause (*see* HEALTH AT MENOPAUSE, p.36).

Medical help

Make an appointment to see your doctor. You should keep a record of your menstrual periods because this information may be useful to your doctor.

If you cannot identify a possible cause for your absence of periods from this chart, make an appointment to see your doctor.

Possible cause

It can take several months for menstruation to become reestablished after childbirth. This delay is likely to be extended if you are breast-feeding your baby frequently (*see* AMENORRHEA, p.735).

Medical help

Make an appointment to see your doctor if your menstrual periods have not restarted within 3 months after the birth if you are not breast-feeding or within 1 month of stopping full-time breast-feeding.

57 Painful menstrual periods

Many women experience mild cramping pain in the lower abdomen during menstruation. This pain is considered normal unless it interferes with daily activities; it can usually be relieved with analgesics. If you regularly have severe pain or if your menstrual periods become more painful than usual, you should consult your doctor.

Start here

How does the pain you are now experiencing compare with that of previous menstrual periods?

- No worse than usual
- Worse than usual

Possible cause
Some menstrual pain is quite normal; it is known as primary DYSMENORRHEA (p.736).

Self-help
Take an analgesic. Make an appointment to see your doctor if pain interferes with normal activities.

Have you had an unusual vaginal discharge between menstrual periods?

- No discharge
- Discharge

Possible cause
You could have an infection (*see* PELVIC INFLAMMATORY DISEASE, p.741).

Medical help

Call your doctor within 24 hours.

Have you had any of the following symptoms?

- Lower abdominal pain
- Low back pain
- Fever
- None of the above

Do you have an intrauterine contraceptive device (IUD)?

- IUD
- No IUD

Possible cause
An increase in menstrual pain is often a side effect of IUDs (*see* CONTRACEPTION, p.69).

Medical help

Make an appointment to see your doctor.

Have your menstrual periods become heavier or longer as well as more painful?

- Heavier
- Longer
- Neither

Possible causes
You may possibly have a gynecological disorder such as FIBROIDS (p.745) or ENDOMETRIOSIS (p.742).

Medical help

Make an appointment to see your doctor.

If you cannot identify a possible cause for your painful menstrual periods from this chart, make an appointment to see your doctor.

58 HEAVY MENSTRUAL PERIODS

If you bleed between periods, see chart 59

Some women lose more blood than others during their menstrual periods. If normal sanitary protection is not sufficient, clots are passed, or bleeding lasts longer than 5 days, the bleeding is probably excessive. If you are concerned about heavy menstrual periods, consult your doctor.

START HERE

How does the bleeding of your most recent menstrual period compare with your usual menstrual periods?

- ABOUT THE SAME → Possible cause (menorrhagia)
- HEAVIER OR LONGER → Do you have an intrauterine contraceptive device (IUD)?

Do you have an intrauterine contraceptive device (IUD)?

- IUD → Possible cause (IUDs)
- NO IUD → Have you had a single heavy menstrual period that was also later than usual?

POSSIBLE CAUSE
Some IUDs can cause heavy menstrual periods (*see* CONTRACEPTION, p.69).

MEDICAL HELP
Make an appointment to see your doctor.

Have you had a single heavy menstrual period that was also later than usual?

- YES → Possible causes (miscarriage)
- NO → Are your menstrual periods more painful than they used to be?

Are your menstrual periods more painful than they used to be?

- MORE PAINFUL → Possible causes (fibroids, endometriosis)
- THE SAME OR LESS PAINFUL → If you cannot identify a possible cause...

POSSIBLE CAUSES
Heavy, painful menstrual periods may indicate the presence of FIBROIDS (p.745) or ENDOMETRIOSIS (p.742).

MEDICAL HELP

Make an appointment to see your doctor.

POSSIBLE CAUSE
Some women regularly have heavy menstrual periods (*see* MENORRHAGIA, p.735).

MEDICAL HELP
Make an appointment to see your doctor. You could be susceptible to IRON-DEFICIENCY ANEMIA (p.447).

POSSIBLE CAUSES
Late menstrual periods may also be heavier than usual. However, there is a possibility that you have had an early MISCARRIAGE (p.791).

MEDICAL HELP
Make an appointment to see your doctor if you think that you might have been pregnant.

If you cannot identify a possible cause for heavy menstrual periods from this chart, make an appointment to see your doctor.

59 ABNORMAL VAGINAL BLEEDING

Vaginal bleeding is considered abnormal if it occurs outside the normal menstrual cycle, during pregnancy, or after menopause. Although there is often a simple explanation, you should always see your doctor if you have any abnormal vaginal bleeding. If you are pregnant and you are bleeding, you should consult your doctor or nurse/midwife at once.

WARNING **BLEEDING IN PREGNANCY**

If you have any vaginal bleeding during pregnancy, you should contact your doctor or nurse/midwife urgently. Although most causes of bleeding are not serious, it is important to rule out MISCARRIAGE (p.791) or a problem such as a low-lying placenta (*see* PLACENTA PREVIA, p.798) or partial separation of the placenta from the wall of the uterus (*see* PLACENTAL ABRUPTION, p.799).

START HERE

Are you pregnant?

- MORE THAN 14 WEEKS PREGNANT
- LESS THAN 14 WEEKS PREGNANT
- NOT PREGNANT

POSSIBLE CAUSE
Bleeding at this stage of pregnancy could be due to a problem with the placenta (*see* VAGINAL BLEEDING IN PREGNANCY, p.791).

MEDICAL HELP
URGENT! Call your doctor or nurse/midwife immediately! Rest in bed until you receive medical advice.

Is the bleeding like that of a normal menstrual period?

- LIKE A PERIOD
- DIFFERENT

Do you have unaccustomed pain in the lower back or abdomen?

- LOWER BACK PAIN
- ABDOMINAL PAIN
- NEITHER

POSSIBLE CAUSES
You may be experiencing a MISCARRIAGE (p.791) or you may have an ECTOPIC PREGNANCY (p.790).

MEDICAL HELP
URGENT! Call your doctor or nurse/midwife immediately! Rest in bed until you receive medical advice.

POSSIBLE CAUSE
Bleeding at this stage of pregnancy could be the first sign of a threatened MISCARRIAGE (p.791).

MEDICAL HELP
URGENT! Call your doctor or nurse/midwife immediately! Rest in bed until you receive medical advice.

How long is it since your last menstrual period?

- LESS THAN 6 MONTHS
- MORE THAN 6 MONTHS

Does either of the following apply?

- YOU HAVE ONLY RECENTLY STARTED MENSTRUATING
- YOU ARE OVER 40
- NEITHER

POSSIBLE CAUSE
Irregular menstrual periods are fairly common in the first year or so of menstruation.

MEDICAL HELP
Make an appointment to see your doctor if you are concerned.

POSSIBLE CAUSE
Having an occasional irregular menstrual period is unlikely to indicate a serious problem if the period was normal in other respects.

MEDICAL HELP
Make an appointment to see your doctor if you are concerned or if your pattern has not returned to normal within 2 months.

POSSIBLE CAUSE
As you approach menopause your menstrual periods may become irregular (*see* HEALTH AT MENOPAUSE, p.36).

MEDICAL HELP
Make an appointment to see your doctor if you are concerned.

WARNING HORMONAL CONTRACEPTIVES
In the first few menstrual cycles after either starting hormonal contraception or changing to a different type of contraceptive pill, spotting is fairly common (*see* CONTRACEPTION, p.69). If abnormal bleeding persists or develops when there have previously been no problems, you should consult your doctor. He or she may examine you and change the dosage or type of hormonal contraceptive that has been prescribed.

Have you had sexual intercourse in the past 3 months?

- INTERCOURSE
- NO INTERCOURSE

Have you noticed bleeding within a few hours of intercourse?

- BLEEDING AFTER INTERCOURSE
- BLEEDING UNRELATED TO INTERCOURSE

POSSIBLE CAUSES
You may have an abnormality of the cervix (*see* CERVICAL DYSPLASIA, p.749; CERVICAL ECTROPION, p.749; and CANCER OF THE CERVIX, p.750).

MEDICAL HELP

Make an appointment to see your doctor.

POSSIBLE CAUSES
Bleeding, especially if it is accompanied by pain in the lower abdomen, may be the first sign of an ECTOPIC PREGNANCY (p.790) or of an impending MISCARRIAGE (p.791), even if you were not aware of being pregnant.

MEDICAL HELP

URGENT! Call your doctor immediately!

POSSIBLE CAUSES
Bleeding after menopause may be caused by a minor problem affecting the vagina or cervix, such as CERVICAL EROSION (p.749), but the possibility of CANCER OF THE UTERUS (p.748) needs to be ruled out.

MEDICAL HELP
Make an appointment to see your doctor.

If you cannot identify a possible cause for your abnormal bleeding from this chart, make an appointment to see your doctor.

60 LOWER ABDOMINAL PAIN IN WOMEN

First refer to chart 35, ABDOMINAL PAIN

Several disorders specific to women can cause discomfort or pain in the lower abdomen. Many of these are related to the reproductive tract (ovaries, uterus, or fallopian tubes) or to pregnancy. Abdominal pain that occurs during pregnancy should always be taken seriously.

WARNING ABDOMINAL PAIN IN PREGNANCY

Intermittent mild abdominal pains are common throughout pregnancy due to stretching of the muscles and ligaments of the abdomen. Abdominal pain that occurs in early pregnancy can be due to complications, such as MISCARRIAGE (p.791) or an ECTOPIC PREGNANCY (p.790). In later pregnancy, pain is most commonly caused by the onset of labor. Rarely, partial separation of the placenta from the uterine wall may occur (*see* PLACENTAL ABRUPTION, p.799). If you develop severe pain call your doctor immediately.

START HERE

Do you have pain when you urinate?

- YES → Possible cause: cystitis
- NO → Are you pregnant?

POSSIBLE CAUSE

You may have CYSTITIS (p.709).

MEDICAL HELP

Call your doctor within 24 hours. Meanwhile, drink plenty of water and take an analgesic.

Are you pregnant?

- MORE THAN 14 WEEKS PREGNANT → Possible causes: late miscarriage or placental abruption
- LESS THAN 14 WEEKS PREGNANT → Possible causes: threatened miscarriage or ectopic pregnancy
- DO NOT THINK SO → Have you had sexual intercourse in the past 3 months?

POSSIBLE CAUSES

You could be having a late MISCARRIAGE (p.791) or the placenta may have partly separated from the wall of the uterus (*see* PLACENTAL ABRUPTION, p.799).

MEDICAL HELP

URGENT! Call your doctor immediately! Rest in bed until you receive medical advice.

POSSIBLE CAUSES

Pain at this stage of pregnancy may indicate a threatened MISCARRIAGE (p.791) or an ECTOPIC PREGNANCY (p.790).

MEDICAL HELP

URGENT! Call your doctor immediately! Rest in bed until you receive medical advice.

Have you had sexual intercourse in the past 3 months?

- YES → Did your last menstrual period occur on time?
- NO → (continued on next page)

Did your last menstrual period occur on time?

- ON TIME → (continued on next page)
- MISSED OR LATE → (continued on next page)

Do you have any of the following symptoms?

- ABNORMAL VAGINAL DISCHARGE
- FEVER
- PAIN DURING INTERCOURSE
- NONE OF THE ABOVE

POSSIBLE CAUSE

PELVIC INFLAMMATORY DISEASE (p.741) is a possible cause of these symptoms.

MEDICAL HELP

Call your doctor within 24 hours.

Do you have an IUD?

- IUD
- NO IUD

Is the pain related to your menstrual cycle?

- OCCURS JUST BEFORE AND/OR DURING MENSTRUAL PERIOD
- OCCURS BRIEFLY IN MIDCYCLE
- UNRELATED

Have you passed menopause?

- PREMENOPAUSAL
- POSTMENOPAUSAL

POSSIBLE CAUSE

This form of CONTRACEPTION (p.69) often causes increased menstrual pain, particularly for the first few cycles after it has been inserted.

MEDICAL HELP

Make an appointment to see your doctor.

POSSIBLE CAUSE

Some women regularly have pain associated with ovulation.

MEDICAL HELP

Make an appointment to see your doctor to rule out other possible causes.

POSSIBLE CAUSE

Normal menstrual pain is known as primary DYSMENORRHEA (p.736).

SELF-HELP

Take an analgesic. Make an appointment to see your doctor if the pain interferes with normal activities.

POSSIBLE CAUSE

There is a possibility of an ECTOPIC PREGNANCY (p.790).

MEDICAL HELP

URGENT! Call your doctor immediately!

If you cannot identify a possible cause for your lower abdominal pain from this chart, make an appointment to see your doctor.

65 DIARRHEA IN CHILDREN

For children of 12 and over, see chart 39

Diarrhea is the passage of loose or watery feces more often than normal. Breast-fed babies may pass loose feces several times a day, and this is normal. To avoid dehydration your child should drink plenty of fluids that do not contain milk. If symptoms do not improve, consult your child's doctor.

DANGER SIGNS

Call an ambulance if your child's diarrhea is accompanied by any of the following symptoms:

- Drowsiness or lethargy.
- Severe and prolonged abdominal pain.
- No urine passed during the day for 3 hours (if under 1 year) or 6 hours (in an older child).
- Refusal to drink or feed (in babies) for over 6 hours.
- Blood in the feces.
- More than eight bowel movements in a day.

START HERE

How long has your child had diarrhea?

- LESS THAN 3 DAYS
- 3 DAYS OR OVER

Does your child have any of the following symptoms?

- ABDOMINAL PAIN
- TEMPERATURE OF 38°C (100°F) OR ABOVE
- VOMITING
- NONE OF THE ABOVE

POSSIBLE CAUSE

Your child may have GASTROENTERITIS (p.628).

MEDICAL HELP

URGENT! Call your child's doctor immediately if your child is under 6 months old. If your child is older, follow the self-help advice for PREVENTING DEHYDRATION (p.627). Consult your child's doctor if your child is no better in 24 hours.

Is your child gaining weight and growing normally (see GROWTH CHARTS, pp.40–43)?

- YES
- NO

Was your child constipated before the onset of diarrhea?

- CONSTIPATED
- NOT CONSTIPATED

POSSIBLE CAUSE

Persistent constipation can lead to overflow soiling, which can be mistaken for diarrhea (*see* CONSTIPATION IN CHILDREN, p.865).

MEDICAL HELP

Call your child's doctor within 24 hours.

What is the appearance of your child's feces?

- UNIFORMLY RUNNY
- CONTAINS RECOGNIZABLE PIECES OF FOOD

POSSIBLE CAUSES

It is possible that your child has a condition affecting the digestive tract, such as FOOD INTOLERANCE (p.657) or CELIAC DISEASE (p.658).

MEDICAL HELP

Make an appointment to see your child's doctor.

How old is your child?

- UNDER 12 MONTHS
- 12 MONTHS – 3 YEARS
- OVER 3 YEARS

Was your baby given any of the following before the onset of diarrhea?

- UNFAMILIAR FOODS
- SUGARY FOODS OR SWEETENED DRINKS
- PRESCRIBED OR OVER-THE-COUNTER MEDICINES
- NONE OF THE ABOVE

POSSIBLE CAUSE
Foods that are new to your baby may be the cause of digestive upsets.

SELF-HELP
Withhold the food that seems to be causing the trouble for at least 1 week. Consult your baby's doctor if your baby is no better in 24 hours or develops other symptoms.

POSSIBLE CAUSE
Sugar in food and drink can cause diarrhea in babies.

SELF-HELP
Avoid giving your baby sweetened foods and drinks. Consult your baby's doctor if your baby is no better in 24 hours or develops other symptoms.

POSSIBLE CAUSE
Young children often fail to chew and digest food properly, which can lead to toddler's diarrhea (*see* VOMITING AND DIARRHEA, p.864).

SELF-HELP
No special action is needed provided that your child is well. Consult your child's doctor if your child develops other symptoms.

POSSIBLE CAUSE
Your baby's symptoms may be a side effect of the drug.

MEDICAL HELP
Call your baby's doctor within 24 hours. Stop giving over-the-counter medicines but continue to give any prescribed medication unless advised to stop by your baby's doctor.

POSSIBLE CAUSE
A digestive tract infection is the most likely cause of diarrhea in babies (*see* GASTROENTERITIS, p.628).

MEDICAL HELP
URGENT! Call your baby's doctor immediately if your baby is under 6 months old. For older babies, follow the self-help measures for PREVENTING DEHYDRATION (p.627) and consult your baby's doctor if your baby is no better in 24 hours or develops other symptoms.

Is your child experiencing unusual stress, anxiety, or excitement?

- STRESS OR ANXIETY
- EXCITEMENT
- NEITHER

POSSIBLE CAUSE
Psychological stress or unusual excitement can cause diarrhea.

SELF-HELP
The diarrhea should stop as soon as the cause has disappeared. Consult your child's doctor if there is a long-term cause for anxiety in your child's life or if your child develops other symptoms.

If you cannot identify a possible cause for your child's diarrhea from this chart, call your child's doctor within 24 hours.

66 FEVER IN CHILDREN

For children of 12 and over, see chart 6

A fever is a temperature of 38°C (100°F) or above. If your child is not well you should take his or her temperature because a high fever may need urgent treatment. If a feverish child becomes unresponsive, call an ambulance. In all cases, follow the advice for BRINGING DOWN A FEVER (p.287).

DANGER SIGNS

Call an ambulance if your child's temperature rises above 39°C (102°F) and he or she has any of the following symptoms:

- Abnormally rapid breathing (*see* CHECKING YOUR CHILD'S BREATHING RATE, p.205).
- Drowsiness.
- Severe headache.
- Dislike of bright light.
- Refusal to drink.
- Reluctance to move arm or leg.

START HERE

How old is your child?

- UNDER 2 MONTHS
- 2 MONTHS OR OVER

POSSIBLE CAUSE
Fever in babies younger than 2 months is unusual; it may indicate a serious illness.

MEDICAL HELP
URGENT! Call your baby's doctor immediately!

Does your child have a rash?

- RASH
- NO RASH

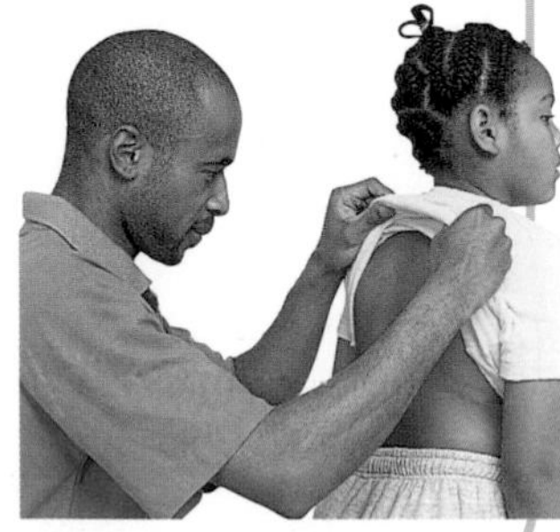

Go to chart 21
RASH WITH FEVER

Does your child have any of the following symptoms?

- SEVERE HEADACHE
- ABNORMAL DROWSINESS, IRRITABILITY, OR CONFUSION
- DISLIKE OF BRIGHT LIGHT
- NECK PAIN ON BENDING THE HEAD FORWARD
- NONE OF THE ABOVE

POSSIBLE CAUSE
Meningitis (*see* MENINGITIS IN CHILDREN, p.848) is a possible cause of these symptoms.

MEDICAL HELP
EMERGENCY! Call an ambulance!

Is your child reluctant to move an arm or leg?

- YES
- NO

POSSIBLE CAUSE
Your child could have an infection in a bone or joint (*see* OSTEOMYELITIS, p.372, and SEPTIC ARTHRITIS, p.381).

MEDICAL HELP
URGENT! Call your child's doctor immediately!

POSSIBLE CAUSE
Your child may have an infection of the middle ear (*see* ACUTE OTITIS MEDIA IN CHILDREN, p.860).

MEDICAL HELP

Call your child's doctor within 24 hours.

Possible causes
Your child could have a respiratory infection, such as PNEUMONIA (p.490), or he or she may be suffering from asthma (*see* ASTHMA IN CHILDREN, p.839) combined with an infection.

Medical help
 EMERGENCY! Call an ambulance!

Is your child's breathing abnormally noisy or rapid (*see* CHECKING YOUR CHILD'S BREATHING RATE, p.205)?

- ABNORMALLY RAPID
- NOISY
- NEITHER

Does either of the following apply?

- YOUR CHILD HAS BEEN PULLING AT ONE EAR
- YOUR CHILD HAS COMPLAINED OF EARACHE
- NEITHER

Does your child have either of the following symptoms?

- COUGH
- RUNNY NOSE
- NEITHER

Does your child have a sore throat?

- SORE THROAT
- NO SORE THROAT

Does your child have either of the following symptoms?

- PAIN ON URINATION
- DIARRHEA WITH OR WITHOUT VOMITING
- NEITHER

If you cannot identify a possible cause for your child's fever from this chart, call your child's doctor within 24 hours.

Possible cause
A viral illness, such as a severe cold (*see* COMMON COLD, p.286) or INFLUENZA (p.287), is the most likely cause of your child's symptoms.

Self-help
See the advice for BRINGING DOWN A FEVER (p.287). Consult your child's doctor if your child's symptoms worsen, if your child is no better in 2 days, or if he or she develops other symptoms.

Possible cause
Your child could be suffering from a throat infection, such as TONSILLITIS (p.843).

Medical help
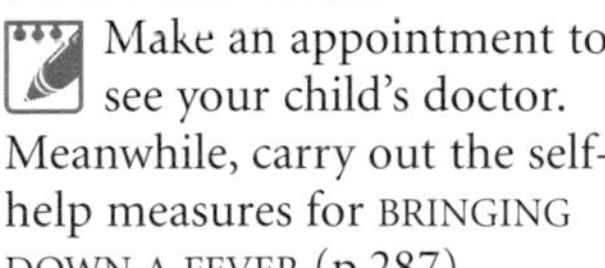 Make an appointment to see your child's doctor. Meanwhile, carry out the self-help measures for BRINGING DOWN A FEVER (p.287).

Possible cause
A URINARY TRACT INFECTION (p.871) is a possibility.

Medical help
 Call your child's doctor within 24 hours.

Possible cause
It is possible that your child has GASTROENTERITIS (p.628).

Medical help
URGENT! Call your child's doctor immediately if your child is under 6 months old. For older children, follow the self-help measures (*see* VOMITING AND DIARRHEA, p.864) and consult your child's doctor if your child is no better in 24 hours or if he or she develops other symptoms.

68 COUGHING IN CHILDREN

For children of 12 and over, see chart 29

Coughing is a normal reaction to irritation in the throat or lungs. Coughing is unusual in babies under 6 months old and may indicate a serious lung infection. Most coughs are caused by minor infections of the nose and/or throat, but the sudden onset of coughing may be caused by choking.

DANGER SIGNS

Call an ambulance if your child is coughing and has any of the following symptoms:

- Bluish lips or tongue.
- Drowsiness.
- Inability to swallow, talk, or produce sounds.
- Excessively rapid breathing (*see* CHECKING YOUR CHILD'S BREATHING RATE, p.205).

START HERE

How long has your child been coughing?

- STARTED SUDDENLY A FEW MINUTES AGO
- STARTED MORE THAN A FEW MINUTES AGO

Is is possible that your child is choking on food or a small object?

- POSSIBLE
- UNLIKELY

POSSIBLE CAUSE
An inhaled foreign body may be the cause of the coughing.

MEDICAL HELP
EMERGENCY! Call an ambulance! While waiting for medical help, follow the first-aid advice for CHOKING (pp.980–981).

How old is your child?

- 6 MONTHS OR OVER
- UNDER 6 MONTHS

POSSIBLE CAUSE
There is a possibility that your baby may be suffering from a serious lung infection (*see* BRONCHIOLITIS, p.841).

MEDICAL HELP
URGENT! Call your baby's doctor immediately!

Is your child's breathing abnormally rapid (*see* CHECKING YOUR CHILD'S BREATHING RATE, p.205) or noisy?

- ABNORMALLY RAPID
- NOISY
- NEITHER

Go to chart 67
BREATHING PROBLEMS IN CHILDREN

Does the cough have either of these characteristics?

- COMES IN FITS ENDING WITH A WHOOP
- IS ACCOMPANIED BY VOMITING
- NEITHER

POSSIBLE CAUSE
PERTUSSIS (p.492) may be the cause of your child's cough.

MEDICAL HELP

Call your child's doctor within 24 hours.

Does your child have a runny nose?

- MOST OF THE TIME OR VERY OFTEN
- HAS DEVELOPED A RUNNY NOSE WITHIN THE PAST FEW DAYS
- NO RUNNY NOSE

POSSIBLE CAUSES
Your child may have an allergy (*see* ALLERGIC RHINITIS, p.466) or ENLARGED ADENOIDS (p.842), both of which may cause these symptoms.

MEDICAL HELP
 Make an appointment to see your doctor.

Does your child have a fever – a temperature of 38°C (100°F) or above?

- FEVER
- NO FEVER

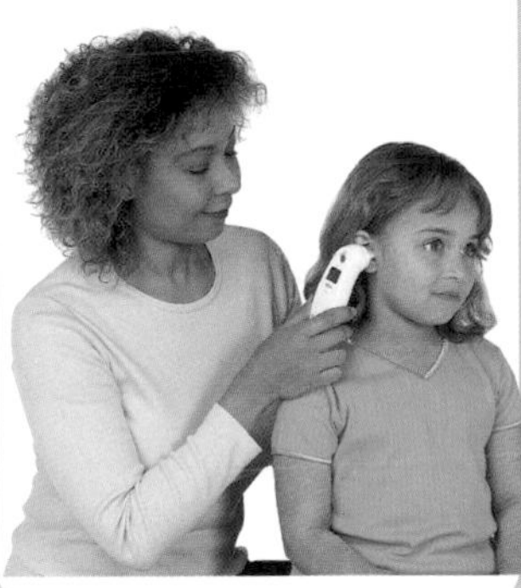

POSSIBLE CAUSE
A viral illness, such as a COMMON COLD (p.286) or INFLUENZA (p.287), is the most likely cause of your child's symptoms.

SELF-HELP
See the advice for BRINGING DOWN A FEVER (p.287). Consult your child's doctor if symptoms worsen, if your child is no better in 2 days, or if other symptoms develop.

POSSIBLE CAUSE
Your child probably has a COMMON COLD (p.286).

SELF-HELP
INHALING MOIST AIR (p.475) may help relieve the cough. Consult your child's doctor if symptoms worsen, if your child is no better in 2 days, or if other symptoms develop.

When does the coughing occur?

- MAINLY AT NIGHT
- AFTER EXERCISE
- WHEN OUT IN THE COLD
- NONE OF THE ABOVE

POSSIBLE CAUSE
There is a possibility that your child has asthma (*see* ASTHMA IN CHILDREN, p.839).

MEDICAL HELP
 Call your doctor within 24 hours.

Are there smokers in the home or might your child have been smoking?

- SMOKERS IN THE HOME
- CHILD MIGHT SMOKE
- NEITHER

POSSIBLE CAUSE
Your child's cough may be a response to being in a smoky atmosphere or to smoking.

SELF-HELP
Make sure that no one smokes in the house and avoid taking your child into a smoky atmosphere. If you suspect your child may be smoking, encourage him or her to stop.

If you cannot identify a possible cause for your child's cough from this chart, call your child's doctor within 24 hours.

69 ABDOMINAL PAIN IN CHILDREN

For children of 12 and over, see chart 35

Every child suffers from abdominal pain at some time, and some children have recurrent episodes. Usually the cause is minor, and the pain subsides in a few hours without treatment. In rare cases, abdominal pain is a symptom of a serious disorder that requires prompt medical attention.

DANGER SIGNS

Call an ambulance if your child's abdominal pain has been continuous for more than 4 hours and is accompanied by any of the following symptoms:

- Greenish yellow vomit.
- Pain in the groin or scrotum.
- Blood in the feces.

START HERE

Does your child have severe pain in either of the following places?

- GROIN
- SCROTUM
- NEITHER

POSSIBLE CAUSES (Groin / Scrotum)
A strangulated inguinal hernia (*see* HERNIAS, p.661) or TORSION OF THE TESTIS (p.719) is possible.

MEDICAL HELP
EMERGENCY! Call an ambulance!

Does your child have any of the following symptoms? (Neither)

- CONTINUOUS PAIN FOR MORE THAN 4 HOURS
- BLOOD IN THE FECES
- GREENISH YELLOW VOMIT
- NONE OF THE ABOVE

POSSIBLE CAUSE (Continuous pain for more than 4 hours)
Continuous abdominal pain for this length of time could be an indication of a serious abdominal condition, such as APPENDICITIS (p.664).

MEDICAL HELP
URGENT! Call your child's doctor immediately!

POSSIBLE CAUSES (Blood in the feces)
Abdominal pain accompanied by blood in the feces could indicate INTUSSUSCEPTION (p.864) in a young child. In older children, the cause of these symptoms may be an intestinal infection due to FOOD POISONING (p.629).

MEDICAL HELP
URGENT! Call your child's doctor immediately!

POSSIBLE CAUSE (Greenish yellow vomit)
An INTESTINAL OBSTRUCTION (p.663) is possible.

MEDICAL HELP
URGENT! Call your child's doctor immediately!

Does your child have diarrhea? (None of the above)

- NO DIARRHEA
- DIARRHEA

Has pain been relieved by either of the following?

- VOMITING
- PASSING GAS OR FECES
- NEITHER

Does your child have any of the following symptoms?

- SORE THROAT
- COUGH
- RUNNY NOSE
- NONE OF THE ABOVE

POSSIBLE CAUSE
Young children often have abdominal pain in association with an upper respiratory tract infection, such as a COMMON COLD (p.286).

SELF-HELP
INHALING MOIST AIR (p.475) may help. Call an ambulance if your child develops danger signs (opposite page).

POSSIBLE CAUSE
Your child could have a digestive tract infection (*see* GASTROENTERITIS, p.628).

MEDICAL HELP
URGENT! Call your child's doctor immediately if your child is under 6 months old. For older children, follow the advice on PREVENTING DEHYDRATION (p.627) and consult your child's doctor if your child is no better in 24 hours or if other symptoms develop.

Does your child have any of the following symptoms?

- PAIN ON URINATION
- TEMPERATURE OF 38°C (100°F) OR ABOVE
- RENEWED BEDWETTING OR DAYTIME "ACCIDENTS"
- NONE OF THE ABOVE

POSSIBLE CAUSE
Your child may have a URINARY TRACT INFECTION (p.871).

MEDICAL HELP

Call your child's doctor within 24 hours.

Has your child suffered from similar bouts of abdominal pain over the past few weeks?

- PREVIOUS ABDOMINAL PAIN
- NO PREVIOUS PAIN

POSSIBLE CAUSE
Recurrent abdominal pain in children can sometimes be related to anxiety.

MEDICAL HELP

Make an appointment to see your child's doctor.

If you cannot identify a possible cause for your child's abdominal pain from this chart, call your child's doctor within 24 hours.

70 WEIGHT PROBLEMS IN CHILDREN

For children of 12 and over, see charts 3 or 4

Check your child is within healthy limits by regularly measuring his or her weight and height (*see* GROWTH CHARTS FOR CHILDREN, pp.42–43). An abnormality in a child's weight may be due to disease. A long-term weight problem may increase your child's risk of future health problems.

WARNING

SPECIAL DIETS

The dietary needs of children differ from those of adults. An unbalanced diet can adversely affect growth and development. You should not put your child on a reducing diet or restrict specific food groups except on the advice of your child's doctor.

START HERE

What is your concern about your child's weight?

- OVERWEIGHT FOR HEIGHT
- UNDERWEIGHT FOR HEIGHT

POSSIBLE CAUSES

Your child may be eating more than is needed for the amount of exercise he or she is getting. Rarely, weight gain is due to a hormonal disorder or to prescribed drugs such as CORTICOSTEROIDS (p.930).

MEDICAL HELP

Make an appointment to see your child's doctor.

Has your child been underweight for long?

- YES
- NO

POSSIBLE CAUSE

It is likely that your child's thinness is constitutional, particularly if either you or your partner is thin.

MEDICAL HELP

Make an appointment to see your child's doctor to confirm that there is no additional medical cause.

How is your child's appetite?

- GOOD
- POOR

Does your child have either of the following symptoms?

- DIARRHEA
- INCREASED THIRST AND URINATION
- NEITHER OF THE ABOVE

POSSIBLE CAUSES

Your child may be unable to absorb food properly due to a condition such as LACTOSE INTOLERANCE (p.657) or CELIAC DISEASE (p.658).

MEDICAL HELP

Call your child's doctor within 24 hours.

POSSIBLE CAUSE

Your child could have DIABETES MELLITUS (p.687), particularly if he or she has also had recurrent infections and been generally unwell.

MEDICAL HELP

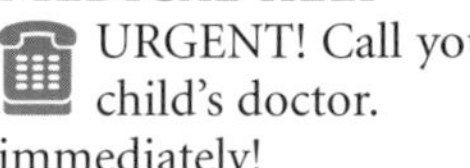
URGENT! Call your child's doctor. immediately!

If you cannot identify a possible cause for your child's loss or gain in weight, make an appointment to see your child's doctor.

Looking for Disease

There are numerous medical tests available that are routinely used for investigating disease. This section describes the most common screening and diagnostic procedures and explains why and when they are used. It begins with what to expect when visiting your doctor and what kind of test samples may be taken. The section then examines how the most common imaging and viewing techniques work and explains how they are used.

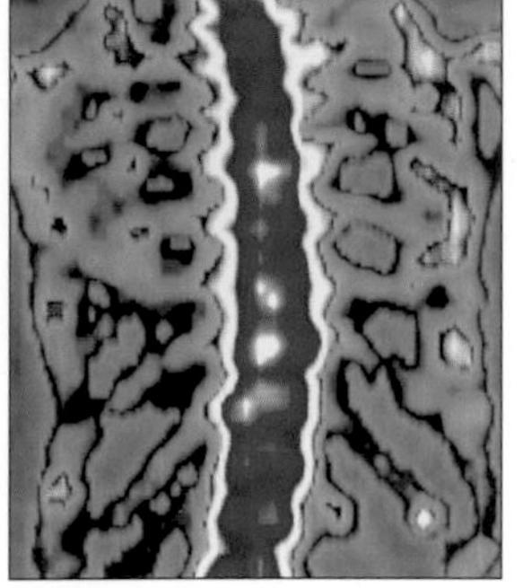

Bone scan of the chest
Radionuclide scanning is often used to detect cancer that has spread to the bones, visible here as light areas along the spine.

INTRODUCTION

THE DIAGNOSTIC METHOD IS THE PROCESS by which a doctor identifies the disease or disorder that is causing symptoms. This may include finding the underlying agent, such as a virus or bacteria. The doctor may use various tests to confirm or eliminate a particular diagnosis or help decide among alternative diagnoses. Some tests are used for screening. Screening methods test large groups of people for early signs of a disease or look for risk factors that may increase their chance of developing a disease, such as cancer, in the future.

There are a number of different reasons for visiting a doctor. You may have a pain or other sensation that worries you, have noticed a change in your body's appearance, or simply be anxious about your general physical or mental state. At other times, you may want a routine health checkup, or an insurance company may require a full medical examination.

If you have a particular health problem, your doctor will try to make a diagnosis based on your symptoms, medical history, a physical examination, and possibly some tests. If you are having a routine health checkup, you will have a comprehensive physical examination, which typically includes measurement of your weight, temperature, respiratory and pulse rates, and blood pressure. Your doctor will examine you from head to toe to look for signs of a disorder, such as enlargement of the liver or abnormal sounds in the heart or lungs. He or she may recommend screening tests that are appropriate to your age, gender, and lifestyle.

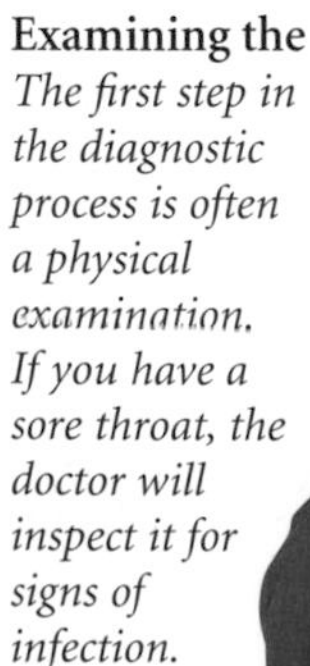

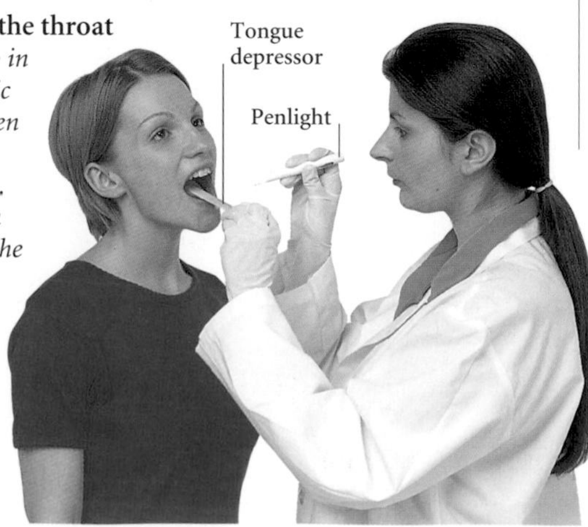
Tongue depressor
Penlight

Examining the throat
The first step in the diagnostic process is often a physical examination. If you have a sore throat, the doctor will inspect it for signs of infection.

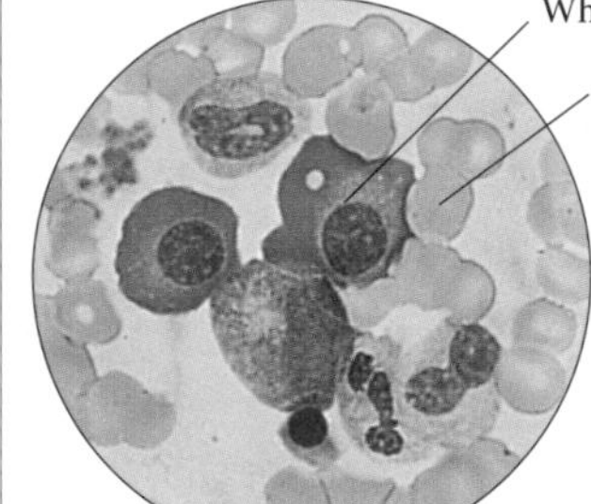
White blood cell
Red blood cell

Blood smear
Examination of a blood sample under a microscope can help the doctor make a diagnosis. On this smear, there are more white blood cells than normal, suggesting that the body is responding to an infection.

WHY TESTS ARE DONE

When you visit your doctor with a health problem, he or she begins the diagnostic process by asking you questions about your general health and any specific symptoms you may have. The next step is to take a complete medical history. This may involve asking you questions about past illnesses, family history of disease, lifestyle, personal relationships, and occupation. You will also have a physical examination. If you have symptoms or signs characteristic of a common disease or disorder, your doctor may be able to arrive at an immediate diagnosis. If he or she is unable to do this, you may be asked to have some tests.

When you see your doctor for a checkup, he or she may advise you to have a screening test. Screening uses some of the same tests as diagnosis, but, because the aim is to detect diseases before symptoms develop, not all tests are appropriate. People having tests because they are ill are usually prepared to tolerate a degree of discomfort or an element of risk. However, a person being screened has no current concerns about his or her health and would not tolerate tests that are risky, painful, or generally uncomfortable.

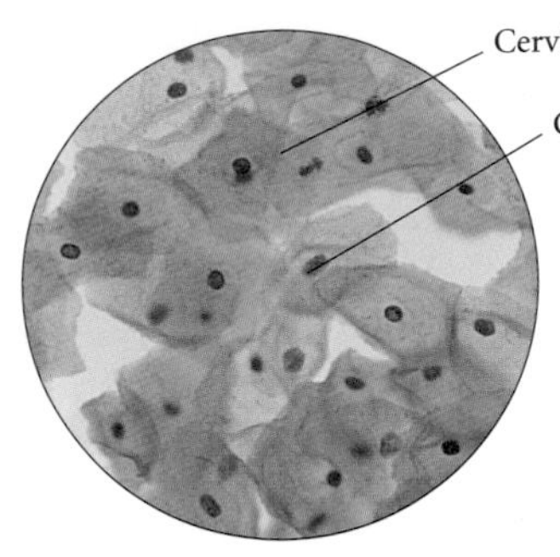
Cervical cell
Cell nucleus

Pap test result
A Pap test is used for detecting abnormal cells of the cervix that might become cancerous. This common screening test enables appropriate treatment to be done at an early stage. The cells shown here are healthy.

Types of tests

Medical tests can be simple enough to be carried out in your doctor's office or more complex, requiring sophisticated equipment in a hospital or laboratory. Tests may be done on samples of body fluids, such as urine or blood, or on tissue, such as cells from the cervix. Viewing tests involve the use of instruments such as endoscopes, viewing tubes through which a doctor can look directly into the body, usually through a natural opening such as the mouth or nose. Imaging tests, such as MRI, CT scanning, and ultrasound, use complex equipment to create images of internal body structures in order to detect abnormalities. Certain tests, such as mammography (X-rays of the breasts), can be used for both diagnosis and screening.

Your doctor will choose an appropriate medical test to answer a specific diagnostic question or to screen for a particular disorder. You and your doctor will balance the medical value and reliability of the test against any health risks, financial costs, and discomfort.

Reliability

Some tests, such as diagnostic tests on tissue samples, are extremely accurate, but most are less reliable. There may be inaccuracies in the test equipment, the procedure, or in the interpretation of results. These and other human errors can lead to false results. A false positive result indicates the presence of disease in a person who is really healthy. A false negative result indicates that a person is free of the disease when he or she actually has it. False positive results cause anxiety and necessitate further tests to confirm or reject the diagnosis. A false negative result may delay diagnosis until symptoms develop, at which stage treatment may be less effective. Good tests give only a small proportion of false positive and false negative results. Since most tests are not totally reliable, results must be carefully assessed and always considered in the context of a person's medical history and examination.

(COMPARISON) Imaging techniques

Many imaging techniques use radiation, which may be from an outside source, as in plain and contrast X-rays, or injected into the body, as in PET scanning and other types of radionuclide scanning. Some techniques, such as MRI and ultrasound scanning, do not use radiation, thus avoiding the risks associated with it. The particular technique a doctor chooses depends on what he or she is looking for. Although MRI produces highly detailed information about internal tissues, fractures are better detected by a simple X-ray. The images here show how different types of information about structures in the head can be obtained using different imaging techniques.

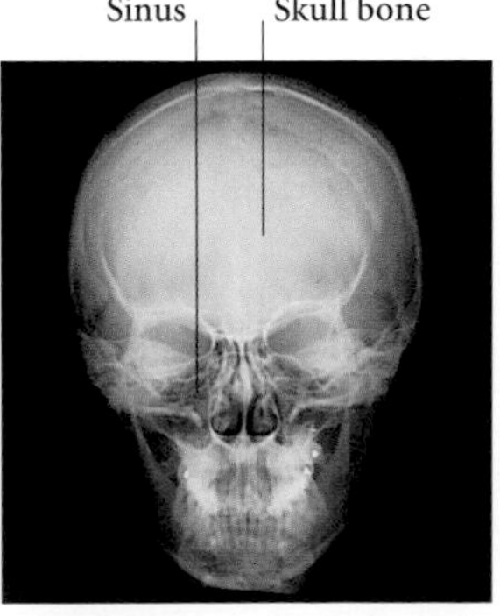
Sinus
Skull bone

X-ray
Plain X-rays can produce clear images of dense structures, such as bones, and air-filled cavities, such as the sinuses in the skull.

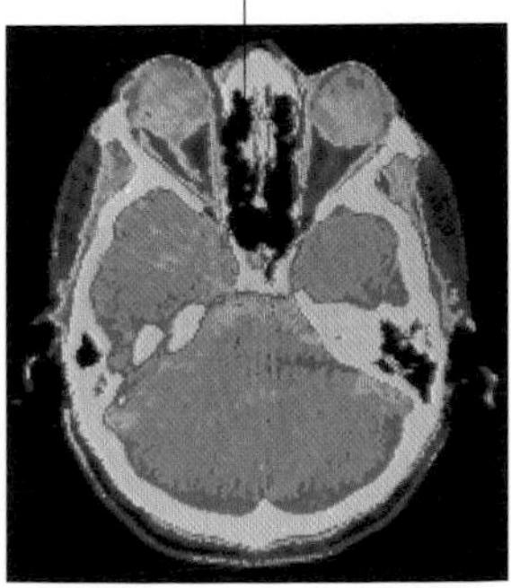
Nasal cavity

CT scan
The cross-sectional images obtained by CT scanning are used to detect a brain tumor or investigate after a stroke.

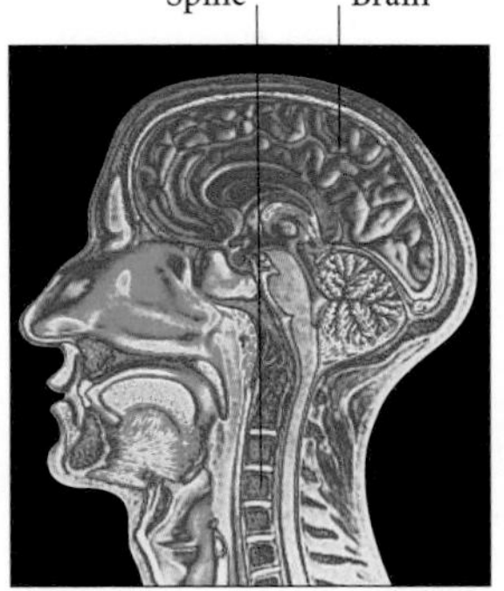
Spine
Brain

MRI scan
Magnetic resonance imaging (MRI) uses magnetic fields to gives detailed structural images without using radiation.

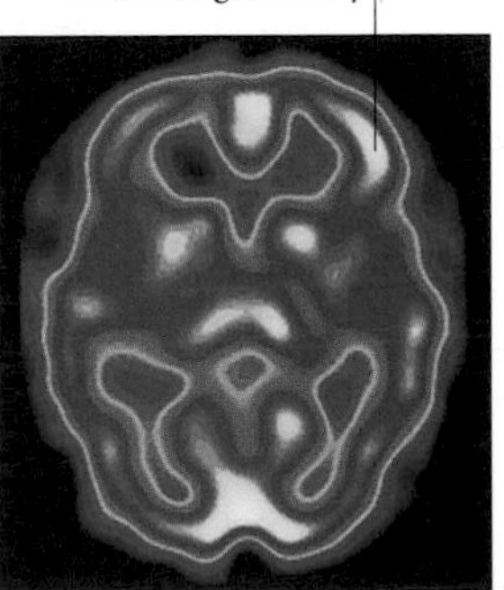
Area of high activity

PET scan
Positron emission tomography (PET) uses injected radioactive substances, which are taken up and reflect the activity in tissues.

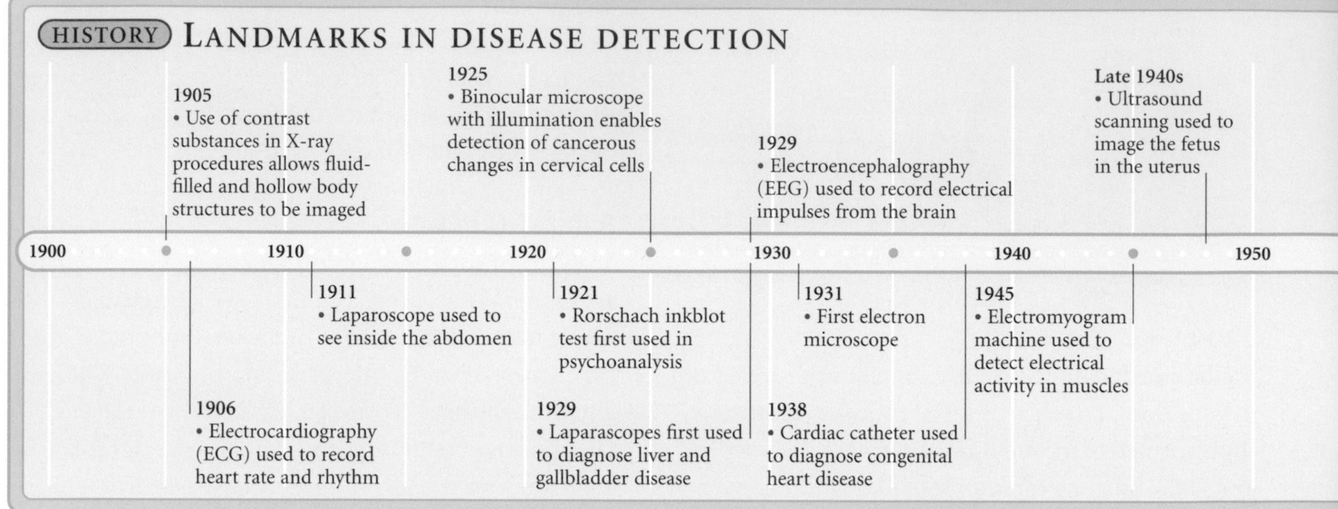
HISTORY
LANDMARKS IN DISEASE DETECTION
1900
1910
1920
1930
1940
1950
1905
• Use of contrast substances in X-ray procedures allows fluid-filled and hollow body structures to be imaged
1906
• Electrocardiography (ECG) used to record heart rate and rhythm
1911
• Laparoscope used to see inside the abdomen
1921
• Rorschach inkblot test first used in psychoanalysis
1925
• Binocular microscope with illumination enables detection of cancerous changes in cervical cells
1929
• Laparascopes first used to diagnose liver and gallbladder disease
1929
• Electroencephalography (EEG) used to record electrical impulses from the brain
1931
• First electron microscope
1938
• Cardiac catheter used to diagnose congenital heart disease
1945
• Electromyogram machine used to detect electrical activity in muscles
Late 1940s
• Ultrasound scanning used to image the fetus in the uterus

Trends in disease detection during the 20th century
Diagnostic and screening tests have become safer, more accurate, and less invasive with the growth of computer technology. The mortality rates of some diseases, such as cervical cancer, have been greatly reduced as a result of efficient screening programs.

Costs, risks, and acceptability

In addition to the cost of the test itself, having a test may involve less obvious expenses. For example, the results of a diagnostic test may affect your life insurance status. Some tests also carry health risks. For example, coronary angiography, which is used to view blood vessels to diagnose coronary artery disease, carries a very small risk of causing a stroke or heart attack. In addition to these costs and risks, the degree of discomfort or pain that the test causes must also be considered. However, the drawbacks of a test need to be weighed against the potential usefulness of the test result. A risky or painful test may still be justified medically and be acceptable to the person having it if it yields information that could be lifesaving.

Viewing with an endoscope
During endoscopy, a rigid or flexible tube is inserted into the body so that a doctor can view internal organs. The technique is particularly useful because if an abnormality is found, a small sample can be removed for analysis.

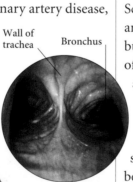

Wall of trachea

Bronchus

ENDOSCOPIC VIEW

Bronchoscope
The tube of a flexible bronchoscope is inserted through the nose or mouth and extends to the lungs

Screening

Screening tests can have one of three basic aims. Many are used to identify people who already have a disease but who have not yet developed symptoms. This type of test is used only if there is a treatment available for an early stage of the disease that can improve the outcome. For example, breast cancer screening is a routine procedure because early detection gives the best chance of a complete cure. On the other hand, screening for Alzheimer's disease is not routine because no effective treatment is currently available.

A second type of screening test looks for risk factors or a genetic predisposition to developing a disease. A typical test might look for high blood cholesterol, associated with coronary artery disease, or for the genes associated with breast cancer. Screening may also be used to detect healthy carriers of abnormal genes, which may be passed on to children. These tests may be offered to couples who are planning to have children and pregnant women who have a family history of a genetic disorder.

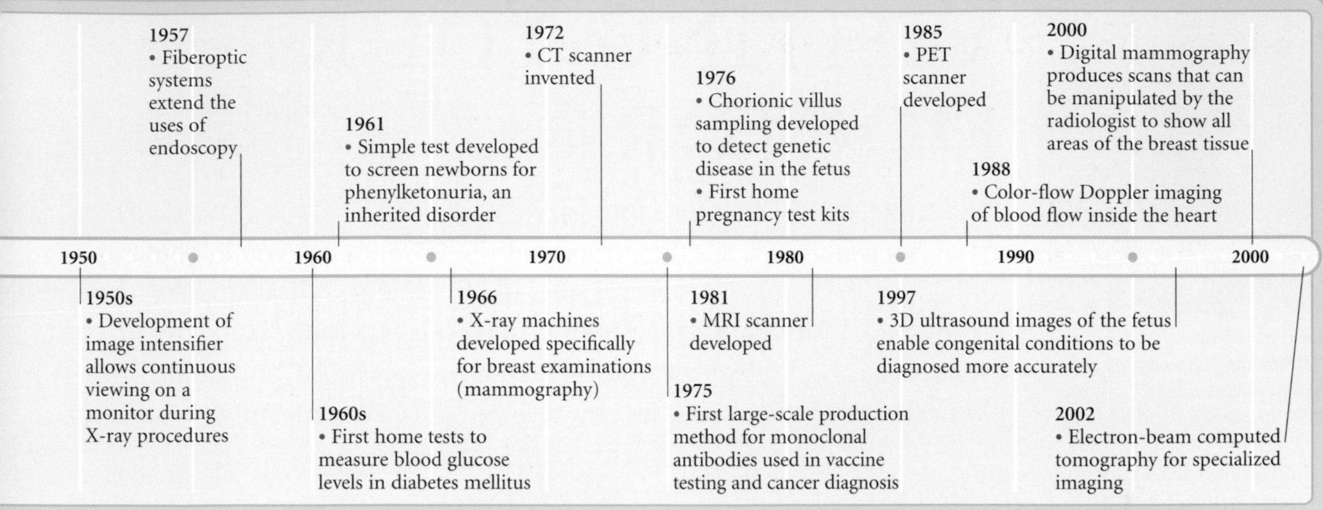
1950
1950s
• Development of image intensifier allows continuous viewing on a monitor during X-ray procedures
1957
• Fiberoptic systems extend the uses of endoscopy
1960
1960s
• First home tests to measure blood glucose levels in diabetes mellitus
1961
• Simple test developed to screen newborns for phenylketonuria, an inherited disorder
1966
• X-ray machines developed specifically for breast examinations (mammography)
1970
1972
• CT scanner invented
1975
• First large-scale production method for monoclonal antibodies used in vaccine testing and cancer diagnosis
1976
• Chorionic villus sampling developed to detect genetic disease in the fetus
• First home pregnancy test kits
1980
1981
• MRI scanner developed
1985
• PET scanner developed
1988
• Color-flow Doppler imaging of blood flow inside the heart
1990
1997
• 3D ultrasound images of the fetus enable congenital conditions to be diagnosed more accurately
2000
2000
• Digital mammography produces scans that can be manipulated by the radiologist to show all areas of the breast tissue
2002
• Electron-beam computed tomography for specialized imaging

Successful screening relies on the careful selection of the population that is to be tested. If the disorder being screened is rare, the proportion of false positive test results tends to be high even if the test is relatively precise. As well, there is little point in testing many people at great expense when few are likely to have the disease. To be both reliable and cost-effective, screening programs must be targeted at those groups that are considered to be at increased risk. For example, routine mammograms usually start for women at age 50, the age at which the test is more reliable and women are at increased risk for breast cancer.

Trends in Disease Detection

Technological advances, such as endoscopy and increasingly sophisticated imaging tests, are making diagnosis safer and less invasive. Computerization is also making the analysis, storage, and retrieval of test results quicker and more reliable.

In addition, various reliable home tests are now available, such as tests for blood sugar (necessary in diabetes) and blood pressure monitors. Used under the supervision of the doctor, these tests can help you take responsibility for your own health and monitor chronic illnesses and the effects of treatments.

ORGANIZATION How this part of the book is organized

This part of the book tells you what happens when you visit the doctor with a problem, including the consultation, physical examination, and taking of samples for testing. Laboratory testing of samples and the technology and uses of imaging tests are then described. Tests specific to a body system or organ are described with the relevant system.

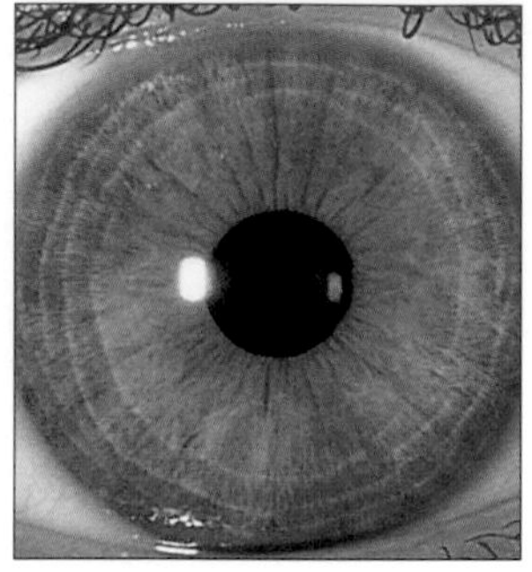
View of the eye
Your doctor may examine your eyes when you have a routine physical examination.

VISITING YOUR DOCTOR

THERE ARE SEVERAL reasons for visiting your doctor. You may need advice about symptoms or health issues, or your doctor may ask you to come in for regular checkups or to discuss ongoing treatment. What happens during the consultation depends on its purpose, but your doctor usually assesses your health by observation, asking you questions, and doing a physical examination. Samples may also be collected for testing.

You may decide to visit your doctor because you feel ill or because you are concerned about a physical change, such as a swelling or stiffness in a joint. You may need advice about a lifestyle change, such as losing weight. If you have a chronic disease, such as diabetes mellitus, you will need to have regular checkups. Even if you are healthy, your doctor may ask you to come in for a health checkup (p.40) at regular intervals, increasing in frequency as you become older.

PREPARING FOR A VISIT

Whatever your reason for visiting your doctor, you may find it helpful to think about what you want to discuss before the appointment. For example, if you have specific symptoms, you should think about how often they occur and whether certain activities bring the symptoms on or relieve them. Your doctor also needs to know about medications or supplements you are taking, allergies you have to particular treatments, and alternative therapies you are currently using.

THE CONSULTATION

There are many ways in which your doctor can assess your health. First of all, he or she will note your general appearance, such as your weight, and look for signs of anxiety or depression in your demeanor. Your doctor will then ask you a series of questions, known as taking your medical history, before he or she performs a physical examination. The questions that you are asked and the extent of the physical examination depend on the purpose of the consultation.

Family history
Some disorders may run in your family. Your doctor needs to know about these to help make a diagnosis.

If you are visiting a doctor for the first time, he or she may take a full medical history, including details of diseases that run in your family, illnesses you have had in the past, and lifestyle factors such as your diet. If your doctor already has your medical record, he or she may refer to it. If you have specific symptoms, the doctor will concentrate on them in order to make a diagnosis.

A full physical examination is usually given only in a general checkup, such as for health insurance or preventive care. If you have symptoms, the doctor usually checks only relevant areas of your body. Even if you are not given a full examination, your doctor may inspect certain parts of your body, such as your skin and nails, to assess your general health.

Your doctor may need to collect a sample, such as blood. Samples are tested to confirm a diagnosis or to monitor a disease. Simple tests can often be done in the doctor's office, but more complex procedures are done in a laboratory. The doctor may ask you to call for the results or return to the office to discuss them, or they may be summarized in a brief note.

(EQUIPMENT) THE DOCTOR'S BASIC EQUIPMENT

Your doctor may use one or more basic pieces of equipment when performing a physical examination. Each has a specific function. Some instruments enable your doctor to examine certain parts of the body more closely. Others are used to listen for abnormal sounds or to check the reflexes.

Aids to examination
An ophthalmoscope and otoscope are used to look at eyes and ears. Reflexes are tested with a hammer, and sounds, such as the heartbeat, can be heard with a stethoscope.

OTOSCOPE

STETHOSCOPE

OPHTHALMOSCOPE

REFLEX HAMMER

SETTING THE DOCTOR'S OFFICE

The office is designed to make the visit as efficient and comfortable as possible. The main part, the consultation room, provides privacy so that you can talk freely to the doctor. There is usually a separate area where basic information, such as height, can be gathered by a doctor, nurse, or physician's assistant. The examination may be performed in a different room containing all the necessary equipment, or the interview and exam may be done in the same room.

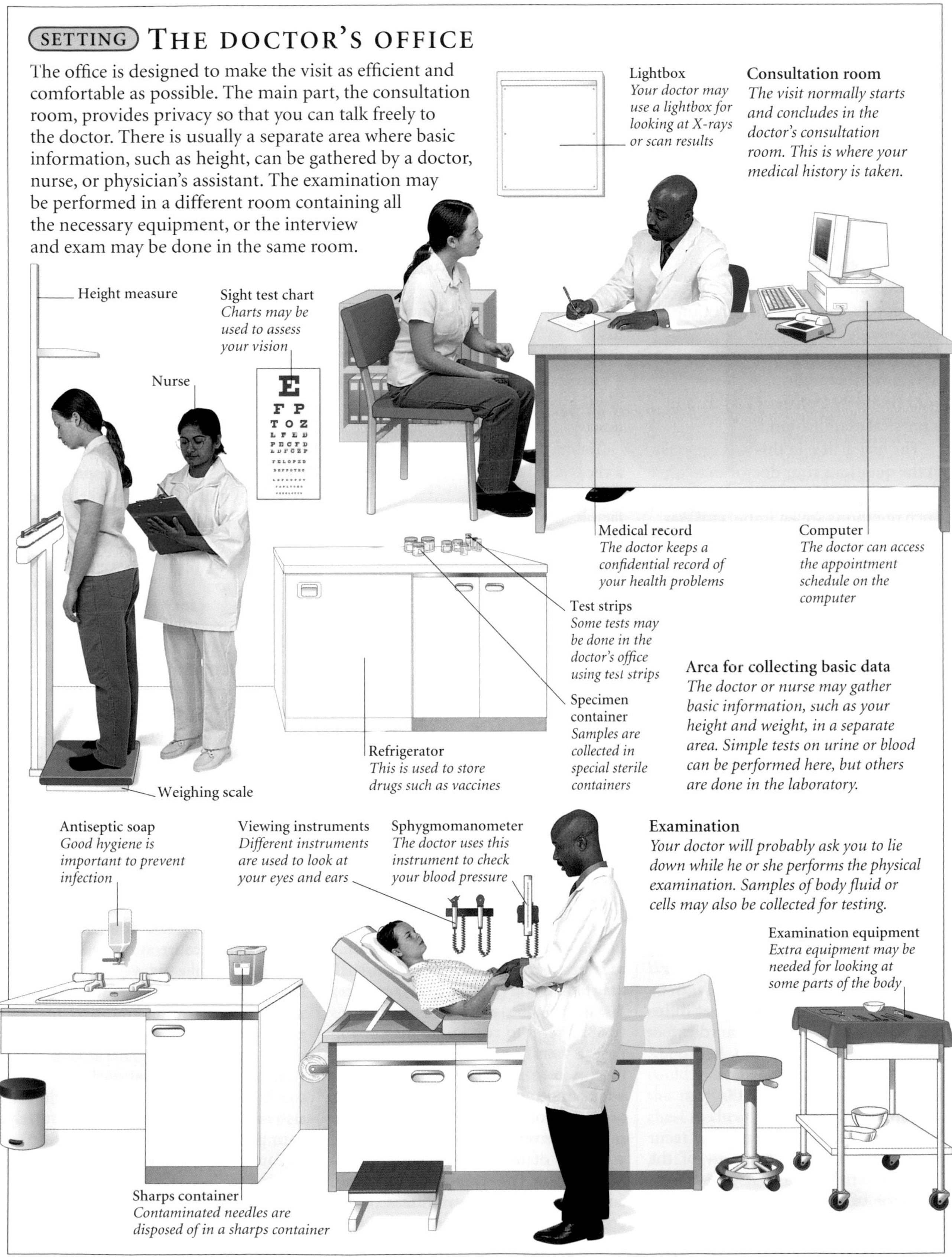
Lightbox
Your doctor may use a lightbox for looking at X-rays or scan results
Consultation room
The visit normally starts and concludes in the doctor's consultation room. This is where your medical history is taken.
Height measure
Sight test chart
Charts may be used to assess your vision
E
F P
T O Z
Nurse
Medical record
The doctor keeps a confidential record of your health problems
Computer
The doctor can access the appointment schedule on the computer
Test strips
Some tests may be done in the doctor's office using test strips
Specimen container
Samples are collected in special sterile containers
Area for collecting basic data
The doctor or nurse may gather basic information, such as your height and weight, in a separate area. Simple tests on urine or blood can be performed here, but others are done in the laboratory.
Refrigerator
This is used to store drugs such as vaccines
Weighing scale
Antiseptic soap
Good hygiene is important to prevent infection
Viewing instruments
Different instruments are used to look at your eyes and ears
Sphygmomanometer
The doctor uses this instrument to check your blood pressure
Examination
Your doctor will probably ask you to lie down while he or she performs the physical examination. Samples of body fluid or cells may also be collected for testing.
Examination equipment
Extra equipment may be needed for looking at some parts of the body
Sharps container
Contaminated needles are disposed of in a sharps container

(PROCEDURE) HAVING A BLOOD SAMPLE TAKEN

Blood samples can be used to screen for or diagnose a variety of different disorders. In adults, blood is usually taken from a vein on the inside of the elbow. The blood is drawn up through a needle and collected into one or more tubes, depending on the tests needed. The blood is then usually sent to a laboratory to be tested. Once blood has been taken, pressure is applied to the wound to prevent the vein from leaking, which may cause a bruise to develop.

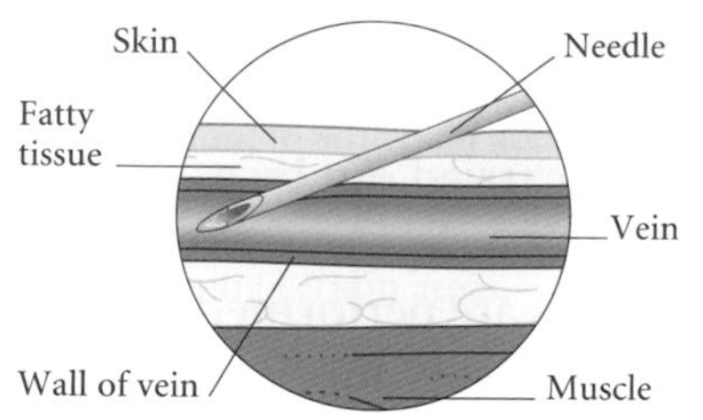
Skin
Needle
Fatty tissue
Vein
Wall of vein
Muscle

INSIDE THE VEIN

During the procedure
The skin around the vein is cleaned. A hollow needle attached to a syringe or vacuum tube is inserted into the vein and blood is taken.

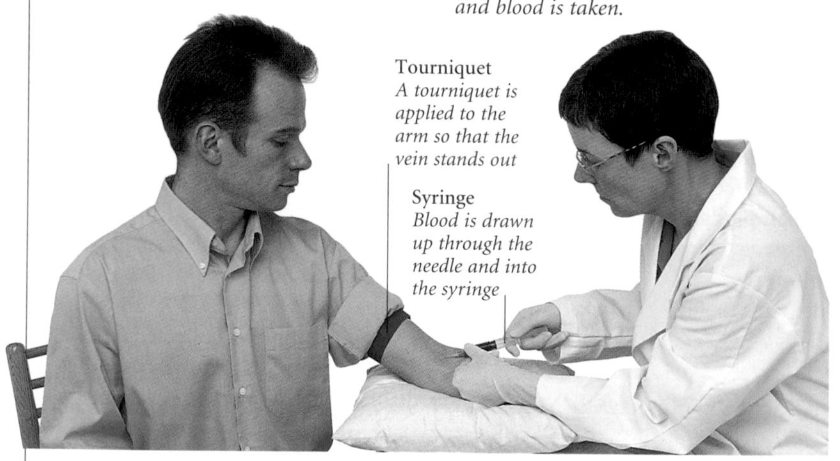

Tourniquet
A tourniquet is applied to the arm so that the vein stands out

Syringe
Blood is drawn up through the needle and into the syringe

laboratory. These may include tests for microorganisms (pp.234–235), chemical tests (pp.229–233), and genetic tests (pp.238–241), as well as tests designed to look at the different types and numbers of blood cells and their function (*see* TESTS ON BLOOD STRUCTURE AND FUNCTION, pp.226–228).

Urine samples

Quantities of urine collected to investigate the function of different body systems, particularly the kidneys and urinary tract

You may be asked to provide a urine sample when you visit the doctor for a health checkup (p.40) or if you have symptoms, such as frequent urination, that need investigation. Urine tests can provide information about the condition of the urinary tract to help your doctor confirm a diagnosis. The urine also reflects changes in blood chemistry associated with disorders of other systems, such as diabetes mellitus (p.687).

HOW ARE SAMPLES OBTAINED?

When you arrive at the doctor's office, the nurse may give you a container in which to collect a small sample of urine. Alternatively, you may be provided with a sterile container and asked to collect a urine sample at home.

Before you collect a urine sample, you should clean your genital area thoroughly with soap and water. You should then pass a small amount of urine into the toilet and stop urinating. When you start to urinate again, collect some of the urine in the sterile container. The first few drops of urine are not collected because they can become contaminated with bacteria as they pass from the normally sterile bladder through the urethra to the outside of the body. For some tests, you may need to collect all the urine that you pass during a 24-hour period.

If you need to collect a urine sample from a baby or a small child, your doctor may give you an adhesive bag and a sterile container. You should wash your child's genital area and attach the bag around his or her genitals. As soon as your child has urinated, you should transfer the urine sample to the sterile container. Alternatively, the doctor may use a catheter to take a urine sample. The catheter is passed through the urethra and up into the child's bladder. The catheter is removed when enough urine has been collected.

Your doctor may make a preliminary assessment of your urine in his or her office by doing simple tests to detect evidence of infection or traces of protein or blood (*see* DIPSTICK TESTING OF URINE, p.231). However, in many cases, the sample needs to be sent to the laboratory for further analysis (*see* ROUTINE URINE CHEMISTRY, p.230, and TESTS FOR MICROORGANISMS, pp.234–235).

Fecal samples

Small amounts of feces that are collected to screen for or diagnose disorders affecting the digestive system

Your doctor may ask you to provide a fecal sample if you have symptoms, such as diarrhea, that suggest a digestive condition, especially if they are likely to have been caused by an infection. In adults over age 50, a fecal sample may be required for an annual screening test designed to detect early signs of colorectal cancer (p.665).

In order to provide a fecal sample, you should defecate into a clean, wide-mouthed receptacle and then transfer a small sample to a container. Your doctor may give you a special container that has a spoon fixed to the inside of the lid to make this process easier. Try not to contaminate the sample with urine and avoid putting toilet paper in the container. If you pass liquid feces, you should collect both solid and liquid material together. If you need to collect a fecal sample from a baby, do not use the contents of a diaper because liquid feces will have been absorbed.

Some samples can be tested by the doctor in his or her office, but most are sent to a laboratory. Tests are most commonly done to look for microscopic amounts of blood in the feces (*see* FECAL OCCULT BLOOD TEST, p.233) or for evidence of infection (*see* TESTS FOR MICROORGANISMS, pp.234–235).

Samples of body fluids

Secretions and other body fluids obtained to diagnose a wide range of disorders

Some body fluids have a protective role, such as the mucus lining the respiratory tract and the fluid that surrounds the spinal cord. Other body fluids, such as pus from a wound or fluid surrounding a lung, form or increase in volume as a result of disease.

Most body fluids are collected to look for evidence of infection or for cancer. However, certain body fluids may be collected for other purposes. For example, the amniotic fluid that surrounds and protects a fetus in the womb contains shed fetal skin cells that can be used for genetic tests (*see* PRENATAL GENETIC TESTS, p.787), and semen can be analyzed to assess a man's fertility (*see* SEMEN ANALYSIS, p.777).

HOW ARE SAMPLES OBTAINED?

You can collect some samples yourself, including sputum, saliva, and semen. Your doctor may provide you with a sterile container for the sample. Other fluids, particularly those within body cavities or from a wound, are usually collected by a nurse or doctor.

Fluids or secretions from the skin surface or from mucous membranes, such as those lining the throat or the vagina, are usually collected on sterile cotton swabs (*see* HAVING A THROAT SWAB, below). In order to collect fluids from body cavities or internal organs, the doctor uses a hollow needle and a syringe. In some cases, local anesthesia is needed for this procedure. Particular techniques for collecting specific body fluids are covered in the section on your body and disease with the relevant body system. For example, joint aspiration (p.380), in which a small sample of fluid is taken from a swollen joint to determine the cause of swelling, is described in the section on joint disorders.

Fluid samples are usually sent to a laboratory for analysis. They may be examined for infection (*see* TESTS FOR MICROORGANISMS, pp.234–235), or the cells in the fluid may be separated and examined to detect other abnormalities (*see* CELL TESTS, p.236).

Cell and tissue samples

Individual cells or pieces of tissue obtained for screening or diagnostic tests

Cell and tissue samples are often used to diagnose disorders such as cancer. Collecting cell samples is a safe and usually painless procedure performed by a doctor or nurse. However, taking a tissue sample can sometimes involve a small risk of bleeding or damage to the surrounding organs and is often done in the hospital. Removal of a sample of tissue for examination is known as a biopsy. Tissue samples are usually taken only when other tests have failed to confirm a diagnosis or when a serious disease, such as cancer, is thought to have developed in a particular organ.

HOW ARE SAMPLES OBTAINED?

Samples of cells can sometimes be extracted from urine or other body fluids. For example, a urine sample may be spun at high speed in a machine called a centrifuge to separate the cells present in urine from the liquid. Cells may also be scraped painlessly from the tissue surfaces of a body cavity, such as the mouth or vagina. The Pap test (p.749), which screens for early signs of cancer of the cervix, analyzes cells scraped from the surface of the cervix and is the most common procedure using this technique. Cells can also be taken from a solid structure, such as a lump in the breast, with a needle and syringe (*see* ASPIRATION OF A BREAST LUMP, p.756).

In some circumstances, a larger piece of tissue is needed. Tissue samples may be taken from almost anywhere in the body, and the procedure used depends on the site. For example, samples of skin tissue are removed using a scalpel (*see* SKIN BIOPSY, p.344), and cores of tissue the size of a match may be removed from internal organs using a biopsy needle. For example, if cirrhosis of the liver is suspected, a sample of liver tissue is taken and analyzed to confirm the diagnosis and determine the severity of the disease (*see* LIVER BIOPSY, p.647). Tissue samples may also be obtained when tissue is removed for the treatment of a disorder.

Cell and tissue samples are examined under a microscope in a laboratory to look for abnormal cells (*see* CELL AND TISSUE TESTS, pp.236–237).

PROCEDURE HAVING A THROAT SWAB

If you have a sore throat, you may need to have a throat swab taken to see if you have a bacterial infection. The doctor or nurse holds your tongue down with a depressor and uses a plastic stick with a sterile cotton end (swab) to collect a fluid sample from your throat. The swab is then sent to a laboratory. The procedure can be carried out quickly in the doctor's office and is not painful. However, you may gag briefly when the swab touches your throat.

Swab
Tongue depressor
Tongue depressor
Back of throat
Palate
Tonsil
Swab
VIEW OF THROAT

During the procedure
The doctor holds your tongue down with a depressor and wipes a swab over your tonsils and the back of your throat.

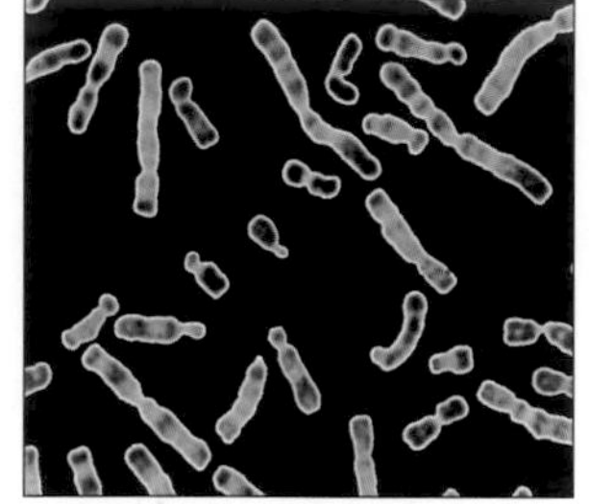
Magnified chromosomes
Chromosomes can be isolated from blood or cell samples in order to detect genetic disorders.

TESTING SAMPLES

TESTS CAN BE DONE on almost any body fluid or tissue. Most samples, such as blood and urine, are easy to obtain and are used for a wide range of tests, including some that you can carry out yourself at home. Other samples, such as tissue, are more difficult to collect and are usually taken only if other tests cannot provide enough information. Test results may be used to confirm a diagnosis, assess the extent of a disorder, screen for disease, or monitor a chronic condition or the effects of treatment.

Tests on samples are often the simplest and the quickest way for your doctor to confirm a suspected diagnosis or to assess your health. Having taken your medical history and examined you, your doctor may be left with certain questions. For example, he or she may want to know if particular organs have been affected by an illness.

The sample needed and the types of tests to be carried out depend on the information that is required. Blood and urine tests can check the function of various organs. Tests on feces may identify disorders of the digestive tract. Sputum or other body fluids, cells, or tissues may be tested to look for various diseases, such as cancer.

Sometimes, several tests are needed. For example, if a kidney or a liver disorder is suspected, a blood test may be done. If the result is abnormal and scans or other noninvasive techniques are inconclusive, a tissue sample may be taken to look for the cause. Often, just one type of test is used to monitor a chronic condition, such as diabetes mellitus, or to screen for disease, but it may be repeated at periodic intervals.

COMPARISON DIFFERENT TESTS AND SAMPLES

The test and sample chosen depend on the information that your doctor needs. Some samples, such as blood or urine, can be used for almost any test. For example, blood can be tested to assess levels of chemicals, search for infection, and assess numbers and types of blood cells. Other samples, such as tissue, are used for only a few tests, such as to look for cancer.

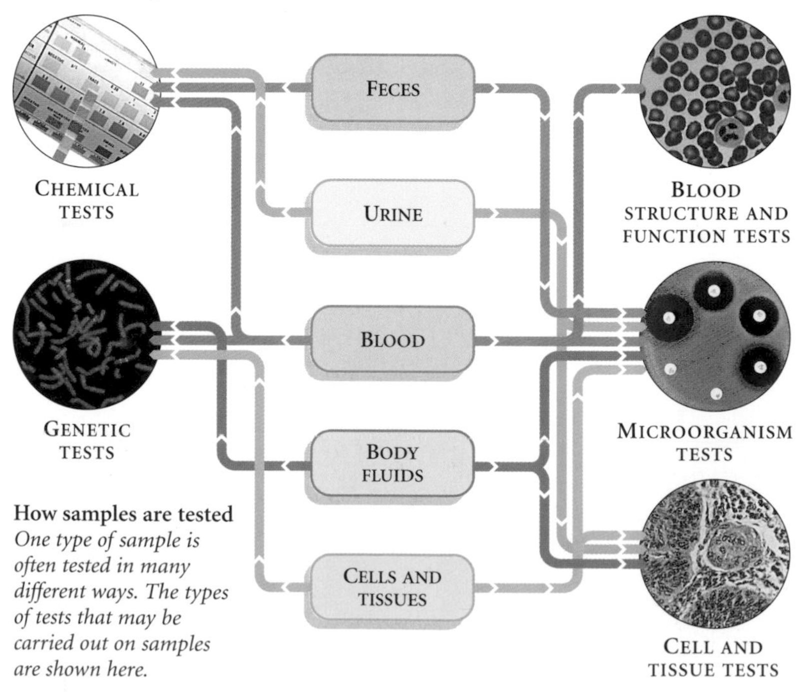
FECES
URINE
BLOOD
BODY FLUIDS
CELLS AND TISSUES
CHEMICAL TESTS
GENETIC TESTS
BLOOD STRUCTURE AND FUNCTION TESTS
MICROORGANISM TESTS
CELL AND TISSUE TESTS

How samples are tested
One type of sample is often tested in many different ways. The types of tests that may be carried out on samples are shown here.

TYPES OF TESTS

Many test results are measurements, such as the amount of a chemical in a sample. These tests are often done by automated machines that produce precise data rapidly, often in minutes. Such machines usually measure several substances in one sample and often process many samples at once.

Other tests rely on observations made by a trained technologist. These may include the presence of abnormal cells in a sample or the identification of a microorganism. Such tests require the samples to be carefully prepared before they are interpreted, and it may take up to 6 weeks to obtain a result.

A few tests, such as monitoring blood sugar levels in diabetes mellitus, can be carried out by yourself at home.

INTERPRETING RESULTS

When the test results are returned to your doctor, he or she assesses them to see if the tests have answered his or her questions. Occasionally, additional tests on samples may be needed. In other cases, further investigations, such as imaging tests, may be required. However, results of tests on samples often provide enough information to enable your doctor to make a diagnosis, assess the severity of a disorder, or decide on the best form of treatment.

SETTING THE MEDICAL LABORATORY

Laboratories contain a wide range of equipment, but they often specialize in one area of testing. For example, some laboratories contain automated machines that analyze blood and urine. Other laboratories may be used to examine tissue samples or to grow microorganisms from samples and examine them under the microscope. Three different types of laboratories are shown here.

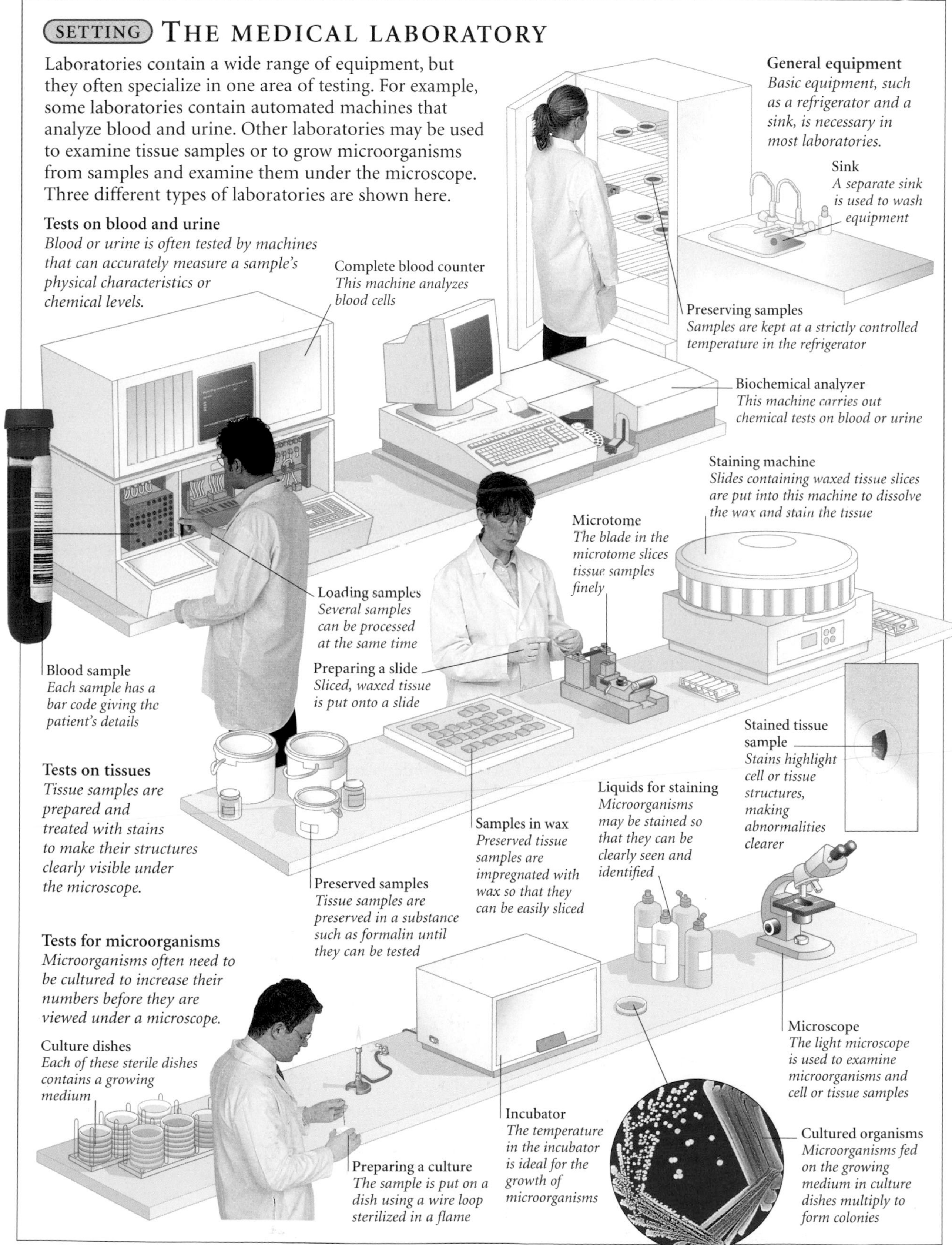

General equipment
Basic equipment, such as a refrigerator and a sink, is necessary in most laboratories.
Sink
A separate sink is used to wash equipment
Tests on blood and urine
Blood or urine is often tested by machines that can accurately measure a sample's physical characteristics or chemical levels.
Complete blood counter
This machine analyzes blood cells
Preserving samples
Samples are kept at a strictly controlled temperature in the refrigerator
Biochemical analyzer
This machine carries out chemical tests on blood or urine
Staining machine
Slides containing waxed tissue slices are put into this machine to dissolve the wax and stain the tissue
Microtome
The blade in the microtome slices tissue samples finely
Loading samples
Several samples can be processed at the same time
Blood sample
Each sample has a bar code giving the patient's details
Preparing a slide
Sliced, waxed tissue is put onto a slide
Stained tissue sample
Stains highlight cell or tissue structures, making abnormalities clearer
Tests on tissues
Tissue samples are prepared and treated with stains to make their structures clearly visible under the microscope.
Liquids for staining
Microorganisms may be stained so that they can be clearly seen and identified
Samples in wax
Preserved tissue samples are impregnated with wax so that they can be easily sliced
Preserved samples
Tissue samples are preserved in a substance such as formalin until they can be tested
Tests for microorganisms
Microorganisms often need to be cultured to increase their numbers before they are viewed under a microscope.
Microscope
The light microscope is used to examine microorganisms and cell or tissue samples
Culture dishes
Each of these sterile dishes contains a growing medium
Incubator
The temperature in the incubator is ideal for the growth of microorganisms
Cultured organisms
Microorganisms fed on the growing medium in culture dishes multiply to form colonies
Preparing a culture
The sample is put on a dish using a wire loop sterilized in a flame

TESTS ON BLOOD STRUCTURE AND FUNCTION

Tests on the composition of blood are some of the most common methods used to look for disease, and may also be done routinely to assess general health. They may be carried out on any blood components: red blood cells, white blood cells, tiny cells called platelets, and proteins, all of which are carried in liquid plasma.

This section describes the tests most commonly performed on a blood sample to measure the amounts of the various blood components and investigate their structures. Tests that measure the chemicals carried in the blood are discussed elsewhere (*see* CHEMICAL TESTS, pp.229–233).

The first article discusses tests that measure the number of the different types of cells in the blood and look at their structure to help diagnose a wide range of diseases and disorders.

Proteins attached to red blood cells determine a person's blood group, and these proteins can be identified using blood typing tests, which are discussed next. Blood typing is done on donated blood and on people before surgical procedures to ensure that if a blood transfusion is needed, blood of the correct group is given.

Blood clotting tests, which are used to diagnose disorders in which blood either does not clot properly or clots too readily, are also covered. These tests assess the time it takes for blood to clot. They also measure the levels of proteins in the blood called clotting factors and levels of platelets, both of which are necessary for blood clotting. Finally, immune function tests, which assess the immune system's strength and identify immune disorders, are discussed. These tests measure blood components that fight infection, such as antibodies and white blood cells.

Examining blood
In a laboratory, scientists use automated machines to perform tests on blood to assess health and diagnose disease.

Blood cell tests

Studies to detect abnormalities in the numbers or structure of blood cells

Blood contains three main cell types: red blood cells containing hemoglobin (an oxygen-carrying pigment); white blood cells, which help protect the body against disease; and platelets, which are tiny cells that play a role in blood clotting. Blood cell tests can help doctors diagnose diseases of the blood or bone marrow (where blood cells are made). The tests may also be used to look for evidence of infection or inflammation because both involve an immune reaction that increases the number of white blood cells in the circulation.

WHAT MIGHT BE STUDIED?

The different types of cells in a known volume of blood may be counted by an automated machine to give a complete blood count. The structure of the blood cells may also be examined by smearing a drop of blood onto a glass slide and looking at it under a microscope.

COMPLETE BLOOD COUNT In this test, a machine counts the numbers of red and white blood cells and platelets in a cubic milliliter of blood. A complete blood count also measures the sizes of the cells, the proportion of the blood that is made up of red blood cells (the hematocrit), and the hemoglobin level in the red blood cells.

If a lower than normal number of red blood cells or a low level of hemoglobin is found, a diagnosis of anemia (p.446) may be made. The average size of the red blood cells may give a clue to the cause of anemia. For example, if the red blood cells are small and pale, the anemia may be due to a deficiency in iron, which is needed to make hemoglobin. Red blood cells that are larger than normal may indicate that vitamin deficiency is a more likely cause of the anemia.

A much higher than normal number of white blood cells may be caused by the bone marrow disorder leukemia (p.453). However, a moderately raised number of white blood cells is usually due to infection or inflammation in the body. There are many different types of white blood cells, and an increase in one type may indicate the cause of the infection or inflammation. For example, an increase in the number of white blood cells known as neutrophils may be a sign of bacterial infection, and an increase in the number of cells called eosinophils may be a sign of an allergy.

If the total number of white blood cells is lower than normal, the immune system may be weakened. This may be

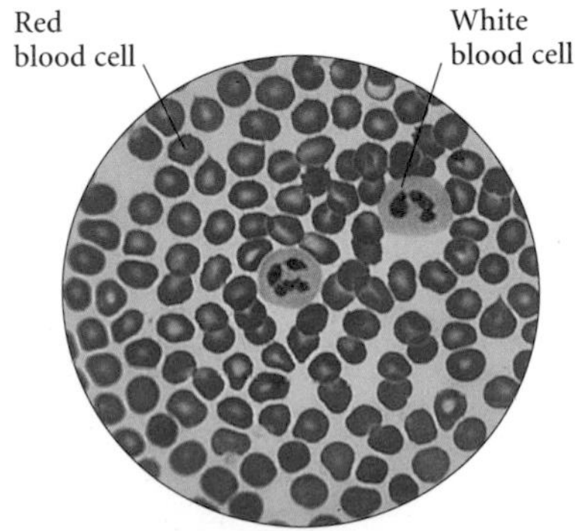
Red blood cell
White blood cell

Cells in a blood smear
This highly magnified view of a drop of blood smeared on a slide shows normal red and white blood cells.

the result of chemotherapy (p.278), malnutrition, or HIV infection (*see* HIV INFECTION AND AIDS, p.295).

Platelets play an important part in preventing bleeding by helping blood clots form. A lower than normal number of platelets present in the blood is a condition known as thrombocytopenia (p.453), which can lead to excessive bruising or internal bleeding.

BLOOD SMEAR If information about the structure of blood cells is needed, a drop of blood is smeared onto a slide to form a thin film called a blood smear. The blood is stained with special dyes to make the cells more visible, and the slide is examined under a microscope by a trained technologist. A blood smear may be used to detect parasites in the blood, such as those that cause malaria (p.305). A blood smear can also identify cells with abnormal shapes that cannot be detected in an automated cell count, such as sickle-shaped red blood cells, which are a characteristic feature of sickle-cell anemia (p.448).

WILL I NEED FURTHER TESTS?

If blood cell tests indicate anemia, you may have chemical tests (pp.229–233) to measure the levels of vitamins and minerals in your blood that are needed for the production of red blood cells. If there is an abnormal number of white blood cells, your doctor may arrange for immune function tests (p.228) that assess the immune system's strength or tests for microorganisms (pp.234–235) to identify possible infections. You may also have tests that examine the bone marrow to see if blood cell production is impaired (*see* BONE MARROW ASPIRATION AND BIOPSY, p.451).

Blood typing

Identifying proteins on red blood cells to establish a person's blood group

Blood typing is a method of identifying your blood group, which is determined by proteins, called antigens, on the surfaces of the red blood cells (*see* BLOOD GROUPS, p.441). The fluid part of the blood (the plasma) contains antibodies that will react with antigens of a different blood group, causing the red blood cells to stick together. The clumps of red blood cells are then attacked by the immune system, which may lead to internal bleeding or hemolytic anemia (p.450). Blood typing is therefore an essential test for safe blood transfusions and is carried out before surgery in case a blood transfusion (p.447) is needed during the operation. If you donate blood, your blood group is identified through blood typing so that it can be used in someone of the correct blood group. Blood typing may also be used to help determine paternity.

WHAT MIGHT BE STUDIED?

There are at least 20 ways of classifying blood. The major blood types, which are the ones tested for most often, are ABO and Rh (Rhesus). Testing blood for minor blood types is not normally necessary. However, if you have regular blood transfusions, you may develop antibodies to one of the minor blood group antigens, and your blood may need to be tested for these.

ABO TYPES This blood typing system consists of four blood groups: A, B, AB, and O. Type A is the most common in white North Americans (found in about 45 percent of people), followed by type O (43 percent), type B (8 percent), and type AB (4 percent). These proportions vary among different ethnic groups. For example, type O blood group is found in 50 percent of African–Americans.

RH TYPES Blood is classified as either Rh positive or Rh negative, although in reality the system is more complex. About 3 in 20 people in Canada are Rh negative. The Rh system is tested for during pregnancy because, if the mother is Rh negative and the fetus is Rh positive, the mother may produce antibodies against Rh factor in the fetal blood (*see* RHESUS INCOMPATIBILITY, p.795).

HOW IS IT DONE?

There are many different blood typing tests, but they are all based on the reaction between antibodies and antigens. Antibodies against the different blood groups are added to a blood sample. The blood group can be determined by seeing if the cells then form visible clumps or not. For example, if a blood sample forms clumps only when it is mixed with antibodies to type A blood, the blood group is A. If clumps form when the blood sample is mixed with antibodies to both type A and B blood, the blood group is AB.

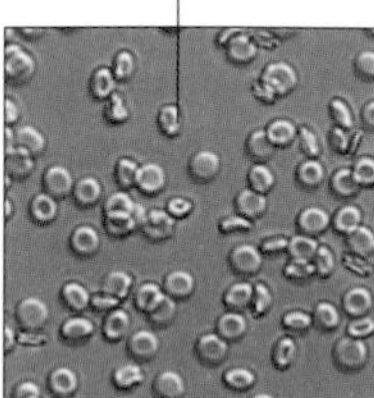
Separate red blood cell

NO REACTION

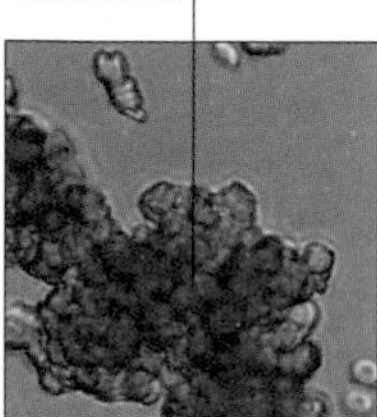
Clumped red blood cells

REACTION

Identifying blood groups
Blood groups are identified by mixing samples of blood with antibodies against known blood groups and watching for a reaction that makes the red blood cells stick together to form a clump.

WILL I NEED FURTHER TESTS?

If a transfusion is needed during an operation, a small amount of the blood that is to be transfused is mixed with a sample of your own blood. This test is called cross-matching and is used to exclude the small possibility that the transfused blood is incompatible with yours because of a reaction between antibodies and antigens of one of the minor blood groups.

Blood clotting tests

Tests that are used to identify and assess abnormalities in the blood clotting process

When blood vessels are damaged, clots normally form in order to stop bleeding. Clots start to form when platelets (very small blood cells) clump together and stick to the lining of the damaged blood vessel. These clumped platelets release chemicals that act on dissolved proteins in the blood known as clotting factors. This process leads to the formation of a clot that seals the vessel and prevents further bleeding. Other substances in blood, known as anticlotting factors, stop the blood from clotting spontaneously in undamaged vessels. Blood clotting tests will be performed if you have symptoms that suggest your blood is clotting either more slowly than is usual (*see* BLEEDING DISORDERS, p.451) or more readily than is usual (*see* HYPERCOAGULABILITY, p.453).

enzyme gamma glutamyl transferase is an especially reliable measure of liver damage due to alcohol (*see* ALCOHOL-RELATED LIVER DISEASE, p.646).

Other blood tests to look for liver damage measure the levels of chemicals in the blood that are usually broken down by the liver or proteins produced by the liver. One test measures bilirubin, which is formed when red blood cells break down and is excreted by the liver in bile. A high blood level of bilirubin may indicate that the liver is not working properly or that there are blockages, such as gallstones, in the bile ducts (*see* JAUNDICE, p.643). Measuring blood levels of albumin, one of the proteins made by the liver, is an important means of detecting long-standing damage to the liver because often there are no symptoms until the damage is irreversible (*see* CIRRHOSIS, p.647).

TESTS FOR MUSCLE DAMAGE These tests can detect chemicals that are released when skeletal or heart muscle is damaged. When skeletal muscle is damaged, an enzyme called creatine kinase leaks into the blood. Raised blood levels may indicate damage due to many different disorders that affect skeletal muscle, ranging from muscle tears to muscular dystrophy (p.826). The tests are therefore of limited use in making a definite diagnosis. However, a particular type of creatine kinase occurs only in the heart muscle, and measurements can indicate if a heart attack (*see* MYOCARDIAL INFARCTION, p.410) has occurred. Levels of this chemical peak about 24 hours after a heart attack and remain high for about 3 days following the attack.

Another substance that can be measured is troponin, a protein that occurs exclusively in heart muscle and enters the blood only when the heart muscle is damaged. Since troponin is released into the blood within a few hours of a heart attack, it often provides the earliest confirmation of a heart attack. The amount of troponin detected provides a measure of the amount of damage caused to heart muscle by a heart attack.

TESTS FOR BONE MINERALS Most of the calcium and phosphate in the body is found in the bones, with a tiny amount in the blood. These minerals constantly move between the bones and the blood, and this movement is regulated by parathyroid hormone and vitamin D.

Tests for bone minerals help diagnose disorders that result in higher than normal levels of minerals being released from the bones, such as bone tumors and overactivity of the parathyroid gland (*see* HYPERPARATHYROIDISM, p.682). One test measures the enzyme alkaline phosphatase because high levels are associated with conditions in which bone is broken down and built up again at an increased rate, such as Paget's disease of the bone (p.370).

WILL I NEED FURTHER TESTS?

If routine blood tests are abnormal, you may need further tests before a diagnosis can be made. For example, X-rays (p.244) or ultrasound scanning (p.250) may be done to image the organ that is thought to be affected. A tissue sample may be taken for examination under a microscope. If a heart attack is suspected, you may require an ECG (p.406), during which heart rate and rhythm are recorded. After a heart attack, blood tests may be repeated at regular intervals to monitor your progress.

TECHNIQUE ANALYSIS OF BLOOD OR URINE

Most chemical tests on blood or urine are carried out by a machine called a biochemical analyzer, which can measure a range of substances. Tests on blood are carried out on the liquid part (the plasma) after all of the cells have been removed. The sample is mixed with a chemical that changes color according to how much of a substance is in the sample. The machine measures the intensity of color with a light beam.

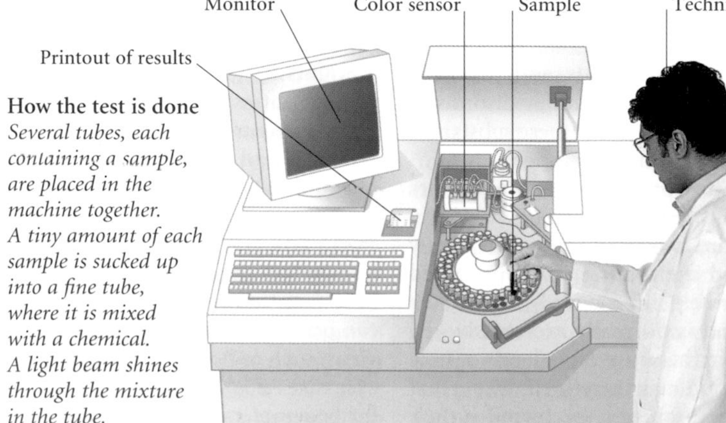
Monitor
Color sensor
Sample
Technician
Printout of results

How the test is done
Several tubes, each containing a sample, are placed in the machine together. A tiny amount of each sample is sucked up into a fine tube, where it is mixed with a chemical. A light beam shines through the mixture in the tube.

Routine urine chemistry

Measurement of chemicals in urine that may reflect the health of certain body systems, particularly the urinary tract

Urine consists of waste products filtered from the blood by the kidneys in a mixture with water, salts, and other chemicals. Abnormal levels of chemicals or salts in the urine, or the presence of substances not normally found in urine, may indicate a problem with the filtering ability of the kidneys. In addition, some hormonal disorders alter body chemistry and may affect the composition of urine. Urine tests can be used to help in making a diagnosis or in monitoring such disorders.

Most urine tests are quick and painless, simply requiring a urine sample and the appropriate dipstick test (*see* DIPSTICK TESTING OF URINE, opposite page). They can be easily done in the doctor's office and are usually the first tests to be performed. More detailed urine testing (*see* ANALYSIS OF BLOOD OR URINE, left) may be helpful in the assessment of some hormonal and kidney disorders. Occasionally, your doctor may wish to monitor a kidney problem by measuring the amount of a chemical, such as protein, excreted in the urine over a period of 24 hours.

TECHNIQUE DIPSTICK TESTING OF URINE

By using a special test dipstick, a sample of urine can quickly be tested in the doctor's office for a range of chemicals, including glucose, blood, enzymes, and protein. Nitrites from bacteria can also be detected. Squares of chemically impregnated paper along a stick change color when they react with one of the test substances. The intensity of the color change shows the amount of substance that is present in the urine.

Test stick
Each square on the stick tests for a different chemical

Urine sample

Color chart
The chart has several rows of colors, showing possible results of the tests

Test stick
The stick is held against the chart to find a color match

1 *The test stick is introduced into the urine. Chemicals in the squares along the stick react to give a color change.*

2 *After specified amounts of time, the colors of the squares on the stick are compared to the chart. The colors on the stick indicate the concentration of different substances in the urine sample.*

WHAT MIGHT BE STUDIED?

Substances commonly measured using a dipstick in urine are glucose, proteins, calcium, and creatinine. In addition to chemical tests, a urine sample may also be examined under the microscope to look for microorganisms (*see* TESTS FOR MICROORGANISMS, p.234–235), blood cells, and other elements that can provide evidence of underlying disease.

GLUCOSE Although glucose is not usually found in urine, some may appear if the glucose level in blood is abnormally high. The presence of glucose in urine may indicate diabetes mellitus (p.687), although the appearance of glucose in urine can be normal during pregnancy.

PROTEINS Healthy people do not usually excrete proteins in urine because they are too large to be filtered from the blood by the kidneys. Proteins may be found in the urine if there is a problem with the filtering units of the kidneys, as in glomerulonephritis (p.699).

CALCIUM To maintain the balance of calcium in the body, small amounts are normally excreted in urine. Hormone disorders, such as hyperparathyroidism (p.682), disturb this balance. Such disorders often result in an increased level of calcium in the urine because of a high level of calcium in the blood.

CREATININE Tests for creatinine levels in the urine can show if the kidneys are filtering this waste product out of the blood effectively. If the kidneys are not functioning normally, there will be a low level of creatinine in the urine and a high level in the blood. The creatinine clearance test compares the level of creatinine in a blood sample (*see* ROUTINE BLOOD CHEMISTRY, p.229) with the level in urine collected over 24 hours.

WILL I NEED FURTHER TESTS?

If the results of urine tests are abnormal, other tests, such as blood tests, will probably be needed in order to confirm a diagnosis or to monitor treatment. If protein is detected in the urine, further tests may be needed to determine how much protein is excreted and diagnose the underlying disorder.

If urine tests suggest a problem with your kidneys, you may need to undergo imaging procedures, such as ultrasound scanning (p.250) or MRI (p.248), to look for kidney abnormalities.

Blood cholesterol tests

Measurement of the levels of cholesterols and other lipids (fatty substances), such as triglycerides, in the blood

Blood cholesterol tests are carried out to measure levels of the lipids (fatty substances) cholesterol and triglycerides in the blood. Although lipids are necessary for the normal functioning of the body, a high level of these substances in the blood increases the risk that they will form fatty deposits in arteries (*see* ATHEROSCLEROSIS, p.402). These fatty deposits narrow the arteries, restricting blood flow, and may result in coronary artery disease (p.405) and stroke (p.532).

Some medical organizations recommend that everyone over age 20 should have a blood cholesterol test at least every 5 years (*see* SCREENING, p.42). This is particularly important if you are at increased risk of heart disease or stroke because you smoke, are overweight, have diabetes mellitus (p.687), or have a family history of heart disease or elevated lipid levels (*see* INHERITED HYPERLIPOPROTEINEMIAS, p.692).

WHAT MIGHT BE STUDIED?

Blood cholesterol tests measure the total level of cholesterol, other lipids such as triglycerides, and the amounts of two types of cholesterol in the blood, known as HDL (high-density lipoprotein) and LDL (low-density lipoprotein). HDL seems to have a protective effect against atherosclerosis, whereas a high blood level of LDL is a risk factor (*see* HYPERCHOLESTEROLEMIA, p.691).

If your blood cholesterol levels are high, the test may be repeated after an overnight fast to make sure that the high cholesterol level was not partly due to a recent meal. If you are found to have an unexpectedly high cholesterol level, your doctor may carry out other blood tests in order to exclude the possibility that an underlying disorder such as diabetes mellitus (p. 687) or hypothyroidism (p.680) is the cause of the condition.

HOW ARE THE RESULTS INTERPRETED?

Your doctor will take into account your other risk factors for coronary artery disease when discussing the results of the cholesterol tests with you.

Your doctor may also measure the triglycerides in the blood. Depending on the results of the test, your doctor may advise you about making changes to your diet or may prescribe lipid-lowering drugs (p.935) to reduce excessive levels of lipids, or both.

Hormone tests

Measurement of chemicals produced by the endocrine glands

Hormones are a group of chemicals that are mainly secreted by glands of the endocrine system, particularly the pituitary gland, thyroid gland, adrenal glands, ovaries, and testes. Hormone tests measure the levels of these chemicals to determine whether a gland is producing abnormal amounts of hormones. The tests may be performed if you have symptoms, such as fatigue, a change in weight, or menstrual problems, that could be the result of a hormonal disorder. Hormone tests may also be carried out to investigate the cause of infertility, abnormal growth in children, or early or delayed puberty. A common reason for having a hormone test is to confirm a pregnancy.

Most hormone tests are carried out on blood samples. However, in some cases, tests measure the amount of a hormone excreted in the urine over 24 hours or the level of a specific hormone in the urine. Measurements of hormones are usually performed automatically by a machine in the laboratory (*see* ANALYSIS OF BLOOD OR URINE, p.230). However, pregnancy tests can be done easily at home by using an over-the-counter test kit (*see* HOME PREGNANCY TEST, below).

WHAT ARE THE TYPES?

In some cases, a diagnosis can be made by using a basic test, in which the level of hormones produced by a gland is measured. If basic tests are insufficient to make a diagnosis, you may need hormone stimulation tests, which establish whether a disorder is caused by faulty control of a gland rather than by an abnormality in the gland itself.

BASIC HORMONE TESTS Sometimes, a diagnosis can be made by detecting or measuring the level of one hormone only. For example, the placental hormone human chorionic gonadotropin (HCG) is usually produced only during pregnancy, and therefore its presence is diagnostic of pregnancy. However, the level of hormones produced by one gland is often controlled by hormones that are made by the pituitary gland or hypothalamus in the brain. In some cases, tests that measure the level of the controlling hormone also need to be done. For example, in suspected thyroid disorders, it is routine to measure the level of thyroid stimulating hormone (TSH), the pituitary hormone that stimulates the thyroid gland to produce thyroxine. The level of thyroxine may also be analyzed to determine if the gland is still secreting this hormone. Analysis of TSH levels provides the doctor with additional information about the underlying cause of a thyroid hormone imbalance and helps him or her choose the appropriate treatment.

HORMONE STIMULATION TESTS These tests are used to make a diagnosis when it is known that there is a disorder of hormone production, but the underlying cause needs to be identified. For example, if low levels of both thyroid hormones and TSH have been found, the pituitary gland may be responsible. To establish whether the fault is with the pituitary gland, you may be given a drug that should stimulate a healthy pituitary gland to produce TSH. If the gland fails to produce TSH in response to the drug, your doctor will know that a pituitary gland disorder is responsible for the hormonal imbalance.

TECHNIQUE HOME PREGNANCY TEST

Pregnancy testing kits are available from pharmacies and allow pregnancy testing to be carried out at home. All of the kits test for the hormone human chorionic gonadotropin (HCG) in a sample of urine. This hormone is normally produced only by a developing placenta, and therefore the tests are extremely accurate, even early in pregnancy. Details for using a test vary among different brands.

1 *The test stick, which has been treated with a chemical that reacts with HCG, is dipped into a sample of urine, usually collected first thing in the morning. Make sure that you follow the manufacturer's instructions.*

Result window

Chemically treated part of test stick

Urine

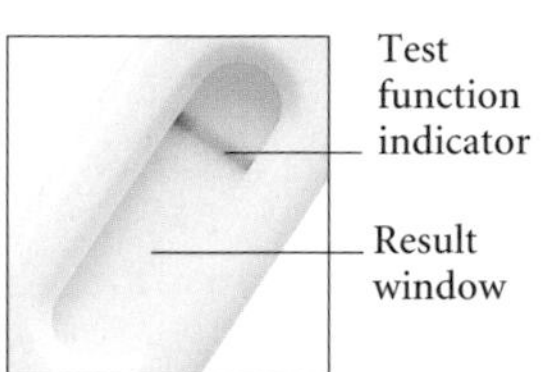
Test function indicator
Result window

NEGATIVE RESULT

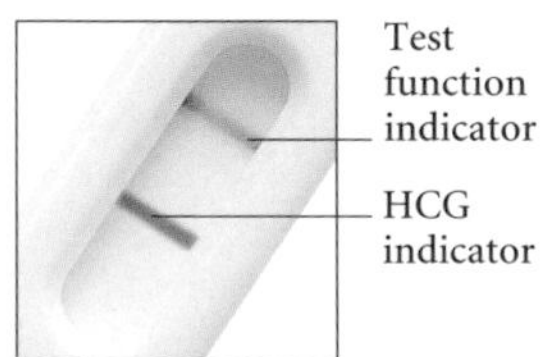
Test function indicator
HCG indicator

POSITIVE RESULT

2 *The result is obtained a few minutes later. In the test shown here, a thick line becomes visible in the result window if the test has worked. Another line appears in the window if HCG is present.*

Tests for inflammation

Measurement of chemicals in blood that change in response to inflammation

The body responds to inflammation caused by damage or infection by producing higher than normal amounts of particular proteins, the inflammatory proteins. The common tests for inflammation are based on assessment of the levels of these proteins in the blood.

Tests for inflammation are often the first tests that may be carried out when you see your doctor with unexplained symptoms. The tests are used to detect inflammation in the body that would otherwise not be apparent, such as that caused by an infection. The tests may also be used to monitor the progression of certain inflammatory disorders, such as rheumatoid arthritis (p.377), and to assess their response to treatment.

WHAT ARE THE TYPES?

One of the most specific indicators of inflammation is the inflammatory protein C-reactive protein. Measuring the level of this protein in the blood is therefore an important means of finding out whether inflammation is present and assessing its severity. C-reactive protein may be measured directly by a machine (*see* ANALYSIS OF BLOOD OR URINE, p.230). Since inflammatory proteins increase the clumping together of red blood cells (erythrocytes), this effect can be observed as an indirect means of measuring levels of these proteins.

C-REACTIVE PROTEIN MEASUREMENTS

The level of C-reactive protein in the blood rises and falls rapidly in association with the severity of inflammation. Therefore, testing for C-reactive protein is useful for assessing a response to treatment because the levels may fall following an effective treatment even before any symptoms of inflammation have started to subside.

ERYTHROCYTE SEDIMENTATION TEST

This test measures the rate at which red blood cells settle to the bottom of a sample of blood, leaving the liquid part of the blood at the top. If inflammation is present, the red blood cells clump together and settle more rapidly than usual. The speed at which the red blood cells settle, called the erythrocyte sedimentation rate (ESR), is related to the severity of inflammation.

WILL I NEED FURTHER TESTS?

Tests for inflammation may indicate the severity of the inflammation, but they do not diagnose the cause or reveal the site. If the result of a test for inflammation is positive, a variety of different disorders could be the cause, including infections due to bacteria or viruses, an autoimmune disorder, or widespread cancer. You may need to provide a further blood sample or a urine sample so that they can be tested for infection (*see* TESTS FOR MICROORGANISMS, p.234) or an autoimmune disease, such as rheumatoid arthritis (*see* IMMUNE FUNCTION TESTS, p.228). Imaging procedures, such as X-rays (p.244), radionuclide scanning (p.251), or MRI (p.248), may also be needed to find a tumor or detect the site of inflammation, such as an abscess.

Tumor marker tests

Measurements of blood proteins that are produced by cells in tumors

A few cancerous tumors produce substances, such as proteins or hormones, that can be detected in blood and, in some cases, in urine. These substances are known as tumor markers. Tumor marker tests are used to detect the levels of these substances in a person with cancer or in someone who is suspected of having cancer as a result of symptoms or other diagnostic tests.

Tumor marker measurements are usually carried out automatically by a machine in the laboratory (*see* ANALYSIS OF BLOOD OR URINE, p.230).

WHY AM I HAVING THE TESTS?

Tumor marker tests are usually used to assess the response of a tumor to treatments such as chemotherapy (p.278) and surgery. The level of a marker can indicate whether the tumor has been completely removed or eradicated or if cancer had spread to other areas of the body before treatment. Repeated measurements of tumor marker levels may be used to monitor how the cancer is responding to courses of treatment. A sudden rise in the marker levels may indicate a recurrence of the tumor.

WHAT MIGHT BE STUDIED?

Some of the tumor markers most commonly tested for are present in small amounts in healthy people. For example, although prostate cancer (p.726) is often associated with a rise in the blood level of prostate specific antigen (PSA), this protein is found at low levels in the blood of all men. The hormone human chorionic gonadotropin (HCG) is normally produced by the placenta during pregnancy. However, HCG is also associated with cancer of the testis (p.719) and choriocarcinoma (p.748), a cancer that develops in the uterus.

WILL I NEED FURTHER TESTS?

In most cases, tumor marker tests are repeated at intervals in order to monitor the effects of treatment. Blood tests and imaging tests, such as MRI (p.248), CT scanning (p.247), or radionuclide scanning (p.251), may be used to detect the spread of the cancer.

Fecal occult blood test

A test on a sample of feces to detect small amounts of blood that are not visible to the naked eye

A fecal occult blood test detects small amounts of blood invisible to the naked eye that may be contained in a sample of feces. Nonvisible (occult) blood may be due to a disorder that causes bleeding in the digestive tract, such as polyps in the colon (p.660), gastritis (p.640), or colorectal cancer (p.665).

WHY AM I HAVING THE TEST?

Annual testing for fecal occult blood may be recommended as a screening test for colorectal cancer in anyone over age 50 (*see* SCREENING, p.42). You may also have the test if you have symptoms such as abdominal pain or if you have anemia (p.446) due to unrecognized blood loss. There are various causes of this kind of anemia, and a fecal occult blood test can show if the blood is being lost from your digestive system. However, the test cannot identify which part of the digestive tract is bleeding.

HOW IS IT DONE?

The test is performed by smearing a sample of feces onto a piece of paper or stool card and adding a chemical to the sample. If a color change occurs, occult blood is present. The doctor may perform the test in his or her office or send the sample to be tested in a laboratory, or you may be asked to apply stool samples to indicator cards and bring them to the doctor. Over-the-counter tests are also available from the pharmacy for home use. These tests work in a similar way to the laboratory tests.

WILL I NEED FURTHER TESTS?

The test is usually repeated three times over several days. This is because blood may not appear in every fecal sample. If blood is present, further tests will be carried out to look for the cause. An endoscope (viewing tube) may be used to examine the digestive tract and identify the cause of the bleeding (*see* ENDOSCOPY, p.255). Alternatively, contrast X-rays (p.245) are sometimes used to image the digestive tract to look for disorders, such as ulcers or tumors, that may cause bleeding.

TESTS FOR MICROORGANISMS

Although many diseases due to microorganisms can be prevented by immunization or effectively treated by drugs, infectious diseases are still a major cause of illness and death worldwide. Identifying microorganisms responsible for disease is an essential step in the diagnosis and treatment of infectious illnesses.

Tests to identify microorganisms that cause infections play an increasingly important role in medicine today. Tests for bacteria may also play a part in diagnosing noninfectious diseases. For example, one specific species of bacterium, *Helicobacter pylori*, is a key cause of peptic ulcers.

This section begins by discussing traditional tests to identify organisms, such as cultures and microscopy. Some organisms are becoming resistant to the drugs used to treat them, especially antibiotics, and drug sensitivity tests used to detect this are also covered.

More modern techniques identify microorganisms using proteins on the surface of the organism, known as antigens, or specific antibodies made by the body in response to infection. Other tests use the organism's genetic material. These tests are covered last and can identify an infectious organism within hours or even minutes.

Examining a culture
Laboratories use special culture plates containing nutrients to grow large numbers of organisms from a sample. The organisms can then be identified.

Microscopy for infectious agents

Microscopic examination to detect or identify harmful microorganisms

Most microorganisms, such as bacteria, fungi, and viruses, are too small to see without a microscope. In microscopy, highly magnified images of organisms are produced using a microscope so that the microorganisms can be seen and identified. Microscopy can be done on any type of sample from the body, such as blood, urine, or other body fluids.

Sometimes, a test sample is examined immediately in the doctor's office or in the laboratory. For example, a sample of urine may be examined under a microscope to identify bacteria. However, a sample often contains so few organisms that they cannot be found easily. In these cases, the microorganisms may be grown (cultured) in order to increase their numbers before microscopy or other tests are performed (*see* CULTURE AND TESTS FOR DRUG SENSITIVITY, right).

HOW IS IT DONE?

Different microscopes are used to identify different organisms. For example, bacteria are usually identified using a light microscope. Viruses, much smaller than bacteria, are examined with a more powerful electron microscope.

Most samples are treated with stains before viewing to aid the detection and identification of any microorganisms they contain. The Gram stain is one of the most commonly used stains for differentiating between the different types of bacteria. Samples to be examined using an electron microscope have to be set in wax, thinly sliced, and coated with metals beforehand.

When the samples have been prepared, any microorganisms present are studied under a microscope. Different types of microorganisms can be recognized by their size, their shape, and how they react with the stains.

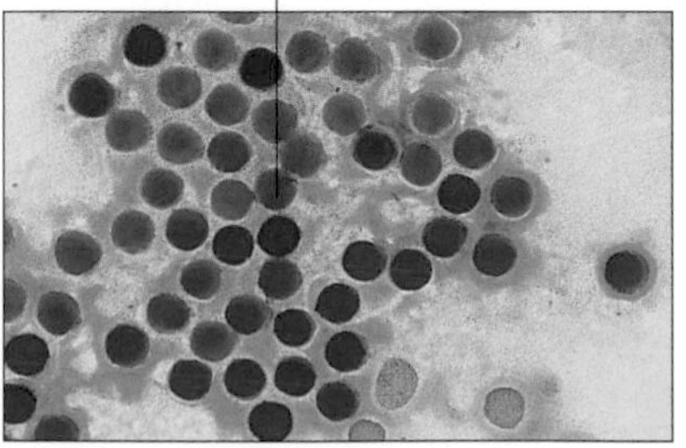
Hepatitis A virus

Highly magnified viruses
Tiny organisms, such as viruses, can be seen only with an electron microscope. This image shows a highly magnified cluster of hepatitis A viruses.

Culture and tests for drug sensitivity

Methods of increasing the numbers of microorganisms to aid their identification and test for sensitivity to antibiotics

Many tests require large numbers of microorganisms, and, to obtain these, the organisms are cultured. Culturing encourages the organisms to reproduce. Most double in number every 20–30 minutes. The organisms generally form clusters, known as colonies. Although it usually takes up to 18 hours to obtain a result, some organisms, such as the bacterium that causes tuberculosis, may take up to 6 weeks to grow sufficient numbers to be easily identified. After they have been cultured, bacteria may be tested to determine which antibiotics are most effective against them.

HOW ARE THEY DONE?

Most microorganisms are grown in a sterile plastic dish containing a nutrient gel on which they feed. The sample to be cultured is spread onto the gel. If a particular organism is thought to be present, the culture is set up specifically to encourage that microorganism while suppressing others. Viruses and some other organisms can be grown only in

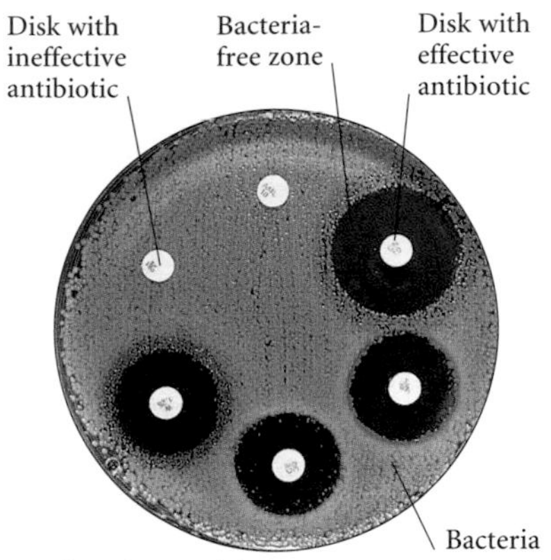
Disk with ineffective antibiotic
Bacteria-free zone
Disk with effective antibiotic
Bacteria

Antibiotic sensitivity test
Paper disks containing different antibiotics have been placed on this culture plate to see which drug can halt bacterial growth.

cultures of living cells. The culture plate is kept at a suitable temperature until colonies of microorganisms have grown, and it is then examined. Some microorganisms have specific features that may identify them. For example, the bacterium *Staphylococcus aureus* forms small, golden yellow colonies when cultured.

After culturing, a small portion of the colony may be carefully removed from the dish, stained, and examined under a microscope to identify the organisms present (*see* MICROSCOPY FOR INFECTIOUS AGENTS, opposite page).

When bacteria have been identified, drug sensitivity tests may be performed. Paper disks containing different types and concentrations of antibiotics are added to the bacterial culture. After 24 hours, the culture is examined to see which antibiotics have been most effective in destroying bacteria.

Tests for antigens and antibodies

Tests on samples of body fluids to detect antigens and antibodies in the body

Every microorganism that enters the body has proteins on its surface, known as antigens, that the immune system recognizes as foreign. When they detect a foreign antigen, white blood cells of the immune system produce antibodies that will exactly fit onto that particular antigen and help destroy the organism. Since every microorganism has an antigen that no other organism has, and one antibody will lock onto only one particular antigen, doctors can use tests for antigens and antibodies to identify microorganisms quickly and accurately.

Antibody tests are usually done on blood samples because antibodies are made by white blood cells. Antigen tests may be done on any type of body fluid.

WHY ARE THEY DONE?

Antigen tests are useful when a rapid diagnosis is needed or when there are not enough microorganisms in a sample to be visible under a microscope. For example, finding the antigen of the bacterium that causes bacterial meningitis (p.527) in a sample of the fluid that surrounds the brain can provide a diagnosis in minutes.

Testing for antibodies is useful for diagnosing a persistent infection, such as HIV infection (*see* HIV INFECTION AND AIDS, p.295), or for confirming your immunity from a previous infection, such as rubella (p.292). Antibody tests are not useful for diagnosing recent infections because the immune system takes about 10 days to make an antibody against a new microorganism.

HOW ARE THEY DONE?

Antigens and antibodies cannot be seen separately, but when they join together they form a large clump that can be seen by the naked eye. In antigen tests, small beads or red blood cells may be coated with an antibody that reacts with the antigens on one particular microorganism. The sample that is to be tested is then added to the antibody-coated beads. If the suspected organism is present in the sample, its antigens will become attached to the antibody beads and make them clump together.

In antibody tests, antigens from a known microorganism may be coated onto small beads. A sample of body fluid is then added to the beads. If the immune system has produced antibodies against the organism, the antibodies will attach to the antigen beads, producing visible clumping.

Although the clumps of antigen and antibody may be seen without a microscope, they can be made even easier to detect by attaching a fluorescent or radioactive marker to either the antigens or the antibodies before they are added to the test sample.

Gene tests for microorganisms

Identifying infectious microorganisms using their genetic material

Gene tests are relatively new techniques for identifying microorganisms. The tests can be done on samples of body fluid, such as blood or urine, and give a diagnosis within a few hours.

Gene tests can give a positive diagnosis even when there are few organisms in a sample. This allows a diagnosis to be made very early in the course of a disease, which is important in people who cannot fight infections because their immune system is damaged, such as people with HIV infection (*see* HIV INFECTION AND AIDS, p.295).

HOW ARE THEY DONE?

Microorganisms can be identified using gene probes or genetic fingerprinting. The basis of these tests is that each microorganism has a different sequence of chemicals in its genetic material, which can be DNA (deoxyribonucleic acid) or, rarely, RNA (ribonucleic acid).

A gene probe is a strand of DNA with a sequence of chemicals that will join to the DNA of just one microorganism. The test sample is treated to extract a small amount of DNA or RNA from the microorganisms. The probe is added to this genetic material and will join to it only if it is an exact match. The probe is radioactively labeled so that it can be detected after joining to the DNA. This test shows if a suspected organism is present in the sample.

In genetic fingerprinting, DNA from the microorganisms in the sample is cut into different-sized pieces by using enzymes. DNA from a known organism is treated in the same way. The two sets of DNA are placed in a gel through which an electric current is passed. The current causes the cut pieces of DNA to separate into patterns. If the patterns match, the two organisms are the same.

Although gene tests can be done with a small number of organisms, the amount of DNA can be increased using a process called polymerase chain reaction. This process takes about 5 hours and makes millions of copies of the microorganism's DNA or RNA.

CELL AND TISSUE TESTS

Microscopic studies of individual cells (cytology) or of a larger sample of tissue containing a variety of different cells (histology) are among the most important and definitive tests carried out. Other tests, such as blood tests or imaging tests, may suggest an abnormality, but in many cases the diagnosis is determined definitively by direct examination of the cells or tissues involved.

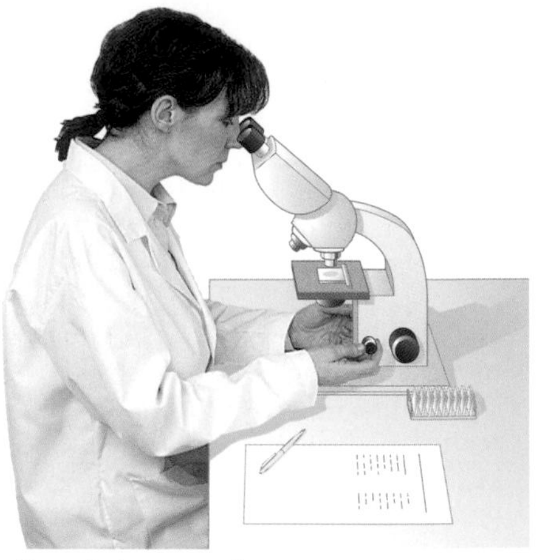

Examining samples
Highly trained technologists and doctors can obtain detailed information about the structure of cells or tissues using powerful microscopes in the laboratory.

Each type of tissue in the body is made up of different cells, all of which have characteristic differences that enable them to be identified when they are examined under a microscope. Many disorders, such as cancer, can cause individual cells to look abnormal. In other diseases, the tissues may contain cells that would not normally be there. For example, infected or damaged tissues may contain inflammatory cells that are not normally present.

In this section, tests on cells are discussed first. These tests are often done at an earlier stage than other tests because they are easy to perform and the samples can be collected easily. Some cell tests, such as the Pap test (p.749), are used for routine screening to detect precancerous cells or cancer cells at an early stage. If such cells are found, treatment can be given early when it is most effective.

The second article covers tissue tests. Tissue tests are not carried out as often as cell tests because the samples are not as easy to obtain and require more preparation before being examined. However, a tissue test may provide more information than a cell test alone, because a tissue sample can show the proportion of abnormal cells within the tissue and therefore the extent of the disease.

Other cell tests are covered elsewhere. These include tests on blood structure and function (pp.226–228) and tests for genetic diseases (*see* GENETIC TESTS, pp.238–241).

Cell tests

Examination of cells under a microscope to detect abnormal changes

The study of cells under a microscope is known as cytology. Samples of cells can be examined to detect abnormalities in the appearance of individual cells or to detect cells that are not normally present in healthy tissue.

WHY AM I HAVING THE TESTS?

Cell tests are commonly used to screen for cancer. Such tests detect precancerous or cancerous cells before symptoms develop and are therefore used to detect certain common cancers at an early stage. For example, cells taken during a Pap test (p.749) are examined under the microscope to look for abnormal cells in the cervix (*see* CANCER OF THE CERVIX, p.750). If abnormal cells are found, treatment can be started early, when it is most likely to be successful.

Your doctor may also arrange for a cell test if you develop symptoms that could be caused by cancer. For example, a small sample of cells may be taken from a swelling in your breast (*see* ASPIRATION OF A BREAST LUMP, p.756). The cells will then be analyzed in the laboratory to determine whether or not the breast lump is cancerous.

HOW ARE THEY DONE?

Samples of cells may be obtained by scraping cells off tissue surfaces such as the lining of the cervix or by washing them off surfaces such as the lining of the lungs (*see* BRONCHOSCOPY, p.504). Individual cells can also be taken from solid tissue using a needle and syringe. In other cases, samples of cells may be obtained from certain body fluids, such as urine or sputum.

Individual cells taken from the surface of a tissue or obtained from solid tissue are usually transferred to a glass slide immediately. However, cells that are obtained from a fluid sample, such as urine, need to be separated from the fluid. By spinning the fluid sample at high speed in a special machine called a centrifuge, cells are pushed to the bottom of the liquid, which can then be drained off. The separated cells are then placed on a glass slide.

Before being examined, the cells are treated with preservative. They are then stained with a dye to make them easier to see. The cells are viewed under a high-powered light microscope.

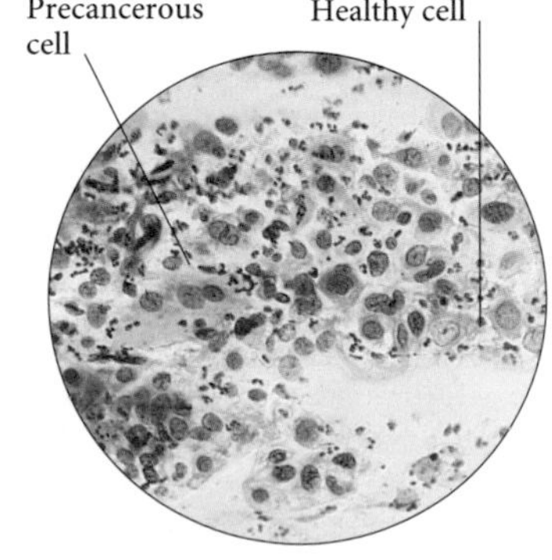
Precancerous cell
Healthy cell

Cells from a Pap test
This highly magnified view through a microscope shows both normal and abnormal (precancerous) cells taken from the surface of the cervix.

How are the results interpreted?

The cells are studied by a cytologist, a technician or doctor trained to analyze cell structures, who looks for abnormal changes suggesting cancer. He or she may also look for other signs of disease, such as inflammatory cells.

The extent to which abnormal cells are different from healthy cells indicates whether the cells are cancerous or likely to become cancerous. Training and experience are needed in order to make an accurate diagnosis and to determine the likelihood that the cancer will spread. Research is currently being carried out on the use of computers to perform preliminary surveys on the cells before the cytologist makes a more detailed analysis.

Will I need further tests?

Cell tests cannot show the proportion of abnormal cells in a tissue or how widely the affected cells are distributed. Therefore, if abnormal cells are found, you may need a tissue test (below) to determine the extent of the disease.

Tissue tests

Examination of tissue samples under a microscope to diagnose or assess the severity of a condition

Some disorders disrupt the proportion of different types of cells within an organ or cause the individual cells to look abnormal. These changes can be detected by tissue tests, in which small samples of tissue are examined under a microscope. Such tests may enable doctors to make a diagnosis or to assess the severity of a disorder.

Why am I having the tests?

Your doctor may arrange for a tissue test if other tests have not established a diagnosis. Tissue tests are often used to distinguish between certain disorders that have similar symptoms, such as the inflammatory bowel conditions ulcerative colitis (p.659) and Crohn's disease (p.658). Tests on a small sample of the inflamed colon may be able to distinguish between the two conditions.

In addition to confirming a diagnosis, tissue tests may also be used to look for a cause. For example, a tissue test on a sample of liver tissue may confirm a diagnosis of cirrhosis (p.647), in which fibrous tissue develops, and suggest a cause from the distribution of the cells.

If a diagnosis has been made, a tissue test may be able to show the extent of disease. For example, if you have had an area of skin removed because of a tumor, a tissue test may show whether the edges of removed skin are free of abnormal cells (indicating that the entire tumor has been removed) or if cancerous cells have reached the edges of the removed tissue, indicating the possibility that the tumor may have spread beyond the margins of the sample.

Finally, tissue tests may help your doctor decide on the most appropriate treatment. For example, if a tissue test shows that cancer has spread from the original site of the tumor, more extensive treatment may be needed.

How are they done?

Samples of tissue are often obtained by a biopsy. During this procedure, a small piece of tissue is removed specifically in order to make a diagnosis. In other cases, the tissue sample may have been removed as part of a particular treatment. For example, part of the colon may be removed during treatment for colorectal cancer (p.665).

The tissue sample is immersed in a preservative substance such as formalin. The sample is then thinly sliced and stained to highlight the different structures in the tissue. Preparation of the tissue may take several days.

Samples are usually examined under a light microscope, but some changes may be seen only with a more powerful electron microscope. For example, a sample of kidney tissue from a person with nephrotic syndrome (p.700) may appear normal under a light microscope, but an electron microscope may reveal abnormalities.

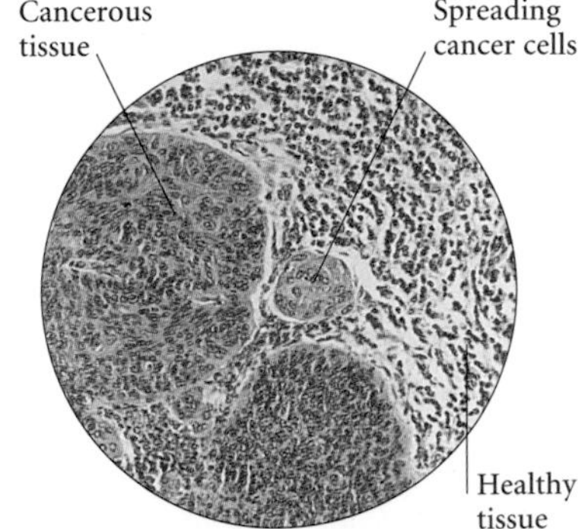
Cancerous tissue
Spreading cancer cells
Healthy tissue

Tissue sample from the cervix
This highly magnified tissue sample taken from the cervix shows cancerous cells spreading into healthy tissue.

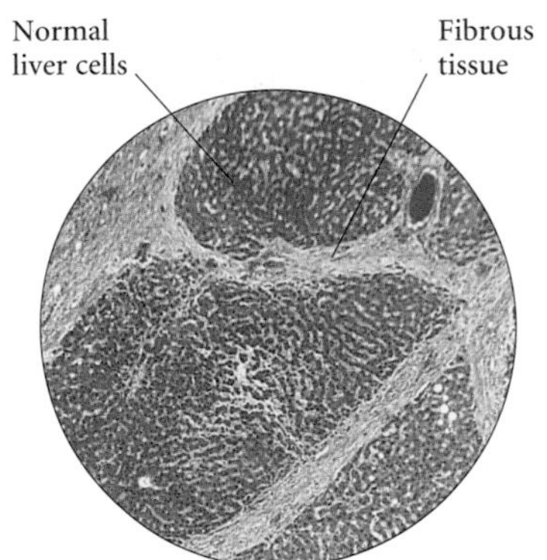
Normal liver cells
Fibrous tissue

Liver tissue sample
This highly magnified view of a tissue sample from the liver shows excess fibrous tissue compressing the normal liver cells. This condition is known as cirrhosis.

How are the results interpreted?

A pathologist, a doctor who is specially trained to analyze tissue samples, usually examines several slides prepared from a single biopsy sample or from different areas of a surgically removed piece of tissue. He or she looks for the presence of abnormal cells or an abnormal balance of cells. The extent to which the tissue is different from healthy tissue indicates the severity of the disease. The slides are usually retained in case they need to be reviewed later.

Will I need further tests?

Tissue tests provide a definitive diagnosis for many conditions in which tissue is damaged. However, further tests may be necessary to determine whether other areas of the body are affected. For example, if tissue tests have already confirmed that a growth from your intestine is cancerous, you may have CT scanning (p.247) or MRI (p.248) of your liver to look for evidence of metastases or tumor spread.

Occasionally, you may need to have repeated tissue tests to monitor disease progression or response to treatment. For example, repeated tissue samples may be taken from an organ transplant to detect early signs of rejection.

GENETIC TESTS

Although genetic tests are less frequently performed than other types of tests, the results may have profound effects on your life. Knowledge of your genetic makeup gives you the information you need to make decisions about your lifestyle. If you know that you carry a faulty gene that could be passed on, you may want to take this into consideration before starting a family.

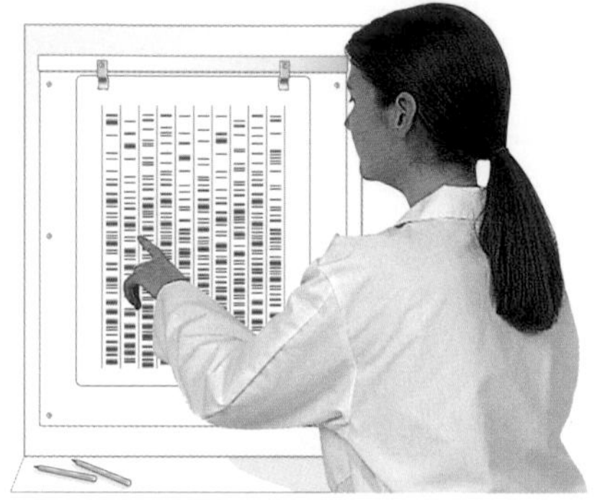

Looking for abnormal genes
Scientists now use techniques that enable small amounts of genetic material to be replicated and studied to look for abnormal genes.

Genes are sets of chemical instructions that control the function of cells in the body. They are located in the nuclei of each body cell in structures called chromosomes (*see* GENES AND INHERITANCE, pp.262–267). Occasionally, genes or chromosomes are faulty, resulting in a disorder or increased susceptibility to a disorder. With the development of more sophisticated tests, an increasingly wide range of genetic abnormalities can now be identified.

Tests for genetic abnormalities either look directly for faulty chromosomes, faulty genes, or the chemical effects that these produce within body cells. This section starts by describing tests that look for abnormalities in chromosome number or structure and tests to detect abnormal genes. Tests designed to look at the effects that certain abnormal chromosomes and genes have on body chemistry are then discussed.

You may be offered genetic tests if you develop symptoms of a genetic disorder, members of your family have a genetic disorder (*see* YOUR FAMILY MEDICAL HISTORY, p.24), or you are at increased risk of a particular genetic disorder. Tests may also be performed prenatally if there is a higher than average risk of a disorder such as Down syndrome. You should discuss the test results with a professional counselor (*see* GENETIC COUNSELING, p.270).

Tests for chromosome abnormalities

Studies of chromosomes to detect abnormalities in number or structure

Chromosomes are threadlike structures within the nucleus of every cell in the body that carry genetic information. Abnormalities can occur in the number of chromosomes or in the structure of individual chromosomes, resulting in a variety of disorders.

Normally, cells in the body contain 22 pairs of ordinary chromosomes and two sex chromosomes, which determine whether a person will be male or female. The complete set of chromosomes contained in a cell is called a karyotype. In chromosome tests, the karyotype is analyzed to determine whether there are any abnormalities. Abnormalities in number are the most common types of chromosome abnormalities. Less commonly, one part of a particular chromosome may be in the wrong place, may be missing, or may be duplicated.

Chromosome abnormalities are usually due to a fault in the way that the chromosomes are divided during the formation of egg and sperm cells, but, occasionally, they may arise during the early stages of cell division following the fertilization of an egg cell (*see* CHROMOSOME DISORDERS, p.268).

In many cases, chromosome abnormalities result in miscarriage (p.791). If a fetus survives, there may be multiple physical abnormalities and/or mental retardation (p.854). A minor alteration in the structure of a chromosome may not cause any obvious abnormalities. However, the structural defect can be passed on and may result in symptoms in the next generation. Abnormalities in the number of chromosomes are not likely to recur in a family.

WHY ARE THEY DONE?

A chromosome test or karyotype analysis may be carried out to determine whether a condition could be caused by a chromosome abnormality. For example, tests may be performed on a baby who has been born with physical characteristics that suggest a chromosome disorder, such as Turner syndrome (p.823). Slow development or learning difficulties in an older child may also prompt the doctor to recommend chromosome analysis.

Chromosome tests may be performed during pregnancy. For example, they are done on women identified by ultrasound scanning (*see* ULTRASOUND SCANNING IN PREGNANCY, p.793) and/or blood tests as being at high risk of having a baby with Down syndrome (p.821). This includes routine ultrasound scans during a pregnancy that

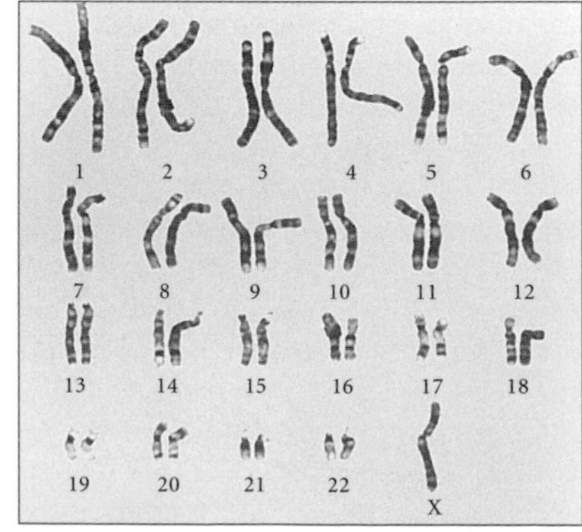
1
2
3
4
5
6
7
8
9
10
11
12
13
14
15
16
17
18
19
20
21
22
X

Karyotype
This set of chromosomes (karyotype) from a female with Turner syndrome shows only one X chromosome rather than the two that are normal for a female.

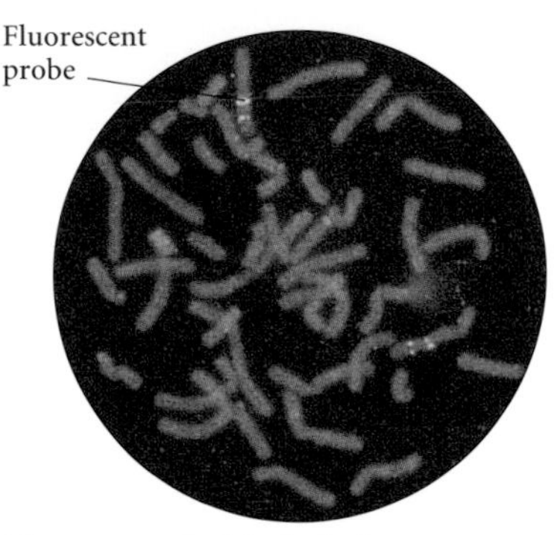
Fluorescent probe

Fluorescently labeled chromosomes
Chromosomes occur in pairs and can be highlighted by probes to detect if any are missing or duplicated. This normal result shows two matching chromosomes.

suggest that a fetus has a physical problem that could be the result of a chromosome abnormality. Karyotype analysis may also be carried out on the parents of a child with a chromosome abnormality in order to predict the chance that any subsequent children they may have will also be affected.

How are they done?

Karyotype analysis on a fetus is done on fetal skin cells taken from the fluid that surrounds the fetus or on fetal cells taken from the placenta (*see* Prenatal genetic tests, p.787). For adults and children, the test is commonly done on white blood cells taken from a routine blood sample or on cells scraped from the inside of the cheek.

To obtain chromosomes for examination, the cells are placed in a nutrient liquid, where they start to divide. The cells are treated with a chemical to stop them dividing at a stage when the chromosomes can be easily seen. The cells can then be examined in several ways.

In one technique, the chromosomes are stained so that they can be identified under the microscope. All of the chromosomes from a cell are arranged in matching pairs to find out whether there are any extra or missing chromosomes or if part of a chromosome is missing, duplicated, or misplaced. The complete set of chromosomes from the cell (the karyotype) can then be photographed to form a permanent record.

Another technique enables chromosome abnormalities to be detected by using fluorescent or radioactive probes that attach themselves to specific areas of chromosomes. This test allows particular chromosomes to be targeted, and abnormalities that are too small to be seen by other techniques to be identified.

How are the results interpreted?

In a fetus or a child found to have a chromosome abnormality, the test results may help doctors predict how severe a disability will be and the course that the disorder may take. If a fetus has a chromosome abnormality that is likely to cause considerable disability, parents may wish to discuss with their doctor whether or not to continue the pregnancy. Parents may benefit from genetic counseling (p.270) in this situation.

Tests for abnormal genes

Tests used to find abnormal genes known to cause a disease or to increase a person's susceptibility to a disease

Within every cell are many thousands of genes that control the cell's structure and functions. If a gene is abnormal, the structure of the cell or the way that it carries out its chemical processes may be altered. The result may be a genetic disorder or increased susceptibility to a disorder. Tests can identify some abnormal genes that are known to cause a disorder or that are linked with a greater than average susceptibility to a disorder.

Genes are located on 23 pairs of structures called chromosomes that are found in the nucleus of a cell. Each gene consists of a length of DNA (deoxyribonucleic acid) made up of individual molecules linked by chemicals arranged in specific sequences. Abnormal changes to the sequence of DNA within a gene can occur, and these are known as mutations. Most mutations consist of a missing segment of DNA or a change in the sequence of chemicals (*see* Genes and inheritance, pp.262–267).

For certain genetic conditions, such as cystic fibrosis (p.824) and the blood disorder sickle-cell anemia (p.448), the abnormality in the DNA sequence and the way in which the abnormality is inherited are known (*see* Gene disorders, p.269). For other disorders, the precise gene abnormality is not known. However, the position of the relevant gene on a chromosome has been established, and this information can be used to help predict a person's chance of inheriting the genetic disorder.

Why are they done?

Tests for mutated genes may be performed to confirm a suspected diagnosis of a genetic disorder. Tests may also be offered to the relatives of a person with a disorder, who may want to find out if they have the abnormal gene and are at risk of developing symptoms and/or passing the abnormal gene on to their children. Many genetic disorders occur only if both parents are carriers of a defective gene. Carriers do not have symptoms themselves. However, if two carriers have children, their children are at 25% risk of inheriting an abnormal gene from each parent and developing the disorder. In these circumstances, genetic tests may be done on couples before they decide to have children or on the fetus in early pregnancy.

How are they done?

Tests for an adult or a child are usually performed on white blood cells from a blood sample or on cells collected by gently scraping the inside of the cheek. For a fetus, tests are done on fetal skin cells taken from the fluid that surrounds the fetus (amniotic fluid) or on fetal cells taken from the placenta (*see* Prenatal genetic tests, p.787).

A cell sample usually contains only a small amount of DNA. A technique called PCR (polymerase chain reaction) can provide enough DNA for a test by making millions of copies of the specific gene of interest. If the precise chemical sequence of a gene has been established, direct identification of mutations may be possible, but, for other genetic disorders, an indirect method of testing for the mutated gene may be needed.

Direct tests These tests are used to look for an abnormal gene when the chemical sequence of the normal gene is known. In one technique, the DNA in the sample is cut into fragments, and the fragments are separated according to their size. Abnormal genes produce differently sized fragments from those of normal genes. These fragments can

PROCEDURE LOOKING FOR ABNORMAL GENES

Genes control every cell in the body, and a defect in the structure of a gene can cause disease. Tests look for abnormalities in the chemical composition of the DNA that makes up the genes. By comparing a DNA sample with the DNA of a control (normal) gene, abnormalities can be identified. The tests work because changes in the chemical sequence of the DNA can cause variations in the sizes of gene fragments when the DNA is cut up. Radioactive probes designed to match a specific gene are used to label the abnormal fragments and the fragments from the normal genes so that they can be seen and compared. In another method, a radioactive chemical makes all the fragments visible so that they can be studied.

1 Cells are scraped painlessly from the lining of the mouth or taken from a blood sample. For prenatal tests, cells come from the fluid around the fetus or from the placenta.

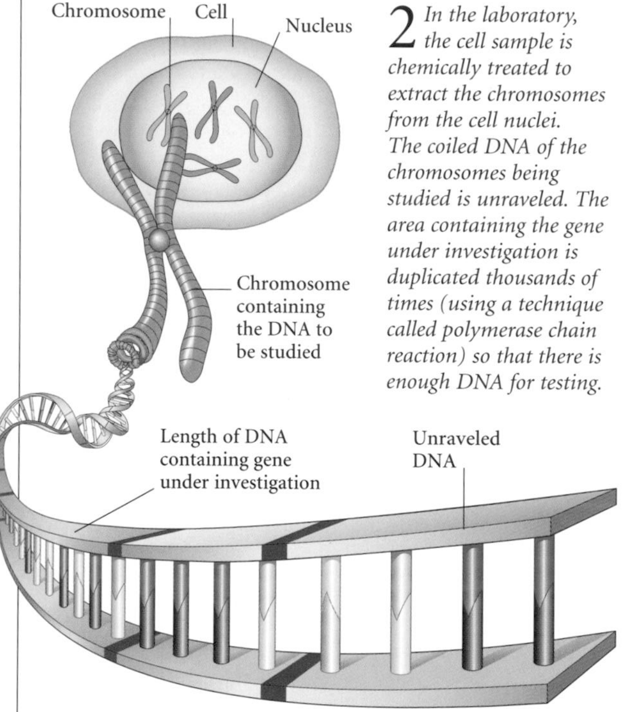

Chromosome
Cell
Nucleus
Chromosome containing the DNA to be studied
Length of DNA containing gene under investigation
Unraveled DNA

2 In the laboratory, the cell sample is chemically treated to extract the chromosomes from the cell nuclei. The coiled DNA of the chromosomes being studied is unraveled. The area containing the gene under investigation is duplicated thousands of times (using a technique called polymerase chain reaction) so that there is enough DNA for testing.

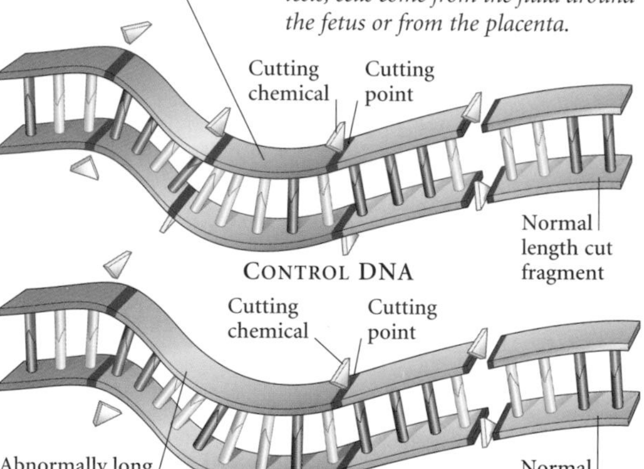

Normal length DNA fragment containing gene under study
Cutting chemical
Cutting point
Normal length cut fragment
CONTROL DNA
Cutting chemical
Cutting point
Abnormally long fragment containing gene under study
TEST DNA
Normal length cut fragment

3 A chemical that cuts the unraveled DNA at specific places is added to the sample and also to a control (normal) sample. If the chemical sequence of the DNA in a gene is abnormal, it will be cut in different places from that of the control DNA, creating abnormally long or short fragments of DNA.

Control DNA
Test DNA
Long fragment
Test fragment under study
Control fragment under study
Short fragment
Direction of movement
Sheet of gel

4 DNA fragments are placed on the surface of a sheet of gel. An electric current is passed through the gel, causing the fragments of DNA to separate according to size. Short fragments move farther along the gel than long ones.

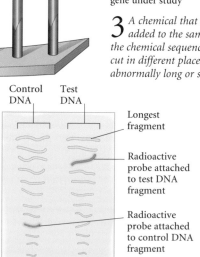

Control DNA
Test DNA
Longest fragment
Radioactive probe attached to test DNA fragment
Radioactive probe attached to control DNA fragment
Shortest fragment

5 After separation, the DNA of the gene under study is located by adding DNA probes, which are pieces of DNA that match the chemical sequence of the gene and bind to it. A radioactive or fluorescent label attached to the probe makes it visible.

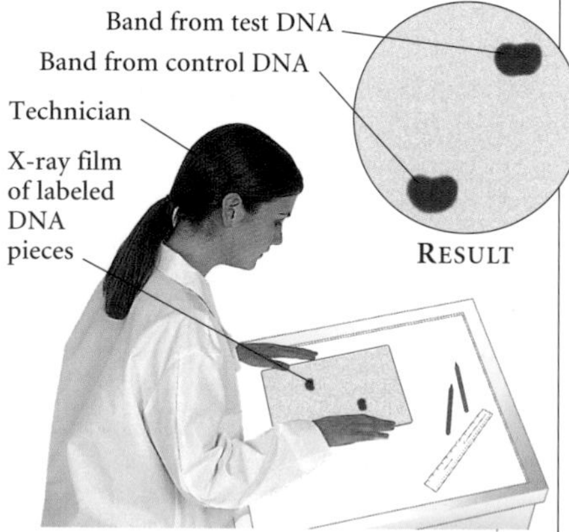

Band from test DNA
Band from control DNA
Technician
X-ray film of labeled DNA pieces
RESULT

6 The radioactive probes are exposed to X-ray film and produce visible bands on the film. If the bands from the two samples are in the same positions, the gene is normal. If the positions are different, the gene is abnormal.

be detected either by adding radioactivity to all the fragments to make them visible or else by using a radioactive DNA probe that is designed to stick to a specific abnormal gene (*see* LOOKING FOR ABNORMAL GENES, opposite page).

INDIRECT TESTS When the exact gene abnormality that causes a disorder has not been identified, indirect tests may be used. The technique, known as linkage analysis, depends on the use of markers, distinctive sequences of DNA that are almost always inherited with an abnormal gene because they are close to it on the same chromosome. A DNA probe is designed to label the marker rather than the abnormal DNA itself.

In order to find a suitable marker for a genetic disorder, relatives with the disorder and unaffected relatives are asked to provide samples from which DNA can be extracted. The DNA is analyzed to detect a DNA sequence that occurs only in affected relatives. This sequence is likely to be closely linked to (found very near) the abnormal gene on a chromosome and can be used as a marker. A relative with this marker is likely to have inherited the abnormal gene.

HOW ARE THE RESULTS INTERPRETED?

Direct testing shows definitely whether an abnormal gene is present or not. If indirect tests show a genetic marker, the likelihood that an abnormal gene is present depends on how closely linked the marker and the gene are. The closer they are on the chromosome, the more likely that both the marker and the abnormal gene have been co-inherited.

People shown to have an abnormal gene may have a disorder; they may be at risk of developing one; or they may have no personal risk of disease but be symptomless carriers. The implications of having an abnormal gene vary according to whether the gene is dominant or recessive. Mutated genes that are inherited in a dominant fashion usually cause disease in most or all the people with the abnormal gene, and there is a 1 in 2 chance of this gene being passed on to any children they may have. Mutations in recessive genes usually cause no symptoms in carriers, but the children of two carriers of a recessive gene are at risk.

Tests for gene products

Identifying an abnormal gene by analyzing its effects on body chemistry

A gene is a length of DNA (deoxyribonucleic acid). The chemical sequence of DNA in each gene contains the necessary instructions to make a protein that controls a specific cell function. If a gene is faulty, a cell may not function properly, leading to a genetic disorder.

The protein coded for by a gene is known as the gene product. In some genetic disorders, it is possible to measure the gene product directly. In others, direct measurement of the gene product is not possible or is very difficult. However, the abnormality affects chemical processes in the cell, leading to abnormal amounts of other substances. Sometimes, it is possible to measure the levels of these substances, as an indirect means of detecting genetic disorders.

WHY ARE THEY DONE?

The tests may be done to confirm a suspected diagnosis if you have symptoms that indicate a genetic disorder. In some cases, tests may be used to look for carriers of an abnormal gene. Carriers do not have symptoms of a disorder but can pass the gene on to their children, who may develop the disorder.

Since tests for biochemical substances are often easier and cheaper than tests for gene products, they are often used to screen large groups of people. For example, newborn babies are routinely screened for phenylketonuria (p.867), a disorder that can cause brain damage if not detected early. Routine screening may also be available to members of certain ethnic groups with a higher than average risk of inheriting a disorder.

WHAT MIGHT BE STUDIED?

The levels of a gene product or a related biochemical substance are often measured by analyzing a sample of blood. Often, only a very small amount of blood is needed for testing. The tests are done in a laboratory, usually by means of an automated machine, which can measure a range of substances (*see* ANALYSIS OF BLOOD OR URINE, p.230).

GENE PRODUCTS Chemicals that may be present in abnormal amounts as a result of a genetic disorder include hormones, blood proteins, and enzymes. For example, in the disorder hemophilia (*see* HEMOPHILIA AND CHRISTMAS DISEASE, p.452), an abnormal gene results in a reduced amount of a protein that is necessary for normal blood clotting. The level of this protein, called Factor VIII, can be measured directly in a blood sample. Another condition that can be diagnosed by measuring levels of a gene product is alpha$_1$-antitrypsin deficiency (p.489). Affected people have a low level of the enzyme antitrypsin, which may cause lung and liver damage.

BIOCHEMICAL SUBSTANCES The way that the chemical processes of a cell are disrupted determines the type of substance that can be used as a biochemical marker. For example, in the disorder phenylketonuria, phenylalanine (a chemical that is found naturally in many foods) accumulates because the enzyme that normally breaks it down is missing. Chemical tests can detect high levels of phenylalanine in the blood of babies born with this condition.

Some genetic abnormalities result in damage to body tissues, causing them to release certain substances into the blood. For example, muscles damaged or weakened as a result of the inherited disorder muscular dystrophy (p.826) release an enzyme called creatine kinase. High levels of creatine kinase are found in the blood of people who have muscular dystrophy.

HOW ARE THE RESULTS INTERPRETED?

Gene products are often unique to a particular illness, in which case test results provide a definite diagnosis. However, a test for a biochemical substance may sometimes only suggest the presence of an abnormality. For example, the blood level of creatine kinase is raised in people with muscular dystrophy, but it is also high in people with other conditions causing muscle damage. In these cases, it may be necessary to examine the gene itself, if possible. Family medical history also needs to be taken into account to assess an individual's risk of having or developing a particular disease.

IMAGING TECHNIQUES

The aim of imaging is to provide detailed and reliable pictorial information about structures within the body with the minimum risk and discomfort. Most imaging is now highly computerized and has largely replaced exploratory surgery in establishing the presence and extent of disease. Recent techniques are also able to indicate how well a tissue or organ is functioning.

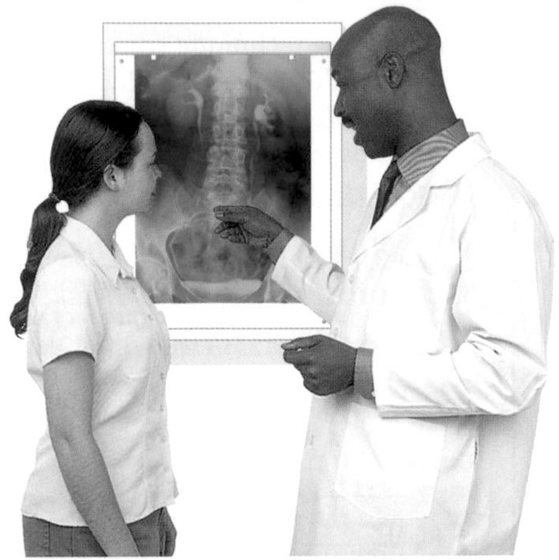

Looking at imaging results
Your doctor may show you your X-ray or scan and explain the results by pointing out the various structures that are visible along with any areas of abnormality.

The first imaging techniques used were based on X-rays, a form of high-energy radiation that is able to pass through body tissues. Some X-rays require particular substances, called contrast media, to improve the visibility of certain structures.

Over the last 30–40 years, a range of new techniques has been introduced, most of which involve the use of computers that control the imaging equipment and are able to create images in three dimensions.

This section begins by explaining the basic imaging methods that use X-rays, including ordinary and contrast X-rays and CT scanning. Other imaging techniques are then covered, including MRI and ultrasound scanning, which do not involve the use of radiation, and different types of radionuclide scanning.

X-rays

Images produced using high-energy radiation; especially suitable for looking at bone and some soft tissues

X-rays have been used in imaging since they were discovered in 1895. Ordinary X-rays, called plain X-rays, are mainly used for imaging bones and certain soft tissues, such as the breasts. Structures that are hollow or fluid-filled, such as the digestive tract or blood vessels, do not show up well on ordinary X-rays and are more successfully imaged using contrast X-rays (opposite page).

Ordinary X-rays are still commonly used in imaging, despite the development of more sophisticated techniques, such as CT scanning (p.247) and MRI (p.248). This is because X-rays are inexpensive, quick, simple to perform, and usually provide the doctor with sufficient information to make a diagnosis.

HOW DO THEY WORK?

X-rays are a form of radiation similar to light waves but with a higher energy. This high energy enables X-rays to pass through body tissues. The ability of X-rays to penetrate structures depends on the tissue's density. X-rays easily penetrate soft tissues but do not easily pass through dense tissue, such as bone. X-rays blacken photographic film. If a single beam of X-rays is focused onto the body, the parts that allow X-rays through, such as air in the lungs, appear black on the film. Soft tissues, such as skin, fat, and muscle, appear as varying shades of gray. Dense substances, such as bone, are seen as white. As a result of these differences, the final image of the body created by the X-rays on the film looks like a photographic negative.

X-rays only create two-dimensional images, which means that occasionally two or more X-rays must be taken from different angles to pinpoint a condition. For example, to determine the position of a tumor in the lung, X-rays would be taken of the body from the front and from the side or at a slanting angle.

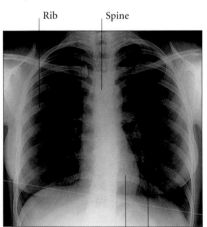

Rib
Spine
Breast
Heart
Lung

Chest X-ray
In this X-ray of a healthy woman's chest, bones appear white, soft tissue appears as shades of gray, and air appears black.

WHAT ARE THEY USED FOR?

Ordinary X-rays produce clear images of bone and are often used to look for fractures (*see* HAVING AN X-RAY, opposite page). Chest X-rays (p.490) may be done to look for an enlarged heart or damaged lung tissue in someone with symptoms, such as chest pain, that may be due to heart or lung disease.

At lower doses, X-rays are useful for examining soft tissues, such as those of the breast, in detail, and they are widely used to screen for breast cancer (*see* MAMMOGRAPHY, p.759). Bone densitometry (p.369) uses low-dose X-rays to measure bone density. This technique may be used to screen for and diagnose osteoporosis (p.368), a common condition in postmenopausal women.

WHAT ARE THE RISKS?

There are no immediate risks from having ordinary X-rays, but there is some risk that radiation may damage body cells, which may possibly lead to cancer later in life. This risk increases if you are repeatedly exposed to X-ray radiation

PROCEDURE HAVING AN X-RAY

X-rays are ideal for looking for fractures in bone and imaging certain soft tissues. You are positioned on or against a special table or surface so that the part of your body to be imaged lies between a drawer containing a film cassette and the X-ray source. After positioning the X-ray machine, the radiographer stands behind a screen. You are exposed to X-rays for a fraction of a second, and the whole procedure takes only a few minutes.

During the procedure
The source of the X-rays is positioned directly above the area being examined. You have to keep still so that the X-ray image is clear. In some cases, a second X-ray may be taken from a different angle to give more information.

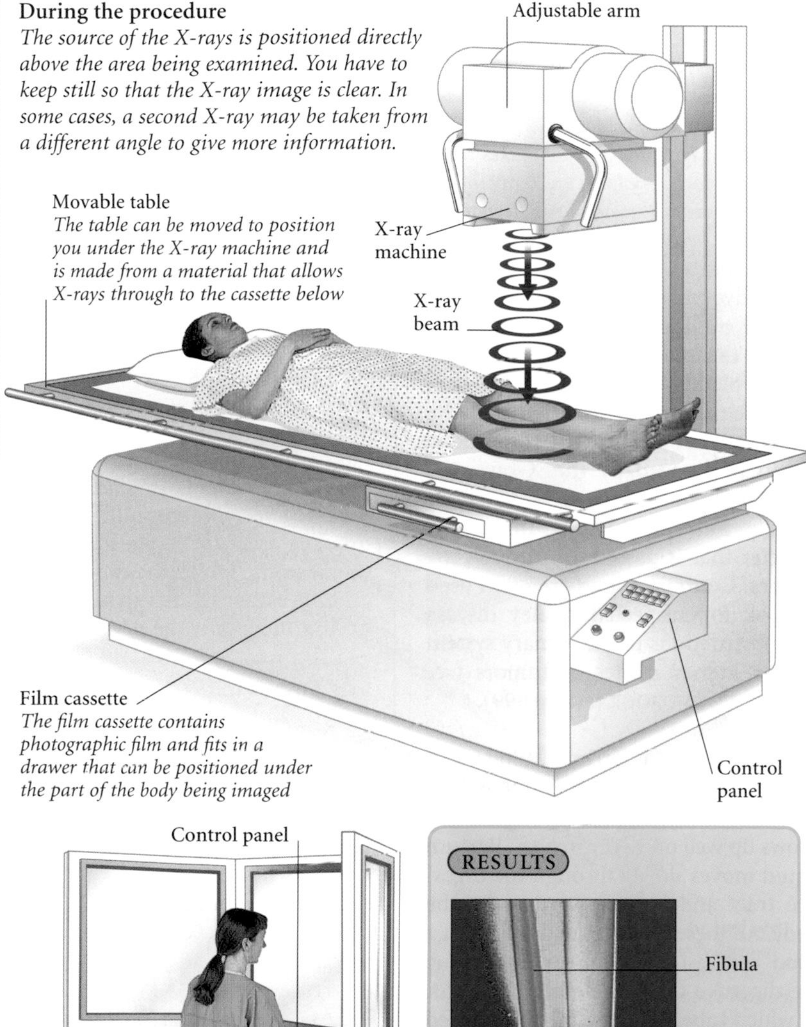
Adjustable arm
X-ray machine
X-ray beam
Control panel

Movable table
The table can be moved to position you under the X-ray machine and is made from a material that allows X-rays through to the cassette below

Film cassette
The film cassette contains photographic film and fits in a drawer that can be positioned under the part of the body being imaged

Control panel
Lead screen
Radiographer

Operating the X-ray machine
The radiographer stands behind a protective screen to minimize his or her exposure to X-rays.

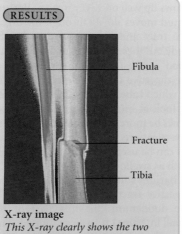

RESULTS

Fibula
Fracture
Tibia

X-ray image
This X-ray clearly shows the two bones of the lower leg, the tibia and the fibula. The main bone, the tibia, has an obvious fracture.

(*see* RADIATION DOSES, p.246). The earlier in life you are exposed to radiation, the greater the risk. Radiographers always try to use the minimum amount of radiation when taking X-rays, and modern equipment makes it possible to produce good-quality images with lower doses of radiation than in the past.

During X-ray procedures, areas that are not being imaged may be shielded. For example, when X-raying the pelvis, special care is often taken to shield the reproductive organs to avoid damage to sperm or eggs. Women are always asked if they may be pregnant before having an X-ray because radiation may cause fetal abnormalities in early pregnancy. Radiographers are always protected by a lead apron or screen to avoid repeated exposure to radiation.

Contrast X-rays

Images produced using radiation and a substance that makes hollow or fluid-filled structures visible

Hollow or fluid-filled body structures, such as the intestines or blood vessels, do not show up well on an ordinary X-ray image (*see* X-RAYS, opposite page). A substance called a contrast medium can be introduced into these structures to make them visible. Contrast media absorb radiation in the same way as dense body tissue, such as bone. X-rays cannot pass through the media, and the areas that contain these substances will appear white on an X-ray image.

The contrast medium is injected into the body or introduced orally or rectally, depending on the structure to be imaged. This procedure is generally straightforward, but it may cause discomfort and involve some risks, such as an adverse reaction to the dye. Contrast X-ray procedures are increasingly being replaced by other techniques, in particular CT scanning (p.247), MRI (p.248), and ultrasound scanning (p.250), all of which cause less discomfort and involve fewer risks to health.

WHAT ARE THEY USED FOR?

Contrast X-rays can produce images of various hollow or fluid-filled structures that do not show up well on ordinary X-rays. Contrast X-rays are often used to image the blood vessels, urinary system,

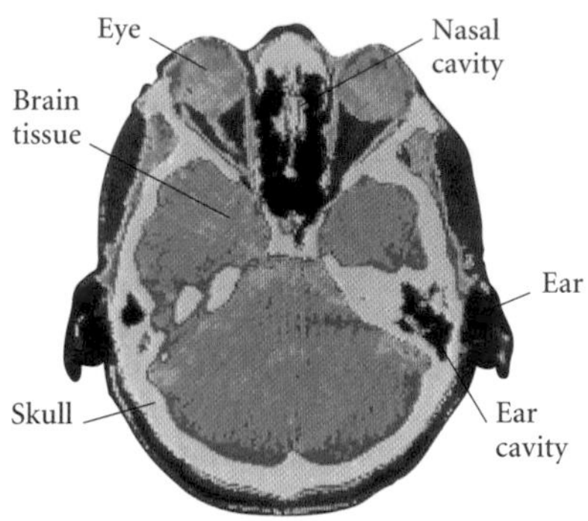

Eye
Nasal cavity
Brain tissue
Ear
Skull
Ear cavity

CT scan of the head
This normal CT scan of the head viewed from above clearly shows the different structures and cavities within the skull.

that are impossible to see using ordinary X-rays, including fibrous tissue in solid organs such as the liver. Instead of sending one beam of radiation through your body, the X-ray source inside a CT scanner emits a succession of narrow beams as it moves through an arc. The X-ray detector then picks up the radiation after it has passed through various body tissues (*see* HAVING A CT SCAN, p.247). After each arc is completed, the bed is moved forward a small distance.

The information from the detector is then sent to the computer, which builds up cross-sectional images of the body and displays them on a monitor. These resulting images can be stored either as computer files or on conventional X-ray film. More sophisticated computers can produce three-dimensional images from standard CT data.

Newer CT scanners use the spiral (or helical) technique, in which the scanner rotates around you as the bed moves forward slowly so that the X-ray beams follow a spiral course. This type of CT scanning produces three-dimensional images and reduces the time taken for the scans to be completed.

WHAT IS IT USED FOR?

The CT scans performed most often are those of the head and the abdomen. CT scanning of the head is a valuable technique that is commonly used to investigate the brain following a stroke (p.532) or if a brain tumor (p.530) is suspected. Abdominal CT scans are frequently used to detect tumors and to diagnose disorders in which organs are enlarged or inflamed, such as polycystic kidney disease (p.704).

CT scans can also be used to investigate the lungs and to guide biopsy procedures, in which cells or tissue are taken from internal organs for examination.

CT scanning produces clear images of bone. Blood vessels and areas of high blood flow, such as the lungs, can also be imaged. These images may be enhanced by using a contrast medium (a substance that makes a hollow or fluid-filled structure visible on the image).

WHAT ARE THE RISKS?

Imaging techniques that use radiation may damage body cells, which may increase the risk of cancer in the long term (*see* RADIATION DOSES, p.246). The dose for a CT procedure depends on the number of cross sections imaged. Scanning time is reduced for spiral CT scans, but the dose is the same as in a normal CT scan. Radiation exposure during CT scans is generally quite low.

MRI

A radiation-free, computer-assisted imaging technique that uses a strong magnetic field and radio waves

The technique of magnetic resonance imaging (MRI) has been used since the early 1980s to provide highly detailed sectional images of internal organs and structures. These images are created by a computer using information received from a scanner. MRI does not involve radiation; instead, it works by using magnets and radio waves.

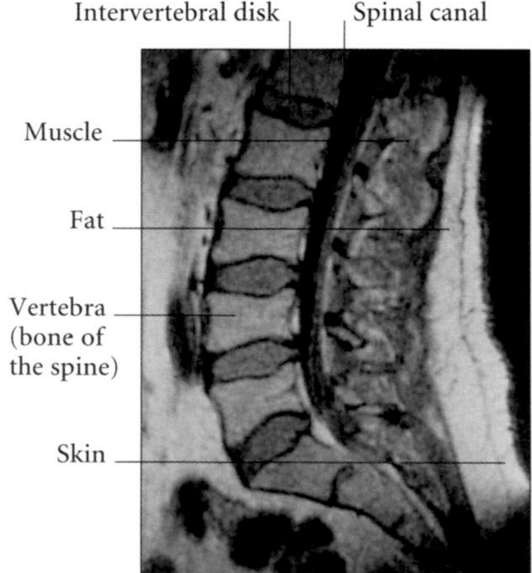

Intervertebral disk
Spinal canal
Muscle
Fat
Vertebra (bone of the spine)
Skin

MRI of the lower spine
This MRI scan of a healthy person's lower spine clearly shows the different structures, including muscle, skin, and bone.

Although MRI is a relatively expensive procedure and MRI scans tend to take longer than other techniques, it does have several advantages. Images from MRI are similar to those produced by CT scanning (p.247), but MRI can distinguish abnormal tissue, such as a tumor, from normal tissue much more clearly. MRI scans can also be taken at a greater range of planes through the body than is possible with CT scanning and therefore can be used to image any part of the body. MRI is radiation-free and is considered to be one of the safest imaging techniques available.

HOW DOES IT WORK?

During an MRI scan, you lie inside a scanner surrounded by a large, powerful magnet. A receiving magnet is then placed around the part of your body that is to be investigated. If large areas, such as the abdomen, are to be imaged, the receiving magnet is fitted inside the MRI scanner; for smaller areas, such as a joint, a magnet may be placed around the part to be scanned (*see* HAVING AN MRI SCAN, opposite page).

Your body, like everything else, is made up of atoms. When the atoms in your body are exposed to a strong magnetic field from the large magnet in the scanner, they line up parallel to each other. Short pulses of radio waves from a radiofrequency magnet then briefly knock the atoms out of alignment. As they realign, the atoms emit tiny signals, which are detected by the receiving magnet. Information about these signals is then passed on to a computer, which builds up an image based on the signals' strength and location.

MRI images can be enhanced by the use of a contrast medium to highlight particular structures in the body, such as tumors and blood vessels.

WHAT IS IT USED FOR?

MRI can provide clear images of any part of the body. This type of scanning is especially useful for looking at the brain and for detecting brain tumors (p.530). MRI is also valuable for looking at the spinal cord and may be used to investigate lower back pain (p.381). Sports injuries (p.391), especially in the knee (*see* TORN KNEE CARTILAGE, p.395), are increasingly being examined using MRI. In a small number of cases, MRI

(PROCEDURE) Having an MRI scan

MRI scanning is most commonly used to investigate the brain but is also used for looking at the spine and, increasingly, for sports injuries. You are positioned on a motorized bed and a receiving magnet is placed around the part of your body being examined. You are then moved into the tunnel of the scanner. Several individual scans will be taken. You will have to lie within the scanner for up to an hour, and therefore it is important that you are as comfortable as possible. You may be given earplugs or headphones because the scanner can be noisy. Your doctor may give you a sedative if you are anxious or claustrophobic.

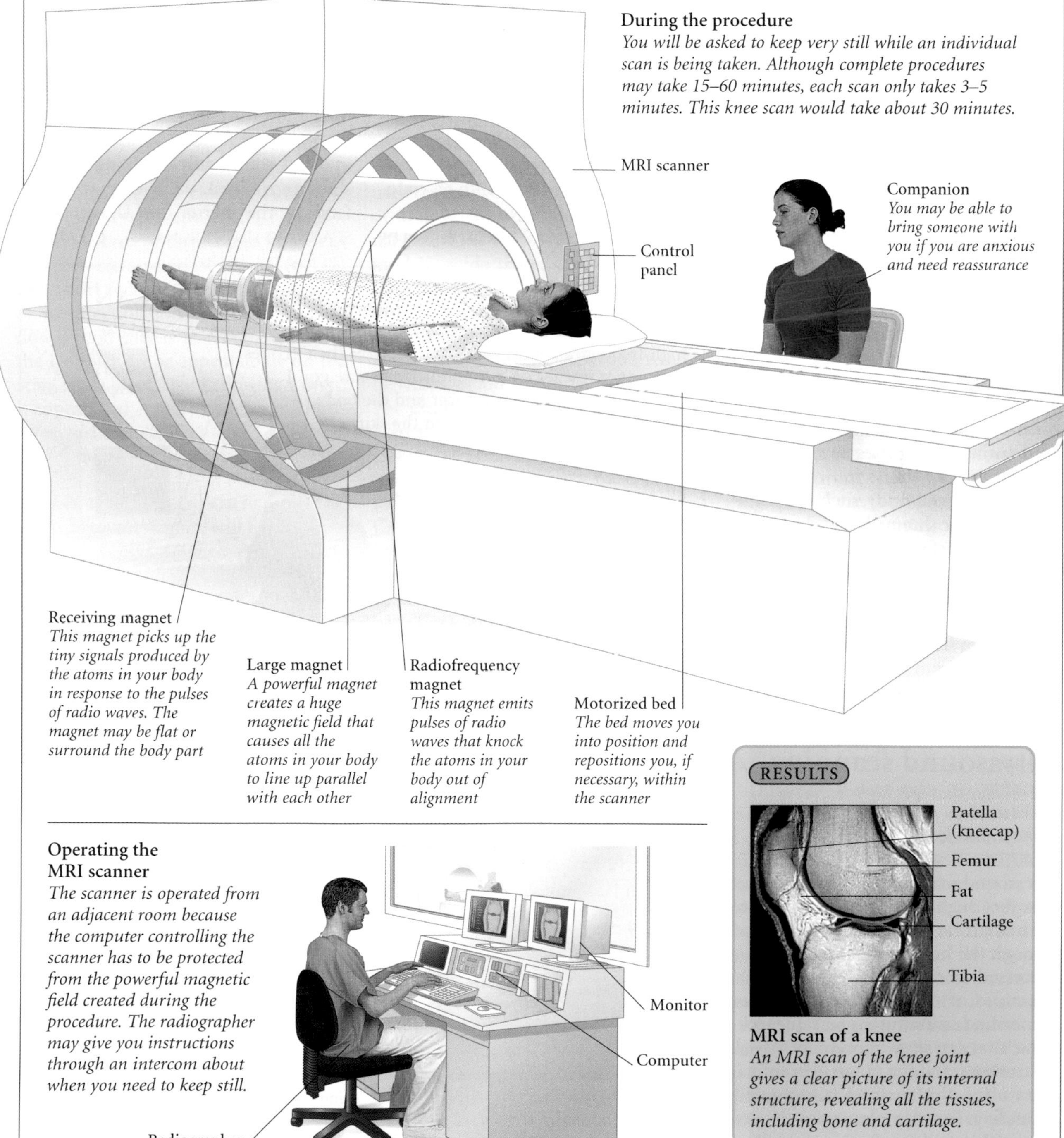
MRI scanner
Control panel
Radiographer
Monitor
Computer
RESULTS
Patella (kneecap)
Femur
Fat
Cartilage
Tibia

During the procedure
You will be asked to keep very still while an individual scan is being taken. Although complete procedures may take 15–60 minutes, each scan only takes 3–5 minutes. This knee scan would take about 30 minutes.

Companion
You may be able to bring someone with you if you are anxious and need reassurance

Receiving magnet
This magnet picks up the tiny signals produced by the atoms in your body in response to the pulses of radio waves. The magnet may be flat or surround the body part

Large magnet
A powerful magnet creates a huge magnetic field that causes all the atoms in your body to line up parallel with each other

Radiofrequency magnet
This magnet emits pulses of radio waves that knock the atoms in your body out of alignment

Motorized bed
The bed moves you into position and repositions you, if necessary, within the scanner

Operating the MRI scanner
The scanner is operated from an adjacent room because the computer controlling the scanner has to be protected from the powerful magnetic field created during the procedure. The radiographer may give you instructions through an intercom about when you need to keep still.

MRI scan of a knee
An MRI scan of the knee joint gives a clear picture of its internal structure, revealing all the tissues, including bone and cartilage.

VIEWING TECHNIQUES

Viewing structures or organs in the body is often important for screening, diagnosis, or monitoring disease. Structures that are easily accessible, such as the ears, may be viewed directly using basic viewing instruments; those deeper inside the body are usually viewed indirectly, using complex optical instruments called endoscopes to transmit images onto a monitor screen.

Some viewing techniques may be done as part of a routine examination. For example, your doctor can look at your ears, eyes, and throat simply and quickly in his or her office. Each of the instruments used is designed to view a particular part of the body. For example, an otoscope is used to look at the ears and an ophthalmoscope to look at the eyes. The first article covers these basic viewing techniques.

To view other organs deeper within the body, your doctor may arrange for an endoscopic investigation. Endoscopy is discussed in the second article. An endoscope is a tubelike viewing device through which body cavities or hollow internal organs can be inspected. Endoscopes may be flexible or rigid and vary in length and diameter. Each type of endoscope is designed to view a particular part of the body.

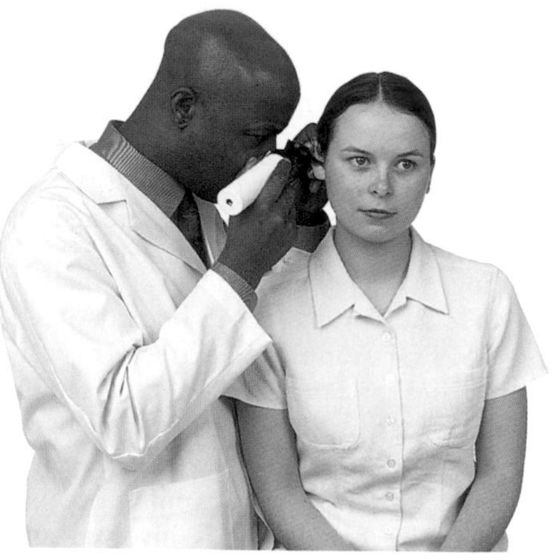

Inspecting the ear
During a routine checkup, your doctor may use a special viewing device called an otoscope to look inside the ear and examine the ear canal and eardrum.

Basic viewing techniques

The use of simple instruments to look at tissues near the surface of the body

Instruments used to view body structures and organs directly have been developed and improved considerably over the past 100 years. Some of these instruments have been replaced by endoscopes (*see* ENDOSCOPY, opposite page). However, basic viewing instruments are still frequently used in a doctor's office as part of a routine examination because they are simple to use and cause little discomfort.

HOW DO THEY WORK?

To examine the interior of a natural opening, such as the ear canal, your doctor will usually need a source of light that can be focused on the area to be examined and some form of magnification. These two elements are often incorporated into a single viewing instrument, such as an otoscope, which is used for inspecting the ear.

For other natural openings, such as the vagina or nose, your doctor may also need to use an additional instrument, called a speculum, to hold the passage open and keep other structures out of the way during viewing. In some cases, a speculum may also be used to make access easier and to enable the doctor to take tissue samples.

External ear canal

Middle ear bone

Eardrum

View through an otoscope
This view shows a healthy eardrum and ear canal as a doctor would see it using an otoscope. One of the bones of the middle ear is visible through the eardrum.

In the eye, the light-sensitive retina at the back of the eye can be viewed from the outside through the pupil. The instrument used to do this, known as an ophthalmoscope, incorporates magnifying lenses and a light.

WHAT ARE THEY USED FOR?

Your doctor may use basic viewing techniques as part of a routine physical examination to assess a particular area of the body or to investigate symptoms in that area. For example, if you have earache, your doctor may examine your ear (*see* OTOSCOPY, p.597), and to investigate hoarseness your doctor may look at your larynx and vocal cords (*see* MIRROR LARYNGOSCOPY, p.481). Basic viewing techniques can also form part of a screening procedure. For example, if you have a chronic disorder such as diabetes mellitus (p.687), your doctor may examine your eyes by means of ophthalmoscopy (p.578) and slit-lamp examination (p.574) so that he or she can detect eye damage at an early stage. In addition, some types of tissue samples, such as tissue from the cervix, can be taken with the help of a viewing instrument (*see* COLPOSCOPY, p.750).

In some cases, it is possible to take photographs through basic viewing instruments, such as an ophthalmoscope. Photographs taken at different times can be compared to monitor improvement or deterioration in a condition.

WHAT ARE THE RISKS?

An examination using basic viewing techniques is completely safe and may be repeated as often as necessary to monitor or screen for a disorder. Most of the examinations cause little or no discomfort, and anesthesia is not usually necessary. However, when viewing the larynx and throat, a local anesthetic spray may be used to numb the throat.

PROCEDURE FLEXIBLE ENDOSCOPY

Flexible endoscopy uses a specially designed viewing instrument to investigate organs and structures inside the body. Before you undergo an endoscopic examination, you may be given an anesthetic or sedative. The endoscope is inserted through a natural opening, such as the mouth, and is guided to the appropriate area by the specialist. A tiny camera at the tip of the endoscope sends views back to the eyepiece and monitor. Very fine surgical instruments may be passed down the endoscope, allowing minor procedures, such as the removal of tissue samples, to be carried out.

During the procedure
For an investigation of the stomach and duodenum, you will be asked to lie on your side. You may be sedated or have local anesthetic sprayed on the back of your throat. A flexible endoscope is then passed into your digestive tract through your mouth.

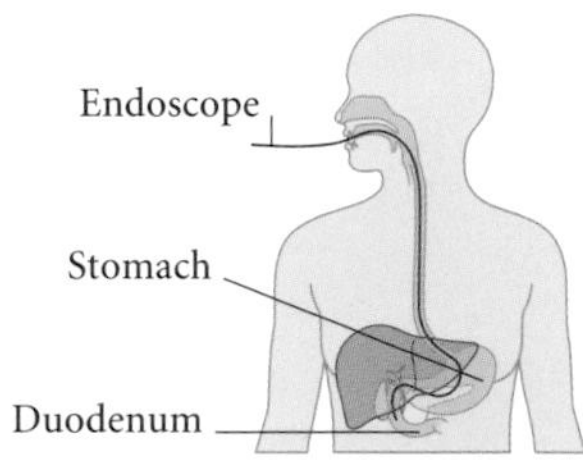
Endoscope
Stomach
Duodenum
ROUTE OF ENDOSCOPE

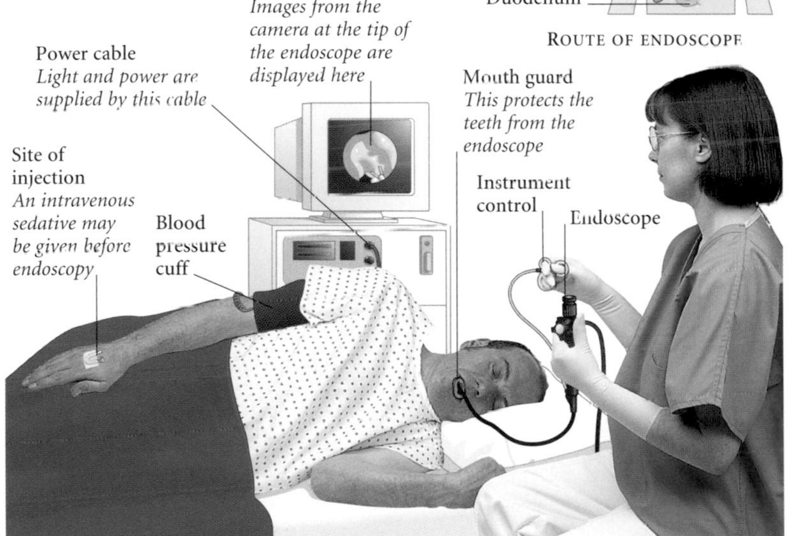
Monitor
Images from the camera at the tip of the endoscope are displayed here
Power cable
Light and power are supplied by this cable
Mouth guard
This protects the teeth from the endoscope
Site of injection
An intravenous sedative may be given before endoscopy
Blood pressure cuff
Instrument control
Endoscope

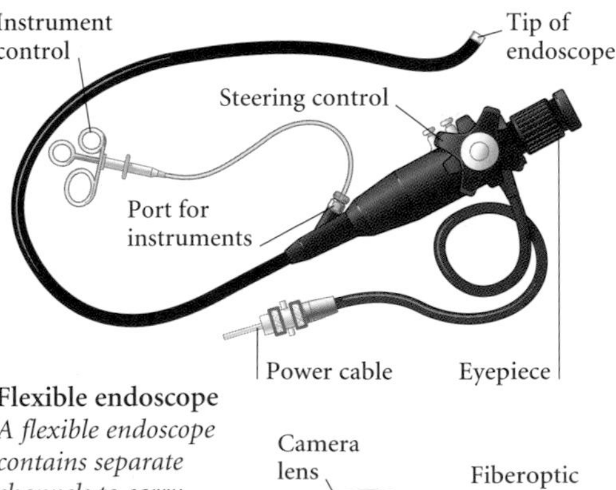
Instrument control
Tip of endoscope
Steering control
Port for instruments
Power cable
Eyepiece

Flexible endoscope
A flexible endoscope contains separate channels to carry water, air, a camera lens, instruments, and optical fibers. A steering control guides the tip around bends in the structure to be viewed.

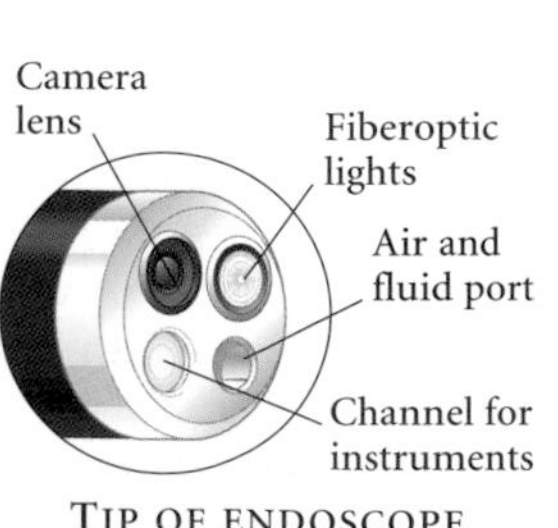
Camera lens
Fiberoptic lights
Air and fluid port
Channel for instruments
TIP OF ENDOSCOPE

VIEW

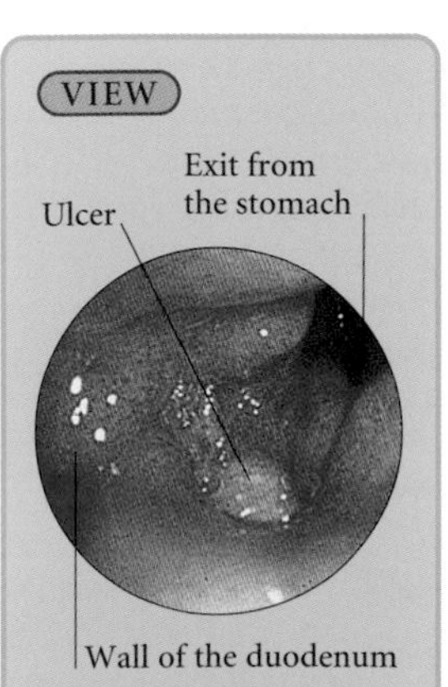
Ulcer
Exit from the stomach
Wall of the duodenum

Endoscopic view of the duodenum
This endoscopic view shows the inside of the duodenum. An ulcer is visible on the wall.

Endoscopy

The use of tubelike instruments to look at organs or structures deep within the body

During endoscopy, a tubelike optical instrument known as an endoscope is introduced deep into the body so that internal structures can be examined visually. Access into the body is usually through a natural opening, such as the mouth or anus, although some endoscopes are introduced through small incisions made in the skin.

The first endoscopes were rigid, but various flexible instruments have been developed since the 1960s. Although most endoscopes now in routine use are flexible, rigid types are preferred in certain cases, including investigations in which there is a short distance from the skin to the structure being viewed, such as in an examination of the knee joint.

HOW DO THEY WORK?

There are many types of endoscope, each specifically designed to investigate a particular part of the body. Flexible and rigid forms of endoscopes are different in appearance, but they share many of the same features. For example, both flexible and rigid endoscopes use light, reflection, and magnification to show body structures clearly.

FLEXIBLE ENDOSCOPES The development of flexible endoscopes has been made possible by the invention of fiberoptics. Fiberoptics use thin, flexible fibers of glass or plastic (optical fibers) that transmit light along their length by internal reflections. The main part of a flexible endoscope consists of a long, thin tube containing several channels that run along its length. Some channels in the endoscope carry optical fibers to provide light or transmit the image back up to the eyepiece. Other channels contain wires to control the direction of the endoscope. Channels may also be used to pump or suck air or fluid into or out of the area being examined. Other channels may be used to pass down various instruments, such as biopsy forceps or scissors.

Most flexible endoscopes now have a miniature camera built into their tip, and the view recorded by the camera is displayed on a monitor. This facility

PROCEDURE RIGID ENDOSCOPY

Rigid endoscopes can be used to examine several internal organs and structures, especially joints and the external surfaces of organs within the abdominal cavity, such as the ovaries. The most frequently investigated joint is the knee, primarily because damage to it is common. Investigations using rigid endoscopes are often done under general anesthesia. The endoscope is inserted through a small incision in the skin. Further small incisions may be made for other instruments, such as forceps. The internal structures may be viewed on a monitor or through an eyepiece.

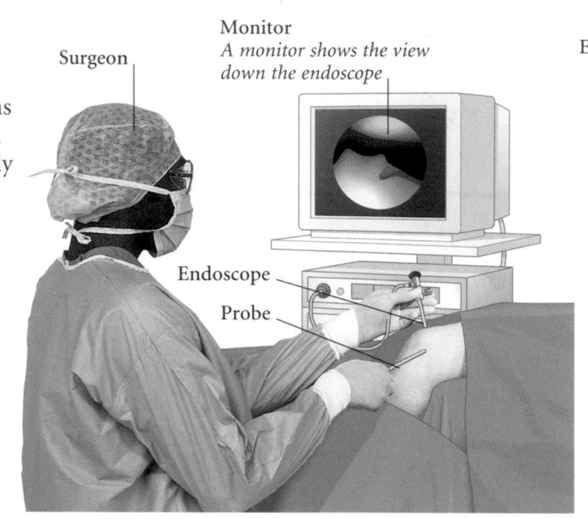
Surgeon
Monitor
A monitor shows the view down the endoscope
Endoscope
Probe

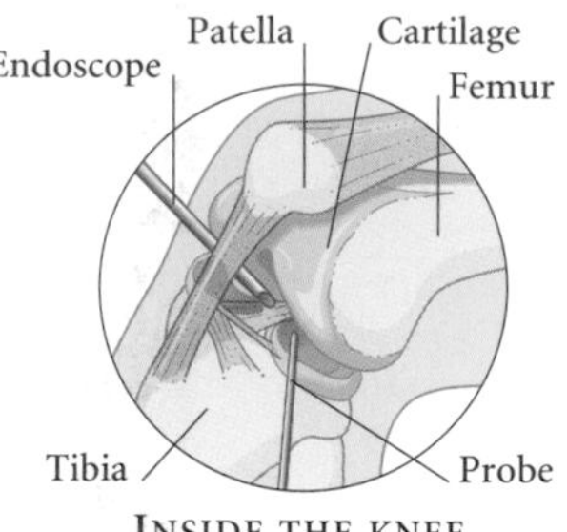
Endoscope
Patella
Cartilage
Femur
Tibia
Probe

INSIDE THE KNEE

During the procedure
For endoscopy of the knee joint, you will be given a general anesthetic. Small incisions are made on either side of the knee through which the endoscope and other instruments are passed.

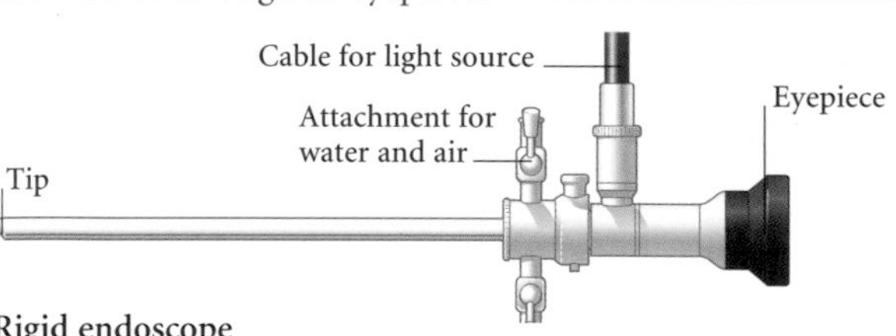
Cable for light source
Attachment for water and air
Tip
Eyepiece

Rigid endoscope
A rigid endoscope is a straight, narrow metal tube with an eyepiece at one end to which a camera can be attached if necessary. A light source is connected to the endoscope and illuminates the structure or organ. Water and air can be pumped down the tube if necessary.

VIEW

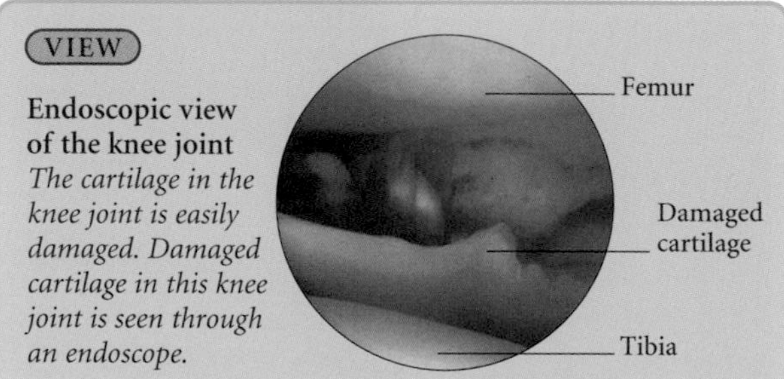
Femur
Damaged cartilage
Tibia

Endoscopic view of the knee joint
The cartilage in the knee joint is easily damaged. Damaged cartilage in this knee joint is seen through an endoscope.

allows the doctor and his or her colleagues, and sometimes the patient, to observe an investigation together and makes it possible for a videotaped record to be kept for reference.

RIGID ENDOSCOPES These endoscopes are normally much shorter than flexible endoscopes and are usually inserted through an incision in the skin. Like flexible endoscopes, rigid endoscopes use a fiberoptic light source. However, other instruments, such as those used to hold tissues out of the way or to perform a surgical procedure, are passed through a separate incision rather than down the endoscope.

To allow the surfaces of the different organs or structures to be seen clearly, investigations using rigid endoscopes often involve expanding the organ or body cavity with gas or fluid to separate tissue surfaces. For example, air may be pumped into the abdomen during a laparoscopy (p.742) so that the abdominal organs can be examined.

WHAT ARE THEY USED FOR?

Flexible endoscopes are particularly useful for looking at the digestive and respiratory tracts, which bend in places (*see* FLEXIBLE ENDOSCOPY, p.255). For example, nasendoscopes are very thin, short, flexible endoscopes that are used to inspect the nasal cavity and the surrounding sinuses (*see* ENDOSCOPY OF THE NOSE AND THROAT, p.476). Rigid endoscopes are used to investigate the abdominal cavity and joints (*see* RIGID ENDOSCOPY, above), where the structure to be viewed is near the skin surface.

If an abnormality is discovered during endoscopy, samples can be taken and, in some cases, treatment can be performed immediately. Instruments may be passed either down the channels of an endoscope or through small incisions in the skin and enable the doctor to perform certain procedures such as taking tissue samples or removing foreign bodies. An endoscope can also be used to introduce a contrast medium into a particular site so that detailed images can then be produced on X-rays (*see* ERCP, p.653).

Some surgical procedures, such as removal of the gallbladder, that used to require a lengthy operation and a large incision can now be performed far more quickly and easily using instruments together with a rigid endoscope (*see* ENDOSCOPIC SURGERY, p.948).

WHAT ARE THE RISKS?

Endoscopy is generally very safe, but, in rare cases, the endoscope may perforate nearby tissue. For example, if the endoscope is in the stomach it may pierce the digestive tract. Immediate surgery will then be needed to repair the damage. If a tissue sample is taken, there may be some bleeding from the site.

For some endoscopic investigations, general anesthesia or sedation may be required (*see* HAVING A GENERAL ANESTHETIC, p.944), and these carry risks of their own. Your doctor will therefore make sure that your health is sufficiently good to undergo the procedure.

Your Body and Disease

This section covers a comprehensive range of diseases and disorders arranged mainly by body system. The normal anatomy and functioning of each body system is explained first, followed by articles on the disorders that affect that body system. Each article investigates the causes, symptoms, diagnosis, treatment options, and prognosis of the disorder concerned. Most of the articles direct you to online sites where further information can be found.

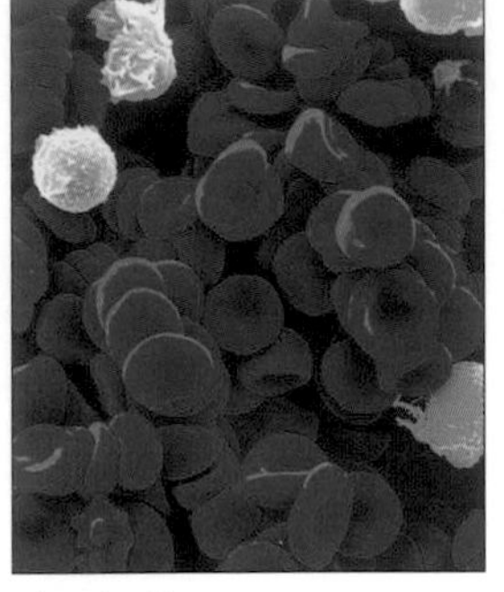

Blood cells
Two components of blood that are essential to health are white blood cells to fight disease and red blood cells to carry oxygen.

INTRODUCTION

HUMAN BEINGS ARE ROBUST AND ADAPTABLE, able to survive in a wide range of environments and to endure physical and psychological stress. The body's design incorporates systems that renew and repair it continually and others that protect it from harm. Many trivial injuries or potential illnesses heal themselves or are controlled before we are even aware of them. However, throughout a lifetime, we are exposed to a relentless stream of minor and more serious diseases and injuries with a wide variety of effects on the body.

You become ill when something disrupts the normal healthy working of your body. Why you become ill at any particular time is a question with multiple answers, many of which focus on your genes. Some rare diseases are caused by an inherited faulty gene, but genes are also a contributing factor in many other illnesses. In particular, they predict to some extent your chance of developing some of the major diseases of adult life, such as cancer and stroke. Genes also help determine your susceptibility to many mental health problems. Other factors that affect your chance of falling ill include age, environment, and the way you live.

One hundred years ago, people were most at risk from infectious diseases. New drugs, immunizations, and advances in hygiene and public sanitation have dramatically reduced mortality from infectious diseases in the developed world, although they remain a major threat in the developing world. Today, the major causes of death in Canada are heart disease, cancer, stroke, and unintentional injuries. Each one is strongly associated with lifestyle, and the risk can be reduced by changes in behavior. As a result, doctors now recognize that prevention is as important as treatment.

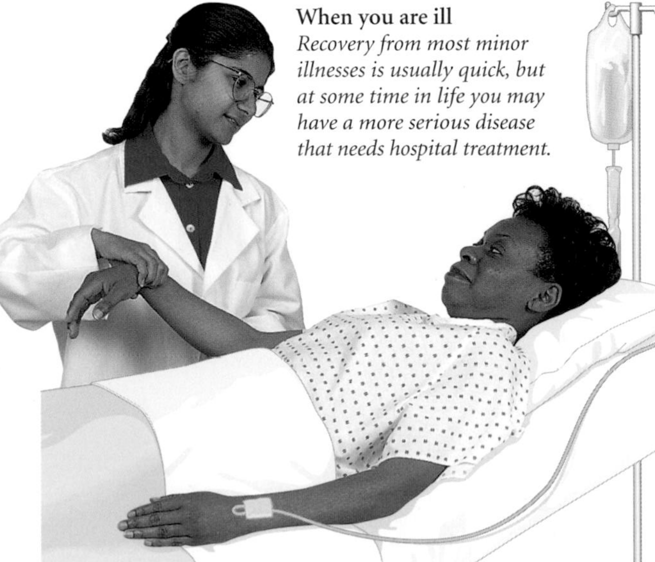

When you are ill
Recovery from most minor illnesses is usually quick, but at some time in life you may have a more serious disease that needs hospital treatment.

UNDERSTANDING THE BODY

The body can be divided into a number of major systems that carry out vital functions. For example, the immune system protects you from infection and some diseases. The bones, muscles, nerves, skin, blood, and other tissues that make up body systems are made of billions of connected cells. Each cell is a specialized, fully functioning unit, and all its activities are controlled by the genetic code contained in the DNA (deoxyribonucleic acid) in its nucleus.

In this book, most diseases and disorders are grouped in sections under the body system that they affect. Each section begins with a description of the normal anatomy and physiology of a body system to help you understand the disorders that follow. However, diseases can also be categorized according to the mechanisms by which they damage the body.

EFFECTS OF DISEASE

The different ways in which diseases damage the body are called disease processes. Several body systems may be damaged by the same process. For example, the major cause of disability and death in Canada, coronary artery disease, is an ischemic disease.

STRUCTURE AND FUNCTION THE HUMAN BODY

The body consists of various systems that interact with each other. Making up these systems are organs and tissues that work together to carry out a specific body function, such as digestion. The different types of tissues that make up organs and other body parts are highly specialized. For example, the stomach has muscular walls for churning food and a mucosa lining that secretes gastric juices and protective mucus. The interconnected cells that make up these tissues each contain genes that program cell activities.

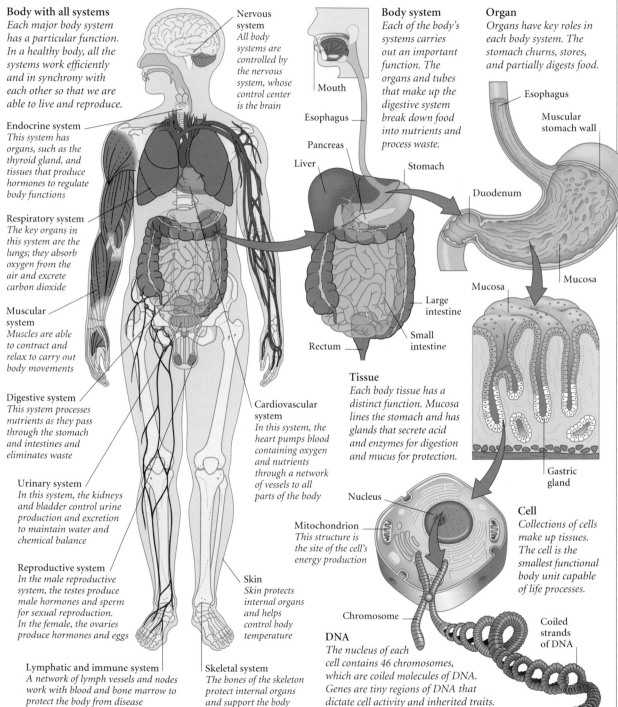

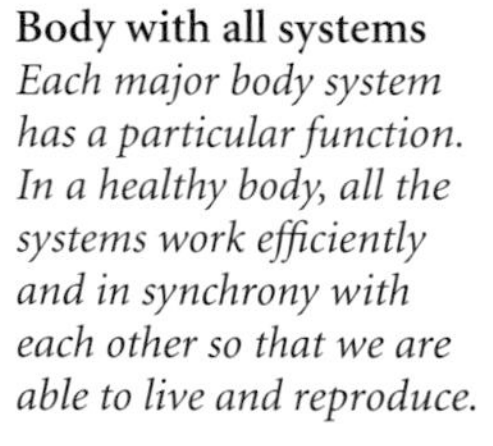
Body with all systems
Each major body system has a particular function. In a healthy body, all the systems work efficiently and in synchrony with each other so that we are able to live and reproduce.
Nervous system
All body systems are controlled by the nervous system, whose control center is the brain
Endocrine system
This system has organs, such as the thyroid gland, and tissues that produce hormones to regulate body functions
Respiratory system
The key organs in this system are the lungs; they absorb oxygen from the air and excrete carbon dioxide
Muscular system
Muscles are able to contract and relax to carry out body movements
Digestive system
This system processes nutrients as they pass through the stomach and intestines and eliminates waste
Urinary system
In this system, the kidneys and bladder control urine production and excretion to maintain water and chemical balance
Reproductive system
In the male reproductive system, the testes produce male hormones and sperm for sexual reproduction. In the female, the ovaries produce hormones and eggs
Lymphatic and immune system
A network of lymph vessels and nodes work with blood and bone marrow to protect the body from disease
Cardiovascular system
In this system, the heart pumps blood containing oxygen and nutrients through a network of vessels to all parts of the body
Skin
Skin protects internal organs and helps control body temperature
Skeletal system
The bones of the skeleton protect internal organs and support the body
Mouth
Esophagus
Pancreas
Liver
Stomach
Large intestine
Small intestine
Rectum
Body system
Each of the body's systems carries out an important function. The organs and tubes that make up the digestive system break down food into nutrients and process waste.
Organ
Organs have key roles in each body system. The stomach churns, stores, and partially digests food.
Esophagus
Muscular stomach wall
Duodenum
Mucosa
Mucosa
Gastric gland
Tissue
Each body tissue has a distinct function. Mucosa lines the stomach and has glands that secrete acid and enzymes for digestion and mucus for protection.
Nucleus
Mitochondrion
This structure is the site of the cell's energy production
Cell
Collections of cells make up tissues. The cell is the smallest functional body unit capable of life processes.
Chromosome
Coiled strands of DNA
DNA
The nucleus of each cell contains 46 chromosomes, which are coiled molecules of DNA. Genes are tiny regions of DNA that dictate cell activity and inherited traits.

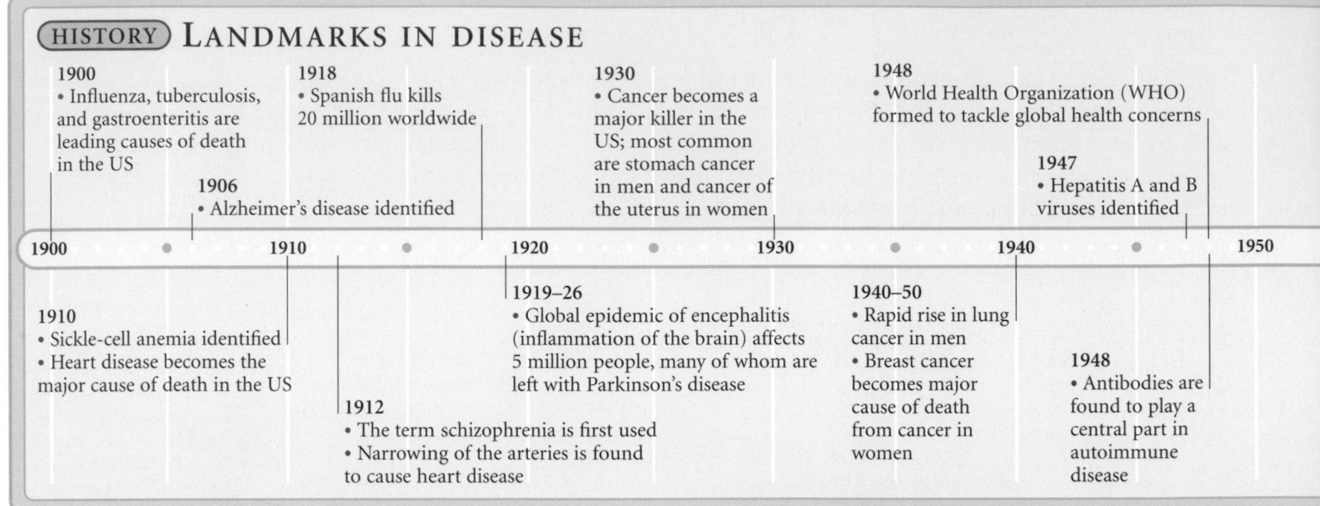
HISTORY LANDMARKS IN DISEASE
1900
• Influenza, tuberculosis, and gastroenteritis are leading causes of death in the US
1918
• Spanish flu kills 20 million worldwide
1930
• Cancer becomes a major killer in the US; most common are stomach cancer in men and cancer of the uterus in women
1948
• World Health Organization (WHO) formed to tackle global health concerns
1906
• Alzheimer's disease identified
1947
• Hepatitis A and B viruses identified
1900
1910
1920
1930
1940
1950
1910
• Sickle-cell anemia identified
• Heart disease becomes the major cause of death in the US
1912
• The term schizophrenia is first used
• Narrowing of the arteries is found to cause heart disease
1919–26
• Global epidemic of encephalitis (inflammation of the brain) affects 5 million people, many of whom are left with Parkinson's disease
1940–50
• Rapid rise in lung cancer in men
• Breast cancer becomes major cause of death from cancer in women
1948
• Antibodies are found to play a central part in autoimmune disease

The rise and fall of disease
The decline, control, and, in some cases, eradication of infectious diseases during the past 100 years was countered by a steady rise in heart disease, cancers, and stroke. These major causes of death in the developed world are now becoming global health problems.

SUSCEPTIBILITY TO DISEASE

Your genes, ethnicity, age, and social and geographical environment all contribute to your chance of becoming ill. However, you can help reduce your risk by following the guidelines for healthy living (*see* TAKING CONTROL OF YOUR HEALTH, pp.15–86).

Most illnesses can occur at any age, but there are stages of life when people are vulnerable to particular types of illness or behave in a way that makes them susceptible to accidents and injury. At certain ages, people may find themselves under the kind of pressures that could lead to psychological disorders.

Babies are susceptible to infectious disease because their immune systems are not fully developed and they have not had previous exposure to infections. Young children tend to have frequent accidents while their physical skills are still developing.

In their teens and in early adulthood, people have a relatively small chance of developing a serious illness and are more likely to injure themselves. Adolescents are prone to eating disorders, depression, and substance abuse. Many eat unhealthily, do insufficient exercise, smoke, and drink too much alcohol, factors that contribute to many of the major diseases, such as heart disease, that are increasingly common after middle age. As people age, the incidence of chronic illness and disability increases, and, for some people, poor physical health leads to mental health problems. Susceptibility to disease is closely linked to social factors. In Canada, rates of chronic illness are much higher in poor families than in those with a reasonable standard of living.

CHANGING DISEASE PATTERNS

During the past 50 years, many major infectious diseases have been brought under control. However, AIDS, a deadly new disease caused by HIV infection, has emerged and is now a leading cause of death.

For most of the 20th century, cardiovascular disease, cancer, and stroke were major causes of death in developed areas. Their high incidence is due in part to the increasing average age of the population. As the number of people over 65 is predicted to double by the year 2025, and the proportion of younger people is predicted to fall, these chronic diseases are likely to continue to be major global threats to health.

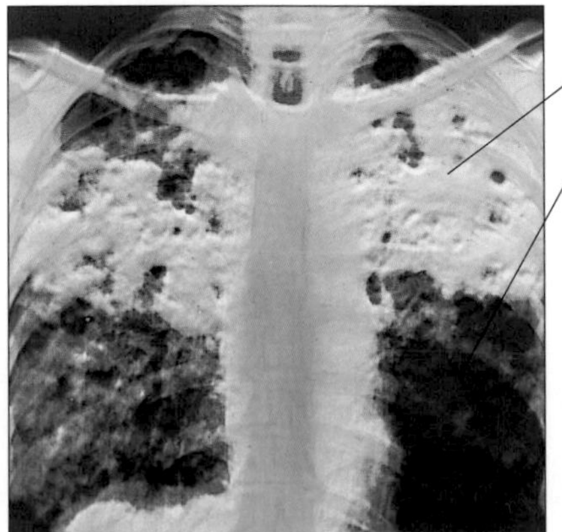
Infected lung tissue
Normal lung tissue

Lungs damaged by tuberculosis
AIDS has increased the incidence of tuberculosis around the world.

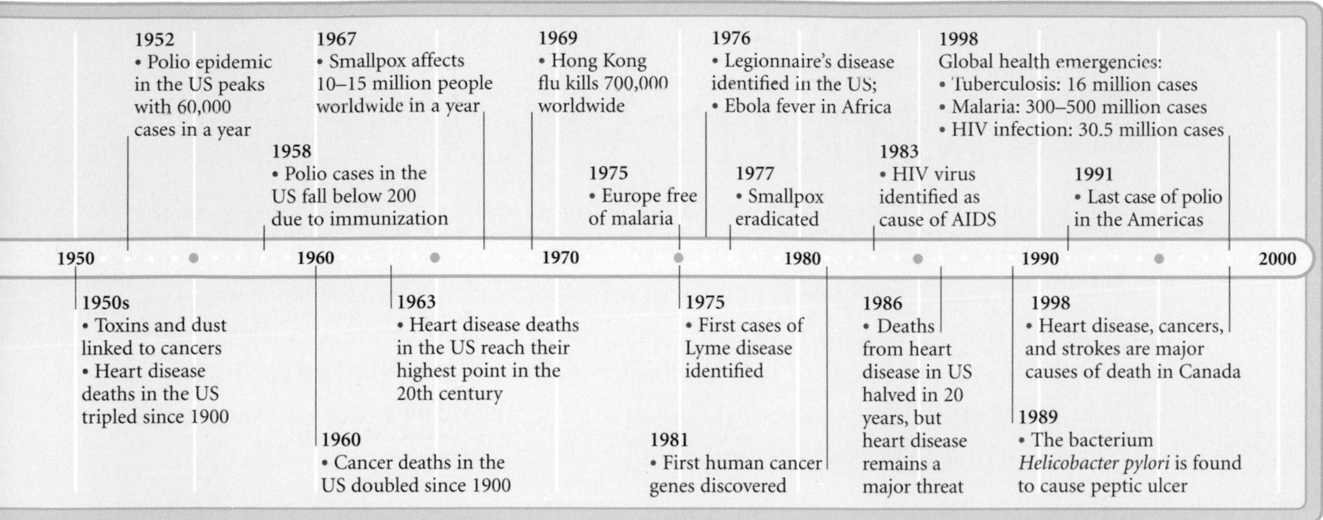
1952
• Polio epidemic in the US peaks with 60,000 cases in a year
1967
• Smallpox affects 10–15 million people worldwide in a year
1969
• Hong Kong flu kills 700,000 worldwide
1976
• Legionnaire's disease identified in the US;
• Ebola fever in Africa
1998
Global health emergencies:
• Tuberculosis: 16 million cases
• Malaria: 300–500 million cases
• HIV infection: 30.5 million cases
1958
• Polio cases in the US fall below 200 due to immunization
1975
• Europe free of malaria
1977
• Smallpox eradicated
1983
• HIV virus identified as cause of AIDS
1991
• Last case of polio in the Americas
1950
1960
1970
1980
1990
2000
1950s
• Toxins and dust linked to cancers
• Heart disease deaths in the US tripled since 1900
1963
• Heart disease deaths in the US reach their highest point in the 20th century
1975
• First cases of Lyme disease identified
1986
• Deaths from heart disease in US halved in 20 years, but heart disease remains a major threat
1998
• Heart disease, cancers, and strokes are major causes of death in Canada
1960
• Cancer deaths in the US doubled since 1900
1981
• First human cancer genes discovered
1989
• The bacterium *Helicobacter pylori* is found to cause peptic ulcer

ORGANIZATION HOW THIS PART OF THE BOOK IS ORGANIZED

Most of this part of the book is organized into major body systems. Each of these sections begins with an illustrated guide to the structure and function of the system and its organs, followed by articles on the diseases affecting that system. There are separate sections on infections, which can affect any body system, serious multi-system injuries, and the principles of cancer. Disorders related to sex and reproduction and pregnancy and childbirth have their own sections, as do problems that exclusively affect children or problems that have different effects in children.

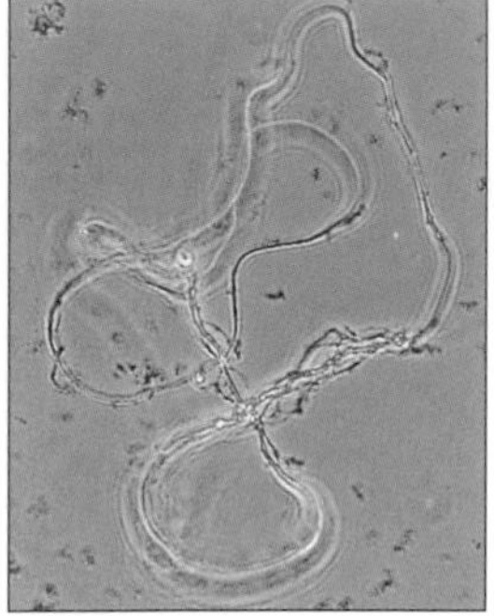

DNA
Genes are made of DNA, a double-stranded helical molecule that is found in the nucleus of cells.

GENES AND INHERITANCE

GENES CONTROL THE GROWTH, REPAIR, AND FUNCTIONS of cells in the human body. Genes are made of DNA (deoxyribonucleic acid), which is found in the nucleus of cells as threads called chromosomes. The DNA provides the cells with all the necessary instructions for building proteins. Proteins are needed for the development and growth of all the body's organs and structures, and genes are the means by which physical and mental characteristics are passed on to children.

There are about 5 trillion cells in the adult human body, and all of them, except red blood cells, have a set of genes made of DNA. This chemical has a double helix shape and consists of two strands of molecules joined together in the center by a series of nucleotide bases. The DNA is coiled into structures called chromosomes that are stored in the nucleus of cells.

GENE ORGANIZATION

Human genes are arranged on 22 pairs of matching chromosomes, plus two sex chromosomes. One chromosome in each pair is inherited from each parent. Therefore, body cells contain two copies of genes, with the genes for the same characteristic carried on the matching chromosomes in a pair. Egg and sperm cells, called sex cells, have 23 single chromosomes so that a paired set of genes is created when a sperm cell fertilizes an egg.

There are about 30,000 pairs of genes in a human body cell. Every gene has one function, to act as a recipe that provides the cell with the information it needs to make specific proteins when needed. The order of nucleotide bases along the DNA provides this information. Each body cell contains the same genes, but each tissue or organ needs to make different proteins. For this reason, many genes in an individual body cell are permanently switched off, and a system exists to turn on genes only when they are required.

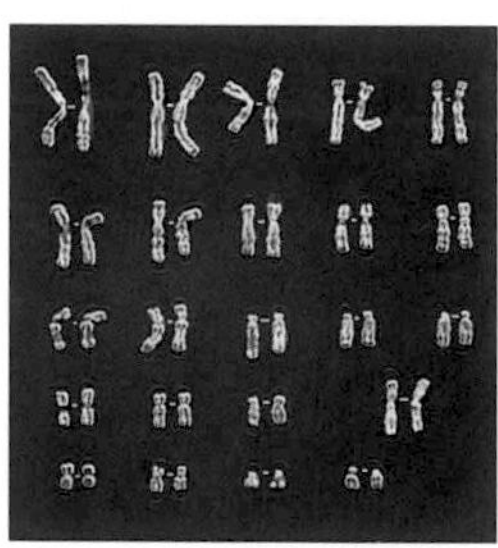

Human chromosomes
Human body cells contain 46 chromosomes, which can be organized in 23 pairs.

Often, both of the genes in a matching pair are identical. However, some matching genes occur in slightly different forms called alleles. Some genes may have two to several hundred different alleles. These different forms account for differences among individuals, such as the shade of hair color or the length of the nose. Differences in just 0.1 percent of our DNA create all our unique features.

Most of the differences that occur between genes do not affect function. For example, blue eyes work as well as brown ones. However, some genetic differences have important effects. For example, inherited diseases, such as cystic fibrosis, are caused by different forms of abnormal genes. Genes may also play a part in disorders such as coronary artery disease and some cancers, such as colorectal and breast cancer.

COPYING GENES

Every time a cell divides into two during growth or repair, its genes are duplicated so that each new cell has a full set. When sperm or egg cells are made, the chromosomes join together and exchange genes between each other before the cell divides. This ensures that when an egg and a sperm fuse, the new child is different from both its parents and from its siblings.

STRUCTURE THE HUMAN GENOME

The human genome contains about 30,000 pairs of genes. In 1990 the Human Genome Project was set up to identify each gene and its sequence of nucleotide bases. The information will give a better understanding of how disorders are passed from parent to child and may aid the development of treatments for inherited disorders. One of the major goals of the project was to better understand the role of genetics in common diseases. Many genes for disorders, including those on the X chromosome such as those shown at right, have already been identified.

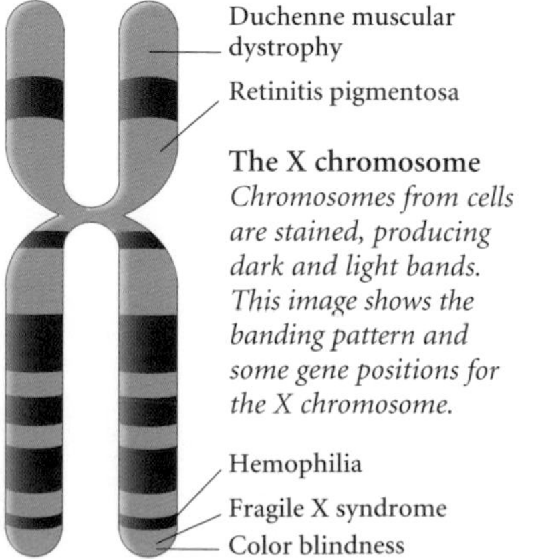
Duchenne muscular dystrophy
Retinitis pigmentosa
Hemophilia
Fragile X syndrome
Color blindness

The X chromosome
Chromosomes from cells are stained, producing dark and light bands. This image shows the banding pattern and some gene positions for the X chromosome.

STRUCTURE — STRUCTURE OF GENETIC MATERIAL

Genes are made up of DNA, which is shaped like a twisted ladder with rungs made of molecules called nucleotide bases linked together in specific pairs. The arrangement of these bases along the DNA provides the cell with instructions on making proteins. DNA is tightly coiled into rod-shaped structures called chromosomes, which are stored in the nucleus of the cell. There are 22 pairs of chromosomes in each body cell plus two sex chromosomes.

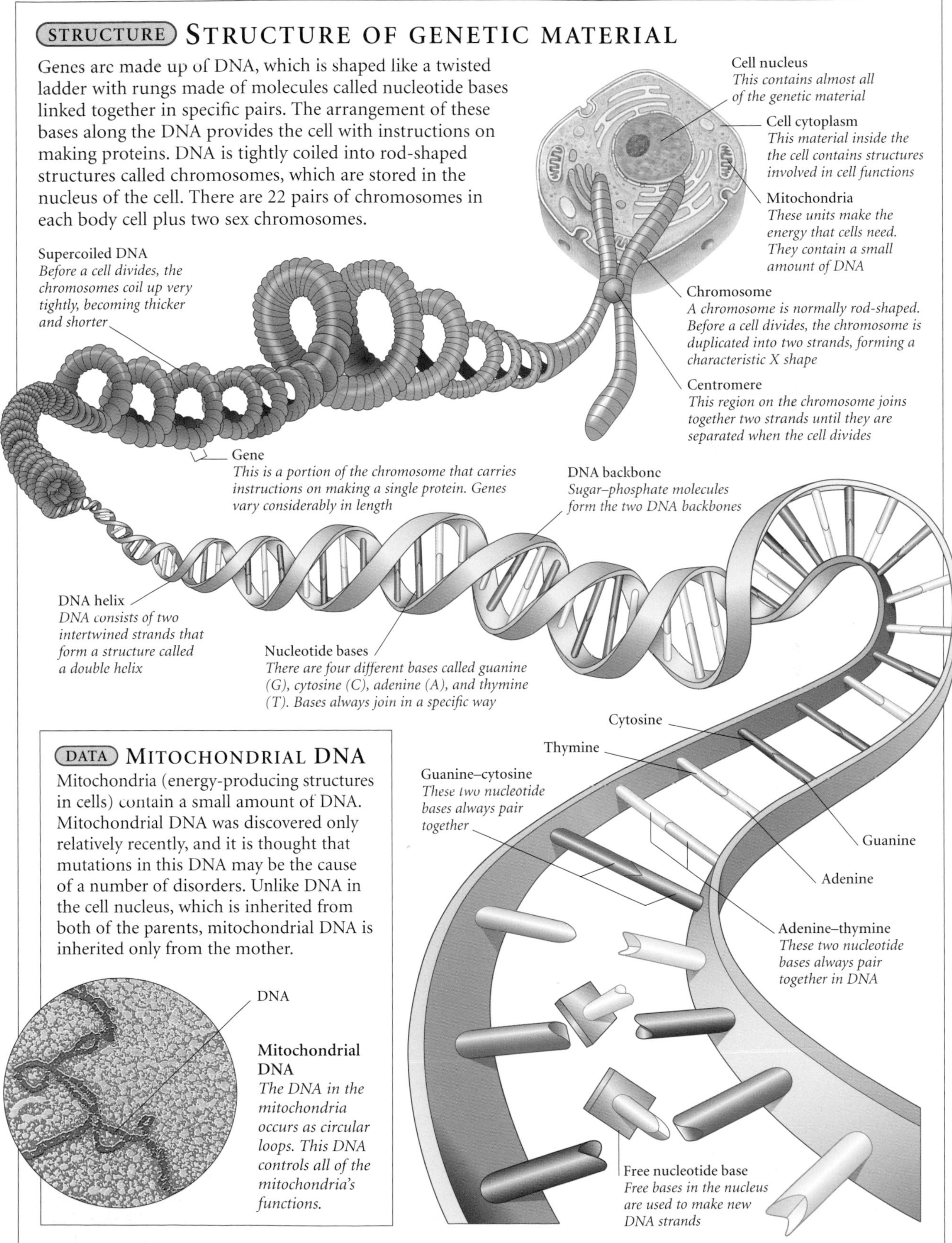
Cell nucleus
This contains almost all of the genetic material
Cell cytoplasm
This material inside the the cell contains structures involved in cell functions
Mitochondria
These units make the energy that cells need. They contain a small amount of DNA
Supercoiled DNA
Before a cell divides, the chromosomes coil up very tightly, becoming thicker and shorter
Chromosome
A chromosome is normally rod-shaped. Before a cell divides, the chromosome is duplicated into two strands, forming a characteristic X shape
Centromere
This region on the chromosome joins together two strands until they are separated when the cell divides
Gene
This is a portion of the chromosome that carries instructions on making a single protein. Genes vary considerably in length
DNA backbone
Sugar–phosphate molecules form the two DNA backbones
DNA helix
DNA consists of two intertwined strands that form a structure called a double helix
Nucleotide bases
There are four different bases called guanine (G), cytosine (C), adenine (A), and thymine (T). Bases always join in a specific way
Cytosine
Thymine
Guanine–cytosine
These two nucleotide bases always pair together
Guanine
Adenine
Adenine–thymine
These two nucleotide bases always pair together in DNA
Free nucleotide base
Free bases in the nucleus are used to make new DNA strands
DNA
Mitochondrial DNA
The DNA in the mitochondria occurs as circular loops. This DNA controls all of the mitochondria's functions.

DATA — MITOCHONDRIAL DNA

Mitochondria (energy-producing structures in cells) contain a small amount of DNA. Mitochondrial DNA was discovered only relatively recently, and it is thought that mutations in this DNA may be the cause of a number of disorders. Unlike DNA in the cell nucleus, which is inherited from both of the parents, mitochondrial DNA is inherited only from the mother.

FUNCTION THE ROLE OF DNA

DNA contains instructions for making proteins, which have many roles in the body. Some make up body structures, such as skin and hair; others are hormones or enzymes that control cell activities. Proteins are made from amino acids, of which there are 20 types, and are made according to instructions relayed by messenger RNA (mRNA). An mRNA strand is a copy of a gene. mRNA has four bases; three are the same as those of DNA, one is unique to mRNA.

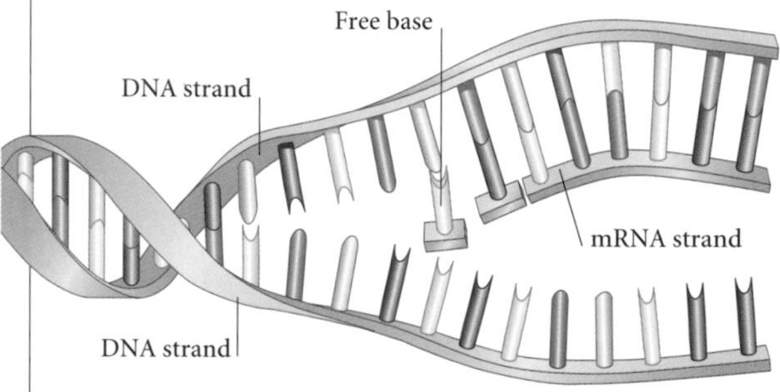
Free base
DNA strand
mRNA strand
DNA strand

1 Strands of DNA separate along a stretch of the molecule. Free bases attach to corresponding bases on one DNA strand to make mRNA. The newly formed mRNA carries the instructions for making a protein and moves into the cytoplasm.

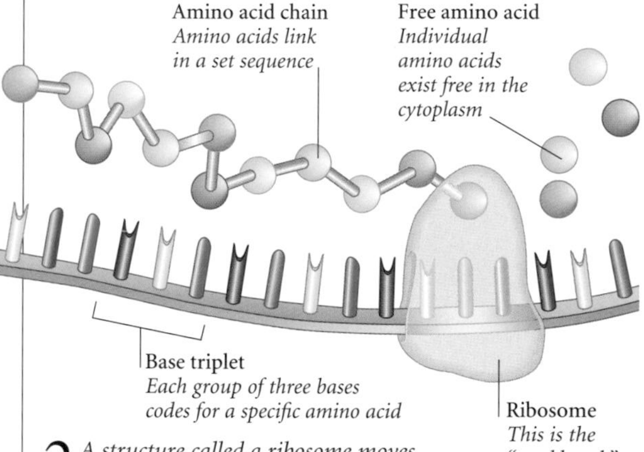
Amino acid chain
Amino acids link in a set sequence
Free amino acid
Individual amino acids exist free in the cytoplasm
Base triplet
Each group of three bases codes for a specific amino acid
Ribosome
This is the "workbench" on which amino acids are built up

2 A structure called a ribosome moves along the strand of mRNA three bases at a time. The ribosome brings specific amino acids into place according to the sequence of bases in the mRNA triplets.

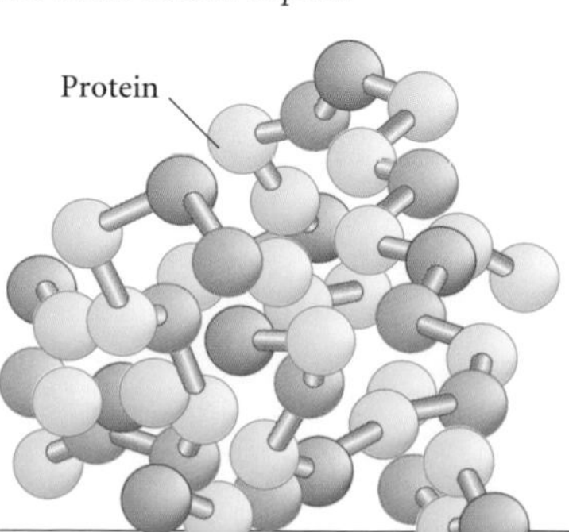
Protein

3 When the ribosome reaches the end of the mRNA strand, it detaches itself from the assembled chain of amino acids. The chain then folds up to form the newly completed protein.

PROCESS CELL DIVISION

The process of growth requires body cells to divide and multiply constantly. Cells also divide to replace those that have become worn out. When a cell divides, its genetic material is copied. This type of cell division is called mitosis. A slightly different process of cell division, called meiosis, results in the production of egg and sperm cells. In this process, the resulting cells have only half the amount of DNA and the genes are rearranged to create a mix of genetic information.

REPLICATION OF DNA

Before a cell can divide to make new body cells or egg and sperm cells, the DNA in the cell must be copied. Each of the two strands in the original DNA acts as a template against which two new strands are built.

1 The original DNA double helix splits open at several points along its length. This process produces areas where there are two separate single strands.

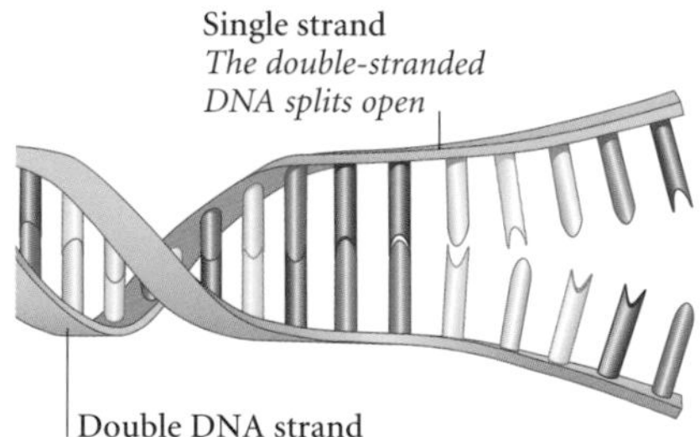
Single strand
The double-stranded DNA splits open
Double DNA strand

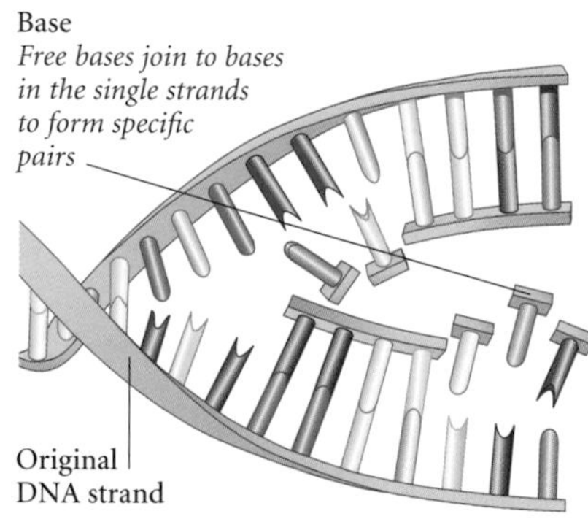
Base
Free bases join to bases in the single strands to form specific pairs
Original DNA strand

2 New free bases (units of DNA) are attached to both of the single strands of DNA. The order in which the bases join to the single DNA strands is determined by the DNA bases that are already present on the single strand.

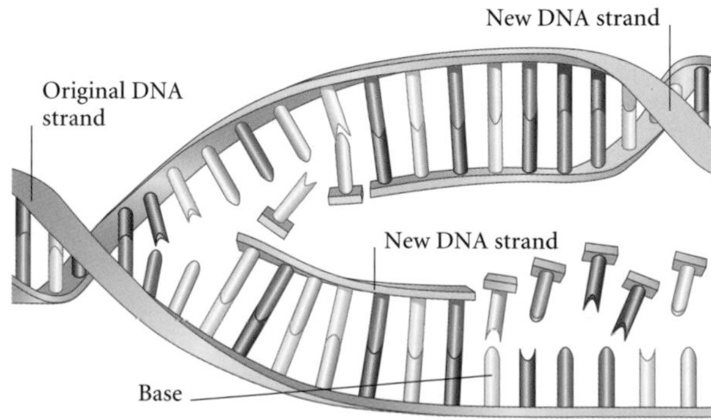
New DNA strand
Original DNA strand
New DNA strand
Base

3 While the bases attach to the strand, each of the two newly formed double strands start to twist. The process continues along the whole length of the DNA, eventually producing two identical double DNA strands.

Mitosis

When body cells divide, their genetic material has to be duplicated so that each new cell has a complete set of genes. This process of division is called mitosis and results in cells identical to the original cell. In the diagram below, only four chromosomes are shown for simplicity.

1 *The DNA in the chromosomes is copied to form two identical strands joined in the center by a structure called the centromere.*

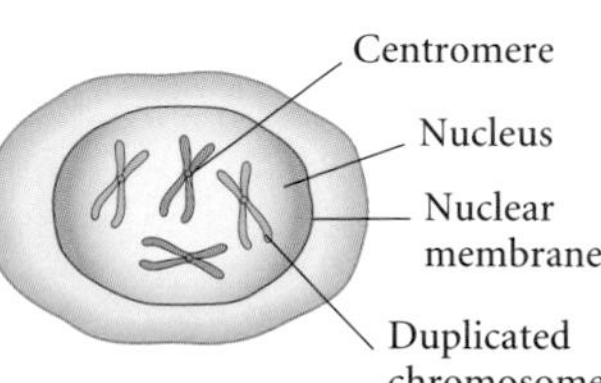
Centromere
Nucleus
Nuclear membrane
Duplicated chromosome

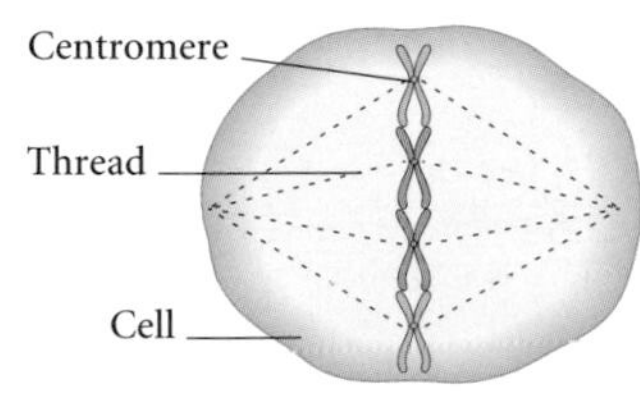
Centromere
Thread
Cell

2 *The membrane around the nucleus breaks down and threads form across the cell. The chromosomes line up on the threads.*

3 *The duplicated chromosomes are pulled apart by the threads. The single chromosomes move to opposite sides of the cell.*

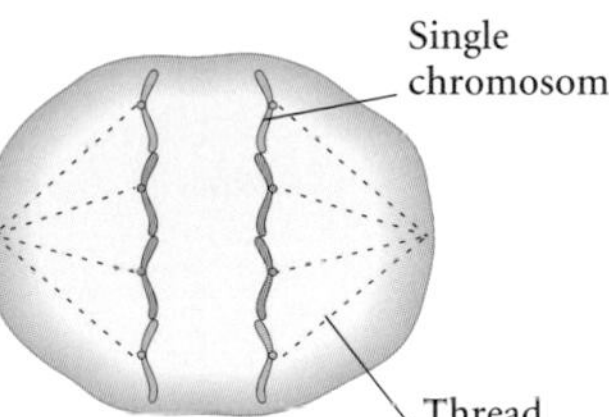
Single chromosome
Thread

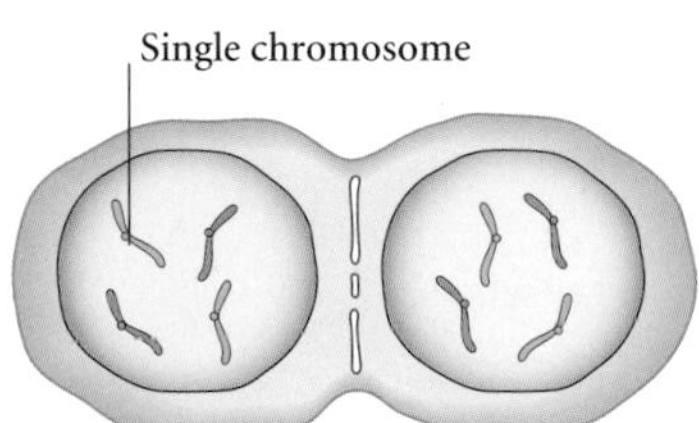
Single chromosome

4 *A nuclear membrane forms around each set of single chromosomes. The cell begins to divide into two new cells.*

5 *Two new cells form. Each cell has a central nucleus containing an identical set of chromosomes.*

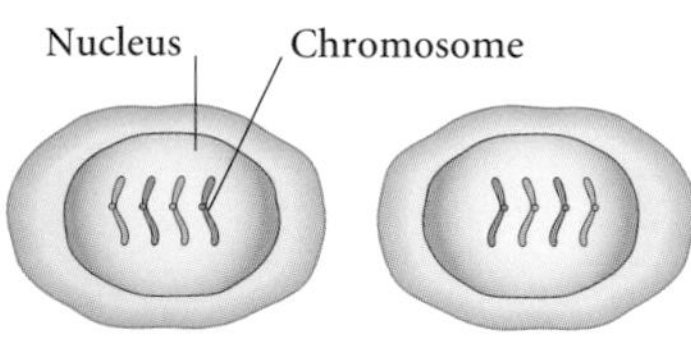
Nucleus
Chromosome

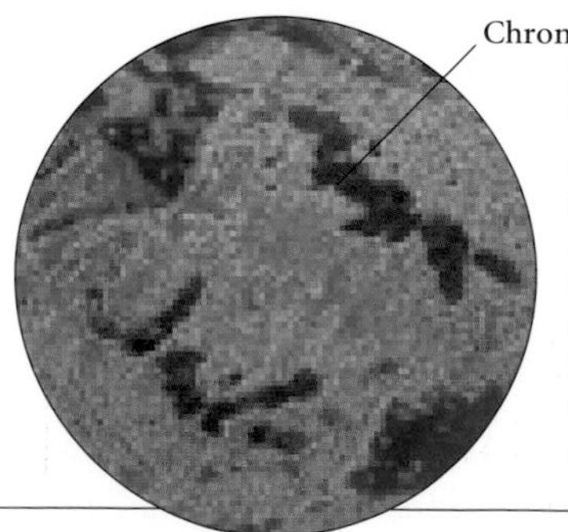
Chromosomes

Dividing cell
This highly magnified image shows a body cell dividing by mitosis. Separated chromosomes can be seen in the middle of each of the new cells.

Meiosis

Sperm cells in males and egg cells in females are produced by a form of cell division called meiosis. In this process, the amount of genetic material in the new cells is halved during two stages of cell division. This process ensures that a complete set of genes is obtained when an egg and sperm fuse. During meiosis, matching pairs of chromosomes exchange genetic material randomly. Each of the resulting sperm or egg cells then has a slightly different mixture of genes from each other.

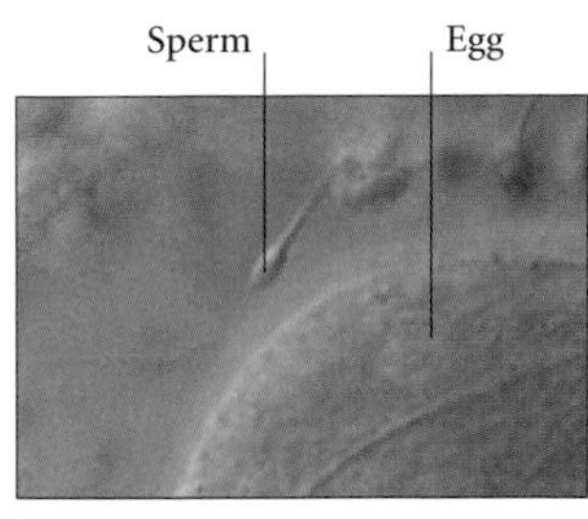
Sperm
Egg

Sperm and egg
This magnified view shows an egg and sperm just before fertilization. Each of these sex cells is made by a process of division called meiosis.

1 *DNA in the chromosomes is duplicated to form X-shaped double chromosomes. Each of these is joined in the center by a structure called a centromere.*

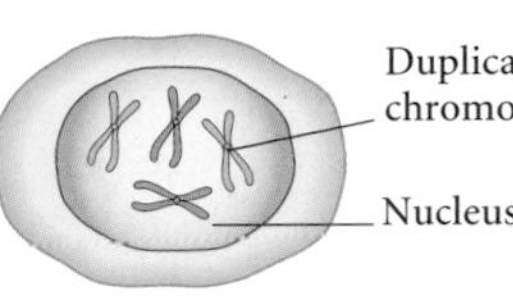
Duplicated chromosome
Nucleus

Matching pair of chromosomes
DNA may be exchanged where the chromosomes come into contact

2 *The membrane around the nucleus disappears. Matching chromosomes touch in random places and may exchange genetic material.*

3 *Each of the duplicated chromosomes has a mixture of genetic material. Threads form in the cell to pull the pairs of chromosomes apart.*

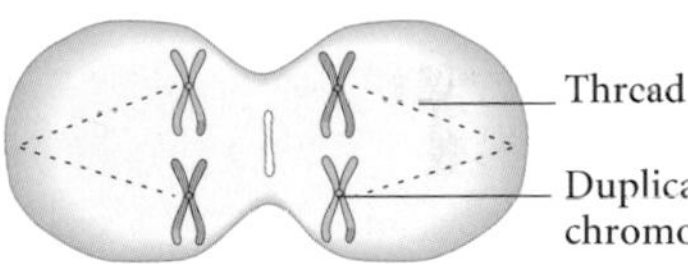
Thread
Duplicated chromosome

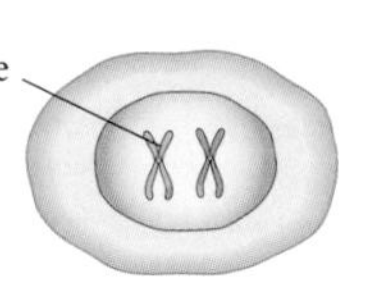
Duplicated chromosome

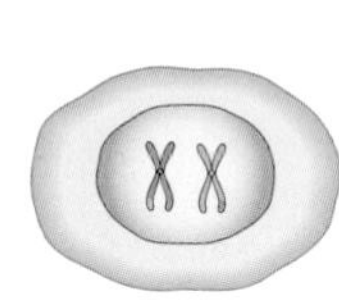

4 *The cell divides to produce two new cells. Each new cell has a full set of 23 duplicated chromosomes from the original cell.*

5 *The duplicated chromosomes line up. More threads attach to each chromosome. Each duplicated chromosome is pulled apart to form two single chromosomes.*

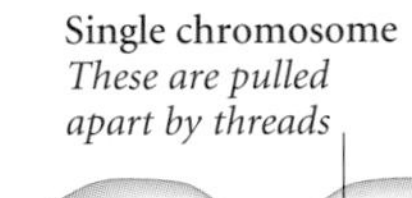

Single chromosome
These are pulled apart by threads

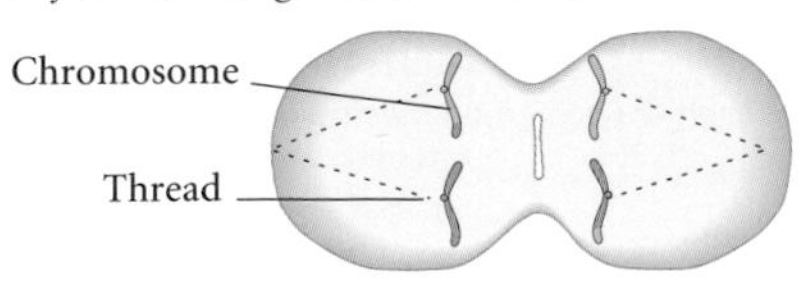
Chromosome
Thread

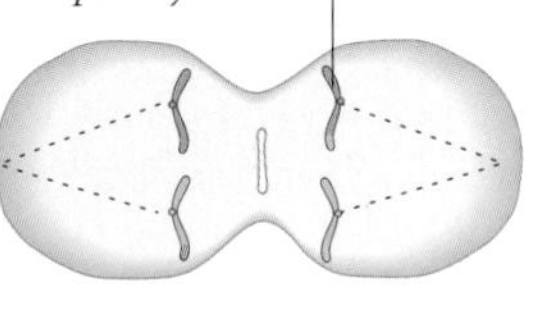

6 *The two cells divide to produce four cells from the original single cell, each with half the amount of genetic material. Each cell has a slightly different mixture of genes.*

Chromosome

Nucleus

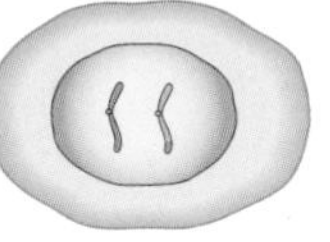

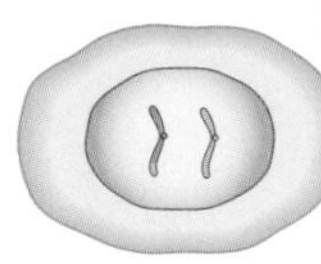

STRUCTURE AND FUNCTION INHERITANCE

Physical characteristics, many disorders, and some aspects of behavior are at least partly determined by genes passed from parents to children. Genes for each characteristic are always found at the same place on the same chromosome. At fertilization, each of the 23 single chromosomes in an egg cell and a sperm cell matches up into pairs, making a full set of 46 chromosomes that contains two copies of each gene.

HOW GENES ARE INHERITED

Half of a child's genes are inherited from its mother and half from its father. In turn, the child's parents inherited half of their genes from each of their own parents. Therefore, approximately one-quarter of a child's genes has been inherited from each of its grandparents.

GRANDPARENTS

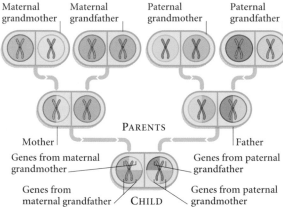

Maternal grandmother
Maternal grandfather
Paternal grandmother
Paternal grandfather
PARENTS
Mother
Father
Genes from maternal grandmother
Genes from paternal grandfather
Genes from maternal grandfather
CHILD
Genes from paternal grandmother

Child's genetic makeup
A child's genes are a mix of genes from his or her parents and grandparents. About one-quarter of each child's genes are inherited from each grandparent.

HOW GENDER IS DETERMINED

There are two sex chromosomes, X and Y, that determine gender. Females have two X chromosomes and males have an X and a Y chromosome, in addition to the 22 other chromosomes. Therefore, all eggs have an X chromosome, while sperm may contain an X or a Y chromosome. The gender of a child depends on whether the sex chromosome in the sperm that fertilizes the egg is X or Y.

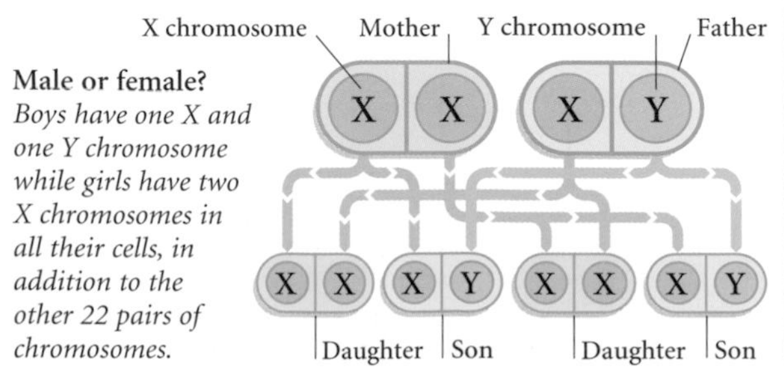
X chromosome
Mother
Y chromosome
Father
X
X
X
Y
X X
X Y
X X
X Y
Daughter
Son
Daughter
Son

Male or female?
Boys have one X and one Y chromosome while girls have two X chromosomes in all their cells, in addition to the other 22 pairs of chromosomes.

DOMINANT AND RECESSIVE INHERITANCE

Most physical characteristics are determined by many pairs of genes. Each gene in a pair may produce a dominant or recessive trait. A dominant trait overrides a recessive trait, with the result that a recessive characteristic occurs only if no dominant genes are present. For example, assume that blue eye color is recessive and brown eye color is dominant, as shown below.

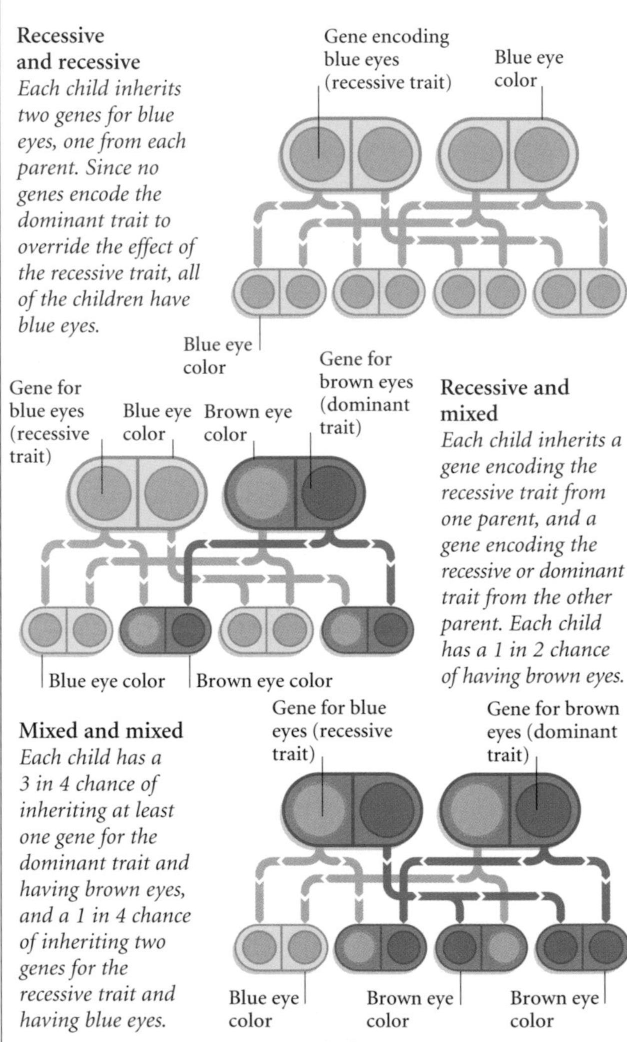
Gene encoding blue eyes (recessive trait)
Blue eye color
Blue eye color
Gene for blue eyes (recessive trait)
Blue eye color
Brown eye color
Gene for brown eyes (dominant trait)
Blue eye color
Brown eye color
Gene for blue eyes (recessive trait)
Gene for brown eyes (dominant trait)
Blue eye color
Brown eye color
Brown eye color

Recessive and recessive
Each child inherits two genes for blue eyes, one from each parent. Since no genes encode the dominant trait to override the effect of the recessive trait, all of the children have blue eyes.

Recessive and mixed
Each child inherits a gene encoding the recessive trait from one parent, and a gene encoding the recessive or dominant trait from the other parent. Each child has a 1 in 2 chance of having brown eyes.

Mixed and mixed
Each child has a 3 in 4 chance of inheriting at least one gene for the dominant trait and having brown eyes, and a 1 in 4 chance of inheriting two genes for the recessive trait and having blue eyes.

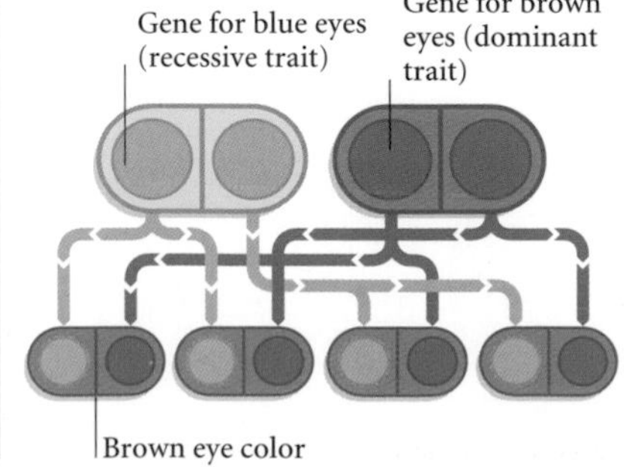
Gene for blue eyes (recessive trait)
Gene for brown eyes (dominant trait)
Brown eye color

Dominant and recessive
Each child inherits a gene encoding the recessive trait from one parent and the dominant trait from the other parent. Since the recessive trait is overridden, all of the children will have brown eyes.

SEX-LINKED INHERITANCE

Sex-linked traits and disorders are usually due to genes on the X chromosome. These characteristics and conditions therefore have different patterns of inheritance in females and males. Females with one recessive gene are called carriers and do not usually display the trait. In males, the change in the gene behaves as if it is a dominant trait since there is only one X chromosome. One example of an X-linked disorder is red-green color blindness. Its inheritance is illustrated in the diagram below.

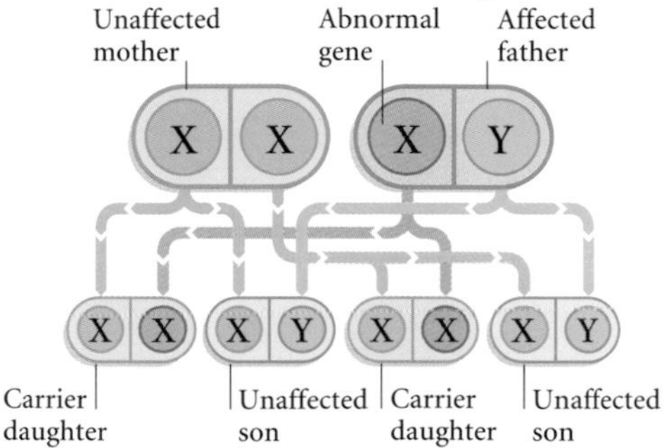
Unaffected mother
Abnormal gene
Affected father
X X X Y
X X X Y X X X Y
Carrier daughter
Unaffected son
Carrier daughter
Unaffected son

Color-blind father and unaffected mother
A color-blind father passes the affected gene on his X chromosome to all his daughters. These daughters are not color blind, although they can pass the gene on to the next generation. Sons inherit the X chromosome from their mother and are not color blind.

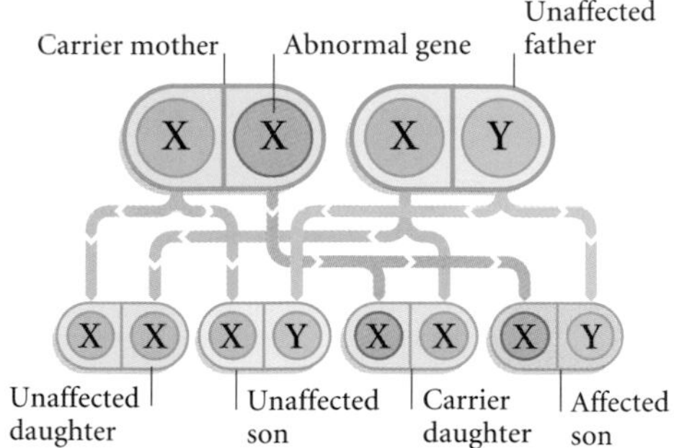
Carrier mother
Abnormal gene
Unaffected father
X X X Y
X X X Y X X X Y
Unaffected daughter
Unaffected son
Carrier daughter
Affected son

Carrier mother and unaffected father
Each child of a carrier mother has a 1 in 2 chance of inheriting the affected gene. Sons who inherit the gene are color blind as they have no other X chromosome. Daughters who inherit the gene are carriers.

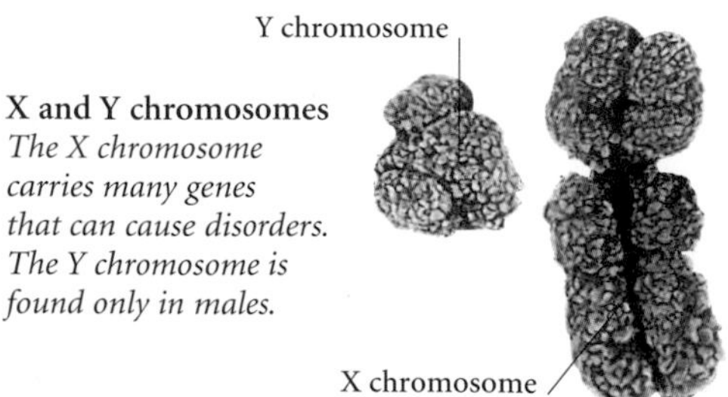
Y chromosome
X chromosome

X and Y chromosomes
The X chromosome carries many genes that can cause disorders. The Y chromosome is found only in males.

PROCESS MUTATIONS

When DNA is duplicated, errors may occur that result in a change in a gene. These changes are called mutations and may have a dramatic effect on cell function. Mutations occur in egg or sperm cells or in body cells but can only be inherited when they are in eggs or sperm. Mutations are important for three reasons: they form the basis of evolution by providing a species with a better chance of survival if the mutation is beneficial; they account for hundreds of inherited disorders; and some mutations occurring over a person's lifetime, which cannot be inherited, sometimes cause cells to become cancerous.

HOW MUTATIONS OCCUR

Most mutations involve a change in just one base (unit of DNA). Mutations may occur spontaneously as random errors in copying or may be caused by exposure to UV light, such as in sunlight, certain chemicals (mutagens), and radiation.

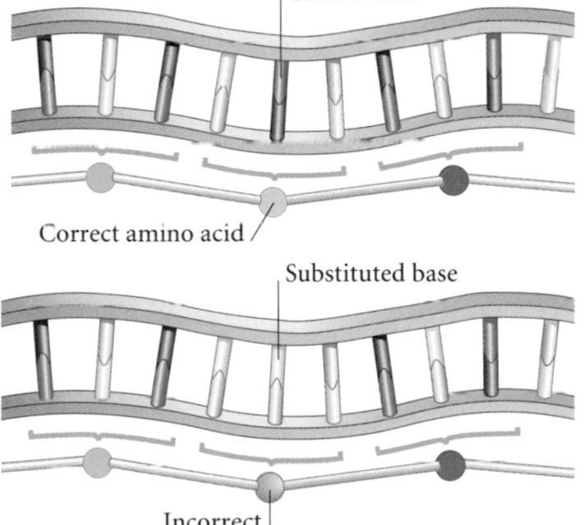
Correct base
Correct amino acid
Substituted base
Incorrect amino acid

Normal gene
The sequence of bases in a gene provides the cell with the correct sequence of amino acids that are needed to make a functioning protein.

Mutated gene
If a base in a gene is incorrect, the wrong amino acid sequence may be used to make the new protein. The resulting protein may function poorly or not at all.

MUTATIONS IN EGGS AND SPERM

A mutation in an egg or sperm cell is transmitted to a child at fertilization, and it then exists in every cell in the child's body. Some of these inherited mutations are harmless, but some may cause abnormalities or illness in the child.

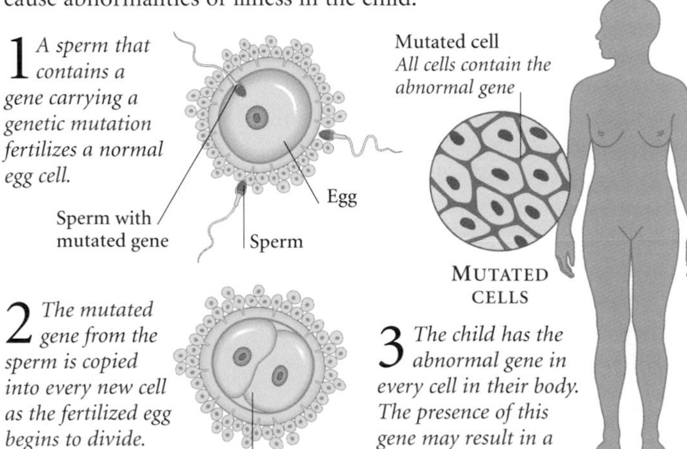
Sperm with mutated gene
Egg
Sperm
New cell
Mutated cell
All cells contain the abnormal gene
MUTATED CELLS

1 *A sperm that contains a gene carrying a genetic mutation fertilizes a normal egg cell.*

2 *The mutated gene from the sperm is copied into every new cell as the fertilized egg begins to divide.*

3 *The child has the abnormal gene in every cell in their body. The presence of this gene may result in a genetic disorder.*

GENETIC DISORDERS

Genes play a part in the cause of almost all common diseases, such as asthma and diabetes mellitus. In these diseases, a number of genes interact with factors in the environment. However, some rarer disorders are caused solely by defective genes or abnormal chromosomes and may be passed on from parent to child.

This section discusses the principles of chromosome and gene disorders and explains how these disorders may be inherited.

The first article discusses the way in which chromosome abnormalities cause physical and intellectual differences in those who are born with them. The most common and well-known pattern of features is Down syndrome, in which a child has one extra chromosome in every cell. Since the extra chromosome is present in every cell, it often causes problems in many systems of the body. The second article describes single gene disorders, which may be passed on through a family or may occur without a family history as the result of a gene mutation. People who have a family history of a gene disorder may find genetic counseling useful. Information about genetic testing is given elsewhere (*see* GENETIC TESTS, pp.238–241).

KEY ANATOMY

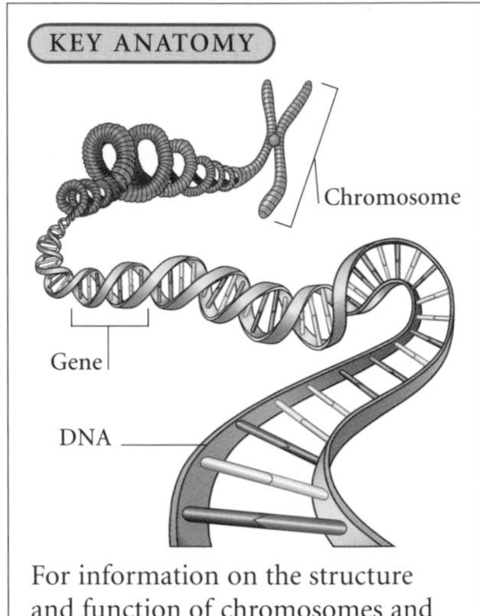
Chromosome
Gene
DNA

For information on the structure and function of chromosomes and genes, *see* pp.262–267.

Chromosome disorders

Disorders that result from inheriting an incorrect number of structurally altered chromosomes

 AGE Always present at birth but effects may not become apparent until later

 GENDER Risk factors depend on the type

 LIFESTYLE Not a significant factor

About 1 in 150–200 babies is born with a chromosome abnormality. Most chromosome abnormalities cause multiple problems, including physical differences and intellectual difficulties. About 50–60 percent of all miscarriages are the result of chromosome disorders. However, there are many chromosome disorders, such as Turner syndrome (p.823), Klinefelter syndrome (p.822), and Down syndrome (p.821), that are compatible with life.

Every cell in the human body, apart from eggs and sperm, carries 46 chromosomes arranged in 22 pairs plus the two sex chromosomes. One of each pair is inherited from each parent. The sex chromosomes determine a person's gender. Males have one X and one Y chromosome; females have two X chromosomes. The other 22 pairs are known as autosomes. The set of chromosomes in each cell is estimated to contain about 30,000 pairs of genes, which provide instructions for making proteins that are involved in the growth, multiplication, and function of the body's cells.

Chromosome abnormalities are usually due to a fault in the division of chromosomes that occurs when eggs and sperm are formed. This process, called meiosis, involves a halving of the number of chromosomes in other body cells so that each sex cell has only 23 chromosomes. Occasionally, a chromosome abnormality can arise in the early stages of division of the fertilized egg. Chromosome abnormalities usually have major physical and/or mental effects on the individual.

Several factors increase the likelihood of a couple having a child with a chromosome abnormality, such as already having a child with a chromosome disorder or a maternal age of over 35 years.

WHAT ARE THE TYPES?

A chromosome abnormality involves either an incorrect number of chromosomes or a defect in the structure of a chromosome. These abnormalities can affect any one of the 44 autosomal chromosomes or one of the sex chromosomes. Disorders that are caused by autosomal chromosome abnormalities are usually more severe.

NUMERICAL ABNORMALITIES Mistakes occasionally occur in the way chromosome pairs are divided between the new egg or sperm cells during meiosis, with one cell having too many chromosomes while the other has too few. If an egg containing an extra chromosome is fertilized by a normal sperm, the fetus will have an extra chromosome in every cell in its body. Alternatively, if a sperm with a missing chromosome fertilizes a normal egg, the fetus will have one less chromosome in each of its cells. About two-thirds of all chromosome disorders are caused by cells that contain the wrong number of chromosomes.

Extra or missing autosomal chromosomes usually result in miscarriage of the embryo. An exception to this is the inheritance of an extra chromosome 21, known as trisomy 21. Although fetuses with this extra chromosome are often miscarried, a number survive, and they have Down syndrome. Abnormalities in the number of sex chromosomes tend to have a less severe effect on the embryo and, in some cases, there are no obvious signs of a disorder at birth. About 1 in 500 babies is born with an extra X or Y chromosome. Boys who are born with an extra X chromosome (XXY) have a disorder called Klinefelter syndrome, a condition in which there is under-development of normal male

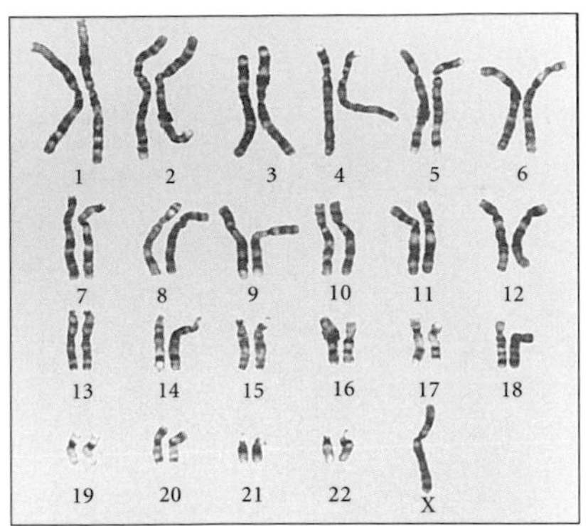
1
2
3
4
5
6
7
8
9
10
11
12
13
14
15
16
17
18
19
20
21
22
X

Chromosomes in Turner syndrome
This set of chromosomes (karyotype) from a female with Turner syndrome shows only one X chromosome rather than the two that are normal for a female.

secondary sexual characteristics. About 1 in 2,500 girls is born with only one X chromosome instead of the usual two X chromosomes, a condition known as Turner syndrome. Girls with this condition have short stature and, if they do not receive treatment, may fail to develop normal secondary sexual characteristics at puberty. Women with Turner syndrome and men with Klinefelter syndrome are usually infertile.

STRUCTURAL ABNORMALITIES There is a natural exchange of genetic material between pairs of chromosomes during meiosis. This mixing ensures that the genetic makeup of each egg and sperm is slightly different. Occasionally, faults occur during this process, resulting in a structural chromosome abnormality. A small section of chromosome may be deleted, duplicated, or inserted the wrong way around (inverted). These types of structural abnormalities in the chromosome may result in miscarriage or birth defects, ranging from mild to extremely severe. The effect on the fetus depends on the amount and type of genetic material that is altered. Material may also be exchanged between two different chromosomes following breaks in each one. This process is known as translocation. If no genetic material is gained or lost during this process, it is known as a balanced translocation. Balanced translocations are carried by about 1 in 500 people. A translocation rarely causes health problems in the affected person. However, when a person with a translocation has a child of his or her own, serious chromosome abnormalities may occur in the child as a result of inheriting too much or too little chromosomal material.

MOSAICISM In this situation, a person has some body cells that contain a normal set of chromosomes and other cells that contain an abnormal set of chromosomes. Mosaicism occurs when there is a fault in cell division in the embryo soon after fertilization occurs. Mosaicism can often be detected by analysis of a blood sample. The effects of mosaicism depend on the proportion and type of cells containing abnormal chromosomes.

How are they diagnosed?

Many chromosome disorders are obvious either at birth or once symptoms appear. The diagnosis of a chromosome disorder can be confirmed with a blood test (*see* TESTS FOR CHROMOSOME ABNORMALITIES, p.238).

During a pregnancy, chromosome abnormalities can be detected by looking at and analyzing the chromosomes in a sample of fetal cells (*see* PRENATAL GENETIC TESTS, p.787). Prenatal genetic tests may be offered to women at increased risk of having an affected baby due to advanced maternal age or when there are ultrasound findings that suggest the possibility of a chromosome abnormality. Certain prenatal screening tests carried out in early pregnancy may also indicate an increased risk of a chromosome abnormality. In such cases, pregnant women may be offered specific prenatal genetic tests, such as amniocentesis or chorionic villus sampling, which can confirm the diagnosis of a chromosome abnormality in a fetus.

What is the treatment?

There is no cure for disorders caused by chromosome abnormalities. However, surgery may rectify physical abnormalities, such as intestinal abnormalities or heart defects, and some people with sex chromosome disorders are treated with hormone replacement. For example, girls with Turner syndrome can be given hormones to induce puberty and increase height.

When there is a history of chromosome abnormality within the family or if multiple miscarriages have occurred in the past, prospective parents may wish to consider genetic counseling (p.270), in order to assess the risk of having a child with a chromosome disorder and also to learn about prenatal testing options, before beginning a pregnancy.

(WWW) ONLINE SITES: p.1032

Gene disorders

Disorders that result from inheriting a faulty gene or genes

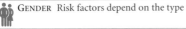

AGE Always present at birth but effects may not become apparent until later

GENDER Risk factors depend on the type

LIFESTYLE Can play a role in common disorders with a genetic basis.

Genes provide instructions to the cells to make enzymes and other proteins that the body needs to grow and function. A defective gene may have mild, moderate, or potentially fatal consequences or no effect at all, depending on the role of the protein for which the gene codes. The development of many common disorders, such as diabetes mellitus (p.687) and asthma (p.483), is linked with genetic factors but is also influenced by environment and lifestyle.

Several thousand disorders are the result of abnormalities in single genes, but the majority of these conditions are extremely rare. The most common single gene disorders are cystic fibrosis (p.824), sickle-cell anemia (p.448), and thalassemia (p.449). About 1 in 100 babies is born with a disorder that is caused by a single faulty gene.

Some communities have particularly high frequencies of abnormal genes for certain disorders. For example, the abnormal gene that produces Tay-Sachs disease (p.868), an inherited condition that leads to progressive brain damage, is more common among Ashkenazi Jews, and the gene for thalassemia is more commonly found in people from Mediterranean countries.

Some gene disorders are obvious soon after birth or in the first few months of life. Other disorders caused by a single abnormal gene, such as Huntington's disease (p.538), may not become apparent until adult life when the symptoms first appear.

What are the causes?

In most single gene disorders, an individual has the defective gene in all cells of the body from the first stages in the development of the embryo. There are two possible reasons for the presence of the abnormal gene. First, the defective gene may have been passed on from parent to child. Second, a normal gene may have become faulty (mutated) during meiosis, the process of division by which eggs and sperm form. Certain single gene disorders are likely to occur without any previous family history of this condition.

What are the types?

Genes occur in pairs; one of each pair is inherited from the mother, the other from the father. Genes are found on the 22 pairs of chromosomes that are known as autosomes and also on the X and Y sex chromosomes (predominantly on the X chromosome). Single gene disorders are classified by their pattern of inheritance: autosomal dominant, autosomal recessive, or X-linked. In addition, many common disorders are brought about by an interaction between genes, environmental factors, and lifestyle. These are known as multifactorial disorders.

AUTOSOMAL DOMINANT DISORDERS In these disorders, an abnormal gene needs to be inherited from only one parent to lead to a disorder. A normal gene inherited from the other parent does not mask the effect of the abnormal gene. If a person has an autosomal dominant disorder, each of his or her children has a 1 in 2 chance of inheriting the abnormal gene and developing the condition. Familial hypercholesterolemia is one of the most common disorders to follow this pattern of inheritance (*see* INHERITED HYPERLIPOPROTEINEMIAS, p.692). In this disorder, there are high levels of blood cholesterol, leading to increased risk of early coronary artery disease (p.405). About 1 person in 500 has this gene and is affected by the disorder.

AFFECTED PARENT
UNAFFECTED PARENT
Abnormal gene
Normal gene

AFFECTED CHILDREN
UNAFFECTED CHILDREN

Autosomal dominant inheritance
In this example, one of the parents has the abnormal gene and the other parent is unaffected. Each child has a 1 in 2 chance of inheriting the faulty gene and therefore developing the disorder.

AUTOSOMAL RECESSIVE DISORDERS A person must inherit two copies of a faulty gene, one from each parent, to develop an autosomal recessive disorder. If a person inherits one copy of the faulty gene but the gene from the other parent is normal, the person is a carrier. A carrier does not develop the disease but may pass the gene on to his or her children. Since two abnormal genes, one inherited from each parent, are necessary to produce the disease, autosomal recessive disorders are rare. Cystic fibrosis, a disease that affects certain glands, is the most common of these gene disorders in white people of North American and European origin. About 1 in 20 people is a carrier of the disease. The chance of one cystic fibrosis carrier having children with another carrier is about 1 in 400, and, since 1 in 4 children has two faulty genes, cystic fibrosis affects 1 in 1,600 people. In African–Americans, the most common autosomal recessive gene disease is sickle-cell anemia, for which 1 in 10 people is a carrier and about 1 in 400 has the disorder.

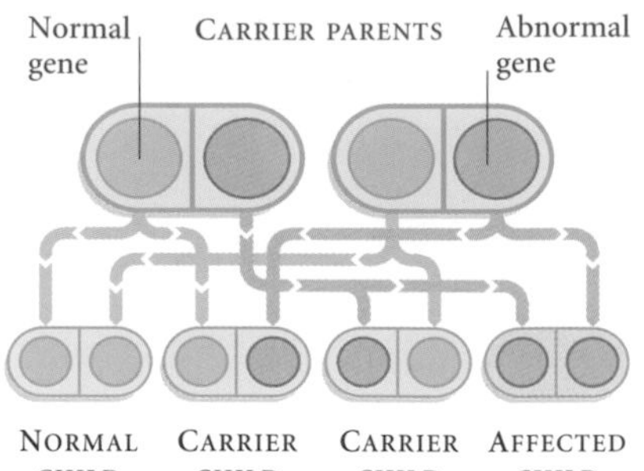
Normal gene
CARRIER PARENTS
Abnormal gene
NORMAL CHILD
CARRIER CHILD
CARRIER CHILD
AFFECTED CHILD

Autosomal recessive inheritance
In this example, both parents carry the abnormal gene but do not have the disease. Their children may be unaffected (1 in 4 chance), may be carriers of the faulty gene (1 in 2), or may have the disease (1 in 4).

X-LINKED RECESSIVE DISORDERS In a disorder of this type, such as hemophilia, the faulty gene is carried on the X chromosome. Women who have just one faulty gene are unaffected carriers because they have a second X chromosome that almost always carries a normal gene and compensates for the presence of the abnormal one. However, they may pass on the abnormal gene to their children. Since each child inherits one X chromosome from the mother, each child of a carrier has a 1 in 2 chance of inheriting the abnormal gene. If a boy inherits the abnormal gene, he will definitely develop the disorder because he cannot inherit a second X chromosome. The girls are carriers because the X chromosome inherited from their father carries the normal gene. An affected man will pass on the faulty gene only to his daughters but not to his sons.

TEST GENETIC COUNSELING

Genetic counseling can assist people in planning their families if there is a history of an inherited disease. Counselors use the most up-to-date information and test results to estimate the chance that a given single gene disorder will recur in the same family. They may discuss the options available for reducing the risk of a child being born with the particular disorder.

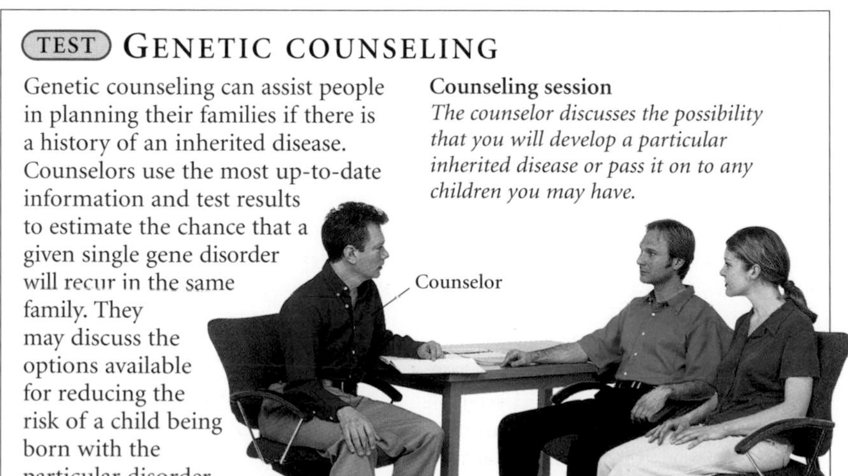
Counselor

Counseling session
The counselor discusses the possibility that you will develop a particular inherited disease or pass it on to any children you may have.

CARRIER MOTHER UNAFFECTED FATHER

Abnormal X chromosome Normal X chromosome Normal Y chromosome

CARRIER DAUGHTER AFFECTED SON UNAFFECTED DAUGHTER AND SON

X-linked recessive inheritance
In this example, a mother carries the abnormal gene on the X chromosome but is unaffected. Their sons have a 1 in 2 chance of inheriting the disease; their daughters have a 1 in 2 chance of being carriers but will not have the disease.

MULTIFACTORIAL DISORDERS There are many common disorders, such as asthma, that run in families but for which no single gene appears to be responsible. In these disorders, it is likely that several different genes interact with each other to cause the disease and that environmental factors and lifestyle also play a role. Certain disorders are known to be associated with a group of proteins called HLAs. These proteins form part of the body's immune system and determine a person's tissue type. HLAs are inherited, and each individual has a unique combination of them. In some people, particular HLAs increase susceptibility to certain disorders, such as ankylosing spondylitis (p.378) and systemic lupus erythematosus (p.461).

What might be done?

The underlying cause of single gene disorders cannot be treated, although gene therapy, in which the products of abnormal genes are replaced by the normal gene product, is currently an area of intense research. The symptoms of many gene disorders can be treated successfully. People who have hemophilia and are unable to produce an important protein involved in blood clotting, called factor VIII, are treated with regular injections of the missing protein (*see* DRUGS THAT PROMOTE BLOOD CLOTTING, p.903). Similarly, over the past 20 years, better treatment of cystic fibrosis, including physiotherapy (p.961) and antibiotics (p.885), has resulted in an improved life expectancy. Some single gene disorders, such as Huntington's disease, are not easily treated and are eventually fatal.

Can they be prevented?

People who have a blood relative with an inherited disorder may be able to have testing to determine whether they have the faulty gene (*see* GENETIC TESTS, pp.238–241). Testing is available only for certain disorders, such as cystic fibrosis and sickle-cell anemia, in which the faulty gene has been identified. Screening may be offered to whole communities in which there is a high incidence of a faulty gene. For example, Ashkenazi Jews may be screened for Tay–Sachs disease, which is common in this group. A couple with a family history of a gene disorder may opt for genetic counseling (opposite page) before conceiving or have prenatal genetic tests (p.787) for fetal abnormalities.

(WWW) ONLINE SITES: p.1032

Single gene disorders (examples)

Autosomal dominant disorders

Achondroplasia p.833
A disorder of bone growth, resulting in short stature and abnormal proportions

Huntington's disease p.538
A brain disorder that causes abnormal movements and dementia in adulthood

Inherited hyperlipoproteinemias p.692
Excessive levels of lipids in the blood, of which the most common form is familial hypercholesterolemia

Marfan syndrome p.824
A rare disorder that mainly affects the skeleton, heart, and eyes

Neurofibromatosis p.827
A disorder in which numerous swellings develop on the covering of nerves

Polycystic kidney disease (in adults) p.704
A disorder in which fluid-filled cysts replace normal kidney tissue

Porphyria p.693
A disorder in which chemicals called porphyrins build up in the body, causing psychological and physical symptoms

Von Willebrand disease p.452
A bleeding disorder due to a deficiency of a substance needed for blood clotting

Autosomal recessive disorders

Albinism p.868
A lack of the pigment melanin, which gives color to the skin, hair, and eyes

Cystic fibrosis p.824
Abnormally thick secretions, leading to digestive and respiratory problems

Galactosemia p.868
Inability to break down a form of sugar, leading to its accumulation in the blood

Hemochromatosis p.692
A condition in which too much iron is deposited in various organs

Phenylketonuria p.867
Deficiency of an enzyme needed to digest a component of protein-containing foods

Polycystic kidneys (in children) p.704
A disorder in which fluid-filled cysts replace normal kidney tissue, usually apparent at birth

Retinitis pigmentosa p.581
Progressive degeneration in the retina, the light-sensitive membrane at the back of the eye, leading to loss of vision

Sickle-cell anemia p.448
A blood disorder in which red blood cells become an abnormal shape and blood flow through vessels is impeded

Tay–Sachs disease p.868
A severe disorder in which harmful substances build up in the brain

Thalassemia p.449
A blood disorder in which production of hemoglobin, the oxygen-carrying component of red blood cells, is abnormal

X-linked disorders

Red-green color blindness p.591
Impaired ability to distinguish between red and green

Fragile X syndrome p.822
A disorder that produces intellectual handicap and a characteristic appearance

Hemophilia and Christmas disease p.452
Disorders in which the blood does not clot normally due to a clotting factor deficiency

Muscular dystrophy p.826
A disorder causing progressive weakness and wasting of muscles

Inheritance of single gene disorders
This table lists the major single gene disorders that are covered in this book. Some disorders exist in more than one form, with different inheritance patterns. The most common pattern is indicated.

CANCER

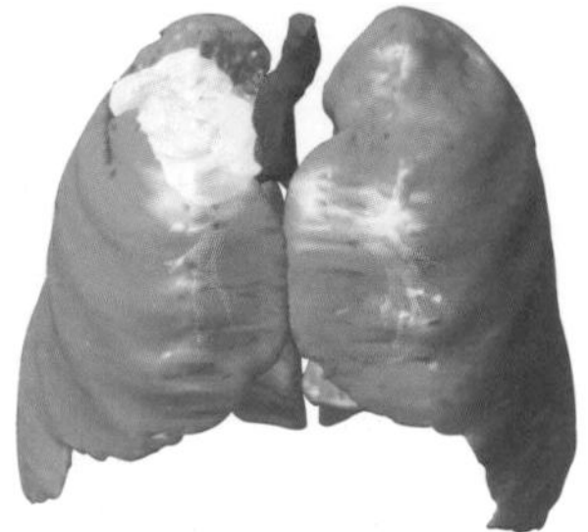

Lung cancer
The yellow and white area in this color-enhanced CT scan of the lungs is a cancerous tumor, probably caused by smoking.

CANCER IS A DISEASE in which body cells grow uncontrollably because their normal regulatory controls have been damaged. Of the many types of cancers, the majority form solid tumors in a specific part of the body, commonly the skin, breast, lung, bowel, or prostate gland. The disease may then spread within the body through the blood and lymphatic systems. As our understanding of cancer has advanced during the past 20 years, changes in lifestyle, efficient screening programs, and new types of therapies have improved prevention and treatment of the disease.

The term "cancer" comes from the Greek word for crab. The ancient Greek physician Hippocrates likened a spreading cancerous tumor to the shape of a crab's claw. Although our understanding of the disease has advanced dramatically since then, the description is still apt. An important feature of a cancerous tumor is its ability to spread within the body.

GENETIC BASIS OF CANCER

The discovery in the late 1970s that damage to genetic material underlies cancer was one of the most important breakthroughs in cancer research. Every cell contains genetic information in the form of about 35,000 pairs of genes that control the activities of cells. A cell may become cancerous when certain genes that control vital processes such as cell division become damaged. These faulty genes may be inherited or caused by carcinogens (cancer-causing agents), such as sunlight and tobacco smoke. Cells are continually exposed to carcinogens, but they rarely become cancerous for several reasons: cells can usually repair their damaged genes; more than one gene must be damaged before cancer develops; and the body's immune system normally destroys any abnormal cells before they are able to multiply enough to form a tumor.

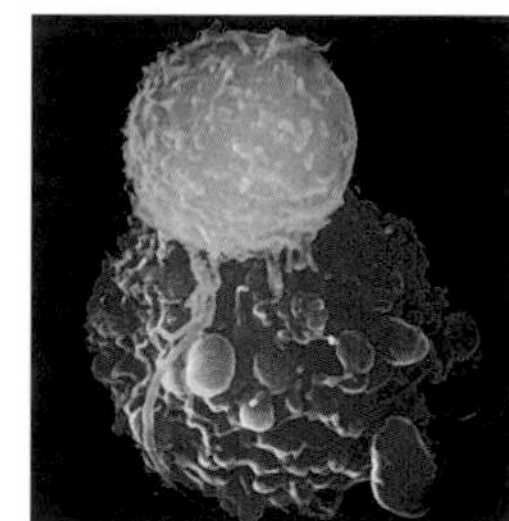

Destroying cancer cells
In this highly magnified image, a white blood cell is chemically destroying the larger cancerous cell.

AGING AND CANCER

Cancer is most common among older people, largely because their cells have had more time to accumulate genetic damage, but also because the body's defenses against cancer, particularly the cells and proteins of the immune system, gradually become less efficient with age. In addition, a cancer that began earlier in life may not be diagnosed until old age because it often takes many years for some types of tumors to grow large enough to produce noticeable symptoms. Since life expectancy increased significantly in developed countries during the second half of the 20th century, cancer has now become one of the most common causes of death in the US, second only to coronary heart disease.

TREATING CANCER

For 2,000 years, doctors have attempted to cure cancer by surgically removing visible tumors. This approach is often successful if the cancer has not spread to lymph nodes or distant sites in the body. For certain cancers, including those that have spread around the body, treatment with anticancer drugs, known as chemotherapy, and radiation therapy may be used instead of or in combination with surgery.

New therapies for the treatment of cancer that are currently being assessed include inactivating damaged genes and boosting the immune system's ability to destroy cancerous cells. However, as with many other diseases, the most effective ways to lower the number of deaths are through prevention (maintaining a healthy lifestyle) and screening to detect cancer early.

DATA CAUSES OF CANCER

Although most cancers appear to be caused by several factors, including inherited ones, a main environmental cause can often be identified for a particular cancer. The most common carcinogens (cancer-causing agents), such as tobacco smoke, are avoidable. Smoking has caused a major lung cancer epidemic throughout the world in the twentieth century.

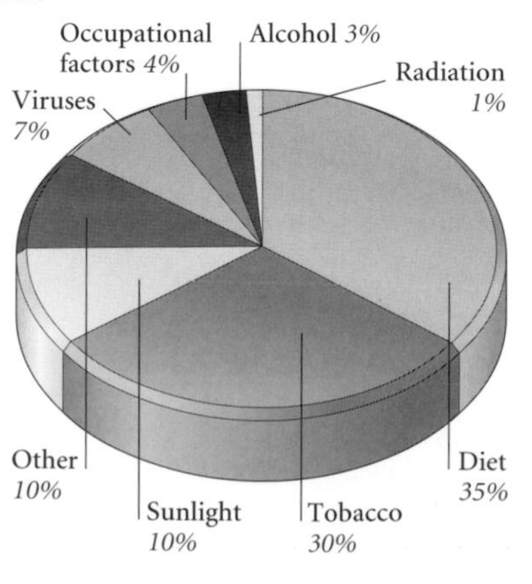
Occupational factors 4%
Alcohol 3%
Radiation 1%
Viruses 7%
Other 10%
Sunlight 10%
Tobacco 30%
Diet 35%

Carcinogens in the environment
Although radiation other than sunlight is commonly cited as a cause of cancer, its contribution is actually very small.

STRUCTURE CANCEROUS TUMORS

A cancerous (malignant) tumor is a collection of many abnormal cells, most of which divide uncontrollably. Cancerous tumors infiltrate neighboring tissues by forcing their way between normal cells and can spread to distant body parts through blood or lymph vessels. Cancerous cells are extremely irregular in shape and size and often bear little resemblance to the cells from which they arose. This characteristic irregular appearance of cancerous cells is often used to help diagnose cancer.

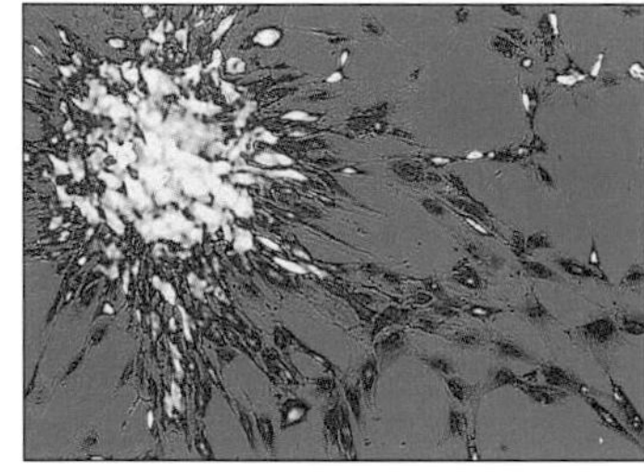

Migration of cancerous cells
In this magnified image, cancerous cells are migrating after becoming detached from a tumor. Some of these cells will settle at new sites and then divide to form tumors.

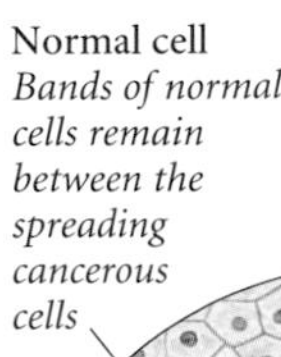

Normal cell
Bands of normal cells remain between the spreading cancerous cells

Dividing cell
Cancerous cells often divide more frequently than normal cells

Cancerous cell
Cancerous cells have large nuclei and tend not to resemble the cells from which they originated

Epithelial layer
Tumors often form in epithelial tissue, which covers the body and lines body cavities and organs

Ulcerated area
The tumor may erode the epithelial layer completely

Bleeding
Inside the tumor, bleeding often occurs because fast-growing cancer cells breach blood vessel walls

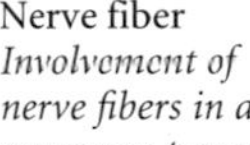

Nerve fiber
Involvement of nerve fibers in a cancerous tumor may cause pain

Dead tissue
Inside the tumor, cancerous cells may die if the tumor has outgrown its blood supply

Calcium deposits
Calcium deposits build up in some tumors and may be visible on X-rays

Blood vessel
Involvement of blood vessels in a tumor provides a route for distant spread of cancer

Lymph vessel
Involvement of lymph vessels in a cancerous tumor provides a route for the spread of cancer to nearby lymph nodes

Tumor outgrowth
The tumor cells form outgrowths that spread into surrounding tissue

STRUCTURE NONCANCEROUS TUMORS

Noncancerous (benign) tumors are common and include lipomas, which are fatty lumps beneath the skin, and many other skin lesions. These types of tumors do not invade tissue but they may compress nearby structures as they grow. Noncancerous tumors do not spread around the body.

Structure of a noncancerous tumor
A noncancerous tumor has an outer fibrous capsule that separates it from the surrounding normal tissue.

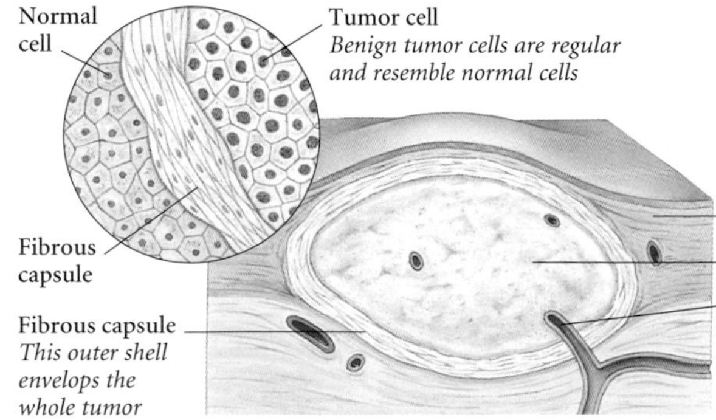
Normal cell
Tumor cell
Benign tumor cells are regular and resemble normal cells
Fibrous capsule
Fibrous capsule
This outer shell envelops the whole tumor
Tissue layer
Surrounding tissue layers may be distorted but are not breached by the tumor
Tumor
Blood vessel
Engulfed blood vessels supply the tumor with oxygen and nutrients

(PROCESS) HOW CANCER STARTS

Cells are continually bombarded by carcinogens (cancer-causing agents such as sunlight and certain viruses). Carcinogens damage specific genes (sections of DNA that control specific cell functions), known as oncogenes, that regulate vital processes such as cell division. Most damaged genes are repaired, but this process occasionally fails. Progressive damage to oncogenes may cause the cell to function abnormally and eventually become cancerous.

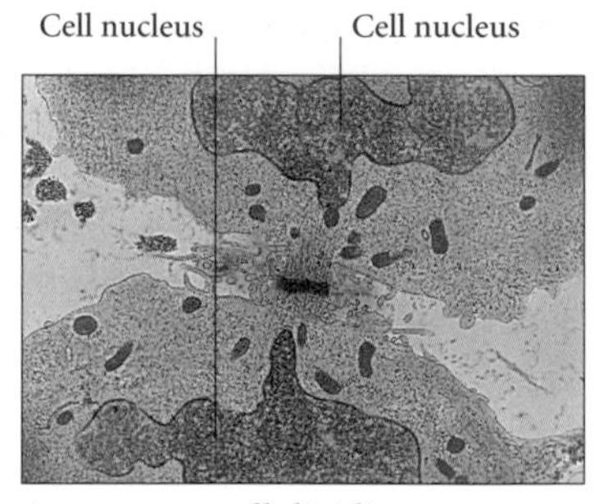
Cell nucleus
Cell nucleus

A cancerous cell dividing
In this magnified image, a cancerous cell is dividing to form two cells that contain damaged genetic material.

GENETIC DAMAGE

Oncogenes regulate the rate at which a cell divides. They also repair damaged genes and program faulty cells to self-destruct. Over time, carcinogens may cause irreparable damage to a cell's oncogenes. As damage accumulates, the oncogenes may start to function abnormally, causing the cell to become cancerous. If a faulty oncogene is inherited, a cell may become cancerous much more quickly.

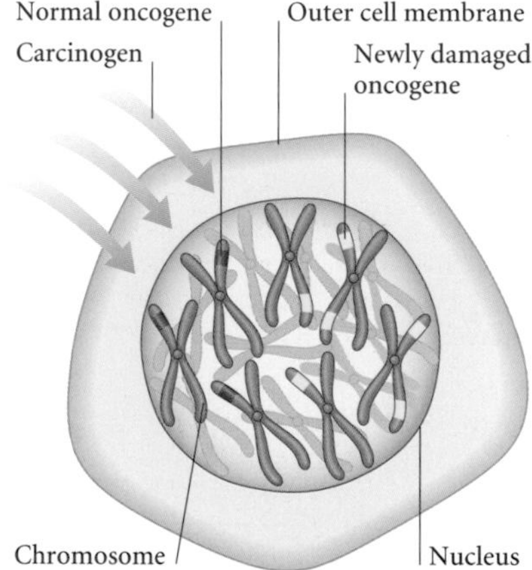
Normal oncogene
Outer cell membrane
Carcinogen
Newly damaged oncogene
Chromosome
Nucleus

1 *Carcinogens penetrate the cell and cause repeated damage to oncogenes on the chromosomes. Most newly damaged oncogenes are repaired.*

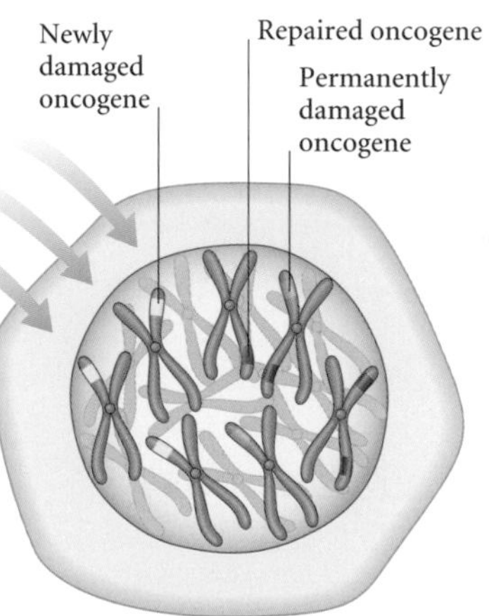
Newly damaged oncogene
Repaired oncogene
Permanently damaged oncogene

2 *The damage and repair of oncogenes continues. With time, some of the oncogenes in the cell become permanently damaged and cannot be repaired.*

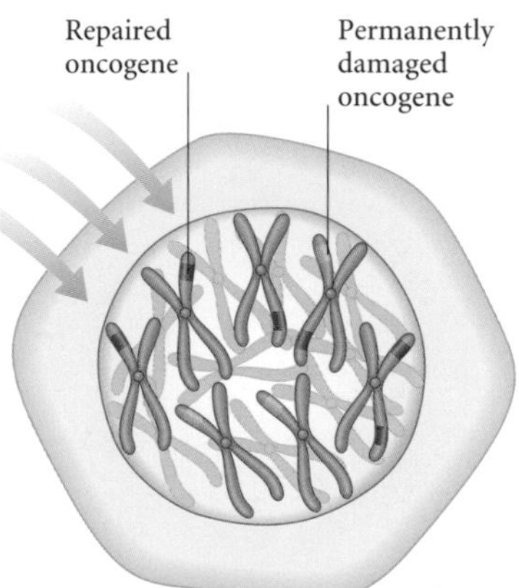
Repaired oncogene
Permanently damaged oncogene

3 *If a number of oncogenes controlling key cell functions are permanently damaged, the cell no longer functions normally and becomes cancerous.*

FORMATION OF A TUMOR

A cancerous tumor begins as a single cell. If the cell is not destroyed by the body's immune system, it will multiply uncontrollably, dividing to form two cells, which in turn divide to form four, and so on. Tumor growth rates are measured by the time taken for the number of cells in a tumor to double (the "doubling time"). The doubling time of a tumor generally varies from about 1 month to 2 years.

Doubling time
A solid tumor can usually be detected after 25–30 doublings. At this stage in its growth a tumor contains about a billion cells and has a diameter of about ½ in (1.3 cm).

Tumor growth
After only four cell divisions, a cancerous tumor contains 16 cells. The cells double in number regularly, causing the tumor to grow larger.

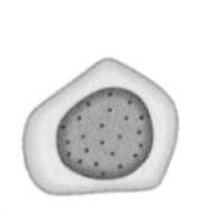

CANCEROUS CELL

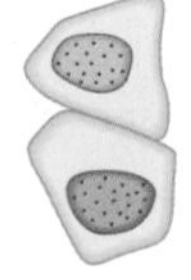

FIRST DOUBLING

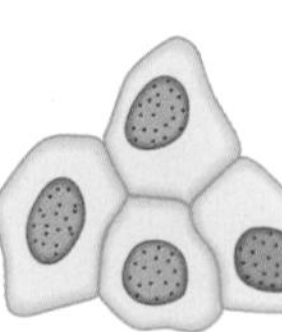

SECOND DOUBLING

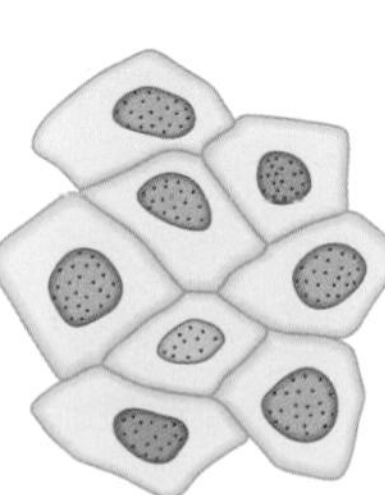

THIRD DOUBLING

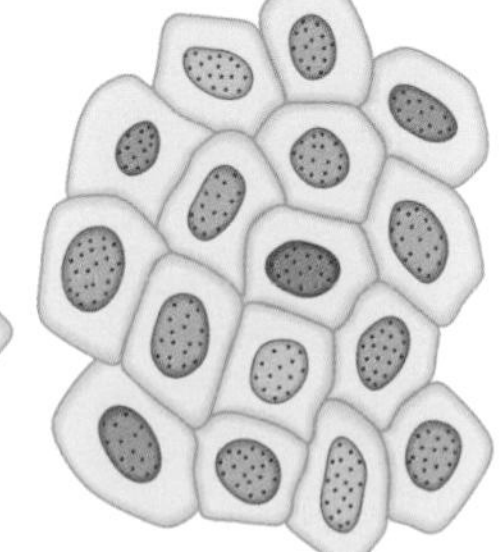

FOURTH DOUBLING

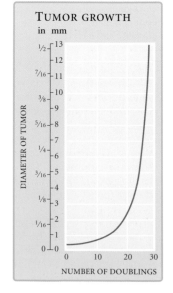

TUMOR GROWTH

in mm

DIAMETER OF TUMOR: 0, 1/16, 1/8, 3/16, 1/4, 5/16, 3/8, 7/16, 1/2 in; 0–13 mm

NUMBER OF DOUBLINGS: 0, 10, 20, 30

(PROCESS) HOW CANCER SPREADS

The defining feature of a cancerous tumor is its ability to spread not only locally but also to distant sites in the body by a process called metastasis. In metastasis, a cancerous cell detaches from a tumor and travels in the blood or lymph to a new location. The cell must overcome many obstacles if it is to settle successfully in a new site and form a secondary tumor, also known as a metastasis. It must survive attacks from the immune system and stimulate the growth of blood vessels (angiogenesis) to provide oxygen and nutrients.

SPREAD IN THE LYMPH FLUID

Cancerous cells may spread into the lymphatic system, which is a network of vessels that drains lymph fluid to nearby lymph nodes, where the fluid is filtered. A cell may become trapped in a lymph node and multiply to form a tumor. Immune cells in the lymph node attack the tumor and may halt the progression of the cancer.

1 As a tumor grows, it invades surrounding tissues and can enter nearby lymph vessels. If some of the cancerous cells from the tumor detach themselves in the lymph vessel, they may be carried along the vessel until they reach and settle in a lymph node.

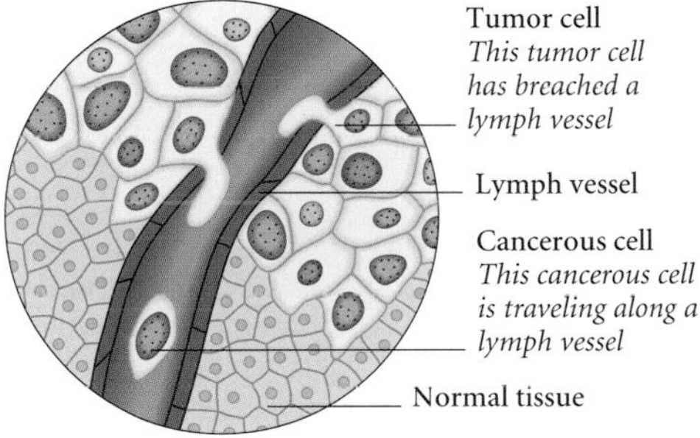
Tumor cell
This tumor cell has breached a lymph vessel
Lymph vessel
Cancerous cell
This cancerous cell is traveling along a lymph vessel
Normal tissue

2 A cancerous cell enters a local lymph node, where it begins dividing to form a tumor. The tumor usually remains within the node, and the cells of the immune system may temporarily stop it from spreading to other parts of the body.

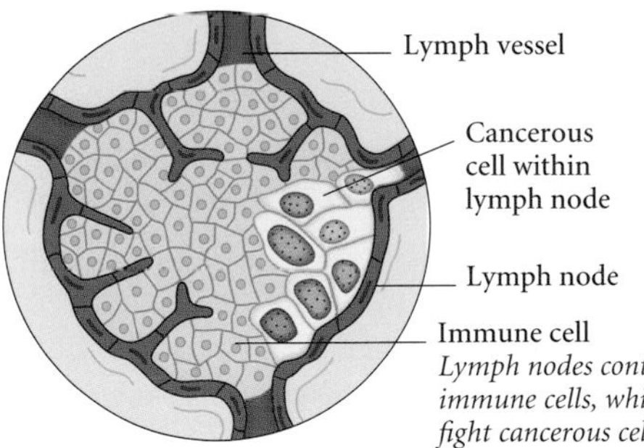
Lymph vessel
Cancerous cell within lymph node
Lymph node
Immune cell
Lymph nodes contain immune cells, which fight cancerous cells

SPREAD IN THE BLOOD

Primary cancer often spreads to sites in the body that have a good blood supply, such as the liver, lungs, bone, and brain. The liver is a particularly common site since it receives blood from the heart and intestines. When cancerous cells reach very small blood vessels, they pass through the walls to invade tissues.

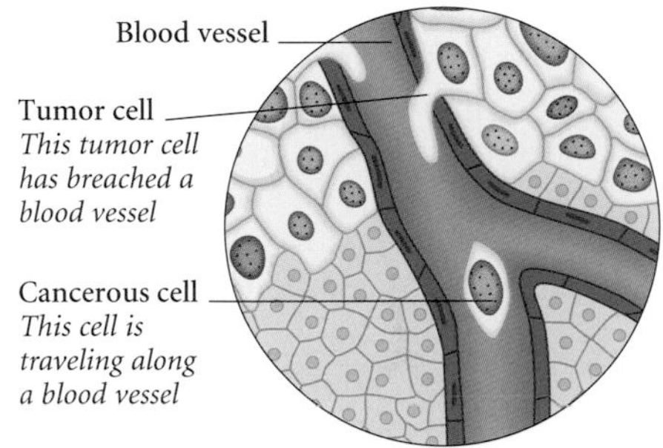
Blood vessel
Tumor cell
This tumor cell has breached a blood vessel
Cancerous cell
This cell is traveling along a blood vessel

1 The growing tumor ruptures the walls of nearby blood vessels. Some cancerous cells detach from the tumor and pass through blood vessel walls into the blood circulation.

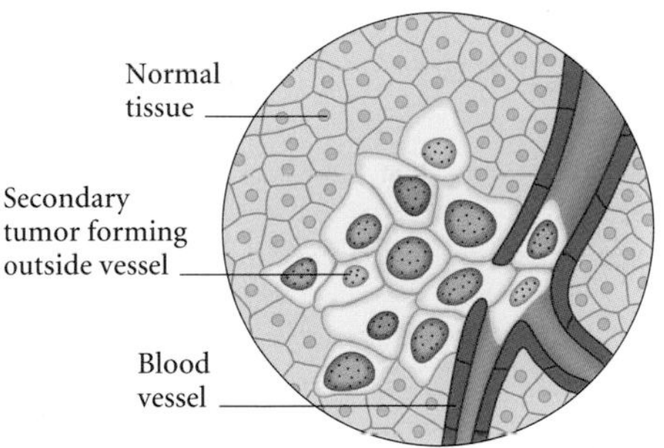
Normal tissue
Secondary tumor forming outside vessel
Blood vessel

2 A cancerous cell flows in the bloodstream until it becomes lodged in a capillary (tiny blood vessel) at a distant site. The cell starts dividing to form a secondary tumor.

HOW TUMORS OBTAIN NUTRIENTS

A cancerous cell obtains oxygen and nutrients from surrounding blood vessels by diffusion across its outer membrane, in the same way as normal cells. As the tumor enlarges, its inner cells are starved of nutrients. Enlarging tumors use two methods of acquiring nutrients – by invading existing blood vessels and by angiogenesis, the process by which a tumor stimulates new blood vessels to form. To survive and grow, a tumor must be able to stimulate angiogenesis successfully.

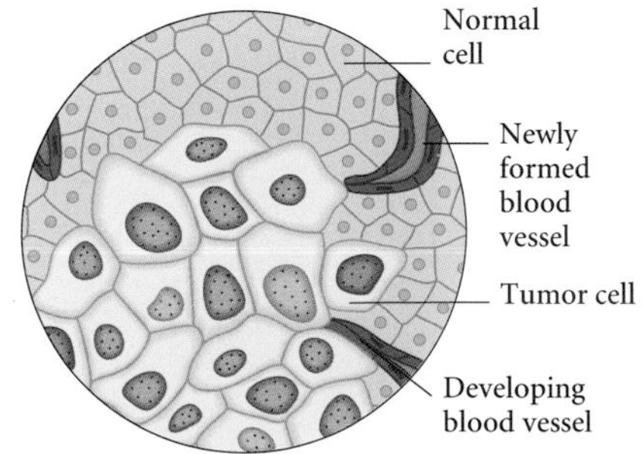
Normal cell
Newly formed blood vessel
Tumor cell
Developing blood vessel

Angiogenesis
In angiogenesis, tumor cells produce chemicals that stimulate the growth of blood vessels toward the tumor.

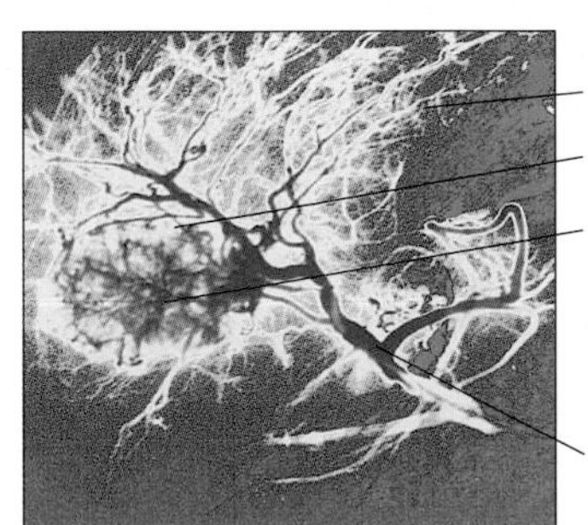
Normal tissue
Tumor
Mass of new vessels within tumor
Normal blood vessel

Angiogram of a liver tumor
This contrast X-ray of a tumor within the liver shows a large number of new blood vessels in the area of the tumor.

LIVING WITH CANCER

In recent years, improved techniques in the early diagnosis and treatment of cancer have led to more cures than ever before. However, cancer is primarily a disease of old age, and, as life expectancy increases, so does the proportion of people who will eventually develop some form of cancer in later life.

Cancer is not a single disease. Tumors arising in different tissues behave in different ways and respond differently to treatment. However, all cancers have some elements in common, such as their invasive growth.

The aim of this section is to look at the general principles applied to the diagnosis, treatment, and aftercare of all cancers. Research is ongoing into new treatments and cures for cancers. Some modern cancer treatments are still experimental but will probably eventually increase the proportion of people who survive. Even if a cancer cannot be cured, many treatments are available to relieve symptoms and improve quality of life.

Cancers that arise in a specific part of the body are covered in the relevant body system section. For example, lung cancer (p.503) is covered in the section on lung disorders, and breast cancer (p.759) in the breast disorders section.

KEY ANATOMY

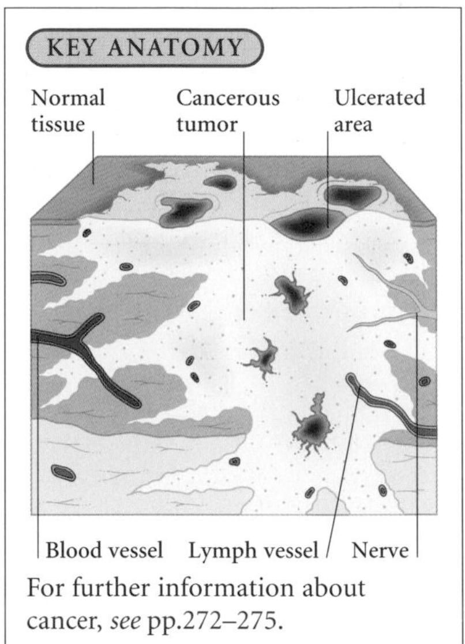
Normal tissue
Cancerous tumor
Ulcerated area
Blood vessel
Lymph vessel
Nerve

For further information about cancer, *see* pp.272–275.

Cancer and its management

The different causes of cancer and its management

AGE GENDER GENETICS LIFESTYLE
Risk factors depend on the type

Cancer is the second most common cause of death after heart disease in most western countries. In some countries, it is the leading cause of death. Although about 1 in 3 people develops cancer at some stage in life, many people can be cured because of advances in diagnosis and treatment.

Many types of cancers produce a solid tumor that forms in an organ, such as the breast, intestine, or bladder. If not detected and treated, these cancers may spread to other body tissues. Other cancers are often widespread from early on, such as cancer of the lymph nodes (*see* LYMPHOMA, p.459) or cancer of blood-forming cells in the bone marrow (*see* LEUKEMIA, p.453).

WHAT ARE THE CAUSES?

Cancer occurs when cells divide and grow in an uncontrolled manner. Cell division and cell functioning are controlled by genes, and defects in some of these genes can lead to a cell becoming cancerous. In both children and adults, these defects (mutations) in the genes may be caused by environmental factors such as chemicals (especially from smoking), viruses, ultraviolet light, or other types of radiation. In some cases, an abnormal gene is inherited from a parent. The main causes of cancer vary in different age groups.

Children and adults with reduced immunity, such as those with AIDS (*see* HIV INFECTION AND AIDS, p.295) or people who are taking immunosuppressants (p.906), have an increased risk of developing certain types of cancers. In such people, agents such as viruses are more likely to cause cancer.

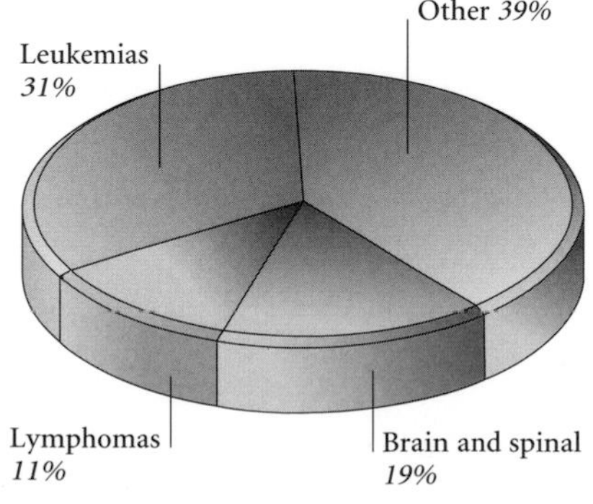
Other *39%*
Leukemias *31%*
Lymphomas *11%*
Brain and spinal *19%*

Cancer in children
Approximately 16 in 100,000 children in Canada develop cancer, the most common being the various types of leukemia.

CANCER IN CHILDREN Cancers in children are rare in Canada, but in some countries they are a leading cause of death. The most common cancers in children are leukemia and tumors of the brain and spinal cord (*see* BRAIN AND SPINAL CORD TUMORS IN CHILDREN, p.850).

The cause of most types of cancers in children is not known. Some cancers, such as a neuroblastoma (p.850), occur primarily in children. A neuroblastoma develops in an adrenal gland or the nervous system from tissue that normally disappears during fetal development. Cancers of this type are most common during infancy. Other types of childhood cancers, such as primary bone cancer (p.373), affect older children.

Occasionally, cancer is caused by an abnormal gene or genes. About half of all cases of the eye cancer retinoblastoma (p.858) and some cases of kidney cancer (*see* WILMS TUMOR, p.872) are primarily genetic in origin. In such cases, one or more family members may be affected by the same cancer.

The risk of cancer is increased in some genetic disorders. For example, children with Down syndrome (p.821) are 10–20 times more likely than other children to develop leukemia.

Some cancers in children may be caused by environmental factors. For example, certain viruses, such as the Epstein–Barr virus, are known to cause some types of cancers, including one type of childhood lymphoma.

CANCER IN ADULTS Cancer occurs much more commonly in adults than in children. In Canada, about 2 in 5 men and 1 in 3 women develops cancer at some time in their adult lives. The most common types of cancers adults have are skin cancer (p.344), lung cancer (p.503), breast cancer (p.759), prostate cancer (p.726), and colorectal cancer (p.665).

Many cancers in adults under age 40 have a significant inherited factor. Up to 1 in 10 cases of cancer of the ovary (p.744), breast cancer, prostate cancer, and colorectal cancer are due in part to the inheritance of abnormal genes. In older people, a combination of several factors eventually leads to cancer. The most common factors are carcinogens (cancer-causing agents), which include certain chemicals (particularly those found in tobacco smoke), dietary factors, some viruses, and specific types of radiation, including the ultraviolet light in natural sunlight.

In adults over age 50, the total number of newly diagnosed cancer cases roughly doubles each decade. Therefore, an 80-year-old person is eight times more likely to have cancer than a 50-year-old person. Some cancers, such as certain types of skin cancers and prostate cancer, are very common in old age, but these cancers may often be present without causing serious problems.

What are the symptoms?

Sometimes, a cancer is detected before it causes symptoms, often during a routine screening test. However, cancer is more often discovered when symptoms gradually develop and become noticeable over a period of weeks or months, prompting a person to visit a doctor. The symptoms of cancer may include:

- A lump, which is often firm and painless, in or beneath the skin.
- Changes in the appearance of a mole.
- A nonhealing wound.
- Blood in the urine or sputum.
- Changes in bowel habits.
- A blood-stained discharge from the bowel or vagina.
- Persistent abdominal pain.
- Hoarseness or changes in the voice.
- Difficulty swallowing.
- Severe, recurrent headaches.

Many cancers also produce more general symptoms, which may include:

- Weight loss.
- Fatigue.
- Loss of appetite and nausea.

If you experience or notice one or more of these symptoms, you should consult your doctor.

How is it diagnosed?

Routine screening (p.42) is constantly improving the early diagnosis of cancer. Screening aims to detect disease before symptoms are present. An example is examination of the large intestine, with a colonoscopy (p.661) or a rectal examination, to look for colorectal cancer. Other screening tests that are commonly used include mammography (p.759) to check for breast cancer

(TEST) Staging cancer

If you are diagnosed with cancer, your doctor will need to know if the cancer has spread from its primary site to nearby lymph nodes or to other parts of the body. This assessment of the spread of a cancer is known as staging and may involve surgery and imaging tests. Staging allows doctors to plan the best treatment and to determine the prognosis.

Size and local spread

The first part of staging involves measuring the size of the tumor and assessing the extent of its invasion into nearby tissues. A biopsy may be performed, in which a sample of tissue is taken from the tumor and examined, or the whole tumor may be removed for examination.

Biopsy sample of a tumor
This biopsy sample taken from an abnormal area of the colon confirms the presence of cancerous tissue. The junction between normal and cancerous tissue is clearly visible.

Normal tissue

Cancerous tissue

Lymph node involvement

If a cancer spreads, it often first affects nearby lymph nodes, causing them to enlarge. Cancer in lymph nodes can be detected by examination under a microscope after surgical removal or by imaging techniques such as CT scanning (p.247).

Enlarged mass of lymph nodes

Spine

Kidney

Cancer in the lymph nodes
This CT scan of the abdominal cavity shows an enlarged mass of cancerous lymph nodes. In this case, the cancer has spread from a testis.

Distant spread

If cancer cells enter the bloodstream, metastases (secondary tumors) may develop in other parts of the body. Imaging of the most common sites of metastases, such as the liver, lungs, and bones, may therefore be performed after a primary tumor is diagnosed.

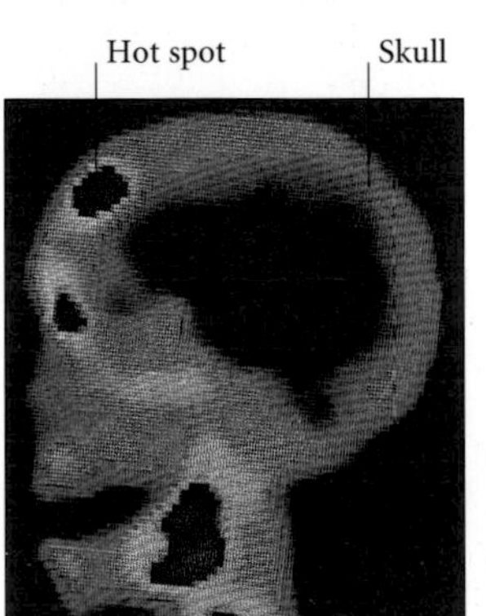
Hot spot
Skull

Bone metastases
In this radionuclide scan of the skull, "hot spots" show areas of increased cell activity. Such areas indicate the presence of cancer that has spread from elsewhere in the body.

and the Pap test (p.749) to look for precancerous cells that may eventually lead to cancer of the cervix (p.750).

Alternatively, cancer may be diagnosed as a result of tests to investigate symptoms. Such tests may include imaging tests, such as X-rays (p.244), ultrasound scanning (p.250), CT scanning (p.247), or MRI (p.248). In a few cases blood tests may be performed. For example, one test looks for proteins that indicate a particular type of tumor (*see* TUMOR MARKER TESTS, p.233). To confirm a diagnosis, it may be necessary to have a biopsy, in which a sample of abnormal tissue is removed and tested to find out if cancer is present (*see* CELL AND TISSUE TESTS, p.236). If cancer is present, further tests will identify the type of cell in the tissue that has become cancerous, which can give an indication of how fast the tumor is likely to grow and the best way to treat it. Once a diagnosis of cancer has been made, you will probably have tests to investigate how far the cancer has spread from its original site (*see* STAGING CANCER, p.277).

WHAT ARE THE TREATMENTS?

Although cancer can develop at many different sites around the body, the general principles of treatment are the same. The chances of a cancer being curable are highest if it is detected by screening at a sufficiently early stage before it causes symptoms.

The three main techniques used to treat cancer are surgery, chemotherapy (right), and radiation therapy (opposite page). Other treatments include biological and hormonal therapies.

Depending on the type and the stage of cancer, treatment may be intended to cure the cancer, slow the growth of the cancer, or be palliative (in which treatment is intended to help a person live as comfortably as possible rather than attempt to cure the cancer).

In most cases, curative treatment involves the surgical removal of a tumor. In addition to surgery, nonsurgical treatments, such as chemotherapy and radiation therapy, are often given with the aim of destroying any spread of the cancer beyond the obvious solid tumor. Nonsurgical treatments may also be used if a cure is not possible with the aim of slowing the growth of certain types of cancer rather than curing them. Palliative care can control the symptoms of cancer, maximize quality of life, and provide psychological help for you and your family as you come to terms with the process of dying.

Treatment is tailored to the type and the extent of the cancer, your age, your general health, and your wishes after discussing the prognosis and options with doctors and family. For example, attempts to cure a cancer may not be appropriate in extreme old age because of the adverse effects of the treatment. Instead, treatment may be offered to relieve symptoms and to improve quality of life (*see* CARING FOR A TERMINALLY ILL PERSON, p.965).

SURGERY Surgical removal of a tumor is the main treatment for most common solid tumors at an early stage. During surgery, it is usual to remove some normal tissue surrounding the tumor to maximize the chances that all cancerous cells are removed from the body. Sometimes, the lymph nodes near the tumor are also removed because cancer often spreads to these nodes first. Less commonly, surgery may aim to remove tumors that have spread to more distant sites in the body.

Surgery may not be appropriate if a tumor is inaccessible. For example, surgery to remove a tumor deep inside the brain may cause great damage to healthy brain tissue. Surgery may also not be the best treatment if the cancer has already spread to other parts of the body. In such cases, other treatments, including chemotherapy or radiation therapy, may be appropriate.

Surgery may be used as a palliative treatment for certain types of cancers (*see* PALLIATIVE SURGERY FOR CANCER, p.280). For example, surgery may be used to remove a tumor blocking the bowel or bile duct or to treat fractures of bones that have been weakened by cancer (*see* BONE METASTASES, p.373).

TREATMENT WITH ANTICANCER DRUGS Chemotherapy (below) consists of anticancer drugs (p.907) that are used to kill cancerous cells. Chemotherapy is the principal treatment for leukemias and early stage solid tumors (for example, breast tumors) so that a recurrence can be prevented. The treatment may also be used for solid tumors and other cancers that have spread to other parts of the body or to reduce the risk of further spread. Like surgery, chemotherapy may be used to cure cancer or as a palliative treatment. However, it can cause many side effects, such as nausea and vomiting, temporary hair loss, constipation, diarrhea, fatigue, and rarely kidney damage or anemia (p.446). You may be offered various treatments in order to relieve some of these side effects, such as antiemetic drugs (p.922) for nausea and vomiting or blood transfusions (p.447) for anemia. The

TREATMENT CHEMOTHERAPY

Treatment of cancer with anticancer drugs (p.907) is known as chemotherapy. The drugs may be taken orally but are often given directly into the bloodstream by injection into a vein. You may need to take the drugs daily, weekly, or every month at a doctor's office or sometimes in the hospital.

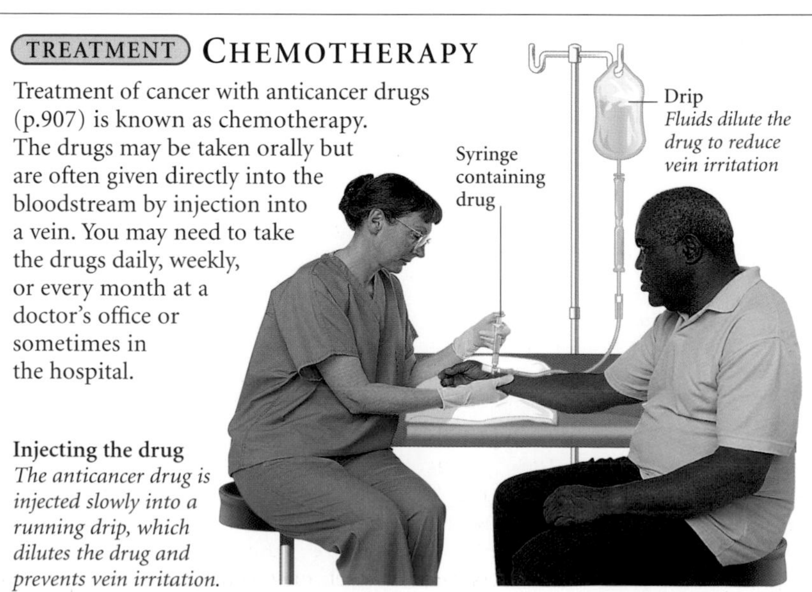
Drip
Fluids dilute the drug to reduce vein irritation
Syringe containing drug

Injecting the drug
The anticancer drug is injected slowly into a running drip, which dilutes the drug and prevents vein irritation.

TREATMENT RADIATION THERAPY

During radiation therapy, cancer cells are destroyed by using high-intensity radiation. Treatment can be either external or internal depending on the site of the tumor. The dose and position of the radiation is carefully calculated so that normal cells receive as little radiation as possible, allowing them to recover with little or no long-term damage. The treatment is painless at the time, but side effects such as nausea may develop as treatment continues. Radiation therapy may be used alone or with other cancer treatments.

EXTERNAL RADIATION

External radiation is often carried out using a linear accelerator, which produces X-rays, gamma rays, or electron beams. The type of radiation used depends on the type of cancer. The skin is usually marked with ink to outline the area to be treated. Treatment may be given once, several times a week, or several times a day, depending on the cancer and type of radiation used.

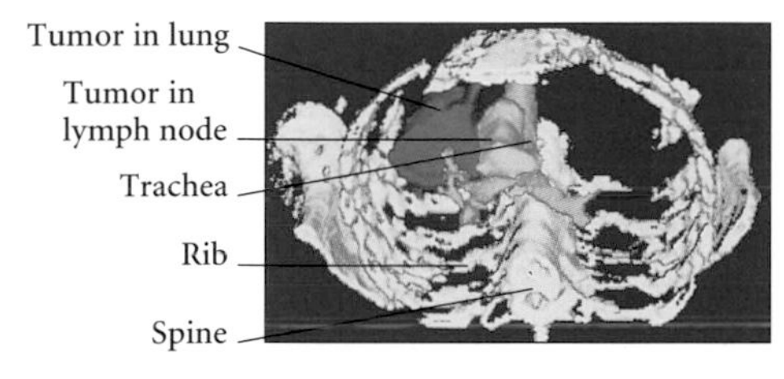
Tumor in lung
Tumor in lymph node
Trachea
Rib
Spine

Lung tumor
Multiple CT scans are taken at different angles and used to construct a 3-D computer map of the tumors in a lung and a nearby lymph node. Such maps are used to accurately plan the area that will receive radiation.

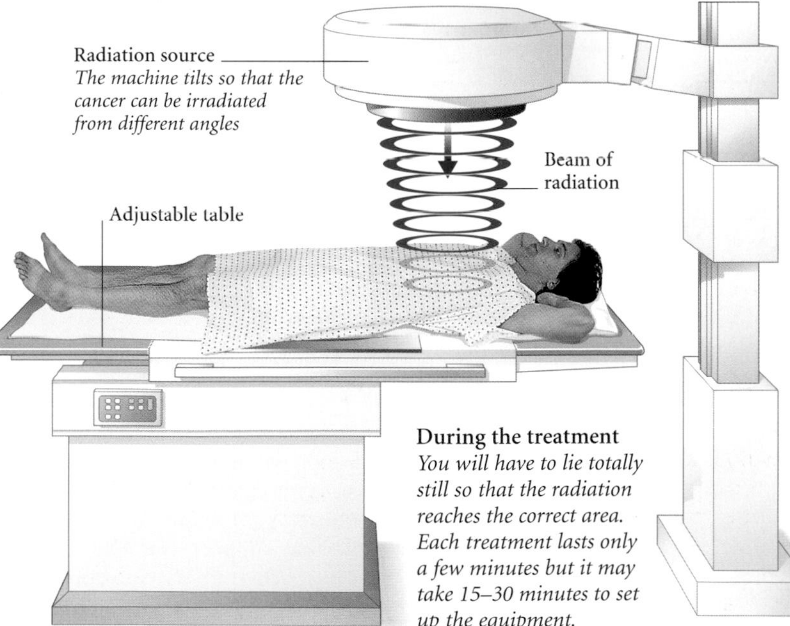
Radiation source
The machine tilts so that the cancer can be irradiated from different angles
Beam of radiation
Adjustable table

During the treatment
You will have to lie totally still so that the radiation reaches the correct area. Each treatment lasts only a few minutes but it may take 15–30 minutes to set up the equipment.

INTERNAL RADIATION

During this procedure, radioactive materials are placed directly into or around the cancer. For example, temporary radioactive implants may be placed within hollow organs, such as the uterus or vagina. Occasionally, a radioactive substance may be taken orally or injected into a body cavity. In some instances, small radioactive seeds may be placed directly into the affected organ and left in place while they gradually release radiation.

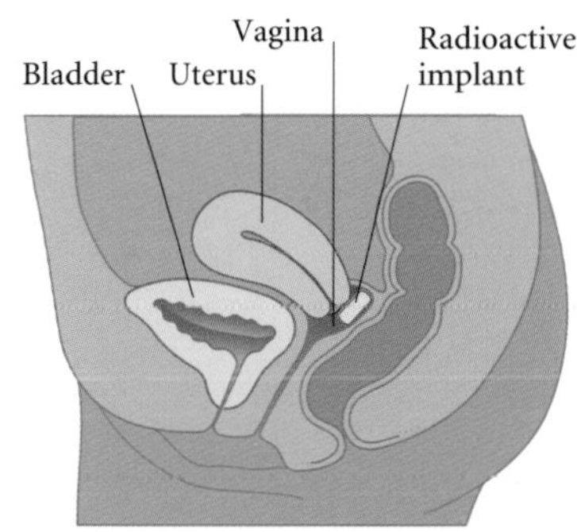
Vagina
Radioactive implant
Bladder
Uterus

Radioactive implants in the vagina
Implants containing radioactive substances are sometimes used to treat cancers of the uterus, the cervix, and the vagina.

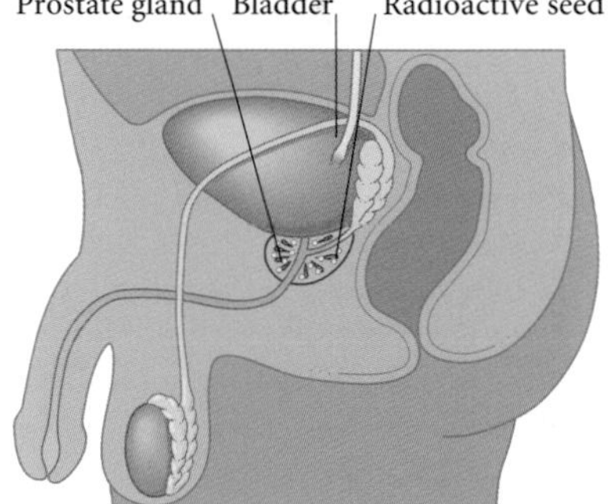
Prostate gland
Bladder
Radioactive seed

Radioactive seeds in the prostate
Prostate cancer may be treated by the insertion of radioactive seeds. The seeds emit radiation for several months.

duration of treatment varies depending on the type of cancer and the aim of the treatment.

TREATMENT WITH RADIATION In this technique, carefully focused radiation is used to destroy or to slow the growth of cancerous tissue (*see* RADIATION THERAPY, above). Common side effects vary from person to person and may include reddened or painful skin at the site of treatment, loss of appetite, nausea and vomiting, and fatigue. If you have radiation therapy to the head or neck, you may temporarily lose your hair (*see* ALOPECIA, p.358) and experience pain in the throat and a permanently dry mouth. Radiation therapy to the large bowel may cause inflammation and persistent diarrhea. Many of these side effects can be relieved using drugs and clear up when treatment has been completed. Radiation therapy can be used either curatively or palliatively.

HORMONAL THERAPIES Certain types of hormones affect the cell growth and replication of some cancers. For example, the female sex hormone estrogen is known to stimulate the growth of most

TREATMENT PALLIATIVE SURGERY FOR CANCER

The aim of palliative surgery is to relieve the symptoms or to prevent complications rather than to cure the cancer. Palliative surgery may be performed to remove an unsightly growth; to relieve or remove an obstruction that is due to a tumor, particularly within the digestive or respiratory tract; to cut nerves that transmit pain signals; or to prevent fractures of bones that are weakened by cancerous deposits. Two common examples of palliative surgery for cancer are described below.

RELIEVING AN OBSTRUCTION

If a narrowing of an airway or of the intestine is causing symptoms, a rigid incompressible tube, known as a stent, can help keep the passage unblocked. Under general anesthesia, the stent is pushed through the obstruction in order to open up or widen the affected passage.

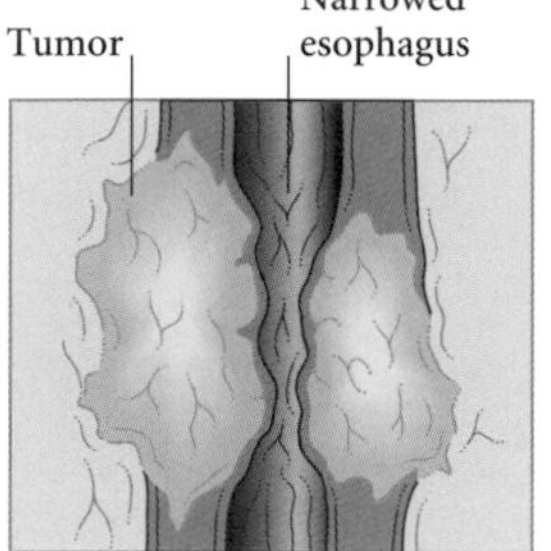
Tumor
Narrowed esophagus

BEFORE SURGERY

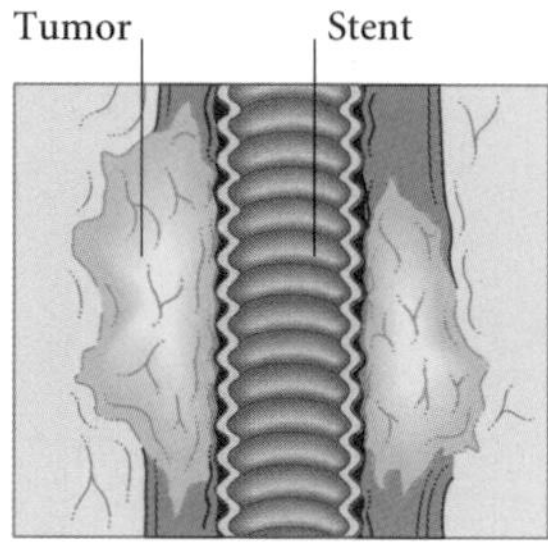
Tumor
Stent

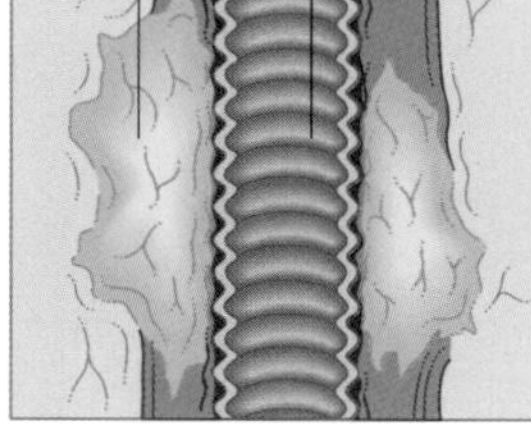

AFTER SURGERY

LOCATION

Esophageal stent
The esophagus has become narrowed by a tumor, which makes swallowing difficult. A rigid plastic tube (stent) inserted to widen the esophagus makes swallowing easier.

PREVENTING FRACTURES

If cancer spreads from elsewhere in the body to an area of the bone, the affected bone becomes weak and thin and may eventually fracture. To help prevent fractures from occurring and allow a person to remain as active as possible, the bone may be pinned using a metal rod.

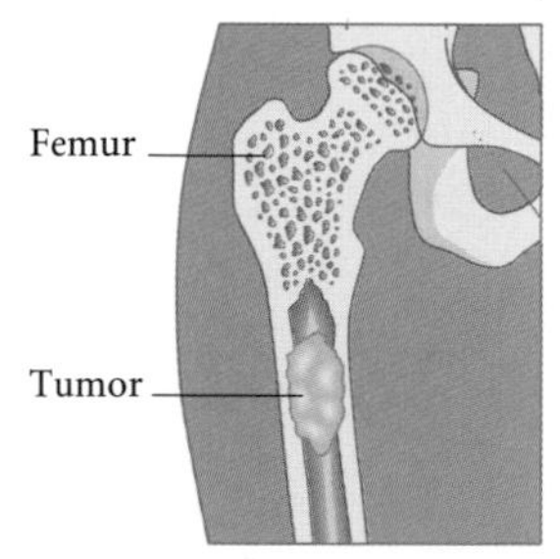
Femur
Tumor

BEFORE SURGERY

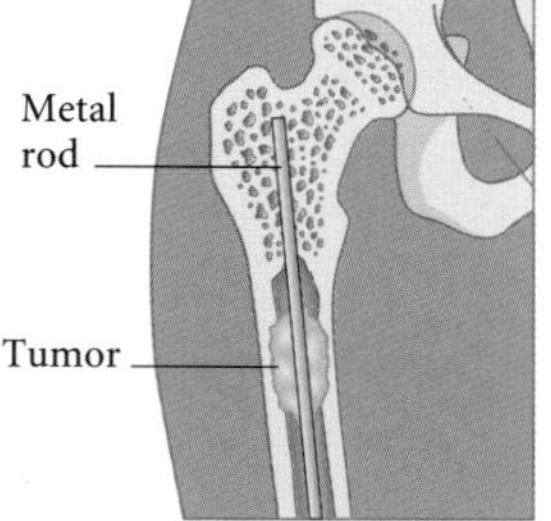
Metal rod
Tumor

AFTER SURGERY

LOCATION

Pinning the femur
Cancer has spread to the femur from elsewhere in the body. The metal rod supports the affected area of bone to prevent a fracture.

breast cancers and also suppress the growth of prostate cancer. Treatment with sex hormones plays an important part in the management of these types of cancers (*see* SEX HORMONES AND RELATED DRUGS, p.933).

BIOLOGICAL THERAPIES These newer types of treatments are currently under investigation and are not yet used for most cancers. Biological therapies may involve taking drugs known as "cancer vaccines" to stimulate the immune system, which is the body's natural defense mechanism. For example, substances such as interferons, which trigger some types of white blood cells to attack abnormal cells, can be manufactured synthetically and given as interferon drugs (p.907). You may also be given synthetically created antibodies (proteins that recognize and attack foreign cells or particles in the body) that deliver a radioactive substance or anticancer drug directly to a cancer.

Two promising experimental biological therapies are gene therapy and angiogenesis inhibition. Gene therapy involves introducing a gene into the genetic material of cancerous cells by using a virus. The new gene is responsible for producing a natural substance that can help destroy the cancerous cells. Experiments using animals have shown that this approach can shrink small tumors. In angiogenesis inhibition, drugs are given to halt the growth of new blood vessels that allow a tumor to continue to grow. When starved of an adequate supply of nutrients and oxygen, the tumor shrinks.

Biological therapies have now been used successfully to treat kidney cancer (p.704), malignant melanoma (p.346), and certain types of lymphomas and leukemias. These treatments may cause side effects such as fever, muscle aches, vomiting, and fatigue.

SUPPORTIVE CARE A diagnosis of cancer and its treatment can be stressful and frightening. The aim of supportive care is to make life continue as normally as possible. You will be offered relief for the symptoms of cancer, such as pain (*see* PAIN RELIEF FOR CANCER, opposite page). Side effects due to cancer treatments, such as vomiting, will also be treated. You and your family will probably be offered psychological support and advice from the medical team involved in your treatment. These specialists will help you understand and cope with the diagnosis and treatment of the cancer. You may wish to see a counselor to obtain advice and psychological support (*see* COUNSELING, p.971). Such support can boost your emotional well-being and self-esteem, which may be particularly affected if treatment has caused obvious physical changes, such as removal of a breast or hair loss. Research appears to show that people with a positive mental attitude survive longer than those who simply resign themselves to the disease.

Sharing problems with people who have had similar personal experiences can be reassuring, and it may be possible to join a support group for people with cancer and their families.

WHAT IS THE PROGNOSIS?

The earlier a cancer is diagnosed, the more likely it is that treatment will be successful and the cancer can be cured. The prognosis is usually expressed in terms of a 5-year survival rate (the percentage of people alive 5 years after the diagnosis of cancer is made). For most types of cancers, the prognosis has been greatly improved during the last few decades, especially in children.

These days, as many as 7 in 10 children and 1 in 2 adults diagnosed with cancer are alive 5 years later (*see* SURVIVING CANCER, below). Even in cases where the cancer cannot be cured, there is still a good chance of long-term survival with a fairly good quality of life, often for many years after the diagnosis.

(WWW) ONLINE SITES: p.1028

Surviving cancer

An overview of the features of life after successful treatment for cancer

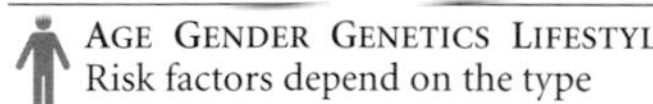
AGE GENDER GENETICS LIFESTYLE
Risk factors depend on the type

Cure rates may be higher than 9 in 10 for some types of cancers and lower than 1 in 10 for others. The chances of cancer being cured depend on various factors, including the age and general health of the affected person, the type of cancer, the stage it has reached, and the effectiveness of treatment (*see* CANCER AND ITS MANAGEMENT, p.276). Complete remission occurs when all symptoms disappear and there is no evidence of any cancerous cells in the body. For many, but not all, cancers if cancer does not recur for 5 years, there is a good chance that it has been cured. A relapse may be indicated by the return of symptoms or by evidence of cancer from follow-up tests.

Sometimes, treatment may damage the immune system. Radiation therapy (p.279) and chemotherapy (p.278) may increase the chance of a second type of cancer developing in previously normal tissue. For example, chemotherapy may increase the risk that leukemia (p.453) or lymphoma (p.459) will develop.

ARE THERE COMPLICATIONS?

Cancer treatment often causes physical changes that may be psychologically difficult to deal with. For example, a breast may have been removed because of breast cancer (p.759). Mental abilities may also be affected, especially after treatment for brain tumors (p.530).

Emotional problems after treatment may understandably include a fear that the cancer is going to recur. You may also become depressed as a reaction to the physical changes caused by the treatment (*see* DEPRESSION, p.554).

You may encounter discrimination at work. Some employers may be reluctant to employ or promote you if you have been treated for cancer. They may be unwilling to invest money in you, assume that you are going to die soon or that you will claim large amounts of money from pension and health insurance plans. Employers may also have an unfounded belief that survivors of cancer are unproductive workers and may fear that you will need a long time off work. However, there are organizations that can offer you emotional support and legal advice if you face discrimination after cancer treatment.

WHAT MIGHT THE DOCTOR DO?

You will be advised to visit the doctor for follow-up evaluations once the cancer has gone into remission. Follow-up involves routine checkups at intervals after treatment. These checkups may involve having imaging tests, such as X-rays (p.244) or CT scanning (p.247), endoscopy (p.255), or blood tests (*see* TUMOR MARKER TESTS, p.233). Some cancers can be successfully treated if a recurrence is detected early enough.

WHAT CAN I DO?

You should attend any recommended follow-up appointments and try not to feel too anxious or fearful about these checkups. They will be scheduled less frequently over time and are often required only annually after 5 years. Follow-up is done to maximize the chances of diagnosing and successfully treating any recurrence of cancer early.

Once your cancer has been cured, you may feel the need to improve the quality of your life by making a change in your priorities. Many cancer survivors decide to leave or change their jobs in order to fulfill lifelong ambitions or to spend more time with their families. You and your family may also wish to join a self-help organization, usually run by cancer survivors, which can offer support and advice to other survivors and their families.

If you develop cancer before age 50, it may have a genetic cause. If this genetic cause has been inherited then other family members may also be at increased risk of developing the same cancer. For example, about 1 in 10 cases of colorectal cancer (p.665), breast cancer, cancer of the ovary (p.744), and prostate cancer (p.726), clearly has an inherited genetic cause.

If your family has a higher than normal incidence of a particular type of cancer, it is important for relatives at risk to be regularly screened for that cancer (*see* SCREENING, p.42).

(WWW) ONLINE SITES: p.1028

(TREATMENT) PAIN RELIEF FOR CANCER

It should be possible to control pain due to cancer by using analgesics (p.912). Drugs of increasing strength can be prescribed and most are taken orally as pills or liquids, or applied as skin patches. If pain is severe and not controlled by these types of drugs, morphine or other powerful analgesics may be injected continuously at home using a portable syringe driver, which allows a person to pursue normal activities.

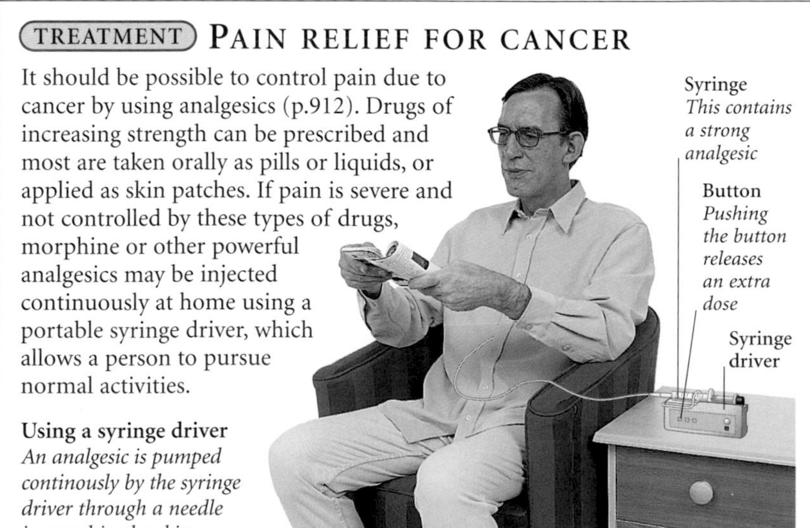
Syringe
This contains a strong analgesic
Button
Pushing the button releases an extra dose
Syringe driver

Using a syringe driver
An analgesic is pumped continously by the syringe driver through a needle inserted in the skin.

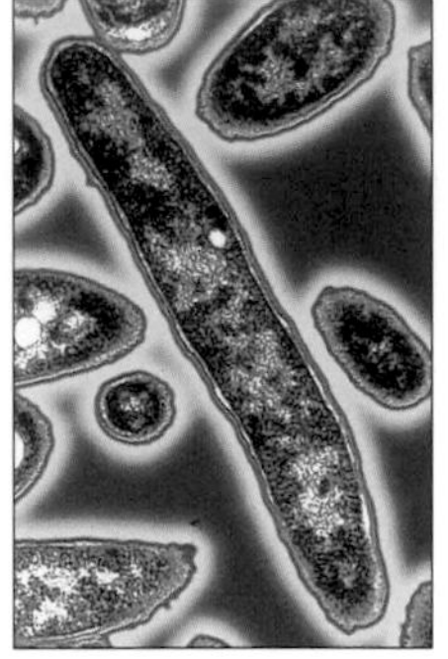

Legionella bacteria
These bacteria, which can cause pneumonia, are sometimes found in air conditioners.

INFECTIONS AND INFESTATIONS

THE MOST COMMON CAUSE OF DISEASE is infection by microorganisms that find their way into internal body tissues, where they multiply and disrupt normal cell function. These organisms, which are commonly known as germs, take a wide range of forms and contain the groups classified broadly as viruses, bacteria, protozoa, and fungi. Disease can also be caused by larger, more complex organisms, such as parasitic worms and their larvae, which may infest various parts of the body, especially the intestine.

The likelihood of serious illness from infectious disease is largely influenced by the environment. In the developed world, most infections can be treated effectively or prevented. However, in the developing world, where children are often malnourished, many of the common infections, such as measles, can be fatal. People living in temperate regions are rarely affected by cholera, malaria, or parasitic worms, but in the tropics such disorders are frequent causes of ill health and death.

Sometimes, an infectious disease spreads rapidly worldwide. Influenza, for example, tends to occur in annual outbreaks in all countries. Future global health threats include several newly emerged diseases, such as AIDS, and long-established diseases, such as tuberculosis, in which organisms have become resistant to common drugs.

HOW INFECTIONS ARE TRANSMITTED

The organisms that cause disease enter the body in a variety of ways. Some are breathed in or swallowed in food and water; others may gain entry through a break in the skin or be transmitted during sexual contact. An infection may spread throughout the body, affecting several organs at once. However, certain infectious organisms target and damage only one particular organ or part of the body, such as the liver, respiratory tract, or intestine.

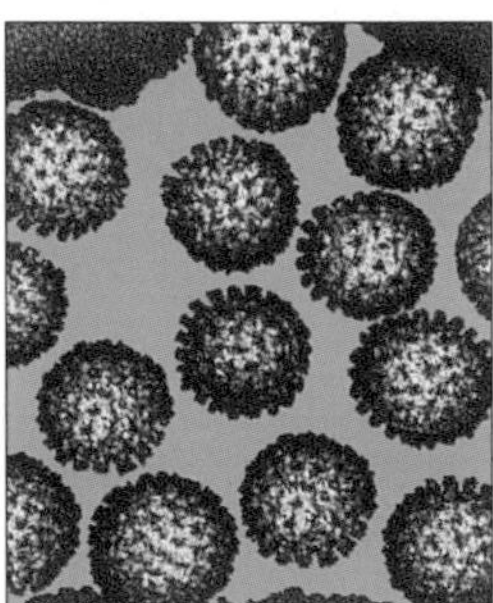

Rotaviruses
These wheel-shaped viruses are a common cause of gastrointestinal infections.

Infections are more likely to develop if the number of infecting organisms is large or if a person's resistance to disease is reduced. Reduced resistance may be due to factors such as extremes of age, poor nutrition, or an immune system already weakened by disease.

CONTROLLING INFECTION

Over the last 100 years, great advances have been made in the control of infections, largely due to improvements in diet, housing, and hygiene. In addition, the increasing availability of routine immunizations and drugs such as antibiotics have made it possible to cure or even wipe out many infectious diseases. International programs to monitor the occurrence of infections have also helped check the spread of many often fatal diseases.

COMPARISON SIZES OF ORGANISMS

There is a vast range in size between the different infectious organisms. However, the size of an organism does not determine the severity of a disease. For example, a microscopic virus can lead to a life-threatening illness, and a tapeworm 20 ft (6 m) long may cause only mild symptoms.

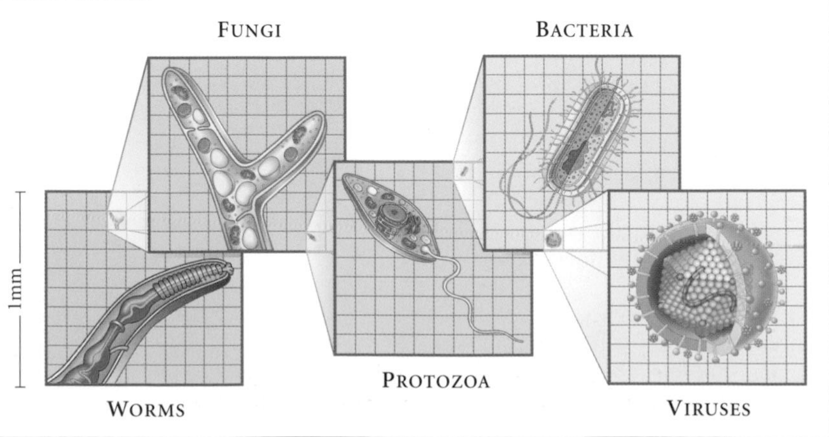
FUNGI
BACTERIA
1mm
PROTOZOA
WORMS
VIRUSES

Relative dimensions of organisms
Worms are the largest disease-causing organisms. In this diagram, each successive picture after worms represents a 100-fold magnification. The smallest disease-causing organisms are the viruses.

STRUCTURE AND FUNCTION VIRUSES

Viruses are the smallest infectious organisms, and they are so tiny that millions of them could fit inside a single human cell. Viruses are only capable of reproduction inside a living cell, called a host cell, that they invade. A virus consists of little more than a single or double strand of genetic material surrounded by a protein shell. However, some types of viruses also have a protective outer envelope.

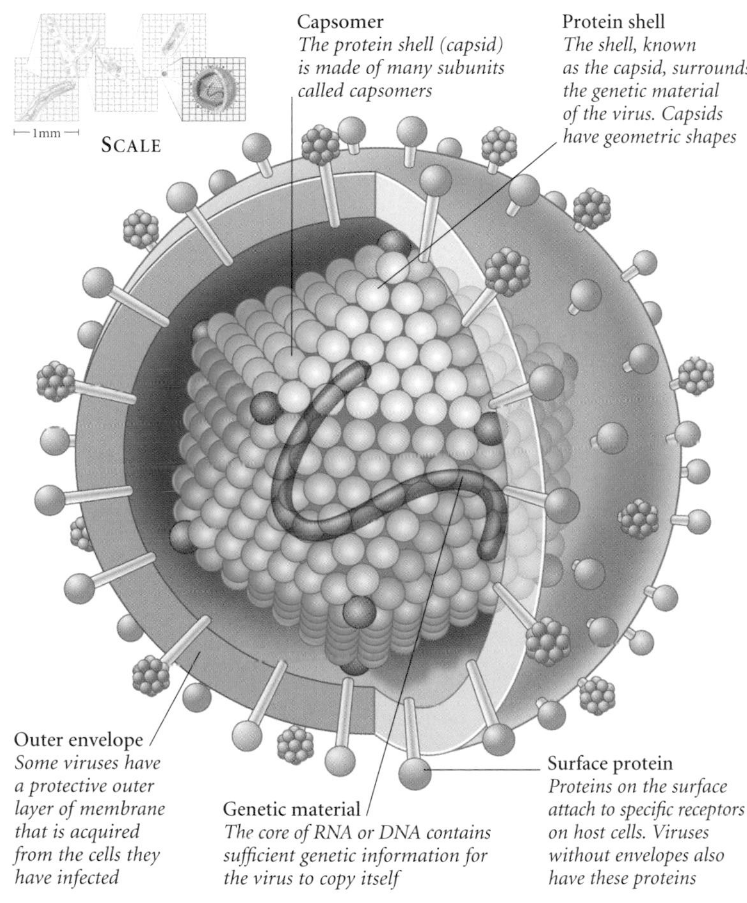
1mm
SCALE

Capsomer
The protein shell (capsid) is made of many subunits called capsomers

Protein shell
The shell, known as the capsid, surrounds the genetic material of the virus. Capsids have geometric shapes

Outer envelope
Some viruses have a protective outer layer of membrane that is acquired from the cells they have infected

Genetic material
The core of RNA or DNA contains sufficient genetic information for the virus to copy itself

Surface protein
Proteins on the surface attach to specific receptors on host cells. Viruses without envelopes also have these proteins

CHANGES IN VIRUSES

The immune system recognizes viruses by the proteins that are on their surfaces (antigens). When viruses reproduce, the antigens on the new viruses may become slightly different to prevent the immune system from recognizing the virus. This is known as antigenic drift. Much larger changes (antigenic shifts) may result in epidemics.

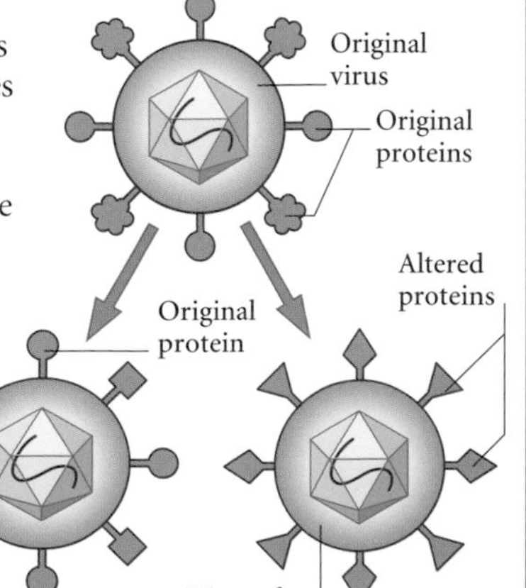
Original virus
Original proteins
Altered proteins
Original protein
Virus after antigenic drift
Altered protein
Virus after antigenic shift

Antigenic drift and shift
A minor change to a virus is known as antigenic drift; a larger change is known as an antigenic shift.

HOW VIRUSES REPRODUCE

To survive, viruses must reproduce inside living cells. The genetic material from an infecting virus takes over the functions of the host cell to make millions of new virus particles.The new viruses leave the host cell by bursting out of the cell or by budding out from the cell surface.

1 *Proteins on the virus attach to specific receptors on the surface of a host cell. The virus may enter the cell by being engulfed by the cell membrane or by fusing into the cell membrane.*

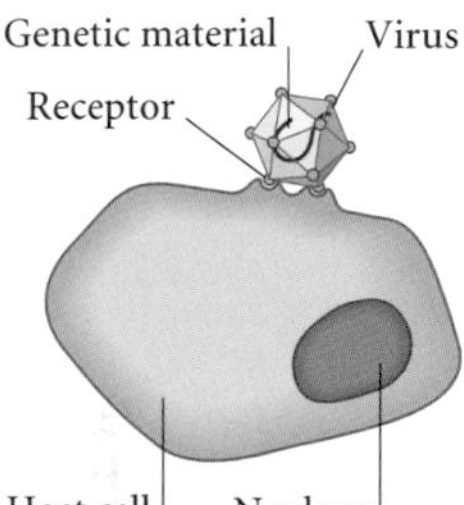
Genetic material
Virus
Receptor
Host cell
Nucleus

2 *When inside the cell, the virus sheds its protein shell. The genetic material of the virus reproduces, using substances from inside the cell.*

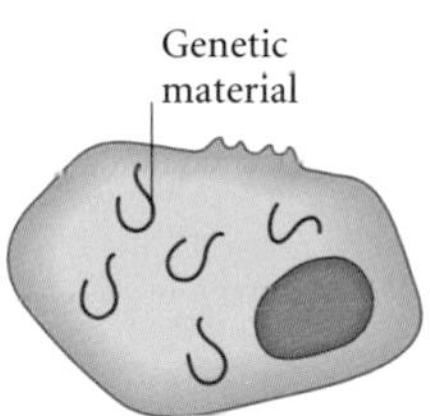
Genetic material

3 *Each new copy of the genetic material programs the formation of a new protein shell. Once the shells have formed, the new viruses are complete.*

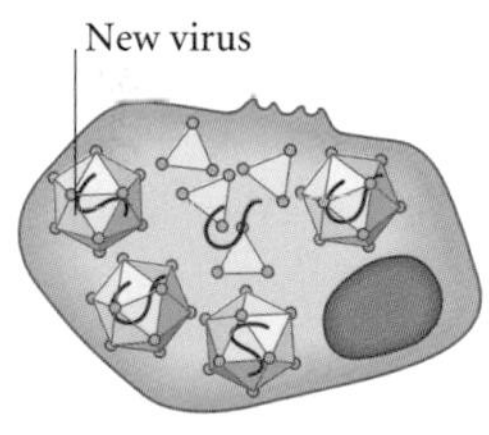
New virus

4 *The viruses leave the cell either by suddenly rupturing the cell membrane, which destroys the host cell, or by slowly budding out from the surface of the cell membrane.*

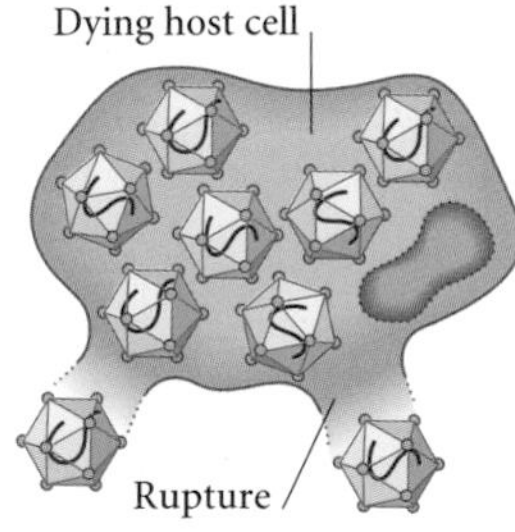
Dying host cell
Rupture

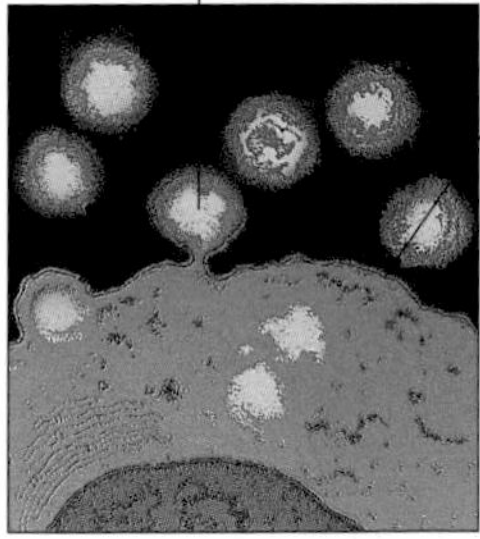
Budding virus
Host cell membrane

Budding viruses
When certain viruses bud out from their host cell, they envelop themselves in host cell surface membrane.

STRUCTURE AND FUNCTION BACTERIA

Bacteria are microscopic single-celled organisms that are found in every environment. Some bacteria live in or on our bodies without causing disease. There are thousands of different types of bacteria, but relatively few of these cause disease in humans. Bacteria have a variety of shapes that are broadly classified as cocci (spheres), bacilli (rods), and spirochetes and spirilla (curved forms).

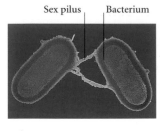

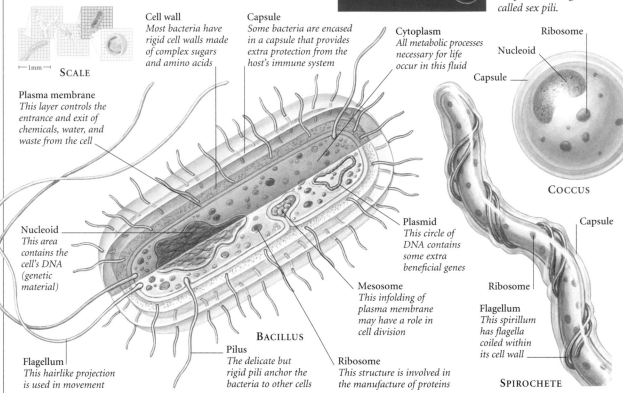

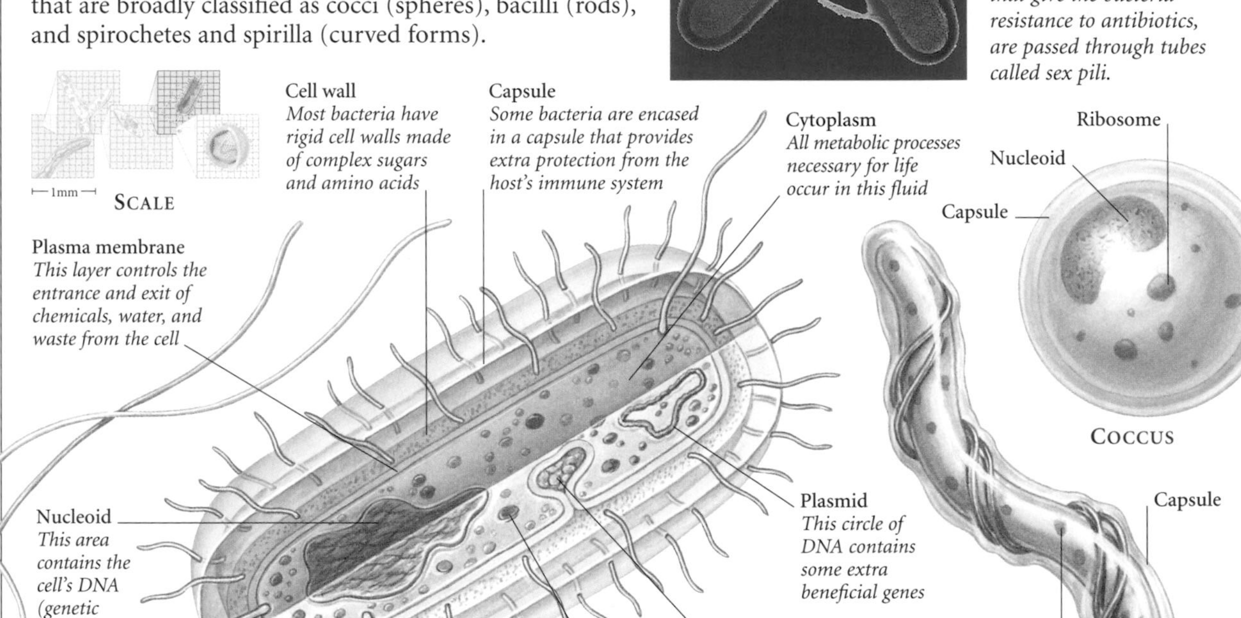
Sex pilus
Bacterium
Conjugation
Bacteria may exchange genes in a process called conjugation. Plasmids, which may contain genes that give the bacteria resistance to antibiotics, are passed through tubes called sex pili.
1mm
SCALE
Cell wall
Most bacteria have rigid cell walls made of complex sugars and amino acids
Capsule
Some bacteria are encased in a capsule that provides extra protection from the host's immune system
Cytoplasm
All metabolic processes necessary for life occur in this fluid
Ribosome
Nucleoid
Capsule
Plasma membrane
This layer controls the entrance and exit of chemicals, water, and waste from the cell
COCCUS
Capsule
Plasmid
This circle of DNA contains some extra beneficial genes
Nucleoid
This area contains the cell's DNA (genetic material)
Mesosome
This infolding of plasma membrane may have a role in cell division
Ribosome
Flagellum
This spirillum has flagella coiled within its cell wall
BACILLUS
Pilus
The delicate but rigid pili anchor the bacteria to other cells
Flagellum
This hairlike projection is used in movement
Ribosome
This structure is involved in the manufacture of proteins
SPIROCHETE

EFFECTS OF TOXINS

Some bacteria cause disease by producing poisonous chemicals known as toxins. These chemicals may destroy specific body cells or enter cells and alter their chemical processes. Some toxins are released from bacteria when they die and may cause shock and fever.

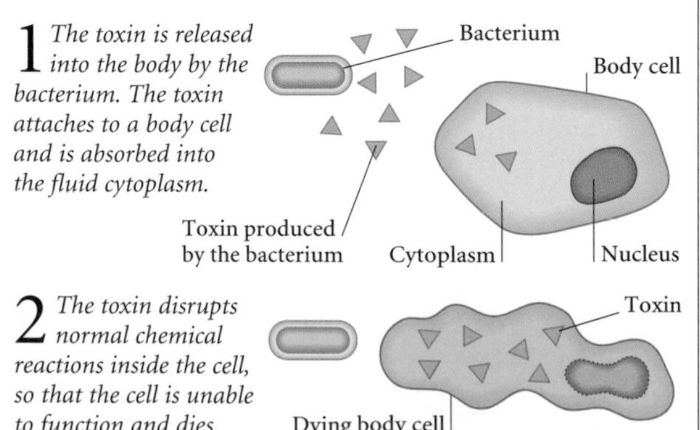
1 *The toxin is released into the body by the bacterium. The toxin attaches to a body cell and is absorbed into the fluid cytoplasm.*
Bacterium
Body cell
Toxin produced by the bacterium
Cytoplasm
Nucleus
2 *The toxin disrupts normal chemical reactions inside the cell, so that the cell is unable to function and dies.*
Toxin
Dying body cell

BACTERIAL INVASION OF A CELL

A few bacteria damage tissues in the human body not by secreting toxins but by directly invading the cells. Once inside body cells, the bacteria reproduce and eventually burst out, rupturing the cell membrane.

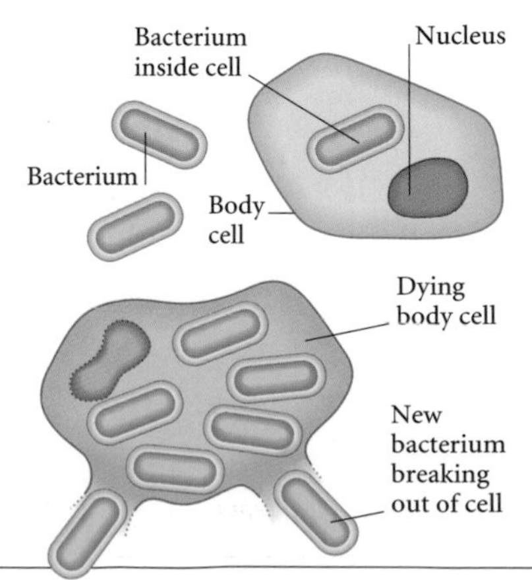
1 *Different bacteria are specifically attracted to certain body cells. Bacteria enter the cell through the membrane and use the cell nutrients.*
Bacterium inside cell
Nucleus
Bacterium
Body cell
2 *The bacteria multiply rapidly in the cell. They kill the cell by breaking its membrane then spread to other areas of the body.*
Dying body cell
New bacterium breaking out of cell

STRUCTURE PROTOZOA

Protozoa are single-celled organisms that feed by scavenging for particles and other microorganisms, such as bacteria, or by absorbing nutrients from their environment. Many types of protozoa live in moist places, such as soil, water, or sewage, and some of these may infect humans and other animals, causing disease. Other types of disease-causing protozoa depend on bloodsucking insects, such as mosquitoes, to spread them among human hosts. Most cases of protozoal infections occur in the tropical regions of the world.

1mm

SCALE

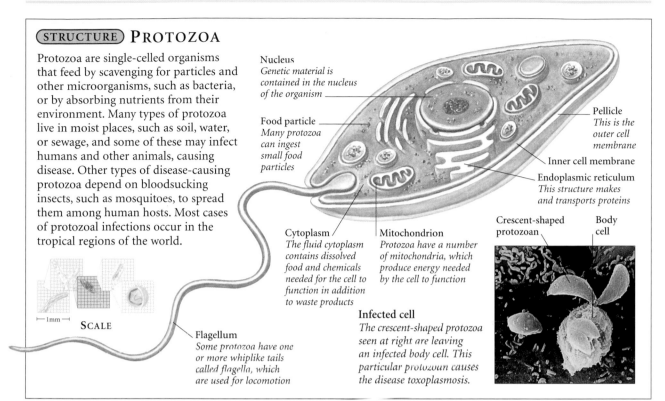

Nucleus
Genetic material is contained in the nucleus of the organism

Food particle
Many protozoa can ingest small food particles

Pellicle
This is the outer cell membrane

Inner cell membrane

Endoplasmic reticulum
This structure makes and transports proteins

Cytoplasm
The fluid cytoplasm contains dissolved food and chemicals needed for the cell to function in addition to waste products

Mitochondrion
Protozoa have a number of mitochondria, which produce energy needed by the cell to function

Flagellum
Some protozoa have one or more whiplike tails called flagella, which are used for locomotion

Crescent-shaped protozoan

Body cell

Infected cell
The crescent-shaped protozoa seen at right are leaving an infected body cell. This particular protozoan causes the disease toxoplasmosis.

STRUCTURE FUNGI

Disease-causing fungi can be divided into two broad groups: the filamentous fungi, which grow as branching threads called hyphae; and the single-celled yeasts. Some fungi have features of both groups. Fungi may form spores that remain dormant for years before causing disease.

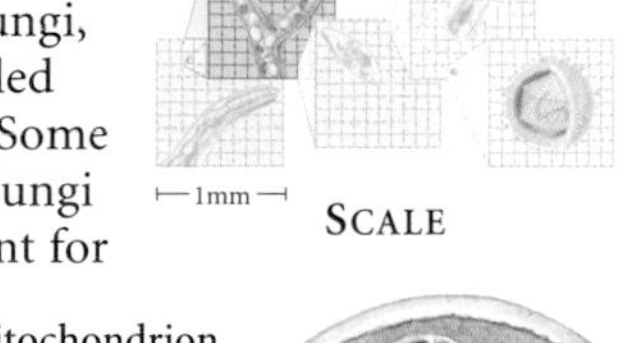
1mm
SCALE

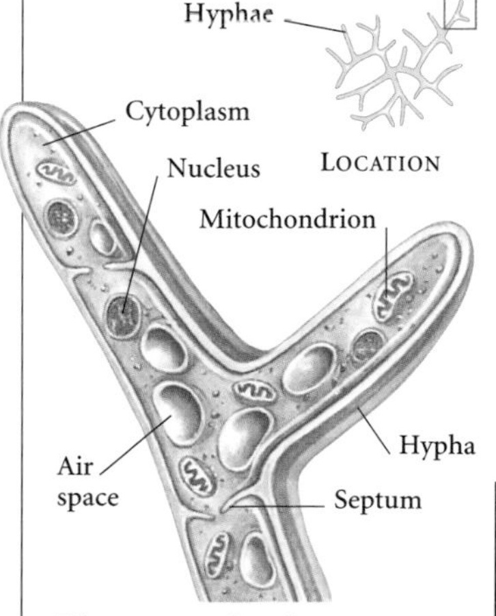
Hyphae
LOCATION
Cytoplasm
Nucleus
Mitochondrion
Air space
Hypha
Septum

Filamentous fungi
These fungi form long tubular branches known as hyphae that may be divided into segments by cross walls called septa.

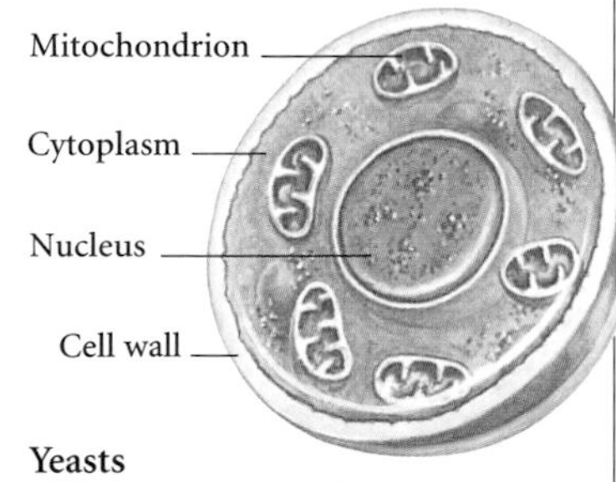
Mitochondrion
Cytoplasm
Nucleus
Cell wall

Yeasts
These types of fungi live in colonies of spherical or ovoid single cells. They multiply by cell division and budding.

Fungal spores
Various types of fungi, including aspergillus fungi (left), produce dormant forms called spores that may cause illness if inhaled.

STRUCTURE WORMS

Worms are complex organisms that range in size from microscopic to several feet long. There are two types, flatworms and roundworms, that are adapted to infest humans. Adult worms or immature larvae infest various parts of the body, including the intestines and blood vessels.

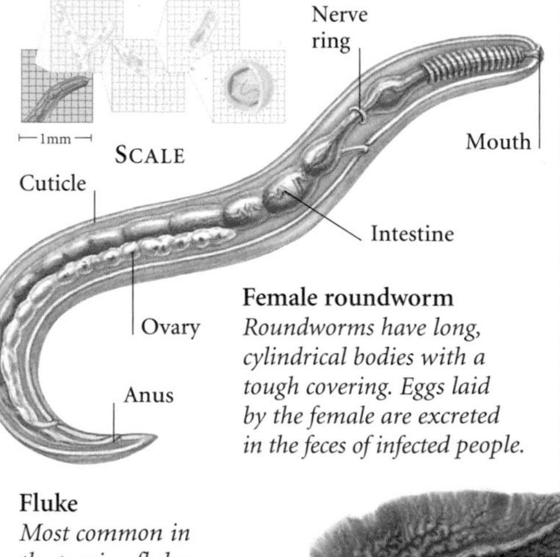
1mm
SCALE
Nerve ring
Mouth
Cuticle
Intestine
Ovary
Anus

Female roundworm
Roundworms have long, cylindrical bodies with a tough covering. Eggs laid by the female are excreted in the feces of infected people.

Fluke
Most common in the tropics, flukes are flat and leaf-shaped or elongated parasitic flatworms.

VIRAL INFECTIONS

Some of the most familiar minor illnesses, such as coughs, sore throats, and attacks of diarrhea and vomiting, are often caused by viral infections. However, viruses are responsible not only for minor infections but also for potentially fatal diseases, such as rabies and HIV infection and AIDS.

The first articles discuss common viral infections such as the common cold and influenza, the related infections chickenpox and herpes zoster, and herpes simplex infections. The next articles describe the once-common viral infections of childhood, measles, mumps, and rubella. As a result of immunization, these diseases are now rare in developed countries. However, some of these viruses can still affect adults who have not been immunized, producing symptoms that are often severe. Articles follow on a number of viral diseases, including yellow fever, that may be encountered in the developing world. HIV infection and AIDS, now common throughout the world, is discussed in the following article. Smallpox, eradicated through vaccination but currently a concern as a potential weapon of bioterrorists, is next discussed. The section ends with articles on severe acute respiratory syndrome (SARS) and West Nile virus.

Viral infections that affect only one body system are covered elsewhere in the book. For example, chronic hepatitis (p.644) is covered in liver and gallbladder disorders.

KEY STRUCTURES

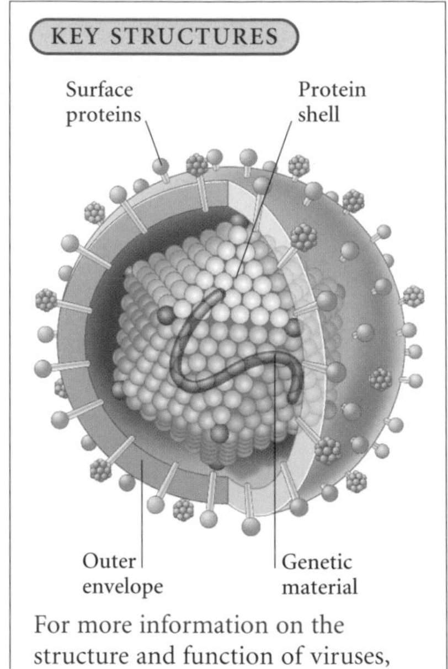
Surface proteins
Protein shell
Outer envelope
Genetic material

For more information on the structure and function of viruses, *see* pp.282–285.

Common cold

An infection of the nose and throat that may be caused by many different viruses

 AGE More common in children

 GENDER GENETICS LIFESTYLE Not significant factors

There are at least 200 highly contagious viruses that can cause the common cold. These viruses are easily transmitted in minute airborne droplets from the coughs or sneezes of infected people. In many cases, the viruses are also spread to the nose and throat by way of hand-to-hand contact with an infected person or by way of objects that have become contaminated with the virus, such as a cup or towel.

Colds can occur at any time of the year, although infections are more frequent in the fall and winter. About half of the population of North America and Europe develops at least one cold each year. Children are more susceptible to colds than adults because they have not yet developed immunity to the most common viruses and also because viruses spread very quickly in communities such as nurseries and schools.

WHAT ARE THE SYMPTOMS?

The initial symptoms of a cold usually develop between 12 hours and 3 days after infection. Symptoms usually intensify over 24–48 hours, unlike those of influenza (opposite page), which worsen rapidly over a few hours. If you have a cold, symptoms may include:

- Frequent sneezing.
- Runny nose with a clear watery discharge that later becomes thick and green colored.
- Mild fever and headache.
- Sore throat and sometimes a cough.

Airborne droplets

Spreading the cold virus
Cold viruses are easily spread by coughs and sneezes. This specialized photograph shows how far droplets are sprayed by a sneeze, even when a handkerchief is used.

In some people, a common cold may be complicated by a bacterial infection such as an infection of the chest (*see* ACUTE BRONCHITIS, p.486) or of the sinuses (*see* SINUSITIS, p.475). Bacterial ear infections, which may cause earache, are a common complication of colds (*see* OTITIS MEDIA, p.597, and ACUTE OTITIS MEDIA IN CHILDREN, p.860).

WHAT CAN I DO?

Most people recognize their symptoms as those of a common cold and do not seek medical advice.

Despite a great deal of scientific research, there is no cure for the common cold, but over-the-counter drugs (*see* COLD AND FLU REMEDIES, p.910) can help relieve the symptoms. These drugs include analgesics (p.912) to relieve a headache and reduce a fever, decongestants (p.909) to clear a stuffy nose, and cough remedies (p.909) to soothe a tickling throat. It is also important to drink plenty of cool fluids, particularly if you have a fever (*see* BRINGING DOWN A FEVER, opposite page). Many people take large quantities of vitamin C to prevent infection and treat the common cold, but any benefit from this popular remedy is unproved.

If your symptoms do not improve in a week or your child is no better in 2 days, you should consult a doctor. If you have a bacterial infection, your doctor may prescribe antibiotics (p.885), although they are ineffective against cold viruses.

The common cold usually clears up without treatment within 2 weeks, but a cough may last longer.

(WWW) ONLINE SITES: p.1033

Influenza

An infection of the upper respiratory tract (airways), commonly known as flu

AGE GENDER GENETICS LIFESTYLE
Not significant factors

Influenza, also known as flu, is a highly contagious viral disease that tends to occur in epidemics during the winter. The infection mainly affects the upper respiratory tract (airways) and can be transmitted easily in airborne droplets from the coughs and sneezes of infected people. Influenza viruses can also be transmitted from person to person through direct contact.

Many different viral infections can result in mild flulike symptoms, but true influenza is caused by two principal types of influenza viruses: A and B. The type A virus, in particular, frequently changes its structure (mutates) and produces new strains to which few people have immunity.

The number of influenza cases varies from year to year, but particularly virulent strains have spread worldwide and caused millions of deaths. Such major outbreaks, called pandemics, occurred in 1918 with Spanish flu, in 1957 with Asian flu, in 1968 with Hong Kong flu, and in 1977 with Russian flu.

What are the symptoms?

The symptoms of influenza develop 24–48 hours after infection. Many people think they have influenza when they have only a common cold (opposite page), but the symptoms of influenza are far more severe than those of a cold. The first symptom may be slight chills. Other symptoms, which develop later and worsen rapidly in just a few hours, may include the following:

- High fever, sweating, and shivering.
- Aching muscles, especially in the back.
- Severe exhaustion.
- Frequent sneezing, stuffy or runny nose, sore throat, and cough.

Following an attack of flu, fatigue and depression are often experienced after other symptoms have disappeared.

The most common complications are bacterial infections of the airways (*see* ACUTE BRONCHITIS, p.486) and lungs (*see* PNEUMONIA, p.490). Such infections can be life-threatening in babies, elderly people, those with chronic heart or lung disease, and people with reduced immunity, such as those with AIDS (*see* HIV INFECTION AND AIDS, p.295) or diabetes mellitus (p.687).

What might be done?

For most normally healthy people, the best way to relieve the symptoms of influenza is to rest in bed, drink plenty of cool fluids, and follow the advice for bringing down a fever (below). Analgesics (p.912), such as acetaminophen, and other over-the-counter remedies may help ease aching muscles and other symptoms (*see* COLD AND FLU REMEDIES, p.910). If self-help measures are ineffective, you may be prescribed antiviral drugs (p.886) such as amantadine or oseltamivir, which are effective against influenza viruses provided that they are given within 24 hours of the onset of symptoms.

You should see your doctor immediately if you have difficulty breathing or if your fever lasts for longer than 2 days. He or she may arrange for you to have a chest X-ray (p.490) to rule out a chest infection such as pneumonia. If a bacterial infection is found, your doctor will prescribe antibiotics (p.885). However, these drugs have no effect on the influenza virus itself.

Babies, young children, elderly people, those with chronic heart or lung conditions, and people with reduced immunity are at increased risk of serious complications. A doctor should be consulted immediately when the symptoms of flu first appear in these groups.

What is the prognosis?

If there are no complications, most of the symptoms of influenza usually disappear after 6–7 days, although a cough may persist over 2 weeks. Fatigue and depression may last for even longer. However, for anyone who is in one of the high-risk groups, the complications of influenza may be life-threatening,

(SELF-HELP) Bringing down a fever

A fever is a body temperature that is above 38°C (100°F). If you or your child develops a fever, look at the symptom charts on p.102 and p.202 to check whether medical help is required. Anyone who has a fever should drink plenty of cool fluids and take over-the-counter analgesics (p.912), such as acetaminophen.

Babies who are over 3 months and young children should be given liquid acetaminophen. They may be cooled by a washcloth moistened with tepid water and sometimes by fanning. Young children are susceptible to febrile convulsions (p.849) if they have a high fever and therefore should be watched closely.

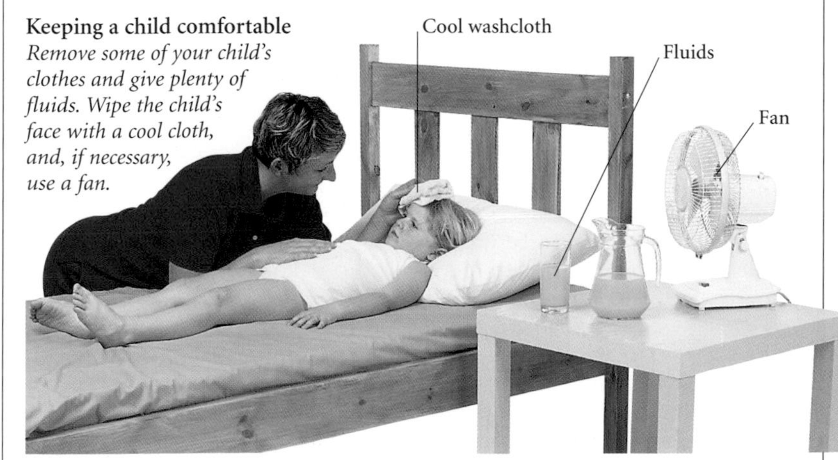
Cool washcloth
Fluids
Fan

Keeping a child comfortable *Remove some of your child's clothes and give plenty of fluids. Wipe the child's face with a cool cloth, and, if necessary, use a fan.*

and, in epidemics, deaths from associated pneumonia are very common.

Immunization is effective protection. It is especially recommended for people in high-risk groups (excluding babies) and people who are particularly likely to be exposed to the virus, such as health workers or carers for elderly people.

Immunization prevents infection in about two-thirds of people who are vaccinated annually. However, the vaccine can never be completely effective because the viruses frequently mutate, and different strains are responsible for outbreaks each year. The World Health Organization recommends what types of vaccines are issued each fall, depending on which strains are expected to be most prevalent in a particular region. However, if a virus mutates substantially, protection from the vaccine will be minimal, and epidemics may occur.

(WWW) ONLINE SITES: p.1033

Chickenpox

A childhood infection that causes a fever and widespread crops of blisters

AGE Mainly affects unimmunized children between the ages of 2 and 10

GENDER GENETICS LIFESTYLE Not significant factors

Chickenpox, sometimes called varicella, is a viral infection that used to be common among young children before routine immunization. The infection, with its characteristic rash of blisters, is caused by the varicella zoster virus, which also causes herpes zoster (right). The virus is transmitted in airborne droplets from the coughs and sneezes of infected people or by direct contact with the blisters. You can catch chickenpox from someone with chickenpox or herpes zoster if you are not immune.

The illness is usually mild in children, but symptoms are more severe in young babies, older adolescents, and adults. Chickenpox can also be more serious in people with reduced immunity, such as those with AIDS (*see* HIV INFECTION AND AIDS, p.295).

WHAT ARE THE SYMPTOMS?

The symptoms of chickenpox appear 1–3 weeks after infection. In children, the illness often starts with a mild fever or headache; in adults, there may be more pronounced flulike symptoms (*see* INFLUENZA, p.287). As infection with the virus progresses, the following symptoms usually become apparent:

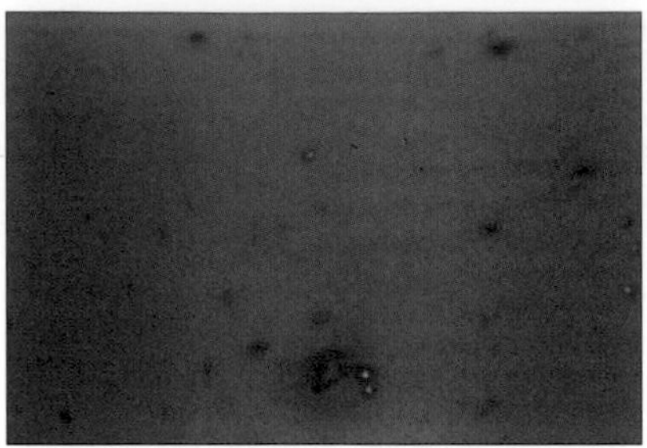

Chickenpox rash
Itchy, fluid-filled blisters are usually widespread all over the head and body in chickenpox. The blisters, seen here on the abdomen, form scabs within 24 hours.

- Rash in the form of crops of tiny red spots that rapidly turn into itchy, fluid-filled blisters. Within 24 hours the blisters dry out, forming scabs. Successive crops occur for 1–6 days. The rash may be widespread or consist of only a few spots, and it can occur anywhere on the head or body.
- Sometimes, discomfort during eating caused by spots in the mouth that have developed into ulcers.

A person is contagious from about 2 days before the rash first appears until it fully crusts over in about 10–14 days.

The most common complication of chickenpox is bacterial infection of the blisters due to scratching. Other complications include pneumonia (p.490), which is more common in adults, and rarely inflammation of the brain (*see* VIRAL ENCEPHALITIS, p.528). Newborn babies and people with reduced immunity are at higher risk of complications. Rarely, if a woman develops chickenpox in early pregnancy, the infection may result in fetal abnormalities.

WHAT MIGHT BE DONE?

Chickenpox can usually be diagnosed from the appearance of the rash. Children with mild infections do not need to see a doctor, and rest and simple measures to reduce fever (*see* BRINGING DOWN A FEVER, p.287) are all that are needed for a full recovery. Calamine lotion (*see* EMOLLIENTS AND BARRIER PREPARATIONS, p.890) may help relieve itching. To prevent skin infections, keep fingernails short and avoid scratching. People at risk of severe attacks, such as babies, older adolescents, adults, and people with reduced immunity, should see their doctor immediately. An antiviral drug (p.886) may be given to limit the effects of the infection, but it must be taken in the early stages of the illness in order to be effective.

Children who are otherwise healthy usually recover within 10–14 days from the onset of the rash, but they may have permanent scars where blisters have become infected with bacteria and then been scratched. Adolescents, adults, and people with reduced immunity take longer to recover from chickenpox.

CAN IT BE PREVENTED?

One attack of chickenpox gives lifelong immunity to the disease. However, the varicella zoster virus remains dormant within nerve cells and may reactivate years later, causing herpes zoster. Immunization against chickenpox is now routine for babies aged 12–18 months and is recommended for children aged 11–12 years who have neither had chickenpox nor been immunized (*see* ROUTINE IMMUNIZATIONS, p.45).

(WWW) ONLINE SITES: p.1033

Herpes zoster

An infection, also known as shingles, that causes a painful rash of blisters along the path of a nerve

AGE Most common between the ages of 50 and 70

GENDER GENETICS LIFESTYLE Not significant factors

Herpes zoster, often known as shingles, is characterized by a painful crop of blisters that erupts along the path of a nerve. The rash commonly occurs on only one side of the body and usually affects the skin on the chest, abdomen, or face. In older people, discomfort may continue for months after the rash has disappeared. This prolonged pain is called postherpetic neuralgia.

Herpes zoster infection is caused by the varicella zoster virus. This virus initially causes chickenpox (left) but then remains dormant in nerve cells. If the virus is reactivated later in life, it causes herpes zoster. The reason for reactivation is unknown, but herpes zoster often occurs at times of stress or ill health.

The disorder most commonly occurs in people aged 50–70 years. People with reduced immunity, such as those with AIDS (*see* HIV INFECTION AND AIDS, p.295) or those undergoing chemotherapy (p.278), are more susceptible to herpes zoster. People with AIDS are particularly likely to have severe outbreaks of herpes zoster.

The varicella zoster virus is easily spread by direct contact with a blister and will cause chickenpox in a person who is not immune to the disease.

WHAT ARE THE SYMPTOMS?

Initially, you may experience tingling, itching, and a sharp pain in an area of skin. After a few days, the following symptoms may also develop:

- Painful rash of fluid-filled blisters.
- Fever.
- Headache and fatigue.

Within 3–4 days, the blisters form scabs. The scabs heal in 10 days but may leave scars in some people. If a nerve that supplies the eye is affected, it may cause inflammation of the cornea (*see* CORNEAL ULCER, p.571). Rarely, infection of a facial nerve causes paralysis of the face (*see* FACIAL PALSY, p.548).

WHAT MIGHT BE DONE?

Herpes zoster can be difficult to diagnose until the rash appears, and severe pain around the ribs can be mistaken for the chest pain of angina (p.407). Your doctor may prescribe antiviral drugs (p.886) to reduce the severity of the symptoms and the risk of postherpetic neuralgia. Immediate treatment with antiviral drugs is important if your eyes are affected or if you have reduced immunity. Analgesics (p.912) may help relieve discomfort, and carbamazepine (*see* ANTICONVULSANT DRUGS, p.914) may help relieve the prolonged pain of postherpetic neuralgia. Most of the people who develop herpes zoster recover within 2–6 weeks, but up to half of the affected people over age 50 develop postherpetic neuralgia.

A single attack of herpes zoster does not provide immunity, and the infection may recur. Immunization against chickenpox in childhood (*see* ROUTINE IMMUNIZATIONS, p.45) stops the virus from establishing itself in the body and gives immunity against herpes zoster in addition to chickenpox.

(WWW) ONLINE SITES: p.1033

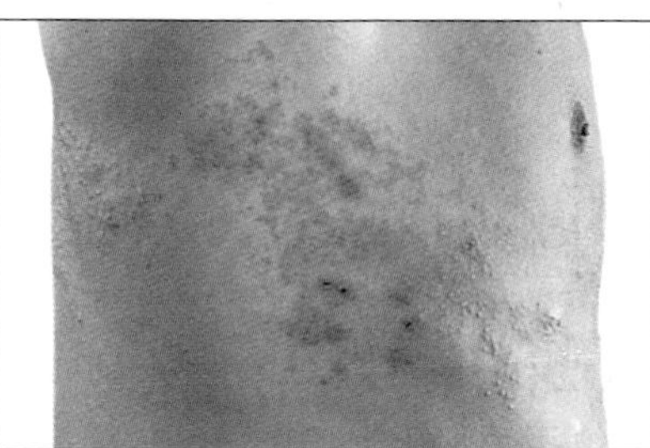

Herpes zoster rash

A rash of blisters develops along the path of a nerve in herpes zoster. The blisters often occur on the skin over the ribs on only one side of the body, as shown here.

Herpes simplex infections

Infections that can cause painful blisters on or around the lips or genitals

LIFESTYLE Unprotected sex with multiple partners is a risk factor for genital herpes

AGE GENDER GENETICS Not significant factors

The highly contagious herpes simplex viruses cause a number of different disorders characterized by small painful blisters on the skin and mucous membranes, most commonly on or around the lips (*see* COLD SORE, p.354) or genital area (*see* GENITAL HERPES, p.767). Herpes simplex virus (HSV) infection is transmitted by contact with a blister.

Infection with HSV does not give immunity against future attacks. The viruses remain dormant in the nerves and may be reactivated at times of stress or illness. Like many viral infections, outbreaks are more frequent and more severe in people with reduced immunity, such as those with AIDS (*see* HIV INFECTION AND AIDS, p.295).

WHAT ARE THE TYPES?

Up to eight types of HSV have been discovered, but only two are common. HSV1 usually causes infections of the lips, mouth, and face, and HSV2 typically causes infections of the genitals.

Most people have been infected with HSV1 by the time they are adults. In most cases, initial infection produces no symptoms. However, some children may develop blisters on the inside of the mouth (*see* STOMATITIS, p.632), and children with the skin disorder eczema may develop eczema herpeticum (*see* ECZEMA IN CHILDREN, p.829). After the initial infection, the virus becomes dormant but may reactivate periodically later in life, causing cold sores.

HSV2 is usually sexually transmitted and causes genital herpes. This condition, like cold sores, tends to recur. HSV2 can also be responsible for a life-threatening infection in a newborn baby who comes into contact with the mother's genital blisters during birth (*see* CONGENITAL INFECTIONS, p.817).

Both HSV1 and HSV2 can affect the eyes, causing herpes keratoconjunctivitis (*see* CONJUNCTIVITIS, p.570). Rarely, they cause severe inflammation of the brain (*see* VIRAL ENCEPHALITIS, p.528).

WHAT MIGHT BE DONE?

HSV infection can be diagnosed from the appearance and site of the blisters. Mild cold sores can usually be treated with over-the-counter topical antiviral drugs (p.886). However, if you have genital herpes or severe or repeated attacks of cold sores, you may be treated with oral antiviral drugs.

(WWW) ONLINE SITES: p.1033

Infectious mononucleosis

An infection causing swollen lymph nodes and a sore throat that is common in adolescence and early adulthood

AGE Most common between the ages of 12 and 20

GENDER GENETICS LIFESTYLE Not significant factors

Infectious mononucleosis is known as the "kissing disease" of adolescence and early adulthood because it is mainly transmitted in saliva. Another name is glandular fever because the symptoms include swollen lymph nodes (glands) and a high temperature. Initially, the illness may be mistaken for tonsillitis (*see* PHARYNGITIS AND TONSILLITIS, p.479), but it is more severe and lasts longer.

WHAT IS THE CAUSE?

Infectious mononucleosis is caused by the Epstein–Barr virus (EBV), which attacks lymphocytes, the white blood cells that are responsible for fighting infection. EBV infection is very common, and about 9 in 10 people have been infected by age 50. More than half of infected people do not develop symptoms and, consequently, are unaware that they have been infected.

What are the symptoms?

If symptoms of infectious mononucleosis develop, they usually do so 4–6 weeks after infection and appear over several days. Symptoms may include:

- High fever and sweating.
- Extremely sore throat, causing difficulty swallowing.
- Swollen tonsils, often covered with a thick, grayish white coating.
- Enlarged, tender lymph nodes in the neck, armpits, and groin.
- Tender abdomen as the result of an enlarged spleen.

These distinctive symptoms are often accompanied by poor appetite, weight loss, headache, and fatigue. In some people, the sore throat and fever clear up quickly, and the other symptoms last less than a month. Other people may be ill longer and may feel lethargic for months after the infection.

What might be done?

Your doctor will probably diagnose the infection from your enlarged lymph nodes, sore throat, and fever. A blood test may be carried out to look for antibodies against EBV in order to confirm the diagnosis. A throat swab may also be taken to exclude bacterial infection, which would need to be treated with antibiotics (p.885).

There is no specific treatment for infectious mononucleosis, but simple measures may help relieve symptoms.

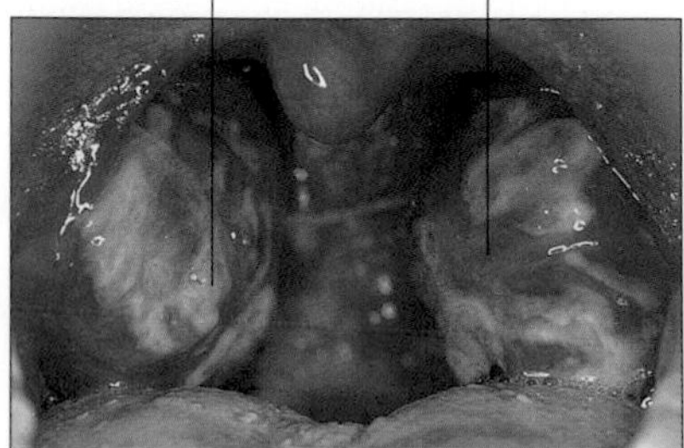
Thick coating
Swollen tonsil

Swollen tonsils
In infectious mononucleosis, the tonsils become swollen, causing a very sore throat. They may also become covered with a thick, grayish white coating.

Drinking plenty of cool fluids and taking over-the-counter analgesics (p.912), such as acetaminophen, may help control the high fever and pain. Contact sports should be avoided while the spleen is enlarged because of the risk of rupture, which causes severe internal bleeding and can be life-threatening.

What is the prognosis?

Almost everyone who has infectious mononucleosis makes a full recovery eventually. However, in some people, recovery may be slow, and fatigue may last for weeks or even months after the symptoms first appear. One attack of the disease, with or without symptoms, provides lifelong protection.

(WWW) ONLINE SITES: p.1033

Cytomegalovirus infection

An infection that usually produces no symptoms but can cause fatal illness in people with reduced immunity

 Gender More common in males

 Age Genetics Lifestyle Not significant factors

Infection with cytomegalovirus (CMV) is very common and affects most adults at some time in their lives. However, most people do not develop symptoms and never know that they have been infected with the virus, although they will carry CMV for life in an inactive form. CMV is a type of herpesvirus.

People with reduced immunity, such as those who have AIDS (*see* HIV infection and AIDS, p.295), are at risk of serious illness from a first infection, and CMV can also be reactivated in this group. In addition, the virus can seriously affect a fetus if a woman becomes infected during pregnancy (*see* Congenital infections, p.817).

The virus can be passed in saliva, in minute droplets from the coughs or sneezes of infected people; during sexual intercourse; through a blood transfusion; during an organ transplant; and across the placenta to a fetus if the mother becomes infected during pregnancy. In developed countries, blood that is used for transfusion to high-risk groups is screened for CMV.

What are the symptoms?

CMV infection can produce widely differing symptoms, depending on the age and general health of the person affected. Most people have no symptoms from a first infection with the virus. If symptoms are present, they are often vague and may include:

- Fatigue.
- Fever.
- Enlarged lymph nodes.

In teenagers and young adults, symptoms may resemble those of infectious mononucleosis (p.289).

The symptoms of CMV infection are more severe in people with reduced immunity. In such cases, first infection or reactivation of the virus can result in a fever lasting for 2–3 weeks, a nonitchy rash, and inflammation of the liver (*see* Acute hepatitis, p.644), which causes yellowing of the skin and whites of the eyes (*see* Jaundice, p.643). In addition, the virus can cause inflammation of the brain (*see* Viral encephalitis, p.528) and the lungs (*see* Pneumonia, p.490). In people with reduced immunity, CMV can also cause retinitis, inflammation of the light-sensitive cells at the back of the eye, which may result in blindness.

If a woman is infected with the virus during the first 24 weeks of pregnancy, there is a 1 in 7 risk that the baby will develop abnormalities, such as deafness. The baby may also be seriously ill at birth with jaundice, liver enlargement, and certain blood disorders.

What might be done?

In a person who is otherwise healthy, CMV infection usually goes unnoticed, causes no problems, and is not treated. If your symptoms are severe and your doctor suspects CMV infection, he or she may arrange for a blood test to look for antibodies against the virus. The symptoms are often relieved by early treatment with antiviral drugs (p.886).

For people with reduced immunity, complications from infection with CMV can be life-threatening. These people may be given antiviral drugs to protect against infection or, if a blood test shows that the virus is already present, to prevent symptoms from developing. Drugs may also be given to a pregnant woman who has the infection, in order to protect the fetus.

(WWW) ONLINE SITES: p.1033

Measles

A childhood illness that causes fever and a widespread nonitchy rash

AGE Mainly affects unimmunized children between the ages of 1 and 5

GENDER GENETICS LIFESTYLE Not significant factors

Measles is a highly contagious viral illness that causes a distinctive rash and fever and mainly affects young children. Rare in the developed world because of routine immunization, the disease kills up to 1 million unimmunized children in the developing world each year.

The measles virus is easily transmitted in minute airborne droplets from the coughs and sneezes of infected people. A child who has measles may feel very sick, and there is a small risk of complications, especially if the child has reduced immunity or is severely malnourished. Measles is contagious for 1–2 days before the rash appears and for about 5 days afterward.

What are the symptoms?

Symptoms of measles usually develop 10 days after infection and may include:

- Fever.
- Tiny white spots with a red base, known as Koplik spots, on the insides of the cheeks.
- After 3–4 days, a red, nonitchy rash that starts on the head and spreads downward. At first, the rash consists of separate flat spots. The spots then merge to give a blotchy appearance.
- Painful, red, watery eyes (*see* CONJUNCTIVITIS, p.570).
- Stuffy or runny nose.
- Hacking cough.

The most common complications of measles are bacterial infections of the middle ear (*see* ACUTE OTITIS MEDIA IN CHILDREN, p.860) and the lungs (*see* PNEUMONIA, p.490). In about 1 in 1,000 cases, the brain is affected (*see* VIRAL ENCEPHALITIS, p.528), a serious complication that starts 7–10 days after the appearance of the rash.

What might be done?

Your doctor will probably be able to diagnose measles from the combination of symptoms. In most children, rest and simple measures to reduce a fever (*see* BRINGING DOWN A FEVER, p.287) are all that are needed for a full recovery. If there are no complications, symptoms usually disappear in 7 days. Antibiotics (p.885) may be prescribed if a bacterial infection develops.

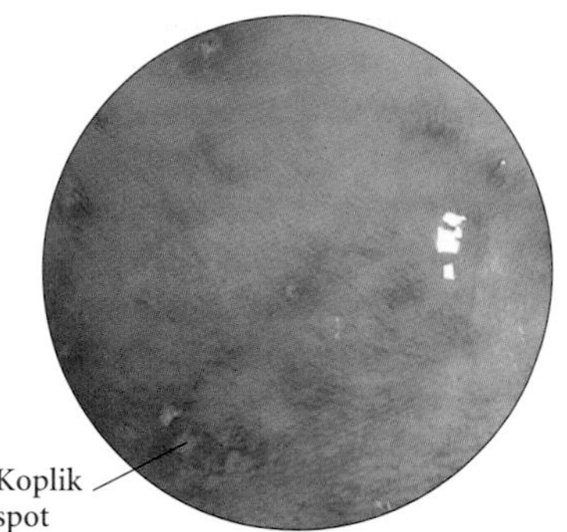
Koplik spot

Koplik spots in measles

These tiny white spots may develop on the insides of the cheeks when the symptoms of measles first begin, a few days before the onset of the rash on the head and body.

Can it be prevented?

Babies are immunized against measles with the measles, mumps, and rubella vaccine, given at age 12–15 months and again at 4–6 years (*see* ROUTINE IMMUNIZATIONS, p.45). Immunization or an attack of measles provides lifelong immunity to the disease.

(WWW) ONLINE SITES: p.1033

Mumps

An illness causing swelling of the salivary glands on one or both sides of the jaw

AGE Mainly affects unimmunized schoolchildren and young adults

GENDER GENETICS LIFESTYLE Not significant factors

Mumps is a mild viral infection that was common among schoolchildren until routine immunization was introduced. The mumps virus is spread in saliva and in minute airborne droplets from the coughs and sneezes of infected people. The virus causes swelling and inflammation of one or both of the parotid salivary glands, which are situated below and just in front of the ears. If both glands are affected, the child's face may have a hamsterlike appearance. In adolescent boys and men, the mumps virus may affect one or both testes; rarely, this effect may result in problems with fertility.

What are the symptoms?

Up to half of all people with mumps develop no symptoms, and in most other people the symptoms are mild. The main symptoms appear 2–3 weeks after infection and may include:

- Pain and swelling on one or both sides of the face, below and just in front of the ear, lasting about 3 days.
- Pain when swallowing.

You may also have a sore throat and fever, and the salivary glands under your chin may become painful. A person who is infected with the mumps virus is contagious for up to 7 days before symptoms first appear and for about 10 days afterward.

About 1 in 4 adolescent boys or adult men with mumps also develops painful inflammation of one or both testes (*see* EPIDIDYMO-ORCHITIS, p.718). Rarely, the inflammation may result in infertility. A few people who develop mumps also develop viral meningitis (p.527), in which the membranes that surround the brain and spinal cord become inflamed. Inflammation of the pancreas (*see* ACUTE PANCREATITIS, p.652) is a rare complication of mumps.

What might be done?

Your doctor will probably diagnose the disorder from the distinctive swelling of the parotid glands. There is no specific treatment, but drinking plenty of cool fluids and taking over-the-counter analgesics (p.912), such as acetaminophen, may help relieve discomfort. Most people recover without further treatment, although adolescent boys and men with severe inflammation of the testes may be prescribed a stronger analgesic. If complications develop, other treatments may be recommended.

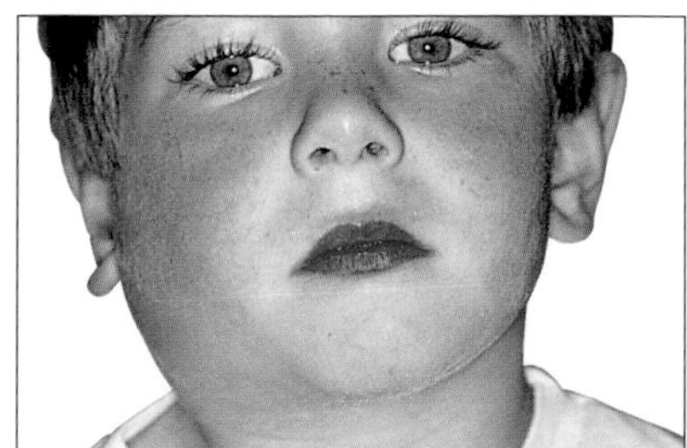

Inflamed parotid gland

The parotid glands are situated below and just in front of each ear. In the viral infection mumps, one (as shown above) or both parotid glands may become swollen.

CAN IT BE PREVENTED?

Babies are routinely immunized against mumps as part of the measles, mumps, and rubella immunization given at age 12–15 months and again at 4–6 years (*see* ROUTINE IMMUNIZATIONS, p.45). Immunization or an attack of mumps give lifelong immunity against the virus.

(WWW) ONLINE SITES: p.1033

Rubella

An illness, also known as German measles, that is usually mild but can severely damage a developing fetus

AGE GENDER GENETICS LIFESTYLE
Not significant factors

Rubella, also called German measles, usually causes little more than a mild rash. However, it can cause serious birth defects in a fetus if the mother contracts the illness during early pregnancy and unimmunized pregnant women should avoid contact with infected people. The disease is caused by the highly contagious rubella virus, which is easily transmitted in airborne droplets from the coughs and sneezes of infected people. Rubella has become less common in the developed world because of routine immunization in early childhood.

WHAT ARE THE SYMPTOMS?

The symptoms of rubella appear from 2–3 weeks after infection and may include all or some of the following:

- Swollen lymph nodes at the back of the neck and behind the ears. In some cases, lymph nodes throughout the body are swollen, including those in the armpits and groin.
- After 2–3 days, a pink, nonitchy rash, first on the face and then the body, that usually disappears within 3 days.

Children may have mild fever, but adolescents and adults can develop high fever and headache. Rarely, several joints may become inflamed for a short time (*see* REACTIVE ARTHRITIS, p.379). A person who has rubella is highly infectious from up to 10 days before the pink rash appears to about 10 days afterward.

ARE THERE COMPLICATIONS?

If you contract rubella in early pregnancy, your baby is at serious risk of being born with abnormalities, such as congenital deafness (p.859), congenital heart disease (p.836), clouding of the lens in the eye (*see* CATARACT, p.573), and the nervous system disorder cerebral palsy (p.846). The greatest risk is during the first 4 months of pregnancy, and the earlier rubella occurs, the more likely the baby will be seriously affected.

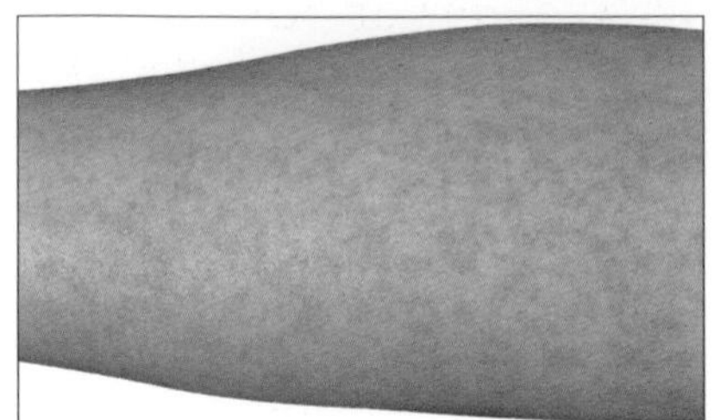

Rubella rash

The light pink rash of rubella is shown here on an arm. The rash usually first develops on the face and gradually spreads to the trunk and then to the limbs.

WHAT MIGHT BE DONE?

Your doctor may suspect rubella from the symptoms, but the rash is not distinctive and other viral infections can produce similar symptoms. He or she may arrange for a blood test to confirm the diagnosis. There is no specific treatment, but drinking plenty of cool fluids and taking over-the-counter analgesics (p.912), such as acetaminophen, may help reduce fever and ease discomfort. Most affected people recover in about 10 days, and one attack gives lifelong immunity against the virus.

If you are pregnant and have rubella or have been in contact with someone with the disease, you may wish to discuss with your doctor the risk to the fetus and how best to proceed.

CAN IT BE PREVENTED?

Babies are routinely immunized against rubella as part of the standard measles, mumps, and rubella immunization that is given at 12–15 months and again at 4–6 years (*see* ROUTINE IMMUNIZATIONS, p.45). Immunization or an attack of the disease provides lifelong immunity against the rubella virus.

Ideally, all unimmunized women who are planning a pregnancy should be tested for antibodies against rubella and should receive advice about immunization (*see* HEALTH IN PREGNANCY AND AFTER CHILDBIRTH, p.33).

(WWW) ONLINE SITES: p.1033

Parvovirus infection

An infection that causes a rash and inflammation of the joints

AGE GENDER GENETICS LIFESTYLE
Not significant factors

In children, parvovirus infection, also called fifth disease, is a mild illness with a fever that often goes unnoticed. However, adults who have the virus may have severe pain in the joints. Parvovirus is transmitted in airborne droplets from the coughs and sneezes of infected people, and infection occurs most frequently in spring. It is occasionally transmitted by a blood transfusion. Infection causes a brief halt in the production of red blood cells by the bone marrow, and, for this reason, may have serious consequences in people with anemia (p.446).

WHAT ARE THE SYMPTOMS?

Many children do not develop symptoms; in others, these symptoms may appear within 7–14 days of infection:

- Bright red rash on the cheeks that may spread to the trunk and limbs.
- Mild fever.
- In rare cases, mild inflammation of the joints (*see* ARTHRITIS, p.374).

Adults tend to develop more severe symptoms that may include:

- Rash on the palms and soles.
- Severe inflammation and pain in the joints of the knees, wrists, and hands.

Some women develop a serious form of arthritis that can last for up to 2 years.

In people with reduced immunity, such as those taking immunosuppressant drugs (p.906) or those with AIDS (*see* HIV INFECTION AND AIDS, p.295), the infection may become chronic and cause anemia. In people who already have anemia, parvovirus infection may exacerbate the condition. If a pregnant woman becomes infected during the first 6 months of pregnancy, there is a risk of miscarriage (p.791).

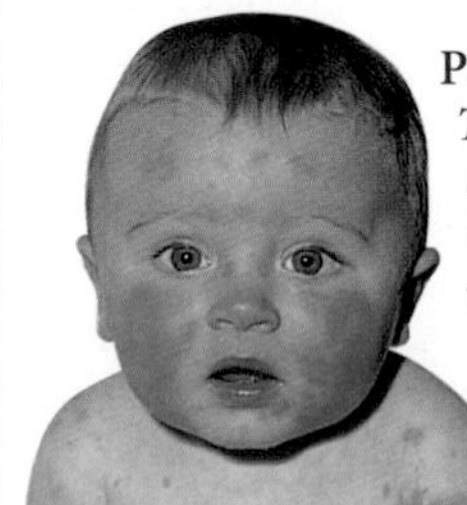

Parvovirus rash

The bright red rash on this baby's face is due to infection with parvovirus. The condition is also known as slapped cheek disease.

WHAT MIGHT BE DONE?

Your doctor may be able to diagnose parvovirus infection from your symptoms. If the diagnosis is not clear, he or she may arrange for a blood test to detect antibodies against the virus. If you have painful joints, your doctor may arrange for further blood tests and for X-rays (p.244) of the joints to exclude other causes of arthritis. In most people, the infection clears up within 2 weeks without treatment. However, people at risk of severe anemia may need hospital treatment. One attack of parvovirus infection provides lifelong immunity.

(WWW) ONLINE SITES: p.1033

Poliomyelitis

A rare infection, commonly known as polio, that can affect the nervous system

AGE Mainly affects unimmunized children but can affect unimmunized adults

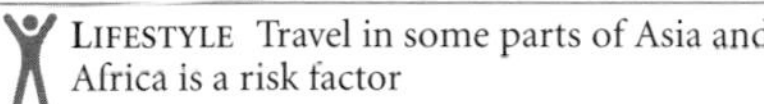
LIFESTYLE Travel in some parts of Asia and Africa is a risk factor

GENDER GENETICS Not significant factors

Poliomyelitis is a highly infectious disease that varies in severity from a mild condition with few or no symptoms to a severe disorder affecting the nervous system. In a few instances, the disease can lead to paralysis. Poliomyelitis is caused by infection with the polio virus, which is transmitted by contact with the feces of an infected person, through contaminated food and drinking water, or in contaminated swimming pools.

Since routine immunization began in the 1950s, polio has become rare in developed countries. However, in some parts of Africa and Asia, the disease remains a serious risk for travelers who do not have up-to-date immunization.

WHAT ARE THE SYMPTOMS?

For most infected people, polio produces no symptoms or results in a mild illness with a slight fever and sore throat that develops 3–21 days after infection. In about 1 in 500 infected people, the brain and spinal cord become inflamed, and symptoms include a high fever, severe headache, backache, and a stiff neck. In a few cases, one or more limbs may be paralyzed, and in addition the muscles of the respiratory system may be affected, causing breathing problems.

WHAT MIGHT BE DONE?

In most cases, polio is undiagnosed and untreated. If it is suspected from the symptoms, the diagnosis can be confirmed by tests to look for the presence of the virus in feces. There is no specific treatment, but mild symptoms can be relieved with analgesics (p.912) and bed rest. People who have severe symptoms are admitted to the hospital, and mechanical ventilation may be given if the respiratory muscles are paralyzed.

Most people make a full recovery. Of those who become paralyzed, many improve within 6 months. Physiotherapy (p.961) can help people recover the use of weakened limbs, but in some people affected muscles may become permanently weakened and affected limbs may become wasted. In other people, muscle pain and weakness may recur many years after the illness. This recurrence is known as postpolio syndrome.

CAN IT BE PREVENTED?

Polio vaccine provides complete protection against the disease. The vaccine, which used to be made with live virus, is now being made with killed virus to eliminate the small risk of spreading polio to unimmunized people. Immunization against the disease is routine in childhood (*see* ROUTINE IMMUNIZATIONS, p.45). Before traveling to a part of the world where infection with polio is still a risk, adults should have a booster (*see* TRAVEL IMMUNIZATIONS, p.86).

(WWW) ONLINE SITES: p.1033, p.1037

Viral hemorrhagic fevers

A group of infections that cause abnormal bleeding and may be fatal

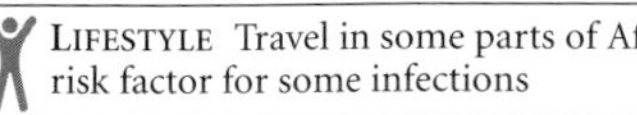
LIFESTYLE Travel in some parts of Africa is a risk factor for some infections

AGE GENDER GENETICS Not significant factors

Viral hemorrhagic fevers, which cause severe abnormal bleeding, occur predominantly in Africa and rarely reach the developed world. Hantavirus infection is the only one of these fevers that is native to some parts of the US and Europe. The other fevers, which include Marburg fever, Ebola fever, and Lassa fever, occur only in localized outbreaks in Africa. African hemorrhagic fevers have made international news headlines in recent years because there is a slight risk that travelers may be infected with these potentially fatal diseases and spread them to the developed world.

Hantavirus and Lassa fever virus are carried by rodents, such as rats, and are spread to people through contact with the animals' urine, feces, or saliva. Marburg fever virus is carried by monkeys, and the animal carrier of Ebola fever virus is unknown. All of these viruses can be transmitted in body secretions and are highly contagious.

WHAT ARE THE SYMPTOMS?

The symptoms of viral hemorrhagic fevers develop slowly from 1 to 3 weeks after infection and may include:

- Flulike symptoms, including headache, fever, sore throat, and fatigue.
- Rash, which causes peeling skin in Ebola fever.
- Abnormal bleeding from the skin and mucous membranes.

Hantavirus infection symptoms vary from mild to severe. Lassa fever may produce no symptoms at all. Ebola and Marburg fevers produce severe symptoms. The complications of Ebola and Marburg fevers include acute kidney failure (p.706), serious breathing difficulties, and shock (p.414).

WHAT MIGHT BE DONE?

Viral hemorrhagic fevers are diagnosed from the symptoms and a blood test to look for antibodies against the virus. There is no specific treatment for Hantavirus infection, Marburg fever, or Ebola fever. However, Lassa fever may respond to antiviral drugs (p.886) such as ribavirin, if the drugs are given in the first week. Most people with these infections are admitted to the hospital for treatment and to limit the spread of the virus. Dialysis (p.707) may be necessary if kidney function is impaired, and mechanical ventilation is required for serious breathing difficulties.

The prognosis depends on the type of virus and the medical care available. Lassa fever is fatal in up to 1 in 50 cases; Hantavirus infection has a death rate of up to 1 in 10; Marburg fever is fatal in about 1 in 4; and Ebola fever has a death rate of up to 9 in 10 cases.

(WWW) ONLINE SITES: p.1033, p.1037

Yellow fever

An infection, mainly confined to Africa, that is transmitted by mosquitoes

LIFESTYLE Travel to Africa and South and Central America is a risk factor

AGE GENDER GENETICS Not significant factors

The tropical viral infection yellow fever was given its name because it can cause severe jaundice (p.643), in which the skin turns bright yellow. The virus is transmitted by mosquitoes from monkeys to humans and then by mosquitoes from person to person. More than 9 in 10 cases occur in Africa; the remainder occur mainly in South and Central America. The disease has become less common with routine immunization, but epidemics still occur in Africa.

The symptoms of yellow fever appear suddenly, 3–6 days after a bite from an infected mosquito. In some cases, there may be a mild flulike illness. However, in others there may be abnormal bleeding, liver failure (p.650), or kidney failure (p.705). Severe bleeding may lead to shock (p.414). Rarely, the infection may lead to convulsions and coma (p.522).

Diagnosis is based on the symptoms and confirmed by a blood test to look for antibodies against the virus. There is no specific treatment for yellow fever, and the disease is fatal in 2–5 out of 10 people. An attack provides lifelong immunity. Immunization gives protection for 10 years and is recommended for people traveling to high-risk areas (*see* TRAVEL IMMUNIZATIONS, p.86).

(WWW) ONLINE SITES: p.1033, p.1037

Dengue fever

An infection, also known as breakbone fever, that is spread by mosquitoes

LIFESTYLE Travel to tropical countries is a risk factor

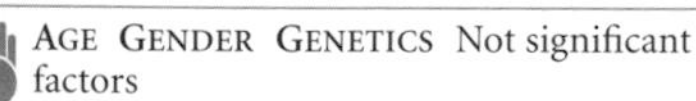
AGE GENDER GENETICS Not significant factors

Dengue fever occurs in many tropical areas of the world, and an estimated 40–80 million people, including many travelers, become infected each year. The dengue fever virus is carried and transmitted by the mosquito *Aedes aegypti*, which inhabits suburban and rural areas and usually bites during the daytime. The disease causes severe pain in the muscles and joints, and for this reason it is also known as "breakbone fever."

The symptoms of dengue fever appear 4–8 days after a bite from an infected mosquito. They include a high temperature, headache, severe backache, muscle pain and weakness, and joint pain. Small red spots may also develop on the skin during the first few days of the illness. The fever often subsides for 3–4 days but then recurs before subsiding again. In severe cases, abnormal bleeding may occur from areas such as the gums and nose, and from injection sites.

WHAT MIGHT BE DONE?

Dengue fever can usually be diagnosed from the symptoms. There is no specific treatment, but it is important to rest and drink plenty of cool fluids. Over-the-counter analgesics (p.912), such as acetaminophen, may relieve symptoms and reduce fever. Severely affected people may need observation and treatment in the hospital, but life-threatening complications are uncommon. Recovery usually takes several weeks.

An attack of dengue fever gives immunity for only about a year, and there is no vaccine against the virus. Travelers to areas where it is common should use mosquito repellents and wear clothing that completely covers the arms and legs (*see* TRAVEL HEALTH, p.85).

(WWW) ONLINE SITES: p.1033, p.1037

Rabies

A serious infection of the nervous system, usually transmitted in saliva from a bite by an infected animal

LIFESTYLE Travel to Africa, Asia, and South and Central America is a risk factor

AGE GENDER GENETICS Not significant factors

The rabies virus mainly affects animals but can be passed to humans by an animal bite or a lick over a break in the skin. After entering the wound, the virus can travel along nerves to the brain and cause potentially fatal inflammation. Immunization against the virus and prompt medical treatment give complete protection against the disease, but, if left untreated, about half of all people bitten by a rabid animal develop rabies and almost inevitably die.

Rabies is very rare in developed countries, although only a few, including the UK, Japan, and Australia, are completely free from the disease. Africa and many parts of Asia are high-risk areas. In the US, most cases are due to bites from bats, and worldwide most cases result from bites by dogs that have been infected by wild animals. Some animals infected with the rabies virus act aggressively and salivate excessively.

WHAT ARE THE SYMPTOMS?

An infected person may develop symptoms within 10 days to 2 months of a bite, although rarely the virus can lie dormant for several years. Rabies usually starts with flulike symptoms (*see* INFLUENZA, p.287) that last for about 2–7 days, followed by:

- Paralysis of face and throat muscles.
- Extreme thirst.
- Painful throat spasms leading to an inability to drink and a fear of water.
- Disorientation and agitation.
- Loss of consciousness.
- Paralysis of limbs.

Once symptoms have developed, the condition is usually fatal.

WHAT MIGHT BE DONE?

Wash all suspect animal bites immediately with soap and water. Seek medical advice without delay because treatment must be started at once to be effective. Treatment consists of injections of antibodies against the rabies virus around the wound site, followed by a rabies vaccination to stimulate production of more antibodies. If possible, the animal that inflicted the bite should be captured and observed for 10 days. If the animal is symptom-free, treatment can stop; if it is rabid, treatment is continued and the animal is destroyed. Alternatively, it may be destroyed immediately and then examined for evidence of the virus.

There is no cure once the symptoms have developed. Diagnosis may not be obvious from the symptoms, and blood and saliva tests are usually done to confirm the presence of the virus.

Rabies can be prevented by a vaccine, which is recommended for people working with animals in high-risk areas (*see* TRAVEL IMMUNIZATIONS, p.86). All travelers in these areas should avoid contact with stray animals.

(WWW) ONLINE SITES: p.1033, p.1037

HIV infection and AIDS

A chronic infection that, left untreated, results in reduced immunity to other infections

 LIFESTYLE Intravenous drug use and unprotected sex with multiple partners are risk factors

 AGE GENDER GENETICS Not significant factors

Infection with the human immunodeficiency virus (HIV), which in many cases leads to acquired immunodeficiency syndrome (AIDS), has been the most written about, most researched, and most feared infection of the past two decades. Despite the development of highly effective drugs to limit the disease, there is still no vaccine against the virus, and the number of people with HIV infection continues to rise, especially in developing countries.

HIV is believed to have originated in Africa, where a similar virus is carried by some species of primates. The virus is thought to have spread from monkeys to humans through saliva in bites, then around the world from person to person in body fluids. The first recognized cases of AIDS in the US occurred in 1981, when there was an outbreak of unusual cases of pneumonia and skin cancer in young homosexual men in Los Angeles. Two years later, the virus was isolated and identified as HIV.

HIV infects and gradually destroys cells in the immune system, weakening the response to infections and cancers. People infected with HIV may have no symptoms for many years, or they may experience frequent or prolonged mild infections. When the immune system becomes severely weakened, an infected person is said to have AIDS. A person with AIDS develops serious infections caused by organisms that are normally harmless to healthy people and is also susceptible to certain cancers.

WHO IS AFFECTED?

By the end of 2002, there were up to 56,000 people in Canada who had HIV infection, with 4000 new cases a year. Worldwide, over 42 million people were thought to be infected, 9 in 10 of whom were unaware that they had the condition. As a result of developments in drug treatment, deaths due to AIDS have fallen dramatically in the developed world since 1995. However, in the US, AIDS is still the leading cause of death among African–Americans and Hispanics between the ages of 25 and 44, who have less access to these advanced drug therapies. The problem of AIDS is much greater in developing countries, where most people with HIV infection live and where the new drugs are unavailable or unaffordable.

HOW IS HIV TRANSMITTED?

HIV is carried in body fluids, including blood, semen, vaginal secretions, saliva, and breast milk. It is most commonly transmitted sexually, by vaginal, anal, or oral intercourse. You are more susceptible to HIV infection and more likely to transmit the virus if you have another sexually transmitted disease.

You are also at increased risk of HIV infection if you use intravenous drugs and share or reuse needles contaminated with the virus. Medical workers are also at risk from contaminated needles or from contact with infected body fluids, but the risk is low.

HIV infection can be passed from an infected woman to the fetus or to the baby at birth (*see* CONGENITAL INFECTIONS, p.817) or by breast-feeding. The virus can also be transmitted through organ transplants or blood transfusions. However, in developed countries screening of blood, organs, and tissues for HIV is now routine, making the risk of infection extremely low.

HIV infection cannot be transmitted by everyday human contact, such as shaking hands, or by coughs or sneezes, and there is no risk to your health from working or living with someone who is infected with the virus.

Cell surface

New HIV viruses

Human immunodeficiency virus
This highly magnified view of a white blood cell known as a CD4 lymphocyte shows tiny newly formed HIV viruses budding out of the cell's uneven surface.

WHAT IS THE CAUSE?

HIV enters the bloodstream and infects cells with a special structure known as the CD4 receptor on their surfaces. The cells include a type of white blood cell known as a CD4 lymphocyte, which is responsible for fighting infection. The virus reproduces rapidly within the cells and destroys them in the process.

At first, the immune system is able to function normally despite the infection, and symptoms may not develop for years. However, especially if the infection is untreated, the number of CD4 lymphocytes eventually begins to fall, causing increased susceptibility to other infections and some types of cancers.

WHAT ARE THE SYMPTOMS?

The first symptoms of HIV infection usually appear within 6 weeks of infection. Some people experience a flulike illness that may include some or all of the following symptoms:

- Swollen lymph nodes.
- Fever.
- Fatigue.
- Rash.
- Aching muscles.
- Sore throat.

These symptoms usually clear up after a few weeks, and many people with HIV infection feel completely healthy. However, in some people, any of the following minor disorders may develop:

- Persistent, swollen lymph nodes.
- Mouth infections such as thrush (*see* CANDIDIASIS, p.309).
- Gum disease (*see* GINGIVITIS, p.617).
- Severe, persistent herpes simplex infections (p.289), such as cold sores (p.354).
- Extensive genital warts (p.768).
- Itchy, flaky skin (*see* SEBORRHEIC DERMATITIS, p.335).
- Weight loss.

The time between infection with HIV and the onset of AIDS varies from person to person, but it can be anywhere between 1 and 14 years. Often people are totally unaware for years that they are infected with HIV until they develop one or more serious infections or cancers known as AIDS-defining illnesses.

ARE THERE COMPLICATIONS?

The single complication of HIV infection is the development of AIDS. A person infected with HIV is said to have developed AIDS if the CD4 lymphocyte count falls below a certain level or if he or she develops a particular AIDS-defining illness. These illnesses include opportunistic infections (infections that occur only in people who have reduced immunity), certain cancers, and problems with the nervous system that may result in dementia (p.535), confusion, behavior changes, and memory loss.

OPPORTUNISTIC INFECTIONS These infections may be caused by protozoa, fungi, viruses, or bacteria, and they can often be life-threatening.

One of the most common illnesses in people with AIDS is a severe infection of the lungs by the parasite *Pneumocystis carinii* (*see* PNEUMOCYSTIS INFECTION, p.308). Other common diseases are the protozoal infections cryptosporidiosis (p.307), which results in prolonged diarrhea, and toxoplasmosis (p.307), which can affect the brain.

Candida albicans is a fungus that causes mild superficial infections in healthy people but may produce much more serious infections in people who have AIDS (*see* CANDIDIASIS, p.309). The cryptococcus fungus (*see* UNCOMMON FUNGAL INFECTIONS, p.308) may cause fever, headaches, and lung infections.

People with AIDS suffer from severe bacterial and viral infections. Bacterial infections include tuberculosis (p.491) and listeriosis (p.300), which may lead to blood poisoning (*see* SEPTICEMIA, p.298). Viral infections include those caused by the herpesviruses. Herpes simplex infections can affect the brain, causing meningitis and viral encephalitis (p.528). Cytomegalovirus infection (p.290) may cause a number of severe conditions, including pneumonia, viral encephalitis, and a type of eye inflammation that can result in blindness. However, people who have AIDS are not more susceptible to common infections such as colds.

CANCERS The most common type of cancer that affects people with AIDS is Kaposi's sarcoma (p.346), a skin cancer that can also affect the inside of the mouth and internal organs, especially the lungs. Other types of cancer that commonly develop in people with AIDS include lymphomas (p.459), such as non-Hodgkin's lymphoma. Cancer of the cervix (p.750) is an AIDS-defining illness in women infected with HIV.

HOW IS IT DIAGNOSED?

If you suspect that you may have been exposed to HIV infection, you should have a blood test to check for antibodies against the virus. The blood test may also be performed if you have symptoms that suggest HIV infection, and it is often offered as part of prenatal care. Consent is always obtained before the test, and counseling is given both before and afterward to discuss the implications of a positive result.

If your HIV test result is negative, you may be advised to have another test in 3 months because antibodies can take time to develop. HIV infection can also be difficult to diagnose in the baby of an infected woman because the mother's antibodies may remain in the baby's blood for up to 18 months.

AIDS is diagnosed when an AIDS-defining illness, such as pneumocystis infection, develops or when a blood test shows that the CD4 lymphocyte count has dropped below a certain level.

WHAT IS THE TREATMENT?

If your HIV test result is positive, you will probably be referred to a special center where you will receive monitoring, treatment, and advice from a team of health-care professionals.

Drug treatment may be started when you are diagnosed with HIV infection or when CD4 lymphocyte levels start to fall. Advances in the use of combinations of specific antiviral drugs that prevent HIV from replicating have made it possible to prevent progression of HIV infection to AIDS and to suppress the viral infection to undetectable levels in some people (*see* DRUGS FOR HIV INFECTION AND AIDS, p.887).

Once AIDS has developed, opportunistic infections are dealt with as they occur, and, in some cases, there may also be long-term preventive treatment against the most common infections. Emotional support and practical advice can be obtained from the many groups and charitable organizations that help people with HIV infection and AIDS.

WHAT IS THE PROGNOSIS?

There is no cure for HIV infection, but the drug treatments available in the developed world have made it possible to regard the condition as a chronic illness rather than a rapidly fatal one. In the 2 years following the introduction of antiviral drug combination therapies in 1995, deaths from AIDS fell by 47 percent in the US. However, for most of the people with HIV who live in the developing world, the prognosis is bleak. Few have access to up-to-date treatment, and, left untreated, half of all people infected with the virus develop AIDS within 10 years and die.

CAN IT BE PREVENTED?

HIV infection can be prevented by teaching everyone about the risks of infection from an early age. The two main precautions that everyone can take to avoid sexual transmission are to use a condom during sexual intercourse and to avoid sex with multiple partners (*see* SEX AND HEALTH, p.67). It is also recommended that both partners have an HIV test before having unprotected sex in a new relationship. Specific groups also need to take special precautions. For example, if you inject drugs intravenously, you must use a clean needle every time.

People who are HIV positive need to take special care to prevent others from coming into contact with their blood or body fluids and should always inform dental or medical staff that they have HIV infection. If you are HIV positive and pregnant, antiviral drugs may be given to reduce the risk of transmission to the fetus. You may also be advised to have a cesarean section (p.802) and avoid breast-feeding to reduce the risk of transmitting the virus to your baby.

Medical professionals take many steps to prevent transmission of HIV, including screening all blood products and tissues for transplant and using disposable or carefully sterilized equipment.

Extensive research is being carried out either to develop a vaccine against HIV or to prevent the development of AIDS. However, although researchers are optimistic they will succeed, there will inevitably be millions more deaths worldwide before an affordable cure is found and made available to everyone.

(WWW) ONLINE SITES: p.1032, p.1033

Smallpox

A highly contagious viral infection characterized by a rash, now eradicated through immunization

AGE GENDER GENETICS LIFESTYLE Not significant factors

Smallpox is caused by the variola virus. Once spread, by the coughs of infected people, it always causes infection.

The disease was a major cause of death worldwide until its eradication by vaccination in 1977.

Several repositories of the virus remain in controlled laboratories such as the CDC. There is concern that unauthorized stores of virus might be used for bioterrorism activities.

WHAT ARE THE SYMPTOMS?

There are two forms of the disease: variola major and variola minor. The major form causes significant illness, and the minor form only rarely does so. A 12-day incubation period is followed by flulike symptoms such as fever, headache, back pain, fatigue, vomiting, and occasionally diarrhea, followed 2 days later by a rash.

In most cases, the rash is of multiple pus-filled blisters. It starts on the tongue, palate, and face and spreads to the trunk and extremities; the more prominent the rash, the higher the mortality. (The smallpox rash is similar to that of chickenpox; however, the chickenpox rash appears in crops and affects central areas, especially the trunk, more than the face and extremities.)

WHAT MIGHT BE DONE?

The diagnosis is usually based upon the appearance of the rash, and confirmed by blood tests and culture. Treatment is of the symptoms, but vaccination during the first week of incubation may reduce the severity in some cases.

Vaccination of those who might come in contact with infected individuals is the most effective way to limit the spread of the disease. Routine vaccination for smallpox in Canada was discontinued in 1972, and it is unclear if people who were immunized are still protected. With the current concerns about bioterrorism, large-scale immunization is being reconsidered. However, this also carries risk, with an expected mortality rate of one to two people for every million who are vaccinated. Thus, immunizing the entire population may present a greater risk than that of the virus itself.

WHAT IS THE PROGNOSIS?

The outcome depends on the severity of the disease. In variola major, the overall mortality rate is 2 in 10. In variola minor, the mortality rate is less than 1 in 100. Blindness from corneal scarring, limb deformities, and pockmarks are common complications.

(WWW) ONLINE SITES: p.1027

West Nile virus

A viral infection transmitted from animals to humans by mosquitoes

LIFESTYLE Visiting or living in areas where the disease occurs is a risk factor

AGE GENDER GENETICS Not significant factors

West Nile virus was first recognized in Africa over 70 years ago but in 1999 the virus was reported in New York City. The virus lives in mosquitoes and birds but can also infect humans. Most infections are acquired from bites from infected mosquitoes. Transmission through blood transfusions and infected transplanted organs is also thought to be probable but otherwise person–to–person transmission does not occur.

WHAT ARE THE SYMPTOMS?

Mild illness usually disappears without treatment and is hard to distinguish from other viral infections. After an incubation period of 3–15 days symptoms may develop, including:

- Fever.
- Headache.
- Muscle aches.

One in five infected people will develop a nonitchy rash on the chest, back, and arms.

The most serious form of the illness, involving the central nervous system, occurs in 1 in 150 people. Additional symptoms then include stiff neck, dislike of bright light, and a depressed level of consciousness.

WHAT MIGHT BE DONE?

West Nile virus is usually diagnosed from the symptoms. Additional tests such as lumbar puncture (p.527), may be done for those whose central nervous system may be affected. Treatment is usually directed at relieving the symptoms, since there are no drugs available to kill the virus.

Avoiding mosquito bites by using mosquito repellents containing DEET is the only way to prevent the disease. Draining standing water will reduce the numbers of mosquitoes and thereby reduce the risk of infection.

Severe acute respiratory syndrome

A potentially serious viral infection, sometimes causing pneumonia

LIFESTYLE Visiting or living in areas where the disease occurs is a risk factor

AGE GENDER GENETICS Not significant factors

Sudden acute respiratory syndrome (SARS) is believed to have originated in the Guangdong Province of China in November 2002 and has spread to affect areas around the world. A new strain of coronavirus is believed to be the cause of the disease.

WHAT ARE THE SYMPTOMS?

After an incubation period of about 2–7 days, symptoms appear, including a fever sometimes accompanied by chills, aching muscles, and headache. After a further 3–7 days, a dry, nonproductive cough may develop, accompanied by shortness of breath that may become severe.

WHAT MIGHT BE DONE?

Initially, tests to exclude other causes of pneumonia, such as chest X-ray and sputum microscopy, may be performed. Reliable tests to detect the presence of the virus itself are being developed. Treatment is usually supportive and includes oxygen therapy, with artificial ventilation if necessary.

WHAT IS THE PROGNOSIS?

Most people recover without any specific treatment. However, in many cases the illness is fatal. Because there is no vaccine or curative treatment, control of the disease depends on physical measures, such as facemasks, hand washing, and isolation of infected individuals.

BACTERIAL INFECTIONS

A large group of diseases is caused by bacteria entering the body and multiplying too fast to be destroyed by the immune system. Some types of bacteria also release powerful poisons, known as toxins, that rapidly damage tissues. In the past, bacterial diseases were a major cause of death; today, most serious infections can be treated effectively with antibiotics.

Each of the bacterial infections covered in this section affects many areas of the body simultaneously. The most serious of these infections is septicemia, described in the first article, which can be due to almost any bacterium. The diseases in the following articles are caused only by particular bacteria. They include both recently identified infections, such as toxic shock syndrome, and those that have long been recognized, such as plague. The following articles describe illnesses caused by the rickettsiae bacteria. The final article discusses anthrax, caused by a bacterium that may be used as a biological weapon.

Many other bacterial infections, such as pneumonia (p.490), tuberculosis (p.491), and meningitis (p.527), cause damage to certain organs, and for this reason they are covered in the sections on specific body systems.

Bacterial skin infections, such as boils, are discussed in skin infections and infestations (pp.351–355).

KEY STRUCTURES

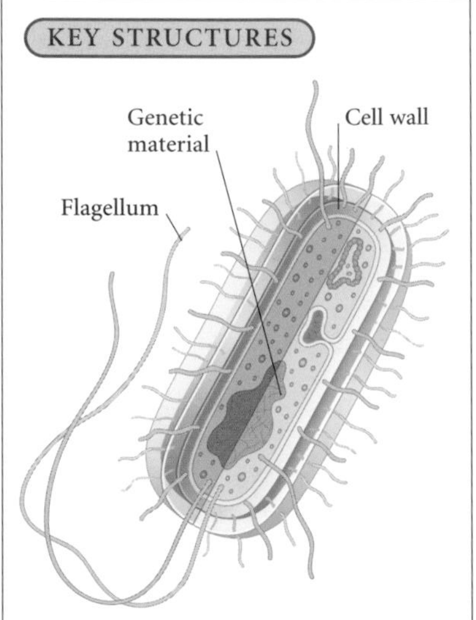
Genetic material
Cell wall
Flagellum

For information on the structure and function of bacteria, *see* pp. 282–285.

Septicemia

An infection, also known as blood poisoning, in which bacteria multiply in the bloodstream

 AGE More common in children and elderly people

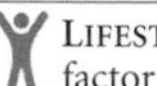 LIFESTYLE Intravenous drug use is a risk factor

 GENDER GENETICS Not significant factors

Septicemia, also known as blood poisoning, is a potentially fatal condition in which bacteria multiply rapidly in the bloodstream. It is common for bacteria to enter the bloodstream in small numbers through sites such as a breach in the skin or through the mouth when the teeth are brushed. The bacteria are usually destroyed by the immune system and cause no symptoms. However, if bacteria enter the bloodstream in large numbers from a major source of infection, such as a kidney infection (*see* PYELONEPHRITIS, p.698), blood poisoning can result. Septicemia can develop as a complication of almost all types of serious infectious diseases.

The infection is more likely to occur in people with reduced immunity due to disorders such as diabetes mellitus (p.687) or HIV infection (*see* HIV INFECTION AND AIDS, p.295) or due to treatment with chemotherapy (p.278) or immunosuppressant drugs (p.906). Young children and elderly people are also more susceptible. Others at increased risk are intravenous drug users, who may introduce bacteria into their blood from contaminated needles.

WHAT ARE THE SYMPTOMS?

The symptoms of septicemia develop suddenly and include:

- High fever.
- Chills and violent shivering.

If septicemia is left untreated, the bacteria may produce toxins that damage blood vessels, causing a drop in blood pressure and widespread tissue damage. In this dangerous condition, called septic shock, symptoms may include:

- Faintness.
- Cold, pale hands and feet.
- Restlessness and irritability.
- Rapid, shallow breathing.
- In many cases, delirium and eventual loss of consciousness.

In some people, bacteria may lodge on the heart valves, especially if the heart has previously been damaged by disease. This serious condition is called infective endocarditis (p.426). Rarely, septicemia may result in a lack of the blood cells involved in blood clotting (*see* THROMBOCYTOPENIA, p.453), which increases the risk of excessive bleeding.

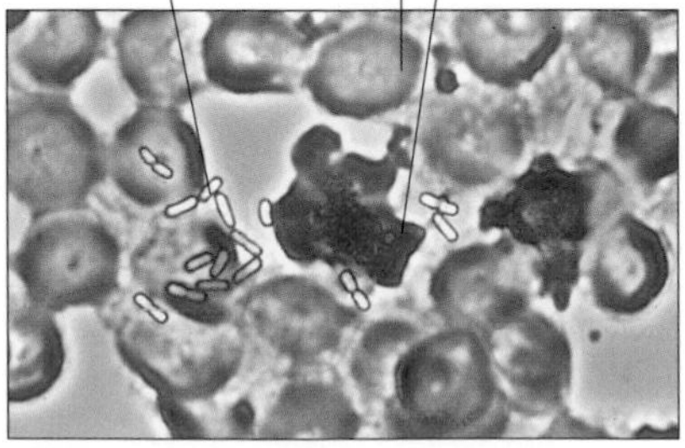

Bacterium Red blood cell White blood cell

Bacteria in blood
This magnified blood sample from a person with septicemia shows small, rod-shaped bacteria among the blood cells.

WHAT MIGHT BE DONE?

If your doctor suspects that you have septicemia, you will be admitted to the hospital for immediate treatment. Intravenous antibiotics (p.885) are given without delay, and then blood tests are done to identify the bacterium causing the infection. Once the bacterium has been identified, specific antibiotics are given. With prompt treatment, most affected people make a complete recovery.

(WWW) ONLINE SITES: p.1033

Toxic shock syndrome

A rare but serious condition caused by staphylococcal or streptococcal toxins

 AGE Most common between the ages of 15 and 20

 GENDER More common in females

 LIFESTYLE Using tampons may be a risk factor

 GENETICS Not a significant factor

First recognized in the late 1970s, toxic shock syndrome is an uncommon but potentially fatal infection. The condition is caused by a toxin produced by *Staphylococcus aureus* and some streptococcal bacteria, which enter the bloodstream from a localized site of infection.

Toxic shock syndrome mainly affects young adults, and about half of all cases occur in menstruating women. The infection may be linked to use of tampons, which can provide a site for bacterial growth in the vagina, particularly if a tampon is left in place longer than the recommended time.

The symptoms start suddenly and may include fever, vomiting, diarrhea, and severe muscular aches and pains. A widespread red, sunburnlike rash may appear, and confusion may occur. More serious complications can also develop, such as acute kidney failure (p.706).

Toxic shock syndrome requires immediate treatment in the hospital with intravenous antibiotics (p.885). Treated promptly, 9 in 10 people recover fully.

(WWW) ONLINE SITES: p.1033, p.1037

Scarlet fever

A rare streptococcal infection causing a red rash and a sore throat

 AGE Most common between the ages of 6 and 12

 GENDER GENETICS LIFESTYLE Not significant factors

Once a common and dangerous childhood disease, scarlet fever has become rare in developed countries since the introduction of antibiotics (p.885). This infection is caused by the bacterium *Streptococcus pyogenes*, transmitted in microscopic droplets from coughs and sneezes. A prominent feature of the condition is a widespread scarlet rash.

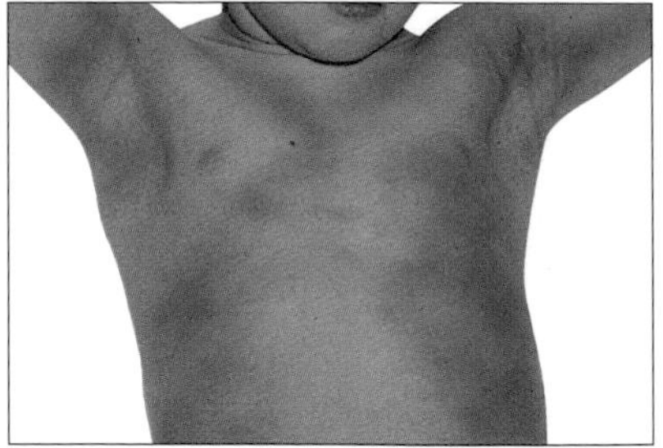

Scarlet fever
The characteristic red rash of scarlet fever begins on the trunk and is often most obvious in the armpits.

WHAT ARE THE SYMPTOMS?

About 1–3 days after infection, the following symptoms may develop:

- Sore throat and headache.
- Fever and vomiting.
- Raised, red rash, spreading rapidly on the neck, trunk, armpits, and groin.

A thick, white coating may develop on the tongue, disappearing in a few days to leave the tongue bright red with a pimpled "strawberry" appearance.

WHAT MIGHT BE DONE?

Scarlet fever is usually diagnosed from the symptoms. To confirm the diagnosis, a throat swab may be taken.

Scarlet fever is treated with antibiotics, and the symptoms usually begin to improve within 24–48 hours. Most people recover completely within a week.

(WWW) ONLINE SITES: p.1033

Diphtheria

A rare throat infection that can cause breathing difficulties

 AGE More common in children

 GENDER GENETICS LIFESTYLE Not significant factors

Now rare in developed countries, diphtheria was a common cause of death in children until immunization became routine. In this disease, the bacterium *Corynebacterium diphtheriae* multiplies in the throat and may release toxins into the blood. The infection is usually transmitted through airborne droplets from coughs or sneezes of infected people.

Diphtheria bacteria may also infect the skin. This form of the disease, cutaneous diphtheria, is more common in tropical countries, but there has been an increasing number of cases reported in the US in recent years. Outbreaks of diphtheria tend to occur among overcrowded communities.

WHAT ARE THE SYMPTOMS?

The symptoms of diphtheria develop 1–4 days after infection and include:

- Sore throat.
- Fever.
- Swollen lymph nodes in the neck.
- In many cases, a gray membrane that grows across the throat, causing difficulty breathing.

In the cutaneous form of the disorder, deep sores may develop. If diphtheria is not treated, bacterial toxins may spread in the blood and cause potentially fatal complications such as acute heart failure (p.412) and paralysis.

WHAT MIGHT BE DONE?

Diphtheria may be diagnosed from the symptoms, but a throat swab is taken for confirmation. Most people recover fully if treated immediately with antibiotics (p.885) and antitoxin injections in the hospital. Routine immunization (p.45) in children and boosters in adults provide protection against the disease.

(WWW) ONLINE SITES: p.1033

Brucellosis

A rare infection, contracted from farm animals and dairy products, that may cause recurrent illness

 LIFESTYLE Working with farm animals is a risk factor

 AGE GENDER GENETICS Not significant factors

Brucellosis is caused by various types of brucella bacteria, which can be transmitted to humans through contact with infected farm animals and in unpasteurized milk and other dairy products. The disease rarely occurs in developed countries, where domestic animals are normally free of the infection.

The symptoms of brucellosis vary considerably from person to person. In some cases, depression and weight loss are the only signs of infection, although many people develop fever with night sweats, fatigue, headache, and pain in the joints. Left untreated, the illness can become chronic, recurring at intervals over months or sometimes years.

WHAT MIGHT BE DONE?

A lack of specific symptoms makes brucellosis difficult to diagnose, although the bacteria can be identified by a blood test. It is usually treated with antibiotics (p.885), which are sometimes given with corticosteroids (p.930). With treatment, most people recover within 2–3 weeks.

WWW ONLINE SITES: p.1033

Listeriosis

An uncommon infection transmitted through contaminated food

 LIFESTYLE Eating certain foods, such as soft cheeses and meat pâté, is a risk factor

 AGE GENDER GENETICS Not significant factors

The bacterium that causes listeriosis, *Listeria monocytogenes*, is widespread in the soil and is present in most animal species. It can pass to humans through food products, particularly soft cheeses, milk, meat pâtés, and prepackaged salads. The risk of listeriosis is increased by incorrect storage of these foods. The bacteria multiply in the intestines and may spread in the blood (*see* SEPTICEMIA, p.298) and affect other organs.

The symptoms vary from one person to another. The infection often goes unnoticed in healthy adults, although some may develop flulike symptoms such as fever, sore throat, headache, diarrhea, and aching muscles.

In elderly people and people with reduced immunity, such as those with HIV infection (*see* HIV INFECTION AND AIDS, p.295) or those taking immunosuppressant drugs (p.906), listeriosis can lead to meningitis (p.527), a potentially fatal inflammation of the membranes covering the brain. In pregnant women, infection can pass to the fetus, causing miscarriage (p.791) or stillbirth (p.805).

WHAT MIGHT BE DONE?

Listeriosis is usually diagnosed from a blood test. In otherwise healthy people, mild listeriosis clears up without treatment in a few days. People with serious infection, especially during pregnancy, need urgent treatment in the hospital with intravenous antibiotics (p.885).

Hygienic handling and storage of food reduces the risk of listeriosis (*see* HOME SAFETY AND HEALTH, p.77).

WWW ONLINE SITES: p.1033, p.1036

Typhoid and paratyphoid

Infections caused by salmonella bacteria that result in high fever followed by a rash

 LIFESTYLE Visiting or living in areas where the disease occurs is a risk factor

 AGE GENDER GENETICS Not significant factors

Typhoid and paratyphoid are almost identical diseases that are caused by the bacteria *Salmonella typhi* and *S. paratyphi*, respectively. The bacteria multiply in the intestines and spread to the blood and to other organs, such as the spleen, gallbladder, and liver. The diseases are transmitted through infected feces and most commonly occur in areas where hygiene and sanitation are poor. Infection is commonly due to food or water contaminated by unwashed hands.

WHAT ARE THE SYMPTOMS?

Symptoms of both diseases appear 7–14 days after infection and may include:

- Headache and high fever.
- Dry cough.
- Abdominal pain and constipation, usually followed by diarrhea.
- Rash of rose-colored spots appearing on the chest, abdomen, and back.

Both infections can lead to serious complications, such as intestinal bleeding and perforation of the intestines.

WHAT MIGHT BE DONE?

Typhoid and paratyphoid can be diagnosed by testing blood or fecal samples for the bacteria. The diseases are usually treated with antibiotics (p.885) in the hospital. Symptoms usually subside 2–3 days after treatment is begun, and most people recover fully in a month.

Even with treatment, the bacteria are excreted for about 3 months after the symptoms have disappeared. Some people who do not undergo treatment may become lifelong carriers of the bacteria and transmit the infection to others, although they appear to be healthy.

Good hygiene is the best protection against infection (*see* TRAVEL HEALTH, p.85). Several vaccines are available, and, if you intend to travel to a developing country, immunization may be advisable (*see* TRAVEL IMMUNIZATIONS, p.86).

WWW ONLINE SITES: p.1033, p.1037

Cholera

An intestinal infection that causes profuse, watery diarrhea

 LIFESTYLE Visiting or living in areas where the disease occurs is a risk factor

 AGE GENDER GENETICS Not significant factors

Cholera typically occurs in epidemics and has caused millions of deaths over the centuries. It is due to infection of the small intestine by the bacterium *Vibrio cholerae*. Usually associated with areas of poor sanitation, cholera can be spread through contaminated water or food.

The illness starts suddenly, 1–5 days after infection, with vomiting and profuse, watery diarrhea. In some cases, fatal dehydration develops.

WHAT MIGHT BE DONE?

Cholera is usually diagnosed from the characteristic "rice water" appearance of the diarrhea. To confirm the diagnosis, a fecal sample may be checked for the presence of the bacteria.

Urgent hospital treatment is needed to replace lost fluids and minerals, which are given orally or intravenously. Antibiotics (p.885) may be given to reduce the risk of passing the infection to others. If treated without delay, most people make a complete recovery.

Cholera vaccines are relatively ineffective. In regions where cholera may occur, good hygiene is the best protection (*see* TRAVEL HEALTH, p.85).

WWW ONLINE SITES: p.1033, p.1037

Botulism

A rare, life-threatening form of poisoning in which a bacterial toxin in food damages the nervous system, causing paralysis

 LIFESTYLE Eating home-preserved food is a risk factor

 AGE GENDER GENETICS Not significant factors

The toxin that causes botulism is one of the most dangerous poisons known to humanity. This toxin is produced by the bacterium *Clostridium botulinum*, which can multiply rapidly in canned or preserved foods. If a contaminated food is eaten, absorption of even minute amounts of toxin can cause severe damage to the nervous system.

Strict controls on commercial canning have made botulism caused by store-bought products rare. The foods most commonly affected are home-preserved vegetables, fish, and fruit. Babies, who are especially susceptible to the effects of the toxin, may develop botulism after being given contaminated honey.

What are the symptoms?

The symptoms of botulism appear very suddenly, 8–36 hours after eating contaminated food. In the initial stages, the symptoms usually include:

- Nausea and constipation.
- Dry mouth.

Within 24 hours, these symptoms are followed by muscle weakness that starts in the eyes, causing blurry vision, and then progresses down the body. Without treatment, the respiratory muscles may become paralyzed, causing suffocation.

What might be done?

Botulism needs immediate treatment in the hospital with antitoxin drugs. For people whose breathing is affected, mechanical ventilation may be necessary. If given treatment without delay, 9 in 10 people make a full recovery.

To reduce the risk of poisoning, you should pressure-cook home-preserved food for at least 30 minutes at 120°C (250°F) and ensure that all containers are sterilized. Babies under the age of 12 months should not be given honey.

(WWW) ONLINE SITES: p.1033

Tetanus

A wound infection, caused by a bacterial toxin, that produces severe muscle spasms

AGE GENDER GENETICS LIFESTYLE Not significant factors

Tetanus is caused by a toxin produced by the bacterium *Clostridium tetani*, which lives in soil and in the intestines of humans and other animals. If the bacteria enter a wound, they multiply, and an infection may develop that acts on the nerves controlling muscle activity. The condition, also called lockjaw, is rare in developed countries because most people have been immunized.

The symptoms of tetanus usually appear 5–10 days after infection. Fever, headache, and muscle stiffness in the jaw, arms, neck, and back are typical. As the condition progresses, painful muscle spasms may develop. In some people, the muscles of the throat or chest wall are affected, leading to breathing difficulties and possible suffocation.

What might be done?

Diagnosis of tetanus is based on details of the injury and on the symptoms. The disease needs immediate treatment in the hospital with antitoxin injections, antibiotics (p.885), and sedatives (*see* ANTIANXIETY DRUGS, p.916) to relieve muscle spasm. Mechanical ventilation may be necessary to aid breathing. If given prompt treatment, most people make a complete recovery. If treatment is delayed, tetanus is usually fatal.

To reduce the risk of tetanus, you should thoroughly clean wounds, especially those contaminated with soil, and treat them with antiseptic. Deep puncture wounds, which are especially likely to become infected, should be seen by your doctor, who may give you antibiotics to prevent infection.

Vaccination against tetanus, usually given in early childhood (*see* ROUTINE IMMUNIZATIONS, p.45), is highly effective. Boosters should be given every 10 years to maintain protection.

(WWW) ONLINE SITES: p.1033

Hansen's disease

An infection, also known as leprosy, that affects nerves and skin, causing numbness and disfigurement

AGE GENDER GENETICS LIFESTYLE Not significant factors

Hansen's disease, commonly known as leprosy, is a chronic infection caused by the bacterium *Mycobacterium leprae*, which damages the skin and nerves. The limbs and face, in particular, may be affected. Infection is thought to be transmitted in airborne droplets produced when an infected person coughs or sneezes and through skin contact. Contrary to popular belief, the disease is not easily transmitted from person to person. Only people who live in prolonged, close contact with an infected person are at risk of infection, and most people are naturally resistant to the bacteria. The disease is rare in developed countries and is most common in Asia, Africa, and South America.

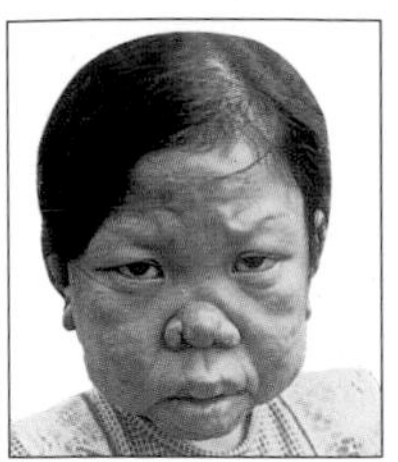

BEFORE TREATMENT

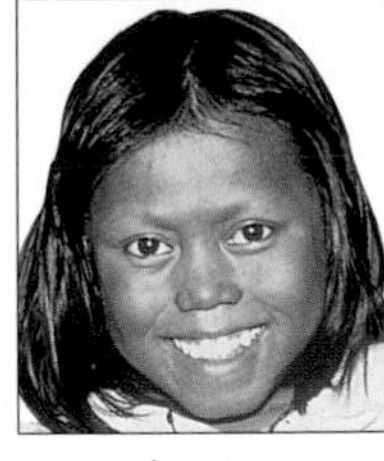

AFTER TREATMENT

Hansen's disease

At age 7, this girl had severely thickened facial skin due to Hansen's disease. After 2 years of treatment with antibiotics, her appearance had improved dramatically.

Hansen's disease develops very slowly, the first symptoms appearing 3–5 years after infection. Initially, nerve damage causes numbness of the skin on the face, hands, and feet. The affected skin may also become thickened and discolored. Hansen's disease is infectious only while these early symptoms are developing. Lack of sensation may lead to injury or even loss of fingers and toes.

Diagnosis is based on the symptoms and examination of a skin tissue sample to identify the bacterium. Treatment with antibiotics (p.885), usually for 2 years or longer, prevents further nerve damage and reduces areas of thickened skin. However, nerve damage that has already occurred is irreversible.

(WWW) ONLINE SITES: p.1033

Leptospirosis

A group of infections transmitted to humans by rats and other animals

LIFESTYLE Working on farms or with sewage is a risk factor

AGE GENDER GENETICS Not significant factors

Infections caused by different types of *Leptospira* bacteria are known generally as leptospirosis. The bacteria are carried by animals such as rats or foxes and excreted in their urine. Infection is usually transmitted to humans by contact with contaminated water or soil. In most cases the infection causes a flulike illness, but, in its most severe form, which is known as Weil's disease, leptospirosis may be life-threatening.

Leptospirosis most commonly occurs in farmers and sewage workers, but the disease can affect anyone who comes into contact with contaminated water, such as swimmers. In the US, 50–100 cases of leptospirosis are reported each year, often during the summer months.

WHAT ARE THE SYMPTOMS?

The symptoms of leptospirosis usually appear abruptly 2–20 days after infection. They may include:

- Fever.
- Intense headache and muscle pain.
- Flat, red rash.
- Inflammation of the eyes and eyelids (*see* CONJUNCTIVITIS, p.570).

The symptoms tend to disappear after a few days but may recur if immediate treatment is not given. If the disease goes untreated, it frequently causes a potentially dangerous inflammation of the membranes covering the brain (*see* MENINGITIS, p.527).

About 1 in 10 infected people develops Weil's disease. This disorder leads to widespread internal bleeding, damage to the kidneys and liver, and jaundice (p.643), which causes the skin and the whites of the eyes to turn yellow.

WHAT MIGHT BE DONE?

To diagnose leptospirosis, your doctor may arrange for blood and urine tests to check for the presence of bacteria. If treated with antibiotics (p.885) at an early stage, most people recover fully.

As a preventive measure, workers at particular risk of infection are usually given antibiotics after minor injuries such as cuts and scrapes.

WWW ONLINE SITES: p.1033

Lyme disease

An infection transmitted by ticks that causes a rash and flulike symptoms

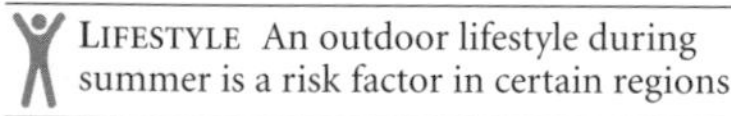
LIFESTYLE An outdoor lifestyle during summer is a risk factor in certain regions

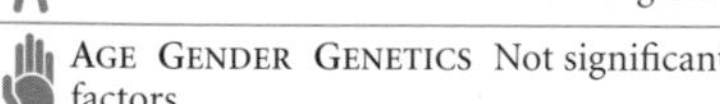
AGE GENDER GENETICS Not significant factors

Named after Old Lyme, the town in Connecticut where the disease was first recognized, Lyme disease is caused by a bacterium called *Borrelia burgdorferi*. The infection is transmitted to humans by ticks that usually live on deer. If a person is bitten by an infected tick that remains embedded in his or her skin, bacteria can enter the bloodstream and may then spread throughout the body.

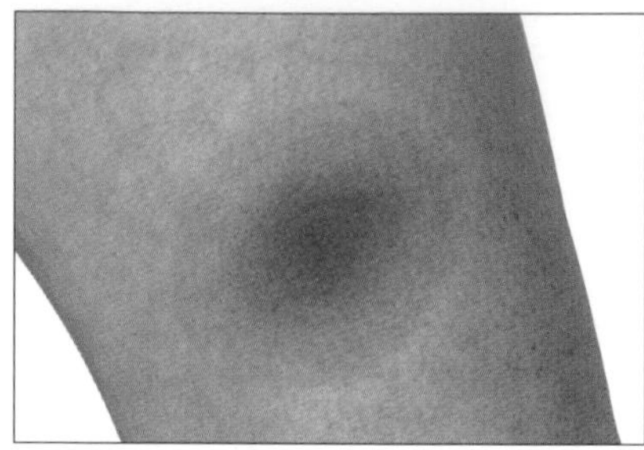

Lyme disease
A bite from a tick infected with the bacterium that causes Lyme disease typically produces an expanding circular red rash, as seen here on the thigh.

A tick may be infected with more than one type of bacterium, and as a result a single bite may cause other, similar infections, such as ehrlichiosis (right), to be transmitted at the same time.

Most reports of Lyme disease have been documented in the northeastern coastal states of the US. The disease also occurs in northern and western states, in Europe, and in Central Asia. People who go camping or walking in wooded areas during the summer months are most at risk of being bitten by a tick carrying Lyme disease bacteria.

WHAT ARE THE SYMPTOMS?

A bite from an infected tick usually produces a red lump with a scab on the skin, although some people who have been bitten may not notice this initial sign. Within 2 days to 4 weeks after the bite, the following symptoms may develop:

- Spreading circular rash at the site of the bite that may clear in the center.
- Fatigue.
- Flulike chills and fever.
- Headache and joint pains.

If the infection is left untreated, these symptoms may persist for several weeks. In some people who have Lyme disease, dangerous complications may develop up to 2 years later that may affect the heart, nervous system, and joints.

WHAT MIGHT BE DONE?

Your doctor may suspect from your symptoms that you have Lyme disease and may also arrange for a blood test to confirm the diagnosis.

If they are given prompt treatment with antibiotics (p.885), most people make a complete recovery. Nonsteroidal anti-inflammatory drugs (p.894) can help relieve joint pain. Complications are extremely rare. Vaccines are now available that offer 70 percent protection against Lyme disease. Vaccination needs to be repeated every 2 years.

In regions known to be tick-infested, you should cover your arms and legs to reduce the risk of bites and promptly remove any ticks that you find on your skin (*see* FIRST AID: TICK BITES, p.995).

WWW ONLINE SITES: p.1033

Ehrlichiosis

An infection transmitted by animal ticks that causes a flulike illness

LIFESTYLE An outdoor lifestyle during summer is a risk factor in certain regions

AGE GENDER GENETICS Not significant factors

Ehrlichiosis is an uncommon infection caused by ehrlichia bacteria, which are transmitted to humans by bites from animal ticks. The disease may occur at the same time as other similar tick-borne infections, such as Lyme disease (left), because a single bite may transmit more than one type of bacterium.

Most cases have been reported in the southern, central, and Atlantic coast states of the US. People who walk or camp in wooded areas during the summer are at the greatest risk of infection.

The symptoms of ehrlichiosis usually appear 7–10 days after infection and include severe headache, chills and fever, and joint pains. Sometimes there is nausea and vomiting, and occasionally a spotted rash appears. Rarely, serious complications develop, causing anemia (p.446) and damage to the liver, kidneys, lungs, and nervous system.

WHAT MIGHT BE DONE?

Ehrlichiosis can be difficult to diagnose from the symptoms, particularly if you have Lyme disease at the same time. Your doctor may arrange for a blood test to confirm the diagnosis so that appropriate antibiotics (p.885) can be given. Prompt treatment usually relieves the symptoms in 24–48 hours.

In tick-infested regions, you should cover your arms and legs to reduce the risk of bites and promptly remove any ticks that attach themselves to your skin (*see* FIRST AID: TICK BITES, p.995).

WWW ONLINE SITES: p.1033

Plague

A serious infection carried by rodents and transmitted to humans by flea bites

AGE GENDER GENETICS LIFESTYLE Not significant factors

Plague is the result of infection by the bacterium *Yersinia pestis,* which usually affects rodents but can be transmitted to humans through flea bites. During the Middle Ages, the disease caused pandemics (widespread epidemics), one of the largest of which was the so-called Black Death of the 14th century, which killed over 25 million people in Europe. Today, small outbreaks occur in Asia, Africa, and South America, but plague is rare in developed countries. There are only 10–12 cases a year in the US.

There are two main forms of plague: bubonic plague, which affects the lymph nodes, and pneumonic plague, affecting the lungs. The symptoms of both forms develop rapidly and include fever and chills. In bubonic plague, swollen lymph nodes in the groin and armpits are typical. Pneumonic plague causes a severe cough and shortness of breath.

Plague is diagnosed from the symptoms and by a blood test. People treated promptly with antibiotics (p.885) usually recover fully. However, if treatment is delayed, the disease is often fatal.

WWW ONLINE SITES: p.1033

Rocky Mountain spotted fever

A rickettsial infection, transmitted to humans by animal ticks, that causes fever and a spotted rash

LIFESTYLE An outdoor lifestyle during summer is a risk factor in certain regions

AGE GENDER GENETICS Not significant factors

Despite its name, Rocky Mountain spotted fever occurs most often in the mountains and hills of the south and central US and South America. The disease is caused by a bacterium called *Rickettsia rickettsii,* which is transmitted to humans through bites from animal ticks. People who go camping or walking in wooded areas during the summer months are at greatest risk of becoming infected.

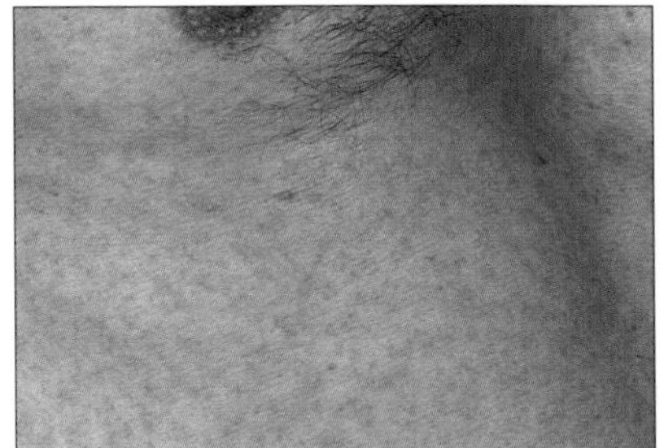

Rocky Mountain spotted fever
The rash of Rocky Mountain spotted fever often begins on the limbs and spreads over the body, as seen here on the chest.

The initial symptoms appear suddenly about a week after infection and may include severe headache, muscle pains, chills, and fever. Within a few days, a pink spotted rash develops on the limbs and spreads over the entire body. This rash gradually becomes darker in color. If the condition is left untreated, fatal complications, such as acute kidney failure (p.706), may develop.

Rocky Mountain spotted fever can usually be diagnosed from the characteristic rash of tiny pink spots. If given immediate treatment with antibiotics (p.885), most people who have the disease make a rapid recovery.

In regions that are infested with ticks, you should keep your arms and legs covered to reduce your risk of being bitten and promptly remove any ticks that attach themselves to your skin (*see* FIRST AID: TICK BITES, p.995).

WWW ONLINE SITES: p.1033

Q fever

A rickettsial infection transmitted to humans by contact with farm animals

LIFESTYLE Working with farm animals or meat is a risk factor

AGE GENDER GENETICS Not significant factors

Labeled Q for Queensland, Australia, Q fever is caused by the rickettsial bacterium *Coxiella burnetti.* The bacteria are carried by livestock such as cattle and can be transmitted in urine, feces, milk, or airborne tissue particles from infected animals.

Within 2–3 weeks of infection, a high fever, severe headache, muscle pain, and cough may suddenly occur. The symptoms usually disappear in 1–2 weeks, but, in some people, infection spreads and damages the heart valves (*see* INFECTIVE ENDOCARDITIS, p.426) and the liver (*see* ACUTE HEPATITIS, p.644).

Q fever is diagnosed by a blood test and is usually treated successfully with antibiotics (p.885). Vaccines give some protection against it for several years and are available for people at high risk, such as farmers and slaughterhouse workers.

WWW ONLINE SITES: p.1033

Typhus

A serious rickettsial infection transmitted to humans by lice, fleas, or mites

LIFESTYLE Living in overcrowded, unhygienic conditions is a risk factor

AGE GENDER GENETICS Not significant factors

There are three main forms of typhus, all of which are caused by different types of rickettsial bacteria.

Epidemic typhus is transmitted by body lice, usually in overcrowded conditions, and has resulted in hundreds of thousands of deaths in times of war or famine. Today, the disease is rare except in some areas of tropical Africa and South America. Endemic typhus, which is also known as murine typhus, is a rare disease that can be transmitted from rats to humans by fleas; a few cases occur each year in North and Central America. Scrub typhus, which is transmitted by mites, has been reported in India and Southeast Asia.

The first sign of infection with scrub typhus is a black scab over the site of the bite. In all types of typhus, flulike symptoms may develop within 1–3 weeks of infection, followed a few days later by a widespread, blotchy pink rash. In more severe cases of typhus, delirium and coma (p.522) occur. If the disease is not treated, dangerous complications such as pneumonia (p.490) or kidney failure (p.705) are also likely to develop.

WHAT MIGHT BE DONE?

Diagnosis is often made from the symptoms, but a blood test may also be done. In most cases, prompt treatment with antibiotics (p.885) is effective. Without treatment, the bacteria can lie dormant in the body for years before being reactivated and causing the disease to recur.

WWW ONLINE SITES: p.1033

Anthrax

A rare bacterial infection with the potential to be misused by bioterrorists

LIFESTYLE Working on farms is a risk factor

AGE GENDER GENETICS Not significant factors

Anthrax is an uncommon infection in the United States but gained notoriety in the months following the September 11, 2001 terrorist attack on New York and Washington, DC. Twenty-two infections were reported in New York, Washington, New Jersey, and Florida, most connected to exposure to a powder containing the bacteria that had been sent through the mail. The last human case in Canada, a cutaneous infection, occurred in 1990.

Anthrax is caused by the bacterium *Bacillus anthracis*, normally found in the soil, where it can remain dormant for long periods of time. It can spread to grazing animals such as goats and then to humans who are exposed to infected animals or their products, such as goat hair used in the textile industry. In 1882, French biologist and chemist Louis Pasteur developed the first antibacterial vaccine to anthrax from altered strains of the bacterium.

Anthrax can cause three major syndromes depending on the way in which the bacterium enters the body. These are: inhalational, cutaneous (through the skin), or gastrointestinal. Of the cases that occurred in 2001, 11 were the inhalational form, and 11 were the cutaneous form. All but two of the infections were thought to be caused by the powder that was sent through the mail. Two cases of inhalational anthrax were fatal.

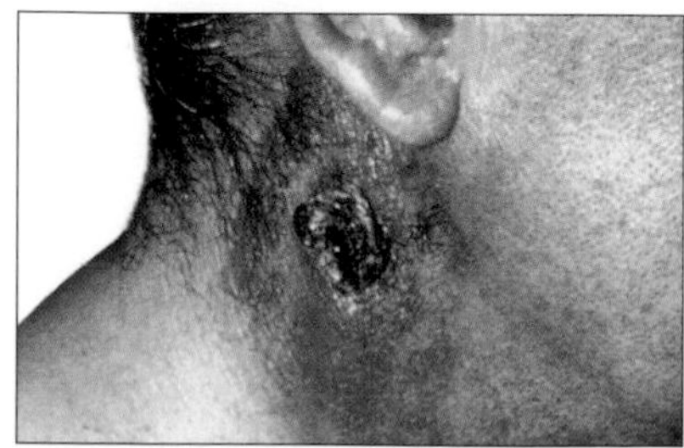

Skin lesion
Typical of cutaneous anthrax, this lesion has ulcerated after a couple of days and formed a large scab.

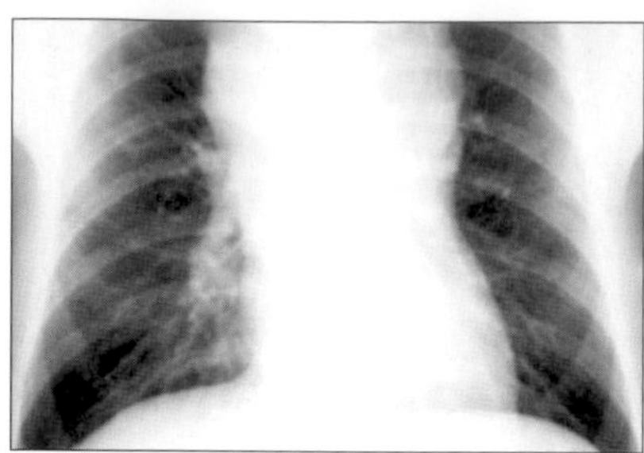

Chest X-ray
The enlarged lymph nodes characteristic of inhalational anthrax can be seen on an X-ray of the chest.

WHAT ARE THE SYMPTOMS?

Symptoms of anthrax usually appear within seven days of exposure to the anthrax bacterium. However, for inhalation anthrax, symptoms may take up to two months to appear.

In cutaneous anthrax, the disease starts as small, painless, but itchy papules with a large amount of swelling surrounding the lesions. The lesions then enlarge, become filled with fluid and then ulcerate and form scabs within two days. Fever and enlargement of the local lymph nodes can develop. The rash usually occurs on exposed areas such as the face, neck, arms, and hands.

In inhalational anthrax, also known as wool sorters' disease, the bacterial spores are breathed into the lungs. Once inhaled, the spores multiply in the lymph nodes in the center of the chest and cause inflammation and hemorrhage. The first symptoms of inhalation anthrax are:

- Fever.
- Fatigue.
- Achiness.

The infection then spreads and can result in infection in the blood and the tissues surrounding the brain (*see* MENINGITIS, p.527). Occasionally the infection causes pneumonia (p.490). Several days after the first symptoms, those infected become sicker and develop shortness of breath and low blood oxygen levels. When the infection spreads to the blood, the blood pressure drops and there can be bleeding into the space around the brain.

In gastrointestinal anthrax, the infection is introduced to the pharynx or gastrointestinal tract by eating infected meat or by other exposure to the gastrointestinal tract. When the pharynx is infected, the symptoms include:

- Fever.
- Sore throat.
- Neck swelling.
- Sores with scabs can be seen in the throat.

Gastrointestinal anthrax can cause severe abdominal pain and swelling of the abdomen due to bloody fluid in the abdominal cavity.

WHAT MIGHT BE DONE?

The bacterium that causes the infection can be cultured in a laboratory and seen under the microscope after it is stained. The infection can also be identified by measurement of the genetic material of the organism.

If anthrax is suspected, your doctor may be able to identify the cutaneous form by examining the skin. Chest X-ray (p.244) and CT scan (p.247) of the chest may be done if inhalational anthrax is suspected. These tests show enlargement in the lymph nodes in the center of the chest. Blood samples for culture, lumbar puncture (p.527) to obtain spinal fluid, and sampling of fluid in the abdominal cavity might also be done to identify the bacteria.

If you develop any of the signs of anthrax infection, you will most likely be hospitalized and treated with a lengthy course of antibiotics (p.885). Occasionally, corticosteroids (p.930) are given for inhalational anthrax. Supportive measures to treat discomfort and help maintain blood pressure and the proper functioning of vital organs are important.

A vaccine for anthrax has been developed and is administered to certain military personnel, but it is not available to the general public. If you have been exposed to anthrax but are not yet infected, your doctor may treat you with preventive doses of antibiotics for two months and possibly longer.

WHAT IS THE PROGNOSIS?

Cutaneous anthrax can cause serious illness but is usually curable with appropriate antibiotic treatment. Although inhalational anthrax was previously thought to be nearly always fatal, treatment was successful in a number of cases in 2001.

(WWW) ONLINE SITES: p.1027

PROTOZOAL AND FUNGAL INFECTIONS

Protozoa and fungi are simple organisms, capable of living in many different habitats. Some protozoa and fungi are parasites of humans. They acquire all their food from our bodies and often cause disease. One protozoal infection, malaria, affects hundreds of millions of people worldwide each year and is often fatal.

Protozoal infections are discussed first, starting with malaria, the most important health hazard for visitors to the tropics. The subsequent articles deal with other protozoal infections, including diseases that are common causes of diarrhea, such as amebiasis and cryptosporidiosis. The protozoal infection trichomoniasis, which is transmitted sexually, is covered with other such sexually transmitted diseases (*see* TRICHOMONIASIS, p.767).

Fungal infections are discussed next. Like most protozoal infections, fungal infections may be serious in people with reduced immunity, such as those who have AIDS. Some fungal infections, such as histoplasmosis, may be severe in otherwise healthy people as well as those with reduced immunity. Common fungal infections that affect particular areas of the body, such as the skin and vagina, are covered in the sections on specific body systems.

KEY STRUCTURES

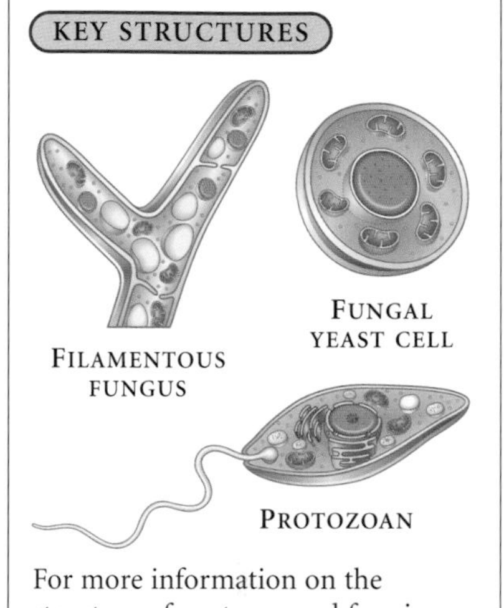
FILAMENTOUS FUNGUS
FUNGAL YEAST CELL
PROTOZOAN

For more information on the structure of protozoa and fungi, *see* pp.282–285.

Malaria

A parasitic infection of red blood cells spread by mosquitoes

 LIFESTYLE Visiting or living in areas where the disease occurs are risk factors

 AGE GENDER GENETICS Not significant factors

More than 1 in every 3 people worldwide are affected by malaria, a parasitic infection that leads to the destruction of red blood cells. In tropical countries, about 10 million new cases of malaria and 2 million deaths due to the disease occur every year. Most of those who die of malaria are children. The disease is the most serious health threat to North Americans who visit tropical countries. In Canada, about 600 cases of malaria are reported each year.

The World Health Organization has been trying to control malaria for many years but with only intermittent success. Malarial parasites are transmitted to humans by mosquitoes of the anopheles group, which have now become resistant to a number of insecticides. In many areas, the malarial parasite itself has now also become resistant to the common antimalarial drugs (p.888). Currently, no effective vaccine has been developed to protect against infection with the malarial parasite.

If you live in a region where malaria is common, you may have several mild episodes of infection that increase your resistance, making you less likely to develop a serious infection. However, this protection is lost within a year in a malaria-free region. Therefore, if you emigrate from a malaria-affected area and later return for a vacation, you will need to take preventive measures (*see* PREVENTING MALARIA, right). If you become ill after a visit to the tropics, you should tell your doctor where you have been and when you went there.

WHAT ARE THE TYPES?

The characteristics of malaria have been known for over 2,000 years. However, the cause of the disease was only identified in 1880. Four species of protozoal parasites from the plasmodium group cause malaria in humans, each species causing a different type of malaria. The most dangerous type of malaria is falciparum malaria, caused by *Plasmodium falciparum.* This type of malaria results in the most deaths and is often fatal within 48 hours of the first symptoms if it is left untreated. The other three types of malaria, caused by *Plasmodium malariae, Plasmodium ovale,* and *Plasmodium vivax,* are less severe.

All types of malarial parasites are transmitted to humans by a bite from an infected mosquito. Initially, the parasites multiply in the liver and are then released into the bloodstream, where they penetrate red blood cells. After 48–72 hours, depending on the species of parasite, the infected cells rupture, releasing parasites that invade other red blood cells. If a noninfected mosquito bites the infected person, the insect itself

SELF-HELP PREVENTING MALARIA

If you plan to visit an area where malaria occurs, your doctor will be able to give you up-to-date advice about antimalarial drugs (p.888) for that area. You may need to start taking the drugs several days before you leave and continue taking them during and after your visit. To protect yourself against mosquito bites, you should:

- Keep your body well covered.
- Sleep under a mosquito net that is already impregnated with insect repellent.
- Use insect repellent on clothes and exposed skin.

These measures against mosquito bites are especially important between dusk and dawn, when malaria-carrying mosquitoes bite.

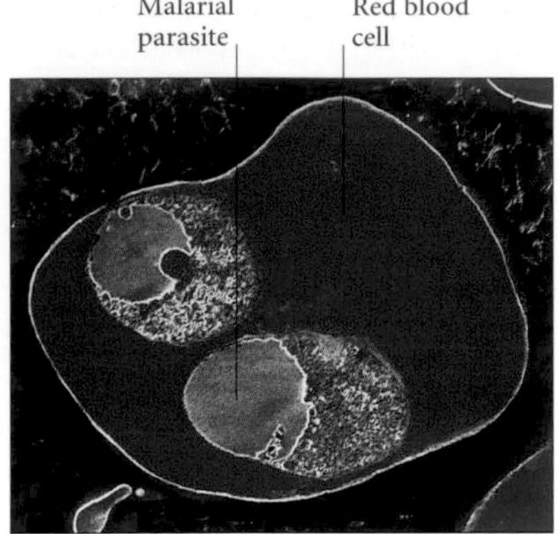
Malarial parasite
Red blood cell

Infected red blood cell
The protozoa that cause malaria infect red blood cells. Attacks of the disease occur when the protozoa burst out of the cells.

becomes infected and can then spread the disease to other people. In all types of malaria, the disease can pass from an infected pregnant woman to her fetus.

What are the symptoms?

The symptoms of malaria usually begin between 10 days and 6 weeks after being bitten by an infected mosquito. However, in some cases, symptoms may not develop for months or years, especially if preventive drugs were being taken at the time of infection.

If not treated, malaria due to *P. vivax*, *P. ovale*, and *P. malariae* causes recurrent attacks of symptoms with each episode of red blood cell destruction by the parasites. Each attack usually lasts for 4–8 hours and may occur at intervals of 2 or 3 days, depending on the species of parasite. Symptoms of an attack include:

- High fever.
- Shivering and chills.
- Heavy sweating.
- Confusion.
- Fatigue, headaches, and muscle pain.

Between each attack, extreme fatigue may be the only symptom.

Falciparum malaria causes a continuous fever that may be mistaken for influenza (p.287). It is more severe than the other types, and attacks may lead to loss of consciousness and kidney failure (p.705) and may be fatal.

What might be done?

Your doctor may suspect malaria if you have an unexplained fever within a year after a trip to a region where the infection occurs. Diagnosis is confirmed by identifying the malarial parasite in a blood smear under a microscope.

If you are diagnosed with malaria, you should be given antimalarial drugs (p.888) as early as possible to avoid complications. Treatment depends on the type of malaria, how resistant the parasite is to drugs, and the severity of the symptoms. If you have falciparum malaria, you may be treated in the hospital with oral or intravenous antimalarial drugs. Treatment may also involve a blood transfusion (p.447) to replace destroyed red blood cells or kidney dialysis (p.707) if kidney function is impaired. Other types of malaria are usually treated on an outpatient basis with oral antimalarial drugs.

If treated early, the prognosis is usually good, and most people make a full recovery. Malaria caused by *P. vivax* and *P. ovale* may recur after treatment.

Preventive measures, including taking antimalarial drugs, should be taken against malaria when visiting an area where the disease is known to occur.

(WWW) ONLINE SITES: p.1033, p.1037

Amebiasis

An intestinal infection that causes diarrhea and may spread to the liver

LIFESTYLE Visiting or living in the tropics and poor personal hygiene are risk factors

AGE GENDER GENETICS Not significant factors

The intestinal infection amebiasis is caused by the protozoan parasite *Entamoeba histolytica.* Worldwide, amebiasis is very common, affecting about 500 million people. It is most common and severe in the tropics but is rare in Canada. In most cases, infection results from drinking water or eating food contaminated with the parasite, which is excreted in the feces of infected people. In severe cases, ulcers develop in the walls of the intestine, and the condition is then called amebic dysentery.

What are the symptoms?

Most infected people do not develop symptoms or have only mild, intermittent symptoms, which may include:

- Diarrhea.
- Mild abdominal pain.

If you develop amebic dysentery, the symptoms usually first appear between 5 days and several weeks after the initial infection. Symptoms may include:

- Watery, bloody diarrhea.
- Severe abdominal pain.
- Fever.

In some cases, dehydration and anemia (p.446) may develop. In addition, there is a risk of infection spreading through the bloodstream to the liver, causing high fever, painful liver abscesses, extreme fatigue, and loss of appetite.

What might be done?

Diagnosis of amebiasis is usually made from examination of a sample of feces under a microscope to look for the parasite. Your doctor may also arrange for you to have a blood test to look for antibodies that are produced by the body in response to the parasite. If your doctor suspects that you have liver abscesses, he or she will arrange for you to have imaging tests, such as CT scanning (p.247) or ultrasound scanning (p.250). Amebiasis can be successfully treated with antibiotics (p.885), which usually kill the parasite within a few days. With drug treatment, most affected people make a full recovery from the infection within a few weeks.

Can it be prevented?

There are several preventive measures you can take against amebiasis if you visit a region where the disease is common. You should drink only bottled or thoroughly boiled water to be certain that it is safe (*see* TRAVEL HEALTH, p.85). You should also avoid eating raw vegetables, salads, or fruits with skins that cannot be peeled because their skins may be contaminated with the parasite.

(WWW) ONLINE SITES: p.1030, p.1033, p.1037

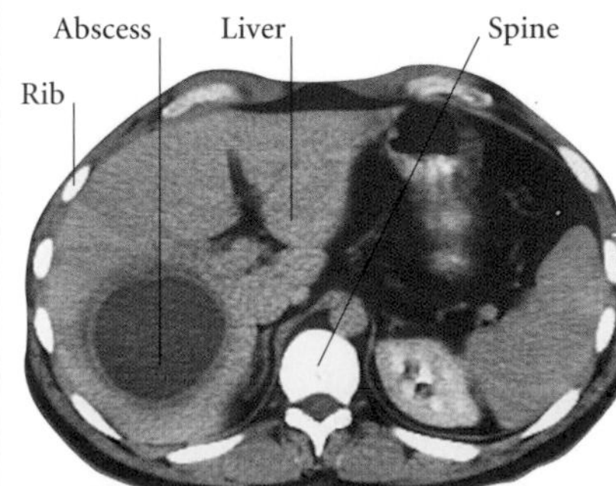
Abscess
Liver
Spine
Rib

Liver abscess due to amebiasis
In some people with amebiasis, infection spreads to the liver and forms an abscess, as seen in the CT scan above.

Giardiasis

An intestinal infection with a protozoal parasite, often leading to diarrhea

 AGE More common in early childhood

 LIFESTYLE Poor personal hygiene is a risk factor

 GENDER GENETICS Not significant factors

Giardiasis is caused by the minute parasite *Giardia lamblia,* which infects the small intestine. Cysts (dormant stages) of the parasite are excreted in the feces of infected people and animals. In most cases, the disease occurs as a result of drinking water contaminated with cysts. The infection may also spread as a result of poor personal hygiene.

Infections are more serious in people with reduced immunity due to disorders such as HIV infection and AIDS (p.295) or treatment with immunosuppressant drugs (p.906).

Giardiasis occurs mainly in developing countries. In developed countries, the infection usually affects children, hikers who drink from contaminated streams, and people who have returned from traveling in developing countries.

WHAT ARE THE SYMPTOMS?

Some people may not have symptoms, but, if symptoms do develop, they usually appear within 2 weeks of infection with the parasite and may include:

- Diarrhea.
- Excessive flatulence and belching.
- Bloating and abdominal pain.
- Nausea.

If the symptoms last longer than one week, the infection may cause damage to the lining of the small intestine, preventing the absorption of food and vitamins. If this happens, weight loss and, in some cases, the blood disorder anemia (p.446) may occur.

WHAT MIGHT BE DONE?

If your doctor suspects that you have giardiasis, you will probably be asked to provide a sample of feces, which will be examined for the parasite cysts. If no parasites are found but your doctor still suspects you have the disease from your symptoms, he or she may recommend that you undergo upper digestive tract endoscopy (p.641) to examine the inside of the small intestine. A sample of tissue or contents from the intestine may be removed during the procedure and examined under the microscope for evidence of infection. If giardiasis is diagnosed, your doctor will prescribe antibiotics (p.885), which usually kill the parasite in a few days. However, the infection may recur.

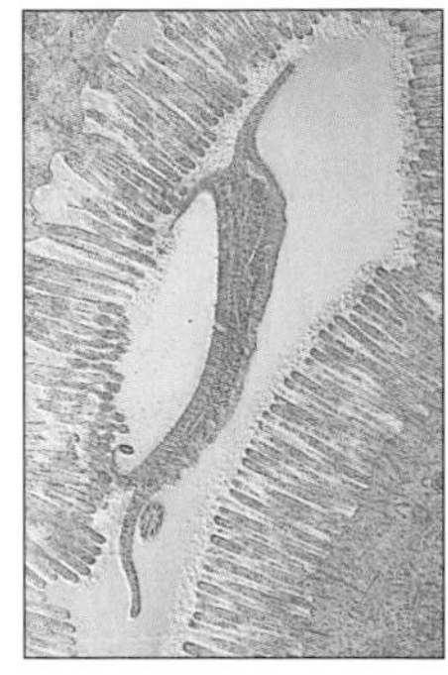

Parasite in body tissue *This highly magnified image shows the parasite* Giardia lamblia *in a sample of tissue taken from the small intestine of a person with giardiasis.*

CAN IT BE PREVENTED?

If you are visiting a region where giardiasis occurs, you can prevent infection by boiling your drinking water for at least 10 minutes to kill the cysts. You should also follow strict standards of personal hygiene, such as washing hands thoroughly after bowel movements and before preparing food, should help prevent the spread of the infection.

(WWW) ONLINE SITES: p.1030, p.1033, p.1037

Cryptosporidiosis

An intestinal infection caused by a protozoal parasite, often leading to watery diarrhea and fever

 AGE More common in children

 LIFESTYLE Poor personal hygiene is a risk factor

 GENDER GENETICS Not significant factors

Cryptosporidiosis is caused by a protozoal parasite known as *Cryptosporidium parvum.* It is an intestinal infection that is spread through contact with infected people or animals or by eating food or drinking water that has been contaminated with the parasite. Poor personal hygiene may help spread infection. The disease occurs throughout the world. In developed countries, local outbreaks may be due to contamination of reservoirs. Cryptosporidiosis is often severe in people with reduced immunity, such as those with AIDS (*see* HIV INFECTION AND AIDS, p.295). In the 1990s, cryptosporidiosis became a more common cause of diarrhea, especially in children.

In some cases, there are no symptoms. In other cases, watery diarrhea, abdominal pain, fever, nausea, and vomiting may develop about a week after infection. These symptoms usually last 7–10 days. People with reduced immunity may have chronic symptoms and develop severe malnutrition and dehydration, which can be fatal.

WHAT MIGHT BE DONE?

Cryptosporidiosis is usually diagnosed by examining a sample of feces under a microscope for the parasite. There is no effective treatment to cure this infection, but, if your symptoms are severe, you may need hospital treatment with intravenous fluids and antidiarrheal drugs (p.924). If a local outbreak of the disease occurs, you should boil all of your drinking water to kill the parasite.

(WWW) ONLINE SITES: p.1030 p.1033

Toxoplasmosis

A protozoal infection that causes serious illness in fetuses and people who have reduced immunity

 LIFESTYLE Contact with cats and eating raw or undercooked meat are risk factors

 AGE GENDER GENETICS Not significant factors

The protozoal infection toxoplasmosis is caused by *Toxoplasma gondii.* Cysts (dormant stages) of the parasite are excreted in the feces of cats and can be passed to people by direct contact with cats or by handling cat litter. Another source of infection is the raw or undercooked meat of animals that have eaten cysts from the feces of infected cats.

In most people, the infection does not cause symptoms because the protozoal cysts are dormant. However, people with reduced immunity, such as those with AIDS (*see* HIV INFECTION AND AIDS, p.295), may become seriously ill either from the initial infection or if dormant cysts are reactivated. If a woman develops toxoplasmosis while she is pregnant, the parasites may infect the fetus and cause abnormalities (*see* CONGENITAL INFECTIONS, p.817).

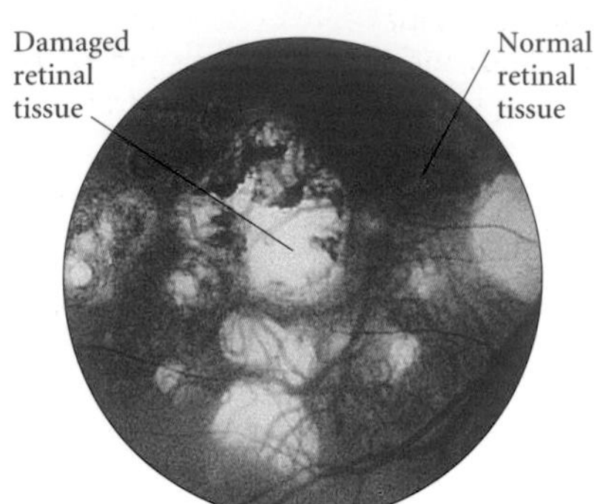
Damaged retinal tissue
Normal retinal tissue

Toxoplasmosis affecting the retina
Areas of damage, caused by the protozoan Toxoplasma gondii, *are visible in this view of the retina as seen through an ophthalmoscope (a viewing instrument).*

What are the symptoms?

Most otherwise healthy people do not develop symptoms. However, in some, mild symptoms appear 1–3 weeks after the initial infection and include:

- Painless, enlarged lymph nodes, usually in the neck.
- Fatigue.
- Fever and headache.

The heart, muscles, skin, and eyes may become damaged by the infection, and, in people with reduced immunity, it may affect the brain. In such cases, the symptoms may develop suddenly or over several weeks and include:

- Fever and headache.
- Paralysis affecting a limb or one side of the body.
- Partial loss of vision.
- Confusion.
- Lethargy.

In some people with reduced immunity, toxoplasmosis causes seizures. If a fetus is infected, toxoplasmosis may damage the eye and cause blindness.

What might be done?

Toxoplasmosis is diagnosed by microscopic examination of affected tissue or by blood tests. Usually, no treatment is necessary, although pyrimethamine (*see* ANTIMALARIAL DRUGS, p.888) and antibiotics (p.885) may be prescribed for people with reduced immunity or pregnant women. Those people with reduced immunity may need to take the drugs for life to prevent reactivation of cysts.

Infection can be prevented by avoiding contact with cats and by not eating undercooked or raw meat.

(WWW) ONLINE SITES: p.1033, p.1036

Pneumocystis infection

A parasitic infection that is a common cause of pneumonia in people with reduced immunity

 AGE GENDER GENETICS LIFESTYLE Not significant factors

People with reduced immunity, such as those who have AIDS (*see* HIV INFECTION AND AIDS, p.295) or those receiving chemotherapy (p.278), may develop a form of pneumonia called pneumocystis infection, caused by inhaling the *Pneumocystis carinii* parasite. In people with a healthy immune system, the parasite does not cause pneumonia. In developing countries, children who are malnourished often have the infection.

What are the symptoms?

The symptoms of pneumocystis infection generally develop gradually over weeks, but, in some people, they may develop quickly. Symptoms include:

- Fatigue and not feeling well.
- Fever.
- Dry cough.
- Shortness of breath on mild exertion.

As the infection progresses, shortness of breath may develop even at rest.

How is it diagnosed?

Pneumocystis infection is diagnosed by a physical examination, a chest X-ray (p.490), or by examining a sample of sputum for the parasite. Sometimes, the parasite is hard to isolate. In such cases, a bronchoscopy (p.504) may be performed. In this procedure, secretions in the bronchi (the main airways of the lungs) and/or a piece of lung tissue are removed and examined for evidence of pneumocystis infection.

What is the treatment?

Pneumocystis pneumonia is treated with antibiotics (p.885), initially administered intravenously, and then orally, for at least 3 weeks. Your doctor may also prescribe corticosteroids (p.930).

Once the infection clears up, you may need to continue taking low doses of antibiotics, depending on the cause of reduced immunity. If you have AIDS, you may remain on antibiotics for life. If you are undergoing chemotherapy, you may need to keep taking antibiotics until the therapy is finished.

What is the prognosis?

Fewer than 1 in 10 cases of initial pneumocystis infection is fatal. However, without treatment with preventive antibiotics, the infection may recur. In the developed world, many people with HIV infection or AIDS now receive preventive treatment with antibiotics for pneumocystis infection before their immunity becomes seriously impaired.

(WWW) ONLINE SITES: p.1032, p.1033, p.1034

Uncommon fungal infections

Rare fungal infections that occur only in certain regions of the world and can cause serious illness in otherwise healthy people

 LIFESTYLE Visiting or living in areas where the diseases occur are risk factors

 AGE GENDER GENETICS Not significant factors

Many types of fungi cause disease only in people with reduced immunity, such as those with AIDS (*see* HIV INFECTION AND AIDS, p.295). In such people, the fungi spread in the body and cause severe, often fatal illness. Certain rare fungi may also cause serious illness in people who are otherwise healthy. These fungi occur only in certain areas, including parts of Canada, and affect a large proportion of the population. However, only some people develop symptoms.

What are the types?

Described below are four examples of uncommon infections caused by fungi: histoplasmosis, coccidioidomycosis, blastomycosis, and cryptococcosis.

HISTOPLASMOSIS This disease, caused by *Histoplasma capsulatum,* occurs in parts of Canada, the US, and Africa. The fungus is found in soil or in bird and bat feces. People are infected by inhaling spores of the fungus, which may cause symptoms similar to tuberculosis (p.491), such as coughing and fever.

COCCIDIOIDOMYCOSIS Caused by the fungus *Coccidioides immitus,* this disease is also called San Joaquin fever. The fungus occurs in desert areas of the western US and parts of Central and South America. People are infected by inhaling airborne spores of the fungus, which then grow in the lungs, causing coughing and fever. They may produce holes in lung tissue and rarely spreads to other parts of the body.

BLASTOMYCOSIS This disease is caused by the fungus *Blastomyces dermatitidis* and occurs in various regions, including Canada. It may affect the skin, causing nonitchy spots that develop into ulcers with a distinct red margin. It may also affect the lungs, causing fever and cough. In some cases, the infection may cause painful bone swellings.

CRYPTOCOCCOSIS This disease is caused by the fungus *Cryptococcus neoformans*, which is inhaled into the lungs. It mainly affects the brain, causing headache and fever, but can also affect the skin, bones, and lungs.

WHAT MIGHT BE DONE?

Diagnosis is based on the presence of a particular fungus in blood, sputum, or cerebrospinal fluid or by detecting antibodies against the fungus in a blood sample. A chest X-ray (p.490) may also be done. MRI (p.248) of the brain is used to look for signs of cryptococcosis.

Often, no treatment is necessary. However, for severe infections, intravenous antifungal drugs (p.889) are needed. Most people recover fully, but an infection may be fatal for people with reduced immunity.

(WWW) ONLINE SITES: p.1033

Aspergillosis

A fungal infection that can affect the lungs and spread to other organs

 AGE GENDER GENETICS LIFESTYLE Not significant factors

Aspergillosis is caused by spores of the aspergillus fungus, which occur in dust, soil, and decaying plants. The spores are harmless if a healthy person inhales them, but they can cause illness in people who are allergic to them; in those with a chronic lung disease as a result of tuberculosis (p.491) or bronchiectasis (p.496); or in those with reduced immunity. In people who are allergic, the infection may cause symptoms similar to asthma (p.483). In people who already have lung damage, the fungi may grow into masses called "fungus balls" in cavities caused by the disease, and a cough, sometimes with bloody sputum, may develop. The fungus may spread to the brain in people with reduced immunity.

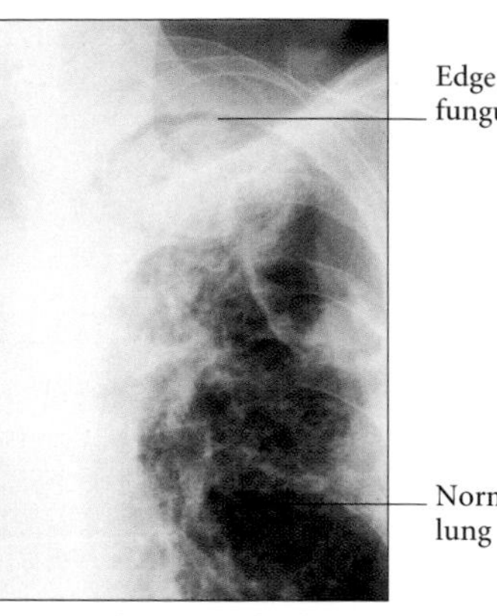
Edge of fungus ball
Normal lung

Aspergillosis in the lungs
In this X-ray, an aspergillus fungus ball can be seen. The fungus ball has formed in a cavity in the top of the lung.

Aspergillosis is diagnosed by testing a sputum sample for the fungi or by a blood test for antibodies. A chest X-ray (p.490) may also be done. Treatment includes antifungal drugs (p.889), but it may be necessary to remove a fungus ball surgically. Aspergillosis is sometimes fatal in people with impaired immunity.

(WWW) ONLINE SITES: p.1033, p.1036

Sporotrichosis

A fungal infection that may produce small lumps below the skin

 LIFESTYLE Working with plants is a risk factor

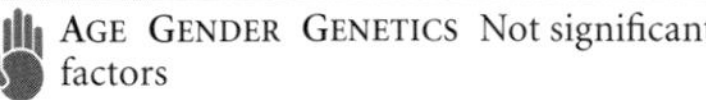 AGE GENDER GENETICS Not significant factors

The fungus that causes sporotrichosis, *Sporothrix schenkii*, normally grows on plants, especially moss and tree bark. Florists and gardeners are at risk of infection, which usually occurs when the fungus enters a wound in the skin. Sporotrichosis is most common in the US but is rare in Europe.

If a wound becomes infected with the fungus, a reddened, painless lump usually develops 1–3 months later. The infection may spread, producing small lumps beneath the skin around the wound. In people with reduced immunity, such as those with AIDS (*see* HIV INFECTION AND AIDS, p.295) or people taking immunosuppressants (p.906), the fungus may spread to other parts of the body, including the lungs and joints.

Diagnosis is usually obvious from the appearance of lumps below the skin and can be confirmed by a skin biopsy. In otherwise healthy people, the infection is usually treated with antifungal drugs (p.889). In some cases, the infection disappears by itself. If infection is widespread in people with reduced immunity, long-term treatment with antifungal drugs is necessary. In such cases, the disease can be difficult to eradicate.

(WWW) ONLINE SITES: p.1033

Candidiasis

A fungal yeast infection that usually affects only one part of the body but can be serious if it spreads around the body

LIFESTYLE Using intravenous drugs is a risk factor

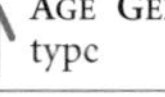 AGE GENDER Risk factors depend on the type

GENETICS Not a significant factor

In healthy people, the yeast *Candida albicans* normally exists on the surface of certain areas of the body, including the mouth, throat, and vagina. Sometimes, the fungus overgrows in localized areas, causing minor forms of candidiasis such as oral thrush (p.862) and vaginal yeast (p.752). In people with reduced immunity, such as those with AIDS (*see* HIV INFECTION AND AIDS, p.295) or diabetes mellitus (p.687), the fungus may spread into the blood and other tissues. Infection that spreads throughout the body may also affect people who have long-term urinary catheters or intravenous catheters, or people who have had prolonged courses of antibiotics or use intravenous drugs.

Widespread candidiasis may be diagnosed by culturing the fungus from a sample of blood or other body fluids or tissue specimens. A chest X-ray (p.490) may also be done to look for signs of infection in the lungs. Antifungal drugs (p.889) may be given either orally or intravenously, depending on the severity of the infection. Untreated, the infection can spread through the body and may eventually be fatal. The prognosis depends on the extent of infection and on the person's general health.

(WWW) ONLINE SITES: p.1033

Worm infestations

Most animals, including humans, can be infested with parasitic worms that derive all their nutrients from their hosts. Most of these worms live in the intestines for at least part of their life cycle. In many cases, worm infestations are chronic diseases that produce few symptoms in their early stages.

Various types of the family of worms known as roundworms can infest humans. Most affect only people in the developing world. However, some roundworms, such as pinworm, commonly affect people in developed countries. The first five articles in this section describe several types of roundworm infestation: pinworm infestation, toxocariasis, ascariasis, hookworm infestation, and tropical worm infestations, such as filariasis.

Infestations in humans that are caused by other types of worms known as flatworms, which include tapeworms and flukes, are covered in the last three articles on schistosomiasis, tapeworm infestation, and hydatid disease.

It is possible to acquire a tropical worm infestation abroad but not to experience symptoms until some months later. If you become ill after visiting the tropics, you should visit a doctor familiar with tropical diseases.

KEY ANATOMY

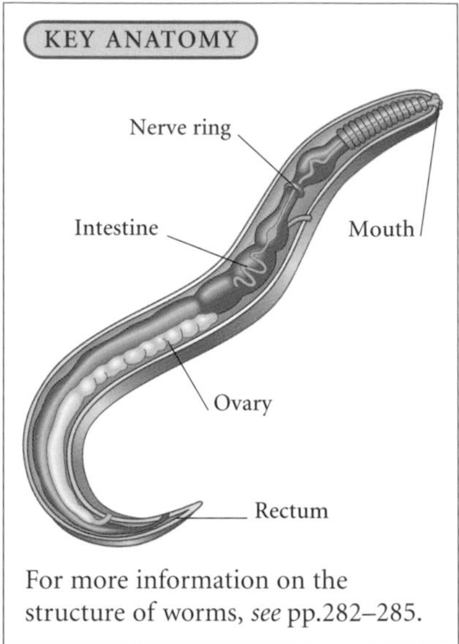
Nerve ring
Intestine
Mouth
Ovary
Rectum

For more information on the structure of worms, *see* pp.282–285.

Pinworm infestation

An infestation of thin worms that lay eggs around the anus, causing intense itching

AGE More common in children

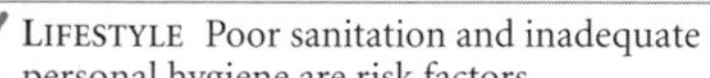
LIFESTYLE Poor sanitation and inadequate personal hygiene are risk factors

GENDER GENETICS Not significant factors

Pinworm infestation is caused by the roundworm *Enterobius vermicularis.* It is the most common parasitic worm infestation affecting humans in Canada. Infestation usually occurs by ingesting worm eggs in contaminated food, on fingers, or in house dust. If swallowed, the eggs develop into adult pinworms in the intestine. At night, female pinworms crawl out of the anus to lay eggs around the anal region, causing itching. Pinworm infestation is very common worldwide, especially in cold climates, and mainly affects children.

What are the symptoms?

In most cases, the symptoms of pinworm infestation include:

- Intense itching in the anal region at night when the worms lay eggs.
- Inflammation of the anus as a result of constant scratching.
- In some cases, mild abdominal pain.

Sometimes tiny white pinworms can be seen wriggling in the feces after a bowel movement. In rare cases, a pinworm infestation causes appendicitis (p.664).

What might be done?

Diagnosis can be confirmed by identification of pinworm eggs in a swab taken from the anal region. Your doctor will probably prescribe a single dose of an anthelmintic drug (p.889) to kill the worms effectively and speed recovery. In most cases, the entire household is treated, and the treatment is repeated after 2 weeks. However, reinfection is common because eggs can be picked up under the fingernails by scratching and then accidentally swallowed, so that the cycle of infestation begins once again. Underwear, nightwear, and bed linen may also become contaminated.

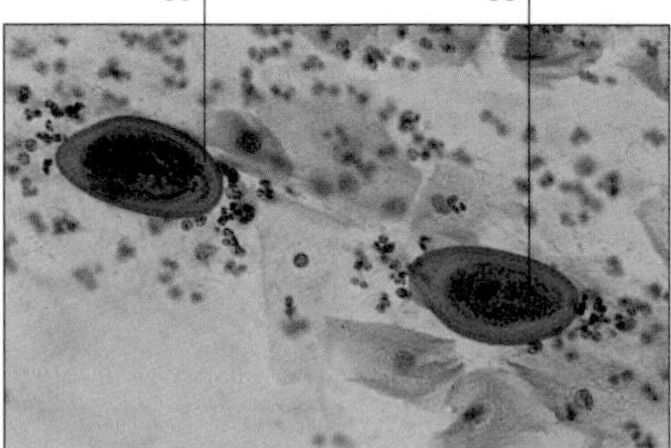
Pinworm egg
Larva inside egg

Pinworm eggs

Adult pinworms infest the intestine and emerge from the anus at night to lay eggs in the anal region, causing itching. Larvae can be seen inside the magnified eggs above.

Pinworm infestation is usually easy to control. It is possible to reduce the risk of reinfection by paying careful attention to personal hygiene, such as not scratching the anal area, washing hands after going to the toilet, and regularly washing clothes and bed linen.

(WWW) ONLINE SITES: p.1033

Toxocariasis

The infestation of various organs with roundworm larvae, which may cause fever

AGE More common in children

LIFESTYLE Owning pet dogs or cats may be a risk factor

GENDER GENETICS Not significant factors

The adults of the roundworms *Toxocara canis* and *Toxocara cati* normally infest dogs and cats, which excrete feces containing worm eggs. However, the larvae (immature forms) of the worms can infest humans, usually as a result of ingestion of soil contaminated with worm eggs. Children are particularly susceptible to the infestation because they are more likely to play in soil and then put their fingers in their mouths.

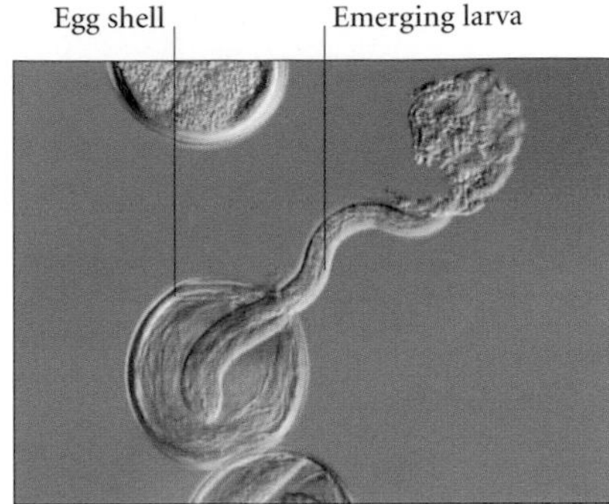
Egg shell
Emerging larva

Toxocariasis
A larva (immature form) of the worm that causes the disease toxocariasis can be seen in this highly magnified image. The larva has just hatched from the egg.

Once the eggs have been swallowed, they hatch in the intestine into tiny larvae, which may then migrate to other parts of the body, including the lungs and liver. In rare cases, the larvae can migrate to the eyes and the brain.

What are the symptoms?

In most cases of toxocariasis, symptoms do not develop. However, in some cases, symptoms may include:

- Mild fever.
- Not feeling well.

A heavy infestation of the larvae in the lungs may cause wheezing and a dry cough. If larvae reach the brain, they may cause epilepsy (p.524), and infestation of the eyes may damage the retina (the light-sensitive membrane at the back of the eye), causing temporary or permanent blindness (p.591).

What might be done?

If your doctor suspects that you or your child has toxocariasis, he or she may arrange for a blood test to confirm the diagnosis. Most people recover completely from the infestation without needing treatment. However, your doctor may prescribe an anthelmintic drug (p.889) to kill the worms. In severe cases in which the brain is affected, anticonvulsant drugs (p.914) will probably be given. Brain or eye damage due to toxocariasis is usually permanent.

It is important to deworm pets regulary to prevent toxocariasis, and dogs or cats should be prevented from defecating in places where children are likely to play, such as in a sandbox.

(WWW) ONLINE SITES: p.1033

Ascariasis

An intestinal roundworm infestation that may cause diarrhea and abdominal pain

AGE More common in children

LIFESTYLE Poor sanitation and inadequate personal hygiene are risk factors

GENDER GENETICS Not significant factors

The roundworm *Ascaris lumbricoides* is responsible for ascariasis, one of the most common parasitic infestations of humans. About 1 in 4 people in the world has ascariasis at some time in his or her life. The disease is most common in tropical and subtropical areas, and children are usually affected more often than adults. Ascariasis is rare in developed countries, such as Canada.

People usually become infested with roundworms by eating food or drinking water contaminated with the worm eggs. Poor sanitation, the use of human excrement as fertilizer, and inadequate personal hygiene all help spread this infestation among humans. Once swallowed, the eggs hatch into larvae in the intestine. The larvae then travel in the blood to the lungs and later return to the intestine, where they develop into adults, breed, and lay eggs.

What are the symptoms?

In most cases, ascariasis does not cause symptoms. However, in large numbers, the roundworms may cause:

- Diarrhea.
- Abdominal pain.

Worm larvae in the lungs may cause wheezing and coughing. A large number of worms in the intestine may cause appendicitis (p.664) or a blockage (*see* INTESTINAL OBSTRUCTION, p.663).

What might be done?

Ascariasis is usually diagnosed by identification of worm eggs in a sample of feces or of the worm itself, which is pale pink with a long cylindrical body approximately 8–12 in (20–30 cm) in length. In most cases, treatment involves taking a single dose of an anthelmintic drug (p.889) to kill the worms. However, the infestation will recur if roundworm eggs are swallowed again after treatment.

(WWW) ONLINE SITES: p.1033

Hookworm infestation

An infestation of small, blood-sucking roundworms that may cause abdominal pain, cough, and fever

AGE More common in children

LIFESTYLE Poor sanitation and inadequate personal hygiene are risk factors

GENDER GENETICS Not significant factors

The two main species of hookworms that can infest humans are *Ancylostoma duodenale* and *Necator americanus.* People are usually infested by direct contact with hookworm larvae (immature forms of the worm), which live in soil and can penetrate human skin. The larvae travel in the bloodstream to the lungs and trachea (windpipe) and then to the intestines, where they develop into adult worms that may reach 1/2 in (1 cm) in length. The adults attach to the intestinal wall by hooklike teeth and feed by sucking blood from the wall. Female worms lay eggs, which pass out in the feces of an affected person and develop into larvae in the soil.

Poor sanitation, inadequate personal hygiene, and the use of human feces as fertilizer may increase the spread of the disorder. Hookworm is very common in tropical areas, affecting up to 1 in 2 people, especially children, at any one time. In the US, people with hookworm have almost always become infested abroad by walking barefoot in water contaminated by sewage.

What are the symptoms?

In the early stages of hookworm infestation, the only symptom may be an itchy rash at the site where the larvae have pierced the skin. As the infestation progresses, symptoms may include:

- Dry cough and mild fever due to the presence of larvae in the lungs.

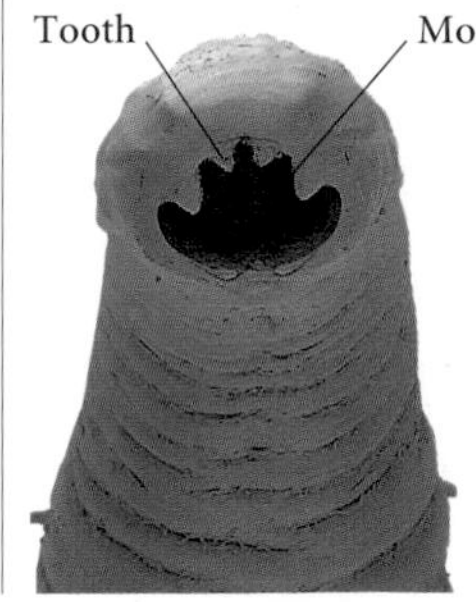
Tooth
Mouth

Hookworm
This magnified image shows the mouth of a hookworm. The "teeth" attach the worm to the wall of the intestine.

- Abdominal pain due to the presence of worms in the intestines.

Left untreated, large numbers of worms in the intestines may cause gradual, heavy blood loss, which may lead to iron-deficiency anemia (p.447). If the anemia is severe, it may in turn cause chronic heart failure (p.413).

WHAT MIGHT BE DONE?

Your doctor will arrange for a sample of your feces to be examined for worm eggs if he or she suspects hookworm infestation. You will be given anthelmintic drugs (p.889) to kill the worms and, if anemia has developed, iron supplements. Rarely, if the anemia is severe, a blood transfusion (p.447) is necessary.

In order to prevent hookworm infestation when traveling in tropical and subtropical regions, you should wear waterproof shoes in villages and other populated areas if the ground is wet.

(WWW) ONLINE SITES: p.1033

Tropical worm infestations

Diseases caused by parasitic roundworms that are widespread in tropical regions

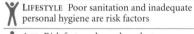

LIFESTYLE Poor sanitation and inadequate personal hygiene are risk factors

AGE Risk factors depend on the type

GENDER GENETICS Not significant factors

Parasitic worms that infest humans are most common in tropical and subtropical regions. Poor sanitation contributes to their spread. Tropical worm infestations are very rare in Canada and usually occur only in people who have visited or lived in the tropics. However, one infestation, trichinosis, also occurs in Canada, especially among northern people.

WHAT ARE THE TYPES?

There are four main types of roundworm infestations that normally affect only people in tropical and subtropical regions, such as Central and South America, Africa, and Southeast Asia.

TRICHINOSIS This disease is caused by a tiny worm called *Trichinella spiralis.* People usually become infested by eating undercooked pork containing cysts (larval stages of the worm). In severe cases, symptoms may include vomiting, diarrhea, abdominal and muscle pains, and fever. In some cases, trichinosis can cause acute heart failure (p.412) or an illness similar to meningitis (p.527).

STRONGYLOIDIASIS The minute worm *Strongyloides stercoralis* causes this condition. Infestation is usually a result of walking barefoot on soil contaminated with larvae. If severe, infestation may result in abdominal pain and diarrhea between periods of constipation and weight loss. Infestations may be present for years without causing symptoms, but symptoms will appear if immunity becomes reduced due to conditions such as HIV infection (*see* HIV INFECTION AND AIDS, p.295).

FILARIASIS Various types of worms or their larvae cause filariasis. The parasites are transmitted to people by certain blood-sucking insects. Different parts of the body are affected, depending on the type of worm. A severe infestation with some types may lead to a massive, painful, disfiguring swelling in the limbs or in the scrotum known as elephantiasis. Infestation with a type of worm known as *Onchocerca volvulus* may result in blindness (p.591).

TRICHURIASIS This infestation is due to *Trichuris trichuria,* also known as whipworm, and it is most common in children. People become infested when they ingest worm eggs. Adult worms live in the intestines, and a severe case of trichuriasis may cause bloody diarrhea, abdominal pain, and weight loss.

WHAT MIGHT BE DONE?

The diagnosis depends on the type of worm but is usually confirmed when eggs, larvae, or adult worms are found in a sample of feces, blood, or tissue. Treatment also varies with the infestation, but anthelmintic drugs (p.889) are commonly prescribed. Most people make a full recovery if treated early, but reinfection is common in tropical countries. Preventive measures include not walking barefoot on soil, not eating undercooked meat or other foods that may be contaminated, and using insect repellents and mosquito nets.

(WWW) ONLINE SITES: p.1033

Schistosomiasis

An infestation of flukes that can damage the liver and bladder

AGE More common in children

LIFESTYLE Swimming in freshwater containing infested snails is a risk factor

GENDER GENETICS Not significant factors

People who bathe in lakes, canals, or unchlorinated freshwater pools in the tropics are at risk of schistosomiasis, also known as bilharzia. The disease is caused by any of five species of flukes (types of flatworms) of the schistosoma group. Freshwater snails release larvae (immature forms) of the parasite, which can penetrate the skin of bathers. Once inside the body, the parasites mature into adults, and the females lay eggs, which may cause inflammation. Schistosomiasis affects about 200 million people worldwide, mainly in developing countries. People in Canada become infested only when visiting tropical regions.

WHAT ARE THE SYMPTOMS?

The symptoms of schistosomiasis vary depending on the species of fluke. Most people experience itching (known as "swimmer's itch") at the site where the parasite has entered the skin. The itching usually occurs within a day of exposure to the parasite. Some people may have no further symptoms, whereas others may develop them within 4–6 weeks. Symptoms may include:

- Fever.
- Muscle pains.
- Diarrhea.
- Coughing and vomiting.
- A burning sensation when urinating and an increased need to urinate.

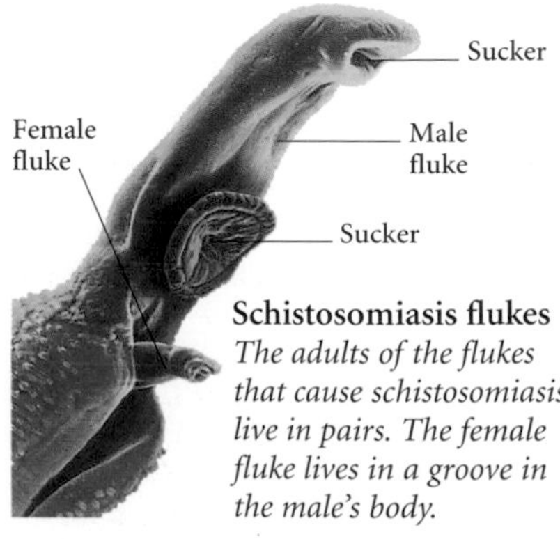
Sucker
Female fluke
Male fluke
Sucker

Schistosomiasis flukes
The adults of the flukes that cause schistosomiasis live in pairs. The female fluke lives in a groove in the male's body.

- Blood in the urine, especially at the end of the stream.

Without treatment, schistosomiasis may eventually damage the liver or the urinary system. In many cases, the damage is life-threatening. A chronic, untreated infestation may lead to colorectal cancer (p.665) and bladder tumors (p.715).

WHAT MIGHT BE DONE?

Schistosomiasis is usually diagnosed by finding fluke eggs in a sample of either urine or feces. Sometimes, the condition is diagnosed by a rectal biopsy, in which a sample of tissue is taken from the rectum and examined under a microscope for eggs. The biopsy is usually accompanied by a blood test to look for antibodies that the body produces against the parasite. In most cases, the infestation is treated with an anthelmintic drug (p.889), which is usually effective in killing the worms. Schistosomiasis can be prevented by not swimming or wading in freshwater in the regions of the world where the infestation is known to occur.

(WWW) ONLINE SITES: p.1033

Tapeworm infestation

An intestinal infestation of ribbon-shaped parasitic flatworms that may cause abdominal pain and diarrhea

LIFESTYLE Eating raw or undercooked meat or fish is a risk factor

AGE GENDER GENETICS Not significant factors

The adults of three types of large tapeworms infest humans. These worms are the pork tapeworm (*Taenia solium*), the beef tapeworm (*Taenia saginata*), and the fish tapeworm (*Diphyllobothrium latum*). Infestation usually occurs by eating raw or undercooked meat or fish that contains larvae (immature stages of the worms). Once in the intestines, the worms mature into adults, which may reach 20–30 ft (6–9 m) in length. Tapeworm eggs are passed out in the feces and, in the case of pork tapeworm, may cause reinfection. Certain other species of tapeworms may live as slow-growing larval cysts in humans (*see* HYDATID DISEASE, right).

Pork and beef tapeworm infestations occur most commonly in developing countries. Fish tapeworm infestation is most common in regions where raw fish dishes, such as sushi, are popular. These regions include Eastern Europe, Scandinavia, and Japan.

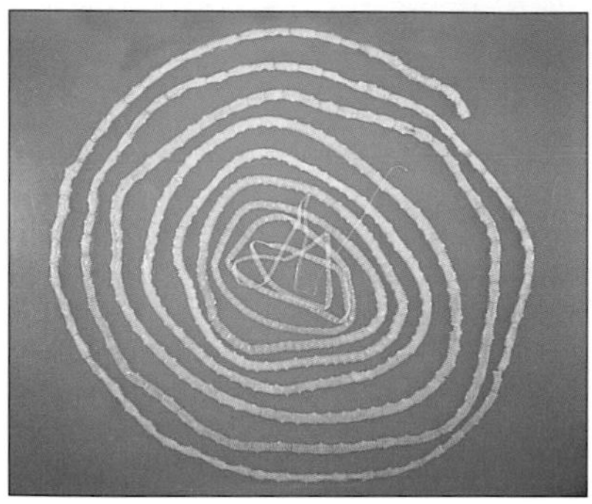

Tapeworm
This coiled beef tapeworm was removed from a human intestine, where it had grown to several feet in length.

WHAT ARE THE SYMPTOMS?

In many people, a tapeworm infestation does not produce any symptoms. However, you may experience:

- Mild abdominal pain.
- Diarrhea.
- In beef and pork tapeworm infestations, an increase in appetite.

If you are infested with beef tapeworm, you may feel segments of the worm wriggling out of your anus. Rarely, fish tapeworms may cause the blood disorder megaloblastic anemia (p.448).

A disorder called cysticercosis may develop if pork tapeworm eggs enter the stomach, either after eating food contaminated with eggs or if an adult worm in the intestine lays eggs that travel to the stomach. Larvae hatch from the eggs and migrate to the intestine. They burrow through the intestinal wall and travel around the body in the blood. Epilepsy (p.524) may result if larvae reach the brain, and, if they infest the eyes, they may cause blindness (p.591).

WHAT MIGHT BE DONE?

A diagnosis is made if tapeworm segments or eggs are present in the feces. To kill the worms, a single dose of an anthelmintic drug (p.889) is prescribed. Tapeworm infestation can be prevented by freezing or cooking meat and fish thoroughly. To prevent reinfection and cysticercosis, wash your hands carefully after a bowel movement.

(WWW) ONLINE SITES: p.1033

Hydatid disease

A rare infestation of tapeworm cysts that may affect the liver, lungs, or bones

AGE Infestation usually occurs in children but normally becomes apparent in adults

LIFESTYLE Owning pet dogs may be a risk factor

GENDER GENETICS Not significant factors

Infestation with cysts that contain the larvae (immature stages) of the tapeworm *Echinococcus granulosus* is called hydatid disease. The cyst stage of the worm normally affects livestock such as sheep. If a dog eats raw offal containing a cyst, the larvae mature into egg-laying adults in the dog's intestines. Worm eggs pass out in the dog's feces and can be transmitted to humans who eat food that has been contaminated with eggs. The eggs hatch into larvae when they reach the human intestine. The larvae then move to different parts of the body, such as the liver, lungs, and bones, where they develop into slow-growing cysts up to 8 in (20 cm) in diameter.

Hydatid disease is rare in Canada. It is usually found in people who have lived in areas where sheepdogs are used, such as Australia and New Zealand.

WHAT ARE THE SYMPTOMS?

Infestation mainly occurs in childhood, but symptoms may not develop until adulthood because the hydatid cysts are so slow-growing. In many cases, there are no symptoms. However, a hydatid cyst in the liver may cause:

- Pain.
- Nausea.
- Yellowing of the skin and whites of the eyes (*see* JAUNDICE, p.643).

A cyst in the lungs may lead to chest pain and coughing, and a cyst in bone may cause pain and fractures (p.392) in the long bones of the limbs.

WHAT MIGHT BE DONE?

Diagnosis is made from the symptoms and by ultrasound scanning (p.250) or X-rays (p.244). The larvae can be killed by an anthelmintic drug (p.889), but surgery is needed to remove the cysts. The spread of hydatid disease can be stopped by deworming dogs regularly and by not feeding them raw offal.

(WWW) ONLINE SITES: p.1033

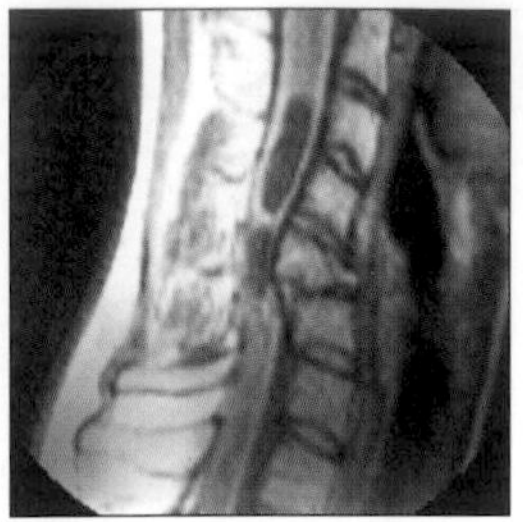

Cervical spine CT scan
This CT scan shows a fractured cervical spine (broken neck), a serious injury after a fall from a height. Such an injury can result in death or cause irreversible paralysis affecting either the whole or parts of the body.

Serious Injuries and Environmental Disorders

Most people know somebody who has experienced a potentially fatal injury or accident, even if they have not been involved in one themselves. Susceptibility to injury is linked to lifestyle, environment, and gender, with more than twice as many men as women sustaining a life-threatening injury. Age is also an important factor, and statistics show that most injuries and accidents tend to happen in adolescence and early adulthood.

Motor vehicle collisions are the major cause of serious injury in North America. In Canada, they account for more than 230,000 injuries and 3,000 deaths each year. In the US, they account for more than 40,000 deaths each year. Many of these deaths are linked to drug and alcohol abuse.

Poisoning is another common cause of death by injury, usually as a result of drug overdose. Many poisoning-related deaths are suicides; these figures are highest in people in middle age.

During childhood, motor vehicle collisions are the leading cause of injury and death, and the numbers of deaths rise dramatically in late adolescence. In babies, a leading cause of death is suffocation caused by choking, while children between age 4 and 8 are more likely to drown or sustain burns possibly leading to death.

Illness and injury that result from environmental factors, such as heat and low temperatures, are becoming much more common. Disorders such as frostbite, hypothermia, and mountain sickness occur when young people, in particular, take risks on vacations in remote areas with extreme climates.

Hypothermia is a particular threat to elderly people because the natural defenses and ability to control body temperature become less effective with old age. However, the most common serious injury in people in old age is a fracture caused by a fall. Weakening of the bones as a result of osteoporosis makes elderly people more susceptible; as many as 1 in 5 people over the age of 80 fractures a bone.

Some accident statistics indicate improving trends. For example, motor vehicle safety features, such as airbags, and the use of seat belts are improving the survival rates for motor vehicle collisions. The medical management of serious injuries has also improved. Paramedics are now able to provide resuscitation at the scene of accidents, patients are taken to the hospital more quickly, critical care units have more effective procedures for dealing with multiple injuries and shock, and trauma centers that specialize in the treatment of patients who are seriously ill have been established.

DATA Death from Motor Vehicle Collisions in Canada

In Canada, more than 3,000 people die every year from injuries resulting from motor vehicle collisions. Death and injury is highest in the age groups 15–19 and 20–24, with almost double the number of deaths occurring in comparison with the general population. More men than women suffer fatal injuries as a result of motor vehicle collisions.

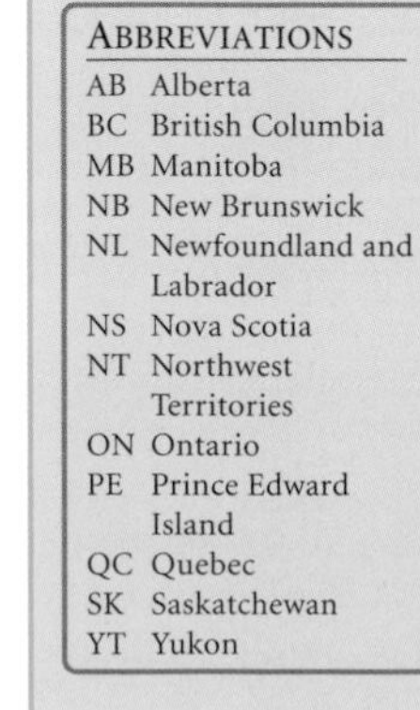

ABBREVIATIONS

AB	Alberta
BC	British Columbia
MB	Manitoba
NB	New Brunswick
NL	Newfoundland and Labrador
NS	Nova Scotia
NT	Northwest Territories
ON	Ontario
PE	Prince Edward Island
QC	Quebec
SK	Saskatchewan
YT	Yukon

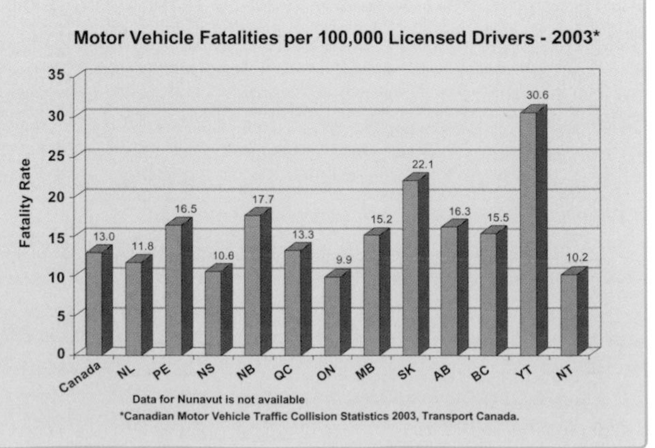
Motor Vehicle Fatalities per 100,000 Licensed Drivers - 2003*
Fatality Rate
35
30
25
20
15
10
5
0
13.0
11.8
16.5
10.6
17.7
13.3
9.9
15.2
22.1
16.3
15.5
30.6
10.2
Canada
NL
PE
NS
NB
QC
ON
MB
SK
AB
BC
YT
NT
Data for Nunavut is not available
*Canadian Motor Vehicle Traffic Collision Statistics 2003, Transport Canada.

Motor vehicle collision-related deaths throughout Canada
Provincial rates for deaths caused by motor vehicle collisions vary widely, with the greatest number found in the Yukon.

DATA SERIOUS INJURIES TO THE BODY

The nature and location of an injury determines its severity. For example, crush injuries to the torso tend to be more serious than those to the limbs because they may damage internal organs. The severity of penetrating injuries depends on the precise location of the wounds and whether major organs or blood vessels are involved. Poisoning and drowning usually affect entire systems and may damage several vital organs.

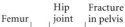

Frostbite of the toes
When toes or fingers freeze, circulation is interrupted, causing damage to tissue. Sometimes, especially when immediate treatment is delayed, amputation will be necessary.

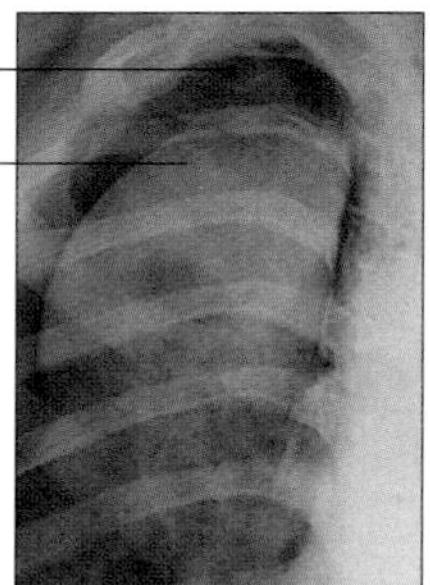
Air outside lung
Collapsed lung

Collapsed lung
This X-ray shows air between the lung and the chest wall following an injury. The lung has collapsed.

Brain
The brain may be damaged when a blow to the head causes internal bleeding and swelling

Skull
The skull is susceptible to fractures. Bone fragments may damage the brain beneath

Trachea (windpipe)
If the trachea is crushed or obstructed by a foreign body, asphyxia (a potentially fatal lack of oxygen) may result

Lung
A lung may collapse following a penetrating wound or become inflamed by inhaled gases or smoke in an accident or fire

Heart
The heart may be directly damaged by physical injuries, such as a stab wound, or its function may be impaired by toxic substances such as in a drug overdose

Spleen
The spleen may rupture when crushed or following a severe blow to the abdomen, resulting in severe internal bleeding

Liver
When the liver is injured by a cut or a blow, a large amount of blood may be lost. Drug overdoses may also damage the liver

Spine
If the spine is injured, the vertebrae may be fractured or displaced and damage the spinal cord, causing paralysis or death

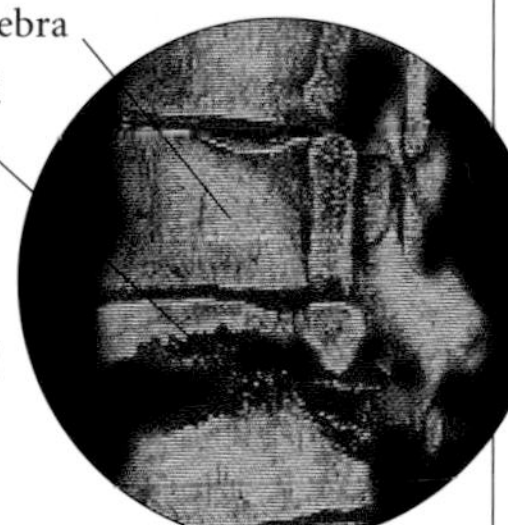
Normal vertebra
Fractured vertebra

Fractured vertebra
This 3D CT scan shows a fractured vertebra in side view. Part of the bone is displaced.

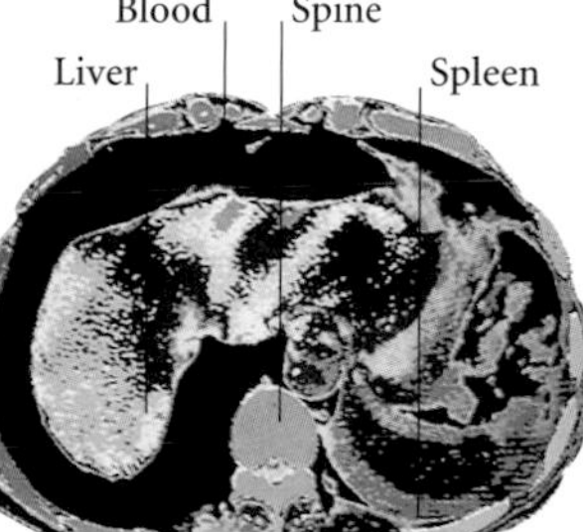
Blood
Spine
Liver
Spleen

Ruptured spleen
The spleen and liver on this CT scan are surrounded by blood. The bleeding is from the spleen, which has been ruptured by a severe blow.

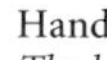

Hand
The hands are vulnerable to injury. In an accident, fingers may be severed, or the skin and tendons may be damaged

Kidney
A lacerated kidney may leak urine into the surrounding tissue, which causes inflammation. An injury that tears the kidney from its blood supply causes profuse bleeding

Skin
The skin's protective layer may be damaged by a burn. Large amounts of body fluids may be lost from the circulation, leading to potentially fatal shock

Intestines
If the intestinal wall is damaged, the contents may leak into the abdomen, causing serious infection

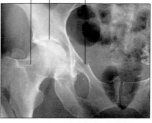

Artery
Bleeding from a severed artery is profuse and life-threatening

Toes
Toes may be crushed or severed by heavy objects. Severe frostbite of the toes may lead to gangrene

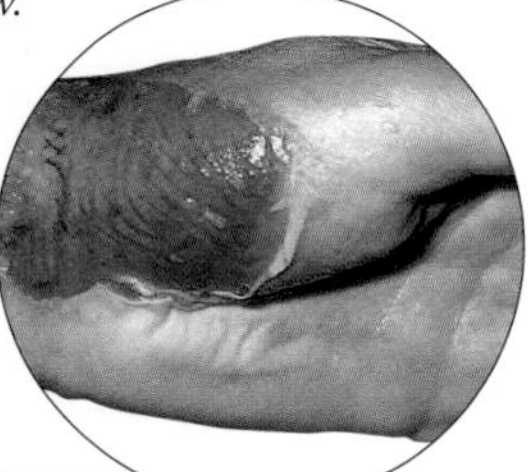

Severe burn
Here, the inside of the wrist has been badly burned. The overlying skin has been lost, leaving a red, raw area.

Femur
Hip joint
Fracture in pelvis

Fractured pelvis
A pelvic fracture can be clearly seen in the X-ray. This type of injury may be caused by a fall.

SERIOUS INJURIES

Injuries can affect any part of the body, but they are most often serious if they affect the head, chest, or abdomen. Such injuries may be the result of an accident or a deliberate act of violence by another person. In addition to their physical impact, serious injuries may have long-term psychological and emotional effects.

This section starts by describing crush injuries, which are the most common form of serious injury and often result from a motor vehicle collision. The number of deaths in Canada from motor vehicle collisions has fallen in recent years, mainly as a result of improved vehicle design and the mandatory use of seatbelts. The next article covers gunshot injuries, which are not common in Canada but can be very serious if they occur.

Stab injuries, covered next, can be deceptive. The skin wound may appear small, yet the internal wound may be very serious. The remaining topics covered in this section deal with more common causes of serious injuries. Burns are extremely common and may result from a wide variety of accidents. Most burns are due to minor accidents around the home. Severe burns often occur in industrial environments and may result in permanent scarring or even death. Electrical injuries are a specific form of burn injury, often causing damage to internal tissues that may not be initially apparent. Such injuries may occur within the home but are often a result of an accident in the electrical or construction industry.

Sexual assault is regarded as one of the most complex serious injuries and may be associated with severe physical injuries. Sexually transmitted diseases may also be contracted, and it may take many years to recover from the effects of the emotional trauma.

Injuries that are specific to one area of the body are covered elsewhere (*see* HEAD INJURIES, p.521, SPINAL INJURIES, p.524, MUSCULOSKELETAL INJURIES, pp.391–395, and EYE INJURIES, p.582).

Crush injuries

Injury to any part of the body caused by compression, most frequently as a result of a motor vehicle collision

 GENDER More common in males

 LIFESTYLE Risk factors depend on the cause

 AGE GENETICS Not significant factors

Crush injuries are most often caused by motor vehicle collisions. In Canada, 10 people per 100,000 of the population die each year in motor vehicle collisions. Accidents in the construction industry, explosions, and falls can also cause compression injuries to any part of the body. These injuries may range in severity from simple bruising to life-threatening damage of internal organs and tissues. Persons who work in the construction business and those who participate in high risk activities are at greatest risk.

WHAT ARE THE TYPES?

Most damage sustained by crushing is internal, and often the only obvious external evidence is bruising. Fractures (p.392) are common, especially to the limbs, and, if the chest is crushed, one or more ribs are likely to be broken and may puncture the lungs. Multiple rib fractures may impair normal breathing. Crush injuries may also lead to a pneumothorax (p.496), in which air is trapped between the two-layered membrane covering the lungs. Damage to the heart can also occur.

If the abdomen has been crushed, the intestines, liver, spleen, or kidneys may be damaged. The contents of a ruptured intestine may leak out into the abdominal cavity and cause an infection (*see* PERITONITIS, p.665). If the spleen or the liver is ruptured, massive internal bleeding may occur.

In addition to specific injuries, more general complications may occur. For example, if a large proportion of the body's tissues is crushed, chemicals released from the damaged tissue may impair kidney function (*see* KIDNEY FAILURE, p.705), which may be fatal.

WHAT MIGHT BE DONE?

Anyone who might possibly have a crush injury should be freed as soon as possible and receive emergency first aid (*see* FIRST AID: ABC OF RESUSCITATION, p.978). If it is possible, an ambulance should be called while first aid is being performed. Once the person reaches the hospital, the treatment depends on the injuries. General measures include emergency resuscitation and the giving of both oxygen and intravenous fluids. Analgesics (p.912) are given as needed, in addition to a blood transfusion (p.447) if bleeding is excessive.

After emergency measures have been carried out, internal damage is assessed using imaging techniques, such as chest X-rays (p.490), CT scanning (p.247), and MRI (p.248). Treatment is then directed at specific injuries. For example, fractures are treated by resetting the broken bones in their correct position and immobilizing the affected part if needed (*see* FRACTURE TREATMENTS, p.393). If limbs are crushed, surgery may be required to repair blood vessels and nerves (*see* MICROSURGERY, p.950). An amputation may be necessary if limb damage is irreparable. A person

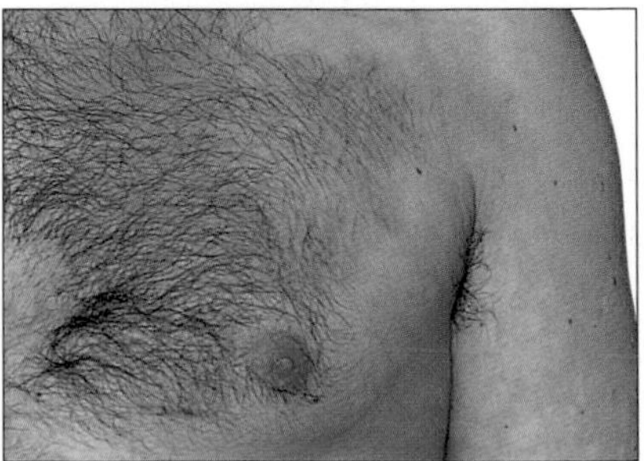

Crush injury
Skin bruising may be the only visible sign of a crush injury. Damage from a crush injury is often internal and may be life-threatening.

with multiple rib fractures may require mechanical ventilation to help breathing (see CRITICAL CARE UNIT, p.958).

If internal bleeding into the abdominal cavity is suspected, a CT scan or a procedure called peritoneal lavage may be performed. A small tube is inserted into the abdominal cavity, and sterile fluid is then introduced into the abdomen. The fluid is then withdrawn, and, if blood is present, surgery is carried out to look for the source of bleeding and to repair it (see ENDOSCOPIC SURGERY, p.948).

Antibiotics (p.885) are prescribed to treat peritonitis and other infections. Additional complications, such as kidney failure, are treated if they arise.

The prognosis depends on the type of injuries, the length of time that the person was crushed, and the speed with which treatment was initiated.

WWW ONLINE SITES: p.1036

Gunshot injuries

Injuries to any part of the body inflicted by a bullet or shotgun pellets

 GENDER More common in males

 LIFESTYLE Hunting as recreation

 AGE GENETICS Not significant factors

Gunshot injuries are not common in Canada, as there are strict gun control laws which restrict gun ownership. However, hunting is a recreational sport in many rural areas. As well, gun ownership is important in rural areas to protect livestock. Guns are often kept in homes, and may lead to unintentional injuries if not stored securely.

The effects of a gunshot injury depend on the site of the injury, the type of weapon and bullets used, and the range from which the weapon was fired. In addition to tissue damage, there is a high risk of infection. Often, wounds to the head or trunk are life-threatening.

WHAT ARE THE TYPES?

A gunshot injury to a limb may damage muscle or cause a fracture (p.392). Damage to vital organs may be life-threatening. For example, a gunshot injury to the chest will probably cause breathing difficulties and may result in a collapsed lung or pneumothorax

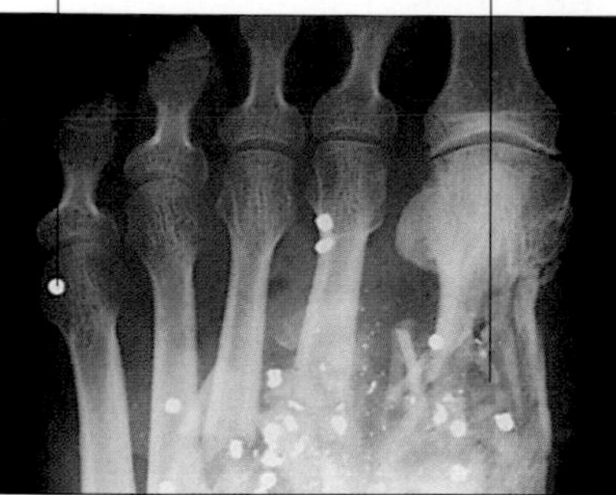
Shotgun pellet
Shattered bone

Gunshot injury
Multiple shotgun pellets can be seen in and between the bones of the toes and foot in this X-ray. The bone at the base of the big toe is also shattered.

(p.496). If the spleen or the liver is damaged, life-threatening bleeding may occur, leading to loss of consciousness and shock (p.414). A gunshot injury to the intestines may cause their contents to leak into the abdominal cavity, which can cause infection (see PERITONITIS, p.665). Gunshot injuries to the heart or the brain are often fatal.

WHAT CAN I DO?

If you are with someone who has been shot, check his or her responsiveness (see FIRST AID: ABC OF RESUSCITATION, p.978) and call an ambulance immediately or ask a bystander to do so. Do not leave the victim alone. Try to stop external bleeding by applying pressure to the affected area (see FIRST AID: SEVERE BLEEDING, p.986). If shock develops, initiate first-aid measures (see FIRST AID: SHOCK, p.987).

WHAT MIGHT THE DOCTOR DO?

Anyone with a gunshot injury needs to be taken to the hospital. Initial measures may include controlling bleeding and administering oxygen and intravenous fluids. If a lot of blood has been lost, a blood transfusion (p.447) may be needed. An injection to prevent tetanus (see VACCINES AND IMMUNOGLOBULINS, p.883) and antibiotics (p.885) to prevent infection are given if necessary.

Following initial measures, the extent of internal tissue damage is investigated using imaging techniques, such as chest X-rays (p.490) and CT scanning (p.247). Almost all gunshot injuries require surgery to repair damaged organs and remove fragments of the bullet, shreds of clothing, and other debris in the wound. Once the wound has been cleaned and bleeding has been stopped, the wound is covered with sterile gauze for 4–5 days to help prevent infection. The wound is then closed.

Specific injuries may need additional treatment. For example, if a pneumothorax develops, a chest tube (p.497) is inserted into the chest cavity to allow the air to escape. If breathing difficulties occur, mechanical ventilation may be necessary (see CRITICAL CARE UNIT, p.958). A gunshot injury to a bone may shatter it, requiring surgery and pinning of the fragments to heal properly.

With prompt treatment, many gunshot injuries do not lead to long-term physical damage. If vital internal organs are affected, the injury may be fatal.

WWW ONLINE SITES: p.1036

Stab injuries

Injuries to any part of the body inflicted by a sharp object

 AGE More common in young adults

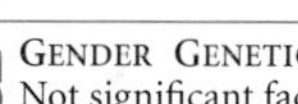 GENDER GENETICS LIFESTYLE Not significant factors

Stab injuries are becoming more common in Canada. Such wounds can be deceptive in their serious nature. Wounds to the chest or abdomen are particularly likely to cause life-threatening internal bleeding. Since visible bleeding is often minor in relation to the seriousness of the internal injuries, medical attention is always essential after a stab wound. Even small stab wounds to the hand can be serious in their consequences. What may appear to be a small puncture wound may in fact hide a severed tendon under the skin. If diagnosis of this injury is delayed, the wound may lead to permanent disability.

WHAT ARE THE TYPES?

Shallow wounds may damage skin and muscle only. Deeper wounds can cause significant internal bleeding, leading to loss of consciousness and shock (p.414). Stab injuries may also cause damage to specific organs. For example, a stab wound to the chest may result in a pneumothorax (p.496), in which air enters the chest cavity, causing breathing difficulties. If the abdomen is wounded, there is a risk of the intestines being punctured and the contents leaking into the abdominal cavity, which can result in infection (*see* PERITONITIS, p.665).

WHAT CAN I DO?

Check level of consciousness (*see* FIRST AID: ABC OF RESUSCITATION, p.978), then call for medical help. Try to stop external bleeding by applying pressure (*see* FIRST AID: SEVERE BLEEDING, p.986). If the stabbing instrument is in the body, leave it in place until doctors can remove it safely.

WHAT MIGHT THE DOCTOR DO?

Shallow wounds may need only stitching. Knife wounds of the skin usually heal well, as the wound edges are sharp and stitch together easily. If the wound is small but to the hand, the doctor may make the cut larger to check for injury to the tendon. An injection to prevent tetanus (*see* VACCINES AND IMMUNOGLOBULINS, p.883) and antibiotics (p.885) to prevent infection may be given.

Deeper injuries need a full assessment to check for internal damage. Emergency measures may include giving oxygen and intravenous fluids or a blood transfusion (p.447). CT scanning (p.247) may be done to look for internal bleeding in the abdomen or chest, and surgery may be performed to locate and repair the site of internal bleeding. If a chest X-ray (p.490) confirms a pneumothorax, a tube is inserted to allow the air to escape (*see* CHEST TUBE, p.497). The prognosis depends on the type of stab injury.

(WWW) ONLINE SITES: p.1036

Burns

Damage to tissue, usually skin, caused by exposure to heat, chemicals, or electricity

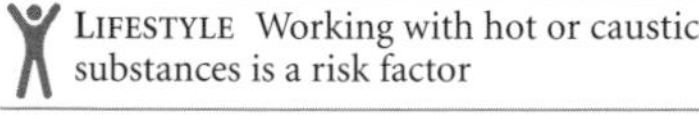
LIFESTYLE Working with hot or caustic substances is a risk factor

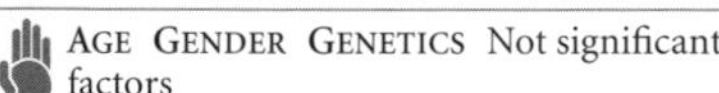
AGE GENDER GENETICS Not significant factors

Burns are a major cause of injury and disability in Canada. Elderly people and young children are especially vulnerable to their effects. Most burns are minor and caused by accidents in the home, such as scalding with hot water. Although almost all minor burns heal quickly, more severe burns often require hospital treatment and some can be life-threatening. The degree of severity depends on how deep the burn extends into tissue and the size of the area affected. Burns to sensitive areas, such as the face, hands, feet, or genitals, can be particularly serious. Scarring left by burns can be disfiguring and interfere with the function of the scarred area.

Burns are usually due to heat, such as that from fire, hot fluids, or sunlight. Caustic chemicals, such as certain paint strippers, and electricity (*see* ELECTRICAL INJURIES, opposite page) can also burn. Burns usually involve the skin, but caustic substances can burn the stomach and esophagus if swallowed, and hot smoke can burn the windpipe and airways.

WHAT ARE THE TYPES?

The skin is made up of two layers: the surface layer, called the epidermis, and the more sensitive dermis underneath. Burns are categorized as first-degree, second-degree, or third-degree, according to the depth of tissue damage.

FIRST-DEGREE BURNS Burns that affect only the epidermis are known as first-degree burns and are the least severe type of burn. The burned area may be red, slightly swollen, and sensitive to the touch, but blisters do not form. Within a few days, the skin heals and the damaged layer of skin may peel off. Sunburn (p.357) is one of the most common causes of first-degree burns.

SECOND-DEGREE BURNS Once the epidermis has been destroyed, the more sensitive lower dermis layer is vulnerable to damage. Damage to both of these two layers is known as a second-degree burn and is usually very painful. The skin becomes red and covered with large blisters filled with clear fluid. After about 3 days, the pain usually decreases, and most second-degree burns should be fully healed within 14 days.

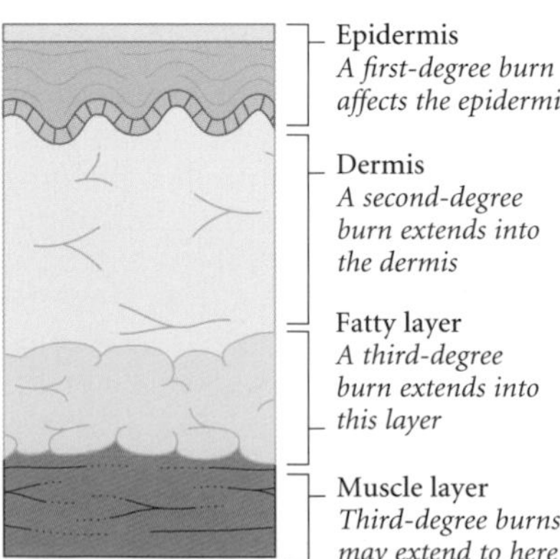
Epidermis
A first-degree burn affects the epidermis
Dermis
A second-degree burn extends into the dermis
Fatty layer
A third-degree burn extends into this layer
Muscle layer
Third-degree burns may extend to here

Degrees of severity of burns
Burns are categorized depending on the extent of damage to the different layers of tissue. The more severe the burn, the more layers of tissue are affected.

THIRD-DEGREE BURNS The most serious and deepest type of burn is known as a third-degree burn, in which the epidermis, dermis, and the underlying fat are destroyed. Sometimes, this damage may extend into the muscle. The area becomes numb, thickened, and discolored. Healing is very slow because the damaged dermis cannot regenerate itself, and new skin can grow only from the edges of the damaged area.

ARE THERE COMPLICATIONS?

In large second-degree and third-degree burns, fluid is lost from the damaged areas, causing shock (p.414) and damage to the kidneys (*see* KIDNEY FAILURE, p.705). Breathing difficulties may arise if the lungs have been damaged by smoke (*see* ASPHYXIATION, p.326).

Burns are particularly susceptible to infection because the damaged skin can no longer act as a barrier against infection. Infection with bacteria is most common after third-degree burns and may delay healing. If bacteria enter the bloodstream, they may multiply and cause septicemia (p.298), commonly known as blood poisoning.

WHAT CAN I DO?

Immediately after a burn or scald the damaged skin should be cooled with cold water (as long as the burned area is small) and first-aid should be started (*see* FIRST AID: MINOR BURNS AND SCALDS, p.988, and FIRST AID: SEVERE BURNS, p.988). Do not put creams on a burn as this may make the burn worse.

Seek medical assistance for anything but minor burns. Large second-degree and all third-degree burns require specialized hospital care. Also seek medical advice if you have any doubt about the severity of a burn. Anyone with serious burns to the face and upper airway may need immediate hospital admittance in case swelling of the tissues causes the airways to close up and makes breathing difficult. Medical attention is also essential if you have inhaled smoke.

TREATMENT SKIN GRAFTING

Skin grafting involves using a section of normal skin from one part of the body (the donor site) to cover another site where the skin has been lost as a result of an injury, such as a burn, or a disorder, such as an ulcer. There are several different methods of skin grafting. The two examples shown here use small donor sites to cover large areas of missing skin.

MESHED GRAFT

A meshed graft is used when a very large area of missing skin needs to be covered and donor sites are limited. The donor skin is removed and made into a mesh using angled cuts. The meshed graft can then be stretched to cover the large area of missing skin.

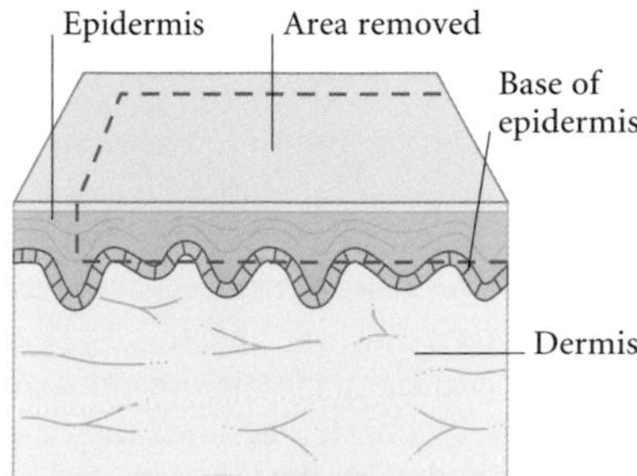
Epidermis
Area removed
Base of epidermis
Dermis

Taking the donor skin
A very thin slice of skin is shaved off the donor site. A sufficient number of cells are left at the base of the epidermis to allow the skin to regrow over the wound.

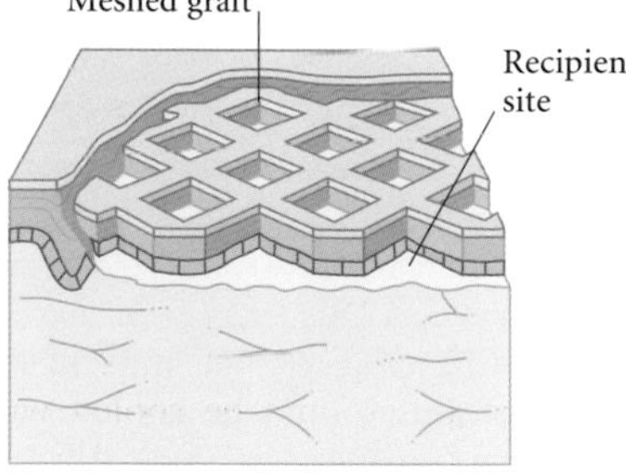
Meshed graft
Recipient site

Positioning the meshed graft
The donor skin is cut and stretched to form a mesh that fits in the larger recipient site. Once in place, new skin grows to fill the spaces around the mesh.

PINCH GRAFTS

Pinch grafts are very small pieces of skin that are often used to help skin ulcers heal. Multiple small grafts are pinched up and removed from the donor site. The pinch grafts are then placed over the larger area of missing skin and grow to cover the area.

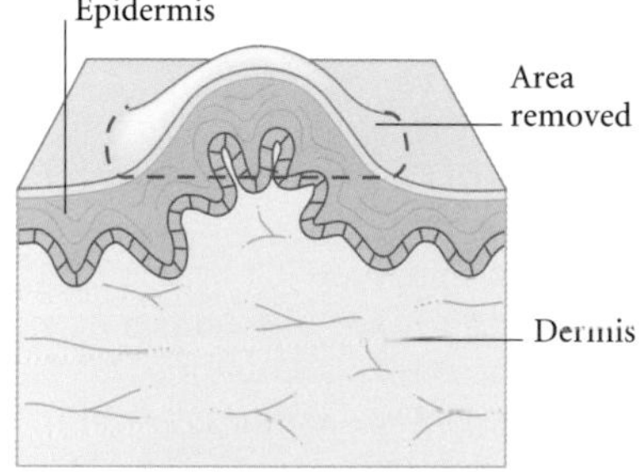
Epidermis
Area removed
Dermis

Taking the pinch grafts
Small sections of skin are pinched up at the donor site and cut using scissors or a scalpel. The donor site can heal because the removed sections are small.

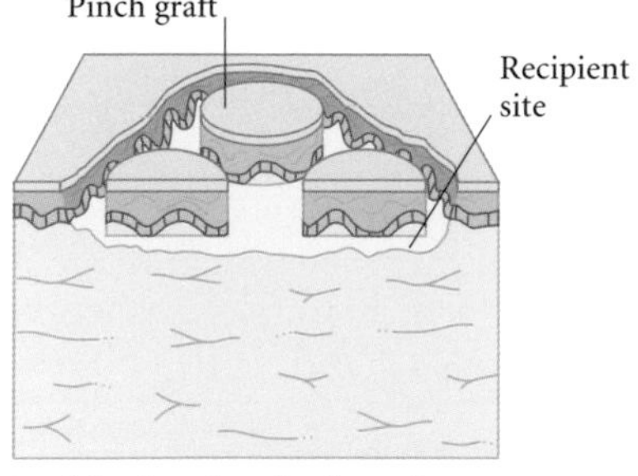
Pinch graft
Recipient site

Positioning the pinch grafts
Multiple small pinch grafts are placed on the recipient site. The grafts will gradually grow outward to form a new sheet of healthy skin in about 10–14 days.

WHAT MIGHT THE DOCTOR DO?

Minor burns are cleaned and dressed. Dressings are usually changed frequently. An antibacterial cream (*see* PREPARATIONS FOR SKIN INFECTIONS AND INFESTATIONS, p.892) may be used to help prevent infection. If an infection does develop, it is usually treated with antibiotics (p.885).

If the burns are extensive, intravenous fluids, analgesics (p.912), and oxygen may be given. Mechanical ventilation (*see* CRITICAL CARE UNIT, p.958) may be needed if breathing problems develop due to smoke inhalation.

Anyone with severe burns will be monitored to make sure that his or her fluid requirements are maintained and that kidney function is not affected. Skin grafting (above) will be considered to aid healing for severe second-degree and third-degree burns.

Scar tissue, which is fragile and sensitive, often develops following severe second-degree and third-degree burns. Scarred areas should be protected from the sun with clothing or sunscreen (*see* SUNSCREENS AND SUNBLOCKS, p.893). Scars may cause itching, which can be relieved with antipruritic drugs (p.891). Scarred areas may also become taut and inflexible, restricting movement if skin over a joint is affected, and skin grafting may therefore be necessary. Physiotherapy (p.961) may help improve movement through exercises and the use of other physical techniques.

WHAT IS THE PROGNOSIS?

With correct treatment, minor burns usually heal within a few days. More severe burns may take several weeks. Third-degree burns may take months to heal even if skin grafts are used, and some scarring may be permanent. Skin that has been severely or repeatedly burned may be at increased risk of developing skin cancer.

(WWW) ONLINE SITES: p.1036

Electrical injuries

Damage to body tissues caused by the passage of an electric current through the body

 GENDER More common in males

 LIFESTYLE Working with electricity is a risk factor

 AGE GENETICS Not significant factors

An electrical current passing through the body can generate intense heat and burn the tissues. Although burns may occur internally, they are often most obvious on the skin (*see* BURNS, opposite page). The current may also disrupt the normal functioning of the heart or brain and may be immediately fatal.

These injuries can be a result of being struck by lightning. Many occur in the home, and the rest occur in workers in the electricity-generating or construction industries. Most electrical injuries result from touching exposed electrical wires, faulty switches, or water that is electrified by a wire or device. The danger of receiving an electrical injury is increased in the presence of water as it is an excellent conductor of electricity.

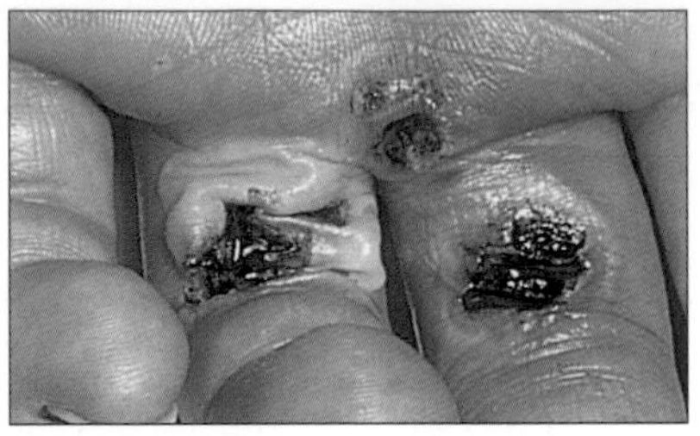

Electrical burns
These two fingers have sustained deep burns as a result of direct contact with an uninsulated electrical cable.

WHAT ARE THE SYMPTOMS?

Symptoms of electrical injuries depend on the voltage, the length of contact, and the route taken by the current through the body. Symptoms common to many electrical injuries may include:

- Loss of consciousness, which may be temporary.
- Dazed, confused behavior.
- Burns on the skin.

The muscles may become rigid during the shock, which may prevent a person from breaking contact with the electrical current. Severe muscle spasms may lead to bone fractures (p.392). Electrical burns seen on the skin may be deceptive in their severity. For example, electrical burns seen on the skin of the hand may give no indication of the extensive damage that has been done to the muscles of the forearm.

Specific symptoms vary depending on the path of the electrical current through the body. For example, if the current passes through the heart, it may disrupt the rhythm of the heartbeat (*see* ARRHYTHMIAS, p.415) and occasionally lead to cardiac arrest (p.419). If the current passes through the brainstem, which controls automatic body functions including breathing, the shock may be fatal (*see* BRAIN DEATH, p.523).

WHAT CAN I DO?

You should call for medical assistance for anything more than a minor shock. If you find someone who has had an electric shock, you must make sure that the electricity is turned off before you attempt to touch him or her in order to prevent risk to you. Check his or her breathing and signs of circulation (*see* FIRST AID: ABC OF RESUSCITATION, p.978) and then start resuscitation measures if necessary. Continue these measures until medical help arrives. You should also carry out these procedures if you come across someone who has an injury as a result of being struck by lightning.

Never attempt to rescue a person who has been injured by high-voltage electricity (more than 1,000 volts) if he or she is still in contact or close to the high-voltage electricity. Instead, call for medical assistance immediately.

You can help prevent electrical burn to a young child by never leaving a loose electrical cord, such as an extension cord, plugged in at an electrical source. A child may put the loose end of the cord in his or her mouth, seriously burning the lips and mouth. This may require plastic surgery and may be permanently disfiguring.

WHAT MIGHT THE DOCTOR DO?

Once the person is in the hospital, a full physical examination will be done and an assessment made of tissue damage. The heartbeat may also be monitored for evidence of an abnormal rhythm. Most people recover if they receive first-aid and medical treatment promptly.

(WWW) ONLINE SITES: p.1036

Sexual assault

Physical and psychological damage resulting from rape or attempted rape

 AGE Most common between the ages of 16 and 24

 GENDER More common in females

 GENETICS LIFESTYLE Not significant factors

The number of reported cases of sexual assault, which includes both rape and attempted rape, has risen in recent years. However, sexual assault still remains one of the most under-reported crimes in Canada, and the true figure is difficult to estimate.

Many people are unwilling to report a sexual assault, especially if they know the perpetrator. However, victims of sexual assault should always seek help. Calling the police and going to the emergency department without delay makes treatment for infection more effective and the gathering of forensic evidence easier. It is best if forensic samples that may be used as evidence against the attacker are collected soon after the assault.

ARE THERE COMPLICATIONS?

Hepatitis B and C (*see* ACUTE HEPATITIS, p.644) and other sexually transmitted diseases, such as HIV infection (*see* HIV INFECTION AND AIDS, p.295) or chlamydial cervicitis (p.765), may be contracted. A victim of sexual assault is also likely to experience severe psychological trauma, and anxiety disorders (p.551), depression (p.554), or post-traumatic stress disorder (p.553) may also develop.

WHAT MIGHT BE DONE?

If you report that you have been sexually assaulted, you will receive treatment for injuries and possible infections. You will also be offered support in order to help you recover from the experience.

The doctor will examine you and note bruises or other injuries. Swabs are taken and tested for infections and the presence of semen or other body fluids that may be used as forensic evidence against the attacker. After you have received counseling, blood samples may be taken to check for HIV infection. Other samples, such as clothes and nail clippings, may be retained for analysis. All examinations and collecting of material for forensic tests are carried out in a supportive environment and only after the doctor has explained what needs to be done and you have agreed.

You will be offered emergency contraception (p.69) if there is a risk of pregnancy. Antibiotics (p.885) are prescribed to prevent sexually transmitted diseases, such as gonorrhea (p.764) and chlamydial cervicitis (p.765). If there is a risk of developing HIV infection, a course of antiviral drugs may be recommended to reduce this risk (*see* DRUGS FOR HIV AND AIDS, p.887).

Follow-up care may be offered after the assault. Subsequent visits to the doctor may be arranged at 6 weeks for syphilis and gonorrhea tests and at 3 and 6 months for repeat HIV and hepatitis B and C testing.

Counseling (p.971) is usually recommended after an attack, and you may also find it helpful to contact self-help organizations that provide emotional support and practical advice for the victims of sexual assault. You may find that you need support for an extended time. Being able to talk about your feelings is likely to hasten recovery.

(WWW) ONLINE SITES: p.1029, p.1036

POISONING AND ENVIRONMENTAL DISORDERS

The natural environment can be hazardous, and, with increased travel and leisure, people today are more likely than ever to be exposed to potentially life-threatening conditions. Health can be affected by environmental factors, such as climate, altitude, sunlight, and the presence of various minerals.

The first article in this section covers deliberate or accidental drug overdose and poisoning. In adults, many drug overdoses are intentional, whereas in children poisoning usually occurs as a result of the accidental ingestion of common household substances.

Disorders caused by extremes of temperature are described next. Heat exhaustion and heatstroke are potential consequences of spending too long in very high temperatures. In hypothermia, the body's temperature falls to life-threatening levels as a result of excessive cold. If the body tissues are cold enough, they may freeze. This condition is known as frostbite and is particularly likely to affect extremities that are inadequately protected.

Illness can also result from exposure to extremes of elevation, and this is described next. Altitude sickness not only affects mountaineers but may also occur in people traveling to cities at high altitudes. Decompression sickness, more commonly known as "the bends," usually results from a rapid decrease in pressure when surfacing too rapidly after a deep dive underwater.

The next articles in this section deal with environmental injuries that affect oxygen supply to the brain. Drowning and near-drowning are both caused by water preventing normal breathing. The more general term of asphyxiation is used to describe oxygen deprivation that results from a wider variety of causes, such as an object in the throat and carbon monoxide poisoning.

The last articles covered here deal with poisoning from snake and spider bites and scorpion stings. Such injuries are painful but rarely serious. Most of these environmental disorders can be easily prevented by simple measures.

Drug overdose and accidental ingestion

Deliberate or unintentional consumption of potentially harmful substances

 AGE Accidental ingestion more common in young children

 GENDER Drug overdose more common in females

 LIFESTYLE Alcohol and drug abuse are risk factors

 GENETICS Not a significant factor

Poisoning in adults is usually a result of an intentional overdose of drugs (*see* ATTEMPTED SUICIDE AND SUICIDE, p.556). Serious illness may also occur when prescription drugs are inadvertently taken inappropriately. Most accidental poisonings occur in the home in children under age 5. Such poisonings are often preventable (*see* HOME SAFETY AND HEALTH, p.77).

Some substances, such as household bleach, are harmful regardless of how much is ingested. Prescribed drugs, such as sleeping drugs (p.915), usually cause harm only if the recommended dose is exceeded. Illegal substances, such as heroin and cocaine, can have unpredictable effects, depending partly on the amount taken and on the person's susceptibility to the drug (*see* DRUGS AND HEALTH, p.65).

WHAT ARE THE SYMPTOMS?

The symptoms vary from mild to severe. They may develop immediately or over a number of days. Some common general symptoms include:

- Nausea and vomiting.
- Abdominal pain.
- Confusion.
- Seizures.
- Loss of consciousness.

There may also be local symptoms, such as burns in the mouth after swallowing caustic substances.

An overdose of certain drugs, such as tricyclic antidepressants (*see* ANTIDEPRESSANT DRUGS, p.916), can disturb the action of the heart and result in an irregular heart rhythm (*see* ARRHYTHMIAS, p.415) and sometimes a feeling of faintness. In some cases, an arrhythmia may even lead to cardiac arrest (p.419). An overdose of an opium-based drug, such as heroin, causes a reduction in the breathing rate, which may be life-threatening. An overdose of certain substances may also damage the liver and kidneys. For example, liver failure (p.650) may be caused by an overdose of acetaminophen (*see* ANALGESICS, p.912). The ingestion of certain poisons can result in anaphylaxis (p.469), a severe allergic reaction, although this is rare.

WHAT CAN I DO?

If the affected person is unconscious, first call for help, then check his or her breathing and pulse rate (*see* FIRST AID: ABC OF RESUSCITATION, p.978). Continue administering first aid until medical help arrives (*see* FIRST AID: SWALLOWED POISONS, p.994).

Even if there are no symptoms and the quantity of poison ingested is small, you should always consult your doctor or poison control center for advice. Try to collect as much information as possible, including what substance was swallowed, how much, how long ago, and the bottle or container and remnants of what has been taken. If the person is unconscious or reluctant to talk, you may be needed to provide vital information. Do not give the person anything to drink or try to induce vomiting unless instructed by a doctor or poison control center to do so.

WHAT MIGHT THE DOCTOR DO?

The doctor needs to know what substance been taken and when. He or she will examine the person and, if a drug overdose has been taken, may arrange for blood tests in order to measure drug levels in the circulation.

Admission to a hospital (p.958) for monitoring and treatment may be required. If tricyclic antidepressants have been taken, the heart rhythm is monitored to detect abnormalities. After an acetaminophen overdose, blood tests are carried out to look for evidence of damage to the liver.

Various methods may be used to try to eliminate the ingested substance from the digestive tract and to prevent the substance from being absorbed into the circulation. A tube may be passed through the mouth into the stomach in order to remove the poison from the stomach with sterile water or a saline solution. If the person is unconscious, a tube may be passed into the windpipe to prevent liquid from entering the lungs as the stomach is emptied.

Activated charcoal may be administered orally. The toxic substance binds to charcoal in the digestive tract and is then passed out in feces.

If very high levels of a substance are present in the circulation, elimination may be increased by filtering the blood (*see* DIALYSIS, p.707). Some substances can be inactivated by giving a specific antidote. For example, naloxone may be given for an opium-based overdose.

Complications are usually treated as they arise. For example, antiarrhythmic drugs (p.898) can be prescribed for an irregular heartbeat. If breathing difficulties are severe, mechanical ventilation may eventually be required.

If an overdose was taken deliberately, a psychiatric assessment will be carried out when the person is stable.

WHAT IS THE PROGNOSIS?

Although poisoning may be fatal, most cases do not cause serious harm. Prognosis depends on the effects of the drug, how much was taken, and the time elapsed before diagnosis. In some cases, such as acetaminophen overdoses, symptoms may appear days after, when damage to the liver and kidneys may already be extensive and irreversible.

(WWW) ONLINE SITES: p.1027, p.1030, p.1031

Heat exhaustion and heatstroke

Exposure to excessive heat, causing loss of fluids and salts and a rise in body temperature

AGE May occur at any age but most common in babies and elderly people

LIFESTYLE Exertion in a hot environment is a risk factor

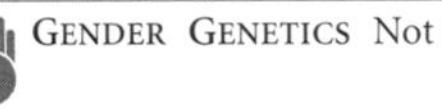
GENDER GENETICS Not significant factors

In a hot environment, the body loses heat by diverting blood to the skin and by sweating. Profuse sweating may lead to an excessive loss of fluids and salts, resulting in heat exhaustion. This condition is rarely serious, but, if exposure to heat continues, heatstroke may occur as the body's normal cooling mechanisms break down and the temperature of the body rises. Heatstroke is a life-threatening medical emergency.

Heat exhaustion and heatstroke most commonly occur above 40°C (104°F). High humidity increases the risk of heatstroke because sweating is ineffective and heat loss is decreased.

EFFECT OF HUMIDITY ON THE RISK OF HEATSTROKE

KEY: EXTREME RISK; HIGH RISK; MODERATE RISK; LOW RISK

RELATIVE HUMIDITY (%): 20, 30, 40, 50, 60, 70, 80, 90, 100

AIR TEMPERATURE: 25, 30, 35, 40, 45, 50, 55 °C; 80, 90, 100, 110, 120, 130 °F

The risk of heatstroke

As the moisture in the atmosphere (the humidity) rises, it becomes more difficult to lose heat by sweating, and heatstroke may occur at lower temperatures.

WHO IS AT RISK?

Heat exhaustion and heatstroke may affect otherwise healthy people, particularly after physical exertion in a hot climate. People who come from temperate climates and travel to the tropics need time to acclimatize to the heat before they can exert themselves without risk of heat exhaustion or heatstroke.

The body's cooling mechanisms are less efficient in babies and elderly people, making them more susceptible to heat exhaustion and heatstroke. Obesity (p.631), diabetes mellitus (p.687), alcohol dependence (p.564), and chronic heart failure (p.413) all decrease the body's ability to lose heat. Diarrhea (p.627) may contribute to dehydration and increase the risk of developing heat exhaustion and heatstroke.

WHAT ARE THE SYMPTOMS?

After prolonged exposure to hot conditions, the following symptoms of heat exhaustion may develop:

- Profuse sweating.
- Fatigue.
- Muscle cramps.
- Nausea and vomiting.
- Faintness and unsteadiness.
- Headache.

If exposure to heat continues, the body temperature rises and heatstroke may develop, causing symptoms such as:

- Fast, shallow breathing.
- Confusion and disorientation.
- Seizures.

Left untreated, heatstroke may progress to coma (p.522). Death may be caused by kidney failure (p.705), acute heart failure (p.412), or direct heat-induced damage to the brain.

WHAT CAN I DO?

Heat exhaustion can be treated easily. The affected person should rest in a cool place, ideally in an air-conditioned building, and sip cool, salty drinks until he or she feels comfortable. If heatstroke is suspected, he or she should seek medical attention as soon as possible.

WHAT MIGHT THE DOCTOR DO?

Once in the hospital, an examination is done, and blood tests are carried out to assess the level of salts in the blood.

Treatment of heatstroke is usually carried out in the Emergency Department or intensive care unit of a hospital.

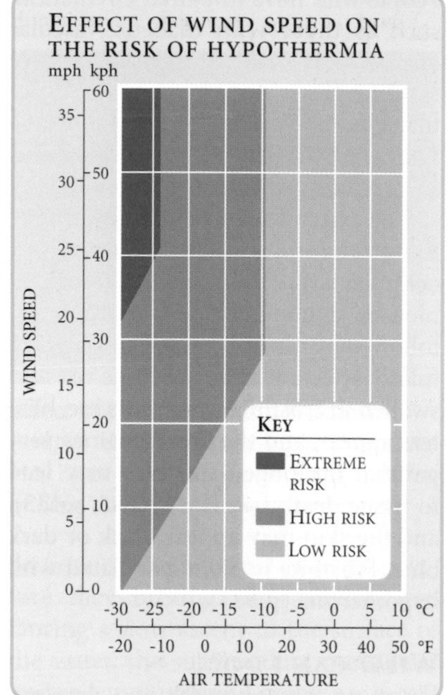
EFFECT OF WIND SPEED ON THE RISK OF HYPOTHERMIA
mph kph
35 30 25 20 15 10 5 0
60 50 40 30 20 10 0
WIND SPEED
KEY
EXTREME RISK
HIGH RISK
LOW RISK
-30 -25 -20 -15 -10 -5 0 5 10 °C
-20 -10 0 10 20 30 40 50 °F
AIR TEMPERATURE

The risk of hypothermia
As the wind speed increases (the windchill factor), heat is lost more rapidly from the body, making hypothermia more likely to occur at warmer temperatures.

The body temperature is lowered by sponging the person with tepid water and placing him or her near a fan. Intravenous fluids are given. Once the body temperature has been reduced to 38°C (100°F), these cooling procedures are stopped to prevent hypothermia (below) from developing. Monitoring is still carried out continuously to make sure that the body temperature returns to normal levels and that the vital organs are functioning normally. In some severe cases, mechanical ventilation may be required to help breathing.

Most people who have suffered from heat exhaustion recover in a few hours if they are moved to a cooler place and fluids are gradually replaced. If heatstroke is treated promptly, most people usually recover within a few days.

CAN THEY BE PREVENTED?

Heat-related disorders can be largely prevented by avoiding strenuous exertion in the heat of the day; spending as much time as possible in the shade, away from direct sunlight; consuming large quantities of liquids; and avoiding alcoholic beverages.

(WWW) ONLINE SITES: p.1036, p.1037

Hypothermia

A fall in body temperature to a dangerously low level

 AGE May occur at any age but most common in babies and elderly people

 LIFESTYLE Homelessness and outdoor activities in cold climates are risk factors

 GENDER GENETICS Not significant factors

Hypothermia occurs when the body's normal temperature of about 37°C (98.6°F) falls below 35°C (95°F). The body normally has various warming mechanisms, including shivering, that help replace lost heat. However, if the environment is too cold or if the body's warming mechanisms fail, hypothermia develops. Hypothermia may be associated with frostbite (p.324) and, if extreme, can be life-threatening.

WHO IS AT RISK?

Hypothermia is particularly common in climbers and walkers who are inadequately dressed for cold weather. People who are homeless in cold weather are also vulnerable. Other people who have a reduced awareness of low temperatures due to alcohol or drug abuse may not realize they need to protect themselves and may develop hypothermia.

Certain disorders increase the risk of developing hypothermia. For example, hypothyroidism (p.680) slows down the body's functions and reduces body temperature. People whose mobility is reduced following a stroke (p.532) or because of a disorder such as arthritis (p.374) generate little body heat and are also at particular risk.

Elderly people are particularly at risk of developing hypothermia. As the body ages, it becomes less able to maintain its normal body temperature in cold conditions. Elderly people are also less aware of the cold and do not always notice if their body temperature drops. In some cases, dementia (p.535) may reduce an elderly person's awareness of temperature changes.

Babies are susceptible to hypothermia because they lose heat rapidly and, like elderly people, cannot easily maintain their body temperature.

In all cases, the rate of heat loss and therefore the risk of hypothermia is increased in high winds or wet conditions, and hypothermia may develop particularly quickly when a person is immersed in cold water.

WHAT ARE THE SYMPTOMS?

The symptoms of hypothermia usually develop gradually over hours or days but may sometimes develop in minutes in someone who is immersed in cold water or exposed to high winds. The person affected may not feel cold. Symptoms may include:

- Fatigue.
- Slow, clumsy movements.
- Confusion, impaired judgment, and slow reactions.

As the body temperature drops further, these symptoms become more obvious. In addition, the lips may turn blue, delirium or loss of consciousness may develop, and the heart may develop an abnormal rhythm (*see* ARRHYTHMIAS, p.415) or, eventually, even stop beating (*see* CARDIAC ARREST, p.419).

(SELF-HELP) AVOIDING HYPOTHERMIA IN ELDERLY PEOPLE

Elderly people are particularly susceptible to hypothermia. If you are elderly, you should take care to protect yourself against the cold. The following measures may help:

- Keep all your windows closed in cold weather.
- Install an easy-to-read wall thermometer. The temperature in the room where you spend most of your time should be at least 20°C (68°F).
- Make sure that your house or apartment is warm before getting out of bed in the morning.
- Have at least one hot meal and several hot drinks each day.
- Try to move around at least hourly to create your own heat.
- Wear several layers of clothing if possible to trap warm air.
- Wear a hat to prevent loss of body heat through the scalp.
- If your clothes get wet, change into dry clothes as soon as possible to prevent the moisture in the clothes from conducting heat away from the body.

ARE THERE COMPLICATIONS?

Lack of oxygen can lead to brain damage and death. Even if breathing is restored, water may cause inflammation of the lungs, leading to acute respiratory distress syndrome (p.506). Debris in the lungs may cause infection and lung damage, impairing the ability of the lungs to function normally.

Inhaled water may alter blood chemistry. If fresh water is inhaled, it passes from the lungs to the bloodstream and destroys the red blood cells. If salt water is inhaled, the salt causes fluids to enter the tissues of the lungs.

A person who has been submerged in cold water has a better chance of being resuscitated because cold water slows down the body's metabolism.

WHAT CAN I DO?

Only attempt to rescue a drowning person if you are sure that you can do so without putting yourself at risk.

If the person is conscious and near you, throw him or her an object that will float, ideally with a rope attached. Alternatively, use a stick, pole, or even an item of clothing. If the person cannot reach the object, swim out only if it is safe. Otherwise, note the position of the person in the water and call for assistance immediately.

If you swim out to the person, basic resuscitation measures will be difficult or impossible to perform while in deep water. Once you are in water shallow enough to stand up in, artificial respiration (pp.982–983) may be started. When you reach land, start full first-aid resuscitation measures, such as rescue breathing, as necessary (*see* FIRST AID: ABC OF RESUSCITATION, p.978).

If the person has fallen into cold water, wrap him or her in warm, dry clothing or blankets to try to reduce the risk of hypothermia. Continue attempting to resuscitate a person who is cold because nearly drowned people can survive far longer if they have hypothermia.

Even if the person seems recovered, medical attention should be sought to make sure there are no complications.

WHAT MIGHT THE DOCTOR DO?

The person will be assessed for vital signs (blood pressure, pulse, and temperature), and for breathing difficulties. Treatment may range from the giving of oxygen to monitoring and care in a critical care unit (p.958). In some cases, the victim may need mechanical ventilation in order to help ease breathing difficulties. Additional treatment will depend on what complications there are. For example, water in the lungs may lead to pneumonia. This may not be apparent immediately, and so the person's condition requires monitoring. In addition, antibiotics (p.885) may be administered in order to counter possible lung infections.

If hypothermia has developed, the person is rewarmed slowly. Body temperature needs to be slowly returned to normal before an assessment for brain damage can be carried out.

WHAT IS THE PROGNOSIS?

The prognosis is improved if the water the person was in is cold, the period of submersion in the water is short, and the person is young and otherwise healthy. Approximately 1 in 20 people who are resuscitated die of a complication. However, those people who do survive may have sustained some permanent brain damage.

(WWW) ONLINE SITES: p.1031, p.1036

Asphyxiation

Failure of oxygen to reach the brain for a variety of reasons

AGE GENDER GENETICS LIFESTYLE
Not significant factors

Asphyxiation is the term that is given to a potentially fatal condition in which oxygen is prevented from reaching the body tissues. If not treated within a few minutes, asphyxiation leads to loss of consciousness, irreversible brain damage, and, subsequently, to death.

WHAT ARE THE CAUSES?

Asphyxiation may be the result of an inability to breathe or insufficient oxygen in the inhaled air.

An inability to breathe can be caused by a variety of factors. One of the most common causes is a foreign object that is lodged in the throat. A severe head injury (p.521) or a drug overdose (*see* DRUG OVERDOSE AND ACCIDENTAL INGESTION, p.321) may also impair breathing.

Severe damage to the wall of the chest (*see* CRUSH INJURIES, p.316) may prevent the lungs from inflating, particularly if one or more of the ribs has been fractured. The neck and upper airway may be compressed by accidental or deliberate strangulation.

Lack of oxygen in the air can occur as a result of carbon monoxide production from a fire or from car exhaust.

WHAT ARE THE SYMPTOMS?

Asphyxiation usually develops rapidly over a few minutes but can occur over several hours, depending on the cause. Most cases of asphyxiation have similar symptoms, including:

- Agitation.
- Confusion.
- Loss of consciousness.

In most cases, the skin, particularly the lips, turns blue. The onset of symptoms of carbon monoxide poisoning may be gradual as the gas competes with the oxygen in the blood, until, finally, the blood oxygen level is dangerously low.

WHAT CAN I DO?

Only go to the aid of a person who is being asphyxiated if you are in no danger from smoke or other gases yourself. Check for an obstruction to breathing (*see* FIRST AID: CHOKING, p.980–981) and carry out emergency resuscitation measures until help arrives (*see* FIRST AID: ABC OF RESUSCITATION, p.978).

WHAT MIGHT THE DOCTOR DO?

Once in the hospital, medical treatment is directed at reversing the cause of the asphyxiation. For example, if the condition is due to a foreign body lodged in the throat, the object will be removed. If the object cannot be removed quickly, an incision may be made in the trachea (the windpipe) and a tube inserted in order to restore breathing until the airway can be cleared. Fractured ribs will be treated and analgesics (p.912) given to help relieve pain. Drug overdoses are treated by eliminating as much of the ingested substance as possible. In some cases, mechanical ventilation (*see* CRITICAL CARE UNIT, p.958) may be needed if the underlying cause of the asphyxiation cannot be treated rapidly.

The shorter the period of oxygen deprivation, the better the prognosis. Following prolonged asphyxiation there may be permanent brain damage.

(WWW) ONLINE SITES: p.1031, p.1036

Snake bites

Penetrating injuries from snakes that may be followed by an injection of venom

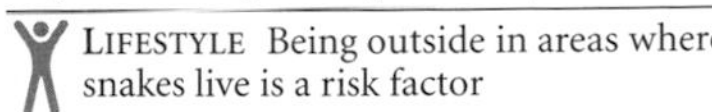

LIFESTYLE Being outside in areas where snakes live is a risk factor

AGE GENDER GENETICS Not significant factors

Most snake bites occur in people hiking or walking outdoors. However, several measures can be taken to avoid being bitten by a venomous snake (*see* AVOIDING BITES AND STINGS, right).

WHAT ARE THE SYMPTOMS?

If there are no fang marks, no venom has been injected and there will be no symptoms. If there is venom in the wound, symptoms occur immediately or over a few hours. Initial symptoms occur around the bite and may include:

- Swelling and discoloration.
- Pain and a burning sensation.

Later, signs of widespread poisoning may begin to appear, including:

- Pale skin and sweating.
- Confusion.
- Eventual loss of consciousness.

Blood pressure may fall, causing shock (p.414). The major organs may also be affected, resulting in respiratory failure (p.507) and acute heart failure (p.412).

WHAT CAN I DO?

If you, or someone with you, are bitten by a snake, remove any clothing or jewelry that may cause constriction if the area around the bite starts to swell. The affected person should move as little as possible, and first aid should be carried out (*see* FIRST AID: POISONOUS BITES AND STINGS, p.994). If possible, you should note the appearance of the snake before going to the hospital. The doctor will need to know the type of snake that bit so that he or she can decide whether an antidote, known as antivenin, is required.

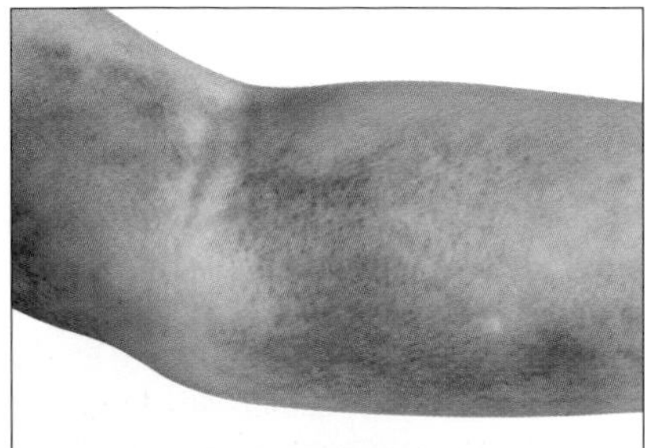

Effect of a snake bite
A bite by a poisonous snake may cause swelling and discoloration of surrounding tissues, obscuring the bite marks.

WHAT MIGHT THE DOCTOR DO?

Hospital treatment may include resuscitation and intravenous fluids. You may also be given antivenin as an antidote. Once your condition has become stable, the area that was bitten will be elevated and immobilized until the swelling goes down. If a snake bite is treated quickly and correctly, recovery usually occurs within a few days and there are no lasting effects.

(WWW) ONLINE SITES: p.1031, p.1036

Spider bites and scorpion stings

Painful penetrating injuries from spiders or scorpions that are accompanied by the injection of venom

LIFESTYLE Being outside in areas where spiders and scorpions live is a risk factor

AGE GENDER GENETICS Not significant factors

Spider bites and scorpion stings can be a hazard when traveling in certain areas of the US. They are most common in hikers and can usually be avoided by preventive measures (*see* AVOIDING BITES AND STINGS, right).

In the US, the two main venomous spiders that bite humans are the black widow spider and the brown recluse spider. The black widow spider is found in the deserts of the Southwest. Its bite rapidly becomes painful, and abdominal cramps, pain in the limbs, faintness, sweating, and difficulty breathing may develop. A bite from the brown recluse spider, which is found in southern and midwestern states, causes a severe burning sensation. An ulcer of dead tissue develops within 24 hours. Rarely, kidney failure (p.705) and yellowing of the skin (*see* JAUNDICE, p.643) may occur. Spider bites cause an average of six deaths each year in the US.

Scorpion stings are usually extremely painful but otherwise harmless. In the US, the exception is the bark scorpion, which is found in the South and Southwest. Its sting initially causes a tingling sensation around the area of the bite. The wound then becomes very painful. Further symptoms may include sweating, restlessness, vomiting, diarrhea, irregular heart rhythms (*see* ARRHYTHMIAS, p.415), and severe muscle spasms. On average, one person dies from a scorpion sting each year in the US.

WHAT MIGHT BE DONE?

Following initial first aid (*see* FIRST AID: POISONOUS BITES AND STINGS, p.994), treatment for bites by a black widow or a brown recluse spider depends on the symptoms. For example, oxygen may be given for breathing difficulties. If symptoms are severe, an antidote may be given to counteract the effects of the venom. A severe ulcer due to a brown recluse spider bite may require removal of dead tissue and skin grafting (p.319).

Most scorpion bites only need application of a cold compress to the wound and analgesics (p.912) for pain. A sting by a bark scorpion may require a local anesthetic (p.914) for pain and a specific antidote to neutralize the venom. Complications are treated as they arise. For example, spasms may be treated with anticonvulsant drugs (p.914).

With the appropriate treatment, most symptoms subside over a few days.

(WWW) ONLINE SITES: p.1031, p.1036

(SELF-HELP) AVOIDING BITES AND STINGS

The chance of being bitten or stung when hiking can be reduced by taking the following steps:

- Apply insect repellent before setting out on a hike.
- Wear a long-sleeved shirt tucked into your waistband and long pants with cuffs tucked into socks.
- Put a rubber band where pants and socks meet to prevent insects from getting under clothing.
- Wear strong hiking boots to protect the entire foot and ankle.
- Stay in the middle of paths when you are hiking and avoid areas of dense undergrowth.
- Make noise as you walk through areas where there may be snakes.
- If you come across a snake, retrace your steps because there may be others in the vicinity.

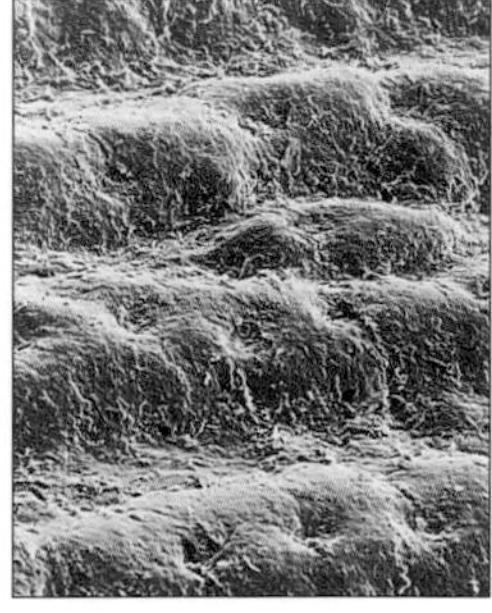

Surface of the skin
This magnified view of the hairless skin of the palm shows sweat pores arranged along ridges. The ridges help us hold on to objects.

SKIN, HAIR, AND NAILS

WITH AN AVERAGE SURFACE AREA of about 2½ sq yd (2 sq m), the skin is one of the largest organs of the body. The skin forms a protective barrier between the harsh environment of the outside world and the body's muscles, internal organs, blood vessels, and nerves. Hair and nails grow from the skin and provide extra protection. The appearance of the skin varies widely, not only changing with factors such as increasing age but also acting as a barometer of our fluctuating emotions and general health.

The skin is a living organ. However, the uppermost layer of the epidermis, which is the outer part of the skin, is made up of dead cells. Although a person sheds about 30,000 of these dead cells every minute, live cells are continually produced in the lower part of the epidermis to replace them. Below the epidermis is the dermis, which contains blood vessels, nerve endings, and glands. A layer of fat lies under the dermis and acts as an insulator, shock absorber, and energy store.

PROTECTING AND SENSING

Even though most parts of it are less than ¼ in (6 mm) thick, the skin is still a robust protective layer. The main component of its surface is a tough, fibrous protein called keratin. This substance can also be found in hair, which provides protection and warmth, and in nails, which cover the delicate ends of the digits.

The skin forms a highly effective barrier against microorganisms and harmful substances, but it is most effective when the surface remains intact. Wounds may become infected and allow bacteria, some of which live on the skin's surface, to enter the bloodstream. Sebum, an oily fluid formed in the sebaceous glands in the dermis, helps keep the skin supple and acts as a water repellent. It is because skin is waterproof that we do not soak up water like a sponge when we bathe.

Our sense of touch comes from receptors in the skin's dermis that respond to pressure, vibrations, heat, cold, and pain. Every second, billions of signals from stimuli received all over the body are sent to the brain, where they are processed to create a sensory "image" and to warn of dangers, such as a hot stove. Some sensory areas, such as the fingertips, have high densities of receptors.

The skin also plays a large part in the regulation of body temperature and, exposed to sunlight, produces vitamin D, which is essential for strong bones.

A RESPONSIVE LAYER

Our skin responds to the life we lead. For example, the skin of a gardener's hands becomes thickened, giving extra protection. The aging process, during which the skin becomes wrinkled and less elastic, can be accelerated by factors such as smoking or excessive sun exposure. Skin can also change color. In direct sunlight, the epidermis and dermis produce extra melanin, a pigment that filters harmful ultraviolet rays and causes the skin to darken. People originating in areas that have a hot climate tend to have darker skin, which does not burn as easily as lighter skin. The skin of people with fair complexions has less melanin and is more susceptible to sunburn.

STRUCTURE PARTS OF A NAIL

Protective plates called nails cover the ends of the fingers and toes. They consist mainly of keratin, the tough protein in hair and skin. Nails grow from the matrix, which lies below a fold of skin called the cuticle, and from the lunula, the crescent-shaped area at the base of the nail.

Nail structures
The most obvious part of a nail is the nail plate. This structure lies on the nail bed, an area rich in blood vessels.

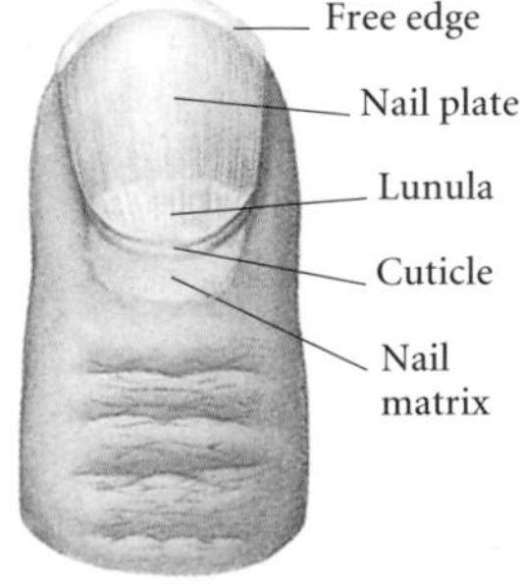
Free edge
Nail plate
Lunula
Cuticle
Nail matrix

EXTERNAL APPEARANCE

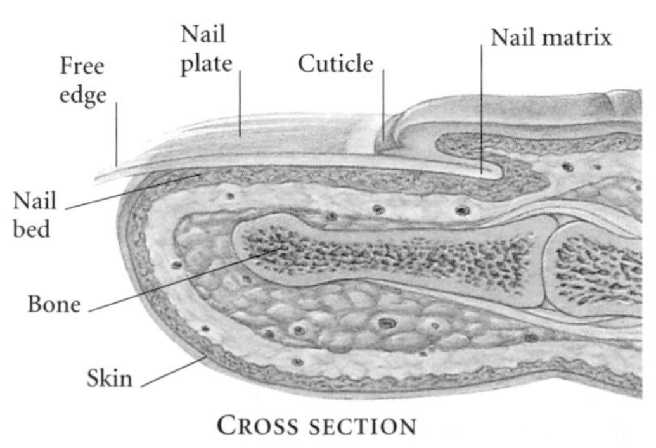
Free edge
Nail plate
Cuticle
Nail matrix
Nail bed
Bone
Skin

CROSS SECTION

(STRUCTURE) SKIN AND HAIR

The skin consists of two basic layers, the thin outer epidermis and the thicker inner dermis. The epidermis consists of sheets of tough, flat cells. Hair grows from hair follicles, which are modified regions of epidermis that reach into the dermis. New hair cells, made in the follicle, eventually die to form the scaly hair shaft. The dermis, which is made of strong, elastic tissue, contains blood vessels, glands, and nerve endings, which respond to stimuli such as heat, pressure, and pain.

Epidermal cell

Sweat pore

Pore surrounded by epidermal cells
Sweat from glands in the dermis reaches the skin's surface through pores such as this one. The large, upright flakes around the pore are dead epidermal cells.

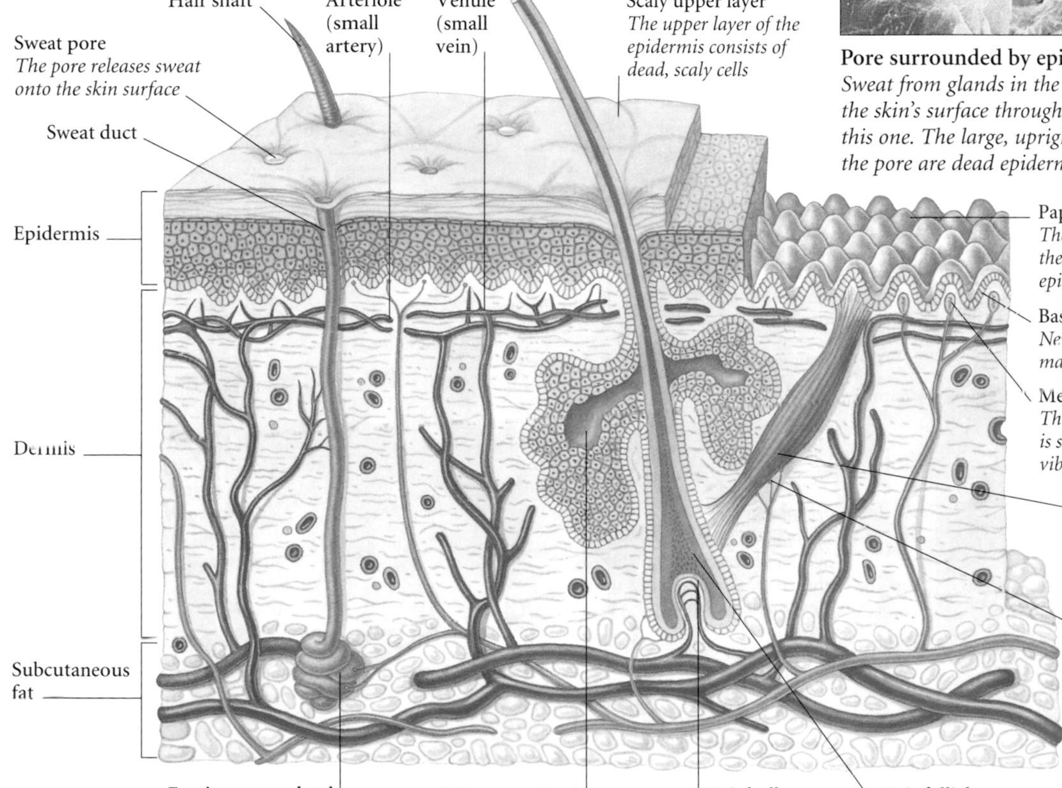
Hair shaft
Arteriole (small artery)
Venule (small vein)
Scaly upper layer
The upper layer of the epidermis consists of dead, scaly cells
Sweat pore
The pore releases sweat onto the skin surface
Sweat duct
Epidermis
Dermis
Subcutaneous fat
Papillae
These lie between the dermis and the epidermis
Basal cell layer
New skin cells are made here
Meissner's ending
This nerve receptor is sensitive to vibration
Erector pili muscle
This muscle tenses to pull the hair upright
Free nerve endings
Different free nerve endings respond to touch, heat, cold, and pain
Eccrine sweat gland
Sweat produced by this gland is carried by the sweat duct up to the skin's surface
Sebaceous gland
Waxy sebum produced by this gland moistens and waterproofs skin
Hair bulb
New hair cells are produced in the hair bulb
Hair follicle
Hairs emerge from the follicle in a continual cycle of growth, rest, and eventual loss

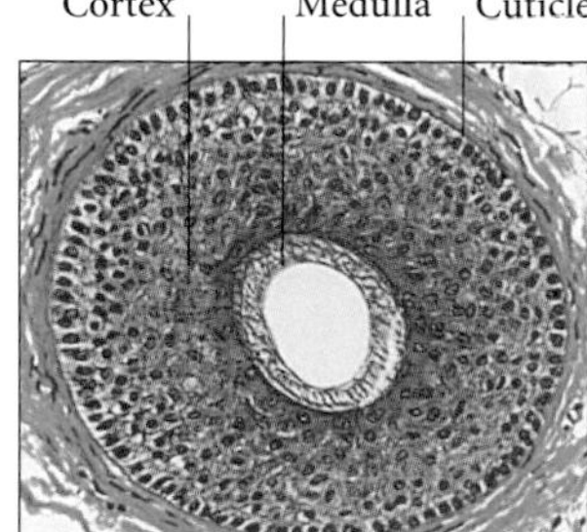
Cortex
Medulla
Cuticle

Magnified section of hair
Hair has three layers: the inner medulla (which is usually hollow), a thick pigmented cortex, and an outer cuticle.

(STRUCTURE) MUCOUS MEMBRANES

Mucous membranes are sheets of cells that protect body areas that must not dry out. These membranes line the mouth and nose; the insides of the eyelids; and the genital, digestive, and respiratory tracts. Special cells in the membranes, called goblet cells, secrete mucus, a sticky protein that lubricates and cleans. At the opening of body cavities, mucous membranes are continuous with the skin.

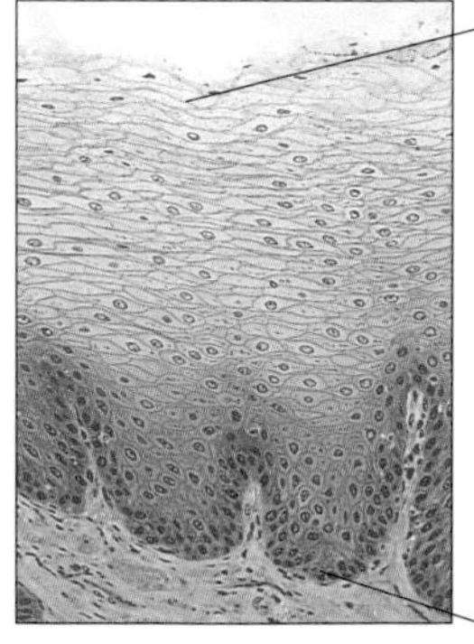
Flat surface cells
Basal cell layer

Membrane layers
The structure of mucous membranes – rapidly dividing cells in the basal layer below the layer of flat cells – is similar to that of the skin's epidermis, but lacks a thick, distinctive outer edge.

GENERALIZED SKIN CONDITIONS

Many skin disorders can affect several or all areas of the body surface at once. Some of these disorders have a strong inherited component, but often the cause of a particular condition is not known. Not all generalized skin problems are curable – some recur intermittently throughout life – but most can be controlled effectively with treatment and self-help measures.

Most generalized skin disorders do not pose a serious threat to health, but chronic conditions, such as psoriasis and eczema, can affect the quality of life and require long-term treatment. Other disorders cause only temporary discomfort and often clear up without treatment. Some conditions are the result of an allergy to substances such as drugs and disappear after the cause has been identified and eliminated.

The articles in this section discuss disorders that can involve several areas of skin at once. Skin disorders that affect particular areas are discussed elsewhere (*see* LOCALIZED SKIN CONDITIONS, pp.340–350, and SKIN INFECTIONS AND INFESTATIONS, pp.351–355). Disorders that affect the skin of children are discussed in a separate section (*see* INFANCY AND CHILDHOOD, pp.828–831). Rashes that affect the skin as part of an infectious disease, such as rubella or measles, are also found elsewhere (*see* INFECTIONS AND INFESTATIONS, pp.282–313).

KEY ANATOMY

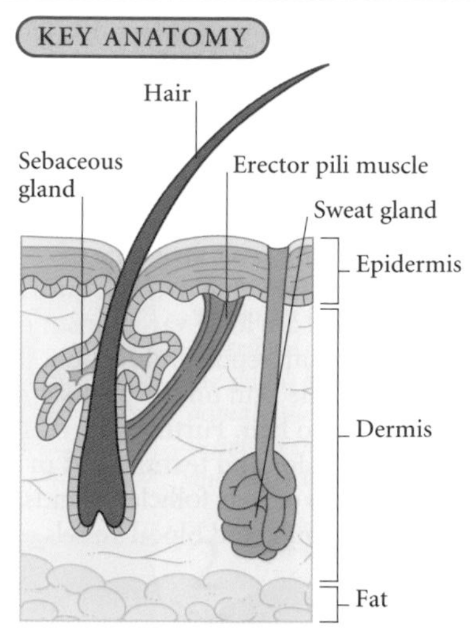
Hair
Sebaceous gland
Erector pili muscle
Sweat gland
Epidermis
Dermis
Fat

For further information on the structure and function of the skin, *see* pp.328–331.

Psoriasis

Plaques of red, thickened, scaly skin, often affecting many areas of the body

 GENETICS Often runs in families

 LIFESTYLE Stress can trigger an attack

 AGE Risk factor depends on the type

 GENDER Not a significant factor

Psoriasis is a common skin condition that is widespread in Western countries and parts of Asia and Africa. There are several types, most of which are difficult to control and flare up throughout life. Red, thickened, scaly skin occurs in all types of psoriasis. The scaly areas do not always itch, but, if the condition affects many parts of the body, psoriasis may cause severe physical discomfort as well as embarrassment in public.

In areas of skin that are affected by psoriasis, new skin cells are produced at a much faster rate than dead cells are shed and the excess skin cells accumulate to form thick patches. The cause is not known, but an episode of psoriasis may be triggered by infection, injury, or stress. The condition often runs in families, which suggests that a genetic factor may be involved; approximately 1 in 3 people with psoriasis has a close relative who has the condition. The use of certain drugs, such as antidepressant drugs (p.916), antihypertensive drugs (p.897), beta blockers (p.898), and antimalarial drugs (p.888), can produce psoriasis in some people.

WHAT ARE THE TYPES?

There are four main types of psoriasis, each of which has a distinctive appearance. Some people may be affected by more than one type of the disorder.

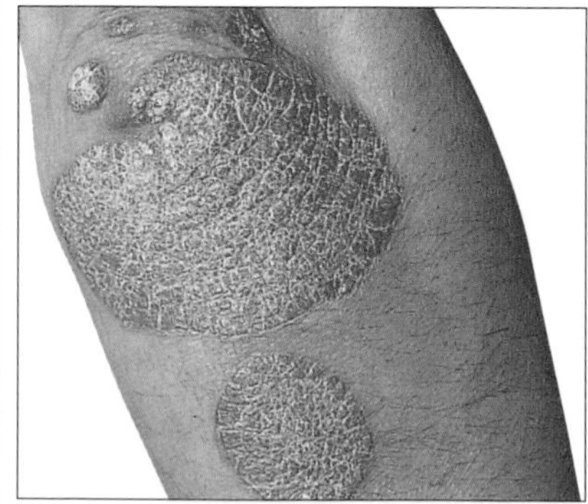

Plaque psoriasis on the elbow
The elbows are a common site for plaque psoriasis. The scaly surfaces of the patches are accumulations of dead skin cells.

PLAQUE PSORIASIS The most common form of psoriasis, plaque psoriasis, is a lifelong disorder that may develop in people of any age. The condition may produce the following symptoms:

- Patches called plaques, consisting of thickened, red skin and scaly surfaces. They usually occur on the knees, elbows, lower back, and scalp; behind the ears; and at the hairline. In some cases, they develop on old scar tissue.
- Intermittent itching of affected areas.
- Discolored nails that are covered with small pits. In severe cases, the nails lift away from the nail beds.

The symptoms of plaque psoriasis tend to continue for weeks or months and may recur intermittently.

GUTTATE PSORIASIS This form most commonly affects children and adolescents and often occurs after a bacterial throat infection. Typical symptoms are:

- Numerous small, pink papules of scaly skin, each about 3/8 in (1 cm) across, mainly on the back and chest.
- Intermittent itching of the affected areas of skin.

These symptoms usually disappear in 4–6 months and do not recur, but more than half of those affected later develop another form of psoriasis.

Guttate psoriasis
The small, pink, scaly papules of guttate psoriasis are often spread over large areas. A typical site is the back, as shown above.

PUSTULAR PSORIASIS This is a rare but potentially life-threatening type of psoriasis that mainly affects adults. The condition may appear abruptly, with the following symptoms:

- Small blisters filled with pus that develop on the palms of the hands and the soles of the feet.
- Widespread areas of red, inflamed, and acutely tender skin.
- Some thickening and scaling of the inflamed areas.

In its most severe form, pustular psoriasis affects the entire body.

INVERSE PSORIASIS Elderly people are commonly affected by this type of psoriasis, in which large, moist, red areas develop in skin folds rather than over widespread body areas. The rash often affects the groin, the skin under the breasts, and sometimes the armpits. Inverse psoriasis usually clears up with treatment but may recur.

ARE THERE COMPLICATIONS?

About 1 in 10 people with psoriasis of any type develops a form of arthritis (p.374) that usually affects the fingers or knee joints. In pustular psoriasis, a massive loss of cells from the surface of the skin may lead to dehydration, kidney failure (p.705), infections, and high fever. If left untreated, the condition can be life-threatening.

WHAT MIGHT BE DONE?

Your doctor should be able to diagnose the type of psoriasis from its appearance. If you have only mild psoriasis that does not cause problems, you may decide not to treat the skin symptoms. Otherwise, you should follow the treatment that your doctor recommends.

TOPICAL TREATMENTS Psoriasis is commonly treated with emollients to soften the skin (*see* EMOLLIENTS AND BARRIER PREPARATIONS, p.890). Other common treatments are preparations containing coal tar or a substance called anthralin, which reduce inflammation and scaling. Coal tar and anthralin are effective but have an unpleasant smell and can stain clothing and bed linen. Anthralin should be applied to affected areas only, because it can irritate healthy skin.

Alternatively, your doctor may prescribe a topical preparation containing the vitamin D derivative calcipotriol (*see* VITAMINS, p.927). The preparation is usually applied twice a day. It has no smell, does not stain skin or clothes, and is normally effective within about 4 weeks. You should follow the advice of your doctor or dermatologist because this treatment should not be used on the face or in the creases of the skin.

Topical corticosteroids (p.892) may also be prescribed. However, the drugs should be used sparingly because they may cause long-term side effects, such as thinning of the skin.

GENERALIZED TREATMENTS For widespread psoriasis that does not respond to topical treatments, therapeutic exposure to ultraviolet (UV) light is often effective. UV therapy is usually given without oral medications. PUVA therapy involves using UV therapy together with psoralen, an oral drug that is taken before the ultraviolet light treatment and helps make the skin more sensitive to the effects of light. This combined treatment slightly increases the risk of skin cancer and is given only under the supervision of a dermatologist.

Regular, short doses of sunlight often help clear up psoriasis. Moderate exposure of affected areas to sunlight can be beneficial during the summer months, but you should adopt sensible precautions when outside to avoid sunburn (*see* SAFETY IN THE SUN, p.80).

In very severe cases of pustular psoriasis, for which topical preparations may not be effective, treatment with oral or intravenous drugs may be recommended. The drugs used for this treatment include retinoids (p.890), methotrexate (*see* ANTICANCER DRUGS, p.907), and cyclosporin (*see* IMMUNOSUPPRESSANTS, p.906). However, both retinoids and methotrexate can cause abnormalities in a developing fetus. For this reason, you should not take either of these drugs if you are pregnant or planning to have a child.

WHAT IS THE PROGNOSIS?

Although there is no cure for psoriasis, treatment normally relieves the symptoms and helps many people with the condition lead a normal life. If psoriasis is a long-term problem, you may find it beneficial to join a self-help group.

(WWW) ONLINE SITES: p.1036

Eczema

Patches of red, blistering, itchy skin, also known as dermatitis

AGE GENDER GENETICS LIFESTYLE
Risk factors depend on the type

The main feature of eczema is red, inflamed, itchy skin that is often covered with small, fluid-filled blisters. In long-standing eczema, the affected skin may become thickened as a result of persistent scratching. Eczema tends to recur intermittently throughout life.

WHAT ARE THE TYPES?

There are several different types of eczema. Some are triggered by particular factors, but others, such as nummular eczema, occur for no known reason.

ATOPIC ECZEMA This is the most common form of eczema. It usually appears first in infancy (*see* ECZEMA IN CHILDREN, p.829) and may continue to flare up during adolescence and adulthood (*see* ATOPIC ECZEMA, p.334). The cause of the condition is not known, but people who have an inherited tendency to allergies, including asthma (p.483), are more susceptible to it.

CONTACT DERMATITIS Direct contact with an irritant substance, or an allergic reaction to a substance, can result in a type of eczema known as contact dermatitis (p.335). It can occur at any age.

SEBORRHEIC DERMATITIS This form of eczema affects both infants and adults. The precise cause of seborrheic dermatitis (p.335) is unknown, although the condition is often associated with a yeastlike organism on the skin.

NUMMULAR ECZEMA Otherwise known as discoid eczema, this form is much more common in men than women. Itchy, coin-shaped plaques develop on the arms or legs, and the affected areas of skin may ooze and become scaly or blistered. The cause is not known.

ASTEATOTIC ECZEMA Most common in elderly people, this is caused by drying of the skin that occurs with aging. The scaly rash is random and cracked.

DYSHIDROTIC ECZEMA This type occurs where the skin is thickest, such as on the fingers, the palms, and the soles of the feet. Numerous itchy blisters develop, sometimes joining to form large, oozing areas. The cause is not known.

WHAT IS THE TREATMENT?

Keep your skin moist with emollients (*see* EMOLLIENTS AND BARRIER PREPARATIONS, p.890), take lukewarm baths, and use mild soaps. Topical corticosteroids (p.892) help reduce inflammation and itching. Nonsteroidal topical treatments, called calcineurin inhibitors, are applied twice a day and are safe for children and adults. Avoid contact with substances that may irritate the skin. If contact dermatitis occurs, patch testing (opposite page) can be done to identify a triggering substance. Most forms of eczema can be controlled successfully.

(WWW) ONLINE SITES: p.1036

Atopic eczema

Itchy inflammation of the skin that appears in patches, usually in skin creases

 AGE Usually first appears in infancy; sometimes persists into adulthood

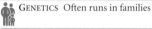

 GENETICS Often runs in families

 LIFESTYLE May be aggravated by extreme temperatures, certain foods, or stress

 GENDER Not a significant factor

The intensely itchy rash that is typical of atopic eczema usually appears first in infancy and often disappears later in childhood (*see* ECZEMA IN CHILDREN, p.829). However, flare-ups of the rash can sometimes occur throughout adolescence and into adulthood. Atopic eczema often affects people with a family history of asthma (p.483) or other allergic disorders, such as hay fever (*see* ALLERGIC RHINITIS, p.466). Flare-ups in adulthood are sometimes linked to stress, temperature change, or an allergic reaction to certain foods. Often, there is no obvious reason for them.

WHAT ARE THE SYMPTOMS?

The rash usually appears in patches, typically on the hands, as well as in skin creases in areas such as the wrists, the backs of the knees, and the insides of the elbows. The symptoms may include:

- Redness and swelling of the skin.
- Small, fluid-filled blisters.
- Itching, especially at night.
- Dry, scaly, and cracked skin.
- Thickened skin as a result of continuous scratching.

Bacterial infection sometimes develops in the affected area, resulting in further swelling and discomfort.

WHAT MIGHT BE DONE?

Your doctor will probably be able to diagnose atopic eczema from the symptoms. He or she may suggest a topical corticosteroid (p.892) to reduce inflammation. Apply this sparingly and reduce the frequency of use when the rash begins to clear up. Avoid using topical corticosteroids on the face unless directed otherwise by your doctor. Topical calcineurin inhibitors can be used safely on the face and elsewhere. Oral antihistamines may help relieve the itching (*see* ANTIPRURITIC DRUGS, p.891). If the rash is infected with bacteria, you will be prescribed oral antibiotics (p.885) or topical antibiotics (*see* PREPARATIONS FOR SKIN INFECTIONS AND INFESTATIONS, p.892).

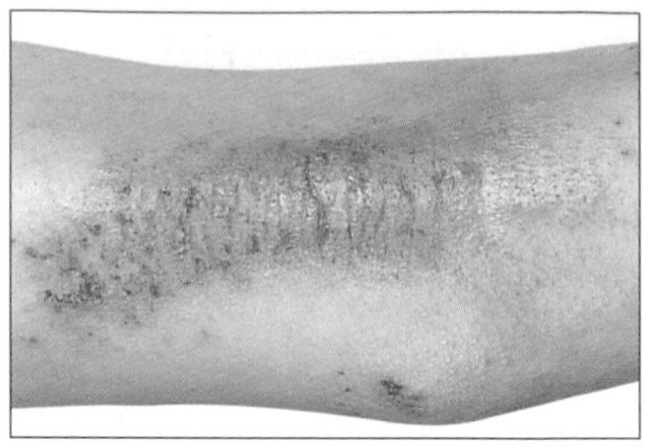

Atopic eczema
The itchy, dry, inflamed rash of atopic eczema typically develops in skin creases, such as the inside of the elbow.

Symptoms can be relieved by using emollients (*see* EMOLLIENTS AND BARRIER PREPARATIONS, p.890) and specially formulated bath oil available over the counter. Self-help measures can be used (*see* MANAGING HAND ECZEMA, below).

WHAT IS THE PROGNOSIS?

Atopic eczema can be controlled but not cured, and new patches of affected skin may appear at any time. However, the condition usually improves with age and is rare in elderly people.

(WWW) ONLINE SITES: p.1036

(SELF-HELP) MANAGING HAND ECZEMA

Eczema on the hands can be particularly persistent, painful, and unattractive. The following tips may help keep your eczema under control and reduce flare-ups:

- Avoid immersing your hands in water for long periods. If possible, wear cotton gloves inside rubber gloves for protection.
- Protect your hands with gloves or an emollient cream before cleaning, gardening, carrying out home repairs, or using irritant substances.
- Remove rings before using detergents or chemicals to prevent these irritant substances from becoming trapped against the skin.
- Use emollient creams frequently during the course of the day, and wash with mild soaps.

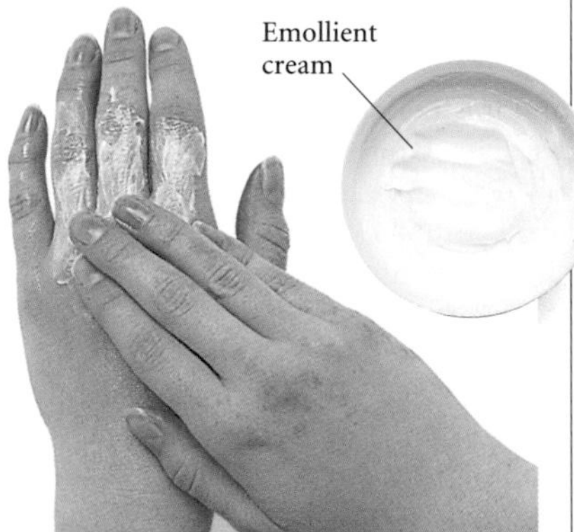
Emollient cream

Applying emollient cream
You can help prevent irritants such as detergents from coming into contact with the skin by applying an emollient cream as a protective barrier before carrying out chores. Emollients should also be used to moisturize the hands after washing.

Contact dermatitis

Plaques of red, itchy, and flaking skin caused by irritation or allergy

LIFESTYLE Work involving exposure to chemicals or detergents is a risk factor

AGE GENDER GENETICS Not significant factors

As its name implies, contact dermatitis is inflammation of the skin caused by contact with a specific substance. There are two types: irritant contact dermatitis, which is caused by primary irritants (substances, such as bleach, that harm anyone's skin); and allergic contact dermatitis, which occurs when a person comes into contact with a particular substance to which he or she has developed a sensitivity over time.

Substances that commonly trigger irritation or allergic reactions include some cosmetics; the nickel contained in jewelry, buttons, earrings for pierced ears, or watch straps; certain chemicals; drugs in skin creams; and some plants, such as poison ivy or ragweed.

WHAT ARE THE SYMPTOMS?

Contact dermatitis usually affects only the area that has been in direct contact with the substance that triggered the reaction. In irritant contact dermatitis, the skin inflammation develops soon after contact with the substance. The severity of the resulting rash depends both on the concentration of the irritant and on the duration of exposure.

Allergic contact dermatitis usually develops slowly over a period of time, and it is possible to have contact with a substance for several years without any skin inflammation occurring. However, once your skin has become sensitive to the substance, even a small amount of it, or a short exposure time, can trigger an allergic reaction.

In either form of contact dermatitis, the symptoms may include:

- Redness and swelling of the skin.
- Water- or pus-filled blisters that may ooze, drain, or become encrusted.
- Flaking skin, which may develop into raw patches.
- Persistent itching.

Consult your doctor if the cause of the contact dermatitis is not obvious or if the inflammation persists for a longer period of time than usual.

WHAT MIGHT BE DONE?

Your doctor will want to know when the skin inflammation developed and whether you have any known allergies. The site of the reaction is often a clue to its cause. For example, a patch of dermatitis on the wrist may be caused by an allergy to nickel in a watch or watch strap. People who handle chemicals at work often develop irritant or allergic contact dermatitis on their hands.

Your doctor may prescribe a topical corticosteroid (p.892) or a calcineurin inhibitor to relieve itching and inflammation. However, even with treatment, contact dermatitis may take a few weeks to clear up.

If you handle chemicals, it is important to find the cause of your allergy. If the cause cannot be identified, you may need to have patch testing (below).

Once the trigger has been identified, you should avoid it as much as possible. If you cannot do so, you may need to use creams (*see* EMOLLIENTS AND BARRIER PREPARATIONS, p.890), protective clothing, or gloves whenever you come into contact with the trigger.

(WWW) ONLINE SITES: p.1036

Seborrheic dermatitis

Patches of red, scaly, itchy skin that occur mainly on the scalp, face, and chest

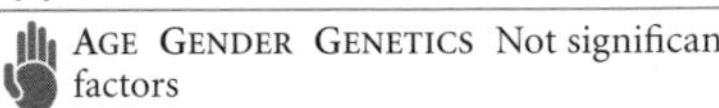

LIFESTYLE Stress can trigger an attack

AGE GENDER GENETICS Not significant factors

Seborrheic dermatitis is a skin rash that commonly occurs in infants and adults. In infants, either the scalp or the diaper area may be affected by the rash (*see* CRADLE CAP, p.829, and DIAPER RASH, p.829). In adults, the rash tends to occur on the central part of the face, the eyebrows, and the scalp, where it often leads to flaking of the skin. Sometimes seborrheic dermatitis also develops in the armpits, the groin, or the middle of the chest. In men, the condition may develop in the beard area.

The cause of seborrheic dermatitis is unknown, but the condition is sometimes associated with the overgrowth of a yeastlike substance that is present naturally on the surface of the skin. Flare-ups of the condition may be triggered by a period of stress or illness.

(TEST) PATCH TESTING

Patch testing is carried out on people with contact dermatitis. The test is performed by a dermatologist to find out which substances provoke an allergic reaction. Possible allergens (substances that can cause an allergic reaction) are diluted and placed on small strips or disks. The test disks are then stuck to the skin using inert (nonallergenic) tape. After 48 hours, the disks are removed and the skin underneath them is examined. A red, inflamed patch indicates a positive reaction to an allergen. The tested area is examined again 2 days later to check for delayed reactions.

Inert tape

Disk of test substance

1 *Minute quantities of test substances are placed on small disks. The disks are stuck with inert tape to an inconspicuous area of the skin, usually on the back.*

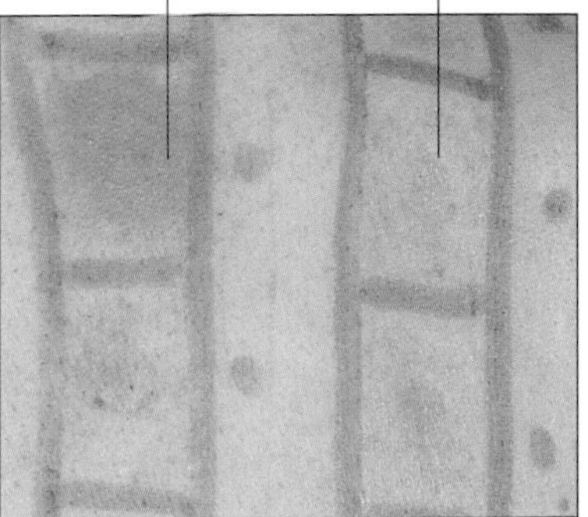
Positive reaction to patch test
Negative reaction to patch test

2 *When the disks are removed from the skin after 48 hours, positive reactions to allergens appear as red patches. In some cases, reactions may take longer to appear.*

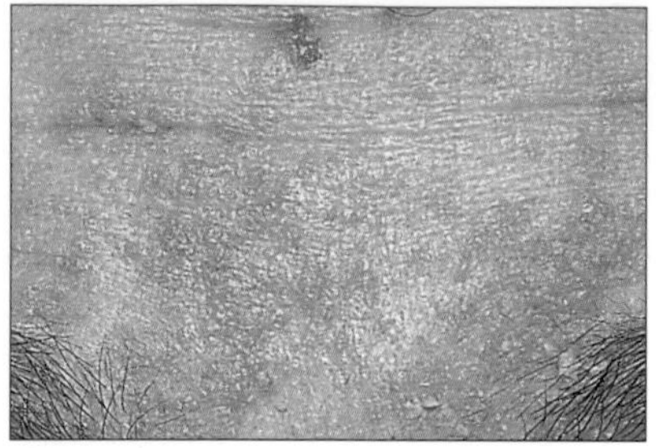

Seborrheic dermatitis on the forehead
The forehead and eyebrows are common sites for seborrheic dermatitis. Flakes of skin may become trapped in the eyebrows.

WHAT ARE THE SYMPTOMS?

The symptoms of seborrheic dermatitis may include the following:

- Scaly, red patches of inflamed skin, often with a yellow crust.
- Eyelids that are sore, red, and crusty (*see* BLEPHARITIS, p.583).
- Excessive dandruff (p.358).
- Occasional itching of affected areas.

This is a recurrent rash that may flare up intermittently over months or years.

WHAT MIGHT BE DONE?

If a yeast overgrowth is diagnosed, your doctor may prescribe a topical corticosteroid (p.892) or an antifungal drug (p.889). If your scalp is affected, he or she may prescribe an antifungal shampoo or recommend you use a coal tar shampoo. Both should produce a rapid improvement in symptoms.

(WWW) ONLINE SITES: p.1036

Blistering diseases

Disorders of various types that cause eruptions of blisters

AGE Risk factor depends on the type

GENETICS Some types are due to an abnormal gene inherited from both parents

GENDER LIFESTYLE Not significant factors

There are several uncommon diseases that produce eruptions of blistering on the surface of the skin. These blistering diseases may either occur in particular sites or cover widespread areas of the body. In contrast to individual blisters (p.357), which are minor skin injuries, blistering diseases can be serious. Left untreated, these diseases may eventually become life-threatening.

WHAT ARE THE TYPES?

Some rare types of blistering diseases are present at birth and are caused by an abnormal gene inherited from both parents in an autosomal recessive manner (*see* GENE DISORDERS, p.269). These diseases cause the skin over the whole body to become very fragile and to blister when touched. They may be fatal.

More commonly, blistering diseases are acquired in adulthood. There are three main types of these diseases; all of them are autoimmune disorders, in which the body produces antibodies that are damaging to the skin.

PEMPHIGOID The most common type of blistering disease is pemphigoid. The disorder usually affects people over age 60. It results in numerous tightly filled blisters, mainly on the legs and trunk, each measuring up to 1¼ in (3 cm) in diameter. Initially, the blisters may itch.

PEMPHIGUS Less common than pemphigoid, pemphigus also usually affects people over age 60. In this condition, blisters may appear on any part of the body but often occur around the eyes and inside the mouth. The blisters are fragile and may rupture spontaneously, leaving patches of raw skin.

DERMATITIS HERPETIFORMIS This disorder is associated with an allergy to gluten, the protein in wheat (*see* CELIAC DISEASE, p.658). The condition results in the eruption of itchy blisters, usually on the elbows, buttocks, and knees.

WHAT MIGHT BE DONE?

In all types of blistering diseases, diagnosis is usually based on a skin biopsy (p.344). This procedure involves taking a sample of skin for examination.

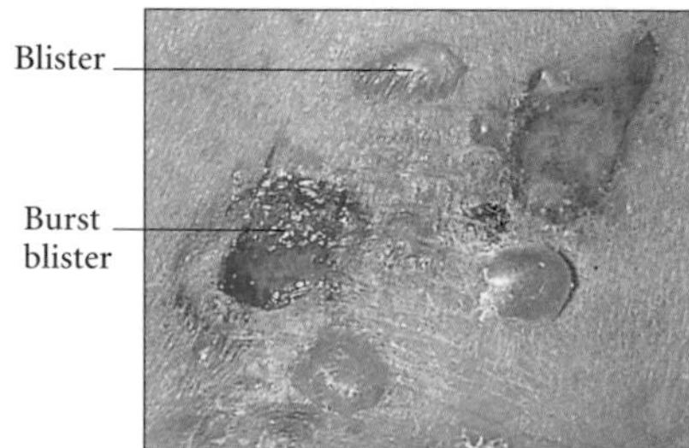
Blister
Burst blister

Blistering caused by pemphigoid
Severe blistering of the skin is the main sign of pemphigoid, an autoimmune disorder usually affecting elderly people.

There is no effective treatment for inherited blistering disorders. Parents of babies who have these diseases may wish to seek genetic counseling (p.270) to discuss the likelihood of further children also being affected.

If you have either pemphigoid or pemphigus, your doctor will prescribe oral corticosteroids (p.930). Some people will also need immunosuppressants (p.906) for several weeks or months. If you have severe pemphigus, you may need immediate treatment in hospital with immunosuppressants.

Introducing a gluten-free diet usually clears up dermatitis herpetiformis, but you may also need the drug dapsone (*see* ANTIBIOTICS, p.885), which helps clear up the blisters.

WHAT IS THE PROGNOSIS?

The blistering diseases that affect adults can often be controlled with treatment, but very few cases can be permanently cured. Although pemphigoid may clear up spontaneously after about 2–5 years, pemphigus often needs lifelong treatment with drugs. The skin condition dermatitis herpetiformis may recur if gluten is reintroduced into the diet.

(WWW) ONLINE SITES: p.1033, p.1036

Lichen planus

An itchy rash consisting of small, raised, flat-topped lesions that are shiny and pink or purple in color

AGE More common in people over age 30

LIFESTYLE Stress may increase the risk

GENDER GENETICS Not significant factors

In lichen planus, small, shiny, itchy lesions appear in a dense cluster. Often, there is no obvious cause, but occasionally the rash may develop as a reaction to certain drugs, such as sulfonamide antibiotics (p.885) or gold-based antirheumatic drugs (p.895). Lichen planus may also be associated with stress. It is more common in people over age 30.

WHAT ARE THE SYMPTOMS?

The rash can develop in patches on the lower back and on the inner surfaces of the wrists, forearms, and ankles. Lichen planus often appears suddenly and may

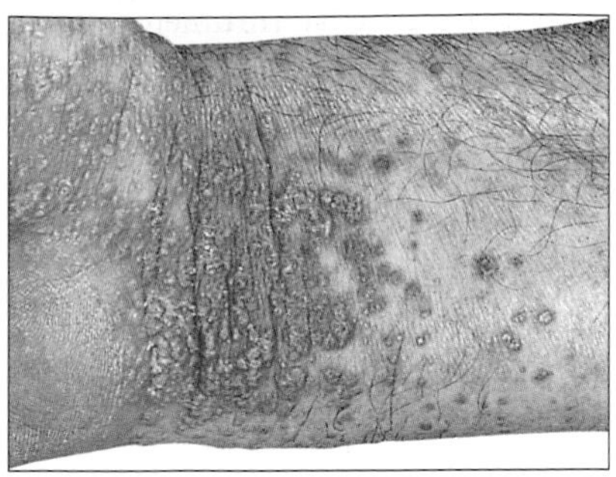

Lichen planus on the wrist
The inner surface of the wrist, shown above, is one of the areas where the itchy lesions of lichen planus may appear.

affect more than one area, but sometimes the rash spreads gradually over a period of a few months. The symptoms of lichen planus include:

- Groups of small, shiny, pink or purple, flat-topped lesions on the skin; the surface of some may be covered by a network of fine white lines.
- Intense itching, particularly at night.

The disorder can also affect the nails and scalp. If lichen planus develops in the nails, they become ridged along their length and, in some cases, fall off (*see* NAIL ABNORMALITIES, p.360). If the scalp is affected, the results may be patchy hair loss with associated scarring of the scalp. The lesions may also appear on the sites of skin injuries such as scratches. Another form of lichen planus affects the mouth (*see* ORAL LICHEN PLANUS, p.634).

WHAT MIGHT BE DONE?

If the diagnosis is not obvious from the appearance of the rash, your doctor may arrange for a skin biopsy (p.344), in which a sample of skin is removed and examined under a microscope. To relieve the itching, the doctor may prescribe a strong topical corticosteroid (p.892). In addition, you can take an over-the-counter oral antihistamine (*see* ANTIPRURITIC DRUGS, p.891) for relief at night. If the rash is widespread and affects your nails or scalp, you may need oral corticosteroid drugs (p.930).

If a drug reaction is suspected, your doctor will advise you to stop taking the drug and may prescribe an alternative. Lichen planus usually persists for 12–18 months and may leave patches of darkened skin where it has healed.

(WWW) ONLINE SITES: p.1036

Erythema multiforme

A red rash forming concentric rings with purplish centers

 AGE Most common in children and young adults

 GENDER More common in males

 GENETICS LIFESTYLE Not significant factors

Erythema multiforme develops rapidly and is characterized by distinctive red spots that grow bigger over a few days. The rash is widespread, and often includes the palms of the hands and the soles of the feet. It may affect the mucous membranes, such as the lining of the mouth and nose. The rash is most common in young people, and affects more males than females. The disorder is not contagious and is usually mild, although a serious form sometimes occurs.

In most cases, the cause of erythema multiforme is unknown, but the rash can be triggered by infection with a virus such as herpes simplex, the virus that produces cold sores (p.354). Other factors that can trigger the rash include taking certain drugs, such as sulfonamide antibiotics (p.885), phenytoin (*see* ANTICONVULSANT DRUGS, p.914), or the vaccine for poliomyelitis (p.293). The rash can also be caused by cancer or by radiation therapy (p.279).

WHAT ARE THE SYMPTOMS?

The symptoms, which usually develop suddenly, may include:

- Numerous small red spots distributed symmetrically over the body. These may enlarge to form red rings with purplish centers, called target lesions. The lesions may blister in the middle.

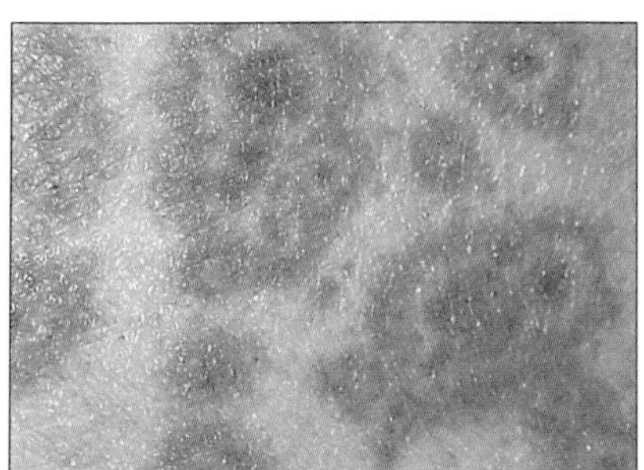

Erythema multiforme
The rash of erythema multiforme usually consists of concentric red rings, often with purplish centers (target lesions).

- Itching of the affected area.
- Painful, inflamed lesions within the mouth and nose.
- Fever, headache, and sore throat.
- Occasionally, diarrhea.

In rare instances, most of the skin and mucous membranes throughout the body become severely inflamed and ulcerated. Such cases require emergency treatment because the condition may be life-threatening if it is left untreated.

WHAT MIGHT BE DONE?

Your doctor will probably make a diagnosis from the appearance of the rash. If the rash appeared shortly after you started taking a prescribed drug, the doctor may prescribe an alternative treatment. If itching is a problem, he or she may suggest an oral antihistamine (*see* ANTIPRURITIC DRUGS, p.891). In a case of severe erythema multiforme, particularly if the mouth is inflamed, you may need treatment in the hospital; intravenous fluids, analgesics (p.912), and corticosteroids (p.930) may be given in the critical care unit.

Erythema multiforme usually disappears over a few weeks. However, there is a possibility that it may recur. If a drug is thought to be the cause, you should avoid taking it in the future.

(WWW) ONLINE SITES: p.1036

Pityriasis rosea

A rash of oval, pink, flat spots, most commonly on the trunk and limbs

 AGE Mainly affects young adults

 GENDER GENETICS LIFESTYLE Not significant factors

Pityriasis rosea produces a scaly, pink rash. The condition most commonly occurs in young adults. It usually affects the trunk, arms, and upper thighs; more rarely, it affects the feet, hands, and scalp. The condition is thought to be caused by a viral infection.

WHAT ARE THE SYMPTOMS?

The symptoms change over time as the condition progresses. They usually develop in the following order:

- An oval patch, $\frac{3}{4}$–$2\frac{1}{2}$ in (2–6 cm) in diameter, known as a herald patch, appears. This patch resembles those that occur in ringworm (p.352).

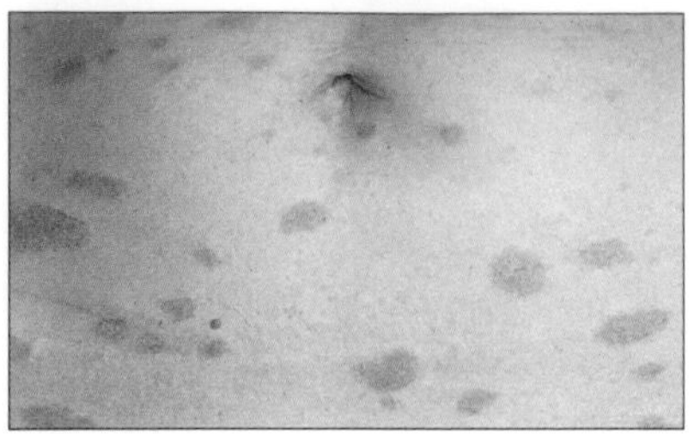

Pityriasis rosea
Oval, pink, scaly spots, as shown here on the abdomen, are typical of pityriasis rosea, commonly seen on the trunk.

- About 3–10 days later, a number of smaller oval, pink, flat spots, 3/8–3/4 in (1–2 cm) in diameter, appears. The rash begins on the trunk, spreading across the abdomen, along the thighs and upper arms, and up toward the neck. The spots on the back usually occur in sweeping lines, resembling the shape of a Christmas tree.
- A scaly margin may appear around the edges of the patches after a week.

Occasionally, mild itching may occur. Although pityriasis rosea is not serious, it is important to consult your doctor to rule out conditions such as psoriasis (p.332) and eczema (p.333).

WHAT MIGHT BE DONE?

The distinctive rash makes the condition easy to diagnose. It usually clears up after about 6–8 weeks without treatment and is unlikely to reappear.

(WWW) ONLINE SITES: p.1036

Photosensitivity

Sensitivity of the skin to ultraviolet light, resulting in redness and discomfort

AGE GENDER GENETICS LIFESTYLE
Not significant factors

Photosensitivity is defined as an abnormal reaction of the skin to the effects of ultraviolet rays in sunlight. The condition is sometimes present at birth and sometimes develops later in life.

Various substances may cause photosensitivity, including drugs such as tetracyclines (*see* ANTIBIOTICS, p.885), diuretics (p.902), and oral contraceptives. Photosensitivity may also result from the use of certain cosmetics. The condition sometimes occurs in people who have systemic lupus erythematosus (p.461), an autoimmune disorder in which the body attacks its own tissues. Sometimes there is no obvious cause. In these cases, the condition is referred to as primary photosensitivity.

WHAT ARE THE SYMPTOMS?

The reaction occurs in areas frequently exposed to sunlight, such as the face and hands. It usually develops shortly after exposure but may be delayed for 24–48 hours. The symptoms include:

- Red, often painful, rash.
- Small, itchy blisters.
- Scaly skin.

At a later stage, the nails may lift from the nail beds. Sometimes, affected people also develop generalized redness on all exposed skin. In rare cases, people with severe photosensitivity are unable to go outdoors in daylight.

WHAT MIGHT BE DONE?

Your doctor will probably make a diagnosis from the appearance of the rash. If the reaction is thought to be caused by a drug, the doctor may prescribe an alternative. You may also need blood tests to check for underlying disorders.

To relieve the symptoms, the doctor may prescribe topical corticosteroids (p.892) or oral antihistamines (*see* ANTIPRURITIC DRUGS, p.891). Severe cases are treated with controlled exposure to ultraviolet light, sometimes combined with drugs, to desensitize the skin.

You can help control the reaction by avoiding sunlight as much as possible. When outdoors, cover your skin, wear a hat, and use a high-factor sunblock (*see* SAFETY IN THE SUN, p.80).

(WWW) ONLINE SITES: p.1036

Drug-induced rashes

Many different kinds of rashes that occur in some people during or after treatment with certain drugs

AGE GENDER GENETICS LIFESTYLE
Not significant factors

Rashes are a common side effect of drug treatment. The reaction is caused by an allergic response to the drug or to substances produced when the drug is broken down by the body.

Reactions to drugs can produce almost any type of rash, including some forms that mimic other disorders, such as lichen planus (p.336) or erythema multiforme (p.337). However, the majority of drug-induced rashes appear as raised areas of skin spread widely over the body. Drug-induced rashes may be accompanied by intense itching. Sometimes, even when a rash is mild, there may be other, more dramatic effects such as wheezing and collapse. Occasionally, people with severe reactions need hospital treatment.

The drugs that most often produce rashes are antibiotics (p.885), such as penicillin, but almost all drug treatments can cause an allergic reaction if a person becomes sensitive to them. Drug-induced rashes usually develop within the first few days of starting treatment but can also occur after a course of treatment has finished.

Sensitivity develops after at least one previous exposure to a drug. It is common for people to take a certain drug for the first time without experiencing any allergic reaction and then to develop a rash when the drug is taken in a subsequent course of treatment.

WHAT MIGHT BE DONE?

If you develop a rash while you are taking a drug, you should consult your doctor before the next dose is due. He or she may then stop the treatment or prescribe another drug.

If you have been taking several drugs and one of these could have caused the rash, you must tell your doctor about all the drugs you have taken recently, including over-the-counter treatments, drugs that have been prescribed in the hospital, and medicines prescribed by another doctor. You should also tell the doctor about any recreational drugs that you may be taking.

Most drug-induced rashes disappear when the drug responsible is stopped. However, the symptoms occasionally continue for weeks afterward. If itching is a problem, your doctor may advise that you apply a topical corticosteroid (p.892) or take an oral antihistamine (*see* ANTIPRURITIC DRUGS, p.891); both types of drugs are available over the counter and by prescription.

Once you know you are allergic to a drug, you should make sure you notify any doctor who treats you in the future. If you have had a severe reaction to a particular drug, you should consider wearing a medical alert tag.

Itching

An irritating sensation in the skin, either localized or widespread

AGE GENDER GENETICS LIFESTYLE
Risk factors depend on the cause

Itching, also known as pruritus, is a very common symptom and is associated with many skin disorders. The irritation may be either restricted to a small area or widespread over the body. Continual scratching, which often damages the skin, aggravates the problem.

WHAT ARE THE CAUSES?

Localized itching can often be the result of an insect bite. Itching may also be associated with a rash. An itchy rash is a common symptom of conditions such as urticaria (p.468), eczema (p.333), lichen planus (p.336), and parasitic skin infestations such as scabies (p.355).

Widespread itching may develop as a result of dry skin, an irritant reaction to particular bath products or detergents, or an allergic reaction to certain drugs (*see* DRUG ALLERGY, p.467). It can also occur as a symptom of a serious underlying disorder, such as liver disease or kidney failure (p.705).

Persistent patches of itchy skin may develop as a result of emotional stress. The itching typically affects the limbs and neck but can also involve other areas of the body. Frequent scratching, often unconsciously, causes the skin to thicken and can increase the itching, leading to a further cycle of scratching and itching. This condition, known as lichen simplex or neurodermatitis, is more common in females.

WHAT CAN I DO?

There are several measures that you can take to relieve itching and stop scratching. Emollients (*see* EMOLLIENTS AND BARRIER PREPARATIONS, p.890) will help moisturize dry and itchy skin, particularly if you apply them after washing or bathing. To relieve severe itching, you may find over-the-counter oral antihistamines (*see* ANTIPRURITIC DRUGS, p.891), calamine, or topical corticosteroids (p.892) to be effective.

As far as possible, you should avoid substances that are likely to irritate the skin, such as scented bath products, detergents, or woolen garments. You may benefit from wearing loose-fitting clothing made of fabric that does not irritate the skin and from keeping your fingernails cut short so that you cannot damage your skin when scratching.

You should contact your doctor if you have persistent itching for which there is no obvious cause.

(WWW) ONLINE SITES: p.1036

Purpura

A group of disorders in which reddish purple spots appear on the skin

AGE GENDER GENETICS LIFESTYLE
Risk factors depend on the cause

In the conditions known as purpura, reddish purple spots or bruiselike areas of discoloration develop on the skin. The spots or bruises, called purpuric spots, result from small areas of bleeding under the skin and may be caused by damaged blood vessels or by an abnormality in the blood. The appearance of the spots varies, and they can range from the size of a pinhead to about 1 in (2.5 cm) in diameter. Unlike many other red rashes, purpuric spots do not fade when they are pressed.

The spots themselves are harmless, but purpura is sometimes a sign of a potentially serious underlying disorder.

WHAT ARE THE TYPES?

The most common type of purpura is senile purpura, which occurs mainly in elderly people. The condition gives rise to dark bruises, typically on the backs of the hands and forearms and on the thighs. Senile purpura is due to weakening of the tissues that support the blood vessels under the skin; these weakened blood vessels become susceptible to damage and bleed easily.

Very small purpuric spots, known as petechiae, often result from a reduction in the number of platelets (cells in the body that help the blood to clot). Platelet deficiency can be associated with many bone marrow disorders, such as leukemia (p.453), or with autoimmune disorders (p.461). The condition may also occur as a side effect of treatment with some drugs, such as diuretic drugs (p.902) or antibiotics (p.885).

Purpuric spots of variable size may be a sign of a serious bacterial infection of the blood (*see* SEPTICEMIA, p.298). In some people, the infection may be due to a type of bacterium called meningococcus, which can result in potentially life-threatening meningitis (p.527). If purpura appears in conjunction with a fever, you should seek emergency medical advice.

Henoch-Schönlein purpura (p.838) is an uncommon type of purpura occurring in childhood and caused by inflammation of small blood vessels. The spots that appear in this condition are unlike those in other forms of purpura and resemble small raised lumps.

WHAT MIGHT BE DONE?

Senile purpura is usually diagnosed from the bruiselike appearance of the spots. The condition is harmless, and no treatment is needed. The spots fade gradually but are likely to recur.

If the cause of the purpura is not obvious, your doctor may arrange for blood tests to find out if the platelet levels in the blood and the ability of the blood to clot are normal. Purpura associated with fever needs urgent medical investigation so that septicemia or meningitis can be excluded.

If blood tests show an abnormality, your doctor may refer you to a specialist for further investigations. If you are found to have a very low platelet count, you may be given platelet transfusions to prevent serious internal bleeding, especially in the brain, until the underlying disorder can be diagnosed and treated. The purpura should disappear once the cause has been successfully treated. If the condition is the result of an autoimmune disorder, your doctor may prescribe corticosteroid drugs (p.930) to clear it up.

(WWW) ONLINE SITES: p.1026, p.1033, p.1036

Senile purpura
These harmless patches resemble purple bruises. They commonly appear on the backs of the hands in elderly people.

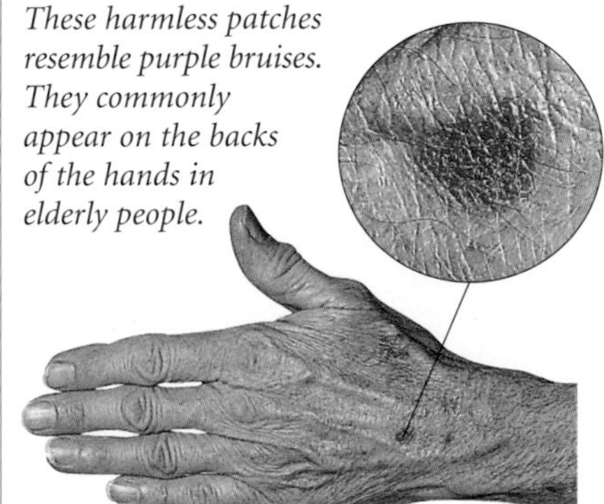

LOCALIZED SKIN CONDITIONS

Localized skin conditions are disorders that affect only one area of the body or a small area of skin. Many of these conditions are related to specific sites because they are associated with areas such as particular glands in the skin, or because of the localized effects of factors such as pressure or exposure to sunlight.

Acne and rosacea, two types of rashes that are usually confined to the face, are described first in this section. The next articles cover conditions that are associated with sweat glands or with under- or overproduction of melanin, the pigment that gives skin its color.

Skin cancers, which are increasingly common, are given extensive coverage. It is important to be able to recognize the signs of cancerous changes in the skin, and the various types of skin cancers are described in detail to help you identify them. Subsequent articles describe several noncancerous forms of swellings and growths. The final articles cover localized skin defects caused by factors such as friction or poor blood circulation.

Localized disorders due to infection are described in another section (*see* SKIN INFECTIONS AND INFESTATIONS, pp.351–355). Skin problems specific to babies are discussed elsewhere in the book (*see* INFANCY AND CHILDHOOD, pp.828–831) as are minor injuries, such as sunburn, (*see* MINOR SKIN INJURIES, pp.356–357).

KEY ANATOMY

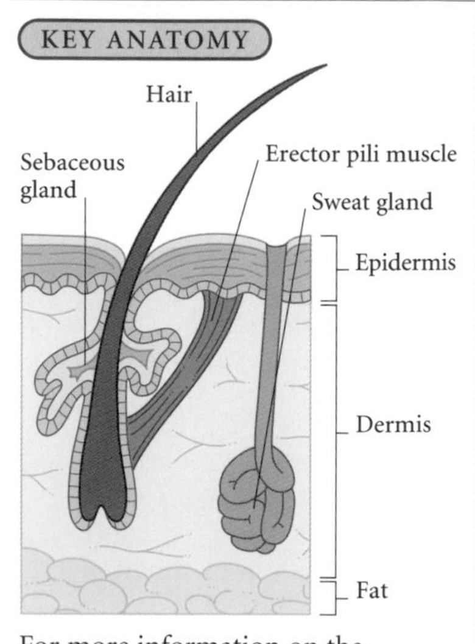
Hair
Sebaceous gland
Erector pili muscle
Sweat gland
Epidermis
Dermis
Fat

For more information on the structure and function of the skin, *see* pp.328–331.

Acne

A rash, mainly on the face, due to blockage and inflammation of glands in the skin

AGE Most common in adolescents

GENDER More common in males

GENETICS Sometimes runs in families

LIFESTYLE Using oil-based cosmetics and exposure to oils at work are risk factors

There are various types of acne. The most common form is acne vulgaris, which is the familiar rash that affects many teenagers. Acne vulgaris tends to be more common and more severe in males. The condition is triggered by hormonal changes at puberty and may appear as early as age 10. The rash usually subsides after adolescence, but in some people it persists after age 30. Acne can cause great psychological distress, and teenagers may feel especially self-conscious about their appearance.

More unusual forms of acne include occupational acne, which results from exposure to certain types of industrial oils, and drug-induced acne, which is caused by some prescribed drugs, such as corticosteroids (p.930).

WHAT ARE THE CAUSES?

Acne vulgaris is caused by the overproduction of sebum, an oily substance secreted by the sebaceous glands in the skin. Normally, the sebum drains into hair follicles and flows out through the follicle openings on the skin's surface, thereby keeping the skin lubricated and supple. However, when the glands produce excess sebum, the hair follicles become blocked. If the sebum remains clogged in the follicle openings, it hardens and becomes dark, forming small plugs called blackheads. In some cases, hair follicles are sealed by an excess of keratin, the tough, fibrous protein that is produced by the skin cells. When this happens, the trapped sebum hardens into small white lumps, called whiteheads, under the surface of the skin. In both types of blockage, bacteria multiply in the sebum, causing inflammation of the surrounding tissues.

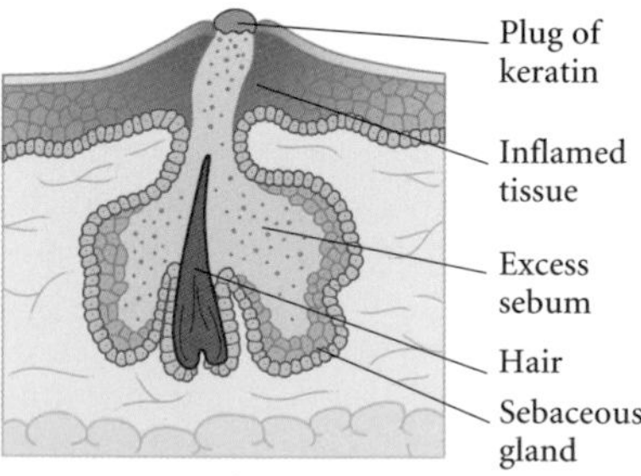
Plug of keratin
Inflamed tissue
Excess sebum
Hair
Sebaceous gland

Formation of acne lesions
Acne develops when excess sebum, and in some cases the protein keratin, blocks hair follicles. Bacteria multiply in the trapped sebum, infecting the surrounding tissues and causing various types of lesions.

Acne that starts at puberty is thought to be the result of oversensitivity to androgens (male sex hormones), which are present in both boys and girls. Androgens cause the sebaceous glands to enlarge and increase their output of sebum. There may be a genetic factor since acne can run in families. The use of steroids to improve performance in sport may also increase the level of androgens. Other causes of acne vulgaris include some disorders, such as Cushing syndrome (p.684), which is due to an excess of corticosteroid hormones.

Acne may become worse in times of stress. In girls, outbreaks may be affected by the hormonal fluctuation that occurs during the menstrual cycle. The condition may also be exacerbated by the use of oil-based cosmetics.

Poor hygiene does not cause acne, although a buildup of oil and dead cells on the skin surface may increase the risk of blocked follicles and allow bacteria to multiply. There is no evidence that fatty foods, candy, or chocolate either cause or aggravate acne.

Occupational acne is usually caused by long-term contact between the skin and oily clothes. The reasons for drug-induced acne are not known.

WHAT ARE THE SYMPTOMS?

Acne vulgaris occurs in areas of skin that have a high density of sebaceous glands. At puberty, the hair, face, and upper trunk normally become greasy due to increased production of sebum. However, in people with acne, oiliness is excessive. Acne tends to appear on the face, but other areas such as the upper back, center of the chest, shoulders, and neck are also commonly affected. The disorder is usually more severe in winter and tends to improve in summer when there is increased exposure to sunlight. Lesions that are caused by occupational acne may appear in those parts of the body that come into close contact with oily clothes, such as the thighs. All forms of acne may produce some or all of the following types of lesions:

- Tiny blackheads.
- Small, firm whiteheads.
- Red pimples, often with yellow pus-filled tips.
- Painful, large, firm, red lumps.
- Tender lumps beneath the skin without obvious heads (cysts).

All of the types of lesions listed above may develop at any one time, but the severity of acne varies greatly from person to person. Deep-seated lesions may leave scars after they have healed.

> SELF-HELP
>
> ### CONTROLLING ACNE
>
> Following these simple self-help measures may help clear up acne and prevent further episodes:
>
> - Wash your skin twice a day with warm water and a mild cleanser. Do not scrub too vigorously.
> - Do not pick at pimples because this may worsen the condition and result in scarring.
> - Apply a benzoyl peroxide cream daily to the affected areas.
> - If you have occupational acne, keep work clothes clean.
>
> 
> Cleanser
>
> **Cleansing your face**
> *Wash your face with warm water and a mild cleanser. Scrubbing hard or using hot water can make the acne worse.*

WHAT IS THE TREATMENT?

Self-help measures may help clear up mild acne and prevent recurrence (*see* CONTROLLING ACNE, left). Your doctor may also recommend a topical drug treatment, such as benzoyl peroxide or retinoid cream (*see* RETINOID DRUGS, p.890) to loosen keratin that is sealing the hair follicles. The doctor may also prescribe topical antibiotics (*see* PREPARATIONS FOR SKIN INFECTIONS AND INFESTATIONS, p.892). Moderate acne is often successfully treated with a low-dose oral antibiotic (p.885), such as tetracycline or erythromycin.

If these treatments fail to provide relief, you may be referred to a dermatologist. He or she may prescribe isotretinoin, an oral retinoid, that acts to loosen keratin and reduce the secretion of sebum. However, the use of isotretinoin is known to result in fetal abnormalities. For this reason, sexually active women should take the drug only if they are using a reliable contraceptive. Some women may be prescribed the combined pill, which may relieve acne by counteracting the action of androgens.

There is no immediate cure for acne. However, scarring may be prevented if treatment is started at an early stage. Individual acne cysts may be treated with corticosteroid injections. If acne has already left noticeable scars, you may wish to consult a plastic surgeon and discuss techniques such as dermabrasion. In this procedure, the top layer of skin is removed under general anesthesia. The raw areas then heal to leave a more even layer of skin.

(WWW) ONLINE SITES: p.1028, p.1036

Rosacea

Long-term, possibly permanent, redness and pimples on the cheeks and forehead

 AGE Most common between the ages of 30 and 55

 GENDER More common in females

 GENETICS Often runs in families

 LIFESTYLE Alcohol, coffee, and spicy foods may trigger attacks

In rosacea, a rash develops on the central area of the face and often results in burning or itching. The cause is unknown, but there may be a genetic factor because rosacea often runs in families. Women between the ages of 30 and 55 are most commonly affected. The rash may be triggered by eating a spicy meal, drinking alcohol, or entering a hot room.

WHAT ARE THE SYMPTOMS?

In most cases, the first symptom is red flushing, which often appears spontaneously on the cheeks, nose, and forehead after exposure to one of the trigger factors. Later, a rash develops, which is intermittent at first but may possibly become permanent. Other symptoms include:

- Red, puffy skin.
- White- or yellow-headed pimples.
- Visible tiny blood vessels.
- Stinging, burning, or itching sensation in the affected area.

If the skin of the nose is affected, it may eventually thicken, swell, and become purplish red. This condition, known as rhinophyma, usually affects only elderly men. In about 1 in 4 people who has rosacea, eye complications such as conjunctivitis (p.570) also occur.

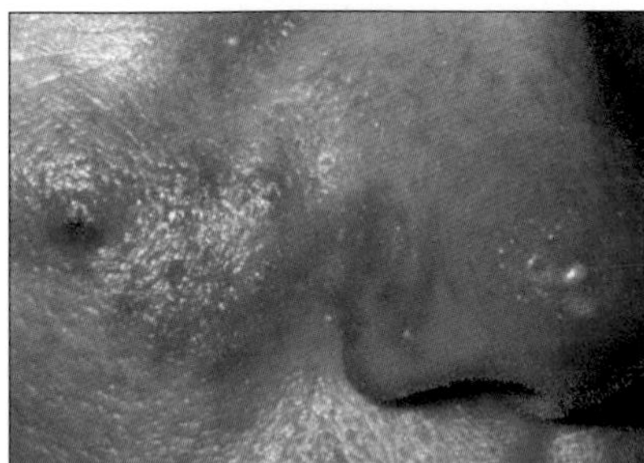

Rosacea pimples on the face
The white- and yellow-headed pimples resemble acne lesions and often appear on the nose and cheeks.

WHAT MIGHT BE DONE?

You should avoid anything that triggers flushing, such as spicy food, alcohol, or coffee. Avoid sunlight and the use of topical corticosteroids on the face, both of which tend to aggravate rosacea.

To treat the condition, your doctor may prescribe metronidazole gel, a topical antibiotic (*see* PREPARATIONS FOR SKIN INFECTIONS AND INFESTATIONS, p.892), which is usually effective. However, if the rosacea does not improve, you may be prescribed the antibiotic tetracycline (*see* ANTIBIOTICS, p.885) or an oral retinoid drug (p.890). You may need several weeks of treatment before the rash eventually clears.

If rhinophyma develops, the area of thickened skin on the nose can be pared away under general anesthesia. Normal skin tissue will then form to cover the treated surface of the nose.

Rosacea usually comes and goes over a period of 5–10 years before finally disappearing. Occasionally, the condition may be lifelong, especially in men.

(WWW) ONLINE SITES: p.1036

Prickly heat

Multiple small, raised, itchy spots that appear in hot conditions

 AGE Most common in infants and children

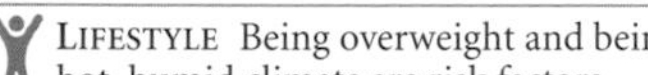 LIFESTYLE Being overweight and being in a hot, humid climate are risk factors

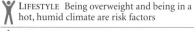

 GENDER GENETICS Not significant factors

Prickly heat is an intensely itchy rash that often occurs in hot weather. It develops when sweat glands are blocked by bacteria and dead skin cells. Sweat trapped in the glands then causes mild inflammation. The rash consists of tiny, red, itchy spots or blisters accompanied by a prickling or burning feeling. The most common sites are the hands, feet, armpits, and chest. Prickly heat often affects overweight people because they tend to become overheated and sweat easily. Infants and children are more likely to have the condition, in which case the rash develops in the diaper area or on the face, chest, or back.

The rash often disappears on its own in a few days. You can help this process by wearing loose clothing made of natural fibers and, in babies, by leaving the diaper off as much as possible. If the rash persists, your doctor may suggest that you buy a mild topical corticosteroid (p.892), but this treatment should not be used on the face. Consult a doctor before using a topical corticosteroid on a baby and always follow the doctor's instructions carefully.

(WWW) ONLINE SITES: p.1036

Hyperhidrosis

Excessive sweating in specific areas or over the whole body

 AGE Most common between the ages of 15 and 30

 GENETICS Sometimes runs in families

 GENDER LIFESTYLE Not significant factors

Frequent, heavy sweating far in excess of normal is known as hyperhidrosis. It usually first appears at puberty and disappears by age 30. Often, no cause can be found, but about half of affected people have a family history of it, suggesting a genetic factor. Hyperhidrosis can be an indication of an underlying problem, such as an overactive thyroid gland (*see* HYPERTHYROIDISM, p.679) or diabetes mellitus (p.687). It may also occur in menopausal women. In some people, sweating attacks are triggered by stress.

Hyperhidrosis may occur in many areas of the body, particularly the feet, armpits, hands, and face. It is often accompanied by an unpleasant odor.

WHAT CAN I DO?

Wash away sweat regularly, and wear loose clothing made from natural fibers that absorb sweat. Antiperspirant may help reduce underarm sweating. If anxiety makes the problem worse, relaxation exercises (p.75) may help. If these methods do not work, consult your doctor.

Your doctor may prescribe a topical treatment containing aluminum chloride to reduce the activity of the sweat glands. If you have hyperhidrosis in the armpits and all treatments have failed, he or she may suggest a minor operation to destroy the nerve centers that control sweating and therefore end the problem permanently. Botulinum toxin can be injected into the skin of armpits and reduces sweating for up to 8 months.

(WWW) ONLINE SITES: p.1036

Vitiligo

Loss of normal pigment from patches of skin, most commonly occurring on the face and hands

 AGE More common in young adults

 GENETICS Sometimes runs in families

 GENDER LIFESTYLE Not significant factors

People who have vitiligo have irregular patches of pale skin caused by the loss of melanin, the pigment that gives the skin its color. The disorder is more obvious in people with dark skin.

In about half of all cases, vitiligo develops before age 20. It does not cause physical discomfort, but some people become distressed by the discolored appearance of their skin.

WHAT IS THE CAUSE?

It is thought that vitiligo is an autoimmune disorder in which the antibodies produced by the body react against its own tissues. In this condition antibodies destroy the cells in the skin that produce melanin. About 1 in 3 people with vitiligo has a family history of the condition. About the same proportion also has another type of autoimmune disorder, such as pernicious anemia (*see* MEGALOBLASTIC ANEMIA, p.448).

WHAT ARE THE SYMPTOMS?

The loss of skin color is gradual, occurring over several months or even years. The symptoms include:

- Depigmented skin patches that may occur on any part of the body but most commonly the face and hands.

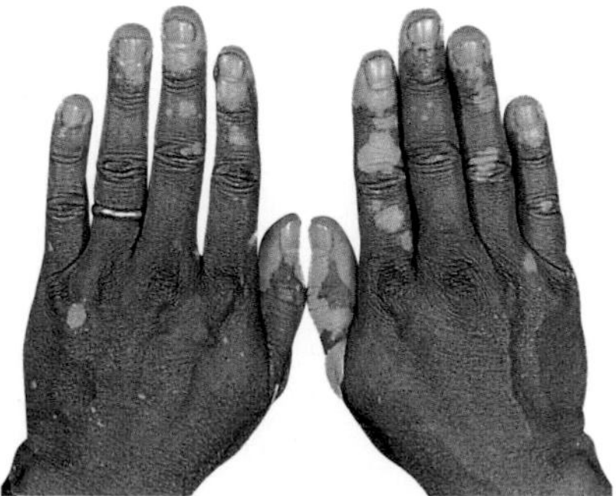

Vitiligo
The pale patches on these hands are due to vitiligo, a condition that causes a gradual loss of the skin pigment melanin.

- In some cases, white hair on affected areas of skin due to loss of pigment from the hair follicles.

In most people with vitiligo, the depigmented patches of skin are distributed symmetrically over the body.

WHAT MIGHT BE DONE?

The diagnosis is usually obvious, but your doctor may arrange for a skin test to exclude pityriasis versicolor (p.353), a fungal infection that may produce discolored patches of skin. Blood tests may be done to make sure you do not have another autoimmune disorder.

In mild vitiligo, the discolored areas can be hidden with cosmetics. No other treatment is needed. The affected areas cannot tan so you should avoid exposure to the sun and use a sunblock in direct sunlight (*see* SAFETY IN THE SUN, p.80). Phototherapy using ultraviolet light can help but takes several months to work. Before treatment, you may be given a drug called psoralen to increase the sensitivity of the skin to light.

Occasionally, people may lose the pigment from extensive areas of skin. In these cases, the rest of the skin may be bleached so that the overall color of the skin appears more even.

There is no cure for vitiligo, and often the depigmented patches continue to enlarge slowly. However, about 3 in 10 affected people regain their natural skin color spontaneously.

(WWW) ONLINE SITES: p.1036

Freckles

Multiple small, brown-colored spots on the skin that are usually harmless

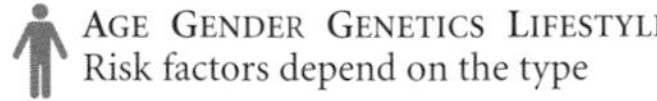

AGE GENDER GENETICS LIFESTYLE Risk factors depend on the type

Freckles result from an overproduction of melanin, the pigment that gives the skin its color. There are two common types of freckles: the small brown spots appearing on areas of skin that are frequently exposed to the sun; and the flat, lighter brown patches that can appear anywhere on the skin and affect most people with increasing age.

The tendency to develop freckles on exposure to the sun is usually inherited. It is more common in people with fair skin, particularly those who have red hair. The patches are harmless and tend to fade during the winter, but they are a sign of sensitivity to sunlight and of increased susceptibility to skin cancer (p.344). Sunscreen should be used daily to help protect your skin against sunburn (*see* SAFETY IN THE SUN, p.80).

The type of patch that develops with age is called an age spot, lentigo, or liver spot. These spots most commonly affect people over the age of 40. They can appear on covered and exposed parts of the body and do not fade in winter.

A lentigo is usually harmless, but it may eventually develop into a malignant melanoma (p.346), particularly if it is on the face. A variation in color may be a warning sign. If raised brown lumps appear on a lentigo, consult your doctor as soon as possible so that he or she can analyze the spot and detect any cancerous changes in the cells.

Moles

Flat or raised growths on the skin that are rough or smooth and vary in color from light to dark brown

AGE Increasingly common in childhood and adolescence

GENETICS Sometimes runs in families

GENDER LIFESTYLE Not significant factors

Moles are caused by an overproduction of pigmented skin cells called melanocytes. They can form anywhere on the skin, and there are several types. Moles may exist from birth (*see* BIRTHMARKS, p.828) or appear during childhood and early adolescence; nearly all adults have about 10–20 moles by the age of 30. Most moles are noncancerous, but in rare cases a mole may undergo changes that make it cancerous (*see* MALIGNANT MELANOMA, p.346). Alterations in the shape, color, or size of moles are not always a sign of cancer, and changes during puberty or pregnancy are usually normal. However, changes in moles should always be evaluated by a doctor.

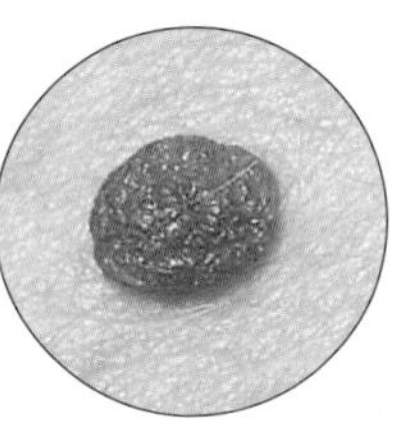

Raised mole
This noncancerous mole appears as a raised, brown spot; the pigmented area may extend deep into the skin.

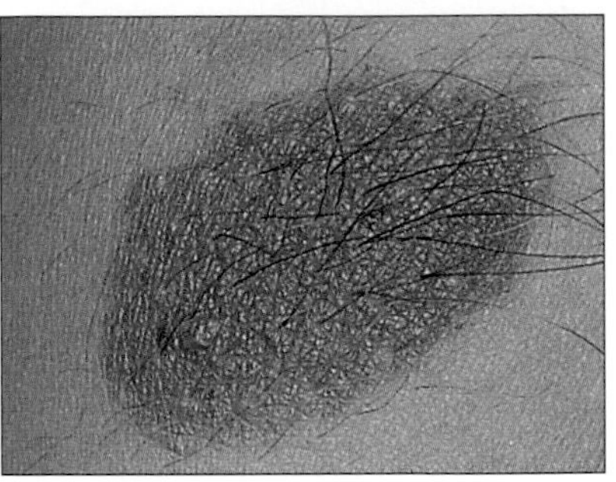

Hairy mole
Moles that are covered in hair, such as the one shown here, or moles with just a few hairs, rarely become cancerous.

WHAT ARE THE TYPES?

Usually, moles are flat or raised growths on the skin that vary in color from light to dark brown and measure less than 3/8 in (1 cm) in diameter. They may be rough or smooth, hairy or hairless.

One type of mole, known as a dysplastic nevus, is larger than usual and unevenly colored. These moles may appear in childhood or old age and may develop from smaller moles. Dysplastic nevi sometimes run in families. Any type of mole may become cancerous, but dysplastic nevi are more likely to undergo cancerous changes than other moles. The risk of such changes is higher in people who have a family history of malignant melanoma or if the mole is frequently exposed to sunlight.

Blue nevi, moles that have a bluish-black color, occur most commonly on the face, arms and legs, and buttocks.

A halo nevus consists of a mole from which pigment is disappearing, leaving a ring of paler skin around a shrinking central dark spot. Eventually the mole may disappear completely.

WHAT MIGHT BE DONE?

You should consult a doctor immediately if you have a mole that is more than 3/8 in (1 cm) in diameter and is growing rapidly, that changes shape or color, that becomes itchy or inflamed, or that starts bleeding.

If your doctor suspects that a mole is cancerous, he or she may recommend that you have it removed and examined for cancerous cells (*see* SKIN BIOPSY, p.344). Noncancerous moles can also be removed, either for cosmetic reasons or if they are being chafed by clothing.

(WWW) ONLINE SITES: p.1036

Skin cancer

Several types of cancer originate in the skin, most of which are associated with prolonged exposure to sunlight

 GENETICS Fair-skinned people are most at risk

 LIFESTYLE Exposure to the sun and the use of tanning booths are risk factors

 AGE GENDER Risk factors depend on the type

Skin cancer is the most common form of cancer in Canada. In recent years, the incidence around the world has escalated, and the condition now affects millions of people worldwide.

The usual cause of skin cancer is prolonged exposure to the harmful ultraviolet radiation in sunlight. The risk of developing skin cancer is higher if you live in or take vacations to areas with intense sun; the closer you are to the equator, the greater the risk. The recent depletion of the Earth's ozone layer is thought to have played a part in increasing the incidence of skin cancer because the ozone layer acts as a protective shield against the sun's harmful ultraviolet light. In addition, tanning booths, which use ultraviolet light, might also cause skin cancer.

If your work involves being outside or you have been sunburned (particularly in childhood), you could be vulnerable to skin cancer. People who have fair skin are especially susceptible to the disease because they have low levels of melanin, the pigment that gives the skin its color and helps protect it from the sun's harmful ultraviolet rays.

To reduce the risk of developing skin cancer, try to avoid exposure to the sun and protect your skin when outside (*see* SAFETY IN THE SUN, p.80). Examine your skin regularly, and ask someone else to check your back and scalp.

WHAT ARE THE TYPES?

There are three main types of skin cancer associated with overexposure to the sun. The most common type is basal cell carcinoma (right). This cancer can be easily treated and rarely spreads. The second most common is squamous cell carcinoma (opposite page). The disease may spread and is occasionally fatal but can be treated if detected early. The third type is malignant melanoma (p.346). Although the incidence is increasing, this form of cancer is still rare. It can spread rapidly to other parts of the body and causes more deaths than other skin cancers.

An uncommon skin cancer, known as Kaposi's sarcoma (p.346), occurs mainly in people with AIDS (*see* HIV INFECTION AND AIDS, p.295).

WHAT MIGHT BE DONE?

Skin cancer can usually be cured if it is diagnosed early. You should consult your doctor promptly if you notice any changes in your skin, such as enlarging lumps or sores that do not heal. You may need to have a skin biopsy (left). During this procedure, a small area of skin is removed and examined under a microscope for abnormal cells.

The type of skin cancer and spread of the disease determines the treatment and prognosis. Sometimes, only the affected area of skin needs to be treated.

Most skin cancers can be removed surgically, but skin grafting (p.319) may be necessary if a cancer has invaded large areas of surrounding skin tissue. If the cancer spreads to other parts of the body, radiation therapy (p.279) or chemotherapy (p.278) may be needed.

(WWW) ONLINE SITES: p.1036

(TEST) SKIN BIOPSY

A skin biopsy is a technique used to diagnose skin diseases, such as cancer. In this procedure a sample of skin is removed from an anesthetized site and sent to a laboratory to be examined under a microscope. A biopsy may be used to cut away a whole lesion from the skin, such as a mole, or to remove a small sample at the edge of a large patch of affected skin.

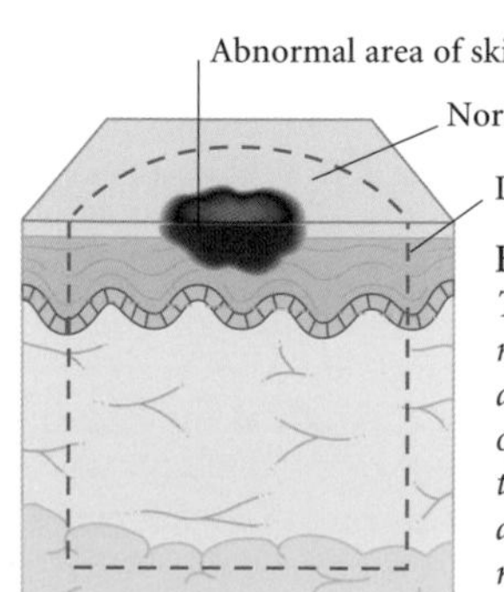
Abnormal area of skin
Normal skin
Line of incision

Biopsy site
The biopsy site is first numbed with a local anesthetic. A section of tissue, including skin that looks abnormal and a surrounding area of normal skin, is then removed for analysis.

(RESULTS)

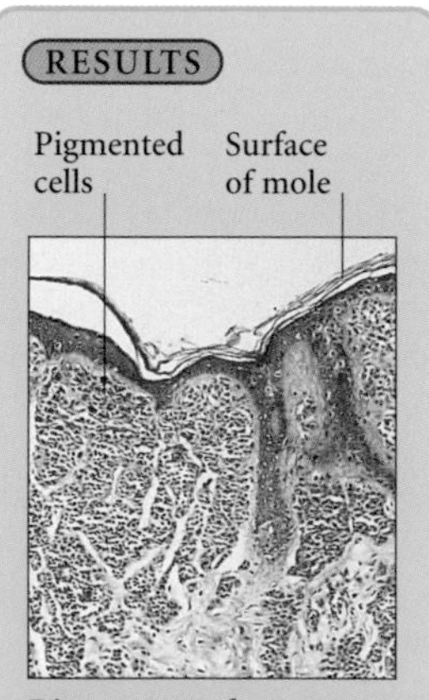
Pigmented cells
Surface of mole

Biopsy sample
This magnified view shows part of a removed mole. The sample confirms that the mole has no cancerous cells.

Basal cell carcinoma

A skin cancer, usually affecting sun-exposed areas, that rarely spreads elsewhere in the body

 AGE Rare in people under age 40; increasingly common over 40

 GENDER More common in males

 GENETICS Fair-skinned people are most at risk

 LIFESTYLE Exposure to the sun and the use of tanning booths are risk factors

The most common type of skin cancer, basal cell carcinoma, is also the least dangerous because it usually remains localized and rarely spreads to other parts of the body. This cancer should not be left untreated because it can destroy bone and surrounding skin.

Basal cell carcinoma is characterized by pearly lesions that can occur on any part of the body but commonly appear on the face, often at the corner of an eye, near the ear, or on the nose.

The condition is usually caused by exposure to strong sunlight, which damages cells just below the surface of the skin. Fair-skinned people over the age of 40 are most susceptible.

You can minimize your risk of developing basal cell carcinoma by avoiding prolonged exposure to sunlight and by protecting your skin when you are outside (*see* SAFETY IN THE SUN, p.80).

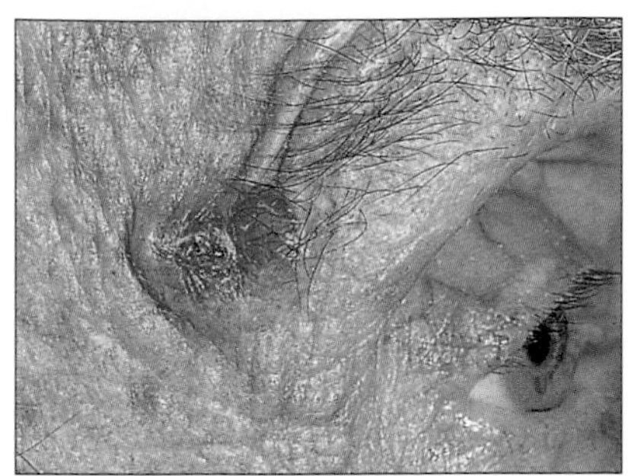

Basal cell carcinoma
This pink, ulcerated lesion, with its waxy, rolled edge and central scab, is an example of an untreated basal cell carcinoma.

What are the symptoms?

Basal cell carcinoma grows slowly over months or even years. A typical lesion develops in the following way:

- A small, painless lump appears; it has a smooth surface, visible blood vessels, a pink to brownish gray color, and a waxy or pearl-like border.
- The lump gradually grows, usually spreading outward and developing a central depression with rolled edges.

An untreated lump may form a shallow ulcer that may bleed intermittently and then form a scab but never fully heals.

If you notice an enlarging skin lump or a sore that fails to heal, you should consult your doctor promptly.

What might be done?

If your doctor suspects basal cell carcinoma, he or she will probably arrange for you to have a skin biopsy (opposite page) to confirm the diagnosis. During this procedure, a small lesion may be scraped away or frozen off. A large lesion may need to be removed surgically. If you have several lesions, or if the affected area is difficult to treat surgically (for example, if it is near the eye), you may need to have radiation therapy (p.279). If the cancer has caused damage to underlying tissue, you may need plastic surgery (p.952).

What is the prognosis?

About 9 in 10 people who develop basal cell carcinoma are successfully treated. There should be no further problems after treatment, but in a few cases the skin cancer may recur.

If you have already had an episode of basal cell carcinoma, you are more likely to develop further cancerous lesions on other parts of your body, usually within a period of 2–5 years. For this reason, you should continue to protect yourself against exposure to sunlight and inspect your skin regularly. Your doctor will probably recommend that you have periodic checkups in order to detect and treat any new lesions that develop while they are still small.

WWW ONLINE SITES: p.1036

Squamous cell carcinoma

A skin cancer that usually affects the face but can spread to other parts of the body

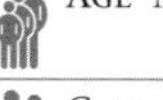
AGE Mainly affects people over age 60

GENDER More common in males

GENETICS Fair-skinned people are most at risk

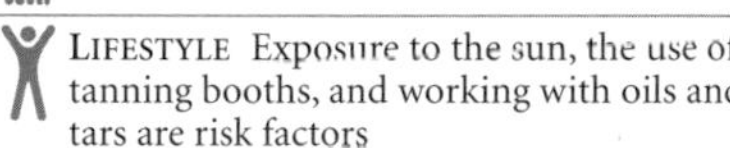
LIFESTYLE Exposure to the sun, the use of tanning booths, and working with oils and tars are risk factors

Squamous cell carcinoma is a common type of skin cancer that usually affects areas that have been exposed to sunlight, but may also occur in other parts of the body, such as the genitals. This type of carcinoma is capable of spreading throughout the body, and for this reason early detection and treatment of the condition are essential.

What are the causes?

Squamous cell carcinoma develops on areas of skin that have been constantly exposed to sunlight over many years. Sometimes this form of skin cancer may develop from scaly growths known as actinic keratoses (p.347). The condition is most common in fair-skinned men over the age of 60.

People who work with some industrial tars and oils are known to have a higher than normal risk of squamous cell carcinoma, but such people are normally protected by adequate health and safety measures.

Most squamous cell carcinomas can be prevented by avoiding prolonged exposure to sunlight. If this is not possible, you should take precautions to protect your skin, such as applying sunblock and wearing a hat, when you are outside (*see* SAFETY IN THE SUN, p.80).

What are the symptoms?

Squamous cell carcinoma begins as an area of thickened, scaly skin. The lesion then develops into:

- A hard, painless, gradually enlarging lump that has an irregular edge and is red to reddish brown in color.
- Subsequently, a recurring ulcer that does not heal.

If you develop an enlarging skin lump or a sore that does not heal on any part of your body, you should consult your doctor as soon as possible.

What might be done?

If your doctor suspects squamous cell carcinoma, he or she may arrange for you to have a skin biopsy (opposite page), in which a small piece of tissue is removed under local anesthesia and examined microscopically for the presence of cancerous cells.

Squamous cell carcinoma can usually be treated surgically if the lesions are detected early on. Sometimes radiation therapy (p.279) is used as an alternative to surgery. If you have several large lesions, or if the cancer has spread to underlying tissues, chemotherapy (p.278) may also be necessary.

What is the prognosis?

If the condition is detected early, about 9 in 10 people with squamous cell carcinoma are treated successfully. Lesions on the face respond particularly well to treatment. If the disease is detected late, the success of the treatment depends on how far the cancer has spread. Some lesions may recur, particularly larger ones, and your doctor will advise you to have regular checkups.

WWW ONLINE SITES: p.1036

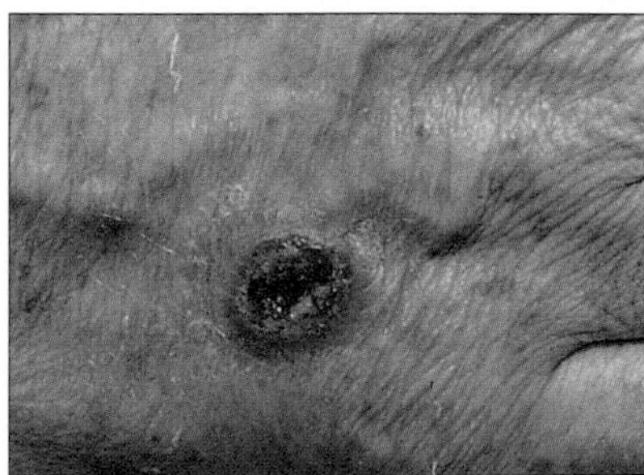

Squamous cell carcinoma
The face and hand are common sites for this carcinoma. Here, a lesion on the back of the hand has developed into a reddish-brown ulcer with a clearly defined edge.

Malignant melanoma

A skin cancer affecting the pigment-producing cells of the skin that can spread rapidly to other parts of the body

 AGE Most common between age 40 and age 60; increasingly common in young adults

 GENDER More common in females

 GENETICS Fair-skinned people are most at risk

 LIFESTYLE Exposure to the sun and the use of tanning booths are risk factors

Malignant melanoma is a rare, serious form of skin cancer. A melanoma may begin as a new growth on normal, healthy skin or may develop from an existing mole. Left untreated, the cancer can spread to other parts of the body and may be fatal. As is the case with most other skin cancers, the main cause is exposure to sunlight.

Worldwide, the number of cases of malignant melanoma, particularly in young adults, has increased dramatically over the past 10 years. This rise is most likely due to the growing popularity of outdoor activities. Malignant melanoma is most common in people aged 40–60 and in women.

WHAT IS THE CAUSE?

Malignant melanoma is thought to result from damage to melanocytes (the skin cells that produce the pigment melanin) by sunlight. The cancer occurs more frequently in people with fair skin than in those with dark skin. People who continually expose themselves to intense sunlight or who live in sunny climates have an increased risk of developing a malignant melanoma. In particular, severe sunburn (p.357) during childhood has been shown to double the chance of developing malignant melanoma in later life. Reducing exposure to the sun can help decrease the risk of developing this type of cancer (*see* SAFETY IN THE SUN, p.80).

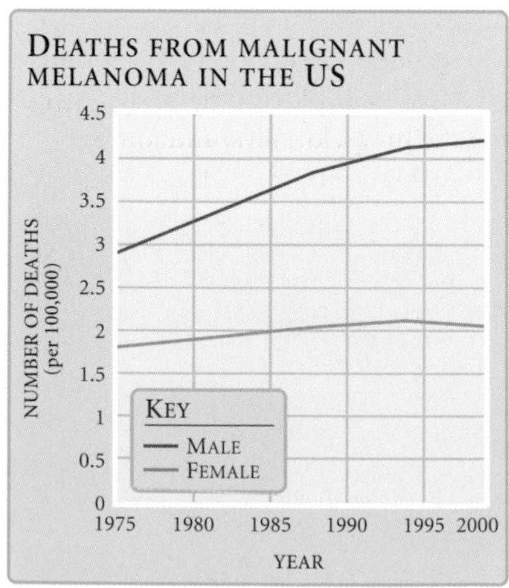
DEATHS FROM MALIGNANT MELANOMA IN THE US
4.5
4
3.5
3
2.5
2
1.5
1
0.5
0
NUMBER OF DEATHS (per 100,000)
1975
1980
1985
1990
1995
2000
YEAR
KEY
MALE
FEMALE

Increasing death rates
In the US, deaths from malignant melanoma have increased since the 1970s. A similar trend in deaths from this cancer is occuring in Canada.

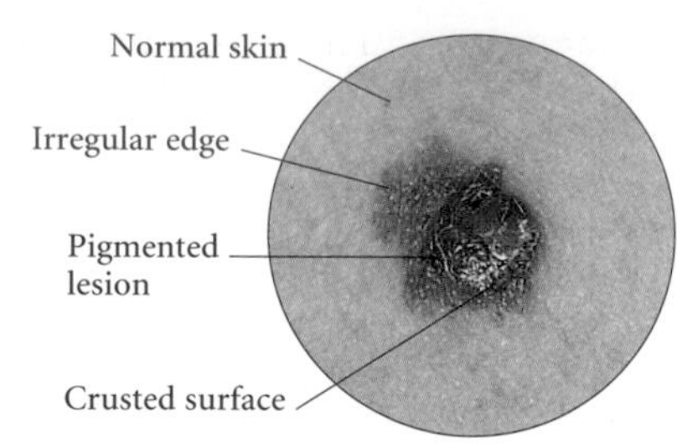
Normal skin
Irregular edge
Pigmented lesion
Crusted surface

Malignant melanoma
The uneven color, irregularly spreading edge, and crusted surface of this raised growth are characteristic features of a malignant melanoma.

WHAT ARE THE SYMPTOMS?

Malignant melanomas can develop on any part of the body but appear most commonly on sun-exposed areas. Some melanomas spread across the skin in irregular flat patches; others appear as fast-growing lumps. In older people, they may occur on the face as freckle-like spots, known as lentigo maligna, that grow slowly over many years. If they are not removed, all of these types of melanomas will grow down into the underlying layers of the skin.

You may have a malignant melanoma if a quickly growing, irregular, dark-colored spot starts to develop on your skin or if you notice any of the following changes in an existing mole:

- Increasing size.
- Irregular and asymmetrical edges.
- Itching, inflammation, or redness.
- Thickening of the surface.
- Bleeding or crusting.
- Variation in shade or color.

You should inspect your skin regularly and note the location and size of any moles. Ask another person to help you examine your back and scalp. Changes in shade or color in existing moles or the appearance of a new and enlarging spot, particularly if it is more than 1/4 in (6 mm) across or starts to vary in shade or color, should be reported to your doctor as soon as possible.

WHAT MIGHT BE DONE?

If your doctor suspects that you have a malignant melanoma, he or she will arrange for a sample to be removed for microscopic examination (*see* SKIN BIOPSY, p.344). If the sample is found to be cancerous, a wider area of skin may then be removed to decrease the risk of malignant cells remaining. If a large portion of skin must be removed, you may need skin grafting (p.319).

Samples may also be taken from the lymph nodes near the melanoma and examined for cancerous cells, the presence of which would indicate that the cancer has spread. If other areas are affected, you may have chemotherapy (p.278) or radiation therapy (p.279).

WHAT IS THE PROGNOSIS?

People who have superficial melanomas and receive early treatment are usually cured, but melanomas are more often fatal in men, possibly because they do not always report symptoms to the doctor immediately. If melanomas are aggressive or penetrate deep into the skin, the outlook is less optimistic, and, if they spread to other parts of the body, they are often fatal.

(WWW) ONLINE SITES: p.1036

Kaposi's sarcoma

A skin cancer, characterized by raised, pinkish-brown lesions, that is most often associated with AIDS

 GENDER More common in males

 LIFESTYLE Unprotected sex with multiple partners and intravenous drug use are risk factors in AIDS-related cases

AGE GENETICS Risk factors depend on the cause

Kaposi's sarcoma used to be a very rare condition, appearing mainly in older men of Mediterranean or Jewish origin. It developed slowly and rarely spread. However, a more rapidly developing form now occurs increasingly in people with AIDS (*see* HIV INFECTION AND AIDS, p.295). In these cases, it is associated with infection by a herpes virus.

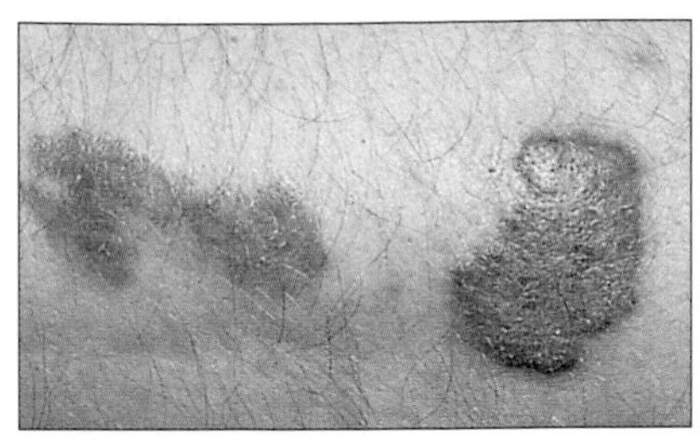

Kaposi's sarcoma
Sharply defined, pinkish-brown raised nodules and flat patches are the first signs of Kaposi's sarcoma. They may develop anywhere on the body.

The sharply defined lesions of Kaposi's sarcoma are pinkish-brown and can occur anywhere on the skin. In AIDS-related cases, the lesions spread quickly; in severe cases, they may affect mucous membranes, especially of the palate and internal organs. Internal lesions can cause severe bleeding.

If detected early, localized Kaposi's sarcoma can be treated effectively with radiation therapy (p.279). If a case is more advanced, chemotherapy (p.278) may be needed. Kaposi's sarcoma is seldom the main cause of death in people with AIDS, although it may be fatal when the internal organs are affected.

(WWW) ONLINE SITES: p.1032, p.1036

Actinic keratosis

A pinkish-red, scaly, rough-textured skin growth, caused by prolonged exposure to sunlight; also called solar keratosis

 AGE More common in people over age 40

 GENDER More common in males

 GENETICS Fair-skinned people are most at risk

 LIFESTYLE Exposure to the sun and the use of tanning booths are risk factors

Actinic keratoses are small, scaly, skin growths usually caused by years of exposure to sunlight. People under age 40 are not often affected, but the risk of developing actinic keratoses increases after this age and is higher than normal in people (usually men) who work outside. The condition is most common in fair-skinned people, who are often particularly sensitive to the sun.

The lesions are pinkish-red and have a rough texture. They most commonly appear on uncovered areas of the skin, such as the face, the backs of the hands, and on bald parts of the scalp. Usually, several lesions appear at the same time. Rarely, an actinic keratosis develops into squamous cell carcinoma (p.345).

WHAT MIGHT BE DONE?

Actinic keratoses should always be removed; they may be frozen or scraped off. If there are many growths in a large area, a cream containing the anticancer drug 5-fluorouracil (*see* ANTICANCER DRUGS, p.907) or imiquimod, an immune modulator cream, may be used. The growths may recur after treatment.

To reduce the risk of developing this condition, protect your skin from exposure to the sun (*see* SAFETY IN THE SUN, p.80). People who are bald or have thin hair should wear a hat outdoors.

(WWW) ONLINE SITES: p.1036

Discoid lupus erythematosus

A disorder in which itchy, red, scaly patches develop, usually on the face and scalp and behind the ears

 AGE Most common between the ages of 25 and 45

 GENDER Much more common in females

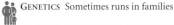

 GENETICS Sometimes runs in families

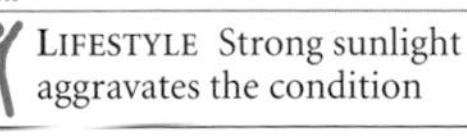 LIFESTYLE Strong sunlight triggers or aggravates the condition

Discoid lupus erythematosus (DLE) is an autoimmune disorder, in which the body attacks its own tissues. It causes a red, itchy, scaly rash to appear, particularly on the face and scalp, behind the ears, and on parts of the body exposed to sunlight. The disorder most commonly occurs in women between the ages of 25 and 45. The cause is unknown, but a genetic factor may be involved because DLE tends to run in families. Exposure to sunlight tends to trigger the onset of the rash or to make it worse. Over several years, DLE may subside and recur with different degrees of severity. Occasionally, it can also affect other organs in the body.

In some cases, the rash disappears, but it can leave behind a scarred area in which the skin is thin and discolored. If DLE occurs on the scalp, the damage to the skin can result in permanent loss of hair and patchy baldness of the scalp (*see* ALOPECIA, p.358).

WHAT MIGHT THE DOCTOR DO?

Your doctor will probably arrange for a small sample of skin to be removed from an affected area (*see* SKIN BIOPSY, p.344) to confirm the diagnosis. If you have DLE, your doctor may prescribe a topical corticosteroid (p.892), which you apply to the affected areas of skin two or three times a day.

If the skin does not heal after corticosteroid treatment, your doctor may prescribe a course of chloroquine sulfate, an antimalarial drug (p.888) that often relieves the symptoms of DLE. You will be advised to have regular eye examinations while on drug therapy because chloroquine may eventually cause damage to the eyes.

WHAT CAN I DO?

You can take steps to control the rash by staying out of the sun or by using a sunscreen to protect your skin (*see* SAFETY IN THE SUN, p.80). Concealing creams may improve the appearance of skin that has become discolored.

WHAT IS THE PROGNOSIS?

Most cases of DLE can be successfully treated with corticosteroids, although scarring can occur. About 1 in 10 people with DLE goes on to develop a related, but frequently more serious, autoimmune disorder called systemic lupus erythematosus (p.461). This condition affects many parts of the body, including the lungs, kidneys, and joints.

(WWW) ONLINE SITES: p.1033, p.1036

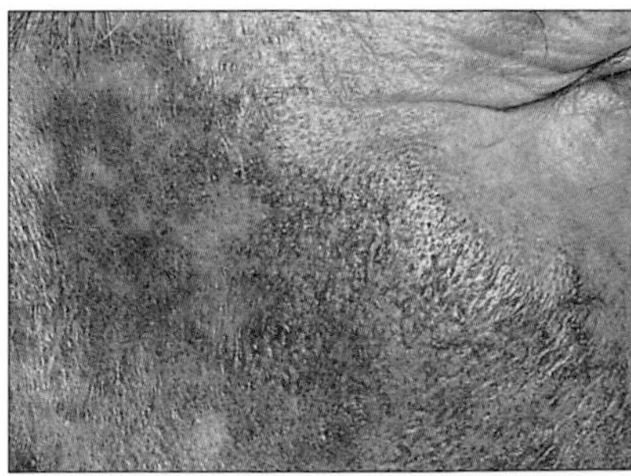

Rash of discoid lupus erythematosus
This red facial rash is characteristic of discoid lupus erythematosus. The distinct, discolored patches are due to scarring from previous episodes of the disorder.

Erythema nodosum

Shiny, tender, red or purple swellings (nodules), usually on the shins

 AGE Most common in young adults

 GENDER More common in females

 GENETICS LIFESTYLE Not significant factors

Many conditions may give rise to erythema nodosum, in which tender red or purple swellings known as nodules develop, usually on the shins.

Erythema nodosum is most common in young adults, and particularly in women. It may be linked with long-standing disorders such as tuberculosis (p.491) and the inflammatory disorder sarcoidosis (p.498). The condition may also be a reaction to drugs, in particular to some types of antibiotics (p.885). In children, it is often associated with a sore throat caused by a streptococcal infection. In some cases, there is no obvious cause for the condition.

WHAT ARE THE SYMPTOMS?

In many cases, erythema nodosum is accompanied by pains in the joints and muscles and by fever. The nodules usually appear on the shins; less commonly they develop on the forearms. They are:

- Shiny and bright red or purple.
- In general, between 3/8 in (1 cm) and 6 in (15 cm) in diameter.
- Very painful and tender.

The nodules fade over a few weeks and may begin to look like bruises.

WHAT MIGHT BE DONE?

A diagnosis is made from the symptoms and appearance of the nodules. There is no specific treatment, but your doctor may advise you to rest in bed and keep your legs raised until the nodules begin to subside. To reduce the swelling, the doctor may also prescribe nonsteroidal anti-inflammatory drugs (p.894) and, occasionally, oral corticosteroids (p.930). In addition, he or she may arrange for blood tests and a chest X-ray (p.490) to be performed to check for an underlying disorder.

Most affected people recover over 4 to 8 weeks. However, in 1 in 5 people, erythema nodosum recurs.

WWW ONLINE SITES: p.1036

Skin tag

A small, harmless flap of skin, usually attached to the neck, trunk, groin, or armpit

 AGE More common with increasing age

 LIFESTYLE Being overweight is a risk factor

 GENDER GENETICS Not significant factors

Tags are tiny flaps of skin, sometimes darker than the surrounding area, that are attached to the body by a stalk. They usually occur spontaneously but sometimes are the result of an imperfectly healed wound. Skin tags are found on any part of the body, typically on the neck and trunk, but they may also occur in the groin or armpit. While skin tags are harmless, they may bleed or become sore if they are rubbed by clothing. Elderly and overweight people are especially prone to skin tags.

Consult your doctor if you are unsure whether a growth is a skin tag, or if a tag is irritated by your clothes. You may have the tag removed under local anesthesia by burning, scraping, or snipping with surgical scissors.

Seborrheic keratosis

A harmless, pigmented wartlike growth that most commonly occurs on the trunk

 AGE More common with increasing age

 GENDER GENETICS LIFESTYLE Not significant factors

Seborrheic keratoses, also called seborrheic warts, are harmless skin growths, usually brown or black in color. The growths usually occur on the trunk but may also affect the head, neck, and, less commonly, the backs of the hands and the forearms. They may appear singly or in groups. Seborrheic keratoses are common in elderly people.

WHAT ARE THE SYMPTOMS?

You may notice a seborrheic keratosis as a crusted patch that appears to be stuck on rather than in the skin. The growth is usually:

- Painless but occasionally itchy; you may find that scratching the growth causes soreness.

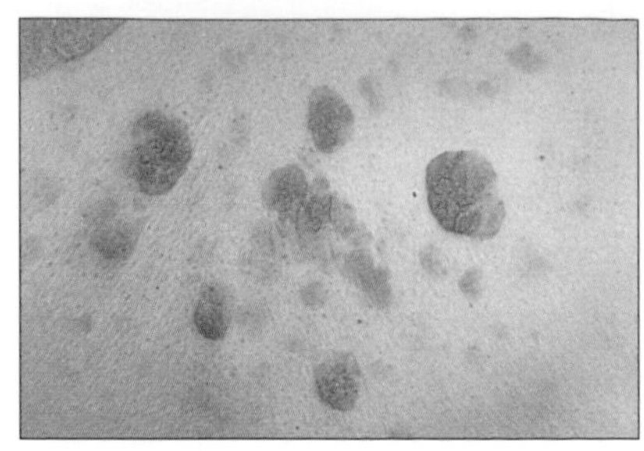

Seborrheic keratoses
Although they vary in color and shape, seborrheic keratoses commonly take the form of rough, brown, raised patches.

- Up to 3/4 in (2 cm) in diameter.
- Greasy and rough on the surface.
- Brown or black in color.
- Either raised or flat.

In rare cases, an individual may have hundreds of seborrheic keratoses.

WHAT MIGHT BE DONE?

If you have a pigmented patch, consult your doctor so that he or she can check that it is not due to a serious condition. If it is a seborrheic keratosis, the doctor may remove it by scraping or cutting it off or by freezing it. This will leave little or no scarring. The lesion is unlikely to recur, but, in a person who is susceptible to seborrheic keratoses, new lesions may develop on other areas of the body.

WWW ONLINE SITES: p.1036

Sebaceous cyst

A harmless swelling under the skin that may become infected

 AGE More common in adults

 GENDER GENETICS LIFESTYLE Not significant factors

A sebaceous cyst is a smooth lump that develops under the skin due to inflammation of a hair follicle. It consists of a sac filled with dead skin cells and sebum, the oily secretion of the sebaceous glands that open into the hair follicle. Some cysts have a dark, central pore.

Sebaceous cysts commonly occur on the scalp, face, trunk, and genitals but may appear on any part of the body. Although harmless, the cysts occasionally grow large and become unsightly. A sebaceous cyst that is infected by bacteria may become inflamed and painful and may eventually burst.

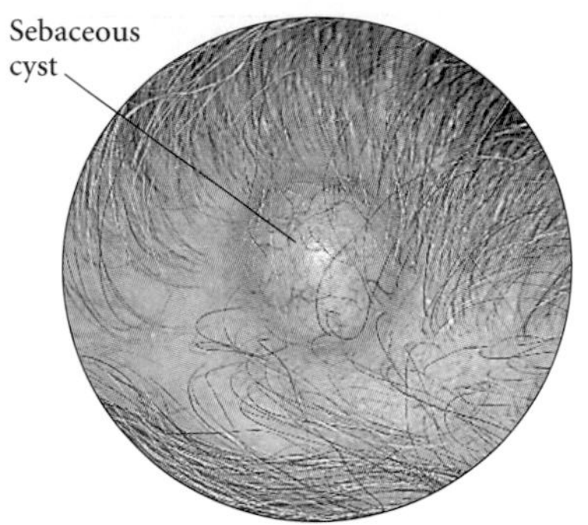
Sebaceous cyst

Sebaceous cyst on the scalp
The scalp is a typical site for a sebaceous cyst, which is a smooth, harmless lump that develops under the skin.

If a sebaceous cyst is not causing you any problems, it can safely be left untreated. However, if the cyst becomes very large or painful, it can be removed under local anesthesia. The cyst will usually be taken out intact because it can recur if the sac and its contents have not been completely removed. If it becomes infected, antibiotics (p.885) or incision and drainage may be required.

(WWW) ONLINE SITES: p.1036

Calluses and corns

Areas of thickened skin on the hands or feet caused by pressure or friction

 LIFESTYLE More common in manual workers, joggers, and musicians

 AGE GENDER GENETICS Not significant factors

If there is prolonged pressure or friction on a small area of the hand or foot, a patch of hard, thickened skin known as a callus may develop to protect the underlying tissues. Calluses are usually painless. They commonly occur on the hands of people such as musicians due to friction. The soles of the feet may become callused by the uneven pressure of body weight during walking.

Corns are patches of thickened skin that occur on the toes. They are usually due to wearing shoes that are too tight. The patches have a hard, clear center and can be painful and persistent.

WHAT IS THE TREATMENT?

If you have a callus, you can remove some of the hardened skin by soaking the area in warm water for 10 minutes and then rubbing the callus gently with a pumice stone. Regular application of moisturizing cream may help keep the skin soft. If possible, keep pressure off the area to aid recovery and to prevent recurrence of the callus. It is difficult to protect calluses that have developed on the sole of the foot, but well-fitting shoes may be of some help.

To relieve pressure on corns, wear shoes that do not press on the toes, and use corn pads (small rings of sponge that are available over the counter).

Your doctor or a podiatrist may reduce the size of a thickened area by paring it down with a scalpel, usually over several sessions. Once the source of pressure has been removed, calluses and corns should not recur.

Calluses or corns may become infected and ulcerated, especially in people with diabetes mellitus (p.687). If infection or ulceration occurs, you should not try to treat the lesions yourself but seek advice from a doctor or podiatrist.

(WWW) ONLINE SITES: p.1036

Keloid

A firm, raised, smooth overgrowth of scar tissue that develops after injury to the skin

 GENETICS May run in families; more common in black people

 AGE GENDER LIFESTYLE Not significant factors

A keloid is an itchy, firm, irregularly shaped overgrowth of scar tissue. Keloids are smooth and shiny, appearing pinkish-red on light skin and brown on dark skin. They usually form on the surface of a wound when a defective healing process causes overproduction of the skin protein collagen. Keloids are more common in black people, and susceptibility to the growths may run in families. If you are prone to these growths, you may find they appear after any kind of skin damage, including cuts, burns, acne, insect bites, tattoos, piercings for jewelry, and minor surgery. Rarely, they form spontaneously with no known cause. Keloids may develop almost anywhere on the body but usually occur on the chest, shoulders, and ear lobes. They are harmless, although large keloids may be unsightly.

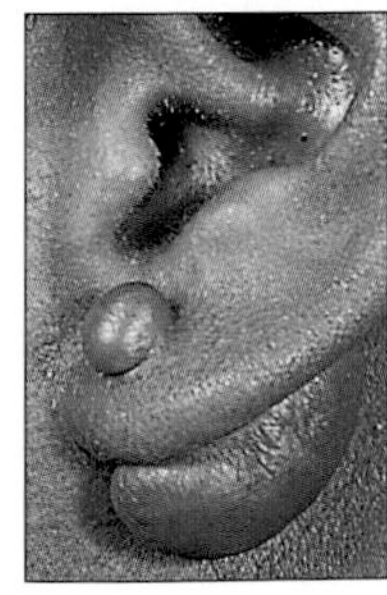

Keloid growth
An overgrowth of scar tissue called a keloid has formed on this earlobe after ear-piercing. Susceptible people may develop keloids after even minor skin damage.

WHAT IS THE TREATMENT?

Your doctor may either inject a corticosteroid (p.930) into the scar tissue, or prescribe a silicone sheet, which can be cut to size, placed over the keloid, and cause the scar to shrink or flatten. Even with treatment, keloids often take up to a year to fade. Surgery and laser treatment usually fail because the new scar tissue created forms another keloid.

(WWW) ONLINE SITES: p.1036

Stretch marks

Pink or purple lines on the skin, most commonly over the abdomen, buttocks, breasts, and thighs

 AGE Sometimes occur as a result of growth spurts at puberty

 GENDER More common in females

 LIFESTYLE More common in pregnant women and overweight people

 GENETICS Not a significant factor

Stretch marks, also called striae, occur when fibers of the skin protein collagen are broken due to rapid stretching of the skin or to hormonal changes that disrupt the fibers. The marks affect 3 in 5 pregnant women and are common in adolescent girls undergoing growth spurts. Overweight people may also develop them, especially if weight gain is rapid. In addition, they occur in people with Cushing syndrome (p.684) and in those using oral corticosteroids (p.930) or topical corticosteroids (p.892).

Stretch marks first appear as pink or purple, raised lines on the abdomen, thighs, breasts, or buttocks. They vary in length and may be between ¼ in (6 mm) and ½ in (12 mm) wide. Over a few months, they usually become pale and flatten, eventually becoming barely noticeable. There are no effective preventive measures or treatments.

(WWW) ONLINE SITES: p.1036

Chilblains

Itchy, painful, reddish-purple swellings on the fingers or toes

 AGE More common in children and elderly people

 GENDER GENETICS LIFESTYLE Not significant factors

Chilblains, also known as pernio, result from excessive narrowing of blood vessels under the skin in cold weather. The reddish-purple swellings, which most commonly affect the fingers and toes, are painful when they are exposed to cold and are intensely itchy once the skin has become warm again.

Chilblains usually disappear without treatment but may recur. If you are susceptible to chilblains and are exposed to cold weather, doing exercise may encourage blood flow to your hands and feet. Children and elderly or inactive people, in particular, should wear sufficient clothing, including gloves, socks, and a hat, to keep warm and help prevent chilblains from developing.

(WWW) ONLINE SITES: p.1036

Leg ulcer

A persistent open sore, usually on the lower part of the leg

 AGE More common in elderly people

 LIFESTYLE People who are of limited mobility or bedridden are at risk

 GENDER GENETICS Not significant factors

A leg ulcer occurs when an area of skin on the lower leg breaks down, usually as a result of poor blood circulation. An open sore may then develop, either spontaneously or following a minor injury, such as a scratch by a fingernail.

An ulcer appears as a shallow, pink area of broken skin, and the surrounding area may be swollen. They are slow to heal, often painful, and most common in older people who have poor circulation or are not very mobile.

What are the types?

There are two main types of leg ulcers: venous ulcers and arterial ulcers. More than 9 in 10 of all leg ulcers are venous ulcers, which are caused by poor blood flow through the veins and therefore often occur in people with varicose veins (p.438). The ulcers usually form just above the ankle and may be surrounded by purplish-brown, scaly skin.

Arterial ulcers develop as a result of poor blood flow through the arteries that supply the limbs. People with diabetes mellitus (p.687) and those with sickle-cell anemia (p.448) are especially susceptible to this type of leg ulcer. Arterial ulcers often form on the foot and may be surrounded by pale, thin skin.

At the first sign of an ulcer, you should consult your doctor. Leg ulcers often become infected, and the infection may spread to the surrounding skin, causing cellulitis (p.352).

What might be done?

Your doctor may recommend Doppler ultrasound scanning (p.432) to assess blood flow in the affected leg. The ulcer should be dressed regularly and firmly bandaged to prevent infection, reduce swelling, and improve blood circulation. Exercising regularly and keeping the leg raised when you are resting can also help improve the circulation of the blood. If you have an arterial ulcer, you may need surgery to improve the blood flow through the arteries.

What is the prognosis?

In susceptible people, leg ulcers may take several months to heal, and they often recur. In rare cases, skin grafting (p.319) may be necessary. If you are susceptible to leg ulcers, you should not neglect even minor wounds and you should consult your doctor at the first signs of soreness in a leg.

(WWW) ONLINE SITES: p.1026, p.1036

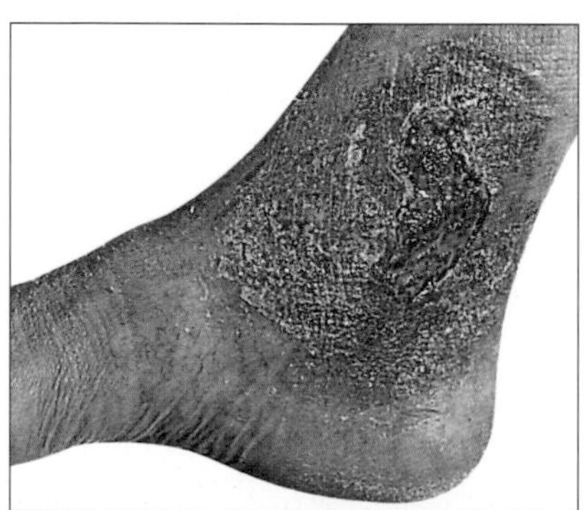

Leg ulcer on the ankle
A venous leg ulcer, such as the one shown here, consists of an open sore that is often surrounded by scaly, purplish-brown skin.

Pressure sores

Skin ulcers that develop in pressure spots, affecting people with limited mobility

 AGE Most common in elderly people

 LIFESTYLE People who are of limited mobility or bedridden are at risk

 GENDER GENETICS Not significant factors

If people are paralyzed or immobile, small areas of their skin are subject to constant pressure from their own body weight. This pressure may restrict the normal supply of blood to the tissues. Sometimes an area of tissue dies, and the skin breaks into open sores, which are called pressure sores or bedsores. Such sores usually affect elderly people, who are more likely to be immobile and have fragile skin. Urinary incontinence (p.710) may contribute to the development of pressure sores if it causes the skin to be continually damp.

What are the symptoms?

Common sites for pressure sores are the shoulders, hips, base of the spine, buttocks, heels, and ankles. The symptoms appear in the following stages:

- Affected areas of skin start to become red and tender.
- Painful areas become purple.
- The skin breaks to form ulcers.

Left untreated, the sores become bigger and deeper and may become infected. Severe pressure sores may sometimes involve muscle, tendon, or bone under the damaged area of skin.

What might be done?

Bedridden people or those with limited mobility should have their skin checked regularly for signs of redness and tenderness. A bedridden person should have his or her position changed at least every 2 hours to relieve compression of the affected areas. It is important to keep the skin clean and dry. If a sore becomes infected, antibiotics (p.885) may be necessary. Usually, they gradually heal with treatment and good nutrition to improve the person's general health, but deep ulcers may take several months to clear up. If they are extensive, plastic surgery (p.952) may be necessary to promote healing.

(WWW) ONLINE SITES: p.1033, p.1036

Skin infections and infestations

The skin surface provides the body with protection from the environment and from infection, but the skin itself may become infected by bacteria, viruses, or fungi. Some of these organisms live naturally on the body and do not normally cause disease unless they breach the barrier of the skin's surface. Infestation of the skin by parasites, such as mites, may also occur.

Infectious organisms can enter the skin in various ways. Natural openings, such as a hair follicle or sweat gland or broken skin at the site of an insect bite or a cut, may provide a gateway for bacteria. Warm and moist areas, such as the skin between the toes, are more susceptible to fungal infections. Some common viral skin infections, such as warts, can be spread from one part of the body surface to another or may be passed from one person to another by direct skin contact.

In this section, bacterial skin infections are described first, followed by fungal and viral infections. The final article covers infestation by the scabies mite.

Diseases such as measles and rubella, in which a skin rash occurs due to an infection that also affects many other areas of the body, are covered elsewhere (*see* INFECTIONS AND INFESTATIONS, pp.282–313). The two common skin infestations, head lice (p.831) and pubic lice (p.768), are also described in other sections of the book.

KEY ANATOMY

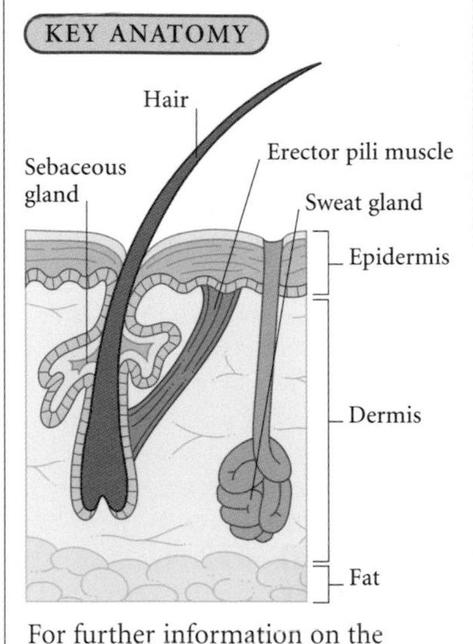
Hair
Sebaceous gland
Erector pili muscle
Sweat gland
Epidermis
Dermis
Fat

For further information on the structure and function of the skin, *see* pp.328–331.

Boil

A red, painful, pus-filled swelling of the skin caused by a bacterial infection

AGE GENDER GENETICS LIFESTYLE Not significant factors

A boil develops when a hair follicle or sebaceous gland (which secretes sebum into the follicle) becomes infected. The infection spreads and pus collects in surrounding tissues. Common sites for boils are moist areas, such as the groin, or areas where friction occurs, such as under a collar. Boils are usually caused by infection with the bacterium *Staphylococcus aureus*, which some people normally carry on the skin or in the nose without symptoms. A cluster of connected boils is called a carbuncle.

Boils are most common in people whose resistance to infection is lowered by a disorder such as diabetes mellitus (p.687) or AIDS (*see* HIV INFECTION AND AIDS, p.295), but they can occur in those without immune problems.

What are the symptoms?

The symptoms develop gradually in the following order over several days:

- A small, red lump appears.
- The area becomes painful and tender.
- The lump and the tissues around it begin to swell as pus accumulates.
- A white or yellow head of pus appears at the center of the boil.
- The affected area feels warm to the touch and throbs.

Boils often clear up without treatment. They may burst and release the pus or gradually subside and then disappear.

What can I do?

You can relieve pain and help the healing process by applying a cotton ball or a clean cloth soaked in hot water to the area for about 30 minutes four times a day. Do not squeeze the boil because this may cause the infection to spread farther. If a boil does not start to heal within a few days or if it becomes very large or painful, consult your doctor.

What might the doctor do?

Your doctor may drain the pus by making a small incision in the center of the boil with a sterile needle. This procedure is usually painless. You may also be prescribed oral antibiotics (p.885) to treat the cause of the infection. Large boils may need to be lanced with a surgical knife under local anesthetic.

If you develop recurrent boils, you may have blood and urine tests to look for an underlying disorder. Your doctor may also recommend that you use antiseptic soap or cream to kill the bacteria (*see* PREPARATIONS FOR SKIN INFECTIONS AND INFESTATIONS, p.892).

WWW ONLINE SITES: p.1033, p.1036

Impetigo

Blistering and crusting of the skin caused by a bacterial infection

AGE More common in children

GENDER GENETICS LIFESTYLE Not significant factors

The blistering skin condition impetigo is caused by bacteria entering broken skin, typically where there is a cut, an area of eczema (p.333), or a cold sore (p.354). The condition is highly contagious and is spread by physical contact. It is more common in children.

What are the symptoms?

Impetigo can appear anywhere on the body but usually occurs on the face, especially around the nose and mouth. The following symptoms usually develop over a period of 1–2 days:

- Initially, the skin reddens and tiny, fluid-filled blisters appear.

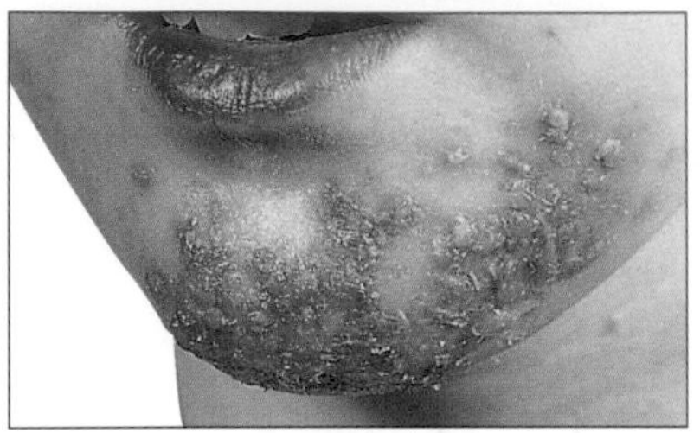

Impetigo on the face
The honey-colored crust covering this child's chin has been formed by impetigo blisters that have burst and dried out.

- The blisters burst soon after they are formed, releasing a yellow fluid.
- The skin underneath the burst blisters becomes red and weeping.
- The blisters dry out to form a honey-colored crust that may become itchy.

The blistered patch often spreads. Left untreated, it may become quite large.

What is the treatment?

Your doctor may prescribe topical antibiotics (*see* PREPARATIONS FOR SKIN INFECTIONS AND INFESTATIONS, p.892) or oral antibiotics (p.885). Soaking the crusts with warm salt water helps remove them and relieve itching. With treatment, impetigo usually clears up in a few days. To avoid spreading the condition to others, wash your hands often, do not share washcloths, and keep an affected child home from school.

(WWW) ONLINE SITES: p.1033, p.1036

Folliculitis

Inflammation of the hair follicles that produces small, yellow, pus-filled pimples

 AGE Most common in adults

 GENDER More common in males

 LIFESTYLE Shaving and hair-plucking are risk factors

 GENETICS Not a significant factor

Inflammation of the hair follicles due to bacterial infection is called folliculitis. The pus-filled pimples produced by this condition may develop on any part of the body but most commonly appear on the limbs and, in men, in the beard area. Shaving or plucking the hairs can increase the risk of inflammation. Folliculitis of the beard area is particularly common in African–American men, whose curly hairs often grow back into the skin, where they may cause infection. The use of topical corticosteroids (p.892) may also cause folliculitis.

Your doctor may prescribe topical antibiotics (*see* PREPARATIONS FOR SKIN INFECTIONS AND INFESTATIONS, p.892) for the infection. Acute, extensive folliculitis is sometimes treated with oral antibiotics. To avoid spreading it, wash regularly with antibacterial soap and do not share razors or towels. Men may find that growing a beard helps prevent folliculitis from developing on the face.

(WWW) ONLINE SITES: p.1033, p.1036

Cellulitis

Bacterial infection of the skin and underlying tissues that causes redness and swelling

 AGE More common in elderly people

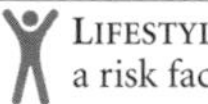 LIFESTYLE Intravenous drug use is a risk factor

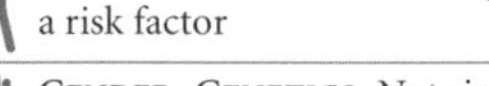

 GENDER GENETICS Not significant factors

In cellulitis, an area of skin and the underlying tissues become infected by bacteria that enter through a small, possibly unnoticed wound. The infection causes redness, pain, and swelling and most commonly affects the legs.

Elderly people are especially vulnerable to cellulitis because many of them have poor circulation, which leads to edema (fluid buildup in the tissues) or leg ulcers (p.350). These problems increase the risk of infection. Others who are at increased risk of cellulitis include intravenous drug abusers and people whose resistance to infection has been lowered by disorders such as diabetes mellitus (p.687) or AIDS (*see* HIV INFECTION AND AIDS, p.295).

What are the symptoms?

The symptoms appear gradually over several hours and include:

- Redness, swelling, and, in some cases, warmth in the affected area of skin.
- Pain and tenderness in the area.
- Occasionally, fever and chills.

If you develop these symptoms, consult your doctor immediately. Untreated, cellulitis may cause septicemia (p.298), a serious blood infection.

What might be done?

If you have an obvious wound, your doctor may take a swab from the area to identify the bacterium that is causing the infection. The doctor will probably prescribe oral antibiotics (p.885), which should take effect within 48 hours. In severe cases, you may need hospital treatment with intravenous antibiotics. If your leg is affected, you should keep it elevated to help reduce the swelling. Cellulitis may recur if you have a persistent immune or circulatory problem.

(WWW) ONLINE SITES: p.1033, p.1036

Ringworm

A fungal infection that produces itchy, red, circular patches on the scalp, groin, or elsewhere on the skin

 AGE GENDER LIFESTYLE Risk factors depend on the type

 GENETICS Not a significant factor

Despite the name, ringworm is caused not by worms but by fungi that infect the skin and cause the itchy, red, ring-shaped patches. Common forms of the disorder are scalp ringworm (tinea capitis), body ringworm (tinea corporis), and ringworm of the groin (tinea cruris), also known as jock itch.

Scalp ringworm, which is more common in children, may spread from one child to another or be acquired from cats and dogs. Jock itch affects mainly men, particularly those who are susceptible to other fungal infections, such as athlete's foot (opposite page). All forms of ringworm are especially common in people with reduced immunity to infection due to disorders such as diabetes mellitus (p.687) or AIDS (*see* HIV INFECTION AND AIDS, p.295).

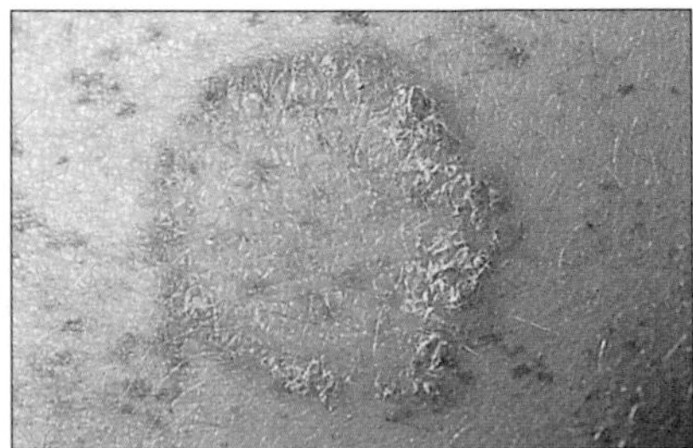

Ringworm on the body
The patch of ringworm shown here has already begun to spread, leaving a scaly, itchy, red ring surrounding normal skin.

WHAT ARE THE SYMPTOMS?

In all forms of ringworm, the following symptoms develop gradually over days or sometimes weeks:

- Initially, a small, round, scaly, itchy, red patch appears.
- After 1–2 weeks more patches appear.
- Each patch grows larger and forms a scaly, red ring around a central area of normal skin.

In scalp ringworm, hairs may break off just above the surface of the skin, leading to irregular patches of stubble (*see* ALOPECIA, p.358). In jock itch, the rash in the groin area occasionally spreads farther to affect the skin on the inside of the thighs and the buttocks.

WHAT MIGHT BE DONE?

Your doctor will probably recognize ringworm from its appearance and may confirm the diagnosis by taking a skin scraping. The removed skin is examined under a microscope to confirm the presence of fungal infection.

Topical antifungal drugs may be obtained by prescription from your doctor or over the counter (*see* PREPARATIONS FOR SKIN INFECTIONS AND INFESTATIONS, p.892). If the ringworm affects your scalp or is widespread, you may be prescribed oral antifungal drugs (p.889), which you will need to take for several weeks or months to clear up the infection completely. If you have jock itch, you can help prevent a recurrence by keeping the groin area clean and dry.

(WWW) ONLINE SITES: p.1033, p.1036

Athlete's foot

A fungal infection of the foot producing cracked, sore, itchy skin between the toes

 AGE Most common in teenagers and young adults; rare in children

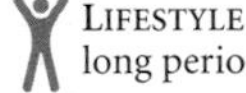

LIFESTYLE Wearing enclosed footwear for long periods is a risk factor

 GENDER GENETICS Not significant factors

Athlete's foot, also called tinea pedis, is a common fungal infection of the feet that particularly affects the skin between the toes. The condition can be caused by several types of fungi that thrive in warm, humid conditions.

Athlete's foot often affects teenagers and young adults, who tend to sweat more and wear enclosed footwear, such as sneakers, for long periods. It is rare in children. Athlete's foot can be picked up by walking barefoot in communal areas that are warm and humid, such as locker rooms and poolsides.

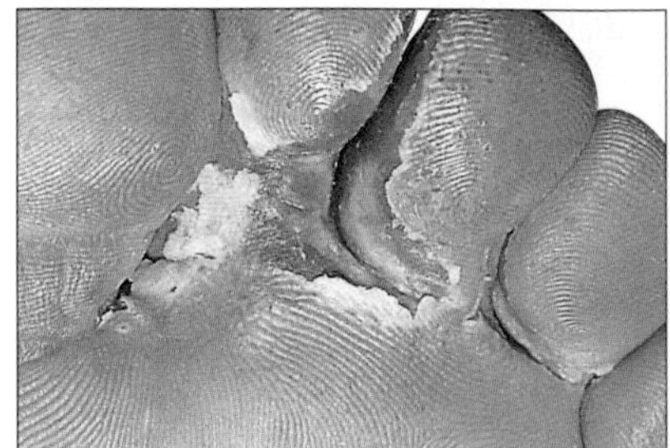

Athlete's foot

Toes affected by the fungal skin infection athlete's foot may become white and soggy, and the skin between and under them may peel away to leave painful raw areas.

WHAT ARE THE SYMPTOMS?

Athlete's foot most commonly occurs between the fourth and fifth toes and produces the following symptoms:

- Cracked, sore, and itchy areas of skin.
- Flaking, white, soggy skin.

Sometimes, the infection spreads onto the sole or the sides of the foot or affects the toenails, which then become yellowish, thickened, and brittle. People who have athlete's foot are more susceptible to ringworm (opposite page) of the groin, another fungal infection.

WHAT IS THE TREATMENT?

The affected area can be treated using an over-the-counter antifungal preparation, which should be applied at least twice a day (*see* PREPARATIONS FOR SKIN INFECTIONS AND INFESTATIONS, p.892). It is important that you continue to apply the preparation to affected areas for a few days after the symptoms have cleared up to make sure that the infection is eradicated. If over-the-counter preparations do not help or you are unsure of the diagnosis, consult your doctor, who can give you further advice about treatment or prescribe a stronger antifungal drug (p.889).

To prevent the infection from recurring, you should wash your feet at least once a day, more frequently if they become sweaty, and dry them thoroughly between the toes. At home, it may help to wear open-toed shoes or go barefoot.

(WWW) ONLINE SITES: p.1033, p.1036

Pityriasis versicolor

A fungal infection that produces patches of discolored skin on the trunk

 AGE More common in people under age 50

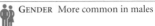

 GENDER More common in males

LIFESTYLE Hot and humid conditions are a risk factor

 GENETICS Not a significant factor

Pityriasis versicolor, also called tinea versicolor, is a patchy skin condition caused by a fungus that lives in the hair follicles of the body. The fungus does not normally produce symptoms, but, in hot and humid conditions, when the skin becomes moist and warm, it grows and colonizes the dead outer layer of skin. Oily skin also encourages the fungus to spread to the surface of the skin. Pityriasis versicolor is more common in men, particularly those under age 50.

WHAT ARE THE SYMPTOMS?

The only symptom is the appearance of scaly, discolored patches on the skin. The upper trunk, including the neck, chest, shoulders, and back, is usually affected. The patches are:

- Of variable size, round, and flat with clearly defined edges.
- Pinkish-brown in color on pale skin, becoming more noticeable if the surrounding skin tans. On dark skin, the patches are pale. In some individuals, the patches are darkly pigmented.

Left untreated, the patches may become widespread and persist indefinitely.

WHAT MIGHT BE DONE?

Your doctor will probably be able to diagnose pityriasis versicolor from the appearance of the patches. Sometimes, skin scrapings may be taken to confirm the presence of the fungus. Treatment usually consists of washing the affected area regularly with an over-the-counter shampoo containing selenium sulfide, an antifungal drug (p.889). With thorough treatment, the infection usually clears up in 2–3 weeks, but it may take several more weeks for your skin to return to its normal color. If you miss a patch of affected skin when applying the shampoo, the infection will recur.

(WWW) ONLINE SITES: p.1033, p.1036

Cold sore

A painful cluster of tiny blisters, usually near the lips, caused by a viral infection

LIFESTYLE Cold wind, sunburn, and stress are risk factors

AGE GENDER GENETICS Not significant factors

Cold sores, also known as fever blisters, are painful clusters of blisters usually caused by herpes simplex virus type 1 (HSV-1). Most people have been infected with HSV-1 by the time they reach adulthood. The initial infection often goes unnoticed but may cause blisters in the mouth. The virus then remains dormant in the nerve cells, but, in some people, it is reactivated and produces cold sores. Trigger factors include wind, sunburn, fatigue, stress, the common cold, menstruation, and fever. Some people have recurrent cold sores.

WHAT ARE THE SYMPTOMS?

Cold sores often develop on the skin around the lips. The symptoms usually appear in the following order:

- The affected site begins to tingle.
- One or more clusters of tiny, painful blisters develop, and the surrounding skin becomes inflamed.
- The blisters burst and become crusty.
- Usually, the blisters subside within 10–14 days.

If cold sores recur, the blisters usually reappear in the same areas on the face.

WHAT MIGHT BE DONE?

You may be able to prevent individual outbreaks by using an antiviral cream such as acyclovir (*see* PREPARATIONS FOR INFECTIONS AND INFESTATIONS, p.892), but you must apply the cream as soon as the first symptoms develop. In some cases, oral antiviral drugs (p.886) may be prescribed. Although prompt treatment can prevent individual outbreaks, the virus remains in the system and symptoms may recur. People who have recurrent cold sores can protect their skin from trigger factors such as sunburn or cold wind. To minimize the risk of spreading the virus, do not touch the blisters and avoid kissing. Sometimes, oral sex can transmit the virus from the mouth to the genitals (*see* GENITAL HERPES, p.767).

(WWW) ONLINE SITES: p.1033, p.1036

Warts

Firm, skin-colored or darker growths on the skin caused by a viral infection

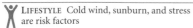

AGE Most common in children and young adults

LIFESTYLE Warm, moist conditions are a risk factor

GENDER GENETICS Not significant factors

Warts, also called verrucas, are small growths caused by human papillomaviruses. The viruses invade skin cells and encourage them to multiply, thus creating thickened areas of skin. Warts usually occur on the hands or feet and are generally harmless. However, some types affect the genitals and are more serious (*see* GENITAL WARTS, p.768).

Warts are transferred by direct contact with an infected person or from virus particles on recently shed flakes of skin. The infection is commonly spread in warm, moist conditions.

Most people have at least one wart by age 20, but some people have recurrent warts. People with reduced immunity due to a disease such as AIDS (*see* HIV INFECTION AND AIDS, p.295) may develop large numbers of warts.

WHAT ARE THE TYPES?

There are three main types of warts. These types are classified according to their appearance and the different sites on the body on which they occur.

COMMON WARTS These warts most frequently occur on the hands. They are:

- Firm with a rough, raised surface.
- Usually round.
- Dotted with tiny, black spots.

The black spots are small blood vessels. Common warts often grow in groups, which are known as crops.

PLANTAR WARTS These warts occur on the soles of the feet. Although plantar warts are the same as common warts, they grow into the skin because they are continually under pressure from the weight of the body. A group of plantar warts that have joined together is called a mosaic wart. Plantar warts are:

- Flattened into the sole of the foot.
- Firm, with a thickened surface.
- Usually painful to walk on.
- Dotted with tiny, black spots.

The virus that causes plantar warts is usually picked up from walking barefoot in communal areas, such as locker rooms and swimming pools.

SELF-HELP TREATING A WART

You can treat common and plantar warts by using over-the-counter gels or lotions containing salicylic acid, which dissolves the thickened layer of skin. Apply the treatment daily for several weeks until the warts have disappeared. Keep equipment used for treating warts away from other bath items to avoid spreading the virus. Do not share bath items.

Pumice stone

Wart

1 *Soak the wart in water to soften it. Then gently rub it with a pumice stone or an emery board to remove as much of the thickened skin as possible.*

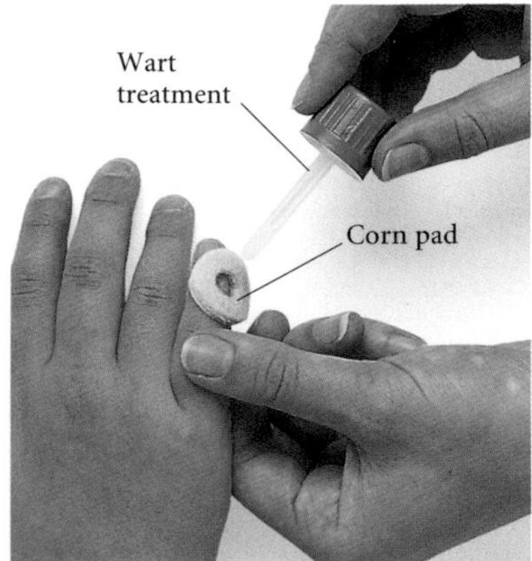
Wart treatment
Corn pad

2 *Shield the surrounding skin with a corn pad or petroleum jelly. Carefully apply the wart treatment to the wart and cover the area with an adhesive bandage.*

Sunburn

Inflammation of the skin caused by overexposure to the sun

 GENETICS More common in fair-skinned people

 LIFESTYLE Outdoor activities are risk factors

 AGE GENDER Not significant factors

Sunburn occurs when the ultraviolet rays in sunlight damage cells in the outer layer of the skin, causing soreness, redness, and blistering. Damage is most likely to occur in the middle of the day when the sun is at its highest point and greatest strength, but sunlight at any time of day can be harmful. It is possible for sunburn to occur even when the sky is overcast because ultraviolet rays can still penetrate the cloud cover. Sunlight reflected off water or snow is especially damaging because its effects are intensified.

Fair-skinned people are more susceptible to sunburn because their skin produces only a small amount of the protective pigment melanin.

WHAT ARE THE SYMPTOMS?

Sunburn can occur after just 30 minutes of exposing the skin to the sun. The symptoms may take a few hours to develop and include:

- Sore, red, hot skin.
- Swelling of the affected area.
- In severe cases, blistering.

A few days after the initial sunburn, the skin may become dry and start to peel. Severe sunburn may be associated with heatstroke, which is a potentially fatal condition (*see* HEAT EXHAUSTION AND HEATSTROKE, p.322).

WHAT IS THE TREATMENT?

If you develop sunburn, stay in the shade and drink plenty of fluids (*see* SAFETY IN THE SUN, p.80). Relief from the burning sensation and other symptoms may be gained by applying bland creams, calamine lotion, or soothing sprays or lotions to the affected areas of skin. Cool baths and compresses may also help relieve the discomfort.

Severe sunburn needs prompt medical attention, and you should consult your doctor as soon as possible. If you are severely burned and you also have heatstroke, you will need to have urgent treatment in the hospital.

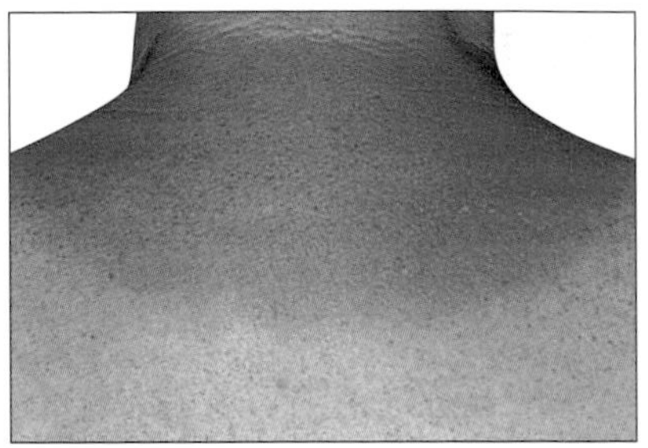

Sunburn
Even a short period of exposure to the sun can damage the surface of the skin, resulting in reddening and soreness.

You can prevent sunburn by avoiding the sun and by protecting your skin when outdoors. Sunburn or long-term exposure to the sun can cause the skin to age prematurely and increase the risk of developing skin cancer (p.344).

 ONLINE SITES: p.1036

Blister

A collection of fluid beneath the surface of the skin

AGE GENDER GENETICS LIFESTYLE Not significant factors

A blister forms when fluid leaks from blood vessels in the skin, usually after minor injury, and collects to form a small, raised area just beneath the outer layer of skin. The most common causes of single blisters are friction, such as that caused by a badly fitting shoe, and burns, including sunburn (left). Widespread blistering may be caused by an allergy (*see* ECZEMA, p.333), or it may occur in some viral infections, such as chickenpox (p.288) and shingles (*see* HERPES ZOSTER, p.288). The bacterial skin infection impetigo (p.351) may cause pus-filled blisters. There are also a number of much less common but potentially life-threatening conditions that cause blistering either on specific areas of skin or over the whole of the body (*see* BLISTERING DISEASES, p.336).

Blistering caused by minor damage usually heals rapidly without treatment. New skin develops beneath the blister, the fluid is gradually absorbed, and the top layer of skin dries and peels away. If the skin is broken, or if the blistered site is likely to be damaged further, you should protect the area with a dry, sterile dressing. Blistering due to disease or infection may need drug treatment.

You should not prick a blister to release the fluid because the skin acts as a barrier against infection. If the blisters are filled with pus or you notice spreading redness in the surrounding skin, consult your doctor.

Bruise

A discolored area of skin caused by bleeding in underlying tissues

 AGE Most common in children and elderly people

 GENDER GENETICS LIFESTYLE Not significant factors

If the blood vessels beneath the skin are damaged by a blow or a fall, blood may leak into the surrounding tissues. This internal bleeding, even if it occurs deep in muscle, will eventually show through the surface of the skin as black or blue patches called bruises. Over a period of a few days after the injury, the red cells in the leaked blood break down and the bruises gradually change color, fading to green, light brown, or yellow. The discoloration normally disappears completely within a week.

After receiving an injury, you can reduce blood loss beneath the skin by applying firm pressure to the area with an ice pack. You should maintain the pressure for at least 5 minutes.

Children and elderly people bruise more easily than young and middle-aged adults. If severe bruising appears for no obvious reason at any age, you should consult your doctor because it may be a sign of a bleeding disorder such as von Willebrand disease (p.452).

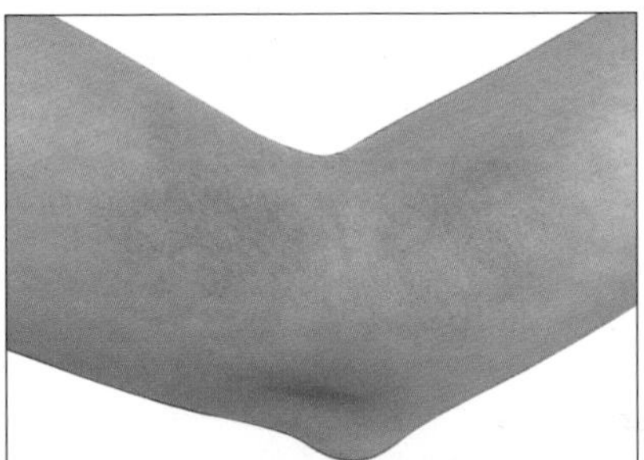

Bruising around the elbow
Prominent areas of the body, such as the elbow and knee, are vulnerable to injury and are common sites for bruises.

Hair and Nail Disorders

Hair and nails, like the outer layers of skin, are made of dead cells that grow from a living base. The dead parts that show above the skin's surface can be cut or damaged without causing pain, but damage to the living roots is painful. The condition of the hair and nails often reflects general health. Changes in the nails, in particular, may indicate an underlying disease.

KEY ANATOMY

Hair
Erector muscle
Sebaceous gland
Hair follicle

HAIR STRUCTURE

Nail
Cuticle
Fingertip
Bone
Nail bed

NAIL STRUCTURE

For more information on the structure and function of hair and nails, *see* pp.328–331.

Most hair and nail disorders are not a health threat but may be unsightly and cause embarrassment. However, some are caused by serious health problems. For example, excessive growth of body hair may be due to a hormonal imbalance, and spoon-shaped nails suggest iron deficiency. In these cases, treating the underlying disorder often improves the condition. Hair disorders may be due to factors such as drug treatments and localized skin diseases. Many nail abnormalities are due to minor injury or infection but can be difficult to treat. Topical preparations do not penetrate the nail, and oral drugs only affect its base. A damaged nail surface will not appear normal until it grows out, and the nails sometimes indicate past more than present health.

This section begins by describing several disorders that affect scalp or body hair. The remaining articles describe abnormalities of the nails and the skin that surrounds them. Some common scalp problems are discussed elsewhere, including head lice (p.831) and seborrheic dermatitis (p.335).

Dandruff

Excessive shedding of flakes of skin from the scalp

AGE More common in young adults

GENDER GENETICS LIFESTYLE Not significant factors

Dandruff is a harmless condition that involves an acceleration in the normal shedding of dead skin cells from the scalp. This dead skin accumulates as white flakes in the hair and sometimes causes itching. The condition is most common in young adults and may be a source of embarrassment.

Dandruff is most often caused by a yeast organism that grows in the scalp. Extensive dandruff is known as seborrheic dermatitis (p.335), a disorder that causes inflammation and scaling of the skin in other areas of the body, such as the face, chest, and back. Dandruff may be associated with inflammation of the eyelids (*see* BLEPHARITIS, p.583).

You can treat dandruff by washing your hair three to four times a week with a tar-based shampoo or a shampoo that contains an antiyeast agent, such as selenium sulfide or ketoconazole (*see* ANTIFUNGAL DRUGS, p.889).

If the dandruff persists despite continued treatment, you should consult your doctor because there is a possibility that you may have developed a skin condition, such as eczema (p.333) or psoriasis (p.332), that also affects the scalp. These disorders may require specific treatment with prescription drugs.

Alopecia

Loss of part or all of the hair, most commonly the hair on the scalp

AGE GENDER GENETICS LIFESTYLE Risk factors depend on the type

Alopecia, or hair loss, can occur in any body area but is particularly noticeable when it affects the scalp. The condition may be localized, in which hair is lost in patches, or generalized, in which there is thinning or total hair loss over the whole scalp. Hair loss can be temporary or permanent. Alopecia is not always associated with ill health, but it may cause embarrassment.

What are the causes?

The most common cause of alopecia in men is oversensitivity to the hormone testosterone, producing a characteristic pattern of hair loss (*see* MALE-PATTERN BALDNESS, opposite page).

Patchy hair loss is usually due to alopecia areata, an autoimmune disorder that causes bald patches to appear on the scalp surrounded by short, broken hairs. The hair will usually regrow within 6 months, but, in rare cases, alopecia areata can cause permanent loss of all body hair.

Hairstyles that pull on the scalp are a common cause of patchy hair loss; if the pulling is continuous, hair loss may be permanent. Patchy hair loss may be the result of a rare psychological disorder in which the hair is compulsively pulled. Burns or skin disorders, such as ringworm (p.352), that scar the scalp may cause permanent patchy hair loss.

Generalized hair loss is normal in elderly people. It may occur temporarily after pregnancy and is a common side effect of chemotherapy (p.278). Other causes of thinning hair include acute illness, stress, and malnutrition.

WHAT IS THE TREATMENT?

Your doctor will probably be able to diagnose alopecia areata by the appearance of your scalp. This condition does not usually require treatment, but corticosteroids injected into the hairless patches may be effective in promoting regrowth. In most other cases of hair loss, the hair usually regrows once the underlying cause has been treated. Hair lost during pregnancy usually regrows about 3 months after childbirth.

If your scalp has patchy scarring, you may need a skin biopsy (p.344) to diagnose the underlying cause. Scarred areas may be treated with topical corticosteroids (p.892) or antifungal drugs (p.889), but if the damage is severe and has affected the hair follicles it is unlikely that new hair will grow.

(WWW) ONLINE SITES: p.1033, p.1036

Male-pattern baldness

Progressive loss of hair from the scalp, often in a characteristic pattern

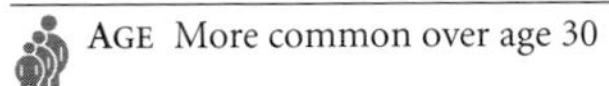
AGE More common over age 30

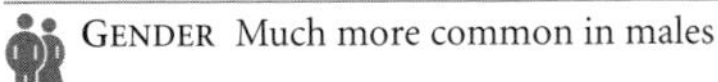
GENDER Much more common in males

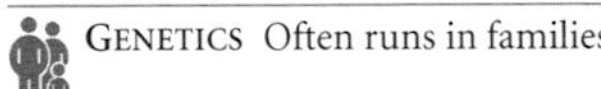
GENETICS Often runs in families

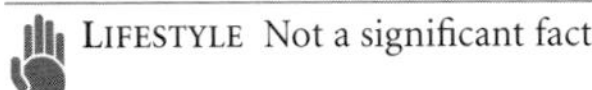
LIFESTYLE Not a significant factor

In male-pattern baldness, also called androgenic alopecia, hair is lost over several years, first from the temples and then from the crown, leaving a rim of hair around the scalp. The condition is very common in men over age 30 but may develop much earlier. In rare cases, it begins during puberty. This type of male-pattern baldness is often progressive and is thought to be caused by hypersensitivity of the follicles to the male sex hormone testosterone. There may be a family history of baldness in male relatives on the mother's side.

Male-pattern baldness also occurs in women but is less common. Hair loss in women is usually due to hormonal disturbances, in particular those that take place after menopause. In these cases, thinning is more generalized.

Your doctor may have you take tests to look for an underlying health problem (*see* ALOPECIA, opposite page). Over-the-counter solutions containing minoxidil may temporarily stimulate regrowth, but the new hair disappears when treatment is stopped. Finasteride, a prescription drug, can help stop hair loss. A more permanent way to replace hair is by having a hair transplant (left).

(WWW) ONLINE SITES: p.1026, p.1034

TREATMENT HAIR TRANSPLANT

Baldness can be treated surgically by several different methods of hair transplantation. In the method shown here, a strip of skin and hair is taken from a donor site, usually at the back of your scalp or behind your ears. The removed hairs and their attached follicles are then inserted into the bald area, the recipient site. You will usually be given a mild sedative, and both the donor and recipient sites on the scalp are anesthetized. The transplant process takes 1–1½ hours.

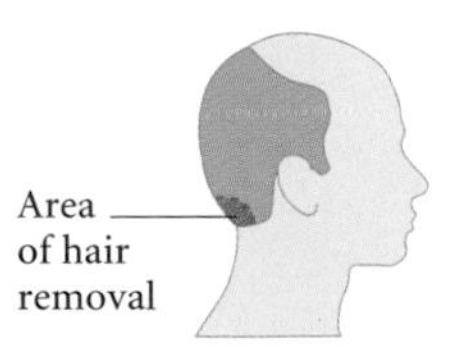
Area of hair removal

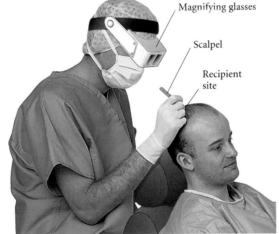

DONOR SITE

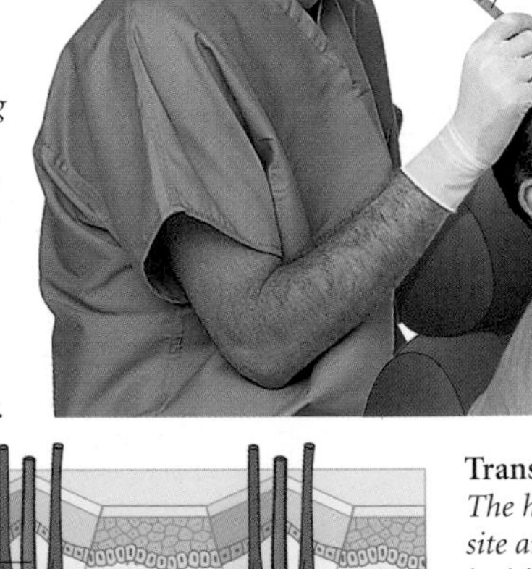
Magnifying glasses
Scalpel
Recipient site

During the procedure
A strip of skin containing hairs with attached follicles is taken from the donor site, usually at the back of the scalp. The surgeon then makes a number of tiny incisions in the area that is to receive transplanted hair.

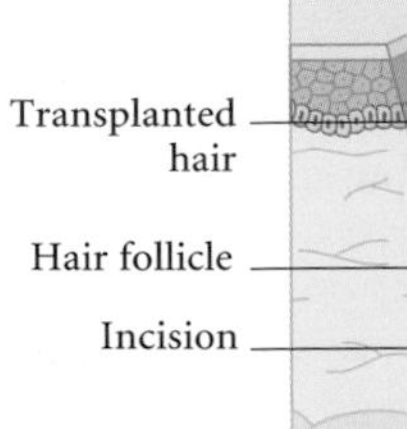
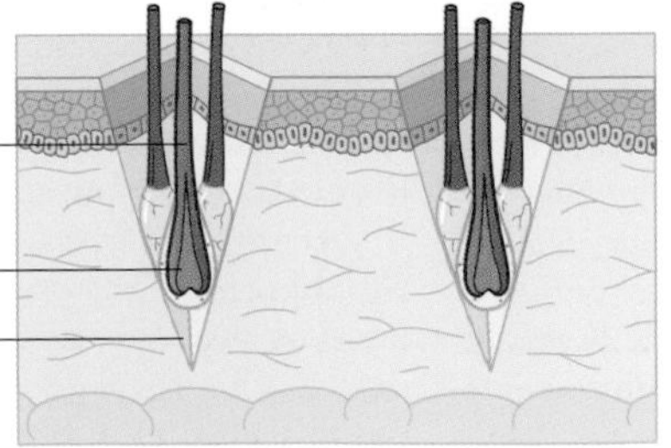
Transplanted hair
Hair follicle
Incision

Transplanted hairs
The hairs from the donor site are inserted into the incisions using tweezers. The hairs themselves fall out shortly afterward, but new hair starts to grow from the follicles 3 weeks to 3 months later. The donor site heals in about 5 days.

Excessive hair

Excessive growth of hair or hair growth in areas that would not normally have hair

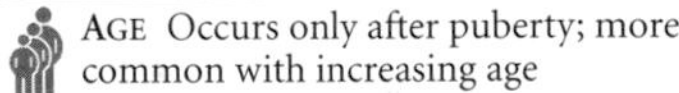
AGE Occurs only after puberty; more common with increasing age

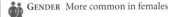

GENDER More common in females

GENETICS Sometimes runs in families

LIFESTYLE Not a significant factor

There are two types of excessive hair growth: hirsutism and hypertrichosis. Hirsutism affects women only. In this condition, excessive hair develops particularly on the face, trunk, and limbs. This type of excessive growth is more common in women over age 60, especially those who are of Mediterranean, Asian, Hispanic, or Arab descent.

The second type of excessive hair growth, hypertrichosis, can affect both males and females. In this condition, hair grows all over the body, even in areas that do not normally have hair.

WHAT ARE THE CAUSES?

Mild hirsutism in women is often considered normal, especially following menopause. In some cases, it may be a result of an increase in normally occurring male hormones in the female body (*see* VIRILIZATION, p.740), which may be caused by disorders such as polycystic ovary syndrome (p.744).

Hypertrichosis can occur with anorexia nervosa (p.562) or as a side effect of immunosuppressants (p.906) or antihypertensive drugs (p.897).

WHAT MIGHT BE DONE?

If you are a young woman with hirsutism, your doctor may arrange for a blood test to measure your male hormone levels. If these levels are high, you may be given a drug to block the hormone's effects and be treated for the underlying disorder. For example, polycystic ovary syndrome may be treated with hormones or surgery. If hypertrichosis occurs as a side effect of a drug, stopping the drug often reverses the condition.

You can deal with excessive hair yourself by bleaching it or by shaving, plucking, waxing, or using depilatory creams. Hair can be removed permanently by electrolysis or laser.

(WWW) ONLINE SITES: p.1033, p1036

Pilonidal sinus

A pit, often containing hairs, at the top of the cleft between the buttocks

 AGE Most common in young adults

 GENDER More common in males

 GENETICS LIFESTYLE Not significant factors

A pilonidal sinus is a small, enclosed pit beneath the skin at the top of the cleft between the buttocks. The condition occurs most commonly in men with a lot of body hair. The exact cause is unknown but may be a defect in the development of that area. Hair growth at the site tends to be directed inward, which may cause infection in the sinus and result in a painful abscess.

Prompt action at the first signs of infection may prevent an abscess from forming. You should soak the area in warm water to relieve discomfort and consult your doctor as soon as possible. You may be prescribed oral antibiotics (p.885) to treat the infection. If pus has built up, the abscess will need to be drained under general anesthesia and left open to heal. In most cases, the infection is unlikely to recur.

Nail abnormalities

Changes in the shape, color, or texture of the nails, often due to injury, infection, or underlying disease

 AGE GENDER GENETICS LIFESTYLE Risk factors depend on the type

The nails are particularly susceptible to damage. Injury is the most common cause of abnormalities in the shape, color, or texture of nails. Changes in general health and in the health of the skin at the nail bed may also lead to abnormalities. In addition, infection of the nail itself may alter its appearance.

WHAT ARE THE TYPES?

Some forms of nail abnormality need treatment only if they are unsightly or painful; others may be signs of underlying health problems that may require medical investigation.

WHITE SPOTS Small white marks that appear on one or more nails occur naturally and are due to minor damage, such as from a knock or blow.

THICKENING Thickening of the nails, a condition known as onychogryphosis, may be due to neglect or a fungal infection or occur for no apparent reason. Distortion of the nail may result. The toenails are most likely to be affected.

RIDGES The occurrence of ridged lines running from the base of the nail to the tip is normal in people who are elderly. In younger people, these ridges may be a sign of rheumatoid arthritis (p.377) or of the skin conditions lichen planus (p.336) and psoriasis (p.332).

PITTING Multiple pits the size of a pinhead on the nail surface often indicate a general skin disorder, such as psoriasis or eczema (p.333). Pitting may also be associated with the hair disorder alopecia areata (*see* ALOPECIA, p.358).

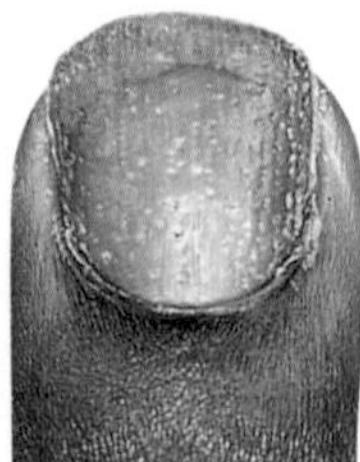

Pitted fingernail
Many small pits can be seen all over the surface of the fingernail. In this case, the pitting is caused by the skin disorder psoriasis.

NAIL SEPARATION If a nail is damaged through injury, it can lift away from the nail bed (a condition called onycholysis) and eventually fall off. Separation of the nail from the nail bed may also occur in some people with the skin conditions psoriasis or lichen planus or those with certain thyroid problems. Nail separation makes the nail bed susceptible to infection, which causes the lifted nail to appear green.

YELLOWING Yellow, crumbly nails may be due to a fungal infection (onychomycosis). Sometimes, heavy smoking causes discoloration of the nails.

CLUBBING Increased curvature of the nails and broadening of the fingertips is called clubbing. This condition often indicates a serious underlying disorder of the lungs, particularly cystic fibrosis (p.824), tuberculosis (p.491), or lung cancer (p.503). Alternatively, clubbing of the nails may be a sign of liver disease, congenital heart disease (p.836), thyroid disease, or certain bowel disorders, such as Crohn's disease (p.658).

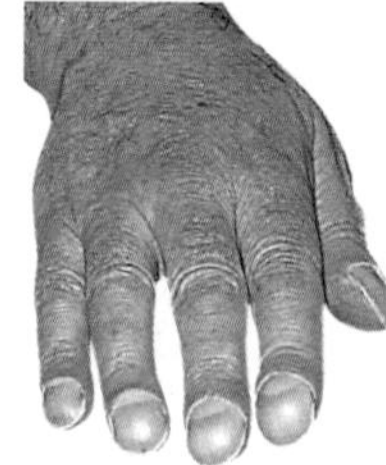

Clubbing of the fingernails
Increased curvature of the nails, known as clubbing, may result in loss of the normal indentation at the nail bed.

SPOON-SHAPED NAILS In this form of abnormality, known as koilonychia, the nails have a concave and spoon-shaped appearance. This condition is usually caused by a severe iron deficiency.

WHAT MIGHT BE DONE?

Minor nail abnormalities that are not associated with underlying disorders, such as white spots caused by minor injury, are unlikely to need treatment. However, if the color, shape, or general condition of your nails changes when no obvious damage has occurred, you should consult your doctor to find out if the problem is caused by a disease. Clubbing that has existed from childhood is probably due to a hereditary defect. This form of clubbing is irreversible and need not be investigated. However, you should consult a doctor if you develop clubbing as an adult. Once the cause of an underlying disorder has been treated, the nails should begin growing normally again, and healthy nail will gradually replace the abnormal tissue. This is a slow process; an abnormal fingernail may take between 6 and 9 months to grow out, and a toenail takes even longer. In the meantime, the appearance of damaged fingernails may be improved by having regular manicures, and a podiatrist may be able to treat distorted toenails.

Paronychia

Infection of the skin fold around a nail, causing a painful swelling

 LIFESTYLE Repeated immersion of the hands in water is a risk factor

 AGE GENDER GENETICS Not significant factors

Infection of the fold of skin surrounding a fingernail or toenail (nail fold) is called paronychia. The infection causes pain and swelling, which may develop either suddenly (acute paronychia) or gradually over several months (chronic paronychia), depending on the underlying cause. One or more nails may be affected by the condition.

What are the causes?

Acute paronychia is usually the result of a bacterial infection entering the nail fold through a cut or break in the skin. Chronic paronychia is common among people such as cooks who repeatedly immerse their hands in water. The skin around the nail separates from the nail, softens, and becomes infected, usually by a yeast organism. A secondary bacterial infection may then occur, resulting in acute paronychia. Some people with decreased resistance to infection, such as those with diabetes mellitus (p.687), are at increased risk of paronychia.

What are the symptoms?

Usually the symptoms of acute paronychia become apparent about 24 hours after infection and include:

- Pain and swelling on one side of the nail fold.
- Buildup of pus around the nail.

If acute paronychia is left untreated, the nail may separate from the nail bed and eventually fall away. The symptoms of chronic paronychia develop over several months. The condition may cause some discomfort and swelling but does not usually produce a buildup of pus. Eventually, the affected nail thickens slightly and develops horizontal ridges and brownish discoloration.

What is the treatment?

Your doctor may prescribe oral antibiotics (p.885) for acute paronychia. In severe cases, pus may be drained under local anesthesia. Although chronic paronychia can sometimes be treated with an over-the-counter cream containing an antifungal drug (p.889), your doctor may prescribe stronger antifungals and oral antibiotics if there is a secondary infection. Acute paronychia often clears up in a few days with treatment. Chronic paronychia may take several weeks.

To prevent chronic paronychia, you should dry your hands thoroughly after washing and wear cotton-lined rubber gloves when your hands are in water.

Ingrown toenail

Painful inward growth of the edges of a toenail into the surrounding skin

 AGE Most common in teenagers and young adults

 GENDER More common in males

 LIFESTYLE Tight or badly fitting shoes increase the risk

GENETICS Not a significant factor

An ingrown toenail curves under on one or both sides and cuts into the surrounding skin, causing inflammation and sometimes infection. The condition, which most commonly affects the big toe, is often due to ill-fitting shoes pressing on an incorrectly cut nail. In some cases, injury can cause the skin around the nail to overgrow and engulf part of the nail. Poor foot hygiene can also increase the risk of infection, leading to inflammation.

What are the symptoms?

The symptoms of an ingrown toenail may include the following:

- Pain, redness, and swelling around the toenail.
- Broken skin at the nail edge, which oozes clear fluid, pus, or blood.

You should consult your doctor as soon as you notice a toenail that has become ingrown because it is possible that your toe may be infected.

What is the treatment?

You can relieve the pain of an ingrown toenail by bathing your foot in warm saltwater daily and by taking analgesics (p.912). You should protect the affected toe by keeping it covered with a clean, dry gauze. If there is no improvement, you should consult your doctor. If your toenail is infected, he or she may prescribe oral antibiotics (p.885) or topical antibiotics (*see* PREPARATIONS FOR SKIN INFECTIONS AND INFESTATIONS, p.892).

To help prevent an ingrown toenail from recurring, keep your feet clean and wear correctly fitting shoes. Your toenails should be cut straight across, rather than along a curve, to prevent them from growing into the skin. If the problem recurs, your doctor may suggest that you have part or all of the toenail removed or destroyed to stop it growing into the toe (*see* REMOVAL OF AN INGROWN TOENAIL, below).

(WWW) ONLINE SITES: p.1036

TREATMENT Removal of an ingrown toenail

Minor surgery may be needed for an ingrown toenail. Your toe will be anesthetized and cleaned with antiseptic, and a tourniquet will be applied to its base. The nail, or part of it, will be removed, and phenol will be applied to the exposed nail bed to kill it and prevent regrowth. You should be comfortable enough to walk within 24 hours of surgery, and the wound should heal within a week.

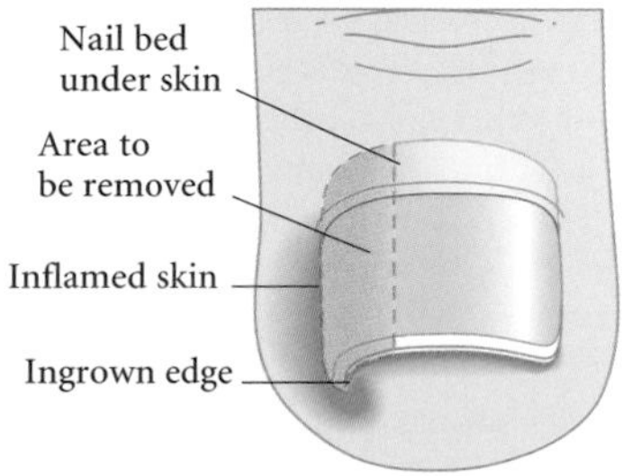
Nail bed under skin
Area to be removed
Inflamed skin
Ingrown edge

The operation
A vertical cut is made along the toenail. The ingrown part is removed and the nail bed treated to prevent regrowth.

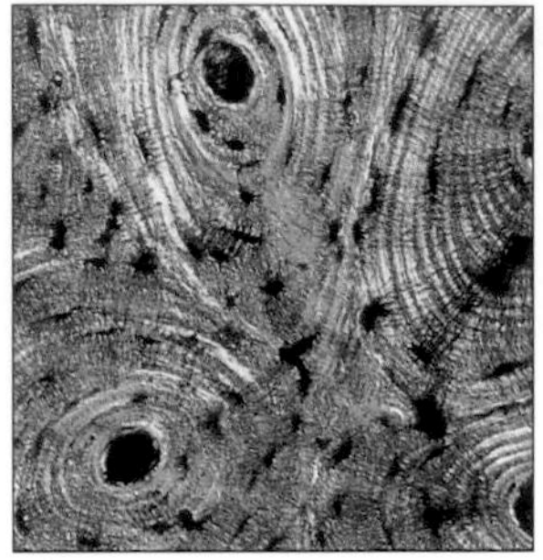
Structure of compact bone
The structural units of compact bone are called osteons (shown here in cross section). Osteons consist of rings of collagen (protein) around central canals.

MUSCULOSKELETAL SYSTEM

EVERY DAY WE USE OUR MUSCLES and joints to carry out voluntary movements. Many of these actions, such as walking, demand very little concentration, but complex tasks, such as playing the piano, require more conscious effort, supported by a subconscious system of coordination learned when the skill was first mastered. All movements are based on mechanical changes in the muscles, which contract or relax, making specific bones pivot, hinge, rotate, or glide at the joints.

Skeletal muscles move the body at its joints by contracting. In addition, they maintain a steady tension, or tone, that gives the body the support it needs to maintain its posture, such as keeping the head upright on the neck. This postural tone is automatic but does require alertness. Unlike horses, people cannot sleep standing up.

There are two other types of muscles in the body: cardiac muscle, found only in the heart, and smooth muscle, occurring in hollow organs such as the intestines. Most smooth muscle is not under conscious control.

TYPES OF BONE

Bones come in many shapes and sizes, ranging from the flat bones found in the skull to the long bones of the limbs. The outer layer of each bone is made of dense, heavy, compact bone. The inner consists of spongy bone that is made up of numerous trabeculae (struts) arranged in such a way that they provide maximum support without excessive weight.

Bone gives the body shape and supports the body's structure. It is a living tissue, which is constantly being renewed. Bone also serves as a reservoir for various minerals, such as calcium and phosphorus. Bone marrow, the soft, fatty substance that fills the cavities in bones, produces most of the body's blood cells (*see* FORMATION OF BLOOD CELLS, p.440).

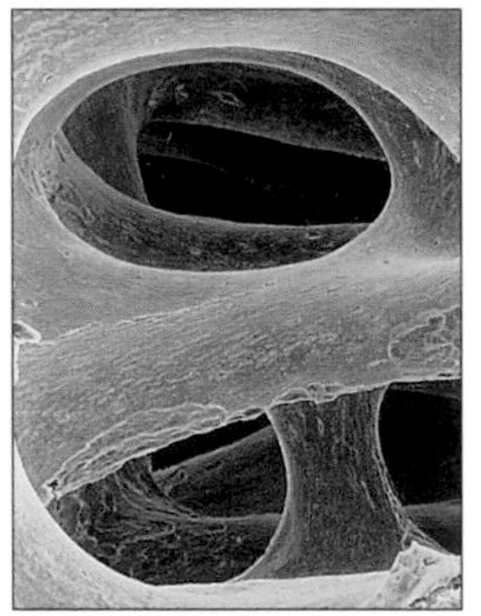
Struts in spongy bone
The trabeculae (struts) that form spongy bone make it light but strong.

MOVEMENT

Joints, which are formed where bones meet, are covered with lubricated cartilage that allows smooth movement. The range of movement of the joints is determined both by their structure and by the ligaments that stabilize and support them; the hip joint, for example, moves less freely than the shoulder. In contrast, the joints in the wrist, foot, and spine sacrifice mobility for stability; their bones are joined by strong, inflexible ligaments that allow little movement. Most of the skull bones fuse together and become immobile once growth has ceased.

FUNCTION HOW THE BODY MOVES

Movement of the body depends on the interaction of muscles, bones, and joints under the organization of the central nervous system. A muscle typically connects two bones and crosses the joint between them. When a muscle contracts, it pulls on the bones to which it is attached and produces movement. Muscles can only pull, not push. Therefore, many muscles are arranged in pairs, one on each side of a joint, so that they produce opposing movements. An example is the pairing of the triceps and biceps muscles in the upper arm.

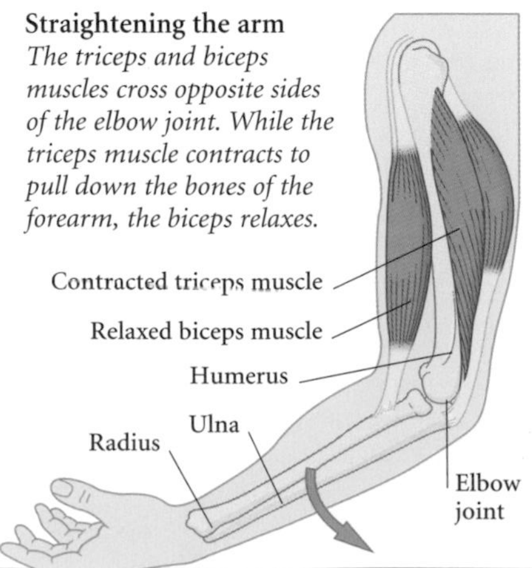
Contracted triceps muscle
Relaxed biceps muscle
Humerus
Ulna
Radius
Elbow joint
Straightening the arm
The triceps and biceps muscles cross opposite sides of the elbow joint. While the triceps muscle contracts to pull down the bones of the forearm, the biceps relaxes.

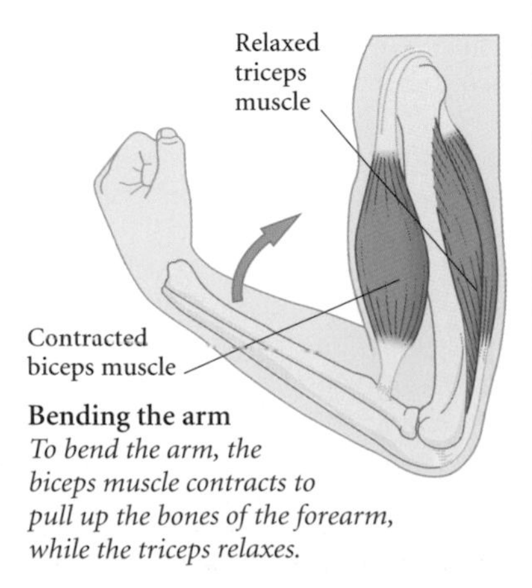
Relaxed triceps muscle
Contracted biceps muscle
Bending the arm
To bend the arm, the biceps muscle contracts to pull up the bones of the forearm, while the triceps relaxes.

STRUCTURE THE BODY'S SKELETON

The adult human skeleton is a bony framework that supports the body and gives it shape. It also protects the internal organs and anchors the body's muscles. The skeleton is composed of 206 bones and is divided into two parts. The axial skeleton – the skull, spine, and rib cage – consists of 80 bones and protects the brain, spinal cord, heart, and lungs. The appendicular skeleton has 126 bones and consists of the bones of the limbs, the collarbones, the shoulder blades, and the bones of the pelvis.

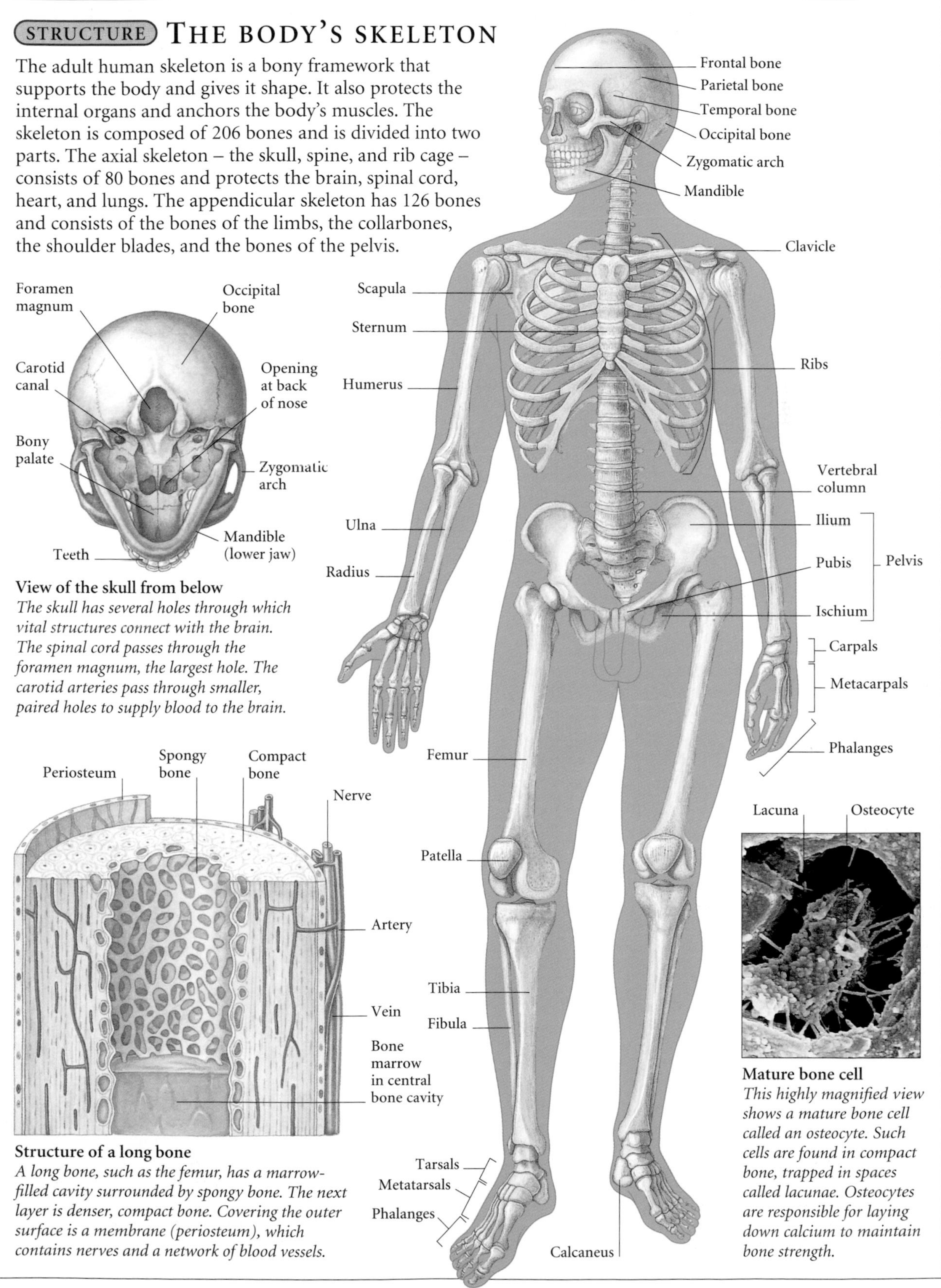

Frontal bone
Parietal bone
Temporal bone
Occipital bone
Zygomatic arch
Mandible
Clavicle
Scapula
Sternum
Ribs
Humerus
Vertebral column
Ulna
Ilium
Pubis
Pelvis
Radius
Ischium
Carpals
Metacarpals
Phalanges
Femur
Patella
Tibia
Fibula
Tarsals
Metatarsals
Phalanges
Calcaneus
Foramen magnum
Occipital bone
Carotid canal
Opening at back of nose
Bony palate
Zygomatic arch
Mandible (lower jaw)
Teeth
Periosteum
Spongy bone
Compact bone
Nerve
Artery
Vein
Bone marrow in central bone cavity
Lacuna
Osteocyte

View of the skull from below
The skull has several holes through which vital structures connect with the brain. The spinal cord passes through the foramen magnum, the largest hole. The carotid arteries pass through smaller, paired holes to supply blood to the brain.

Structure of a long bone
A long bone, such as the femur, has a marrow-filled cavity surrounded by spongy bone. The next layer is denser, compact bone. Covering the outer surface is a membrane (periosteum), which contains nerves and a network of blood vessels.

Mature bone cell
This highly magnified view shows a mature bone cell called an osteocyte. Such cells are found in compact bone, trapped in spaces called lacunae. Osteocytes are responsible for laying down calcium to maintain bone strength.

STRUCTURE THE BACKBONE

The spine, also known as the vertebral column, holds the body upright, supports the head, and encircles the spinal cord. It consists of 33 bones called vertebrae. Joints and disks of fibrous tissue between most of the vertebrae make the spine flexible, while ligaments and muscles stabilize it and control movement.

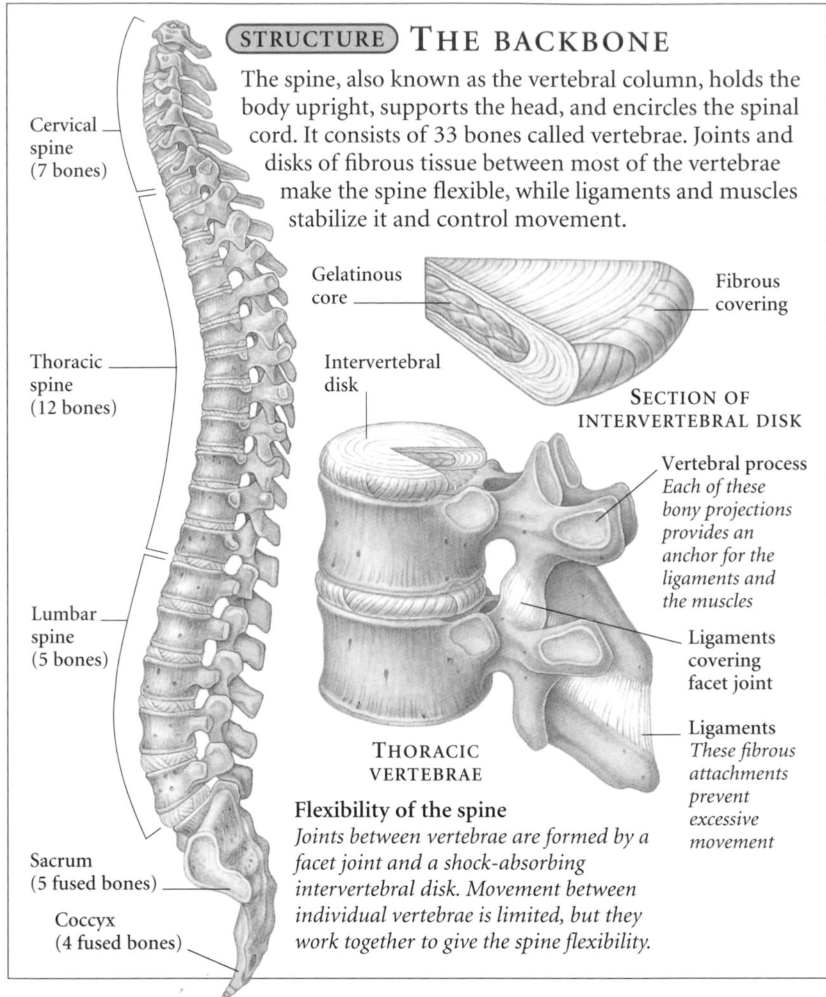

Cervical spine (7 bones)
Thoracic spine (12 bones)
Lumbar spine (5 bones)
Sacrum (5 fused bones)
Coccyx (4 fused bones)
Gelatinous core
Fibrous covering
Intervertebral disk
SECTION OF INTERVERTEBRAL DISK
Vertebral process
Each of these bony projections provides an anchor for the ligaments and the muscles
Ligaments covering facet joint
Ligaments
These fibrous attachments prevent excessive movement
THORACIC VERTEBRAE

Flexibility of the spine
Joints between vertebrae are formed by a facet joint and a shock-absorbing intervertebral disk. Movement between individual vertebrae is limited, but they work together to give the spine flexibility.

FUNCTION HOW BONE REPAIRS ITSELF

A broken bone and any damaged blood vessels start to repair and heal themselves immediately. A fracture in a long bone, such as the collarbone, normally takes about 6 weeks to heal in an adult. However, some injured bones may not regain their full strength for several months, and healing may need to be aided by a plaster or resin cast or by mechanical fixation. In children, fractured bones usually heal more quickly.

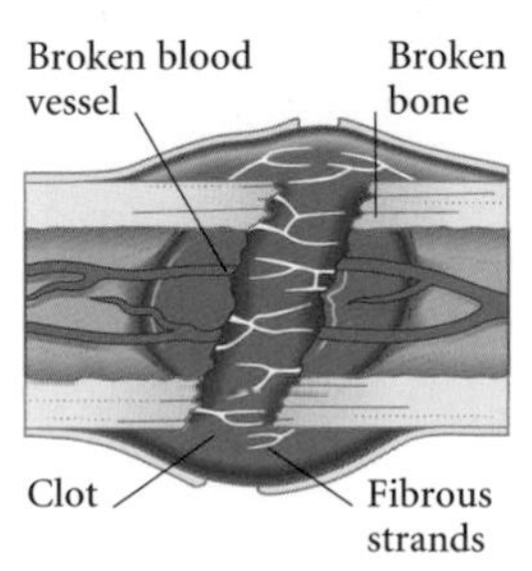

Broken blood vessel
Broken bone
Clot
Fibrous strands

1 *A clot forms to seal broken blood vessels. Gradually, a mesh of fibrous tissue forms and starts to replace the clot.*

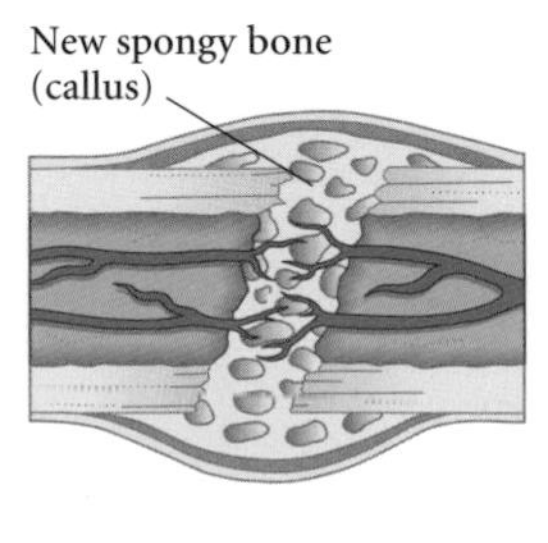

New spongy bone (callus)

2 *New, soft, spongy bone called callus develops on the framework provided by the fibrous tissue, joining the broken ends.*

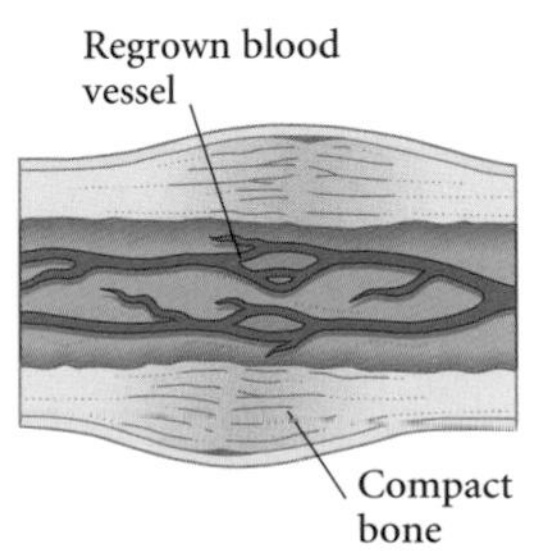

Regrown blood vessel
Compact bone

3 *Dense, compact bone gradually replaces the callus, and blood vessels regrow. Eventually, the bone regains its shape.*

STRUCTURE AND FUNCTION THE JOINTS

Joints are formed where two or more bones meet. Most joints, including those of the limbs, move freely and are known as synovial joints. They are lubricated by synovial fluid secreted by the joint lining. In contrast, semimovable joints, like those in the pelvis and spine, are less flexible but give greater stability. A few joints, such as those of the skull, are fixed and allow no movement.

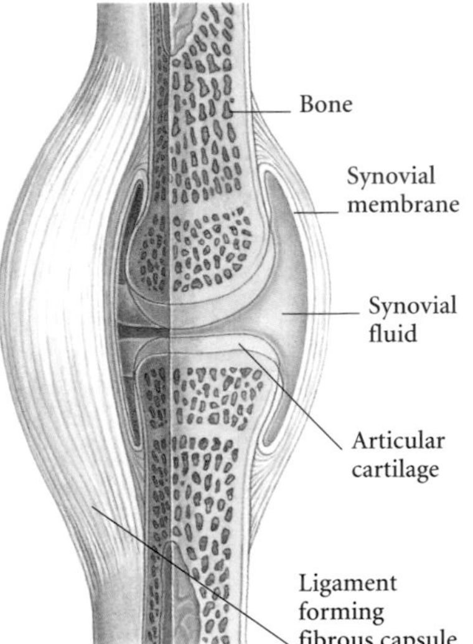

Bone
Synovial membrane
Synovial fluid
Articular cartilage
Ligament forming fibrous capsule

Structure of a synovial joint
The bones of synovial joints are held together by ligaments that form a fibrous capsule. The synovial membrane lining the capsule secretes a lubricating fluid, and articular cartilage on the bone ends provides a smooth surface for movement.

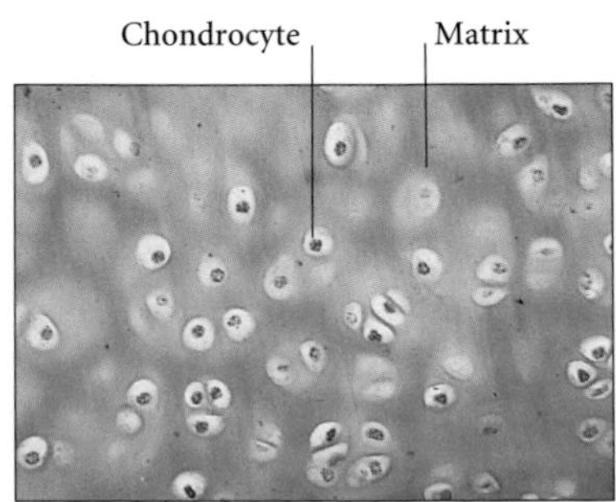

Chondrocyte
Matrix

Composition of articular cartilage
Articular cartilage is composed of cells (chondrocytes) located in cavities in a tough matrix of collagen, forming a smooth, flexible surface.

Types of joints

Shown here are six examples of synovial joints, each of a different type, and a fixed and a semimovable joint. Synovial joints are classified according to the way in which their articular surfaces (where bones meet) fit together and the movements each permits. The diagram that accompanies each synovial joint illustrates its range of movement.

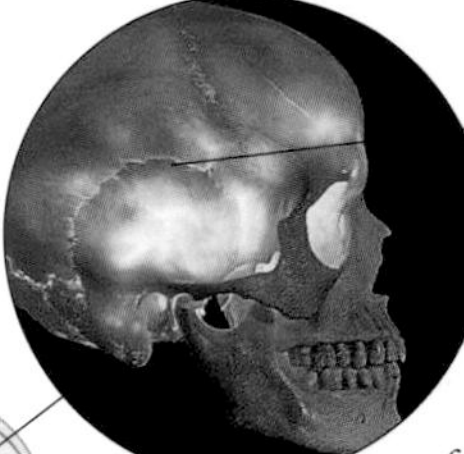
Joint of skull (suture)

Fixed joint

In a fixed joint, the bones are bound together by fibrous tissue, allowing little or no movement. The fixed joints between the bones of the skull are called sutures.

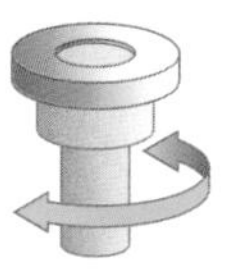
Joint between uppermost bones of neck

Pivot joint

In a pivot joint, one bone rotates within a collar formed by another. The pivot joint between the atlas and the axis, the uppermost bones of the neck, allows the head to turn to either side.

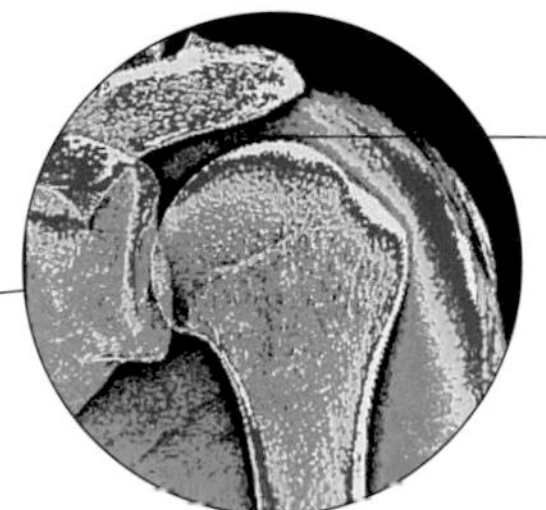
Shoulder joint

Ball-and-socket joint

In a ball-and-socket joint, the ball-shaped end of one bone fits into a cup-shaped cavity in another, allowing movement in all directions. The shoulder and hip are ball-and-socket joints.

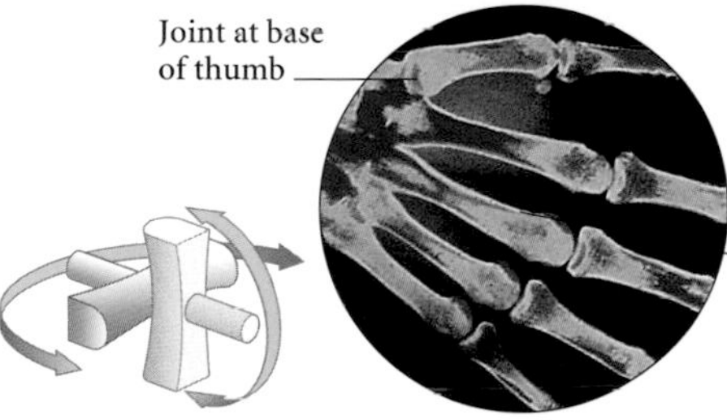
Joint at base of thumb

Saddle joint

Saddle-shaped bone ends that meet at right angles form a saddle joint. The bones can rotate a little and move sideways and back and forth. The body's only saddle joint is at the base of the thumb.

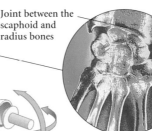

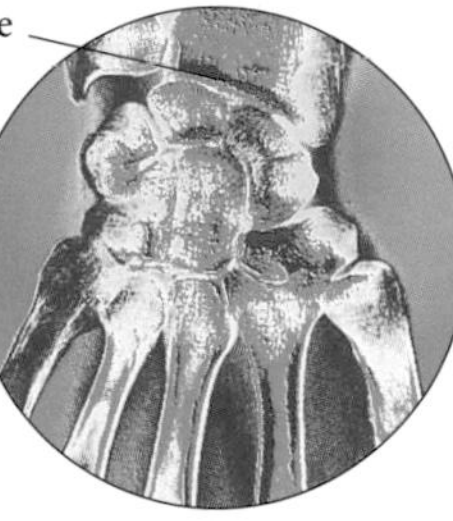
Joint between the scaphoid and radius bones

Ellipsoidal joint

The oval end of one bone fits into the oval cup of another in an ellipsoidal joint, allowing movement in most directions and limited rotation. The wrist is an ellipsoidal joint.

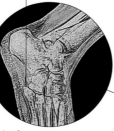

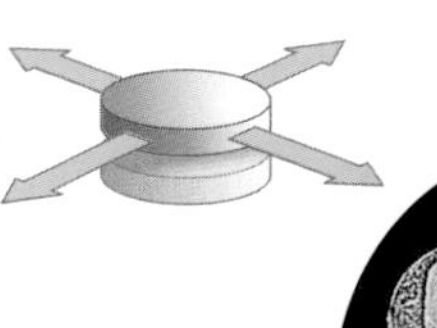
Foot joint

Plane joint

In a plane joint, surfaces that are almost flat slide over each other, back and forth and sideways. Some joints in the foot and wrist are plane joints.

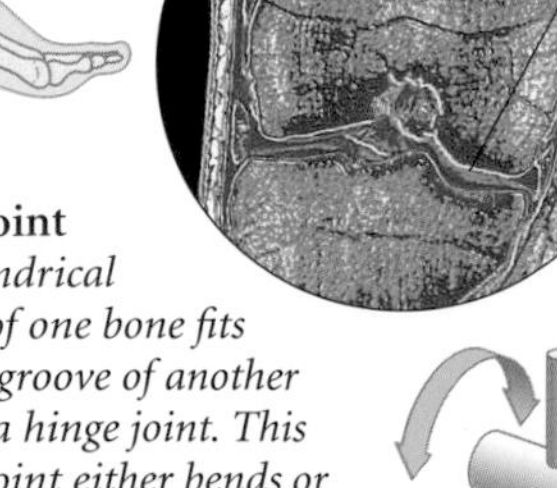
Knee joint

Hinge joint

The cylindrical surface of one bone fits into the groove of another to form a hinge joint. This type of joint either bends or straightens a limb. The knee, elbow, and finger joints are all examples of hinge joints.

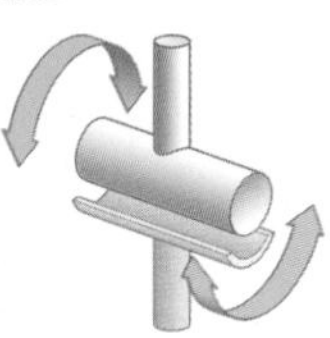

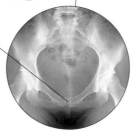

Pubic symphysis joining the pelvis

Semimovable joint

In a semimovable joint, the articular surfaces are fused to a tough pad of cartilage that allows only a little movement. Examples are the pubic symphysis, which joins the two front halves of the pelvis, and the joints of the spine.

STRUCTURE THE BODY'S MUSCLES

Muscles consist of tissue that can contract powerfully to move the body, maintain its posture, and work the various internal organs, including the heart and blood vessels. These functions are performed by three different types of muscles (opposite page), of which skeletal muscle makes up the greatest bulk. (Many of the body's skeletal muscles are identified, right.) Usually each end of a skeletal muscle is attached to a different bone by a tendon, a flexible cord of fibrous tissue. The skeletal muscles may be controlled consciously to produce movement.

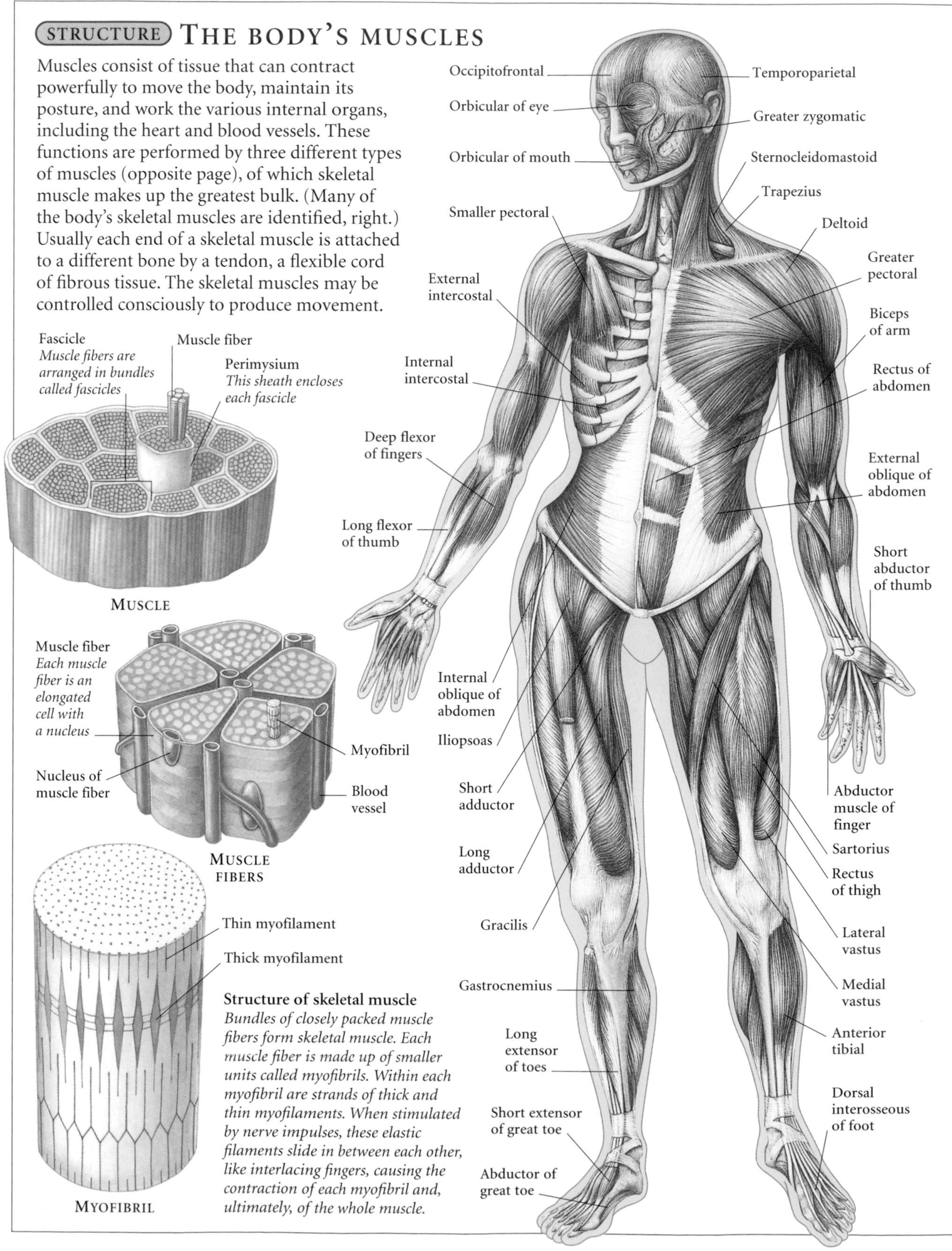
Fascicle
Muscle fibers are arranged in bundles called fascicles
Muscle fiber
Perimysium
This sheath encloses each fascicle
MUSCLE
Muscle fiber
Each muscle fiber is an elongated cell with a nucleus
Nucleus of muscle fiber
Myofibril
Blood vessel
MUSCLE FIBERS
Thin myofilament
Thick myofilament
MYOFIBRIL
Occipitofrontal
Orbicular of eye
Orbicular of mouth
Smaller pectoral
External intercostal
Internal intercostal
Deep flexor of fingers
Long flexor of thumb
Internal oblique of abdomen
Iliopsoas
Short adductor
Long adductor
Gracilis
Gastrocnemius
Long extensor of toes
Short extensor of great toe
Abductor of great toe
Temporoparietal
Greater zygomatic
Sternocleidomastoid
Trapezius
Deltoid
Greater pectoral
Biceps of arm
Rectus of abdomen
External oblique of abdomen
Short abductor of thumb
Abductor muscle of finger
Sartorius
Rectus of thigh
Lateral vastus
Medial vastus
Anterior tibial
Dorsal interosseous of foot

Structure of skeletal muscle
Bundles of closely packed muscle fibers form skeletal muscle. Each muscle fiber is made up of smaller units called myofibrils. Within each myofibril are strands of thick and thin myofilaments. When stimulated by nerve impulses, these elastic filaments slide in between each other, like interlacing fingers, causing the contraction of each myofibril and, ultimately, of the whole muscle.

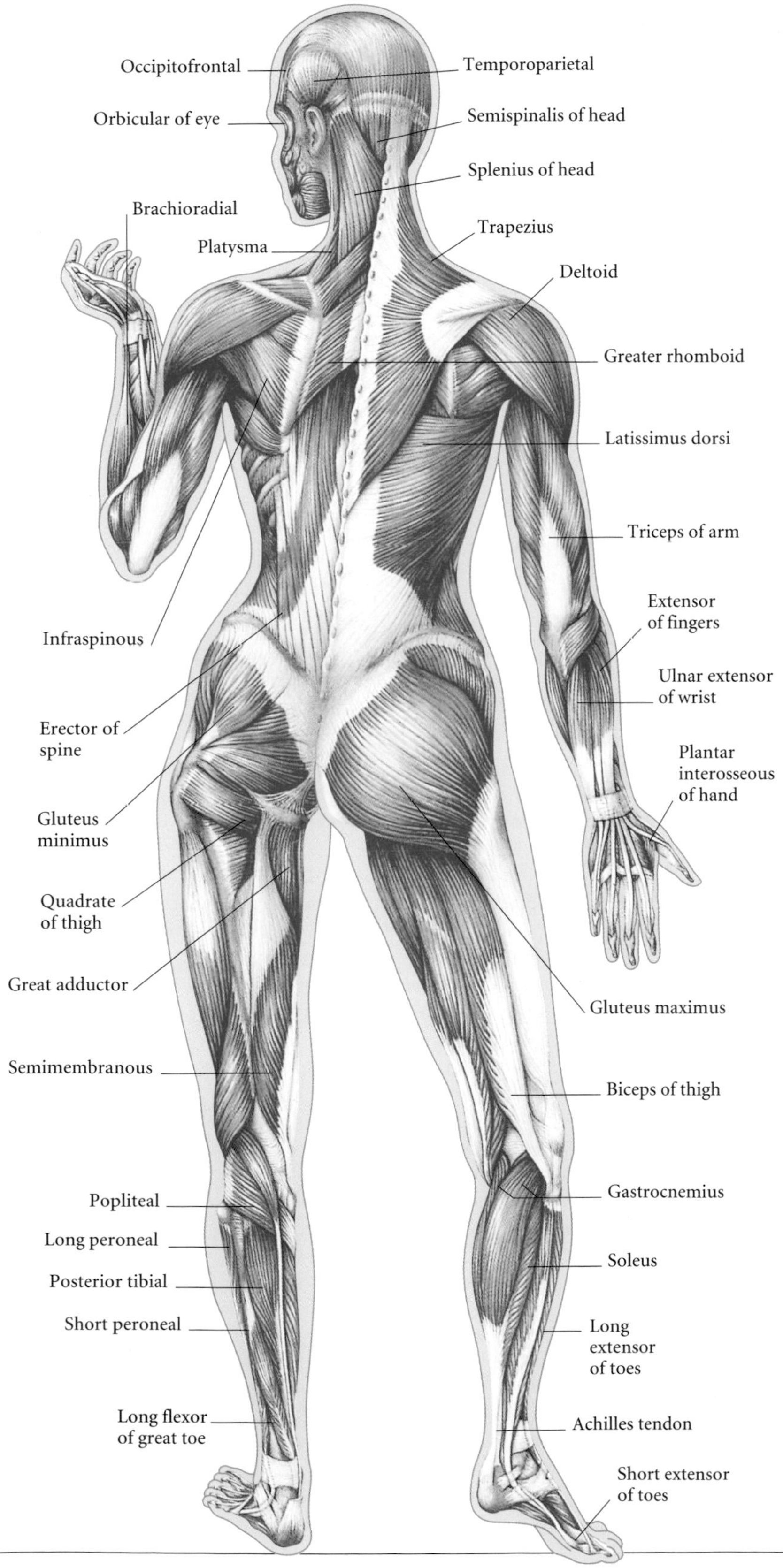

Occipitofrontal
Temporoparietal
Orbicular of eye
Semispinalis of head
Splenius of head
Brachioradial
Platysma
Trapezius
Deltoid
Greater rhomboid
Latissimus dorsi
Triceps of arm
Extensor of fingers
Infraspinous
Ulnar extensor of wrist
Erector of spine
Plantar interosseous of hand
Gluteus minimus
Quadrate of thigh
Great adductor
Gluteus maximus
Semimembranous
Biceps of thigh
Popliteal
Gastrocnemius
Long peroneal
Soleus
Posterior tibial
Short peroneal
Long extensor of toes
Long flexor of great toe
Achilles tendon
Short extensor of toes

TYPES OF MUSCLES

The three types of muscles are skeletal muscle, which covers and moves the skeleton; cardiac (heart) muscle, which pumps blood around the body; and smooth muscle, which is found in the walls of the digestive tract, blood vessels, and the genital and urinary tracts. Smooth muscle performs the unconscious actions of the body, such as propelling food along the digestive tract.

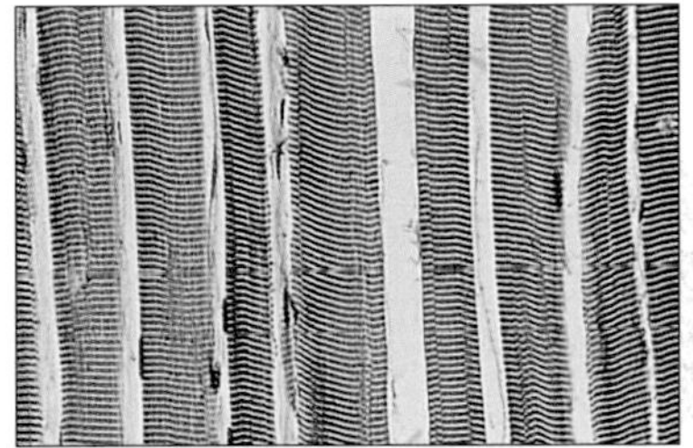

Skeletal muscle
This type of muscle is formed of long, strong, parallel fibers, which are able to contract quickly and powerfully, but can do so only for short periods of time.

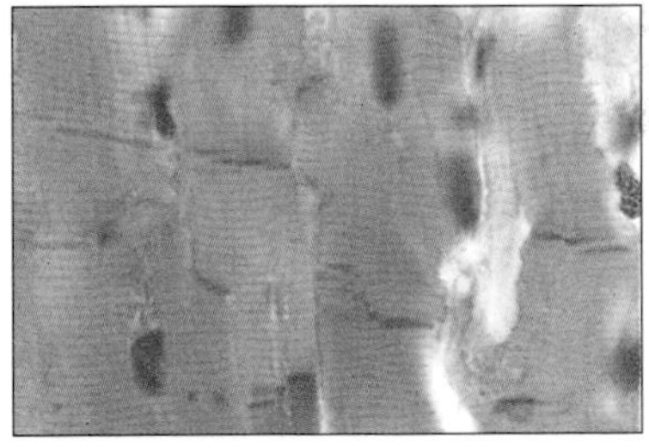

Cardiac muscle
Short, branching, interlinked fibers form a network within the wall of the heart. Cardiac muscle contracts rhythmically and continually without tiring.

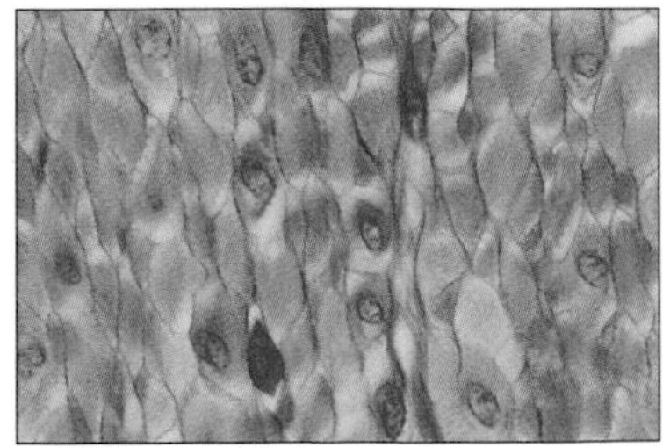

Smooth muscle
These fibers are short, spindle-shaped, and thinner than skeletal muscle fibers. Smooth muscle cells form sheets of muscle that can contract for prolonged periods.

Bone disorders

Bone consists of a resilient protein framework strengthened by calcium and phosphate deposits. While people often think of bone as lifeless and unchanging, it is actually a living tissue, supplied with nerves and blood vessels, that is continually being broken down and rebuilt. Bone can be weakened by nutritional and hormonal factors and by certain long-term disorders.

This section starts by discussing the bone disorder osteoporosis, which is common in elderly people. This disorder affects the natural processes of bone breakdown and replacement, causing bones to become brittle and fracture more easily. The section also covers the other main disorders that affect bone formation, including osteomalacia and rickets, both of which are due to lack of vitamin D, and Paget's disease of the bone, the cause of which has yet to be established. Kyphosis, lordosis, and scoliosis, bone disorders that affect the curvature of the spine, are described next. Further articles discuss the bone infection osteomyelitis and noncancerous and cancerous tumors of the bones. Defects in the bone marrow are covered elsewhere in the book (*see* Blood disorders, pp.446–457).

KEY ANATOMY

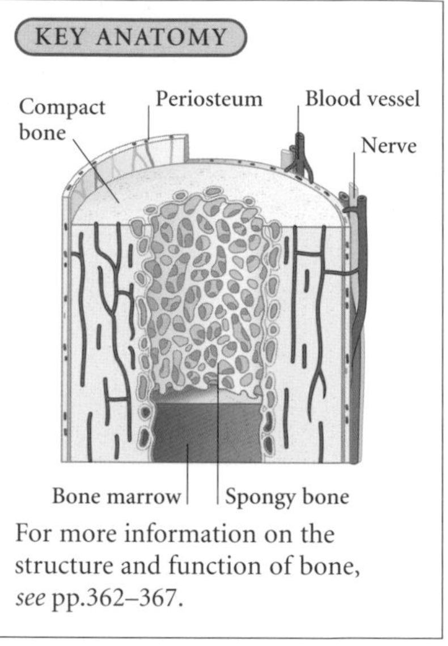
Compact bone
Periosteum
Blood vessel
Nerve
Bone marrow
Spongy bone

For more information on the structure and function of bone, *see* pp.362–367.

Osteoporosis

Loss of bone tissue, resulting in bones that are brittle and susceptible to fracture

AGE Common over age 50

GENDER More common in females

GENETICS Sometimes runs in families; more common in white and Asian people

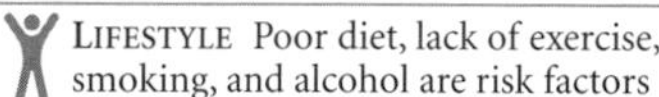
LIFESTYLE Poor diet, lack of exercise, smoking, and alcohol are risk factors

As people get older, their bones become thinner and lighter. By age 70, most people's skeletons are about one-third lighter than they were at age 40. This loss of bone density, known as osteoporosis, is the gradual result of an imbalance between the natural breakdown and the replacement of bone. Eventually, all elderly people are affected by osteoporosis, although the severity of the condition will vary from person to person. People who are thin, who do little exercise, and whose relatives have been affected by osteoporosis are more likely to develop the condition to a greater degree than others.

Many people do not realize that they have osteoporosis until they fracture a wrist or hip as a result of a minor fall. Osteoporosis is a major cause of fractures in people age 65 and older, the hip being the most common fracture site. Hip fractures in elderly people are serious since they are often life-threatening or result in immobility.

What are the causes?

Sex hormones are necessary for bone replacement. In both men and women, osteoporosis begins to develop as sex hormone production declines with age. Any condition that accelerates the decline in sex hormones will increase the severity of age-related osteoporosis. In women, production of the female sex hormone estrogen declines rapidly at menopause. Early menopause is associated with smoking and increases the risk of osteoporosis. In men, untreated hypogonadism (p.729) results in low levels of the sex hormone testosterone early in life and a low bone density.

Osteoporosis may occur as a result of long-term treatment with oral corticosteroids (p.930). People with rheumatoid arthritis (p.377), an overactive thyroid gland (*see* Hyperthyroidism, p.679), or chronic kidney failure (p.706) are also at an increased risk of osteoporosis.

Exercise is essential to maintain bone health. The density of bones declines rapidly in people who are confined to bed and in those whose daily activity is reduced by disorders such as arthritis (p.374) or multiple sclerosis (p.541).

Osteoporosis sometimes runs in families. Women who have a close relative with osteoporosis are more likely to develop the disorder themselves. White and Asian women, especially those who have a slight build, are at increased risk of developing osteoporosis.

Can it be prevented?

Measures to prevent osteoporosis are most effective if started early in life. Teenagers and young adults should eat a balanced diet rich in calcium and vitamin D (*see* A healthy diet, p.48) and maintain it throughout life. Calcium is essential for bone strength, and vitamin

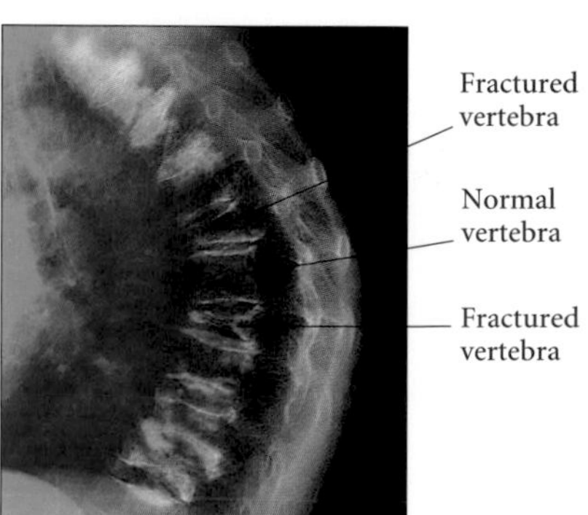
Fractured vertebra
Normal vertebra
Fractured vertebra

Spine affected by osteoporosis
This color-enhanced X-ray shows severe curvature of the upper spine due to compression fractures of vertebrae that have been weakened by osteoporosis.

D aids calcium absorption in the body. Extra calcium is needed during pregnancy, while breast-feeding, and during and after menopause; it may be advisable to take a supplement at such times. Vitamin D is also produced in the skin in response to sunlight. People who are exposed to little sunlight may need to take vitamin D supplements.

Walking and other forms of regular, moderate, weight-bearing exercise can help increase bone density. Not smoking and limiting alcohol consumption also reduce the risk of osteoporosis.

Women may be encouraged to use hormone replacement therapy (p.937) during and after menopause, but there is no clear medical consensus on how long it should be continued.

Anyone thought to have an increased risk of developing osteoporosis, such as having a family history of the condition, should have his or her bone density measured (*see* BONE DENSITOMETRY, below). Bone density testing is often done to check for early signs of osteoporosis in menopausal women or to monitor people who are taking preventive treatment for osteoporosis.

WHAT ARE THE SYMPTOMS?

Some physical changes associated with aging are in fact due to osteoporosis. These include:

- Gradual loss of height.
- Rounding of the back.

For many people the first evidence of osteoporosis is a painful fracture (p.392) of a bone after minor stress or injury. An example is sudden, severe back pain due to a compression fracture of the body of a vertebra (bone of the spine). In severe osteoporosis, a fracture may occur spontaneously.

WHAT MIGHT BE DONE?

The diagnosis will be confirmed using bone densitometry. X-rays (p.244) and blood tests may also be performed to exclude other causes of the symptoms, such as osteomalacia (*see* OSTEOMALACIA AND RICKETS, p.370) and Paget's disease of the bone (p.370), and to look for various disorders that may cause osteoporosis, such as hyperthyroidism.

If you have back pain that is due to a fracture, your doctor may recommend analgesics (p.912) or the use of a heat pad to reduce the pain. Underlying disorders will be treated if possible. For example, you may be prescribed drugs to treat an overactive thyroid gland (*see* DRUGS FOR HYPERTHYROIDISM, p.932).

To slow the progression of osteoporosis, it is important to follow the advice already discussed under preventive measures. Most drug treatments simply slow the rate of bone loss (*see* DRUGS FOR BONE DISORDERS, p.896), although there is evidence that bisphosphonates may actually increase bone density. However, even if these measures are taken, a certain degree of bone loss is inevitable in later life.

(WWW) ONLINE SITES: p.1035

(TEST) BONE DENSITOMETRY

This technique uses low-dose X-rays to measure the density of bone. The test is carried out to screen for and diagnose osteoporosis, a condition that is particularly common in postmenopausal women. The varying absorption of X-rays as they pass through the body is interpreted by a computer and displayed as an image. The computer calculates the average density of the bone and compares it with the normal range for the person's age and sex. The procedure takes about 10–20 minutes and is painless.

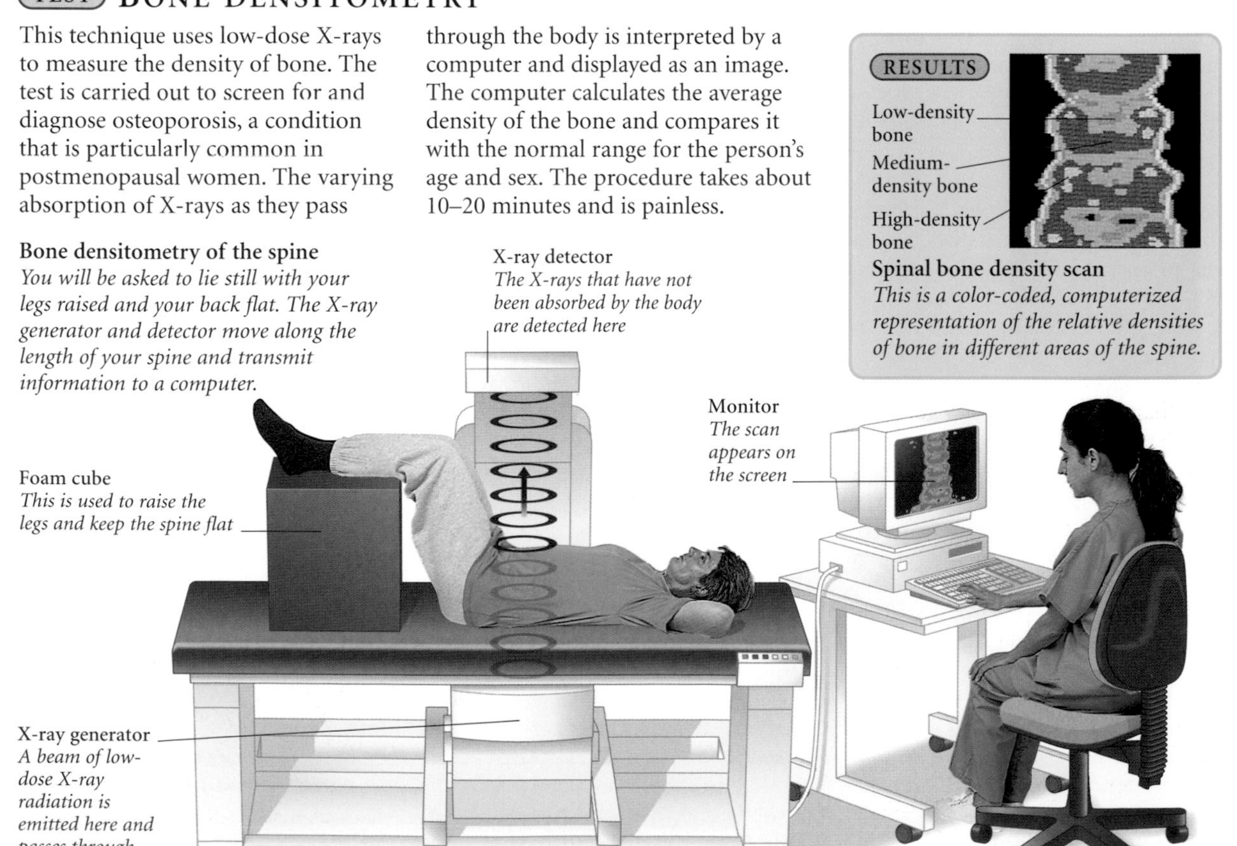
RESULTS
Low-density bone
Medium-density bone
High-density bone
X-ray detector
The X-rays that have not been absorbed by the body are detected here
Monitor
The scan appears on the screen
Foam cube
This is used to raise the legs and keep the spine flat
X-ray generator
A beam of low-dose X-ray radiation is emitted here and passes through the body

Spinal bone density scan
This is a color-coded, computerized representation of the relative densities of bone in different areas of the spine.

Bone densitometry of the spine
You will be asked to lie still with your legs raised and your back flat. The X-ray generator and detector move along the length of your spine and transmit information to a computer.

Osteomalacia and rickets

Disorders due to a lack of vitamin D, resulting in weak, soft bones that become distorted or fracture easily

AGE Osteomalacia develops in adults; rickets develops in children

GENETICS In some cases, the cause is inherited

LIFESTYLE Minimal exposure to sunlight and vegan or fat-free diets are risk factors

GENDER Not a significant factor

The minerals calcium and phosphate give bone its strength and density. A deficiency of vitamin D results in poor absorption of calcium from the diet, leading to weak and soft bones that are easily deformed or fractured. In adults, the condition is called osteomalacia; in children, it is known as rickets.

WHAT ARE THE CAUSES?

Healthy people obtain the vitamin D they need partly from their diet (from eggs, fish, green vegetables, fortified margarine, and milk) and partly from vitamin D production in the skin on exposure to sunlight. A deficiency of vitamin D, therefore, is most common in people who eat a restricted diet and receive little direct sunlight. In tropical countries vitamin D deficiency is almost unknown, except in women who are required to cover their entire bodies. At higher latitudes, deficiency may occur in elderly, housebound people.

Some people cannot absorb vitamin D from food due to intestinal surgery or celiac disease (p.658). Less commonly, osteomalacia and rickets may be caused by inherited disorders of vitamin D metabolism or chronic kidney failure (p.706). Rarely, drugs used to treat epilepsy (*see* ANTICONVULSANT DRUGS, p.914) interfere with vitamin D metabolism and cause osteomalacia or rickets.

WHAT ARE THE SYMPTOMS?

The symptoms of osteomalacia develop over months or years and may include:

- Painful, tender bones, most often the ribs, hips, and bones of the legs.
- Difficulty in climbing stairs or in getting up from a squatting position.
- Bone fractures after a minor injury.

A child with rickets may experience similar symptoms, and may also have:

- Retarded growth.
- Swelling and tenderness at the growing ends of the bones.
- Prominence of the ribs where they join the breastbone.

Left untreated, bowed legs or knock-knees may develop in affected children.

WHAT MIGHT BE DONE?

Your doctor may suspect osteomalacia or rickets from your symptoms and a physical examination. He or she may arrange for blood tests to check for low levels of calcium, phosphate, and vitamin D. A bone biopsy, in which a bone sample is removed for analysis, or X-rays (p.244) may confirm the diagnosis.

If you have a vitamin D deficiency, you should eat foods rich in vitamin D (*see* A HEALTHY DIET, p.48) and increase your exposure to sunlight. If you have a disorder that prevents absorption of the vitamin from food, you may need to have vitamin D injections (*see* VITAMINS, p.927). Calcium supplements (*see* MINERALS, p.929) may also be required.

After treatment, most people make a full recovery, although in children early deformities may be permanent.

(WWW) ONLINE SITES: p.1035

Paget's disease of the bone

A disorder of bone maintenance and repair, leading to weakened, distorted, and occasionally painful bones

AGE Rare under age 40; increasingly common over age 50

GENDER More common in males

GENETICS Sometimes runs in families; rare in people of Asian or African origin

LIFESTYLE Not a significant factor

In a healthy person, bone is continually being broken down and replaced by new bone to maintain the normal bone structure. However, in Paget's disease of the bone (also known as osteitis deformans), the processes involved in the normal breakdown and replacement of bone tissue become disrupted in some parts of the skeleton. The condition may affect any bone in the body, but the pelvis, collarbone, vertebrae (bones of the spine), skull, and the leg bones are those most commonly involved. The affected bones become larger and structurally abnormal, making them weaker and more liable to fracture.

Paget's disease usually develops after the age of 50 and affects 1 in 10 people over age 80. It tends to run in families and affects more men than women. The condition is most common in North America, Europe, and Australia. It is rare in Asia and Africa.

WHAT ARE THE SYMPTOMS?

Frequently, Paget's disease produces no symptoms and may be diagnosed only by chance when an X-ray has been taken for some other reason. If symptoms are present, they may include:

- Bone pain that is worse at night.
- Joint pain, especially in those joints near affected bones.
- Bone deformities, such as bowed legs or enlargement of the skull.
- Fractures (p.392) that occur after a minor injury.

Long-standing Paget's disease may also lead to the following complications:

- Numbness, tingling, or weakness in the affected area if the bone presses on adjacent nerves.
- Hearing loss if abnormal growth of bone compresses nerves to the ear.

In severe cases, increased blood flow through affected bones causes the heart to work harder and may eventually result in chronic heart failure (p.413).

WHAT MIGHT BE DONE?

If your doctor suspects you have Paget's disease, he or she may arrange for you to have X-rays (p.244) to confirm the diagnosis. You may also have blood and urine tests to check for abnormal levels of substances involved in the formation and breakdown of bone. If your hearing is affected, you will probably have hearing tests (p.600).

Treatment may not be necessary if only a small area of bone is affected. If you are in pain, you may be given a nonsteroidal anti-inflammatory drug (p.894). Your doctor may also suggest that you take acetaminophen (*see* ANALGESICS, p.912). If your condition is severe, a bisphosphonate or the hormone calcitonin (*see* DRUGS FOR BONE DISORDERS, p.896) may be prescribed to help slow down progression of the disease. Calcitonin, either in the form of a nasal spray or a self-administered injection, is effective in relieving pain and promoting normal bone formation. Your response to the drug may be monitored by regular blood tests.

Paget's disease of the bone cannot be cured, but treatment is usually effective in helping control the symptoms.

(WWW) ONLINE SITES: p.1035

Kyphosis and lordosis

Excessive outward curvature at the top of the spine (kyphosis) or inward curvature in the lower back (lordosis)

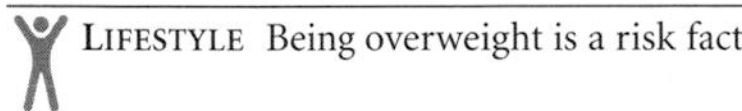

LIFESTYLE Being overweight is a risk factor

AGE GENDER GENETICS Risk factors depend on the cause

Viewed from the side, a normal spine has two main curves along its length. If you have kyphosis or lordosis, these natural curves may become exaggerated. In kyphosis, there is an excessive outward curve at the top of the back, which results in a rounded back, or "humpback." Lordosis affects the spine in the lower back, leading to an exaggerated "hollow back." Kyphosis and lordosis often occur together, resulting in excessive curvature both at the top and in the small of the back.

Disorders that limit mobility, such as osteoarthritis (p.374), or that weaken the vertebrae (bones of the spine), such as osteoporosis (p.368), are the most common causes of kyphosis. Poor posture, especially in people who are very overweight, may also lead to kyphosis.

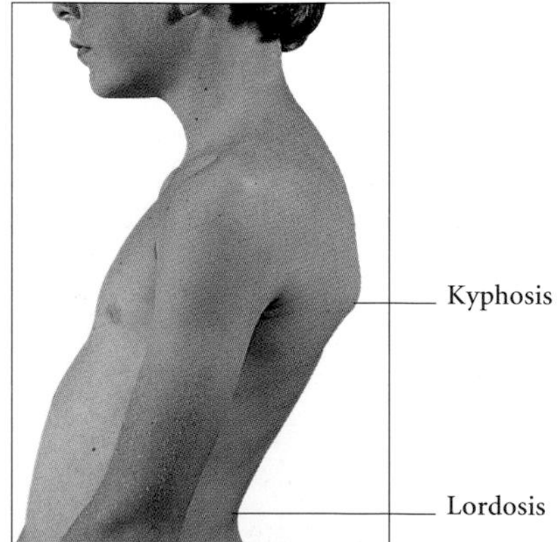
Kyphosis
Lordosis

Kyphosis and lordosis
The child in this photograph has kyphosis, in which the back below the neck is curved out and rounded, and lordosis, in which the lower back is excessively hollow.

Kyphosis often leads to lordosis because the lower spine compensates for the imbalance of the curve at the top of the spine. Lordosis may also develop in people with weak abdominal muscles and poor posture. People who are very overweight are more likely to develop lordosis since they tend to lean backward to improve their balance.

Your doctor may advise you on ways to improve your posture. He or she may also recommend that you avoid strenuous activity and lose any excess weight. Sleeping on a very firm mattress may also help. Physiotherapy (p.961) can improve posture by strengthening the muscles that help support the spine.

People with abnormal curvature of the spine have a predisposition to other spinal problems in later life, such as a prolapsed or herniated disk (p.384).

(WWW) ONLINE SITES: p.1035

Scoliosis

Abnormal curvature of the spine to the left or right

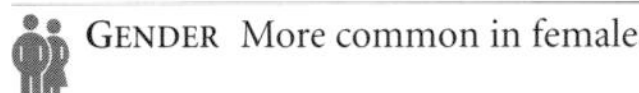

GENDER More common in females

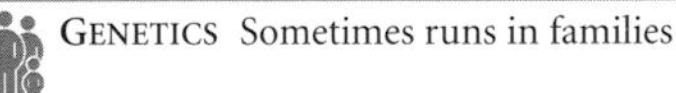

GENETICS Sometimes runs in families

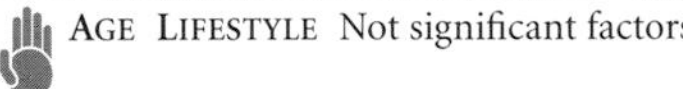

AGE LIFESTYLE Not significant factors

The spine normally forms a straight, vertical line when viewed from the back. Scoliosis is an abnormal sideways curvature of the spine, most commonly affecting the spine in the chest area and the lower back region. Scoliosis is more common in females. Early diagnosis is important because, if left untreated, the deformity tends to become worse.

What are the causes?

In most cases, the cause of scoliosis is unknown. Genetic factors may be involved because the condition tends to run in families. In some cases, scoliosis is congenital (present at birth). Rarely, the curvature is caused by muscle weakness around the spine or by a neuromuscular disease such as cerebral palsy (p.846) or poliomyelitis (p.293).

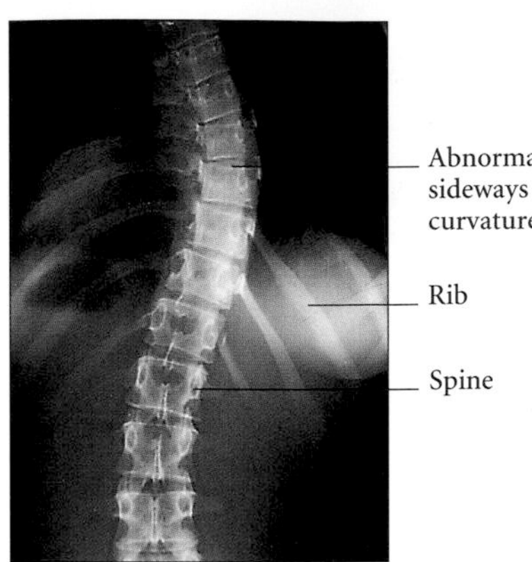
Abnormal sideways curvature
Rib
Spine

Scoliosis
In this X-ray the upper spine curves to one side, a condition known as scoliosis. Left untreated, the curvature will increase.

Scoliosis may also be due to skeletal defects, such as unequal leg length. In rare cases, temporary scoliosis occurs as a result of muscle spasm following a spinal injury (p.524).

What are the symptoms?

Unless the condition is congenital or the result of a spinal injury, the symptoms develop gradually, usually during childhood or adolescence. The symptoms may include:

- Visible curving of the spine to one side, which is more obvious when bending forward.
- Back pain.
- Abnormal gait.

If scoliosis is severe, the rib cage may become deformed, sometimes leading to heart and lung problems.

What might be done?

Your doctor will probably diagnose scoliosis from a physical examination and X-rays (p.244). If possible, treatment is aimed at the underlying cause. For example, if your legs are of unequal length, your doctor may recommend wearing corrective shoes.

If there is no underlying cause and the spinal curvature is slight, you will probably only need regular checkups to monitor your condition. If scoliosis is severe or is progressing rapidly, it may be necessary for you to wear a spinal brace to limit further curvature. Surgery may be necessary to fuse the affected vertebrae or to straighten the spine with metal rods and wires.

(WWW) ONLINE SITES: p.1028, p.1035

Coccydynia

Severe, sharp pain in the coccyx, the small triangular bone at the base of the spine

 LIFESTYLE Poor posture when sitting is a risk factor

 AGE GENDER GENETICS Not significant factors

Pain in the coccyx, or coccydynia, may be due to injury, a baby pushing against the mother's coccyx during birth, or prolonged pressure due to poor posture while sitting. Often, no cause is found.

Before making the diagnosis, your doctor may carry out a rectal examination to rule out a tumor in the rectum. Women may also undergo a vaginal examination to look for a tumor in the uterus. Your doctor may also arrange for you to have an X-ray (p.244) of the lower spine to look for signs of injury.

The pain may be relieved by taking a nonsteroidal anti-inflammatory drug (p.894). Applying heat to the area with a heating pad or applying cold with an ice pack may also help. In some cases, a local injection with a corticosteroid drug (*see* LOCALLY ACTING CORTICOSTEROIDS, p.895), often combined with an anesthetic, can provide relief. Usually no further treatment is necessary, and the pain decreases with time.

(WWW) ONLINE SITES: p.1035

Osteomyelitis

Infection of bone, causing pain and damage to surrounding tissue

 AGE Most common in young children and elderly people but can occur at any age

 LIFESTYLE Use of intravenous drugs is a risk factor

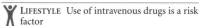

 GENDER GENETICS Not significant factors

Osteomyelitis is infection of bone, usually caused by bacteria. The condition is most common in young children, but elderly people are also at risk. In other age groups, the condition is most common in people with reduced immunity, such as those with sickle-cell anemia (p.448) or diabetes mellitus (p.687). In young children, the vertebrae (spinal bones) or one of the long bones of the limbs are usually affected. In adults, osteomyelitis most commonly affects the vertebrae or the pelvis.

WHAT ARE THE CAUSES?

There are two forms of osteomyelitis: one that comes on suddenly (acute), and the other that develops more gradually and is long-term (chronic).

The acute form of osteomyelitis is usually a consequence of infection with *Staphylococcus aureus* bacteria. These bacteria normally live harmlessly on the skin but they can enter the bloodstream and cause osteomyelitis if they infect the bone tissue as a result of a wound, fracture (p.392), joint replacement (p.377), or intravenous injection with a contaminated needle.

The chronic form of osteomyelitis may be caused by tuberculosis (p.491) or, in rare cases, by a fungal infection. In some cases, acute osteomyelitis may develop into the chronic form.

WHAT ARE THE SYMPTOMS?

The symptoms of the acute form develop suddenly and may include:

- Swelling of the skin and severe pain in the affected area.
- Fever.
- In young children, not wanting to move an affected arm or leg.

Chronic osteomyelitis develops more slowly. Its symptoms include:

- Weight loss.
- Mild fever.
- Persistent pain in the affected bone.

Pus may form in the bone and can make its way to the skin's surface, causing a discharging opening (a sinus).

HOW IS IT DIAGNOSED?

If your doctor suspects that you have osteomyelitis, he or she may arrange for X-rays (p.244), radionuclide scanning (p.251), or MRI (p.248) to locate the infected area of bone. If pus is present, a sample may be aspirated (removed from the bone through a fine needle) for examination to identify the organism that is causing the disease.

WHAT IS THE TREATMENT?

Treatment with intravenous antibiotics (p.885) is usually begun in the hospital and may continue after you return home. You may then need to continue taking antibiotics orally for a period of several months. When osteomyelitis is caused by tuberculosis, antituberculous drugs (p.886) may be prescribed for a period of 12–18 months.

In some cases, surgery may be necessary to remove infected bone. If a large area of bone is removed, you may need a bone graft, in which the infected bone is replaced by new bone taken from elsewhere in the body or from a donor. If the infection is associated with a joint replacement, the artificial joint will be removed, the infection treated, and a new joint put in its place.

The acute form of osteomyelitis is usually treated successfully, but the chronic form may take several months or years to clear up. In some cases, it may be necessary to take antibiotics indefinitely to suppress the infection.

(WWW) ONLINE SITES: p.1035

Noncancerous bone tumors

Noncancerous growths that may cause pain and deformity in a bone

 AGE Most common in childhood or adolescence; rare over age 40

 GENDER GENETICS LIFESTYLE Not significant factors

Noncancerous bone tumors may occur in any part of a bone. These tumors develop most commonly in the long bones of the limbs, such as the femur (thighbone). The bones of the hands are another common site. Noncancerous bone tumors most often develop during childhood or adolescence. They are rare in people over age 40.

Although the presence of a tumor normally causes no symptoms, sometimes there may be pain in the affected area, or the bone may become enlarged and deformed. Affected bone is more

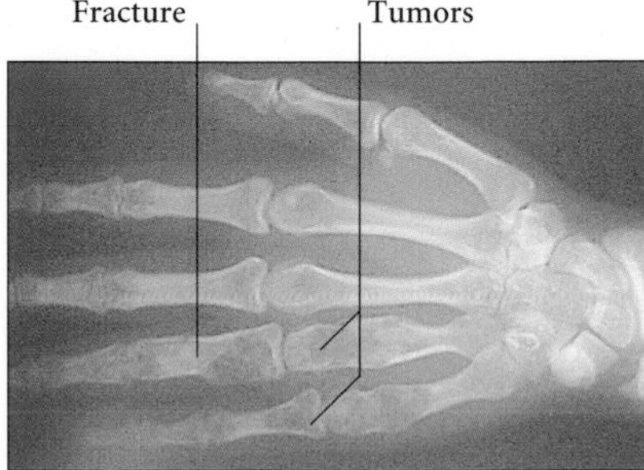
Fracture
Tumors

Noncancerous bone tumors
This X-ray shows several noncancerous tumors in the bones of the fingers. Some bones have become enlarged as a result of the tumors, and one has a fracture.

likely to fracture from even a minor injury. Occasionally, a tumor may press on nerves, causing a tingling sensation or numbness. In some cases, movement may be restricted, or pain may be felt on movement if the tumor presses on nearby tendons (fibrous bands that connect muscles to bones).

A bone tumor is usually diagnosed from X-rays (p.244), MRI (p.248), or radionuclide scanning (p.251). To confirm that the tumor is noncancerous, your doctor may arrange for a biopsy of the bone, in which a small piece of the affected bone is removed for analysis.

A tumor may be removed surgically if it is painful, causes deformity of the bone, or grows rapidly. You may subsequently need a bone graft, in which artificial bone or bone taken from elsewhere in your body or from a donor is used to replace diseased bone. Generally, surgery is successful in removing tumors, although occasionally growths recur and may require further surgery.

(WWW) ONLINE SITES: p.1035

Primary bone cancer

Cancerous tumors that originate within the bone tissue

 AGE Most common in childhood and adolescence

 GENETICS Sometimes runs in families

 GENDER LIFESTYLE Not significant factors

Cancers originating in bone, known as primary bone cancers, are rare. They usually develop in children and teenagers. The causes are unknown, but in some cases are associated with genetic factors. The most common site of primary bone cancer is the leg, either just above or just below the knee.

The first symptom is often painful, tender swelling of the affected area. If the cancer affects a bone in the leg, you may experience pain on standing or while you are at rest, and the pain may become worse at night. The diseased bone may fracture easily.

What might be done?

To confirm the diagnosis, your doctor will probably arrange for you to have X-rays (p.244) and possibly CT scanning (p.247) or MRI (p.248). He or she

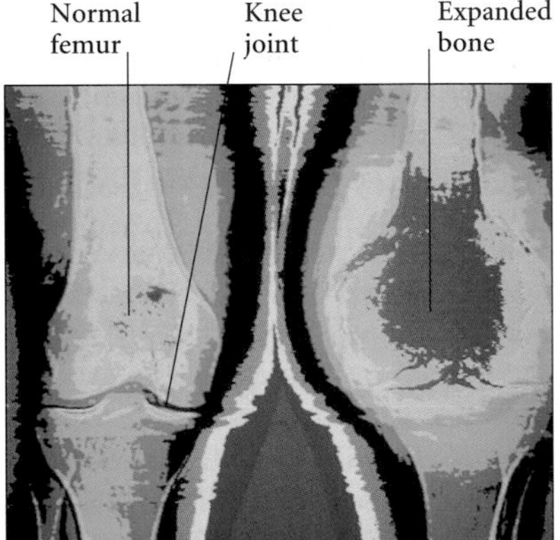
Normal femur
Knee joint
Expanded bone

Primary bone cancer in the leg
This color-coded CT scan of both legs reveals a primary bone cancer of one femur (thighbone) and associated swelling.

may also arrange for you to have chest X-rays (p.490) and radionuclide scanning (p.251) to check if the cancer has spread to other parts of the body.

Radiation therapy (p.279) may reduce the size of the tumor. However, in most cases the tumor is removed surgically. Removed bone is replaced by artificial bone or by bone taken from elsewhere in the body or from a donor.

After surgery, radiation therapy or chemotherapy (p.278) may be given to destroy any remaining cancerous cells. Amputation of a limb is rarely necessary. Most people treated for primary bone cancer have only a small chance of recurrence in the first 5 years. After this period, recurrence is unlikely.

(WWW) ONLINE SITES: p.1028, p.1035

Bone metastases

Cancerous tumors in bone that have spread from a cancer elsewhere in the body

 AGE More common in elderly people

GENETICS Risk factors depend on the type

GENDER LIFESTYLE Not significant factors

Bone metastases, also known as secondary bone cancer, are tumors that have spread from another part of the body. Metastases most often develop in the ribs, pelvis, skull, or spine. The condition is much more common than primary bone cancer, especially in older people, who are more likely to have cancer elsewhere in their body. The cancers that most often spread to bone are those that originate in the breast, the lung, the thyroid gland, the kidney, and the prostate gland.

What are the symptoms?

Bone metastases may cause the following symptoms in addition to those of the main cancer:

- Gnawing bone pain that may become worse at night.
- Swelling of the affected area.
- Tenderness over the affected area.

The affected bones fracture easily, often after minor injury.

What might be done?

If you already have a cancer somewhere else in your body, you may have X-rays (p.244) or radionuclide scanning (p.251) to check whether the cancer has spread to the bones. If the site of the primary cancer is unknown, you may need further tests to find out where the metastasis came from. For example, women may be given a breast X-ray (*see* MAMMOGRAPHY, p.759) to look for evidence of breast cancer.

Your doctor will probably direct treatment at your original cancer. He or she may also arrange for you to have chemotherapy (p.278), radiation therapy (p.279), or hormonal therapy to relieve bone pain.

The prognosis for people with bone metastases usually depends on the site of the original cancer and how successfully it can be treated. However, the best that can usually be achieved after bone metastases is a period of remission.

(WWW) ONLINE SITES: p.1028, p.1035

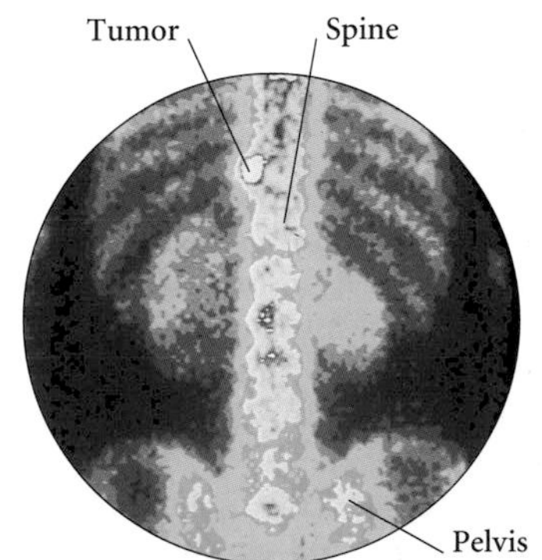
Tumor
Spine
Pelvis

Bone metastases
This radionuclide scan gives a view of the trunk of a person with metastatic bone cancer. The scan reveals a cancerous tumor on a vertebra of the upper spine.

Referred pain (in areas remote from the site of damage but on the same nerve pathway as the affected joint) may develop. For example, an arthritic hip may cause referred pain in the groin, buttock, or knee. The pain may worsen toward the end of the day.

If movement is severely restricted, an affected person may be confined to the home. Lack of mobility may lead to weakness and wasting of muscles and sometimes to weight gain.

WHAT MIGHT THE DOCTOR DO?

Your doctor may suspect that you have osteoarthritis from your symptoms, a history of joint problems, and a physical examination. It is often possible to confirm a diagnosis of osteoarthritis, while at the same time ruling out other types of arthritis, by means of blood tests and X-rays (p.244).

There is no cure for osteoarthritis, and treatment is aimed at relieving the symptoms. Your doctor may recommend that you take acetaminophen (*see* ANALGESICS, p.912) or a nonsteroidal anti-inflammatory drug (p.894). If you experience a severe flare-up of pain and inflammation in a single joint, your doctor may inject a corticosteroid drug directly into the affected joint to reduce swelling and relieve pain (*see* LOCALLY ACTING CORTICOSTEROIDS, p.895).

To improve muscle function around joints affected by osteoarthritis, your doctor may refer you for physiotherapy (p.961). If osteoarthritis is very severe, surgery may be necessary to repair or replace an affected joint (*see* JOINT REPLACEMENT, opposite page).

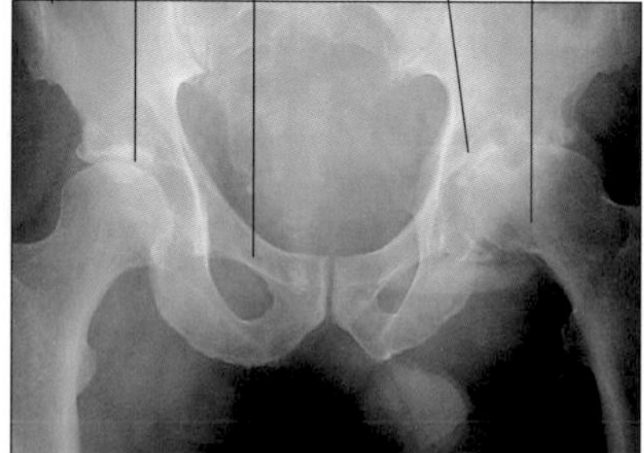
Healthy hip joint
Pelvis
Osteoarthritic hip joint
Femur

Osteoarthritis in a hip joint
In the hip joint seen on the right of this X-ray, the head of the femur (thighbone) has become worn where it fits into the pelvis, causing pain and stiffness.

WHAT CAN I DO?

If you have mild osteoarthritis, you may be able to participate in most everyday activities by adapting your lifestyle (*see* LIVING WITH ARTHRITIS, p.375). If you are overweight, ask your doctor for dietary advice to help you lose weight and reduce further wear on your joints. If possible, do gentle exercises to help lose weight, maintain muscle tone, and delay the progression of the disease. Supportive shoes with rubber soles will absorb shock and reduce further wear. If you have a painful hip or knee, use a cane for support. Massage, warm baths, or a heating pad may also ease joint pain and increase mobility.

(WWW) ONLINE SITES: p.1027, p.1035

Cervical spondylosis

Degeneration of bones and cartilage in the neck, which may lead to pain and stiffness

 AGE Increasingly common over age 45

 GENDER More common in males

 GENETICS LIFESTYLE Not significant factors

Cervical spondylosis is osteoarthritis (p.374) affecting the upper spine. In this disorder, the vertebrae (bones of the spine) and the disks of cartilage between them begin to degenerate. The bones become thickened, and bony outgrowths called osteophytes develop on the vertebrae. Inflamed joints and osteophytes may press on spinal nerves or compress blood vessels in the neck.

The condition is increasingly common over age 45 and affects more men than women. Rarely, it is triggered by injury and affects younger people.

WHAT ARE THE SYMPTOMS?

Many people do not have symptoms or may develop only very mild symptoms. When symptoms do become apparent, they may include:

- Restricted neck movement that may be painful.
- Pain at the back of the head.
- Aching or shooting pain that travels from the shoulders to the hands.
- Numbness, tingling, and muscle weakness in the hands and arms.

Sometimes, if the head is moved too quickly, the deformities in the upper spine may suddenly compress blood vessels that carry blood to the brain, resulting in dizziness, unsteadiness, or double vision (*see* VERTIGO, p.603).

In rare cases, joints that have severely degenerated may put prolonged pressure on the spinal cord, causing tingling and muscle weakness or paralysis in the legs or, sometimes, difficulty controlling bladder or bowel function.

HOW IS IT DIAGNOSED?

Some people do not have symptoms and the condition is only diagnosed when an X-ray (p.244) is taken for another reason. However, if you experience neck pain or dizziness, you should consult your doctor, who may arrange for X-rays to look for signs of cervical spondylosis. If your doctor thinks that your symptoms may not be due solely to cervical spondylosis, he or she may arrange for further tests to look for other causes, such as a prolapsed or herniated disk (p.384). You may also undergo nerve conduction studies and EMG (*see* NERVE AND MUSCLE ELECTRICAL TESTS, p.544) to assess nerve activity in your arms and hands. CT scanning (p.247) or MRI (p.248) may also be carried out to see whether there have been any changes affecting the bones of the spine, the disks of cartilage between them, or the tissues around them.

WHAT IS THE TREATMENT?

Degeneration of the spine cannot be halted, but its effects can be reduced with treatment. To relieve pain in mild cases, your doctor may recommend that you take analgesics (p.912) or prescribe nonsteroidal anti-inflammatory drugs (p.894). Once the initial pain has been relieved, he or she may also suggest neck exercises to maintain mobility and increase muscle strength. In some cases, a cervical collar may be used to give the neck extra support.

If cervical spondylosis has damaged a nerve, surgery may be recommended to prevent the symptoms from getting worse. In this operation, the surgeon widens the natural opening between the vertebrae through which the nerve passes when it branches off the spinal cord. In some cases, surgery may also be carried out to stabilize the spine by fusing together the affected vertebrae.

(WWW) ONLINE SITES: p.1027, p.1035

Rheumatoid arthritis

A chronic disorder that causes the joints to become painful, swollen, stiff, and deformed

AGE Most common between the ages of 40 and 60

GENDER Affects three times more females

GENETICS May run in some families and in some Native American tribes

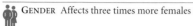

LIFESTYLE Not a significant factor

In rheumatoid arthritis, the affected joints become stiff and swollen as a result of inflammation of the synovial membrane, which encloses each joint. Gradually, the inflammation damages both the ends of the bones and the cartilage that covers them. The tendons and ligaments, which give the joints support, become worn and slack, and deformity of the joints occurs.

In most cases, rheumatoid arthritis affects several joints. The disorder usually appears first in the small joints of the hands and feet but may develop in any joint. Rheumatoid arthritis usually tends to appear in similar areas on both sides of the body. Tissues in other parts of the body, such as the eyes, lungs, heart, and blood vessels, may also be affected by the inflammation.

Rheumatoid arthritis is a chronic disease and usually recurs in episodes lasting for several weeks or months with relatively symptom-free periods in between. Rheumatoid arthritis affects about 1 in 100 people and is three times more common in women than in men. A similar but distinct arthritic disorder can develop in children (*see* JUVENILE RHEUMATOID ARTHRITIS, p.835).

Rheumatoid arthritis is an autoimmune disorder (p.461) in which the body produces antibodies that attack the synovial membrane and, in some cases, other body tissues. A genetic factor may be involved since the condition is common in some families and certain Native American tribes.

WHAT ARE THE SYMPTOMS?

Rheumatoid arthritis usually develops slowly, although the onset is sometimes abrupt. The general symptoms associated with the condition may include fatigue, pale skin, shortness of breath on exertion, and poor appetite. Specific symptoms may include:

- Stiff, painful, and swollen joints.
- Painless, small bumps (nodules) on areas of pressure such as the elbows.

Since the condition can be both painful and debilitating, depression (p.554) is

TREATMENT JOINT REPLACEMENT

Joints that have been severely damaged by a disorder such as arthritis, or by an injury, may be surgically replaced with artificial joints made of metal, ceramic, or plastic. Most joints in the body can be replaced, but the common ones are the hips, knees, and shoulders. During the operation, the ends of damaged bones are removed and the artificial components are fixed in place. The operation usually relieves pain and increases the range of motion in the affected joint.

HIP REPLACEMENT

The most commonly replaced joint is the hip. During the operation, both the pelvic socket and the head of the femur (thighbone), which fits into the socket, are replaced. The operation is carried out under general or spinal anesthesia and involves a short stay in the hospital.

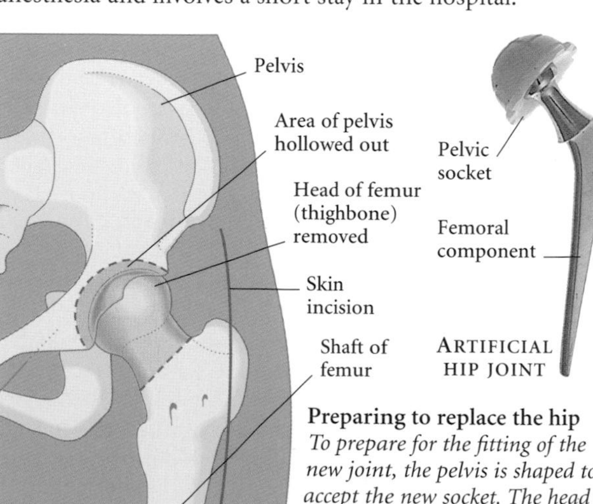
Pelvis
Area of pelvis hollowed out
Head of femur (thighbone) removed
Skin incision
Shaft of femur
Pelvic socket
Femoral component
ARTIFICIAL HIP JOINT

Preparing to replace the hip
To prepare for the fitting of the new joint, the pelvis is shaped to accept the new socket. The head of the femur is removed, and the center of the bone is shaped to fit the femoral component.

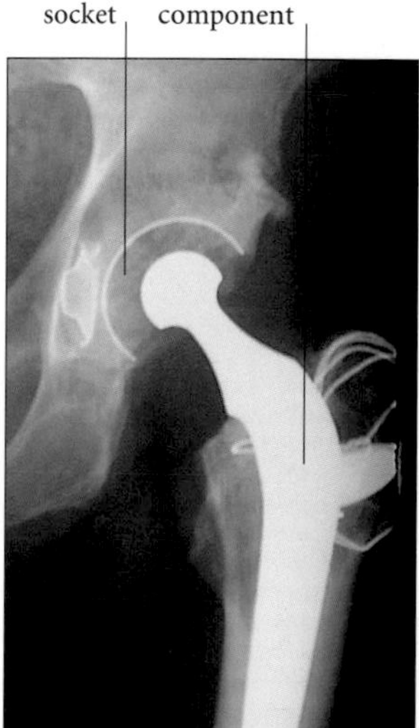
Pelvic socket
Femoral component

Artificial hip in position
This X-ray shows an artificial hip joint in place, with the femoral component fitted into the femur (thighbone) and the socket fitted into the pelvis.

OTHER JOINTS

Many different types of joints in the body can be replaced, from tiny finger joints to large joints such as the knees.

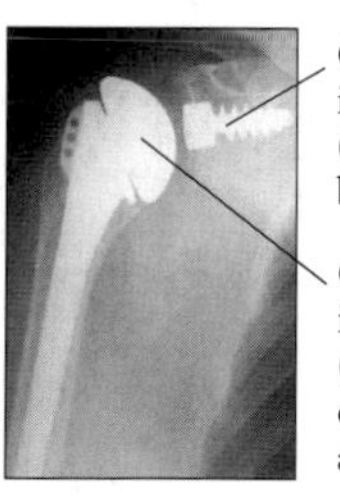
Component in scapula (shoulder blade)
Component in humerus (long bone of upper arm)

Artificial shoulder joint
This replacement shoulder joint has components fitted in the humerus and the scapula.

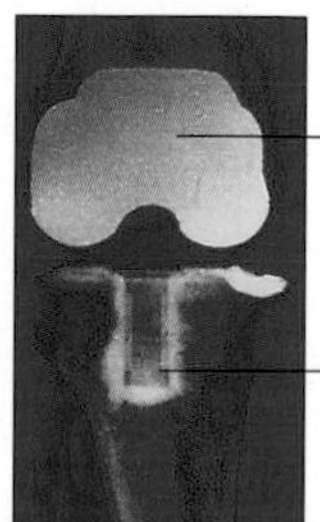
Component in femur (thighbone)
Component in tibia (shinbone)

Artificial knee joint
This replacement knee joint has artificial components in the femur and the tibia.

common in people with rheumatoid arthritis. In women, the symptoms of rheumatoid arthritis may improve during pregnancy but may then flare up again after the baby is born.

ARE THERE COMPLICATIONS?

In time, the bones around the affected joint may lose density as a result of reduced mobility, becoming increasingly brittle and more susceptible to fracture (*see* OSTEOPOROSIS, p.368). In very severe cases, osteoporosis of the whole skeleton may develop.

The general symptoms of rheumatoid arthritis are partly due to anemia (p.446), caused by a failure of the bone marrow to manufacture enough new red blood cells. Bursitis (p.387) may develop, in which one or more of the fluid-filled sacs around a joint become inflamed. Swelling that compresses the median nerve in the wrist may lead to feeling tingling and pain in the fingers (*see* CARPAL TUNNEL SYNDROME, p.547). Inflammation of the walls of the arteries that supply the fingers and toes may constrict those arteries and result in Raynaud's phenomenon (p.436), a condition in which the digits become pale and painful on exposure to cold.

Less commonly, the spleen and the lymph nodes may become enlarged (*see* LYMPHADENOPATHY, p.458). The membranous sac that surrounds the heart may also become inflamed (*see* PERICARDITIS, p.428). In some cases, there may also be inflammation of the white of the eye (*see* SCLERITIS, p.574).

HOW IS IT DIAGNOSED?

The diagnosis is usually based on your medical history and a physical examination. Your doctor may arrange for blood tests to check for the presence of an antibody known as rheumatoid factor, which is usually associated with rheumatoid arthritis. Blood tests may also be done to measure the severity of the inflammation. X-rays (p.244) of the affected joints may be taken to assess the level of bone and joint damage.

WHAT IS THE TREATMENT?

There is no cure for rheumatoid arthritis. The aim of treatment is to control symptoms and reduce further joint damage by slowing the progression of the disease. Different drugs are available, and your doctor's recommendation will depend on the severity and progression of the disease, your age, and your general health.

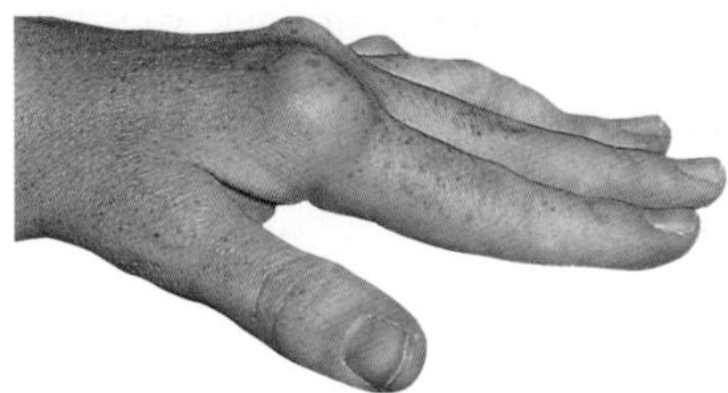

Swelling in rheumatoid arthritis
The swollen knuckles of this hand are caused by rheumatoid arthritis, a condition in which the joints become inflamed and may be damaged.

If you have only mild symptoms, your doctor may simply prescribe a nonsteroidal anti-inflammatory drug (p.894). However, if your symptoms are more severe, he or she may prescribe drugs that slow the disease process (*see* ANTIRHEUMATIC DRUGS, p.895), which should limit permanent joint damage but may have to be taken for several months before the full benefits are felt. An antirheumatic such as sulfasalazine or chloroquine may be given first. If symptoms persist, your doctor may prescribe a drug such as gold, penicillamine, methotrexate, or cyclosporine. Because these drugs can have serious side effects, your condition will be closely monitored by your doctor.

The anemia that is commonly associated with rheumatoid arthritis may be improved by treatment with the hormone erythropoietin.

Your doctor may recommend that you use a splint or brace to support a particularly painful joint and to slow down the development of deformities. Gentle, regular exercise may help keep your joints mobile and prevent muscle weakness. Physiotherapy (p.961) may be given to improve joint mobility and help increase muscle strength. Hydrotherapy and heat or ice treatments may help provide pain relief.

An intensely painful joint may be eased if your doctor injects it with a corticosteroid drug (*see* LOCALLY ACTING CORTICOSTEROIDS, p.895). If a joint is severely damaged, your doctor may suggest that you have surgery to replace the damaged joint with an artificial one (*see* JOINT REPLACEMENT, p.377).

WHAT IS THE PROGNOSIS?

Many people with rheumatoid arthritis are able to lead a normal life (*see* LIVING WITH ARTHRITIS, p.375), but lifelong drug treatment may be needed to control the symptoms. About 1 in 10 people becomes severely disabled as repeated attacks destroy the joints. To monitor progression of the disease and your response to treatment, regular blood tests will be needed. Sometimes, the attacks gradually cease, and the disease is said to have burned itself out, but some permanent disability may remain.

(WWW) ONLINE SITES: p.1027, p.1035

Ankylosing spondylitis

Chronic, progressive joint inflammation and stiffening, usually affecting the spine and pelvis

 AGE Usually begins in late adolescence or early adulthood; onset rare over age 45

 GENDER About four times more common in males

 GENETICS Sometimes runs in families; more common in white people

 LIFESTYLE Not a significant factor

In ankylosing spondylitis, chronic joint inflammation particularly affects the sacroiliac joints at the back of the pelvis and the vertebrae (bones of the spine). If the spine is severely diseased, new bone starts to grow between the vertebrae, which eventually fuse together.

This form of arthritis is four times more common in men than in women, mainly affecting young white men. A variant of the disorder is preceded, in some cases, by the skin disorder psoriasis (p.332) or by inflammatory bowel disease, such as Crohn's disease (p.658).

WHAT ARE THE CAUSES?

The cause of ankylosing spondylitis is unknown, but about 9 in 10 people with the condition have a particular antigen (a substance that is capable of stimulating an immune response in the body) called HLA-B27 on the surface of most cells. This antigen is inherited, which helps explain why ankylosing spondylitis runs in families. Most people with HLA-B27 do not develop the condition, and a bacterial infection is thought to trigger ankylosing spondylitis in those who are predisposed.

What are the symptoms?

The symptoms of ankylosing spondylitis usually appear in late adolescence or early adulthood and develop gradually over a period of months or even years. Men are usually more severely affected. The main symptoms include:

- Lower back pain, which may spread down into the buttocks and thighs.
- Lower back stiffness that may be worse in the morning and improves with exercise.
- Pain in other joints, such as the hips, knees, and shoulders.
- Pain and tenderness in the heels.
- Fatigue, weight loss, and mild fever.

If left untreated, ankylosing spondylitis can distort the spine (*see* KYPHOSIS AND LORDOSIS, p.371), resulting in a stooped posture. If the joints between the spine and the ribs are affected, expansion of the chest becomes restricted. In some people, ankylosing spondylitis causes inflammation or damage to the tissues in areas other than the joints, such as the eyes (*see* UVEITIS, p.574).

How is it diagnosed?

Your doctor may suspect that you have ankylosing spondylitis from the pattern of your symptoms. He or she will perform a physical examination and may arrange for an X-ray (p.244) to look for evidence of fusion in the joints of the pelvis and the spine. Your doctor may also arrange for you to have blood tests to measure the level of inflammation and look for the HLA-B27 antigen.

What is the treatment?

Treatment of ankylosing spondylitis is aimed at relieving symptoms and preventing spinal deformity. Your doctor may prescribe a nonsteroidal anti-inflammatory drug (p.894) to control pain and inflammation. He or she may also refer you for physiotherapy (p.961), which may include breathing exercises and daily exercises to help improve posture, strengthen the back muscles, and prevent deformities of the spine (*see* PREVENTING BACK PAIN, p.382). You may also benefit from regular, gentle physical activity, such as swimming, which may help relieve pain and stiffness. If a joint such as a hip is affected, you may eventually need to have it replaced surgically (*see* JOINT REPLACEMENT, p.377). If your mobility becomes severely reduced, you may need occupational therapy (p.962) and the therapist may suggest that you use specially designed equipment and furniture to help make your life easier.

What is the prognosis?

Although the condition is not curable, most people with ankylosing spondylitis are only mildly affected, causing minimum disruption of their everyday lives. Even in those people with more severe symptoms, the condition tends to become less severe with age. In many cases, early treatment and regular exercise help relieve pain and stiffness of the back and prevent deformity of the spine. However, about 1 in 20 people with ankylosing spondylitis eventually becomes disabled and has difficulty in carrying out many routine activities.

(WWW) ONLINE SITES: p.1035

Reactive arthritis

Inflammation of joints as a result of an abnormal immune response to a recent infection elsewhere in the body

AGE Most common between the ages of 20 and 40

GENDER More common in males

GENETICS Sometimes runs in families

LIFESTYLE Risk factor depend on the cause

Reactive arthritis is a short-term disorder that develops after a bacterial infection of the genital tract, such as chlamydial cervicitis (p.765) or non-gonococcal urethritis (p.765), or the intestinal tract (*see* GASTROENTERITIS, p.628). Either of these infections may stimulate an abnormal immune response that causes tissues in the joints, usually the knee or ankle, to become inflamed. If inflammation also affects the eyes or the genital tract, the condition is known as Reiter syndrome.

About 8 in 10 people who develop Reiter syndrome have a particular antigen (a substance capable of stimulating an immune response in the body) known as HLA-B27. Although Reiter syndrome is induced by infection, it usually develops in people who have a genetic predisposition to it. The disorder may therefore run in families.

What are the symptoms?

Depending on the infection that has triggered reactive arthritis or Reiter syndrome, you may experience symptoms of a genital infection, such as pain on urinating, or symptoms of gastroenteritis, such as diarrhea. However, some people have no initial symptoms.

Both conditions develop 3–30 days after the initial infection has appeared. Symptoms may include:

- Painful, red, tender joints.
- Swelling around the joints.

Although the knees or ankles are most commonly affected, other joints may also be involved. If you have Reiter syndrome, you may also notice:

- Sore, red eyes (*see* CONJUNCTIVITIS, p.570, and UVEITIS, p.574).
- Pain on urinating and a discharge from the penis or vagina.

Less commonly, complications such as mouth ulcers (p.632), inflammation of the penis (*see* BALANITIS, p.722), lower back pain (p.381), and skin lesions on the hands and feet may develop.

What might be done?

Your doctor may diagnose reactive arthritis or Reiter syndrome from your history and symptoms. He or she will probably take swabs from your urethra or cervix or collect a stool sample to try to establish the source of infection. Further tests may include a blood test in order to detect signs of inflammation and an X-ray (p.244) to look for evidence of joint damage.

If you are still affected by a genital or intestinal infection, your doctor may prescribe oral antibiotics (p.885). To relieve pain in your joints, he or she may recommend a nonsteroidal anti-inflammatory drug (p.894). If joint pain is very severe and there is no infection present in the joint itself, your doctor may inject a corticosteroid drug directly into the joint (*see* LOCALLY ACTING CORTICOSTEROIDS, p.895).

What is the prognosis?

The symptoms usually last for less than 6 months, and most people recover fully from reactive arthritis or Reiter syndrome. People who are susceptible to Reiter syndrome can reduce the risk of recurrence by taking care with personal hygiene and practicing safe sex (p.68).

(WWW) ONLINE SITES: p.1027, 1035

Gout

A type of arthritis in which crystalline deposits of uric acid form within joints, particularly at the base of the big toe

AGE Most common between the ages of 30 and 50

GENDER Twenty times more common in males

GENETICS Often runs in families

LIFESTYLE Being overweight and excessive use of alcohol are risk factors

Gout causes sudden pain and inflammation, usually in a single joint. The base of the big toe is the most common site, but any joint may be affected. The disorder affects many more men than women. In women, gout rarely appears before menopause.

What are the causes?

Gout is usually caused by elevated blood levels of uric acid (a waste product of the breakdown of cells and proteins). Excess uric acid may be caused by the overproduction and/or decreased excretion of uric acid and may lead to uric acid crystals being deposited in a joint. The underlying cause of gout is unknown, but the condition is often inherited. A few people with gout also develop kidney stones (p.701) formed from excess uric acid.

Gout may occur spontaneously or be due to surgery, being overweight, drinking alcohol, or excess cell destruction associated with diuretic drugs (p.902) or chemotherapy (p.278).

What are the symptoms?

The symptoms of gout usually flare up suddenly. They may include:

- Redness, tenderness, warmth, and swelling around the affected area.
- Pain, which may be severe, in the affected joint or joints.
- Mild fever.

In long-standing gout, deposits of uric acid crystals may collect in the earlobes and the soft tissues of the hands, forming small lumps called tophi.

What might be done?

Your doctor may suspect gout from the symptoms you have and may arrange for blood tests to measure your uric acid levels. To confirm the diagnosis, he or she may arrange for you to have a joint aspiration (below), in which fluid is withdrawn from the affected joint and examined for uric acid crystals.

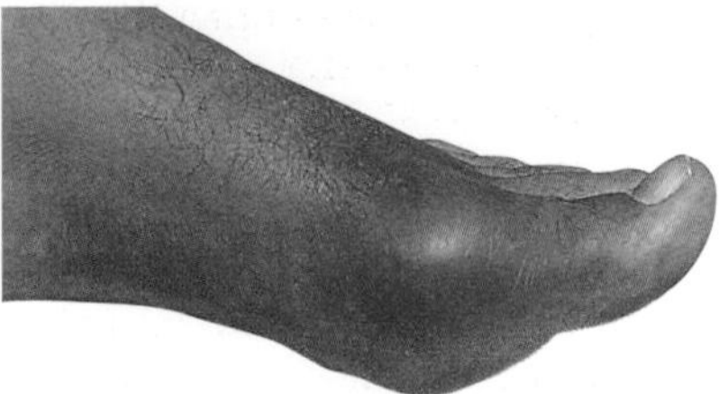

Swelling due to gout
As a result of an acute attack of gout, in which uric acid crystals form in a joint, the joint at the base of this big toe has become painful and swollen.

Gout may subside by itself after a few days. To reduce severe pain and inflammation, you may be treated with a nonsteroidal anti-inflammatory drug (p.894), the antigout drug colchicine, or with oral corticosteroids (p.930). If gout persists, your doctor may give you a corticosteroid injection directly into the affected joint (*see* LOCALLY ACTING CORTICOSTEROIDS, p.895).

If you have recurring gout, you may need lifelong treatment with preventive drugs, such as allopurinol to reduce the production of uric acid or probenecid to increase the excretion of uric acid.

Your doctor may recommend that you reduce your alcohol consumption. In addition, you may be able to reduce the frequency and severity of attacks by keeping fit and losing excess weight (*see* CONTROLLING YOUR WEIGHT, p.53).

What is the prognosis?

Gout can be painful and disrupt normal activities, but attacks often become less frequent and less severe with age. Repeated attacks may damage the joint.

WWW ONLINE SITES: p.1027

TEST AND TREATMENT — JOINT ASPIRATION

During joint aspiration, fluid is withdrawn from a swollen joint with a needle and syringe, possibly under local anesthesia. The fluid is then examined to find the cause of the swelling. Joint aspiration may also be carried out to relieve swelling due to excess fluid, and to diagnose or treat disorders such as gout, pseudogout, and septic arthritis.

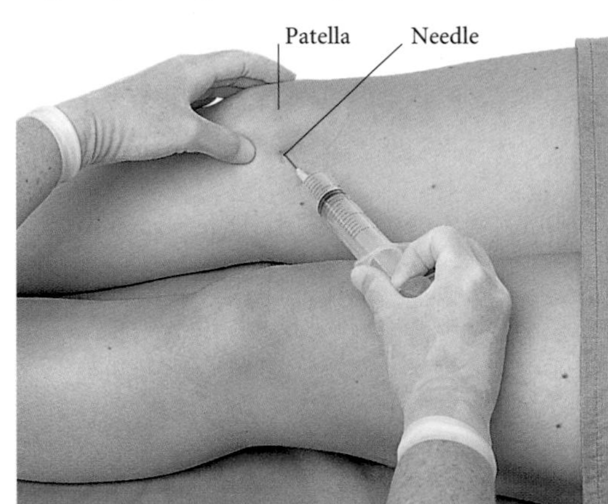
Patella
Needle

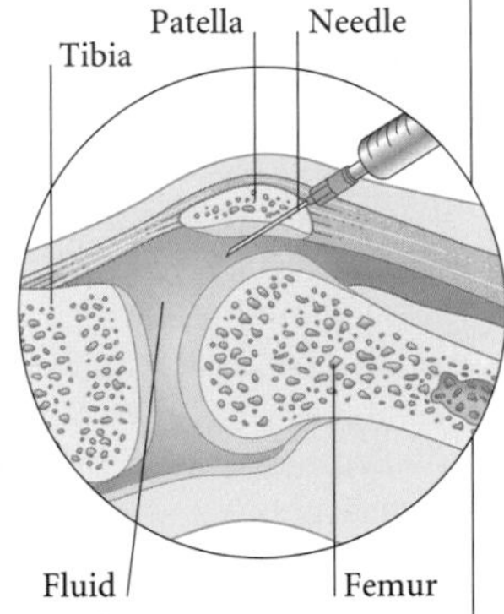
Patella
Needle
Tibia
Fluid
Femur
INSIDE THE JOINT

Knee joint aspiration
You will be asked to keep your knee relaxed so that the needle can be inserted easily. The patella is held still while the needle is passed into the space under the patella and fluid is withdrawn.

RESULTS

Fluid sample
A fluid sample withdrawn from a swollen joint is examined under a microscope. This magnified view of the fluid reveals the presence of uric acid crystals, which are indicative of gout.

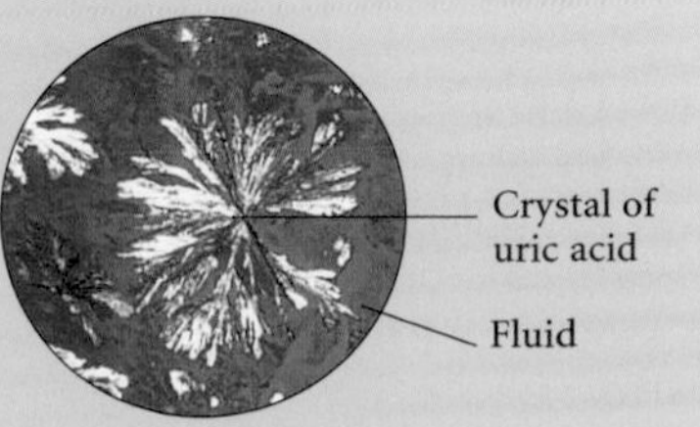
Crystal of uric acid
Fluid

Pseudogout

A type of arthritis in which crystals of calcium pyrophosphate or other chemicals are deposited in joints

 AGE Usually develops over age 60; more common with increasing age

 GENDER More common in females

 GENETICS Sometimes runs in families

 LIFESTYLE Not a significant factor

In this condition, crystals of calcium pyrophosphate or similar chemicals are deposited in joints, causing attacks of pain and stiffness. Usually, a single joint is affected. The most common sites are the knee and wrist, but crystals may be deposited in any joint. Although the process of formation and deposition of the crystals may start earlier, symptoms are less common before the age of 60.

In most people, the cause of pseudogout is unknown, although attacks may be triggered by surgery, infection, or injury. Pseudogout is often associated with other joint disorders, particularly, osteoarthritis (p.374). Pseudogout may also be linked to hyperparathyroidism (p.682), a hormonal condition which leads to high blood levels of calcium, or hemochromatosis (p.692), a disorder in which the body is overloaded with iron. Pseudogout is more commonly found in women and may run in families.

WHAT ARE THE SYMPTOMS?

Symptoms are similar to those of gout (opposite page). Attacks may cause:

- Severe pain, stiffness, swelling, and redness of the affected joint.
- Mild fever.

Some people have no pain between attacks, while others experience persistent pain and stiffness.

WHAT MIGHT BE DONE?

If your doctor suspects pseudogout, he or she may arrange for X-rays (p.244) of the affected joints. You may also need joint aspiration (opposite page), in which fluid is removed from a joint for analysis and to relieve swelling.

The symptoms of pseudogout may be relieved by simply removing fluid from the affected joint. In severe cases, a corticosteroid drug may be injected directly into the joint during the same procedure (*see* LOCALLY ACTING CORTICOSTEROIDS, p.895). You may also need nonsteroidal anti-inflammatory drugs (p.894). Once treatment starts, symptoms usually clear up within 48 hours.

There is no cure for pseudogout, but joint damage is rarely severe and does not often affect daily life. Physiotherapy (p.961) may be necessary to increase the joint mobility and muscle strength.

(WWW) ONLINE SITES: p.1035

Septic arthritis

A type of arthritis resulting from infection of a joint

 AGE Most common in children and elderly people

 LIFESTYLE Intravenous drug use is a risk factor

GENDER GENETICS Not significant factors

Septic arthritis is an infection in the synovial fluid or tissues of a joint, such as a hip or a knee. The condition is caused by bacteria or, less commonly, by viruses or fungi that have entered the joint through an open wound or have traveled through the bloodstream from an infection elsewhere in the body. For example, the bacteria that cause gonorrhea (p.764) may spread from the genital tract through the bloodstream. The risk of septic arthritis is increased in people who have rheumatoid arthritis (p.377), who have been fitted with an artificial joint, or who use intravenous recreational drugs.

WHAT ARE THE SYMPTOMS?

The symptoms of septic arthritis usually appear suddenly and may include:

- Fever.
- Swelling, tenderness, redness, and warmth around the affected joint.
- Severe pain and restricted movement of the affected joint.

If pus builds up in an infected area, the joint may be damaged permanently. If you develop the above symptoms, consult your doctor immediately.

WHAT MIGHT BE DONE?

Your doctor may arrange for a sample of fluid to be taken from the affected joint (*see* JOINT ASPIRATION, opposite page). The fluid is analyzed to look for evidence of infection and also to try and establish the cause.

Septic arthritis caused by bacteria is initially treated with intravenous antibiotics (p.885) for at least 4 weeks. Your doctor may then prescribe oral antibiotics for several weeks or months. If your condition is caused by a virus or fungus, antiviral drugs (p.886) or antifungal drugs (p.889) may be prescribed.

To help relieve pain and inflammation, pus may be drained from the infected joint several times. Your doctor may also prescribe a nonsteroidal anti-inflammatory drug (p.894). You should rest the joint, keeping it immobile until the inflammation has completely subsided. If the infected joint is an artificial joint, it may need to be replaced surgically with a new artificial joint to allow the infection to clear up.

WHAT IS THE PROGNOSIS?

If treatment is started early, the symptoms of septic arthritis should begin to subside within 24 hours. Eventually, the disorder may clear up completely. However, left untreated, the infection may lead to irreversible joint damage.

(WWW) ONLINE SITES: p.1027, p.1035

Lower back pain

Pain in the back, below the waist, that may be sudden and sharp or persistent and dull

 AGE GENDER GENETICS LIFESTYLE Risk factors depend on the cause

Lower back pain affects about 6 in 10 adults during the course of a year. More working days are lost due to back pain than to any other medical condition. In most cases, the pain lasts for only a week or so, but many people find that their problem recurs unless they alter the way they perform daily activities. In a minority of people, persistent lower back pain causes chronic disability.

Lower back pain is usually caused by minor damage to the ligaments and muscles in the back. The lower back is vulnerable to these problems because it supports most of the body's weight and is under continual stress from movements such as bending and twisting. Less commonly, lower back pain may be a result of an underlying disorder such as a prolapsed or herniated disk (p.384) in the spine.

SELF-HELP PREVENTING BACK PAIN

Most people have experienced back pain at some time in their lives, but in many cases the problem could have been avoided. Back pain is often due to poor posture, weak abdominal or back muscles, or sudden muscle strain. You can improve your posture by wearing comfortable shoes, by standing or sitting with your spine properly aligned, and by choosing a supportive mattress for your bed. Gentle, regular exercises may strengthen abdominal and back muscles, and losing excess weight may relieve stress on joints and muscles. Learning how to perform physical tasks safely, including how to lift and carry objects safely, can help prevent back strain. Ask your doctor or physiotherapist to give you advice on posture, exercises, and diet.

CORRECT BODY POSTURE

To break bad postural habits, you should be constantly aware of the way in which you stand, sit, move, and even sleep. The pictures on this page show how to carry out everyday activities comfortably, with minimal strain on your spine and back muscles.

Eyes level with monitor
Back straight
Feet flat on floor

Sitting position
Sit with your back straight and both feet flat on the floor. Use a chair that supports the small of your back. When using a computer, position the monitor so that you can look straight at it.

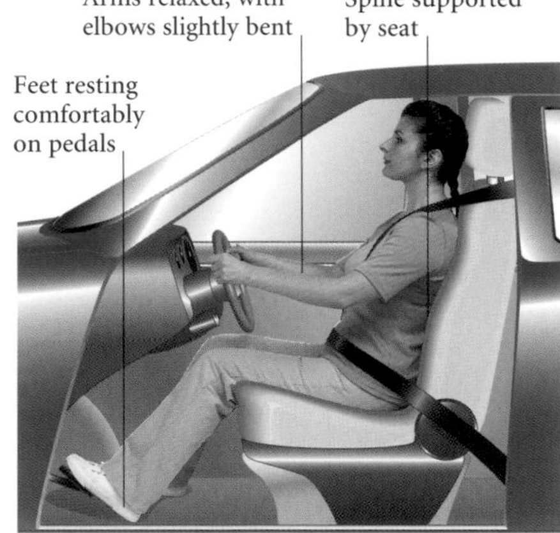

Arms relaxed, with elbows slightly bent
Spine supported by seat
Feet resting comfortably on pedals

Driving position
Angle your seat backward a little to support your spine, and position the seat so that you can reach the hand and foot controls easily.

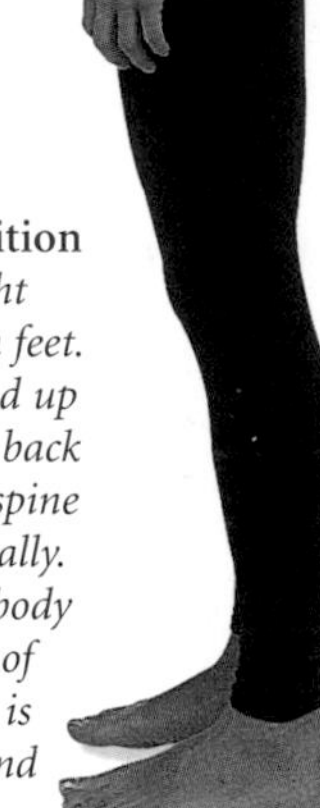

Shoulders pulled back
Trunk held straight
Abdominal muscles tightened
Pelvis tilted slightly to align body

Standing position
Put your weight evenly on both feet. Hold your head up and shoulders back to allow your spine to curve naturally. Balance your body over its center of gravity, which is in the pelvis and lower spine.

LIFTING AN OBJECT

When lifting, pushing, or pulling a heavy object, keep the object close to you so that you can use your full strength to move it. To lift an object, hold the bottom edge so that you support the full weight of the object and keep your body balanced as you lift to avoid straining your spine.

Back straight
Object directly in front
Base of object supported

1 *Squat close to the object with your weight evenly on both feet and the object between your legs. Grasp the base of the object.*

2 *Keep your back straight and lean forward slightly. Stand up in a single, smooth movement, pushing yourself up with your leg muscles and keeping the object close to you.*

Upper body straight

Weight of object balanced over thighs and feet

Legs pushing body straight upward

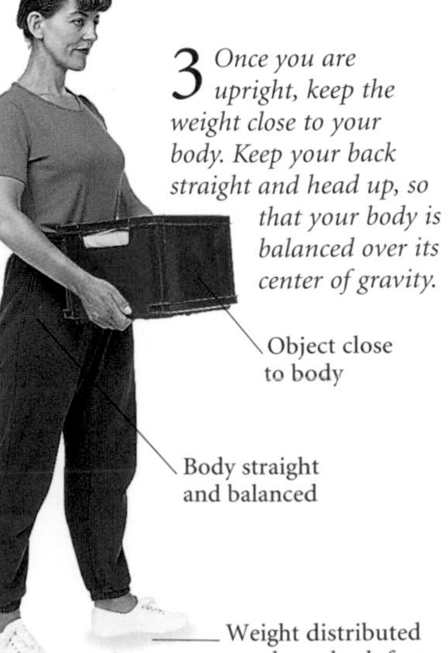

Object close to body
Body straight and balanced
Weight distributed evenly on both feet

3 *Once you are upright, keep the weight close to your body. Keep your back straight and head up, so that your body is balanced over its center of gravity.*

BACK-STRENGTHENING EXERCISES

You can help prevent back pain by gently exercising the muscles in your back and abdomen. Consult a doctor or ask for a referral to a physiotherapist before starting an exercise regimen. You should not continue any exercise that causes you pain.

The movements shown below should make your back muscles stronger and your spine more flexible. Repeat each one 10 times if you can, and try to exercise daily. Do the exercises on a comfortable but firm, flat surface, such as a mat laid on the floor.

Lower back stretch

This stretch may relieve aching joints and muscles in the lower back. Lie on your back with your feet flat on the floor and with your knees bent. Lift your knees toward your body. With your hands, pull your knees into your chest. Hold for 7 seconds and breathe deeply. Keeping your knees bent, lower your feet to the floor one at a time.

Small of back flat on floor
Feet flat on floor
Knees close in to chest
Hands clasped around upper shins
Buttocks lifted slightly off floor

Pelvic tilt

This movement helps to stretch the muscles and ligaments of the lower back. Lie on your back with your knees bent and your feet flat on the floor. Press the small of your back into the floor. Tighten your abdominal and buttock muscles so that your pelvis tilts upward and your buttocks rise slightly off the floor. Hold for 6 seconds and then relax.

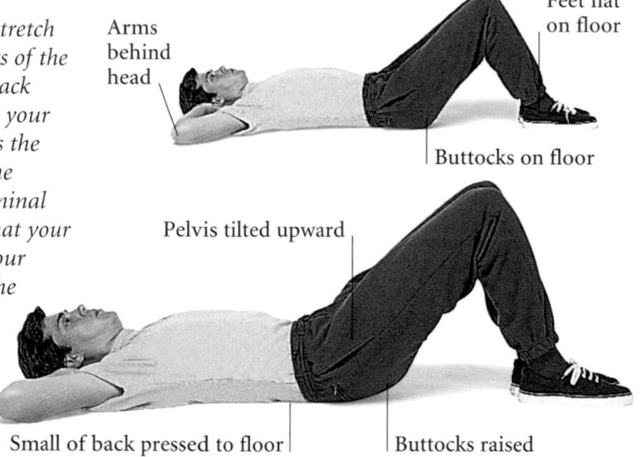
Arms behind head
Feet flat on floor
Buttocks on floor
Pelvis tilted upward
Small of back pressed to floor
Buttocks raised

Hump and sag

The movements in this exercise should increase suppleness in the joints and muscles of the back. Support yourself on your hands and knees with your knees slightly apart. Tuck your chin into your chest, then gently arch your back. Hold for about 5 seconds. Look up, allowing your back to sag, and hold again for about another 5 seconds.

Head tucked between arms
Back arched
Back sagging
Head lifted
Abdominal muscles relaxed
Upper body supported by arms

WHAT ARE THE CAUSES?

Lower back pain may come on suddenly (acute) or develop gradually over a period of weeks (chronic).

Sudden back pain is often caused by a physical injury due to lifting heavy objects or to activities such as digging in the garden. The pain is commonly caused by a strained muscle or tendon. The injury may be aggravated by subsequent activity. In most cases, symptoms subside within 2–14 days.

Back pain that comes on gradually and tends to be more persistent is often caused by poor posture, such as while sitting at a desk or driving a car, or by excessive muscle tension due to emotional stress. Lower back pain may also occur during pregnancy, due both to changes in posture because of the extra weight of the baby and to softening of ligaments supporting the spine caused by hormonal changes.

Another cause of lower back pain is a prolapsed or herniated disk exerting pressure on a spinal nerve or the spinal cord. Back pain of this type may have a gradual or sudden onset and is often accompanied by sciatica (p.546), in which severe pain shoots down the back of one or both legs.

Sometimes, persistent lower back pain is caused by joint disorders. In people over age 45, the most common joint problem is osteoarthritis (p.374), while in younger people the problem may be ankylosing spondylitis (p.378), which affects the joints of the spine. Less often, back pain results from bone disorders, such as Paget's disease of the bone (p.370), or cancer that has spread to bone from a tumor elsewhere in the body (*see* BONE METASTASES, p.373).

In some cases, disorders affecting internal organs can lead to pain in the lower back. Examples include certain disorders of the female reproductive system, such as pelvic inflammatory disease (p.741), and of the urinary system, such as prostatitis (p.724).

WHAT ARE THE SYMPTOMS?

Pain in the lower back can take various forms. You may experience:

- Sharp pain localized to a small area of the back.
- More general, aching pain in the back and buttocks, which is made worse by sitting and relieved by standing.

- Back stiffness and pain on bending.
- Pain in the back that radiates to the buttock and leg, sometimes accompanied by numbness or tingling.

Back pain associated with difficulty in controlling your bowel or bladder may be caused by a disorder putting pressure on the spinal cord. You should consult your doctor immediately if you develop these symptoms.

WHAT CAN I DO?

In most cases, you should be able to treat lower back pain yourself by taking an over-the-counter nonsteroidal anti-inflammatory drug (p.894). If the pain persists, additional relief may be provided by a heating pad or wrapped hot-water bottle and sometimes by ice placed against your back.

If the pain is severe, you may be more comfortable resting in bed, but you should not stay in bed for more than 2 days. Start moving around as soon as possible and gradually return to normal activities. If the pain worsens or is still too severe to allow you to move around after a few days, you should consult your doctor.

Once the pain has subsided, you can help prevent recurrences if you pay attention to your posture, learn to lift correctly, and do regular exercises to strengthen the muscles of your back and make your spine more flexible (*see* PREVENTING BACK PAIN, p.382).

WHAT MIGHT THE DOCTOR DO?

If you need to consult your doctor because of severe or persistent lower back pain, he or she will probably carry out a full physical examination to assess your posture, the range of movement in your spine, and any areas of local tenderness. Your reflexes, the strength of different leg muscles, and the sensation in your legs may also be tested to look for evidence of pressure on spinal nerves or the spinal cord. A pelvic or rectal examination may also be performed to rule out disorders of the internal organs.

You may have various blood tests and X-rays (p.244) to look for underlying causes of the pain, such as joint inflammation or bone cancer. If there is evidence of pressure on the spinal cord or spinal nerves, MRI (p.248) or CT scanning (p.247) may be carried out to detect abnormalities that may require additional treatment, such as a prolapsed or herniated disk.

Unless the physical examination and other tests indicate that there is a serious underlying cause for your back pain, your doctor will probably advise you to continue taking a nonsteroidal anti-inflammatory drug. You may be given physiotherapy (p.961) to mobilize stiff and painful joints between the vertebrae. In some cases, an injection combining a local anesthetic (p.914) with a corticosteroid (*see* LOCALLY ACTING CORTICOSTEROIDS, p.895) is given directly into areas of tenderness.

WHAT IS THE PROGNOSIS?

Most episodes of lower back pain clear up without treatment, but the problem recurs in many people unless poor posture or lifting technique are improved.

In a small number of people, lower back pain may be a long-standing condition, severely disrupting their work and social life and sometimes leading to depression (p.554). Effective pain control is essential in these chronic cases, and many people find that treatment with antidepressants (p.916) also helps them cope with their condition.

(WWW) ONLINE SITES: p.1035

Prolapsed or herniated disk

Protrusion of one of the shock-absorbing pads that lie between the vertebrae of the spine, also known as a "slipped disk"

AGE Most common between the ages of 25 and 45

GENDER Slightly more common in males

LIFESTYLE Being overweight and lifting objects incorrectly are risk factors

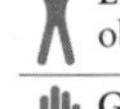
GENETICS Not a significant factor

The shock-absorbing disks between the vertebrae (bones of the spine) consist of a strong, fibrous outer coat and a soft, gelatinous core. A prolapsed disk occurs when the core pushes outward, distorting the shape of the disk. If the outer coat ruptures, the condition is termed a herniated disk. When a disk prolapses or herniates, the surrounding tissues become inflamed and swollen. Then, together with the disk, the tissues may press on a spinal nerve or the spinal cord, causing pain.

Although disks in the lower back are the most commonly affected, damage to the disks in the neck and, very rarely, the upper back can occur. People aged between 25 and 45 are most vulnerable to disk prolapse or herniation. The condition is slightly more common in men.

WHAT ARE THE CAUSES?

From about age 25, the disks begin to dry out. They also become more vulnerable to prolapse or herniation as a result of the normal stresses of daily life and minor injury. Sometimes, damage to a disk is caused by a sharp bending or twisting movement or by lifting a heavy object incorrectly. From about age 45, fibrous tissue forms around the disks, eventually stabilizing them and making them less likely to be damaged.

WHAT ARE THE SYMPTOMS?

Symptoms of a prolapsed or herniated disk may develop progressively over a period of weeks or may appear suddenly. They may include:

- Dull pain in the affected area.
- Muscle spasm and stiffness around the affected area that makes movement difficult.

If the disk presses on a spinal nerve, you may also have the following symptoms:

- Severe pain, tingling, or numbness in a leg (*see* SCIATICA, p.546) or, if the neck is affected, in an arm.
- Weakness or restricted movement in the leg or arm.

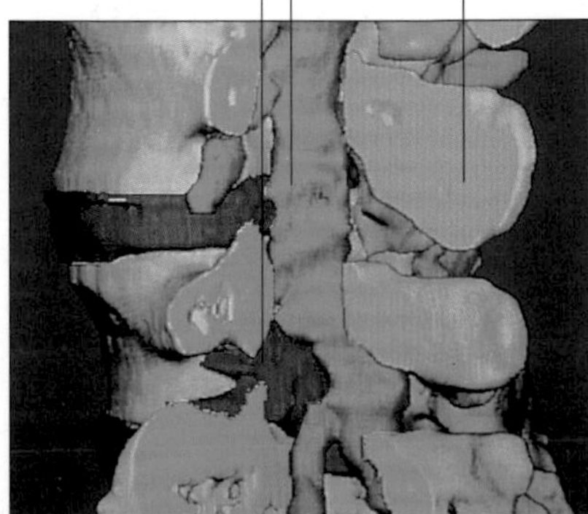
Herniated disk
Spinal cord
Vertebra

Herniated disk
This 3D CT scan shows a herniated disk in the spine. The soft core of the disk is protruding through the fibrous outer coat and pressing against the spinal cord.

TREATMENT **MICRODISKECTOMY**

Microdiskectomy is a surgical procedure used to treat a prolapsed or herniated disk pressing on a spinal nerve or the spinal cord. The protruding part of the disk is removed through an incision in the fibrous outer coat of the disk. The operation is performed under general anesthesia and requires a brief stay in the hospital.

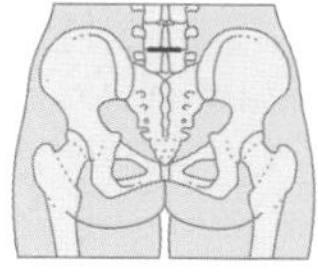

SITE OF INCISION

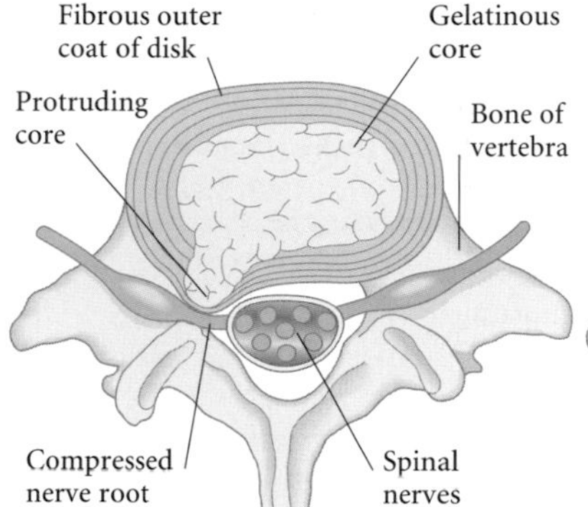
Fibrous outer coat of disk
Gelatinous core
Protruding core
Bone of vertebra
Compressed nerve root
Spinal nerves

Before the operation
The soft core of the disk is pushed outward, distorting (and sometimes rupturing) the outer coat. The protruding tissue presses on a nearby spinal nerve root.

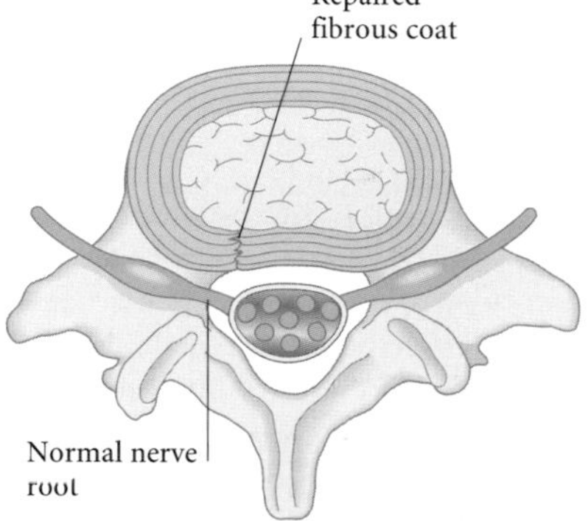
Repaired fibrous coat
Normal nerve root

After the operation
The protruding tissue has been removed, and the incision in the outer coat of the disk has been closed up. The spinal nerve root is no longer compressed.

The pain is often relieved by rest but can be made worse by walking upstairs, sitting, coughing, sneezing, bending, or bowel movements. Since impaired bladder or bowel function may indicate pressure on the spinal cord, you should consult a doctor urgently in such cases.

WHAT MIGHT BE DONE?

Diagnosis is usually made from the symptoms and a physical examination. You may also have an X-ray (p.244) to rule out other causes of back pain, such as osteoarthritis (p.374), and MRI (p.248) or CT scanning (p.247), which can locate the position of the prolapsed or herniated disk accurately.

Although the disk is permanently damaged, the pain usually improves over 6–8 weeks as the swelling subsides. Your doctor will suggest bed rest and medication for pain relief. If you are free of pain, physiotherapy (p.961) and exercises may help reduce muscle spasms and hasten your recovery.

Rarely, pain may be relieved with traction, in which the spine is gently stretched with weights to create more space around a nerve and reduce pressure on it. Some people may benefit from a selective nerve root block, in which a local anesthetic (p.914), sometimes combined with a corticosteroid drug (*see* LOCALLY ACTING CORTICOSTEROIDS, p.895), is injected around the compressed nerve to decrease swelling. If the damaged disk is in the neck, a supportive collar may be helpful.

In a few cases, if bladder or bowel function is impaired due to pressure on a nerve or the spinal cord or if there is severe pain or muscle weakness, urgent surgery on the disk may be required (*see* MICRODISKECTOMY, above).

(WWW) ONLINE SITES: p.1035

Spondylolisthesis

A disorder in which a vertebra (bone of the spine) slips forward over the one beneath it

AGE GENDER GENETICS LIFESTYLE Risk factors depend on the cause

In spondylolisthesis, a vertebra (bone of the spine) slides forward to project over the vertebra below, distorting the spinal cord or the nerves that branch off the cord. Spondylolisthesis usually affects the vertebrae in the lower part of the back. The disorder may be caused by a deformity of the spine present from birth or by ligament damage due to overstretching, especially in athletes such as pitchers and rowers. In elderly people, particularly women, the condition may result from a joint disorder such as osteoarthritis (p.374). In rare cases, it is caused by a severe injury.

Many people with spondylolisthesis have no symptoms. However, sometimes pain and stiffness may be felt in the affected area of the spine. Pressure on the spinal roots of the sciatic nerve may lead to sciatica (p.546), a condition in which pain is felt in the lower back and travels down the leg.

A diagnosis of spondylolisthesis will need to be confirmed by X-rays (p.244). Procedures such as MRI (p.248) or CT scanning (p.247) may also be needed to exclude other possible causes of back pain such as a prolapsed or herniated disk (opposite page). Treatment may include wearing a support, such as a brace, and physiotherapy (p.961), which helps to strengthen the muscles that support the affected vertebrae (*see* PREVENTING BACK PAIN, p.382). Rarely, in severe cases, surgery may be needed to fuse the affected vertebrae together.

Normal activity can often be resumed about 6 months after treatment.

(WWW) ONLINE SITES: p.1035

Frozen shoulder

Pain and restriction of movement in the shoulder joint, commonly due to inflammation

AGE More common over age 40

GENDER More common in females

GENETICS LIFESTYLE Not significant factors

Pain and stiffness in a shoulder joint, severely restricting its movement, is called frozen shoulder. The condition may be due to inflammation resulting from an injury to the shoulder region. Frozen shoulder may also occur if the shoulder is kept immobilized for a long period of time, such as following a stroke (p.532). However, in many cases, frozen shoulder develops for no apparent reason. The condition occurs most frequently in people over age 40 and is more common in women. People with diabetes mellitus (p.687) are also more susceptible to the condition.

What are the symptoms?
The symptoms of frozen shoulder often begin gradually over a period of weeks or months. They may include:
- Pain in the shoulder, which is severe in the early stage of the condition and often worse at night.
- With time, gradually decreasing pain but increasing stiffness and restricted joint movement.
- In severe cases, pain traveling down the arm to the elbow.

If you have pain in the shoulder that lasts for more than a few days, consult your doctor without delay.

What might be done?
Your doctor will probably diagnose frozen shoulder from the symptoms and an examination of your shoulder. An analgesic (p.912) or a nonsteroidal anti-inflammatory drug (p.894) may be prescribed to relieve the pain and reduce inflammation.

If the pain persists or is severe, you may be given a corticosteroid drug by means of a direct injection into the shoulder joint (*see* Locally acting corticosteroids, p.895). You may also be referred for physiotherapy (p.961). Despite these measures, your shoulder may remain stiff for up to a year.

Even when the stiffness has disappeared, recovery is usually slow and may take up to a further 6 months.

(WWW) ONLINE SITES: p.1035

Chondromalacia

Pain in the front of the knee due to an abnormality of the cartilage at the back of the kneecap

 Age Most common in teenagers and young adults

 Genetics Sometimes runs in families

 Lifestyle Strenuous exercise can trigger symptoms

Gender Not a significant factor

Chondromalacia, also referred to as patellofemoral pain syndrome, occurs when the cartilage surface of the back of the patella (kneecap) is damaged. The underlying cause of the condition is not known, but it is often triggered by strenuous exercise or repeated knee injuries. In teenagers, chondromalacia is often caused by increased weight-bearing on the knee joint during a growth spurt. The condition may also be associated with a misaligned or a recurrently dislocated patella or with muscle weakness in the upper leg.

What are the symptoms?
Symptoms vary in severity from person to person but may include:
- Pain in the knee when the leg is bent and straightened (such as when going up or down stairs).
- Stiffness after prolonged sitting.
- Crepitus (a crackling noise) during knee movement.

Chondromalacia usually occurs in only one knee, although the condition does sometimes develop in both knees.

What might be done?
Your doctor will examine your knee and press down on the patella to see if your symptoms worsen. He or she may arrange for X-rays (p.244) of the knee and back of the patella. In severe cases, arthroscopy (below) may be performed to examine the interior of the knee joint and remove damaged cartilage.

Your doctor may advise you to take a nonsteroidal anti-inflammatory drug (p.894) and suggest that you apply ice packs for pain relief. He or she may also advise mild exercise to strengthen thigh and knee muscles and reduce stress on the knee joint. You may be advised to wear a knee support as a temporary measure. In rare cases, surgery is necessary to realign the patella or remove it.

What is the prognosis?
Most people recover from chondromalacia in a few months, although they may have mild recurrences of pain in the knee. Recovery is slower if strenuous exercise is resumed prematurely. Chondromalacia is associated with an increased risk of developing chronic osteoarthritis (p.374) in later life.

(WWW) ONLINE SITES: p.1035

(TEST AND TREATMENT) Arthroscopy

In arthroscopy, the inside of a joint is inspected with a viewing instrument called an arthroscope. The procedure is most commonly used to inspect the inside of the knee joint and to treat disorders such as a damaged cartilage. It is usually performed under general anesthesia. The arthroscope is inserted into the joint through a small incision in the skin. Fine surgical instruments can then be passed down through the arthroscope or through other incisions. While watching the screen, the surgeon can remove or repair tissue, such as damaged cartilage, or shave the surface of the patella (kneecap).

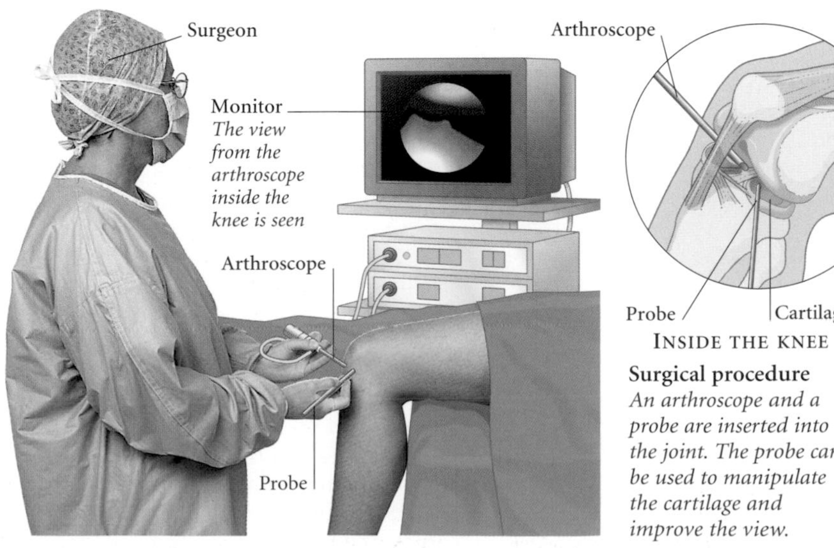
Surgeon
Monitor
The view from the arthroscope inside the knee is seen
Arthroscope
Probe
Arthroscope
Probe
Cartilage
Inside the knee

Surgical procedure
An arthroscope and a probe are inserted into the joint. The probe can be used to manipulate the cartilage and improve the view.

Bursitis

Inflammation of a bursa, one of the fluid-filled sacs located around joints

 AGE More common in adults

 LIFESTYLE Occupations involving repeated stress on a joint are risk factors

 GENDER GENETICS Not significant factors

Bursae act as friction-reducing cushions around joints. Inflammation of a bursa, called bursitis, may occur after prolonged or repeated stress on it. The bursa becomes tender and swollen, and movement of the joint is restricted.

The knee is most commonly affected, especially as a result of frequent kneeling, but the elbow or other joints may also be affected. Bursitis may also follow injury or unaccustomed exercise. Certain joint diseases, such as rheumatoid arthritis (p.377) and gout (p.380), increase the risk of bursitis. Rarely, the condition is due to a bacterial infection.

Your doctor will probably diagnose bursitis from a physical examination. Treatment includes resting the affected joint. Your doctor may also recommend a nonsteroidal anti-inflammatory drug (p.894) and application of ice packs. However, if symptoms persist, he or she may drain the bursa and inject it with a corticosteroid drug (*see* LOCALLY ACTING CORTICOSTEROIDS, p.895) to reduce inflammation. If a bacterial infection is present, antibiotics (p.885) will be prescribed, in which case the symptoms usually subside within 24 hours. If bursitis is persistent or recurrent, surgical removal of the bursa may be necessary.

(WWW) ONLINE SITES: p.1035

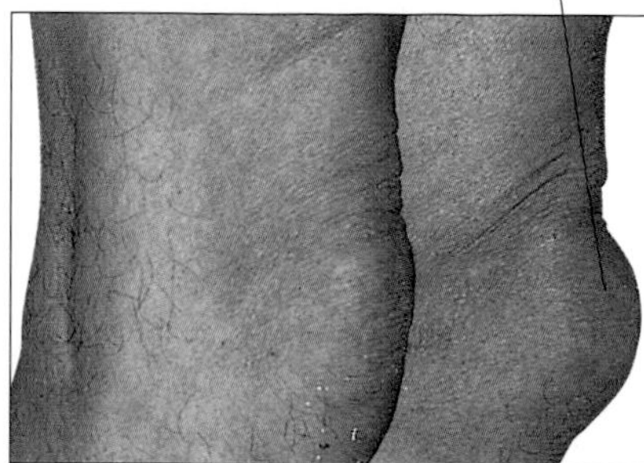
Swollen knee

Bursitis in the knee
The knee seen on the right is swollen due to a fluid-filled, inflamed bursa, which can be caused by prolonged kneeling.

(TREATMENT) BUNION SURGERY

Surgery to treat a bunion is aimed at correcting the underlying bone deformity, known as hallux valgus. One common type of surgical procedure used to treat a bunion involves reshaping and realigning the deformed bone at the base of the big toe. The operation is performed under general anesthesia and may require a brief stay in the hospital. Normal activity can usually be resumed about 6 weeks after surgery.

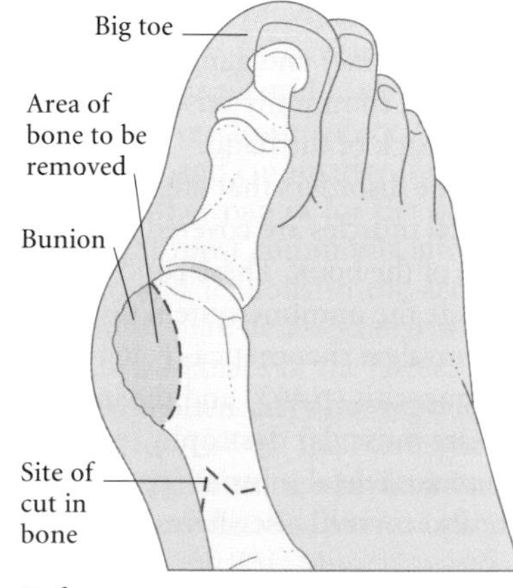
Big toe
Area of bone to be removed
Bunion
Site of cut in bone

Before surgery
The big toe is turned inward toward the other toes. The bone has become obviously deformed, and the soft tissue around it has thickened, forming a painful bunion.

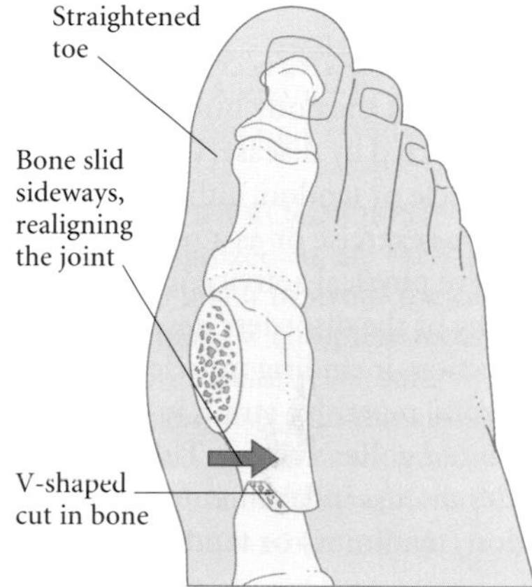
Straightened toe
Bone slid sideways, realigning the joint
V-shaped cut in bone

After surgery
The protruding part of the bone has been removed and a V-shaped cut made in the lower part of the bone. The big toe is straight due to realignment of the bone.

Bunion

Inflamed, thickened soft tissue and bony overgrowth at the base of the big toe

 AGE Most common in young adults and older people

 GENDER More common in females

 GENETICS Sometimes runs in families

 LIFESTYLE Wearing tight, pointed shoes, especially with high heels, is a risk factor

A bunion is a thickened lump at the base of the big toe. It often becomes inflamed and painful, making walking difficult. The underlying cause is usually a minor bone deformity, called hallux valgus, in which the joint at the base of the big toe projects outward while forcing the tip of the toe to turn inward toward the other toes. The cause of hallux valgus itself is not known, but the condition runs in some families. As a result of pressure on the deformity, the surrounding tissues thicken. The term bunion refers to the thickened lump that is due to the combination of the bony deformity and thickening of the soft tissue around it. The condition is particularly common in young women who wear tight, pointed shoes with high heels.

In rare cases, the constant rubbing of tight shoes on the skin over a bunion may cause an abrasion, which then leads to a bacterial infection. People with diabetes mellitus (p.687) are particularly susceptible to bunions because the sensation in their feet is reduced (*see* PERIPHERAL NEUROPATHIES, p.543). In such people, damage to the skin tends to heal more slowly.

Without attention, a bunion may gradually worsen. Pain may be alleviated by wearing comfortable shoes and a special toe pad or corrective sock that straightens the big toe. However, if a bunion causes severe discomfort, your doctor may suggest surgery to correct the underlying deformity by realigning the bone (*see* BUNION SURGERY, above). If the bunion becomes infected, your doctor will prescribe antibiotics (p.885) to treat it. A bunion increases the chance of developing osteoarthritis (p.374) of the toe joint in later life.

(WWW) ONLINE SITES: p.1036

and ultrasound treatment may help relieve symptoms. You may also find that a nonsteroidal anti-inflammatory drug (p.894) helps. If the condition does not improve within 2–6 weeks, your doctor may inject a corticosteroid drug into the affected area (*see* LOCALLY ACTING CORTICOSTEROIDS, p.895). You should seek advice on ways to change your technique before resuming the sport or activity that gave rise to the condition once the symptoms have subsided.

(WWW) ONLINE SITES: p.1031, p.1035, p1036

Tendinitis and tenosynovitis

Painful inflammation of a tendon (tendinitis) or of a tendon sheath (tenosynovitis)

AGE More common in adults

LIFESTYLE More common in athletes

GENDER GENETICS Not significant factors

Tendinitis is inflammation of a tendon, the fibrous cord that attaches a muscle to a bone. Tenosynovitis is inflammation of the sheath of tissues that surrounds a tendon. These two conditions usually occur together. Tendons around the shoulder, elbow, wrist, fingers, thigh, knee, or back of the heel are most commonly affected.

Both conditions may be caused by injury of a particular tendon or, rarely, by an infection. Inflammation of the Achilles tendon between the heel and the calf may be the result of a sports injury (p.391) or of wearing ill-fitting shoes. Tenosynovitis may be associated with rheumatoid arthritis (p.377). In some cases, the cause is unknown.

WHAT ARE THE SYMPTOMS?

You may notice the following symptoms in the affected area, particularly during movement:

- Pain and/or mild swelling.
- Stiffness and restricted movement in the affected area.
- Warm, red skin over the tendon.
- A tender lump over the tendon.

Occasionally, you may feel a crackling sensation (known as crepitus) when the affected tendon moves.

WHAT MIGHT BE DONE?

Diagnosis is based on the symptoms and a physical examination. Your doctor will treat any underlying disorder. To reduce the pain and inflammation, he or she may recommend nonsteroidal anti-inflammatory drugs (p.894). You may also require an injection of a corticosteroid drug (*see* LOCALLY ACTING CORTICOSTEROIDS, p.895) directly into the tendon sheath. If the condition is caused by infection, a course of antibiotics (p.885) will be prescribed. In some cases, a tendon will heal more quickly if it is splinted. Tendinitis and tenosynovitis improve with treatment.

(WWW) ONLINE SITES: p.1031, p.1035

Dupuytren's contracture

Thickening and shortening of tissues in the palm of the hand, resulting in deformity of the fingers

AGE More common over age 50

GENDER Much more common in males

GENETICS Sometimes runs in families

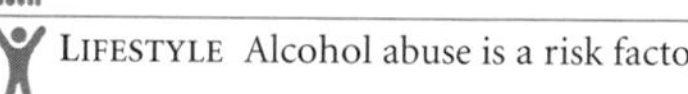
LIFESTYLE Alcohol abuse is a risk factor

In Dupuytren's contracture, the fibrous tissue in the palm of the hand becomes thickened and shortened. As a result, one or more fingers, often the fourth and fifth fingers, are pulled toward the palm into a bent position. Sometimes, painful lumps develop on the palm, and the overlying skin becomes puckered. In about half of all cases, both hands are involved. Rarely, the disorder affects the soles of the feet and the toes.

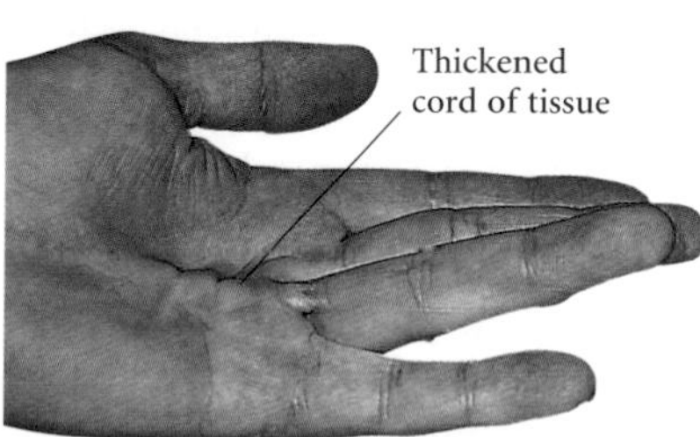
Thickened
cord of tissue

Dupuytren's contracture
The fourth finger of this hand is pulled toward the palm by fibrous tissue that has thickened and shortened. This is known as Dupuytren's contracture.

The tissue changes in Dupuytren's contracture develop slowly over months or years. In severe cases, the condition may interfere with using hands for everyday activities such as washing hands. The cause is unknown, but it is more common in men over age 50, in people with diabetes mellitus (p.687) or epilepsy (p.524), and in people who abuse alcohol. About 1 in 10 people with Dupuytren's contracture has a relative with the disorder.

WHAT MIGHT BE DONE?

In mild cases, no treatment may be needed. If your fingers are slightly bent, you may benefit from stretching exercises or short-term splinting. In severe cases, surgery is the most effective treatment, especially if performed early. Under general or local anesthesia, the thickened tissue in the palm is removed to allow the fingers to straighten. Surgery can restore function to the hand, but does not cure the condition. Further treatment may be needed if the disorder recurs.

(WWW) ONLINE SITES: p.1035

Ganglion

A fluid-filled cyst that most commonly develops on the wrist or back of the hand and sometimes the foot

AGE GENDER GENETICS LIFESTYLE Not significant factors

A ganglion is a cyst that develops under the skin near a joint and is filled with a jellylike fluid. The ganglion is usually an outgrowth from the capsule surrounding a joint or from the sheath of a tendon, the fibrous cord that attaches muscle to bone. The fluid inside the ganglion is derived from the synovial fluid that lubricates tendons and joints.

Ganglia are extremely common and are usually painless. They most commonly occur on the wrist or the back of the hand but occasionally they develop on the foot. They vary in size from that of a small pea to that of a plum.

A ganglion may be felt as a lump under the skin and may be present for several years without causing a problem. However, some ganglia become very uncomfortable or even painful. A ganglion may disappear spontaneously, or it can be removed surgically under local anesthesia. Ganglia sometimes recur.

(WWW) ONLINE SITES: p.1035

MUSCULOSKELETAL INJURIES

The bones, joints, muscles, and connective tissues of the body's musculoskeletal system are susceptible to injury from the stresses and strains placed on them during routine and leisure activities. The healing of minor injuries is usually rapid and complete, but major ones require expert treatment to avoid permanent damage.

Today, many people are aware of the health benefits of exercise and use part of their leisure time to pursue athletic activities. However, such pursuits may lead to musculoskeletal injuries if care is not taken. The first article in this section gives an overview of the main types of sports injuries, the treatment of which has now become a specialized branch of medicine.

Injury may result in bone fractures of various types and these are covered next. The treatment of fractures has changed a great deal in the past 20 years as a result of various technical innovations, particularly for more complicated fractures in which the damaged bone is fragmented.

Injuries occurring in other parts of the musculoskeletal system, including joints, ligaments, muscles, and tendons, are also discussed. As with fractures, these injuries may cause long-term disability if not treated properly.

Damage to the musculoskeletal system may also occur as part of more widespread damage to the body following serious trauma, such as a motor vehicle accident (*see* SERIOUS INJURIES, pp.316–320).

KEY ANATOMY

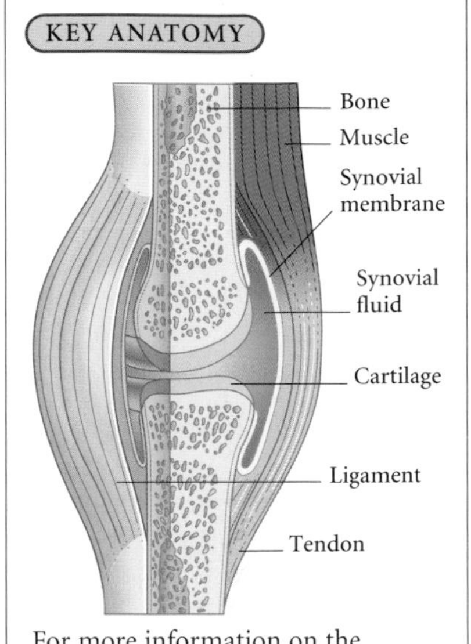
Bone
Muscle
Synovial membrane
Synovial fluid
Cartilage
Ligament
Tendon

For more information on the structure of the musculoskeletal system, *see* pp.362 367.

Sports injuries

Damage to any part of the body as a result of athletic activity

 GENDER More common in males

 AGE Older participants may be more likely to be injured and injuries heal more slowly

 LIFESTYLE Playing sports, especially contact sports, is a risk factor

 GENETICS Not a significant factor

Athletes and other people who exercise vigorously risk injury. Sports injuries often occur in people who are new to a sport, begin to exercise after long inactivity, or do not warm up properly before exercise. Men are at greater risk because they play more contact sports.

What are the types?

Any part of the musculoskeletal system may be injured while playing sports. In some sports, there is an increased risk of injury to a specific part of the body.

BONE INJURIES Many sports activities can cause damage to the bones, either through repetitive actions or as a result of an impact with another person, the ground, or sports equipment, such as a bat or a hard ball. Bones may be broken or cracked (*see* FRACTURES, p.392) during contact sports such as football. The repetitive jarring of bones in the feet of runners may cause stress fractures.

JOINT INJURIES The bones that form a joint may partially or completely pull apart (*see* DISLOCATED JOINT, p.394) during sports that put them under great strain, such as javelin throwing. Dislocation is also a risk in all contact sports. A common injury among football and baseball players is damage to the cartilage pads in the knee joint (*see* TORN KNEE CARTILAGE, p.395).

LIGAMENT AND TENDON INJURIES The fibrous bands of tissue that hold the structures of the musculoskeletal system together are often injured during sports activities. Ligaments, which hold the bones together, may become damaged by a sudden twisting movement or during a fall (*see* LIGAMENT INJURIES, p.394). Tendons, which attach muscle to bone, may become torn during athletic activities such as jumping that involve a sudden muscle contraction (*see* RUPTURED TENDON, p.395).

MUSCLE INJURIES Most sports rely on strength and suppleness of the muscles, and damage to muscles is common in athletes (*see* MUSCLE STRAINS AND TEARS, p.395). For example, calf strain, which is overstretching of the muscles in the calf region, is a common injury in basketball players. Muscle injury is frequently caused by sudden, strenuous movements and lifting heavy objects.

Can they be prevented?

Many sports injuries could be prevented by warming up correctly before starting exercise (*see* WARMING UP AND COOLING DOWN IN YOUR EXERCISE ROUTINE, p.60). Adequate preparation can increase flexibility and reduce stiffness in the muscles and joints. In sports such as running you should start gently, gradually increasing your pace to prevent placing too much strain on your body. Wear clothes and footwear designed for your type of sport and use recommended safety equipment.

What might be done?

Many minor injuries to ligaments, tendons, and muscles can be treated using basic first-aid procedures (*see* FIRST AID: SPRAINS AND STRAINS, p.991) and nonsteroidal anti-inflammatory drugs (p.894). If a sports injury is causing intense or persistent pain, you should consult a doctor. He or she will examine you and may arrange for you to have an X-ray (p.244) to check whether you have sustained a fracture.

If you have a fracture, it may be necessary to immobilize the injured area by using a cast (*see* FRACTURE TREATMENTS, opposite page). Surgery may be required for some injuries, such as a ruptured tendon. You may also need physiotherapy (p.961) from a sports therapist. You should nor participate in any sports until you are free of pain.

(WWW) ONLINE SITES: p.1031, p.1035, p1036

Fractures

Breaks or cracks in bones anywhere in the body from a variety of causes

AGE GENDER GENETICS LIFESTYLE
Risk factors depend on the cause

Any bone in the body can be fractured. Most fractures are caused by an injury such as a direct impact or a twisting movement, which may occur during an athletic activity or a fall.

Susceptibility to fractures increases with the bone disorder osteoporosis (p.368), which mainly affects women after menopause and results in brittle bones. Fractures that occur in bones affected by tumors are known as pathological fractures and may occur after minimal injury or even spontaneously.

The most common sites of fracture in elderly people are the neck of the femur (thighbone) and the end of the radius bone of the forearm near the wrist. A fracture at the end of the radius bone, known as a Colles fracture, may occur if a person trips and breaks his or her fall with an outstretched arm.

WHAT ARE THE TYPES?

There are two main types of fracture: closed (simple), in which the broken bone does not break through the overlying skin; and open (compound), in which the bone pierces the skin and is exposed. Open fractures are more serious because of the risk of infection and an increased risk of damage to nerves and blood vessels. Open and closed fractures may be further subdivided according to their shape and pattern.

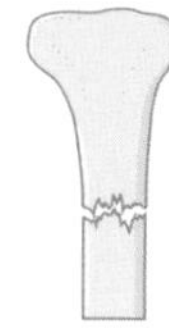

TRANSVERSE FRACTURE In a transverse fracture, there is a straight break across a bone. Transverse fractures, often in a long bone in the arm or leg, are usually due to a powerful blow, such as that sustained in a collision during a traffic accident.

SPIRAL FRACTURE This type of fracture is also known as an oblique fracture. Spiral fractures are usually caused by sudden, violent, rotating movements, such as twisting the leg during a fall. Spiral fractures usually occur in arm and leg bones.

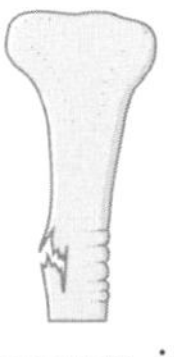

GREENSTICK FRACTURE If a long bone in the arm or leg bends, it may crack on one side only, producing a break called a "greenstick" fracture. This type of fracture occurs in children, whose bones are still growing and flexible.

COMMINUTED FRACTURE In a comminuted fracture, the bone is broken into small fragments, which increases the likelihood of damage to the soft tissues surrounding the broken bone. These fractures are usually caused by severe, direct forces.

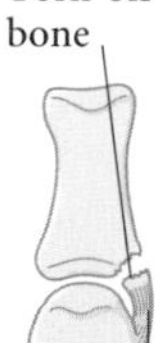
Torn-off bone
Tendon

AVULSION FRACTURE In this type of fracture, a piece of bone is pulled away from the main bone by a tendon, a fibrous band that attaches muscle to a bone. It usually results from a sudden violent twisting injury.

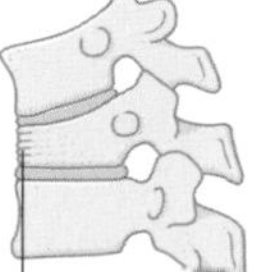
Compression fracture

COMPRESSION FRACTURE A compression fracture occurs if spongy bone, like that in the vertebrae of the spine, is crushed. This type of fracture is often due to osteoporosis.

Fractures caused by repeated jarring of a bone are called stress fractures. They may occur in the feet or shinbones of long-distance runners. In the elderly, fractures may result from minor stress such as a cough, which can break a rib.

WHAT ARE THE SYMPTOMS?

The symptoms of a fracture depend on its type and may include:

- Pain and tenderness, which may limit movement of the affected area.
- Swelling and bruising.
- Deformity in the affected area.
- Crackling noise (crepitus) caused by grating of the ends of the bones on movement or pressure.
- In an open fracture, damage to skin, bleeding, and visible bone.

All fractures cause a certain amount of internal bleeding because of damage to blood vessels in the bone. The broken bone ends may cause further bleeding by damaging tissues and blood vessels in the injured area. In some fractures, blood loss may be severe and can occasionally lead to shock (p.414).

Various complications may be associated with a fracture. For example, if you fracture a rib, there is a risk that the broken rib may puncture a lung (*see* PNEUMOTHORAX, p.496). An open fracture may become infected.

Delay in treating a fracture properly may result in failure of the bone to heal and permanent deformity or disability. Consult a doctor immediately if you think that you have a fracture.

HOW IS IT DIAGNOSED?

Your doctor will arrange for you to have X-rays (p.244) of the affected area to reveal the type and extent of the fracture. CT scanning (p.247) or MRI (p.248) may be needed to investigate complex fractures. If a fracture was not due to injury, your doctor may check for a possible underlying disorder that may have weakened your bones.

WHAT IS THE TREATMENT?

If the broken ends of the bone have been displaced, they will need to be returned to their original position to restore normal shape. This process is known as reduction. Depending on the location and severity of the fracture, a broken bone may be manipulated back into its proper position under local or general anesthesia, either without an incision (closed reduction) or through an incision in the skin (open reduction). The fractured bone may be held in place until it heals by using one of several methods (*see* FRACTURE TREATMENTS, opposite page).

TREATMENT FRACTURE TREATMENTS

Although some broken bones do not need to be immobilized, most have to be returned to their correct position (reduction) and held in place so that the fractured ends are able to heal and join together properly. The method of immobilization chosen for a particular fracture depends on the type, location, and severity of the fracture.

IMMOBILIZATION IN A CAST

The simplest form of immobilization is a cast, a rigid casing that is applied to a limb and left in position for several weeks to hold the fractured bone ends together and prevent movement. Casts are usually made from plaster, plastic, or resin. They are removed using an electric saw, which cuts through the cast.

Resin cast
Resin casts are light, waterproof, and durable. The cast is applied as a bandage to fit the affected limb. It then sets and provides support without restricting the blood supply.

INTERNAL FIXATION

Bones that are severely fractured may require metal plates, screws, nails, wires, or rods to be inserted surgically to hold the broken bone ends together. A cast is not needed. Internal fixation is often used for fractures at the ends of bones.

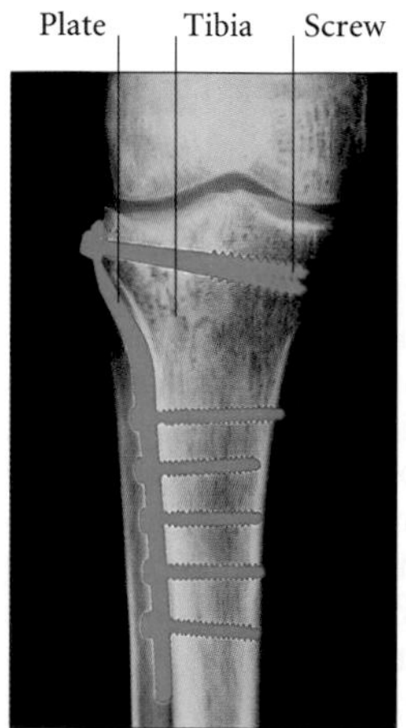
Plate
Tibia
Screw

Plate and screws
A fracture in the tibia (shinbone) may be immobilized by a metal plate secured by screws.

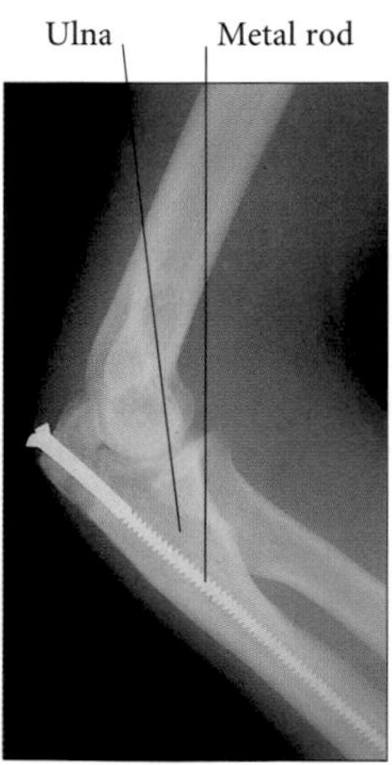
Ulna
Metal rod

Inserted rod
A fractured ulna (lower arm bone) may be held together by a metal rod inserted into the bone.

EXTERNAL FIXATION

A specialized technique known as external fixation is often required to repair bones that are fractured in several places. In this technique, pins are inserted through the skin into the bone fragments. The pins are held in place by an external metal frame, which allows the affected limb to be used normally within a few days. The frame and pins are removed when the bone has healed.

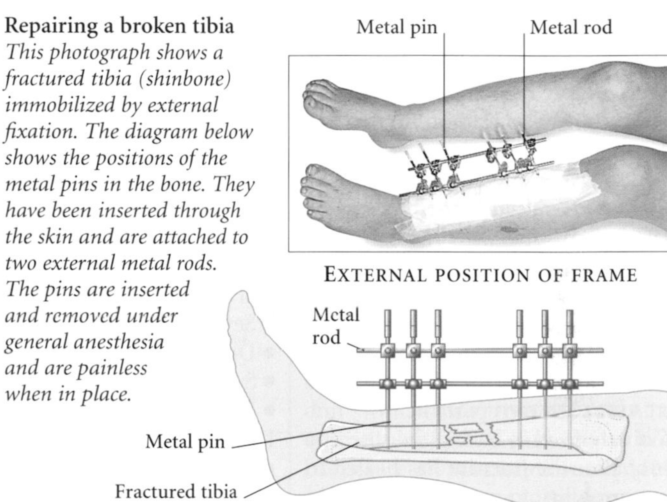
Metal pin
Metal rod
EXTERNAL POSITION OF FRAME
Metal rod
Metal pin
Fractured tibia
INTERNAL POSITION OF FRAME

Repairing a broken tibia
This photograph shows a fractured tibia (shinbone) immobilized by external fixation. The diagram below shows the positions of the metal pins in the bone. They have been inserted through the skin and are attached to two external metal rods. The pins are inserted and removed under general anesthesia and are painless when in place.

TRACTION

Traction is used when the correct position of a bone with a simple fracture, such as a transverse fracture, cannot be maintained by external fixation. It is often used to treat fractures in the shaft of the femur (thighbone). Weights are used to maintain alignment because the powerful muscles in the thigh would normally pull on the ends of the broken bone, forcing them out of alignment.

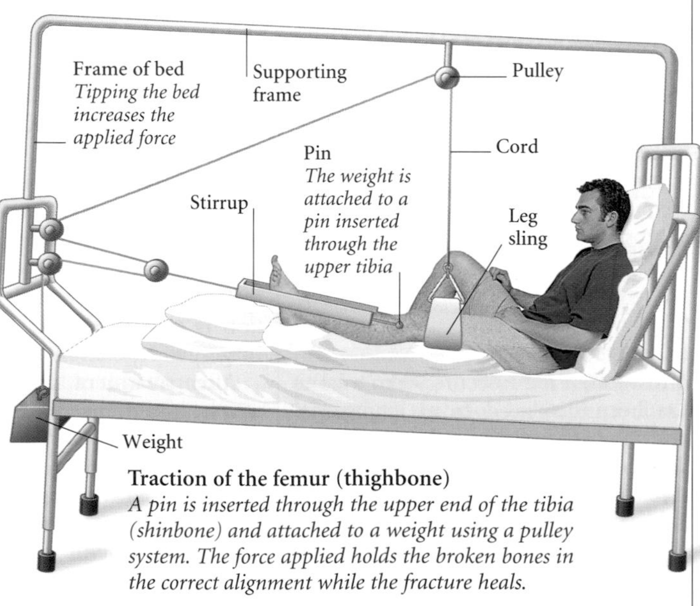
Frame of bed
Tipping the bed increases the applied force
Supporting frame
Pulley
Cord
Pin
The weight is attached to a pin inserted through the upper tibia
Stirrup
Leg sling
Weight

Traction of the femur (thighbone)
A pin is inserted through the upper end of the tibia (shinbone) and attached to a weight using a pulley system. The force applied holds the broken bones in the correct alignment while the fracture heals.

Cardiovascular System

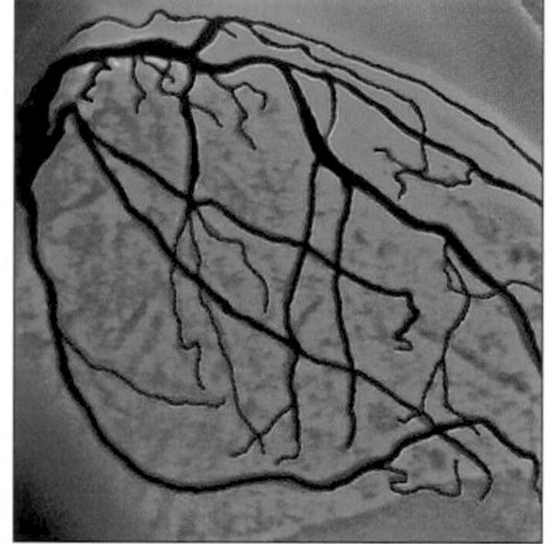

Blood supply to the heart
The extensive network of arteries that surround the heart and supply oxygenated blood to its muscle can be seen in this contrast X-ray.

THE CARDIOVASCULAR SYSTEM and the blood contained in its vessels are the body's transport system. The heart pumps blood around two circuits of blood vessels. The main (systemic) circuit carries blood that contains oxygen, vital nutrients, and hormones to every cell. The second (pulmonary) circuit takes blood to the lungs, where oxygen is absorbed and the waste product carbon dioxide is eliminated. Other waste products are taken to the liver for processing and finally eliminated by the kidneys.

The heart pumps the body's total volume of blood (about 10½ pints or 5 liters) around the entire body about once every minute. In the systemic circulation, blood containing oxygen and vital nutrients is pumped to tissues and organs through blood vessels called arteries. Body cells absorb the oxygen and nutrients, while the blood absorbs waste products from the cells before returning to the heart through blood vessels called veins. The deoxygenated blood is then pumped to the lungs in the pulmonary circulation. After oxygen has been absorbed and carbon dioxide eliminated, the blood returns to the heart. During exercise, the rate of circulation may increase several times to meet the body's demand for oxygen. The blood supply to some muscles may increase twelvefold while that to the digestive system falls by one third.

The heart and its chambers

The heart is a muscular organ about the size of a clenched fist and lies in the center of the chest, slightly to the left. It is divided into two halves, each of which contains an upper chamber (the atrium) and a lower chamber (the ventricle). The atria collect blood from various parts of the body, while the ventricles pump blood out of the heart. Each of the four chambers is joined to one or more blood vessels. The largest of these vessels, the aorta, is about the diameter of a garden hose. Forceful contractions of the ventricles pump blood out of the heart about 70 times per minute at rest. This pumping rate is called the heart rate and is measured in beats per minute. With each beat, a pressure wave travels along the arteries, causing their walls to expand. This wave, or pulse, can be felt where the arteries are close to the skin's surface. Between pulse waves, the elastic walls of the arteries rebound.

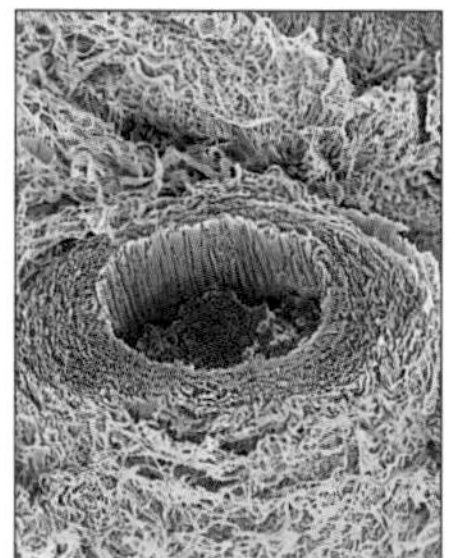

A small artery
The multilayered wall of the artery seen in this highly magnified image contains muscle and elastic fibers. Individual red blood cells inside the artery are also visible.

Heart muscle (myocardium) must work continuously for 24 hours a day without rest. Therefore, myocardial cells contain more and larger energy-producing units (mitochondria) than other types of body cells.

Heart rate and blood pressure

Heart rate is regulated by electrical impulses from the heart's pacemaker, the sinoatrial node, which is a small area of nervous tissue in the wall of the right atrium. Each impulse causes a rapid sequence of contractions, first in the atria and then in the ventricles, that corresponds to one heartbeat.

Blood pressure depends on the rate and force of the heart's contractions, the volume of blood pumped out, and the resistance to blood flow in the blood vessels, which varies with their size. Heart rate and blood pressure are controlled by the nervous system in the short term and by hormones, which act over a longer period.

FUNCTION Blood flow through the heart

Blood flows through veins into the heart's upper chambers (atria) and is pumped into the arteries by the lower chambers (ventricles). Deoxygenated blood collects in the right atrium and flows into the right ventricle, which pumps it to the lungs. Oxygenated blood returns from the lungs to the left atrium. The left ventricle then pumps this blood around the body.

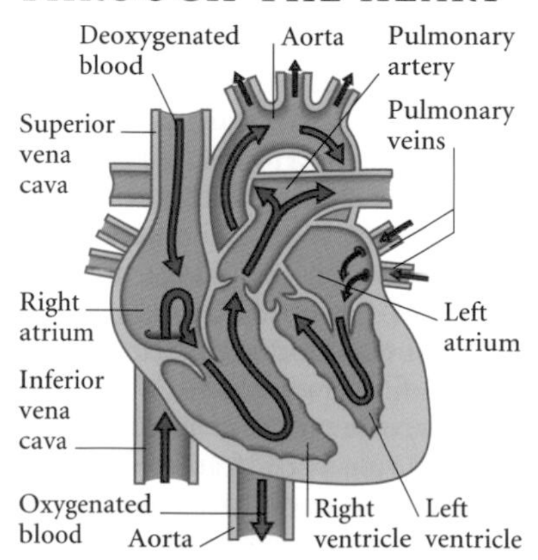
Deoxygenated blood
Aorta
Pulmonary artery
Superior vena cava
Pulmonary veins
Right atrium
Left atrium
Inferior vena cava
Oxygenated blood
Aorta
Right ventricle
Left ventricle

Two sides of the heart
The heart's right side pumps deoxygenated blood from the body to the lungs. The left side pumps oxygenated blood to the body.

STRUCTURE AND FUNCTION

THE BLOOD VESSELS

The cardiovascular system includes three types of blood vessels: arteries, veins, and capillaries. Placed end to end, they would circle the Earth nearly four times. The smallest vessels, the capillaries, make up 98 percent of this length. The largest artery, the aorta, emerges from the heart and branches into a network of progressively smaller arteries that carry blood to every part of the body. The smallest arteries join capillaries, which in turn join a network of tiny veins that merge into larger veins as they return blood to the heart.

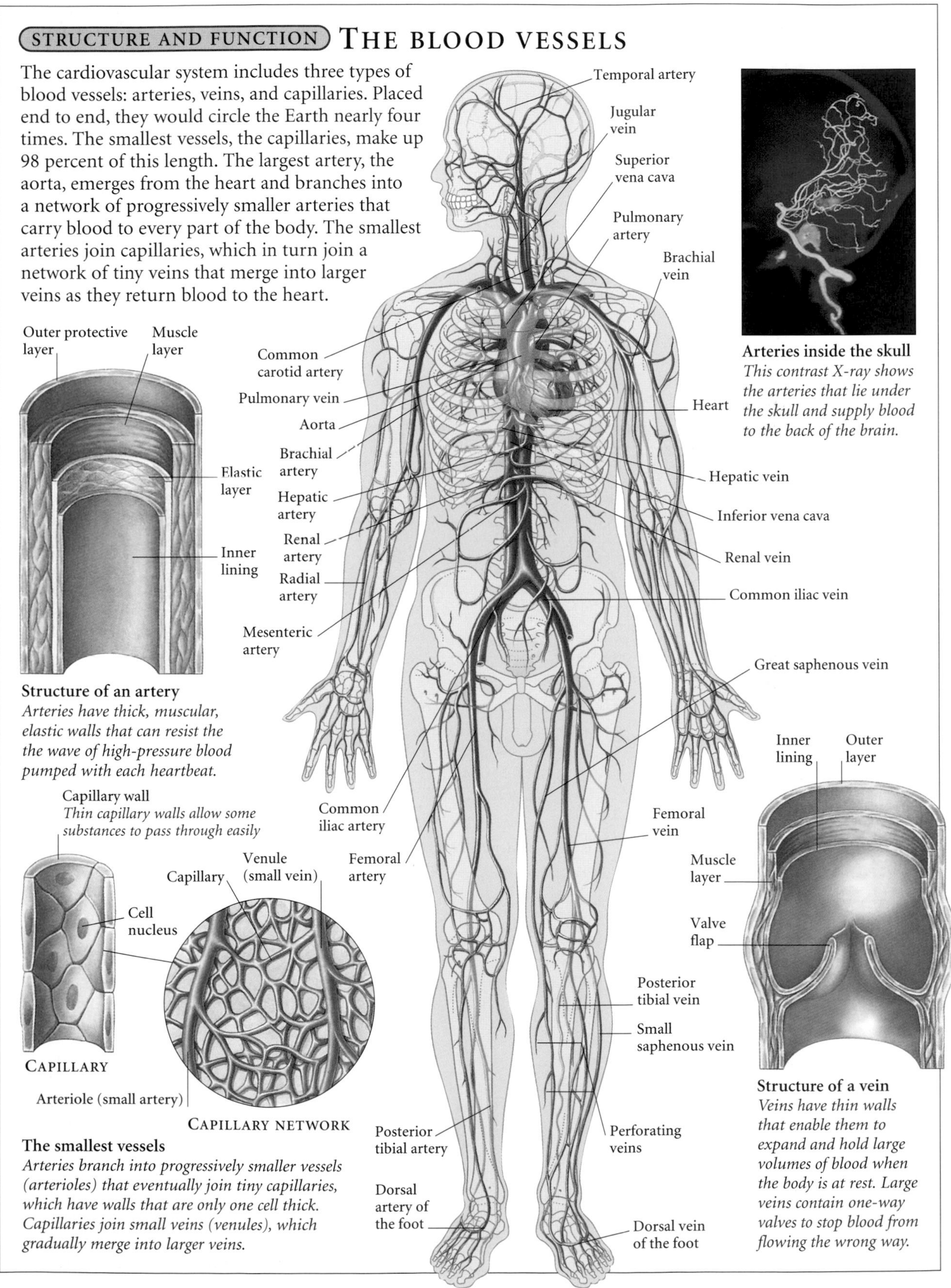
Temporal artery
Jugular vein
Superior vena cava
Pulmonary artery
Brachial vein
Common carotid artery
Pulmonary vein
Aorta
Brachial artery
Hepatic artery
Renal artery
Radial artery
Mesenteric artery
Heart
Hepatic vein
Inferior vena cava
Renal vein
Common iliac vein
Great saphenous vein
Common iliac artery
Femoral artery
Femoral vein
Posterior tibial vein
Small saphenous vein
Perforating veins
Posterior tibial artery
Dorsal artery of the foot
Dorsal vein of the foot
Outer protective layer
Muscle layer
Elastic layer
Inner lining
Capillary wall
Thin capillary walls allow some substances to pass through easily
Cell nucleus
Capillary
Venule (small vein)
Arteriole (small artery)
CAPILLARY
CAPILLARY NETWORK
Inner lining
Outer layer
Muscle layer
Valve flap

Arteries inside the skull
This contrast X-ray shows the arteries that lie under the skull and supply blood to the back of the brain.

Structure of an artery
Arteries have thick, muscular, elastic walls that can resist the the wave of high-pressure blood pumped with each heartbeat.

The smallest vessels
Arteries branch into progressively smaller vessels (arterioles) that eventually join tiny capillaries, which have walls that are only one cell thick. Capillaries join small veins (venules), which gradually merge into larger veins.

Structure of a vein
Veins have thin walls that enable them to expand and hold large volumes of blood when the body is at rest. Large veins contain one-way valves to stop blood from flowing the wrong way.

STRUCTURE — Structure of the heart

The heart is a hollow muscular pump consisting mainly of myocardium, a type of muscle that can work without resting. The interior of the heart is divided into two halves, each of which consists of an upper chamber and a lower chamber (the atrium and the ventricle). Each chamber connects to one or more blood vessels. Blood flow through these chambers is controlled by one-way valves.

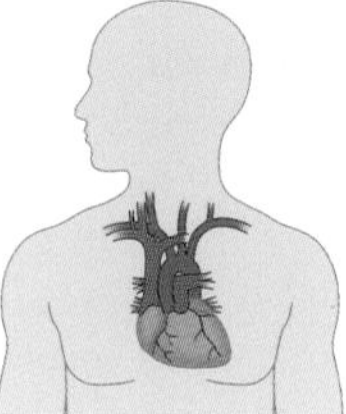

Location

Superior vena cava

Aorta
This is the main artery of the body

Pulmonary artery
Deoxygenated blood is carried to each lung by branches of this artery

Endocardium
This smooth layer lines the interior of the heart and is one cell thick

Pulmonary veins
Oxygenated blood is carried from the lungs to the heart by these veins

Left atrium

Aortic valve
The three leaflets (flaps) of the aortic valve allow one-way blood flow from the left ventricle into the aorta

Mitral valve
This valve has two leaflets; it allows one-way blood flow from the left atrium into the left ventricle

Left ventricle

Myocardium
Heart muscle is three times thicker on the left side, which pumps blood to the body, than on the right

Descending aorta

Inferior vena cava

Pulmonary valve
This valve has three leaflets (flaps); it allows blood to flow from the right ventricle into the pulmonary artery

Right atrium

Tricuspid valve
The three leaflets (flaps) of this valve allow one-way blood flow from the right atrium into the right ventricle

Pericardium
This double-layered membrane separates the heart from the lungs and chest wall

Right ventricle

Chordae tendineae
These fibrous strands attach the heart valve leaflets to the heart wall

Septum
The two sides of the heart are divided by this thick, muscular wall

Mitochondrion

Muscle cell

Heart muscle
The numerous mitochondria (energy-producing units) in heart muscle cells enable the heart to pump without resting.

FUNCTION — Blood supply to the heart

The coronary arteries branch off the aorta and surround and penetrate heart muscle. Arterioles and capillaries branch off from the arteries to supply heart muscle with oxygen-rich blood. Deoxygenated blood drains into the coronary veins, which carry it back into the heart's right atrium.

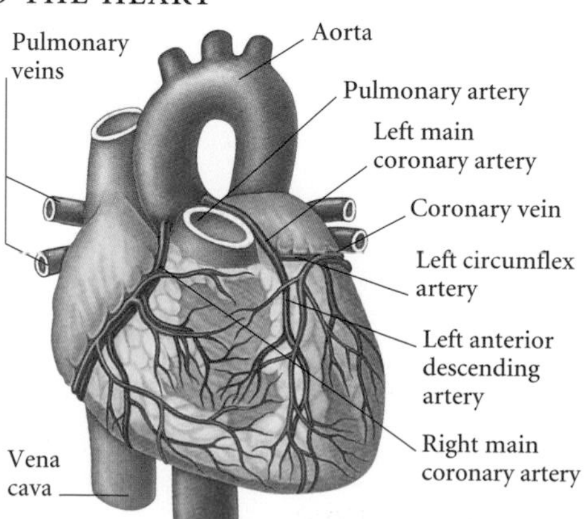
Pulmonary veins
Aorta
Pulmonary artery
Left main coronary artery
Coronary vein
Left circumflex artery
Left anterior descending artery
Right main coronary artery
Vena cava

The coronary arteries
There are two main coronary arteries, the left and the right. The left one branches into the left circumflex artery and the left anterior descending artery.

Valve leaflet

Chorda tendina

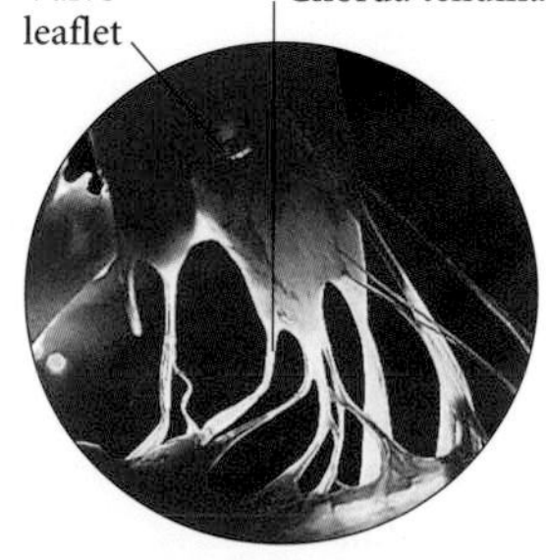

Anchoring the valves
Stringlike chordae tendineae anchor each valve leaflet to the heart wall, preventing it from being turned inside out.

FUNCTION How the heart beats

A single pumping action of the heart is called a heartbeat. A healthy adult heart beats at a rate of 60–80 beats per minute at rest and at up to 200 beats per minute during strenuous exercise. One-way valves inside the heart prevent blood from being pumped in the wrong direction. The rhythmic "lub-dub" sound of the heart is due to the heart valves shutting tightly.

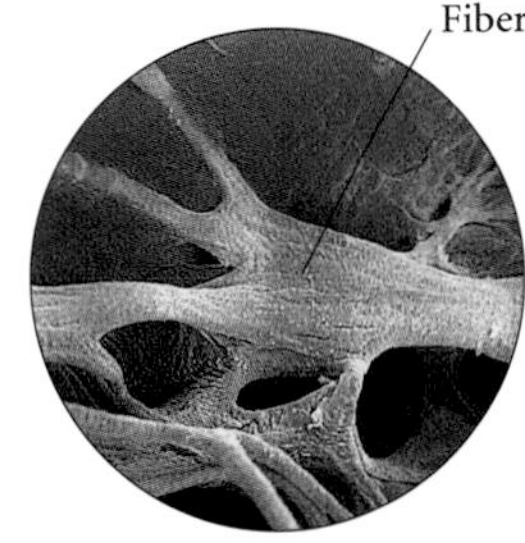
Fiber

Conducting fibers
Specialized muscle fibers in the walls of the heart conduct electrical impulses that regulate the heartbeat.

The heart cycle

A heartbeat has three phases. In diastole, the heart relaxes. During atrial systole, the atria contract, and in ventricular systole, the ventricles contract. The sinoatrial node (the heart's pacemaker) regulates the timing of the phases by sending electrical impulses to the atria and ventricles.

Diastole
The heart muscle relaxes, and blood flows into the atria from the pulmonary veins and vena cava. Near the end of this phase, the sinoatrial node emits an electrical impulse.

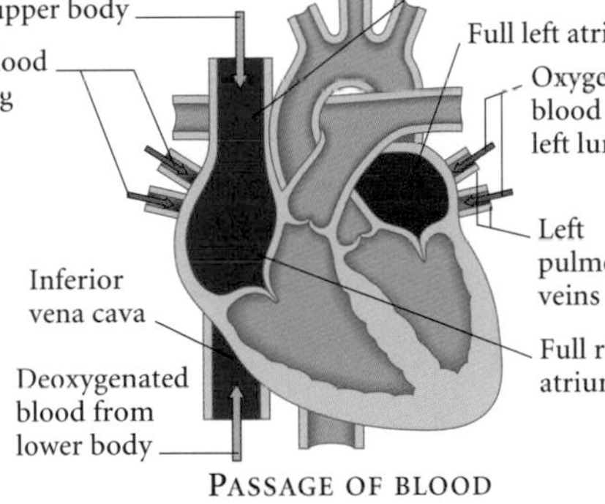
Deoxygenated blood from upper body
Superior vena cava
Oxygenated blood from right lung
Full left atrium
Oxygenated blood from left lung
Left pulmonary veins
Inferior vena cava
Full right atrium
Deoxygenated blood from lower body
PASSAGE OF BLOOD
Sinoatrial node
Electrical impulse
ELECTRICAL ACTIVITY

Atrial systole
The electrical impulse spreads through both atria. The impulse causes their muscular walls to contract and push blood into the ventricles. By the end of atrial systole, the impulse reaches the atrioventricular node, which is in the right atrium.

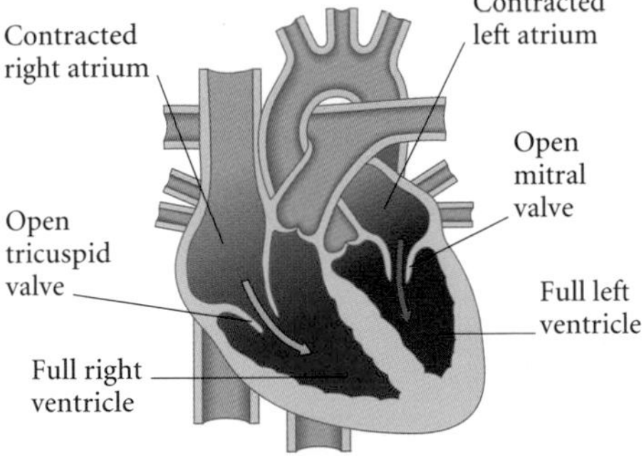
Contracted right atrium
Contracted left atrium
Open mitral valve
Open tricuspid valve
Full left ventricle
Full right ventricle
PASSAGE OF BLOOD

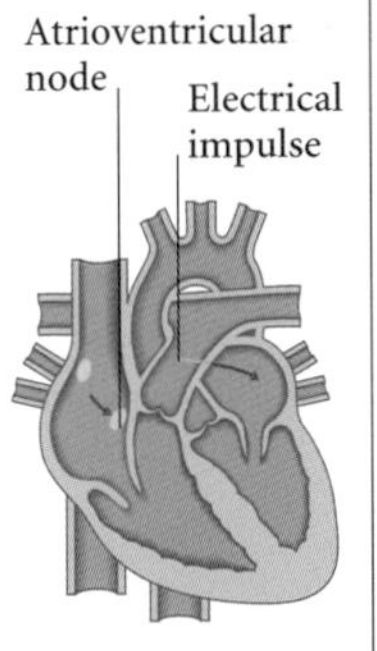
Atrioventricular node
Electrical impulse
ELECTRICAL ACTIVITY

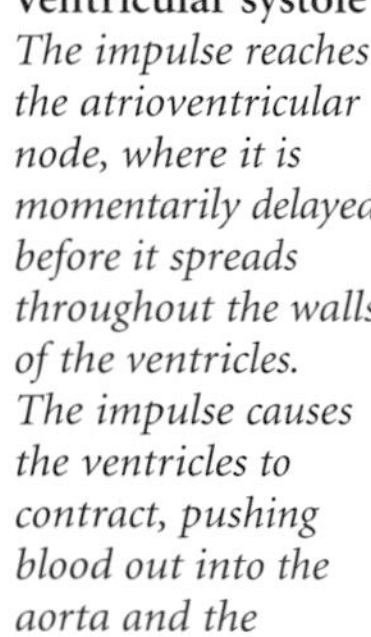

Ventricular systole
The impulse reaches the atrioventricular node, where it is momentarily delayed before it spreads throughout the walls of the ventricles. The impulse causes the ventricles to contract, pushing blood out into the aorta and the pulmonary arteries.

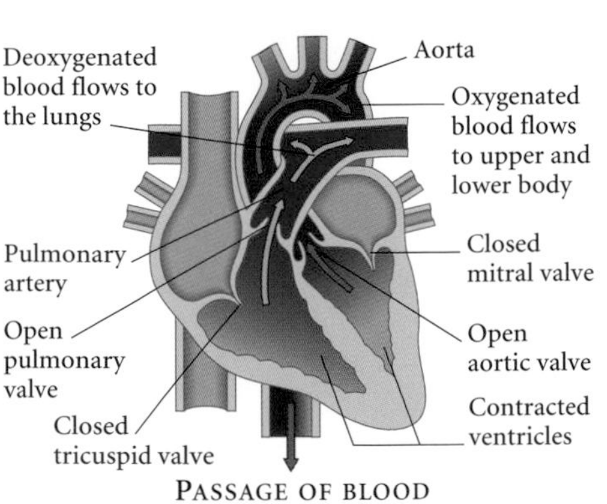
Deoxygenated blood flows to the lungs
Aorta
Oxygenated blood flows to upper and lower body
Pulmonary artery
Closed mitral valve
Open pulmonary valve
Open aortic valve
Closed tricuspid valve
Contracted ventricles
PASSAGE OF BLOOD

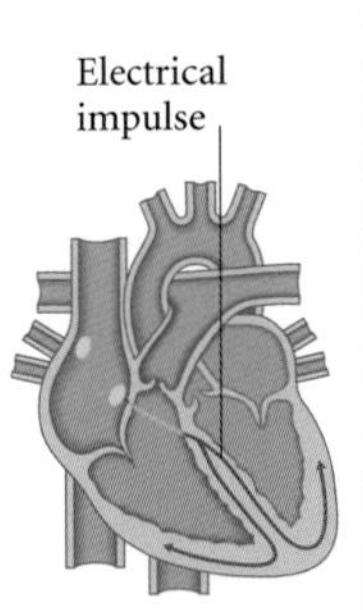
Electrical impulse
ELECTRICAL ACTIVITY

Heart valves

Heart valves consist of two or three cup-shaped leaflets (flaps). The leaflets consist mainly of collagen, a tough protein, and are covered in endocardium, a thin layer of tissue that lines the inside of the heart and joins the lining of the blood vessels.

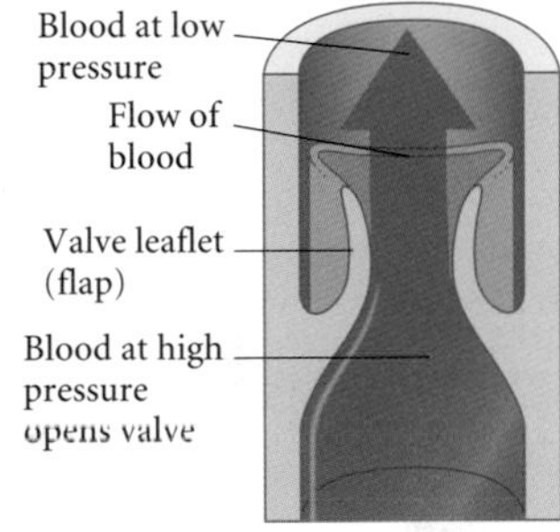
Blood at low pressure
Flow of blood
Valve leaflet (flap)
Blood at high pressure opens valve

Open heart valve
When a heart chamber contracts, the high pressure of the blood inside it pushes open the valve leaflets, and blood flows through to the other side of the valve.

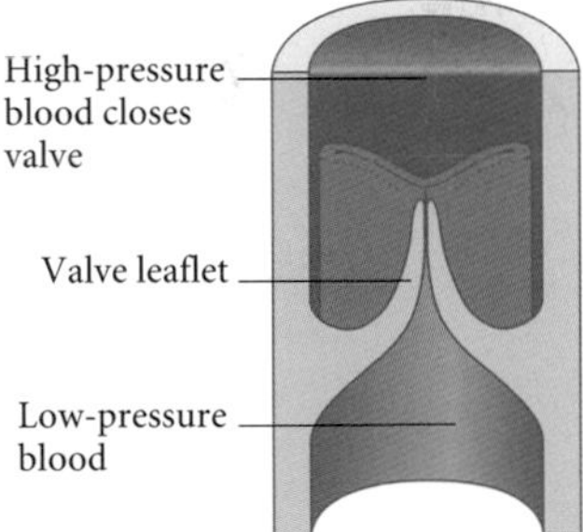
High-pressure blood closes valve
Valve leaflet
Low-pressure blood

Closed heart valve
The pressure of blood on the other side of the valve rises and snaps shut the valve leaflets. The closed valve prevents backflow.

Closed pulmonary valve
The pulmonary valve has three leaflets with rounded undersides that are attached to the inner wall of the pulmonary artery.

FUNCTION THE BLOOD CIRCULATION

Blood circulates in two linked circuits: the pulmonary, which carries blood to the lungs to be oxygenated, and the systemic, which supplies oxygenated blood to the body. Arteries carrying blood from the heart divide into smaller vessels called arterioles and then into capillaries, where nutrient and waste exchange occurs. Capillaries join up to form venules, which in turn join to form veins that carry blood back to the heart. The portal vein does not return blood to the heart but carries it to the liver.

A DOUBLE CIRCUIT

The heart powers the pulmonary and the systemic circulations. In the pulmonary circulation, deoxygenated blood travels to the lungs, where it absorbs oxygen before returning to the heart. This oxygenated blood is pumped around the body in the systemic circulation. Body tissues absorb oxygen, and deoxygenated blood returns to the heart to be pumped to the lungs again.

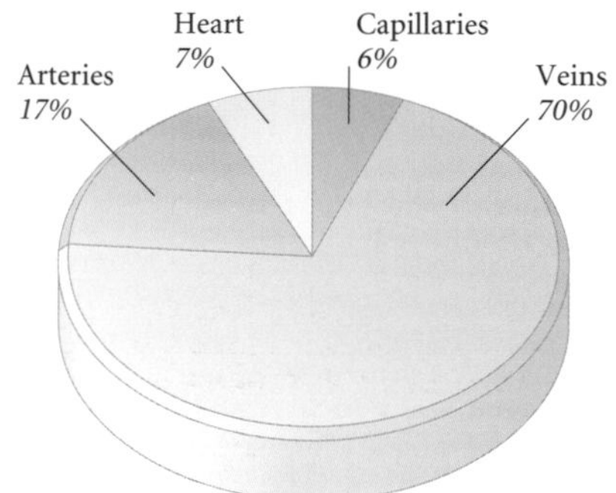

Heart 7%
Capillaries 6%
Arteries 17%
Veins 70%

Distribution of blood in the circulation
At rest, the veins act as a reservoir for blood, holding most of the body's blood volume. If an increase in blood supply is needed, the veins constrict and return more blood to the heart.

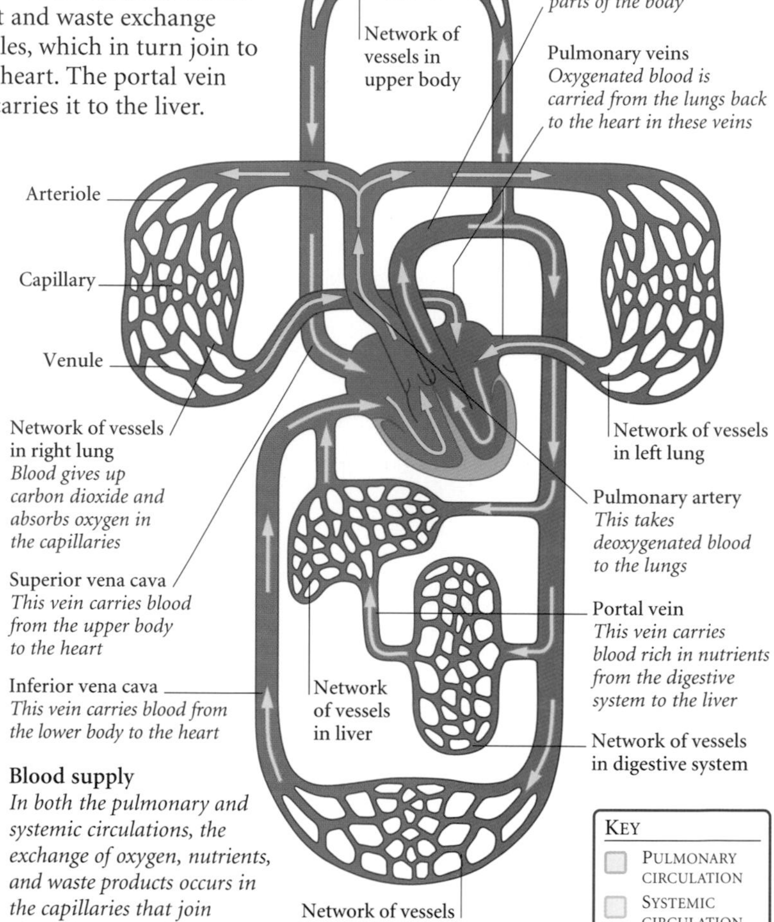

Aorta
This major artery carries oxygenated blood to all parts of the body
Network of vessels in upper body
Pulmonary veins
Oxygenated blood is carried from the lungs back to the heart in these veins
Arteriole
Capillary
Venule
Network of vessels in right lung
Blood gives up carbon dioxide and absorbs oxygen in the capillaries
Network of vessels in left lung
Pulmonary artery
This takes deoxygenated blood to the lungs
Superior vena cava
This vein carries blood from the upper body to the heart
Portal vein
This vein carries blood rich in nutrients from the digestive system to the liver
Inferior vena cava
This vein carries blood from the lower body to the heart
Network of vessels in liver
Network of vessels in digestive system
Network of vessels in lower body
KEY
PULMONARY CIRCULATION
SYSTEMIC CIRCULATION

Blood supply
In both the pulmonary and systemic circulations, the exchange of oxygen, nutrients, and waste products occurs in the capillaries that join arterioles to venules.

VENOUS RETURN

The blood pressure in the veins is about one tenth of that in the arteries. Various physical mechanisms ensure that there is adequate venous return (blood flow back to the heart). Many deep veins lie within muscles. When the muscles contract, they squeeze the veins and force blood back to the heart. The action of inhalation during breathing also draws blood to the heart. In addition, venous return from the upper body is assisted by gravity.

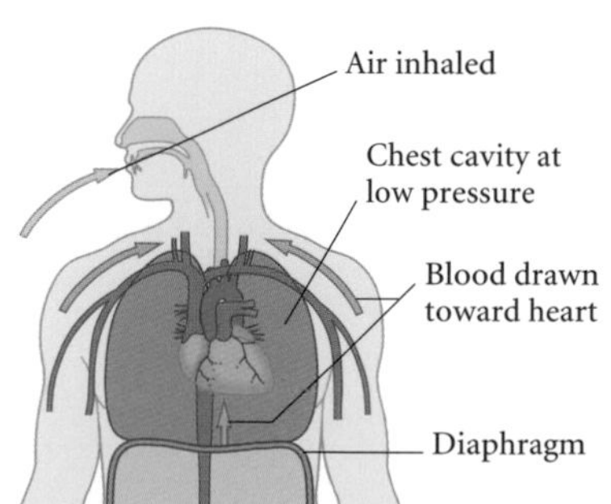

Air inhaled
Chest cavity at low pressure
Blood drawn toward heart
Diaphragm

Respiratory pump during inhalation
While inhaling, the chest cavity expands, lowering the pressure in the chest. The higher pressure in the rest of the body pushes blood in the veins toward the heart.

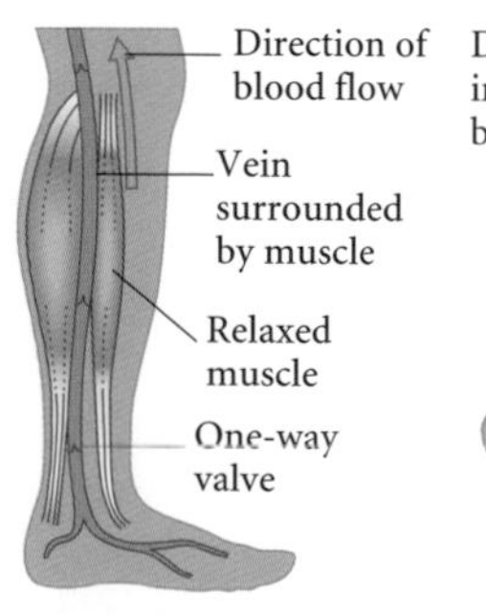

Direction of blood flow
Vein surrounded by muscle
Relaxed muscle
One-way valve

RELAXED MUSCLE

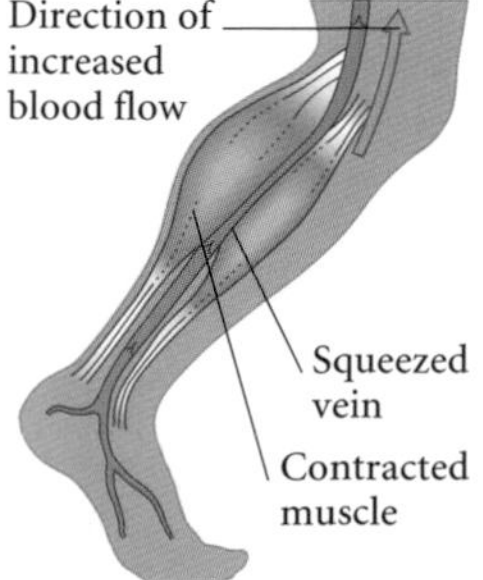

Direction of increased blood flow
Squeezed vein
Contracted muscle

CONTRACTED MUSCLE

Muscular pump
Muscles contract and relax as we move, squeezing the veins that pass through them and pushing blood back to the heart. One-way valves prevent backflow.

FUNCTION CONTROL OF BLOOD PRESSURE

Blood pressure in the arteries must be regulated to ensure an adequate supply of blood, and hence oxygen, to the organs. If arterial blood pressure is too low, not enough blood reaches body tissues. If it is too high, it may damage blood vessels and organs. Rapid changes in blood pressure trigger compensatory responses from the nervous system within seconds. These autonomic nervous responses do not involve the conscious parts of the brain. Longer-term changes are largely regulated by hormones that affect the volume of fluid excreted by the kidneys. Hormonal responses work over several hours.

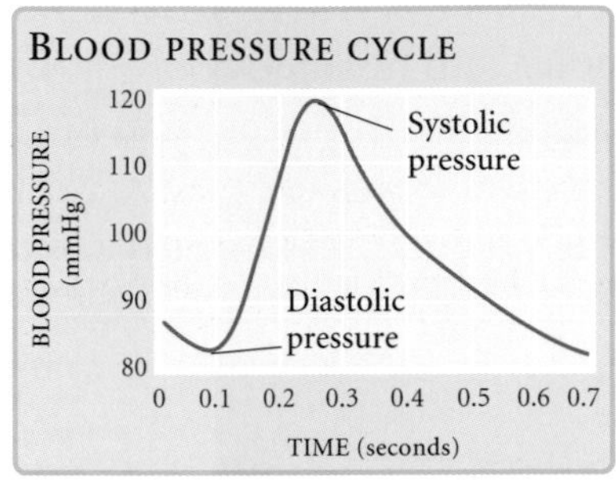
BLOOD PRESSURE CYCLE
BLOOD PRESSURE (mmHg)
120
110
100
90
80
Systolic pressure
Diastolic pressure
0 0.1 0.2 0.3 0.4 0.5 0.6 0.7
TIME (seconds)

Systolic and diastolic pressure
Arterial pressure is low while the heart fills with blood (diastolic pressure) but rises as the heart pumps blood out (systolic pressure). The units of pressure are millimeters of mercury (mmHg).

SHORT-TERM CONTROL OF BLOOD PRESSURE

Heavy bleeding or a sudden change in posture may cause a rapid change in blood pressure, to which the nervous system immediately responds. Baroreceptors (stretch receptors in the walls of the major arteries) detect pressure changes and send signals along sensory nerves to the brain. An autonomic response adjusts the heart rate, volume of blood pumped, and arterial diameter to restore normal pressure.

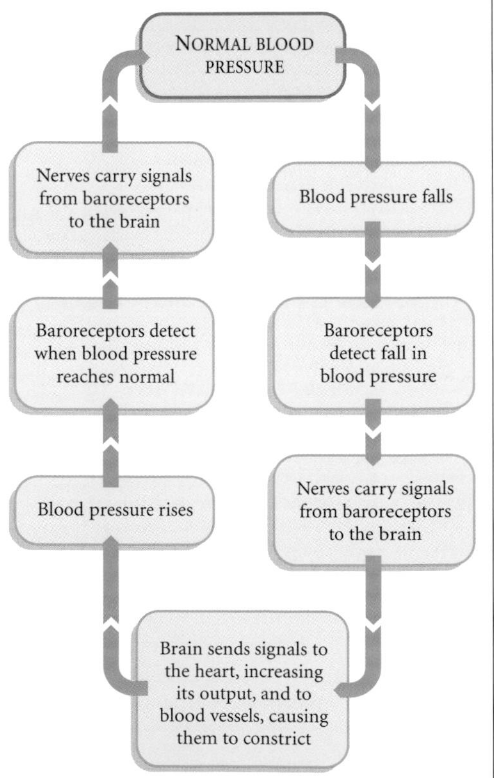
NORMAL BLOOD PRESSURE
Blood pressure falls
Baroreceptors detect fall in blood pressure
Nerves carry signals from baroreceptors to the brain
Brain sends signals to the heart, increasing its output, and to blood vessels, causing them to constrict
Blood pressure rises
Baroreceptors detect when blood pressure reaches normal
Nerves carry signals from baroreceptors to the brain

Response to falling blood pressure
Baroreceptors in the aorta and carotid arteries, which supply the head, detect a fall in blood pressure and send signals to the brain. The brain sends signals to the heart and blood vessels to restore normal pressure.

LONG-TERM CONTROL OF BLOOD PRESSURE

Blood pressure is controlled in the long term by the action of hormones. The kidneys respond to low blood pressure by secreting renin. This hormone is converted into angiotensin, which constricts arteries and raises blood pressure. The adrenal glands, hypothalamus, and heart also respond to high or low pressure by secreting aldosterone, ADH (antidiuretic hormone), and natriuretic hormone, respectively. These hormones alter the amount of fluid excreted by the kidneys, which affects the volume of blood in the body and hence the blood pressure.

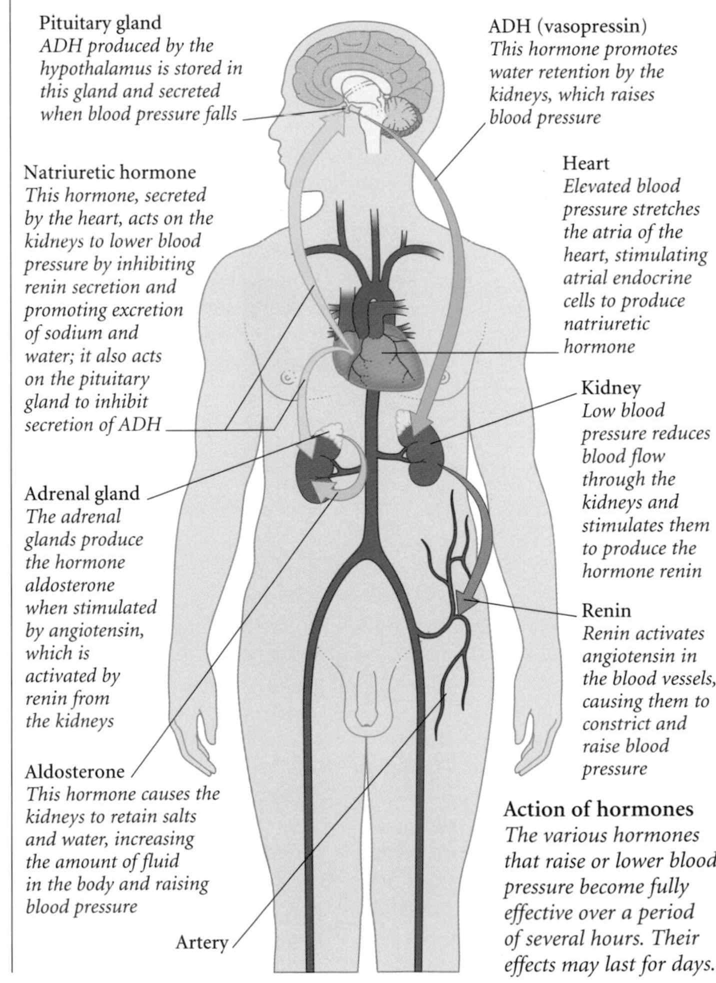
Pituitary gland
ADH produced by the hypothalamus is stored in this gland and secreted when blood pressure falls
ADH (vasopressin)
This hormone promotes water retention by the kidneys, which raises blood pressure
Natriuretic hormone
This hormone, secreted by the heart, acts on the kidneys to lower blood pressure by inhibiting renin secretion and promoting excretion of sodium and water; it also acts on the pituitary gland to inhibit secretion of ADH
Heart
Elevated blood pressure stretches the atria of the heart, stimulating atrial endocrine cells to produce natriuretic hormone
Kidney
Low blood pressure reduces blood flow through the kidneys and stimulates them to produce the hormone renin
Adrenal gland
The adrenal glands produce the hormone aldosterone when stimulated by angiotensin, which is activated by renin from the kidneys
Renin
Renin activates angiotensin in the blood vessels, causing them to constrict and raise blood pressure
Aldosterone
This hormone causes the kidneys to retain salts and water, increasing the amount of fluid in the body and raising blood pressure
Artery

Action of hormones
The various hormones that raise or lower blood pressure become fully effective over a period of several hours. Their effects may last for days.

MAJOR CARDIOVASCULAR DISORDERS

By the middle of the 20th century, heart disease was the leading cause of death in America and northern Europe. In America, the number of deaths caused by heart disease had peaked by the late 1960s. Coronary artery disease was the primary cause, although rheumatic fever and high blood pressure also claimed lives. However, over the last 30 years, there has been a steady decline in the number of deaths from heart disease in many countries.

This section covers the major disorders affecting the heart and the circulation. The first articles overlap to a certain extent because some cardiovascular disorders can lead to the development of others. Smoking, high-fat diets, being overweight, and lack of exercise are risk factors for the development of hypertension (high blood pressure) and atherosclerosis, in which the arteries are narrowed. Narrowing of the coronary arteries that supply the heart muscle can cause coronary artery disease, which itself is the major cause of angina and heart attacks. If the heart is damaged by coronary artery disease or a heart attack, it may be unable to pump blood efficiently around the rest of the body, resulting in heart failure. Heart failure can develop suddenly, or it may be a chronic disorder that develops over a number of years.

The last articles in the section cover hypotension, the medical term for low blood pressure, and shock. Shock is a medical emergency that requires immediate treatment in the hospital.

KEY ANATOMY

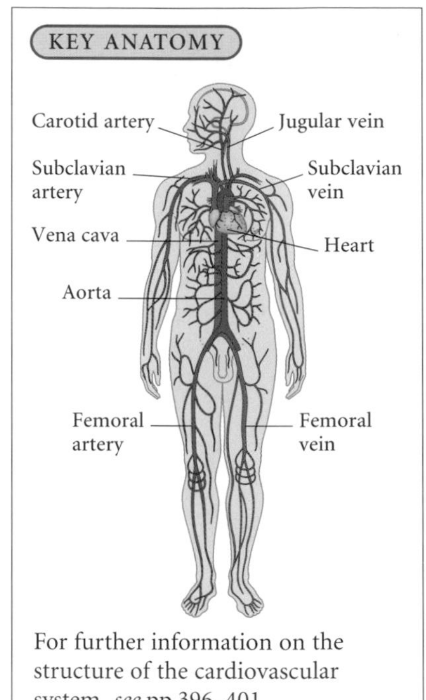
Carotid artery
Jugular vein
Subclavian artery
Subclavian vein
Vena cava
Heart
Aorta
Femoral artery
Femoral vein

For further information on the structure of the cardiovascular system, *see* pp.396–401.

Atherosclerosis

Accumulation of cholesterol and other fatty substances in the walls of arteries, causing them to narrow

 AGE More common with increasing age

 GENDER More common in males until age 60, then equal incidence

 GENETICS Sometimes runs in families

 LIFESTYLE Smoking, a high-fat diet, lack of exercise, and excess weight are risk factors

Atherosclerosis is a disease that results in the arteries becoming narrowed. The condition can affect arteries in any area of the body and is a major cause of stroke (p.532), heart attack (*see* MYOCARDIAL INFARCTION, p.410), and poor circulation in the legs (*see* LOWER LIMB ISCHEMIA, p.434). The arteries become narrowed when fatty substances, such as cholesterol, that are carried in the blood accumulate on the inside lining of the arteries and form yellow deposits called atheroma. These deposits restrict the blood flow through the arteries. In addition, the muscle layer of the artery wall becomes thickened, narrowing the artery even more. Platelets (tiny blood cells responsible for clotting) may collect in clumps on the surface of the deposits and initiate the formation of blood clots. A large clot may then completely block the artery and result in an organ being deprived of oxygen.

Atherosclerosis is much more common in America and northern Europe than in developing countries in Africa and Asia. It also becomes more common with increasing age. In America, autopsies on young men who have died in accidents reveal that nearly all have some atheroma in their large arteries, and most people who die in middle age are found to have widespread atherosclerosis when autopsied. However, the condition rarely causes symptoms until age 45–50, and many people do not realize that they have the condition until they have a heart attack or stroke.

The incidence of atherosclerosis is much lower in women before menopause than in men. By age 60, the risk of women developing it has increased until it is equal with the risk for men.

WHAT ARE THE CAUSES?

The risk of developing atherosclerosis is determined largely by the level of cholesterol in the bloodstream, which depends on dietary and genetic factors. Since cholesterol levels are closely linked with diet, atherosclerosis is most common in Western countries where people eat a diet which is high in fat and calories. Some disorders, such as diabetes mellitus (p.687) can be associated with a high cholesterol level regardless of the person's diet. Certain inherited disorders also result in a high level of fats in the bloodstream (*see* INHERITED HYPERLIPOPROTEINEMIAS, p.692).

In addition to high blood cholesterol levels, factors that make atherosclerosis more likely are smoking, not exercising regularly, having high blood pressure (*see* HYPERTENSION, opposite page), and being overweight, especially if a lot of fat is around the waist.

WHAT ARE THE SYMPTOMS?

There are usually no symptoms in the early stages of atherosclerosis. Later, symptoms are caused by the reduced or total absence of a blood supply to the

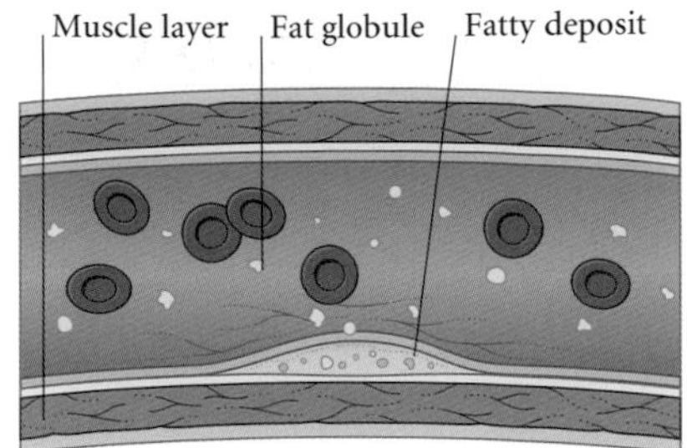
Muscle layer
Fat globule
Fatty deposit

EARLY ATHEROSCLEROSIS

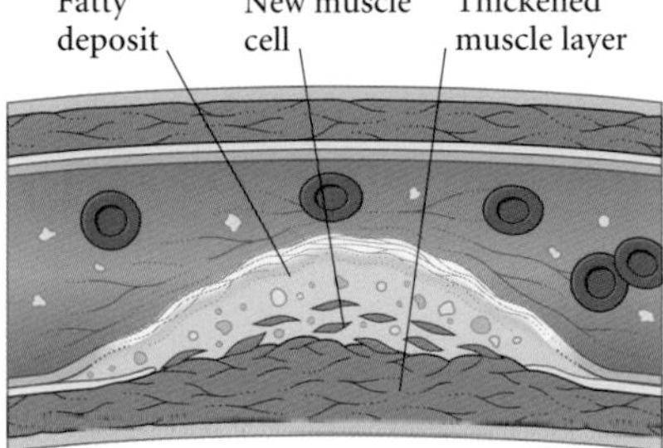
Fatty deposit
New muscle cell
Thickened muscle layer

ADVANCED ATHEROSCLEROSIS

How atherosclerosis develops

Fatty substances gradually accumulate in the lining of the artery wall, and the muscle layer thickens as new muscle cells form in the fatty deposit. As a result, the artery becomes progressively narrowed.

organs supplied by the affected arteries. If the coronary arteries, which supply the heart muscle, are partially blocked, symptoms may include the chest pain of angina (p.407). If there is a complete blockage in a coronary artery, there may be a sudden, often fatal, heart attack. Many strokes are a result of atherosclerosis in the arteries that supply blood to the brain. If atherosclerosis affects the arteries in the legs, the first symptom may be cramping pain when walking caused by poor blood flow to the leg muscles. With some inherited lipid disorders, fatty deposits may develop on tendons or under the skin in visible lumps.

HOW IS IT DIAGNOSED?

Since atherosclerosis has no symptoms until blood flow has been restricted, it is important to screen for the disorder before it becomes advanced and causes damage to the organs of the body. Routine medical checkups include screening for the major risk factors of atherosclerosis, particularly raised blood cholesterol levels, high blood pressure, and diabetes mellitus. Some current recommendations suggest that all adults should have their cholesterol levels measured at intervals of at least every 5 years after age 30.

If you develop symptoms of atherosclerosis, your doctor may arrange tests to assess the damage both to the arteries and to the organs they supply. Blood flow in affected blood vessels can be imaged by Doppler ultrasound scanning (p.432) or coronary angiography (p.408), in which a contrast dye is injected through a catheter, and a series of X-rays taken. If your doctor thinks that the coronary arteries are affected, an ECG (p.406) may be carried out to monitor the electrical activity of the heart and imaging techniques, such as angiography and radionuclide scanning (p.251), may be used to look at the blood supply to the heart. Some of these tests may be done as you exercise in order to check how the heart functions when it is put under stress (*see* EXERCISE TESTING, p.407).

WHAT IS THE TREATMENT?

The best treatment is to prevent atherosclerosis from progressing. Preventive measures include following a healthy lifestyle by eating a low-fat diet, not smoking, exercising regularly, and maintaining the recommended weight for your height. These measures lead to a lower than average risk of developing significant atherosclerosis.

If you are in a good state of health but have been found to have a high blood cholesterol level, your doctor will advise you to adopt a low-fat diet. You may also be offered drugs that decrease your blood cholesterol level (*see* LIPID-LOWERING DRUGS, p.935). For people who have had a heart attack, research has shown that there may be a benefit in lowering blood cholesterol levels, even if the cholesterol level is within the average range for healthy people.

If you have atherosclerosis and are experiencing symptoms of the condition, your doctor may prescribe a drug such as aspirin to reduce the risk of blood clots forming on the damaged artery lining (*see* DRUGS THAT PREVENT BLOOD CLOTTING, p.904).

If you are thought to be at a high risk of severe complications, your doctor may recommend surgical treatment, such as coronary angioplasty (p.409), in which a balloon is inflated inside the artery to widen it and improve blood flow. Alternatively, your doctor may refer you for bypass surgery (*see* CORONARY ARTERY BYPASS GRAFT, p.411) if blockages are serious (*see* CORONARY ARTERY DISEASE, p.405) and not suitable for angioplasty.

WHAT IS THE PROGNOSIS?

A healthy diet and lifestyle can slow the development of atherosclerosis in most people. If you do have a myocardial infarction or a stroke, you can reduce the risk of having further complications by taking preventive measures (*see* LIFE AFTER A HEART ATTACK, p.412).

(WWW) ONLINE SITES: p.1032

Hypertension

Persistent high blood pressure that may damage the arteries and the heart

 AGE More common with increasing age

 GENDER More common in males

 GENETICS Sometimes runs in families

 LIFESTYLE Stress, alcohol abuse, a high-salt diet, and excess weight are risk factors

High blood pressure, a condition also known as hypertension, puts strain on the heart and arteries, resulting in damage to delicate tissues. If it is left untreated, hypertension may eventually affect the eyes and kidneys. The higher the blood pressure, the greater the risk that complications will develop such as heart attack (*see* MYOCARDIAL INFARCTION, p.410), coronary artery disease (p.405), and stroke (p.532).

Blood pressure varies naturally with activity, rising during exercise or stress and falling during rest. It also varies among individuals, gradually increasing with age and weight.

Blood pressure is expressed as two values given in units of millimeters of mercury (mmHg). The blood pressure of a resting, healthy young adult should not be more than 120/80 mmHg. In general, a person is considered to have hypertension when his or her blood pressure is persistently higher than 140/90 mmHg, even at rest.

Hypertension does not usually cause symptoms, but, if your blood pressure is very high, you may have headaches,

TEST BLOOD PRESSURE MEASUREMENT

Blood pressure measurement is a routine part of having a physical examination. A measuring device called a sphygmomanometer gives a blood pressure reading as systolic pressure (the higher figure) when the heart contracts and diastolic pressure when the heart relaxes. A healthy young adult has a blood pressure of about 120/80 mmHg. Your blood pressure may be taken when you are sitting, standing, or lying down.

During the procedure
An inflatable cuff is wrapped around your upper arm and inflated using a bulb. The cuff is slowly deflated while the doctor listens to the blood flow through an artery in your arm using a stethoscope.

Sphygmomanometer

Inflatable cuff

Stethoscope

Bulb
The doctor uses the bulb to inflate and deflate the cuff

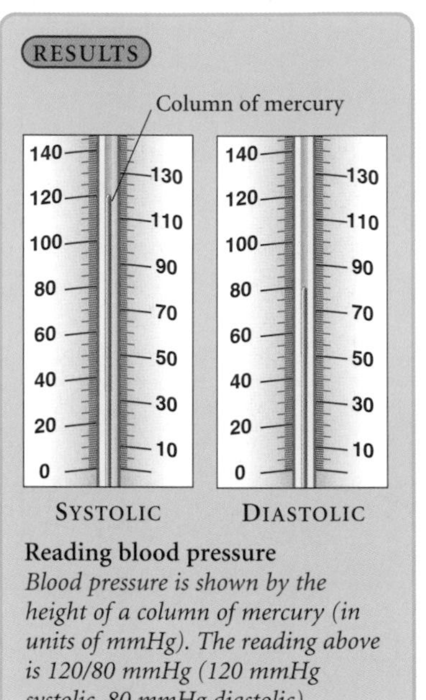
RESULTS
Column of mercury
140
120
100
80
60
40
20
0
130
110
90
70
50
30
10
SYSTOLIC
DIASTOLIC

Reading blood pressure
Blood pressure is shown by the height of a column of mercury (in units of mmHg). The reading above is 120/80 mmHg (120 mmHg systolic, 80 mmHg diastolic).

dizziness, or blurry vision. However, in most cases, the only symptoms that develop are those due to the damage caused by hypertension. By the time these arise and hypertension becomes evident, irreversible damage to arteries and organs has occurred. Hypertension is sometimes called the "silent killer" because individuals may have a fatal stroke or heart attack without warning.

In the last 20 years, health education and screening programs have led to many more people being diagnosed with hypertension at an early stage before symptoms occur. Early diagnosis, together with improved treatments, has substantially reduced the incidence of heart attacks and strokes.

WHAT ARE THE CAUSES?

In about 9 in 10 people with hypertension, there is no obvious cause for the condition. However, both lifestyle and genetic factors may contribute. The condition is found to be most common in middle aged and elderly people. This is because the arteries become more rigid with age. High blood pressure is also more common among men. People who are overweight or drink large amounts of alcohol are more likely to develop hypertension, and a stressful lifestyle may aggravate the condition. For this reason, hypertension occurs most often in developed countries. The condition is rare in countries that have a low-salt diet, suggesting that salt may be a contributing factor. A tendency to develop hypertension may be inherited.

In a minority of cases, an underlying cause of the hypertension is identified, such as kidney disease or a hormonal disorder, such as hyperaldosteronism (p.685) or Cushing syndrome (p.684). Some drugs, such as combined oral contraceptives and corticosteroids (p.930), can cause hypertension.

In pregnant women, hypertension can lead to the development of the potentially life-threatening conditions preeclampsia and eclampsia (p.794). The elevated blood pressure usually returns to normal after the birth.

ARE THERE COMPLICATIONS?

The risk of damage to the arteries, heart, and kidneys increases with the severity of hypertension and the length of time for which it is present. Arteries that have been damaged are at greater risk of becoming narrowed by atherosclerosis (p.402), a disease in which cholesterol and other fatty deposits build up in vessel walls, causing them to narrow and restricting blood flow.

Atherosclerosis is more likely in people who smoke or who have high blood cholesterol levels. Atherosclerosis of the coronary arteries may lead eventually to chest pain (*see* ANGINA, p.407) or to a heart attack. In other arteries in the body, atherosclerosis may result in disorders such as aortic aneurysm (p.430) or stroke. Hypertension puts strain on the heart that may eventually lead to chronic heart failure (p.413).

Damage to the arteries in the kidneys may result in chronic kidney failure (p.706). The arteries in the retina in the eye may also be damaged by hypertension (*see* RETINOPATHY, p.579).

HOW IS IT DIAGNOSED?

It is important that you have your blood pressure measured on an intermittant basis after age 21 (*see* BLOOD PRESSURE MEASUREMENT, above). If your blood pressure measures at more than 140/90 mmHg, your doctor may ask you to return in a few weeks so that he or she can check it again. Some individuals become anxious when visiting their doctor, which may cause a temporary rise in blood pressure. Therefore, a diagnosis of hypertension is usually not made unless you have elevated blood pressure on three separate occasions. If your readings are variable, your doctor may arrange for you to have a portable device so that you can measure your blood pressure regularly at home.

If you have hypertension, your doctor may arrange for tests that check for organ damage. Tests for heart damage include echocardiography (p.425) or electrocardiography (*see* ECG, p.406). Your eyes may be examined to look for damaged blood vessels. You may also have tests to look for other factors, such as a high blood cholesterol level, that may increase your risk of a heart attack.

If you are young or have severe hypertension, your doctor may recommend tests to identify the underlying cause. For example, urine and blood tests and ultrasound scanning (p.250) may be arranged to look for kidney disease or a hormonal disorder.

What is the treatment?

Hypertension cannot usually be cured but can be controlled with treatment. If you have mild hypertension, changing your lifestyle is often the most effective way of lowering your blood pressure. You should reduce your salt and alcohol consumption and try to keep your weight within the ideal range (*see* ARE YOU A HEALTHY WEIGHT?, p.53). If you smoke, you should stop.

If self-help measures are not effective in reducing your blood pressure, your doctor may prescribe antihypertensive drugs (p.897). These drugs work in different ways, and you may be prescribed just one type of drug or a combination of several. The type of drug and the dosage are tailored to the individual, and it may take some time to find the right combination and dosage. If you develop side effects from drug treatment, you should consult your doctor so that the medication can be adjusted.

Some doctors recommend that you regularly measure your blood pressure yourself. Self-monitoring helps your doctor evaluate your drug treatment.

If your hypertension has an obvious underlying medical cause, such as a hormonal disorder, treatment of this disorder may result in your blood pressure returning to a normal level.

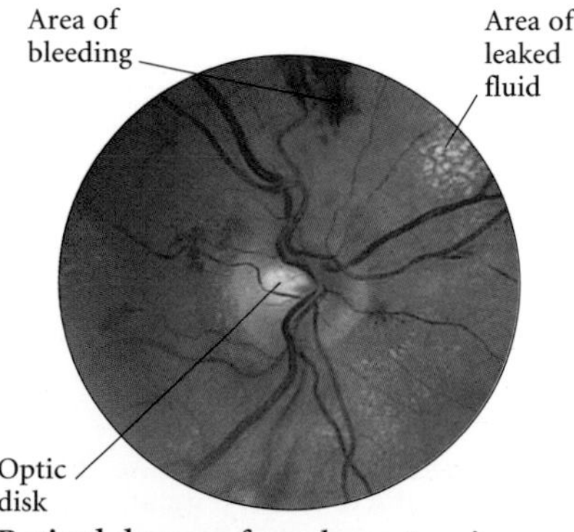
Area of bleeding
Area of leaked fluid
Optic disk

Retinal damage from hypertension
Damage to the small blood vessels in the retina at the back of the eye has resulted in blood and fluid leaking into the retina.

What is the prognosis?

The prognosis depends on how high your blood pressure is and how long it has been high. In most cases, lifestyle changes and drug treatment can control blood pressure and reduce the risk of complications. These measures usually need to be maintained for life.The greatest risk of complications is with long-standing, severe hypertension.

(WWW) ONLINE SITES: p.1032

Coronary artery disease

Narrowing of the coronary arteries that supply the heart muscle with blood, leading to heart damage

 AGE More common with increasing age

 GENDER More common in males until age 60, then equal incidence

GENETICS Sometimes runs in families

LIFESTYLE Smoking, a high-fat diet, lack of exercise, and excess weight are risk factors

The coronary arteries, which branch from the main artery in the body, the aorta, supply the heart muscle with oxygen-rich blood. In coronary artery disease (CAD), sometimes called coronary heart disease, one or more of the coronary arteries is narrowed. Blood flow through the arteries is restricted, which can lead to chest pain or even damage to the heart muscle. Heart disorders, including heart attacks (*see* MYOCARDIAL INFARCTION, p.410) and the chest pain of angina (p.407), are usually caused by CAD. The condition is therefore a leading cause of death in many Western countries. In Canada, approximately 1 in 5 deaths is the result of CAD. The prevalence rates of smoking, high blood pressure, and obesity run parallel to the rates of CAD. However, in many parts of the world, mortality from CAD is rising. This increase is probably a result of changing lifestyle factors.

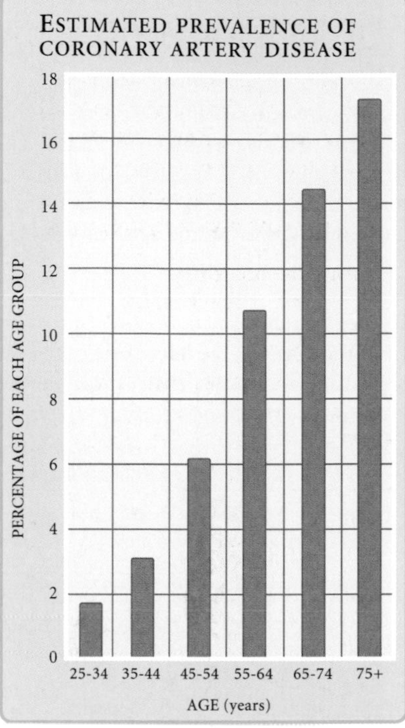
ESTIMATED PREVALENCE OF CORONARY ARTERY DISEASE
PERCENTAGE OF EACH AGE GROUP
0
2
4
6
8
10
12
14
16
18
25-34
35-44
45-54
55-64
65-74
75+
AGE (years)

Prevalence of coronary artery disease
The percentage of people (the prevalence) affected by coronary artery disease, which causes restricted blood supply to the heart, steadily increases with age. More than 1 in 6 people over age 65 is affected.

What are the causes?

Coronary artery disease is usually caused by atherosclerosis (p.402), a disease in which fatty substances carried in the blood accumulate on the inside of the artery walls. These deposits may narrow the arteries, thereby restricting the blood flow through them. If a blood clot forms or lodges in the narrowed area of an artery, that artery can become completely blocked. CAD that is caused by atherosclerosis is more likely if your blood cholesterol level is high and you eat a high-fat diet. CAD has also been linked to smoking, obesity, lack of exercise, diabetes mellitus (p.687), and high blood pressure (*see* HYPERTENSION, p.403).

After menopause, the levels of estrogen drop, and by age 60 women have the same risk of developing CAD as men although their mortality remains lower.

Rarely, the coronary arteries are narrowed by inflammation, which may be due to the autoimmune disorder polyarteritis nodosa (p.465), or Kawasaki disease (p.837), a disorder that affects children. Temporary narrowing can be caused by spasm in the artery wall.

WHAT ARE THE SYMPTOMS?

In the early stages of CAD, there are often no symptoms. In the later stages, the first symptom is usually either pain in the chest on exertion, a condition known as angina, or a heart attack. Some people with CAD may develop an abnormality of the heart rhythm (*see* ARRHYTHMIAS, p.415), causing palpitations (awareness of the heartbeat), lightheadedness, or loss of consciousness. Some severe arrhythmias can cause the heart to stop pumping completely (*see* CARDIAC ARREST, p.419), which accounts for most of the sudden deaths from CAD.

In elderly people, CAD may lead to chronic heart failure (p.413), in which the heart gradually becomes too weak to provide an adequate circulation of blood around the body. Chronic heart failure may then lead to the accumulation of excess fluid in the lungs and tissues, causing additional symptoms such as shortness of breath and swollen ankles.

TEST ECG

ECG (electrocardiography) is used to record the electrical activity of the heart. The procedure is frequently used to diagnose abnormal heart rhythms and to investigate the cause of chest pain. Several electrodes are attached to the skin to transmit the electrical activity of the heart to an ECG machine. Several traces are produced at the same time. Each trace shows electrical activity in different areas of the heart. The test usually takes several minutes to complete and is safe and painless.

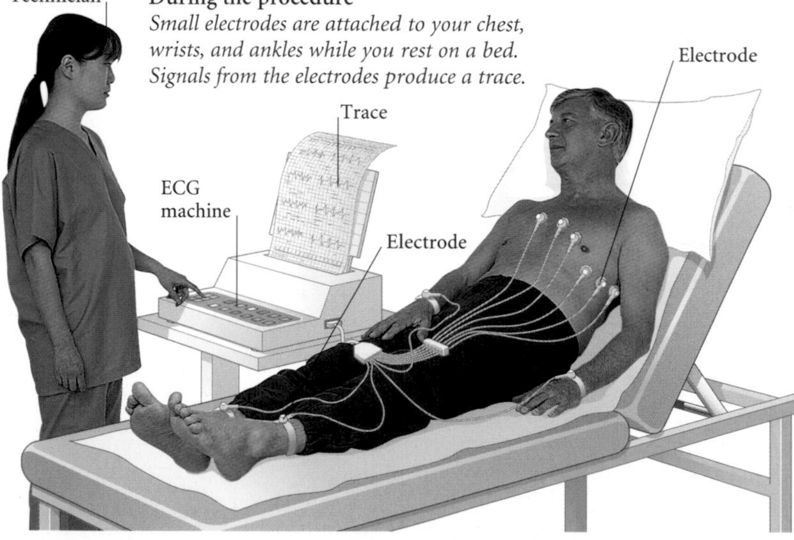
Technician
Electrode
Trace
ECG machine
Electrode

During the procedure
Small electrodes are attached to your chest, wrists, and ankles while you rest on a bed. Signals from the electrodes produce a trace.

RESULTS

ECG tracing
This trace from an ECG machine shows the normal electrical activity produced by one area of the heart as it contracts during three heartbeats.

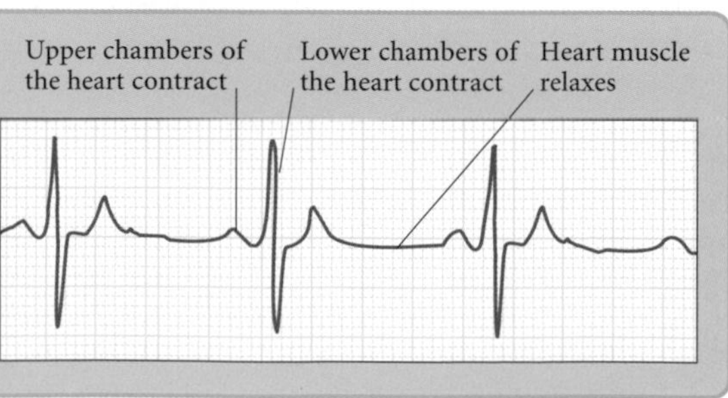
Upper chambers of the heart contract
Lower chambers of the heart contract
Heart muscle relaxes

HOW IS IT DIAGNOSED?

Often, CAD is detected only during a routine health checkup or an assessment of a predisposing disorder, such as high blood pressure. CAD is often diagnosed when symptoms develop. If you have symptoms that suggest CAD, such as chest pain, your doctor may arrange a series of tests to establish the severity of the problem.

These tests include an ECG (left) in order to monitor the heart's electrical activity and radionuclide scanning (p.251) to show whether the blood supply to the heart muscle is adequate. You may also have exercise testing (opposite page) to check how the heart performs under stress, as well as echocardiography (p.425), an ultrasound technique that images the heart muscle and valves. The imaging technique MRI (p.248), which uses magnets and radio waves rather than radiation to provide detailed sectional images of internal organs and structures on a computer, is also increasingly used to detect heart abnormalities.

If these tests suggest that the blood supply to your heart is inadequate, your doctor may refer you for coronary angiography (p.408). In this procedure, a contrast dye is injected into the bloodstream to enable the arteries to be seen on a series of X-rays. Angiography detects blocked or seriously narrowed sections of an artery and provides your doctor with the information he or she needs to decide whether or not you require surgical treatment.

WHAT IS THE TREATMENT?

Treatment for CAD falls into three categories: lifestyle changes to reduce the risk of CAD becoming worse, drug treatments to improve the function of the heart and help relieve symptoms, and surgical procedures, such as coronary angioplasty (p.409), that improve the blood supply to the heart muscle by widening the coronary arteries.

If you are diagnosed as having CAD, you should adopt a healthier lifestyle, with a low-fat diet and regular exercise. If you smoke, you should stop.

The drugs used to treat CAD depend on your symptoms and their severity and on the cause of the disorder. If tests

TEST EXERCISE TESTING

Exercise (stress) testing is usually done when coronary artery disease is suspected. It is used to assess heart function when it is put under stress. The test involves raising your heart rate by exercising, generally using a treadmill with an adjustable slope or an exercise bicycle, and monitoring the heart's function. The exercise is tailored to ensure your heart is tested adequately without putting you at risk. Various methods of monitoring may be used, including radionuclide scanning (p.251), which can image the heart's function, and ECG, which monitors the heart's electrical activity.

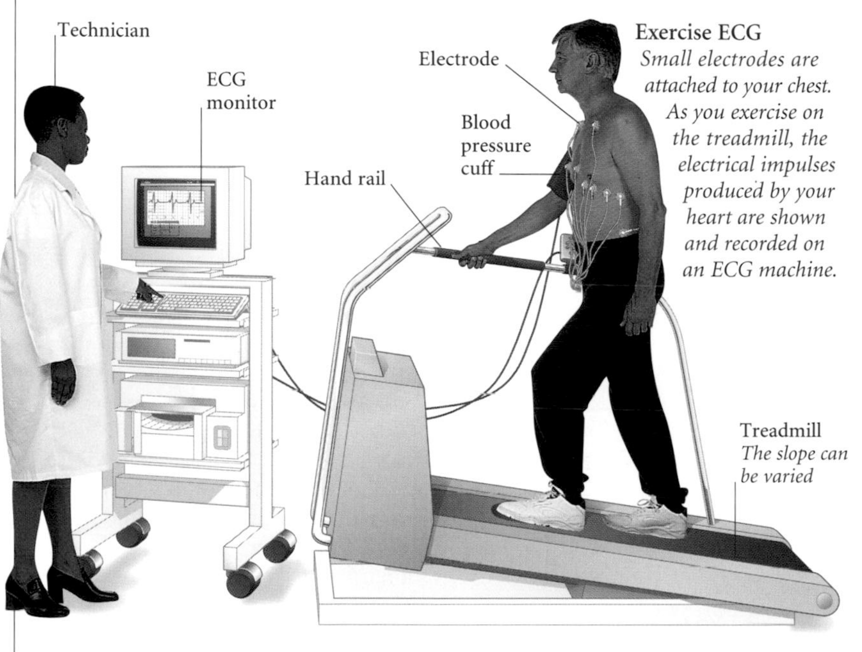
Technician
ECG monitor
Electrode
Blood pressure cuff
Hand rail
Treadmill
The slope can be varied

Exercise ECG
Small electrodes are attached to your chest. As you exercise on the treadmill, the electrical impulses produced by your heart are shown and recorded on an ECG machine.

RESULTS

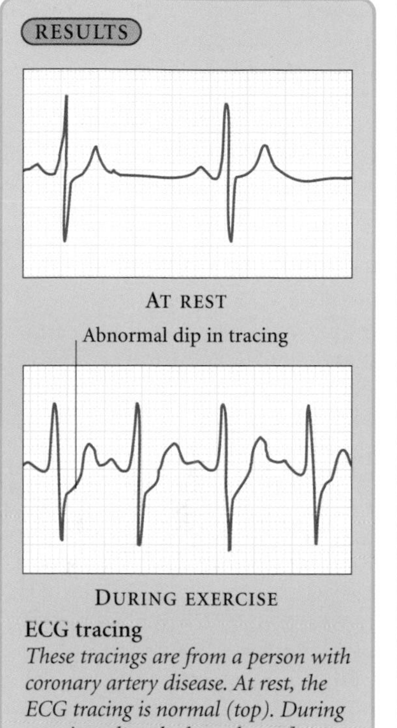
AT REST
Abnormal dip in tracing
DURING EXERCISE

ECG tracing
These tracings are from a person with coronary artery disease. At rest, the ECG tracing is normal (top). During exercise, when the heart beats faster and requires more oxygen, the tracing becomes abnormal (bottom), showing an exaggerated downward dip.

show that you have a high blood cholesterol level, you will be treated with lipid-lowering drugs (p.935).

Angina may be treated with drugs, such as nitrate drugs (p.899) and beta blocker drugs (p.898), that improve the blood flow through the arteries and help the heart pump effectively. An abnormal heart rhythm is often treated using antiarrhythmic drugs (p.898).

If treatment fails to relieve the symptoms or if there is extensive narrowing of the arteries, your doctor will discuss treatment options with you. If small segments of the artery are affected, you may be offered coronary angioplasty, a procedure in which a balloon is inflated in the narrowed area of the affected blood vessel to widen it. During angioplasty, a small hollow tube called a stent may be inserted into the affected artery to keep it open. Alternatively, your doctor may suggest a coronary artery bypass graft (p.411). In this procedure, the blockage is bypassed using the saphenous vein from the leg. It has also become routine to use arteries located in the chest, or occasionally, an artery in the arm.

WHAT IS THE PROGNOSIS?

Coronary artery disease affects people in middle to old age and is more easily prevented than treated. The chance of developing the disease can be reduced by following a healthier lifestyle. More efficient methods of diagnosing CAD and screening for risk factors also make it possible to begin treatment early in the course of the disease. Effective drugs to prevent the progression of CAD and the success of both coronary angioplasty and bypass grafting have greatly improved the prognosis for CAD.

For an individual with CAD, the outlook depends on the number of blood vessels involved and how extensively the heart muscle is damaged when the condition is diagnosed.

WWW ONLINE SITES: p.1032

Angina

Pain in the chest, usually brought on by exertion and relieved by rest

 AGE More common with increasing age

 GENDER More common in males until age 60, then equal incidence

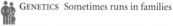

 GENETICS Sometimes runs in families

 LIFESTYLE Smoking, a high-fat diet, lack of exercise, and excess weight are risk factors

Angina is chest pain that originates in the heart muscle during physical activity and is quickly relieved by rest. The pain is due to an inadequate supply of blood to the heart muscle. Angina affects both sexes but is less common in women before menopause. After menopause, the protective effects of the hormone cycle gradually disappear.

Over the last 30 years, angina has become progressively less common in America and western Europe, mainly due to people adopting a healthier lifestyle. At the same time, treatment with drugs and surgery has improved the outlook for people with the condition.

WHAT ARE THE CAUSES?

The most common cause of angina is coronary artery disease (p.405), a narrowing of the arteries that supply the heart muscle. This narrowing is usually the result of fatty deposits building up on the inside of the artery walls (*see* ATHEROSCLEROSIS, p.402). The blood flow through the arteries may be sufficient for the heart while it is at rest but becomes inadequate during exertion. If the supply of oxygen-rich blood is insufficient, the heart muscle is starved of oxygen and toxic substances build up in the heart muscle, causing a constrictive, cramplike pain. People who have a high blood cholesterol level (*see* HYPERCHOLESTEROLEMIA, p.691), persistently high blood pressure (*see* HYPERTENSION, p.403), or diabetes mellitus (p.687) are at greater risk of developing atherosclerosis and angina. Other risk factors for angina include smoking and having a close relative with the disorder.

Angina can also be caused by temporary spasm of the coronary arteries, in which the arteries narrow for a short time, or by a damaged heart valve that causes a reduction in the blood flow to the heart muscle (*see* AORTIC STENOSIS, p.423). A rare cause of angina is anemia, in which the ability of the blood to carry oxygen is impaired. This reduces the supply of oxygen to the heart.

WHAT ARE THE SYMPTOMS?

The chest pain of angina varies from mild to severe. It usually starts during exertion and is relieved after a short rest. The features of angina are:

- A dull, heavy, constricting sensation in the center of the chest.
- A discomfort that spreads into the throat and down one or both arms, more often the left arm.

Angina usually occurs predictably at a particular level of exertion. For example, if you regularly walk uphill or climb stairs, the pain of angina will develop at about the same stage of the activity each time. Angina brought on by outdoor exertion often occurs more rapidly in cold or windy weather.

If you experience this type of chest pain for the first time, or if your angina becomes more frequent or develops at rest, you should contact your doctor immediately. Worsening angina can be a warning that a blood clot has formed in the coronary artery and may completely block it and cause a heart attack (*see* MYOCARDIAL INFARCTION, p.410). A prolonged and very severe attack of angina may be due to a heart attack.

HOW IS IT DIAGNOSED?

Your doctor will usually make a diagnosis of angina from your symptoms. However, in some cases it may be difficult for your doctor to be certain that the pain is angina and is not due to a gastrointestinal problem such as gastroesophageal reflux disease (p.636).

Your doctor will measure your blood pressure to see if you have hypertension (p.403). He or she may also request blood tests to check for anemia or elevated cholesterol levels. You will also probably have an ECG (p.406) to monitor the electrical activity of the heart at rest and exercise testing (p.407) as a comparison. The ECG at rest may show no abnormalities, but the ECG with exercise may be abnormal if you have coronary artery disease. The ECG may confirm that you have had a heart

TEST CORONARY ANGIOGRAPHY

Coronary angiography is used to image the arteries that supply the heart muscle with blood. Angiography can image narrowed or blocked coronary arteries, which are not visible on a normal X-ray. A local anesthetic is injected into the groin, and a fine flexible catheter is passed into the femoral artery, through the aorta, and into a coronary artery. Contrast dye is injected through the catheter, and a series of X-rays is taken. The procedure is painless, but you may feel a flushing sensation as the dye is injected.

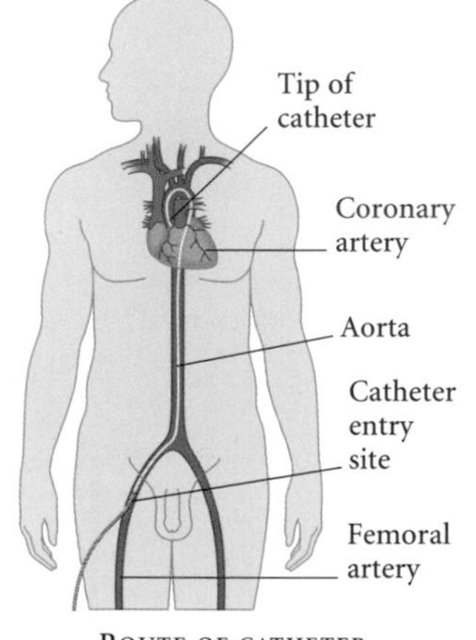
Tip of catheter
Coronary artery
Aorta
Catheter entry site
Femoral artery
ROUTE OF CATHETER

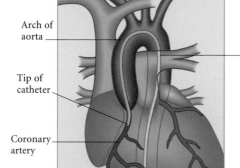

Arch of aorta
Catheter
Tip of catheter
Coronary artery
Aorta

During the procedure
The catheter is positioned in the heart so that its tip rests in a coronary artery and contrast dye is then injected. The artery and the small vessels leading from it are visualized by a series of X-rays. The catheter may be repositioned and the procedure repeated to check all the coronary arteries.

RESULTS

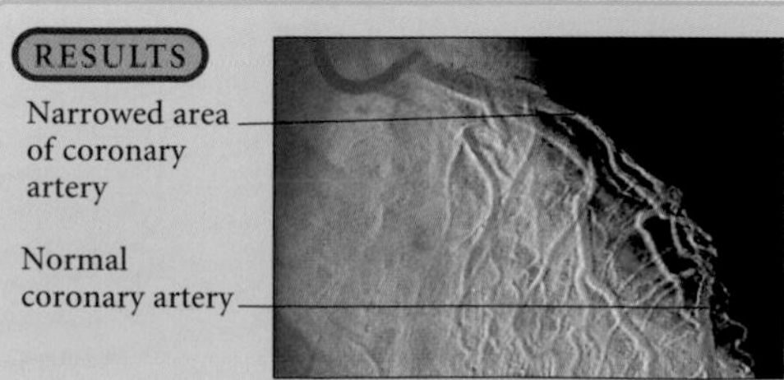
Narrowed area of coronary artery
Normal coronary artery

Coronary artery disease
This angiogram of the heart shows a section of coronary artery that has become narrowed by coronary artery disease, restricting blood flow.

(TREATMENT) CORONARY ANGIOPLASTY

Coronary angioplasty is used to widen coronary arteries narrowed or blocked by fatty deposits. The technique may be carried out at the same time as coronary angiography (opposite page). Under local anesthesia, a guide wire is inserted through the femoral artery in the groin and up into the affected coronary artery. A balloon catheter is passed up the wire, and the balloon is inflated in the narrowed area to widen it. A metal tube called a stent is inserted afterward to keep the artery open.

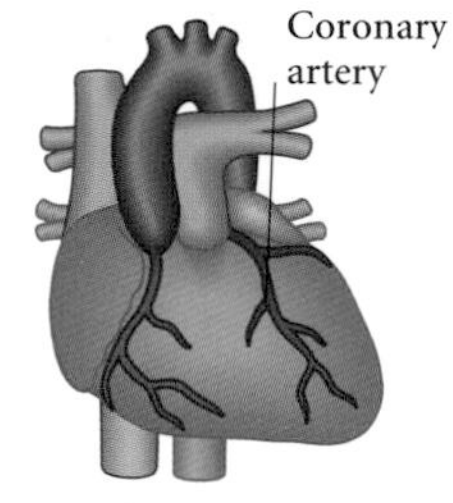
Coronary artery

LOCATION

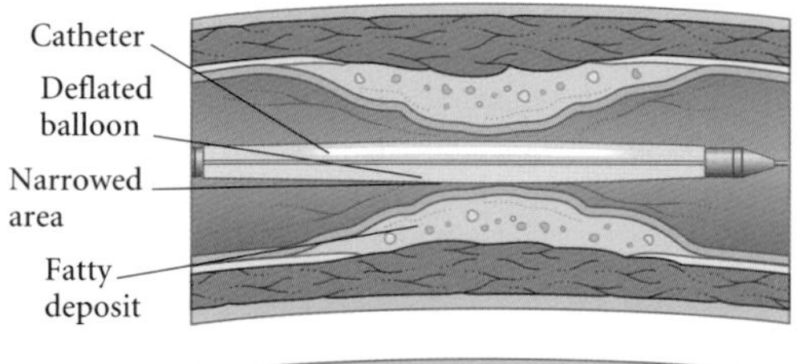
Catheter
Deflated balloon
Narrowed area
Fatty deposit

1 *A catheter with a deflated balloon attached to its tip is threaded into the artery. The catheter is placed precisely so that the balloon is inside the narrowed area of the coronary artery.*

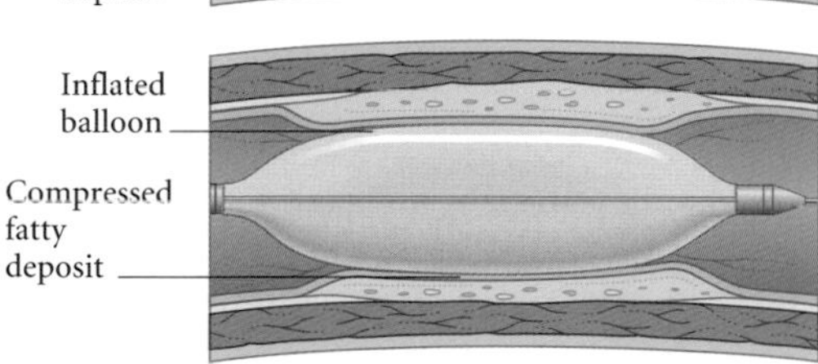
Inflated balloon
Compressed fatty deposit

2 *The balloon is inflated and deflated several times in order to compress the deposits and widen the narrowed area. The catheter is then withdrawn. A small tube (stent) may be inserted to keep the artery open.*

(RESULTS)

Effect of treatment

X-rays using contrast dye are taken before and after coronary angioplasty. These images show that the blocked artery has been widened successfully and blood flow improved.

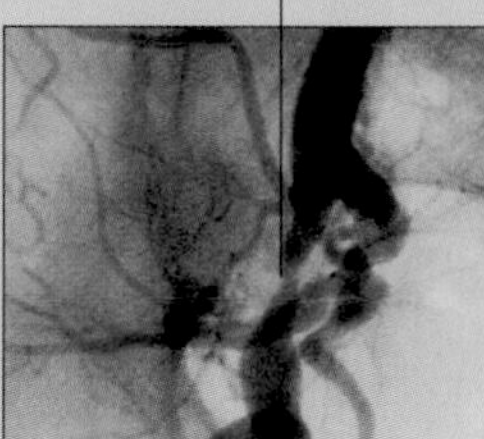
Blocked artery

BEFORE TREATMENT

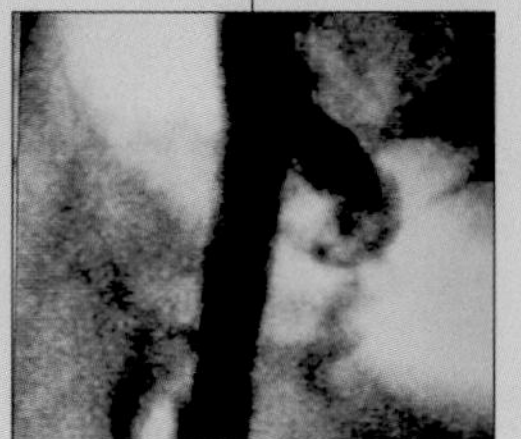
Widened artery

AFTER TREATMENT

attack. If the tests confirm that there is a significant problem with blood flow to the heart, you may need coronary angiography (opposite page), in which dye is injected into the coronary arteries so that narrowed areas may be detected on an X-ray.

WHAT IS THE TREATMENT?

The treatment of angina depends on its severity. Drugs are used to relieve acute episodes of pain and also to reduce the number and severity of attacks. Drug treatment of an acute attack of angina usually includes nitrate drugs (p.899) to widen the coronary arteries. Fast-acting nitrates can be administered in the form of a spray or soluble tablets. Longer-acting nitrates can be taken on a regular basis, usually twice a day, to prevent angina attacks from occurring. In addition, drugs may be used, normally on a long-term basis, to reduce the heart's need for oxygen (*see* BETA BLOCKER DRUGS, p.898). Doctors also advise that a daily low dose of aspirin be taken (*see* DRUGS THAT PREVENT BLOOD CLOTTING, p.904) because this makes the blood less sticky and reduces the risk of clots forming in an artery.

If there is an underlying disorder contributing to the angina, such as aortic stenosis, hypertension, or diabetes mellitus, it will be treated.

Lifestyle changes can prevent the worsening of angina while increasing the level of exercise that you can achieve without experiencing pain. It is imperative that you stop smoking; cutting down is not sufficient. A diet that is low in saturated fat is important, and, if necessary, you should try to lose weight (*see* CONTROLLING YOUR WEIGHT p.53). You may also be prescribed drugs to lower your blood cholesterol level (*see* LIPID-LOWERING DRUGS, p.935), even if the level of lipids in your blood is within the normal range, because this has been shown to slow down the progress of coronary artery disease.

You should also do as much regular exercise as you can tolerate within the limits prescribed by your doctor. Even walking 1–2 miles (1.5–3 km) every day has been shown to reduce the risk of a fatal heart attack.

If the angina becomes more severe despite drug treatment, your doctor may advise you to consider surgery to either widen the arteries or improve the blood flow to the heart. Coronary angioplasty (left) is now used to treat several coronary blockages. If there is extensive atherosclerosis, or if angioplasty is not successful, then bypass surgery (p.411), may be an alternative. The saphenous vein, the vein running the length of the leg, or arteries in the chest are used to bypass the diseased areas in the arteries. Coronary artery bypass grafting is a major surgical procedure requiring a brief stay in a critical care unit (p.958). A stay of about one week in the hospital is usual, and you will then need 2–3 months of convalescence.

WHAT IS THE PROGNOSIS?

The prognosis depends on the extent of coronary artery disease. If you have mild angina, the prognosis is good provided that you make sensible changes to your lifestyle and follow the treatment recommended by your doctor. People with angina often have no further symptoms once they have started treatment and many are able to live a normal life with the exception of some restrictions on exercise.

(WWW) ONLINE SITES: p.1032

Myocardial infarction

Loss of blood supply to part of the heart muscle due to a blockage in a coronary artery, commonly known as heart attack

 AGE More common with increasing age

 GENDER More common in males until age 60, then equal incidence

 GENETICS Sometimes runs in families

 LIFESTYLE Smoking, a high-fat diet, lack of exercise, and obesity increase the risk

Heart attack or "coronary" are common terms for the disorder myocardial infarction, which means, literally, death of part of the heart muscle following a blockage in its blood supply. Myocardial infarction is one of the major causes of death in developed countries such as Canada. However, the mortality rates have fallen significantly since the late 1960s due to recent improvements in treatment and an increasing awareness that following a healthier lifestyle helps prevent heart attacks.

WHAT ARE THE CAUSES?

Myocardial infarction is usually a result of coronary artery disease (p.405). In this condition, the coronary arteries that supply the heart muscle with fresh oxygenated blood become narrowed. This narrowing is usually due to atherosclerosis (p.402), in which droplets of fatty substances, like cholesterol, build up on the inside of the artery wall. These substances form deposits called atheroma, which become covered with a fibrous layer that may rupture or become roughened. Blood cells called platelets can stick to the rough or damaged area and trigger the formation of a blood clot. Once formed, the clot may completely block blood flow through the artery, leading to a heart attack.

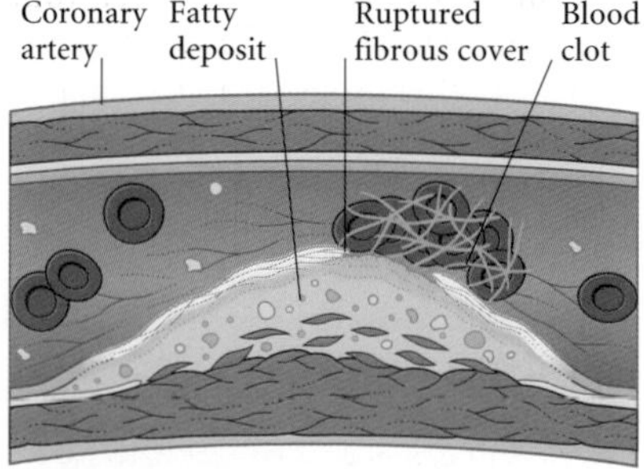
Coronary artery
Fatty deposit
Ruptured fibrous cover
Blood clot

Cause of myocardial infarction
If a coronary artery is narrowed by a fatty deposit, the fibrous cover of the deposit may rupture, triggering the formation of a blood clot. If this clot blocks the artery, blood flow to an area of heart muscle stops, causing a myocardial infarction.

If you have a family history of coronary artery disease (CAD), you are at increased risk of having a heart attack, especially if one or more members of your family developed CAD or had a heart attack before the age of 55.

WHAT ARE THE SYMPTOMS?

The symptoms of a heart attack usually develop suddenly and may include:

- Severe, heavy, crushing pain in the center of the chest that may spread up to the neck and into the arms, especially the left arm.
- Pallor and sweating.
- Shortness of breath.
- Nausea and, sometimes, vomiting.
- Anxiety, sometimes accompanied by a fear of dying.
- Restlessness.

If you develop these symptoms, you should always assume that you are having a heart attack and require urgent medical attention. Do not delay calling an ambulance to "see how things go" because this delay may be fatal. A well-equipped emergency ambulance is the most appropriate means of transportation to the hospital because life-saving treatment may be required on the journey. While waiting for the ambulance, you should chew an aspirin tablet if possible. Aspirin reduces the stickiness of the blood to prevent further clotting.

Sometimes, a myocardial infarction may cause a different pattern of symptoms. If you have been suffering from the chest pain of angina (p.407), your pain may have been getting steadily worse and may have been occurring at rest as well as on exertion. An episode of angina that does not respond to your usual treatment or that lasts longer than 10 minutes may be a myocardial infarction and requires immediate emergency hospital treatment.

About 1 in 5 people experiences no chest pain in a heart attack. However, there may be other symptoms, such as breathlessness, faintness, sweating, and pale skin. This pattern of symptoms is known as a "silent infarction." This type of heart attack is more common in people with diabetes mellitus (p.687) or those with elevated blood pressure (*see* HYPERTENSION, p.403). It is also more common in elderly people.

ARE THERE COMPLICATIONS?

In the first few hours and days after a heart attack, the main risks are the development of an irregular heartbeat, which may be life-threatening, or a cardiac arrest (p.419). Depending on the extent and site of the damaged muscle, other problems may develop. For example, in the weeks or months after the attack, the pumping action of the heart muscle may be too weak, leading to a condition called heart failure. Its symptoms include fatigue, shortness of breath, and swollen ankles. Less common complications include damage to one of the heart valves (*see* MITRAL REGURGITATION, p.423) or inflammation of the membrane covering the heart's surface (*see* PERICARDITIS, p.428), both of which may also lead to the development of heart failure.

HOW IS IT DIAGNOSED?

In many cases, the diagnosis is obvious. An ECG (p.406), which is a tracing of the electrical activity of the heart, often shows changes that confirm myocardial infarction. The ECG can be valuable in assessing which part and how much of the heart muscle has been damaged and will establish whether the heart rhythm is still normal or is irregular. To confirm the diagnosis, blood samples may be taken to measure the levels of particular chemicals that leak into the blood from damaged heart muscle.

WHAT IS THE TREATMENT?

The immediate aims of treatment for myocardial infarction are to relieve pain and restore the blood supply to the heart muscle in order to minimize the amount of damage and prevent further complications. These aims are best achieved by immediate admission to a critical care unit (p.958), where your heart rhythm and vital clinical signs can be monitored continuously. If you have severe chest pain from the heart attack, you will probably be given an injection of a powerful analgesic drug (p.912), such as morphine.

Within the first 6 hours of the attack, you may also be given a thrombolytic drug (p.904) to dissolve the blood clot

TREATMENT CORONARY ARTERY BYPASS GRAFT

During this procedure, one or more narrowed coronary arteries are bypassed using blood vessels from the legs or chest. The operation takes about 2 hours. In most cases, the heart is stopped and a heart–lung machine is used to take over the function of the heart during surgery (*see* SURGERY USING A HEART–LUNG MACHINE, p.953). However, a less invasive technique using endoscopic surgery is now sometimes used. Afterward, you will be monitored in a critical care unit for several days.

THORACIC ARTERY BYPASS GRAFT

If there is only one blockage in a coronary artery, one of the internal thoracic arteries within the chest, usually the left artery, is used to create the bypass. Artery grafts are preferable to vein grafts because they are better able to take the pressure of the blood that normally flows through the coronary arteries and are less likely to become blocked over time.

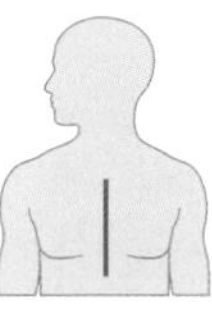

SITE OF INCISION

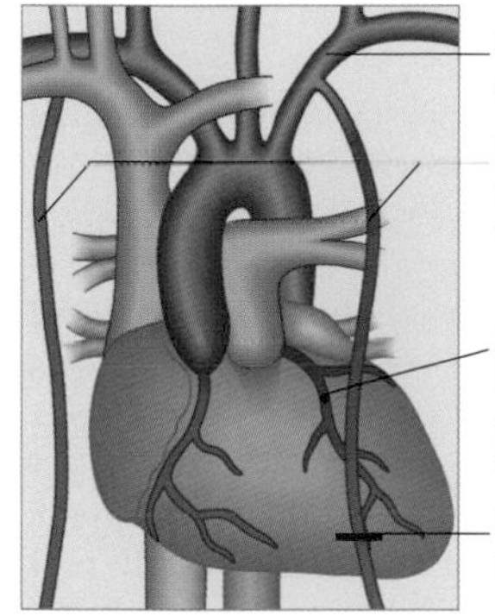
Subclavian artery
Internal thoracic arteries
Blockage in coronary artery
Cutting site

1 *The left internal thoracic artery is cut where shown above. The upper end is left attached to the subclavian artery and the lower end is tied off.*

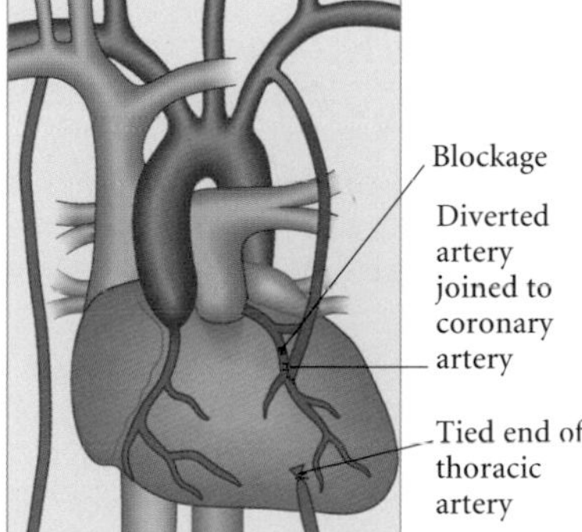
Blockage
Diverted artery joined to coronary artery
Tied end of thoracic artery

2 *The free end of the thoracic artery is connected to the coronary artery at a point beyond the blockage to supply blood to the heart muscle there.*

SAPHENOUS VEIN BYPASS GRAFT

If more than one blockage in a coronary artery needs to be bypassed or if the internal thoracic artery is not suitable, sections of the saphenous vein (the vein that runs the length of the leg) are used after first being reversed. Sometimes, the vein is used in addition to the thoracic artery, although vein grafts tend to become obstructed more quickly than arterial grafts.

SITES OF INCISION

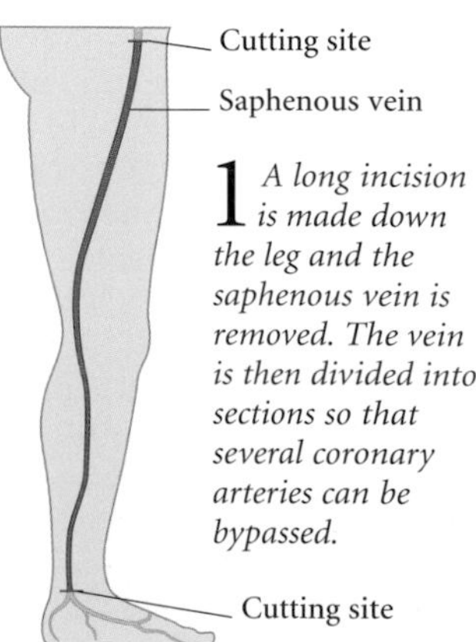
Cutting site
Saphenous vein
Cutting site

1 *A long incision is made down the leg and the saphenous vein is removed. The vein is then divided into sections so that several coronary arteries can be bypassed.*

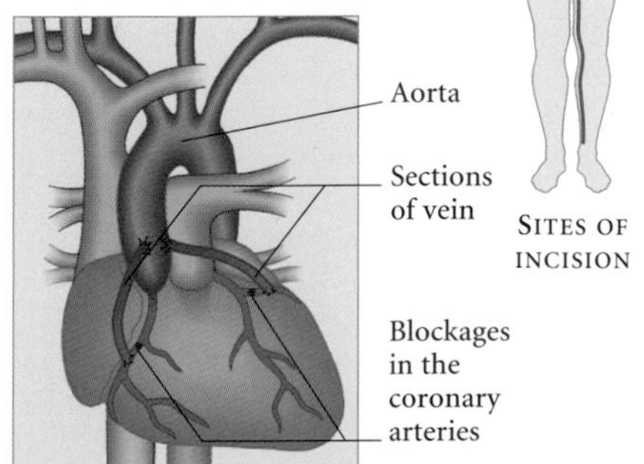
Aorta
Sections of vein
Blockages in the coronary arteries

2 *Sections of the saphenous vein are used to bypass the blockages. One end of each section is attached to the aorta, and the other is attached to the coronary artery beyond a blockage.*

that is blocking the coronary artery. Alternatively, you may have immediate coronary angioplasty (p.409) to open the artery. If the blood flow to the damaged heart muscle can be restored within 6 hours, there is a greater likelihood of full recovery.

While you are in the coronary care unit, your heartbeat is monitored, and treatment is given if arrhythmias or symptoms of heart failure develop. If progress is satisfactory, you should be allowed out of bed briefly after 24–48 hours. Soon afterward, you can begin a program of rehabilitation, during which you are encouraged to spend gradually longer periods out of bed.

Once you have recovered from the attack, the condition of your coronary arteries and heart muscle is assessed. Tests such as exercise electrocardiography (*see* EXERCISE TESTING, p.407) and echocardiography (p.425) are used to help decide on further treatment. For example, if the pumping action of the heart is impaired, you may be prescribed an ACE inhibitor (p.900) and/or a diuretic drug (p.902). If a coronary artery is blocked, you may need angioplasty or bypass surgery (*see* CORONARY ARTERY BYPASS GRAFT, left). If tests reveal that you have a persistent irregular heartbeat, you may need to have a pacemaker implanted in your chest (*see* CARDIAC PACEMAKER, p.419).

Certain drugs taken long-term can reduce the risk of another heart attack, and you may be prescribed a beta blocker drug (p.898) and/or aspirin for this reason. You may also be advised to adopt a low-fat diet and to take lipid-lowering drugs (p.935) to lower your blood cholesterol level. These drugs are beneficial after a heart attack even if your cholesterol level is not elevated.

WHAT CAN I DO?

It is important to follow your doctor's advice about how soon to return to normal activities. It is natural to feel worried about your health, and many people experience some mild depression (p.554). It is important to avoid becoming disabled by the fear of having another heart attack. Many hospitals offer ongoing cardiac rehabilitation programs after discharge from the hospital to help people regain their confidence and share their experiences with others.

WHAT IS THE PROGNOSIS?

If you have not suffered a previous myocardial infarction, you receive treatment quickly, and you do not have any complications as a result of the attack, your prognosis is good. After 2 weeks, the risk of having another heart attack is considerably reduced. The long-term prognosis is better if you stop smoking, reduce your intake of alcohol, exercise regularly, and follow a healthy diet.

If you have experienced a previous myocardial infarction, the prognosis depends on the amount of heart muscle that was damaged during the heart attack and whether or not you have developed any additional complications after the heart attack.

(WWW) ONLINE SITES: p.1032

(SELF-HELP) LIFE AFTER A HEART ATTACK

Making changes in your lifestyle after a heart attack can help speed your recovery and reduce the risk of another attack occurring:

- Stop smoking. This is the single most important factor in preventing a further attack.
- Eat a healthy diet and try to keep your weight within the ideal range for your height and build (*see* DIET AND HEALTH, p.48).
- If you drink alcohol, take only moderate amounts. You should have no more than 1–2 small glasses of wine or beer a day.
- Together with your doctor, agree on a program of increasing exercise until you are able to engage in moderate exercise, such as swimming regularly, for 30 minutes or more at a time.

After a period of recovery, you can make a gradual return to your normal daily routine:

- You will probably be able to return to work within 6 weeks, or sooner if you have a desk job. You might consider working part-time at first.
- Try to avoid stressful situations.
- You should be able to drive a car within 6 weeks.
- You can resume having sexual intercourse about 4 weeks after a heart attack.

Acute heart failure

Sudden deterioration in the pumping action of the heart, usually leading to accumulation of fluid in the lungs

AGE More common over age 65

LIFESTYLE Risk factors depend on the cause

GENDER GENETICS Not significant factors

Heart failure is the term given when the heart's ability to pump efficiently is reduced. In acute heart failure, the condition develops suddenly, usually due to a severe heart attack. In most cases, only the left side of the heart is affected by acute heart failure. This side of the heart receives blood rich in oxygen directly from the lungs and pumps it to the rest of the body. If acute heart failure develops, a backup of blood occurs in the blood vessels leading from the lungs to the heart. Back pressure then causes fluid to accumulate in the lungs. This buildup of fluid is called pulmonary edema, and, if it is not treated immediately, is life-threatening.

WHAT ARE THE CAUSES?

The most common cause of acute heart failure is a severe myocardial infarction (p.410) that damages a large area of heart muscle. The condition may also be caused by an acute infection of a heart valve (*see* INFECTIVE ENDOCARDITIS, p.426). Acute heart failure may develop in people with complete heart block or those with chronic heart failure (opposite page) if the weakened heart is put under more strain. For example, a severe infection, such as pneumonia (p.490), may increase the workload on the heart and lead to acute heart failure.

Right-sided acute heart failure is rare and is usually due to a blood clot blocking the pulmonary artery, which is the blood vessel that leads from the lungs to the right side of the heart (*see* PULMONARY EMBOLISM, p.495).

WHAT ARE THE SYMPTOMS?

The symptoms of acute heart failure usually develop rapidly and include:

- Severe shortness of breath.
- Wheezing.
- Cough with pink, frothy sputum.
- Pale skin and sweating.

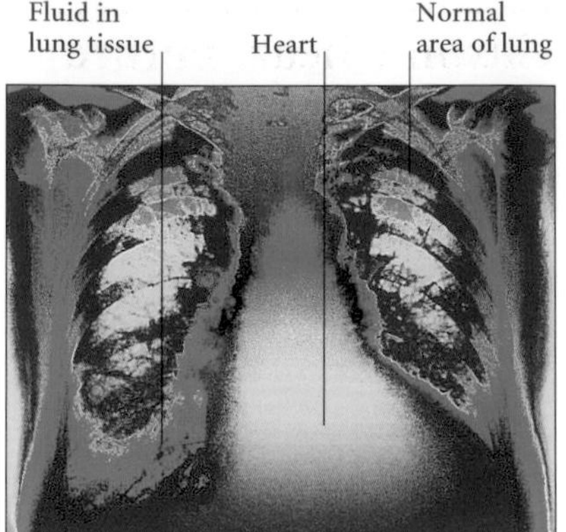
Fluid in lung tissue
Heart
Normal area of lung

Lung edema in acute heart failure
In acute heart failure, fluid accumulates rapidly in both lungs (a condition known as pulmonary edema). This results in extreme shortness of breath.

If acute heart failure is caused by a heart attack, you may have additional symptoms such as intense, prolonged chest pain and feelings of anxiety. If heart failure is caused by a pulmonary embolism, you may cough up blood and have sharp chest pain that is worse when inhaling. If acute heart failure is not treated, it can cause dangerously low blood pressure (*see* SHOCK, p.414), and the condition may then be fatal.

WHAT MIGHT BE DONE?

Acute heart failure is a medical emergency and requires immediate hospital treatment. You will be advised to sit in an upright position to make breathing easier, and oxygen may be given to you through a face mask. Diuretics (p.902) may be administered intravenously to reduce the accumulation of fluid in the lungs and make breathing easier.

You may need electrocardiography (*see* ECG, p.406) and echocardiography (p.425) to evaluate the function of the heart and to look for the cause of heart failure. A chest X-ray (p.490) usually confirms the presence of fluid in the lungs. Once your symptoms are under control, you may also have coronary angiography (p.408) to look for blockages in the coronary arteries supplying the heart muscle.

Prompt treatment usually relieves the symptoms. Long-term treatment depends on the underlying cause. In some cases, the cause cannot be treated and acute heart failure may be fatal.

(WWW) ONLINE SITES: p.1032

Chronic heart failure

Long-standing inefficient pumping action of the heart, leading to poor circulation of blood and accumulation of fluid in tissues

AGE More common over age 65

LIFESTYLE Risk factors depend on the cause

GENDER GENETICS Not significant factors

In chronic heart failure, the heart is unable to pump blood around the body effectively, which leads to a buildup of fluid in the lungs and the body tissues. Chronic heart failure is a progressive condition that may be so mild at first that symptoms go unnoticed. The condition is common and mostly affects people over age 65. The incidence of chronic heart failure in most developed countries is rising because the average lifespan is increasing.

Although the term chronic heart failure implies a life-threatening disorder, it can often be treated, and people with mild chronic heart failure can live for many years. However, the condition may limit physical activity.

Initially, only one side of the heart may be predominantly affected, and the disorder is often referred to as right-sided or left-sided chronic heart failure. Right-sided heart failure may occur on its own and causes fluid to accumulate in the body tissues. The ankles are the areas most noticeably affected. In left-sided heart failure, fluid accumulates in the lungs. Left-sided chronic heart failure is often followed by the failure of the right side of the heart.

What are the causes?

Any condition that damages the heart can lead to chronic heart failure. In 8 in 10 cases, chronic heart failure occurs as a result of coronary artery disease (p.405), in which blood supply to the heart muscle is reduced.

Persistent high blood pressure (*see* HYPERTENSION, p.403) can also lead to chronic heart failure because the heart has to work harder to pump blood through vessels in which the pressure is abnormally high. Other conditions that may cause chronic heart failure include heart valve disorders (p.421), dilated cardiomyopathy (p.427), and chronic obstructive pulmonary disease (p.487). In rare cases, chronic heart failure may be due to anemia (p.446), the hormone disorder hyperthyroidism (p.679), or extreme obesity (p.631). Some people with diabetes mellitus (p.687) may be at risk of developing chronic heart failure.

What are the symptoms?

The symptoms of chronic heart failure develop gradually, are often vague, and may include:

- Fatigue.
- Shortness of breath that is worse during exertion or when lying flat.
- Loss of appetite.
- Nausea.
- Swelling of the feet and ankles.
- In some cases, confusion.

People with chronic heart failure may also have sudden attacks of acute heart failure (opposite page), with symptoms of severe shortness of breath, wheezing, and sweating. These attacks generally occur during the night. Occasionally, acute heart failure develops if the heart is put under additional strain due to a heart attack or an infection. Acute heart failure is a medical emergency and needs immediate hospital treatment.

How is it diagnosed?

If your doctor suspects chronic heart failure, he or she may arrange for you to have electrocardiography (*see* ECG, p.406) to assess the electrical activity of your heart. You may also have echocardiography (p.425) to image the heart and check its function. A chest X-ray (p.490) may show signs of heart failure, such as an abnormally large heart or excess fluid in the lung tissue.

Your doctor may arrange for further tests to investigate the underlying cause of heart failure. For example, you may have coronary angiography (p.408) to diagnose narrowing of the coronary arteries or blood tests to check for anemia or an overactive thyroid gland.

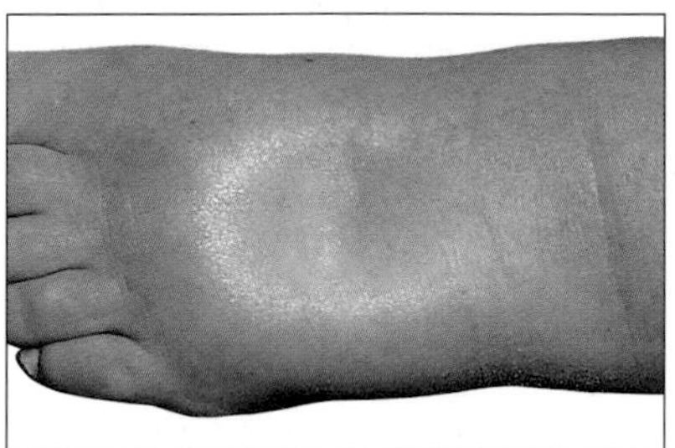

Fluid retention
In chronic heart failure, fluid collects in body tissues, most obviously in the feet. If the skin is pressed, an indentation remains at the site of pressure for a few minutes.

What can I do?

If you have chronic heart failure, you should avoid strenuous exercise and stressful situations. If you smoke, you should stop immediately. Regular gentle exercise, such as walking, may help if you have mild or moderate chronic heart failure. If necessary, you should try to lose excess weight to avoid putting unnecessary strain on your heart (*see* ARE YOU A HEALTHY WEIGHT?, p.53). You should also avoid salty foods, which can encourage your body to retain fluid.

How might the doctor treat it?

Your doctor will probably prescribe diuretic drugs (p.902), which increase urine production, and ACE inhibitor drugs (p.900), which cause blood vessels to widen, thereby reducing the workload on the heart. In addition, drugs that increase the efficiency of the heart, such as digoxin (*see* DIGITALIS DRUGS, p.901) or, in some cases, beta blocker drugs (p.898), may be prescribed. You may also be treated to prevent progression of any underlying cause. For example, if you have coronary artery disease, you may be advised to take a daily dose of aspirin, which has been found to reduce the risk of a heart attack (*see* DRUGS THAT PREVENT BLOOD CLOTTING, p.904). Your doctor will monitor your heart condition and adjust your drug treatments and the dosage as needed.

In some cases, drug treatment may not be effective, and a heart transplant (p.427) may be considered if a person is otherwise in good health.

What is the prognosis?

Treatment of chronic heart failure is usually initially successful in relieving the symptoms and improving the quality of life. However, in most cases, the underlying cause of the condition cannot be treated effectively. As a result, heart failure becomes progressively more severe, and symptoms are then difficult to control with drugs.

(WWW) ONLINE SITES: p.1032

Hypotension

Lower than normal blood pressure due to a variety of causes

AGE GENDER GENETICS LIFESTYLE
Risk factors depend on the cause

Hypotension is the medical term for low blood pressure. The pressure with which the blood is pumped around the circulation varies between individuals and throughout the day. The normal range is that which is adequate to supply all of the organs and body tissues with blood. Blood pressure at the lower end of the normal range is not likely to produce symptoms. However, if the pressure in the circulation falls below the level needed to provide the brain with enough blood, lightheadedness or fainting may occur.

A common type of hypotension is postural hypotension, in which suddenly standing or sitting up leads to lightheadedness and fainting.

WHAT ARE THE CAUSES?

In many people, low blood pressure occurs as a result of dehydration following loss of large amounts of fluid or salts from the body. For example, heavy sweating, loss of blood, or profuse diarrhea may all cause hypotension.

Disorders that reduce the efficiency of the heart's pumping action are common causes of low blood pressure. These disorders include heart failure (*see* ACUTE HEART FAILURE, p.412, and CHRONIC HEART FAILURE, p.413), heart attack (*see* MYOCARDIAL INFARCTION, p.410), and an irregular heartbeat (*see* ARRHYTHMIAS, p.415).

Hypotension may also be caused by an abnormal widening of the blood vessels, which may occur as a result of an infection in the bloodstream (*see* SEPTICEMIA, p.298) or a severe allergic reaction (*see* ANAPHYLAXIS, p.469).

Postural hypotension may be caused by disorders in which the nerve supply to the blood vessels is damaged, such as diabetic neuropathy (p.545) or peripheral neuropathies (p.543). Hypotension may also sometimes be the result of an adverse effect of certain drugs, particularly those used to treat high blood pressure (*see* ANTIHYPERTENSIVE DRUGS, p.897) and certain types of antidepressant drugs (p.916).

WHAT ARE THE SYMPTOMS?

You may not have symptoms of hypotension unless your blood pressure is very low. Symptoms may include:

- Fatigue.
- General weakness.
- Lightheadedness and fainting.
- Blurry vision.
- Nausea.

These symptoms are usually temporary, and blood pressure rises when the cause is treated. However, if blood pressure is too low to provide an adequate blood supply to vital organs, it can be fatal (*see* SHOCK, below).

WHAT MIGHT BE DONE?

Your doctor will measure your blood pressure when lying and standing (*see* BLOOD PRESSURE MEASUREMENT, p.404). The reason for the low blood pressure may be obvious. For example, you may be dehydrated and require treatment with intravenous fluids. If your doctor suspects an underlying disorder, such as a heart condition, you will probably be hospitalized for tests and treatment. If medication is the cause of hypotension, your doctor will probably advise an alteration in the drug or dosage.

(WWW) ONLINE SITES: p.1032

Shock

A severe reduction in blood pressure causing poor blood supply to major organs

AGE Risk factor depends on the cause

GENDER GENETICS LIFESTYLE
Not significant factors

Shock is a life-threatening condition that necessitates immediate medical attention. The medical term shock describes the cold, pale, collapsed state that results from low blood pressure due to serious injury or illness. Left untreated, the reduced blood supply deprives the vital organs and body tissues of oxygen and is eventually fatal.

The condition is unrelated to the mental and emotional distress that may follow a traumatic experience.

WHAT ARE THE CAUSES?

Shock may develop as a result of any situation in which the heart cannot pump blood effectively or in which there is too little blood for the heart to pump. The heart is unable to function normally if it is damaged following a heart attack (*see* MYOCARDIAL INFARCTION, p.410) or if the heart rhythm is abnormal (*see* ARRHYTHMIAS, p.415).

Shock due to insufficient blood circulating around the body may result from major blood loss, such as bleeding from the digestive tract (p.630) or from a serious injury. The volume of blood circulating in the body may also be reduced by fluid loss due to severe burns or profuse diarrhea.

Some conditions, such as an allergic reaction (*see* ANAPHYLAXIS, p.469) or a serious blood infection (*see* SEPTICEMIA, p.298), may cause the blood vessels in the body to widen, resulting in a severe drop in blood pressure and shock.

WHAT ARE THE SYMPTOMS?

Shock may not develop until hours after the injury or illness, but as soon as blood pressure falls, the symptoms develop suddenly. Symptoms may include:

- Confusion or agitation.
- Cold, clammy skin and sweating.
- Rapid, shallow breathing.
- Fast heartbeat.
- Loss of consciousness.

Symptoms of the underlying cause may also be present, such as prolonged chest pain due to a heart attack.

If shock is not treated immediately, the internal organs may be damaged, leading to various disorders including kidney failure (p.705) and acute respiratory distress syndrome (p.506).

WHAT MIGHT BE DONE?

A person in shock requires emergency admission to a critical care unit, where he or she can be treated and carefully monitored. The priority is to restore the blood and oxygen supply to the body's major organs regardless of the cause of shock. Immediate treatment usually includes oxygen therapy and intravenous fluids, blood or blood products, and drugs to increase blood pressure. Once the cause of shock has been established, specific treatment can be given. For example, antibiotics (p.885) may be given to treat septicemia. Surgery may be needed to stop bleeding. For treatment to be successful, the blood supply to the organs must be restored before permanent damage occurs.

(WWW) ONLINE SITES: p.1032

HEART RATE AND RHYTHM DISORDERS

Disorders of heart rate and rhythm are caused by disturbances in the heart's electrical system and are very common, particularly in elderly people. These disorders do not always cause symptoms and are sometimes detected only during a routine health checkup. Treatment usually consists of drugs, although newer techniques that use carefully controlled electric currents are also used.

A healthy adult has a resting heart rate of 60–100 beats per minute, although this rate rises during exercise. Children have a higher resting heart rate, while that of very fit adults and the elderly may be as low as 50 beats per minute. Disorders that affect the pumping action of the heart may increase or decrease the heart rate, alter its rhythm, or, in cardiac arrest, stop the heart pumping altogether. Many of these disorders have coronary artery disease (p.405) as an underlying cause.

The first article in this section describes ectopic beats, which are extra, isolated heartbeats. This article is followed by an overview of arrhythmias, which are abnormal heart rates and rhythms, and a discussion of individual types of arrhythmias. The final article discusses cardiac arrest, which is the sudden and complete failure of the heart to pump blood caused by a disturbance in its electrical system. Cardiac arrest is a potentially fatal condition and requires emergency medical treatment.

KEY ANATOMY

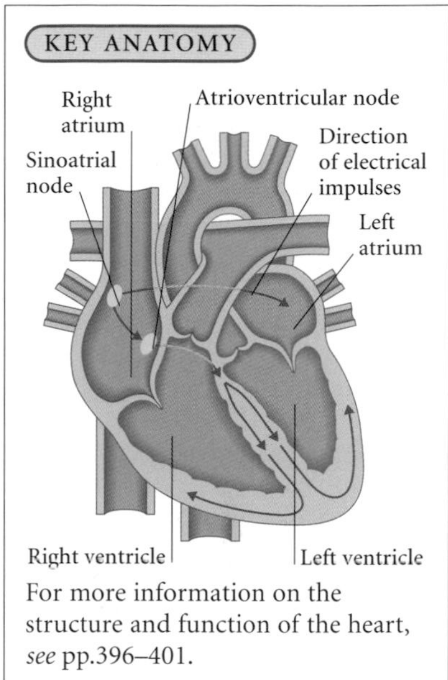
Right atrium
Atrioventricular node
Sinoatrial node
Direction of electrical impulses
Left atrium
Right ventricle
Left ventricle

For more information on the structure and function of the heart, *see* pp.396–401.

Ectopic beats

Contractions of the heart that are out of the normal rhythmic pattern

 AGE More common in young people and elderly people

 LIFESTYLE Smoking and consumption of alcohol and caffeine are risk factors

 GENDER GENETICS Not significant factors

An ectopic beat is an isolated, irregular heartbeat that rapidly follows a normal one. The interval between an ectopic beat and the next normal beat may be longer than usual. Most people experience ectopic beats at some time in their lives. Ectopic beats may originate either in the atria (the upper chambers of the heart) or in the ventricles (the lower chambers of the heart). Atrial ectopic beats are usually harmless. They typically occur in young people and are often associated with the use of nicotine and the consumption of caffeine and alcohol. Ventricular ectopic beats occur less frequently, usually in elderly people, and may indicate the presence of a more serious underlying disorder, such as coronary artery disease (p.405). They may also occur after a heart attack (*see* MYOCARDIAL INFARCTION, p.410).

Ectopic beats may be symptomless or may cause a thumping sensation in the chest as the heart briefly beats more strongly than usual.

WHAT MIGHT BE DONE?

Ectopic beats in young people are likely to be atrial and harmless. They may disappear if you stop smoking and reduce your intake of coffee and alcohol. If they persist, visit your doctor. Ectopic beats that are frequent or accompanied by light-headedness, shortness of breath, or chest pain, or that occur at an older age, are likely to be ventricular. They may have a serious underlying cause, requiring urgent medical attention.

Since ectopic beats are intermittent, your doctor may arrange for your heart to be monitored continuously over 24 hours or longer (*see* AMBULATORY ECG, p.416). Tests may be carried out to look for an underlying cause of the ectopic beats, such as coronary artery disease.

The treatment of ventricular ectopic beats depends on the underlying cause. Antiarrhythmic drugs (p.898) reduce the frequency of the beats and are commonly prescribed. The use of beta blocker drugs lowers the risk of cardiac arrest following a heart attack.

WWW ONLINE SITES: p.1032

Arrhythmias

Abnormal rates and/or rhythms of the heartbeat

 AGE More common in elderly people

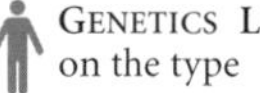 GENETICS LIFESTYLE Risk factors depend on the type

 GENDER Not a significant factor

The normal resting adult heart rate is 60–100 beats per minute. Both heart rate and rhythm may be affected in arrhythmias, which may involve both the atria (upper heart chambers) and the ventricles (lower heart chambers). There are two types of arrhythmias: tachycardias, in which the heart rate is too high, and bradycardias, in which the rate is too low. Tachycardias may arise in the atria or the ventricles and can be regular or irregular. When tachycardias occur in the ventricles, they can deteriorate into ventricular fibrillation, a serious arrhythmia that may lead to cardiac arrest (p.419). Bradycardias include sick sinus syndrome (p.419) and complete heart block (p.418). Most arrhythmias are caused by disorders of the heart and its blood vessels. A heart rate outside the usual range is not always a cause for concern. An elevated heart rate is normal during exercise and pregnancy, and exceptionally fit people have a resting heart rate that is lower than normal.

Arrhythmias may reduce the pumping efficiency of the heart, causing too little blood to reach the brain. Although arrhythmias may cause alarming symptoms, such as a thumping heartbeat, the different types vary in seriousness.

WHAT ARE THE CAUSES?

Most arrhythmias are caused by disorders of the heart or its blood vessels. The most common underlying disorder is coronary artery disease (p.405), which reduces the blood supply to the heart, including the electrical system that controls heart rate. Less common causes of arrhythmias include various heart valve disorders (pp.421–429) and inflammation of the heart muscle (*see* MYOCARDITIS, p.426). Some types of arrhythmias present from birth are due to a defect of the heart, such as an abnormal electrical pathway between the atria and the ventricles. However, these types of arrhythmias may cause symptoms only later in life. Causes of arrhythmias that originate outside the heart include an imbalance of thyroid hormones (*see* HYPERTHYROIDISM, p.679, and HYPOTHYROIDISM, p.680) or of blood chemistry, such as an excess of potassium. Some drugs, such as bronchodilators (p.910) and digitalis drugs (p.901), may cause arrhythmias, as may the use of caffeine and tobacco.

WHAT ARE THE SYMPTOMS?

Symptoms do not always develop, but, if they do, their onset is usually sudden. The symptoms may include:

- Palpitations (awareness of an irregular heartbeat).
- Light-headedness, sometimes leading to loss of consciousness.
- Shortness of breath.
- Pain in the chest or neck.

Stroke (p.532) and heart failure (p.412) are possible complications.

WHAT MIGHT BE DONE?

Your doctor may suspect that you have an arrhythmia from your symptoms and by checking your pulse. In addition, he or she may arrange for you to undergo electrocardiography (*see* ECG, p.406), which shows electrical activity within the heart. Since some arrhythmias occur only intermittently, you may have a continuous ECG over 24 hours or be fitted with an event monitor (*see* AMBULATORY ECG, left). You may also have tests to detect abnormalities that affect the electrical pathways of the heart (*see* CARDIAC ELECTROPHYSIOLOGICAL STUDIES, opposite page).

In some cases, antiarrhythmic drugs (p.898) can be used to treat arrhythmias. In other cases, electric shocks may be administered to restore a normal heartbeat (*see* CARDIOVERSION, p.420). Abnormal electrical pathways in the heart can be destroyed using a technique called radiofrequency ablation, which is done at the same time as electrophysiological studies. If the heart rate is too low, an artificial pacemaker may be inserted to stimulate the heart and restore a normal heartbeat (*see* CARDIAC PACEMAKER, p.419).

The prognosis for an arrhythmia depends on the type. Supraventricular tachycardia usually is not serious and does not affect life expectancy, whereas ventricular fibrillation is fatal without emergency medical treatment.

(WWW) ONLINE SITES: p.1032

(TEST) AMBULATORY ECG

Ambulatory electrocardiography (ECG) utilizes a wearable device called a Holter monitor that records the electrical activity of the heart using electrodes attached to the chest. The device is usually worn for 24 hours and detects intermittent arrhythmias (abnormal heart rates and rhythms). An event monitor is a similar device that can be worn for longer periods but that records only when activated by the user.

Shoulder strap

Marker button *Pressing this button marks the recording*

Electrode

Holter monitor

Using a Holter monitor
You press a button on the device to mark times when symptoms occur. A doctor can check if these markings coincide with periods of arrhythmia.

(RESULT)

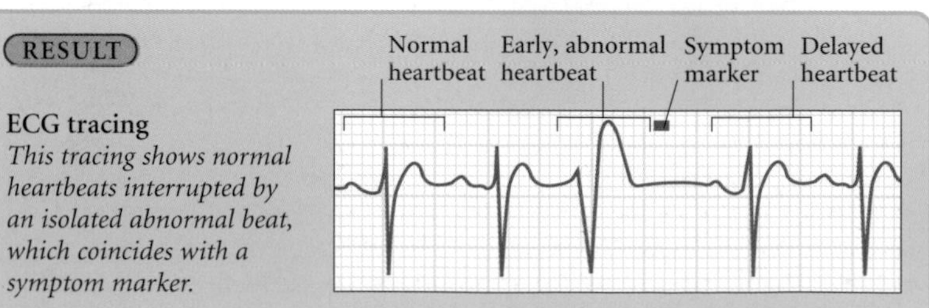
Normal heartbeat
Early, abnormal heartbeat
Symptom marker
Delayed heartbeat

ECG tracing
This tracing shows normal heartbeats interrupted by an isolated abnormal beat, which coincides with a symptom marker.

Supraventricular tachycardia

Recurrent episodes of rapid heart rate arising in the upper chambers of the heart

 AGE Most common in children

 GENETICS Sometimes runs in families

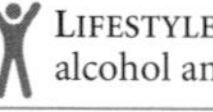 LIFESTYLE Exertion and consumption of alcohol and caffeine may trigger attacks

 GENDER Not a significant factor

Supraventricular tachycardia (SVT) is a type of arrhythmia caused by a fault in the electrical pathway that regulates the heart rate. During an episode of SVT, which may last up to several hours, the heartbeat is rapid but regular. The heart rate rises to 140–180 beats per minute and sometimes climbs even higher. In a heart that is working normally, each heartbeat is triggered by an electrical impulse from the sinoatrial node (the heart's pacemaker), located in the right atrium (one of the heart's upper chambers). The impulse passes to a second node, the atrioventricular node, which relays it to the ventricles. In SVT, the heartbeat is not controlled by the sinoatrial node, either because an abnormal pathway develops, causing an impulse to circulate continuously between the atrioventricular node and the ventricles, or because an extra node develops and sends out pacemaking impulses.

SVT may first appear in childhood or adolescence, although it can occur at any age. In some cases, SVT is caused by an inherited abnormality in the heart's electrical pathways. Episodes generally occur for no apparent reason, but they may be triggered by exertion and by caffeine and alcohol.

WHAT ARE THE SYMPTOMS?

The symptoms of SVT usually develop suddenly. They last from a few seconds to several hours and include:

- Palpitations (awareness of an irregular or abnormally rapid heartbeat).
- Light-headedness.
- Pain in the chest or neck.

Heart failure (p.412) can be a complication of SVT. In rare cases, a long episode of SVT may reduce blood pressure to a life-threatening level.

WHAT MIGHT BE DONE?

If your doctor suspects that you have SVT, you will probably have electrocardiography (*see* ECG, p.406), in order to record the electrical activity of your

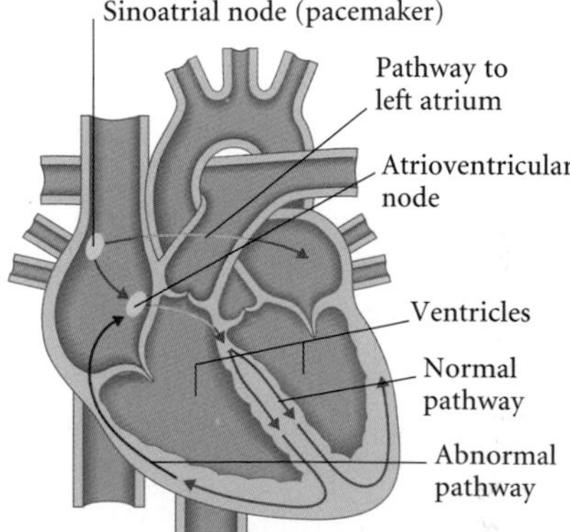
Sinoatrial node (pacemaker)
Pathway to left atrium
Atrioventricular node
Ventricles
Normal pathway
Abnormal pathway

Supraventricular tachycardia (SVT)
Impulses from the sinoatrial node normally control heart rate. One cause of SVT is an abnormal electrical pathway, which allows an impulse to circulate continuously in the heart, taking over from the sinoatrial node.

TEST AND TREATMENT CARDIAC ELECTROPHYSIOLOGICAL STUDIES

Cardiac electrophysiological studies (EPS) are used to pinpoint abnormal pathways in the heart's electrical conducting system. A catheter that has electrodes at its tip is introduced into the heart and manipulated to record the electrical activity at different sites. Once an abnormal pathway is located, it can be destroyed by sending a current through the electrodes in a procedure known as radiofrequency ablation. Radiofrequency ablation can provide a permanent cure for some disorders in about one minute and has a high success rate.

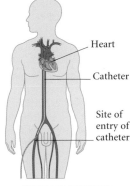

Heart
Catheter
Site of entry of catheter

ROUTE OF CATHETER

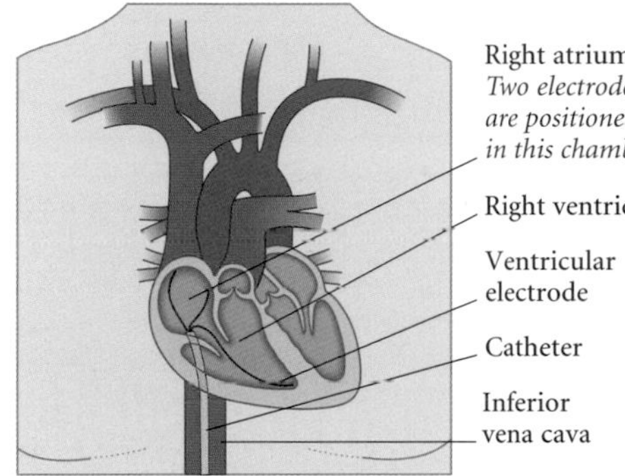
Right atrium
Two electrodes are positioned in this chamber
Right ventricle
Ventricular electrode
Catheter
Inferior vena cava

During EPS
A catheter is inserted into a vein in the groin under local anesthesia and threaded into the heart. Electrodes at the tip of the catheter detect electrical activity and can be used to deliver a current to destroy abnormal pathways.

heart and to detect any arrhythmia (abnormal heart rate and/or rhythm). This investigation may last 24 hours or more (*see* AMBULATORY ECG, opposite page) because SVT occurs only intermittently. You may have to undergo further tests to look for abnormalities in the electrical pathways of the heart (*see* CARDIAC ELECTROPHYSIOLOGICAL STUDIES, above).

A prolonged and severe episode of SVT requires emergency hospital treatment. In the hospital, you may be given oxygen and an intravenous injection of an antiarrhythmic drug (p.898). In some cases, an electric shock may be given to restore the heart to its normal rate (*see* CARDIOVERSION, p.420).

People who have occasional, brief episodes of SVT can control the symptoms by stimulating the vagus nerve, to slow the heart rate. One way to stimulate the nerve is to rub the area over the carotid artery in the neck. Discuss this with your doctor.

Troublesome episodes of SVT may be treated with long-term antiarrhythmic drugs. SVT may be cured by radio-frequency ablation, a treatment carried out during cardiac electrophysiological studies. This treatment destroys abnormal electrical pathways but carries a small risk of causing complete heart block (p.418), in which the heart's electrical system fails, greatly reducing the heart's efficiency. In most cases, SVT does not affect life expectancy.

WWW ONLINE SITES: p.1032

Atrial fibrillation

Rapid, uncoordinated contractions of the atria, the upper chambers of the heart

 AGE Most common in people over age 60

 GENDER More common in males

 LIFESTYLE Smoking, a high-fat diet, alcohol abuse, lack of exercise, and excess weight are risk factors

 GENETICS Not a significant factor

Atrial fibrillation is the most common type of rapid, irregular heart rate. It affects up to 1 in 10 people over age 60 in the US. During atrial fibrillation, the atria contract weakly at 300–500 beats per minute. Only some of the electrical impulses that cause this rapid beating are conducted through the heart to the ventricles (the lower chambers), which also beat faster than normal, at up to 160 beats per minute. Since the atria and ventricles are no longer beating in rhythm, the heartbeat becomes irregular in timing and in strength, leading to less blood being pumped.

The most dangerous complication of atrial fibrillation is stroke (p.532), the risk of which increases with age. Since the atria do not empty properly during contractions, blood stagnates in them and may form a clot. If a part of the clot breaks off and enters the bloodstream, it may block an artery anywhere in the body (*see* THROMBOSIS AND EMBOLISM, p.431). A stroke occurs when part of a clot blocks an artery supplying the brain.

WHAT ARE THE CAUSES?

Atrial fibrillation may occur for no apparent reason, especially in the elderly, but it is usually due to an underlying disorder that causes the atria to enlarge. Such disorders include heart valve disorders (p.421), coronary artery disease (p.405), and high blood pressure (*see* HYPERTENSION, p.403). Smoking, lack of exercise, a high-fat diet, and being overweight are risk factors for many of these disorders. Atrial fibrillation is also common in people with an overactive thyroid gland (*see* HYPERTHYROIDISM, p.679) or low potassium levels in the blood. It may occur in people who drink excessive amounts of alcohol.

WHAT ARE THE SYMPTOMS?

Symptoms do not always develop, but, if they do, their onset is usually sudden. The symptoms may be intermittent or persistent and typically include:

- Palpitations (awareness of an irregular or abnormally rapid heartbeat).
- Light-headedness.
- Shortness of breath.
- Chest pain.

Stroke and heart failure (p.412) are possible complications.

WHAT MIGHT BE DONE?

Your doctor may suspect atrial fibrillation if you have a fast, irregular pulse. To confirm the diagnosis, you will have electrocardiography (*see* ECG, p.406) to check your heartbeat. You may have blood tests to look for an underlying cause such as hyperthyroidism.

If an underlying cause such as hypertension or hyperthyroidism is found, treatment of it often cures the arrhythmia. If atrial fibrillation is diagnosed early, it may be treated successfully using cardioversion (p.420), in which an electric shock is applied to the heart.

Atrial fibrillation is usually treated with antiarrhythmic drugs (p.898), such as beta blocker drugs (p.898) or digitalis drugs (p.901). These drugs slow the conduction of electrical impulses from the atria to the ventricles, giving the ventricles sufficient time to fill with blood between each heartbeat. Other antiarrhythmic drugs are then used to treat the irregular rhythm. You may also be prescribed the anticoagulant drug warfarin, which reduces the risk of blood clot formation (*see* DRUGS THAT PREVENT BLOOD CLOTTING, p.904) and thereby lowers the risk of a stroke.

(WWW) ONLINE SITES: p.1032

Complete heart block

Complete failure of the system that conducts electrical impulses from the upper to the lower heart chambers

AGE More common in elderly people

LIFESTYLE Smoking, a high-fat diet, lack of exercise, and excess weight are risk factors

GENDER GENETICS Not significant factors

In complete heart block, damage to the heart's conductive tissue prevents electrical impulses from the atria (the upper chambers) from reaching the ventricles (the lower chambers), so that the ventricles cannot contract normally. Heart muscle contracts automatically in the absence of a regulating signal. In complete heart block, the ventricles contract at about 40 beats per minute instead of the usual rate of 60–100 beats per minute, which greatly reduces the heart's efficiency. In some cases, the heart stops beating altogether for up to 20 seconds.

The tissue damage that causes complete heart block becomes more likely in elderly people and may be linked with coronary artery disease (p.405), for which lifestyle factors such as smoking increase the risk. Sudden complete heart block, which may be either temporary or permanent, may follow a heart attack (*see* MYOCARDIAL INFARCTION, p.410).

WHAT ARE THE SYMPTOMS?

The symptoms may come on gradually or suddenly and typically include:

- Palpitations (awareness of an irregular heartbeat).
- Light-headedness, and loss of consciousness if the heart stops beating.
- Shortness of breath.
- Chest pain.

If left untreated, complete heart block may lead to heart failure (p.412), stroke (p.532), and shock (p.414).

WHAT MIGHT BE DONE?

Complete heart block is usually suspected if you have a very slow heartbeat and is confirmed by electrocardiography (*see* ECG, p.406). Initial treatment may involve the temporary insertion of a pacing wire into the heart, usually through a vein in the chest or groin. The wire transmits electrical impulses that restore a normal heartbeat until an artificial pacemaker can be permanently fitted (*see* CARDIAC PACEMAKER, opposite page). Pacemakers may successfully restore a normal heart rate, but the overall prognosis depends on whether there is an underlying disorder, such as coronary artery disease.

(WWW) ONLINE SITES: p.1032

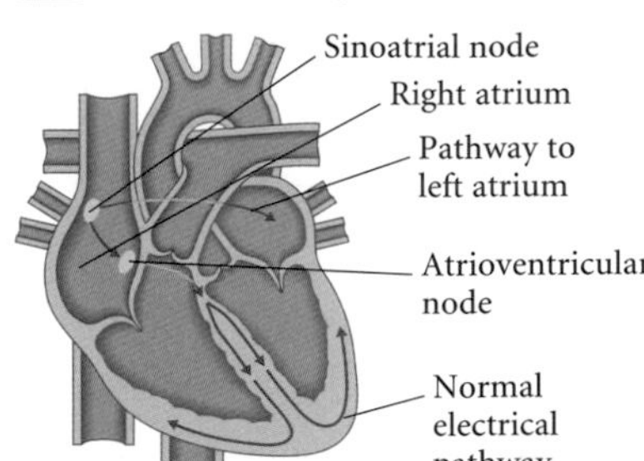
Sinoatrial node
Right atrium
Pathway to left atrium
Atrioventricular node
Normal electrical pathway
NORMAL

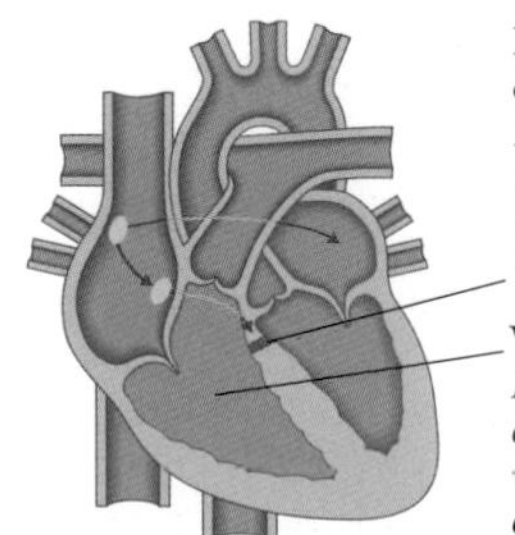
Damaged conductive tissue
Damaged tissue blocks electrical impulses to the ventricles
Ventricles
In the absence of impulses, the ventricles do not contract normally
ABNORMAL

Block in the heart's electrical system
Normally, electrical impulses pass from the sinoatrial node to the atrioventricular node in the right atrium and then to the ventricles. In complete heart block, the impulses cannot reach the ventricles.

TREATMENT CARDIAC PACEMAKER

Cardiac pacemakers stimulate the heart with electrical impulses to maintain a regular heartbeat. Pacemakers are used to treat disorders in which the heart's electrical conducting system is faulty, such as complete heart block. Some pacemakers produce impulses continually; others send an impulse only when the heart rate falls too low. Defibrillator pacemakers deliver an electric shock to the heart when ventricular fibrillation (rapid, uncoordinated contraction of the lower chambers of the heart) occurs to restore the normal rate and rhythm.

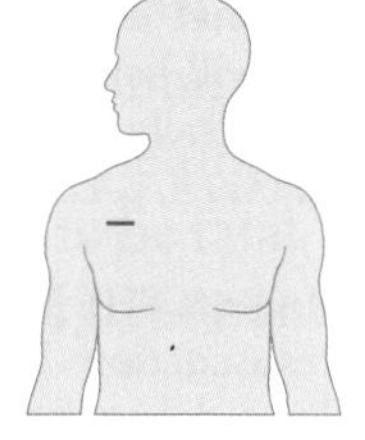

SITE OF INCISION

Insertion of a pacemaker
A pacemaker is inserted just under the skin and stitched into position in the chest wall, usually under local anesthesia. Two wires from the pacemaker are passed into the large vein above the heart (superior vena cava). One wire is guided into the right atrium and the other into the right ventricle.

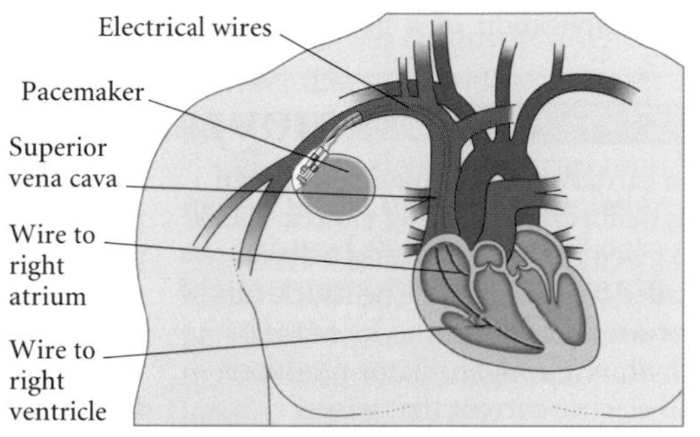
Electrical wires
Pacemaker
Superior vena cava
Wire to right atrium
Wire to right ventricle

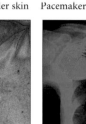

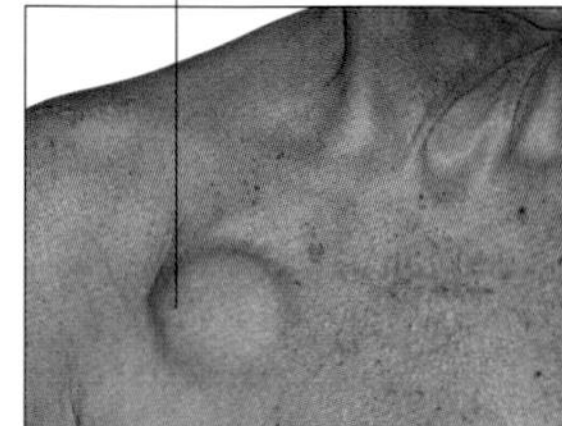
Pacemaker under skin

EXTERNAL VIEW

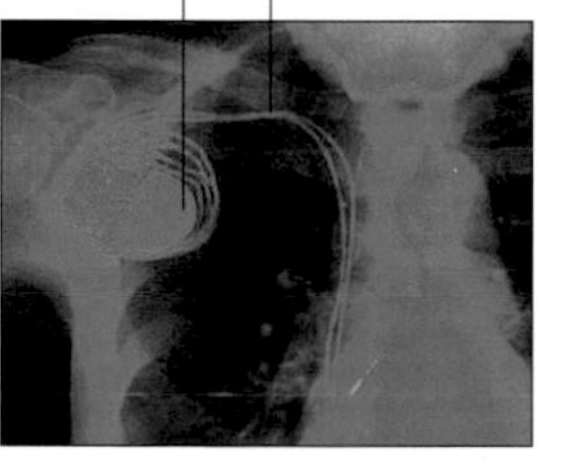
Pacemaker
Electrical wires

X-RAY IMAGE

Pacemaker in place
The pacemaker is implanted into the chest and appears as a small bulge under the skin. An X-ray image reveals the wires that lead from the pacemaker to the right atrium and ventricle of the heart.

Sick sinus syndrome

Abnormal function of the sinoatrial node, the heart's natural pacemaker

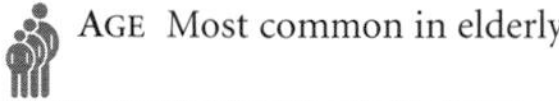
AGE Most common in elderly people

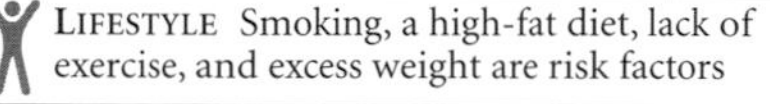
LIFESTYLE Smoking, a high-fat diet, lack of exercise, and excess weight are risk factors

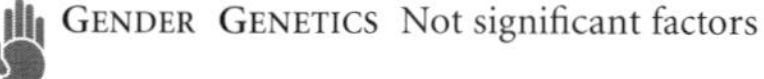
GENDER GENETICS Not significant factors

In sick sinus syndrome, the sinoatrial node, the heart's natural pacemaker, becomes faulty, causing the heart to beat too slowly or to miss a few beats. In some cases, the heart rate alternates between runs of slow and fast beats. Sick sinus syndrome is caused by the degeneration of cells in the sinoatrial node and is most common in elderly people. In most cases, the underlying cause is coronary artery disease (p.405), the risk of which is increased by lifestyle factors such as smoking. Sick sinus syndrome may also be due to heart muscle disease (*see* DILATED CARDIOMYOPATHY, p.427). Typically, sick sinus syndrome is progressive, and episodes become more frequent and prolonged over time.

WHAT ARE THE SYMPTOMS?

Symptoms have a sudden onset and are intermittent. They may include:

- Palpitations (awareness of an irregular heartbeat).
- Brief attacks of light-headedness.
- Loss of consciousness.
- Shortness of breath.

Many of the symptoms are caused by decreased oxygen levels to the brain due to the reduced efficiency of the heart.

WHAT MIGHT BE DONE?

If your doctor suspects that you have sick sinus syndrome, he or she will probably arrange for you to have electrocardiography (*see* ECG, p.406). Since symptoms are intermittent, you may need to have your heartbeat monitored for 24 hours or more while you carry out your everyday activities (*see* AMBULATORY ECG, p.416). Your doctor may also recommend that you have further tests, such as echocardiography (p.425), to look for signs of cardiomyopathy.

Treatment usually involves inserting a pacemaker to stimulate the heart when it is beating too slowly (*see* CARDIAC PACEMAKER, left). If the heart is alternating between fast and slow rates, antiarrhythmic drugs (p.898) may also be given to slow down the fast heart rate. If a pacemaker is required, you will need regular checkups with a doctor or a pacemaker technician.

Sick sinus syndrome can usually be treated successfully with a pacemaker or drugs. However, the overall prognosis depends on the underlying condition.

(WWW) ONLINE SITES: p.1032

Cardiac arrest

Sudden failure of the heart to pump blood, which is often fatal

AGE More common with increasing age

GENDER More common in males

LIFESTYLE Smoking, a high-fat diet, lack of exercise, and excess weight are risk factors

GENETICS Not a significant factor

During cardiac arrest, the heart stops pumping. As a result, the brain and other organs no longer receive oxygenated blood, without which they cannot function. Within 3 minutes of cardiac arrest, the brain will have sustained some damage. Death is likely to occur within 5 minutes if the pumping action of the heart is not restored by emergency treatment or if circulation is not maintained by external cardiac massage.

WHAT ARE THE CAUSES?

Cardiac arrest is commonly caused by one of two types of electrical problems in the heart: ventricular fibrillation, the more common type, and asystole. During ventricular fibrillation, the ventricles (lower chambers of the heart) rapidly contract in an uncoordinated manner, preventing the heart from pumping out

TREATMENT HEART VALVE REPLACEMENT

Heart valves may need to be replaced if daily activities are affected by symptoms and the valve cannot be repaired by surgery. Replacement heart valves made of tissue may come from a human donor or from a pig's heart. Valves may also be mechanical. Replacing heart valves involves open heart surgery. During the operation, the heart is stopped, and its function is taken over by a heart–lung machine (*see* SURGERY USING A HEART–LUNG MACHINE, p.953). You may stay in the hospital for up to 21 days after surgery while you recover. If a mechanical valve is used, drugs that prevent blood clotting (p.904) are taken for life to reduce the risk of clots forming on the valve.

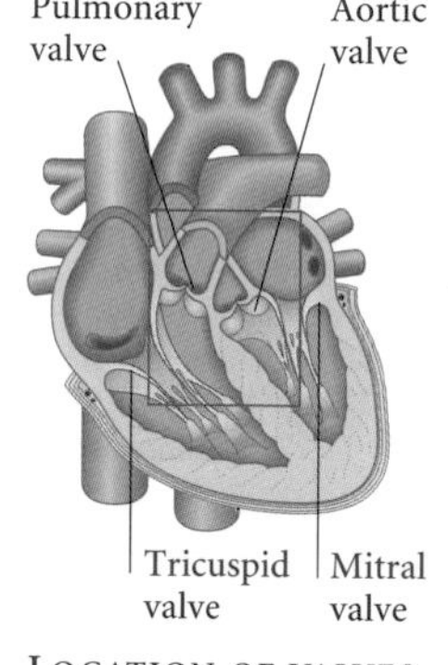
Pulmonary valve
Aortic valve
Tricuspid valve
Mitral valve

LOCATION OF VALVES

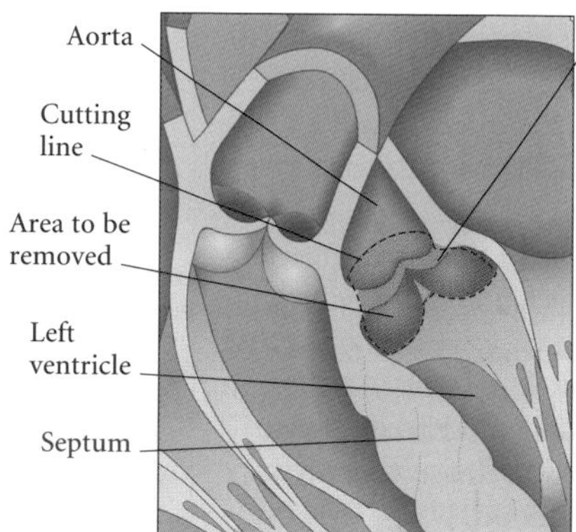
Aorta
Cutting line
Area to be removed
Left ventricle
Septum
Diseased aortic valve

Aortic valve replacement
The aortic valve is the most commonly replaced heart valve. An incision is made in the aorta, the major blood vessel from the heart, to gain access to the valve. The diseased valve is cut out, leaving a ring of tissue to which the replacement aortic valve is then stitched.

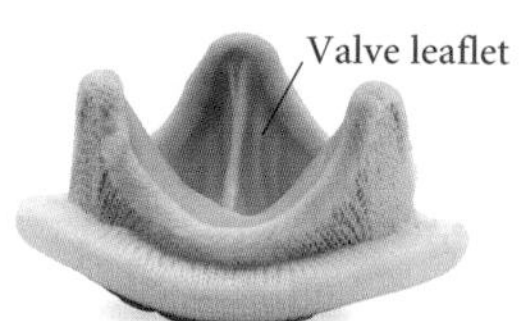
Valve leaflet

TISSUE VALVE

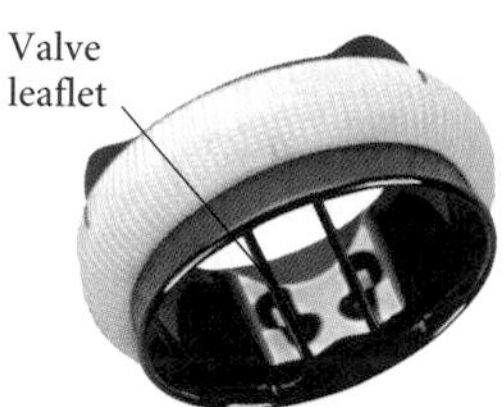
Valve leaflet

MECHANICAL AORTIC VALVE

Replacement valves
Tissue valves have three leaflets that open and close to control blood flow. In one type of mechanical valve, two leaflets open and close to regulate blood flow through the valve.

If treatment is needed, you may be given drugs to strengthen the heartbeat or relieve the symptoms. In severe valve disorders, surgery may be needed to repair or replace the valve (*see* HEART VALVE REPLACEMENT, above). Your doctor may advise you to take a single dose of an antibiotic (p.885) before you have dental treatment or certain operations, such as those on the digestive tract, that could allow infection into the blood.

WWW ONLINE SITES: p.1032

Aortic regurgitation

Leakage of blood back through the aortic valve of the heart

 GENDER More common in males

 GENETICS In some cases, the condition is inherited

 AGE LIFESTYLE Not significant factors

The aortic valve separates the left lower chamber of the heart (the left ventricle) from the aorta, which is the main artery leading from the heart. This valve normally stops blood from flowing back into the heart from the aorta. In aortic regurgitation, the valve leaflets (flaps) do not close tightly, letting blood leak back from the aorta into the heart. As a result, the heart has to pump harder to circulate blood around the body, and this may eventually lead to the development of chronic heart failure (p.413).

WHAT ARE THE CAUSES?

A normal aortic valve has three leaflets. Approximately 2 percent of people are born with an abnormal valve having only two leaflets. On occasion this can lead to aortic regurgitation. Some of these cases are due to the rare genetic disorder Marfan syndrome (p.824). A possible cause of valve damage later in life is infection (*see* INFECTIVE ENDOCARDITIS, p.426). The aortic valve flaps may also become leaky as a result of the rare inflammatory joint disorder ankylosing spondylitis (p.378). Other causes include rheumatic fever (p.429) and syphilis, but these diseases are now rare in many countries due to effective antibiotics. In some developing countries, rheumatic fever is still common.

WHAT ARE THE SYMPTOMS?

If aortic regurgitation is mild, it may not cause symptoms. If aortic regurgitation is severe, then symptoms may develop, including:

- Fatigue.
- Shortness of breath during exertion.
- Awareness of the heart beating strongly.

Heart failure may eventually develop, leading to symptoms such as constant shortness of breath and swollen ankles.

WHAT MIGHT BE DONE?

If there are no symptoms, aortic regurgitation is usually discovered during a routine examination. Your doctor may then arrange for electrocardiography (*see* ECG, p.406) to evaluate the electrical activity of the heart. In addition, the heart may be imaged by echocardiography (p.425). A chest X-ray (p.490) may also be taken to see if the heart has enlarged due to heart failure.

If the condition is mild, often no treatment is needed. If chronic heart failure develops or if you have symptoms, you may need treatment with drugs such as ACE inhibitor drugs (p.900).

If drug treatment fails to relieve your symptoms, surgery may be needed to repair the valve or to replace it with a tissue valve from a human donor or a pig or with a mechanical valve (*see* HEART VALVE REPLACEMENT, above). Surgery is more likely to be successful if it is done before heart failure becomes advanced.

An abnormal or replacement aortic valve is more susceptible to infection than a normal valve. Your doctor may therefore advise you to take a single dose of an antibiotic (p.885) before dental treatment or before operations that carry a risk of introducing bacteria into the bloodstream, such as surgery on the digestive or urinary tracts.

Once the damaged aortic valve has been repaired or replaced, the prognosis for the affected person is good and life expectancy should be normal.

(WWW) ONLINE SITES: p.1032

Aortic stenosis

Narrowing of the aortic valve, reducing the flow of blood into the circulation

 AGE May be present at birth but most common in people over age 70

 GENDER More common in males

 GENETICS LIFESTYLE Not significant factors

The aortic valve separates the left lower chamber (left ventricle) of the heart and the main artery of the body, the aorta. The valve opens to allow blood to flow out of the heart. In aortic stenosis, the opening of the valve is narrowed, reducing the flow of blood through it. The heart then has to pump harder to compensate. Aortic stenosis is the most common valve disorder in the US and is found most often in males.

WHAT ARE THE CAUSES?

In young people in developed countries, aortic stenosis is usually the result of a heart abnormality that is present at birth (*see* CONGENITAL HEART DISEASE, p.836). In elderly people, aortic stenosis is often caused by calcium deposits on the valve, which naturally build up over time. Rheumatic fever (p.429) was once a common cause of aortic stenosis. However, rheumatic fever is now rare in developed countries, mainly due to the use of effective antibiotics.

WHAT ARE THE SYMPTOMS?

In mild cases of aortic stenosis, often there are no symptoms. In some cases of mild stenosis, fatigue may be the only symptom. Other symptoms may develop in more severe cases, such as:

- Dizziness and fainting.
- Chest pain during exertion.
- Shortness of breath.

If the opening through the aortic valve is very narrow, the flow of blood to the coronary arteries that supply blood to the heart muscle is reduced. This eventually leads to breathlessness due to chronic heart failure (p.413). Abnormal heart rhythms may also develop (*see* ARRHYTHMIAS, p.415), and infection of the valves is more likely.

HOW IS IT DIAGNOSED?

Mild aortic stenosis is often detected only during a routine examination. If your doctor suspects that you have aortic stenosis, he or she may arrange for echocardiography (p.425) to image the interior of the heart, including the aortic valve. You may also have a chest X-ray (p.490) because, if there is stenosis, calcium deposits on the valve may be visible on the X-ray. The severity of stenosis can be assessed by a procedure called cardiac catheterization, in which a flexible catheter is inserted into an artery in the arm or groin and passed into the heart. A small device attached to the catheter then measures the pressures on either side of the valve.

WHAT IS THE TREATMENT?

Mild aortic stenosis usually requires no treatment. When breathlessness develops, diuretic drugs (p.902) work by removing excess fluid from the lungs. When aortic stenosis is severe, a heart valve replacement (opposite page) is often needed. You may need a single dose of an antibiotic (p.885) before you have dental treatment or operations that may introduce infection, such as those on the digestive or urinary tracts. The prognosis is good if treatment is given before the heart muscle becomes badly damaged.

(WWW) ONLINE SITES: p.1032

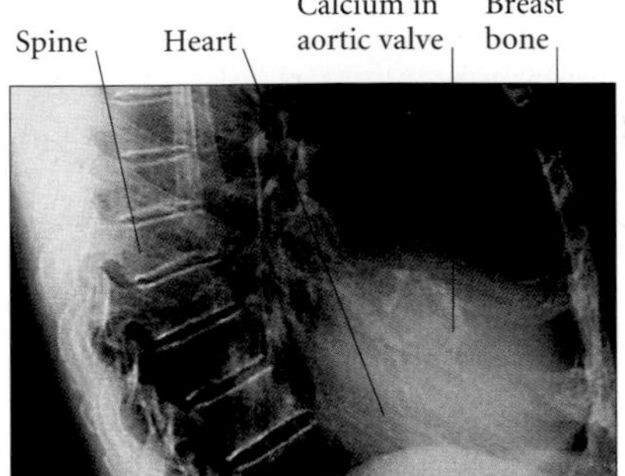
Spine
Heart
Calcium in aortic valve
Breast bone

Aortic stenosis

This chest X-ray taken from the side shows calcium deposits that have formed in a narrowed aortic valve. The deposits make the valve visible on the X-ray.

Mitral regurgitation

Leakage of blood back through the mitral valve of the heart

 GENETICS In some cases, the condition is inherited

 AGE GENDER LIFESTYLE Risk factors depend on the cause

The mitral valve sits between the upper chamber (atrium) and the lower chamber (ventricle) on the left side of the heart. In mitral regurgitation, the valve fails to close properly and allows blood to leak back into the atrium. This increases the pressure in the blood vessels leading to that chamber. The left side of the heart has to work harder to pump blood around the body, and eventually chronic heart failure (p.413) develops. Mitral regurgitation can occur in conjunction with mitral stenosis (p.424).

WHAT ARE THE CAUSES?

In rare cases, mitral regurgitation is present at birth, sometimes as a result of the rare genetic disorder Marfan syndrome (p.824). Any condition that damages the mitral valve can lead to mitral regurgitation. Rheumatic fever (p.429) was once a common cause of the disorder but is now rarely seen in developed countries, mainly due to the use of antibiotics (p.885). A more common cause is an infection of the valve (*see* INFECTIVE ENDOCARDITIS, p.426). Hypertrophic cardiomyopathy (p.428), in which the wall of the left ventricle is thickened, may distort the valve, causing regurgitation. The disorder may also occur as a consequence of a heart attack if the heart muscle attached to the valve is affected (*see* MYOCARDIAL INFARCTION, p.410). In some cases, mitral regurgitation occurs with mitral valve prolapse (p.425).

WHAT ARE THE SYMPTOMS?

Symptoms of mitral regurgitation usually develop gradually over months or years but may appear suddenly if the cause is a heart attack or valve infection. The symptoms include:

- Fatigue.
- Shortness of breath during exertion.
- Palpitations (awareness of an irregular or abnormally rapid heartbeat).

Eventually, symptoms of chronic heart failure may occur, such as shortness of breath at rest as well as during exertion, due to fluid in the lungs. The buildup of fluid in the body tissues also causes swelling of the ankles.

ARE THERE COMPLICATIONS?

The backward blood flow into the left atrium may enlarge it, leading to an irregular heartbeat (*see* ATRIAL FIBRILLATION, p.417). If the atrium is so large that it cannot empty fully with each heartbeat, a blood clot may form. If a clot passes into an artery supplying the brain and blocks it, the result may be a stroke (p.532). Another potential complication is infection of the leaky mitral valve after dental treatment or surgery on the digestive or urinary tracts.

WHAT MIGHT BE DONE?

Your doctor may suspect mitral regurgitation if he or she hears characteristic sounds known as heart murmurs. Tests to assess the function of the heart and lungs may be carried out, including an ECG (p.406) to monitor the electrical activity of the heart and a chest X-ray (p.490). The interior of the heart may be imaged by echocardiography (opposite page) to confirm the diagnosis. This procedure can show the movements of the mitral valve.

If heart failure develops, drugs such as diuretics (p.902) may be prescribed to relieve the symptoms. If the left atrium becomes enlarged, you may also be given drugs that prevent blood clotting (p.904) to lessen the risk of clots in the atrium. Severe mitral regurgitation may need to be treated with surgery to repair the valve or replace the valve (p.422). If you have a damaged or replacement heart valve, you may be advised to take a single dose of an antibiotic (p.885) before dental treatment and surgical procedures such as those on the digestive or urinary tracts.

The prognosis for mitral regurgitation is good if treatment is given before the heart has become badly damaged.

(WWW) ONLINE SITES: p.1032

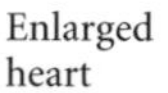

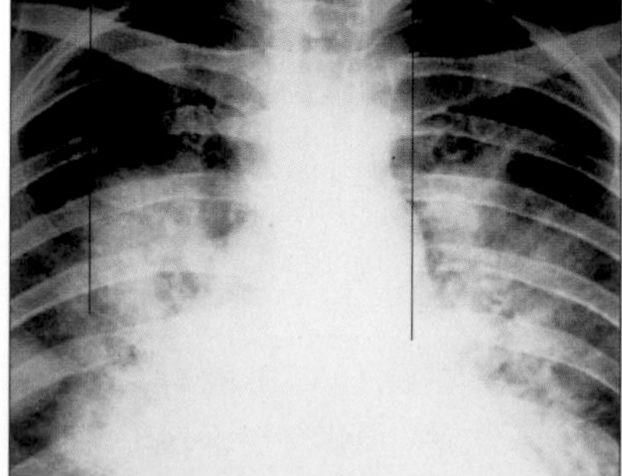
Fluid in lung tissue
Enlarged heart

Effects of mitral regurgitation
Enlargement of the heart and excess fluid in the lungs, which are indications of heart failure caused by mitral regurgitation, can be seen on this chest X-ray.

Mitral stenosis

Narrowing of the mitral valve, resulting in a decrease in blood flow within the heart

 AGE More common after age 40

 GENDER More common in females

 GENETICS LIFESTYLE Not significant factors

The mitral valve sits between the upper chamber (atrium) and lower chamber (ventricle) on the left side of the heart. In mitral stenosis, the opening of this valve is narrowed, restricting the blood flow through the atrium. The heart works harder to pump blood through the narrow valve, and chronic heart failure (p.413) may eventually develop. Mitral stenosis is more common in females and sometimes occurs with mitral regurgitation (p.423).

WHAT ARE THE CAUSES?

Mitral stenosis is almost always due to damage to the valve caused by an earlier attack of rheumatic fever (p.429). This condition is now rare in developed countries, and, in the US, mitral stenosis is most often found in middle-aged or elderly people who had rheumatic fever during their childhood. In rare cases, mitral stenosis is present at birth.

WHAT ARE THE SYMPTOMS?

Symptoms usually develop gradually in adulthood and may include:

- Fatigue.
- Shortness of breath, occurring during exertion at first but later also at rest.
- Palpitations (awareness of an irregular or abnormally rapid heartbeat).

As the stenosis becomes worse, the symptoms of heart failure may develop, including swelling of the tissues, which is most noticeable in the ankles.

ARE THERE COMPLICATIONS?

Sometimes, the atria beat irregularly and rapidly (*see* ATRIAL FIBRILLATION, p.417). Blood clots may also form on the wall of the left atrium because it does not empty fully. If fragments of clots break off, they may block a blood vessel elsewhere in the body. If the clot blocks an artery supplying the brain, the result may be a stroke (p.532).

HOW IS IT DIAGNOSED?

Your doctor will examine you and will probably arrange for an ECG (p.406) to assess the electrical activity of the heart. The inside of the heart may be imaged by echocardiography (opposite page), a technique that shows the movement of the heart valves. You may also have a chest X-ray (p.490). The severity of the stenosis may be assessed by a procedure in which a tube called a cardiac catheter is inserted through blood vessels into the heart. The catheter is attached to a device that measures the pressure on either side of the valve.

WHAT IS THE TREATMENT?

In most cases of mitral stenosis, drug treatment is used to relieve the symptoms. For example, diuretic drugs (p.902) may be prescribed to remove excess fluid from the body and relieve shortness of breath. Antiarrhythmic drugs (p.898) may be given to help correct an abnormal heart rhythm. Drugs that prevent blood clotting (p.904) are often prescribed to reduce the risk of blood clots forming in the heart.

If drug treatment is ineffective, a balloon valvuloplasty may be performed, in which a balloon-tipped catheter is passed into the heart and the balloon briefly inflated inside the stenosed valve to widen it. Alternatively, the valve may be repaired or replaced by surgery (*see* HEART VALVE REPLACEMENT, p.422).

An abnormal or replacement valve is susceptible to infection. For this reason, you may be advised to take a single dose of an antibiotic (p.885) before having dental treatment or operations on the digestive or urinary tracts when bacteria may enter the bloodstream.

Mitral stenosis may recur after a balloon valvuloplasty. If needed, a heart valve replacement is often effective for 10 years or more.

(WWW) ONLINE SITES: p.1032

TEST ECHOCARDIOGRAPHY

Echocardiography is a technique that uses ultrasound waves to image the interior of the heart. The test looks at the size and function of the heart and is used to diagnose disorders of the heart and the heart valves. The test is usually done by using an ultrasound transducer (probe) placed on the skin of the chest directly over the heart. In some cases, a small probe is passed down the esophagus instead so that it is close to the back of the heart. A moving image of the beating heart with its valves and chambers is then produced. The test takes about 20 minutes and is painless.

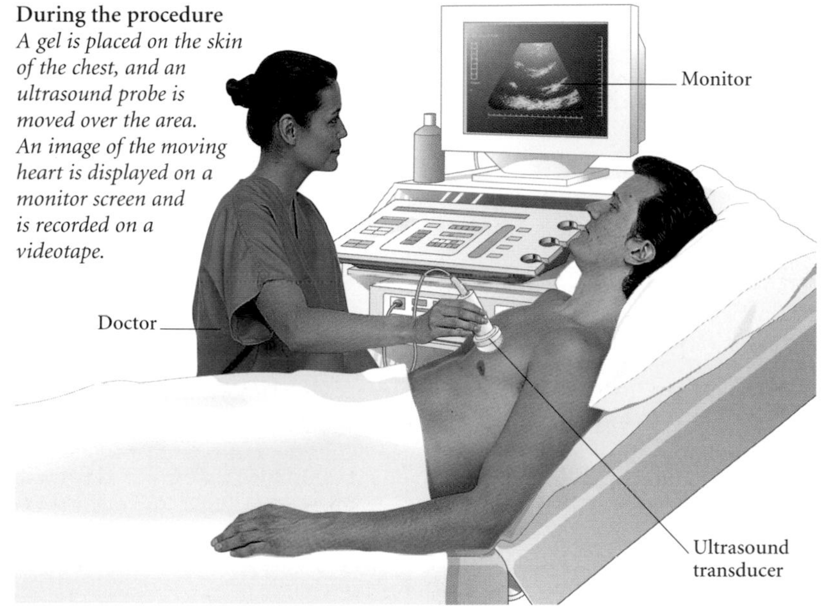
Monitor
Doctor
Ultrasound transducer

During the procedure
A gel is placed on the skin of the chest, and an ultrasound probe is moved over the area. An image of the moving heart is displayed on a monitor screen and is recorded on a videotape.

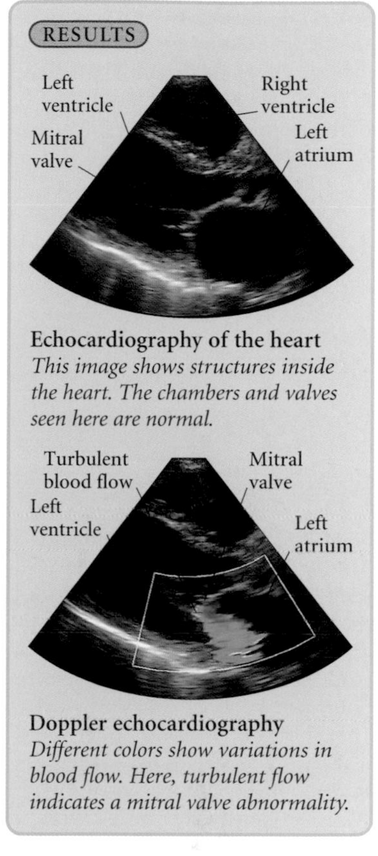
RESULTS
Left ventricle
Right ventricle
Mitral valve
Left atrium
Turbulent blood flow
Mitral valve
Left ventricle
Left atrium

Echocardiography of the heart
This image shows structures inside the heart. The chambers and valves seen here are normal.

Doppler echocardiography
Different colors show variations in blood flow. Here, turbulent flow indicates a mitral valve abnormality.

Mitral valve prolapse

A minor abnormality of the mitral valve, also known as floppy mitral valve

 AGE Most common between the ages of 20 and 40

 GENDER More common in females

 GENETICS In some cases, the condition is inherited

 LIFESTYLE Not a significant factor

The mitral valve sits between the upper chamber (atrium) and the lower chamber (ventricle) on the left side of the heart. This valve normally closes tightly when the heart contracts to pump blood out into the circulation. In the disorder mitral valve prolapse, the valve is slightly deformed and bulges back into the left atrium. This prolapse may allow a small amount of blood to leak back into the atrium (*see* MITRAL REGURGITATION, p.423). Mitral valve prolapse is common, occurring in up to 2 percent of people. The condition occurs most commonly in young or middle-aged women, but often the cause is not known. In some cases, mitral valve prolapse is associated with the rare genetic disorder Marfan syndrome (p.824).

WHAT ARE THE SYMPTOMS?

Mitral valve prolapse usually causes no symptoms, and most people are unaware that they have the condition. If symptoms do occur, they are usually intermittent and may include:

- Light-headedness.
- Fainting.
- Sharp, left-sided chest pains.
- Palpitations (awareness of an irregular or abnormally rapid heartbeat).

There is also an increased chance that a floppy valve may become further damaged by an infection (*see* INFECTIVE ENDOCARDITIS, p.426), particularly following dental procedures or surgery on the digestive or urinary tracts.

HOW IS IT DIAGNOSED?

Your doctor may suspect mitral valve prolapse if he or she hears a characteristic clicking sound when listening to your heart with a stethoscope. Your doctor may arrange for tests to confirm the diagnosis, including an ECG (p.406) to monitor the electrical activity of the heart. The diagnosis is usually confirmed by echocardiography (above), which examines the movements of the valves. If you have palpitations, your heart rhythm may also be monitored over a period of 24 hours while you perform your normal activities (*see* AMBULATORY ECG, p.416).

WHAT IS THE TREATMENT?

Most people with mitral valve prolapse need no treatment. If symptoms such as an irregular heartbeat cause problems, an antiarrhythmic drug (p.898) may be prescribed. You may also be prescribed a single dose of an antibiotic (p.885) before dental treatment or some operations, such as those on the digestive or urinary tracts.

The disorder usually has no effect on life expectancy, but, in very rare cases, mitral regurgitation develops, leading to chronic heart failure (p.413). Heart valve replacement (p.422) may then be needed, but the prognosis is still good.

(WWW) ONLINE SITES: p.1032

Infective endocarditis

Inflammation of the lining of the heart, particularly affecting the heart valves, caused by an infection

LIFESTYLE Intravenous drug abuse increases the risk

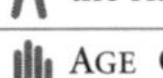
AGE GENDER GENETICS Not significant factors

The internal lining of the heart, the endocardium, may become infected if microorganisms enter the bloodstream and reach the heart. The infection causes the lining, especially over the heart valves, to become inflamed, and bacteria and blood clots can accumulate over the inflamed areas. The valves are particularly prone to infection if they are already damaged or if they are replacement valves (*see* HEART VALVE REPLACEMENT, p.422).

In most cases, infective endocarditis is a chronic disorder that develops over weeks or months and causes only vague symptoms, such as a fever and aching joints. Rarely, endocarditis is an acute disorder that may rapidly damage one or more of the heart valves and within days cause acute heart failure (p.412), which may be life-threatening.

WHAT ARE THE CAUSES?

The most common causes of infective endocarditis are bacteria and, less often, fungi. Microorganisms that are normally harmless may enter the blood during dental procedures, especially tooth extraction, and operations on the digestive or urinary tracts. The condition occasionally also occurs after a medical procedure, such as the insertion of a catheter into the bladder. Rarely, infective endocarditis develops after cardiac surgery, especially if artificial materials, such as replacement heart valves, are inserted into the heart.

People with a suppressed immune system are particularly susceptible to infective endocarditis because the body is less able to fight the infection. For example, anyone with HIV infection or AIDS (p.295) or who is undergoing treatment with anticancer drugs (p.907) is at increased risk of developing infective endocarditis. People who abuse intravenous drugs are also particularly susceptible to the infection, especially if needles are shared, because microorganisms can be injected into the bloodstream and travel to the heart.

WHAT ARE THE SYMPTOMS?

The symptoms of chronic endocarditis are often generalized and unrelated to heart damage. They may include:

- Fatigue.
- Fever and night sweats.
- Aching joints.
- Weight loss.

Infected material from the valve may break off and block a vessel elsewhere in the body. For example, small clots may lodge in veins under the fingernails or skin, causing tiny splinterlike hemorrhages. If a clot blocks an artery that supplies blood to the brain, it may result in a stroke (p.532).

The symptoms of acute endocarditis develop suddenly and may include:

- High fever.
- Palpitations (awareness of an irregular or abnormally rapid heartbeat).

These symptoms can rapidly worsen. If acute heart failure develops, there may be other symptoms, such as shortness of breath and swollen ankles.

HOW IS IT DIAGNOSED?

Chronic infective endocarditis is difficult to diagnose because the symptoms are often unrelated to heart damage. Your doctor may suspect the disorder if he or she hears a new heart murmur or a change in an existing heart murmur. The diagnosis may be confirmed by echocardiography (p.425) to image the interior of the heart and detect infected material on the surface of the valves. Blood tests may be done to identify the organism responsible for the infection.

WHAT IS THE TREATMENT?

If you have infective endocarditis, you will usually need treatment with intravenous antibiotics (p.885) for about 6 weeks. Blood tests are done regularly to confirm that the infection is clearing

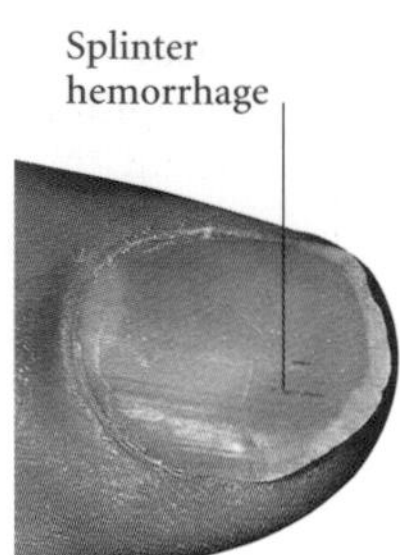
Splinter hemorrhage

Effect of infective endocarditis
Bleeding under the fingernail, resulting in so-called splinter hemorrhages, can occur in association with the heart disorder infective endocarditis.

up. This treatment is successful in up to 4 in 5 cases. If a valve is badly damaged or if the infection cannot be controlled with drugs, heart valve replacement (p.422) may be necessary.

If you have a valve disorder or you already have a replacement heart valve, you should be aware of the possible symptoms of endocarditis and contact your doctor immediately if they appear. Once you have had one episode of the disorder, you have a greater risk of developing it again. To prevent recurrence of endocarditis, you may be prescribed an antibiotic.

You may be prescribed a single dose of an antibiotic before dental treatment or some operations, such as those on the digestive or urinary tracts.

(WWW) ONLINE SITES: p.1032

Myocarditis

Inflammation of the muscle tissue of the heart, usually due to an infection

AGE GENDER GENETICS LIFESTYLE Not significant factors

Myocarditis is inflammation of the heart muscle, usually due to an infection. Frequently, the condition goes unrecognized because there are no obvious symptoms. However, severe inflammation of the heart muscle may develop, causing chest pain and leading eventually to heart enlargement and chronic heart failure (p.413).

The most common cause of the disorder is a viral infection, usually with the coxsackie virus. Myocarditis may also be due to rheumatic fever (p.429), although this is now rare in developed countries, mainly due to the widespread use of antibiotics (p.885). Some autoimmune disorders, such as systemic lupus erythematosus (p.461), in which the body attacks its own tissues, may also cause myocarditis.

WHAT ARE THE SYMPTOMS?

Myocarditis often causes no symptoms. However, if symptoms do occur, they usually develop over a number of hours or days and may include:

- Fever.
- Fatigue.
- Aching in the chest.
- Palpitations (awareness of an irregular or abnormally rapid heartbeat).

Eventually, breathlessness and swelling of the ankles may develop due to heart failure. Rarely, myocarditis causes sudden death during vigorous exertion.

WHAT MIGHT BE DONE?

If your doctor suspects that you have myocarditis, he or she will probably arrange for an ECG (p.406) to monitor the electrical activity of the heart and a chest X-ray (p.490) to see if the heart is enlarged. You may have echocardiography (p.425) to image the interior of the heart. Blood tests may be done to check for infection and for the presence of enzymes that can indicate whether or not the heart muscle is damaged.

Myocarditis is usually mild, and the heart should recover within 2 weeks. If severe heart failure does develop, a heart transplant (right) may give the best chance of a return to normal health.

(WWW) ONLINE SITES: p.1032

Dilated cardiomyopathy

Damaged heart muscle, leading to enlargement of the heart

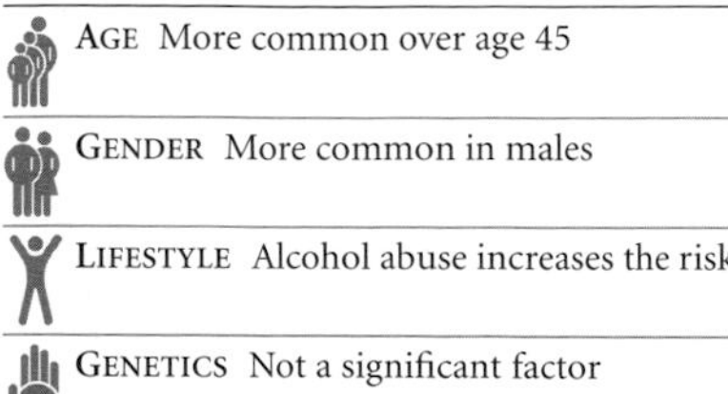
AGE More common over age 45

GENDER More common in males

LIFESTYLE Alcohol abuse increases the risk

GENETICS Not a significant factor

Healthy heart muscle is vital for the heart to pump blood around the body effectively. In dilated cardiomyopathy, the muscular walls of the heart become damaged. The weakened muscle then stretches, making the heart larger. This weakening and the enlargement of the heart muscle reduce the heart's pumping action, leading to chronic heart failure (p.413). In some cases, dilated cardiomyopathy is caused by alcohol abuse. The disorder may also be due to an autoimmune disorder, in which the body attacks its own tissues, or it may occur after a viral illness. Often, the underlying cause is not found.

The symptoms of dilated cardiomyopathy are similar to those of chronic heart failure. Therefore, before making a diagnosis of dilated cardiomyopathy, your doctor may wish to carry out tests that exclude other disorders that cause heart failure, such as coronary artery disease (p.405) and heart valve disorders. Dilated cardiomyopathy is more common over age 45 and among men.

WHAT ARE THE SYMPTOMS?

In many cases of mild dilated cardiomyopathy, there are no symptoms. If symptoms do occur, they usually develop gradually over a number of years and may include:

- Fatigue.
- Shortness of breath during exertion.
- Palpitations (awareness of an irregular or abnormally rapid heartbeat).
- Swelling of the ankles.

As the disorder progresses, the heart's pumping efficiency decreases, causing worsening symptoms, such as shortness of breath at rest.

The heart enlargement may stretch the valves, causing them to become leaky. This may eventually lead to the development of chronic heart failure or an abnormal heart rhythm (*see* ARRHYTHMIAS, p.415). If the chambers in the heart cannot empty fully because they are too large, a blood clot can form, which may break off and block a vessel elsewhere in the body.

HOW IS IT DIAGNOSED?

The diagnosis of dilated cardiomyopathy involves a number of tests, many of which are used to exclude other possible causes of your symptoms, such as coronary artery disease. You may have an ECG (p.406) to monitor the heart's electrical activity and echocardiography (p.425) to image the interior of the heart. You may also have a chest X-ray (p.490) to detect enlargement of the heart. Coronary angiography (p.408) is done to exclude coronary artery disease as a cause of symptoms. To exclude valve disease, a cardiac catheter may be passed into the heart from an artery to measure blood pressure inside the

(TREATMENT) HEART TRANSPLANT

A heart transplant is sometimes the only treatment option if the heart is severely damaged by a disorder such as dilated cardiomyopathy (left). However, there may be a long wait before a suitable donor heart is found. During the operation, the heart's normal function is taken over by a heart–lung machine (*see* SURGERY USING A HEART–LUNG MACHINE, p.953). The operation takes between 3 and 5 hours. You will need lifelong drug treatment to prevent the body from rejecting the donor heart. About 4 in 5 people survive for 5 years or more after having a heart transplant.

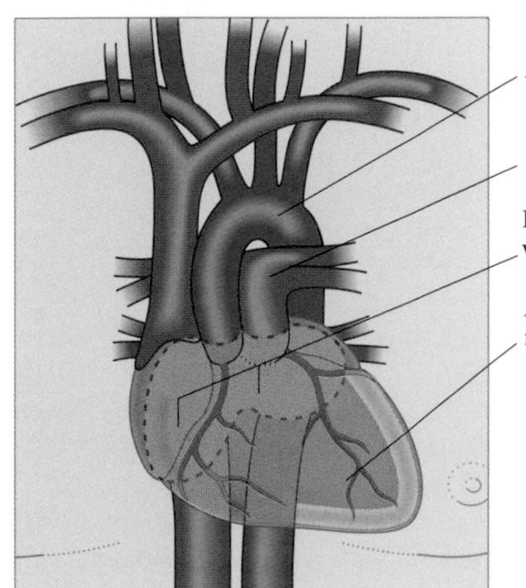
Aorta
Pulmonary artery
Remaining back walls of atria
Area to be replaced

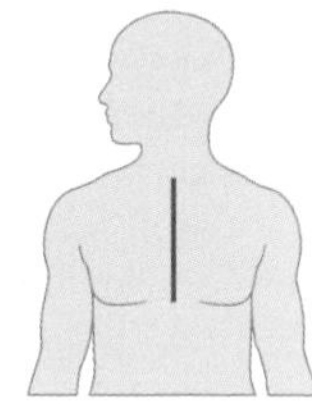

SITE OF INCISION

The procedure

Most of the diseased heart is removed, but the back walls of the upper chambers (atria) are left in place. The lower chambers (ventricles) of the donor heart are then attached to the remaining areas of the recipient's heart.

heart. If you have palpitations, an ECG may be carried out over a period of 24 hours to monitor your heartbeat while you carry out your daily activities (*see* AMBULATORY ECG, p.416).

WHAT IS THE TREATMENT?

If the cause of the dilated cardiomyopathy is unknown, no specific treatment can be given. If the disorder is caused by alcohol abuse, you must stop drinking. Symptoms of heart failure may be relieved by drugs such as digoxin (*see* DIGITALIS DRUGS, p.901) to improve the pumping function of the heart and diuretic drugs (p.902) in order to remove excess fluid. You may also be prescribed drugs that prevent blood clotting (p.904).

If heart failure worsens despite drug treatment, a heart transplant (p.427) may be considered. Prognosis varies depending on the severity and the cause of the cardiomyopathy.

(WWW) ONLINE SITES: p.1032

Hypertrophic cardiomyopathy

Abnormal thickening of the muscular walls of the heart, which reduces its pumping efficiency

AGE Often present from birth, but symptoms usually develop in adolescence

GENETICS In some cases, the condition is inherited

GENDER LIFESTYLE Not significant factors

In hypertrophic cardiomyopathy, the walls of the heart are excessively thick. This thickening prevents the heart from filling properly and may partially block the passage of blood from the heart, both of which reduce the pumping efficiency of the heart. The condition is usually an inherited disorder present at birth, but the exact cause is not known. Hypertrophic cardiomyopathy is one cause of sudden death in apparently healthy, active young people.

WHAT ARE THE SYMPTOMS?

Symptoms of the disorder usually develop in adolescence. They first occur during exertion and may include:

- Fainting.
- Shortness of breath.
- Chest pain.
- Palpitations (awareness of an irregular or abnormally rapid heartbeat).

As the disorder progresses, shortness of breath may be present at rest. In some cases, a life-threatening abnormal heart rhythm develops (*see* ARRHYTHMIAS, p.415). Hypertrophic cardiomyopathy may also distort the valve that sits between the left upper and lower chambers of the heart, causing it to leak (*see* MITRAL REGURGITATION, p.423).

In severe cases, the thickened heart walls may obstruct the blood flow out of the heart, which results in inadequate blood supply to the rest of the body. This situation is potentially fatal.

HOW IS IT DIAGNOSED?

If your doctor suspects that you may have hypertrophic cardiomyopathy, he or she may arrange for you to have an ECG (p.406) to measure the heart's electrical activity. You may also have echocardiography (p.425), which shows the thickness of the heart walls and assesses how much the output of blood from the heart is restricted. You may also have your heart rhythm monitored for 24 hours while you carry out your normal activities (*see* AMBULATORY ECG, p.416).

WHAT IS THE TREATMENT?

Treatment is aimed at improving the filling capacity of the heart using drugs such as beta blockers (p.898) and calcium channel blockers (p.900). If you have an abnormal heart rhythm, it may be treated with antiarrhythmic drugs (p.898). Surgery may be used to remove some of the thickened muscle. Percutaneous septal ablation is an alternative to surgery. This procedure uses a catheter, inserted through the groin and advanced to the heart. In rare cases, a heart transplant (p.427) may be considered. Hypertrophic cardiomyopathy increases your risk of developing an infection of the heart muscle or valve. For this reason, a single dose of an antibiotic (p.885) may be prescribed before dental treatment or some operations.

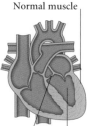

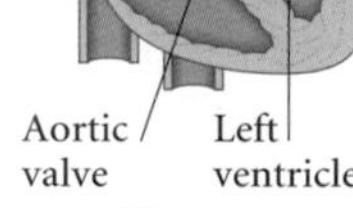
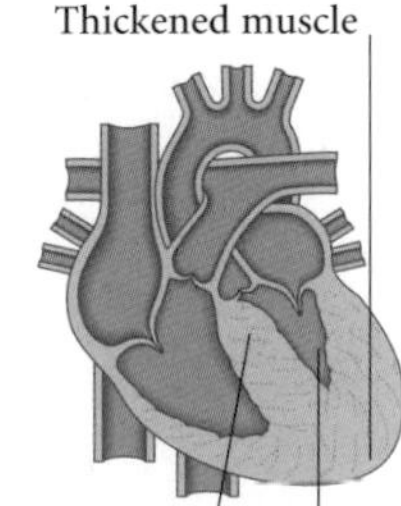
Normal muscle
Thickened muscle
Aortic valve
Left ventricle
Thickened septum
Left ventricle
NORMAL
ABNORMAL

Hypertrophic cardiomyopathy
In this condition, the septum and the muscular wall of the left ventricle become abnormally thick. This thickening prevents the left ventricle from filling properly and obstructs the outflow to the aortic valve.

The disorder is sometimes inherited. For this reason, relatives of anyone with hypertrophic cardiomyopathy should be screened with echocardiography.

About 1 in 25 affected people die each year. The prognosis is better if the symptoms are diagnosed and treated early.

(WWW) ONLINE SITES: p.1032

Pericarditis

Inflammation of the pericardium, the double-layered membrane that envelops the heart

AGE Risk factors depend on the cause

GENDER GENETICS LIFESTYLE Not significant factors

The pericardium is a two-layered membrane that surrounds the heart. In pericarditis, this membrane becomes inflamed, usually due to infection. The inflammation is usually acute, with symptoms that are often mistaken for a heart attack (*see* MYOCARDIAL INFARCTION, p.410). The inflammation usually subsides after about a week. Rarely, the inflammation persists and causes the pericardium to become scarred and thickened and to contract around the heart. As a result, the constricted heart muscle is unable to pump normally. This serious chronic condition is called constrictive pericarditis. In both acute and chronic disorders, fluid may accumulate between the two layers of the pericardium and stop the heart from pumping effectively. This is called a pericardial effusion and may lead to chronic heart failure (p.413).

WHAT ARE THE CAUSES?

In young adults, pericarditis is usually due to a viral infection, although pericarditis may develop as a complication of bacterial pneumonia (p.490). Tuberculosis (p.491) is an important cause of

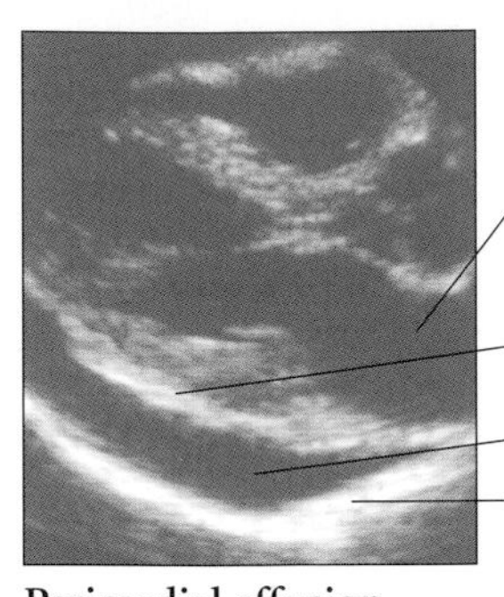
Ventricle of heart
Inner layer of pericardium
Fluid
Outer layer of pericardium

Pericardial effusion
This echocardiogram shows fluid between the two layers of the pericardium, the membrane that surrounds the heart.

pericarditis in some countries. A heart attack (*see* MYOCARDIAL INFARCTION, p.410) can cause pericarditis if the muscle on the surface of the heart is affected. Pericarditis may also develop when a cancerous tumor elsewhere in the body spreads to the pericardium.

Inflammation of the pericardium is also associated with autoimmune disorders, in which the body attacks its own tissues. For example, the conditions rheumatoid arthritis (p.377) and systemic lupus erythematosus (p.461) may sometimes cause pericarditis.

WHAT ARE THE SYMPTOMS?

The symptoms of acute pericarditis develop over a few hours and last for about 7 days. They include:

- Pain in the center of the chest, which worsens when taking a deep breath and is relieved by sitting forward.
- Pain in the neck and shoulders.
- Fever.

In chronic constrictive pericarditis or when excess fluid builds up in the pericardium, the heart may be unable to pump blood around the body effectively. Poor circulation may then lead to further symptoms that develop over a few months, such as breathlessness and swelling of the ankles and abdomen. An irregular heartbeat may also develop (*see* ATRIAL FIBRILLATION, p.417).

WHAT MIGHT BE DONE?

Your doctor will probably arrange for you to have a chest X-ray (p.490) and an ECG (p.406) to monitor the heart's electrical activity. Echocardiography (p.425) may be done to image the interior of the heart. This technique allows the thickness of the pericardium to be measured and can detect fluid around the heart. Blood tests can check for infection or autoimmune disease.

Pericarditis requires treatment in the hospital. You will probably be given nonsteroidal anti-inflammatory drugs (p.894) to relieve chest pain and to help reduce the inflammation.

When pericarditis is caused by a viral infection, the infection should clear up within a week without further treatment. In other cases, the treatment is directed at the underlying cause. For example, antibiotics (p.885) may be prescribed for bacterial infections, corticosteroids (p.930) for autoimmune disorders, and antituberculous drugs (p.886) to treat tuberculosis infection.

Fluid in a pericardial effusion may be withdrawn through a needle passed through the chest wall. If the effusion recurs, a piece of pericardium may be removed, allowing the fluid to drain continuously. In chronic constrictive pericarditis, surgery may be needed to remove most of the pericardium and allow the heart to pump freely.

WHAT IS THE PROGNOSIS?

Most people who have viral pericarditis recover within a week, but about 1 in 10 has a recurrence in the first few months afterward. Pericarditis may also recur if due to an autoimmune disorder. Surgery for chronic constrictive pericarditis is successful in only a minority of cases.

(WWW) ONLINE SITES: p.1032

Rheumatic fever

Inflammation of the heart, joints, and skin following bacterial infection

 AGE Most common in people aged 5–15, but effects often not seen until adulthood

 LIFESTYLE Overcrowded living conditions and inadequate nutrition are risk factors

 GENDER GENETICS Not significant factors

Fifty years ago, rheumatic fever was a major childhood illness in North America and Europe that left thousands of people with damaged heart valves. The effects of the damage are seen in elderly people as heart valve disorders, most commonly as mitral stenosis (p.424). Rheumatic fever is now rare in developed countries, mainly due to the use of antibiotics (p.885) and to improved standards of living and housing. In some parts of the US, however, small outbreaks have recently begun to occur. The disease still affects many people in developing countries.

Rheumatic fever develops after an infection, usually of the throat, caused by streptococcal bacteria. The condition is caused by the immune system attacking the body's own tissues in response to the infection.

WHAT ARE THE SYMPTOMS?

Rheumatic fever develops 1–4 weeks after the sore throat has cleared up. Symptoms may include:

- High fever.
- Aching and swelling of larger joints, such as the knees, elbows, and ankles.
- Characteristic blotchy pink rash on the trunk and limbs.

If the heart muscle is affected, there may be shortness of breath and chest pain for a few weeks until the inflammation settles. Inflammation of a heart valve causes permanent damage that may lead to thickening and scarring of the valve years later. This valve damage causes symptoms such as fatigue.

WHAT MIGHT BE DONE?

If rheumatic fever is suspected, a swab is taken from the throat and a blood test done to look for streptococcal infection. A chest X-ray (p.490) may be taken to look at the size of the heart to see if it is inflamed. An ECG (p.406) may be done to monitor the electrical activity of the heart and echocardiography (p.425) to image the interior of the heart and the valves.

Rheumatic fever is treated with antibiotics to clear up the infection and complete bed rest for about 2 weeks. Nonsteroidal anti-inflammatory drugs (p.894) may be used to reduce fever and joint inflammation, and corticosteroids (p.930) may be prescribed to reduce inflammation of the heart. Low-dose antibiotics often need to be taken for several years to avoid recurrence.

About 1 in 100 people dies during an initial attack of rheumatic fever. The risk of a recurrence is highest in the first 3 years after the initial infection in young adults and people with damaged heart valves. After 10 years, 2 in 3 people have a detectable heart valve disorder.

(WWW) ONLINE SITES: p.1032, p.1033

PERIPHERAL VASCULAR DISORDERS

The peripheral blood vessels carry blood from the heart to the rest of the body and back to the heart, providing oxygen and nutrients to all parts of the body. If the blood vessels are diseased, oxygen supply to the tissues is reduced, leading to possible tissue damage and even tissue death. Many peripheral vascular disorders are more common in people who smoke and have a high-fat diet.

All of the blood vessels that carry blood around the body, apart from those in the heart and the brain, are known collectively as the peripheral vascular system. The peripheral vascular system consists of arteries, which carry blood away from the heart, and veins, which carry blood toward the heart.

This section begins by discussing aortic aneurysm, which is a potentially life-threatening disorder of the largest artery in the body. The second article examines thrombosis and embolism, in which a peripheral artery or vein becomes blocked. The most common cause of these disorders is a buildup of fatty deposits on the artery walls, which is a factor that also contributes to the development of diabetic vascular disease. All of these disorders reduce blood supply to the tissues, leading to conditions such as lower limb ischemia and gangrene. Subsequently, disorders that affect the small blood vessels in the hands and feet are considered.

The section ends with a discussion of disorders of the peripheral veins. The veins may be blocked by a blood clot, as occurs in deep vein thrombosis and superficial thrombophlebitis, or may develop structural abnormalities, as occurs in varicose veins.

KEY ANATOMY

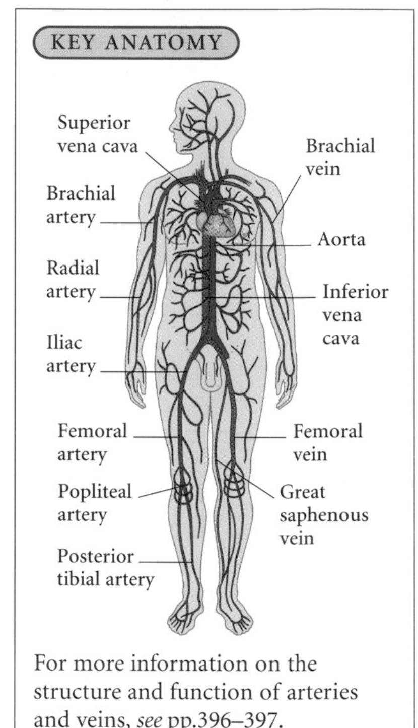
Superior vena cava
Brachial vein
Brachial artery
Aorta
Radial artery
Inferior vena cava
Iliac artery
Femoral artery
Femoral vein
Popliteal artery
Great saphenous vein
Posterior tibial artery

For more information on the structure and function of arteries and veins, *see* pp.396–397.

Aortic aneurysm

Enlargement of a section of the aorta due to weakness in the artery wall

AGE More common after age 65

GENDER More common in males

GENETICS Sometimes runs in families

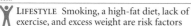

LIFESTYLE Smoking, a high-fat diet, lack of exercise, and excess weight are risk factors

If a section of an artery wall becomes weakened, the pressure of blood in the artery may cause it to bulge out. The bulging section of the artery is called an aneurysm. An aneurysm may occur in any artery in the body, but the aorta, the major artery that transports blood away from the heart, is most commonly involved. Three-quarters of all aortic aneurysms occur in the abdominal section of the aorta below the kidneys, and this type of aneurysm tends to run in families. Aortic aneurysms may also develop in the chest. The risk of having an aneurysm increases with age, and the condition most commonly occurs in men over age 65.

Small aortic aneurysms do not usually produce symptoms, although large ones may cause localized pain. In some enlarged aneurysms, known as dissecting aneurysms, the inner layer of the arterial wall tears and peels away from the outer layer, allowing blood to collect in the space between the two. The larger an aneurysm is, the more likely it is to rupture, causing internal bleeding that can rapidly prove fatal.

WHAT ARE THE CAUSES?

The cause of most aneurysms is uncertain, but they are often associated with atherosclerosis (p.402), in which fatty deposits build up on the artery walls. The risk of developing atherosclerosis is increased by some lifestyle factors, such as smoking, eating a diet high in fat, excess weight, and doing little exercise. Aneurysms are also more common in males and people with high blood pressure (*see* HYPERTENSION, p.403).

In rare cases, an injury or an inherited weakness in the artery wall leads to the development of an aneurysm. For example, the genetic disorder Marfan syndrome (p.824) may lead to the formation of multiple aneurysms.

WHAT ARE THE SYMPTOMS?

Symptoms vary according to the site and usually develop when an aneurysm enlarges. The symptoms of an abdominal aneurysm may include:

- Pain in the abdomen that may spread to the back and can be relieved temporarily by leaning forward.
- Pulsating sensation in the abdomen.

An aneurysm in the chest may produce symptoms such as:

- Pain in the chest, or in the upper back between the shoulder blades.
- Severe cough and wheezing.
- Difficulty swallowing and hoarseness.

If you have symptoms of this kind, you should seek emergency medical help.

ARE THERE COMPLICATIONS?

Sometimes, a blood clot forms at the site of the aneurysm and may obstruct the passage of blood through the aorta. In the case of a dissecting aneurysm, the

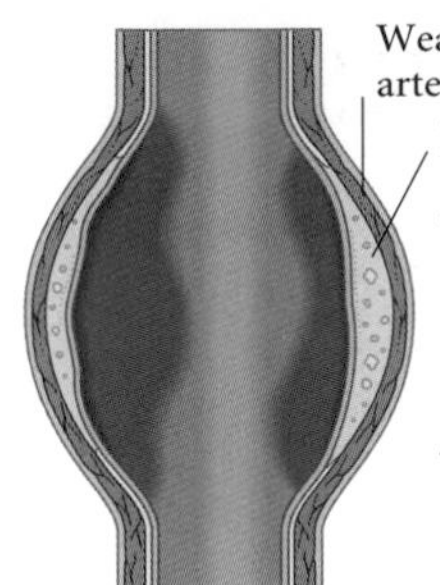
Weakened, bulging artery wall
Fatty deposit

Aneurysm
In an aneurysm, an area of artery wall in which there is a fatty deposit grows weak and bulges due to the pressure of blood in the vessel.

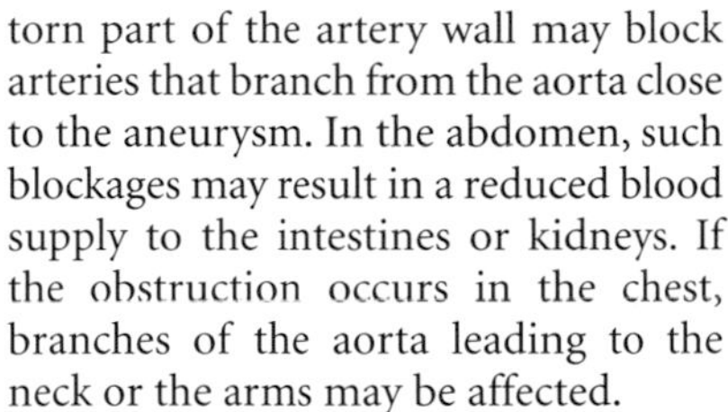
Outer wall
Tear in inner wall
Blood in false channel
Fatty deposit

Dissecting aneurysm
In a dissecting aneurysm, the inner artery wall tears away from the outer wall. Blood then collects in a false channel between the walls.

torn part of the artery wall may block arteries that branch from the aorta close to the aneurysm. In the abdomen, such blockages may result in a reduced blood supply to the intestines or kidneys. If the obstruction occurs in the chest, branches of the aorta leading to the neck or the arms may be affected.

Pressure in the aorta may eventually cause an aneurysm to rupture, allowing blood to leak from the vessel and causing worsening pain. If rupture occurs suddenly, you may have severe pain accompanied by loss of consciousness, a fast pulse, and shock (p.414). Without immediate medical treatment, a ruptured aneurysm is likely to be fatal.

How is it diagnosed?

If there are no symptoms, an aneurysm may be detected during a routine physical examination when a doctor feels a swelling in the abdomen. Sometimes an aneurysm is seen on an X-ray of the chest or abdomen carried out to check for another disorder. In certain cases, screening for abdominal aortic aneurysm may be recommended for men over age 65. If you develop symptoms, ultrasound scanning (p.250) may be performed at regular intervals to measure the diameter of the aorta and see if the aneurysm is enlarging. CT scanning (p.247), MRI (p.248), or angiography (*see* CONTRAST X-RAYS, p.245) may be performed to image the affected arteries.

What is the treatment?

An aneurysm may be treated by surgery, the aim of which is to repair the artery before the aneurysm dissects or ruptures. Your doctor will consider your age and general state of health, as well as the size and site of the aneurysm, when deciding whether surgery is necessary. Surgery for larger aneurysms involves removing the weakened area of arterial wall and replacing it with a graft of synthetic material. To prevent complications from developing while you are waiting for surgery, you may be given beta blocker drugs (p.898) to lower blood pressure in the artery. For a dissecting or ruptured aneurysm, emergency surgery may be necessary.

If you are a smoker, you should give up immediately and completely. For anyone who has had an aneurysm, a low-fat diet (*see* A HEALTHY DIET, p.48) and regular exercise will help slow the progress of atherosclerosis and thus reduce the risk of further aneurysms.

What is the prognosis?

Surgery on an aneurysm offers a good chance of recovery provided the aneurysm has not yet dissected or ruptured. If the aneurysm has dissected or ruptured, between 15 and 50 percent of people survive, depending on the location of the blood vessel affected.

(WWW) ONLINE SITES: p.1032

Thrombosis and embolism

Obstruction of blood flow in a vessel by a blockage that has formed in that vessel or has traveled from elsewhere in the body

GENETICS Rarely, runs in families

LIFESTYLE Smoking, a high-fat diet, lack of exercise, and excess weight are risk factors

AGE GENDER Risk factors depend on the cause

Both thrombosis and embolism may be serious and potentially fatal conditions. In thrombosis, a blood clot, known as a thrombus, forms in a blood vessel and obstructs the flow of blood. Any blood vessel in the body may become blocked by a thrombus, but thrombosis is more serious in arteries and in deep veins in the legs (*see* DEEP VEIN THROMBOSIS, p.437). In embolism, a plug of material called an embolus travels through the bloodstream until it becomes lodged in an artery. Although some emboli consist of substances such as tissue or fat, most are pieces of blood clot that have become detached from a larger clot elsewhere in the body.

If an artery is blocked by either a thrombus or an embolus, and blood cannot reach the tissues beyond the blockage by an alternative route, those tissues are deprived of oxygen. Unlike thrombosis, which often develops gradually, the effects of embolism usually develop immediately and may be severe if the blood vessel becomes completely obstructed. Blockage of the arteries that supply the brain (*see* STROKE, p.532), the lungs (*see* PULMONARY EMBOLISM, p.495), or the heart (*see* MYOCARDIAL INFARCTION, p.410) often proves fatal.

What are the causes?

Blood flowing through an artery is normally under pressure so that clots are unlikely to form. If the flow of blood in an artery slows down, a clot is more likely to develop. Decreased blood flow through an artery may be caused by narrowing of the vessel due to a gradual buildup of fatty deposits in its walls, known as atherosclerosis (p.402). The long-term risk of developing atherosclerosis, and therefore thrombosis in the arteries, is increased by factors such as smoking and a diet high in fat.

Thrombosis is more likely to develop if there is an increase in the natural tendency of the blood to clot, a condition

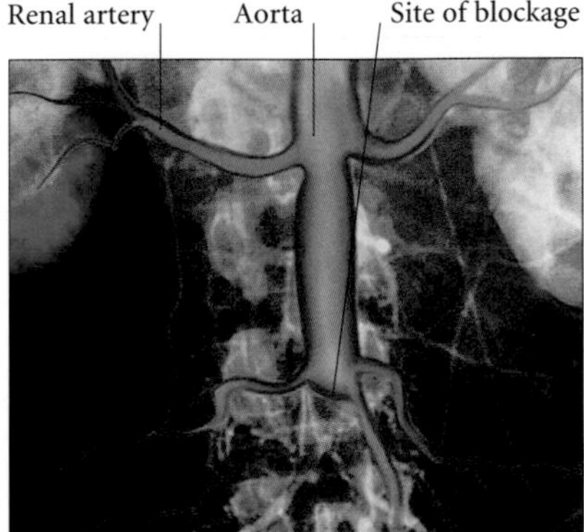
Renal artery
Aorta
Site of blockage

Arterial thrombosis
This contrast X-ray shows blood flow in the aorta and adjacent arteries. A blood clot in the aorta is blocking the flow of blood below the site of the obstruction.

known as hypercoagulability (p.453). In rare cases, the condition is inherited. Hypercoagulability may also occur as a result of taking combined oral contraceptives (*see* CONTRACEPTION, p.69), being pregnant, or having surgery.

Blood clots sometimes form in the heart when the heartbeat is weak and irregular because the upper chambers (atria) are not totally emptied of blood at each beat (*see* ATRIAL FIBRILLATION, p.417). These blood clots may then be released from the atria into the coronary or peripheral arteries.

WHAT ARE THE SYMPTOMS?

The symptoms caused by thrombosis or embolism vary, depending on which blood vessel is blocked. If the blockage affects blood supply to the legs, symptoms may develop within a few hours, and they may be more severe if there is already a chronic reduction in blood supply to this region (*see* LOWER LIMB ISCHEMIA, p.434). Symptoms include:

- Pain in the legs, even at rest.
- Pale, cold feet.

If the arteries supplying the intestines are affected, symptoms may include:

- Severe abdominal pain.
- Vomiting.
- Fever.

Left untreated, the reduction in blood supply may eventually result in tissue death, which may be life-threatening. The affected tissues will change color over several days, eventually becoming black (*see* GANGRENE, p.435). If you develop these symptoms, you should seek emergency medical attention.

WHAT MIGHT BE DONE?

If your doctor suspects that you have thrombosis or embolism, he or she will have you admitted to the hospital immediately for treatment. The blood flow through your blood vessels may be measured using pulse volume recording and imaging such as Doppler ultrasound scanning (right). Angiography (*see* CONTRAST X-RAYS, p.245), sometimes combined with MRI (p.248), may be done to obtain detailed images of the blood vessels and look for obstruction.

Depending on the site and size of the clot, you may be given drugs to dissolve it and prevent further clots from forming (*see* DRUGS THAT PREVENT BLOOD CLOTTING, p.904). Emergency surgery may be necessary to remove the clot or to bypass it using a graft made from synthetic material. Alternatively, the affected artery may be widened by angioplasty, a procedure in which a balloon on the tip of a catheter is passed into the artery and then inflated to widen the obstructed area.

After the thrombosis or embolism has been treated, you may need to continue medication for several months to prevent further blood clots from forming. For example, you may be advised to take a low dose of aspirin daily. If you smoke, you should stop immediately. You should also try to eat a low-fat diet (*see* A HEALTHY DIET, p.48) and exercise regularly. If you are taking a combined oral contraceptive, you should consider using another form of contraception.

(WWW) ONLINE SITES: p.1032

(TEST) DOPPLER ULTRASOUND SCANNING

Doppler ultrasound scanning is an imaging technique commonly used to measure the blood flow through a blood vessel in circulatory disorders such as thrombosis and embolism (p.431). It may also be used to measure blood pressure in the limbs. The technique produces an image of the blood flow through the vessel so that narrowing and blockages of the vessel can be detected. A routine Doppler ultrasound scan can take up to 20 minutes to perform and is completely painless and safe.

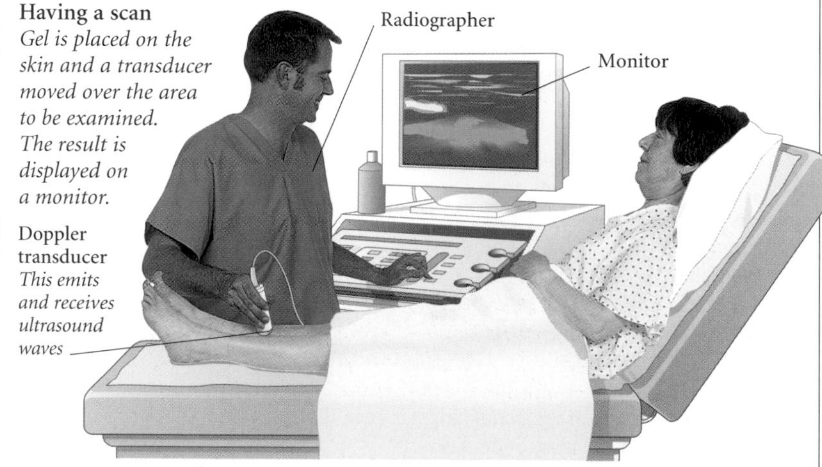
Radiographer
Monitor
Doppler transducer
This emits and receives ultrasound waves

Having a scan
Gel is placed on the skin and a transducer moved over the area to be examined. The result is displayed on a monitor.

(RESULTS)

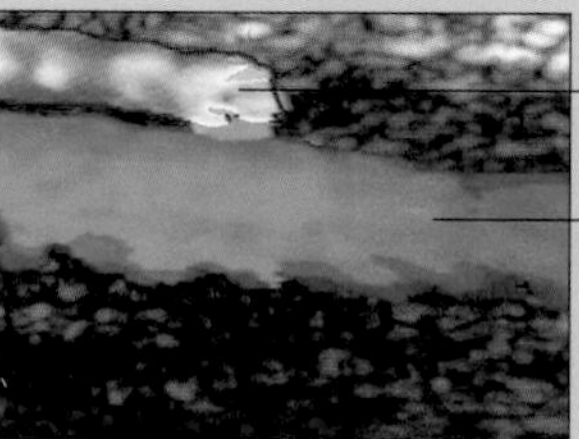
Blocked artery
Healthy vein

Doppler scan
This ultrasound image shows blood flow through vessels in the leg and confirms a blockage in the artery. Doppler ultrasound scans allow the precise position and severity of a blockage to be determined.

Diabetic vascular disease

Damage to large and small blood vessels throughout the body that occurs in people who have diabetes mellitus

 GENETICS The underlying condition sometimes runs in families

LIFESTYLE Smoking, a high-fat diet, lack of exercise, and excess weight are risk factors

 AGE GENDER Not significant factors

Vascular disease is a common long-term complication of diabetes mellitus (p.687), a condition that tends to run in families. There are two types of vascular disease that are more likely to affect people who have diabetes: atherosclerosis (p.402) and small vessel disease.

In atherosclerosis, fatty deposits gradually build up in the walls of larger blood vessels, making these vessels narrower. This condition, which develops to some degree in most people as they become older, is likely to occur earlier and more extensively in people with diabetes.

Diabetic small vessel disease is not fully understood, but it is thought to involve thickening of the walls of the smaller blood vessels as a result of certain chemical changes. This thickening reduces the amount of oxygen passing from blood in the vessels into the surrounding body tissues.

These vascular conditions frequently occur together and each of them may lead to serious complications. The risk of developing either type of diabetic vascular disease is higher the longer a person has had diabetes mellitus. Lifestyle factors such as smoking and a diet that is high in fat increase the risk of developing diabetic vascular disease, as does poor control of blood sugar levels, and it is therefore important that your diabetes is managed effectively (*see* LIVING WITH DIABETES, p.690).

ARE THERE COMPLICATIONS?

Atherosclerosis may eventually lead to blockage of the arteries, causing potentially life-threatening complications, in particular stroke (p.532), heart attack (*see* MYOCARDIAL INFARCTION, p.410), and lower limb ischemia (p.434).

Damage to small blood vessels may occur in many parts of the body. Small blood vessels in the eyes are commonly damaged (*see* DIABETIC RETINOPATHY, p.579), leading to blurry vision and, sometimes, even blindness. If the small vessels in the eyes are damaged, similar changes will have occurred in vessels throughout the body. If the blood vessels in the kidneys are affected, kidney function will be impaired (*see* DIABETIC KIDNEY DISEASE, p.705). Kidney damage sometimes results in high blood pressure (*see* HYPERTENSION, p.403).

Small vessel disease may also lead to nerve damage, most commonly in the feet (*see* DIABETIC NEUROPATHY, p.579). Such damage can reduce sensation in the affected area so that an injury goes unnoticed at first. In addition, the reduced supply of blood slows healing, and persistent skin ulcers (*see* LEG ULCERS, p.350) and even gangrene (p.435) may develop. Some people already have these complications when they are first diagnosed as having diabetes mellitus. In other cases, complications may not develop for many years after diagnosis.

WHAT MIGHT BE DONE?

It is essential that diabetes mellitus is diagnosed promptly and managed well. In order to prevent or reduce the effects of diabetic vascular disease on blood vessels, you should maintain effective control of your blood sugar levels (*see*

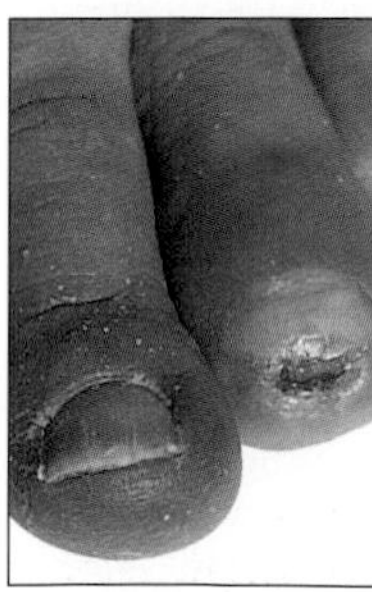

Ulcerated toe
If diabetic vascular disease affects the arteries in the leg, the tissues of the feet may become deprived of oxygen, eventually leading to the formation of a skin ulcer.

(TEST) FEMORAL ANGIOGRAPHY

Femoral angiography is a contrast X-ray technique, sometimes combined with MRI (p.248), that is used to diagnose narrowing or blockage of arteries in the legs. During the procedure, which is carried out under local anesthesia, a contrast medium is injected into the femoral artery. The medium spreads in the circulation to other vessels in the leg. X-rays are then taken of one or more sites. The procedure takes about 30 minutes, and you should be able to return home within 6 hours.

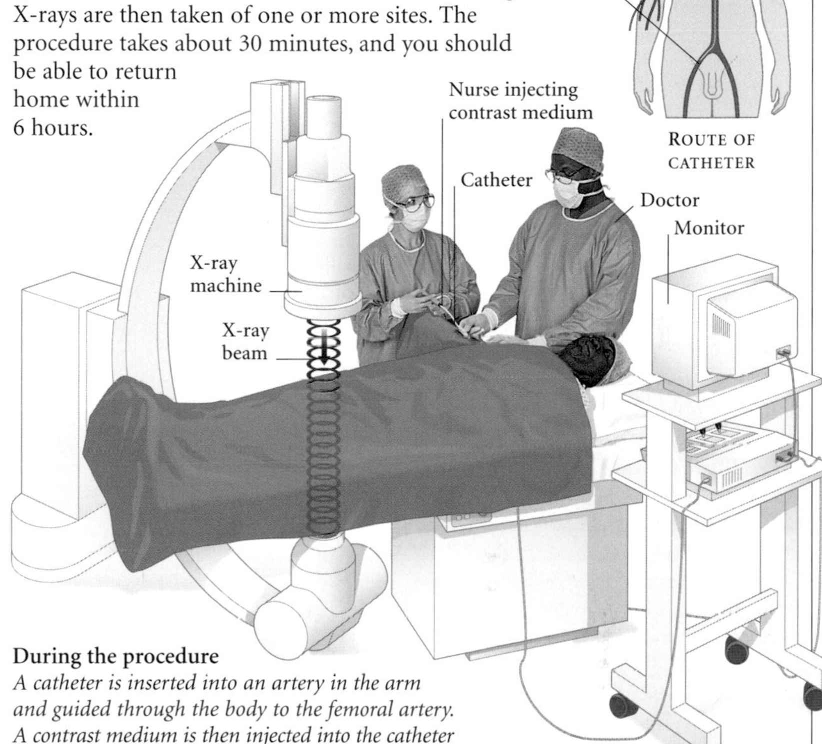

Entry site of catheter
Tip of catheter
ROUTE OF CATHETER
Nurse injecting contrast medium
Catheter
Doctor
Monitor
X-ray machine
X-ray beam

During the procedure
A catheter is inserted into an artery in the arm and guided through the body to the femoral artery. A contrast medium is then injected into the catheter so that the artery can be seen on an X-ray image.

(RESULTS)

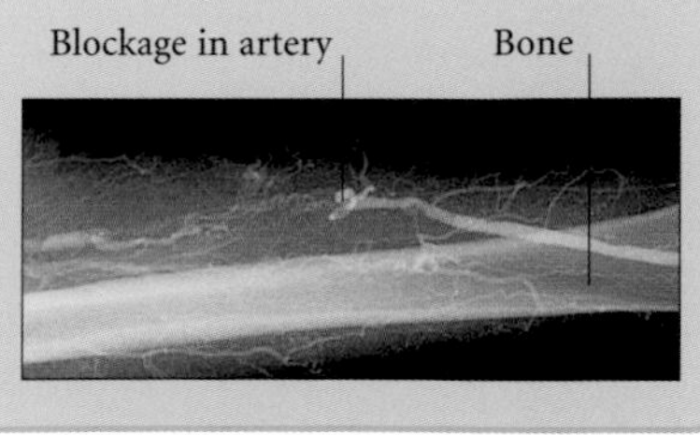

Blockage in artery
Bone

Angiogram of the leg
This contrast X-ray shows a blockage in the main artery in the leg, restricting blood flow to the tissues of the lower leg. If this blockage is not treated, the tissues will be permanently damaged.

MONITORING YOUR BLOOD GLUCOSE, p.689), follow a healthy diet (p.48) that is low in fat, and avoid smoking. If you have diabetes, your doctor will regularly measure your blood pressure (*see* BLOOD PRESSURE MEASUREMENT, p.404) and the level of cholesterol in your blood (*see* BLOOD CHOLESTEROL TESTS, p.231) to assess your susceptibility to atherosclerosis. Your urine may be tested for protein, which is sometimes the first sign of kidney disease, and blood tests may be performed to find out if your kidneys are functioning normally. In addition, regular eye examinations, using ophthalmoscopy (p.578) and, sometimes, retinal photography, are done to ensure that retinal damage is detected as early as possible because early detection increases the chances of successful treatment.

If you have a high blood cholesterol level, your doctor may prescribe drugs to prevent atherosclerosis from worsening (*see* LIPID-LOWERING DRUGS, p.935). If protein is found in your urine, you may be prescribed ACE inhibitor drugs (p.900), which help counteract the progression of small vessel damage in the kidneys. You may also receive treatment for high blood pressure if necessary (*see* ANTIHYPERTENSIVE DRUGS, p.897).

WHAT IS THE PROGNOSIS?

Diabetic vascular disease is the most common cause of death in people who have diabetes mellitus, and the risk of developing it increases with time.

A person with diabetes is about 10 times more likely to develop lower limb ischemia than someone without diabetes, four times more likely to have a heart attack, and twice as likely to have a stroke. Damage to small blood vessels in the eyes occurs in about 8 in 10 people with long-term diabetes. However, eye damage is often reversible if it is treated in the early stages. Kidney damage occurs in about 4 in 10 people who have had diabetes mellitus for longer than 15 years. About 3 in 10 people with diabetes develop nerve damage, but only 1 in 10 has severe symptoms.

If your diabetes mellitus is carefully managed and your blood sugar level is well controlled, the progress of diabetic vascular disease will be slowed and the risk of complications will be reduced.

(WWW) ONLINE SITES: p.1029, p.1032

(TREATMENT) FEMORAL ARTERY BYPASS GRAFT

This procedure is used to treat blocked or narrowed arteries in the leg, which can cause lower limb ischemia (below). During the operation, the blocked artery is bypassed using a section of vein from the same leg or, less commonly, an artificial graft. The blocked artery is left in place, but, because blood can flow freely through the bypass, the blood supply to the limb is restored. The cut ends of the vein used for the graft are tied and remain in place, and blood is diverted up other veins in the leg. The operation is performed in the hospital under general anesthesia.

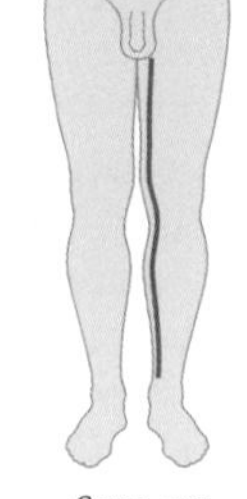

SITE OF INCISION

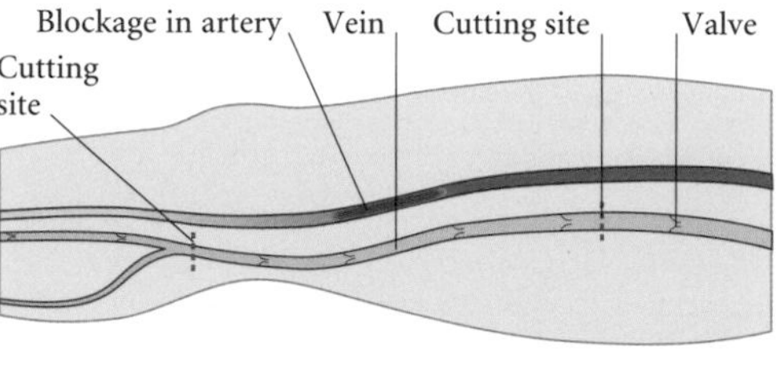
Blockage in artery
Vein
Cutting site
Valve
Cutting site

Before surgery
An obstruction in an artery in the leg prevents blood from reaching the lower leg. A small section of a vein from the same leg can be used to create a bypass around this blockage.

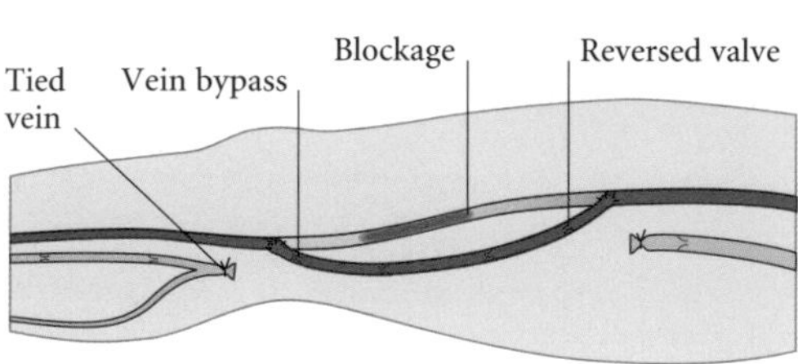
Blockage
Reversed valve
Tied vein
Vein bypass

After surgery
A length of vein has been removed and attached above and below the blockage, forming a bypass channel. The vein is reversed so that its valves allow arterial blood flow.

Lower limb ischemia

A reduced oxygen supply to the tissues of the legs as a result of a poor blood supply

 AGE More common over age 40

 GENDER More common in males

 GENETICS Sometimes runs in families

 LIFESTYLE Smoking, a high-fat diet, lack of exercise, and excess weight are risk factors

If blood flow to the legs is reduced, the leg tissues may become deprived of oxygen, and this may lead to a cramplike pain on exertion called claudication. Reduced blood flow is usually due to atherosclerosis (p.402), a buildup of fatty deposits on artery walls, which often has the most noticeable effects on the lower limbs. People with an inherited tendency toward high blood cholesterol levels (*see* HYPERCHOLESTEROLEMIA, p.691) are more likely to develop atherosclerosis, as are those who have had diabetes mellitus (p.687) for a long time. Lifestyle factors such as a high-fat diet and smoking also increase the risk. About 9 in 10 people with lower limb ischemia smoke.

WHAT ARE THE SYMPTOMS?

The symptoms of lower limb ischemia usually develop gradually over months or years. Symptoms may affect one leg more than the other. In the initial stages of the condition, blood flow to the legs may be adequate to supply the tissues when at rest but not on exertion. The main symptom is a cramplike pain in the legs with the following features:

- Pain that affects one or both calves when walking and may be severe.
- Pain consistently appears after walking the same distance.
- Walking uphill or exposure to cold temperatures causes the pain to come on sooner.
- Pain is relieved by rest and usually disappears after several minutes.

As the disease progresses, the distance a person is able to walk before experiencing pain gradually decreases, so that eventually pain may be present at rest. Additional symptoms of lower limb ischemia may then include:

- Pale, cold feet.
- Persistent leg or foot ulcers.

If a blockage occurs in blood vessels in the pelvic region, blood flow is reduced to the whole of the lower body, and as a result there may be pain in the buttocks or, in men, erectile dysfunction. If the blood vessel becomes completely blocked by a clot (*see* THROMBOSIS AND EMBOLISM, p.431), the symptoms may suddenly worsen. Without immediate treatment, death of tissues in the feet and legs may occur (*see* GANGRENE, right).

WHAT MIGHT BE DONE?

Your doctor may suspect that you have lower limb ischemia from your symptoms and by examining the strength of the pulses in your legs. He or she may arrange for tests such as pulse volume recording and Doppler ultrasound scanning (p.432) to measure the blood flow in your legs and angiography (*see* FEMORAL ANGIOGRAPHY, p.433), which produces detailed images of the vessels, to look for atherosclerosis.

Treatment is aimed at increasing the blood flow to the tissues in the legs. Affected arteries may be widened using a technique known as angioplasty, in which a balloon on the tip of a catheter is passed into the artery and inflated. In some cases, surgery is carried out to bypass affected arteries (*see* FEMORAL ARTERY BYPASS GRAFT, opposite page).

Taking a low dose of aspirin daily may help prevent blood clots from developing. If a clot has formed, you may be given drugs to dissolve it and to prevent more clots from forming (*see* DRUGS THAT PREVENT BLOOD CLOTTING, p.904). In some cases, the clot needs to be surgically removed. If gangrene has developed, amputation of part or all of the affected limb may be necessary.

If you smoke, it is vital that you stop immediately. The nicotine in cigarettes causes blood vessels to constrict, further reducing blood supply to the legs. Even one cigarette can produce a constricting effect that lasts for several hours, and you need to give up smoking completely to improve the outlook once lower limb ischemia is diagnosed. If you continue to smoke, the disease is likely to progress, and surgery may be required. You should follow a healthy diet (p.48) and walk increasing distances each day to build up the amount of exercise you can do without feeling pain (*see* DOING REGULAR EXERCISE, p.57). By adopting these measures, you may be able to prevent the condition from worsening.

(WWW) ONLINE SITES: p.1032

Gangrene

Tissue death as a result of an inadequate blood supply or infection of a wound

LIFESTYLE Smoking, a high-fat diet, lack of exercise, and excess weight are risk factors

AGE GENDER GENETICS Risk factors depend on the cause

Gangrene involves death of the tissues in a particular area of the body, most commonly the legs and feet, and is a potentially life-threatening condition.

There are two types of gangrene: dry and wet. Dry gangrene occurs when the tissues become deprived of oxygen as a result of a reduced blood supply. Tissue death is localized and does not spread from the affected site. Wet gangrene is less common and occurs when tissue that has been damaged by a wound or by dry gangrene becomes infected with bacteria. Infection is often due to clostridia, which are bacteria that thrive in dead tissues where there is no oxygen and produce a foul-smelling gas. The infection may spread to surrounding healthy tissues and can be fatal.

The reduction in blood supply that produces gangrene is most often due to a blood clot forming in an artery (*see* THROMBOSIS AND EMBOLISM, p.431), which may already be narrowed by the accumulation of fatty deposits on vessel walls, known as atherosclerosis (p.402). The tissues in the legs and feet are most commonly affected by these underlying conditions (*see* LOWER LIMB ISCHEMIA, opposite page). The risk of an artery becoming blocked is increased by certain lifestyle factors, such as smoking and a high-fat diet. People who have diabetes mellitus (p.687) are more likely to develop gangrene as a result of progressive damage to the small blood vessels (*see* DIABETIC VASCULAR DISEASE, p.432). Frostbite (p.324) may also lead to the development of gangrene.

WHAT ARE THE SYMPTOMS?

The symptoms of dry gangrene may develop gradually or may appear over a few hours, depending on how quickly the blood supply is reduced. If the legs are affected, symptoms include:

- Pain in the leg and foot.
- Pale, cold skin, which becomes red and hot before turning purple and eventually black over several days.

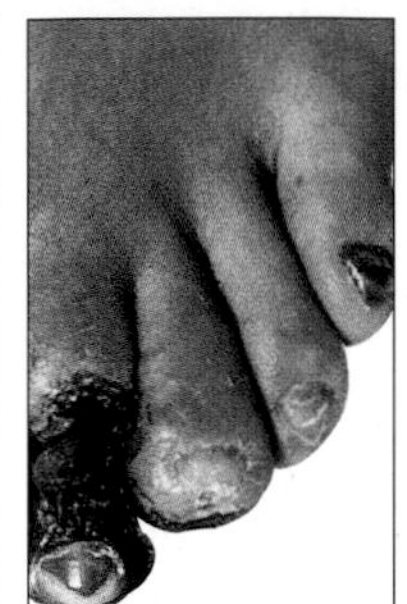

Gangrene
An inadequate supply of blood to the feet may lead to tissue death, also known as gangrene, which causes the toes to turn purple. Left untreated, the dead tissue may become infected.

If the gangrene is due to an infection, additional symptoms may be present, including pus around the affected area and fever. Infection may spread to the bloodstream (*see* SEPTICEMIA, p.298).

WHAT MIGHT BE DONE?

Your doctor will probably be able to diagnose gangrene from its appearance. He or she may arrange for you to have pulse volume recording or Doppler ultrasound scanning (p.432) to measure blood flow in the limb. You may require contrast X-rays (p.245), sometimes combined with MRI (p.248), to look for a blocked artery.

If you have gangrene, you will be admitted to the hospital immediately. Intravenous antibiotics (p.885) will be given to prevent or treat infection and, if possible, the blood supply to the gangrenous tissue will be restored. If an artery is obstructed, the vessel may be widened using angioplasty, in which a balloon on the tip of a catheter is passed into the narrowed area and then inflated. Alternatively, surgery may be carried out to remove or bypass the blockage (*see* FEMORAL ARTERY BYPASS GRAFT, opposite page). The gangrenous tissue will be removed, and, if it has become infected, some of the living tissue around the gangrenous area will also be removed to prevent the infection from spreading. In some cases, amputation of a limb is necessary. If you develop wet gangrene, you may be placed in a chamber containing high-pressure oxygen to destroy the bacteria.

The earlier gangrene is diagnosed, the better the prognosis, because blood supply to the tissues is more likely to be restored. A good blood supply promotes tissue healing after surgery. Gangrene is fatal in about 1 in 5 people, usually because of infection in the bloodstream.

(WWW) ONLINE SITES: p.1032, p.1033

Buerger's disease

Severe inflammation of the small arteries that is triggered by smoking

AGE Most common between the ages of 20 and 40

GENDER Three times more common in males

GENETICS Sometimes runs in families; more common in Asians and Eastern Europeans

LIFESTYLE Smoking is a risk factor; exposure to cold aggravates symptoms

Buerger's disease is a rare condition that most frequently affects men who smoke. The condition tends to run in families and is more common in people of Asian or Eastern European descent. The cause is not fully understood, but it is thought that, in people genetically susceptible to the disease, smoking triggers an autoimmune response, in which the immune system produces antibodies that attack the body's own tissues. The arteries in the legs, and sometimes those in the arms, become inflamed, reducing blood supply to the tissues.

WHAT ARE THE SYMPTOMS?

The initial symptoms of Buerger's disease are often intermittent and include:

- Pale hands or feet, particularly after exposure to the cold.
- Pain in the hands or feet, which may be severe at night and after exercise.
- Numbness, tingling, or a sensation of burning in the fingers or toes.

With time, these symptoms usually become more severe and skin ulcers or gangrene (p.435) may develop on the tips of the toes or fingers.

WHAT MIGHT BE DONE?

If you have the symptoms listed above, your doctor may first take your pulse to check if it is weak or absent. If it is, he or she may suspect Buerger's disease and arrange for angiography (*see* CONTRAST X-RAYS, p.245) and Doppler ultrasound scanning (p.432) to assess blood flow in the small arteries in the hands or feet.

If you are diagnosed with Buerger's disease, the only action you can take to improve the outlook is to stop smoking. In people who continue to smoke, the disease is likely to progress so that amputation of the affected limb may eventually become necessary.

(WWW) ONLINE SITES: p.1032

Raynaud's phenomenon and Raynaud's disease

Sudden, intermittent narrowing of the arteries in the hands or, rarely, the feet

GENDER More common in females

GENETICS Sometimes runs in families

LIFESTYLE Smoking and exposure to cold trigger attacks

AGE Risk factors depend on the cause

During an attack of Raynaud's phenomenon, the arteries in the hands or feet become narrowed as a result of muscle spasm in the artery walls. This narrowing restricts blood supply to the fingers or toes, causing them to become pale. Numbness or tingling may also develop in the affected fingers or toes.

In about half of all people with Raynaud's phenomenon, the condition is the result of an underlying disorder, particularly the autoimmune disorders scleroderma (p.462), rheumatoid arthritis (p.377), or Buerger's disease (left), all of which run in families. In some people with Raynaud's phenomenon, the condition is associated with hand–arm syndrome (right). Certain drugs, such as beta blockers (p.898), are known to produce the symptoms of Raynaud's phenomenon as a side effect.

If there is no apparent cause for the condition, it is known as Raynaud's disease, which is most common in women between the ages of 15 and 45 and is usually mild. Episodes of either condition are triggered by smoking, because the nicotine in cigarettes constricts the arteries. Exposure to cold and handling frozen items can also trigger an attack.

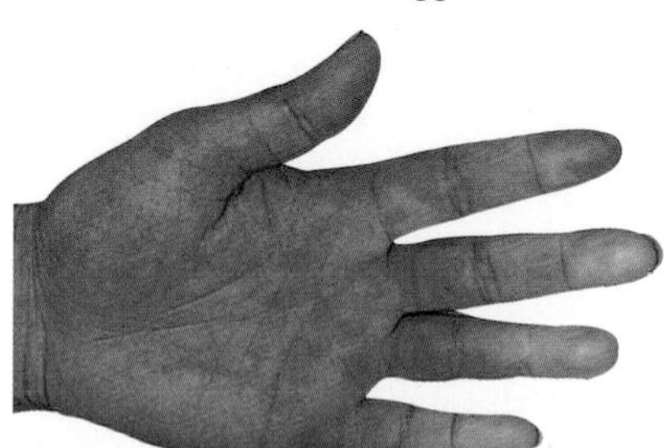

Raynaud's phenomenon
An attack of Raynaud's phenomenon in the hand restricts the blood supply to the tips of the fingers, turning them white.

WHAT ARE THE SYMPTOMS?

The symptoms of Raynaud's phenomenon and Raynaud's disease affect the hands or feet, last from a few minutes to a few hours, and include:

- Numbness and tingling in the fingers or toes that may worsen and progress to a painful burning sensation.
- Progressive change of color in the fingers or toes, which initially turn pale, then blue, and later red again as blood returns to the tissues.

There may be a marked color difference between the affected area and the surrounding tissues. In severe cases, skin ulcers or gangrene (p.435) may form on the tips of the fingers or toes.

WHAT MIGHT BE DONE?

Your doctor will carry out tests to look for an underlying cause of your symptoms. For example, blood tests may be performed to look for evidence of an autoimmune disorder.

Immunosuppressant drugs (p.906) may be prescribed to treat an autoimmune disorder. Your doctor may also recommend that you take drugs that dilate the blood vessels during an attack (*see* CALCIUM CHANNEL BLOCKER DRUGS, p.900). If you smoke, you should stop immediately. Wearing thermal gloves and socks in cold weather helps avoid the onset of symptoms. If symptoms are severe, surgery may be needed to cut the nerves that control arterial constriction.

(WWW) ONLINE SITES: p.1032

Hand–arm syndrome

Painful, pale fingers associated with the use of vibrating tools

GENDER More common in males

LIFESTYLE Affects people who use vibrating machinery; smoking and exposure to cold aggravate symptoms

AGE GENETICS Not significant factors

Hand–arm syndrome, also known as vibration white finger, causes pain and numbness in parts of the body that are repeatedly exposed to intense vibration from machinery. As the name of the condition implies, the hands, arms, and in particular the fingers are most commonly affected. Prolonged exposure to vibration from the use of mechanical tools causes localized constriction of the small blood vessels and nerve damage. Smoking and exposure to cold, which also constrict the small blood vessels, may trigger or aggravate the symptoms of hand–arm syndrome.

About 3 in 100 employed people, mainly men, are exposed to machine vibration that may lead to hand–arm syndrome. In the past, the mining and engineering industries were responsible for the majority of cases. The use of chainsaws in the forestry industry is a common cause in Canada.

What are the symptoms?

The symptoms of hand–arm syndrome do not appear immediately after exposure to vibration but tend to develop slowly over several years of exposure. Symptoms are often more severe in one hand than the other and may include:

- Pain, numbness, and tingling in the fingers, hands, or arms.
- Pale or blue fingers.
- Difficulty manipulating small objects, such as picking up coins, buttoning clothes, or tying shoelaces.

At first, the symptoms of hand–arm syndrome tend to occur intermittently, but they become more frequent and persistent as the condition progresses.

What might be done?

If you have the symptoms described above and you have been working with vibrating machinery, your doctor may suspect hand–arm syndrome. Once the disorder has been diagnosed, you should avoid exposure to vibration. Your doctor may advise you to change jobs. You should also avoid anything that may worsen the symptoms, such as smoking and exposure to cold. There is no specific treatment, but, if the symptoms are severe, your doctor may prescribe calcium channel blocker drugs (p.900), which dilate the blood vessels.

If you use vibrating machinery, make sure that it is in good working order and that you know how to operate it correctly and safely. In addition, you should always wear approved protective gloves. If you manage to avoid further exposure to vibrating machinery, the symptoms of hand–arm syndrome may improve. However, once numbness has developed, the condition is irreversible.

(WWW) ONLINE SITES: p.1032, p.1036

Deep vein thrombosis

Formation of a blood clot within a deep-lying vein

 AGE More common over age 40

 GENDER Slightly more common in females

 GENETICS Sometimes runs in families

 LIFESTYLE Prolonged immobility and excess weight are risk factors

Deep vein thrombosis is a condition in which a blood clot forms in a large vein in a muscle, usually in the leg or pelvic region. It affects 2 million people in the US each year, many of them over age 40.

The formation of a clot in a deep vein is usually not dangerous in itself. However, there is a risk that a fragment of the clot may break off and travel through the heart in the circulation. If the fragment lodges in a vessel supplying the lungs, a potentially fatal blockage called a pulmonary embolism (p.495) occurs.

What are the causes?

Deep vein thrombosis is usually caused by a combination of slow blood flow through a vein, an increase in the natural tendency of the blood to clot, and damage to the wall of the vein.

Several factors may slow blood flow and thus increase the risk of deep vein thrombosis. Long periods of immobility, such as those experienced during airplane or automobile travel or while bedridden, are a common cause of slow blood flow. Other causes include compression of a vein by the fetus during pregnancy or by a tumor. Leg injury may also slow blood flow and may cause a clot to form in the deep veins of the leg.

The blood may clot more easily as a result of an injury, surgery, pregnancy, or taking combined oral contraceptives (*see* CONTRACEPTION, p.69). Some people have an inherited tendency for the blood to clot too readily (*see* HYPERCOAGULABILITY, p.453).

What are the symptoms?

If a blood clot has formed in a deep-lying vein in the leg, it may produce symptoms that include the following:

- Pain or tenderness in the leg.
- Swelling of the lower leg or thigh.
- Enlarged veins beneath the skin.

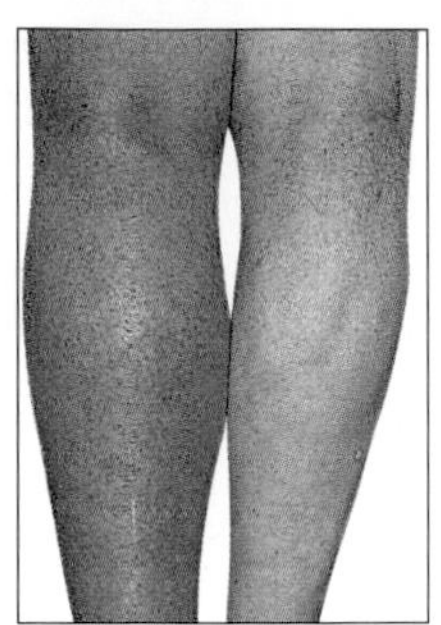

Deep vein thrombosis
The leg on the left is visibly swollen and red compared to the leg on the right, indicating that a blood clot has formed in a deep vein within the leg muscle.

Symptomatic pulmonary embolism occurs in about 1 in 5 cases of deep vein thrombosis. Associated symptoms usually include shortness of breath and chest pain. If the blood supply to the lungs is completely blocked, the condition is life-threatening.

In some cases, thrombosis causes permanent damage to the vein and varicose veins (p.438) may appear later.

What might be done?

Your doctor may need to carry out various tests to confirm the diagnosis of deep vein thrombosis because the symptoms are often similar to those of other conditions, such as cellulitis (p.352). You may have Doppler ultrasound scanning (p.432) to measure blood flow through the veins and sometimes a venogram, in which dye is injected into a vein and then X-rays are taken to reveal blood clots (*see* CONTRAST X-RAYS, p.245). MRI (p.248) may also be used. A sample of your blood may be taken and analyzed to assess how easily it clots.

In severe cases, thrombolytic drugs (p.904) may be prescribed to dissolve the blood clot in the vein and reduce the risk of a pulmonary embolism. You may also be given injections of anticoagulants to prevent further clots. Treatment can take place in the hospital, although you may be able to self-administer anticoagulant drugs at home. Only rarely is surgery required to remove the clot.

After you have had the initial treatment, your doctor will prescribe drugs to reduce the risk that the condition will recur (*see* DRUGS THAT PREVENT BLOOD CLOTTING, p.904).

Can it be prevented?

Certain surgical procedures carry a risk of deep vein thrombosis, and your susceptibility to developing the condition is assessed beforehand. If there is a high risk, you will probably be given low doses of short-acting anticoagulant drugs after surgery in order to prevent the blood from clotting. In addition, your doctor may advise you to wear special elastic stockings for a few days after the operation to help maintain blood flow in the veins of the leg.

It is possible to reduce the risk of deep vein thrombosis by avoiding long periods of inactivity. If you are confined to bed, make sure that you regularly stretch your legs and flex your ankles. Your doctor may also recommend that you wear elastic stockings. During an airplane flight, walk around at least once every hour, and, during a long drive, stop regularly so that you can get out and stretch your legs.

What is the prognosis?

Usually, when deep vein thrombosis is diagnosed in its early stages, treatment with anticoagulant drugs will be successful. However, if the affected vein has been permanently damaged, persistent swelling of the leg or varicose veins may develop. There is also a risk that the condition may recur.

(WWW) ONLINE SITES: p.1032

Varicose veins

Visibly swollen and distorted veins that lie just beneath the skin, mainly in the legs

AGE Rare before age 20; more common in elderly people

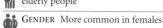

GENDER More common in females

GENETICS Often runs in families

LIFESTYLE Pregnancy, excess weight, and prolonged standing are risk factors

Varicose veins affect approximately 1 in 5 adults and are more common with increasing age. Although the condition may cause discomfort and appear unsightly, varicose veins are not usually harmful to your health.

Varicose veins mainly affect the legs. Normally, blood in the legs collects in the superficial veins just below the skin. These veins empty the blood into deep-lying veins through small perforating veins. The deep-lying veins carry blood back toward the heart. Contraction of the leg muscles helps pump the blood in the veins upward to the heart, even when you are standing, and the veins have one-way valves to stop blood from flowing backward into the legs. If the valves in the perforating vein do not close adequately, the blood flows back into the superficial veins. The pressure of returning blood causes these veins to become swollen and distorted, and they are then known as varicose veins. If left untreated, the condition often worsens.

Varicose veins can develop in other parts of the body as a complication of chronic liver disease, which raises blood pressure in the portal veins (*see* PORTAL HYPERTENSION AND VARICES, p.648). The rise in blood pressure may cause veins to become swollen at the lower end of the esophagus, and, in some cases, around the rectum (*see* HEMORRHOIDS, p.668).

What are the causes?

Varicose veins may be associated with an inherited weakness of the valves in the veins. The female hormone progesterone, which causes the veins to dilate, may encourage the formation of varicose veins, and the condition is therefore more common in women, especially during pregnancy (*see* COMMON COMPLAINTS OF NORMAL PREGNANCY, p.784). In addition, increased pressure is placed on the veins in the pelvic region during pregnancy as the uterus gradually grows larger. Other factors that increase the risk of developing varicose veins include being overweight and having an occupation that involves standing for long periods and little walking.

Sometimes, varicose veins are caused by a blood clot blocking a deep vein (*see* DEEP VEIN THROMBOSIS, p.437).

What are the symptoms?

If you develop varicose veins in the legs, you may have the following symptoms:

- Easily visible, blue, swollen, distorted veins that bulge beneath the skin and are more prominent when standing.

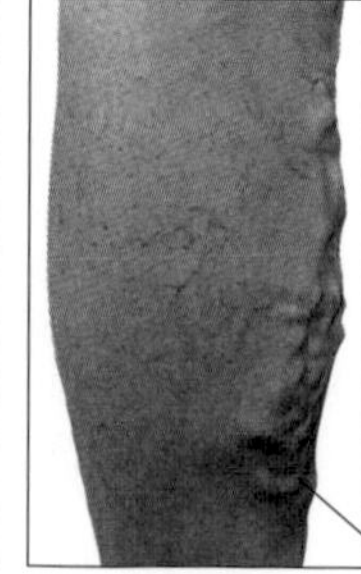
Varicose vein

Varicose veins
Abnormal backflow of blood into the superficial veins that lie just beneath the surface of the skin has caused these veins to become swollen and distorted.

> **SELF-HELP COPING WITH VARICOSE VEINS**
>
> If you have troublesome symptoms caused by varicose veins, the following measures may help:
>
> - Avoid prolonged standing.
> - Take regular walks to exercise the leg muscles and keep blood flowing in the legs.
> - Keep your legs elevated when sitting, if possible.
> - If your doctor has recommended that you wear elastic stockings, put them on before you get out of bed in the morning while your legs are still elevated.
> - Avoid clothing, such as girdles, that may restrict the flow of blood at the top of the legs.
> - If you are overweight, you should try to lose weight.

- Aching or pain in the affected leg, especially after prolonged standing.

In severe cases, the skin over a varicose vein, usually in the ankle area, becomes thin, dry, and itchy. Eventually, ulceration may occur (*see* LEG ULCER, p.350).

How are they diagnosed?

Your doctor will examine the affected area while you are standing, when the veins are usually more prominent and easily visible. You may have Doppler ultrasound scanning (p.432) to assess the direction of blood flow in the veins of the leg. If the veins are varicose, the blood will appear to flow backward.

What is the treatment?

In the majority of cases, varicose veins do not require medical treatment, and you may be able to relieve discomfort using self-help measures (*see* COPING WITH VARICOSE VEINS, above).

Treatment is usually carried out only if the veins become painful or especially unsightly or if the skin becomes ulcerated. There are several ways of treating varicose veins (opposite page), and you may need to discuss these options with your doctor. If your varicose veins are small and below the knee, your doctor may recommend that the veins be injected with a solution to make their walls stick together and thus prevent blood from entering them. For varicose veins above the knee, the usual treatment is to tie off the perforating veins so that blood does not enter the varicose vein. If the entire vein is varicose, it may be surgically removed. Even after surgery, varicose veins may eventually recur, and treatment may need to be repeated.

(WWW) ONLINE SITES: p.1032

Superficial thrombophlebitis

Inflammation of a superficial vein (a vein just beneath the surface of the skin) that may cause a blood clot to form in it

AGE More common after age 20

GENDER More common in females

GENETICS Sometimes runs in families

LIFESTYLE Intravenous drug abuse is a risk factor

In superficial thrombophlebitis, a blood clot develops in an inflamed superficial vein. The condition is rarely serious, but it may be painful. Thrombophlebitis can affect any superficial vein, including varicose veins (opposite page). Superficial thrombophlebitis may run in families and is most common in adult women.

Inflammation leading to clot formation may result from damage to a vein, which may be sustained during intravenous drug injection or surgery. The development of blood clots in superficial veins is more common in people who have cancer. In some cases, superficial thrombophlebitis is associated with an increase in the tendency of blood to clot (*see* HYPERCOAGULABILITY, p.453). For example, blood may clot more easily in women who are pregnant or who take combined oral contraceptives (*see* CONTRACEPTION, p.69). However, in many cases, the cause is unclear.

WHAT ARE THE SYMPTOMS?

The symptoms associated with superficial thrombophlebitis usually develop over 24–48 hours and include:

- Redness of the skin overlying a vein.
- A painful, tender, swollen vein that may feel hard like a cord.
- Mild fever.

Inflammation is usually localized in the area of the blood clot and may spread to the overlying skin. However, in rare cases, thrombophlebitis extends into a deep-lying vein, usually in the leg, leading to deep vein thrombosis (p.437).

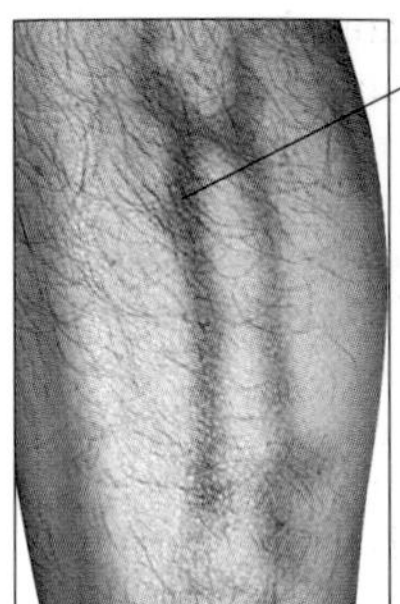
Inflamed vein

Superficial thrombophlebitis *The skin overlying the affected vein is red and inflamed. The outline of the swollen vein can be seen beneath the surface of the skin.*

WHAT MIGHT BE DONE?

Your doctor will probably be able to diagnose superficial thrombophlebitis from your symptoms and the appearance of the vein and the overlying skin.

Most cases improve in a few days without treatment. You may be able to relieve pain by taking an analgesic drug, such as ibuprofen (*see* NONSTEROIDAL ANTI-INFLAMMATORY DRUGS, p.894), and keeping the area rested and elevated. Warm, moist compresses can also ease discomfort. If the condition is due to hypercoagulability or has resulted in a deep vein thrombosis, your doctor may recommend that you take drugs that prevent blood clotting (p.904). Superficial thrombophlebitis is likely to recur in susceptible people.

(WWW) ONLINE SITES: p.1032

(TREATMENT) TREATING VARICOSE VEINS

There are several methods of treating varicose veins, including injection therapy and surgery. Injection therapy is mainly used to treat small varicose veins below the knee, and surgery is performed to treat larger veins. Surgery may be used to divide faulty perforating veins responsible for the formation of the varicose veins or to remove an entire varicose vein. Treatment may need to be repeated if the varicose veins recur.

DIVISION OF PERFORATING VEINS

Blood normally flows from the superficial veins into the deep veins along perforating veins. If the valves in the perforating veins are not working properly, there is a backflow of blood into the superficial veins, which leads to the formation of varicose veins. During the surgical division of faulty perforating veins, these veins are tied off and cut. Surgery is usually performed in the hospital under general anesthesia.

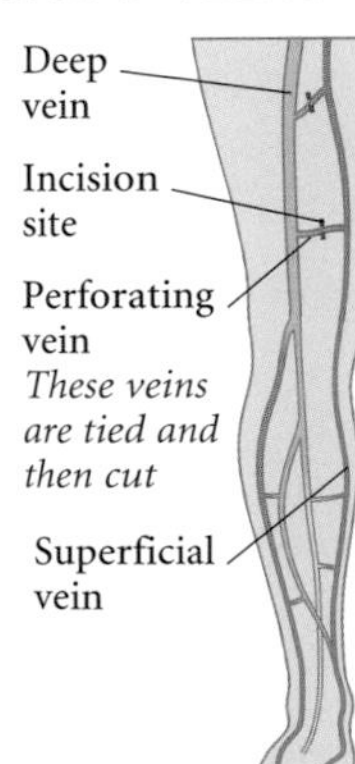
Deep vein
Incision site
Perforating vein
These veins are tied and then cut
Superficial vein

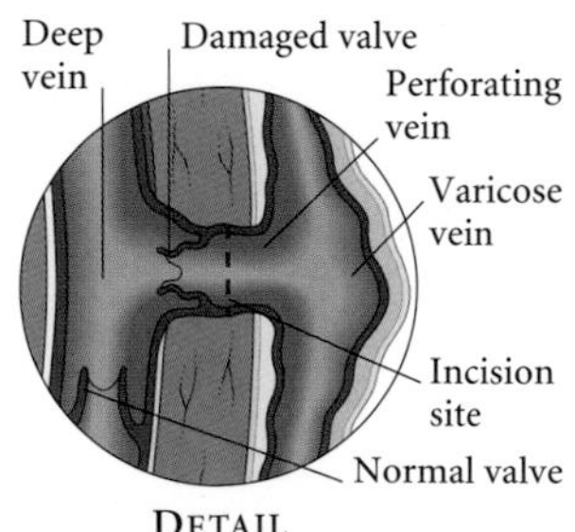
Deep vein
Damaged valve
Perforating vein
Varicose vein
Incision site
Normal valve
DETAIL

During the procedure *Small incisions are made in the leg, usually in the groin, behind the knee, and sometimes also in the lower leg. The perforating veins are then tied and cut.*

INJECTION THERAPY

Injection therapy is used for small varicose veins below the knee. The procedure uses a mild irritant to make the walls of the varicose veins stick together and stop blood from entering them. For a week after the procedure, an elastic bandage is worn around the leg in order to compress the veins and help the vessel walls stick together.

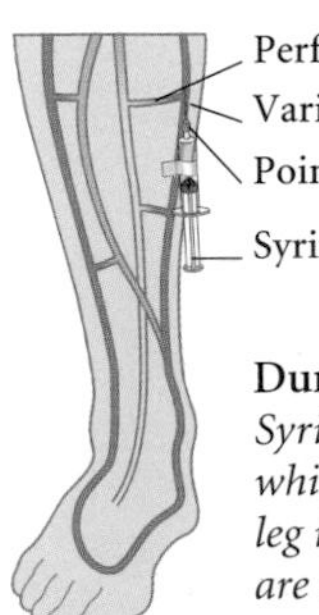
Perforating vein
Varicose vein
Point of injection
Syringe

During the procedure *Syringes are taped in place while you are standing. The leg is elevated and the veins are injected at each site. The syringes are then removed.*

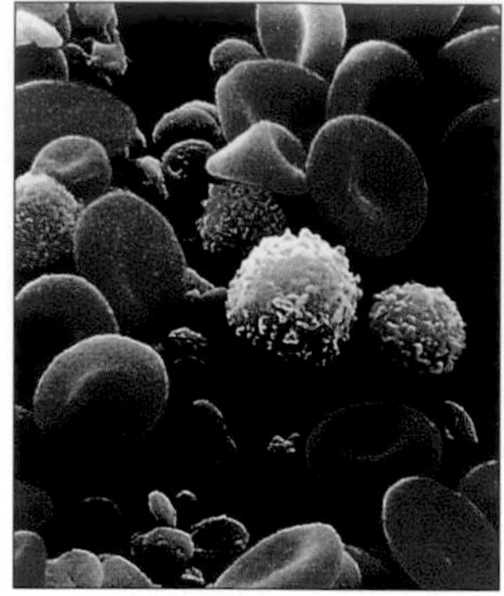

The cells in blood
A magnified view of a drop of blood reveals the various blood cells present: different types of white blood cells, together with red blood cells and platelets.

Blood and the Lymphatic and Immune Systems

Blood is the body's internal transport system, constantly flowing around the body delivering oxygen, nutrients, and other substances to the tissues and removing waste products from them. Running almost parallel with the blood's circulation is the lymphatic system, which collects excess fluid from the tissues and returns it to the blood. Both the blood and the lymphatic system form part of the body's immune system.

Body tissues, such as muscle, brain, heart, and other internal organs, need to have a constant supply of energy to function. The energy is obtained from glucose and oxygen, which are carried to body tissues by the blood in the circulation. Blood circulates around the body in about 1 minute at rest and 20 seconds during vigorous exercise.

Circulatory transport

Glucose, a simple sugar that is derived from the breakdown of many foods, is dissolved in the blood and carried in the circulation to every cell within the body. To release its energy, glucose must be "burned" inside the cells, which requires oxygen (a process known as oxidation). The oxygen is transported by red blood cells from the lungs to the body cells, where it is released.

In addition to glucose, body cells also require proteins, fats, vitamins and minerals, and lipids such as cholesterol. These substances are carried in the plasma, the fluid part of the blood, to every cell within the body.

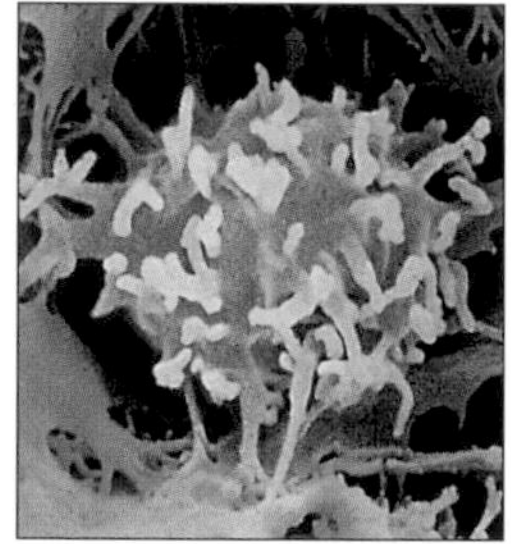

White blood cell
Some white blood cells, such as the one shown, play a particularly important part in the body's defenses.

As body cells carry out their various functions, grow, reproduce, and repair damage, they release waste products into the bloodstream. These waste products include carbon dioxide produced from the oxidation of glucose, protein wastes such as urea, and bilirubin from the breakdown of the pigment hemoglobin. The carbon dioxide is eliminated from the bloodstream in the lungs, while the other wastes are mostly processed in the liver before being excreted in the feces or transported to the kidneys for excretion in the urine.

The body's defenses

Blood contains colorless cells known as white cells. These are the main components of the immune system, which protects the body against infection, against toxins produced by bacteria, and against some cancers.

Other essential components of the immune system transported in the blood are proteins called antibodies, which help destroy microorganisms. Blood also contains billions of small cells called platelets, which seal injured blood vessels through blood clotting.

The lymphatic system also forms part of the immune system and helps protect the body by filtering out and destroying "foreign" particles, such as infectious organisms and cancer cells, that have contaminated body fluids.

FUNCTION Formation of blood cells

Bone marrow, the soft fatty tissue inside bone cavities, is the source of all the red blood cells and platelets and most of the white blood cells. In adults, blood cells are formed mainly in the bone marrow of flat bones, such as the shoulder blades, ribs, breastbone, and pelvis. All the blood cells are derived from a single type of cell called a stem cell. Production of stem cells is controlled by hormones, including erythropoietin, which is produced by the kidneys; thyroid hormones; corticosteroids secreted by the adrenal glands; and growth hormones from the pituitary gland.

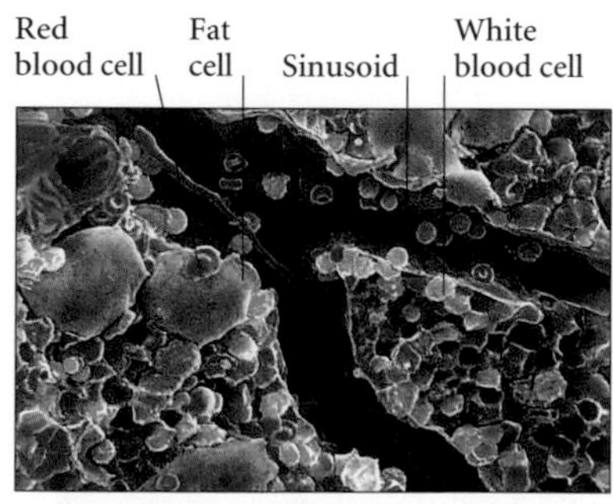
Red blood cell
Fat cell
Sinusoid
White blood cell

Cells in bone marrow
Blood cells, such as red and white cells, and fat cells are found in bone marrow. Tiny blood vessels called sinusoids supply nourishment and carry away wastes.

STRUCTURE COMPONENTS OF BLOOD

The average person has about 11 pints (5 liters) of blood, which consists of cells and fluid (plasma). Red blood cells, the most numerous blood cells, transport oxygen in the body. White blood cells destroy bacterial organisms, cells infected by viruses, and cancer cells. Platelets are the smallest blood cells; after an injury to a blood vessel, they rapidly clump together to seal the damaged lining. Plasma is mostly water but contains other important substances.

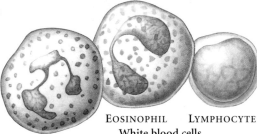

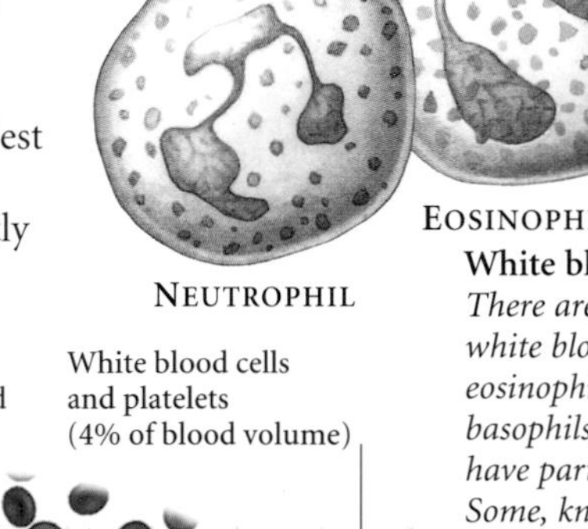

NEUTROPHIL
EOSINOPHIL
LYMPHOCYTE

White blood cells
There are five main types of white blood cells: neutrophils, eosinophils, lymphocytes, basophils, and monocytes. All have particular roles to play. Some, known as phagocytes, destroy foreign organisms.

Dissolved substances (10% of plasma)

Water (90% of plasma)

Plasma (55% of blood volume)

White blood cells and platelets (4% of blood volume)

Plasma
Plasma consists of water, nutrients, salts, hormones, and proteins, including the dissolved protein fibrinogen, which has a key role in blood clotting.

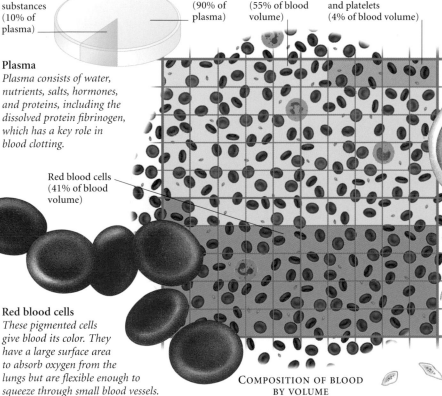

Red blood cells (41% of blood volume)

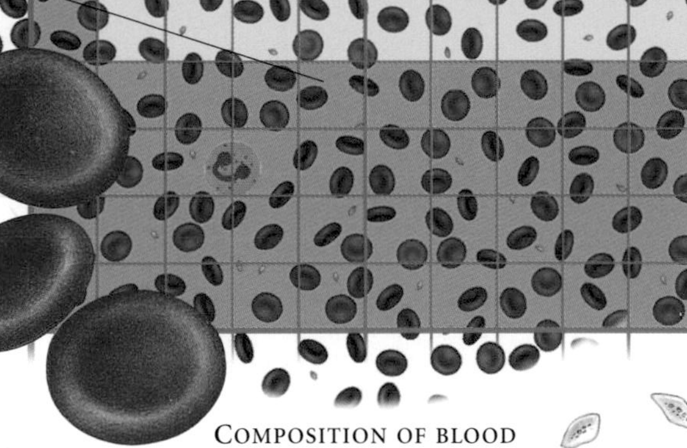

BASOPHIL

MONOCYTE

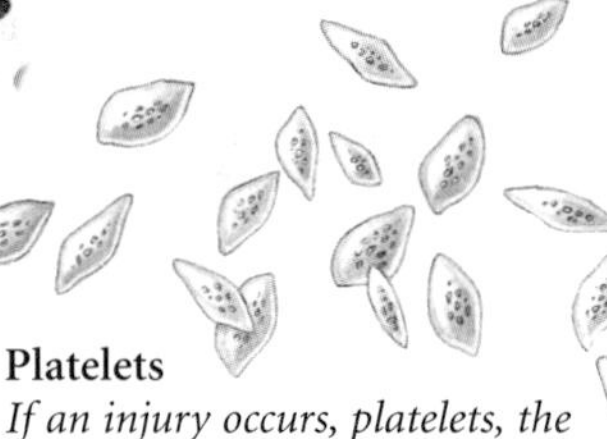

Red blood cells
These pigmented cells give blood its color. They have a large surface area to absorb oxygen from the lungs but are flexible enough to squeeze through small blood vessels.

COMPOSITION OF BLOOD BY VOLUME

Platelets
If an injury occurs, platelets, the smallest blood cells, help stop bleeding by plugging the broken blood vessel wall and releasing chemicals that promote clotting.

STRUCTURE BLOOD GROUPS

Each person's red blood cells have certain proteins called antigens on their surface, which categorize the blood into various groups. Antibodies within the blood are produced against any antigens foreign to the red cells. The ABO blood grouping is important for transfusions; if a recipient's blood contains antibodies to antigens in the donor blood, a reaction will occur between them. The Rhesus (Rh) system is another important method of typing blood.

Blood group A
This group has A antigens on the surface of the red blood cells and anti-B antibodies in the blood.

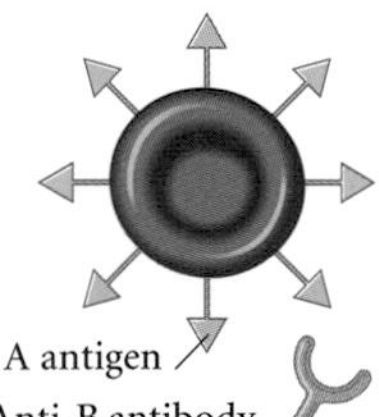

A antigen
Anti-B antibody

Blood group B
People in this group have red blood cells with B antigens, and anti-A antibodies in their blood.

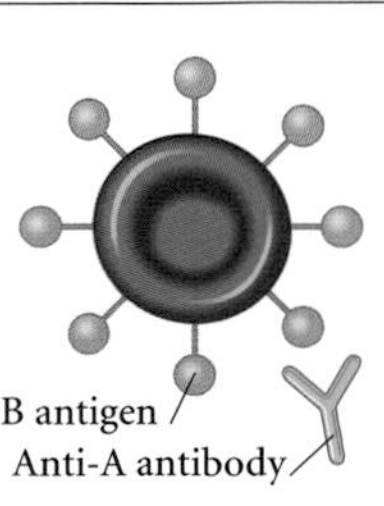

B antigen
Anti-A antibody

Blood group AB
The rarest blood group, AB, has both antigens on the red cells and neither antibody in the blood.

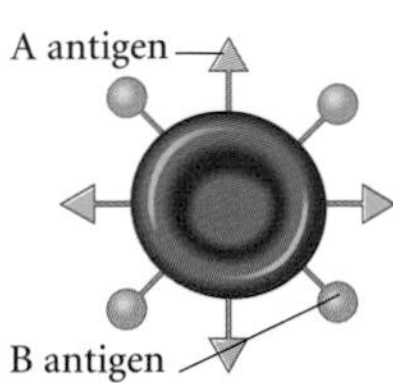

A antigen
B antigen

Blood group O
The most common group, O, has no red cell antigens, and anti-A and anti-B antibodies in the blood.

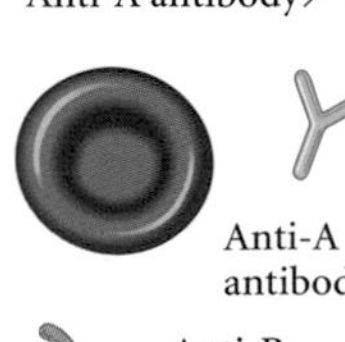

Anti-A antibody
Anti-B antibody

FUNCTION THE ROLES OF BLOOD

One of the main functions of blood is to transport oxygen, cells, proteins, hormones, and other substances around the body to the organs and tissues. Oxygen is carried from the lungs to the body cells, and the waste product carbon dioxide is transported from the cells to the lungs. Blood also has a clotting mechanism that acts to seal damaged blood vessels and prevents internal and external blood loss.

TRANSPORTING OXYGEN

Each red blood cell contains millions of molecules of hemoglobin, each made up of four protein chains (two alpha- and two beta-globin) and four heme, an iron-bearing red pigment. Hemoglobin combines with oxygen from the lungs to give arterial blood its bright red color. Once oxygen is released in the tissues, the blood becomes darker, a distinctive feature of venous blood.

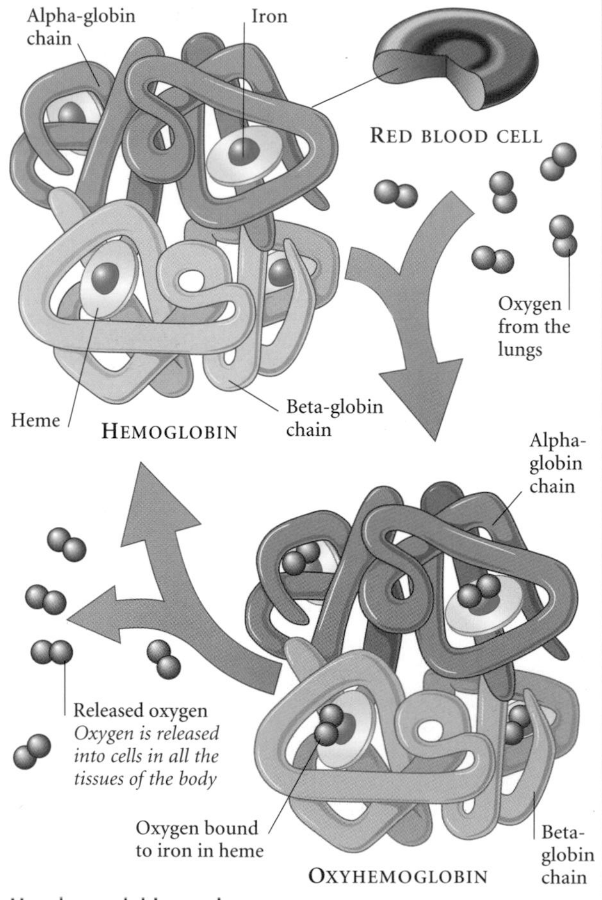
Alpha-globin chain
Iron
RED BLOOD CELL
Oxygen from the lungs
Heme
HEMOGLOBIN
Beta-globin chain
Alpha-globin chain
Released oxygen
Oxygen is released into cells in all the tissues of the body
Oxygen bound to iron in heme
OXYHEMOGLOBIN
Beta-globin chain

How hemoglobin carries oxygen
The oxygen from the lungs enters the red blood cells in the bloodstream. The oxygen then combines chemically with the heme within the hemoglobin to form oxyhemoglobin, which is carried around the body. In areas that need oxygen, the oxyhemoglobin releases its oxygen and reverts to hemoglobin.

BLOOD CLOTTING

When a blood vessel is cut or torn, the damage triggers a series of chemical reactions that lead to the formation of a blood clot to seal the injury. Clot formation depends on blood cells called platelets, which adhere at the site of injury. The platelets then clump together and release chemicals that activate proteins, called clotting factors.

1 *When a blood vessel is damaged, it constricts at once. Platelets that come into contact with the damaged blood vessel walls are activated. They become sticky and start to adhere to the blood vessel walls near the site of the injury.*

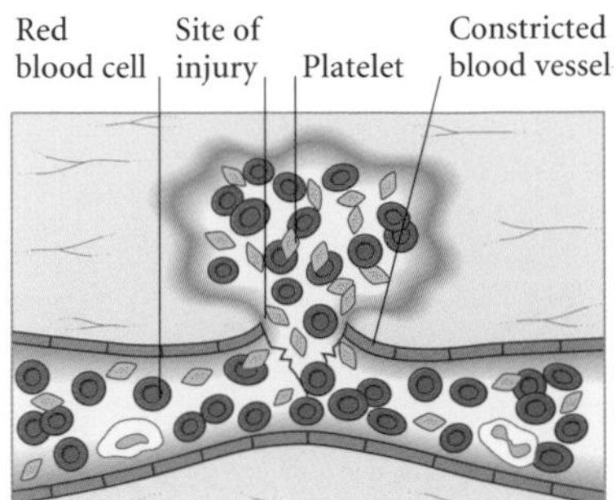
Red blood cell
Site of injury
Platelet
Constricted blood vessel

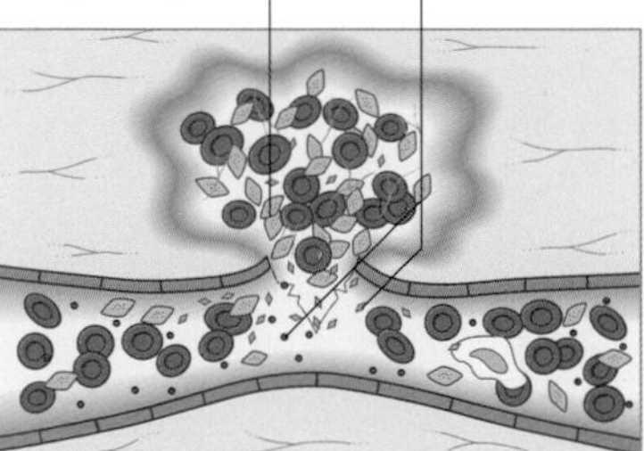
Platelets clumped together
Released chemicals

2 *The platelets clump together. Damaged tissue and activated platelets release chemicals that start a "coagulation cascade," a complex series of reactions involving clotting factors. At each stage, more clotting factors are activated.*

3 *The final stage is conversion of the protein fibrinogen, which is dissolved in the fluid part of the blood, to insoluble fibrin strands. The sticky fibrin threads form a tangled mesh that traps red cells and other blood cells, forming a clot.*

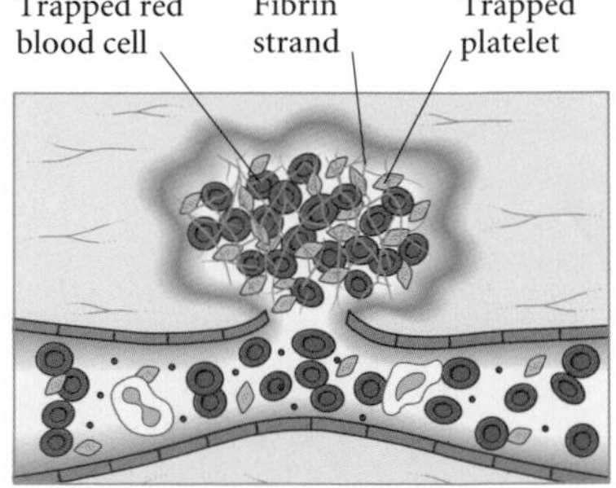
Trapped red blood cell
Fibrin strand
Trapped platelet

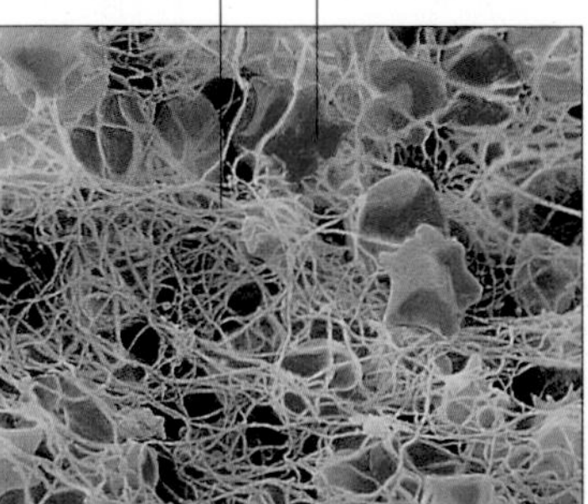
Fibrin strand
Red blood cell

Blood clot
This magnified view shows red blood cells trapped in a mesh of sticky fibrin strands, forming a blood clot. An injured blood vessel is plugged by the clot, which becomes denser as more fibrin strands form. Eventually the clot will solidify.

STRUCTURE THE LYMPHATIC SYSTEM

A network of lymph vessels, lymphatic tissue, and clumps of bean-shaped lymph nodes (glands) makes up the lymphatic system. The lymph vessels collect fluid (lymph) from the body tissues and return it to the blood, maintaining the fluid balance within the body. Lymph filters through the lymph nodes, which are packed with particular types of white blood cells known as lymphocytes. These cells are produced in the bone marrow, spleen, and thymus, and they help protect the body against infection.

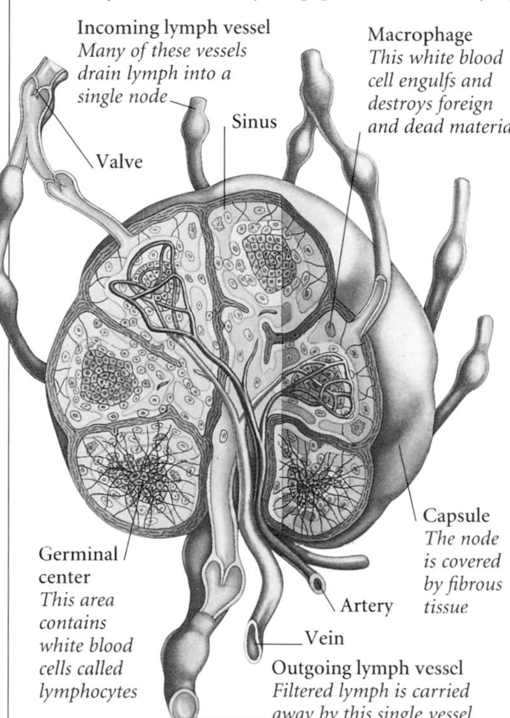
Incoming lymph vessel
Many of these vessels drain lymph into a single node
Valve
Sinus
Macrophage
This white blood cell engulfs and destroys foreign and dead material
Germinal center
This area contains white blood cells called lymphocytes
Capsule
The node is covered by fibrous tissue
Artery
Vein
Outgoing lymph vessel
Filtered lymph is carried away by this single vessel

Inside a lymph node
The flow of lymph slows as it moves through the narrow channels in the spaces, called sinuses, in a node. The reduction in flow allows macrophages time to filter disease organisms from the lymph.

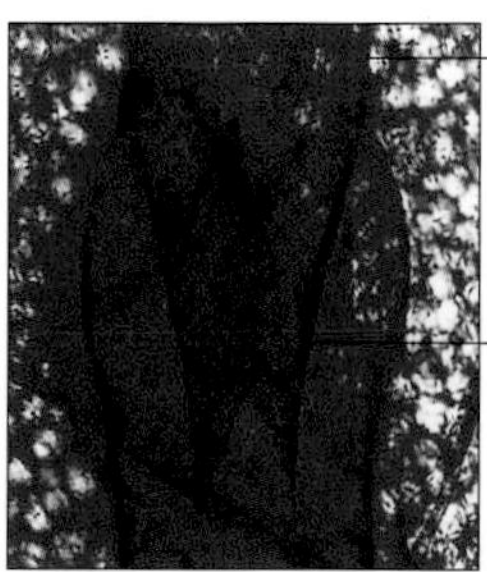
Lymph vessel wall
Thin, specialized walls allow fluid to flow into, but not out of, the vessel
Valve
This structure opens (as here) to let lymph flow through and closes to prevent backflow

Section of a lymph vessel
Lymph vessels have thin walls that allow fluid from the surrounding body tissues (known as lymph) to enter. The lymph is moved through the lymph vessel by the contractions of muscles. Valves in each vessel prevent backflow of fluid.

Fibrous tissue

White blood cell

Lymphatic tissue in a node
This magnified view reveals a fine, fibrous network of lymphatic tissue. White blood cells, a key feature of the body's immune system, are seen entangled within the mesh.

Supratrochlear node

Cervical (neck) nodes
Lymph from the head and neck is filtered here

Axillary (armpit) nodes
These nodes filter lymph from the arms and breasts

Right lymphatic duct
This duct receives lymph that is filtered from the right arm and upper right side of the body

Subclavian vein
This vein, which leads toward the heart, receives filtered lymph from the thoracic and right lymphatic ducts

Thymus gland
The thymus produces vital white blood cells

Spleen
This is the largest lymph organ, in which certain types of lymphocytes (white blood cells) are manufactured

Thoracic duct
This main duct receives lymph from the majority of lymph vessels

Cisterna chyli
This lymph vessel, which narrows into the thoracic duct, receives lymph from the lower body

Peyer's patch
Areas of lymphatic tissue in the intestines are known as Peyer's patches

Deep inguinal (groin) nodes
These nodes filter lymph from the lower part of the body

Popliteal lymph nodes
These nodes, which are situated behind the knees, filter lymph from the legs and feet

Lymph vessel
Many lymph vessels carry lymph from the tissues to the main lymphatic ducts through lymph nodes

FUNCTION

THE BODY'S DEFENSES

Several barriers and responses work together to protect the body against infection and the development of cancer. Physical and chemical barriers and the inflammatory response form the first two lines of defense. If invading organisms break through these general lines of defense, the body's immune system fights back with two extremely effective immune responses that are specific to different invaders.

PHYSICAL AND CHEMICAL BARRIERS

The skin and the mucous membranes, which line the body openings and the internal passages, are effective barriers against invading organisms. Saliva, tears, mucus, sebum, sweat, and acid aid these barriers in protecting the different parts of the body.

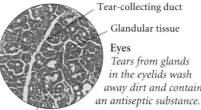

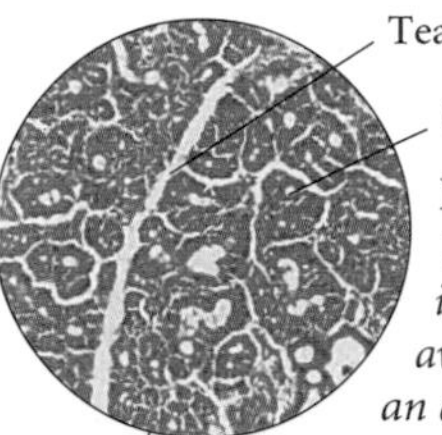
Tear-collecting duct
Glandular tissue

Eyes
Tears from glands in the eyelids wash away dirt and contain an antiseptic substance.

Mucus-secreting cell

Cilia

Respiratory tract
The lining of the respiratory tract produces mucus, which traps organisms. Tiny hairs (cilia) move mucus to the throat.

Enzyme-secreting cells

Mucus-secreting cells

Mouth
Glands in the mouth produce saliva, a mixture of mucus and enzymes that cleans the mouth.

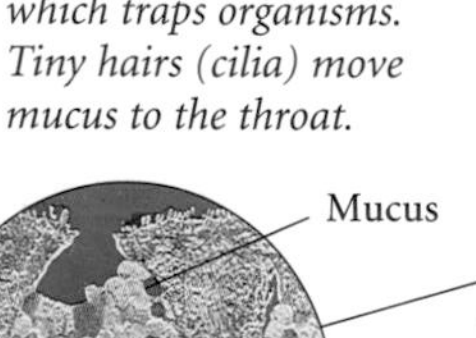
Mucus
Goblet cell

Intestines
Goblet cells in the lining of the intestines produce mucus, which protects the lining from digestive chemicals and harmful organisms.

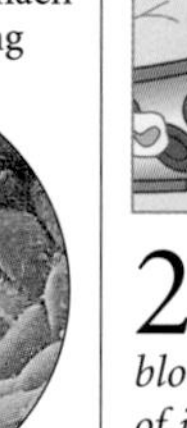
Opening of gastric gland
Stomach lining

Stomach
Glands in the stomach lining produce hydrochloric acid, a powerful agent that kills most invading organisms.

"Harmless" bacteria in the genital tract

Genital and urinary tracts
"Harmless" bacteria within the genital tract and the flushing action of urine in the urinary tract both help prevent the growth of harmful organisms.

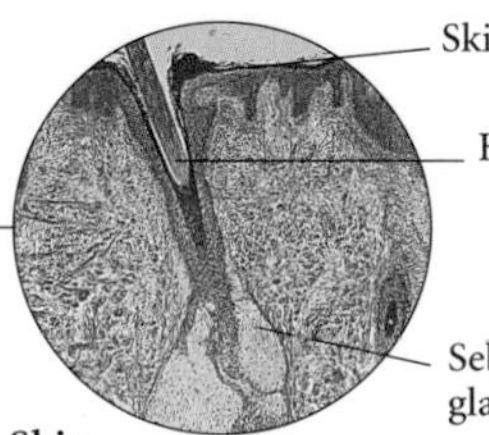
Skin surface
Hair
Sebaceous gland

Skin
The skin is protected by an oily substance, sebum, produced by sebaceous glands, and by sweat. Both of these are mildly antiseptic.

THE INFLAMMATORY RESPONSE

If foreign organisms such as bacteria overcome the body's physical and chemical barriers, the next line of defense is the inflammatory response, characterized by redness, pain, heat, and swelling at the damaged site.

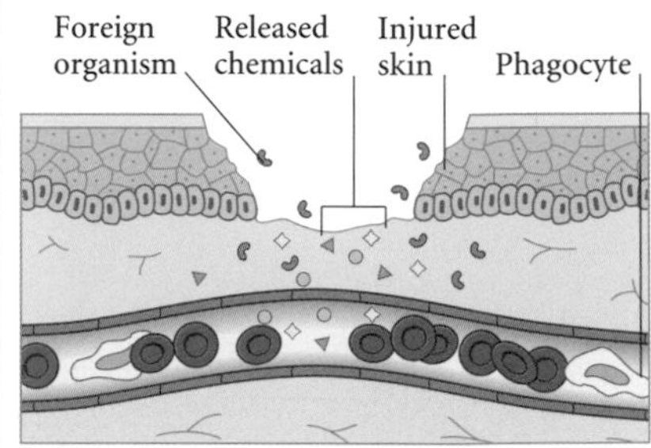
Foreign organism
Released chemicals
Injured skin
Phagocyte

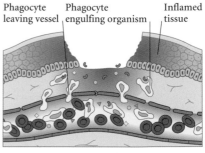

1 *Foreign organisms invade the body through skin that has been broken due to injury. Instantly, the damaged tissue releases specific chemicals that attract specialized white blood cells called phagocytes.*

Phagocyte leaving vessel

Phagocyte engulfing organism

Inflamed tissue

2 *The chemicals cause the underlying blood vessel to widen and the flow of blood to increase, leading to symptoms of inflammation. The vessel walls become slightly porous, allowing phagocytes to reach, engulf, and destroy the foreign organisms.*

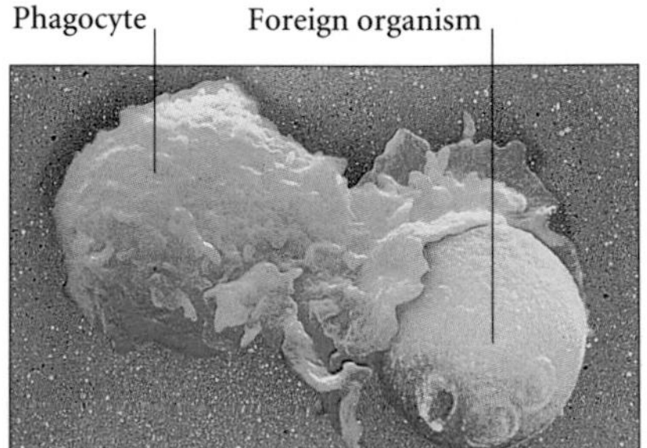
Phagocyte
Foreign organism

Destroying foreign organisms
Here, a white blood cell called a phagocyte has started to engulf a foreign organism. To destroy the organism, the phagocyte releases enzymes that help break it down.

THE ANTIBODY IMMUNE RESPONSE

This specific immune response targets invading bacteria and relies on white blood cells called B lymphocytes or B cells. These cells recognize proteins (antigens) of invading bacteria and multiply to produce antibodies. The antibodies seek out the bacteria and lock onto them, causing their destruction.

1 The bacteria enter the body. Some of them are engulfed by cells called phagocytes that bring the bacterial antigens into contact with B cells, some of which match the antigens.

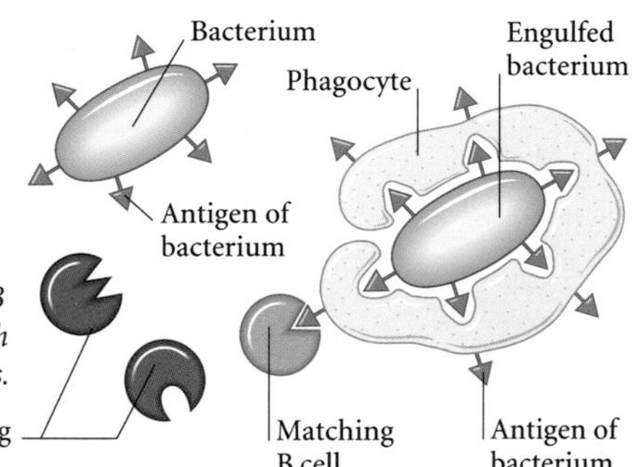

Bacterium
Engulfed bacterium
Phagocyte
Antigen of bacterium
Nonmatching B cells
Matching B cell
Antigen of bacterium

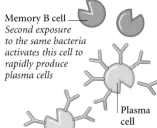

Memory B cell
Second exposure to the same bacteria activates this cell to rapidly produce plasma cells

Plasma cell

Antibody

2 The matching B cell multiplies to produce two types of cells: plasma cells, which produce antibodies to destroy the bacteria, and memory B cells, which are stored in the body for future use.

3 The antibodies that are released by the plasma cells seek out and lock onto bacterial antigens and inactivate the bacteria. The antibodies also attract more phagocytes to the site to destroy the bacteria.

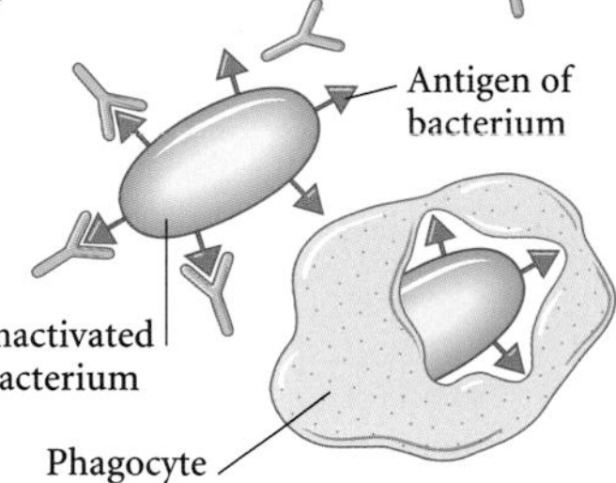

Antibody
Antigen of bacterium
Inactivated bacterium
Phagocyte

THE CELLULAR IMMUNE RESPONSE

This type of specific immune response targets viruses, parasites, and cancer cells. It depends on white blood cells called T lymphocytes or T cells. After recognizing a foreign protein (antigen), T cells multiply and engage in a direct battle against infected cells or cancer cells.

1 Cells that are infected by the invading viruses are engulfed by cells called phagocytes. These bring the viral antigens into contact with T cells, some of which match up with these antigens.

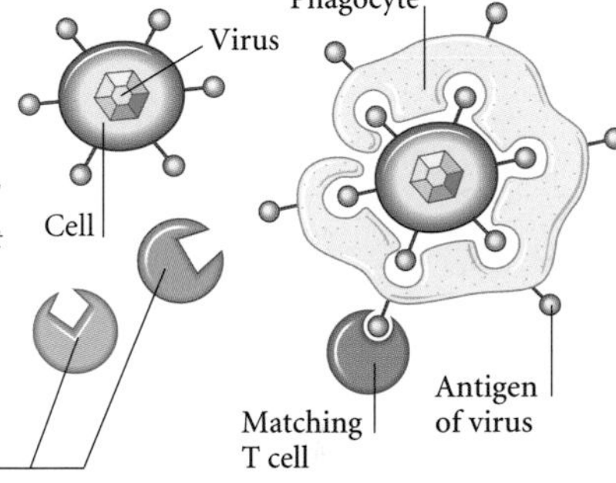

Virus
Phagocyte
Cell
Nonmatching T cells
Matching T cell
Antigen of virus

Memory T cell
Future exposure to the same antigen activates this cell to rapidly produce killer T cells

Toxic protein

Killer T cell

2 The matching T cell multiplies in order to produce different types of cells, including killer T cells, which contain toxic proteins, and memory T cells, stored to protect the body against the virus in the future.

3 Killer T cells lock onto the infected cell bearing the recognized antigen and release their toxic proteins. These proteins then destroy the infected cell. Killer T cells may then go on to seek out other infected cells.

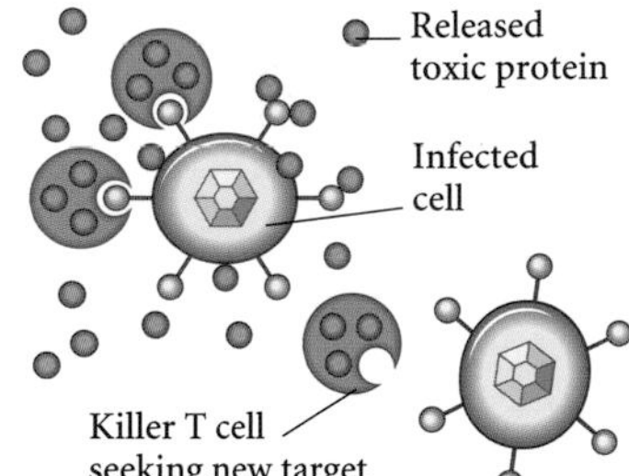

Released toxic protein
Infected cell
Killer T cell seeking new target

FUNCTION ALLERGIC REACTIONS

An allergy is an inappropriate immune response to a normally harmless substance, called an allergen. On initial exposure to the allergen, the immune system becomes sensitized to it. During subsequent exposures, an allergic reaction occurs. Mast cells, located in the skin, nasal lining, and other tissues, are destroyed, releasing a substance called histamine that causes an inflammatory response, irritating body tissues and producing allergy symptoms.

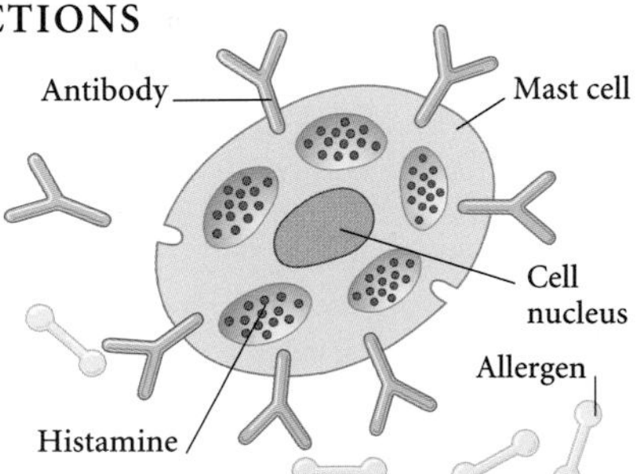

Antibody
Mast cell
Cell nucleus
Allergen
Histamine

1 On repeat exposure to an allergen, antibodies previously produced in response to it bind to the surface of mast cells, which contain histamine.

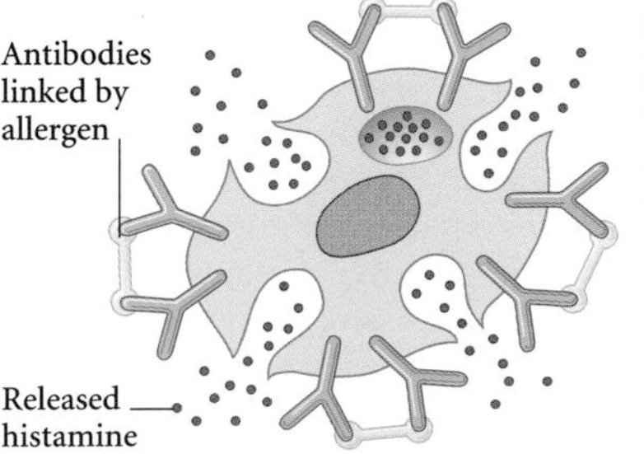

Antibodies linked by allergen
Released histamine

2 The allergens bind to and link two or more antibodies, causing the cell to burst and release the histamine within. Histamine causes the symptoms of allergy.

Blood disorders

Blood transports oxygen and nutrients to all parts of the body and carries away carbon dioxide and other waste materials. Oxygen is carried inside red blood cells, which make up almost half the volume of blood. Other components include white blood cells, which help combat infections, and platelets, tiny cells that help form blood clots to seal any damage to blood vessels.

Disorders of the blood may be caused by an abnormality in the number, content, or form of one or more of the different types of blood cells. The first articles in this section deal with the different types of anemia. In these disorders, hemoglobin, the oxygen-carrying pigment in red blood cells, is deficient or abnormal, or the red cells are destroyed at an accelerated rate. Disorders in which the blood either fails to clot or clots too readily are then discussed. Some of these disorders are inherited, such as hemophilia A, Christmas disease, and von Willebrand disease. In these disorders, the genes that are responsible for producing specific clotting factors are either absent or abnormal. Various cancers of the blood, for example leukemias, are also discussed. These disorders result from an overproduction of white blood cells, which suppresses the production of the normal blood cells in the body. The final article in this section deals with polycythemia, a condition in which too many red blood cells are produced.

KEY ELEMENTS

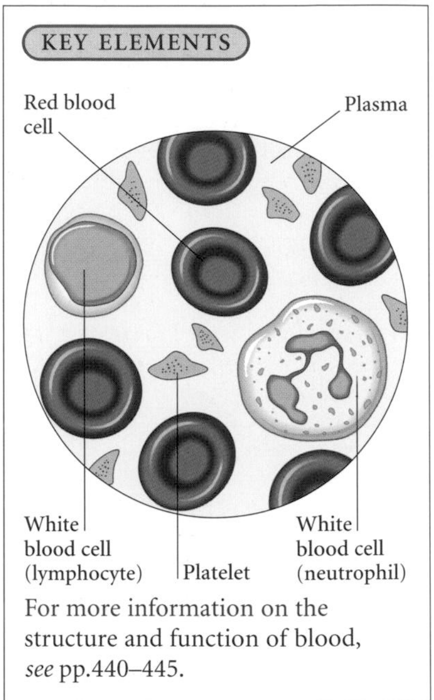
Red blood cell
Plasma
White blood cell (lymphocyte)
Platelet
White blood cell (neutrophil)

For more information on the structure and function of blood, *see* pp.440–445.

Anemia

Disorders in which hemoglobin (the oxygen-carrying pigment in red blood cells) is deficient or abnormal

AGE GENDER GENETICS LIFESTYLE
Risk factors depend on the type

Anemia is a deficiency or an abnormality of hemoglobin, the component of red blood cells that binds with oxygen from the lungs and carries it through the circulation to the body tissues. The oxygen-carrying capacity of the blood is thus reduced, and the tissues of the body may not receive sufficient oxygen.

Red blood cells are manufactured in the bone marrow and circulate in the bloodstream for about 120 days before they are broken down in the spleen. In a healthy person, the production and destruction of red blood cells are balanced. Anemia occurs if this balance is upset, reducing the number of healthy cells, or if the hemoglobin is abnormal.

What are the types?

There are four main types of anemia. The first type is due to a deficiency of one or more of the substances that are essential for the formation of healthy red blood cells. By far the most common form is iron-deficiency anemia (opposite page), which results from low levels of iron in the body. A much rarer form is megaloblastic anemia (p.448), which is usually the result of low levels of either vitamin B_{12} or another vitamin, folic acid, in the body.

The second type of anemia results from inherited abnormalities of hemoglobin production. Examples of this type include sickle-cell anemia (p.448) and thalassemia (p.449). The hemoglobin is abnormal from shortly after birth, but symptoms of anemia may not develop until later in childhood.

The third type of anemia is caused by excessively rapid destruction of red blood cells (hemolysis) and is called hemolytic anemia (p.450).

The fourth type of anemia, called aplastic anemia (p.450), is caused by the failure of the bone marrow to produce enough red blood cells and often all the other types of blood cells as well.

Anemia may be due to a combination of different causes, and sometimes the exact cause is not known. In some cases, anemia develops during a long-term illness, such as various cancers or rheumatoid arthritis (p.377).

What are the symptoms?

If your anemia is mild, your body may be able to make up for a slight reduction in the oxygen-carrying capacity of blood by increasing the blood supply to the tissues. In this case there may not be any symptoms. Symptoms of more severe anemia may include:

- Fatigue and a feeling of faintness.
- Pale skin.
- Shortness of breath on mild exertion.

You may also have a rapid heart rate because the heart has to work harder to increase blood supply to the rest of the body. Stress on the heart may result in chronic heart failure (p.413), common symptoms of which are swollen ankles and increasing shortness of breath.

What might be done?

Anemia is usually confirmed by blood tests to measure the level of hemoglobin and to establish the type and cause of the anemia. A bone marrow aspiration and biopsy (p.451) may be carried out to obtain tissue samples for examination under a microscope.

Many anemias respond well to treatment. Severe cases may require blood transfusion (opposite page).

(WWW) ONLINE SITES: p.1027

(TREATMENT) BLOOD TRANSFUSION

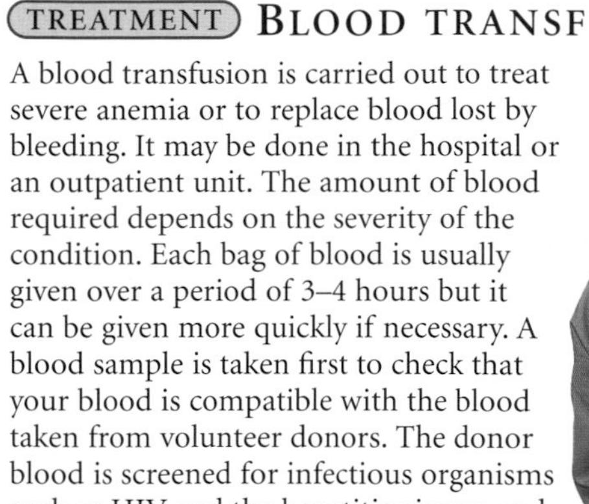

A blood transfusion is carried out to treat severe anemia or to replace blood lost by bleeding. It may be done in the hospital or an outpatient unit. The amount of blood required depends on the severity of the condition. Each bag of blood is usually given over a period of 3–4 hours but it can be given more quickly if necessary. A blood sample is taken first to check that your blood is compatible with the blood taken from volunteer donors. The donor blood is screened for infectious organisms such as HIV and the hepatitis viruses and is stored in blood banks.

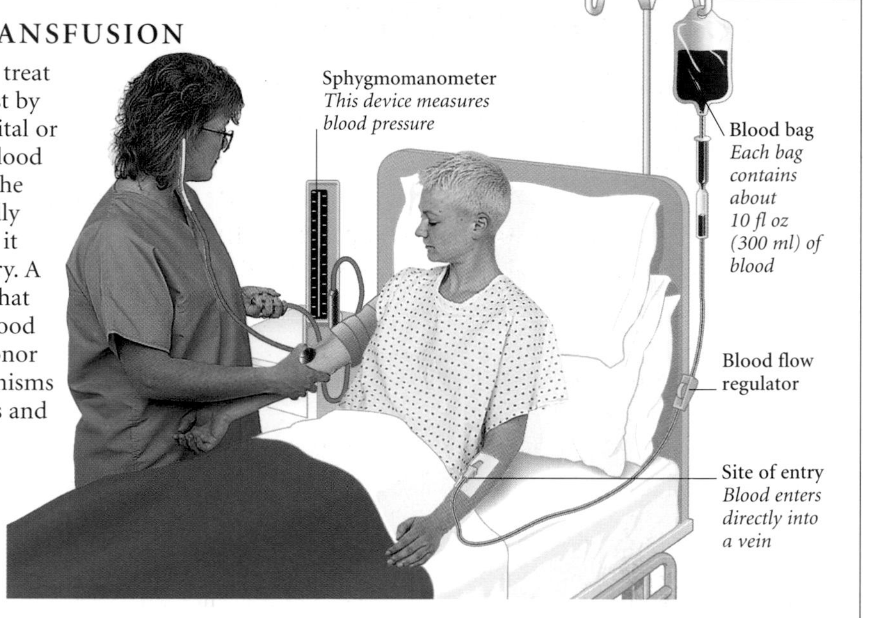
Sphygmomanometer
This device measures blood pressure
Blood bag
Each bag contains about 10 fl oz (300 ml) of blood
Blood flow regulator
Site of entry
Blood enters directly into a vein

Having a transfusion
A nurse will regularly measure your blood pressure, pulse, and temperature while the blood transfusion is given directly into a vein in your arm.

Iron-deficiency anemia

A type of anemia caused by inadequate levels of iron in the body

GENDER More common in females

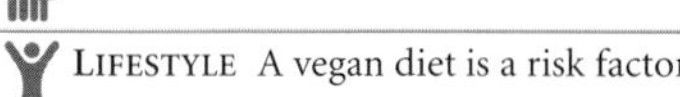
LIFESTYLE A vegan diet is a risk factor

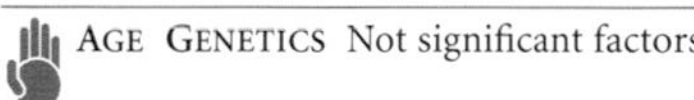
AGE GENETICS Not significant factors

Iron-deficiency anemia is the most common form of anemia (a deficiency of the oxygen-carrying pigment hemoglobin in red blood cells). Iron is an essential component of hemoglobin in the production of blood. If insufficient iron is available, the production of hemoglobin and its incorporation into red blood cells in the bone marrow are reduced. As a result, there is less hemoglobin to bind with oxygen in the lungs and to carry the oxygen to the body tissues. Consequently, the tissues may receive insufficient oxygen.

WHAT ARE THE CAUSES?

Iron-deficiency anemia is most commonly caused by the loss of significant amounts of iron through persistent bleeding. Iron-deficiency anemia occurs mainly in women who experience regular blood loss over a period of time from heavy menstrual bleeding (*see* MENORRHAGIA, p.735). Persistent loss of blood may also be due to stomach ulcers (*see* PEPTIC ULCER, p.640). The prolonged use of aspirin or long-term use of nonsteroidal anti-inflammatory drugs (p.894) is a possible cause of bleeding from the stomach lining. In people over age 60, a common cause of blood loss is cancer of the bowel (*see* COLORECTAL CANCER, p.665). Bleeding in the stomach or upper intestine may go unnoticed, while blood lost from the lower part of the intestine or rectum may be visible in the feces.

The second cause of iron-deficiency anemia is insufficient iron in the diet. People whose diet contains little or no iron, such as vegans, may be at particular risk of developing the condition.

Iron-deficiency anemia is also more likely to develop when the body needs higher levels of iron than normal and these extra demands are not met by the existing diet. For example, women who are pregnant and children who are growing rapidly, especially adolescents, have an increased risk of developing iron-deficiency anemia if their diet does not contain plenty of iron.

Some other causes of iron-deficiency anemia include disorders that prevent absorption of iron from the diet. In the body, iron is absorbed from food while it passes through the small intestine; conditions that damage the small intestine, such as celiac disease (p.658) or surgery on the small intestine, may sometimes result in iron deficiency.

WHAT ARE THE SYMPTOMS?

You may experience the symptoms of an underlying disorder, along with the general symptoms of anemia, such as:

- Fatigue and a feeling of faintness.
- Pale skin.
- Shortness of breath on mild exertion.

You may also have symptoms that are specifically due to a marked deficiency of iron. These may include:

- Brittle, concave-shaped nails.
- Painful cracks in the skin at the sides of the mouth.
- A smooth, reddened tongue.

If your anemia is severe, you may be at risk of chronic heart failure (p.413) because your heart has to work harder to supply blood to the rest of the body.

WHAT MIGHT BE DONE?

Your doctor will arrange for blood tests to measure the levels of hemoglobin and iron in your blood. If the cause of the iron deficiency is not obvious, other laboratory tests may also be necessary. For example, a sample of feces may be tested for signs of intestinal bleeding (*see* FECAL OCCULT BLOOD TEST, p.233).

Your doctor will treat any underlying disorder such as a stomach ulcer. He or she may prescribe iron tablets (syrup for children) or, less commonly, iron infusions for several months to replace iron stores. Severe cases of anemia may require blood transfusion (above).

(WWW) ONLINE SITES: p.1027, p.1035

Megaloblastic anemia

A type of anemia caused by a lack of vitamin B_{12} or folic acid

AGE More common over age 40

GENDER GENETICS LIFESTYLE Risk factors depend on the cause

Two major vitamins, B_{12} and folic acid, play an essential role in the production of healthy red blood cells. Deficiency of either vitamin may lead to megaloblastic anemia, in which large, abnormal red blood cells (megaloblasts) are produced by the bone marrow, and the production of normal red blood cells is reduced. The blood may thus be unable to carry sufficient oxygen to the tissues.

WHAT ARE THE CAUSES?

Lack of vitamin B_{12} is rarely due to a dietary deficiency. The problem is usually due to an autoimmune disorder in which antibodies are produced that damage the stomach lining and prevent it from forming intrinsic factor, which is vital for absorption of vitamin B_{12} from food in the intestines. The resulting anemia, called pernicious anemia, tends to run in families and is more common in women and in people with other autoimmune disorders, such as Hashimoto's thyroiditis (*see* THYROIDITIS, p.681). Intestinal disorders, such as celiac disease (p.658), or surgery on the stomach or intestines, can also interfere with vitamin B_{12} absorption.

Folic acid deficiency is often due to a poor diet. People who abuse alcohol are at particular risk because alcohol interferes with the absorption of folic acid. Pregnant women may also be at risk because folic acid requirements are higher in pregnancy. Disorders causing a rapid turnover of cells, including severe psoriasis (p.332), may also cause folic acid deficiency. In rare cases, the deficiency is a side effect of certain drugs, such as anticonvulsants (p.914) and anticancer drugs (p.907).

WHAT ARE THE SYMPTOMS?

The initial symptoms of megaloblastic anemia, which are common to all anemias, develop slowly and may include:

- Fatigue and a feeling of faintness.
- Pale skin.
- Shortness of breath on mild exertion.

These symptoms of megaloblastic anemia may worsen over time. Although lack of folic acid does not produce additional symptoms, lack of vitamin B_{12} may eventually damage the nervous system, possibly leading to:

- Tingling in the hands and feet.
- Weakness and loss of balance.
- Loss of memory and confusion.

If you have pernicious anemia, you may also notice a yellow tinge to your skin due to jaundice (p.643).

WHAT MIGHT BE DONE?

The diagnosis requires blood tests to look for megaloblasts and to measure the levels of vitamin B_{12} and folic acid. Rarely, you may also have a bone marrow aspiration and biopsy (p.451) to obtain tissue samples for further examination.

Megaloblastic anemia caused by an inability to absorb vitamin B_{12} may be improved by treating the underlying disorder, but some people, such as those with pernicious anemia and malabsorption caused by surgery, need lifelong monthly injections of vitamin B_{12}. Symptoms should begin to subside within days, but existing damage to the nervous system may be irreversible.

If megaloblastic anemia is caused by an inadequate diet, the condition usually disappears with an improved diet and a short course of folic acid tablets.

(WWW) ONLINE SITES: p.1027

Sickle-cell anemia

An inherited type of anemia in which red blood cells become sickle shaped

AGE Present from birth; first symptoms appear after about 4–6 months

GENETICS Due to an abnormal gene inherited from both parents. Mainly affects people of African descent

LIFESTYLE Strenuous exercise, high altitudes, and infections may trigger symptoms

GENDER Not a significant factor

Sickle-cell anemia is the result of an abnormality of hemoglobin, the pigment within the red blood cells that binds to oxygen and carries it away from the lungs to the body tissues. When the amount of oxygen bound to the abnormal hemoglobin drops, the red blood cells become distorted into an elongated sickle shape. Because these sickle cells are rigid and fragile, their flow through narrow blood vessels is hindered and they tend to be destroyed too early. These effects combine to deprive body tissues of oxygen.

Sickle-cell anemia occurs most often in African–American people and less commonly in people from countries around the Mediterranean.

WHAT ARE THE CAUSES?

Sickle-cell anemia is caused by a genetic disorder in which an abnormal gene must be inherited from both parents in an autosomal recessive pattern (*see* GENE DISORDERS, p.269). An abnormal gene inherited from only one parent leads to sickle-cell trait, which usually does not produce symptoms or require treatment. In communities in which sickle-cell anemia is common, genetic testing may be advisable for couples planning to have children. If both partners carry the sickle-cell gene, they should seek genetic counseling (p.270).

WHAT ARE THE SYMPTOMS?

The symptoms of sickle-cell anemia are highly variable, even within the same family. In children and adults, they may include those common to all anemias:

- Fatigue and a feeling of faintness.
- Pale skin.
- Shortness of breath on mild exertion.

Typically, sickle-cell anemia is punctuated by distinct episodes, known as sickle-cell crises, in which the sickle-shaped red blood cells clump together inside small blood vessels, causing blocking of the blood supply to body tissues. These sickle-cell crises may be triggered by infection, strenuous exercise, dehydration, high altitudes, or

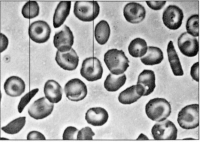

Sickle cell
Normal red cell

Sickle-shaped red blood cells
In sickle-cell anemia, some of the red blood cells become distorted into a distinctive and fragile sickle shape.

general anesthesia. The symptoms of a crisis appear suddenly and may include:

- Severe pain and swelling around the bones and joints, particularly those of the hands and feet in children.
- Abdominal pain.
- Chest pain and shortness of breath.

A severe sickle-cell crisis is potentially fatal and you should obtain medical help without delay if you have a crisis.

ARE THERE COMPLICATIONS?

People with sickle-cell anemia are more susceptible to serious infections, such as pneumococcal infection (*see* PNEUMONIA, p.490), and any infection can trigger a sickle-cell crisis. Gallstones (p.651) sometimes develop when the abnormal red cells are broken down. The abnormal cells also cause problems by blocking and damaging small blood vessels throughout the body and may cause persistent leg ulcers (p.350) or kidney damage (*see* CHRONIC KIDNEY FAILURE, p.706). There is an increased risk of transient ischemic attacks (p.531) and stroke (p.532). Women with sickle-cell anemia who become pregnant face an increased risk of miscarriage (p.791).

WHAT MIGHT BE DONE?

To confirm the diagnosis, your doctor may take a blood sample to look for sickle-shaped cells under the microscope. He or she may also arrange for tests for defective hemoglobin.

If the anemia is mild, folic acid, necessary for the production of red blood cells, may be prescribed. If anemia is more severe, you may require long-term treatment including regular transfusions and sometimes drugs to reduce the number of abnormal cells. You may also need to take a preventive antibiotic (p.885) continually and to be vaccinated against pneumococcal infection.

Immediate hospital admission is often necessary for sickle-cell crises. You may be given intravenous fluids to treat dehydration, analgesics (p.912) to provide pain relief, antibiotics for underlying infections, oxygen if the anemia is severe, and a transfusion. People with recurrent crises may be given exchange transfusions, replacing their blood with healthy blood from a donor. In rare cases, a bone marrow transplant (p.454) from a suitable donor may cure the disease.

WWW ONLINE SITES: p.1027

Thalassemia

An inherited type of anemia affecting production of hemoglobin, the oxygen-carrying pigment in red blood cells

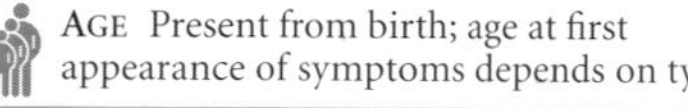

AGE Present from birth; age at first appearance of symptoms depends on type

GENETICS Due to an abnormal gene inherited from one or both parents

GENDER LIFESTYLE Not significant factors

In thalassemia, an inherited genetic defect prevents the normal formation of hemoglobin, the oxygen-carrying pigment inside red blood cells. Red cells containing the defective hemoglobin carry less oxygen than normal and are destroyed prematurely, reducing oxygen transport to the body tissues.

The body tries to compensate by producing additional red blood cells throughout the bone marrow and in the liver and spleen, where blood cells are not normally formed. The marrow expands due to overactivity, which may lead to thickening of the bones of the skull and face. The liver and spleen may become enlarged as they produce and, in the case of the spleen, destroy large numbers of the abnormal red cells. Thalassemia occurs mainly in people from the Mediterranean, the Middle East, Southeast Asia, and Africa.

WHAT ARE THE CAUSES?

A normal hemoglobin molecule contains four protein (globin) chains: two alpha and two beta chains. Different genes are responsible for the production of each type of chain. Thalassemia is caused by one or more genetic defects, and results in a failure to produce sufficient quantities of either the alpha or the beta chains.

Thalassemia due to abnormal beta-chains is more common. If a defective gene for beta-thalassemia is inherited from only one parent, there may be no symptoms. Inheritance of a defective gene from each parent in an autosomal recessive pattern (*see* GENE DISORDERS, p.269) leads to a more severe condition.

There are four genes responsible for hemoglobin alpha chains. People with one to three abnormal genes for alpha-thalassemia usually have no symptoms or only mild ones, but a fetus with four defective genes will die before birth.

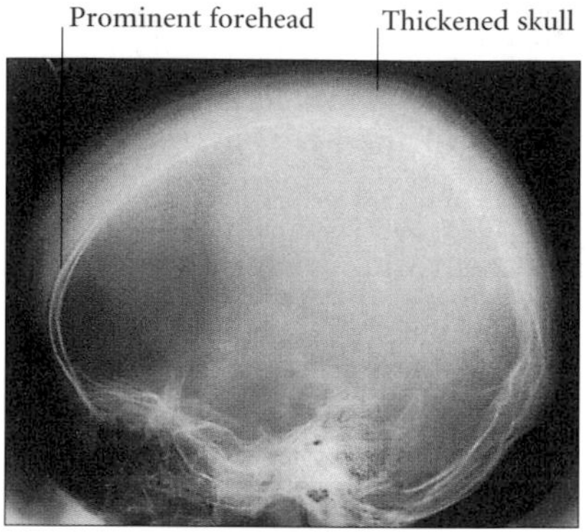
Prominent forehead
Thickened skull

Enlarged skull bones in thalassemia
In severe thalassemia, increased bone marrow activity causes the bones of the skull to expand and become thickened, altering the appearance of the face.

CAN IT BE PREVENTED?

In communities in which thalassemia is common, genetic testing may be offered to couples who are planning to have children. If a defective gene is found, they should seek genetic counseling (p.270). If a woman or her partner are known to have the disorder, tests can be performed to establish whether the fetus has inherited the genetic defect (*see* PRENATAL GENETIC TESTS, p.787).

WHAT ARE THE SYMPTOMS?

In nonfatal alpha-thalassemia, there are usually no symptoms or only mild ones. Mild forms of beta-thalassemia may also be asymptomatic. However, if the defective gene for beta-thalassemia is inherited from both parents, the symptoms of severe anemia typically appear between 4 and 6 months of age. They may include:

- Pale skin.
- Shortness of breath on mild exertion.
- Swelling of the abdomen due to an enlarged spleen and liver.

Affected children have slow growth, and sexual development is delayed. The bones of the skull and face may thicken as the bone marrow expands.

WHAT MIGHT BE DONE?

If your doctor suspects that you have thalassemia, he or she may arrange for you to undergo various blood tests.

If the thalassemia is mild, you may not need treatment, but you may have to take folic acid supplements to help stimulate the production of red blood cells. If the condition is severe, you may

TREATMENT SKIN-TUNNELED VENOUS CATHETER

A skin-tunneled venous catheter ("central line") is a flexible plastic tube passed through the skin of the chest and inserted into the subclavian vein, which leads to the heart. It is used in people with leukemia or other cancers who need regular chemotherapy and blood tests. Using the catheter, drugs can be injected directly into the bloodstream and blood samples can be obtained easily.

The catheter is inserted under local anesthesia and can remain in position for months. The external end is plugged when not in use. Because the catheter is inserted through the skin some distance away from the site of entry into the vein, the risk of infection is reduced.

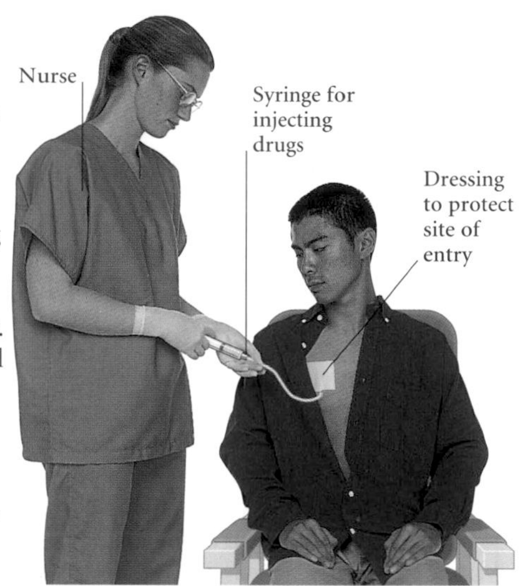
Nurse
Syringe for injecting drugs
Dressing to protect site of entry

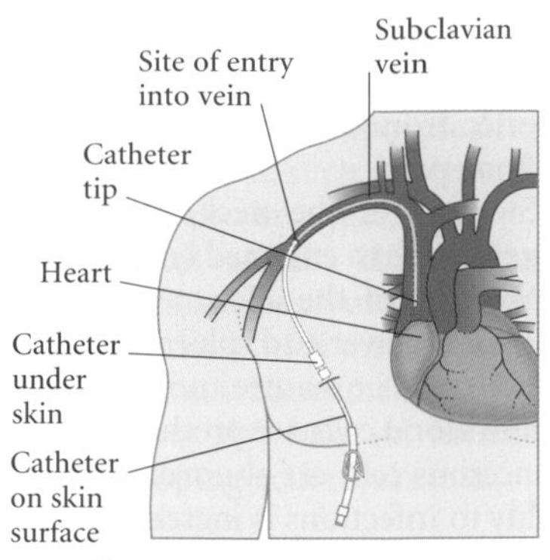
Site of entry into vein
Subclavian vein
Catheter tip
Heart
Catheter under skin
Catheter on skin surface

POSITION OF CATHETER

Using the catheter
The catheter is tunneled under the skin and enters the subclavian vein to lie with its tip in the heart. A syringe can be attached to inject drugs.

WHAT ARE THE CAUSES?

The cause of CML is unknown. In almost all people with the disorder, however, the cancerous cells contain an abnormal chromosome (known as the Philadelphia chromosome), in which part of one chromosome is attached to another. Rarely, CML is linked with past exposure to radiation, such as radiation therapy (p.279).

WHAT ARE THE SYMPTOMS?

There are two phases of CML. In the first, or chronic, phase, lasting for about 3–5 years, symptoms develop slowly and are often mild. In the second, or acute, phase, symptoms of the disease become more severe. In either phase, you may experience:

- Fatigue, pale skin, and shortness of breath on exertion due to anemia.
- Swelling of the abdomen due to an enlarged liver and spleen.
- A sensation of fullness due to the enlarged spleen, resulting in loss of appetite and weight loss.
- Night sweats.
- Abnormal bruising and bleeding.

During the acute phase of CML, you may also experience either or both of the following symptoms:

- Fever and abdominal pain.
- Swollen glands in the neck, armpits, and groin.

Rarely, in the acute phase, skin nodules full of abnormal granulocytes appear.

WHAT MIGHT BE DONE?

CML is usually diagnosed by chance during the chronic phase of the condition when a blood test is carried out for another reason. In other cases, when the condition is suspected from the symptoms, a blood test will be carried out to measure the levels of blood cells. If you have CML, the blood test will show high numbers of granulocytes and low numbers of red cells and platelets. To confirm the diagnosis, you may need to have a bone marrow aspiration and biopsy (p.451), in which tissue samples are taken for examination under a microscope.

The treatment for CML usually involves oral chemotherapy (p.278) with an anticancer drug called imatinib mesylate. This drug works directly on the leukemic cells. Patients who are diagnosed in the chronic phase of CML often achieve complete remission. The blood counts return to normal or near normal for prolonged periods. As well, the spleen decreases towards normal size.

If CML develops into the acute phase, you may be hospitalized for intravenous chemotherapy, in which anticancer drugs are given directly into the blood stream by injection. The drugs may be injected into the bloodstream through a skin-tunneled venous catheter (above).

WWW ONLINE SITES: p.1027, p.1028

Multiple myeloma

A bone marrow cancer in which abnormal antibody-producing white blood cells multiply uncontrollably

AGE Increasingly common over age 40; most common around age 70

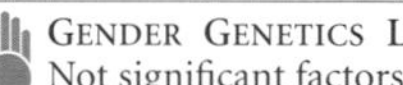
GENDER GENETICS LIFESTYLE Not significant factors

Multiple myeloma is a rare but life-threatening cancer of the bone marrow. The condition affects plasma cells, the white blood cells that normally produce antibodies against infection. In multiple myeloma, a plasma cell undergoes a cancerous change and begins to multiply in an uncontrolled manner, disrupting the usual production of normal red blood cells, normal white blood cells, and platelets.

The abnormal plasma cells produce abnormal antibodies, and the production of normal antibodies is reduced. As a result, people with myeloma are particularly susceptible to infections. The abnormal plasma cells also destroy bone tissue, releasing excess calcium into the bloodstream.

Low numbers of red cells may cause the blood to have a reduced oxygen-carrying capacity (*see* ANEMIA, p.446). Reduced numbers of platelets, which help to seal any damaged blood vessels, may lead to abnormal bleeding (*see* THROMBOCYTOPENIA, p.453).

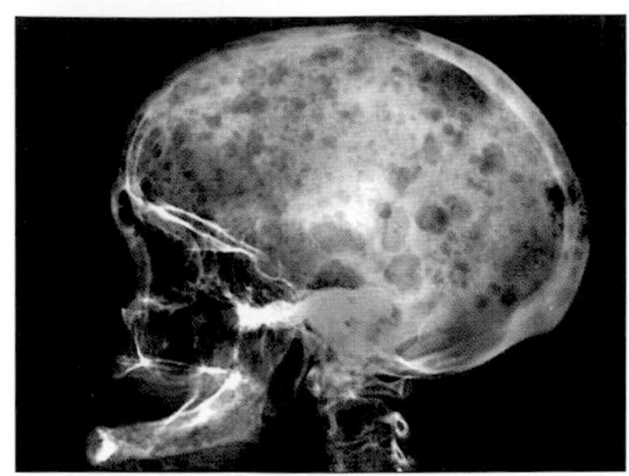

Skull bone loss in multiple myeloma
This X-ray shows the skull of a person with multiple myeloma. The abnormal "pepper-pot" appearance results from areas of localized bone loss.

WHAT ARE THE SYMPTOMS?

The symptoms of multiple myeloma result from the disruption of blood cell production in the bone marrow and the destruction of bone. They include:

- Fatigue, pale skin, and shortness of breath on exertion due to anemia.
- Bone pain, most often in the spine, as the plasma cells multiply within the bone marrow.
- Repeated infections.
- Bleeding from the nose and gums.
- Easy bruising without injury.
- Thirst, frequent urination, and constipation due to high calcium levels in the blood.

The loss of calcium from bone tissue may lead to brittle bones that fracture easily. Increased levels of calcium and abnormal antibodies in the blood may lead to kidney failure (p.705).

WHAT MIGHT BE DONE?

Your doctor may arrange for blood tests to measure levels of blood cells and to look for abnormal antibodies. Because these antibodies are excreted in urine, you may also need to have a urine test. Cells may be taken from the bone marrow and examined (*see* BONE MARROW ASPIRATION AND BIOPSY, p.451). You may have X-rays (p.244) to look for bone loss.

You will probably be treated with chemotherapy (p.278). The intensity of the treatment depends on a person's age and general health. Radiation therapy (p.279) may be given for severe bone pain, and you may have blood transfusions (p.447) for severe anemia. Infections may be treated with antibiotics (p.885). You may be given bisphosphonates (*see* DRUGS FOR BONE DISORDERS, p.896) to treat high calcium levels. Drinking plenty of fluids will also help lower the calcium levels.

The prognosis varies, depending on the severity of the disorder. Most people live for about 3 years after diagnosis, but some have survived for 10 years. An autologous bone marrow transplant may be offered to some patients.

(WWW) ONLINE SITES: p.1027, p.1028

Polycythemia

A blood disorder in which there is an increased concentration of red blood cells

AGE LIFESTYLE Risk factors depend on the type

GENDER GENETICS Not significant factors

In polycythemia, the concentration of red blood cells is increased. The condition may be due to increased red blood cell production or decreased volume of the fluid part of blood (plasma), leading to a high concentration of red cells.

WHAT ARE THE TYPES?

There are three types of polycythemia: primary, secondary, and stress.

In primary polycythemia, which is also known as true polycythemia or polycythemia vera, the production of red blood cells in the bone marrow is increased for no known reason. This is a rare disorder, which usually only affects people over the age of 60.

In secondary polycythemia, there is also increased production of red cells by the bone marrow. In this case the cause is a low oxygen level in the blood, which can occur for several reasons. For example, it can develop in people living at high altitudes, where oxygen levels are naturally low. It may also occur if the uptake of oxygen by the blood is impaired due to heavy smoking or lung disorders such as chronic obstructive pulmonary disease (p.487).

In stress polycythemia, production of red cells is normal but the volume of blood plasma is decreased. This change in the composition of blood may result from dehydration. It may also occur in people who are obese or abuse alcohol.

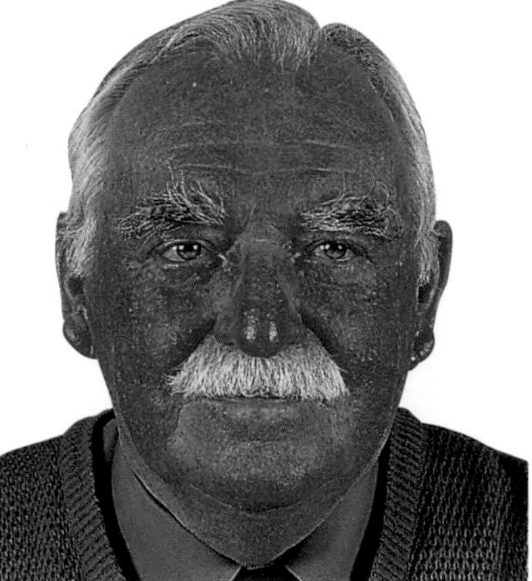

Effect of polycythemia
This man's ruddy complexion is due to polycythemia, an abnormally high concentration of red cells in the blood.

WHAT ARE THE SYMPTOMS?

All types of polycythemia produce similar symptoms due to thickening of the blood. They may include:

- A ruddy complexion, together with bloodshot eyes.
- Headache and ringing in the ears (*see* TINNITUS, p.602).
- Blurry vision and dizziness.

Primary polycythemia may also produce itching, especially after a hot bath. The spleen may enlarge as it attempts to deal with the increased number of red blood cells, causing abdominal discomfort. There may also be prolonged bleeding or increased blood clotting.

WHAT MIGHT BE DONE?

Your doctor may arrange for a blood test to measure the concentrations of red cells in the blood, and a bone marrow aspiration and biopsy (p.451) to look for increased red cell production. You may also have a lung function test (p.488) to look for an underlying cause.

If you have secondary or stress polycythemia, treatment is directed at eliminating the underlying cause.

Phlebotomy (needle puncture of a vein) may be used to treat primary polycythemia. At least 10 fl oz (300 ml) of blood are removed from the circulation weekly until the levels of red cells are normal. Hydroxyrea chemotherapy (p.278) may be prescribed to reduce red cell production. With treatment, most people live for 10–15 years after diagnosis. However, primary polycythemia may develop into another bone marrow disorder, such as acute leukemia (p.454).

(WWW) ONLINE SITES: p.1027

DISORDERS OF THE LYMPHATIC SYSTEM

The lymphatic system consists of lymph nodes, or glands, connected by a network of lymphatic vessels that extends to all parts of the body. The system drains a fluid called lymph from the body's tissues back into the bloodstream. It also protects the body against infection and the development of cancer by filtering out infectious organisms and cancerous cells from the lymph.

Lymph, a fluid that contains white blood cells called lymphocytes, fats, and protein, flows along the network of lymphatic vessels and ultimately reenters the bloodstream from which it originally came. Along the way, lymph is filtered through the lymph nodes, which are located in clusters close to the skin's surface in the neck, armpits, and groin. Nodes are also found deep within the abdomen and chest. The lymph nodes contain large numbers of cells and antibodies of the immune system that trap and destroy infectious organisms and cancerous cells that have entered the lymph from the blood and body tissues.

The first article in this section covers lymphadenopathy, in which the lymph nodes become enlarged. A painful swelling of the lymph nodes is not often a cause for concern, but painless swelling may be a sign of a serious underlying disorder, such as cancer. The next articles cover lymphangitis, in which lymphatic vessels are inflamed, and lymphedema, in which lymph cannot drain from a limb, causing the limb to swell. In developed countries, a common cause of lymphedema is surgery or radiation therapy for cancer. The final article discusses lymphoma, a group of cancers that often develop in one or more lymph nodes.

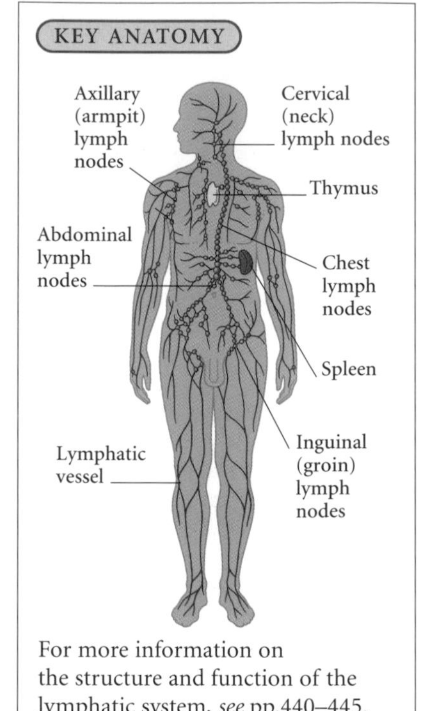
KEY ANATOMY
Axillary (armpit) lymph nodes
Cervical (neck) lymph nodes
Thymus
Abdominal lymph nodes
Chest lymph nodes
Spleen
Lymphatic vessel
Inguinal (groin) lymph nodes

For more information on the structure and function of the lymphatic system, *see* pp.440–445.

Lymphadenopathy

Enlarged lymph nodes, also known as swollen glands, which often develop as a response to infection

AGE GENDER GENETICS LIFESTYLE
Risk factors depend on the cause

Swelling of the lymph nodes is a common symptom of many conditions. A single node, a group of nodes, or all the lymph nodes may be affected. Lymph nodes most commonly become swollen in response to a bacterial or viral infection. You are more likely to notice a swollen lymph node in the neck, groin, or armpit, because the nodes in these areas lie closest to the skin.

Swelling of a single node or group of lymph nodes is often due to a localized bacterial infection. For example, swollen lymph nodes in the neck are commonly caused by throat infections. In most cases of lymphadenopathy due to an infection, the swelling usually subsides when the infection clears up. Swollen lymph nodes that are the result of an infection are often painful.

Long-term infections, such as tuberculosis (p.491) and HIV infection (*see* HIV INFECTION AND AIDS, p.295), are a common cause of persistent lymphadenopathy. Less commonly, persistent swelling of many, or all, of the lymph nodes may be a result of some types of cancer, such as breast cancer (p.759), leukemia (p.453), or lymphoma (opposite page). Swollen lymph nodes due to cancer are not normally painful.

You should consult your doctor if a swelling is persistent or if you are worried about other symptoms.

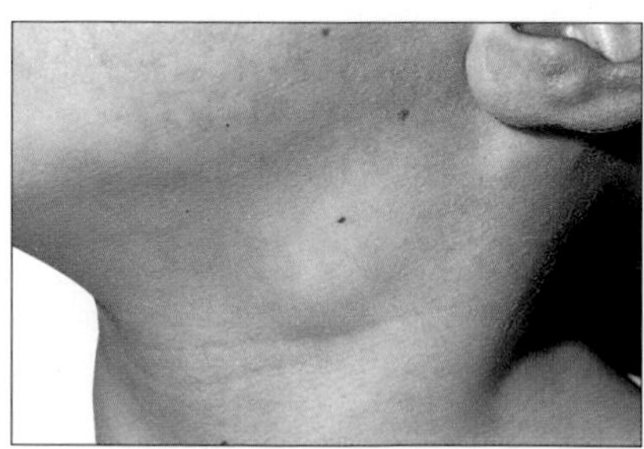

Lymphadenopathy in the neck
A throat infection may cause swelling of the lymph nodes. Here, a swollen lymph node is clearly visible on the side of the neck.

Lymphangitis

Inflammation of the lymphatic vessels as a result of a bacterial infection

AGE GENDER GENETICS LIFESTYLE
Not significant factors

Lymphangitis develops when bacteria spread into lymphatic vessels close to the site of an infection, possibly as a result of an injury. The condition usually affects lymphatic vessels in an arm or a leg and may be accompanied by fever, headache, and a general sense of not feeling well. The infected vessels become inflamed and tender, and hot, red streaks may appear on the skin over the inflamed vessels. Lymph nodes near to the affected area sometimes become swollen (*see* LYMPHADENOPATHY, left). If you develop any of these symptoms following an injury, you should consult your doctor immediately.

In some cases, ulcers form in the skin over an infected lymph vessel. Without treatment, the infection may spread into the blood (*see* SEPTICEMIA, p.298), which can be life-threatening.

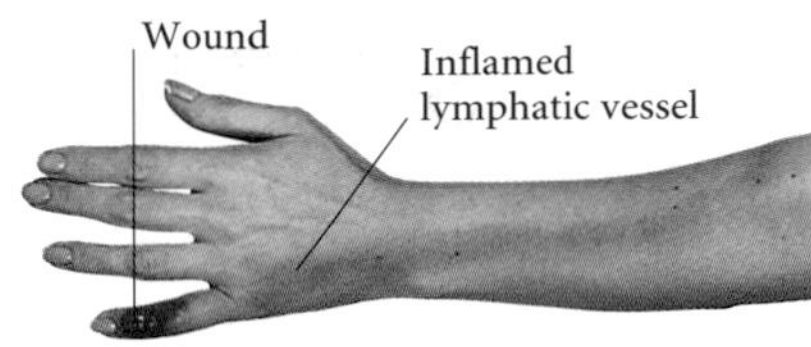
Wound
Inflamed lymphatic vessel

Lymphangitis of the arm
Inflamed lymphatic vessels (lymphangitis) have caused a red streak on the skin. The inflammation is due to bacteria that have spread from a wound on the finger.

If your doctor suspects that you have lymphangitis from your symptoms and after a physical examination, he or she may take a sample of your blood, which will be tested in the laboratory to determine whether the infection has spread into the blood. Antibiotics (p.885) will be prescribed to treat the lymphangitis. The symptoms of the condition usually begin to clear up within 24 hours of starting antibiotic treatment.

Lymphedema

A localized accumulation of fluid in the lymphatic vessels, causing painless swelling of a limb

 GENDER More common in females

 GENETICS Sometimes runs in families

 AGE LIFESTYLE Not significant factors

Lymphedema occurs when a defect in the lymphatic vessels prevents drainage of lymph from a limb. Most commonly, lymphedema is caused by damage to the lymphatic vessels following surgery or radiation therapy (p.279), for example in the treatment of breast cancer (p.759). Rarely, the condition may be due to blockage of a lymphatic vessel by a cancerous growth in a lymph node.

Lymphedema can be inherited, in which case it results from incomplete development of the lymphatic vessels. This type is more common in women.

Although the symptoms of lymphedema may be present from birth, they usually first occur at puberty. The main symptom is painless swelling of a limb. The skin over the affected limb often becomes rough and thickened. Injury to a limb affected by lymphedema may result in a rapid spread of infection through the tissues. You should contact your doctor immediately if you injure a limb affected by lymphedema.

In most cases, lymphedema is a lifelong disorder and treatment is aimed at relieving the symptoms. You can reduce swelling by keeping the affected limb elevated, and wearing an elastic stocking or sleeve helps prevent further swelling.

Lymphoma

Any of several types of cancer arising in the lymphatic system

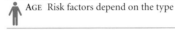

 GENDER More common in males

 GENETICS Sometimes runs in families

 AGE Risk factors depend on the type

LIFESTYLE Not a significant factor

The lymphomas are a group of diseases in which immune cells become cancerous and multiply uncontrollably in a lymph node. Initially, a single node may be affected, but the cancer may spread to other nodes and also to other tissues, such as the bone marrow.

Lymphomas are divided into two main categories: Hodgkin's and non-Hodgkin's lymphomas. In Hodgkin's lymphoma, a particular type of cancer cell is present. All the other lymphomas, of which there are many types, are classified as non-Hodgkin's lymphomas. Non-Hodgkin's lymphoma is three times more common than Hodgkin's lymphoma and usually develops in people over the age of 50. Hodgkin's lymphoma is most common in people belonging to the age groups 15–30 and 55–70. Different types of lymphomas grow and spread at different rates.

WHAT ARE THE CAUSES?

The cause of lymphoma is not known but the condition sometimes runs in families, suggesting that there may be a genetic factor. Lymphomas are more common if immunity is reduced, such as in people with AIDS (*see* HIV INFECTION AND AIDS, p.295) or in those who are taking immunosuppressant drugs (p.906). Some lymphomas may be triggered by a viral infection. For example, Burkitt's lymphoma, which is common in children in equatorial Africa, is associated with the Epstein–Barr virus.

WHAT ARE THE SYMPTOMS?

The symptoms of lymphoma, common to all types, may include:

- One or more persistent and painless swellings caused by enlarged lymph nodes in the neck, armpits, or groin.
- Fever and sweating at night.
- Weight loss.
- Abdominal swelling and discomfort due to enlarged lymph nodes or an enlarged spleen.

Some people with lymphoma develop anemia (p.446), resulting in symptoms such as fatigue, pale skin, and shortness of breath on mild exertion.

WHAT MIGHT BE DONE?

Your doctor may suspect lymphoma from your symptoms and following a physical examination. He or she may arrange for a blood test to check for anemia. A tissue sample may also be taken from a swollen node to find out whether cancerous cells are present.

If lymphoma is diagnosed, further tests may be needed to find out how far the disease has progressed. These may include imaging techniques, such as CT scanning (p.247), to assess the size of lymph nodes in the chest and abdomen. You may also have bone marrow aspiration and biopsy (p.451) to determine whether your bone marrow is affected.

Treatment depends on the type of lymphoma and how far it has spread. If only one node or one group of nodes is affected, the lymphoma may be treated with local radiation therapy (p.279) alone. When more than one group of nodes is affected, the usual treatment is chemotherapy (p.278), sometimes combined with radiation therapy. Monoclonal antibody drugs are also used. In refractory disease, a bone marrow transplant is considered.

WHAT IS THE PROGNOSIS?

The prognosis of lymphoma depends on the type, the patient's age, his or her general health, and how widespread the disease is at the time of diagnosis. If the cancer is not detectable following treatment, the disease is said to have gone into remission. However, lymphomas sometimes recur, and a second course of treatment may be necessary. If remission continues for 5 years or more, the risk of recurrence is small.

(WWW) ONLINE SITES: p.1028

People who have SLE may have widely varying symptoms. For example, some people suffer from mild symptoms that appear gradually, whereas others report a wide range of more severe symptoms that develop far more rapidly.

The most common symptoms experienced by people with the disorder are the following:

- Aching, swollen joints, which may become increasingly painful.
- Skin rashes, one of which is a raised, red, butterfly-shaped rash on the nose and cheeks.
- Increased sensitivity to sunlight.
- Fatigue and fever.

Additionally, there may be less common symptoms of SLE, which include:

- Shortness of breath and chest pain if the membrane covering the lungs is inflamed (*see* PLEURISY, p.493).
- Headaches, seizures, or strokes due to involvement of the nervous system.
- Constant chest pain if the membrane covering the heart is inflamed (*see* PERICARDITIS, p.428).
- Hair loss.
- Mouth ulcers.

Women who have SLE may find that their symptoms become worse while they are taking an oral contraceptive pill or during pregnancy, as a result of hormonal imbalances.

ARE THERE COMPLICATIONS?

SLE may cause damage to the kidneys, which can lead to high blood pressure (*see* HYPERTENSION, p.403) and eventually kidney failure (p.705). In severe cases, problems with painful, swollen joints may cause deformity. SLE may occur in association with polymyositis and dermatomyositis (opposite page).

Although many women with SLE have successful pregnancies, the risk of having a miscarriage (p.791) increases if the SLE is active during pregnancy. If you have SLE and are planning a pregnancy, visit your doctor to ask for advice.

WHAT MIGHT BE DONE?

Since the symptoms of SLE are so varied, they often mimic those of other disorders. However, if your doctor suspects you may have SLE from your symptoms, he or she may arrange for blood tests to look for antibodies associated with the condition. You may also be given specific tests to determine if the function of particular organs has been affected by the disorder.

There is no cure for SLE; treatment is aimed at relieving the symptoms and slowing the progression of the condition. However, if you have an SLE-like condition that is triggered by a particular drug, your doctor will prescribe an alternative drug, and your symptoms should gradually disappear within a few weeks or months.

If your joints are painful, your doctor may recommend a nonsteroidal anti-inflammatory drug (p.894). You may also be given the drug hydroxychloroquine (*see* ANTIMALARIAL DRUGS, p.888), which is often used to control symptoms of SLE. A corticosteroid (p.930) may be given to suppress severe inflammation. If the condition fails to respond to corticosteroids, an immunosuppressant drug (p.906) may be prescribed. Physiotherapy (p.961) may be suggested for joint problems. Your doctor may also advise you to avoid direct exposure to the sun and to ensure that infections are treated without delay.

Most people with SLE can lead an active life. Only in the most severe cases may life expectancy be shortened.

(WWW) ONLINE SITES: p.1033

Scleroderma

Thickening and hardening of the connective tissues in the skin, joints, and internal organs

AGE Most common between the ages of 20 and 50

GENDER More common in females

GENETICS Sometimes runs in families; more common in African–Americans

LIFESTYLE Not a significant factor

Scleroderma, also known as systemic sclerosis, is a rare disorder in which the connective tissues that hold together the structures of the body become inflamed, damaged, and thickened. The tissues, particularly those in the skin, then contract and harden.

This condition is an autoimmune disorder in which the immune system and cells that make connective tissue do not properly regulate themselves. The reason for this is unknown, but genetic factors may play a part. Scleroderma is approximately four times more common in women than it is in men and occurs most commonly in adults under age 50.

WHAT ARE THE SYMPTOMS?

Scleroderma commonly affects the skin and the joints, but other organs may be involved. Symptoms vary from mild to severe and may include:

- Fingers or toes that are sensitive to the cold, becoming white and painful (*see* RAYNAUD'S PHENOMENON AND RAYNAUD'S DISEASE, p.436).
- Ulcers and small, hardened areas that appear on the fingers.
- Swollen fingers or hands.
- Pain in the joints, especially the joints in the hands.
- Thickening and tightening of the skin, which is most severe on the limbs but may affect the trunk and face.
- Muscle weakness.
- Difficulty swallowing due to stiffening of the tissues of the esophagus (the tube that runs from the mouth to the stomach).

If the lungs are affected, shortness of breath may develop. In some people, scleroderma causes high blood pressure (*see* HYPERTENSION, p.403) and eventually kidney failure (p.705).

WHAT MIGHT BE DONE?

Your doctor may be able to make a diagnosis from your symptoms and from a physical examination. He or she may also arrange for blood tests to look for certain antibodies. A small skin sample may also be taken for examination.

There is no cure for scleroderma, but treatment can slow the progression of the condition, reducing the damage to body organs and relieving symptoms. Thickening of the skin may be slowed

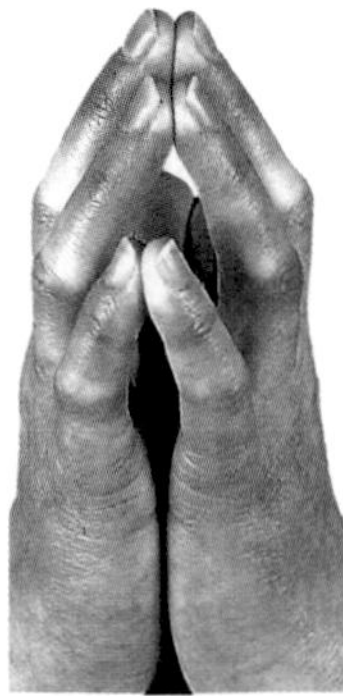

Effects of scleroderma
In a person with scleroderma, the skin on the fingers and hands may become thickened and swollen, making it difficult to straighten the fingers.

down by drugs such as penicillamine (*see* ANTIRHEUMATIC DRUGS, p.895). If the lungs are affected, an immunosuppressant (p.906) may be prescribed. Calcium channel blockers (*see* ANTIHYPERTENSIVES, p.897) may be used to treat Raynaud's phenomenon. Your doctor may advise you to dress warmly and wear gloves and socks to protect your fingers and toes against the cold.

The course of scleroderma is variable. The condition may remain mild or, having been severe, may improve spontaneously. In rare cases, scleroderma progresses rapidly and is fatal.

(WWW) ONLINE SITES: p.1033

Sjögren syndrome

Damage to glands, including the tear and salivary glands, causing dryness of the eyes and mouth

 AGE Most common between the ages of 40 and 60, but may occur at any age

 GENDER More common in females

 GENETICS Sometimes runs in families

 LIFESTYLE Not a significant factor

Sjögren syndrome is a chronic disorder in which damage to the tear and salivary glands causes the eyes and mouth to become very dry. Glands that lubricate the skin, nasal cavity, throat, and vagina may also be affected.

The syndrome is an autoimmune disorder in which gland tissues are attacked by the body's own antibodies and become inflamed and damaged. The cause is not known, but genetic factors may play a role. The condition is nine times more common in women and usually occurs between the ages of 40 and 60.

The main symptoms usually develop over several years and include gritty, dry eyes and dry mouth. Lack of saliva often leads to difficulty swallowing dry foods and to dental problems (*see* DENTAL CARIES, p.609). Some people develop joint problems similar to rheumatoid arthritis (p.377).

WHAT MIGHT BE DONE?

Your doctor may be able to make a diagnosis from your symptoms and an examination. He or she may arrange for blood tests to look for antibodies. You may also need to have tests to measure the quantity of tears your eyes produce, and a small sample of tissue may be removed from your lip or salivary glands to look for damaged cells.

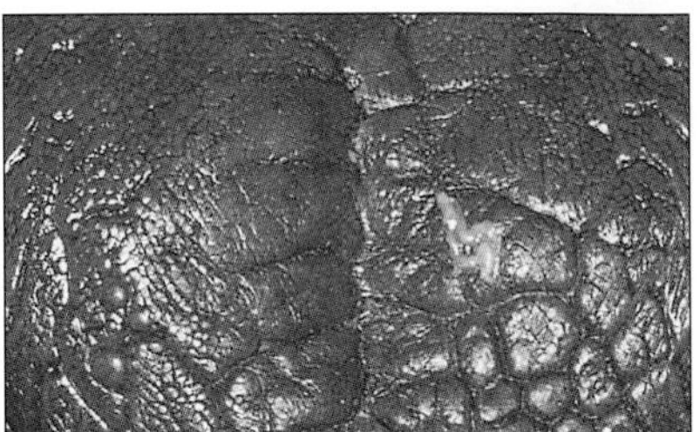

Dry tongue in Sjögren syndrome

The salivary glands become inflamed in Sjögren syndrome, preventing normal saliva production. As a result, the mouth and the tongue become very dry.

There is no cure for this disorder but symptoms can be controlled, usually with lifelong treatment. Artificial tears may be prescribed or, occasionally, tear ducts will be plugged by an ophthalmologist to decrease tear drainage. You will be advised to drink frequently and to visit your dentist regularly. If symptoms are severe, a corticosteroid (p.930), an immunosuppressant (p.906), or the drug hydroxychloroquine (*see* ANTIMALARIAL DRUGS, p.888) may be given to reduce the inflammation.

(WWW) ONLINE SITES: p.1033

Polymyositis and dermatomyositis

Muscle inflammation (polymyositis), sometimes with a rash (dermatomyositis)

 AGE Most common in children aged 5–15 and adults aged 40–60

 GENDER More common in females

 GENETICS Sometimes runs in families

 LIFESTYLE Not a significant factor

In polymyositis, inflammation causes muscle weakness and wasting, particularly around the shoulders and pelvis. If the symptoms are accompanied by a rash, the disorder is known as dermatomyositis. Both of these conditions are rare autoimmune disorders in which tissues are attacked by the body's own antibodies. The cause of the abnormal reaction is unknown, although its onset may be triggered by a viral infection. In adults, particularly in men, these diseases may be associated with cancer. They can also occur in association with other autoimmune disorders such as systemic lupus erythematosus (p.461). Sometimes polymyositis and dermatomyositis run in families, suggesting that genetic factors may be involved. Both are more common in women than in men, and in childhood and middle age.

WHAT ARE THE SYMPTOMS?

The symptoms of polymyositis and dermatomyositis may develop rapidly, particularly in children; in adults the symptoms usually develop over several weeks. Symptoms may include:

- Weakness of affected muscles, leading, for example, to difficulty raising the arms or getting up from a sitting or squatting position.
- Painful, swollen joints.
- Fatigue.
- Difficulty swallowing if the muscles of the throat are affected.
- Shortness of breath if the heart or chest muscles are involved.

In dermatomyositis, the above symptoms may be preceded, accompanied, or followed by these symptoms:

- A red rash, often on the face, chest, or backs of the hands over the knuckles.
- Swollen, pink-violet eyelids.

About half of all children affected with dermatomyositis develop skin ulcers.

WHAT MIGHT BE DONE?

If polymyositis or dermatomyositis is suspected, your doctor may arrange for blood tests to investigate inflammation and to look for antibodies that are specific to these conditions. You may also have electromyography (*see* NERVE AND MUSCLE ELECTRICAL TESTS, p.544) to measure electrical activity in the muscle, and a muscle biopsy, in which a tissue sample is removed for examination. An ECG (p.406) may be necessary to check for involvement of the heart muscle. You may also have a chest X-ray (p.490) and other tests to exclude the possibility of an underlying cancer.

There is no cure for polymyositis or dermatomyositis. However, the symptoms can usually be controlled. You will probably be prescribed high doses of corticosteroids (p.930) to help reduce the inflammation. If there is no marked improvement, an immunosuppressant drug (p.906) or a drug that is normally used to treat cancer (*see* ANTICANCER DRUGS, p.907) may be given to slow the progression of the disorder. If dermatomyositis fails to respond to these drugs, intravenous injections of immunoglobulins (antibodies) may be given. Physiotherapy (p.961) may help prevent muscle stiffness and restore muscle strength.

WHAT IS THE PROGNOSIS?

The outlook for both polymyositis and dermatomyositis is better in children than in adults. About 7 in 10 affected children recover completely in 2 years. Adults with polymyositis or dermatomyositis may need corticosteroid drugs for several years. In people who have cancer, the autoimmune disorder may improve if the cancer can be treated.

(WWW) ONLINE SITES: p.1033

Polymyalgia rheumatica

Pain and stiffness in the muscles around the shoulders and hips

 AGE Rare under age 50

 GENDER Twice as common in females

 GENETICS Sometimes runs in families

 LIFESTYLE Not a significant factor

In polymyalgia rheumatica, inflammation of tissues causes pain and stiffness in the shoulder and hip muscles and may be associated with a general sense of not feeling well and loss of energy.

Polymyalgia rheumatica is an autoimmune disorder in which there is inflammation in connective tissue and around blood vessels. The condition is rare, can run in families, and is more common in older women. It may occur in association with the disorder temporal (giant cell) arteritis (right).

WHAT ARE THE SYMPTOMS?

The symptoms usually appear over a few weeks but sometimes develop suddenly. They may include:

- Painful, stiff muscles, often causing difficulty getting out of bed.
- Fatigue.
- Persistent or intermittent fever and night sweats.
- Weight loss.

The symptoms may be accompanied with those of temporal arteritis, such as severe headaches on one or both sides of the head and tenderness of the scalp.

WHAT MIGHT BE DONE?

Your doctor will probably be able to make a diagnosis based on a physical examination and the results of blood tests done to look for inflammation. In some cases, additional blood tests will be performed to exclude other disorders, such as rheumatoid arthritis (p.377).

Your doctor will prescribe an oral corticosteroid (p.930) to reduce the inflammation. If you also have temporal arteritis, the initial doses of this drug may be higher. In either case, the dose will be gradually reduced to a maintenance level as the symptoms subside.

Symptoms are usually relieved soon after starting corticosteroid treatment. However, polymyalgia rheumatica may persist for a longer period, in which case you need to continue taking low doses to control symptoms.

(WWW) ONLINE SITES: p.1033

Temporal (giant cell) arteritis

Inflammation of the blood vessels on the temples

 AGE Rare under age 55; increasingly common with age

 GENDER More common in females

 GENETICS Sometimes runs in families; more common in white people

 LIFESTYLE Not a significant factor

In temporal arteritis, also called giant cell arteritis, particular arteries become inflamed and narrowed, reducing the blood flow through them. The disorder mainly affects the temporal arteries, the blood vessels on the sides of the forehead. In some cases, other arteries that supply blood to the head and neck may also be affected by the condition.

The cause of temporal arteries is not known, but it may be due to an autoimmune reaction, in which the immune system attacks the arteries. Temporal arteritis may be accompanied by polymyalgia rheumatica (left) and sometimes runs in families, suggesting that genetic factors may be involved. It occurs more commonly in women and older people.

WHAT ARE THE SYMPTOMS?

If you have temporal arteritis, you may notice the following symptoms:

- Severe headaches affecting either one or both sides of the head.
- Tenderness of the scalp.
- Pain in the sides of the face, which becomes worse on chewing.
- Prominent, tender temporal arteries.
- Fatigue.
- Loss of appetite and weight loss.

These symptoms may occur with those of polymyalgia rheumatica, such as pain and stiffness in the muscles of the shoulders and pelvis. Rarely, a stroke (p.532) may occur. If you also develop visual disturbances, you should consult your doctor at once because untreated temporal arteritis may lead to loss of an area of vision or even blindness.

WHAT MIGHT BE DONE?

Your doctor may be able to diagnose temporal arteritis from your description of the headache and by a physical examination. He or she may arrange for an urgent blood test to look for inflammation. You may also have a biopsy of the temporal artery, in which a tissue sample is taken for examination.

To reduce inflammation, a high dose of an oral corticosteroid (p.930) will be prescribed immediately. The symptoms usually improve within 24 hours of starting treatment. Once the condition begins to improve, the initial high dose of corti-

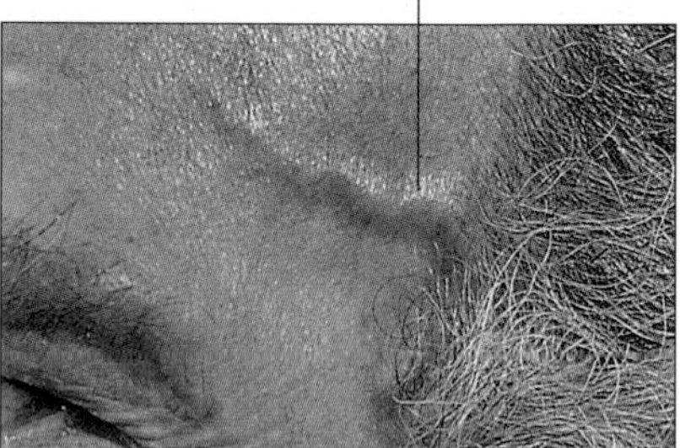
Temporal artery

Temporal (giant cell) arteritis
The temporal artery shown above is prominent and inflamed due to temporal arteritis. Headaches and tenderness of the scalp are common with this disorder.

costeroid will be reduced, although it may be necessary for you to continue taking smaller doses for 2–3 years.

Your doctor will probably recommend that you have regular blood tests to monitor the course of the disorder. He or she may prescribe an immunosuppressant (p.906) as an alternative drug if there is little or no improvement in your condition or if you develop side effects with the corticosteroid.

WHAT IS THE PROGNOSIS?

Usually, temporal arteritis clears up completely with treatment, although the symptoms may recur. If your vision has already been impaired because of temporal arteritis, your sight is not likely to improve by undergoing treatment. However, treatment may prevent further impairment of your vision.

(WWW) ONLINE SITES: p.1033

Polyarteritis nodosa

Widespread tissue damage as a result of patchy inflammation of the arteries

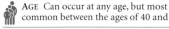

 AGE Can occur at any age, but most common between the ages of 40 and 60

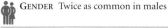

 GENDER Twice as common in males

 GENETICS LIFESTYLE Not significant factors

In polyarteritis nodosa, segments of small- to medium-sized arteries are inflamed, reducing the blood supply to muscles, joints, and many of the internal organs. If the arteries that supply the heart or kidneys are affected, the condition may be life-threatening.

Polyarteritis nodosa is an autoimmune disorder in which the immune system attacks the body's own arteries. The cause of the abnormal immune reaction is not known, but the hepatitis B and C viruses (*see* ACUTE HEPATITIS, p.644) have been found in some people who have polyarteritis nodosa, suggesting that these viruses may trigger the disorder. Polyarteritis nodosa is more common in middle-aged men.

WHAT ARE THE SYMPTOMS?

The number and severity of symptoms vary depending on which organs are affected. The symptoms may include:

- Fatigue.
- Weight loss.

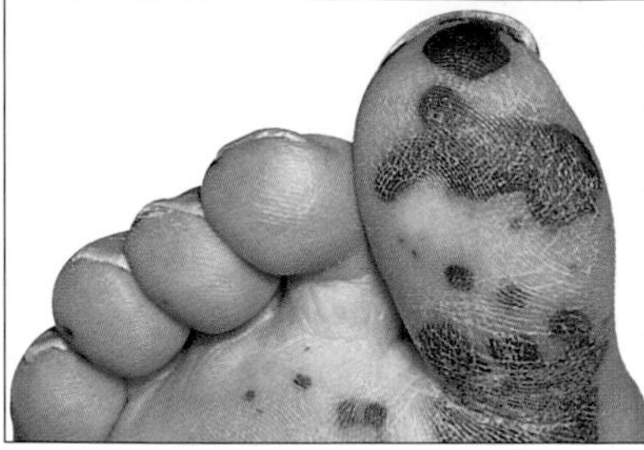

Rash of polyarteritis nodosa

This rash is due to polyarteritis nodosa, in which the blood vessels are inflamed and blood flow to tissues is restricted.

- Fever.
- Abdominal pain or discomfort.
- Joint pain and muscle weakness.
- Tingling and numbness in the fingers and toes.
- A red-purple patchy rash on the skin that does not fade with pressure.
- Skin ulcers.

Polyarteritis nodosa commonly leads to increased blood pressure (*see* HYPERTENSION, p.403). In some people, there is severe damage to the kidneys, leading to kidney failure (p.705). Less commonly, polyarteritis may cause lung damage, a heart attack (*see* MYOCARDIAL INFARCTION, p.410), or a stroke (p.532).

HOW IS IT DIAGNOSED?

Your doctor may arrange for blood tests to check for inflammation and to look for the hepatitis B or C viruses. To confirm the diagnosis, you may have a biopsy, in which a sample of an affected artery or organ is removed and examined under a microscope. You may also have angiography (*see* FEMORAL ANGIOGRAPHY, p.433), in which an X-ray of the arteries is taken to look for abnormal areas in the blood vessels.

WHAT IS THE TREATMENT?

Polyarteritis nodosa cannot be cured; the aim of treatment is to relieve symptoms and prevent tissue injury. Your doctor may initially prescribe a high dose of a corticosteroid (p.930), which will be reduced once the symptoms subside. If there is no improvement, an immunosuppressant drug (p.906) may be prescribed. Left without treatment, the condition may be life-threatening. With treatment, life expectancy is normal in about half of all cases.

(WWW) ONLINE SITES: p.1033

Behçet syndrome

An inflammatory disorder producing recurrent mouth and genital ulcers

 AGE Most common between the ages of 20 and 40

 GENDER More common in males

 GENETICS Sometimes runs in families; more common in some ethnic groups

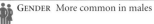

LIFESTYLE Not a significant factor

Behçet syndrome is a rare disorder that varies in severity. The effects range from difficulty eating to significant disability. Painful ulcers usually recur in the mouth and on the genitals. Other symptoms include eye inflammation (*see* UVEITIS, p.574), an acnelike rash, and/or small, tender lumps on the shins. The brain, spinal cord, and joints (*see* ARTHRITIS, p.374) may be affected, and there is an increased tendency for the blood to clot.

Behçet syndrome is an autoimmune disorder in which the body produces antibodies against its own tissues. The cause of the abnormal immune reaction is unknown, but it may be triggered by viral infection. The syndrome can develop in members of the same family and occurs more often in people of Japanese or Mediterranean origin, suggesting that genetic factors may be involved. Behçet syndrome is twice as common in men and occurs most frequently in adults under age 40.

WHAT MIGHT BE DONE?

Your doctor may suspect Behçet syndrome from your symptoms and a physical examination. It may take some time to confirm the diagnosis because there are no specific tests for the condition and many other disorders with similar symptoms need to be excluded. Some of the symptoms may disappear of their own accord, but your doctor may prescribe a topical corticosteroid (p.892) for the ulcers and eyedrops (*see* DRUGS ACTING ON THE EYE, p.919) for eye inflammation. In severe cases, oral corticosteroids (p.930) and/or immunosuppressants (p.906) may be needed.

Behçet syndrome is a chronic condition with symptom-free periods that may last weeks, months, or even years. It rarely affects life expectancy.

(WWW) ONLINE SITES: p.1033

ALLERGIES

An allergy is an abnormal reaction of the body's immune system to a foreign substance. In most people, the substance produces no symptoms, but in a susceptible person it triggers an allergic reaction. Most allergies are mild and merely unpleasant, and they are easily treated with drugs and self-help remedies. However, sometimes allergies can be life-threatening.

In this section, allergic reactions due to foreign substances such as pollen, food, and certain drugs are discussed first. The trigger substance, called an allergen, causes no symptoms on initial contact. However, the body's immune system begins to form antibodies against the allergen, and certain types of white blood cells become sensitive to it. Later contact with the allergen may then stimulate specialized cells called mast cells to release histamine, the chemical that triggers the allergic response. Allergic reactions may cause either urticaria or angioedema, which are discussed next. The last article covers anaphylaxis, a severe and potentially life-threatening allergic reaction to an allergen.

Allergies often develop in childhood and may either persist or disappear in adulthood. Conditions such as asthma (p.483) and eczema (p.333), which may have an allergic basis, are dealt with in the sections of the book that cover the relevant body systems.

KEY STRUCTURES

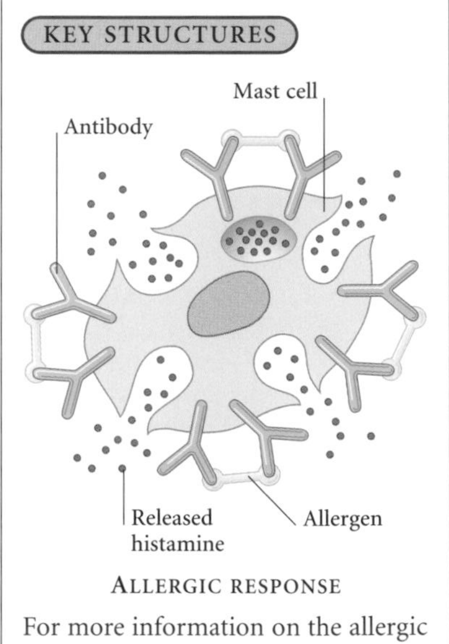
Mast cell
Antibody
Released histamine
Allergen

ALLERGIC RESPONSE

For more information on the allergic response, *see* p.445.

Allergic rhinitis

Inflammation of the membrane lining the nose and throat due to an allergic reaction

 GENETICS Sometimes runs in families

 AGE GENDER LIFESTYLE Not significant factors

Allergic rhinitis is a condition in which the membrane lining the nose and the throat is inflamed. It affects people who experience an allergic reaction after they inhale specific airborne substances (allergens). Allergic rhinitis may occur only during the spring and summer, in which case it is known as seasonal allergic rhinitis or hay fever, or it may be perennial and occur all year round. Allergic rhinitis is more common in people who also have other allergic disorders, such as asthma (p.483).

WHAT ARE THE CAUSES?

Seasonal allergic rhinitis is usually due to grass, tree, flower, or weed pollens; it occurs mostly in the spring and summer when pollen counts are high. The most common allergens that provoke perennial allergic rhinitis include house dust and dust mites, animal fur and dander, feathers, and mold spores.

WHAT ARE THE SYMPTOMS?

The symptoms of both forms of allergic rhinitis usually appear soon after contact with the allergen but tend to be more severe in hay fever. They include:

- Itchy sensation in the nose.
- Frequent sneezing.
- Blocked, runny nose.
- Itchy, red, watery eyes.

Some people may develop a headache. If the lining of the nose is severely inflamed, nosebleeds may occur.

WHAT MIGHT BE DONE?

Your doctor will probably recognize allergic rhinitis from your symptoms, particularly if you are able to identify the substance that triggers a reaction.

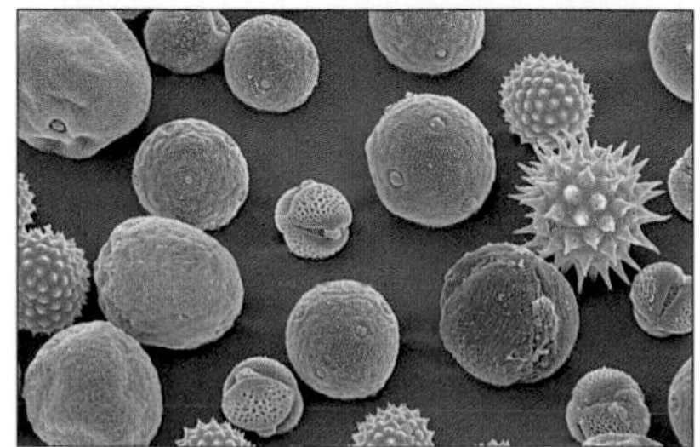

Possible allergens in allergic rhinitis
This magnified view reveals a variety of grain pollens that can cause seasonal allergic rhinitis in susceptible people.

A skin prick test (p.468) may be performed in order to identify the allergen that causes the allergic rhinitis. In some cases, the allergen cannot be found.

If you can avoid the allergens that affect you, your symptoms will subside (*see* PREVENTING ALLERGIC RHINITIS, opposite page). Many antiallergy drugs (p.905) are available over-the-counter or by prescription. For example, allergies can be blocked by nasal sprays that contain cromolyn sodium. Alternatively, corticosteroids (*see* CORTICOSTEROIDS FOR RESPIRATORY DISEASE, p.911) are effective for hay fever but may take a few days to work. Nasal sprays containing decongestants (p.909) can relieve symptoms but should not be used regularly. Oral antihistamines (p.906) are often combined with decongestants to relieve inflammation and itching. Eyedrops may help relieve eye symptoms. Rarely, if symptoms are severe, your doctor may prescribe an oral corticosteroid (p.930).

The most specific treatment for allergic rhinitis is immunotherapy, in which you are injected with gradually increasing doses of allergen with the aim of desensitizing the immune system. This treatment, which typically takes as long as 3–4 years, is often successful.

(WWW) ONLINE SITES: p.1027

SELF-HELP PREVENTING ALLERGIC RHINITIS

The following measures are all aimed at maintaining an allergen-free environment in your home. Tips on preventing perennial allergic rhinitis include:

- Avoid keeping furry animals as pets if you are allergic to them.
- Replace pillows and quilts containing animal materials such as duck feathers with those containing synthetic stuffing.
- Cover mattresses with plastic.
- Remove dust-collecting items such as upholstered furniture and curtains if possible.

To help prevent the symptoms of seasonal allergic rhinitis, also known as hay fever, the following measures may be effective:

- Avoid areas with long grass or where grass is being cut.
- In summer, keep doors and windows closed and spend as much time as possible in air-conditioned buildings.
- Try to stay inside during late morning and early evening when the pollen count is highest.
- Make sure your car is fitted with an effective pollen filter.
- When outside, wear sunglasses to help prevent eye irritation.

Food allergy

An abnormal reaction of the immune system to certain foods

 AGE Affects all ages, but most common in infants and children

 GENETICS Sometimes runs in families

 GENDER LIFESTYLE Not significant factors

Food allergy is an uncommon condition in which the immune system reacts in an inappropriate or an exaggerated way to a specific food or foods, causing the development of various symptoms such as an itchy rash. This condition should not be confused with food intolerance (p.657), which often causes abdominal discomfort and indigestion but does not involve the immune system.

WHAT ARE THE CAUSES?

Although allergic reactions can occur with any food, ground nuts (especially peanuts) and tree nuts are probably the most common cause. Other relatively common causes of food allergy include seafood, strawberries, and eggs. Food colorings and preservatives rarely cause allergic reactions. However, intolerance to the food additive monosodium glutamate (MSG) is common.

Wheat may cause a condition known as celiac disease (p.658) and an allergic reaction to the protein in cow's milk is especially common in infants and young children (*see* COWS' MILK PROTEIN ALLERGY, p.864). Both of these conditions differ from immediate sensitivity to nuts or other foods in that they are more chronic conditions.

Food allergy is more commonly found in people who have other allergy-related conditions such as asthma (p.483), eczema (p.333), or allergic rhinitis (opposite page).

WHAT ARE THE SYMPTOMS?

Symptoms may appear almost immediately after eating the food or develop over a few hours. They may include:

- Itching and swelling affecting the lips, mouth, and throat.
- An itchy, red rash anywhere on the body (*see* URTICARIA, p.468).
- Nausea, vomiting, and diarrhea.

If you have a severe reaction, the following symptoms may also be present:

- Nonitchy swelling anywhere on the body, especially the face, mouth, and throat (*see* ANGIOEDEMA, p.469).
- Shortness of breath or wheezing.

Sometimes, a food allergy may lead to anaphylaxis (p.469), a life-threatening allergic response that causes sudden difficulty in breathing and collapse. If you develop the symptoms of a severe reaction, call an ambulance.

WHAT MIGHT BE DONE?

You may be able to diagnose food allergy yourself if the symptoms occur consistently soon after you eat a particular food. However, you should still consult with your doctor. If he or she is unsure what is responsible for the reaction, you may be advised to take a painless skin prick test (p.468).

Your doctor may also recommend an exclusion diet. By eating a restricted diet for 1 or 2 weeks, you may avoid the foods that cause your symptoms. If your symptoms improve substantially while on the diet, you may have one or more food allergies. You can gradually add other foods to your diet but if symptoms recur when a particular food is eaten, you should avoid it in the future. You should not embark on an exclusion diet without first consulting your doctor. Nor should you follow a nutritionally restricted diet for more than 2 weeks. Interpreting the results of an exclusion diet is often difficult.

Avoiding the problem food is the only effective treatment. Always ask about ingredients when eating out, and check labels on packaged foods. Consult a diet or nutrition counselor if you need to exclude a food that is a major part of a normal diet, such as wheat. If a major permanent dietary change is needed, be sure to maintain a balanced diet.

WHAT IS THE PROGNOSIS?

Many food allergies, particularly nut allergies, are permanent, and people must avoid the relevant foods throughout their lives. Some food allergies may disappear. Children under age 4 who completely avoid problem foods such as wheat for 2 years have an excellent chance of outgrowing their allergy.

WWW ONLINE SITES: p.1027, p.1035

Drug allergy

An abnormal reaction to a drug, most commonly an antibiotic

 AGE GENDER GENETICS LIFESTYLE Not significant factors

Both over-the-counter and prescription drugs can cause various problems. Most symptoms, such as nausea or diarrhea, are not allergies but side effects that can affect anyone. A drug allergy occurs when the immune system produces an abnormal reaction to a specific drug. Often the reactions are mild, but some can be life-threatening.

WHAT ARE THE CAUSES?

A drug may provoke an allergic reaction the first time you use it. You may also develop an allergic reaction to a drug that you have been taking for some time. In the latter case, your body gradually becomes more and more

FUNCTION BREATHING AND RESPIRATION

Air constantly enters and leaves the lungs, enabling the tissues of the body to receive an adequate supply of oxygen and to dispose of their waste product, carbon dioxide. Breathing is controlled by the respiratory center in a part of the brain known as the medulla. The respiratory center stimulates the intercostal muscles around the chest cavity to contract and relax so that we breathe in and out.

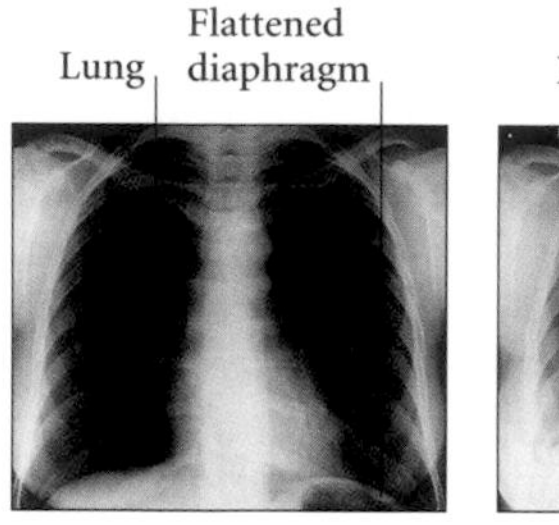

Lung
Flattened diaphragm

INHALATION

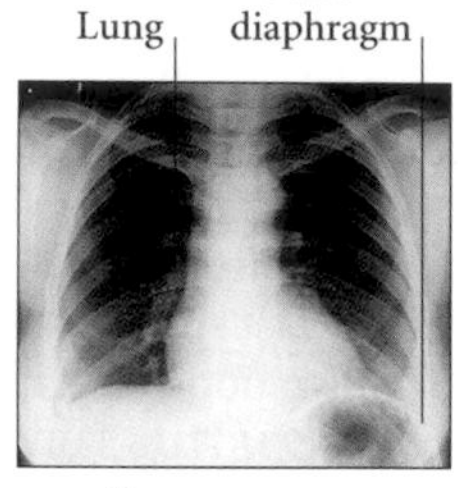

Lung
Domed diaphragm

EXHALATION

Chest X-rays
These normal chest X-rays show the volume of air in the lungs during inhalation and exhalation, which is achieved by changes in the position of the ribs and diaphragm.

HOW BREATHING WORKS

During breathing, air moves from areas of high pressure to areas of low pressure. When the pressure in the lungs is lower than the pressure in the atmosphere, air enters the airways. If the pressure in the lungs increases, air moves out of the lungs and is then exhaled.

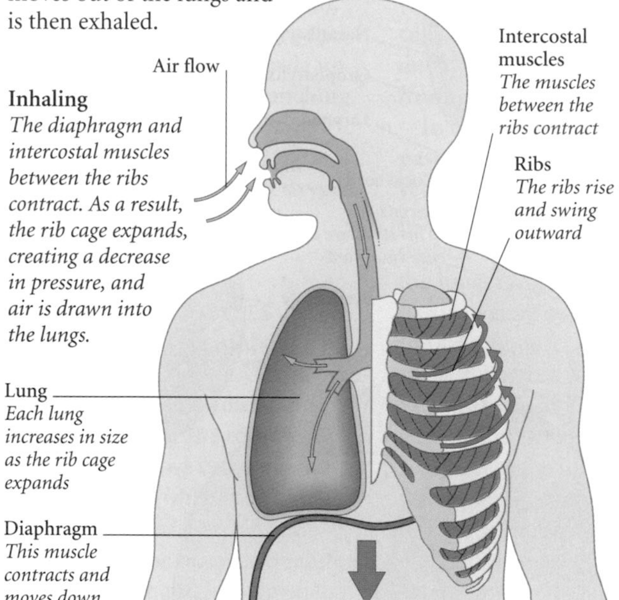

Air flow
Inhaling
The diaphragm and intercostal muscles between the ribs contract. As a result, the rib cage expands, creating a decrease in pressure, and air is drawn into the lungs.
Intercostal muscles
The muscles between the ribs contract
Ribs
The ribs rise and swing outward
Lung
Each lung increases in size as the rib cage expands
Diaphragm
This muscle contracts and moves down

Exhaling
After breathing in, the diaphragm and intercostal muscles relax and the rib cage contracts. Pressure inside the lungs increases and air moves out of the lungs in order to be exhaled.

Air flow

Lung
Each lung decreases in size as the rib cage contracts

Diaphragm
This muscle relaxes and moves up

Intercostal muscles
The muscles between the ribs relax

Ribs
The ribs move downward and inward

FUNCTION HOW BREATHING IS REGULATED

Even while we sleep, our basic breathing rhythm is controlled by a collection of nerve cells in the brain called the respiratory center. From there, messages travel down nerves to the diaphragm and rib muscles and stimulate them so that we continue breathing. As activity changes, so does the amount of carbon dioxide in the blood. Receptors in some of the large arteries detect the changes and send instructions to the brain.

How carbon dioxide influences breathing
Nerve cells in arteries and in the respiratory center in the brain are sensitive to changes in the blood levels of carbon dioxide. A slight rise in the carbon dioxide level increases the breathing rate and corrects the level.

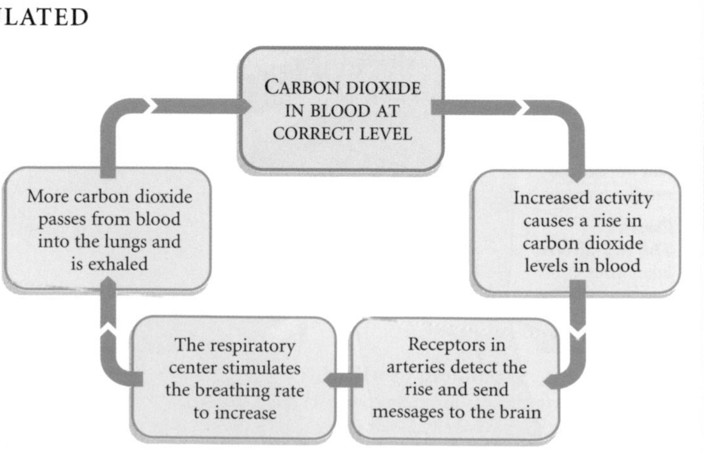

CARBON DIOXIDE IN BLOOD AT CORRECT LEVEL
Increased activity causes a rise in carbon dioxide levels in blood
Receptors in arteries detect the rise and send messages to the brain
The respiratory center stimulates the breathing rate to increase
More carbon dioxide passes from blood into the lungs and is exhaled

Gas exchange in the body

The exchange of oxygen and carbon dioxide gases occurs constantly throughout the body. In the lungs, oxygen crosses the delicate walls of the alveoli (air sacs) and enters tiny blood vessels (capillaries), where it binds to the molecule hemoglobin in the red blood cells. At the same time, carbon dioxide is released from the blood into the alveoli and exhaled through the mouth or nose. In tissue cells, blood from the lungs exchanges its supply of oxygen for carbon dioxide.

Exchange of gases
Body cells require a constant supply of oxygen in order to obtain energy to survive. In addition, waste products from the body cells, mainly carbon dioxide, must be transported away from the cells.

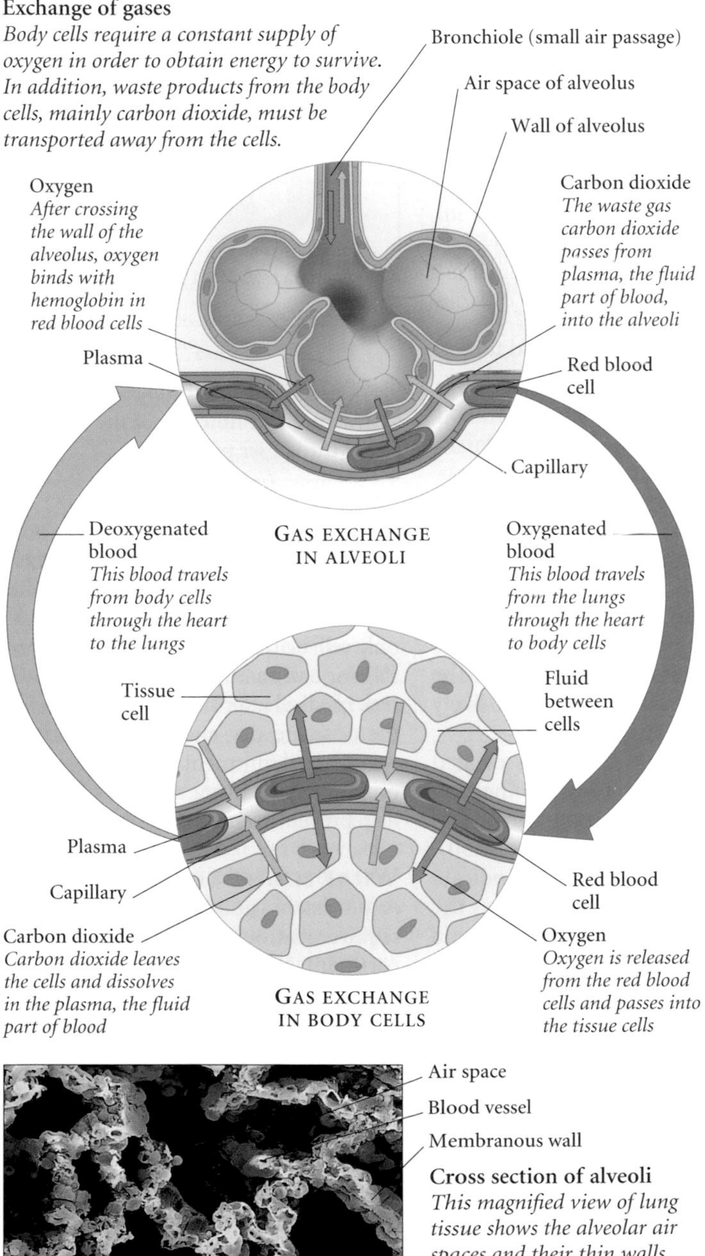
Bronchiole (small air passage)
Air space of alveolus
Wall of alveolus
Oxygen
After crossing the wall of the alveolus, oxygen binds with hemoglobin in red blood cells
Carbon dioxide
The waste gas carbon dioxide passes from plasma, the fluid part of blood, into the alveoli
Plasma
Red blood cell
Capillary
Deoxygenated blood
This blood travels from body cells through the heart to the lungs
GAS EXCHANGE IN ALVEOLI
Oxygenated blood
This blood travels from the lungs through the heart to body cells
Tissue cell
Fluid between cells
Plasma
Capillary
Red blood cell
Carbon dioxide
Carbon dioxide leaves the cells and dissolves in the plasma, the fluid part of blood
GAS EXCHANGE IN BODY CELLS
Oxygen
Oxygen is released from the red blood cells and passes into the tissue cells
Air space
Blood vessel
Membranous wall

Cross section of alveoli
This magnified view of lung tissue shows the alveolar air spaces and their thin walls. The tiny holes seen in the walls are blood vessels.

(FUNCTION) Speech

The larynx (voice box) is responsible for voice production. Sounds are made when air from the lungs passes across two fibrous bands within the larynx, known as vocal cords. The sounds produced by the vibrating cords are formed into speech by the mouth and tongue.

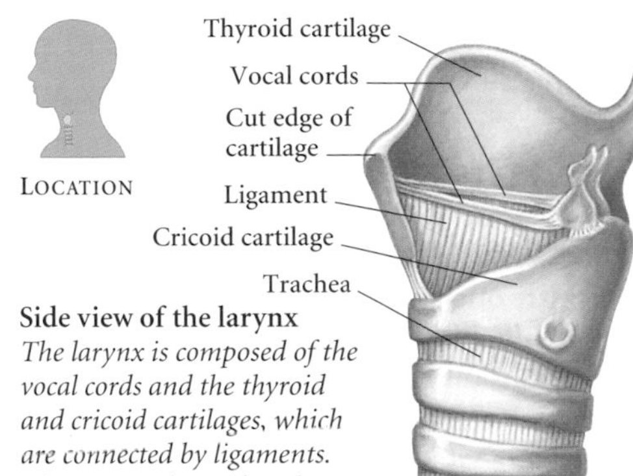
Thyroid cartilage
Vocal cords
Cut edge of cartilage
LOCATION
Ligament
Cricoid cartilage
Trachea

Side view of the larynx
The larynx is composed of the vocal cords and the thyroid and cricoid cartilages, which are connected by ligaments. The organ is located in the neck, above the trachea.

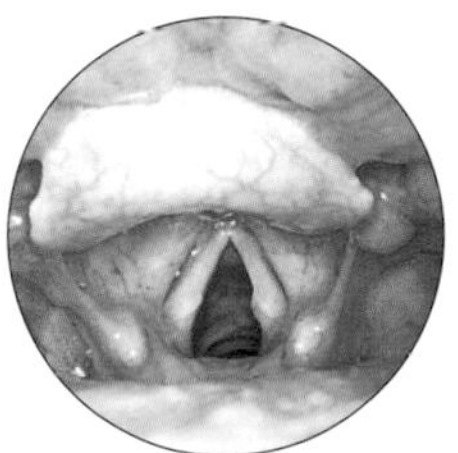

OPEN VOCAL CORDS

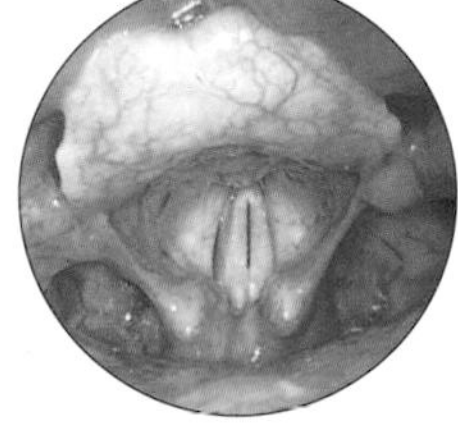

CLOSED VOCAL CORDS

Movements of the vocal cords
The vocal cords are held open during breathing, but during speech they pull together and vibrate as air from the lungs passes between them. Sounds vary according to the exact position of the cords.

(FUNCTION) The cough reflex

If substances such as dust or excess mucus irritate the lungs or airways, they may be removed by the familiar reaction known as a cough. The irritation stimulates nerve cell receptors in the airways, sending signals to the brain, which then triggers the cough reflex.

The cough
During a cough, air, moisture, and foreign particles are noisily and forcefully expelled. This reflex action helps clear irritant material from the airways, preventing it from causing damage.

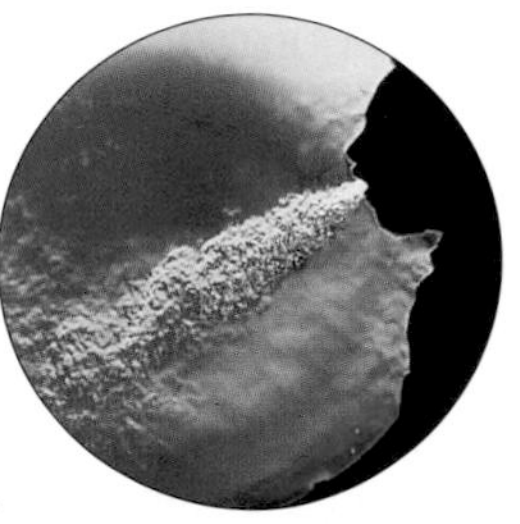

TEST ENDOSCOPY OF THE NOSE AND THROAT

Endoscopy can be used to look at the internal structures of the nose and throat as well as to diagnose disorders such as nasal polyps or cancer of the larynx. During the procedure, a flexible endoscope is inserted up each nostril in turn and into the nasal cavity. If necessary, it is passed down farther in order to look at the larynx. Endoscopy takes only a few minutes to perform. The procedure is carried out under local anesthesia in the doctor's office and can be repeated easily to monitor the progress of a disorder or treatment.

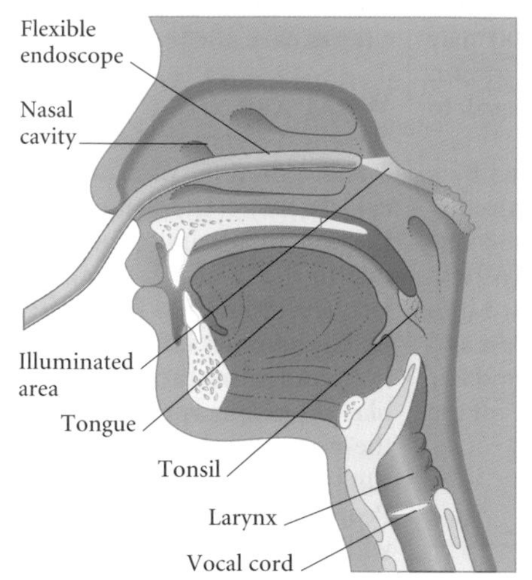
Flexible endoscope
Nasal cavity
Illuminated area
Tongue
Tonsil
Larynx
Vocal cord

During the procedure
The endoscope is used to examine the nasal cavity and sometimes also the larynx. Instruments inserted through the endoscope can collect tissue samples or remove minor abnormalities, such as polyps.

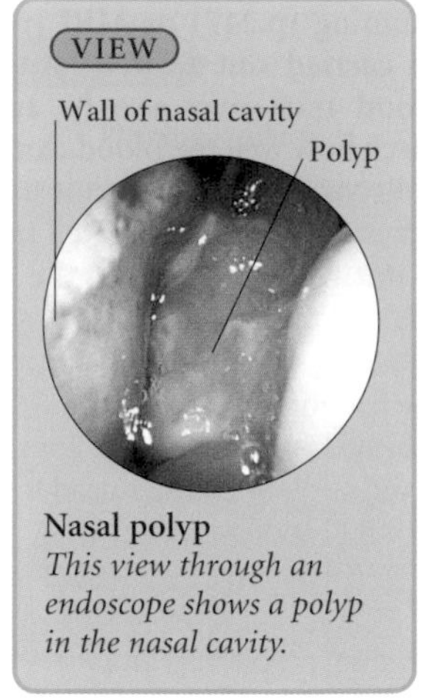
VIEW
Wall of nasal cavity
Polyp

Nasal polyp
This view through an endoscope shows a polyp in the nasal cavity.

Deviated nasal septum

An abnormality of the partition that separates the nostrils

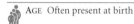

 AGE Often present at birth

 GENDER More common in males

 LIFESTYLE Playing contact sports, such as football, is a risk factor

 GENETICS Not a significant factor

Sometimes, the wall of cartilage and bone that divides the nostrils, called the nasal septum, is slightly misshapen or bent without causing problems. However, in some people the nasal septum is very misshapen, or deviated, and blocks one side of the nose, which impairs breathing. The defect may also cause snoring (opposite page).

A mildly deviated nasal septum is most often present from birth. In other cases, the condition results from a blow to the nose, usually due to a fall or an athletic injury. Men are more likely to have a deviated septum because they participate more often in contact sports that may lead to this type of injury. A severely deviated nasal septum may increase the risk of infections in the sinuses (*see* SINUSITIS, p.475).

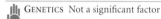

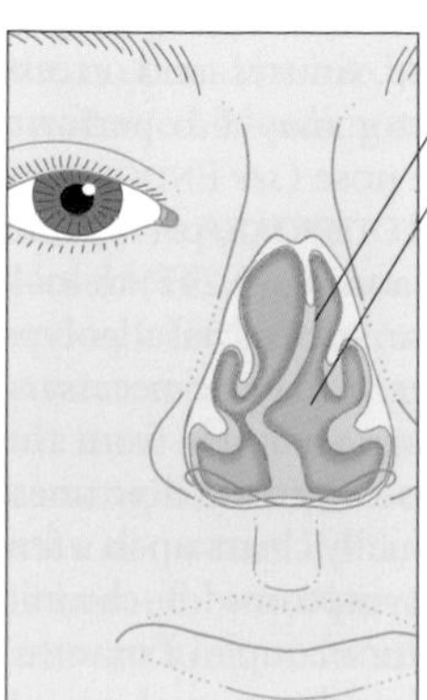
Misshapen septum
Nasal cavity

Deviated nasal septum
A misshapen nasal septum is not usually a problem, but a severe deviation may obstruct breathing.

If you experience recurrent sinusitis or breathing difficulties, your doctor may recommend surgery. The deviated septum is straightened by realigning the cartilage and bone or by removing them. Both operations are carried out in the hospital under local or general anesthesia and are usually successful.

(WWW) ONLINE SITES: p.1030

Nasal polyps

Fleshy growths of the mucus-secreting lining of the nose

 AGE More common in adults

 GENETICS Risk factors depend on the cause

 GENDER LIFESTYLE Not significant factors

Growths that develop in the mucus-secreting lining of the nose are known as nasal polyps. The exact cause of nasal polyps is not known. However, they are more common in people who have asthma (p.483) or rhinitis, a condition in which the membrane that lines the nose and throat becomes inflamed. Although polyps rarely occur in children, they do sometimes develop in children who have the inherited condition cystic fibrosis (p.824).

WHAT ARE THE SYMPTOMS?

The symptoms of nasal polyps often develop gradually over months. The severity of the symptoms depends on the number and the size of the polyps. Symptoms may include:

- Blocked nose due to obstruction by the polyps.
- Decreased sense of smell.
- In some cases, a runny nose due to excess secretion of mucus.

Nasal polyps may lead to recurrent sinusitis (p.475) if the narrow channels that drain mucus from the sinuses become blocked by the polyps and the sinuses become inflamed.

WHAT MIGHT BE DONE?

If your doctor suspects that you have nasal polyps but cannot see them easily, he or she may arrange for you to have endoscopy of the nose (*see* ENDOSCOPY OF THE NOSE AND THROAT, above). You may also have CT scanning (p.247) if the number and size of the polyps cannot be assessed with an endoscope. If there is a single polyp, a small sample of the polyp may be removed and examined under a microscope in order to exclude cancer.

Small nasal polyps may be treated by using a corticosteroid spray, which shrinks the polyps over a few weeks.

Larger polyps may be removed during an endoscopic procedure. A corticosteroid spray may also be necessary for several months after surgery to prevent the polyps from recurring. In more severe cases, a course of oral corticosteroids (p.930) may also be prescribed.

(WWW) ONLINE SITES: p.1030

Snoring

Noisy breathing during sleep, which may be a symptom of the more serious disorder sleep apnea

 AGE Most common in children and in adults between the ages of 30 and 50

 GENDER More common in males

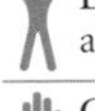 LIFESTYLE Being overweight, drinking alcohol, and smoking are risk factors

GENETICS Not a significant factor

Snoring is the sound made by the vibration of the soft palate (the rear of the roof of the mouth). Although it is often considered just an insignificant or entertaining problem, the disturbance caused by snoring can at times be distressing both to those affected and to their partners. Loud snoring may also be an early symptom of sleep apnea (right). The condition is most common in children and in men between the ages of 30 and 50.

WHAT ARE THE CAUSES?

Vibration of the soft palate may be caused by an obstruction or narrowing of the nasopharynx (the passage leading from the back of the nasal cavity to the throat). For example, the nasopharynx may become obstructed if you are overweight. Sleeping on your back can also worsen snoring because the nasopharynx is more likely to become partly blocked if you lie in this position. Other causes of snoring include narrowing of the nasopharynx caused by relaxation or swelling of the tissues of the soft palate. Relaxation may be the result of drinking alcohol or taking sedatives. Swelling may be caused by a throat infection or irritation of the soft palate by tobacco smoke.

Snoring also occurs because of congestion due to a common cold (p.286). In some cases, an anatomical abnormality such as a deviated nasal septum (opposite page) causes an obstruction in the nose, which results in snoring. In children, the condition usually occurs as a result of enlarged adenoids (p.842).

WHAT CAN I DO?

If you have other symptoms, such as daytime sleepiness or lack of concentration, you should consult your doctor in case you have sleep apnea. Otherwise, you can try the following self-help measures. You may be able to prevent snoring by making it uncomfortable to sleep on your back. This may be done by sewing a small object, such as a tennis ball, into the back of your sleepwear. If you are overweight, it will help to lose weight. You should also try to avoid taking sedatives at night and give up smoking, excessive alcohol consumption, and drinking alcohol at night.

(WWW) ONLINE SITES: p.1030, p.1037

Sleep apnea

Repeated temporary interruption of breathing during sleep

 AGE Most common in children and in adults between the ages of 30 and 50

 GENDER More common in males

 LIFESTYLE Being overweight, drinking alcohol, and smoking are risk factors

 GENETICS Not a significant factor

In sleep apnea, breathing stops during sleep for at least 10 seconds at least 5 times an hour. Mild sleep apnea causes few symptoms, but the condition may lead to low oxygen levels, which can be life-threatening. Sleep apnea is more common in people who smoke, drink alcohol, or are overweight. It may also occur in people at high altitudes.

(TEST) SLEEP STUDIES

Sleep studies monitor the changes in body processes during a period of normal sleep. Variables that are usually monitored during sleep include oxygen levels in the blood, brain activity, heart rate, blood pressure, airflow in the respiratory passages, and movement of the chest wall and the abdomen. If you undergo testing in a sleep laboratory, you may need to stay overnight.

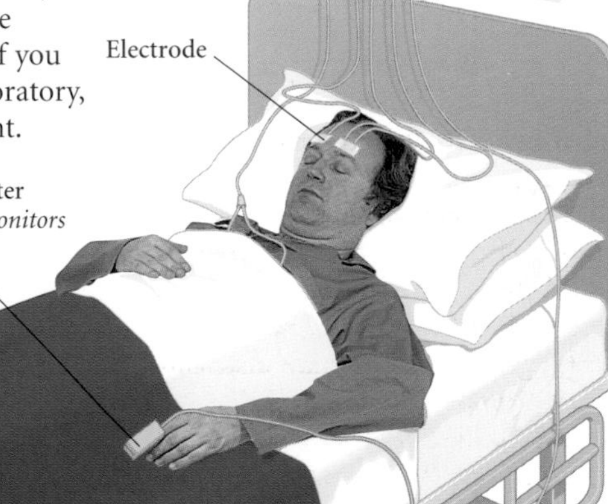
Monitor
Control panel
Electrode
Oximeter
This monitors oxygen levels

In the sleep laboratory *You will be attached to instruments that will continuously monitor various body functions while you are sleeping.*

(RESULTS)

Tracing indicating sleep apnea *The tracing shows oxygen levels falling repeatedly as breathing temporarily stops during 2.5 minutes of sleep, indicating sleep apnea. In response to the lower oxygen levels, the heart rate rises.*

Oxygen level (%) — Heart rate (beats/min) — Time (minutes)

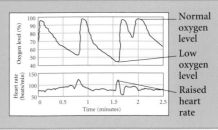

Normal oxygen level

Low oxygen level

Raised heart rate

What are the types?

Sleep apnea can be divided into two types: obstructive sleep apnea (OSA), which is common and due to blockage of the airway, and central sleep apnea, which is rare and caused by a problem with the nerves that control breathing. In some cases, a mixture of both types of sleep apnea may occur.

OBSTRUCTIVE SLEEP APNEA This condition mainly affects men aged between 30 and 50. OSA occurs when the air passages in the upper respiratory tract become obstructed during sleep. Most commonly, obstruction is caused by the soft tissue of the pharynx relaxing and blocking the flow of air. The obstruction prevents breathing until the low levels of oxygen in the blood cause a person to respond by waking up and taking a deep, snorting breath. Being overweight (particularly around the neck area) or having a large tongue or a small mouth can also cause or contribute to the obstruction. In children, enlarged tonsils (*see* TONSILLITIS, p.843) or enlarged adenoids (p.842) are the most common causes of obstruction that can lead to OSA.

CENTRAL SLEEP APNEA In this rare type of sleep apnea, the region of the brain and the nerves that regulate breathing do not function normally and this causes breathing to be impaired. Causes of central sleep apnea include brain damage following a head injury (p.521) or a stroke (p.532).

What are the symptoms?

The symptoms of OSA develop gradually. Central sleep apnea may develop suddenly, depending on the cause. It may be a partner or another member of your family who first notices your disturbed sleep, rather than yourself. Symptoms of both types may include:

- Restless, unrefreshing sleep.
- Daytime sleepiness.
- Poor memory and concentration.
- Headache in the morning.
- Loud snoring (p.477).
- Change in personality.
- In men, erectile dysfunction (p.770).
- Frequent urination during the night.

In severe cases, daytime sleepiness may result in accidents, such as when driving. Taking sleeping drugs (p.915) and drinking alcohol may aggravate the symptoms. Left untreated, complications may develop, such as an irregular heartbeat (*see* ARRHYTHMIAS, p.415) and pulmonary hypertension (p.505). There is also an increased risk of high blood pressure developing (*see* HYPERTENSION, p.403). Severe sleep apnea may eventually be life-threatening.

How is it diagnosed?

If your doctor suspects that you have sleep apnea, he or she will probably examine your nose and throat to look for an obvious cause of obstruction to your breathing. You may also have an endoscopy of the nose and throat (p.476) and X-rays (p.244) or CT scanning (p.247) of the head and neck. To confirm the diagnosis, you may have to undergo sleep studies (p.477), in which variables such as your breathing, oxygen levels in your blood, and your heart rate are measured while you are asleep. Sleep studies may also help in assessing the severity of sleep apnea.

What is the treatment?

If you have mild OSA, you should avoid sleeping drugs and alcohol. If you are overweight, losing weight often helps. You should also try to sleep on your side, which may relieve the symptoms. If caused by high altitudes, sleep apnea should disappear when you acclimatize or return to lower altitudes.

If OSA is caused by enlarged tonsils or adenoids, surgery may be necessary to remove them (*see* TONSILLECTOMY AND ADENOIDECTOMY, p.843). In some cases, OSA is treated by surgically reconstructing the soft palate. If the cause is not treatable, or if you do not wish to have surgery, positive pressure ventilation (below) may help and is often the first treatment offered. In this procedure, air is steadily pumped through a tight-fitting nasal mask. The increased air pressure keeps the airways open so that breathing is easier. The treatment is easy to use, but some people have difficulty tolerating the mask. Drugs that stimulate breathing may help people with central sleep apnea.

Treatment for OSA is usually successful. Central sleep apnea is more difficult to cure because the underlying causes are less likely to be reversed.

(WWW) ONLINE SITES: p.1030, p.1037

(TREATMENT) Positive pressure ventilation

During positive pressure ventilation, a steady supply of air is pumped to the nose during sleep through a tube and mask. The high pressure of the pumped air keeps the upper airways open. Positive pressure ventilation may be used to treat people with sleep apnea, in which breathing repeatedly ceases for short periods of time during sleep. The treatment needs to be carried out every night during sleep and it can be easily done at home.

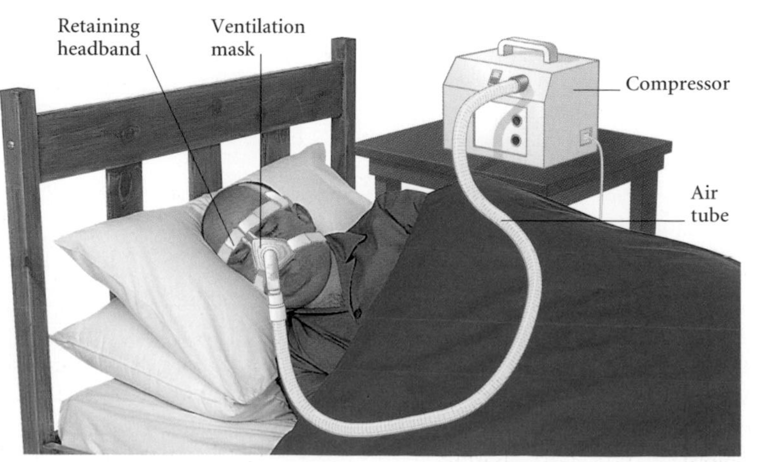
Retaining headband
Ventilation mask
Compressor
Air tube

Wearing the mask
A compressor supplies a flow of air at high pressure to the nose through a tube and mask. The mask is held in place by straps around the back of the head above and below the ears.

Pharyngitis and tonsillitis

Inflammation of the pharynx (throat) and/or the tonsils

AGE Pharyngitis more common in adults; tonsillitis more common in children

GENDER GENETICS LIFESTYLE Not significant factors

Pharyngitis and tonsillitis are common conditions often described as sore throat. The pharynx connects the back of the mouth and nose to the esophagus and larynx. The tonsils lie at the top of the pharynx and help defend the body against infection. Tonsils are large in children but shrink with age. As a result, tonsillitis (p.843) is more common in children, while adults tend to get pharyngitis. However, pharyngitis and tonsillitis may occur together in both adults and children.

WHAT ARE THE CAUSES?

Pharyngitis and tonsillitis are usually the result of a viral infection, such as a common cold (p.286) or infectious mononucleosis (p.289). Other causes include bacterial infections, such as with streptococcal bacteria, and fungal infections, such as candidiasis (p.309). Smoking, drinking alcohol, and straining the voice, often when shouting, may lead to pharyngitis in adults.

WHAT ARE THE SYMPTOMS?

Pharyngitis and tonsillitis have similar symptoms, which become worse over about 12 hours. Symptoms may include:

- Sore throat.
- Difficulty swallowing.

Tongue
Inflamed tonsil

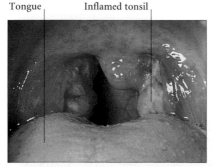

Tonsillitis
The tonsils shown here have become inflamed and covered with a white coating, a condition known as tonsillitis.

- Pain in the ear, which may be worse on swallowing.
- Enlarged and tender lymph nodes in the neck.

Pharyngitis and tonsillitis may also be associated with a fever and not feeling well, especially if the conditions are caused by a bacterial infection.

ARE THERE COMPLICATIONS?

In severe cases, the pharynx and/or the tonsils may become so swollen that difficulties with breathing gradually develop. Occasionally, an abscess may also form next to a tonsil, a condition known as a peritonsillar abscess. Rarely, if pharyngitis and/or tonsillitis is caused by a streptococcal infection, the kidney disorder glomerulonephritis (p.699) may develop some weeks later.

WHAT MIGHT BE DONE?

There are several self-help measures that you can take to ease a sore throat, such as drinking plenty of hot or very cold fluids and eating ice cream (*see* SOOTHING A SORE THROAT, below).

Both pharyngitis and tonsillitis usually clear up with self-help measures after a few days. However, if the pain is severe or has not improved after 48 hours, or if you have difficulty breathing or swallowing, you should consult a doctor. The doctor may take a throat swab to find the cause of the infection. You may also have a blood test for infectious mononucleosis.

Your doctor may prescribe antibiotics (p.885) if he or she suspects a bacterial infection. A peritonsillar abscess may be treated with intravenous antibiotics, or it may need to be drained under local or general anesthesia. In some cases, it may also be necessary to remove the tonsils.

Tonsillitis rarely recurs in adults but may do so in children. In contrast, pharyngitis may recur throughout life.

(WWW) ONLINE SITES: p.1030

(SELF-HELP) SOOTHING A SORE THROAT

A sore throat may be due to pharyngitis, tonsillitis, or both. The following steps may help relieve the discomfort:

- Drink plenty of fluids, especially hot or very cold drinks.
- Eat ice cream and popsicles.
- Gargle warm saltwater or, for adults, a single dose of soluble aspirin dissolved in water (*see* ANALGESICS, p.912).
- Take pain medications or, for adults, throat lozenges containing a local anesthetic.
- Install a humidifier or place bowls of water near radiators to keep the air moist.

Laryngitis

Inflammation of the larynx (voice box), usually caused by infection and producing hoarseness

LIFESTYLE Smoking and drinking alcohol are risk factors

AGE GENDER GENETICS Not significant factors

The larynx lies between the throat and trachea (windpipe) and contains the vocal cords. Laryngitis is rarely serious and may be acute, lasting a few days, or chronic, persisting for months. The condition can cause breathing difficulties in children (*see* CROUP, p.841).

Acute laryngitis is almost invariably caused by a viral infection, such as a common cold (p.286), but it may also occur after prolonged use of the voice. Chronic laryngitis may be caused by smoking and long-term overuse of the voice, which may eventually damage the larynx. Drinking alcohol, especially hard liquor, may aggravate laryngitis.

WHAT ARE THE SYMPTOMS?

The symptoms of laryngitis usually develop over 12–24 hours and vary depending on the underlying cause. Symptoms may include:

- Hoarseness.
- Gradual loss of the voice.
- Pain in the throat, especially when using the voice.

Sometimes laryngitis is associated with vocal cord nodules (p.480).

WHAT CAN I DO?

Acute laryngitis that is caused by a viral infection usually clears up without treatment. There is no specific treatment for chronic laryngitis. For both forms of the condition, resting your voice can help relieve pain and avoid further damage to the vocal cords.

Inhaling moist air while under a towel may also help relieve symptoms (*see* INHALING MOIST AIR, p.475). To prevent a recurrence of chronic laryngitis, avoid overusing your voice. If you smoke, try to stop completely, and, if you drink heavily, reduce your intake of alcohol.

Since hoarseness can be a symptom of cancer of the larynx (opposite page), consult your doctor if a voice change persists for more than 4 weeks. He or she may examine your throat using mirror laryngoscopy (opposite page) or flexible fiberoptic endoscopy (*see* ENDOSCOPY OF THE NOSE AND THROAT, p.476) to look for signs of cancer.

(WWW) ONLINE SITES: p.1030

Vocal cord nodules

Small, noncancerous lumps on the vocal cords, causing hoarseness

 GENDER More common in boys and adult females

 LIFESTYLE Excessive use of the voice is a risk factor

 AGE GENETICS Not significant factors

Constant strain on the voice may eventually lead to the formation of small, grayish white nodules on the vocal cords of the larynx (voice box). The size of these nodules ranges from that of a pinhead to a grape seed. Although these nodules are noncancerous, they may cause scarring of the vocal cords.

The condition is common in singers and other people who overuse their voices over a long period. It can also affect people who do a lot of speaking, such as teachers, and may occur in persistently noisy children, especially boys.

The symptoms include increasing hoarseness, which may develop suddenly or gradually, and rapid voice loss when speaking. Drinking alcohol and smoking may aggravate the symptoms. You should consult a doctor if symptoms last over 4 weeks because some types of cancer of the larynx (opposite page) have similar symptoms.

WHAT MIGHT BE DONE?

Your doctor will probably look at your throat using mirror laryngoscopy (opposite page) or an endoscope (p.476). You may also undergo a biopsy, in which a sample of tissue is removed using an

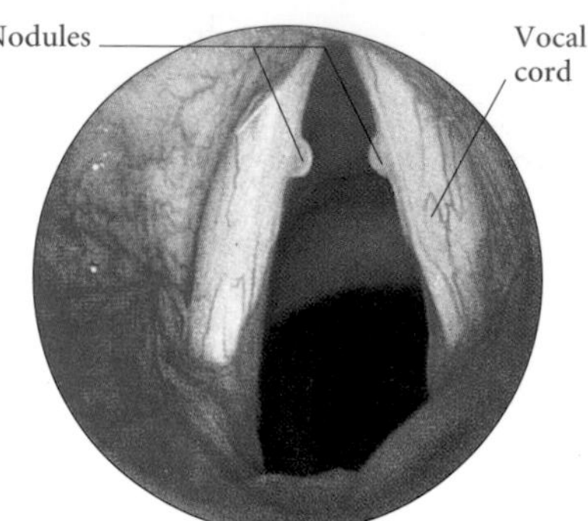
Nodules
Vocal cord

Vocal cord nodules
This view of the larynx (voice box) through an endoscope shows the vocal cords. A nodule can be seen on each vocal cord.

endoscope (*see* ENDOSCOPY OF THE NOSE AND THROAT, p.476) and examined for signs of cancer. If the nodules are small, you may have speech therapy (p.963), which can cause the nodules to shrink or disappear. Your doctor may suggest that larger nodules be removed using laser treatment (p.951) or microsurgery (p.950). The condition may recur.

(WWW) ONLINE SITES: p.1030

Cancer of the nasopharynx

A cancerous growth in the nasopharynx, the passage connecting the back of the nose to the throat

 AGE Most common between the ages of 50 and 60

 GENETICS More common in Chinese people

 LIFESTYLE Smoking, eating salted fish, and inhaling some dusts are risk factors

GENDER Not a significant factor

Cancer of the nasopharynx is a rare condition in which a tumor originates in the nasopharynx, the passage connecting the nasal cavity to the throat. This type of cancer occurs most frequently in Chinese people. The precise reasons for this are unknown, but it may involve genetic factors or certain chemicals present in foods such as salted fish and fermented dishes.

Other factors that may increase the risk of having cancer of the nasopharynx include smoking or using snuff, alcohol abuse, or a viral infection, especially with the Epstein–Barr virus (*see* INFECTIOUS MONONUCLEOSIS, p.289). People who inhale hardwood dust or nickel dust over a long period may also be at risk. If cancer of the nasopharynx is diagnosed early, it is usually easily treated. However, if the cancer is not diagnosed early, it may spread to the lymph nodes of the neck and to other parts of the body and may be fatal.

WHAT ARE THE SYMPTOMS?

Cancer of the nasopharynx may not initially cause symptoms, and it may not be noticed until the tumor spreads to a lymph node, causing a painless swelling in the neck. If early symptoms do develop, they may include:

- Repeated nosebleeds.
- Blocked or runny nose, usually affecting one nostril only.
- Discomfort on swallowing.

In addition, you may experience symptoms that include:

- Repeated infection and inflammation of the sinuses (*see* SINUSITIS, p.475).
- Facial pain and swelling.
- Earache and loss of hearing.
- Loss of sense of smell.

Left untreated, the cancer may spread to other areas such as nearby nerves, causing your voice to change or one side of your face to become paralyzed.

WHAT MIGHT BE DONE?

You may have endoscopy of the nose and throat (p.476) and, if a tumor is found, you may have a biopsy, in which a sample of the growth is removed and examined for signs of cancer. You may also have CT scanning (p.247) or MRI (p.248) to assess the size of the tumor and to see if the cancer has spread.

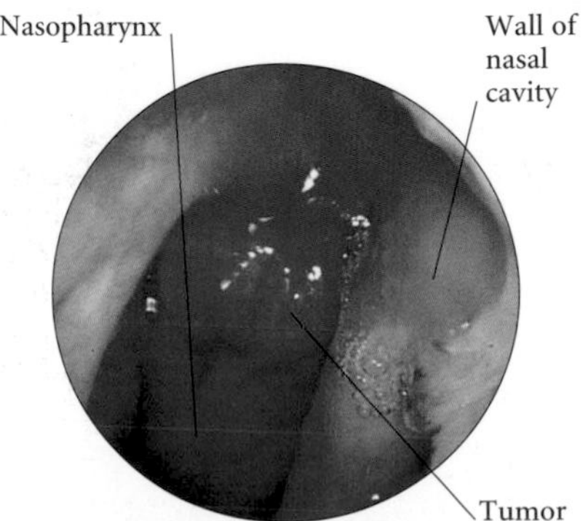
Nasopharynx
Wall of nasal cavity
Tumor

Cancer of the nasopharynx
This view through an endoscope shows a tumor in the nasopharynx, the passage connecting the nasal cavity and throat.

If cancer is diagnosed before it has spread, a cure is possible. You may have surgery to remove the tumor or radiation therapy (p.279) if surgery is not practical. Both procedures may also be used to relieve symptoms. The prognosis depends on how far the cancer has advanced. If treated early, one-third of people survive more than 5 years.

(WWW) ONLINE SITES: p.1028, p.1030

Cancer of the larynx

Cancer of the larynx (voice box), often causing persistent hoarseness

AGE Most common between the ages of 55 and 65

GENDER Five times more common in males

LIFESTYLE Smoking and alcohol abuse are risk factors

GENETICS Not a significant factor

Cancer of the larynx accounts for about 1 in 100 cases of cancer in men, usually in those aged 55–65. In about 6 in 10 cases, the cancer develops on the vocal cords; the remainder begin above or below the cords. If the cancer is on the cords, symptoms develop early, allowing prompt diagnosis and treatment. If the cancer develops elsewhere, it is more likely to be advanced at the time of diagnosis.

The cause of laryngeal cancer is not known, but it may be associated with smoking, particularly when combined with alcohol abuse. Without treatment, cancer of the larynx may spread to the lymph nodes in the neck and eventually to other parts of the body.

What are the symptoms?

If a tumor develops on the vocal cords, the first noticeable symptom is hoarseness. If the tumor is not detected, it may spread above and below the vocal cords, causing symptoms such as:

- Loud breathing.
- Difficulty breathing.
- Difficult and painful swallowing.

These symptoms may also occur if cancer develops above or below the vocal cords, although often these tumors do not produce symptoms at first. Tumors developing anywhere in the larynx may spread to the lymph nodes in the neck, causing them to become enlarged.

How is it diagnosed?

Your doctor will examine your throat (*see* MIRROR LARYNGOSCOPY, below, and ENDOSCOPY OF THE NOSE AND THROAT, p.476). You may also have a biopsy, in which tissue from the larynx is removed through an endoscope and examined for cancer. If the lymph nodes in the neck are enlarged, fine needle aspiration may be performed. In this procedure, a tissue sample is removed from a lymph node using a needle attached to a syringe. CT scanning (p.247) or MRI (p.248) may also be done to see the extent of the cancer.

What is the treatment?

Treatment will depend on how far the cancer has spread. You may be offered surgery to remove part or all of the larynx and/or radiation therapy (p.279). If surgery to remove the entire larynx is necessary, you will need a permanent laryngectomy, in which a hole (stoma) is made in the windpipe (trachea) to maintain an airway for breathing. A temporary tracheostomy may be necessary while you are having radiation therapy, but it can be reversed after treatment has been completed.

If the larynx is removed, ordinary speech will not be possible. However, several techniques have been developed to allow speech without a larynx. A small device known as a tracheoesophageal implant may be fitted to help you speak. Speech therapy (p.963) may enable you to speak using your esophagus, or you may be able to learn to speak with the help of a handheld electromechanical device that generates sounds when held against the neck.

In more than 9 in 10 cases, treatment is successful if the tumor develops on the vocal cords and is detected and treated early. If the cancer originates elsewhere in the larynx, the chances of a cure are reduced because symptoms appear later and the cancer may have already spread. In these cases, treatment may be given only to relieve symptoms, and survival rates are much reduced.

(WWW) ONLINE SITES: p.1028, p.1030

(TEST) Mirror laryngoscopy

Mirror laryngoscopy is simple, quick, and painless and is used to detect disorders of the larynx (voice box), such as vocal cord nodules and cancer of the larynx. The procedure, which is performed under local anesthesia, involves viewing the larynx by shining a light onto an angled mirror held at the back of the palate. You should not drink or eat afterward until the anesthetic has worn off to avoid inhaling food or fluids. If tissue samples need to be taken, you may need direct laryngoscopy (*see* ENDOSCOPY OF THE NOSE AND THROAT, p.476).

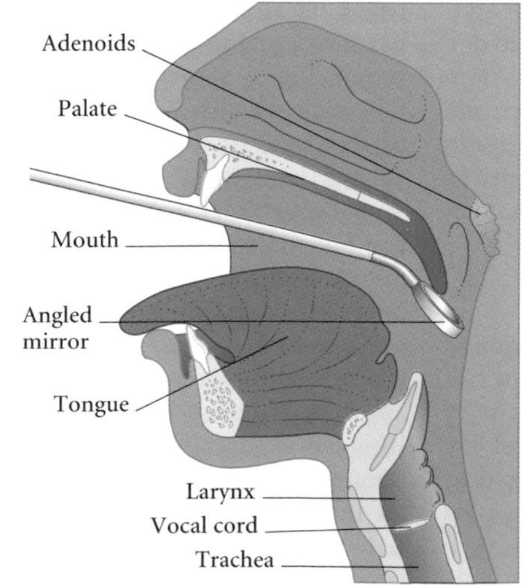
Adenoids
Palate
Mouth
Angled mirror
Tongue
Larynx
Vocal cord
Trachea

Viewing the larynx
After spraying your throat with a local anesthetic, the doctor places an angled mirror at the back of the palate so that he or she can examine the larynx and vocal cords to see if they are normal.

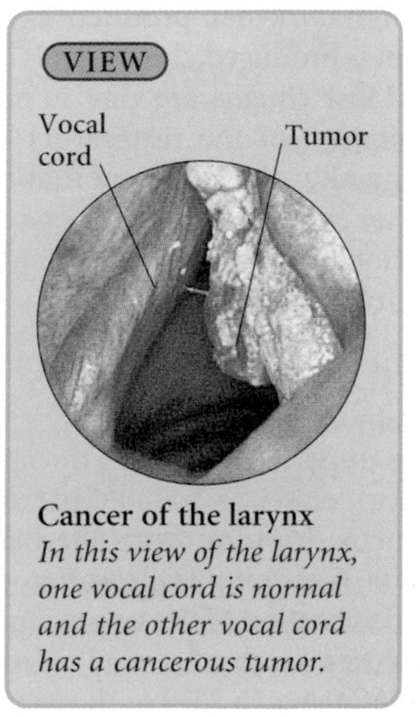
VIEW
Vocal cord
Tumor

Cancer of the larynx
In this view of the larynx, one vocal cord is normal and the other vocal cord has a cancerous tumor.

Factors that can provoke attacks in a person with asthma include cold air, exercise, smoke, and occasionally emotional stress. Although pollution from industry and motor vehicles does not normally cause asthma, it does appear to worsen symptoms in people with existing asthma and may trigger the condition in susceptible people.

In some cases, a substance that is inhaled regularly in the work environment can cause a previously healthy person to develop asthma. This is called occupational asthma and is one of the few occupational lung diseases (p.499) that is still increasing in incidence. If you develop wheezing and shortness of breath that improve when you are not in the work environment, you may have occupational asthma. This disorder can be difficult to diagnose because a person may be regularly exposed to the particular trigger substance for weeks, months, or even years before the symptoms of asthma begin to appear. There are currently about 200 substances used in the workplace that are known to trigger symptoms of asthma, including glues, resins, latex, and some chemicals, especially isocyanate chemicals that are used in spray-painting.

What are the symptoms?

The symptoms of asthma may develop gradually and may not be noticed until a trigger provokes the first severe attack. For example, exposure to an allergen or a respiratory tract infection may cause the following symptoms:

- Wheezing.
- Painless tightening in the chest.
- Shortness of breath.
- Difficulty exhaling.
- Dry, persistent cough.
- Feelings of panic.
- Sweating.

These symptoms often become considerably worse at night and in the early hours of the morning.

Some people find that they develop mild wheezing during the course of a common cold or a chest infection, but in most cases this does not indicate asthma. The main feature that distinguishes asthma from other respiratory conditions is its variability.

If asthma becomes severe, the following symptoms may develop:

- Wheezing that is inaudible because so little air flows through the airways.
- Inability to complete a sentence due to shortness of breath.
- Blue lips, tongue, fingers, and toes due to lack of oxygen.
- Exhaustion, confusion, and coma.

If you are with someone who is having a severe attack of asthma or your own symptoms continue to worsen, you need to call an ambulance.

How is it diagnosed?

If you have had breathing problems recently but are free of symptoms when you consult the doctor, he or she will ask you to describe your symptoms and will examine you. Your doctor may also arrange for you to have various tests, such as spirometry, to measure how efficiently your lungs work (*see* Lung function tests, p.488). As part of these tests, your doctor may attempt to induce a mild attack of asthma, either by giving you drugs or by getting you to exercise. If you do have an attack, you will be given medication to relieve it.

If you are having a mild attack when you consult your doctor, he or she may measure the speed at which you exhale using a device called a peak flow meter (*see* Monitoring your asthma, left), then ask you to inhale a bronchodilator drug (p.910), which relaxes the airways. Your doctor may be able to diagnose asthma if your peak flow rate increases substantially after you have inhaled the bronchodilator drug.

If you have a severe attack of shortness of breath, you may be treated and sent to the hospital for assessment. Once you are in the hospital, the oxygen level in your blood may be assessed (*see* Measuring blood gases, p.501), and you may have a chest X-ray (p.490) to rule out other serious lung disorders, such as a pneumothorax (p.496).

If you are diagnosed with asthma, your doctor may suggest that you have tests at a later date to check for allergies to substances that could trigger attacks. If your doctor suspects that you have occupational asthma, he or she will try to identify and confirm a specific trigger substance at your workplace.

TEST Monitoring your asthma

At times, you may want to monitor your asthma, for example, in order to determine if medications are effective. The best way to do this is with a peak flow meter, which can be used to measure the maximum rate at which you can exhale in liters per minute. The reading indicates whether the airways are narrowed. You should record your peak flow each morning and evening and plot the results on a chart.

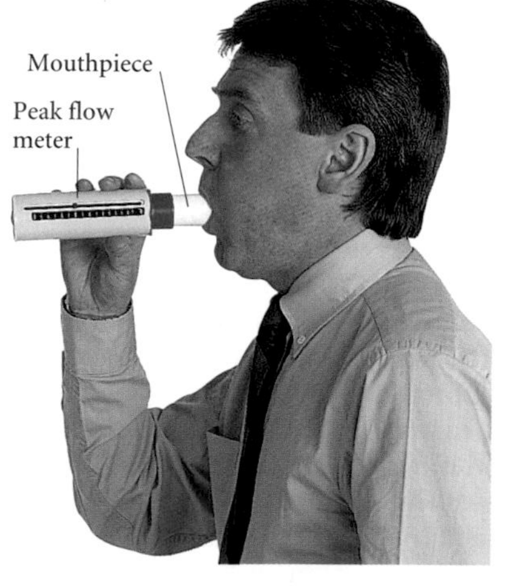
Mouthpiece
Peak flow meter

Using a peak flow meter
You should take a full breath in, seal your lips around the mouthpiece, and exhale as hard as you can. The pointer on the side of the meter shows your peak flow result.

RESULTS

Charting your peak flow
This chart shows twice-daily peak flow readings with marked variations between the morning and evening readings. These variations indicate that the asthma is poorly controlled.

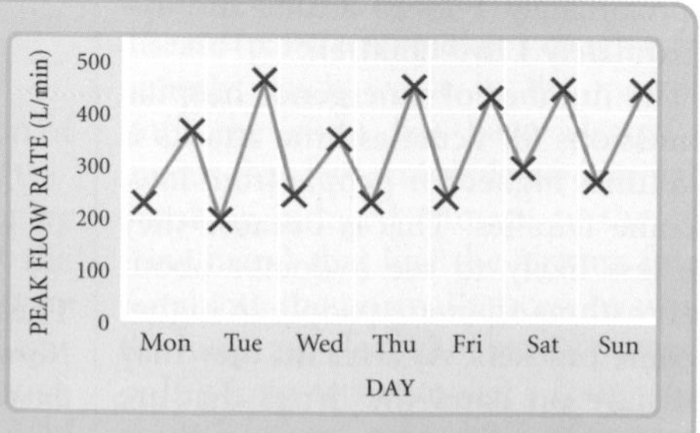
PEAK FLOW RATE (L/min)
500
400
300
200
100
0
Mon
Tue
Wed
Thu
Fri
Sat
Sun
DAY

SELF-HELP TAKING INHALED ASTHMA DRUGS

Inhaled drugs reach the lungs quickly and have few side effects because only a small amount of drug enters the circulation. There are several forms of inhaled asthma drugs. For example, a metered-dose inhaler delivers a precise dose when the inhaler is pressed.

A spacer can be used to hold the dose before it is inhaled. In cases where hand-breath co-ordination is difficult, a nebulizer may be used. Different devices are available for children (*see* GIVING INHALED DRUGS TO CHILDREN, p.839).

Using a nebulizer

A nebulizer creates a fine mist of drugs by forcing compressed air or oxygen through a liquid dose of the drug. The drug in mist form is then inhaled, through either a mouthpiece or a face mask.

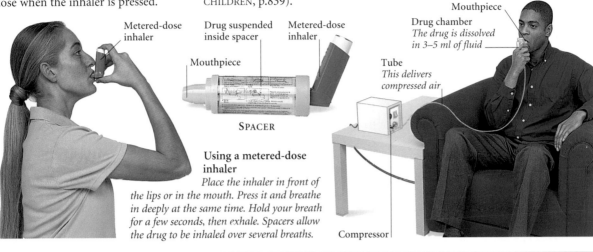

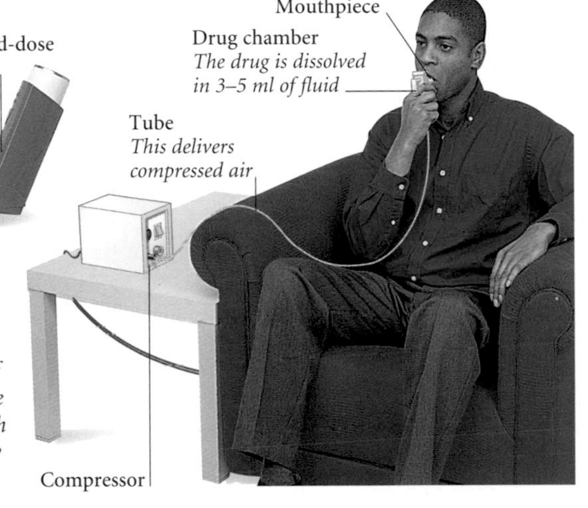
Mouthpiece
Drug chamber
The drug is dissolved in 3–5 ml of fluid
Tube
This delivers compressed air
Compressor

Metered-dose inhaler

Drug suspended inside spacer

Metered-dose inhaler

Mouthpiece

SPACER

Using a metered-dose inhaler

Place the inhaler in front of the lips or in the mouth. Press it and breathe in deeply at the same time. Hold your breath for a few seconds, then exhale. Spacers allow the drug to be inhaled over several breaths.

WHAT IS THE TREATMENT?

Some people with asthma do not need treatment if they manage to avoid the factors that trigger their symptoms (*see* LIVING WITH ASTHMA, p.486). However, there are so many triggers that it is very difficult to avoid them all, and for this reason treatment is often necessary.

The regular use of preventer (controller) drugs reduces the number of asthma attacks and the need for reliever (rescue) drugs. The current approach to asthma treatment is to give you the knowledge and confidence to manage the condition yourself in partnership with your doctor on a day-to-day basis. The most important aspects of controlling your asthma effectively are careful planning of drug treatment and regular monitoring of your condition.

The aim of all drug treatment of asthma is to eliminate symptoms and reduce the frequency and severity of attacks so that visits to the emergency room are no longer needed. Severe, potentially fatal attacks of asthma rarely develop without warning. Being able to recognize a serious change in your condition and taking prompt action by adjusting your drugs or contacting your doctor are essential to stop an attack from occurring.

TYPES OF DRUGS The drugs used to treat asthma fall into two distinct categories: reliever (rescue) drugs and preventer (controller) drugs. Attacks of wheezing are usually treated with reliever drugs called bronchodilators. There are several different types of bronchodilators, all of which relax the muscles that narrow the airways and treat breathing problems as they occur. Reliever drugs are usually effective within a few minutes if inhaled. However, the effect of these drugs lasts for only a few hours.

The second category of drugs used to treat asthma are preventers (controller), which help prevent attacks. Most preventers of asthma are corticosteroid drugs (*see* CORTICOSTEROIDS FOR RESPIRATORY DISEASE, p.911), which slow the production of mucus, reduce inflammation in the airways, and make the airways less likely to narrow on exposure to a trigger substance. In some cases, nonsteroidal preventers, such as cromolyn sodium (*see* ANTIALLERGY DRUGS, p.905), may be used to lessen the allergic response and prevent the airways from narrowing. Leukotriene antagonists are specifically aimed at controlling the inflammation of asthma. They are tablets, convenient to use, but their role in the management of asthma is not fully understood. Preventers must be used daily and can take several days to become effective.

Bronchodilator drugs that have a long (12-hour) duration of action are of value. In combination with an inhaled steroid, these drugs are most effective in poorly controlled asthma. The drugs are often combined in the same inhaler device.

People with long-term severe asthma may be given controllers in the form of low-dose oral corticosteroids instead of inhaled drugs. Oral corticosteroids may also be given to treat severe attacks.

DAY-TO-DAY MANAGEMENT Adults with asthma are given a lot of responsibility to manage the condition themselves. Many doctors provide patients with an agreed-upon management plan. The key to managing asthma is regular monitoring of symptoms and self-assessment using a peak flow meter, which can help you to determine the rate at which you are able to exhale and whether or not your airways are narrowed. Asthma may vary in severity from day to day or over longer periods. For this reason, your doctor will develop a treatment plan especially for your asthma.

In this plan, your asthma treatment will move up a level, down a level, or remain unchanged, depending on your most recent symptoms and peak flow readings. A different level of treatment may involve altering a drug dosage; taking the drug in another way, such as orally instead of by inhaling; taking a different drug; and/or using drugs more or less frequently. If one level of treatment is not controlling your asthma, you move up to the next level.

If you are an adult newly diagnosed with asthma, your treatment may start with reliever drugs only. Preventers (controllers) may gradually be added if you find that you need to use reliever drugs more than a few times a week. Your doctor will closely monitor your progress over an agreed period of time in order to determine whether your treatment plan needs to be changed. If you use your peak flow meter to monitor your asthma every day, you will get an early warning sign of worsening of your condition and can then adapt your treatment in accordance with the prescribed plan. Discuss your treatment plan with your doctor and ensure that you understand it. Your plan should include specific advice on what you should do if you experience a severe acute attack of asthma.

EMERGENCY TREATMENT If you have a sudden, severe attack of asthma, you should take your reliever drugs as instructed by your doctor. If the treatment does not appear to be working, call for an ambulance immediately. You should try to stay calm and sit in a comfortable position. Place your hands on your knees to help support your back; do not lie down. Try to slow down the rate of your breathing to prevent yourself from becoming exhausted.

Once you are in the hospital, you will probably be given oxygen and corticosteroids, initially by injection and then orally. In addition, you will probably be given bronchodilators at a high dose, either through a nebulizer or by continuous intravenous infusion.

Rarely, when emergency drug measures are not immediately effective, mechanical ventilation may be necessary to force oxygen-enriched air into the lungs. Mechanical ventilation may have to be continued until the drugs can take effect and the airways relax. Once your condition is stable, you may have chest physiotherapy (p.962), which includes chest clapping and breathing exercises, to help displace mucus trapped in the airways so that it can be coughed up.

WHAT IS THE PROGNOSIS?

The majority of children and adults with asthma are able to lead normal lives if they receive medical advice for their condition and then follow their treatment plans. Asthma that begins in childhood disappears by age 20 in at least half of all cases. The outlook for adults with asthma who are otherwise healthy is excellent if they are careful to monitor their condition.

Despite this excellent outlook for people with asthma, more than 500 people still die from severe asthma attacks every year in Canada. In most of these cases, the cause of death is a delay in recognizing the severity of an asthma attack and consequently a delay in getting to the hospital.

WWW ONLINE SITES: p.1027

SELF-HELP LIVING WITH ASTHMA

Without doubt, the single most important aspect of controlling your asthma is the careful and planned use of drug treatments. However, there are several things that you can do to reduce your risk of an attack and to decrease the severity of your symptoms:

- Do not smoke and try to avoid polluted or smoky atmospheres.
- Do regular exercise to improve your stamina. Swimming is a particularly beneficial form of exercise. Be careful when you exercise outside in cold weather as the cold may provoke an attack.
- Avoid substances that are likely to provoke an allergic response; do not keep furry animals as pets if you are allergic to them.
- Always carry an inhaler, and be sure that you take medication with you on vacations.
- If your attacks are triggered by stress, try to practice relaxation exercises (p.75).

Acute bronchitis

Short-term inflammation of the airways, most often due to a viral infection

 AGE More common in adults

 LIFESTYLE Smoking and air pollution are risk factors

 GENDER GENETICS Not significant factors

Acute bronchitis occurs as a complication of respiratory infection in healthy adults. It is also a recurrent problem for people with chronic obstructive pulmonary disease (opposite page), who often experience several episodes each winter. In acute bronchitis, the lining of the bronchi, the main airways of the lungs, becomes inflamed, often due to infection. The inflammation produces a large amount of mucus, which is usually coughed up as sputum. In adults who are otherwise well, acute bronchitis does not usually cause permanent damage. However, in older people or those with a heart or lung disorder, infection may spread farther into the lungs, causing pneumonia (p.490).

Acute bronchitis is often caused by a viral infection, such as a common cold (p.286), that has spread from the nose, throat, or sinuses. Smokers, people who have an existing lung disorder, or those who are exposed to high levels of air pollution are more prone to attacks.

WHAT ARE THE SYMPTOMS?

The symptoms of acute bronchitis usually develop quickly over 24–48 hours and may include the following:

- Irritating, persistent cough that produces clear sputum.
- Central chest pain on coughing.
- Tightness of the chest and wheezing.
- Mild fever.

If you have a chronic heart or lung disease and develop these symptoms or if you cough up discolored sputum, indicating a possible bacterial infection, contact your doctor promptly.

WHAT MIGHT BE DONE?

In a person who is otherwise in good health, acute bronchitis caused by a viral infection usually clears up in a few days without specific medical treatment. Taking an over-the-counter analgesic (p.912), such as acetaminophen, may help bring down your temperature. If you smoke, you should stop immediately and completely.

If your doctor suspects that you have developed a secondary bacterial infection, he or she will probably prescribe oral antibiotics (p.885), and you should make a full recovery within 2 weeks of starting treatment. If acute bronchitis persists, your doctor may arrange for you to have additional investigations, such as a chest X-ray (p.490), to look for an underlying lung disorder.

(WWW) ONLINE SITES: p.1033, p.1034

Chronic obstructive pulmonary disease

Progressive damage to the lungs, usually caused by smoking, resulting in wheezing and shortness of breath

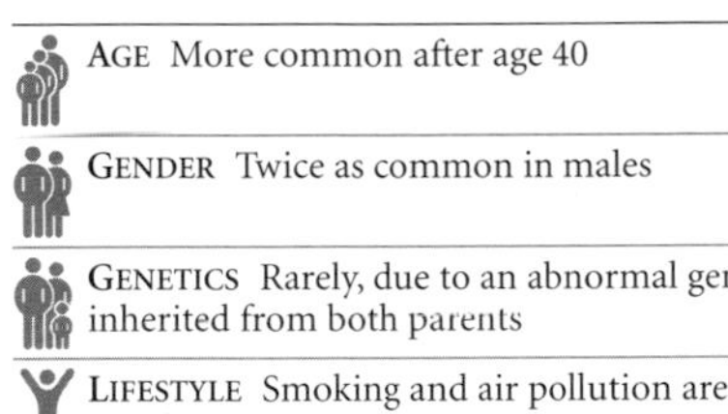

AGE More common after age 40

GENDER Twice as common in males

GENETICS Rarely, due to an abnormal gene inherited from both parents

LIFESTYLE Smoking and air pollution are risk factors

In chronic obstructive pulmonary disease (COPD), the airways and tissues of the lungs gradually become damaged over time, causing increasing shortness of breath. Some people with COPD eventually become so short of breath that they are seriously disabled and are unable to carry out even simple daily living activities. In nearly all cases of COPD, the cause is smoking.

People with COPD usually have two separate lung conditions, chronic bronchitis and emphysema, and either one of these conditions may be dominant. In chronic bronchitis, the bronchi (airways) become inflamed, congested, and narrowed, and this obstructs the flow of air through them. In emphysema, the alveoli (air sacs) in the lungs become enlarged and damaged, making them less efficient in transferring oxygen from the lungs to the bloodstream. The damage to the lungs that is caused by both bronchitis and emphysema is usually irreversible. In Canada, approximately 500,000 people over the age of 35 have been diagnosed with COPD, and many are not diagnosed until the disease is well advanced.

What are the causes?

The main cause of both chronic bronchitis and emphysema, and hence of COPD, is smoking. One quarter of smokers develop COPD. Atmospheric pollution also contributes to the disorder. Occupational exposure to dust, noxious gases, or other lung irritants can worsen existing COPD.

In chronic bronchitis, the linings of the airways of the lungs respond to smoke irritation by becoming thickened, narrowing the passages that carry air into and out of the lungs. Mucus glands in the bronchial linings multiply so that more mucus is produced, and the normal mechanism for clearing the airways and coughing up excess mucus as sputum is impaired. As the disease progresses, retained mucus in the airways easily becomes infected, which may lead to further damage. Repeated infections eventually cause the linings of the airways to become permanently thickened and scarred.

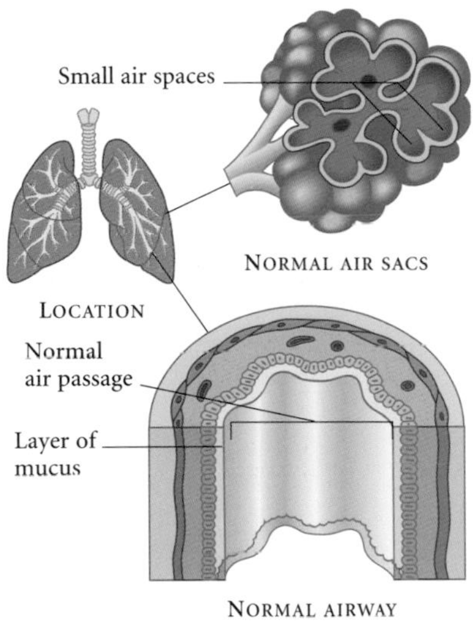
Small air spaces
Normal air sacs
Location
Normal air passage
Layer of mucus
Normal airway
Normal lung

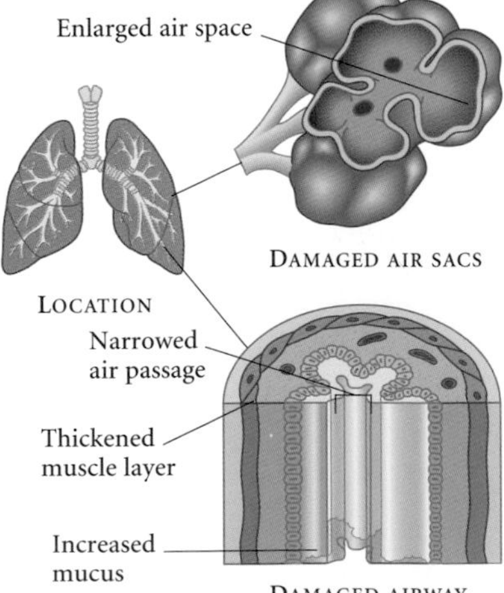
Enlarged air space
Damaged air sacs
Location
Narrowed air passage
Thickened muscle layer
Increased mucus
Damaged airway
Damaged lung

Damage to the lungs from COPD

In chronic obstructive pulmonary disease, the lungs are damaged in two ways. The air sacs of the lungs become stretched, reducing the area over which oxygen is absorbed, and the air passages narrow due to thickened walls and increased mucus.

In emphysema, tobacco smoke and other airborne pollutants damage the tissues of the air sacs. The sacs eventually lose their elasticity, and the lungs become distended. Eventually, the air sacs tear and merge together, reducing their total surface area, and air becomes trapped in the dilated sacs. As a result, the amount of oxygen that enters the blood with each breath is reduced. In rare cases, the main cause of emphysema is an inherited condition called alpha$_1$-antitrypsin deficiency (p.489). In such cases, damage occurs whether or not the person smokes, but smoking accelerates the disease.

What are the symptoms?

The symptoms of COPD may take several years to develop. When they appear, symptoms often occur in the following order:

- Coughing in the morning that produces sputum.
- Coughing throughout the day.
- Increasing production of sputum.
- Frequent chest infections, especially in the winter months, producing yellow or green sputum.
- Wheezing, especially after coughing.
- Shortness of breath on mild exertion, becoming progressively worse so that eventually shortness of breath occurs even when at rest.

Cold weather and infections, such as influenza (p.287), cause symptoms of COPD to worsen. Some people who have emphysema develop a barrel-shaped chest as the lungs become distended. Respiratory failure (p.507) may develop, in which lack of oxygen causes the lips, tongue, fingers, and toes to turn blue. Eventually, swelling of the ankles caused by chronic heart failure (p.413) may occur.

Some people who have COPD unconsciously compensate for their lung

TEST LUNG FUNCTION TESTS

Two tests are used to detect airflow problems in the lungs: spirometry, which measures how quickly the lungs fill and empty, and the lung volume test, which show how much air the lungs can hold. Other tests not shown here include gas transfer tests, which use a small amount of inhaled carbon monoxide to determine how fast a gas is absorbed from the lungs into the blood. Tests to measure blood gases (p.501) show the blood level of oxygen and other gases.

SPIROMETRY

A spirometer is used to measure the volume of air (in liters) that you can inhale and exhale over a period of time. The results show whether the airways are narrowed as a result of lung disorders such as asthma. Spirometry can also be used to monitor the effectiveness of certain treatments for lung disorders, such as bronchodilator drugs, which widen the airways.

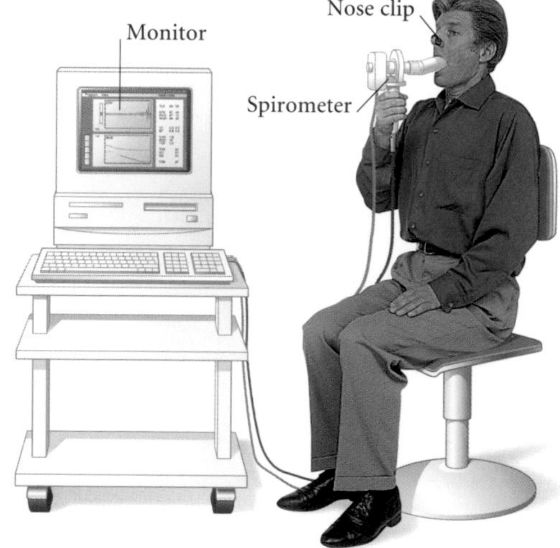
Nose clip
Monitor
Spirometer

Using the spirometer
You will be asked to inhale and exhale fully through a mouthpiece several times. The volume of air inhaled and exhaled is displayed on the monitor.

RESULTS

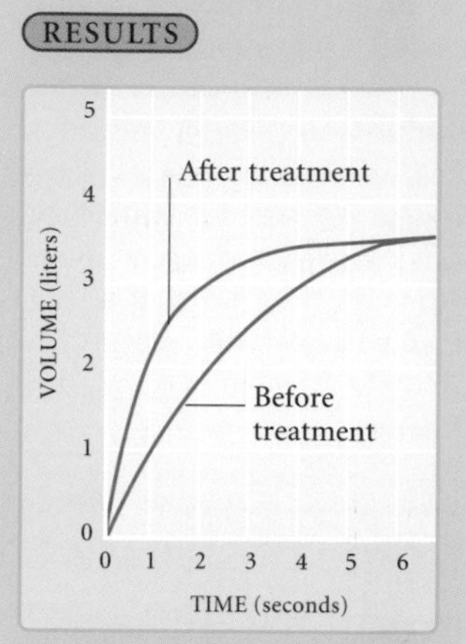
5
4
3
2
1
0
VOLUME (liters)
After treatment
Before treatment
0 1 2 3 4 5 6
TIME (seconds)

Spirometry graph
This graph shows the effect of drug treatment to widen the air passages in a person with asthma. The volume of air that is exhaled in 1 second rises from about 1 liter to 2 liters soon after the drugs have been taken.

LUNG VOLUME TEST

This test measures the volume of air (in liters) that can be taken in with a full breath and the volume of air that remains in the lungs when the breath is fully exhaled. The lung volume test is used to help diagnose disorders such as chronic obstructive pulmonary disease that affect the volume of air retained by the lungs after breathing out.

During the test
You will be asked to sit in an airtight booth and breathe in and out through a tube as fully as you can. The volume of air you can inhale and exhale is displayed as a graph on a monitor.

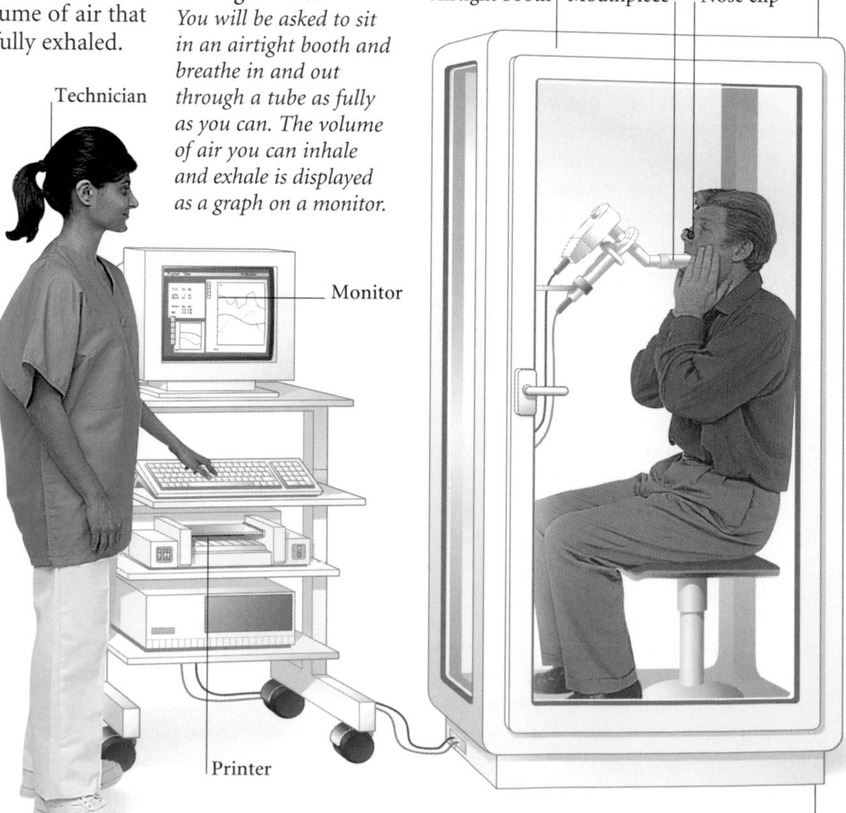
Airtight booth
Mouthpiece
Nose clip
Technician
Monitor
Printer

RESULTS

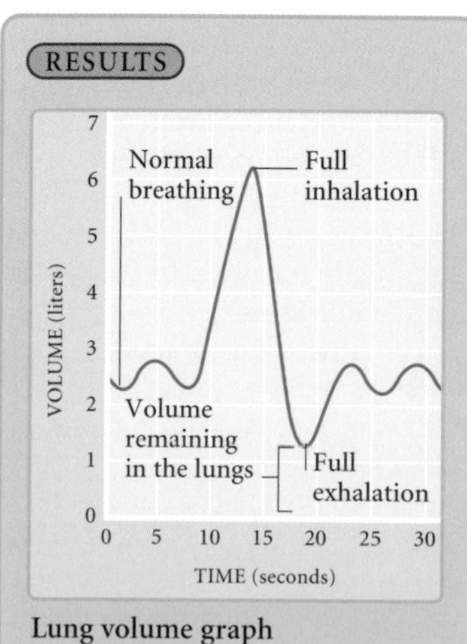
7
6
5
4
3
2
1
0
VOLUME (liters)
Normal breathing
Full inhalation
Volume remaining in the lungs
Full exhalation
0 5 10 15 20 25 30
TIME (seconds)

Lung volume graph
This graph shows the amount of air exhaled and inhaled when lungs are functioning normally.

problems by breathing rapidly to get more oxygen into their blood, and, as a result, they have a rosy flush to their skin. Other people affected by COPD are unable to compensate in this manner and tend to have a blue complexion instead, which is caused by lack of oxygen. These people often have tissue swelling in the feet and legs, which is due to heart failure.

If you are a smoker and notice symptoms that indicate you may have COPD, you should consult your doctor as soon as possible.

How is it diagnosed?

If you have a history of smoking, the doctor may suspect COPD from your symptoms and a physical examination. He or she will arrange for you to have lung function tests (opposite page) to assess the extent of damage to the lungs. You may have a chest X-ray (p.490) or CT scanning (p.247) to exclude other disorders and look for evidence of lung tissue damage. Part of the assessment of lung function may involve taking samples of your blood to check the levels of both oxygen and carbon dioxide (*see* MEASURING BLOOD GASES, p.501).

If members of your family have developed COPD before the age of 50, you may need a blood test to check the levels of the enzyme alpha$_1$-antitrypsin to look for a deficiency. Your doctor may take a sample of sputum to check for infection, and you may also have electrocardiography (*see* ECG, p.406) or echocardiography (p.425) to see if your heart is working unusually hard to pump blood through the lungs.

Chronic asthma (p.483) can produce symptoms that are very similar to those of COPD. If your doctor suspects that you have asthma, he or she may prescribe a course of corticosteroid drugs (*see* CORTICOSTEROIDS FOR RESPIRATORY DISEASE, p.911). Marked improvement of your symptoms suggests that you may have asthma rather than COPD.

What can I do?

If you develop COPD and you smoke, giving up smoking permanently is the only action that can delay the progress of COPD. Your environment should be kept as free as possible from smoke, pollution, dust, dampness, and cold. If possible, you should take part in a rehabilitation program, in which exercise, relaxation breathing, and energy conservation are major components.

How might the doctor treat it?

The damage caused by COPD is largely irreversible, but there are treatments that may help to ease the symptoms. Your doctor may prescribe an inhaler that contains a bronchodilator drug (p.910) in order to ease shortness of breath. Bronchodilators open up the airways of the lungs by relaxing muscle in the bronchial walls. There are two types of bronchodilators: one type produces instant relief, and the other has a slower but more prolonged effect. Inhaled corticosteroids are only of help to a small number of people with COPD. If your doctor confirms that you have a continuously low blood oxygen level, treatment will likely involve the use of continuous home oxygen therapy (p.507).

If you have swollen ankles, your doctor may prescribe diuretics (p.902) in order to reduce the buildup of fluid. Antibiotics (p.885) may be prescribed if you develop a chest infection. In COPD, the natural defense mechanisms against chest infections do not function properly. Learn the symptoms and signs of chest infection, and consult your doctor right away if you think you have one. Even a mild chest infection should be treated without delay. It is advisable that you are vaccinated against influenza each winter, and you may also be given a further vaccine to protect against infection with the bacterium *Streptococcus pneumoniae.*

What is the prognosis?

If your COPD is mild and has been diagnosed at an early stage, you may be able to avoid severe, progressive lung damage by stopping smoking at once. However, most people with COPD do not realize they have the condition until it is well advanced. For these people, the prognosis is poor. They often need to retire from work early and may become inactive and housebound by shortness of breath. Although about 3 in 4 people with COPD survive for 1 year after diagnosis, fewer than 1 in 20 survives for longer than 10 years.

(WWW) ONLINE SITES: p.1034

Alpha$_1$-antitrypsin deficiency

A rare inherited disorder that results in damage to the lungs and liver

AGE Present from birth, but effects usually appear after age 50

GENETICS Due to an abnormal gene inherited from both parents

LIFESTYLE Smoking and drinking alcohol may hasten onset of symptoms

GENDER Not a significant factor

The enzyme alpha$_1$-antitrypsin prevents other enzymes in the body from destroying tissues, mainly those in the lungs and liver. People with alpha$_1$-antitrypsin deficiency are missing this protective enzyme. The disorder is rare and is inherited in an autosomal recessive pattern, meaning that a person must inherit one abnormal gene from each parent in order to develop it (*see* GENE DISORDERS, p.269).

In severe cases, alpha$_1$-antitrypsin deficiency may cause jaundice in newborn babies (*see* NEONATAL JAUNDICE, p.817). However, the effects most often appear after age 50 and include damage to the air sacs (alveoli) in the lungs (*see* CHRONIC OBSTRUCTIVE PULMONARY DISEASE, p.487) and, less often, inflammation of the airways (*see* BRONCHIECTASIS, p.496). Liver cirrhosis (p.647) may also develop.

What might be done?

The diagnosis is made by measuring levels of the enzyme in the blood, and a blood test should establish if you have the abnormal gene. Other family members may also need to be tested. If you intend to start a family, you may wish to consult your doctor about having genetic counseling (p.270).

At present, no specific treatment for alpha$_1$-antitrypsin deficiency is available, but trials of enzyme replacement therapy are in progress. Your doctor may prescribe inhaled bronchodilator drugs (p.910) to help your breathing. People with severe lung or liver disease may be helped by an organ transplant. You should not smoke or drink alcohol if you have alpha$_1$-antitrypsin deficiency because these activities may cause lung and liver disease to worsen.

(WWW) ONLINE SITES: p.1032, p.1034

Pneumonia

Inflammation of the alveoli (air sacs) of the lungs, often resulting from infection

AGE Most common in infants, children, and elderly people

LIFESTYLE Smoking, alcohol abuse, and malnutrition are risk factors

GENDER GENETICS Not significant factors

In pneumonia, some of the alveoli (air sacs) in the lungs become inflamed and filled with white blood cells and fluid. As a result, it is harder for oxygen to pass across the walls of the alveoli into the bloodstream. Usually, only a proportion of one lung is affected, but, in some severe cases, pneumonia affects both lungs and can be life-threatening.

The cause of the inflammation is often a bacterial infection, but other organisms, including viruses, protozoa, and fungi, may also cause pneumonia. Less commonly, inhaling certain substances, such as chemicals or vomit, causes inflammation, which may lead to a serious condition called acute respiratory distress syndrome (p.506).

Pneumonia used to be a major cause of death in young adults, but the great majority of people with the disorder now recover completely due to more effective antibiotics. However, pneumonia is still fatal in elderly people or people with another illness and results in thousands of deaths each year in Canada. Some forms of pneumonia are becoming more difficult to treat due to the increasing resistance to antibiotics of some of the organisms responsible for the disease. For this reason, pneumonia is now the most common fatal infection acquired in the hospital.

Infants, elderly people, and people who are already seriously ill or have a chronic disease, such as diabetes mellitus (p.687), are at the greatest risk of developing pneumonia. Other people more likely to develop pneumonia are those who have lowered immunity as a result of a serious disease such as AIDS (*see* HIV INFECTION AND AIDS, p.295). Impaired immunity can also occur during treatment with immunosuppressant drugs (p.906) or chemotherapy (p.278). People who smoke, drink excessive amounts of alcohol, or are malnourished are more likely to develop pneumonia.

WHAT ARE THE CAUSES?

Most cases of pneumonia in adults are caused by infection with a bacterium, most commonly *Streptococcus pneumoniae.* This type of pneumonia may develop as a complication of a viral infection in the upper respiratory tract, such as a common cold (p.286). Other common causes of bacterial pneumonia in healthy adults include infection with the bacteria *Haemophilus influenzae* and *Mycoplasma pneumoniae.*

The bacterium known as *Legionella pneumophila* causes a form of pneumonia called Legionnaires' disease, which can be spread through air-conditioning systems. Legionnaires' disease may also lead to liver and kidney disorders.

Pneumonia caused by the bacterium *Staphylococcus aureus* usually affects people who are already in the hospital with another illness, especially very young children and the elderly. This type of pneumonia can also develop as a serious complication of influenza (p.287). Other causes of pneumonia that are often acquired in the hospital include infection with klebsiella and pseudomonas bacteria. Viral causes of pneumonia include the organisms that cause influenza and chickenpox (p.288).

In some cases, pneumonia is due to other organisms, such as fungi and protozoa. These infections tend to be rare and mild when they occur in otherwise healthy adults but are more common and potentially fatal in those with weakened immune systems. For example, *Pneumocystis carinii* may live harmlessly in healthy lungs but may cause severe pneumonia in people with AIDS (*see* PNEUMOCYSTIS INFECTION, p.308).

TEST CHEST X-RAY

A chest X-ray is often one of the first tests used to investigate lung and heart conditions because it is painless, quick, and safe. To create the image, X-rays are passed through your chest onto photographic film. Dense tissues, such as the bones, absorb X-rays and appear white; soft tissues appear gray; and air appears black. Damaged or abnormal lung tissue or excess fluid in the chest shows up as a white area because it does not contain air as it should. Chest X-rays are usually taken from behind, but in some cases side views may also be required.

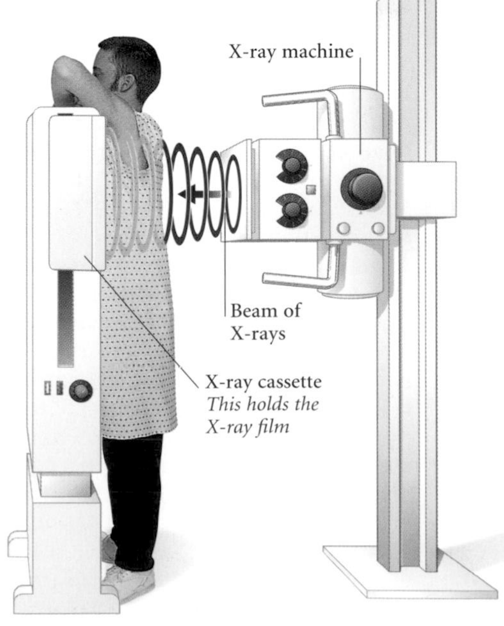
X-ray machine
Beam of X-rays
X-ray cassette
This holds the X-ray film

Having a chest X-ray
You will be asked to raise your arms to move your shoulder blades away from your lungs and to take a deep breath. While the X-ray is being taken, you must remain still to prevent the image from blurring.

RESULTS

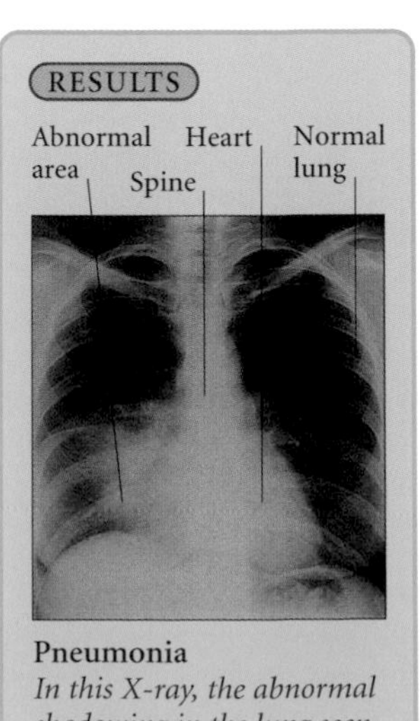
Abnormal area
Heart
Spine
Normal lung

Pneumonia
In this X-ray, the abnormal shadowing in the lung seen on the left is due to infection in the lung tissue.

A rare type of pneumonia, known as aspiration pneumonia, may be caused by accidental inhalation of vomit. Aspiration pneumonia is most likely to occur in people who have no cough reflex, often because they are unconscious after consuming an excessive amount of alcohol, taking a drug overdose, or sustaining a head injury (p.521).

WHAT ARE THE SYMPTOMS?

Bacterial pneumonia usually has a rapid onset, and severe symptoms generally develop within a few hours. You may experience the following symptoms:

- Cough that may produce rust-colored or bloody sputum.
- Chest pain that becomes worse when you inhale.
- Shortness of breath at rest.
- High fever, delirium, or confusion.

Pneumonia caused by organisms other than bacteria causes less specific symptoms that may develop more gradually. You may feel generally unwell for several days and develop a fever, and you may lose your appetite. Coughing and shortness of breath may be the only respiratory symptoms that you experience.

In infants, children, and elderly people, the symptoms associated with all types of pneumonia are often less obvious. Infants may initially vomit and can develop a high fever that may cause a convulsion. Elderly people may not experience respiratory symptoms but often become progressively confused.

ARE THERE COMPLICATIONS?

Inflammation as a result of pneumonia may spread from the alveoli in the lungs to the pleura (the two-layered membrane that separates the lungs from the chest wall), causing pleurisy (p.493). Fluid may accumulate between the two pleura (*see* PLEURAL EFFUSION, p.494), compressing the underlying lung and making breathing difficult.

In severe cases, the microorganism that initially caused the infection may enter the bloodstream, leading to blood poisoning (*see* SEPTICEMIA, p.298). In some vulnerable people, such as young children, elderly people, or those with a weakened immune system, the inflammation caused by pneumonia may spread widely into the lung tissue and result in respiratory failure (p.507), which is a life-threatening condition.

HOW IS IT DIAGNOSED?

If your doctor suspects pneumonia, the diagnosis may be confirmed by a chest X-ray (opposite page), which will show the extent of infection in the lung. A sample of sputum may be collected and tested to identify the organism that has caused the infection. The doctor may also arrange for blood tests to be done to help reach a precise diagnosis.

WHAT IS THE TREATMENT?

If you are otherwise healthy and have a mild form of pneumonia, you can probably be treated at home. Analgesics (p.912) should help reduce your fever and chest pain. If a bacterial infection is the cause of the pneumonia, your doctor will treat it with antibiotics (p.885). If the pneumonia is caused by a fungus, antifungal drugs (p.889) may be prescribed. No drug treatment is usually needed for mild viral pneumonia.

Hospital treatment will probably be needed in severe cases of bacterial or fungal pneumonia and for infants, children, elderly people, and people whose immune systems are suppressed. In all these cases, drug treatment is essentially the same as for people treated at home. Severe pneumonia caused by a viral infection, such as by the varicella zoster virus responsible for chickenpox, may be treated with oral or intravenous acyclovir (*see* ANTIVIRAL DRUGS, p.886).

If the oxygen levels in your blood are low or if you are short of breath, you will be given oxygen through a face mask. Less commonly, you may require mechanical ventilation in a critical care unit (p.958). You may also have chest physiotherapy (p.962) regularly while in the hospital to help loosen excess mucus in the airways so that it can be coughed up as sputum.

WHAT IS THE PROGNOSIS?

Young people who are in good health are generally able to recover from most types of pneumonia within 2–3 weeks, and there is no permanent damage to the lung tissue. Recovery from bacterial pneumonia usually begins within a few hours of starting treatment with antibiotics. However, some severe types of pneumonia, such as Legionnaires' disease, may be fatal, especially in people whose immune systems are weakened.

(WWW) ONLINE SITES: p.1033, p.1034

Tuberculosis

A bacterial infection that most often affects the lungs but may also affect many other parts of the body

AGE Most common in children and in adults over age 60

LIFESTYLE Overcrowded conditions and malnutrition are risk factors

GENDER GENETICS Not significant factors

Tuberculosis (TB) is a slow-developing bacterial infection that usually begins in the lungs but can spread to many other parts of the body. TB can now be treated very effectively using oral antibiotics (*see* ANTITUBERCULOUS DRUGS, p.886), but, left untreated, it may cause chronic ill-health and can be fatal.

Worldwide, TB causes more deaths among adults than any other bacterial infection. The disease is still especially common in developing countries. Canadians travelling in these countries should have TB tests before they go. In developed countries, TB was once common, but the number of cases steadily decreased during most of the 20th century due to improved health care, diet, and housing. However, since 1985 there has been a worldwide increase in the number of cases of TB. This rise is associated with the spread of strains of TB bacteria that are resistant to antibiotic treatment and the increase in HIV infection and AIDS (p.295), in which immunity is lowered, making people more susceptible to infection.

WHAT IS THE CAUSE?

The bacterium *Mycobacterium tuberculosis* causes TB. It is usually transmitted in airborne droplets that are produced when an infected person coughs. Although many people are infected with the bacterium at some point in their lives, only a small proportion of these people develop TB.

When the bacteria are inhaled, an initial minor infection develops in the lungs. The outcome of this initial lung infection depends on the strength of a person's immune system. In many healthy people, the infection does not progress. However, some TB bacteria lie dormant in the lungs, and the disease may be reactivated years later if a person's immunity is reduced.

In some cases, the bacteria enter the bloodstream and spread to other sites in the body. Rarely, the infection does not begin in the lungs but in another part of the body. For example, TB may affect the gastrointestinal tract if a person drinks unpasteurized milk from a cow infected with TB.

WHO IS AT RISK?

People with reduced immunity are more likely to develop TB. This includes people who are infected with HIV, those who have diabetes mellitus (p.687), and those who are taking immunosuppressant drugs (p.906). Others at risk of TB include those who have chronic lung disease and people who live in overcrowded and unsanitary housing or who have a poor diet. Generally, elderly people and children are more susceptible.

WHAT ARE THE SYMPTOMS?

During the initial infection, many people have no symptoms. However, some people may experience:

- Cough, which may be dry.
- Generally feeling unwell.

If the disease progresses, further symptoms usually appear over 2–6 weeks, but progression may be more rapid. Later symptoms may include:

- Persistent cough, which may produce greenish or yellowish sputum that is sometimes bloodstreaked.
- Chest pain when inhaling deeply.
- Shortness of breath.
- Fever.
- Poor appetite and weight loss.
- Excessive sweating at night.
- Fatigue.

Abnormal area in right lung

Heart

Normal left lung

Chest X-ray in tuberculosis

This X-ray image shows an abnormal area at the top of the right lung caused by an infection with tuberculosis.

Left untreated, TB that begins in the lungs can spread directly to the tissue covering the lungs (*see* PLEURAL EFFUSION, p.494). The infection may also spread through the bloodstream to the brain (*see* MENINGITIS, p.527), the bones, and many other parts of the body.

The onset of TB in areas of the body other than the lungs is very slow, and symptoms are not specific, making the condition very difficult to diagnose. For example, the symptoms of gastrointestinal tuberculosis may be similar to those of Crohn's disease (p.658).

HOW IS IT DIAGNOSED?

Your doctor may suspect TB from your symptoms and a physical examination. He or she may also arrange for you to have a chest X-ray (p.490) and possibly CT scanning (p.247) to look for evidence of lung damage.

If you are coughing up sputum, a sample will be sent to the laboratory so that it can be examined for bacteria and tested for sensitivity to particular drugs (*see* CULTURE AND TESTS FOR DRUG SENSITIVITY, p.234). In the meantime, you will be treated with antituberculous drugs.

Sometimes, a bronchoscopy (p.504) may be necessary to obtain lung tissue samples for examination. In addition, if your doctor suspects that you may have infection in a part of the body other than the lungs, samples of tissue from these areas may be taken to look for TB.

People who have recently come into close contact with an infected individual need to be screened. A chest X-ray may be done to look for signs of infection, along with a TB skin test, in which a substance extracted from TB bacteria is injected under the skin. The site of injection is checked for a reaction 2 or 3 days later. A reaction indicates that you have been exposed to TB, and you may be treated with antituberculous drugs.

WHAT IS THE TREATMENT?

In people who have been exposed to TB, prevention of active disease can be achieved by taking one antituberculosis drug for several months. If you are diagnosed with active TB, you will probably be able to receive treatment at home unless you are very unwell. Your doctor will prescribe a combination of antituberculous drugs, which should be taken for at least 6 months. By using a combination of drugs, the development of bacterial resistance to antibiotics can be avoided. The drugs used will depend on the severity of the infection, the sensitivity and resistance of the bacteria to different antituberculous drugs, and whether the infection has spread to other areas of the body. TB affecting areas that drugs do not easily penetrate, such as bone, will generally need treatment for a longer period.

It is important that you take the full course of the drugs. If remembering to take them is a problem, ask your doctor about directly observed therapy, in which you are given your drugs regularly under medical supervision at a health center.

While you are undergoing treatment for TB, you will probably need to have chest X-rays and blood tests repeated on a regular basis to make sure that the infection is responding to treatment and to detect side effects of the drugs.

A vaccine against TB is available, but immunization is not routinely carried out in Canada. Immunization may be carried out in areas where the risk of contracting the disease is high.

WHAT IS THE PROGNOSIS?

Most people can make a full recovery from TB if antituberculous drugs are taken as directed. However, in people who have a type of TB resistant to two or more drugs, in those whose immunity is severely weakened, or in people with widespread TB, the disease may be fatal.

(WWW) ONLINE SITES: p.1033, p.1034

Pertussis

A bacterial infection, also called whooping cough, that causes bouts of coughing

AGE Can occur at any age but more common under age 5

GENDER GENETICS LIFESTYLE Not significant factors

Pertussis is a distressing and extremely infectious disease that is caused by the *Bordetella pertussis* bacterium, which infects and inflames the trachea (windpipe) and the bronchi (airways) in the lungs. The bacteria are transmitted in the airborne droplets that are produced when infected people cough and sneeze. Pertussis brings about violent fits of coughing that often end in a characteristic high-pitched "whoop" when the affected person inhales.

Pertussis is most serious in children under the age of 12 months, when the disease can be life-threatening. Before the introduction of a vaccine, pertussis alone was responsible for more childhood deaths in Canada than all the other infectious diseases combined. The incidence of pertussis has been greatly reduced by routine courses of childhood immunization.

WHAT ARE THE SYMPTOMS?

The first symptoms usually appear 2–3 weeks after infection. These symptoms are mild and resemble those of a common cold, typically a dry cough, runny nose, and sneezing. During this initial stage, which lasts about 7–14 days, the disease is highly infectious. Following this period, symptoms worsen and may include the following:

- Attacks of coughing followed by a sharp intake of breath that may produce a whooping sound. Bouts of coughing are often much worse during the night.
- Production of large amounts of sputum during coughing fits.
- Vomiting, which is caused by severe, repeated fits of coughing.

Episodes of prolonged coughing may cause small blood vessels to burst, resulting in a rash, especially around the face, hairline, and eyes. Nosebleeds may also occur if vessels in the nose burst.

Complications include pneumonia (p.490) and bronchiectasis (p.496), in which the airways become abnormally widened. Infants may stop breathing temporarily after a severe coughing spasm, and the resulting lack of oxygen may cause seizures and brain damage.

WHAT MIGHT BE DONE?

The doctor will probably be able to diagnose the condition in a child from the characteristic sound of the cough. However, in adults, symptoms may not be so obvious. The diagnosis can be confirmed by taking nose or throat swabs to look for pertussis bacteria under the microscope. Pertussis is normally treated with antibiotics (p.885). Antibiotics are effective in fighting the infection only when they are given early in its course. However, when given in the later stages, antibiotics are still useful because they ensure that infection cannot be passed to others. Seriously ill children need to be admitted to the hospital for monitoring, and they may be given oxygen therapy and intravenous fluids along with antibiotics. To prevent the infection from spreading further, antibiotics may be prescribed for people who have been in close contact with an infected person.

The symptoms of pertussis usually improve within 4–10 weeks if there are no complications, but a dry cough may persist for several months.

CAN IT BE PREVENTED?

The pertussis vaccine is usually given routinely in early childhood as part of the DTP (diphtheria, tetanus, and pertussis) triple vaccine (*see* VACCINES AND IMMUNOGLOBULINS, p.883).

Pertussis immunization may carry a very small risk of inflammation of the brain, and your doctor will advise you if he or she believes your child is at risk of developing this condition. It should be kept in mind that the disease itself presents a far greater risk than the risks of immunization. It is important that your child should receive the complete course of immunization, including the preschool dose.

(WWW) ONLINE SITES: p.1033, p.1034

Pleurisy

Inflammation of the pleura, the two-layered membrane separating the lungs from the chest wall

AGE GENDER GENETICS LIFESTYLE
Risk factors depend on the cause

Normally, when people breathe, the two layers of the pleura (the membrane that separates the lungs from the chest wall) slide over each other, allowing the lungs to inflate and deflate smoothly. In pleurisy, inflammation of the pleura prevents the layers from moving over each other easily, and they grate as they rub against each other, causing sharp, severe chest pain when inhaling.

WHAT ARE THE CAUSES?

Pleurisy may be caused by a viral illness, such as influenza (p.287), or tuberculosis (p.491). However, the disorder is often a reaction to damage to the lung just beneath the pleura. This lung damage may be due to pneumonia (p.490) or pulmonary embolism (p.495), in which the blood supply to part of the lung is blocked by a blood clot. The pleura can also be affected by primary lung cancer (p.503). Occasionally, an autoimmune disorder, such as rheumatoid arthritis (p.377) or systemic lupus erythematosus (p.461), in which the immune system attacks healthy tissues, affects the pleura and leads to pleurisy.

WHAT ARE THE SYMPTOMS?

If an infection or a pulmonary embolism is the cause of the inflammation, the symptoms usually develop rapidly over 24 hours. In other cases, the symptoms occur gradually. They may include:

- Sharp chest pain that causes you to catch your breath on inhaling.
- Feeling that it is difficult to breathe.

The pain is often restricted to the side of the chest affected by the underlying inflamed pleura. In some cases, fluid accumulates between the layers of the pleura (*see* PLEURAL EFFUSION, p.494). This condition may actually lessen the pain because it eases the movements of the pleural layers over each other.

WHAT MIGHT BE DONE?

If you suspect that you have pleurisy, you should consult your doctor within 24 hours. He or she may be able to hear the layers of the pleura rubbing against each other when listening to your chest with a stethoscope. You may need a chest X-ray (p.490) to check for a problem in the underlying lung or for the presence of a pleural effusion.

You may be prescribed nonsteroidal anti-inflammatory drugs (p.894) to relieve the pain and inflammation. You may also find that holding the affected side while coughing helps relieve the discomfort. In addition, you will probably need treatment for the underlying condition that is causing the pleurisy. For example, if a lung infection is the cause, you may be prescribed a course of antibiotics (p.885). If you have a pulmonary embolism, you will probably be given anticoagulant drugs (*see* DRUGS THAT PREVENT BLOOD CLOTTING, p.904). In the majority of affected people, the condition clears up within 7–10 days of the start of treatment.

(WWW) ONLINE SITES: p.1034

Pleural effusion

An accumulation of fluid between the layers of the pleura, the membrane that separates the lungs from the chest wall

AGE GENDER GENETICS LIFESTYLE
Risk factors depend on the cause

A pleural effusion occurs when fluid accumulates between the layers of the pleura, the two-layered membrane separating the lungs from the chest wall. As fluid accumulates, the lung underneath becomes compressed, gradually causing shortness of breath. In some cases, the amount of fluid accumulated may be as much as 4–6 pints (2–3 liters).

WHAT ARE THE CAUSES?

In most cases of pleural effusion, the pleura itself is inflamed and produces fluid (*see* PLEURISY, p.493). The inflammation may be due to a lung infection, such as pneumonia (p.490) or tuberculosis (p.491), or to other disorders that affect the lung, such as lung cancer (*see* PRIMARY LUNG CANCER, p.503). Less often, the cause may be an autoimmune disorder, such as rheumatoid arthritis (p.377) or systemic lupus erythematosus (p.461), in which the immune system attacks the body's own tissues.

In some cases, the pleura itself is not the cause of the effusion. Instead, fluid may leak into the space between the pleural layers as a result of a serious underlying disorder such as heart failure (*see* ACUTE HEART FAILURE, p.412, and CHRONIC HEART FAILURE, p.413). In these cases, a pleural effusion is often associated with the accumulation of fluid elsewhere in the body, which may be responsible for swelling in areas such as the ankles or abdomen.

A pleural effusion that produces little fluid may not cause symptoms. In severe cases, compression of the lungs due to the presence of a large amount of fluid between the pleural layers may result in shortness of breath.

WHAT MIGHT BE DONE?

Your doctor may be able to detect a pleural effusion while examining your chest. You may also have a chest X-ray (p.490) to confirm the diagnosis and to assess the severity of the effusion. In order to identify the underlying cause, your doctor may take a sample of fluid by inserting a needle through the chest wall under local anesthesia. A sample of the pleura may also be removed. The sample is examined under a microscope to look for evidence of infection or cancer. A sample of blood may be taken for testing to exclude other problems, such as kidney disorders.

Shortness of breath due to a severe pleural effusion may be relieved by removing some of the fluid through a tube inserted into the chest under local anesthesia. Your doctor may prescribe antibiotics (p.885) if a bacterial infection is the cause of the effusion. Diuretic drugs (p.902) may be given to reduce the volume of fluid in the body. An effusion

(TEST) RADIONUCLIDE LUNG SCANNING

Radionuclide lung scanning is used to diagnose pulmonary embolism. It involves two scans that are performed simultaneously: one to assess blood flow through the lungs and the other, which is called a ventilation scan, to assess airflow. A diagnosis can be made by comparing the ventilation scan and the blood flow scan because many lung disorders disrupt the flow of both blood and air in a specific area, whereas a pulmonary embolism disrupts only blood flow. The procedure usually takes about 20 minutes to perform.

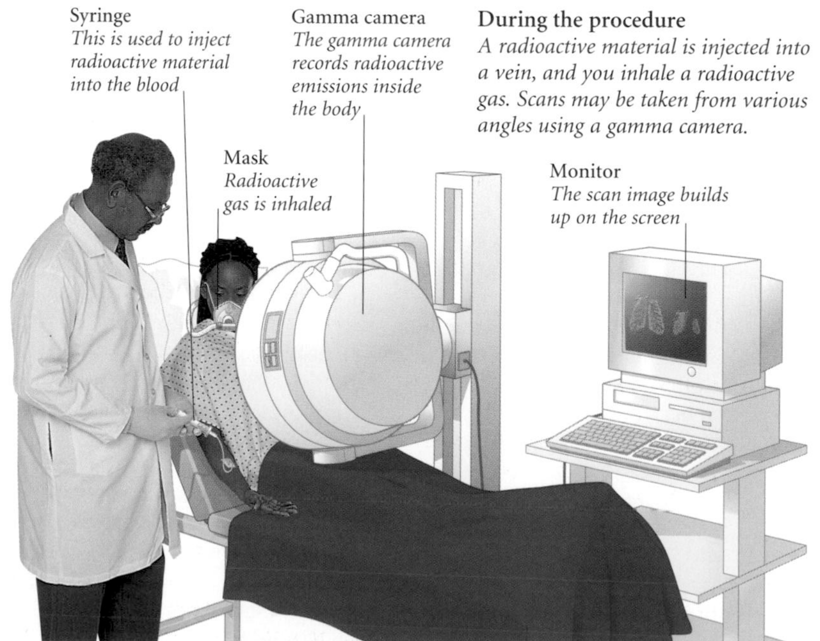
Syringe
This is used to inject radioactive material into the blood
Gamma camera
The gamma camera records radioactive emissions inside the body
Mask
Radioactive gas is inhaled
Monitor
The scan image builds up on the screen

During the procedure
A radioactive material is injected into a vein, and you inhale a radioactive gas. Scans may be taken from various angles using a gamma camera.

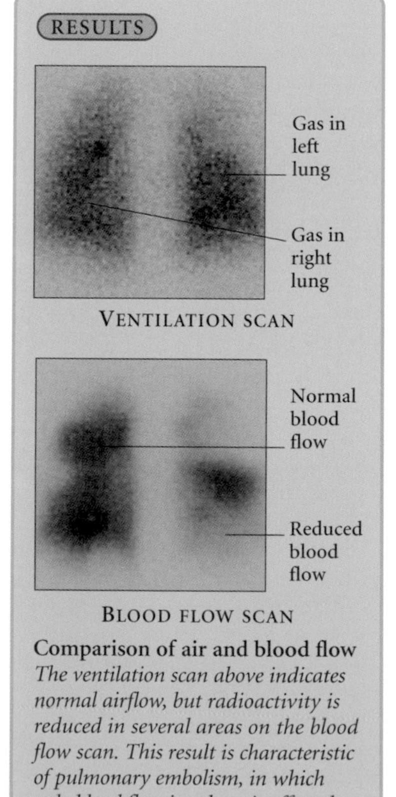
RESULTS
Gas in left lung
Gas in right lung
VENTILATION SCAN
Normal blood flow
Reduced blood flow
BLOOD FLOW SCAN

Comparison of air and blood flow
The ventilation scan above indicates normal airflow, but radioactivity is reduced in several areas on the blood flow scan. This result is characteristic of pulmonary embolism, in which only blood flow in a lung is affected.

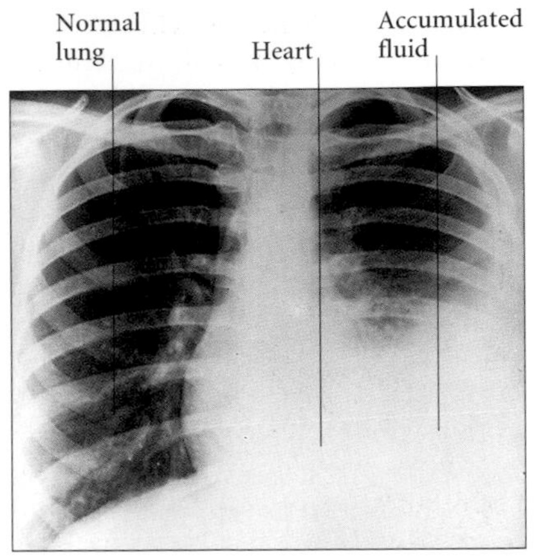
Normal lung
Heart
Accumulated fluid

Pleural effusion
In this X-ray, the left lung (on the right of the image) is partly obscured by the accumulated fluid of a pleural effusion.

associated with cancer may be treated by radiation therapy (p.279) or by chemotherapy (p.278), in which anticancer drugs are injected between the two layers of the pleura. In most cases, excess fluid slowly disappears once the underlying cause has been treated.

In some people, particularly those who have lung cancer, pleural effusion may recur. If the effusion does recur, a chemical can be injected into the chest cavity to make the two layers of the pleura stick together.

WWW ONLINE SITES: p.1034

Pulmonary embolism

Obstruction of the blood flow to the lungs by one or more blood clots

 AGE Rare in children

 GENDER More common in females

 GENETICS Sometimes runs in families

 LIFESTYLE Smoking, using oral contraceptives, and long periods of immobility are risk factors

In pulmonary embolism, a piece of a blood clot (embolus) becomes lodged in an artery in the lungs and partially or completely blocks blood flow in the affected area. Usually, the clot has broken off from a larger clot in the veins of the legs or the pelvic region (*see* DEEP VEIN THROMBOSIS, p.437) and traveled to the lungs in the bloodstream. Pulmonary embolism may be mild if the blocked artery is small, but blockage of a major artery may suddenly cause severe symptoms and can be fatal. Rarely, small clots can block numerous small arteries in the lungs over months or years, and symptoms may not appear for some time. This condition is called recurrent pulmonary embolism.

Pulmonary embolism is most likely to occur in people who have developed deep vein thrombosis as a result of a period of immobility, such as that following childbirth or surgery (especially repair of fractures or pelvic surgery) or rarely during a long trip. A tendency to develop blood clots (*see* HYPERCOAGULABILITY, p.453) increases the risk of deep vein thrombosis, as does smoking and taking oral contraceptives.

WHAT ARE THE SYMPTOMS?

The symptoms depend on the extent of blockage to the blood flow. Massive pulmonary embolism, in which a large blood clot blocks a major pulmonary artery, may cause sudden death with no warning. Single small clots sometimes produce no symptoms. However, in most cases symptoms develop over only a few minutes and may include:

- Shortness of breath.
- Sharp chest pain that is often much worse when inhaling.
- Coughing up blood.
- Feeling faint.
- Palpitations.

In recurrent pulmonary embolism, the only symptom may be shortness of breath that worsens over months. Eventually, so many blood vessels may be blocked that pressure in the pulmonary arteries is increased (*see* PULMONARY HYPERTENSION, p.505). Chronic heart failure (p.413) may then develop.

HOW IS IT DIAGNOSED?

If your doctor suspects that you have pulmonary embolism, you will be admitted to the hospital as an emergency. You may have tests to measure the levels of oxygen and carbon dioxide in your blood (*see* MEASURING BLOOD GASES, p.501). You may also have a chest X-ray (p.490) to exclude other lung conditions and radionuclide lung scanning (opposite page) to look at the blood flow in the lungs. The blood flow in veins in your legs may be measured by using Doppler ultrasound scanning (p.432). If the diagnosis is not clear, you may have a contrast X-ray to image the blood vessels in the lungs in order to pinpoint the exact location of blockages and confirm the diagnosis. Blood tests may be carried out to check if you have a clotting disorder.

WHAT IS THE TREATMENT?

Treatment depends on the severity of the blockage. You may have a continuous intravenous infusion or injections of heparin, an anticoagulant drug that acts immediately to prevent the existing clots from enlarging and new clots from developing (*see* DRUGS THAT PREVENT BLOOD CLOTTING, p.904). At the same time, you may be started on an oral anticoagulant drug, such as warfarin, which also prevents further clotting by thinning the blood but takes a few days to have an effect. Anticoagulant drug treatment may last for 3–6 months if pulmonary embolism followed a single period of immobility. If the embolism is due to a long-term condition, such as hypercoagulability, you may need drug treatment indefinitely. Treatment is usually monitored with regular blood tests to check your blood clotting, and the drug dosage is altered as necessary.

In severe cases, thrombolytic drugs (p.904) may be used to dissolve the clot. If the main artery to the lungs is affected, emergency surgery to remove the clot may be life-saving. If clots recur despite anticoagulant drug therapy, you may have surgery in which a filter to trap blood clots is placed in the main vein that leads from the lower half of the body to the heart.

WHAT IS THE PROGNOSIS?

Massive pulmonary embolism is fatal in about 1 in 3 cases. However, if you survive the first few days, you are likely to make a full recovery. People who have recurrent pulmonary embolism may remain short of breath.

If you have already had pulmonary embolism, you have a higher than average risk of further episodes and should avoid periods of prolonged immobility, such as sitting down continually during a long trip. You may also need to have preventive treatment, such as heparin injections, following an operation that may require a period of immobility.

WWW ONLINE SITES: p.1034

Bronchiectasis

Abnormal widening of the larger airways in the lungs (bronchi), causing a persistent cough with large amounts of sputum

AGE May begin in childhood but may not become apparent until after age 40

GENETICS In some cases, the underlying cause is inherited

GENDER LIFESTYLE Not significant factors

In bronchiectasis, the larger branches of the airways in the lungs (the bronchi) become abnormally wide, and their lining is damaged. Bronchiectasis usually starts in childhood as a result of a lung infection, but the symptoms of the condition may not develop until after age 40. The main symptoms are a chronic cough with large amounts of sputum and increasing shortness of breath. The disorder was once fairly common, but it is now rare in the developed world due to the greatly reduced incidence of childhood lung infections.

What are the causes?

Childhood infections such as whooping cough (*see* PERTUSSIS, p.492) and measles (p.291) were once very common causes of bronchiectasis. Today, the main cause is repeated bacterial infections of the lungs in people with the inherited condition cystic fibrosis (p.824), in which the mucus produced by the lining of the airways is thicker than normal and tends to collect in the lungs. The repeated infections damage the bronchi, which become distorted so that small pockets form in the tissue. Stagnant mucus then builds up in the pockets, where it may become infected. Bronchiectasis that is confined to one area of the lung may develop as a result of a blockage in one of the bronchi. The blockage may be due to an inhaled foreign body, such as a peanut.

What are the symptoms?

The symptoms of bronchiectasis gradually worsen over a period of several months or years and may include:

- A persistent cough that produces very large quantities of dark green or yellow sputum. The cough is often worse when lying down.
- Coughing up blood.
- Bad breath.

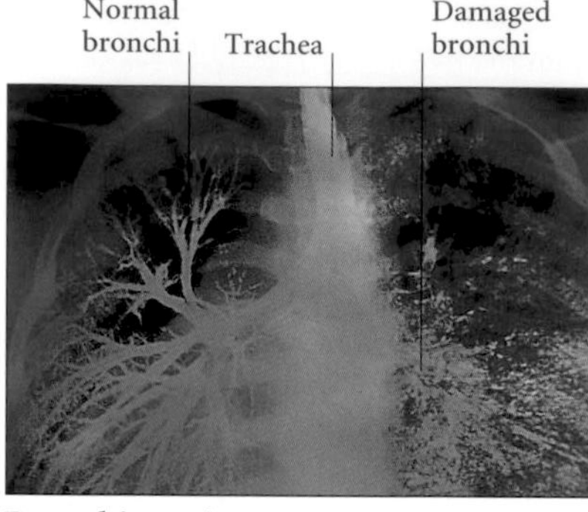
Normal bronchi
Trachea
Damaged bronchi

Bronchiectasis
In this specialized X-ray, obtained using radiopaque dye to visualize the airways, the bronchi (large airways) seen on the right have become damaged and distorted.

- Wheezing and shortness of breath.
- Enlarged fingertips with abnormal fingernails, known as clubbing (*see* NAIL ABNORMALITIES, p.360).

Eventually, an affected person will experience the effects of long-term infection, such as weight loss and anemia (p.446). Bronchiectasis may affect an increasing number of bronchi, causing extensive damage to a large area of the lung tissue, and may finally lead to respiratory failure (p.507).

How is it diagnosed?

Your doctor may suspect that you have bronchiectasis from the large amount of sputum that you cough up. Your sputum may be tested in order to identify an infection, and you may also have a chest X-ray (p.490) and lung function tests (p.488). CT scanning (p.247) may be used to assess airway damage.

What might be done?

If you have bronchiectasis, you should not smoke, and you should avoid smoke and dust. A family member or friend may be taught how to give you chest physiotherapy (p.962), which ideally should be carried out on a daily basis. This technique helps mucus drain from the lungs. It involves lying on a bed or other flat surface with your head and chest hanging over the edge so that mucus can drain into your windpipe, while your relative or friend taps your back with cupped hands to free the mucus in your lungs. Keeping the lungs as clear of mucus as possible reduces the risk of infections that may cause further lung damage.

You may be given inhaled bronchodilator drugs (p.910) to help you breathe more easily. If an infection develops, it will be treated with antibiotics (p.885). Surgery to remove a single affected area of the lung may cure the condition. In severe cases, a heart and lung transplant may be considered.

(WWW) ONLINE SITES: p.1034

Pneumothorax

Presence of air between the layers of the pleura, the two-layered membrane that separates the lungs from the chest wall

AGE Most common in young people

GENDER Much more common in males

GENETICS Sometimes runs in families

LIFESTYLE Not a significant factor

In a pneumothorax, air enters between the two layers of the pleura, the membrane that separates the lungs from the chest wall. A pneumothorax may cause the lung beneath it to collapse, which can then lead to chest pain and shortness of breath. The air that causes a pneumothorax can come from within the lungs or outside the body, depending on the cause. The condition often affects only one side of the chest.

The amount of air between the layers of the pleura may be small, and in such cases breathing is not severely affected.

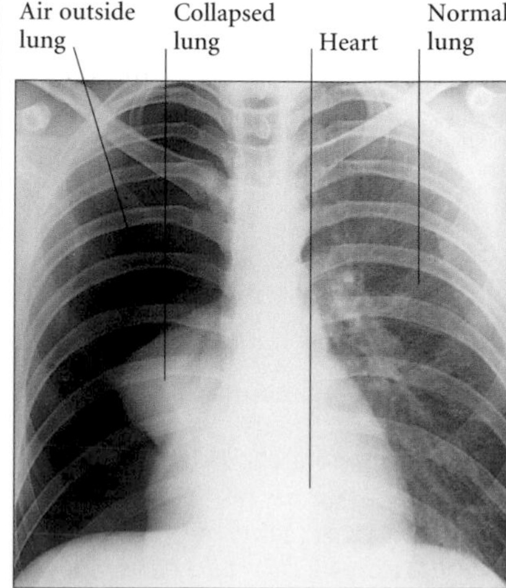
Air outside lung
Collapsed lung
Heart
Normal lung

Pneumothorax
A large volume of trapped air can be seen on the left side of this X-ray image. It has caused the lung beneath it to collapse.

CHEST TUBE

A chest tube is used to treat a pneumothorax, in which air enters between the layers of the pleura (the membrane that separates the lungs from the chest wall). It may also be needed following chest surgery. The tube is inserted between the layers of the pleura, allowing air to escape. The tube may be connected to a pump that extracts the air. A chest tube must remain in place until the lung heals, which often takes at least 2 days.

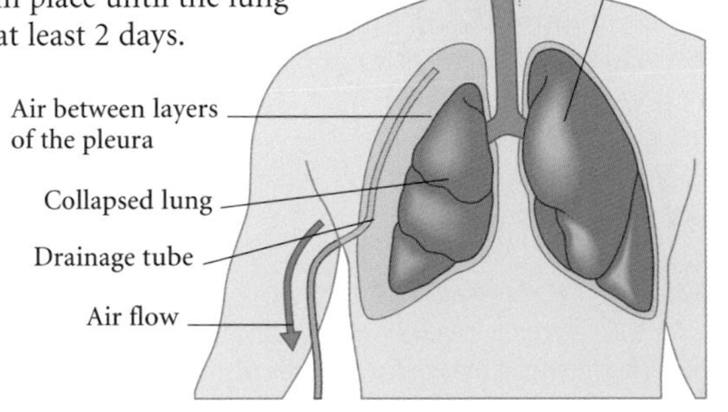
Normal lung
Air between layers of the pleura
Collapsed lung
Drainage tube
Air flow

Insertion of a chest tube
Under local anesthesia, an incision is made in the chest wall. The chest tube is then inserted through the incision. It may have a one-way valve to control airflow.

However, a large pneumothorax may cause severe shortness of breath. In a tension pneumothorax, air that enters between the layers of the pleura cannot get back out and causes the pressure inside the pleural layers to rise. This condition also causes severe shortness of breath and can be fatal. It requires immediate medical treatment.

WHAT ARE THE CAUSES?

In most cases, the cause of a pneumothorax is the spontaneous rupture of an abnormally dilated alveolus (air sac), known as a bulla, on the surface of the lung. Most bullae are present from birth. Rupture of a bulla is often caused by doing vigorous exercise but can sometimes occur at rest. A pneumothorax due to the rupture of a bulla occurs most frequently in tall, thin young men.

A pneumothorax may develop as a complication of lung disorders such as asthma (p.483) and chronic obstructive pulmonary disease (p.487). Repeated pneumothoraces may be associated with Marfan syndrome (p.824), a rare inherited disorder that affects connective tissue and results in abnormalities of the skeleton, heart, and eyes.

Other possible causes of a pneumothorax include a penetrating chest wound that allows air to enter between the layers of the pleura from outside the body, fractured ribs that tear the lung beneath them, or surgical procedures performed on the chest.

WHAT ARE THE SYMPTOMS?

Symptoms of a pneumothorax usually develop rapidly and may include:

- Chest pain, which may be felt as sudden and sharp or may cause only slight discomfort.
- Shortness of breath or a sudden worsening of preexisting shortness of breath in someone with a long-term respiratory disorder.
- Tightness across the chest.

In a tension pneumothorax, there is severe pain and shortness of breath. The high pressure caused by a tension pneumothorax prevents blood from returning to the heart from the lungs, which in turn causes low blood pressure, fainting, and shock (p.414).

WHAT MIGHT BE DONE?

If your doctor suspects that you have a pneumothorax, a chest X-ray (p.490) will be done to confirm the diagnosis. A small pneumothorax will usually disappear over the course of a few days as the leak that created it heals and the air is gradually absorbed by the body. If the pneumothorax is larger or an underlying lung disorder is involved, you may need hospital treatment. A drainage tube may be inserted through the chest wall under local anesthesia to enable air to escape (*see* CHEST TUBE, above).

A tension pneumothorax is a medical emergency. It is treated by inserting a large, hollow needle directly into the affected side of the chest to allow air to escape. This procedure provides immediate relief of symptoms.

If an air leak persists or returns, a technique known as pleurodesis may be used to prevent further lung collapse. This procedure involves introducing a chemical between the two layers of the pleura through a chest tube. The chemical causes widespread inflammation of the pleura and makes the layers of the pleural membrane stick to each other. However, pleurodesis is not always successful. If it fails, surgery may be needed to repair the damaged area or in rare cases to obliterate the pleural space. With treatment, most people who have had a pneumothorax recover completely.

(WWW) ONLINE SITES: p.1034

Interstitial fibrosis

Progressive thickening of the walls of the air sacs of the lungs, resulting in shortness of breath

 AGE Usually occurs after age 40 but is most common over age 60

 GENDER Twice as common in males

 GENETICS LIFESTYLE Not significant factors

Inflammation and thickening of the walls of the alveoli (air sacs) in the lungs is called interstitial fibrosis. As a result of this condition, it is difficult for oxygen to pass into the bloodstream, and the level of oxygen in the blood falls. In addition, the alveoli begin to lose their elasticity, causing shortness of breath.

Usually, interstitial fibrosis is chronic, developing over months or years. Rarely, an acute form develops over a few days or weeks. Both forms usually become progressively worse and are difficult to treat successfully. The disorder is most common in people over age 60 and is more common in men than in women.

WHAT ARE THE CAUSES?

In some cases, interstitial fibrosis is the result of an autoimmune disorder, in which the immune system attacks the body's own healthy tissues. For example, the condition may be associated with rheumatoid arthritis (p.377) or systemic lupus erythematosus (p.461). Other causes include radiation therapy (p.279) of organs in the chest and certain drugs that are used to treat cancer (*see* CHEMOTHERAPY, p.278). However, in about half of all cases, no cause can be found, and the condition is then known as idiopathic pulmonary fibrosis.

WHAT ARE THE SYMPTOMS?

In the chronic form of interstitial fibrosis, the symptoms gradually become worse over months or years, whereas in the acute form symptoms worsen over a few days. In either case, symptoms may include the following:

- Shortness of breath.
- Persistent, dry cough.
- Joint pains.

As the condition progresses, breathing becomes increasingly difficult, especially during vigorous exercise, and the nails often become abnormally shaped. In severe cases, there is a risk of respiratory failure (p.507) and chronic heart failure (p.413). Some people with the disorder are more susceptible to lung cancer (*see* PRIMARY LUNG CANCER, p.503).

HOW IS IT DIAGNOSED?

Your doctor may suspect that you have interstitial fibrosis from your symptoms and medical history and from listening to your chest with a stethoscope. You may have a chest X-ray (p.490) or CT scanning (p.247) to look for thickened lung tissue. Your doctor may also arrange for you to have a blood test to check the levels of oxygen and carbon dioxide in your blood (*see* MEASURING BLOOD GASES, p.501) and lung function tests (p.488) to see how well your lungs are working. The diagnosis may be confirmed by examining a piece of lung tissue, which can be obtained during a bronchoscopy (p.504) or surgery.

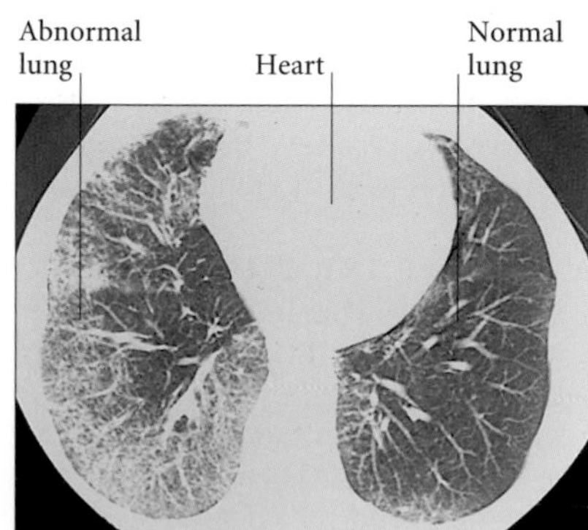
Abnormal lung
Heart
Normal lung

Interstitial fibrosis
In this horizontal CT scan through the chest, the lung on the left shows multiple areas of thickening within the lung tissue.

WHAT IS THE TREATMENT?

Sometimes, interstitial fibrosis remains stable for months or years and does not need treatment. In this case, it will be monitored regularly. If it is progressing, high-dose corticosteroids (*see* CORTICOSTEROIDS FOR RESPIRATORY DISEASE, p.911), combined with other immunosuppressant drugs (p.906), may be used to suppress the immune system and slow the progress of the lung damage. These drug treatments are effective in only about 1 in 4 cases. A lung transplant may be recommended for some people. Home oxygen therapy (p.507) may help breathing.

WHAT IS THE PROGNOSIS?

Interstitial fibrosis usually progresses, making breathing increasingly difficult. Only about half of those with the condition survive longer than 5 years. For some people, a lung transplant may be life-saving. About 1 in 10 people with the condition develops lung cancer.

(WWW) ONLINE SITES: p.1034

Sarcoidosis

Inflammation of tissue in one or many parts of the body, most often affecting the lungs, lymph nodes, skin, and eyes

 AGE Most common in young adults

 GENDER More common in females

 GENETICS Sometimes runs in families; more common in African–Americans

 LIFESTYLE Not a significant factor

In sarcoidosis, multiple areas of inflammation develop in or on the body, frequently in the lungs. Sometimes, only a single type of tissue is affected. In other cases, the condition may affect several different organs at the same time. Sarcoidosis is thought to be caused by an abnormal, exaggerated response of the immune system. The trigger for this response is not fully understood, but it is thought that the cause may be an infection.

Sarcoidosis may not produce symptoms. If symptoms do develop, they either appear suddenly over a few days (acute sarcoidosis) or progress slowly over several years (chronic sarcoidosis). There is no cure for sarcoidosis, but symptoms usually disappear spontaneously. The disorder, especially in its acute form, is five times more common in women than in men. In addition, sarcoidois sometimes runs in families.

WHAT ARE THE SYMPTOMS?

Some people who have sarcoidosis never develop symptoms. However, in acute sarcoidosis, there may be symptoms, which include the following:

- Cough.
- Fever and excessive sweating at night.
- Weight loss.
- Fatigue.
- Pain in the joints.
- Painful red lesions on the shins (*see* ERYTHEMA NODOSUM, p.348).

People who have chronic sarcoidosis may initially experience no symptoms but gradually develop:

- Increasing shortness of breath.
- Cough.

Both acute and chronic sarcoidosis may cause redness of the eyes, blurry vision (*see* UVEITIS, p.574), and skin lesions on the nose and face. Sarcoidosis may also cause high levels of calcium in the blood and/or urine, which may result in nausea and constipation and eventually lead to kidney damage.

HOW IS IT DIAGNOSED?

If there are no symptoms, chronic sarcoidosis is usually discovered only after a chest X-ray (p.490) has been taken for another reason. Sarcoidosis may also be diagnosed by an X-ray taken to investigate symptoms such as weight loss or fever. The X-ray usually shows swollen lymph nodes in the chest or shadows on the lungs. Sarcoidosis may also be diagnosed by the presence of skin lesions. The diagnosis may be confirmed by an examination of affected tissue, usually from a skin sample or cells taken from the lung during bronchoscopy (p.504). In addition, you may have lung function tests (p.488) and blood tests to measure your calcium levels.

WHAT IS THE TREATMENT?

There is no cure for sarcoidosis, but your symptoms may be treated with corticosteroids (*see* CORTICOSTEROIDS FOR RESPIRATORY DISEASE, p.911). These drugs are usually effective, although you may need low-dose treatment for several years if you have chronic sarcoidosis.

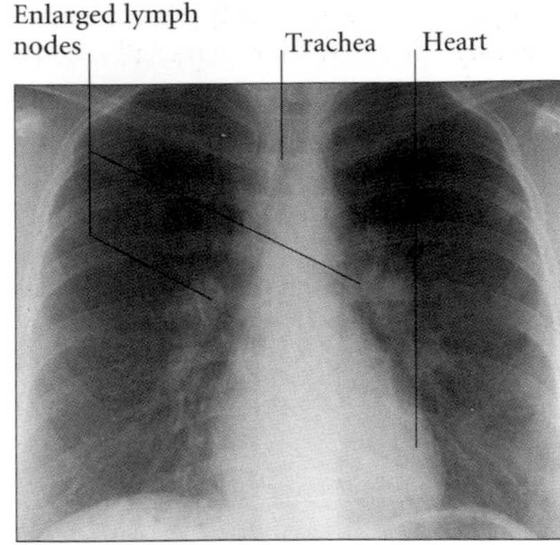
Enlarged lymph nodes
Trachea
Heart

Sarcoidosis
This chest X-ray shows enlarged lymph nodes due to sarcoidosis, a disorder causing inflammation of various body tissues.

Oral corticosteroids (p.930) may be used for serious complications such as uveitis. You may need regular blood tests, chest X-rays, and lung function tests to monitor your response to treatment.

WHAT IS THE PROGNOSIS?

In about 8 in 10 people, most commonly those with acute sarcoidosis, the disorder clears up spontaneously within 3 years. In a further 1 in 10 cases, it does not progress. Only 1 in 10 people has progressive disease, but sarcoidosis is fatal in only 2 in 100 people.

(WWW) ONLINE SITES: p.1034

Occupational lung diseases

A variety of disorders caused by inhaling damaging dusts or gases at work

 AGE More common over age 40

 GENDER More common in males due to increased risk of occupational exposure

 LIFESTYLE Smoking causes some disorders to progress more quickly

 GENETICS Not a significant factor

In developed countries, the number of cases of most occupational lung diseases is decreasing. This is partly due to the improved measures now used to protect workers, such as masks and protective clothing. In addition, regulations are in place that limit the maximum exposure levels for inhaled substances. A decline in the number of workers in industries such as mining in developed countries has also led to a reduction in occupational lung diseases. However, the diseases are still common in developing countries where workers are less likely to have adequate protection.

Occupational lung diseases are initiated by the body's reaction to small solid particles or gases that are breathed into the lungs while a person is in the workplace. The nature of the lung disorder depends on the type and amount of particles that are inhaled.

WHAT ARE THE TYPES?

Occupational lung diseases associated with mineral dusts include coalworkers' pneumoconiosis (right), silicosis (p.500), and asbestosis (*see* ASBESTOS-RELATED DISEASES, p.501). In the most severe cases, these disorders can result in irreversible scarring of lung tissue. Asbestos can also cause thickening of the pleura (the two-layered membrane that separates the lungs from the chest wall) and mesothelioma, a form of cancer that affects the pleura. Silicosis and coalworkers' pneumoconiosis are rare in developed countries. However, the incidence of mesothelioma is still increasing because it takes many years for symptoms to develop. Workers who have been exposed to asbestos before the introduction of safer working practices are still at risk of developing the disease at a later date.

Exposure to certain biological dusts, spores, and chemicals may induce allergic reactions, causing inflammation of the alveoli (air sacs) inside the lungs (*see* HYPERSENSITIVITY PNEUMONITIS, p.502) or asthma (p.483). Although occupational asthma has probably been occurring for centuries, doctors have only recently begun to recognize the extent of the disorder. There is a growing list of substances known to trigger asthma and an increasing number of reported cases each year.

WHAT MIGHT BE DONE?

If you have respiratory symptoms, such as shortness of breath or chronic cough, you should consult your doctor. Tell the doctor if your past or current occupation has involved working with dust or other irritants that could be causing your symptoms. He or she may arrange for you to have a chest X-ray (p.490) and lung function tests (p.488) to look for evidence of lung damage.

It is vital that you avoid the substance that is causing your symptoms. If this is not possible, you may have to consider changing your occupation to prevent a deterioration in your condition.

If your doctor thinks that you have occupational asthma, he or she will need to identify a specific trigger substance and confirm its presence in your workplace. Apart from avoiding the triggers, occupational asthma is usually managed using drug treatment in the same way as other forms of asthma.

(WWW) ONLINE SITES: p.1034, p.1036

Coalworkers' pneumoconiosis

Scarring of the lung tissue caused by long-term exposure to coal dust, also known as black lung

 AGE More common over age 40

 GENDER More common in males due to increased risk of occupational exposure

 LIFESTYLE Caused by exposure to coal dust; smoking aggravates the disease

 GENETICS Not a significant factor

Coalworkers' pneumoconiosis is a serious lung disorder caused by inhaling coal dust. The dust causes a gradual buildup of scar tissue in the lungs over many years, which leads to progressive and disabling shortness of breath. The severity of the condition depends on the degree to which a person has been exposed to coal dust. Pneumoconiosis was once a common disease in coal-mining areas. However, the decline of the coal industry and improved safety practices have made it increasingly rare in developed countries.

WHAT ARE THE CAUSES?

In pneumoconiosis, minute particles of coal dust are inhaled into the lungs, where they reach the alveoli (air sacs). Over many years of exposure, the dust causes irritation of the lung tissue. This form of the disorder is known as simple pneumoconiosis. Continuing exposure to the dust results in a serious complication known as progressive massive fibrosis (PMF). In this condition, lung

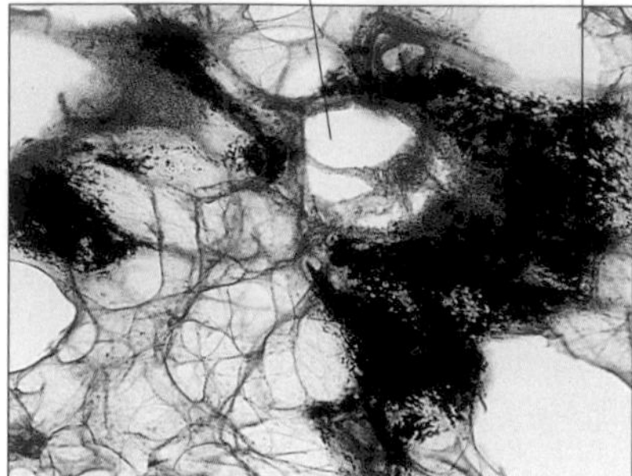
Air sac
Coal dust deposit

Coalworkers' pneumoconiosis
This magnified view of lung tissue shows black deposits of coal dust in and around the alveoli (air sacs). Eventually, the coal dust deposits cause scarring of lung tissue.

tissue becomes heavily scarred. The disorder is likely to be worse if the coal dust contains a high level of silica (*see* SILICOSIS, right). Smoking causes the condition to progress more rapidly.

WHAT ARE THE SYMPTOMS?

Simple pneumoconiosis initially produces no symptoms. Later symptoms of simple pneumoconiosis and PMF include the following:

- Coughing up black sputum.
- Shortness of breath on exertion that becomes progressively worse.

People with simple pneumoconiosis or PMF are also more susceptible to many other lung disorders, including chronic bronchitis (*see* CHRONIC OBSTRUCTIVE PULMONARY DISEASE, p.487) and tuberculosis (p.491). Coalworkers who also have rheumatoid arthritis (p.377) may develop Caplan syndrome, in which inflamed nodules form in the lungs.

As simple pneumoconiosis or PMF progresses, breathing difficulties may become so severe that respiratory failure (p.507) develops.

HOW IS IT DIAGNOSED?

Your doctor will probably base the diagnosis on your occupational history and symptoms. He or she may arrange for a chest X-ray (p.490) and lung function tests (p.488) to confirm the diagnosis and assess existing damage to the lungs. You will probably also have tests that measure the levels of oxygen and carbon dioxide in your blood (*see* MEASURING BLOOD GASES, opposite page). These tests show how effectively oxygen from your lungs is reaching the bloodstream.

WHAT IS THE TREATMENT?

You should not smoke and should avoid further exposure to coal dust as far as possible. If you have simple pneumoconiosis and are no longer exposed to the dust, no treatment is necessary because the disease will not progress. If you have PMF, the symptoms may get worse even after exposure to the dust has stopped. Although there is no complete cure for PMF, your doctor may prescribe bronchodilator drugs (p.910) and oxygen therapy (*see* HOME OXYGEN THERAPY, p.507) to help relieve your symptoms. You may also need to have chest physiotherapy (p.962) regularly to help remove mucus from the airways, and a friend or member of the family may be taught how to do this.

CAN IT BE PREVENTED?

In most developed countries, there are regulations governing the coal-mining industry that require adequate ventilation in the workplace and other safety measures. Appropriate face masks and equipment to control dust may also be needed for people who work underground. Workers exposed to coal dust should have a chest X-ray every few years to detect the presence of simple pneumoconiosis before PMF develops.

(WWW) ONLINE SITES: p.1034, p.1036

Silicosis

Scarring of the lung tissue caused by inhaling dust containing silica

 AGE More common over age 40

 GENDER More common in males due to increased risk of occupational exposure

 LIFESTYLE Caused by exposure to silica dust; smoking aggravates the disease

 GENETICS Not a significant factor

Once common in developed countries, silicosis is a disorder that leads to irreversible lung damage. It tends to affect people who work with sandstone, granite, slate, and coal, as well as potters, foundry workers, and sandblasters. Silicosis affects millions of workers worldwide, and remains an important occupational health hazard.

Most people with silicosis have the chronic form of the disease, which usually develops following 20–30 years of exposure to silica dust. The acute form of silicosis, which tends to develop suddenly after only a few months' exposure to a high level of silica dust, can lead to death in less than a year.

Unlike most other dust particles that are breathed into the lungs, silica dust causes a strong inflammatory response in lung tissue. Over time, the inflammation causes thickening and scarring, and the lungs become less efficient in supplying oxygen to the blood. Symptoms of silicosis may be more severe and the condition may progress more rapidly in people who smoke.

WHAT ARE THE SYMPTOMS?

The symptoms of chronic and acute silicosis are the same but develop over different time periods. They include:

- Coughing up sputum.
- Shortness of breath on exertion.
- Tightness of the chest.

A complication of both forms of silicosis is an increased susceptibility to tuberculosis (p.491). Even without further exposure to silica dust, silicosis may progress and may eventually lead to respiratory failure (p.507).

WHAT MIGHT BE DONE?

You should tell your doctor if your past or current occupation has involved handling materials that produce silica dust. He or she will probably arrange for a chest X-ray (p.490) and for lung function tests (p.488) to assess the level of damage to the lungs. There is no treatment for silicosis, but avoiding further exposure to the dust may slow the progress of the disease. If you have silicosis, you should not smoke, and, if you cannot avoid exposure to silica dust at work, your doctor may advise you to change your job. If you have severe silicosis, you may receive home oxygen therapy (p.507) to ease your breathing.

CAN IT BE PREVENTED?

If you think that you are at risk from silicosis, you should discuss the matter with your doctor and your employer. It is very important that you and your employer take immediate measures to decrease the amount of silica dust that you may inhale. Appropriate ventilation, dust-control facilities, face masks, and showers should all be used.

(WWW) ONLINE SITES: p.1034, p.1036

Asbestos-related diseases

Serious lung disorders that develop as a result of inhaling asbestos fibers many years earlier

 AGE Rare under age 40; more common with increasing age

 GENDER More common in males due to increased risk of occupational exposure

 LIFESTYLE Caused by exposure to asbestos in the workplace or at home

 GENETICS Not a significant factor

Asbestos is a fibrous mineral that can cause serious lung damage if inhaled. Inhaling even very small numbers of asbestos fibers can lead to problems decades later, but those with the heaviest exposure are at greatest risk. The damage caused by inhaling asbestos fibers is irreversible, and preventing exposure to the dust is very important. The families of people who are exposed to asbestos at work may also be at risk of developing asbestos-related diseases because fibers from the workplace may be brought into the home on clothing.

The use of asbestos has declined over the past 25 years. However, there is a time lag of up to 50 years between first exposure to asbestos and the development of lung disease, with the result that, despite the recent introduction of safe working practices, the number of people with asbestos-related diseases is continuing to rise.

What is the cause?

Asbestos fibers are needle-shaped. They are therefore drawn deep into the lungs when inhaled, where they can penetrate the lung tissue. The asbestos fibers then trigger a reaction from the defensive white blood cells in the lungs, which try to engulf the fibers. However, the fibers usually destroy the white blood cells, and inflammation and eventual scarring of lung tissue may follow.

Asbestos fibers are divided into three main types: white, blue, and brown, all of which are dangerous. White asbestos is the type most commonly used for commercial purposes. Blue and brown asbestos fibers are less common, but they are particularly dangerous and are the most likely to trigger the development of asbestos-related diseases.

What are the types?

The inhalation of asbestos fibers can result in three different types of disease: asbestosis, diffuse pleural thickening (in which the pleura, the membrane that separates the lungs from the chest wall, becomes abnormally thickened), and mesothelioma, a cancerous tumor of the pleura. Often, more than one type of asbestos-related disease occurs at the same time in one person.

ASBESTOSIS In this condition, widespread fine scarring occurs in the lung tissue. The disease may progress even when exposure to asbestos is discontinued. Asbestosis tends to develop among people who have been heavily exposed to asbestos, such as asbestos miners, people who work in asbestos factories, and workers who regularly handle insulation materials that contain asbestos.

The period of time from first exposure to asbestos until development of symptoms is usually at least 20 years and often longer. The main symptom is increasing shortness of breath on exertion, which may eventually become disabling. Other symptoms include a dry cough, an abnormality in the shape of the fingernails known as clubbing (*see* NAIL ABNORMALITIES, p.360), and a bluish tinge to the complexion that is due to too little oxygen in the blood.

DIFFUSE PLEURAL THICKENING Pleural thickening may develop after only a brief exposure to asbestos. Usually, the condition produces no obvious symptoms and is detected only if a chest X-ray (p.490) is done for another reason. However, in some cases, pleural thickening is severe and widespread, and the ability of the lungs to expand is restricted, causing shortness of breath.

MESOTHELIOMA This disorder is a cancerous tumor of the pleura or less often of the peritoneum (the thin membrane that lines the abdominal cavity). Mesotheliomas most commonly result from working with blue or brown asbestos. It may be 30–50 years from the initial exposure until symptoms first appear.

TEST Measuring blood gases

Measuring the levels of oxygen and carbon dioxide in the blood helps in the diagnosis and monitoring of many lung disorders. To measure these gases, a blood sample is taken from an artery, usually in the wrist. This test also measures blood acidity (pH), which may be abnormal in conditions such as diabetes mellitus and in some forms of poisoning. Oxygen levels in the blood can also be measured continuously using a pulse oximeter, which detects changes in the amount of light that blood absorbs.

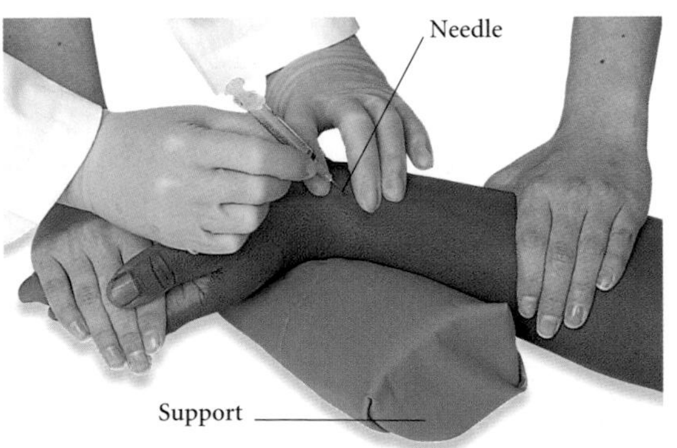
Needle
Support

Taking blood
To obtain a blood sample, the skin is cleaned and local anesthesia may be given before the blood is withdrawn from an artery with a needle and syringe. The procedure may be uncomfortable, but it is quick. Pressure must be applied for a few minutes afterward to prevent bleeding.

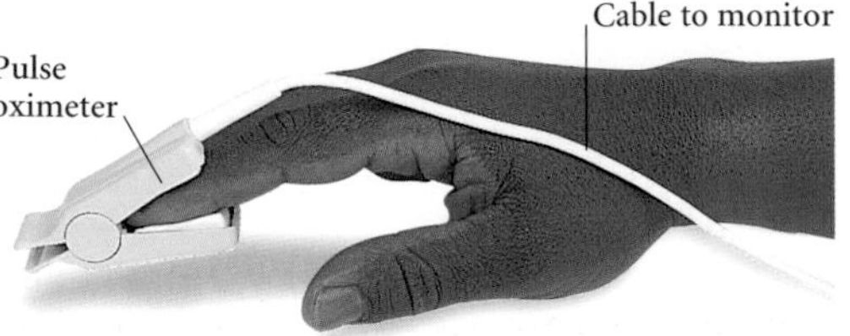
Cable to monitor
Pulse oximeter

Pulse oximeter
A machine called a pulse oximeter shines a light through the soft tissues of the finger or earlobe to measure oxygen levels in the blood painlessly.

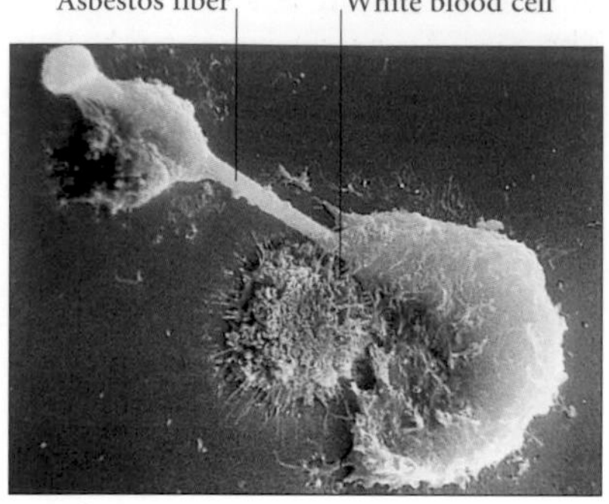
Asbestos fiber
White blood cell

Asbestos fiber in the lungs
Fibers of asbestos inhaled into the lungs are engulfed by white blood cells, as shown above, but destroy the cells. The result is scarring of the lungs called asbestosis.

Mesotheliomas that affect the pleura usually cause chest pain and shortness of breath. A mesothelioma in the peritoneum may cause intestinal obstruction (p.663), which leads to abdominal pain, vomiting, and weight loss.

ARE THERE COMPLICATIONS?

People with asbestos-related diseases are particularly susceptible to developing primary lung cancer (opposite page). People who smoke and who also have an asbestos-related disease are considered 75–100 times more likely to develop lung cancer than people with neither factor. Asbestos-related diseases may also increase a person's susceptibility to other serious lung conditions, including tuberculosis (p.491) and chronic obstructive pulmonary disease (p.487).

HOW IS IT DIAGNOSED?

If your doctor suspects that you have an asbestos-related disease, he or she will ask you about your current occupation and work history. Asbestos-related disease is usually diagnosed using a chest X-ray (p.490) to look for signs of thickening of the pleura. Your doctor may also listen to your chest for abnormal sounds and may arrange for lung function tests (p.488) to assess the extent of your breathing problems. A sample of sputum from the lungs may be examined for evidence of asbestos fibers. If a mesothelioma is suspected, CT scanning (p.247) or MRI (p.248) may be performed. To confirm the diagnosis of mesothelioma, a sample of tissue may be taken from the pleura under local anesthesia to check for cancerous cells.

WHAT IS THE TREATMENT?

No treatment can reverse the progress of an asbestos-related disease. However, further exposure to asbestos may cause the condition to worsen more rapidly and should be avoided. If you have asbestosis, you may be prescribed oxygen (*see* HOME OXYGEN THERAPY, p.507) to relieve shortness of breath. Diffuse pleural thickening requires no specific treatment because the condition rarely causes severe symptoms. Mesothelioma cannot be treated effectively, but radiation therapy (p.279) may relieve pain.

CAN IT BE PREVENTED?

The only way to prevent asbestos-related diseases is to minimize your exposure to asbestos fibers in the workplace and at home. Since the 1970s, the use of asbestos has been severely restricted, and industries that use asbestos have improved fiber-control measures. Most cases of asbestos-related diseases now being diagnosed are the result of working practices that were in effect before the 1970s. If you are carrying out repair work on a house that was constructed before 1970, you should check for the presence of asbestos, and, if you find any, you should seek professional advice before you continue the work.

WHAT IS THE PROGNOSIS?

About 4 in 10 people with asbestosis or diffuse pleural thickening will eventually die of lung cancer, and smoking should be avoided to lower the risk. Only a few people with asbestos-related mesothelioma survive for longer than 2 years after the diagnosis.

(WWW) ONLINE SITES: p.1034, p.1036

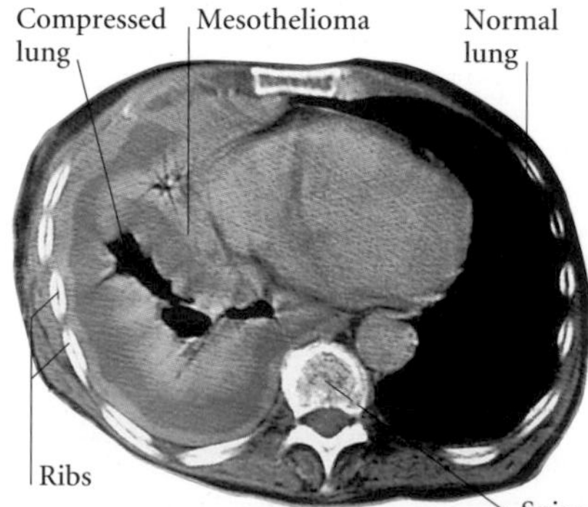
Compressed lung
Mesothelioma
Normal lung
Ribs
Spine

CT scan of mesothelioma
The lung seen on the left is completely encased in a mesothelioma, which consists of a large mass of thickened pleura.

Hypersensitivity pneumonitis

An allergic reaction to inhaled dusts or chemicals, causing cough and fever

 AGE More common in adults

 GENDER More common in males due to increased risk of occupational exposure

 LIFESTYLE Exposure to certain organic dusts and chemicals is a risk factor

 GENETICS Not a significant factor

In some people, inhaling certain dusts or chemicals containing organic substances, such as proteins and fungal spores, triggers an allergic reaction that causes inflammation of lung tissue and shortness of breath. This condition is known as hypersensitivity pneumonitis. The dusts, fungal spores, and chemicals that cause it may be found in the workplace and can affect people in a variety of different occupations.

WHAT ARE THE CAUSES?

Many substances in the workplace can trigger the allergic response that results in hypersensitivity pneumonitis. There are several forms of the disorder, which tend to be named for the occupation that typically causes them. For example, in farmer's lung, the reaction is triggered by fungal spores from moldy hay. If particles from bird droppings are the cause, the disorder is known as bird fancier's lung. Other substances that can trigger hypersensitivity pneumonitis include cheese mold, coffee dust, mushroom soil, and certain chemicals used in manufacturing products such as insulation and packing materials. Certain microorganisms that may be present in air-conditioning systems, hot tubs, and humidifiers can trigger the disorder in office environments.

The allergic reaction causes inflammation of the alveoli (air sacs) and small airways in the lungs. The walls of the alveoli thicken, reducing their efficiency in transferring oxygen to the blood, and the airways narrow. Not everyone who is exposed to these dusts and chemicals will develop an allergic reaction if they inhale them. However, some people are particularly susceptible to allergies, and, in such people, exposure to these substances provokes an acute attack. If exposure to the trigger substance continues after the allergy has become established, some people may go on to develop a chronic form of the disorder, which may cause permanent damage to the lungs.

What are the symptoms?

The symptoms of an acute attack of hypersensitivity pneumonitis resemble symptoms of influenza. They usually develop within 4–8 hours after initial exposure and may include:

- Fever and chills.
- Coughing and wheezing.
- Tightness in the chest and, in some people, shortness of breath.

If exposure to the substance stops at once, these symptoms usually begin to clear up spontaneously within 12–24 hours and often disappear completely within 48 hours. However, if further exposure to the substance occurs, acute attacks are eventually followed by continuous symptoms.

The symptoms of chronic hypersensitivity pneumonitis include:

- Coughing that may become progressively worse over time.
- Progressive shortness of breath.
- Loss of appetite and weight loss.

In chronic hypersensitivity pneumonitis, symptoms may continue even after exposure to the substance has stopped. If exposure to the substance continues, progressive lung damage may eventually lead to respiratory failure (p.507).

What might be done?

Your work or hobbies may alert your doctor to the diagnosis, which can be confirmed by blood tests to look for antibodies against the substance causing the allergic reaction. Your doctor may also arrange for a chest X-ray (p.490) and lung function tests (p.488) to look for evidence of lung damage.

If you have a severe, acute attack of hypersensitivity pneumonitis, you may be given corticosteroids (*see* CORTICOSTEROIDS FOR RESPIRATORY DISEASE, p.911) to help reduce inflammation in the lungs and bronchodilator drugs (p.910) to help widen the airways. If the lung damage is severe, you may also be given oxygen (*see* HOME OXYGEN THERAPY, p.507). In most acute cases, the symptoms clear up once exposure to the dust has stopped. In chronic cases, long-term treatment that includes corticosteroids may be necessary even after exposure has stopped.

Can it be prevented?

If you become sensitive to substances in your workplace, you should wear a protective mask. Employers should store materials safely and ensure that air conditioners are serviced regularly. You may consider changing your lifestyle or finding alternative employment to prevent the allergy from becoming chronic.

(WWW) ONLINE SITES: p.1034

Primary lung cancer

A cancerous tumor that develops in the tissue of the lungs

AGE Most common between the ages of 50 and 70

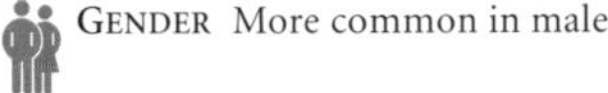

GENDER More common in males

LIFESTYLE Smoking and certain occupations are risk factors

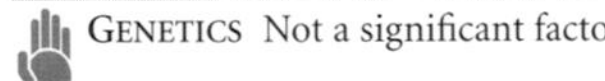

GENETICS Not a significant factor

Since 1900, the number of cases of primary lung cancer has risen faster than that of any other form of cancer. Primary lung cancer, in which a tumor develops in lung tissue, is now the most common type of cancer after skin cancer. Although more prevalent in men, it is the most common cause of death due to cancer in both men and women. It usually develops in people between the ages of 50 and 70. A minority of people diagnosed with primary lung cancer live for longer than 5 years. In Canada, about 22,000 new cases occur each year.

Smoking is the main cause of lung cancer. The rise in the incidence of the disease over the last hundred years is largely due to a dramatic increase in the number of smokers. Although smoking is becoming less common in developed countries, the incidence of lung cancer in these countries is not expected to decrease for some decades because lung cancer can take many years to develop. The more cigarettes you smoke, the sooner you may develop cancer. For example, if you smoke 20 cigarettes a day, you may develop lung cancer 20 years later; if you smoke 40 a day, you may develop the disease after only 10 years.

What are the types?

The type of cancer depends on the type of cell in the lungs that becomes cancerous (*see* HOW CANCER STARTS, p.274). Most lung cancers fall into one of four categories. The most common types are squamous cell carcinoma and small cell carcinoma, with adenocarcinoma and large cell carcinoma accounting for the remainder. Most of these cancers begin in the cells that line the bronchi, the airways that lead to the lungs.

Each type of cancer has a different growth pattern and response to treatment. In general terms, squamous cell carcinoma grows more slowly than other types of lung cancer and spreads to other parts of the body late in the course of the disease. Small cell carcinoma is the most highly malignant (cancerous) type; this type of cancer grows rapidly and spreads very quickly

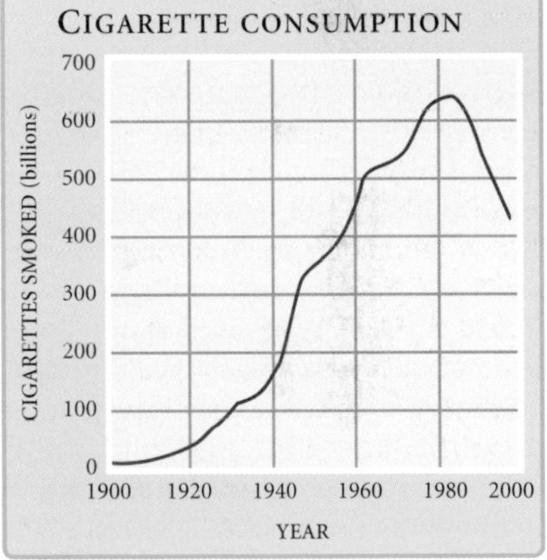
CIGARETTE CONSUMPTION
CIGARETTES SMOKED (billions)
700
600
500
400
300
200
100
0
1900
1920
1940
1960
1980
2000
YEAR

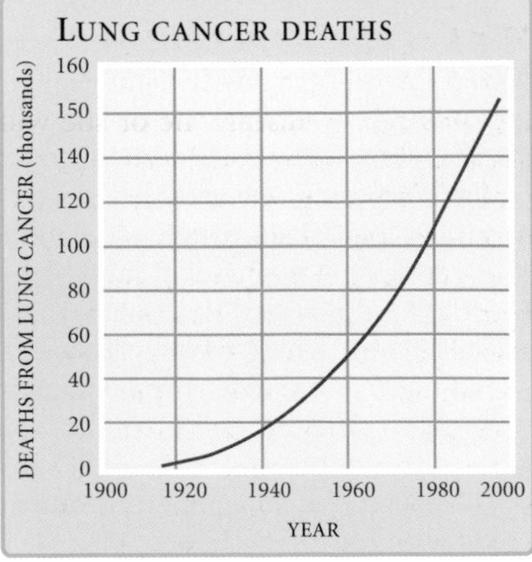
LUNG CANCER DEATHS
DEATHS FROM LUNG CANCER (thousands)
160
150
140
120
100
80
60
40
20
0
1900
1920
1940
1960
1980
2000
YEAR

Lung cancer

These graphs show the link between cigarettes smoked and deaths from lung cancer in the US. Despite a recent fall in smoking, deaths are still rising because lung cancer may take years to develop.

throughout the body. Adenocarcinoma and large cell carcinoma both develop at a rate somewhere between that of squamous and small cell carcinomas.

Lung metastases (opposite page) are cancers that have spread to the lung from a tumor in another part of the body. Lung tissue is a common site for metastases because all circulating blood passes through the lungs, allowing cancerous cells to pass into lung tissue.

What are the causes?

Smoking is the cause of lung cancer in approximately 80–90 percent of cases, and about 1 in 7 smokers is likely to develop the disease by age 70. The risk is greatest for people who have smoked more than 20 cigarettes a day since early adulthood. For people who have never smoked, the risk of lung cancer is small, but it increases slightly for anyone who may be exposed to other people's cigarette smoke on a regular basis.

Working with particular substances, such as radioactive materials, asbestos (*see* Asbestos-related diseases, p.501), chromium, and nickel, may lead to an increased risk of lung cancer, especially when the exposure is combined with smoking. Exposure to radon, a radioactive gas that is released slowly from granite rock, also leads to a slightly increased risk for people who live in areas that have a lot of granite. Living in an environment with a high level of air pollution may be a factor in some cases of lung cancer, but it is far less important as a cause than smoking.

What are the symptoms?

The symptoms of lung cancer depend on how far advanced the tumor is, but initial symptoms may include:

- A new, persistent cough or change in a long-standing cough, sometimes with blood-streaked sputum.
- Chest pain, which may be felt as a dull ache or as a sharp pain that is worse on inhaling.
- Shortness of breath.
- Wheezing, if the tumor is positioned so that it blocks an airway.
- Abnormal curvature of the fingernails, known as clubbing (*see* Nail abnormalities, p.360).

Some lung cancers produce no symptoms until they are advanced, when they may cause shortness of breath.

You should consult your doctor as soon as possible if you develop a new cough that is persistent, experience a change in a long-term cough, or develop any of the other symptoms associated with lung cancer listed above.

Are there complications?

In some cases, pneumonia (p.490) may develop in an area of the lung if an airway is blocked by a tumor. This may be the first indication of lung cancer. A tumor may also cause fluid to accumulate between the layers of the pleura, the thin membrane that separates the lungs from the wall of the chest (*see* Pleural effusion, p.494), which may lead to increased shortness of breath. Later, as the disease progresses, loss of appetite followed by weight loss and weakness may develop. A tumor at the top of the lung may affect the nerves that supply the arm, making it painful or weak. Small cell carcinomas may produce hormonelike chemicals that cause endocrine disorders such as Cushing syndrome (p.684).

There may also be symptoms from tumors that have spread from the lungs to other parts of the body. For example, headaches may result from cancer that has spread to the brain.

Test and Treatment: Bronchoscopy

Bronchoscopy can be used to diagnose or treat various lung disorders, such as lung cancer and tuberculosis. A rigid or flexible instrument called a bronchoscope is used to view the bronchi (airways). The rigid type is passed through the mouth into the lungs under general anesthesia. The flexible type is passed through the nose or mouth into the lungs under local anesthesia. Instruments can be used to remove tissue samples and to carry out laser surgery.

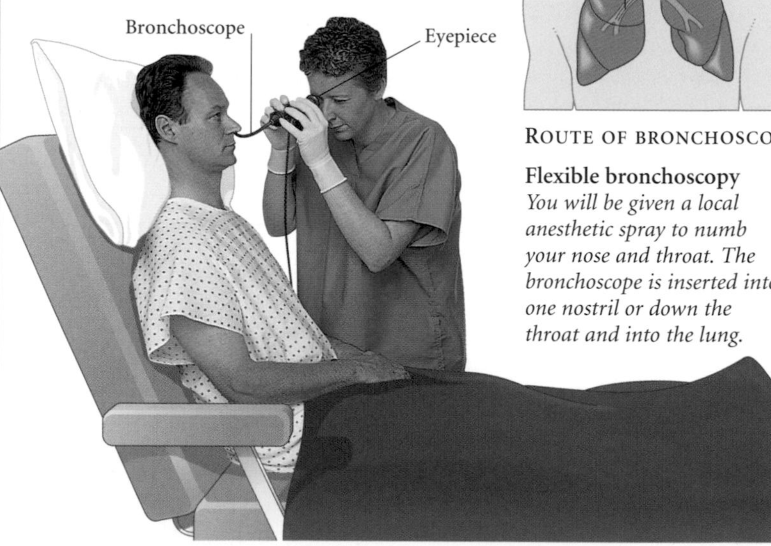
Bronchoscope
Eyepiece
Bronchus
Flexible bronchoscope

Route of bronchoscope

Flexible bronchoscopy
You will be given a local anesthetic spray to numb your nose and throat. The bronchoscope is inserted into one nostril or down the throat and into the lung.

Results

Tumor in the bronchus
This view down a bronchoscope clearly shows a tumor almost completely blocking a bronchus. During the procedure, cell and tissue samples can be taken through the bronchoscope for laboratory analysis.

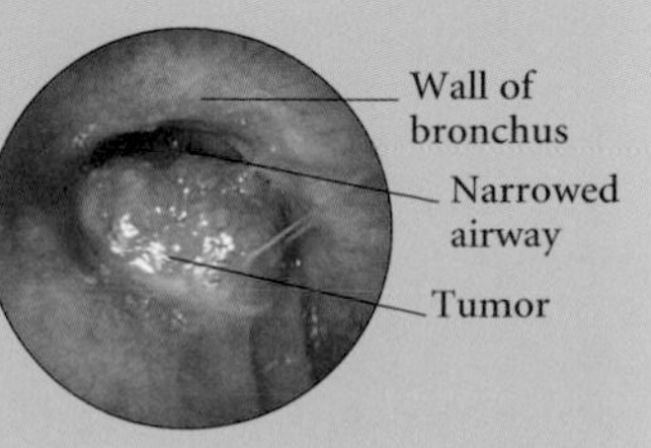
Wall of bronchus
Narrowed airway
Tumor

HOW IS IT DIAGNOSED?

A chest X-ray (p.490) is often one of the first investigations to be done in anyone with a lung problem. A tumor is usually visible as a shadow on the X-ray.

Samples of sputum may be taken to look for cancerous cells, and your doctor may also perform a bronchoscopy (opposite page) to examine your airways. If a tumor is found during the procedure, a sample will be removed and examined under the microscope. If the tumor is cancerous, tests may be done to determine whether cancerous cells have spread to other parts of the body. In addition to blood tests, CT scanning (p.247) and MRI (p.248) of the brain, chest, and abdomen may be arranged to assess the extent of cancer spread. Radionuclide scanning (p.251) may be done to see if the cancer has spread to the bones.

WHAT IS THE TREATMENT?

Treatment of lung cancer depends on the type of cancer and whether it has spread to other parts of the body.

Surgery to remove a tumor in the lung is an option only if the cancer has not spread. Surgery normally involves removal of the whole lung or a major part of it. However, in 4 out of 5 cases, the cancer has already spread to other organs, and surgery is not an option. Small cell carcinoma is rarely treated with surgery because it is highly malignant and has usually spread beyond the lungs by the time it is diagnosed. This cancer is usually treated with chemotherapy (p.278), and radiation therapy (p.279) is used to treat metastases from the lung. In other cases, surgery may not be advised due to the size or location of the tumor or the presence of another serious disorder, such as chronic obstructive pulmonary disease (p.487).

If a tumor cannot be removed surgically and is not small cell carcinoma, radiation therapy is usually given initially. This does not destroy all the cancerous cells but slows tumor growth.

WHAT IS THE PROGNOSIS?

The prognosis is best for people whose cancer is detected early. Only about 1 in 20 people with lung cancer survives for 5 years or more after it is diagnosed. About 3 in 4 people who have surgery to remove a tumor survive for 2 years.

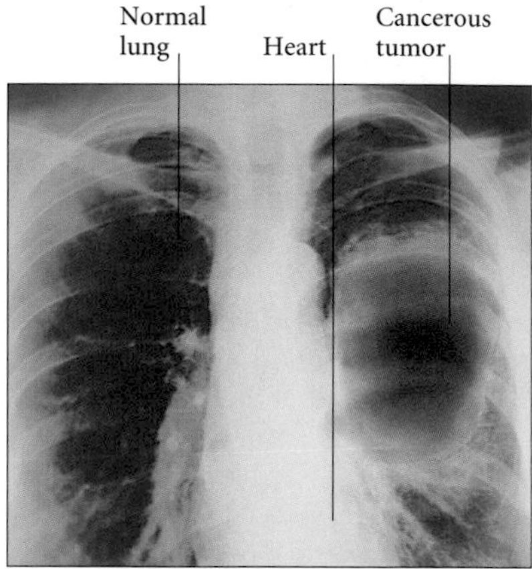
Normal lung
Heart
Cancerous tumor

Lung cancer
In this color-enhanced chest X-ray, a large cancerous tumor can be seen in the lung on the right of the image.

People with small cell carcinoma usually survive for 2 to 10 months after diagnosis. Surgery, radiation therapy, and chemotherapy may not prolong life in all cases, but they can alleviate symptoms and improve quality of life.

CAN IT BE PREVENTED?

Lung cancer is closely linked to smoking. People who stop smoking greatly improve their chances of avoiding lung cancer, and long-term ex-smokers have only a slightly greater risk of developing lung cancer than nonsmokers.

(WWW) ONLINE SITES: p.1028, p.1034

Lung metastases

Cancerous tumors in lung tissue that have spread from another part of the body

 AGE Most common between the ages of 50 and 70

 GENDER More common in females

 GENETICS LIFESTYLE Risk factors depend on the cause

Lung metastases, also known as secondary lung cancers, are cancers that have spread to the lungs from other parts of the body. Lung tissue is a very common site for metastases because all circulating blood passes through the lungs, allowing cancerous cells to be carried into lung tissue from other parts of the body. The primary (original) cancers that spread most often to the lungs include cancers of the breast, colon, and prostate gland.

Secondary lung cancers may not cause symptoms. However, if many secondary tumors have formed in the lung, you may feel short of breath. You may also develop a cough, which can produce blood if a tumor is blocking an airway.

WHAT MIGHT BE DONE?

If cancer has already been diagnosed elsewhere in your body, your doctor may arrange for you to have a chest X-ray (p.490) to check whether the cancer has spread to your lungs. If the site of the original cancer has not been confirmed, further tests may be done to locate the original tumor. For example, women will probably be given a breast X-ray (*see* MAMMOGRAPHY, p.759) to look for evidence of a breast tumor.

Treatment is aimed at destroying the primary cancer. Chemotherapy (p.278), radiation therapy (p.279), or hormonal treatment (*see* ANTICANCER DRUGS, p.907) may be used, depending on the type and extent of the primary tumor.

By the time lung metastases have been detected, there are usually several tumors, and treatment of the cancer is difficult. The best outcome that can usually be achieved is relief of symptoms.

(WWW) ONLINE SITES: p.1028, p.1034

Pulmonary hypertension

Abnormally high pressure in the blood vessels supplying the lungs

 AGE More common over age 40

 LIFESTYLE Risk factors depend on the cause

 GENDER GENETICS Not significant factors

Blood is normally pumped through the lungs by the heart at a lower pressure than blood is pumped around the rest of the body. In pulmonary hypertension, the pressure of the blood in the arteries supplying the lungs is abnormally high. Consequently, the right side of the heart, which pumps the blood through the lungs, must contract much more vigorously than normal in order to maintain an adequate flow of blood through the arteries of the lungs. This causes enlargement of the muscle wall on the right side of the heart.

WHAT ARE THE CAUSES?

There are various lung and heart conditions that may result in pulmonary hypertension. For example, in chronic obstructive pulmonary disease (p.487), resistance to blood flow in the lungs is caused by destruction of lung tissue. In diseases that cause extensive scarring of the tissue in the lungs, such as interstitial fibrosis (p.497), blood vessels in the lungs are destroyed, making blood flow more difficult. Blood clots in the lungs (*see* PULMONARY EMBOLISM, p.495) may obstruct the flow of blood, leading to pulmonary hypertension. Narrowing of the mitral valve prevents blood from leaving the lungs, causing back pressure in the lungs (*see* MITRAL STENOSIS, p.424) and pulmonary hypertension.

In some forms of congenital heart disease (p.836), the heart pumps more blood than is normal into the lungs, and as a result the pressure rises.

Rarely, sleep apnea (p.477) leads to pulmonary hypertension. Occasionally, there is no obvious cause for the condition, and it is then known as primary pulmonary hypertension.

WHAT ARE THE SYMPTOMS?

Many people who develop pulmonary hypertension already have symptoms of a chronic heart or lung disorder. The additional symptoms associated with pulmonary hypertension may include:

- Shortness of breath that tends to become worse on exertion.
- Fatigue.

As the disease progresses, shortness of breath becomes increasingly severe until it may occur at rest. Eventually, the right side of the heart, which pumps blood through the lungs, may fail, leading to tissue edema (swelling caused by fluid buildup), especially around the ankles.

WHAT MIGHT BE DONE?

If you have an existing chronic heart or lung disorder and your symptoms suddenly become worse, your doctor may suspect that you are developing pulmonary hypertension. He or she may arrange for a chest X-ray (p.490) to look for enlarged arteries. An echocardiogram (*see* ECHOCARDIOGRAPHY, p.425) and an electrocardiogram (*see* ECG, p.406) may be done to look for signs of heart disease, and lung function tests (p.488) are useful to assess the extent of lung damage. If the diagnosis is still unclear, a procedure called right heart catheterization may be performed. This involves passing a tube through a vein in the arm or leg into the right side of the heart to measure blood pressure there.

If you have already developed pulmonary hypertension, treatment will initially be directed at the underlying cause if one is found. Your doctor may advise long-term home oxygen therapy (opposite page) if you have low oxygen levels due to a disorder such as chronic obstructive pulmonary disease. Drugs that prevent blood clotting (p.904) may be prescribed if the blood vessels in the lungs have become blocked by clots. You may also be prescribed drugs to dilate blood vessels in the lungs and lower the pressure in them. If heart failure has developed, you may be given diuretic drugs (p.902) to reduce excess fluid.

WHAT IS THE PROGNOSIS?

If the underlying cause of pulmonary hypertension is identified and can be treated successfully, it is possible that the condition may improve. However, in most cases, pulmonary hypertension becomes progressively worse.

In primary pulmonary hypertension and cases in which the underlying cause is untreatable, the disorder may progress to chronic heart failure (p.413), which may be life-threatening. For this reason, if you have pulmonary hypertension, are under age 55, and are otherwise in good health, you may be considered for a heart and lung transplant.

(WWW) ONLINE SITES: p.1034

Acute respiratory distress syndrome

Inflammatory response of the lungs to severe disease or injury

AGE GENDER GENETICS LIFESTYLE
Not significant factors

Acute respiratory distress syndrome (ARDS) is a serious lung disorder that develops suddenly as a result of severe damage either to the lungs or elsewhere in the body. In ARDS, the tiny blood vessels (capillaries) in the lungs leak fluid into the alveoli (air sacs), reducing the amount of oxygen that reaches the blood and preventing the lungs from expanding fully. This in turn can lead to the failure of other vital organs, including the kidneys and liver. ARDS can be a life-threatening disorder that requires emergency medical treatment.

WHAT ARE THE CAUSES?

ARDS can develop after any serious illness or injury. One-third of cases result from widespread bacterial infection of the blood (*see* SEPTICEMIA, p.298). In other cases, major trauma such as multiple fractures, crushed internal organs, or severe burns are the cause. Less commonly, ARDS results from pneumonia (p.490), obstetric emergencies, inhaling vomit, or an overdose of an opioid drug such as heroin. How these conditions and emergencies cause leakage in the lungs remains unclear.

WHAT ARE THE SYMPTOMS?

The symptoms of ARDS usually begin 24–48 hours after the injury or disease that brings about the condition and may include the following:

- Severe shortness of breath.
- Wheezing.
- Mottled blue skin.
- Confusion or unconsciousness.

These symptoms develop in addition to those related to the underlying disorder that has caused the lung damage. As well as being a possible cause of ARDS, pneumonia may develop as a complication. Other complications, such as acute kidney failure (p.706), may also occur.

WHAT MIGHT BE DONE?

A doctor will probably suspect ARDS if a person who is already seriously ill develops sudden, unexpected breathing difficulties. The diagnosis can often be confirmed by a chest X-ray (p.490), which is used to look for evidence of fluid in the alveoli, and analysis of the oxygen levels in the blood (*see* MEASURING BLOOD GASES, p.501).

People with ARDS are usually treated in an intensive care unit (p.958). High concentrations of oxygen are given using mechanical ventilation in order to increase the amount of oxygen that passes from the lungs into the blood. Diuretic drugs (p.902) may be given to reduce the amount of fluid in the lungs. The underlying cause and any complications are treated, and the condition of major organs is monitored.

WHAT IS THE PROGNOSIS?

Only 1 in 2 people who develop ARDS survive. In those who recover, symptoms usually improve over 7–10 days. There is often little or no permanent damage to the lungs, and the majority of people who do make a recovery experience no further problems.

(WWW) ONLINE SITES: p.1034

Respiratory failure

Abnormally low levels of oxygen in the blood, resulting from lung damage

AGE GENDER GENETICS LIFESTYLE
Not significant factors

Respiratory failure occurs if the amount of oxygen that enters the bloodstream from the lungs is greatly reduced, leading to severe shortness of breath and eventually to profound confusion or unconsciousness. Simultaneously, there may be an excess of carbon dioxide in the blood. Respiratory failure is a life-threatening condition that should be treated promptly to prevent damage to other organs, such as the heart, which need an adequate supply of oxygen to maintain their function.

WHAT ARE THE CAUSES?

There are two broad groups of conditions that lead to respiratory failure. In the first group of disorders, there is no difficulty in moving air into and out of the lungs, but less oxygen than normal is transferred to the blood as a result of damage to the alveoli (air sacs) in the lungs. The most common causes of this type of respiratory failure are chronic lung disorders such as interstitial fibrosis (p.497). Less commonly, the alveoli may become filled with fluid, as occurs in acute respiratory distress syndrome (opposite page). In this case, levels of oxygen in the blood are low, but carbon dioxide levels are usually normal.

The second group of conditions consists of ventilation disorders, in which a person cannot move sufficient air into and out of the lungs. A ventilation disorder may develop suddenly after a stroke (p.532) or an injury to the area of the brain that controls breathing. A drug overdose (*see* DRUG OVERDOSE AND ACCIDENTAL INGESTION, p.321) or injury to the chest wall may also reduce breathing. In addition, breathing difficulties may result from particular disorders, such as myasthenia gravis (p.549), in which the muscles involved in breathing become progressively weakened. Ventilation problems usually lead to low levels of oxygen and high levels of carbon dioxide in the blood.

WHAT ARE THE SYMPTOMS?

Disorders that involve damage to the alveoli are nearly always chronic conditions, and symptoms develop gradually. In ventilation disorders, symptoms of respiratory failure may develop either suddenly or gradually over a period of time, depending on the cause.

Whatever the underlying cause, the symptoms of respiratory failure are mainly due to low levels of oxygen in the blood and may include:

- Shortness of breath.
- A bluish tinge to the lips and tongue, a condition known as cyanosis.
- Anxiety.
- Agitation.
- Confusion.
- Sweating.

In addition to the symptoms listed above, ventilation disorders cause further symptoms, such as headache and drowsiness, due to the high levels of carbon dioxide in the blood.

WHAT MIGHT BE DONE?

Respiratory failure can usually be diagnosed from the symptoms, and its severity can be assessed by measuring the levels of oxygen and carbon dioxide in blood (*see* MEASURING BLOOD GASES, p.501). If the cause is not obvious, you may need further tests.

Respiratory failure due to permanent damage to the alveoli cannot be treated except with a lung transplant. However, symptoms of respiratory failure may be relieved by long-term home oxygen therapy (below), which needs to be used continuously for at least 15 hours a day to prevent chronic heart failure (p.413).

If you develop respiratory failure caused by a ventilation disorder, you may need help from a ventilation mask or tube to breathe. If long-term ventilation is required, it may be possible to continue treatment at home.

If respiratory failure occurs suddenly due to a ventilation disorder, recovery is possible if the underlying cause can be treated successfully. Cases of gradual respiratory failure are less likely to improve significantly, but the symptoms can be controlled effectively with long-term oxygen therapy.

(WWW) ONLINE SITES: p.1034

(TREATMENT) HOME OXYGEN THERAPY

Oxygen therapy can be used at home to relieve the consequences of low blood oxygen levels due to many lung disorders. You can use either oxygen cylinders or an oxygen concentrator. In people with chronic respiratory failure, the treatment can delay the development of complications and prolong life if used for at least 15 hours per day. Smaller, portable oxygen cylinders can be used when outside, enabling you to move around freely while receiving extra oxygen.

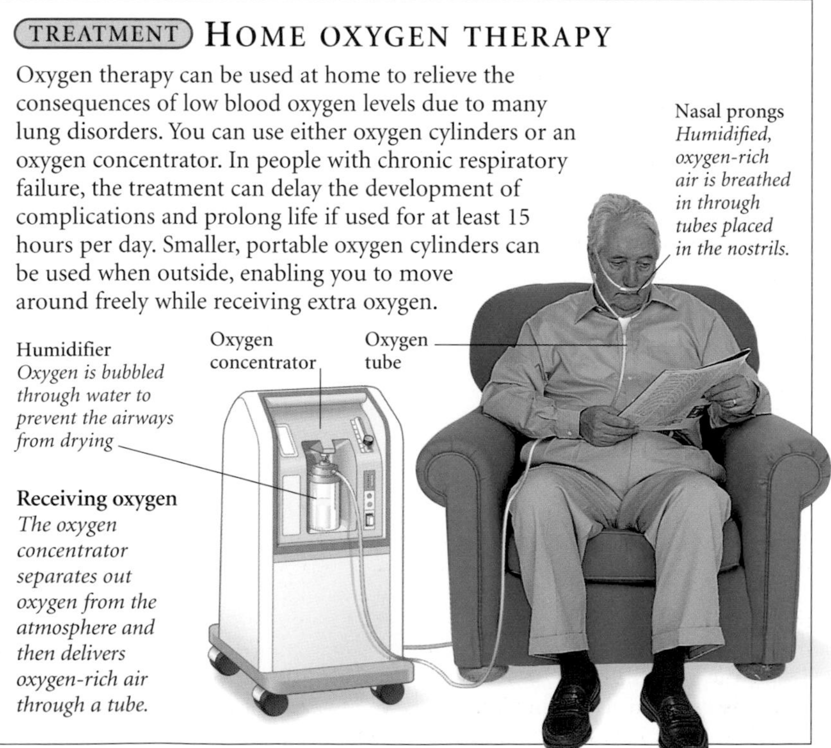
Nasal prongs
Humidified, oxygen-rich air is breathed in through tubes placed in the nostrils.
Humidifier
Oxygen is bubbled through water to prevent the airways from drying
Oxygen concentrator
Oxygen tube

Receiving oxygen
The oxygen concentrator separates out oxygen from the atmosphere and then delivers oxygen-rich air through a tube.

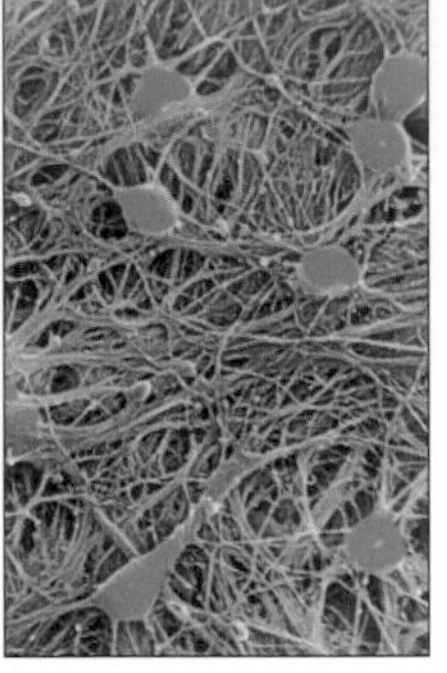
Nerve fibers
Brain tissue largely consists of networks of nerve fibers that carry electrical signals.

Nervous System and Mental Function

The nervous system is the most complex system in the body and regulates hundreds of activities simultaneously. It is the source of our consciousness, intelligence, and creativity and allows us to communicate and experience emotions. It also monitors and controls almost all bodily processes, ranging from automatic functions of which we are largely unconscious, such as breathing and blinking, to complex activities that involve thought and learning, such as playing a musical instrument and riding a bicycle.

The nervous system has two parts: the central nervous system (CNS), which consists of the brain and spinal cord; and the peripheral nervous system (PNS), which consists of all the nerves that emerge from the CNS and branch throughout the body. Nerve signals are processed and coordinated by the CNS, while the PNS transmits nerve signals to and from the CNS and other parts of the body.

The nervous system has immediate control over our voluntary actions, such as walking, and our automatic bodily functions, such as salivation. The longer-term control of automatic activities, such as maintaining normal blood pressure and temperature, is aided by some of the hormones produced by the endocrine system.

How the nervous system works

The activity of the nervous system is largely performed by cells called neurons. Each neuron typically has a long projection known as a nerve fiber (axon), which carries information in the form of electrical signals. When a signal reaches the end of a nerve fiber, it is carried in chemical form to the next neuron or to another kind of cell. In the PNS, nerve fibers form bundles called nerves, and these carry messages concerning the outside world and the inside of the body. For example, data about sound are detected by sensory receptors in the ear and converted into nerve impulses. These signals travel along nerve fibers toward the brain. In response to these nerve impulses, the CNS then transmits signals to the motor nerves in the PNS, which communicate with glands, organs, or muscles to produce an appropriate response to the original stimuli. The CNS also receives a constant stream of information from other sensory organs throughout the body concerning the inner organs and bodily functions, such as blood pressure and body temperature. These data are all monitored and elicit appropriate responses, often without input from the conscious mind.

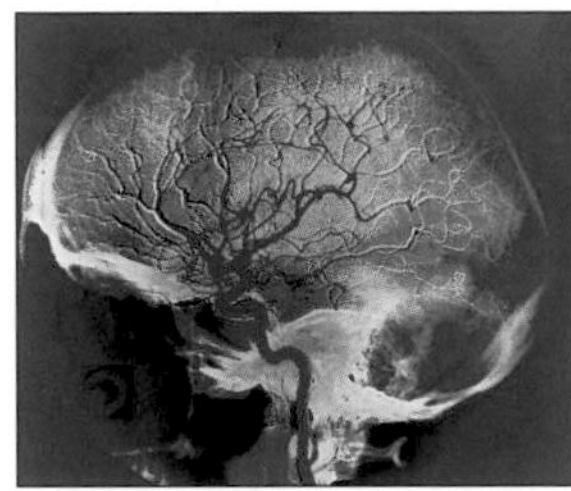
Arteries supplying the brain
Four arteries branch at the base of the brain to supply it with about one-fifth of the body's total supply of blood.

Complex activities

Many complex functions, including creativity and logic, involve conscious thought. Other activities, such as the coordination of complex physical tasks, are regulated unconsciously. For example, when first learning to ride a bicycle, you make a conscious effort, but you eventually learn and memorize the necessary skills so that you can cycle without conscious thought. However, you still remain conscious of sensory stimuli, such as sight and sound, that aid navigation while riding the bicycle.

FUNCTION Nervous system organization

The nervous system is divided into two parts: the central nervous system (CNS), which regulates bodily activity; and the peripheral nervous system (PNS), which transmits signals between the body and the CNS. The PNS is divided into nerves that control voluntary actions and autonomic nerves that regulate the body's internal environment.

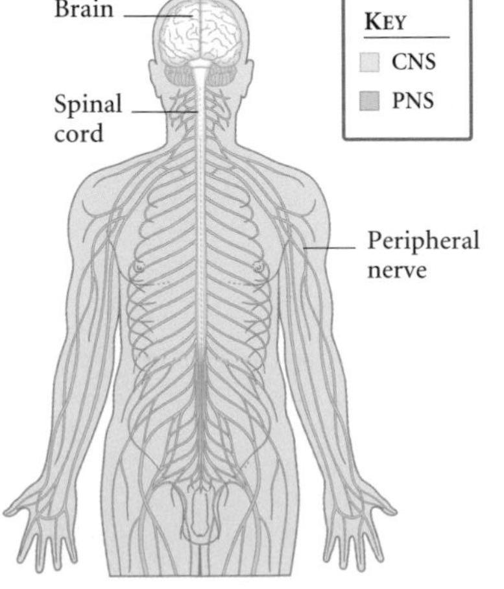
Brain
Spinal cord
Key
CNS
PNS
Peripheral nerve
Nerve links between brain and body
Nerve fibers leave the brain and enter the spinal cord to form a thick bundle of nerves. Individual nerves then emerge from the spinal cord and branch out through the body, supplying every tissue.

STRUCTURE NERVOUS SYSTEM

The brain and spinal cord form the central nervous system and are protected by the bones of the skull and the vertebral column. Inside these hard outer coverings, further protection is provided by three membranes called the meninges and a clear liquid known as cerebrospinal fluid. The cranial nerves emerge directly from the brain, and the spinal nerves from the spinal cord. Together, these form the peripheral nerves that branch to every part of the body.

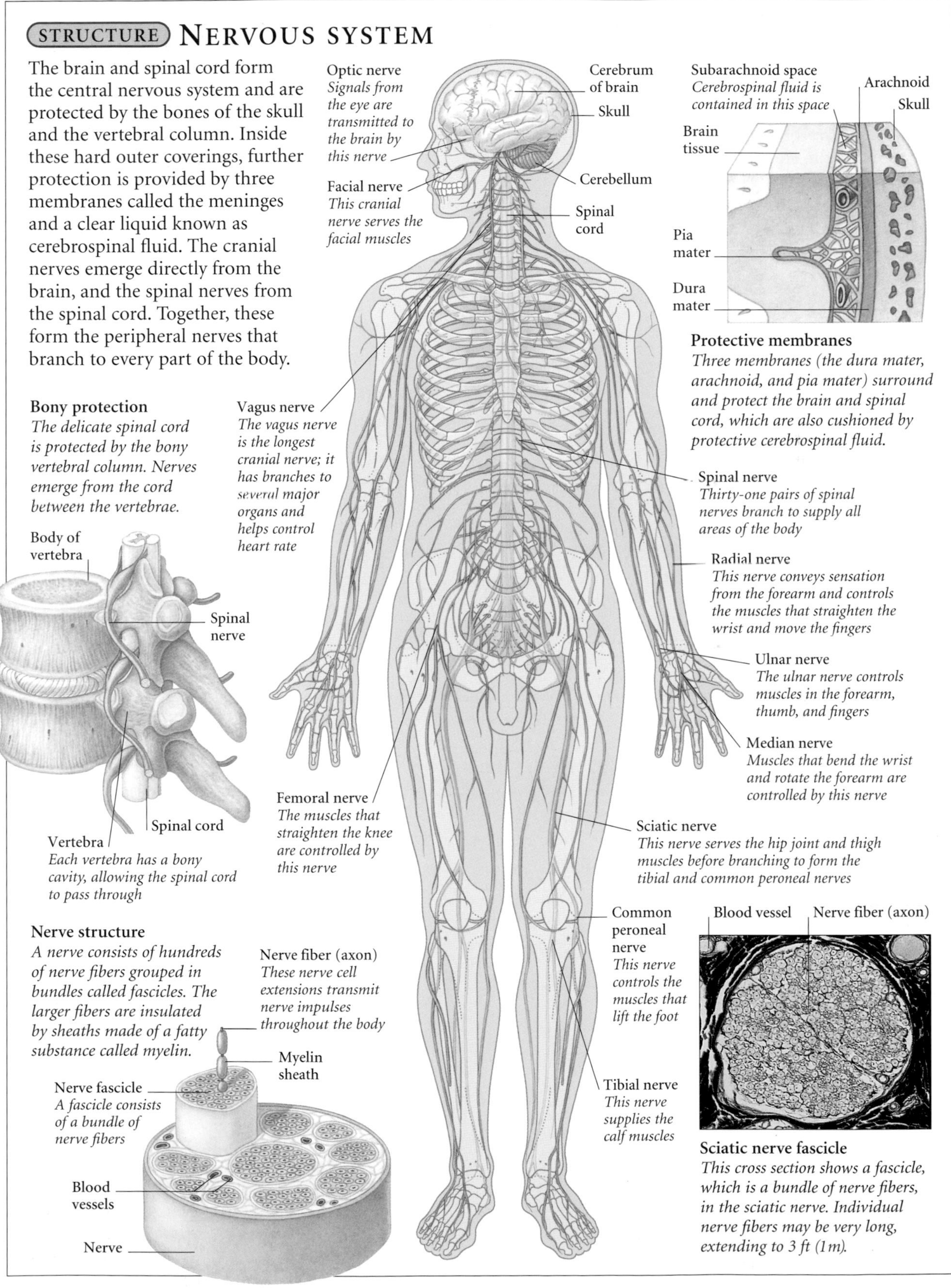
Optic nerve
Signals from the eye are transmitted to the brain by this nerve
Cerebrum of brain
Skull
Cerebellum
Facial nerve
This cranial nerve serves the facial muscles
Spinal cord
Subarachnoid space
Cerebrospinal fluid is contained in this space
Arachnoid
Skull
Brain tissue
Pia mater
Dura mater
Protective membranes
Three membranes (the dura mater, arachnoid, and pia mater) surround and protect the brain and spinal cord, which are also cushioned by protective cerebrospinal fluid.
Bony protection
The delicate spinal cord is protected by the bony vertebral column. Nerves emerge from the cord between the vertebrae.
Vagus nerve
The vagus nerve is the longest cranial nerve; it has branches to several major organs and helps control heart rate
Spinal nerve
Thirty-one pairs of spinal nerves branch to supply all areas of the body
Body of vertebra
Spinal nerve
Radial nerve
This nerve conveys sensation from the forearm and controls the muscles that straighten the wrist and move the fingers
Ulnar nerve
The ulnar nerve controls muscles in the forearm, thumb, and fingers
Median nerve
Muscles that bend the wrist and rotate the forearm are controlled by this nerve
Spinal cord
Vertebra
Each vertebra has a bony cavity, allowing the spinal cord to pass through
Femoral nerve
The muscles that straighten the knee are controlled by this nerve
Sciatic nerve
This nerve serves the hip joint and thigh muscles before branching to form the tibial and common peroneal nerves
Nerve structure
A nerve consists of hundreds of nerve fibers grouped in bundles called fascicles. The larger fibers are insulated by sheaths made of a fatty substance called myelin.
Nerve fiber (axon)
These nerve cell extensions transmit nerve impulses throughout the body
Myelin sheath
Nerve fascicle
A fascicle consists of a bundle of nerve fibers
Blood vessels
Nerve
Common peroneal nerve
This nerve controls the muscles that lift the foot
Tibial nerve
This nerve supplies the calf muscles
Blood vessel
Nerve fiber (axon)
Sciatic nerve fascicle
This cross section shows a fascicle, which is a bundle of nerve fibers, in the sciatic nerve. Individual nerve fibers may be very long, extending to 3 ft (1 m).

STRUCTURE AND FUNCTION BRAIN, SPINAL CORD, AND NERVES

The brain contains more than 100 billion neurons and weighs about 3 lb (1.4 kg). The brain and spinal cord contain two main types of tissue: gray matter, which originates and processes nerve impulses; and white matter, which transmits them. The largest structure in the brain is the cerebrum, which is divided into two halves or hemispheres. Other structures include the cerebellum, the brain stem, and a central region that includes the thalamus and hypothalamus. The spinal cord is an extension of the brain stem and continues downward from the base of the skull.

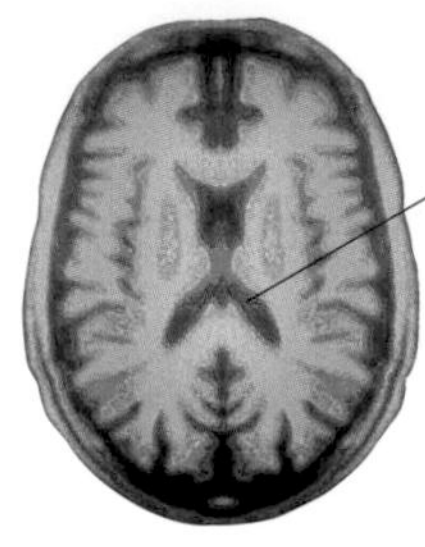

Lateral ventricles
The left and right lateral ventricles appear X-shaped when viewed in cross section

MRI scan of the brain
Protective cerebrospinal fluid is made in four ventricles, or cavities, in the brain. This section of the brain shows the lateral ventricles.

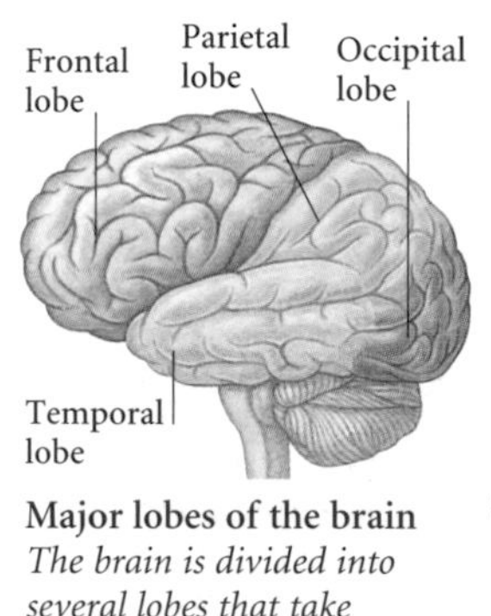
Frontal lobe
Parietal lobe
Occipital lobe
Temporal lobe

Major lobes of the brain
The brain is divided into several lobes that take their names from the skull bones that cover them.

Cerebrum
The cerebrum consists of gray and white matter. It is the largest part of the brain and links to every part of the body

Meninges
Surrounding the brain and the spinal cord are three protective membranes called the meninges

Cerebral cortex
This outer layer of the cerebrum governs higher brain functions, including thought. It receives and processes sensations and initiates movement

Subarachnoid space
This region contains cerebrospinal fluid, which protects and nourishes the brain and spinal cord as it circulates around them before draining back into the venous sinuses

Arachnoid granulation
Cerebrospinal fluid is absorbed from here into the blood

Skull

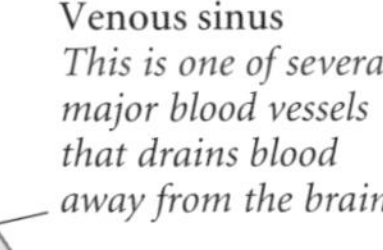

Venous sinus
This is one of several major blood vessels that drains blood away from the brain

Corpus callosum
This large bundle of about 300 million nerve fibers connects the two cerebral hemispheres

Choroid plexus
This area is involved in producing cerebrospinal fluid

Hypothalamus
The hypothalamus controls the endocrine system. It regulates sleep, sexual function, body temperature, and water content

Thalamus
Sensory nerve impulses pass through the thalamus on their way to the cerebral cortex

Pituitary
This gland regulates other glands throughout the body

Cerebellum
This area is involved in balance and the control of muscle movement

Midbrain
Pons
Medulla

Brain stem
The brain stem relays nerve impulses between the spinal cord and the brain; it controls vital functions such as heart rate and breathing

Spinal cord
Nerve impulses sent between the brain and the peripheral nerves travel along nerve fibers that run through tracts (pathways) in the spinal cord

Gray matter
Gray matter consists mainly of neuron cell bodies, from which nerve impulses originate

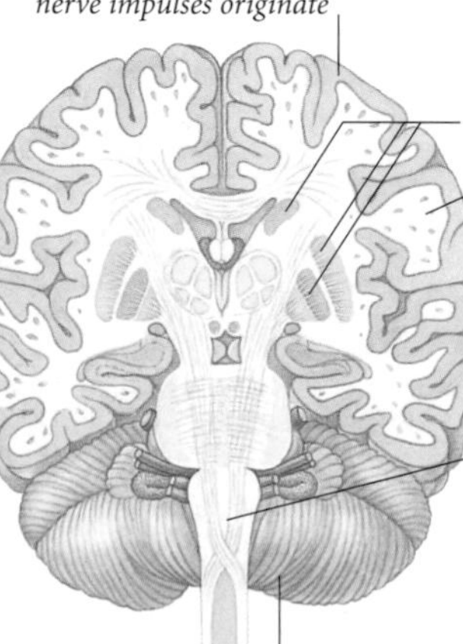
Cerebellum

Basal ganglia
These islands of gray matter help coordinate movement

White matter
White matter consists largely of nerve fibers; its main role is to transmit nerve impulses

Brain stem
The main motor pathways cross over in the brain stem to the opposite sides of the spinal cord

Brain tissue
The outer layer of the brain, the cerebral cortex, is made of gray matter. Beneath are white matter and islands of gray matter.

Cranial nerves

Twelve pairs of cranial nerves emerge directly from the underside of the brain. Most of these nerves supply the head, face, neck, and shoulders. Certain organs in the chest and abdomen, including the heart, lungs, and much of the digestive system, are supplied by the vagus nerve.

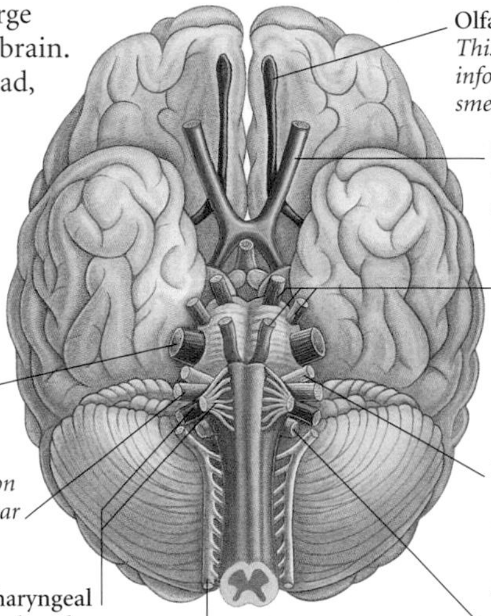

Trigeminal nerve
Signals from the face are relayed by this nerve, which also controls muscles used in chewing

Vestibulocochlear nerve
Fibers in this nerve carry information about sound and balance from the ear

Olfactory nerve
This nerve relays information about smell from the nose

Optic nerve
This nerve transmits information about visual images

Oculomotor, trochlear, and abducent nerves
These nerves supply muscles that move the eyes

Facial nerve
This nerve transmits information from the taste buds and controls facial expression

Glossopharyngeal and hypoglossal nerves
These nerves carry information about taste in addition to controlling movements of the tongue

Spinal accessory nerve
This nerve controls some movements of the head and shoulder muscles

Vagus nerve
This nerve performs many roles, such as regulation of heart rate and speech

Cranial nerve functions
The cranial nerves contain sensory and/or motor fibers, which control various conscious and unconscious functions.

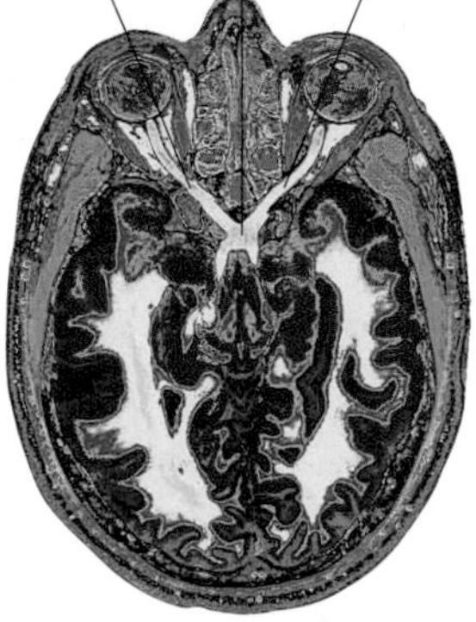

Left optic nerve

Crossover point

Right optic nerve

MRI scan of optic nerves
The optic nerves from the left and the right eyes merge and then diverge in the center of the brain so that each cerebral hemisphere receives data from both eyes.

Spinal nerves

Thirty-one pairs of spinal nerves emerge from the spinal cord and extend through the protective, bony spinal column. These nerves divide to supply all parts of the torso and the limbs. Before reaching the limbs, bundles of nerves converge to form braidlike plexuses, called the brachial and lumbar plexuses, which then branch farther along.

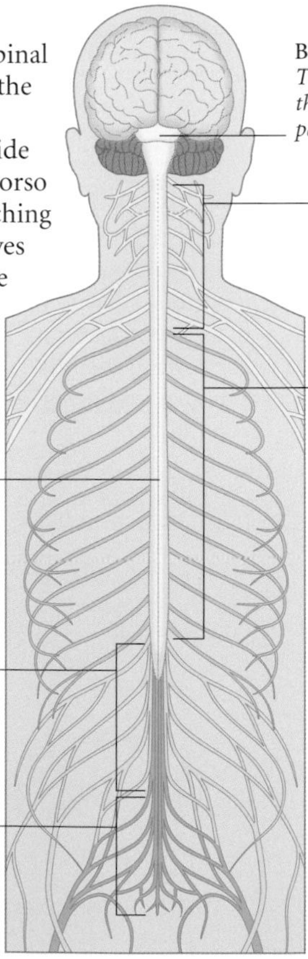

Brain stem
The brain stem connects the spinal cord to other parts of the brain

Cervical nerves
Eight pairs of cervical nerves supply the head, neck, shoulders, arms, and hands

Thoracic nerves
The twelve pairs of thoracic nerves connect to parts of the upper abdomen and to muscles in the back and chest

Spinal cord
Nerve impulses are carried between the spinal nerves and the brain along this column of nervous tissue

Lumbar nerves
Five pairs of lumbar nerves supply the area of the lower back and the legs

Sacral region
Five pairs of sacral nerves and a pair of coccygeal nerves supply the buttocks, legs, feet, anal, and genital areas

Role of the spinal nerves
The spinal nerves (shown here from the front) carry sensory nerve impulses toward the spinal cord and brain. They also carry motor nerve impulses from the brain to the rest of the body.

Structure of the spinal cord

The spinal cord has a core of gray matter containing nerve cell bodies, dendrites, and supporting cells. Surrounding the gray matter is white matter containing columns of nerve fibers that carry signals to and from the brain along the length of the spinal cord.

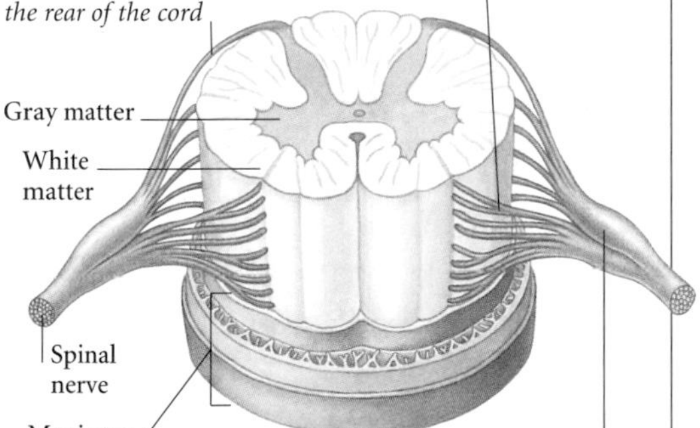

Sensory nerve root
These sensory fibers carry data about sensations and enter the rear of the cord

Motor nerve root
These motor nerve fibers control movement and leave the front of the spinal cord

Gray matter

White matter

Spinal nerve

Meninges
These membranes protect the spinal cord

Ganglion
This nodule contains the cell bodies of sensory nerve fibers

Nerve root pathways
Each spinal nerve has motor and sensory nerve roots. The sensory nerve roots enter the back of the spinal cord to join fibers that lead to the brain. Nerve fibers carrying signals from the brain join motor nerve roots leaving the front of the cord.

STRUCTURE AND FUNCTION NERVE CELLS

Neurons are nerve cells that originate, process, transmit, and receive nerve impulses. They are connected to other neurons or to cells in muscles, organs, or glands. Nerve impulses travel electrically along the neuron and are transmitted by chemical messengers (neurotransmitters) to the next neuron across a tiny gap, called a synapse, between the neuron and the adjacent cell, which is known as the target cell. In addition to neurons, the nervous system contains large numbers of other types of cells, called neuroglia, which protect, nourish, and support neurons.

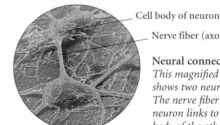

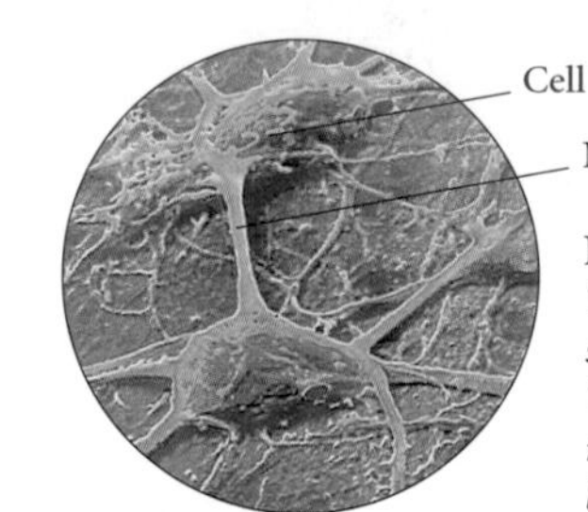
Cell body of neuron
Nerve fiber (axon)

Neural connection
This magnified image shows two neurons. The nerve fiber of one neuron links to the cell body of the other.

NEURONS

In addition to features common to all cells, such as a nucleus, neurons have specialized projections, known as nerve fibers (axons), that carry nerve signals. Neurons in the brain form densely packed clusters. Neurons in the spinal cord and around the body form long communication tracts.

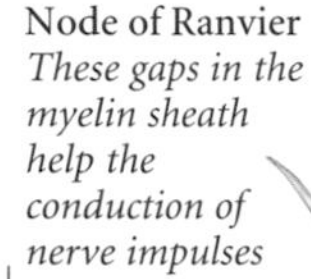
Nerve fiber (axon)
Nerve fibers may link to the cell bodies or the dendrites of other neurons or to other cells
Dendrite
A neuron may have up to 200 of these short, branching projections
Node of Ranvier
These gaps in the myelin sheath help the conduction of nerve impulses
Myelin sheath
Some fibers have this fatty coating, which speeds up nerve impulse transmission
Synapse
This gap separates a fiber's end bulb from an adjacent cell body or a dendrite
Synaptic end bulb
This swelling at the end of the nerve fiber holds chemicals able to travel across the synapse
Nucleus
Neuron cell body

Neuron structure
A typical neuron has one or two long nerve fibers and many dendrites. Nerve fibers carry signals away from a neuron's cell body, and dendrites carry signals toward it.

CONDUCTION OF NERVE SIGNALS

Nerve impulses travel along neurons in the form of electrical signals. These signals cross the synapses (tiny gaps) between one neuron and the next in chemical form before being transmitted again in electrical form. Signals are also chemically transmitted to other target cells, such as those in muscles, which make appropriate responses.

Electrical and chemical conduction
When an electrical signal arrives at the end of a nerve fiber, it triggers the release of neurotransmitter molecules, which transmit the signal in chemical form to the next cell.

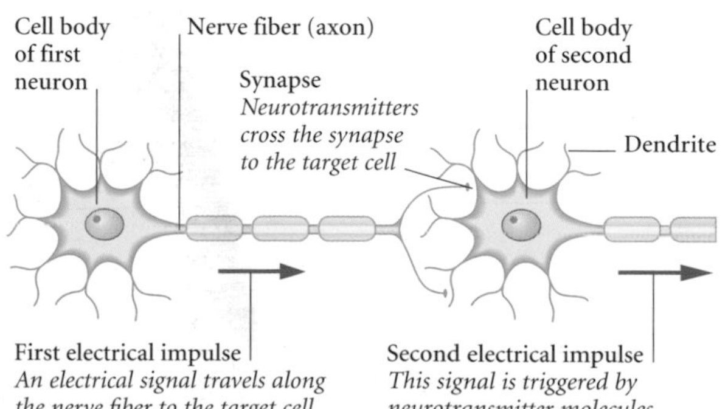
Cell body of first neuron
Nerve fiber (axon)
Synapse
Neurotransmitters cross the synapse to the target cell
Cell body of second neuron
Dendrite
First electrical impulse
An electrical signal travels along the nerve fiber to the target cell
Second electrical impulse
This signal is triggered by neurotransmitter molecules

HOW NEUROTRANSMITTERS WORK

More than 50 neurotransmitters have been identified. Their task is to carry nerve impulses across the synapse (a tiny gap) between neurons and target cells. Neurotransmitters either stimulate or inhibit electrical impulses in target cells.

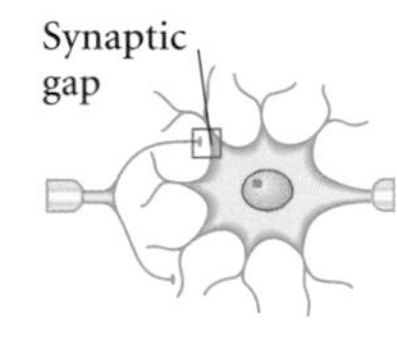
Synaptic gap

LOCATION

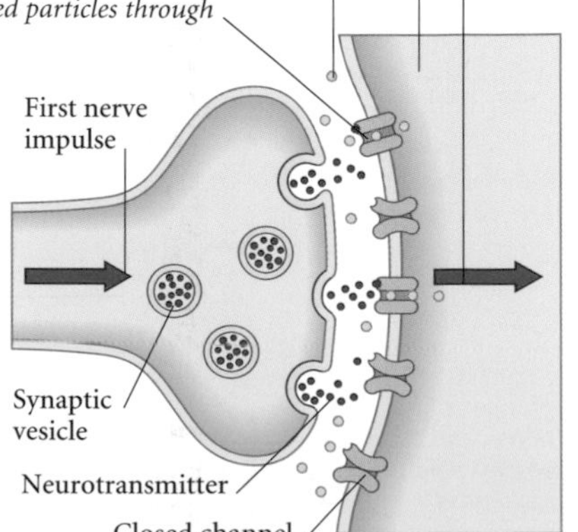
Open channel
Neurotransmitters open channels in the target cell to let charged particles through
Charged particle
Target cell
Second impulse
First nerve impulse
Synaptic vesicle
Neurotransmitter
Closed channel

Crossing the synapse
Arrival of a nerve impulse stimulates the release of neurotransmitters from vesicles. They pass across the synapse and open channels in the target cell. Charged particles can then enter and trigger a second impulse.

STRUCTURE AND FUNCTION SENSORY RECEPTORS

Sensory receptors respond to stimuli and transmit data about them to the brain. In the skin, receptors detect touch, pressure, vibration, temperature, and pain. Elsewhere in the body, more specialized receptors detect light (*see* HOW THE EYE WORKS, p.568), sound (*see* THE MECHANISM OF HEARING, p.594), smell, and taste. Internal receptors called proprioceptors detect the position of body parts relative to each other and in space.

TOUCH

Touch receptors are found all over the body. The most common are free nerve endings, which sense pain, pressure, and temperature in addition to touch. Other touch receptors include Merkel's and Meissner's corpuscles, which detect light touch, and Pacinian corpuscles, which sense deep pressure and vibration.

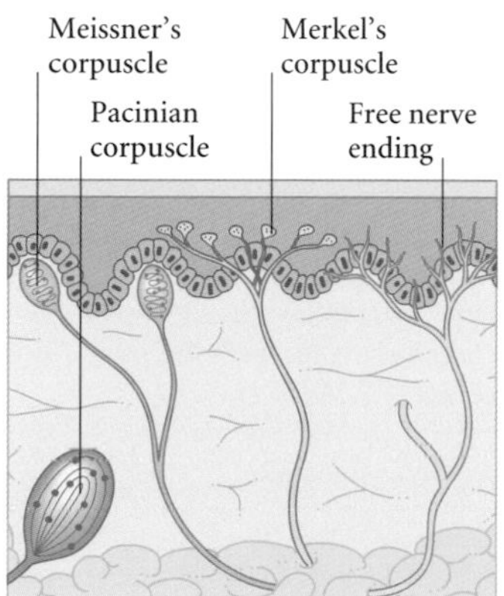
Meissner's corpuscle
Merkel's corpuscle
Pacinian corpuscle
Free nerve ending

Receptors in the skin
Merkel's, Meissner's, and Pacinian corpuscles end in a capsule. Free nerve endings are uncovered.

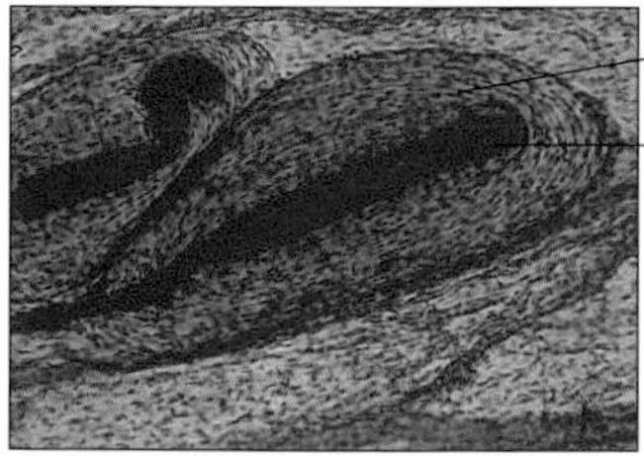
Capsule of layered membranes
Nerve ending

Pacinian corpuscle
This receptor consists of a nerve ending surrounded by layered membranes. Pacinian corpuscles are found in the palms, soles, genitals, and nipples.

SMELL

Olfactory receptors in the roof of the nasal cavity are stimulated by odors. Nerve impulses from these receptors travel to the olfactory bulb (the end of the olfactory nerve) and then to the olfactory centers in the brain. Our sense of smell is thousands of times more sensitive than our sense of taste, and we can detect more than 10,000 odors.

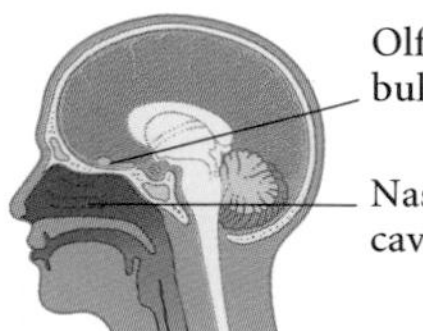
Olfactory bulb
Nasal cavity
LOCATION

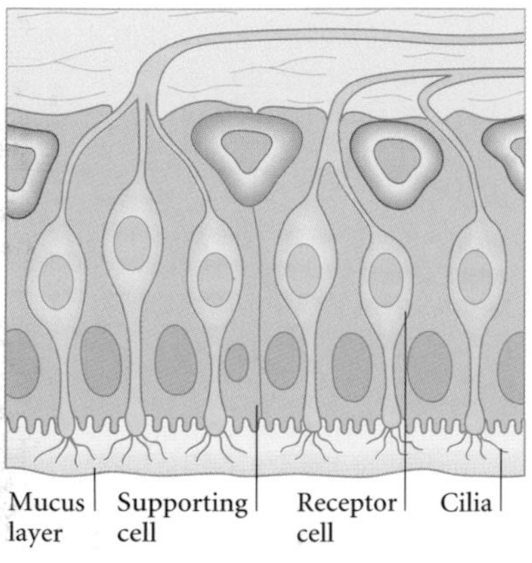
Mucus layer
Supporting cell
Receptor cell
Cilia

Olfactory receptors
When odor molecules enter the nose, they stimulate the cilia (tiny hairs) attached to receptor cells, causing nerve impulses to travel to the olfactory bulb and then onward to the brain.

TASTE

There are about 10,000 taste buds on the upper surface of the tongue. Each bud contains about 25 sensory receptor cells, on which tiny taste hairs are exposed to drink and food dissolved in saliva. Buds in different parts of the tongue sense the four basic tastes: bitter, sour, salty, and sweet. A combination of odors and these basic tastes produce more subtle tastes.

Taste bud structure
Substances in the mouth come into contact with taste hairs on the tongue. These tiny hairs generate nerve impulses that travel along nerve fibers to a specialized area of the brain.

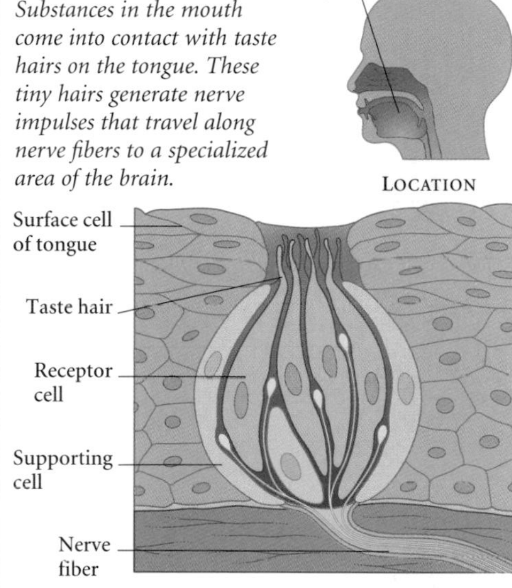
Tongue
LOCATION
Surface cell of tongue
Taste hair
Receptor cell
Supporting cell
Nerve fiber

PROPRIOCEPTORS

Proprioceptors are types of internal sensory receptors that monitor the degree of stretch of muscles and tendons around the body. This information gives us our sense of balance and our awareness of the position of various parts of the body in relation to each other.

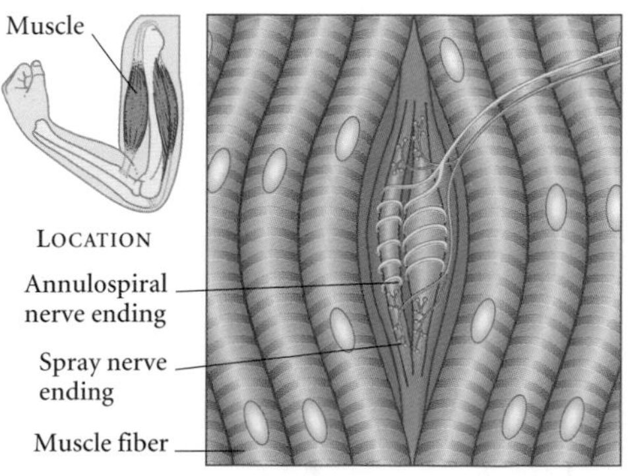
Muscle
LOCATION
Annulospiral nerve ending
Spray nerve ending
Muscle fiber

Muscle proprioceptors
Two types of muscle proprioceptor are annulospiral sensory endings, which wind around the muscle fibers, and spray endings, which lie on top of the fibers.

FUNCTION VOLUNTARY AND INVOLUNTARY RESPONSES

The responses of the nervous system to stimuli may be voluntary or involuntary. Voluntary responses are mainly under conscious control, but some voluntary movements, such as walking, require less conscious attention. There are two types of involuntary response, autonomic and reflex. Autonomic responses regulate the body's internal environment. Reflexes mainly affect those muscles that are normally under voluntary control.

VOLUNTARY RESPONSES

All voluntary activities involve the brain, which sends out the motor impulses that control movement. These motor signals are initiated by thought and most also involve a response to sensory stimuli. For example, people use sight and sense of position to help them coordinate the action of walking.

Voluntary pathways
The sensory impulses that trigger voluntary responses are dealt with in many parts of the brain.

Cerebral cortex *The cortex processes sensory data and sends impulses to the muscles*

Cerebellum *The cerebellum monitors all sensory data, fine-tuning motor nerve impulses from the cerebral cortex to produce coordinated movement*

Basal ganglia *These masses of gray matter help control coordinated movements, such as walking*

Sensory nerve impulse

Motor nerve impulse

Spinal cord

Nerve–muscle junction
At this junction, a nerve fiber transmits signals to produce a response from muscle fibers.

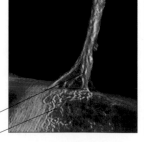

Nerve fiber

Muscle fiber

AUTONOMIC RESPONSES

The autonomic nervous system controls the body's internal environment without conscious intervention and helps regulate vital functions, such as blood pressure. The two types of autonomic nerves, sympathetic and parasympathetic, have opposing effects but balance each other most of the time. At certain times, such as during stress or exercise, one system dominates.

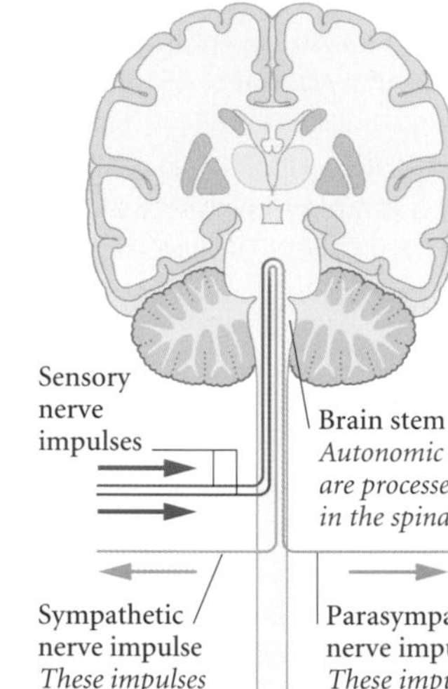
Sensory nerve impulses
Brain stem
Autonomic responses are processed here or in the spinal cord
Sympathetic nerve impulse
These impulses are carried by spinal nerves
Parasympathetic nerve impulse
These impulses are mainly carried by cranial nerves
Spinal cord

Autonomic pathways
Information collected by internal receptors travels along sensory nerves to the spinal cord and the brain stem for processing. Sympathetic and parasympathetic response signals have separate pathways.

DIVISIONS OF THE AUTONOMIC SYSTEM		
AFFECTED ORGAN	SYMPATHETIC RESPONSE	PARASYMPATHETIC RESPONSE
Eyes	Pupils dilate	Pupils constrict
Lungs	Bronchial tubes dilate	Bronchial tubes constrict
Heart	Rate and strength of heartbeat increase	Rate and strength of heartbeat decrease
Stomach	Enzymes decrease	Enzymes increase
Liver	Releases glucose	Stores glucose

Two types of responses
Sympathetic and parasympathetic nerves each produce different responses in a particular organ. The sympathetic responses prepare the body to cope at times of stress. Parasympathetic responses help conserve or restore energy.

REFLEXES

A reflex is an involuntary response to a stimulus, such as withdrawing your hand from a hot surface before you become aware of the heat. Most reflexes are processed in the spine, although some, such as blinking, are processed in the brain. In a spinal reflex, the stimulus signal travels along a sensory nerve to the spinal cord, and a response signal travels back by means of a motor nerve.

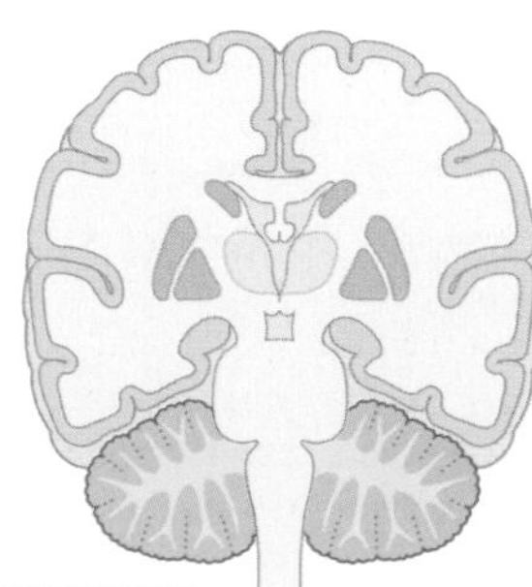

Sensory nerve impulse

Motor nerve impulse

Spinal cord *Each sensory nerve impulse is processed in the spinal cord, which sends a response signal directly to the correct muscle*

Spinal reflex pathway
Spinal reflexes involve the simplest nerve pathways: the sensory and motor neurons are directly linked together in the spinal cord.

FUNCTION INFORMATION PROCESSING

Different types of sensory information are processed in different parts of the nervous system, which sends out appropriate response signals. Complex information, such as data about music and emotion, is processed in the cerebral cortex, which is known as the "higher" part of the brain. Some specialized functions, such as the interpretation of language, are processed mainly in one side of the brain, the "dominant hemisphere." The left hemisphere is dominant in more than 9 out of 10 people.

Broca's area in right hemisphere

Broca's area in left hemisphere

Wernicke's area in left hemisphere

Language interpretation in the brain
The colored areas in this PET scan show the regions of the brain that are most active while interpreting language. There is more activity in the left dominant hemisphere than in the right hemisphere.

PROCESSING HIGHER FUNCTIONS

Neuroscientists can now pinpoint those parts of the brain's cortex that process nerve impulses concerned with higher human functions, such as intellect and memory. Areas of the cortex that are mainly concerned with detecting nerve impulses are known as primary areas; those that are concerned with analyzing impulses are known as association areas.

Motor cortex
The motor cortex sends signals to muscles to cause voluntary movements

Premotor cortex
This part of the cortex coordinates complex movement sequences, such as piano playing

Prefrontal cortex
The prefrontal cortex deals with various aspects of behavior and personality

Broca's area
This area is vital for the formation of speech

Primary auditory cortex
This area detects discrete qualities of sound, such as pitch and volume

Auditory association cortex
This area analyzes data about sound. Data about individual sounds are combined, so that words or melodies can be recognized

Primary sensory cortex
This area receives data about sensations in skin, muscles, joints, and organs

Sensory association cortex
Data about sensations are analyzed here

Visual association cortex
Images are formed once visual data have been analyzed here

Primary visual cortex
This part of the cortex receives nerve impulses from the eye

Wernicke's area
This area interprets spoken and written language

The brain map
Different areas of the cortex have specific functions. Many areas of the cortex are involved in complex functions such as learning.

MOVEMENT AND TOUCH

Each side of the brain has its own motor and sensory cortices, which control movement and sense touch in the opposite side of the body. Movement signals are processed by a particular region at the top of the cerebrum in the motor cortex. An adjacent area, known as the sensory cortex, processes touch signals. Movements that involve great complexity or body parts that are extremely sensitive to touch are allocated a larger proportion of motor or sensory cortex. In general, those parts of the body capable of complex movement are also highly sensitive to touch.

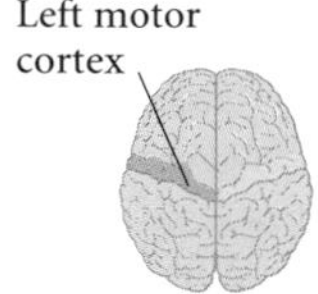
Left motor cortex
TOP VIEW

Motor map of the brain
Areas of the body that require great skill and precision of movement, such as the hands, are allocated relatively large areas of the motor cortex.

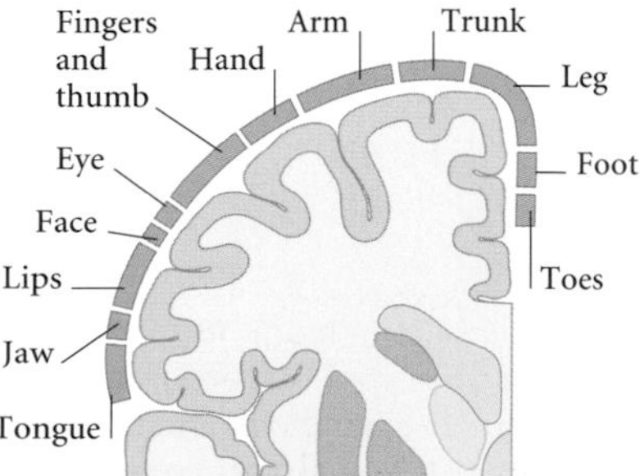
Fingers and thumb
Hand
Arm
Trunk
Leg
Foot
Toes
Eye
Face
Lips
Jaw
Tongue

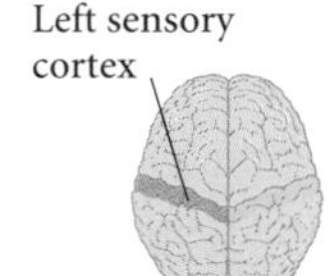
Left sensory cortex
TOP VIEW

Touch map of the brain
Very sensitive areas of the body, such as the fingers, lips, and genitals have disproportionately large areas of the sensory cortex allocated to them.

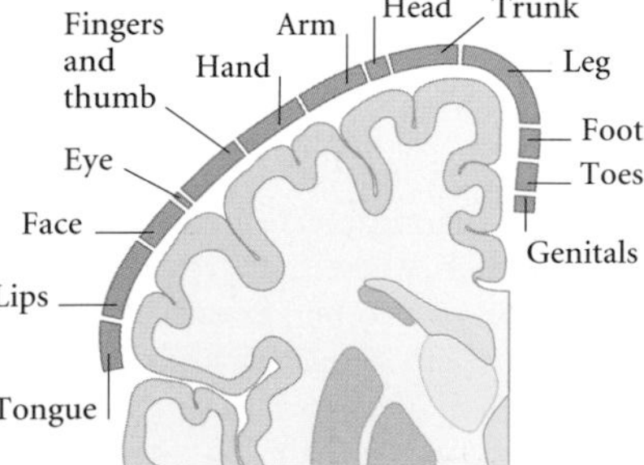
Fingers and thumb
Hand
Arm
Head
Trunk
Leg
Foot
Toes
Genitals
Eye
Face
Lips
Tongue

GENERAL NERVOUS SYSTEM DISORDERS

The nervous system is composed of the brain and spinal cord, together known as the central nervous system, and a vast array of peripheral nerves that transmit information to and from these central structures. The nervous system may be damaged in various ways, such as by infection, injury, or vascular problems. However, many of the general disorders have no obvious underlying cause.

KEY ANATOMY

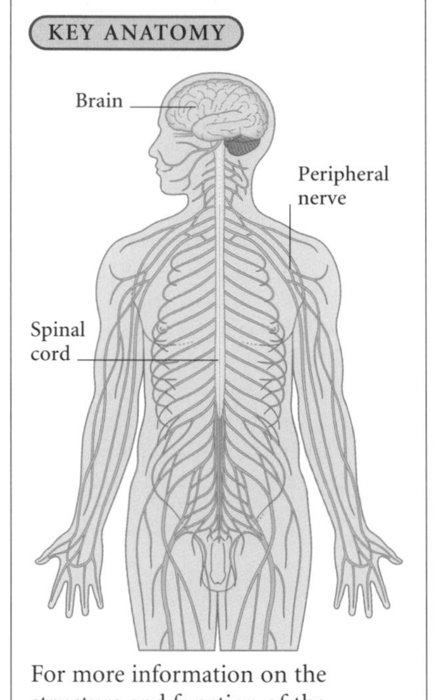
Brain
Peripheral nerve
Spinal cord

For more information on the structure and function of the nervous system, *see* pp.508–515.

The first article in this section deals with pain. Most people feel pain when injured, and it is a common symptom of many disorders. A description of the pain, including information about where it occurs and its nature, often helps in the diagnosis of a disorder. Fortunately, the advent of effective analgesics and new treatments, such as transcutaneous electrical nerve stimulation (TENS), means that prolonged unbearable pain can be effectively treated and/or controlled.

The different types of headaches are discussed next. Tension headaches cause discomfort and pain to millions of people every year, often due to stress or tension. Migraine is also relatively common, while cluster headaches are a severe but less common type of headache that occur in a characteristic pattern. A headache can be a sign of an underlying disorder, and persistent or severe headaches associated with other symptoms, such as nausea, should be assessed by a doctor without delay.

The final article in this section discusses chronic fatigue syndrome, a complex and debilitating condition.

Headaches and migraine in children are covered elsewhere (*see* INFANCY AND CHILDHOOD, pp.844–850).

Pain

An unpleasant sensation often felt as a result of tissue disease or damage

AGE GENDER GENETICS LIFESTYLE
Not significant factors

Pain is the body's response to injury or disease that results in tissue damage. Pain usually functions as a protective warning mechanism, helping prevent further damage, although chronic pain often seems to serve no useful function. Everyone has experienced pain at some time, but its severity and character depend to some extent on the cause. For example, the pain experienced as the result of an athletic injury may be less severe than that of a similar injury caused by a violent assault. Mood and personality also affect the way we perceive pain. For example, fear or anxiety can make pain worse, and relaxation may relieve it to a certain extent.

The brain and spinal cord produce their own painkillers, known as endorphins, in response to pain. Endorphins are natural chemicals that are closely related to morphine and act as highly effective pain relievers for short periods but are less effective for chronic pain.

Most forms of pain can now be controlled as a result of improvements in treatment, and it is rare for someone to have to live with persistent pain.

WHAT ARE THE CAUSES?

When tissue is damaged by trauma, infection, or a problem with its blood supply, specialized nerve endings called pain receptors are stimulated. Electrical signals travel along the nerves and through the spinal cord to the brain, which interprets them as pain. While this is happening, the damaged tissues release chemicals known as prostaglandins, which leads to inflammation and swelling. The prostaglandins further stimulate the pain receptors. The skin and other sensitive parts of the body, such as the tongue and the eyes, have a large number of pain receptors and are therefore very sensitive to painful stimuli. The internal organs of the body have fewer pain receptors and are insensitive to most types of injury.

WHAT ARE THE TYPES?

Although each individual may describe the character or the site of pain in a different way, there are some types of pain that usually result from specific problems. For example, throbbing pain is often due to increased blood flow, either as a result of widening of the blood vessels, as may occur in migraine (p.518), or because of an increase in blood flow through injured tissues. Severe shooting pains, such as sciatica (p.546), can be caused by pressure or irritation of the nerve at the point that it emerges from the spinal cord. Colicky pain is caused by intermittent stretching and contraction of muscles in the walls of the intestines or other parts of the body, such as the bile ducts, which lead from the liver to the intestine.

The location of the pain usually acts as a good guide to its source. However, in some cases, overlapping nerve pathways can result in a confused message, causing pain to be felt in a different area of the body than exactly where it originates. This type of pain is known as referred pain and occurs when the nerves carrying the sensation of pain merge with other nerves before they reach the brain. For example, hip problems may be felt as knee pain, while problems with a tooth may be felt as earache. Heart problems can cause pain across the chest, into the neck, and in one or both arms. Pain due to problems in the intestines tends to be felt in the center of the abdomen at first and is felt locally only when the wall of the abdomen is affected, as in the later stages of appendicitis (p.664).

Sudden, severe pain may be associated with other symptoms, such as pale skin, sweating, nausea or vomiting, rapid pulse, and dilated pupils. Prolonged periods of severe pain that continue for weeks or months may lead to depression (p.554), loss of weight as a result of decreased appetite, and disturbed sleeping patterns (*see* INSOMNIA, p.554).

TREATMENT PAIN RELIEF USING TENS

Transcutaneous electrical nerve stimulation (TENS) is sometimes useful for relieving severe, persistent pain, such as back pain. In TENS, electrical impulses are relayed from an impulse generator to electrodes placed on the skin in the area of the pain. After about 30 minutes, pain is usually significantly reduced. Relief may last for several hours. TENS can be used while pursuing normal activities.

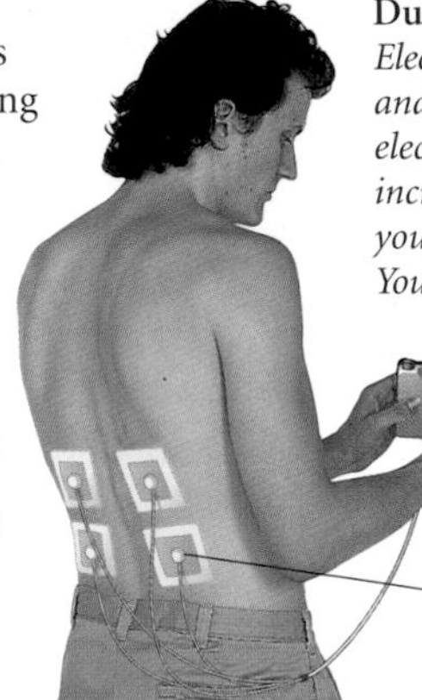
Impulse generator
This battery-operated device can be clipped onto a belt
Electrode
The electrodes can be left on the skin between treatments

During TENS
Electrodes are placed on the skin, and a portable device generates electrical impulses. You can increase the level of stimulation yourself until the pain is relieved. You may feel a tingling sensation.

WHAT MIGHT BE DONE?

If you experience severe or recurrent unexplained pain, you should see your doctor who may be able to establish the cause of pain after a physical examination. Further investigations, including blood tests and imaging tests, such as ultrasound scanning (p.250), may be necessary if there is no obvious cause.

Since it is difficult to assess the severity of pain, your doctor may ask how the pain affects your sleep and your ability to cope with daily activities. You may also be asked to describe the severity of the pain on a scale of 1 to 10, using 1 for slight discomfort and 10 for almost unbearable pain.

The most effective remedy for pain is treatment of the underlying cause, if possible. However, pain relief is important at the same time until treatment of the cause takes effect. There are many different ways to relieve pain, including drugs and physical methods. The form of pain relief chosen depends on the cause and type of pain you experience.

Since pain, in particular persistent pain, is influenced by other factors such as stress and personality, treatment has to be tailored to the individual.

DRUG TREATMENT The vast majority of short-lived pain and much long-term pain can be relieved successfully by analgesics (p.912). Pain is often caused partly by local prostaglandin release. In this case, treatment with nonsteroidal anti-inflammatory drugs (p.894) often works well because these drugs block the release of prostaglandins.

Opioid analgesics, such as morphine and codeine, act directly on the part of the brain that perceives pain and are usually highly effective. Opioid analgesics may be needed to relieve intense pain, such as that following surgery and the severe pain associated with some cancers (*see* PAIN RELIEF FOR CANCER, p.281). The risk of addiction to these drugs is small when they are used for short periods, and dependence is not a cause for concern when they are used in caring for a terminally ill person (p.965).

In addition to analgesics, other drugs may be given for certain types of pain. These include local anesthetics (p.914) and drugs that affect the transmission of nerve impulses, such as antidepressant drugs (p.916) and anticonvulsant drugs (p.914). Pain caused by muscle tension may be treated using antidepressant drugs, and anticonvulsant drugs are often used to help relieve pain associated with trigeminal neuralgia (p.546) and other painful neuropathies.

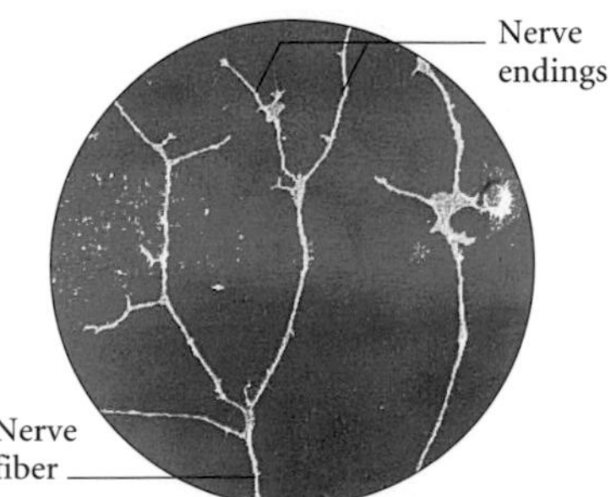
Nerve endings
Nerve fiber

Nerve endings
Branching nerve endings, as shown here, may respond to tissue damage by sending electrical signals to the brain. These signals are then interpreted as pain.

PHYSICAL TREATMENT A wide range of nondrug therapies is available to help relieve pain, including gentle massage and the use of hot or cold compresses. These treatments both alter blood flow through damaged tissues and stimulate other nerve endings, blocking pain.

Acupuncture (p.973) is helpful for some types of pain and may be used to relieve pain after operations and persistent pain that does not respond to other types of treatments. Acupuncture is believed to work by causing the brain to release endorphins or by stimulating nerve endings near the site of the pain so that they stop sending pain messages.

If you have pain due to damaged ligaments or muscles, your doctor may suggest ultrasound treatment, in which sound waves produce vibrations in the tissues and generate heat. TENS (*see* PAIN RELIEF USING TENS, above) uses electric impulses to block pain sensation by stimulating the nerves. TENS is sometimes used for lower back pain (p.381) or during labor.

WHAT IS THE PROGNOSIS?

Almost all pain can be relieved to some degree, even if the underlying cause of the pain cannot be definitively treated. However, chronic pain is often more difficult to control than acute pain.

(WWW) ONLINE SITES: p.1035

Headache

Pain in the head of variable severity due to a variety of causes

 AGE More common over age 20

 GENDER More common in females

 LIFESTYLE Stress is a risk factor

 GENETICS Not a significant factor

Headache is very common in Canada, and most common in women. The majority of headaches last for only a few hours, but some can persist for weeks.

Pain may occur in only one part of the head, such as above the eyes, or it may involve the entire head. The type of pain experienced varies; it may be constant and dull or sudden and sharp. Sometimes, other symptoms, such as nausea, occur at the same time.

WHAT ARE THE CAUSES?

There are many possible causes of headache that determine the site and nature of the pain. Quite commonly, headaches are caused by tension in the scalp or neck muscles. Tension headaches (right) tend to recur frequently and cause moderate pain that affects both sides of the head. Other types of headaches, including migraine (right) and cluster headaches (opposite page), have a variety of possible causes.

Very few headaches have a serious underlying cause (*see* SYMPTOM CHART: HEADACHE, p.110), but those that do require urgent medical attention. For example, a severe headache may be a sign of meningitis (p.527), a condition in which the membranes covering the brain and spinal cord become infected, or of subarachnoid hemorrhage (p.534), in which bleeding occurs between the membranes covering the brain. In elderly people, a headache with tenderness of the scalp or temple may be due to temporal arteritis (p.464), in which blood vessels in the head become inflamed. Occasionally, headache results from prolonged use of strong analgesics (p.912).

If your headache is severe, lasts more than 24 hours, or is accompanied by other symptoms, such as problems with your vision or vomiting, you should seek medical help without delay.

WHAT MIGHT BE DONE?

Your doctor will do a physical examination. If he or she suspects an underlying disorder is causing your headache, you may require tests, such as CT scanning (p.247) or MRI (p.248) of your brain.

Treatment depends on the cause of the headache. For example, a tension headache will usually clear up with rest and analgesics. Cluster headaches and migraine headaches can be treated with specific drugs, such as sumatriptan (*see* ANTIMIGRAINE DRUGS, p.913).

(WWW) ONLINE SITES: p.1032

Tension headaches

Moderate or severe pain, affecting one or more areas around the head, often as a result of stress

 AGE More common over age 20

 GENDER More common in females

 LIFESTYLE Stress is a risk factor

 GENETICS Not a significant factor

Tension headaches are often the result of stress (p.74) or bad posture, which causes a tightening of the muscles in the neck and scalp. Tension headaches usually last only a few hours, but some people may have chronic headaches that continue for several days or weeks. Recurrent tension headaches often affect people with depression (p.554) or those who are under continuous stress due to difficulties at work or at home. Tension headaches are often made worse by noise and hot, stuffy environments. This type of headache occurs mostly in women over age 20.

WHAT ARE THE SYMPTOMS?

Symptoms often begin late in the morning or in the early afternoon and may persist for several hours. They include:

- Pain that is usually constant and may be throbbing. Pain is felt above the eyes or more generally over the head.
- Feeling of pressure behind the eyes.
- Tightening of neck muscles.
- Feeling of tightness around the head.

People who have persistent headaches may find it difficult to sleep (*see* INSOMNIA, p.554). They may also become depressed and feel depleted of energy.

WHAT CAN I DO?

Self-help measures, such as taking over-the-counter analgesics (p.912), may help relieve a tension headache. However, the prolonged use of analgesics may eventually cause headaches. If you have a severe headache that lasts for more than 24 hours, does not respond to self-help measures, or is associated with other symptoms, such as vomiting or blurry vision, consult your doctor immediately.

WHAT MIGHT THE DOCTOR DO?

Your doctor will ask about the severity and frequency of your headaches and may look for signs of stress or depression. A diagnosis of tension headache is often clear from the symptoms, but you may need further tests, such as MRI (p.248) or CT scanning (p.247) of the brain, to check for an underlying cause.

Your doctor may recommend ways for you to deal with stress, such as yoga or relaxation exercises (p.75). If you are suffering from depression, he or she may prescribe antidepressant drugs (p.916). Once stress or depression has been relieved, tension headaches usually clear up, but they may recur in the future.

(WWW) ONLINE SITES: p.1032

Migraine

A severe headache often associated with visual disturbances and nausea or vomiting

 AGE First attack usually occurs by age 30; incidence decreases with age

 GENDER More common in females

 GENETICS Often runs in families

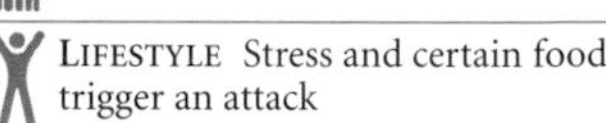 LIFESTYLE Stress and certain foods can trigger an attack

It is estimated that 3.2 million adults in Canada experience migraine headaches. Migraine is more common in women, and people usually have their first attack before age 30. First attacks rarely occur in people over age 40, but they can occur in children as young as 3 years old (*see* MIGRAINE IN CHILDREN, p.847). Migraine headaches recur at intervals of varying length. Some people have attacks several times a month; others have less than one a year. Most people find that migraine attacks occur less frequently and become less severe as they get older.

There are two major types of migraine headache: migraine with an aura and migraine without an aura. An aura is a group of symptoms, mainly visual, that develops before the onset of the main headache. Migraine with aura accounts for about 1 in 5 of all migraine cases. Some people experience both types of migraine at different times.

What are the causes?

The underlying cause of migraine is unknown, but increased blood flow as a result of widening of the blood vessels in the brain is known to occur during a migraine. About 8 in 10 people who have migraine have a close relative with the disorder. Stress (p.74) and depression (p.554) may be trigger factors, as may the relief of stress, such as relaxing after a difficult day. Other potential migraine triggers are missed meals, lack of sleep, and certain foods, such as cheese or chocolate. Many women find that their migraines often occur around the time of menstruation.

What are the symptoms?

Migraine headaches, either with or without aura, are sometimes preceded by a group of symptoms that are collectively known as a prodrome. These prodrome symptoms tend to appear about an hour before the main symptoms begin. The prodrome often includes:

- Anxiety or mood changes.
- Altered sense of taste and smell.
- Either an excess or a lack of energy.

People who have a migraine with aura experience a number of further symptoms before the migraine, including:

- Visual disturbances, such as blurry vision and bright flashes.
- Pins and needles, numbness, or a sensation of weakness on the face or on one side of the body.

The main symptoms, common to both types of migraine, then develop. These symptoms include:

- Headache that is severe, throbbing, made worse by movement, and usually felt on one side of the head, over one eye, or around one temple.
- Nausea or vomiting.
- Dislike of bright light or loud noises.

A migraine may last from a few hours to a few days but eventually clears up. After a migraine, you may feel tired and unable to concentrate.

What might be done?

Your doctor will usually be able to diagnose a migraine from your symptoms. Rarely, tests such as MRI (p.248) or CT scanning (p.247) of the brain may be done to rule out more serious causes such as a brain tumor (p.530).

Once migraine has been diagnosed, you may be prescribed drugs that reduce the duration of attacks, help treat symptoms, or prevent further occurrences. For example, your doctor may prescribe an antimigraine drug (p.913), such as sumatriptan, that, if taken in the early stages of an attack, will usually prevent the migraine from developing further. Ergotamine, another antimigraine drug, may also help relieve an attack but should not be taken for long periods of time.

If a full-blown migraine develops, analgesics (p.912) or nonsteroidal anti-inflammatory drugs (p.894) may help relieve the pain. If you also experience nausea and vomiting, antiemetic drugs (p.922) may provide relief.

Self-help measures may be useful in preventing further migraine attacks (*see* PREVENTING A MIGRAINE, below). If you have severe migraine more than twice a month, your doctor may prescribe a drug such as propranolol (*see* BETA BLOCKER DRUGS, p.898) to take every day to prevent attacks. Antiepileptic drugs or antidepressants may be used.

(WWW) ONLINE SITES: p.1032

(SELF-HELP) PREVENTING A MIGRAINE

Many factors are known to trigger a migraine. You need to identify the ones that affect you. Avoiding these factors may help reduce the frequency and severity of attacks.

- Keep a diary for a few weeks to help pinpoint trigger factors.
- Avoid any food you find brings on an attack. Common dietary triggers of migraine include red wine, cheese (especially matured cheese), and chocolate.
- Eat regularly, because missing a meal may trigger an attack.
- Follow a regular sleep pattern if possible, because changing it may trigger an attack.
- If stress is a trigger, try doing relaxation exercises (p.75).

Cluster headaches

Severe short-lived headaches that recur over a few days

 AGE Rare under age 30

 GENDER More common in males

 LIFESTYLE Smoking and drinking alcohol are risk factors

 GENETICS Not a significant factor

Cluster headaches consist of brief periods of pain, often excruciating, in one part of the head. They occur in a characteristic pattern, usually between one and four times a day, and there may be gaps of months or years between each group of headaches. However, a small number of people have chronic cluster headaches that occur at regular intervals with very few remission periods between attacks. Like migraines (opposite page), cluster headaches are likely to be related to an increase in blood flow as a result of widening of the blood vessels in the brain. Cluster headaches affect about 1 million people in the US, 9 in 10 of whom are men. Smoking cigarettes and drinking alcohol increase the risk.

What are the symptoms?

Cluster headaches often develop early in the morning. The major symptoms, which appear suddenly and affect one side of the head or face, include:

- Severe pain around one eye or temple.
- Watering and redness of the eye.
- Drooping of the eyelid.
- Stuffiness in the nostril and, sometimes, a runny nose on one side.
- Flushing of one side of the face.

Individual episodes of pain may last from a few minutes to 3 hours. The average attack lasts 15–30 minutes. If you have a sudden, severe headache for the first time or if you have symptoms that are different from those of previous headaches, you should consult your doctor at once so that a more serious underlying cause can be excluded.

What might be done?

Your doctor may prescribe an antimigraine drug (p.913), which will help reduce the length of a cluster attack and decrease the severity of the headaches. Antimigraine drugs should be taken as

Spinal injuries

Damage to the back or neck that may involve the spinal cord

 AGE More common under age 30

 GENDER More common in males

 LIFESTYLE Drinking and driving and certain sports are risk factors

 GENETICS Not a significant factor

Injuries to the neck and back are most commonly caused by traffic accidents. The areas most often damaged are the muscles of the back and neck, the bones of the spine (vertebrae), and the ligaments that hold the bones together. Injuries to the spine may also damage the spinal cord, which lies in a narrow canal in the vertebrae and carries all the major nerve pathways connecting the limbs and trunk to and from the brain. Damage to the spinal cord may cause numbness and weakness in part of the body. If damage is severe, it can lead to paralysis, which may be permanent and even life-threatening. Spinal injuries tend to occur more commonly in young men due to lifestyle factors.

What are the types?

The most common type of spinal injury is whiplash, also called neck sprain or strain, in which the ligaments and muscles of the neck are damaged. The spinal cord is not usually affected by this type of injury. Whiplash is caused by sudden, extreme bending of the spine when the neck is "whipped" back, usually as the result of a motor vehicle crash.

A spinal injury may dislocate or fracture one or more of the vertebrae. The vertebrae may be damaged by an impact, such as being hit by a car, or by compression, usually due to a fall from a height. The spinal cord may be damaged by fractured or dislocated vertebrae or by a penetrating injury.

What are the symptoms?

Symptoms of a spinal injury depend on the type and severity of the damage and on which part is injured. A whiplash injury may lead to one or more of the following symptoms:

- Headache.
- Neck pain and stiffness.
- Swelling of the affected area.
- Shoulder pain.

Displacement or damage to vertebrae, including compression of a disk, may produce pain and inflammation. If the spinal cord is damaged, symptoms occur in other parts of the body. These symptoms may include:

- Loss of sensation.
- Weakness.
- Inability to move the affected part.
- Problems with control of the bladder and bowel.
- Difficulty breathing.

The areas of the body that are affected by symptoms depend on which part of the spinal cord has been damaged. The higher up the spinal cord the damage is, the more parts of the body will be affected. For example, damage to the midchest area of the spine may cause weakness and numbness in the legs but will not affect the arms. If the spinal cord is severely damaged in the neck area, there may be total paralysis of all four limbs (quadriplegia), the trunk, and the muscles that control breathing, and death may result.

Anyone who has a suspected neck or spinal injury must not be moved without medical supervision. Emergency first-aid measures should be carried out (*see* FIRST AID: SPINAL INJURY, p.990) and medical help sought at once.

How are they diagnosed?

Once in the hospital, a full neurological assessment will be carried out, including measuring the person's responses to different kinds of stimuli. This examination helps the doctor assess whether the spinal cord has been damaged. If there is damage, CT scanning (p.247 or MRI (p.248) may be used to determine its nature and extent. If a fracture of the vertebrae is suspected, X-rays (p.244) of the spine may be taken.

What is the treatment?

If there is ligament and muscle damage, but the vertebrae are undamaged and unlikely to become displaced, bed rest and regular monitoring will probably be the only treatments that are needed. Nonsteroidal anti-inflammatory drugs (p.894) may be used to relieve pain and swelling of tissues. Physiotherapy (p.961) may help strengthen the damaged muscles. If the injury has caused vertebrae to become displaced or damaged, the affected bones will need to be stabilized. Surgery may be carried out to realign damaged vertebrae and prevent possible damage to the spinal cord. People who have irreversible damage to the spinal cord may be paralyzed. In some people, early treatment with drugs reduces inflammation and limits the extent of the damage. Long-term physiotherapy is necessary to maintain muscle strength.

What is the prognosis?

Recovery from a back injury involving only muscles and ligaments is likely to take 4–6 weeks. Fractures usually heal in 6–8 weeks. If the spine is stable and there is no damage to the spinal cord, the person usually makes a complete recovery. When paralysis occurs, a long period of rehabilitation is needed. If there is no improvement after 6 months, the paralysis is likely to be permanent.

(WWW) ONLINE SITES: p.1035, p.1036

Epilepsy

A disorder of brain function causing recurrent seizures

 AGE Usually develops in children and young adults

 GENETICS Some types run in families

 GENDER LIFESTYLE Not significant factors

In a person who has epilepsy, recurrent seizures or brief episodes of altered consciousness are caused by abnormal electrical activity in the brain. Epilepsy is a common disorder in Canada.

The condition usually develops in childhood and may be gradually outgrown. However, elderly people are also at risk of developing epilepsy because they are more likely to have conditions that can cause it, such as stroke (p.532).

Many people with epilepsy lead normal lives. However, people who have recurrent seizures may have to limit their lifestyle to some degree.

What are the causes?

In 6 out of 10 people with epilepsy, the underlying cause of the disorder is not clear, although it is thought that a genetic factor may be involved. In other cases, recurrent seizures may be the result of disease or damage to the brain caused by an infection, such as meningitis (p.527), a stroke, a brain tumor (p.530), or scarring following a severe head injury (p.521).

In people with epilepsy, seizures may be triggered by lack of sleep or by missing a meal. Other trigger factors may include excessive alcohol consumption, flashing lights, and flickering television and computer screens.

A single seizure may not be caused by epilepsy. For example, high fevers in children can result in febrile convulsions (p.849). People who abuse alcohol over a long period may have a seizure, either while drinking heavily or during withdrawal from alcohol (*see* ALCOHOL DEPENDENCE, p.564). Very low blood glucose levels, which can occur as a result of treatment for diabetes mellitus (p.687), can also trigger a seizure.

What are the types?

Epileptic seizures may be generalized or partial, depending on how much of the brain is affected by abnormal electrical activity. During a generalized seizure, all areas of the brain are affected at the same time, whereas during a partial seizure only one part of the brain is affected. Generalized seizures can be further divided into either tonic–clonic or absence seizures. Partial seizures can be divided into simple partial seizures and complex partial seizures. Both simple partial and complex partial seizures can become generalized.

TONIC–CLONIC SEIZURES This type of seizure may be preceded by a warning of an attack, known as an aura. This aura lasts for a few seconds and gives people an opportunity to sit or lie down before they lose consciousness and fall. Auras may consist of a sensation of fear or unease. During the first 30 seconds of a seizure, the body stiffens and breathing may become irregular or stop briefly. This stage is followed by several minutes of uncontrolled movement of the limbs and trunk. After the seizure, consciousness is regained, breathing returns to normal, and muscles relax. Relaxation of the muscles in the bladder can cause incontinence. The person may be confused and disoriented for a few hours afterward and may develop a headache. After a tonic–clonic seizure, the person affected usually has no memory of what has happened.

Status epilepticus is a serious condition in which a person has repeated tonic–clonic seizures without regaining consciousness in between each seizure. The condition can be life-threatening, and medical attention should be sought.

ABSENCE SEIZURES These seizures are also known as petit mal seizures. They start in childhood and may continue into adolescence. Absence seizures are rare in adults. During an attack, the child loses touch with his or her surroundings and may be accused of daydreaming because his or her eyes remain open and staring. Each separate attack lasts for between 5 and 30 seconds, and the child is usually unaware afterward that anything was wrong. Since the seizures are almost never associated with falling down or other abnormal movements, they may not be noticed. However, frequent attacks can affect school performance.

SIMPLE PARTIAL SEIZURES During simple partial seizure, the affected person remains conscious. The head and the eyes may turn to one side, the hand, arm, and one side of the face may

TEST EEG

Electroencephalography (EEG) is used to diagnose conditions, such as epilepsy, that are associated with abnormal electrical activity in the brain. Electrodes are attached to a person's scalp, and recordings are made of brain activity with the eyes open and closed. A strobe light may be switched on for short periods to see if brain activity changes. The procedure takes approximately 20–30 minutes and is painless.

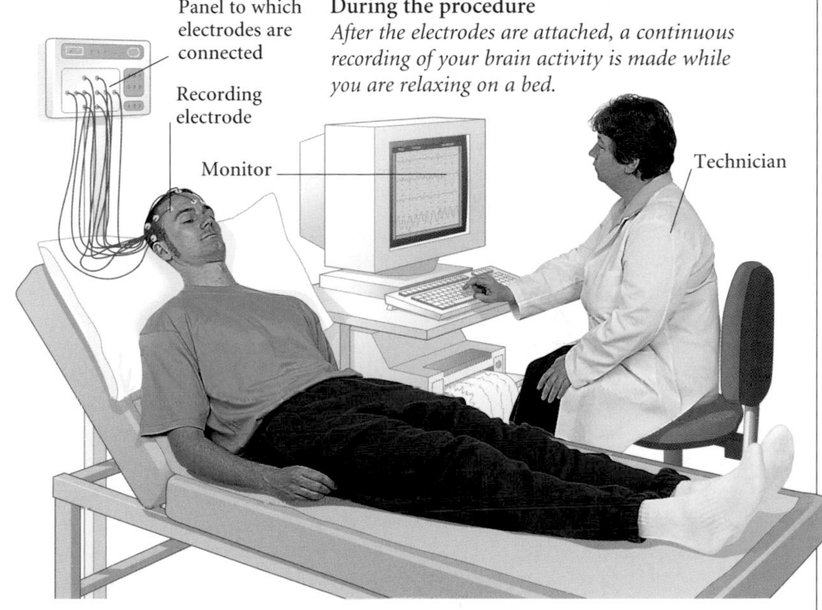
Panel to which electrodes are connected
Recording electrode
Monitor
Technician

During the procedure
After the electrodes are attached, a continuous recording of your brain activity is made while you are relaxing on a bed.

RESULTS

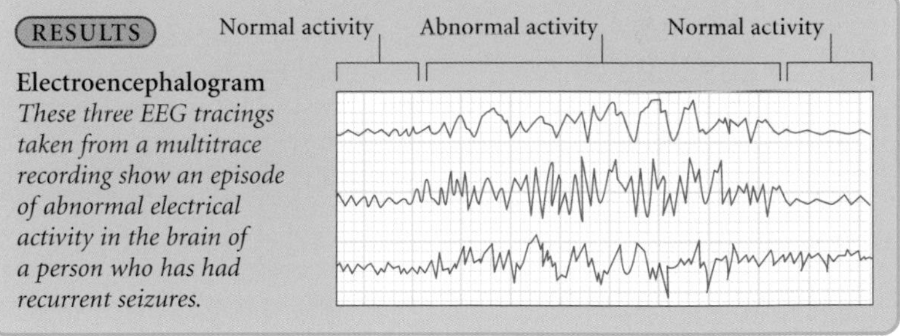
Normal activity
Abnormal activity
Normal activity

Electroencephalogram
These three EEG tracings taken from a multitrace recording show an episode of abnormal electrical activity in the brain of a person who has had recurrent seizures.

twitch, or the person may feel a tingling sensation in some of these areas. Temporary weakness or paralysis of one side of the body may follow an attack. The person may also experience odd smells, sounds, and tastes.

COMPLEX PARTIAL SEIZURES Prior to this type of seizure, the affected person may experience odd tastes or smells or have a feeling of having already experienced what is happening. He or she then enters a dreamlike state and is uncommunicative for a few minutes. During the attack, the person may smack his or her lips, grimace, or fidget. After the seizure, there is no memory of what has happened. Sometimes, a generalized seizure occurs soon afterward.

How is it diagnosed?

You should consult a doctor if you lose consciousness for an unknown reason or if someone witnesses you having a seizure. If your child has a seizure, you should also seek medical advice immediately. It is helpful if you can obtain full details of your seizure from a witness so you are able to give the doctor a full picture of what happened. He or she may arrange for you to have tests to look for an underlying cause of the seizure, such as a brain tumor or an infection such as meningitis. If no cause is found or if you have recurrent seizures, you may have an EEG (p.525) to look for abnormal electrical activity in the brain. An EEG also helps diagnose the particular type of epilepsy because some forms produce a distinctive pattern of electrical activity. Your doctor may also arrange for CT scanning (p.247) or MRI (p.248) of the brain to look for structural abnormalities that may be causing epilepsy.

> **SELF-HELP LIVING WITH EPILEPSY**
>
> If you have recently been diagnosed as having epilepsy, the following points may be helpful:
>
> - Avoid anything that has previously triggered or may trigger a seizure, such as flashing lights.
> - Learn relaxation exercises (p.75) to help you cope with stress, which may trigger seizures.
> - Try to eat at regular times.
> - Avoid drinking too much alcohol.
> - Check with your doctor before taking medications that may interact with anticonvulsant drugs you are taking.
> - Make sure that you have someone with you if you are swimming or playing water sports.
> - Wear protective headgear when participating in contact sports.
> - Talk to your doctor about possible restrictions before applying for a driving license.
> - Consult an adviser before choosing a career because some types of employment may not be suitable.
> - Consult your doctor if you are planning a pregnancy.

How might the doctor treat it?

If only one seizure has occurred, treatment may not be needed. However, an underlying problem, such as poor control of diabetes, may need to be treated. If you have had recurrent seizures, you will probably be treated with anticonvulsant drugs (p.914). Your doctor will usually prescribe the drugs in gradually increasing doses until the seizures are controlled. Occasionally, a second anticonvulsant may be needed.

You will probably have regular blood tests to monitor drug levels. If you have no seizures for 2–3 years, drug treatment may be reduced or even stopped. However, any changes in dosage should be carried out only under medical supervision. Up to 1 in 2 people who stop taking anticonvulsant drugs have seizures again within 2 years. If drugs do not control the seizures and a small area of brain tissue is found to be their cause, it may be removed surgically.

People with status epilepticus need to be admitted to the hospital without delay, where intravenous drugs will be given to control the seizures.

What can I do?

If you have epilepsy, you should try to avoid anything that triggers an attack, such as stress or lack of sleep (*see* LIVING WITH EPILEPSY, left). You should also carry some form of identification that will alert others to your condition in case you have a seizure.

If you witness someone having an epileptic seizure, you can help by turning the person onto his or her side and protecting him or her from self-injury (*see* FIRST AID: MAJOR SEIZURES, p.989). If the seizure lasts for more than 5 minutes, you should call an ambulance.

What is the prognosis?

About 1 in 3 people who have a single seizure will have another one within 2 years. The risk of recurrent seizures is highest during the first few weeks. However, the prognosis for most people with epilepsy is good, and more than 7 in 10 people go into long-term remission within 10 years.

WWW ONLINE SITES: p.1031

Narcolepsy

An extreme tendency to fall asleep during normal waking hours

AGE Usually develops before age 20

GENETICS Sometimes runs in families

GENDER LIFESTYLE Not significant factors

People with narcolepsy fall asleep at any time of the day, often when carrying out a monotonous task. Sleep may also occur at inappropriate times, such as while eating. People affected can be awakened easily but may fall asleep again soon afterward. Narcolepsy can seriously interfere with daily life.

Some people with narcolepsy have vivid hallucinations just before falling asleep. Others find that they cannot move as they are going to sleep or waking up (sleep paralysis).

About 3 in 4 people who have narcolepsy also have cataplexy, in which a temporary loss of strength in the limbs causes the person to fall to the ground. Cataplexy may sometimes be triggered by strong emotions, such as fear.

The cause of narcolepsy is unknown, but it sometimes runs in families. It affects about 1 in 3,000 people in the US, usually developing before age 20.

What might be done?

Your doctor will probably diagnose narcolepsy from your symptoms. EEG (p.525) may also be used to record the electrical activity of your brain.

You should take regular, short naps during the day and keep busy while you are awake. Your doctor may prescribe amphetamines (*see* CENTRAL NERVOUS SYSTEM STIMULANT DRUGS, p.918) to help you keep awake. Certain tricyclic antidepressant drugs (p.916) are helpful in treating people with cataplexy.

Narcolepsy is usually a lifelong condition, but it may sometimes improve spontaneously over time.

WWW ONLINE SITES: p.1035, p.1037

Meningitis

Inflammation of the meninges, the membranes that cover the brain and spinal cord, due to an infection

 AGE LIFESTYLE Risk factors depend on the cause

 GENDER GENETICS Not significant factors

In meningitis, the membranes, known as the meninges, that cover the brain and spinal cord are inflamed. The disease is most often caused by a viral or bacterial infection. The viral form of meningitis is the more common of the two and is usually not as severe as bacterial meningitis. The bacterial form is less common but can be life-threatening. Both viral and bacterial meningitis can occur in people of any age. However, bacterial meningitis occurs predominantly in children (*see* MENINGITIS IN CHILDREN, p.848), and viral meningitis is most common in young adults. Meningitis may also be caused by a fungal infection, although this is rare. This type of infection predominately affects people who have AIDS (*see* HIV INFECTION AND AIDS, p.295).

TEST LUMBAR PUNCTURE

A lumbar puncture is usually carried out to look for evidence of meningitis or other nervous system disorders, such as multiple sclerosis. The procedure is done under local anesthesia and takes about 15 minutes. During the procedure, the pressure of the cerebrospinal fluid is checked, and a sample is taken for analysis. You should remain lying down and rest for an hour afterward to prevent a severe headache.

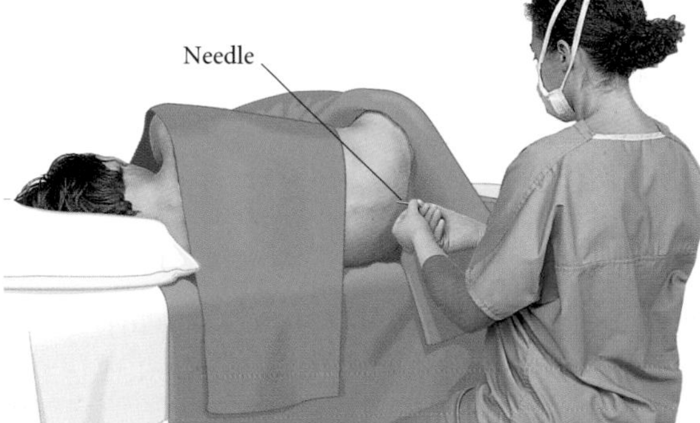
Cerebro-spinal fluid
Spinal cord
Needle
Vertebra
CROSS SECTION
Needle

During the procedure
A hollow needle is inserted between two vertebrae near the base of the spine and into the cerebrospinal fluid. A small sample of the fluid is removed for analysis.

RESULTS

Evidence of meningitis
This magnified view of a sample of cerebrospinal fluid shows several meningococcal bacteria, which confirm meningitis. The large numbers of white blood cells are a response to the infection.

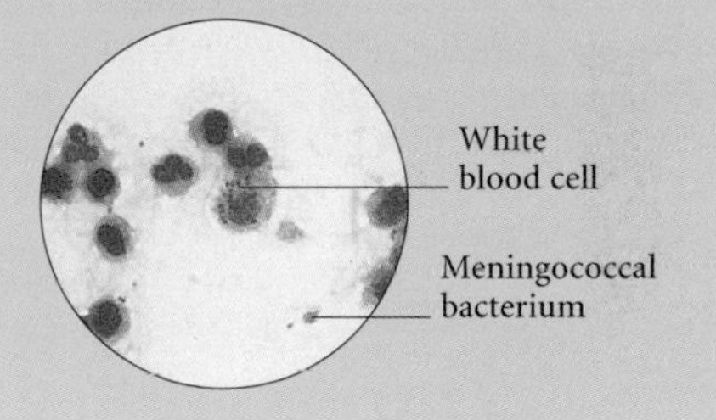
White blood cell
Meningococcal bacterium

WHAT ARE THE CAUSES?

Many different viruses can result in meningitis. Among the most common are enteroviruses, such as the coxsackie virus that can cause sore throats or diarrhea, and, more rarely, the virus that causes mumps (p.291). Viral meningitis tends to occur in small outbreaks, most commonly in summer.

Bacterial meningitis usually occurs for no detectable reason in a healthy child or teenager. Less often, bacterial meningitis may occur as a complication of an infection elsewhere in the body that spreads to the meninges through the bloodstream. For example, the bacterium *Streptococcus pneumoniae*, the most common cause of meningitis in adults in Canada, can spread from the lungs, where it causes pneumonia, to the meninges. Another bacterium, called *Neisseria meningitidis*, causes meningococcal meningitis. There are three types of these bacteria. Type B is the most common in Canada, while types A and C have caused epidemics in South America and Africa. Many people carry *Neisseria meningitidis* bacteria in the back of their throats, but for unknown reasons only a tiny fraction of these develop meningitis. The bacterium that causes tuberculosis (p.491) can also infect the meninges.

Bacterial meningitis usually occurs as single cases only. However, there may be small outbreaks, especially in institutions such as schools and colleges. This form of meningitis is most common during the winter.

People who have a weakened immune system as a result of an existing illness or a particular treatment, such as people with HIV infection or those having chemotherapy (p.278), are at increased risk of developing meningitis.

WHAT ARE THE SYMPTOMS?

Initially, meningitis may produce vague flulike symptoms, such as mild fever and aches and pains. More pronounced symptoms may then develop. Symptoms are the most severe in bacterial meningitis and may develop rapidly, often within a few hours.

The symptoms of viral meningitis may take a few days to develop, while in fungal and tuberculosis meningitis, symptoms develop slowly and may take several weeks to become pronounced.

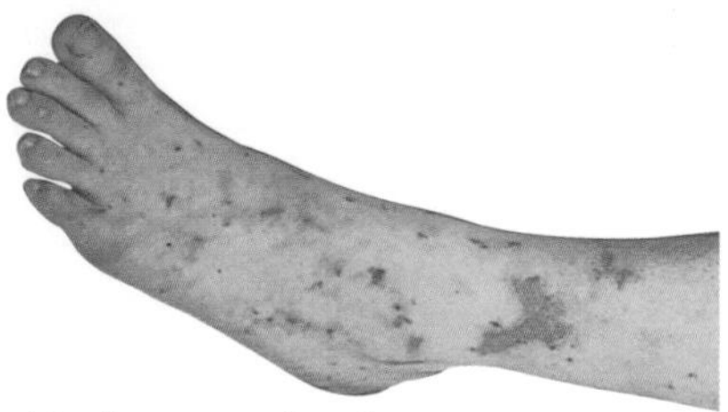

Meningococcal rash
In meningococcal meningitis, bacteria in the bloodstream may cause dark red or purple spots that develop into blotches. This rash does not fade when pressed.

The main symptoms of meningitis may include the following:

- Severe headache.
- Fever.
- Stiff neck.
- Dislike of bright light.
- Nausea and vomiting.
- In meningococcal meningitis, a rash of flat, reddish purple lesions, varying in size from pinheads to large patches, that do not fade when pressed (*see* CHECKING A RED RASH, p.129).

Unless prompt treatment is given, bacterial meningitis may lead to seizures, drowsiness, and coma (p.522). In some cases, pus collects (*see* BRAIN ABSCESS, opposite page), resulting in compression of nearby tissue.

WHAT MIGHT BE DONE?

If meningitis is suspected, immediate medical attention and admission to the hospital is necessary. A sample of fluid will be removed from around the spinal cord and tested for evidence of infection (*see* LUMBAR PUNCTURE, p.527). Antibiotics (p.885) given intravenously are started immediately. CT scanning (p.247) or MRI (p.248) may also be done to look for a brain abscess.

If bacterial meningitis is confirmed by lumbar puncture results, antibiotics are continued for at least a week. If meningitis is found to be caused by tuberculosis bacteria, antituberculous drugs (p.886) will be given. In cases of bacterial meningitis, continuous monitoring in a critical care unit (p.958) is often needed. Intravenous fluids, anticonvulsant drugs (p.914) and drugs to reduce inflammation in the brain, such as corticosteroids (p.930), may be given.

There is no specific treatment for viral meningitis. As long as bacterial meningitis has been excluded by tests, people with viral meningitis are usually allowed to go home providing they are well enough. They may be given drugs to relieve symptoms, such as analgesics (p.912) for headaches. Fungal meningitis is treated with intravenous antifungal drugs (p.889) in the hospital.

WHAT IS THE PROGNOSIS?

Recovery from viral meningitis is usually complete within 1–2 weeks. It may take weeks or months to make a complete recovery from bacterial meningitis. Occasionally, long-term problems may occur, such as impaired hearing or memory impairment due to damage to a part of the brain. About 1 in 10 people with bacterial meningitis dies despite treatment. Deaths most commonly occur in infants and elderly people.

CAN IT BE PREVENTED?

People in close contact with someone with meningococcal meningitis, such as family members, are usually given antibiotics for 2 days as a precaution. This treatment kills the meningococcal bacteria that may be present at the back of the throat and prevents their spread to other people. Children are now routinely vaccinated against *Haemophilus influenza* type b (*see* ROUTINE IMMUNIZATIONS, p.45), an important cause of meningitis in childhood.

People traveling to high-risk areas, such as Africa, may be vaccinated against other types of meningococcal bacteria.

(WWW) ONLINE SITES: p.1033, p.1035

Viral encephalitis

Inflammation of the brain as a result of a viral infection

AGE Most common in young children and elderly people

GENDER GENETICS LIFESTYLE Not significant factors

Viral encephalitis is a rare condition in which the brain becomes inflamed as a result of a viral infection. About 20,000 people in the US develop the condition every year. Viral encephalitis varies in severity. Cases can be mild and cause virtually no symptoms, but occasionally the disorder is serious and even life-threatening. The condition is most common in babies and elderly people, who are more susceptible to infections.

WHAT ARE THE CAUSES?

Many different viruses can cause viral encephalitis. Mild cases are sometimes the result of infectious mononucleosis, (p.289). In addition, viral encephalitis still occurs as a complication of some childhood infections, such as measles (p.291) and mumps (p.291), although these disorders have become much less frequent due to routine immunization.

The most common cause of life-threatening viral encephalitis is the herpes simplex virus (*see* HERPES SIMPLEX INFECTIONS, p.289). The disorder may also be a result of HIV infection (*see* HIV INFECTION AND AIDS, p.295); in tropical countries, it is sometimes caused by mosquito- and tick-borne infections, such as yellow fever (p.294).

In the past, the disorder was frequently caused by infection with the polio virus. However, this disease is now rare in developed countries as a result of routine immunization (p.45).

WHAT ARE THE SYMPTOMS?

Mild cases of viral encephalitis usually develop gradually over several days and may cause only a slight fever and mild headache. However, in severe cases, the symptoms usually develop quickly over 24–72 hours and may include:

- High fever.
- Intense headache.
- Nausea and vomiting.
- Problems with speech, such as slurring of words.
- Weakness or paralysis in one or more parts of the body.
- Memory impairment.
- Hearing loss.

If the membranes that surround the brain (meninges) become inflamed, other symptoms may develop, such as a stiff neck and intolerance of bright

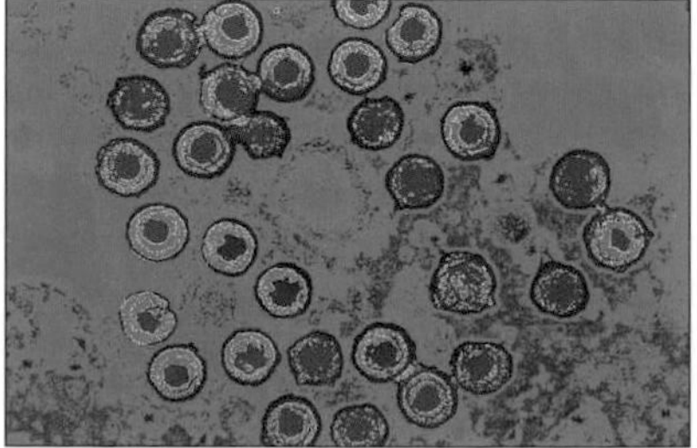

Herpes simplex virus
This highly magnified view shows the herpes simplex virus, the most common cause of life-threatening viral encephalitis.

light (*see* MENINGITIS, p.527). Seizures may also occur. In some cases, there is confusion, which may then progress to drowsiness, a gradual loss of consciousness, and coma (p.522).

HOW IS IT DIAGNOSED?

If viral encephalitis is suspected, you will be admitted to the hospital. Your doctor may arrange for a blood test to look for signs of viral infection. You may also have CT scanning (p.247) or MRI (p.248) to look for areas of brain swelling due to inflammation and to exclude other possible reasons for the symptoms, such as a brain abscess (right). A sample of the fluid surrounding the brain and spinal cord may be taken (*see* LUMBAR PUNCTURE, p.527) to look for evidence of infection. You may also have an EEG (p.525) to look at electrical activity in the brain, which is often abnormal in viral encephalitis. Less commonly, a sample of tissue may be taken from the brain under general anesthesia and then examined under a microscope to confirm the diagnosis.

WHAT IS THE TREATMENT?

Viral encephalitis that is caused by the herpes simplex virus can be treated with intravenous doses of acyclovir (*see* ANTIVIRAL DRUGS, p.886) and possibly also with corticosteroids (p.930) to reduce inflammation of the brain. In severe cases, intravenous acyclovir may be given, even if the cause has not been identified. Anticonvulsant drugs (p.914) may be prescribed if seizures develop. Severely affected people may need to be treated in a critical care unit (p.958).

WHAT IS THE PROGNOSIS?

It is often difficult to predict the prognosis of viral encephalitis. People who have mild encephalitis usually make a full recovery over several weeks, but occasional headaches may occur for a few months. However, in severe cases, the condition may be fatal. Encephalitis caused by the herpes simplex virus often produces long-term effects, such as memory problems or muscle weakness. In children, herpes simplex viral encephalitis may cause learning difficulties. The effects of this type of viral encephalitis can usually be minimized if treatment is begun early.

(WWW) ONLINE SITES: p.1033, p.1035

Brain abscess

A pus-filled swelling in the brain caused by bacterial or fungal infection

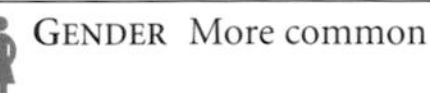
GENDER More common in males

LIFESTYLE Intravenous drug abuse is a risk factor

AGE GENETICS Not significant factors

Brain abscesses are collections of pus. They are rare but, if left untreated, can be life-threatening. Pus may collect to form a single abscess or may form several abscesses in different parts of the brain. Brain tissue around the abscess or abscesses becomes compressed, and the brain itself may swell, increasing pressure inside the skull.

People with impaired immunity, including those with HIV infection (*see* HIV INFECTION AND AIDS, p.295) and those having chemotherapy (p.278), are more likely to develop a brain abscess. The risk of a brain abscess is also higher in intravenous drug users than in other people because reused needles may be contaminated with infectious microorganisms. Men are twice as likely as women to develop a brain abscess.

WHAT ARE THE CAUSES?

Most brain abscesses are caused by a bacterial infection that has spread to the brain from an infection in nearby tissues in the skull. For example, the infection may spread from a dental abscess (p.611) or from an infection in the sinuses (*see* SINUSITIS, p.475). If the skull is penetrated (*see* HEAD INJURIES, p.521), bacteria may enter the brain and cause infection. Bacterial infection can also be carried in the bloodstream to the brain from an infection in another part of the body, such as the lungs (*see* PNEUMONIA, p.490).

Occasionally, a brain abscess may be the result of a fungal infection. In 1 out of 10 cases, the source of the bacterial infection cannot be found.

WHAT ARE THE SYMPTOMS?

The symptoms of a brain abscess may develop in a few days or gradually over a few weeks. They may include:

- Headache.
- Fever.
- Nausea and vomiting.

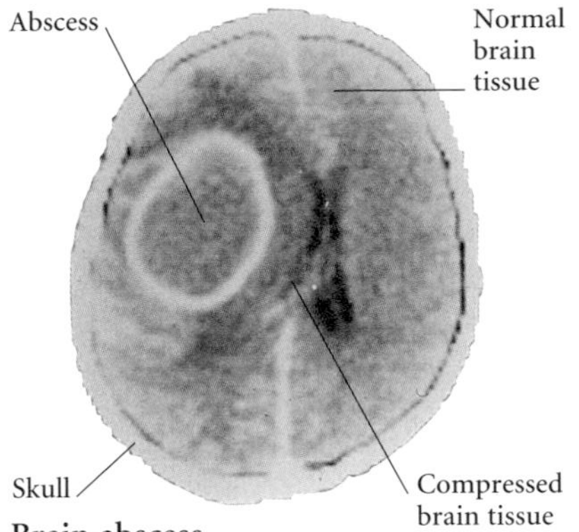
Abscess
Normal brain tissue
Skull
Compressed brain tissue

Brain abscess
This CT scan shows a large brain abscess caused by bacterial infection compressing and displacing brain tissue.

- Stiff neck.
- Seizures.

Other symptoms, including speech and vision problems or weakness of one or more limbs, depend on which part of the brain is affected. Without treatment, other symptoms may develop, including impaired consciousness that may eventually lead to coma (p.522).

WHAT MIGHT BE DONE?

If your doctor suspects that you have a brain abscess, you will be admitted to the hospital immediately. The diagnosis can be confirmed by MRI (p.248) or CT scanning (p.247) of the head. You may also have blood tests to identify the infecting organism and X-rays (p.244) to look for possible sources of infection.

Brain abscesses caused by bacterial infections are treated with high doses of antibiotics (p.885), given intravenously at first and then orally for about 6 weeks. In some cases, a small hole is drilled through the skull to allow pus to drain. The pus is then analyzed to identify the infecting organism. Swelling of the brain may need to be controlled by corticosteroids (p.930), and anticonvulsant drugs (p.914) may be given to reduce the risk of seizures. In severe cases, mechanical ventilation in a critical care unit (p.958) may be needed.

WHAT IS THE PROGNOSIS?

Up to 8 in 10 people recover from a brain abscess if treatment is begun early. However, some will have problems that persist after treatment, such as seizures, slurred speech, or weakness of a limb.

(WWW) ONLINE SITES: p.1033, p.1035

Brain tumors

Abnormal growths developing in brain tissue or the coverings of the brain

AGE Most common between the ages of 40 and 60. Some types occur only in children

GENDER More common in males

GENETICS LIFESTYLE Not significant factors

Brain tumors may be cancerous or noncancerous. However, unlike most tumors elsewhere in the body, cancerous and noncancerous brain tumors may be equally serious. The seriousness of a brain tumor depends on its location, size, and rate of growth. Both types of tumors can compress nearby tissue, causing pressure to build up inside the skull.

Tumors that arise from brain tissue or from the meninges, the membranes that cover the brain, are called primary tumors and may be cancerous or noncancerous. Most primary tumors arise from nerve cells. Less commonly, tumors may develop from the cells of the meninges. Primary brain tumors that develop in the pituitary gland at the base of the brain are discussed in the article on pituitary tumors (p.676).

Secondary brain tumors (metastases) can also occur. They are always cancerous, having developed from cells that have spread to the brain from cancers in other areas, such as the breast. Several secondary tumors may develop simultaneously.

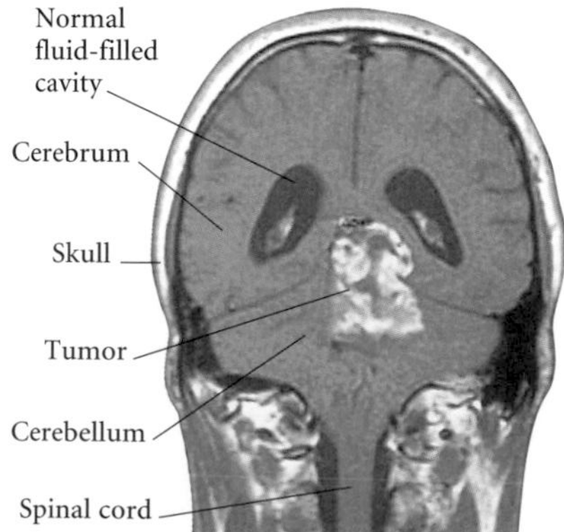
Normal fluid-filled cavity
Cerebrum
Skull
Tumor
Cerebellum
Spinal cord

Brain tumor

This MRI scan shows a brain tumor in the cerebellum, the part of the brain that helps maintain posture and control movement. Balance and coordination are affected when the cerebellum is damaged.

Brain tumors are slightly more common in males and usually develop between age 40 and 60. Certain types of tumors, such as neuroblastomas, affect only children (*see* BRAIN AND SPINAL CORD TUMORS IN CHILDREN, p.850).

What are the symptoms?

Symptoms usually occur when a primary tumor or a metastasis compresses part of the brain or raises the pressure inside the skull. They may include:

- Headache that is usually more severe in the morning and is worsened by coughing or bending over.
- Nausea and vomiting.
- Blurry vision.

Other symptoms tend to be related to whichever area of the brain is affected by the tumor and may include:

- Slurred speech.
- Strabismus (misalignment of the gaze of the eyes) due to partial paralysis of the eye muscles.
- Difficulty reading and writing.
- Change of personality.
- Numbness and weakness of the limbs on one side of the body.

A tumor may also cause seizures (*see* EPILEPSY, p.524). Sometimes, a tumor blocks the flow of the cerebrospinal fluid that circulates in and around the brain and spinal cord. As a result, the pressure inside the ventricles (the fluid-filled spaces inside the brain) increases and leads to further compression of brain tissue. Left untreated, drowsiness can develop, which may eventually progress to coma (p.522) and death.

How are they diagnosed?

If your doctor suspects a brain tumor, he or she will suggest immediate assessment by a neurologist. You will have CT scanning (p.247) or MRI (p.248) of the brain to look for a tumor and check its location and size. If these tests suggest that the tumor has spread from a cancer elsewhere, you may need other tests such as mammography (p.759) or chest X-rays (p.490) to check for tumors in the breasts or lungs. Cerebral angiography (p.533) may be performed to show the blood flow around the tumor. You may also need to have a brain biopsy, in which a sample of the tumor is removed and examined under a microscope in order to identify the type of cell from which the tumor has developed.

What is the treatment?

Treatment for brain tumors depends on whether there is one tumor or several, the precise location of the tumor, and the type of cell affected. Primary brain tumors are commonly treated surgically. The aim of surgery is to remove the entire tumor, or as much of it as possible, with minimal damage to surrounding brain tissue. Surgery will probably not be an option for tumors located deep within the brain tissue. Radiation therapy (p.279) may be used in addition to surgical treatment, or as an alternative to it, for both cancerous and noncancerous primary tumors.

As brain metastases are often multiple, surgery is not usually an option. However, in cases where there is a single metastasis, surgical removal may be successful. Multiple tumors are usually treated with radiation therapy or, less commonly, with chemotherapy (p.278).

Other treatments may be necessary to treat the effects of brain tumors. For example, the drug dexamethasone (*see* CORTICOSTEROIDS, p.930) may be given to reduce the pressure inside the skull, and anticonvulsant drugs (p.914) may also be prescribed to prevent or treat seizures. If a tumor blocks the flow of cerebrospinal fluid in the brain so that the fluid builds up in the ventricles, a small tube may be inserted through the skull to bypass the blockage.

You may also benefit from treatments for the physical effects of the tumor, such as physiotherapy (p.961) to help with mobility problems or speech therapy (p.963) for speech problems.

What is the prognosis?

The prognosis is usually better for slow-growing noncancerous tumors, and many people with such a tumor can be completely cured. For other tumors, the prognosis depends on the type of cell affected and whether the tumor can be surgically removed. About 1 in 4 people is alive 2 years after the initial diagnosis of a primary cancerous brain tumor, but few people live longer than 5 years. Most people with brain metastases do not live longer than 6 months, although in rare cases, a person with a single metastatic tumor may be cured. All types of brain tumor carry a risk of permanently damaging nearby brain tissue.

(WWW) ONLINE SITES: p.1028

Transient ischemic attacks

Episodes of temporary loss of function in one area of the brain resulting from a reduced blood supply to the brain

AGE More common over age 45

GENDER More common in males

GENETICS Sometimes runs in families

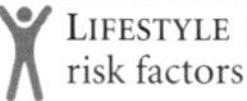
LIFESTYLE Smoking and a high-fat diet are risk factors

In a transient ischemic attack, part of the brain suddenly and briefly fails to function properly because it is temporarily deprived of oxygen by blockage of its blood supply. Transient ischemic attacks can last for anything from a few minutes to 1 hour and have no aftereffects. However, if the symptoms persist for longer than 24 hours, the attack is classified as a stroke (p.532).

Transient ischemic attacks are more common in people over the age of 45, and attacks are three times more common in men than they are women. Without treatment, about 1 in 3 people who has a transient ischemic attack has a stroke later on. It is important that a transient ischemic attack not be ignored because there is a strong possibility that it may be followed by a stroke.

WHAT ARE THE CAUSES?

Two conditions can lead to blockage of an artery supplying the brain. A blood clot, called a thrombus, may develop in the artery, or a fragment from a blood clot, called an embolus, may detach elsewhere in the body and travel in the blood to block an artery in the brain (*see* THROMBOSIS AND EMBOLISM, p.431).

A thrombus usually forms in blood vessels that are affected by atherosclerosis (p.402), a condition in which fatty deposits build up in the vessel wall. People at increased risk of atherosclerosis include smokers and those who have a high-fat diet. People with an inherited tendency toward high levels of fat (*see* INHERITED HYPERLIPOPROTEINEMIAS, p.692) or who have diabetes mellitus (p.687) are at risk. High blood pressure (*see* HYPERTENSION, p.403) also increases the risk of atherosclerosis.

The emboli that cause transient ischemic attacks usually originate in the heart, the aorta (the main artery of the body), or the carotid arteries in the neck. Blood clots are more likely to form in the heart if it has been damaged by a heart attack (*see* MYOCARDIAL INFARCTION, p.410), if the heartbeat is irregular (*see* ATRIAL FIBRILLATION, p.417), or if the heart valves are damaged or have been replaced (*see* HEART VALVE DISORDERS, p.421). Sickle-cell anemia (p.448) also increases the risk of transient ischemic attacks because abnormally shaped red blood cells tend to clump together and block blood vessels.

WHAT ARE THE SYMPTOMS?

The symptoms of a transient ischemic attack usually develop suddenly and are often short-lived, lasting for only a few minutes. Symptoms vary depending on which part of the brain is affected and may include the following:

- Loss of vision in one eye or blurry vision in both.
- Slurred speech.
- Difficulty finding the right words.
- Problems understanding what other people are saying.
- Numbness on one side of the body.
- Weakness or paralysis on one side of the body, affecting one or both limbs.

TEST CAROTID DOPPLER SCANNING

Carotid Doppler scanning uses ultrasound to look at the flow of blood through blood vessels in the neck. The procedure is generally used to investigate disorders such as transient ischemic attacks or stroke. Ultrasound waves from a transducer produce a picture of the blood flow, which can reveal narrowing of the carotid blood vessels in the neck. The procedure takes about 20 minutes and is painless and safe.

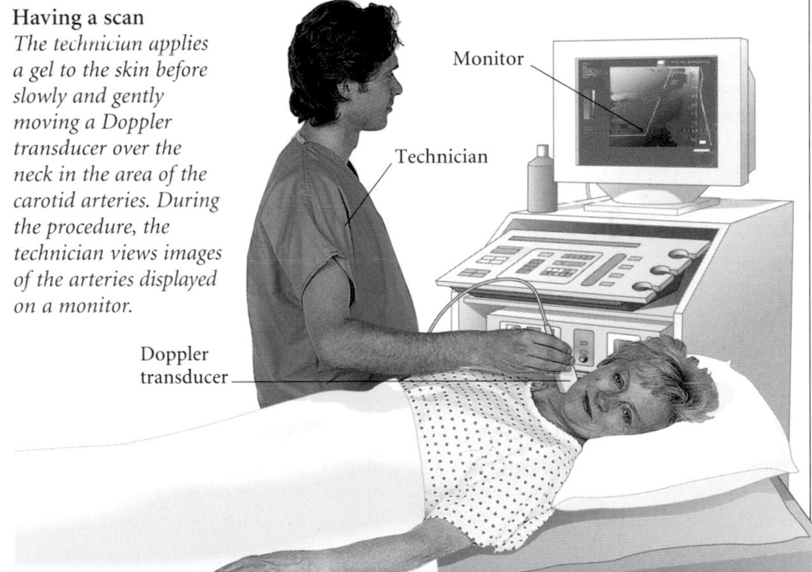
Monitor
Technician
Doppler transducer

Having a scan
The technician applies a gel to the skin before slowly and gently moving a Doppler transducer over the neck in the area of the carotid arteries. During the procedure, the technician views images of the arteries displayed on a monitor.

RESULTS

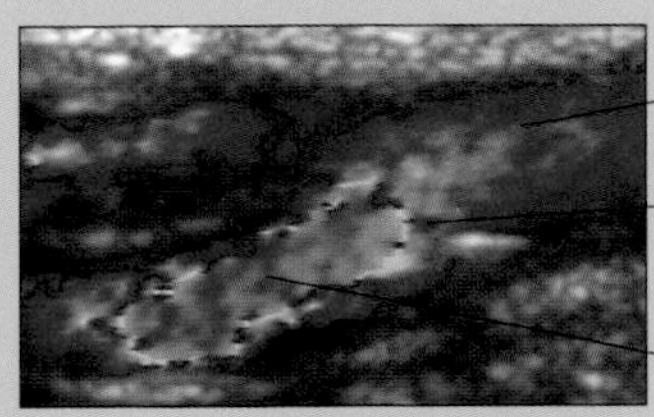
Normal blood flow
Narrowed area
Turbulent blood flow

Carotid Doppler scan
This ultrasound image shows the blood flow through a branched carotid artery. After the blood passes through a narrowed section of the artery, the flow becomes disrupted.

- Feeling of unsteadiness and general loss of balance.
- Loss of consciousness.

Although the symptoms of transient ischemic attacks usually disappear within an hour, attacks tend to recur. People may have a number of attacks in one day or over several days. Sometimes, several years may elapse between attacks.

How are they diagnosed?

Your doctor will carry out a physical examination, which will include checking your blood pressure, heart rhythm, and neurological function. He or she may arrange for CT scanning (p.247) or MRI (p.248) of your brain to look for other causes of your symptoms. You might also have ultrasound scanning of the arteries in your neck (*see* CAROTID DOPPLER SCANNING, p.531) to look for narrowing. If these arteries are significantly narrowed, further imaging tests will be done to assess the severity of the narrowing. For example, you may have cerebral angiography (opposite page), in which X-rays are taken of the arteries that supply the brain.

Tests to look for the source of the blood clots include echocardiography (p.425), which is used to look at the structure of your heart and the movement of its valves. Your heart rate may also be monitored for 24 hours to look for irregularities in your heart rhythm (*see* AMBULATORY ECG, p.416).

You may have blood tests to look for other factors that increase the risk of having a transient ischemic attack, such as diabetes mellitus and hyperlipoproteinemias. Blood tests may also be done to check for blood disorders that may increase the risk of a clot forming.

What is the treatment?

Once a transient ischemic attack has been diagnosed, the aim of treatment is to reduce your risk of having a stroke in the future. You will be advised to reduce the amount of fat in your diet and, if you smoke, you should stop. If you have diabetes mellitus, you should make sure your blood glucose levels are well controlled. Your doctor will prescribe appropriate drugs to treat high blood pressure (*see* ANTIHYPERTENSIVE DRUGS, p.897) or an irregular heartbeat (*see* ANTIARRHYTHMIC DRUGS, p.898) if you have either of these conditions. Treatment after a transient ischemic attack can be as simple as taking a daily aspirin to help prevent blood clots from forming inside blood vessels. Other drugs that help prevent blood clotting (p.904), such as warfarin, may be prescribed if emboli originate from clots that have formed in the heart.

If your doctor finds that the arteries in your neck are severely narrowed, he or she may recommend a surgical procedure called a carotid endarterectomy to clear fatty deposits from the narrowed arteries. Alternatively, you may be referred for a surgical procedure known as a balloon angioplasty, in which a small balloon is inserted into the affected artery or arteries. Once in place, the balloon is inflated to open up the narrowed section of artery. Both of these procedures increase the diameter of the blood vessel and improve the blood supply to the brain.

What is the prognosis?

Transient ischemic attacks may occur intermittently over a long period or they may stop spontaneously. Of those people who have a transient ischemic attack, about 1 in 5 will have a stroke within a year. The more frequently you have transient ischemic attacks, the higher your risk of having a stroke in the future. However, if you take appropriate steps to change aspects of your lifestyle, such as stopping smoking and adopting a low-fat diet, you will reduce the risk of having further transient ischemic attacks or a stroke.

(WWW) ONLINE SITES: p.1037

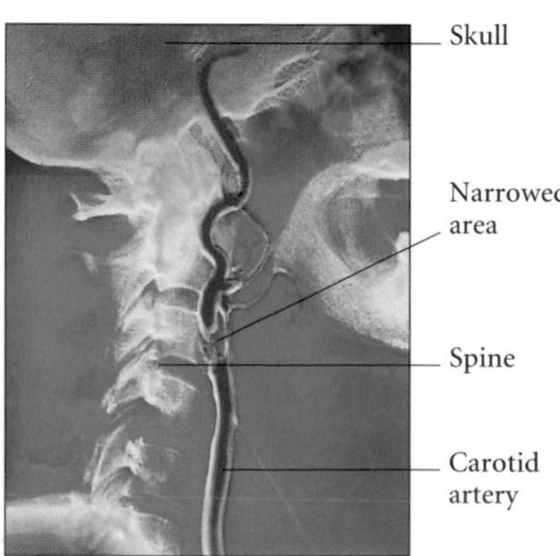
Skull
Narrowed area
Spine
Carotid artery

Narrowed carotid artery
In this color-enhanced X-ray, a narrowed area, possibly due to fatty deposits, is visible in the carotid artery supplying the brain. This may lead to transient ischemic attacks.

Stroke

Damage to part of the brain caused by an interruption in its blood supply, sometimes called a brain attack

 AGE More common over age 70

 GENDER More common in males

 LIFESTYLE Smoking and a high-fat diet are risk factors

 GENETICS Risk factors depend on the cause

If the blood supply to part of the brain is interrupted, the affected region no longer functions normally. This condition is called a stroke, although today it is often described as a "brain attack" to highlight the need for urgent medical attention. A stroke may be due to either a blockage or a leak in one of the arteries supplying the brain.

There is usually little or no warning of a stroke. Immediate admission to the hospital for assessment and treatment is essential if there is to be a chance of preventing permanent brain damage. The aftereffects of a stroke vary depending on the location and extent of the brain tissue affected. They range from mild, temporary symptoms, such as blurry vision, to lifelong disability or death.

If the symptoms disappear within 24 hours, the condition is known as a transient ischemic attack (p.531), which is a warning sign of a possible future stroke and so, although it has no aftereffects, should not be ignored.

How common is it?

Stroke accounts for 7 percent of all deaths in Canada each year. The condition is more common in men and in older people. Although the number of deaths from stroke has fallen over the last 50 years, stroke is still the third most common cause of death after heart attacks and cancer in Canada.

What are the causes?

About half of all strokes occur when a blood clot forms in an artery in the brain, a process called cerebral thrombosis. Other major causes are cerebral embolism and cerebral hemorrhage (bleeding). Cerebral embolism occurs when a fragment of a blood clot that has formed elsewhere in the body, such

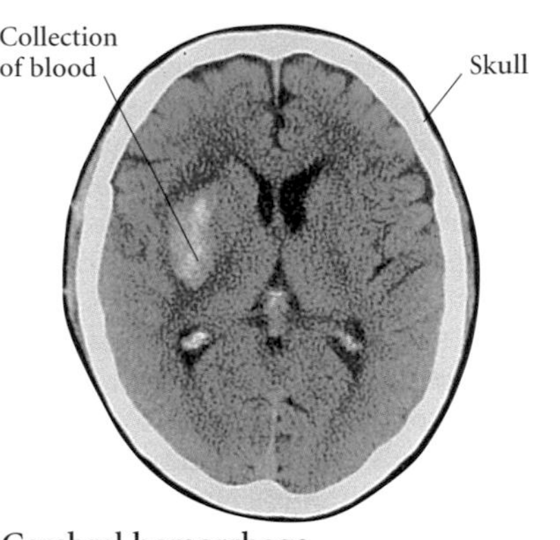
Collection of blood
Skull

Cerebral hemorrhage
Bleeding into the brain tissue, as shown in this CT brain scan, is known as a cerebral hemorrhage and is one cause of stroke.

as in the heart or the main arteries of the neck, travels in the blood and lodges in an artery supplying the brain. Cerebral hemorrhage, which causes about one-fifth of all strokes, occurs when an artery supplying the brain ruptures and blood seeps out into the surrounding tissue.

The blood clots that lead to cerebral thrombosis and cerebral embolism are more likely to form in an artery that has been damaged by atherosclerosis (p.402), a condition in which fatty deposits build up in artery walls. Factors that increase the risk of atherosclerosis are a high-fat diet, smoking, diabetes mellitus (p.687), and high lipid levels in the blood (*see* INHERITED HYPERLIPOPROTEINEMIAS, p.692).

Cerebral embolism may be a complication of heart rhythm disorders (*see* ARRHYTHMIAS, p.415), heart valve disorders (p.421), and recent myocardial infarction (p.410), all of which can cause blood clots to form in the heart. The risk of cerebral embolism, thrombosis, or hemorrhage is increased by high blood pressure (*see* HYPERTENSION, p.403). Sickle-cell anemia (p.448), an abnormality of the red blood cells, also increases the risk of cerebral thrombosis because abnormal blood cells tend to clump together and block blood vessels. Less commonly, thrombosis is caused by narrowing of the arteries supplying the brain due to inflammation. The inflammation may be due to an autoimmune disorder, such as polyarteritis nodosa (p.465), in which the immune system attacks the body's own healthy tissues.

What are the symptoms?

In most people, the symptoms develop rapidly over a matter of seconds or minutes. The exact symptoms depend on the area of the brain affected. The symptoms may include:

- Weakness or inability to move on one side of the body.
- Numbness on one side of the body.
- Tremor, clumsiness, or loss of control of fine movements.
- Visual disturbances, such as blurry vision or loss of vision in one eye.
- Slurred speech.
- Difficulty in finding words and understanding what others are saying.
- Vomiting, difficulty in maintaining balance, and vertigo (p.603).

If the stroke is severe, the affected person may become unconscious. In these circumstances, there may be a decline into coma (p.522) and death.

How is it diagnosed?

If you suspect that a person has had a stroke, he or she should be taken to the hospital immediately to find the cause and start treatment. Imaging of the brain, such as CT scanning (p.247) or MRI (p.248), may be done to find out whether the stroke was due to bleeding or a blockage in a vessel.

Once any emergency treatment has been performed, cerebral angiography (below) or carotid Doppler scanning (p.531) may be used to help identify

TEST Cerebral angiography

Cerebral angiography uses X-rays to look for abnormalities of the arteries supplying the brain. It is often used to investigate transient ischemic attacks and stroke. Under local anesthesia, a thin, flexible tube called a catheter is inserted into an artery, usually at the groin or elbow, and guided to an artery in the neck. When the catheter is in position, a special dye that shows up on X-rays is injected through it. The outline of the blood flow through the arteries is then seen with X-ray, MRI, or CT angiogram.

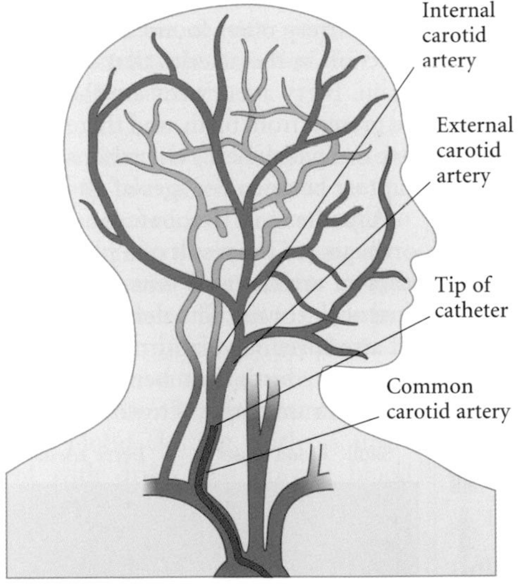
Internal carotid artery
External carotid artery
Tip of catheter
Common carotid artery

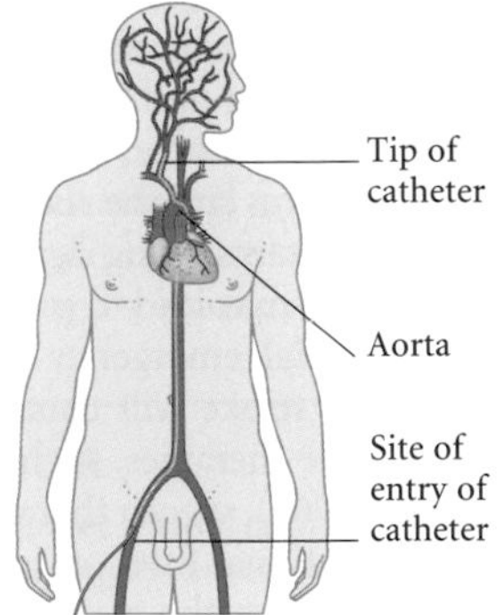
Tip of catheter
Aorta
Site of entry of catheter
ROUTE OF CATHETER

The procedure
The tip of the catheter is guided through the arteries and into the common carotid artery. Dye is injected, and X-rays are taken.

RESULTS

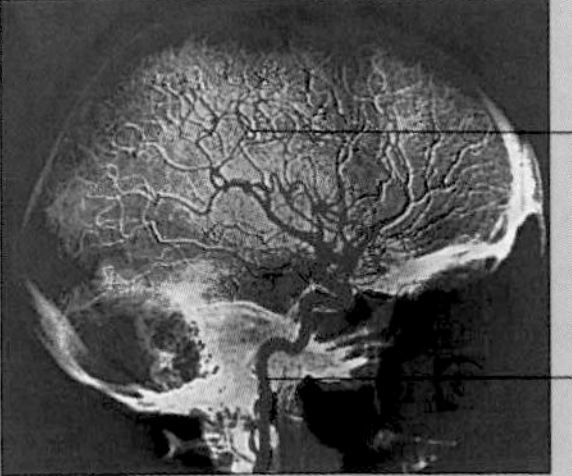
Cerebral blood vessels
Internal carotid artery

Angiogram
This color-enhanced contrast angiogram, using X-ray, shows the internal carotid artery, a main artery supplying the brain, branching into many smaller blood vessels. In this angiogram, the artery is normal.

about 1 in 10 people in Canada over age 65 affected to some degree. Although dementia is usually progressive and is not treatable, in some cases, the underlying cause can be treated. An elderly person with severe depression (p.554) may appear to have dementia because the conditions share a number of similar features, such as forgetfulness.

What are the causes?

The underlying abnormality in dementia is a decline in the number of brain cells, resulting in shrinkage of brain tissue. Alzheimer disease (right), which occurs mainly in people over age 65, is the most common cause of dementia. Alzheimer disease has a tendency to run in families. In multi-infarct dementia (opposite page), blood flow in the small vessels of the brain is blocked by blood clots. Less common causes of dementia include other brain disorders, such as Huntington's disease (p.538), Creutzfeldt–Jakob disease (p.540), and Parkinson's disease (p.539).

Dementia may also occur in young people. For example, people with AIDS (*see* HIV INFECTION AND AIDS, p.295) may eventually develop AIDS-related dementia. People who abuse alcohol over a long period of time are at risk of dementia. This is partly due to direct damage to the brain tissue and partly to a poor diet leading to vitamin B_1 deficiency. Severe deficiency may lead to the brain disorder Wernicke–Korsakoff syndrome (p.538). In pernicious anemia (*see* MEGALOBLASTIC ANEMIA, p.448), there is a deficiency of vitamin B_{12} due to impaired absorption in the digestive tract. If the deficiency is very severe, it can result in dementia. Dementia may also follow a severe head injury (p.521).

Certain drugs, such as anticonvulsant drugs (p.914) and mood-stabilizing drugs (p.918), may cause memory impairment similar to that of dementia.

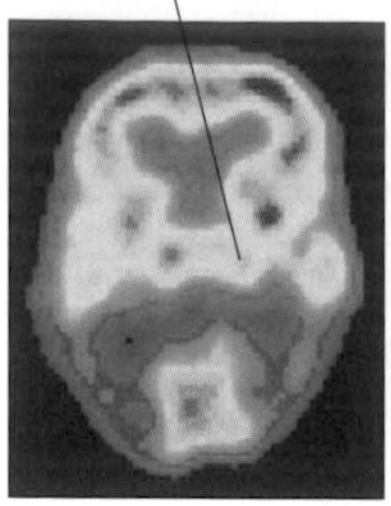
Area of normal activity
NORMAL BRAIN

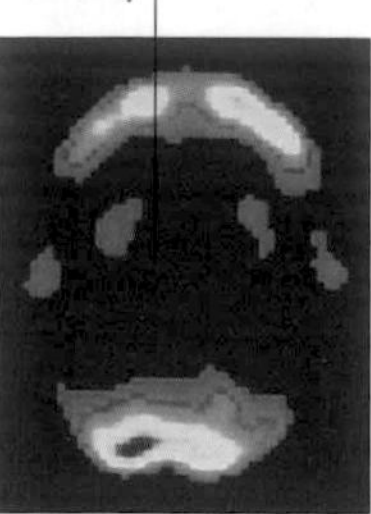
Area of reduced activity
BRAIN IN DEMENTIA

Brain activity in dementia
These PET scans show a large area of normal activity in the brain of a normal person compared to reduced activity in the brain of a person who has dementia.

> **SELF-HELP Caring for someone with dementia**
>
> If you are taking care of someone with dementia, you need to balance his or her needs with your own. In the early stages, it is important to allow the person to remain as independent and active as possible. As the disorder progresses, there are several measures you can take to help compensate for the person's failing memory, loss of judgment, and unpredictable behavior:
>
> - Put up a bulletin board with a list of things that need to be done during each day.
> - If wandering is a problem, persuade the person to wear a badge with your contact details and phone number on it.
> - Place notes around the house to help the person remember to turn off appliances.
> - Consider installing bath aids to make washing easier.
> - Try to be patient. It is common for people with dementia to have frequent mood changes.
> - Give yourself a break whenever you can by finding someone who can help for a few hours.
> - Join a caregivers' support group and investigate day centers or alternative respite care.

What are the symptoms?

The symptoms may develop over a period of months or years, depending on the cause. They may include:

- Impairment of memory, particularly when trying to recall recent events.
- Gradual loss of intellect, affecting reasoning and understanding.
- Difficulty engaging in conversations.
- Reduced vocabulary.
- Emotional outbursts.
- Wandering and restlessness.
- Neglect of personal hygiene.

In the early stages of the disorder, a person is likely to become anxious (*see* ANXIETY DISORDERS, p.551) or depressed due to awareness of the memory loss. As the dementia gets worse, the person may become more dependent on others.

What might be done?

Tests may be performed to look for the underlying cause and to exclude other disorders. If memory loss is due to vitamin B_1 deficiency or pernicious anemia, injections of vitamin supplements may be given. Symptoms caused by certain drugs may improve with a change in medication. Most other causes cannot be treated, but drugs may relieve some symptoms. For example, depression may be treated with antidepressants (p.916).

A person who has dementia usually needs support at home and may eventually need full-time care in a nursing home. Caregivers may also need support (*see* CARING FOR SOMEONE WITH DEMENTIA, left, and HOME CARE, p.960).

WWW ONLINE SITES: p.1026, p.1033, p.1035

Alzheimer disease

A progressive deterioration in mental ability due to degeneration of brain tissue

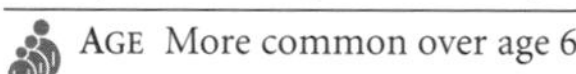

AGE More common over age 65

GENETICS Sometimes runs in families

GENDER LIFESTYLE Not significant factors

It is normal to become mildly forgetful with increasing age, but severe impairment of short-term memory may be a sign of Alzheimer disease. In this disorder, brain cells gradually degenerate and deposits of an abnormal protein build up in the brain. As a result, the brain tissue shrinks, and there is a progressive loss of mental abilities, known as dementia (p.535).

Alzheimer disease is the most common cause of dementia. In Canada, the condition affects about 1 in 13 people over age 65 and 1 in 3 people over age 85. Sometimes, younger people are affected by the disease. The underlying cause of the tissue destruction is unknown, although genetic factors may be involved. Studies have found that 15 in 100 people with Alzheimer disease have a parent affected by the disorder.

What are the symptoms?

The first symptom of Alzheimer disease is usually forgetfulness. The normal deterioration of memory that occurs in old age becomes much more severe and begins to affect intellectual ability. Memory loss is eventually accompanied by other symptoms, which may include:

- Poor concentration.
- Difficulty understanding both written and spoken language.
- Wandering and getting lost, even in familiar surroundings.

In the early stages of the disease, people frequently become aware that they have become more forgetful. This may lead to depression (p.554) and anxiety (*see* Anxiety disorders, p.551). Over a period of time, the existing symptoms may get worse and additional symptoms may develop, including:

- Slow movements and unsteadiness when walking.
- Rapid mood swings from happiness to tearfulness.
- Personality changes, aggression, and feelings of persecution.

Sometimes people find it difficult to sleep (*see* Insomnia, p.554) and become restless at night. After several years, most people with the disease cannot look after themselves and need full-time care.

How is it diagnosed?

There is no single test that can be used to diagnose Alzheimer disease. The doctor will discuss the symptoms with the affected person and his or her family. Tests may be arranged to exclude other possible causes of dementia. For example, blood tests may be carried out to check for vitamin B deficiencies. CT scanning (p.247), PET scanning (p.253), or MRI (p.248) may be done to exclude other possible brain disorders, such as multi-infarct dementia (below), subdural hematoma (p.535), or a brain tumor (p.530). An assessment of mental ability, which may include memory and writing tests, may be done to determine the severity of the dementia.

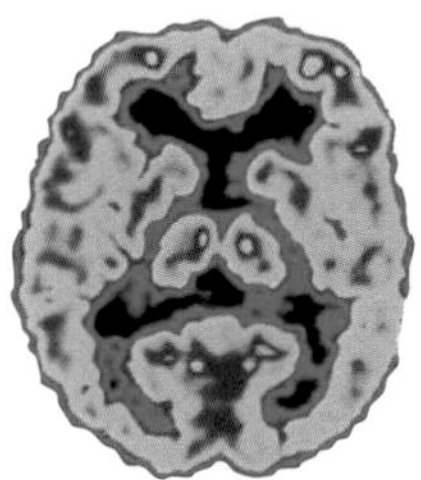

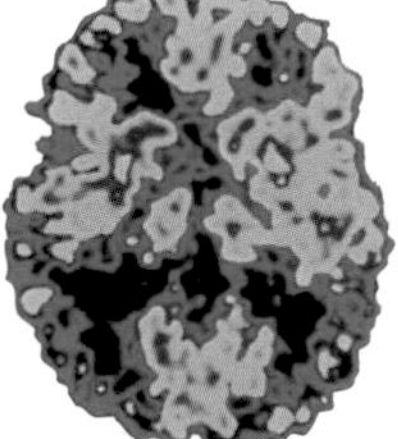

Normal brain

Brain in Alzheimer disease

Effect of Alzheimer disease

PET scans show a pattern of large, bright areas of high activity and small, dark areas of low activity in a normal brain compared to patchy activity in the brain of a person with Alzheimer disease.

What is the treatment?

There is no cure for Alzheimer disease, but drugs such as donepezil may slow the loss of mental function in mild to moderate cases. Some of the symptoms that are sometimes associated with Alzheimer disease, such as depression and sleeping problems, can be relieved by antidepressant drugs (p.916). A person who is agitated may be given a sedative drug to calm him or her down.

Eventually, full-time care may be necessary, either at home (*see* Home care, p.960, and Caring for someone with dementia, opposite page) or in a nursing home. Caring for a person who has Alzheimer disease is often stressful and many caregivers need practical and emotional support, especially if the affected person starts to become hostile and aggressive. Support groups can help people cope with caring for an elderly relative with the disease. Most people with Alzheimer disease survive for up to 10 years from the time of diagnosis.

(WWW) ONLINE SITES: p.1027

Multi-infarct dementia

A deterioration in mental ability due to blood clots in small blood vessels in the brain that cause tissue damage

Age More common over age 60

Gender More common in males

Lifestyle Smoking and a high-fat diet are risk factors

Genetics Not a significant factor

Multi-infarct dementia, also known as vascular dementia, occurs when blood flow in the small blood vessels supplying the brain is obstructed by blood clots. Each of these clots prevents oxygen from reaching a small part of the brain, and this causes tissue death (infarcts) in the affected parts. Infarcts occur in a number of distinct episodes. People who have multiple small infarcts are at increased risk of a major stroke (p.532), which can be life-threatening.

The risk of multi-infarct dementia is increased by atherosclerosis (p.402), in which fatty deposits build up in the artery walls, causing them to become narrowed and increasing the risk of clots forming. The risk of atherosclerosis is increased if a person has high blood pressure (*see* Hypertension, p.403). Lifestyle factors, such as eating a high-fat diet and smoking, can also contribute to the development of atherosclerosis. Multi-infarct dementia is more common in men and is more likely to occur in people over age 60.

What are the symptoms?

Symptoms of multi-infarct dementia vary from one individual to another because they depend on the part of the brain affected. Unlike other types of dementia, multi-infarct dementia gets incrementally worse following each separate episode. Symptoms are similar to those that occur with other forms of dementia and include:

- Poor memory, particularly when trying to recall recent events.
- Difficulty in making decisions.
- Problems with simple, routine tasks, such as getting dressed.
- Tendency to wander and get lost in familiar surroundings.

It is common for a person with multi-infarct dementia to develop depression (p.554) and have episodes of agitation. There may be other symptoms, depending on which part of the brain is affected. These may include partial loss of sight and slow, sometimes slurred, speech. Some people begin to walk with very small steps, or they develop a weakness or partial paralysis in one leg that makes walking difficult.

What might be done?

Diagnosis of multi-infarct dementia is usually possible from the symptoms, although various tests, such as blood tests, may also be done to rule out other types of dementia. The doctor may also arrange for CT scanning (p.247) or MRI (p.248) of the brain to look for evidence of multiple small infarcts.

Although the dementia itself cannot be cured, treatment can help prevent further infarcts that would make the condition worse. Anyone with multi-infarct dementia should eat a low-fat diet and exercise regularly. Smokers should stop smoking immediately. Antihypertensive drugs (p.897), which help control raised blood pressure, and a daily dose of aspirin, which reduces the risk of blood clot formation, may be prescribed.

Weakness and loss of movement may be treated with physiotherapy (p.961), and speech problems alleviated with speech therapy (p.963). Antidepressant drugs (p.916) and/or counseling (p.971) may help treat depression.

WHAT IS THE PROGNOSIS?

Many people with multi-infarct dementia find that their symptoms improve for short periods of time but later become worse again. Early recognition of the condition and treatment of risk factors, such as high blood pressure, may prevent further progression of the disorder and increasing disability and also reduce the risk of a future, potentially fatal stroke.

(WWW) ONLINE SITES: p.1026, p.1035

Wernicke–Korsakoff syndrome

A brain disorder caused by severe vitamin B_1 deficiency, usually the result of chronic alcohol abuse

 AGE More common over age 45

 GENDER More common in males

 LIFESTYLE Long-term alcohol abuse is a risk factor

 GENETICS Not a significant factor

Wernicke–Korsakoff syndrome is a rare disorder of the brain, causing dementia, abnormal eye movements, and abnormal gait. The condition develops rapidly and is due to a severe deficiency of vitamin B_1. It is a medical emergency. If untreated, coma (p.522) and death may occur. About 2 in 10 individuals with the disorder die within 5 days. Vitamin B_1 deficiency is usually caused by many years of severe alcohol abuse, but it may be due to extreme malnutrition or starvation. The condition is most common in people over age 45 and affects more men than women.

WHAT ARE THE SYMPTOMS?

Symptoms may start gradually or suddenly, sometimes after heavy drinking, and are easily mistaken for drunkenness. They include the following:

- Abnormal movements of the eyes, which often result in double vision.
- Unsteadiness when walking.
- Confusion and restlessness.

Unless the individual is given urgent treatment, he or she will develop severe memory loss, become drowsy, go into a coma, and eventually die.

WHAT MIGHT BE DONE?

A person with Wernicke–Korsakoff syndrome needs immediate admission to the hospital for intravenous treatment with high-dose vitamin B_1. Once treated, many of the symptoms may be reversed within days, but memory loss may persist. If untreated, the disorder is fatal.

(WWW) ONLINE SITES: p.1027, p.1035

Huntington's disease

An inherited brain disorder that causes personality changes, involuntary movements, and dementia

 AGE More common over age 30

 GENETICS Due to an abnormal gene inherited from one parent

 GENDER LIFESTYLE Not significant factors

Huntington's disease is an inherited disorder that causes degeneration of a particular part of the brain. Also known as Huntington's chorea, the condition causes jerky, involuntary movements, clumsiness, and progressive dementia. Huntington's disease is rare. The symptoms commonly develop in adults between the ages of 30 and 50.

Huntington's disease is caused by an abnormal dominant gene. To develop the disease, an affected person needs to inherit the abnormal gene from only one of his or her parents (*see* GENE DISORDERS, p.269). People who have the gene have a 1 in 2 chance of passing it on to each of their children. Since the symptoms of Huntington's disease do not develop until later in life, an abnormal gene may be passed on to children before the affected parent becomes aware that he or she has Huntington's disease. However, a genetic test can be carried out at any age to find out if an individual has inherited the abnormal gene from his or her parents (*see* TESTS FOR ABNORMAL GENES, p.239).

WHAT ARE THE SYMPTOMS?

Symptoms develop gradually over a period of months or years. Initially, they may include the following:

- Jerks and spasms of the face, arms, and trunk.
- Clumsiness.
- Mood swings, including outbursts of aggressive antisocial behavior.
- Poor memory, especially for events that have occurred recently.

As the disease progresses, further symptoms of dementia, such as losing the ability to think rationally, may develop. There may be difficulty speaking and swallowing, and problems with urinary incontinence (p.710). Anxiety and depression (p.554) may also occur.

WHAT MIGHT BE DONE?

Unless the condition has already been diagnosed in a family, it may not be recognized during its early stages. Usually, a member of the affected person's family first realizes that there is a problem. The affected person may be suspicious of others and refuse help. Diagnosis is usually made from the symptoms and by CT scanning (p.247) or MRI (p.248) of the brain, which may show distinct patterns of tissue degeneration. A blood test for the abnormal gene may be performed after genetic counseling.

There is no cure for Huntington's disease, but drugs may be used to relieve certain symptoms. For example, antipsychotic drugs (p.917) help control jerks and spasms. Speech therapy (p.963) for speech problems and occupational therapy (p.962) may help affected people lead as normal a life as possible.

Sometimes, nursing-home care may be necessary if the person is unable to live at home or when caregivers need a period of respite. Family members may decide to have genetic tests to determine if they have the abnormal gene themselves. The results of these tests are likely to have a bearing on whether or not they decide to have children.

The disease progresses slowly, and a person may live with it for 15–20 years after the onset of symptoms.

(WWW) ONLINE SITES: p.1032, p.1035

Parkinson's disease and parkinsonism

A progressive brain disorder causing shaking and problems with movement

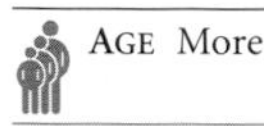
AGE More common over age 60

GENDER More common in males

GENETICS Sometimes runs in families

LIFESTYLE Not a significant factor

Parkinson's disease results from degeneration of cells in a part of the brain called the basal ganglia, which controls the smoothness of muscle movements. The cells affected usually produce a neurotransmitter (a chemical that transmits nerve impulses) called dopamine, which acts with acetylcholine, another neurotransmitter, to fine-tune muscle control. In Parkinson's disease, the level of dopamine relative to acetylcholine is reduced, adversely affecting muscle control.

Although the cause of Parkinson's disease is not known, genetic factors may be involved. About 3 in 10 people with the disorder have an affected family member. About 1 in 100 people over the age of 60 in the US have Parkinson's disease. Parkinson's disease is slightly more common in men.

Parkinsonism is the term given to the symptoms of Parkinson's disease when they are due to another underlying disorder. Certain drugs, including some antipsychotic drugs (p.917) used to treat severe psychiatric illness, may cause parkinsonism, as may repeated head injuries (p.521).

What are the symptoms?

The main symptoms of Parkinson's disease begin gradually over a period of months or even years. Parkinsonism may start gradually or suddenly depending on the cause. Symptoms include:

- Tremor of one hand, arm, or leg, usually when resting and later occurring on both sides.
- Muscle stiffness, making it difficult to start moving.
- Slowness of movement.
- Shuffling walk.
- Expressionless or masklike face.
- Stooped posture.

Later, stiffness, immobility, and a constant tremor of both hands can make daily tasks difficult to perform. Speech may become slow and hesitant, and swallowing may be difficult.

Many people with Parkinson's disease develop depression (p.554). About 3 in 10 people with the condition eventually develop dementia (p.535).

How is it diagnosed?

Since Parkinson's disease begins gradually, it is often not possible to diagnose the condition immediately. Your doctor will examine you and may arrange for you to have tests such as CT scanning (p.247) or MRI (p.248) to exclude other possible causes. Sometimes, it is only a positive response to antiparkinsonism drugs that confirms the diagnosis. If a specific underlying disorder is found to be causing symptoms, you will be diagnosed as having parkinsonism rather than Parkinson's disease.

How might the doctor treat it?

Although there is no specific cure for Parkinson's disease, drugs, surgery, and physical treatments may relieve the symptoms. If you have parkinsonism due to medications, your doctor may change your drugs. Symptoms may then disappear in about 8 weeks. If the symptoms do not resolve, treatment with antiparkinsonism drugs may be needed.

DRUG TREATMENT The aim of drug treatment is to restore the balance of dopamine and acetylcholine in the brain. For mild to moderate symptoms, two main types of drugs are prescribed. Drugs such as levodopa increase the activity of dopamine, while anticholinergic drugs, such as trihexyphenidyl, decrease acetylcholine activity. These drugs help reduce shaking and muscle stiffness, and levodopa and anticholinergic drugs improve mobility.

Amantadine may be effective for only a few months. It has side effects that include nausea, loss of appetite, and occasionally hallucinations. Levodopa is usually effective for several years. At first, its side effects are mainly nausea and vomiting, although in some cases involuntary movements and hallucinations may occur. Long-term use of levodopa sometimes results in abrupt changes of symptoms, known as motor fluctuations and dyskinetic movements. Mobility is also impaired by involuntary movements such as tics, spasms, and writhing. Levodopa is always prescribed in combination with a drug called carbidopa, which reduces side effects. Carbidopa prevents the breakdown of levodopa so that smaller doses of levodopa provide the same effect. Other drugs that are similar to dopamine, such as bromocriptine, and newer agonist drugs are used to relieve symptoms of Parkinson's disease.

Anticholinergic drugs can be effective for several years. However, side effects may include vision problems, difficulty urinating, and a dry mouth.

If you experience any change in your symptoms, it is important to consult your doctor because your drug regimen may need to be altered.

PHYSICAL TREATMENT The doctor may arrange physiotherapy (p.961) to help you with mobility problems or speech therapy (p.963) for speech and swallowing problems. If you are finding it difficult to cope at home, occupational therapy (p.962) may be useful. The therapist may suggest certain changes, such as installing grab-rails in your home, to make it easier for you to move around.

SURGICAL TREATMENT Younger people may have surgery if the tremor cannot be controlled by drugs and they are otherwise in good health. Surgery for Parkinson's disease involves destroying a part of the brain tissue responsible for the tremor. Recent therapies include stem cell research (experimental) and deep brain stimulation with electrical impulses to reduce tremor. Deep brain stimulation may be very helpful.

What can I do?

It is important to continue to exercise and take care of your general health. Try to take a walk each day. Doing stretching exercises can help you maintain your strength and mobility. However, you should also rest during the day to avoid getting tired. Encouragement and emotional support from your family and friends, and help from support groups is also important.

What is the prognosis?

The course of the disease is variable, but drugs may be effective in treating the symptoms and improving quality of life. The disease may shorten lifespan, but people can lead active lives for many years after being diagnosed. However, most people eventually need daily help, and their symptoms may be increasingly hard to control with drugs.

(WWW) ONLINE SITES: p.1035

Creutzfeldt–Jakob disease

A progressive, degenerative disease of brain tissue due to an infection

 AGE More common over age 50

 GENETICS Sometimes runs in families

 LIFESTYLE Risk factors depend on the cause

 GENDER Not a significant factor

Creutzfeldt–Jakob disease (CJD) is a rare condition in which brain tissue is progressively destroyed by an unusual infectious agent. The disorder leads to a general decline in all areas of an individual's mental and physical ability and will ultimately result in death.

What is the cause?

CJD is caused by an infectious agent known as a prion, which replicates in the brain and causes brain damage. One type of CJD, accounting for 15 in 100 cases, has been found to run in families.

Most people who develop CJD are over age 50. Usually, the source of the infection is unknown, but in about 1 in 20 people it can be traced to previous treatment with products derived from human tissue. Before the use of artificial growth hormone to treat growth disorders, one source of infection was human growth hormone injections.

In the mid 1990s, a new and rare variant of CJD that affects people in their teens or 20s was discovered in the UK. This form of the disease is believed to be linked with eating contaminated meat from cattle with a disease called bovine spongiform encephalopathy (BSE). No cases of this variant of CJD have been reported in Canada.

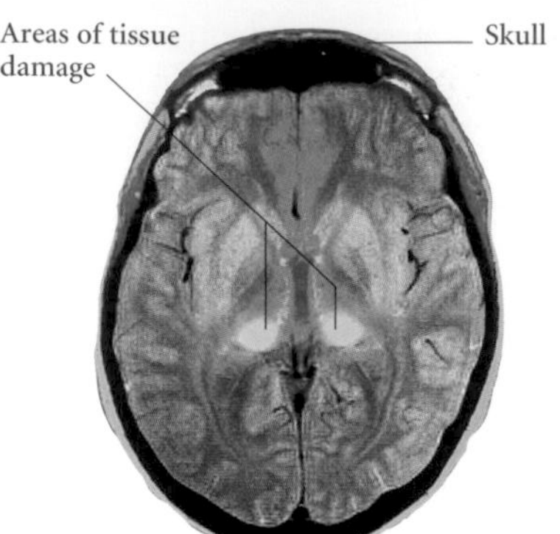
Areas of tissue damage
Skull

Brain in Creutzfeldt–Jakob disease
This color-enhanced MRI scan of a brain affected by Creutzfeldt–Jakob disease shows generalized shrinkage of brain tissue and areas of particular damage.

What are the symptoms?

It is thought that CJD is present for between 2 and 15 years before symptoms start to appear. Early symptoms develop gradually and may include:

- Depression.
- Poor memory.
- Unsteadiness and poor coordination.

Other symptoms develop as the condition progresses and include:

- Sudden muscle contractions.
- Seizures.
- Weakness or paralysis on one side of the body.
- Progressive dementia.
- Impaired vision.

Eventually, an affected person may become unable to move and talk. People with late-stage CJD who are confined to bed are also prone to serious lung infections (*see* PNEUMONIA, p.490).

What might be done?

CJD is usually diagnosed from the symptoms because no specific test is yet available. However, anyone suspected of having CJD will undergo extensive tests, such as MRI (p.248), to exclude other treatable causes. In addition, a brain biopsy may be performed. In this procedure, a small piece of tissue is surgically removed for examination. CJD cannot be cured, but drugs can relieve some of the symptoms. For example, symptoms of depression may be treated with antidepressant drugs (p.916), and muscle contractions may be controlled by muscle relaxants (p.896). The disorder is usually fatal within 3 years.

(WWW) ONLINE SITES: p.1033, p.1035

Motor neuron disease

Progressive degeneration of the nerves in the brain and spinal cord that control muscular activity

 AGE More common over age 40

 GENDER More common in males

 GENETICS Sometimes runs in families

 LIFESTYLE Not a significant factor

Motor neuron disease affects 6 per 100,000 people in Canada. In this disease, also known as amyotrophic lateral sclerosis, degeneration of the nerves that are involved in muscular activity results in progressive wasting of the muscles and weakness. There are several types of motor neuron disease. Some affect mainly the spinal nerves, while other types also affect the brain. The condition is not painful, does not affect bowel or bladder function, and does not usually affect the intellect or the senses, such as sight.

The cause of motor neuron disease is unknown. It is thought that genetic factors may be involved because, in about 1 in 10 cases, the disease runs in the family. It is slightly more common in males and usually develops after age 40.

What are the symptoms?

Initially, weakness and wasting develop over a few months and usually affect muscles of the hands, arms, or legs. Other early symptoms may include:

- Twitching movements in the muscles.
- Stiffness and muscle cramps.
- Difficulty performing twisting movements, such as unscrewing bottle tops and turning keys.

As the disease progresses, other symptoms may include:

- Dragging one foot or a tendency to stumble when walking.
- Difficulty climbing stairs or getting up from low chairs.

Less commonly, the muscles of the mouth and throat are involved, and symptoms may include slurred speech, hoarseness, and difficulty swallowing.

An affected person may have mood swings and may become anxious and depressed. If the muscles involved in breathing and swallowing are affected, small particles of food may enter the lungs and cause recurrent chest infections and possibly pneumonia (p.490). The head may fall forward because the muscles in the neck are too weak to support it. Eventually, weakness of the muscles that control respiration may cause difficulty in breathing.

How is it diagnosed?

There is no specific test to diagnose motor neuron disease. However, electromyography (*see* Nerve and muscle electrical tests, p.544) may be done to look for a decrease in electrical activity in the muscles. Additional tests may be carried out to exclude other possible causes of the symptoms. For example, MRI (p.248) of the neck may be done to exclude cervical spondylosis (p.376).

What is the treatment?

At present, no treatment can significantly slow down the progression of motor neuron disease, although a new drug called riluzole may have a small effect. Treatment for symptoms may include antidepressants (p.916) to relieve depression and antibiotics (p.885) to treat chest infections. If the person is having difficulty swallowing, a gastrostomy may be created surgically. This is an opening through which a permanent feeding tube is inserted directly into the stomach or the small intestine.

Usually, a team of specialists will be available to provide support and care for an affected person and members of his or her family. Counseling (p.971) may be offered to both, and the affected person may be given physiotherapy (p.961) to help keep joints and muscles supple. An occupational therapist (*see* Occupational therapy, p.962) may provide special aids for activities such as eating and walking. In addition, a speech therapist (*see* Speech therapy, p.963) may provide help with speech difficulties and give advice on how to deal with swallowing problems. People who have motor neuron disease and their families may wish to join a self-help group for advice and support.

The prognosis for motor neuron disease is variable, with approximately 2 in 10 affected people alive 5 years after diagnosis. About 1 in 10 affected people survives more than 10 years.

(WWW) ONLINE SITES: p.1035

Multiple sclerosis

A progressive disease of nerves in the brain and spinal cord causing weakness and problems with sensation and vision

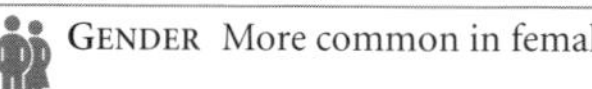
Age Usually develops between the ages of 20 and 40

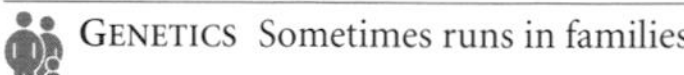
Gender More common in females

Genetics Sometimes runs in families

Lifestyle Stress and heat may aggravate symptoms

Multiple sclerosis (MS) is the most common nervous system disorder affecting young adults. In this condition, nerves in the brain and spinal cord are progressively damaged, causing a wide range of symptoms that affect sensation, movement, body functions, and balance. Specific symptoms may relate to the particular areas that are damaged and vary in severity between individuals. For example, damage to the optic nerve may cause blurry vision. If nerve fibers in the spinal cord are affected, it may cause weakness and heaviness in the legs or arms. Damage to nerves in the brain stem, the area of the brain that connects to the spinal cord, may affect balance.

In many people with MS, symptoms occur intermittently and may be followed by long periods of remission. However, some people have chronic symptoms that gradually get worse.

An estimated 50,000 Canadians have MS. People who have a close relative with MS are more likely to develop the disorder. The condition is much more common in the northern hemisphere, which suggests that environmental factors also play a part. MS is more common in females than in males and more likely to develop between early adulthood and middle age.

What are the causes?

MS is an autoimmune disorder, in which the body's immune system attacks its own tissues, in this case those of the nervous system. Many nerves in the brain and spinal cord are covered by a protective insulating sheath of material called myelin. In MS, small areas of myelin are damaged, leaving holes in the sheath, a process known as demyelination. Once the myelin sheath has been damaged, impulses cannot be conducted normally along nerves to and from the brain and spinal cord. At first, damage may be limited to one nerve, but myelin covering other nerves may be damaged over time. Eventually, damaged patches of myelin insulation are replaced by scar tissue.

It is thought that MS may be triggered by external factors such as a viral infection during childhood in genetically susceptible individuals.

What are the types?

There are two types of MS. In the most common, known as relapsing–remitting MS, symptoms last for days or weeks and then clear up for months or even years. However, some symptoms may eventually persist between the attacks. About 3 in 10 people with MS have a type known as chronic–progressive MS, in which there is a gradual worsening of symptoms with no remission. A person with relapsing–remitting MS may go on to develop chronic–progressive MS.

What are the symptoms?

Symptoms may occur singly in the initial stages and in combination as the disorder progresses. They may include:

- Blurry vision.
- Numbness or tingling in any part of the body.
- Fatigue, which may be persistent.
- Weakness and a feeling of heaviness in the legs or arms.
- Problems with coordination and balance, such as an unsteady gait.
- Slurred speech.

Stress and heat sometimes make symptoms worse. About half of the

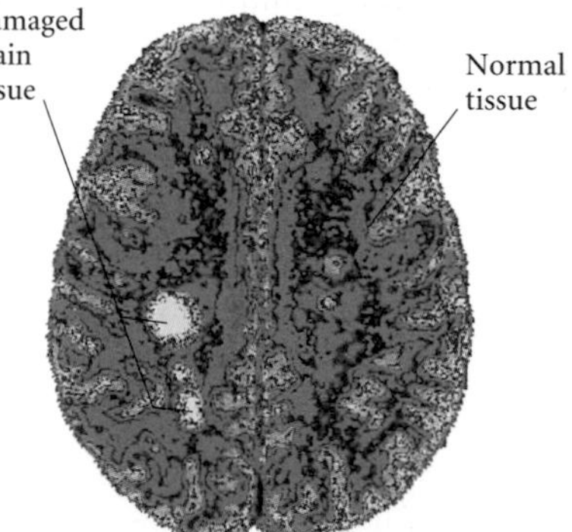
Damaged brain tissue
Normal tissue

Damage due to multiple sclerosis
This MRI scan of the brain of a person with multiple sclerosis shows damaged brain tissue caused by the destruction of the sheaths that surround nerve fibers.

people who have MS find it hard to concentrate and experience memory lapses. Depression (p.554) is common in advanced multiple sclerosis. Later in the course of the disease, some people with muscle weakness develop painful muscle spasms. Nerve damage can also lead to urinary incontinence (p.710), and men may find it is increasingly difficult to achieve an erection (*see* ERECTILE DYSFUNCTION, p.770). Eventually, damage to myelin covering nerves in the spinal cord may cause partial paralysis, and an affected person may need a wheelchair.

HOW IS IT DIAGNOSED?

There is no single test to diagnose MS, and, because symptoms are so wide-ranging, a diagnosis is only made once other possible causes of the symptoms have been excluded. Your doctor will take your medical history and do a physical examination. If you are having visual problems, such as blurry vision, you may be referred to an ophthalmologist, who will examine the optic nerve, which is commonly affected in the early stages of the disorder (*see* OPTIC NEURITIS, p.581). Your doctor may arrange for tests to find out how quickly your brain receives messages when particular nerves are stimulated. The most common test measures damage to the visual pathways (*see* VISUAL EVOKED RESPONSES, right). You will probably also have an imaging test of the brain, such as MRI (p.248), to see if there are areas of demyelination.

Your doctor may arrange for a lumbar puncture (p.527), a procedure in which a small amount of the fluid that surrounds the spinal cord is removed for microscopic analysis. Abnormalities in this fluid may confirm the diagnosis.

WHAT IS THE TREATMENT?

There is no cure for MS, but there are several new immunomodulatory drugs (*see* INTERFERON DRUGS, p.907), which may help lengthen remission periods and shorten the length of attacks. Your doctor may prescribe corticosteroids (p.930) to shorten the duration of a relapse. Mitoxantrone, a drug used to treat leukemia, may be used to treat MS.

Many of the more common symptoms that occur in all types of MS can be relieved by drugs. For example, your doctor may treat muscle spasms with a drug that relaxes muscles (*see* MUSCLE RELAXANTS, p.896). Similarly, incontinence can often be improved by drugs (*see* DRUGS THAT AFFECT BLADDER CONTROL, p.939). Problems in getting an erection may be helped by a drug treatment such as sildenafil. If you have mobility problems, your doctor may arrange for you to have physiotherapy (p.961). Occupational therapy (p.962) may make day-to-day activities easier.

WHAT CAN I DO?

If you are diagnosed with MS, you and your family will need time and possibly counseling (p.971) to come to terms with the disorder. You should minimize stress in your life and avoid exposure to high temperatures if heat tends to make your symptoms worse. Regular, gentle exercise, such as swimming, will help keep your muscles strong without risk of overstraining them.

WHAT IS THE PROGNOSIS?

The progression of MS is extremely variable. About 7 in 10 people with MS have active lives with long periods of remission between relapses. However, some people, particularly those with chronic–progressive MS, become increasingly disabled. Half of all people with MS are still leading active lives 10 years after diagnosis, and the average lifespan from diagnosis is 25–30 years.

(WWW) ONLINE SITES: p.1035

(TEST) VISUAL EVOKED RESPONSES

A visual evoked response test measures the function of the optic nerve, the nerve that transmits messages from the eye to the brain. The test is most often used in the diagnosis of multiple sclerosis and can detect abnormalities before visual symptoms become apparent. The test records brain activity in response to a visual stimulus to find out the speed at which messages from the eye reach the brain. The test takes 20–30 minutes.

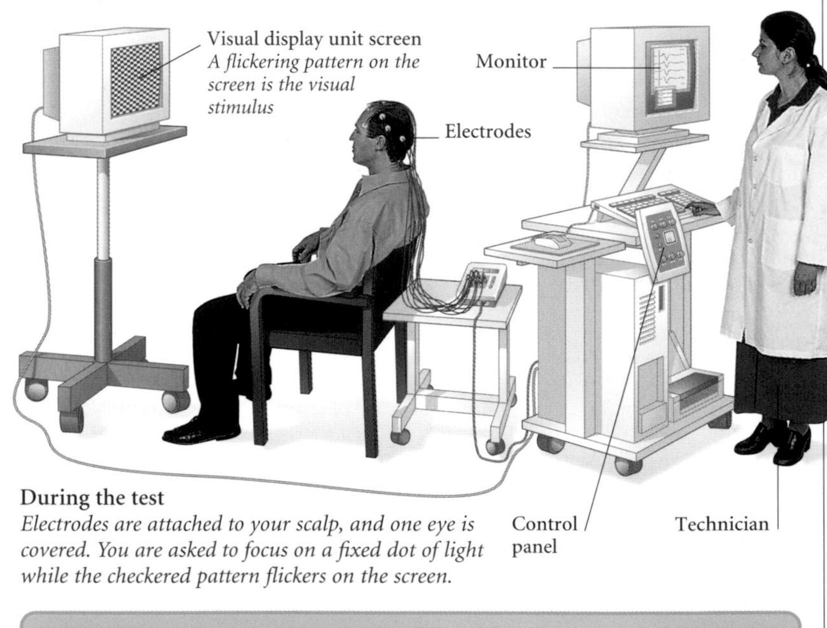
Visual display unit screen
A flickering pattern on the screen is the visual stimulus
Monitor
Electrodes
Control panel
Technician

During the test
Electrodes are attached to your scalp, and one eye is covered. You are asked to focus on a fixed dot of light while the checkered pattern flickers on the screen.

(RESULTS)

Visual evoked responses
This normal tracing shows electrical activity in an area of the brain as it receives messages from the eye. The first spike on the trace shows the moment of visual stimulus. The time taken for the signal to reach the brain is measured.

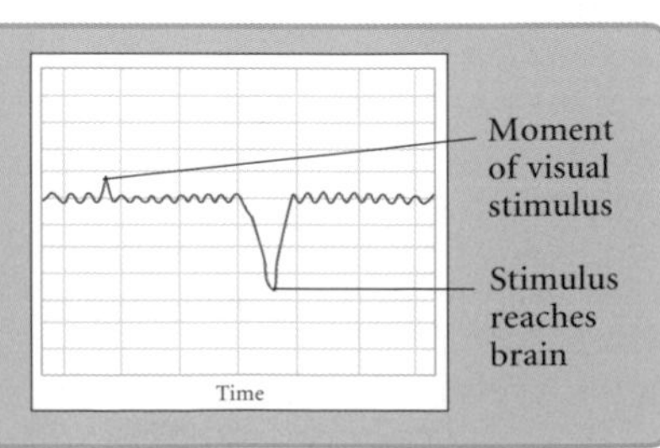
Moment of visual stimulus
Stimulus reaches brain
Time

PERIPHERAL NERVOUS SYSTEM DISORDERS

The peripheral nervous system is composed of nerves that branch from the brain and spinal cord and then divide repeatedly to supply every part of the body. The nerves transmit information necessary for sensation, muscle stimulation, and the regulation of unconscious functions. Disorders of these nerves may be painful, cause loss of sensation, or lead to paralysis.

This section starts with an overview of peripheral neuropathies, in which one or more peripheral nerves are damaged. Peripheral neuropathies are relatively common and have many causes, including injuries, infection, nutritional deficiencies, and disorders such as diabetes mellitus. Diabetic neuropathy, the most common cause of peripheral nerve damage, is covered next. This is followed by an article on nutritional neuropathies, in which deficiencies of essential nutrients in the diet, especially vitamin B complex, cause nerve damage.

The next articles cover disorders such as sciatica, carpal tunnel syndrome, and facial palsy, all of which may be caused by compression of a nerve. Rarer disorders that affect peripheral nerves are covered next. Such disorders include myasthenia gravis, in which the body's immune system affects its ability to transmit impulses from the nerves to muscles, and Guillain–Barré syndrome, which is the result of an abnormal response of the immune system after an infection. The final article covers nervous tics, which are often caused by stress.

KEY ANATOMY

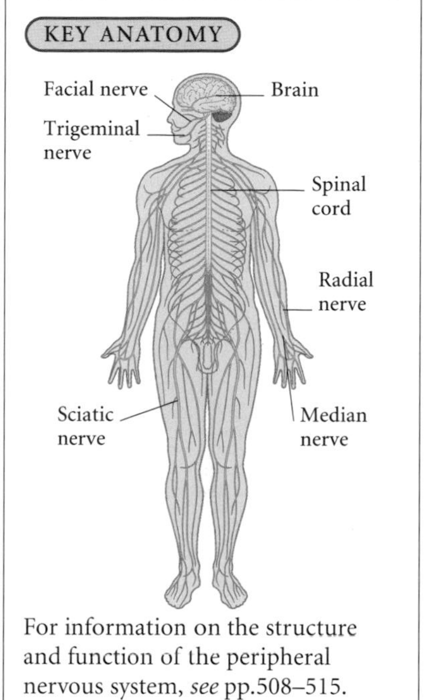
Facial nerve
Brain
Trigeminal nerve
Spinal cord
Radial nerve
Sciatic nerve
Median nerve

For information on the structure and function of the peripheral nervous system, *see* pp.508–515.

Peripheral neuropathies

Disorders of one or more of the nerves outside the brain and spinal cord, known as the peripheral nerves

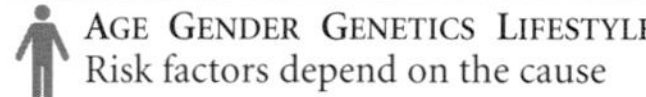
AGE GENDER GENETICS LIFESTYLE
Risk factors depend on the cause

Disorders of the peripheral nerves, the nerves that branch from the brain and spinal cord to the rest of the body, are called neuropathies. Depending on the nerves affected, peripheral neuropathies may affect sensation, movement, or automatic functions, such as bladder control. Rarely, a peripheral neuropathy may be life-threatening.

WHAT ARE THE CAUSES?

The most common cause of peripheral nerve damage in developed countries is diabetes mellitus (*see* DIABETIC NEUROPATHY, p.545). Vitamin B complex deficiencies and some other nutritional disorders may also result in nerve damage (*see* NUTRITIONAL NEUROPATHIES, p.545). In the developed world, nutritional neuropathy is often the result of a poor diet in people who abuse alcohol. Drinking too much alcohol may also damage peripheral nerves directly.

Damage to a single nerve may occur as a result of an injury (*see* PERIPHERAL NERVE INJURIES, p.548) or because of compression. For example, in carpal tunnel syndrome (p.547), the median nerve, which supplies part of the hand, is compressed at the wrist.

Neuropathy may also be associated with an infection, such as Hansen's disease (p.301) or HIV infection (*see* HIV INFECTION AND AIDS, p.295). Guillain–Barré syndrome (p.550), one particular peripheral neuropathy, is caused by an abnormal immune response that sometimes occurs following an infection.

Autoimmune disorders such as systemic lupus erythematosus (p.461), in which the immune system attacks the body's tissues, may cause nerve damage. Occasionally, a disorder such as polyarteritis nodosa (p.465) may damage nerves by causing inflammation of the blood vessels that supply them. Neuropathy may also result from certain cancers, particularly primary lung cancer (p.503) and lymphoma (p.459). Occasionally, neuropathy is caused by amyloidosis (p.693), in which an abnormal protein is deposited in the body.

Some drugs, such as isoniazid (*see* ANTITUBERCULOUS DRUGS, p.886), may cause nerve damage, as may exposure to certain toxic substances such as lead. In some cases, the cause is unknown.

WHAT ARE THE TYPES?

Peripheral neuropathies may affect the nerves that transmit sensory information (sensory nerves), the nerves that stimulate the muscles (motor nerves), and/or the nerves that control automatic functions (autonomic nerves).

SENSORY NERVE NEUROPATHIES These neuropathies first affect the feet, then hands, and then spread toward the center of the body. The symptoms may include tingling, pain, and numbness in the affected area. If the fingertips are numb, everyday tasks may become difficult. This type of neuropathy is most often caused by nutritional disorders or drugs.

MOTOR NERVE NEUROPATHIES If the motor nerves are damaged, the muscles they supply become weak, and muscle wasting eventually occurs. In severe cases, mobility may be restricted, and, very rarely, breathing may have to be assisted by mechanical ventilation (*see* CRITICAL CARE UNIT, p.958). Lead poisoning may result in a neuropathy that affects the motor nerves only.

AUTONOMIC NERVE NEUROPATHIES If a neuropathy affects one or more autonomic nerves, symptoms may include fainting due to low blood pressure (*see* HYPOTENSION, p.414), diarrhea (p.627), constipation (p.628), urinary incontinence (p.710), or erectile dysfunction (p.770). This type is often caused by long-standing diabetes mellitus.

WHAT MIGHT BE DONE?

Your doctor may be able to tell which nerves are affected from your symptoms and an examination. If the cause of your neuropathy is not clear, he or she will probably arrange for blood tests to look for evidence of an underlying disorder, such as nutritional deficiencies or an autoimmune disorder. If there is evidence of compression of a nerve, you may also have CT scanning (p.247) or MRI (p.248) to assess the severity and extent of nerve damage. Special tests to assess the function of the nerves (*see* NERVE AND MUSCLE ELECTRICAL TESTS, below) may also be done.

Treatment of a peripheral neuropathy depends on the cause and the type of nerve affected. For example, careful control of diabetes mellitus may keep

TEST NERVE AND MUSCLE ELECTRICAL TESTS

Nerve and muscle electrical tests consist of nerve conduction studies and electromyography (EMG). Nerve conduction studies are used to assess how well a nerve is conducting electrical impulses. They are often followed by EMG to see whether symptoms, such as weakness, are due to a disorder of the muscle or the nerve supplying it. Both tests are usually done on an outpatient basis. Each takes about 15 minutes and may cause discomfort.

NERVE CONDUCTION STUDIES

Nerve conduction studies are used to measure nerve damage in disorders such as peripheral neuropathies. A single nerve is stimulated by an electrical impulse, and the response to the stimulus and the speed at which this response travels along the nerve indicates whether the nerve is damaged and what the degree of damage is.

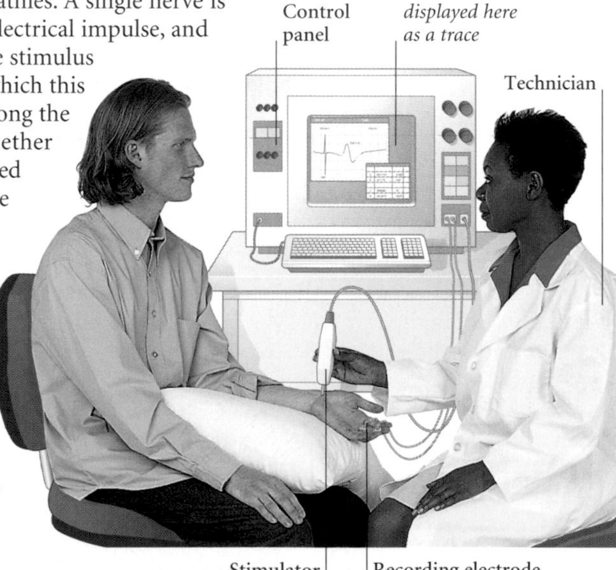
Monitor
The results are displayed here as a trace
Control panel
Technician
Stimulator
Recording electrode

During the procedure
A probe is held against the skin to stimulate the nerve to be tested. The signal that is produced by the nerve is picked up by a recording electrode placed further along the nerve on the skin.

RESULTS

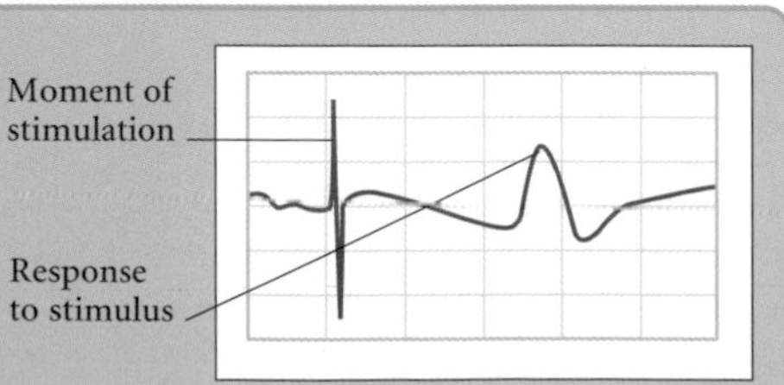
Moment of stimulation
Response to stimulus

Nerve conduction trace
This tracing shows a normal electrical impulse through a nerve. The nerve is stimulated, and the speed at which the impulse travels through the nerve is measured.

ELECTROMYOGRAPHY

EMG is used to differentiate between nerve and muscle disorders and to diagnose disorders such as muscular dystrophy. A fine needle is used to record the electrical activity of a muscle at rest and when contracting. The results are recorded on a tracing.

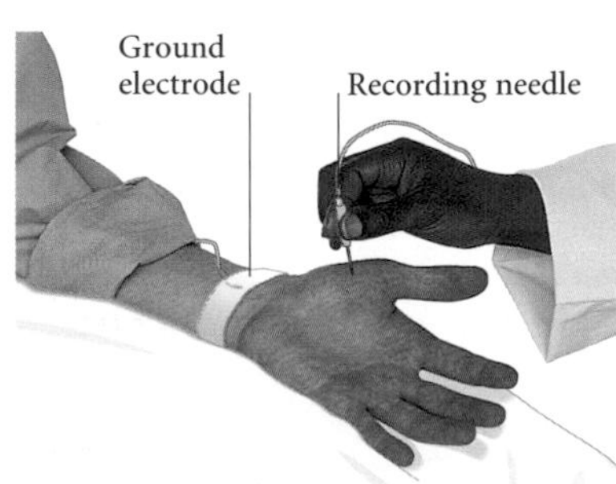
Ground electrode
Recording needle

During the procedure
A needle placed in or on the muscle records electrical activity at rest and when you contract the muscle. A ground electrode eliminates background electrical activity.

RESULTS

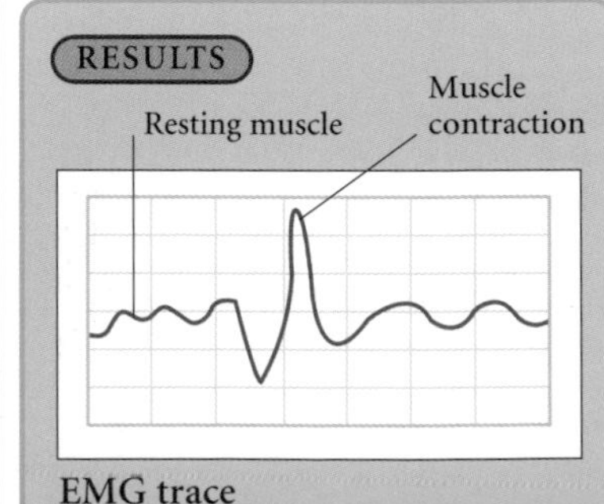
Resting muscle
Muscle contraction

EMG trace
This tracing shows normal patterns of electrical activity in a muscle at rest and when contracting.

diabetic neuropathy from worsening, and vitamin B complex injections (*see* VITAMINS, p.927) may help a nutritional neuropathy. If motor nerves are affected, your doctor may recommend physiotherapy (p.961) to maintain muscle tone and strength. If the underlying cause can be treated, the condition may improve or disappear, but chronic nerve damage may be irreversible.

(WWW) ONLINE SITES: p.1035

Diabetic neuropathy

Damage to one or more of the peripheral nerves caused by diabetes mellitus

AGE More common over age 40

GENETICS Diabetes mellitus sometimes runs in families

LIFESTYLE Poor control of diabetes mellitus and smoking are risk factors

GENDER Not a significant factor

In diabetic neuropathy, one or more of the peripheral nerves that branch from the brain and spinal cord to the rest of the body are damaged as a result of diabetes mellitus (p.687). Diabetic neuropathy is the most common cause of peripheral neuropathy in developed countries. If diabetes is poorly controlled, the resulting high levels of glucose in the blood damage the peripheral nerves directly and the blood vessels that supply them (*see* DIABETIC VASCULAR DISEASE, p.432). Good control of diabetes reduces this risk by up to half.

About 3 in 10 people with diabetes mellitus have damage to one or more peripheral nerves, but only 1 of these 3 people develops significant symptoms.

People with diabetes mellitus who smoke increase the risk of damaging the blood vessels that supply the nerves.

What are the symptoms?

The symptoms of diabetic neuropathy usually develop slowly over a number of years. Rarely, they develop rapidly over days or weeks. Symptoms vary depending on which of the nerves are involved, but the feet are often affected. Less commonly, diabetic neuropathy may affect the larger nerves, mainly in the thighs. Symptoms may include:

- Pins and needles.
- Numbness.
- Pain, which is often worse at night.
- Muscle weakness and wasting.

If sensation is lost, a minor injury to the foot, such as rubbing by badly fitting shoes, may not be noticed. Slow healing due to poor blood supply may lead to infection. If left untreated, ulcers may develop (*see* LEG ULCER, p.350) and, in severe cases, gangrene (p.435) occurs.

Eventually, diabetic neuropathy may also affect the autonomic nerves, which regulate automatic body functions such as blood pressure and passage of food through the intestines. Damage to these nerves causes symptoms such as dizziness when standing, diarrhea (p.627), and erectile dysfunction (p.770).

What might be done?

Careful control of diabetes reduces the risk of developing diabetic neuropathy. However, if you develop symptoms of nerve damage, you should consult your doctor promptly. He or she will probably be able to diagnose the condition from your symptoms. However, nerve conduction tests may need to be done at the hospital to confirm which nerves are affected and to assess the severity of the damage (*see* NERVE AND MUSCLE ELECTRICAL TESTS, opposite page).

The goal of treatment of diabetic neuropathy is to prevent further nerve damage and the development of complications. Your doctor will help you monitor your blood sugar level carefully and advise you about good foot care (*see* LIVING WITH DIABETES, p.690). For example, you should check your feet regularly for cuts or abrasions, particularly if you have been wearing new shoes. You should avoid wearing open-toed sandals or walking barefoot. If you smoke, you should try to stop.

To relieve pain, particularly at night, anticonvulsant drugs (p.914) such as carbamazepine and gabapentin, or an antidepressant drug (p.916), such as amitriptyline, may be prescribed.

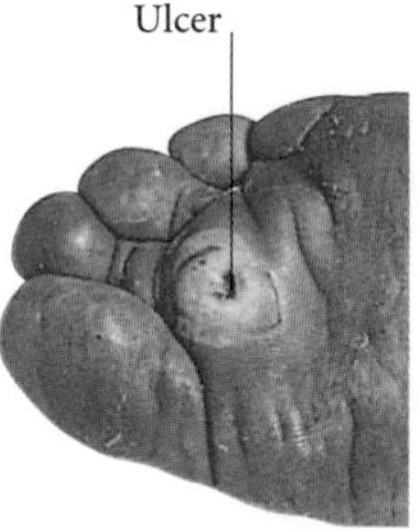
Ulcer

Foot ulcer
If nerves are damaged as a result of diabetic neuropathy, a painless ulcer, such as shown here on the sole, may develop.

What is the prognosis?

Good control of blood glucose levels in diabetes mellitus not only reduces the risk of developing diabetic neuropathy but may also halt further progression of the disease. However, in most cases, nerve damage is irreversible.

(WWW) ONLINE SITES: p.1029

Nutritional neuropathies

Damage to peripheral nerves caused by a nutritional deficiency

LIFESTYLE Poor diet and excessive alcohol consumption are risk factors

AGE GENDER GENETICS Not significant factors

In nutritional neuropathies, the peripheral nerves, which branch from the brain and spinal cord, are damaged by deficiencies of essential nutrients, particularly those of the vitamin B complex (*see* NUTRITIONAL DEFICIENCIES, p.630).

Worldwide, nutritional neuropathies are mainly caused by malnutrition. In developed countries, such neuropathies are more commonly associated with excessive alcohol consumption. People who drink heavily often also have a poor diet, which can cause a vitamin B_1 deficiency. In addition, alcohol may directly damage the peripheral nerves. The risk of a nutritional neuropathy developing increases greatly in those people who have been drinking heavily for 10 years or more.

Nutritional deficiencies may occur in people with eating disorders, such as anorexia nervosa (p.562). People with chronic conditions that affect absorption of nutrients from the intestines (*see* MALABSORPTION, p.655) may also develop nutritional deficiencies.

What are the symptoms?

Nutritional neuropathies usually first affect the tips of the fingers and the toes. The symptoms appear gradually over several months or years and slowly progress up the limbs to the trunk. Symptoms may include:

- Loss of sensation.
- Pins and needles.
- Pain in the feet and/or the hands.

Walking may be clumsy as a result of the loss of sensation in the feet and legs.

If motor nerves, which stimulate the muscles, are affected, muscle weakness and wasting may gradually occur and further affect the ability to walk.

WHAT MIGHT BE DONE?

Your doctor will examine you by checking your reflexes and your ability to feel sensation, such as a pinprick. He or she may arrange for blood tests to look for a vitamin deficiency or for evidence of liver damage caused by excessive alcohol consumption. Your doctor may also arrange for tests to determine the extent of the nerve damage (*see* NERVE AND MUSCLE ELECTRICAL TESTS, p.544).

Nutritional neuropathies are treated by replacing the nutrients that are missing, either by giving a course of oral supplements or, in some cases, by injections (*see* VITAMINS, p.927). Pain can usually be relieved by analgesics (p.912). Occasionally, if analgesics are not successful in relieving pain, your doctor may prescribe anticonvulsant drugs (p.914) or antidepressants (p.916).

Nerve damage is often irreversible, but with treatment the progression of the disease can usually be halted.

(WWW) ONLINE SITES: p.1027, p.1035

Trigeminal neuralgia

Severe pain on one side of the face due to compression, inflammation, or damage to the trigeminal nerve

 AGE More common over age 50

 GENDER More common in males

 GENETICS Risk factors depend on the cause

 LIFESTYLE Not a significant factor

The trigeminal nerve transmits sensation from parts of the face to the brain and controls some of the muscles that are involved in chewing. Damage to this nerve causes repeated bursts of sharp, stabbing pain, known as trigeminal neuralgia, in the lip, gum, or cheek on one side of the face. The attacks may last for a few seconds or several minutes and may become more frequent over time. In severe cases of trigeminal neuralgia, the pain may be so intense that the affected person is unable to do anything during the attack. Afterward, pain usually disappears completely. An attack may occur spontaneously or be triggered by certain facial movements, such as chewing, or by touching a trigger spot on the face. Attacks rarely occur at night.

The disorder is more common in men over age 50. The most common cause of trigeminal neuralgia is a dilated blood vessel. However, in people under age 50, symptoms may be an early sign of multiple sclerosis (p.541), a disorder that sometimes runs in families. Rarely, the nerve is compressed by a tumor.

WHAT MIGHT BE DONE?

There are no specific tests to diagnose trigeminal neuralgia. Your doctor will examine you to rule out any other causes of facial pain, such as toothache or sinusitis (p.475). He or she may also arrange for you to have MRI (p.248) to look for the presence of a tumor.

You may be given analgesics (p.912), such as acetaminophen, to relieve the pain. However, if the pain persists, your doctor may prescribe anticonvulsant drugs (p.914), such as carbamazapine, or certain antidepressants (p.916), all of which have proved effective in treating trigeminal neuralgia. Unlike analgesics, which are taken only when the pain is present, both anticonvulsants and antidepressants must be taken every day to prevent attacks of trigeminal neuralgia from occurring.

If a tumor is found, surgery may be necessary to remove it. Surgery may also be used to separate the trigeminal nerve from a blood vessel if the vessel is compressing the nerve. People who have chronic severe pain that does not respond to drugs may be offered treatment to numb the face. Occasionally, the pain can be alleviated by using a special heated probe to destroy the nerve.

If you have had treatment to numb the face, trigeminal neuralgia may recur. You must avoid hot food or drinks that could burn you. In other people, attacks of neuralgia may stop spontaneously, become more frequent, or persist without change for months or years. However, symptoms usually improve significantly with treatment.

(WWW) ONLINE SITES: p.1035

Sciatica

Pain in the buttock and down the back of the leg, occurring when the sciatic nerve is compressed or damaged

 AGE GENDER LIFESTYLE Risk factors depend on the cause

 GENETICS Not a significant factor

Sciatica is a form of nerve pain that may be felt anywhere along the course of one of the sciatic nerves, the two largest nerves in the body and the main nerve in each leg. The sciatic nerves are formed from nerve roots from the lower part of the spinal cord. They run from the base of the spine down the backs of the thighs to above the knees, where they divide into branches that supply the soles and outer sides of the feet. The pain of sciatica is caused by compression of or damage to the sciatic nerve, usually where it leaves the spinal cord. Often, only one leg is affected. In most cases, the pain disappears gradually over about 1–2 weeks, but it may recur.

WHAT ARE THE CAUSES?

In some cases, the cause of sciatica is unknown. However, in people between the ages of 20 and 40, the most common cause is a prolapsed or herniated disk (p.384) in the spinal column that presses on a spinal nerve root, causing pain in the affected leg. A prolapsed

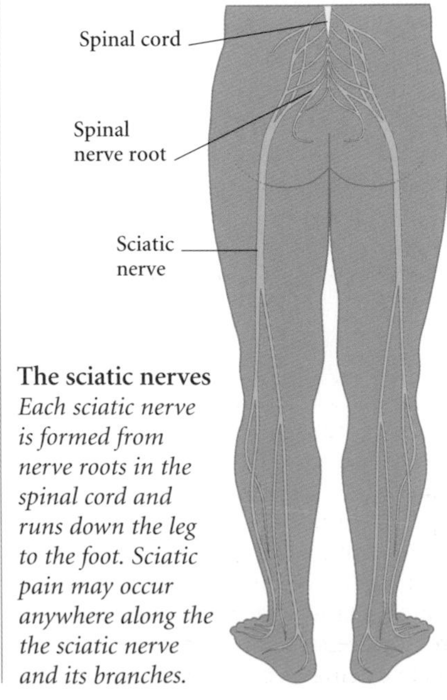
Spinal cord
Spinal nerve root
Sciatic nerve

The sciatic nerves
Each sciatic nerve is formed from nerve roots in the spinal cord and runs down the leg to the foot. Sciatic pain may occur anywhere along the the sciatic nerve and its branches.

disk may often occur as a result of straining to lift a heavy object. In older people, sciatica may be caused by bony changes in the spine as a result of various conditions, such as osteoarthritis (p.374). Pregnant women may develop sciatica during the last few months of pregnancy because of postural changes that cause increased pressure on the sciatic nerve (*see* COMMON COMPLAINTS OF NORMAL PREGNANCY, p.784).

Muscle spasm and sitting in an awkward position for long periods of time are relatively common causes of brief episodes of sciatica in all age groups.

Less commonly, sciatica may be the result of an injection into the buttock muscles that was mistakenly given too close to one of the sciatic nerves. Rarely, a tumor on the spinal cord may press on the sciatic nerve roots.

WHAT ARE THE SYMPTOMS?

The symptoms can be mild or severe, with spasmodic or persistent pain in the affected leg. Symptoms may include:

- Pain that is made worse by movement or by coughing.
- Tingling or numbness.
- Muscle weakness.

If sciatica is severe, you may have difficulty lifting the foot on the affected side because of muscle weakness, and you may be unable to stand upright. Some people have difficulty walking.

WHAT MIGHT BE DONE?

The doctor will examine you and test your leg reflexes, muscle strength, and sensation. He or she may advise you to rest in bed on a firm mattress for a couple of days and may also prescribe analgesics (p.912) to relieve the pain. If symptoms persist, you may have tests, such as CT scan (p.247) or MRI (p.248) of the spine, to look for bony changes or a prolapsed disk.

Sciatica as a result of pregnancy will usually disappear after childbirth. Pain caused by muscle spasm or sitting awkwardly also usually clears up without treatment. Occasionally, the condition can be helped by physiotherapy (p.961), exercise (*see* PREVENTING BACK PAIN, p.382), or chiropractic (p.973) treatments. However, sciatica can recur. Rarely, surgery may be necessary to relieve pressure on the nerve.

(WWW) ONLINE SITES: p.1035

Carpal tunnel syndrome

Tingling and pain in the hand and forearm due to a compressed nerve at the wrist

AGE Most common between the ages of 40 and 60

GENDER More common in females

LIFESTYLE Work that involves repetitive hand movements is a risk factor

GENETICS Not a significant factor

The carpal tunnel is the narrow space formed by the bones of the wrist (carpal bones) and the strong ligament that lies over them. In carpal tunnel syndrome, the median nerve, which controls some hand muscles and conveys sensation from nerve endings in part of the hand, is compressed where it passes through the tunnel. This compression causes painful tingling in the hand, wrist, and forearm. Carpal tunnel syndrome is a common disorder, especially in women aged 40–60, and often affects both hands.

WHAT ARE THE CAUSES?

In most cases, the underlying cause of nerve compression is not known. In others, it occurs because the soft tissues within the carpal tunnel swell, compressing the median nerve at the wrist. Such swelling may be due to diabetes mellitus (p.687), or it may occur during pregnancy. The carpal tunnel may also be narrowed by a joint disorder, such as rheumatoid arthritis (p.377), or a wrist fracture. The syndrome is associated with occupations that involve repetitive hand movements, such as keyboarding, which can lead to inflammation of the tendons in the wrist (*see* TENDINITIS AND TENOSYNOVITIS, p.390).

WHAT ARE THE SYMPTOMS?

Symptoms mainly affect specific areas of the hand, such as the thumb, the first and middle fingers, the inner side of the ring finger, and the palm of the hand. Symptoms initially may include:

- Burning and tingling in the hand.
- Pain in the wrist and up the forearm.

As the condition worsens, other symptoms may gradually appear including:

- Numbness of the hand.
- Weakened grip.

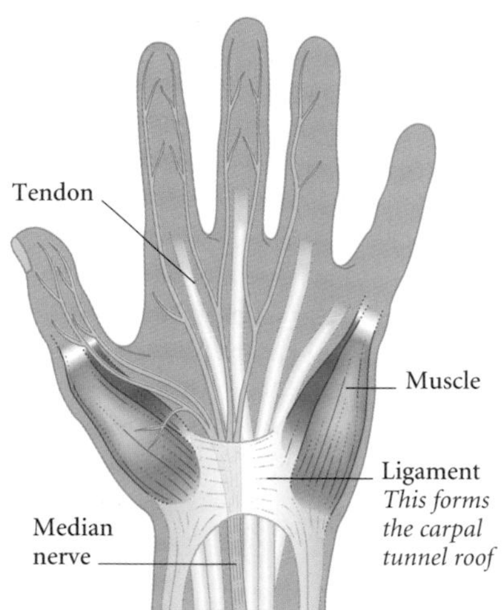
Tendon
Muscle
Ligament
This forms the carpal tunnel roof
Median nerve

Carpal tunnel
The carpal tunnel is formed by the bones of the wrist and the ligament over them. Compression of the median nerve in the tunnel causes carpal tunnel syndrome.

- Wasting of some hand muscles, particularly at the base of the thumb.

Symptoms may be more severe at night, and pain may interrupt sleep. Shaking the affected arm may temporarily relieve symptoms, but the numbness may become persistent if left untreated.

WHAT MIGHT BE DONE?

Your doctor may suspect carpal tunnel syndrome from your symptoms. He or she will examine your wrists and hands and may tap the inside of your wrists to check if a tingling sensation occurs. Nerve conduction tests (*see* NERVE AND MUSCLE ELECTRICAL TESTS, p.544) may be performed to confirm the diagnosis. If pregnancy is the cause of carpal tunnel syndrome, the symptoms usually disappear after childbirth. In other cases, treating the cause, if it can be identified, usually relieves symptoms.

The symptoms of carpal tunnel syndrome may be relieved temporarily by nonsteroidal anti-inflammatory drugs (p.894) or by wearing a wrist splint, particularly at night. In some cases, a corticosteroid injection (*see* LOCALLY ACTING CORTICOSTEROIDS, p.895) under the ligament may reduce swelling. If symptoms persist or recur, surgery may be recommended to cut the ligament under local anesthesia and release pressure on the nerve. After surgery, most people have no further symptoms.

(WWW) ONLINE SITES: p.1035

Facial palsy

Weakness or paralysis of the facial muscles on one side of the face due to damage to one of the facial nerves; often called "Bell's palsy"

AGE GENDER GENETICS LIFESTYLE
Not significant factors

The facial nerve controls the muscles of expression and emotion in the face and carries taste sensations from the front of the tongue to the brain. In facial palsy, one of the two facial nerves is damaged, compressed, or inflamed, and this results in weakness of the facial muscles. The eyelid is unable to close and the corner of the mouth droops on one side of the face. People with facial palsy are often worried that they have had a stroke (p.532), but this is unlikely if only the face is affected because a stroke is usually also associated with muscle weakness in other parts of the body.

Facial palsy is usually temporary, but a full recovery may take several months. The disorder affects about 1 in 4,000 people in Canada each year.

WHAT ARE THE CAUSES?

Often, the cause of facial palsy cannot be established, and in this case the condition is known as Bell's palsy. It is thought that a viral infection may be responsible for this type of palsy. Known causes of damage to the facial nerve include the viral infection shingles (*see* HERPES ZOSTER, p.288) and the bacterial infection Lyme disease (p.302). The facial nerve may also become inflamed due to a middle-ear infection (*see* OTITIS MEDIA, p.597). Rarely, the facial nerve may be compressed by a tumor called an acoustic neuroma (p.605).

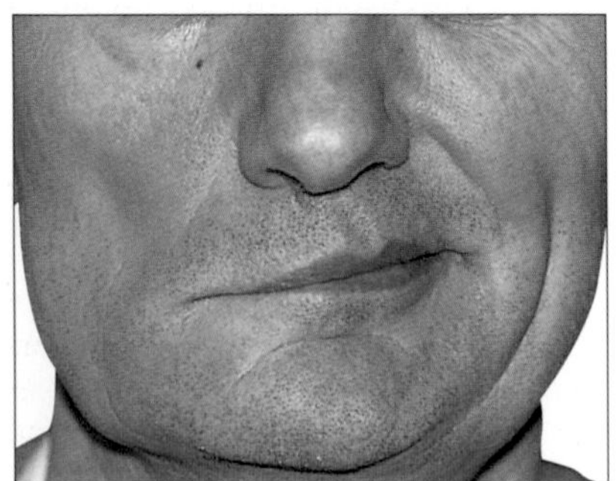

Facial palsy
Facial palsy caused by nerve damage has affected the muscles on the right side of this man's face, causing a lopsided smile.

Facial nerve damage can also result from progressive diseases of the nervous system, such as multiple sclerosis (p.541), and salivary gland tumors (p.635).

WHAT ARE THE SYMPTOMS?

In some cases, such as Bell's palsy, the symptoms of facial palsy appear suddenly over about 24 hours. In other cases, including facial palsy caused by an acoustic neuroma, symptoms may develop slowly. The symptoms include:

- Partial or complete paralysis of the muscles on one side of the face.
- Pain behind the ear on the affected side of the face.
- Drooping of the corner of the mouth, sometimes associated with drooling.
- Inability to close the eyelid on the affected side and watering of the eye.
- Impairment of taste.

If facial palsy is very severe, you may have difficulty speaking and eating, and, occasionally, sounds may seem unnaturally loud in the ear on the affected side. If the eyelid cannot be closed, the eye may become infected, leading to ulceration of the cornea, the transparent front part of the eye. In facial palsy due to shingles, you will also have a rash of crusting blisters on your ear.

HOW IS IT DIAGNOSED?

Your doctor will probably be able to diagnose facial palsy from your symptoms alone. A rapid onset over about 24 hours suggests Bell's palsy. Symptoms that develop more slowly usually indicate another cause.

If your doctor suspects a tumor may be compressing the facial nerve, he or she may arrange for you to have CT scanning (p.247) or MRI (p.248). Nerve and muscle electrical tests (p.544) may also be arranged in order to assess nerve damage. If you live in a part of the US where Lyme disease is common, you may have a blood test to look for evidence of this disorder.

WHAT MIGHT BE DONE?

If your symptoms have appeared in the last 48 hours, your doctor may prescribe corticosteroids (p.930) for up to 2 weeks to reduce inflammation of the nerve and may recommend analgesics (p.912) to relieve pain. To prevent damage to the cornea, you may be given artificial tears (*see* DRUGS ACTING ON THE EYE, p.919) and will probably be advised to tape the affected eye shut when you go to sleep.

Bell's palsy usually clears up without further treatment. If facial palsy has an underlying cause, it will be treated if possible. For example, if facial palsy is due to shingles, antiviral drugs (p.886), such as acyclovir, will be prescribed. Treatment with acyclovir should begin as soon as the rash appears. Acyclovir may be prescribed even in the absence of a rash. If you have an acoustic neuroma, it will be removed surgically to relieve compression of the facial nerve.

If muscle paralysis persists, plastic surgery (p.952) may be used to reroute another nerve to the face. Facial exercises and massage may help maintain tone (*see* PHYSIOTHERAPY, p.961).

WHAT IS THE PROGNOSIS?

With appropriate treatment, facial palsy usually improves in about 2 weeks. However, a full recovery may take up to 3 months. Some people are left with weakness, and facial palsy may recur.

(WWW) ONLINE SITES: p.1035

Peripheral nerve injuries

Damage to a nerve outside the brain or spinal cord as a result of physical injury

AGE GENDER GENETICS LIFESTYLE
Not significant factors

Any of the peripheral nerves, which connect the brain and the spinal cord to the rest of the body, may be damaged by physical injury. This damage may cause weakness and loss of sensation in the part of the body the nerve supplies. A peripheral nerve may be partially or completely severed, or it may be compressed. Damage may not be permanent because peripheral nerves can regenerate if they are not completely severed.

WHAT ARE THE SYMPTOMS?

The part of the body affected depends on which peripheral nerves are damaged. Symptoms usually include:

- Tingling and numbness.
- Muscle weakness or paralysis.
- Eventually, muscle wasting.

The severity of the symptoms depends on whether the nerve is damaged or completely severed.

WHAT MIGHT BE DONE?

Your doctor will check for loss of sensation, test your reflexes, and assess the strength of your muscles. You may also have nerve and muscle electrical tests (p.544), in which the function of the affected nerve is tested to assess how severely it has been damaged.

Treatment is often unnecessary if a peripheral nerve is only compressed or partially severed. After a few weeks, nerve and muscle tests may be repeated to see if there has been an improvement in your condition. If the nerve is totally severed, it cannot regenerate by itself, and you may be offered microsurgery (p.950) to try to repair it. After the operation, you may have physiotherapy (p.961) to help regain lost muscle strength and coordination.

However, even with skilled surgery, full recovery may not be possible, and you may continue to have symptoms.

(WWW) ONLINE SITES: p.1035

Myasthenia gravis

Chronic muscle weakness, especially of the muscles of the face, the throat, and around the eyes, due to an immune disorder

AGE Most common between the ages of 20 and 40 in females and 50 and 70 in males

GENDER More common in females

LIFESTYLE Stress and fatigue may aggravate the symptoms

GENETICS Not a significant factor

Myasthenia gravis is a rare autoimmune disorder in which the immune system produces antibodies that attack and slowly destroy the receptors in muscles that receive nerve impulses. As a result, the affected muscles fail to respond or they respond only weakly to nerve impulses. The muscles of the face, the throat, and around the eyes are those most often affected, causing speech and vision problems. However, other muscles may be affected, including those in the arms and legs. Rarely, the respiratory muscles are also affected.

Myasthenia gravis is a chronic condition that varies in severity. It is more common in women, especially in those between the ages of 20 and 40. In men, the condition most commonly occurs between the ages of 50 and 70.

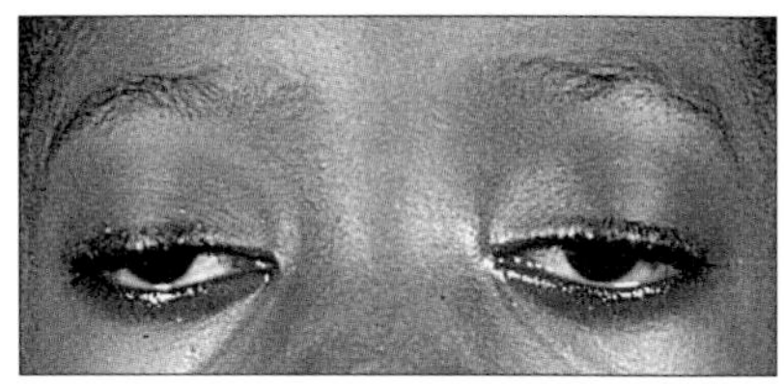

Myasthenia gravis
The rare immune disorder myasthenia gravis has affected the muscles controlling the eyelids, causing them to droop.

WHAT ARE THE CAUSES?

In most cases, the cause of the autoimmune disorder is not known. However, about 3 in 4 people have an abnormality of the thymus gland, which forms part of the immune system and is located at the base of the neck just underneath the breastbone. In some of these people, myasthenia gravis is associated with a thymoma, a noncancerous tumor of the thymus gland. Certain drugs, such as penicillamine (*see* ANTI-RHEUMATIC DRUGS, p.895), may cause myasthenia gravis. The condition may also be associated with other autoimmune disorders, such as the joint disorder rheumatoid arthritis (p.377).

WHAT ARE THE SYMPTOMS?

The symptoms of myasthenia gravis usually develop gradually over several weeks or months and tend to fluctuate. In some cases, symptoms appear suddenly. Symptoms may include:

- Drooping eyelids.
- Double vision.
- Slurred speech.
- Lack of facial expression.
- Difficulty chewing and swallowing.
- Weakness in the arm and leg muscles.

Symptoms usually improve with rest but worsen when the affected muscles are used. Symptoms may also be made worse by stress and, in women, by menstruation. Rarely, if respiratory muscles are weakened, life-threatening breathing difficulties may develop. About 1 in 7 babies born to mothers who have myasthenia gravis develops symptoms immediately after birth, but these usually disappear over a few weeks.

HOW IS IT DIAGNOSED?

Your doctor may suspect myasthenia gravis from your symptoms. To confirm the diagnosis, you will probably be given an injection that increases the levels of neurotransmitters, the chemicals responsible for conveying nerve impulses from nerves to muscle receptors. If the injection results in a rapid but temporary improvement in muscle strength, you probably have myasthenia gravis. You may also have blood tests to look for the particular antibodies that attack the receptors in muscles and electromyography (*see* NERVE AND MUSCLE ELECTRICAL TESTS, p.544) to look for muscle weakness by measuring electrical activity. CT scanning (p.247) of the chest should be carried out to look for a thymoma.

WHAT IS THE TREATMENT?

Your doctor may prescribe drugs that raise the levels of the neurotransmitters. If your symptoms are mild, this treatment may control your symptoms sufficiently for you to resume normal activities. If the symptoms persist, you may be prescribed oral corticosteroids (p.930) or other immunosuppressant drugs (p.906), such as azathioprine, to reduce antibody production. Treatment with oral corticosteroids may be started in the hospital because initially the drugs may have an adverse effect, and symptoms may become worse.

In severe cases, regular plasmapheresis may be necessary. In this procedure, plasma (the fluid part of the blood) is taken from the body, treated to remove the abnormal antibodies, and replaced. If breathing becomes difficult, mechanical ventilation may be necessary (*see* CRITICAL CARE UNIT, p.958).

If a tumor of the thymus is found, surgery will be performed to remove the thymus gland. Some people under age 45 with severe symptoms but no thymoma may also benefit from surgical removal of the thymus gland.

People who have myasthenia gravis should avoid extremes of temperature, infections, stress, and fatigue, all of which may intensify muscle weakness.

WHAT IS THE PROGNOSIS?

About 8 in 10 people with myasthenia gravis can be cured or their symptoms substantially improved with treatment. In a few people, the symptoms disappear spontaneously after about a year. Rarely, if the respiratory muscles are involved, the disorder may be fatal.

(WWW) ONLINE SITES: p.1033, p.1035

Guillain–Barré syndrome

A rare disorder in which damage to the peripheral nerves results in weakness that spreads upward from the legs

AGE GENDER GENETICS LIFESTYLE
Not significant factors

Guillain–Barré syndrome is a rare and potentially life-threatening disorder, causing a progressive loss of feeling and weakness that can rapidly lead to paralysis. The condition is caused by an abnormal immune response that may develop 2–3 weeks after certain infections, such as with *Campylobacter jejuni* bacteria (*see* FOOD POISONING, p.629). Rarely, Guillain–Barré syndrome may also develop as a complication following an immunization.

In Guillain–Barré syndrome, antibodies that are produced in response to an infection or vaccine attack the peripheral nerves, causing the nerves to become inflamed. Initially, the legs are affected, followed by the trunk, arms, and head. The condition is often mild, but, if severe, Guillain–Barré syndrome may cause difficulty in swallowing and breathing. In these cases, artificial feeding and mechanical ventilation may sometimes be necessary. In Canada, about 1 in 100,000 people is affected with Guillain–Barré syndrome each year.

WHAT ARE THE SYMPTOMS?

The symptoms may develop in a few days or weeks and include:

- Weakness in the legs, which may spread up the trunk and to the arms.
- Numbness and tingling of the limbs.

Usually, no further symptoms develop, but, in severe cases, symptoms become progressively worse and include:

- Paralysis of the limbs.
- Difficulty speaking and swallowing.

If the muscles of the rib cage and diaphragm are affected, serious breathing difficulties may develop.

HOW IS IT DIAGNOSED?

Your doctor will probably diagnose Guillain–Barré syndrome from your symptoms. However, you may have tests to confirm the diagnosis, including nerve conduction studies (*see* NERVE AND MUSCLE ELECTRICAL TESTS, p.544). You may also have a lumbar puncture (p.527), in which a sample of fluid from around the spinal cord is removed under local anesthesia for analysis.

WHAT IS THE TREATMENT?

During the early stages of Guillain–Barré syndrome, you will be admitted to the hospital for continuous monitoring. If breathing difficulties develop, mechanical ventilation may be necessary (*see* CRITICAL CARE UNIT, p.958). If you have problems swallowing, you may be given fluids intravenously or through a tube. Severe episodes have been found to respond to intravenous immunoglobulin. An alternative treatment is plasmapheresis, in which plasma (the fluid part of the blood) is withdrawn, treated to remove the abnormal antibodies, and then replaced. During recovery, you may have physical therapy (p.961) to maintain muscle tone.

WHAT IS THE PROGNOSIS?

Most people with Guillain–Barré syndrome recover without needing specific treatment. Mild symptoms usually disappear in a few weeks, but people with severe symptoms may take several months to recover and may be left with some weakness in affected areas. The syndrome is fatal in 3 in 100 cases.

(WWW) ONLINE SITES: p.1033, p.1035

Nervous tics

Involuntary repeated contraction of one or more muscles

AGE More common in children

GENDER More common in males

LIFESTYLE Stress is a risk factor

GENETICS Risk factors depend on the cause

Nervous tics occur when a muscle or a group of muscles controlled by peripheral nerves contracts repeatedly and involuntarily. The condition most often affects the facial muscles, but sudden, uncontrolled movements of the limbs and sounds such as grunts and throat clearing can also occur. Typical nervous tics include repetitive blinking, mouth twitching, and shrugging. Tics are common, recurrent, and painless. However, they may result in self-consciousness or teasing by others. Nervous tics usually develop during childhood and occur more commonly in boys than girls.

Often, the cause is unknown, but tics may be associated with stress. They are more common in children who are tired or upset. In Tourette's syndrome, a rare genetic disorder that occurs more frequently in boys, uncontrolled movements of the head, arms, and legs occur together with repetitive shouts, noises, grimaces, and spoken obscenities.

WHAT ARE THE SYMPTOMS?

A tic usually lasts only a fraction of a second. The muscle contraction may occur repeatedly and may cause:

- Rapid, uncontrolled blinking.
- Twitching of the muscles around the mouth.
- Shrugging of the shoulders or jerking movements of the neck.
- Involuntary contractions of the diaphragm, causing grunting or hiccups.

Nervous tics may be suppressed for a short period, but, in doing this, people often become more tense. When children are absorbed in an activity or asleep, tics usually disappear. Tourette's syndrome may be associated with phobias (p.552) and learning disabilities.

WHAT MIGHT BE DONE?

You should consult your doctor if you or your child has persistent nervous tics. Often, no treatment is necessary. In other cases, your doctor may suggest you try one or more different psychological therapies (pp.968–971) to help relieve stress. If symptoms are severe, your doctor may prescribe an anti-anxiety drug (p.916) for short periods of time. In some cases, nervous tics produced by Tourette's syndrome may be suppressed by tetrabenazine (p.1022). Treatment of some of the problems associated with Tourette's syndrome, such as phobias and learning disabilities, often requires specialized psychological help.

Nervous tics, especially those that occur in children, will usually disappear within about a year of the development of the symptoms. However, in a few children, childhood tics tend to persist into adulthood. Tourette's syndrome is always a lifelong condition.

(WWW) ONLINE SITES: p.1035

MENTAL HEALTH DISORDERS

Few people hesitate to seek treatment for a physical illness, but many find it hard to accept that they have a mental health problem. However, disorders such as depression, anxiety, and irrational fears are common, well understood, and, in many cases, treatable. No one need feel embarrassed about a mental illness or believe that he or she must deal with it alone.

This section begins with anxiety disorders, which are among the most common mental health problems in Canada. Feeling worried is a natural reaction to problems and stress. However, persistent anxiety, often with no obvious cause, needs treatment to prevent it from becoming a long-term problem. Phobias, irrational fears of anything from spiders to confined spaces, can dominate many areas of a person's life. Other anxiety-related illnesses include post-traumatic stress disorder, a response to events such as serious accidents and natural disasters.

Insomnia, a symptom of many mental illnesses, particularly anxiety and depression, is covered next. Depression, a very common disorder that affects 1 in 3 people at some time in their lives, is described in the article that follows. The condition requires prompt treatment to relieve symptoms and prevent chronic feelings of despair and possibly even suicide. The two eating disorders described next, anorexia nervosa and bulimia, are most common in teenage girls, but they are also being diagnosed at a younger age and in boys, too.

The common factor in the next group of disorders, which includes somatization and hypochondriasis, is the relationship between the mind and physical symptoms. Discussion of schizophrenia, a severe mental illness that may cause disturbed emotions and a break with reality, follows.

The final articles focus on drug and alcohol dependence and compulsive gambling. Treatment for these disorders begins when a person is able to acknowledge that there is a problem and is motivated to overcome it.

Anxiety disorders

Intense apprehension that may or may not have an obvious cause

 GENDER More common in females

 GENETICS Some types run in families

 LIFESTYLE Stress is a risk factor

 AGE Risk factors depend on the type

Temporary feelings of nervousness or worry in stressful situations are natural and appropriate. However, when anxiety becomes a general response to many ordinary situations and causes problems in coping with normal, everyday life, it is diagnosed as a disorder.

Anxiety disorders occur in a number of different forms. The most common is generalized anxiety disorder or persistent anxiety state, characterized by excessive and persistent anxiety that is difficult to control. Another type of anxiety disorder is panic disorder, in which there are recurrent panic attacks of intense anxiety and alarming physical symptoms. These attacks occur unpredictably and usually have no obvious cause. Panic attacks may also feature in generalized anxiety disorder. In another type of anxiety disorder known as phobia, severe anxiety is provoked by an irrational fear of a situation, creature, or object (*see* PHOBIAS, p.552).

Generalized anxiety disorder affects about 1 in 25 people in any one year in Canada. The condition usually begins in middle age, and women are more commonly affected than men. Sometimes, anxiety disorders exist alongside other mental health disorders, such as depression (p.554) or schizophrenia (p.560).

WHAT ARE THE CAUSES?

An increased susceptibility to anxiety disorders may be inherited or may be due to experiences in childhood. For example, poor bonding between a parent and child and abrupt separation of a child from a parent have been shown to play a part in some anxiety disorders. Generalized anxiety disorder may develop after a stressful life event, such as the death of a close relative. However, frequently the anxiety has no particular cause. Similarly, panic disorder often develops for no obvious reason.

WHAT ARE THE SYMPTOMS?

People with generalized anxiety disorder and panic disorder experience both psychological and physical symptoms. However, in generalized anxiety disorder, the psychological symptoms tend to be persistent while physical symptoms are intermittent. In panic attacks, both psychological and physical symptoms come on together suddenly and unpredictably. The psychological symptoms of generalized anxiety disorder include:

- A sense of foreboding with no obvious reason or cause.
- Being on edge and unable to relax.
- Impaired concentration.
- Repetitive worrying thoughts.
- Disturbed sleep (*see* INSOMNIA, p.554) and sometimes nightmares.

In addition, you may have symptoms of depression, such as early waking or a general sense of hopelessness. Physical symptoms of the disorder, which occur intermittently, include:

- Headache.
- Abdominal cramps, sometimes with diarrhea, and vomiting.
- Frequent urination.
- Sweating, flushing, and tremor.
- A feeling of something being stuck in the throat.

Psychological and physical symptoms of panic attacks include the following:

- Shortness of breath.
- Sweating, trembling, and nausea.
- Palpitations (awareness of an abnormally rapid heartbeat).
- Dizziness and fainting.

- Fear of choking or that death may be imminent.
- A sense of unreality and fears about loss of sanity.

Many of these symptoms can be misinterpreted as signs of a serious physical illness, and this may increase your level of anxiety. Over time, fear of having a panic attack in public may lead you to avoid situations such as eating out in restaurants or being in crowds.

WHAT MIGHT BE DONE?

You may be able to find your own ways of reducing anxiety levels, including relaxation exercises (p.75). If you are unable to deal with or identify a specific cause for your anxiety, you should consult your doctor. It is important to see a doctor as soon as possible after a first panic attack to prevent repeated attacks. There are several measures you can try to help control a panic attack, such as breathing into a bag (*see* COPING WITH A PANIC ATTACK, below). For any anxiety disorder, your doctor may suggest counseling (p.971) to help you manage stress. You may also be offered cognitive therapy (p.970) or behavior therapy (p.969), to help you control anxiety. A self-help group may also be useful.

If you are coping with a particularly stressful period in your life or a difficult event, your doctor may prescribe a benzodiazepine (*see* ANTIANXIETY DRUGS, p.916), but these drugs are usually prescribed for only a short period of time because there is a danger of dependence. You may be prescribed beta blocker drugs (p.898) to treat the physical symptoms of anxiety. If you have symptoms of depression, you may be given antidepressant drugs (p.916), some of which are also useful in treating panic attacks.

In most cases, the earlier that anxiety disorders are treated, the quicker their effects can be reduced. Without treatment, an anxiety disorder may develop into a life-long condition.

(WWW) ONLINE SITES: p.1029, p.1034

SELF-HELP COPING WITH A PANIC ATTACK

Rapid breathing in a panic attack reduces carbon dioxide levels in the blood and may cause tingling in the fingers. You can control these symptoms by breathing through the mouth into a paper bag. By doing this, you rebreathe air with more carbon dioxide and restore the body's levels to normal.

Paper bag
The paper bag should be held tightly to the mouth

Rebreathing from a bag
Breathe in and out slowly into a paper bag about 10 times and then breathe normally for 15 seconds. Continue until you no longer need to breathe rapidly.

Phobias

Persistent and irrational fears of, and a compelling desire to avoid, particular objects, activities, or situations

 AGE Most commonly develops from late childhood to early adulthood

 GENDER GENETICS Risk factors depend on the type

 LIFESTYLE Not a significant factor

Many people have particular fears, such as a fear of dogs or heights, that are upsetting occasionally but do not disrupt their everyday activities. A phobia is a fear or anxiety that has been carried to extremes. A person with a phobia has such a compelling desire to avoid contact with a feared object or situation that it interferes with normal life.

Being exposed to the subject of the phobia causes a panic reaction of severe anxiety, sweating, and a rapid heartbeat. A person with a phobia is aware that this intense fear is irrational but still feels anxiety that can be alleviated only by avoiding the feared object or situation. The need to do this may disrupt routines and limit the person's capacity to take part in new experiences. About 1 in 20 people in Canada has a phobia. Phobias usually develop in late childhood, adolescence, or early adult life.

WHAT ARE THE TYPES?

Phobias take many different forms, but they can be broadly divided into two types: simple and complex phobias.

SIMPLE PHOBIAS Phobias specific to a single object, situation, or activity, such as a fear of spiders, heights, or air travel, are called simple phobias. For example, claustrophobia, a fear of enclosed spaces, is a simple phobia. A fear of blood is a common simple phobia that affects more men than women.

COMPLEX PHOBIAS More complicated phobias that have a number of component fears are described as complex phobias. Agoraphobia is an example of a complex phobia that involves multiple anxieties. These fears may include being alone in an open space or being trapped in a public area with no exit to safety. The kind of situations that provoke agoraphobic anxiety include riding on public transportation, using elevators, and visiting crowded stores. Tactics to avoid these situations may disrupt work and social life, and a person with severe agoraphobia may eventually become housebound. Agoraphobia may occasionally develop in middle age and is more common in women.

Social phobias are also classified as complex phobias. People with a social phobia have an overwhelming fear of embarrassing themselves or of being humiliated in front of other people in social situations, such as when they are eating or speaking in public.

WHAT ARE THE CAUSES?

Often, no explanation can be found for the phobia. However, occasionally a simple phobia may be traced to an experience earlier in life. For example, being trapped temporarily in a confined enclosed space during childhood may lead to claustrophobia in later life. Simple phobias appear to run in families, but this is thought to be because children often "learn" their fear from a family member with a similar phobia.

The causes of complex phobias, such as agoraphobia and social phobia, are unclear, but they may develop from a general tendency to be anxious. Agoraphobia sometimes develops after an unexplained panic attack. Some people recall a stressful situation as the trigger for their symptoms and then become conditioned to be anxious in these circumstances. Most social phobias also begin with a sudden episode of intense anxiety in a social situation, which then becomes the main focus of the phobia. A person who is lacking in self-esteem is also more likely to develop agoraphobia or a social phobia.

WHAT ARE THE SYMPTOMS?

Exposure to or simply thinking about the object, creature, or situation, that generates the phobia leads to intense anxiety accompanied by:

- Dizziness and feeling faint.
- Palpitations (awareness of an abnormally rapid heartbeat).
- Sweating, trembling, and nausea.
- Shortness of breath.

A factor that is common to every phobia is avoidance. Activities may become limited because of fear of unexpectedly encountering the subject of the phobia, and this may lead to depression (p.554). Anxiety and panic attacks (*see* ANXIETY DISORDERS, p.551) may develop. Sometimes, a person with a phobia attempts to relieve fear by drinking too much alcohol or abusing drugs.

WHAT MIGHT BE DONE?

If you have a phobia that interferes with your life, you should seek treatment. Many simple phobias can be treated effectively using a form of behavior therapy (p.969), such as desensitization (*see* DESENSITIZATION THERAPY, p.969). During treatment, a therapist gives support while you are safely and gradually exposed to the object or situation that you fear. Inevitably, you will experience some anxiety, but exposure is always kept within bearable limits.

Members of your family may be given guidance on how to help you cope with your phobic behavior. If you have symptoms of depression, your doctor may prescribe antidepressant drugs (p.916).

WHAT IS THE PROGNOSIS?

A simple phobia often resolves itself as a person gets older. However, complex phobias, such as social phobias and agoraphobia, tend to persist unless they are treated. More than 9 in 10 people with agoraphobia are treated successfully with desensitization therapy.

(WWW) ONLINE SITES: p.1029, p.1034

Post-traumatic stress disorder

A prolonged emotional response to an extreme personal experience

 AGE Most common in children and elderly people

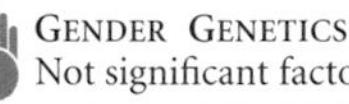 GENDER GENETICS LIFESTYLE Not significant factors

Post-traumatic stress disorder (PTSD) occurs when a person is involved in a stressful event that triggers persistent intense emotions for some time afterward. Experiencing an event in which life and personal safety are perceived to be at risk or simply witnessing a traumatic event is often enough to trigger the disorder. The kind of events that result in PTSD include natural disasters, accidents, and being assaulted.

About 1 in 10 people has PTSD at some time in life. Children and elderly people are more susceptible, as are people who lack support or who have a history of anxiety disorders (p.551).

WHAT ARE THE SYMPTOMS?

The symptoms of PTSD occur soon after the event or develop weeks, months, or, rarely, years later. They may include:

- Involuntary thoughts about the experience and repeated reliving of events.
- Daytime flashbacks of the event.
- Panic attacks with symptoms such as shortness of breath and fainting.
- Avoidance of reminders of the event and refusal to discuss it.
- Sleep disturbance and nightmares.
- Poor concentration.
- Irritability.

A person with PTSD may feel emotionally "numb," detached from events, and estranged from family and friends. He or she may also lose interest in normal day-to-day activities. Other psychological disorders, such as depression (p.554) or anxiety (p.551), may coexist with PTSD. Occasionally, the disorder leads to alcohol or drug abuse.

WHAT MIGHT BE DONE?

The doctor will assess the severity of symptoms and ask whether there have been mental health problems in the past. Counseling (p.971) may encourage the person to talk about his or her experiences, and support for the individual and family members is often an important part of treatment. Drugs such as antidepressants (p.916) may be used with counseling, and this approach often produces an improvement within 8 weeks. Drugs may need to be taken for at least a year. PTSD often disappears after a few months of treatment, but some symptoms may persist. In some cases, PTSD may last for years. After a person has experienced PTSD, there is an increased likelihood of the disorder recurring after other traumatic events.

(WWW) ONLINE SITES: p.1029, p.1034

Obsessive–compulsive disorder

Uncontrollable thoughts that are often accompanied by irresistible urges to carry out acts or rituals to relieve anxiety

 AGE Usually develops in adolescence

 GENETICS Sometimes runs in families

 LIFESTYLE Stress is a risk factor

 GENDER Not a significant factor

A person with obsessive–compulsive disorder feels dominated by unwanted thoughts that enter the mind repeatedly. Obsessive thoughts are frequently accompanied by a form of compulsive ritual, in which a behavior or action, such as checking that keys are still in a pocket, is repeated again and again. The person affected does not want to perform these actions but feels driven to do so. Thoughts may be concerns about hygiene, personal safety, or security of

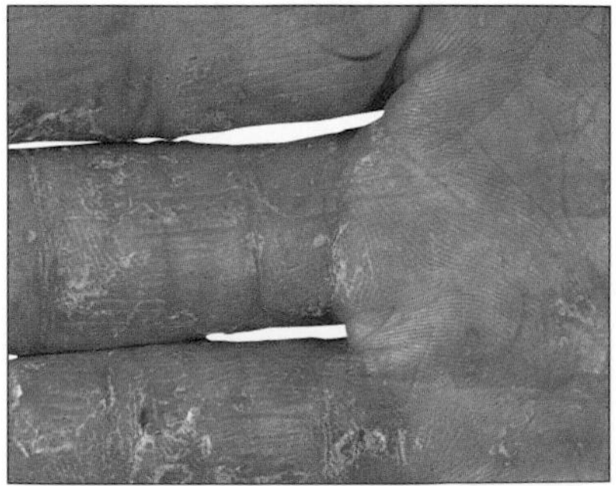

Effects of compulsive handwashing
Repeated handwashing in a person with obsessive–compulsive disorder has made the skin of the hands raw and chapped.

possessions. Alternatively, there may be violent and obscene thoughts that are completely out of character. Examples of common compulsions include hand-washing, checking that windows and doors are locked, and arranging objects on a desk in precise patterns. Carrying out the ritual brings short-lived relief, but, in severe cases, the ritual is done hundreds of times a day and interferes with work and social life.

About 3 in 100 people in Canada have obsessive–compulsive disorder, which sometimes runs in families. Having an obsessive–compulsive personality (*see* PERSONALITY DISORDERS, p.561) tends to increase the risk of the disorder. Stressful life events may trigger the condition.

WHAT ARE THE SYMPTOMS?

An obsession or compulsion can focus on any object, event, or idea. The most common symptoms include:

- Intrusive, irrational mental images.
- Repeated attempts to resist thoughts.
- Repetitive behavior.

The person may be aware that the behavior is irrational and be distressed by it but cannot control the compulsions.

TEST PSYCHOLOGICAL ASSESSMENT

To help diagnose a mental health disorder, your doctor may arrange for you to have a psychological assessment. You will be asked a series of questions to establish the nature of your problem and its effect on your life. Areas of discussion include your family, your history, how life was before you became ill, and factors that might have triggered the disorder, such as a bereavement.

Having an assessment
Although questions are intimate and personal, they are part of a standard assessment procedure. The doctor usually records answers on a checklist.

WHAT MIGHT BE DONE?

Your doctor will probably be able to diagnose obsessive–compulsive disorder from your symptoms. To help you confront your compulsion to carry out rituals, your doctor may suggest treatment with a form of psychotherapy, such as behavior therapy (p.969). He or she may prescribe an antidepressant drug (p.916) because drugs combined with psychotherapy usually offer the best chance of success. Initially, behavior therapy may make your anxiety and compulsion to perform rituals worse, but, given time, therapy may help you resist compulsive urges.

As part of your treatment, you may want to involve a family member or friend to encourage you. You should also try to identify stress factors that may contribute to your condition and seek ways to reduce them. Many people find joining a self-help group is beneficial.

More than 9 in 10 people begin to improve within a year of starting treatment. Other people, particularly those who already have an obsessive–compulsive personality, have a chronic illness that fluctuates in severity.

(WWW) ONLINE SITES: p.1029, p.1034

Insomnia

A regular inability to fall asleep or stay asleep, leading to excessive fatigue

 AGE More common in elderly people

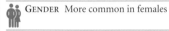

 GENDER More common in females

LIFESTYLE Drinking excess caffeine or alcohol and stress are risk factors

 GENETICS Not a significant factor

At some point in their lives, about 1 in 3 people in Canada experiences regular difficulty in sleeping, known as insomnia. The problem may be in falling asleep or in waking up and being unable to get back to sleep. Insomnia is distressing and may lead to excessive fatigue and a general inability to cope. Sleep problems are more common in women and in elderly people of both sexes.

Sleeping difficulties most commonly start when a person is worried or anxious. A high intake of caffeine or alcohol during the day may also lead to sleeplessness. Often, not sleeping properly then becomes persistent because good sleep habits are lost. Insomnia may be caused by an illness with symptoms that cause problems at night, such as asthma (p.483) or the metabolic disorder hyperthyroidism (p.679). Insomnia is often associated with mental health problems, such as depression (p.554) and anxiety disorders (p.551).

WHAT MIGHT BE DONE?

Your doctor will first treat any physical and mental problems that may be causing your insomnia. For example, if you are depressed, the doctor may prescribe antidepressant drugs (p.916). However, if there is no obvious cause for your insomnia, your doctor may arrange for you to be assessed during sleep at a sleep clinic. Tests often show that people actually sleep more hours than they think they do but wake frequently. Reassurance that you are getting sufficient sleep may be all that is needed.

Your doctor may suggest changes to your lifestyle, such as doing more exercise or cutting out caffeinated drinks (*see* SLEEP, p.73). Elderly people in particular may be advised to avoid taking daytime naps because they reduce the need for sleep at night. Rarely, the doctor may prescribe sleeping drugs (p.915) for a few days to help restore a normal sleep pattern. Sleeping drugs should not be taken for a longer period because of the risk of dependence.

(WWW) ONLINE SITES: p.1034, p.1037

Depression

Feelings of sadness, often accompanied by loss of interest in life as a whole and reduced energy

 AGE More common from the late 20s onward

 GENDER More common in females

 GENETICS Sometimes runs in families

 LIFESTYLE Social isolation is a risk factor

Sadness is an expected reaction to adversity or personal misfortune and may last for a considerable time. Depression exists when feelings of unhappiness intensify and daily life becomes difficult. Depression is one of the most common mental health disorders in Canada. It affects about 1 in 5 people at some time in life, more commonly from the late 20s onward. Women are twice as likely to have depression as men. In some people, depression lifts spontaneously after days or weeks. However, others may need professional help and support. In severe depression, hospital admission may be necessary to protect people from neglect or self-harm.

Depression is often accompanied by symptoms of anxiety (*see* ANXIETY DISORDERS, p.551). For example, there may be a persistent sense of foreboding and repetitive, worrying thoughts.

What are the causes?

Depression may develop when a person has to face one or more stressful life events. The trigger factor is often some form of loss, such as the breakdown of a close relationship or a bereavement.

A traumatic experience in childhood, such as the death of a parent, may increase susceptibility to depression later. In addition, a tendency toward depression sometimes runs in families. There are several physical disorders that may cause depression. These include some infections, such as infectious mononucleosis (p.289); neurological disorders, such as Parkinson's disease (p.539); and hormonal disorders, such as Cushing syndrome (p.684). Hormonal changes at menopause or after childbirth may also cause depression (*see* DEPRESSION AFTER CHILDBIRTH, p.807).

A number of mental health disorders may lead to depression. They include phobias (p.552), the eating disorder anorexia nervosa (p.562), alcohol dependence (p.564), and drug dependence (p.564). Some people feel generally low and become depressed only during the winter months, a condition known as seasonal affective disorder. Depression can also be a side effect of certain drugs, such as oral contraceptives and beta blocker drugs (p.898). However, depression often has no identifiable cause.

What are the symptoms?

A typical sign of depression is a feeling of sadness, even misery, that is worse in the morning and lasts for most of the day. Other common symptoms include:

- Loss of interest in and enjoyment of work and leisure activities.
- Diminished energy levels.
- Poor concentration.
- Reduced self-esteem.
- Feelings of guilt.
- Tearfulness.
- Inability to make decisions.
- Early waking and inability to resume sleep (*see* INSOMNIA, opposite page) or an excessive need to sleep.
- Loss of hope for the future.
- Recurrent thoughts of death.
- Weight loss or increase in weight.
- Decreased sex drive (p.769).

In an elderly person, other symptoms may occur, including confusion, forgetfulness, and personality changes, that may be mistakenly attributed to dementia (p.535). Neglect of personal hygiene and diet in an elderly person may also be an indication of underlying depression. Sometimes, depressive illness manifests itself as a physical symptom, such as fatigue (*see* SOMATIZATION, p.559), or may lead to a physical problem, such as constipation or headache.

Severely depressed people may see or hear things that are not there. Irrational delusions may also occur. For instance, a depressed person may become convinced that his or her partner is having a sexual relationship with someone else.

Depression may also alternate with periods of euphoria in a person who has manic depression (*see* BIPOLAR AFFECTIVE DISORDER, p.557).

Are there complications?

Rarely, if the condition is not treated, a depressive stupor may develop, in which speech and movement are greatly reduced. Left untreated, depression can delay recovery from a physical illness and intensify pain whatever the cause, which then increases the depression. A person who is severely depressed may contemplate or attempt suicide (*see* ATTEMPTED SUICIDE AND SUICIDE, p.556).

What might be done?

If your depression is mild, your symptoms may disappear spontaneously if you are given sympathy and support from those close to you. However, if you do need help for depression, it is not a sign of weakness. Depression can almost always be treated effectively, and you should not put off seeing your doctor if you continue to feel low. He or she may examine you and arrange for blood tests to make sure that your low energy levels and mood are not caused by a physical illness. You may be asked to have a psychological assessment (opposite page) in case there are other mental health problems that may be causing or contributing to your depression.

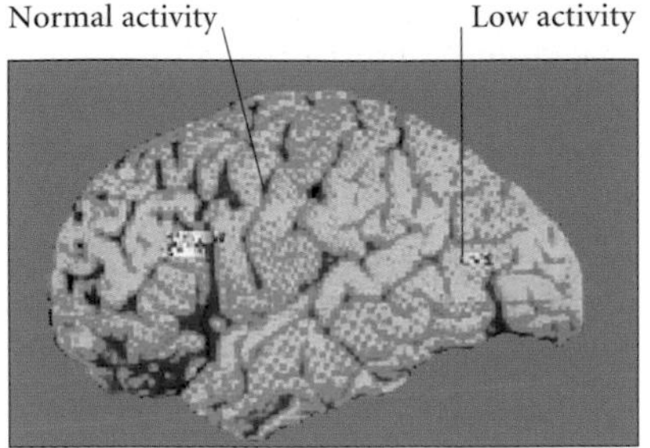
Normal activity
Low activity

BRAIN OF NORMAL PERSON

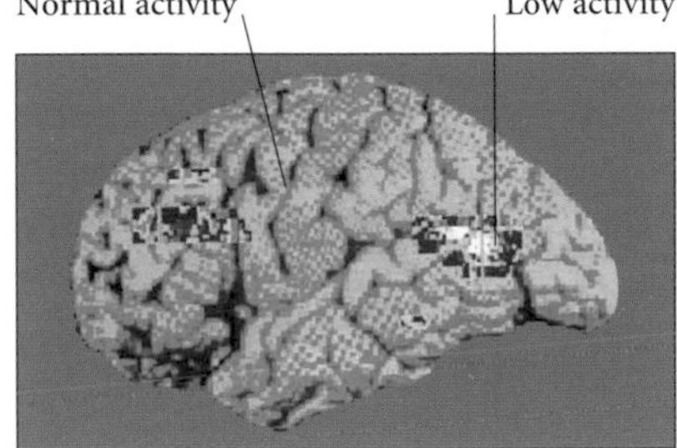
Normal activity
Low activity

BRAIN OF DEPRESSED PERSON

Reduced brain activity in depression
These images show large areas of low activity in the brain of a depressed person compared with small areas of low activity in the brain of a normal person.

If depression is diagnosed, you may be treated with drugs, psychotherapy, or a combination of therapy and drugs. Rarely, a severe case of depression is treated with electroconvulsive therapy.

DRUG TREATMENTS The doctor usually prescribes a course of antidepressant drugs (p.916). There are several different types, and your doctor will choose the one most suitable for your needs. Although some have undesirable side effects, other side effects may be useful. For example, an antidepressant drug that is mildly sedating may relieve a sleeping problem. Your mood usually improves after you have been taking an antidepressant for 2–4 weeks, although some of your symptoms may improve more quickly. If your depression shows little improvement after a month or if you have troublesome side effects from your treatment, your doctor may adjust the dosage or prescribe an alternative drug. Once your depression has lifted, you should continue taking antidepressants for as long as your doctor suggests. Treatment usually lasts for a minimum of 6 months, but the length of time depends on how quickly the depression responds to treatment and whether you have had previous episodes of depression. There is no risk of addiction with antidepressant drugs, but depression may recur if they are stopped suddenly.

PSYCHOLOGICAL TREATMENTS While you are feeling depressed, support and encouragement from your doctor or other health professionals are essential. Your doctor may refer you to a therapist for treatments such as cognitive therapy (p.970) to help you change negative patterns of thinking or psychoanalytic-based psychotherapies (p.968) to look into the reasons for your depression. Counseling (p.971), either on an individual basis or as part of a group, may help you make sense of your feelings.

ELECTROCONVULSIVE THERAPY In rare cases, treatment with electroconvulsive therapy (ECT) may be given. In this procedure, which is carried out under general anesthesia, an electrical stimulus that causes a brief seizure in the brain is given by placing two electrodes on the head. Between 6 and 12 treatments may be given to the affected person over approximately a month. ECT is particularly useful for treating depression that is accompanied by delusions. Following treatment with ECT, antidepressants are prescribed for at least a few months to prevent relapse.

SELF-HELP RECOVERING FROM DEPRESSION

There are a number of strategies that can help someone rebuild self-confidence and regain control of life after recovery from depression:

- Make a list of things to do each day, beginning with the most important.
- Tackle each task one at a time, and reflect on what you have achieved when each is done.
- Set aside a few minutes each day to relax by breathing deeply or stretching (*see* RELAXATION EXERCISES, p.75).
- Exercise regularly to help reduce feelings of stress (*see* EXERCISE AND HEALTH, p.55).
- Eat a healthy diet (p.48).
- Take up a pastime or hobby that distracts you from worries.
- Join a support group to meet other people who have shared similar experiences.

WHAT IS THE PROGNOSIS?

Antidepressant drugs help to relieve many symptoms of depression. They are effective in treating about 3 in 4 people with this condition. When drug treatments and psychological therapy are used in combination, the symptoms of depression can often be relieved completely over a period of 2–3 months. Of those people who are treated with ECT, about 9 in 10 make a successful recovery. However, for some people, depression can last for years or recur with no obvious trigger.

(WWW) ONLINE SITES: p.1029, p.1034

Attempted suicide and suicide

An attempt to end one's life that may have a nonfatal or fatal outcome

AGE More young people attempt suicide, but more elderly people die from an attempt

GENDER More females attempt suicide, but more males die from an attempt

LIFESTYLE Social isolation and living in urban areas are risk factors

GENETICS Not a significant factor

Most people who attempt suicide are in their teens or are elderly. Among those who attempt suicide, some are certain that they wish to die while others use the attempt to signal their desperation rather than end their lives. Over half of all suicides and suicide attempts involve drug overdoses (*see* DRUG OVERDOSE AND ACCIDENTAL INGESTION, p.321), most commonly of an analgesic (p.912) such as acetaminophen.

Suicide rates vary according to age groups, gender, and province. Women are three times more likely than men to attempt suicide. However, men are four times more likely to die as a result of a suicide attempt because the methods they use generally have a greater potential to kill. The actual number of suicides is unknown because some are recorded as deaths from other causes. Nevertheless, suicide is estimated as a leading cause of "years of life lost", as it so commonly involves young people.

WHAT ARE THE CAUSES?

The majority of suicides in people of all ages are associated with an underlying mental health disorder. About half of all suicide attempts are a consequence of depression (p.554) or bipolar affective disorder (opposite page).

Teenage suicide attempts are often impulsive and may follow family quarrels or the breakup of a relationship. These attempts rarely indicate a determined wish to die, but a fatal dose of pills may be taken by mistake. Youth suicide attempts using guns are usually fatal. Suicide in elderly people is often the result of depression caused by bereavement and loneliness. Incurable, painful physical illnesses lead to 1 in 5 suicides among people over age 65.

Other mental health disorders associated with suicide are schizophrenia (p.560), drug dependence (p.564), and alcohol dependence (p.564).

WHAT MIGHT BE DONE?

If suicide has been attempted, admission to the hospital is necessary for assessment and treatment. In the case of an overdose, as much of the ingested substance as possible is removed from the body to prevent it from being absorbed. If the substance is identifiable, an antidote will be given if there is one available. Any physical effects of an attempted suicide, such as cuts to the wrists, are treated appropriately.

Treatment for underlying psychiatric problems is particularly important to prevent future suicide attempts. Drugs such as antidepressants (p.916) may be prescribed, and a form of psychotherapy or counseling (*see* PSYCHOLOGICAL THERAPIES, pp.968–971) may be recommended. Any problems that may have precipitated the suicide attempt will be identified and help offered to resolve and overcome them. After a first suicide attempt, there is an increased risk of future attempts.

CAN IT BE PREVENTED?

Some people talk about their wish to kill themselves before they attempt suicide, and these threats should be taken seriously. Family and friends should try to remove any available means and seek professional help urgently. If there is a high risk of suicide, it may be necessary to admit the person to the hospital, possibly without his or her consent.

After a suicide attempt, treatment for underlying disorders and problems, and family support and vigilance may prevent further attempts. However, a person who has a strong desire to die may try to prevent discovery during an attempt and is more likely to choose a method that will prove fatal.

(WWW) ONLINE SITES: p.1029, 1034

Bipolar affective disorder

A disorder in which mood fluctuates between extremes of highs and lows

AGE Usually develops in the early 20s

GENETICS Sometimes runs in families

GENDER LIFESTYLE Not significant factors

About 1 in 100 people in Canada has bipolar affective disorder, also known as manic depression. In this disorder, episodes of elation and abnormally high activity levels (mania) tend to alternate with episodes of low mood and abnormally low energy levels (depression). More than half of all people with bipolar affective disorder have repeated episodes. Trigger factors for manic and depressive episodes are not generally known, although they are sometimes brought on in response to a major life-event, such as a marital breakup or bereavement. Bipolar affective disorder usually develops in the early 20s and can run in families, but exactly how it is inherited is not known.

WHAT ARE THE SYMPTOMS?

Symptoms of mania and depression tend to alternate, each episode of symptoms lasting an unpredictable length of time. Between periods of mania and depression, mood and behavior are usually normal. However, a manic phase may occasionally be followed immediately by depression. Sometimes, either depression or mania predominates to the extent that there is little evidence of a pattern of changing moods. Occasionally, symptoms of depression and mania are present during the same period. During a manic episode of the disorder, the symptoms may include:

- Elated, expansive, or sometimes irritable mood.
- Inflated self-esteem, which may lead to delusions of great wealth, accomplishment, creativity, and power.
- Increased energy levels and decreased need for sleep.
- Distraction and poor concentration.
- Loss of social inhibitions.
- Unrestrained sexual behavior.
- Spending excessive sums of money on luxuries and vacations.

Speech may be difficult to follow because the person tends to speak rapidly and change topic frequently. At times, he or she may be aggressive or violent and may neglect diet and personal hygiene.

During an episode of depression, the main symptoms include:

- Feeling generally low.
- Loss of interest and enjoyment.
- Diminished energy level.
- Reduced self-esteem.
- Loss of hope for the future.

While severely depressed, an affected person may not care whether he or she lives or dies. About 1 in 10 people with bipolar disorder eventually attempts suicide (*see* ATTEMPTED SUICIDE AND SUICIDE, opposite page).

In more severe cases of bipolar disorder, delusions of power during manic episodes may be made worse by hallucinations. When manic, the person may hear voices that are not there praising his or her qualities. In his or her depressive phase, these imaginary voices may describe the person's inadequacies and failures. In such cases, the disorder may resemble schizophrenia (p.560).

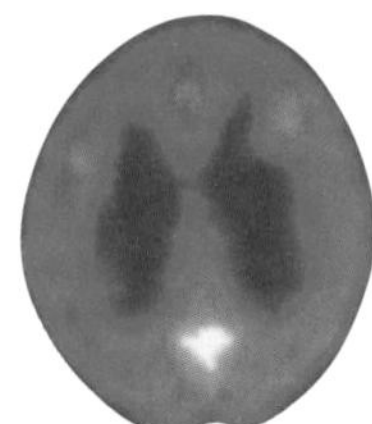

BRAIN IN NORMAL PERIODS

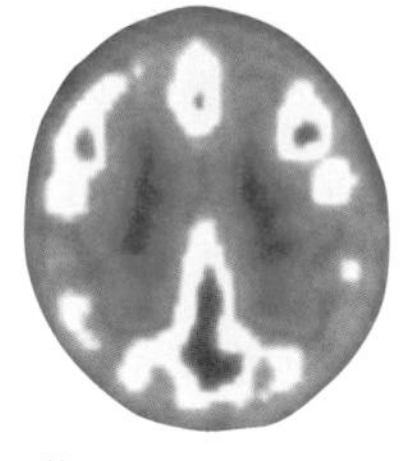

BRAIN IN MANIC PHASE

Increased brain activity in bipolar affective disorder

These PET scans of the brain of a person with bipolar affective disorder show high levels of activity during a manic episode.

WHAT MIGHT BE DONE?

During a manic phase, people usually lack insight into their condition and may not know that they are ill. Often a relative or friend observes erratic behavior in a person close to him or her and seeks professional advice. A diagnosis of bipolar affective disorder is based on the full range of the person's symptoms, and treatment will depend on whether the person is in a manic or a depressive phase. For the depressive phase, antidepressants (p.916) are prescribed, but their effects have to be monitored to ensure that they do not precipitate a manic phase. During the first days or weeks of a manic phase, symptoms may be controlled by antipsychotic drugs (p.917).

Some people may need to be admitted to the secure environment of a hospital for assessment and treatment during a manic phase or a severe depressive phase. They may feel creative and energetic when manic and may be reluctant to accept long-term medication because it makes them feel "flat."

Most people make a good recovery from manic-depressive episodes, but recurrences are common. For this reason, initial treatments for depression and mania may be gradually replaced with lithium (*see* MOOD-STABILIZING DRUGS, p.918), a drug that has to be taken continuously to prevent relapse. If lithium is not fully effective, other types of drugs, including certain anticonvulsant drugs (p.914), may be given. In severe cases in which drugs have no effect, electroconvulsive therapy (ECT) may be used to relieve symptoms by inducing a brief seizure in the brain under general anesthesia.

Once symptoms are under control, the person will need regular follow-ups to check for signs of mood changes. A form of psychotherapy (*see* PSYCHOLOGICAL THERAPIES, pp.968–971) can help the person come to terms with the disorder and reduce stress factors in his or her life that may contribute to it.

(WWW) ONLINE SITES: p.1029, p.1034

Mental problems due to physical illness

One or more psychological conditions resulting from a physical illness

 LIFESTYLE Unsettled domestic or financial circumstances are risk factors

 AGE GENDER GENETICS Not significant factors

Changes in mental state are a common response to a physical illness. A serious physical illness may cause anxiety (*see* ANXIETY DISORDERS, p.551), depression (p.554), anger, or denial of the problem. Usually, reactions are transient and disappear when the person adjusts to the change in his or her physical condition. However, illnesses that may be fatal or chronic disorders that involve lengthy or unpleasant treatment may cause persistent mood problems. People who have had previous psychiatric disorders are more at risk, as are people who are subject to additional stresses, such as an unstable home life or financial problems or who generally find it hard to deal with adversity.

Mood problems are sometimes a recognized symptom of a physical illness. For example, anxiety is a symptom of the hormonal disorder hyperthyroidism (p.679), and depression is associated with multiple sclerosis (p.541) and also Parkinson's disease (*see* PARKINSON'S DISEASE AND PARKINSONISM, p.539).

What are the symptoms?

The psychological symptoms that may result from a physical illness include:

- Feelings of anxiety, ranging from mild apprehension to fear and panic.
- Depressive symptoms, such as a sense of hopelessness and worthlessness.
- Irritability and anger.

In extreme cases, there may be social withdrawal and drug or alcohol abuse.

What might be done?

If your doctor thinks you are at risk of developing a psychological problem as a result of illness, you will be offered support and counseling (p.971) to help you adjust. If there are signs that you are avoiding coming to terms with an illness, your doctor will encourage you to ask questions and talk about possible anxieties. Home and work problems may be discussed, and your doctor will want to know if you have a history of depression or anxiety disorders.

A person who has developed psychological problems as a result of illness may not be aware of the fact, and it may be a family member or friend who first contacts the doctor. The doctor may prescribe antidepressant drugs (p.916). Less commonly, an antianxiety drug (p.916) may be prescribed for a short time. The person may be referred to a psychiatrist, who will encourage a problem-solving approach to illness that concentrates on developing solutions rather than focusing on difficulties.

The prognosis for a mental problem resulting from physical illness depends on a person's ability to cope with the demands of his or her illness and its severity. Given continued support, most people are able to recognize and deal with mood problems and find that they gradually diminish as a result.

(WWW) ONLINE SITES: p.1029, p.1034

Munchausen syndrome

A condition in which medical care is sought repeatedly for nonexistent or self-induced symptoms

 AGE Usually begins in early adulthood

 GENDER More common in males

 LIFESTYLE Working in a health-related profession is a risk factor

 GENETICS Not a significant factor

Munchausen syndrome is a rare condition in which a person claims to have symptoms of illness and may repeatedly seek treatment from a number of hospitals. Common symptoms that are complained of include abdominal pain, blackouts, and fever. This unexplained desire to assume the role of a patient is seen as an attempt to escape from everyday life and be cared for and protected.

The syndrome usually develops in early adulthood and is more common in men. Those affected tend to have some knowledge of symptoms and hospital procedures, which may have been acquired through working in a health-related profession. For this reason, their bogus claims to illness may not be detected until test results prove negative or exploratory surgery is carried out. People with the condition often try to conceal personal details or may offer an extraordinary account of their circumstances. If challenged, they may accuse doctors of being incompetent and leave the hospital to avoid discovery.

In factitious disorder, a variant of Munchausen syndrome, a person may aggravate an existing condition or cause deliberate self-injury. The disorder occurs most often in health professionals.

In another related condition called Munchausen syndrome by proxy, a parent, often the mother, repeatedly claims her child is ill and in need of treatment.

What are the symptoms?

Munchausen syndrome and factitious disorder have similar typical patterns of behavior, which may include :

- Dramatic presentation of symptoms and their history.
- Histrionic and argumentative behavior toward medical staff.
- Wide knowledge of medical terms and medical procedures.

There may be evidence of multiple surgical operations, such as a number of scars on the abdomen. An affected person may demand strong pain relievers, possibly because he or she has an addiction. In cases of Munchausen syndrome by proxy, the parent may fake physical signs of illness in a child and give a false description of symptoms. The child may be repeatedly admitted to the hospital for unnecessary tests or treatment.

What might be done?

Treatment is difficult because as soon as staff begin to suspect that a person is feigning symptoms, the person leaves the hospital. Munchausen syndrome is

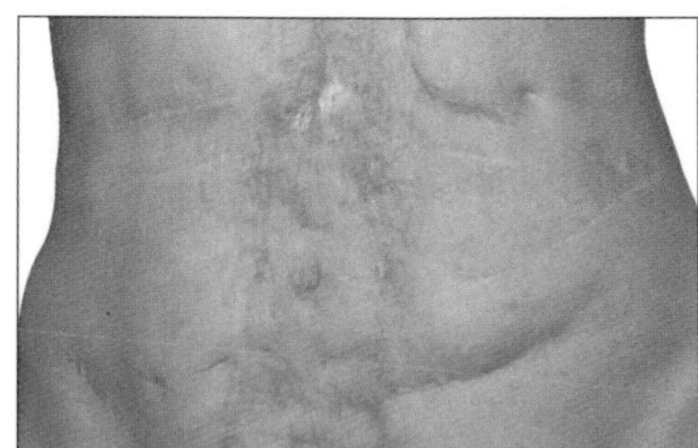

Scars due to Munchausen syndrome
The numerous scars on the abdomen of this person with Munchausen syndrome are the result of multiple operations to investigate fictitious symptoms.

frequently identified only with hindsight after the person has left.

It is often difficult to treat Munchausen syndrome and related conditions because deception is a characteristic of the disorders. The doctor will try to prevent further unnecessary treatments and tests by building a calm and supportive relationship with the person. In cases of Munchausen syndrome by proxy, a social worker should be alerted in case a child needs to be placed in foster care.

WWW ONLINE SITES: p.1034

Somatization

The expression of psychological problems as physical symptoms

AGE Usually develops in adolescence or early adulthood

GENDER More common in females

LIFESTYLE Stress is a risk factor

GENETICS Not a significant factor

Somatization describes a disorder in which a psychological problem manifests itself as a physical symptom or a range of physical symptoms. Although occasionally bizarre, these symptoms are not fabricated and may be frightening if they are interpreted as signs of a progressive or potentially fatal disease. The condition is related to hyponchondriasis (right), a condition in which there are constant, unfounded worries that minor symptoms are caused by a serious underlying disorder. However, in somatization, psychological problems generate actual physical changes, which cause debilitating symptoms.

People with somatization may make repeated visits to their doctor to ask for investigations into their symptoms and treatment. When test results are normal, and reassurance is given that there is no underlying physical illness, an affected person feels no relief and may consult other doctors to find a physical cause for the symptoms. In extreme cases of somatization, life is continually disrupted by numerous follow-up medical visits, and health is placed at risk by invasive tests and investigations.

Several psychiatric illnesses may be associated with somatization, including anxiety disorders (p.551) and depression (p.554). There may also be an underlying personality disorder (p.561) marked by self-absorption and reliance on others. Somatization usually develops in adolescence or early adult life and is more common in women. The disorder is often associated with stress and may become a life-long problem.

What are the symptoms?

A person who has a somatization disorder may have a long history of varying physical symptoms that fluctuate in severity and have no identifiable medical cause. Symptoms that sometimes have psychological causes include:

- Headaches.
- Chest pain, often accompanied by shortness of breath and palpitations.
- Abdominal pain and nausea.
- Fatigue.
- Itching of the skin.
- Partial weakness of a limb.
- Difficulty swallowing.

In addition, there may be psychological symptoms of anxiety, depression, and substance abuse. Severely affected people may attempt suicide (*see* ATTEMPTED SUICIDE AND SUICIDE, p.556).

What might be done?

The doctor will first carry out a physical examination and may arrange for blood and urine tests to exclude a physical illness. Medical records will give a picture of past symptoms and investigations.

Treating somatization is often difficult because the person affected may be convinced there is a physical illness in spite of normal test results. The doctor may prescribe treatment for symptoms, such as analgesics (p.912) for headaches, but will try to avoid further tests and investigations by offering reassurance that physical symptoms are taken seriously and explaining how they may be caused by psychological problems.

The doctor may recommend a psychological assessment (p.554) to look for an underlying mental health disorder, but this may be resisted by the person. However, it is only by addressing underlying psychological problems that physical symptoms will be relieved.

If depression is causing somatization, it may be treated with antidepressant drugs (p.916) and a form of psychological therapy (pp.968–971).

WWW ONLINE SITES: p.1029, 1034

Hypochondriasis

A deep, worrying, and unfounded suspicion of being seriously ill

AGE Most common between the ages of 20 and 30

LIFESTYLE Chronic illness in childhood, proximity to serious illness, and stress are risk factors

GENDER GENETICS Not significant factors

People who suffer from hypochondriasis are constantly anxious about their health and interpret all symptoms, no matter how minor, as indications of serious illness. They may be concerned about a combination of symptoms or a single symptom, such as a headache.

Inevitably, the disorder leads to frequent visits to the doctor to have tests. Even when the results are negative, people affected by hypochondriasis remain convinced that they are seriously ill. They may reject the doctor's findings and react with strong feelings of frustration and hostility. Frequently, their anxiety about illness causes problems with relationships, work, and social life.

Somatization (left) is a related condition in which psychological problems are expressed as physical symptoms.

Hypochondriasis is more common between the ages of 20 and 30 and may be a complication of other psychological disorders, such as depression (p.554) or anxiety (*see* ANXIETY DISORDERS, p.551). In other cases, the cause is unknown, but people who were very ill in childhood or who have prolonged contact with someone who is chronically ill are more susceptible. Stress increases the risk of the disorder developing.

What might be done?

The doctor will first look for and treat any underlying psychological disorders. For example, he or she may prescribe antidepressant drugs (p.916) for depression. The doctor will avoid unnecessary tests by reassuring the person that he or she does not have a serious illness and will explain normal body reactions if the person is mistaking responses, such as rapid heartbeats during exercise, for signs of serious illness. A patient doctor can relieve hypochondriasis by being open to regular visits for reassurance.

WWW ONLINE SITES: 1034

Schizophrenia

A serious mental disorder, in which there is a loss of the sense of reality and an inability to function socially

 AGE Usually develops in males aged 18–25 and females aged 26–45

 GENETICS Sometimes runs in families

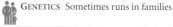

 LIFESTYLE Stressful life events are risk factors

 GENDER Not a significant factor

Schizophrenia is a severe and disruptive mental illness that occurs in all cultures and affects about 1 in 100 people worldwide. Although the term is sometimes mistakenly used to refer to a split personality, schizophrenia is actually an impairment of a person's sense of reality that leads to irrational behavior and disturbed emotional reactions. People with schizophrenia may hear voices, and this may contribute to their bizarre behavior. In addition, they are usually unable to function at work or maintain relationships with other people.

Without proper support and treatment, people with schizophrenia are likely to neglect or harm themselves. About 1 in 10 people with the condition commits suicide (*see* ATTEMPTED SUICIDE AND SUICIDE, p.556).

WHAT ARE THE CAUSES?

No single cause of schizophrenia has been identified, but genetic factors are known to play a part. A person who is closely related to someone with schizophrenia has a significantly increased risk of developing the disorder. In addition, a stressful life event, such as a serious illness or a bereavement, may trigger the disorder in a person who is susceptible. Evidence also points to abnormalities in brain structure, such as enlarged fluid-filled cavities, that suggest loss of brain tissue.

WHAT ARE THE SYMPTOMS?

Schizophrenia tends to develop in men during their teens or early twenties, but the onset may be 10–20 years later in women. The condition usually begins gradually, with the person losing energy and personal motivation and becoming increasingly withdrawn over a period of months or years. In other cases, the illness is more sudden and may be a response to an episode of stress. Some people have clear-cut episodes of illness and recover completely in between. In other cases, the disorder is more or less continuous. Symptoms may include:

- Hearing imaginary voices.
- Having irrational beliefs, in particular that thoughts and actions are being controlled by an outside force.
- Delusions of being a great figure, such as Napoleon, or that trivial objects and events have deep significance.
- Expression of inappropriate emotions, such as laughing at bad news.
- Rambling speech with rapid switching from one topic to another.
- Impaired concentration.
- Slow movement and thought.
- Agitation and restlessness.

A person with schizophrenia may be depressed, lethargic, and socially withdrawn. He or she may begin to neglect personal care and become increasingly isolated. In rare cases, violence toward other people may occur.

Area of low activity
Area of high activity
Area of low activity
NORMAL BRAIN
BRAIN IN SCHIZOPHRENIA

Brain activity in schizophrenia
PET scans show a distinctive pattern of large areas of low activity in the brain of a person with schizophrenia when compared with the brain of an unaffected person.

HOW IS IT DIAGNOSED?

If you are worried that a close friend or family member is suffering from schizophrenia, you should contact a doctor. Normally, the doctor will look for evidence of a profound break with reality, disturbed emotions, and strange beliefs lasting for several months before considering a diagnosis of schizophrenia. He or she will carry out a full physical examination, and blood or urine tests may be arranged to exclude other possible causes of abnormal behavior, such as abuse of alcohol or drugs. The doctor may arrange for imaging of the brain by CT scanning (p.247) or MRI (p.248) to exclude an underlying physical disorder, such as a brain tumor (p.530).

WHAT IS THE TREATMENT?

If schizophrenia is suspected, it will be necessary to admit the person to the hospital for further assessment and to begin treatment. Antipsychotic drugs (p.917) are prescribed to help calm the affected person. About 3 weeks of treatment may be needed to reduce the more obvious symptoms of schizophrenia. Some drugs may cause serious side effects, such as tremors, and doses may have to be reduced or other drugs prescribed to minimize these effects.

Treatment with adjusted doses of drugs usually continues after the major symptoms have subsided because of the likelihood that symptoms will recur.

After assessment and treatment, people with schizophrenia are usually sent home, but it is essential that they have support and a calm and unthreatening home environment. People who have schizophrenia need to be protected from stressful situations because anxiety may trigger symptoms. They also need frequent, regular contact with community mental health service workers, who will supervise their progress and well-being after they leave the hospital.

Counseling (p.971) may be offered both to the person with schizophrenia and family members. People close to the affected person should watch for signs of relapse and indications that the person is sinking into a general state of apathy and self-neglect.

WHAT IS THE PROGNOSIS?

For most affected people, schizophrenia is a long-term illness. However, about 1 in 5 of those affected have one sudden episode from which they recover and lead a normal life. The majority have a number of episodes of severe symptoms that may require hospital stays, interspersed with periods of recovery. Drugs have improved the prognosis for people with schizophrenia, but adequate community care and support is essential to prevent relapse. The prognosis is worse for people who develop schizophrenia gradually while they are young.

(WWW) ONLINE SITES: p.1034

Delusional disorders

The development of one or more persistent delusions of persecution or jealousy

 AGE More common from age 40

 GENDER More common in females

 LIFESTYLE Stress may be a risk factor

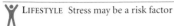

 GENETICS Not a significant factor

Delusional disorders are rare, affecting only about 3 in 10,000 people worldwide. The main characteristic of these disorders is an irrational belief or set of beliefs that is not associated with other symptoms or caused by another mental illness, such as schizophrenia (opposite page). These beliefs or delusions persist in spite of all rational arguments and clear evidence to the contrary. However, apart from behavior related to the delusion, the person appears well, and work and relationships may not be affected.

There are several different types of delusions, the most common of which is persecutory. People who have this type of delusional disorder believe they are being hounded, chased, or spied upon. Extreme jealousy, in which a person believes his or her partner is being unfaithful, is another common form.

Major life events, such as moving to another country, and long-term stress factors, such as poverty, may contribute to the development of delusions. A person who has a paranoid personality (*see* PERSONALITY DISORDERS, right) is at an increased risk of delusions, as is a person who is alcohol dependent (p.564).

Delusional disorders usually develop suddenly, most commonly in middle age or late in life, and are slightly more common in women.

WHAT MIGHT BE DONE?

People with a delusional disorder are often suspicious or dismissive of others who are trying to help them. They may be reluctant to discuss their beliefs and unable to recognize that their delusions are irrational. Family members often seek medical advice on their behalf.

The doctor will look for additional symptoms in case delusions are being caused by another psychological illness, such as schizophrenia. The doctor will try to find out how firmly held or "fixed" the delusions are and whether the person is likely to act on them. If there is a risk of violence or self-harm, the person may need to be admitted to the hospital, possibly without his or her consent.

Occasionally, an antipsychotic drug (p.917) is used to reduce the intensity of severe delusions. Counseling (p.971) may bring about a shift in perspective. Generally, delusional disorders tend to persist but without causing major disruption in a person's life.

(WWW) ONLINE SITES: p.1029, 1034

Personality disorders

A group of disorders in which fixed patterns of thought and behavior cause persistent life problems

 AGE Usually develop in adolescence or early adulthood

 GENDER GENETICS LIFESTYLE Risk factors depend on the type

People with personality disorders have ingrained patterns of thought and behavior that prevent them from fitting in with society. An affected person often fails to see that his or her personality is unusual but is aware that it is causing problems in daily life. Although many people have strong personalities, this is not the same as a personality disorder. People with personality disorders are inflexible and unable to adapt.

Personality disorders tend to develop in adolescence and early adulthood but may not be diagnosed until adult life. The cause of most of these disorders is unknown, but they are probably due to a combination of genetic influences and difficult experiences in childhood.

WHAT ARE THE TYPES?

Personality disorders are divided into three broad groups: emotional or erratic, eccentric or odd, and anxious or fearful. Each group has its own pattern of thought processes and behavior.

EMOTIONAL OR ERRATIC This personality disorder further divides into four different types: antisocial, borderline, histrionic, and narcissistic.

An antisocial personality is typified by impulsive, destructive behavior that often disregards the feelings and rights of others. People who have an antisocial personality lack a sense of guilt and cannot tolerate frustration. They may have problems with relationships and are frequently in trouble with the law.

A person with a borderline personality has multiple abnormalities that may include an uncertainty about personal identity and an inability to form stable relationships. People who have this disorder are habitually bored and may indulge in promiscuity, reckless spending, or substance abuse. They may harm themselves or threaten suicide.

People with a histrionic personality have emotions that are exaggerated and shallow. They are self-centered, inconsiderate, and easily bored and constantly demand reassurance and approval.

People with a narcissistic personality believe themselves to be unique, special and superior to others. They constantly seek attention and admiration and lack concern for the problems of others.

ECCENTRIC OR ODD This group of disorders can be further divided into three separate types of personality: paranoid, schizoid, and schizotypal.

A person with a paranoid personality tends to be mistrustful, jealous, and self-important. He or she readily interprets other people's actions as hostile and may feel continually rebuffed.

People who have a schizoid personality are emotionally cold and indifferent to others. They tend to be prone to fantasy and ill at ease in company. This disorder is not related to the mental illness schizophrenia (opposite page).

People with a schizotypal personality display eccentric and suspicious behavior, often accompanied by odd ideas, such as a belief in magic or telepathy. They may have an unkempt appearance and vague, abstract speech patterns and may talk to themselves.

ANXIOUS OR FEARFUL The four different types of personality that make up the anxious or fearful group of disorders are: avoidant, passive–aggressive, obsessive–compulsive, and dependent.

A person with an avoidant personality is timid, oversensitive to rejection, and cautious of new experiences and responsibilities. He or she is generally ill at ease in social situations.

People with a passive–aggressive personality react to any demands made on

Drug dependence

Compulsive use of drugs, producing withdrawal symptoms when stopped

AGE Usually develops in adolescence

GENDER More common in males

LIFESTYLE Stress, some social factors, and peer pressure are risk factors

GENETICS Not a significant factor

Drug dependence, or addiction, is the excessive and compulsive use of drugs for their effects on mental state. Often, increasing quantities of the drug are needed to produce the desired effect, and physical symptoms may develop if use stops or is delayed. Some drugs, such as LSD, do not cause this physical addiction but may cause psychological craving (*see* DRUGS AND HEALTH, p.65).

Drugs that may produce dependence include those obtained illegally, such as heroin and cocaine, and drugs that are prescribed by a doctor, such as barbiturates (*see* SLEEPING DRUGS, p.915) and analgesics (p.912). Two common forms of dependence are nicotine dependence (*see* TOBACCO AND HEALTH, p.63) and alcohol dependence (right). Although nicotine dependence rarely affects work and social life, alcohol dependence is often damaging. Drug addictions may lead to debt, loss of work, and breakdown in close relationships.

WHAT ARE THE CAUSES?

Initially, drugs may be taken for the psychological "high" they produce and because they relieve symptoms such as anxiety (*see* ANXIETY DISORDERS, p.551) and insomnia (p.554). People who find it difficult to cope with stress may be more susceptible, as may people who have a parent who has abused drugs or alcohol. Dependence is more common in men than in women. Peer pressure in adolescence and readily available illegal drugs make young people particularly susceptible. The risk of dependence developing depends on which drug is taken. For example, heroin may cause dependence after only a few doses.

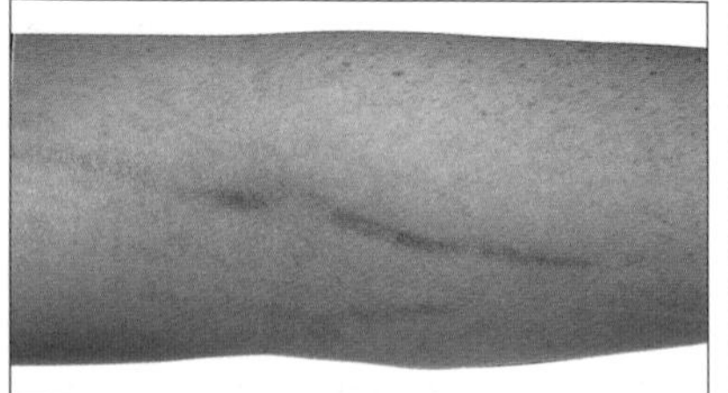

Needle tracks from drug injections
When a drug-dependent person repeatedly injects drugs, the veins can be damaged. In this picture, the damage is visible as needle tracks on the inside of the arm.

WHAT ARE THE SYMPTOMS?

There are different symptoms for each drug. However, certain areas of behavior tend to be altered by most drugs that cause dependence. Symptoms of drug dependence often include:

- Mood changes.
- Changes in concentration levels.
- Altered energy levels.
- Faster or slower speech rate.
- Increased or decreased appetite.

Typically, withdrawal symptoms develop within 12 hours of last using or taking a drug. Effects range from mild to extremely severe and may include:

- Anxiety and restlessness.
- Overheating and sweating, alternating with chills and shivering.
- Confusion and hallucinations.
- Muscle aches and abdominal cramps.
- Diarrhea and vomiting.
- Seizures.

Rarely, withdrawal from opioid analgesics, such as heroin, may lead to coma (p.522). If drugs are injected, sharing needles may transmit diseases such as HIV infection (*see* HIV INFECTION AND AIDS, p.295) and hepatitis B and C (ACUTE HEPATITIS, p.644). Drug dependence often leads to depression (p.554).

WHAT MIGHT BE DONE?

People who are dependent on drugs may not accept that they need help, and a member of their family or a friend may consult a doctor. The doctor will ask which drugs are used and about the length and pattern of use.

Once a person has accepted that he or she needs treatment, withdrawal from the drug can begin. If the symptoms of withdrawal are likely to be severe or if there have been failed attempts in the past, admission to a hospital or a drug rehabilitation center will be arranged. Otherwise, withdrawal may be closely supervised at home. Withdrawal symptoms are usually treated with substitute drugs that cause less dependence. For example, benzodiazepines (*see* ANTI-ANXIETY DRUGS, p.916) may be used to treat symptoms of withdrawal from barbiturates. The doctor will offer support and recommend specialized drug services for long-term counseling (p.971).

WHAT IS THE PROGNOSIS?

Treatment of drug dependence is difficult and often unsuccessful. Sometimes there are several withdrawal attempts before dependence is overcome. Success is most likely if the person is strongly motivated and has good support from family, friends, and counseling services. Joining a support group also increases the chance of overcoming dependence.

(WWW) ONLINE SITES: p.1029 , p.1030

Alcohol dependence

Compulsive regular consumption of alcohol, producing withdrawal symptoms when intake is stopped

AGE Most common between the ages of 20 and 40

GENDER More common in males

GENETICS Sometimes runs in families

LIFESTYLE Stress and occupations that are associated with social drinking are risk factors

A person who is dependent on alcohol has an irresistible compulsion to drink, which takes priority over almost everything else in life. This craving for drink, coupled with withdrawal symptoms when drinking stops, is what separates alcohol dependence from alcohol abuse, a term used to describe regular drinking to excess (*see* ALCOHOL AND HEALTH, p.62). About 1 million people in Canada abuse or are dependent on alcohol. Drinking problems are more common in men, particularly between the ages of 20 and 40. In addition to causing damage to the liver and brain, the need to drink to excess regularly is damaging to mental health and may destroy a person's family and social life and career.

WHAT ARE THE CAUSES?

Alcohol dependence is often the result of a combination of factors. Sometimes alcohol dependence runs in families, partly as a result of children growing up in an environment of heavy drinking and partly because of an inherited predisposition. People who are shy, anxious, or depressed may rely heavily on alcohol. Working as a bartender or in an occupation that is associated with social drinking increases the risk of dependence. Stressful life events may turn a moderate drinker into a heavy one.

WHAT ARE THE SYMPTOMS?

Alcohol dependence may develop after a number of years of moderate to heavy drinking. Symptoms may include:

- A compulsion to drink and loss of control over the amount consumed.
- Increased tolerance to the effects of alcohol, leading to greater consumption to achieve the desired effects.
- Withdrawal symptoms, such as nausea, sweating, and tremor, which start a few hours after the last drink.

In severe cases, withdrawal seizures develop after alcohol is stopped. After a few days without alcohol, delirium tremens may develop with symptoms of fever, shakes, seizures, disorientation, and hallucinations. Symptoms last for 3 to 4 days and are usually followed by a deep, prolonged sleep. In extreme cases, shock (p.414) occurs and may be fatal.

ARE THERE COMPLICATIONS?

Alcohol has direct effects on the body and may cause many diseases. Long-term alcohol dependence is the most common cause of severe liver disease (*see* ALCOHOL-RELATED LIVER DISEASE, p.646) and may damage the digestive system, causing peptic ulcers (p.640).

Heavy drinkers often have a poor diet, which may lead to a deficiency in vitamin B_1 (thiamine) that may eventually cause dementia (p.535). Rarely, severe thiamine deficiency leads to Wernicke–Korsakoff syndrome (p.538), a severe brain disorder that causes confusion and amnesia and may lead to coma. If excessive drinking continues for a prolonged period of time, damage to vital organs may be life-threatening.

Psychiatric disorders associated with alcohol dependence include anxiety (*see* ANXIETY DISORDERS, p.551), depression (p.554), and suicidal behavior (*see* ATTEMPTED SUICIDE AND SUICIDE, p.556). Generally, a person with alcohol dependence becomes self-centered and lacks concern for family and friends.

HOW IS IT DIAGNOSED?

Before the doctor can make a diagnosis, a person may need to be persuaded to seek help. The doctor will ask about the extent of the person's drinking and look for evidence of dependence. Blood tests to assess possible damage to the liver and other organs may be arranged.

WHAT IS THE TREATMENT?

Gradual reduction of alcohol intake or limiting alcohol consumption to social drinking is rarely possible. Instead, the person will be asked to stop drinking completely. In mild to moderate cases, withdrawal can take place at home, provided that adequate support is available. Antianxiety drugs (p.916), such as a benzodiazepine, may be prescribed for a short time to reduce agitation and other physical effects of withdrawal.

When heavy drinking is stopped suddenly, withdrawal seizures or delirium tremens may develop. The symptoms of delirium tremens are potentially life-threatening and require admission to the hospital or a special detoxification unit. Withdrawal symptoms are usually treated with antianxiety drugs.

Treatment for physical problems as a result of long-term alcohol dependence includes ulcer-healing drugs (p.923) for peptic ulcers and vitamin B_1 injections for a thiamine deficiency.

When the symptoms of withdrawal have been treated, the doctor may prescribe drugs that reduce cravings for alcohol or cause unpleasant reactions when it is consumed. Support is given to help prevent a relapse. Individual counseling (p.971) or group therapy (p.970) may help people address the problems that contribute to alcohol dependence.

WHAT IS THE PROGNOSIS?

Accepting that there is a problem and receiving emotional support during the effort to give up drinking greatly improve a person's chance of recovery. Attending a self-help group, such as Alcoholics Anonymous, reduces the risk of relapse. However, after a long period of dependence, several attempts at detoxification may be needed before a person abstains from alcohol altogether.

In about 1 in 5 cases in which delirium tremens develops and is untreated, the condition proves fatal.

(WWW) ONLINE SITES: p.1027, p.1029

Compulsive gambling

Frequent gambling that dominates a person's life

 AGE Usually develops by age 25

 GENDER More common in males

 LIFESTYLE Exposure to gambling in adolescence is a risk factor

 GENETICS Not a significant factor

In compulsive gambling or pathological gambling, a person has an intense urge to gamble that dominates his or her life. Compulsive gamblers continually increase their spending to achieve their desired intensity of excitement. They build up large debts and may lie, steal, and defraud to continue gambling. This behavior continues regardless of its effects on family and social life and jeopardizes work and relationships.

Compulsive gambling is more common in men and usually develops before age 25. Growing up with a parent who gambles compulsively or is dependent on alcohol has been shown to increase the risk. Adolescents who gamble are at an increased risk of developing a gambling problem. A person who gambles compulsively often appears optimistic, lively, and full of confidence. However, compulsive gambling may be associated with mood disorders, such as anxiety (*see* ANXIETY DISORDERS, p.551) and depression (p.544), and with an antisocial personality disorder (p.561).

WHAT MIGHT BE DONE?

If a person is gambling excessively, a family member or friend may consult the doctor. The person will be assessed and treated for any underlying psychological disorders, such as anxiety or depression. Most self-help groups offer valuable support and encouragement, and a number of groups also give support to family and friends in their efforts to help a compulsive gambler.

Psychological therapies (pp.968–971) may be beneficial once the person has managed to refrain from gambling for a period of at least 3 months. Generally, therapy works best when a person has managed to gain some control over the compulsion to gamble.

(WWW) ONLINE SITES: p.1029, 1034

STRUCTURE AND FUNCTION

How the eye works

When you look at an object, light rays reflected from the object hit the transparent cornea at the front of your eye. The rays are partly focused and pass through the pupil, which enlarges or constricts depending on light conditions. The lens varies its focusing power for near and distant objects and fine-focuses the rays to create a sharp image on the fovea, the most responsive area of the light-sensitive retina at the back of the eye.

The mechanism of vision

Light rays focused by the cornea and lens produce an image on the retina that is upside down. Electrical signals from stimulated cells in the retina travel along the optic nerve to the brain, where the image is interpreted as being upright.

Action of the pupil

In dim conditions, the pupil widens (dilates) to allow the maximum amount of light to reach the light-sensitive retina. In bright light, the pupil constricts. Two sets of muscles in the colored iris control these processes.

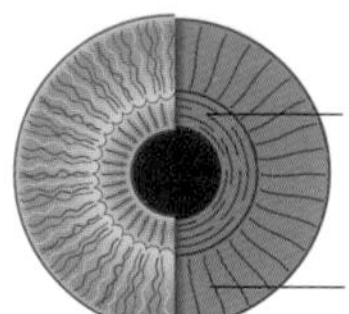
Contracted circular muscles
Relaxed radial muscles

CONSTRICTED

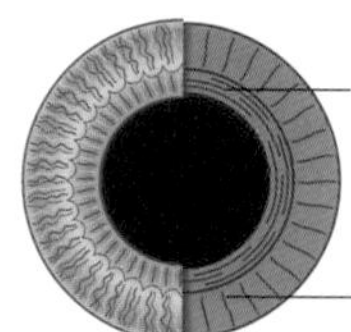
Relaxed circular muscles
Contracted radial muscles

DILATED

Changes in pupil size
To make the pupil constrict, the circular muscles contract; and to widen (dilate) it, the radial muscles contract.

Blood vessel
Retinal arteries and veins supply nutrients and remove waste from the retina

Ciliary body
The muscles of the ciliary body control the shape and focusing power of the lens

Lens
The lens provides fine focusing of light rays

Cornea
Incoming light rays are initially refracted (bent) by the cornea

Object
Light reflected from an object travels in all directions. Some rays enter the eye

Pupil
Light rays enter the pupil to reach the retina

Iris
The ring of muscles in the iris controls the pupil's size to allow in more or less light

Retina
Light-sensitive cells (rods and cones) in the retina transform light into nerve signals

Macula
The macula, the area of the retina surrounding the fovea, is responsible for detailed vision

Fovea
The fovea contains the highest density of cells

Optic nerve
Fibers of the optic nerve carry impulses from the retina to the brain

Inverted image
The image on the retina is upside down

Light rays
Rays of light from the object cross in the eye and are focused on the retina

Accommodation

The eye adjusts for near and distant vision by changing the shape of its lens. This varies the extent to which incoming light is refracted (bent). To create a sharp image on the retina, light rays from near objects must be bent more than those from distant objects. This process is called accommodation.

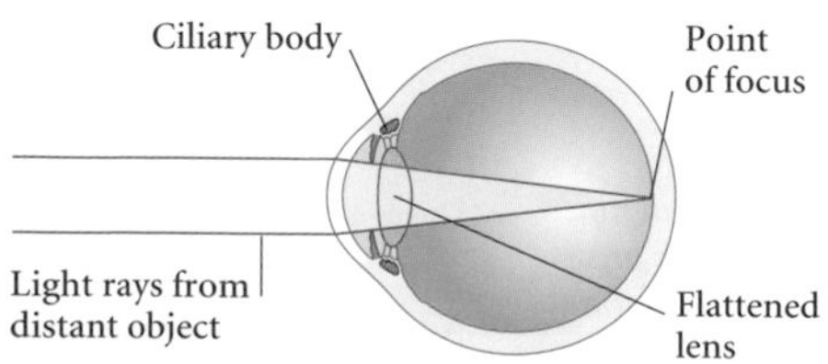
Ciliary body
Point of focus
Light rays from distant object
Flattened lens

Focusing for distant objects
When you look at an object in the distance, muscles in the ciliary body relax and the lens assumes a flatter shape.

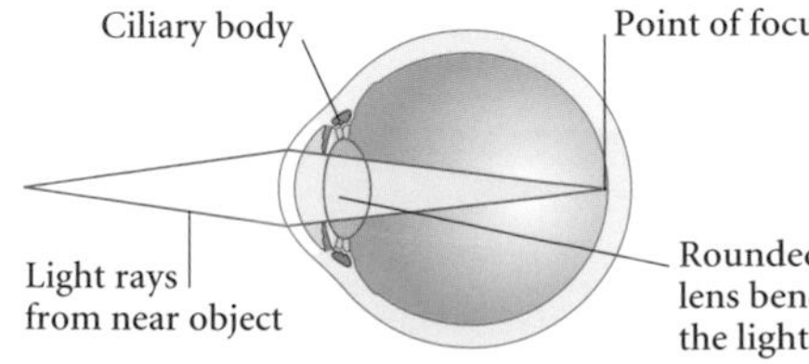
Ciliary body
Point of focus
Light rays from near object
Rounded lens bends the light

Focusing for near objects
When you look at a close object, muscles in the ciliary body contract, allowing the elastic lens to spring into a more spherical shape.

VISUAL PATHWAYS

Electrical signals from each retina pass along the optic nerves, which meet at a junction called the optic chiasm. Here, half of the nerve fibers from the left eye cross to the right side and vice versa, and the fibers continue along the optic tracts to the brain. Information from the right half of each retina passes to the right visual cortex; information from the left half of each retina goes to the left visual cortex. The brain then integrates these messages into a complete visual picture.

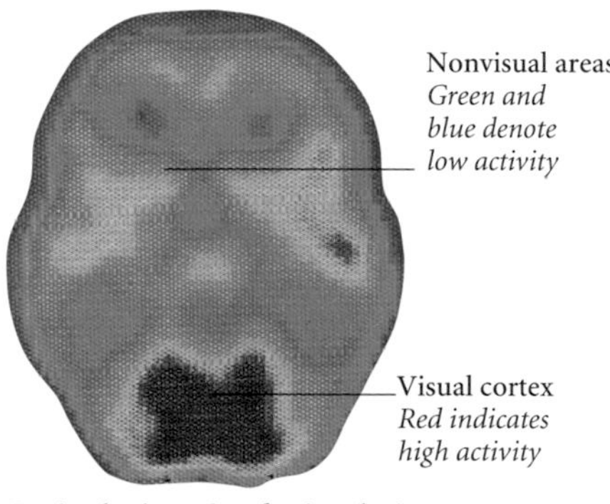
Nonvisual areas
Green and blue denote low activity
Visual cortex
Red indicates high activity

Brain during visual stimulation
The visual cortex, which is located at the back of the brain, exhibits high activity compared with the rest of the brain when a detailed colored picture is observed.

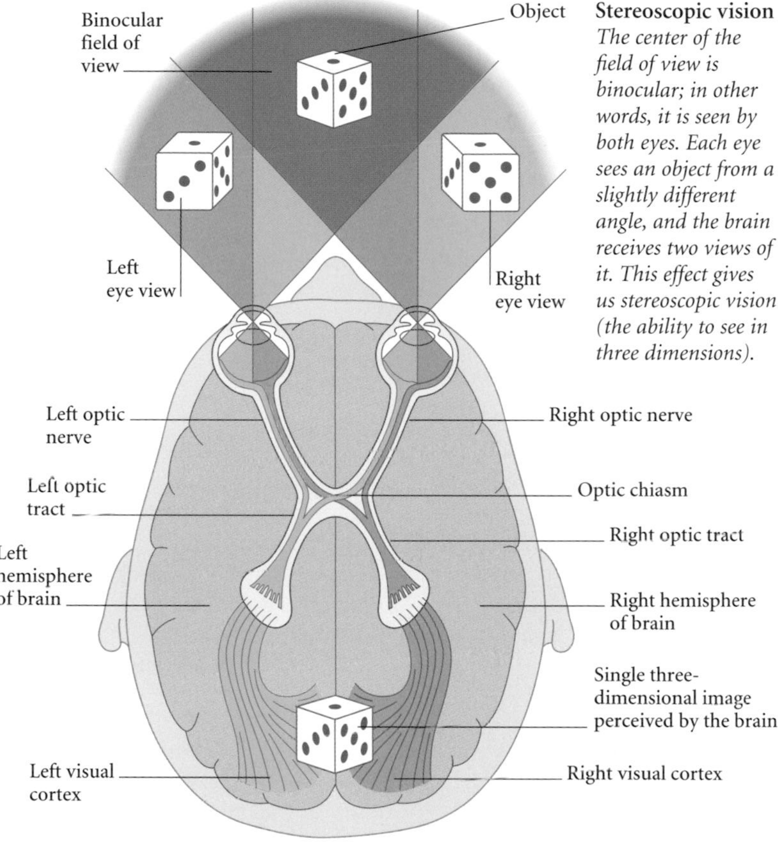
Binocular field of view
Object
Left eye view
Right eye view
Left optic nerve
Right optic nerve
Left optic tract
Optic chiasm
Right optic tract
Left hemisphere of brain
Right hemisphere of brain
Single three-dimensional image perceived by the brain
Left visual cortex
Right visual cortex

Stereoscopic vision
The center of the field of view is binocular; in other words, it is seen by both eyes. Each eye sees an object from a slightly different angle, and the brain receives two views of it. This effect gives us stereoscopic vision (the ability to see in three dimensions).

RODS AND CONES

There are two types of light-sensitive cells in the retina: rods and cones. Up to 120 million rods are distributed throughout the retina. Although rods are sensitive to all visible light, they contain only one type of pigment and cannot distinguish colors. They are therefore responsible mainly for night vision. In contrast, the 6.5 million cones provide detailed and color vision. Every cone responds to red, green, or blue light, working only in bright light. They are most concentrated in the central part of the retina, the fovea.

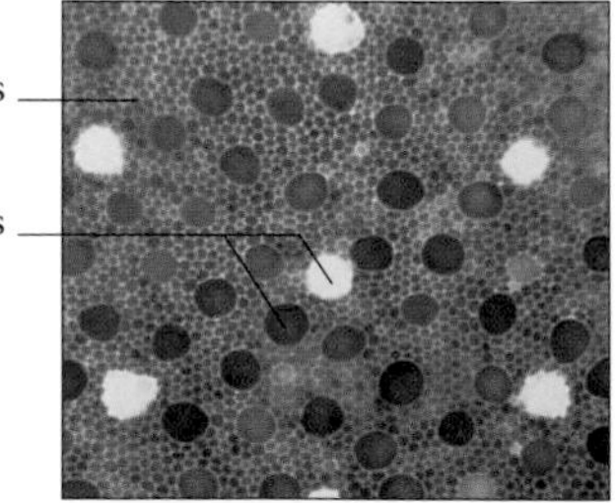
Rods
Cones

Rods and cones
This magnified view of the retina shows that rods greatly outnumber cones. Here, the cones are shown in two colors.

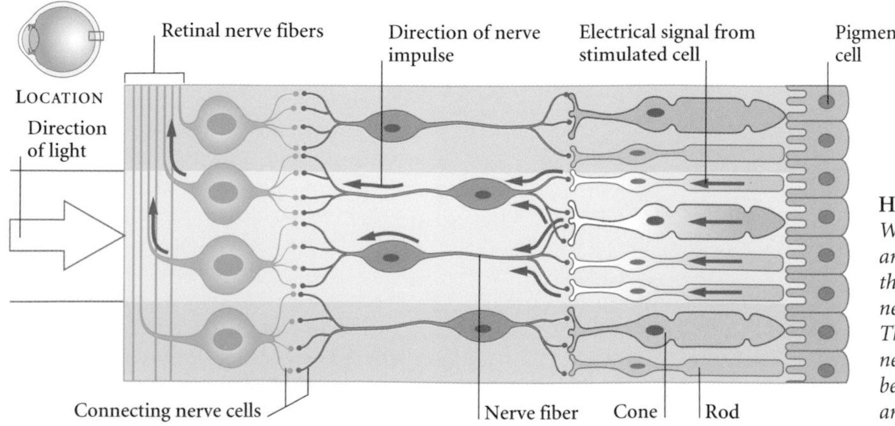
LOCATION
Direction of light
Retinal nerve fibers
Direction of nerve impulse
Electrical signal from stimulated cell
Pigment cell
Connecting nerve cells
Nerve fiber
Cone
Rod

How the retina responds to light
When light strikes the retina, the rods and cones produce electrical signals that trigger further impulses in the nerve cells to which they are connected. These signals travel along the optic nerve to the brain. Pigment cells behind the rods and cones absorb light and prevent reflection inside the eye.

EYE DISORDERS

The eye is a complex organ made up of several highly specialized components. Many eye disorders do not threaten sight, but a few serious conditions may damage the eye's components and lead to loss of vision. Eye disorders are very common, but early diagnosis usually leads to successful treatment.

This section covers disorders caused by disease, structural abnormality, or injury to the eye. Conditions that involve the front covering of the eye (the conjunctiva and cornea) are described first, followed by disorders that affect the front chamber of the eye and the structures within it, including the iris and lens.

The next group of articles discusses disorders of the light-sensitive retina at the back of the eye and conditions affecting the optic nerve, which carries nerve signals from the retina to the brain. The final articles in this section cover conditions in which the eye is displaced or injured in some way.

Impaired vision, whether occurring in healthy eyes or as a consequence of serious underlying causes, is described separately (*see* VISION DISORDERS, pp.586–591), as are disorders of the eyelid and tear system (pp.583–585) and eye disorders that usually or only affect children. These include congenital blindness (p.856), cancer of the retina (*see* RETINOBLASTOMA, p.858), and misalignment of the gaze of the eyes (*see* STRABISMUS, p.857).

Many major eye disorders that in the past would have ultimately progressed to blindness can now be treated successfully if detected early. For example, diabetic retinopathy is often now treated by laser surgery to prevent further sight loss. Regular eye examinations are therefore important, particularly for people over age 40.

KEY ANATOMY

Retina
Lens
Macula
Iris
Optic nerve
Conjunctiva
Cornea

For more information on the structure and function of the eye, *see* pp.566–569.

Conjunctivitis

Inflammation of the conjunctiva, the membrane covering the white of the eye and the inside of the eyelids

LIFESTYLE Wearing contact lenses and using cosmetics or eyedrops are risk factors

GENETICS Risk factors depend on the type

AGE GENDER Not significant factors

Conjunctivitis, also called pink eye, is a common condition in which the conjunctiva, the clear membrane covering the white of the eye and lining the eyelids, becomes inflamed. The affected eye becomes red and sore and may look alarming, but the condition is rarely serious. One or both of the eyes may be affected, and in some cases it begins in one eye then spreads to the other.

WHAT ARE THE CAUSES?

Conjunctivitis may be caused by a bacterial or viral infection, or it may result from an allergic reaction or irritation of the conjunctiva for example, by smoke, pollution, or ultraviolet light.

Bacterial conjunctivitis, which is common, may be caused by any of several types of bacteria. Viral conjunctivitis can be caused by one of the viruses responsible for the common cold (p.286). It may also be due to the herpes simplex virus that causes cold sores (p.354). Conjunctivitis due to a bacterial or viral infection can be spread by hand-to-eye contact and is usually highly contagious.

Newborn babies sometimes develop conjunctivitis. This can happen if an infection is transmitted to the baby's eyes from the mother's vagina during the birth. This form of conjunctivitis is usually caused by the microorganisms responsible for certain sexually transmitted diseases, including chlamydial cervicitis (p.765), gonorrhea (p.764), and genital herpes (p.767).

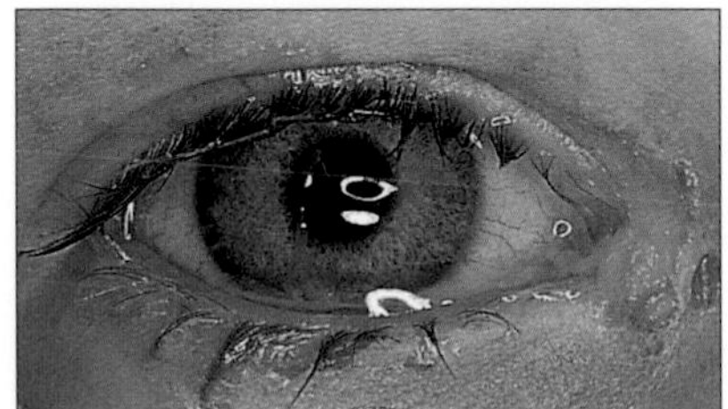

Conjunctivitis
This eye shows signs of conjunctivitis, including swollen eyelids, a discharge, and redness over the white of the eye.

Allergic conjunctivitis is a common feature of hay fever and of allergy to dust, pollen, and other airborne substances (*see* ALLERGIC RHINITIS, p.466). The condition may also be triggered by chemicals found in eyedrops, cosmetics, or contact lens solutions. Allergic conjunctivitis often runs in families.

WHAT ARE THE SYMPTOMS?

The symptoms of conjunctivitis usually develop over a few hours and are often first experienced on waking. The symptoms generally include:

- Redness of the white of the eye.
- Gritty and uncomfortable sensation in the eye.
- Swelling and itching of the eyelids.
- Discharge that may be yellowish and thick or clear and watery.

The discharge may dry out during sleep and form crusts on the eyelashes and eyelid margins. As a result, the eyelids sometimes stick together on waking.

WHAT CAN I DO?

The symptoms of conjunctivitis can be relieved by bathing the eye with artificial tears. To avoid spreading infection, wash your hands after touching the eye and do not share towels or washcloths. Once the conjunctivitis has cleared up, vision is rarely affected.

If you are susceptible to allergic conjunctivitis, avoid exposure to triggering substances. Antiallergy eyedrops can be used to ease the symptoms (*see* DRUGS ACTING ON THE EYE, p.919). If an eye becomes painful and red, you should consult your doctor to rule out the possibility of a more serious condition.

WHAT MIGHT THE DOCTOR DO?

Your doctor will probably make a diagnosis from your symptoms and examining your eye. If infection is suspected, he or she may take a sample of the discharge to identify the cause.

Bacterial conjunctivitis is treated by applying antibiotic drops or ointment. In such cases, the symptoms usually improve within 48 hours. However, the treatment should be continued for several days, even if the symptoms improve, to ensure the infection is eradicated. Although most types of viral conjunctivitis cannot be treated, their symptoms usually clear up within 2–3 weeks. Your doctor may prescribe eyedrops or oral antiallergy drugs if you have allergic conjunctivitis. You may be referred to an allergy specialist to determine a cause.

(WWW) ONLINE SITES: p.1027, p.1031, p.1033

Subconjunctival hemorrhage

Bleeding between the white of the eye and the conjunctiva, the membrane covering the white of the eye and lining the eyelids

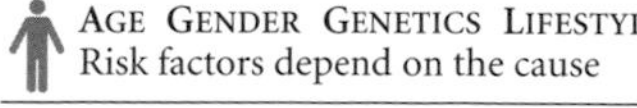

AGE GENDER GENETICS LIFESTYLE Risk factors depend on the cause

Ruptured blood vessels in the conjunctiva, the clear membrane covering the white of the eye and lining the eyelids, cause bleeding under the membrane. The condition, called subconjunctival hemorrhage, is common because the blood vessels in the conjunctiva are easily injured. The bleeding causes a red area over the white of the eye.

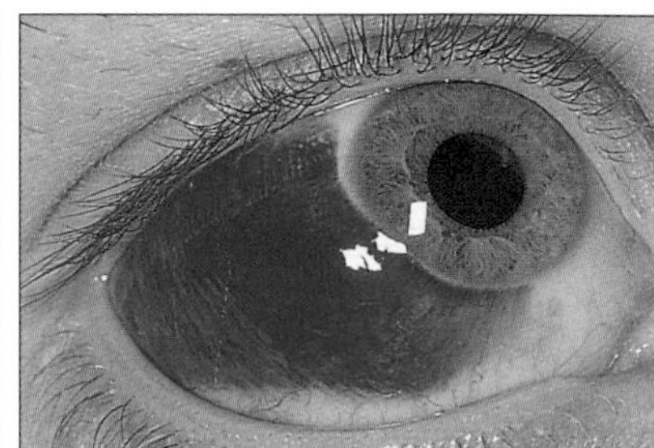

Subconjunctival hemorrhage
The red area on this eye is caused by bleeding under the conjunctiva, the outer membrane covering the white of the eye.

The condition most often results from a minor eye injury (p.582), sneezing, coughing, or rarely, a bleeding disorder (p.451). It can also be spontaneous, especially in elderly people. Although the hemorrhage looks dramatic, it is generally painless and usually clears up without treatment within 2–3 weeks. If the eye is painful or the redness persists, you should consult your doctor.

Corneal abrasion

A scratch on the surface of the cornea, the transparent front part of the eye

LIFESTYLE Wearing contact lenses is a risk factor

AGE GENDER GENETICS Not significant factors

The cornea, situated at the front of the eye, is susceptible to minor damage. For example, if it is scraped by the edge of a newspaper or by a foreign particle such as a speck of dirt, an injury known as a corneal abrasion may occur. People who wear soft contact lenses and rub their eyes excessively are particularly at risk of injury because tiny particles can become stuck behind the lenses and scratch the surface of the cornea.

WHAT ARE THE SYMPTOMS?

The symptoms of a corneal abrasion usually occur suddenly. They include:

- Pain in the eye.
- Redness and watering of the eye.
- Blurry vision.
- Sensitivity to bright light.
- Frequent blinking.

A corneal abrasion is not usually serious. However, there is a risk that the abrasion may become infected and a corneal ulcer (right) may develop.

WHAT MIGHT BE DONE?

You should consult your doctor or go to the emergency room for tests and treatment. The doctor will place fluorescein dye in your eyes and examine them with an opthalmoscope, or an instrument called a slit lamp (*see* SLIT-LAMP EXAMINATION, p.574) in order to have a magnified look at the cornea. If an abrasion is very painful, your doctor may recommend an eye patch and may also prescribe antibiotic eyedrops to prevent infection and ulceration (*see* DRUGS ACTING ON THE EYE, p.919). A corneal abrasion usually takes only a few days to heal.

(WWW) ONLINE SITES: p.1031, p.1036

Corneal ulcer

A deep erosion in the cornea, the transparent front part of the eye

LIFESTYLE Wearing contact lenses is a risk factor

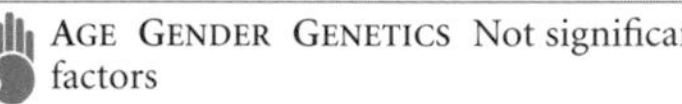

AGE GENDER GENETICS Not significant factors

An erosion in the cornea, the transparent outer part of the front of the eye, is called a corneal ulcer. These ulcers can be very painful and, if they are left untreated, may cause scarring and lead to permanently impaired vision, blindness (p.591), or even loss of the eye. People who wear contact lenses are at increased risk of corneal ulcers.

WHAT ARE THE CAUSES?

Corneal ulcers may be caused by an eye injury, an infection, or a combination of both. A relatively small injury such as a corneal abrasion (left), can develop into a corneal ulcer if the damaged area becomes infected. A more severe injury,

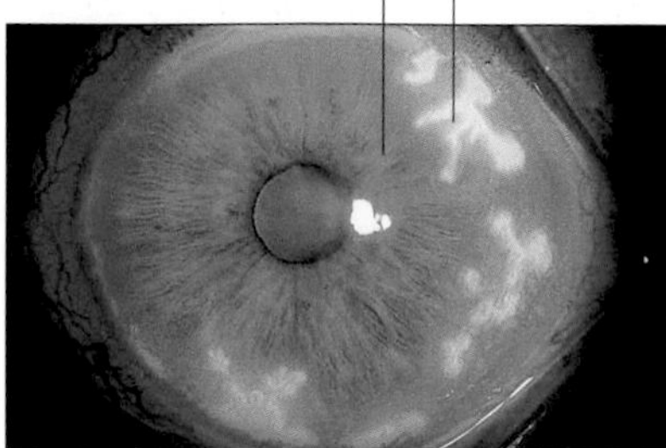
Normal area of the cornea
Ulcerated area

Corneal ulcer
Fluorescein placed in this eye revealed ulceration in the cornea. This ulcer is due to a herpes simplex infection.

such as that caused by a caustic chemical, can produce an ulcer in the absence of infection. However, an ulcer that becomes infected may enlarge and penetrate more deeply into the cornea. Only rarely do infections cause corneal ulcers without prior injury. The most common of these infections are herpes zoster (p.288), known as shingles, and herpes simplex infections (p.289).

WHAT ARE THE SYMPTOMS?

If you have a corneal ulcer, you may experience the following symptoms:

- Intense pain in the eye.
- Redness and discharge from the eye.
- Blurry vision.
- Increased sensitivity to light.

With an untreated infected ulcer, the infection may spread and permanently damage the vision in that eye and the eye itself. Consult your doctor immediately if you develop a painful, red eye along with blurry vision.

WHAT MIGHT BE DONE?

Your doctor may place fluorescein in the affected eye and examine it. A slit lamp (*see* SLIT-LAMP EXAMINATION, p.574) is required to have a magnified look at the cornea. If the dye reveals an ulcer, you may be given antibiotic or antiviral eyedrops to treat the infection (*see* DRUGS ACTING ON THE EYE, p.919). Even severe corneal ulcers usually clear up within 1–2 weeks of treatment, but they can leave scars that permanently affect vision.

(WWW) ONLINE SITES: p.1031, p.1033

Hyphema

A pool of blood in the front chamber of the eye, behind the transparent cornea

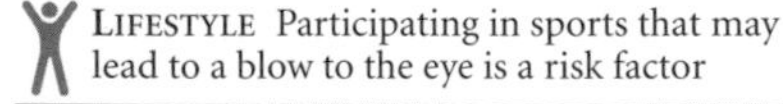
LIFESTYLE Participating in sports that may lead to a blow to the eye is a risk factor

AGE GENDER GENETICS Not significant factors

A blow to the eye may rupture a blood vessel in the iris (the colored part of the eye) or in the ciliary body, the ring of muscle behind the iris. The damaged blood vessel may bleed into the chamber between the lens and the cornea, the transparent front part of the eye, forming a pool of blood called a hyphema. Initially, the blood mixes with the clear fluid behind the cornea, resulting in severely blurry vision, but within a few hours the blood cells sink to the bottom of the chamber, which enables the vision to return to normal.

If you have an eye injury, first take the correct emergency action (*see* FIRST AID: EYE WOUND, p.993). If you experience blurry vision, consult your doctor immediately or go to the hospital. Hyphema blood usually disappears in less than a week, but restricting your activities may stop further bleeding. If bleeding recurs, the pressure in the eye can rise and cause acute glaucoma (p.575), which needs urgent treatment.

(WWW) ONLINE SITES: p.1031

Trachoma

A persistent eye infection that often causes damage to the cornea, the transparent front part of the eye

AGE Particularly common in children

LIFESTYLE Living in an area with limited water and poor hygiene is a risk factor

GENDER GENETICS Not significant factors

Trachoma is a serious, persistent eye infection that often causes permanent scarring of the cornea, the transparent front part of the eye. Although rare in developed countries, trachoma is one of the world's main causes of blindness. It affects about 400 million people, of whom about 6 million are blind.

Trachoma is due to the bacterium *Chlamydia trachomatis*, which is spread to the eyes by direct contact with contaminated hands or by flies. Trachoma is common in poor parts of the world, particularly in hot, dry countries that have poor sanitation and limited water supplies. Overcrowding encourages the spread of the trachoma infection.

To avoid becoming infected in a high-risk area, you should wash your hands and face regularly and avoid touching your eyes with dirty fingers.

WHAT ARE THE SYMPTOMS?

Initially, trachoma causes inflammation of the conjunctiva, the membrane that covers the white of the eye and lines the eyelids (*see* CONJUNCTIVITIS, p.570). Later symptoms include:

- Thick discharge from the affected eye that contains pus.
- Redness of the white of the eye.
- Gritty sensation in the eye.

Over time, repeated episodes of trachoma can cause scarring on the inside of the eyelids. The scars may pull the eyelids inward and cause the eyelashes to rub against the delicate cornea (*see* ENTROPION, p.584). Left untreated, the condition can lead to blindness.

WHAT IS THE TREATMENT?

In the early stages, trachoma is treated with antibiotic eyedrops or ointment (*see* DRUGS ACTING ON THE EYE, p.919). If the cornea has become scarred, sight may be restored by an operation called a corneal graft, in which a cornea from a donor is used to replace the scarred one.

(WWW) ONLINE SITES: p.1031, p.1033

Keratoconus

Progressive change in the shape of the cornea, the transparent front part of the eye, causing blurry vision

AGE Usually develops around puberty

GENDER More common in females

GENETICS Sometimes runs in families

LIFESTYLE Not a significant factor

In keratoconus, the central area of the transparent cornea at the front of the eye grows abnormally and becomes cone-shaped and thin. This rare, sometimes inherited condition, also known as conical cornea, is more common in females and usually begins at puberty.

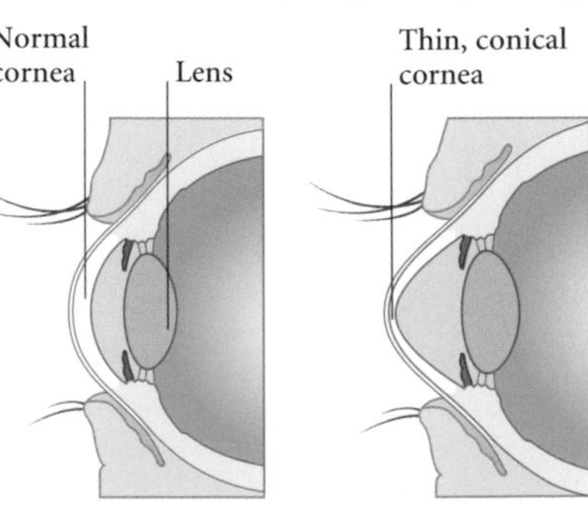
Normal cornea
Lens
Thin, conical cornea
NORMAL EYE
KERATOCONUS

Effects of keratoconus

The normal cornea has an even, spherical curvature. Keratoconus causes the cornea to grow abnormally, becoming thinner and bulging forward in a conical shape.

The condition may affect one or both eyes. As the shape of the cornea changes, vision becomes blurry, and nearsightedness develops (*see* MYOPIA, p.586). These symptoms worsen, in some cases quite rapidly, as the distortion of the cornea progresses.

WHAT MIGHT BE DONE?

A slit lamp may be used to examine your eyes (*see* SLIT-LAMP EXAMINATION, p.574). If your doctor detects keratoconus in its early stages, your vision can be corrected by glasses or hard contact lenses (*see* GLASSES AND CONTACT LENSES, p.588). However, if your vision has seriously deteriorated, your doctor may suggest a corneal graft, an operation in which the abnormal cornea is replaced with a healthy one from a donor. This operation will usually restore normal vision permanently.

(WWW) ONLINE SITES: p.1031

Cataract

Clouding of the lens of the eye, causing loss of vision

 AGE Most common after age 75 but may be present from birth

 GENETICS Sometimes due to an abnormal chromosome

 LIFESTYLE Contact sports and frequent exposure to the sun are risk factors

 GENDER Not a significant factor

If you have a cataract, the normally transparent lens of the eye is cloudy as a result of changes in protein fibers in the lens. The clouding affects the transmission and focusing of light entering the eye, reducing clarity of vision.

If cataracts are present from birth, total loss of vision (*see* CONGENITAL BLINDNESS, p.856) may result. However, cataracts do not usually affect children or young adults. Most people over age 75 have some cataract formation, but visual loss is often minimal as only the outer edges of the lens are affected.

Cataracts usually develop in both eyes, but generally one eye is more severely affected. A cataract in the central part of the lens or one that affects the whole lens can cause total loss of clarity and detail in vision. However, the affected eye will still be able to detect light and shade.

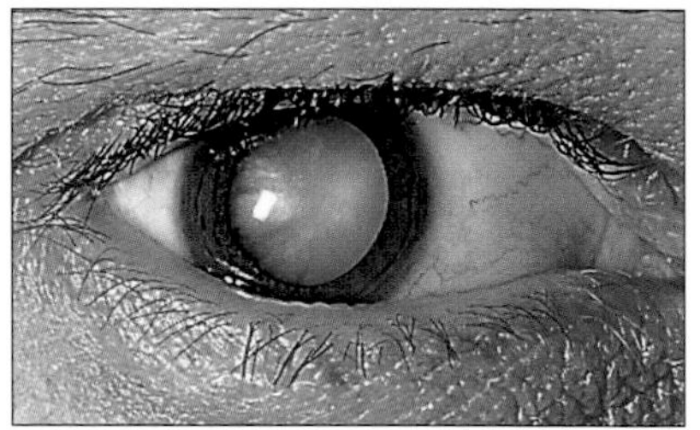

Severe cataract
This cataract, seen as a cloudy area behind the pupil, affects a large part of the lens. Cataracts cause visual impairment.

WHAT ARE THE CAUSES?

All cataracts occur as a result of structural changes to protein fibers within the lens. These changes cause part or all of the lens to become cloudy.

Changes in the protein fibers are a normal part of the aging process, but cataracts that develop earlier in life may occur because of an eye injury (p.582) or from prolonged exposure to sunlight. They may occur due to diabetes mellitus (p.687), uveitis (p.574), or long-term treatment with corticosteroid drugs (p.930) and are common in people with the chromosome abnormality Down syndrome (p.821).

WHAT ARE THE SYMPTOMS?

Cataracts usually develop over a period of months or years. In most cases, they are painless and usually cause only visual symptoms, such as:

- Blurry or distorted vision.
- Star-shaped scattering of light from bright lights, particularly at night.
- Altered color vision: objects appear reddish or yellow.
- Temporary improvement in near vision in people who were farsighted.

A severe cataract may make the pupil of the eye appear cloudy.

WHAT MIGHT BE DONE?

Your doctor may examine your eyes with a slit lamp (*see* SLIT-LAMP EXAMINATION, p.574) and an ophthalmoscope (*see* OPHTHALMOSCOPY, p.578). If your vision is affected significantly, he or she may recommend that the cataract is removed surgically and an artificial lens put in the eye (*see* CATARACT SURGERY, below). If there is no other reason for your visual deterioration, your sight should improve greatly after the operation. However, you may still need to wear glasses afterward.

(WWW) ONLINE SITES: p.1027, p.1031

(TREATMENT) CATARACT SURGERY

A cataract is an opaque region in the lens of the eye causing loss of vision. During cataract surgery, the affected lens is removed and replaced with an artificial lens. The operation is usually performed under local anesthesia, and you will probably be able to go home the same day. In the technique shown here, the lens is first softened by an ultrasound probe. The softened tissue is extracted, and a new lens is inserted.

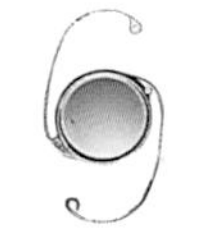

ARTIFICIAL LENS (actual size)

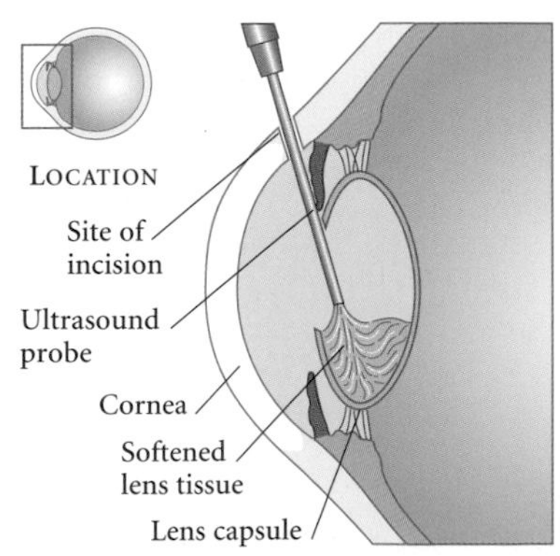
LOCATION
Site of incision
Ultrasound probe
Cornea
Softened lens tissue
Lens capsule

1 *An ultrasound probe is inserted into the lens through a small incision in the cornea. The probe softens the lens by emitting sound waves and the softened tissue is then sucked out.*

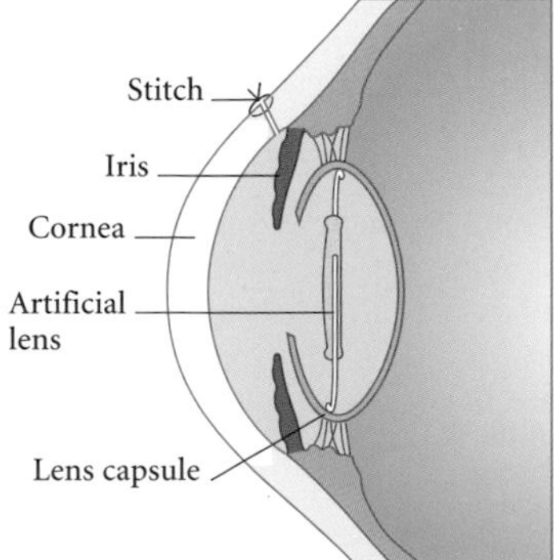
Stitch
Iris
Cornea
Artificial lens
Lens capsule

2 *The back of the natural lens capsule is left in place, and an artificial lens is placed inside it. The incision in the cornea is either closed with surgical stitches or will gradually heal on its own.*

Scleritis

Inflammation of the sclera, the tough, white, outer covering of the eye

GENDER More common in females

GENETICS May run in families if associated with rheumatoid arthritis

AGE LIFESTYLE Not significant factors

Scleritis is a rare, serious condition in which the sclera (the white outer coat of the eye) becomes inflamed. The condition is more common in women and is frequently associated with inflammatory disorders, such as rheumatoid arthritis (p.377). The main symptoms are severe pain in the eye, redness of the white of the eye, and excessive watering. If the scleritis is linked with rheumatoid arthritis, you may have repeated attacks. Rarely, severe cases of scleritis may cause perforation of the sclera and blindness (p.591) of the affected eye.

If you have any of these symptoms, contact your doctor immediately. Mild cases may need only anti-inflammatory eyedrops (*see* DRUGS ACTING ON THE EYE, p.919), but if rheumatoid arthritis is the cause, immunosuppressant drugs (p.906) can help both conditions.

(WWW) ONLINE SITES: p.1031

Uveitis

Inflammation of any part of the uveal tract, which is a group of connected structures inside the eye

AGE GENDER GENETICS LIFESTYLE Risk factors depend on the cause

The uveal tract consists of several connected structures: the iris (the colored part of the eye); the ciliary body (a ring of muscle behind the iris); and the choroid (a layer of tissue that supports the light-sensitive retina). Inflammation of any part of the uveal tract is called uveitis. The condition may involve the iris (iritis), the ciliary body (anterior uveitis or iritis), the retina, or the choroid. If you develop uveitis and it is not treated, your vision can become seriously impaired.

What are the causes?

Uveitis is most commonly caused by an autoimmune disorder, in which the body attacks its own tissues, such as juvenile rheumatoid arthritis (p.377). There may be links with inflammatory disorders, such as ankylosing spondylitis (p.378) and sarcoidosis (p.498). The condition may also occur with certain infectious diseases, including tuberculosis (p.491) and syphilis (p.766).

What are the symptoms?

Uveitis may affect only one eye. Symptoms may include:

- Redness and watering of the eye.
- Sensitivity to bright light.
- Blurry vision.
- Aching in the eye.
- Spots or haziness in the visual field.

It is important that you consult your doctor without delay if your eye becomes red and painful or if you develop blurry vision.

The main danger in iritis is that the inflamed iris may stick to the lens. This prevents normal drainage of fluid through the pupil and increases the pressure inside the eye (*see* ACUTE GLAUCOMA, opposite page). If this rise in pressure inside the eye is not treated promptly, it can lead to blindness (p.591). Uveitis may also increase the risk of developing a cataract (p.573), in which the normally transparent lens of the eye becomes clouded, reducing clarity of vision. Repeated attacks of uveitis can also lead to permanent damage to the iris and deterioration in vision.

Occasionally, when the retina is involved, parts may be damaged irreversibly by posterior uveitis, resulting in partial or total loss of vision in the affected eye.

(TEST) Slit-lamp examination

The slit lamp is used to examine structures at the front of the eye: the transparent cornea, which covers the front part of the eye; the colored iris; the lens; and the front chamber, which lies between the cornea and the lens. The slit lamp produces a long, narrow beam of brilliant light that is focused onto the eye. Although the examination is painless, eye drops used to dilate the pupil may make your vision blurry for a few hours afterward.

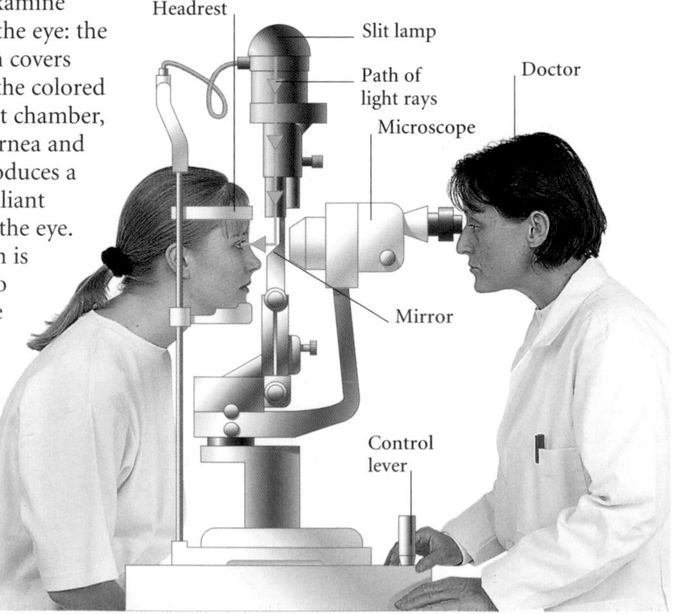
Headrest
Slit lamp
Path of light rays
Doctor
Microscope
Mirror
Control lever

During the examination
As the doctor moves the light beam across your eye using a control lever, a headrest and chin support keep your head still.

(VIEW)

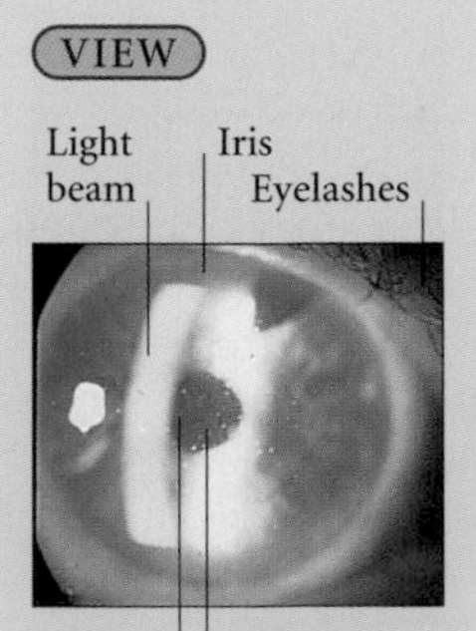
Light beam
Iris
Eyelashes
Pupil
Opaque areas

Eye during slit-lamp examination
Many tiny opaque areas (white dots) were seen on the cornea as the light beam moved across the eye. These areas indicate inflammation and may cause blurry vision.

WHAT MIGHT BE DONE?

If uveitis is suspected, you may have a slit-lamp examination (opposite page) and ophthalmoscopy (p.578), which examines the inside of your eye. If this is your first attack of uveitis, you will probably have other diagnostic tests to establish the underlying cause.

Your doctor may prescribe eyedrops to dilate the pupil and stop the iris from sticking to the lens, or corticosteroid eyedrops to reduce the inflammation (*see* DRUGS ACTING ON THE EYE, p.919). Treatment of uveitis is usually effective, but the condition tends to recur.

(WWW) ONLINE SITES: p.1031, p.1033

Glaucoma

Abnormally high pressure of the fluid inside the eye

 AGE Rare under age 40; most common over age 60

 GENETICS Some types run in families

 GENDER LIFESTYLE Not significant factors

Fluid continually moves into and out of the eye to nourish its tissues and maintain its shape. In glaucoma, the flow of fluid out of the eye becomes blocked and pressure inside the eye rises. This high pressure may permanently damage nerve fibers in the light-sensitive retina and in the optic nerve, which carries nerve signals from the retina to the brain. Glaucoma becomes more common with age, and mainly affects people over age 60. If untreated, the condition may cause blindness (p.591).

WHAT ARE THE TYPES?

There are two common types (acute and chronic) and two rare types (congenital and secondary) of glaucoma. Acute glaucoma (right) develops suddenly, causing rapid loss of vision and severe eye pain. In contrast, chronic glaucoma (p.576) develops slowly and painlessly, often over many years. It may not cause noticeable symptoms until the eyes are badly damaged. Both types can run in families.

Secondary glaucoma occurs because of an underlying disorder, such as uveitis (opposite page), or from using certain drugs such as corticosteroid eyedrops (*see* DRUGS ACTING ON THE EYE, p.919). The other rare form, congenital glaucoma, is due to a defect in the drainage apparatus of the eye. Congenital glaucoma is present from birth and can lead to blindness (*see* CONGENITAL BLINDNESS, p.856). Secondary glaucoma can also result in blindness.

Glaucoma is diagnosed by measuring pressure in the eye using an instrument called a tonometer (*see* APPLANATION TONOMETRY, p.576). Treatment should always be given urgently. Eyedrops are used first, to reduce pressure in the eye (*see* DRUGS FOR GLAUCOMA, p.920). In some cases, surgery is then necessary to increase drainage of fluid and prevent the buildup of pressure in the eye (*see* LASER IRIDOTOMY, p.576, and TRABECULECTOMY, p.577). Correct treatment normally prevents further vision loss.

(WWW) ONLINE SITES: p.1031

Acute glaucoma

An abrupt blockage of the drainage system in the eye, causing a painful, rapid rise in fluid pressure

 AGE Rare under age 40; most common over age 60

 GENETICS Sometimes runs in families; more common in people of African or Asian descent

 GENDER LIFESTYLE Not significant factors

Normally, the fluid that is secreted into the front of the eye to maintain the eye's shape and nourish the tissues drains away continuously. However, in acute (narrow-angle) glaucoma, the drainage system suddenly develops a blockage, and the fluid pressure inside the eye rises rapidly. Acute glaucoma is a medical emergency that requires prompt treatment. Left untreated, the eye can swiftly become damaged and a permanent reduction in vision can result.

WHAT ARE THE CAUSES?

The fluid in the front part of the eye is produced continuously by a ring of tissue called the ciliary body, behind the eye's colored iris. Normally the fluid flows out through the pupil and drains away through the trabecular meshwork, which surrounds the iris. This sievelike meshwork is situated behind the drainage angle, which is found between the outer rim of the iris and the edge of the cornea. In acute glaucoma, the iris bulges forward and closes the drainage angle, so that fluid is trapped within the eye. The pressure inside the eye rises as more fluid is secreted. As the pressure rises, it may damage the nerves in the light-sensitive retina and in the optic nerve, which carries nerve signals to the brain, causing reduced vision.

Having an eyeball that is smaller than normal is a common cause of farsightedness (*see* HYPEROPIA, p.586) and increases the risk of developing acute glaucoma. The disorder is more common in older people because the lens of the eye thickens throughout life and may eventually press against the iris. Fluid then builds up behind the iris, which bulges forward and blocks the drainage angle. Occasionally, acute glaucoma may be triggered when dim light causes the pupil to widen. The iris then thickens and the drainage angle can close. Acute glaucoma sometimes runs in families and is more common in people of African and Asian descent.

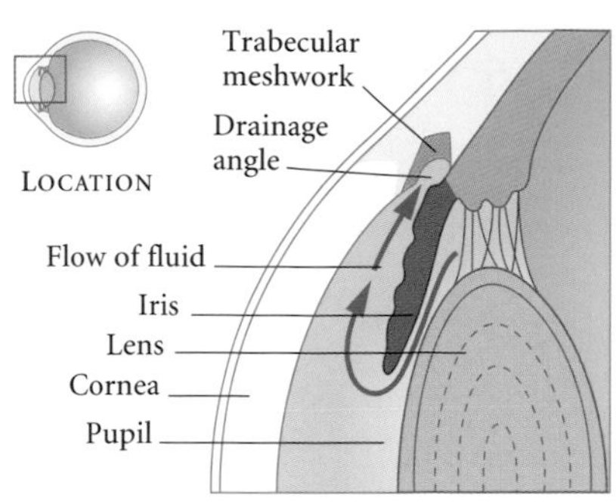
Trabecular meshwork
Drainage angle
LOCATION
Flow of fluid
Iris
Lens
Cornea
Pupil

NORMAL EYE

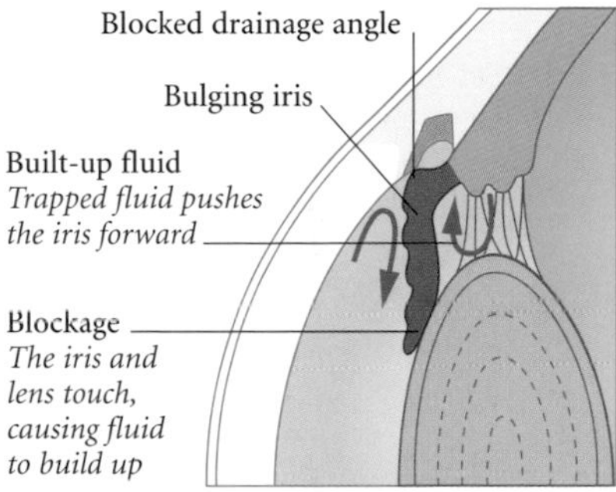
Blocked drainage angle
Bulging iris
Built-up fluid
Trapped fluid pushes the iris forward
Blockage
The iris and lens touch, causing fluid to build up

ACUTE GLAUCOMA

Mechanism of acute glaucoma

Fluid normally flows out through the pupil and drains out of the meshwork at the back of the drainage angle. If the iris and lens touch, fluid becomes trapped and the iris bulges forward. This blocks the drainage angle, causing acute glaucoma.

TEST APPLANATION TONOMETRY

The eye condition glaucoma, in which the pressure inside the eye is elevated, can be detected using an instrument called an applanation tonometer. Anesthetic drops are put into your eye, then the tonometer is pressed gently against the cornea, the transparent front part of the eye, and the force needed to flatten the cornea is measured. The test takes only a few seconds and is painless.

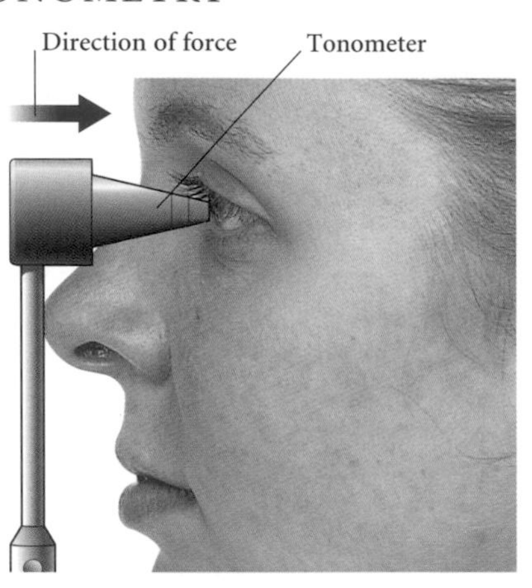
Direction of force
Tonometer

During the test
The tonometer is held against the cornea. As the internal pressure is measured, the pressure on your eye will increase slightly.

WHAT ARE THE SYMPTOMS?

A full-blown attack of acute glaucoma may be preceded by mild attacks in the weeks before. Mild attacks usually take place in the evening. Symptoms include pain in the eyes and haloes appearing around lights and are relieved by sleeping. If you have these symptoms, you should consult your doctor at once. Full-blown attacks develop suddenly. Symptoms include:

- Rapid deterioration of vision.
- Intense pain in the eye.
- Redness and watering of the eye.
- Sensitivity to bright light.
- Haloes appearing around lights.
- Nausea and vomiting.

If you develop a painful eye or your vision deteriorates suddenly, go to a hospital emergency room or consult your doctor immediately.

WHAT MIGHT BE DONE?

The pressure inside the eye is measured using a technique such as applanation tonometry (above). If acute glaucoma is detected, you will be given immediate drug treatment by intravenous injection, as eyedrops, and possibly also by mouth to reduce the pressure in the eye (*see* DRUGS FOR GLAUCOMA, p.920). Laser iridotomy (below) will probably be performed as soon as the pressure falls. In this technique, a laser is used to make a small hole in the iris so that fluid can be released. The unaffected eye may also be treated as a precaution.

After surgery, most people are symptom-free, but some loss of the outer edges of vision may remain. Long-term drug treatment or a second operation may be needed to prevent loss of sight.

WWW ONLINE SITES: p.1031

Chronic glaucoma

A gradual, painless increase in the fluid pressure inside the eye

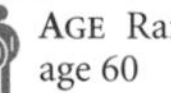

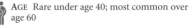

AGE Rare under age 40; most common over age 60

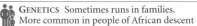

GENETICS Sometimes runs in families. More common in people of African descent

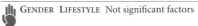

GENDER LIFESTYLE Not significant factors

Chronic glaucoma is also known as open-angle glaucoma. The condition causes a gradual deterioration of sight due to a progressive buildup of fluid pressure inside the eye over a period of several years. There are often no symptoms until late in the disease, and loss of vision is permanent. Although the condition can lead to total blindness (p.591), early treatment can prevent severe damage. In most cases, both eyes are affected, although symptoms may only occur in one eye initially.

WHAT ARE THE CAUSES?

Fluid is continually secreted into the front of the eye to nourish the tissues and maintain the eye's shape. Normally, this fluid drains away through the trabecular meshwork, a sievelike structure at the back of the angle that is formed between the iris and the edge of the cornea (called the drainage angle).

However, in chronic glaucoma, a gradual blockage develops in the meshwork. Although the drainage angle remains open, fluid is prevented from draining normally, and the pressure in the eye gradually rises. The increasing

TREATMENT LASER IRIDOTOMY

This technique is used to treat acute glaucoma, in which pressure in the eye rises suddenly due to blockage in the outflow of fluid. The pressure is reduced using eyedrops, intravenous drugs, and, sometimes, oral drugs. Anesthetic eyedrops are then put into the eye, and a thick contact lens is placed in front of it to focus a laser beam onto the bulging iris. The laser cuts a small hole in the iris, releasing the fluid behind it. The iris flattens, opening the drainage angle and letting trapped fluid out. The hole remains in the eye with no ill effects.

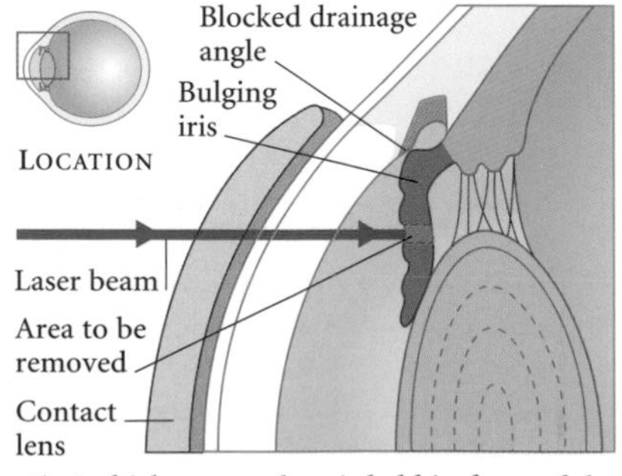
LOCATION
Blocked drainage angle
Bulging iris
Laser beam
Area to be removed
Contact lens

1 *A thick contact lens is held in front of the eye, and a laser beam is focused through it onto the bulging iris. The laser then cuts a small hole right through the iris.*

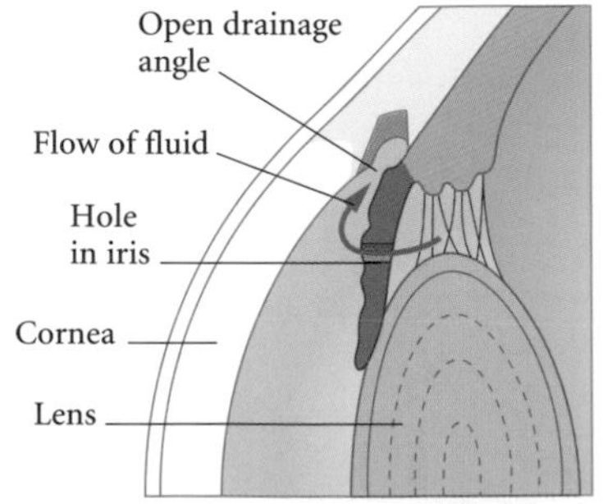
Open drainage angle
Flow of fluid
Hole in iris
Cornea
Lens

2 *Fluid trapped behind the iris flows through the hole. The iris returns to its normal shape, and the drainage angle opens, allowing the eye to drain normally.*

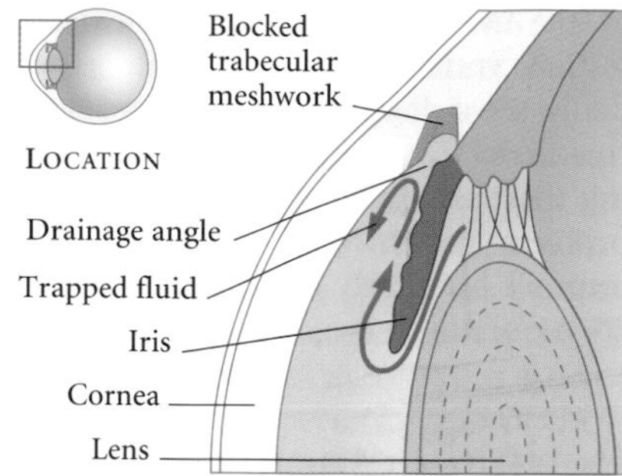
Blocked trabecular meshwork
LOCATION
Drainage angle
Trapped fluid
Iris
Cornea
Lens

Fluid flow in chronic glaucoma
Normally, fluid flows out of the eye through the meshwork around the iris. In chronic glaucoma the meshwork is blocked, and pressure builds up.

fluid pressure progressively damages the nerve fibers situated in the light-sensitive retina at the back of the eye and in the optic nerve, which carries nerve signals from the retina to the brain, causing loss of vision.

The underlying reason for the problem in the drainage system is not yet fully understood. Genetic factors may be involved and the condition sometimes runs in families. It is also more common in people of African descent. There is also an increased risk of developing chronic glaucoma if you are very nearsighted (*see* MYOPIA, p.586).

WHAT ARE THE SYMPTOMS?

Chronic glaucoma often has no symptoms until late in the disease, by which time it is probable that your vision has been permanently affected. During the later stages, the symptoms may include:

- Bumping into objects because of loss of the outer edges of vision (peripheral vision).
- Eventual blurring of objects that are straight ahead.

Always consult your doctor promptly if you notice a change in your vision. Because the risk of chronic glaucoma increases beyond middle age, everyone over age 40 should be tested for the condition every 2 years. If you are in a high-risk group, you should be tested regularly whatever your age.

HOW IS IT DIAGNOSED?

Chronic glaucoma can be detected at an early stage during a routine eye examination. Ophthalmologists and optometrists often use a technique known as applanation tonometry (opposite page) to measure the pressure inside the eye. The retina may also be examined using ophthalmoscopy (p.578), a technique that may reveal damage to the optic nerve resulting from the high pressure. Your ophthalmologist or optometrist may perform a visual field test (p.590) to check for loss of peripheral vision.

WHAT IS THE TREATMENT?

If chronic glaucoma is diagnosed early, eyedrops to reduce the pressure in the eye will probably be prescribed (*see* DRUGS FOR GLAUCOMA, p.920). You will probably have to continue using these eyedrops for the rest of your life.

If the condition is advanced, or if eyedrops do not lower the pressure sufficiently, surgery may be needed to make a drainage channel in the white of the eye (*see* TRABECULECTOMY, below). In another surgical technique, called laser trabeculoplasty, a laser beam is used to create tiny holes in the trabecular meshwork, allowing fluid to drain away. Both procedures usually succeed in eliminating the symptoms and preventing sight loss. If the condition affects only one eye, the other will probably also need treatment eventually.

(WWW) ONLINE SITES: p.1031

Floaters

Dark specks that appear to float and move in front of the eye

AGE GENDER GENETICS LIFESTYLE
Not significant factors

It is quite common to see small specks, known as floaters, that appear to float in the field of vision. Although floaters seem to lie in front of the eyes, they are in fact fragments of tissue in the jelly-like vitreous humor that fills the back of the eye. These fragments cast shadows on the light-sensitive retina at the back of the eye. They move rapidly with any eye movement, but, when the eyes are still, they drift slowly.

The reason for most floaters is not known. They rarely affect vision, but you should consult your doctor immediately if floaters suddenly appear in large numbers or interfere with vision. A sudden increase in the number of floaters may indicate a serious eye disorder that requires urgent treatment, such as the separation of the retina from its underlying tissue (*see* RETINAL DETACHMENT, p.578), or a leakage of blood into the vitreous humor (*see* VITREOUS HEMORRHAGE, p.578).

TREATMENT TRABECULECTOMY

This surgical technique is used to treat chronic glaucoma, in which the pressure in the eye gradually rises due to a blockage of the trabecular meshwork, a sievelike structure through which the fluid in the eye normally drains. Trabeculectomy is usually done under local anesthesia and involves cutting out a section of the blocked meshwork so that fluid can flow freely out of the eye. Your doctor may advise you to wear an eye shield for a day while the eye is healing. You should also avoid strenuous activity for several weeks after the procedure.

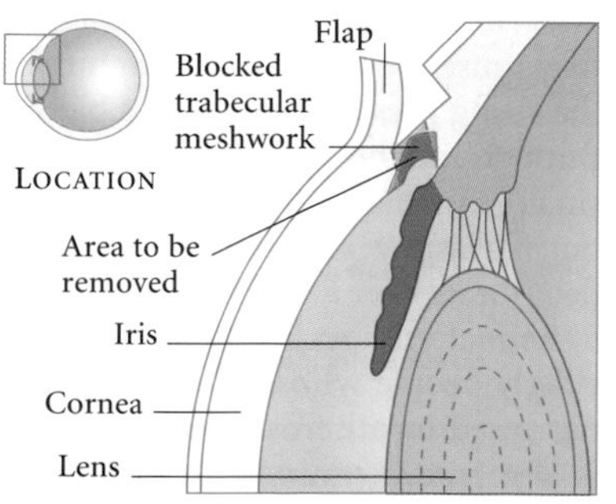
Flap
Blocked trabecular meshwork
LOCATION
Area to be removed
Iris
Cornea
Lens

1 *An incision is made in the white of the eye over the area where fluid normally drains away. The flap is pulled back to expose the trabecular meshwork, and a section of the blocked meshwork is cut out.*

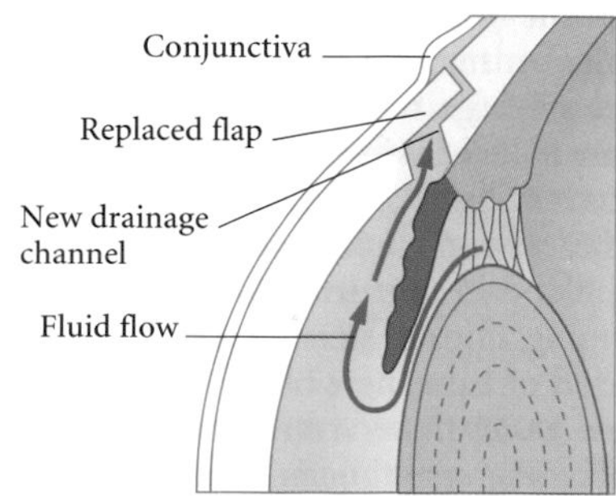
Conjunctiva
Replaced flap
New drainage channel
Fluid flow

2 *The flap in the white of the eye is replaced. Fluid can now drain around the edges of the flap and under the clear conjunctiva that covers the white of the eye. Pressure in the eye is then relieved.*

blepharitis recurs repeatedly, see your doctor, who may prescribe topical antibiotics (*see* DRUGS ACTING ON THE EYE, p.919) or a corticosteroid (p.930). The condition often clears up after 2 weeks of treatment, but it may recur. Allergic blepharitis usually improves on its own, but you should try to avoid contact with the trigger substance.

(WWW) ONLINE SITES: p.1036

Chalazion

A swelling in the eyelid that may be painless

AGE GENDER GENETICS LIFESTYLE
Not significant factors

If an oil-secreting gland in the eyelid becomes blocked, the gland enlarges, creating a swelling called a chalazion. A chalazion may at first look like a stye (p.583), but, unlike a stye, it is not on the eyelid margin. Usually, the pain and redness associated with a chalazion disappear after a few days. However, if the swelling is large, it may cause long-term discomfort, and pressure on the front of the eye can interfere with vision.

WHAT MIGHT BE DONE?

If your doctor diagnoses a chalazion, he or she will probably wait for several weeks before arranging any treatment because it will probably disappear on its own. Meanwhile, if the chalazion is painful or irritating, holding a clean, warm, damp cloth against it may help.

A persistent chalazion can be treated by a simple operation in which a small cut is made in the inner surface of the eyelid and the contents of the swelling removed. The procedure is performed under local anesthesia and is painless.

(WWW) ONLINE SITES: p.1031

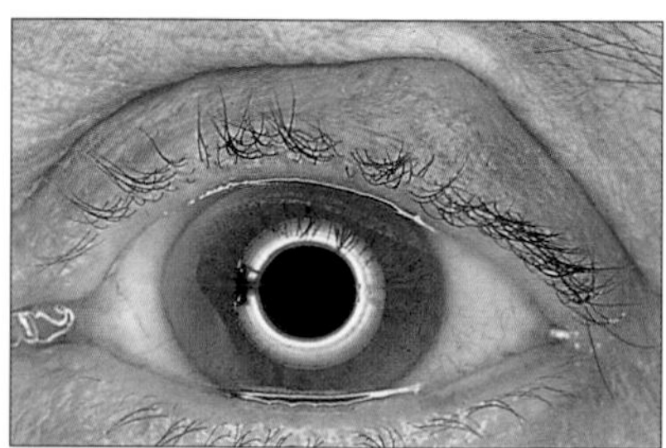

Chalazion
The swelling in the upper eyelid of this eye is a chalazion, caused by blockage of an oil-secreting gland.

Ptosis

Abnormal drooping of one or both upper eyelids

AGE GENDER HEREDITY LIFESTYLE
Risk factors depend on the cause

Drooping of the upper eyelid due to weakness of the muscle that raises it is called ptosis. The condition may be the result of a problem with the muscle or nerve that controls the eyelid. The sagging lid may partly or totally close the eye. One or both eyes may be affected.

Ptosis is occasionally present from birth. If a baby's eyelid droops and it covers the pupil, his or her vision may not develop normally (*see* AMBLYOPIA, p.858) and early treatment is vital.

Ptosis in adults can occur as a part of the aging process, or it may be a symptom of myasthenia gravis (p.549), which causes progressive muscle weakness. If ptosis starts suddenly, it may be due to a brain tumor (p.530) or a defective blood vessel in the brain. If you develop ptosis, see your doctor to rule out a serious underlying disorder.

WHAT IS THE TREATMENT?

Ptosis in babies can be corrected by surgically tightening the eyelid muscle. If treatment is carried out early, the child's vision should develop normally.

In adults, surgery for ptosis should be carried out only after any possible significant underlying disorders have been ruled out. Surgery is very effective for ptosis caused by the aging process.

(WWW) ONLINE SITES: p.1031, p.1035

Entropion

Inward turning of the margin of the upper or lower eyelid or both

AGE More common in elderly people

GENDER GENETICS LIFESTYLE
Not significant factors

In entropion, the eyelid turns inward. The eyelashes rub against the cornea (the transparent front part of the eye) and the conjunctiva (which covers the white of the eye). Although the conjunctiva also lines the eyelids, this area is unaffected. Typical symptoms of the condition are pain in the eye area, watery eye (opposite page) and irritation. Left untreated, the cornea may be damaged (*see* CORNEAL ULCER, p.571), ultimately leading to loss of vision.

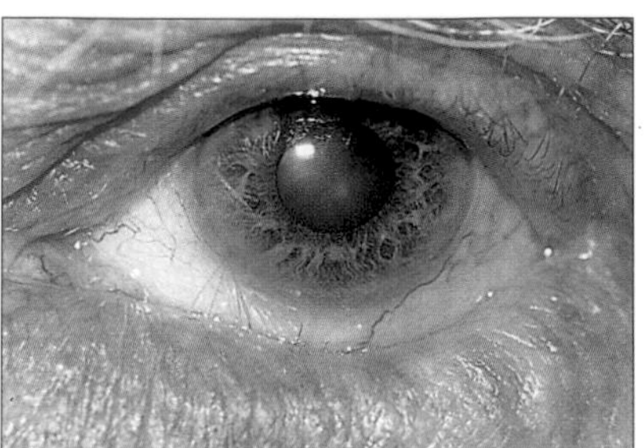

Entropion
This eye's lower lid has turned inward, causing the eyelashes to rub against the eye. This condition is called entropion.

In developed countries, entropion mainly affects elderly people because of the natural laxity of the eyelids that takes place with increasing age. In developing countries, entropion most often follows bouts of the eye infection trachoma (p.572), which causes scar tissue to form on the inner surface of the eyelids. Eventually, this tissue may shrink, making the eyelids turn inward.

A minor operation can be carried out to realign the eyelid in entropion. If the cornea is scarred, it can be replaced with a healthy one from a donor. This procedure is called a corneal graft.

(WWW) ONLINE SITES: p.1026, p.1031, p1033

Ectropion

Outward turning of the margin of the lower eyelid

AGE More common in elderly people

GENDER GENETICS LIFESTYLE
Not significant factors

If the edge of the lower eyelid turns outward and the eyelid hangs away from the eye, the exposed inner surface of the lid becomes dry and sore. This condition is known as ectropion and may stop tears from entering the nasolacrimal duct, which runs from the eye to the nose, causing the eye to water continuously. Because the eyelids cannot close fully, the transparent cornea at the front of the eye is constantly exposed and may become damaged (*see* CORNEAL ABRASION, p.571) or repeatedly infected. The condition most often occurs in elderly people as a result of laxity of the lower eyelid that may occur with increasing age. Both eyes are usually affected. Ectropion may also be caused by contraction of a scar on the eyelid or cheek or by facial palsy (p.548), in which the muscles around the eye (and other facial muscles on the affected side) are paralyzed. In these cases, only one eye is usually involved.

WHAT IS THE TREATMENT?

If you think that you have ectropion, you should consult your doctor as soon as you can, because treatment of the disorder is most successful when it is carried out early. Your doctor will probably recommend a straightforward surgical operation, performed under local anesthesia, in which the skin and muscles around the eyelid are tightened. In severe cases, more complex plastic surgery may be necessary.

(WWW) ONLINE SITES: p.1026, p.1031, p1035

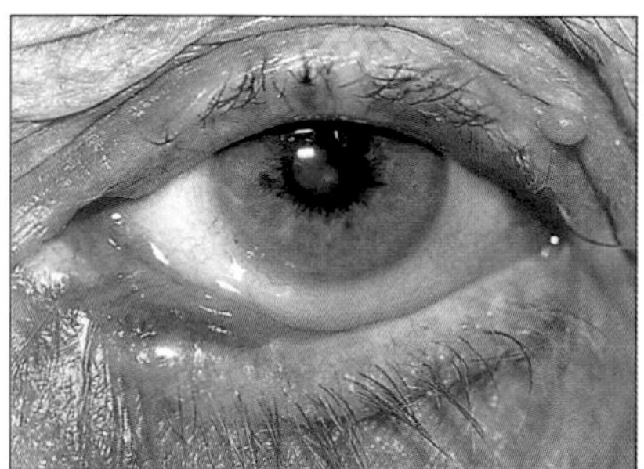

Ectropion
The lower eyelid of this eye has turned outward (ectropion), exposing the inner surface and preventing drainage of tears.

Watery eye

Overflow of tears from the eye due to overproduction or poor drainage

 AGE Most common in babies and elderly people

 GENDER GENETICS LIFESTYLE Not significant factors

Watery eye usually results from irritation of the eye by a foreign body such as a particle of dirt. Older people often have watery eye as a result of entropion (opposite page), in which the eyelashes rub against the eye, or ectropion (opposite page), in which tears do not drain away normally. The watering usually stops when the irritant is removed or the underlying condition is corrected. Watery eye may also occur as a result of a blocked nasolacrimal system (which drains tears), possibly caused by an infection of the eye or sinus infection.

Babies may have watery eyes because the nasolacrimal system is underdeveloped. Gently massaging between the corner of the eyelid and the nose may help. The condition usually corrects itself by age 6 months. Persistent blockages, at any age, must be treated by a doctor, who may clear the blockage by inserting a fine probe into the tear duct.

Dacryocystitis

Painful swelling of the lacrimal (tear) sac, into which fluid drains from the surface of the eye

 AGE Most common in babies and elderly people

 GENDER GENETICS LIFESTYLE Not significant factors

Normally, tears from the eyes drain into the lacrimal sacs on either side of the nose. An infection of the lacrimal sacs is known as dacryocystitis. The condition is usually caused by a bacterial infection and most commonly results from a blockage in the nasolacrimal duct, which normally carries tears from the lacrimal sac to the nose. Nasolacrimal blockage is common in babies because the ducts are not fully developed until a year after birth. Elderly people may develop a blockage with no apparent cause, although it may be due to previous injury or inflammation.

Dacryocystitis usually starts with a red, watery eye. The area beside the nose just below the eye then becomes tender, red, and swollen. Pus may be discharged into the eye. Dacryocystitis usually affects only one eye at a time, but it can recur in either eye.

WHAT MIGHT BE DONE?

In adults, warm compresses and oral antibiotics (p.885) may help clear the infection. If the problem continues, a probe may be inserted to clear the nasolacrimal duct or surgery may be required to correct the damage. In babies, gentle massage of the lacrimal sac may help relieve the condition and antibiotics may also be given. As with adults, the blockage may be cleared by the insertion of a tiny probe.

(WWW) ONLINE SITES: p.1031

Keratoconjunctivitis sicca

Persistent dryness of the eye due to insufficient production of tears, also known as dry eye

 AGE Increasingly common over age 35

 GENDER More common in females

 GENETICS LIFESTYLE Not significant factors

Insufficient tear production, known as keratoconjunctivitis sicca or dry eye, results from damage to the lacrimal (tear) glands. The condition causes eye irritation and often leads to eye infections (*see* CONJUNCTIVITIS, p.570). In severe cases, corneal ulcers (p.571) may develop. Dry eye affects more women than men and is more common over age 35. The condition may be linked to autoimmune disorders, such as Sjögren syndrome (p.463), in which the body attacks its own tissues.

Your doctor will prescribe artificial tears to restore moisture to the eye. He or she may also investigate and treat an underlying cause. Sometimes, surgery may be performed to plug the channel through which the tears normally drain.

(WWW) ONLINE SITES: p.1031, p.1033

Xerophthalmia

Dryness of the eye due to a dietary deficiency of vitamin A

 AGE More common in children but can occur at any age

 LIFESTYLE Caused by a diet low in vitamin A

 GENDER GENETICS Not significant factors

Xerophthalmia, which occurs mainly in developing countries, means dryness of the eye. The condition is caused by a dietary deficiency of vitamin A (*see* NUTRITIONAL DEFICIENCIES, p.630).

Left untreated, xerophthalmia leads to chronic infection and the cornea (the transparent part of the front of the eye) may soften and perforate. Infection may then spread inside the eye and blindness (p.591) may result. Artificial tears may relieve dryness, but the main treatment is large doses of vitamin A.

TREATMENT GLASSES AND CONTACT LENSES

Most refractive errors can be corrected by wearing glasses or, for older children and adults, contact lenses. Glasses are suitable for most refractive errors, are comfortable to wear, and do not cause complications. Contact lenses are also available for many refractive errors, but they are most effective for myopia (p.586) and hyperopia (p.586). All contact lenses require careful cleaning to reduce the chance of an infection of the transparent cornea over which they are placed.

HOW LENSES WORK

Glasses and contact lenses correct refractive errors in the eye by altering the angle of light rays before the rays reach the surface of the cornea, the transparent front part of the eye. The cornea at the front of the eye and the lens can then focus the rays correctly on the retina. Concave lenses make the light rays diverge (bend apart) and convex lenses make the light rays converge (bend together).

Divergent light rays
Light rays focused on retina
Light rays from distant object
Concave lens
Cornea
Lens

LENS TO CORRECT MYOPIA

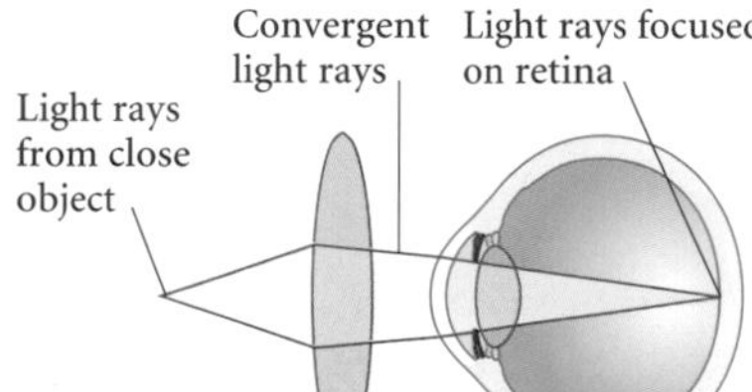
Convergent light rays
Light rays focused on retina
Light rays from close object
Convex lens

LENS TO CORRECT HYPEROPIA

Myopia and hyperopia
Myopia is corrected by concave lenses, which make light rays diverge, so that they are focused on the retina and not in front of it. Hyperopia requires a convex lens to make light rays converge, focusing them on the retina and not behind it.

CONTACT LENSES

Three types of contact lenses are available: rigid, gas-permeable, and soft. Soft lenses are the most widely used and rigid the least. Some soft lenses are worn only once or for a few days. Nondisposable lenses should be disinfected daily unless worn for an extended period of time (not usually recommended). If an eye becomes red or painful, stop wearing your lenses and consult your ophthalmologist immediately.

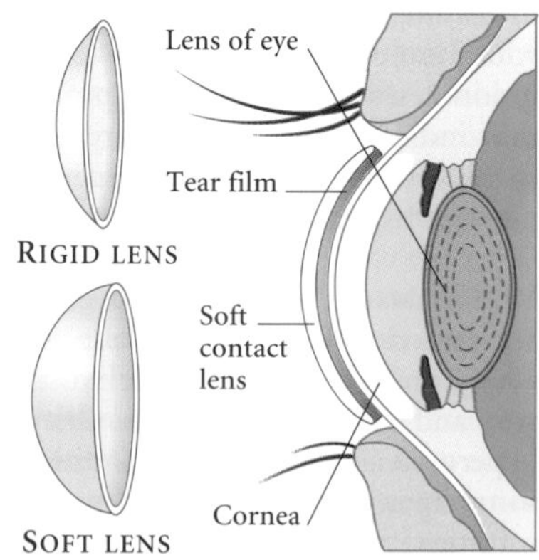
Lens of eye
Tear film
RIGID LENS
Soft contact lens
Cornea
SOFT LENS

Rigid and soft lenses
A contact lens floats on the tear film on the front of the eye. Soft lenses cover the whole cornea; rigid and gas-permeable lenses cover only the central part of the cornea.

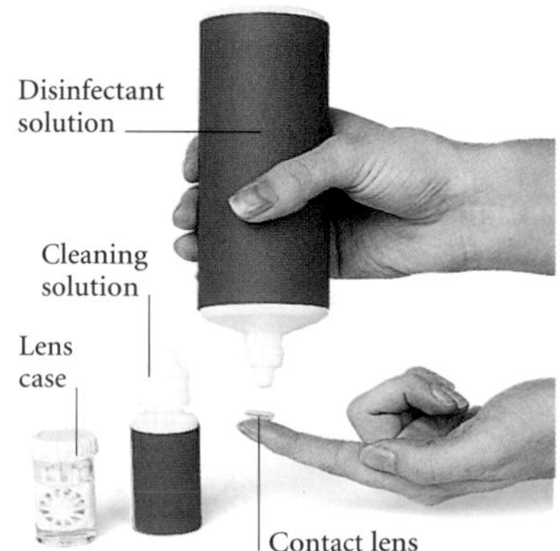
Disinfectant solution
Cleaning solution
Lens case
Contact lens

Contact lens care
Good lens hygiene prevents eye infections. Nondisposable lenses must be carefully cleaned before and after use and soaked overnight in disinfectant solution.

LENSES, left). The focusing power of the lens decreases gradually with age, and your prescription may need to be updated regularly. Some people who have hyperopia may be helped by laser treatment, which reshapes the surface of the cornea by laser beam to increase its focusing power (*see* SURGERY FOR REFRACTIVE ERRORS, opposite page).

Hyperopia does not cause complications, but people who have it are more prone to acute glaucoma (p.575), a serious condition that must be treated promptly. You should therefore see an ophthalmologist regularly, so that any problems can be treated immediately.

WWW ONLINE SITES: p.1031

Astigmatism

Distorted vision caused by an uneven curvature of the transparent cornea at the front of the eye

GENETICS Sometimes runs in families

AGE GENDER LIFESTYLE Not significant factors

In people with astigmatism, the transparent cornea at the front of the eye is unevenly curved and refracts (bends) the light rays striking different parts of it to differing degrees. The lens is then unable to bring all the rays into focus on the light-sensitive retina at the back of the eye, and vision becomes blurry. Astigmatism can run in families and often occurs in combination with myopia (p.586) or hyperopia (p.586).

WHAT ARE THE CAUSES?

The most common form of astigmatism is present from birth and is due to a slight buckling of the cornea in both eyes. Instead of being round like a basketball, the cornea is shaped like a football, with a steep curvature in one direction and a shallow curvature in the other. This type may worsen slowly with age. Less often, astigmatism is due to an eye disorder such as keratoconus (p.572) or an eye injury that causes a corneal ulcer (p.571) to develop.

WHAT ARE THE SYMPTOMS?

The majority of people have a slight degree of astigmatism. If you are only slightly affected, you probably will not notice much wrong with your vision.

TREATMENT SURGERY FOR REFRACTIVE ERRORS

Surgery can correct some refractive errors permanently. Two main surgical techniques are laser-assisted in-situ keratomileusis (LASIK) and photorefractive keratectomy (PRK). LASIK, a procedure in which the cornea is reshaped by removing part of the cornea by a laser, causes minimal scarring and is most widely used. PRK, a procedure in which the cornea is reshaped by a laser on the surface of the cornea without raising a flap, is the original laser corrective measure.

LASIK treatment of myopia
After a thin flap has been created by a surgical lathe, a laser beam, guided by computer, removes part of the cornea. The reshaped cornea is flatter, and light rays are focused to form a sharp image on the retina.

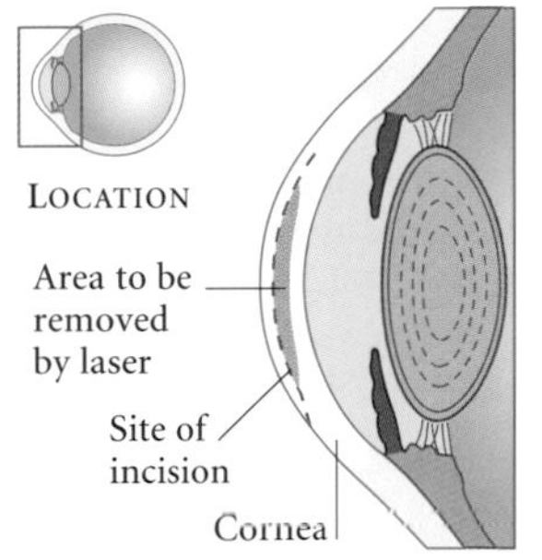
LOCATION
Area to be removed by laser
Site of incision
Cornea
BEFORE TREATMENT

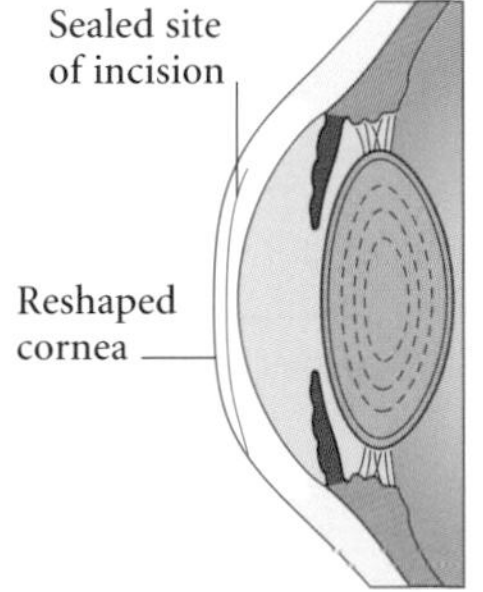
Sealed site of incision
Reshaped cornea
AFTER TREATMENT

More severe astigmatism, however, may lead to significant visual problems.

Astigmatism can affect vision in a number of different ways. Symptoms may include the following:

- Blurring of small print, causing difficulty in reading.
- Inability to see both near and distant objects clearly.

If you are experiencing difficulty in seeing objects clearly at any distance, it is important to visit your ophthalmologist to have a vision test (p.587).

WHAT IS THE TREATMENT?

In people with astigmatism, vision can usually be corrected by glasses that have special lenses that compensate for the unevenly shaped cornea. Rigid contact lenses are also effective because they smooth out the surface of the cornea. Conventional soft contact lenses mold to the shape of the cornea and can normally correct only mild astigmatism. However, soft contact lenses (known as toric lenses), which are designed to correct the condition, are also available.

In some people, astigmatism may be corrected by surgical treatment that reshapes the cornea (*see* SURGERY FOR REFRACTIVE ERRORS, above). One of the most widely used and least intrusive forms of surgical treatment for this condition is laser surgery, which tends to cause only minimal scarring.

WWW ONLINE SITES: p.1031

Presbyopia

Gradual age-associated loss of the eye's ability to focus on near objects

 AGE Generally develops after age 40

 GENDER GENETICS LIFESTYLE Not significant factors

After about age 40, almost everyone starts to notice increased difficulty in reading small print because of the development of presbyopia. A person with normal vision is able to see close objects clearly because the elastic lens of the eye changes shape, becoming thicker and more curved when focusing on near objects. The thicker lens brings light rays from close objects into sharp focus on the light-sensitive retina at the back of the eye in a process called accommodation. As we age, the lens becomes less elastic and the power of accommodation is reduced. Eventually, light rays from near objects can no longer be focused on the retina and the objects we see appear blurry.

WHAT ARE THE SYMPTOMS?

Since presbyopia develops very slowly, most people are unaware of the initial stages of this condition. However, the symptoms usually become noticeable between the ages of 40 and 50. Farsighted people (*see* HYPEROPIA, p.586) may have noticeable symptoms from an earlier age. Common symptoms of presbyopia include:

- The need to hold newspapers and books at arm's length so that you can read them.
- Increased difficulty focusing on near objects in poor light.
- If you are nearsighted (*see* MYOPIA, p.586), the need to take off your glasses to see near objects clearly.

If you develop any of these problems, consult your ophthalmologist.

WHAT IS THE TREATMENT?

Presbyopia can be corrected by wearing glasses with convex (outward-curved) lenses, which bring light rays from near objects into focus on the retina. If you are also farsighted, nearsighted, or have astigmatism (opposite page), you may be prescribed glasses with a different power in different parts of the lens. For example, bifocals have an upper lens to correct distance vision and a lower lens to correct presbyopia. Progressive lenses that gradually alter the focusing power from top to bottom are also available. Presbyopia can sometimes be corrected with contact lenses, but glasses may still be necessary for reading.

Presbyopia tends to worsen with age, and you will probably need to have your lens prescription updated every few years. You should therefore see your eye doctor regularly in order to have vision tests. The condition eventually stabilizes at about age 60 by which time little natural focusing power is left. By this stage most of the focusing work is done by glasses instead of the eye.

WWW ONLINE SITES: p.1026, p.1031

Double vision

Seeing two separate images of a single object instead of one

 AGE GENDER GENETICS LIFESTYLE Risk factors depend on the cause

People with double vision see two images of one object. The images are separate but often clearly focused. The disorder can be due to a number of causes and it usually disappears when one eye is closed. You should consult your doctor immediately if you start to experience double vision because it may indicate that you have a serious underlying disorder.

What are the causes?

The most common cause of double vision is weakness or paralysis of one or more of the muscles that control the movements of one eye. The movement of the affected eye is impaired, causing crossed eyes (*see* Strabismus, p.857). Two different views of the same object are received by the visual system and the brain cannot combine them. Tilting or turning the head may briefly correct the problem. However, not all types of crossed eyes cause double vision.

Many serious conditions that affect the brain and nervous system may cause impaired eye movements, leading to double vision. Potential causes include multiple sclerosis (p.541), head injuries (p.521), brain tumors (p.530), and bulging of an artery inside the head due to a weakness in the vessel wall (called an aneurysm). In older people, impaired eye movement resulting in double vision may be linked with diabetes mellitus (p.687) and, rarely, with atherosclerosis (p.402) and high blood pressure (*see* Hypertension, p.403).

Double vision can also occur as a result of a tumor or blood clot behind one of the eyes, causing the movement of that eye to be affected.

How is it diagnosed?

Your doctor may ask you to shut one eye at a time to see whether the double vision disappears. He or she may also ask you to describe the double images, or ask if they appear side by side or one on top of the other or whether one of the images appears to be tilted. Your doctor will probably observe the movements of your eyes closely in order to establish whether any of the eye muscles are weak or paralyzed. He or she may also carry out special vision tests to identify weak eye movement.

If double vision has come on suddenly, or if no obvious cause can be found, urgent CT scanning (p.247) or MRI (p.248) may be done to check for any abnormality in the eye sockets or brain that might be affecting the alignment of the eyes. You may also have a neurological examination.

What is the treatment?

Treatment of double vision is aimed at the underlying cause. A serious disorder such as an aneurysm may need hospital treatment. Double vision caused by diabetes mellitus will usually disappear over time, but, if it does not, your doctor may advise wearing a patch over one eye to eliminate the second image. Muscle surgery is also useful if double vision has been present for some time.

(WWW) ONLINE SITES: p.1031, p.1035

(TEST) VISUAL FIELD TEST

Visual field testing (perimetry) is used to check the whole area that each eye can see (the visual field). The development of blank sections in the visual field may be caused by various underlying disorders (*see* Visual field defects, right). Many eye disorders cause characteristic visual field defects that can develop without being noticed. Testing allows early detection and treatment.

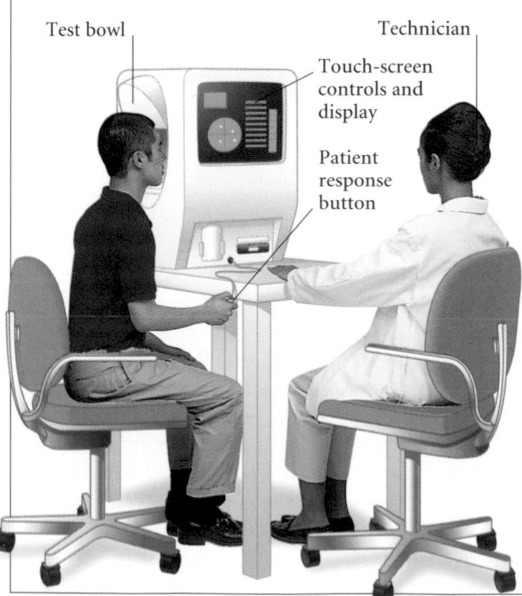
Test bowl
Technician
Touch-screen controls and display
Patient response button

Visual field test
One eye is covered while you look at a central target inside the test bowl. When you see lights flashing in different parts of your visual field, you press a response button.

(RESULTS)

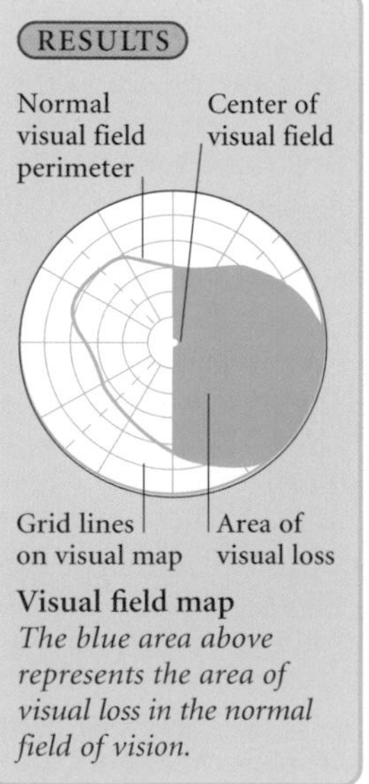
Normal visual field perimeter
Center of visual field
Grid lines on visual map
Area of visual loss

Visual field map
The blue area above represents the area of visual loss in the normal field of vision.

Visual field defects

Loss of part of the normal area of vision in one or both eyes

Age Gender Genetics Lifestyle
Risk factors depend on the cause

Visual field defects take different forms, ranging from loss of areas at the outer edges of vision (peripheral vision) or small blind spots to loss of most of the area that you normally see (the visual field). If you notice a loss of vision, you should seek urgent medical advice because visual field defects sometimes indicate a serious underlying disorder. Regular vision tests (p.587) are important because visual field defects may develop slowly without being noticed.

What are the causes?

Visual field defects may be caused by damage to the light-sensitive retina at the back of the eye; the optic nerve, which carries nerve signals from the retina to the brain; or the parts of the brain involved with vision.

Several eye disorders cause characteristic patterns of visual field loss. For example, the gradual increase in fluid pressure in the eye (*see* Chronic glaucoma, p.576) can damage nerve fibers in the retina, causing loss of peripheral vision. If glaucoma is left untreated, only a narrow area of central vision will remain (tunnel vision). Inflammation of the optic nerve (*see* Optic neuritis, p.581) can cause various visual field defects, and a pituitary tumor (p.676) often causes loss of the outer half of the visual field in each eye. Brain damage due to a stroke (p.532) or tumor (*see* Brain tumor, p.530) may result in loss of the right or left half of the visual field in both eyes. Migraine (p.518) can cause temporary visual field defects.

WHAT ARE THE SYMPTOMS?

Visual field defects usually appear gradually and often remain unnoticed. In other cases, depending on the type of defect, symptoms may include:

- Bumping into objects on one side.
- Missing whole sections of text while you are reading.
- Being able to see only straight ahead (tunnel vision).

The majority of visual field defects can be detected during routine vision tests. However, you should see your doctor immediately if you notice a change in your normal field of vision.

WHAT MIGHT BE DONE?

Your doctor may carry out a visual field test (opposite page) to assess the pattern and extent of the defect.

The treatment for the defect depends on the underlying cause. For example, if you have chronic glaucoma, you will be given drugs to reduce the pressure in the eye (*see* DRUGS FOR GLAUCOMA, p.920). Existing defects are usually permanent, but treatment of the underlying condition may prevent further deterioration. Many people who have a visual field defect become used to it, but it may affect their lifestyle or choice of occupation. For example, if you have tunnel vision, you should not drive.

(WWW) ONLINE SITES: p.1031, p.1035

Eyestrain

Temporary discomfort or aching in or around the eyes

 AGE GENDER GENETICS LIFESTYLE Not significant factors

Eyestrain is neither a medical term nor a diagnosis. In contrast to widespread belief, you cannot damage or strain your eyes by using them under difficult conditions, such as reading small print in poor light or wearing glasses of the wrong strength. Although aching and discomfort are commonly attributed to eyestrain, they are often headaches that are caused by tension or fatigue of the muscles around the eye as a result of frowning or squinting.

The symptoms normally attributed to eyestrain do not require treatment and normally disappear on their own, but, if the problem worsens or persists, you should consult your doctor.

Color blindness

Below-normal ability to distinguish between colors

 AGE Usually present from birth

 GENDER More common in males

 GENETICS Usually due to an abnormal gene inherited from the mother

 LIFESTYLE Not a significant factor

Color blindness is the reduced ability to tell certain colors apart. It is due to a defect in the cones, the specialized cells in the light-sensitive retina at the back of the eye. There are three types of cone cells, each of which is sensitive to blue, green, or red light. If one or more type of cell is faulty, color blindness results. Color blindness is usually inherited.

WHAT ARE THE TYPES?

The most common type of color blindness, red–green color blindness, affects far more males than females, and may take one of two forms. In one form, people cannot distinguish between pale reds, greens, oranges, and browns. The other form makes shades of red appear dull and indistinct. Red–green color blindness is caused by an abnormal gene carried on the X chromosome. It mainly affects men because women have a second X chromosome that usually masks the effect of the abnormal gene (*see* GENE DISORDERS, p.269). However, the abnormal gene may be passed on by women to their children.

Another, much rarer, type of color blindness makes it difficult to distinguish between blues and yellows. This form of the condition can be inherited, but because it is not linked to the X chromosome, it affects both females and males in equal numbers. Macular degeneration (p.580) and other eye disorders may cause color blindness. The toxic effects of various drugs, including chloroquine (*see* ANTIMALARIAL DRUGS, p.888), may also cause color blindness.

WHAT MIGHT BE DONE?

Color blindness is usually noticed during routine vision testing in childhood (*see* VISION TESTS IN CHILDREN, p.857). It may also be detected during medical tests for jobs requiring normal color vision, such as flying airplanes. The test is done by checking your ability to see numbers in patterns of colored dots.

Color blindness rarely causes serious problems. Inherited forms are untreatable, but, if the condition is caused by eye disorders or drugs, the underlying cause can sometimes be treated.

(WWW) ONLINE SITES: p.1031, p.1032

Blindness

Severe to total loss of vision that cannot be rectified by corrective lenses

 AGE GENDER GENETICS LIFESTYLE Risk factors depend on the cause

Complete or almost complete loss of sight, usually termed blindness, affects at least 40 million people worldwide. The risk of blindness increases with age, with 1 in 9 adults experiencing a vision loss by age 65. The condition can be present from birth (*see* CONGENITAL BLINDNESS, p.856).

WHAT ARE THE CAUSES?

Blindness may be caused by disorders of the eyes, the nerves that connect the eyes to the brain, or the areas of the brain that process visual information.

In developed countries, blindness most often results from damage to the light-sensitive retina due to diabetic retinopathy (p.579) or macular degeneration (p.580), elevated fluid pressure in the eye due to glaucoma (p.575), or clouding of the lens due to cataracts (p.573). In developing countries, the most common causes of blindness are the eye infection trachoma (p.572) and vitamin A deficiency (*see* XEROPHTHALMIA, p.585).

WHAT MIGHT BE DONE?

Early diagnosis can help some underlying disorders that cause blindness to be treated to preserve vision. For example, if you have glaucoma, you will be given drugs to reduce the pressure in the eye (*see* DRUGS FOR GLAUCOMA, p.920).

If you are legally blind or visually handicapped, you should check if you are eligible for certain benefits and services. You may also find that visual aids, such as magnifying glasses, are helpful when you are carrying out some of your daily tasks.

(WWW) ONLINE SITES: p.1031

The cochlea in the inner ear
Resembling the shell of a snail, the cochlea is a coiled tubular structure in the inner part of the ear. The central duct of the cochlea contains the spiral organ of Corti, the receptor for hearing.

EARS, HEARING, AND BALANCE

OUR EARS PROVIDE US with two vital but very different senses: hearing and balance. Sound detected by the ears provides essential information about our external surroundings and allows us to communicate in highly sophisticated ways, such as through speech and music. In addition, our ears contribute to our sense of balance, the largely unconscious understanding of the body's orientation in space that allows us to maintain an upright posture and move without falling over.

The ear contains separate organs of hearing and balance, which detect sound from the world around us and internal information about our posture and movement. Sensory structures inside our ears convert the different forms of information into nerve impulses, which travel along nerves to various parts of the brain where the information is analyzed. Our ability to interpret sounds and use information about balance develops during infancy and childhood.

THE QUALITIES OF SOUND

Sound is actually a vibration of the molecules in the air all around us. The pitch of a noise (how "high" or "low" it sounds) is determined by a property of sound waves called the frequency. Frequency is the number of vibrations per second and is measured in units called hertz (Hz). The higher the frequency, the higher the pitch.

The intensity or loudness of a sound depends on the power of the sound waves and is measured in units called decibels (dB). For every 10 dB increase in power, our ears hear double the loudness, so noises at 90 dB sound twice as loud as those at only 80 dB. Conversation is typically about 60 dB, and sound from nearby traffic is usually about 80 dB. Even brief exposure to noises over 120 dB can damage our hearing.

We all vary in the acuity of our hearing (how loud a sound has to be for us to hear it) and in our ability to analyze complex sounds such as music. The human ear can normally detect sounds with frequencies between about 30 Hz and 20,000 Hz, but our ability to hear high-frequency sounds tends to decline with age. Animals such as bats and dogs can hear sounds with frequencies much higher than the normal human range.

BALANCE AND MOVEMENT

The structures of the inner ear that are concerned with balance have two functions: awareness of the head's orientation – where it is in space – and detection of the head's rotation and movement in all directions. The brain combines information from the ears with that from position sensors in the muscles, tendons, and joints and visual information from the eyes. Taken together, this information enables us to move in many different ways without losing our balance.

(STRUCTURE) CONNECTING PASSAGEWAYS

Although the ears may appear to be isolated structures, they are directly linked to the nose and throat. The visible part of the ear, the pinna, is connected to the ear canal, which ends at the eardrum. Beyond this membrane lies the middle ear, an air-filled space connected to the back of the nasal cavity and to the throat by a channel called the eustachian tube. This tube ensures that the air pressure is the same on both sides of the eardrum. The structures of the inner ear lie deep within the skull and contain the sensory organs for sound and balance.

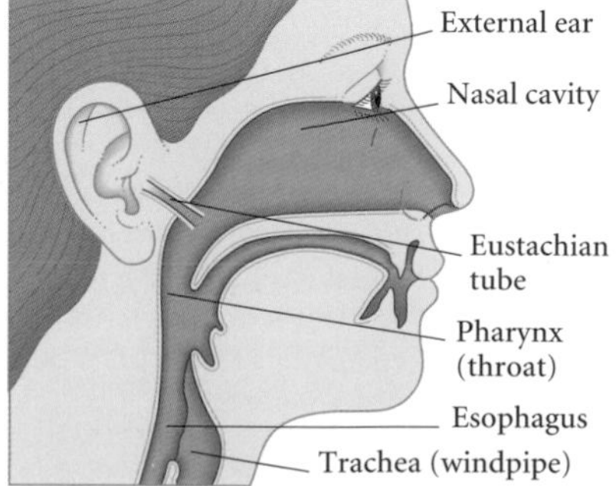
External ear
Nasal cavity
Eustachian tube
Pharynx (throat)
Esophagus
Trachea (windpipe)

Link between the ear, nose, and throat
The eustachian tube connects the ear to the nasal cavity and throat and maintains equal air pressure on both sides of the eardrum.

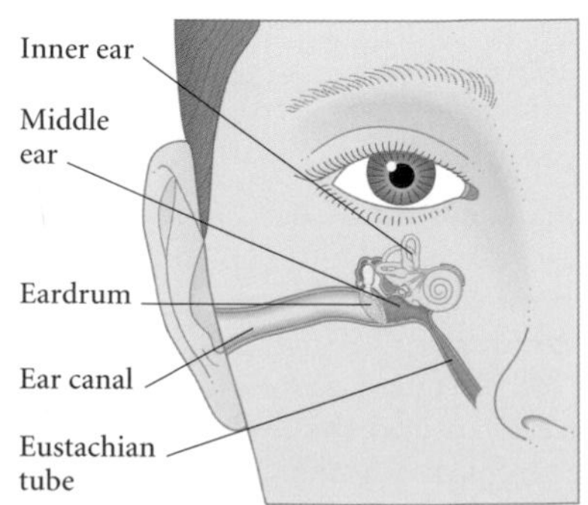
Inner ear
Middle ear
Eardrum
Ear canal
Eustachian tube

Internal components of the ear
The ear canal runs from the external ear to the middle and inner ear, which are situated inside the skull.

STRUCTURE Components of the ear

The ear is made up of the outer, middle, and inner ear. The outer ear consists of the visible pinna and the ear canal. This air-filled tube ends at the eardrum, which vibrates in response to sound. Beyond the eardrum lies the middle ear, also filled with air, which contains three tiny bones called the auditory ossicles – the malleus, incus, and stapes. These bones transmit vibrations from the eardrum to the membrane of the oval window, which separates the middle ear from the inner ear. In the fluid-filled inner ear is the cochlea, which contains the sensory receptor for hearing together with other structures that detect movement and balance.

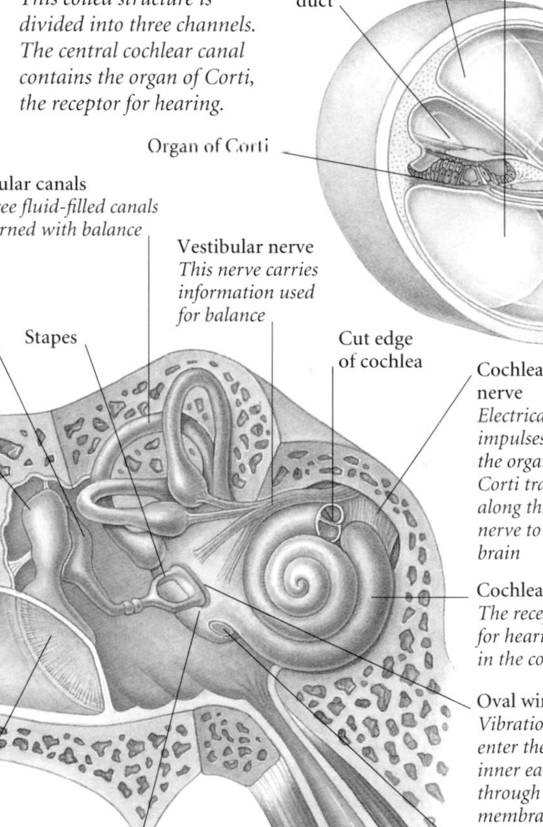
Outer ear
The pinna and ear canal are parts of the outer ear
Inner ear
This contains the cochlea and semicircular canals
Middle ear
The auditory ossicles transmit sound across this space
LOCATION
Cochlea
This coiled structure is divided into three channels. The central cochlear canal contains the organ of Corti, the receptor for hearing.
Cochlear duct
Vestibular canal
Tympanic canal
Organ of Corti
Cartilage
The ear's pinna derives shape and strength from the cartilage inside it
Muscle
Skull bone
Semicircular canals
These three fluid-filled canals are concerned with balance
Vestibular nerve
This nerve carries information used for balance
Incus
This is the middle of the three bones in the middle ear
Stapes
Malleus
Cut edge of cochlea
Cochlear nerve
Electrical impulses from the organ of Corti travel along this nerve to the brain
Cochlea
The receptor for hearing lies in the cochlea
Oval window
Vibrations enter the inner ear through this membrane
Eardrum
This membrane separates the outer ear from the middle ear
Vestibule
Structures in this fluid-filled cavity detect the head's position
Round window
Vibrations leave the cochlea of the inner ear through this membrane.
Ear canal
Sound waves travel down this channel to the eardrum
Eustachian tube
This connects the middle ear to the back of the nose and throat
Ear canal
Malleus
This bone is visible through the eardrum
Eardrum
Pinna
The pinna is shaped to funnel sound waves into the ear canal

Eardrum
Sound causes this membrane to vibrate. These vibrations pass to the malleus, a tiny bone in the middle ear.

Stapes
This stirrup-shaped bone is one of the three tiny bones in the middle ear. It is the smallest bone in the body.

OUTER- AND MIDDLE-EAR DISORDERS

The outer ear consists of the visible part called the pinna, which is composed of skin and cartilage, and the ear canal, the channel that leads to the eardrum. Behind the eardrum is the air-filled middle ear, which contains three tiny, delicate bones. The middle ear is directly linked to the respiratory system by the eustachian tube, the passage connecting the ear to the nose and throat.

This section covers disorders of the visible parts of the ear and of the ear canal, followed by conditions that affect the eardrum and middle ear. Outer- and middle-ear disorders have a number of causes, including injury, infections, obstruction, damage from atmospheric pressure changes, and inherited disease. The symptoms of these disorders include irritation, discomfort, pain, and, in some cases, partial hearing loss.

Most outer- and middle- ear problems are more easily treatable than those affecting the inner ear and are less likely to lead to permanent loss of hearing. Most causes of hearing loss are covered elsewhere (*see* HEARING AND INNER-EAR DISORDERS, pp.599–605), as are disorders of the middle ear that particularly affect children (*see* ACUTE OTITIS MEDIA IN CHILDREN, p.860, and CHRONIC SECRETORY OTITIS MEDIA, p.860).

KEY ANATOMY

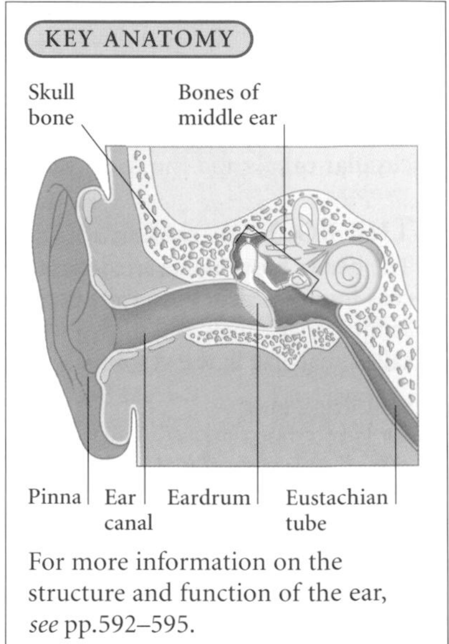
Skull bone
Bones of middle ear
Pinna
Ear canal
Eardrum
Eustachian tube

For more information on the structure and function of the ear, *see* pp.592–595.

Outer-ear injury

Damage to the visible part of the ear, sometimes leading to deformity

LIFESTYLE Playing contact sports is a risk factor

AGE GENDER GENETICS Not significant factors

If the visible part of the outer ear is injured, blood may collect between the skin of the ear and its underlying cartilage, leading to pain and swelling. The collected blood (hematoma) may cut off the supply of blood to the cartilage, which may break down and be gradually replaced by scar tissue. Severe or repeated injury may result in a "cauliflower ear," a deformity that sometimes occurs in boxers and other athletes.

You can reduce the discomfort of an injured ear by applying an ice pack. If the ear is severely swollen, you should consult your doctor. He or she may drain a hematoma under local anesthesia or apply a pressure bandage to help reduce swelling. Plastic surgery may be necessary to correct a deformity.

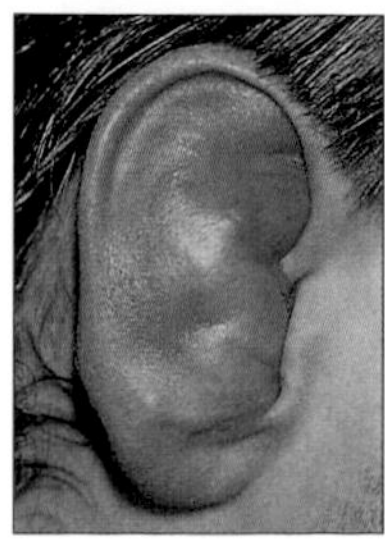

Outer-ear injury *The visible part of this ear is swollen and distorted due to a large collection of blood under the skin. The injury was caused by a blow to the ear.*

When playing contact sports, make sure you wear headgear to protect your ears (*see* EXERCISING SAFELY, p.59).

WWW ONLINE SITES: p.1030, p.1036

Otitis externa

Inflammation of the ear canal, commonly known as "swimmer's ear"

LIFESTYLE Swimming or wearing a hearing aid or earplugs are risk factors

AGE GENDER GENETICS Not significant factors

In otitis externa, the ear canal becomes inflamed, usually because of bacterial, viral, or fungal infection. Otitis externa often develops after swimming because persistent moisture within the ear canal increases the risk of infection. The condition can also affect people who work in a hot and humid environment or who wear a hearing aid or earplugs. Scratching the ear with a cotton swab or fingernail is another cause of otitis externa. Less commonly, the infection occurs as a reaction to chemicals such as those in eardrops or hair dye.

WHAT ARE THE SYMPTOMS?

The symptoms of otitis externa usually appear over 1–2 days and may include:

- Itching and/or pain within the ear canal at the affected site.
- Discharge of pus from the ear.

If pus blocks the canal, see your doctor rather than trying to remove it yourself.

WHAT MIGHT BE DONE?

Your doctor will examine your ear with an otoscope (*see* OTOSCOPY, opposite page). If there is pus present, indicating infection, he or she may take a swab to identify the organism responsible. The ear canal may also be cleaned out using a suction device. Depending on the type of infection present, your doctor may prescribe eardrops that contain an antibiotic or antifungal and/or a corticosteroid (*see* DRUGS ACTING ON THE EAR, p.921). An oral analgesic (p.912) may be given to relieve pain.

If you have a severe bacterial infection, your doctor may prescribe oral antibiotics (p.885). Most viral infections are treated solely with analgesics. However, if the condition is caused by the herpes virus, you may be prescribed an oral antiviral drug (p.886), sometimes with a corticosteroid (p.930). The disorder usually clears up in a few days.

WWW ONLINE SITES: p.1030, p.1033

Wax blockage

Blockage of the ear canal by earwax, often causing a feeling of fullness and irritation in the ear

AGE GENDER GENETICS LIFESTYLE Not significant factors

Earwax, produced by glands in the ear canal, cleans and moistens the canal. Usually, wax is produced in small quantities and emerges naturally from the ear. However, if the canal becomes blocked with wax, it causes a feeling of fullness and discomfort and sometimes hearing loss. A common cause of wax blockage is insertion of a cotton swab or finger into the canal in an attempt to remove the wax. This action usually pushes the wax deeper into the canal. Excessive secretion of wax may also lead to blockage.

Wax blockage can be treated with over-the-counter eardrops, which usually dissolve the earwax in about 4–10 days. If the ear remains blocked, you should consult your doctor. He or she will probably use a viewing instrument to inspect the ear canal (*see* OTOSCOPY, right). You may have the wax removed with a probe or suction device, or the ear may be gently flushed out with warm water from a syringe. Wax blockage sometimes recurs after treatment.

(WWW) ONLINE SITES: p.1030

Otitis media

Inflammation of the middle ear, usually as a result of a bacterial or viral infection

AGE More common in children but can occur at any age

GENDER GENETICS LIFESTYLE Not significant factors

In otitis media, tissues lining the middle ear are inflamed, and pus and fluid accumulate in the middle ear, causing pain and partial hearing loss. The condition occurs when a viral infection, such as a common cold (p.286) or influenza (p.287), or a bacterial infection spreads from the throat to the middle ear. The infection may cause a ruptured eardrum (right). Otitis media is common in children because their eustachian tubes, which connect the ear to the back of the nose and throat and ventilate the middle ear, are immature and may easily be blocked by large structures, such as adenoids (*see* ACUTE OTITIS MEDIA IN CHILDREN, p.860). In some children, a sticky fluid persistently collects in the middle ear, impairing hearing (*see* CHRONIC SECRETORY OTITIS MEDIA, p.860).

WHAT ARE THE SYMPTOMS?

The symptoms of otitis media often develop over a few hours and include:

- Pain in the ear, which may be severe.
- Partial hearing loss.
- Fever.

If the eardrum ruptures, there may be a bloodstained discharge from the ear and a decrease in pain. Untreated otitis media may become a chronic infection with a constant discharge of pus from the ear. Rarely, the infection results in a cholesteatoma, a collection of skin cells and debris, in the middle ear. This complication may damage the middle ear and rarely the inner ear, causing permanent loss of hearing.

WHAT MIGHT BE DONE?

Your doctor will examine your ear with an otoscope (*see* OTOSCOPY, below) to check if your eardrum is inflamed and if there is pus in the middle ear. You may be prescribed oral antibiotics (p.885) and may be given analgesics (p.912) to relieve pain. In most cases, the pain subsides in a few days, but mild hearing loss may sometimes last for a week or two in adults, longer in children. If a cholesteatoma has developed, it is usually necessary for it to be removed by surgery.

(WWW) ONLINE SITES: p.1030, p.1033

Ruptured eardrum

A tear or hole in the membrane between the outer and middle ear

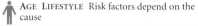

AGE LIFESTYLE Risk factors depend on the cause

GENDER GENETICS Not significant factors

Rupture of the eardrum most commonly results from an acute bacterial infection of the middle ear (*see* OTITIS MEDIA, left). Pus or other fluid produced by the infection builds up inside the middle ear and eventually bursts through the eardrum. Less commonly, a rupture occurs when an object, such as a cotton swab or hairpin, is poked into the ear. In some cases, the eardrum suddenly ruptures because there is an imbalance between the pressures inside the middle ear and the outer ear. Such an imbalance of pressure in different parts of the ear may occur after a blow to the ear, an explosion, a head injury (p.521), or when flying or diving (*see* BAROTRAUMA, p.598).

WHAT ARE THE SYMPTOMS?

The symptoms usually last for only a few hours and may include:

- Sudden, sometimes intense pain in the affected ear.
- Bloodstained discharge from the ear.
- Partial hearing loss.

If you suspect that you have a ruptured eardrum, keep the affected ear dry and consult your doctor as soon as possible.

(TEST) OTOSCOPY

The ear canal and eardrum can be examined directly by using an otoscope, a viewing instrument that illuminates and magnifies the inside of the ear. Otoscopy is used to diagnose disorders such as otitis media (left) and ruptured eardrum (above).

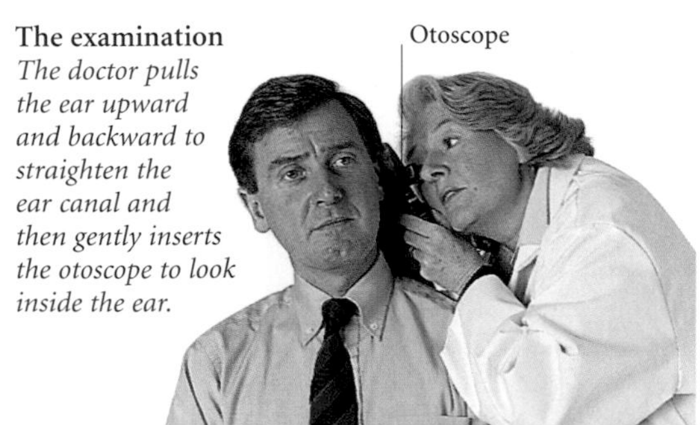
Otoscope

The examination
The doctor pulls the ear upward and backward to straighten the ear canal and then gently inserts the otoscope to look inside the ear.

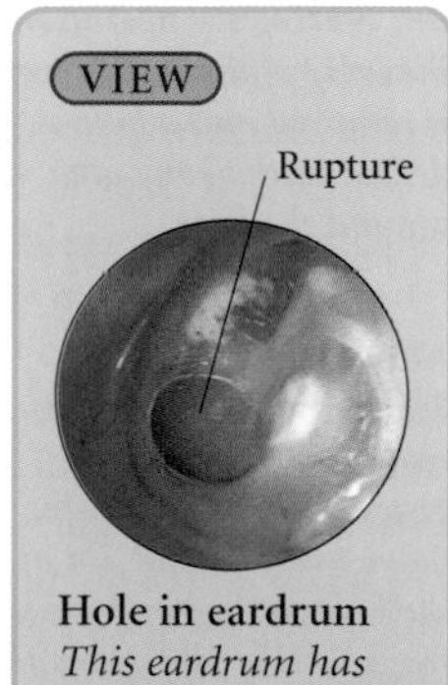
VIEW
Rupture

Hole in eardrum
This eardrum has ruptured as a result of a long-standing bacterial infection of the middle ear.

TEST HEARING TESTS

Your doctor may recommend hearing tests if you have difficulty hearing speech or if you work in a noisy environment. He or she may perform some of the tests in the office and may refer you to a hearing specialist for others. Some tests determine the type of hearing loss, while others assess how well you can hear sounds of varying frequency and volume. The screening of school-age children or any child with speech delay is appropriate (*see* HEARING TESTS IN CHILDREN, p.859).

PRELIMINARY TESTS

A tuning fork is used to distinguish conductive hearing loss, due to a disorder of the outer or middle ear, from sensorineural loss, caused by a disorder of the inner ear or of the nerves or parts of the brain that process auditory information.

Vibrating tuning fork

Weber test
A vibrating tuning fork is held against your forehead. If you have conductive hearing loss, the sound will seem louder in the more affected ear. In sensorineural loss, it is louder in the less affected ear.

Vibrating tuning fork

Rinne test
A vibrating tuning fork is held near your ear and then against a bone behind the ear. If it sounds louder in the second position, you have conductive hearing loss. If it is louder in the first position, either the ear is healthy or the hearing loss is sensorineural.

TYMPANOMETRY

Detailed information about the movements of the eardrum and bones of the middle ear in response to sound can be obtained by tympanometry. The test can also differentiate between different types of hearing loss. Unlike other hearing tests, the results do not depend on your responses and are therefore highly reliable.

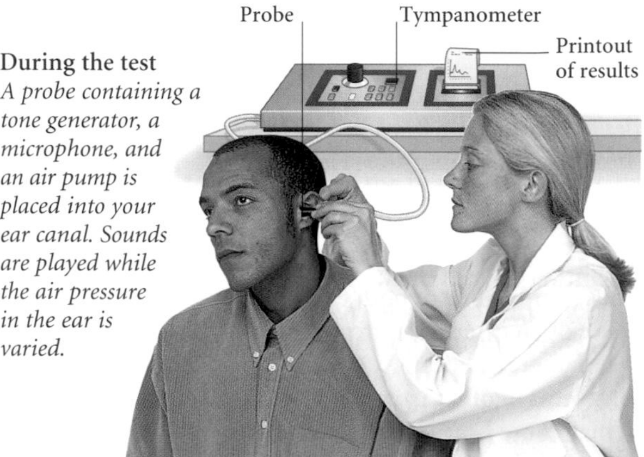
Probe
Tympanometer
Printout of results

During the test
A probe containing a tone generator, a microphone, and an air pump is placed into your ear canal. Sounds are played while the air pressure in the ear is varied.

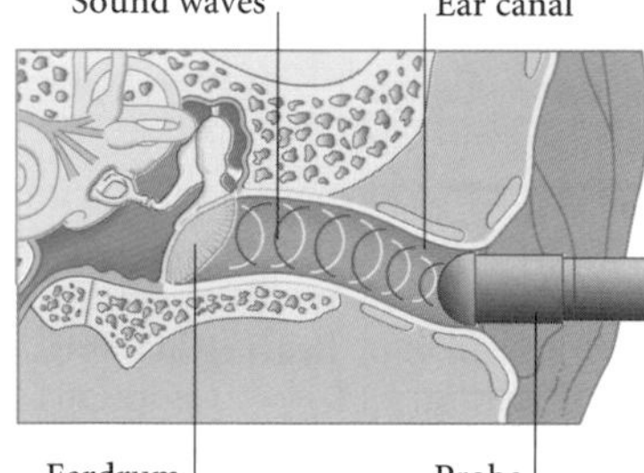
Sound waves
Ear canal
Eardrum
Probe

How the test works
The sounds bounce off the eardrum and are picked up by a microphone. The pattern of reflected sound varies at different air pressures and shows whether the eardrum is moving normally.

AUDIOMETRY

This test measures how loud a sound has to be for you to hear it. Sounds of varying frequency are transmitted to one ear at a time through headphones. For each frequency, the volume is increased until you hear it, and the results are charted. The test is repeated with a speaker held against a bone behind the ear.

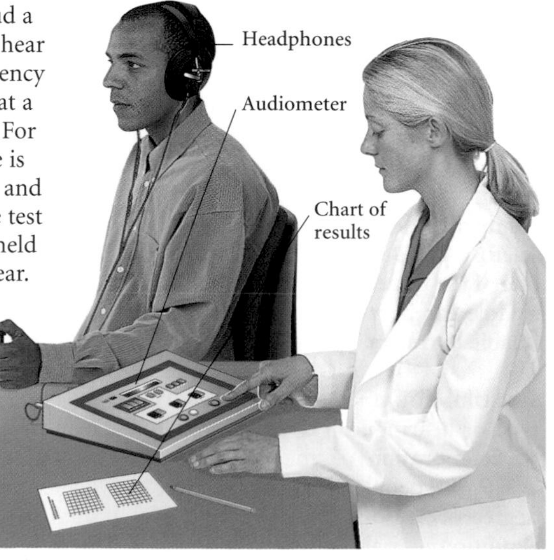
Headphones
Audiometer
Chart of results
Response button

During the test
You will be asked to press a button when you hear a sound in either ear. The softest sound that you can hear at each frequency will be charted.

RESULTS

HEARING LOSS (dB): -20, 0, 20, 40, 60, 80, 100
FREQUENCY (hertz): 125, 250, 500, 1000, 2000, 4000, 8000
Left ear
Right ear

Audiometry trace
This tracing is from a person with normal hearing in the left ear and sensorineural hearing loss in the right. At higher frequencies, the right ear can detect sound only if the sound level is much higher than normal.

TREATMENT HEARING AIDS

Hearing aids amplify sounds, improving hearing in people with most types of hearing loss. These devices have a tiny microphone, amplifier, and speaker, all powered by batteries. The range of sounds amplified by a hearing aid is tailored to the individual's pattern of hearing loss.

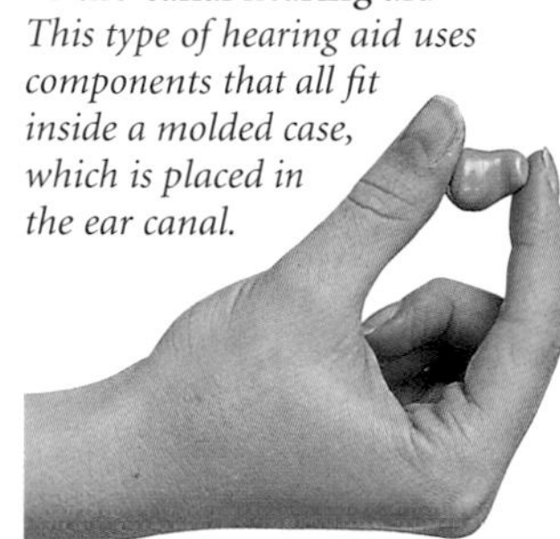

In-the-canal hearing aid
This type of hearing aid uses components that all fit inside a molded case, which is placed in the ear canal.

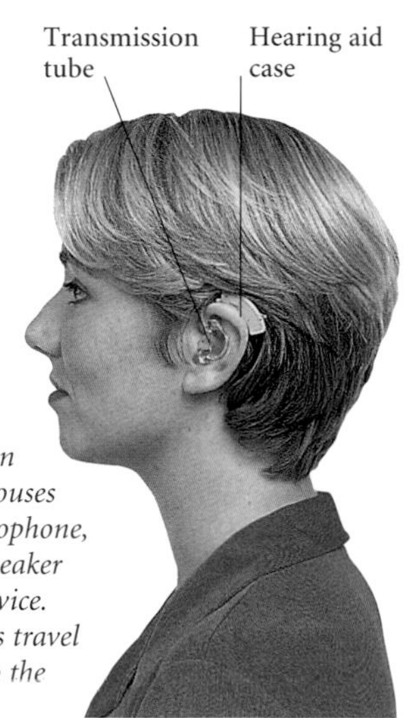
Transmission tube
Hearing aid case

Behind-the-ear hearing aid
A small case worn behind the ear houses the battery, microphone, amplifier, and speaker of this type of device. Amplified sounds travel along a tube into the ear canal.

Presbycusis

Gradual loss of hearing that develops as a natural part of aging

 AGE More common over age 50

 GENDER More common in males

 GENETICS Sometimes runs in families

 LIFESTYLE Prior damage due to excessive noise exposure may increase the severity

Many people over age 50 notice that they cannot hear quiet or high-pitched sounds very well and that conversation is sometimes hard to understand, particularly in the presence of background noise, such as music. Over a period of years, sounds of all pitches may become increasingly difficult to hear. This progressive decline in hearing is known as presbycusis and is a common feature of the normal process of aging.

Presbycusis occurs in about 1 in 5 people aged 50–60, 1 in 3 people aged 60–70, and half of all people over age 70. The condition is more common and severe in men and may run in families.

WHAT ARE THE CAUSES?

The body's sensory receptor for hearing, located within the cochlea in the inner ear, is lined with sensory hair cells. Presbycusis occurs when these sensory hair cells degenerate and die with age. The condition is sometimes more severe in people whose hearing has already been damaged by exposure to excessive levels of noise (see NOISE-INDUCED HEARING LOSS, right).

WHAT ARE THE SYMPTOMS?

The symptoms of presbycusis develop gradually, often over many years, and may include:

- Loss of hearing, initially of high-pitched sounds and gradually of lower pitches.
- Difficulty hearing speech, especially with noise in the background.
- Loss of sound clarity, so that even loud speech is difficult to understand.
- Tinnitus (p.602), a ringing or buzzing sound in one or both ears.

Both ears are usually affected, although not always equally. The severity and progression of hearing loss vary from person to person. Severe hearing loss sometimes leads to feelings of isolation, loneliness, and depression (p.554).

WHAT MIGHT BE DONE?

Your doctor will examine your ears with a viewing instrument called an otoscope (see OTOSCOPY, p.597) and may arrange for hearing tests to determine the type and degree of hearing loss (see HEARING TESTS, opposite page). There is no cure for presbycusis. However, a hearing aid (above) may greatly improve your ability to hear and communicate, although it may take time to adjust to using one.

WWW ONLINE SITES: p.1026, p.1032

Noise-induced hearing loss

Hearing loss caused by prolonged exposure to excessive noise or by brief exposure to intensely loud noise

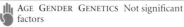

 LIFESTYLE A noisy workplace and using a portable stereo are risk factors

AGE GENDER GENETICS Not significant factors

Persistent exposure to extremely loud noise or a single intensely loud sound can both damage the delicate sensory hair cells that line the receptor for hearing within the inner ear. Temporary or permanent hearing loss may result.

Your risk of noise-induced hearing loss is increased if there is excessive noise in your workplace, if you listen to loud music, or if you regularly attend rock concerts. A single excessively loud noise, such as an explosion, may cause immediate hearing loss and can also lead to a ruptured eardrum (p.597).

A few simple steps, such as using earplugs, can reduce your risk of noise-induced hearing loss (see PROTECTING YOUR HEARING, p.602).

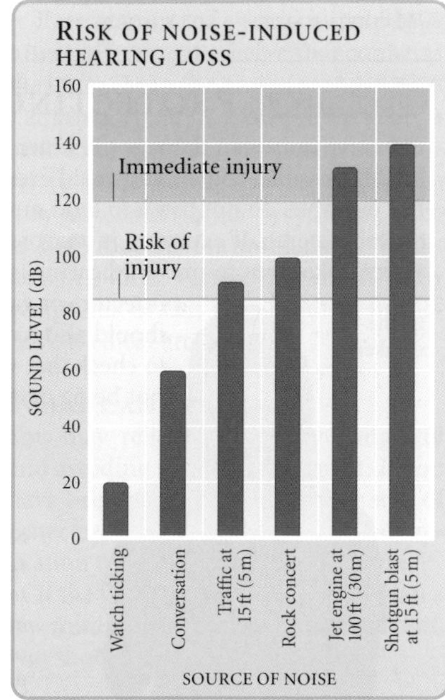
RISK OF NOISE-INDUCED HEARING LOSS
SOUND LEVEL (dB)
160
140
120
100
80
60
40
20
0
Immediate injury
Risk of injury
Watch ticking
Conversation
Traffic at 15 ft (5 m)
Rock concert
Jet engine at 100 ft (30 m)
Shotgun blast at 15 ft (5 m)
SOURCE OF NOISE

Noise levels and damage to hearing
The intensity of sound is measured in decibels (dB). A 10 dB increase doubles the loudness, so that 90 dB sounds twice as loud as 80 dB. As shown in this graph, noises above 85 dB can damage hearing.

check the function of the vestibular apparatus. A neck X-ray (p.244) may be done to look for cervical spondylitis. If you also have tinnitus, you may have CT scanning (p.247) or MRI (p.248) to rule out a tumor pressing on the brain.

Your doctor may recommend drugs to relieve the symptoms of vertigo (*see* ANTIEMETIC DRUGS, p.922, and ANTIHISTAMINES, p.906). If vertigo is a side effect of an antibiotic, you may be given an alternative drug. Other treatment will be aimed at the underlying cause. Rarely, vertigo is caused by a bacterial infection of the vestibular apparatus and may be treated with antibiotics.

(WWW) ONLINE SITES: p.1035

Motion sickness

A range of symptoms, generally including nausea, caused by motion during travel by road, sea, or air

 AGE Can occur at any age; most common in children aged 3–12

 GENDER GENETICS LIFESTYLE Not significant factors

Most people experience some degree of motion sickness at some time in their lives. The condition is especially common in children. Motion sickness occurs when the brain receives messages from the organs of balance in the inner ear and from the eyes that conflict with one another. For example, when you travel in a vehicle, the inner ear senses the motion, but, if you look at the interior of the vehicle, the eyes may perceive it as still. The conflicting messages that the brain receives may lead to a feeling of nausea.

WHAT ARE THE SYMPTOMS?

In its mildest form, motion sickness may produce only a feeling of uneasiness. However, the initial symptoms of motion sickness usually include:

- Nausea.
- Headache and dizziness.
- Lethargy and fatigue.

If the motion continues after the onset of symptoms, the initial symptoms typically get worse and other symptoms, such as pale skin, excessive sweating, yawning, hyperventilation (abnormally deep or rapid breathing), and vomiting may occur. Poor ventilation in the vehicle may make the symptoms worse.

WHAT CAN I DO?

Before traveling, you should eat only small amounts and not drink alcohol. When traveling, you should try to sit in a cool, well-ventilated position. You should also avoid reading or looking at nearby objects. Instead, try to look at the horizon or a distant object in the direction of travel.

There are many drugs, both over-the-counter and prescription, available to prevent or treat motion sickness (*see* ANTIEMETIC DRUGS, p.922, and ANTIHISTAMINES, p.906). To prevent symptoms the medication should be taken before traveling, but, if you are driving, you should avoid certain drugs that may cause drowsiness. Many of these drugs may also increase the effects of alcohol.

Motion sickness remedies based on ginger plant stems, which are thought to prevent nausea, are available in health-food stores. Motion sickness may be reduced by wearing special wristbands that work by acupressure, a method derived from acupuncture (p.973).

(WWW) ONLINE SITES: p.1037

Labyrinthitis

Inflammation of the labyrinth of the inner ear, which contains the organs of balance and the receptor for hearing

 AGE GENDER GENETICS LIFESTYLE Not significant factors

The labyrinth of the inner ear consists of the vestibular apparatus, which is composed of the organs of balance, and the cochlea, which contains the receptor for hearing. Inflammation of the labyrinth, known as labyrinthitis, can therefore affect both balance and hearing. Labyrinthitis can be mild, but more often it is extremely unpleasant. The condition is not painful and rarely has serious consequences.

WHAT ARE THE CAUSES?

The most common cause of labyrinthitis is a viral infection. Viral labyrinthitis may develop as a result of a viral infection of the upper respiratory tract, such as a common cold (p.286) or influenza (p.287). Less commonly, labyrinthitis is due to a bacterial infection, usually a complication of a middle-ear infection (*see* OTITIS MEDIA, p.597) or, rarely, an infection elsewhere in the body.

WHAT ARE THE SYMPTOMS?

The symptoms of labyrinthitis usually develop rapidly and are most severe in the first 24 hours. They may include:

- Dizziness and a loss of balance (*see* VERTIGO, p.603).
- Nausea and vomiting.
- Ringing and buzzing noises in the ears (*see* TINNITUS, p.602).

The symptoms may gradually decrease as the brain compensates for the disturbance to the vestibular apparatus, but you should consult your doctor immediately if you develop symptoms of labyrinthitis. Left untreated, bacterial infection of the labyrinth may cause severe damage to the cochlea, possibly leading to permanent hearing loss, or it may spread to the membranes covering the brain, causing meningitis (p.527).

WHAT MIGHT BE DONE?

Labyrinthitis can be diagnosed from your symptoms. Your doctor may prescribe an antiemetic drug (p.922) to ease the nausea. He or she may also advise you to lie in a darkened room with your eyes closed. Viral labyrinthitis often clears up without specific treatment, but, if you have bacterial labyrinthitis, your doctor will prescribe antibiotics (p.885). It may take several weeks to recover completely from labyrinthitis.

(WWW) ONLINE SITES: p.1030

Ménière's disease

A disorder of the inner ear causing sudden episodes of severe dizziness, nausea, and hearing loss

 AGE Most common between the ages of 20 and 60

 GENETICS Sometimes runs in families

 LIFESTYLE A high-salt diet may increase the frequency of attacks

 GENDER Not a significant factor

Ménière's disease is a rare disorder in which the amount of fluid in the inner ear increases intermittently. The raised pressure in the inner ear disturbs the organs of hearing and balance, causing sudden attacks of distorted hearing and dizziness so severe that the affected person may fall to the ground.

Usually only one ear is affected, but both ears can become involved. The

condition is most common in people aged 20–60 years and sometimes runs in families. The underlying cause of Ménière's disease is unknown, but a high-salt diet may increase the frequency of attacks. The disorder may lead to permanent hearing loss.

WHAT ARE THE SYMPTOMS?

Attacks of Ménière's disease occur suddenly and may last from a few minutes to several days before gradually subsiding. The symptoms may include:

- Sudden, severe dizziness and loss of balance (*see* VERTIGO, p.603).
- Nausea and vomiting.
- Abnormal, jerky eye movements.
- Ringing or buzzing noises in the affected ear (*see* TINNITUS, p.602).
- Loss of hearing, particularly of low-pitched sounds.
- Feeling of pressure or pain in the affected ear.

The time between attacks of Ménière's disease ranges from a few days to years. Tinnitus may be constant or occur only during an attack. Between attacks, vertigo and nausea cease and hearing may improve. With repeated attacks, hearing often deteriorates progressively.

HOW IS IT DIAGNOSED?

Your doctor may arrange for hearing tests (p.600) to assess your hearing loss. He or she may also arrange for a caloric test, in which the ear is filled with water at different temperatures to check the functioning of the organs of balance. Ménière's disease produces symptoms similar to those of a tumor affecting the nerve that connects the ear to the brain (*see* ACOUSTIC NEUROMA, right); your doctor may therefore arrange for you to have tests such as CT scanning (p.247) or MRI (p.248) to rule out a tumor.

WHAT IS THE TREATMENT?

You may be prescribed drugs to relieve nausea (*see* ANTIEMETIC DRUGS, p.922). Your doctor may also recommend an antihistamine (p.906) to give further relief from nausea and vertigo and to reduce the frequency of the episodes. In addition, sedative drugs such as diazepam may be prescribed to relieve vertigo (*see* ANTIANXIETY DRUGS, p.916). In some cases, oral corticosteroids (p.930) and diuretic drugs (p.902) may be used to help prevent further attacks.

There are a few simple steps you can take to help yourself if you have Ménière's disease. During an attack, lie still with your eyes closed and avoid noise, perhaps by wearing earplugs. Between attacks, try to avoid stress. Relaxation techniques and a low-salt diet may also be helpful.

Despite treatment, some people who have Ménière's disease have constant, severe, and disabling vertigo. For these people, the doctor may recommend one of a number of possible surgical approaches to treatment.

WHAT IS THE PROGNOSIS?

The symptoms of Ménière's disease are usually improved with medication. The frequency and severity of the episodes tend to decrease over a period of years. However, hearing usually worsens progressively with each successive attack, and permanent hearing loss may eventually result. If the deafness becomes total, the other symptoms of the disease will usually disappear.

(WWW) ONLINE SITES: p.1030, p.1035

Acoustic neuroma

A noncancerous tumor affecting the vestibulocochlear (acoustic) nerve, which connects the ear to the brain

 AGE Most common between the ages of 40 and 60

 GENETICS One type runs in families

GENDER LIFESTYLE Not significant factors

An acoustic neuroma is a rare tumor affecting the vestibulocochlear (acoustic) nerve, which carries auditory and balance information from part of the inner ear to the brain. The tumor usually affects the vestibulocochlear nerve on one side of the head only, but it may affect both nerves. The tumor is noncancerous but can cause severe nerve and brain damage. If detected early, it can be removed by surgery.

The cause of acoustic neuroma is unknown but, if the tumor affects both acoustic nerves, it may be associated with the inherited condition neurofibromatosis (p.827), in which multiple tumors grow from the sheaths around nerves. Acoustic neuroma is most common between the ages of 40 and 60.

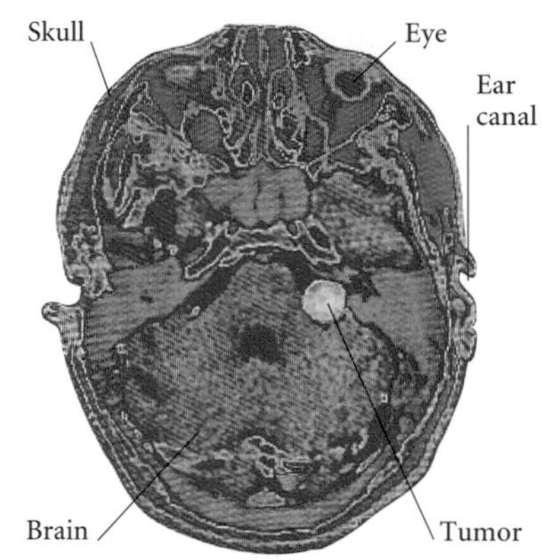
Skull
Eye
Ear canal
Brain
Tumor

Acoustic neuroma
This MRI scan of the head shows an acoustic neuroma, a tumor of the nerve that connects the ear to the brain.

WHAT ARE THE SYMPTOMS?

The symptoms of an acoustic neuroma usually develop slowly, almost always affect only one ear, and may include:

- Progressive hearing loss.
- Ringing or buzzing noises in the ear (*see* TINNITUS, p.602).
- Headache and pain in the ear.
- Dizziness and a loss of balance (*see* VERTIGO, p.603).

An acoustic neuroma is slow-growing, but as it enlarges it may press on part of the brain, causing lack of coordination of body movements. The tumor may also compress the nerves that supply the face, causing weakness of the facial muscles (*see* FACIAL PALSY, p.548) and pain. Left untreated, a neuroma may cause permanent nerve damage.

WHAT MIGHT BE DONE?

If you have symptoms of an acoustic neuroma, your doctor may arrange for imaging tests such as MRI (p.248) to look for a tumor and hearing tests (p.600) to check for hearing loss.

An acoustic neuroma can usually be removed by surgery, and the earlier this treatment is carried out, the better the outcome. Many of the symptoms disappear with surgery, and, if the tumor is small, hearing may be restored in the affected ear. However, removal of a large tumor may damage the vestibulocochlear or facial nerves. If these nerves are damaged, there may be permanent hearing loss in the affected ear, combined with numbness, weakness, or paralysis of part of the face.

(WWW) ONLINE SITES: p.1035

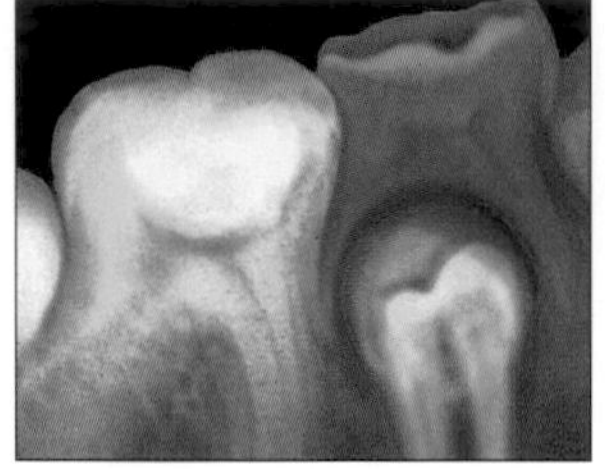

Tooth eruption
In this color-enhanced X-ray of a child's lower jaw, a secondary tooth that has not yet erupted can be seen below a primary tooth.

Teeth and Gums

The primary function of teeth is to break down food ready for digestion. Teeth also help us pronounce sounds clearly and give the face shape and definition. Each of us grows two sets of teeth in a lifetime, the second set gradually replacing the first during childhood. The gums help keep the teeth firmly in the jaw and protect the roots from decay. Both teeth and gums are vulnerable to buildup of plaque (a sticky mixture of bacteria, mucus, and food particles), which causes decay and gum disease.

At the beginning of the 20th century, it was common for people to have lost all of their secondary (adult) teeth by age 60 as a result of tooth decay and gum disease. Today, because of the advances that have been made in dental health care, improvements in nutrition, and widespread fluoridation of water, many people keep their secondary teeth throughout their lives.

The structure of the teeth

The part of the tooth that protrudes from the gum is called the crown; the part beneath the gumline is called the root. The crown is covered with a protective layer of enamel, the hardest substance in the body. Enamel is composed of rod-shaped calcium salt crystals and cannot renew itself. As a result, the enamel may eventually become worn down from abrasion, or it may be damaged by acid present in food and drinks or produced by bacteria in plaque. If the enamel is worn through, a cavity is formed. This can be repaired with a dental filling.

Beneath the enamel layer lies the dentin, a hard ivory-like substance that surrounds the pulp cavity. This central cavity contains nerves and blood vessels that extend through tiny channels into the dentin, making the dentin sensitive to heat, cold, and pain. About two-thirds of a tooth is made up of the root, buried below the gumline in a deep socket in the jaw. Each root is attached to the jawbone by a periodontal ligament, which cushions the root in its socket while the teeth are grinding down food.

Tooth enamel
This magnified image of tooth enamel shows the many tiny, rod-shaped calcium crystals that lie at right angles to the surface of the tooth.

Teeth have various shapes and sizes to enable them to hold, cut, tear, and chew food efficiently. For example, to enable teeth to grind down food effectively, the contoured chewing surfaces of the upper and lower back teeth meet and are similar in shape. The actions of the teeth are controlled by the upper and lower jaws, which are able to clamp the teeth together with great force – up to 7,000 lb/sq. in (500 kg/sq. cm) – with the help of four powerful sets of muscles.

The role of the gums

The bone and periodontal ligaments that support the teeth in the jaw are covered by a layer of protective tissue known as the gums or gingiva. Healthy gums are pink or brown and firm. They form a tight seal around the neck of the tooth, preventing food particles and plaque from invading underlying tissues and the root of the tooth.

STRUCTURE Development of teeth

Our first set of 20 teeth appears between the ages of 6 months and 3 years. These teeth are known as primary, deciduous, or milk teeth. As the jaw grows, a set of 32 secondary (adult or permanent) teeth appears between the ages of 6 and 21. As the secondary teeth erupt, they eventually displace the primary teeth, which usually fall out by age 13. In some cases, the third molars, also known as wisdom teeth, never erupt.

Patterns of eruption
The primary and secondary teeth usually erupt in a specific order (as indicated here by the numbers in parentheses).

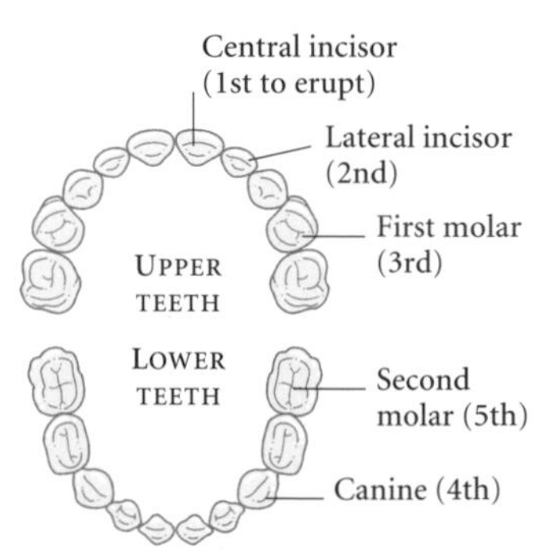

Central incisor (1st to erupt)
Lateral incisor (2nd)
First molar (3rd)
Upper teeth
Lower teeth
Second molar (5th)
Canine (4th)
Primary teeth

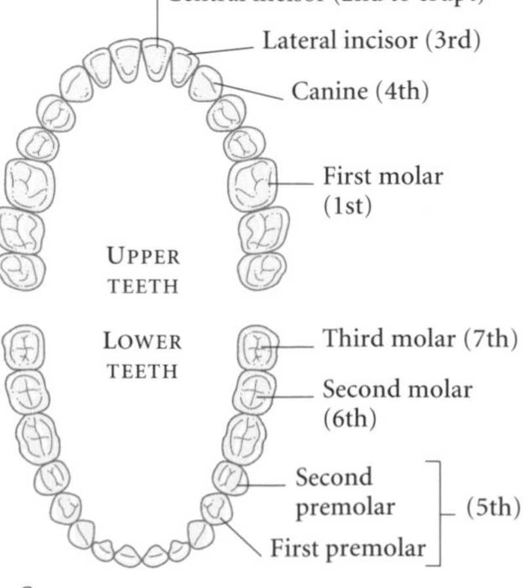
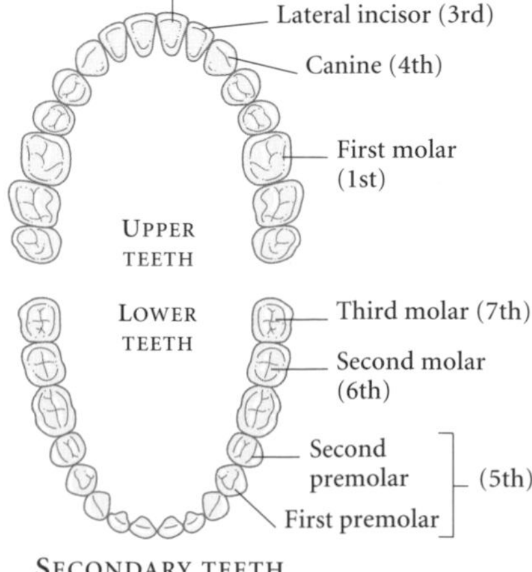

Central incisor (2nd to erupt)
Lateral incisor (3rd)
Canine (4th)
First molar (1st)
Upper teeth
Lower teeth
Third molar (7th)
Second molar (6th)
Second premolar
First premolar
(5th)
Secondary teeth

STRUCTURE TEETH AND GUMS

Teeth vary in shape and size but have an identical structure. Each tooth consists of a hard shell that surrounds a cavity of soft tissue, known as pulp. The crown (the exposed part of the shell) is coated in a tough layer of enamel, beneath which is a layer of a yellowish substance similar to ivory, called dentin. The dentin and pulp form long, pointed roots that extend into the jawbone and are covered by a layer of firm, fleshy tissue called the gums.

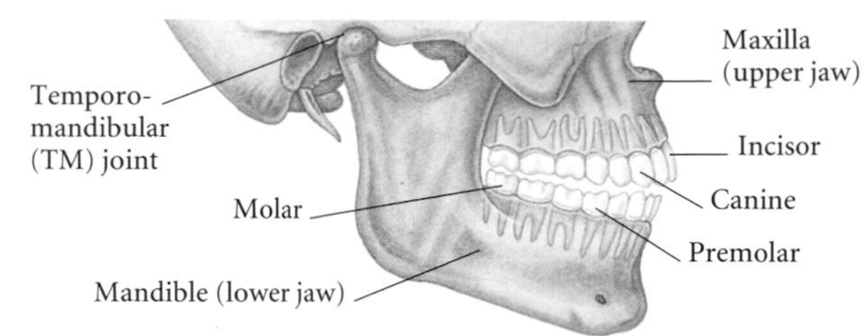

Temporo-mandibular (TM) joint
Maxilla (upper jaw)
Incisor
Canine
Molar
Premolar
Mandible (lower jaw)

SIDE VIEW OF THE JAWS AND TEETH

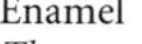

Crown
The crown is the part of the tooth exposed above the gumline

Neck
The part of the tooth that narrows slightly at the gumline is called the neck

Root
The root is the long pointed part of the tooth embedded in the jawbone; incisors and canines have one root, premolars one or two, and molars three or four

Incisor
The sharp chisel-like incisors, situated at the front of the mouth, cut and hold food.

Canine
Canines are longer and more pointed than incisors; they are used for tearing food.

Premolar
Premolars have two prominences (cusps) on their biting surfaces and are used for grinding food.

Molar
Molars, the largest teeth, are used for grinding. They have five or six cusps on their chewing surfaces.

Enamel
The crown is coated in enamel, an insensitive, nonliving substance

Dentin
Dentin is a tough, ivory-like material supplied with blood and nerves from the pulp tissue

Gum (gingiva)
This layer of protective tissue fits tightly around the base of the crown and covers the roots of the tooth

Pulp
At the center of a tooth lies the soft pulp tissue, containing nerves and blood vessels

Periodontal ligament
This ligament joins the tooth to the jawbone and gums

Cementum
This layer of hard tissue covers the roots and anchors the fibers of the periodontal ligament

Jawbone
Deep sockets in the jawbone encase the roots of the tooth

Nerve
Nerves supply the periodontal ligament, pulp, gums, and jaw

Blood vessel
These blood vessels supply nutrients to the pulp tissue, bone, and gums

FUNCTION USING THE JAWS

The actions of biting and chewing require the lower jaw to move in all directions. This range of movement is made possible by the temporomandibular joint, a complex but exceptionally flexible type of hinge joint that attaches the lower jaw to the skull.

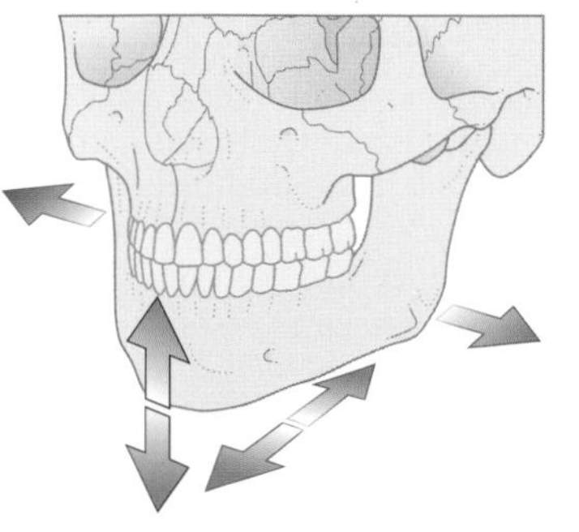

Moving the lower jaw
The lower jaw moves in six directions, side to side, up and down, and backward and forward. This mobility is essential for biting off and chewing food.

The upper surface of a molar
This magnified image shows the normal undulations on the chewing surface of a molar tooth.

Disorders of the Teeth

Teeth are necessary for chopping food into small pieces to make digestion easier. Each person has two sets of teeth: the primary teeth, which emerge in infancy, and the secondary teeth, which gradually replace the primary teeth in late childhood. Both sets are protected from damage and decay by a hard coating of enamel and by the gums, which cover the roots.

Good oral hygiene is essential because without regular brushing and flossing of the teeth and gums, tooth disease may develop. Improved oral hygiene and the addition of fluoride to water in many parts of the world in order to harden teeth have made tooth disease far less common today than it was several decades ago.

The first articles in this section deal with tooth disorders that are usually caused by neglect of oral hygiene, such as toothache and tooth decay. If left untreated, tooth decay may spread to the central parts of the teeth and cause pulpitis. Pus may eventually build up at the root of a tooth due to infection, resulting in a dental abscess. Poor oral hygiene can also cause teeth to become discolored. Malocclusion caused by teeth that have grown unevenly or become overcrowded is covered next. Sometimes teeth are missing, or are broken or lost due to injury. Problems of the temporomandibular joint are covered in the last article of this section. Teething (p.819) in babies is discussed in the children's section.

KEY ANATOMY

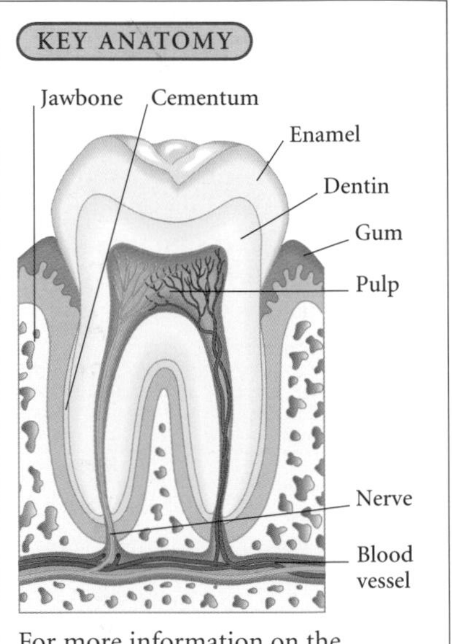
Jawbone
Cementum
Enamel
Dentin
Gum
Pulp
Nerve
Blood vessel

For more information on the structure and function of teeth, *see* pp.606–607.

Toothache

Pain or discomfort in one or more teeth or in the gums

LIFESTYLE Poor oral hygiene and a diet high in sugar are risk factors

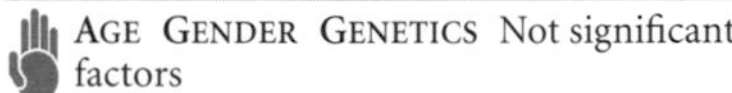

AGE GENDER GENETICS Not significant factors

Pain in one or more teeth is usually a symptom of an underlying problem with the teeth or gums. Depending on the cause, the pain may range from a dull ache to a severe throbbing sensation. Toothache may last only a few minutes, or it may be continuous.

What are the causes?

A sharp pain triggered by biting or consuming hot, cold, or sweet foods and drinks may be a symptom of the early stages of tooth decay (*see* DENTAL CARIES, opposite page). A fractured tooth (p.614), receding gums (p.619), or advanced gum disease (*see* PERIODONTITIS, p.618) may also result in toothache. A dull pain in the teeth while chewing may be due to inflammation of the gums (*see* GINGIVITIS, p.617) following a buildup of plaque (a deposit of food particles, mucus, and bacteria). Dull pain may also be caused by food trapped between the teeth.

A continuous, severe, throbbing pain is usually the result of advanced tooth decay (*see* PULPITIS, p.611), in which the pulp, or central part of the tooth containing the nerves and blood vessels, becomes inflamed. If the pain changes so that the tooth becomes tender to touch, it may indicate that pulpitis has developed into a dental abscess (p.611) at the root, with infection and death of the pulp tissues. The infection may spread to surrounding tissues and be accompanied by fever and occasionally facial swelling. The lymph nodes in the neck may also become enlarged and tender.

Pain and tenderness at the back of the mouth may be due to emerging wisdom teeth. The gums may be particularly painful if the wisdom teeth only partially emerge or grow in the wrong direction (*see* IMPACTED TEETH, p.613).

In some cases, toothache occurs as a result of a disorder elsewhere in the body, such as sinusitis (p.475), an ear infection (*see* OTITIS MEDIA, p.597), or a problem in the joint between the jaw and the skull (*see* TEMPOROMANDIBULAR JOINT DISORDER, p.616).

What can I do?

If you have toothache, you should consult your dentist as soon as possible. If you have a fever and/or a swollen face in addition to toothache, you should see a dentist immediately.

Analgesics (p.912), such as aspirin and acetaminophen, can help relieve toothache while you are waiting for an appointment. Rinsing your mouth with warm saltwater may also help. Oil of cloves, available over the counter, may also help soothe the pain when applied to the tooth. However, the only permanent remedy is for the affected tooth to be treated by a dentist.

What might be done?

Your dentist will ask you about your symptoms and examine your teeth and gums. He or she may also take X-rays of your mouth to look for decay.

If toothache is caused by decay, your dentist will remove the decayed areas and may put in an ordinary filling to stop the pain and prevent further decay (*see* TOOTH FILLING, p.611). If you have gingivitis, your dentist will probably remove the plaque by scaling the teeth. He or she may also prescribe antibiotics (p.885) for an infection. If tooth decay is advanced and you have pulpitis or a dental abscess, you may need root canal treatment (p.612), in which the soft tissues within the tooth are removed. The cavity is sterilized to clear up the infection, and the root canals and decayed area are filled permanently. A tooth that is very badly damaged or decayed and painful, impacted wisdom teeth may be extracted. If your toothache is due to a condition such as sinusitis or an ear infection, you may need to consult your doctor for the necessary treatment.

To prevent toothache, you should brush and floss your teeth and gums regularly (*see* CARING FOR YOUR TEETH AND GUMS, p.610). You should also have regular dental checkups (below).

WWW ONLINE SITES: p.1029

Dental caries

Cavities in a tooth or teeth, commonly known as tooth decay

AGE More common under age 25 and over age 65

LIFESTYLE Poor oral hygiene and a diet high in sugar are risk factors

GENDER GENETICS Not significant factors

Gradual, progressive decay of a tooth is known as dental caries. This condition usually starts as a small cavity in the enamel (the hard, protective outer covering of a tooth). If left untreated, the decay eventually penetrates the outer layer of enamel and attacks the dentin, the softer material that makes up the bulk of a tooth. As the tooth decay progresses, the pulp (the living core of the tooth that contains the nerves and blood vessels) may be affected (*see* PULPITIS, p.611). If the pulp is exposed to decay and becomes infected, it may die.

Most people develop dental caries at some time in their lives. In younger age groups, tooth decay most often occurs on the chewing surfaces of the upper and lower teeth and on the surfaces where the teeth touch each other. In older people, tooth decay is more common at the gum margins where the teeth meet the gums.

In developed countries, the number of teeth lost as a result of dental caries has fallen considerably in recent years, particularly among children. This fall is

TEST DENTAL CHECKUP

In order to keep your teeth and gums healthy, you should consult your dentist at least once every 6 months for a checkup. He or she will examine your teeth for signs of decay and your gums for evidence of gum disease. If you have not been to the dentist for some time, you may have X-rays to look for evidence of decay between the back teeth and under existing fillings. Your dentist may also clean and polish your teeth and will advise you on good oral hygiene.

LOOKING AT THE TEETH AND GUMS

Your teeth and gums will be examined for signs of disease while you lie in a dental chair under a bright light. Your dentist will also check that all the teeth are present and aligned correctly and that teeth still emerging are not likely to become impacted.

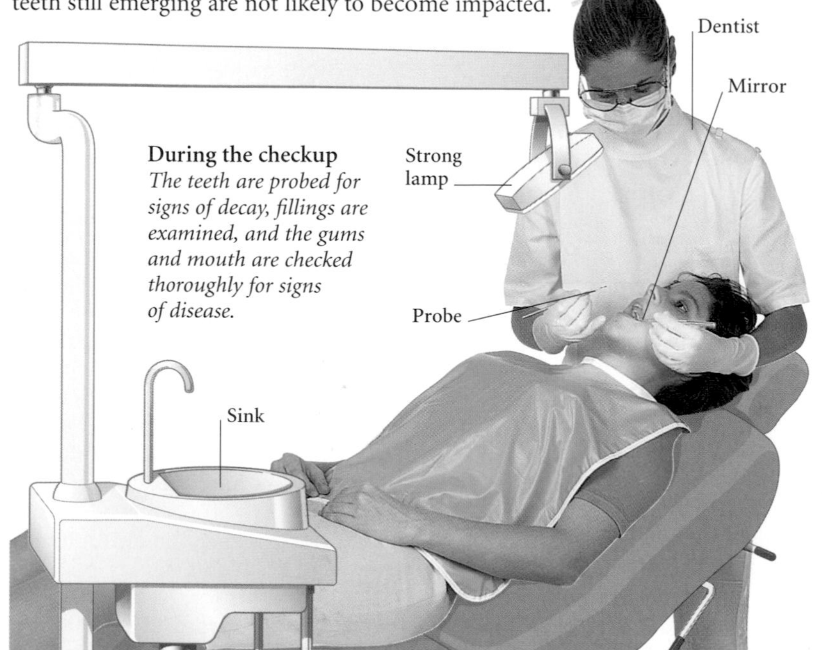
Dentist
Mirror
Strong lamp
Probe
Sink

During the checkup
The teeth are probed for signs of decay, fillings are examined, and the gums and mouth are checked thoroughly for signs of disease.

BITE-WING X-RAY

A bite-wing X-ray is used to look for decay. The X-ray film is held between the teeth while the X-ray machine is placed near your cheek. An X-ray may be taken on both sides of the face.

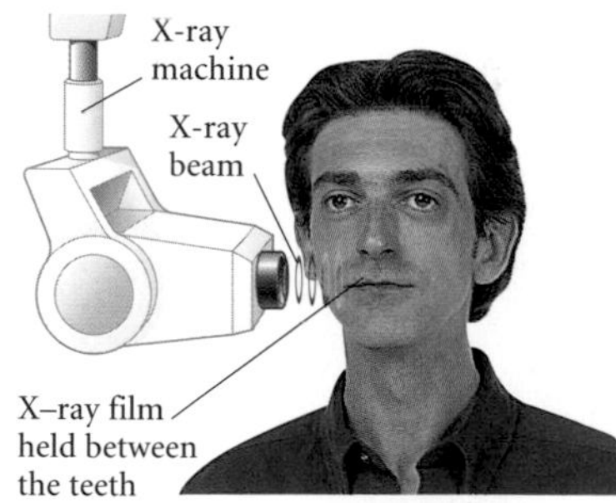
X-ray machine
X-ray beam
X–ray film held between the teeth

Having an X-ray
The X-ray film is placed in the cheek and held between the teeth using the wing attached to the film. An X-ray is taken.

RESULTS

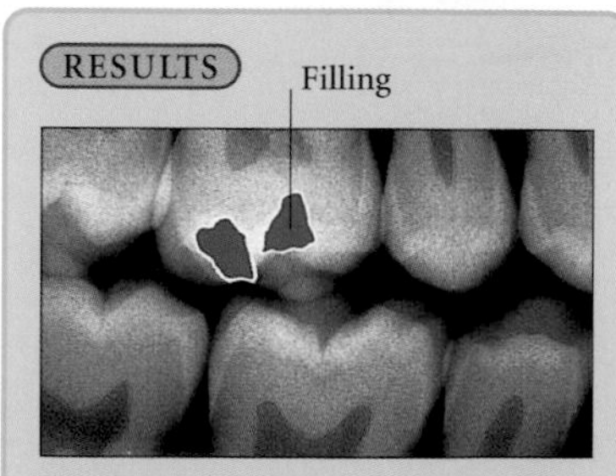
Filling

Bite-wing X-ray
This color-enhanced X-ray shows two fillings in an upper molar tooth. No decay is present.

SELF-HELP CARING FOR YOUR TEETH AND GUMS

Daily care of your teeth is as important as having regular dental checkups. If you adopt a simple routine of regular brushing and flossing, you can prevent food particles and bacteria from building up on the surface of your teeth and reduce the risk of tooth decay and gum disease. If you cannot clean your teeth between meals, chewing sugar-free gum may help. You should avoid sugary foods and drinks, which contribute to tooth decay. If your water does not contain fluoride, which helps strengthen teeth, consult your dentist about whether to use fluoride tablets or drops.

BRUSHING YOUR TEETH

Your teeth need brushing at least twice a day for 2 minutes and, if possible, after every meal. Use a small-headed, soft toothbrush and fluoride toothpaste. Make sure that you clean all the surfaces of all your teeth, especially where they meet the gum. You should replace your toothbrush every 2–3 months.

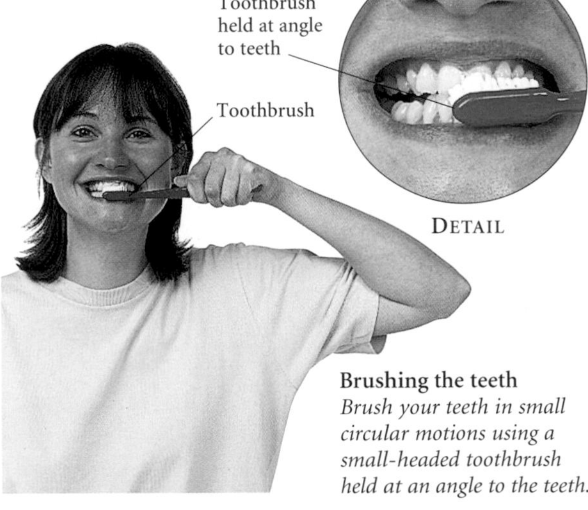
Toothbrush held at angle to teeth
Toothbrush
DETAIL

Brushing the teeth
Brush your teeth in small circular motions using a small-headed toothbrush held at an angle to the teeth.

CLEANING BETWEEN TEETH

Dental floss or dental tape is used to clean between the teeth and remove food particles and bacteria from areas between the teeth that cannot be reached easily with a toothbrush. Toothpicks and small interdental brushes are also often used. You should clean between each tooth in turn in a regular pattern so that no teeth are missed.

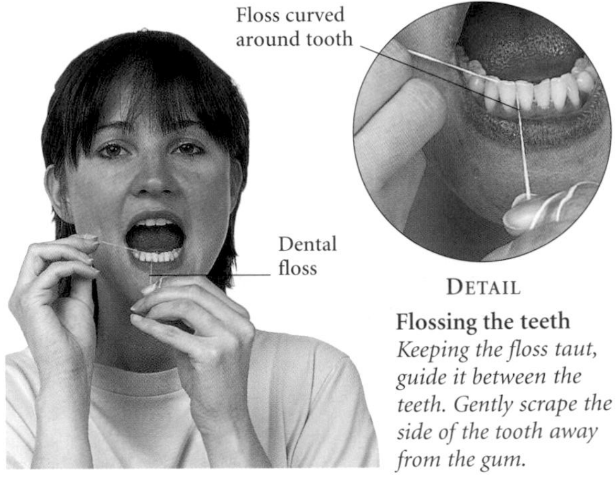
Floss curved around tooth
Dental floss
DETAIL

Flossing the teeth
Keeping the floss taut, guide it between the teeth. Gently scrape the side of the tooth away from the gum.

FOOD AND DRINK

You should avoid consuming foods and drinks that have a high sugar content, such as desserts and sodas, particularly if you cannot clean your teeth immediately. If you cannot brush soon after eating sugary foods, chew sugar-free gum.

Sugarless snacks
Snacking on foods such as nuts, celery, carrots, and cheese is better for your teeth than eating sugary foods.

partly due to the addition of fluoride to drinking water in some areas and to the widespread use of fluoride toothpaste, both of which help harden the teeth, making them more resistant to decay.

WHAT ARE THE CAUSES?

Tooth decay is usually caused by a buildup of plaque (a deposit of food particles, mucus, and bacteria) on the surface of the teeth. The bacteria in plaque break down the sugar in food to produce an acid that erodes the tooth enamel. If sugary foods are eaten regularly and the teeth are not cleaned thoroughly soon afterward, eventually a cavity is likely to form.

The condition is especially common in children, adolescents, and young adults because they are more likely to have a diet high in sugar and fail to clean their teeth regularly. Babies who frequently fall asleep with a bottle of juice or milk in their mouths may also develop severe caries, especially in the front teeth.

WHAT ARE THE SYMPTOMS?

There may be no signs of dental caries in the early stages, but the symptoms develop gradually as the decay progresses and may include:

- Toothache, which may be constant or sharp and stabbing and triggered by hot, cold, or sweet foods or drinks.
- Persistent, throbbing pain in the jaw and occasionally in the ear and face, which may be worse when chewing.
- Bad breath.

Pain in a tooth can take several forms. It may be persistent, recurrent, or set off by extremes of hot or cold or pressure on the tooth. You should see your dentist as soon as possible after pain first appears and make an immediate appointment if the pain ends abruptly because this may indicate that the nerves and blood vessels have died. Delaying a visit to your dentist may result in the spread of infection, and an abscess may eventually form (*see* DENTAL ABSCESS, opposite page).

WHAT MIGHT BE DONE?

Your dentist will examine your teeth with a probe and a mirror to look for areas of tooth decay. An X-ray may also be taken to look for decay that may be developing beneath the surfaces of the teeth (*see* DENTAL CHECKUP, p.609).

If you have superficial dental caries restricted to the surface of the enamel, your dentist may only apply fluoride to the affected area and advise you to be more careful about oral hygiene.

If tooth decay has penetrated further into the enamel, or if it has affected the dentin, your dentist will probably need to fill the affected tooth (*see* TOOTH FILLING, right). An injection of local anesthetic is often used to numb the tooth and nearby gum to prevent you from feeling pain. When the area is numb, the decayed parts of the tooth are drilled out, and the cavity is cleaned and filled to prevent further decay. If you have pulpitis and the pulp cannot be saved, you may need root canal treatment (p.612).

CAN IT BE PREVENTED?

Your teeth and gums should be brushed and flossed regularly to keep them clean (*see* CARING FOR YOUR TEETH AND GUMS, opposite page). You can also help prevent dental caries from developing by avoiding sweet foods and drinks.

(WWW) ONLINE SITES: p.1029

Pulpitis

Inflammation of the pulp, the living core of a tooth

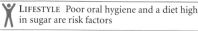

LIFESTYLE Poor oral hygiene and a diet high in sugar are risk factors

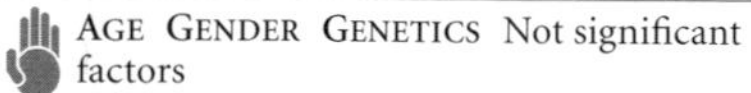

AGE GENDER GENETICS Not significant factors

The soft central part (the pulp) of a tooth contains the blood vessels and nerves. If tooth decay (*see* DENTAL CARIES, p.609) becomes advanced, it will gradually progress to invade the pulp and cause pulpitis. Pulpitis may also develop if the pulp becomes exposed after hard contact results in a fractured tooth (p.614). Grinding the teeth at night may inflame the pulp.

There are two varieties of pulpitis: reversible and irreversible. In reversible pulpitis, the decay has not affected the entire pulp, and the remaining tissue with its nerves and blood vessels can be saved. Left untreated, reversible pulpitis may eventually become irreversible, in which the decay is so severe that the remaining pulp, nerves, and vessels die and have to be removed. Eventually the tooth may become discolored (*see* DISCOLORED TEETH, p.612).

The principal symptom of pulpitis is toothache. If it only occurs while eating or drinking, pulpitis is likely to be reversible. In irreversible pulpitis, pain tends to be more constant until the tissues in the pulp die. You may also notice pain if you tap the tooth with a finger. Left untreated, an abscess may form (*see* DENTAL ABSCESS, right).

WHAT MIGHT BE DONE?

Your dentist will examine your teeth and may take an X-ray to look for decay (*see* DENTAL CHECKUP, p.609). He or she will probably treat reversible pulpitis by removing the decayed area and filling the tooth to prevent further damage (*see* TOOTH FILLING, below). If the pulpitis is irreversible, you will probably need root canal treatment (p.612), in which the pulp is removed and the root canals are filled. It is unlikely that the tooth will be extracted.

(WWW) ONLINE SITES: p.1029

Dental abscess

A pus-filled sac in or around the root of a tooth

LIFESTYLE Poor dental hygiene and a diet high in sugar are risk factors

AGE GENDER GENETICS Not significant factors

An accumulation of pus in or around the root of a tooth is known as a dental abscess. An abscess usually develops as a complication of dental caries (p.609), which gradually destroys the layer of enamel on the outside of the tooth and the inner dentin, allowing bacteria to invade the soft central core, or pulp, of the tooth (*see* PULPITIS, left). Eventually, a dental abscess may form. The pulp may also become infected if a tooth is damaged by a blow to the mouth (*see* FRACTURED TOOTH, p.614).

An abscess may also form as a result of certain forms of gum disease (*see* PERIODONTITIS, p.618). Periodontitis is usually caused by a buildup of dental plaque (a deposit including food particles, mucus, and bacteria) in a pocket that forms between a tooth and gum.

A dental abscess can be extremely painful and may cause the affected tooth to loosen in its socket.

TREATMENT TOOTH FILLING

Teeth are usually filled because of tooth decay. White fillings are used in front teeth and white fillings or amalgam (a mixture of silver, tin, and mercury) in back teeth. Local anesthesia may be used to make the tooth and gum numb. When they are numb, the decayed area of the tooth is drilled away and the hole is shaped to secure the filling. The filling is then bonded or packed into the tooth as a soft paste that will harden within a few hours.

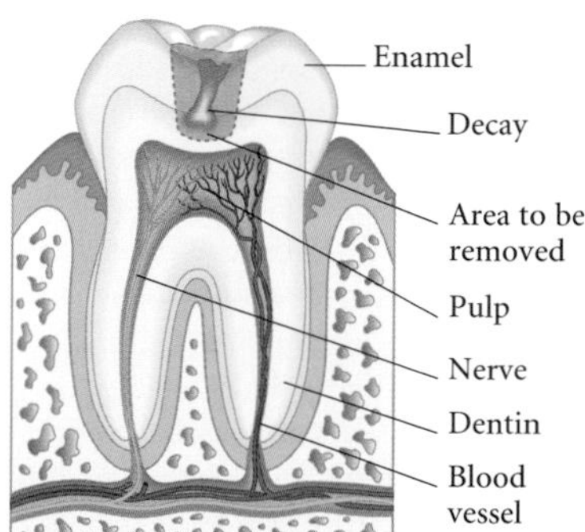
Enamel
Decay
Area to be removed
Pulp
Nerve
Dentin
Blood vessel

Before treatment
Tooth decay has penetrated the hard enamel covering of the tooth and invaded the dentin, the softer material that makes up the bulk of the tooth.

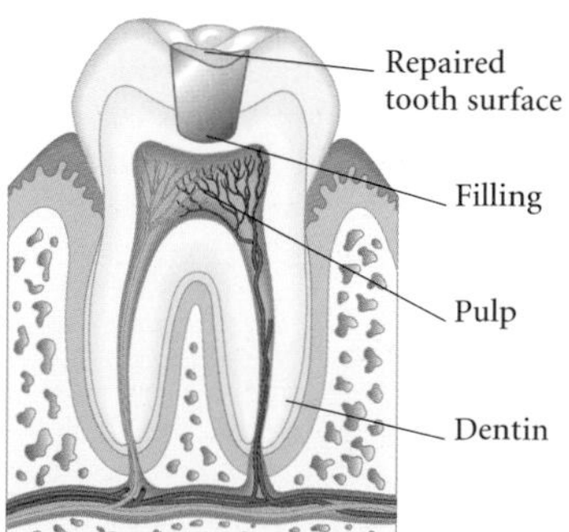
Repaired tooth surface
Filling
Pulp
Dentin

After treatment
The decayed area of the tooth has been drilled out and the hole carefully shaped to hold a filling. The filling has been put in to prevent further tooth decay.

WHAT ARE THE SYMPTOMS?

The main symptoms of a dental abscess develop gradually and may include:

- Dull aching around either or both of the cheekbones.
- Severe pain on touching the affected tooth and on biting or chewing.
- Loosening of the affected tooth.
- Red, tender swelling of the gum over the root of the tooth.
- Release of pus into the mouth.

If the abscess is not treated, the infection may make a channel from the tooth to the surface of the gum, and a painful swelling, known as a gumboil, may form. If the gumboil bursts, foul-tasting pus is released and the pain decreases. In some cases, the channel may persist, leading to a chronic abscess that discharges pus periodically. If the infection spreads to surrounding tissues, your face may become swollen and painful, and you may also develop a fever. If you suspect that you have a dental abscess, you should consult your dentist as soon as possible.

WHAT CAN I DO?

If there is a delay before you are able to see your dentist, you can try taking analgesics (p.912), such as acetaminophen, to relieve the pain. Rinsing your mouth with warm saltwater may also help decrease pain and encourage a gumboil to burst. If a gumboil does burst, wash away the pus thoroughly with more warm saltwater.

WHAT MIGHT THE DENTIST DO?

Your dentist will ask you about your symptoms and examine your teeth and gums. He or she may take an X-ray of your mouth to confirm the diagnosis (*see* DENTAL CHECKUP, p.609).

If the abscess has been caused by decay, your dentist may try to save the tooth. Under local anesthesia, a hole is drilled through the top of the tooth to release the pus and relieve the pain. If there is a gumboil, a small cut may be made in the boil to drain the pus. The cavity is then cleaned with an antiseptic solution. A small tube may be left in place for a few days to allow any remaining pus to drain, and you will probably be given a course of antibiotics (p.885). Once the infection has cleared up, you will probably need root canal treatment (above). If it is not possible to save the tooth, it will be extracted.

To treat an abscess caused by gum disease, your dentist may use a probe to scrape out the plaque from the pocket between the affected tooth and gum. Afterward, the pocket is washed out with an antiseptic solution. In severe cases, the tooth may be extracted.

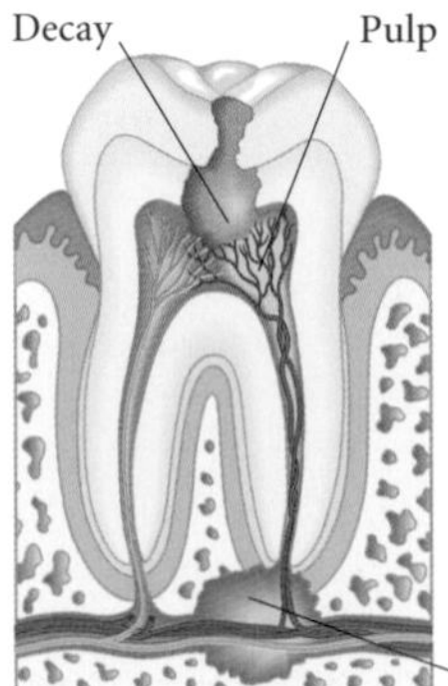
Decay
Pulp
Pus

Dental abscess
Tooth decay and infection has spread through the tooth, and pus has gathered at the root of the tooth. If not treated, the tooth will have to be extracted.

(TREATMENT) ROOT CANAL TREATMENT

Sometimes, decay invades the pulp, the center of the tooth, and root canal treatment may be performed. The pulp is removed, as well as the nerves and blood vessels, and an antiseptic solution is used to sterilize the cavity. If infection within the tooth is severe, a temporary filling may be inserted for a few days before the cavity is sterilized again. The root canals and the decayed area of the tooth are then filled.

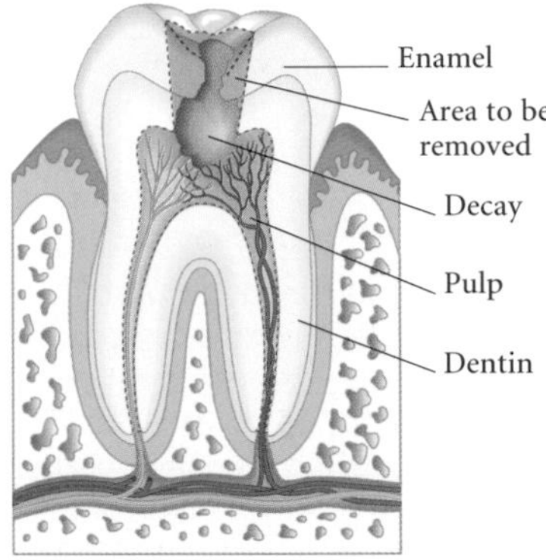
Enamel
Area to be removed
Decay
Pulp
Dentin

Before treatment
Tooth decay has penetrated the enamel and the dentin and has reached the pulp, the core of the tooth that contains the blood vessels and nerves.

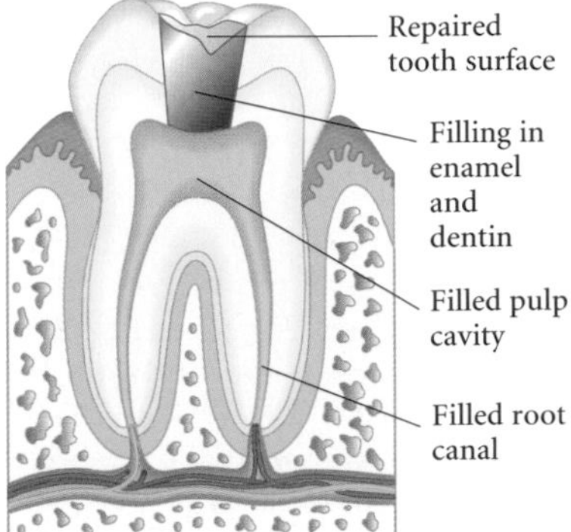
Repaired tooth surface
Filling in enamel and dentin
Filled pulp cavity
Filled root canal

After treatment
The decayed area of the tooth and pulp have been removed, and the pulp cavity has been sterilized. The decayed area, pulp cavity, and root canals have been filled.

WHAT IS THE PROGNOSIS?

Most treatment is successful, but a small area of infection may persist and further treatment may be required.

To help prevent the formation of a dental abscess, brush and floss your teeth and gums regularly (*see* CARING FOR YOUR TEETH AND GUMS, p.610).

(WWW) ONLINE SITES: p.1029

Discolored teeth

Abnormal coloring of the teeth, which may be due to a number of factors

AGE More common with increasing age

LIFESTYLE Poor oral hygiene, using tobacco, and drinking coffee and tea are risk factors

GENDER GENETICS Not significant factors

Tooth color varies from person to person, and the secondary teeth are usually darker than the primary teeth. Teeth also normally darken slightly with age. However, abnormal discoloration may occur because of changes in the teeth.

WHAT ARE THE CAUSES?

A common cause of discoloration is the buildup of dental plaque (a deposit of food particles, mucus, and bacteria) on the surface of the teeth. Plaque-stained teeth are often yellowish brown, but children's teeth may be black or green. Drinking tea and coffee and chewing or smoking tobacco may also stain the surface of the teeth, as may some liquid medicines that contain iron.

The teeth may also become discolored if children are given certain drugs

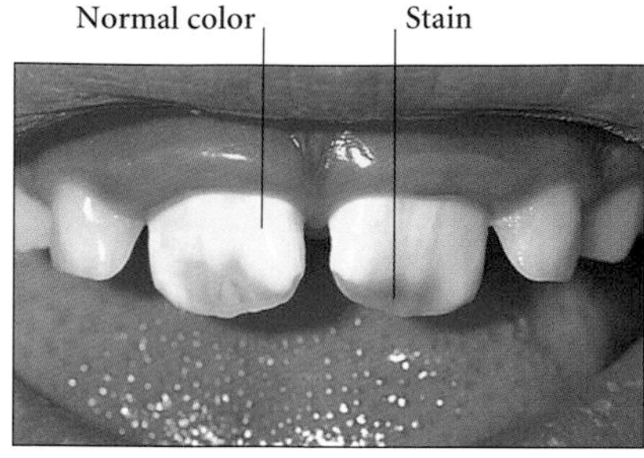
Normal color
Stain

Discolored teeth
The brown areas of discoloration on this child's two front teeth have been caused by excess amounts of fluoride. This condition is called fluorosis.

while their secondary teeth are developing. For example, if tetracycline (*see* ANTIBIOTICS, p.885) is given to babies or children under age 10, it may cause a yellow discoloration of the secondary teeth. If the drug is given to a pregnant woman, her baby's primary teeth may be discolored when they emerge.

Fluorosis, in which the teeth develop a mottled color, is due to an excess of natural fluoride in the water in some parts of the world. However, where fluoride is added to the water to reduce tooth decay, the concentration is too low to cause fluorosis. Fluorosis may also develop if children are given too high a dose of fluoride drops or pills.

A tooth may become darker than normal following irreversible pulpitis (*see* PULPITIS, p.611), when the soft center, or the pulp, of the tooth dies. Root canal treatment (opposite page) may cause a tooth to darken if the material used to fill the tooth is dark in color.

WHAT MIGHT BE DONE?

Staining on the surface of the teeth is routinely removed by scaling and polishing of teeth by your dentist or oral hygienist. If staining is severe, the teeth can be bleached. If a single tooth is discolored as a result of a condition such as pulpitis or following root canal treatment, a porcelain or plastic veneer may be bonded to the front of the tooth, or the top of the tooth can be replaced by a crown (*see* CROWNS AND REPLACEMENT TEETH, p.615).

Most discoloration of teeth can be prevented by brushing and flossing the teeth and gums regularly (*see* CARING FOR YOUR TEETH AND GUMS, p.610).

(WWW) ONLINE SITES: p.1029

Impacted teeth

Failure of teeth to emerge completely from the gum and grow into their normal position, usually due to lack of room

AGE More common under age 25

GENDER GENETICS LIFESTYLE Not significant factors

Teeth usually become impacted when there is not enough room in the mouth for them to grow into their correct positions. Impacted teeth may remain entirely buried in the jawbone, with few or no symptoms, or only partly erupt through the gum. Impaction may also occur if a tooth starts to grow in the wrong direction and pushes against other teeth or the jawbone.

Wisdom teeth are most likely to become impacted, followed by the upper canines. These teeth emerge at a later stage of life than other teeth, and frequently there is insufficient room in the mouth for them to erupt normally. Impacted teeth most frequently occur in adolescents and young adults when the teeth are still emerging.

Impacted teeth may cause pain and inflammation. A partly erupted tooth may be covered by a flap of gum under which plaque (a deposit including food particles, mucus, and bacteria) accumulates, leading to inflammation of the gum and gradual decay of the tooth (*see* DENTAL CARIES, p.609).

WHAT MIGHT BE DONE?

Your dentist will check at each visit (*see* DENTAL CHECKUP, p.609) whether any emerging teeth are likely to become impacted. He or she may also take X-rays to look at unerupted teeth. One or more teeth may be extracted to allow room for other teeth to come through. You may also need orthodontic treatment (p.614) to straighten the teeth.

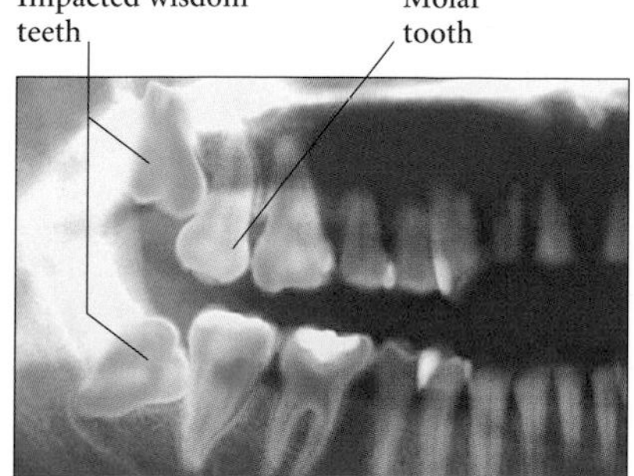
Impacted wisdom teeth
Molar tooth

Impacted teeth
This X-ray shows two wisdom teeth that are growing at an angle and have impacted on the roots of adjacent molars.

Wisdom teeth that appear likely to become impacted are often extracted to avoid complications. If canines are impacted, they may be fully exposed by removing gum tissue. An orthodontic device is then applied to guide the teeth into position.

(WWW) ONLINE SITES: p.1029

Malocclusion

Unsatisfactory contact between the upper and lower teeth

AGE Most common between the ages of 6 and 14

GENETICS Often runs in families

LIFESTYLE Poor oral hygiene and thumb sucking beyond age 6 are risk factors

GENDER Not a significant factor

Ideally, the upper front teeth should slightly overlap the lower front teeth and the molars should meet evenly. However, perfect teeth are rare and most people have some teeth that are out of position. Imperfections are not usually a pressing problem unless appearance is adversely affected or biting and chewing are impaired.

Malocclusion may occur when the teeth are crooked because they are crowded and overlap each other or when the upper front teeth protrude too far in front of the lower front teeth. Less commonly, the lower teeth protrude in front of the upper front teeth. Sometimes, the back teeth prevent the front teeth from meeting properly, a condition known as an open bite.

WHAT ARE THE CAUSES?

Malocclusion often runs in families and usually develops in childhood when the teeth and jaws are growing. The condition is usually caused by a discrepancy between the number and size of the teeth and the growth of the jaws. Protrusion of the front teeth may also be caused by children who persistently suck their thumbs beyond about age 6.

If the primary teeth are lost early (before age 9 or 10) because of decay

TREATMENT ORTHODONTIC TREATMENT

Orthodontics is the correction of crowded or unevenly spaced teeth. Orthodontic treatment is usually performed on older children and adolescents while their teeth are still developing, although adults can also benefit. Casts of the teeth are taken before an orthodontic appliance, or brace, is applied either to move or straighten the teeth gradually. In some cases, it is necessary to extract one or more teeth in order to make room for others. The treatment usually takes several months or years to complete and necessitates regular visits to the orthodontist for checkups.

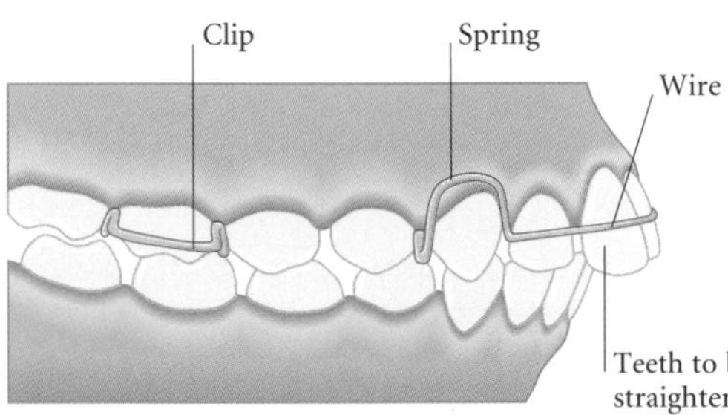
Clip
Spring
Wire
Teeth to be straightened

Removable appliances
Removable braces consist of a plastic plate, which fits into the roof of the mouth and clips into place. Springs and wires exert pressure on the teeth. To increase the amount of pressure, the brace may be connected to a headcap that is worn while sleeping.

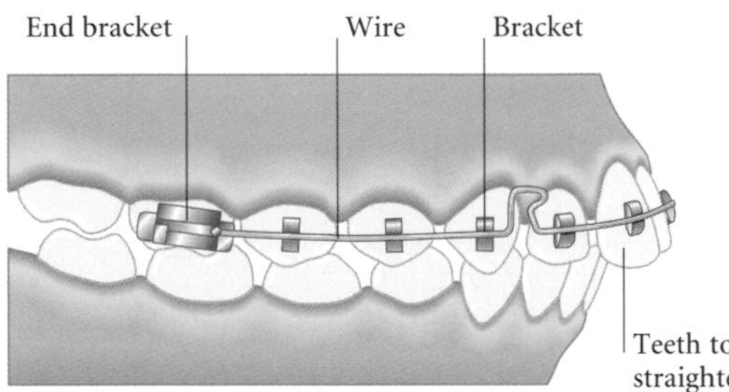
End bracket
Wire
Bracket
Teeth to be straightened

Fixed appliances
Fixed braces consist of wires and springs carried by brackets that are fixed to the teeth with dental adhesive. These braces can exert greater pressure than removable appliances and produce more complex movements of the teeth.

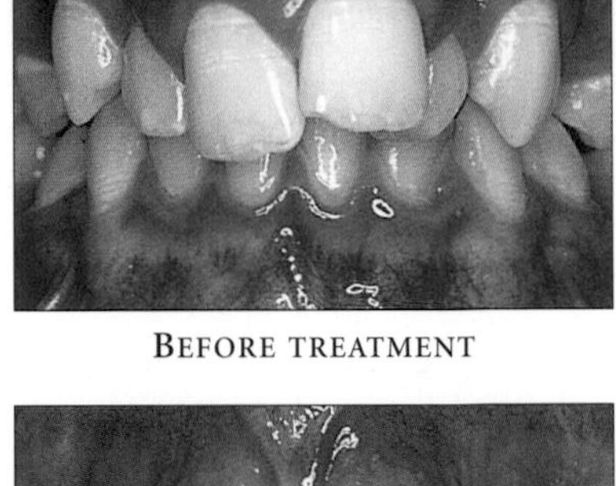

BEFORE TREATMENT

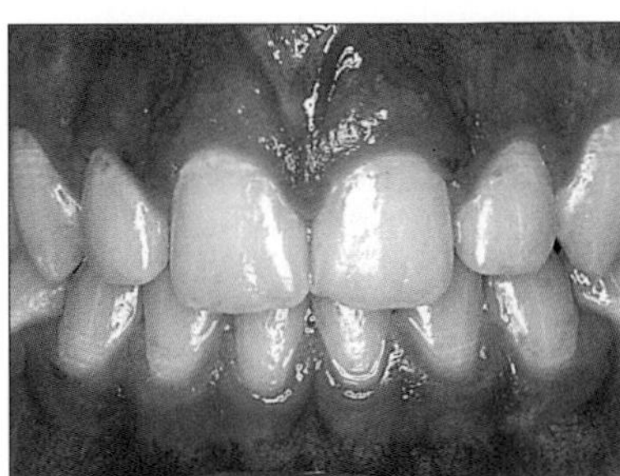

AFTER TREATMENT

Orthodontic treatment
These two photographs show a set of teeth before and after orthodontic treatment. The irregular teeth have been brought into line by the treatment.

(*see* DENTAL CARIES, p.609), the secondary molars that are already in position may move forward to take up some of the space meant for the new teeth. The new teeth then become crowded and misaligned.

WHAT ARE THE SYMPTOMS?

The symptoms develop gradually from about age 6 onward. They may include:

- Out-of-line, crowded, or abnormally spaced teeth.
- Excessive protrusion of the upper teeth in front of the lower, or a protruding lower jaw.
- Front teeth that do not meet.

Some children have mild symptoms, but these are often temporary and tend to result from a growth spurt.

Speech and chewing are affected in severe cases of malocclusion. An abnormal bite may be painful and may also affect the appearance, particularly the lower-jaw profile. Arthritis may develop in the temporomandibular joint (*see* TEMPOROMANDIBULAR JOINT DISORDER, p.616) in rare cases.

WHAT MIGHT BE DONE?

The dentist will look for malocclusion as part of a dental checkup (p.609). If found, a specialist dentist called an orthodontist may take casts of the teeth to study the bite in detail. The orthodontist may also take X-rays, especially if some of the teeth have not erupted.

Treatment is usually necessary only if malocclusion is severe and causing difficulties when eating and speaking or affecting appearance. If the teeth are overcrowded, some of them may be extracted. Rough or irregular teeth are often reshaped or capped. If required, the teeth may then be aligned using an orthodontic appliance (*see* ORTHODONTIC TREATMENT, above). Surgery is necessary only in rare cases.

It is best to treat malocclusion during childhood, when the teeth and jaw bones are still developing. However, if malocclusion is caused by a severe mismatch in the size of the jaws and teeth, surgery may be needed and treatment may be delayed until adulthood.

WWW ONLINE SITES: p.1029

Fractured tooth

A tooth that is cracked, chipped, or broken, often as a result of a blow to the mouth

 AGE More common under age 30

 GENDER More common in males

 LIFESTYLE Playing contact sports is a risk factor

 GENETICS Not a significant factor

A hard blow to the mouth, often while playing sports, is the most common cause of a fractured tooth. Young men are more likely to damage their teeth in this way because they are more likely to participate in contact sports. Protruding front teeth or teeth weakened by heavy filling are particularly susceptible to breaking.

The enamel, the hard outer covering of the crown, is most often damaged, but this does not usually produce symptoms. Sensitivity to heat or cold and pain when biting may occur if the dentin beneath the enamel is affected. Pain and bleeding may indicate that the pulp containing the nerves and blood vessels is damaged. You should consult your dentist within 24 hours if the damaged tooth is sensitive or bleeding because the pulp may become infected (*see* PULPITIS, p.611) and a dental abscess (p.611) may form. Soft dental wax can be placed over a damaged tooth before seeing your dentist.

WHAT MIGHT BE DONE?

Treatment depends on the severity of the damage. Chipped enamel may only be treated for cosmetic reasons. A large fracture may be filled (*see* TOOTH FILLING, p.611), or a crown may be fitted (*see* CROWNS AND REPLACEMENT TEETH, right). A tooth with an extensive fracture may be splinted to neighboring teeth for 1–2 weeks. If the pulp is infected or has died, you may need root canal treatment (p.612). Severely damaged teeth may have to be extracted.

(WWW) ONLINE SITES: p.1029

Missing teeth

The lack of one or more secondary, or adult, teeth

AGE More common with increasing age

GENDER More common in males

GENETICS In some cases, the cause is inherited

LIFESTYLE Poor oral hygiene and playing contact sports are risk factors

Total absence of many or all of the secondary teeth is very rare. Failure of one or more teeth to develop is more common. Of all the teeth, the wisdom teeth are most likely to be absent, which may be an advantage because it reduces the risk of impaction (*see* IMPACTED TEETH, p.613). The emergence of some teeth may be delayed in people with Down syndrome (p.821), by the effects of chemotherapy (p.278) and radiation therapy (p.279), or for genetic reasons. A delay may also be due to impaction caused by overcrowding.

Teeth may be lost following tooth decay caused by neglect of oral hygiene (*see* DENTAL CARIES, p.609). Teeth may also be lost due to injury (*see* AVULSED TOOTH, p.616). The risk of tooth loss is

TREATMENT CROWNS AND REPLACEMENT TEETH

If a tooth is damaged but the root and main body of the tooth are healthy, a new biting surface, or crown, may be attached. The crown is colored to match the surrounding natural teeth. If a tooth is extracted or lost, it may be replaced by an artificial tooth or teeth. There are several methods for replacing missing teeth. The method used depends on the circumstances as well as the number of teeth that have been lost.

CROWNS

Up to two or three visits to your dentist may be necessary for a crown to be fitted. White porcelain is usually used for crowns at the front of the mouth. Crowns at the back of the mouth are often made of gold or porcelain fused to a metal alloy.

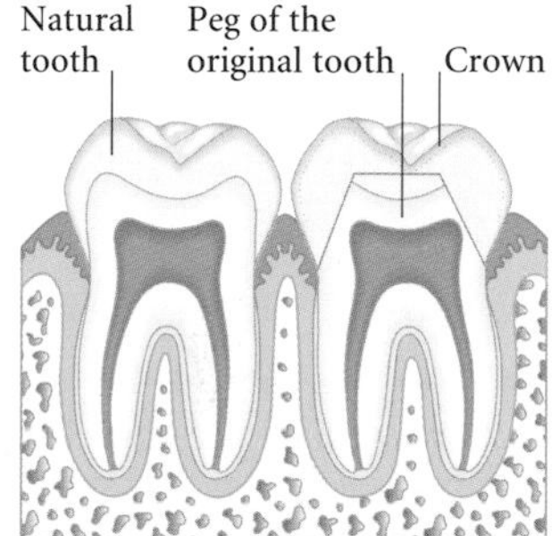
Natural tooth
Peg of the original tooth
Crown

Fitting a crown
The tooth is shaped into a peg and an impression of the peg is taken. A temporary crown is made to fit over the peg while a final crown is made. The final crown is then cemented into place.

REPLACEMENT TEETH

If one or more teeth have to be extracted, or if they are lost, they can be replaced by one of three different types of artificial teeth: a bridge, a dental implant, or dentures. Bridges and dental implants are nonremovable and are used to replace only one or two teeth at a time. Dentures can be removed and are used when many teeth need to be replaced.

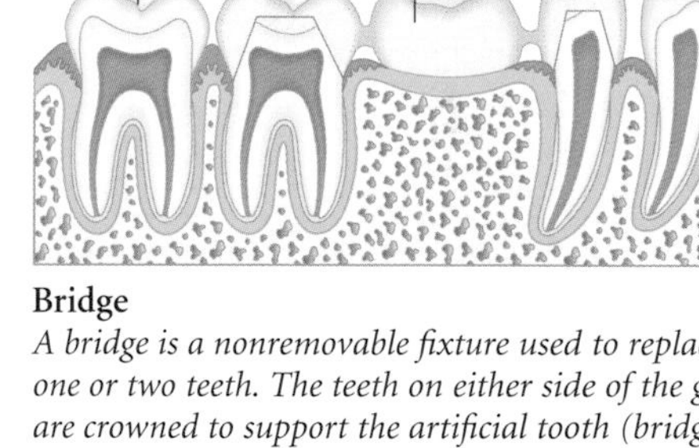
Natural tooth
Crowned tooth
Bridge
Crowned tooth
Natural tooth

Bridge
A bridge is a nonremovable fixture used to replace one or two teeth. The teeth on either side of the gap are crowned to support the artificial tooth (bridge).

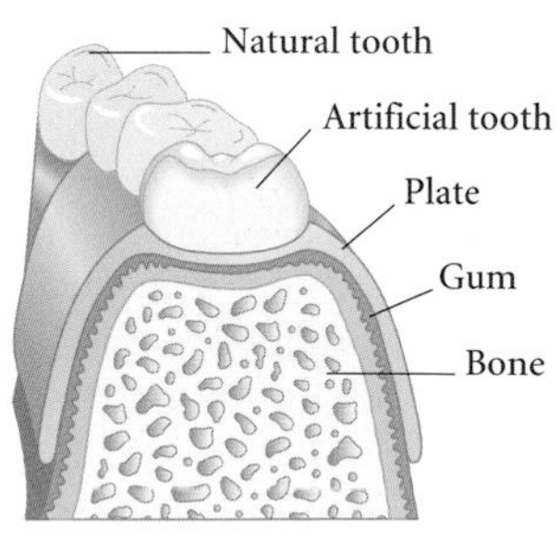
Natural tooth
Artificial tooth
Plate
Gum
Bone

SECTION ACROSS DENTURE

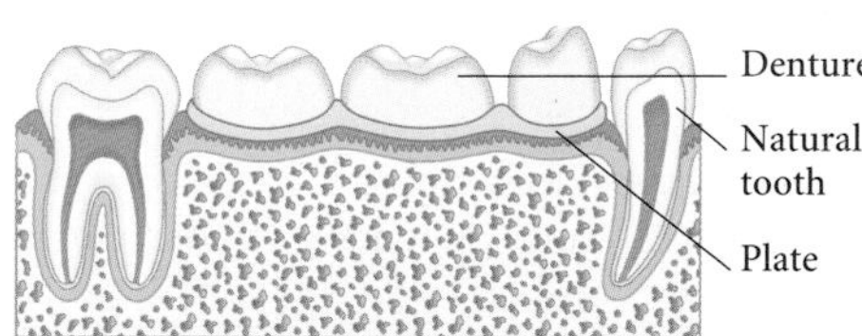
Denture
Natural tooth
Plate

SECTION ALONG DENTURE

Dentures
A denture can be removed and may replace any number of teeth. Dentures have a metal or plastic baseplate and stay in place by resting on the gum ridges or by clasps that fit the natural teeth.

Implants
An implant is a nonremovable method of replacing a single tooth. A hole is drilled in the jaw at the site of the missing tooth, and an implant, usually titanium, is placed into the hole. The implant must heal for 4–6 months before an artificial tooth is attached to the top of the implant.

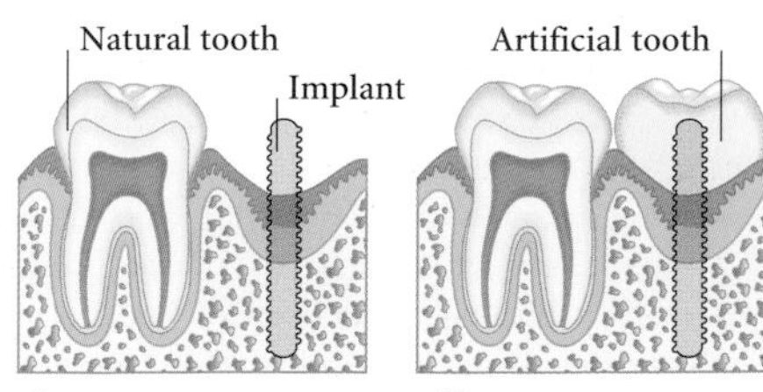
Natural tooth
Implant
Artificial tooth

IMPLANT IN PLACE   TOOTH IN PLACE

higher in men because they participate more frequently in contact sports such as hockey and football. If the secondary (adult) teeth are not present in the mouth, adjacent teeth tend to grow into the remaining spaces, which may cause uneven teeth or malocclusion (p.613).

What might be done?

The dentist will check the teeth during each visit in childhood to make sure that all the teeth emerge. If one or more teeth are missing, he or she may arrange to take X-rays to see if the teeth are absent or still within the jaw (*see* DENTAL CHECKUP, p.609). If you lose a tooth, you should consult a dentist or visit an emergency room immediately.

Treatment depends on how many and which teeth are affected. If the teeth are held back or delayed by overcrowding, one or two teeth may be removed to make room for the others. A brace may be needed to move teeth into place or keep them locked in position until missing teeth have emerged and are established (*see* ORTHODONTIC TREATMENT, p.614). Lost teeth can sometimes be reattached. If a tooth has failed to develop or one or more teeth have been lost, the missing tooth or teeth may be replaced (*see* CROWNS AND REPLACEMENT TEETH, p.615). Missing wisdom teeth are not replaced.

(WWW) ONLINE SITES: p.1029

Avulsed tooth

A tooth that has been partly or completely knocked out of its socket as a result of a powerful impact to the jaw

 AGE More common in children

 GENDER More common in males

 LIFESTYLE Playing contact sports is a risk factor

 GENETICS Not a significant factor

Although teeth are commonly lost in childhood accidents, an avulsed tooth is really a problem only if a secondary (adult) tooth is lost, because primary (baby) teeth are eventually replaced by secondary teeth. Avulsed teeth are much more common in men because they play more contact sports. The front teeth are most often involved.

If you have a tooth that is dislodged or knocked out, you should consult a dentist or visit your local emergency room immediately. If your tooth has been completely knocked out, you should put it back into the socket if possible. Alternatively, put the tooth in a glass of milk or saltwater, or wrap it in a clean, damp cloth. In 9 out of 10 cases, a tooth will reattach itself to the jaw if it is replaced in the socket within 30 minutes of being knocked out.

What might be done?

The dentist will replace the tooth and splint it to other teeth to immobilize it for 10–14 days. Complete avulsion usually kills the pulp (containing nerves and blood vessels), in which case you may need root canal treatment (p.612) when the tooth has been replaced.

If you have lost a tooth and may have inhaled it, a chest X-ray (p.490) may be done to ensure that the tooth is not lodged in your airways or lungs. A lost or damaged tooth may have to be replaced with an artificial tooth (*see* CROWNS AND REPLACEMENT TEETH, p.615).

(WWW) ONLINE SITES: p.1029

Temporomandibular joint disorder

Problems in the joint between the jaw and skull, causing headaches or pain in the face

 GENDER Much more common in females

 LIFESTYLE Stress may be a risk factor

 AGE GENETICS Not significant factors

The temporomandibular joint connects the mandible (lower jawbone) to the part of the skull known as the temporal bone. The joint allows the lower jaw to move in all directions so that the teeth can be used to bite off and chew food efficiently. In temporomandibular joint disorder, the joint and the muscles and ligaments that control the joint do not work together properly, causing pain. The condition is three times more common in women than in men.

Temporomandibular joint disorder is most commonly caused by spasm of the chewing muscles, often as a result of clenching the jaw or grinding the teeth. Clenching the jaw and grinding the teeth may be increased by stress. A poor bite (*see* MALOCCLUSION, p.613) places stress on the muscles and may also cause temporomandibular joint disorder, as may an injury to the head, jaw, or neck that causes displacement of the joint. In rare cases, arthritis (p.374) is a cause of the condition.

What are the symptoms?

If you have temporomandibular joint disorder, you may notice one or more of the following symptoms:

- Headaches.
- Tenderness in the jaw muscles.
- Aching pain in the face.
- Severe pain near the ears.

In some cases, pain is caused by chewing or by opening the mouth too widely when yawning. There may be difficulty in opening the mouth, locking of the jaw, and clicking noises from the joint as the mouth is opened or closed.

What might be done?

Your dentist may take a panoramic X-ray of your mouth and jaws. He or she may also arrange for you to have an MRI (p.248) of the joint.

Treatment is aimed at eliminating muscle spasm and tension and relieving the pain. There are several self-help measures that you can take, including applying a warm, wet towel to the face, massaging the facial muscles, eating only soft foods, and using a device that fits over the teeth at night to prevent you from clenching or grinding your teeth. Taking analgesics (p.912), such as aspirin and acetaminophen, may also help relieve pain. Your doctor may prescribe muscle relaxants (p.896) if tension of the muscles used for chewing is severe. If stress is a major factor, relaxation exercises (p.75) may help.

If your bite needs to be adjusted, your dentist may recommend wearing a fixed or removable orthodontic appliance for a specified period of time (*see* ORTHODONTIC TREATMENT, p.614).

What is the prognosis?

In about 3 in 4 people, the symptoms improve within 3 months of treatment. However, if symptoms do not improve, surgery may be required to repair the temporomandibular joint.

(WWW) ONLINE SITES: p.1029

GUM DISORDERS

The gums form a layer of connective tissue that surrounds the base of each tooth and covers part of the jawbones. Healthy gum forms a tight seal around the crown of a tooth and protects the sensitive root area below from bacterial infection and corrosion. If the gums are damaged, the teeth are more likely to decay. Most gum disorders can be prevented by good oral hygiene.

Most adults have some degree of gum disease which, if left untreated, may eventually lead to loss of teeth. Good oral hygiene is essential to help prevent gum disorders. During regular dental checkups, most dentists and oral hygienists provide information on the correct way to brush and floss teeth and on general mouth care.

The first topics covered here are gum disorders such as gingivitis and periodontitis, which may be caused by poor oral hygiene. Inadequate teeth cleaning leads to buildup of plaque (a deposit of food particles, mucus, and bacteria) on the surfaces of the teeth. If the plaque is not removed, it causes the gums to become inflamed. In more serious cases, the teeth may be affected and loosen or come out, either because the periodontal tissues are inflamed and detach from the teeth or because the gums recede, exposing the roots and leading to tooth decay. The final article in this section discusses dry socket, a condition in which a tooth socket becomes inflamed after the tooth has been extracted.

KEY ANATOMY

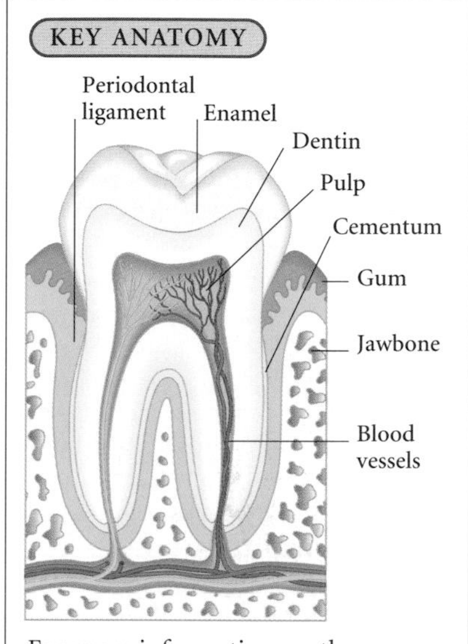
Periodontal ligament
Enamel
Dentin
Pulp
Cementum
Gum
Jawbone
Blood vessels

For more information on the structure and function of the gums, *see* pp.606–607.

Gingivitis

Inflammation of the gums, usually caused by poor oral hygiene

 GENDER More common in females

 LIFESTYLE Poor oral hygiene is a risk factor

 AGE GENETICS Not significant factors

Mild gingivitis, also known as gum disease, is a very common disorder and occurs in about 9 in 10 adults. Healthy gums are pink or brown and firm. In gingivitis, the gums become purple-red, soft, and shiny and bleed easily, especially when brushed. The condition is usually caused by buildup of dental plaque (a deposit of food particles, mucus, and bacteria) where the gum meets the base of the tooth.

Gingivitis can be made worse by taking some drugs, such as phenytoin (*see* ANTICONVULSANTS, p.914) and some immunosuppressants (p.906) and antihypertensives (p.897). These drugs may cause overgrowth of the gums, making the removal of dental plaque difficult. Some contraceptive drugs can also make the symptoms worse. Pregnant women are particularly susceptible to gingivitis because of dramatic changes in their hormone levels.

If gingivitis develops suddenly, it is known as acute necrotizing ulcerative gingivitis (ANUG) or "trench mouth." ANUG usually occurs in teenagers and young adults. The condition sometimes develops from chronic gingivitis and is caused by an abnormal growth of the bacteria that normally exist harmlessly within the mouth. ANUG is more common in people who are stressed or run down and in people with AIDS (*see* HIV INFECTION AND AIDS, p.295).

WHAT ARE THE SYMPTOMS?

The symptoms of gingivitis develop gradually and usually include:

- Purple-red, soft, shiny, swollen gums.
- Gums that bleed when brushed.

If gingivitis is not treated, the gum eventually pulls away from the tooth, causing a pocket to develop between the tooth and the gum in which more dental plaque can form. Bacteria in the plaque may cause the inflammation to spread. Eventually, chronic periodontitis (p.618) or receding gums (p.619) may develop. In severe cases, one or more teeth may be lost.

Symptoms of ANUG usually develop over 1–2 days and may include:

- Bright red gums that are covered with a grayish deposit.
- Craterlike ulcers on the gums.
- Gums that bleed easily.
- Bad breath and a metallic taste in the mouth.
- Pain in the gums.

As ANUG progresses, the lymph glands in the neck may become enlarged, and you may develop a fever.

WHAT IS THE TREATMENT?

If you have gingivitis, your dentist will probably scale your teeth to remove the plaque and calculus (hardened plaque). The procedure involves using an ultrasonic scaler to remove the calculus and scraping away at resistant areas with a hand tool. After scaling, the teeth are polished. Regular follow-up visits to the dentist may be necessary to monitor the condition of your gums. Your dentist may also recommend using a mouthwash containing hydrogen peroxide, which aids cleaning and helps prevent buildup of plaque.

If you have ANUG, your dentist will clean carefully around all the teeth. He or she will also prescribe antibiotics

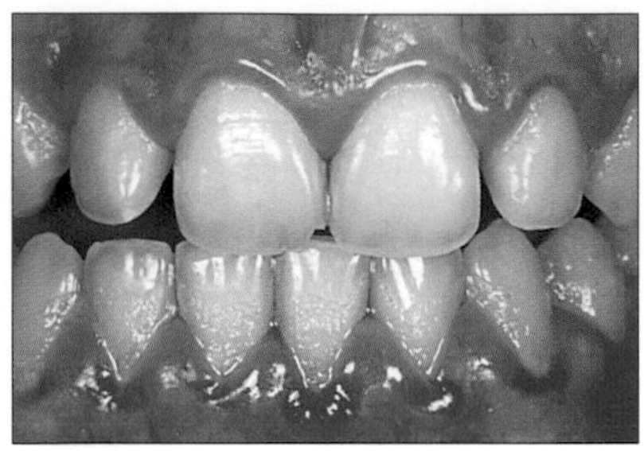

Gingivitis
In gingivitis, the gums become inflamed and soft due to buildup of plaque on the teeth. The gums also bleed easily.

(p.885) and an antiseptic mouthwash. Analgesics (p.912) may be prescribed to relieve pain. Once your teeth have been scaled and cleaned, your gums will gradually return to normal.

You can prevent gingivitis by adopting good oral hygiene (*see* CARING FOR YOUR TEETH AND GUMS, p.610).

(WWW) ONLINE SITES: p.1029

Periodontitis

Inflammation of the tissues that support the teeth

 AGE More common over age 55

 GENETICS In rare cases, the cause is inherited

 LIFESTYLE Poor oral hygiene is a risk factor

 GENDER Not a significant factor

Periodontitis affects many people overage 55 and is one of the major causes of tooth loss. In this condition, the bone and ligaments that secure teeth in their sockets become inflamed and shrink, and the teeth could loosen. The damage from periodontitis is irreversible, but further inflammation can be prevented with treatment and by improving oral hygiene (*see* CARING FOR YOUR TEETH AND GUMS, p.610).

WHAT ARE THE CAUSES?

The most common form of periodontitis is chronic periodontitis, which often develops as a complication of gingivitis (p.617), an inflammation of the gums caused by poor oral hygiene. If toothbrushing is neglected, plaque (a deposit of food particles, mucus, and bacteria) and calculus (hardened plaque) build up on the teeth, causing the gums to become inflamed. Over time, the gums pull away from the teeth, leaving pockets in which more plaque can collect. As gingivitis develops, the bacteria in the plaque attack the periodontal tissues, causing them to become inflamed and detach from the teeth. The inflammation also results in the loss of bone supporting the teeth. The teeth become loose in their sockets and may fall out.

Retrograde periodontitis is another form of periodontitis that is caused by tooth decay (*see* DENTAL CARIES, p.609), usually as a result of poor oral hygiene. If tooth decay is left untreated, the hard enamel that covers the tooth and the dentin underneath will eventually be destroyed, allowing bacteria to enter the pulp, or central part, of the tooth (*see* PULPITIS, p.611). Bacteria may then spread to the root tip and into the surrounding tissues, causing the socket of the tooth to become inflamed.

Rare genetic disorders, such as juvenile periodontitis, result in particularly severe forms of periodontitis that occur in children or young adults.

WHAT ARE THE SYMPTOMS?

In the early stages of periodontitis, you may not notice any symptoms. If there are symptoms of chronic periodontitis, they may include:

- Red, soft, shiny gums that bleed easily and may recede (*see* RECEDING GUMS, opposite page).
- An unpleasant taste in the mouth and bad breath.
- Toothache when hot, cold, or sweet foods or drinks are consumed.

In the late stages of chronic periodontitis, there may be loosening of the teeth.

The symptoms of retrograde periodontitis may include:

- Toothache in a specific area, especially when biting.
- Loosening of a tooth.
- Swelling of the jaw.

In some cases, a dental abscess (p.611) forms. If any of these symptoms occur, consult your dentist promptly.

WHAT MIGHT BE DONE?

Your dentist will examine your teeth and gums and check the depth of the pockets between them using a special probe. He or she will probably take dental X-rays (*see* DENTAL CHECKUP, p.609) to see how much of the bony support around the teeth has been lost.

Chronic periodontitis is treated by removing plaque and calculus from the teeth in a procedure known as scaling. In some cases, a flap procedure (surgical trimming of the gums) may also be performed to reduce the size of the pockets between the gums and teeth. The diseased lining of the pockets may be removed to allow healthy tissue to attach itself to the teeth. After surgery, an antiseptic mouthwash to kill bacteria may be prescribed. If periodontitis is severe, antibiotics (p.885) may be prescribed, or an antibiotic paste or pellet may be pushed into the deep pockets between the teeth and gums. Loose teeth may be fixed to other teeth to prevent their loss. Occasionally, grafting materials are used to regenerate the periodontal tissues and reduce the depth of the pockets.

Retrograde periodontitis is treated by removing the bacteria from the tooth and carrying out root canal treatment (p.612). A tooth that cannot be saved may need to be extracted.

After treatment, your dentist will advise that you brush and floss your teeth at least twice a day to prevent further buildup of plaque and calculus.

WHAT IS THE PROGNOSIS?

If you have chronic periodontitis, scaling the teeth, mouthwashes, and proper brushing and flossing should stop the gums from receding and prevent further loosening of the teeth. If you have retrograde periodontitis, a root canal filling should prevent further infection.

(WWW) ONLINE SITES: p.1029

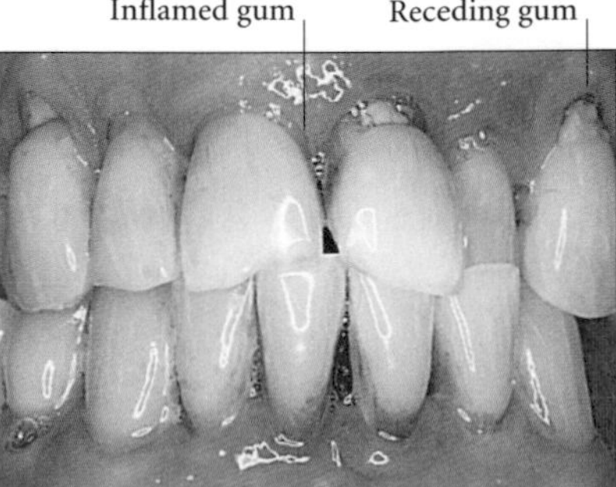
Inflamed gum
Receding gum

Periodontitis
The gums and tissues securing the teeth have become inflamed, and the gums have receded, leaving the teeth unsupported. The condition is known as periodontitis.

Receding gums

Withdrawal of the gums from around the teeth, exposing part of the roots

 AGE Usually develops after age 35

 LIFESTYLE Poor oral hygiene and abrasive toothbrushing are risk factors

 GENDER GENETICS Not significant factors

Healthy gums form a tight seal around the tooth where the crown of the tooth meets the root. If the gums recede, the root of the tooth becomes exposed, causing the attachment between the tooth and the socket to weaken. Eventually, the tooth may become loose and, in severe cases, may have to be extracted by the dentist.

If the roots are exposed, the teeth may be sensitive to hot, cold, or sweet substances. Since the roots are softer than the enamel on the crown of the tooth, they are also more susceptible to decay (*see* DENTAL CARIES, p.609).

WHAT ARE THE CAUSES?

Severely receding gums are usually a symptom of chronic gingivitis (p.617) or periodontitis (opposite page). These disorders are usually a result of poor oral hygiene and a buildup of plaque (a deposit of food particles, mucus, and bacteria) and calculus (hardened plaque) between the base of the teeth and the gums. The gums will eventually become inflamed and recede, exposing the roots of the teeth. Vigorous, abrasive toothbrushing along the margins of the gums, particularly in a horizontal direction with a hard toothbrush, may also cause the gums to recede.

WHAT MIGHT BE DONE?

Once you have receding gums, grafting procedures may be used to help cover exposed root surfaces and prevent further recession of the gums. Improving your oral hygiene (*see* CARING FOR YOUR TEETH AND GUMS, p.610) is also important in order to stop the gums from receding further.

Your dentist will probably use a procedure known as scaling to remove plaque and calculus from your teeth. Scaling should help prevent your gums from receding further. He or she will also advise you on your toothbrushing and flossing techniques to avoid further damage to the exposed roots. Your dentist or oral hygienist may also suggest that you use a desensitizing toothpaste or fluoride mouthwash, which will also reduce the risk of decay. If your teeth are very sensitive, the dentist may treat them with a desensitizing varnish or an adhesive filling material. If severely receding gums cause any of your teeth to become loose, they can sometimes be fixed to teeth that are more firmly anchored in the jawbone.

(WWW) ONLINE SITES: p.1029

Gingival hyperplasia

Enlargement and swelling of the gums due to various causes

LIFESTYLE Poor oral hygiene is a risk factor

 AGE GENDER GENETICS Not significant factors

The gums most commonly enlarge and swell, a condition known as gingival hyperplasia, as a result of the common gum disease gingivitis (p.617). This condition is due to poor oral hygiene, which allows plaque (a deposit of food particles, mucus, and bacteria) and calculus (hardened plaque) to build up where the gums meet the teeth. The gums become inflamed and bleed easily, especially when brushed.

Gingival hyperplasia can also be a side effect of some drugs, such as antihypertensives (p.897), anticonvulsants (p.914), and certain immunosuppressants (p.906). The condition may occur during pregnancy because of hormonal changes. Rarer causes include scurvy and acute leukemia (p.454).

To treat gingival hyperplasia, your dentist will probably scale your teeth to remove the plaque and advise you to brush and floss your teeth regularly (*see* CARING FOR YOUR TEETH AND GUMS, p.610). In some cases, excess gum tissue may be removed. If you are taking drugs associated with gingival hyperplasia, alternatives will be given. An underlying disorder, such as acute leukemia, will be treated if possible, and the condition of your gums should improve. Gingival hyperplasia due to pregnancy should clear up after the birth as hormone levels return to normal.

(WWW) ONLINE SITES: p.1029

Dry socket

Inflammation of a tooth socket that will not heal after extraction of the tooth

 LIFESTYLE Smoking and taking oral contraceptives are risk factors

 AGE GENDER GENETICS Not significant factors

After a tooth has been extracted, the tooth socket fills up with blood. The blood clots and provides the framework for healing the socket. If this clot is washed away for some reason, for example, by over-vigorous rinsing, or if the clot becomes infected, the bony lining of the socket can become inflamed, a condition known as "dry socket" or post-extraction alveolitis.

Dry socket occurs in about 1 in 25 tooth extractions and is most common following a difficult extraction of a molar tooth from the lower jaw. The condition occurs more frequently in people who smoke, as well as in women taking oral contraceptives.

There are a number of symptoms of dry socket, including a severe throbbing pain that commonly radiates to the ear 2–4 days after the tooth has been extracted, a bad taste in the mouth, and bad breath. The tooth socket may only partly heal, and, occasionally, small pieces of bone may come out of the tooth socket.

WHAT MIGHT BE DONE?

If, a few days after the extraction of the tooth, the socket is not healing, or you are feeling increasing pain, make an appointment to see your dentist as soon as possible. While waiting for the appointment, you may wish to take over-the-counter analgesics (p.912), which will help relieve the pain.

To treat dry socket, your dentist may first wash out the tooth socket with warm saltwater or a dilute antiseptic solution. He or she will then pack the socket with antiseptic paste. This treatment is repeated every 2–3 days until the tooth socket begins to heal. Your dentist may also suggest that you use hot saltwater mouthwashes at home to help reduce the inflammation. The socket should start to heal within a few days, and complete healing should occur in a few weeks.

(WWW) ONLINE SITES: p.1029

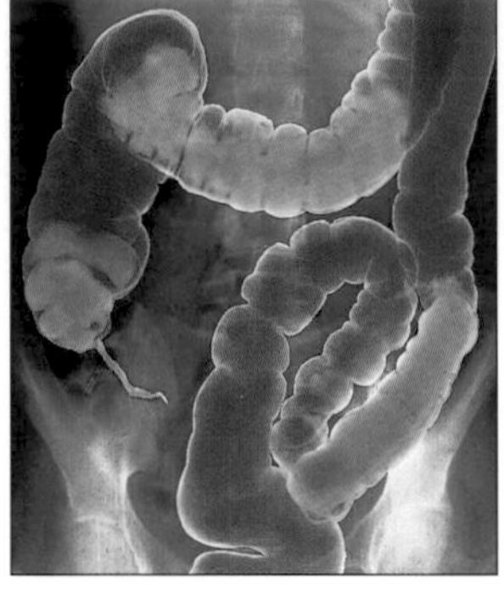

Colon
The colon is a looped tube about 4 ft (1.3 m) long that makes up most of the large intestine.

Digestive System

THE DIGESTIVE SYSTEM breaks down food into simple components that the body's cells can absorb and eliminates remaining waste. Food is propelled by muscular contractions through the digestive tract, the long tube that runs from the mouth to the anus. Digestion begins in the mouth, where saliva moistens and dissolves the food and the chewing action of the teeth and tongue breaks up large particles. The process of digestion is completed when nutrients (the useful parts of food) have been absorbed into the bloodstream and waste has passed out of the anus. The body uses nutrients for energy, growth, and tissue repair.

The digestive system consists of a long, convoluted, muscular tube or tract, which extends from the mouth to the anus, and a number of other digestive organs. These associated organs include the salivary glands, liver, and pancreas. The digestive tract is made up of a series of hollow organs, which includes the stomach and the small and large intestines.

The functions of the digestive system are to ingest food, break it down, extract the useful components, or nutrients, and dispose of the remaining waste as feces. Food can take many hours to pass through the tract. However, the esophagus and stomach enable us to swallow a large amount of food quickly and digest it at leisure. In an average person's lifetime, the digestive system processes 66,000 lb (30,000 kg) of food. The digestive system can process a variety of diets, from a typical meat-based Canadian diet to a Japanese diet consisting mainly of rice and fish.

Food breakdown

Most food molecules are too large to pass through cell membranes and must be broken down before they can be absorbed. Organs of the digestive system secrete juices containing enzymes (proteins that speed up chemical reactions) and acids that help convert large molecules into small, absorbable units. Chewing physically breaks down food into small particles, exposing a large surface area to the action of enzymes. In the stomach, food is churned with digestive juices to make chyme, a semiliquid mixture.

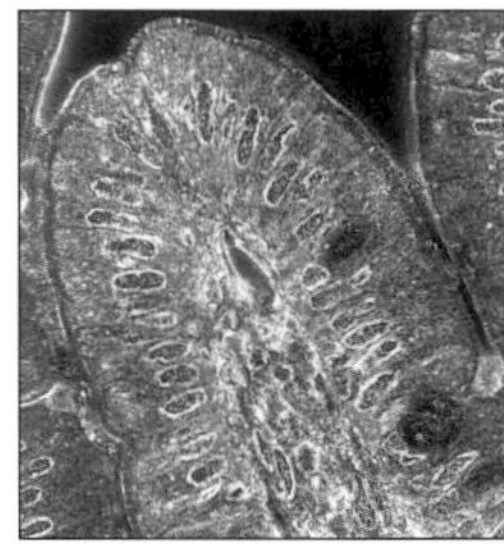

Villus
A villus is one of many, tiny, fingerlike projections lining the small intestine.

Absorption

By the time food reaches the end of the small intestine, most large nutrient molecules have been broken down into smaller molecules. These are absorbed into the blood through tiny pores in the villi, the fronds that project from the intestinal wall. The blood carries nutrients to the liver, then to the body's cells. Indigestible matter passes into the large intestine, where some water is absorbed before the remainder is expelled from the anus as feces.

Regulating digestion

The nervous and hormonal systems work together to ensure that digestive juices are secreted at the right time in different parts of the digestive tract. For example, when food enters the stomach or intestines, local glands release hormones that activate the production of digestive juices. These systems also control the action of the muscular walls of the digestive tract.

PROCESS Hunger and appetite

How much and how often we eat is determined by both hunger and appetite. When the body needs food or at times of day when it expects a routine meal, the nervous and hormonal systems cause the stomach to contract, resulting in hunger pangs. Appetite is a pleasurable sensation caused by the production of digestive juices in the mouth and stomach.

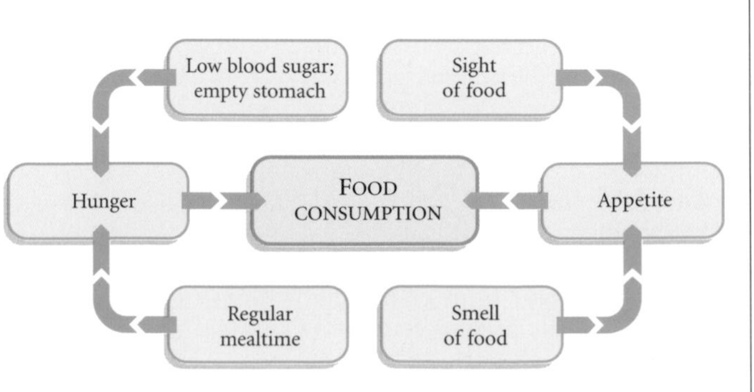
Low blood sugar; empty stomach
Sight of food
Hunger
Food consumption
Appetite
Regular mealtime
Smell of food

Stimulating hunger and appetite
Hunger is stimulated by the body's need for food or by the routine of mealtimes. The anticipation of food stimulates the appetite. Both sensations trigger a desire to eat.

STRUCTURE AND FUNCTION THE DIGESTIVE SYSTEM

The digestive system consists of the digestive tract and its associated organs. The digestive tract is a tube about 24 ft (7 m) long through which food passes while it is broken down. The tract consists of the mouth and pharynx (throat), esophagus, stomach, the small and large intestines, and the anus. The associated digestive organs include three pairs of salivary glands, the liver, the pancreas, and the gallbladder.

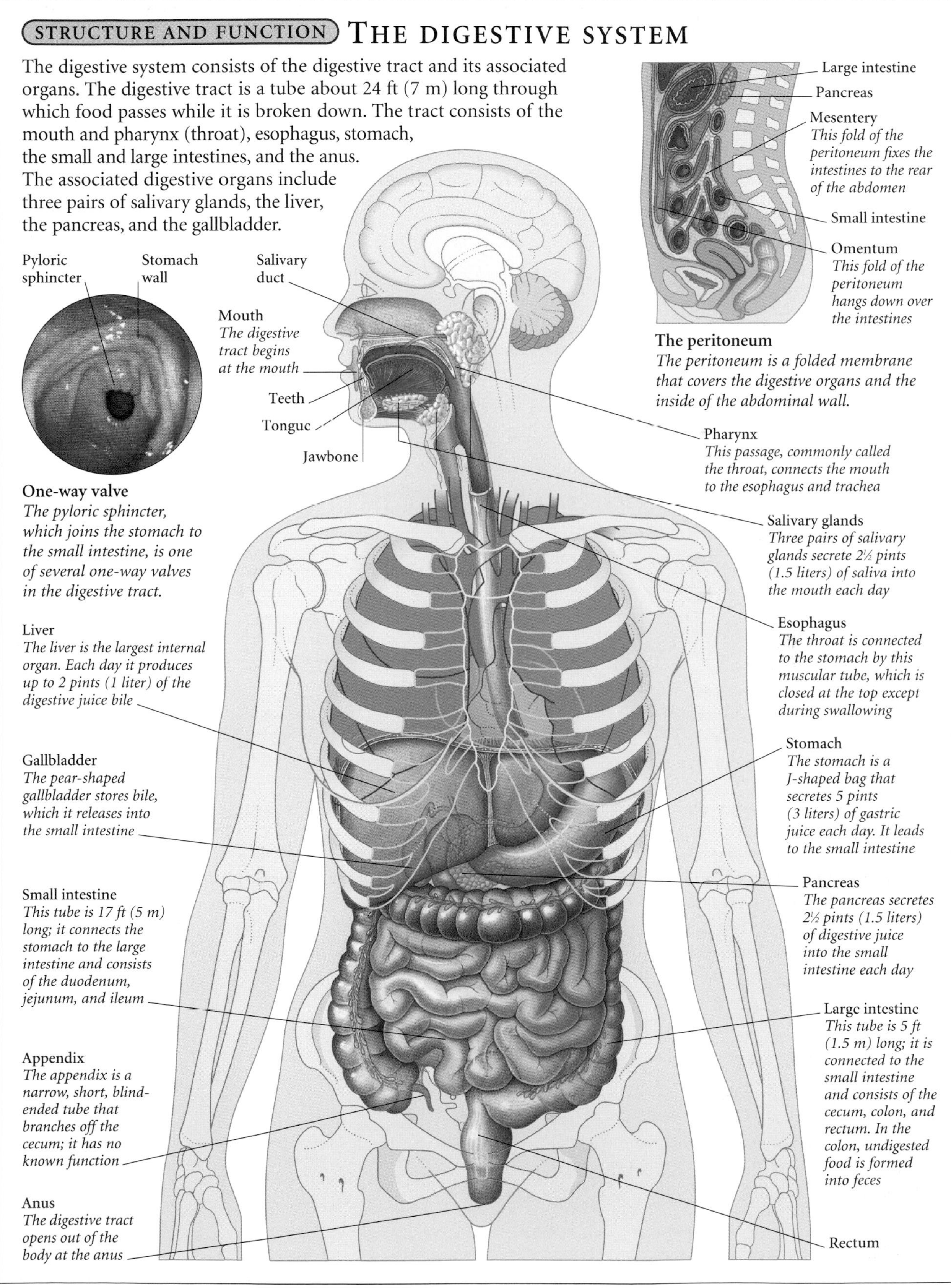
Pyloric sphincter
Stomach wall
Salivary duct
Mouth
The digestive tract begins at the mouth
Teeth
Tongue
Jawbone
Large intestine
Pancreas
Mesentery
This fold of the peritoneum fixes the intestines to the rear of the abdomen
Small intestine
Omentum
This fold of the peritoneum hangs down over the intestines
Pharynx
This passage, commonly called the throat, connects the mouth to the esophagus and trachea
Salivary glands
Three pairs of salivary glands secrete 2½ pints (1.5 liters) of saliva into the mouth each day
Esophagus
The throat is connected to the stomach by this muscular tube, which is closed at the top except during swallowing
Stomach
The stomach is a J-shaped bag that secretes 5 pints (3 liters) of gastric juice each day. It leads to the small intestine
Pancreas
The pancreas secretes 2½ pints (1.5 liters) of digestive juice into the small intestine each day
Large intestine
This tube is 5 ft (1.5 m) long; it is connected to the small intestine and consists of the cecum, colon, and rectum. In the colon, undigested food is formed into feces
Rectum
Liver
The liver is the largest internal organ. Each day it produces up to 2 pints (1 liter) of the digestive juice bile
Gallbladder
The pear-shaped gallbladder stores bile, which it releases into the small intestine
Small intestine
This tube is 17 ft (5 m) long; it connects the stomach to the large intestine and consists of the duodenum, jejunum, and ileum
Appendix
The appendix is a narrow, short, blind-ended tube that branches off the cecum; it has no known function
Anus
The digestive tract opens out of the body at the anus

One-way valve
The pyloric sphincter, which joins the stomach to the small intestine, is one of several one-way valves in the digestive tract.

The peritoneum
The peritoneum is a folded membrane that covers the digestive organs and the inside of the abdominal wall.

STRUCTURE AND FUNCTION

THE DIGESTIVE TRACT

The digestive tract is a series of hollow organs – the mouth, esophagus, stomach, small and large intestines, and anus – connected to form a long tube. The tract has muscular walls that rhythmically propel food along the tube (*see* PERISTALSIS, opposite page), breaking it down and mixing it with digestive juices. Muscular activity is controlled by a network of nerves that covers the tract. Several muscular valves control the passage of food and prevent it from moving backward.

MOUTH

The tongue, teeth, and saliva work together to start digestion and aid swallowing. Teeth chop and grind food, increasing the surface area over which digestive enzymes in saliva can act. Saliva also softens food so that the tongue can mold it into a bolus, or ball, for swallowing.

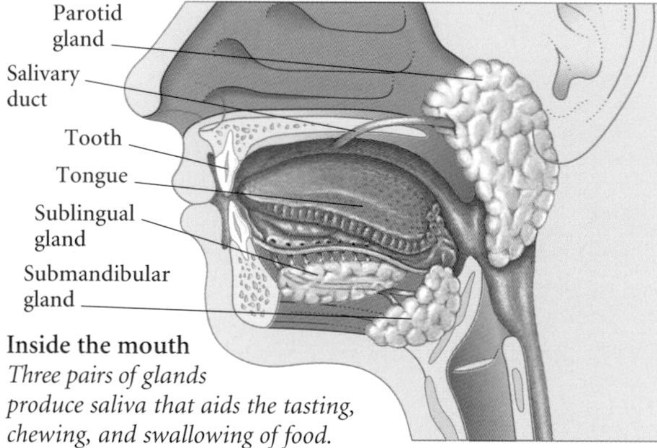
Parotid gland
Salivary duct
Tooth
Tongue
Sublingual gland
Submandibular gland

Inside the mouth
Three pairs of glands produce saliva that aids the tasting, chewing, and swallowing of food.

FUNCTION

SWALLOWING

Swallowing begins when you voluntarily push a bolus (ball of food) toward the esophagus with your tongue. This action triggers two involuntary events: the soft palate, the back of the roof of the mouth, closes off the nasal cavity, and the epiglottis, a flap of cartilage, tilts downward to seal the trachea (windpipe).

1 *In their normal positions, the soft palate and the epiglottis allow air to pass from the nasal cavity into the trachea.*

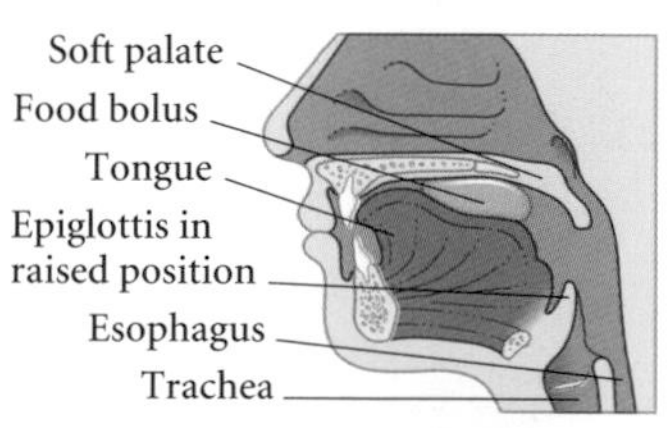
Soft palate
Food bolus
Tongue
Epiglottis in raised position
Esophagus
Trachea

2 *While swallowing, the epiglottis tilts to seal the trachea, the soft palate lifts to close off the nasal cavity, and the bolus enters the esophagus.*

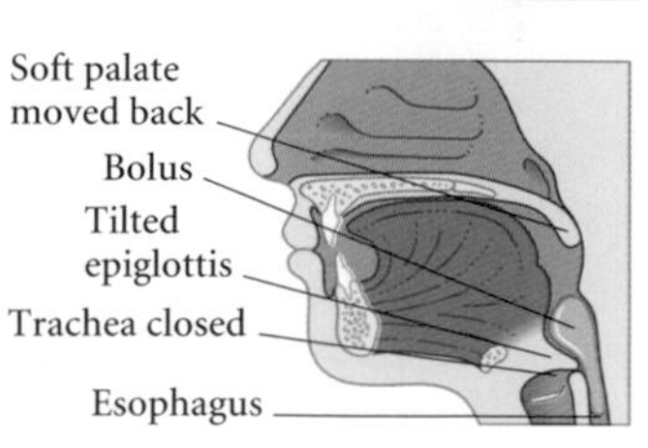
Soft palate moved back
Bolus
Tilted epiglottis
Trachea closed
Esophagus

ESOPHAGUS AND STOMACH

The throat opens into the esophagus, a muscular tube that propels food to the stomach. In the stomach, solid food spends up to 5 hours being churned to a pulp and mixed with gastric juice to form chyme before being squirted into the small intestine. Liquids pass from the mouth to the intestine in a matter of minutes.

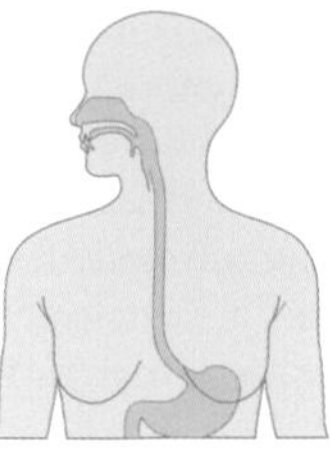

LOCATION

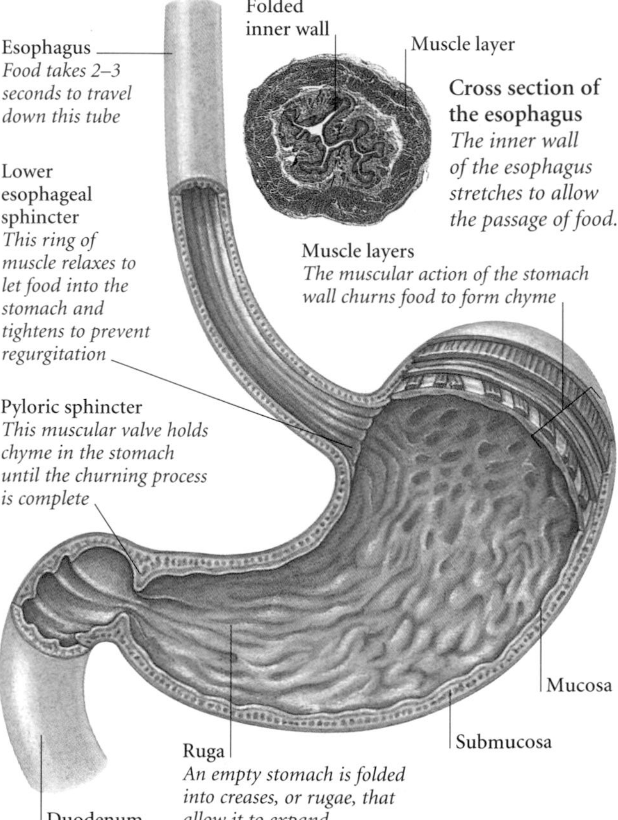
Esophagus
Food takes 2–3 seconds to travel down this tube
Folded inner wall
Muscle layer
Lower esophageal sphincter
This ring of muscle relaxes to let food into the stomach and tightens to prevent regurgitation
Muscle layers
The muscular action of the stomach wall churns food to form chyme
Pyloric sphincter
This muscular valve holds chyme in the stomach until the churning process is complete
Mucosa
Submucosa
Ruga
An empty stomach is folded into creases, or rugae, that allow it to expand
Duodenum

Cross section of the esophagus
The inner wall of the esophagus stretches to allow the passage of food.

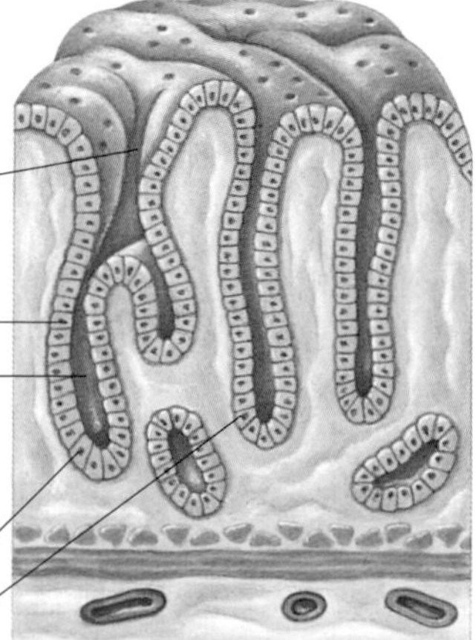
Gastric pit
The bases of these pits contain gastric glands
Mucus-producing cell
Gastric gland
Within each ruga, there are many gastric glands, which secrete acid and enzymes that make up gastric juice
Enzyme-producing cell
Acid-producing cell

Section of the stomach lining
The stomach is lined by mucosa, which secretes mucus to prevent the stomach from digesting itself.

Small and large intestines

At about 22 ft (6.5 m) in length, the intestines form the longest part of the digestive tract. In the small intestine, which consists of the duodenum, jejunum, and ileum, food mixes with digestive juices, and nutrients and water are absorbed into the blood. In the large intestine, which is divided into the cecum, colon, and rectum, feces are formed before passing out of the anus.

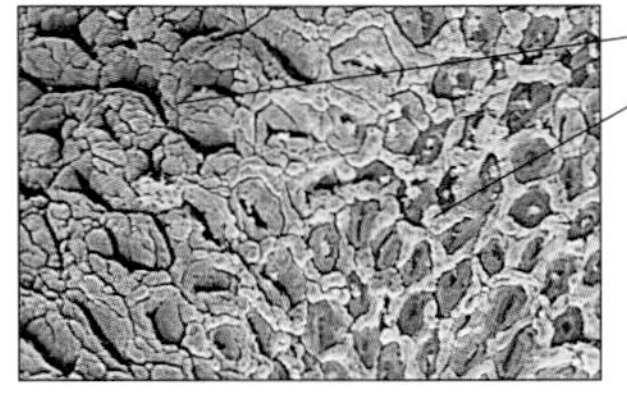
Lining of small intestine
Lining of large intestine

Intestinal junction
The small intestine has a folded lining to absorb nutrients; the lining of the large intestine is flatter.

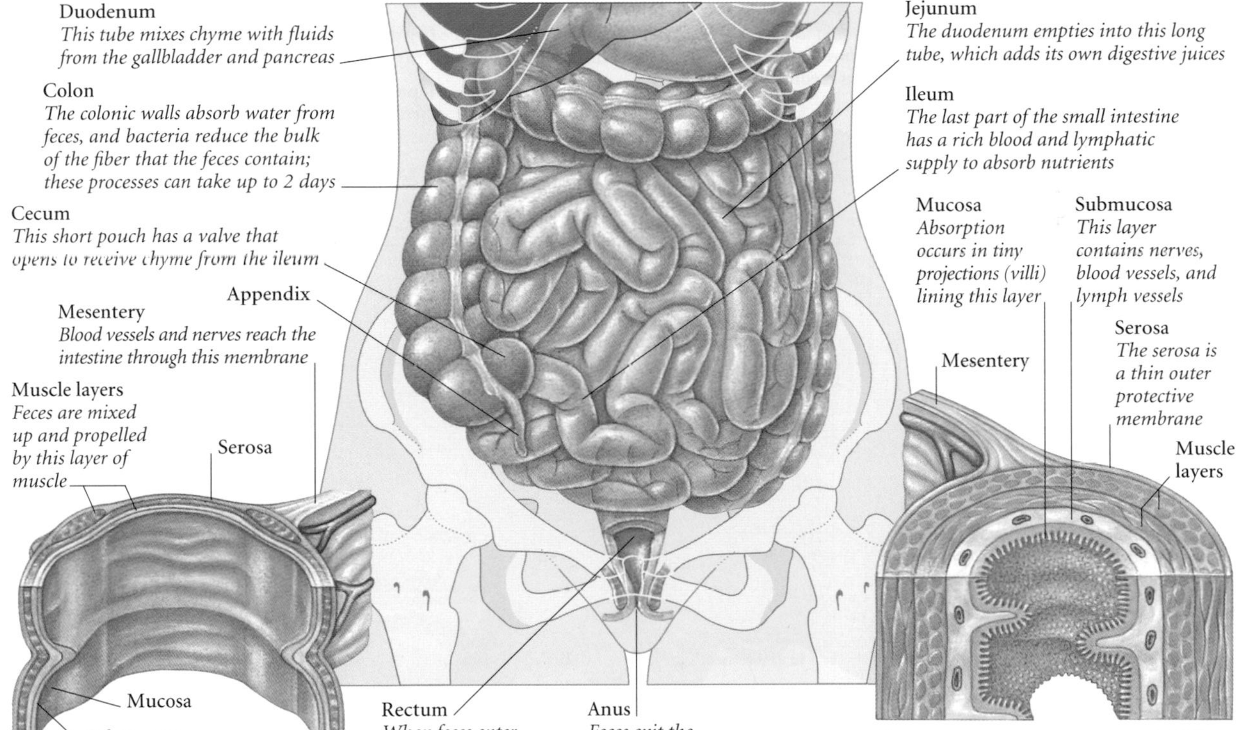
Duodenum
This tube mixes chyme with fluids from the gallbladder and pancreas
Colon
The colonic walls absorb water from feces, and bacteria reduce the bulk of the fiber that the feces contain; these processes can take up to 2 days
Cecum
This short pouch has a valve that opens to receive chyme from the ileum
Appendix
Mesentery
Blood vessels and nerves reach the intestine through this membrane
Muscle layers
Feces are mixed up and propelled by this layer of muscle
Serosa
Mucosa
Submucosa
Jejunum
The duodenum empties into this long tube, which adds its own digestive juices
Ileum
The last part of the small intestine has a rich blood and lymphatic supply to absorb nutrients
Mucosa
Absorption occurs in tiny projections (villi) lining this layer
Submucosa
This layer contains nerves, blood vessels, and lymph vessels
Mesentery
Serosa
The serosa is a thin outer protective membrane
Muscle layers
Rectum
When feces enter the rectum, they trigger an urge to defecate; this urge can be overridden voluntarily
Anus
Feces exit the digestive tract through the anus; a ring of muscle controls this action

Cross section of the large intestine
The large intestine wall has a wider diameter and less developed muscle layers than the small intestine.

Cross section of small intestine

(FUNCTION) Peristalsis

Food is propelled along the digestive tract by a sequence of muscular contractions called peristalsis. The muscular wall behind a piece of food squeezes to push it forward into the next part of the tract, where the muscle is relaxed. Other types of muscular action churn food in the stomach and form feces in the colon.

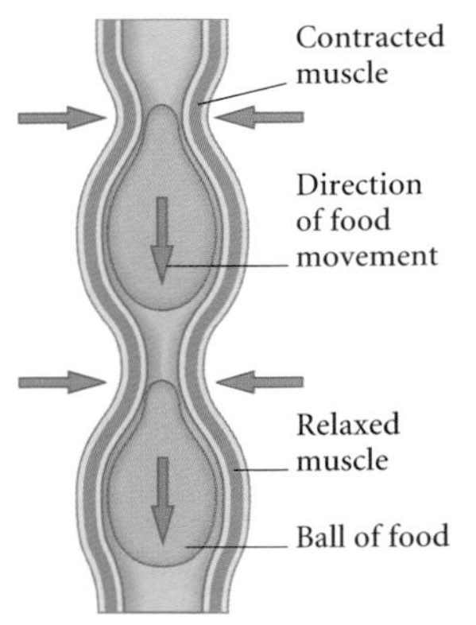
Contracted muscle
Direction of food movement
Relaxed muscle
Ball of food

The peristaltic wave
The muscular action of the digestive tract moves food continuously in an action known as a "peristaltic wave."

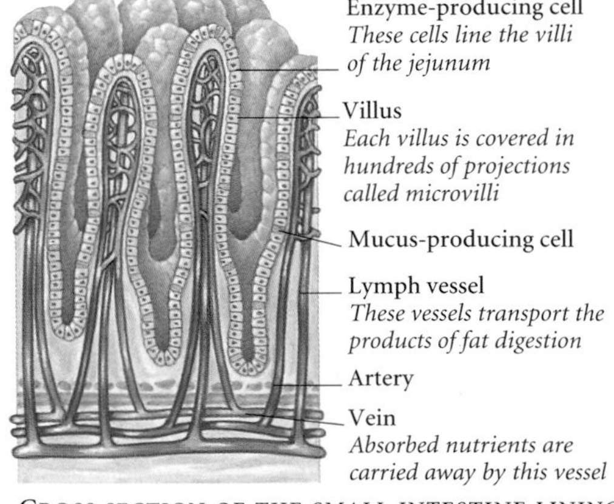
Enzyme-producing cell
These cells line the villi of the jejunum
Villus
Each villus is covered in hundreds of projections called microvilli
Mucus-producing cell
Lymph vessel
These vessels transport the products of fat digestion
Artery
Vein
Absorbed nutrients are carried away by this vessel

Cross section of the small intestine lining

Villi of the small intestine
The mucosa, the inner layer of the small intestine, has millions of fingerlike fronds called villi covered in smaller fronds called microvilli. These fronds provide a surface area the size of a tennis court for nutrient absorption.

GENERAL DIGESTIVE AND NUTRITIONAL PROBLEMS

Most common digestive problems cause short-term symptoms, such as indigestion, diarrhea, and constipation. However, chronic symptoms affecting the digestive system sometimes reflect a more serious underlying disorder.

The first part of this section looks at indigestion (dyspepsia), the abdominal discomfort that most people feel at some time. Occasionally, as is described in the second article, discomfort may be more vague and persist without an identifiable cause, in which case it is known as functional dyspepsia.

The next articles cover diarrhea and constipation. These problems often clear up on their own. If they persist, you should seek medical advice because there may be an underlying disorder that needs treatment. Diarrhea may be a result of gastroenteritis or food poisoning, both of which can be serious in elderly people and young children.

Bleeding from the digestive tract can indicate a serious disorder and is discussed in the next article. New techniques developed in the last 25 years have enabled most cases of digestive tract bleeding to be diagnosed and treated without the need for surgery.

The final articles look at nutritional deficiencies, which are rare in Canada, and obesity, a condition increasingly common among Canadians.

KEY ANATOMY

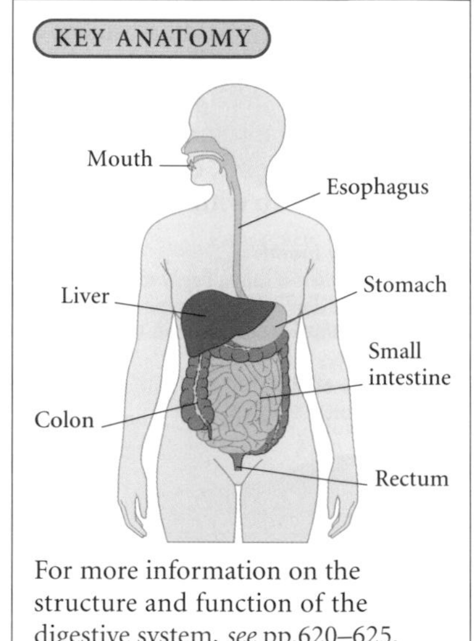
Mouth
Esophagus
Liver
Stomach
Small intestine
Colon
Rectum

For more information on the structure and function of the digestive system, *see* pp.620–625.

Indigestion

Pain or discomfort in the upper abdomen that is brought on by eating

 AGE More common in adults

 LIFESTYLE Stress, being overweight, smoking, and certain dietary habits are risk factors

 GENDER GENETICS Not significant factors

The medical term for indigestion is dyspepsia, which means "pain in the upper abdomen." The condition is more common in adults. Smoking and being overweight increase the risk. Most cases are not serious.

Usually, indigestion will occur after a meal, especially one that included rich, fatty, or heavily spiced food. As well, overeating, consuming too much alcohol, coffee, or tea, and eating too quickly can cause discomfort, as can stress and drugs such as aspirin that irritate the digestive tract.

If indigestion persists or increases in severity, or if you start to vomit, lose your appetite, or lose weight, consult your doctor. These symptoms may be a sign of a more serious disorder such as gastroesophageal reflux disease (p.636), a peptic ulcer (p.640), or, in rare cases, stomach cancer (p.642).

Antacids (p.923) can usually relieve mild indigestion. There are also some self-help measures that you can follow to avoid future attacks (*see* PREVENTING INDIGESTION, opposite page).

(WWW) ONLINE SITES: p.1030

Functional dyspepsia

Pain or discomfort in the upper abdomen that is not associated with a structural abnormality

 AGE More common in adults

 GENDER More common in males

 LIFESTYLE Stress, being overweight, smoking, and certain dietary habits are risk factors

 GENETICS Not a significant factor

Functional dyspepsia describes recurrent and persistent indigestion (left) that occurs without an identifiable cause or abnormality of the digestive tract. The condition occurs more commonly in adults, especially women, and may be worsened by factors such as stress, being overweight, smoking, and a poor diet. The symptoms may include pain in the upper abdomen, often made worse by eating, and nausea, particularly in the morning. People with the condition often have these symptoms several times a week for months. If you have such symptoms, consult your doctor because they could be a sign of a more serious underlying disorder, such as a peptic ulcer (p.640) or stomach cancer (p.642).

WHAT MIGHT BE DONE?

Your doctor will probably arrange for you to have tests in order to exclude other disorders. For example, you may be given a blood test to check for the presence of antibodies against the bacterium *H. pylori,* which may indicate an infection of the stomach lining (*see* HELICOBACTER PYLORI INFECTION, p.639). In addition, upper digestive tract endoscopy (p.641) or contrast X-rays (p.245) may be done to look for abnormalities in the digestive tract. If the tests do not reveal an underlying disorder, you will be diagnosed as having functional dyspepsia.

There are measures that you can take to try to reduce the frequency and severity of symptoms (*see* PREVENTING INDIGESTION, above). If these measures

SELF-HELP PREVENTING INDIGESTION

Some measures can be taken to prevent or reduce the frequency of episodes of indigestion. You may find some of the following helpful:

- Eat small portions of food at regular intervals without rushing or overfilling your stomach.
- Avoid eating in the 3 hours before going to bed at night to allow your body enough time to digest food.
- Reduce or eliminate your intake of alcohol, coffee, and tea.
- Avoid rich, fatty foods such as butter and fried foods.
- Keep a food diary to help identify foods that cause indigestion.
- Learn to overcome stress, which can often trigger episodes of indigestion (*see* RELAXATION EXERCISES, p.75).
- Try to lose excess weight and avoid tight-fitting clothing.
- If possible, avoid taking medicines that irritate the digestive tract, such as aspirin and nonsteroidal anti-inflammatory drugs (p.894).

do not resolve the problem, your doctor may prescribe medication that will neutralize or reduce stomach acid production (*see* ACID-SUPPRESSIVE DRUGS, p.923, and ANTACIDS, p.923).

WWW ONLINE SITES: p.1030

Diarrhea

The passage of loose or watery stools and/or an increase in the frequency of bowel movements

 LIFESTYLE Poor food hygiene is a risk factor

 AGE GENDER GENETICS Not significant factors

Diarrhea is the production of stools that are more watery, more frequent, or greater in volume than is normal for a particular individual. Although it is not a disease itself, diarrhea may be a symptom of an underlying disorder.

In some cases, diarrhea is accompanied by abdominal pain, bloating, loss of appetite, and vomiting. Severe diarrhea can also lead to dehydration that may be life-threatening, particularly in babies (*see* VOMITING AND DIARRHEA, p.864) and elderly people.

Short episodes of diarrhea, especially if they are associated with vomiting, are often due to gastroenteritis (p.628) or food poisoning (p.629). Diarrhea that lasts more than 3–4 weeks usually indicates that there is an intestinal disorder and requires medical attention.

WHAT ARE THE CAUSES?

Diarrhea that starts abruptly in a person who is otherwise healthy is often caused by contaminated food or water and may last a few hours to 10 days. This sort of diarrhea often occurs during travel in a developing country, where food hygiene and sanitation may be poor. Diarrhea may also be caused by a viral infection that is spread by close personal contact. Such infectious gastroenteritis is the most common cause of diarrhea in babies and young children.

People with reduced immunity, such as those with AIDS (*see* HIV INFECTION AND AIDS, p.295), are more susceptible to infectious gastroenteritis, which also tends to be more severe in these people. People taking drugs such as antibiotics (p.885) may develop sudden diarrhea if the drugs disturb the normal balance of bacteria in the colon.

Persistent diarrhea may be a result of chronic inflammation of the intestine due to disorders such as Crohn's disease (p.658) or ulcerative colitis (p.659) or some conditions in which the small intestine cannot absorb nutrients (*see* MALABSORPTION, p.655). Lactose intolerance (p.657), a disorder in which lactose (a natural sugar present in milk) cannot be broken down and absorbed, can also cause diarrhea.

Infections with protozoal parasites, such as giardiasis (p.307) and amebiasis (p.306), may lead to chronic diarrhea. Irritable bowel syndrome (p.656) may produce abnormal contractions of the intestine, which result in alternating episodes of diarrhea and constipation.

WHAT MIGHT BE DONE?

In most cases, diarrhea clears up within a day or two. Other symptoms that can accompany diarrhea, such as headache, weakness, and lethargy, are most often caused by dehydration. The symptoms of dehydration disappear as soon as lost fluids and salts are replaced (*see* PREVENTING DEHYDRATION, below).

If your diarrhea lasts longer than 3–4 days, you should consult your doctor, who may request a sample of feces to look for evidence of either infection or unabsorbed nutrients. If your diarrhea persists for more than 3–4 weeks or if blood is in the feces, your doctor will probably arrange for you to have investigative procedures, such as contrast X-rays (p.245) of the intestines, sigmoidoscopy, or colonoscopy (p.661).

Specific treatments given for diarrhea depend on the underlying cause. If you need to curtail your diarrhea quickly, your doctor may prescribe an antidiarrheal drug (p.924), such as loperamide. However, antidiarrheal drugs should usually be avoided if your diarrhea is due to an infection because they may prolong the infection. Antibiotics are only needed to treat persistent diarrhea that has a known bacterial cause.

WWW ONLINE SITES: p.1030

SELF-HELP PREVENTING DEHYDRATION

For normal body functioning, the body's water and salt content must be kept at a constant level. During an attack of diarrhea or vomiting, the body can become dehydrated due to loss of large amounts of fluids and salts. Babies, children, and elderly people are particularly vulnerable to dehydration, which can be reversed or prevented by following these simple measures:

- Drink plenty of fluids, such as flat soda, weak sweet tea, or premixed rehydration solution, which is available in bottles over the counter.
- Ensure that you drink at least 1 pint (500 ml) of fluid every 1–2 hours while symptoms last.
- Do not give children milk because it may perpetuate the diarrhea. However, if a breast-feeding baby is affected, continue to breast-feed and give the baby additional fluids.
- Stay out of the sun and try to keep cool in order to prevent further loss of fluids in sweat.

Constipation

Difficult and infrequent passage of small, hard stools

 AGE Most common in children and elderly people

 GENDER More common in females

 LIFESTYLE A low-fiber diet is a risk factor

 GENETICS Risk factors depend on the cause

If your stools are small and hard or if you have to strain to pass them, you are probably constipated. How frequently you pass stools is less important because healthy people have bowel movements at widely differing intervals. Usual intervals range from three times a day to three times a week. Most people tend to have a regular routine, and bowels usually function best if they are allowed to follow a consistent pattern.

Harmless bouts of constipation are common, but occasionally there is an underlying disorder that needs to be investigated. You should consult your doctor if you have recently developed constipation that is severe or lasts more than 2 weeks, particularly if it first occurs after age 50 or if blood is present in the feces. Persistent constipation may lead to fecal impaction, in which hard feces remain in the rectum. Liquid feces may leak around the partial obstruction, resulting in diarrhea (p.627).

What are the causes?

A diet that is low in fiber and fluids is the most common cause of constipation. Drinking too much alcohol or drinks containing caffeine, which may lead to dehydration, can also make feces hard and difficult to pass. Other factors that decrease the frequency of bowel movements are doing too little exercise and long periods of immobility. Several disorders, such as the metabolic disorder hypothyroidism (p.680) and depression (p.554), may also lead to constipation. In addition, the condition is associated with disorders that affect the large intestine, such as diverticulosis (p.663).

People recovering from abdominal surgery and people with anal disorders, such as hemorrhoids (p.668) or a tear in the anal canal, may find it painful to defecate and then develop constipation. Certain drugs, including some analgesics (p.912), some antidepressants (p.916), and antacids (p.923) containing aluminum and calcium carbonate, may cause constipation.

Poor toilet training in infants (*see* CONSTIPATION IN CHILDREN, p.865) and increasing immobility in elderly people make constipation much more common in these age groups. For unknown reasons, it is more common in women.

What might be done?

If constipation is associated with your lifestyle, there are several measures you can take to relieve it and prevent recurrence (*see* PREVENTING CONSTIPATION, below). If constipation persists, consult your doctor, who will perform tests to look for an underlying cause. He or she will probably first examine your abdomen and check your rectum by inserting a gloved finger. You may be asked to give a fecal sample, which will be examined for the presence of blood (*see* FECAL OCCULT BLOOD TEST, p.233).

If further tests are necessary, you may have your large intestine examined with a viewing instrument (*see* COLONOSCOPY, p.661) or have contrast X-rays (p.245) of your intestines to reveal abnormalities. If your doctor finds an underlying cause, its treatment should relieve constipation. Your doctor will prescribe an alternative drug if a particular drug is the cause of constipation.

You may have an enema, in which liquid is passed through a tube into the rectum to stimulate bowel movements. This treatment should be followed by a change in diet to include more fiber.

Constipation linked to a painful anal disorder may be relieved with a soothing ointment or suppositories.

(WWW) ONLINE SITES: p.1030, p.1035

> **SELF-HELP PREVENTING CONSTIPATION**
>
> There are some simple steps you can take to prevent or reduce the severity of constipation:
>
> - Increase your daily fiber intake. Fiber-rich foods include bran, wholegrain bread, cereals, fruit, leafy vegetables, potato skins, beans, and dried peas.
> - Reduce your intake of highly refined and processed foods, such as cheese and white bread.
> - Increase your daily fluid intake, but avoid drinks containing caffeine or alcohol.
> - Do not use stimulant laxatives (p.924) persistently because the colon may eventually be unable to function without them.
> - Do not ignore the urge to defecate. The longer that feces remain in the colon, the drier and harder they become.
> - Try to achieve a regular routine in which you go to the toilet at the same time of day.

Gastroenteritis

Inflammation of the lining of the stomach and intestines, usually due to infection

 AGE Most common in babies and children but can occur at any age

 LIFESTYLE Poor food hygiene or insanitary conditions are risk factors

 GENDER GENETICS Not significant factors

Gastroenteritis usually starts suddenly, causing symptoms of vomiting, diarrhea (p.627), and fever. Outbreaks commonly occur within families and among people who are in close contact, such as schoolchildren. Most people recover from the disorder without problems, but gastroenteritis may be serious in elderly people and very young children (*see* VOMITING AND DIARRHEA, p.864) because there is a risk of dehydration. In these age groups in developing countries, gastroenteritis is a common cause of death.

What are the causes?

Gastroenteritis is usually due to a viral or bacterial infection that inflames the lining of the stomach and intestines. The infection may be acquired from contaminated food or water (*see* FOOD POISONING, p.629), or it may be spread among people who are in close contact, especially if hygiene is poor.

Viral gastroenteritis is often caused by rotaviruses or astroviruses, particularly in young children, and by the Norwalk virus in older children and adults. Most people acquire immunity to these viruses by the time they are adults. Bacterial causes of gastroenteritis include salmonella and *Escherichia coli*.

WHAT ARE THE SYMPTOMS?

The symptoms of gastroenteritis often develop rapidly over 1–2 hours and may vary in severity. They include:

- Nausea and vomiting.
- Cramping abdominal pain.
- Fever, often with headache.
- Diarrhea.

In some people, vomiting or diarrhea may lead to dehydration. Babies and elderly people are much more susceptible to the effects of dehydration, which are often difficult to recognize. Babies may become listless and cry feebly, and an elderly person may become confused. Consult your doctor promptly if you are not able to keep fluids down or have not urinated for over 6 hours, especially if you have a chronic illness, such as diabetes mellitus (p.687) or kidney disease. Without the appropriate treatment, dehydration may be life-threatening.

WHAT MIGHT BE DONE?

A mild attack of gastroenteritis usually clears up without treatment, but you should follow self-help measures and drink plenty of fluids every few hours (*see* PREVENTING DEHYDRATION, p.627). Over-the-counter antidiarrheal drugs (p.924) are useful when you need to curtail symptoms quickly. However, these remedies are best avoided because they may prolong gastroenteritis by retaining the infective organism inside the gastrointestinal tract.

If your symptoms are severe or prolonged, you should consult your doctor. You may be asked to provide a sample of feces, which will be tested for an infection. Antibiotics (p.885) are rarely needed unless a bacterial infection is identified. Severe dehydration requires emergency treatment in the hospital to replace fluids and salts intravenously.

WHAT IS THE PROGNOSIS?

Most people recover rapidly from gastroenteritis with no long-lasting effects. Occasionally, short-term damage to the intestine may reduce its ability to digest lactose, the natural sugar present in milk (*see* LACTOSE INTOLERANCE, p.657). This disorder occurs particularly in infants and often results in diarrhea that can persist for days or weeks. In rare cases, gastroenteritis may trigger irritable bowel syndrome (p.656).

WWW ONLINE SITES: p.1030, p.1033

Food poisoning

Sudden illness caused by consuming food or drink contaminated by a toxin or infectious organism

LIFESTYLE Poor food hygiene is a risk factor

AGE GENDER GENETICS Not significant factors

Food poisoning is the term used to describe a sudden illness that is caused by consuming food or drink that may taste normal but is contaminated with a toxin or infectious organism.

The diagnosis of food poisoning is easily made if a group of people all develop the same symptoms, usually vomiting and diarrhea, after they have consumed the same food or drink. The symptoms may start hours or days after consuming the food or drink.

Usually, the symptoms are confined to the gastrointestinal tract. However, some food poisoning may cause more widespread symptoms. For example, the *Clostridium botulinum* bacterium causes muscle weakness and paralysis (*see* BOTULISM, p.301), and listeriosis (p.301) may cause flulike symptoms and lead to meningitis (p.527).

Food poisoning is becoming increasingly common in Canada. However, it can usually be avoided by the careful preparation, storage, and cooking of food (*see* FOOD HYGIENE, p.79). Drinks should be given the same attention.

WHAT ARE THE CAUSES?

Most cases of food poisoning result from contamination of food or water by bacteria, viruses, or, less commonly, protozoal parasites. Poor food hygiene can enable microorganisms to multiply. In some cases of bacterial food poisoning, it is not the presence of bacteria themselves that cause poisoning but the effect of toxins produced by the bacteria.

If infectious organisms are ingested with the food, they can multiply in the digestive tract. If the food poisoning is caused by bacterial toxins, they may be produced in the food before it is eaten.

Most types of food poisoning cause diarrhea and/or vomiting, often with abdominal pain. The severity of symptoms, the speed at which they develop, and the duration of the illness depend on the cause of food poisoning.

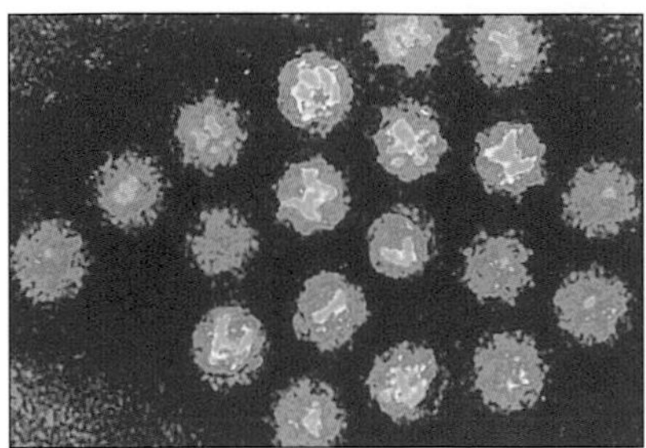

Norwalk virus
This magnified image shows particles of Norwalk virus, which often contaminates shellfish and causes food poisoning.

STAPHYLOCOCCI BACTERIA A number of foods, such as poultry, eggs, and previously prepared sandwiches and pâté, can be infected by staphylococci bacteria. These bacteria produce toxins that are ingested with food. The toxins usually produce diarrhea and/or vomiting within 4 hours. In most cases, symptoms clear up within 24 hours.

ESCHERICHIA COLI BACTERIA Certain types of *E. coli* can contaminate meat and water and produce toxins of varying potency. Types of *E. coli* are usually responsible for causing traveler's diarrhea, which is usually mild. However, some types of *E. coli* may cause a severe illness because they produce a potent type of toxin that can damage blood cells and lead to kidney failure (p.705).

SALMONELLA BACTERIA Salmonellosis is a disease caused by salmonella bacteria, which infect eggs and poultry. Salmonellosis typically causes symptoms such as vomiting, mild fever, and severe diarrhea that may be blood-stained. The symptoms usually begin 12–72 hours after eating the contaminated food and last for 1–3 days.

CAMPYLOBACTER BACTERIA These bacteria are one of the most common causes of diarrhea. They may contaminate meat and more rarely water or unpasteurized milk. Symptoms usually develop about 2–5 days after eating the contaminated food and may include severe, watery diarrhea. The diarrhea may contain blood and/or mucus. In most cases, the symptoms will subside within 2–3 days, although there may be bacteria present in the feces for as long as 5 weeks after infection.

OTHER INFECTIONS Viral infections can be contracted from contaminated food or water. Shellfish are also a common source of viral contamination, especially with the Norwalk virus. Symptoms often start suddenly after eating contaminated food, but recovery is usually rapid. Protozoal infections that may be contracted from contaminated food include cryptosporidiosis (p.307), amebiasis (p.306), and giardiasis (p.307). Cryptosporidiosis may cause symptoms such as vomiting and loose, watery diarrhea that develop about a week after consuming contaminated food or water. The symptoms of amebiasis may include watery, often bloody, diarrhea that persists for several days or weeks. In giardiasis, there may be diarrhea with bloating and flatulence that often lasts more than a week.

NONINFECTIOUS CAUSES In some cases, food poisoning may be caused by poisonous mushrooms or contamination of fruit or vegetables with high concentrations of pesticides. Symptoms may include vomiting and diarrhea.

WHAT MIGHT BE DONE?

Usually, symptoms disappear without treatment. If your symptoms are mild, use self-help measures to prevent dehydration (*see* PREVENTING DEHYDRATION, p.627). If the symptoms are severe or last more than 3–4 days, consult your doctor. If an elderly person or child is affected, you should consult a doctor immediately. Keep a sample of any remaining food in addition to the feces, which can be tested for the presence of infectious microorganisms. If the cause is noninfectious, such as poisonous mushrooms, you may need to be treated urgently to eliminate the poison from the body.

Treatment of food poisoning is usually aimed at preventing dehydration. In severe cases, fluids and salts may be administered intravenously in the hospital. Antibiotics (p.885) are used only if specific bacteria are identified. People usually recover rapidly from a bout of food poisoning and rarely experience long-lasting consequences.

In rare cases, there is a risk of septicemia (p.298) if bacteria spread into the bloodstream. Both dehydration and septicemia can lead to shock (p.414), a condition that may be fatal.

(WWW) ONLINE SITES: p.1030, p.1033

Bleeding from the digestive tract

Loss of blood from the lining of the digestive tract, sometimes resulting in bloodstained feces or vomit

AGE GENDER GENETICS LIFESTYLE
Risk factors depend on the cause

Bleeding can occur in any part of the digestive tract and should always be investigated because there may be a serious underlying cause. In some cases, only small amounts of blood are lost over a long period of time and go unnoticed. In other cases, severe, sudden bleeding from the digestive tract may result in blood being vomited or passed out of the anus in the feces. You should seek medical help if you notice any bleeding.

WHAT ARE THE CAUSES?

The causes of bleeding in the digestive tract include inflammation of or damage to the tract's lining and tumors.

Bleeding from the upper tract, which includes the esophagus, stomach, and duodenum, may occur when stomach acid damages the lining of these organs. This is a common complication of gastroesophageal reflux disease (p.636) and peptic ulcers (p.640). Severe bleeding is sometimes due to enlargement of veins in the esophagus, a complication of chronic liver diseases (*see* PORTAL HYPERTENSION AND VARICES, p.648).

Most cases of bleeding from the lower digestive tract, which includes the colon, rectum, and anus, are due to minor disorders, such as hemorrhoids (p.668) or anal fissure (p.669) caused by straining to defecate. However, bleeding may be a sign of colorectal cancer (p.665). Diverticulosis (p.663) and other disorders of the colon can also lead to the presence of blood in the feces.

WHAT ARE THE SYMPTOMS?

The symptoms vary according to the site and the severity of the bleeding. If the bleeding is mild, blood loss may go unnoticed, but it may eventually cause symptoms of anemia (p.446), such as pale skin and shortness of breath. Severe bleeding from the esophagus, stomach, or duodenum may cause:

- Vomit containing bright red blood or resembling coffee grounds.
- Light-headedness.
- Black, tarry stools.

If there is a heavy loss of blood from the lower part of the tract, there will probably be visible blood in the stools. When there is severe blood loss from any part of the tract, shock (p.414) may develop. Shock causes symptoms that include fainting, sweating, and confusion and requires immediate hospital treatment.

WHAT MIGHT BE DONE?

Minor bleeding may be detected only during an investigation for anemia or screening to detect colorectal cancer. If the bleeding is severe, you may need intravenous fluids and a blood transfusion (p.447) to replace lost blood. You will be examined to detect the location of the bleeding, usually by endoscopy through the mouth (*see* UPPER DIGESTIVE TRACT ENDOSCOPY, p.641) or anus (*see* COLONOSCOPY, p.661).

Treatment for bleeding depends on the underlying cause. For example, peptic ulcers are treated with antibiotics (p.885) and ulcer-healing drugs (p.923), but colorectal cancer needs surgery. It may be possible to stop bleeding by a treatment done during endoscopy, such as laser surgery (*see* LASER TREATMENT, p.951), making open surgery unnecessary. Treatment is usually successful if the cause is identified and treated early.

(WWW) ONLINE SITES: p.1030

Nutritional deficiencies

Deficiencies of one or more nutrients essential for normal body function

AGE More common in children

LIFESTYLE Alcohol dependence and extreme dieting are risk factors

GENDER GENETICS Not significant factors

Nutritional deficiencies occur when the body lacks essential elements that are obtained from food. In developing countries, such deficiencies are usually the result of poverty and insufficient food supplies. In Canada, nutritional deficiencies are due mainly to disorders that limit the body's intake or absorption of nutrients or to self-imposed dietary restrictions. Deficiencies may be noticed when nutritional needs increase, such as in growth spurts in childhood.

WHAT ARE THE TYPES?

There are two main types of nutritional deficiencies: a general deficiency of calories and all nutrients and deficiencies of specific nutrients. A general deficiency may be the result of poor eating because of severe illness or surgery. It may also be due to extreme dieting or deliberate starvation, as occurs in the eating disorder anorexia nervosa (p.562). Some people may neglect their diet because of other psychological problems, such as depression (p.554) or alcohol dependence (p.564). result from poor absorption of food in the small intestine (*see* MALABSORPTION, p.655). Symptoms may include weight loss, muscle weakness, and fatigue.

Specific nutritional deficiencies may occur if people limit their diets because of certain beliefs. In some cases, malabsorption causes deficiency of a specific nutrient. For example, the bowel disorder Crohn's disease (p.658) can affect the last section of the small intestine, through which vitamin B_{12} is absorbed. Specific nutritional deficiencies result in a variety of disorders. These include iron-deficiency anemia (p.447) and the bone disorders osteomalacia and rickets (p.370), which are caused by a lack of calcium or vitamin D.

WHAT MIGHT BE DONE?

If your doctor suspects that you have a nutritional deficiency, he or she will weigh you and make an assessment of your diet. You may also have blood tests to look for anemia and to measure levels of specific nutrients. Investigations, such as intestinal biopsies or contrast X-rays (p.245) of the gastrointestinal tract, may be done to detect underlying disorders.

If the deficiency is severe, you will be admitted to the hospital and given nutrients using a tube passed through the nose into the stomach or through a drip directly into the bloodstream.

If the deficiency is a result of a treatable physical problem, it should resolve with treatment. Changing your diet should resolve the problem if poor eating is the cause. Psychological problems will also require treatment. In some cases, such as Crohn's disease, long-term vitamin and mineral supplements (p.927) may be required. In celiac disease, a lifelong gluten-free diet will be prescribed.

WWW ONLINE SITES: p.1030, p.1035

Obesity

A condition in which there is an accumulation of excess body fat

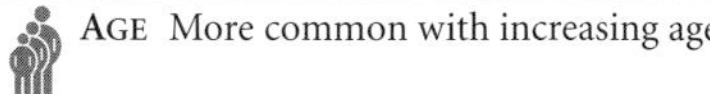

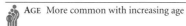

AGE More common with increasing age

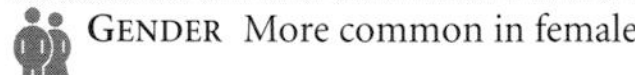

GENDER More common in females

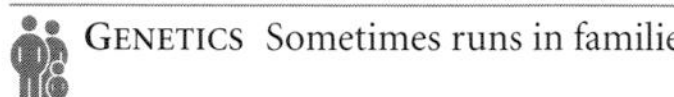

GENETICS Sometimes runs in families

LIFESTYLE Overeating and a sedentary lifestyle are risk factors

A person is considered obese if he or she weighs at least 20 percent more than the maximum healthy weight for his or her height (*see* ARE YOU A HEALTHY WEIGHT?, p.53). About 3 in 10 people in Canada are overweight, and the condition is becoming increasingly common.

Obesity can cause many health problems due to the strain it puts on organs and joints. For example, back pain, painful hips and knees, and shortness of breath are common problems. Obesity increases the risk of some widespread and potentially fatal disorders, such as coronary artery disease (p.405), stroke (p.532), and high blood pressure (*see* HYPERTENSION, p.403). Obesity may also lead to psychological problems, including depression (p.554).

WHAT ARE THE CAUSES?

Obesity occurs when food taken into the body provides more energy than is used. The main causes of obesity are overeating and a sedentary lifestyle. Obesity may run in families as a result of learned eating habits in addition to inherited factors. In rare cases, obesity may be a symptom of a hormonal disorder, such as hypothyroidism (p.680). Some drugs, particularly corticosteroids (p.930), can also lead to obesity. Occasionally, obesity may be a result of an underlying psychological problem.

ARE THERE COMPLICATIONS?

Obesity increases the risk of various chronic health problems. For example, obese people are more likely to have high blood cholesterol levels (*see* HYPERCHOLESTEROLEMIA, p.691). High cholesterol in turn increases the risk of atherosclerosis (p.402), in which fatty deposits build up on the inner linings of the arteries. Atherosclerosis may contribute to high blood pressure and coronary artery disease. Arterial thrombosis and embolism (p.431), which is blockage of a blood vessel by a blood clot, occurs more often in obese people. Obese adults are at greater risk of gallstones (p.651) and are more likely to develop diabetes mellitus (p.687). Certain cancers, such as prostate cancer (p.726), breast cancer (p.759), and cancer of the uterus (p.748), are also more common in obese people.

Excess weight can put strain on joints. Osteoarthritis (p.374) is common in obese people, especially in the hips and knees. Sleep apnea (p.477), a respiratory disorder, is also associated with obesity.

WHAT MIGHT BE DONE?

Your doctor will probably measure your weight and height and discuss your diet with you (*see* A HEALTHY DIET, p.48). He or she will probably also ask you how much exercise you do (*see* EXERCISE AND HEALTH, pp.55–61). Tests may be performed to measure blood sugar levels (to look for diabetes) and cholesterol levels (*see* BLOOD CHOLESTEROL TESTS, p.231). Rarely, you may have blood tests to check for a hormonal disorder.

Obesity is most commonly treated by a weight-reduction diet and increased exercise. Calorie intake per day is usually reduced to 500–1,000 calories less than the average requirement for a person of your age, sex, and height (*see* CONTROLLING YOUR WEIGHT, p.53). This type of eating plan is designed to produce slow, sustainable weight loss. The diet may be formulated by your doctor or a dietitian, although you may also choose to join a self-help group. Moderate and regular exercise is essential in losing weight.

Appetite suppressant drugs are available but many are not recommended because of side effects. However, newer drugs with fewer side effects are under development. Sibutramine controls the appetite by affecting neurotransmitters in the brain. Drugs that reduce fat absorption from the digestive tract, such as orlistat, may also help. Rarely, surgery is used to treat obesity. For example, the stomach may be stapled to reduce its size so that you feel full after small meals.

Changes in diet and lifestyle need to be maintained throughout life. Support from your family, doctor, and a self-help group should help you follow your weight-loss plan successfully.

WWW ONLINE SITES: p.1030, p.1035

DISORDERS OF THE MOUTH, TONGUE, AND ESOPHAGUS

Digestion begins in the mouth, where food is chewed by the teeth and mixed by the tongue with saliva secreted by the salivary glands. Swallowing forces the food into the esophagus, where it progresses to the stomach by coordinated muscle contractions. The mouth, tongue, and esophagus are constantly exposed to irritants and infection from food and airborne particles.

The first half of this section deals with disorders that affect the mouth and tongue. These range from mouth ulcers, which are relatively mild yet common, through the more serious disease mouth cancer. This part of the section also includes disorders that cause inflammation, such as glossitis, and disorders that cause white patches in the mouth, such as oral leukoplakia.

Two disorders affecting the salivary glands are described next. Salivary gland stones may be painful but can usually be removed successfully. The majority of salivary gland tumors are not cancerous, and their prognosis is generally good, but they may recur.

The last part of the section covers disorders of the esophagus, the most common being gastroesophageal reflux disease; cancer of the esophagus, which is much rarer, is also described.

For disorders specifically affecting the teeth and gums, *see* pp.606–619.

KEY ANATOMY

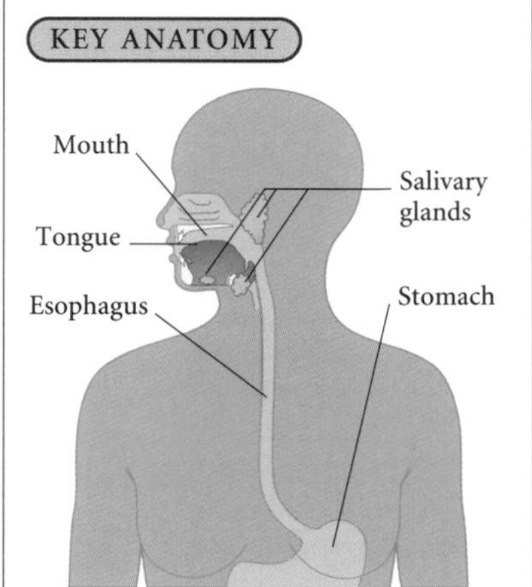
Mouth
Tongue
Esophagus
Salivary glands
Stomach

For more information concerning the structure and function of the mouth, tongue, and esophagus, *see* pp.620–625.

Mouth ulcers

Painful sores in the lining of the mouth, also called aphthous ulcers or canker sores

 AGE Most common in adolescents and young adults

 GENDER Slightly more common in females

 GENETICS Sometimes run in families

 LIFESTYLE More likely to occur when under stress, run down, or ill

Mouth ulcers are shallow, gray-white pits with a red border. They can cause pain, particularly when you are chewing spicy, hot, or acidic food. Mouth ulcers are extremely common and may occur singly or in clusters anywhere in the mouth. They may recur several times a year, but they usually disappear without treatment within 2 weeks.

The cause of mouth ulcers is not known, but they tend to occur in people who are run down or ill and before menstruation in women. Mouth ulcers are often stress-related. Injuries to the lining of the mouth caused by ill-fitting dentures, a roughened tooth, or careless toothbrushing can also result in the development of mouth ulcers.

Rarely, recurrent mouth ulcers may be the result of anemia (p.446), a deficiency of either vitamin B_{12} or folic acid, intestinal disorders such as Crohn's disease (p.658) or celiac disease (p.658). In rare cases, it is due to the autoimmune disorder, Behçet syndrome (p.465).

Ulcers may also occur as a result of specific infections, such as herpes simplex infections (p.289). Rarely, an ulcer that enlarges slowly and does not heal may be mouth cancer (p.634).

Mouth ulcers usually heal without treatment. If you are prone to them, avoid possible irritants, including spicy foods, and use a mouthwash of salt water. Over-the-counter preparations containing a corticosteroid to reduce inflammation combined with an anesthetic are available in lozenge, gel, and paste form. The most suitable preparation depends on the site of the ulcer.

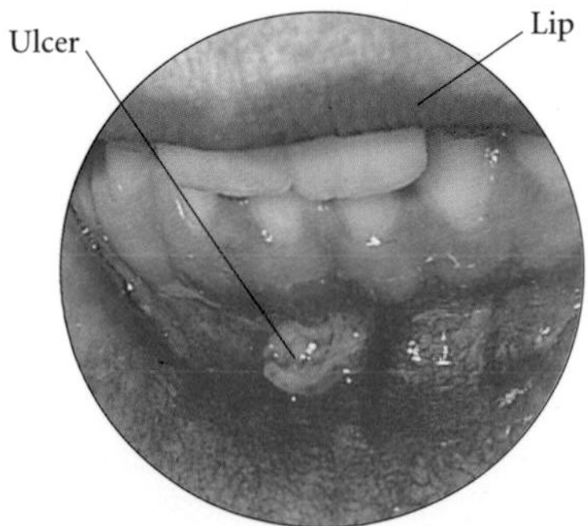
Ulcer
Lip

Mouth ulcer
The typical gray-white pit of a mouth ulcer has developed on the lower gum of the mouth shown above.

Consult a doctor about a mouth ulcer that does not heal within 3 weeks. He or she may do tests for an underlying cause.

(WWW) ONLINE SITES: p.1029

Stomatitis

Inflammation of the lining of the mouth that may be mild or severe

 AGE May occur at any age but most common in children and elderly people

 LIFESTYLE Poor oral hygiene, smoking, and a diet deficient in iron are risk factors

 GENDER GENETICS Not significant factors

Stomatitis is a general inflammation of the lining of the mouth including the tongue. The disorder is usually caused by an infection. If the inflammation affects the tongue, it is called glossitis (opposite page); if it affects the gums, it is called gingivitis (p.617). Mouth ulcers (left) are another form of stomatitis.

Whichever part of the mouth is affected, stomatitis is usually a short-lived disorder and, although it may be painful, it does not usually cause serious problems.

WHAT ARE THE CAUSES?

The most common causes of stomatitis are infections with viruses, bacteria, or fungi, and a poor diet. Smoking may also cause the condition.

Viral stomatitis is mainly caused by the herpes simplex virus (*see* HERPES SIMPLEX INFECTIONS, p.289) and the coxsackie virus. Viral stomatitis occurs most commonly in childhood.

Bacterial stomatitis, particularly gingivitis, usually results from neglected dental problems and poor oral hygiene, such as ineffective toothbrushing. Oral bacterial infections are also more likely when saliva production is reduced, such as in Sjögren syndrome (p.463).

Stomatitis may also result from the fungal infection candidiasis (p.309), in which a fungus that is normally present in the mouth overgrows and causes inflammation. Candidiasis occurs most commonly in infants, elderly people, those who wear dentures, and pregnant women. People who have reduced immunity are also susceptible to candidiasis, such as those with diabetes mellitus (p.687) and people with AIDS (*see* HIV INFECTION AND AIDS, p.295). Candidiasis may also occur in people who are taking antibiotics (p.885) and in those who use inhaled steroids to treat asthma (*see* CORTICOSTEROIDS FOR RESPIRATORY DISEASE, p.911) and do not rinse their mouth thoroughly afterward.

The most common deficiency causing stomatitis is a shortage of iron, which also leads to anemia (*see* IRON-DEFICIENCY ANEMIA, p.447). Deficiency of vitamin B_{12} or folic acid in the diet may also cause stomatitis.

WHAT ARE THE SYMPTOMS?

The symptoms of stomatitis may range from mild to severe and include:

- Sore mouth.
- Bad breath.
- In some cases, mouth ulcers.
- In severe cases, fever.

In gingivitis, the gums may be sore and swollen and may bleed during toothbrushing. Chronic gingivitis and poor oral hygiene may lead to teeth loosening and eventually falling out.

WHAT MIGHT BE DONE?

If your doctor cannot make an immediate diagnosis from your symptoms, a swab may be taken from the affected area of the mouth and sent to a laboratory for testing. If stomatitis is due to infection, antibiotics or antifungal drugs (p.889) may be prescribed. Most viral infections clear up spontaneously, and treatment is usually aimed at relieving symptoms such as pain. Antiviral drugs (p.886) may also be prescribed.

To relieve the symptoms, you should keep your mouth clean by using salt-water mouthwashes regularly. If eating and drinking are particularly causing you pain, your doctor may prescribe a pain-relieving mouthwash or a local anesthetic gel to apply to the inside of your mouth before meals. If children are unable to drink, they may be admitted to the hospital to be given fluids intravenously to rehydrate them.

Gingivitis can be prevented by good oral hygiene (*see* CARING FOR YOUR TEETH AND GUMS, p.610). Once it has developed, more extensive treatment by your dentist or dental hygienist may be necessary in order to control the progression of the condition.

WWW ONLINE SITES: p.1029

Glossitis

Inflammation of the tongue, making it smooth, red, and swollen

 LIFESTYLE Alcohol abuse and smoking are risk factors

 AGE GENDER GENETICS Not significant factors

Glossitis, inflammation of the tongue, is usually a temporary condition that heals quickly with treatment. The most common cause of glossitis is an injury to the tongue, which can be due to ill-fitting dentures, roughened teeth, or scalding liquids. Smoking, eating spicy foods, and excessive alcohol intake may cause mild irritation and inflame the tongue. Glossitis may also be the primary symptom of a fungal infection such as candidiasis (p.309) or a viral infection such as herpes simplex infection (p.289). In some cases, the tongue becomes inflamed as a result of a deficiency of iron, vitamin B_{12}, or folic acid in the diet. Rarely, some people find that particular oral hygiene products, such as mouthwashes, breath fresheners, and toothpastes, cause an allergic reaction in the mouth, which leads to inflammation of the tongue.

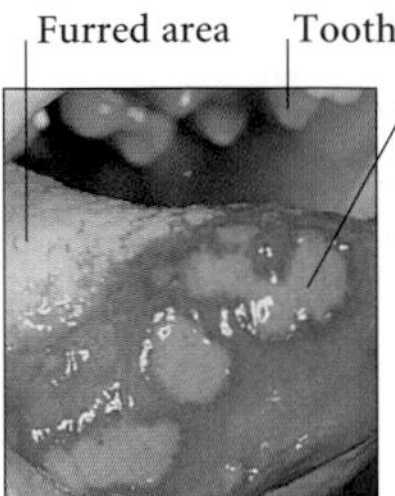
Furred area
Tooth
White patch

Glossitis
Herpes simplex infection has caused inflammation of this tongue (glossitis), along with thick furring and smooth, white patches.

WHAT ARE THE SYMPTOMS?

In many cases, the symptoms of glossitis develop gradually. With time, the tongue may become:

- Painful, swollen, and tender.
- Smooth and red.
- Furred.
- Dotted with multiple small ulcers.
- Cracked.

In cases of glossitis caused by damage from scalding liquids, a viral infection, or an allergic reaction, the symptoms often develop rapidly. Swallowing and speaking may become painful. Other symptoms may also be present in addition to a swollen tongue, depending on the cause. For example, you may have smooth, white patches on your tongue if you have a herpes simplex infection, or if you have candidiasis, you may have sore, creamy yellow, raised patches.

WHAT MIGHT BE DONE?

Your doctor may take swabs from the tongue to identify an infection. A blood sample may also be taken to look for mineral or vitamin deficiencies.

Whatever the cause, you can relieve the discomfort by rinsing your mouth regularly with a salt solution and antiseptic or pain-relieving mouthwashes. It should also help to stop smoking and to avoid acidic and spicy foods that exacerbate the soreness. In many cases, the symptoms clear up without a cause being identified. However, if a clear diagnosis is made, specific treatment for the infection is usually effective. For example, if your condition is caused by candidiasis, you may be prescribed an antifungal drug (p.889), such as clotrimazole in an oral paste form.

WWW ONLINE SITES: p.1029, p.1030

Oral lichen planus

White patches in the mouth, sometimes associated with an itchy skin rash

AGE Most common between the ages of 30 and 60

GENDER More common in females

GENETICS LIFESTYLE Not significant factors

Oral lichen planus is a rare condition in which small, white patches develop on the inside of the cheeks and sometimes elsewhere in the mouth. The patches often have a lacy pattern. In most people these white patches are painless, but sometimes they develop into chronic ulcers that can be very painful.

Oral lichen planus usually occurs in episodes that may last months or even years and frequently recurs after treatment. The condition occurs most often in people between the ages of 30 and 60 and affects more women than men. A small number of people who have oral lichen planus may also develop the general skin condition lichen planus (p.336), in which an itchy rash appears on the skin, most commonly on the inner surfaces of the wrists.

What are the causes?

Often no cause can be found, but oral lichen planus may be due to an abnormal immune response and may occur with other immune disorders, such as systemic lupus erythematosus (p.461). Oral lichen planus is sometimes due to an adverse reaction to amalgam tooth fillings or particular drugs, including gold-based antirheumatic drugs (p.895) and some of the drugs used to treat diabetes mellitus (p.687). Stress sometimes triggers the symptoms.

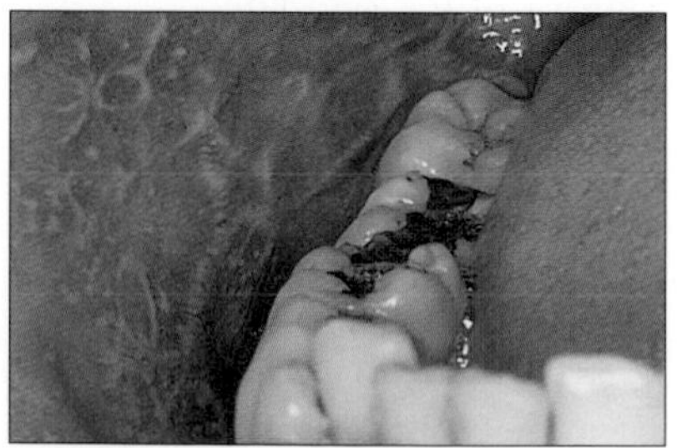

Oral lichen planus
The distinctive lacy pattern of oral lichen planus can be seen clearly here on the lining of the inside of the cheek.

What might be done?

If you have any white patches in your mouth that last longer than 3 weeks, you should consult your doctor. He or she may make a diagnosis from your symptoms. However, to confirm the diagnosis and exclude other disorders, a sample of tissue from the affected area may be taken under local anesthetic and examined microscopically.

If the symptoms are mild, no treatment may be necessary. However, a topical corticosteroid in an oral paste may be given to relieve pain. Oral lichen planus sometimes disappears spontaneously after several years.

(WWW) ONLINE SITES: p.1030

Oral leukoplakia

Small, thickened, white patches on the lining of the mouth or tongue

AGE Nearly all cases occur after age 40

LIFESTYLE Smoking, chewing tobacco, and alcohol abuse are risk factors

GENDER GENETICS Not significant factors

In oral leukoplakia, thickened white patches develop on the lining of the mouth or on the tongue. The patches develop slowly and painlessly, starting most often on the sides of the tongue. Unlike the white patches in the mouth caused by oral thrush (*see* CANDIDIASIS, p.309), leukoplakia patches cannot be scraped off. Sometimes, these patches harden, causing the surface to crack.

What are the causes?

Occasionally, the condition is caused by repeated mild damage to one area of the mouth, such as by a roughened tooth. Often, however, the cause is unknown. If there is no obvious cause, there is a 1 in 20 chance that the patch may eventually become cancerous (*see* MOUTH CANCER, right). The risk is higher if the patch is on the floor of the mouth or is ulcerated. Oral leukoplakia occurs much more frequently in smokers and people who chew tobacco. The risk of the disorder is increased if they also drink excessive amounts of alcohol. The condition nearly always occurs in people over age 40.

A form of leukoplakia called hairy leukoplakia, in which the patches have a furred surface, occurs in people with reduced immunity, especially people with AIDS (*see* HIV INFECTION AND AIDS, p.295). Hairy leukoplakia does not usually become cancerous.

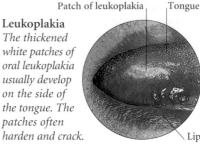

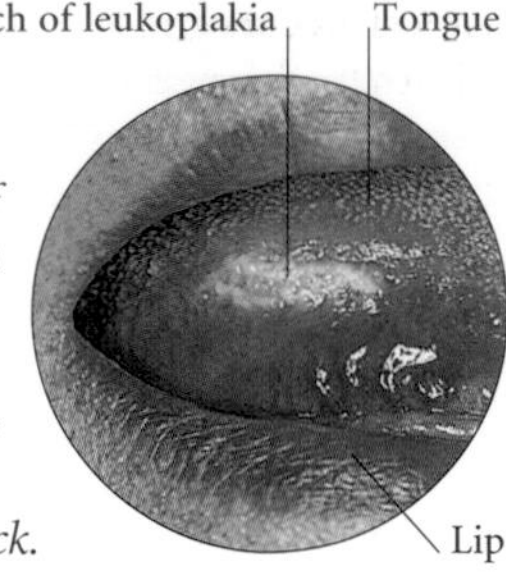
Patch of leukoplakia
Tongue
Lip

Leukoplakia
The thickened white patches of oral leukoplakia usually develop on the side of the tongue. The patches often harden and crack.

What might be done?

An obvious cause for the patches, such as damage from dentures, can be treated, and the patches may then disappear.

If no cause is found or the condition persists, your doctor or dentist may take a tissue sample from your mouth to exclude mouth cancer. Persistent patches may be removed by surgery or laser treatment (p.951). Even with treatment, oral leukoplakia may recur and needs to be monitored regularly.

(WWW) ONLINE SITES: p.1030

Mouth cancer

Cancerous tumor of the lips, tongue, or lining of the mouth

AGE Most common over age 60; rare under age 40

GENDER Twice as common in males

LIFESTYLE Smoking, chewing tobacco, alcohol abuse, and excessive exposure to sunlight are risk factors

GENETICS Not a significant factor

About half of all cancerous tumors of the mouth occur on either the tongue or the lower lip. The gums, inside of the cheeks, floor of the mouth, and palate are less commonly affected.

In developed countries, mouth cancer is one of the less common forms of cancer. In developing countries such as India, where people chew tobacco, betel leaves, and nuts, mouth cancer is the most common type of cancer. Worldwide, the disease is twice as common in men as it is in women, although mouth cancer is on the increase in women. The cancer occurs most commonly in people over the age of 60 and is rare in those under age 40. The prognosis for lip cancer is good. The prognosis is poorer for other forms of mouth cancer but is improved with early diagnosis.

WHAT ARE THE CAUSES?

In half of all people with mouth cancer, the tumor develops from oral leukoplakia (opposite page), a condition in which thickened white patches appear on the lining of the mouth or on the tongue. The main factor that encourages the growth of leukoplakia and mouth tumors is smoking, particularly pipes and cigars, and chewing tobacco. The risk of mouth cancer is increased further when tobacco use is combined with excessive alcohol consumption.

Diet may also play a part, particularly if the diet is deficient in vitamins A, C, and E and iron. In addition, lip cancer is strongly associated with repeated unprotected exposure to strong sunlight.

WHAT ARE THE SYMPTOMS?

If you have mouth cancer, you may experience the following symptoms:

- An ulcer that enlarges slowly and fails to heal, occurring on the lining of the mouth or on the tongue.
- A swelling that develops anywhere inside the mouth or on the lips.

Left untreated, mouth cancer usually spreads from the mouth to nearby tissues, the lymph nodes in the neck, and from there to other parts of the body.

HOW IS IT DIAGNOSED?

Cancerous tumors in the mouth are often detected early by a dentist during a checkup. If your doctor suspects that a lump or nonhealing ulcer in the mouth is a tumor, a small sample of tissue may be taken for examination. If cancer is found, further tests will be performed to see how far cancer has spread (*see* STAGING CANCER, p.277).

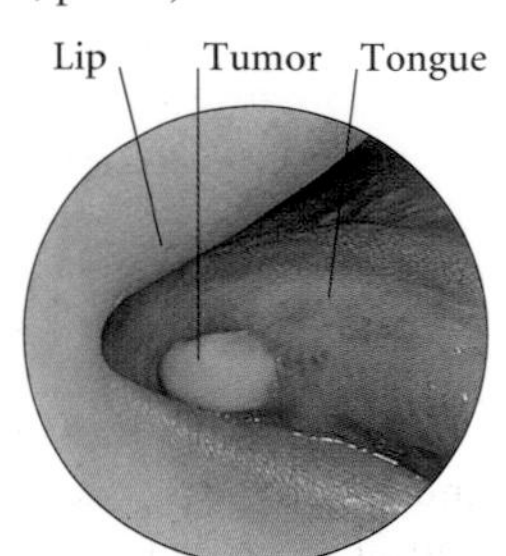
Lip
Tumor
Tongue

Mouth cancer
A cancerous tumor can be seen here in the form of a small, white lump that has developed on the right side of the tongue.

WHAT IS THE TREATMENT?

A small cancerous tumor that is discovered early may be removed by surgery or laser treatment (p.951). In about 8 in 10 people, surgery is successful and the cancer does not recur after the tumor has been removed. If the tumor is large, it will be removed surgically, and plastic surgery (p.952) may be necessary to restore a more normal facial appearance. Following surgery, radiation therapy (p.279) may be done to ensure that all cancerous cells have been destroyed and the cancer does not recur.

WHAT IS THE PROGNOSIS?

Tumors that are found early and are in an easily accessible part of the mouth can usually be treated successfully. The prognosis is best for lip cancer, which is the most accessible site. For cancers within the mouth, less than half of the affected people survive for 5 years.

(WWW) ONLINE SITES: p.1028

Salivary gland stones

Stones that form in the ducts of the salivary glands

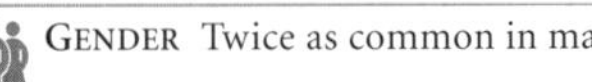
AGE More common over age 40

GENDER Twice as common in males

GENETICS LIFESTYLE Not significant factors

There are three pairs of salivary glands in the mouth, and sometimes the salivary ducts (tubes through which saliva enters the mouth) become blocked by stones. The stones are composed of calcium salts and vary in size. They either partially or, rarely, completely block the duct. The salivary gland then becomes swollen and feels painful during eating because saliva cannot escape from the gland into the mouth. In most cases, no cause can be found. Stones are twice as common in men, and occur most frequently in people over age 40.

WHAT ARE THE SYMPTOMS?

In most cases, the symptoms of salivary gland stones include:

- A visible swelling on the outside of the mouth or a sensation of a lump inside the mouth.
- Pain during or after a meal due to a buildup of saliva behind the stone.

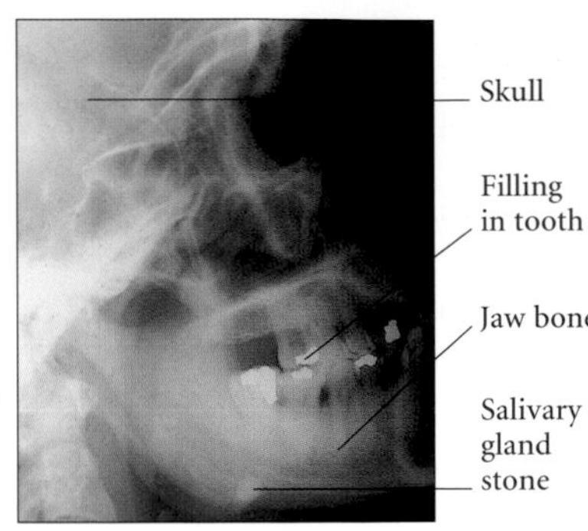
Skull
Filling in tooth
Jaw bone
Salivary gland stone

Salivary gland stone
In this X-ray, a salivary gland stone shows up as a white mass. The stone is blocking the duct of the gland beneath the jaw bone.

A blocked salivary duct is liable to become infected, causing the swelling to become red and inflamed with possible leakage of pus into the mouth.

WHAT MIGHT BE DONE?

If your doctor suspects that you have a salivary gland stone, he or she may arrange for imaging tests, such as X-rays (p.244) or CT scanning (p.247). If the location of the stone is not clear, you may have a test called a sialogram, in which a dye is injected directly into the blocked duct and an X-ray is taken.

The doctor may be able to use his or her fingers to tease the stone out of the duct. Failing this, the stone can be removed under local anesthesia. Salivary gland stones may recur after treatment.

(WWW) ONLINE SITES: p.1030

Salivary gland tumors

Noncancerous or cancerous tumors in the salivary glands

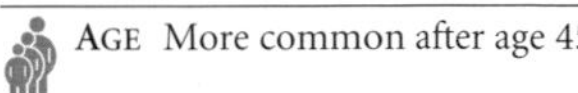
AGE More common after age 45

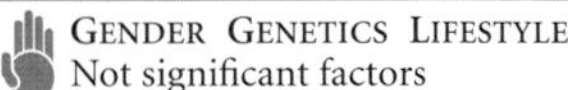
GENDER GENETICS LIFESTYLE Not significant factors

Tumors that affect the salivary glands are rare, particularly in people under the age of 45. Three-quarters of the tumors occur in one of the two parotid salivary glands that lie behind the angles of the jaw. Only about 1 in 5 salivary gland tumors is cancerous.

The symptoms of a salivary gland tumor depend on whether or not it is a cancerous tumor, but in all cases there is a lump that may be felt either protruding inside the mouth or on the

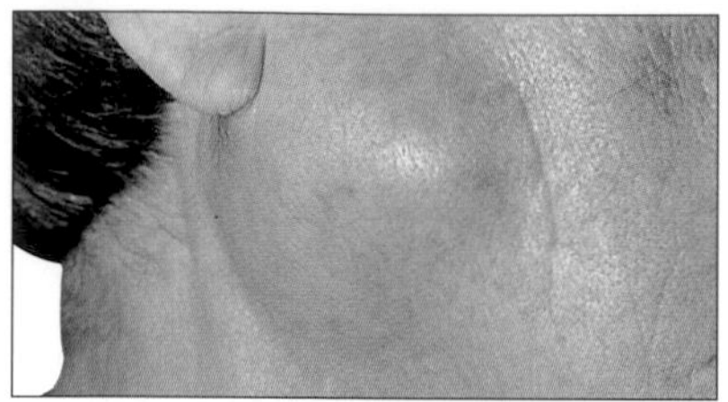

Salivary gland tumor
This swelling close to the ear and over the angle of the jawbone is caused by a noncancerous tumor of a salivary gland.

outside. Noncancerous tumors are usually painless, rubbery in consistency, and movable when touched. These benign tumors grow slowly and usually stay the same size for years.

Cancerous tumors of the salivary gland usually grow quickly, feel hard, and are sometimes painful. The facial nerve, which passes through the gland, may be affected as the cancer develops, leading to paralysis of part of the face (*see* FACIAL PALSY, p.548). If the tumor is left untreated, the cancer may spread to nearby lymph nodes in the neck and from there to other parts of the body, such as the chest and liver.

WHAT IS THE TREATMENT?

Treatment for a noncancerous tumor of the parotid gland is an operation to remove the affected part of the gland. This is a very delicate procedure and there is a risk that the facial nerve may be damaged. If damage does occur, the mouth may droop as a result. The nerve sometimes recovers, but in other cases the damage may be permanent.

If a tumor is cancerous, all of the affected gland is removed. If the tumor has spread to the lymph nodes in the neck, these nodes may also need to be removed. After surgery, radiation therapy (p.279) may be performed to destroy remaining cancerous cells.

WHAT IS THE PROGNOSIS?

Noncancerous tumors can usually be treated but may recur. Untreated, up to 1 in 10 become cancerous over 20 years.

Most people with cancerous tumors survive for more than 5 years after diagnosis. However, the earlier the diagnosis and treatment, the greater the chance of a cure. If the disease spreads beyond the salivary glands, it may be fatal.

(WWW) ONLINE SITES: p.1028, p.1030

Gastroesophageal reflux disease

Regurgitation of acidic stomach juices into the esophagus, causing pain in the upper abdomen and chest

 LIFESTYLE Obesity, a high-fat diet, drinking too much coffee or alcohol, and smoking are risk factors

 AGE GENDER GENETICS Not significant factors

Gastroesophageal reflux disease (GERD), commonly known as acid reflux, is probably the most common cause of attacks of indigestion (p.626). The discomfort is due to acidic juices from the stomach flowing back up into the esophagus (the tube leading from the throat down to the stomach). The lining of the esophagus does not have adequate defense against the harmful effects of stomach acid, which causes inflammation and a burning pain known as heartburn.

Attacks of GERD are usually brief and relatively mild but if they are persistent, the lining of the esophagus may be permanently damaged or scarred. In some cases, GERD causes bleeding from the digestive tract (p.630).

SELF-HELP MANAGING GASTROESOPHAGEAL REFLUX DISEASE

The following steps either relieve the symptoms of gastroesophageal reflux disease (GERD) or prevent the symptoms from recurring:

- Take antacids (p.923) to help neutralize stomach acids.
- Avoid spicy, acidic, tomato-based foods and high-fat foods such as chocolate and cream.
- Avoid alcohol, colas, and coffee.
- Stop smoking.
- Lose excess weight.
- Eat smaller amounts of food to avoid overfilling the stomach and do not eat late at night.
- After eating, do not exercise or lie down since both may lead to food being regurgitated.
- Raise the head of your bed or sleep on extra pillows so that your head is higher than your feet during the night.

WHAT ARE THE CAUSES?

A double-action valve mechanism keeps stomach contents out of the esophagus. One part of the mechanism is the lower esophageal sphincter, the muscular ring at the lower end of the esophagus. The other part is the effect of the diaphragm muscle on the esophagus as it passes through a narrow opening in the muscle, called the hiatus. These mechanisms provide an effective one-way valve.

GERD may develop as a result of several factors acting together to make the valve leak. These factors include poor muscle tone in the sphincter; increased abdominal pressure due to pregnancy; obesity; or a weakness in the hiatus that allows part of the stomach to slide into the chest (a hiatus hernia). Many people develop mild attacks of GERD after eating certain foods or drinks, especially pickles, fried or fatty meals, carbonated soft drinks, alcohol, or coffee. Smoking may also worsen symptoms.

WHAT ARE THE SYMPTOMS?

The main symptoms of GERD are usually most noticeable immediately after eating a large meal or when bending over. They may include:

- Burning pain or discomfort in the chest behind the breastbone, known as heartburn.
- Acidic taste in the mouth due to regurgitation of acidic fluid into the throat or mouth.
- Persistent cough.
- Belching.
- Nausea.
- Blood in the vomit or feces.
- Hoarseness of voice.

GERD that persists over many years can cause scarring in the esophagus, which may eventually be severe enough to cause a stricture (narrowing). A stricture can make swallowing very difficult and may lead to weight loss. Chronic GERD may lead to Barrett's esophagus, in which part of the esophageal lining is replaced by the stomach lining. People with this condition are at increased risk of developing cancer of the esophagus (p.638).

If you have recently developed pain in the center of your chest that seems unrelated to eating or drinking, you should seek immediate medical help because the far more serious condition angina (p.407) is sometimes mistaken for the pain of severe heartburn.

TEST BARIUM SWALLOW

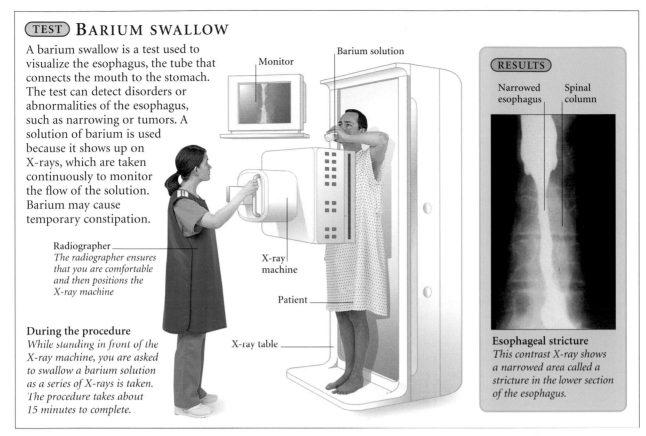

A barium swallow is a test used to visualize the esophagus, the tube that connects the mouth to the stomach. The test can detect disorders or abnormalities of the esophagus, such as narrowing or tumors. A solution of barium is used because it shows up on X-rays, which are taken continuously to monitor the flow of the solution. Barium may cause temporary constipation.

Monitor

Barium solution

X-ray machine

Patient

X-ray table

Radiographer
The radiographer ensures that you are comfortable and then positions the X-ray machine

During the procedure
While standing in front of the X-ray machine, you are asked to swallow a barium solution as a series of X-rays is taken. The procedure takes about 15 minutes to complete.

RESULTS

Narrowed esophagus

Spinal column

Esophageal stricture
This contrast X-ray shows a narrowed area called a stricture in the lower section of the esophagus.

WHAT MIGHT BE DONE?

Self-help measures often relieve many of the symptoms of heartburn (*see* MANAGING GASTROESOPHAGEAL REFLUX DISEASE, opposite page). However, if your heartburn is troublesome and persistent, consult your doctor about the problem.

The doctor may arrange for contrast X-rays that can show any abnormalities in the esophagus (*see* BARIUM SWALLOW, above). You may also undergo endoscopy (p.255), in which a flexible viewing tube is used to examine the lining of the esophagus. During this procedure, a small sample of tissue may be removed from the esophagus for examination under a microscope.

If self-help measures do not relieve your symptoms, your doctor may prescribe a drug that reduces the stomach's acid production (*see* ULCER-HEALING DRUGS, p.923). The rate at which the stomach is emptied may be increased by taking a drug such as domperidone (*see* ANTISPASMODIC DRUGS AND MOTILITY STIMULANTS, p.926), making GERD less likely. In most cases, the symptoms of GERD disappear with treatment. If they do not, you may need surgery to return the stomach to its normal position and tighten the lower esophageal sphincter muscle. The operation may be carried out by means of laparoscopic surgery (p.742), in which surgical instruments are manipulated through tiny incisions in the abdomen.

WWW ONLINE SITES: p.1030

Achalasia

Difficulty swallowing due to a muscle disorder of the esophagus

AGE Most common between the ages of 20 and 40; rare in childhood

GENDER GENETICS LIFESTYLE Not significant factors

In people with achalasia, the passage of food and drink into the stomach from the esophagus is delayed or prevented. The problem is caused by poor relaxation of the lower esophageal sphincter (the ring of muscle at the lower end of the esophagus), which normally relaxes to allow food and drink to pass into the stomach during swallowing, as well as poor muscle coordination in the esophagus. As the lower part of the esophagus is progressively distorted and widened over a period of months or years, swallowing becomes increasingly difficult. The condition usually occurs between the ages of 20 and 40.

WHAT ARE THE SYMPTOMS?

Symptoms of achalasia usually develop slowly and include the following:

- Difficulty swallowing.
- Chest pain or a feeling of discomfort behind the breastbone, which may be related to eating.
- Regurgitating undigested food during meals or some hours afterward, especially at night.
- Possibly repeated chest infections due to regurgitation.
- Eventually, weight loss.

If achalasia is left untreated, the risk of developing cancer of the esophagus (p.638) is slightly increased.

HOW IS IT DIAGNOSED?

If your doctor suspects achalasia, a chest X-ray (p.490) may be done to look for widening and distortion of the esophagus. The diagnosis may be apparent from a barium swallow (above), in which the action of muscles in the esophagus can be observed. Your doctor may look down your esophagus using a flexible viewing instrument called an endoscope (*see* ENDOSCOPY, p.255), in order to confirm the diagnosis and eliminate other possible disorders, such as cancer of the esophagus. Esophageal manometry may be arranged, in which a flexible tube is passed down the esophagus in order to measure pressures. Normally, the procedure shows changing pressures as a result of the alternate contractions and relaxations of the muscles that propel the food toward the stomach. In achalasia, these pressure changes are absent, and the overall pressure is high due to incomplete muscle relaxation.

WHAT IS THE TREATMENT?

Several different effective treatments are available for achalasia. The choice of treatment depends on your age and general health in addition to the severity and duration of your symptoms.

The simplest treatment is for your doctor to prescribe drugs called calcium channel blockers (p.900), which temporarily relax the lower esophageal sphincter muscle. However, for longer-term relief, the treatment most often used is to pass a small balloon down to the esophageal sphincter. Once the balloon is in place, it is inflated with either air or water to stretch the sphincter and is then removed. This procedure is successful in at least half of all people with the disorder. However, in a few people, it may have to be repeated over periods varying from 6 months to several years.

An alternative treatment is the injection of botulin toxin into the sphincter. In small doses, this toxin paralyzes the affected muscles, causing them to relax and allow food and liquids to pass. This effect typically lasts a little over a year and may need to be repeated.

If none of these methods is successful, endoscopic surgery (p.948) may be performed using instruments passed down an endoscope. Some of the muscle at the lower end of the esophagus may be cut to allow food to pass into the stomach. In about 1 in 10 cases this procedure leads to the stomach contents flowing back up the esophagus, which must also be treated (*see* GASTROESOPHAGEAL REFLUX DISEASE, p.636).

WWW ONLINE SITES: p.1030

Cancer of the esophagus

Cancerous tumor in the tissue of the esophagus

AGE Most common between the ages of 60 and 70; rare before age 50

GENDER About 2–3 times more common in males

LIFESTYLE Smoking and alcohol abuse are risk factors

GENETICS Not a significant factor

In Canada, cancer of the esophagus is uncommon and accounts for about 1 in 100 of all cancers. It is much more common in countries such as Iran and parts of China. The disease is more than twice as common in men than women, occurring most frequently in people between the ages of 60 and 70. Death rates from cancer of the esophagus are high because the tumor is often present for some time before it causes symptoms. As a result, by the time medical help is sought, the cancer has often spread to other parts of the body.

WHAT ARE THE CAUSES?

The exact cause of cancer of the esophagus is unknown, but factors known to increase the risk of developing it include smoking and excessive alcohol consumption. In China, fungal toxins in food are thought to be responsible for the high rate of the cancer. People who have certain disorders of the esophagus, such as gastroesophageal reflux disease (p.636), achalasia (p.637), and Barrett's esophagus (in which stomach lining replaces part of the esophageal lining), are more likely to develop cancer of the esophagus. Those people with chronic esophageal disease should have regular endoscopy (p.255) in order to look for early evidence of cancerous growths affecting the esophagus.

Tumor

Wall of esophagus

Esophageal cancer *This endoscopic view shows a cancerous tumor on the lining of the esophagus.*

WHAT ARE THE SYMPTOMS?

Early in the disease, there are often no symptoms, but, when they develop, they do so slowly over weeks or months as the esophagus becomes obstructed. The symptoms may include:

- Pain and difficulty swallowing solid foods, particularly bread and meat.
- Difficulty swallowing liquids.
- Regurgitation of recently eaten food.
- Cough as a result of food spilling into the lungs.
- Loss of appetite and weight loss.

If the tumor spreads to involve the trachea, you may develop shortness of breath and may cough up blood.

HOW IS IT DIAGNOSED?

Your doctor may arrange for a tissue sample to be taken during endoscopy, which involves passing a flexible viewing tube into the esophagus (see UPPER DIGESTIVE TRACT ENDOSCOPY, p.641). A barium swallow (p.637) may be performed to detect an obstruction in the esophagus. Once the diagnosis has been confirmed, tests such as CT scanning (p.247) of the chest or of the abdomen may be done to determine if the tumor has spread beyond its original site (*see* STAGING CANCER, p. 277).

WHAT IS THE TREATMENT?

The treatment depends on whether the cancer is limited to the esophagus or has spread to the structures around it. A localized cancer can be removed, but the operation is a major procedure and only a small proportion of patients are diagnosed at an early enough stage to make attempting surgery worthwhile.

If the cancer has already spread or if general health is not good enough for major surgery, treatment is given to relieve the symptoms. Insertion of a rigid tube into the esophagus in the narrowed area can relieve swallowing difficulties (*see* PALLIATIVE SURGERY FOR CANCER, p. 280). Additional treatment may involve radiation therapy (p.279) and chemotherapy (p.278).

WHAT IS THE PROGNOSIS?

About 1 in 4 people in whom curative surgery is attempted survive for more than 5 years. However, people in whom curative surgery was not an option usually survive for less than a year.

WWW ONLINE SITES: p.1028

DISORDERS OF THE STOMACH AND DUODENUM

The stomach and the duodenum (the first part of the intestine) are exposed to many potentially damaging substances, including acid produced by the stomach to aid food digestion, alcohol, and irritative foods such as spices. The stomach and duodenum have a natural defense mechanism that protects against damage, but sometimes this mechanism fails, leading to disease.

The first article in this section covers infection with the *Helicobacter pylori* bacterium, which was only discovered in the early 1980s. It is now estimated that about half the world's population is infected with *H. pylori.* In most cases, there are no symptoms. However, *H. pylori* is known to be associated with the disorders of the stomach and duodenum discussed in this section: gastritis, which is inflammation of the lining of the stomach; peptic ulcer, which is an area of the stomach lining or the duodenum that has been eroded by acidic digestive juices; and stomach cancer. Both gastritis and peptic ulcer are common disorders of the digestive system that affect tens of thousands of North Americans every year. However, if either of these disorders occurs with *H. pylori* infection, it can be treated successfully with drugs. The final article in this section covers stomach cancer, now rare in many developed countries. General problems that may involve the stomach or another part of the upper digestive tract are covered elsewhere (*see* INDIGESTION, p.626; FUNCTIONAL DYSPEPSIA, p.626; and GASTRO-ESOPHAGEAL REFLUX DISEASE, p.636).

KEY ANATOMY

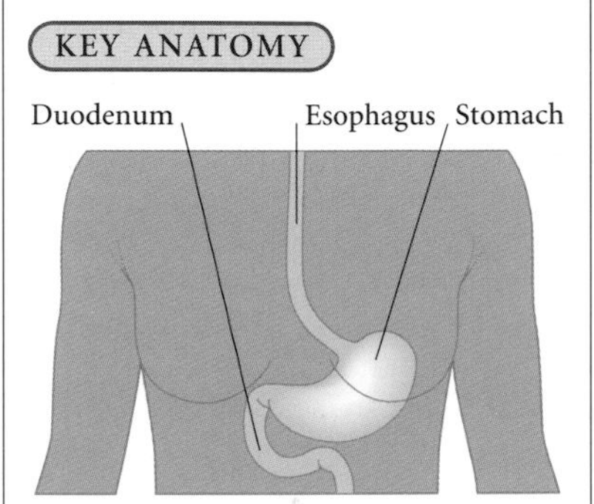
Duodenum
Esophagus
Stomach

For further information about the structure and function of the stomach and duodenum, *see* pp.620–625.

Helicobacter pylori infection

A common bacterial infection, which may lead to inflammation or ulceration in the upper digestive tract

AGE Often contracted in childhood, but symptoms can develop at any age

GENDER More common in males

LIFESTYLE Living in overcrowded, unsanitary conditions is a risk factor

GENETICS Not a significant factor

The *Helicobacter pylori* bacterium was discovered in the early 1980s. Research since then has shown that about half of the world's population is infected. The infection is usually contracted during childhood and, in most cases, causes no symptoms. However, in some people, *H. pylori* infection may lead to the development of gastritis (p.640), in which the stomach lining becomes inflamed, or to a peptic ulcer (p.640), in which an area of the lining of the stomach or the duodenum is eroded by the action of the acidic digestive juices.

The *H. pylori* bacterium can lead to peptic ulcers or gastritis when it damages the mucus layer of the stomach or duodenum. The mucus usually protects the lining of the stomach and the duodenum from acidic digestive juices, and the lining may become inflamed or eroded in areas where the mucus layer is damaged. Chronic infection with *H. pylori* may also increase the risk of developing stomach cancer (p.642).

The exact way in which *H. pylori* is transmitted is unknown. It is believed that the bacterium may be carried in feces and saliva and is most readily passed on by close contact with others, especially among people living in overcrowded, unsanitary conditions. The infection is more common in males.

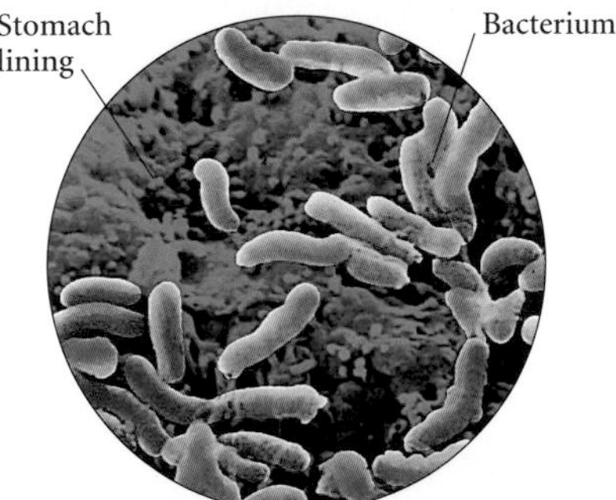
Stomach lining
Bacterium

Helicobacter pylori
A number of Helicobacter pylori *bacteria can be seen in this magnified view of the mucus lining of the stomach.*

HOW IS IT DIAGNOSED?

If you have discomfort or pain in the upper abdomen, your doctor may suspect that you have a peptic ulcer. He or she may arrange for tests to check for *H. pylori* infection. You may have a blood test to check for the presence of antibodies against *H. pylori* (*see* TESTS FOR ANTIGENS AND ANTIBODIES, p.235). A positive result will confirm that you have had the infection at some time. Alternatively, you may be given a breath test that involves drinking a substance that is broken down by *H. pylori.* If these bacteria are present, the substance is broken down into a chemical that can be detected with a breathalyzer. Your doctor may also arrange for you to have an upper digestive tract endoscopy (p.641), in which the stomach or duodenum is examined with a flexible viewing tube. At the same time, a small piece of the lining may be taken for examination under a microscope.

WHAT IS THE TREATMENT?

Treatment for *H. pylori* is given only if the infection has led to a disorder such as a peptic ulcer (below). Your doctor will prescribe a combination of antibiotics (p.885) to treat the infection and other drugs to suppress the production of stomach acid (*see* ULCER-HEALING DRUGS, p.923). In about 9 in 10 cases, infection with *H. pylori* bacteria can be successfully treated. The infection may recur in a small number of cases.

(WWW) ONLINE SITES: p.1030

Gastritis

Inflammation of the lining of the stomach, which may be acute or chronic

 AGE More common over age 50; rare in children

 GENETICS Sometimes runs in families

 LIFESTYLE Alcohol abuse and smoking are risk factors

 GENDER Not a significant factor

Gastritis, which is inflammation of the stomach lining, is a common disorder in North America. More than half of the population over age 50 have gastritis, although in most cases there are no symptoms. The disorder may be acute and have a sudden onset, but it is more frequently chronic, developing gradually over months or years. Symptoms, if present, commonly include discomfort in the upper abdomen.

Some types of gastritis run in families. However, in the 1980s, *Helicobacter pylori* infection (p.639) was found to be a major cause of gastritis. This discovery has led to effective treatment for many cases of the disorder.

WHAT ARE THE CAUSES?

Acute gastritis may occur when the stomach lining is suddenly damaged by drinking an excessive amount of alcohol or by taking aspirin or nonsteroidal anti-inflammatory drugs (p.894), such as ibuprofen. Acute gastritis can also develop after serious illness, such as blood poisoning (*see* SEPTICEMIA, p.298).

Chronic gastritis is often caused by infection with *H. pylori* bacteria, which are found in the stomach lining of about half of the population. The bacterium damages the mucus layer that protects the stomach lining from acidic digestive juices, allowing acid to attack the lining. Chronic gastritis may also occur in the inflammatory disorder Crohn's disease (p.658), which may cause digestive tract inflammation. Long-term use of alcohol, tobacco, aspirin, or nonsteroidal anti-inflammatory drugs may also lead to chronic gastritis.

One type of chronic gastritis, known as atrophic or autoimmune gastritis, is caused by an abnormal reaction of the immune system in which the body produces antibodies that attack the tissues of the stomach lining.

WHAT ARE THE SYMPTOMS?

Chronic gastritis rarely causes any symptoms. The onset of symptoms in acute gastritis is much faster and the symptoms are more severe. The symptoms of both types of gastritis may include the following:

- Discomfort or pain in the stomach area, often after eating.
- Nausea and vomiting.
- Loss of appetite.

In chronic gastritis, bleeding from the lining of the stomach rarely if ever occurs, except when the gastritis is caused by nonsteroidal anti-inflammatory drugs or alcohol. In the first case, if bleeding occurs, it is usually such a small amount of blood at any one time that it may go unnoticed until it leads to low iron in the blood and then to anemia (p.446). In the second case, bleeding is usually more acute and can cause vomiting of blood or passage of black tarry stools (see BLEEDING FROM THE DIGESTIVE TRACT, p.630).

Atrophic gastritis is usually painless, and the only symptoms may be those of pernicious anemia due to a deficiency of vitamin B_{12}. Atrophic gastritis damages the stomach so that it cannot make intrinsic factor, a substance that is essential for the absorption of this vitamin. People with atrophic gastritis also have an increased risk of developing stomach cancer (p.642).

WHAT CAN I DO?

The symptoms of mild gastritis can be treated with over-the-counter antacids (p.923), which neutralize the excess acid in the stomach. You may also find that your symptoms are relieved by eating small and regular meals, reducing alcohol intake, and stopping smoking. If the symptoms persist or are severe, or if you are losing weight, you should consult your doctor.

WHAT MIGHT BE DONE?

Your doctor will ask you about your smoking, drinking, and dietary habits, and your use of medications. You may be given a blood or breath test to look for *H. pylori* infection. You may also have a blood test for anemia to see if there has been bleeding from the stomach lining. Your doctor may arrange for you to have endoscopy (*see* UPPER DIGESTIVE TRACT ENDOSCOPY, p.641) to examine the stomach lining.

If infection with *H. pylori* is confirmed, a combination of antibiotics (p.885) and ulcer-healing drugs (p.923) may be prescribed. If you have gastritis and need to take aspirin (*see* ANALGESICS, p.912) or one of the nonsteroidal anti-inflammatory drugs (p.894) for a period of time, you may also be advised to take a drug called misoprostol. This reduces the production of stomach acid and helps protect the stomach lining.

Gastritis often improves with lifestyle changes, such as reducing alcohol intake.

(WWW) ONLINE SITES: p.1030

Peptic ulcer

An eroded area of the tissue lining the stomach or the duodenum, the first part of the small intestine

 AGE Stomach ulcers are more common over age 50; duodenal ulcers are most common in people between the ages of 20 and 45

 GENDER Duodenal ulcers are more common in males

 GENETICS Sometimes runs in families

 LIFESTYLE Stress, excess alcohol, smoking, and unsanitary conditions are risk factors

The lining of the stomach and duodenum normally has a barrier of mucus to protect it from the effects of acidic digestive juices. If this barrier is damaged, the acid may cause inflammation and erosion of the lining. The resulting eroded areas are known as peptic ulcers.

There are two different types of peptic ulcers: duodenal ulcers and gastric (stomach) ulcers. Duodenal ulcers are more common than gastric ulcers and usually occur in people between the age of 20 and 45. Men are particularly susceptible. Gastric ulcers are more common in people over the age of 50. Peptic ulcers are common, and it is estimated that about 1 in 10 people in the US develops an ulcer at some time.

WHAT ARE THE CAUSES?

Peptic ulcers are most commonly associated with *Helicobacter pylori* infection (p.639). This bacterium, which is thought to be transmitted most easily in unsanitary living conditions, releases substances that reduce the protective effectiveness of the mucus layer of the stomach or duodenum. Acidic digestive juices are then able to erode the lining of the stomach or the duodenum, allowing peptic ulcers to develop.

Peptic ulcers may sometimes result from the use of aspirin or nonsteroidal anti-inflammatory drugs (p.894), such as ibuprofen, that are known to cause damage to the lining of the stomach. Other factors that may play a role in peptic ulcers include smoking, alcohol, and possibly caffeine.

It is currently thought that psychological stress is most likely not one of the primary causes of peptic ulcers; however, stress may play a part in making an existing ulcer worse.

WHAT ARE THE SYMPTOMS?

Many people with a peptic ulcer do not experience symptoms or dismiss their discomfort as indigestion (p.626). Those with persistent symptoms may notice:

- Pain or discomfort that is felt in the upper abdomen.
- Loss of appetite and weight loss.
- A feeling of fullness in the abdomen.
- Nausea and sometimes vomiting.

Pain is often present for several weeks and then disappears for months or even years. The pain from a duodenal ulcer can be worse before meals when the stomach is empty. This pain may be quickly relieved by eating but usually recurs a few hours afterward. By contrast, pain caused by a gastric ulcer is often aggravated by food.

ARE THERE COMPLICATIONS?

The most common complication of a peptic ulcer is bleeding as the ulcer becomes deeper and erodes into nearby blood vessels (*see* BLEEDING FROM THE DIGESTIVE TRACT, p.630). Minor bleeding from the digestive tract may cause no symptoms except those of anemia (p.446), such as pale skin, fatigue, and a feeling of faintness. Bleeding from the digestive tract may lead to vomiting of blood. Alternatively, blood may pass through the digestive tract, resulting in black, tarry stools. In some cases, an ulcer perforates all the layers of the stomach or duodenum, allowing gastric juices to enter the abdomen and causing severe pain (*see* PERITONITIS, p.665). Bleeding from the digestive tract and perforation of the stomach or the duodenum may be life-threatening and require immediate medical attention.

In rare cases, stomach ulcers may result in narrowing of the stomach outlet into the duodenum, which prevents the stomach from emptying fully. Symptoms may then include bloating after meals, vomiting undigested food hours after eating, and weight loss.

WHAT MIGHT BE DONE?

If your doctor suspects that you have a peptic ulcer, he or she may schedule an endoscopy (*see* UPPER DIGESTIVE TRACT ENDOSCOPY, below) to view the stomach and duodenum. During endoscopy, a sample of the stomach lining may be taken to look for evidence of *H. pylori* infection and exclude stomach cancer (p.642), which may cause similar symptoms. Your doctor may also arrange for you to have blood tests to detect antibodies against the *H. pylori* bacterium and to check for evidence of anemia.

TEST AND TREATMENT: UPPER DIGESTIVE TRACT ENDOSCOPY

This technique involves passing a flexible viewing tube through the mouth to examine the esophagus, stomach, and duodenum (the first part of the small intestine) to look for disorders such as peptic ulcers. Diathermy (a heat treatment) or laser therapy can be performed or injections of drugs given to stop any bleeding.

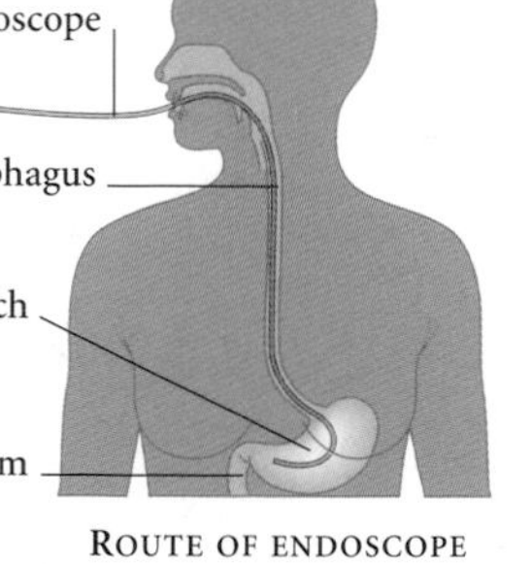
Endoscope
Esophagus
Stomach
Duodenum

ROUTE OF ENDOSCOPE

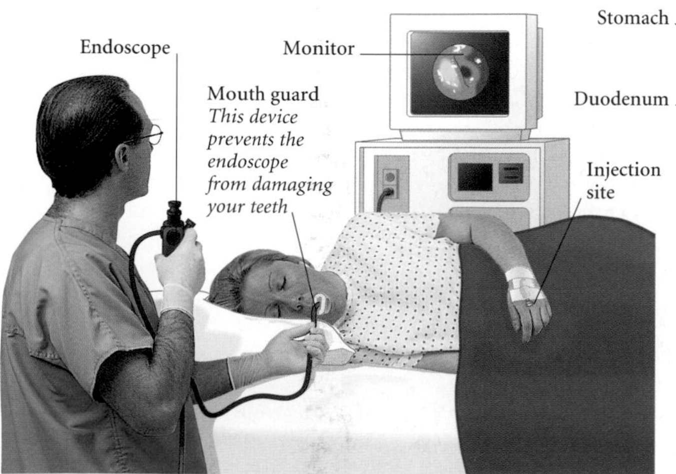
Endoscope
Monitor
Injection site

Mouth guard *This device prevents the endoscope from damaging your teeth*

During the procedure *You may have a local anesthetic spray to numb the back of your throat and, if necessary, some sedation. You then swallow the endoscope, through which the doctor views your upper digestive tract. The procedure usually takes about 15 minutes.*

VIEW

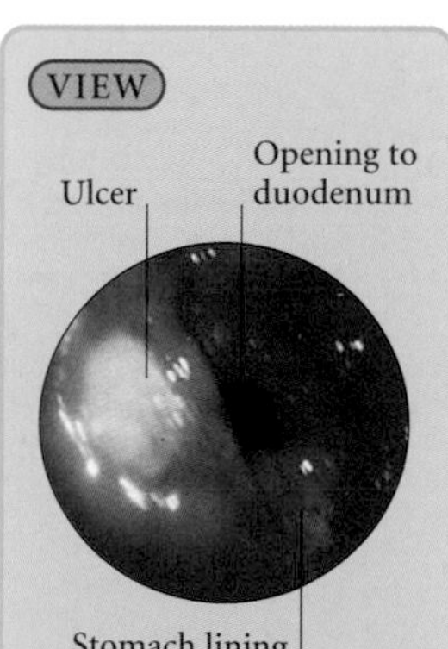
Ulcer
Opening to duodenum
Stomach lining

Gastric ulcer *In this view through an endoscope, a gastric ulcer is clearly visible in the mucous membrane lining the stomach. Close by is the opening from the stomach into the duodenum.*

Treatment of a peptic ulcer is designed to heal the ulcer and to prevent it from recurring. You will be advised to make some lifestyle changes, such as giving up smoking and drinking less alcohol.

If *H. pylori* is found, a combination of antibiotics (p.885) and ulcer-healing drugs (p.923) will usually be prescribed. Ulcer-healing drugs are usually given to maximize the chance of healing even if tests for *H. pylori* prove negative.

If long-term treatment with aspirin or a nonsteroidal anti-inflammatory drug is the cause, your doctor may prescribe an alternative drug or an additional drug, such as misoprostol, to protect the lining of the stomach and duodenum.

A bleeding or perforated ulcer requires urgent hospital admission. If blood loss is severe, a transfusion (p.447) may be needed. Endoscopy may be done to view the stomach lining; during this, bleeding blood vessels may be treated with diathermy, a technique that uses heat to seal them. Alternatively, an injection of drugs may be given to stop bleeding. If bleeding is severe or the ulcer is perforated, surgery is usually necessary.

If treated, about 19 in 20 peptic ulcers disappear within months. However, the ulcer may recur if lifestyle changes are not made, if the *H. pylori* infection was not successfully treated, or if NSAIDs are taken without a drug to prevent the ulcer.

(WWW) ONLINE SITES: p.1030

Stomach cancer

A cancerous tumor in the lining of the stomach wall

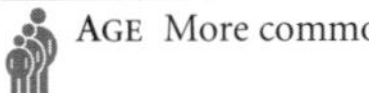

AGE More common over age 50

GENDER Twice as common in males

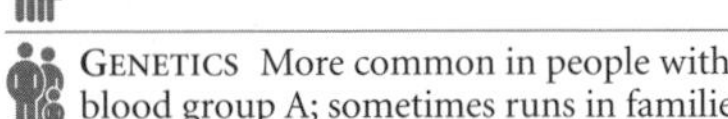

GENETICS More common in people with blood group A; sometimes runs in families

LIFESTYLE Certain foods, smoking, and a high alcohol intake are risk factors

Worldwide, stomach cancer is the second most common cancer after lung cancer. It is a particular problem in Japan and China, possibly because of dietary factors. In most other countries, the disease is now less common, a change thought to be due to less smoked and salted foods in the diet. There are about 2,800 new cases of stomach cancer each year in Canada. Few cases occur before age 50, but the incidence increases after that age. Stomach cancer occurs twice as often in males. It is more common in people of blood group A and sometimes runs in families, suggesting a genetic factor.

In most cases, stomach cancer develops in the stomach lining. The cancer may spread rapidly to other parts of the body. Early diagnosis is rare because the symptoms are usually mild, and by the time people seek medical help, the cancer has often spread.

What are the causes?

The causes of stomach cancer are not fully understood, but there are a number of factors. Chronic gastritis due to infection with the *H. pylori* bacterium (*see* HELICOBACTER PYLORI INFECTION, p.639) as well as chronic atrophic gastritis increase the risk of stomach cancer. Certain diets may increase the risk, such as a diet with a high intake of salt, pickled and smoked foods, and a low intake of fresh fruit and green vegetables. As well, smoking and a high intake of alcohol are risk factors.

What are the symptoms?

The early symptoms of stomach cancer are mild and vague, and many people ignore them. They may include:

- Discomfort in the upper abdomen.
- Pain in the stomach after eating.
- Loss of appetite and weight loss.
- Nausea and vomiting.

In many people, anemia (p.446) develops due to minor bleeding from the stomach lining. Later on, swelling may be felt in the upper abdomen.

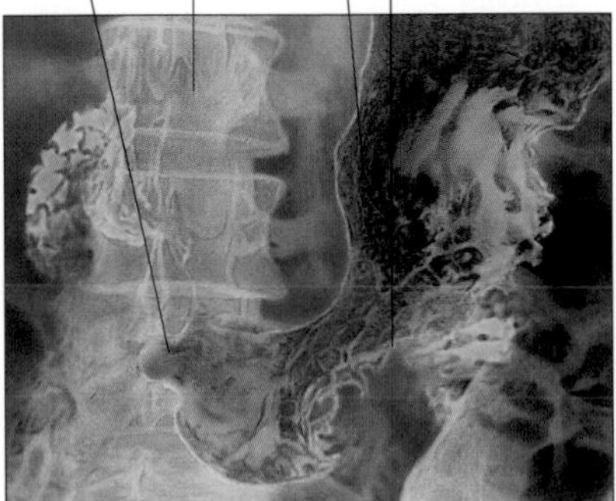
Stomach outlet
Spine
Stomach
Outline of tumor

Cancer in the lower stomach
In this X-ray, barium has been used to outline the stomach. The lining of the stomach has an irregular area where there is a large tumor.

How is it diagnosed?

Your doctor may arrange for you to have upper digestive tract endoscopy (p.641), in which a thin, flexible viewing tube is used to examine the lining of the stomach. Samples of tissue are taken from abnormal areas of the stomach lining during the procedure and tested to look for the presence of cancerous cells. You may also have a barium meal (*see* CONTRAST X-RAYS, p.245), in which a liquid barium mixture is swallowed to show the stomach clearly on an X-ray. The doctor may arrange blood tests for anemia, which may show that there has been bleeding from the stomach lining.

If a diagnosis of stomach cancer is confirmed, further investigations, such as CT scanning (p.247) and blood tests, may be performed to check whether the cancer has spread to other organs (*see* STAGING CANCER, p.277).

What is the treatment?

The only effective treatment for stomach cancer is early surgery to remove the tumor. However, this option is only suitable in about 2 in 10 cases because in others the cancer has already spread too widely to be operable. The operation involves the removal of part or all of the stomach. The surrounding lymph nodes are also removed since they are possible sites of cancerous spread. In cases where the cancer has spread to other parts of the body, surgery may help improve life expectancy, although in some cases the operation may be performed in order to relieve the symptoms rather than to attempt definitive cure. Radiation therapy (p.279) and chemotherapy (p.278) are used to slow the progress of the disease and to relieve pain. Strong analgesics (p.912) may help relieve severe discomfort.

What is the prognosis?

If detected and treated early, stomach cancer has a good cure rate. Some countries in which stomach cancer is common, such as Japan, have efficient screening programs to detect the cancer early. In these countries, about 8 in 10 people are alive 5 years after diagnosis, following surgery. However, the prognosis worldwide is generally poor, with only about 2 in 10 affected people surviving for 5 years after diagnosis.

(WWW) ONLINE SITES: p.1028, p.1030

Disorders of the liver, gallbladder, and pancreas

One of the main functions of the liver and pancreas is to aid food digestion. The liver makes the digestive fluid bile, which is stored in the gallbladder. The pancreas makes digestive enzymes. These organs have other vital functions. The liver uses digestion products to make new substances such as proteins and fats, and the pancreas produces hormones that control the level of glucose in the blood.

The yellow discoloration of the skin and eyes known as jaundice is a sign of liver disease but also has other causes, which are discussed in the first article in this section. In Western countries, excessive alcohol consumption is the main cause of liver disease, while hepatitis due to viral infection is more prevalent in the rest of the world. The next articles describe viral and other forms of hepatitis. They are followed by a discussion of alcoholic liver disease and the serious complications of cirrhosis and portal hypertension and varices. Liver cancer is described next. Cancer originating in the liver is less common in Western countries than the spread of cancer from other organs to the liver (liver metastases). Liver failure, which may be fatal unless treated with liver transplantation, is also discussed.

Gallstones do not usually cause symptoms and need no treatment, as explained in the next articles, but may lead to gallbladder inflammation, called cholecystitis. The following articles in the section describe the inflammatory conditions, acute and chronic pancreatitis. The final article covers pancreatic cancer, which is becoming more common in Western countries.

KEY ANATOMY

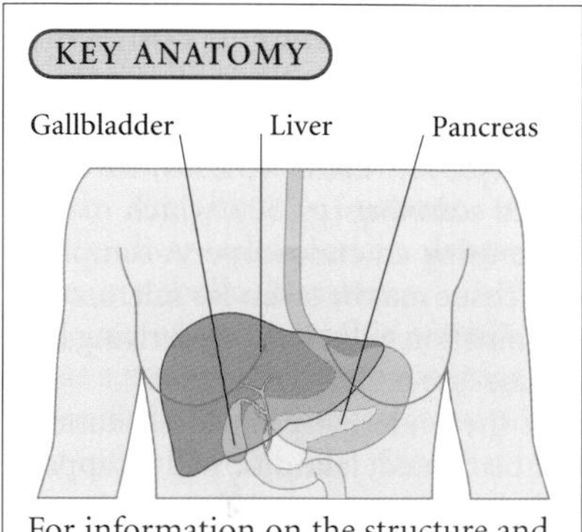
Gallbladder
Liver
Pancreas

For information on the structure and function of the liver, gallbladder, and pancreas, *see* pp.620–625.

Jaundice

Yellow discoloration of the skin and the whites of the eyes

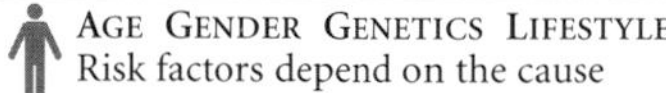
AGE GENDER GENETICS LIFESTYLE
Risk factors depend on the cause

Jaundice, a yellow discoloration of the skin and the whites of the eyes, is a symptom of many disorders of the liver, gallbladder, or pancreas. It may also be caused by some blood disorders. Jaundice results from excessively high blood levels of the pigment bilirubin, a breakdown product of red blood cells. Bilirubin is processed by the liver and then excreted as a component of the digestive fluid bile.

Jaundice always requires investigation because the underlying disorder may be serious. A few days after birth, many babies develop a form of jaundice that is usually harmless and disappears quickly (*see* NEONATAL JAUNDICE, p.817).

What are the causes?

Levels of bilirubin in the blood can increase if the amount of bilirubin produced is too great for the liver to process. Damaged liver cells or obstruction of the bile ducts, which carry bile from the liver to the gallbladder and small intestine, can also lead to high levels of bilirubin in the blood.

EXCESS RED BLOOD CELL BREAKDOWN In a healthy person, red blood cells have a lifespan of about 120 days, after which they are removed from the blood and broken down by the spleen to produce bilirubin. The bilirubin then passes to the liver. If the number of red blood cells being broken down is above normal, the liver cannot process the large amounts of bilirubin produced. This is known as hemolytic jaundice and may result from disorders such as hemolytic anemia (p.450), in which the lifespan of red blood cells is shorter than normal. It may be accompanied by other symptoms, such as fatigue.

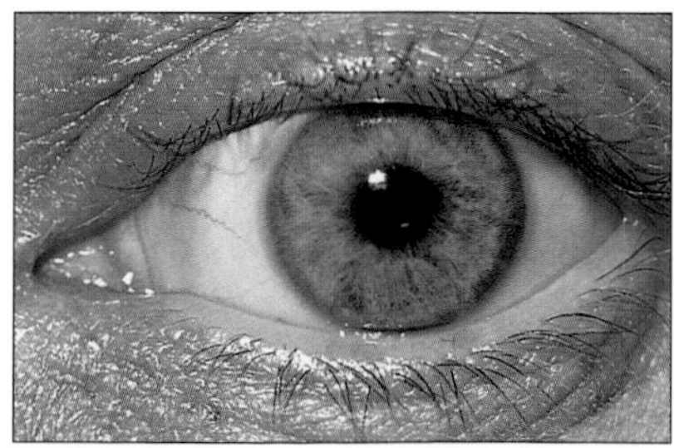

Jaundice
The skin and the white of the eye have become yellow. These symptoms, known as jaundice, can occur as a result of many disorders, including liver disease.

LIVER CELL DAMAGE If the liver is damaged, its ability to process bilirubin is reduced. Liver cell damage may occur for a variety of reasons, including viral infection (*see* ACUTE HEPATITIS, p.644), alcohol abuse (*see* ALCOHOL-RELATED LIVER DISEASE, p.646), and an adverse reaction to some drugs. Jaundice due to liver cell damage is sometimes accompanied by nausea, vomiting, pain in the abdomen, and a swollen abdomen.

BILE DUCT OBSTRUCTION An obstruction in the bile ducts, the channels through which bile leaves the liver, may result in jaundice. Obstruction may be due to disorders such as pancreatic cancer (p.654) or gallstones (p.651). If bile ducts are blocked, bile builds up in the liver, and bilirubin is forced back into the blood. This type of jaundice may be accompanied by itching, dark-colored urine, and pale-colored feces.

connect the digestive tract to the liver. This pressure may lead to bleeding into the digestive tract (*see* PORTAL HYPERTENSION AND VARICES, p.648). In some cases, cirrhosis can result in liver failure, which may be fatal.

WHAT MIGHT BE DONE?

Your doctor will do a physical examination and arrange for blood tests to evaluate your liver function and to look for causes of the hepatitis. He or she may use an imaging technique such as ultrasound scanning (p.250). To confirm the diagnosis, and to determine the nature and severity of liver damage, a liver biopsy (opposite page), in which a small piece of liver is removed for microscopic examination, may also be done.

Chronic hepatitis caused by infection with the hepatitis B or C viruses may respond to treatment with particular antiviral drugs (p.886), such as ribavirin, or interferon alpha (*see* INTERFERON DRUGS, p.907). These drugs are usually taken long term to prevent hepatitis from recurring. They can cause significant side effects; monitoring is needed.

People with chronic hepatitis caused by an autoimmune reaction are usually treated indefinitely with corticosteroids (p.930), which may be combined with immunosuppressant drugs (p.906). If the liver has been damaged by a drug, it should recover slowly as long as the drug is stopped. If chronic hepatitis is due to a metabolic disorder, treatment of that underlying disorder may slow the progress of liver damage.

WHAT IS THE PROGNOSIS?

The prognosis depends on the cause of the hepatitis. Chronic viral hepatitis usually progresses slowly, and it may take years before problems such as cirrhosis and liver failure develop, if ever. People with chronic hepatitis are at increased risk of developing liver cancer, particularly if hepatitis is due to infection with the hepatitis B or C virus.

Without treatment, approximately 1 in 2 people who have autoimmune chronic hepatitis develop liver failure after 5 years. Hepatitis due to a metabolic disorder tends to get progressively worse, often ending in liver failure. In the case of liver failure, a liver transplant (p.650) may be considered.

(WWW) ONLINE SITES: p.1027, p.1033, p.1034

Alcohol-related liver disease

Short-term or progressive liver damage due to excessive alcohol consumption

 AGE More common over age 30

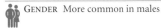

 GENDER More common in males

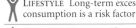

 LIFESTYLE Long-term excessive alcohol consumption is a risk factor

 GENETICS Not a significant factor

The most common cause of severe long-term liver disease in developed countries is excessive alcohol consumption (*see* ALCOHOL AND HEALTH, p.62, and ALCOHOL DEPENDENCE, p.564). More men than women have alcohol-related liver disease because more men drink heavily. However, women are more susceptible to liver damage from alcohol because of differences in the way that men and women metabolize alcohol. Regular excessive alcohol consumption is more likely to cause damage to the liver than sporadic heavy drinking. The longer excessive alcohol consumption continues, the greater the likelihood of developing liver disease. Long-term alcohol-related liver disease is known to increase the risk of developing liver cancer (p.649).

WHAT ARE THE TYPES?

Alcohol may cause three types of liver disease: fatty liver, alcoholic hepatitis, and cirrhosis (opposite page). Typically, these conditions occur in sequence, but this is not always the case. Over a number of years, most heavy drinkers develop a fatty liver, in which fat globules develop within liver cells. If alcohol consumption continues, hepatitis or inflammation of the liver develops. With continued drinking, cirrhosis develops. In this condition, liver cells that are damaged by alcohol are replaced by fibrous scar tissue. If cirrhosis has developed, liver damage is irreversible. It is not known why some heavy drinkers go on to develop hepatitis or cirrhosis while others do not.

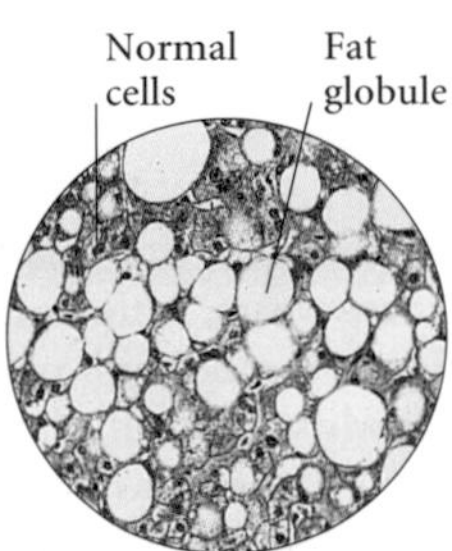
Normal cells
Fat globule

Fatty liver
Excessive alcohol consumption can damage the liver, causing fat globules to form in liver cells, as seen in this magnified view.

WHAT ARE THE SYMPTOMS?

In many cases, fatty liver does not cause symptoms and often remains undiagnosed. However, in about 1 in 3 affected people, the liver becomes enlarged, which may lead to discomfort in the right upper abdomen.

Alcoholic hepatitis also may not produce symptoms, but after about 10 years of heavy drinking in men and sooner in women, the first symptoms usually develop. These may include:

- Nausea and occasional vomiting.
- Discomfort in the upper right side of the abdomen.
- Weight loss.
- Fever.
- Yellowing of the skin and the whites of the eyes (*see* JAUNDICE, p.643).
- Swollen abdomen.

Cirrhosis may often cause no symptoms for a number of years or only mild symptoms, including:

- Poor appetite and weight loss.
- Nausea.
- Muscle wasting.

In some cases, severe cirrhosis may lead to a serious condition in which there is bleeding into the digestive tract from abnormal blood vessels that develop in the wall of the esophagus (*see* PORTAL HYPERTENSION AND VARICES, p.648). Severe alcoholic hepatitis and cirrhosis can lead to liver failure (p.650), which may result in coma (p.522) and death.

HOW IS IT DIAGNOSED?

A history of heavy alcohol consumption is essential for the diagnosis of alcohol-related liver disease. It is important that you be honest and tell your doctor exactly how much you drink. However, many people who drink heavily are reluctant to do this.

Your doctor may arrange for blood tests to evaluate your liver function. You may also have a liver biopsy (opposite page), a procedure in which a hollow needle is inserted into the liver to obtain a sample of liver tissue. The sample is then examined under a microscope to look for cell abnormalities.

TEST LIVER BIOPSY

In a liver biopsy, a sample of tissue is removed from the liver to diagnose a variety of disorders, including cirrhosis, hepatitis, and cancer. This procedure is performed in the hospital under local anesthesia and the sample is sent to a laboratory for microscopic examination. You will need to remain in bed for up to 6 hours afterward, lying on your right side at first to prevent bleeding. The biopsy site may be tender for a few days.

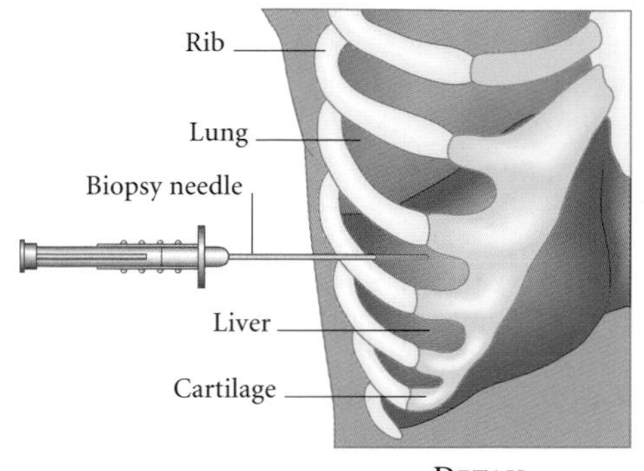
Rib
Lung
Biopsy needle
Liver
Cartilage

DETAIL

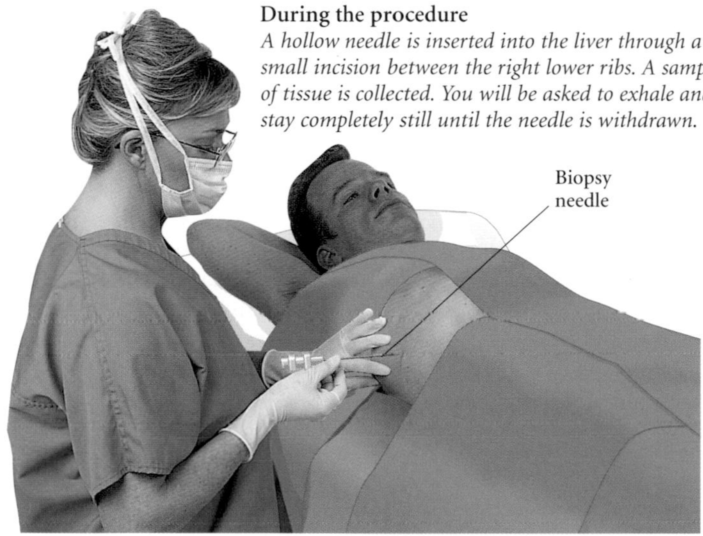
Biopsy needle

During the procedure
A hollow needle is inserted into the liver through a small incision between the right lower ribs. A sample of tissue is collected. You will be asked to exhale and stay completely still until the needle is withdrawn.

RESULTS

Cirrhosis
This magnified view of a sample of liver tissue shows normal liver cells surrounded by bands of fibrous scar tissue. Such an appearance is typical of the damage caused by cirrhosis.

Normal cells — Fibrous tissue

WHAT IS THE TREATMENT?

People who have alcohol-related liver disease must stop drinking completely and forever. Many people need professional help to achieve this. If drinking continues, the disease will progress and may be fatal. If drinking stops, the prognosis is likely to improve.

Fatty liver often disappears after 3–6 months of abstinence from alcohol. Some people with alcoholic hepatitis who stop drinking recover completely. However, in most cases damage to the liver is irreversible, and the condition progresses to cirrhosis. Severe alcoholic cirrhosis can cause a number of serious complications, which in some cases may be fatal. About half of all people who have cirrhosis die from liver failure within 5 years. More than 1 in 10 people with cirrhosis go on to develop liver cancer. People with alcohol-related liver disease who have no other serious health problems and have stopped drinking may be candidates for a liver transplant (p.650).

Many of the symptoms and some of the complications of alcohol-related liver disease can be treated with some success. For example, swelling of the abdomen, which results from fluid accumulation in the abdominal cavity, may be decreased by diuretic drugs (p.902) and a diet that is low in salt. Nausea can frequently be relieved by antiemetic drugs (p.922).

WWW ONLINE SITES: p.1027, p.1034

Cirrhosis

Irreversible scarring of the liver, occurring in the late stages of various liver disorders

AGE More common over age 40

GENDER More common in males

GENETICS In some cases, the underlying cause is inherited

LIFESTYLE Long-term excessive alcohol consumption is a risk factor

In cirrhosis, normal liver tissue is destroyed and replaced by fibrous scar tissue. The condition may be caused by several different disorders, including viral infections and excessive alcohol consumption. The liver damage is irreversible and prevents the liver from functioning properly. Some people with cirrhosis may feel well for years despite having severe liver damage. However, with time they may develop complications, such as liver failure (p.650) and liver cancer (p.649).

In developed countries, cirrhosis is the third most common cause of death in people aged 45–65, after coronary artery disease and cancer. In the US, cirrhosis is much more common in men than in women and accounts for about 30,000 deaths each year.

WHAT ARE THE CAUSES?

There are various causes of cirrhosis. Worldwide, the most common cause is infection with a hepatitis virus, particularly the hepatitis B and C viruses (*see* CHRONIC HEPATITIS, p.645). However, in developed countries cirrhosis is most frequently caused by excessive alcohol consumption (*see* ALCOHOL-RELATED LIVER DISEASE, opposite page). Another cause, which is more common in women than in men, is the autoimmune disorder primary biliary cirrhosis. Bile, a liquid produced by the liver to aid digestion, normally leaves the liver through the bile ducts. In primary biliary cirrhosis, the bile ducts become inflamed, blocking the flow of bile from the liver.

This causes bile to build up, damaging the liver tissue. Cirrhosis may also be caused by sclerosing cholangitis, a condition in which the bile ducts inside the liver become inflamed. The cause of this condition is not known, although it can be associated with some inflammatory bowel diseases, such as ulcerative colitis (p.659) and Crohn's disease (p.658). Cirrhosis may also develop after bile duct surgery or as a result of a blockage of the bile ducts by gallstones (p.651). In addition, certain inherited disorders, such as hemochromatosis (p.692), may cause cirrhosis to develop.

WHAT ARE THE SYMPTOMS?

Cirrhosis often produces no symptoms and is detected only during a routine examination for another condition. If there are symptoms, they may include:

- Poor appetite and weight loss.
- Fatigue.
- Nausea.
- Yellowing of the skin and the whites of the eyes (*see* JAUNDICE, p.643).

In the long term, life-threatening complications may arise. For example, cirrhosis can lead to high pressure in veins in the esophagus, which causes them to be fragile and bleed easily (*see* PORTAL HYPERTENSION AND VARICES, right). Malnutrition may also develop from being unable to absorb fats and certain vitamins. Eventually, cirrhosis can lead to liver cancer or liver failure. The symptoms of liver failure include a swollen, fluid-filled abdomen and visible spiderlike blood vessels in the skin, known as spider nevi. A failing liver may result in abnormal bleeding and easy bruising because of reduced production of blood clotting factors in the liver.

WHAT MIGHT BE DONE?

If your doctor suspects that you have cirrhosis from your symptoms, he or she will take blood samples to assess liver function and look for hepatitis viruses. You may also have ultrasound scanning (p.250), CT scanning (p.247), or MRI (p.248) to assess the liver. To confirm the diagnosis, you may have a liver biopsy (p.647), in which a small sample of tissue is removed from your liver for microscopic examination.

Damage to the liver caused by cirrhosis is always irreversible. However, if the underlying cause can be treated, further deterioration may be prevented. Whatever the cause of the cirrhosis, you should not drink alcohol. Nutritional deficiencies can be corrected by taking supplements and altering your diet. If the condition worsens but you are otherwise in good health, you may be suitable for a liver transplant (p.650).

WHAT IS THE PROGNOSIS?

The prognosis for cirrhosis is extremely variable and depends on the degree of liver damage, whether complications have developed, and whether further damage can be prevented. If the condition is mild, people may live for many years. About 7 in 10 people survive for more than a year after a liver transplant.

(WWW) ONLINE SITES: p.1027, p.1034

Portal hypertension and varices

Elevated pressure in the vein carrying blood to the liver, leading to distended veins, particularly in the esophagus

AGE More common in adults, especially those over age 40

GENDER More common in males

LIFESTYLE Excessive alcohol consumption is a risk factor

GENETICS Not a significant factor

In a liver damaged by disease, normal blood flow may become obstructed. This obstruction leads to portal hypertension, in which the pressure is increased in the portal vein, a large vein that carries blood from the digestive tract to the liver. The high pressure forces blood through other smaller veins of the digestive tract. These veins then become distended and fragile and are known as varices.

In most cases, varices develop at the lower end of the esophagus. They are prone to rupture, and heavy bleeding from them can be life-threatening. In some cases, varices develop in other areas of the body, such as in the skin over the abdomen and in the rectum.

Portal hypertension occurs mainly in adults and is more common in men. The condition is often associated with excessive consumption of alcohol (*see* ALCOHOL AND HEALTH, p.62).

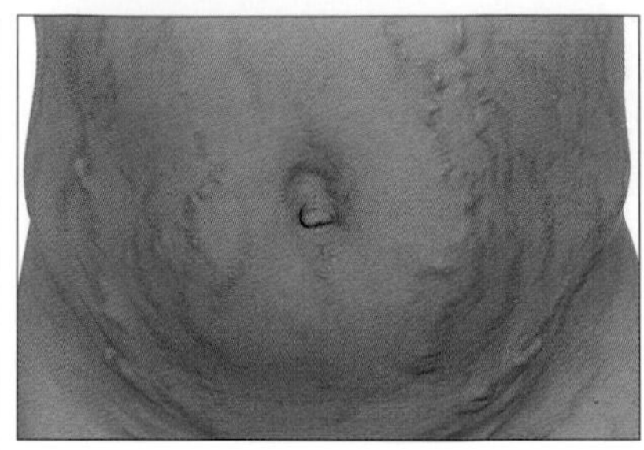

Effect of portal hypertension
Increased pressure in the portal vein, which carries blood from the digestive tract to the liver, can cause distended veins in the skin over the abdomen, as shown here.

WHAT ARE THE CAUSES?

In Western countries, about 8 in 10 cases of portal hypertension are associated with cirrhosis (p.647), which is often due to chronic hepatitis (p.645) or long-term alcohol abuse (*see* ALCOHOL-RELATED LIVER DISEASE, p.646). A blood clot blocking the portal vein, schistosomiasis (p.312), and rarely congenital liver disorders may also cause portal hypertension.

WHAT ARE THE SYMPTOMS?

Portal hypertension is usually undetected until complications develop. If symptoms develop, they may include:

- Swollen abdomen due to accumulation of fluid.
- Visible swelling of the veins in the skin over the abdomen, sometimes around the navel.

In about 1 in 3 of people with varices in the esophagus, the veins eventually rupture. The bleeding is usually sudden and massive and leads to vomiting of blood and later passage of black, tarry feces that contain partly digested blood (*see* BLEEDING FROM THE DIGESTIVE TRACT, p.630). Loss of large volumes of blood can result in shock (p.414). If not treated immediately, shock may cause damage to internal organs and lead to disorders such as acute kidney failure (p.706) and liver failure (p.650).

WHAT MIGHT BE DONE?

Your doctor will check for signs of portal hypertension if you have chronic hepatitis. Ultrasound scanning (p.250) or CT scanning (p.247) may be done to detect enlarged veins or endoscopy may be used to visualize them (*see* UPPER DIGESTIVE TRACT ENDOSCOPY, p.641).

Usually, once portal hypertension has developed, liver damage is irreversible. However, beta blocker drugs (p.898) may be prescribed to lower pressure in the portal vein and decrease the risk of bleeding from varices.

Ruptured varices require urgent treatment in the hospital with intravenous fluids and a blood transfusion (p.447) to replace lost blood. The source of bleeding will be investigated using endoscopy. If possible, the varices will be injected through the endoscope with a chemical that causes the blood vessel to close and therefore stops bleeding. The drug vasopressin may be given to reduce bleeding.

If these measures do not succeed in stopping bleeding, a tube encircled by a deflated balloon may be passed through the mouth into the esophagus. The balloon is inflated to compress the varices and is left in place until bleeding stops. In some cases, a procedure is carried out to allow blood from the digestive tract to bypass the liver. This may involve using X-rays to view and direct the insertion of a tube that connects the portal vein directly to the hepatic vein, through which blood normally leaves the liver.

What is the prognosis?

The prognosis depends on whether or not varices develop and bleed and also on the severity of bleeding. About 7 in 10 people survive ruptured varices, but in over half of them bleeding will recur.

(WWW) ONLINE SITES: p.1027, p.1034

Liver cancer

A cancerous tumor that originates in the cells of the liver

AGE More common with increasing age

GENDER Up to four times more common in males

LIFESTYLE Alcohol abuse and intravenous drug abuse are risk factors

GENETICS Not a significant factor

Worldwide, liver cancer is one of the most common cancers, accounting for half of all cancer cases. However, in developed countries, the disease is less common and most cases occur following longstanding cirrhosis (p.647) due to long-term alcohol abuse or viral infection. In developing countries, liver cancer is closely linked with viral hepatitis, especially that due to the hepatitis B and C viruses (*see* CHRONIC HEPATITIS, p.645), which account for about 7 in 10 cases. People with hemochromatosis (p.692), a condition in which excess iron builds up in the liver, are also at high risk of developing liver cancer.

Another cause of liver cancer is food contaminated by carcinogens (cancer-causing agents) such as aflatoxin, a toxin produced by a fungus that grows on stored grain and peanuts. Rarely, liver cancer results from infection with a form of liver fluke (a parasitic worm) common in the Far East or exposure to certain chemicals in the workplace.

What are the symptoms?

People with liver cancer may experience the following symptoms:

- Weight loss and fever.
- Pain in the upper right side of the abdomen.
- Yellowing of the skin and the whites of the eyes (*see* JAUNDICE, p.643).
- Symptoms of liver failure (p.650).

As the disease progresses, the abdomen may become swollen due to an accumulation of fluid.

What might be done?

Your doctor may suspect liver cancer from your symptoms if you already have cirrhosis. You may have blood tests to look for signs of cancer and to assess liver function. Imaging tests, such as ultrasound scanning (p.250), CT scanning (p.247), or MRI (p.248), may be done to confirm the diagnosis. You may also have a liver biopsy (p.647), in which a piece of tissue is removed and tested for cancer cells.

Surgery offers the only chance of a cure. A liver transplant (p.650) is rarely done because in many cases the cancer is likely to recur. More commonly, the aim is to slow the progress of the disease with treatments that include injection of chemicals into the tumor, chemotherapy (p.278), and blocking the blood supply to the tumor, causing it to shrink.

What is the prognosis?

The prognosis for people with liver cancer is poor. Many people do not respond to treatment and survive less than a year after diagnosis.

(WWW) ONLINE SITES: p.1027, p.1028, p.1034

Liver metastases

Cancerous tumors in the liver that have spread from other parts of the body

AGE More common with increasing age

GENDER GENETICS LIFESTYLE Not significant factors

Metastases are cancerous tumors in the liver that originate from cancers elsewhere in the body, commonly those of the lung, breast, colon, pancreas, and stomach. Other types of cancer, such as leukemia (p.453) and lymphoma (p.459), may also spread to the liver. Liver metastases form when cancerous cells separate from the original cancer, circulate in the blood, and settle in the liver, where they multiply. Several metastases of varying size may develop.

In developed countries, liver metastases occur more commonly than liver cancer (left). The disease is also more common in elderly people.

What are the symptoms?

People may already have symptoms due to the original cancer, but sometimes this cancer is not apparent. The symptoms of liver metastases may be the only warning of illness. They include:

- Weight loss.
- Reduced appetite.
- Fever.
- Pain in the upper right side of the abdomen.
- Yellowing of the skin and the whites of the eyes (*see* JAUNDICE, p.643).

As the disease progresses, the abdomen may become swollen due to enlargement of the liver or fluid accumulation.

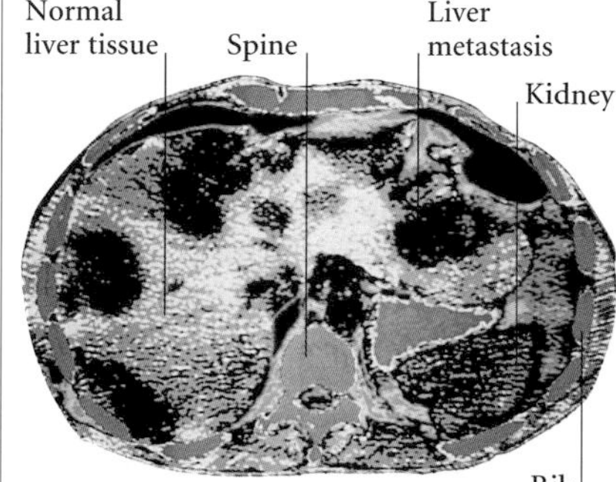
Normal liver tissue
Spine
Liver metastasis
Kidney
Rib

Liver metastases
The dark areas in the liver shown in this CT scan are metastases, which are cancerous tumors that have spread from a cancer elsewhere in the body.

WHAT ARE THE CAUSES?

Chronic pancreatitis is most commonly caused by long-term alcohol abuse. Less commonly, the condition may be associated with very high blood levels of fats (*see* INHERITED HYPERLIPOPROTEINEMIAS, p.692) or very high levels of iron in the tissues (*see* HEMOCHROMATOSIS, p.692). In some cases, the cause of chronic pancreatitis is unclear.

WHAT ARE THE SYMPTOMS?

Symptoms usually develop over several years and vary in severity depending on the extent of damage to the pancreas. Most people do not experience symptoms during the early stages, but, as the disease progresses, they may develop symptoms such as:

- Persistent upper abdominal pain, often radiating to the back.
- Nausea and vomiting.
- Loss of appetite.

Complications result mainly from the reduced production of enzymes and hormones. A reduced level of pancreatic enzymes causes malabsorption (p.655), which may lead to greasy, bulky stools, vitamin deficiencies, and weight loss. Diabetes mellitus (p.687) may result if the production of insulin is reduced.

HOW IS IT DIAGNOSED?

There is no simple test to diagnose chronic pancreatitis. Your doctor may arrange for X-rays (p.244), ultrasound scanning (p.250), or MRI (p.248) to look for calcium deposits in the pancreas, which are an indication that the pancreas has been inflamed. Other tests may include ERCP (p.653), in which a tubelike instrument called an endoscope is used to inject a contrast dye into the pancreatic duct to look for abnormalities. You may also have ultrasound scanning, which may be done through an endoscope, to look for gallstones. In addition, you may have blood tests to determine blood sugar levels.

WHAT IS THE TREATMENT?

Your doctor will probably advise you to avoid alcohol and fatty foods. You may need drugs to replace the hormones and enzymes that should be produced by the pancreas. Enzymes in pill or powder form can be taken with each meal to aid digestion. Regular insulin injections may also be necessary to control blood sugar levels and will probably be needed for life. If pain is severe, strong opiate analgesics (p.912) are given. In some cases, pain may be relieved by a nerve block. In this procedure, an injection is used to destroy the nerves that carry pain sensations from the pancreas to the spinal cord.

WHAT IS THE PROGNOSIS?

The symptoms of chronic pancreatitis may recede over time, but in some cases the disorder worsens and symptoms become more severe. People who have chronic pancreatitis are more likely to develop pancreatic cancer (below).

(WWW) ONLINE SITES: p.1027, p.1030

Pancreatic cancer

A cancerous tumor of the pancreas that may be symptomless in its early stages

AGE More common over age 50

GENDER Almost twice as common in males

GENETICS More common in certain ethnic groups

LIFESTYLE Smoking, a high-fat diet, and alcohol abuse are risk factors

Pancreatic cancer is a relatively rare disorder, accounting for about 1 in 50 cases of all cancers in Canada. However, the disease, which mainly affects people over the age of 50, is becoming more common as life expectancy increases. Pancreatic cancer occurs almost twice as frequently in men as it does in women and has also been found to be more common in certain ethnic groups.

People with pancreatic cancer usually have few symptoms until the disorder reaches an advanced stage and often not until it has spread to other parts of the body, typically the lymph nodes in the abdomen and the liver. The disease is nearly always fatal and is one of the most common causes of death from cancer in North America.

Little is known about the causes of pancreatic cancer, but it has been linked with diet, in particular with fatty foods and high alcohol consumption. A higher incidence of the cancer in certain ethnic groups indicates that genetic factors may be involved. The risk of the disease is greater in people who smoke and in those with chronic pancreatitis (p.653).

WHAT ARE THE SYMPTOMS?

Symptoms often develop gradually over a few months and may include:

- Pain in the upper abdomen that radiates to the back.
- Loss of weight.
- Reduced appetite.

Many pancreatic tumors cause obstruction of the bile ducts through which the digestive liquid bile leaves the liver. Such blockage leads to jaundice (p.643), in which the skin and whites of the eyes turn yellow. Jaundice may be accompanied by itching, dark-colored urine, and lighter than normal feces.

HOW IS IT DIAGNOSED?

Imaging techniques, such as ultrasound scanning (p.250), CT scanning (p.247), or MRI (p.248), are normally used to diagnose pancreatic cancer. In addition, specialized imaging procedures such as ERCP (p.653) and ultrasound scanning through an endoscope may be used to look for abnormalities in the bile and pancreatic ducts. To confirm the diagnosis, a sample of pancreatic tissue may be taken for microscopic examination.

WHAT IS THE TREATMENT?

Surgery to remove part or all of the pancreas offers the only chance of cure. However, the cancer has usually spread by the time it is diagnosed. In such cases, surgery to relieve symptoms may be possible. For example, if the bile duct is obstructed by a tumor, a rigid tube known as a stent may be inserted to keep the duct open. This procedure is usually done during ERCP and helps reduce jaundice. Treatment such as chemotherapy (p.278) and radiation therapy (p.279) may be used to slow the progress of the disease.

Pain can often be relieved with analgesics (p.912). Severe pain may be treated by a nerve block, a procedure using an injection of a chemical to inactivate the nerves supplying the pancreas.

WHAT IS THE PROGNOSIS?

In many cases, pancreatic cancer is not diagnosed until it is far advanced, at which time the prognosis is poor. Fewer than 2 in 100 people survive more than 5 years. Even with surgery, only 10 in 100 people survive more than 5 years. Most people survive for less than a year.

(WWW) ONLINE SITES: p.1028, p.1034

DISORDERS OF THE INTESTINES, RECTUM, AND ANUS

The intestines, rectum, and anus are exposed to infectious agents and toxins in food, and disorders involving these organs are common. Often the causes are unknown, although diet is a factor in some conditions. Many of the disorders cause changes in the consistency of feces and in the frequency of bowel movements.

The first articles in this section deal with disorders in which the body has difficulty absorbing nutrients from food, such as lactose intolerance and celiac disease. The next two articles describe the inflammatory bowel disorders Crohn's disease and ulcerative colitis. Digestive disorders in which the movement of the intestinal contents may be affected, such as hernias and intestinal obstruction, are then looked at. This section also covers the common disorders appendicitis and irritable bowel syndrome. Finally, colorectal cancer, a common cause of death in North America, and disorders of the rectum and anus, such as hemorrhoids and anal cancer, are described.

Diarrhea (p.627) and constipation (p.628) are included with general digestive and nutritional problems. Intestinal infections (*see* INFECTIONS AND INFESTATIONS, pp.282–313) and intestinal disorders in children (*see* INFANCY AND CHILDHOOD, pp.862–865) are covered elsewhere in the book.

KEY ANATOMY

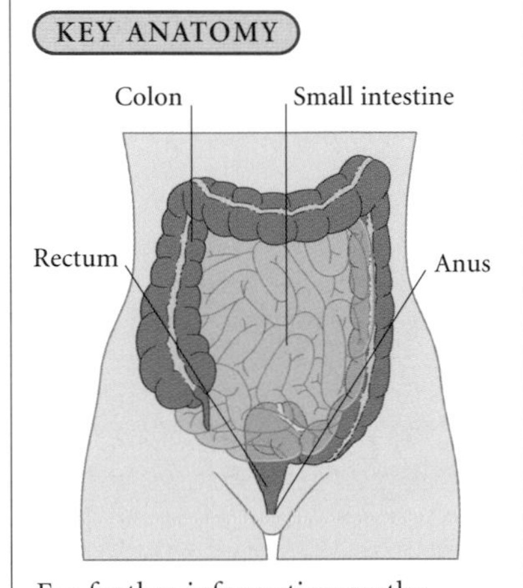
Colon
Small intestine
Rectum
Anus

For further information on the structure and function of the intestines, rectum, and anus, *see* pp.620–625.

Malabsorption

Impaired absorption of nutrients from the small intestine

 GENETICS Sometimes runs in families

 AGE GENDER LIFESTYLE Risk factors depend on the cause

Malabsorption occurs when the small intestine cannot absorb nutrients from food passing through it. The disorder may cause various symptoms, including diarrhea and weight loss. If malabsorption is left untreated, certain nutritional deficiencies (p.630) can develop, which may lead to further problems, such as anemia (p.446) or nerve damage (*see* NUTRITIONAL NEUROPATHIES, p.545).

WHAT ARE THE CAUSES?

Malabsorption is due to disorders that result in inadequate breakdown of food during digestion, damage to the lining of the small intestine, or impairment of motility, which is the ability of the muscular intestinal walls to contract.

In some cases, the small intestine cannot break down food because digestive enzymes or juices are missing or in short supply. For example, disorders affecting the pancreas, the organ that produces digestive juices, may prevent the breakdown of food. Such disorders include chronic pancreatitis (p.653) and cystic fibrosis (p.824). Sometimes, there is a problem in breaking down a specific nutrient. For example, people with lactose intolerance (p.657) lack an enzyme in the intestine needed to break down the sugar lactose from milk.

Damage to the intestinal lining may result from inflammation due to disorders such as celiac disease (p.658) and Crohn's disease (p.658) and particular infections, such as giardiasis (p.307). As a result, nutrients are unable to cross the lining and enter the bloodstream. In the autoimmune disorder scleroderma (p.462), changes in the structure of the intestinal walls affect motility and lead to malabsorption of nutrients. Diabetes mellitus (p.687) may cause abnormal motility and malabsorption by damaging the nerves that supply the muscles in the intestinal walls.

WHAT ARE THE SYMPTOMS?

The most common symptoms of malabsorption include:

- Bulky, pale, foul-smelling feces.
- Flatulence and abdominal bloating.
- Weight loss.
- Abdominal pain with cramps.
- Fatigue and weakness.

Left untreated, malabsorption can lead to deficiencies in vitamin B_{12} and iron, which may result in anemia (p.446), the symptoms of which include pale skin and shortness of breath.

HOW IS IT DIAGNOSED?

Your doctor may arrange for you to have a variety of blood tests to look for anemia, vitamin deficiencies, and other signs of malabsorption. If the doctor suspects that your pancreas is damaged, he or she will probably arrange for additional tests to assess its function. A test may also be carried out in order to confirm the enzyme deficiency that causes lactose intolerance.

Your doctor may also arrange for further tests to be carried out so that he or she can check for other disorders of the small intestine. For example, you may have a blood test to look for the particular antibodies that are present in celiac disease. A special X-ray in which barium is used to highlight the inside of the small intestine (*see* CONTRAST X-RAYS, p.245) may need to be done to look for damage to the digestive tract caused by Crohn's disease. You may also require an endoscopy (p.255) to obtain a sample of intestinal tissue for microscopic analysis.

What is the treatment?

If possible, the underlying cause of malabsorption is treated. Celiac disease can usually be treated with a special diet, and Crohn's disease usually responds to corticosteroids (p.930) or sulfasalazine (*see* 5-AMINOSALICYLATE DRUGS, p.924). If the cause of malabsorption is giardiasis, antiprotozoal drugs (p.888) will be prescribed. Specific nutritional deficiencies can be corrected by taking vitamin and mineral supplements (*see* VITAMINS, p.927, and MINERALS, p.929).

If you are severely malnourished, you may need treatment in the hospital and feeding with intravenous nutrients or special liquid food supplements.

Most disorders that lead to malabsorption can be treated effectively, and the majority of affected people recover fully from the condition.

(WWW) ONLINE SITES: p.1030, p.1035

Irritable bowel syndrome

A combination of intermittent abdominal pain, constipation, and/or diarrhea

 AGE Most commonly develops between the ages of 20 and 30

 GENDER Twice as common in females

 GENETICS Sometimes runs in families

 LIFESTYLE Stress and certain foods may make symptoms worse

Irritable bowel syndrome (IBS) accounts for more referrals to gastroenterologists than any other disorder, although many people with the problem never consult a doctor. The condition most commonly develops in people between the ages of 20 and 30 and is twice as common in women as in men. As many as 2 in 10 people have symptoms of irritable bowel syndrome at some time in their lives. The symptoms, which include abdominal pain, constipation, and/or diarrhea, tend to be intermittent, typically persisting for many years. Although irritable bowel syndrome can be distressing, it does not lead to serious complications.

SELF-HELP Living with irritable bowel syndrome

Some people learn to control the symptoms of irritable bowel syndrome by making dietary and lifestyle changes. The symptoms may improve if you follow a diet that is high in fiber and low in fat (*see* DIET AND HEALTH, p.48). You may need to try several different approaches before finding one that helps you. Try the following:

- Keep a food diary. Try to eliminate any food or beverage that seems to bring on an attack of irritable bowel syndrome.
- Avoid large meals; spicy, fried, fatty foods; and milk products.
- If constipation is a problem, try gradually increasing your fiber intake. If bloating and diarrhea are particular problems, reduce your fiber intake.
- Cut out or reduce your intake of tea, coffee, milk, cola, and beer.
- Eat at regular times.
- Stop smoking.
- Try relaxation exercises (p.75) to alleviate stress, which is often a contributing factor.

What are the causes?

The precise cause of irritable bowel syndrome is unknown. It may result from abnormal contractions of the muscles in the intestinal walls. An increased sensitivity to certain foods, including fruit, sorbitol (an artificial sweetener), and fat, may also be a contributory factor.

Irritable bowel syndrome sometimes develops after a gastrointestinal infection (*see* GASTROENTERITIS, p.628). The problem may run in families, which suggests that genetic factors are involved. Often, stress, anxiety, or depression is associated with the syndrome and can worsen existing symptoms.

What are the symptoms?

The symptoms are typically intermittent but usually recur for many years and often persist into old age. They vary widely among people and with each episode. The main symptoms include:

- Abdominal bloating combined with excessive quantities of gas.
- Abdominal pain, often on the lower left side, that may be relieved by defecation or passing gas.
- Diarrhea, which may be most severe on waking and sometimes alternates with bouts of constipation that may produce "rabbit pellet" stools.
- Feeling that the bowel has not been emptied completely.
- Passage of mucus during defecation.
- Nausea and vomiting.
- Feeling of fullness and difficulty finishing meals.

Many people have symptoms unrelated to the digestive tract, such as fatigue, headache, back pain, and an increased urge to urinate. In women, sexual intercourse may be painful, and symptoms may be worse before menstrual periods.

You should consult your doctor if the symptoms are severe, persistent, or recurrent or if you have unexpectedly lost weight. If you are over 40 when the symptoms first develop, you should seek medical advice so that serious disorders with similar symptoms, such as colorectal cancer (p.665), can be ruled out.

How is it diagnosed?

The number and types of tests done for irritable bowel syndrome depend on your age. There is no single test that can diagnose the disorder. Instead, your doctor will want to make sure that you have no other serious condition.

If your symptoms suggest that you may have an inflammatory bowel disorder such as Crohn's disease (p.658), or if you are over the age of 40, your doctor will probably want to investigate your symptoms further. You may have a blood test to check for inflammation, which can indicate the presence of Crohn's disease. If the result is positive or if your doctor suspects a colorectal tumor, you will probably have a contrast X-ray (p.245) of the intestines or undergo a colonoscopy (p.661). You may also have tests to exclude food intolerance (opposite page) and lactose intolerance (opposite page), which cause symptoms similar to those of irritable bowel syndrome.

What is the treatment?

Although the symptoms can be severe, irritable bowel syndrome is not a serious condition. You should usually be able to control your symptoms yourself with a combination of a change in diet and relaxation techniques (*see* LIVING WITH IRRITABLE BOWEL SYNDROME, opposite page). However, if symptoms are troublesome enough to interfere with daily routines, then you should consult your doctor for advice on treatment. He or she may prescribe antispasmodic drugs to relax the contractions of the digestive tract and help relieve abdominal pain (*see* ANTISPASMODIC DRUGS AND MOTILITY STIMULANTS, p.926).

Antidiarrheal drugs (p.924) may help alleviate diarrhea, especially in people who have diarrhea on waking. If constipation is a problem, bulk-forming agents (*see* LAXATIVES, p.924) may help.

If you have psychological symptoms such as anxiety in addition to irritable bowel syndrome, you should ask your doctor to refer you to a therapist for advice on how to control anxiety.

Irritable bowel syndrome tends to be a chronic disorder, often lasting into old age. However, attacks usually become less frequent and severe with time.

(WWW) ONLINE SITES: p.1030

Food intolerance

Symptoms that are related to eating a specific food

AGE GENDER GENETICS LIFESTYLE
Not significant factors

If you develop troublesome symptoms such as stomachache each time you eat a particular food, you may have food intolerance. The condition is difficult to prove and may be very rare. The cause of food intolerance is usually unknown, although in some cases there is a definite abnormality, such as an enzyme deficiency (*see* LACTOSE INTOLERANCE, right). Food intolerance is different from food allergy (p.467), in which the immune system reacts inappropriately to a specific food.

WHAT ARE THE SYMPTOMS?

The symptoms of food intolerance vary among individuals. Symptoms are usually related to a particular type of food, such as milk or wheat flour. They may occur within minutes or hours of eating and include the following:

- Nausea and vomiting.
- Abdominal pain.
- Diarrhea.

WHAT MIGHT BE DONE?

In most cases of food intolerance, the diagnosis is based on your symptoms. Tests will then be performed to confirm the diagnosis. In some cases, endoscopy (*see* UPPER DIGESTIVE TRACT ENDOSCOPY, p.641) is carried out to examine the digestive tract and to look for evidence of an intestinal disorder such as celiac disease (p.658). During the procedure, a small piece of tissue may be taken from the intestinal wall for examination under a microscope.

Frequently, the only way to diagnose food intolerance is to exclude the suspect food from your diet for a time to see if your symptoms improve. The food is later reintroduced into your diet, and you are monitored to see if your symptoms worsen. An exclusion diet, especially one for a child, should be undertaken only under the supervision of a doctor and a dietitian because restricted diets can cause vitamin and mineral deficiencies.

Once the cause of your intolerance has been identified, you should avoid eating those foods that have been found to aggravate the problem. You will probably need to consult a dietitian, who will help you devise a diet that excludes the foods to which you are intolerant while providing all the nutrients you need to maintain a healthy diet.

(WWW) ONLINE SITES: p.1030, p.1035

Lactose intolerance

An inability to digest lactose, the natural sugar found in milk

AGE Most commonly develops from adolescence onward

GENETICS More common in certain ethnic groups

GENDER LIFESTYLE Not significant factors

A person who is lactose intolerant is unable to digest lactose, a natural sugar that is found in milk and dairy products. As a result, the lactose remains undigested in the intestines. In an affected person, lactose can cause abdominal pain and diarrhea. Lactose intolerance usually develops in adolescence or adulthood. The condition only rarely affects babies. It also is more likely to develop in non-Caucasians than in Caucasians.

WHAT ARE THE CAUSES?

Normally, the enzyme lactase breaks down lactose in the intestines to form the sugars glucose and galactose, which are easily absorbed through the intestinal wall. If this enzyme is absent, the unabsorbed lactose ferments in the large intestine and produces symptoms. Although high levels of lactase are present at birth, in many racial groups the levels can drop with increasing age, becoming very low by adolescence so that milk can no longer be digested.

In children, lactose intolerance can sometimes occur temporarily following an attack of gastroenteritis (p.628), an inflammation that causes short-term damage to the lining of the intestine.

WHAT ARE THE SYMPTOMS?

The symptoms of lactose intolerance usually develop a few hours after eating or drinking products containing milk. They may include the following:

- Abdominal bloating and cramping.
- Diarrhea.
- Vomiting.

The severity of the symptoms will depend on the degree of lactase deficiency. One person may experience symptoms only after drinking several glasses of milk while another may feel discomfort after consuming only a small amount of a dairy product.

WHAT MIGHT BE DONE?

Your doctor may be able to diagnose lactose intolerance from your symptoms. He or she will probably ask you to keep a diary of all the foods you eat and the symptoms that occur. You may then have a specialized test to confirm lactose intolerance. Alternatively, your doctor may ask you to eliminate all dairy products from your diet for a few days. If your symptoms improve but return when dairy products are reintroduced into your diet, the diagnosis of lactose intolerance is confirmed.

Lactose intolerance is usually a permanent condition in adults. However, if you are affected, you can completely relieve the symptoms by eliminating lactose from your diet. It is important to remember to avoid milk and all dairy products, such as cheese, cream, and butter, all of which contain lactose. If milk is excluded from the diet, calcium supplements should be considered.

Most people who have lactose intolerance can usually tolerate a few ounces of milk 2–3 times a day. In children whose lactose intolerance is caused by gastroenteritis, milk and dairy products may be gradually reintroduced into their diets a few weeks after the infection, as the intestine recovers.

(WWW) ONLINE SITES: p.1030, p.1035

Celiac disease

Malabsorption due to the intestine being damaged by a reaction to gluten, a protein found in many foods

 AGE Usually occurs in the first year of life but can occur at any age

 GENDER More common in females

 GENETICS Sometimes runs in families

 LIFESTYLE Not a significant factor

Celiac disease, commonly called sprue, is a condition caused by the protein gluten, found in wheat, rye, barley, and to some extent in oats. In people with the disease, the lining of the small intestine is damaged so that food cannot be properly absorbed (*see* MALABSORPTION, p.655). The exact mechanism of damage is uncertain, but it seems to be due to an abnormal immune response in which antibodies against gluten are produced. The resulting malabsorption leads to a deficiency of many nutrients that are vital for good health. Celiac disease sometimes runs in families, which suggests that genetic factors are involved.

In the US, celiac disease affects about one person out of 133. The condition is very rare in Africa and Asia.

What are the symptoms?

In babies, the symptoms first appear soon after cereals are introduced into the diet, usually at 3 or 4 months. In adults, they usually develop gradually and include:

- Bulky, loose, foul-smelling feces that look greasy.
- Abdominal bloating and flatulence.
- Weight loss.
- Weakness and fatigue.
- In some cases, a persistent, itchy rash on the knees, buttocks, elbows, and across the shoulders.
- In many cases, there may not be any symptoms.

In babies and children, the following symptoms may also occur:

- Diarrhea.
- Failure to grow or gain weight.
- Muscle wasting, especially around the buttocks.

Vitamin and mineral deficiencies may lead to disorders such as iron-deficiency anemia (p.447) and osteoporosis (*see* OSTEOPOROSIS p.368), which is due to a lack of vitamin D and calcium. Untreated, celiac disease may increase the risk of cancers, particularly cancer of the small intestine.

How is it diagnosed?

Your doctor may suspect celiac disease from your symptoms, from your family history, or if you have unexplained iron deficiency and/or osteoporosis. A blood test to look for antibodies may also help support the diagnosis. The doctor may suspect the condition in a baby if symptoms developed soon after solid foods were introduced.

Diagnosis is confirmed by removing a small sample of tissue from the lining of the small intestine. This procedure is performed using an endoscope inserted through the mouth (*see* UPPER DIGESTIVE TRACT ENDOSCOPY, p.641). When the tissue is examined under a microscope, the intestinal lining appears flattened. You may also have blood tests to look for evidence of anemia.

What is the treatment?

The disease is treated by removing gluten from your diet. The recommended diet can be complicated, and it is advisable to see a dietitian for guidance. You should avoid foods that contain wheat, rye, and barley. Of the cereals, only rice, corn, and possibly oats are suitable. It is not advisable to eat mustard, pasta, salad dressing, and some margarines because they contain wheat or wheat extracts, and you should avoid drinking beer. Initially, you may also need to take supplements of vitamins (p.927) and minerals (p.929).

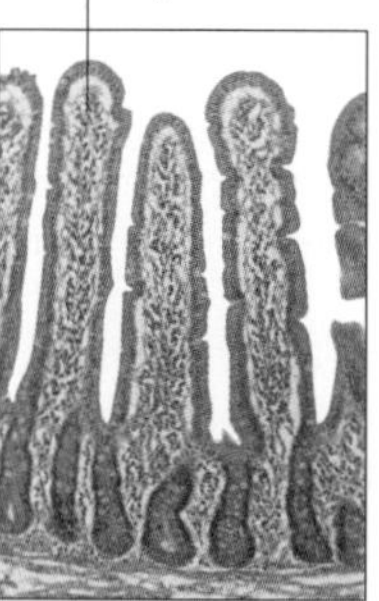

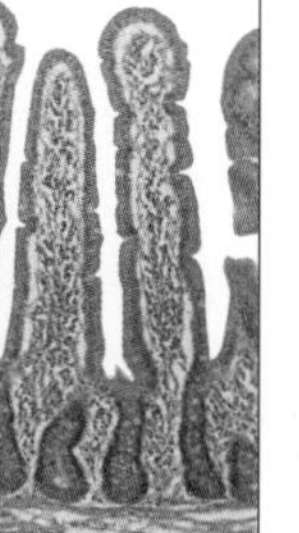

Projection
NORMAL INTESTINE

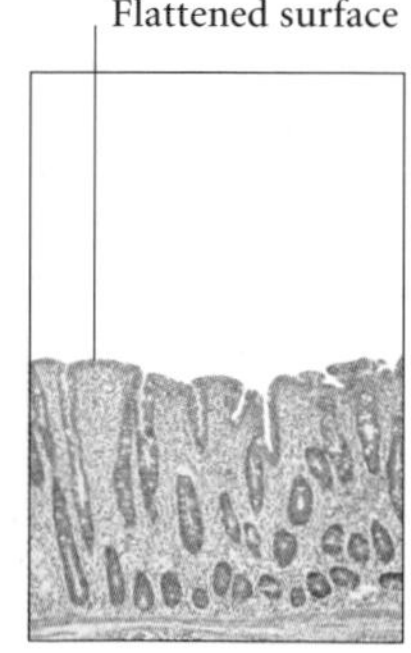

Flattened surface
DISEASED INTESTINE

Intestine in celiac disease

These magnified sections of small intestine show the effects of celiac disease. The fingerlike projections that normally absorb nutrients are flattened in celiac disease.

Removing gluten from the diet usually produces a substantial and rapid improvement, and eventually the symptoms may totally disappear. However, celiac disease is a chronic condition and may reappear if gluten is reintroduced into the diet. Since celiac disease sometimes runs in families, relatives of an affected person may be screened for the disorder by having a blood test to check for antibodies produced in the disease.

(WWW) ONLINE SITES: p.1030, p.1035

Crohn's disease

A long-term inflammatory disease that can affect any part of the digestive tract

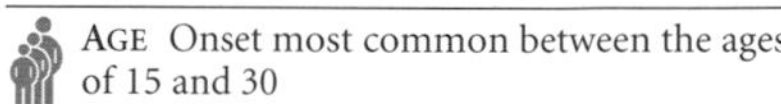 AGE Onset most common between the ages of 15 and 30

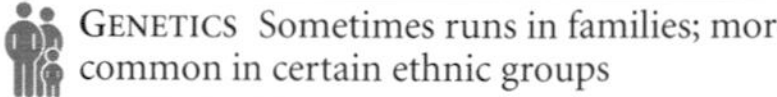 GENETICS Sometimes runs in families; more common in certain ethnic groups

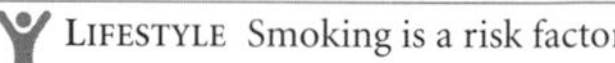 LIFESTYLE Smoking is a risk factor

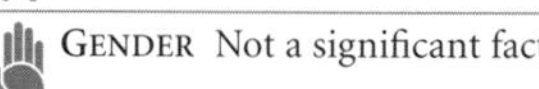 GENDER Not a significant factor

Crohn's disease is a chronic illness that usually begins in early adulthood and may cause serious ill health throughout life. In this condition, areas of the digestive tract become inflamed, causing a range of symptoms that include diarrhea, abdominal pain, and weight loss. The disorder can occur in any part of the digestive tract from the mouth to the anus. However, the parts most frequently affected are the ileum (the last part of the small intestine) and the colon (the major part of the large intestine). Inflammation often occurs in more than one part of the digestive tract, with unaffected or mildly affected areas between the inflamed areas.

Crohn's disease is an uncommon disorder. In Europe and North America, the condition most commonly affects white people, especially those of Jewish origin, and its onset usually occurs between the ages of 15 and 30. Crohn's disease tends to recur despite treatment, and in most cases the condition is lifelong and often requires surgery.

The exact cause of Crohn's disease is unknown. Genetic factors are likely to contribute since about 1 in 10 affected people has one or more relatives with Crohn's disease or another inflammatory bowel disorder. Smoking may also play a part; smokers are three times more likely to develop Crohn's disease.

WHAT ARE THE SYMPTOMS?

The symptoms of Crohn's disease vary between individuals. The disorder usually recurs at intervals throughout life. Episodes of the disease may be severe, lasting weeks or several months, before settling down to periods with mild or no symptoms. The symptoms include:

- Diarrhea.
- Abdominal pain.
- Fever.
- Weight loss.
- General feeling of malaise.

If the colon is affected, symptoms may also include the following:

- Diarrhea, often containing blood.
- Bloody discharge from the anus.

About 1 in 10 people also develops other disorders associated with Crohn's disease. These other conditions may occur even in mild cases of Crohn's disease and include arthritis (*see* ANKYLOSING SPONDYLITIS, p.378), eye disorders (*see* UVEITIS, p.574), kidney stones (p.701), gallstones (p.651), and a rash (*see* ERYTHEMA NODOSUM, p.348).

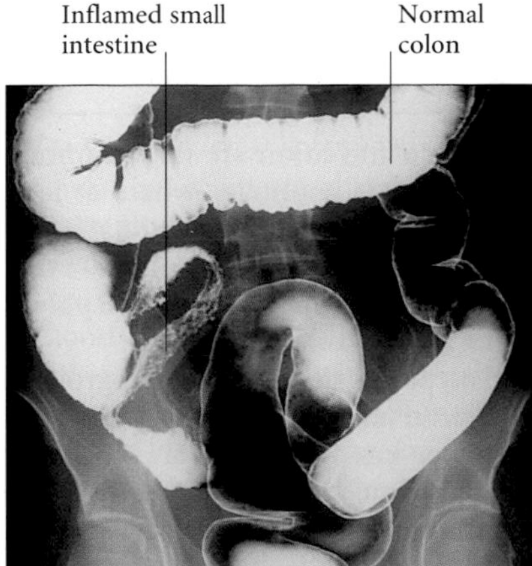
Inflamed small intestine
Normal colon

Crohn's disease
This contrast X-ray shows a normal colon and an area of small intestine that has become inflamed as a result of the chronic condition Crohn's disease.

ARE THERE COMPLICATIONS?

Complications of Crohn's disease may include pus-filled cavities near the anus (*see* ANAL ABSCESS, p.669). These cavities can develop into abnormal passages between the anal canal and the skin around the anus, called anal fistulas.

Intestinal obstruction (p.663) caused by thickening of the intestinal walls is a fairly common complication of Crohn's disease. Damage to the small intestine may prevent the absorption of nutrients (*see* MALABSORPTION, p.655) and thus lead to anemia (p.446) or vitamin deficiencies. Inflammation of the colon over a long period of time may also be associated with an increased risk of developing colorectal cancer (p.665).

HOW IS IT DIAGNOSED?

If your doctor suspects that you have Crohn's disease, he or she may arrange for a colonoscopy (p.661), in which the intestine is examined and tissue samples are taken from affected areas for microscopic examination. If the small intestine is affected, you may have a contrast X-ray (p.245) of the intestine, known as a small bowel enema study, to look for abnormalities.

Blood tests may be done to check for anemia and to assess how severely the intestine is inflamed. If your doctor suspects that you have gallstones or kidney stones, you may have imaging tests.

WHAT IS THE TREATMENT?

Mild attacks of Crohn's disease can often be treated with antidiarrheal drugs (p.924) and analgesics (p.912). For an acute attack, your doctor may prescribe oral corticosteroids (p.930). As soon as symptoms subside, the dosage will be reduced to avoid the risk of side effects. If your symptoms are very severe, you may need hospital treatment with intravenous corticosteroids. In all cases, once the dosage of corticosteroids has been reduced, your doctor may recommend oral sulfasalazine or mesalamine (*see* 5-AMINOSALICYLATE DRUGS, p.924) to prevent recurrent attacks. He or she may also give you an immunosuppressant drug (p.906), such as azathioprine.

You may need dietary supplements, such as extra protein and vitamins (p.927), to counteract malabsorption. During severe attacks, nutrients may have to be given intravenously.

Many people who have Crohn's disease need surgery at some stage. The procedure involves removing the diseased area of the intestine and rejoining the healthy ends (*see* COLECTOMY, p.665). However, surgery is not usually performed until it is absolutely necessary because further affected regions may develop in the remaining intestine.

WHAT IS THE PROGNOSIS?

Crohn's disease is a recurring disorder. Most affected people learn to live reasonably normal lives, but 7 in 10 people eventually need surgery. Complications and repeated surgery can occasionally reduce life expectancy. Crohn's disease may increase the risk of colorectal cancer, and, for this reason, your doctor may advise you to have regular checkups that include colonoscopy.

(WWW) ONLINE SITES: p.1030

Ulcerative colitis

Chronic, intermittent inflammation and ulceration of the rectum and colon

 AGE Onset most common between the ages of 15 and 35

 GENETICS Sometimes runs in families; more common in white people and in certain ethnic groups

 LIFESTYLE More common in nonsmokers and ex-smokers

 GENDER Not a significant factor

Ulcerative colitis is a chronic, intermittent inflammatory condition that most commonly develops in young adults. The disorder causes ulceration of the rectum and the colon (the major part of the large intestine). It may either affect the rectum alone (*see* PROCTITIS, p.667) or extend from the rectum farther up the colon. In some cases, the disorder involves the entire colon.

Ulcerative colitis affects about 1 in 1,000 people. It occurs most frequently in white people, particularly those of Jewish descent. Smoking may give some protection against the disease.

WHAT IS THE CAUSE?

The exact cause of ulcerative colitis is unknown. However, there is some evidence that genetic factors are involved, since about 1 in 10 people with ulcerative colitis has a close relative with the

pain and vomiting. Immediate surgery is essential to prevent the intestine from becoming gangrenous.

Occasionally, hernias occur in other areas. Hiatus hernias develop when part of the stomach protrudes into the chest cavity through a weakened area in the diaphragm (the sheet of muscle that lies beneath the lungs and is involved in breathing) and may be accompanied by gastroesophageal reflux disease (p.636).

What are the types?

Hernias are classified according to the site where they occur in the body. Some types occur more often in men; others are more frequently found in women.

INGUINAL HERNIA This type of hernia occurs when a portion of the intestine pushes through into the inguinal canal,

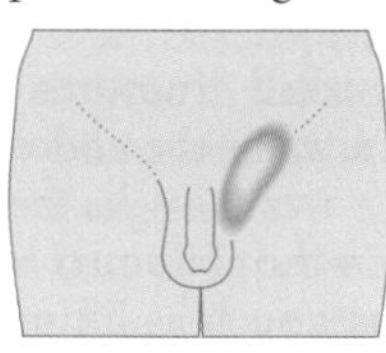

which is a weak spot in the abdominal muscle wall. The hernia causes a visible bulge in the groin or scrotum. These hernias usually affect men, but sometimes occur in women.

FEMORAL HERNIA This type of hernia occurs in the part of the groin where the femoral vein and artery pass from

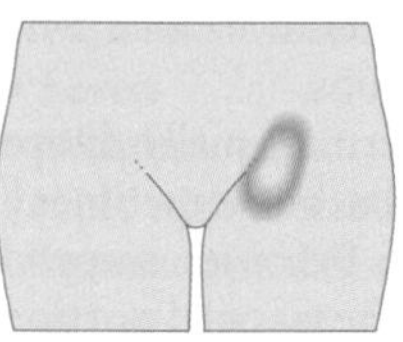

the lower abdomen to the thigh. Women who are overweight or who have had several pregnancies are at increased risk of these hernias because their abdominal muscles are weakened.

UMBILICAL HERNIA Babies may be born with an umbilical hernia, which develops behind the navel due to a weakness

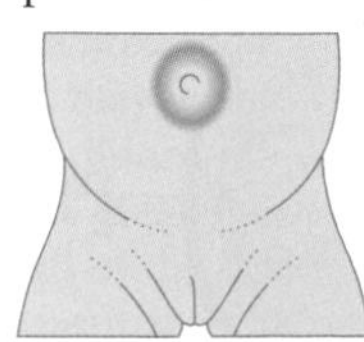

in the abdominal wall. Hernias that develop near the navel are known as paraumbilical hernias and are most common in women who are overweight or have had several pregnancies.

OTHER TYPES OF HERNIA Epigastric hernias develop in the midline between the navel and the breastbone and are three times more common in men. Incisional hernias may develop after abdominal surgery if there is weakness around the scar. Risk factors include being overweight and having several operations through the same incision.

What are the symptoms?

The symptoms may come on suddenly, but more often they develop over a period of several weeks or months. They may include the following:

- Lump in the abdomen or groin, which may disappear when you lie down and reappear whenever you cough or strain to defecate.
- Dragging or aching sensation in the abdomen or groin.

It is important to consult a doctor if you think that you have a hernia. Seek immediate medical advice for a hernia that cannot be pushed back through the abdominal wall or one in which the skin is tender or inflamed because these symptoms suggest a strangulated hernia.

What might be done?

Your doctor may be able to feel a hernia by examining the abdomen or groin. Even small hernias eventually need to be repaired (*see* HERNIA REPAIR, below) because, if they are left untreated, they may become strangulated. The type of operation depends largely on the size of the hernia and on your age and general health. Some procedures are done under local anesthesia as day surgery. Umbilical hernias in babies can usually be left untreated since they tend to disappear naturally by the age of 5.

Surgery is usually effective. However, there is a risk that the hernia will recur in the same place or elsewhere. After a hernia repair, you may be advised to avoid strenuous activity for a few weeks. You can help prevent a recurrence by losing excess weight, doing gentle exercise, and avoiding constipation.

(WWW) ONLINE SITES: p.1030

(TREATMENT) Hernia repair

A hernia repair is a simple operation, often performed as day surgery. Local or general anesthesia will be given depending on the size and location of the hernia. The procedure may be done either as open surgery, in which a 1–2 in (3–5 cm) incision is made over the hernia, or by endoscopic surgery (p.948). In both types of operation, the contents of the hernia are eased back into place and the weakened muscle is repaired. After the operation, the area is likely to be painful at first, but you will be given analgesics for relief. You can resume most normal activities within 7 days, but you should avoid lifting heavy objects for up to 3 months.

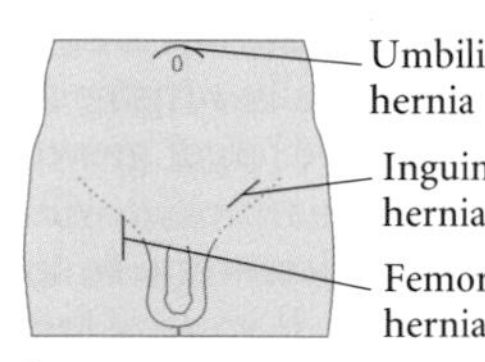
Umbilical hernia
Inguinal hernia
Femoral hernia

SITES OF INCISIONS

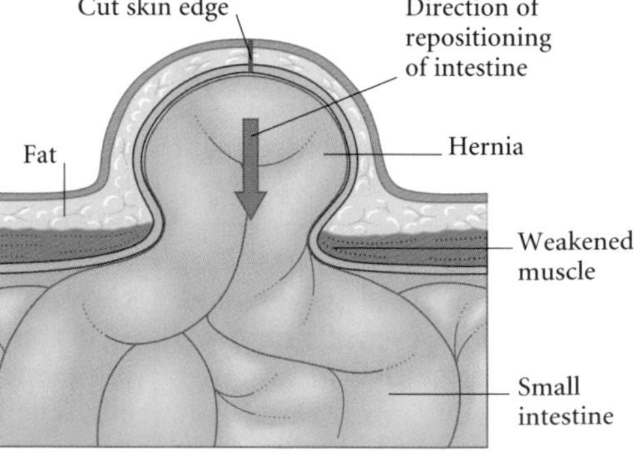
Cut skin edge
Direction of repositioning of intestine
Fat
Hernia
Weakened muscle
Small intestine

1 *An incision is made through the layers of skin and fat to uncover the hernia. The intestine is then gently pushed back into the abdominal cavity.*

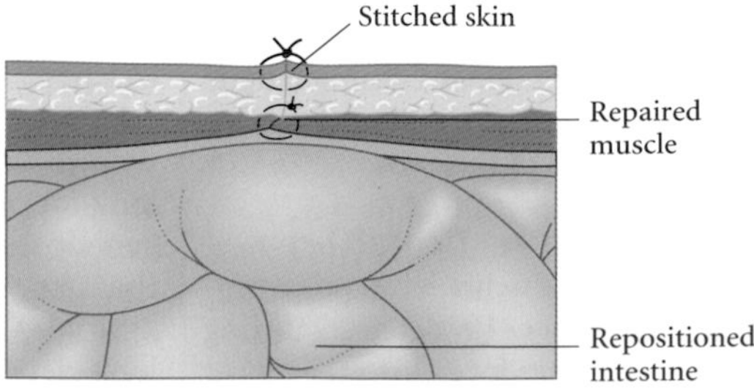
Stitched skin
Repaired muscle
Repositioned intestine

2 *Once the hernia has been repositioned, the weakened area is repaired, usually by suturing the muscle. However, in some cases, a repair may have to be reinforced with a piece of synthetic mesh placed over the abdominal muscle.*

Intestinal obstruction

Failure of partly digested material to move through the intestine due to a blockage or paralysis of the intestinal muscles

AGE GENDER GENETICS LIFESTYLE Risk factors depend on the cause

In intestinal obstruction, a section of the intestine is partially or totally blocked (mechanical obstruction) or the muscles in the intestinal walls stop contracting (functional obstruction). In both circumstances, the intestinal contents are unable to move along the digestive tract normally. Left untreated, the condition can be life-threatening.

What are the causes?

Many disorders can cause mechanical obstruction. For example, the intestine may be blocked by a tumor inside it or by external compression from a growth in another organ. Obstruction may also be due to narrowing of the intestine as a result of inflammation, which occurs in Crohn's disease (p.658). In addition, an obstruction can be the result of a strangulated hernia, in which a small part of the intestine protrudes through a weakened area in the muscles of the abdominal wall and becomes trapped (*see* HERNIAS, p.661). After abdominal surgery, scar tissue can form between loops of intestine and cause an obstruction months or even years later.

Functional obstruction, when the intestinal muscles fail to contract properly, may be a complication of some disorders, such as the serious abdominal inflammation peritonitis (p.665), or it may follow major surgery.

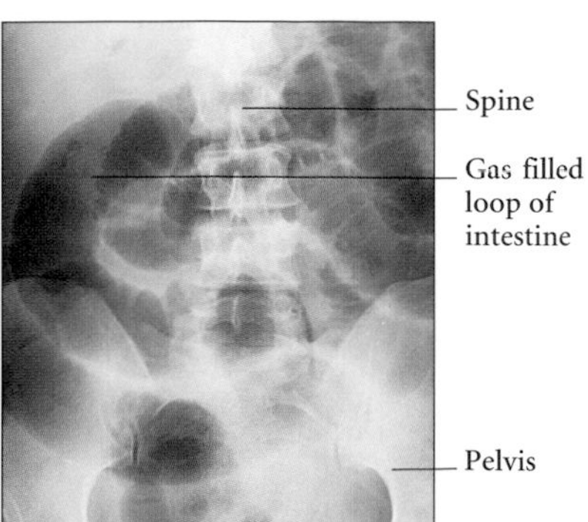
Spine
Gas filled loop of intestine
Pelvis

Intestinal obstruction
This abdominal X-ray shows enlarged loops of gas-filled intestines due to an obstruction in the colon.

What are the symptoms?

The symptoms of intestinal obstruction may appear suddenly or develop gradually depending on the cause. In all cases, symptoms may include:

- Vomiting fluid that may be greenish yellow, or brown with a fecal odor.
- Severe constipation.
- Abdominal bloating.
- Pain, usually occurring in waves that may later become continuous.
- Total absence of flatulence, implying a complete intestinal obstruction.

Repeated vomiting may cause dehydration due to fluid loss. The intestinal wall may tear due to increased pressure and leak its bacteria-rich contents into the abdomen, causing peritonitis.

What might be done?

If your doctor suspects that you have an intestinal obstruction, you will be hospitalized immediately. You will have abdominal X-rays (p.244), which can confirm the diagnosis and determine the nature and position of the obstruction. A tube may be inserted through your nose and down into your stomach to remove digestive juices and prevent vomiting. You will probably be given intravenous fluids to prevent further dehydration. Surgery is often needed to relieve an obstruction. If the cause is Crohn's disease or peritonitis, treating the inflammation may relieve the condition. If a blockage occurs after major surgery, the intestinal wall usually starts to contract normally after a few days.

(WWW) ONLINE SITES: p.1030

Diverticulosis

The presence of small pouches known as diverticula in the wall of the colon

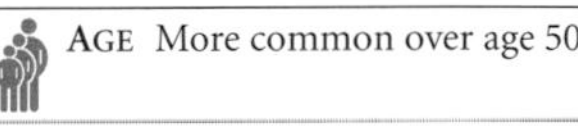

AGE More common over age 50

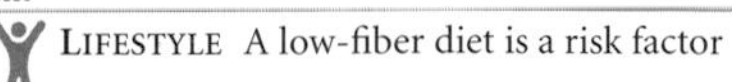

LIFESTYLE A low-fiber diet is a risk factor

GENDER GENETICS Not significant factors

In diverticulosis, pea-sized or grape-sized pouches (diverticula) protrude from the wall of the large intestine, usually from the part of the colon that is closest to the rectum. The pouches form when parts of the wall of the intestine bulge outward through weakened areas, often close to an artery. In many cases, the bulging of the intestinal wall is associated with chronic constipation (p.628) and occurs when the pressure inside the intestine increases as the person strains to defecate. Sometimes, one or more of the pouches become inflamed, a condition known as diverticulitis.

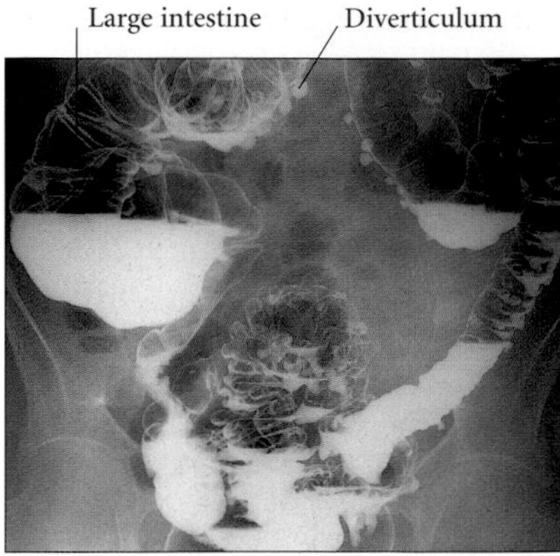
Large intestine
Diverticulum

Diverticulosis
In this special X-ray, a contrast dye shows small pouches (diverticula) protruding from the wall of the large intestine.

Approximately 1 in 3 people between the ages of 50 and 60 has diverticulosis, and it becomes progressively more common after age 60. However, most people who are affected by the condition have no symptoms.

Diverticulosis is strongly associated with a low-fiber diet, which can lead to constipation. For this reason, the formation of diverticula is very rare in developing countries, where fiber comprises a large part of most diets.

What are the symptoms?

More than three-quarters of all people with diverticulosis do not know that they have the condition because there are no symptoms. If symptoms are present, they may include the following:

- Episodes of abdominal pain, especially in the lower left abdomen.
- Intermittent episodes of constipation and diarrhea.
- Occasional bright red bleeding from the rectum, which may be painless.

If diverticulitis develops, the symptoms may become worse, and they may be accompanied by:

- Severe lower abdominal pain and tenderness in the abdomen.
- Fever.
- Nausea and vomiting.

If you notice any change in your bowel habits or you have rectal bleeding, you should consult your doctor immediately because these symptoms may indicate a more serious underlying disease, such as colorectal cancer (p.665).

ARE THERE COMPLICATIONS?

If an inflamed diverticulum bursts, feces and bacteria can spill into the abdominal cavity. As a result, an abscess may form next to the colon, or peritonitis (opposite page), an inflammation of the membrane that lines the abdominal cavity, may develop. Peritonitis is a potentially life-threatening condition.

In some women, an abnormal channel called a fistula may develop between a diverticulum and the vagina, causing fecal material to be discharged through the vagina. A fistula may also develop between a diverticulum and the bladder, causing pain, a more frequent urge to urinate, or recurrent bladder infections (*see* CYSTITIS, p.709). An inflamed diverticulum may also cause intestinal obstruction (p.663).

HOW IS IT DIAGNOSED?

If your doctor suspects that you have diverticulosis, he or she may arrange for you to have a contrast X-ray (p.245), in which a barium enema is used to highlight the shape of the intestines. If your symptoms include rectal bleeding, a colonoscopy (p.661) may be carried out to examine the colon and exclude colorectal cancer. Sometimes, diverticulosis is found during an investigation for another disease.

If your symptoms develop suddenly, you may be admitted to the hospital for investigative tests. You may have X-rays and a colonoscopy. In addition, CT scanning (p.247) or ultrasound scanning (p.250) may be done.

WHAT IS THE TREATMENT?

Often, a high-fiber diet with plenty of fluids is the only treatment needed for diverticulosis. You may also be given antispasmodic drugs (*see* ANTISPASMODIC DRUGS AND MOTILITY STIMULANTS, p.926) to relieve abdominal pain.

If you develop severe diverticulitis, you will be admitted to the hospital, where you will be given intravenous fluids and antibiotics (p.885) to treat bacterial infection.

Following a severe attack of diverticulitis, most people improve without any further treatment. However, surgery is sometimes necessary if you have severe rectal bleeding or if an abscess or a fistula has developed. Anyone who has two or three attacks of diverticulitis within a few years is also likely to need surgery. The most common operation is a partial colectomy (p.665), which involves removing the diseased part of the colon and rejoining the healthy ends of the intestine. At the same time, a temporary colostomy (p.666) may be done to aid in the healing of the rejoined ends.

WHAT IS THE PROGNOSIS?

The prognosis for diverticulosis is generally good. If a high-fiber diet is begun early enough, it is unlikely that the condition will progress. Among people with diverticulitis, 2 in 3 have only one attack. However, in others, the attack recurs, and surgery may be needed. Approximately 2 in 10 people who experience bleeding will have a recurrence within the next few months to a year unless the problem is treated surgically.

(WWW) ONLINE SITES: p.1030

Appendicitis

Inflammation of the appendix, leading to severe abdominal pain

AGE More common under age 40, especially among adolescents

GENDER Slightly more common in males

LIFESTYLE A low-fiber diet is a risk factor

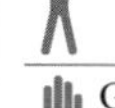
GENETICS Not a significant factor

Appendicitis is inflammation affecting the appendix, the small, blind-ended tube attached to the first section of the large intestine. The disorder is common, especially among adolescents, affecting about 1 in 500 people every year. In Canada, appendicitis is a common cause of sudden, severe pain in the abdomen, and removal of the appendix is one of the most commonly performed emergency operations. Inflammation of the appendix occurs most commonly in developed countries.

In most cases of appendicitis, no cause is detected, but in some instances the inflammation is the result of a blockage inside the appendix. Blockages sometimes occur when a lump of fecal material passes from the large intestine into the appendix and becomes lodged there. The closed end of the appendix beyond the obstruction then becomes infected with bacteria and inflamed.

WHAT ARE THE SYMPTOMS?

Symptoms differ from one person to another. The early symptoms usually develop over a few hours and include:

- Sudden onset of intermittent pain that is first felt in the upper abdomen or around the navel.
- Nausea with or without vomiting.

Less often, there may be:

- Diarrhea.
- Mild fever.
- Loss of appetite.
- Frequent urination.

After a few hours, the pain shifts to the lower right abdomen. If treatment is delayed, the appendix may rupture, and intestinal matter containing a high concentration of bacteria can leak into the abdomen. The result may be peritonitis (opposite page), a potentially serious condition in which the membrane that lines the abdominal cavity becomes inflamed. If the appendix ruptures, the pain becomes widespread and severe.

WHAT MIGHT BE DONE?

Your doctor will first ask you about the development of your symptoms. He or she will then examine your abdomen and may also insert a gloved finger into the rectum to determine whether there is tenderness in the area around the appendix. You may also have a blood test to measure the white blood cell count. An elevated white cell count may be a sign of inflammation. If your doctor suspects that you have appendicitis, you will be admitted to the hospital immediately, where imaging with ultrasound scanning (p.250) or CT scanning (p.247) may confirm the diagnosis.

The usual treatment is removal of the appendix by minimally invasive surgery (*see* ENDOSCOPIC SURGERY, p.948) or by conventional open surgery. The operation is relatively simple and is done under general anesthesia. There are usually no long-term adverse effects following either type of operation, and recovery normally takes only 3–4 days.

(WWW) ONLINE SITES: p.1030

Peritonitis

Inflammation of the peritoneum, the membranous lining of the abdomen

 GENDER More common in males

 AGE GENETICS LIFESTYLE Not significant factors

Inflammation of the peritoneum, the membrane that surrounds the organs in the abdomen and lines the inner wall of the abdominal cavity, is called peritonitis. The condition usually occurs as a complication of another abdominal disorder, such as appendicitis (opposite page). Severe peritonitis may be fatal if not treated rapidly.

WHAT ARE THE CAUSES?

The most common cause of peritonitis is a bacterial infection that has spread from elsewhere in the abdomen. For example, bacteria from the intestine may escape into the abdominal cavity if the intestine is perforated. Possible causes of a perforation include a severe flare-up of a chronic inflammatory condition, such as ulcerative colitis (p.659); intestinal obstruction (p.663); or surgery on the intestine.

A less common cause of peritonitis is irritation of the peritoneum. For example, stomach acid may leak out into the abdominal cavity and cause irritation if a peptic ulcer (p.640) perforates the wall of the stomach or the duodenum (the first part of the small intestine). Peritonitis may also develop if bile leaks from an inflamed gallbladder into the abdominal cavity (*see* CHOLECYSTITIS, p.652). Occasionally, the condition is caused by leakage of digestive enzymes into the abdominal cavity as a result of acute pancreatitis (p.652).

WHAT ARE THE SYMPTOMS?

The symptoms of peritonitis usually develop rapidly. They may include:

- Severe constant pain in the abdomen.
- Fever.
- Abdominal swelling.
- Nausea and vomiting.

In severe cases, dehydration and shock (p.414) may also occur. Rarely, after an attack of peritonitis, adhesions may develop, in which fibrous bands of scar tissue grow between loops of intestine, causing the loops to stick together. Adhesions may cause acute abdominal pain months after the attack.

If you believe that you may have peritonitis, you should seek medical attention without delay.

WHAT MIGHT BE DONE?

It is important that peritonitis is diagnosed and treated as soon as possible. If your doctor suspects that you have peritonitis, you will be admitted to the hospital immediately. At the hospital, a doctor will examine your abdomen to check for pain or tenderness and you will have X-rays (p.244) of the abdomen. In addition, you may need a procedure called a laparoscopy (p.742), in which the abdominal cavity is examined for abnormalities.

If peritonitis is the result of a bacterial infection, you will be given antibiotics (p.885). You may also need intravenous fluids to treat dehydration and shock. Your doctor will treat the underlying cause of the peritonitis. For example, a perforated peptic ulcer will be repaired or a ruptured appendix removed.

If peritonitis is treated immediately, recovery is usually rapid and long-term problems, such as adhesions, are rare.

(WWW) ONLINE SITES: p.1030

Colorectal cancer

A cancerous tumor of the lining of the colon or rectum

 AGE Rare under age 40; becomes increasingly common over age 40

 GENDER Rectal cancer is more common in males; colon cancer is more common in females

 GENETICS In some cases, the condition is inherited

 LIFESTYLE A high-fat, low-fiber diet, alcohol abuse, and obesity are risk factors

Colorectal cancer is the third most common cause of cancer deaths in Canada. It is also one of the few cancers that may be detected at an early stage by screening people thought to be at risk (*see* SCREENING, p.12, and COLONOSCOPY, p.661). When it is detected early enough, the disease can often be successfully treated by surgery.

Colorectal cancer is rare under age 40 and most cases occur in people over age 60. In general, rectal cancer is more common in men, and colon cancer is more common in women. Cancer can occur anywhere in the colon or rectum, but about 6 in 10 tumors develop in the part of the colon nearest the rectum.

(TREATMENT) COLECTOMY

A colectomy is an operation in which part or all of the large intestine (the colon and the rectum) is removed under general anesthesia. Usually, the operation is performed to treat inflammatory conditions, such as Crohn's disease, or cancer of the colon. In most cases, the cut ends of the colon are rejoined once the diseased area has been removed, but sometimes a colostomy (p.666) is needed. You will have to stay in the hospital for at least a week depending on the extent of the surgery.

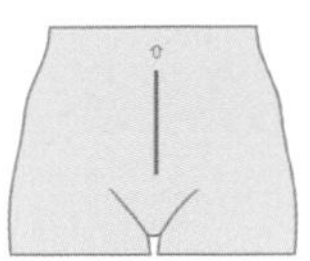
SITE OF
INCISION

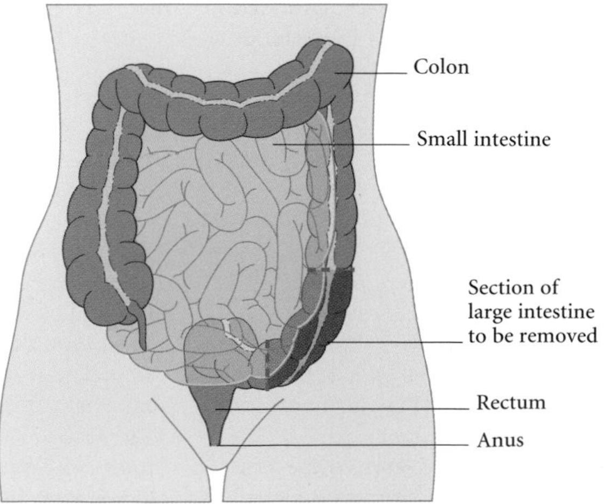
Colon
Small intestine
Section of large intestine to be removed
Rectum
Anus

Partial colectomy
During the procedure, the abnormal section of the colon is cut out, and the healthy ends of the remaining intestine are joined together. A colostomy is performed only in a minority of partial colectomies.

WHAT ARE THE CAUSES?

In less affluent countries, where people traditionally live on a high-fiber diet consisting mainly of cereals, fruit, and vegetables, colorectal cancer is rare. However, a typical western diet, which tends to be high in meat and animal fats and low in fiber, seems to increase the risk of developing colorectal cancer. It is not known how or if fiber in the diet reduces the risk of the disorder. A possible explanation is that dietary fiber shortens the time it takes for waste matter to pass through the intestines. As a result, potentially cancer-causing substances (known as carcinogens) in food are expelled from the body at a faster rate. Other lifestyle factors, such as excessive alcohol consumption, obesity, and lack of exercise, may also contribute to the risk of developing colorectal cancer. The reasons for this increased risk are also unknown.

About 1 in 8 cases of colorectal cancer is hereditary. Most of these cases are caused by inheritance of an abnormal gene. People who have this gene are at increased risk of developing a form of the cancer known as hereditary nonpolyposis colorectal cancer (HNPCC). Rarely, colorectal cancer may be caused by the inherited disorder familial adenomatous polyposis (FAP), in which polyps (growths of tissue) form inside the large intestine (*see* POLYPS IN THE COLON, p.660). In FAP, there is a 9 in 10 chance that some of the polyps will become cancerous over time.

Inflammatory disorders affecting the large intestine, such as ulcerative colitis (p.659) or Crohn's disease (p.658), can also increase the risk of developing colorectal cancer if they are long-standing.

TREATMENT COLOSTOMY

In a colostomy, part of the colon opens onto the skin of the abdominal wall to form an artificial opening called a stoma. Feces are expelled through the stoma into a disposable bag. A colostomy is performed following a colectomy (p.665) and may be either temporary or permanent. A temporary colostomy may be done if part of the colon has been removed and allows the rejoined ends to heal without feces passing through the site. A permanent colostomy is needed when the rectum and anus have been removed with part of the colon.

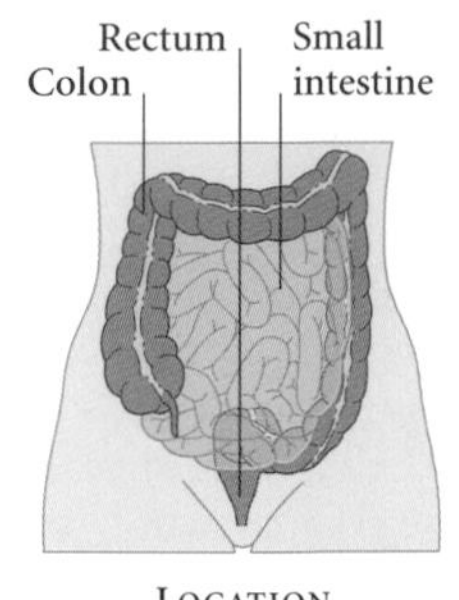
Rectum
Colon
Small intestine
LOCATION

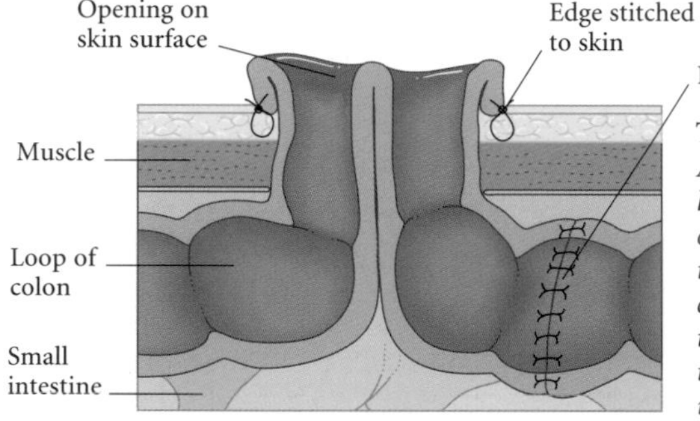
Opening on skin surface
Edge stitched to skin
Healing colectomy site
Muscle
Loop of colon
Small intestine

Temporary colostomy
An incision is made in a loop of colon and the edges of the loop are stitched to the skin surface. When the colectomy site has healed, the colostomy is closed and the colon is then returned under the skin.

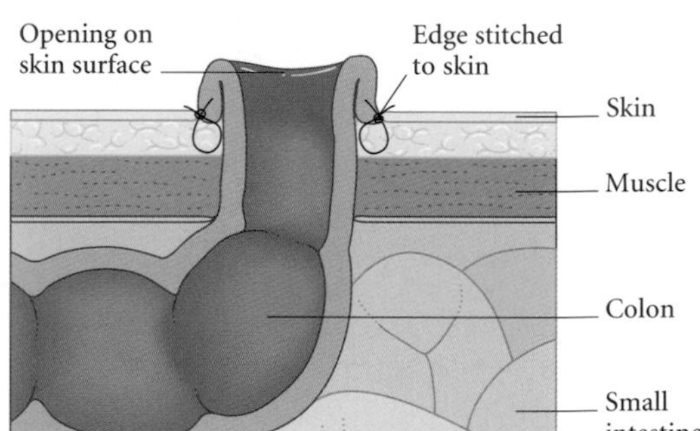
Opening on skin surface
Edge stitched to skin
Skin
Muscle
Colon
Small intestine

Permanent colostomy
The cut end of the colon is passed through the abdominal wall. The edges are then stitched to the skin surface to create a permanent opening onto the skin. Normal defecation is no longer possible.

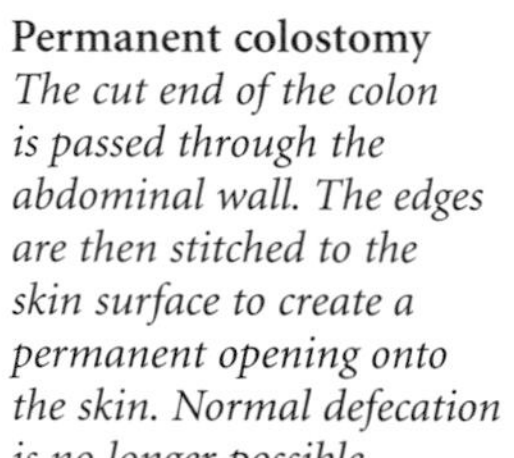

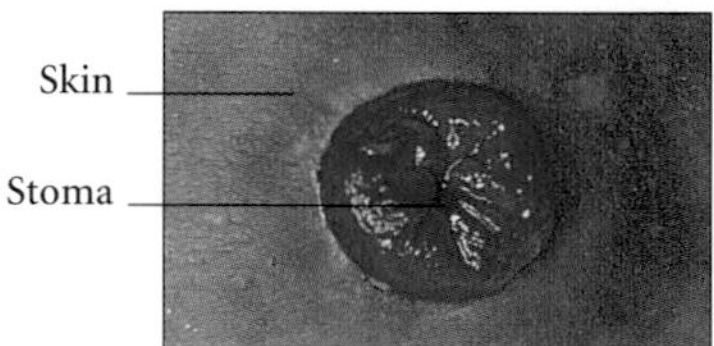
Skin
Stoma

Permanent stoma
An artificial opening (stoma) can be seen on the surface of the abdomen. Feces discharged from the intestine are collected in a disposable bag fitted over the stoma.

WHAT ARE THE SYMPTOMS?

The symptoms of colorectal cancer vary depending on the site of the tumor. They may include the following:

- Changes in the frequency of bowel movements or in the general consistency of the feces.
- Abdominal pain.
- Blood in the feces.
- Rectal discomfort or a sensation of incomplete emptying of the rectum.
- Loss of appetite.

The symptoms of colorectal cancer may be mistaken for the symptoms of a less serious disorder, such as hemorrhoids (p.668). If there is heavy loss of blood from the rectum, iron-deficiency anemia (p.447) may result. This condition produces symptoms such as pale skin, headaches, and fatigue. As the tumor grows bigger, it may eventually cause intestinal obstruction (p.663).

You should consult your doctor without delay if you notice an obvious change in your bowel habits or blood in your feces. Left untreated, colorectal cancer will eventually spread via the bloodstream to the lymph nodes, liver, and other organs in the body.

HOW IS IT DIAGNOSED?

Colorectal cancer is often diagnosed during screening before symptoms have developed. If you do have symptoms, your doctor may first feel your abdomen to detect swelling. A rectal examination, in which a gloved finger is inserted into the rectum, may also be done to see if a tumor can be felt, and a stool sample is tested for the presence of blood (*see* FECAL OCCULT BLOOD TEST, p.233). A blood sample may be tested for anemia.

The rectum may be examined visually with a viewing instrument inserted through the anus. Your doctor may also arrange for a colonoscopy, in which a flexible viewing instrument is used to examine the entire colon. A biopsy may be taken (in which a small sample of tissue is removed for microscopic examination) during the procedure. You may also have a contrast X-ray (p.245) in which a barium enema is used to detect an abnormality of the rectum or colon. If a cancerous tumor is detected, you will probably need to have CT scanning (p.247) to see if the cancer has spread to the lymph nodes in the abdomen or to the liver.

An annual fecal occult blood test is advised for people over age 50, in addition to sigmoidoscopy (a form of colonoscopy), every 3 to 5 years. People with a family history of colorectal cancer should be screened from age 40.

WHAT IS THE TREATMENT?

Treatment of colorectal cancer depends on the site of the tumor. In most cases of early cancer, the affected part of the intestine can be removed and the cut ends rejoined (*see* COLECTOMY, p.665). In a few cases, if most of the rectum has been removed, a permanent colostomy (opposite page) may be necessary. In this procedure, an opening is created on the surface of the abdomen for the discharge of feces. If the cancer cannot be cured, treatment is aimed at relieving symptoms. For example, surgery may be done to remove a tumor obstructing the bowel. If cancer has spread to other parts of the body, chemotherapy (p.278), radiation therapy (p.279), or both may be necessary to treat the disease.

About 9 in 10 people treated at an early stage live at least 5 years free from cancer. Surgical removal of affected tissue at a more advanced stage of the disease gives the person a 3 in 4 chance of living 5 years free from cancer. If the cancer has spread, the outlook is poor.

(WWW) ONLINE SITES: p.1028, p.1030

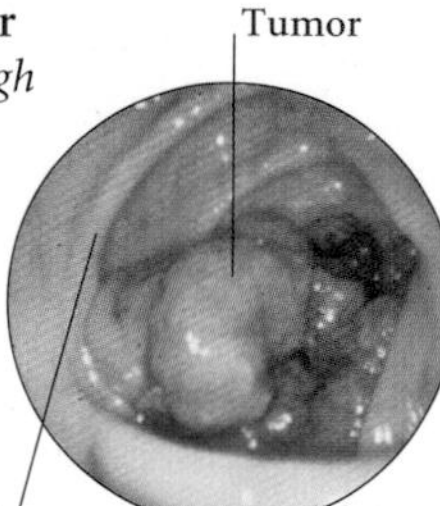

Tumor
Wall of colon

Colorectal cancer
In this view through a colonoscope, a tumor can be seen growing from the wall of the colon.

Proctitis

Inflammation of the rectum, most often due to ulcerative colitis

 AGE Rare in childhood

 GENDER LIFESTYLE Risk factors depend on the cause

 GENETICS Not a significant factor

In proctitis, the lining of the anus and the rectum becomes inflamed. The disorder most commonly develops as part of ulcerative colitis (p.659), a condition that can either be restricted to the rectum or be a more widespread disease that also affects the colon.

Proctitis may also result from an infection of the lining of the rectum. Unprotected anal sex increases the risk of sexually transmitted infections (STIs), such as herpes simplex infection (p.289) or gonorrhea (p.764). Anal sex may also lead to proctitis by causing physical injury to the rectum. Proctitis is more common, therefore, in homosexual men. Other possible causes of proctitis include the gastrointestinal infection amebic dysentery (*see* AMEBIASIS, p.306) and radiation therapy (p.279) used to treat cancers close to the rectum, such as prostate cancer (p.726).

WHAT ARE THE SYMPTOMS?

In most cases, the symptoms of proctitis include the following:

- Blood, mucus, or pus in the feces.
- Discomfort and pain in the anus and rectum that becomes more severe with a bowel movement.
- Diarrhea or constipation.
- An increased urge to defecate.

Inflammation due to an STI may be accompanied by fever and pelvic pain. If the rectum is inflamed, there may also be an increased risk of acquiring or transmitting STIs, such as HIV infection (*see* HIV INFECTION AND AIDS, p.295), through unprotected anal sex.

In some cases, proctitis is complicated by the presence of an anal fissure (p.669) or an anal abscess (p.669).

HOW IS IT DIAGNOSED?

Your doctor may ask for a stool sample or take a rectal swab to look for infection. He or she may also examine your rectum by using a viewing instrument called a proctoscope to determine the extent of the inflammation. A small sample of rectal tissue may be taken for examination under the microscope.

WHAT IS THE TREATMENT?

Treatment of proctitis depends on the cause. However, pain and inflammation, whatever the cause, may be eased with analgesics (p.912) and drugs to soften the feces (*see* LAXATIVES, p.924). If the cause is ulcerative colitis, sulfasalazine (*see* 5-AMINOSALICYLATE DRUGS, p.924) or corticosteroids (p.930) are usually given to reduce inflammation.

Antibiotics (p.885) are usually given to treat a bacterial STI. Topical corticosteroids (p.892) can be used to reduce rectal inflammation caused by injury. Avoiding anal intercourse will also help speed up the healing process. Antibiotics may be given to treat amebic dysentery, while proctitis due to radiation therapy is often treated with corticosteroids. Treatment is usually successful.

(WWW) ONLINE SITES: p.1030, p.1036

Rectal prolapse

Protrusion of the lining of the rectum outside the anus

 AGE Most common in young children and in elderly people

 GENDER More common in males

 LIFESTYLE A low-fiber diet is a risk factor

 GENETICS Not a significant factor

Rectal prolapse is an uncommon condition in which the lining of the rectum protrudes through the anus. It is usually associated with a low-fiber diet and constipation (p.628). The condition is more common in males and in elderly people and may be a recurrent problem in those with weak pelvic floor muscles. In addition, rectal prolapse may sometimes occur temporarily in very young children during toilet-training.

WHAT ARE THE SYMPTOMS?

If you have a rectal prolapse, you may experience symptoms after straining to defecate. These include:

- Bleeding and discharge of mucus from the anus.
- Pain or discomfort on defecation.

- The sensation of a lump protruding from the anus.

If the prolapse is large, there may also be some fecal incontinence.

WHAT MIGHT BE DONE?

Your doctor may examine the prolapse with a gloved finger and gently push the rectum back into place. Further treatment is used to relieve the underlying cause, such as a high-fiber diet to relieve constipation. If the prolapse recurs and you have persistent constipation, your doctor may arrange for tests, such as colonoscopy (p.661) or contrast X-rays (p.245), to look for an underlying disease, such as colorectal cancer (p.665).

In children, rectal prolapse will usually disappear when measures are taken to prevent constipation. Elderly people may require surgery to fix the rectum in position permanently.

(WWW) ONLINE SITES: p.1030

Hemorrhoids

Swollen veins inside the rectum and around the anus, also known as piles

 AGE More common in adults

 GENDER More common in females during pregnancy and after childbirth

 LIFESTYLE Being overweight and a low-fiber diet are risk factors

 GENETICS Not a significant factor

Hemorrhoids are a common problem, affecting up to half of all people at some time in their lives. In this disorder, veins in the soft tissues around the anus and inside the lower part of the rectum become swollen. Swellings around the anus are called external hemorrhoids, and those within the rectum are called internal hemorrhoids. Internal hemorrhoids that protrude outside the anus are known as prolapsing hemorrhoids.

Hemorrhoids often cause bleeding, itching, and discomfort. However, these symptoms are usually intermittent, and the condition is not in itself serious.

WHAT ARE THE CAUSES?

Hemorrhoids most commonly occur as a result of constipation, when a person strains to pass stools. Straining in this way increases the pressure inside the abdomen, which in turn causes blood vessels around the rectum to swell. Constipation is often due to a low-fiber diet. Being overweight also exerts pressure on blood vessels and increases the risk of hemorrhoids. During pregnancy, the growing fetus has the same effect, frequently causing hemorrhoids.

WHAT ARE THE SYMPTOMS?

The symptoms of hemorrhoids commonly develop following constipation. They may include:

- Fresh blood on toilet paper or in the toilet after a bowel movement.
- Increasing discomfort on defecation.
- Discharge of mucus from the anus, sometimes leading to itching.
- Visible swellings around the anus.
- Feeling that the bowels have not been fully emptied.

A prolapsing hemorrhoid may protrude through the anus after a bowel movement and may then retract or can be pushed back inside with a finger. In some cases, a blood clot (thrombus) may form within a prolapsing hemorrhoid, causing severe pain and a visible, tender, blue, grape-sized swelling.

If you have bleeding from the anus, you should consult your doctor without delay, especially if you are over 40, since it may indicate a more serious disorder, such as colorectal cancer (p.665).

WHAT MIGHT BE DONE?

Your doctor will probably examine your rectum by inserting a gloved finger into it, and, if there has been bleeding that suggests a serious underlying disease, may arrange for colonoscopy (p.661).

Small hemorrhoids do not usually need treatment. Hemorrhoids due to pregnancy usually disappear soon after the birth. A high-fiber diet helps prevent constipation, and laxatives (p.924) may help ease defecation. Over-the-counter topical corticosteroids (p.892) and corticosteroid suppositories can reduce swelling and itching, and anesthetic sprays may relieve pain. If these measures do not help within a few days, consult your doctor, who may consider surgery.

Small internal hemorrhoids may be treated by sclerotherapy, in which the affected area is injected with a solution that causes the veins to shrink. Alternatively, the doctor may place a band around the base of an internal hemorrhoid, causing it to shrink and fall off (*see* BANDING HEMORRHOIDS, below).

Persistent, painful, bleeding hemorrhoids can be destroyed by electrical, laser, or infrared heat treatment. They can also be removed surgically.

Hemorrhoids may recur, although treatment is usually successful.

(WWW) ONLINE SITES: p.1030

(TREATMENT) BANDING HEMORRHOIDS

Large or prolapsing hemorrhoids can be successfully treated by using a procedure called banding, in which a rubber band is placed around the base of the hemorrhoid. As a result, the hemorrhoid gradually shrinks over a period of several days and eventually drops off. Before the procedure, you may need a laxative to ensure that the rectum is empty. The procedure is often carried out in the doctor's office and is usually painless, although the treated area may be sore for a few days afterward.

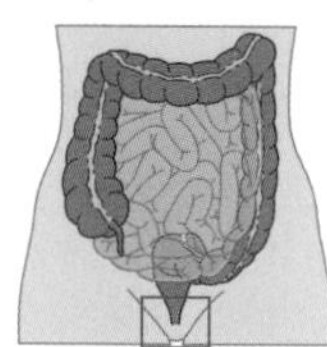

LOCATION

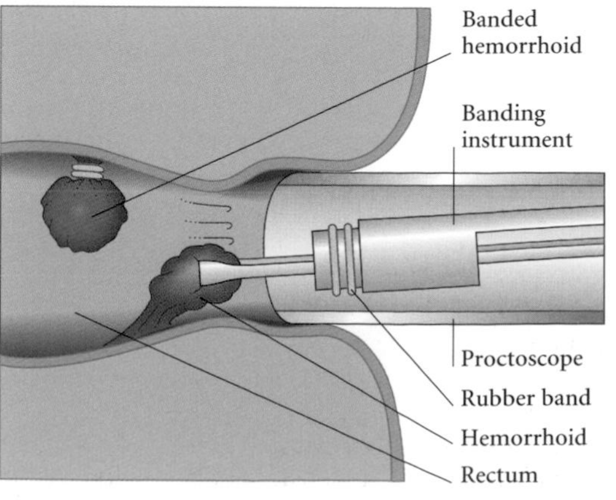
Banded hemorrhoid
Banding instrument
Proctoscope
Rubber band
Hemorrhoid
Rectum

During the procedure
Using a short viewing tube called a proctoscope, the doctor takes hold of the hemorrhoid with forceps and places a rubber band around the base using a banding instrument.

Anal abscess

An infected, pus-filled cavity in the anal or rectal area

 GENDER More common in males

 LIFESTYLE Anal sex is a risk factor

 AGE GENETICS Not significant factors

An anal abscess is a pus-filled cavity that develops when bacteria enter a mucus-secreting gland in the anus or rectum and multiply. The abscess may be deep within the rectum or close to the anus.

Inflammatory disorders of the colon, such as Crohn's disease (p.658), can be associated with anal abscesses. Anal sex also increases the risk.

You should consult a doctor if you have swelling or redness in the anal area or have a throbbing pain that worsens with defecation. If the infection spreads from the anal area, you may also have a fever and feel generally unwell.

An anal abscess is usually diagnosed by a physical examination. Treatment involves draining the abscess through an incision under local anesthesia. Drainage of deep or large abscesses may need general anesthesia. You may be prescribed oral antibiotics (p.885) and advised to soak the affected area in warm water three or four times a day. An abscess may take weeks to heal.

(WWW) ONLINE SITES: p.1030

Anal fissure

A tear in the lining of the anus that is usually a result of constipation

 LIFESTYLE A low-fiber diet is a risk factor

 AGE GENDER GENETICS Not significant factors

The most common cause of an anal fissure is the passage of a large, hard stool due to constipation (p.628). The stool can tear the anal lining so that subsequent defecation is extremely painful. You may also notice bright red blood on your feces or the toilet paper.

Your doctor will diagnose an anal fissure during an examination of the anus. In some cases, the doctor views the anal lining using a viewing instrument called an anuscope.

Self-help measures to relieve constipation, such as using laxatives (p.924) and eating a high-fiber diet, may help the anal fissure heal. However, further episodes of constipation may cause the fissure to recur. Persistent or recurrent anal fissures may eventually require surgery to loosen or stretch the ring of muscle around the anus.

(WWW) ONLINE SITES: p.1030

Anal itching

Irritation in or, more commonly, around the anus

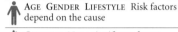

 AGE GENDER LIFESTYLE Risk factors depend on the cause

GENETICS Not a significant factor

Anal itching (pruritus ani) is rarely a serious condition, although it may be embarrassing and hard to treat. Itching may be either localized around the anus or part of a generalized itching disorder (*see* ITCHING, p.339). It may be worse in older people because their skin is drier, less elastic, and more easily irritated.

Localized itching may be caused by poor personal hygiene, hemorrhoids (opposite page), or pinworm infestation (p.310). Generalized itching around the anal area may be a symptom of a skin disease, such as psoriasis (p.332) or eczema (p.333), or be due to an allergic reaction to a substance such as laundry detergent or washing soap.

WHAT MIGHT BE DONE?

There are several measures you can take to relieve anal itching. It is important to keep the anal area clean by washing and drying carefully after a bowel movement. Avoid using soaps that irritate the skin, and try not to scratch because it will worsen the itching. A warm bath or shower before bed may soothe nighttime itching. Loose underclothes made of natural fibers are less likely than synthetic materials to cause irritation. An over-the-counter cream containing a topical corticosteroid (p.892) may give relief. Itching that lasts for longer than 3 days should be assessed by a doctor.

Your doctor may examine your anus and arrange for tests to look for causes that need treatment. For example, hemorrhoids may need to be removed.

(WWW) ONLINE SITES: p.1036

Anal cancer

Cancer of the anus or anal canal, which may cause pain and bleeding

 AGE More common with increasing age

 GENDER More common in males

 GENETICS LIFESTYLE Not significant factors

Cancer of the anus or the anal canal (the passage from the rectum to outside the body) is very rare. Although the cause is not known, there may be a link between anal cancer and human papillomaviruses, which cause genital warts (p.768) and are also associated with cancer of the cervix (p.750).

WHAT ARE THE SYMPTOMS?

The symptoms of anal cancer usually develop gradually and include:

- Bleeding from the anus.
- Itching or discomfort in the anal area.
- A frequent desire to defecate.
- A lump in or near the anus.

If you have any of these symptoms, you should consult your doctor to determine the cause. Left untreated, anal cancer may spread to nearby tissues and eventually to other parts of the body.

WHAT MIGHT BE DONE?

Your doctor will first examine the anus and then insert a gloved finger into the rectum to feel for lumps. Under local anesthesia, your doctor may remove a sample of tissue from the anal canal for examination under a microscope.

If anal cancer is diagnosed, you will need further tests to look for cancer spread. These tests include blood tests and CT scanning (p.247) or MRI (p.248) of the abdomen and pelvis.

The usual treatment is chemotherapy (p.278) accompanied by radiation therapy (p.279). In about 2 in 3 people, this treatment causes the tumor to shrink so that surgery is not needed. In most people, treatment is curative. However, in rare cases, surgery is necessary to remove the anus and part of the rectum.

If the cancer has already spread to other parts of the body, the prognosis is poor. However, surgery in combination with radiation therapy may relieve the symptoms and prolong life.

(WWW) ONLINE SITES: p.1028, p.1030

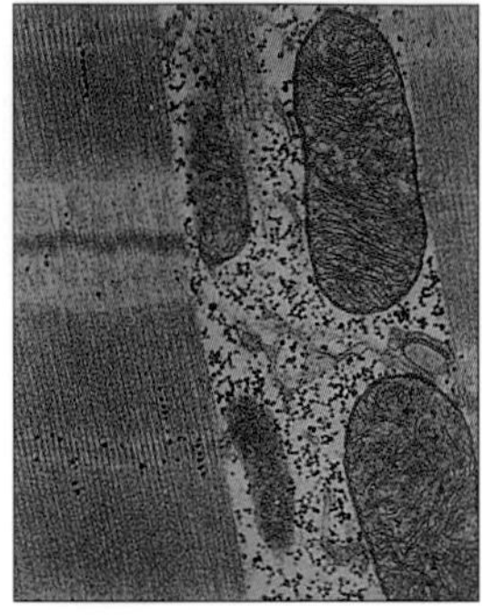

Glycogen in muscles
Glycogen stores, which break down into glucose to supply energy, appear as black dots in this view of muscle cells.

HORMONES AND METABOLISM

THE WORD HORMONE is derived from a Greek term meaning "to excite" or "to spur on." Hormones are chemical messengers that alter the activity of or "excite" targeted cells. They are produced in various specialized glands and cells throughout the body and are transported in the bloodstream to their specific sites of action. Hormones regulate many important body processes and functions, including growth, reproduction, and metabolism, the collective term for all the chemical reactions that occur in the body.

Hormones are produced by a number of different glands and cells that are described collectively as the endocrine system. The major endocrine glands – the pituitary, thyroid, parathyroid, and adrenal glands and the pancreas, ovaries, and testes – are all primarily dedicated to the production of various hormones. However, other organs in the body with major functions of their own also contain cells that produce hormones. For example, the main function of the kidneys is to filter the blood, but they also contain endocrine cells that secrete hormones.

Hormones are transported in the bloodstream to their target tissues, which may then be stimulated to produce other hormones in a chain reaction. For example, the pituitary gland produces thyroid-stimulating hormone (TSH), which in turn stimulates the thyroid gland to produce another hormone, thyroxine.

Hormones also regulate the balance of certain substances in the blood. If there is too much or too little of a substance, a feedback mechanism restores the correct levels. The pituitary, a pea-sized gland regulated by a part of the brain called the hypothalamus, has overall control of most hormone production.

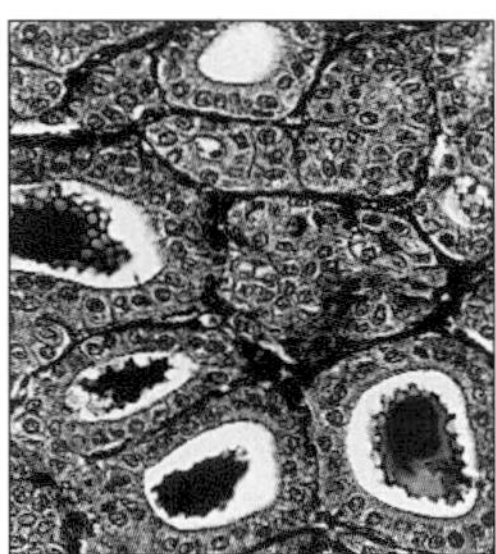

Thyroid gland tissue
This image shows hormone-secreting cells in the thyroid gland. The red areas are stores of hormones.

Some hormones work on cells throughout the body. For example, thyroxine influences metabolic rate. Others have specific target cells, such as antidiuretic hormone (ADH), which acts only on specific cells in the kidneys to regulate the concentration of urine.

When we are under stress or excited, the two adrenal glands increase production of hormones that affect our blood pressure, circulation, and breathing, creating the heightened states that form part of our "fight or flight" response to danger.

Throughout life, hormone levels rise and fall. For example, during puberty sex hormones rise sharply, and in women the levels fall after menopause.

PROCESS FEEDBACK MECHANISM

Hormone secretion is regulated by feedback mechanisms in order to maintain correct levels of substances in the blood. For example, a drop in the calcium level in the bloodstream stimulates an increase in the secretion of parathyroid hormone (PTH), which acts on various parts of the body to raise calcium levels. When calcium reaches the normal level, PTH secretion decreases.

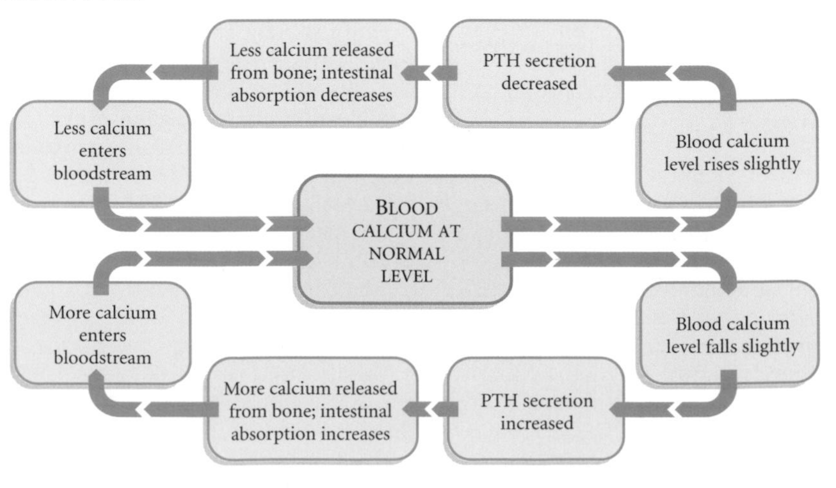
Less calcium released from bone; intestinal absorption decreases
PTH secretion decreased
Less calcium enters bloodstream
Blood calcium level rises slightly
BLOOD CALCIUM AT NORMAL LEVEL
More calcium enters bloodstream
Blood calcium level falls slightly
More calcium released from bone; intestinal absorption increases
PTH secretion increased

Maintaining blood calcium levels
The parathyroid glands detect fluctuations in calcium levels in the blood and secrete appropriate amounts of parathyroid hormone (PTH) to correct them.

STRUCTURE AND FUNCTION

HORMONE-SECRETING GLANDS AND CELLS

Most endocrine cells are grouped together in organs, such as the pituitary, thyroid, and adrenal glands, whose only purpose is to produce hormones. However, hormone-secreting cells are also present in many other tissues that have a different primary function. For example, the kidneys secrete hormones that stimulate red blood cell production, although their main role is to filter the blood. New chemical substances that act as hormones are still being discovered and their specific roles in the body clarified.

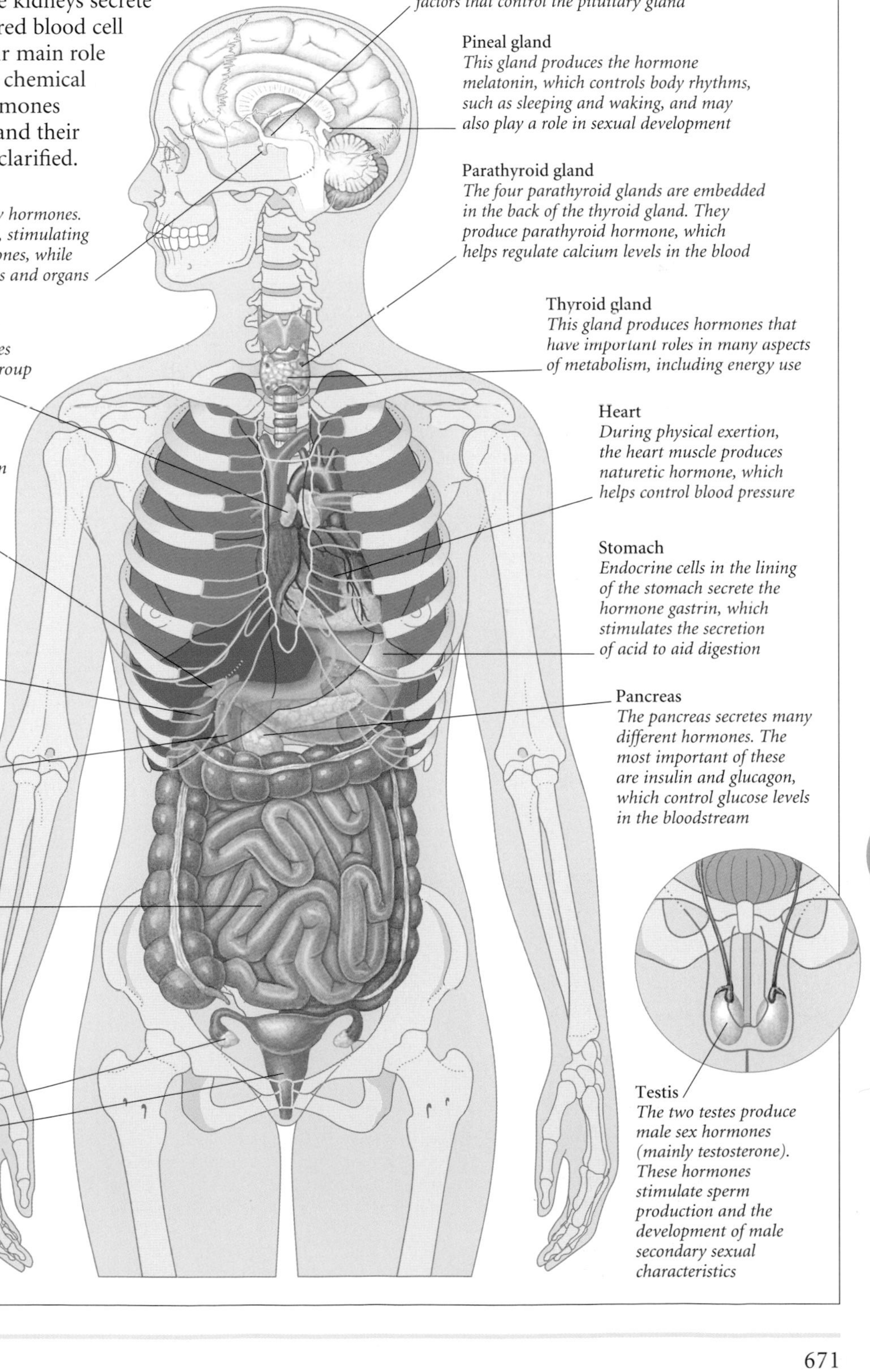

Pituitary gland
The pituitary gland secretes many hormones. Some of these act on other glands, stimulating them to produce their own hormones, while others act directly on target tissues and organs
Thymus
This gland is part of the immune system but also produces hormones that control the production of a group of white blood cells called T cells
Adrenal gland
The two adrenal glands produce hormones that control metabolism and hormones involved in the body's responses to stress
Kidney
The main role of the kidneys is to filter blood, but they also produce erythropoietin, which stimulates red blood cell production
Duodenum
The duodenum secretes hormones that act on other digestive organs, such as the gallbladder
Intestines
Endocrine cells in the lining of the intestines release several hormones that are involved in digestion
Ovary
The two ovaries produce progesterone and estrogen, two hormones involved in the menstrual cycle. Estrogen also plays a part in the development of female secondary sexual characteristics
Placenta
During pregnancy, the placenta, which forms in the uterus, produces certain hormones that are essential for fetal development
Hypothalamus
Although not strictly part of the endocrine system, the hypothalamus acts as the link between the nervous system and the endocrine system. It produces hormones called releasing factors that control the pituitary gland
Pineal gland
This gland produces the hormone melatonin, which controls body rhythms, such as sleeping and waking, and may also play a role in sexual development
Parathyroid gland
The four parathyroid glands are embedded in the back of the thyroid gland. They produce parathyroid hormone, which helps regulate calcium levels in the blood
Thyroid gland
This gland produces hormones that have important roles in many aspects of metabolism, including energy use
Heart
During physical exertion, the heart muscle produces naturetic hormone, which helps control blood pressure
Stomach
Endocrine cells in the lining of the stomach secrete the hormone gastrin, which stimulates the secretion of acid to aid digestion
Pancreas
The pancreas secretes many different hormones. The most important of these are insulin and glucagon, which control glucose levels in the bloodstream
Testis
The two testes produce male sex hormones (mainly testosterone). These hormones stimulate sperm production and the development of male secondary sexual characteristics

STRUCTURE AND FUNCTION PITUITARY GLAND

Also known as the master gland, the pituitary controls the activities of many other endocrine glands and hormone-producing cells. The pituitary gland has two parts, the anterior and posterior lobes, which are under the control of a part of the brain known as the hypothalamus. The hypothalamus secretes releasing chemicals that pass through blood vessels to the pituitary's anterior lobe and trigger the production of hormones that control other glands. Nerve cells in the hypothalamus produce two hormones that pass down nerve fibers to be stored in the posterior lobe until they are needed.

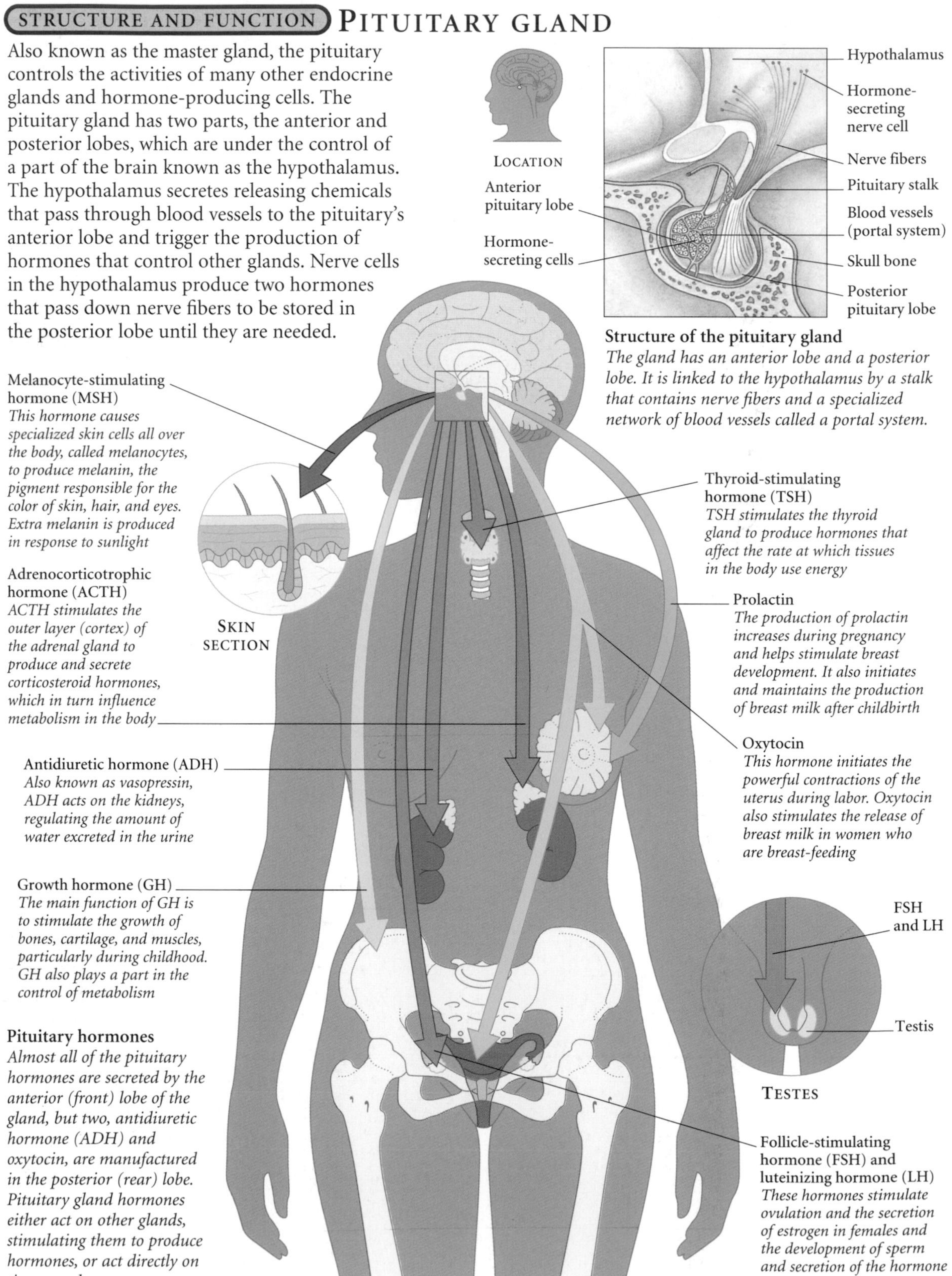

LOCATION
Anterior pituitary lobe
Hormone-secreting cells
Hypothalamus
Hormone-secreting nerve cell
Nerve fibers
Pituitary stalk
Blood vessels (portal system)
Skull bone
Posterior pituitary lobe
SKIN SECTION
TESTES
FSH and LH
Testis

Structure of the pituitary gland
The gland has an anterior lobe and a posterior lobe. It is linked to the hypothalamus by a stalk that contains nerve fibers and a specialized network of blood vessels called a portal system.

Melanocyte-stimulating hormone (MSH)
This hormone causes specialized skin cells all over the body, called melanocytes, to produce melanin, the pigment responsible for the color of skin, hair, and eyes. Extra melanin is produced in response to sunlight

Adrenocorticotrophic hormone (ACTH)
ACTH stimulates the outer layer (cortex) of the adrenal gland to produce and secrete corticosteroid hormones, which in turn influence metabolism in the body

Antidiuretic hormone (ADH)
Also known as vasopressin, ADH acts on the kidneys, regulating the amount of water excreted in the urine

Growth hormone (GH)
The main function of GH is to stimulate the growth of bones, cartilage, and muscles, particularly during childhood. GH also plays a part in the control of metabolism

Thyroid-stimulating hormone (TSH)
TSH stimulates the thyroid gland to produce hormones that affect the rate at which tissues in the body use energy

Prolactin
The production of prolactin increases during pregnancy and helps stimulate breast development. It also initiates and maintains the production of breast milk after childbirth

Oxytocin
This hormone initiates the powerful contractions of the uterus during labor. Oxytocin also stimulates the release of breast milk in women who are breast-feeding

Follicle-stimulating hormone (FSH) and luteinizing hormone (LH)
These hormones stimulate ovulation and the secretion of estrogen in females and the development of sperm and secretion of the hormone testosterone in males

Pituitary hormones
Almost all of the pituitary hormones are secreted by the anterior (front) lobe of the gland, but two, antidiuretic hormone (ADH) and oxytocin, are manufactured in the posterior (rear) lobe. Pituitary gland hormones either act on other glands, stimulating them to produce hormones, or act directly on tissues and organs.

STRUCTURE AND FUNCTION THYROID AND PARATHYROID GLANDS

The thyroid and parathyroid glands are situated close to each other in the front of the neck. The thyroid gland produces the hormone thyroxine (T_4) and its more active form, T_3, which act on body cells to regulate metabolism (the chemical reactions continually occurring in the body). Some thyroid cells secrete the hormone calcitonin, which lowers calcium in the blood. The parathyroid glands produce parathyroid hormone (PTH), the main regulator of calcium.

LOCATION

Structure of the thyroid and parathyroid glands
The thyroid gland is wrapped around the front of the trachea. The four parathyroid glands are at the back of the thyroid gland.

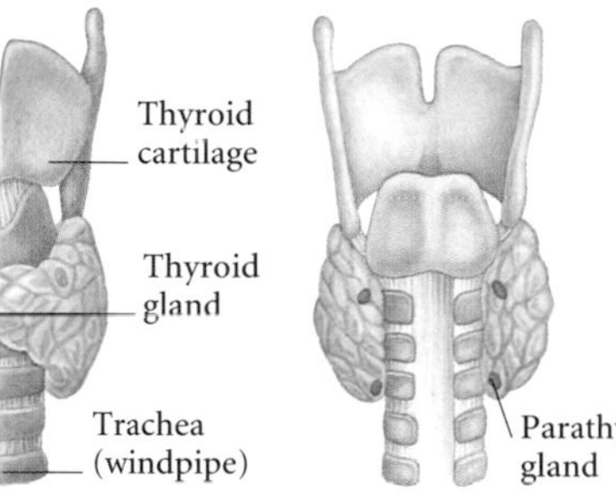
Thyroid cartilage
Thyroid gland
Trachea (windpipe)
Parathyroid gland
FRONT VIEW
BACK VIEW

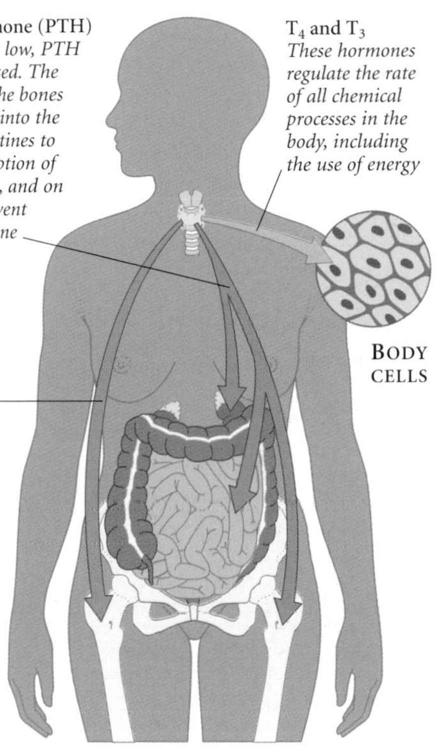
Parathyroid hormone (PTH)
If blood calcium is low, PTH secretion is increased. The hormone acts on the bones to release calcium into the blood, on the intestines to increase the absorption of calcium from food, and on the kidneys to prevent calcium loss in urine
T_4 and T_3
These hormones regulate the rate of all chemical processes in the body, including the use of energy
Calcitonin
This hormone inhibits calcium release from the bones if blood calcium levels are high
BODY CELLS

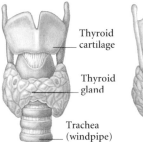

Thyroid and parathyroid hormones
Iodine from the diet is used to make the hormones T_4 and T_3. These hormones are produced by the thyroid gland and regulate body metabolism. Parathyroid hormone (PTH) and, to a lesser extent, calcitonin regulate levels of calcium and phosphate.

STRUCTURE AND FUNCTION ADRENAL GLANDS

Each adrenal gland has two parts. The cortex (outer layer) is controlled by the pituitary gland and secretes several corticosteroid hormones, the most important of which affect metabolism and blood pressure. The cortex also produces very small amounts of male sex hormones (androgens). The medulla (core) influences the autonomic nervous system by releasing the hormones epinephrine and norepinephrine, which increase heart activity and blood flow in response to excitement or stress.

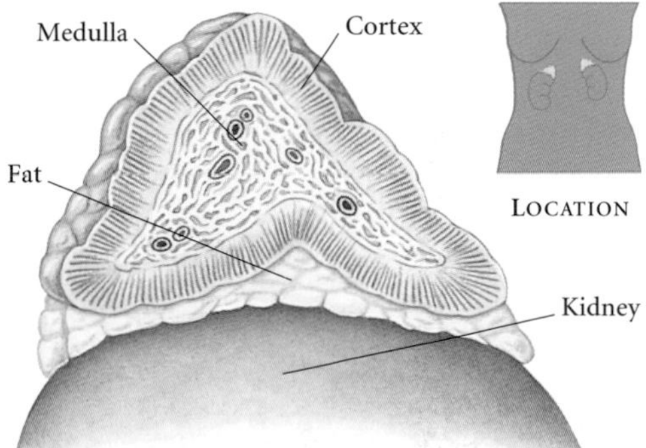
Medulla
Cortex
Fat
Kidney
LOCATION

Structure of the adrenal gland
The adrenal glands rest on pads of fat above the kidneys. Each gland has an outer cortex, which makes up 90 percent of its weight, and an inner medulla.

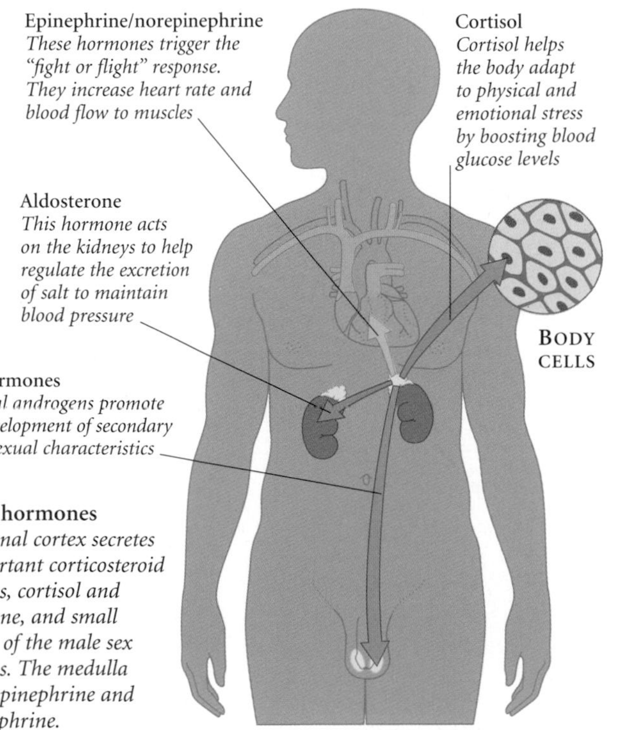
Epinephrine/norepinephrine
These hormones trigger the "fight or flight" response. They increase heart rate and blood flow to muscles
Cortisol
Cortisol helps the body adapt to physical and emotional stress by boosting blood glucose levels
Aldosterone
This hormone acts on the kidneys to help regulate the excretion of salt to maintain blood pressure
Sex hormones
Adrenal androgens promote the development of secondary male sexual characteristics
BODY CELLS

Adrenal hormones
The adrenal cortex secretes the important corticosteroid hormones, cortisol and aldosterone, and small amounts of the male sex hormones. The medulla secretes epinephrine and norepinephrine.

STRUCTURE AND FUNCTION

PANCREAS

The pancreas has two functions. It plays a major role in digestion, releasing enzymes that break down fat, starch, and proteins through the pancreatic ducts into the intestine. It also contains clusters of cells, called islets of Langerhans, that secrete hormones directly into the bloodstream. These cells secrete insulin and glucagon, two hormones that regulate glucose levels in the body, and other digestive hormones.

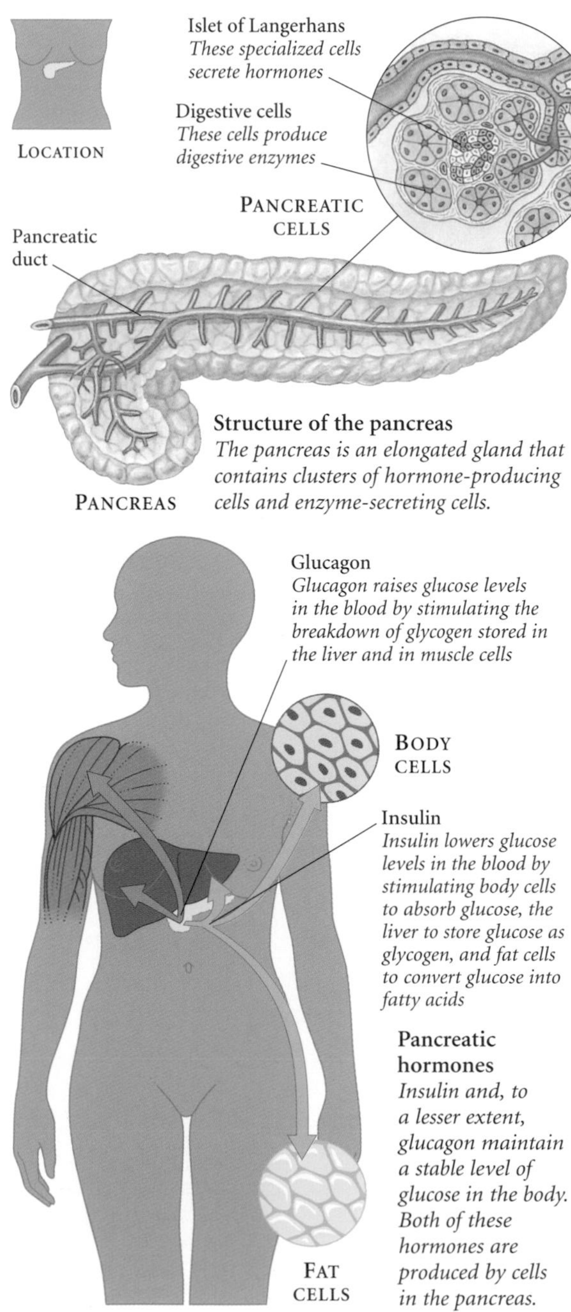

LOCATION
Islet of Langerhans
These specialized cells secrete hormones
Digestive cells
These cells produce digestive enzymes
PANCREATIC CELLS
Pancreatic duct
PANCREAS
Glucagon
Glucagon raises glucose levels in the blood by stimulating the breakdown of glycogen stored in the liver and in muscle cells
BODY CELLS
Insulin
Insulin lowers glucose levels in the blood by stimulating body cells to absorb glucose, the liver to store glucose as glycogen, and fat cells to convert glucose into fatty acids
FAT CELLS

Structure of the pancreas
The pancreas is an elongated gland that contains clusters of hormone-producing cells and enzyme-secreting cells.

Pancreatic hormones
Insulin and, to a lesser extent, glucagon maintain a stable level of glucose in the body. Both of these hormones are produced by cells in the pancreas.

PROCESS

METABOLISM

Thousands of chemical reactions and conversions take place continuously in body cells to keep the body alive and healthy and to generate energy. Metabolism is the collective term for all these chemical processes. The raw materials for metabolic processes are obtained from nutrients in food, which are broken down into simple molecules during digestion. These molecules are either recycled and built up into new complex molecules that can be used to repair or make new cells (anabolism) or are further broken down to release energy (catabolism).

ANABOLISM AND CATABOLISM

In anabolic processes, body cells are built up and repaired, or complex substances are constructed out of simpler ones. In catabolic processes, complex molecules are broken down into simple molecules, such as glucose and amino acids, and these simple molecules are broken down to supply the cells with energy and materials for renewing cell structures.

Metabolic activity
Anabolic and catabolic processes take place simultaneously in cells throughout the body, to build complex molecules and to provide energy.

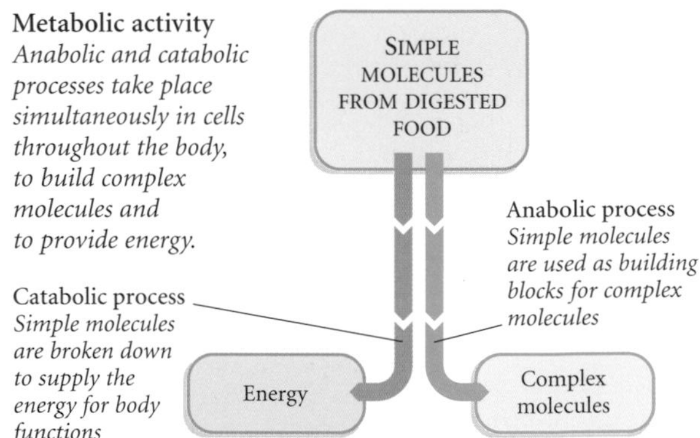

SIMPLE MOLECULES FROM DIGESTED FOOD
Anabolic process
Simple molecules are used as building blocks for complex molecules
Catabolic process
Simple molecules are broken down to supply the energy for body functions
Energy
Complex molecules

BASAL METABOLIC RATE

The amount of energy a person uses for essential functions, such as maintaining body heat, breathing, and heart rate, is called the basal metabolic rate (BMR). BMR decreases naturally with age, but it is raised in the short term by factors such as illness, pregnancy, breast-feeding, and menstruation. All forms of exercise increase the body's use of energy above the BMR.

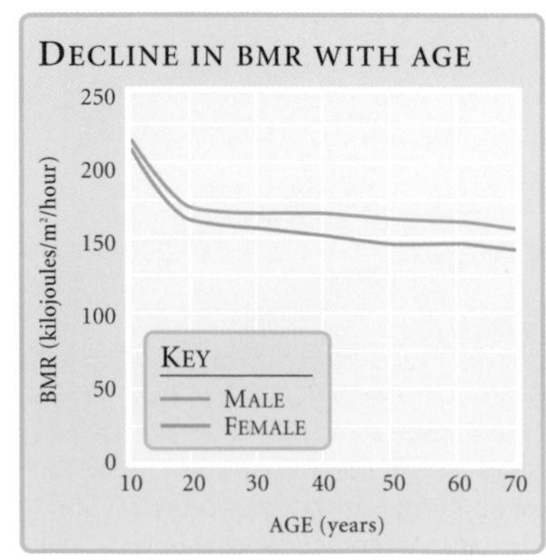

DECLINE IN BMR WITH AGE
BMR (kilojoules/m²/hour)
250
200
150
100
50
0
10
20
30
40
50
60
70
AGE (years)
KEY
MALE
FEMALE

Basal metabolic rate (BMR)
After about age 10, basal metabolic rate decreases with age and tends to be lower in females than in males. BMR is measured at rest and is often expressed as kilojoules used per square meter of body surface per hour (1 kilojoule equals about 4 kilocalories).

How the body uses food

Every living body cell depends on essential nutrients in food. Carbohydrates, proteins, and fats are converted into glucose, amino acids, and fatty acids respectively during digestion. These molecules enter the lymphatic system and the bloodstream and are converted into a usable form (metabolized) in the liver and in all body cells. Glucose is used to produce energy, as are fatty acids when glucose is in short supply. Amino acids are used to build the complex proteins needed to make and repair cells.

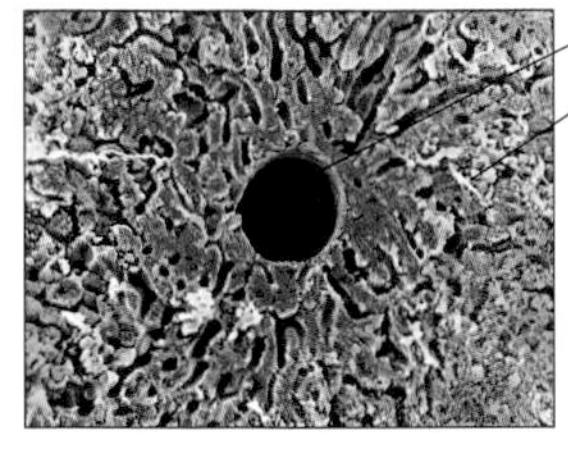
Blood vessel
Hepatocyte

Liver tissue
The liver has a rich blood supply. This magnified view of liver tissue shows a blood vessel surrounded by large liver cells (hepatocytes).

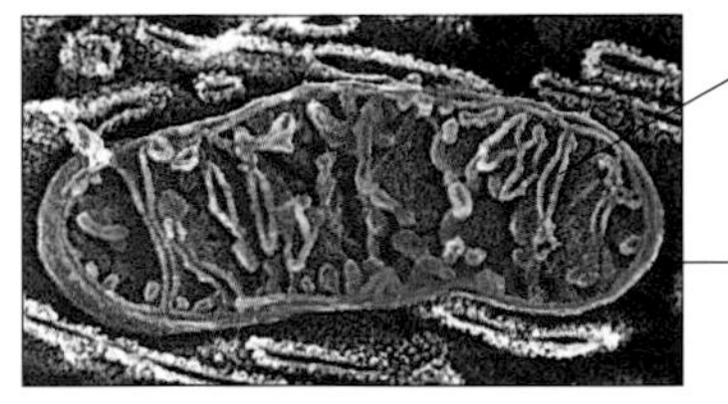
Crista
Outer membrane

Mitochondrion
Each body cell contains many mitochondria. This magnified image of a mitochondrion, the cell "powerhouse," shows the folds (cristae) where energy-producing reactions take place.

Digestion
During digestion, complex carbohydrates are converted into simple sugars, such as glucose; fats and oils are broken down into fatty acids and glycerol; and proteins are broken down into amino acids. The bloodstream transports these nutrients to the liver, the body's major metabolic site, and then to all body cells.

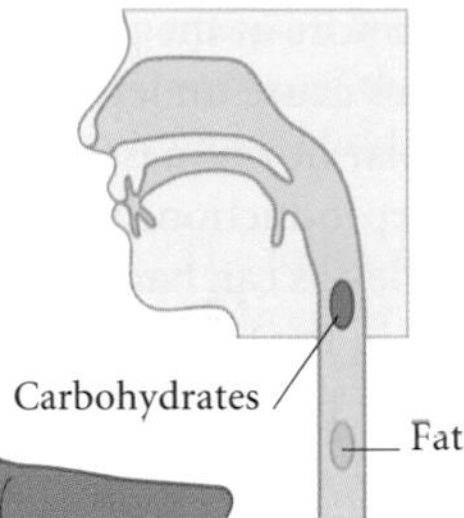
Carbohydrates
Fats
Proteins
Stomach
Glucose
Fatty acids and glycerol
Amino acids
Liver
Body cells

Energy production
The food we eat is mainly used for energy. The breakdown of glucose is the body's preferred source of energy, but fatty acids can be converted into energy if glucose is unavailable. In extreme cases, amino acids in the tissues may be used for energy.

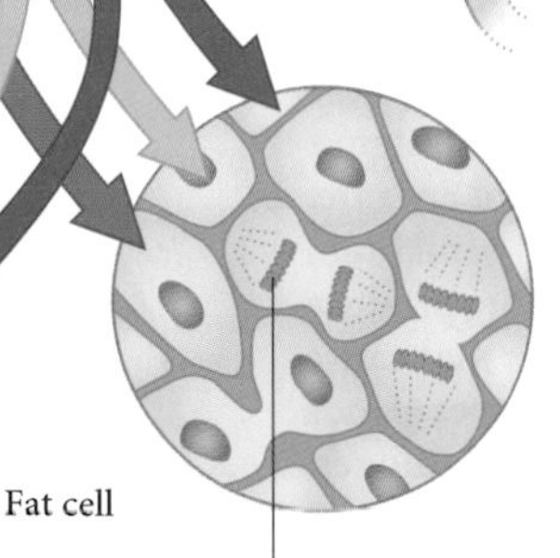
Dividing cell
Fat cell

How materials are used
Glucose provides energy for cell growth and repair. Fats are mainly used to build cell walls. Amino acids are built up into complex proteins, which are used in cell division and the repair of damaged cells.

Liver tissue
Muscle cell

Glycogen storage
Fat storage

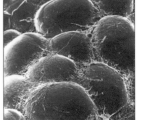

Storage of materials
Surplus glucose is stored in the liver and muscle cells as glycogen. This substance can be broken down into glucose and used for instant energy. Excess fats are stored as fatty acids in fat cells. Excess amino acids cannot be stored, but they can be converted into fatty acids for storage in fat cells. If glycogen stores are full, excess glucose is also converted into fatty acids for storage.

Layer of fat cells
Fats are deposited in oval storage cells known as fat cells. These cells, also called adipocytes, form a layer of varying thickness beneath the skin to insulate the body. A thin layer of adipose tissue surrounds the heart, kidneys, and other internal organs.

Hypopituitarism

Insufficient production initially of some and eventually of all pituitary hormones

AGE GENDER GENETICS LIFESTYLE
Not significant factors

Hypopituitarism is a rare condition in which the pituitary gland secretes inadequate amounts of one or more of its hormones. In many cases, the disorder is progressive, ultimately causing underproduction of all pituitary hormones.

Hypopituitarism is usually caused by a pituitary tumor that damages normal tissue in the gland as it grows. The disorder may also be due to other factors that damage the pituitary gland or the hypothalamus, the part of the brain lying directly above the pituitary gland. Such factors include surgery or radiation therapy (p.279) to treat a pituitary tumor or other head or neck tumor, head injuries (p.521), or heavy blood loss that deprives the gland of oxygen.

WHAT ARE THE SYMPTOMS?

The symptoms may appear suddenly but more commonly develop gradually and can go unrecognized for months or years. They may include:

- Loss of interest in sex.
- Lack of menstrual periods in women.
- Loss of facial hair and shrinking of the testes in men.
- Loss of underarm and pubic hair.
- Dizziness, nausea, and vomiting.
- Paleness of the skin.
- Fatigue, constipation, weight gain, and intolerance to cold.

Untreated, hypopituitarism can eventually lead to coma. It can also be fatal because the body is unable to increase the output of hormones that respond to infection or stress.

WHAT MIGHT BE DONE?

If your doctor suspects that you have hypopituitarism, he or she will probably arrange for blood tests to check your hormone levels. You may also need to undergo tests in the hospital to determine hormone production in response to various chemical stimulants, and you may have MRI (p.248) or CT scanning (p.247) to look for a pituitary tumor.

If a tumor is detected, you may have surgery to remove it, followed by radiation therapy to prevent a recurrence. Hypopituitarism can be treated with lifelong hormone-replacement drugs. These drugs do not usually replace pituitary hormones; they replace hormones, such as thyroid hormones and corticosteroids, that are produced by other glands stimulated by the pituitary.

You may need additional doses of corticosteroid drugs (p.930) in times of stress or illness. It is important for you to carry identification that provides information about the drugs you need in case a medical emergency arises.

(WWW) ONLINE SITES: p.1033

Diabetes insipidus

Inadequate production of, or resistance to the effects of, the pituitary hormone involved in controlling water balance

AGE GENDER GENETICS LIFESTYLE
Risk factors depend on the type

Diabetes insipidus is a rare condition in which the kidneys produce large volumes of dilute urine. The condition is not related to diabetes mellitus (p.687), although both conditions cause thirst and excessive urination.

In diabetes insipidus, the body lacks or cannot fully respond to antidiuretic hormone (ADH). This hormone is produced by the hypothalamus, the part of the brain directly above the pituitary gland. However, ADH is stored and secreted by the pituitary gland, which is why it is usually considered a pituitary hormone. The role of ADH is to maintain the water balance of the body by controlling urine production.

WHAT ARE THE TYPES?

Diabetes insipidus occurs in two forms: the more common form, called central diabetes insipidus, and a form known as nephrogenic diabetes insipidus.

Central diabetes insipidus is due to the reduced secretion of ADH. Possible causes of this condition include a pituitary tumor (p.676), a tumor near the hypothalamus, surgery, radiation therapy (p.279), or head injuries (p.521). In some cases, the cause is not known.

Nephrogenic diabetes insipidus is a condition in which the kidneys fail to respond to normal levels of ADH. In some cases, the disorder is present from birth and is permanent. In these cases, it is more common in males than in females because it is due to an inherited recessive gene carried on the X chromosome (*see* GENE DISORDERS, p.269). The disorder may also be due to chronic kidney failure (p.706) or to kidney damage resulting from the use of drugs such as certain antibiotics (p.885) or lithium, a mood-stabilizing drug (p.918). In such cases, the condition may be reversible.

WHAT ARE THE SYMPTOMS?

Symptoms of both forms of diabetes insipidus usually develop over days or weeks, but they may appear suddenly if the pituitary gland has been damaged. Symptoms may include:

- Excessive urination.
- Insatiable thirst.
- Disturbed sleep due to the need to urinate frequently.

If water lost from the body is not replaced, dehydration will occur. Severe dehydration may need immediate hospital treatment with intravenous fluids.

WHAT MIGHT BE DONE?

If your doctor suspects that you have diabetes insipidus, he or she may first measure your urine concentration and volume. Initially, urine output is measured after you have been deprived of fluids for several hours. If you have diabetes insipidus, you will continue to produce a large volume of urine. Next, your response to synthetic ADH is measured. If ADH lowers your output of urine, you probably have central diabetes insipidus; if output remains high, you probably have the nephrogenic form. If a tumor is suspected as the cause of the central form, you may also undergo imaging such as MRI (p.248).

Central diabetes insipidus is most commonly treated with synthetic ADH (*see* PITUITARY DRUGS, p.934). If there is an underlying cause, such as a pituitary tumor, it will also be treated.

Nephrogenic diabetes insipidus that is inherited is usually treated with a low-sodium diet and thiazide diuretics (p.902), which reduce urine volume. Treatment must be continued for life. Nephrogenic diabetes due to kidney damage may clear up as the kidneys recover; otherwise, drug treatment is needed. If you have diabetes insipidus, carry identification to alert others to the fact in an emergency.

(WWW) ONLINE SITES: p.1033

THYROID AND PARATHYROID GLAND DISORDERS

The thyroid and parathyroid glands are situated in the neck, where they produce and secrete hormones into the bloodstream. There are two types of thyroid hormones, both of which help control the rate of metabolism (the chemical reactions constantly occurring in the body). The four small parathyroid glands produce a hormone that controls calcium levels in the blood.

Thyroid disorders are common, but their onset is often gradual and they may not be detected or diagnosed for months or even years. Low levels of thyroid hormones at birth can prevent normal development of the brain and, for this reason, a thyroid function test is one of the first tests to be performed on a newborn baby (see SCREENING FOR METABOLIC DISORDERS, p.867). Over- and underactivity of the thyroid gland are the most common thyroid disorders and are discussed first. Swellings and growths are covered next, followed by disorders in which there is over- or underproduction of hormones by the parathyroid gland.

The last article describes multiple endocrine neoplasia, a rare inherited condition in which tumors develop in several endocrine glands, including the thyroid and parathyroid glands.

KEY ANATOMY

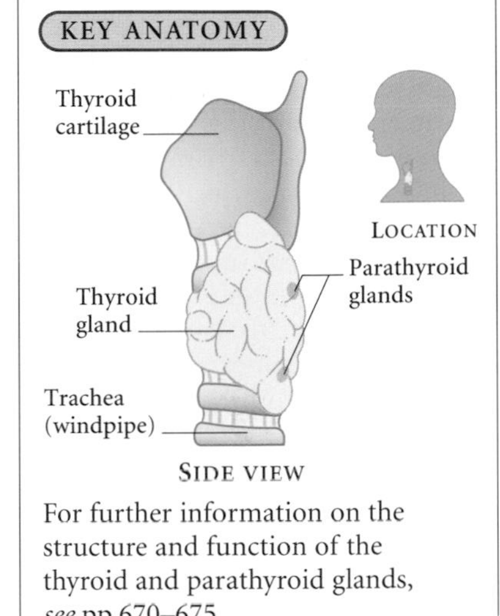
Thyroid cartilage
Location
Parathyroid glands
Thyroid gland
Trachea (windpipe)
Side view

For further information on the structure and function of the thyroid and parathyroid glands, see pp.670–675.

Hyperthyroidism

Overproduction of thyroid hormones, causing many body functions to speed up

 AGE Most common between the ages of 20 and 50

 GENDER More common in females

 GENETICS Sometimes runs in families

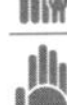 LIFESTYLE Not a significant factor

When the thyroid gland produces an excess of hormones, many of the body's functions are stimulated by these hormones and speed up. This condition is known as hyperthyroidism and is one of the most common hormonal disorders. Hyperthyroidism is 7–10 times more common in women and usually develops between the ages of 20 and 50.

About 3 in 4 cases of the condition are due to Graves' disease, an autoimmune disorder in which the immune system produces antibodies that attack the thyroid gland, resulting in overproduction of thyroid hormones. Graves' disease tends to run in families and is thought to have a genetic basis. In rare cases, hyperthyroidism may be associated with other autoimmune disorders, in particular the skin disorder vitiligo (p.342), and pernicious anemia, a disorder of the blood (see MEGALOBLASTIC ANEMIA, p.448). In some cases, thyroid nodules (p.681) that secrete hormones lead to hyperthyroidism. Inflammation of the thyroid gland (see THYROIDITIS, p.681) may also temporarily produce the symptoms of hyperthyroidism.

WHAT ARE THE SYMPTOMS?

In most cases, symptoms of hyperthyroidism develop gradually over several weeks and may include:

- Weight loss despite increased appetite and food consumption.
- Rapid heartbeat, which is sometimes also irregular.
- Tremor (persistent trembling) affecting the hands.
- Warm, moist skin as a result of excessive sweating.
- Intolerance to heat.
- Anxiety and insomnia.
- Frequent bowel movements.
- Swelling in the neck caused by an enlarged thyroid (see GOITER, p.680).
- Muscle weakness.
- In women, irregular menstruation.

People with hyperthyroidism caused by Graves' disease may also have bulging eyes (see EXOPHTHALMOS, p.582).

HOW IS IT DIAGNOSED?

If your doctor suspects you have hyperthyroidism, he or she may arrange for a blood test to check for abnormally high levels of the thyroid hormones and for antibodies that can attack the thyroid gland. Your doctor will also feel around your neck for lumps caused by general enlargement of the gland. If swelling is detected in the area of the thyroid gland, you may have radionuclide scanning (p.251) to check for a nodule.

WHAT IS THE TREATMENT?

Symptoms of hyperthyroidism can initially be relieved by beta blocker drugs (p.898), which reduce tremor and anxiety but do not affect thyroid hormone levels. There are three main treatments aimed at reducing the production of thyroid hormones. The most common is antithyroid drugs (see DRUGS FOR HYPERTHYROIDISM, p.932), which are used when hyperthyroidism is due to Graves' disease and work by suppressing production of thyroid hormones. These drugs need to be taken daily for 12–18 months, after which the thyroid gland often functions normally. Radioactive iodine may be the most effective treatment for thyroid nodules that secrete hormones and involves drinking a dose of radioactive iodine in solution. The iodine is absorbed and accumulates in the thyroid gland, destroying part of it. Rarely, if drug treatments are ineffective, surgical removal of part of the thyroid gland may become necessary.

WHAT IS THE PROGNOSIS?

Many people recover fully following treatment. However, hyperthyroidism may recur, particularly in people who have Graves' disease. If the treatment involves surgery or radioactive iodine, the remaining part of the thyroid may not be able to produce sufficient hormones (*see* HYPOTHYROIDISM, below). It is therefore important for thyroid hormone levels to be monitored regularly after treatment so that hormone supplements can be given if needed.

(WWW) ONLINE SITES: p.1033

Hypothyroidism

Underproduction of thyroid hormones, causing many body functions to slow down

 AGE Most common over age 40

 GENDER More common in females

 GENETICS Sometimes runs in families

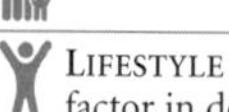 LIFESTYLE Dietary iodine deficiency is a risk factor in developing countries

In hypothyroidism, the thyroid gland does not produce enough thyroid hormones. These hormones are important in metabolism (the chemical reactions constantly occurring in the body). A deficiency causes a slowing down of many of the body's functions. The disorder is more common in women, particularly in those over age 40.

WHAT ARE THE CAUSES?

A common cause of hypothyroidism is thyroiditis (opposite page). The most common type of thyroiditis that leads to hypothyroidism is an autoimmune disorder known as Hashimoto's thyroiditis, which runs in families. In Hashimoto's thyroiditis, the body produces antibodies that attack the thyroid gland, damaging it permanently. Other forms of thyroiditis may lead to temporary or permanent hypothyroidism.

Treatments for an overactive thyroid gland that involve radioactive iodine or surgery (*see* HYPERTHYROIDISM, p.679) can also lead to permanent hypothyroidism. These treatments destroy part of the gland, and the remaining tissue may not produce sufficient hormones.

Insufficient dietary iodine, which is essential for the production of thyroid hormones, can cause hypothyroidism but is rare in developed countries.

In rare cases, hypothyroidism is due to the pituitary gland releasing insufficient amounts of thyroid-stimulating hormone (TSH), which stimulates the thyroid gland to secrete its own hormones. The underproduction of TSH is often due to a pituitary tumor (p.676).

WHAT ARE THE SYMPTOMS?

The symptoms of hypothyroidism vary in severity, usually develop slowly over months or years, and may initially go unnoticed. Symptoms include:

- Fatigue, which may make even minimal physical activity difficult.
- Weight gain.
- Constipation.
- Hoarseness of the voice.
- Intolerance to cold.
- Swelling of the face, puffy eyes, and dry, thickened skin.
- Generalized hair thinning.
- In women, heavy menstrual periods.

Some people with hypothyroidism develop a swelling in the neck due to an enlarged thyroid (*see* GOITER, right).

WHAT MIGHT BE DONE?

Your doctor may arrange for you to have blood tests to measure the levels of thyroid hormones and to check for antibodies that act against the thyroid gland.

Treatment is aimed at the underlying cause. Permanent hypothyroidism may be treated with synthetic thyroid hormones, which you will need to take for life (*see* DRUGS FOR HYPOTHYROIDISM, p.932). The symptoms should begin to improve about 3 weeks after drug treatment starts. Hormone treatment must be monitored regularly to ensure that the correct dosage is maintained. If a pituitary tumor (p.676) is the cause, it will be removed surgically or treated with radiation therapy (p.279).

Temporary hypothyroidism does not usually need to be treated. A deficiency in dietary iodine can be treated with supplements or an improved diet.

(WWW) ONLINE SITES: p.1033

Goiter

A swelling in the neck due to enlargement of the thyroid gland

 AGE GENDER GENETICS LIFESTYLE Risk factors depend on the cause

If the thyroid gland enlarges, it causes a swelling in the neck known as a goiter. A goiter can range in size from a barely noticeable lump to a swelling the size of a grapefruit. In rare cases, a large goiter may press on the esophagus and trachea (windpipe), causing difficulty in swallowing and breathing.

WHAT ARE THE CAUSES?

The thyroid gland may enlarge without any disturbance of its function at puberty, during pregnancy, or at other times when there is no apparent cause. Disorders that may be associated with goiter include hyperthyroidism (p.679), hypothyroidism (left), a thyroid nodule (opposite page), and certain types of thyroiditis (opposite page). Goiter is a known side effect of drugs such as lithium (*see* MOOD-STABILIZING DRUGS, p.918), which is used to treat bipolar affective disorder (p.557). Iodine deficiency may also cause goiter, mainly in developing countries. Rarely, goiter is due to thyroid cancer (opposite page).

WHAT MIGHT BE DONE?

Your doctor will examine your neck to assess the size and shape of the gland. You may have a blood test to check thyroid hormone levels and radionuclide scanning (p.251) to assess gland activity. Needle aspiration of the thyroid gland (p.682) may be done to look for cancer in a suspicious area of the gland.

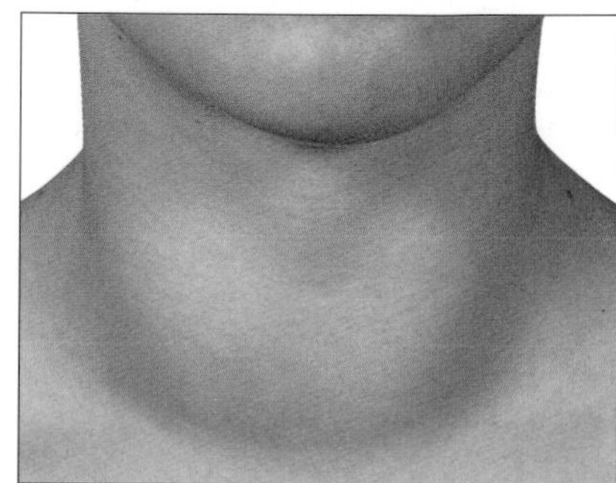

Goiter

This swelling in the neck, called a goiter, is due to enlargement of the thyroid gland. Most goiters are painless.

Treatment is directed at the underlying cause. Radioactive iodine, antithyroid drugs (*see* DRUGS FOR HYPERTHYROIDISM, p.932), or surgery are sometimes successful in shrinking a goiter in people with hyperthyroidism. Surgery may also be necessary if breathing or swallowing is obstructed or if thyroid cancer is suspected. A small goiter that has no effect on thyroid function may not require treatment and may decrease in size or disappear completely with time.

(WWW) ONLINE SITES: p.1033

Thyroiditis

Inflammation of the thyroid gland, causing permanent or temporary damage

 AGE More common in adults; rare in children

 GENDER GENETICS Risk factors depend on the type

 LIFESTYLE Not a significant factor

Inflammation of the thyroid gland is known as thyroiditis. This disorder can disrupt thyroid activity, causing underactivity (*see* HYPOTHYROIDISM, opposite page) or overactivity (*see* HYPERTHYROIDISM, p.679) of the thyroid gland. The under- or overproduction of thyroid hormones that results from this disruption in thyroid activity is usually temporary, but it can be permanent.

What are the types?

Thyroiditis may take a number of different forms, depending on its cause. The three most common types of thyroiditis are described below.

HASHIMOTO'S THYROIDITIS The most common type of thyroid inflammation is Hashimoto's thyroiditis, an autoimmune disorder in which the body produces antibodies that attack the thyroid gland. It often causes underactivity of the thyroid gland (*see* HYPOTHYROIDISM, opposite page) and sometimes a swelling in the neck due to an enlarged thyroid (*see* GOITER, opposite page). Hashimoto's thyroiditis is eight times more common in women. It sometimes runs in families and may be associated with other autoimmune disorders, such as the skin condition vitiligo (p.342) or the blood disorder pernicious anemia (*see* MEGALOBLASTIC ANEMIA, p.448).

VIRAL THYROIDITIS This form of thyroiditis can sometimes be mistaken for a throat infection because it causes pain on swallowing. There may be pain in the jaws or ears, fever, and weight loss. The condition can cause overactivity followed by underactivity of the gland.

POSTPARTUM THYROIDITIS About 1 in 10 women develops postpartum thyroiditis within a few months of giving birth. It is thought that this condition results from certain changes that occur in a woman's immune system during pregnancy. Symptoms are uncommon but may include those associated with hyperthyroidism followed by those of hypothyroidism. Postpartum thyroiditis usually clears up after a few months but may recur after future pregnancies.

What might be done?

Your doctor may arrange for a blood test to check your thyroid hormone levels and look for specific antibodies that attack the thyroid gland. Radionuclide scanning (p.251) may also be necessary to assess the level of thyroid activity.

If you have Hashimoto's thyroiditis, you will usually need lifelong treatment with synthetic thyroid hormones (*see* DRUGS FOR HYPOTHYROIDISM, p.932). In severe cases of viral thyroiditis, corticosteroids (p.930) or aspirin may be used to relieve inflammation. Postpartum thyroiditis is usually temporary and does not need treatment.

(WWW) ONLINE SITES: p.1033

Thyroid nodules

Cancerous or noncancerous growths in the thyroid gland

 AGE Most common between the ages of 40 and 60

 GENDER More common in females

 GENETICS LIFESTYLE Not significant factors

Thyroid nodules are abnormal growths in the thyroid gland. They are generally small and occur as single or multiple hard nodules or cysts. Some nodules produce excess thyroid hormones (*see* HYPERTHYROIDISM, p.679). All types of thyroid nodules are most common in people aged 40–60 and are three times more common in women.

What are the symptoms?

Nodules may have no symptoms, but some people may develop the following:

- Lump or swelling in the neck.
- Difficulty in swallowing or breathing.

If nodules cause hyperthyroidism, additional symptoms may develop, such as rapid heartbeat and loss of weight.

What might be done?

Imaging of the thyroid gland with ultrasound scanning (p.250) or radionuclide scanning (p.251) may be necessary to diagnose a thyroid nodule. Needle aspiration of the thyroid gland (p.682) may be done to establish whether a nodule is solid or a cyst or if it is cancerous. If the nodule is found to be cancerous, further investigation and treatment are necessary (*see* THYROID CANCER, below).

Noncancerous thyroid nodules that do not cause symptoms may not require treatment but should be monitored regularly. In some cases, radioactive iodine is used to treat a nodule that secretes excess thyroid hormones (*see* DRUGS FOR HYPERTHYROIDISM, p.932).

(WWW) ONLINE SITES: p.1033

Thyroid cancer

An uncommon, cancerous tumor occurring in the thyroid gland

 AGE More common over age 40

 GENDER More common in females

 GENETICS Risk factor depends on the type

 LIFESTYLE Previous exposure to radiation is a risk factor

Abnormal growths in the thyroid gland can sometimes be cancerous. Thyroid cancer is rare and accounts for only 1 in 100 of all cancers, but it is twice as common in women as men. The condition generally occurs after age 40, and evidence suggests that previous exposure to radiation increases the risk. The cure rates of most types of thyroid cancers are among the highest of all cancers.

What are the types?

There are three main types of thyroid cancer, each arising from different cell types in the gland: papillary, follicular, and medullary. About 7 in 10 thyroid cancers are papillary, and this type of

TEST NEEDLE ASPIRATION OF THE THYROID GLAND

Needle aspiration of the thyroid gland is used to determine the cause of a lump and, if the lump is a cyst, to drain it. During the procedure, cells are removed from the abnormal area using a fine hollow needle attached to a syringe. Ultrasound guidance may be used if a lump is inaccessible. The sample is examined in a laboratory for the presence of cancerous cells. This procedure is almost painless and can be carried out in the doctor's office.

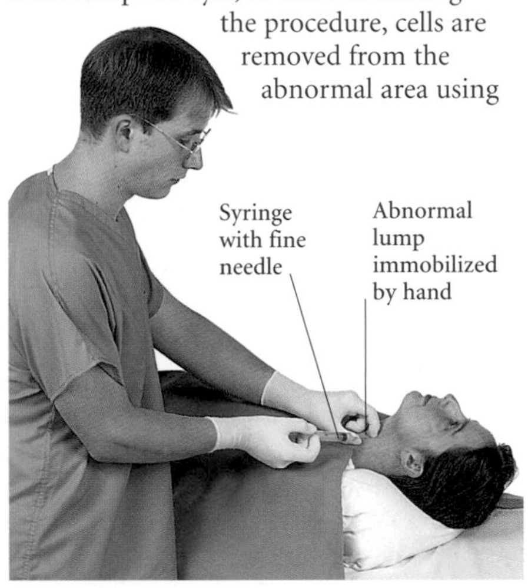
Syringe with fine needle
Abnormal lump immobilized by hand

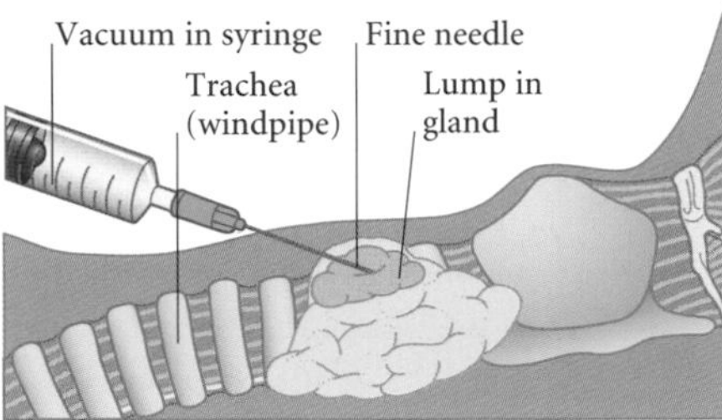
Vacuum in syringe
Fine needle
Trachea (windpipe)
Lump in gland

INSIDE THE NECK

Taking a sample
A pillow is placed under your neck to raise the thyroid area. The doctor withdraws cells from the abnormal area using a syringe with a fine needle.

RESULTS

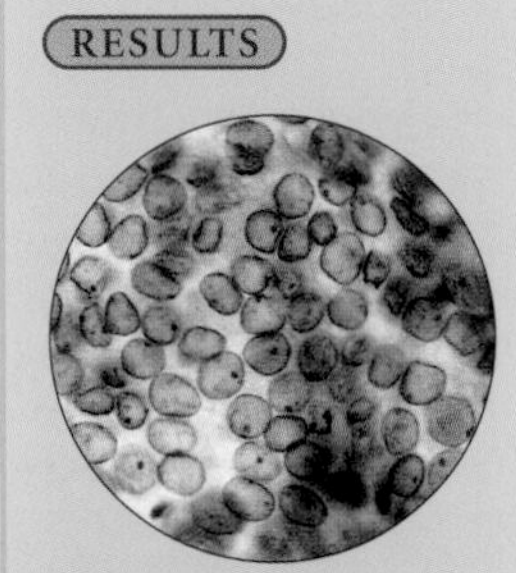

Cancerous thyroid cells
Abnormal thyroid cells obtained using needle aspiration are viewed through a microscope in the laboratory by a specialist. These cells, taken from an abnormal lump, are all cancerous.

thyroid cancer spreads most often to the lymph nodes. Exposure to radiation increases the risk of developing papillary cancer. Follicular thyroid cancer is less common and may spread to the lungs or the bones. Medullary cancer of the thyroid is rare and is usually associated with multiple endocrine neoplasia (opposite page), an inherited condition.

What are the symptoms?

The symptoms depend on the type of thyroid cancer, but they often include:

- Painless, hard lump in the neck.
- Difficulty swallowing.
- Hoarseness.

The first symptom of papillary thyroid cancer may be a lump in the side of the neck due to enlarged lymph nodes.

What might be done?

If you develop a lump in your neck, your doctor will examine you and may arrange for a blood test to measure thyroid hormone levels. The thyroid gland may be imaged using ultrasound scanning (p.250) or radionuclide scanning (p.251). Your doctor may carry out a needle aspiration of the thyroid gland (above) to remove cells from the lump. The extracted cells are then examined to see if they are cancerous.

Thyroid cancer is usually treated by surgical removal of the whole thyroid gland. Further treatment often involves drinking a dose of radioactive iodine in solution. The iodine accumulates in the remaining thyroid tissue and destroys cancer cells that may still be present. After treatment you will need to take thyroid hormone drugs for the rest of your life (*see* DRUGS FOR HYPOTHYROIDISM, p.932). If thyroid cancer is diagnosed and treated early, the survival rate after 5 years is as high as 95 percent.

WWW ONLINE SITES: p.1028, p.1033

Hyperparathyroidism

Overproduction of parathyroid hormone, which may lead to a high level of calcium in the blood

 AGE More common over age 50

 GENDER More common in females

 GENETICS In some cases, the condition is inherited

 LIFESTYLE Not a significant factor

Parathyroid hormone (PTH), which is produced by four pea-sized parathyroid glands embedded in the thyroid tissue, helps regulate levels of calcium in the body. Overproduction of PTH is called hyperparathyroidism and leads to high calcium levels in the blood. The condition rarely develops before age 50 and is four times more common in women.

What are the causes?

The most common cause of hyperparathyroidism is a tumor in one or more of the four parathyroid glands. In some cases, development of parathyroid tumors is associated with the inherited disorder multiple endocrine neoplasia (opposite page), in which tumors form in several endocrine glands. Parathyroid tumors are rarely cancerous.

The parathyroid glands may become enlarged and overproduce PTH in an attempt to compensate for disorders that cause a low level of calcium in the blood, such as chronic kidney failure (p.706). In these cases, the condition is called secondary hyperparathyroidism.

What are the symptoms?

A slightly raised level of calcium in the blood due to hyperparathyroidism may not cause obvious symptoms. However, people with a very high calcium level may develop the following symptoms:

- Abdominal pain.
- Nausea and vomiting.
- Constipation.
- Increased urination and thirst.
- Depression.

An abnormally high level of calcium in the blood may also lead to dehydration, confusion, and unconsciousness and can be life-threatening. Serious complications of hyperparathyroidism include the formation of kidney stones (p.701), due to a buildup of calcium, and bone fractures (p.392), resulting from calcium gradually leaking out of the bone into the bloodstream.

WHAT MIGHT BE DONE?

If you develop the symptoms of hyperparathyroidism, your doctor is likely to arrange for you to have blood tests to assess kidney function and to check for elevated levels of calcium and PTH. If you have not experienced symptoms, hyperparathyroidism is usually detected by chance during a routine checkup. Sometimes, the condition is diagnosed during investigations to look for the cause of kidney stones.

You may not require treatment if the level of calcium in your blood is only slightly elevated; however, your blood calcium level and kidney function will need to be monitored annually. If your calcium levels are very high, you will be given fluids and drugs intravenously in the hospital to lower blood calcium.

If a parathyroid tumor is accompanied by high blood calcium levels, the affected parathyroid gland will need to be surgically removed. You may require calcium supplements immediately after surgery, but body calcium levels usually return to normal after a few days. If possible, the cause of secondary hyperparathyroidism will be treated; otherwise, some of the parathyroid glands may be surgically removed.

(WWW) ONLINE SITES: p.1033

Hypoparathyroidism

Underproduction of parathyroid hormone, which may lead to a low level of calcium in the blood

 GENDER More common in females

 GENETICS Sometimes runs in families

 AGE LIFESTYLE Not significant factors

Hypoparathyroidism occurs when the parathyroid glands produce an inadequate amount of parathyroid hormone (PTH), which regulates the amount of calcium in the body. A lack of PTH results in an abnormally low level of calcium in the blood and may lead to disorders of the muscles and nerves, which need calcium in order to function properly. In rare cases, hypoparathyroidism is present from birth. It is twice as common in women as men and sometimes runs in families.

Muscular spasm
A muscular spasm has caused this hand to turn inward, the fingers to bend, and the thumb to turn across the palm. This spasm, due to low calcium levels, is a symptom of hypoparathyroidism.

WHAT ARE THE CAUSES?

Damage to the parathyroid glands during surgery on the thyroid gland is the most common cause of hypoparathyroidism. In this case, the disorder tends to develop suddenly. Hypothyroidism is sometimes associated with autoimmune disorders, in which the body attacks its own tissues, and with the blood disorder pernicious anemia (*see* MEGALOBLASTIC ANEMIA, p.448).

WHAT ARE THE SYMPTOMS?

If hypoparathyroidism develops after thyroid surgery, symptoms appear within a few hours. In other cases, symptoms develop gradually and are usually less severe. In either case, symptoms are due to low calcium levels and include:

- Tetany (muscular spasm) in the feet, the hands, and sometimes the throat.
- Tingling and numbness in the hands, the feet, and around the mouth.
- Seizures.

If the condition is left untreated, long-term complications, such as cataracts (p.573), may develop.

WHAT MIGHT BE DONE?

Your doctor will probably arrange for blood tests in order to measure the levels of PTH and calcium in your blood.

If the symptoms are severe, you may require emergency hospital treatment, including intravenous injections of calcium to relieve extreme muscle spasms. Lifelong treatment with supplements of calcium (*see* MINERALS, p.929) and vitamin D (*see* VITAMINS, p.927) may be necessary, as well as regular tests to monitor your blood calcium level.

(WWW) ONLINE SITES: p.1033

Multiple endocrine neoplasia

A rare inherited condition in which tumors develop in several of the endocrine glands

 GENETICS Due to an abnormal gene inherited from one parent

 AGE GENDER LIFESTYLE Not significant factors

In the rare condition known as multiple endocrine neoplasia (MEN), tumors form in several of the endocrine glands around the body. The condition exists in many forms, each caused by a different abnormal gene. In each case, this abnormal gene is inherited in an autosomal dominant manner, which means that the condition can be inherited from just one parent (*see* GENE DISORDERS, p.269). Each child of an affected person has a 1 in 2 chance of inheriting the abnormal gene. MEN may appear at any age, but some people with the abnormal gene never develop the disorder.

Tumors may occur in several glands at the same time or at different times over a period of years. In the most common type of MEN, tumors develop in the pancreas, parathyroid glands, and pituitary gland (*see* PITUITARY TUMORS, p.676). Less commonly, MEN causes tumors to develop in the adrenal glands (*see* PHEOCHROMOCYTOMA, p.686) and the thyroid gland. Thyroid tumors may be cancerous (*see* THYROID CANCER, p.681), but tumors that form in the other endocrine glands are usually noncancerous. The affected glands may produce excess hormones.

WHAT MIGHT BE DONE?

If your doctor detects an abnormality in one gland, he or she may arrange for you to have blood tests to check the function of the other endocrine glands. If you have MEN, your family may be offered screening tests (*see* TESTS FOR ABNORMAL GENES, p.239). Those who have the abnormal gene can be monitored to detect tumors at an early stage.

Tumors are usually removed surgically. After treatment, you will probably be monitored periodically to check for endocrine abnormalities. If endocrine tumors are diagnosed early, they can usually be treated successfully.

(WWW) ONLINE SITES: p.1032, p.1033

ADRENAL GLAND DISORDERS

The body has two adrenal glands, one sitting above each kidney. Hormones produced by the adrenal glands are vital in controlling body chemistry. If adrenal hormone levels become imbalanced, the effects can be serious, widespread throughout the body, and even life-threatening. However, these disorders are rare.

KEY ANATOMY

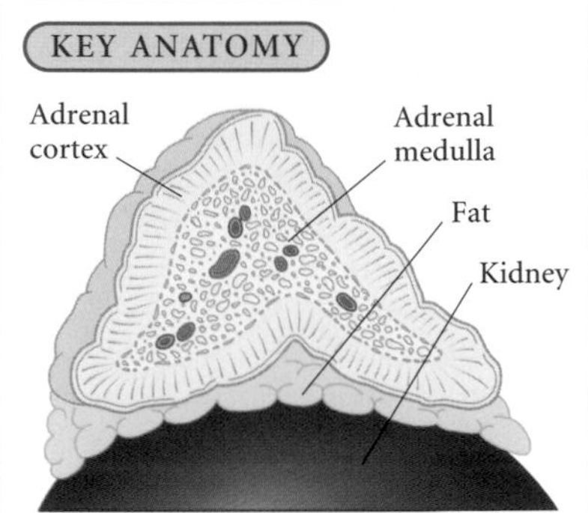
Adrenal cortex
Adrenal medulla
Fat
Kidney

For more information about the structure and function of the adrenal glands, *see* pp.670–675.

Adrenal gland disorders may involve either the over- or underproduction of adrenal hormones. This section first discusses disorders in which adrenal hormones are overproduced. The overproduction of adrenal hormones is most commonly due to the presence of an adrenal tumor. These tumors are usually noncancerous and can often be removed by means of surgery.

The final article discusses Addison's disease, a disorder in which the adrenal gland underproduces hormones. The lack of adrenal hormones is frequently caused by an autoimmune disorder that damages the gland. Addison's disease is often treated successfully with synthetic hormones.

Adrenal disorders are sometimes caused by changes in the levels of the hormones that are produced by the pituitary gland (*see* PITUITARY GLAND DISORDERS, pp.676–678). There is also an extremely rare adrenal disorder that is caused by a genetic defect (*see* CONGENITAL ADRENAL HYPERPLASIA, p.866). Disorders that are due to the abnormal production of sex hormones by the adrenal glands are described elsewhere in the book (*see* MALE HORMONAL DISORDERS, pp.728–729, and MENSTRUAL, MENOPAUSAL, AND HORMONAL PROBLEMS, pp.734–740).

Adrenal tumors

Tumors in the adrenal glands, usually noncancerous, that may produce excess adrenal hormones

AGE GENDER GENETICS LIFESTYLE
Risk factors depend on the type

Tumors of the adrenal glands are rare, and in 9 in 10 cases they are noncancerous. The tumors almost always occur in only one adrenal gland, and their effects depend on which part of the gland is affected. Most adrenal tumors secrete excessive amounts of one of the adrenal hormones, which can upset metabolism (the chemical reactions that are constantly occurring in the body) and water balance. The hormones may also alter the body's response to stress.

WHAT ARE THE TYPES?

Adrenal tumors can develop in either the cortex (outer layer) or the medulla (center) of the adrenal gland.

Adrenal tumors in the cortex may secrete corticosteroids, aldosterone, or androgens (sex hormones). The overproduction of corticosteroids causes changes in physical appearance as well as in body chemistry (*see* CUSHING SYNDROME, right) and may lead to serious complications. An excess of the hormone aldosterone, a condition known as hyperaldosteronism (opposite page), disturbs the body's salt and water balance and is a rare cause of high blood pressure (*see* HYPERTENSION, p.403). A high level of androgens in women may lead to the development of male characteristics (*see* VIRILIZATION, p.740); in males, an excess often goes unnoticed.

Tumors in the adrenal medulla are known as pheochromocytomas (p.686). They produce large amounts of either or both of the hormones epinephrine and norepinephrine. These excessive levels cause sweating, high blood pressure, and palpitations.

WHAT MIGHT BE DONE?

Adrenal tumors are usually diagnosed by detecting abnormal levels of adrenal hormones in the blood. Imaging tests, such as MRI (p.248) and CT scanning (p.247), may also be carried out to look for abnormalities in the adrenal glands.

Most adrenal tumors can be treated by surgical removal. In the rare cases in which an adrenal tumor is found to be cancerous, further treatment with radiation therapy (p.279) or chemotherapy (p.278) may also be necessary.

WWW ONLINE SITES: p.1028, p.1033

Cushing syndrome

Changes in body chemistry and physical appearance caused by excessive amounts of corticosteroid hormones

GENDER More common in females

AGE GENETICS LIFESTYLE
Not significant factors

Corticosteroid hormones are involved in the regulation of metabolism (the chemical reactions that continually occur in the body) and play a part in the control of salt and water balance and blood pressure. In Cushing syndrome, an excess of corticosteroids causes disruption of these control mechanisms. The distribution of fat around the body and the growth of body hair are affected, resulting in significant changes in physical appearance. Depression and other psychological problems may also occur. Cushing syndrome is more common in women than in men.

WHAT ARE THE CAUSES?

The most common cause of Cushing syndrome is long-term treatment with oral corticosteroid drugs (p.930), such as prednisone, which are used to treat rheumatoid arthritis (p.377) and other inflammatory conditions. These drugs exaggerate the effects of corticosteroids produced by the adrenal glands. Less commonly, Cushing syndrome is due to overproduction of corticosteroids by the adrenal glands. This may be caused by a hormone-secreting tumor in one of the adrenal glands (*see* ADRENAL TUMORS, opposite page) or in the pituitary gland, which controls the production of hormones in the adrenal glands (*see* PITUITARY TUMORS, p.676).

Some cancers, such as primary lung cancer (p.503), may produce substances that act like pituitary hormones, some of which can cause Cushing syndrome.

WHAT ARE THE SYMPTOMS?

The symptoms appear gradually and become increasingly obvious over a period of weeks or months. Any of the following symptoms may develop:

- Changes in the face, which may become red and rounded.
- Weight gain concentrated around the chest and abdomen.
- Excessive growth of facial or body hair (more noticeable in women).
- In women, irregular menstruation. Eventually, menstruation may stop.
- Reddish-purple stretch marks on the abdomen, thighs, and arms.
- Pads of fat between the shoulder blades at the base of the neck.
- Difficulty climbing stairs, associated with muscle wasting and weakness of the legs. Arms may also be affected.
- Tendency to bruise easily, especially on the limbs.
- Acne.
- Lack or loss of sexual drive; men may become impotent.
- Depression and mood swings.

If the disorder is left untreated, it may lead to complications such as high blood pressure (*see* HYPERTENSION, p.403), thinning of the bones (*see* OSTEOPOROSIS, p.368), diabetes mellitus (p.687), and chronic heart failure (p.413).

HOW IS IT DIAGNOSED?

If you have been taking large doses of corticosteroid drugs, your doctor will probably be able to diagnose Cushing syndrome from your symptoms. Otherwise, a blood test may be carried out to look for elevated levels of natural corticosteroids. Abnormally high levels of corticosteroids may indicate that you have an adrenal tumor or that your adrenal glands are being overstimulated by the pituitary gland.

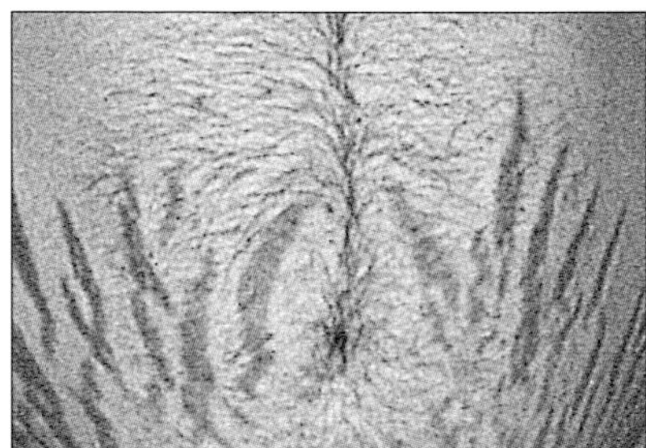

Stretch marks in Cushing syndrome
Large, reddish purple stretch marks on the trunk, especially the abdomen, are often seen in people with Cushing syndrome.

Once the diagnosis is confirmed, the cause will be investigated in more detail. You may require hospital tests to distinguish between raised hormone levels that may be due to a pituitary tumor and those possibly due to an adrenal tumor. MRI (p.248) or CT scanning (p.247) of the adrenal glands may be performed.

WHAT IS THE TREATMENT?

The treatment of Cushing syndrome depends on the underlying cause. If you are on a long-term course of corticosteroid drugs, your doctor may reduce your dosage or, if possible, discontinue the treatment. However, you should never stop taking corticosteroid drugs without first consulting your doctor.

If the cause is a tumor in one of the adrenal glands, your doctor may initially prescribe drugs to lower corticosteroid levels. After that, it may be necessary to have the affected adrenal gland surgically removed.

If the adrenal glands have been overstimulated by a pituitary tumor, this tumor may be surgically removed. In most cases the surgery is successful but radiation therapy (p.279) or chemotherapy (p.278) may be necessary to destroy any remaining abnormal cells.

You may need to take small doses of corticosteroid drugs for several months after surgery until your adrenal gland or glands adapt and produce normal amounts of hormones. In rare cases, if both adrenal glands are removed, you will need to take corticosteroid drugs for life. The symptoms of Cushing syndrome should then gradually improve.

WWW ONLINE SITES: p.1033

Hyperaldosteronism

Changes in body chemistry caused by an excess of the hormone aldosterone

AGE More common over age 30

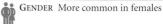

GENDER More common in females

GENETICS LIFESTYLE Not significant factors

Aldosterone is a hormone that is produced by the outer layers of the adrenal glands and acts on the kidneys to regulate salt balance and blood pressure. Overproduction of aldosterone by one or both adrenal glands is called hyperaldosteronism and leads to a high level of salt in the body and loss of the mineral potassium in the urine. High salt levels cause high blood pressure (*see* HYPERTENSION, p.403), but fewer than 2 in 100 people with high blood pressure have hyperaldosteronism.

Hyperaldosteronism is usually due to a noncancerous tumor in the adrenal cortex. It may also result from other conditions, such as chronic heart failure (p.413), cirrhosis (p.647), and nephrotic syndrome (p.700). Hyperaldosteronism due to an adrenal tumor is more common after age 30 and in women.

WHAT ARE THE SYMPTOMS?

Hyperaldosteronism does not always produce noticeable symptoms. Sometimes, however, symptoms do develop and may include:

- Muscle weakness and cramps.
- Frequent passage of large amounts of urine, accompanied by thirst.

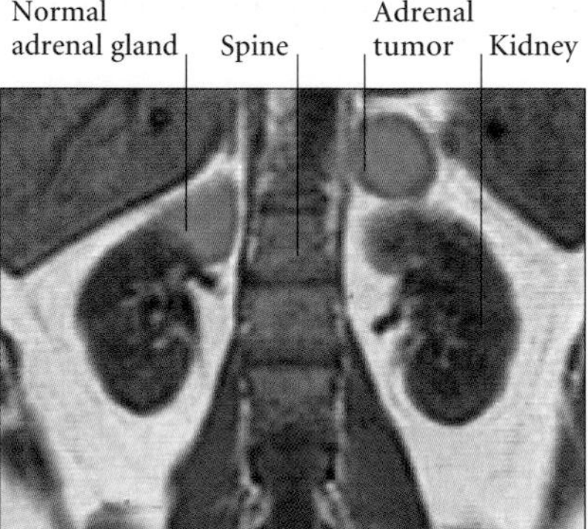
Normal adrenal gland
Spine
Adrenal tumor
Kidney

Aldosterone-producing tumor
This vertical CT scan through the upper abdomen shows an adrenal tumor. Such tumors may cause hyperaldosteronism.

Hyperaldosteronism also causes high blood pressure, which rarely produces noticeable symptoms but may be detected during a checkup.

WHAT MIGHT BE DONE?

Your doctor may arrange for blood tests to measure salt, potassium, and aldosterone levels and CT scanning (p.247) to look for a tumor. If a tumor is found, the adrenal gland may be removed surgically. Treatment may include drugs to block the action of excess aldosterone and drugs to control blood pressure (*see* ANTIHYPERTENSIVE DRUGS, p.897).

(WWW) ONLINE SITES: p.1033

Pheochromocytoma

A tumor in the center of the adrenal gland that produces an excess of the hormones epinephrine and norepinephrine

 AGE Most common between the ages of 30 and 60 but may occur at any age

 GENETICS Sometimes runs in families

 GENDER LIFESTYLE Not significant factors

A pheochromocytoma is a tumor that develops in the medulla (center) of one of the adrenal glands. Pheochromocytomas produce excessive amounts of the hormones epinephrine and norepinephrine, which are normally secreted by the adrenal glands and act to prepare the body for action or stress.

Pheochromocytomas are rare. Only 1 in 10 is cancerous. Such tumors may develop as part of multiple endocrine neoplasia (p.683), an inherited condition in which tumors occur in several glands of the endocrine system.

WHAT ARE THE SYMPTOMS?

Exercise, emotion, or even a change in body position can trigger the tumor to release hormones into the blood. When this happens you may experience the following symptoms:

- Palpitations (awareness of an abnormally fast or irregular heartbeat).
- Pale, cold skin, and profuse sweating.
- Nausea and vomiting.
- Feelings of intense anxiety.
- Headache.

Raised levels of epinephrine and norepinephrine also lead to a rise in blood pressure (*see* HYPERTENSION, p.403).

WHAT MIGHT BE DONE?

If your doctor suspects a pheochromocytoma, he or she may ask you to collect your urine for 24 hours so that tests can be performed on it. Chemicals in the urine provide information about levels of epinephrine and norepinephrine in your body. If the levels of these hormones are higher than normal, you will probably have MRI (p.248) or CT scanning (p.247) to look for a tumor.

At first, drug treatment is used to lower your blood pressure. The tumor is then removed surgically. People who have had a noncancerous pheochromocytoma removed usually make a full recovery. However, cancerous tumors are more likely to recur.

(WWW) ONLINE SITES: p.1028, p.1033

Addison's disease

Insufficient levels of corticosteroid hormones in the blood, causing changes in body chemistry

 GENDER Twice as common in females

 GENETICS Sometimes runs in families

 AGE LIFESTYLE Not significant factors

Corticosteroids are adrenal hormones involved in metabolism (the chemical reactions constantly occurring in the body). They also help control blood pressure and salt and water balance in the body. In the rare illness Addison's disease, underproduction of corticosteroids leads to changes in body chemistry. Twice as common in women as in men, the disorder sometimes runs in families.

The usual cause of Addison's disease is damage to an adrenal gland by an autoimmune disorder (p.461), in which the body attacks its own tissues. Less common causes of the disorder include HIV infection and AIDS (p.295), tuberculosis (p.491), lack of stimulation from the pituitary gland (*see* HYPOPITUITARISM, p.678), and sudden, severe low blood pressure (*see* SHOCK, p.414).

Corticosteroid secretion is also suppressed if you take corticosteroid drugs (p.930) long-term for another disorder. If you suddenly stop treatment, undergo surgery, or become ill for any reason, the levels of natural corticosteroids fall rapidly and become dangerously low.

WHAT ARE THE SYMPTOMS?

The symptoms of Addison's disease appear gradually but become increasingly obvious over a period of several weeks or months. You may develop:

- Vague feeling of ill health.
- Fatigue and weakness.
- Gradual loss of appetite.
- Weight loss.
- Skin pigmentation similar to suntan, especially in the creases of the palms and on knuckles, elbows, and knees.

People with Addison's disease usually develop low blood pressure (*see* HYPOTENSION, p.414). If the corticosteroid levels become very low, a crisis may occur, particularly during an illness or after an injury. The crisis is caused by an excessive loss of salt and water and results in dehydration, extreme weakness, abdominal pain, vomiting, and confusion. Left untreated, a crisis may lead to coma (p.522) and death.

HOW IS IT DIAGNOSED?

Diagnostic tests are not usually needed if you have suddenly stopped taking corticosteroid drugs. If your doctor suspects Addison's disease, he or she may arrange for a blood test to measure salt and potassium levels. Further tests may include a blood test to check levels of corticosteroid hormones. You may also be given an injection of a substance that normally stimulates the adrenal glands to produce the corticosteroid hormone hydrocortisone. If blood tests then show that your hydrocortisone levels have not increased, you probably have Addison's disease.

WHAT IS THE TREATMENT?

Addison's disease is usually treated with oral corticosteroid drugs (p.930). Injections of corticosteroids may be needed to treat severe episodes or when you are unable to take drugs orally. You may also need extra oral corticosteroids in times of stress or illness. If there is an underlying cause, it will be treated.

A very low level of corticosteroid hormones needs emergency treatment with intravenous fluids, glucose, and injections of corticosteroids. If you are taking corticosteroid drugs continually for any reason, you should carry a card or wear an identity bracelet with this information in case of a crisis.

(WWW) ONLINE SITES: p.1033

METABOLIC DISORDERS

The chemical processes that take place in the body are known collectively as metabolism. These processes are largely controlled by hormones, and either overproduction or underproduction of a particular hormone can have wide-ranging effects on the body's internal chemistry. Metabolic disorders may also be caused by underlying conditions affecting major organs that regulate metabolism, such as the liver and the kidneys.

One important group of metabolic disorders is due to faulty or blocked chemical pathways, which cause the buildup of a chemical that is usually eliminated from the body. As the chemical accumulates, it may damage organs such as the brain and the liver. Many of these disorders, such as hemochromatosis, are due to genetic defects, some of which may run in families. If you have a close relative with one of these disorders, you may be at increased risk of developing the metabolic disorder yourself (*see* GENE DISORDERS, p.269).

Most metabolic disorders can be diagnosed using blood or urine tests to measure levels of hormones or other specific chemicals. If the disorders are recognized early, they can sometimes be treated by a change in diet or the replacement of missing hormones or other chemicals. The sooner treatment is started, the better the prospects are for avoiding permanent damage.

In this section, the opening article describes diabetes mellitus, the most common metabolic disorder. The next discusses hypoglycemia, a condition sometimes associated with treatment for diabetes. The final articles cover disorders, including amyloidosis, in which abnormal levels of particular chemicals collect in the body.

Certain metabolic disorders are also disorders of particular endocrine (hormone-secreting) glands and are described elsewhere (*see* PITUITARY GLAND DISORDERS, pp.676–678; THYROID AND PARATHYROID GLAND DISORDERS, pp.679–683; and ADRENAL GLAND DISORDERS, pp.684–686).

Diabetes mellitus

Inability of the body to use glucose for energy due to inadequate amounts of or loss of sensitivity to the hormone insulin

GENETICS Sometimes runs in families

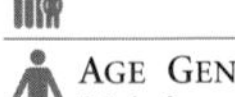
AGE GENDER LIFESTYLE Risk factors depend on the type

Diabetes mellitus is one of the most common chronic diseases occurring in the US, affecting more than 1 in 20 people. In this disorder, either the pancreas produces insufficient amounts of the hormone insulin or body cells become resistant to the hormone's effects.

Normally, insulin is produced by the pancreas and enables the body's cells to absorb the sugar glucose (their main energy source) from the bloodstream. In diabetes mellitus, the cells have to use other sources of energy, which may lead to a buildup of toxic by-products in the body. Unused glucose accumulates in the blood and urine, causing symptoms such as excessive urination and thirst.

Treatment is designed to control glucose levels in the blood. Among people treated for diabetes mellitus, 1 in 10 depends on self-administered injections of insulin for life. The rest need a carefully managed diet and often oral drugs. These measures enable most affected people to lead normal lives. However, in many cases, complications eventually develop, although their onset may be delayed by treatment. Complications include problems with the eyes, kidneys, cardiovascular system, and nervous system. Diabetes mellitus also weakens the immune system and thus increases susceptibility to infections such as cystitis (p.709). The condition is usually permanent, and there is no known cure.

WHAT ARE THE TYPES?

There are two main forms of diabetes mellitus, designated as type 1 diabetes and type 2 diabetes.

TYPE 1 DIABETES This form of diabetes occurs when the pancreas produces far too little insulin or produces none at all. The disorder usually develops suddenly in childhood or adolescence. Although dietary measures are also important, it must be treated with insulin injections. About 80,000 people in Canada have this type of diabetes.

TYPE 2 DIABETES Type 2 is by far the most common form of diabetes. In this condition, the pancreas continues to secrete insulin, but cells in the body become resistant to its effects. This form of diabetes mainly affects people over age 40 and is more common in overweight people. It develops slowly and is often unnoticed for many years. Sometimes the condition may be treated with dietary measures alone, but oral drugs and sometimes insulin injections may become necessary. About 750,000 people in Canada have type 2 diabetes.

Diabetes mellitus can sometimes develop during pregnancy (*see* DIABETES DEVELOPING IN PREGNANCY, p.788). This condition is called gestational diabetes and is usually treated with insulin to maintain the health of the mother and baby. Gestational diabetes usually disappears after childbirth; however, women who have had it are at increased risk of developing type 2 diabetes in later life.

WHAT ARE THE CAUSES?

Type 1 diabetes is usually caused by an abnormal bodily reaction, in which the immune system destroys insulin-secreting cells in the pancreas. The trigger of the abnormal reaction is unknown, but it may be a viral infection. In some cases, destruction of the insulin-secreting tissues occurs after inflammation of the pancreas (*see* ACUTE PANCREATITIS, p.652).

Genetics may also play a role, but the pattern of inheritance is complicated.

SELF-HELP Injecting insulin

If you need regular injections of insulin, you will be shown how to inject yourself. You can use a syringe and needle, but many people prefer insulin pens, which are easier to use and more discreet. Insulin can be injected into any fatty area, such as the upper arms, abdomen, or thighs. Insert the needle quickly into a pinch of skin and then inject the insulin slowly. You should try not to use exactly the same site each time for the injection.

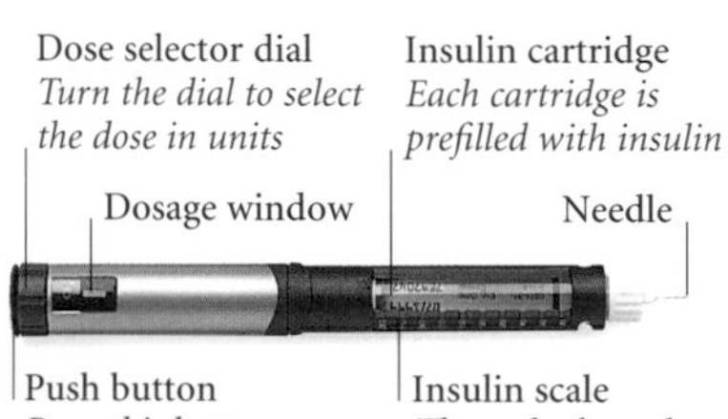
Dose selector dial
Turn the dial to select the dose in units
Insulin cartridge
Each cartridge is prefilled with insulin
Dosage window
Needle
Push button
Press this button to release the insulin
Insulin scale
The scale shows how many units are left

Insulin pen
This device for carrying and delivering insulin holds an insulin cartridge and has a dial that lets you set the required dose. Disposable needles attach to one end.

Learning to inject
After about age 10, children with diabetes can be taught how to inject themselves.

Injection site
For children, the thigh is often an easy site for injection

The child of a person who has type 1 diabetes is at greater risk of developing the same type of diabetes. However, most affected children do not have a parent with diabetes.

The causes of type 2 diabetes are less well understood, but genetics and obesity are important factors. About 1 in 3 affected people has a relative with the same type of diabetes. Type 2 diabetes is a growing problem in societies that are becoming more affluent. In such societies, food intake increases, leading to a rise in the number of overweight people and the prevalence of this condition.

Diabetes can also be caused by corticosteroid drugs (p.930) or excess levels of natural corticosteroid hormones (*see* Cushing syndrome, p.684), which oppose the action of insulin.

What are the symptoms?

Although some of the symptoms of both forms of diabetes mellitus are similar, type 1 diabetes tends to develop more quickly and become more severe. The symptoms of type 2 may not be obvious or may go unnoticed until a routine medical checkup. The main symptoms of both forms may include:

- Excessive urination.
- Thirst and a dry mouth.
- Insufficient sleep because of the need to urinate at night.
- Lack of energy.
- Blurry vision.

Type 1 diabetes may also cause weight loss. In some people, the first sign of the disorder is ketoacidosis, a condition in which toxic chemicals called ketones build up in the blood. These chemicals are produced when body tissues are unable to take up glucose from the blood, due to inadequate production of insulin, and have to use fats for energy. Ketoacidosis can also occur in people with type 1 diabetes who are taking insulin if they miss several doses or develop another illness (because any form of illness increases the body's requirement for insulin). The symptoms of ketoacidosis may include:

- Nausea and vomiting, sometimes with abdominal pain.
- Deep breathing.
- Acetone smell to the breath (like nail-polish remover).
- Confusion.

The development of these symptoms is a medical emergency because they can lead to severe dehydration and coma (p.522) if not treated urgently. Emergency treatment for ketoacidosis includes intravenous infusion of fluids to correct dehydration and restore the chemical balance in the blood and insulin injections to enable cells to absorb glucose from the blood.

Are there complications?

Diabetes mellitus may give rise to both short-term and long-term complications. Short-term problems are usually easy to remedy, but long-term complications are hard to control and can lead to premature death.

SHORT-TERM COMPLICATIONS Poorly controlled or untreated type 1 diabetes may lead to ketoacidosis, the symptoms of which are described at left.

One very common complication of insulin treatment for either type of diabetes is hypoglycemia (p.691), a disorder in which the blood sugar falls to abnormally low levels. Hypoglycemia is often caused by an imbalance between food intake and the dose of insulin. The disorder is more common in people with type 1 diabetes but may also affect people with type 2 diabetes who take sulfonylurea drugs (*see* Drugs for diabetes mellitus, p.931). If untreated, it can cause unconsciousness and seizures.

LONG-TERM COMPLICATIONS Certain long-standing problems pose the main health threat to people with diabetes and eventually affect even people with well-controlled diabetes. Close control of the blood sugar level reduces the risk of developing these problems, and early recognition of complications helps in their control. For these reasons, all affected people should see their doctor at least four times a year (*see* Living with diabetes, p.690). Type 2 diabetes is often not diagnosed until years after its onset. As a result, complications may be evident at the time of initial diagnosis.

People with diabetes are at increased risk of cardiovascular disorders (*see* Diabetic vascular disease, p.432). Large blood vessels may be damaged by atherosclerosis (p.402), which is a major cause of coronary artery disease (p.405) and stroke (p.532). Elevated levels of cholesterol in the blood (*see* Hypercholesterolemia, p.691), which accelerates the development of atherosclerosis, is more common in people with diabetes. Diabetes is also associated with hypertension (p.403), another risk factor for cardiovascular disease.

Other long-term complications result from damage to small blood vessels throughout the body. Damage to blood vessels in the light-sensitive retina at the back of the eye may cause diabetic retinopathy (p.579). Diabetes also increases the risk of developing cataracts (p.573) in the eyes. People with diabetes mellitus should have their eyes examined yearly by an ophthalmologist.

If diabetes affects blood vessels that supply nerves, it may cause nerve damage (*see* DIABETIC NEUROPATHY, p.545). There may be a gradual loss of sensation, starting at the hands and feet and sometimes gradually extending up the limbs. Symptoms may also include dizziness upon standing and erectile dysfunction (p.770) in men. Loss of feeling, combined with poor circulation, makes the legs more susceptible to ulcers (*see* LEG ULCERS, p.350) and gangrene (p.435).

Damage to small blood vessels in the kidneys (*see* DIABETIC KIDNEY DISEASE, p.705) may lead to chronic kidney failure (p.706) or end-stage kidney failure (p.708), which requires lifelong dialysis (p.707) or a kidney transplant (p.708).

How is it diagnosed?

Your doctor will first ask you to provide a urine sample, which will be tested for glucose. The diagnosis is confirmed by a blood test to check for a high glucose level. If the level is borderline, you may undergo another blood test after fasting overnight. Your blood may also be tested for glycosylated hemoglobin, an altered form of the pigment in red blood cells, which increases in concentration when the blood glucose level has been high for several weeks or months.

What is the treatment?

For anyone with diabetes mellitus, the aim of treatment is maintain the level of glucose in the blood within the normal range without marked fluctuations. This aim may be achieved with dietary measures, a combination of diet and insulin injections, or diet and pills that lower blood glucose levels. Treatment is usually lifelong, and you will have to take responsibility for the daily adjustment of your diet and medication.

TYPE 1 DIABETES This form of diabetes mellitus is nearly always treated with insulin injections. Oral drugs alone are ineffective. Insulin is available in various forms, including short-acting, long-acting, and combinations of both forms (*see* DRUGS FOR DIABETES MELLITUS, p.931). Treatment regimens need to be individually tailored and they may include combinations of insulin and oral drugs. Your doctor will talk to you about your needs and arrange for you to learn how to inject yourself (*see* INJECTING INSULIN, opposite page). You will also have to control your diet and monitor your blood glucose as described below. If the diabetes is difficult to control, you may be given an insulin pump, which dispenses insulin through a catheter that is inserted into your skin.

The only way to cure type 1 diabetes is by a pancreas transplant, but this surgery is not routinely offered because the body may reject the new organ and because lifelong treatment with immunosuppressant drugs (p.906) is needed afterward. However, some people are given a pancreas transplant at the same time as a kidney transplant. A method is currently being devised to transplant insulin-secreting cells isolated from a normal pancreas, but this technique is still at an experimental stage.

TYPE 2 DIABETES Many people with this form of diabetes can control their blood glucose levels by exercising regularly and following a healthy diet to maintain ideal weight.

You should follow general guidelines for a healthy diet (*see* DIET AND HEALTH, pp.48–54) and seek the guidance of a dietitian if necessary. Try to keep fat intake low, and obtain energy from complex carbohydrates (such as bread and rice) to minimize fluctuations in the blood glucose level. The diet should have a fixed calorie content. The proportions of protein, carbohydrate, and fat must be consistent to keep a balance between food intake and medication.

TEST Monitoring your blood glucose

You can monitor your blood glucose level using a digital meter. The method of use varies, depending on the type of meter, but usually involves applying a drop of blood to a test strip impregnated with a chemical that reacts with glucose. Checking your blood glucose at least once a day or as often as your doctor recommends allows you to monitor your treatment to confirm that it is effective and to alter it as necessary.

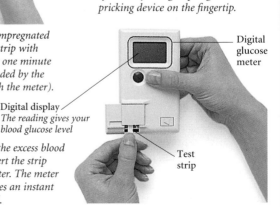

Pricking device

1 Before starting, wash your hands thoroughly and dry them. Once your hands are clean, obtain a drop of blood by using a spring-loaded pricking device on the fingertip.

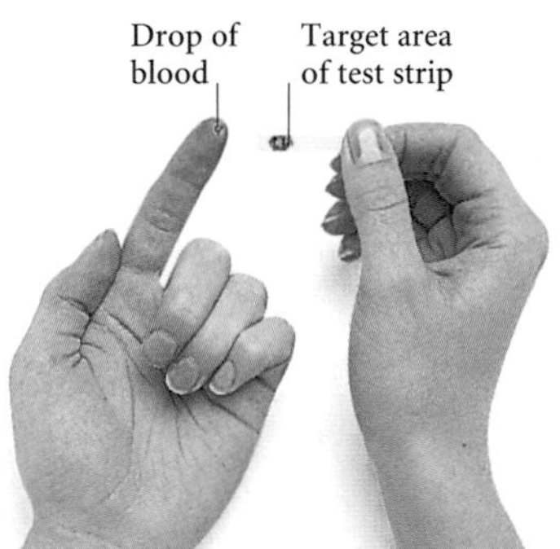
Drop of blood
Target area of test strip

2 Cover the chemically impregnated target area of the test strip with the drop of blood. Wait for one minute (or as long as is recommended by the instructions that come with the meter).

Digital glucose meter

Digital display
The reading gives your blood glucose level

Test strip

3 Finally, wipe or wash the excess blood from the strip and insert the strip into the digital glucose meter. The meter analyzes the blood and gives an instant reading of the glucose level.

SELF-HELP LIVING WITH DIABETES

People with diabetes mellitus can lead normal lives, and they can continue to exercise and to eat most foods. However, it is very important to eat a healthy diet, maintain fitness, and, if necessary, lose weight. Following a healthy regimen helps minimize the risk of developing complications over time, including heart disease, circulatory problems, and kidney failure.

A HEALTHY DIET

For some people with diabetes, a healthy diet and weight loss are enough to keep blood glucose levels normal. Your diet should be high in complex carbohydrates, such as rice, pasta, and legumes, and low in fats, particularly fats of animal origin.

Complex carbohydrates
Rice, pasta, legumes, and other complex carbohydrates are the basis of a healthy diet.

DRINKING AND SMOKING

Alcohol in moderation is safe for most people, but in excess it may lower blood glucose levels. In addition, it is high in calories and may cause weight gain. Smoking is very harmful because it greatly increases the risk of long-term complications, such as heart disease and stroke.

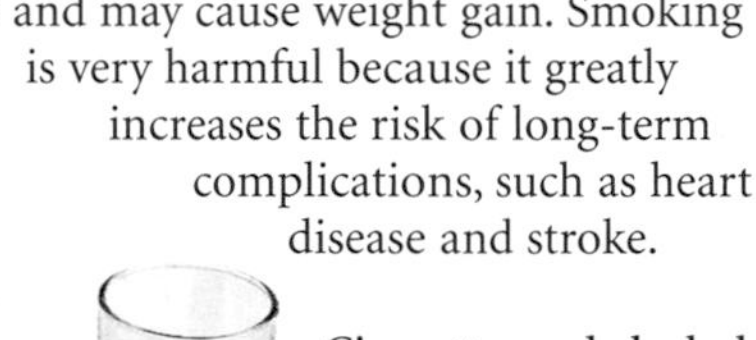

Cigarettes and alcohol
If you have diabetes and smoke, you should stop. If you drink alcohol, you can continue to do so, but you should make sure that you drink in moderation.

SPECIAL CARE FOR YOUR FEET

Diabetes can increase the risk of skin infections and ulcers on the feet. You can reduce the risk by wearing shoes that fit comfortably, visiting a podiatrist regularly, not walking barefoot, and cutting your toenails straight across. You should inspect and clean your feet daily and consult your doctor promptly if you develop a sore on your foot.

Foot care
Wash and dry your feet carefully. If the skin is dry, use a moisturizer every day.

EXERCISE AND SPORTS

Regular exercise makes you feel healthier, reduces the risk of heart disease, stroke, and high blood pressure, and can help if you need to lose weight. If you have insulin-dependent diabetes, you may need to monitor your blood glucose before, during, and after exercise to check how the activity affects your requirements for both insulin and food.

Strenuous exercise
Blood glucose levels usually drop during strenuous exercise. You may need to adjust your dose of insulin or eat more before strenuous activity.

Moderate exercise
Regular moderate exercise reduces the chance of developing coronary artery disease and may improve the control of your diabetes.

YOUR MEDICAL CHECKUP

You should visit your doctor every few months so that the doctor can detect problems related to diabetes at an early stage and treat them effectively. Management includes a neurological exam, an examination of your pulse and blood pressure, and a formal eye exam at least once a year. Your levels of blood sugar and glycosylated hemoglobin will be tested. Your urine will be tested to check for kidney disease.

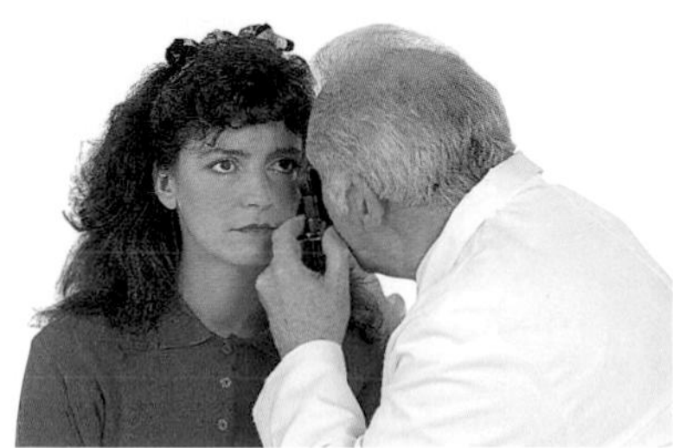

Eye examination
Inspection of the retina (the light-sensitive membrane at the back of the eye) can detect retinal damage caused by diabetes.

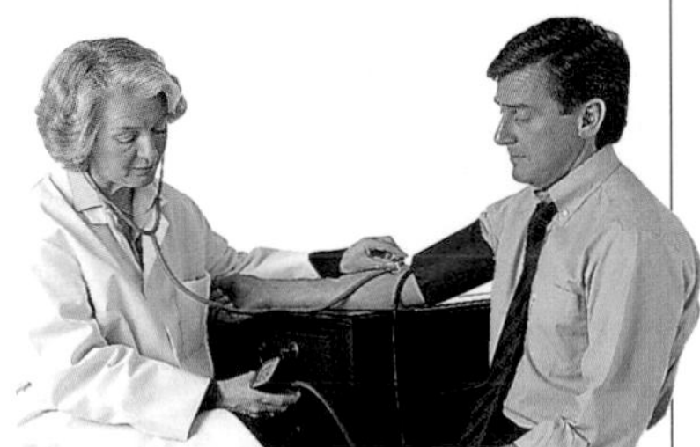

Blood pressure measurement
People with diabetes mellitus have an increased risk of high blood pressure, and regular monitoring is important.

You must also check your blood glucose regularly (*see* MONITORING YOUR BLOOD GLUCOSE, p.689). If the glucose level is higher or lower than recommended, you may need to alter your diet or adjust your insulin or drug dose with the help of your doctor. Effective monitoring is especially important if you develop another illness, such as influenza (p.287), and in other situations, such as exercising or planning to eat a larger meal than usual.

When diet is not sufficient to control your blood sugar, one or more medications may be prescribed (*see* DRUGS FOR DIABETES MELLITUS, p.931). You will probably begin with oral drugs, such as sulfonylureas, which stimulate the pancreas to release insulin, or metformin, which helps body tissues absorb glucose. You may also be given acarbose, which slows the absorption of glucose from the intestine and prevents fluctuations in the blood level. If oral drugs are ineffective, you may need insulin injections.

WHAT IS THE PROGNOSIS?

Diabetes mellitus can cause premature death, usually due to cardiovascular complications. However, advances in monitoring blood glucose levels, combined with a healthy lifestyle, have made diabetes easier to control, allowing people to lead a more normal life. Self-help groups exist for affected people.

(WWW) ONLINE SITES: p.1029

Hypoglycemia

An abnormally low level of glucose in the blood, depriving body cells of glucose

AGE GENDER GENETICS LIFESTYLE Risk factors depend on the cause

In hypoglycemia, the body's cells are deprived of glucose, which is their main source of energy. Symptoms of hypoglycemia include nausea, sweating, and anxiety. The condition is usually temporary and occurs most frequently as a side effect of insulin treatment for type 1 diabetes (*see* DIABETES MELLITUS, p.687). It is less common in people who have type 2 diabetes and rare in those who do not have diabetes. Vague feelings of faintness or nausea that some people attribute to hypoglycemia are usually due to other disorders or to fatigue or stress (p.74).

WHAT ARE THE CAUSES?

In people who have type 1 diabetes, hypoglycemia is usually due to a dose of insulin that is excessive in relation to food intake and that lowers glucose levels in the blood too much. People taking insulin must balance their insulin dosage with food intake, which raises blood glucose levels, and physical activity, which lowers blood glucose. If the balance is disturbed and the glucose level falls, hypoglycemia may result.

Hypoglycemia in people with type 2 diabetes and impaired kidney function may be due to the gradual buildup of glucose-lowering drugs in the blood (*see* DRUGS FOR DIABETES MELLITUS, p.931).

The rare cases occurring in people without diabetes are usually due to serious medical problems. Such problems include severe liver disease, adrenal failure, or very rarely an insulin-secreting tumor of the pancreas. In babies, especially in newborns, hypoglycemia may develop because the liver does not yet contain sufficient stores of glucose.

WHAT ARE THE SYMPTOMS?

When blood glucose levels become low, the symptoms of hypoglycemia develop rapidly. Some people may get warning signs of an attack, which may include:

- Sweating, nausea, and anxiety.
- Rapid, forceful heartbeat.

If blood glucose continues to fall, further symptoms may develop, including:

- Confusion.
- Slurred speech and unsteady movements, similar to drunkenness.
- Seizures (particularly in children).

Unconsciousness may result. If not treated promptly, the condition may cause permanent brain damage or death.

WHAT IS THE TREATMENT?

If you have diabetes mellitus and experience the above symptoms, take food or drink containing sugar immediately. Always carry candy with you and wear a bracelet to warn people that you have diabetes. If you develop hypoglycemia for any reason and lose consciousness, you will need an immediate injection of glucagon, a hormone that restores consciousness by raising blood glucose levels. If the treatment fails or is not available, you will need emergency treatment with intravenous glucose.

(WWW) ONLINE SITES: p.1029

Hypercholesterolemia

Elevated levels of cholesterol in the blood, which increase the risk of developing cardiovascular disease

AGE More common with increasing age

GENDER More common in males

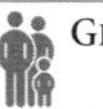
GENETICS Sometimes runs in families

LIFESTYLE A diet high in saturated fats, obesity, and lack of exercise are risk factors

In hypercholesterolemia, blood cholesterol levels are elevated. High cholesterol levels have been shown to be associated with an increased risk of coronary artery disease (p.405) and stroke (p.532) due to atherosclerosis (p.402).

Cholesterol is a substance known as a lipid. It is used in the manufacture of cell walls and in the production of bile acids (which aid the digestion of fat) and hormones. Most of the body's supply of cholesterol is produced in the liver, but some cholesterol is also derived from food, particularly from eggs, meat, and shellfish. The level of cholesterol in the body can be affected by diet (*see* DIET AND HEALTH, p.48) and other lifestyle factors.

Cholesterol is carried in the bloodstream in the form of lipid–protein molecules called lipoproteins. There are two main types of these molecules: low-density lipoproteins (called LDLs) and high-density lipoproteins (known as HDLs). LDLs carry larger amounts of cholesterol than HDLs and deposit the cholesterol around the body. A high level of LDLs in the blood increases the risk of arterial disease. The reason is that excess LDLs form fatty deposits on the walls of arteries. As these deposits grow, they restrict blood flow and can cause the formation of clots that block the vessels. HDLs pick up free molecules of cholesterol and return them to the liver to be broken down. A high level of HDLs in the blood thus protects against arterial disease.

WHAT ARE THE CAUSES?

Your cholesterol level is determined by a combination of genetic and lifestyle factors, including diet, weight, smoking, and exercise. A high cholesterol level is associated with a diet that is high in fats, particularly saturated fats (*see* CHOOSING HEALTHY FATS, p.50). Being overweight and doing little exercise also lead to high cholesterol levels. Although hypercholesterolemia almost always runs in families, about 1 in 10 people have one of the specific inherited disorders called inherited hyperlipoproteinemias (right), which affect lipid metabolism and are associated with especially elevated cholesterol levels.

A high cholesterol level does not usually cause symptoms until it leads to the development of another disorder, such as coronary artery disease.

HOW IS IT DIAGNOSED?

Regular screening to measure cholesterol levels (*see* COMMON SCREENING TESTS, p.44) depends on your age, sex, and risk factors. Testing is recommended every 5 years in males age 40–70 and females age 50–70. Testing is recommended yearly in people with several other risk factors. In people who have a family history of high cholesterol levels, heart disease, or stroke, screening may begin earlier.

The optimal range of blood cholesterol for a middle-aged North American is 115–200 mg/dL (3–5.2 mmol/L). If the total cholesterol level is over 200 mg/dL (5.2 mmol/L), your doctor may carry out a further blood test to check your levels of LDL and HDL cholesterol.

WHAT IS THE TREATMENT?

Whether or not you need treatment depends on how high your cholesterol level is and whether you have other risk factors for coronary artery disease, such as high blood pressure (*see* HYPERTENSION, p.403) or smoking. In addition, even if your blood cholesterol level falls within the normal range, you may be given treatment to lower cholesterol if you are already known to have heart disease or atherosclerosis.

If you are found to have an excessively high blood cholesterol level, your doctor may initially advise you about changes in diet and exercise habits that should lower the level. If these measures fail to lower your cholesterol level sufficiently, you may be given drugs, which you will need to take for life (*see* LIPID-LOWERING DRUGS, p.935).

(WWW) ONLINE SITES: p.1032, p.1035

Inherited hyperlipoproteinemias

Inherited conditions in which the blood contains abnormally high levels of cholesterol and/or triglycerides

AGE Present from birth, but usually become apparent in early adulthood

GENETICS Due to an abnormal gene inherited from one or both parents

LIFESTYLE A diet high in fats and lack of exercise aggravate the conditions

GENDER Not a significant factor

Many people have elevated levels of cholesterol in their blood (*see* HYPERCHOLESTEROLEMIA, p.691). In 1 in 10 affected people, blood levels of cholesterol and of lipids called triglycerides are high due to distinct genetic disorders called hyperlipoproteinemias. These disorders create especially high levels of lipoproteins and tend to produce symptoms earlier in adulthood than other hypercholesterolemias. Elevated blood levels of lipids (especially cholesterol) increase the risk of developing complications of atherosclerosis (p.402), such as coronary artery disease (p.405).

There are several forms of inherited hyperlipoproteinemias. The most common form affects about 1 in 500 people of European descent, who inherit one copy of an abnormal gene. Affected people have a cholesterol level two or three times higher than normal. There is a one in a million risk that people will inherit the abnormal gene from both parents. If two copies of the gene are inherited, the cholesterol level is six to eight times higher than normal. Affected people have a high probability of a heart attack (*see* MYOCARDIAL INFARCTION, p.410), which may occur even in childhood.

WHAT ARE THE SYMPTOMS?

Very high cholesterol levels associated with inherited hyperlipoproteinemias may cause some of the following symptoms, which develop gradually over a period of several years:

- Yellow swellings under the skin (xanthomas) on the back of the hands.
- Swellings on the tendons around the ankle and wrist joints.
- Yellow swellings on the skin of the eyelids (xanthelasmas).
- Pale yellow ring around the iris (the colored part of the eye).

Raised triglyceride levels do not usually produce any symptoms but do increase the risk of acute pancreatitis (p.652).

Men with these disorders can develop symptoms of coronary artery disease, such as chest pain (*see* ANGINA, p.407), as early as their 20s or 30s. In women, estrogen usually gives protection from these problems until after menopause.

WHAT MIGHT BE DONE?

There is no cure for inherited hyperlipoproteinemias, but symptoms can be treated with a combination of exercise, a diet that is low in cholesterol and saturated fats (*see* CHOOSING HEALTHY FATS, p.50), and lipid-lowering drugs (p.935). The prognosis varies, but early treatment can reduce the risk of a heart attack. Relatives of an affected person should have screening for the disorder.

(WWW) ONLINE SITES: p.1032, p1035

Hemochromatosis

An inherited disorder affecting body chemistry, in which iron is deposited in body tissues, causing damage to them

AGE Present from birth but does not usually become apparent until age 40

GENDER Much more common in males

GENETICS Due to an abnormal gene inherited from both parents

LIFESTYLE Excessive alcohol intake aggravates the condition

In hemochromatosis, the level of iron in the blood is too high. Excess iron gradually accumulates in organs such as the liver, pancreas, and heart. This gradual buildup of iron damages these organs. Hemochromatosis is an inherited condition that affects about 3 in 1,000 people in Canada. Men are much more likely to develop symptoms than women, who lose iron when menstruating.

WHAT ARE THE CAUSES?

Hemochromatosis is the result of an abnormal gene that causes the body to absorb too much iron from food. The gene is inherited in an autosomal recessive manner; a person must inherit one abnormal gene from each parent for symptoms to develop. If both parents are carriers (people who have just one abnormal gene instead of a pair), there is a 1 in 4 chance of their children having the disease. Carriers do not develop symptoms of the disorder. About 1 in 10 people is thought to be a carrier.

What are the symptoms?

The symptoms develop gradually and usually do not appear until after age 40. Initial symptoms may include:

- Weakness and lack of energy.
- Abdominal pain.
- Shrinking of the testes in men and loss of interest in sex.
- Pain or stiffness in the joints, particularly in the hands.
- Bronzing of the skin.

Symptoms occur earlier in people who drink excessive alcohol because alcohol increases the amount of iron that is absorbed by the intestines.

As the disease progresses, damage to organs can lead to chronic heart failure (p.413), diabetes mellitus (p.687), cirrhosis (p.647), and liver cancer (p.649).

How is it diagnosed?

Hemochromatosis is diagnosed by testing blood for an abnormally high iron level. CT scanning (p.247) or ultrasound scanning (p.250) may be used to look for liver damage. A liver biopsy (p.647) may also be carried out in order to check for iron deposits in the liver. Members of an affected person's family should have screening (p.42) for the condition. A blood test to detect the abnormal gene is available.

What is the treatment?

Treatment is aimed at removing some of the excess iron from the body. About 1 pint (500 ml) of blood is removed each week until the iron levels are normal. Thereafter, blood needs to be removed less often. If you have hemochromatosis, you should avoid alcohol and iron-rich foods. You may also need treatment for complications such as diabetes mellitus.

What is the prognosis?

Early treatment, before liver damage has occurred, can prevent the disease from reducing life expectancy. If severe organ damage has occurred, hemochromatosis is potentially life-threatening. In some cases, a heart transplant (p.427) or liver transplant (p.650) may be necessary.

(WWW) ONLINE SITES: p.1032, p.1033

Amyloidosis

A group of disorders in which abnormal proteins accumulate in internal organs

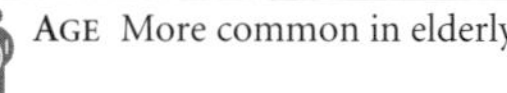
AGE More common in elderly people

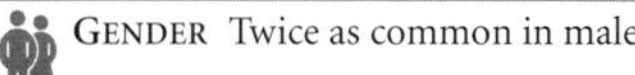
GENDER Twice as common in males

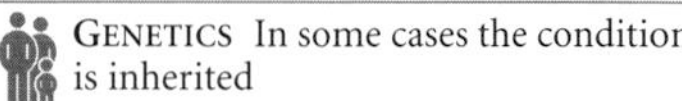
GENETICS In some cases the condition is inherited

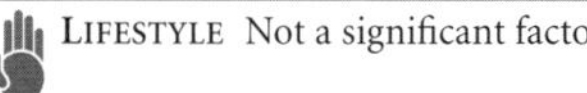
LIFESTYLE Not a significant factor

The various rare conditions known as amyloidosis develop when deposits of abnormal proteins, called amyloid, collect in organs and interfere with their function. There are various forms of amyloidosis, each of which is caused by a different type of amyloid. The condition mainly affects elderly people and is twice as common in men as in women.

Amyloidosis may be due to an abnormal gene or have no apparent cause; in these cases it is called primary amyloidosis. More commonly, it occurs as a complication of another disorder and is therefore called secondary amyloidosis. The condition may result from disorders that include chronic infections, inflammatory disorders such as rheumatoid arthritis (p.377), and the bone marrow cancer multiple myeloma (p.456).

What are the symptoms?

There are often no symptoms in the earliest stages. Over months or years, various symptoms develop, depending on which organs and body tissues are affected. Diseased organs such as the kidneys, heart, liver, and nerves often become enlarged and cannot function properly. Resulting complications may include chronic kidney failure (p.706), chronic heart failure (p.413), chronic liver failure (p.650), or nerve damage (*see* PERIPHERAL NEUROPATHIES, p.543).

What might be done?

Amyloidosis is diagnosed by examining a sample of tissue from an affected organ under a microscope in order to detect protein deposits. In secondary amyloidosis, treating the underlying cause may halt or even reverse the disorder. However, amyloidosis that is associated with myeloma usually progresses rapidly, and the prognosis is poor. In cases of primary amyloidosis, immunosuppressant drugs (p.906) or drugs that are more commonly used to treat cancer (*see* ANTICANCER DRUGS, p.907) may be prescribed. If amyloidosis has already caused the failure of an organ, a transplant may be an option, but the replacement organ will also be affected if the disease is not controlled.

(WWW) ONLINE SITES: p.1033

Porphyria

A set of rare disorders in which chemicals called porphyrins accumulate in tissues

GENETICS Some types are inherited

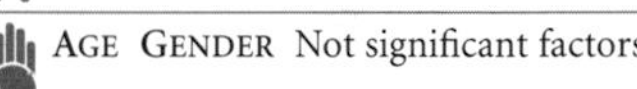
LIFESTYLE Excessive alcohol intake is a risk factor

AGE GENDER Not significant factors

As the body makes hemoglobin, the red pigment in blood, it forms chemicals called porphyrins. Normally, porphyrins are turned into hemoglobin, but in porphyria this change is blocked and they build up in the body. There are several forms of porphyria. Most forms are due to inherited abnormal genes. The most common is inherited in an autosomal dominant manner (*see* GENE DISORDERS, p.269). Some forms may be associated with liver diseases, excessive alcohol use, or AIDS (*see* HIV INFECTION AND AIDS, p.295). In susceptible people, porphyria may be a side effect of some drugs.

What are the symptoms?

Each type of porphyria causes different symptoms. In some, the symptoms are chronic; in others, they are intermittent and may be triggered by sunlight, alcohol, or drugs. Symptoms may include:

- Dark, purplish urine.
- Rashes or blisters in areas that are exposed to sunlight.
- Abdominal pain.
- Pain or weakness in the arms or legs.

Severe intermittent porphyria can cause psychiatric problems such as delusions.

What might be done?

Porphyria is diagnosed by testing blood, feces, or urine for porphyrins. There is no cure, but avoiding triggers may reduce the frequency of attacks. In some forms, intravenous glucose may help prevent attacks or limit their severity.

(WWW) ONLINE SITES: p.1032, p.1033

URINARY SYSTEM

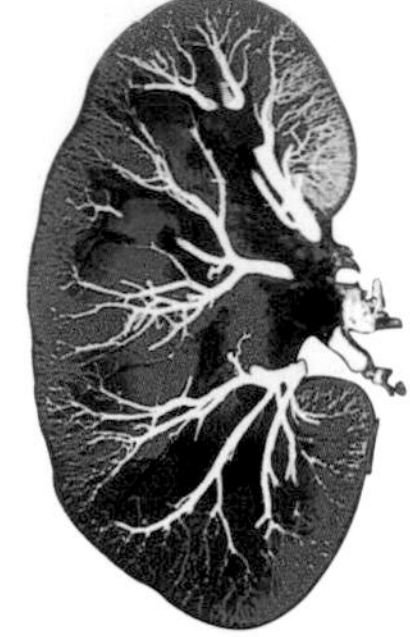

Rich blood supply
Numerous blood vessels supply the kidney with blood.

THE URINARY SYSTEM, also known as the urinary tract, acts as a filtering unit for the body's blood, excreting waste products and excess water as urine. The system consists of a pair of kidneys; the bladder; the ureters, which connect each kidney to the bladder; and the urethra, through which urine leaves the body. As the urinary system filters the blood, it regulates body water levels and maintains the balance of body fluids. The kidneys also produce hormones, one of which helps control blood pressure. Every day, the body's entire volume of blood passes through the kidneys over 300 times – a flow of about 440 gallons (1,700 liters).

Every action of our daily lives, from eating and breathing to walking and running, is made possible by chemical reactions in our body cells. Waste and water produced as a result of these reactions collect in the blood. To remain healthy, these wastes and excess fluid must be filtered out and excreted. This is the main function of the urinary system.

The kidneys are connected to the aorta, the body's main artery that runs directly from the heart. When the body is at rest, the kidneys receive about one-quarter of the blood pumped by the heart. Filtered blood is returned to the heart through the inferior vena cava, the largest vein in the body.

BLOOD FILTRATION

Each kidney contains about 1 million nephrons, mini-filtering units that consist of a knot of capillaries called the glomerulus and a long, thin tube called the renal tubule. Pores in the glomerulus allow only some of the molecules in the blood to pass through, depending on their size and shape. For example, red blood cells and proteins are much too large to pass through these pores and do not enter the filtered fluid. Smaller molecules pass into the renal tubule, where useful substances, such as glucose, are reabsorbed into the bloodstream. The fluid remaining in the tubule is called urine, a mixture of wastes, such as urea, and other substances that are not required by the body, such as excess water and salts.

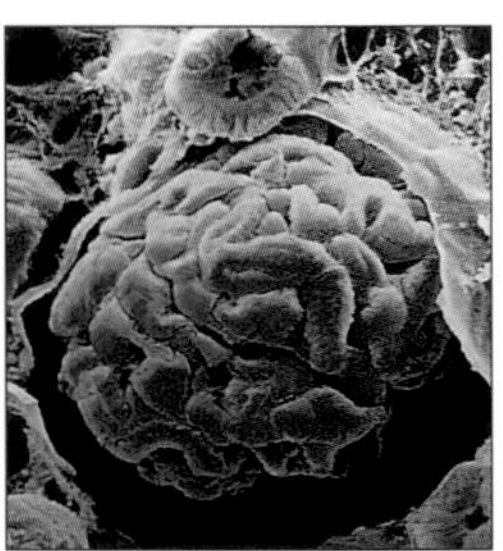

A glomerulus
This knot of capillaries is the glomerulus, which filters blood in the kidney.

This constant filtration of blood not only removes harmful wastes from the body but also helps regulate water levels. If, for example, you drink more water than is necessary for your body's requirements, the excess is excreted in urine. However, if you need to conserve water, the kidneys make the urine more concentrated and excrete as little water as possible. Furthermore, if your blood becomes too acidic or too alkaline, the kidneys change the urine's acidity level to restore the correct balance.

HORMONE PRODUCTION

The kidneys produce a number of hormones, each with different roles. Their functions include stimulating the formation of blood cells and controlling blood pressure by helping regulate blood flow through arteries.

STRUCTURE SEXUAL DIFFERENCES

The lower part of the urinary tract is different in males and females. The urethra from the male bladder passes through the prostate gland, carrying either urine or semen to the opening at the tip of the penis. The female bladder sits under the uterus, and the urethra carries urine to the opening in the front of the vagina. In both sexes, urination is partly controlled by muscles in the neck of the bladder.

Length of the urethra
The male urethra is usually about 8 in (20 cm) long. In females, the urethra is about 1½ in (4 cm) long.

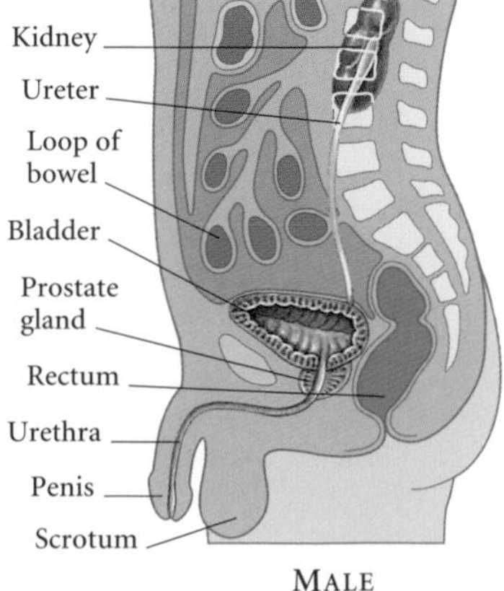
Kidney
Ureter
Loop of bowel
Bladder
Prostate gland
Rectum
Urethra
Penis
Scrotum

MALE

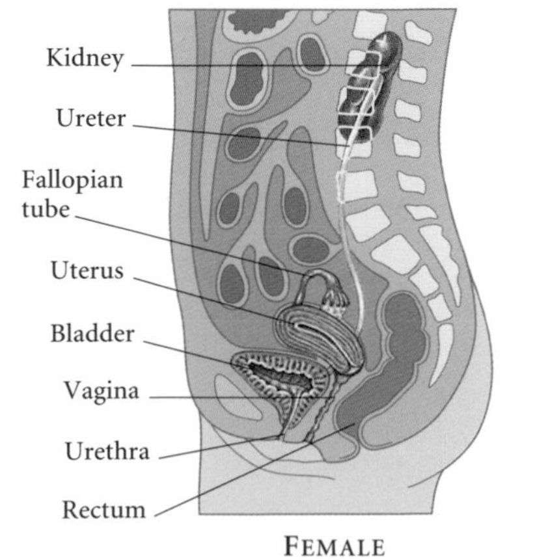
Kidney
Ureter
Fallopian tube
Uterus
Bladder
Vagina
Urethra
Rectum

FEMALE

STRUCTURE URINARY SYSTEM

The urinary system consists of two kidneys, each linked by a ureter to the bladder, and a urethra, which connects the bladder to the outside of the body. The kidneys lie at the back of the abdomen, on either side of the spine. They are red-brown, bean-shaped organs, about 4–5 in (10–12.5 cm) long and 2–3 in (5–7.5 cm) wide. The ureters are thin, muscular tubes about 10–12 in (25–30 cm) long, and the bladder is a hollow, muscular organ located in the pelvis. The bladder's lower opening is surrounded by muscle that helps control the release of urine through the urethra.

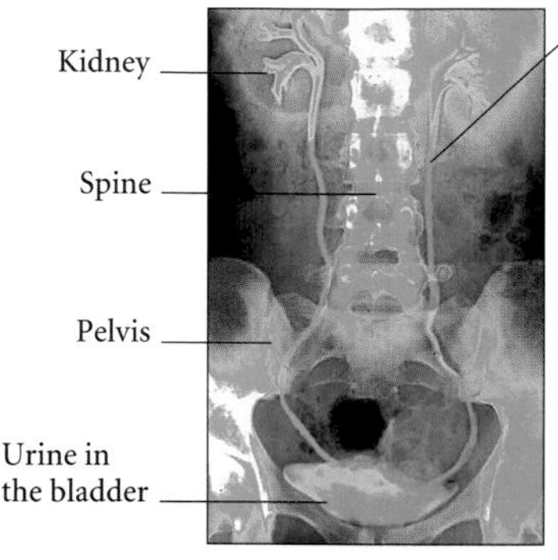
Kidney
Spine
Pelvis
Urine in the bladder
Ureter

X-ray of urinary system
This specialized X-ray, known as an intravenous urogram (IVU), is used to highlight structures of the urinary system. Part of the kidneys, the ureters, which lie at either side of the spine, and the bladder are clearly visible. No abnormalities are seen.

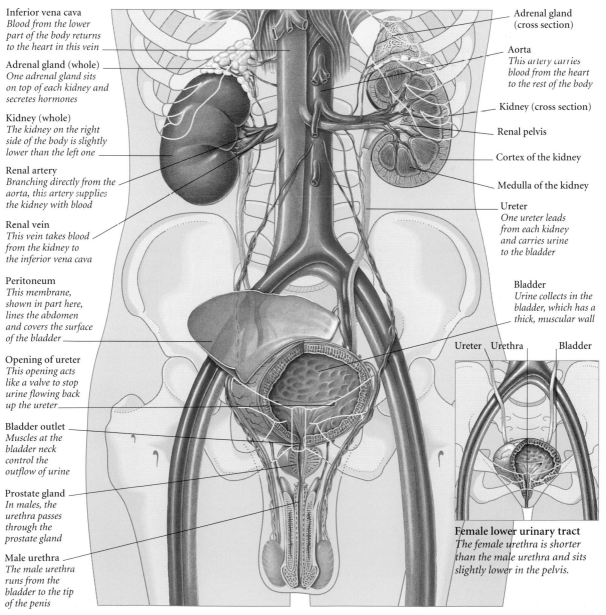

Inferior vena cava
Blood from the lower part of the body returns to the heart in this vein

Adrenal gland (whole)
One adrenal gland sits on top of each kidney and secretes hormones

Kidney (whole)
The kidney on the right side of the body is slightly lower than the left one

Renal artery
Branching directly from the aorta, this artery supplies the kidney with blood

Renal vein
This vein takes blood from the kidney to the inferior vena cava

Peritoneum
This membrane, shown in part here, lines the abdomen and covers the surface of the bladder

Opening of ureter
This opening acts like a valve to stop urine flowing back up the ureter

Bladder outlet
Muscles at the bladder neck control the outflow of urine

Prostate gland
In males, the urethra passes through the prostate gland

Male urethra
The male urethra runs from the bladder to the tip of the penis

Adrenal gland (cross section)

Aorta
This artery carries blood from the heart to the rest of the body

Kidney (cross section)

Renal pelvis

Cortex of the kidney

Medulla of the kidney

Ureter
One ureter leads from each kidney and carries urine to the bladder

Bladder
Urine collects in the bladder, which has a thick, muscular wall

Ureter
Urethra
Bladder

Female lower urinary tract
The female urethra is shorter than the male urethra and sits slightly lower in the pelvis.

STRUCTURE THE KIDNEY

The kidney has three regions: the cortex, the medulla, and the renal pelvis. The outer layer, the cortex, contains filtering units called nephrons, each consisting of a glomerulus and a renal tubule. The middle layer, the medulla, consists of cone-shaped groups of urine-collecting ducts. The inner region, the renal pelvis, branches into cavities called major and minor calyces. Each minor calyx gathers urine from the medulla; the urine is then collected in major calyces and funneled into the ureter.

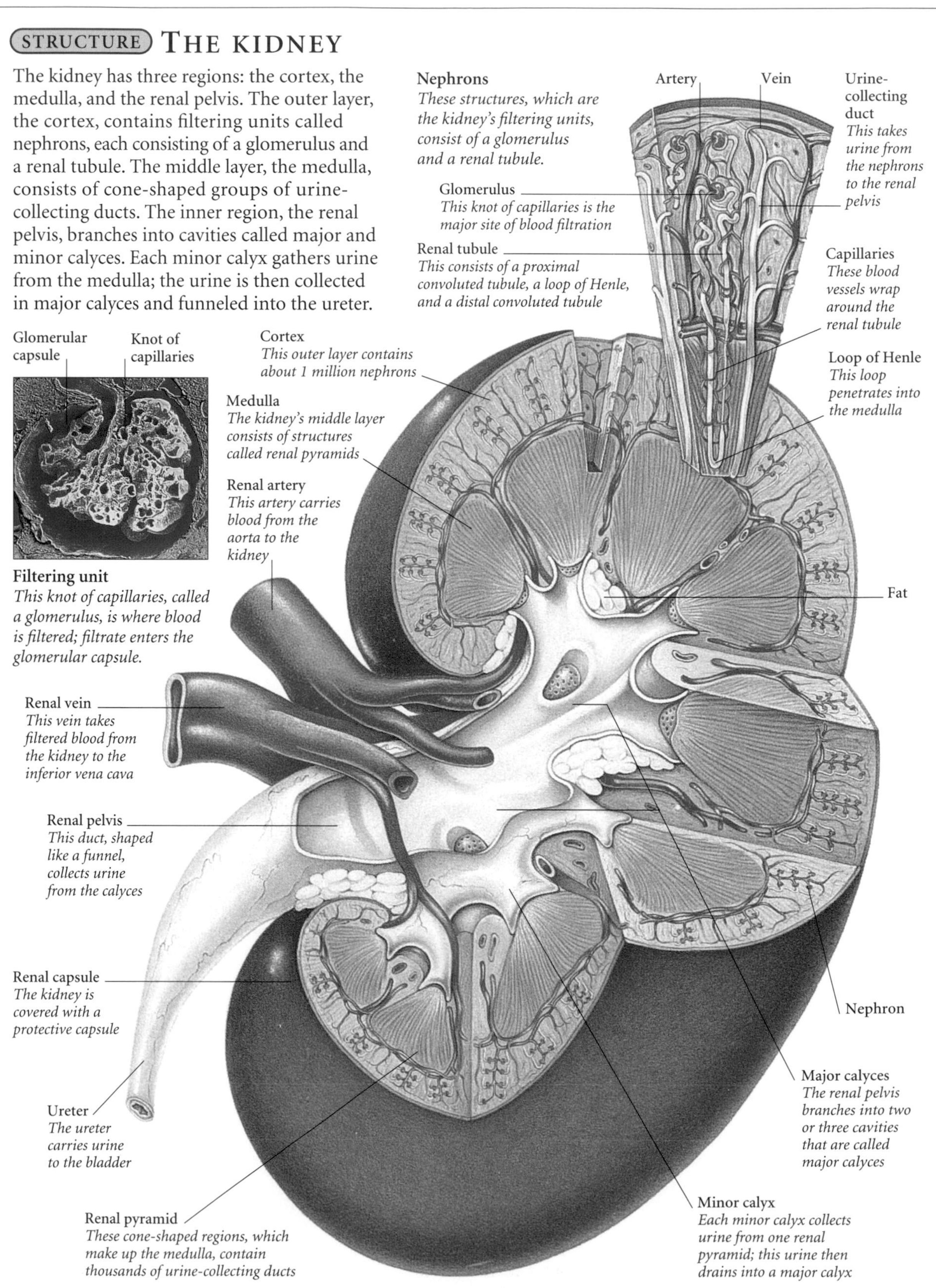
Nephrons
These structures, which are the kidney's filtering units, consist of a glomerulus and a renal tubule.
Artery
Vein
Urine-collecting duct
This takes urine from the nephrons to the renal pelvis
Glomerulus
This knot of capillaries is the major site of blood filtration
Renal tubule
This consists of a proximal convoluted tubule, a loop of Henle, and a distal convoluted tubule
Capillaries
These blood vessels wrap around the renal tubule
Glomerular capsule
Knot of capillaries
Cortex
This outer layer contains about 1 million nephrons
Loop of Henle
This loop penetrates into the medulla
Medulla
The kidney's middle layer consists of structures called renal pyramids
Renal artery
This artery carries blood from the aorta to the kidney
Filtering unit
This knot of capillaries, called a glomerulus, is where blood is filtered; filtrate enters the glomerular capsule.
Fat
Renal vein
This vein takes filtered blood from the kidney to the inferior vena cava
Renal pelvis
This duct, shaped like a funnel, collects urine from the calyces
Renal capsule
The kidney is covered with a protective capsule
Nephron
Ureter
The ureter carries urine to the bladder
Major calyces
The renal pelvis branches into two or three cavities that are called major calyces
Renal pyramid
These cone-shaped regions, which make up the medulla, contain thousands of urine-collecting ducts
Minor calyx
Each minor calyx collects urine from one renal pyramid; this urine then drains into a major calyx

FUNCTION URINE FORMATION AND EXCRETION

Urine is composed of unwanted substances that have been filtered from the blood by nephrons, the functional units of the kidneys. The urine formed in the kidneys passes through the ureters and is temporarily stored in the bladder. From here it is emptied, normally under voluntary control, through the urethra. A healthy adult excretes 1–4 pints (0.5–2 liters) of urine each day.

HOW A NEPHRON MAKES URINE

Blood entering the nephron is filtered through a cluster of capillaries called the glomerulus. The filtrate then enters the renal tubule, along which a complex process of secretion and reabsorption occurs. Useful substances such as glucose are reabsorbed, the acidity of the blood is regulated, and water levels are adjusted. The resulting fluid is called urine.

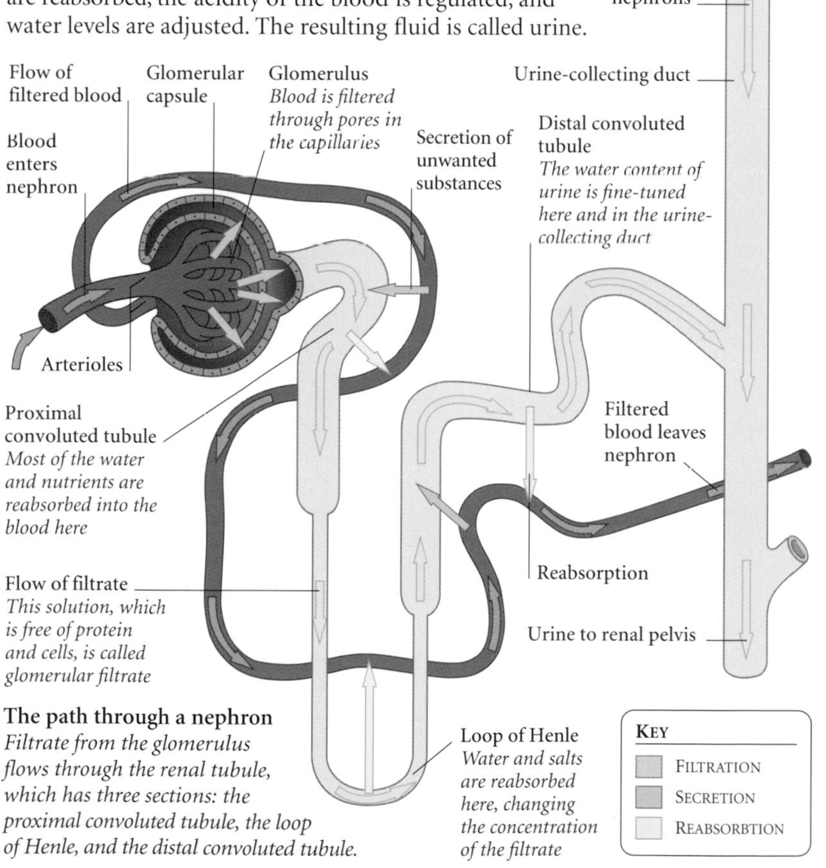

Urine from other nephrons
Urine-collecting duct
Flow of filtered blood
Glomerular capsule
Glomerulus
Blood is filtered through pores in the capillaries
Secretion of unwanted substances
Distal convoluted tubule
The water content of urine is fine-tuned here and in the urine-collecting duct
Blood enters nephron
Arterioles
Proximal convoluted tubule
Most of the water and nutrients are reabsorbed into the blood here
Filtered blood leaves nephron
Reabsorption
Flow of filtrate
This solution, which is free of protein and cells, is called glomerular filtrate
Urine to renal pelvis
Loop of Henle
Water and salts are reabsorbed here, changing the concentration of the filtrate
KEY
FILTRATION
SECRETION
REABSORBTION

The path through a nephron
Filtrate from the glomerulus flows through the renal tubule, which has three sections: the proximal convoluted tubule, the loop of Henle, and the distal convoluted tubule.

WHAT IS URINE MADE OF?

Urine consists of a mixture of waste products and other substances. The mixture is balanced so that the body's internal environment remains constant. The water content of urine depends on whether there is too much or too little water in the body.

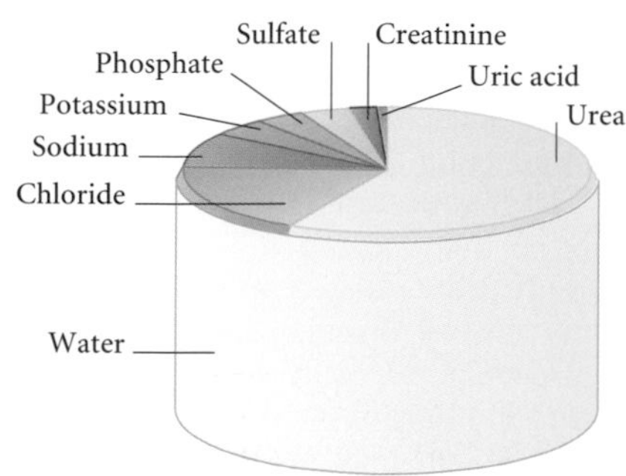

Sulfate
Creatinine
Phosphate
Uric acid
Potassium
Urea
Sodium
Chloride
Water

Mainly water
Urine is about 95 percent water. The remainder includes wastes and other substances not needed by the body.

HOW URINATION IS CONTROLLED

When the bladder is full, nerves in the bladder wall send signals to the spinal cord. Signals are then sent back to the bladder, making it contract and expel urine. In older children and adults, the timing of urination can be regulated because this process is controlled by the brain. Infants lack this control, and the bladder empties when full.

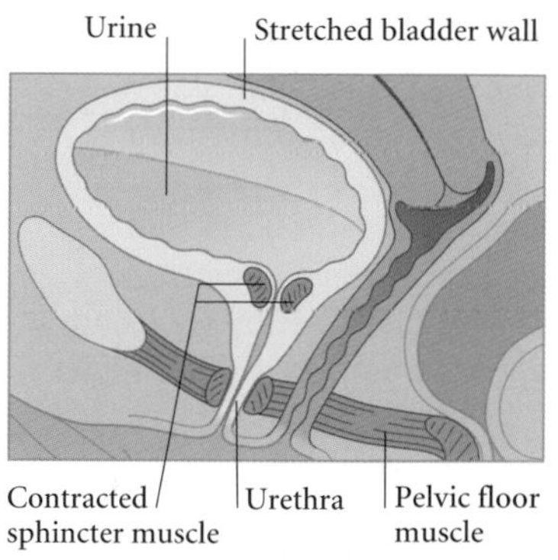

Urine
Stretched bladder wall
Contracted sphincter muscle
Urethra
Pelvic floor muscle

FULL BLADDER

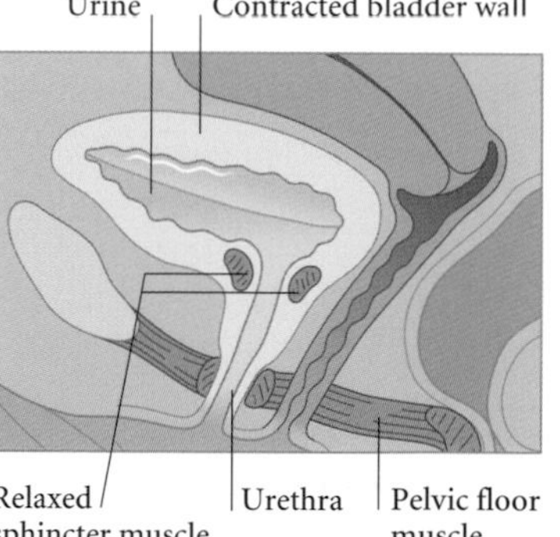

Urine
Contracted bladder wall
Relaxed sphincter muscle
Urethra
Pelvic floor muscle

EMPTYING BLADDER

Emptying the bladder
To empty the bladder, muscles in the bladder wall contract and the sphincter muscles relax, forcing urine out of the bladder and down the urethra.

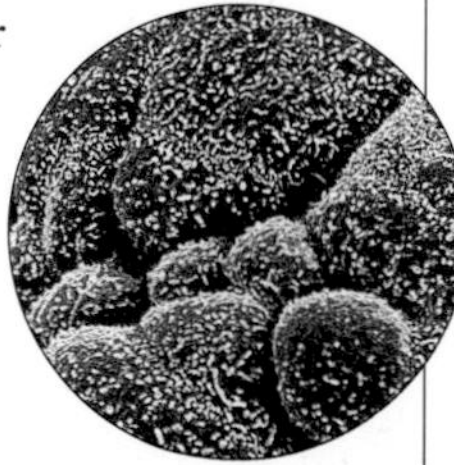

Inside the bladder
This highly magnified view shows the folds in the lining of the bladder wall. The folds in the wall stretch out as the bladder fills.

KIDNEY DISORDERS

The kidneys keep the body's chemistry in balance by removing waste products and excess water. They also regulate blood pressure, stimulate red blood cell production, and help maintain bone balance. Although the body can stay healthy with only a single kidney, it is important that kidney disorders are treated promptly because some disorders progress rapidly, often affecting both kidneys.

The first article in this section covers pyelonephritis, a common disorder in which kidney tissue becomes inflamed, usually due to a bacterial infection. Glomerulonephritis, which develops when inflammation damages the glomeruli (the kidneys' filtering units), is discussed in the second article. This condition is most often the result of an abnormal response of the immune system rather than infection.

The next articles discuss stones and cysts in the kidneys. Kidney stones are often treated by a technique called lithotripsy, in which shock waves are used to pulverize the stones. Cysts are usually harmless, but multiple cysts resulting from a genetic disorder may cause kidney failure. The final articles cover cancer of the kidneys and kidney failure. The latter disorder may occur suddenly, especially if it results from a reduction in the blood flow to the kidneys, but it more often develops gradually due to a long-term disease such as diabetes mellitus. Kidney infections in children as well as a rare kidney cancer called Wilms tumor (p.872) are discussed in the section on infancy and childhood (pp.870–872).

KEY ANATOMY

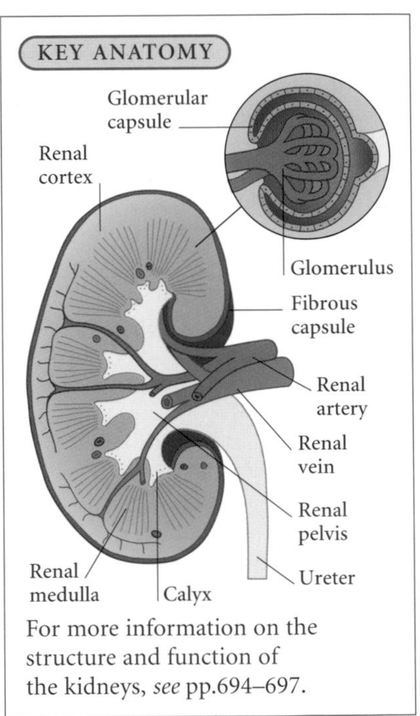
Glomerular capsule
Renal cortex
Glomerulus
Fibrous capsule
Renal artery
Renal vein
Renal pelvis
Ureter
Renal medulla
Calyx

For more information on the structure and function of the kidneys, *see* pp.694–697.

Pyelonephritis

Inflammation of one or both kidneys, usually due to bacterial infection

AGE Most common between the ages of 16 and 45

GENDER Much more common in females

LIFESTYLE May be related to sexual activity in females

GENETICS Not a significant factor

Pyelonephritis is one of the most common kidney disorders, particularly in young and middle-aged adults. In this condition, one or both of the kidneys become inflamed, usually as a result of a bacterial infection. In adults, pyelonephritis causes intense pain around the kidneys. The condition can usually be promptly diagnosed and treated and, for this reason, rarely leads to long-term damage to the kidneys. However, the symptoms of pyelonephritis may be less obvious in children. As a result, it may go unnoticed and lead to serious kidney damage (*see* URINARY TRACT INFECTIONS IN CHILDREN, p.871), possibly resulting in kidney failure in later life.

WHAT ARE THE CAUSES?

Pyelonephritis may be caused by bacteria entering the urinary tract through the urethra (the passage from the bladder to the outside of the body). Often the bacteria migrate from an infection in the bladder (*see* CYSTITIS, p.709). Urinary infections, and therefore pyelonephritis, are much more common in females since the female urethra is shorter than that of the male, and its opening is nearer the anus. Bacteria from the anal area may enter the urethra during sex or if the area is wiped from back to front after a bowel movement. People with diabetes mellitus (p.687) are more likely to have urinary infections, partly because glucose in the urine may encourage bacterial growth.

In both sexes, pyelonephritis is more likely to develop if there is a physical obstruction anywhere in the urinary tract that prevents the normal flow of urine. In these cases, if bacteria have already contaminated the urine, they are not flushed through the urinary tract as would normally happen. Instead, they multiply in the stagnant urine. An obstruction may result from pressure on parts of the urinary tract. Possible causes of blockage include the expanding uterus in pregnant women or an enlarged prostate gland (p.725) in men. Normal urine flow may also be obstructed by bladder tumors (p.715) or kidney stones (p.701). In addition, kidney stones may harbor bacteria and can therefore predispose affected people to infection in the urinary tract. All of these conditions are likely to lead to recurrent episodes of pyelonephritis.

Bacteria may also enter the bladder during bladder catheterization (p.713), a procedure in which a tube is passed up the urethra into the bladder to drain urine. In addition, bacteria may be carried in the bloodstream from elsewhere in the body to the kidneys.

WHAT ARE THE SYMPTOMS?

The symptoms of pyelonephritis may appear suddenly, often over a period of a few hours, and include:

- Intense pain that begins in the back just above the waist and then moves to the side and groin.
- Fever over 38°C (100°F), resulting in shivering and headache.
- Painful and frequent urination.
- Cloudy, bloodstained urine.

- Foul-smelling urine.
- Nausea and vomiting.

If you develop these symptoms, consult your doctor immediately.

How is it diagnosed?

If your doctor suspects pyelonephritis, he or she will probably examine a sample of your urine to find out whether it contains bacteria. If there is evidence of infection, the urine sample will be sent for laboratory analysis to establish which type of bacterium has caused the infection. Men and children may need further tests to detect an underlying cause after a single episode of the disorder. Pyelonephritis is more common in women. For this reason, further tests are carried out for women only if they have recurrent episodes or if the doctor suspects an underlying cause.

Further investigations may include a blood test to assess the function of the kidneys. Imaging procedures, such as ultrasound scanning (p.250), CT scanning (p.247), or intravenous urography (below), may also be carried out to check for signs of kidney damage or a disorder such as kidney stones.

What is the treatment?

Pyelonephritis is usually treated with a short course of oral antibiotics (p.885), and symptoms often improve within 2 days of treatment. When the course is finished, further urine tests may be done to confirm that the infection has cleared up. However, if you are vomiting, in pain, pregnant, or seriously ill, you may be admitted to the hospital and given intravenous fluids and antibiotics.

If you experience repeated episodes of pyelonephritis, you may be advised to take low-dose antibiotics over a prolonged time period to reduce the frequency of the attacks. If you have an underlying disorder, such as kidney stones, this may also need to be treated.

What is the prognosis?

In most cases, prompt treatment of pyelonephritis is effective, and the condition causes no permanent damage to the kidneys. However, in rare cases, frequent episodes of pyelonephritis may lead to scarring of the kidneys and result in irreversible damage (*see* END-STAGE KIDNEY FAILURE, p.708).

WWW ONLINE SITES: p.1037

Glomerulonephritis

Inflammation of the glomeruli, the tiny filtering units of the kidney

AGE Most common in children and young adults

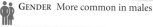

GENDER More common in males

GENETICS LIFESTYLE Not yet well understood

Glomerulonephritis is an uncommon disorder in which many of the tiny filtering units of the kidneys, known as glomeruli, become inflamed. As a result, the kidneys are unable to carry out their usual function of removing waste products and excess water from the body efficiently. In addition, blood cells and protein molecules, which normally remain in the blood, leak through the glomeruli into the urine.

Glomerulonephritis can be acute or chronic. An acute episode of the disorder is usually followed by complete recovery, but in severe cases damage to the glomeruli may be permanent. In some people, chronic glomerulonephritis develops after an acute attack of

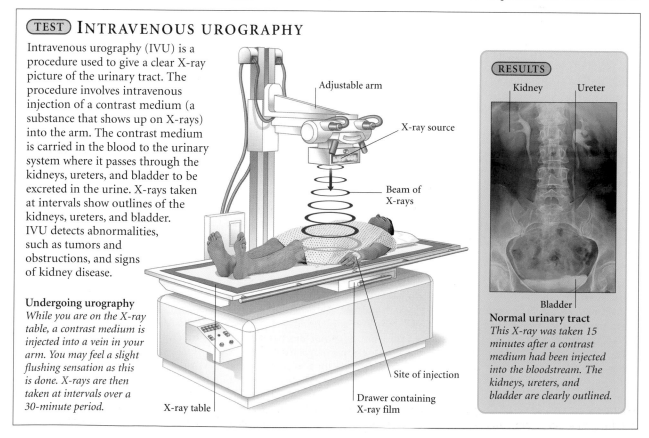

TEST INTRAVENOUS UROGRAPHY

Intravenous urography (IVU) is a procedure used to give a clear X-ray picture of the urinary tract. The procedure involves intravenous injection of a contrast medium (a substance that shows up on X-rays) into the arm. The contrast medium is carried in the blood to the urinary system where it passes through the kidneys, ureters, and bladder to be excreted in the urine. X-rays taken at intervals show outlines of the kidneys, ureters, and bladder. IVU detects abnormalities, such as tumors and obstructions, and signs of kidney disease.

Adjustable arm
X-ray source
Beam of X-rays
Site of injection
Drawer containing X-ray film
X-ray table

Undergoing urography
While you are on the X-ray table, a contrast medium is injected into a vein in your arm. You may feel a slight flushing sensation as this is done. X-rays are then taken at intervals over a 30-minute period.

RESULTS
Kidney
Ureter
Bladder

Normal urinary tract
This X-ray was taken 15 minutes after a contrast medium had been injected into the bloodstream. The kidneys, ureters, and bladder are clearly outlined.

the condition. Progressive kidney damage then occurs over several months or years as a result of continual inflammation. However, most of the people who develop glomerulonephritis have no previous history of kidney disease.

Although glomerulonephritis affects both kidneys, not all the glomeruli are affected at the same time.

WHAT ARE THE CAUSES?

Acute glomerulonephritis sometimes occurs as a complication of certain infectious diseases. The antibodies that are produced by the immune system to fight the infection attack the glomeruli in the kidneys, causing inflammation and damage. A common cause of acute glomerulonephritis, especially in children, is a bacterial throat infection, such as a streptococcal infection. Occasionally, acute glomerulonephritis develops after a viral infection, such as infectious mononucleosis (p.289). In developing countries, the disorder may occur as a result of parasitic diseases, such as malaria (p.305).

Chronic glomerulonephritis is usually caused by an abnormal reaction of the immune system, in which antibodies attack only the kidney tissues. Often, the reason for this reaction is not known. However, chronic glomerulonephritis may be associated with an autoimmune disorder that affects many organs in the body, such as systemic lupus erythematosus (p.461).

WHAT ARE THE SYMPTOMS?

In acute glomerulonephritis, symptoms develop rapidly over a few days. In contrast, the initial symptoms of chronic glomerulonephritis develop slowly and may only become apparent when the kidneys have already been severely damaged. The symptoms of both forms of the disorder may include:

- Frequent urination.
- Frothy or cloudy urine.
- Blood in the urine.
- Puffiness of the face, with swelling around the eyes in the morning.
- Swollen feet and legs.
- Shortness of breath.
- Loss of appetite.

A serious complication of glomerulonephritis is high blood pressure (*see* HYPERTENSION, p.403), which may result in further damage to the kidneys.

HOW IS IT DIAGNOSED?

In the initial stages of chronic glomerulonephritis, there may be no symptoms and the condition may be discovered during routine screening tests or investigations for another disorder. If you do develop symptoms of acute or chronic glomerulonephritis, the doctor may test a urine sample to detect blood and protein. Further urine tests and a blood test are necessary to assess kidney function. In addition, your doctor may arrange for imaging tests to assess the size of your kidneys because the kidneys are likely to become larger in cases of acute glomerulonephritis and to shrink in chronic glomerulonephritis. Assessment is usually performed using X-rays (p.244) or ultrasound scanning (p.250) and by intravenous urography (p.699), a form of X-ray in which the urinary tract is highlighted with a contrast dye. However, the use of this dye is avoided in people with suspected serious kidney problems. A kidney biopsy (opposite page) may also be done to determine the extent of kidney damage.

WHAT IS THE TREATMENT?

Treatment depends on the severity and, if known, the cause of the disorder. Some cases are so mild that they do not need treatment and are simply monitored. However, if the disorder follows a bacterial infection, antibiotics (p.885) and sometimes corticosteroids (p.930) may be prescribed. Glomerulonephritis due to an autoimmune disorder can usually be treated with immunosuppressants (p.906) and corticosteroids. If the condition is accompanied by high blood pressure, this will be treated at the same time. For chronic glomerulonephritis, a low-salt diet with reduced fluid intake may be recommended to prevent fluid retention in body tissues.

WHAT IS THE PROGNOSIS?

In most cases, the symptoms of acute glomerulonephritis disappear after 6–8 weeks. However, the prognosis is variable. In some people, kidney function is reduced but does not deteriorate further. Other people may develop chronic kidney failure (p.706), which can lead to end-stage kidney failure (p.708), an irreversible loss of kidney function that may be fatal if not treated promptly.

(WWW) ONLINE SITES: p.1037

Nephrotic syndrome

A group of symptoms resulting from kidney damage that causes loss of protein into the urine and swelling of body tissues

 AGE Most common in young children but can affect people of any age

 GENDER LIFESTYLE GENETICS Not significant factors

The urine of a healthy person does not normally contain protein because the molecules are too large to pass across the glomeruli (the blood-filtering units in the kidneys). However, if the delicate glomeruli are damaged, large amounts of protein can leak into the urine from the blood. Eventually, this leakage results in low protein levels in the blood, an accumulation of fluid in body tissues, and widespread swelling.

WHAT ARE THE CAUSES?

Nephrotic syndrome can be due to various kidney diseases, most commonly glomerulonephritis (p.699) and diabetic kidney disease (p.705). It may also be a complication of infection elsewhere in the body, such as hepatitis B (*see* ACUTE HEPATITIS, p.644). Rarely, it can be due to amyloidosis (p.693). Other possible causes include reactions to drugs and chemicals, as well as certain autoimmune disorders (in which the body attacks its own tissues), such as systemic lupus erythematosus (p.461).

WHAT ARE THE SYMPTOMS?

The symptoms of nephrotic syndrome may appear gradually or rapidly over days or weeks and worsen as more and more protein is lost. You may notice:

- Frothy urine.
- Decreased urine production.
- Puffiness of the face, with swelling around the eyes in the morning.
- Swollen feet and legs.
- Swelling in the scrotum in men.
- Shortness of breath.
- Loss of appetite and weight loss.
- Swelling of the abdomen.

If you develop these symptoms, you should see a doctor immediately.

WHAT MIGHT BE DONE?

If your doctor suspects nephrotic syndrome, he or she will test your urine for the presence of protein and will also ask you to collect the urine you produce over a 24-hour period so that daily protein loss can be measured. A blood test may be done to measure your protein levels and assess kidney function. You may also need a kidney biopsy (right) to determine the cause of the condition.

Your doctor may prescribe diuretics (p.902) to help remove excess fluid from your body, and he or she may also recommend a low-salt diet to prevent further fluid retention. If your symptoms are severe, you may need treatment in the hospital. You may also be given corticosteroids (p.930) and immunosuppressants (p.906). If possible, the underlying disorder will be treated.

WHAT IS THE PROGNOSIS?

The prognosis of nephrotic syndrome depends on the cause and extent of the damage to the kidneys. Children usually respond well to corticosteroids and often make a full recovery, but adults may experience recurrent episodes of the disorder or fail to respond to treatment. In the most severe cases, chronic kidney failure (p.706) and eventually end-stage kidney failure (p.708), an irreversible loss of kidney function, may develop.

(WWW) ONLINE SITES: p.1037

(TEST) KIDNEY BIOPSY

A kidney biopsy is a procedure that is used to identify the exact nature and extent of the damage to a kidney and is usually carried out in the hospital. During the procedure, a small piece of kidney tissue is removed. This sample is then sent to a laboratory for examination under a microscope. After the biopsy is completed, you will be advised to rest for about 4–6 hours so that the risk of bleeding from the kidney is minimized.

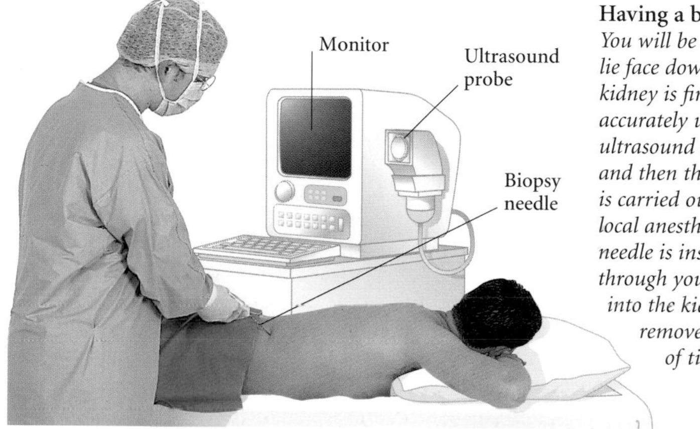
Monitor
Ultrasound probe
Biopsy needle

Having a biopsy
You will be asked to lie face down. The kidney is first located accurately using ultrasound scanning and then the biopsy is carried out. Under local anesthesia, a needle is inserted through your skin into the kidney to remove a sliver of tissue.

(RESULTS)

Normal kidney tissue
This highly magnified view shows healthy kidney tissue. Several of the filtering units of the kidney, known as glomeruli, and the kidney tubules that lead from them are clearly visible.

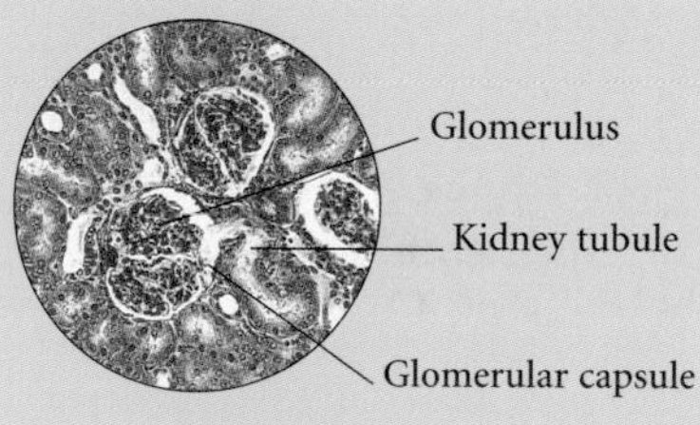
Glomerulus
Kidney tubule
Glomerular capsule

Kidney stones

Crystal deposits of varying sizes that form in the kidney

AGE Most common between the ages of 30 and 50

GENDER More common in males

GENETICS In some cases, the cause is inherited

LIFESTYLE Certain diets and living in a hot climate are risk factors

Normally, the waste products of the body's chemical processes pass out of the kidneys in the urine. Kidney stones occur when the urine is saturated with waste products that are able to crystallize into stonelike structures or when the chemicals that normally inhibit this crystallization process are not present. Kidney stones can take years to form.

If the stones are small, they may become dislodged from the kidney and move through the urinary tract, eventually passing out of the body in the urine. Larger stones stay in the kidney but may occasionally move into the ureter (the tube that takes urine from the kidney to the bladder). If a stone becomes lodged in the ureter, it can cause severe pain. A large stone in the kidney is not usually painful, but it can increase the risk of urinary infection.

WHAT ARE THE CAUSES?

The risk of stones forming in the kidneys is greatest when there is a high concentration of dissolved substances in the urine. Inadequate intake of fluid increases the risk of kidney stones. When there is too little water in the body, the kidneys conserve water by forming less urine, and as a result the urine they produce is highly concentrated. People who live in hot climates may be susceptible to kidney stones if they do not drink enough to replace the fluid lost through perspiration.

Different types of kidney stones can form, depending on the waste products that crystallize out of the urine. Most are made of calcium salts. These stones may be associated with a diet containing foods rich in calcium or a substance called oxalic acid. They may also develop if your body produces too much parathyroid hormone (*see* HYPERPARATHYROIDISM, p.682), a process causing high levels of calcium to build up in the bloodstream. A small percentage of stones contain uric acid and may occur in people who have gout (p.380).

Kidney stones may also result from a long-standing urinary tract infection. In such cases, the stones can grow into a staghorn shape and fill the central cavity of the kidney. Rarely, they are formed from cystine, a substance present in abnormally high levels in people who have the inherited disorder cystinuria. Kidney stones are also associated with some drugs, such as indinavir, which is used to treat HIV infection (*see* DRUGS FOR HIV INFECTION AND AIDS, p.887).

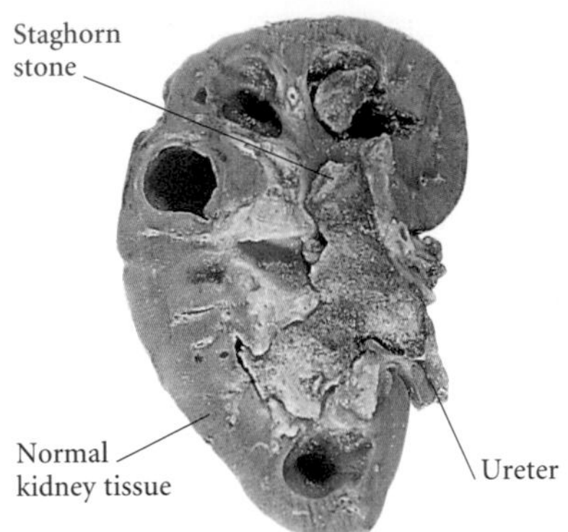
Staghorn stone
Normal kidney tissue
Ureter

Staghorn kidney stone
Named for its shape, this staghorn kidney stone has enlarged over many years to fill the entire center of the kidney.

What are the symptoms?

Very small kidney stones may pass unnoticed in the urine. Larger stones or small fragments of stones that pass into the ureter may cause painful spasms of the ureter wall. The symptoms usually appear suddenly and may include:

- Excruciating pain that starts in the back, spreads to the abdomen and groin, and may be felt in the genitals.
- Frequent, painful urination.
- Nausea and vomiting.
- Blood in the urine.

If a kidney stone is passed in the urine, the pain will subside rapidly. However, if a stone lodges in a ureter, it may cause a buildup of urine, which will then lead to swelling of the kidney (*see* HYDRONEPHROSIS, opposite page).

How is it diagnosed?

If your doctor suspects that you have kidney stones, he or she will take a specimen of urine to look for blood, crystals, and evidence of an underlying infection. Stones that have been passed in the urine may be collected and analyzed so that their composition can be determined. An ordinary X-ray (p.244) may be used to look for calcium stones; other types of kidney stone can be detected by taking specialized X-rays of the urinary tract (*see* INTRAVENOUS UROGRAPHY, p.699). You may also have blood and urine tests to assess kidney function by measuring the levels of calcium, uric acid, and other substances in your blood and urine. These tests can be done in an outpatient unit. They enable the doctor to determine the presence and the composition of kidney stones remaining in the urinary tract.

What is the treatment?

If the stones are small and remain in the kidney, you may simply be advised to rest, take analgesics (p.912) to relieve discomfort, and drink plenty of fluids to help flush the stones into the urine. In some instances, kidney stones that have become lodged in the lower part of the ureter can be removed during cystoscopy (p.715). In this procedure, a viewing tube is passed into the ureter through the urethra and bladder. Forceps are then passed through the tube to crush or remove the stone.

If a stone moves into the ureter, it usually causes severe pain that can last for several hours. You may need to go to the hospital for strong analgesics. You may also be given intravenous fluids to increase the volume of urine and help flush the stone out of the ureter. The most frequently used treatment for kidney stones is lithotripsy (below), in which shock waves are used to break the stones into powder that can be passed easily in the urine. Surgical removal of kidney stones is needed only if they are very large. In rare cases, a staghorn stone is so large that the entire kidney must be surgically removed.

The underlying cause needs to be treated to prevent a recurrence of kidney stones. Your doctor will probably recommend that you drink at least 4–6 pints (2–3 liters) of fluids a day and avoid foods that may encourage the formation of stones (*see* PREVENTING KIDNEY STONES, opposite page).

(TREATMENT) LITHOTRIPSY

Lithotripsy is a procedure that is usually carried out in the hospital. It uses high-energy shock waves to disintegrate stones in the kidneys, ureters, or bladder. You will then pass the fragmented stones in the urine. Analgesics are given before the procedure because there may be some discomfort; children are usually given general anesthesia. For a few days after lithotripsy, you may have blood in your urine, and the treated area will feel bruised and tender. However, serious complications are uncommon.

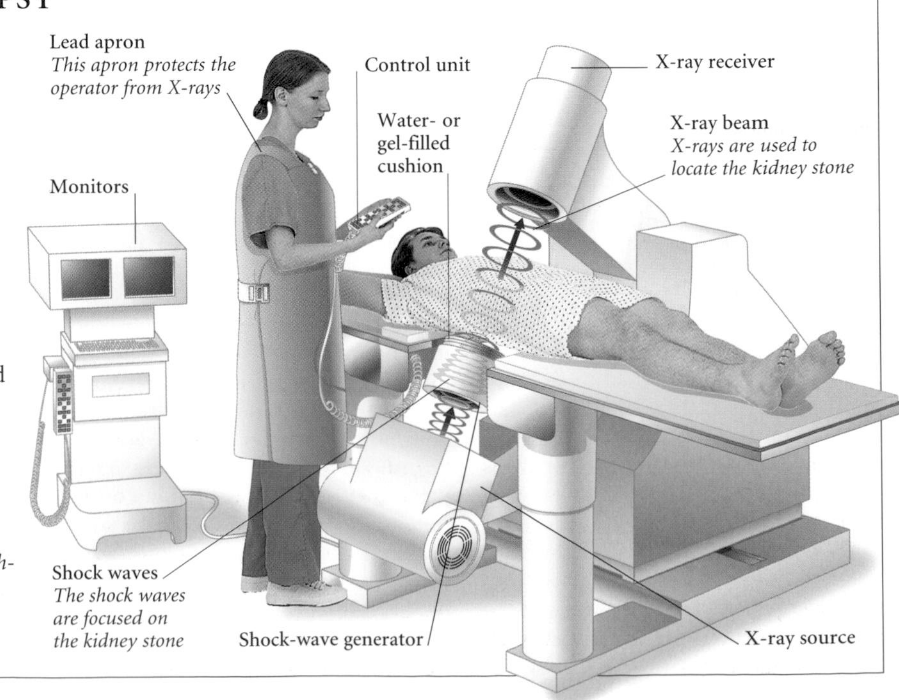
Lead apron
This apron protects the operator from X-rays
Control unit
X-ray receiver
Water- or gel-filled cushion
X-ray beam
X-rays are used to locate the kidney stone
Monitors
Shock waves
The shock waves are focused on the kidney stone
Shock-wave generator
X-ray source

Undergoing lithotripsy
The stone is located using X-rays. A machine called a lithotripter focuses high-energy ultrasonic shock waves onto the stone through a water- or gel-filled cushion, placed under the back.

SELF-HELP PREVENTING KIDNEY STONES

If you have kidney stones, these dietary precautions may help prevent their recurrence:

- Drink 4–6 pints (2–3 liters) of fluids daily.
- Drink fluids before you sleep to ensure that urine production continues overnight.
- Drink more fluids in hot weather, after strenuous exercise, or if you have a fever.
- Check with your doctor about eating fewer dairy products and avoiding calcium-based antacids. If you live in a hard-water area, use a softener on drinking water.
- To prevent oxalate stones, avoid rhubarb, spinach, and asparagus.

WHAT IS THE PROGNOSIS?

More than half the people treated for a kidney stone develop another within about 7 years. However, the self-help measures above may reduce the risk of recurrence. Kidney stones rarely cause permanent damage to the kidneys.

WWW ONLINE SITES: p.1037

Hydronephrosis

Swelling of the kidney due to a blockage of the urinary tract

AGE Most common in very young children and elderly people

GENDER GENETICS LIFESTYLE Not significant factors

In hydronephrosis, a blockage in the urinary tract prevents urine from flowing normally through the system. As a result, the kidney becomes swollen with urine and pressure builds up within it, preventing normal function. The condition can affect one or both kidneys and may occur suddenly or gradually.

WHAT ARE THE CAUSES?

The blockage that causes hydronephrosis may be due to an abnormality of the urinary tract that is present at birth or to narrowing of the ureter (the tube that takes urine from the kidney). This narrowing may develop as a result of pressure from outside the ureter, such as that caused by a tumor or by the enlargement of the uterus during pregnancy. Hydronephrosis may also occur if a ureter is blocked by a kidney stone (p.701) moving toward the bladder.

In addition, the disorder can be due to blockage of the urethra (the passage that leads from the bladder to outside the body). A blocked urethra is usually due to a urethral stricture (p.714) or an enlarged prostate gland (p.725).

WHAT ARE THE SYMPTOMS?

If hydronephrosis results from a sudden obstruction in the urinary tract, the following symptoms may develop:

- Severe pain in the abdomen.
- Acute lower back pain.
- Nausea and vomiting.

However, hydronephrosis that develops gradually over a long period of time does not usually produce the symptoms listed above. In these cases, kidney failure (p.705) may be the first sign that the condition exists.

People with hydronephrosis have an increased risk of urinary tract infection because bacteria are likely to multiply in urine that is not flowing freely.

HOW IS IT DIAGNOSED?

If your doctor suspects that you have hydronephrosis, he or she may arrange for blood tests and urine tests to find out how well your kidneys are functioning. The doctor may also arrange for imaging tests, including ultrasound scanning (p.250) and intravenous urography (p.699). These tests will enable the blockage in your urinary tract to be located and the cause of the obstruction determined. In some instances, hydronephrosis is detected only when another disorder, such as an enlarged prostate gland, is being investigated.

WHAT IS THE TREATMENT?

Initially, the aim of treatment is to prevent permanent damage to the kidney by relieving the pressure that has built up inside it as soon as possible. If there is a blockage in the urethra, a tube will be inserted into the bladder to drain the urine (*see* BLADDER CATHETERIZATION, p.713). If the blockage is higher in the urinary tract, a tube may be inserted directly into the affected kidney to drain the urine. Once the pressure in the kidney has been relieved, your doctor can treat the cause of the blockage.

Hydronephrosis that is associated with pregnancy is usually mild and does not require treatment. The condition should improve spontaneously after the birth.

WHAT IS THE PROGNOSIS?

If hydronephrosis is detected early, the affected kidney tissue normally recovers once the cause has been treated. However, in rare cases, hydronephrosis may lead to permanent kidney damage, and chronic kidney failure (p.706) may develop if both kidneys are affected.

WWW ONLINE SITES: p.1037

Kidney cyst

A fluid-filled swelling within the cortex, the outer part of the kidney

AGE More common over age 50

GENDER GENETICS LIFESTYLE Not significant factors

Kidney cysts form in the cortex (outer layer) of the kidney. They often occur singly, but sometimes three or four cysts may occur. Kidney cysts are very common; up to half of all people over age 50 have at least one cyst, often without realizing it. The cause is not known.

Unlike the multiple cysts that occur in polycystic kidney disease (p.704), kidney cysts do not affect kidney function and are usually harmless. In most cases, they cause no symptoms. Rarely, a kidney cyst may become large enough to cause back pain, or it may bleed, causing blood to appear in the urine.

WHAT MIGHT BE DONE?

A kidney cyst is often detected by chance during ultrasound scanning (p.250), CT scanning (p.247), or intravenous urography (p.699) performed to investigate another condition. In some cases, a fluid sample may be taken from the cyst through a hollow needle to be examined for cancerous cells. This procedure is done under local anesthesia and uses ultrasound to locate the cyst.

A simple kidney cyst does not usually require treatment unless symptoms develop. However, if the cyst becomes painful, you may be sent to the hospital to have fluid removed using a needle and syringe. Alternatively, the cyst can be removed surgically.

WWW ONLINE SITES: p.1037

Polycystic kidney disease

An inherited disorder in which multiple fluid-filled cysts gradually replace the tissue in both kidneys

 AGE Juvenile form usually evident at birth; adult form usually apparent by age 45

 GENETICS Due to an abnormal gene inherited from one or both parents

 GENDER LIFESTYLE Not significant factors

Polycystic kidney disease is an inherited condition in which the kidneys have a honeycomb appearance as a result of the presence of numerous fluid-filled cysts. The cysts gradually replace normal tissue so that the kidneys become larger and progressively less able to function until eventually they fail completely (*see* END-STAGE KIDNEY FAILURE, p.708). Polycystic kidney disease is not the same as simple kidney cysts (p.703), which are generally harmless.

Polycystic kidneys may affect adults or, rarely, infants. Adult polycystic kidney disease does not usually become apparent until about age 45, although symptoms can appear as early as age 20. In children, the condition is known as juvenile polycystic kidney disease and can sometimes be fatal.

WHAT ARE THE CAUSES?

Polycystic kidney disease is caused by an abnormal gene. In the form that affects adults, the gene is inherited in an autosomal dominant manner, and as a result the disease can be inherited from just one affected parent (*see* GENE DISORDERS, p.269). Each child of such a parent has a 1 in 2 chance of developing the disorder. The juvenile form is inherited in an autosomal recessive way; both parents must pass the faulty gene to the child for the disorder to develop. When both parents have one copy each of the faulty gene, each child has a 1 in 4 chance of developing the disorder.

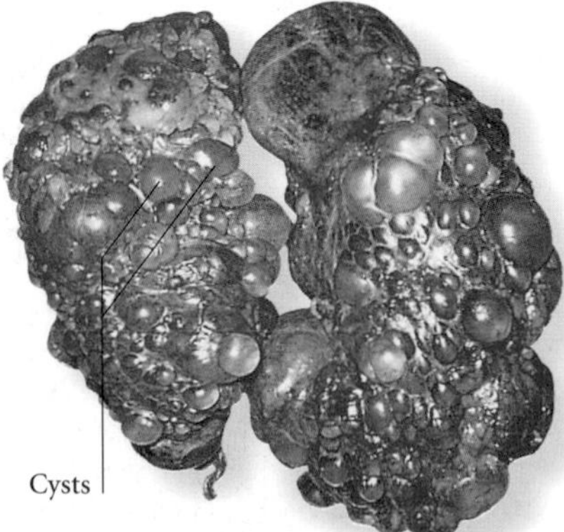
Cysts

Polycystic kidneys
Multiple fluid-filled cysts have replaced the normal tissue in both of these kidneys. As a result, the kidneys have become very large and irregularly shaped.

CAN IT BE PREVENTED?

The gene responsible for polycystic kidneys in adults has been identified, and genetic counseling (p.270) is available for people who have a family history of the disease. If both parents are aware that they carry the gene that is responsible for the juvenile form, they will also need counseling. Otherwise, it is possible to check the kidneys of a fetus for signs of the disorder using ultrasound scanning (*see* ULTRASOUND SCANNING IN PREGNANCY, p.793). If an ultrasound scan reveals polycystic kidneys in the fetus, the parents can discuss the options available with the doctor.

WHAT ARE THE SYMPTOMS?

The symptoms of adult polycystic kidney disease may not appear for many years. The main symptoms are:

- Vague discomfort in the abdomen or aching in the lower back.
- Episodes of severe and sudden pain in the abdomen or lower back.
- Blood in the urine.

A baby with juvenile polycystic disease will have a very swollen abdomen due to enlargement of the kidneys.

In adults, as the disease progresses, high blood pressure (*see* HYPERTENSION, p.403) may develop, which can lead to further kidney damage. Occasionally, one or more of the kidney cysts become infected, resulting in pain and fever. Sometimes, cysts develop in other organs, such as the pancreas and liver.

If you have abdominal pain and notice blood in your urine, you should consult your doctor as soon as possible.

WHAT MIGHT BE DONE?

In many people, adult polycystic kidney disease is first discovered during a routine physical examination. It may also be detected when family members are screened because a relative already has polycystic kidney disease. Blood and urine tests may be performed to assess kidney function, and ultrasound scanning (p.250) or CT scanning (p.247) may be done to confirm the diagnosis. It is advisable for healthy children of people with polycystic kidney disease to have periodic ultrasound scans to check for the development of the disorder.

If it has not been detected in the fetus, juvenile polycystic kidney disease may be obvious at birth because the baby will have a very swollen abdomen. Doctors can then confirm the diagnosis by using ultrasound scanning to look for enlarged kidneys with cysts.

There is no effective way to prevent the cysts forming, but careful control of high blood pressure may slow the rate of the kidney damage. If the fluid in the cysts is infected, antibiotics (p.885) may be prescribed. If end-stage kidney failure occurs, dialysis (p.707) or a kidney transplant (p.708) will be needed.

WHAT IS THE PROGNOSIS?

The progression of polycystic kidney disease in adults varies considerably. However, members of the same family who have the condition tend to have a similar prognosis. About 7 in 10 of the people who have polycystic kidney disease develop kidney failure by age 65.

In a child who has juvenile polycystic kidney disease, the kidneys will fail, and eventually the child will need dialysis or a kidney transplant. Some affected infants may die at only a few months of age due to kidney failure.

(WWW) ONLINE SITES: p.1032, p.1037

Kidney cancer

Cancerous tumors that either originate in the kidney or have spread from a cancer elsewhere in the body

AGE GENDER GENETICS LIFESTYLE Risk factors depend on the cause

In most cases of kidney cancer, a tumor develops within the kidney tissue itself. Rarely, cancer may spread to the kidney from other organs in the body.

There are three main types of kidney cancer. The most common type, adenocarcinoma, develops from the cells that make up the main body of the kidneys. A second, rare form, known as transitional cell carcinoma, develops from

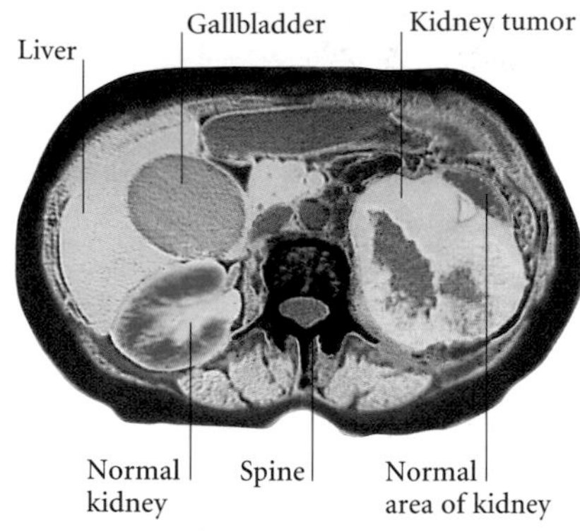
Liver
Gallbladder
Kidney tumor
Normal kidney
Spine
Normal area of kidney

Kidney cancer
This CT scan through the abdomen shows a large kidney tumor that has grown to replace most of the normal kidney tissue.

the cells that line the urine-collecting system within the kidney, bladder, and ureters (the tubes that carry urine from the kidneys to the bladder). This form is more common in people who smoke, because tobacco contains carcinogens (cancer-inducing substances), and in people who have been exposed to other carcinogens, such as chemical dyes, even many years previously. A third type, called Wilms tumor (p.872), is usually either present at birth or develops during the first 5 years of life.

What are the symptoms?

There are often no symptoms in the early stages of kidney cancer. If symptoms do develop, they may include:

- Painful, frequent urination.
- Blood in the urine.
- Pain in the back or sides.
- Weight loss.

If you notice blood in your urine (indicated by a red, dark, or tea color), consult your doctor immediately.

What might be done?

If your doctor suspects kidney cancer, he or she may image the kidneys using ultrasound scanning (p.250), CT scanning (p.247), or intravenous urography (p.699). Where possible, the tumour or the affected kidney will be surgically removed. If the cancer has spread to other areas, you may need to have chemotherapy (p.278). The natural hormone progesterone (*see* SEX HORMONES AND RELATED DRUGS, p.933) and cancer treatments such as interleukin-2 (*see* ANTICANCER DRUGS, p.907) have also been successful in treating some cases.

About 7 in 10 people who have a kidney tumor removed survive more than 5 years, even if the tumor was large. If the cancer has spread to other organs before it is diagnosed, the chance of survival decreases. However, treatments such as radiation therapy (p.279) may slow the spread of cancer and relieve pain.

(WWW) ONLINE SITES: p.1028, p.1037

Diabetic kidney disease

Damage to the filtering units of the kidneys that occurs in people who have diabetes mellitus

 AGE Usually occurs in adults who have had diabetes mellitus for many years

 GENETICS Diabetes mellitus sometimes runs in families

LIFESTYLE Poor control of diabetes mellitus is a risk factor

 GENDER Not a significant factor

Long-term diabetes mellitus (p.687) may result in damage to various organs in the body. Kidney damage caused by diabetes mellitus is known as diabetic kidney disease. The disorder develops in about 4 in 10 of the people who have had diabetes for over 15 years.

Diabetes mellitus affects small blood vessels in the glomeruli (the filtering units of the kidney). Damage to these vessels causes protein to leak into the urine and reduces the kidneys' ability to remove wastes and excess water from the body. Symptoms do not usually appear until kidney damage is severe, and they may then include vomiting, drowsiness, and shortness of breath (*see* CHRONIC KIDNEY FAILURE, p.706, and NEPHROTIC SYNDROME, p.700). Many people with long-term diabetes mellitus also have high blood pressure (*see* HYPERTENSION, p.403), which may cause further damage to the kidneys.

What might be done?

People who have diabetes mellitus are monitored regularly by their doctor so that complications such as kidney damage can be detected at an early stage. The doctor may look for the first signs of diabetic kidney disease by having your urine tested to detect protein, and blood tests may be done to check how well the kidneys are functioning. Once the condition has been diagnosed, the primary aim of treatment will be to slow the progression of the disease to kidney failure. In some cases, control of blood glucose levels and blood pressure can prevent kidney function from deteriorating. ACE inhibitors (p.900) may help counteract the progression of kidney damage in people with diabetes mellitus. However, even if diabetes is controlled, diabetic kidney disease may still lead to damage. The outcome may be end-stage kidney failure (p.708), in which there is a complete loss of kidney function.

End-stage kidney failure due to diabetic kidney disease can usually be treated with dialysis (p.707) or a kidney transplant (p.708). It is sometimes possible to combine a kidney transplant with a transplant of the pancreas, treating both kidney failure and diabetes mellitus at the same time. However, the surgery involved is complex and is only carried out in certain specialty centers.

(WWW) ONLINE SITES: p.1029, p.1037

Kidney failure

Loss of the normal function of both kidneys due to a variety of causes

 AGE GENDER GENETICS LIFESTYLE Risk factors depend on the cause

In kidney failure, the kidneys cease to function normally, and waste products and excess water build up in the body, disrupting the chemical balance of the blood. The condition may take one of three forms: acute kidney failure (p.706), chronic kidney failure (p.706), or end-stage kidney failure (p.708).

Acute kidney failure is a sudden, drastic loss of kidney function that can be fatal if not treated rapidly. Chronic kidney failure is a gradual reduction in function of the kidneys over months or years. Some people have the condition for years without knowing it. End-stage kidney failure is a permanent and almost total loss of kidney function and is the last stage of chronic kidney failure. Left untreated, the condition is fatal.

Treatment for kidney failure involves first reversing or slowing the damage, then restoring the chemical balance of the blood and treating the underlying disorder. Methods of treatment for kidney failure may include drugs, dialysis (p.707), or a kidney transplant (p.708).

(WWW) ONLINE SITES: p.1037

Acute kidney failure

Sudden loss of the function of both kidneys, which is potentially life-threatening

AGE GENDER GENETICS LIFESTYLE Risk factors depend on the cause

Acute kidney failure occurs when both kidneys suddenly cease their normal function of filtering waste products and excess water from the blood into the urine. The waste substances build up to dangerous levels in the body, and the chemical balance of the blood is upset. The condition is life-threatening and requires immediate hospital treatment.

What are the causes?

The kidneys will stop working properly if their blood supply is greatly reduced. This reduction may be due to a fall in blood pressure associated with shock (*see* HYPOTENSION, p.414), such as after severe bleeding, serious infection, or a heart attack (*see* MYOCARDIAL INFARCTION, p.410). Kidney failure may also result from damage by disorders such as glomerulonephritis (p.699), by toxic chemicals, or by drugs. Another cause may be a blockage in the urinary tract that causes both kidneys to swell with urine (*see* HYDRONEPHROSIS, p.703).

What are the symptoms?

The symptoms of acute kidney failure may appear rapidly, sometimes over a period of hours, and include:

- Greatly reduced urine volume.
- Nausea and vomiting.
- Drowsiness and headache.
- Back pain.

If you develop these symptoms, you should call your doctor immediately. Without treatment, acute kidney failure may be fatal within a few days.

How is it diagnosed?

If your doctor suspects acute kidney failure, he or she will have you admitted to the hospital for emergency treatment and tests to find the cause. In some cases, there may be an obvious cause, such as severe bleeding. In other cases, ultrasound scanning (p.250) or CT scanning (p.247) may be performed to look for a blockage of the urinary tract. A kidney biopsy (p.701) may also be performed to examine kidney tissue.

What is the treatment?

If you have acute kidney failure, you will need immediate treatment for the disorder and any associated conditions. You may be treated in a critical care unit (p.958). You may have to undergo dialysis (opposite page) for a short time so that the excess fluid and waste products can be removed from your bloodstream while the doctors investigate the cause of the kidney failure. If you have lost a large amount of blood, you may need to have a blood transfusion (p.447) to restore your normal blood volume. If an underlying disorder is diagnosed, treatment with drugs may be necessary. Finally, if there is a blockage anywhere in your urinary tract, you may need to undergo surgery to have the obstruction removed.

What is the prognosis?

If your kidneys have not yet been damaged irreversibly, there is a good chance that you will make a complete recovery, which may take up to 6 months. However, in some cases, the resulting damage is not completely reversible, and in this situation chronic kidney failure (below) may develop. If chronic kidney failure eventually progresses to end-stage kidney failure (p.708), in which there is a permanent and almost total loss of kidney function, you will need treatment involving long-term dialysis or a kidney transplant (p.708) to replace (dialysis) or restore normal kidney function.

(WWW) ONLINE SITES: p.1037

Chronic kidney failure

Gradual and progressive loss of function in both kidneys

AGE Some causes are increasingly common with age

GENDER GENETICS Risk factors depend on the cause

LIFESTYLE Not a significant factor

In chronic kidney failure, progressive damage gradually reduces the ability of the kidneys to remove excess water and wastes from the blood for excretion as urine. As a result, waste substances start to build up in the body and cause problems. In many cases, kidney function is reduced by over 60 percent before the buildup begins; by this time, often after months or perhaps years, the kidneys may be irreversibly damaged. Dialysis (opposite page) or a kidney transplant (p.708) may therefore become necessary.

What are the causes?

Chronic kidney failure can be due to disorders that progressively damage kidney tissue, such as polycystic kidney disease (p.704) or glomerulonephritis (p.699). The condition may also be the result of generalized disorders, such as diabetes mellitus (p.687) or high blood pressure (*see* HYPERTENSION, p.403). People who have sickle-cell anemia (p.448) are at risk of developing chronic kidney failure if abnormal blood cells block the small vessels that supply the kidneys. Chronic kidney failure can also follow prolonged blockage of the urinary tract, such as that caused by an enlarged prostate gland (p.725).

What are the symptoms?

The initial symptoms of chronic kidney failure appear gradually over weeks or months and are often vague, such as fatigue and loss of appetite. Obvious symptoms may then develop, including:

- Frequent urination, particularly during the night.
- Pale, itchy, and easily bruised skin.
- Shortness of breath.
- Poor concentration.
- Nausea and vomiting.
- Muscular twitching.
- Pins and needles.
- Cramps in the legs or hands.

The condition is associated with a number of complications, such as high blood pressure, which may be an effect as well as a cause of kidney failure; bone thinning (*see* OSTEOPOROSIS, p.368); and anemia (p.446), in which the oxygen-carrying capacity of the blood is reduced. Disturbance in blood chemistry caused by kidney failure may lead to conditions such as hyperparathyroidism (p.682).

How is it diagnosed?

If you have symptoms of chronic kidney failure, your doctor will probably have samples of your blood and urine tested to detect abnormal levels of waste products. You may also have ultrasound scanning (p.250), radionuclide scanning (p.251), or CT scanning (p.247) to assess the size of the kidneys; abnormally small kidneys are often a

TREATMENT DIALYSIS

Dialysis is used to treat kidney failure by replacing the functions of the kidneys, which filter out wastes and excess water from the blood. It can be a temporary treatment for acute kidney failure (opposite page) or a long-term measure used in end-stage kidney failure (p.708). There are two forms: peritoneal dialysis, in which the peritoneal membrane in the abdomen is used as a filter; and hemodialysis, in which a kidney machine filters the blood.

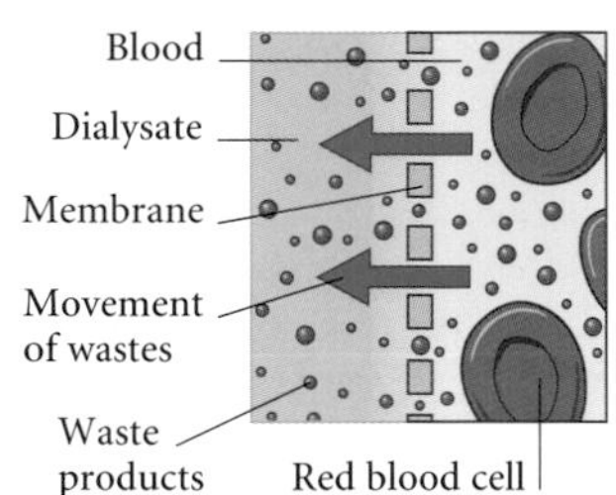
Blood
Dialysate
Membrane
Movement of wastes
Waste products
Red blood cell

How dialysis works
During dialysis, excess water and waste products from the blood pass across a membrane into a solution (the dialysate), which is then discarded.

PERITONEAL DIALYSIS

In peritoneal dialysis, the peritoneum, the membrane that surrounds the abdominal organs, is used instead of the kidneys to filter the blood. A procedure called an exchange is carried out four times a day at home. During an exchange, dialysis fluid that was flowed into the abdomen 4–6 hours earlier is drained out of the peritoneum through a catheter in the abdominal wall. The fluid is replaced with fresh solution, then the equipment is disconnected, and you can carry out normal activities. Between exchanges, wastes and excess water pass continually from the peritoneal blood vessels into the dialysis fluid.

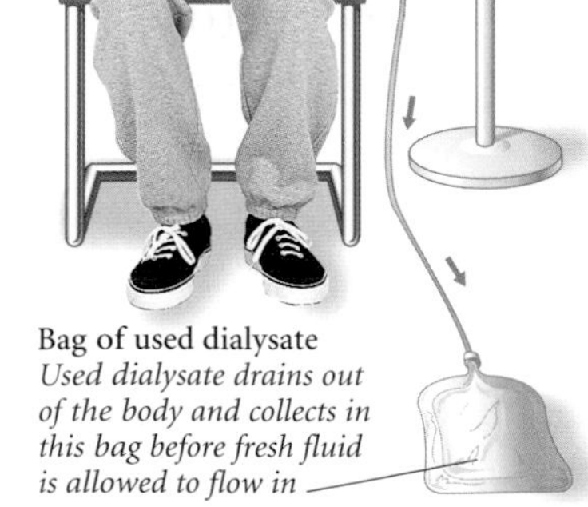
Dialysate tubing

Fresh dialysate
The bag of fresh dialysate is slowly emptied into the peritoneal cavity

Bag of used dialysate
Used dialysate drains out of the body and collects in this bag before fresh fluid is allowed to flow in

Undergoing peritoneal dialysis
In peritoneal dialysis, dialysis fluid is changed at regular intervals and is continually present in the abdomen. Once a fluid exchange has taken place, the bags and tubing are detached, and you can move freely.

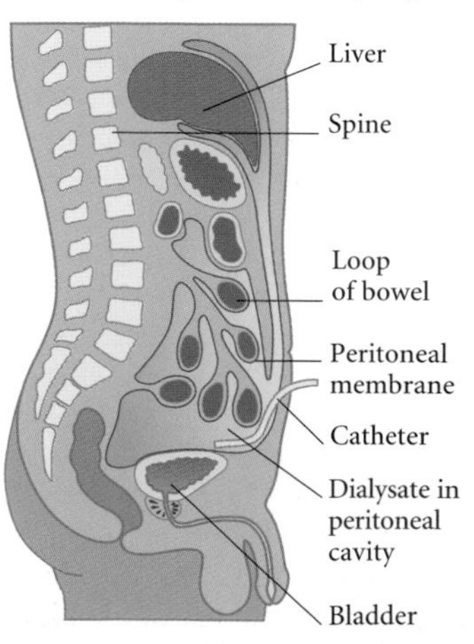
Liver
Spine
Loop of bowel
Peritoneal membrane
Catheter
Dialysate in peritoneal cavity
Bladder

Using the peritoneum as a filter
The abdominal organs are covered by a peritoneal membrane, which is rich in blood vessels. In peritoneal dialysis, waste products and water pass from the blood across the membrane and into dialysate fluid in the abdomen.

HEMODIALYSIS

In hemodialysis, blood is pumped by a kidney machine through a filter attached to the side of the machine. Inside the filter, blood flows on one side of a membrane and dialysis fluid flows on the other. Waste products and water pass from the blood across the membrane and into the dialysate fluid, and the filtered blood returns to the body. Each treatment takes 3–4 hours and is required about three times a week.

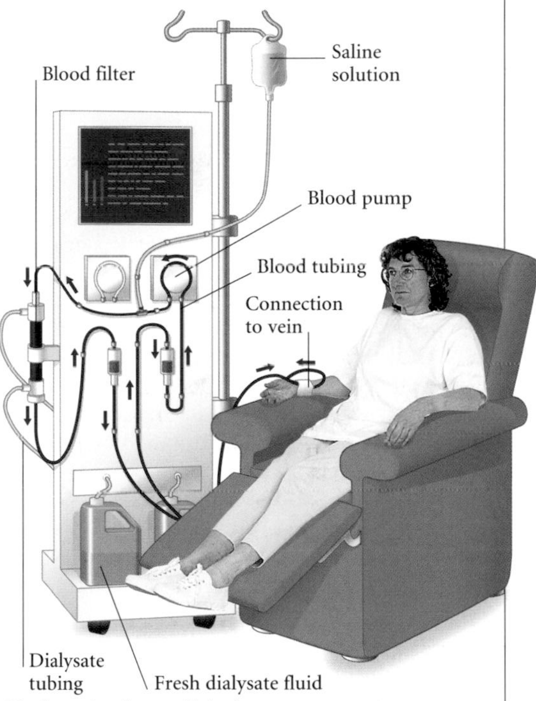
Saline solution
Blood filter
Blood pump
Blood tubing
Connection to vein
Dialysate tubing
Fresh dialysate fluid

Undergoing hemodialysis
During hemodialysis, you are attached to the kidney machine for several hours while waste products and water are removed from your blood. Hemodialysis is usually carried out in dialysis centers, but some people are able to treat themselves at home.

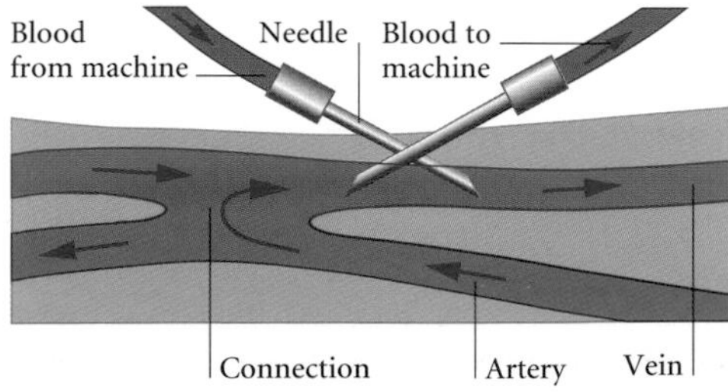
Blood from machine
Needle
Blood to machine
Connection
Artery
Vein

Access to the bloodstream
Dialysis requires fast blood flow. A vein and an artery near the skin surface are surgically joined so that the vein carries blood at high pressure. This vein can then be used for access to the circulatory system.

sign of chronic kidney failure. In addition, you may need to undergo a kidney biopsy (p.701), a procedure in which a small piece of kidney tissue is removed and examined under a microscope to determine the nature of kidney damage.

What is the treatment?

Treatment is directed at the underlying cause. Corticosteroids (p.930) may be used to treat some forms of glomerulonephritis. Drugs for high blood pressure (*see* Antihypertensive drugs, p.897) may also be given, whether the condition is a cause or a result of chronic kidney failure. If there is an obstruction in the urinary tract, you will probably need surgery to relieve it. In addition, your doctor will monitor the progress of the disease and the effectiveness of your treatment with regular checkups.

What is the prognosis?

The prognosis for chronic kidney failure depends on the cause and severity of the kidney damage. If your doctor is able to treat the cause and prevent further damage to your kidneys, you may not need dialysis. However, in many cases, treatment only slows the rate of deterioration. After several months or even years, chronic kidney failure may develop into end-stage kidney failure (below), in which the damage is irreversible. At this stage, dialysis or a kidney transplant operation is required.

(WWW) ONLINE SITES: p.1037

Treatment: Kidney transplant

End-stage kidney failure may be treated with a kidney transplant, which can take over the function of both diseased kidneys. An organ may be donated by a living relative or spouse or by someone who has consented to the use of their organs after death. The new kidney is placed in the pelvis during the operation; the diseased ones are usually left in place. A kidney transplant avoids the need for dialysis and often allows a normal lifestyle.

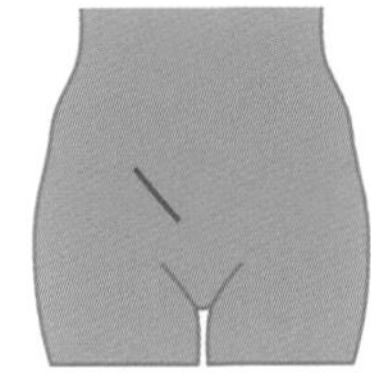

Site of incision

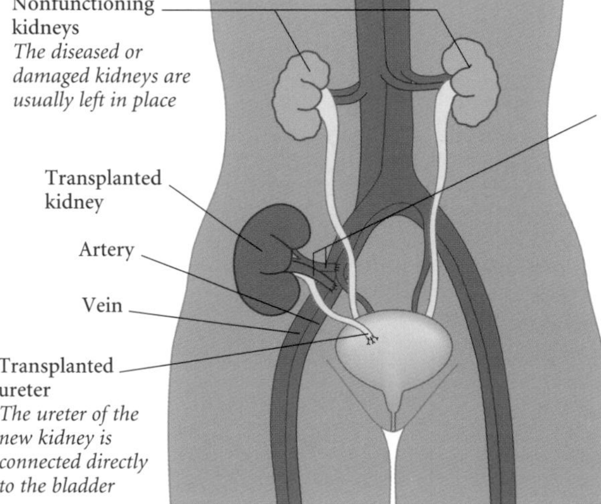
Nonfunctioning kidneys
The diseased or damaged kidneys are usually left in place
Transplanted kidney
Artery
Vein
Transplanted ureter
The ureter of the new kidney is connected directly to the bladder
Transplanted artery and vein
The artery and vein of the new kidney are attached to blood vessels in the pelvis

The operation
The new kidney is placed in the pelvis through an incision in the abdomen. The kidney is carefully positioned so that it can be connected easily to a nearby vein and artery and to the bladder.

End-stage kidney failure

Irreversible loss of the function of both kidneys, which is often life-threatening

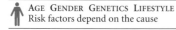

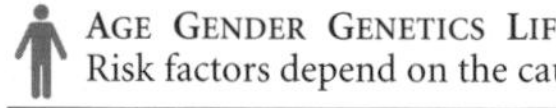
Age Gender Genetics Lifestyle
Risk factors depend on the cause

In end-stage kidney failure, the kidneys have permanently lost more than 90 percent of their normal function. They are therefore unable to filter waste products and excess water out of the blood for excretion as urine. End-stage kidney failure usually progresses from chronic kidney failure (p.706). If prompt action is not taken to replace the function of the failed kidneys with dialysis (p.707) or a kidney transplant (above), the condition is inevitably fatal.

What are the symptoms?

The main symptoms of end-stage kidney failure usually include:

- Greatly reduced volume of urine.
- Swelling of the face, the limbs, and the abdomen.
- Severe lethargy.
- Weight loss.
- Headache and vomiting.
- Hand and leg cramps.
- Very itchy skin.

Many people who have end-stage kidney failure also have breath that smells like ammonia, an odor similar to that of household bleach.

How is it diagnosed?

If your doctor suspects end-stage kidney failure, he or she will first arrange for urine tests and blood tests to detect abnormal levels of waste products in these body fluids. If the cause of kidney failure has not already been identified, you may also have to undergo imaging procedures such as ultrasound scanning (p.250), CT scanning (p.247), or radionuclide scanning (p.251), to detect abnormalities in your kidneys.

What is the treatment?

Kidney dialysis, the usual treatment for end-stage kidney failure, takes over the function of filtering harmful waste products from the blood and controlling the water balance of the body. However, long-term dialysis may lead to complications such as gradual weakening of the bones (*see* Osteoporosis, p.368). Anemia (p.446), in which the oxygen-carrying capacity of the blood is reduced, may develop due to a lack of the hormone erythropoietin, which is made in the kidneys and stimulates red blood cell production. However, anemia is easily treated by injections of erythropoietin.

A kidney transplant offers the best hope of returning to a normal lifestyle. The main drawback of a transplant is that you will need to take immunosuppressants (p.906) for the rest of your life to prevent your immune system rejecting the donor organ. Occasionally, a second transplant is needed if the first kidney stops functioning. If you do not have a kidney transplant, you will need dialysis for the rest of your life.

(WWW) ONLINE SITES: p.1037

DISORDERS OF THE BLADDER AND URETHRA

Urinary disorders are very common. The symptoms may include an increased need to empty the bladder, urinary leakage, blood in the urine, and pain during and after urination. These symptoms can often disrupt daily routine. However, most disorders of the bladder and urethra (the passage from the bladder to the outside of the body) are curable or at least controllable by treatment.

The first article in this section deals with cystitis, a condition in which the bladder becomes inflamed. Cystitis is often due to infection by bacteria from the skin around the anus. Women are particularly susceptible because the female urethra is short and close to the anus, allowing bacteria to enter easily. In men, bladder infections are most likely to develop because of incomplete emptying of the bladder due to an enlarged prostate gland.

The next three articles cover urinary incontinence, which is the inability to control bladder function. There are several types of incontinence, all of which are more common in women and in older people of both sexes. Structural disorders are discussed next; they include stones that form in the bladder and strictures that narrow the urethra, making urination difficult.

The final article discusses cancerous and noncancerous bladder tumors, which are often detected after blood is found in the urine. Early diagnosis usually leads to successful treatment.

Sexually transmitted infections that affect the male urethra are discussed elsewhere in the book (*see* SEXUALLY TRANSMITTED INFECTIONS, pp.764–768). Urinary tract problems in children are covered in the section on infancy and childhood (pp.870–872).

KEY ANATOMY

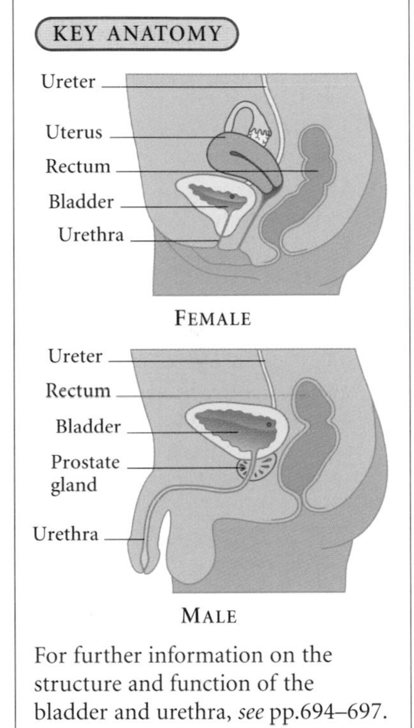
Ureter
Uterus
Rectum
Bladder
Urethra
FEMALE
Ureter
Rectum
Bladder
Prostate gland
Urethra
MALE

For further information on the structure and function of the bladder and urethra, *see* pp.694–697.

Cystitis

Inflammation of the bladder lining, causing painful, frequent urination

 AGE Rare in children; more common in teenage girls and women of all ages

 GENDER Much more common in females

 LIFESTYLE For some women, sexual intercourse may bring on an episode

 GENETICS Not a significant factor

In cystitis, the lining of the bladder becomes inflamed, resulting in a frequent need to urinate and pain during urination. In most cases, the condition is due to a bacterial infection.

Cystitis affects women much more commonly than men. About half of all women have at least one attack of bacterial cystitis in their lifetime and some women have recurrent attacks. In men, cystitis is rare and is usually associated with a disorder of the urinary tract. In children, cystitis can be the result of an anatomical or structural problem and can damage the kidneys (*see* URINARY TRACT INFECTIONS IN CHILDREN, p.871).

WHAT ARE THE TYPES?

There are several types of cystitis. The most common form is bacterial cystitis, which is often caused by *Escherichia coli*, a bacterium that normally lives in the intestines. Cystitis usually occurs when bacteria from the anal or vaginal areas enter the bladder through the urethra (the tube from the bladder to the outside of the body), often during sex or when the anus is wiped after a bowel movement. Women are at much greater risk of infection than men because the female urethra is shorter than that of the male and the opening is nearer the anus. The risk of bacterial cystitis is increased if the bladder cannot be emptied. Incomplete emptying causes urine to be retained in the bladder, and the trapped urine can harbor bacteria.

Postmenopausal women are especially prone to bacterial cystitis because they have reduced levels of the hormone estrogen, which leaves their urethral lining vulnerable. Women who use a diaphragm and spermicide as a method of contraception are at increased risk because a diaphragm, which has to stay in place for several hours, can prevent complete bladder emptying, and spermicide may encourage the growth of bacteria in the vagina. In addition, people with diabetes mellitus (p.687) are also susceptible for several reasons: there may be glucose in their urine, which encourages the growth of bacteria; they may have reduced immunity to infection; or they may have nerve damage that prevents the bladder from emptying completely. Other disorders that prevent complete bladder emptying include an enlarged prostate gland (p.725) and urethral stricture (p.714).

Interstitial cystitis is a rare, chronic inflammation of the lining and tissues of the bladder that may lead to ulceration. The cause is unknown.

In radiation cystitis, the bladder lining is damaged as a result of radiation therapy (p.279) to treat prostate cancer (p.726) or cancer of the cervix (p.750).

Some women have repeated bouts of painful, frequent urination but with no bacteria in the urine. These symptoms are known as urethral syndrome. Minor bruising following sexual intercourse is sometimes a factor, particularly in postmenopausal women whose genital tissues may be thin and easily damaged.

What are the symptoms?

The main symptoms of all types of cystitis are the same and include:

- Burning pain when urinating.
- Frequent and urgent need to urinate, with little urine passed each time.
- A feeling of incomplete emptying of the bladder.

If the cause of the cystitis is a bacterial infection, you may also notice the following symptoms:

- Pain in the lower abdominal region and sometimes in the lower back.
- Fever and chills.

A bladder infection can spread upward to a kidney, causing severe pain in the back (*see* PYELONEPHRITIS, p.698). In some severe cases of cystitis, complete or partial loss of control over bladder function can occur as a result of irritation of the muscle in the bladder wall (*see* URGE INCONTINENCE, p.712).

SELF-HELP Preventing bacterial cystitis

If you have had bacterial cystitis, the following measures can help you avoid further attacks:

- Drink 4–6 pints (2–3 liters) of fluids per day.
- Empty your bladder frequently.
- After a bowel movement, wipe yourself from front to back to prevent bacteria around the anus from entering the urethra.
- Wash your genital area before sexual intercourse. Make sure your partner washes, too.
- Urinate shortly after having sexual intercourse.
- Use unperfumed toiletries and avoid vaginal deodorants.
- Do not use a diaphragm or spermicide for contraception.

What might be done?

If you develop the symptoms of cystitis, arrange to see your doctor. Meanwhile, you may be able to relieve symptoms by drinking 1 pint (1/2 liter) of fluid every hour for 4 hours. Drinking cranberry juice can relieve the burning sensation when urinating and analgesics (p.912) may reduce the pain. To prevent a recurrence, follow self-help measures (*see* PREVENTING BACTERIAL CYSTITIS, left).

Your doctor may arrange for you to undergo urine tests to detect any evidence of infection. While awaiting the results, he or she may prescribe antibiotics (p.885). Almost all attacks of bacterial cystitis are cured by a single course of antibiotics. Recurrent attacks of cystitis in women or a single episode in men need further investigation, for example, specialized imaging studies such as ultrasound or cystoscopy (p.715), in which a viewing instrument is used to look for underlying conditions. If there is no evidence of a disorder, but the cystitis still recurs, particularly after sexual intercourse, your doctor may prescribe a long course of low-dose antibiotics. Women may be given a single high dose of antibiotics to be taken after intercourse or at the first sign of symptoms.

If urine tests show no infection but you continue to have recurrent attacks of pain and frequent urination, your doctor may suspect urethral syndrome. However, bacteria may be difficult to detect, and your doctor may prescribe antibiotics even though no infection has been found. He or she may suggest self-help measures like those for bacterial cystitis. Some postmenopausal women find hormone replacement therapy (p.937) or estrogen-containing creams helpful.

If the attacks continue, you may have interstitial cystitis. Your doctor may arrange for cystoscopy to view inside the bladder, and a sample of bladder tissue may be taken. If these investigations reveal interstitial cystitis, your doctor may suggest a procedure that stretches the bladder by filling it with water. This procedure, carried out under general anesthesia, often relieves symptoms.

WWW ONLINE SITES: p.1037

Urinary incontinence

Complete or partial loss of voluntary control over bladder function

 AGE More common with increasing age

 GENDER More common in females

 GENETICS LIFESTYLE Risk factors depend on the type

Normally, muscles in the bladder wall squeeze the urine out of the bladder, while muscles in the neck of the bladder and pelvic floor control the opening and closing of the bladder outlet. Any disorder affecting these muscles or their nerve supply can result in a partial or complete loss of bladder control.

Urinary incontinence becomes more common with increasing age. The condition is more common in women than in men. It sometimes accompanies dementia (p.535) or stroke (p.532).

What are the types?

There are four main types of incontinence: stress, urge, overflow, and total. The symptoms and treatment are different for each type.

The most common type of incontinence is stress incontinence (opposite page), in which small amounts of urine are expelled involuntarily.

People who have urge incontinence (p.712) feel an unexpected and urgent need to urinate due to an involuntary contraction of the bladder, resulting in the uncontrollable and sudden passing of large amounts of urine.

In overflow incontinence, the bladder cannot empty because of a blockage at the bladder neck or in the urethra (the tube that leads from the bladder to the outside of the body) or because of a weak bladder muscle. As a result, pressure builds up in the bladder while it fills, causing a continual dribble of urine. The outflow of urine may be obstructed by bladder stones (p.714), urethral stricture (p.714), or in men by an enlarged prostate gland (p.725) that constricts the urethra. Weakness of the bladder muscle may be caused by an untreated obstruction, diabetes mellitus (p.687), or pelvic surgery.

In total incontinence there is no control of bladder function. The condition usually results from a disorder of the

TEST URODYNAMIC STUDIES

Urodynamic studies are carried out to investigate problems with bladder control, including incontinence and restricted urine flow. In these studies, probes are inserted into the urethra, bladder, and rectum or vagina to monitor pressure changes while the bladder is filling and emptying. At the same time, a contrast medium (a dye that shows up on X-rays), passed into the bladder through a catheter, enables the doctor to view the shape of the bladder on an X-ray monitor. You will be asked to cough as the bladder fills, which will cause leakage of urine if you have stress incontinence.

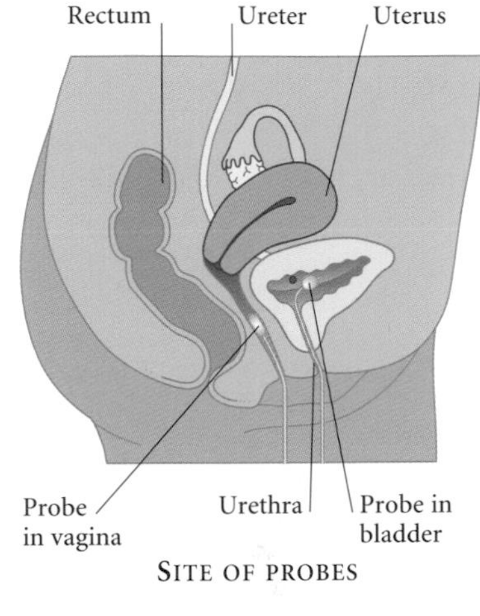
Rectum
Ureter
Uterus
Probe in vagina
Urethra
Probe in bladder

SITE OF PROBES

X-ray monitoring
During the procedure, you will need to stand against an upright X-ray table for continuous X-ray video monitoring. The appearance of the urethra and bladder can then be compared with pressure changes.

X-ray monitor
X-ray table
Solution containing contrast medium
X-ray machine
Pressure trace
Lead from electronic diaper
Lead from vaginal probe
Lead from bladder probe
Catheter to bladder

RESULTS

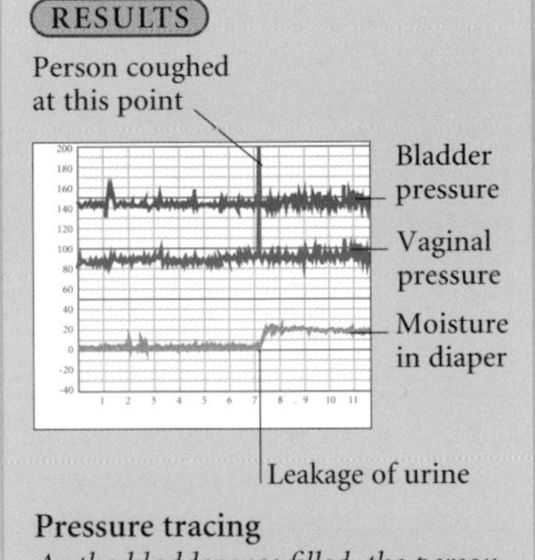
Person coughed at this point
Bladder pressure
Vaginal pressure
Moisture in diaper
Leakage of urine

Pressure tracing
As the bladder was filled, the person was asked to cough. This action increased pressure in and around the bladder, causing a leakage of urine into an electronic diaper. This is typical of stress incontinence.

nervous system, such as dementia, or neurologic trauma, such as spinal injury (p.524). Surgery to treat pelvic cancers can also cause incontinence by damaging the nerves that supply the bladder.

WHAT MIGHT BE DONE?

Urodynamic studies (above) can be done to determine the type of incontinence. In minor incontinence, absorbent pads can be worn to protect the clothes, and physiotherapy (p.961), Kegel exercises (p.712), or surgery may improve the tone of the pelvic floor muscles. Incontinence that is due to a long-term nerve problem may be relieved by bladder catheterization (p.713) to drain the urine.

WWW ONLINE SITES: p.1026, p.1037

Stress incontinence

Involuntary loss of small amounts of urine during exertion, coughing, or sneezing

 AGE More common with increasing age

 GENDER Almost exclusively affects females

 GENETICS LIFESTYLE Not significant factors

Stress incontinence results from weakness of the pelvic floor muscles. These muscles support the bladder and help control the opening and closing of the bladder outlet during urination. Weakness of the pelvic floor muscles allows the bladder neck to drop, resulting in involuntary loss of urine when pressure in the abdomen is increased.

In mild stress incontinence, a small amount of urine leaks out of the bladder during strenuous activities, such as running. In severe cases, urine escapes during activities such as coughing or lifting. Stress incontinence is the most common type of incontinence and affects women almost exclusively.

The disorder commonly occurs during and after pregnancy; after surgery in the pelvic area; during menopause, when a reduced level of the hormone estrogen causes the pelvic muscles to lose elasticity; and with increasing age. Stress incontinence may also be associated with a prolapse of the uterus and

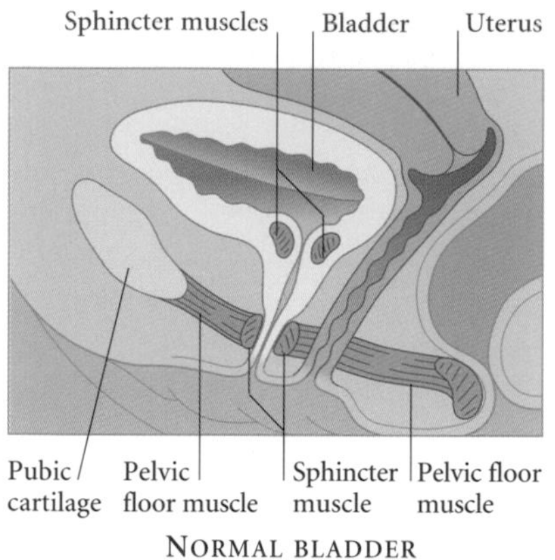
Sphincter muscles
Bladder
Uterus
Pubic cartilage
Pelvic floor muscle
Sphincter muscle
Pelvic floor muscle

NORMAL BLADDER

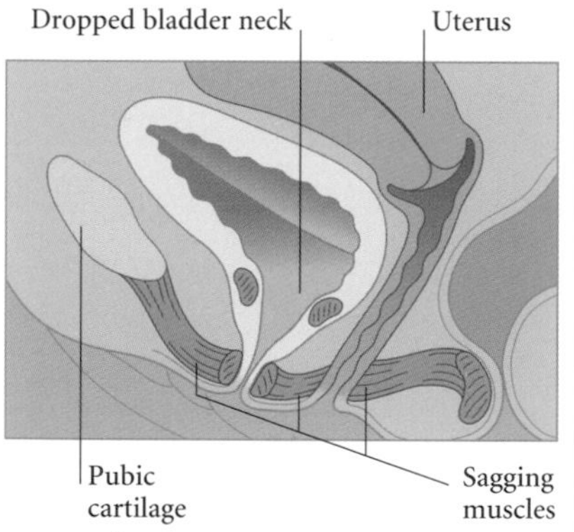
Dropped bladder neck
Uterus
Pubic cartilage
Sagging muscles

INCONTINENT BLADDER

Cause of stress incontinence

In stress incontinence, the muscles in the pelvic floor cannot support the bladder. The bladder neck drops, and the sphincter muscles become unable to keep it closed.

vagina (p.747), rectal prolapse (p.667), or a prolapsed bladder. You are more likely to develop the condition if you are overweight or have a chronic cough.

HOW IS IT DIAGNOSED?

Your doctor may diagnose stress incontinence after asking about your fluid intake, how frequently you urinate, the amount of urine you pass, and when you leak urine. He or she will perform a pelvic examination to check your pelvic floor muscles and find out if you have a prolapsed bladder or uterus. The doctor may arrange for urodynamic studies (p.711) to assess your bladder function.

WHAT IS THE TREATMENT?

Strengthening the pelvic floor muscles by doing Kegel exercises (right) is an effective form of self-help treatment for stress incontinence, whatever the cause. If the condition occurs after childbirth, muscle tone will gradually return, but Kegel exercises can be used to hasten the process of recovery. For postmenopausal women, hormone replacement therapy (p.937) may be recommended to help counteract loss of muscle tone in the pelvic floor. If you are overweight, your doctor may recommend a weight loss diet (*see* CONTROLLING YOUR WEIGHT, p.53). Surgery can relieve severe incontinence by tightening the muscles that have stretched and may restore near-normal bladder control. Periurethral injection of collagen can be used to treat some types of severe stress incontinence.

(WWW) ONLINE SITES: p.1026, p.1037

Urge incontinence

Repeated episodes of involuntary loss of urine preceded by a sudden, urgent need to empty the bladder

 AGE More common with increasing age

 GENDER More common in females

 GENETICS LIFESTYLE Not significant factors

A person with urge incontinence feels a sudden, urgent need to urinate that is followed by involuntary loss of urine. This condition varies in severity. At its mildest, the person is able to get to a toilet before the bladder empties. If the condition is severe, it can be impossible to stop the flow of urine voluntarily once the bladder begins to empty.

WHAT ARE THE CAUSES?

Urge incontinence is most commonly caused by irritability of the muscle that forms the bladder wall. When irritated, the muscle contracts involuntarily and empties the bladder of urine. Bladder irritability can be associated with infection or inflammation of the bladder lining (*see* CYSTITIS, p.709).

Urge incontinence can be caused by neurologic conditions such as stroke (p.532), multiple sclerosis (p.541), or spinal injury (p.524). As well, some cases are thought to be associated with anxiety disorders (p.551).

WHAT MIGHT BE DONE?

Your doctor may ask you to keep a record of the frequency and amount of urine you pass and how much fluid you drink. He or she may carry out a physical examination in order to look for an underlying disorder, and you may also be asked to provide a urine sample, which will then be sent to the laboratory and checked for infection. Your doctor may also arrange for you to undergo cystoscopy (p.715) and/or urodynamic studies (p.711) to assess your bladder function.

Any underlying cause of urge incontinence should be treated first. If no underlying disorder is identified, there are several self-help measures you can take that may improve the condition. For example, you can learn to control your bladder function by gradually extending the intervals between the times when you pass urine. Kegel exercises (below) will strengthen those muscles that control the bladder outlet. You should also try to avoid drinks containing caffeine and alcohol, which increase urine production and worsen incontinence. In addition, you may be given an antispasmodic drug (*see* ANTISPASMODIC DRUGS AND MOTILITY STIMULANTS, p.926) to reduce irritability of the bladder wall.

(WWW) ONLINE SITES: p.1037

(SELF-HELP) KEGEL EXERCISES

Kegel exercises help strengthen the pelvic floor muscles, which support the bladder, uterus, and rectum. If done regularly, they can help in the treatment and prevention of urinary incontinence.

You can perform Kegel exercises sitting, standing, or lying down. Try to do the exercises as often as you can, at least once every hour throughout the day.

In order to identify the pelvic floor muscles, imagine that you are urinating and have to stop suddenly midstream. The muscles that you feel tighten around your vagina, urethra, and rectum are the pelvic floor muscles. To strengthen these muscles, go through the following exercises:

- Contract the pelvic floor muscles and hold them for 10 seconds.
- Relax the muscles slowly.
- Repeat 5 to 10 times, as often as you can.

Urinary retention

Inability to empty the bladder completely or at all

AGE More common over age 50

GENDER More common in males

GENETICS LIFESTYLE Not significant factors

Urinary retention may be either acute or chronic. In acute retention, the bladder cannot be emptied at all despite a desperate urge to do so, and a sudden and painful buildup of urine occurs. In chronic retention, some urine can be passed with difficulty, but the bladder cannot be emptied completely, and as a result, a gradual and painless buildup of urine occurs. Both forms of urinary retention are more common in men than they are women.

WHAT ARE THE CAUSES?

Anything that exerts pressure on the urethra (the tube from the bladder to the outside of the body) can restrict the flow of urine, causing acute or chronic urinary retention. The most common cause in men is an enlarged prostate gland (p.725). Sometimes, the flow of urine is restricted by a narrowed urethra (*see* URETHRAL STRICTURE, p.714). In women, retention may occur during early pregnancy due to pressure by the enlarging uterus on the urethra but may disappear later as the uterus rises up into the abdomen. In both sexes, urinary retention may be caused by constipation because feces in the rectum can press on the urethra. Occasionally, the flow of urine from the bladder is restricted by conditions in which the neck of the bladder is obstructed, such as bladder stones (p.714) and bladder tumors (p.715).

Damage to the nerves supplying the bladder muscles can also cause urinary retention. Damage may occur in disorders such as multiple sclerosis (p.541) and diabetes mellitus (p.687) or it may be caused by spinal injury (p.524).

In some cases, chronic urinary retention can become acute because of a sudden increase in the amount of urine produced, which can be triggered by diuretic drugs (p.902), cold weather, or alcohol consumption. In other cases, acute urinary retention is a side effect of antidepressant drugs (p.916), drugs for Parkinson's disease (*see* PARKINSON'S DISEASE AND PARKINSONISM, p.539), or cold and flu remedies (p.910).

WHAT ARE THE SYMPTOMS?

Symptoms of acute urinary retention develop over a few hours and include:

- Abdominal pain.
- A distressing and painful urge to urinate without being able to do so.

In contrast to acute retention, chronic retention is unlikely to cause any pain, although the condition can be uncomfortable. The symptoms tend to develop more slowly and include:

- A frequent urge to urinate.
- Swelling of the abdomen.
- Difficulty starting to urinate.
- A weak flow of urine that ends in a dribble. In some cases, there may be involuntary dribbling of urine between visits to the toilet.

Urinary retention can cause kidney damage if urine cannot drain from the kidneys (*see* HYDRONEPHROSIS, p.703).

WHAT MIGHT BE DONE?

If you have acute urinary retention, you will probably need to have your bladder emptied in the hospital (*see* BLADDER CATHETERIZATION, below). In order to identify the underlying cause, you may have a rectal or pelvic examination and specialized tests (*see* URODYNAMIC STUDIES, p.711, and CYSTOSCOPY, p.715).

Chronic urinary retention may be suspected if a routine medical examination reveals you have an enlarged bladder. Diagnostic tests are the same as those for acute retention. The cause of the retention is treated if possible and, in most cases, bladder function returns to normal. If the condition results from nerve damage, permanent or intermittent catheterization to drain the urine may be necessary. You may be taught how to catheterize yourself.

Urinary retention that occurs during pregnancy usually disappears when the uterus enlarges and moves up and out of the pelvis into the abdominal area, relieving pressure on the urethra.

(WWW) ONLINE SITES: p.1037

(TREATMENT) BLADDER CATHETERIZATION

In this procedure, a catheter is inserted into the bladder through the urethra (urethral catheterization) or through an incision in the abdomen (suprapubic catheterization). The catheter allows urine to drain out of the body if urination is not possible, if a person is incontinent, or if urine flow needs to be measured for diagnostic reasons. The catheter is held in place by a small, water-filled balloon and may be removed after urine has been drained or left in permanently. Some people may be taught to insert a catheter themselves several times a day to drain urine.

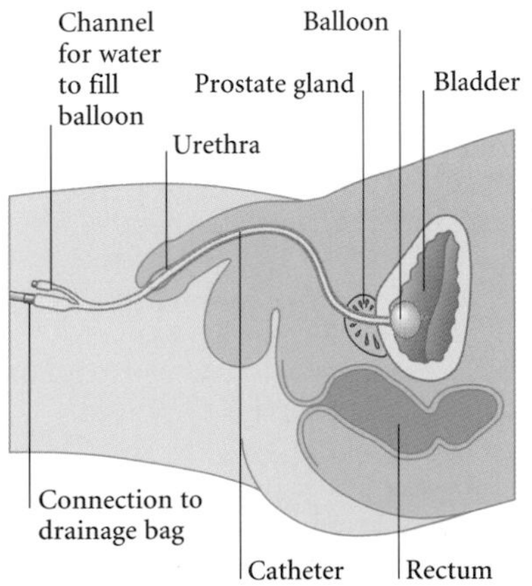
Channel for water to fill balloon
Balloon
Prostate gland
Bladder
Urethra
Connection to drainage bag
Catheter
Rectum

Urethral catheterization
The catheter is inserted along the urethra and into the bladder. Urine passes down the catheter into a drainage bag attached to a stand or worn around the thigh.

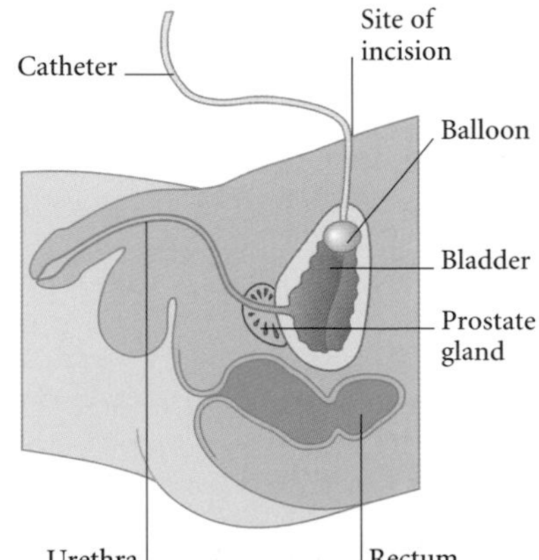
Catheter
Site of incision
Balloon
Bladder
Prostate gland
Urethra
Rectum

Suprapubic catheterization
This technique is used if the urethra is blocked. The catheter enters the bladder through an incision in the abdomen and the urine is collected in a drainage bag.

Urethral stricture

Abnormal narrowing of part of the urethra, the passage from the bladder to the outside of the body

 AGE Most common in young adults and people over age 50

 GENDER Almost exclusively affects males

 LIFESTYLE Unprotected sex with multiple sexual partners is a risk factor

 GENETICS Not a significant factor

In urethral stricture, scar tissue forms within the wall of the urethra, causing narrowing of the urethra and difficulty urinating. In developed countries, scar tissue usually results from damage to the area during certain medical procedures, such as bladder catheterization (p.713), cystoscopy (opposite page), or partial prostatectomy (p.725). Scarring from these procedures usually affects people over 50 years old. Worldwide, the most common causes of scarring are persistent urethral inflammation due to sexually transmitted infections, such as gonorrhea (p.764), and accidental injury to the genital area. Such conditions usually affect young adults.

What are the symptoms?

The symptoms of stricture gradually worsen over time and may include:

- Painful and difficult urination.
- Poor flow of urine.
- Dribbling after urination.
- The sensation that the bladder has been only partly emptied.
- Frequent need to urinate.
- Painful ejaculation.

An untreated stricture may block the flow of urine from the bladder, causing urinary retention (p.713). Incomplete emptying of the bladder can result in cystitis (p.709). In a few cases, it may cause an abnormal buildup of pressure in the urinary tract that can damage the kidneys (*see* HYDRONEPHROSIS, p.703).

What might be done?

Your doctor will first give you a physical examination to find out if your bladder is enlarged. He or she may then arrange for you to have specialized X-rays of the urinary tract in order to establish whether your bladder empties completely on urination as well as to look for any bladder abnormalities. An urethral stricture may be suspected if the X-rays reveal slow bladder emptying and an abnormally large volume of retained urine. Further studies may be carried out to investigate bladder control (*see* URODYNAMIC STUDIES, p.711), and these may show whether or not a stricture exists. In addition, cystoscopy may be used to locate the narrowed area of stricture in the urethra.

If a stricture is detected, the first step in treatment is usually urethral dilation (widening). In this procedure performed under local anesthesia, a slim, flexible instrument is passed into the urethra to stretch the narrowed area gently.

Urethral dilation is usually successful, but, if symptoms persist, the scar tissue may be surgically cut during cystoscopy. If there is substantial scarring, the narrowed section may be removed and the urethra then reconstructed using plastic surgery techniques.

(WWW) ONLINE SITES: p.1037

Bladder stones

Ball-like masses of variable size, made of chemical deposits, that gradually form within the bladder

 AGE Can affect adults of any age but much more common over age 45

 GENDER More common in males

 GENETICS LIFESTYLE Not significant factors

Stones can form in the bladder if waste products in the urine crystallize. About 8 in 10 stones consist of calcium, which comes from excess salts in the urine. Most are between 1/16 in (2 mm) and 3/4 in (2 cm) in diameter, although some will grow much larger. The occurrence of bladder stones is approximately three times more common in men than it is in women and is much more common in people over 45 years old.

The condition may develop if urine stagnates in the bladder as a result of incomplete emptying (*see* URINARY RETENTION, p.713).

What are the symptoms?

A small bladder stone may not cause any symptoms. However, as a stone increases in size, it may start to irritate the bladder lining, causing some or all of the following symptoms:

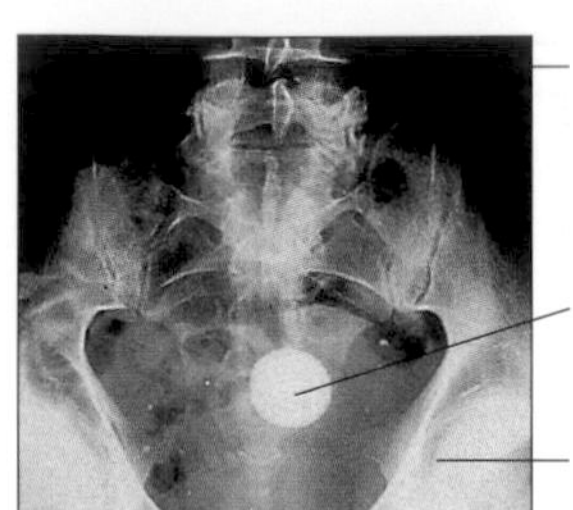
Spine
Bladder stone
Pelvis

Bladder stone
A large bladder stone can be seen in this X-ray. Stones in the bladder, especially if large, can cause painful, difficult urination.

- Painful and difficult urination.
- Frequent and sometimes urgent need to urinate.
- Blood in the urine.

If you develop any of these symptoms, you should consult your doctor without delay. These symptoms are not unique to bladder stones, however. They may also indicate a bladder infection or cancer. Left untreated, a stone may irritate the muscles in the bladder wall, causing urge incontinence (p.712). A stone that blocks the bladder outlet can cause urinary retention or cystitis, which may be intensely painful.

What might be done?

If your doctor suspects that there are stones in your bladder, he or she may arrange for you to have an abdominal X-ray (p.244) or specialized X-rays of the urinary tract (*see* INTRAVENOUS UROGRAPHY, p.699). The doctor also may have your urine analyzed for signs of infection. In addition, cystoscopy (opposite page) may be carried out in order to examine the lining of your bladder for abnormalities.

If bladder stones are detected, they can usually be broken into fragments during cystoscopy or by using a form of ultrasound (*see* LITHOTRIPSY, p.702). The pulverized stones will be excreted in the urine shortly after the procedure, and there may also be some blood in your urine. However, if the bladder stones are very large in size, abdominal surgery may be necessary to remove them. Bladder stones may recur, especially if the underlying cause, such as incomplete bladder emptying, is not corrected. You can have regular urine tests to monitor your condition.

(WWW) ONLINE SITES: p.1037

Bladder tumors

Cancerous or noncancerous growths that develop in the lining of the bladder

AGE Rare under age 50; more common with increasing age over age 50

GENDER More common in males

GENETICS May be a significant factor

LIFESTYLE Smoking and some occupations using chemicals are risk factors

Tumors in the bladder are almost all cancerous. Most of these tumors begin as superficial, wartlike growths, called papillomas, which grow from the lining of the bladder and project into the bladder cavity. Bladder tumors are about three times more common in men than in women.

WHAT ARE THE CAUSES?

More than half of all bladder tumors have been found to develop in people who smoke. About 1 in 6 tumors occurs in people who are exposed to certain industrial chemicals. These people are susceptible to tumors because they handle carcinogens (cancer-causing substances), which are absorbed by the body and excreted in the urine. Carcinogens therefore come into contact with the bladder lining, where they can trigger the growth of abnormal tissue.

In some tropical regions, a common cause of bladder tumors is the parasitic infestation schistosomiasis (p.312).

WHAT ARE THE SYMPTOMS?

Bladder tumors, cancerous or noncancerous, initially cause no symptoms, but the following may develop over time:

- Blood in the urine.
- Dull ache in the lower abdomen.
- Difficulty urinating.

Large tumors may block the bladder outlet, causing urinary retention (p.713). If the bladder is unable to empty completely with urination, the remaining urine stagnates and often becomes infected (see CYSTITIS, p.709). Blockage can also cause the ureters to swell and infection to spread up to the kidney, causing flank pain. If not treated, a cancerous tumor may spread to nearby areas, such as the intestine or rectum. Cancerous cells can also pass through the bloodstream to other body tissues.

TEST AND TREATMENT CYSTOSCOPY

During cystoscopy, a thin, hollow viewing tube, known as a cystoscope, is inserted into the urethra and then into the bladder to look for tumors and other abnormalities affecting the urethra and bladder. The cystoscope may be rigid or flexible. Instruments to take tissue samples or destroy or remove tumors and stones can be inserted through the cystoscope as required. Cystoscopy may be carried out under local or general anesthesia.

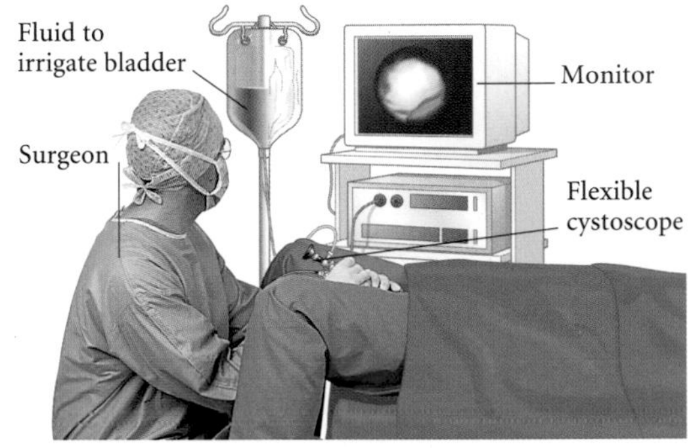
Fluid to irrigate bladder
Monitor
Surgeon
Flexible cystoscope

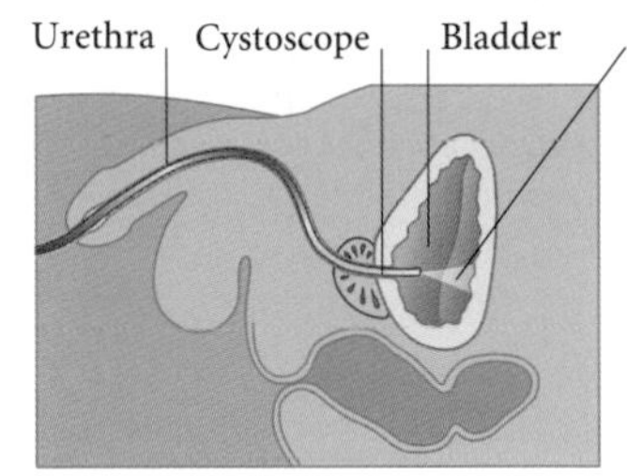
Urethra
Cystoscope
Bladder
Illuminated area
CROSS SECTION

During the procedure
An illuminated and magnified view of part of the bladder lining is transmitted from the cystoscope to a monitor.

VIEW

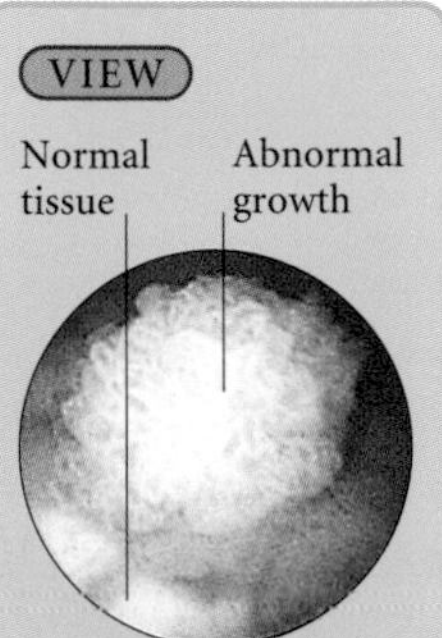
Normal tissue
Abnormal growth

Bladder lining
This magnified view through a cystoscope shows a growth in the lining of the bladder. Samples taken from such a growth may be analyzed under a microscope to look for cancerous cells.

WHAT MIGHT BE DONE?

Your doctor will probably have a sample of your urine tested in the laboratory for blood and cancer cells. Ultrasound scanning (p.250) or intravenous urography (p.699) may be used to image the bladder and reveal any abnormalities. Your doctor may also arrange for you to undergo cystoscopy (above), in which a viewing instrument is used to examine the bladder lining. If a tumor is found, surgical instruments may be inserted through the cystoscope to take a tissue sample, remove the tumor, or destroy it by heat treatment. Tumors may also be treated by drugs delivered directly into the bladder through a catheter.

If a tumor is large or has spread deep into the tissues of the bladder, abdominal surgery may be recommended to remove the tumor along with part or all of the bladder. In some cases, the bladder can be repaired and may function normally again. However, in other cases, the entire bladder needs to be removed. It may be possible for a new bladder to be created from a part of the intestine. Rather than urine draining into an external collecting bag that is attached to the abdominal wall, the collection bag is internal and can be catheterized by the person affected when convenient. Radiation therapy (p.279) and chemotherapy (p.278) may be used for tumors that would be difficult to treat with cystoscopy or surgery.

WHAT IS THE PROGNOSIS?

Bladder tumors diagnosed at an early stage can usually be treated successfully. However, regular monitoring will be necessary because further bladder tumors are likely to develop.

If you smoke, giving up will greatly reduce your risk of developing a bladder tumor. Once you have had a tumor treated, giving up smoking will reduce the risk of recurrence. If you currently work with high-risk chemicals or have done so in the past, you should see your doctor for regular checkups because tumors can develop many years after exposure to carcinogenic chemicals.

(WWW) ONLINE SITES: p.1028, p.1037

MALE REPRODUCTIVE SYSTEM

Sperm
Each sperm has a long tail that enables it to swim inside the female reproductive tract.

MEN REACH THEIR PEAK of sexual activity at about age 16–18 just after they reach puberty. Since they are able to produce sperm continuously from puberty onward, men remain fertile for a much longer period than women; some men can still become fathers at age 70 or older. In addition to producing sperm and delivering them to the female reproductive system, the male reproductive system manufactures male sex hormones that are essential for the production of sperm and for normal sexual development at puberty.

The male reproductive system begins to develop before a male baby is even born. The only visible parts of the male reproductive system are the penis and the scrotum, but inside the body there is a complicated network of ducts, glands, and other tissues that work together to make the production and transport of sperm possible.

SPERM PRODUCTION

Once puberty is reached, sperm are manufactured continuously in the two testes at a rate of about 125 million each day. Since sperm production is not efficient at body temperature, the testes are kept cool by being suspended outside the body in a sac of skin called the scrotum. Mature sperm leave each testis through an epididymis, a long coiled tube that lies above and behind each testis. The sperm are stored in the epididymis and mature there before going to the vas deferens, the tube that connects an epididymis to an ejaculatory duct. During sexual activity, each vas deferens contracts and pushes sperm toward the urethra (the tube that connects the bladder to the outside of the body). The sperm are ejaculated during sexual activity or are reabsorbed into the body. Some dribble through the upper end of the vas deferens into the urethra and are later washed away in the urine.

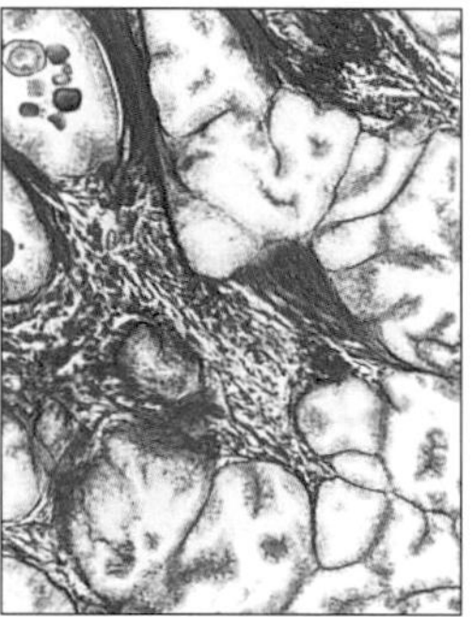

Prostate gland
The prostate gland secretes a milky fluid that helps the sperm swim.

The sperm are carried in a fluid consisting of secretions from various glands. Most of these secretions are produced by glands called seminal vesicles as the sperm leave the vas deferens. Fluid is also added by the prostate gland. In addition to acting as a vehicle for the sperm to help them swim, the fluid provides nutrients that help keep the sperm healthy. Together, these secretions and sperm form semen, containing about 50 million sperm per milliliter.

In order for reproduction to take place, sperm must enter the female reproductive system (*see* SEX AND REPRODUCTION, pp.762–763). During arousal, the penis becomes enlarged and firm. Muscular contractions at the base of the penis then force sperm through the male urethra and into the vagina during male orgasm.

MALE HORMONES

The main male sex hormone, testosterone, is produced throughout life. Testosterone plays an important part in the development of the genitalia and of male sexual characteristics. At puberty, there is a rapid increase in the level of testosterone. This increase triggers the growth of the genitalia and the development of secondary male sexual characteristics, such as body and facial hair, deepening of the voice, and muscle development.

PROCESS PUBERTY

Puberty is the process of sexual development. In boys, puberty usually occurs between ages 12 and 15 and lasts for 3–4 years. Hormones secreted by the pituitary gland cause levels of the male sex hormone testosterone to rise, stimulating changes such as genital growth and the development of secondary sexual characteristics.

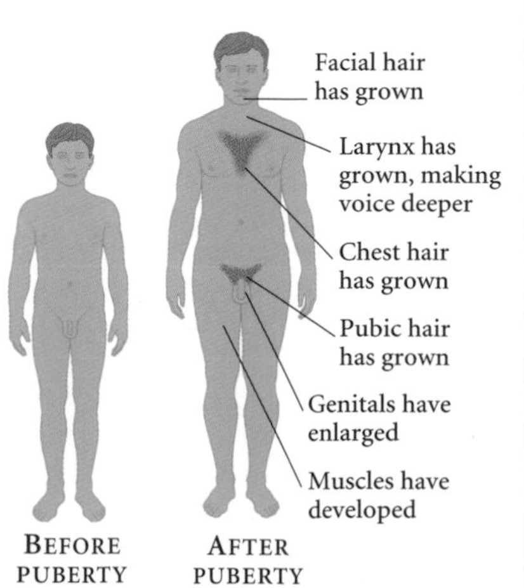
Facial hair has grown
Larynx has grown, making voice deeper
Chest hair has grown
Pubic hair has grown
Genitals have enlarged
Muscles have developed
BEFORE PUBERTY
AFTER PUBERTY

Physical development
During puberty, the penis, scrotum, and testes enlarge, and pubic hair grows. Hair also appears on the face and other parts of the body. Rapid growth occurs, the muscles develop, and the voice deepens.

STRUCTURE MALE REPRODUCTIVE SYSTEM

The male genitals consist of the penis, scrotum, and the two testes, which are suspended in the scrotum. Above and behind each testis is an epididymis, a coiled tube that leads to another tube called the vas deferens. The upper end of each vas deferens is joined by a duct draining from a gland called the seminal vesicle. This duct and a vas deferens together form an ejaculatory duct. The two ejaculatory ducts then join the urethra where it is surrounded by the prostate gland, and the urethra passes through the penis to the outside.

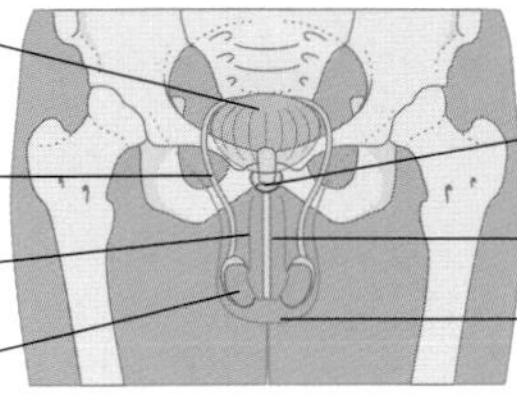

Bladder
Vas deferens
Penis
Testis
Prostate gland
Urethra
Scrotum

FRONT VIEW

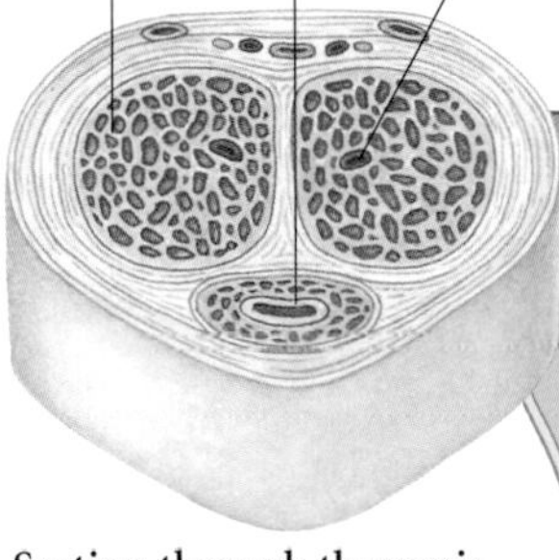

Spongy erectile tissue
Urethra
Artery

Section through the penis
The penis contains three columns of spongy tissue and many blood vessels.

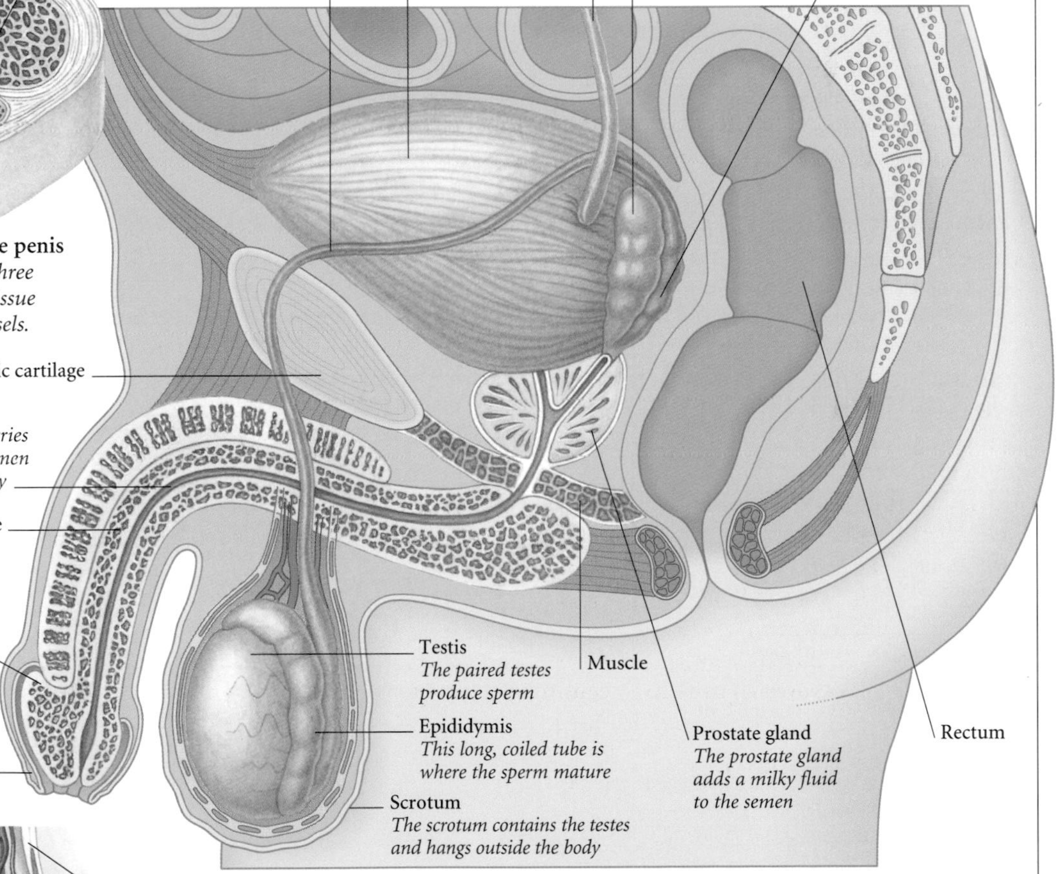

Vas deferens
This tube carries sperm to one of the ejaculatory ducts

Bladder

Ureter

Seminal vesicle
Each seminal vesicle adds fluid and nutrients to sperm

Ejaculatory duct
Each of these ducts joins one vas deferens to the urethra

Pubic cartilage

Urethra
This tube carries urine and semen from the body

Spongy erectile tissue

Glans penis
This forms the bulbous end of the penis

Foreskin
The foreskin covers and protects the head of the penis

Testis
The paired testes produce sperm

Muscle

Epididymis
This long, coiled tube is where the sperm mature

Scrotum
The scrotum contains the testes and hangs outside the body

Prostate gland
The prostate gland adds a milky fluid to the semen

Rectum

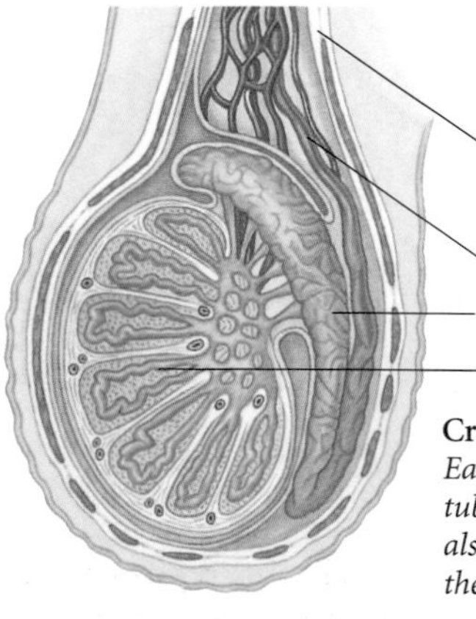

Spermatic cord
This cord contains muscle, blood vessels, nerves, and the vas deferens

Vas deferens

Epididymis

Seminiferous tubule

Cross section of the testis
Each testis is packed with seminiferous tubules, which make sperm. The testes also contain Leydig cells that manufacture the sex hormone testosterone.

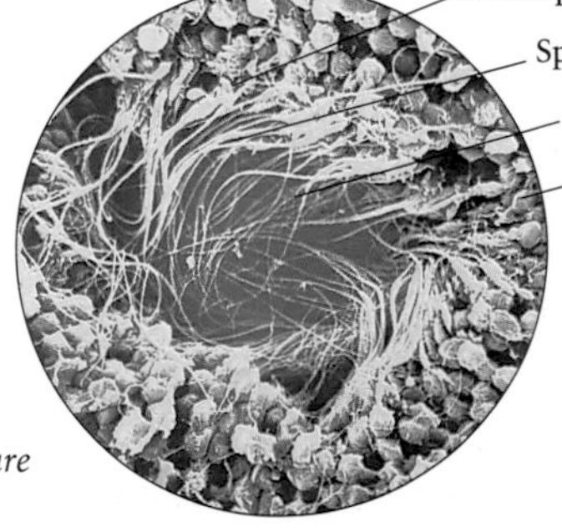

Developing sperm
Sperm tails
Center of tubule
Tubule wall

Sperm production
This magnified image shows maturing sperm in a seminiferous tubule. The tails of developing sperm are near the center.

DISORDERS OF THE TESTES, SCROTUM, AND PENIS

Most of the male reproductive system – the penis, scrotum, and testes – is outside the abdomen. Consequently, symptoms of disorders in these structures are usually obvious at an early stage. Such symptoms should not be ignored out of embarrassment since most genital disorders can be cured by prompt treatment.

In this section, disorders that affect the epididymis (the coiled tube that carries sperm away from each testis) and the testes are described first. These disorders range from epididymal cysts, which are harmless collections of fluid, to cancer of the testis.

The next articles discuss disorders of the scrotum, the sac in which the testes are suspended. These disorders are usually not serious and include varicose veins in the scrotum, known as varicocele, and hydrocele, in which fluid collects around the testis.

Disorders caused by inflammation of the penis and foreskin are covered next, followed by two disorders of erectile function of the penis. The final article in this section discusses cancer of the penis, a rare but distressing disorder that, if diagnosed early, responds well to treatment.

Skin conditions that may affect the penis and scrotum are discussed elsewhere (*see* SKIN, HAIR, AND NAILS, pp.328–361), as are male hormonal disorders (pp.728–729) including abnormal puberty, sexual problems (pp.769–773) such as erectile dysfunction, infertility (pp.774–777), and sexually transmitted infections (pp.764–768). Conditions that develop in the male genitals during childhood are covered in disorders of the urinary and reproductive systems (*see* INFANCY AND CHILDHOOD, pp.870–872).

KEY ANATOMY

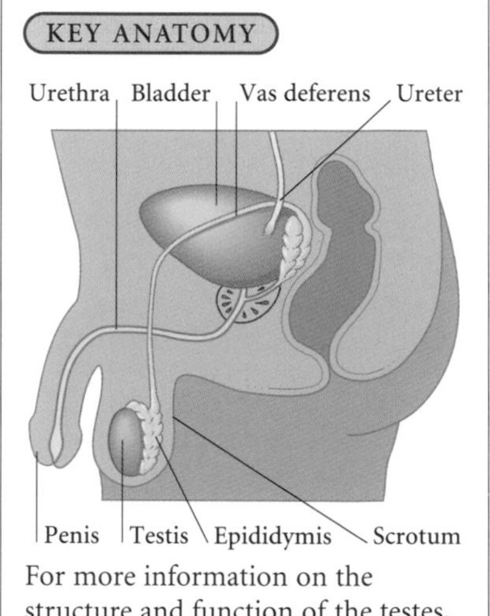
Urethra
Bladder
Vas deferens
Ureter
Penis
Testis
Epididymis
Scrotum

For more information on the structure and function of the testes, scrotum, and penis, *see* pp.716–717.

Epididymal cysts

Swellings in the epididymis, the coiled tube inside the scrotum that stores and transports sperm

AGE More common over age 40

GENETICS LIFESTYLE Not significant factors

Epididymal cysts, or spermatoceles, are harmless fluid-filled sacs that form in the epididymis, which stores and transports sperm away from the testis. Small epididymal cysts are common, particularly in men over 40. The cysts develop slowly and are usually painless.

In many cases, there are multiple cysts, which can be felt as distinct, painless swellings like a tiny bunch of grapes on top of and behind the testis. Both of the epididymal tubes may be affected by cysts at the same time.

If you detect a swelling on one or both sides of your scrotum, you should consult your doctor to rule out a serious condition, such as cancer of the testis (opposite page). He or she will probably be able to make a diagnosis from a physical examination, but further tests such as ultrasound scanning (p.250) may be necessary.

Epididymal cysts normally remain small and do not need treatment. Rarely, they become large and cause discomfort, in which case they can be removed.

(WWW) ONLINE SITES: p.1034

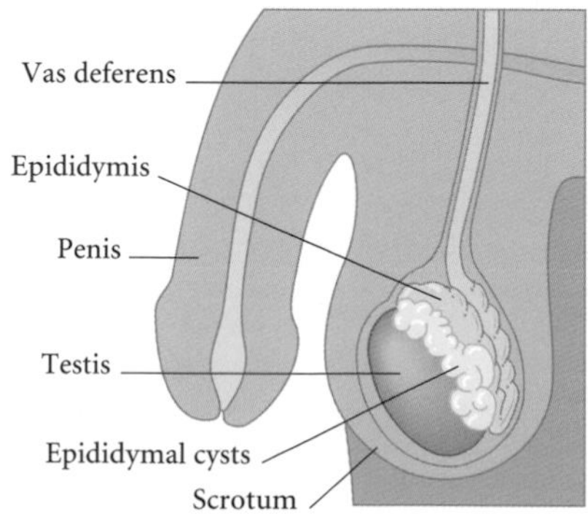
Vas deferens
Epididymis
Penis
Testis
Epididymal cysts
Scrotum

Epididymal cysts
Fluid-filled cysts that develop next to the testis in the epididymis are known as epididymal cysts and are usually painless.

Epididymo-orchitis

Inflammation of the epididymis, the coiled tube inside the scrotum that stores and transports sperm, and of the testis

AGE More common after puberty

GENETICS LIFESTYLE Not significant factors

Infection of the testis and epididymis (the coiled tube that stores and transports sperm away from the testis) can lead to inflammation called epididymo-orchitis. This condition usually causes painful swelling of one testis and may be accompanied by fever.

WHAT ARE THE CAUSES?

Epididymo-orchitis is usually caused by bacteria that have traveled from the urinary tract along the spermatic duct (vas deferens) to the epididymis. In men under age 35, a common cause is a sexually transmitted infection (STI), such as nongonococcal urethritis (p.765). In older men, a urinary tract infection or prostatitis (p.724) is more likely to be a cause of the condition. In rare cases, an infection that is transmitted through the bloodstream, such as tuberculosis (p.491), can lead to the development of epididymo-orchitis.

In boys and young men, the most common cause of the condition used to be inflammation due to mumps (p.291). However, mumps has become less common since the introduction of routine immunization against the mumps virus.

WHAT ARE THE SYMPTOMS?

The symptoms of epididymo-orchitis usually develop over a period of several hours and may include:

- Swelling, redness, and tenderness of the scrotum on the affected side.
- In severe cases, extreme pain in the scrotum, with fever and chills.

You may also have some symptoms of the underlying disorder, such as painful and frequent urination in the case of a urinary tract infection.

The symptoms of epididymo-orchitis are similar to those of a more serious condition called torsion of the testis (right). For this reason, you should consult your doctor immediately if you have any of the symptoms listed above.

WHAT MIGHT BE DONE?

Your doctor may ask you to provide a urine sample to be tested for evidence of infection. If the doctor suspects an STI, he or she may also take a swab from your urethra. If there is any doubt about the diagnosis, ultrasound scanning (p.250) may also be performed to check for torsion of the testis. In some cases, an exploratory operation may be necessary.

Your doctor will probably prescribe antibiotics (p.885) unless the inflammation is caused by infection with the mumps virus, in which case antibiotics are ineffective. He or she may advise you to rest in bed and drink plenty of fluids. Taking analgesics (p.912) may help ease the pain, and using an ice pack may reduce the swelling and pain in the scrotum. An athletic supporter can be worn to support the scrotum and cushion it from sudden movements.

Pain is usually relieved in 1–2 days, but the swelling of the scrotum may take several weeks to subside.

(WWW) ONLINE SITES: p.1033, p.1034

Torsion of the testis

Twisting of the testis within the scrotum, causing severe pain

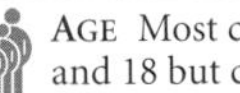 AGE Most common between the ages of 12 and 18 but can occur at any age

GENETICS LIFESTYLE Not significant factors

Each testis is suspended in the scrotum on a spermatic cord. The spermatic duct (vas deferens) and the blood vessels that supply the testis are contained in the spermatic cord. If it is twisted, blood flow to the testis is restricted, causing severe pain in the scrotum.

Torsion of the testis usually affects only one testis. It sometimes occurs after strenuous activity. However, the condition may also develop for no apparent reason, even during sleep. Once you have had torsion in one testis, you are at increased risk of developing it in the other testis.

WHAT ARE THE SYMPTOMS?

Symptoms of torsion of the testis usually appear suddenly. They may include:

- Sudden pain in the scrotum that increases in severity.
- Pain in the groin and lower abdomen.
- Redness and extreme tenderness of the scrotum on the affected side.

The severity of the pain can cause nausea and vomiting. Torsion of the testis is a potentially serious condition that may cause permanent damage to the testis if not treated immediately.

WHAT MIGHT BE DONE?

Torsion of the testis needs immediate medical attention. Your doctor may arrange for an urgent ultrasound scanning (p.250) of the scrotum to exclude other disorders that cause similar symptoms, such as epididymo-orchitis (opposite page). If you have torsion of the testis, a minor operation is carried out to untwist the spermatic cord. Each testis is then anchored in the scrotum with stitches to prevent recurrence of the disorder. If the operation is performed promptly, the testis is usually undamaged. However, a testis that is irreversibly damaged must be removed.

Occasionally, the spermatic cord will untwist spontaneously. If your symptoms disappear, you should still consult your doctor because they may recur.

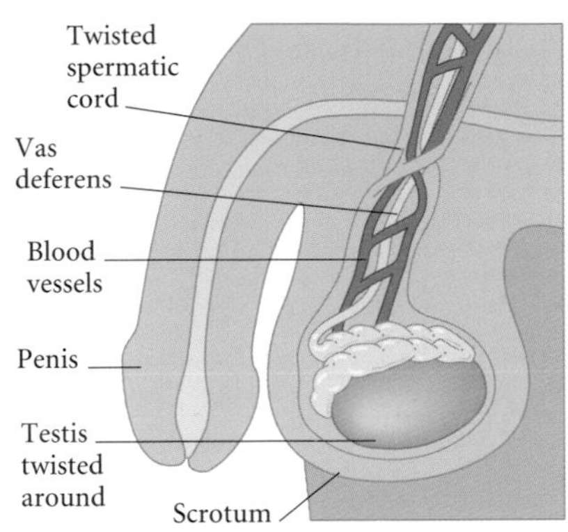
Twisted spermatic cord
Vas deferens
Blood vessels
Penis
Testis twisted around
Scrotum

Torsion of the testis

Torsion of the testis causes the spermatic cord, from which the testis hangs, to become twisted, which restricts the blood flow to and from the testis.

WHAT IS THE PROGNOSIS?

The testis is usually undamaged if the spermatic cord is untwisted within 6–12 hours. Removal of one testis does not normally affect fertility because the remaining one can produce sufficient sperm. A testis can be replaced by an artificial implant for cosmetic reasons.

(WWW) ONLINE SITES: p.1034

Cancer of the testis

A cancerous tumor that develops within a testis

 AGE Most common between the ages of 20 and 40

 GENETICS Sometimes runs in families

 LIFESTYLE Not a significant factor

Although cancer of the testis is a rare condition, it is one of the most common forms of cancer diagnosed in men between the ages of 20 and 40. It is also one of the most easily cured cancers if discovered at an early stage. However, cancer of the testis may spread to the lymph nodes and eventually to other parts of the body if left untreated, and it may ultimately be fatal. The condition usually affects only one testis.

Most testicular tumors develop in the sperm-producing cells of the testis. There are four types of tumors: seminoma, embryonal carcinoma, teratoma, and choriocarcinoma. Seminomas are the most common type of testicular tumor, and they are usually found in men aged 35–45 years.

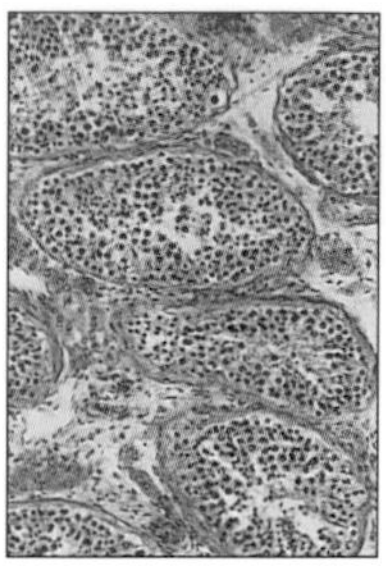
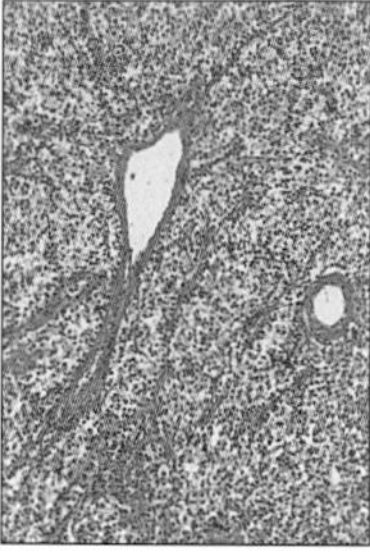

NORMAL ABNORMAL

Cancer of the testis

These tissue samples from testes compare normal tissue structures in a healthy testis with the disordered tissue structures that are found in a cancerous testis.

WHAT ARE THE CAUSES?

The causes of cancer of the testis are not known, but certain factors increase the risk, such as having had an undescended testis (p.870), a condition in which a testis fails to descend into the scrotum before birth.

WHAT ARE THE SYMPTOMS?

You may not notice the symptoms of cancer of the testis unless you examine your testes regularly (*see* EXAMINING YOUR TESTES, below). The symptoms may include the following:

- Hard, pea-sized, painless lump in the affected testis.
- Change in the usual size and texture of the testis.
- Dull ache in the scrotum.
- Rarely, a sudden, sharp pain in the affected testis.

Self-examination of your testes is vital for early detection and treatment of cancer. If you find any changes, you should consult your doctor immediately.

HOW IS IT DIAGNOSED?

Your doctor may examine the affected testis and arrange for ultrasound scanning (p.250) of the testes. He or she may also order a special blood test to look for evidence of cancer (*see* TUMOR MARKER TESTS, p.233). If a tumor is found, further blood tests, CT scanning (p.247), and MRI (p.248) may be performed to determine whether the cancer has spread to other parts of the body.

WHAT IS THE TREATMENT?

If cancer of the testis is diagnosed, the affected testis will have to be surgically removed. If the cancer has not spread beyond the testis, no further treatment may be needed. However, even after the testis has been removed, blood tests to check tumor marker levels will usually be done every 6 months to make sure that the cancer has not begun to spread.

If the cancer has spread to tissues in other parts of the body, you may need to undergo further treatment, which may include surgery, radiation therapy (p.279), and chemotherapy (p.278). If the cancer has spread to the lymph nodes in the abdomen, surgery may be required to remove the affected nodes. Of the four types of tumors, seminomas are the most easily treated by surgery and radiation therapy.

WHAT IS THE PROGNOSIS?

The prognosis depends on the type of cancer and the stage at which it is diagnosed. Cancer of the testis has a very high cure rate. About 4 in 10 testicular cancers are seminomas, which have a survival rate of more than 9 in 10, but, if the cancer has spread to other tissues, this drops to 8 in 10.

Surgical removal of a testis is not likely to affect sexual function or fertility if they were normal before the testis was removed. However, both chemotherapy and radiation therapy reduce sperm production, and fertility may be temporarily or permanently affected by these treatments. If desired, semen containing normal sperm can be frozen before treatment is started.

(WWW) ONLINE SITES: p.1028, p.1034

SELF-HELP EXAMINING YOUR TESTES

Cancer of the testis is one of the most easily treated cancers if it is diagnosed early. For this reason, all men should examine their testes regularly to check for lumps or swellings. An early cancerous tumor can usually be felt as a hard, pea-sized lump embedded in the surface of the testis. This lump is not usually tender when pressed. Soft swellings may be harmless cysts, and painful swellings are often due to infection. You should also check for changes in the skin of the scrotum. If you detect any changes in your testes or scrotum, you should consult your doctor immediately.

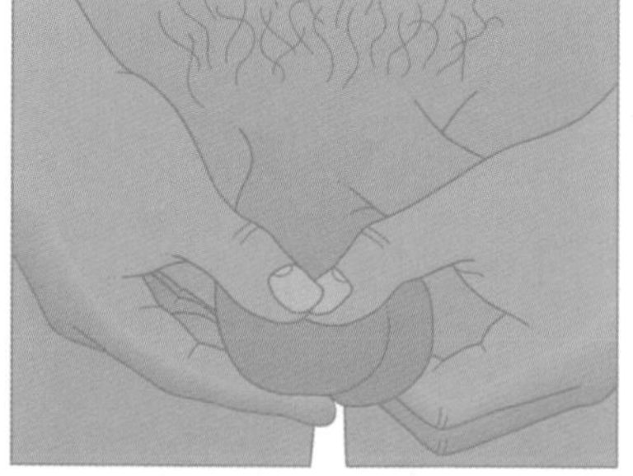

How to examine your testes

After a bath or shower, when the scrotum is relaxed, carefully feel across the entire surface of each testis by rolling each one slowly between fingers and thumb. Check for lumps or swellings and be thorough.

Varicocele

A collection of varicose veins in the scrotum

AGE GENETICS LIFESTYLE Not significant factors

A varicocele is a knot of dilated veins in the scrotum. The condition is caused by leaking valves in the testicular veins, which drain blood away from the testes. There is usually no identifiable cause. Rarely, a varicocele can be caused by pressure on a vein, usually in the pelvis, which prevents blood from draining efficiently from the testis. This pressure may be caused by a tumor in a kidney. Varicoceles usually occur on the left-hand side of the scrotum because blood does not drain as easily from the left testis as from the right one.

If you develop a varicocele, you may notice some swelling of your scrotum and a dragging, aching discomfort. The affected side of your scrotum may hang lower than normal, and the swelling may feel like a bag of worms.

WHAT MIGHT BE DONE?

Your doctor will probably be able to make a diagnosis by examining your scrotum while you are standing up and again while you are lying on your back. If the swelling is caused by a varicocele, it should disappear when you lie down because the veins will empty.

Small, painless varicoceles do not need to be treated because they usually cause no other symptoms and often disappear. Wearing an athletic supporter or close-fitting underwear can relieve mild discomfort. If the varicocele is due to a kidney tumor, all or part of the kidney will be removed surgically.

Although a varicocele may reduce your fertility, sexual performance is not impaired. If tests reveal a low sperm count or if you have persistent discomfort, surgery may be needed to divide and tie off the swollen veins. A varicocele may sometimes recur.

(WWW) ONLINE SITES: p.1034

Hydrocele

An abnormal accumulation of fluid between the double-layered membrane that surrounds the testis

 AGE Most common in infants and elderly males

 GENETICS LIFESTYLE Not significant factors

The double-layered membrane that surrounds each testis normally contains a small amount of fluid. If an excessive amount of fluid accumulates within this membrane, the swelling that forms is called a hydrocele. In most cases, there is no apparent cause, but hydroceles have been linked to infection, inflammation, or injury to the testis.

A hydrocele usually occurs as a painless swelling in the scrotum that is accompanied by a heavy, dragging sensation due to the increased size of the scrotum. The condition is most common in infant boys and elderly men.

What might be done?

If you have symptoms that lead you to think that you have a hydrocele, consult your doctor. He or she may first try to detect a hydrocele by holding a flashlight against the scrotum. If the swelling is caused by fluid, light will shine through the swelling. Ultrasound scanning (p.250) may also be used to confirm the diagnosis.

Hydroceles that develop in infants often subside without requiring treatment. In all cases, if the swelling becomes uncomfortable or painful, it may be treated with a minor operation. In very elderly men who are not able to undergo an operation, a procedure may be carried out, under local anesthesia, in which the fluid is drained away using a hollow needle. A fluid called a sclerosant may then be injected between the two layers of the membrane to help them stick together and prevent the hydrocele from recurring.

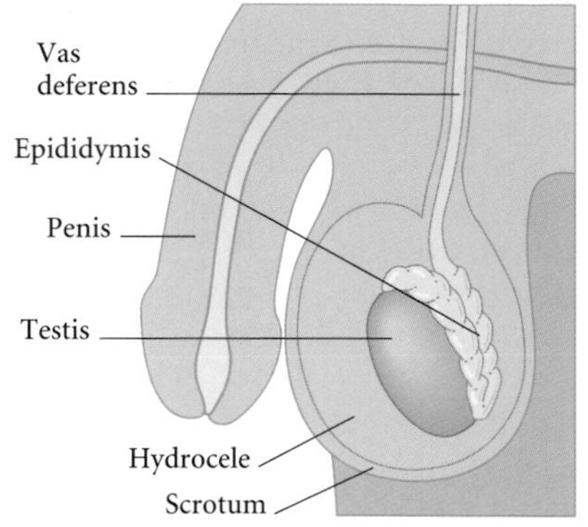
Vas deferens
Epididymis
Penis
Testis
Hydrocele
Scrotum

Hydrocele
If fluid accumulates in the double-layered membrane enclosing the testis, it forms a swelling in the scrotum called a hydrocele.

If the hydrocele has been caused by a bacterial infection, an antibiotic (p.885) may be prescribed. Once the underlying infection has been treated, the hydrocele is unlikely to recur.

(WWW) ONLINE SITES: p.1034

Phimosis

An abnormally small opening at the tip of the foreskin, preventing the foreskin from being retracted over the head of the penis

 AGE More common in children

 GENETICS LIFESTYLE Not significant factors

In phimosis, the foreskin cannot be retracted (pulled back) over the head of the penis (the glans) because the opening at the tip of the foreskin is too narrow. Difficulty in cleaning the head of the penis thoroughly may be the result, and subsequently, infections may occur under the foreskin (*see* BALANITIS, p.722). Phimosis may also cause pain with erection.

What are the causes?

Phimosis may be present at birth or it may become apparent during childhood. The cause of the condition in children is unknown.

By the time a boy is 12 months old, it is usually possible to retract the foreskin. If it is not possible to pull a boy's foreskin back over the glans by age 5,

(TREATMENT) Vasectomy

Vasectomy is a method of male sterilization. Counseling is given to make sure the man and his partner do not wish to have children in the future. The procedure has no effect on sex drive or ejaculation, but the semen no longer carries sperm, which are reabsorbed in each testis. Additional contraception is needed until 12–16 weeks later, when semen is tested to ensure sperm are no longer present.

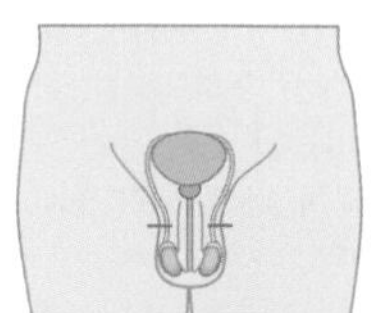

SITES OF INCISIONS

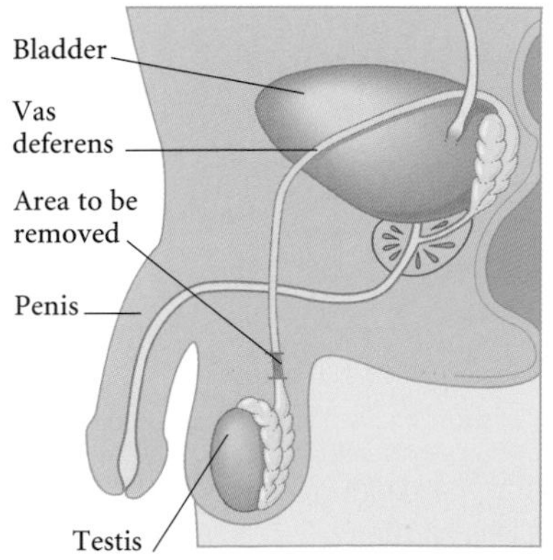
Bladder
Vas deferens
Area to be removed
Penis
Testis

The procedure
A small section of each vas deferens (spermatic duct) is removed through small incisions on either side of the scrotum.

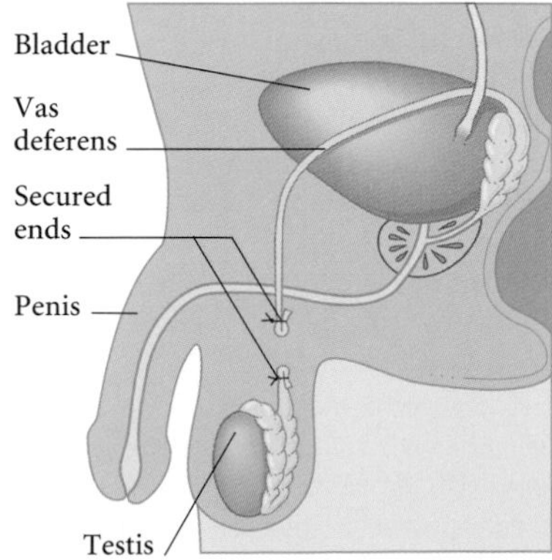
Bladder
Vas deferens
Secured ends
Penis
Testis

After the procedure
The open ends of the vas deferens have been turned back and secured with a stitch to prevent them from rejoining.

he has phimosis and probably needs treatment. In older children and adults, scarring caused by episodes of balanitis may result in phimosis.

What are the symptoms?

The only symptom of phimosis may be an inability to pull back the foreskin, but this may be accompanied by:

- Weak urinary stream.
- Gradual ballooning of the foreskin during urination.
- Painful erection.

If bacteria become trapped behind the foreskin, other complications, including balanitis and recurrent urinary tract infections, may occur.

A complication of phimosis called paraphimosis may occur. In this condition, it is not possible for a foreskin that has been retracted to be rolled forward again. The condition needs immediate medical attention because it constricts the flow of blood to the head of the penis, causing the area to become swollen and extremely painful.

What might be done?

Boys under age 5 will probably not need treatment because the condition is likely to improve by itself. If the condition has resulted in a urinary tract infection or difficulty urinating, or if it occurs in adolescent boys or men, the doctor will probably recommend that surgical removal of the foreskin (*see* Circumcision, below) is carried out. Paraphimosis needs immediate treatment. The doctor may ease the foreskin forward by applying an ice pack to the penis and then squeezing the head. Alternatively, the doctor may make a small incision in the foreskin to enable it to be pulled forward. Circumcision is often required to prevent recurrence.

(WWW) ONLINE SITES: p.1028, p.1034

Balanitis

Inflammation of the head of the penis and foreskin

 Age More common in children

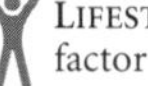 Lifestyle Not being circumcised is a risk factor

 Genetics Not a significant factor

In balanitis, the head of the penis (the glans) and the foreskin become itchy, sore, and inflamed. In addition, discharge and a rash may develop.

The disorder can be caused by a bacterial infection, a fungal infection such as yeast (*see* Candidiasis, p.309), or an allergic reaction. It may also be due to a sexually transmitted infection, such as the protozoal infection trichomoniasis (p.767). A tighter than normal foreskin (*see* Phimosis, p.721) may also increase the risk of infection by preventing effective cleaning of the head of the penis.

Men with diabetes mellitus (p.687) are more susceptible to the condition because their urine contains high levels of glucose, which can encourage the growth of microorganisms. This leads to infection and inflammation at the opening of the urethra. Excessive use of antibiotics (p.885) can increase the risk of a fungal infection by temporarily lowering the body's natural defenses against this type of infection. Children are especially vulnerable to balanitis.

The condition may also occur as a result of sensitivity of the penis to certain chemicals, such as those found in some condoms, contraceptive creams, detergents, and laundry soaps.

What might be done?

If the head of your penis or your foreskin is inflamed, you should consult your doctor. He or she will examine the area and probably take a swab to look for evidence of infection. The doctor may also test your urine to check for the presence of glucose.

The treatment of balanitis depends on the cause. For example, if you have a bacterial infection, antibiotics may be prescribed, and, if the infection is due to a tight foreskin, circumcision (below) may be recommended to prevent balanitis from recurring. If the condition is the result of a sexually transmitted infection (STI), your partner should be checked for evidence of infection and treated if necessary to prevent recurrence (*see* Preventing STIs, p.765). If the cause seems to be sensitivity to a

(TREATMENT) Circumcision

Circumcision is the surgical removal of the foreskin, which is the skin covering the head of the penis (the glans). The operation may be done if the foreskin is too tight to be pulled back over the glans (*see* Phimosis, p.721). Circumcision may also be carried out for religious reasons or, less often now, for hygienic purposes. In boys and men, circumcision is usually performed under general anesthesia. However, in newborn boys it is more often done under local anesthesia. In the operation, the inner and outer layers of the foreskin are cut away and their edges are then stitched together. No dressing is needed while the wound heals.

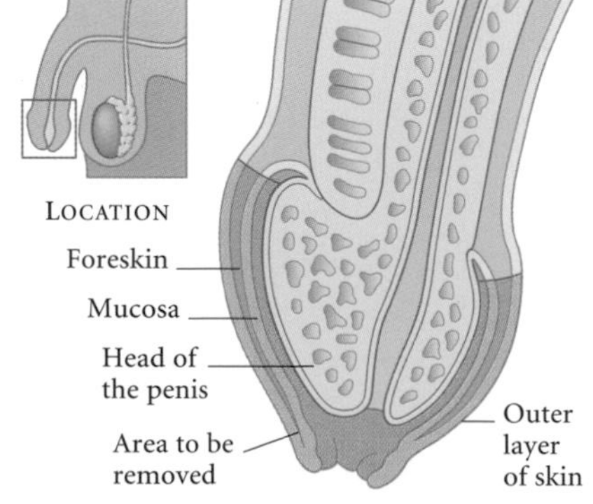
LOCATION
Foreskin
Mucosa
Head of the penis
Area to be removed
Outer layer of skin

The operation
The foreskin, which covers the head of the penis, consists of an inner layer of mucosa and an outer layer of skin. During the operation, both layers are removed.

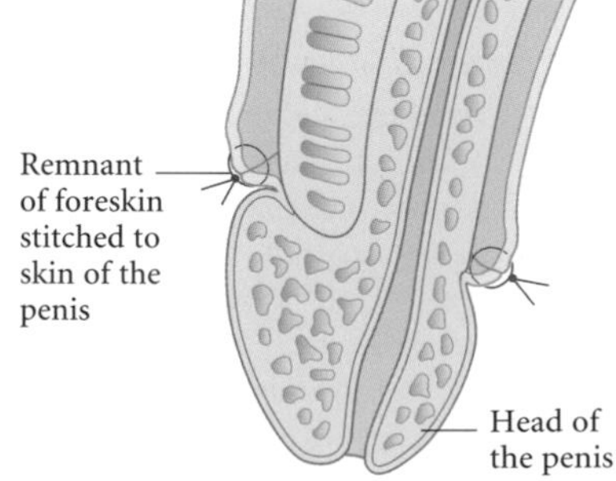
Remnant of foreskin stitched to skin of the penis
Head of the penis

After the operation
The remnant of the foreskin has been stitched to the skin just behind the head of the penis, leaving the head of the penis uncovered. These stitches either dissolve or fall out after a few days.

chemical, the irritant should be identified, if possible, so that you can avoid it.

The inflamed area should be kept clean, dry, and free of irritants. Most cases of balanitis clear up rapidly once the cause has been found and treated.

(WWW) ONLINE SITES: p.1028, p.1034

Priapism

Prolonged, painful erection of the penis not related to sexual desire

 AGE More common in young adults

 GENETICS LIFESTYLE Not significant factors

Priapism is a persistent erection of the penis for 4 hours or more without any accompanying sexual arousal. The condition is usually painful and urgent hospital treatment is necessary in order to avoid permanent damage to the erectile tissues of the penis.

Priapism develops if blood cannot drain from the erect penis. The causes include damage to the nerves controlling the supply of blood to the penis; blood disorders, including sickle-cell anemia (p.448), leukemia (p.453), and polycythemia (p.457); and, in some instances, prolonged sexual intercourse.

Priapism may also occur as a side effect of medical treatment with certain antipsychotic drugs (p.917). However, treatments for erectile dysfunction (p.770), whether they consist of oral drugs, such as the erectile dysfunction medication sildenafil, or of drugs that are injected into the penis, rarely result in priapism if they are used properly.

WHAT MIGHT BE DONE?

If you have a painful and very prolonged erection, particularly one that is not a result of sexual arousal, you must consult your doctor or go to your nearest emergency room immediately. In most cases of priapism, the doctor will be able to rapidly drain the blood from the erectile tissues of the penis with the use of a syringe. This will be followed by the irrigation of the erectile tissues. However, surgery may be necessary if treatment has been significantly delayed.

In all cases of priapism, there is a risk that full erection of the penis may be adversely affected in the future.

(WWW) ONLINE SITES: p.1034

Peyronie's disease

An abnormality of the shape of the penis, causing it to bend at an angle when erect

 AGE More common over age 40

 GENETICS Sometimes runs in families

 LIFESTYLE Not a significant factor

In Peyronie's disease, fibrous tissue of the penis develops, causing the penis to bend during erection. It may bend so much that sexual intercourse is difficult and painful. Peyronie's disease occurs in about 1 in 100 men, most commonly in those men over age 40.

Often no cause of the disorder can be identified, although previous damage to the penis may be a risk factor. Peyronie's disease is also associated with Dupuytren's contracture (p.390), a condition in which fibrous tissue develops in the palm of the hand, causing the fingers to become deformed, bending inward. Peyronie's disease can run in families, which suggests that a genetic factor is involved.

WHAT ARE THE SYMPTOMS?

The symptoms of Peyronie's disease develop gradually and may include:

- Curvature of the penis to one side during an erection.
- Pain in the penis on erection.
- Thickened area within the penis that can usually be felt as a firm nodule when the penis is flaccid.

Eventually, the thickened region of the penis may extend to include parts of the erectile tissue. In this case, Peyronie's disease may lead to erectile dysfunction, also known as impotence (p.770).

WHAT IS THE TREATMENT?

Peyronie's disease usually improves without treatment. In mild cases, in which painless intercourse is still possible, no treatment is necessary. However, in other cases, the condition continues to worsen if left untreated.

For ongoing symptoms of the disorder that either prevent or make sexual intercourse difficult, various surgical procedures, including penile prosthetics, can be used with success.

(WWW) ONLINE SITES: p.1034

Cancer of the penis

A rare, cancerous tumor that usually occurs on the head of the penis

 AGE More common over age 40

 LIFESTYLE Smoking and not being circumcised are risk factors

 GENETICS Not a significant factor

Cancer of the penis is a rare disorder that almost exclusively occurs in uncircumcised men, particularly those in whom the foreskin does not retract (*see* PHIMOSIS, p.721). Infection with the human papilloma virus, which causes genital warts (p.768), is thought to increase the risk of developing the cancer. Smoking also seems to be a risk factor.

The tumor usually develops on the head of the penis (the glans). It appears as a wartlike growth or flat painless sore that may be hidden by the foreskin. Sometimes the growth may bleed or produce an unpleasant-smelling discharge. The cancer usually grows slowly, but, if left untreated, it may eventually spread to the lymph nodes in the groin.

A sore area on the penis should be examined by a doctor immediately.

WHAT MIGHT BE DONE?

Your doctor will carry out a physical examination and may take a swab to check for infections that can produce similar symptoms. He or she may also arrange for a biopsy (*see* SKIN BIOPSY, p.344), in which a sample of the growth is removed and examined under a microscope for evidence of cancer.

If detected early, a tumor on the penis can often be treated successfully with surgery, radiation therapy (p.279), or a combination of both. Surgery involves either a partial or a complete amputation of the penis. In certain cases, penile reconstruction may be possible following complete amputation. Radiation therapy may be recommended as the first choice of treatment because it offers the chance of curing the cancer without loss of the penis.

The prognosis depends on how far the disease has advanced before diagnosis and treatment. More than 8 in 10 men who have been treated for penile tumors survive for 5 years or more.

(WWW) ONLINE SITES: p.1028, p.1034

PROSTATE DISORDERS

The prostate gland is a firm, round organ about the size of a chestnut. It surrounds the upper part of the urethra (the tube through which urine is emptied from the bladder) and lies underneath the bladder and directly in front of the rectum. The secretions that are produced by the prostate gland are added to semen, the fluid that contains sperm.

Disorders affecting the prostate gland are very common and usually occur in men over age 30. Prostatitis, in which the prostate gland is inflamed, is the first disorder discussed in this section. Enlargement of the prostate gland is covered next. Some degree of prostate enlargement occurs in most men over age 50 and is often viewed as a natural part of aging. The final article covers prostate cancer. In many cases, prostate cancer is not life-threatening, and in older men it may not need treatment because the tumor is often slow-growing and life expectancy may not be affected. However, prostate cancer in younger men may spread more quickly and can be life-threatening. Current research is therefore aimed at developing tests that detect prostate cancer before the symptoms start to appear. However, although these tests can help identify prostate cancer in its early stages, they cannot identify which cancers are more likely to spread and will require early treatment.

KEY ANATOMY

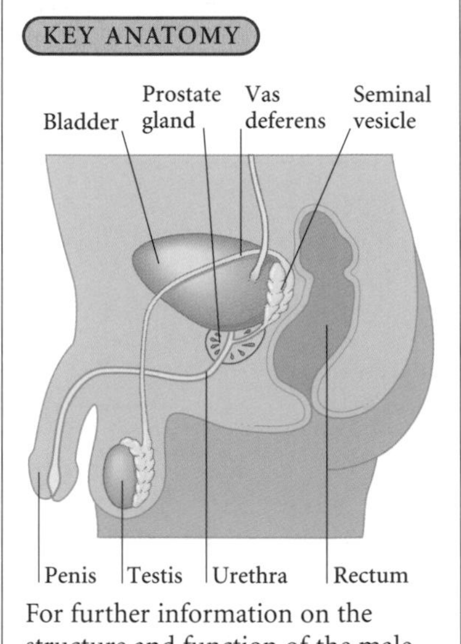
Bladder
Prostate gland
Vas deferens
Seminal vesicle
Penis
Testis
Urethra
Rectum

For further information on the structure and function of the male reproductive system, *see* pp.716–717.

Prostatitis

Inflammation of the prostate gland, sometimes due to infection

 AGE Most common between the ages of 30 and 50

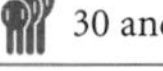 LIFESTYLE Unprotected sex with multiple partners is a risk factor

 GENETICS Not a significant factor

Inflammation of the prostate gland, known as prostatitis, may be acute or chronic. Acute prostatitis is uncommon and usually produces sudden, severe symptoms that clear up rapidly. Chronic prostatitis, by contrast, may cause mild symptoms for a long period of time and may be difficult to treat. Both types of prostatitis are most common in sexually active men aged 30–50.

WHAT ARE THE CAUSES?

In most instances of acute and chronic prostatitis, the cause cannot be determined for certain. However, both forms of the condition can be the result of organisms that spread from the urinary tract to the prostate gland. Inflammation of the prostate may also develop in association with sexually transmitted diseases (pp.764–768).

WHAT ARE THE SYMPTOMS?

The symptoms of acute prostatitis are usually severe and develop suddenly. They may include:

- Fever and chills.
- Pain around the base of the penis.
- Lower back pain.
- Pain during bowel movements.
- Frequent, urgent, painful urination.

Acute prostatitis sometimes causes urinary retention (p.713), painful swelling behind the testes, or the formation of an abscess in the prostate.

Chronic prostatitis may not produce symptoms. If symptoms do occur, they develop gradually and may include:

- Pain and tenderness at the base of the penis and in the testes, groin, pelvis, or back.
- Pain on ejaculation.
- Blood in the semen.
- Frequent, painful urination.

If you suspect that you have either acute or chronic prostatitis, you should consult your doctor immediately.

HOW IS IT DIAGNOSED?

Your doctor will perform a digital rectal examination, in which he or she inserts a finger into the rectum to feel the prostate. The doctor may also ask you for a urine sample and may obtain a sample of prostate gland secretions by massaging the prostate through the rectum and collecting the secretions from the urethra. Both the sample of urine and the prostate gland secretions will then be sent to a laboratory to be tested for the presence of infectious organisms. Ultrasound scanning (p.250) and/or CT scanning (p.247) may also be carried out to check for an abscess.

WHAT IS THE TREATMENT?

If an infection is found, your doctor will prescribe a course of antibiotics (p.885). It may take several months for the infection to disappear. In the meantime, your doctor may recommend that you take analgesics (p.912) to relieve pain. If your symptoms are severe, he or she may suggest bed rest.

Prostatitis that is not caused by an infection may be treated with analgesics and drugs to relax the muscle at the exit of the bladder (*see* DRUGS FOR PROSTATE DISORDERS, p.938). To help relieve the symptoms of chronic prostatitis, you may need repeated massage of the prostate gland.

Although most affected men recover fully, both types of prostatitis can recur.

(WWW) ONLINE SITES: p.1036

Enlarged prostate gland

Noncancerous enlargement of the prostate gland, causing problems with urination

 AGE Rare before age 40; increasingly common after age 50

 GENETICS LIFESTYLE Not significant factors

Most men over age 50 have some enlargement of the prostate gland. This condition is known as benign prostatic hyperplasia. It is noncancerous and is distinct from prostate cancer (p.726). If the degree of enlargement of the prostate is minor, it is seen as a natural part of the aging process. The cause of benign prostatic hyperplasia is unknown.

What are the symptoms?

As the prostate gland grows larger, it constricts and distorts the urethra (the tube from the bladder to the outside of the body). At first, this enlargement does not cause symptoms. However, if the prostate gland continues to enlarge,

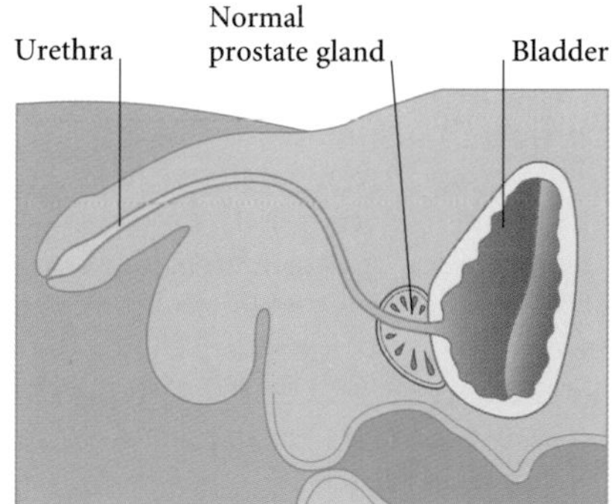
Urethra
Normal prostate gland
Bladder

NORMAL PROSTATE

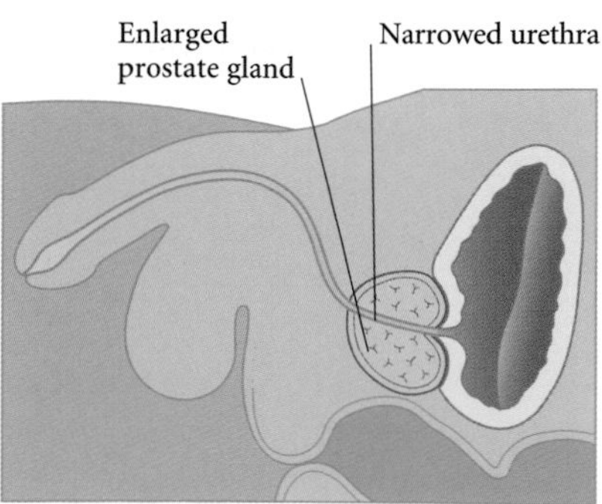
Enlarged prostate gland
Narrowed urethra

ENLARGED PROSTATE

Prostate enlargement
The prostate gland encircles the upper part of the urethra. An enlarged prostate may constrict the urethra, making urination difficult, and indent the base of the bladder, preventing it from emptying completely.

TREATMENT PARTIAL PROSTATECTOMY

There are several different operations to treat an enlarged prostate gland. The most common type is a partial or transurethral prostatectomy, in which only part of the prostate gland is removed. The operation is performed under general or spinal anesthesia and requires a stay in the hospital of about 3 days. Although the procedure is usually successful, it may need to be repeated if symptoms recur. After the operation, sperm pass into the bladder on ejaculation in 7 out of 10 men. Although this causes infertility, orgasm is normal. Rarely, the operation may cause erectile dysfunction.

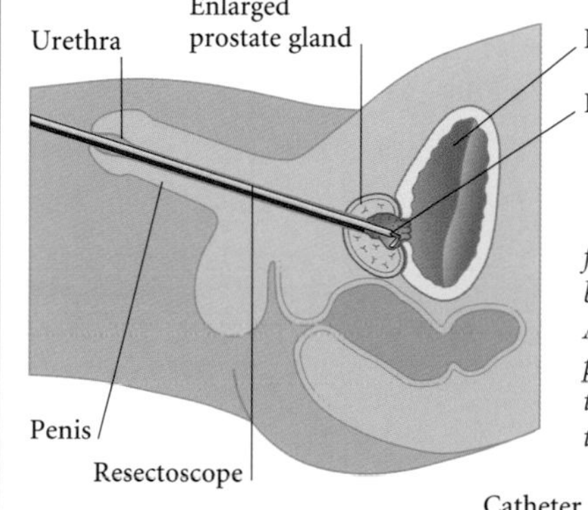
Urethra
Enlarged prostate gland
Bladder
Diathermy wire
Penis
Resectoscope

1 *A viewing tool called a resectoscope is passed along the urethra (the tube from the bladder to the outside of the body) until it reaches the prostate gland. A heated wire (diathermy wire) is then pushed along the resectoscope and used to cut away the excess prostate tissue, thereby widening the urethra.*

Catheter
Widened urethra
Bladder
Attachment for irrigation system
Balloon to hold catheter in place

2 *The diathermy wire and the resectoscope are withdrawn. A catheter is passed along the urethra into the bladder to drain urine. An irrigation system is attached to the catheter to wash out prostate tissue and keep blood clots from forming. The catheter is left in place for 2–3 days.*

urination may be affected and symptoms may develop, including:

- Frequent urination, day and night.
- Delay in starting to urinate, especially at night or if the bladder is full.
- Weak, intermittent flow of urine.
- Dribbling at the end of urination.
- Feeling that the bladder has not completely emptied.

The symptoms may be worsened by cold weather; drinking large volumes of fluids (especially alcohol); taking drugs that increase urine production, such as diuretics (p.902); or taking drugs that may cause urinary retention, such as antispasmodics (*see* ANTISPASMODICS AND MOTILITY STIMULANTS, p.926).

If the bladder does not empty completely, it may enlarge and make the abdomen swell visibly. Urine may also collect in the bladder and stagnate. If the condition is not treated, the urinary tract may become infected (*see* CYSTITIS, p.709) and there is an increased risk of bladder stones (p.714). Rarely, retained urine can produce a buildup of backward pressure from the bladder to the kidneys, leading to kidney damage (*see* HYDRONEPHROSIS, p.703). In some cases, kidney failure (p.705) may develop. Occasionally, an enlarged prostate may suddenly block urine outflow completely (*see* URINARY RETENTION, p.713), causing rapidly increasing pain. This problem needs emergency treatment.

How is it diagnosed?

Your doctor will perform a digital rectal examination, in which he or she inserts a finger into the rectum to feel the prostate gland. The doctor may also arrange for blood tests to assess kidney function and exclude prostate cancer and urine tests to look for infection. Ultrasound scanning (p.250) may be done to measure the amount of urine in your bladder after urination and check that your kidneys are not abnormally enlarged. Urine flow may also be assessed (*see* URODYNAMIC STUDIES, p.711).

WHAT IS THE TREATMENT?

The choice of treatment depends on factors such as age, general health, the extent of the prostate enlargement, and whether the bladder and kidneys are affected by an obstruction to urination. Treatment may affect sexual function, and you should discuss the available treatments with your doctor in detail.

If your symptoms are mild, your doctor may simply advise you not to drink fluids in the evening so that urinary frequency is decreased at night. If the symptoms persist, drugs, surgery, or catheterization may be necessary.

Drugs, such as an alpha blocker, or an alpha-blocker plus a 5-alpha reductase inhibitor, are commonly used to treat prostate gland enlargement and can relieve the symptoms in many cases (*see* DRUGS FOR PROSTATE DISORDERS, p.938). If drug treatment is not successful, your doctor may recommend a partial prostatectomy (p.725), in which part of the prostate is removed through the urethra. Only tissue that is obstructing urine flow is removed. Rarely, if the prostate is very enlarged and excess tissue cannot be removed through the urethra, most of the gland is removed through an abdominal incision. This operation may result in infertility. It may also cause erectile dysfunction (p.770), especially in older men. Laser surgery and shrinkage of the prostate using microwaves are alternative treatments currently being developed.

If surgery is unsuitable, as it may be for frail, ill men, a catheter may be left in permanently to drain the urine (*see* BLADDER CATHETERIZATION, p.713).

WHAT IS THE PROGNOSIS?

The prognosis varies greatly. Mild cases may be treated with drugs, but in more serious cases surgery is more effective. About 1 in 7 men needs a second partial prostatectomy after 8–10 years.

(WWW) ONLINE SITES: p.1036

Prostate cancer

Cancerous tumor arising from the glandular tissue of the prostate gland

 AGE Rare under age 40; increasingly common over age 65

 GENETICS Sometimes runs in families; more common in African–Americans

 LIFESTYLE Not a significant factor

Prostate cancer is the most commonly diagnosed cancer in men in Canada and is the second most common cause of death from cancer in men after lung cancer. The disorder is more common in African–Americans but is rare in men from Asian countries. The number of cases identified in Canada has been rising since the 1970s, not only in elderly men, in whom it is most common, but also in men in their 40s and 50s. Increased identification has been largely due to a new screening test that measures the level of a protein known as prostate-specific antigen, secreted by the prostate gland. Although prostate cancer is an important cause of death, many tumors grow slowly, especially in elderly men, and may never cause symptoms. Treatment is more likely to be necessary in younger men.

WHAT ARE THE CAUSES?

It is not known what causes prostate cancer, although the male sex hormone testosterone, produced by the testes, is known to influence the growth and spread of the tumor. In approximately 1 in 10 cases, the cancer is partly due to an inherited abnormal gene. In these cases, it is more likely to occur before age 60. Although there has been concern that having had a vasectomy (p.721) increases the risk of prostate cancer, there is currently no strong evidence to support this view.

WHAT ARE THE SYMPTOMS?

Prostate cancer may not cause symptoms, particularly in elderly men. If symptoms do occur, they are likely to develop when the tumor starts to constrict the urethra (the tube from the bladder to the outside of the body). The symptoms may then include:

- Weak urinary stream or inability to urinate normally.

TEST PROSTATE GLAND BIOPSY

A prostate gland biopsy is used to diagnose prostate cancer. In the most common type of biopsy, an ultrasound probe is inserted into the rectum in order to visualize the prostate. A hollow needle attached to the probe is gently pushed through the rectal wall and into the prostate several times, removing pieces of tissue for examination. After the biopsy, urine and semen may contain blood for a few days.

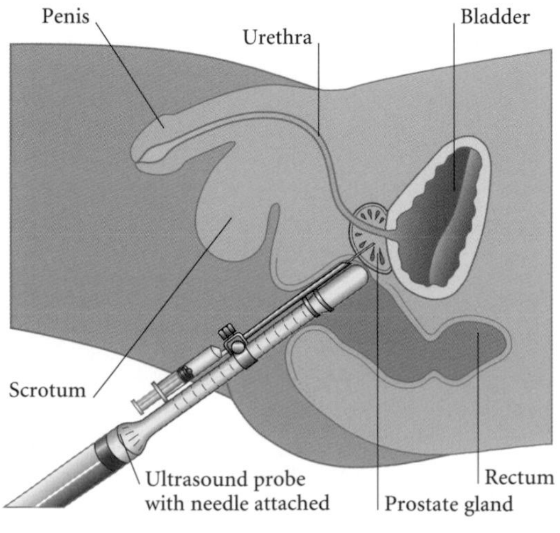
Penis
Urethra
Bladder
Scrotum
Ultrasound probe with needle attached
Prostate gland
Rectum

The procedure
A slight pricking sensation may be felt as each biopsy sample is taken, but anesthesia is usually not required.

RESULTS

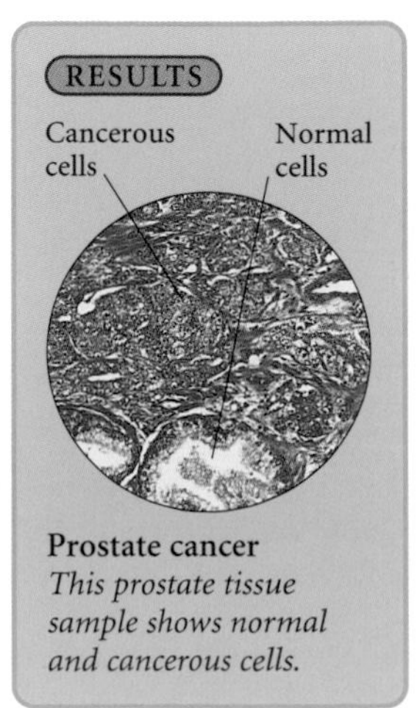
Cancerous cells
Normal cells

Prostate cancer
This prostate tissue sample shows normal and cancerous cells.

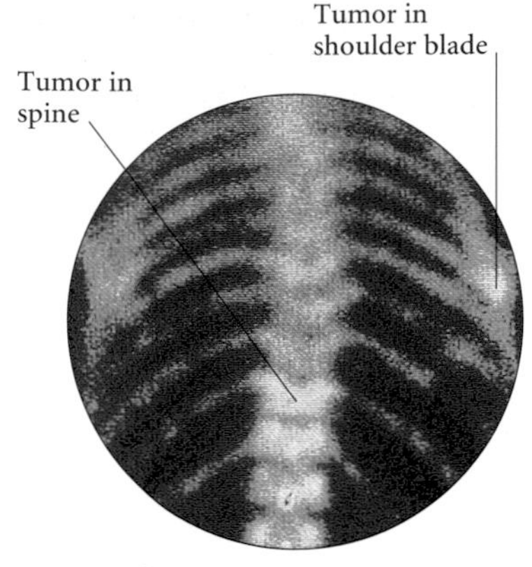
Tumor in shoulder blade
Tumor in spine

Metastatic cancer
This radionuclide bone scan of the chest shows hotspots in the spine and in the shoulder blade due to metastases from a primary prostate cancer.

- Frequent urge to urinate, especially during the night.
- Rarely, blood in the urine.

In some men, the initial symptoms of prostate cancer are due to the metastasis (spreading) of the cancer to other parts of the body, especially the bones, lymph nodes, and lungs. In these cases, the symptoms may include back pain, enlarged lymph nodes, shortness of breath, and significant weight loss.

How is it diagnosed?

If you develop the symptoms of prostate cancer, or if the disorder runs in your family, you should consult your doctor. The doctor will perform a digital rectal examination, in which he or she inserts a finger into the rectum to feel the prostate gland. Your doctor may also arrange for a blood test to measure your prostate-specific antigen levels.

A type of ultrasound scanning may be performed in which an ultrasound probe is inserted into the rectum to visualize the prostate gland. The size of the gland and the presence of any abnormalities in the prostate can then be assessed. During scanning, a prostate gland biopsy (opposite page) may also be carried out. In this procedure, cells are removed from areas of the gland that appear abnormal and are examined under a microscope. If prostate cancer is diagnosed, you may need imaging tests, such as MRI (p.248) and radionuclide scanning (p.251), to check whether the prostate cancer has spread to other parts of the body.

What is the treatment?

Prostate cancer treatment depends on whether the cancer has spread, your age, and your general health. If the cancer is confined to the prostate gland and your health is otherwise good, your doctor may recommend that all of the prostate gland be removed, along with some of the surrounding tissues (*see* Radical prostatectomy, below). Alternatively, radiation therapy (p.279) may be given. This therapy may involve either having a radioactive implant or radioactive seeds placed in the prostate gland or undergoing external radiation therapy over several weeks. In elderly men in whom the cancer is confined to a small area of the prostate gland, no immediate treatment may be recommended, but the course of the disease will be closely monitored.

If the cancer has spread beyond the prostate, a cure may not be possible. However, progress of the disease can be slowed significantly with hormone therapy. In this treatment, drugs that block the release or actions of testosterone may be given to suppress the effects of the hormone on the cancer (*see* Drugs for prostate disorders, p.938). In some cases, both of the testes may be surgically removed to stop the production of testosterone. Treatments that block the actions or production of testosterone may sometimes result in a loss of interest in sex.

What is the prognosis?

A diagnosis of cancer of the prostate gland does not necessarily mean that the cancer will cause symptoms or be life-threatening. Sometimes the best policy, especially in elderly men, is to defer treatment and begin regular checkups to monitor the disease. Men with certain types of small tumors need no treatment and are likely to live for several years with no symptoms before dying from some other cause. For men who have had surgery for a tumor confined to the prostate, the prognosis is good, with over 9 in 10 men surviving for 5 years after diagnosis. Unfortunately, surgery may result in erectile dysfunction and urinary incontinence in some men.

Cancer that has spread beyond the prostate gland cannot be cured completely, but hormone therapy often controls the symptoms for many years.

(WWW) ONLINE SITES: p.1036

(TREATMENT) Radical prostatectomy

A radical prostatectomy may be done to treat prostate cancer if the cancer has not spread beyond the gland. The procedure is performed under general anesthesia and usually requires a hospital stay of about 3–5 days. The operation completely removes the cancer in most men, but afterward about 1 in 2 men will be impotent, and some will have a degree of urinary incontinence.

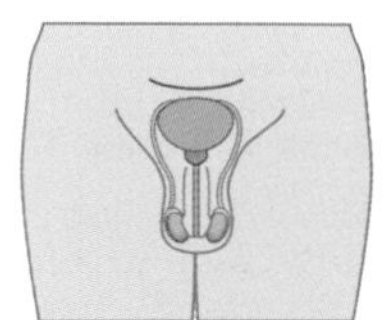

Site of incision

Area to be removed
Neck of bladder
Prostate tumor
Seminal vesicle

The procedure
The tumor is removed, together with the entire prostate gland, the seminal vesicles, and the neck of the bladder.

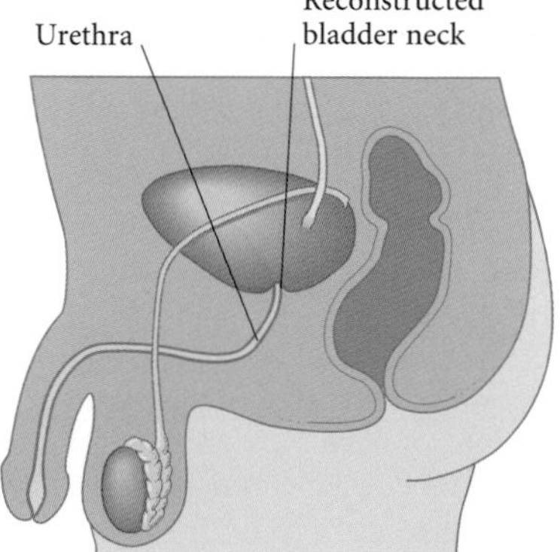
Urethra
Reconstructed bladder neck

After the procedure
The bladder neck has been reconstructed and rejoined to the urethra (the tube from the bladder to the outside of the body).

MALE HORMONAL DISORDERS

The most important male sex hormone is testosterone, which influences sperm production, fertility, and sex drive. Male sex hormones also promote the development of secondary sexual characteristics at puberty. Over- or underproduction of male sex hormones may be caused by a variety of factors, including inherited disorders, chronic illnesses, tumors, or lifestyle factors.

Male sex hormones, or androgens, are produced mainly by the testes but also by the adrenal glands. The production of male sex hormones is controlled by hormones secreted by the pituitary gland. In turn, the pituitary gland is under the control of a part of the brain called the hypothalamus.

The changes that occur at puberty are controlled by the sex hormones. This section starts by discussing early or late onset of puberty in boys, which may be a symptom of under- or overproduction of male sex hormones.

Hypogonadism, in which male sex hormones are underproduced, is covered next. In boys, this condition can suppress sexual development; in men, hypogonadism lowers sperm production and fertility. The final article discusses gynecomastia, a common disorder causing breast enlargement that temporarily affects nearly half of all boys during puberty.

Male hormonal disorders may lead to sexual problems (pp.769–773) and can sometimes be a cause of infertility (*see* MALE INFERTILITY, p.777).

KEY ANATOMY

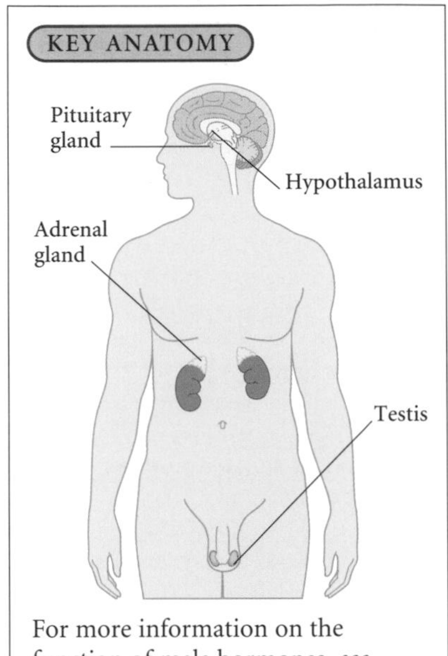
Pituitary gland
Hypothalamus
Adrenal gland
Testis

For more information on the function of male hormones, *see* pp.670–675 and pp.716–717.

Abnormal puberty in males

Very early or late onset of puberty, usually due to a hormonal imbalance

AGE Occurs before or after the normal age range for puberty

GENETICS Sometimes runs in families; rarely due to a chromosomal abnormality

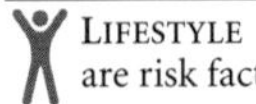
LIFESTYLE Excessive exercise and a poor diet are risk factors

The natural process of sexual development and maturation that takes place over several years is known as puberty (p.716). In boys, puberty is normally characterized by a growth spurt; deepening of the voice; enlargement of the genitals; and the development of hair on the face, in the armpits, and in the pubic region. Puberty in boys usually begins between the ages of 10 and 15. Abnormal puberty starts either earlier than normal (precocious puberty) or later (delayed puberty).

Precocious puberty is rare and is usually an indication of an underlying hormonal disorder. Delayed puberty is more common and less likely to indicate a serious underlying condition.

WHAT ARE THE CAUSES?

In boys, puberty is controlled by male sex hormones produced by the testes and adrenal glands. The production of these hormones is controlled by hormones from the pituitary gland and from the hypothalamus (the part of the brain that regulates the pituitary gland). Disorders in these organs may lead to abnormal early or late puberty.

Precocious puberty is caused by the overproduction of male sex hormones in a young boy. For example, congenital adrenal hyperplasia (p.866), in which the adrenal glands produce excessive amounts of male sex hormones, may lead to precocious puberty.

Boys in whom puberty is delayed are usually just late developers, a tendency that often runs in families. However, delayed puberty may also be caused by an underproduction of male sex hormones. Rarely, there is a more serious underlying cause, such as a brain tumor that is pressing on the hypothalamus or pituitary gland, or a chromosomal disorder, such as Klinefelter syndrome (p.822), in which the sex organs do not develop normally. Some chronic illnesses, such as Crohn's disease (p.658), kidney failure (p.705), cystic fibrosis (p.824), and diabetes mellitus (p.687), can also cause delayed puberty and growth. Lifestyle factors, such as excessive exercise and an inadequate diet, may delay puberty. Rarely, a pituitary tumor (p.676) may lead to either precocious or delayed puberty.

WHAT MIGHT BE DONE?

Early or late puberty should be investigated by a doctor. He or she will carry out a physical examination to see if puberty has started or how far it has progressed. A blood test may also be needed to measure hormone levels and check for a chromosomal abnormality. X-rays (p.244) of the wrist and hand may be used to assess bone maturity, and ultrasound scanning (p.250) of the testes or adrenal glands may also be carried out to look for abnormalities. If a pituitary tumor is suspected, MRI (p.248) or CT scanning (p.247) of the brain may be arranged.

If tests identify an underlying cause, it will be treated. For example, precocious puberty may be treated with drugs that inhibit the action of the male sex hormones. These drugs may be given as injections, implants under the skin, or nasal sprays.

If delayed puberty runs in the family, treatment may not be needed. In many other cases, puberty is induced with injections of testosterone (*see* SEX HORMONES AND RELATED DRUGS, p.933). Some boys benefit from counseling for psychological problems caused by precocious or late puberty.

Abnormal puberty is often treatable, but lifelong treatment may be needed. Future fertility depends on the cause.

WWW ONLINE SITES: p.1028, p.1033, p.1034

Hypogonadism in males

Underactivity of the testes, resulting in low levels of the sex hormone testosterone and impaired production of sperm

 GENETICS Sometimes due to a chromosomal abnormality

 LIFESTYLE Alcohol abuse is a risk factor

 AGE Not a significant factor

Reduced activity of the testes, known as hypogonadism, results in underproduction of the male sex hormone testosterone and impaired sperm production. In boys yet to reach puberty, it often slows growth, and may delay sexual development. It is uncommon.

Abnormal development of the testes due to a chromosomal disorder, such as Klinefelter syndrome (p.822), may cause hypogonadism, as may failure of the pituitary gland to produce sufficient hormones, which may be due to a pituitary tumor (p.676). A number of different disorders may damage the testes and lead to hypogonadism, such as torsion of the testis (p.719) and mumps (p.291). Alcohol abuse, chemotherapy (p.278), and radiation therapy (p.279), can also cause hypogonadism. Serum testosterone does decrease slowly with age. In some aging men this may produce symptoms – a condition called 'andropause'.

WHAT ARE THE SYMPTOMS?

If hypogonadism occurs after puberty, its only effect may be infertility (*see* MALE INFERTILITY, p.777) due to the reduced production of sperm. However, the following symptoms may also be evident:

- Erectile dysfunction.
- Reduction in the size of the genitals.
- Lowered sex drive.
- Reduced growth of facial, underarm, and pubic hair.
- Reduced muscle strength.

When hypogonadism develops before adolescence, it may result in late onset of puberty (*see* ABNORMAL PUBERTY IN MALES, opposite page).

WHAT MIGHT BE DONE?

The doctor will do a physical examination to assess whether the genitals are normal and to look for secondary sexual characteristics. He or she may arrange for a blood test to measure levels of testosterone and other hormones and look for a chromosomal abnormality.

Treatment is aimed at the underlying cause. Synthetic male hormones (*see* SEX HORMONES AND RELATED DRUGS, p.933) may be used to treat disorders of the testes. If underactivity of the pituitary gland is the cause, pituitary hormones may be given (*see* PITUITARY DRUGS, p.934). A pituitary tumor may require surgical removal. In boys, hormonal treatment stimulates puberty, including growth and sexual development. In adults, hormones encourage muscle strength, facial hair growth, potency, and sex drive. Side effects may include temporary breast development (*see* GYNECOMASTIA, below) and acne.

If the genitals are normal, sexual potency and fertility may be restored, but if hypogonadism is caused by a testicular disorder, fertility is rarely restored.

WWW ONLINE SITES: p.1032, p.1033, p.1034

Gynecomastia

Noncancerous enlargement of one or both breasts in males

 AGE Most common in newborn babies and adolescents

 LIFESTYLE Alcohol abuse and being overweight are risk factors in adults

 GENETICS Not a significant factor

All males produce small amounts of the female sex hormone estrogen. If too much estrogen is produced, breast enlargement (gynecomastia) occurs. One or both breasts may be affected. The condition is common in newborn boys and affects 1 in 2 male adolescents. It is usually temporary in both age groups. Older men can also be affected.

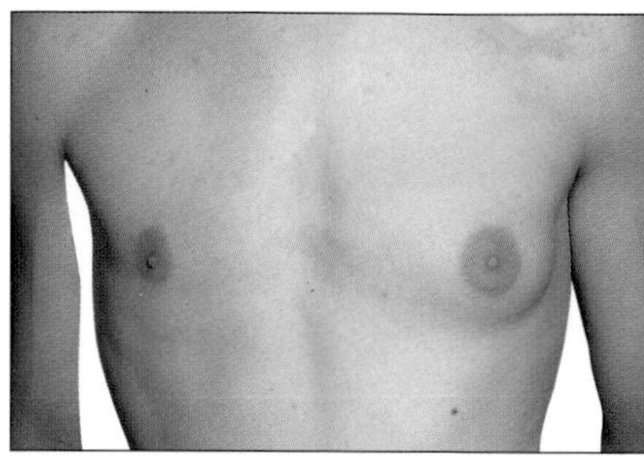

Gynecomastia
An excess of the female sex hormone estrogen in the blood may cause one or both male breasts to enlarge, as seen here.

WHAT ARE THE CAUSES?

Gynecomastia in the newborn occurs when the fetus has been exposed to the mother's estrogen within the uterus. Increased levels of estrogen, resulting in breast enlargement, are also common during puberty. In adults, alcohol abuse and being overweight are the most common causes of gynecomastia.

Drugs that affect levels of female sex hormones, such as spironolactone (*see* DIURETIC DRUGS, p.902) and corticosteroids (p.930), may lead to breast enlargement. Some drugs for prostate cancer (*see* DRUGS FOR PROSTATE DISORDERS, p.938) may have the same effect.

WHAT ARE THE SYMPTOMS?

The symptoms of gynecomastia may include the following:

- Tender and swollen breast or breasts.
- Firm or rubbery button of tissue that can be felt underneath the nipple.
- Discharge from the nipple.

One breast may enlarge more than the other. The symptoms listed here should always be investigated because they are similar to those of breast cancer (p.759).

WHAT MIGHT BE DONE?

Newborn boys do not need treatment, and gynecomastia usually disappears in a few weeks. In most adolescents, the condition disappears in less than 18 months without treatment. In older men, the doctor will ask about lifestyle factors and carry out an examination. He or she may arrange for tests to measure hormone levels and look for signs of breast cancer. The treatment and prognosis depend on the underlying cause, but, if gynecomastia persists, excess tissue may be removed surgically.

WWW ONLINE SITES: p.1032, p.1033, p.1034

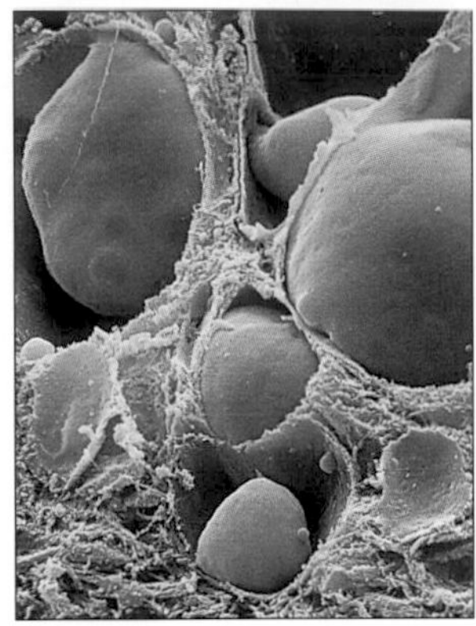

Developing egg follicles
A woman's eggs mature in fluid-filled follicles in the ovaries. This magnified image shows follicles at various stages of development.

FEMALE REPRODUCTIVE SYSTEM

THE CENTRAL ROLE of the female reproductive system is carried out by the ovaries, which produce sex cells, called ova or eggs, containing genetic material. When an egg fuses with a male sex cell, called a sperm, it has the potential to develop into a fetus. The ovaries also secrete sex hormones that control sexual development and the menstrual cycle. The breasts play a part in sexual arousal and produce milk after childbirth.

The only visible parts of the female reproductive system are the tissues that make up the vulva. The labia are folds of skin that protect the entrance to the vagina, which is lined with cells that produce a slightly acidic fluid to prevent infection. The vagina leads from the outside of the body to the uterus, the thick-walled organ in which a fetus develops. Two fallopian tubes lead from the uterus to the two ovaries, where eggs are stored.

FEMALE FERTILITY

Newborn girls are born with a supply of about 150,000 immature eggs, which have developed in their ovaries before birth. The eggs are stored in the ovaries but do not begin to mature until a rise in female sex hormones at puberty triggers the start of monthly menstrual cycles.

Once a month, an egg matures for 14 days in its follicle and is released from the ovary into the fallopian tube in a process called ovulation.The egg survives for 24 hours after ovulation and can only be fertilized by a sperm during this time. It takes about 5–6 days for the egg, fertilized or not, to pass along the tube to the uterus. If fertilized, the egg eventually implants in the lining of the uterus, which becomes thicker after ovulation, ready for an egg to implant. The egg then grows into an embryo. If not fertilized, the egg passes out of the vagina, along with the uterine lining. This blood loss is called menstruation.

Inside the fallopian tube
Hair-like projections (cilia) in the fallopian tube propel the egg toward the uterus.

The cycle of egg maturation, ovulation, and menstrual bleeding occurs at intervals of, on average, 28 days during a woman's reproductive lifespan. At menopause, which usually occurs between the ages of 45 and 55, eggs stop maturing and are no longer released by the ovaries. Menstruation stops, and the reproductive phase of a woman's life comes to an end.

PROCESS PUBERTY

Puberty is the period during which visible sexual characteristics develop and sexual organs mature. In girls, this period starts between the ages of about 10 and 14 and lasts for about 3–4 years. Puberty can be up to 2 years earlier in African–Americans, and girls in general usually enter puberty about 1–2 years before boys.

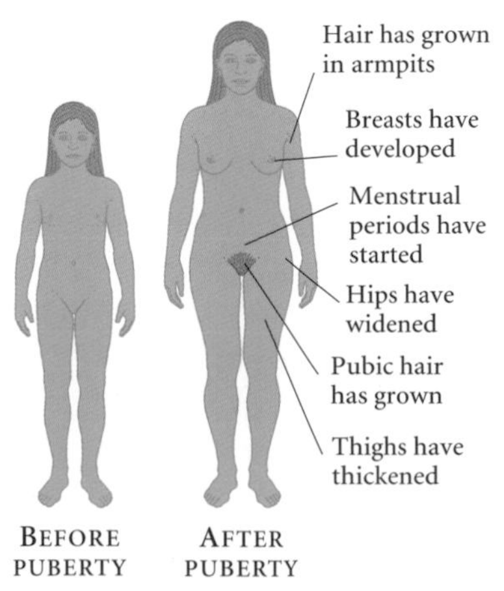
Hair has grown in armpits
Breasts have developed
Menstrual periods have started
Hips have widened
Pubic hair has grown
Thighs have thickened
BEFORE PUBERTY
AFTER PUBERTY

Physical development
During puberty, the breasts start to develop, pubic hair grows, and there is a rapid increase in height. The hips also widen, hair grows in the armpits, and menstruation begins.

FEMALE HORMONES

The ovaries produce the female sex hormones estrogen and progesterone, but secretion of these hormones is controlled by follicle-stimulating hormone and luteinizing hormone, which are produced in the pituitary gland, a tiny structure just below the brain. Sex hormones control sexual development at puberty, the menstrual cycle, and fertility. Estrogen also stimulates the fat distribution that results in a woman's rounded shape. Changes in hormone levels during the menstrual cycle and at menopause may affect mood and behavior.

STRUCTURE FEMALE REPRODUCTIVE SYSTEM

The internal organs of the female reproductive system are all located in the lower third of the abdomen. The ovaries store and release eggs, which pass along the fallopian tubes into the uterus. The vagina connects the uterus to the outside of the body. The visible external organs are collectively known as the vulva and consist of the sexually sensitive clitoris surrounded by folds of skin called the labia, which protect the entrances to the vagina and the urethra. Just inside the entrance to the vagina lie the two Bartholin's glands, which secrete a fluid for lubrication during sexual intercourse.

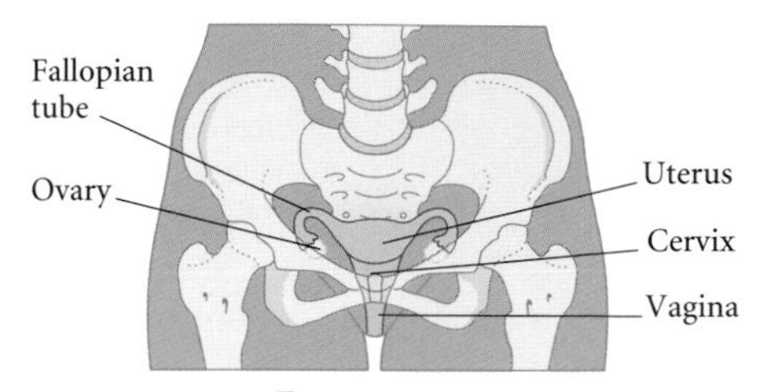

Fallopian tube
Ovary
Uterus
Cervix
Vagina

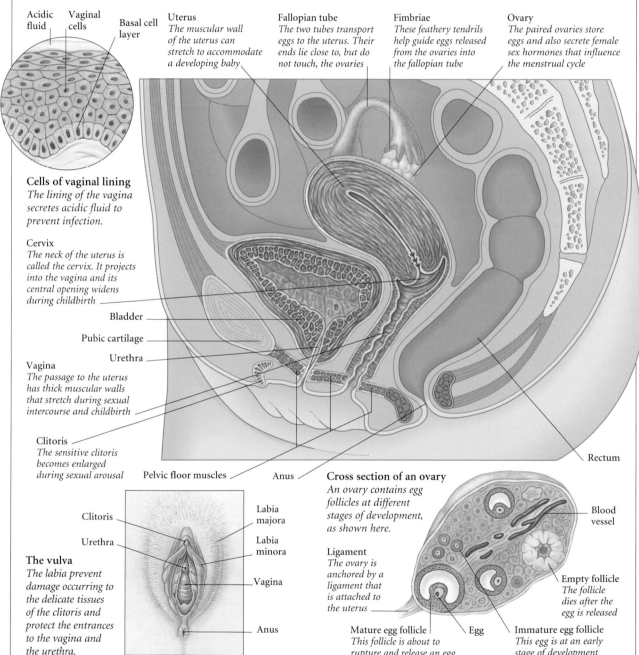

FRONT VIEW

Acidic fluid

Vaginal cells

Basal cell layer

Cells of vaginal lining
The lining of the vagina secretes acidic fluid to prevent infection.

Uterus
The muscular wall of the uterus can stretch to accommodate a developing baby

Fallopian tube
The two tubes transport eggs to the uterus. Their ends lie close to, but do not touch, the ovaries

Fimbriae
These feathery tendrils help guide eggs released from the ovaries into the fallopian tube

Ovary
The paired ovaries store eggs and also secrete female sex hormones that influence the menstrual cycle

Cervix
The neck of the uterus is called the cervix. It projects into the vagina and its central opening widens during childbirth

Bladder

Pubic cartilage

Urethra

Vagina
The passage to the uterus has thick muscular walls that stretch during sexual intercourse and childbirth

Clitoris
The sensitive clitoris becomes enlarged during sexual arousal

Pelvic floor muscles

Anus

Rectum

Clitoris

Urethra

Labia majora

Labia minora

Vagina

Anus

The vulva
The labia prevent damage occurring to the delicate tissues of the clitoris and protect the entrances to the vagina and the urethra.

Cross section of an ovary
An ovary contains egg follicles at different stages of development, as shown here.

Ligament
The ovary is anchored by a ligament that is attached to the uterus

Blood vessel

Empty follicle
The follicle dies after the egg is released

Mature egg follicle
This follicle is about to rupture and release an egg

Egg

Immature egg follicle
This egg is at an early stage of development

PROCESS MENSTRUAL CYCLE

Each month between puberty and menopause, a woman's body goes through the menstrual cycle in preparation for conception and pregnancy. A mature egg is released, and the lining of the uterus (the endometrium) becomes thicker, ready for a fertilized egg to implant. If the egg is not fertilized, it passes out of the body during menstruation. The menstrual cycle lasts 28 days on average but may not be the same length every month and varies from woman to woman. The cycle is regulated by a complex interaction between four female sex hormones. Follicle-stimulating hormone (FSH) and luteinizing hormone (LH) are produced in the pituitary gland, and estrogen and progesterone are secreted by the ovaries.

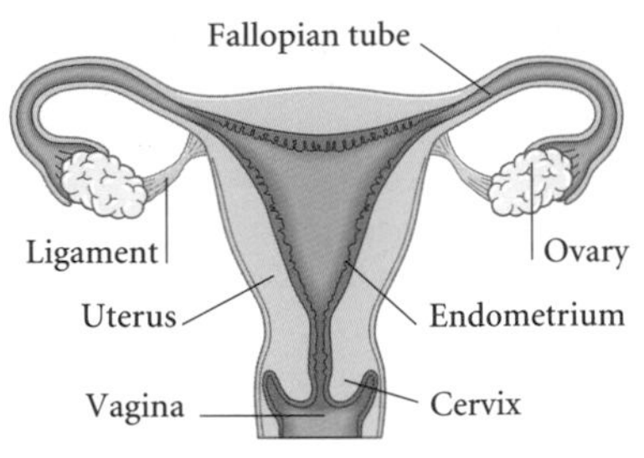

Fallopian tube
Ligament
Ovary
Uterus
Endometrium
Vagina
Cervix

FEMALE REPRODUCTIVE SYSTEM

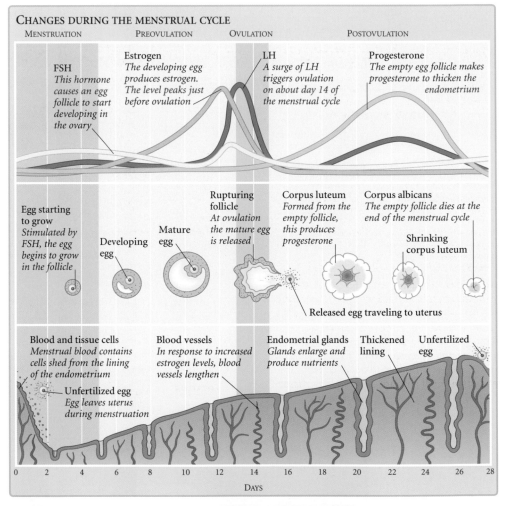

Hormones
Once a month, FSH causes an egg to mature and LH triggers its release. Just before ovulation, estrogen levels peak. A rise in progesterone causes the lining of the uterus to thicken.

Inside the ovary
The cycle begins with an egg developing inside a follicle in the ovary. The mature egg is released into the fallopian tube, leaving the empty follicle, called the corpus luteum, in the ovary.

Endometrium
Hormones cause the endometrium to double in thickness, to about ¼ in (6 mm). If fertilization does not occur, some of the endometrial cells are shed as menstrual blood, together with the unfertilized egg.

CHANGES DURING THE MENSTRUAL CYCLE

MENSTRUATION PREOVULATION OVULATION POSTOVULATION

FSH *This hormone causes an egg follicle to start developing in the ovary*

Estrogen *The developing egg produces estrogen. The level peaks just before ovulation*

LH *A surge of LH triggers ovulation on about day 14 of the menstrual cycle*

Progesterone *The empty egg follicle makes progesterone to thicken the endometrium*

Egg starting to grow *Stimulated by FSH, the egg begins to grow in the follicle*

Developing egg

Mature egg

Rupturing follicle *At ovulation the mature egg is released*

Corpus luteum *Formed from the empty follicle, this produces progesterone*

Corpus albicans *The empty follicle dies at the end of the menstrual cycle*

Shrinking corpus luteum

Released egg traveling to uterus

Blood and tissue cells *Menstrual blood contains cells shed from the lining of the endometrium*

Unfertilized egg *Egg leaves uterus during menstruation*

Blood vessels *In response to increased estrogen levels, blood vessels lengthen*

Endometrial glands *Glands enlarge and produce nutrients*

Thickened lining

Unfertilized egg

0 2 4 6 8 10 12 14 16 18 20 22 24 26 28

DAYS

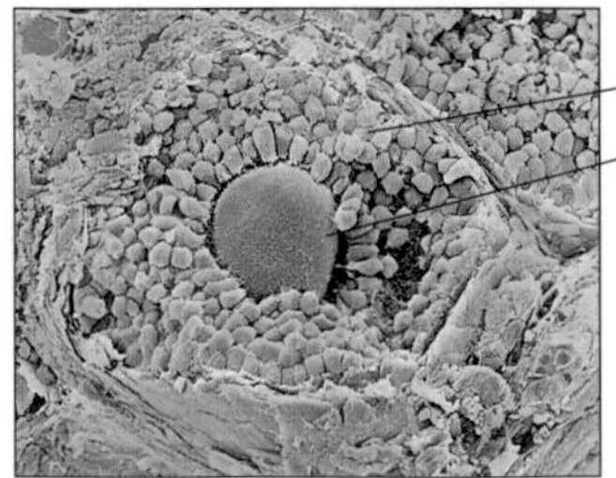

Nourishing cells in the follicle

Immature egg

Developing follicle
By absorbing nutrients from cells inside the follicle, an immature egg is able to develop and grow to maturity.

Fold of thickened endometrial tissue

Endometrium
After ovulation, the thickened endometrium tissue looks spongy and is ready to receive the fertilized egg.

FUNCTION CHANGES DURING MENOPAUSE

Menopause occurs between the ages of 45 and 55, when a woman's ovaries stop responding to follicle-stimulating hormone (FSH) and produce less of the female sex hormones estrogen and progesterone. This permanent drop in hormone levels brings an end to ovulation and menstruation. In the years just before and after menopause, hormone changes produce physical symptoms such as mood swings, hot flashes, vaginal dryness, and night sweats. Menopause may be associated with long-term physical changes, such as osteoporosis.

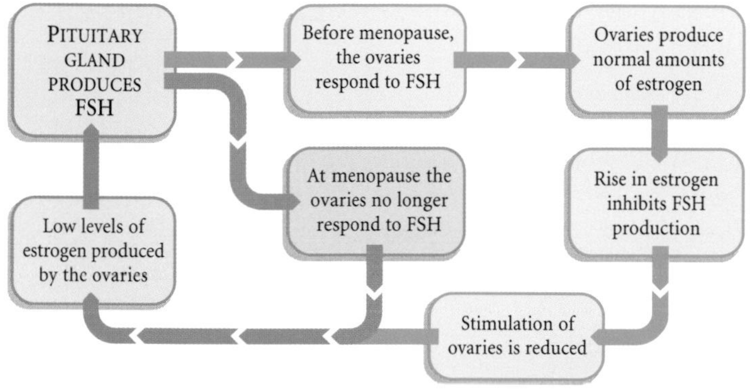
PITUITARY GLAND PRODUCES FSH
Before menopause, the ovaries respond to FSH
Ovaries produce normal amounts of estrogen
At menopause the ovaries no longer respond to FSH
Rise in estrogen inhibits FSH production
Low levels of estrogen produced by the ovaries
Stimulation of ovaries is reduced

Hormone cycle
At menopause, the ovaries no longer respond to FSH and produce little estrogen. The pituitary gland reacts by increasing its production of FSH. The raised levels of FSH are associated with symptoms such as flashes.

KEY
BEFORE MENOPAUSE
AT MENOPAUSE

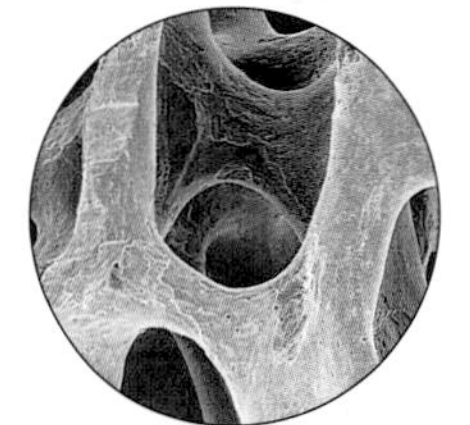
BEFORE MENOPAUSE

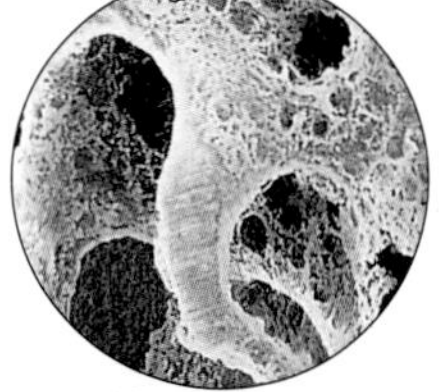
AFTER MENOPAUSE

Osteoporosis in bone tissue
Estrogen is needed to give bones strength. After menopause, when estrogen levels are low, osteoporosis can develop. Bones lose density and may become thin and brittle, as shown in the microscopic images above.

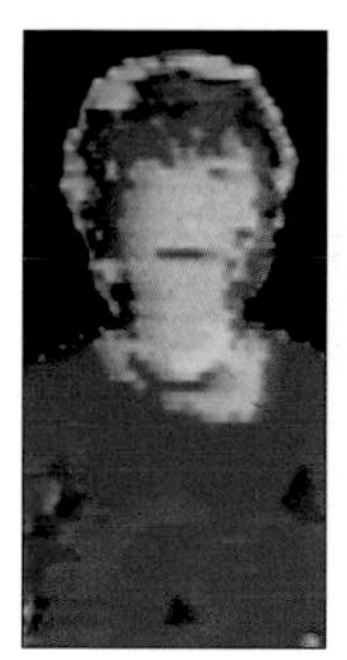
NORMAL

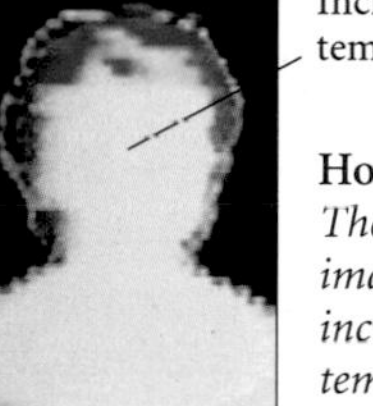
Increased skin temperature
HOT FLASH

Hot flashes
These thermal images show increased skin temperature in a hot flash, a symptom of menopause related to high FSH levels.

FUNCTION ROLE OF THE BREASTS

Breasts have a role in sexual arousal, but their main function is to produce and deliver milk to a newborn baby. Hormonal changes in late pregnancy stimulate the production of milk in glands called lobules, which lead to ducts that converge and then open onto the surface of the nipple. The remaining breast tissue is mostly fat, with a small amount of connective tissue that helps support the breasts. The wide variety in size and shape of breasts is determined by genetic factors, fat content, and muscle tone.

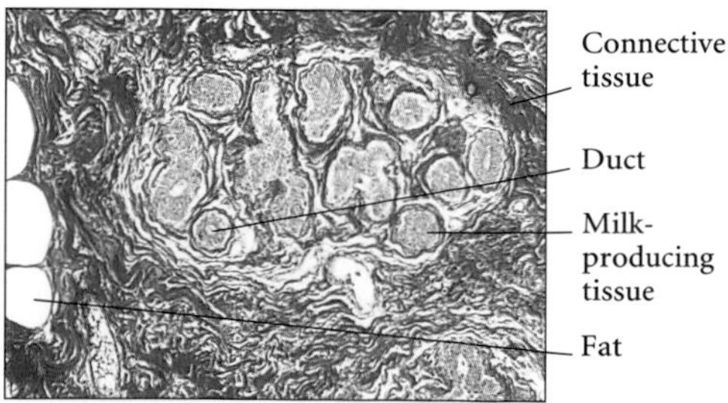
Connective tissue
Duct
Milk-producing tissue
Fat

Breast tissue
A milk-producing lobule of the breast and the drainage ducts leading from it are shown here. Each lobule is surrounded by fat and connective tissue.

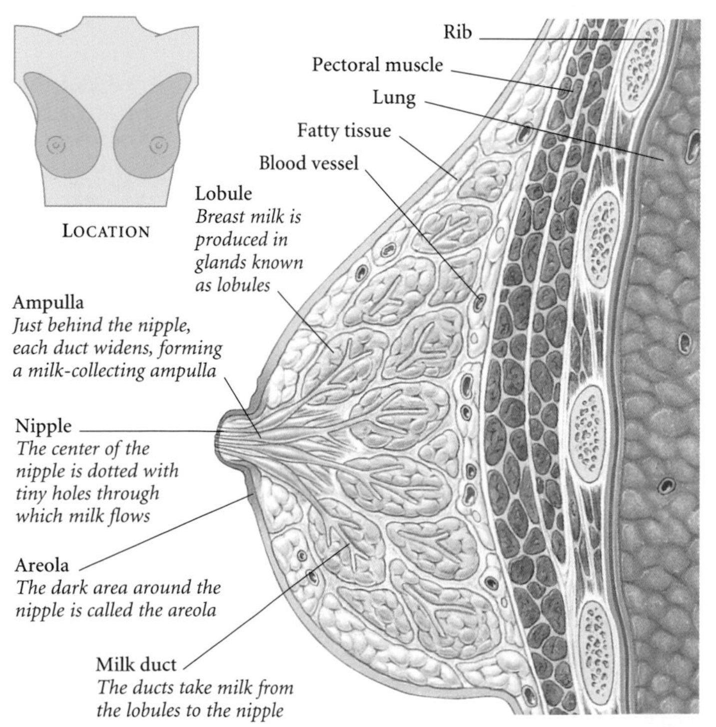
LOCATION
Rib
Pectoral muscle
Lung
Fatty tissue
Blood vessel
Lobule
Breast milk is produced in glands known as lobules
Ampulla
Just behind the nipple, each duct widens, forming a milk-collecting ampulla
Nipple
The center of the nipple is dotted with tiny holes through which milk flows
Areola
The dark area around the nipple is called the areola
Milk duct
The ducts take milk from the lobules to the nipple

MENSTRUAL, MENOPAUSAL, AND HORMONAL PROBLEMS

Menstruation usually starts at puberty and ceases at menopause. These two stages in a woman's life are determined by the levels of female sex hormones in the body. The menstrual cycle itself is also governed by a combination of hormones, all of which are produced at varying levels throughout the cycle. Many conditions or disorders may upset the balance of these hormones.

This section begins by discussing some common menstrual disorders. Several of these disorders are still not fully understood, but advances in diagnostic techniques have made investigation easier, and modern surgical methods have improved treatment. The articles that follow cover health problems associated with menopause and other disorders caused by an imbalance of the sex hormones. The widespread use of hormonal treatment has helped relieve many of these disorders.

Related disorders that affect the female reproductive system are dealt with in other sections (*see* DISORDERS OF THE FEMALE REPRODUCTIVE ORGANS, pp.741–753, and SEX AND REPRODUCTION, pp.762–777), as are disorders involving hormones other than the sex hormones (*see* HORMONES AND METABOLISM, pp.670–693).

KEY ANATOMY

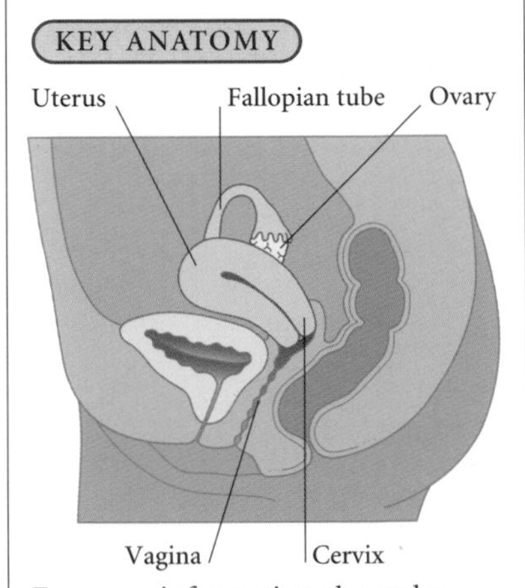
Uterus
Fallopian tube
Ovary
Vagina
Cervix

For more information about the structure and function of the female reproductive system, *see* pp.730–733.

Irregular menstrual periods

A menstrual cycle that has wide variations in the length of time between periods

 AGE Most common just after puberty and just before menopause

 LIFESTYLE Stress, excessive exercise, and being underweight are all risk factors

 GENETICS Not a significant factor

Menstrual periods start at puberty and continue until menopause. The average menstrual cycle lasts 28 days, but menstrual periods may occur as often as every 24 days or as infrequently as every 35 days. After puberty, most women develop a regular menstrual cycle with a relatively consistent length of time between periods, but in some women menstrual periods may remain irregular. Menstrual bleeding normally lasts between 2 and 7 days, with the average length of bleeding being 5 days.

WHAT ARE THE CAUSES?

Variations in the length of the menstrual cycle are usually the result of a temporary hormonal imbalance. At puberty, normal changes in hormone levels mean that menstrual periods are often irregular when they first start, and wide variations in a woman's normal pattern of bleeding are common in the first few months after childbirth and with the approach of menopause.

Hormonal imbalances at other times may be created by factors such as stress, depression, and severe or chronic illness. Excessive exercise and extreme weight loss (*see* ANOREXIA NERVOSA, p.562) are also common causes of hormonal disturbance that can cause menstruation to become irregular.

Occasionally, irregular menstruation may be a symptom of a disorder of the ovaries or of the uterus. In particular, polycystic ovary syndrome (p.744), in which there is an imbalance of the sex hormones, or endometriosis (p.742), in which fragments of the tissue that normally lines the uterus are displaced and attached to other pelvic organs, may disrupt menstrual periods.

In some cases, an unsuspected pregnancy may produce irregular vaginal bleeding that could easily be mistaken for a menstrual period. A single, late, heavy period may in fact be due to a miscarriage (p.791). A late menstrual period that is accompanied by severe abdominal pain should receive urgent medical attention because it may be due to an ectopic pregnancy (p.790). In some cases, the cause of irregular menstrual periods is unknown.

WHAT MIGHT BE DONE?

Irregular menstruation due to the normal hormonal changes that follow puberty or childbirth usually becomes more regular with time. In women who are approaching menopause, irregular periods will eventually cease altogether. In all of these cases, treatment is not usually necessary. However, if the problem persists and interferes with lifestyle, drugs may be prescribed to regulate menstruation. These drugs include oral contraceptives for younger women and hormone replacement therapy (p.937) for women approaching menopause.

If there is no obvious cause for your irregular periods and no apparent pattern to menstrual bleeding, tests may be performed to look for an underlying disorder. These tests may include a pregnancy test, blood tests to measure hormone levels, and ultrasound scanning (p.250) to look at the ovaries and uterus. If an underlying disorder is discovered, treatment of that disorder should regulate periods in most cases.

(WWW) ONLINE SITES: p.1037

Amenorrhea

The absence of menstrual periods for at least 3 months in women who would otherwise be menstruating

AGE Occurs between puberty and menopause

GENETICS In some cases, due to a chromosomal abnormality

LIFESTYLE Stress, excessive exercise, and being underweight are all risk factors

There are two types of amenorrhea, primary and secondary. Primary amenorrhea is the term used to describe menstruation that has not started at all by age 16. Once menstruation has started at puberty, it is normal for it to stop during pregnancy, for a few months following childbirth, while breast-feeding, after ceasing to take oral contraceptive pills, and permanently at menopause. If menstrual periods suddenly stop at any other time for at least 3 continuous months, the condition is known as secondary amenorrhea.

WHAT ARE THE CAUSES?

Amenorrhea is often caused by a disturbance in the female sex hormones, which may be brought on by factors such as stress or depression. Excessive exercise and extreme or sudden weight loss (*see* ANOREXIA NERVOSA, p.562) may also lead to such hormonal disturbances and are common causes of amenorrhea in athletes, gymnasts, and ballet dancers. Hormonal changes may lead to primary or secondary amenorrhea, depending on when they occur.

Primary amenorrhea is a characteristic feature of delayed puberty (*see* ABNORMAL PUBERTY IN FEMALES, p.739), and may be caused by a chromosomal abnormality. The failure of menstrual periods to start at puberty may also be due to a condition in which the hymen (the thin membrane over the vagina) has no opening, and menstrual blood cannot leave the body. In rare cases, the uterus is absent from birth, and therefore no menstruation can occur.

Secondary amenorrhea may be due to a pituitary gland disorder, such as a pituitary tumor (*see* PROLACTINOMA, p.677), or it may be due to premature menopause, in which menstrual periods cease before age 35. Other possible causes are disorders of the ovaries, such as polycystic ovary syndrome (p.744), and treatments such as chemotherapy (p.278) and radiation therapy (p.279), that can result in damage to the ovaries.

WHAT MIGHT BE DONE?

Treatment is not needed if amenorrhea occurs for a few months after stopping oral contraceptives or during pregnancy or breast-feeding. Menstruation usually resumes within a few months of giving birth if you are not breast-feeding or within a month of stopping breast-feeding. If you are near menopause, amenorrhea will be permanent.

Amenorrhea that occurs at any other time should be investigated. Your doctor will examine you and may do a pregnancy test. You may also need to have blood tests to measure hormone levels, ultrasound scanning (p.250) of the ovaries and uterus, and CT scanning (p.247) of the pituitary gland.

Treatment of the underlying disorder induces menstruation in most cases. If the cause cannot be treated, hormonal treatments may be used to start menstruation. Amenorrhea due to weight loss, stress, or excessive exercise should clear up once the problem is overcome.

(WWW) ONLINE SITES: p.1037

Menorrhagia

Menstrual periods that are heavier than normal

AGE More common over age 40

LIFESTYLE Being overweight is a risk factor

GENETICS Not a significant factor

Some women have heavier menstrual periods than others. However, if menstrual bleeding lasts for longer than 7 days, cannot be controlled by sanitary napkins or tampons, or includes large blood clots, it is classed as menorrhagia. In some cases, this condition may be associated with a dragging pain in the lower abdomen. Menstruation may also be irregular (*see* IRREGULAR MENSTRUAL PERIODS, opposite page). Severe bleeding may lead to iron deficiency anemia (p.447), causing lightheadedness and fatigue. About 1 in 20 women has menorrhagia regularly. It is more common approaching menopause.

WHAT ARE THE CAUSES?

Heavy menstrual bleeding is a symptom of various disorders of the uterus, such as fibroids (p.745), uterine polyps (p.746), or cancer of the uterus (p.748). Menorrhagia is also a well-known side effect of using an intrauterine contraceptive device (IUD). A single heavy period that is late may be due to a miscarriage (p.791). Menorrhagia may also be due to a hormonal disorder, such as hypothyroidism (p.680). The condition is more common in overweight women.

In some cases, there is no apparent cause. If your periods have always been heavy, there is probably no cause for concern. However, you should consult your doctor so that he or she can check that there is no underlying disorder.

HOW IS IT DIAGNOSED?

Your doctor will examine you and may arrange for blood tests to measure your hormone levels and look for evidence of anemia. Further investigations, such as ultrasound scanning (p.250) to look for fibroids or polyps in the uterus, may be necessary. You may also have hysteroscopy (p.745), in which a viewing instrument is introduced through the cervix to inspect the uterus. A small sample of the endometrium (the lining of the uterus) may be taken for analysis (*see* ENDOMETRIAL SAMPLING, p.738).

WHAT IS THE TREATMENT?

Treatment depends on the cause, your age, and the severity of bleeding. If no cause can be found, drugs may initially be given to reduce bleeding. You should consider changing your method of contraception if you use an IUD. If you are overweight, losing weight may help.

If initial treatments are not effective or menorrhagia is severe, you may need a procedure to remove or destroy the lining of the uterus by laser (p.951) or heat treatment (endometrial ablation), or to remove the uterus (*see* HYSTERECTOMY, p.747). These procedures are irreversible and are only offered to women who do not want to have children in the future. Removal of the endometrium is a minor procedure, but carries a small risk that problems will recur if endometrial tissue remains. A hysterectomy is a major operation but ensures that menorrhagia will not recur.

(WWW) ONLINE SITES: p.1037

Dysmenorrhea

Lower abdominal pain and discomfort experienced just before or during menstruation

 GENETICS Sometimes runs in families

 AGE LIFESTYLE Risk factors depend on the type

Up to three-quarters of women have menstrual period pain, also known as dysmenorrhea, at some time. In about one-fifth of these women, the pain is severe and can seriously disrupt normal activities. Pain is usually experienced in the 24 hours before menstruation or over the first few days of the period.

WHAT ARE THE TYPES?

There are two types of dysmenorrhea: primary, which has no obvious cause; and secondary, which is the result of a disorder of the reproductive organs.

PRIMARY DYSMENORRHEA This form of dysmenorrhea usually appears in the early teens. The pain is associated with the hormones involved in the monthly release of eggs from the ovaries. Periods often become painful 1–2 years after the start of menstruation when ovulation begins to occur. A rise in the level of hormonelike substances, known as prostaglandins, occurs some days after ovulation and makes the uterine muscles contract. This muscle contraction interferes with the blood supply to the uterus and causes period pain. This type of menstrual pain tends to lessen after age 25, often disappearing by age 30, and usually becomes less severe following childbirth, probably because the blood supply to the uterus increases.

Women with close female relatives who have had primary dysmenorrhea are more likely to develop it, suggesting that genetic factors are involved.

SECONDARY DYSMENORRHEA Painful periods in women who have not had menstrual pain before or have only experienced mild pain is called secondary dysmenorrhea. This type of period pain usually affects women aged 20–40. The cause is often endometriosis (p.742), in which fragments of the tissue that normally lines the uterus are attached to other pelvic organs, or a disorder of the uterus, such as fibroids (p.745). A chronic infection of the reproductive organs (*see* PELVIC INFLAMMATORY DISEASE, p.741) and use of an intrauterine contraceptive device (IUD) may also cause painful periods.

WHAT ARE THE SYMPTOMS?

The symptoms of dysmenorrhea begin either just before or at the start of menstruation and are worst when bleeding is heaviest. The pain may be described as either or both of the following:

- Cramping lower abdominal pain that comes in waves, radiating to the lower back and down the legs.
- Dragging pain in the pelvis.

The pain may be accompanied by any of the symptoms of premenstrual syndrome (right), such as headache, breast tenderness, and abdominal bloating.

WHAT CAN I DO?

You may find certain over-the-counter analgesics (p.912), such as ibuprofen, helpful in alleviating the pain. Relaxing in a hot bath and applying a source of heat, such as a hot water bottle, to your abdomen may also provide pain relief. However, consult your doctor if you are experiencing menstrual period pain for the first time or if it becomes severe.

WHAT MIGHT THE DOCTOR DO?

Your doctor will ask if your menstrual periods have always been painful and may examine you, especially if you have secondary dysmenorrhea. Various tests may be done, including a cervical swab to look for infection, ultrasound scanning (p.250) of your lower abdomen, or examination of the uterus by using an endoscope (*see* HYSTEROSCOPY, p.745).

Treatment depends on the type of dysmenorrhea. For primary dysmenorrhea, you may be given a nonsteroidal anti-inflammatory drug (p.894) or an antispasmodic drug to reduce cramping pain. Your doctor may prescribe oral contraceptive pills, which relieve period pain by preventing ovulation and can also decrease menstrual blood loss. Once ovulation has been suppressed, primary dysmenorrhea should improve, but the pain may recur at any time if you stop treatment. Secondary dysmenorrhea usually disappears once the underlying condition is treated.

(WWW) ONLINE SITES: p.1037

Premenstrual syndrome

Varying symptoms that may affect women in the days leading up to menstruation

 AGE Usually develops in late adolescence; may occur in all menstruating females

 GENETICS Sometimes runs in families

 LIFESTYLE Stress and certain foods may aggravate symptoms

As many as 1 in 3 women experience premenstrual syndrome (PMS) as their menstrual period approaches. In up to 1 in 20 women, the symptoms may be severe enough to disrupt lifestyle.

The cause of PMS is disputed, but it is thought that the symptoms are triggered by the action of the female sex hormones estrogen and progesterone before menstruation. Stress may make the symptoms worse, as may an excessive consumption of chocolate and caffeine-containing drinks, such as coffee and cola. Women are more likely to

(SELF-HELP) PREVENTING PREMENSTRUAL SYNDROME

The following self-help measures may help either prevent or relieve premenstrual syndrome. If these measures do not help and you have persistent symptoms, visit your doctor for advice.

- Relax as much as possible and try to avoid stress.
- Try taking up a light, relaxing exercise, such as yoga.
- Take warm baths.
- Eat little and often, making sure your diet includes plenty of carbohydrates and fiber.
- Try to reduce your salt intake.
- Avoid eating excessive amounts of chocolate.
- Avoid drinks containing large amounts of caffeine, such as coffee, tea, and cola.
- A vitamin B_6 supplement may be helpful, although very high doses may be harmful.
- Evening primrose oil capsules are often effective, especially in relieving breast tenderness.

experience severe symptoms of PMS if their close female relatives have had similar problems, although no genetic factors have as yet been identified.

WHAT ARE THE SYMPTOMS?

The symptoms of PMS can vary among women, and some women find that they also differ from month to month. Symptoms may appear just a few hours before a menstrual period begins, but they can start up to 14 days beforehand. In most affected women, symptoms disappear by the time menstruation has finished, or a few days afterward. The symptoms may include:

- Tenderness or generalized lumpiness of the breasts.
- A feeling of bloating caused by retention of fluid.
- Mood changes, including feelings of tension, irritability, depression, anxiety, and fatigue.
- Difficulty concentrating and making everyday decisions.
- Headaches, including migraine.
- Backache and muscle stiffness.
- Disruption of normal sleep patterns.
- Unusual food cravings.

Less commonly, nausea, vomiting, cold sweats, lightheadedness, and hot flashes may also be experienced.

WHAT MIGHT BE DONE?

The diagnosis of PMS is usually easily made from the timing of your symptoms. Your doctor may ask you to keep a record of symptoms to confirm that they are related to menstruation.

There are a number of self-help measures you can take to try to prevent PMS (*see* PREVENTING PREMENSTRUAL SYNDROME, opposite page). If these are not effective or symptoms are severe, you should seek medical advice. Some analgesics (p.912), such as ibuprofen, help relieve headaches and muscle stiffness. If you experience mood swings, your doctor may prescribe antidepressant drugs (p.916) which may be more effective if taken throughout the menstrual cycle. Diuretic drugs (p.902) may help relieve fluid retention. Your doctor may prescribe treatment with the hormone progesterone (*see* SEX HORMONES AND RELATED DRUGS, p.933). No treatment is consistently successful, but the symptoms can usually be relieved.

(WWW) ONLINE SITES: p.1037

Abnormal vaginal bleeding

Vaginal bleeding that is not related to menstruation

 AGE LIFESTYLE Risk factors depend on the cause

GENETICS Not a significant factor

Normally, vaginal bleeding occurs only during a menstrual period. Any bleeding that occurs outside menstruation is abnormal. In women under the age of 35, abnormal vaginal bleeding is often the result of starting oral contraceptives. Abnormal bleeding caused by a disorder of the reproductive organs is more common in women over this age.

WHAT ARE THE CAUSES?

Light bleeding between menstrual periods, or spotting, is common in the first few menstrual cycles after starting oral contraceptives or changing to a different type of pill. Spotting is usually brought on by the body adjusting to changes in hormone levels, but it may also occur if you have an intrauterine contraceptive device (IUD).

Abnormal bleeding, especially within a few hours of sexual intercourse, may indicate a cervical disorder, such as cervical ectropion (p.749) or cancer of the cervix (p.750). In older women, sex may damage the walls of the vagina, which become thinner and more fragile after menopause, causing vaginal bleeding.

Abnormal vaginal bleeding that is not associated with sexual intercourse or contraception may be caused by a disorder such as endometriosis (p.742) or uterine polyps (p.746). Loss of blood from the uterus can also occur in early pregnancy and could indicate a miscarriage (p.791). Various disorders of the female reproductive organs may cause postmenopausal bleeding (p.738), such as cancer of the uterus (p.748).

If you notice abnormal bleeding, you should see your doctor immediately so that the cause can be investigated.

WHAT MIGHT BE DONE?

Your doctor may be able to identify the cause of the problem from the timing of the bleeding, but he or she will probably examine you. You may need more tests, such as a Pap test (p.749) to check for disorders of the cervix, ultrasound scanning (p.250) to look at the uterus, or endoscopy to view the inside of the uterus (*see* HYSTEROSCOPY, p.745).

The treatment for abnormal vaginal bleeding varies depending on the cause. Spotting caused by oral contraceptives may be prevented by changing the dose or type of pill. Hormone treatments can be used to restore the elasticity in fragile vaginal walls. Surgery may be required to treat more serious underlying conditions. In most cases, abnormal vaginal bleeding disappears once the cause has been treated.

(WWW) ONLINE SITES: p.1037

Menopausal problems

Symptoms associated with the normal changes that take place in a woman's body as her period of fertility ends

 AGE Most common between the ages of 45 and 55

 GENETICS Sometimes runs in families

 LIFESTYLE Smoking lowers the age at which menopause occurs

Menopause, the time at which a woman stops menstruating, is a normal consequence of the aging process. More than 8 in 10 women experience only mild problems at menopause, or none at all, but some women have severe symptoms that can affect their lifestyle.

Menopause usually occurs between the ages of 45 and 55, although some women experience symptoms before or after this time. Smoking lowers the age at which menopause occurs. A woman is usually considered to be menopausal if she has not had a menstrual period for 6 months and there is no other underlying cause. The tendency to have either an early or a late menopause sometimes runs in families.

WHAT ARE THE CAUSES?

As women age, their ovaries gradually become less active and produce smaller amounts of the sex hormone estrogen. Menopause occurs as a result of this reduction in ovarian activity. As levels of estrogen in the body decline, the pituitary gland begins to secrete more follicle-stimulating hormone (FSH) to try to stimulate the ovaries. Most of the symptoms associated with menopause are a consequence of the reduced levels of estrogen or increased levels of FSH. These symptoms tend to be more severe when menopause takes place prematurely or abruptly. A sudden menopause can be brought about by surgical removal of the ovaries or anti-cancer treatments that can damage the ovaries, such as chemotherapy (p.278) and radiation therapy (p.279).

WHAT ARE THE SYMPTOMS?

Menopausal symptoms may begin up to 5 years before menstruation finally stops and usually last for a year or two. Many women find that one of the first signs of menopause is irregularity in their menstrual cycle. Menstrual bleeding may also become heavier (*see* MENORRHAGIA, p.735). Increased levels of FSH cause many of the other common symptoms that can occur during menopause. These symptoms include:

- Hot flashes, in which the head, chest, and arms become red and feel hot, lasting from a couple of minutes to as long as an hour.
- Heavy sweating, which is often especially troublesome at night.
- Feelings of anxiety, panic, or depression, which may be made worse if menopause coincides with a stressful life event such as the departure of adult children from the home.

The longer-term effects of a decline in estrogen levels include:

- Drying and wrinkling of the skin.
- Vaginal dryness and discomfort during sexual intercourse as a result of thinning of the lining of the vagina.
- Urinary infections that occur due to thinning of the lining of the urethra (the passage leading from the bladder to outside the body).

The decline in estrogen levels following menopause may also increase your risk of developing certain long-term conditions, such as coronary artery disease (p.405) and age-related thinning of the bones (*see* OSTEOPOROSIS, p.368).

WHAT MIGHT BE DONE?

Hormone replacement therapy (p.937), known as HRT, may help relieve many of the symptoms of menopause by boosting the level of estrogen in the body and reducing the production of FSH. Your doctor may prescribe HRT as pills, skin gel or patch, vaginal cream, vaginal ring, or injections. HRT is usually given for the shortest period to alleviate menopausal symptoms, usually less than 5 years. However, its use may have risks, and you should discuss these with your doctor.

Alternative treatments are available in the form of vaginal creams and rings, which control vaginal dryness and discomfort, and the drug clonidine, which can help relieve hot flashes. Some women find complementary therapies, such as homeopathy (p.974), helpful.

The process of menopause normally lasts between 1 and 5 years, after which symptoms usually disappear naturally.

(WWW) ONLINE SITES: p.1026, p.1037

Postmenopausal bleeding

Bleeding from the uterus occurring at least 6 months after menstruation has stopped

 AGE Occurs after menopause

 GENETICS LIFESTYLE Not significant factors

Menstrual bleeding should cease at the menopause. Postmenopausal bleeding is normal only with certain forms of hormone replacement therapy (p.937) that cause withdrawal bleeding once a month. Other postmenopausal bleeding may be a sign of a serious disorder, such as cancer of the reproductive tract, and should be investigated by a doctor. Postmenopausal bleeding is usually painless and may range from light spotting to a heavier flow of blood.

WHAT ARE THE CAUSES?

Postmenopausal bleeding is associated with numerous disorders of the vulva, vagina, cervix, and uterus. The most common and least serious cause of bleeding is atrophic vaginitis, in which the vagina becomes inflamed following a decline in estrogen after menopause (*see* VULVOVAGINITIS, p.752).

Postmenopausal bleeding could be caused by a disorder of the cervix, or cancer of the cervix (p.750). In these disorders, bleeding from the cervix may be more likely to occur after sexual

TEST ENDOMETRIAL SAMPLING

During endometrial sampling a small sample of tissue is removed from the endometrium (the lining of the uterus) to investigate symptoms such as heavy vaginal bleeding and to rule out cancer of the uterus. The sample is sent to a laboratory for microscopic examination. The procedure may be slightly uncomfortable but usually lasts for only a few minutes and does not require anesthesia.

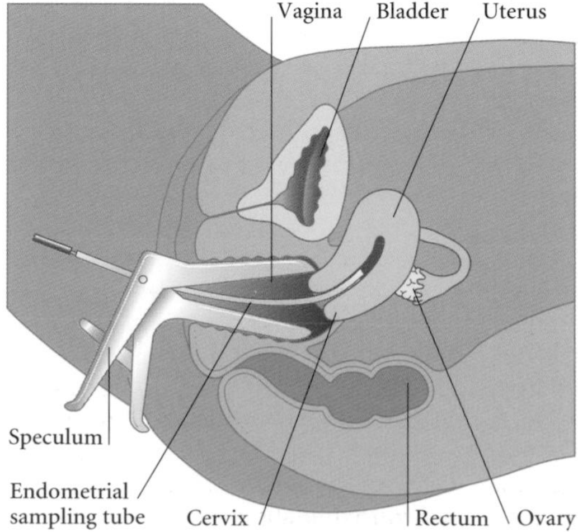
Vagina
Bladder
Uterus
Speculum
Endometrial sampling tube
Cervix
Rectum
Ovary

During the procedure
An instrument called a speculum is used to hold the vagina open while a thin, flexible tube is inserted into the uterus. A small sample of tissue is then drawn into the tube by vacuum suction.

RESULTS

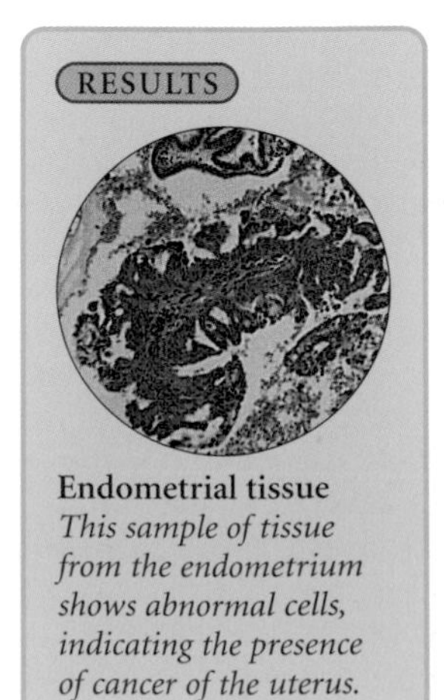

Endometrial tissue
This sample of tissue from the endometrium shows abnormal cells, indicating the presence of cancer of the uterus.

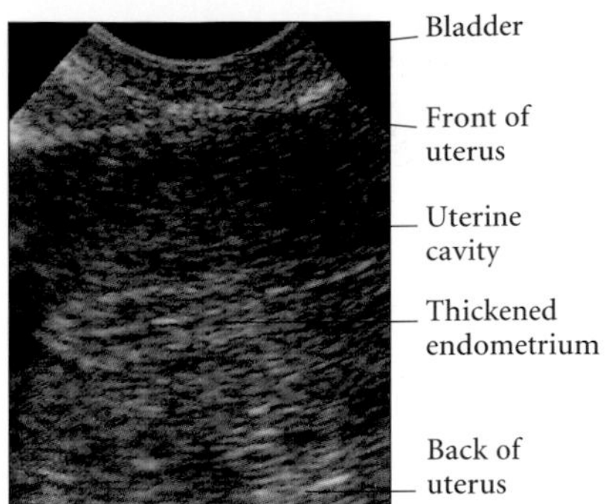
Bladder
Front of uterus
Uterine cavity
Thickened endometrium
Back of uterus

Thickened endometrium
This ultrasound scan of the uterus shows that the endometrium (the lining of the uterus) is thickened. This may be a cause of postmenopausal bleeding.

intercourse. Postmenopausal bleeding may also be the result of a thickened endometrium (the lining of the uterus) or cancerous or noncancerous growths in the uterus (*see* CANCER OF THE UTERUS, p.748, and UTERINE POLYPS, p.746). Cancer of the vulva and of the vagina (p.753) may also lead to postmenopausal bleeding, although both these disorders are very rare.

WHAT MIGHT BE DONE?

Your doctor will examine the vagina and cervix to look for abnormalities. If abnormal areas are seen in the vagina, a small sample of tissue may be taken for examination under the microscope. Your doctor may also perform a Pap test (p.749) to check for abnormal cells in the cervix. In some cases, a small sample of the endometrial tissue may be taken for analysis (*see* ENDOMETRIAL SAMPLING, opposite page).

Ultrasound scanning (p.250) may be carried out to image the uterus and to measure the thickness of the lining. You may need endoscopy to view inside the uterus (*see* HYSTEROSCOPY, p.745).

The treatment for postmenopausal bleeding varies depending on the underlying cause of the condition. Estrogen creams that are applied to the vagina may be prescribed to help relieve atrophic vaginitis. Surgery may be necessary to remove cancerous growths and to treat disorders of the cervix and uterus, such as uterine polyps and a thickened endometrium. Postmenopausal bleeding should cease once the underlying disorder has been treated.

(WWW) ONLINE SITES: p.1026, p.1037

Hypogonadism in females

Underactivity, developmental failure, or absence of the ovaries, leading to low levels of female sex hormones

 GENETICS In some cases, due to a chromosomal abnormality

 AGE LIFESTYLE Risk factors depend on the cause

Female sex hormones control sexual development and the menstrual cycle. Underactivity of the ovaries, known as hypogonadism, leads to low levels of these hormones in the body. Decreased levels of female sex hormones are natural during menopause, but may also be characteristic of other conditions. Hypogonadism may cause distressing symptoms but is often treatable.

WHAT ARE THE TYPES?

There are two types of hypogonadism, primary and secondary. Either type can occur at any age. Primary hypogonadism is often caused by a disorder or failure of the ovaries, which may result from a chromosomal abnormality such as Turner syndrome (p.823). It may also be caused by the surgical removal of the ovaries. However, in most cases primary hypogonadism occurs as a natural consequence of menopause.

Secondary hypogonadism is caused by an abnormality of the pituitary gland or hypothalamus in the brain that leads to underproduction of the hormones that stimulate the ovaries to function. This abnormality may be due to a disorder such as a pituitary tumor (p.676) or, in rare cases, to damage of the pituitary gland or the hypothalamus as a result of a head injury (p.521) or an infection such as viral encephalitis (p.528). Sometimes it results from excessive exercise or sudden weight loss.

WHAT ARE THE SYMPTOMS?

The symptoms depend on the age at which hypogonadism develops and the amount of sex hormones produced. If the onset occurs before puberty, hypogonadism causes abnormal puberty in females (right). If the onset occurs after puberty, symptoms may include:

- Reduced or absent menstruation (*see* AMENORRHEA, p.735).
- Reduced fertility.
- Hot flashes, sweating, anxiety, and additional symptoms associated with menopause (*see* MENOPAUSAL PROBLEMS, p.737).
- Rarely, the pubic hair may recede and the breasts may become smaller.

There may also be other symptoms depending on the underlying cause.

WHAT MIGHT BE DONE?

Your doctor may arrange for you to have blood tests to measure your hormone levels. You may also have CT scanning (p.247) of the brain to look for a pituitary abnormality, or ultrasound scanning (p.250) of the ovaries.

Treatment depends on the cause of the problem. For example, a pituitary tumor may be removed by surgery. If the condition is due to weight loss, gaining weight may help. Hormonal treatment may be prescribed to induce puberty. For menopausal women, hormone replacement therapy (p.937) may be prescribed to relieve menopausal symptoms and help prevent diseases associated with low levels of sex hormones, such as osteoporosis (p.368) and coronary artery disease (p.405).

(WWW) ONLINE SITES: p.1032, p.1033, p.1037

Abnormal puberty in females

Very early or late start of puberty, usually due to a hormonal imbalance

 AGE Occurs before or after the normal age range for puberty

 LIFESTYLE Excessive exercise and weight loss are risk factors

 GENETICS In some cases, due to a chromosomal abnormality

Puberty is the period during which sexual development occurs (*see* PUBERTY, p.730). In girls, puberty is characterized by a growth spurt, hair growth in the armpits and pubic region, the development of the breasts and reproductive organs, and the onset of menstruation. Although there is considerable variation in the age of onset of puberty, girls tend to start this process between age 10 and 14. Puberty may be considered abnormal if it starts either earlier than normal (precocious) or later (delayed). Early puberty occurs if a girl develops breasts before age 8 or if menstruation starts before age 10. In extreme cases, puberty may begin at age 4. Puberty is delayed if menstruation has not started by age 16 (*see* AMENORRHEA, p.735) or breast development is absent at age 14.

Early puberty is rare and may be a sign of an underlying hormonal disorder. Delayed puberty is more common. There may be an underlying cause, but many girls who have not menstruated by age 16 are simply late developers, a tendency that often runs in families.

Abnormal puberty can be disturbing for a girl and her family because physical and sexual development will not coincide with that of her peers. Medical advice should be sought as soon as abnormal puberty is suspected.

WHAT ARE THE CAUSES?

Puberty in girls is controlled by female sex hormones produced by the ovaries. The production of these hormones is controlled by hormones from the pituitary gland in the brain and from the hypothalamus (the part of the brain that regulates the pituitary). Disorders of any of these organs may lead to an abnormally early or late puberty.

Precocious puberty may be due to an underlying disorder that leads to a premature rise in female sex hormones. For example, an ovarian cyst (p.743) that develops in childhood may produce sex hormones, causing early sexual development. A tumor of the hypothalamus or damage to the pituitary gland as the result of a head injury (p.521) or an infection such as meningitis (p.527) may also lead to early puberty.

Delayed puberty may be caused by certain chromosomal disorders, such as Turner syndrome (p.823), or less commonly by a pituitary tumor (p.676). Excessive weight loss or exercise may create a temporary hormonal imbalance that can lead to delayed puberty.

In many cases of abnormal puberty no underlying cause is found.

WHAT MIGHT BE DONE?

The doctor will do a physical examination to determine whether puberty has started or how far it has progressed. A blood test may be arranged to measure hormone levels or check for a chromosome abnormality. You may have MRI (p.248) or CT scanning (p.247) of the brain if a pituitary tumor is suspected, or ultrasound scanning (p.250) of the ovaries to look for cysts.

If there is an underlying condition, it will be treated. For example, an ovarian cyst will be removed. Hormonal treatment may be prescribed to suspend precocious puberty or to promote sexual development if puberty is delayed. Delayed puberty may be associated with infertility (*see* FEMALE INFERTILITY, p.775) and further evaluation and treatment may be required in the future if a woman who has had a delayed puberty wants to have children.

Sometimes, puberty is simply late and treatment is not necessary. Gaining weight and reducing strenuous activity may help if delayed puberty has been caused by weight loss or exercise.

(WWW) ONLINE SITES: p.1028, p.1037

Virilization

Development of male characteristics in a female due to a hormonal imbalance

 AGE May be present at birth, but usually develops later in life

 GENETICS In some cases, the cause is inherited

 LIFESTYLE Not a significant factor

Low levels of male sex hormones are normally present in females, and these are produced by the adrenal glands and ovaries. However, if the production of these hormones increases significantly, various male characteristics begin to develop, a condition called virilization. Virilization most commonly occurs in adulthood, causing symptoms such as deepening of the voice, excessive hair growth on the face and body, and thinning of the hair on the temples and crown. These symptoms often cause psychological distress. Rarely, the condition is present at birth. If present at birth, virilization is usually due to a genetic disorder which causes abnormal hormone levels (*see* CONGENITAL ADRENAL HYPERPLASIA, p.866).

WHAT ARE THE CAUSES?

When virilization develops later in life, the possible causes include abnormalities of the ovaries, such as certain types of ovarian cysts (p.743), cancer of the ovary (p.744), and polycystic ovary syndrome (p.744). Hormone levels can also be increased by adrenal tumors (p.684) and the use of certain male hormone supplements by athletes.

WHAT ARE THE SYMPTOMS?

Symptoms appear gradually as male sex hormone levels rise. They include:

- Excessive growth of hair on the face and body.
- Less regular or absent menstruation (*see* AMENORRHEA, p.735).
- Reduction in breast size or in rare cases failure of the breasts to develop.
- Enlargement of the clitoris.
- Irreversible enlargement of the larynx (Adam's apple), causing the voice to deepen.
- Thinning of the hair around the temples and crown (*see* MALE PATTERN BALDNESS, p.359).

The hormonal imbalance may lead to increased muscular development, producing a male body shape.

WHAT MIGHT BE DONE?

Your doctor will examine you and may arrange for tests to determine the cause of your symptoms. These tests include blood tests to measure hormone levels, MRI (p.248) or CT scanning (p.247) to look for an adrenal tumor, and ultrasound scanning (p.250) to evaluate the ovaries. Treatment of the cause, such as removal of a tumor, should reverse some of the changes. If no cause is found, oral contraceptives may be given to suppress hormone production by the ovaries and reduce male sex hormone levels. You may be given advice on how to manage excessive hair, perhaps by using electrolysis, waxing, or laser treatment.

(WWW) ONLINE SITES: p.1032, p.1033, p.1037

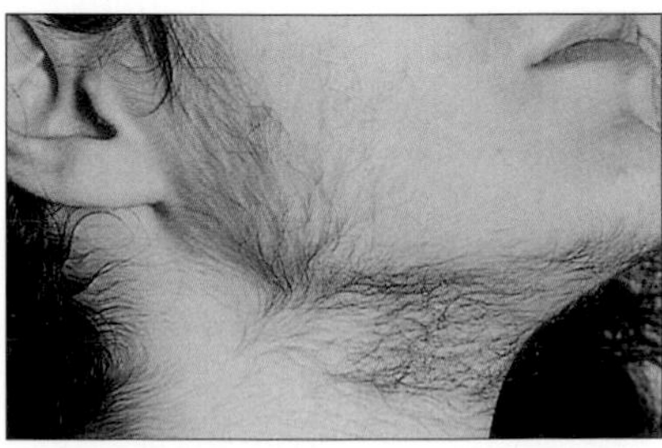

Excessive facial hair

This young woman has excessive facial hair, a common symptom of virilization, a condition caused by the excess production of male sex hormones.

DISORDERS OF THE FEMALE REPRODUCTIVE ORGANS

The female reproductive organs are the ovaries, fallopian tubes, uterus, cervix, vagina, and vulva. Since the combined primary function of these organs is reproduction, disorders affecting these organs often result in infertility and should be treated as soon as possible if children are planned. Such disorders may be caused by infections, physical damage, or hormonal imbalances.

The first two articles in this section discuss pelvic inflammatory disease and endometriosis, disorders that may affect more than one female reproductive organ. The next articles discuss disorders of the ovaries, uterus, and cervix. Disorders affecting the vagina and vulva are covered last.

Many disorders affecting the female reproductive organs are common, and most women will develop one or more of them during their lifetime. Many of these disorders are easily treated.

Disorders affecting menstruation, menopause, or sexual development are covered elsewhere in other sections (*see* MENSTRUAL, MENOPAUSAL, AND HORMONAL PROBLEMS, pp.734–740), as are sexual disorders of both sexes (*see* SEXUALLY TRANSMITTED DISEASES, pp.764–768, INFERTILITY, pp.774–777, and SEXUAL PROBLEMS, pp.769–773).

KEY ANATOMY

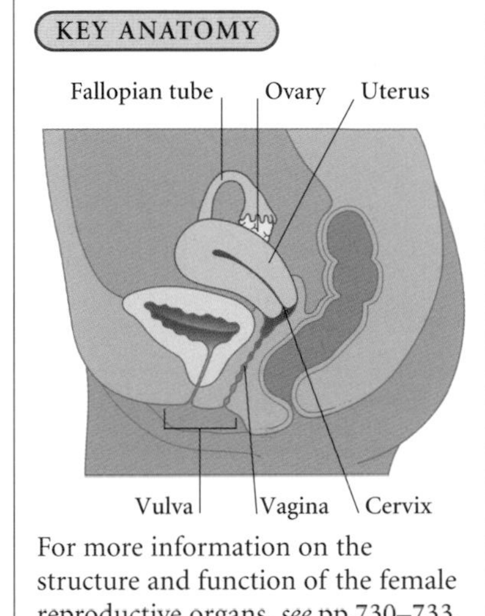
Fallopian tube
Ovary
Uterus
Vulva
Vagina
Cervix

For more information on the structure and function of the female reproductive organs, *see* pp.730–733.

Pelvic inflammatory disease

Inflammation of the female reproductive organs, most often due to a sexually transmitted disease

 AGE Most common between the ages of 15 and 24; rare before puberty

 LIFESTYLE Risk factors depend on the cause

 GENETICS Not a significant factor

Pelvic inflammatory disease (PID) is a common cause of pain in the pelvic region in women. In this condition, some of the female reproductive organs become inflamed, usually as a result of an infection. Young and sexually active women are most likely to be affected. Since PID sometimes has no obvious symptoms, it may be diagnosed only during investigations for infertility (*see* FEMALE INFERTILITY, p.775).

PID is usually caused by a sexually transmitted infection, such as chlamydia (p.765) or gonorrhea (p.764). PID may also be caused by an infection after a termination of pregnancy (p.789) or after childbirth. In rare cases, the infection is tuberculosis (p.491).

The infection spreads upward from the vagina to the uterus and fallopian tubes. The ovaries may also be affected. An intrauterine contraceptive device (IUD) makes this spread of infection more likely. When PID is discovered during investigations for the possible causes of infertility, the original cause may remain unknown.

WHAT ARE THE SYMPTOMS?

PID may have no obvious symptoms, especially when caused by chlamydia. If there are symptoms, they may include:

- Pain in the pelvic region.
- Fever.
- An abnormal vaginal discharge.
- Heavy or prolonged menstrual periods (*see* MENORRHAGIA, p.735).
- Pain during sexual intercourse.
- Fatigue.

If PID develops suddenly, you may experience severe pain, nausea, and vomiting, and urgent admission to a hospital is required.

If the condition is not diagnosed and is left untreated, the fallopian tubes may become damaged, causing infertility and increasing the risk of a future ectopic pregnancy (p.790). The infection may also spread to other organs in the pelvis and the abdomen.

WHAT MIGHT BE DONE?

If your doctor suspects that you have PID, he or she will carry out a pelvic examination. Swabs may also be taken from the cervix and the vagina to identify the organisms that are causing the infection. Ultrasound scanning (p.250) of the pelvis may be performed. If you have severe symptoms, you will be admitted to the hospital, and a laparoscopy (p.742) may be performed to view the abdominal and pelvic cavities.

Your doctor will probably prescribe antibiotics (p.885), which may have to be given intravenously in the hospital. You may also receive analgesics (p.912).

You should not have sexual intercourse until your recovery is complete. Your sexual partner should have tests to look for sexually transmitted diseases and should be treated if necessary to prevent a reinfection (*see* PREVENTING STDS, p.765). If you use an IUD, you may be advised to change to a different method of contraception.

If PID is detected and treated early, you should make a complete recovery. Tests for chlamydia and gonorrhea may be done every year after you become sexually active. Treatment of infection can then be carried out before PID develops.

(WWW) ONLINE SITES: p.1034, p.1036, p.1037

Endometriosis

A condition in which endometrial tissue, which normally lines the uterus, becomes attached to other organs in the abdomen

AGE Most common between the ages of 30 and 45

GENETICS Sometimes runs in families

LIFESTYLE Not having had children is a risk factor

The lining of the uterus, known as the endometrium, is normally shed once a month during menstruation and then regrows. In endometriosis, some pieces of the lining become attached to organs in the pelvic cavity, such as the ovaries and the lower intestine. The misplaced pieces of lining react to the hormones of the menstrual cycle and bleed during menstrual periods. The blood cannot leave the body through the vagina and causes irritation of the surrounding tissues, leading to pain in the abdomen and eventually scarring. Irritation of the ovaries may lead to painful cysts.

Endometriosis is a common condition, affecting as many as 1 in 5 women of childbearing age. Women who delay having children until they are in their 30s and those who do not have children are more likely to develop the condition. Severe endometriosis often causes problems with fertility in women (*see* FEMALE INFERTILITY, p.775).

The exact cause of endometriosis is not known, but there are many theories. One theory is that fragments of endometrium shed during menstruation do not leave the body in the usual way through the vagina. Instead, they travel along the fallopian tubes, from where they may pass into the pelvic cavity and become attached to the surfaces of nearby organs.

WHAT ARE THE SYMPTOMS?

Endometriosis may not produce symptoms. If symptoms do develop, their severity varies from woman to woman. Symptoms may also vary depending on which organs are affected by the condition. They may include:

- Pain in the lower abdomen, which is often most severe immediately before and during menstrual periods (*see* DYSMENORRHEA, p.736).
- Irregular menstrual periods or very heavy menstrual bleeding.
- Pain during sexual intercourse.
- Painful urination.

If the endometrium grows on the lower intestine, you may develop diarrhea or constipation, pain during bowel movements, and in rare cases bleeding from the rectum during menstruation.

WHAT MIGHT BE DONE?

In women who do not have symptoms, endometriosis may only be suspected following investigations for infertility. To help confirm a diagnosis, your doctor will carry out a pelvic examination. The diagnosis may be confirmed by a laparoscopy (left), in which the organs in the pelvic and abdominal cavities are examined using a viewing instrument.

There are many different treatments for endometriosis, and the one chosen depends on your age, which organs are affected, the severity of symptoms, and whether you wish to have children in the future. You may be offered hormonal or surgical treatment. In mild cases, treatment may not be necessary.

If symptoms are troublesome, your doctor may prescribe one of several different hormonal treatments in order to stop menstruation for several months. These drugs may include the synthetic hormone gonadorelin or gonadorelin analogs, such as danazol (*see* SEX HORMONES AND RELATED DRUGS, p.933), all of which suppress production of the female sex hormone estrogen, which has the effect of stopping menstruation. Alternatively, you may be given the combined oral contraceptive pill. This treatment is usually given for about 6–12 months, during which time

TEST AND TREATMENT LAPAROSCOPY

During laparoscopy, a rigid viewing instrument called a laparoscope is used to view the inside of the pelvis and the abdomen through small abdominal incisions. Laparoscopy may be done to look for disorders of the female reproductive organs, such as endometriosis, and to investigate other abdominal disorders, such as appendicitis. Some types of surgery, such as tubal ligation (opposite page), may also be done during the procedure. Laparoscopy is performed under general anesthesia. Recovery is faster than after normal surgery because of the smaller incisions.

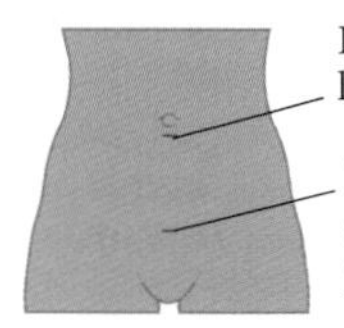
Incision for laparoscope
Incision for manipulating probe

SITES OF INCISIONS

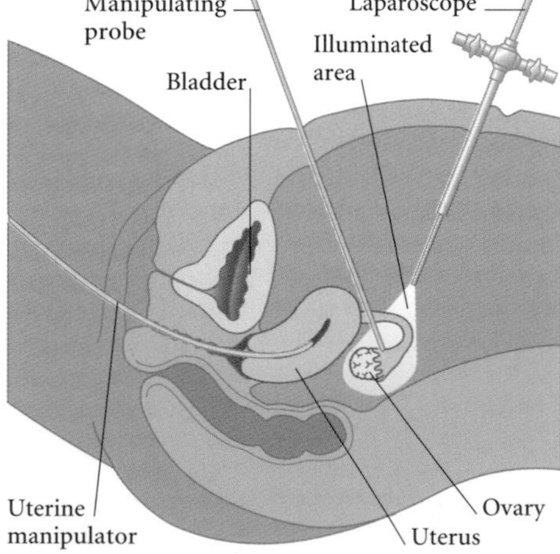
Manipulating probe
Laparoscope
Illuminated area
Bladder
Uterine manipulator
Ovary
Uterus

The procedure
The laparoscope and a tool to manipulate the internal organs are inserted through incisions. Gas is pumped through the laparoscope so that the organs separate and can be seen clearly. In women, a second tool may be inserted through the vagina.

VIEW

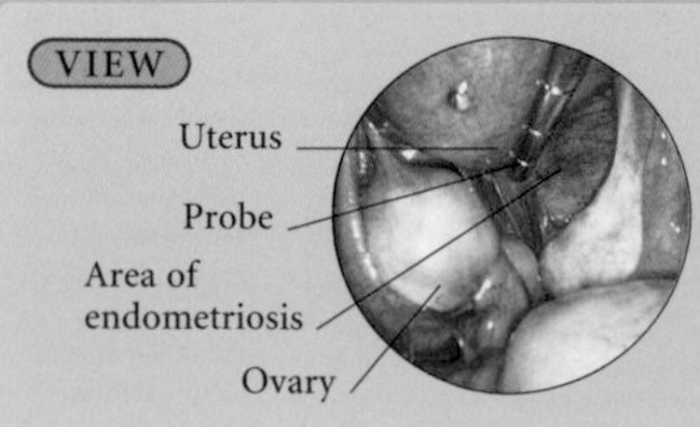
Uterus
Probe
Area of endometriosis
Ovary

Endometriosis
This view through a laparoscope shows areas of endometriosis on the lining of the pelvic cavity next to the uterus. The tip of a manipulating probe and one of the ovaries can also be seen.

TREATMENT TUBAL LIGATION

Tubal ligation is a permanent method of contraception suitable for women who do not want any more children or for whom pregnancy would be harmful. The operation seals the fallopian tubes, usually by cutting and tying them. In some cases, clips may be used. Sperm then cannot travel through the tubes to fertilize eggs. The operation may be done through small incisions in the abdomen (laparoscopic sterilization) or through a single incision made in the pubic area (minilaparotomy).

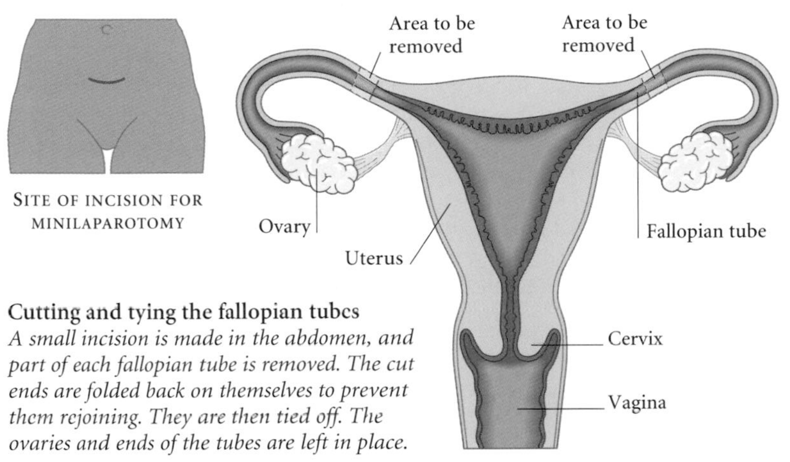

SITE OF INCISION FOR MINILAPAROTOMY
Area to be removed
Area to be removed
Ovary
Uterus
Fallopian tube
Cervix
Vagina

Cutting and tying the fallopian tubes
A small incision is made in the abdomen, and part of each fallopian tube is removed. The cut ends are folded back on themselves to prevent them rejoining. They are then tied off. The ovaries and ends of the tubes are left in place.

the condition should improve. If endometriosis recurs after treatment, it is usually milder than before.

Small fragments of endometrial tissue that do not respond to a period of hormonal treatment may be destroyed by laser surgery during a laparoscopy. However, endometriosis sometimes recurs after this treatment, and further operations may be necessary.

If you have severe endometriosis and you do not plan to have children or you are past menopause, your doctor may recommend that you have a hysterectomy (p.747) to remove the uterus surgically. Both ovaries may also need to be removed, together with other areas that are affected by endometriosis. If the ovaries are removed before you have reached menopause naturally, you will develop symptoms of menopause and your doctor will probably recommend hormone replacement therapy (p.937) to alleviate these symptoms.

WHAT IS THE PROGNOSIS?

Although treatment is usually successful, endometriosis may recur until menopause, when the menstrual cycle ends. However, endometriosis is unlikely to recur if the ovaries are removed.

WWW ONLINE SITES: p.1037

Ovarian cysts

Fluid-filled swellings that grow on or in one or both ovaries

 AGE Most common between the ages of 30 and 45

 GENETICS LIFESTYLE Not significant factors

Ovarian cysts are fluid-filled sacs that grow on or in the ovaries. Most ovarian cysts are noncancerous and not harmful, but a cyst may sometimes become cancerous (*see* CANCER OF THE OVARY, p.744). Cancerous cysts are more likely to develop in women over age 40.

WHAT ARE THE TYPES?

There are many types of ovarian cysts. The most common type is a follicular cyst, in which one of the follicles, where eggs develop, grows and fills with fluid. This type of ovarian cyst may grow to 2 in (5 cm) in diameter. Follicular cysts usually occur singly. Multiple small cysts that develop in the ovaries are caused by a hormonal disorder, and this condition is known as polycystic ovary syndrome (p.744).

Less commonly, cysts may form in the corpus luteum, the yellow tissue that develops from a follicle after the release of an egg. These cysts fill with blood and can grow to 1¼ in (3 cm).

A dermoid cyst is a cyst that contains cells that are normally found elsewhere in the body, such as skin and hair cells. A cystadenoma is a cyst that grows from one type of cell in the ovary. In rare cases, a single cystadenoma can fill the entire abdominal cavity.

WHAT ARE THE SYMPTOMS?

Most ovarian cysts do not usually cause symptoms, but when there are symptoms, they may include:

- Discomfort in the abdomen.
- Pain during sexual intercourse.
- Irregular menstrual periods, sometimes with heavy blood loss.
- Postmenopausal bleeding (p.738).

Large cysts can put pressure on the bladder, leading to urinary retention (p.713) or a frequent need to urinate.

ARE THERE COMPLICATIONS?

If an ovarian cyst ruptures or becomes twisted, severe abdominal pain, nausea, and fever may develop. Cysts may grow so large that the abdomen is distended. In rare cases, a cyst producing the sex hormone estrogen may develop before puberty, bringing on the development of puberty (*see* ABNORMAL PUBERTY IN FEMALES, p.739). Some ovarian cysts produce male sex hormones, which can cause the development of male characteristics, such as growth of facial hair (*see* VIRILIZATION, p.740).

WHAT MIGHT BE DONE?

Sometimes, ovarian cysts are only discovered when a pelvic examination is carried out during a routine checkup. Otherwise, if you have symptoms of a cyst, your doctor will perform a pelvic

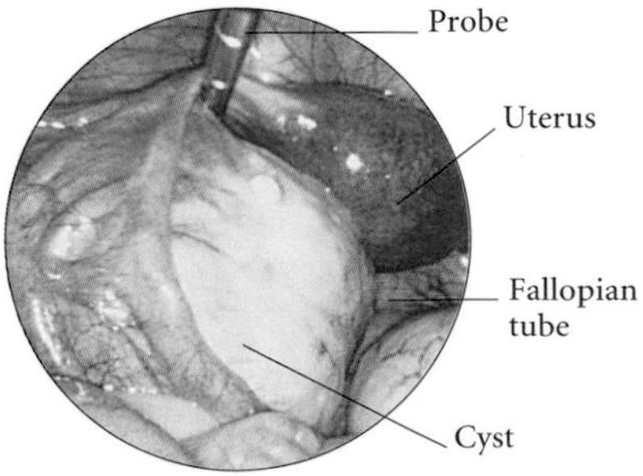

Probe
Uterus
Fallopian tube
Cyst

Ovarian cyst
This view through a laparoscope shows a large ovarian cyst next to the uterus. Most ovarian cysts are noncancerous.

examination. You may also be sent for ultrasound scanning (p.250) or laparoscopy (p.742) to confirm the diagnosis and determine the size and position of the cyst. You may also have blood tests to see if a cyst may be cancerous.

Ovarian cysts may disappear without treatment, although the size of a cyst may be monitored with regular ultrasound scans. Large or persistent cysts may be drained or removed. If there is a chance that the cyst is cancerous, it will be removed, leaving the ovary and fallopian tube if possible. Ovarian cysts may recur if the ovary is not removed.

(WWW) ONLINE SITES: p.1037

Polycystic ovary syndrome

A sex hormone imbalance often associated with multiple, small, fluid-filled cysts in the ovaries

 AGE Affects females of childbearing age

 GENETICS Sometimes runs in families

 LIFESTYLE Not a significant factor

In polycystic ovary syndrome, both of the ovaries become enlarged with multiple, fluid-filled cysts. The condition is thought to be caused by an imbalance of sex hormones, sometimes with a relative excess of luteinizing hormone, produced by the pituitary gland, and of the male sex hormone testosterone. This imbalance may prevent ovulation (egg release), thus reducing fertility (*see* FEMALE INFERTILITY, p.775), and sometimes leading to the excessive growth of body hair (*see* VIRILIZATION, p.740).

Polycystic ovary syndrome is the most common reproductive disorder in women, affecting about 5 in 100 women of childbearing age. The condition sometimes runs in families.

What are the symptoms?

The symptoms of polycystic ovary syndrome are variable. The condition may go unnoticed until a woman is tested for infertility because she has difficulty conceiving. Typical symptoms include:

- Infrequent or absent menstruation.
- Obesity.
- Excessive hair growth.

Women who have polycystic ovary syndrome are at an increased risk of developing resistance to the action of the hormone insulin and this resistance may lead to diabetes mellitus (p.687). Women who are affected by the condition are also at increased risk of developing cancer of the uterus (p.748).

What might be done?

If your doctor suspects that you have polycystic ovary syndrome, he or she will take blood samples to measure your levels of sex hormones and see if you have an imbalance. You may also have ultrasound scanning (p.250) to look for ovarian cysts.

The treatment depends on the severity of your symptoms and whether you want to conceive. Infertility can be treated with drugs, such as clomiphene (*see* DRUGS FOR INFERTILITY, p.936) or metformin (p.931). If you do not want children, abnormal menstrual periods can be treated with a combined oral contraceptive pill.

To treat insulin resistance and reduce your risk of developing diabetes mellitus, your doctor may prescribe drugs such as metformin (*see* DRUGS FOR DIABETES MELLITUS, p.931), which may also help regularize menstrual periods and aid weight loss. Excess hair can be removed by electrolysis or laser treatment.

(WWW) ONLINE SITES: p.1037

Cancer of the ovary

A cancerous tumor that can develop in one or both ovaries

 AGE Most common between the ages of 50 and 70; rare under age 40

 GENETICS Sometimes runs in families

LIFESTYLE Not having had children is a risk factor

Cancer of the ovary is the fifth leading cause of cancer deaths among Canadian women, causing 1,500 deaths per year in Canada. This high death rate is usually explained by the fact that symptoms do not develop until late in the disease, delaying the diagnosis and treatment.

The cause of cancer of the ovary is not known, although the tumor sometimes develops from an ovarian cyst (p.743). However, there seem to be hormonal and genetic risk factors. Women

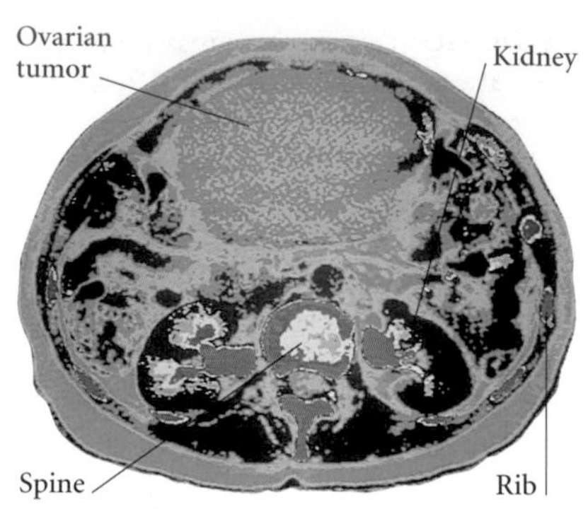
Ovarian tumor
Kidney
Spine
Rib

Cancer of the ovary
Most of the abdominal cavity seen in this color-enhanced CT scan is filled by a large cancerous ovarian tumor.

who have never had children or have had a late menopause are more likely to develop cancer of the ovary. As well, those women with a close relative who developed ovarian cancer before age 50 are at greater risk of the disease.

What are the symptoms?

Ovarian cancer rarely produces symptoms in the early stages, although there may be symptoms similar to those of an ovarian cyst, such as irregular menstrual periods. In most cases, symptoms occur only if the cancer has spread to other organs and may include:

- Pain in the lower abdomen.
- Swelling in the abdomen caused by excess fluid.
- Frequent urination.
- Rarely, abnormal vaginal bleeding.

There may also be general symptoms of cancer, such as loss of weight, nausea, and vomiting, or change in bowel habits. Left untreated, the cancer may spread to other organs in the body, such as the liver or lungs.

How is it diagnosed?

If a close relative has had cancer of the ovary, you should consult your doctor about screening for this type of cancer. Screening may detect cancerous changes before symptoms develop and will allow for treatment to be given in the early stages of the disease. You may be offered ultrasound scanning through the vagina to look for a tumor or blood tests to look for a specific protein that is produced by ovarian cancer. Otherwise, if your doctor suspects cancer of the ovary, he or she will examine your abdomen for the presence of swellings or lumps. Your doctor may also arrange for you to have an ultrasound scan of your ovaries or to have a laparoscopy (p.742). Other tests that may be carried out include a chest X-ray (p.490) and CT scanning (p.247) of the lungs or liver to see if the disease has spread.

What is the treatment?

If cancer of the ovary is diagnosed in a woman who wishes to have children, the affected ovary and fallopian tube are usually removed. If the cancer has spread to other parts of the reproductive tract, or the woman does not wish to conceive, it may be necessary to perform surgery in which the uterus, fallopian tubes, and ovaries are all removed. Surgery may be followed by chemotherapy (p.278) to kill any remaining cancer cells. If the cancer has spread to other organs in the body, radiation therapy (p.279) may be given. After treatment, blood tests and physical examinations are carried out regularly to check for recurrence.

What is the prognosis?

A complete recovery from cancer of the ovary is only possible if the condition is diagnosed and treated while in the early stages. However, the disease has spread in up to 3 in 4 women by the time of diagnosis. In these women, chemotherapy can prevent further spread of the cancer, sometimes for years, but it can rarely eliminate the cancer completely.

(WWW) ONLINE SITES: p.1028, p.1037

Fibroids

Common, noncancerous tumors that grow slowly within the muscular wall of the uterus

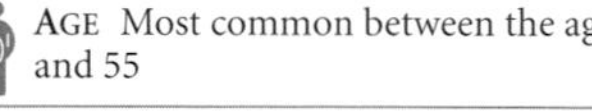
AGE Most common between the ages of 35 and 55

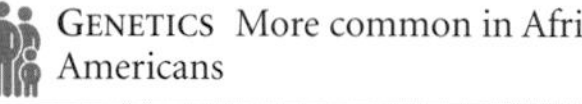
GENETICS More common in African–Americans

LIFESTYLE Not a significant factor

Fibroids are abnormal growths in the uterus that are made of muscular and fibrous tissue. Fibroids are found in up to 1 in 2 women in the US and are more common in African–American women. Fibroids may occur singly or in groups and may be as small as a pea or as big as a grapefruit. Small fibroids may not cause problems, but larger ones may affect menstruation or cause infertility (*see* FEMALE INFERTILITY, p.775).

What is the cause?

The cause of fibroids is unknown, but they are thought to be related to an abnormal response by the uterus to the female sex hormone estrogen. Fibroids do not occur before puberty, when the ovaries begin to increase estrogen production, and they usually stop growing after menopause. They also increase in size at times when there are increased levels of estrogen in the body, such as during pregnancy and when taking the combined contraceptive pill or hormone replacement therapy (p.937).

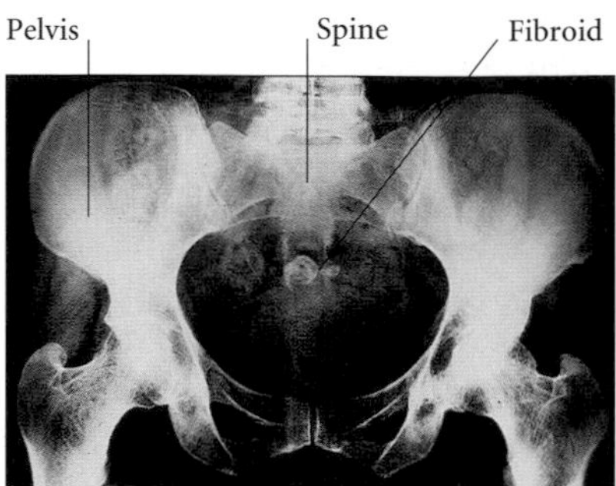
Pelvis
Spine
Fibroid

Fibroid in the uterus
A noncancerous tumor, known as a fibroid, can be seen within the wall of the uterus in this X-ray of the pelvis.

What are the symptoms?

Most small fibroids do not cause symptoms, but the common symptoms of larger fibroids include:

- Prolonged menstrual bleeding.
- Pain during menstrual periods (*see* DYSMENORRHEA, p.736).
- Heavy menstrual periods (*see* MENORRHAGIA, p.735).

Heavy blood loss may lead to anemia (p.446), causing fatigue. Large fibroids may distort the uterus, which can often result in infertility or in recurrent miscarriages (p.791). During pregnancy, a large fibroid may cause the fetus to lie in an abnormal position in the uterus (*see* ABNORMAL PRESENTATION, p.800). Fibroids may also press on the bladder, causing a need to urinate often, or on the rectum, causing back pain. Rarely, a fibroid may become twisted, causing sudden pain in the lower abdomen.

TEST AND TREATMENT — Hysteroscopy

A hysteroscope is an instrument used to see inside the uterus and fallopian tubes. Hysteroscopy is done to diagnose disorders such as uterine polyps and can be performed under general or local anesthesia. Minor surgery, such as removal of fibroids, may be carried out. Although the procedure may be uncomfortable, it usually lasts 15 minutes or less and may be done in the doctor's office.

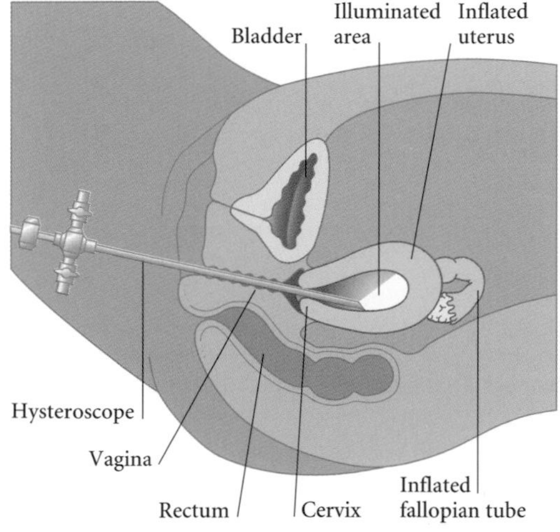
Bladder
Illuminated area
Inflated uterus
Hysteroscope
Vagina
Rectum
Cervix
Inflated fallopian tube

The procedure
The hysteroscope is inserted through the vagina into the uterus. The uterus and fallopian tubes are filled with fluid passed through the hysteroscope to allow them to be seen easily. Light provides a clear view.

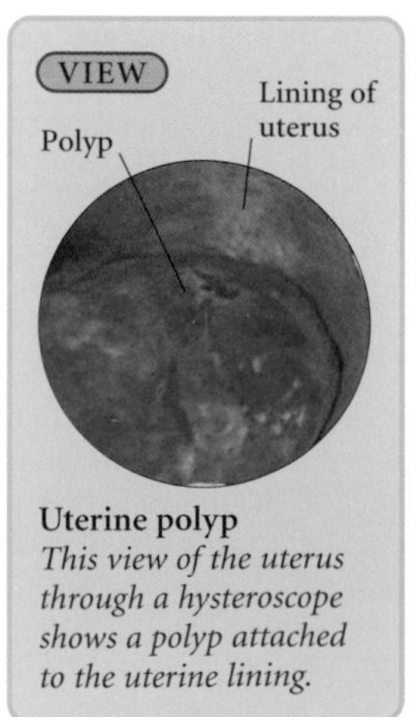
VIEW
Polyp
Lining of uterus

Uterine polyp
This view of the uterus through a hysteroscope shows a polyp attached to the uterine lining.

How are they diagnosed?

The doctor will perform a pelvic examination. You may also have ultrasound scanning (p.250) of the uterus or a hysteroscopy (p.745), in which a viewing instrument is inserted through the cervix in order to examine the inside of the uterus. A sample of the fibroid will be taken during the hysteroscopy to check that the growth is not cancerous. Sometimes fibroids show up on X-rays (p.244) taken for other reasons.

What is the treatment?

Small fibroids often do not need treatment but should be checked regularly by your doctor to make sure that they have not grown. If treatment is necessary, they may be removed during a hysteroscopy if they are on an inner wall. Very occasionally, fibroids may be treated by blocking the blood vessels to them by an injection. When the blood supply is blocked, the fibroid shrinks.

Large fibroids can be removed via an incision in the abdomen. Before having the surgery, you may be prescribed hormones that suppress the production of estrogen so that the fibroids shrink. If you have persistent, large fibroids and do not want children, you may consider having a hysterectomy (opposite page).

Removal of fibroids usually results in regained fertility, but in about 1 in 10 women fibroids recur. Fibroids usually shrink after menopause, when estrogen levels in the body start to fall.

(WWW) ONLINE SITES: p.1037

Uterine polyps

Noncancerous growths that develop in the uterus or the cervix

 AGE Most common between the ages of 30 and 50

 LIFESTYLE Not having had children is a risk factor

 GENETICS Not a significant factor

Uterine polyps are painless growths that are attached to the cervix or to the inside of the uterus. The polyps may occur singly or in groups and vary in length up to about 1 in (3 cm). Polyps are usually harmless, but they may become cancerous in rare cases. Uterine polyps are common, especially in premenopausal women over age 30.

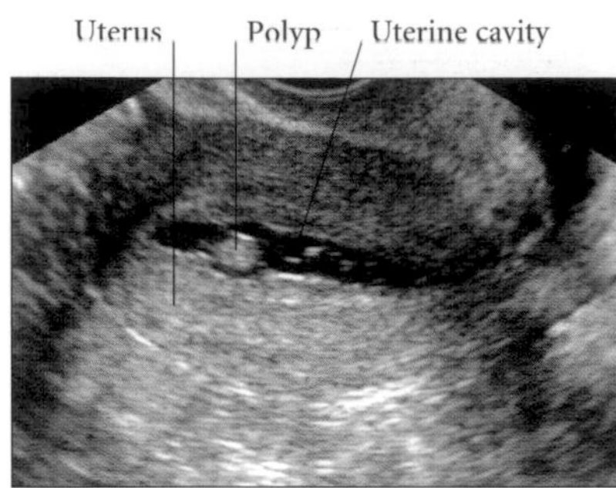
Uterus
Polyp
Uterine cavity

Uterine polyp
This ultrasound scan of the pelvis shows a single polyp in the uterine cavity that has grown from the lining of the uterus.

The reason why uterine polyps form is unknown, but they may develop on the cervix if it is affected by cervical ectropion (p.749), in which the cells on the surface of the cervix are more delicate than usual. Polyps may also form on the cervix after an infection of the cervix. Women who have not had children are more likely to develop uterine polyps for reasons that are not known.

Symptoms of uterine polyps include a watery, bloodstained discharge from the vagina and bleeding between menstrual periods, after sexual intercourse, or after menopause. Such bleeding may be a sign of a more serious disorder, such as cancer of the cervix (p.750).

What might be done?

Your doctor will usually be able to see polyps on the cervix by looking at the cervix while holding your vagina open with an instrument called a speculum. If polyps in the uterus are suspected, further investigations will be arranged, such as ultrasound scanning (p.250) or hysteroscopy (p.745), in which a viewing instrument is inserted through the cervix to view the inside of the uterus.

Treatment of polyps is usually quick and easy. Polyps on the cervix may be removed surgically while looking at the cervix through the speculum, and uterine polyps can be removed during a hysteroscopy. Mild pain and slight vaginal bleeding are likely for a few days after surgery. Tissue samples from the polyps are examined under a microscope to make sure that there are no cancerous cells. Uterine polyps may recur after treatment, and further surgery is usually required.

(WWW) ONLINE SITES: p.1037

Retroverted uterus

A usually harmless condition in which the uterus is tilted backward

 LIFESTYLE Having had children is a risk factor

 AGE GENETICS Not significant factors

The uterus is normally inclined upward and forward. In about 1 in 10 women the uterus is tilted backward, lying close to the rectum. This condition is known as a retroverted uterus and is a harmless variation of the normal position. There is often no cause for retroverted uterus, although the condition may occur after childbirth or because an ovarian cyst (p.743) pushes the uterus backward.

A retroverted uterus usually causes no symptoms and does not affect fertility, pregnancy, or childbirth. However, you may feel pain during sexual intercourse or have low backache, especially during menstrual periods.

What might be done?

Your doctor may be able to feel that the uterus is retroverted during a pelvic examination. If an underlying disorder is thought to be causing the condition, laparoscopy (p.742) may be carried out to view the pelvis and abdominal cavity. Mild analgesics (p.912) may relieve backache, and pain during intercourse may be relieved through trying a different sexual position. If there is an underlying cause, such as a cyst, this may be treated, allowing the uterus to return to its normal position.

(WWW) ONLINE SITES: p.1037

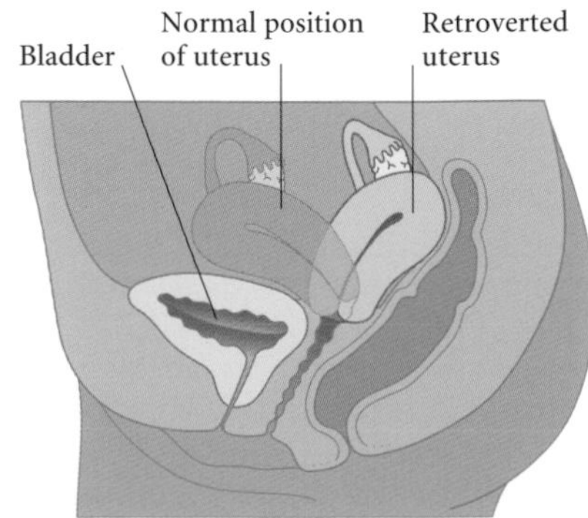
Bladder
Normal position of uterus
Retroverted uterus

Retroverted uterus
The uterus usually tilts forward, resting close to and just above the bladder. A retroverted uterus tilts backward so that it lies close to the rectum.

Prolapse of the uterus and vagina

Downward displacement of the uterus and/or wall of the vagina

AGE More common after menopause

GENETICS More common in white people

LIFESTYLE Being overweight and having had children are risk factors

The uterus and vagina are held in place by ligaments and muscles in the pelvis. If these supporting structures become weakened or stretched, often as a result of childbirth, the uterus and/or vaginal walls may be displaced. Prolapse usually occurs only after menopause, when reduced levels of the hormone estrogen lead to weakening of the ligaments. The risk of prolapse is increased by conditions that put extra pressure on the muscles and ligaments in the pelvis, such as obesity, a chronic cough, or straining when having bowel movements. For unknown reasons, prolapse is more common in white people.

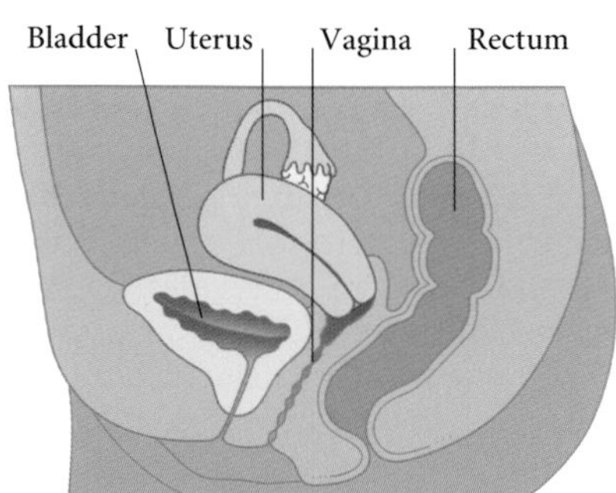
Bladder
Uterus
Vagina
Rectum
NORMAL

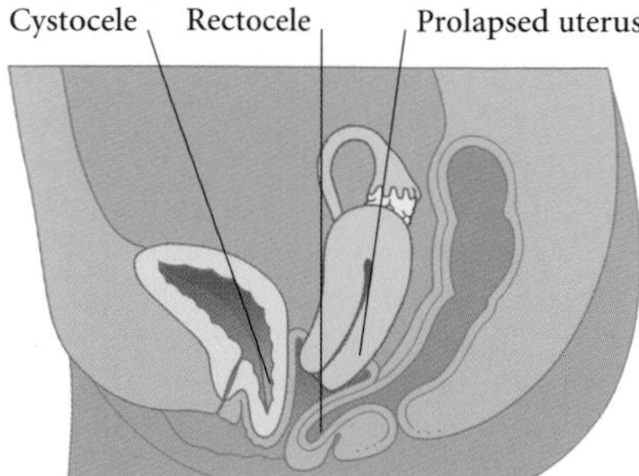
Cystocele
Rectocele
Prolapsed uterus
PROLAPSE

Prolapse of the uterus and vagina
In this prolapse, the uterus is displaced, the bladder bulges into the front vaginal wall (cystocele), and the rectum bulges into the back vaginal wall (rectocele).

TREATMENT HYSTERECTOMY

A hysterectomy is an operation involving the uterus. A total hysterectomy is removal of the uterus (which includes the cervix). A subtotal hysterectomy is removal of the uterus excluding the cervix. A total hysterectomy and salpingo-oophorectomy is removal of the tubes and ovaries, along with the uterus (which includes the cervix). The operation may be carried out through an incision in the abdomen or through the vagina and is done under general anesthesia in the hospital. The upper end of the vagina is then repaired by stitching.

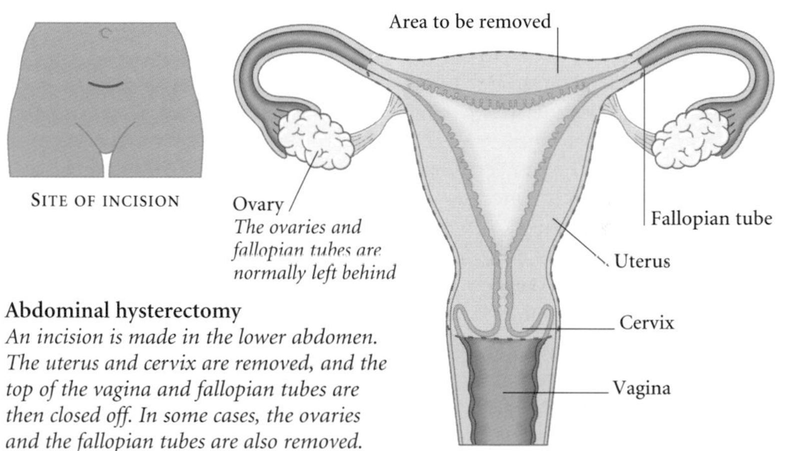
SITE OF INCISION
Area to be removed
Ovary
The ovaries and fallopian tubes are normally left behind
Fallopian tube
Uterus
Cervix
Vagina

Abdominal hysterectomy
An incision is made in the lower abdomen. The uterus and cervix are removed, and the top of the vagina and fallopian tubes are then closed off. In some cases, the ovaries and the fallopian tubes are also removed.

WHAT ARE THE TYPES?

In uterine prolapse, the uterus moves down into the vagina. The amount of movement ranges from slight displacement into the vagina to projection of the uterus outside the vulva.

There are two main types of vaginal prolapse: cystocele and rectocele. In a cystocele, the bladder presses inward against the weak front vaginal wall. In a rectocele, the rectum bulges against the weakened back vaginal wall. Both types of vaginal prolapse may occur together with or without uterine prolapse.

WHAT ARE THE SYMPTOMS?

The symptoms of any type of uterine or vaginal prolapse may include:

- A feeling of fullness in the vagina.
- A lump protruding into or even out of the vagina.
- A dragging sensation or mild pain in the lower back.
- Difficulty urinating or defecating.
- Increased frequency of urination.

A cystocele can cause leakage of urine when laughing or coughing (*see* STRESS INCONTINENCE, p.711). It also increases the risk of an infection in the bladder (*see* CYSTITIS, p.709) because the bladder may not empty properly.

WHAT MIGHT BE DONE?

Your doctor may be able to see that you have a prolapse by looking at the position of the uterus and the walls of the vagina while using a speculum to hold the vagina open. He or she may ask you to cough or strain so that the prolapse can be assessed. A sample of urine may also be taken to check for infection.

Exercises that strengthen the pelvic floor muscles can help treat a mild prolapse (*see* KEGEL EXERCISES, p.712). Practicing the exercises before and after childbirth can help prevent a prolapse.

If you are past menopause and have a mild prolapse your doctor may prescribe estrogen hormones, either orally or as a cream that can be applied to the vaginal wall (*see* SEX HORMONES AND RELATED DRUGS, p.933). This hormone helps strengthen the supporting tissues. In some women with uterine prolapse, a plastic device called a ring pessary may be inserted into the vagina to help keep the uterus in place. Surgical techniques may also be used. For example, if a uterine prolapse is severe and you do not want to have children in the future, a hysterectomy (above) to remove the uterus may be recommended.

(WWW) ONLINE SITES: p.1037

Cancer of the uterus

A cancerous tumor that grows in the lining of the uterus

 AGE Most common between the ages of 55 and 65

 LIFESTYLE Being overweight and not having had children are risk factors

 GENETICS Not a significant factor

Cancer of the uterus is the most common cancer of the female reproductive organs in Canada, with over 1,300 new cases each year. Most uterine cancers develop in the endometrium (the lining of the uterus). Rarely, cancer occurs in the muscular wall of the uterus.

WHAT ARE THE CAUSES?

The causes of cancer of the uterus are unclear. However, the disorder is more common in women aged 55–65 and in women who have or have previously had higher levels than usual of the female sex hormone estrogen. Estrogen levels may be raised by being overweight and by certain disorders, such as polycystic ovary syndrome (p.744). The disorder is also more likely in women who have had a late menopause (after age 52) or who have not had children.

WHAT ARE THE SYMPTOMS?

The symptoms of cancer of the uterus vary depending on whether it develops before or after menopause. Common symptoms may include:

- In premenopausal women, heavier than normal menstrual periods (*see* MENORRHAGIA, p.735) or bleeding between menstrual periods or after sexual intercourse.
- In postmenopausal women, vaginal bleeding that may vary from spotting to heavier bleeding.

Left untreated, cancer of the uterus may spread to the fallopian tubes and the ovaries and to other organs, including the lungs and sometimes the liver.

HOW IS IT DIAGNOSED?

If your doctor suspects cancer of the uterus from your symptoms, he or she will perform a pelvic examination. In addition, a sample of tissue may be taken from the endometrium to check for the presence of cancerous cells (*see* ENDOMETRIAL SAMPLING, p.738). Your doctor may also arrange for ultrasound scanning (p.250), using a probe inserted into the vagina to measure the thickness of the uterus lining. A thicker than normal lining may indicate cancer.

If these tests are not conclusive, a D and C (dilatation and curettage) may be done to remove a larger amount of tissue from the uterus. In this procedure, the cervix is dilated (stretched open), and the endometrium is scraped away with a spoon-shaped instrument passed through the cervix. Samples of the endometrial tissue are then examined for cancerous cells. Hysteroscopy may be done at the same time as a D and C, to look inside the uterus.

If cancer of the uterus is diagnosed, tests will be carried out to see if the cancer has spread. For example, you may have a chest X-ray (p.490) or MRI (p.248) of the chest to examine the lungs. You may also have blood tests to assess the function of the liver.

WHAT IS THE TREATMENT?

The treatment depends on the stage at which the cancer is diagnosed and whether it has spread elsewhere in the body.

In most women, the tumor can be treated by a hysterectomy (p.747), in which the uterus is surgically removed. Usually, the ovaries and the fallopian tubes are removed at the same time. In addition, samples from nearby pelvic lymph nodes are usually taken and examined under a microscope to see if the disease has spread and if further treatment is required. Surgery may be followed by radiation therapy (p.279) to destroy cancer cells that remain.

If cancerous cells are found in the lymph nodes, you will be treated with chemotherapy (p.278) and the female hormone progesterone (*see* SEX HORMONES AND RELATED DRUGS, p.933), which slows down the growth of cancer cells. After treatment, you will have regular tests to look for signs of cancerous changes in samples of cells taken from the top of the vagina.

The prognosis for cancer of the uterus depends on whether the tumor is treated at an early stage before the condition has spread to other parts of the body. About 8 in 10 women who are treated when the cancer is at an early stage survive for 5 years or longer.

(WWW) ONLINE SITES: p.1028, p.1037

Choriocarcinoma

A cancerous tumor that develops from the placenta after a pregnancy

 AGE Affects females of childbearing age

 GENETICS LIFESTYLE Not significant factors

A choriocarcinoma is a rare cancerous tumor that occurs in 1 in every 20,000 pregnancies. The tumor develops from placental tissue and usually arises from a noncancerous placental tumor called a hydatidiform mole (*see* MOLAR PREGNANCY, p.790). A choriocarcinoma may also occur after an ectopic pregnancy (p.790) or rarely after childbirth or termination of pregnancy (p.789). Occasionally, the tumor may not develop until months or even years after pregnancy. The main symptom of a choriocarcinoma is persistent vaginal bleeding. If left untreated, the tumor grows quickly, and the disease spreads first to the walls of the uterus and then to other organs such as the liver.

WHAT MIGHT BE DONE?

Choriocarcinoma is usually diagnosed by blood or urine tests to measure levels of the hormone human chorionic gonadotropin (HCG). HCG is ordinarily produced by the placenta, but abnormally high levels of the hormone are associated with a choriocarcinoma. Women who have had a molar pregnancy and are at particular risk of the disease are usually given regular tests to measure the levels of HCG. Women who have had persistent bleeding after childbirth, a termination, or an ectopic pregnancy may also have their HCG levels checked. If HCG is detected, ultrasound scanning (p.250), using a probe inserted into the vagina, will be scheduled to look for a tumor. If choriocarcinoma is confirmed, further tests, such as CT scanning (p.247) of the abdomen and blood tests to assess liver function, may be arranged to check if the disease has spread.

Choriocarcinoma is usually treated with chemotherapy (p.278), whether or not the disease has spread to other organs. Rarely, a hysterectomy (p.747) may be necessary. Most women recover completely following treatment.

(WWW) ONLINE SITES: p.1028, p.1036, p.1037

Cervical ectropion

Extension of cells that normally line the inside of the cervical canal onto the surface of the cervix

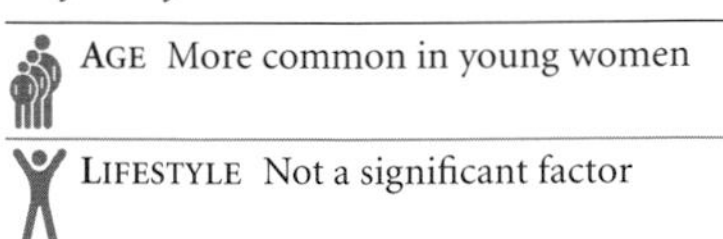

AGE More common in young women

LIFESTYLE Not a significant factor

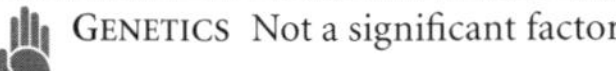

GENETICS Not a significant factor

In cervical ectropion, the layer of delicate cells that line the cervical canal extend onto the outer surface of the cervix, which is usually covered with stronger tissue. This does not lead to an actual loss of cervical tissue. Instead, since the cervix is now covered with delicate rather than with strong tissue, it is more easily damaged than it normally would be, and it therefore has a tendency to bleed.

There is no obvious reason for cervical ectropion. In many cases, the condition does not result in evident symptoms and is discovered only after microscopic examination of cell tissue. However, a few women may notice increased vaginal discharge and bleeding between menstrual periods or after sexual intercourse due to the delicacy of cells on the surface of the cervix.

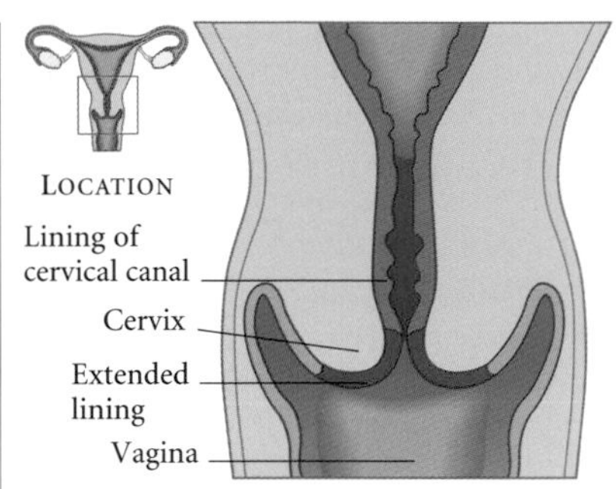
LOCATION
Lining of cervical canal
Cervix
Extended lining
Vagina

Cervical ectropion
In cervical ectropion, the delicate cells that line the inside of the cervical canal extend onto the surface of the cervix.

WHAT MIGHT BE DONE?

Cervical ectropion is often detected during examination for a routine Pap test (below) when cells are collected from the cervix and then microscopically examined. Treatment for the condition is often not necessary, as an ectropion is usually considered to be a variation of normal. However, if you develop symptoms and have a pelvic examination as a result, your doctor will arrange for you to have tests in order to rule out other possible causes of those symptoms. Cervical ectropion usually disappears by the time a woman reaches menopause.

(WWW) ONLINE SITES: p.1037

Cervical dysplasia

Changes in the surface cells of the cervix that may become cancerous

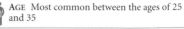

AGE Most common between the ages of 25 and 35

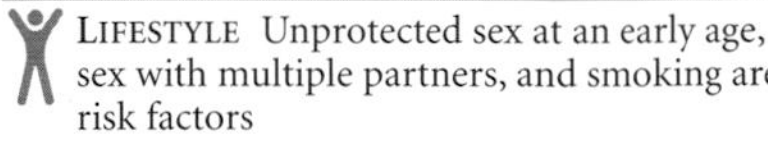

LIFESTYLE Unprotected sex at an early age, sex with multiple partners, and smoking are risk factors

GENETICS Not a significant factor

In some women, the cells of the cervix gradually change from normal to a cancerous state. The condition between these two extremes, when the cells are abnormal with the potential to become cancerous, is known as cervical dysplasia. There are two grades of dysplasia: low grade and high grade. Low grade dysplasia may return to a normal state, but high grade dysplasia may progress to cancer of the cervix (p.750) if not treated.

Many developed countries, including Canada, have established screening programs to check for cervical dysplasia using the Pap test (below). Regular testing, which helps ensure that cervical dysplasia is diagnosed and treated at an early stage before the abnormal cells become cancerous, has led to a dramatic fall in the total number of cases of cancer of the cervix.

(TEST) PAP TEST

A Pap test is a painless procedure used to detect abnormal cells on the cervix. Cells are collected from the cervix using a spatula or brush and are sent away to be examined under a microscope. Pap tests are performed within 6 months of first having sexual intercourse, and are then repeated at regular intervals. More frequent tests may be necessary if abnormal cells are detected on the cervix. Early treatment of some cervical abnormalities helps prevent the development of cancer of the cervix (*see* TREATING CERVICAL DYSPLASIA, p.751).

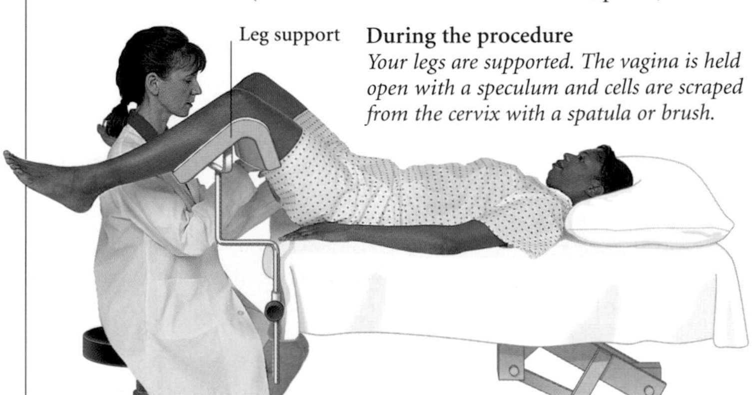
Leg support

During the procedure
Your legs are supported. The vagina is held open with a speculum and cells are scraped from the cervix with a spatula or brush.

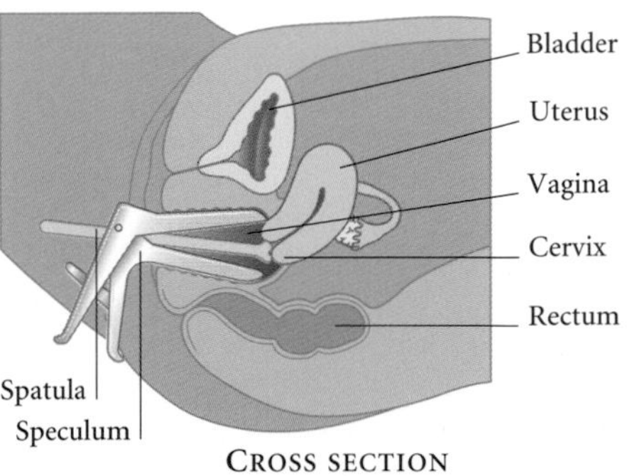
Bladder
Uterus
Vagina
Cervix
Rectum
Spatula
Speculum

CROSS SECTION

(RESULTS)

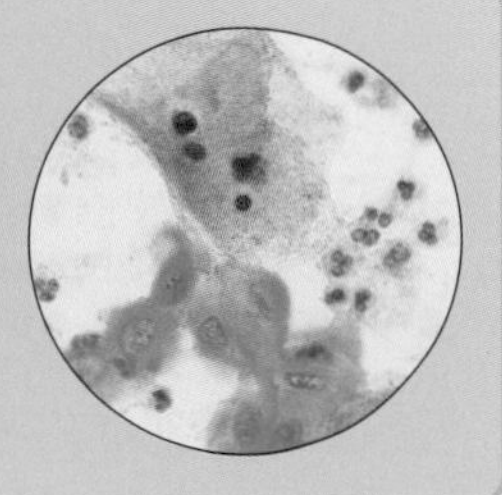

Normal cervical cells
This highly magnified image shows cervical cells of regular shape and size. This pattern of cells indicates a normal Pap test result.

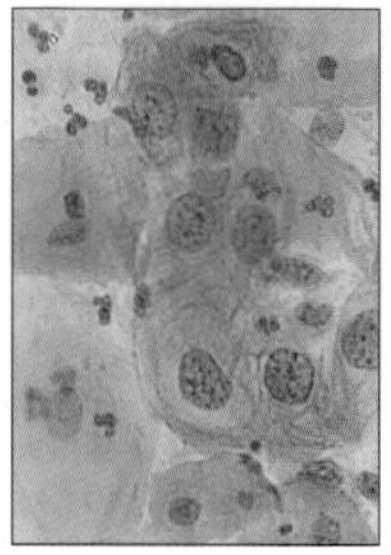
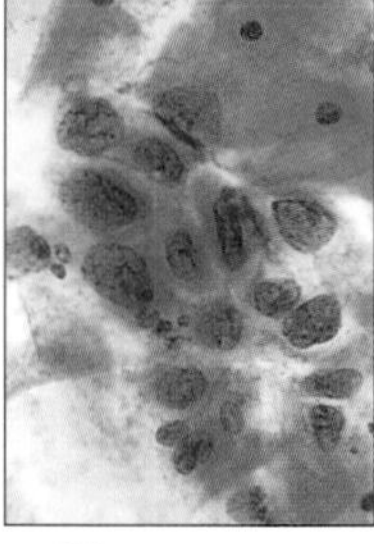

LOW GRADE HIGH GRADE

Cervical dysplasia
These highly magnified images of cells taken from the cervix illustrate the various degrees of cell distortion present in low grade and high grade cervical dysplasia.

WHAT ARE THE CAUSES?

The exact cause of cervical dysplasia is not known, but a number of different risk factors have been identified. For example, the risk of developing it appears to be higher after exposure to those types of human papilloma virus that are associated with genital warts (p.768). Other risk factors for the development of cervical dysplasia include unprotected sex at an early age, unprotected sex with many partners, and becoming pregnant before age 20. However, exactly how these risk factors are connected to cervical dysplasia is unknown. Smoking markedly increases the risk of developing cervical dysplasia.

HOW IS IT DIAGNOSED?

Cervical dysplasia does not produce symptoms. The condition is only normally diagnosed after a Pap test, during which a sample of cells is taken from the cervix and sent for examination under a microscope. If you are found to have abnormal cells, your doctor may arrange for you to have a colposcopy (right), so that the cervix can be seen through an instrument and examined for abnormal-looking areas. A small sample of tissue may also be removed from the cervix and examined under the microscope for abnormalities.

WHAT IS THE TREATMENT?

If you are diagnosed with cervical dysplasia, the treatment depends on the degree of abnormality of the cells. Low grade dysplasia may not require treatment because the abnormal cells revert to normal in up to 4 in 10 cases. However, the disorder will be monitored by colposcopy and Pap tests every 6 months. If cervical dysplasia persists or worsens, treatment to destroy or remove the abnormal cells will be needed (*see* TREATING CERVICAL DYSPLASIA, opposite page). After treatment, you may have a bloodstained discharge for a few weeks.

WHAT IS THE PROGNOSIS?

In many cases of cervical dysplasia, the cells of the cervix will return to normal after treatment. However, your condition will be monitored for the next few years to ensure that no further abnormalities develop. In the first year after diagnosis, a Pap test and colposcopy are performed every 4–6 months, followed by yearly Pap tests. The risk of developing cancer of the cervix is greater in cases of high grade cervical dysplasia.

(WWW) ONLINE SITES: p.1037

Cancer of the cervix

A cancerous growth occurring in the lower end of the cervix

AGE Most common between the ages of 45 and 65

LIFESTYLE Unprotected sex at an early age, sex with multiple partners, and smoking are risk factors

GENETICS Not a significant factor

Cancer of the cervix is one of the most common cancers affecting women. In Canada, there are 1,300 new cases each year. However, it is also one of the few cancers that can be prevented by regular screening before symptoms appear. Cancer of the cervix usually develops slowly. In the precancerous stage, cells in the cervix gradually change from

TEST AND TREATMENT COLPOSCOPY

A colposcope is a binocular viewing instrument used to magnify the cervix for examination. Colposcopy is often performed after an abnormal Pap test (p.749) to look for evidence of cervical dysplasia. During the procedure, which is painless and lasts for 5–10 minutes, your doctor may paint solutions onto the cervix to highlight abnormal areas. A sample of cervical tissue may also be taken, or abnormal areas of the cervix may be treated (*see* TREATING CERVICAL DYSPLASIA, opposite page).

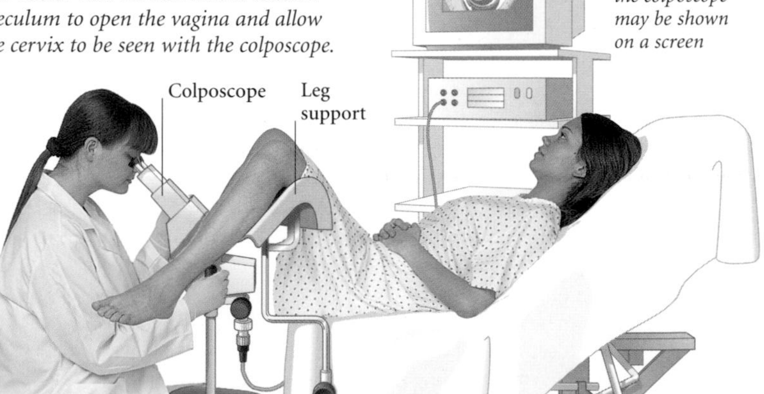
Monitor
The view through the colposcope may be shown on a screen
Colposcope
Leg support

During the procedure
You will need to put your legs in supports. The doctor uses an instrument called a speculum to open the vagina and allow the cervix to be seen with the colposcope.

VIEW

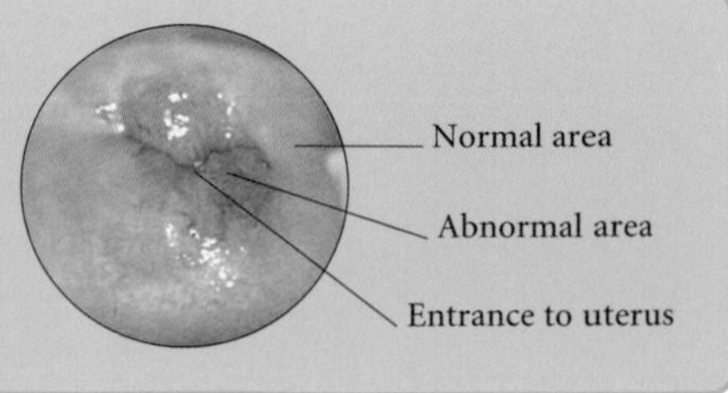
Normal area
Abnormal area
Entrance to uterus

View of the cervix
Normal and abnormal areas of tissue can be seen on this cervix. The abnormal area close to the center of the cervix proved to be due to high grade cervical dysplasia.

TREATMENT TREATING CERVICAL DYSPLASIA

Treatment depends on the severity and location of the lesion. Low grade dysplasia is monitored by colposcopy and Pap tests. High grade dysplasia is treated with laser; cryotherapy, a technique that destroys cells by freezing them; loop electrosurgical excision procedure (LEEP); or knife cone biopsy. All treatment is done through the vagina. You may have a bloodstained discharge for a few weeks afterward.

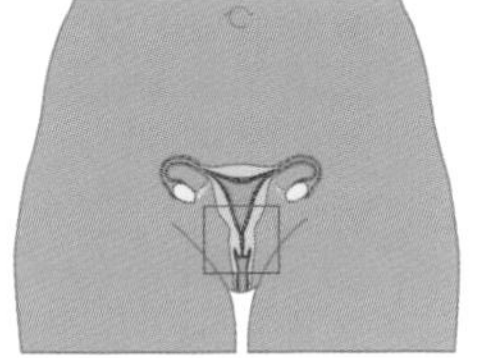

LOCATION

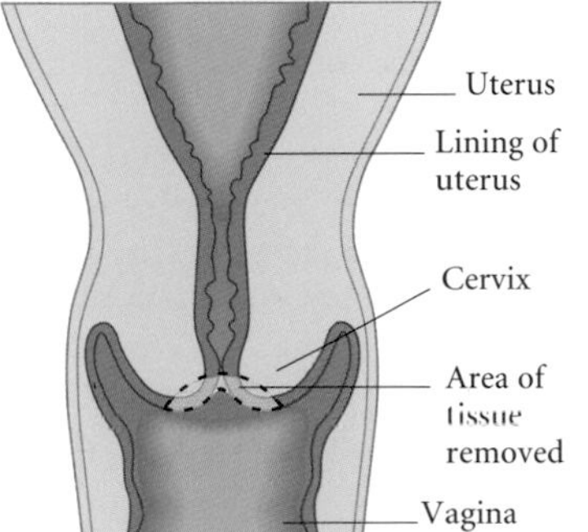
Uterus
Lining of uterus
Cervix
Area of tissue removed
Vagina

Removal of a small area
In high grade cervical dysplasia, a small area of abnormal cells together with surrounding tissue may be removed from the cervix. Treatment is carried out under local anesthesia and takes 15–20 minutes.

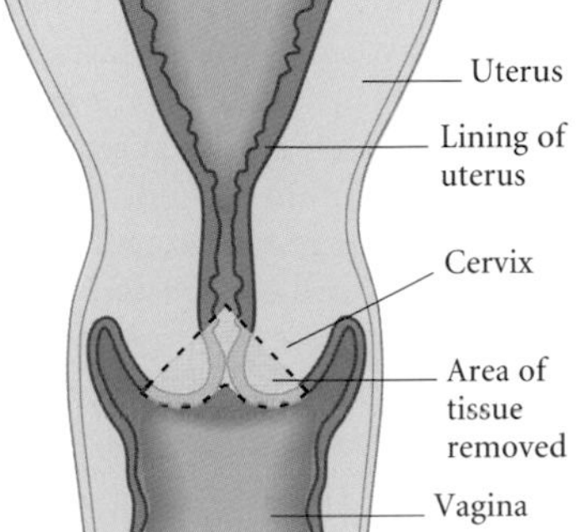
Uterus
Lining of uterus
Cervix
Area of tissue removed
Vagina

Knife cone biopsy
In instances where the abnormal or dysplastic tissues extend into the cervical canal, a knife cone biopsy is performed, often under general anesthesia, and the wound is then left to heal on its own.

being mildly to extremely abnormal, a condition known as cervical dysplasia (p.749). These changes in the cells can be detected using a Pap test (p.749), allowing treatment to be carried out before cancer of the cervix develops.

WHAT ARE THE CAUSES?

The cause of cancer of the cervix is not clear, but there is evidence that changes in cells in the cervix are associated with the types of human papilloma virus (HPV) that can cause genital warts (p.768). The virus is transmitted through unprotected sexual intercourse, and the risk of cervical cancer is increased if you have unprotected sex from an early age or with many partners. Smoking is a significant risk factor for cervical cancer. Women with reduced immunity or who are taking immunosuppressant drugs (p.906) are at increased risk of developing cancer of the cervix.

WHAT ARE THE SYMPTOMS?

Cancer of the cervix does not always cause symptoms. However, in some women, there may be some abnormal vaginal bleeding, especially after sexual intercourse. As the cancer progresses, further symptoms may include:

- A watery, bloodstained, and offensive-smelling vaginal discharge.
- Pelvic pain.
- Pain during intercourse.

If left untreated, cancer of the cervix may spread to the uterus and then to the lymph glands in the pelvis. Eventually, cancer may spread to other parts of the body, such as the liver and lungs.

HOW IS IT DIAGNOSED?

If your doctor suspects that you have cancer of the cervix from your symptoms, he or she may do a Pap test. If the test shows abnormal cells, your doctor may arrange for you to have a colposcopy (opposite page) to view the cervix through a magnifying instrument and check for abnormal areas. A small sample of tissue will probably be taken from the cervix at the same time and examined under a microscope for evidence of cancerous cells.

If cancer of the cervix is diagnosed, you may have further tests to see if the condition has spread to other parts of the body. These tests may include a chest X-ray (p.490) or MRI (p.248) of the chest to look at the lungs and blood tests and CT scanning (p.247) of the abdomen to assess liver function.

WHAT IS THE TREATMENT?

The treatment for cancer of the cervix depends on the stage of the disease and your individual circumstances.

If the cancer is confined to the cervix and you want children, it may be possible to remove only the affected section of the cervix. More often, a hysterectomy (p.747) to remove the cervix and the uterus will be performed. If the disease has spread to the uterus, it may be necessary to remove not only the uterus but also the fallopian tubes, the ovaries, the top of the vagina, and the lymph nodes. In women who are premenopausal, the ovaries are left if possible because they produce sex hormones and removing them causes premature menopause. If cancer of the cervix has spread to other organs, radiation therapy (p.279) and sometimes chemotherapy (p.278) may be needed.

WHAT IS THE PROGNOSIS?

If cancer of the cervix is diagnosed and treated early, almost all women recover completely. However, if the disease has spread beyond the cervix, the disease is fatal in 4 out of 10 women.

Routine Pap tests and the treatment of abnormal cells before they become cancerous have dramatically cut the incidence of cancer of the cervix in the developed world. In addition to having regular Pap tests, some women may consider trying to reduce the risks of cervical cancer by not smoking and by using barrier contraception (p.69).

(WWW) ONLINE SITES: p.1028, p.1037

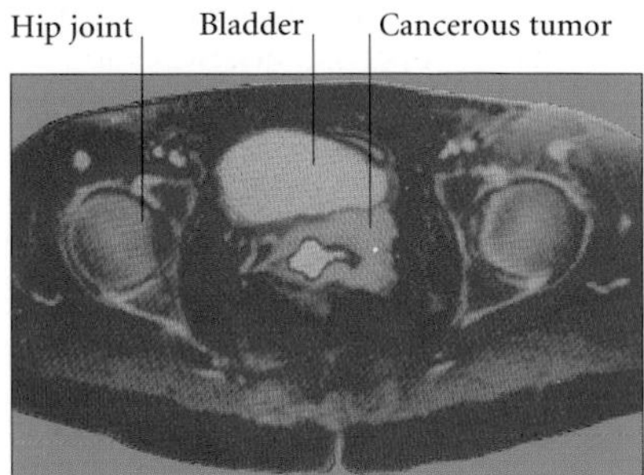
Hip joint
Bladder
Cancerous tumor

Cancer of the cervix
This color-enhanced MRI through the pelvis shows a large cancerous tumor of the cervix lying just behind the bladder.

Vulvovaginitis

Inflammation of the vulva and vagina, causing itching and soreness

 AGE LIFESTYLE Risk factors depend on the cause

 GENETICS Not a significant factor

Vulvovaginitis is a very common disorder affecting most women at some time during their lifetime. In this condition, the vulva and the vagina become inflamed, itchy, and sore. There may also be pain during sexual intercourse and a discharge from the vagina. The condition can also affect children.

WHAT ARE THE CAUSES?

Most cases of vulvovaginitis are caused by an infection, usually either with the fungus *Candida albicans*, which causes vaginal yeast (right), or with the protozoan *Trichomonas vaginalis*, which leads to the sexually transmitted disease trichomoniasis (p.767). Women who have diabetes mellitus (p.687) have an increased risk of fungal vulvovaginitis. Overgrowth of harmless bacteria that normally live in the vagina (*see* BACTERIAL VAGINOSIS, opposite page) may also lead to vulvovaginitis.

In some cases, vulvovaginitis may be caused by irritation from perfumed bath products, laundry detergents, deodorants, or contraceptive creams. After menopause, the disorder may develop as the vaginal tissues become thinner, drier, and more susceptible to irritation. These changes in the tissues of the vagina are caused by low levels of estrogen. Rarely, vulvovaginitis may be the result of cancerous changes in the cells that line the surface of the vulva or the vagina (*see* CANCER OF THE VULVA AND VAGINA, opposite page).

In children, the cause of the disorder is often unclear. In some cases, a foreign body in the vagina or, rarely, sexual abuse may be the cause.

WHAT MIGHT BE DONE?

Your doctor will take a swab from the inflamed area to look for an infection and to identify the causative organism. If you have repeated episodes of fungal vulvovaginitis, your urine may also be tested for glucose to exclude diabetes mellitus. If cancerous changes are suspected, a tissue sample will be taken and examined for abnormal cells.

Treatment of vulvovaginitis depends on the cause of the inflammation. If you have bacterial vaginosis, you will be prescribed antibiotics (p.885) or a vaginal cream; your sexual partner may also need to be treated to prevent reinfection. Hormone replacement therapy (p.937) or topical creams containing estrogen can relieve vulvovaginitis caused by the low levels of estrogen after menopause. If vulvovaginitis is caused by a bath product, laundry detergent, deodorant, or contraceptive cream, you should change to another product.

Your doctor will advise you to avoid sexual intercourse until your symptoms have cleared up. Most affected people recover completely after treatment but the condition may recur.

(WWW) ONLINE SITES: p.1033, p.1037

Vaginal yeast

Inflammation of the vagina caused by infection with the candida fungus

 AGE Most common in females of childbearing age

 LIFESTYLE Stress may trigger the condition

 GENETICS Not a significant factor

Vaginal yeast affects many women at some point in their adult lives, most commonly at some time during the childbearing years, and can recur regularly. The condition develops when a fungus called *Candida albicans*, which can occur naturally in the vagina, grows more rapidly than usual. Vaginal yeast is not serious, but it may cause unpleasant itching of the vulva and vagina and a discharge. Candida infections may occur in other areas, such as the mouth (*see* ORAL THRUSH, p.862).

WHAT ARE THE CAUSES?

The candida fungus is found in the vagina of about 1 in 5 women and does not usually cause disease. The growth of the fungus is suppressed by both the immune system and harmless bacteria that normally live in the vagina. If these bacteria are destroyed by antibiotics or spermicides, the fungus can multiply, which may lead to symptoms. Harmless bacteria in the vagina may also be destroyed as a result of changes in levels of female sex hormones. Such changes may occur during pregnancy or before menstrual periods or may be due to drugs that affect female sex hormone levels, such as the oral contraceptive pill. Vaginal yeast may also develop after having sexual intercourse with a partner who has candida.

Women who have diabetes mellitus (p.687) are more susceptible to vaginal yeast. Sometimes stress can trigger an episode of the condition.

WHAT ARE THE SYMPTOMS?

The symptoms usually develop gradually over several days and may include:

- Intense irritation and itching of the vagina and vulva (*see* VULVOVAGINITIS, left).
- Thick, white vaginal discharge that is cheesy in appearance.

If left untreated, vulvovaginitis may lead to redness and eventually cracking of the delicate skin of the vulva.

WHAT CAN I DO?

If you are confident that your symptoms are caused by vaginal yeast because you have had the condition before, you can start treating yourself by using

> **SELF-HELP PREVENTING VAGINAL YEAST**
>
> If you often have vaginal yeast, the following self-help measures may help you prevent further episodes of infection:
>
> - Wash the vaginal area with water only. Try to avoid using bath additives, perfumed soaps, or vaginal deodorants or douches.
> - Avoid spermicidal creams, lubricants, and latex condoms if you find they irritate the vagina.
> - Avoid scented sanitary napkins or tampons, change tampons frequently, and use sanitary napkins instead of tampons as often as possible.
> - Keep your external genital area clean, dry, and cool. Wear cotton underwear and loose-fitting clothes if possible.
> - If yeast seems to be triggered by stress, try to avoid stressful situations whenever possible.

over-the-counter drugs. Antifungal drugs (p.889) are readily available and come in a variety of forms, including vaginal suppositories and creams or pills.

It is advisable not to have sexual intercourse for the next few days until your symptoms have cleared up.

If you get vaginal yeast regularly, there are some simple steps that you can take to help you prevent the condition, such as avoid perfumed products (*see* PREVENTING VAGINAL YEAST, opposite page). If you are not sure about the cause of your symptoms or if over-the-counter treatment does not help, you should consult your doctor.

WHAT MIGHT THE DOCTOR DO?

Your doctor may diagnose yeast from the vaginal discharge. He or she will perform a pelvic examination and may take a swab from your vagina for examination. If vaginal yeast is diagnosed, your doctor may advise you on self-help measures or prescribe a stronger antifungal drug. Although treatment for vaginal yeast is usually successful, the condition tends to recur.

(WWW) ONLINE SITES: p.1033, p.1037

Bacterial vaginosis

Bacterial infection of the vagina that sometimes causes an abnormal discharge

 AGE Can affect sexually active females of any age

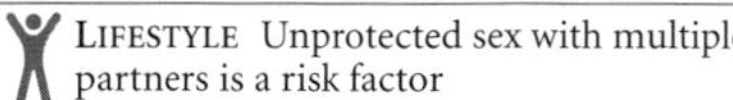 LIFESTYLE Unprotected sex with multiple partners is a risk factor

 GENETICS Not a significant factor

Bacterial vaginosis is caused by excess growth of some of the bacteria that normally live in the vagina, particularly *Gardnerella vaginalis* and *Mycoplasma hominis*. As a result, the natural balance of organisms in the vagina is altered. The reason for this excess growth is unknown, but the condition is more common in sexually active women and often, but not always, occurs in association with sexually transmitted diseases. Vaginal infections can also be caused by an overgrowth of the candida fungus (*see* VAGINAL YEAST, opposite page) and the protozoan *Trichomonas vaginalis* (*see* TRICHOMONIASIS, p.767).

Bacterial vaginosis often causes no symptoms. However, some women may have a grayish white vaginal discharge with a fishy or musty odor and vaginal or vulval itching. Rarely, the disorder leads to pelvic inflammatory disease (p.741), in which some of the reproductive organs become inflamed.

WHAT MIGHT BE DONE?

Your doctor may be able to diagnose bacterial vaginosis from your symptoms. Swabs of any discharge may be taken and tested to confirm the diagnosis. Vaginosis is usually treated with antibiotics (p.885), either orally or as cream inserted into the vagina. Sexual partners should also be checked for infection and treated if necessary. Vaginosis usually clears up completely within 2 days of starting treatment, but the condition tends to recur.

(WWW) ONLINE SITES: p.1036, p.1037

Bartholin gland infection

Infection of one or both Bartholin's glands, located in the vulva, and/or of their ducts

 AGE More common after puberty

 LIFESTYLE Poor hygiene and unprotected sex with multiple partners are risk factors

 GENETICS Not a significant factor

Bartholin's glands are two pea-sized glands with ducts that open into the vulva. The glands produce a fluid that helps lubricate the genital area during sexual intercourse. One or both glands and/or ducts can become infected, called bartholinitis. In some cases, the disorder is caused by bacteria entering the glands as a result of poor hygiene after a bowel movement or by a sexually transmitted disease. The infection causes swelling in the surrounding tissues and may lead to a painful abscess. One or both ducts may also become blocked, causing a painless swelling called a Bartholin's cyst.

Your doctor will prescribe antibiotics (p.885) to treat bartholinitis; it should clear up in a few days. Analgesics (p.912) may help relieve discomfort. An abscess may be drained under local anesthesia. Bartholin's cysts are not usually removed unless they are very large or cause discomfort. Bartholinitis may recur.

(WWW) ONLINE SITES: p.1036, p.1037

Cancer of the vulva and vagina

Cancerous growths occurring on the vulva or in the vagina

 AGE More common over age 60

 LIFESTYLE Unprotected sex at an early age, sex with multiple partners, and smoking are risk factors

 GENETICS Not a significant factor

Cancers of the vulva and vagina are rare and usually affect women over age 60. They account for about 1 in 20 cancers of the female reproductive organs. Although these cancers do not usually occur together, they may both be associated with certain types of the human papilloma virus that cause genital warts (p.768). Smoking may also be a risk factor. If not treated, both cancers may spread to the pelvic lymph nodes and from there to other parts of the body.

Cancer of the vulva may cause vulval itching, but often the first symptom is a hard lump or ulcer on the vulva. If the ulcer is not treated, it may produce an offensive, bloody discharge. Cancer of the vagina often causes no symptoms until the tumor is at an advanced stage, although bleeding and pain may occur after sexual intercourse. If you develop any one of these symptoms, you should consult your doctor at once.

WHAT MIGHT BE DONE?

Your doctor may make a diagnosis of cancer of the vulva or vagina from your symptoms. A sample of tissue may also be removed from the affected area and examined to look for cancerous cells.

Cancer of the vulva is usually treated surgically by removing all of the affected area. The nearby lymph nodes are also usually removed and examined to see if the disease has spread and if further treatment is necessary. Cancer of the vagina is usually treated with radiation therapy (p.279). However, it may also be necessary to remove part of the vagina and the nearby lymph nodes.

The prognosis for these cancers depends on the extent to which they have spread. If they are diagnosed and treated early, there is often a full recovery.

(WWW) ONLINE SITES: p.1028, p.1037

BREAST DISORDERS

The breasts consist of fatty tissue that gives them their size and shape, lobules that secrete milk after childbirth, and milk ducts that carry the milk to the nipple during breast-feeding. The nipples are sensitive to touch and play a role in sexual arousal. Most disorders of the breasts are not serious, although breast cancer is becoming increasingly common in developed countries.

Throughout life, the breasts change size and shape in response to varying levels of female sex hormones. The breasts usually enlarge during puberty, before menstrual periods, and during pregnancy and breast-feeding. This enlargement can be associated with breast pain and generalized lumpiness.

This section opens with an overview of the causes of breast lumps, both normal and abnormal. Many women associate a breast lump with breast cancer, but in fact most lumps are noncancerous. Two common causes of noncancerous lumps in the breasts, fibroadenomas and breast cysts, are discussed next in this section.

The following articles cover breast pain, abnormalities in breast size, and problems that affect the nipples. The final article deals with breast cancer. Since the early diagnosis of breast cancer significantly improves the chances of survival, this section includes information about screening techniques and how to examine your breasts so that you notice any abnormalities as soon as possible.

KEY ANATOMY

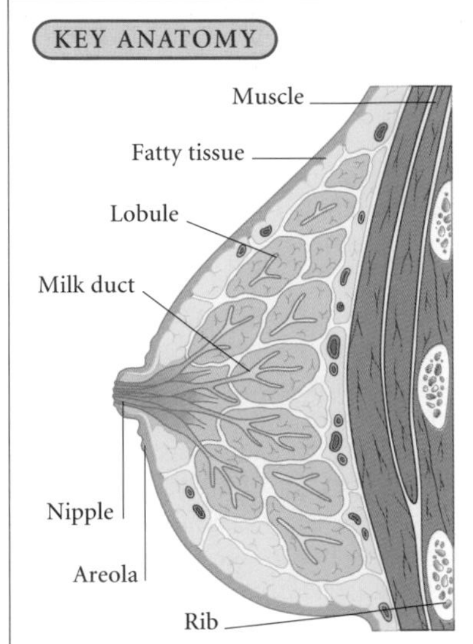
Muscle
Fatty tissue
Lobule
Milk duct
Nipple
Areola
Rib

For more information about the structure and function of the breast, *see* pp.730–733.

Breast lumps

Any masses or swellings that can be felt in the breast tissue

AGE GENETICS LIFESTYLE
Risk factors depend on the cause

Breast lumps are a common problem. Many women notice generalized breast lumpiness, especially when the breasts enlarge during puberty and pregnancy and before menstruation. This generalized lumpiness can usually be regarded as a variation in normal breast development and does not increase the risk of breast cancer. Discrete breast lumps may cause concern, but in fact only 2 in 10 breast lumps are due to cancer.

WHAT ARE THE CAUSES?

Generalized lumpiness in the breasts, often with associated breast tenderness, is thought to be related to the hormonal changes that occur during the menstrual cycle. The lumpiness usually becomes worse just before a menstrual period, and this worsening may be due to oversensitivity of the breast tissue to female sex hormones at this time.

A discrete lump is often a fibroadenoma (right). This noncancerous lump is caused by the overgrowth of one or more breast lobules (the structures that produce milk). Breast cysts (opposite page) are fluid-filled sacs in the breast tissue. One or more cysts may be present, and both breasts may be affected. Occasionally, a breast lump is caused by an infection that has developed into an abscess. A breast abscess may develop if mastitis (p.809), which is most common in women who are breast-feeding, is not treated. An abscess may be associated with inflammation and localized pain. A lump in the breast may also be a symptom of breast cancer (p.759).

WHAT MIGHT BE DONE?

You should check your breasts regularly (*see* BREAST SELF-EXAMINATION, opposite page), so that you become familiar with their normal appearance and texture. Always consult your doctor if you notice a new lump or a change in an existing lump. He or she will perform a physical examination of your breasts and may arrange for ultrasound scanning (p.250) or mammography (p.759) to investigate a breast lump. Your doctor may also take a sample of cells from the lump (*see* ASPIRATION OF A BREAST LUMP, p.756) to look for cancerous cells.

Many noncancerous breast lumps do not need treatment. Generalized lumpiness tends to decrease after menopause, but may continue if you take hormone replacement therapy (p.937). However, breast cysts are usually treated by draining. Modern screening techniques and treatments mean that breast cancer can often be diagnosed early and treated successfully. If a tumor is found in your breast, you will be referred to a specialist.

(WWW) ONLINE SITES: p.1037

Fibroadenoma

A firm, round, noncancerous growth in the breast tissue

AGE Most common between the ages of 15 and 30

GENETICS Not a significant factor

LIFESTYLE Not a significant factor

A fibroadenoma is an overgrowth of a breast lobule (the part of the breast that produces milk) and surrounding connective tissue. Although the cause of this condition is not fully understood, the development of a fibroadenoma is thought to be linked to the sensitivity of

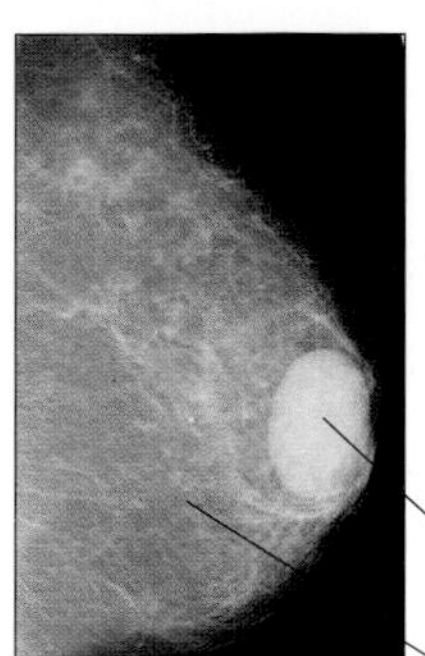
Fibroadenoma
Normal breast tissue

Fibroadenoma
A fibroadenoma can be seen in the breast tissue in this color-enhanced mammogram (breast X-ray).

breast tissue to female sex hormones. The lumps tend to grow more quickly during pregnancy (pp.778–809), probably because of the increase in female sex hormone levels. Fibroadenomas occur most commonly in women who are between the ages of 15 and 30.

A fibroadenoma is usually painless. Fibroadenomas may occur anywhere in the breast, but they are most commonly found in the upper, outer part and are usually about ½–2 in (1–5 cm) in size. There is often more than one lump and both breasts may be affected. In some cases, multiple fibroadenomas develop together with a generalized thickening of the breast tissue.

It is important to carry out a regular breast self-examination (right) to look for any changes in the appearance or texture of your breasts. Fibroadenomas are harmless, but, if you find a lump in your breast, you should consult your doctor so that the possibility of breast cancer (p.759) can be ruled out.

What might be done?

Your doctor will examine your breasts and may arrange for breast X-rays (*see* MAMMOGRAPHY, p.759) or ultrasound scanning (p.250) of the breast tissue to confirm the diagnosis. A sample of cells may be removed from the lump (*see* ASPIRATION OF A BREAST LUMP, p.756) to be examined for cancerous cells.

Small fibroadenomas do not usually need treatment. About 1 in 3 fibroadenomas becomes smaller or disappears completely within 2 years. If you are worried about the fibroadenoma, or if it grows larger, your doctor may recommend surgical removal. After removal, the lump will be examined under the microscope for the presence of cancerous cells. In most cases, fibroadenomas do not recur after treatment.

(WWW) ONLINE SITES: p.1037

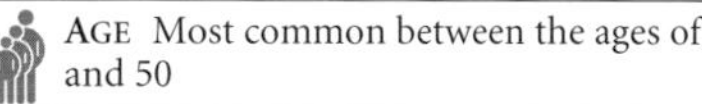

Breast cyst

A firm, round, fluid-filled swelling within the breast tissue

AGE Most common between the ages of 30 and 50

GENETICS LIFESTYLE Not significant factors

A breast cyst is a firm, round lump in the breast tissue that forms when a lobule (the part of the breast that produces milk) fills with fluid. The development of cysts is influenced by levels of female sex hormones. Breast cysts most often affect women aged 30–50, particularly women approaching menopause.

A cyst may be felt just under the skin or may occur deeper within the breast tissue. The lump is usually not painful.

Breast cysts may occur singly, but in about half of all cases there is more than one cyst, and both breasts may be affected. Some women also have generalized lumpiness of the breast tissue.

You should always consult your doctor if you detect a lump during breast self-examination (below) so that the possibility of breast cancer (p.759) can be ruled out. In rare cases, cancerous cells may be found in the wall of a cyst.

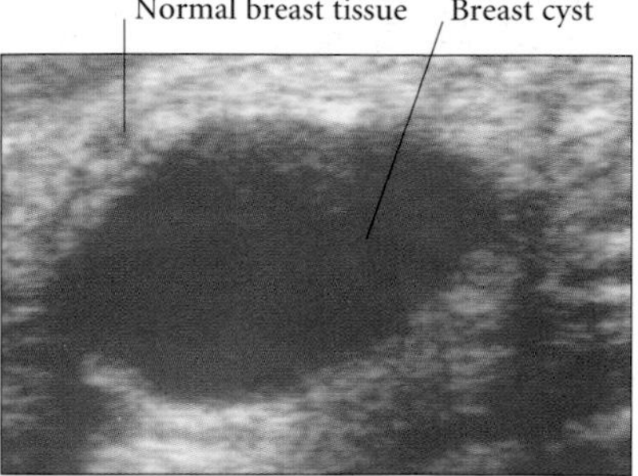
Normal breast tissue
Breast cyst

Breast cyst
This ultrasound scan of a breast shows a fluid-filled breast cyst, visible as a dark area within the breast tissue.

What might be done?

If your doctor suspects a cyst after examining your breast, he or she may arrange for breast X-rays (*see* MAMMOGRAPHY, p.759) or ultrasound scanning (p.250).

Breast cysts are treated by draining the fluid they contain (*see* ASPIRATION OF A BREAST LUMP, p.756). This fluid can then be examined for cancerous cells. A cyst usually disappears after aspiration, but it may recur and require further drainage. If a cyst recurs several times, or if it is found to contain cancerous cells, it will be surgically removed.

(WWW) ONLINE SITES: p.1037

SELF-HELP BREAST SELF-EXAMINATION

Regular examination of your breasts helps you become familiar with their normal feel and appearance, so that you will notice if a change occurs. The best time to examine your breasts is just after your menstrual period. If you detect a new lump, changes in a long-standing lump, a change in nipple shape, or a change in the skin overlying the breast, you should consult your doctor. In many cases, breast lumps are harmless, but they are sometimes caused by a cancerous tumor.

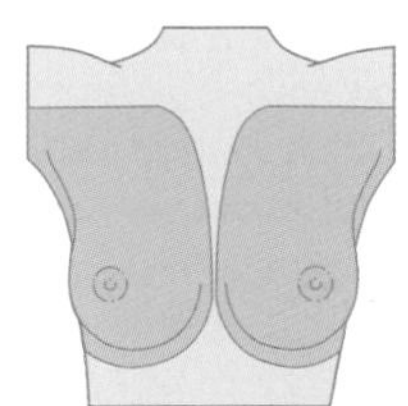

AREA TO BE EXAMINED

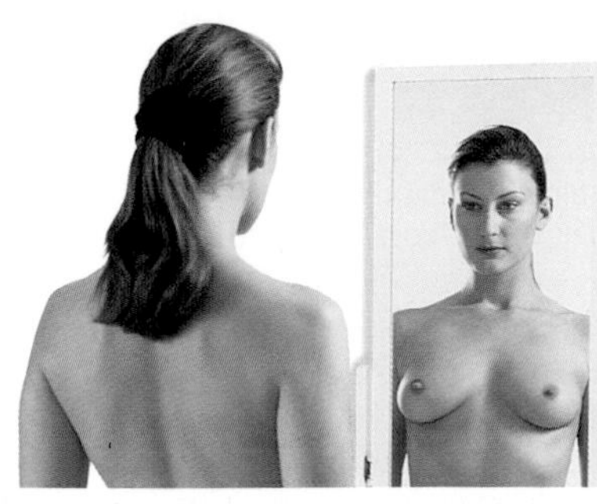

1 *Look at the appearance of your breasts in a mirror. Look closely for dimpled skin and any changes to your nipples or to the size and shape of your breasts.*

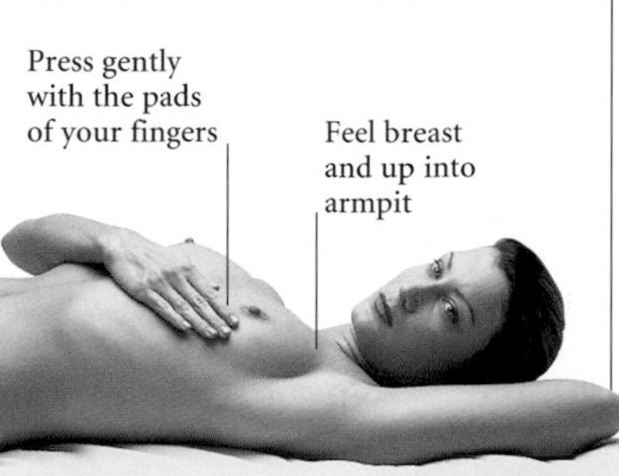
Press gently with the pads of your fingers
Feel breast and up into armpit

2 *With one arm behind your head, gently but firmly press the breast with small circular movements. Feel around the entire breast, armpit area, and nipple.*

TEST AND TREATMENT ASPIRATION OF A BREAST LUMP

Aspiration of a breast lump is used to diagnose and to treat breast cysts. The procedure, which is done in a doctor's office, is a relatively simple one. First, fluid is withdrawn to drain the cyst. The fluid is then examined under a microscope to check for cancer cells. If there is no fluid in a breast lump, it is not a cyst. Although aspiration may be uncomfortable, the procedure usually takes only a few minutes.

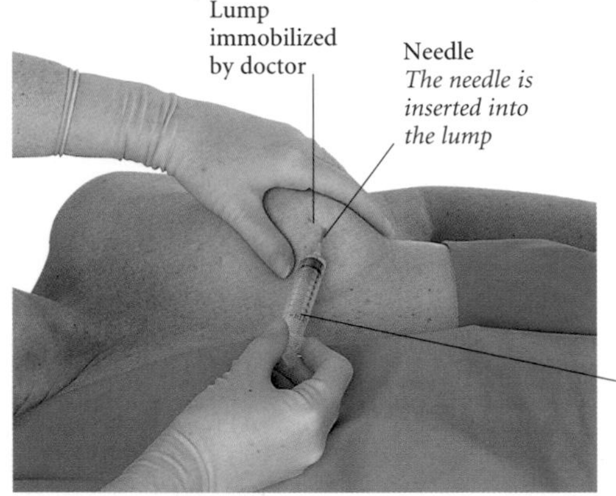
Lump immobilized by doctor
Needle
The needle is inserted into the lump
Syringe
The syringe is used to withdraw cells and/or fluid from the lump

During the procedure
The doctor holds the breast lump still with one hand. He or she then inserts a needle attached to a syringe into the breast lump and withdraws cells or fluid for analysis.

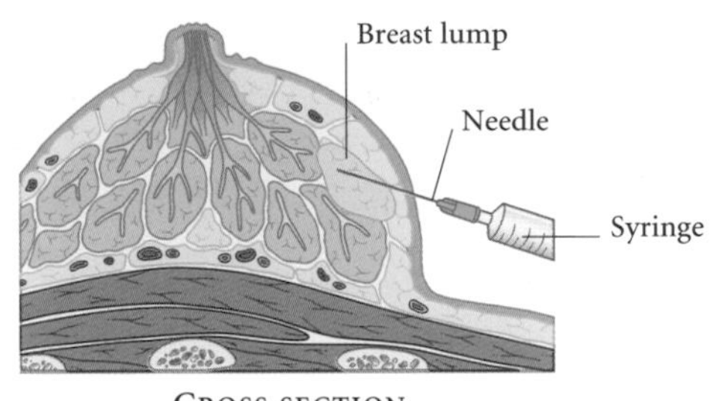
Breast lump
Needle
Syringe

CROSS SECTION

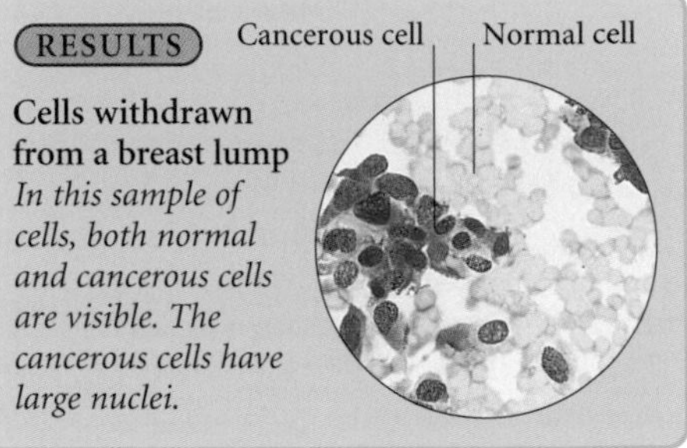
Cancerous cell
Normal cell

RESULTS

Cells withdrawn from a breast lump
In this sample of cells, both normal and cancerous cells are visible. The cancerous cells have large nuclei.

Breast pain

Pain or discomfort usually affecting one or both breasts

 AGE Most common between the ages of 15 and 50

 GENETICS LIFESTYLE Risk factors depend on the cause

Breast pain is an extremely common problem. In most women, the pain is cyclical, varying in severity in response to the hormonal changes of the menstrual cycle. This cyclical pain is usually most severe before menstrual periods and tends to affect both breasts.

Cyclical breast pain affects as many as 1 in 2 women and is commonly a chronic problem. In some women, the pain is severe. Women who experience cyclical breast pain often also have generalized breast lumpiness, which tends to become worse before a menstrual period. The pain may be aggravated by stress and by caffeine in certain drinks.

In some women, breast pain is not related to menstruation. Muscle strain may result in noncyclical breast pain. Rarely, pain is caused by a breast cyst (p.755) or breast cancer (p.759). Breast pain may also be due to an acute problem, such as an infection that causes inflammation of the breast tissue (*see* MASTITIS, p.809) or engorgement of the breast with milk after childbirth (*see* BREAST ENGORGEMENT, p.808). Sometimes, the cause of breast pain is not known. If you have large breasts, you are more likely to suffer from both cyclical and noncyclical breast pain.

WHAT MIGHT THE DOCTOR DO?

Your doctor will ask you about your breast pain to see if there is a pattern. He or she will examine your breasts to look for an underlying cause, such as a breast cyst or any tender areas in the surrounding muscles. If it is apparent from the consultation and examination that you do not have an underlying disorder, your doctor may ask you to keep a record of when you experience breast pain to help confirm that the pain is cyclical. If your doctor suspects that an underlying disorder may be causing the pain, he or she will probably arrange for mammography (p.759) or ultrasound scanning (p.250) in order to detect abnormalities in the breast.

Mild cyclical pain does not normally require treatment. However, in about 1 in 10 women, the pain is so severe that it can interfere with everyday life. Taking large doses of evening primrose oil has been reported to reduce the response of the breast tissue to female sex hormones. However, if this treatment is ineffective or the pain is severe, your doctor may prescribe danazol, a drug that reduces the effects of female sex hormones acting on the breast (*see* SEX HORMONES AND RELATED DRUGS, p.933). Although this drug is effective in relieving pain, it may have side effects such as acne and weight gain. Cyclical breast pain tends to ease after menopause. If you take hormone replacement therapy (p.937), the pain may continue after menopause, but it often improves after a few months.

If your breast pain is noncyclical, the cause will be treated if necessary. Cysts are usually drained (*see* ASPIRATION OF A BREAST LUMP, above) and antibiotics (p.885) can be used to treat infection. Nonsteroidal anti-inflammatory drugs (p.894) may help relieve muscle pain.

WHAT CAN I DO?

Breast pain may be eased by wearing a bra that supports your breasts properly. If your breasts are heavy and the pain is severe, you may need to wear a bra at night. Cyclical pain may be relieved by cutting down on caffeine, practicing relaxation exercises (p.75) to help control stress, and trying to lose weight to reduce the size of the breasts. Some women find that taking vitamin E supplements is also helpful, but this effect is not supported by scientific studies.

WWW ONLINE SITES: p.1037

Abnormality of breast size

Abnormally large, small, or asymmetrical breasts

AGE Develops during puberty

GENETICS LIFESTYLE Not significant factors

There is considerable natural variation in breast size among women. A slight asymmetry in the size of the breasts in an individual woman is also very common. However, having abnormally large, small, or asymmetrical breasts can lead to emotional distress and, in the case of abnormally large breasts, may result in pain and discomfort.

Breasts that grow to an abnormally large size often develop rapidly during puberty and are thought to be caused by oversensitivity of the breast tissue to the female sex hormone estrogen. Large breasts may lead to pain in the back, shoulders, and neck, and in some cases a skin infection may develop under the breast. Women who have abnormally large breasts may experience discomfort when running or playing sports and have difficulty finding clothes that fit.

In some women, the breasts develop to only a very small size. A woman who has very small breasts may find her appearance unfeminine. However, having small breasts does not cause any physical problems and does not affect a woman's ability to breast-feed.

Occasionally, there is a marked difference in size between the two breasts because one breast develops more than the other at puberty. This asymmetry may cause embarrassment and anxiety.

WHAT MIGHT BE DONE?

Women who have large breasts can benefit from a well-fitting, supportive bra. You may also find that wearing a bra at night makes you feel more comfortable. If this does not relieve your discomfort or distress, you may wish to consider the possibility of a surgical operation to permanently reduce the size of your breasts (*see* BREAST REDUCTION, below).

Women with small breasts may find that a padded bra boosts their confidence and improves their body shape under clothes. The only permanent way to enlarge small breasts is by surgically inserting an implant behind the breast tissue. In the past, these implants were usually filled with a silicone gel, but implants that contain other substances, such as saltwater, are now available.

Some women who experience distress as a result of having abnormally large, small, or asymmetrical breasts may benefit from counseling (p.971).

(WWW) ONLINE SITES: p.1037

TREATMENT BREAST REDUCTION

Breast reduction operations relieve permanently the discomfort of very large, heavy breasts. The procedure takes place under general anesthesia and involves a short hospital stay. During the operation, some skin and breast tissue are removed, and the breast is reshaped. The nipple and areola may be moved up and made smaller. After breast reduction surgery, your breasts will be smaller and firmer. The scarring is usually minimal and is mostly hidden under the breast. However, sensation in the nipple will be reduced, and breast-feeding will not be possible.

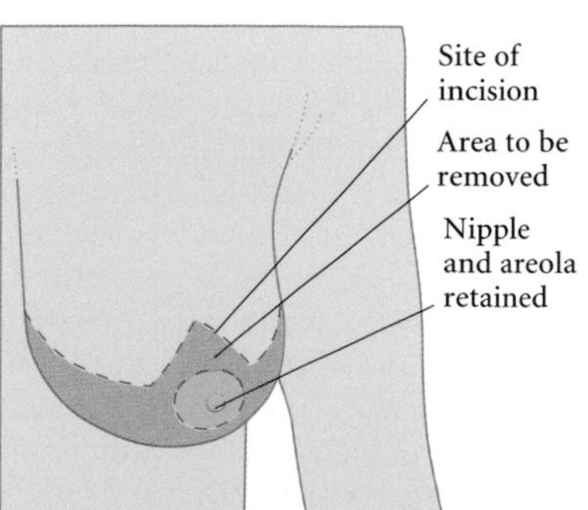
Site of incision
Area to be removed
Nipple and areola retained

1 *A substantial area of skin and tissue is removed from the lower part of the breast. The nipple and areola are preserved, along with the blood vessels and some of the nerves that supply the area.*

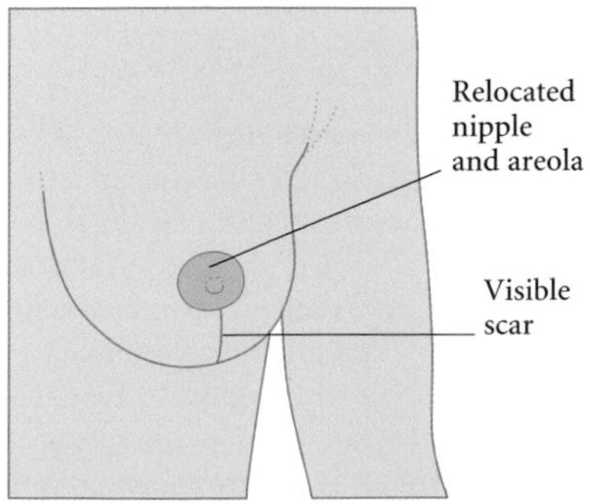
Relocated nipple and areola
Visible scar

2 *The nipple and areola are repositioned higher up, and the V-shaped part of the incision is sewn together below it. The remaining skin edges are rejoined under the breast and are not visible.*

Abnormal nipples

Change in the shape or skin of a nipple or the area around it (areola)

AGE GENETICS LIFESTYLE Risk factors depend on the cause

There are two main types of nipple abnormality: retraction into the breast (nipple inversion) and disorders affecting the skin on or around the nipple. Although these abnormalities are most often caused by minor problems that are easily treatable, any changes in the condition of the nipples should receive medical attention because, in rare cases, they may indicate breast cancer (p.759).

WHAT ARE THE CAUSES?

Inversion of the nipples may occur during puberty when the breasts develop. This type of inversion is usually harmless, although it may later make breast-feeding difficult. Nipple inversion may also occur in a previously normal breast as a result of inflammation of the milk ducts behind the nipple (*see* MASTITIS, p.809). This condition most often affects women who are breast-feeding. Changes in the structure of the breasts as they age may cause the nipple to be drawn into the breast in older women. Less commonly, nipple inversion that develops in adulthood may be due to breast cancer.

Many women develop fine cracks and tender areas on their nipples during the first few weeks of breast-feeding (*see* CRACKED NIPPLES, p.808). These cracks are most often the result of the baby not taking the whole nipple into his or her mouth properly when feeding. Leaving your nipples wet after a feed can also cause them to become sore and cracked. Cracked nipples often cause stabbing or burning pain as the baby starts or stops feeding and may become infected, causing inflammation of the breast tissue.

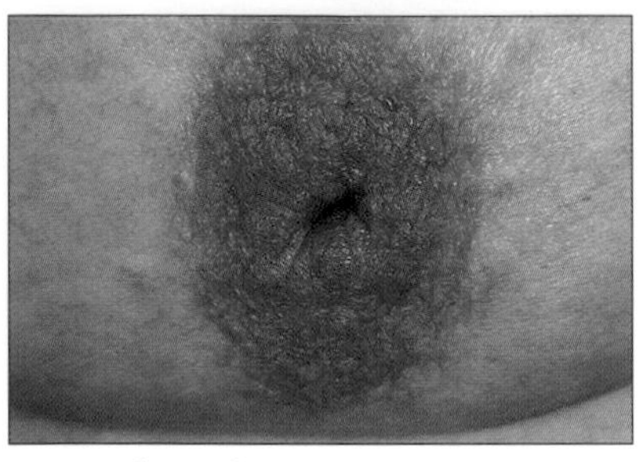

Inverted nipple
This nipple has been drawn into the breast (become inverted), which may be a result of inflammation of the milk ducts.

Dry, flaky, sometimes blistering patches of skin that occur on or around both nipples may be due to eczema (p.333). Eczema is usually itchy and tends to occur in several sites on the body. However, occasionally, skin changes on the nipples that resemble eczema are in fact caused by Paget's disease of the breast, a rare form of cancer that originates in the milk ducts. As it may resemble other skin conditions, diagnosis may be difficult. Unlike eczema, Paget's disease rarely develops on both nipples and does not heal. This type of breast cancer often causes soreness and bleeding from the nipple and is often associated with a breast lump.

WHAT MIGHT BE DONE?

Your doctor will examine your breasts, paying particular attention to your nipples. If nipple inversion has occurred in adulthood but is not related to breast-feeding, your doctor may arrange for ultrasound scanning (p.250) or breast X-rays (*see* MAMMOGRAPHY, opposite page) to look for breast abnormalities. If a breast lump is found, cells or fluid may be taken from it using a needle and syringe (*see* ASPIRATION OF A BREAST LUMP, p.756) and examined under the microscope for cancerous cells. If you have a persistent rash on or around a nipple, your doctor may take a skin sample to look for cancerous cells.

If your nipples have become cracked, washing and drying them carefully and applying a moisturizer may help. Make sure that you wash the moisturizer off before breast-feeding. You should also avoid plastic-lined breast pads which may become damp and encourage infection. Infection is usually treated with antibiotics (p.885) and eczema can be improved by hydrocortisone cream (*see* TOPICAL CORTICOSTEROIDS, p.892).

If cancer of the breast is discovered, you will be referred to a specialist for treatment, and further tests, including blood tests and X-rays (p.244), may be done to find out if the cancer has spread to other body organs. If Paget's disease is diagnosed, the affected skin will be surgically removed along with the surrounding tissue. Treatment of Paget's disease will depend on whether the cancer cells have spread to surrounding breast tissue, and how much of the breast is affected. If a lump is present, treatment can include surgery, radiation therapy (p.279), and/or chemotherapy (p.278).

(WWW) ONLINE SITES: p.1037

Nipple discharge

Discharge of fluid from one or both nipples

AGE GENETICS LIFESTYLE Risk factors depend on the cause

It is normal for women to release milk from their nipples during the late stages of pregnancy and while breast-feeding. At any other time, nipple discharge may be a normal result of a change in hormone levels or a symptom of a minor disorder. However, because nipple discharge may be a sign of a more serious condition, such as breast cancer (opposite page), you should see your doctor if you notice an unusual nipple discharge.

WHAT ARE THE TYPES?

Many different types of fluid may be discharged from the nipples. The color and consistency of this fluid depends on the underlying cause.

CLEAR, WATERY DISCHARGE In some women, a clear, watery discharge from both nipples occurs just before a menstrual period. This type of discharge is particularly common in women who are using the combined oral contraceptive pill and may also occur in the early stages of pregnancy. In most cases, a clear discharge is harmless.

MILKY DISCHARGE A profuse, watery, milky discharge in a woman who is not pregnant or breast-feeding is known as galactorrhea. Galactorrhea is caused by the overproduction of prolactin, a hormone that stimulates milk secretion. The condition is often associated with certain other endocrine disorders, such as hyperthyroidism (p.679) and a noncancerous tumor of the pituitary gland called a prolactinoma (p.677).

BLOODSTAINED DISCHARGE A bloodstained discharge from the nipples may be caused by a noncancerous tumor of the milk ducts or, less commonly, by a cancerous tumor of the breast.

DISCHARGE CONTAINING PUS A discharge from the nipple that contains pus is usually caused by an infection within the breast, such as mastitis (p.809), an inflammation of breast tissue in one or both breasts. Breast infections are most common in women who are breast-feeding.

WHAT MIGHT BE DONE?

Your doctor will ask you questions about the nipple discharge and carry out a physical examination of your breasts. He or she may also take a sample of the discharge to be examined for evidence of infection or cancerous cells. X-rays of the breast (*see* MAMMOGRAPHY, opposite page) as well as ultrasound scanning (p.250) may be performed. In addition, blood samples are likely to be taken in order to measure hormone levels.

A clear nipple discharge does not normally need treatment. Galactorrhea can often be treated using the drug bromocriptine (*see* SEX HORMONES AND RELATED DRUGS, p.933), which reduces production of the hormone prolactin by the pituitary gland. However, if galactorrhea is caused by a tumor in the pituitary gland, surgery and/or radiation therapy (p.279) may be required. A bloodstained nipple discharge that has been caused by a noncancerous tumor of the milk duct is normally treated by surgically removing the affected milk duct. A nipple discharge of pus usually clears up after the infection that caused it has been treated with antibiotics (p.885).

If initial tests reveal that your nipple discharge has been caused by a cancerous growth in the breast, your doctor will arrange for you to see a specialist for further tests and treatment.

(WWW) ONLINE SITES: p.1037

Breast cancer

A cancerous growth that originates in the breast

 AGE Risk increases with age

 GENETICS In some cases, due to an abnormal gene

 LIFESTYLE Being overweight and delaying having children are risk factors

In Canada, about 21,000 women develop cancer of the breast each year. The disease can also occur in men, although cancer of the male breast accounts for less than 1 in 100 breast cancer cases.

The risk of breast cancer increases with age, doubling every 10 years. The disease is most commonly diagnosed in women over age 50. Very few women under age 30 develop breast cancer. The number of cases diagnosed in Canada is increasing by about 1 percent per year. Despite the rise in incidence, there has been a small drop in the number of deaths from cancer of the breast in recent years, and only about one-fifth of cases prove fatal. This reduction is due to improvements in treatment and the increased use of mammography for screening, which means that tumors can be detected early, when they often respond well to treatment. Screening may reduce the number of breast cancer deaths in women over age 50 by up to 3 in 10. In Canada, guidelines recommend that women age 50 and over have a mammogram every 2 years. Discuss this with your doctor.

Breast cancer normally arises from the breast ducts. Less commonly (10%), it arises from the breast lobules. A tumor that originates in one duct may lead to Paget's disease of the breast (*see* ABNORMAL NIPPLES, p.757), a rare cancer. Tumors may spread to other organs in the body, such as the lungs, liver, or bones, before being detected.

WHAT ARE THE CAUSES?

The underlying cause of most breast cancers is still unclear. However, some risk factors have been identified, many of which suggest that the female hormone estrogen is an important factor in the progress of the disease once it has developed. It is known that women who have their first menstrual period before age 12, or who have a late menopause, seem to be at increased risk of developing breast cancer. The number of menstrual cycles a woman has before her first pregnancy is also a significant factor. A woman who has her first child after the age of 30 or who never has children is twice as likely to develop breast cancer as is a woman who has her first child before the age of 20. Breast-feeding is thought to have an additional protective effect.

Obesity is a risk factor, particularly in older women. Artificial estrogen used in certain hormone medications may

TEST MAMMOGRAPHY

A mammogram is an X-ray of the breast and is used to screen for signs of breast cancer and to investigate lumps in the breast. Mammograms can show precancerous cells as well as tumors but may not detect every case of breast cancer. For this reason, it is important to examine your breasts regularly. You should have routine mammograms from age 50 because the risk of developing breast cancer increases with age. The procedure is slightly uncomfortable but lasts only a few seconds. Two pictures are taken of each breast.

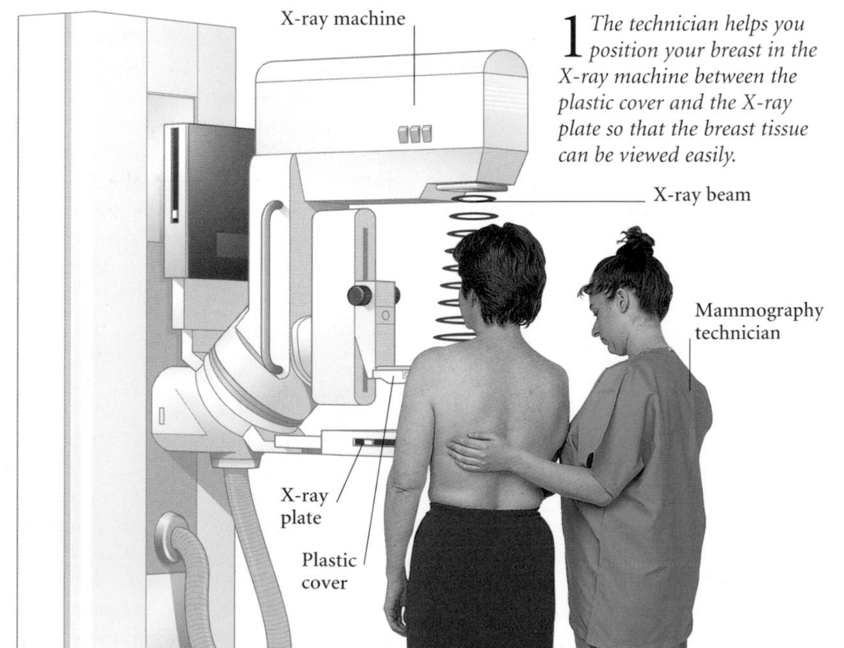
X-ray machine
X-ray beam
Mammography technician
X-ray plate
Plastic cover

1 The technician helps you position your breast in the X-ray machine between the plastic cover and the X-ray plate so that the breast tissue can be viewed easily.

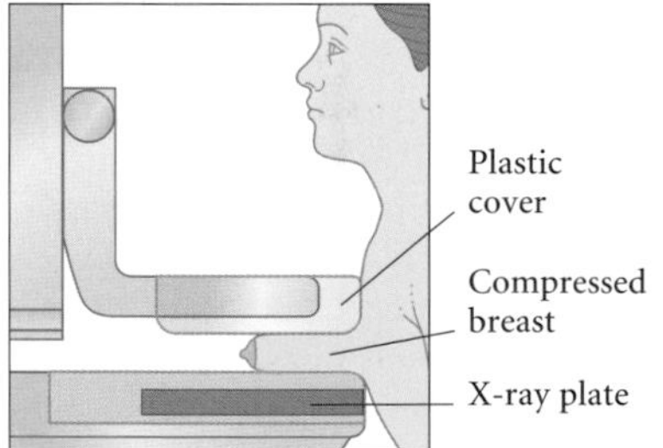
Plastic cover
Compressed breast
X-ray plate

2 The breast is firmly compressed between the plastic cover and the X-ray plate. X-rays pass down through the breast and onto the X-ray plate.

RESULTS

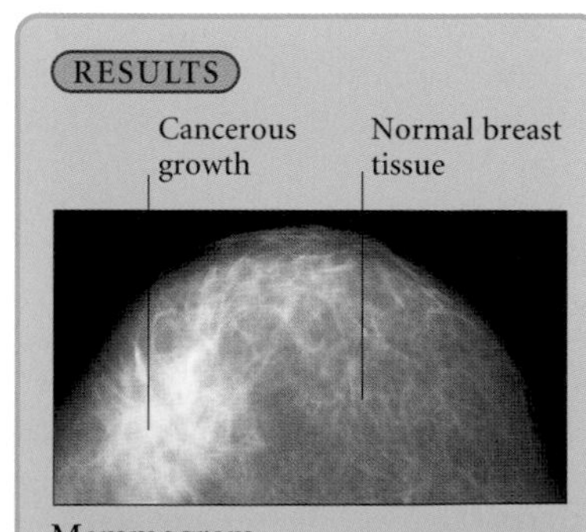
Cancerous growth
Normal breast tissue

Mammogram
In this X-ray image, a tumor is visible within the breast tissue. The tumor is denser than normal breast tissue and appears opaque on the X-ray.

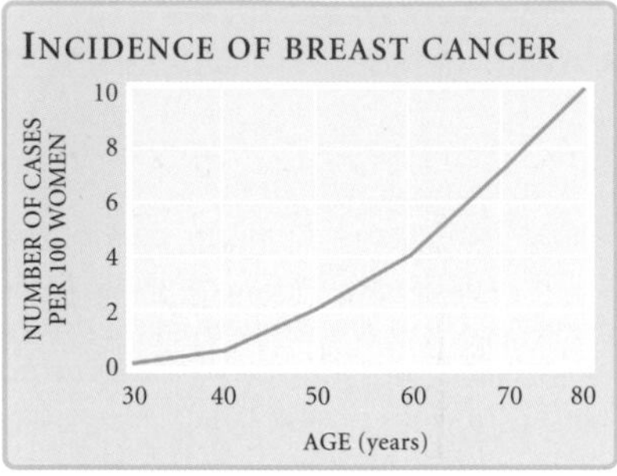
INCIDENCE OF BREAST CANCER
NUMBER OF CASES PER 100 WOMEN
10
8
6
4
2
0
30
40
50
60
70
80
AGE (years)

Increased risk of breast cancer with age
This graph shows that breast cancer is 10 times more common in women aged 80 than it is in those aged 30.

also influence susceptibility to breast cancer. Many cancerous tumors are estrogen-sensitive, and estrogen encourages these tumors to grow once they have formed. The type and duration of postmenopausal hormone replacement therapy (p.937) should be discussed with your doctor.

Up to 1 in 20 cases of breast cancer is linked to an abnormal gene, and several of these genes have now been identified. Breast cancer with a genetic basis most commonly affects women in their 30s and 40s and may also affect men. If you have a close relative who had breast cancer before the age of 45, you may have a breast cancer gene. Genetic testing will enable you to find out if you have the gene (*see* TESTS FOR ABNORMAL GENES, p.239). If close members of your family have had breast cancer after the age of 45, you have only a slightly increased risk of developing the disease. In many cases, there is no family history of cancer of the breast.

The occurrence of noncancerous breast lumps has not been found to increase the risk of breast cancer.

WHAT ARE THE SYMPTOMS?

It is very unusual for breast cancer to produce symptoms in its early stages. When symptoms do occur, they usually affect only one breast and may include:

- A lump in the breast, which is usually painless and may be situated deep in the breast or just under the skin.
- Dimpling of the skin in the area of the lump.
- Inversion or change in direction of the nipple.
- A bloodstained nipple discharge.

In Paget's disease, the only symptom may be a patch of dry, flaky skin on the nipple. Although these symptoms most often result from noncancerous conditions, you should consult your doctor if you notice a change in the appearance or texture of your breasts. If breast cancer is not treated, it can spread to the lymph nodes in the armpit and then to other organs, such as the lungs, liver, or bones, causing additional symptoms.

HOW IS IT DIAGNOSED?

Breast screening programs are available in all Canadian provinces. Professional breast examination, as well as breast self-examination teaching and access to mammography, is provided through these programs or by your doctor. You should check your breasts regularly (*see* BREAST SELF-EXAMINATION, p.755) to look for lumps and other abnormalities. Screening for breast cancer using mammography (p.759) enables cancerous tumors to be detected before symptoms or a lump have appeared.

If you visit your doctor because you have noticed a lump or other abnormality of your breast, he or she will do a breast examination. Mammography or ultrasound scanning (p.250) may be performed. A sample of cells from the lump or the area of abnormality found on the mammogram may be removed using a variety of techniques and then examined for cancerous cells.

If the diagnosis of breast cancer is confirmed, your doctor will arrange for you to undergo further tests to find out whether the cancer is sensitive to estrogen and to see if it has spread. Certain blood tests and ultrasound may indicate whether the cancer has spread to the liver. Chest X-rays (p.490) may be taken to look for evidence of spread of the cancer to the lungs, and a bone scan (*see* RADIONUCLIDE SCANNING, p.251) may be done to find out whether the bones have been affected.

WHAT IS THE TREATMENT?

The extent of the cancerous growth within the breast, whether it has spread to other parts of the body, and whether it is estrogen-sensitive are the main considerations when deciding on the most appropriate course of treatment. Once a full assessment has been made, your doctor will discuss your treatment options with you. Treatment of breast cancer may include surgery, radiation therapy, chemotherapy, hormone therapy, or, most often, a combination of these. Counseling may help you come to terms with your diagnosis, and certain complementary therapies can be used to promote a sense of well-being.

SURGERY Surgery is normally the first stage of breast cancer treatment. There are many possible types of operations used to treat breast cancer (*see* SURGERY FOR BREAST CANCER, opposite page).

If the tumor is small, a lumpectomy may be done, in which the tumor and a small amount of surrounding tissue are removed. A larger tumor is treated by a quadrantectomy, in which about one-quarter of the breast tissue is removed.

In some cases, all of the tissue from the affected breast is surgically removed in a procedure known as a mastectomy. Some women choose to have a mastectomy because they want to make sure that all the tumor has been removed. However, medical studies have shown that this operation is not necessary for most single, small tumors.

During surgery, a number of lymph nodes from the armpit on the same side as the affected breast may be removed. After removal, cells from these lymph nodes are examined to look for signs of cancer. If the lymph nodes are found to be free of cancerous cells, the cancer has probably not spread from the tumor site.

Surgery will affect the appearance of your breast. If one breast looks smaller after surgery, you may want the other breast reduced to the same size. After a mastectomy, some women choose to have a breast reconstruction, which can either be done at the same time as the mastectomy or at a later time.

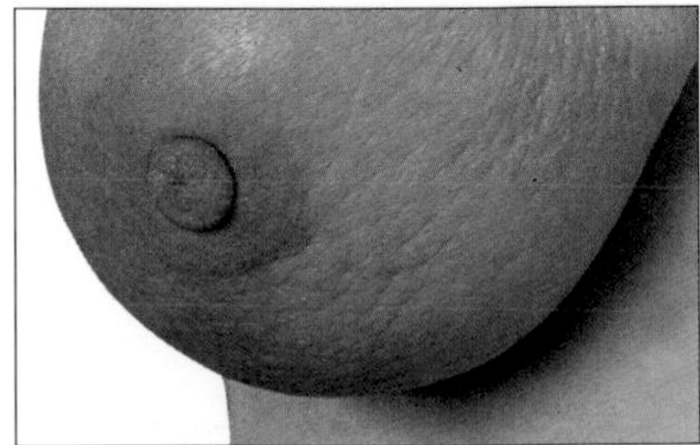

Appearance of the skin in breast cancer
A cancerous growth in this breast has caused the overlying skin to develop the texture of an orange peel

RADIATION THERAPY Treatment with radiation therapy (p.279) is frequently given following surgery, especially if a lumpectomy has been performed, a large tumor has been removed, or if the cancer has spread to the lymph nodes. Treatment usually begins after surgery or upon completion of chemotherapy and is given 5 days a week for about 4–6 weeks. The aim is to destroy any remaining cancer cells after the tumor has been removed, reducing the risk of the cancer recurring or spreading.

DRUG TREATMENTS Estrogen-sensitive tumors usually respond to drug treatments that block the action of estrogen, whereas chemotherapy (p.278) is often effective for all types of tumors.

Tamoxifen (*see* SEX HORMONES AND RELATED DRUGS, p.933) is used to inhibit the effects of estrogen so that the tumor becomes smaller or does not grow as quickly. Tamoxifen is usually taken for up to 5 years following diagnosis. The drug has also been found effective in decreasing the chance of breast cancer development in women who are at increased risk. However, tamoxifen may produce symptoms associated with menopause, and it is therefore most suitable for postmenopausal women. Anastrozole is a new drug that shows promise for treating breast cancer.

Chemotherapy involves using combinations of drugs that destroy rapidly dividing cancerous cells. Treatment is usually given at monthly intervals for about 4–6 months following diagnosis. Some of these drugs also kill normal rapidly dividing cells, such as blood-producing cells in the bone marrow, causing increased risk of infection.

COMPLEMENTARY THERAPIES Women with breast cancer may choose to complement conventional treatments with other therapies, such as relaxation exercises (p.75), homeopathy (p.974), or acupuncture (p.973). Counseling (p.971) may also be helpful. Such therapies should not replace conventional medical treatments.

WHAT IS THE PROGNOSIS?

If breast cancer is diagnosed before it has spread to other body organs, treatment is more likely to be successful and the cancer is less likely to recur after treatment. Combining drug treatment with surgery has been found to improve the chances of long-term survival.

Following treatment, you will have follow-up examinations with your doctor and regular mammograms to check for recurrence of the disease. Cancer may recur close to the site of the original tumor or in a different area. There is an increased risk of developing breast cancer in the other breast. Any recurrence requires further treatment.

About 9 in 10 women who receive treatment for breast cancer in its early stages survive for 10 years or more.

(WWW) ONLINE SITES: p.1028

(TREATMENT) SURGERY FOR BREAST CANCER

The aim of breast cancer surgery is to remove all cancerous tissue. The procedure varies depending on the size and position of the tumor. Two operations are described here: lumpectomy, commonly used to treat small tumors, and mastectomy, sometimes used to treat larger or multiple tumors. Usually, the doctor also removes a number of lymph nodes from the armpit. These are examined to see whether the cancer has spread out of the breast.

LUMPECTOMY

In a lumpectomy, the small area of breast tissue that contains the tumor is removed, along with a small number of lymph nodes from the armpit. The procedure takes place under general anesthesia. After the operation, the basic shape of the breast is essentially unchanged.

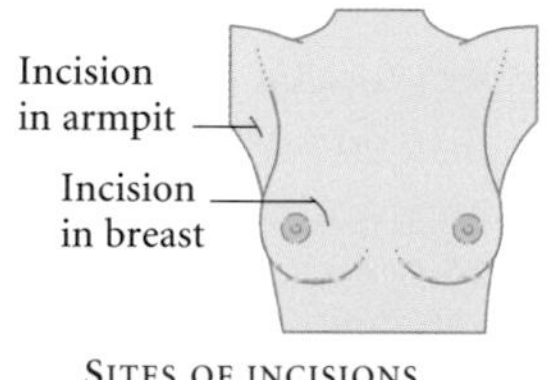
Incision in armpit
Incision in breast

SITES OF INCISIONS

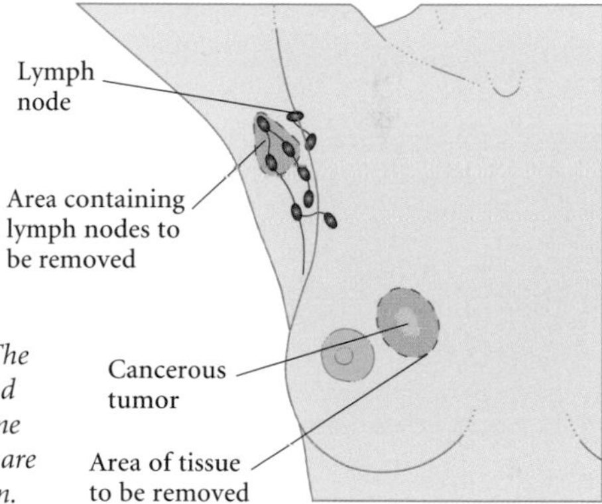
Lymph node
Area containing lymph nodes to be removed
Cancerous tumor
Area of tissue to be removed

During the procedure
An incision is made in the breast. The tumor, some surrounding tissue, and the overlying skin are removed. Some of the lymph nodes from the armpit are removed through a separate incision.

MASTECTOMY

In a mastectomy, the whole breast is removed. This operation is used to treat large or multiple cancerous breast tumors. The procedure takes place under general anesthesia, and you will need to stay in the hospital for several days. You may choose to have plastic surgery to reconstruct your breast at the same time as the mastectomy or at a later time.

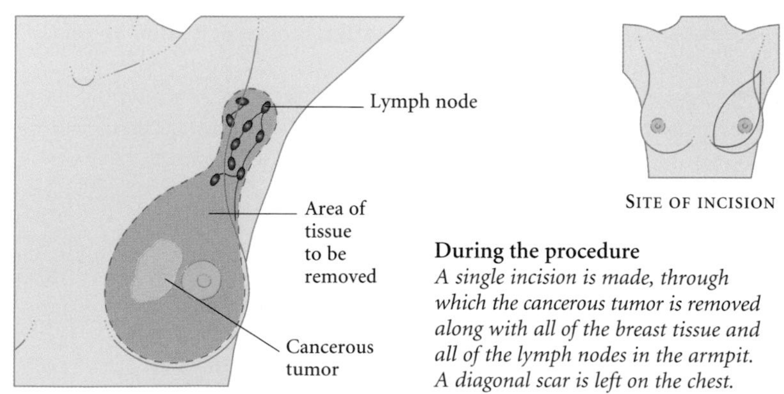
Lymph node
Area of tissue to be removed
Cancerous tumor

SITE OF INCISION

During the procedure
A single incision is made, through which the cancerous tumor is removed along with all of the breast tissue and all of the lymph nodes in the armpit. A diagonal scar is left on the chest.

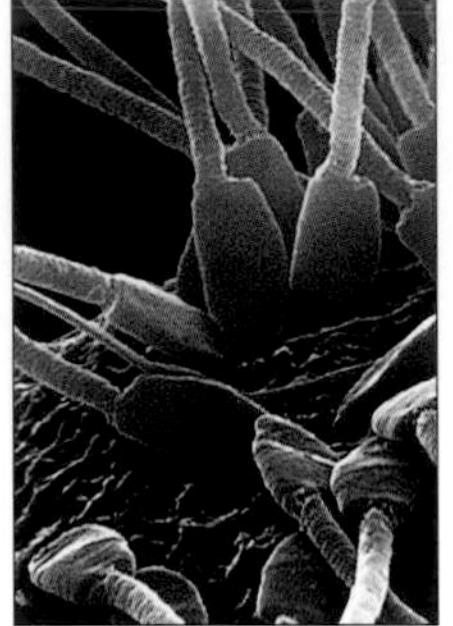

Sperm meet egg
Many sperm attempt to penetrate the surface of an egg to fertilize it.

SEX AND REPRODUCTION

IN BIOLOGICAL TERMS, the urge to reproduce is one of the strongest basic human drives. Producing a new generation to ensure the continuation of the species fulfills one of the primary functions of the human body. In humans, sexual intercourse is not only the means by which males and females reproduce but also an outlet for emotional expression. A sexual relationship can therefore play an important role in creating and maintaining the bond between partners.

All living organisms maintain their populations by reproduction. Most simple organisms, such as bacteria, reproduce asexually, usually by cell division, resulting in offspring that are genetically identical.

In humans, reproduction is sexual, involving the fusion of two cells, a sperm and an egg. Eggs are produced by the ovaries in women, and sperm are produced by the testes in men. These cells are normally brought into contact through sexual intercourse. If a sperm succeeds in fertilizing an egg, DNA (genetic material) from each parent combines to create a unique individual.

Sexual reproduction results in an infinite variety of offspring. The only exceptions are identical twins, which develop when a fertilized egg divides equally to produce two individuals with the same genetic makeup.

HUMAN SEXUALITY

In many animals, the urge to reproduce is largely instinctive, but, in humans, many social and psychological factors also significantly influence sexuality and reproduction. Changing social attitudes toward sexual behavior in the last few decades have enabled both men and women to express their sexual needs more freely to each other.

Sex drive, or libido, varies widely among individuals of both sexes and ranges from a complete lack of sexual interest to very powerful urges. The ease with which sexual arousal can be achieved varies between individuals.

Human beings are probably unique among animals in seeking to engage in sexual intercourse as a pleasurable experience separate from the act of reproduction. Most people have a preference for a sexual partner of the opposite sex (heterosexual). Others have a preference for members of the same sex (homosexual), and some people may experience attraction to members of either sex (bisexual).

FERTILITY

Reproduction depends on an egg being fertilized and embedding in the uterus of the woman. Sexual behavior and fertility affect the likelihood that these events will occur. If a fertile man and a woman at the fertile stage of her menstrual cycle have sex without contraception, a sperm has about a 1 in 5 chance of fertilizing an egg.

With medical advances, the process of reproduction can increasingly be controlled. Couples can choose to prevent conception by using a form of contraception. On the other hand, if a couple is unable to conceive naturally, conception can be assisted in a number of ways.

FUNCTION SEXUAL RESPONSE

Sexual thoughts, the sight of a partner's body, and foreplay all contribute to sexual arousal. Excitement makes breathing quicken, heart rate increase, and blood pressure rise. In a male, the penis becomes firm and erect. In a female, the labia and clitoris swell, the vagina lengthens and becomes lubricated, and the breasts enlarge. The time taken for the development of arousal varies between men and women.

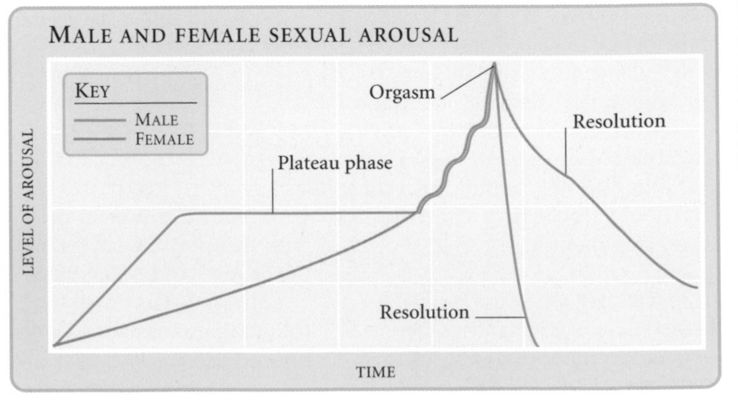
MALE AND FEMALE SEXUAL AROUSAL
KEY
MALE
FEMALE
Orgasm
Resolution
Plateau phase
Resolution
LEVEL OF AROUSAL
TIME

Phases of sexual arousal
In men, sexual excitement rises rapidly to reach a plateau; in women, arousal is more gradual. In both sexes, arousal peaks at orgasm, which may not occur simultaneously, and wanes in the resolution phase.

FUNCTION SEXUAL INTERCOURSE

When a couple is sexually aroused (*see* SEXUAL RESPONSE, opposite page), the man's penis becomes erect and the woman's vagina is lubricated. During sexual intercourse, also called coitus, the penis is inserted into the vagina and the man begins thrusting pelvic movements. At orgasm, which the partners may experience simultaneously or at different times, intense, pleasurable sensations spread throughout the body. The woman's vaginal walls contract rhythmically and the man ejaculates, releasing sperm.

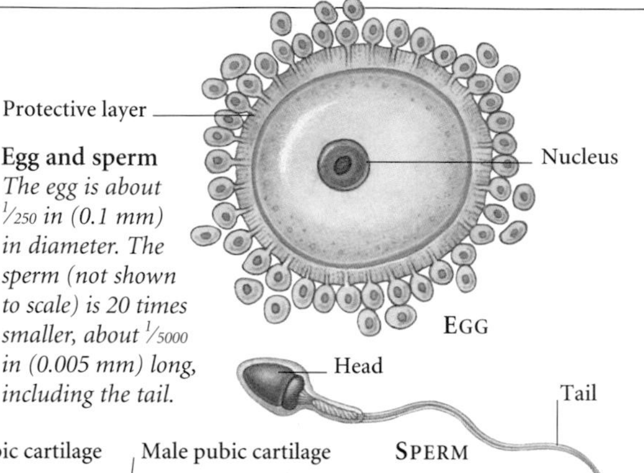
Protective layer
Nucleus
EGG
Head
Tail
SPERM

Egg and sperm
The egg is about 1/250 in (0.1 mm) in diameter. The sperm (not shown to scale) is 20 times smaller, about 1/5000 in (0.005 mm) long, including the tail.

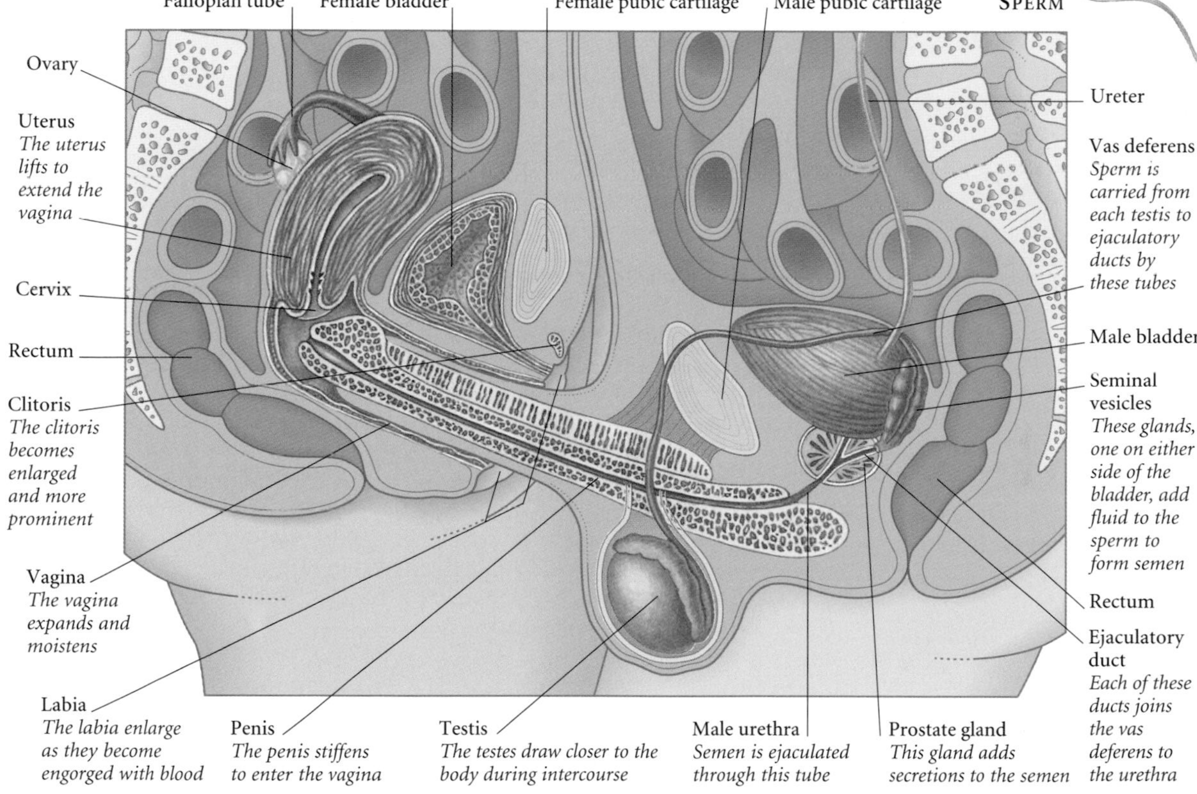
Fallopian tube
Female bladder
Female pubic cartilage
Male pubic cartilage
Ovary
Uterus
The uterus lifts to extend the vagina
Cervix
Rectum
Clitoris
The clitoris becomes enlarged and more prominent
Vagina
The vagina expands and moistens
Labia
The labia enlarge as they become engorged with blood
Penis
The penis stiffens to enter the vagina
Testis
The testes draw closer to the body during intercourse
Male urethra
Semen is ejaculated through this tube
Prostate gland
This gland adds secretions to the semen
Ureter
Vas deferens
Sperm is carried from each testis to ejaculatory ducts by these tubes
Male bladder
Seminal vesicles
These glands, one on either side of the bladder, add fluid to the sperm to form semen
Rectum
Ejaculatory duct
Each of these ducts joins the vas deferens to the urethra

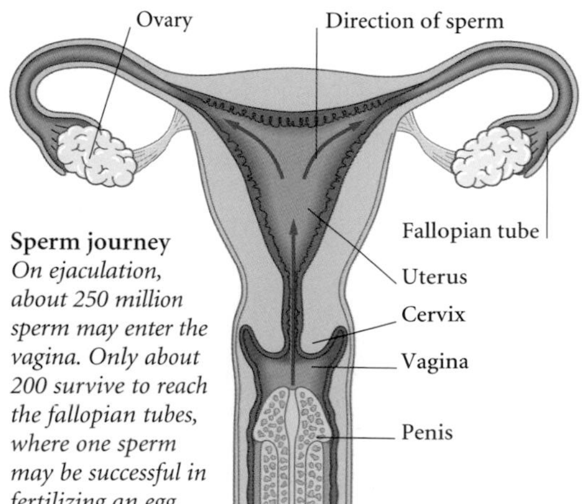
Ovary
Direction of sperm
Fallopian tube
Uterus
Cervix
Vagina
Penis

Sperm journey
On ejaculation, about 250 million sperm may enter the vagina. Only about 200 survive to reach the fallopian tubes, where one sperm may be successful in fertilizing an egg.

FUNCTION FERTILIZATION

Fertilization takes place in one of the fallopian tubes. Many sperm reach the egg and try to penetrate its outer covering. If a sperm succeeds, its head enters the egg and its tail is then shed. A membrane then rapidly forms around the egg, creating a barrier to prevent other sperm from entering. Fertilization occurs when the head of the sperm fuses with the nucleus of the egg.

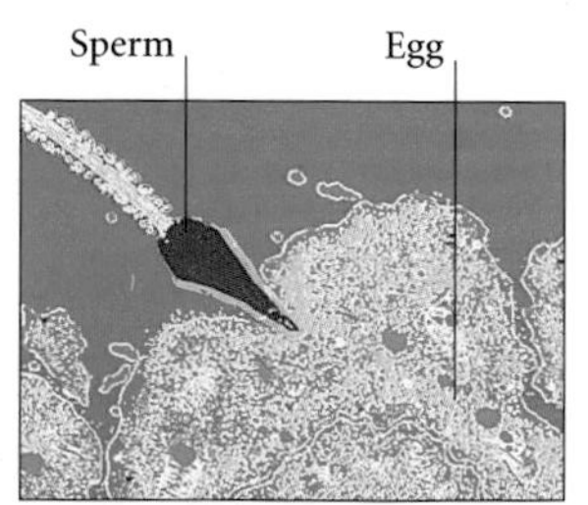
Sperm
Egg

Moment of fertilization
The sperm enters the egg, and fertilization takes place as it fuses with the egg's nucleus.

Sexually Transmitted Diseases

Sexually transmitted diseases (STDs), also called sexually transmitted infections (STIs), are passed primarily from person to person during sexual activity. Many people delay seeking medical help for STDs because of embarrassment, but early diagnosis often prevents complications. Most STDs can be treated with modern drugs.

The diseases covered in this section are arranged according to the type of organism that causes each of them. The first few articles discuss bacterial infections such as gonorrhea. The next article covers the protozoal infection trichomoniasis, and the following articles deal with viral infections, such as genital warts. Finally, parasitic infestation with pubic lice is described.

Early treatment of STDs is essential because some, such as chlamydia, may cause infertility. Sexually active people should have routine tests because some STDs may not cause symptoms and people may be unaware that they have an STD. Syphilis, a progressive and once fatal disease, can now usually be fully cured if it is treated when the initial symptoms appear.

STDs such as genital herpes and genital warts can recur. Genital warts increase the risk of cancer of the cervix; infected women, or those whose partners have warts, need regular cervical screening. Pregnant women with STDs must be carefully monitored because some STDs can pass to the baby through the birth canal or the umblical cord.

HIV infection and AIDS (p.295) and certain forms of hepatitis (pp.644–645) are viral infections that can also be transmitted by sexual contact.

The risk of contracting an STD can be reduced by using safe sex practices, which are covered in detail elsewhere (*see* SEX AND HEALTH, pp.67–70).

Gonorrhea

A bacterial infection that causes genital inflammation and discharge

AGE Can affect sexually active people of any age

GENDER More frequent in males

LIFESTYLE Unprotected sex with multiple partners is a risk factor

GENETICS Not a significant factor

The bacterium *Neisseria gonorrhoeae* (gonococcus), which causes gonorrhea, can be transmitted by various forms of sexual contact, including vaginal, oral, and anal sex. The infection is usually confined to the site where the bacteria enter the body, such as the vagina or the mouth, but can spread through the bloodstream to other parts of the body, such as the joints. A newborn baby who is exposed to the infection in the birth canal during delivery may develop neonatal ophthalmia, a severe eye infection that can sometimes result in blindness (*see* CONGENITAL INFECTIONS, p.817).

Gonorrhea is less widespread now than it has been in the past. Part of the decline may result from the increasing practice of safe sex (p.68). Gonorrhea is now the third most common sexually transmitted disease (STD) after nongonococcal urethritis (opposite page) and genital herpes (p.767).

What are the symptoms?

Gonorrhea often causes no symptoms. If symptoms occur, they usually appear 1–14 days after sex with an infected person. In men, they may include:

- Discharge of pus from the penis.
- Pain on urinating.

Without treatment, the symptoms may start to disappear after about 2 weeks, but the person remains infectious.

Symptoms are present in about half of all infected women. They may include:

- Yellowish green discharge of pus from the vagina.
- Pain on urinating.
- Lower abdominal pain.
- Irregular vaginal bleeding.

In both sexes, if gonorrhea occurs as a result of anal intercourse, the anus and the rectum may become inflamed (*see* PROCTITIS, p.667). If the infection has been transmitted during oral sex, the first symptom may be a sore throat.

Are there complications?

In men, gonorrhea may lead to inflammation of the testes and epididymides (the tubes that carry sperm from the testes), a condition called epididymo-orchitis (p.718). Gonorrhea may also result in inflammation of the prostate gland (*see* PROSTATITIS, p.724) or of the bladder (*see* CYSTITIS, p.709). Rarely, gonorrhea in men results in urethral stricture (p.714), in which scarring and blockage of the urethra (the tube from the bladder to the outside of the body) causes difficulty urinating.

In women, the infection may spread up from the vagina into the fallopian tubes, resulting in pelvic inflammatory disease (p.741). Left untreated, this disorder can make women infertile (*see* FEMALE INFERTILITY, p.775).

Occasionally, gonorrhea may spread in the bloodstream, causing fever, rash, and, rarely, infection of the joints (*see* SEPTIC ARTHRITIS, p.381).

What might be done?

If you suspect that you or your partner has gonorrhea, consult your doctor or go to a clinic specializing in STDs. To confirm the diagnosis, a swab is taken from areas likely to be infected and tested for the bacteria. You will probably

Bacterium

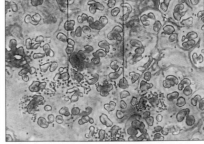

Vaginal cell

Cells infected by gonorrhea bacteria
The cells in this image are surrounded by clusters of Neisseria gonorrhoeae*, the bacterium that causes gonorrhea.*

also be tested for other STDs, such as chlamydial cervicitis (right). Gonorrhea is treated with antibiotics (p.885) and usually clears up within 3–4 days. If bacteria have spread throughout the body, treatment with intravenous antibiotics in the hospital is necessary. All sexual partners should be tested and treated even if they have no symptoms.

Can it be prevented?

You can take steps to reduce your risk of contracting gonorrhea (*see* PREVENTING STDs, right). If you are infected, avoid sex until you and your partner have finished treatment and your doctor says that you are free of infection.

(WWW) ONLINE SITES: p.1036

Nongonococcal urethritis

Inflammation of the urethra in men that may be caused by several different organisms

 AGE Can affect sexually active males of any age

 GENDER Affects males only

 LIFESTYLE Unprotected sex with multiple partners is a risk factor

 GENETICS Not a significant factor

Inflammation of the male urethra (the tube leading from the bladder to the tip of the penis) that is not due to the bacterium that causes gonorrhea (opposite page) is known as nongonococcal urethritis (NGU). Worldwide, NGU is one of the most common sexually transmitted diseases (STDs) in men.

What are the causes?

Nearly half of all cases of NGU are due to the bacterium *Chlamydia trachomatis.* However, NGU can also be caused by organisms such as the bacterium *Ureaplasma urealyticum;* the protozoan *Trichomonas vaginalis,* which can also cause trichomoniasis (p.767); and the fungus *Candida albicans,* which can also cause candidiasis (p.309). The viruses that cause genital warts (p.768) and genital herpes (p.767) can also result in NGU if they affect the urethra. However, in one-quarter of all cases no cause for the disorder is found.

What are the symptoms?

About 1–6 weeks after you have become infected with NGU, the following group of symptoms may develop:

- Pain on urinating, especially the first time in the morning.
- Discharge from the penis.
- Redness and soreness at the opening of the urethra.

If you have any of these symptoms, you should consult your doctor or go to a clinic specializing in STDs.

Are there complications?

Various complications may result from NGU, including inflammation of the prostate gland (*see* PROSTATITIS, p.724), which causes pain around the rectum and anus, in the genitals, and on ejaculation. Occasionally, the testes and the epididymides (the tubes carrying sperm from the testes) may become inflamed (*see* EPIDIDYMO-ORCHITIS, p.718). If the bacteria spread in the bloodstream, inflammation of the joints may occur (*see* REACTIVE ARTHRITIS, p.379).

What might be done?

Your doctor will take a swab from your urethra, together with a urine sample, to check for the presence of an infectious organism that could cause NGU. Tests for other STDs will probably be carried out at the same time.

Depending on the organism found, your doctor may then prescribe antibiotics (p.885), antifungal drugs (p.889), or antiviral drugs (p.886). With treatment, NGU usually clears up in about a week; however, it sometimes returns, and treatment may need to be repeated. You can also be reinfected if your sexual partner has the disease. Sexual partners must be tested and treated even if they have no symptoms because in women the infection causes chlamydial cervicitis (right), which can lead to infertility (*see* FEMALE INFERTILITY, p.775).

Can it be prevented?

The risk of contracting NGU can be reduced by following safe sex measures (*see* PREVENTING STDs, right). To avoid spreading the infection, it is important that you do not have sexual contact until you and your partner have finished your treatment and your doctor confirms that you are no longer infected.

(WWW) ONLINE SITES: p.1036

SELF-HELP

Preventing STDs

There are several safe sex measures that you can follow to reduce the risk of acquiring an STD:

- Avoid sex with multiple partners.
- For sexual intercourse of any kind, you should use a condom in conjunction with a spermicide containing nonoxynol 9, which may have an antiviral effect.
- If you use lubricants, use water-based types; oil-based lubricants damage the rubber in condoms.
- Avoid sexual activity that may split a condom or sex that causes breaks in the skin or the tissues of the vagina or anus.

If you suspect that you or your partner has an STD, you should both consult a doctor or an STD clinic. Complete the course of treatment and avoid sexual contact until your doctor confirms that you are free of infection (*see* SEX AND HEALTH, pp.67–70).

Chlamydial cervicitis

An infection of the genital tract in women that is often symptomless

 AGE Can affect sexually active females of any age

 GENDER Affects females only

 LIFESTYLE Unprotected sex with multiple partners is a risk factor

 GENETICS Not a significant factor

The most common sexually transmitted disease (STD) in Canada is infection of the genital tract with the bacterium *Chlamydia trachomatis.* In women, the infection is called chlamydial cervicitis. In men, it is the most common cause of nongonococcal urethritis (left). A baby exposed to infection in the birth canal is at risk of acquiring serious eye infections (*see* CONGENITAL INFECTIONS, p.817).

What are the symptoms?

Many women remain symptom-free. If symptoms do occur, they may include:

- Abnormal vaginal discharge.
- Frequent urge to urinate.

- Pain in the lower abdomen.
- Pain on deep penetration during sex.

Left untreated, chlamydial cervicitis can sometimes lead to pelvic inflammatory disease (p.741), which is a major cause of infertility in women. If the infection enters the bloodstream, the disorder may also lead to a form of arthritis (*see* REACTIVE ARTHRITIS, p.379).

WHAT MIGHT BE DONE?

Chlamydial cervicitis may not be suspected until inflammation shows up in a Pap test (p.749) or a partner is tested for an STD. The disorder may also first be suspected during investigations for infertility, which is a complication of untreated chlamydial infection. Screening is recommended for sexually active women at high risk, including those who have been treated previously for an STD or who have multiple partners.

If you think that you or your partner has a chlamydial infection you should consult your doctor or go to a clinic that specializes in STDs. In women, diagnosis is confirmed by taking a swab from the cervix. Tests for other STDs may be performed at the same time.

Chlamydial cervicitis is treated with antibiotics (p.885). In a few cases, the infection recurs, and you may need to take a further course of drugs. Sexual partners should be tested even if free of symptoms and treated if necessary.

CAN IT BE PREVENTED?

The risk of contracting chlamydial cervicitis can be reduced by practicing safe sex (*see* PREVENTING STDs, p.765). You and your partner should not have sex until you have finished the antibiotics.

(WWW) ONLINE SITES: p.1036

Normal cell

Infected cell

Bacteria in membrane

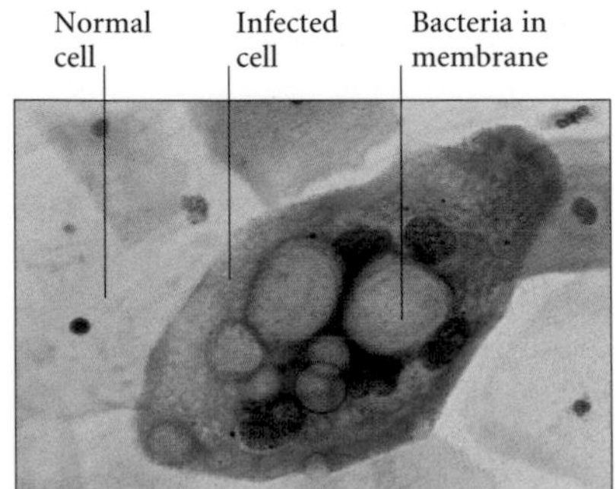

Cervical cell infected by chlamydia

The magnified view of a cervical specimen shows an infected cell in which chlamydia bacteria are enclosed within a membrane.

Syphilis

A bacterial infection initially affecting the genitals that, left untreated, can damage other parts of the body years later

AGE Can affect sexually active people of any age

LIFESTYLE Unprotected sex with multiple partners is a risk factor

GENDER GENETICS Not significant factors

Syphilis is caused by the bacterium *Treponema pallidum.* This organism enters the body through the mucous membranes of the genital area or the skin. Left untreated, the disease may be fatal.

Although it was once widespread throughout the world, syphilis became less common with the introduction of the antibiotic penicillin in the 1940s. Today, this sexually transmitted disease rarely progresses as far as the tertiary (third) stage. However, since the 1980s, there has been a resurgence of syphilis infection in Canada.

A pregnant woman with syphilis can pass the disease to the fetus, causing it to develop congenital syphilis (*see* CONGENITAL INFECTIONS, p.817). However, screening during pregnancy has now made congenital syphilis very rare.

WHAT ARE THE SYMPTOMS?

The symptoms of syphilis develop in three stages. The primary and secondary stages are infectious for up to 2 years. However, the tertiary stage of syphilis is not infectious.

PRIMARY STAGE Within 1–12 weeks after contact with an infected person, the following symptoms may develop:

- Hard, painless, and highly infectious sore known as a chancre. The chancre usually appears on the penis or vulva but may occur in the mouth or rectum as a result of oral or anal sex.
- Painless enlargement of the lymph nodes in the groin or neck.

The chancre may go unnoticed and disappears after 1–6 weeks.

SECONDARY STAGE About 6–24 weeks after the appearance of the chancre, the following symptoms develop:

- Nonitchy, contagious rash over the whole body, including the palms of the hands and soles of the feet.

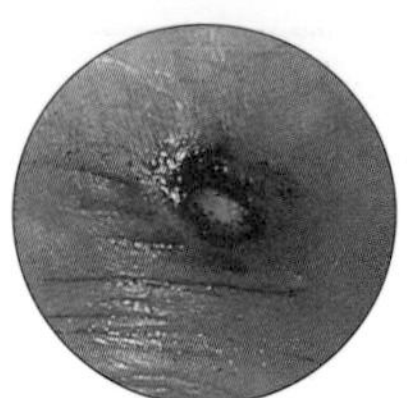

Chancre on penis

In primary stage syphilis, a hard, painless sore, called a chancre, appears. It usually develops on the genitals.

- Thickened, gray or pink, moist, wart-like patches in the skin folds of the genitals and anus.
- In rare cases, patchy hair loss.
- Fever and fatigue.
- Headaches and muscle pain.

After 4–12 weeks, these symptoms disappear, and the disease then enters a symptomless stage of indefinite length.

TERTIARY STAGE Some people remain without further symptoms for the rest of their lives. However, if treatment is not given, 1 in 3 people develops tertiary syphilis 10–20 years after the initial infection. The symptoms vary and may include personality changes; mental illness; meningitis (p.527); tabes dorsalis (destruction of the spinal cord), which leads to weakness and difficulty walking; and aortic aneurysm (p.430).

WHAT MIGHT BE DONE?

If you think you or your partner has syphilis, consult your doctor or go to a clinic specializing in STDs. In the primary stage, your doctor may take a swab of the chancre for microscopic examination. Diagnosis of both primary and secondary syphilis may be confirmed by a blood test. At the same time you will probably be tested for other STDs. If tertiary syphilis is suspected, a lumbar puncture (p.527) may be done to look for antibodies to the bacterium in the cerebrospinal fluid.

Syphilis is treated with injections of antibiotics (p.885). In the primary or secondary stages, treatment usually results in complete recovery. Damage due to tertiary syphilis may be permanent.

CAN IT BE PREVENTED?

The risk of contracting syphilis can be reduced by practicing safe sex (*see* PREVENTING STDs, p.765). If you have the disease, or your partner has it, avoid sexual contact until you have both finished your treatment and your doctor confirms that you are free of infection.

(WWW) ONLINE SITES: p.1036

Trichomoniasis

A genital tract infection that is often symptomless but may cause a discharge

 AGE Can affect sexually active people of any age

 LIFESTYLE Unprotected sex with multiple partners is a risk factor

 GENDER GENETICS Not significant factors

Trichomoniasis is an infection of the genital area caused by the protozoan *Trichomonas vaginalis.* In women, the infection may cause vulvovaginitis (p.752), inflammation in and around the vagina, which may lead to cystitis (p.709), an inflammation of the bladder lining. In men, the infection sometimes causes mild inflammation of the urethra (the tube from the bladder to the outside of the body) and occasionally may result in nongonococcal urethritis (p.765). In most cases, trichomoniasis is transmitted through sexual intercourse.

WHAT ARE THE SYMPTOMS?

Some women have no symptoms, and the infection is often detected only on a routine Pap test (p.749). If symptoms of trichomoniasis do occur, they may include the following:

- Profuse, yellow, frothy, and offensive-smelling discharge from the vagina.
- Painful inflammation of the vagina.
- Itching and soreness of the vulva (the skin around the vagina).
- Burning sensation on urinating.
- Discomfort during intercourse.

Men, too, may not have symptoms, but if present, they may include:

- Discomfort on urinating.
- Discharge from the penis.

If you or your partner develop any of these symptoms, consult your doctor or go to a clinic specializing in STDs.

WHAT MIGHT BE DONE?

Swabs will be taken from infected areas and tested for the presence of the protozoan. You will probably also be tested for other STDs at the same time.

If you have trichomoniasis, antibiotics (p.885) will be prescribed by your doctor. Sexual partners and babies born to infected mothers should also be tested even if they have no symptoms and should be treated if necessary.

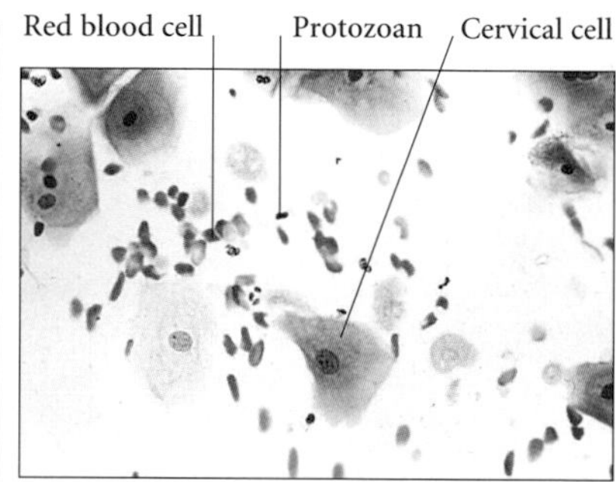
Red blood cell
Protozoan
Cervical cell

Trichomoniasis protozoan
This magnified image of cells from the cervix shows the presence of Trichomonas vaginalis, *the protozoan responsible for causing trichomoniasis.*

CAN IT BE PREVENTED?

You can reduce your own risk of contracting trichomoniasis by practicing safe sex (*see* PREVENTING STDs, p.765). If you or your partner becomes infected, you should avoid spreading the infection further by abstaining from sexual contact until you have both finished your course of drug treatment and your doctor has confirmed that the infection has completely cleared.

(WWW) ONLINE SITES: p.1036

Genital herpes

A viral infection that causes painful recurring blisters on and around the genitals

 AGE Can affect sexually active people of any age

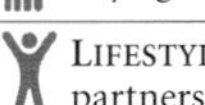 LIFESTYLE Unprotected sex with multiple partners is a risk factor

 GENDER GENETICS Not significant factors

Genital herpes is a common sexually transmitted disease (STD). The disease is caused by the herpes simplex virus, of which there are two forms: type 1 (HSV-1) and type 2 (HSV-2). Genital herpes is usually due to type 2; type 1 mainly causes blisters around the mouth (*see* COLD SORE, p.354). However, oral sex with a person who has cold sores can lead to HSV-1 being transmitted from the mouth to the genitals and can produce genital herpes.

The disease tends to recur, especially in the first few years after the initial attack. In women, it tends to occur 5–12 days before a menstrual period and tends to clear up in 5–10 days. The symptoms are generally milder in following attacks, but the condition is still infectious. The herpes simplex virus can cause serious illness in a baby who is exposed to it during birth (*see* CONGENITAL INFECTIONS, p.817).

WHAT ARE THE SYMPTOMS?

The first attack of genital herpes is usually the most severe and occurs within 5 days of contact with an infected person. The symptoms may include:

- Painful, fluid-filled blisters on the genitals. Blisters may occur on the thighs and buttocks and, rarely, in the mouth or rectum due to oral or anal sex.
- Tingling, burning, soreness, and redness of the affected area.
- Enlarged and painful lymph nodes in the groin.
- Pain on urinating.
- Headache, fever, and muscle aches.
- In women, vaginal discharge.

After 10–21 days the symptoms usually disappear, but further attacks are likely to occur, often affecting the same areas.

WHAT MIGHT BE DONE?

If you suspect genital herpes in yourself or your partner, consult your doctor or go to a clinic specializing in STDs. The doctor will probably be able to make a diagnosis from your symptoms and a physical examination. He or she may take swabs of the blisters to test for the virus. You may also be tested for other STDs. Partners should be tested for infection even if they have no symptoms.

Genital herpes cannot be cured. Your doctor may prescribe acyclovir or another antiviral drug (p.886) during an attack. If acyclovir is taken early, it usually reduces the severity of symptoms. Regular preventive treatment can decrease the number of attacks.

WHAT IS THE PROGNOSIS?

Once you have genital herpes, the virus remains in your body and the infection may flare up at any time. About 2 in 10 infected people have only one attack.

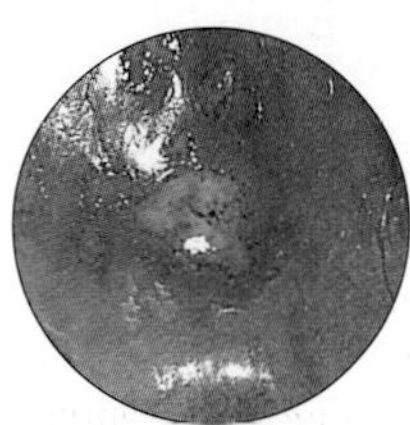

Genital blisters
The fluid-filled blisters shown in this close-up of a penis are caused by the genital herpes virus.

Others have a few attacks a year for several years. In most people, symptoms are less severe in subsequent attacks and the time between attacks increases.

CAN IT BE PREVENTED?

The risk of contracting genital herpes can be reduced by practicing safe sex (*see* PREVENTING STDs, p.765). However, a condom may not always provide total protection since areas apart from the genitals may be infected, and the virus can be passed on even if no blisters are present. If you have an attack, avoid sex until the symptoms have gone.

If a pregnant woman has an attack of genital herpes just before delivery, a cesarean section may be done so that the infection does not pass to the baby. Infected women may also have been exposed to HPV, which may be associated with cancer of the cervix (p.750).

(WWW) ONLINE SITES: p.1036

Genital warts

Fleshy, painless growths on and around the genitals caused by a virus

 AGE Can affect sexually active people of any age

 LIFESTYLE Unprotected sex with multiple partners is a risk factor

 GENDER GENETICS Not significant factors

Genital warts are skin growths that are caused by the human papillomavirus (HPV). The condition is reported more frequently by men than by women, probably because warts are more visible on the penis. However, an infected person can transmit the virus to sexual partners even if he or she has no symptoms. Women are at greater risk than men if their infection is unnoticed because HPV is associated with cancer of the cervix (p.750).

The warts appear from a few weeks to as long as 20 months after infection. They are soft with a rough surface and are usually painless. Genital warts enlarge rapidly, and in some instances the growths cluster together in one area.

In men, warts may occur on the shaft of the penis or less commonly on the foreskin, the glans (head of the penis), and around the anus. In women, the growths may appear on the vulva (the external part of the female genitals), inside the vagina, on the cervix, and around the anus. The warts may also occur in the rectum as a result of infection through anal intercourse, and in the mouth following oral sex. If a pregnant woman has genital warts, there is a risk that the infection will be transmitted to her baby during delivery (*see* CONGENITAL INFECTIONS, p.817), causing problems for the newborn baby.

WHAT MIGHT BE DONE?

If you or your partner has genital warts, or if you have been exposed to infection, you should consult your doctor or go to a clinic that specializes in STDs. Diagnosis of genital warts is usually based on a physical examination. Tests may also be performed to check for other STDs.

Genital warts may be treated in different ways. You may be prescribed the liquid chemicals imiquimod, podophyllin, or condylox, which are used on external genital areas and are applied directly to the warts. The treatment is repeated until the warts have gone. Other methods include cryotherapy, in which warts are removed by freezing; electrocautery, which burns them off; laser treatment; surgical removal; or injecting each wart with interferon drugs (p.907), proteins that stimulate the body's immunity to the virus. Despite treatment, HPV infection cannot be cured, and warts often recur.

In women, the presence of HPV increases the risk of developing cancer of the cervix. A woman who has genital warts, or whose partner has the infection, should have a Pap test (p.749) yearly to look for abnormal cells.

CAN IT BE PREVENTED?

You can reduce your risk of contracting genital warts by practicing safe sex (*see* PREVENTING STDs, p.765). People are often advised to avoid sexual contact when warts are visible. However, since HPV infection cannot be cured and because it may be transmitted even if a person has no warts, the risk of infecting sexual partners remains.

Condoms may not give complete protection from the disease since they may not cover all affected areas. Researchers are developing preventative measures such as vaccines.

(WWW) ONLINE SITES: p.1036

Pubic lice

Infestation of pubic hair by a type of small wingless insect, causing irritation

 AGE Can affect sexually active people of any age

 LIFESTYLE Sex with multiple partners is a risk factor

 GENDER GENETICS Not significant factors

Pubic lice, often called "crabs," are usually spread by sexual contact. The lice live in pubic hair, where they feed on blood and lay eggs called nits. About 3 million cases of infestation with pubic lice are treated in the US each year.

The most common symptom is itching in the pubic area and around the anus, especially at night. Some people have no symptoms and only realize that they are infested when they see the nits or the tiny insects. Normal washing does not remove the nits since they are firmly stuck to the hair.

If you think that you or your partner has pubic lice, you should consult your doctor or go to a clinic specializing in sexually transmitted diseases (STDs).

WHAT MIGHT BE DONE?

Your doctor will probably prescribe a preparation containing lindane or permethrin to apply to affected areas (*see* PREPARATIONS FOR SKIN INFECTIONS AND INFESTATIONS, p.892). A second application is needed about 10 days after the first to destroy freshly hatched lice.

To prevent the spread of lice, sexual partners should be checked and treated if necessary. The clothing and sheets used by an infested person should be machine-washed in hot water.

(WWW) ONLINE SITES: p.1036

Pubic louse
This highly magnified image shows a pubic louse attached to a human hair. Lice are about 1/12 in (2 mm) in width.

SEXUAL PROBLEMS

Most men and women experience a sexual problem at some time in their lives. Some problems, such as decreased sex drive and pain during intercourse, may be experienced by either partner, while others, such as erectile dysfunction (impotence) and vaginismus, are specific to men or women. Sexual problems have many causes, such as physical and psychological disorders and some drug treatments.

The most common sexual problem that affects both sexes is decreased sex drive. This is often a natural response to changing hormone levels, although there are many other causes. Other common problems include failure of orgasm in women, and, in men, erectile dysfunction (impotence) and premature ejaculation. A sexual problem may begin with an underlying physical cause, but anxiety about sexual performance can often develop and compound the original problem. Sometimes, a sexual problem experienced by one partner may be caused by the response or the behavior of the other partner. For these reasons, doctors and sex therapists generally prefer to involve both partners in discussions and therapy sessions to promote mutual understanding and appreciation. This is particularly important when the recommended treatment involves exercises to be practiced at home by both partners.

A variety of treatments is currently available, and there are many doctors and therapists who specialize in treating sexual problems. Sources of specialized help include urologists, gynecologists, and sex therapists. For some problems, assistance from a psychiatrist or psychologist may be helpful. Treatments for sexual problems have a high success rate.

Decreased sex drive

A temporary or long-term reduction of interest in sex

 AGE More common with increasing age

 GENETICS In rare cases, due to an extra chromosome

 LIFESTYLE Physical and mental stress and the use of certain drugs may be risk factors

 GENDER Not a significant factor

Someone whose sex drive has decreased loses interest in sex, does not fantasize about sex, and feels little or no pleasure during sexual activity. It is common for a person to experience a temporary loss of sex drive, or libido, at some point in his or her life. However, a long-term decrease in a person's sex drive may become a problem if it causes distress either to the individual concerned or to his or her sexual partner.

Sex drive is partly controlled by sex hormones, which decrease gradually as you grow older. As a result, sex drive also declines naturally with age. However, men and women have different patterns of sexual desire. Sex drive is most intense in young men in their teens and 20s, whereas most women reach their sexual peak later in life, often not until their 30s. Different people have different levels of sex drive and activity. For this reason, a decrease in your sex drive should be judged only in comparison with your own normal sex drive and activity, not in comparison with the claims of other people.

WHAT ARE THE CAUSES?

Many women experience a temporary decline in sex drive after childbirth or gynecological surgery, and some women are affected during pregnancy. Menopausal women may also be affected, partly because of fluctuations in the levels of sex hormones and partly due to emotional responses to menopause. Many women experience regular fluctuations in sexual desire that reflect the normal changes in hormone levels occurring during the menstrual cycle.

A number of psychological problems may trigger a loss of interest in sex in either men or women. Such problems may include anxiety disorders (p.551), depression (p.554), stress (p.74), and general problems with the relationship.

A reduction in sex drive may be a side effect of certain drugs, including certain antidepressant drugs (p.916); and certain antihypertensive drugs (p.897), such as beta blockers (p.898). Heavy drinking of alcohol may also decrease sex drive.

Other possible causes include illness and fatigue as well as a few rare genetic disorders, such as Klinefelter syndrome (p.822), which affects only males and results in low levels of sex hormones.

WHAT CAN I DO?

You may be able to identify the reason for your loss of sex drive. If you suspect that stress or heavy drinking may be the cause, try changing your lifestyle. If you think that the cause is an underlying problem in your relationship, it may help to discuss the issue with your partner (*see* COMMUNICATING YOUR SEXUAL NEEDS, p.770). If you cannot improve the situation, consult your doctor.

WHAT MIGHT THE DOCTOR DO?

Your doctor may discuss your lifestyle and relationship with you to determine which factors are contributing to the problem. If your doctor suspects that there is a physical condition underlying your decreased sex drive, he or she may examine you and arrange for tests to look for a disorder. For example, blood tests may be useful in men to check for abnormally low hormone levels. If your decreased sex drive is due to the side effects of a particular drug, your doctor may give you a different medication. The doctor may also suggest changes in your lifestyle, such as reducing stress or cutting down on alcohol intake. If the cause seems to be psychological, your doctor may recommend that you and your partner have sex therapy (p.773).

Most people who consult a doctor about a decrease in their sex drive can be treated successfully.

(WWW) ONLINE SITES: p.1034, p.1036, p.1037

Failure of orgasm

Inability to reach the peak of sexual excitement

 AGE Can affect sexually active people of any age

 GENDER Common in females; rare in males

 LIFESTYLE Stress, alcohol, and the use of certain drugs are risk factors

 GENETICS Not a significant factor

Failure to reach orgasm, the peak of sexual excitement, is called anorgasmia. The causes are usually psychological. Anorgasmia is the most frequently reported sexual problem in women and affects up to half of all women at some time in their lives. Fewer than 1 in 10 men report failure to reach orgasm.

What are the causes?

Psychological factors that can inhibit orgasm include anxiety about sexual performance, fear of pregnancy, a previous unpleasant sexual experience, and sexual inhibitions as a result of a strict upbringing regarding sex or physical or mental abuse during childhood.

Poor sexual technique on the part of one or both partners may lead to failure of orgasm. Most often, insufficient time is allowed for the woman to become fully aroused. Poor sexual technique is common between new partners who know little about each other's sexual responses. The problem may also be due to inexperience or a lack of communication between partners.

Some chronic disorders that result in damage to nerves, including diabetes mellitus (p.687), may lead to failure of orgasm. Certain drugs, such as particular antidepressants (p.916) and some antihypertensive drugs (p.897), including beta blockers (p.898), can cause a decreased sex drive (p.769) that may result in anorgasmia. Heavy drinking may also cause failure of orgasm.

What might be done?

If you or your partner repeatedly fail to reach orgasm, it is important to discuss the matter together (*see* COMMUNICATING YOUR SEXUAL NEEDS, right). Your doctor should be consulted if the situation does not improve. If the problem is psychological or due to poor sexual technique, you will probably be referred to a sex therapist (*see* SEX THERAPY, p.773). If the problem is caused by drug treatment, the doctor may change your medication. However, if you have nerve damage, the problem is usually permanent and cannot be treated.

Sex therapy is effective in most cases, but, if you or your partner have deep-rooted problems such as difficulties due to abuse in childhood, some form of psychological therapy (pp.968–971) may be needed. Failure of orgasm can be treated successfully in many people.

(WWW) ONLINE SITES: p.1034, p.1036, p.1037

Erectile dysfunction

Inability to achieve or sustain an erection, also known as impotence

 AGE More common with increasing age

 LIFESTYLE Smoking, alcohol, stress, and the use of certain drugs are risk factors

 GENETICS Not a significant factor

Most men experience temporary difficulty in achieving or maintaining an erection at some time in their lives. Such occasional erectile dysfunction is normal. Persistent, long-term difficulty achieving an erection may indicate a physical cause and should prompt you to seek medical advice. Erectile dysfunction over a long period often results in distress for both the individual and his partner. Despite this, only 1 in 10 men with the condition seeks medical advice.

What are the causes?

Erectile dysfunction can be due to a physical or a psychological disorder and in many cases may be a combination of the two. Anxiety disorders (p.551) and depression (p.554) can lead to the condition, and may be a reflection of stress in a man's life, a relationship difficulty, or fear of sexual failure. It may occur as a side effect of drugs, including antidepressants (p.916) and antihypertensives (p.897). The risk of erectile dysfunction can be increased by factors such as fatigue, heavy drinking, and smoking.

The condition is more common in middle-aged and elderly men and often has a physical cause. The most common cause is a vascular disease, such as atherosclerosis (p.402), that reduces the blood supply to the penis. It can also result if the nerves supplying the penis are damaged due to surgery, such as operations on the prostate gland (*see* PARTIAL PROSTATECTOMY, p.725, and RADICAL PROSTATECTOMY, p.727), or to chronic conditions such as multiple sclerosis (p.541) or diabetes mellitus (p.687). Rarely, erectile dysfunction is due to low levels of the sex hormone testosterone.

Episodes of sudden and intermittent erectile dysfunction usually have psychological causes. Erectile dysfunction that develops gradually and is persistent or progressive is primarily due to physical causes.

What might be done?

If you have persistent problems with erectile dysfunction, you should consult your doctor. He or she will ask if you have full morning erections. If you do, it is more likely that the condition has a psychological cause. Your doctor will also ask about your lifestyle and about any medication that you use to see if there are factors contributing to your problem that can be altered.

Your doctor may give you a physical examination. He or she may also take a

> SELF-HELP
>
> **COMMUNICATING YOUR SEXUAL NEEDS**
>
> Many people feel that the sexual side of their relationship could be better. The key to improving your sex life is communication with your partner and mutual understanding. Bear the following points in mind when you discuss your problems with your partner:
>
> - Think carefully about your words and timing to avoid sounding hostile or critical.
> - Talk about the positive aspects of your sex life.
> - Suggest things that you would like to do or would like to spend more time on; watch your partner's reaction carefully.
> - Keep your comments open and your suggestions positive.
> - Listen to what your partner says.
> - Create an action plan together and include the points that you would both like to work on.

sample of blood to check for diabetes mellitus and to measure your level of testosterone. In addition, Doppler ultrasound scanning (p.432) may be done to assess the blood flow to your penis.

If the blood vessels to the penis are narrowed due to atherosclerosis, surgery may restore normal blood flow and allow you to achieve an erection. Your doctor may change your medication if drug treatment is a likely cause. If you have diabetes, your doctor should make sure that it is well controlled to prevent further nerve damage.

If your doctor suspects that an aspect of your lifestyle is causing your erectile dysfunction, he or she may suggest changes that you can make, such as reducing stress or your alcohol intake.

If the erectile dysfunction appears to have a psychological basis or if you have difficulties in your relationship, your doctor may suggest that you and your partner consult a sex therapist or a counselor (*see* SEX THERAPY, p.773).

For cases in which the cause cannot be treated, a variety of drug treatments and physical aids are available.

DRUG TREATMENTS The oral medications sildenafil and tadalafil have proved effective in many men. The drugs relax the muscles of the penis and the walls of the arteries that supply blood to the penis. As a result more blood flows into the penis, and an erection can more easily occur when the penis is stimulated. It is important to consult your doctor before using one of these drugs because you may have a medical condition or may be taking a particular drug for another condition that makes these drugs inadvisable.

The drug alprostadil may also help you achieve an erection. This drug can be inserted into the urethra. Alternatively, the drug can be injected directly into the penis. However, alprostadil can sometimes have serious side effects, and you should seek medical advice before using it. For the small number of men with low testosterone levels, testosterone injections may be effective.

PHYSICAL TREATMENTS There are many physical aids that can help you achieve and maintain an erection. The vacuum constriction device consists of a plastic cylinder that is fitted over the penis. A handheld pump is used to create a vacuum in the cylinder, causing the penis to fill with blood and become erect. The cylinder is then removed and the erection is maintained by a special rubber band applied to the base of the penis.

An alternative is a penile prosthesis, which is surgically implanted into the penis. One type consists of paired rods that enable the position of the penis to be adjusted manually. However, once the rods are implanted, the size of the penis cannot be altered. Another device is the inflatable penile implant, which consists of paired cylinders and a small pump. The pump can be triggered to inflate the cylinders, which then hold the penis erect. When not in use, this implant enables the erection to subside.

The outlook for erectile dysfunction is good. In many men, the cause can be treated; if it is not treatable, drugs and physical aids are usually effective.

(WWW) ONLINE SITES: p.1034, p.1036

Premature ejaculation

Release of seminal fluid from the penis that occurs before or immediately after penetration and with minimal stimulation

 AGE Most common in young, sexually inexperienced males

 LIFESTYLE Early sexual encounters in rushed conditions may be a risk factor

 GENETICS Not a significant factor

Premature ejaculation is a very common sexual problem, particularly for young men. Ejaculation is considered to be premature when semen is released from the penis before or very shortly after penetration and with minimal sexual stimulation. Most sex therapists agree that the experience of premature ejaculation is part of the normal sexual learning curve for men, and inexperienced men, particularly if they are young, often ejaculate prematurely. The problem may also occur in experienced men when they have intercourse after a period of abstinence from sex.

Recurrent premature ejaculation can be a frustrating problem, and repeated episodes may make a man anxious about his performance, possibly resulting in erectile dysfunction (opposite page). If premature ejaculation occurs repeatedly, medical advice should be sought.

WHAT ARE THE CAUSES?

The causes of premature ejaculation are usually psychological. These may include anxiety about performance or early sexual experiences in which there was a fear of being discovered. Some men are unable to recognize the physical sensations that they experience immediately before they ejaculate and therefore cannot control the timing of their orgasm. Premature ejaculation is more common during the early stages of a sexual relationship, when the partners may lack confidence and may be nervous about their performance.

Rarely, premature ejaculation may be caused by a physical disorder such as inflammation of the prostate gland (*see* PROSTATITIS, p.724) or may result from damage to the spinal cord.

WHAT MIGHT BE DONE?

If you experience recurrent problems with premature ejaculation, you should discuss the matter with your doctor. You will have an examination to look for a physical cause, and any underlying disorder will be treated.

(SELF-HELP) SQUEEZE TECHNIQUE

The squeeze technique can be used to prevent premature ejaculation. Just before ejaculation, the shaft of the penis is firmly squeezed between the thumb and forefinger. The squeezing causes the erection to be partially lost, thus preventing ejaculation. Repeated regularly, the exercise can dramatically improve control of ejaculation.

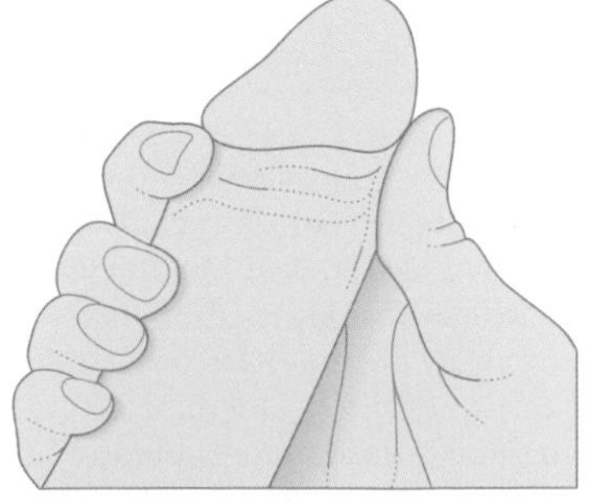

Applying pressure
The thumb and forefinger are used to apply pressure just behind the head of the penis, on the upper and lower sides. This pressure prevents ejaculation.

If premature ejaculation does not have a physical cause, treatment of the disorder is aimed at teaching you how to recognize and control sexual arousal. Your doctor will probably recommend that you see a sex therapist, who can teach you exercises for managing arousal (*see* SEX THERAPY, opposite page).

Exercises may include the start/stop technique, in which the man's penis is stimulated by his partner. When the man feels that he is close to ejaculation, he asks his partner to stop stimulating him. After a few minutes, stimulation is resumed by his partner and then stopped again. When the stop/start exercise is repeated many times over a period of weeks, it can help men achieve better control. The squeeze technique (p.771) can be used together with the start/stop technique or used separately.

Some antidepressant drugs (p.916), such as sertraline, have the side effect of delaying ejaculation. These drugs may be prescribed as a short-term measure to treat premature ejaculation because delaying ejaculation can boost confidence and assist in solving the problem.

The outlook is excellent, and most men who seek help gain vastly improved control over the timing of ejaculation.

(WWW) ONLINE SITES: p.1034, p.1036

Painful intercourse in men

Pain experienced in the genital area during sexual intercourse

AGE Can affect sexually active males of any age

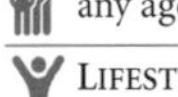
LIFESTYLE Unprotected sex is a risk factor

GENETICS Not a significant factor

Painful sexual intercourse, known as dyspareunia, is rare in men. The cause is usually physical, but in some cases it may be psychological. Pain occurring in the penis during intercourse may be accompanied by a burning sensation both during and after ejaculation.

What are the causes?

The most common cause of painful intercourse in men is an infection of the genitals, the prostate gland, or the urethra (the tube through which urine and semen leave the body). These infections, which include conditions such as genital herpes (p.767) and nongonococcal urethritis (p.765), are often transmitted through unprotected sexual intercourse. Friction on the penis during sexual intercourse can aggravate the pain of an infection. Other causes of pain during intercourse may include inflammation of the head of the penis (*see* BALANITIS, p.722) and chronic inflammation of the prostate gland (*see* PROSTATITIS, p.724), which may result in pain on ejaculation. Dyspareunia may also be a result of Peyronie's disease (p.723), a condition in which the shape of the penis is abnormal when erect. A tight foreskin is another possible cause of painful intercourse (*see* PHIMOSIS, p.721).

In some instances, discomfort during penetration results from skin irritation caused by an allergic reaction to a particular brand of condom or spermicide. Less commonly, sharp pain during penetration can be caused by threads of an intrauterine contraceptive device that protrude from the woman's cervix (*see* USING CONTRACEPTIVES, p.70). Rarely, there may be a psychological reason, such as sexual abuse in childhood.

What might be done?

If you think that the pain is due to an allergy to condoms or spermicide, try changing to another brand. If the pain persists, consult your doctor. The doctor will examine you and may take a swab from the tip of the penis to test for infection. If you have an infection, the doctor may prescribe antibiotics (p.885) for both you and your partner so that you do not reinfect each other, or he or she may refer you to a clinic that specializes in sexually transmitted diseases.

Any disorder that interferes with the erection of the penis may require surgery if it is causing pain. If your partner has an intrauterine contraceptive device that causes you discomfort, your doctor may trim its threads so that they do not protrude as far through the cervix.

If no physical cause is found, your doctor may refer you to a sex therapist, who will help you work through any psychological problems together with your partner (*see* SEX THERAPY, opposite page). Painful sexual intercourse in men can usually be treated successfully.

(WWW) ONLINE SITES: p.1034, p.1036

Painful intercourse in women

Pain experienced in the genital area or the lower abdomen during sexual intercourse

AGE Can affect sexually active females of any age

LIFESTYLE Unprotected sex is a risk factor

GENETICS Not a significant factor

Many women experience painful sexual intercourse, known as dyspareunia, at some point in their lives. The pain may be superficial, in the vulva or vagina, or deep in the pelvis. It may have either a psychological or a physical cause.

What are the causes?

For many women, superficial pain during sexual intercourse may be caused by psychological factors, such as anxiety disorders (p.551), guilt, or fear of sexual penetration. These factors can also result in vaginismus (opposite page).

There are many physical causes of superficial pain during intercourse. A fairly common cause is vaginal dryness. This problem may result from insufficient arousal before penetration. It may also be a side effect of drugs, such as some antidepressants (p.916), or it may be due to hormonal changes following childbirth or menopause (*see* MENOPAUSAL PROBLEMS, p.737). Many women find intercourse painful for some time after giving birth, especially if they had a vaginal tear. Pain during a woman's first sexual experience is common, particularly if the hymen is intact.

Superficial pain during intercourse may also be caused by infections of the urinary tract or the genitals, including cystitis (p.709), trichomoniasis (p.767), and candidiasis (p.309). In rare cases, an abnormally shaped vagina may make sexual intercourse painful.

Pain that is felt deep within the pelvis during intercourse may be due to a disorder of the pelvic cavity or of the pelvic organs, such as pelvic inflammatory disease (p.741), fibroids (p.745), or endometriosis (p.742). Another possible cause of pain may be an intrauterine contraceptive device that is incorrectly positioned in the uterus (*see* USING CONTRACEPTIVES, p.70).

Despite common belief, a large penis does not make sex painful, although certain positions can cause pain in the vagina and vulva or deep in the pelvis.

WHAT CAN I DO?

If your pain is due to vaginal dryness caused by lack of arousal, you may need to talk to your partner about spending more time on foreplay (*see* COMMUNICATING YOUR SEXUAL NEEDS, p.770). It may be helpful to use a lubricant, particularly after childbirth and during and after menopause. If using condoms, use only vaginal lubricants that are compatible. If certain sexual positions cause discomfort, try other ones.

WHAT MIGHT THE DOCTOR DO?

Your doctor may take swabs from your vagina and cervix to test for infection and may arrange for ultrasound scanning (p.250) and CT scanning (p.247) of the pelvis to look for abnormalities. If pain is due to an underlying disorder, it will be treated if possible. If the pain is due to vaginal dryness caused by a drug, your doctor may give you an alternative drug. If no physical cause is found, your doctor may refer you for sex therapy (right) with your partner. In most cases, the pain ceases following treatment.

(WWW) ONLINE SITES: p.1036, p.1037

Vaginismus

Spasm of the muscles around the entrance to the vagina, making sexual intercourse painful or impossible

AGE Can affect sexually active females of any age

GENETICS LIFESTYLE Not significant factors

In vaginismus, the pelvic floor muscles go into painful involuntary spasm and reduce the size of the vaginal opening. As a result, sexual intercourse may be very painful and vaginal penetration can often be impossible. The condition varies in severity for different women. Some women are affected by vaginismus to such an extent that they cannot insert even a finger or a tampon into the vagina and may need anesthesia for a vaginal examination. Other women may be able to tolerate a vaginal examination by a doctor or nurse but cannot tolerate sexual intercourse.

WHAT ARE THE CAUSES?

Vaginismus is usually psychological in origin and often occurs in women who fear that penetration may be painful. This fear may result from a previous traumatic sexual experience, such as a rape or sexual abuse in childhood. Another cause of vaginismus may be the fear of pregnancy. Anxiety or guilt concerning sex may also be a contributing factor to this condition.

Certain physical disorders can also lead to vaginismus. Inflammation of the vagina (*see* VULVOVAGINITIS, p.752) may make intercourse painful and lead to vaginismus. Some women develop the condition because they expect that sex will be painful after childbirth or that they will experience sexual difficulties during or after menopause (*see* MENOPAUSAL PROBLEMS, p.737).

WHAT MIGHT BE DONE?

Your doctor will examine you gently to look for any physical condition that could make penetration painful or difficult. If there is an underlying cause, he or she will treat it. If the problem is psychological, you may need some form of psychological therapy (pp.968–971) or, alternatively, you may be referred to a sex therapist (*see* SEX THERAPY, below). The sex therapist will explain that the vaginal wall is elastic and may teach you relaxation exercises. He or she may then show you how a small dilator can be inserted into the vagina. By practicing this technique and gradually using larger dilators, you should lose your fear that penetration will be painful. Treatment for vaginismus is successful in about 9 in 10 women.

(WWW) ONLINE SITES: p.1036, p.1037

(TREATMENT) SEX THERAPY

Sex therapy is often helpful when a sexual problem has a psychological basis rather than a physical cause. The type of therapy used depends on your problem but often involves discussions with a sex therapist. To overcome particular problems, the therapist may set exercises for you to practice at home, either by yourself or with your partner.

DISCUSSION SESSIONS

Discussing sexual problems with a trained sex therapist or counselor can often help a couple analyze and understand their relationship and sexual needs more clearly. It is important that both partners attend the therapy sessions. Each visit lasts about 1 hour, and several sessions may be necessary.

Counseling
Talking with a counselor can help you understand your relationship and deal with sexual problems.

EXERCISES

A sex therapist may assign you exercises to practice at home to improve the way in which you and your partner communicate. Exercises may include techniques such as sensate focus. This technique involves experiencing your partner simply through touch and is helpful for problems stemming from anxiety about performance.

Sensate focus technique
This technique involves discovering pleasure in your own body and that of your partner by means of touch rather than sexual intercourse.

INFERTILITY

Infertility affects 1 in 7 couples who want children. Fertility declines in both sexes after age 30, and because more and more couples are delaying starting a family until their 30s, infertility is becoming more common in the developed world. If conception has not occurred after a year of unprotected, regular sex, one or both partners may have a fertility problem.

About 8 in 10 couples trying to have a child conceive over a period of a year. This figure rises to 9 in 10 couples over 2 years. A problem conceiving may be temporary, or it may prevent a couple from ever having children unless they seek infertility treatment. Infertility problems can also affect couples who have already had children.

It is important that both partners visit the doctor together if they are worried about an inability to conceive. In about half of all couples, the problem lies with the female partner, and, in about one-third of couples, with the male. In some couples, problems may be found in both partners, and in others, no cause can be found.

In this section, the advice a doctor might give to a couple who are having difficulties conceiving is discussed in the first article. The following two articles describe infertility problems specific to either women or men. Each article discusses tests that your doctor may perform to identify fertility disorders and how specific problems may be treated. Other conditions that can lead to infertility are discussed in other sections of the book. They include polycystic ovary syndrome (p.744) and endometriosis (p.742) in women and varicocele (p.720) and hypogonadism in males (p.729).

In many couples, the cause of infertility can be identified and treated. If a specific cause cannot be found or is untreatable, assisted conception may be advised. This section discusses the techniques in current use, including the recent sophisticated developments.

Problems conceiving

When pregnancy does not result after a couple have had regular unprotected sex for more than a year

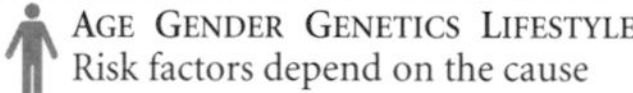
AGE GENDER GENETICS LIFESTYLE
Risk factors depend on the cause

The average time taken by a couple who are trying to conceive is 6 months, and 8 in 10 couples will be successful within 1 year. It is very common for a couple to feel anxious if pregnancy does not occur in the first few months, but most young couples are advised to continue trying for a year before seeking medical help. Older couples, especially those in whom the woman is over age 35 and the male is over age 40, may decide to ask for medical help earlier because fertility declines naturally with age, especially in women.

WHAT MIGHT BE DONE?

If you are having problems conceiving, you and your partner should consult a doctor together. The doctor will ask about your sex life and whether you are having any specific difficulties with sexual intercourse (*see* SEXUAL PROBLEMS, pp.769–773). He or she will also ask if you have been having intercourse on the optimum days preceding the middle of the menstrual cycle, during which your chances of conceiving are best.

Your doctor will also take a medical history from both of you because previous illnesses or operations may be relevant to your problem. You will be asked how often you drink alcohol, whether you smoke, and if you use any prescribed or recreational drugs. You may also be given a physical examination, including an examination of your genitals.

If you are both relatively young and there is no obvious problem, your doctor may give you advice about measures that you can take to improve your likelihood of conceiving (*see* MAXIMIZING YOUR CHANCE OF CONCEPTION, right) and suggest you keep trying. If you have not had preconception counseling for advice on a healthy pregnancy, the doctor may discuss your health, diet, and lifestyle with you.

If your doctor suspects there may be a problem preventing conception, or if the female partner is over 35, you may be referred to a specialist for a series of tests (*see* FEMALE INFERTILITY, opposite page, and MALE INFERTILITY, p.777).

WHAT IS THE PROGNOSIS?

For most couples, it is only a matter of time before they conceive, and 9 in 10 couples are successful within 2 years.

If a problem is detected, the treatment and outlook will depend on the cause. Assisted conception (p.776) or artificial insemination (opposite page) may be suitable for some couples if no cause is discovered or if the problem cannot be treated successfully.

(WWW) ONLINE SITES: p.1034

(SELF-HELP) MAXIMIZING YOUR CHANCE OF CONCEPTION

The overall health of both partners has an important effect on fertility. You may find that following the self-help measures below improves your chance of conception:

- Make sure your weight is in or near the normal range (*see* ARE YOU A HEALTHY WEIGHT? p.53).
- Eat a healthy diet.
- Do not smoke.
- Cut down on alcohol, which is known to reduce the sperm count and can damage the fetus if pregnancy occurs.
- Have sex every 2 days at the woman's most fertile time, in the middle of the menstrual cycle.
- Try not to worry because stress can alter your ovulations. Learn relaxation exercises (p.75) to lower your stress levels.
- Men should avoid hot baths, saunas, and hot tubs.

Female infertility

Inability of a woman to conceive with a partner of normal fertility

AGE Increases with age; more common over age 35

GENETICS In rare cases, may be due to a chromosomal abnormality

LIFESTYLE Stress, excessive exercise, and low or excess body weight are risk factors

About half of couples who experience difficulties conceiving do so as a result of female infertility. Fertility in women decreases with age and is generally lower by age 35, making conception more difficult for women over this age.

For conception to occur, all of the following steps must take place: ovulation (the production and release of a mature egg by an ovary), fertilization of the egg by a sperm, transport of the fertilized egg along the fallopian tube to the uterus, and implantation of the fertilized egg in the lining of the uterus. If any stage is interrupted or does not occur, conception cannot take place.

What are the causes?

There are a number of fertility problems in females that may affect one or more of the processes required for conception. The problems can develop at different stages of conception.

PROBLEMS WITH OVULATION A common cause of female infertility is the ovaries' failure to release a mature egg during every monthly cycle. Ovulation is controlled by a complex interaction of hormones produced by the hypothalamus (an area of the brain), the pituitary and thyroid glands, and the ovaries. A common and treatable cause of female infertility is polycystic ovary syndrome (p.744), which may cause a hormone imbalance that prevents ovulation from taking place. Disorders of the thyroid gland, such as hypothyroidism (p.680), may also cause a hormonal imbalance that can affect the frequency of ovulation. Pituitary gland disorders, such as prolactinoma (p.677), a noncancerous tumor, may cause a similar imbalance. In some women, ovulation does not always occur, for reasons that are unclear. In some cases, women who have been using oral contraceptives for a number of years may take time to reestablish a normal hormonal cycle after discontinuing them. Excessive exercise, stress, and obesity or low body weight may affect hormone levels and cause temporary infertility.

Site of fallopian tube blockage
Distorted fallopian tube

Damaged fallopian tubes
In this X-ray, a contrast dye has been used to show female reproductive organs. One fallopian tube is blocked and is not visible; the other is narrowed and distorted.

Premature menopause also results in a failure to ovulate. It can occur with no apparent cause or may be the result of surgery, chemotherapy (p.278), or radiation therapy (p.279). In rare cases, the ovaries do not develop normally due to a chromosomal abnormality, such as Turner syndrome (p.823).

PROBLEMS WITH EGG TRANSPORT AND FERTILIZATION The passage of the egg from the ovary to the uterus may be impeded by damage to one of the fallopian tubes. This damage may be due to pelvic infection (*see* PELVIC INFLAMMATORY DISEASE, p.741), which may in turn result from a sexually transmitted infection such as chlamydial cervicitis (p.765). Such infections may exist with no symptoms and may be detected only if you have difficulty conceiving.

Endometriosis (p.742), a condition that can lead to the formation of scar tissue and cysts within the pelvis, may also damage the fallopian tubes, preventing the passage of an egg.

In some women, the egg cannot be fertilized because the mucus produced naturally by the cervix is too thick or contains antibodies that destroy the partner's sperm before reaching the egg.

PROBLEMS WITH IMPLANTATION If the lining of the uterus has been damaged by an infection, such as gonorrhea (p.764), the implantation of a fertilized egg may not be possible. Hormonal problems may also result in the uterine lining not being adequately prepared for successful implantation. Noncancerous tumors that distort the uterus (*see* FIBROIDS, p.745) and, rarely, structural abnormalities present from birth may make it impossible for a fertilized egg to embed itself in the uterine lining.

TREATMENT ARTIFICIAL INSEMINATION

Artificial insemination is a simple procedure to introduce sperm into a woman's vagina or uterus. Sperm from the woman's partner or from a donor is drawn into a syringe and injected into the top of the vagina or through the cervix into the uterus. The procedure is painless and takes only minutes, and the woman can go home after 30 minutes of rest.

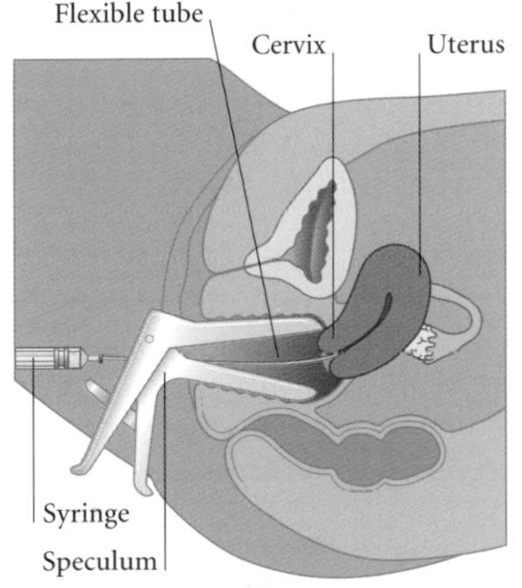
Flexible tube
Cervix
Uterus
Syringe
Speculum

Artificial insemination
The vagina is held open by a speculum so that sperm can be injected into the top of the vagina or into the uterus.

What might be done?

Your doctor will ask you about your general state of health, your lifestyle, your medical and menstrual history, and your sex life before recommending particular tests and treatments.

Most causes of female infertility can now be identified through testing. You can find out if and when you ovulate by using an ovulation prediction kit, available over the counter, or by recording your body temperature daily (*see* USING CONTRACEPTIVES, p.70). If your doctor suspects that you are not ovulating regularly, you may have repeated blood tests during your menstrual cycle to assess the level of the hormone progesterone (which normally rises after ovulation). Repeated ultrasound scanning (p.250) of the ovaries during the cycle may also be done to check if and when ovulation occurs. In addition, a tissue sample may be taken from the uterus and examined for abnormalities (*see* ENDOMETRIAL SAMPLING, p.738).

If tests show that you are not ovulating, you may need further blood tests to check the levels of thyroid hormones and other hormones, and drugs may be prescribed to stimulate ovulation (*see* DRUGS FOR INFERTILITY, p.936). However, if you are ovulating, the next step is to find out whether your partner is producing sufficient normal sperm by analyzing two or more semen samples (*see* SEMEN ANALYSIS, opposite page).

If you are ovulating normally and your partner's sperm are normal, your doctor will check if there is a problem preventing the egg and sperm from meeting. For example, you and your partner may be asked to have sex during the time that you are ovulating so that a sample of your cervical mucus (collected within a few hours of intercourse) can be tested for antibodies to sperm. If analysis of the sample of cervical mucus shows antibodies to sperm, there is a method of treatment. Your partner's semen may be injected directly into your uterus to avoid contact with the mucus (*see* ARTIFICIAL INSEMINATION, p.775). If these steps are not successful, your doctor may recommend assisted conception (right).

If the cause of the infertility has still not been found, your doctor may arrange for further investigations to look for a blockage in the fallopian tubes or an abnormality of the uterus. One such test is laparoscopy (p.742), in which an endoscope containing a camera is inserted through the abdomen. Another is hysterosalpingography, in which a dye is injected through the cervix and X-rays are taken as the dye enters the reproductive organs. The treatment depends on the problem. For example, a tubal blockage may be corrected by microsurgery (p.950), and endometriosis may be treated with drugs (*see* SEX HORMONES AND RELATED DRUGS, p.933).

TREATMENT ASSISTED CONCEPTION

Infertility treatments that involve mixing eggs and sperm outside the body include in-vitro fertilization (IVF), gamete intrafallopian transfer (GIFT), and zygote intrafallopian transfer (ZIFT). IVF is also used to treat some genetic disorders because the embryo can be tested for abnormalities before implantation.

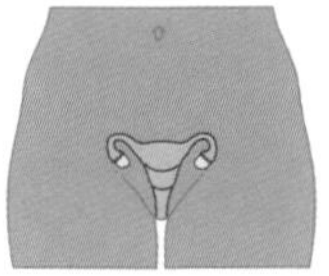

LOCATION

IN-VITRO FERTILIZATION

IVF may be performed if the cause of infertility cannot be determined or treated or if there is a blockage in a fallopian tube. Successful pregnancies occur in about 15 percent of IVF attempts.

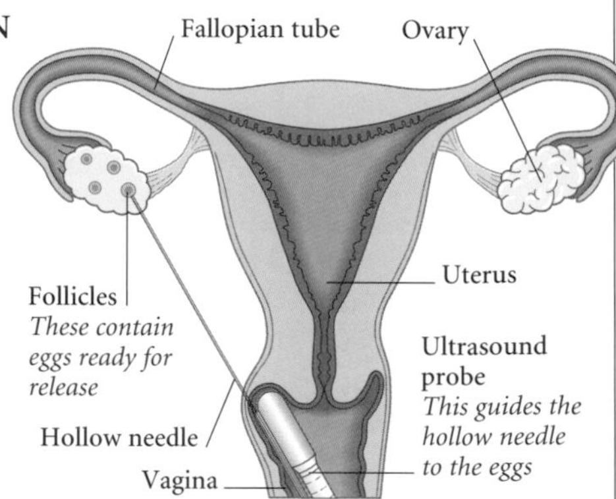
Fallopian tube
Ovary
Uterus
Follicles
These contain eggs ready for release
Ultrasound probe
This guides the hollow needle to the eggs
Hollow needle
Vagina

1 *Drugs are given to stimulate several eggs to mature in the ovaries. Under ultrasound guidance, the eggs are collected with a needle inserted through the vaginal wall.*

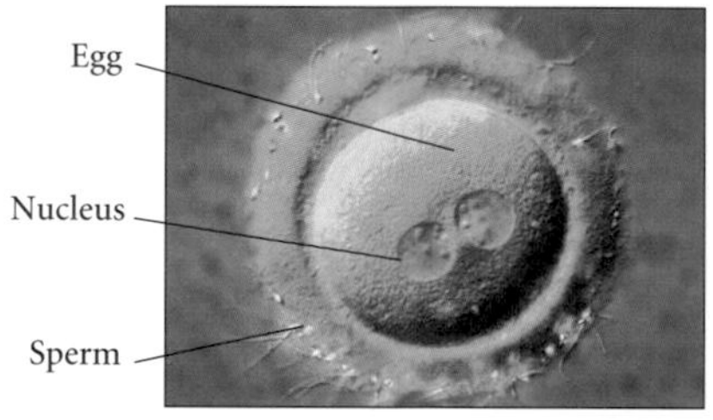
Egg
Nucleus
Sperm

2 *A sperm sample, provided by the woman's partner, is combined with the collected eggs and the mixture is incubated for 48 hours at normal body temperature (98.6°F or 37°C) to allow fertilization to take place.*

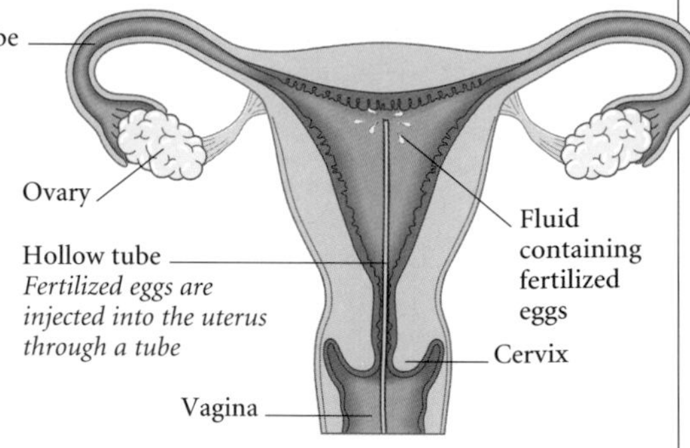
Fallopian tube
Ovary
Hollow tube
Fertilized eggs are injected into the uterus through a tube
Fluid containing fertilized eggs
Cervix
Vagina

3 *The fertilized eggs are introduced into the woman's uterus. Up to three eggs are injected through a thin tube that is fixed to a syringe and passed through the cervix. This procedure takes around 20 minutes. If one or more fertilized eggs implant, conception occurs.*

OTHER METHODS

The techniques GIFT and ZIFT may help couples who have unexplained infertility. In each method, eggs are collected as in IVF but are returned to the fallopian tube rather than the uterus. The success rate for both methods is 25–30 percent.

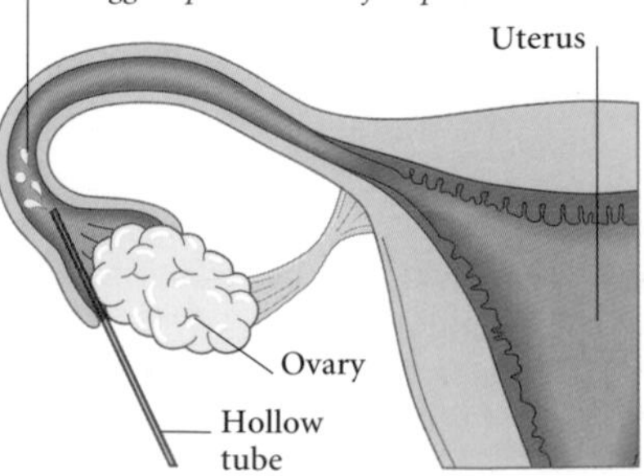
Fluid in fallopian tube
Fluid containing fertilized eggs or sperm and eggs is placed in the fallopian tube
Uterus
Ovary
Hollow tube

GIFT and ZIFT replacement methods
In GIFT, eggs are mixed with sperm and then returned to the fallopian tube before fertilization. In ZIFT, the eggs are fertilized and returned to the fallopian tube.

WHAT IS THE PROGNOSIS?

Treatments for female infertility have greatly increased the chance of pregnancy. Success rates vary, depending on the cause of the infertility and the type of treatment. Fertility drugs stimulate ovulation in 2 in 3 women, but there is a risk of multiple pregnancy. Microsurgery to clear obstructed fallopian tubes is sometimes successful but increases the risk of ectopic pregnancy (p.790). Success rates for assisted conception methods range from 15 to 50 percent per individual treatment.

(WWW) ONLINE SITES: p.1034

Male infertility

Inability of a man to produce or deliver sufficient numbers of healthy sperm to achieve fertilization

 GENETICS In rare cases, may be due to a chromosomal abnormality

 LIFESTYLE Smoking and drinking alcohol are risk factors

 AGE A significant factor after age 40

In about 1 in 3 couples who have difficulty conceiving, the problem results from male infertility. In males, fertility depends partly on the production of enough normal sperm to make it likely that one will fertilize an egg and partly on the ability to deliver the sperm into the vagina during sexual intercourse. If either of these factors is adversely affected, infertility may result.

WHAT ARE THE CAUSES?

Unlike the causes of female infertility, which are more easily identifiable, the cause of infertility can be difficult to find in some men. A cause is discovered in only 1 in 3 men investigated.

PROBLEMS WITH SPERM PRODUCTION A low sperm count or the production of abnormal sperm may have various causes. Normally, the testes have a temperature of about 4°F (2°C) lower than the rest of the body. Any factors that raise the temperature of the testes can reduce the number of sperm produced.

Aspects of your lifestyle that may impair sperm production include smoking, drinking alcohol, using certain medications and recreational drugs, and even wearing tight pants. Sperm production can be adversely affected by some long-term illnesses, such as chronic kidney failure (p.706), and by some infections, such as mumps (p.291), that occur after puberty. Conditions affecting the urethra, such as hypospadias (p.870), or the scrotum, such as a varicocele (p.720), may also reduce fertility. In addition, fertility problems may occur if the testes are damaged by medical procedures such as surgery, chemotherapy (p.278), or radiation therapy (p.279) for disorders such as cancer (p.719).

Low sperm production may also be due to a hormonal or chromosomal deficiency. Insufficient production of the sex hormone testosterone by the testes (*see* HYPOGONADISM IN MALES, p.729) can cause a low sperm count. Since the pituitary gland controls testosterone secretion, pituitary disorders, such as a tumor (*see* PROLACTINOMA, p.677), may also lead to reduced sperm production. Rarely, low testosterone levels are due to a chromosomal abnormality such as Klinefelter syndrome (p.822). The most common cause of a low sperm count is idiopathic oligospermia, in which there is a reduced sperm count for no identifiable reason. There is no effective cure.

PROBLEMS WITH SPERM DELIVERY A number of factors may prevent sperm from reaching the vagina. The most easily identifiable is erectile dysfunction (p.770), the inability to achieve or maintain an erection. Other factors include damage to the epididymides and vas deferens (tubes that transport sperm). Damage is often due to a sexually transmitted infection such as gonorrhea (p.764). It may also be caused by retrograde ejaculation, in which semen flows back into the bladder when the bladder valves do not close properly. This condition can occur after prostate surgery (*see* PARTIAL PROSTATECTOMY, p.725, and RADICAL PROSTATECTOMY, p.727).

WHAT MIGHT BE DONE?

Your doctor will ask about your health, medical history, and sex life and give you a physical examination, including an examination of your genitals. You may also need to provide semen samples (*see* SEMEN ANALYSIS, right). If your sperm count is low or your sperm are abnormal, further investigations will be done, such as blood tests to check hormone levels. Treatment depends on the diagnosis. Low testosterone levels can be treated with hormone injections (*see* SEX HORMONES AND RELATED DRUGS, p.933). Artificial insemination (p.775) may be used in cases of erectile dysfunction or retrograde ejaculation; for the latter, the sperm may be taken from urine. Damage to the epididymis or vas deferens may be treated by microsurgery (p.950).

If you have only a few healthy sperm, a sample may be taken from an epididymis or testis by microsurgery and a process called intracytoplasmic sperm injection (ICSI) may be used with IVF to fertilize an egg with a single sperm.

WHAT IS THE PROGNOSIS?

If the infertility is treatable, the chance of regaining fertility is high. With artificial insemination, the chance of conceiving in one menstrual cycle is about 10–15 percent, and the treatment usually works within 6 months. Each attempt at assisted conception (IVF with ICSI) is successful in 25–50 percent of cases, depending on the technique.

(WWW) ONLINE SITES: p.1034

(TEST) SEMEN ANALYSIS

Microscopic examinations of several samples of a man's semen are carried out to investigate male infertility. If there are too few sperm, or many are abnormally formed or dead, fertility will be reduced. A smaller-than-normal volume of semen also indicates that there may be a problem.

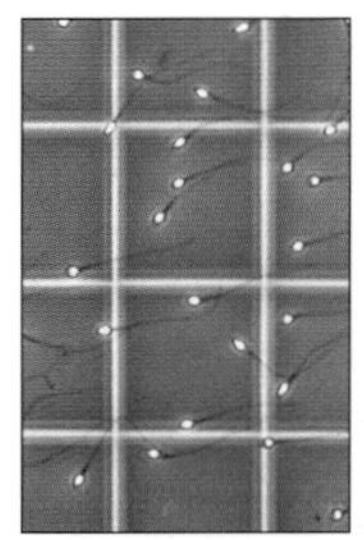

NORMAL SPERM COUNT

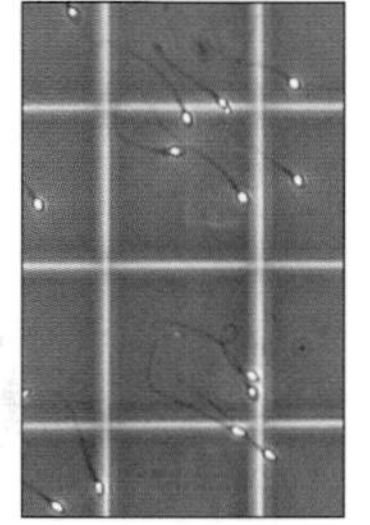

LOW SPERM COUNT

The sperm count

Each milliliter of normal semen has at least 20 million sperm, the majority of which are healthy. A low sperm count contains fewer than 20 million sperm.

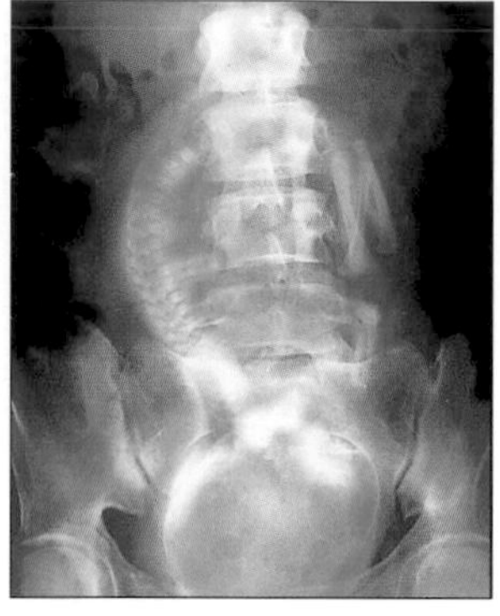

A fully grown fetus
This X-ray shows the skeleton of a fetus at full term. Its head is low in the mother's pelvis.

PREGNANCY AND CHILDBIRTH

FROM THE MOMENT OF CONCEPTION, when an egg is fertilized, to the moment of birth, complex changes take place within a pregnant woman's body. Genetic material from the father and the mother fuses together and then grows to form a new, genetically different individual. During this time, the mother provides a nourishing and protective environment in which the fetus can develop. When the baby is born, he or she is able to survive outside the mother's body and begin a separate existence.

About a week after fertilization, the egg embeds itself securely into the lining of the uterus, at which stage it is known as an embryo. Only 8 weeks later, the embryo is taking on a form and has developed all its vital organs, including the heart and brain. From this stage onward, it is called a fetus and begins a spurt of rapid growth. Between 8 and 12 weeks, its weight increases by up to 15 times. By the time the baby is born, it weighs just over 7 lb (3 kg) on average.

THE PREGNANT WOMAN

Alterations in the mother's hormone levels control the physical changes necessary for a healthy pregnancy and for birth. First, menstruation ceases, and then the ligaments and the joints in the mother's pelvis begin to soften and become more flexible in preparation for the birth of the baby. In addition, the mother's breasts enlarge as their milk-producing glands increase in number, ready for breast-feeding the newborn baby.

Each new pregnancy runs a slightly different course. Many prospective mothers feel well throughout their pregnancies. Others experience uncomfortable symptoms such as nausea, vomiting, heartburn, indigestion, and fatigue. These are a result of the biological changes, such as pressure of the fetus on surrounding organs and hormone changes, occurring in the body as the fetus grows. Such symptoms develop at various different stages during the pregnancy.

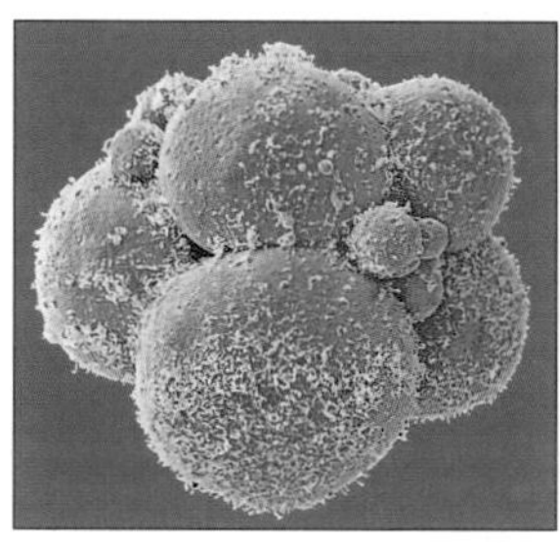

Cell division
In the days after fertilization, the egg has divided to form a cluster of cells called a morula.

THE BABY'S BIRTH

After about 36 weeks, the fetus is fully formed and is able to survive outside its mother's body. Around the 40th week, a change in the mother's hormones triggers the first of the three stages of labor. After the baby is born, the mother begins to produce breast milk in preparation for breast-feeding, and her body gradually returns to its state before pregnancy.

PROCESS FROM EGG TO EMBRYO

Pregnancy begins when an egg is fertilized by a sperm. This event takes place in the outer third of one of the fallopian tubes, when a single sperm meets and fuses with an egg following sexual intercourse. Within 2 days of fertilization, the egg starts its journey toward the uterus, propelled by the muscular action of the fallopian tube. As the egg travels, its cells gradually divide to form a cluster of cells known as a morula. After 5–7 days, the egg arrives in the uterus and then embeds securely in the uterine lining. From this moment onward, the pregnancy is properly established, and the fertilized egg is known as an embryo.

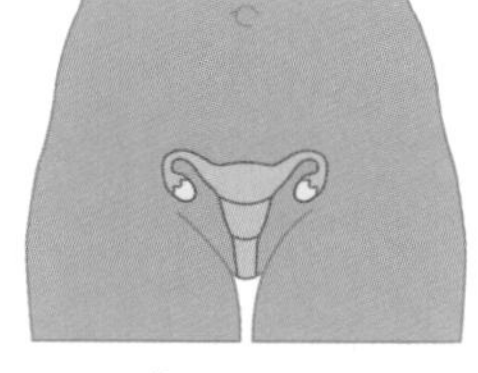

LOCATION

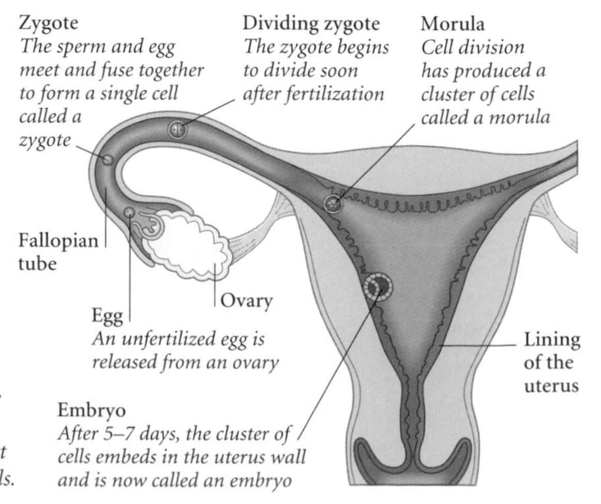
Zygote
The sperm and egg meet and fuse together to form a single cell called a zygote
Dividing zygote
The zygote begins to divide soon after fertilization
Morula
Cell division has produced a cluster of cells called a morula
Fallopian tube
Ovary
Egg
An unfertilized egg is released from an ovary
Lining of the uterus
Embryo
After 5–7 days, the cluster of cells embeds in the uterus wall and is now called an embryo

The beginning of life
After fertilization, the egg begins to move along the fallopian tube, its cells doubling in number every 12 hours. By the time the egg arrives in the uterus, it consists of hundreds of cells.

STRUCTURE AND FUNCTION PREGNANCY

Inside the uterus, the fetus is surrounded by a protective, fluid-filled bag known as the amniotic sac. Nourishment is provided through the placenta, an organ attached to the wall of the uterus and connected to the fetus by the umbilical cord. As the fetus grows, the uterus increases in size and weight and gradually expands into the mother's abdomen. Many of the mother's organs, such as the bladder and the intestines, are pushed out of their normal positions by the enlarged uterus. By the end of pregnancy, the fetus is usually tightly curled up with its head pointing downward toward the mother's pelvis.

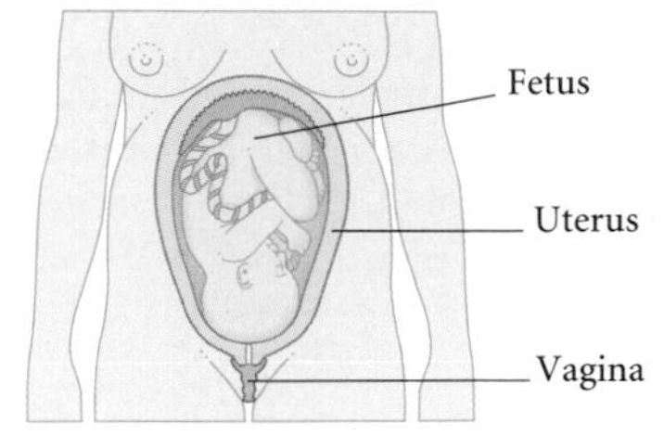
Fetus
Uterus
Vagina

LOCATION

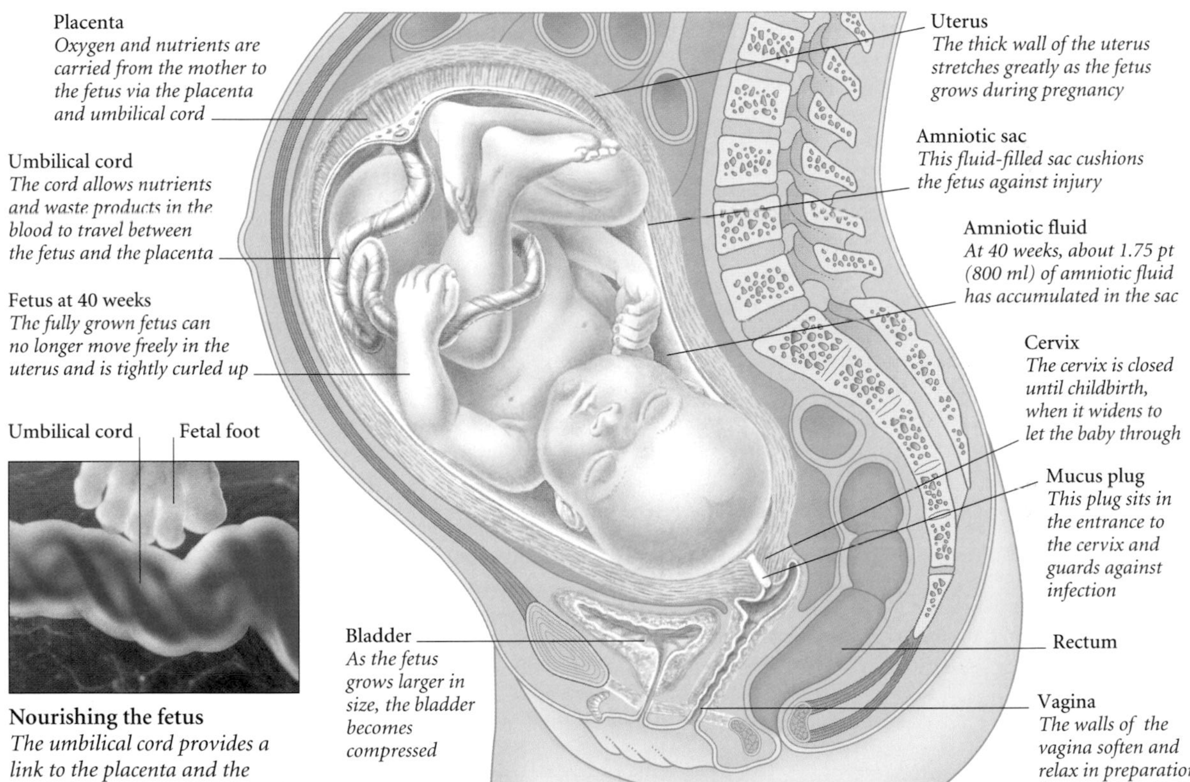
Placenta
Oxygen and nutrients are carried from the mother to the fetus via the placenta and umbilical cord
Umbilical cord
The cord allows nutrients and waste products in the blood to travel between the fetus and the placenta
Fetus at 40 weeks
The fully grown fetus can no longer move freely in the uterus and is tightly curled up
Umbilical cord
Fetal foot
Uterus
The thick wall of the uterus stretches greatly as the fetus grows during pregnancy
Amniotic sac
This fluid-filled sac cushions the fetus against injury
Amniotic fluid
At 40 weeks, about 1.75 pt (800 ml) of amniotic fluid has accumulated in the sac
Cervix
The cervix is closed until childbirth, when it widens to let the baby through
Mucus plug
This plug sits in the entrance to the cervix and guards against infection
Rectum
Vagina
The walls of the vagina soften and relax in preparation for the baby's birth
Bladder
As the fetus grows larger in size, the bladder becomes compressed

Nourishing the fetus
The umbilical cord provides a link to the placenta and the mother's nourishing blood supply.

PROCESS MULTIPLE PREGNANCY

Most multiple pregnancies produce twins; three or more babies are a rare occurrence. The majority of twins are nonidentical and develop when two eggs are released from an ovary and fertilized by two separate sperm. These twins may or may not be the same sex. Less commonly, fertilization of a single egg takes place as normal, but the fertilized cell divides to form two identical, same-sex embryos.

Twins in the uterus
Nonidentical twins develop in their own amniotic sacs and have their own separate placentas. Identical twins may share an amniotic sac, or a placenta, or both. Twins can lie in any position in the uterus.

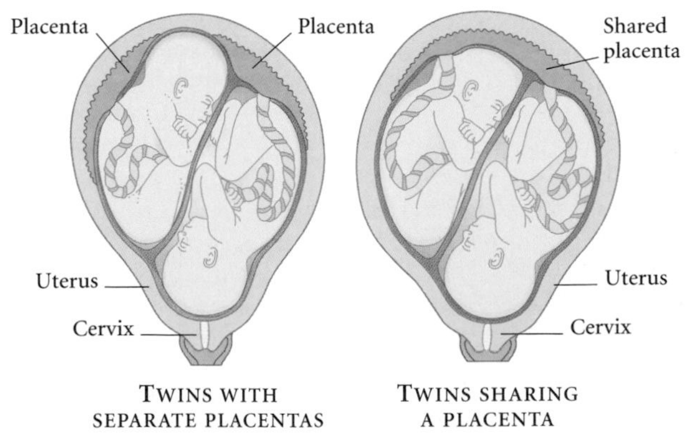
Placenta
Placenta
Uterus
Cervix
Shared placenta
Uterus
Cervix

TWINS WITH SEPARATE PLACENTAS

TWINS SHARING A PLACENTA

PROCESS STAGES OF PREGNANCY

Pregnancy is divided into three stages, or trimesters, each about 3 months in duration. Each trimester brings about significant changes in the mother's body and progressive development and growth of the baby. During the first 8 weeks of pregnancy, the developing baby is called an embryo. After 8 weeks it is called a fetus.

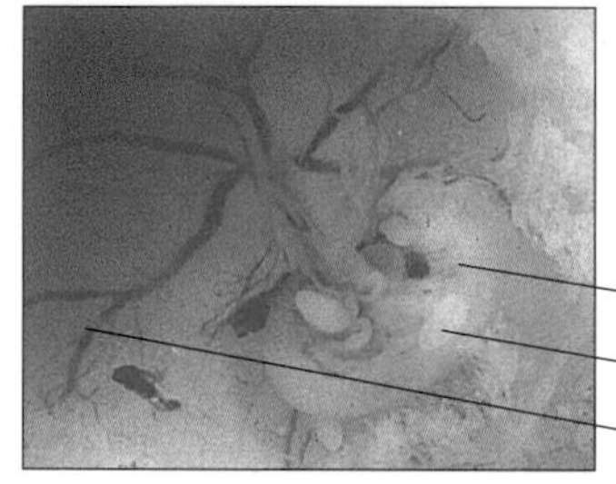
Developing eye
Developing arm
Placental blood vessel

Embryo at 4 weeks
At 1 month old, the embryo has bulges on either side of its head where the eyes are beginning to form.

FIRST TRIMESTER (WEEKS 1–12)

There are few visible changes in the mother's body during this trimester. However, her heart rate increases by about 8 beats per minute to increase the blood circulation. Most of the growing fetus's major organs, such as the heart and the brain, become fully developed during the first 3 months.

From embryo to fetus
The first trimester is crucial in the baby's development; 8 weeks after fertilization, the embryo has developed most of its organs and is now called a fetus. In the 3rd month it more than doubles in length.

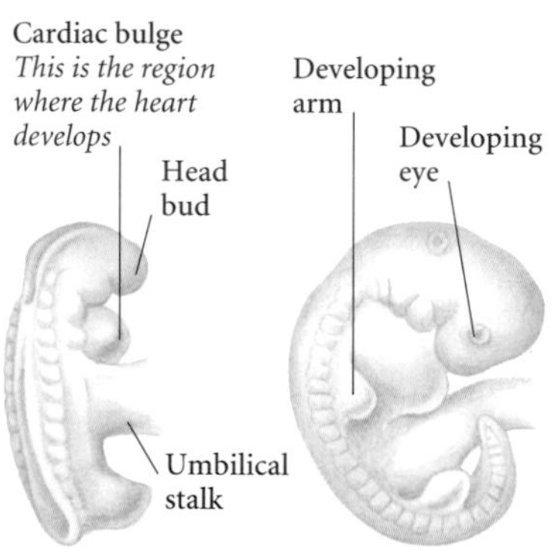
Cardiac bulge
This is the region where the heart develops
Head bud
Umbilical stalk
Developing arm
Developing eye
Ear
The shapes of the ears are now visible
Eye
The eyes are developing. The eyelids are closed
Leg
The limbs are now quite well developed
20 DAYS
1/8 in (3 mm) long
4 WEEKS
5/16 in (7 mm) long
8 WEEKS
1 in (2.5 cm) long

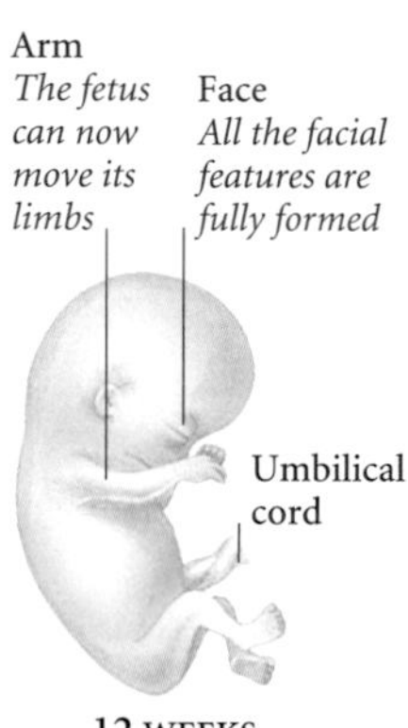
Arm
The fetus can now move its limbs
Face
All the facial features are fully formed
Umbilical cord
12 WEEKS
2 1/2 in (6 cm) long

The mother at 12 weeks
At 12 weeks, the mother's waistline is only slightly thickened. The breasts are tender and the areola, the area around the nipple, becomes darker in color.

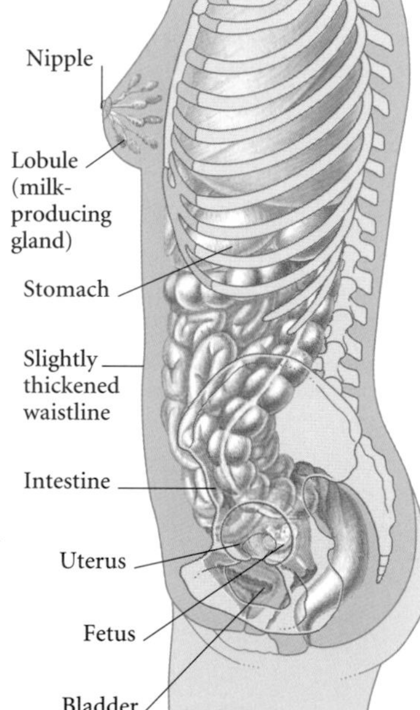
Nipple
Lobule (milk-producing gland)
Stomach
Slightly thickened waistline
Intestine
Uterus
Fetus
Bladder

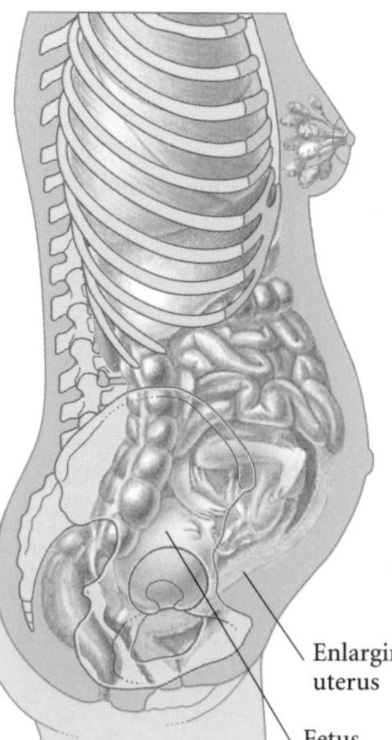
Enlarging uterus
Fetus

SECOND TRIMESTER (WEEKS 13–28)

The mother may experience backache as she copes with the growing weight of the fetus. Her appetite tends to increase. The fetus starts moving at 18–20 weeks, producing sensations of fluttering in the mother's abdomen.

The mother at 24 weeks
The mother's abdomen swells as the fetus grows. There may be discharge from the nipples, caused by enlarging lobules (milk-producing glands) in the breasts.

The fetus
The fetus grows in size and accumulates a layer of fat, and its internal organs become more complex. Its sense of hearing is now developed.

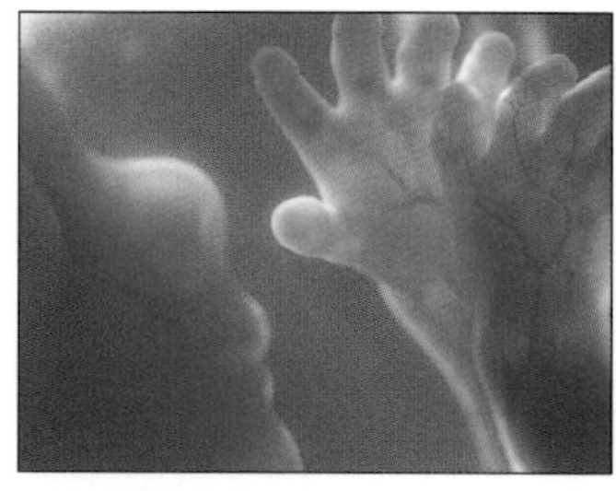

Fetus at 20 weeks
At this stage, the hands are well developed and the fetus is able to flex its fingers. The fetus now has recognizable features and the profile of the face shows the forehead, nose, lips, and chin.

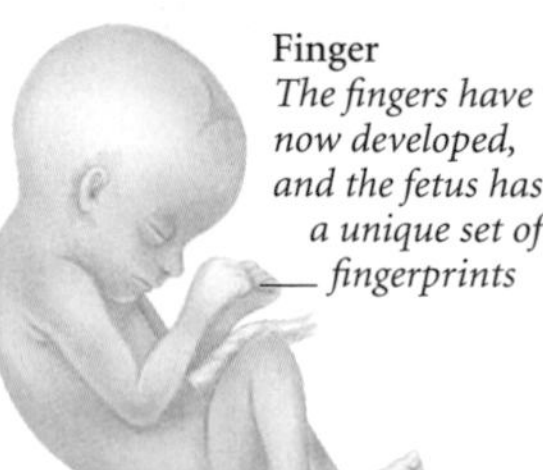
Finger
The fingers have now developed, and the fetus has a unique set of fingerprints
16 WEEKS
7 in (18 cm) long

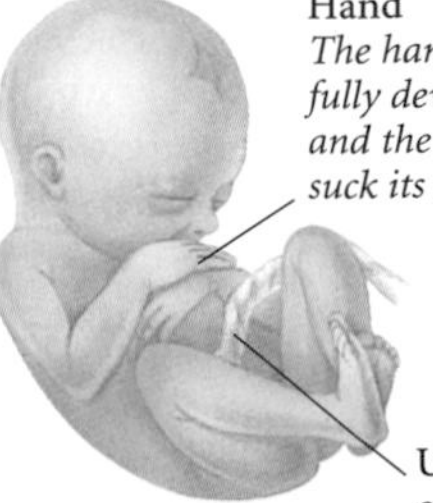
Hand
The hands are fully developed, and the fetus can suck its thumb
Umbilical cord
28 WEEKS
12 in (30.5 cm) long

THIRD TRIMESTER (WEEKS 29–40)

During the third trimester, the mother rapidly gains weight as the fetus undergoes a growth spurt. The top of the uterus is high in the abdomen, almost to the level of the breastbone. This can cause slight shortness of breath due to compression of the mother's lungs.

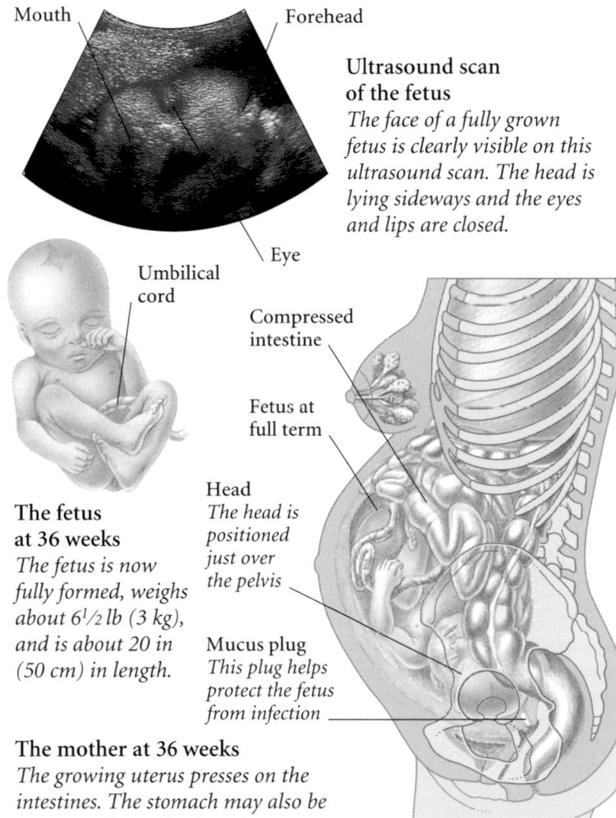
Mouth
Forehead
Eye
Umbilical cord
Compressed intestine
Fetus at full term

Ultrasound scan of the fetus
The face of a fully grown fetus is clearly visible on this ultrasound scan. The head is lying sideways and the eyes and lips are closed.

The fetus at 36 weeks
The fetus is now fully formed, weighs about 6½ lb (3 kg), and is about 20 in (50 cm) in length.

Head
The head is positioned just over the pelvis

Mucus plug
This plug helps protect the fetus from infection

The mother at 36 weeks
The growing uterus presses on the intestines. The stomach may also be compressed, causing heartburn.

PROCESS ENGAGEMENT

A few weeks before labor begins, the head of the fetus moves down to sit snugly in the pelvis. The head is then said to be engaged. In women who have given birth before, this process may not occur until labor begins.

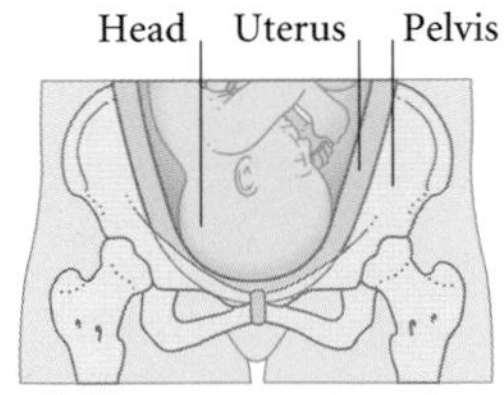
Head
Uterus
Pelvis

BEFORE ENGAGEMENT

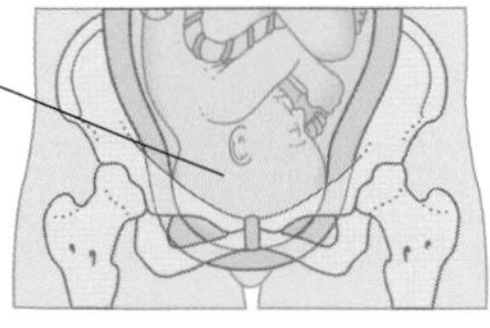
Head sits in pelvis

AFTER ENGAGEMENT

Fetus at 40 weeks
In preparation for the birth, the fetus drops lower in the mother's abdomen so that its head sits low in her pelvic cavity.

PROCESS NOURISHING THE FETUS

The growing fetus is dependent on the mother for nourishment and oxygen. These substances are transferred from the mother's blood to the fetus's blood inside the placenta, an organ attached to the uterus and connected to the fetus by the umbilical cord. About 1.3 pt (600 ml) of maternal blood passes through the placenta every single minute, carrying a continuous supply of nutrients.

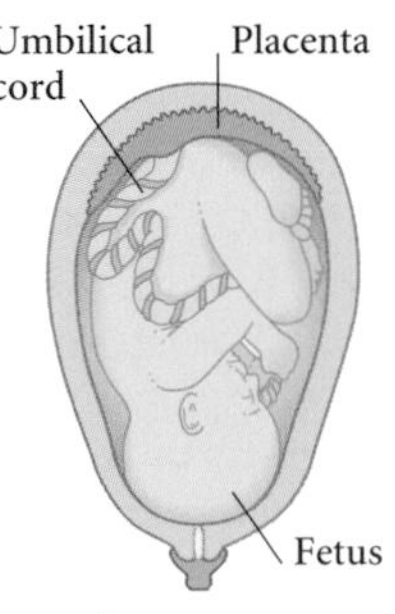
Umbilical cord
Placenta
Fetus

LOCATION

Maternal artery
This artery circulates blood, which contains oxygen and nutrients for the fetus, around the chorionic villi

Chorionic villus
Tiny projections, called villi, form from a thin membrane called the chorion and contain the fetal blood vessels

Flow of oxygen and nutrients

Wall of uterus

Maternal vein
This vein carries waste products away from the fetus

Lining of uterus (endometrium)

Flow of wastes

Pool of mother's blood

Umbilical vein
Blood, oxygen, and nutrients pass to the fetus in this vein

Umbilical artery
This artery carries waste products away from the fetus

Amniotic fluid

Umbilical cord

Blood vessels of the placenta
Inside the placenta, substances are exchanged between the blood supplies of the mother and the fetus through a thin membrane called the chorion. Oxygen, nutrients, and antibodies pass from the mother's blood to the fetus's blood, and waste products pass in the opposite direction.

Lining of the uterus
The placenta is firmly attached to the uterine lining

Fetal blood vessel
The blood vessels of the fetus are surrounded by the mother's blood

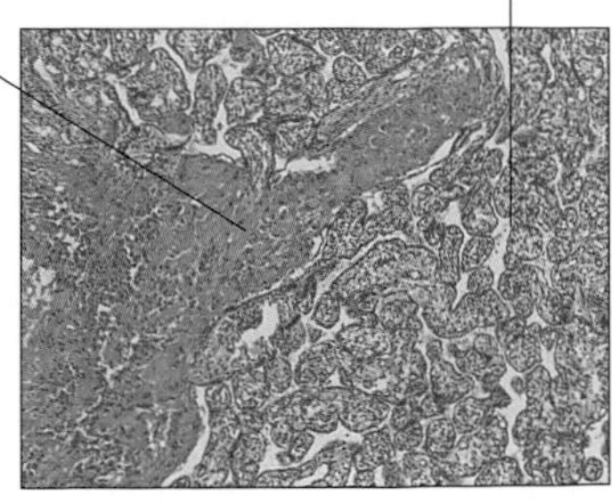

Placental tissue
This magnified image of a section of placenta shows tissue from both the mother and the fetus. In the placenta, their blood circulations do not mix but are in very close proximity.

PROCESS CHILDBIRTH

The process of childbirth, known as labor, begins at about the 40th week of pregnancy. There are three distinct stages of labor: first, the contractions in the uterus and the widening of the cervix; second, the birth of the baby; and finally, the delivery of the placenta. The length of each stage varies between women and often depends on the number of previous pregnancies.

THE FIRST SIGNS OF LABOR

Labor begins when contractions start. The passing of the mucus plug from the cervix occurs up to 10 days before the start of contractions. In addition, the amniotic sac surrounding the baby ruptures either shortly before or at any time in the first stage of labor. The first stage of labor lasts on average 6–12 hours.

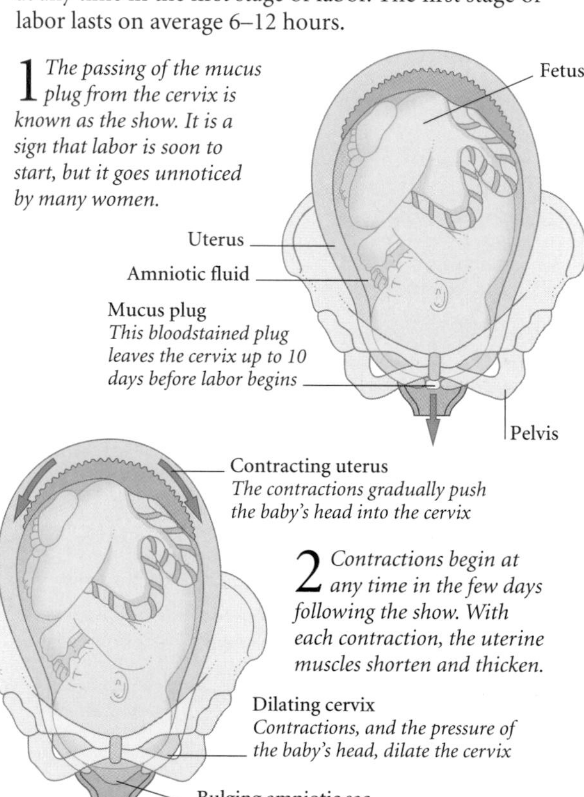
Fetus
Uterus
Amniotic fluid
Mucus plug
This bloodstained plug leaves the cervix up to 10 days before labor begins
Pelvis
Contracting uterus
The contractions gradually push the baby's head into the cervix
Dilating cervix
Contractions, and the pressure of the baby's head, dilate the cervix
Bulging amniotic sac

1 The passing of the mucus plug from the cervix is known as the show. It is a sign that labor is soon to start, but it goes unnoticed by many women.

2 Contractions begin at any time in the few days following the show. With each contraction, the uterine muscles shorten and thicken.

Contracting uterus
The uterus continues to contract, pushing the baby down

Dilated cervix
The cervix has a diameter of about 4 in (10 cm) when fully dilated

3 The contractions gradually become stronger and more regular. By this stage, the amniotic sac has usually burst.

DELIVERY OF THE BABY

During the second stage of labor, the baby travels from the uterus down the vagina and is born. This stage is much quicker than the first stage and usually lasts 1–2 hours. The cervix is fully dilated, and the uterine contractions are very strong and usually painful. The baby's head presses down on the pelvic floor, which causes the mother to have an overwhelming urge to push down. Once the baby's head is visible at the vaginal opening, the birth is imminent.

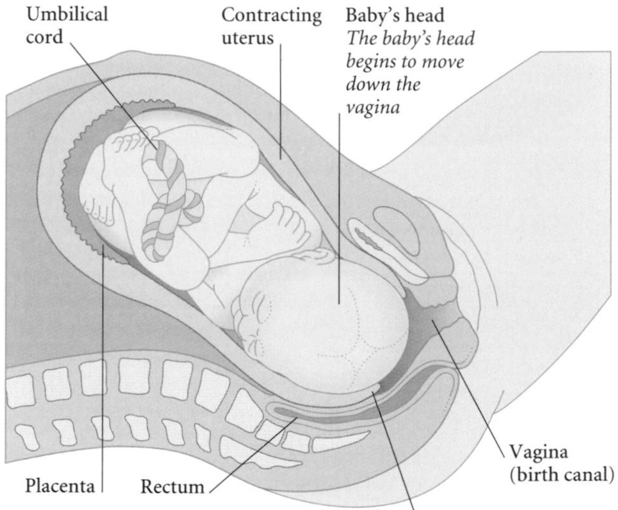
Umbilical cord
Contracting uterus
Baby's head
The baby's head begins to move down the vagina
Placenta
Rectum
Vagina (birth canal)
Dilated cervix
The cervix is fully dilated to allow the baby's head to pass through

1 As the mother starts to push, the baby turns toward the mother's back and begins to move out of the uterus, with its head bent onto its chest. The vagina, or birth canal, stretches as the baby descends.

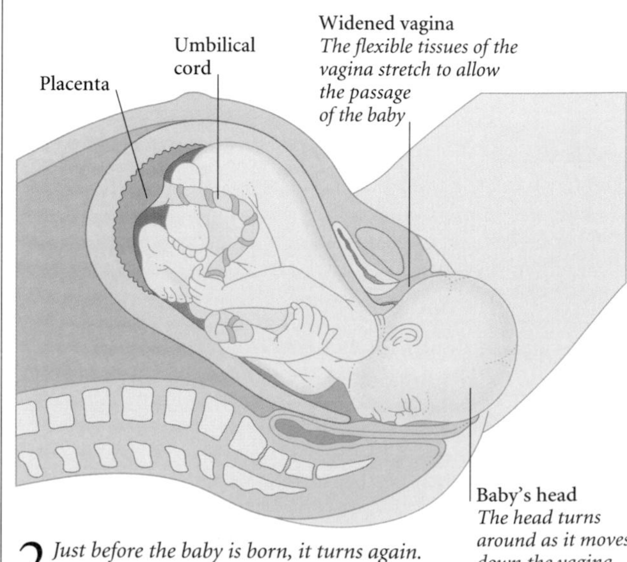
Placenta
Umbilical cord
Widened vagina
The flexible tissues of the vagina stretch to allow the passage of the baby
Baby's head
The head turns around as it moves down the vagina and is the first part of the baby to appear at delivery

2 Just before the baby is born, it turns again. The head rotates so that it can negotiate the bend in the vagina. The baby's face usually faces the mother's anus as the baby leaves the vagina.

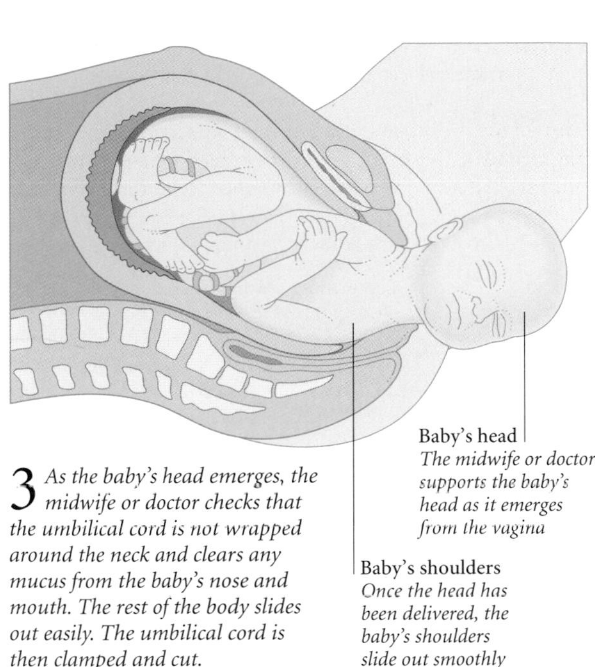

3 *As the baby's head emerges, the midwife or doctor checks that the umbilical cord is not wrapped around the neck and clears any mucus from the baby's nose and mouth. The rest of the body slides out easily. The umbilical cord is then clamped and cut.*

Baby's head
The midwife or doctor supports the baby's head as it emerges from the vagina

Baby's shoulders
Once the head has been delivered, the baby's shoulders slide out smoothly

Delivery of the placenta

During the third stage of labor, the placenta is expelled from the uterus. Sometimes the mother is injected with a drug to help the uterus contract and speed up this stage. Blood vessels in the uterus also contract to stop bleeding. The placenta peels away from the lining of the uterus and is pulled gently through the vagina and out of the body.

Uterus
The uterus resumes mild contractions shortly after the baby is born

Placenta
The placenta separates from the uterus 5–15 minutes after delivery

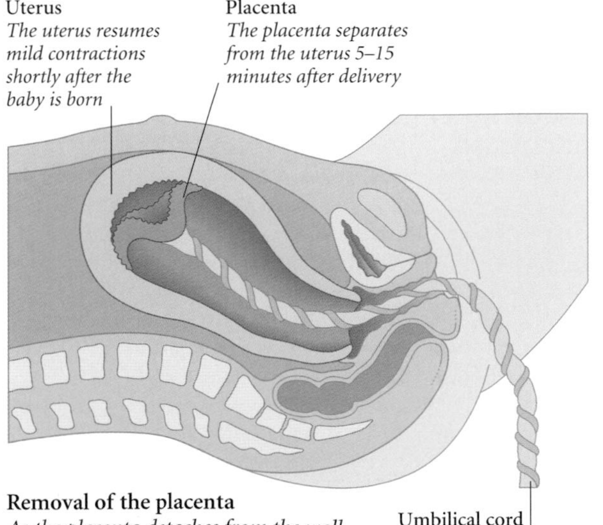

Removal of the placenta
As the placenta detaches from the wall of the uterus and moves down the vagina, the doctor gently pulls on the cord. Any bleeding vessels in the uterus are sealed as the uterus contracts.

Umbilical cord
Once the placenta has separated from the uterus, it is eased out by gently pulling on the cord

PROCESS After the birth

After birth, the mother's breasts produce colostrum, a fluid rich in nutrients and antibodies, before milk production begins. The mother's uterus, cervix, vagina, and abdomen, which enlarged during pregnancy, begin to return to their normal sizes.

Preparing for lactation

During pregnancy, the lobules (milk-producing glands), which are dormant in nonpregnant women, gradually become able to produce milk in preparation for nourishing the newborn baby. At the same time, they increase in number in order to produce enough milk.

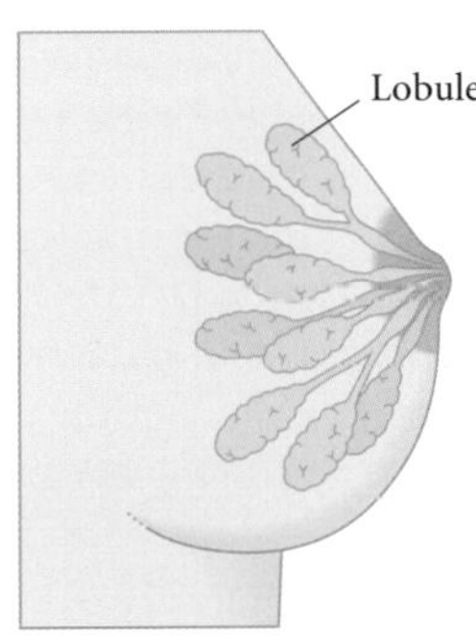
Lobule

Before pregnancy

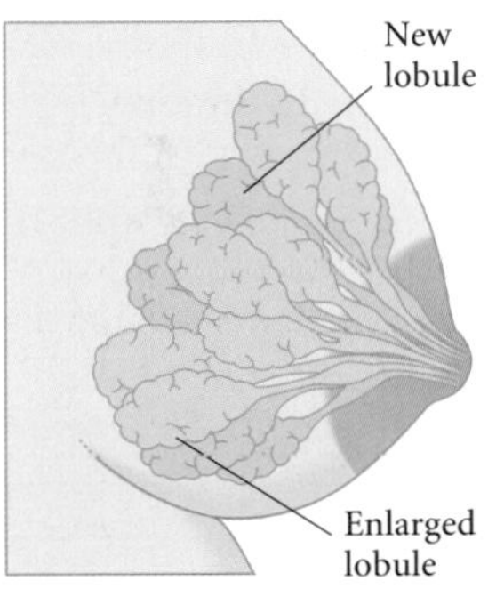
New lobule
Enlarged lobule

During pregnancy

Changes in the breasts
The number of lobules (milk-producing glands) in the breasts increases during pregnancy. After 3 months, they are able to produce colostrum, and after the baby is born, they can produce around 2 pints (1 liter) of milk per day.

The uterus returns to normal

The uterus begins to shrink right after the birth and continues to decrease in size for the next 6–8 weeks, helped by hormones circulating in the mother's body. There may be some mild pains as the uterus shrinks, but these usually disappear a few weeks after delivery.

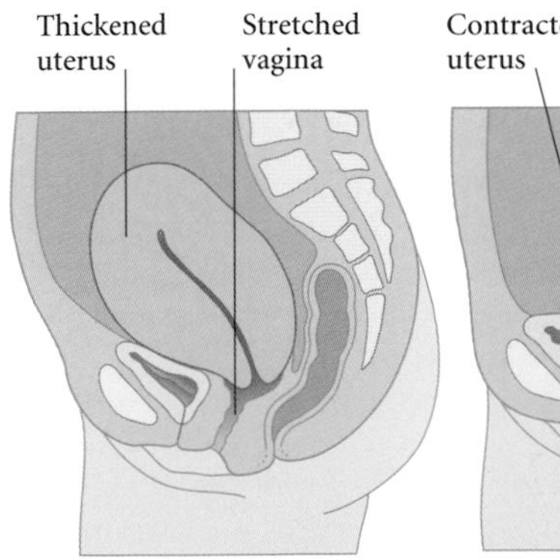
Thickened uterus
Stretched vagina

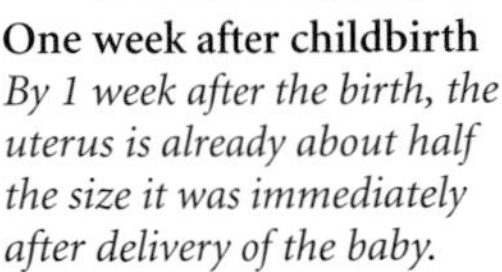

One week after childbirth
By 1 week after the birth, the uterus is already about half the size it was immediately after delivery of the baby.

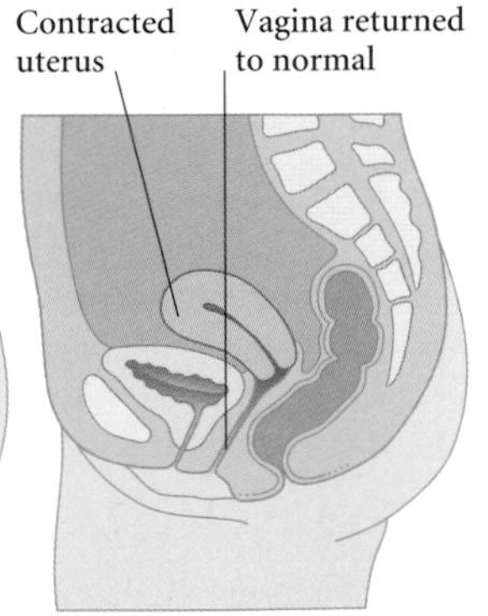
Contracted uterus
Vagina returned to normal

Six weeks after childbirth
After 6 weeks, the uterus has contracted, although not quite to its original size, and returned to its usual position.

PROBLEMS IN PREGNANCY

Pregnancy normally lasts about 40 weeks dating from the first day of the woman's last menstrual period. During this time, a single fertilized cell develops into a fully grown fetus that is able to survive outside the uterus. For the fetus to develop, it must be protected in the uterus and nourished by the mother. Although this process usually progresses smoothly, problems may develop.

Problems during pregnancy may affect the mother, the fetus, or both. Many of the most common disorders are mild and short-lived, but others may be severe or even life-threatening to the mother or the fetus.

The first article in this section deals with common complaints that occur at some time during most pregnancies. These complaints are usually minor and often relieved by simple self-help measures. High-risk pregnancies and preexisting conditions that should be taken into consideration if planning a pregnancy are discussed next. The remaining articles in this section cover various problems that may occur at different stages of pregnancy.

In developed countries, pregnancy is no longer a major health risk for most women. In some cases, problems in pregnancy can be averted by good prenatal care and a healthy lifestyle before and during pregnancy. Advice about healthy eating and exercise during pregnancy can be found elsewhere (*see* HEALTH IN PREGNANCY AND AFTER CHILDBIRTH, p.33).

KEY ANATOMY

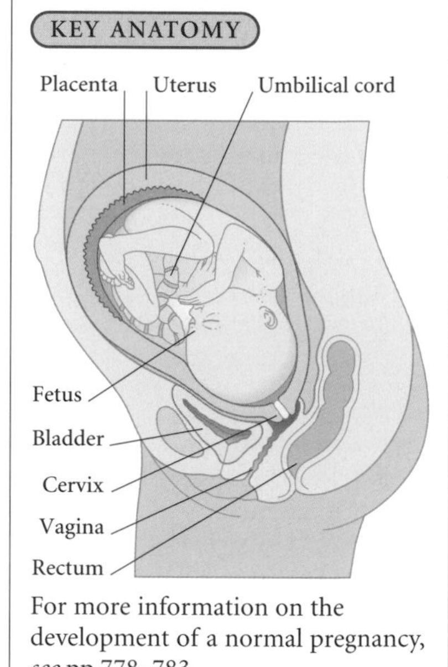
Placenta
Uterus
Umbilical cord
Fetus
Bladder
Cervix
Vagina
Rectum

For more information on the development of a normal pregnancy, *see* pp.778–783.

Common complaints of normal pregnancy

Minor problems commonly experienced during pregnancy

 AGE GENETICS LIFESTYLE Not significant factors

Most of the common complaints that occur during pregnancy are not serious and are a result of the normal changes in the body that take place as the pregnancy progresses. Some problems are caused by changes in the levels of sex hormones in the mother, others by the weight and pressure of the developing fetus on the organs around the uterus. Although many pregnant women experience some or all of these complaints, others have only a few problems, and some feel even healthier than usual.

WHAT ARE THE SYMPTOMS?

Some symptoms that occur in pregnancy are due to the hormonal changes taking place in the body. They often develop early and may include:

- Breast tenderness.
- Nausea, often with vomiting (known as morning sickness).
- Constipation (p.628).
- Heartburn (*see* GASTROESOPHAGEAL REFLUX DISEASE, p.636).
- Skin changes, such as increased pigmentation and dry skin.

The weight and pressure of the growing fetus and surrounding fluid may also cause symptoms. These usually develop later in pregnancy than those due to hormonal changes and may include:

- An increased urge to urinate.
- Increased constipation, which sometimes leads to hemorrhoids (p.668).
- Swollen ankles.
- Varicose veins (p.438).
- Stretch marks (p.349).
- Backache.
- Sciatica (p.546).
- Shortness of breath.
- Difficulty sleeping due to discomfort.

You may also feel very tired, feel faint on occasion, and have headaches.

It is normal to have several different symptoms during pregnancy and often to have more than one problem at a time. If you are worried about a specific symptom, you should obtain medical advice. You should also speak to your doctor if you are having problems with severe vomiting and cannot keep any food or fluids down (*see* HYPEREMESIS, p.789). If you find it painful to urinate or your urine appears cloudy, you should consult your doctor to make sure that you do not have a urinary tract infection, such as cystitis (p.709).

WHAT CAN I DO?

There is little that you can do to relieve some of the symptoms associated with pregnancy, such as breast tenderness. However, some other complaints may be eased by various self-help measures (*see* COPING WITH PREGNANCY, opposite page). For example, you may be able to relieve morning sickness by eating before you get out of bed. Eating small snacks throughout the day rather than a few larger meals and sleeping propped up by several pillows may help reduce nausea and heartburn. If heartburn is severe, you may be prescribed medication to help reduce the acidity of the stomach (*see* ANTACIDS, p.923).

It is important that you check with your doctor before you take any over-the-counter drugs because there are several common medications, such as laxatives and analgesics, that can harm a developing baby and should not be taken at any time during pregnancy.

(WWW) ONLINE SITES: p.1036

SELF-HELP COPING WITH PREGNANCY

It is normal to experience a variety of complaints during pregnancy. These are usually caused by hormonal changes within the body and by the increasing weight of the fetus. Although such complaints may cause discomfort, they are usually not serious. Many symptoms can be relieved by self-help measures, but you should consult your pharmacist or doctor before using any drugs and see your doctor if symptoms are severe.

DIGESTIVE COMPLAINTS

A healthy diet is important throughout pregnancy. It not only provides the fetus with the correct nutrients for growth but also helps prevent digestive complaints, such as nausea, vomiting, heartburn, and constipation. Avoid eating spicy foods because they can cause heartburn, and always have something plain available to eat in case you feel hungry.

Milk
Drinking milk may help ease heartburn

Fruit
Eating fruit may reduce constipation

Eating during pregnancy
Small, frequent meals may help reduce nausea, and milky drinks may ease heartburn. Plenty of fruit, vegetables, and other fiber-rich foods in your diet should help reduce constipation.

CIRCULATORY COMPLAINTS

Increased pressure on the blood vessels in the pelvis may lead to varicose veins, swollen ankles, and feeling faint in late pregnancy. To relieve symptoms, avoid standing still for long and sit or lie down whenever you feel faint. Support panty hose may help relieve varicose veins.

Support for back

Feet raised above hip level

Pillow under legs

Sitting comfortably
Try to rest and put your feet up whenever possible. Support your back and always try to elevate your feet above the level of your hips.

BACKACHE AND SCIATICA

Backache is an increasingly common problem as pregnancy progresses, and poor posture may place pressure on the sciatic nerve, causing a shooting pain from the buttock down one leg (sciatica). Both of these problems may be eased by adopting good posture when standing, using a chair with good back support, sleeping on a firm mattress, and wearing flat shoes.

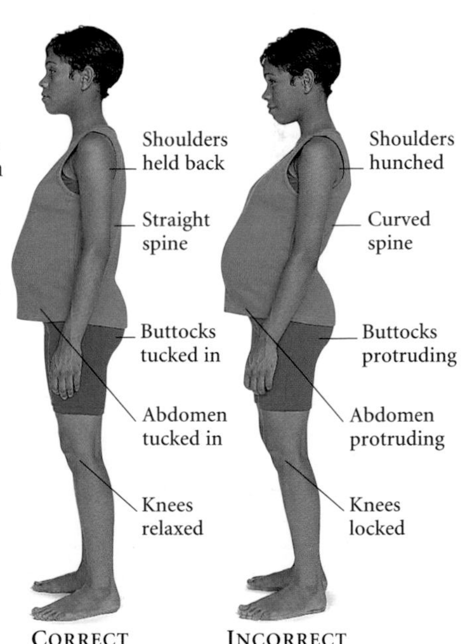
Shoulders held back
Straight spine
Buttocks tucked in
Abdomen tucked in
Knees relaxed
CORRECT
Shoulders hunched
Curved spine
Buttocks protruding
Abdomen protruding
Knees locked
INCORRECT

Standing correctly
Stand with your feet apart and your weight equally balanced on each foot. Hold your back straight and your shoulders back. Tuck in your buttocks and abdomen and relax your knees.

FATIGUE AND DIFFICULTY SLEEPING

You will probably feel tired from early pregnancy onward. As your pregnancy progresses and your abdomen enlarges, you may also find it more difficult to get into a comfortable position in which to sleep. Before going to bed, try to relax, have a warm bath and a milky drink, and watch television, listen to the radio, or read until you feel sleepy.

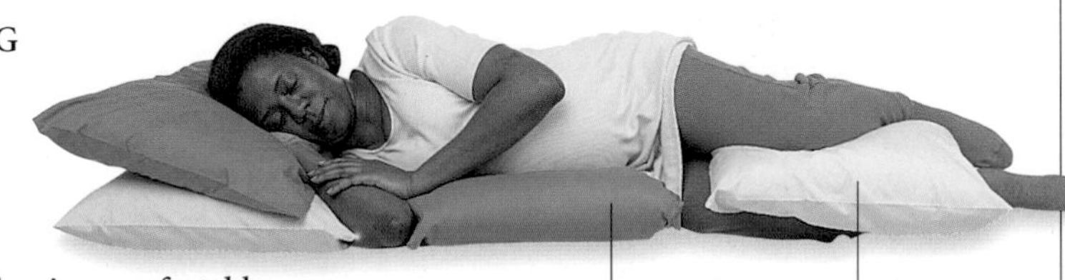

Supporting pillow under abdomen

Pillow between legs

Sleeping comfortably
Try to sleep on your side, with a pillow between your legs. You may feel more comfortable if you place another pillow under your abdomen.

High-risk pregnancy

A pregnancy with a higher than average risk for the mother or fetus

AGE Most common under age 15 or over age 35

LIFESTYLE Smoking and alcohol or drug abuse during pregnancy are risk factors

GENETICS Risk factors depend on the cause

For most women, pregnancy progresses well except for some minor problems (*see* COMMON COMPLAINTS OF NORMAL PREGNANCY, p.784), which are usually not serious. However, pregnancy is not without risks, and, although the overall risk of death for both mother and fetus is low, it increases in certain situations. Some women are at higher risk of developing problems in pregnancy, and one of the functions of routine prenatal care (below) is to identify these women so that they can be monitored and receive additional treatment if needed.

WHAT ARE THE RISK FACTORS?

There are many different factors that lead to a high-risk pregnancy. Women under age 15 or over age 35 are more likely to have problems in pregnancy as are women with a small build. Other risk factors in pregnancy include certain lifestyle factors, such as smoking, a history of problems in previous pregnancies, and preexisting illnesses.

AGE Women under age 15 who become pregnant are at increased risk of going into labor before the end of pregnancy (*see* PRETERM LABOR, p.798). They are also at risk of developing certain complications during their pregnancy, such as preeclampsia and eclampsia (p.794), in which blood pressure is elevated.

Women over age 35 are more likely to have preexisting disorders, such as noncancerous tumors in the uterus (*see* FIBROIDS, p.745) or diabetes mellitus (p.687). They are also more likely to develop preeclampsia or diabetes while pregnant (*see* DIABETES DEVELOPING IN PREGNANCY, p.788). All of these problems may place the pregnancy at greater risk. There is also an increased risk of the fetus having a chromosome disorder, such as Down syndrome (p.821), if the mother is over age 35.

PHYSICAL FACTORS Women who have a small build and a small pelvis are at greater risk of a delayed first stage of labor (p.801), especially if they are carrying a large baby who cannot easily fit through the pelvis.

Underweight women who weigh less than 105 lb (47.5 kg) before pregnancy are more likely to have small babies. Conversely, women who are overweight are more likely to develop diabetes during pregnancy, which increases their risk of having a large baby. Overweight women are at greater risk of high blood pressure (*see* HYPERTENSION, p.403).

LIFESTYLE FACTORS A poor diet, smoking, and alcohol and drug abuse during pregnancy all increase the risk of various problems, including miscarriage (p.791), preterm labor (p.798), and the baby being small for gestational age (p.796).

PROBLEMS IN PREVIOUS PREGNANCIES Any problems in a previous pregnancy, such as a preterm labor or a stillbirth (p.805), tend to increase the risk for the current pregnancy. A woman who had a small baby in a previous pregnancy will be more likely to have another baby who is underweight.

PREEXISTING ILLNESSES Any preexisting disorder (*see* PREEXISTING DISEASES IN PREGNANCY, p.788), such as diabetes mellitus, epilepsy (p.524), or preexisting high blood pressure, may lead to

(TEST) ROUTINE PRENATAL CARE

Prenatal care is essential to make sure that a pregnancy is progressing well. Regular prenatal visits include one or more ultrasound scans of the developing fetus. Occasionally, prenatal genetic tests (opposite page) may also be carried out to look for disorders in the fetus.

Routine tests
Prenatal care starts at about 11 weeks. Follow-up occurs monthly at first; every 2 weeks from 28 to 36 weeks; and every week after 36 weeks.

WHEN DONE	TYPE OF TEST	REASON FOR TEST
First visit	Medical history and examination	To look for preexisting risk factors, such as chronic illnesses
	Pap test (p.749)	To check for cervical dysplasia (p.749)
	Urine tests	To check the urine for glucose, which may indicate diabetes developing in pregnancy (p.788), and for protein, which may indicate preexisting kidney disease
	Blood tests	To determine blood type and look for anemia (p.446), antibodies to rubella (p.292), and infectious diseases, such as hepatitis B and, after discussion, HIV infection (p.295)
	Weight and blood pressure	To provide initial measurements against which later ones are compared
Between 11 and 20 weeks	Ultrasound scans (one or more)	To check the age of the fetus and look for fetal abnormalities (*see* ULTRASOUND SCANNING IN PREGNANCY, p.793)
Follow-up visits at regular intervals from 11 weeks to delivery	Weight and examination	To assess the growth of the fetus and to see which way it is lying in the uterus
	Urine tests	To detect diabetes or preeclampsia (*see* PREECLAMPSIA AND ECLAMPSIA, p.794)
	Blood pressure	To detect developing preeclampsia
	Blood tests (at some visits only)	To look for anemia and, in combination with ultrasound scanning, to assess the risk of fetal abnormalities, such as neural tube defects (p.844) or Down syndrome (p.821). A test to screen for diabetes mellitus may also be needed

TEST PRENATAL GENETIC TESTS

If you are at increased risk of having a baby with a gene or chromosome disorder, possibly because of your age, you may be offered one of two tests: chorionic villus sampling or amniocentesis. The tests are outpatient procedures and take approximately 30 minutes each. Both of these tests increase the risk of miscarriage, and you will be given counseling to help you decide whether or not you wish to have the test.

CHORIONIC VILLUS SAMPLING

This test is usually carried out between weeks 8 and 11 of pregnancy. Tissue from the edge of the placenta (chorionic villi) is taken and then analyzed for a chromosomal or gene abnormality. The risk of miscarriage is highest in early pregnancy and is increased slightly by the test.

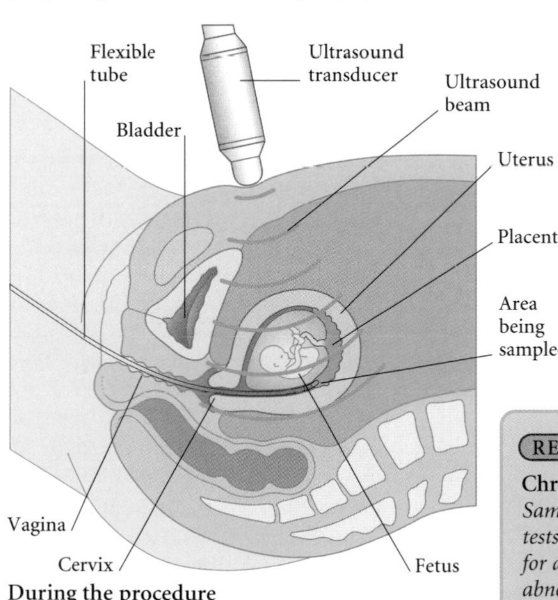
Flexible tube
Ultrasound transducer
Ultrasound beam
Bladder
Uterus
Placenta
Area being sampled
Vagina
Cervix
Fetus

During the procedure
A flexible tube is inserted through the cervix using ultrasound as a guide, and a small sample of the placenta is removed by gentle suction. Sometimes a needle is inserted through the abdominal wall instead. Mild discomfort or cramping may be felt.

AMNIOCENTESIS

Amniocentesis is usually carried out between weeks 14 and 18 of pregnancy. A small sample of the amniotic fluid surrounding the fetus is removed and analyzed for genetic abnormalities. The procedure is associated with a very small risk of miscarriage (about 1 in 200 women).

During the procedure
Ultrasound is used to guide a needle into the sac containing the fetus and the amniotic fluid. A small sample of fluid is then withdrawn using a syringe. A slight pricking sensation may be felt.

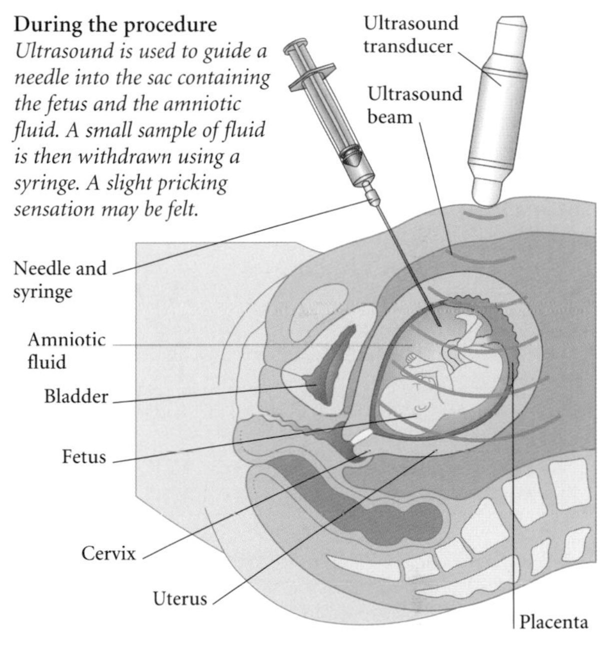
Ultrasound transducer
Ultrasound beam
Needle and syringe
Amniotic fluid
Bladder
Fetus
Cervix
Uterus
Placenta

RESULTS

Chromosome analysis
Samples from genetic tests are analyzed to look for a chromosomal abnormality. This test result shows one extra chromosome number 21, indicating Down syndrome in the fetus.

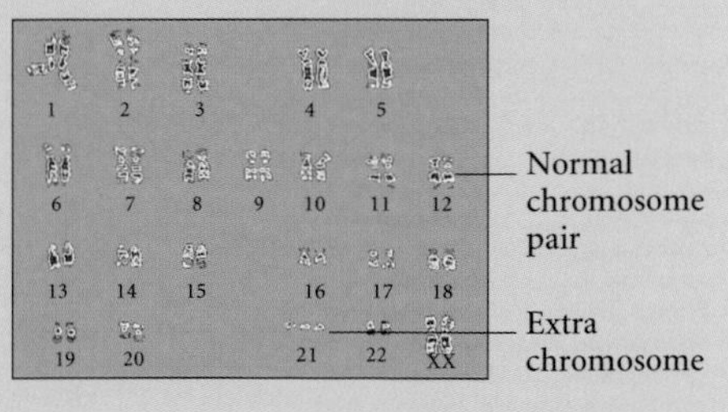
1
2
3
4
5
6
7
8
9
10
11
12
13
14
15
16
17
18
19
20
21
22
XX
Normal chromosome pair
Extra chromosome

certain problems for both mother and fetus. Changes to the mother's current medication and additional monitoring of mother and fetus may be necessary before and during pregnancy.

WHAT MIGHT BE DONE?

At your first prenatal visit, your doctor or midwife will examine you and ask you questions to determine whether or not you are at increased risk. If you are, you will need additional monitoring and possibly specialized treatment during your pregnancy or labor.

If you have a high-risk pregnancy, you will probably need more frequent prenatal visits than usual to make sure that the pregnancy is progressing normally. You may also be offered additional tests if you are at increased risk of having a baby with a gene or chromosome disorder (*see* PRENATAL GENETIC TESTS, above). Frequent blood tests may be needed to monitor any preexisting diseases, and additional ultrasound scans may be required to monitor the development and growth of the fetus (*see* ULTRASOUND SCANNING IN PREGNANCY, p.793). You may be supervised by several doctors, including specialists, who will work together to maximize your chances of a successful pregnancy.

WHAT IS THE PROGNOSIS?

With careful monitoring and appropriate delivery techniques, the majority of problems in pregnancy can be treated successfully. Although complications are still more likely to occur in a high-risk pregnancy, modern treatments have significantly improved the outlook.

(WWW) ONLINE SITES: p.1036

Preexisting diseases in pregnancy

Chronic preexisting diseases that could affect the progress of pregnancy or the health of the fetus

AGE More common over age 35

GENETICS LIFESTYLE Not significant factors

Although many women who become pregnant are healthy, others have a preexisting disease that may require them to have specialist care throughout pregnancy and labor. Preexisting conditions that could adversely affect pregnancy or the health of the fetus are more common in women over age 35.

Chronic preexisting conditions and their treatments may affect the progress of the pregnancy. For example, women who have diabetes mellitus (p.687) are susceptible to preterm labor (p.798) if their diabetes is not controlled properly in pregnancy. Changes in hormone levels during pregnancy can have a variety of effects depending on the chronic disease present. Whereas diabetes mellitus often worsens in pregnancy, some women who have mild asthma (p.483) find that their condition improves.

The fetus may also be affected by preexisting diseases in the mother. For example, a mother who has high blood pressure (*see* HYPERTENSION, p.403) is at an increased risk of having a smaller than average baby (*see* SMALL FOR GESTATIONAL AGE, p.796). A baby who is born to a woman with diabetes mellitus may have low blood sugar levels immediately after the birth.

If you have a chronic condition, you should consult your doctor for advice before you become pregnant. Your condition and that of your fetus will need careful monitoring, and your regular doctor will work with your obstetrician to ensure that you receive the best care.

WHAT MIGHT BE DONE?

If you have a chronic disease, your doctor will review your condition before you become pregnant to make sure that it is as well controlled as possible.

Your usual treatment may need to be altered while you are pregnant because some drugs can affect the fetus. For example, if you normally take pills to control your diabetes mellitus, you will have to change to insulin injections (*see* DRUGS FOR DIABETES MELLITUS, p.931). The dose of some treatments may also need to be altered, and additional measures may be required. For example, women who have epilepsy (p.524) and are taking anticonvulsant drugs (p.914) will usually be prescribed a higher than normal dose of folic acid to reduce the risk of their medication causing neural tube defects (p.844) in the fetus.

You may have prenatal checkups at more frequent intervals than usual, and your doctor may refer you to an obstetrician specializing in your condition. Additional tests may be necessary, including extra ultrasound scanning (*see* ULTRASOUND SCANNING IN PREGNANCY, p.793). Extra monitoring may be necessary during labor, and after the delivery your baby may have tests to ensure that he or she is healthy.

WHAT IS THE PROGNOSIS?

With monitoring and treatment, preexisting conditions in pregnancy can be controlled and carry little risk for the mother or the fetus. Changes in the disorder as a result of the pregnancy are normally reversed soon after delivery.

(WWW) ONLINE SITES: p.1036

Diabetes developing in pregnancy

Inability of the tissues to absorb glucose from the bloodstream during pregnancy due to a lack of the hormone insulin

AGE More common over age 30

GENETICS A family history of diabetes mellitus is a risk factor

LIFESTYLE Being overweight is a risk factor

During the course of pregnancy, up to 1 in 50 women temporarily develops diabetes mellitus (p.687). The condition is called gestational diabetes. Normally, the hormone insulin, which is produced by the pancreas, enables body cells to absorb glucose from the bloodstream. During pregnancy, additional hormones, which have an anti-insulin effect, are produced by the placenta. If the body does not produce enough insulin to counter this effect, the result is high levels of glucose in the blood and gestational diabetes.

Diabetes developing in pregnancy is more common in women over age 30, women who are overweight, and those who have a family history of diabetes mellitus. Gestational diabetes can usually be controlled by a special diet.

In almost all cases, gestational diabetes disappears soon after the birth of the baby, but about 1 in 3 women who have had gestational diabetes develops permanent type 2 diabetes mellitus, often within 5 years of her pregnancy.

WHAT ARE THE SYMPTOMS?

Many women with gestational diabetes do not develop symptoms. Others may develop symptoms that include:

- Fatigue.
- Increased thirst and appetite.
- Passing large amounts of urine.

If gestational diabetes is not controlled, the fetus may gain an excessive amount of weight and may have difficulty passing through the mother's pelvis. Labor may then be particularly difficult (*see* DELAYED FIRST STAGE OF LABOR, p.801). Babies born to mothers with gestational diabetes are also at risk of having low blood sugar levels at birth. Women whose diabetes cannot be controlled have a greater risk of a stillbirth (p.805).

HOW IS IT DIAGNOSED?

Your urine will be tested for glucose at each prenatal visit. If glucose is found, your doctor may arrange for a glucose tolerance test, in which you are given a sugar solution to drink and a sample of blood is tested. If your blood shows higher glucose levels than would normally be anticipated, the diagnosis is confirmed. Your doctor may also suggest that you have this test if you had an unexplained stillbirth in the past or have given birth to a larger than average baby or if diabetes mellitus runs in your family. This test may be performed routinely during weeks 24–28 of pregnancy.

WHAT IS THE TREATMENT?

If you have gestational diabetes, your doctor will recommend that you follow a modified diet that includes less sugar than normal and greater amounts of fiber and starchy carbohydrates. Some women also need insulin injections.

You will need to have a blood test at least once every 2 weeks to check your blood sugar levels. You may also be advised to test your blood sugar levels at home (*see* MONITORING YOUR BLOOD GLUCOSE, p.689) and check your urine daily for glucose. More frequent prenatal visits than normal may be necessary, and you may also need to have extra ultrasound scanning (*see* ULTRASOUND SCANNING IN PREGNANCY, p.793).

For most women with gestational diabetes, pregnancy progresses safely to about 40 weeks, and vaginal delivery is possible. However, if diabetes becomes difficult to control, early induction of labor (p.797) may be necessary. If the fetus is very large, the doctor may consider a cesarean section (p.802) to avoid a difficult vaginal delivery.

After delivery, your blood sugar levels and those of your baby will be monitored carefully. If the baby's blood sugar level is low, he or she may need to be admitted to a neonatal care unit (p.959) for treatment. Since you may be at risk of developing permanent diabetes mellitus after pregnancy, you will be given a glucose tolerance test at your 6-week postnatal checkup.

WHAT IS THE PROGNOSIS?

Usually, glucose levels return to normal soon after delivery of the baby, and you should be able to resume your normal diet. If you were having insulin injections, they can be stopped. However, you are likely to develop diabetes during future pregnancies.

(WWW) ONLINE SITES: p.1029, p.1036

Hyperemesis

Severe vomiting associated with early pregnancy

LIFESTYLE Stress may aggravate the condition

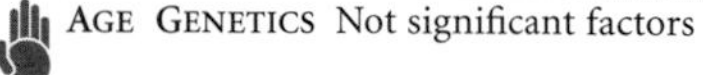

AGE GENETICS Not significant factors

In hyperemesis, vomiting in early pregnancy is so severe that no food or fluids can be kept down. Hyperemesis is more severe than common morning sickness (*see* COMMON COMPLAINTS OF NORMAL PREGNANCY, p.784), in which nausea and vomiting during early pregnancy are usually not serious and can often be relieved by a few simple measures. When morning sickness occurs in pregnancy, the mother continues to gain weight steadily. In contrast, a mother who has hyperemesis will lose weight. Excessive vomiting eventually leads to dehydration, which, in turn, decreases urination and causes an imbalance of chemicals in the blood. Allowed to continue without treatment, dehydration may become a life-threatening condition for both the mother and the fetus.

The cause of hyperemesis is usually not known, although it is thought that very high amounts of human chorionic gonadotropin (HCG), a hormone that occurs in pregnancy, may contribute to excessive vomiting in the mother. High levels of HCG occur if there is more than one fetus present (*see* MULTIPLE PREGNANCY AND ITS PROBLEMS, p.792) or, less commonly, if a tumor develops from part of the placenta (*see* MOLAR PREGNANCY, p.790). Occasionally, psychological factors, such as stress, may aggravate the condition.

WHAT MIGHT BE DONE?

If you are unable to keep any food or fluids down, you need to be admitted to the hospital. You may have blood tests to assess the degree of dehydration. You may also have ultrasound scanning (*see* ULTRASOUND SCANNING IN PREGNANCY, p.793) to investigate the possibility of a multiple or molar pregnancy.

Usually, dehydration is treated with intravenous fluids. You may be given drugs that help stop vomiting (*see* ANTIEMETIC DRUGS, p.922) and possibly sedatives to help you relax.

Once the vomiting has been treated, you should be able to start eating small quantities of plain food and gradually build up to a normal diet. However, vomiting often recurs, and further hospital stays may be necessary to prevent dehydration. Hyperemesis usually subsides after the 14th week of pregnancy, although the condition is likely to recur in subsequent pregnancies.

(WWW) ONLINE SITES: p.1036

TREATMENT TERMINATION OF PREGNANCY

A termination of pregnancy (therapeutic abortion) may be carried out early in pregnancy with minimal risk or side effects. All types of termination cause some abdominal pain for a few hours and a brown discharge for several days. Sexual intercourse should be avoided for 2 weeks.

Methods of termination

There are several different methods of termination, depending on the stage of the pregnancy. Most terminations are carried out using suction between 6 and 14 weeks.

WHEN DONE	WHERE DONE	PROCEDURE USED
Before 7 weeks	Available at some clinics in urban centers	Medical methods for an early termination of pregnancy are undergoing clinical trials. Where this method is available, it involves medications that cause the placenta to detach from the uterus. After 36–48 hours a prostaglandin suppository is placed in the vagina in order to encourage the uterus to contract and expel the embryo. Monitoring is carried out for a further 6–8 hours
At 6–14 weeks	At a clinic or hospital. No overnight stay is required	A suction device is inserted through the cervix and into the uterus under general anesthesia or, in some centers, local anesthesia. A vaginal device may be used first to gently dilate the cervix. The fetus is then removed
After 14 weeks	In the hospital. An overnight stay is usually required	A prostaglandin drug is given to stimulate uterine contractions, which expel the fetus. The drug may be given as an intravenous infusion, a vaginal suppository, or an injection through the abdomen into the uterus. Pain relief (*see* ANALGESICS, p.912) and mild sedatives may be needed

Molar pregnancy

A rare condition in which part of the placenta develops into a tumor

AGE More common over age 35

GENETICS More common in Asian women

LIFESTYLE Not a significant factor

In about 1 in 2,000 pregnancies, part of the placenta develops into a hydatidiform mole, a tumor that looks similar to a small bunch of grapes. Although a hydatidiform mole is noncancerous, in a few cases it develops into a cancerous tumor. In a molar pregnancy, there are higher than normal levels of a hormone called human chorionic gonadotropin (HCG), which is normally produced in pregnancy. In most molar pregnancies, the tumor prevents a fetus from developing, but occasionally an abnormal fetus develops. Placental cells left after a miscarriage or pregnancy may also develop into a hydatidiform mole.

In about 1 in 10 molar pregnancies, a hydatidiform mole invades the wall of the uterus. In about 3 in 100 cases, a hydatidiform mole becomes cancerous (*see* CHORIOCARCINOMA, p.748) and may spread. Molar pregnancy occurs more often in women over age 35 and tends to be far more common in Asian women, but the cause is unknown.

WHAT ARE THE SYMPTOMS?

A hydatidiform mole exaggerates some of the symptoms of a normal pregnancy, such as fatigue. Other symptoms may include the following:

- Bleeding from the vagina and passing material that looks like grapes.
- Extreme nausea and vomiting (*see* HYPEREMESIS, p.789).

A hydatidiform mole grows faster than a normal fetus, making the uterus larger than normal for the stage of pregnancy. If the pregnancy progresses, additional problems, including preeclampsia (*see* PREECLAMPSIA AND ECLAMPSIA, p.794) and anemia (p.446), may develop.

WHAT MIGHT BE DONE?

If you are experiencing severe nausea and vomiting, or if your uterus appears much larger than normal for the stage of your pregnancy, your doctor may suspect a molar pregnancy. He or she will arrange for an ultrasound scan (*see* ULTRASOUND SCANNING IN PREGNANCY, p.793) to look for signs of a molar pregnancy, and your blood will be tested to measure levels of HCG. If a hydatidiform mole is diagnosed, the abnormal tissue will be removed from the uterus under general anesthesia.

WHAT IS THE PROGNOSIS?

Most women recover fully and need no further treatment once the molar pregnancy has been removed. However, a choriocarcinoma sometimes develops and further treatment, such as chemotherapy (p.278), is needed.

All women who have had a molar pregnancy should have regular blood tests for at least 2 years to measure HCG levels and ensure that any further tumors are detected early. It is advisable not to conceive for at least 1 year after receiving treatment for a hydatidiform mole because it can often be difficult to distinguish a molar pregnancy from a normal pregnancy in the early stages. In up to 3 in 100 subsequent pregnancies, a hydatidiform mole recurs.

(WWW) ONLINE SITES: p.1036

Ectopic pregnancy

A pregnancy that develops outside the uterus, usually in one fallopian tube

AGE Most common between the ages of 20 and 29

LIFESTYLE Use of an intrauterine contraceptive device is a risk factor

GENETICS Not a significant factor

About 1 in 100 pregnancies is ectopic. In an ectopic pregnancy, a fertilized egg becomes implanted in the tissues outside the uterus instead of implanting in the lining of the uterus. The egg then begins to develop into an embryo. In most cases, the fertilized egg lodges in one of the fallopian tubes. Rarely, the egg implants in the cervix, in one of the two ovaries, or in the abdominal cavity. The fetus is not able to grow normally in an ectopic pregnancy and will not survive.

If the placenta develops inside a fallopian tube and the fetus grows, the fallopian tube will eventually rupture, causing life-threatening bleeding into the mother's abdominal cavity. Ectopic pregnancies need to be removed surgically or dealt with medically as soon as possible after detection because of the serious risk to the mother.

WHAT ARE THE CAUSES?

Ectopic pregnancy is more common in women aged 20 to 29, but the cause is not always known. However, previous damage to one of the two fallopian tubes may obstruct the passage of a fertilized egg along the tube to the uterus. The egg then implants in the wall of the tube instead of in the uterus. This prior damage may have been caused by an unsuccessful or a reversed sterilization procedure (*see* TUBAL LIGATION, p.743) or a fallopian tube infection (*see* PELVIC INFLAMMATORY DISEASE, p.741). Ectopic pregnancies may be more common in women using an intrauterine contraceptive device (*see* CONTRACEPTION, p.69), partly because these devices increase the risk of a pelvic infection in women who are exposed to sexually transmitted diseases (p.764).

WHAT ARE THE SYMPTOMS?

An ectopic pregnancy usually produces symptoms in the first 6–7 weeks of pregnancy, sometimes even before the woman realizes that she is pregnant. However, most women who have an ectopic pregnancy will have missed a menstrual period. The symptoms of an ectopic pregnancy may include:

- Pain that is low down on one side of the abdomen.
- Irregular vaginal bleeding that may be confused with menstruation.

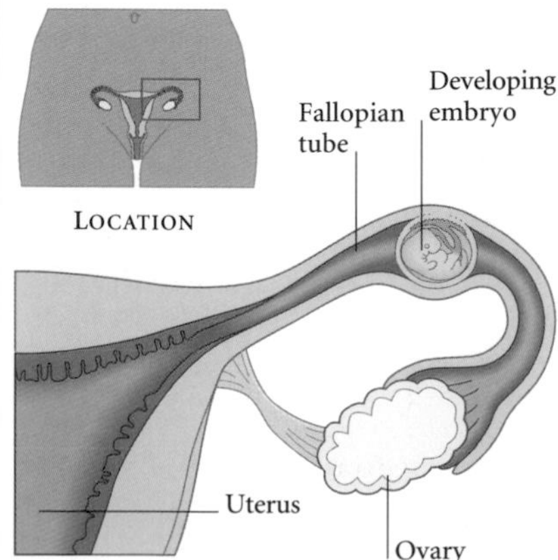
LOCATION
Fallopian tube
Developing embryo
Uterus
Ovary

Ectopic pregnancy
In most ectopic pregnancies, the fertilized egg implants in a fallopian tube and starts to develop there, rather than in the uterus.

If the ectopic pregnancy is not detected and a fallopian tube ruptures, further symptoms may develop that include:

- Sudden, severe pain that gradually spreads throughout the abdomen.
- Shoulder pain (referred pain due to overlapping nerve pathways).

Sudden internal bleeding follows the rupture of the fallopian tube and may cause shock (p.414). If you are in shock, you may sweat profusely and feel faint. It is important to see your doctor at once if you have abdominal pain or vaginal bleeding and might be pregnant. If you experience severe pain and shock, call an ambulance immediately.

WHAT MIGHT BE DONE?

If you are not sure whether or not you are pregnant, a pregnancy test will be performed. If the test is positive, your doctor may arrange for you to have an ultrasound scan using a probe through your vagina to find out the position of the embryo. You may also have a blood test to measure blood levels of human chorionic gonadotropin (HCG), a hormone that is produced in lower amounts than normal in ectopic pregnancies. To confirm the diagnosis, an examination of the inside of the abdominal cavity may be performed under general anesthesia (*see* LAPAROSCOPY, p.742).

If an ectopic pregnancy is confirmed, the embryo and surrounding tissue are surgically removed. A damaged fallopian tube will be repaired if possible, but, if it is badly damaged, the tube may be removed to prevent another ectopic pregnancy from occurring at the same site. An early ectopic pregnancy may be treated with the drug methotrexate, taken orally, instead of surgery.

WHAT IS THE PROGNOSIS?

Although ectopic pregnancy will recur in 1 in 10 affected women, most women can have normal pregnancies even if one fallopian tube has been removed. If both fallopian tubes have been damaged, in-vitro fertilization treatment (*see* ASSISTED CONCEPTION, p.776) may help a woman become pregnant.

In subsequent pregnancies, an ultrasound scan (*see* ULTRASOUND SCANNING IN PREGNANCY, p.793) may be done at an early stage to check that the fetus is developing in the uterus.

(WWW) ONLINE SITES: p.1036

Vaginal bleeding in pregnancy

Bleeding from the vagina at any time during pregnancy

AGE GENETICS LIFESTYLE Not significant factors

If you experience vaginal bleeding in pregnancy, you should seek immediate advice from your doctor. If you develop heavy bleeding, particularly late in pregnancy, you should call an ambulance. Emergency care is necessary because severe bleeding may be life-threatening for both you and your baby.

WHAT ARE THE CAUSES?

The causes of vaginal bleeding in pregnancy vary, depending on the stage of the pregnancy. Some common conditions can cause bleeding at any stage. These include noncancerous growths on the cervix (*see* UTERINE POLYPS, p.746) and cervical ectropion (p.749), in which cells on the inner lining of the cervix extend onto its surface.

BLEEDING BEFORE 14 WEEKS Bleeding in early pregnancy is often caused by a miscarriage (right) and may be accompanied by cramping, period-like pain. Light to heavy bleeding accompanied by severe pain at 6–7 weeks may be due to a pregnancy outside the uterus (*see* ECTOPIC PREGNANCY, opposite page).

Rarely, light, painless vaginal bleeding called spotting persists during the first 14 weeks of pregnancy. In most cases, the pregnancy continues.

BLEEDING AT 14–24 WEEKS After week 14 of pregnancy, bleeding may be due to a late miscarriage, the causes of which can include a weak cervix (*see* CERVICAL INCOMPETENCE, p.794). Bleeding due to miscarriage at this stage may be painful.

BLEEDING AFTER 24 WEEKS After the 24th week of pregnancy, painful, light to heavy vaginal bleeding is most often caused by placental abruption (p.799), in which the placenta becomes partially separated from the wall of the uterus. Painless vaginal bleeding after 24 weeks may be due to placenta previa (p.798), in which the placenta covers some or all of the opening of the cervix.

WHAT MIGHT BE DONE?

A manual examination is rarely carried out, particularly if you are in late pregnancy, because the examination could damage the placenta if it is lying low in the uterus. Using a speculum to hold open the vagina, your doctor will examine your cervix to investigate the cause of the bleeding. You may also have ultrasound scanning (*see* ULTRASOUND SCANNING IN PREGNANCY, p.793). If you are in the late stages of pregnancy, the fetus's heartbeat may be monitored (*see* FETAL MONITORING, p.803).

Treatment depends on the cause and extent of the bleeding and the stage of your pregnancy. If you have light to moderate bleeding in the early stages of pregnancy, your doctor may suggest bed rest. Many of these pregnancies continue. However, surgery may be required in some cases of miscarriage or if the cause of the bleeding is an ectopic pregnancy. If you have heavy vaginal bleeding later in your pregnancy, your baby may have to be delivered by emergency cesarean section (p.802). If you have lost a large amount of blood, you may need to have a blood transfusion (p.447).

(WWW) ONLINE SITES: p.1036

Miscarriage

The spontaneous end of a pregnancy before week 24, also known as a spontaneous abortion

AGE Most common under age 16 and over age 35

GENETICS In some cases, due to a genetic or chromosomal abnormality in the fetus

LIFESTYLE Smoking and alcohol or drug abuse during pregnancy are risk factors

More than 1 in 4 of all pregnancies end in miscarriage, the loss of a fetus before the 24th week of pregnancy. Most miscarriages occur in the first 14 weeks of pregnancy, and some occur so early that the woman may not be aware that she is pregnant. Generally, women who miscarry have abnormal vaginal bleeding and abdominal cramps.

WHAT ARE THE CAUSES?

About 6 in 10 miscarriages in the first 14 weeks of pregnancy are caused by a genetic disorder or an abnormality in the fetus. An early miscarriage may also result from lower than normal levels of the hormone progesterone. Early miscarriage is more common in multiple pregnancies (*see* MULTIPLE PREGNANCY AND ITS PROBLEMS, right).

Later miscarriages (between weeks 14 and 24) may be due to a weak cervix (*see* CERVICAL INCOMPETENCE, p.794) or to a severe infection in the mother. An abnormally shaped uterus or noncancerous tumors in the wall of the uterus (*see* FIBROIDS, p.745) may also cause a late miscarriage. Smoking and alcohol or drug abuse in pregnancy are also risk factors. Women who have diabetes mellitus (p.687) are at increased risk of a late miscarriage.

Any one of the above factors may cause recurrent miscarriages. Generally, miscarriage is more common in women under age 16 or over age 35. There is frequently concern that stress or minor injuries may lead to a miscarriage, but there is no evidence to support this.

WHAT ARE THE TYPES?

A miscarriage can be classified into one of several different types: threatened, inevitable, and missed miscarriage.

In a threatened miscarriage, the fetus is alive and the cervix remains closed. There is some vaginal bleeding, which is usually painless, but the pregnancy often continues for its full term of about 40 weeks. However, sometimes a threatened miscarriage develops into an inevitable miscarriage.

In an inevitable miscarriage, the fetus is usually dead and the cervix is open. An inevitable miscarriage is frequently painful because the uterus contracts to expel the fetus. Pain varies from mild menstrual period-type pains to severe pain, and there may be heavy vaginal bleeding with clots. An inevitable miscarriage may be either complete (all the contents of the uterus are expelled) or incomplete (some contents remain in the uterus after the miscarriage).

In a missed miscarriage, the fetus is dead, but there is usually no bleeding or pain. The uterus does not contract, and the cervix is closed with the fetus still inside. Although pregnancy symptoms, such as nausea, come to an end, a missed miscarriage is often not detected until a routine ultrasound scan is carried out (*see* ULTRASOUND SCANNING IN PREGNANCY, opposite page).

You should consult your doctor if you have vaginal bleeding or pain in pregnancy. If bleeding or pain is severe, call an ambulance immediately.

HOW IS IT DIAGNOSED?

Your doctor will look at your cervix using a speculum to hold open your vagina. If your cervix is closed, there is a chance that the pregnancy will continue. An ultrasound scan will usually be done to make sure that the fetus is alive. If the cervix is open and miscarriage is inevitable, an ultrasound scan may be done to find out if all the contents of the uterus have been expelled.

HOW MIGHT THE DOCTOR TREAT IT?

If you have a threatened miscarriage, your doctor may suggest that you rest for a few days until the bleeding has stopped. Your doctor will treat any identifiable cause, such as an infection. In the event of an inevitable miscarriage, your treatment will depend on whether the miscarriage is complete or incomplete. Normally, no further medical treatment is needed for a complete miscarriage, although you may be prescribed analgesics (p.912) if you are in pain. If your miscarriage was incomplete, you need to be admitted to the hospital so that any tissue left behind in the uterus can be removed surgically to prevent an infection from developing. The same procedure is used for an early missed miscarriage. If a missed miscarriage occurs in later pregnancy, you may require induction of labor (p.797).

WHAT CAN I DO?

The loss of a baby is always distressing, and you should take time to grieve and talk about your feelings. You may want to discuss your concerns about future pregnancies with your doctor. If you want to become pregnant again, it is best to wait several months to give yourself time to recover from your loss.

WHAT IS THE PROGNOSIS?

Most women who have a miscarriage do not have problems with subsequent pregnancies. Some women have recurrent miscarriages, but with specialist investigation and treatment they may eventually have a successful pregnancy.

(WWW) ONLINE SITES: p.1029, p.1036

Multiple pregnancy and its problems

The presence of more than one fetus in the uterus and the problems that may arise

 AGE Multiple pregnancy more common over age 30

 GENETICS Multiple pregnancy sometimes runs in families

 LIFESTYLE Not a significant factor

Multiple pregnancy occurs when more than one fetus develops in the uterus. Although most multiple pregnancies progress smoothly, the risk of problems is increased for both mother and fetuses.

Nonidentical fetuses may develop if two or more eggs are fertilized at the same time, whereas two or more identical fetuses may develop if an egg splits after fertilization. Fetuses may share a placenta or each fetus may have its own.

In Canada, twins occur naturally in about 1 in 90 births and triplets occur in about 1 in 8,000 births. Natural pregnancies of more than three fetuses are extremely rare, but there has been a dramatic increase in multiple pregnancies as a result of fertility treatment.

You are more likely to have nonidentical twins if you are over age 30 or if there are multiple births in your family history on your mother's side. However, these factors do not increase your chance of having identical twins.

WHAT ARE THE CAUSES OF MULTIPLE PREGNANCY?

Multiple pregnancies may occur naturally, but 2 in 3 pregnancies with three or more fetuses result from infertility treatments (*see* ASSISTED CONCEPTION,

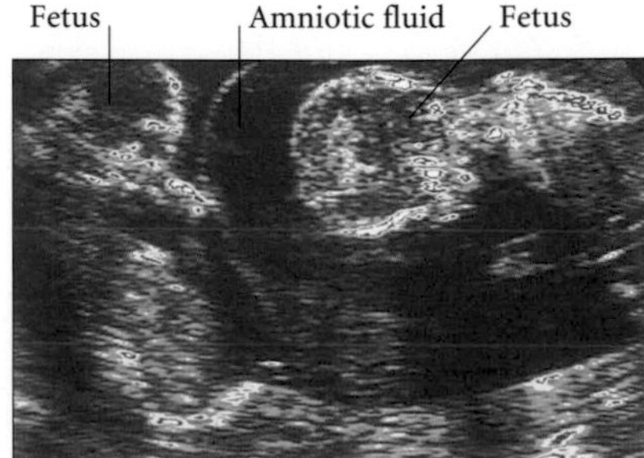
Fetus
Amniotic fluid
Fetus

Twins in the uterus
Two fetuses, each in its own sac of fluid, can be seen lying at right angles to each other in this color-enhanced ultrasound scan.

p.776). This is because drugs for infertility (p.936) stimulate the ovaries to release more than one egg each month, and more than one egg is inserted into the uterus during in-vitro fertilization.

WHAT ARE THE PROBLEMS?

The common problems associated with normal pregnancy (*see* COMMON COMPLAINTS OF NORMAL PREGNANCY, p.784) are sometimes more severe in a multiple pregnancy. This is partly because of the increased size of the uterus and partly because the placenta or placentas produce a higher level of hormones.

Women who are carrying more than one fetus are more likely to have certain problems, such as high blood pressure during pregnancy (*see* PREECLAMPSIA AND ECLAMPSIA, p.794). Such women are also more likely to develop excessive vomiting during early pregnancy (*see* HYPEREMESIS, p.789), have greater than normal amounts of fluid surrounding the fetus (*see* POLYHYDRAMNIOS, p.795), and have a low-lying placenta or placentas (*see* PLACENTA PREVIA, p.798). Iron-deficiency anemia (p.447) is more likely because the mother must supply iron to more than one fetus.

A multiple pregnancy is more likely to result in a miscarriage (p.791) or in preterm labor (p.798). The fetuses in a multiple pregnancy are usually smaller than single babies, and there is a greater risk of one baby not being in the normal position for labor (*see* ABNORMAL PRESENTATION, p.800). Since there may be more than one placenta, bleeding after the delivery may be heavy (*see* POSTPARTUM HEMORRHAGE, p.806).

WHAT MIGHT BE DONE?

Your doctor may suspect a multiple pregnancy if your abdomen is larger than would be expected for the stage of the pregnancy. The diagnosis is usually confirmed by ultrasound scanning (*see* ULTRASOUND SCANNING IN PREGNANCY, below). You may be monitored with ultrasound scans every month, possibly together with Doppler ultrasound scanning every 2 weeks to check that each fetus is receiving adequate blood. Some centers have multiple pregnancy clinics.

Additional treatment may be needed if problems develop. For example, you may be prescribed iron supplements to prevent anemia. You should rest often, especially after the 28th week, to help reduce the risk of a preterm labor. Multiple fetuses are usually delivered in the hospital because of the risks of a difficult or preterm labor. Twins may be delivered vaginally if the first baby is in the head-down position. A cesarean section (p.802) is usually necessary for the delivery of three or more babies.

Since the babies are often preterm and small, they may need to be looked after in a neonatal care unit (p.959).

(WWW) ONLINE SITES: p.1036

(TEST) ULTRASOUND SCANNING IN PREGNANCY

Ultrasound scanning uses sound waves to produce an image of the internal organs. The procedure is routinely used during pregnancy to assess the health of the fetus, determine the fetus's age, and measure fetal growth. Scanning may also be used to investigate problems, such as vaginal bleeding, and diagnose fetal abnormalities. For example, the procedure may identify neural tube defects and can sometimes detect heart disease. A scan takes about 20–30 minutes and is painless and safe. Doppler scanning may be used to measure blood flow to the fetus.

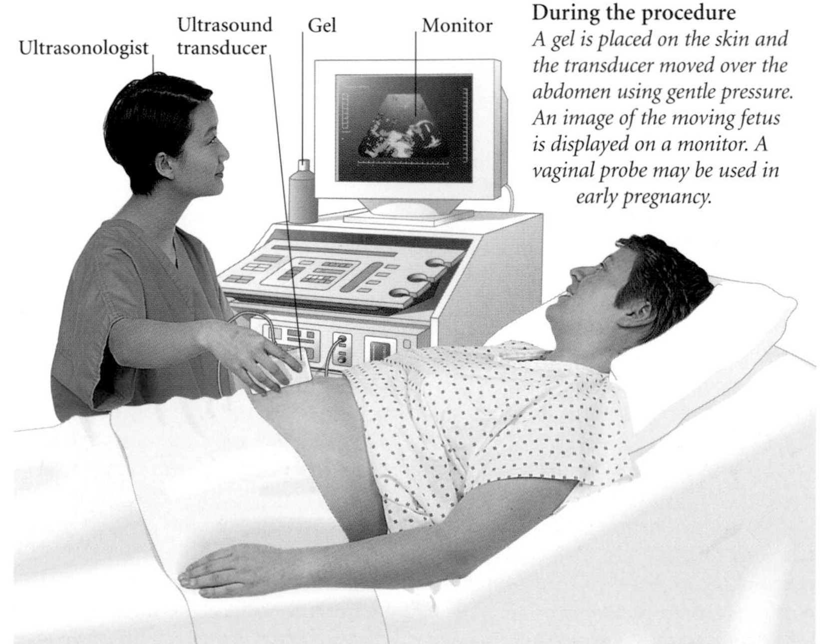
Ultrasonologist
Ultrasound transducer
Gel
Monitor

During the procedure
A gel is placed on the skin and the transducer moved over the abdomen using gentle pressure. An image of the moving fetus is displayed on a monitor. A vaginal probe may be used in early pregnancy.

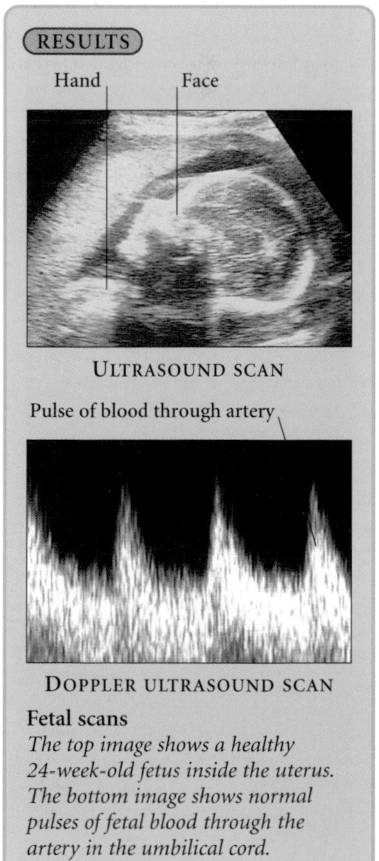
RESULTS
Hand
Face
ULTRASOUND SCAN
Pulse of blood through artery
DOPPLER ULTRASOUND SCAN

Fetal scans
The top image shows a healthy 24-week-old fetus inside the uterus. The bottom image shows normal pulses of fetal blood through the artery in the umbilical cord.

Cervical incompetence

Weakness of the cervix, which may result in a late miscarriage

 AGE GENETICS LIFESTYLE Not significant factors

The cervix normally stays closed until labor begins. However, if the cervix has been weakened, a condition known as cervical incompetence, the weight of the growing fetus and its surrounding amniotic fluid may cause the cervix to open early, resulting in a miscarriage (p.791). Cervical incompetence is the cause of about 1 in 4 miscarriages after the 14th week of pregnancy.

The cervix may be weakened by previous surgery, such as a cone biopsy (*see* TREATING CERVICAL DYSPLASIA, p.751), or by any procedure that involves artificial opening of the cervix. For example, a woman who has had more than three terminations of pregnancy (p.789) at an early stage is more likely to develop cervical incompetence.

Often there are no symptoms of cervical incompetence before miscarriage occurs. At this stage, the mother may feel pressure in the lower abdomen or a "lump" in the vagina.

WHAT MIGHT BE DONE?

If you have had a previous miscarriage after the 14th week of pregnancy, your doctor will probably suggest that you have ultrasound scanning (p.250) to look for evidence of cervical incompetence. The scan is performed through the vagina to measure the thickness of the cervix and may be carried out at an early stage in your next pregnancy or, if possible, when you are planning a pregnancy. If you are at high risk of cervical incompetence, possibly because of previous surgery on the cervix, you may also be investigated for cervical incompetence before or early in pregnancy.

If the cervix is weak, a stitch can be inserted in it to hold it closed. The procedure is usually done under general or epidural anesthesia between week 12 and week 16 of pregnancy. The stitch will be removed at 37 weeks, before the beginning of labor. If labor starts while the stitch is still in place, it will be removed immediately to prevent the cervix from becoming torn. If the stitch fails to prevent a miscarriage, another pregnancy may be successful if a stitch is inserted higher in the cervix.

Cervical incompetence is likely to be a problem in subsequent pregnancies. The cervix may need to be stitched each time to prevent miscarriage.

(WWW) ONLINE SITES: p.1036

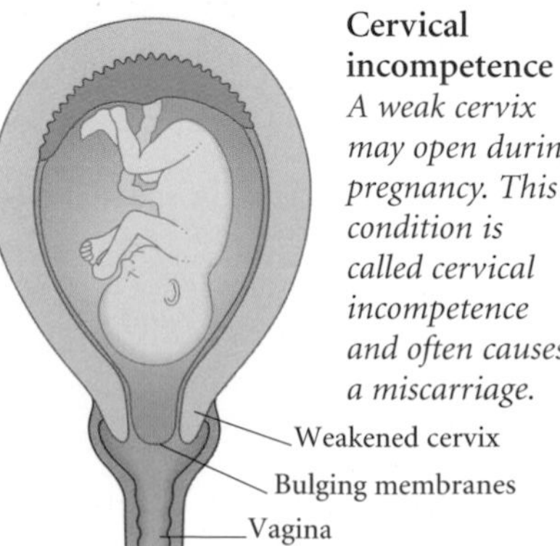
Weakened cervix
Bulging membranes
Vagina

Cervical incompetence
A weak cervix may open during pregnancy. This condition is called cervical incompetence and often causes a miscarriage.

Preeclampsia and eclampsia

High blood pressure, fluid retention, and protein in the urine in pregnancy, which may lead to seizures and coma

 AGE Most common under age 19 or over age 35

 GENETICS Sometimes runs in families

 LIFESTYLE Being overweight is a risk factor

Preeclampsia, also called preeclamptic toxemia, occurs in about 5–10 in 100 pregnancies, usually in the second half of pregnancy. The condition is a combination of high blood pressure with excessive fluid retention and/or protein in the urine. Mild preeclampsia is common in the last weeks of pregnancy and is usually easy to treat. However, severe preeclampsia may threaten the life of the mother and/or the fetus. Untreated, severe preeclampsia may lead to a dangerous disorder called eclampsia that causes seizures and may bring on a coma (p.522). Eclampsia may be fatal.

The cause of preeclampsia is not yet understood, but it may be due in part to the mother developing an immune reaction to the fetus. The condition is most likely to develop in a first pregnancy, a subsequent pregnancy with a new father, or a multiple pregnancy. Preeclampsia can run in families and is most common in women under age 19 or over age 35. There is an increased risk of preeclampsia in women who are overweight and in women who have chronic kidney disease, diabetes mellitus (p.687), or preexisting high blood pressure (*see* HYPERTENSION, p.403).

WHAT ARE THE SYMPTOMS?

Initially, preeclampsia may produce no symptoms. As the condition progresses, the symptoms tend to develop gradually, but occasionally they develop very rapidly. Symptoms may include:

- Swollen feet, ankles, and hands and excessive weight gain due to retention of fluid.
- Headaches.
- Visual disturbances, such as blurry vision and seeing flashing lights.
- Vomiting.
- Upper abdominal pain.

You should consult your doctor immediately if you develop any of the above symptoms during pregnancy. Without treatment, the condition may develop into the more serious eclampsia.

HOW IS IT DIAGNOSED?

Your doctor will examine you for evidence of preeclampsia at every prenatal checkup. He or she will examine you for signs of fluid retention, take your blood pressure, and test your urine for evidence of protein. If your doctor suspects preeclampsia, he or she may also arrange for various blood tests, including tests to check your kidney function.

WHAT IS THE TREATMENT?

Treatment for preeclampsia depends on the stage of your pregnancy and the severity of your symptoms. If you have mild to moderate preeclampsia and are less than 36 weeks pregnant, you will probably be advised to rest in bed. Your blood pressure will be taken frequently to make sure that it is not elevated. In some women, bed rest and regular monitoring in the hospital may be needed.

If preeclampsia becomes severe and the fetus is mature enough to survive early delivery, induction of labor (p.797) or a cesarean section (p.802) may be recommended. Before an early delivery, you may have injections of corticosteroids to help the lungs of the fetus mature ready for the birth. Very rarely, severe preeclampsia that develops before the 24th week requires a termination of pregnancy (p.789) to save the mother.

Regardless of the severity, if you have preeclampsia more than 36 weeks into your pregnancy, your doctor will probably recommend that labor be induced at once or a cesarean section be performed to deliver the baby.

If eclampsia develops, you will be given antihypertensive drugs (p.897) to lower your blood pressure and intravenous anticonvulsant drugs (p.914) to stop seizures. Delivery by emergency cesarean section is then essential.

WHAT IS THE PROGNOSIS?

If preeclampsia is treated before it becomes severe, the prognosis is usually good. If eclampsia develops, the lives of the mother and fetus are at risk.

High blood pressure usually returns to normal within about 1 week of delivery, but there is an increased risk of the mother developing high blood pressure in later life. About 1 in 10 women has preeclampsia in a future pregnancy.

(WWW) ONLINE SITES: p.1036

Polyhydramnios

An excessive amount of amniotic fluid surrounding the fetus in the uterus

GENETICS Risk factors depend on the cause

AGE LIFESTYLE Not significant factors

Normally the amount of amniotic fluid surrounding the fetus does not exceed 3 pints (1.5 liters). In polyhydramnios, more than 4 pints (2 liters) of amniotic fluid build up, causing abdominal discomfort or pain in the mother.

Excess fluid makes it easier for the fetus to move around in the uterus. For this reason, the fetus may not lie in the normal head-down position at the end of pregnancy (*see* ABNORMAL PRESENTATION, p.800). Excessive amounts of fluid also increase the likelihood of a preterm labor (p.798) or of premature rupture of membranes (p.797).

WHAT ARE THE TYPES?

There are two types of polyhydramnios: chronic, in which the amniotic fluid accumulates slowly over several weeks; and acute, in which the amniotic fluid accumulates over a few days.

Chronic polyhydramnios is the more common form. It develops from about week 32 of pregnancy and causes gradual abdominal discomfort. Breathing difficulties, indigestion, and retention of fluid also sometimes occur. In many women, no cause is found for chronic polyhydramnios. However, the condition occurs more often in mothers with preexisting diabetes mellitus (p.687) and in women carrying more than one fetus (*see* MULTIPLE PREGNANCY AND ITS PROBLEMS, p.792). The disorder is more likely if the fetus has a developmental defect, such as spina bifida (*see* NEURAL TUBE DEFECTS, p.844).

The acute form of polyhydramnios develops from 22 weeks and is typically associated with an identical twin pregnancy. The symptoms are similar but more severe than those of chronic polyhydramnios. Frequently, there is severe abdominal pain, nausea, and vomiting.

WHAT MIGHT BE DONE?

Your doctor may suspect that you have polyhydramnios if your abdomen is larger than would be expected for the stage of your pregnancy. You will probably have ultrasound scanning (*see* ULTRASOUND SCANNING IN PREGNANCY, p.793) to confirm the diagnosis and look for fetal abnormalities. You may also need a blood test to check whether you have diabetes mellitus.

Usually, chronic cases can be treated by bed rest. If troublesome symptoms occur late in pregnancy, induction of labor (p.797) may be recommended.

If you have acute polyhydramnios, your doctor may recommend induction of labor if the fetus or fetuses are mature enough. If the fetus is immature, you may be given corticosteroid injections to help the lungs of the fetus mature so that it can be delivered early. Abdominal pain may be relieved temporarily by removing some of the amniotic fluid from the uterus using a needle inserted into the abdomen. If required, the procedure can be repeated.

If you have diabetes mellitus, polyhydramnios may recur in subsequent pregnancies. However, careful control of your diabetes should reduce this risk. If you have polyhydramnios due to other causes, you are not at increased risk in future pregnancies.

(WWW) ONLINE SITES: p.1036

Rhesus incompatibility

A mismatch between the Rh blood group of a pregnant woman and that of her fetus

GENETICS Due to incompatibility of genetically determined blood groups

AGE LIFESTYLE Not significant factors

One of the systems for classifying blood is the Rhesus (Rh) group. This system classifies blood according to the presence or absence of certain proteins on the surface of red blood cells. About 17 in 20 people in Canada have Rh proteins on the surface of their red blood cells and are Rh positive. The remaining 3 in 20 people do not have these proteins and are therefore Rh negative.

Rh incompatibility occurs when a mother is Rh negative and her fetus is Rh positive. The situation rarely causes problems in a first pregnancy. However, the mother may develop antibodies if stray blood cells from the baby enter her circulation. These antibodies may attack red blood cells in an Rh-positive fetus in a future pregnancy. The destruction of fetal blood cells may result in severe anemia (p.446) in the fetus and in anemia and yellowing of the skin and whites of the eyes (*see* NEONATAL JAUNDICE, p.817) in the newborn baby.

Women with Rh-incompatible pregnancies now routinely have treatment to prevent antibodies from developing, and fewer than 1 in 100 women has problems in future pregnancies.

WHAT IS THE CAUSE?

Blood groups are inherited from both parents. A baby who is Rh positive can be born to an Rh-negative mother only if the baby's father is Rh positive. The circulatory systems of the mother and the fetus are separate, and the red blood cells do not usually cross from one to the other. However, there are circumstances in which stray red blood cells from the fetus can enter the mother's circulation. The fetus's blood cells may leak into the mother's system during delivery, miscarriage (p.791), or termination of pregnancy (p.789). There is also a risk of blood mixing when an amniocentesis test is carried out (*see* PRENATAL GENETIC TESTS, p.787) or after a placental abruption (p.799), in which part or all of the placenta detaches from the uterus before delivery. The mother's immune system reacts by producing antibodies to destroy the fetal red blood cells in her circulation. In future pregnancies in which the fetus is Rh positive, these antibodies cross the placenta and destroy fetal red blood cells. Untreated, these effects become increasingly severe in each subsequent Rh-incompatible pregnancy.

WHAT ARE THE EFFECTS?

The mother remains well and is usually unaware that there is a problem. The effects on the fetus depend on the level of antibodies present and when in the pregnancy they are produced.

The fetus may develop swelling and progressive anemia, in which destruction of the red blood cells leads to low levels of oxygen-carrying pigment in the blood. Rarely, a severely anemic fetus develops acute heart failure (p.412) and may die in the uterus (*see* STILLBIRTH, p.805). After an Rh-incompatible pregnancy, a baby may be born with severe anemia. Jaundice in the newborn baby occurs due to buildup of bilirubin, a pigment produced from the destruction of fetal red blood cells. Rarely, severe jaundice may cause brain damage.

WHAT MIGHT BE DONE?

If Rh antibodies develop, treatment depends on the amount of antibodies and their effect on the fetus. A sample of the fluid in the uterus is tested for evidence of high bilirubin in the fetus. Additional ultrasound scanning (*see* ULTRASOUND SCANNING IN PREGNANCY, p.793) may be used to check whether the fetus is swollen. If antibody levels are low, the pregnancy may continue until labor is induced at 38 weeks (*see* INDUCTION OF LABOR, opposite page); if levels are high, labor may be induced earlier. A fetus that is too immature for delivery may have a blood transfusion of Rh-negative blood into the umbilical cord or abdominal cavity. After birth, the baby may need more transfusions and treatment for jaundice.

CAN PROBLEMS BE PREVENTED?

All women are tested at their first prenatal visit to determine their Rh blood group. If you are Rh negative, you will have a blood test at about 28 weeks to see if you have developed antibodies. You will also be given an injection of antibodies against Rh-positive blood at about week 28 and soon after the birth to destroy any fetal red blood cells in your blood. This prevents you from developing antibodies that might react against future Rh-positive fetuses. You may also have this injection after a miscarriage or other procedure that causes fetal and maternal blood to mix. With this treatment, you are very unlikely to develop antibodies that will cause problems in the future.

(WWW) ONLINE SITES: p.1036

Small for gestational age

Failure of the fetus to grow properly in the uterus so that it is smaller than expected throughout the pregnancy

AGE Most common under age 17 or over age 34

LIFESTYLE Smoking, alcohol or drug abuse, and an inadequate diet during pregnancy are risk factors

GENETICS Risk factors depend on the cause

Approximately 1 in 20 babies are small for gestational age. This condition occurs when, during pregnancy, a fetus fails to put on sufficient weight. On average, a baby weighs just over 7 lb (3 kg) at full term. A baby small for gestational age is one who weighs less than 5½ lb (2.5 kg) at full term. A baby with this condition is usually thinner than average rather than shorter in length. Underweight and thin babies are more commonly born to mothers who are under the age of 17 or over the age of 34.

WHAT ARE THE CAUSES?

Poor fetal growth is usually caused by lack of nourishment, which may be due to a disorder in the mother or a factor in her lifestyle. The condition may also be caused by a problem with the placenta or a fetal abnormality.

Maternal disorders that may affect the function of the placenta and lead to malnourishment of the fetus include preeclampsia (*see* PREECLAMPSIA AND ECLAMPSIA, p.794), in which high blood pressure and other symptoms develop during pregnancy, chronic high blood pressure (*see* HYPERTENSION, p.403), or preexisting kidney failure (p.705). Poor fetal growth can also be caused by a serious infection in the mother, such as rubella (p.292). In addition, several factors in the mother's lifestyle may be linked to the condition. Smoking, abusing alcohol or drugs, and eating an inadequate diet may all affect levels of nutrients that pass across the placenta in order to nourish the fetus.

In addition, there are problems with the placenta itself that may lead to fetal malnourishment. For example, part of the placenta may separate from the wall of the uterus (*see* PLACENTAL ABRUPTION, p.799). In rare cases, an inherited or a chromosomal abnormality in the fetus, such as Down syndrome (p.821), will lead to the fetus being small for the gestational age.

WHAT MIGHT BE DONE?

You will probably have no symptoms, but your doctor may be concerned if measurements of your abdomen during pregnancy show that your uterus is not increasing in size at the normal rate. You will have regular ultrasound scans to monitor the rate of growth of the fetus and may be given scans that measure blood flow through the umbilical cord to the fetus (*see* ULTRASOUND SCANNING IN PREGNANCY, p.793).

If small for gestational age is diagnosed, you may need to be admitted to the hospital for bed rest. You will be treated for any underlying condition, if possible. For example, you may be given drugs to treat high blood pressure. If your diet is inadequate, you may be offered dietary advice. The fetus's heartbeat will probably be monitored twice daily. If the fetus continues to grow slowly, it may be delivered early, either by induction of labor (opposite page) or by cesarean section (p.802).

WHAT IS THE PROGNOSIS?

After they are born, small babies may initially need monitoring and special care in a neonatal care unit (p.959) because they tend to be more susceptible to problems such as infections, low blood glucose, and low body temperature (hypothermia). Most small babies gain weight rapidly and reach a normal size. Having a small baby slightly increases the risk of your next baby also being small. However, each new baby tends to be larger than the last.

(WWW) ONLINE SITES: p.1036

Premature rupture of membranes

Rupture of the membrane sac surrounding the fetus that is not closely followed by labor or that occurs before labor is due

LIFESTYLE Smoking is thought to be a risk factor

AGE GENETICS Not significant factors

The fetus is protected in the uterus inside a fluid-filled bag called the amniotic sac. The membranes that form this sac normally rupture during or just before the start of labor, but in about 1 in 14 women they rupture early.

It is not known exactly what causes the membranes to break early, although smoking during pregnancy appears to increase the risk. In some pregnancies, premature rupture of the membranes may be due to an infection that spreads upward to the uterus from the vagina.

Rupture of the membranes causes the amniotic fluid to leak from the vagina. The amount of fluid lost varies from a light trickle to a heavy gush. If your membranes break at night, you may wake in a pool of liquid, which can easily be mistaken for urine. If you think that your membranes have broken, you should contact your doctor.

ARE THERE COMPLICATIONS?

If labor does not commence within a few hours of the membranes rupturing, there is a risk of the uterus or the fetus becoming infected. There is also a possibility of a cord prolapse, in which the umbilical cord drops into the cervix or vagina. If this occurs, the blood supply to the fetus may be reduced, depriving it of oxygen (*see* FETAL DISTRESS, p.804). In women who have not yet reached week 37 of pregnancy, premature rupture of the membranes may lead to preterm labor (p.798). In this event, the risk to the fetus of an early delivery must be balanced against the risk of an infection developing if labor is stopped.

WHAT MIGHT BE DONE?

You may need to be admitted to the hospital and monitored for evidence of an infection. Your doctor will feel your abdomen and examine you internally using a speculum to hold the vagina open. He or she will also take your temperature because a fever may indicate an infection. Your doctor may also take a vaginal swab and arrange for blood tests to look for signs of an infection. If there is an infection, you will be treated with antibiotics (p.885). The heart rate of the fetus may be monitored (*see* FETAL MONITORING, p.803) to look for indications of fetal distress. If you are at least 37 weeks into your pregnancy, labor usually begins within 24 hours of the rupture of the membranes. Labor will be induced (*see* INDUCTION OF LABOR, below) if it fails to start.

If you are 36 weeks pregnant or the fetus is mature enough for delivery, labor may be induced; otherwise, you may be kept in the hospital and monitored for signs of infection. If you are less than 34 weeks pregnant, you may be given injections of corticosteroids to help the fetus's lungs mature.

After the birth, the baby may need monitoring in a neonatal care unit (p.959), but most babies are healthy and have no ill effects from early delivery.

WWW ONLINE SITES: p.1036

TREATMENT INDUCTION OF LABOR

If a pregnancy continues beyond 42 weeks, or if the health of the mother or fetus is at risk, labor may need to be artificially induced. Various methods are used depending on the stage of labor: a suppository may be inserted into the vagina to encourage the cervix to open, the membranes containing the fetus may be ruptured, or a hormone may be given intravenously to stimulate uterine contractions. In some cases, all three methods need to be used. The last two methods may also be used to speed up labor if it is delayed.

Closed cervix
Suppository

Insertion of a suppository
If the cervix is closed, a prostaglandin suppository is placed at the top of the vagina to soften the cervix, which then thins and begins to open.

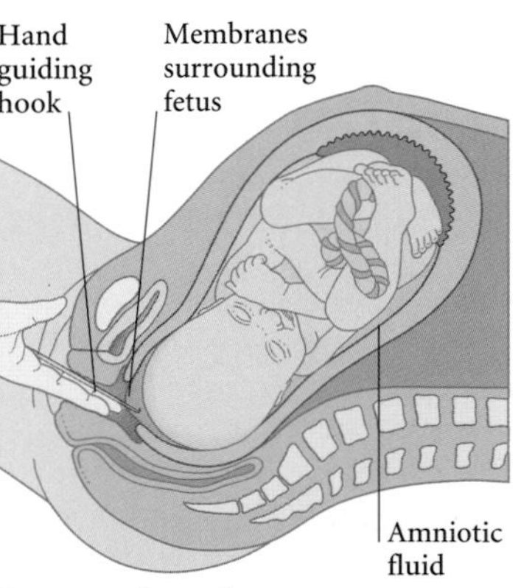
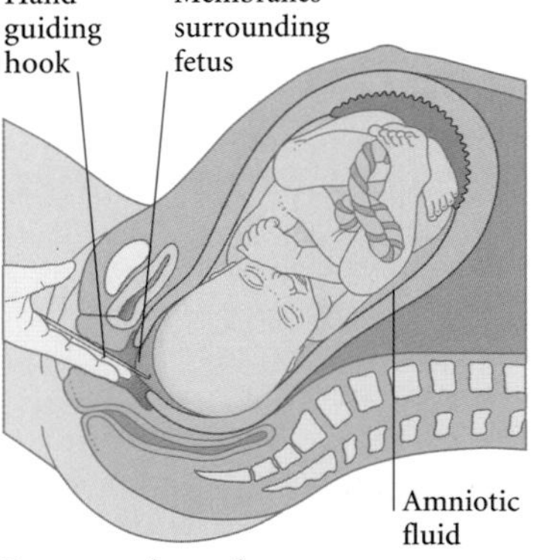
Hand guiding hook
Membranes surrounding fetus
Amniotic fluid

Rupture of membranes
If the cervix is already open, a small hook may be used to rupture the membranes that contain the fetus and its surrounding amniotic fluid.

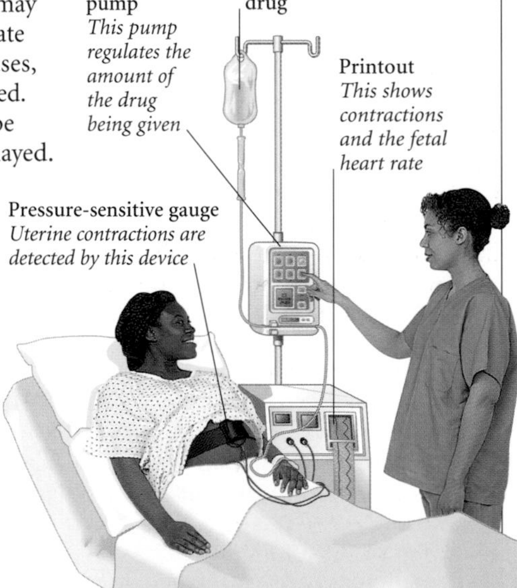
Infusion pump
This pump regulates the amount of the drug being given
Drip containing drug
Printout
This shows contractions and the fetal heart rate
Pressure-sensitive gauge
Uterine contractions are detected by this device

Stimulating uterine contractions
If the cervix is open and the membranes have ruptured, a drug may be given intravenously to encourage the uterus to contract. The contractions and the fetal heart rate will be monitored.

Preterm labor

The onset of labor before the 37th week of pregnancy

AGE Most common under age 17 or over age 35

LIFESTYLE Smoking and alcohol or drug abuse during pregnancy are risk factors

GENETICS Not a significant factor

The normal duration of pregnancy is about 40 weeks. Labor that starts before 37 weeks is known as preterm. Preterm labor carries few extra risks for the mother, but preterm babies often have problems because of their small size and immaturity (*see* PROBLEMS OF THE PRETERM BABY, p.816).

If preterm labor is diagnosed early, there is a chance that it can be stopped and that the pregnancy will continue. If labor cannot be stopped completely, it may often be delayed for a day or two so that corticosteroids (p.930) can be given to help the fetus mature. Preterm labor occurs in about 1 in 10 births and is more common in very young mothers and those who are over age 35.

What are the causes?

The cause of preterm labor is unknown in about half of all cases. The remainder are triggered by a variety of factors.

A multiple pregnancy often results in preterm labor, possibly because the uterus is stretched (*see* MULTIPLE PREGNANCY AND ITS PROBLEMS, p.792). An excessive amount of fluid around the fetus (*see* POLYHYDRAMNIOS, p.795) has the same effect. An infection of the urinary tract (*see* CYSTITIS, p.709) or of the vagina (*see* BACTERIAL VAGINOSIS, p.753) may also trigger preterm labor.

Factors that increase the chance of preterm labor occurring include smoking and alcohol or drug abuse during pregnancy, heavy work, stress, a previous preterm labor, and chronic disorders such as diabetes mellitus (p.687).

What are the symptoms?

The symptoms of preterm labor may be mistaken initially for the backache and painless irregular contractions that can occur in late pregnancy. They include:

- Intermittent pain in the lower back.
- Tightenings felt in the abdomen that become regular painful contractions.
- A discharge of blood and mucus from the vagina.

If you think you are going into preterm labor, you should contact your doctor immediately. The earlier preterm labor is diagnosed, the greater the chances of stopping it. You may be admitted to the hospital and transferred to a maternity center with a neonatal care unit (p.959) in case it is impossible to stop labor and you deliver your baby early.

What might be done?

Your doctor will examine you to make sure that you are in labor and to assess how far it has advanced. The uterine contractions and the heartbeat of the fetus will be monitored regularly (*see* FETAL MONITORING, p.803). Tests may also be carried out to try to find the cause of the preterm labor.

If your pregnancy is not advanced far enough for the fetus to be mature enough to be delivered safely, your doctor may try to stop labor. You may be given an intravenous infusion of drugs (*see* DRUGS FOR LABOR, p.938) that sometimes stop the uterus from contracting. You should rest completely during your treatment because movement encourages contractions.

If your labor cannot be stopped, the doctor may try to postpone it for a couple of days so that you can be given two injections of corticosteroid drugs, which help the lungs of the fetus mature. This procedure reduces the risk of breathing problems in the baby after delivery. The fetus will be monitored for signs of fetal distress (p.804). In many cases, a carefully monitored vaginal delivery is possible, but, if there are risk factors such as a multiple pregnancy, it may be necessary to carry out a cesarean section (p.802).

What is the prognosis?

In many cases, labor can be stopped and the pregnancy then progresses to about 40 weeks. Otherwise, postponing labor for a day or two allows time for corticosteroid treatment to improve the fetus's chance of survival. Babies born before 37 weeks may need to be cared for and monitored in a neonatal care unit (p.959) until they are more mature. Preterm labor often recurs in subsequent pregnancies.

(WWW) ONLINE SITES: p.1036

Placenta previa

A condition in which the placenta covers or partially covers the opening of the cervix into the uterus

AGE More common over age 35

GENETICS LIFESTYLE Not significant factors

In some pregnancies, the placenta is implanted lower down in the uterus and closer to the cervix than is normal. Although usually a placenta that is lying low will gradually move upward as the uterus expands, the placenta may remain in this position and cover some or all of the opening of the cervix. This condition, known as placenta previa, occurs in about 1 in 200 pregnancies and is more common in women over age 35. Placenta previa causes up to 1 in 5 cases of vaginal bleeding that occurs after week 24 of pregnancy.

The severity of this condition is related to how much of the opening of the cervix is covered by the placenta. In marginal placenta previa, the placenta lies low in the uterus and just reaches the edge of the cervix. When complete placenta previa occurs, the entire cervix is covered. Symptoms caused by the condition vary, and mild cases may cause no adverse effects. In other cases, light to heavy painless vaginal bleeding occurs intermittently from week 24 of pregnancy onward. Complete placenta previa may cause severe bleeding that can be life-threatening to the mother

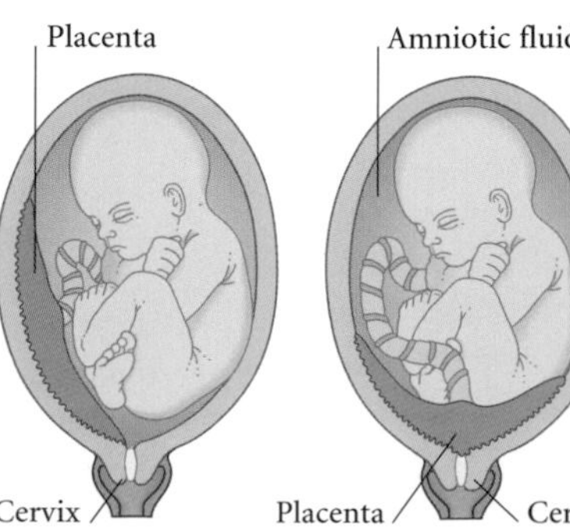
Placenta
Amniotic fluid
Cervix
Placenta
Cervix
MARGINAL PLACENTA PREVIA
COMPLETE PLACENTA PREVIA

Placenta previa

In marginal placenta previa, the placenta implants low down in the uterus but only just reaches the opening of the cervix. In complete placenta previa, the placenta covers the entire opening of the cervix.

and/or fetus. Women who have placenta previa are at increased risk of developing postpartum hemorrhage (p.806) because the lower part of the uterus may not be able to contract sufficiently to constrict the blood vessels of the uterus and stop bleeding after birth.

WHAT ARE THE CAUSES?

There is an increased risk of placenta previa in women who have had several pregnancies or if the uterus has been scarred in previous surgery, such as a cesarean section (p.802). The placenta may also develop low in the uterus if there are noncancerous tumors present (*see* FIBROIDS, p.745). The risk of placenta previa is increased in a multiple pregnancy because there may be more than one placenta or because the placenta may be larger than in a normal pregnancy (*see* MULTIPLE PREGNANCY AND ITS PROBLEMS, p.792).

WHAT MIGHT BE DONE?

Usually, placenta previa is detected after week 20 by routine ultrasound scanning (*see* ULTRASOUND SCANNING IN PREGNANCY, p.793). If the placenta is lying low, you will be given follow-up scans to monitor its position. The problem may disappear because in most cases the placenta moves upward and away from the cervix by the 32nd week of pregnancy.

If the placenta remains low and you develop vaginal bleeding, you will be admitted to the hospital. If you have light bleeding, you may need only bed rest; if bleeding is heavy, you may need an emergency cesarean section and possibly a blood transfusion (p.447) to replace the blood you have lost.

Even if there are no problems, when placenta previa is complete you will normally be admitted to the hospital for monitoring at about the 30th week of pregnancy because of the risk of bleeding. Your baby will then be delivered by cesarean section at 38 weeks. A cesarean section is usually necessary even if there is marginal placenta previa because of the risk of hemorrhage.

WHAT IS THE PROGNOSIS?

With close monitoring, the pregnancy is usually successful. Placenta previa may recur in a future pregnancy if an underlying cause cannot be treated.

(WWW) ONLINE SITES: p.1036

Placental abruption

Separation of the placenta from the wall of the uterus before the baby is delivered

LIFESTYLE Smoking and alcohol or drug abuse during pregnancy are risk factors

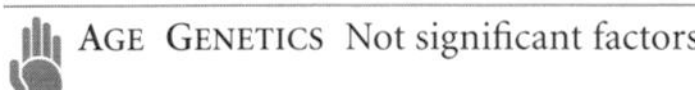

AGE GENETICS Not significant factors

The placenta normally separates from the wall of the uterus after the baby has been born. In placental abruption, part or all of the placenta separates from the uterus before the baby has been delivered. The condition occurs in about 1 in 120 pregnancies and is potentially life-threatening, particularly for the fetus. Placental abruption is the most common cause of vaginal bleeding in pregnancy after the 28th week.

There are two basic types of placental abruption: revealed and concealed. A revealed placental abruption causes mild to severe vaginal bleeding. In a concealed placental abruption, there is no visible bleeding from the vagina because blood collects between the placenta and the wall of the uterus.

WHAT ARE THE CAUSES?

The exact cause of placental abruption is not known. However, the condition appears to be more common in women who have chronic high blood pressure (*see* HYPERTENSION, p.403). The risk is also increased if a woman smokes during pregnancy, drinks large amounts of alcohol, and/or abuses drugs. The disorder occurs more often after several previous pregnancies or in women who have had a placental abruption in a previous pregnancy. Abdominal injury sometimes leads to placental abruption.

WHAT ARE THE SYMPTOMS?

Symptoms usually occur suddenly and depend on how much of the placenta has separated from the wall of the uterus. If only a small part of the placenta has pulled away, bleeding may be minor, but a large separation can cause severe hemorrhage. In increasing order of severity, symptoms may include:

- Slight to heavy vaginal bleeding.
- Abdominal cramps or backache.
- Severe, constant abdominal pain.
- Reduced fetal movements.

If you develop vaginal bleeding at any stage of pregnancy, you should consult your doctor immediately. If the bleeding is heavy, it is advisable to call an ambulance without delay because you may need emergency care.

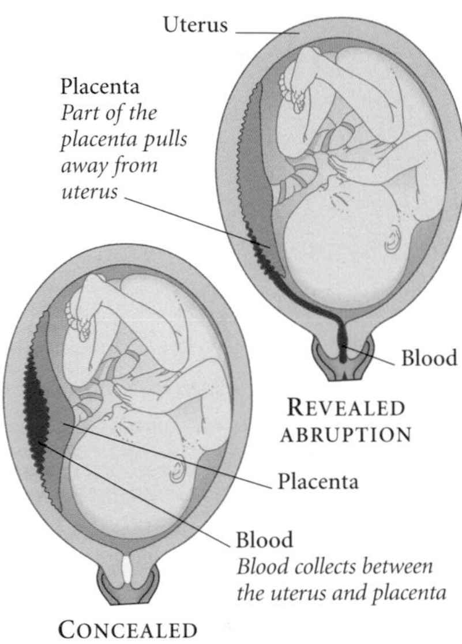

Uterus
Placenta
Part of the placenta pulls away from uterus
Blood
REVEALED ABRUPTION
Placenta
Blood
Blood collects between the uterus and placenta
CONCEALED ABRUPTION

Placental abruption
In a placental abruption, part of the placenta separates from the uterine wall before birth. A revealed abruption causes vaginal bleeding; in a concealed abruption blood collects behind the placenta.

WHAT MIGHT BE DONE?

Your doctor will examine you internally using a speculum, which is an instrument that holds the vagina open. You may also have ultrasound scanning (*see* ULTRASOUND SCANNING IN PREGNANCY, p.793), and the fetal heartbeat will probably be checked. A small separation may be treated by bed rest in the hospital, where the fetal heartbeat can be monitored (*see* FETAL MONITORING, p.803).

If bleeding does not stop or restarts, labor may be induced (*see* INDUCTION OF LABOR, p.797). After a large placental abruption, an emergency cesarean section (p.802) is often needed to save the fetus. You may be given a blood transfusion (p.447) if you lose a lot of blood.

The prognosis varies depending on the degree of separation. With appropriate treatment, the mother is not usually in danger. If the condition is minor, the pregnancy often progresses, although the fetus may be at risk of being small for gestational age (p.796). Severe cases may lead to death of the fetus.

(WWW) ONLINE SITES: p.1036

PROBLEMS IN LABOR

Labor is the process of birth, from the first strong contractions of the uterus to the delivery of the baby and placenta. Labor may last up to 24 hours for a first pregnancy but tends to be shorter in subsequent pregnancies. In most cases, the stages of labor progress smoothly. When problems do occur, they are rarely serious if they are identified and treated promptly.

Improvements in monitoring and more effective pain relief have made labor a safer and much less traumatic experience than it once was. In the past, little relief was available to help mothers cope with the extreme pain of a difficult labor, and complications often threatened the life of the mother or baby, or sometimes both.

The first article in this section looks at abnormal presentation, a condition in which the fetus is not lying in the normal position in the uterus, which is the easiest position for delivery. Problems that may complicate labor and delivery, usually because the fetus is unable to pass through the mother's pelvis, are covered next.

Two relatively rare conditions are discussed in the final part of this section. Fetal distress arises when the fetus is deprived of sufficient oxygen for its needs. This condition may occur at any stage of pregnancy, but is more common during labor. The final article discusses stillbirth, an extremely rare and distressing situation that occurs when a fetus dies in the womb later than 20 weeks into a pregnancy or, more rarely, a baby dies during labor.

KEY ANATOMY

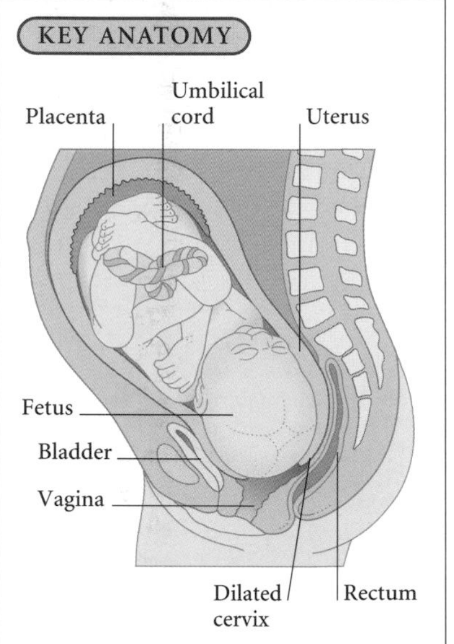
Placenta
Umbilical cord
Uterus
Fetus
Bladder
Vagina
Dilated cervix
Rectum

For more information on pregnancy and the stages of childbirth, *see* pp.778–783.

Abnormal presentation

Any deviation from the normal position of the fetus for delivery

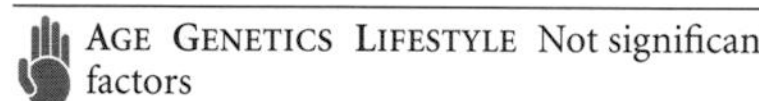
AGE GENETICS LIFESTYLE Not significant factors

In most normal pregnancies, the fetus settles into the mother's pelvic cavity from week 36 onward, ready for labor and birth. About 8 in 10 fetuses settle head downward, facing the mother's back, with the chin resting on the chest. In this position, the fetus is in the optimum position for birth, and a normal vaginal delivery is usually possible. All other fetal positions are considered to be abnormal presentations and may cause problems during labor.

When a fetus is lying in an abnormal position in the uterus, a vaginal delivery may be possible, but the labor may be prolonged (*see* PROBLEMS DURING DELIVERY, p.802). If the fetus becomes stuck, it may need an assisted delivery (p.805) or cesarean section (p.802).

Most abnormal presentations can be diagnosed before labor begins, and arrangements to deliver the fetus safely can be discussed in advance.

WHAT ARE THE CAUSES?

Abnormal presentation may occur if the fetus is able to move more freely within the uterus than usual, either because the fetus is small and does not fit closely into the pelvis (*see* PRETERM LABOR, p.798) or because there is excess amniotic fluid surrounding the fetus (*see* POLYHYDRAMNIOS, p.795). There is also an increased risk of an abnormal presentation when there is more than one fetus in the uterus (*see* MULTIPLE PREGNANCY AND ITS PROBLEMS, p.792).

Occasionally, the fetus cannot settle into the pelvic cavity because of an obstruction, such as the placenta lying low in the uterus (*see* PLACENTA PREVIA, p.798) or a noncancerous growth in the uterine wall (*see* FIBROIDS, p.745). An unusually shaped uterus may also contribute to an abnormal presentation.

WHAT ARE THE TYPES?

The most common abnormal presentations are the breech position and the occipitoposterior position. Rarer types include face, compound, brow, and shoulder presentations, named according to which parts of the fetus are over the dilated cervix at delivery.

BREECH In a breech birth, the fetus presents buttocks first. Many fetuses lie in a breech position before week 32 of pregnancy but most turn by 36 weeks. The 3 in 100 that do not turn are in one of three types of breech presentation. A complete breech is one in which the fetus is curled up. In a frank breech, the legs are extended and the feet are close to the face. In a footling breech, one or both feet are positioned over the cervix. Often one twin fetus is a breech.

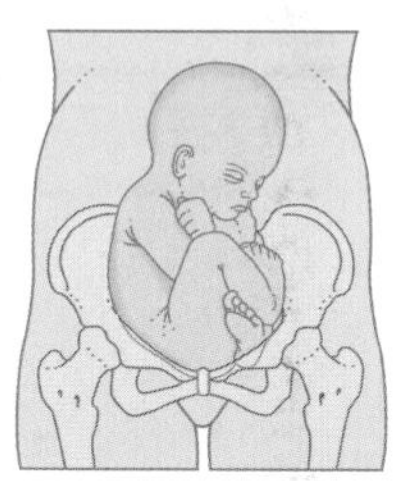

OCCIPITOPOSTERIOR At the beginning of labor, about 1 in 5 fetuses lies in an occipitoposterior position, head-down but facing the mother's abdomen instead of her back. Most fetuses will turn at some stage during labor, but 2 in 100 do not and are still in this presentation when they are delivered.

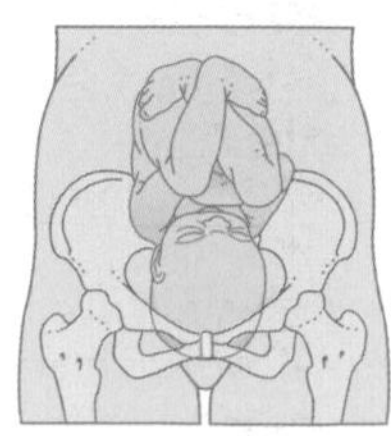

RARE PRESENTATIONS In a face presentation, the neck of the fetus is bent backward so that the face is over the cervix. This presentation occurs in about 1 in every 400 births. In a compound presentation, which occurs in 1 in every 700 births, an arm or leg lies over the cervix in addition to the head or buttocks. In a brow presentation, occurring in about 1 in every 1,000 births, the fetus's head is bent slightly backward with the brow over the cervix. A shoulder or oblique presentation, in which the fetus lies across the uterus with its shoulder over the cervix, occurs in about 1 in every 2,500 births.

ARE THERE COMPLICATIONS?

If the fetus lies in an abnormal position just before delivery, there may be complications that place both the fetus and mother at risk. A fetus in the normal head-down position blocks the cervix and prevents the umbilical cord from passing out of the uterus before the fetus. Some abnormal presentations leave space for the cord to drop through the cervix when the membranes surrounding the fetus rupture. When this occurs, the cord may be compressed by the fetus, or, rarely, its blood vessels may go into spasm because of the drop in temperature outside the uterus. As a result, the fetus may be deprived of oxygen (*see* FETAL DISTRESS, p.804). This may cause brain damage or fetal death.

A breech delivery may cause problems if the legs and body of the fetus are able to pass through the cervix when it is not completely dilated, but the head becomes stuck. If, in a footling breech, one foot drops through the cervix, this may prompt the mother to try to push too early. An abnormal presentation may also increase the risk of the cervix or vagina being torn during delivery.

HOW IS IT DIAGNOSED?

Normally, the position of the fetus in the uterus is assessed at each prenatal visit. Your doctor will usually be able to tell if your baby is lying in an abnormal position at the end of your pregnancy. A fetal stethoscope determines where the heartbeat is loudest, and this helps identify the approximate position of the fetus in the uterus. If your doctor suspects an abnormal presentation, you will be given ultrasound scanning to confirm the position (*see* ULTRASOUND SCANNING IN PREGNANCY, p.793).

WHAT IS THE TREATMENT?

Abnormal presentation is usually diagnosed toward the end of a pregnancy, and, if necessary, a cesarean section is arranged. A vaginal birth may be possible for some breech or occipitoposterior presentations. Sometimes, a mother with a fetus in a breech presentation is offered a procedure to turn the fetus around after week 36 of pregnancy. The doctor attempts to manipulate the fetus into the correct position by pushing gently on the wall of the abdomen. This technique is performed using ultrasound guidance. It is not painful for the mother or fetus, and the mother does not require anesthesia.

If the abnormal presentation was due to a structural problem, such as an unusually shaped uterus, there is an increased risk of recurrence in a subsequent pregnancy. However, if the presentation was caused by a condition associated with that particular pregnancy, such as placenta previa, the risk of recurrence is not increased.

(WWW) ONLINE SITES: p.1036

Delayed first stage of labor

Prolonged or complicated labor in the predelivery stage of labor

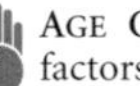

AGE GENETICS LIFESTYLE Not significant factors

The first stage of labor begins with the onset of regular, strong contractions of the uterus and ends when the cervix is fully dilated. In this period, the cervix widens until it is 4 in (10 cm) in diameter to allow the fetus to pass into the vagina. The average length of the first stage of labor is 6–12 hours, but it can take much longer in a first pregnancy.

(TREATMENT) EPIDURAL ANESTHESIA IN LABOR

Epidural anesthesia is one method of pain relief in labor. The anesthetic is given through a catheter inserted between two of the vertebrae (bones in the spine) in the lower back. The tip of the catheter is put into the epidural space formed by membranes surrounding the spinal cord. The other end is taped to the shoulder, so that further doses can be given. The anesthetic numbs nerves from below the waist, including those from the uterus. Intravenous fluids are given, and the baby's heart rate is checked by fetal monitoring.

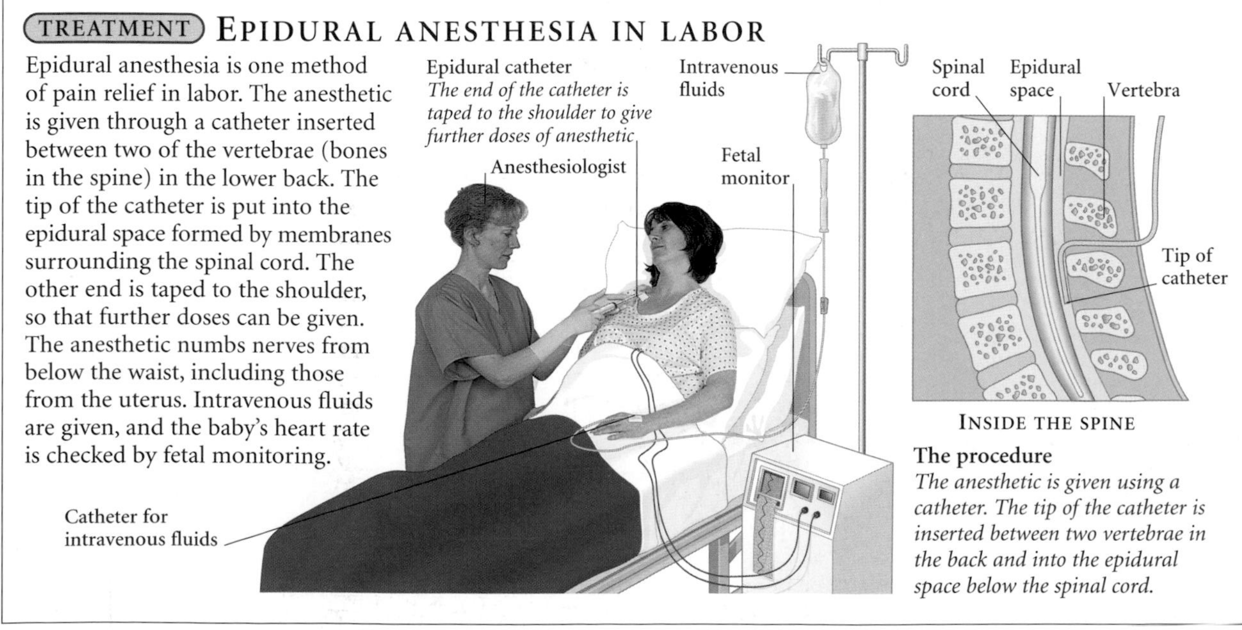
Epidural catheter
The end of the catheter is taped to the shoulder to give further doses of anesthetic
Anesthesiologist
Intravenous fluids
Fetal monitor
Catheter for intravenous fluids
Spinal cord
Epidural space
Vertebra
Tip of catheter
INSIDE THE SPINE

The procedure
The anesthetic is given using a catheter. The tip of the catheter is inserted between two vertebrae in the back and into the epidural space below the spinal cord.

TREATMENT CESAREAN SECTION

In a cesarean section, the baby is delivered through an incision in the mother's abdomen rather than through the vagina. The operation is carried out when circumstances make it safer than a vaginal birth for the mother and baby. A general anesthetic or an epidural anesthetic, injected into the lower back to numb the body below the waist (*see* EPIDURAL ANESTHESIA IN LABOR, p.801), is given. An incision is made in the lower abdomen and the baby and placenta are delivered within a few minutes. The mother stays in the hospital for about 4 days afterward.

During the procedure

A cesarean section may be performed under epidural anesthesia so that you can remain awake. Your partner can be with you during the operation, and you can hold the baby immediately afterward.

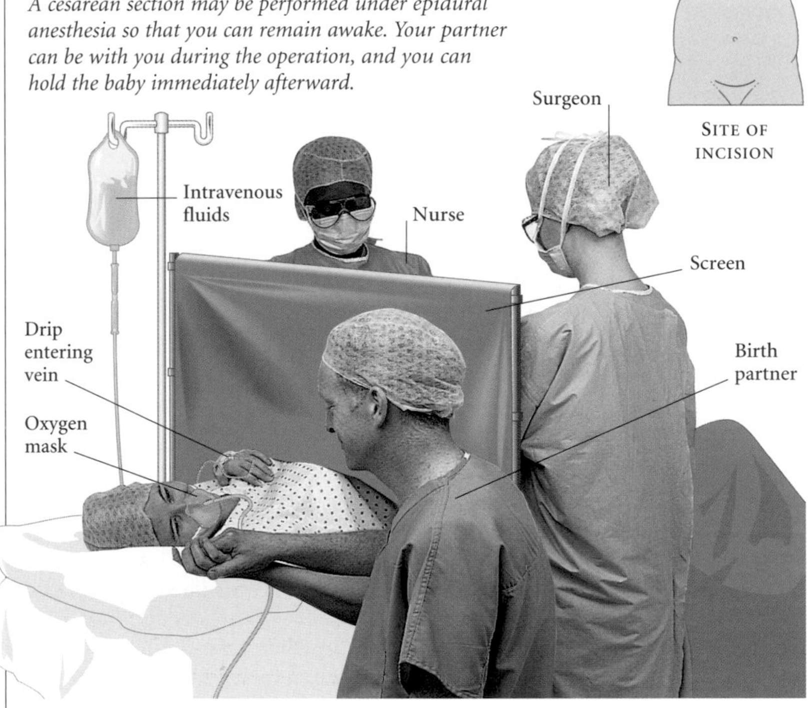
Surgeon
Site of incision
Intravenous fluids
Nurse
Screen
Drip entering vein
Birth partner
Oxygen mask

Labor is delayed when the first stage of labor is prolonged and the cervix is not dilating normally. A prolonged labor occurs in about 3 in 10 first births and about 1 in 8 subsequent births.

When it has been recognized that the first stage of labor is not progressing, the problem can usually be treated successfully with modern techniques and monitoring. The mother is likely to find a long first stage of labor exhausting and this may cause problems during delivery (right). If left untreated, a delay in the first stage may threaten the life of the mother and/or the fetus.

WHAT ARE THE CAUSES?

A delay in the first stage of labor may be due to uterine contractions that are too weak to fully dilate the cervix. In first pregnancies, weak uterine contractions are especially common, and dilation of the cervix is often slower than normal. Drugs that are given to relieve pain in labor, such as epidural anesthesia (*see* EPIDURAL ANESTHESIA IN LABOR, p.801), may also weaken contractions.

Sometimes, the cervix fails to dilate because it is scarred from surgery. In some labors, the fetus is in an unusual position and cannot put enough pressure on the cervix to assist dilation (*see* ABNORMAL PRESENTATION, p.800).

WHAT CAN I DO?

If your labor is taking an abnormally long time, try to keep walking around because gentle movement encourages the uterus to contract more effectively, and gravity increases the pressure from the fetus on the cervix. If you cannot get out of bed, try to sit upright. A prolonged labor can be exhausting and may cause dehydration. It is important that you keep your fluid intake up by drinking plenty of water.

WHAT MIGHT THE DOCTOR DO?

At regular intervals during your labor, a nurse will measure your blood pressure and check the dilation of your cervix. Your contractions and the heart rate of the fetus will be monitored continuously (*see* FETAL MONITORING, opposite page). If the heart rate is abnormal, a blood sample may be taken from the fetus's scalp to check for signs of fetal distress. An intravenous drip is used to maintain fluid levels if you are dehydrated. If your uterine contractions cannot dilate the cervix effectively, your doctor may be able to speed up labor using a number of different methods (*see* INDUCTION OF LABOR, p.797). If labor is still delayed, you may need to have a cesarean section (left).

WHAT IS THE PROGNOSIS?

With careful monitoring and management, a delayed first stage of labor is unlikely to cause problems.

The chance of having a delayed first stage of labor in future pregnancies depends on the cause. Weak or ineffective uterine contractions are less likely to occur in subsequent pregnancies, and dilation of the cervix is usually quicker. However, if the cervix has been scarred by surgery or damaged by a difficult delivery, a cesarean section may be necessary in future births.

(WWW) ONLINE SITES: p.1036

Problems during delivery

Any problem that prolongs the second stage of labor or prevents normal delivery

 AGE GENETICS LIFESTYLE Not significant factors

The delivery of a baby, called the second stage of labor, begins as soon as the mother's cervix has fully dilated to 4 in (10 cm) and ends when the baby is born. About 4 in 10 mothers experience problems during delivery, and the risk is higher for a first pregnancy. With careful management, it may be possible to carry out a normal vaginal delivery,

TEST FETAL MONITORING

Fetal monitoring, also known as cardiotocography, is used to detect fetal distress, usually as a result of oxygen deficiency. During labor, changes in the fetal heart rate in response to uterine contractions are recorded. An abnormal heart rate is a sign of fetal distress. If the fetus is distressed, a more accurate reading may be taken using a probe attached to the fetus's head. A blood sample may be taken from the fetus's scalp to check the level of oxygen. Monitoring normally takes place during labor but may also be used to detect problems during pregnancy.

External fetal monitoring
Two devices are strapped to your abdomen: an ultrasound transducer to detect the fetus's heartbeat and a pressure-sensitive gauge to measure your contractions.

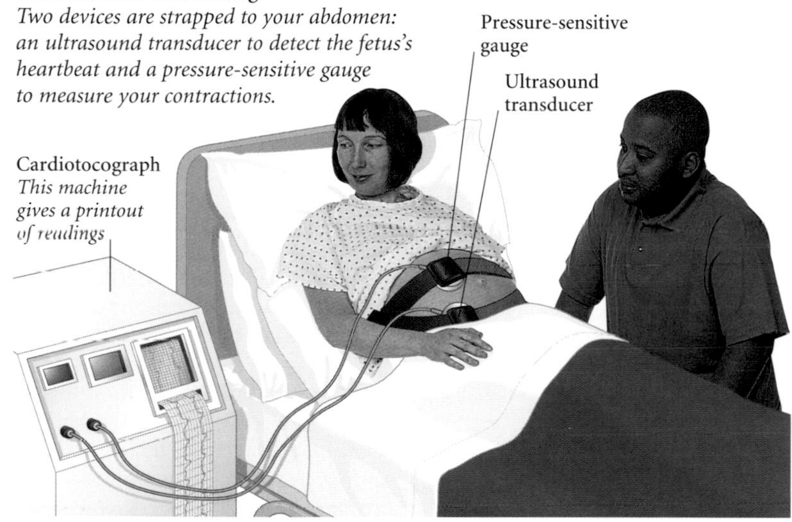
Pressure-sensitive gauge
Ultrasound transducer
Cardiotocograph
This machine gives a printout of readings

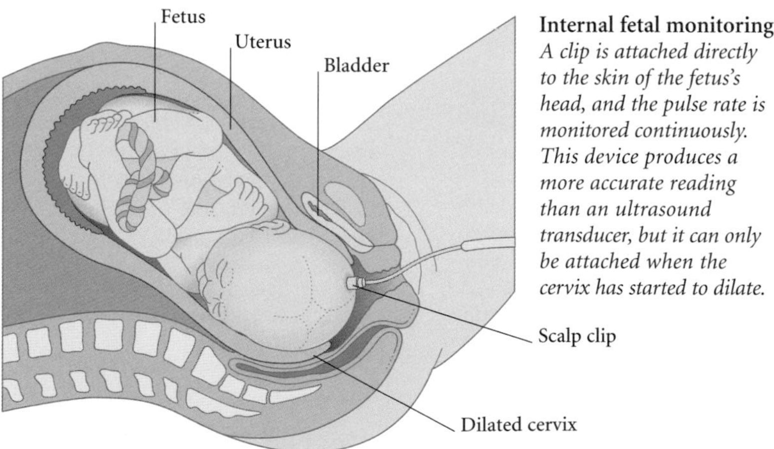
Fetus
Uterus
Bladder
Scalp clip
Dilated cervix

Internal fetal monitoring
A clip is attached directly to the skin of the fetus's head, and the pulse rate is monitored continuously. This device produces a more accurate reading than an ultrasound transducer, but it can only be attached when the cervix has started to dilate.

RESULTS

Cardiotocograph during labor
Readings from the two devices around the mother's abdomen are converted into tracings on a cardiotocograph. The heart rate of a healthy fetus speeds up at the start of a contraction, as the peaks in the graph show, then rapidly returns to a normal level.

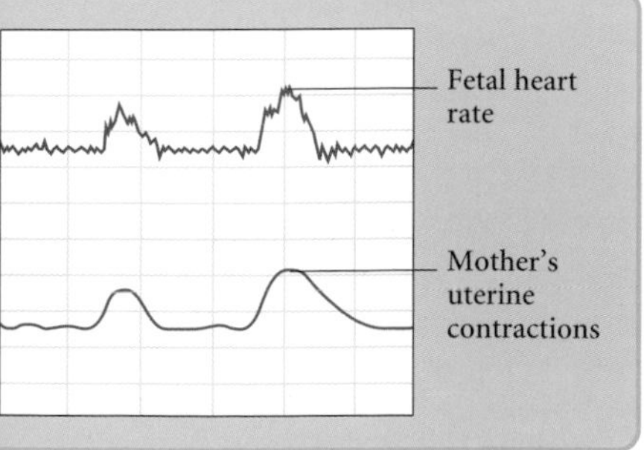
Fetal heart rate
Mother's uterine contractions

but if the second stage of labor is long, and the supply of oxygen to the fetus is insufficient, there is an increased risk of fetal distress (p.804). The doctor may then carry out an assisted delivery (p.805) using vacuum suction or forceps, or a cesarean section (opposite page).

WHAT ARE THE CAUSES?

Any of the problems that cause a delayed first stage of labor (p.801) can prevent a normal delivery. However, even if the first stage has progressed smoothly, a problem may arise at the second stage.

Weak or ineffective uterine contractions may slow down the delivery. Pain relief, such as epidural anesthesia during labor (p.801), may also affect the strength of contractions. If the mother is exhausted as a result of a long first stage of labor or because of poor general health, contractions may be weak and delivery may be difficult.

There may be a delay in the baby passing through the cervix and vagina if the baby is not in the normal position (*see* ABNORMAL PRESENTATION, p.800). Normal delivery may also be difficult if the baby cannot pass easily through the pelvis, either because the baby is large or because the mother has a narrow or irregularly shaped pelvis.

Once the baby has reached the vaginal opening, there may be problems in delivery if the surrounding tissues cannot stretch enough to let the head out.

HOW IS IT DIAGNOSED?

When your cervix has dilated fully and the second stage of labor begins, your doctor will monitor the baby's passage through the cervix and into the vagina and will check the heartbeat (*see* FETAL MONITORING, left) for signs of distress. The strength and frequency of uterine contractions are monitored. This information is then used to help determine whether a vaginal delivery is possible.

WHAT IS THE TREATMENT?

If your uterine contractions are too weak, the doctor may give an intravenous drip of oxytocin, a hormone that stimulates strong contractions (*see* INDUCTION OF LABOR, p.797). When a baby is slow to pass through the cervix and vagina, your doctor may perform an assisted delivery using forceps or vacuum suction. Just before an assisted delivery, an incision, called an episiotomy (right), is usually made in the tissue between the vagina and the anus. This cut eases the baby's passage and prevents the tissues around the vaginal opening from tearing. An episiotomy is also used to help delivery when a mother's vaginal opening is too small for the baby's head to pass through.

A cesarean section will be necessary if the baby cannot pass easily through your pelvis or if an assisted delivery would put either of you at risk.

WHAT IS THE PROGNOSIS?

You may feel disappointed if you need an assisted delivery, a cesarean section, or an episiotomy, but these methods are only used to ensure that your baby is delivered safely. Your ability to have normal vaginal deliveries in the future is not usually affected by these procedures. Many women who have a difficult first birth have no problems with subsequent births. However, if there is a physical reason why normal childbirth is difficult for you, such as an abnormally shaped pelvis or one that is too narrow, a cesarean birth will usually be required for future pregnancies.

(WWW) ONLINE SITES: p.1036

Fetal distress

Physical stress experienced by a fetus due to a lack of oxygen

AGE GENETICS LIFESTYLE Not significant factors

Fetal distress develops when there is an insufficient oxygen supply reaching the fetus. Although this condition usually occurs during labor or after week 28 of pregnancy, it may develop at any time in pregnancy. Fetal distress occurs in about 1 in 20 pregnancies, but the fetus is usually delivered before lasting harm occurs. If left untreated, fetal distress may cause fetal brain damage or death.

WHAT ARE THE CAUSES?

A common cause of fetal distress in pregnancy is a problem with the placenta, the organ that supplies oxygen and nutrients via the umbilical cord to the fetus. The function of the placenta may be affected if the mother develops preeclampsia (*see* PREECLAMPSIA AND ECLAMPSIA, p.794). The oxygen supply to the fetus may also be reduced if part or all of the placenta separates from the uterus during pregnancy (*see* PLACENTAL ABRUPTION, p.799).

Frequently, the cause of fetal distress during labor is unknown. There may be a placental abruption during labor, or the umbilical cord may become tangled, preventing oxygen from reaching the fetus. Another, less common, cause of fetal distress is cord prolapse. This condition may develop if the fetus is not securely fitted into the mother's pelvis because it is not lying in the normal head-down position facing the mother's back (*see* ABNORMAL PRESENTATION, p.800). An abnormal position may create space for the umbilical cord to drop through the cervix into the vagina. Once it is outside the uterus, the blood vessels in the cord may become compressed or, rarely, may go into spasm. Both of these situations can reduce the oxygen supply to the fetus.

The risk of fetal distress is increased if the fetus is weak or smaller than average (*see* SMALL FOR GESTATIONAL AGE, p.796) or if your labor starts before the 37th week of pregnancy (*see* PRETERM LABOR, p.798).

HOW IS IT DIAGNOSED?

If your doctor is concerned that there is a risk of fetal distress during your pregnancy, he or she may decide to refer you for an additional ultrasound scan (*see* ULTRASOUND SCANNING IN PREGNANCY, p.793). This scan enables your doctor to observe fetal movements and also to look at the blood flow in the vessels carrying blood from the placenta to the fetus. Reduced fetal movements may indicate oxygen deficiency. Your doctor may also recommend fetal monitoring (p.803). This monitors the fetus's heart rate, which may be abnormal if it is not getting enough oxygen.

During labor, the heartbeat of the fetus is continuously monitored, and a tiny sample of blood may be taken from the fetus's scalp to measure blood oxygen levels. The amniotic fluid from the uterus may be examined regularly for signs of staining from fetal feces (meconium), which are sometimes released from the fetus when it is under stress.

WHAT IS THE TREATMENT?

Treatment for fetal distress depends on the underlying cause, the severity of the distress, whether it occurs before or in labor, and how far labor has progressed.

If there are signs of even mild fetal distress during late pregnancy or early labor, your doctor will probably recommend a cesarean section (p.802). If labor is advanced and the fetus is experiencing only mild levels of distress, an assisted delivery (opposite page) may be a possible option. However, if fetal distress is severe, or there is a cord prolapse, your doctor will probably advise an emergency cesarean section.

WHAT IS THE PROGNOSIS?

If fetal distress is diagnosed and treated promptly, there is a good chance that your baby will be delivered safely and with no permanent harm. However, in some circumstances, babies need special care after birth (*see* NEONATAL CARE UNIT, p.959). This is often the case when a baby is born preterm (*see* PROBLEMS OF THE PRETERM BABY, p.816).

(WWW) ONLINE SITES: p.1036

TREATMENT EPISIOTOMY

An episiotomy is an incision made in the perineum (the area of tissue between the vagina and anus) to enlarge the birth opening and prevent a ragged tear. The cut may be used before an assisted delivery or if the perineum fails to stretch sufficiently for the baby's head.

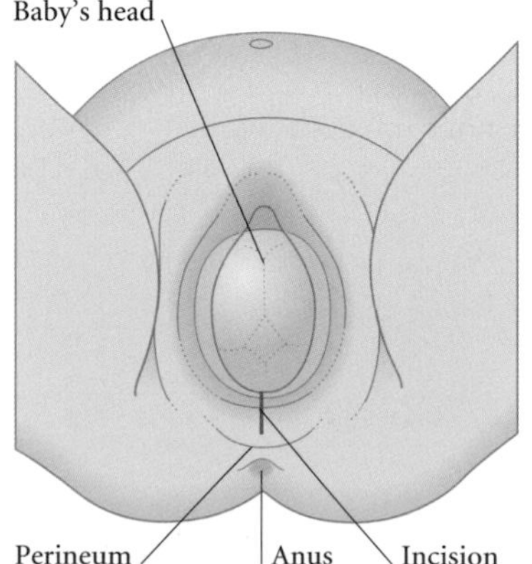
Baby's head
Perineum
Anus
Incision

Having an episiotomy
A local anesthetic is injected into the perineum and a small cut is made during a contraction. The cut follows a direct vertical line toward, but not as far as, the anus, enabling the baby's head to pass through the vaginal opening easily.

TREATMENT ASSISTED DELIVERY

When a vaginal delivery does not progress smoothly, a baby may need an assisted delivery. This sometimes occurs if the mother is too exhausted to push the baby out or the baby becomes stuck or distressed. In these circumstances, the doctor may use vacuum suction or forceps to assist the delivery. An episiotomy (opposite page) to enlarge the birth opening is usually carried out just before an assisted delivery. Vacuum suction and forceps procedures are used in about 1 in 10 vaginal births.

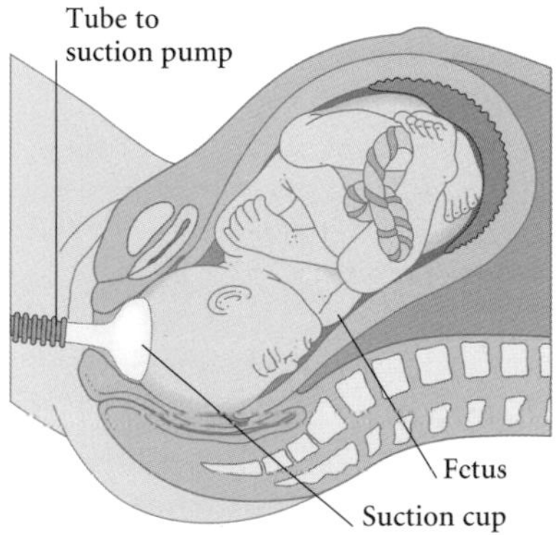
Tube to suction pump
Fetus
Suction cup

Vacuum suction delivery
A suction cup is placed on the baby's scalp, and the baby is assisted out while the mother pushes. The suction cup leaves a temporary swelling on the baby's head.

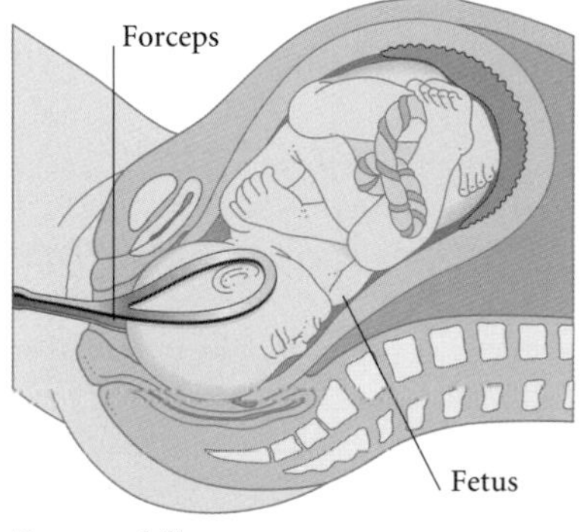
Forceps
Fetus

Forceps delivery
Metal forceps are inserted into the vagina and placed on each side of the baby's head. The doctor pulls with the forceps as the mother pushes the baby out.

Stillbirth

The delivery of a dead fetus after week 20 of pregnancy

 AGE More common over age 35

 LIFESTYLE Smoking and alcohol or drug abuse during pregnancy are risk factors

 GENETICS Risk factors depend on the cause

The death of a fetus in the uterus or during birth is a very distressing event. Bereaved parents may experience confused feelings of anger, shock, guilt, and inadequacy, in addition to overwhelming grief. Stillbirths are extremely rare. Their incidence has decreased dramatically in developed countries during the past 50 years, and fewer than 6 in 1,000 babies are now stillborn in Canada each year. Stillbirth is slightly more common in mothers over age 35.

WHAT ARE THE CAUSES?

Often, the precise cause of fetal death is unknown. The death may be caused by a reduction in the fetus's oxygen supply (*see* FETAL DISTRESS, opposite page) due to a problem with the umbilical cord or placenta. For example, the umbilical cord may be tangled or knotted, or the placenta may separate from the uterus before the baby is born (*see* PLACENTAL ABRUPTION, p.799). If the mother has very high blood pressure or poorly controlled diabetes mellitus (p.687), the risk of stillbirth is increased.

Stillbirth may occur if the fetus has a severe genetic disorder or, rarely, if the blood groups of the mother and fetus are not compatible (*see* RHESUS INCOMPATIBILITY, p.795). Certain infectious diseases that pass from the mother to the fetus, such as listeriosis (p.300), may harm the fetus and, if they are severe, may cause death. Women who smoke or abuse drugs or alcohol are at greater risk of a stillbirth.

WHAT MIGHT BE DONE?

The first sign that a fetus may have died in the uterus is the absence of movement. If, after week 20 of pregnancy, you are aware that fetal movements have decreased or ceased altogether, you should call your doctor without delay. The doctor will listen for the fetal heartbeat and then confirm his or her findings with an ultrasound scan (*see* ULTRASOUND SCANNING IN PREGNANCY, p.793). In most cases, the results of the scan will confirm that the fetus is well and the pregnancy is progressing normally. Rarely, if the fetus has died and labor has not started, induction of labor (p.797) will probably be necessary.

If there is no immediate risk to your health, such as an infection, you may be given time to come to terms with the loss of your child before the baby is delivered. A cesarean section is not usually used to deliver the baby because of the risks associated with any operation and the small risk of the scar reopening during a subsequent vaginal delivery. In the rare event of a baby dying during labor, delivery will continue.

Parents are encouraged to see and hold their stillborn baby after the birth as part of the grieving process. After the delivery, the mother and baby undergo tests to determine the cause of death. In addition, the mother will be given advice before she leaves the hospital on how to ease breast engorgement (p.808).

Your doctor may recommend professional counseling to help you recover from the loss of your baby (*see* LOSS AND BEREAVEMENT, p.76). You should not be afraid to seek support from family members and friends and may find it helpful to join a self-help group of people who have been through a similar experience. A funeral ceremony may be comforting to some people. About 6 weeks after the birth, your doctor will review the results of tests and the postmortem with you and discuss the cause of the death, if it is known.

WHAT IS THE PROGNOSIS?

After a stillbirth, you may feel strongly that you want to begin another pregnancy right away. However, it may be better to wait until you are emotionally ready for a new baby and are fully recovered from your pregnancy. If you do decide on another pregnancy, your doctor will ensure that you are given extra care because you will be considered to be at high risk (*see* HIGH-RISK PREGNANCY, p.786). The risk of having another stillbirth depends on the original cause, if one can be found, but most subsequent pregnancies are successful. As with all grief, the pain of losing a baby lessens with time.

WWW ONLINE SITES: p.1029, p.1036

PROBLEMS AFTER CHILDBIRTH

Childbirth is an exhilarating experience for many women, but it can also be difficult and painful. In addition to recovering from physical trauma, the body has to adapt to the abrupt changes in hormone levels after the birth. These hormone changes often lead to emotional swings and always cause physiological changes, particularly in the breasts in preparation for breast-feeding.

KEY ANATOMY

Uterus after delivery
Rectum
Cervix
Bladder
Vagina
Nipple
Milk duct
Lobule
Areola

REPRODUCTIVE ORGANS

BREAST

For more information on the physical changes during and after a normal pregnancy, *see* pp.778–783.

Once the baby and the placenta have been delivered, the uterus starts to revert to its size before pregnancy. This process takes about 6 weeks. However, it may take several months for muscle tone to be regained in the abdomen, and any excess weight gained while pregnant will have to be lost through a careful diet and exercise. The breasts remain enlarged while breast-feeding and only return to their normal size once the baby has been weaned.

The first article in this section covers excessive bleeding occurring after childbirth or in the first few weeks following delivery of the baby. This condition is now relatively rare due to developments in drug treatment over the past few decades.

Depression, which is covered next, is very common after the birth of a baby. Feelings may range from mild baby blues to severe depression that requires hospital treatment. The last articles in this section cover breast disorders that can occur after childbirth, often in association with breast-feeding.

Postpartum hemorrhage

Excessive loss of blood immediately after delivery or in the first few weeks after childbirth

AGE More common over age 35

GENETICS LIFESTYLE Not significant factors

Almost all women have some degree of blood loss over the 3 or 4 days after childbirth, and most women have some light vaginal bleeding for up to 4 weeks afterward. Postpartum hemorrhage is defined as the loss of more than 1 pint (500 ml) of blood after childbirth.

After delivery of the baby, the placenta normally separates from the wall of the uterus and is then expelled from the body through the vagina. The site where the placenta was attached continues to bleed until strong contractions of the uterus constrict the blood vessels in the wall of the uterus and gradually stop the flow of blood. The majority of postpartum hemorrhages, especially if severe, are the result of bleeding from the uterus. However, bleeding may also come from the cervix or the vagina.

Postpartum hemorrhage occurs in about 1 in 50 births, usually immediately after delivery (early postpartum hemorrhage). Only a few women have a late postpartum hemorrhage, in which bleeding occurs more than 1 day after delivery. Although a severe postpartum hemorrhage may be life-threatening to the mother, it is now uncommon due to the routine injection of drugs after childbirth to help the uterus contract.

WHAT ARE THE CAUSES?

In most cases, early postpartum hemorrhage occurs because the uterus is unable to contract sufficiently to constrict the blood vessels of the uterus. This may be due to exhaustion of the muscles of the uterus after a long labor, overstretching of the uterus due to a multiple pregnancy (*see* MULTIPLE PREGNANCY AND ITS PROBLEMS, p.792), excess amniotic fluid (*see* POLYHYDRAMNIOS, p.795), or a large baby.

Contraction of the uterus may also be impaired by noncancerous growths of tissue in the uterus (*see* FIBROIDS, p.745) or if some or all of the placenta remains in the uterus after birth. Occasionally, general anesthesia given for a cesarean section (p.802) can impair contractions. Early postpartum hemorrhage may also occur if the placenta has implanted in the lower uterus (*see* PLACENTA PREVIA, p.798). In this case, muscles in the lower uterus may not contract sufficiently to stop bleeding.

Less commonly, an early postpartum hemorrhage may be due to a tear to the cervix or the vagina in childbirth. Tears are more likely to occur if the baby is born very rapidly, is not born head first (*see* ABNORMAL PRESENTATION, p.800), or is delivered with either forceps or suction (*see* ASSISTED DELIVERY, p.805).

Late postpartum hemorrhage is usually caused by fragments of the placenta left in the uterus or by an infection.

WHAT ARE THE SYMPTOMS?

The main symptom of early postpartum hemorrhage is bright red excessive vaginal bleeding shortly after delivery.

A late postpartum hemorrhage may occur between 24 hours and 6 weeks after the birth. Symptoms may include:

- Sudden, heavy vaginal bleeding that is bright red in color.

- Lower abdominal pain.
- Fever.

Sudden, severe postpartum hemorrhage may lead to shock (p.414). Postpartum hemorrhage almost always occurs while you are hospitalized. If you are not in the hospital and you develop severe vaginal bleeding after delivery, you should contact your doctor immediately.

How is it diagnosed?

If you are not already in the hospital, you will usually be admitted immediately. Your pulse and blood pressure will be monitored to look for evidence of shock. If an early postpartum hemorrhage has occurred, your doctor will feel your lower abdomen to see if the uterus is contracted. The placenta will be checked to ensure that it is complete. If the uterus appears to be contracted but bleeding continues, your cervix and vagina will be examined. This may be carried out under general anesthesia or epidural anesthesia.

If you are having a late postpartum hemorrhage, your doctor may arrange for a special ultrasound scan, using a probe inserted into the vagina, to check for remaining pieces of placenta in the uterus. A vaginal swab may be taken to check for evidence of infection.

What is the treatment?

If an early postpartum hemorrhage is due to poor contraction of the uterus, you may be given an injection to help the uterus contract. Your doctor may also massage your abdomen. If these measures do not work, further drugs may be given to help the uterus contract. If bleeding continues, surgery may be required. In rare cases, a hysterectomy (p.747) may be necessary. Bleeding caused by a retained placenta is treated by manually removing the remaining placenta through the vagina. If the blood loss is due to tears in the cervix or vagina, these will be stitched.

If a late postpartum hemorrhage is the result of an infection, antibiotics (p.885) will be prescribed. If the bleeding continues, surgery may be needed to examine the uterus and remove any remaining fragments of placenta.

Blood lost due to a postpartum hemorrhage may have to be replaced by a blood transfusion (p.447).

(WWW) ONLINE SITES: p.1036

Depression after childbirth

Depressive feelings or psychological disturbances in the first few weeks or months after childbirth

GENETICS Sometimes runs in families

LIFESTYLE Lack of emotional support and additional stressful life events are risk factors

AGE Not a significant factor

It is very common for a new mother to feel low or miserable during the first few days or weeks after childbirth. A new baby leads to major changes in lifestyle and adjustments will need to be made. This mild mood change is commonly known as the "baby blues" and affects up to 8 in 10 women following the birth of a child.

More severe postpartum depression is a relatively common disorder in the first few weeks or months after childbirth and affects about 1 in 10 women. About 1 in 1,000 women develops a serious psychiatric condition known as postpartum psychosis that requires immediate treatment in the hospital.

What are the causes?

Baby blues are thought to be caused by the sudden fall in hormone levels (particularly of estrogen and progesterone) that occurs after a baby is born. These hormonal changes may also cause postpartum depression and possibly also postpartum psychosis.

Some women who have postpartum depression have had depression (p.554) before, or postpartum depression may run in their families. Other factors, such as feelings of isolation and inadequacy and concerns about the new responsibilities of motherhood, can cause stress and contribute to depression. Lack of sleep due to caring for the baby, exhaustion from a long labor, or painful wounds, such as tears in the vagina or scars from a cesarean section, may aggravate the problem. Some mothers who experience postpartum depression have also reported a difficult labor. Any extra stresses or problems with a partner may also make feelings of depression worse. Some women experience anxiety after childbirth and they may have panic attacks with palpitations and shortness of breath (*see* ANXIETY DISORDERS, p.551). If recurrent panic attacks are untreated, they may lead to postpartum depression.

Although the precise cause of postpartum psychosis is not understood, a previous history of episodes of depression that alternate with episodes of mania (*see* BIPOLAR AFFECTIVE DISORDER, p.557) greatly increases the risk. Some women who have postpartum psychosis also have close relatives with a medical history of bipolar affective disorder or severe depression.

What are the symptoms?

The symptoms of baby blues start 3–10 days after giving birth. They are often worse about day 5 and include:

- Dramatic mood swings.
- Weeping.
- Fatigue and irritability.
- Lack of concentration.

Postpartum depression may begin any time in the first 6 months after childbirth. The condition is similar to baby blues but much more severe, and unlike baby blues it can interfere with the mother's ability to carry out day-to-day activities. The symptoms include:

- Constantly feeling exhausted.
- Having little interest or no interest at all in the new baby.
- Sense of anticlimax.
- Feeling inadequate and overwhelmed by new responsibilities.
- Difficulty sleeping.
- Loss of appetite.
- Feelings of guilt.

The symptoms of postpartum psychosis usually develop rapidly about 2–3 weeks after childbirth. They often include:

- Insomnia and overactivity.
- Extreme mood swings from depression to mania.
- False beliefs of being disliked and persecuted by people.
- Hallucinations.
- Confusion.

Sometimes, threats of suicide or of harming the baby may be made.

What can I do?

You should try to get as much support as possible from medical staff, friends, and family after childbirth. Make sure you are not left alone until you feel happy caring for your baby, and rest as

STRUCTURE AND FUNCTION THE DEVELOPING BODY

A child's body grows and changes continuously from birth to adulthood through processes that are largely controlled by hormones. The most dramatic changes take place during infancy, when rapid growth occurs, and during puberty, when the body is approaching sexual maturity. At certain times, some parts of the body develop faster than others, which is why body proportions change throughout childhood. A child's brain is almost fully grown by age 6, while the rest of the body remains relatively undeveloped.

CHANGING BODY PROPORTIONS

At birth, a baby's head is as wide as the shoulders and appears large in relation to the rest of the body. The head continues to grow quickly, and by age 2, the brain is already four-fifths of its adult size. As the child grows older, the rate of growth of the head decreases compared with the rest of the body. Eventually, usually by age 18, the proportion of the head with the rest of the body stays the same and growth stops.

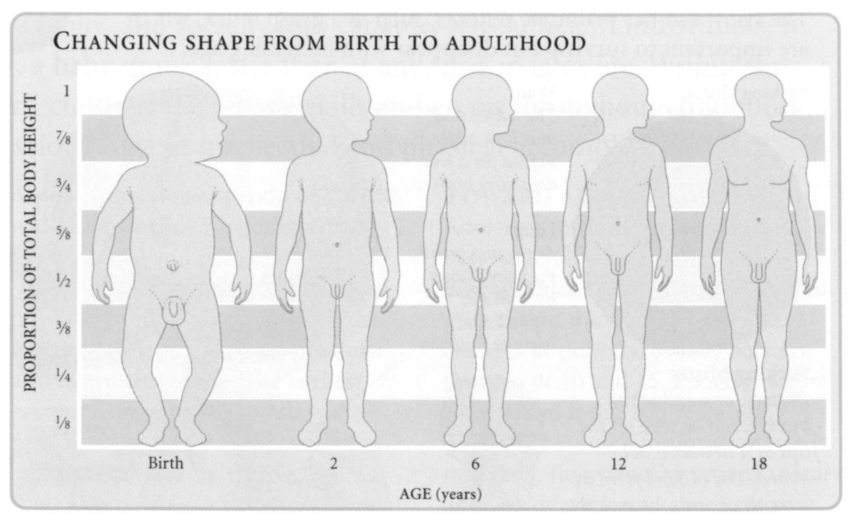
CHANGING SHAPE FROM BIRTH TO ADULTHOOD
PROPORTION OF TOTAL BODY HEIGHT
1
7/8
3/4
5/8
1/2
3/8
1/4
1/8
Birth
2
6
12
18
AGE (years)

How proportions change
A newborn baby's head makes up about one-quarter of total body length, and the legs three-eighths. By age 18, proportions have changed; the head is one-eighth of total body length and the legs one-half.

HOW BONES DEVELOP

Hard-bone formation (ossification) commences before birth at sites in the bone shafts known as primary ossification centers. In a newborn baby, only the shafts (diaphyses) are ossified. The ends of these bones (epiphyses) consist of tissue called cartilage, which is gradually replaced by bone that develops from secondary ossification centers. Between the shaft and the ends is a zone called the growth plate, which produces more cartilage to elongate the bones.

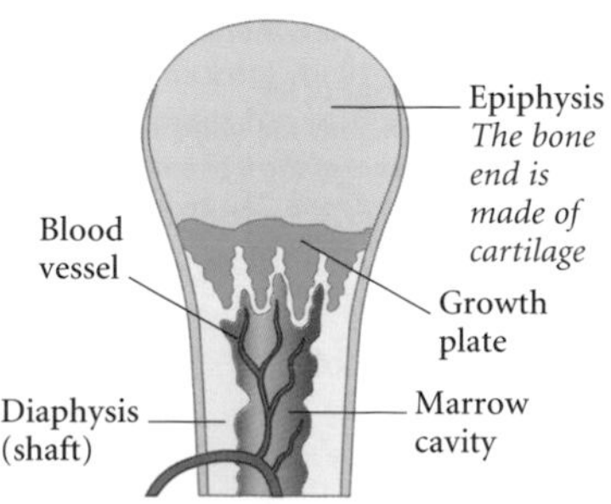
Epiphysis
The bone end is made of cartilage
Blood vessel
Growth plate
Diaphysis (shaft)
Marrow cavity

Long bone of a newborn baby
The shaft (diaphysis) is mostly bone, while the ends (epiphyses) are made of cartilage that gradually hardens.

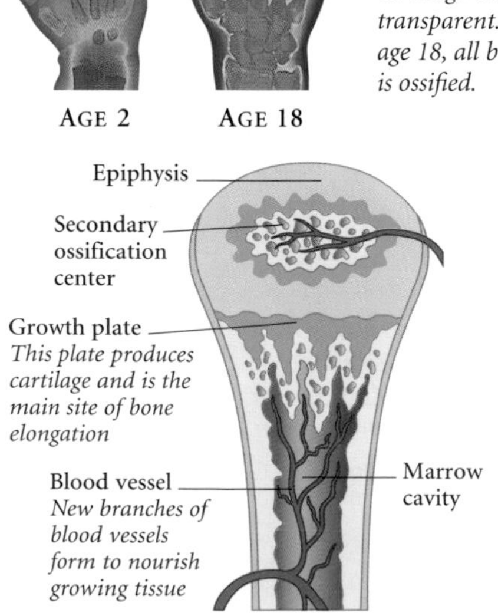
AGE 2
AGE 18
Epiphysis
Secondary ossification center
Growth plate
This plate produces cartilage and is the main site of bone elongation
Blood vessel
New branches of blood vessels form to nourish growing tissue
Marrow cavity

Hand growth
At age 2, ossified hand bone shafts look opaque on an X-ray. The growing cartilage looks transparent. By age 18, all bone is ossified.

Long bone of a child
The epiphyses contain secondary ossification centers from which bone forms. A growth plate near the ends produces new cartilage.

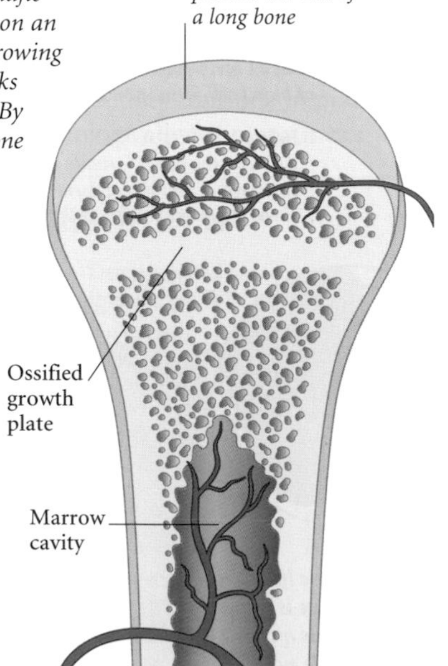
Articular cartilage
This smooth tissue protects the end of a long bone
Ossified growth plate
Marrow cavity

Long bone of an adult
Bone growth is complete by age 18, when the shafts, growth plates, and epiphyses have all ossified and fused into continuous bone.

How the skull and brain develop

At birth, a newborn's brain has its full complement of billions of neurons (nerve cells) that transmit and receive messages along axons (nerve fibers). At first, these neural networks are partially developed. During the first 6 years, the networks expand, and the brain grows rapidly to allow children to learn new skills. The skull expands to accommodate this growth. From age 6 to 18, neural pathways develop at a slower rate.

How the brain and skull grow
During infancy, the part of the skull around the brain (cranium) grows rapidly at the seams (sutures) and soft gaps (fontanelles) between the bone plates. By age 6, the brain is almost full size.

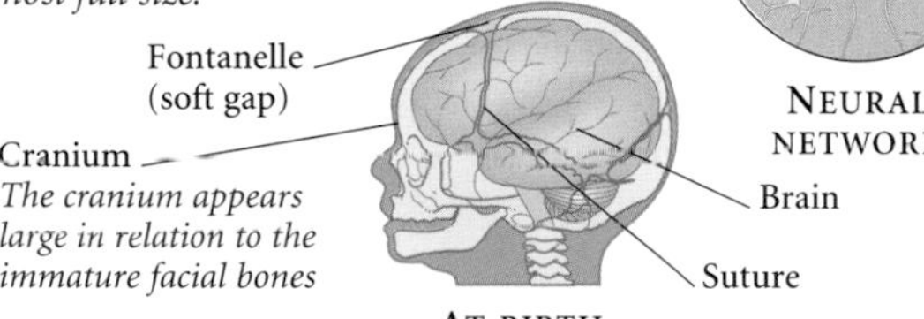
Fontanelle
(soft gap)
Cranium
The cranium appears large in relation to the immature facial bones
Brain
Suture
Neural network
At birth

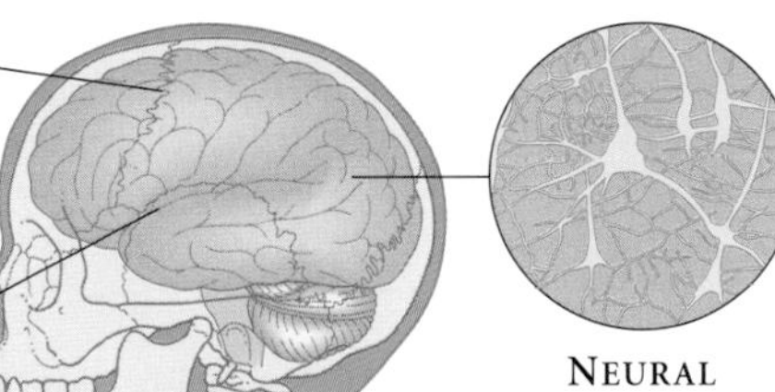
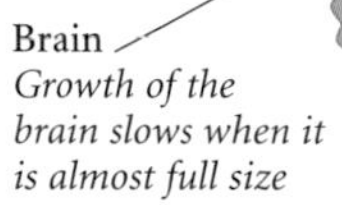
Suture (seam)
Skull plates are fixed at the sutures, and the fontanelles have closed.Growth continues at a slower rate
Brain
Growth of the brain slows when it is almost full size
Neural network
At 6 years

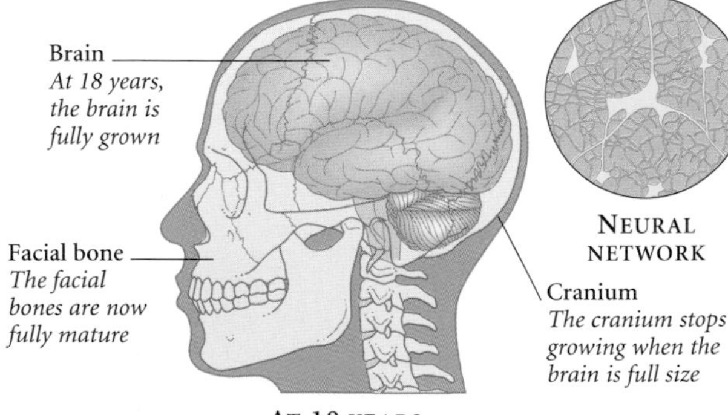
Brain
At 18 years, the brain is fully grown
Facial bone
The facial bones are now fully mature
Neural network
Cranium
The cranium stops growing when the brain is full size
At 18 years

Axon (nerve fiber)
Neuron cell body

Neural network
This highly magnified view of adult brain tissue shows neurons within a complex network of neural pathways.

How nerves develop

Early in life, most nerve fibers (axons) become wrapped in insulating sheaths made of a fatty substance known as myelin. This insulation speeds up nerve transmission by as much as 100 times and is essential for the body to grow and function normally.

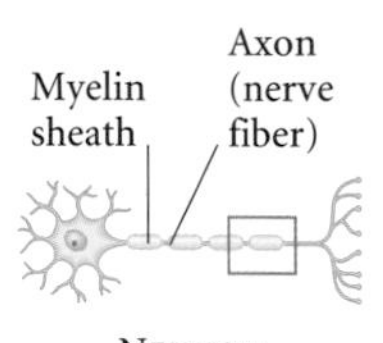
Myelin sheath
Axon (nerve fiber)
Neuron

Supportive cell · Axon · Nucleus of supportive cell

1 *Supportive cells, composed mainly of fatty material known as myelin, wind around an axon to form a protective and insulating sheath.*

2 *The axon is now wrapped in sections of myelin sheath separated by gaps (nodes of Ranvier). Nerve signals jump from one gap to the next.*

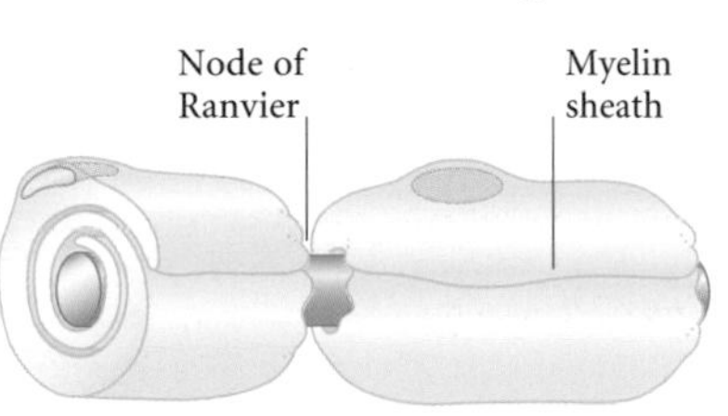
Node of Ranvier
Myelin sheath

Factors affecting growth

A child's potential maximum growth is determined by his or her genes, but achieving the maximum depends on a number of other factors, such as nutrition and general health. Girls and boys have similar patterns of yearly growth in childhood (below). A growth spurt at puberty is triggered by sex hormones, which also speed up the fusion of growth plates in the bone. Growth is complete by about age 18.

Why boys grow taller than girls
Boys go through puberty a bit later than girls, which gives them more time to grow in childhood before a final spurt completes their full growth.

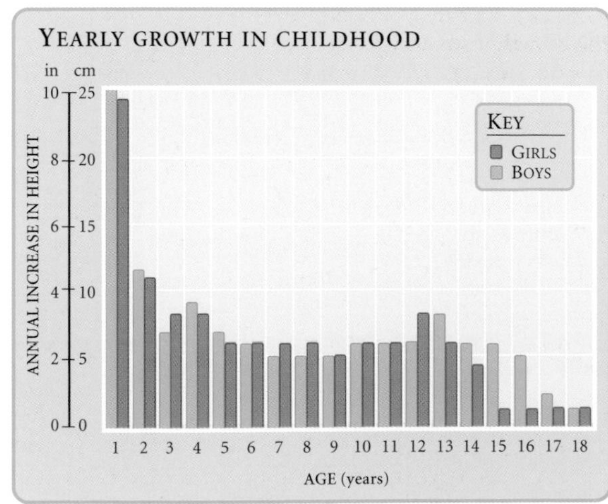
Yearly growth in childhood
in cm
10 25
8 20
6 15
4 10
2 5
0 0
Annual increase in height
Key
Girls
Boys
1 2 3 4 5 6 7 8 9 10 11 12 13 14 15 16 17 18
AGE (years)

DATA GAINING SKILLS DURING THE FIRST FIVE YEARS

During their first 5 years, children learn the basic skills necessary for their future development. The four main areas are physical skills, manual dexterity, language, and social skills. Although children progress at different rates, developmental milestones occur in a predictable order. This is partly because the ability to learn particular skills depends upon the maturity of the child's nervous system. In addition, for some complex skills, children need to develop a lesser skill first; for example, babies must learn to stand before they can walk.

DEVELOPMENTAL MILESTONES

AGE (years): 0, 1, 2, 3, 4, 5

Physical skills
Babies first master control of their body posture and head, then go on to develop physical skills, including standing, crawling, and walking.

- Can lift head to 45°
- Can roll over
- Can bear weight on legs
- Can sit unsupported
- Can crawl
- Can stand by hoisting up own weight
- Can stand without help
- Can walk holding on to furniture
- Can walk without help
- Can walk up stairs without help
- Can throw a ball
- Can kick a ball
- Can pedal a tricycle
- Can balance on one foot for a second
- Can catch a bounced ball
- Can hop on one leg

Manual dexterity and vision
Children have to coordinate their movement and vision to perform manipulative tasks, such as picking up objects or drawing.

- Holds hands together
- Reaches out for a rattle
- Passes rattle from hand to hand
- Plays with feet
- Can grasp object between finger and thumb
- Can pick up a small object
- Likes to scribble
- Can build a tower of four bricks
- Can draw a straight line
- Can copy a circle
- Can draw rudimentary likeness of a person
- Can copy a square

Hearing and language
Early on, babies turn toward voices and respond to sounds by cooing. At about 1 year, children speak their first word.

- Startled by loud sounds
- Squeals
- Turns toward voice
- Makes cooing noises
- Says "dada" and "mama" to anyone
- Says "dada" and "mama" to parents
- Starts to learn single words
- Can point to parts of the body
- Can put two words together
- Knows first and last names
- Can talk in full sentences
- Can name a color
- Can define seven words

Social behavior and play
Self-care begins with basic skills, such as dressing and toilet training. Social skills range from smiling to making the first new friends.

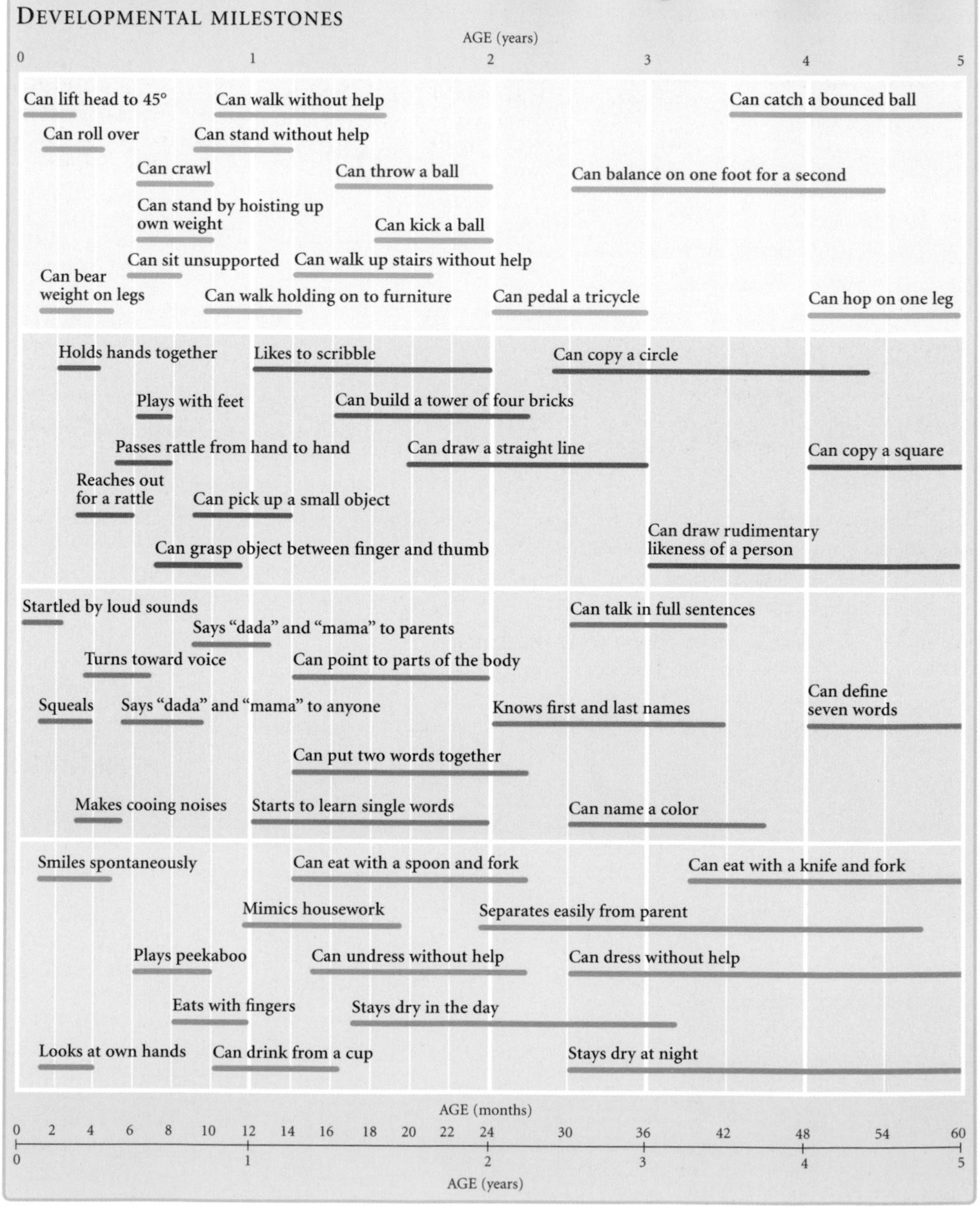

- Smiles spontaneously
- Looks at own hands
- Plays peekaboo
- Eats with fingers
- Can drink from a cup
- Mimics housework
- Can eat with a spoon and fork
- Can undress without help
- Stays dry in the day
- Separates easily from parent
- Can dress without help
- Stays dry at night
- Can eat with a knife and fork

AGE (months): 0, 2, 4, 6, 8, 10, 12, 14, 16, 18, 20, 22, 24, 30, 36, 42, 48, 54, 60

AGE (years): 0, 1, 2, 3, 4, 5

FUNCTION PUBERTY

Puberty is a period of rapid growth and physical change, during which adolescents become sexually mature. The age at which puberty begins and the rate of growth are influenced by genetics, general health, and weight. Puberty begins when the pituitary gland, located at the base of the brain, secretes hormones that stimulate the production of sex hormones. Within about 2 years of the start of puberty, sexual reproduction is possible, but it takes longer for adolescents to become mature enough emotionally for adult relationships.

CHANGES IN GIRLS DURING PUBERTY

In girls, puberty begins between the ages of 10 and 14, when luteinizing hormone (LH) and follicle-stimulating hormone (FSH) stimulate the ovaries to secrete the sex hormones estrogen and progesterone. These hormones prompt physical changes and, later, stimulate ovulation, menstruation, and increased sex drive.

RISE IN ESTROGEN

High

ESTROGEN LEVEL

Low

8 10 12 14 16 18

AGE (years)

The rise in estrogen at puberty
Estrogen levels rise sharply between about age 11 and 14 years. After this period, estrogen levels out until the menopause, when it decreases.

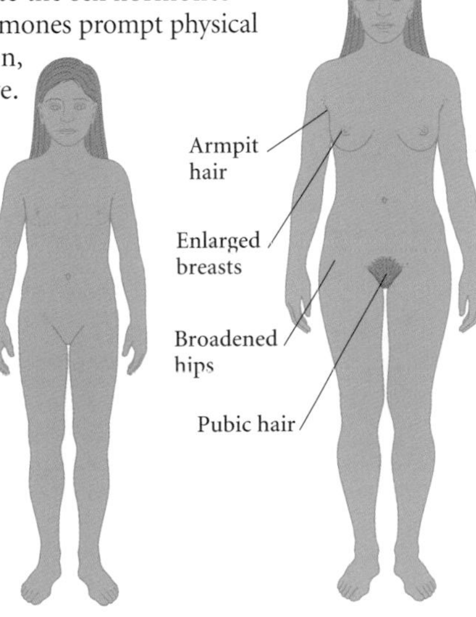
Armpit hair
Enlarged breasts
Broadened hips
Pubic hair

BEFORE PUBERTY

AFTER PUBERTY

Milk duct

Milk-producing cells

Magnified breast tissue
At puberty, the breasts start to enlarge as they develop the milk glands and ducts that supply milk after a baby is born.

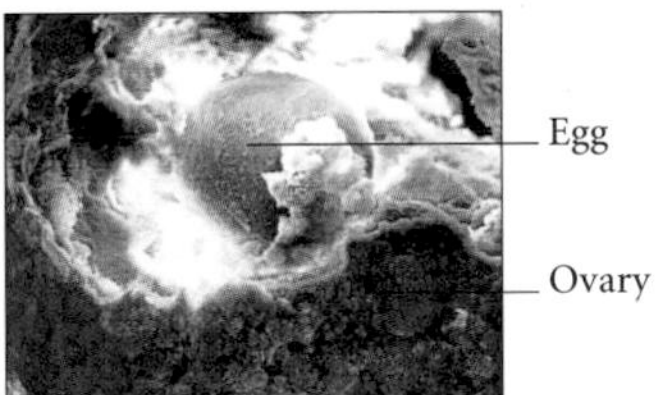
Egg
Ovary

Ovulation
During puberty, ovulation begins; every month an egg is released from the ovary (as shown here) and travels to the uterus.

CHANGES IN BOYS DURING PUBERTY

In boys, puberty begins between the ages of about 12 and 15. During this time, the pituitary gland starts to secrete the hormones LH and FSH. These hormones stimulate the testes to secrete the male sex hormone testosterone, which prompts physical changes and, later, sperm production and increased sex drive.

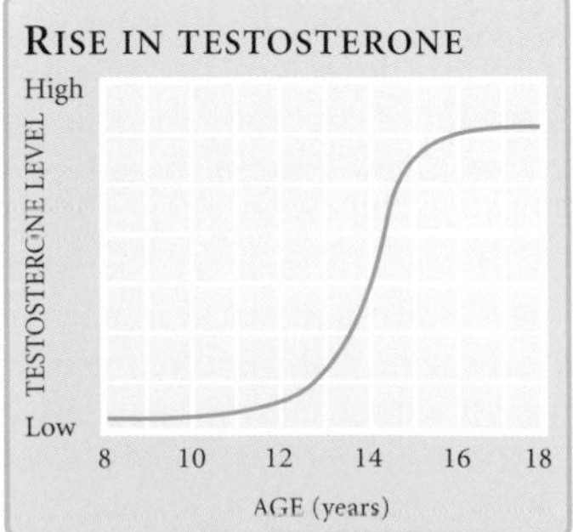
RISE IN TESTOSTERONE
High
TESTOSTERONE LEVEL
Low
8 10 12 14 16 18
AGE (years)

The rise in testosterone at puberty
Testosterone levels rise sharply between about age 13 and 16 years. After this period, testosterone levels out until old age, when it gradually decreases.

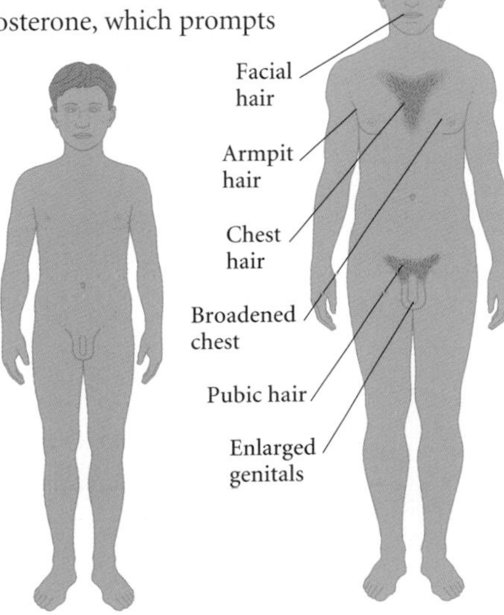
Facial hair
Armpit hair
Chest hair
Broadened chest
Pubic hair
Enlarged genitals

BEFORE PUBERTY

AFTER PUBERTY

Hair shaft

Facial hair
Hair on the face is part of the typical male pattern of hair growth triggered by increasing levels of testosterone.

Tubule
Developing sperm cells

Cross section of testis tissue
In each testis, there are about 1,000 tubules. During puberty, these tubules begin to produce sperm cells.

PROBLEMS IN BABIES

Many problems in babies are associated with their immaturity and the adjustment to a new environment. Preterm babies are at particular risk of life-threatening conditions, but medical advances have greatly increased the number of babies that survive.

The first article in this section covers the problems experienced by preterm babies. Preterm babies are born more than 3 weeks early and may have special problems as a result of their immaturity. The article that follows discusses congenital infections, which are transmitted from the mother to the fetus either during pregnancy or at birth as the baby passes through the birth canal. Although these infections are rare, they may have serious effects. Neonatal jaundice, which is discussed next, occurs in many newborn babies. In most cases, the jaundice is normal, but rarely there is a serious cause, such as the underdevelopment of the baby's bile ducts in the liver. Problems experienced with sleeping, feeding, crying, colic, and teething are also covered. These minor problems can be stressful for parents but rarely require medical treatment. The section ends with an article on sudden infant death syndrome (SIDS), which is also known as crib death, and advice on how to prevent it. The cause of SIDS is not known, but the incidence of it has decreased since parents have been advised to position babies on their backs to sleep. Other conditions that affect babies from birth are discussed in chromosome and gene disorders (pp.821–827) and endocrine and metabolic disorders (pp.866-869).

Problems of the preterm baby

Problems experienced by babies born more than three weeks earlier than their expected birth date

 AGE Present from birth

 GENDER GENETICS LIFESTYLE Not significant factors

Pregnancy usually lasts about 40 weeks. Babies born before 37 weeks of pregnancy (*see* PRETERM LABOR, p.798) are called preterm, and these babies may have problems because of their small size and immaturity. The severity of these problems will depend on how far the pregnancy has progressed and the baby's weight at birth. With specialist care, babies born as early as 23 weeks now have a chance of survival.

WHAT ARE THE PROBLEMS?

All preterm babies lose heat easily because they are smaller than full-term babies and have thin skin and little fat. In addition, respiratory problems may occur because the lungs are immature and may not produce enough surfactant, a chemical that is required for the lungs to function properly. This problem is known as respiratory distress syndrome. Irregular breathing is a common problem and is due to immaturity of the brain. Preterm babies are also very vulnerable to injury and infection.

The trauma of birth, lack of oxygen, and infection can all affect the developing brain. In very preterm babies (those under 28 weeks), tiny blood vessels in the brain may rupture and bleed. There are usually no lasting problems, but specific learning disabilities (p.854) and problems with movement and posture (*see* CEREBRAL PALSY, p.846) may occur.

About 8 in 10 preterm babies are affected by neonatal jaundice (opposite page), due to immaturity of the liver. In this condition, there is yellowing of the skin and whites of the eyes.

WHAT MIGHT BE DONE?

The doctor will assess your baby's condition at birth and start treatment if necessary. A baby who is only a few weeks preterm may not need specialist care. However, you will be advised to feed your baby frequently and to make sure he or she is kept warm.

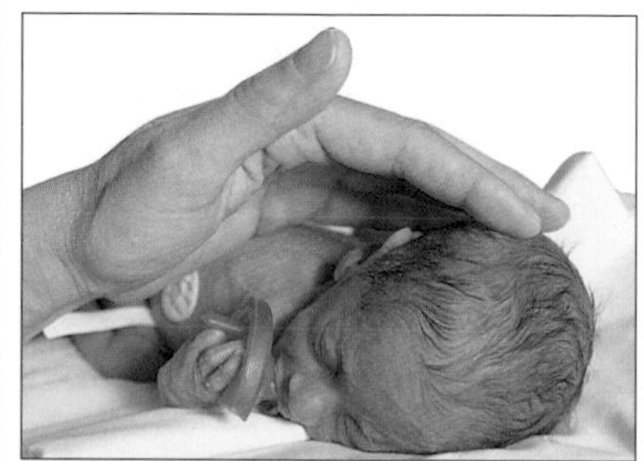

A preterm baby
This baby was born preterm and is much smaller than normal. Preterm babies need specialist care and monitoring.

Other preterm babies may be looked after in a special neonatal care unit and placed in an incubator so that the environment can be carefully controlled. They may also be given fluids and fed intravenously or through a tube passed through the nose into the stomach. A preterm baby may need to spend several weeks or months in the unit, and parents will be encouraged to take part in the baby's care. Tests may also be performed, such as ultrasound scanning (p.250) of the brain and chest X-rays (p.490), to look for abnormalities that may need treatment.

If your baby has respiratory distress syndrome, mechanical ventilation may be necessary, and surfactant will probably be given directly into the airways to help the lungs function properly. A ventilated baby may be given sedatives to make him or her more comfortable. However, the high levels of oxygen that are sometimes necessary to treat respiratory problems in preterm babies may cause irreversible damage to the retina, the light-sensitive cells at the back of the eye, resulting in visual impairment.

A baby who has jaundice may have treatment with a specific wavelength of fluorescent light (*see* PHOTOTHERAPY, p.818). Antibiotics (p.885) may also be given to treat or prevent infection.

When your baby leaves the hospital, the doctor will continue to give you advice and support. Your baby may be given a vision test to look for retinal damage (*see* VISION TESTS IN CHILDREN, p.857) and also a hearing test (*see* HEARING TESTS IN CHILDREN, p.859) to check for hearing loss. Growth and development will be carefully monitored.

WHAT IS THE PROGNOSIS?

Successful treatment depends on how early the baby was born and the weight at birth. About 4 in 10 babies born at 23–24 weeks survive, but they may have long-term problems, such as visual impairment, chronic lung disorders, or cerebral palsy. Babies born after 30 weeks usually develop normally with no long-term problems. Preterm babies are more susceptible to sudden infant death syndrome (p.820), thought to be linked with abnormal breathing patterns.

WWW ONLINE SITES: p.1036

Congenital infections

Infections contracted before or at birth from the mother

 AGE Present from birth

 LIFESTYLE Risk factors depend on the cause

 GENDER GENETICS Not significant factors

Most infections contracted by a mother during pregnancy do not affect the fetus, but some cross the placenta and cause harm. These infections are often brief, minor illnesses for the pregnant mother, and she may be unaware of them. Chronic infections such as HIV (*see* HIV INFECTION AND AIDS, p.295) may also be passed on.

The effect on the baby depends on the stage of pregnancy at which the infection occurs. In early pregnancy, the development of organs may be disrupted, and a miscarriage (p.791) may occur. Infections in later pregnancy may result in preterm labor (p.798) and a baby who is seriously ill at birth. Infections may also be transmitted as the baby passes through the birth canal.

WHAT ARE THE CAUSES?

In the first 3 months of pregnancy, the viral disease rubella (p.292) can lead to heart abnormalities (*see* CONGENITAL HEART DISEASE, p.836) and impaired hearing and vision. Cytomegalovirus (CMV) infection (p.290), parvovirus infection (p.292), and toxoplasmosis

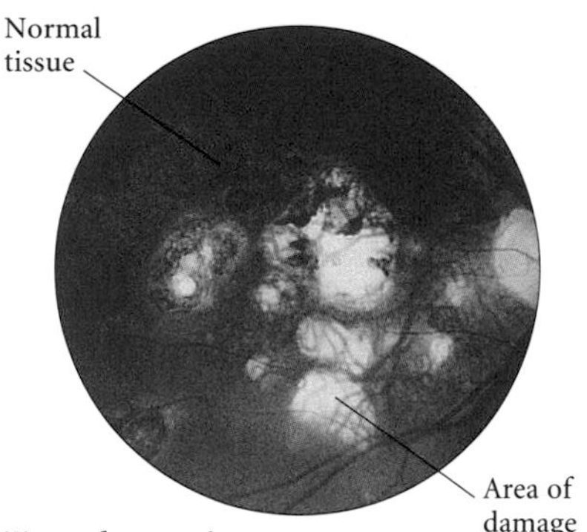
Normal tissue
Area of damage

Toxoplasmosis
The pale patches in this view of the retina, at the back of a baby's eye, indicate the congenital infection toxoplasmosis.

(p.307), caused by a protozoal parasite found in the feces of cats, may cause miscarriage or malformations in early pregnancy. CMV is the leading cause of congenital deafness (p.859) and toxoplasmosis can damage the retina. Later in pregnancy, these infections may cause preterm labor, stillbirth (p.805), and serious illness in the newborn. Listeriosis (p.300), a bacterial infection that can be contracted from eating soft cheese and pâté, may cause miscarriage or stillbirth.

Chronic viral infections that can be passed from mother to fetus include HIV infection and hepatitis B and C (*see* CHRONIC HEPATITIS, p.645). The bacterial infection syphilis (p.766) may also be passed on to the fetus. These infections do not always produce symptoms at birth but can cause serious illness later in life.

Infections that can be transmitted from mother to baby during labor and cause acute and sometimes fatal illness in the newborn include herpes simplex virus infections (*see* GENITAL HERPES, p.767) and bacterial streptococcal infections. The risk of transmission is greater if the mother's waters break prematurely (*see* PREMATURE RUPTURE OF MEMBRANES, p.797).

WHAT MIGHT BE DONE?

If a baby is seriously ill at birth and a congenital infection is suspected, blood and urine samples are taken to identify the infection. Babies are usually nursed in a neonatal care unit and treated intravenously with appropriate drugs. Ultrasound scanning (p.250) may be used to image the baby's brain and echocardiography (p.425) may be arranged if there is a heart problem. If the mother is known to be infected with the hepatitis B virus, the baby is given antibodies against the virus.

CAN THEY BE PREVENTED?

Pregnant women can minimize the risk of contracting many of these infections (*see* HEALTH IN PREGNANCY AND AFTER CHILDBIRTH, p.33). Women can ensure that they are immune to rubella before conception. During pregnancy, they can avoid handling cat litter to prevent toxoplasmosis and avoid eating foods that may cause listeriosis. Pregnant women with HIV infection may be given antiviral drugs to reduce the risk of transmission to the baby. Delivery by cesarean section (p.802) is usually advised for women with HIV infection or active genital herpes.

Mild congenital infections may have no lasting effect on the baby, but severe infections can be life-threatening. Congenital abnormalities may also result in long-term health and learning problems.

WWW ONLINE SITES: p.1033, p.1036

Neonatal jaundice

Yellow discoloration of the skin and the whites of the eyes in a newborn baby

 AGE Present from or shortly after birth

 GENETICS Risk factors depend on the cause

 GENDER LIFESTYLE Not significant factors

More than half of all newborn babies develop slight yellowing of the skin in the first week of life, giving them a tanned appearance. This condition is known as neonatal jaundice. In most cases, neonatal jaundice is normal, lasts only a few days, and does not indicate a serious underlying illness.

Neonatal jaundice is caused by high levels of a yellow-green pigment in the blood known as bilirubin, which is a breakdown product of red blood cells. The liver, which removes bilirubin, may not function properly in a newborn baby for several days. As a result, the level of bilirubin rises as fetal red blood cells are broken down. Breast-feeding may make neonatal jaundice worse, but a mother can continue to breast-feed without harming the baby.

to feel the emerging tooth if you stroke the gum with your finger. Symptoms such as fever, vomiting, or diarrhea are not due to teething and suggest that an infection may be present. You should take your baby to see his or her doctor if these symptoms appear.

WHAT CAN I DO?

Babies who are teething often seem to like chewing on a cold hard object such as a teething ring. Over-the-counter local anesthetic gels are available and can be soothing if gently applied to the affected gums. Babies over the age of 3 months can also be given liquid acetaminophen to relieve the pain (*see* ANALGESICS, p.912).

You should avoid using sweet drinks to comfort your baby. Begin to clean his or her teeth with a soft baby toothbrush and fluoride toothpaste as soon as the first tooth appears. Regular brushing will help prevent decay and establish a routine of good oral hygiene (*see* CARING FOR YOUR TEETH AND GUMS, p.610).

(WWW) ONLINE SITES: p.1028

SELF-HELP POSITIONING YOUR BABY FOR SLEEP

It is important to position your baby for sleep in a way that minimizes the risk of sudden infant death syndrome (SIDS). You should make sure that your baby sleeps on his or her back near the foot of the crib so that he or she cannot wriggle under the bedcovers. The crib should have a firm mattress but no pillow. The number of bedcovers should be appropriate for the room temperature.

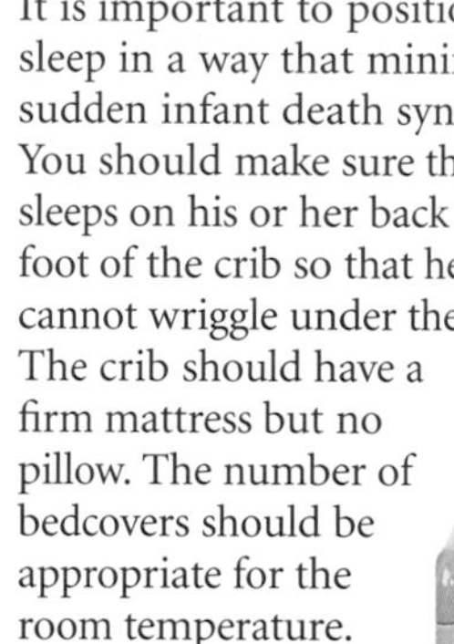

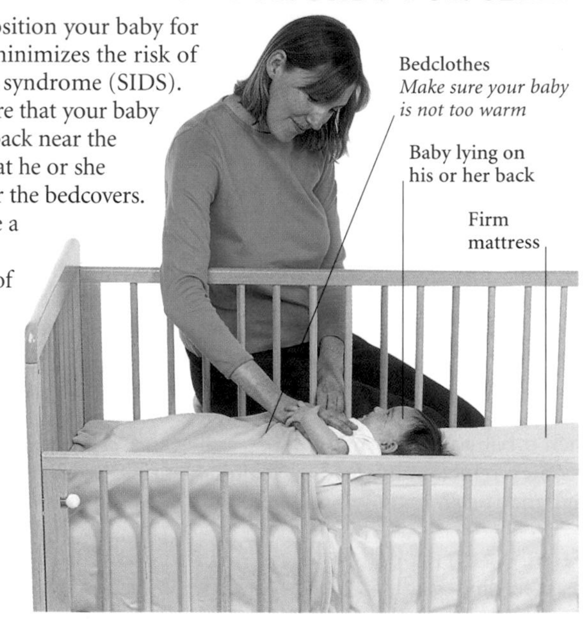
Bedclothes
Make sure your baby is not too warm
Baby lying on his or her back
Firm mattress

Reducing the risk
Lay your baby down on his or her back to sleep at the foot of the crib so that the face cannot be covered by bedding. Do not overwrap your baby.

Sudden infant death syndrome

The sudden and unexpected death of a baby for which no cause can be found

 AGE Most common between the ages of 1 and 6 months

 GENDER Slightly more common in boys

 LIFESTYLE Parental smoking and drug abuse are risk factors

 GENETICS Not a significant factor

Sudden infant death syndrome (SIDS), also known as crib death, is devastating for parents of an affected baby. SIDS occurs when healthy babies are put to bed and later found dead for no identifiable reason. In Canada, 150 babies die each year of SIDS, although the frequency of SIDS has declined since parents have been advised to put babies to sleep on their backs.

WHAT ARE THE CAUSES?

The cause of SIDS is unknown but may be associated with abnormal breathing patterns. Several risk factors have been recognized, such as parental smoking and drug abuse, but in most cases the death is unexplained. Evidence suggests that putting babies to sleep on their fronts and bottle-feeding increase the risk. Babies who are overwrapped, particularly during an illness, may become overheated and may be at increased risk. Parents sometimes report minor symptoms of infection in the hours or days beforehand, but whether these symptoms are significant is not known. The risk of SIDS is slightly higher for siblings of an infant who has died of SIDS and is more common in babies born before 37 weeks (*see* PROBLEMS OF THE PRETERM BABY, p.816).

WHAT MIGHT BE DONE?

If possible, parents should begin resuscitation immediately after calling for an ambulance (*see* CARDIOPULMONARY RESUSCITATION FOR INFANTS, p.985). On arrival at the hospital, the doctors will attempt to resuscitate the baby, but they are rarely successful. Very occasionally, an infant will be revived, and tests will be done to try to discover the cause. The baby will receive follow-up care and monitoring to prevent a recurrence.

The sudden death of a baby is a very distressing and shocking event. Bereaved parents need support from doctors, family, and friends and may also receive professional counseling (*see* LOSS AND BEREAVEMENT, p.76). A postmortem examination of the baby is always performed to exclude other causes of death and reassure the family that the death could not have been prevented. During this period, everyone concerned may experience intense emotions, including guilt, and family relationships can be disrupted. These feelings are quite normal. Bereaved parents usually find it helpful to contact a support group that allows them to discuss their feelings with other families who have experienced crib death. If the parents decide to have another child, the doctor will provide advice and support and arrange for special monitoring.

CAN IT BE PREVENTED?

Many parents feel that SIDS is a threat over which they have no control, but there are ways to reduce the risk. All babies should be placed on their backs to sleep, and pillows should not be used until a baby is over age 1 (*see* POSITIONING YOUR BABY FOR SLEEP, above). Ensure that your baby has a smoke-free environment. You may feel more confident if you know cardiopulmonary resuscitation. Alarms that alert parents if a baby stops breathing are available, but there is no firm evidence that these devices reduce the risk of SIDS.

(WWW) ONLINE SITES: p.1029

CHROMOSOME AND GENE DISORDERS

The 46 chromosomes in human cells contain about 90,000 pairs of genes, but only a few rare disorders are directly the result of a defect in a gene or a chromosome abnormality. Many children affected by such genetic disorders can be easily recognized because their disorders cause a distinctive physical appearance.

This section covers a few examples of chromosome and gene disorders that affect many body systems and become apparent during childhood. Some of these conditions are caused by an extra or absent chromosome or by an abnormality in a gene. For example, Down syndrome is due to an extra chromosome, and Turner syndrome, a rare disorder that affects only girls, is due to an absent chromosome. The other disorders covered in this section, including cystic fibrosis, muscular dystrophy, and neurofibromatosis, are caused by defective genes.

Genetic disorders that mainly affect one part of the body, such as polycystic kidney disease (p.704), are covered in the relevant sections of the book. The principles of chromosome and gene disorders, including how and why they occur and patterns of inheritance, are discussed elsewhere (*see* GENETIC DISORDERS, pp.268–271).

KEY ANATOMY

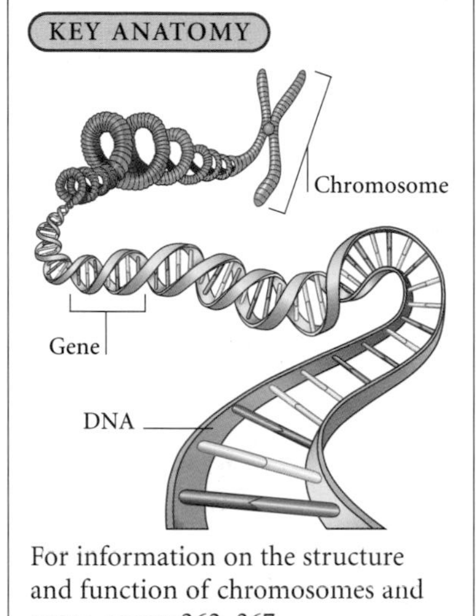
Chromosome
Gene
DNA

For information on the structure and function of chromosomes and genes, *see* pp.262–267.

Down syndrome

A chromosome disorder affecting mental development and physical appearance

 AGE Present at birth

 GENETICS Due to an extra chromosome

 GENDER LIFESTYLE Not significant factors

Down syndrome, also known as trisomy 21, is the most common chromosome abnormality. In Canada, approximately 1 in 700 pregnancies is affected. The condition usually occurs because a baby has three copies of chromosome 21 instead of the normal two copies, giving a total of 47 chromosomes instead of the usual 46. In most cases, the extra chromosome is inherited from the mother due to an abnormality in the egg. Less commonly, the extra chromosome is inherited from the father due to a sperm abnormality. Children with Down syndrome have a characteristic physical appearance and learning disabilities (*see* MENTAL RETARDATION, p.854).

The risk of a baby having Down syndrome becomes greater with increasing age of the mother. In women who conceive at age 20, there is a risk of 1 in 1,500 that the baby will have the condition. For women aged 37, the risk of Down syndrome rises to 1 in 100. A woman who has already had an affected child has an increased risk of having other children with the condition in subsequent pregnancies.

WHAT ARE THE SYMPTOMS?

Many of the physical characteristics of Down syndrome are present at birth and may include:

- Floppy limbs.
- Round face with full cheeks.
- Eyes that slant up at the outer corners with folds of skin covering the inner corners of the eyes.
- Protruding tongue.
- Flattening of the back of the head.
- Excess skin on the back of the neck.
- Short, broad hands that have a single transverse crease on the palm.

Children with Down syndrome have abnormalities that vary in degree of severity. They are slow in learning to walk and talk, have learning disabilities ranging from mild to severe, and are typically short in stature. They are usually cheerful and affectionate.

ARE THERE COMPLICATIONS?

More than 1 in 3 children with Down syndrome also have an abnormality of the heart (*see* CONGENITAL HEART DISEASE, p.836), usually a hole in the wall (septum) that divides the main chambers of the left and right sides of the heart. Sometimes, abnormalities can occur in the digestive tract, causing the tract to become narrow or blocked. Affected children are also more likely to have ear infections and accumulation of fluid in the ear, which may lead to impaired hearing (*see* CHRONIC SECRETORY OTITIS MEDIA, p.860). Instability of the joints in the neck may develop, which can prevent children with Down syndrome from taking part in certain sports. Children with Down syndrome also have an increased risk of developing cancer of the white blood cells (*see* ACUTE LEUKEMIA, p.454) and a higher than average risk of developing an underactive thyroid gland (*see* HYPOTHYROIDISM, p.680). From about age 40, people with Down syndrome are at increased risk of developing Alzheimer's disease (p.536), a progressive brain disorder that results in a gradual decline in mental abilities.

HOW IS IT DIAGNOSED?

Most pregnant women are offered a blood test at 15–18 weeks of pregnancy to screen for an increased risk of Down syndrome in the fetus. If the test shows an increased risk, amniocentesis will be offered (*see* PRENATAL GENETIC TESTS, p.787). An ultrasound scan will probably be performed at about 16 weeks to look for evidence of abnormalities in the fetus, such as heart defects. If a pregnant woman is over age 35, prenatal testing may be offered regardless of blood test and ultrasound results. If the test results are positive, parents may wish to discuss with their doctor how to proceed.

Sometimes, Down syndrome is not diagnosed until after the baby is born. The condition is usually recognized by the distinctive appearance of the face. The diagnosis is confirmed by taking a small sample of the baby's blood and performing a blood test to look for an extra copy of chromosome 21. Tests, such as ultrasound scanning of the heart (*see* ECHOCARDIOGRAPHY, p.425) or a contrast X-ray (p.245) of the intestine, known as a barium enema, may also be done to look for complications.

WHAT IS THE TREATMENT?

In the past, many children with Down syndrome were given institutional care and lacked stimulation and support to maximize their mental development. Today, with improved facilities, care of affected children combines making the most of their mental capabilities with treatment for physical problems. In many cases, children are able to remain in their home environment.

Children with Down syndrome and their families usually receive medical care and long-term support from a team of professionals. Specialized care may include physiotherapy (p.961) and speech therapy (p.963). Special educational programs will help affected children to develop intellectually as much as possible. Surgery may be necessary to correct abnormalities of the heart or intestine. Sometimes, surgery is also used to change the characteristic facial appearance. Parents of affected children may find it helpful to contact support groups to obtain advice.

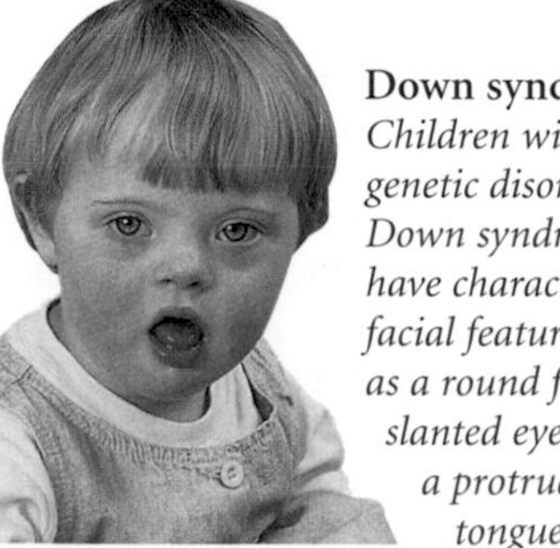

Down syndrome *Children with the genetic disorder Down syndrome have characteristic facial features, such as a round face, slanted eyes, and a protruding tongue.*

WHAT IS THE PROGNOSIS?

Most children with Down syndrome lead happy and fulfilling lives. Although intellectual ability varies widely, affected children are now able to achieve much more because of the improvement in teaching methods. Some children learn to read and write and may acquire sufficient skills to enable them to work later in life. However, most are unable to live independently and will need long-term supervision, provided either by parents or in a residential home. Although many survive into middle age, about 1 in 5 children with Down syndrome dies in childhood, often as a result of congenital heart disease. Some people with Down syndrome live long lives, but of these about 1 in 7 develops Alzheimer's disease from about age 40.

(WWW) ONLINE SITES: p.1030

Fragile X syndrome

A defect in a specific gene on the X chromosome causing learning difficulties

 AGE Present at birth

 GENDER Much more common in boys

 GENETICS Due to an abnormal gene on the X chromosome

 LIFESTYLE Not a significant factor

Fragile X syndrome is a common cause of learning difficulties in boys and is associated with a characteristic physical appearance. The condition is caused by an abnormality of a specific gene on the X chromosome, one of the two sex chromosomes. In Canada, about 1 in 2,000 boys is affected; the condition is far less common in girls.

Girls who have fragile X syndrome have mild symptoms because they have a second copy of the X chromosome that is normal and compensates for the abnormality in the other chromosome. However, even mildly affected women can pass on the abnormal gene to sons who may develop the disorder.

WHAT ARE THE SYMPTOMS?

The initial symptoms are learning disabilities, which vary in severity and become more obvious as the child grows older (*see* MENTAL RETARDATION, p.854). The characteristic physical features of fragile X syndrome often do not appear until puberty and include:

- Above average height.
- Large head and a long, thin face with a prominent jaw and large ears.
- In boys, large testes.

Affected children are also susceptible to seizures and behavior problems (*see* AUTISM SPECTRUM DISORDERS, p.852).

WHAT MIGHT BE DONE?

If your child's doctor suspects fragile X syndrome, he or she will arrange for a blood test to look for the gene abnormality on the X chromosome. Although the condition cannot be treated, affected children can benefit from speech therapy (p.963), specialized teaching, and in some cases help from a psychologist for behavior problems. Some affected children will need to take anticonvulsant drugs (p.914) to prevent seizures. Parents of an affected child may find it helpful to join a support group.

Genetic counseling (p.270) is offered to couples who already have a child with fragile X syndrome to assess the risk of having another child with this condition. Prenatal testing can be performed in subsequent pregnancies (*see* PRENATAL GENETIC TESTS, p.787).

The life expectancy for affected children is normal, but boys usually require lifelong care, either from their parents or in a residential home.

(WWW) ONLINE SITES: p.1034

Klinefelter syndrome

A chromosome abnormality in boys causing tall stature and small genitals

 AGE Present at birth

 GENDER Affects only boys

 GENETICS Due to an extra chromosome

 LIFESTYLE Not a significant factor

Klinefelter syndrome affects only boys. In Canada, about 1 in every 1,000 boys is diagnosed as having the condition, but it is thought that many cases are never detected. Affected boys have two copies of the X chromosome instead of the usual one, and this may lead to insufficient levels of the male sex hormone testosterone in the body.

What are the symptoms?

A boy with Klinefelter syndrome often appears normal at birth. However, as he reaches puberty, the physical characteristics of the condition become more obvious and include:

- Tall stature.
- Long legs.
- Small penis and testes.

In some cases, enlarged breasts develop (*see* GYNECOMASTIA, p.729). All boys with Klinefelter syndrome are infertile because they cannot produce sperm. Rarely, some boys with the condition have learning disabilities (*see* MENTAL RETARDATION, p.854).

What might be done?

Klinefelter syndrome is often suspected from an affected boy's physical characteristics. The diagnosis is confirmed by a blood test to look for the extra X chromosome. If the condition is diagnosed in childhood, treatment with a testosterone supplement may help the development of male characteristics. Most boys with Klinefelter syndrome lead a normal life, although in adulthood they cannot father children. If gynecomastia develops and causes psychological distress, an operation may be done to reduce breast size. Genetic counseling (p.270) is available to parents who have an affected child and plan to have more children.

(WWW) ONLINE SITES: p.1032

Turner syndrome

A chromosome disorder in which a girl has only one X chromosome

 AGE Present at birth

 GENDER Affects only girls

 GENETICS Due to an absent chromosome

 LIFESTYLE Not a significant factor

Normally, girls have two copies of the X sex chromosome. In Turner syndrome, only one X chromosome is present, giving a total of 45 chromosomes instead of the normal complement of 46 chromosomes. Girls without a second X chromosome have ovaries that do not function normally. As a result of this disorder, some of the hormones that are needed for normal growth and sexual development, such as estrogen and progesterone, are not produced. Turner syndrome is rare, affecting only about 1 in 2,500 girls in Canada.

What are the symptoms?

Some symptoms of Turner syndrome may be present at birth and include:

- Puffy hands and feet.
- Difficulty feeding.
- Broad chest.
- Short, broad neck.
- Low-set ears.

However, in some girls, there may be no symptoms except short stature, which does not become apparent until late childhood. In some cases, Turner syndrome is recognized only when a girl fails to reach puberty at the normal age (*see* ABNORMAL PUBERTY IN FEMALES, p.739). If the condition is recognized and treated before puberty, a girl is more likely to attain a greater height and develop female sexual characteristics, such as breasts and menstrual periods.

Are there complications?

About 1 in 10 girls with Turner syndrome also has an abnormal narrowing of the aorta, the main artery of the body (*see* CONGENITAL HEART DISEASE, p.836). About 1 in 2 girls with Turner syndrome has abnormally formed kidneys. Hearing impairment is common and is usually due to a buildup of fluid in the middle ear (*see* CHRONIC SECRETORY OTITIS MEDIA, p.860). In later life, other complications include infertility (*see* FEMALE INFERTILITY, p.775) and possibly osteoporosis (p.368), in which the bones become thin and brittle.

Girls with Turner syndrome are of normal intelligence, but some may have minor learning disabilities, especially with respect to mathematics and activities requiring hand–eye coordination. Psychological problems may also arise when a girl becomes aware of her sexual immaturity and short stature.

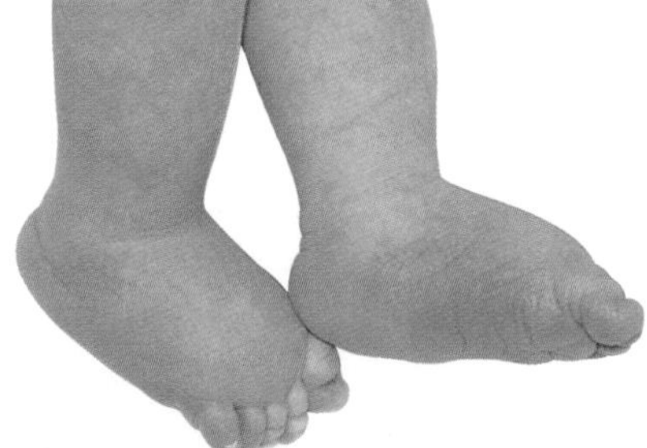

Turner syndrome
Newborn baby girls with the chromosome disorder Turner syndrome are sometimes born with temporary puffiness of the feet.

How is it diagnosed?

In rare cases, Turner syndrome may be diagnosed in the fetus during routine ultrasound scanning in pregnancy (p.793). The diagnosis can be confirmed by performing further prenatal tests (*see* PRENATAL GENETIC TESTS, p.787). If the condition is suspected in infancy or childhood due to short stature, a blood test will be done to analyze the chromosomes. Turner syndrome may also be suspected in later childhood if puberty and menstruation do not occur.

What might be done?

There is no cure for Turner syndrome, but treatment is aimed at relieving the symptoms. Growth hormone and estrogen may be given to encourage growth, allow normal puberty, and prevent the early onset of osteoporosis. Growth hormone is usually given only until the child reaches the usual age of puberty. Estrogen is then given from this age and is continued for life.

Other treatments center on associated complications. Ears will be checked regularly for fluid buildup. Narrowing of the aorta and kidney problems are corrected surgically if necessary. Women with Turner syndrome cannot conceive naturally, but pregnancy may be possible using in-vitro fertilization (*see* ASSISTED CONCEPTION, p.776).

Genetic counseling (p.270) is usually offered to the parents of a daughter with Turner syndrome, although the risk of having another affected child is low. Parents and affected individuals may also find it helpful to contact support groups to obtain advice.

What is the prognosis?

Although affected girls do not grow to the average height for their age, most should be able to have a normal childhood and eventually become healthy and independent women. Even serious complications that are associated with Turner syndrome, such as a narrowed aorta, can now be treated successfully.

(WWW) ONLINE SITES: p.1032

Marfan syndrome

An inherited condition in which a protein is lacking, resulting in tall stature and defects of the eyes, heart, and arteries

 AGE Present at birth

 GENETICS Due to an abnormal gene inherited from one parent

 GENDER LIFESTYLE Not significant factors

In Marfan syndrome, a protein that is a component of the connective tissue between the structures and organs of the body is deficient. The condition usually affects the muscles, bones, eyes, heart, and main arteries of the body. Marfan syndrome is due to an abnormal gene that is usually inherited in an autosomal dominant manner (*see* GENE DISORDERS, p.269). However, not everyone with this disorder is affected to the same extent. About 1 in 15,000 children in Canada has the condition.

WHAT ARE THE SYMPTOMS?

The symptoms of Marfan syndrome usually appear at about age 10 but may be seen earlier. They may include:

- Very tall stature.
- Long, thin limbs, fingers, and toes.
- Weak joints and ligaments.
- Inward curving of the chest.
- Curvature of the spine.
- Impaired vision.

The risk of complications depends on which tissues are affected and the severity of abnormalities. Most people with Marfan syndrome are nearsighted (*see* MYOPIA, p.586), and some have other eye defects such as an incorrectly placed lens. Marfan syndrome can lead to heart valve disorders (p.421). The aorta, the main artery of the body, may also become weakened and may swell and rupture (*see* AORTIC ANEURYSM, p.430). This condition is life-threatening.

WHAT MIGHT BE DONE?

Marfan syndrome is usually diagnosed only when the visible features of the condition begin to appear. There is no cure, but an affected child is monitored carefully, and complications are treated as they arise. Almost all affected children need glasses and should have an eye test once a year. Some people with the condition are given beta blockers (p.898) to help prevent weakening of the aorta. Rarely, girls under age 10 are given hormone therapy to promote the early onset of puberty and to stop growth sooner, avoiding excessive height. Many children have surgery to correct defects in the heart valves or aorta. Affected children and their families may wish to join a support group.

WHAT IS THE PROGNOSIS?

In the past, people with the disorder were restricted in their activities and often died before age 35. Today, because of advances in heart surgery, most affected people lead normal active lives, but many do not live beyond age 50.

(WWW) ONLINE SITES: p.1032

Cystic fibrosis

An inherited condition that causes body secretions to be thick and abnormal

 AGE Present at birth

 GENETICS Due to an abnormal gene inherited from both parents

 GENDER LIFESTYLE Not significant factors

Cystic fibrosis is the most common severe inherited disease in people of North American and European origin. The condition is much rarer in other ethnic groups. In Canada, about 1 in 2,500 children is born with cystic fibrosis. All the fluid- and mucus-secreting glands in the body are affected and this leads to thick, abnormal secretions, especially in the lungs and pancreas. As a result, children who are affected may experience recurrent chest infections and have problems absorbing nutrients from food.

In the past, severe chest infections were a major cause of death in children with cystic fibrosis. Today, with better understanding of the disease and recent advances in treatment, most children who are affected by cystic fibrosis survive into adulthood.

WHAT ARE THE CAUSES?

Cystic fibrosis is caused by an abnormal gene, which is carried by about 1 in 25 people and inherited in an autosomal recessive manner (*see* GENE DISORDERS, p.269). The abnormal gene occurs on chromosome number 7. Over 300 different mutations (abnormalities) in the gene have now been identified. Of these, the most common is called delta 508, and this is the cause of more than 1 in 7 cases of cystic fibrosis in the US.

WHAT ARE THE SYMPTOMS?

Sometimes, a newborn baby with cystic fibrosis may have a swollen abdomen and does not pass feces for the first few days after birth. Other symptoms of cystic fibrosis usually develop later in infancy and may include:

- Failure to put on weight or grow at the normal rate.

(TEST) SWEAT TESTING

A sweat test is used to diagnose cystic fibrosis by measuring the levels of salt in sweat. The procedure is painless and is performed in the hospital on an outpatient basis. The production of sweat is stimulated for about 3 minutes using two electrodes. The electrodes are then replaced with a pad, which collects the sweat for the next 30 minutes.

Technician

Electrical source

Electrodes

During the test
A small electrical current passes to gel-filled electrodes on the arm to stimulate sweat production.

TREATMENT ANTIBIOTIC DELIVERY SYSTEM

This system enables the easy and regular delivery of intravenous antibiotics and is particularly useful for children with cystic fibrosis (opposite page). Under general anesthesia, the internal part of the system is placed on the chest wall just under the skin so that it does not interfere with the child's normal activities. A catheter carries the injected antibiotics from the injection site to a vein in the chest just above the heart. The external part of the system is removable.

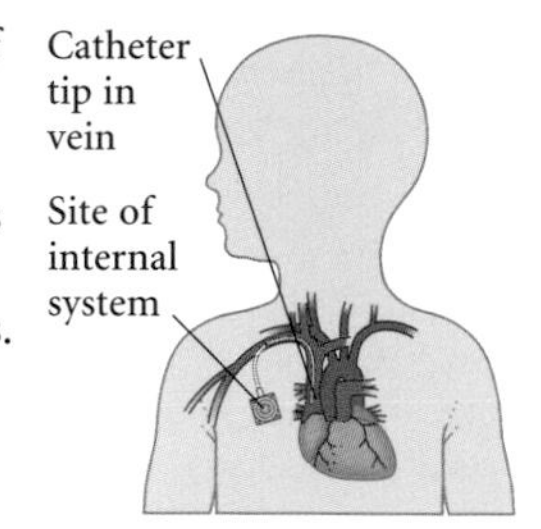
Catheter tip in vein
Site of internal system

POSITION OF SYSTEM

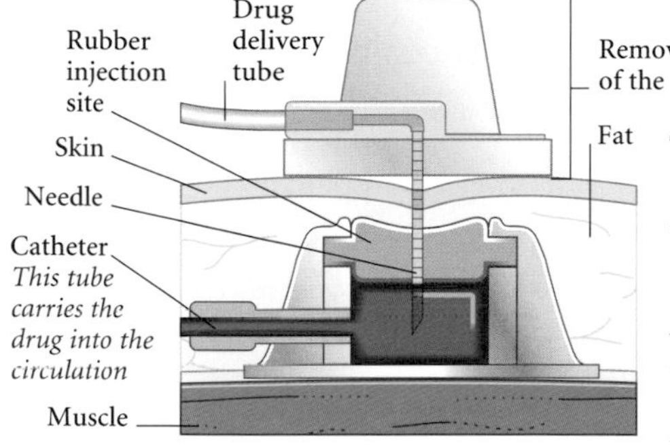
Drug delivery tube
Rubber injection site
Skin
Needle
Catheter
This tube carries the drug into the circulation
Muscle
Removable external part of the injection system
Fat

COMPLETE DELIVERY SYSTEM

The injection procedure
The external part of the injection system is positioned over the internal part so that the sterile needle pierces the injection site. Antibiotics are injected into the delivery tube and pass through the catheter into the circulation. Local anesthetic cream is often used to numb the skin beforehand.

- Pale, greasy feces that float and have a particularly offensive smell.
- Recurrent chest infections.

In many cases of cystic fibrosis, a constant cough develops, producing large amounts of sticky mucus.

ARE THERE COMPLICATIONS?

As cystic fibrosis progresses, the lung disorder bronchiectasis (p.496) may occur, in which the main airways are abnormally widened. Abscesses may also form in the lungs. Further complications may include liver damage (*see* CIRRHOSIS, p.647) and chronic inflammation of the sinuses (*see* SINUSITIS, p.475). About 3 in 100 children with cystic fibrosis develop diabetes mellitus (p.687). In all affected children, abnormally high levels of salt are excreted in the sweat, which may lead to dehydration during hot weather.

Children with cystic fibrosis sometimes develop psychological problems because of the difficulties that are commonly associated with chronic illness. Affected children may also be unable to participate in normal childhood and school activities due to continual bad health and may therefore feel isolated.

In later life, almost all males with cystic fibrosis and about 1 in 5 affected females are infertile because the mucus secretions produced by the reproductive organs are abnormally thick. Infertility in males with the disorder is also sometimes caused by a birth defect, in which the two vas deferens (the tubes through which sperm are propelled) are absent.

HOW IS IT DIAGNOSED?

An early diagnosis improves the long-term prognosis by helping prevent damage to the lungs in infancy. If the doctor suspects that a child has the condition at birth or later in infancy, a sweat test (opposite page) may be done to look for high levels of salt in the baby's sweat. A blood test may also be performed to look for the abnormal gene. If the result is positive, siblings of the affected child can also be tested.

WHAT IS THE TREATMENT?

Treatment for cystic fibrosis is aimed at slowing the progression of lung disease and maintaining adequate nutrition.

Chest physiotherapy (p.962) is usually performed twice a day to remove secretions from the lungs. Parents and older affected children are often taught how to do this procedure at home. If an affected child develops a chest infection, he or she will require immediate treatment with antibiotics (p.885). In addition, long-term use of antibiotics may be necessary to prevent other chest infections from developing. Older children sometimes require regular courses of intravenous antibiotics to treat bacteria that become established in the lung secretions. In these situations, under general anesthesia, a permanent catheter may be inserted under the chest wall so that the antibiotics can be administered more easily (*see* ANTIBIOTIC DELIVERY SYSTEM, left). Some affected children are helped by inhaled drugs that reduce the stickiness of the secretions. In some cases, it may be possible to carry out a heart–lung transplant if the lungs are severely damaged and suitable organs become available for transplant.

A high-calorie diet helps ensure that a child with cystic fibrosis grows normally. He or she may also need to take pancreatic enzymes and vitamin supplements with every meal.

An affected child and his or her family will receive psychological support, particularly during adolescence when chronic illness is especially difficult to cope with. Family members may find it helpful to join a support group.

CAN IT BE PREVENTED?

Genetic testing means that carriers can be identified and that the disorder can be detected prenatally. Genetic testing may be offered to adults with a family history of cystic fibrosis and partners of people who have the disease. If these test results are positive, the couple will be offered genetic counseling (p.270). A couple at risk may opt to use assisted conception (p.776), which enables the embryo to be tested for the abnormal gene before it is implanted by in-vitro fertilization. Pregnant women may be offered prenatal genetic tests (p.787).

In the future, cystic fibrosis may be treated with gene therapy, in which a normal gene is introduced into relevant tissues to prevent cystic fibrosis from developing. The results of research in this field are promising.

WHAT IS THE PROGNOSIS?

The average life expectancy of a person with cystic fibrosis has increased over the past 30 years. With specialized treatment, children with the disorder who were born in the 1990s are now likely to live into their 40s.

WWW ONLINE SITES: p.1032

Muscular dystrophy

A group of genetic conditions in which muscles become weak and wasted

 AGE Present at birth

 GENDER Almost always affects boys

 GENETICS Due to an abnormal gene on the X chromosome

 LIFESTYLE Not a significant factor

The two main types of muscular dystrophy almost exclusively affect boys. The most common type of this condition is Duchenne muscular dystrophy, which causes serious disability from early childhood. A second, much rarer type of the disorder is Becker muscular dystrophy, which affects only about 1 in 25,000 boys. The onset of this condition is slower, and the symptoms start later in childhood. Other extremely rare forms of muscular dystrophy can affect girls and boys.

What are the causes?

Both Duchenne and Becker muscular dystrophies are caused by an abnormal gene carried on the X sex chromosome (*see* GENE DISORDERS, p.269). Girls may carry the defective gene but do not usually have the disorder because they have two X chromosomes, and the normal X chromosome compensates for the defect in the gene on the other.

Normally, the gene is responsible for the production of a protein called dystrophin, which is necessary for healthy muscles. In Duchenne and Becker muscular dystrophies, the gene is abnormal, resulting in a deficiency of the protein and damage to muscle. In Duchenne muscular dystrophy, almost no dystrophin is produced. However, in Becker muscular dystrophy some dystrophin is present, accounting for the difference in severity between the two conditions.

What are the symptoms?

The symptoms of Duchenne muscular dystrophy usually appear around the time a child would begin to walk. Late walking is common; often an affected child does not begin to walk until about 18 months and then will fall more frequently than other children. The more obvious symptoms of the disorder may not appear until the child reaches age 3–5 and may include:

- Waddling gait.
- Difficulty climbing stairs.
- Difficulty getting up from the floor. Characteristically, a child will use his or her hands to "walk up" the thighs.
- Large calf muscles and wasted muscles at the tops of the legs and arms.
- Mild learning disabilities.

The symptoms are progressive, and a child may be unable to walk by age 12. The symptoms of Becker muscular dystrophy are similar but usually do not appear until about age 11 or later. The disease progresses more slowly; many of those affected are still able to walk until their late 20s or later.

Are there complications?

In Duchenne muscular dystrophy, the heart muscle may become thickened and weakened (*see* HYPERTROPHIC CARDIOMYOPATHY p.428). The limbs may also become deformed, and abnormal curvature of the spine may develop (*see* SCOLIOSIS, p.371). In the later stages of the disease, a child may also have difficulty breathing, and there may be an increased risk of chest infections that can be life-threatening.

How is it diagnosed?

If a pregnant woman is a known carrier, she may be offered prenatal testing to find out if the fetus is affected (*see* PRENATAL GENETIC TESTS, p.787).

In most cases, muscular dystrophy is suspected only when symptoms begin to appear. A blood test may then be carried out to look for evidence of muscle damage. Electromyography (*see* NERVE AND MUSCLE ELECTRICAL TESTS, p.544), which records electrical activity in muscles, may be performed. A small piece of muscle may be removed under general anesthesia for microscopic examination. In addition, tests may be done to find out if the heart is affected, including recording electrical activity in the heart (*see* ECG, p.406) and ultrasound scanning (*see* ECHOCARDIOGRAPHY, p.425).

What is the treatment?

The treatment for muscular dystrophy is aimed at keeping an affected child mobile and active for as long as possible. A team of professionals, such as a physiotherapist, doctor, and social worker, can provide support for the whole family. Physiotherapy (p.961) is important to keep limbs supple, and supportive splints may be used. Some children with muscular dystrophy need equipment, such as leg braces or a wheelchair, to aid mobility. If a child has severe scoliosis, surgery may be required to straighten the spine.

Children with muscular dystrophy and their families require a lot of psychological support. Genetic counseling (p.270) is offered to parents of an affected child who are thinking about having another child and to sisters of boys affected by the disorder.

Duchenne muscular dystrophy may be fatal before age 20. Becker muscular dystrophy has a better prognosis; people often survive into their 40s or later.

(WWW) ONLINE SITES: p.1032

Congenital immunodeficiency

Defects of the immune system present from birth, leading to recurrent infection and failure of normal growth

 AGE Present at birth

 GENETICS Due to an abnormal gene

 GENDER Risk factors depend on the type

 LIFESTYLE Not a significant factor

In immunodeficiency, the immune system is defective and therefore unable to combat infections effectively. As a result, infections are more frequent and severe and may be life-threatening. A child's growth may also be affected. In children, immunodeficiency is usually caused by an underlying illness (*see* ACQUIRED IMMUNODEFICIENCY, p.460). In rare cases, the condition is inherited and is present at birth, in which case it is called congenital immunodeficiency.

What are the types?

Congenital immunodeficiencies are either linked with the X chromosome or are due to an abnormal gene inherited in an autosomal recessive manner (*see* GENE DISORDERS, p.269). The type of immunodeficiency depends on which part of the immune system is affected.

The most common type of immunodeficiency is agammaglobulinemia, which affects only boys. In this condition, severe bacterial infections, especially of the chest, frequently occur because the production of antibodies is abnormal. Other less serious types of immunodeficiency may be caused by failure of the immune system to produce some specific types of antibodies.

Chronic granulomatous disease is another type of congenital immunodeficiency. In this disease, the phagocytes, which are the white blood cells that are responsible for engulfing and killing bacteria and fungi, are unable to function properly. As a consequence, a child who has this disorder may have frequent bacterial and fungal infections, especially of the skin, lungs, and bones.

Severe combined immunodeficiency (SCID) is a disorder in which a child is unable to fight most forms of infection because both the antibodies and the white blood cells are deficient.

What might be done?

It is possible to screen for congenital immunodeficiency during pregnancy if the fetus is thought to be at risk (*see* PRENATAL GENETIC TESTS, p.787). More often, congenital immunodeficiency is suspected when a child has persistent unusual infections or fails to grow normally. The child's doctor may then do blood tests to measure the levels of antibodies and white blood cells and assess the function of the immune system. Sometimes, it is possible to detect the abnormal gene by a blood test.

All infections in a child with a congenital immunodeficiency should be treated as soon as possible. Antibiotics (p.885) will be given if appropriate. If antibodies are deficient, they may be replaced intravenously every few weeks. In some severe types of congenital immunodeficiency, such as SCID, a bone marrow transplant (p.454) may be necessary if a suitable donor can be found. If the transplant is successful, the transplanted bone marrow starts to produce normal white blood cells that can fight infection.

If treatment for congenital immunodeficiencies is started sufficiently early, many children affected with these disorders can lead a normal life and enjoy an average life expectancy.

In the future, treatment of congenital immunodeficiency may include gene therapy. The aim of this new treatment is to correct the genetic defects that affect the function of the immune system.

Genetic tests (p.238) may be offered to relatives of affected people. Genetic counseling (p.270) is offered to couples who know that they have an abnormal gene or who have an affected child and plan to have more children.

(WWW) ONLINE SITES: p.1032, p.1033

Neurofibromatosis

The development of noncancerous tumors along nerve fibers

 AGE Present at birth

 GENETICS Due to an abnormal gene inherited from one parent

 GENDER LIFESTYLE Not significant factors

Neurofibromatosis is a rare inherited condition that causes numerous soft, noncancerous growths, known as neurofibromas, to appear throughout the body. The tumors grow from nerve tissue and develop along nerve pathways. If the condition is severe, it can be disfiguring and may be distressing for the affected child and his or her family.

There are two types of neurofibromatosis. The more common of the two, known as neurofibromatosis 1, affects about 1 in every 3,000 children. The other type, neurofibromatosis 2, is very rare, and the symptoms do not usually appear until adulthood. Both types are caused by an abnormal gene that is inherited in an autosomal dominant manner (*see* GENE DISORDERS, p.269). The abnormal gene for neurofibromatosis 1 is located on chromosome 17, and the gene for neurofibromatosis 2 is located on chromosome 22.

What are the symptoms?

The symptoms of neurofibromatosis 1 usually appear during early childhood. They may include:

- Numerous pale-brown, flat patches with irregular edges, known as café au lait spots, developing on the skin.
- Soft growths under the skin, ranging in size from hardly noticeable to large and disfiguring.
- Freckles in the armpit and groin areas.

Adults with neurofibromatosis 2 may develop tumors in the inner ear, which can affect hearing, but rarely develop tumors on the skin.

Are there complications?

Complications may occur when growing tumors press on the surrounding organs or nerves. For example, vision may be affected if a tumor develops on the optic nerve, which connects the eye to the brain. Tumors can also cause curvature of the spine (*see* SCOLIOSIS, p.371). Some children with neurofibromatosis may develop epilepsy (p.524) or have learning disabilities. In rare cases, tumors become cancerous.

What might be done?

Neurofibromatosis 1 is normally diagnosed in children when the symptoms appear. The doctor may arrange for a child to have CT scanning (p.247) or MRI (p.248) of the brain to look for tumors. The child's hearing and vision may also be tested. Neurofibromatosis 2 is usually diagnosed in adulthood.

There is no cure for the disease, and its progression cannot be slowed. As a result, long-term care is often required for severely affected children. Large, painful, or disfiguring tumors can often be surgically removed. Complications are treated as they arise. For example, a child with learning disabilities may need special education. Parents of an affected child who want more children may have genetic counseling (p.270).

In mild cases of neurofibromatosis, life expectancy is normal, but, if tumor growth is extensive and cancer develops, life expectancy may be reduced.

(WWW) ONLINE SITES: p.1032, p.1035

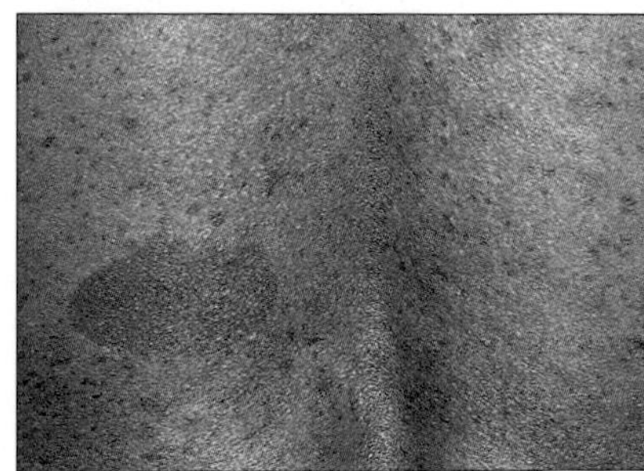

Café au lait spot in neurofibromatosis
This pale-brown, flat patch on the skin is known as a café au lait spot. The development of patches such as this is typical of neurofibromatosis.

SKIN AND HAIR DISORDERS

Young skin is sensitive and particularly susceptible to irritation or allergies. Most skin disorders in children are minor, affect only a small area of skin, and disappear as the child grows older. Many skin and hair disorders that affect children can be treated successfully at home with over-the-counter preparations.

Skin and hair disorders that mainly or exclusively affect children include a number of rashes and viral infections. The section begins with disorders that may affect young babies: birthmarks, which are present at birth or develop soon afterward, and two skin rashes, cradle cap and diaper rash. The next article discusses the more serious rash eczema, which is sometimes caused by an allergy and may persist for many years. Viral infections that cause a rash and affect only young children are also included. The section finishes with an article on infestation with head lice. Children are especially vulnerable to infestation with head lice due to close contact with other children at school.

Skin and hair disorders that affect people of any age are covered either in the main section on skin, hair, and nails (pp.328–361) or, if the disorders are caused by viruses, in the section on viral infections (pp.286–297).

KEY ANATOMY

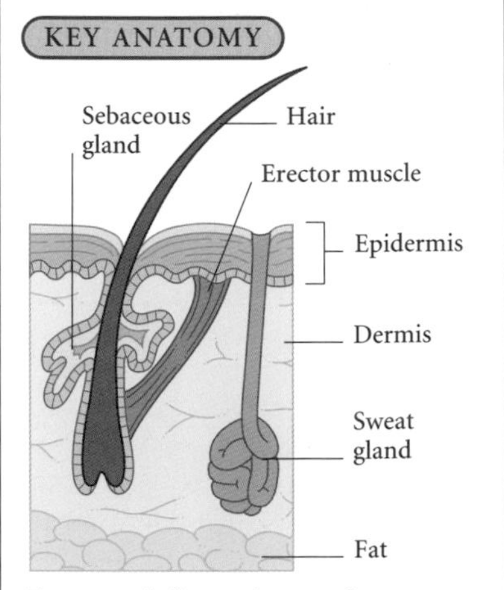
Sebaceous gland
Hair
Erector muscle
Epidermis
Dermis
Sweat gland
Fat

For more information on the structure and function of the skin and hair, *see* pp.328–331.

Birthmarks

Colored patches of skin that are present at birth or appear soon afterward

 AGE Present at or shortly after birth

 GENETICS Risk factors depend on the type

 GENDER LIFESTYLE Not significant factors

Many babies have patches of colored skin, known as birthmarks, that may be present at birth or appear during the first weeks of life. Although they may be unsightly and distressing to the parents, most birthmarks are not harmful and rarely cause discomfort.

WHAT ARE THE TYPES?

Birthmarks are usually divided into two groups: hemangiomas, which form from small blood vessels just under the skin; and pigmented nevi, which form from densely pigmented skin cells.

HEMANGIOMAS This group of birthmarks includes stork marks, strawberry hemangiomas, and port-wine stains.

Stork marks are very common birthmarks and can occur in up to 5 in 10 babies at birth. A stork mark appears as a flat, pale-pink patch usually between the eyebrows or on the nape of the neck. The birthmark usually disappears by the age of 18 months.

Strawberry hemangiomas are common birthmarks, occurring in about 1 in every 50 babies. The hemangioma appears as a small, flat, red spot at birth. It enlarges rapidly and becomes raised during the first year of life, but usually disappears completely by the time the child is aged about 5 years.

Port-wine stains occur in about 1 in 3,000 babies and are usually permanent. The birthmark is visible as an irregularly shaped, red patch and may be distressing, particularly if the mark is on the baby's face. In rare cases, a port-wine stain on the face is associated with abnormal blood vessels in the brain that can cause epilepsy (p.524).

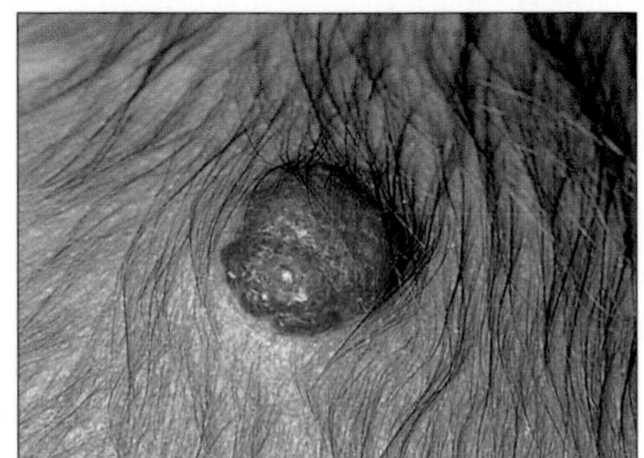

Strawberry hemangioma on scalp
This bright-red swelling, known as a strawberry hemangioma, is a common birthmark but usually disappears by age 5.

PIGMENTED NEVI This group of birthmarks includes Mongolian blue spots and moles. Mongolian blue spots are irregular, bluish areas on the skin. They are commonly seen at birth over the backs and buttocks of black and Asian babies and may be mistaken for bruises. The spots usually disappear by the time the child is aged 10 years.

A mole is a permanent, raised, dark-brown patch on the skin. The presence of a mole at birth is unusual. In very rare cases, such birthmarks may become cancerous in later life.

WHAT MIGHT BE DONE?

Most birthmarks fade as the baby grows. However, a strawberry hemangioma on the eyelid is usually treated within a few weeks of birth before it can enlarge and affect the baby's vision. Corticosteroids (p.930) may be given orally or injected into the hemangioma to shrink it, or it may be removed with laser treatment (p.951). Permanent birthmarks, such as port-wine stains, can also be treated with laser surgery, usually during infancy to minimize scarring. All moles should be checked for changes in size, shape, and color. If moles cause concern, they can be removed surgically. Treatment for permanent birthmarks usually gives good cosmetic results.

(WWW) ONLINE SITES: p.1028, p.1036

Cradle cap

A thick scaly rash that appears on the scalp during the first months of life

 AGE Most common between the ages of 1 month and 1 year

 GENDER GENETICS LIFESTYLE Not significant factors

Babies with cradle cap have reddened skin and thick yellowish scales on the scalp. Scaly areas may also appear on the baby's forehead and eyebrows, as well as behind his or her ears. Although it may look unpleasant, cradle cap is harmless. The cause of cradle cap is unknown. Rarely, the rash may become infected with bacteria (*see* IMPETIGO, p.351), causing blistering and crusting of the skin, or with fungi (*see* CANDIDIASIS, p.309). Also in rare instances, the rash may become inflamed.

WHAT MIGHT BE DONE?

Cradle cap eventually disappears on its own without any treatment. However, washing your baby's hair and scalp regularly will help prevent scale buildup. You can also massage mineral oil into your baby's scalp at night and then brush out the softened scales in the morning.

You should consult your child's doctor if these measures do not improve the condition or if the rash becomes infected or inflamed. An infected rash may be treated with topical antibiotics or antifungal drugs (*see* PREPARATIONS FOR SKIN INFECTIONS AND INFESTATIONS, p.892) and an inflamed rash with topical corticosteroids (p.892). Cradle cap will start to improve within a few weeks of treatment but may take longer to disappear altogether.

(WWW) ONLINE SITES: p.1028, p.1036

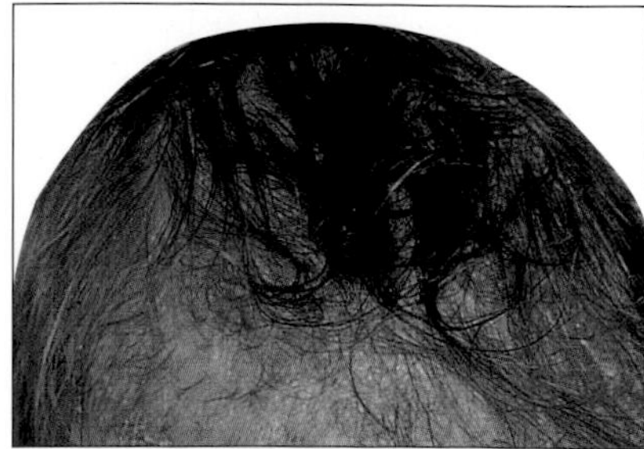

Cradle cap
The reddened skin and thick patches of yellowish scales on top of this baby's head are typical of cradle cap.

Diaper rash

A red rash in the area covered by a diaper, caused by irritation or infection

 AGE May affect babies from birth until they stop wearing diapers

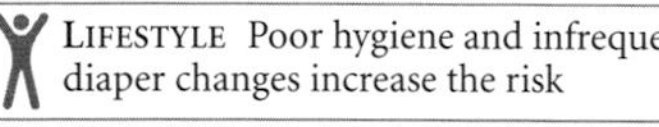 LIFESTYLE Poor hygiene and infrequent diaper changes increase the risk

 GENDER GENETICS Not significant factors

Nearly all babies are affected by diaper rash at some time. The rash causes inflammation and soreness in the area of skin covered by a diaper, and the discomfort can make a baby irritable.

WHAT ARE THE CAUSES?

Diaper rash is most commonly caused by urine or feces irritating the skin. It usually occurs only where the skin and soiled diaper have been in direct contact and does not spread to creases in the baby's skin. It is made worse if the baby's diaper is not changed frequently or the diaper area is not cleaned thoroughly. Perfumed skin products and some laundry soaps used to wash fabric diapers can cause a similar rash.

A fungal skin infection such as candidiasis (p.309) or, less commonly, a bacterial infection such as impetigo (p.351) can also cause diaper rash. A rash caused by infection will affect the whole diaper area, including creases in the baby's skin. Sometimes, a scaly rash similar to cradle cap (left) develops in the baby's diaper area (*see* SEBORRHEIC DERMATITIS, p.335).

WHAT MIGHT BE DONE?

Your baby's diaper rash will usually clear up within a few days without any medical treatment if you follow the simple self-help measures suggested for managing diaper rash (right).

You should take your baby to the doctor if these self-help measures do not work or you think the diaper rash is infected. Your baby's doctor will examine the diaper rash, and he or she may prescribe topical corticosteroids (p.892) to reduce the inflammation. Oral or topical antibiotics (p.885) may be prescribed to treat a bacterial infection, and topical antifungal drugs may be given to treat candidiasis (*see* PREPARATIONS FOR SKIN INFECTIONS AND INFESTATIONS, p.892).

SELF-HELP MANAGING DIAPER RASH

Diaper rash can usually be managed successfully using the measures described below, which also help prevent recurrence.

- Change your baby's diapers often to prevent skin irritation.
- When changing diapers, clean the diaper area gently with water and allow it to dry thoroughly.
- Use an emollient cream, such as zinc and castor oil cream.
- Avoid perfumed skin products.
- Leave your baby without a diaper as much as possible.
- Wash fabric diapers in enzyme-free laundry soap and rinse the diapers thoroughly.
- Use absorbent diaper liners with fabric diapers.

An infected rash should improve with treatment and clear up completely within a week. Diaper rash may recur if preventive self-help measures are not followed regularly throughout the time your child is wearing diapers.

(WWW) ONLINE SITES: p.1028, p.1036

Eczema in children

Itching and inflammation of the skin, sometimes accompanied by scaling

 AGE Can occur at any age but most commonly develops under age 18 months

 GENETICS Sometimes runs in families

 LIFESTYLE Exposure to irritants aggravates the condition

 GENDER Not a significant factor

Eczema affects over 1 in 10 children in Canada. The condition may last for many years but usually disappears in late childhood. A child with eczema has red, inflamed, itchy skin that may make him or her irritable.

WHAT ARE THE CAUSES?

The cause of eczema in children is not fully understood, but an allergic reaction to something in the child's diet or environment is often a factor. Common allergens (substances that provoke an allergic reaction) include cows' milk

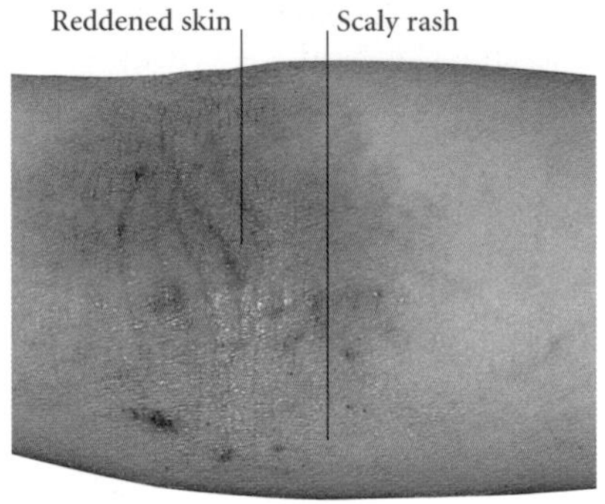
Reddened skin
Scaly rash

Eczema in children
A red, scaly eczema rash is seen here on the inside of a child's elbow. The inflamed skin is often very itchy and uncomfortable.

(*see* COWS' MILK PROTEIN ALLERGY, p.864), soy, wheat, and eggs (*see* FOOD ALLERGY, p.467). Affected children are also susceptible to allergic conditions such as hay fever (*see* ALLERGIC RHINITIS, p.466) and asthma (*see* ASTHMA IN CHILDREN, p.839). Close relatives may have the same allergic disorders, suggesting a genetic factor may be involved.

WHAT ARE THE SYMPTOMS?

The symptoms of eczema vary in severity and usually affect particular areas of the body. Symptoms may include:

- Red, scaly rash.
- Intense itching.
- Gradual thickening of the skin.

In babies, the eczema rash tends to occur on the face and neck and then on the knees and elbows as the children begin to crawl. In older children, the rash usually appears on the insides of the elbows and wrists and on the backs of the knees. The intense itching causes children to scratch the rash, which may break the skin and lead to bacterial infection. If an infection does occur, the inflammation becomes more severe, and weeping blisters develop.

A rare but serious complication of eczema is eczema herpeticum, which occurs if a child with eczema is also infected with a type of herpes simplex virus (*see* HERPES SIMPLEX INFECTIONS, p.289). Eczema herpeticum causes a widespread rash with blisters and fever.

HOW IS IT DIAGNOSED?

Your child's doctor will probably diagnose eczema from the inflamed, itchy rash. In some cases, he or she may arrange for a blood test and a skin prick test (p.468) to try to identify a specific food or substance to which your child is allergic. The doctor may also take swabs of the eczema rash to check for signs of bacterial infection.

WHAT IS THE TREATMENT?

Parents play a major part in treating children with eczema and preventing the affected skin from becoming dry (*see* MANAGING ECZEMA IN CHILDREN, below). Your child's doctor will advise you on day-to-day care and how best to moisturize your child's skin with unperfumed emollients, such as bath oils and creams (*see* EMOLLIENTS AND BARRIER PREPARATIONS, p.890). He or she may prescribe a topical corticosteroid (p.892) to reduce inflammation and oral antibiotics (p.885) or antibiotic creams (*see* PREPARATIONS FOR SKIN INFECTIONS AND INFESTATIONS, p.892) if the rash is infected. Your child may also be prescribed an oral antihistamine (p.906) to take at night to reduce itching and act as a sedative.

In very rare cases, a child with severe eczema may be hospitalized. Treatment usually consists of applying corticosteroid cream to the inflamed rash and wrapping affected areas in bandages soaked in emollient cream.

If your child develops eczema herpeticum, he or she will be admitted to the hospital and treated with intravenous antiviral drugs (p.886).

If the cause of eczema is found to be related to something your child eats, elimination of the food from the diet should improve the eczema. However, you should give your child a special diet only under medical supervision. In babies, breast-feeding can help protect against future food allergies.

Since eczema is a chronic disorder with no reliable cure, you may wish to try alternative treatments such as evening primrose oil or herbs. The doctor may be able to suggest treatments that have been effective in some cases, and he or she may warn against products, such as some Chinese herbal remedies, that may have serious side effects.

SELF-HELP MANAGING ECZEMA IN CHILDREN

Parents play an important role in managing eczema in their children, and the following measures may help control symptoms and keep your child comfortable.

- Avoid perfumed skin products.
- Wash your child with emollient cream instead of soap.
- Bathe your child at least once a day using moisturizing bath oil.
- After washing, moisturize your child's skin with a chilled emollient cream.
- Use prescribed ointments as needed on the affected areas of skin.
- If your child scratches, make sure his or her fingernails are cut short and he or she wears cotton mittens at night.

WHAT IS THE PROGNOSIS?

Eczema may last throughout childhood. Although there is no reliable cure, the symptoms of eczema can usually be controlled. Eczema usually disappears without scarring by adolescence, but in a few cases, the rash continues to flare up (*see* ATOPIC ECZEMA, p.334). About half of all affected children develop another allergic disorder later in life.

(WWW) ONLINE SITES: p.1028, p.1036

Roseola infantum

A viral infection that causes a high fever followed by a rash of tiny pink spots

 AGE Most common between the ages of 6 months and 2 years

 GENDER GENETICS LIFESTYLE Not significant factors

Roseola infantum is a common illness in early childhood that affects about 3 in 10 children in Canada. The infection is most common in spring and fall and is caused by strains of the herpesvirus that are spread by close contact with other children. One attack of the infection gives lifelong immunity.

WHAT ARE THE SYMPTOMS?

The symptoms of roseola infantum occur in two stages. The first symptoms appear 5–15 days after infection and develop rapidly over a few hours. They include some or all of the following:

- High fever.
- Mild diarrhea.
- Dry cough.

- Swollen lymph nodes in the neck and back of scalp.
- Earache.

In some children, the high fever causes febrile convulsions (p.849). After about 4 days, the fever vanishes and tiny pink spots appear on the face and trunk. The rash usually disappears after 4 days.

WHAT MIGHT BE DONE?

Roseola infantum does not require specific treatment, and your child will feel better as soon as his or her temperature drops and the spots appear. You should contact the doctor at once if the self-help measures for bringing down a fever (p.287) do not work, if a baby under 6 months is feverish, if your child has a febrile convulsion, or if he or she seems ill even after the fever has been reduced.

WWW ONLINE SITES: p.1028, p.1036

Hand, foot, and mouth disease

A common viral infection that causes small blisters in the mouth and blisters on the hands and feet

AGE More common in children under age 4

GENDER GENETICS LIFESTYLE Not significant factors

Hand, foot, and mouth disease is a common childhood infection that occurs in epidemics during the summer and early fall. The infection is caused by the coxsackie virus and lasts a few days.

WHAT ARE THE SYMPTOMS?

The symptoms develop 3–5 days after infection and may include:

- Blisters inside the mouth that may develop into painful ulcers.
- Blisters on the hands and feet that typically develop 1–2 days after those in the mouth and disappear spontaneously after 3–4 days.
- Fever.

Children often seem well but may not want to eat if mouth ulcers develop.

WHAT MIGHT BE DONE?

There is no specific treatment for hand, foot, and mouth disease, but self-help measures should relieve the symptoms. Ensure that your child drinks enough fluid, such as chilled milk. Fruit juices should be avoided because they are acidic and can aggravate mouth ulcers. Liquid acetaminophen or ibuprofen (*see* ANALGESICS, p.912) will help to bring down a fever (p.287) and reduce discomfort. If your child is reluctant to drink, watch for signs of dehydration, such as abnormal drowsiness, and consult the doctor immediately if you are worried.

You should also consult a doctor if your child has severe symptoms of hand, foot, and mouth infection. Your child's doctor may prescribe a medicated mouthwash to soothe the ulcers and prevent bacterial infection. Blisters clear up in a few days, but ulcers can persist for up to 4 weeks.

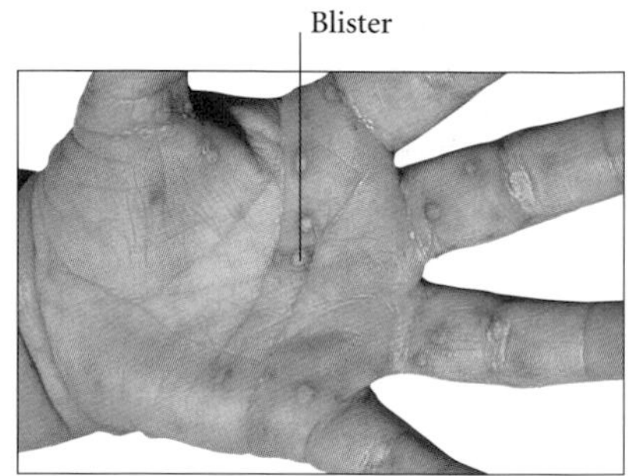
Blister

Hand, foot, and mouth disease
The small blisters on this child's hand are characteristic of the viral infection hand, foot, and mouth disease.

WWW ONLINE SITES: p.1028, p.1033

Head lice

Infestation of tiny wingless insects on the scalp that may cause intense itching

AGE Most common between the ages of 5 and 11

GENDER More common in girls

GENETICS LIFESTYLE Not significant factors

Infestation with head lice is common among young schoolchildren, particularly girls, between the ages of 5 and 11 years. These tiny, almost transparent insects are transmitted by close contact and by sharing combs and hats. Head lice prefer clean hair and skin and are not a result of poor hygiene.

The insects live by sucking blood from the scalp and may be seen as they fall off a child's head when the hair is washed or combed. The eggs, known as nits, are visible as tiny white specks attached to the bases of the hairs. An infestation of head lice usually causes intense itching, but there may be no other obvious symptoms.

WHAT CAN I DO?

If you think that your child has head lice, check for eggs at the bases of hairs and comb the hair over a piece of white paper to see if adult lice fall out. If head lice are present, you should check the rest of the family for infestation and alert your child's school.

You can usually treat head lice using over-the-counter lotions or shampoos that contain an insecticide (*see* PREPARATIONS FOR SKIN INFECTIONS AND INFESTATIONS, p.892). You should use the type that is currently recommended because head lice develop resistance to insecticides. If your child is under age 2 or has allergies or asthma, discuss treatment with his or her doctor. To avoid reinfestation, wash bedlinen and combs in very hot water and discourage your child from sharing combs and hats.

WWW ONLINE SITES: p.1028

SELF-HELP TREATING HEAD LICE

Infestations of head lice can be treated with an over-the-counter lotion or shampoo, and the lice can then be removed with a nit comb. Hair conditioner may make it easier for you to comb out the dead lice and eggs, especially if your child's hair is long, thick, or curly. All combs and towels should be washed in very hot water after use to prevent reinfestation.

Fine-toothed nit comb

Removing head lice
After applying a recommended lotion or shampoo, carefully comb your child's hair with a fine-toothed nit comb to remove the dead lice and eggs.

MUSCULOSKELETAL DISORDERS

In addition to everyday injuries and fractures, most bone, muscle, and joint problems in children fall into two broad categories: problems that are present at birth and those associated with the changes that occur during the growth spurt of puberty. Early treatment of most of these conditions improves the likelihood of recovery and reduces the risk of complications.

This section begins with articles on three conditions that may be present at birth: congenital hip dysplasia, clubfoot, and achondroplasia, which is caused by an abnormal gene. These are followed by conditions that may develop later in childhood and around puberty. These conditions include two that affect the femur (thighbone), Perthes disease and slipped femoral epiphysis, and Osgood–Schlatter disease, which causes inflammation of the tibia (shinbone). Minor foot and leg problems, such as flat feet and bowlegs, which are often part of normal development, are also covered. The final article discusses the joint disorder juvenile rheumatoid arthritis. Musculoskeletal disorders that affect adults in addition to children are included in the main section on the musculoskeletal system (pp.362–395).

KEY ANATOMY

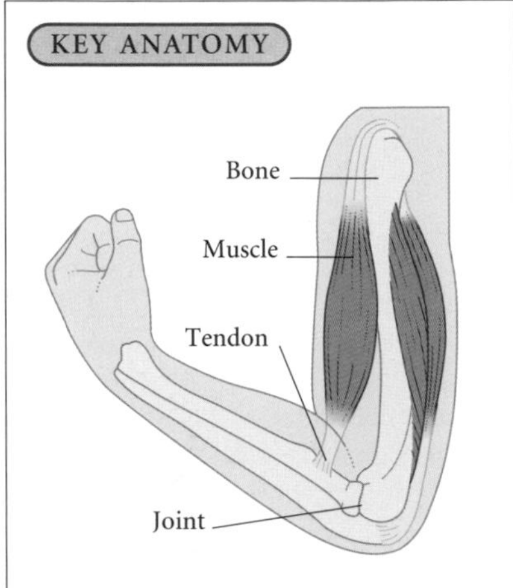
Bone
Muscle
Tendon
Joint

For more information on the structure and function of the musculoskeletal system, *see* pp.362–367.

Congenital hip dysplasia

Problems affecting the hip joint, ranging from mild looseness to dislocation

 AGE Present at birth

 GENDER Six times more common in girls

 GENETICS Sometimes runs in families

 LIFESTYLE Rarely persists in babies who are carried astride the mother's back

Congenital hip dysplasia is a term that covers a range of problems with the hip joint in the newborn. In mild cases, the hip joint moves excessively when manipulated. In moderate cases, the head of the femur (thighbone) slips out of the hip socket when manipulated but can be eased back in. In severe cases, the dislocation is permanent, and the head of the femur lies outside the hip socket.

Mild cases are the result of loose ligaments, but in moderate and severe cases the dislocation is related to abnormal development of the hip socket. Hip dysplasia occurs more often in the left hip and rarely affects both hips. About 1 in 250 babies is affected. Babies regularly carried astride the mother's back rarely have persistent dysplasia.

Congenital hip dysplasia is more common in girls and in babies who are born in the breech position. It may also be associated with clubfoot (p.833).

The cause of hip dysplasia is not fully understood. In about 1 in 5 babies there is a family history of hip dysplasia, suggesting a genetic factor. The condition may also be due to the effect of maternal hormones that relax the mother's own ligaments in preparation for labor.

WHAT ARE THE SYMPTOMS?

Mild forms of congenital hip dysplasia may have no symptoms. In severe cases, the symptoms may include:

- Asymmetrical creases in the skin on the backs of the baby's legs.
- Inability to turn the affected leg out fully at the hip.
- Shorter appearance of the affected leg.
- Limping when older.

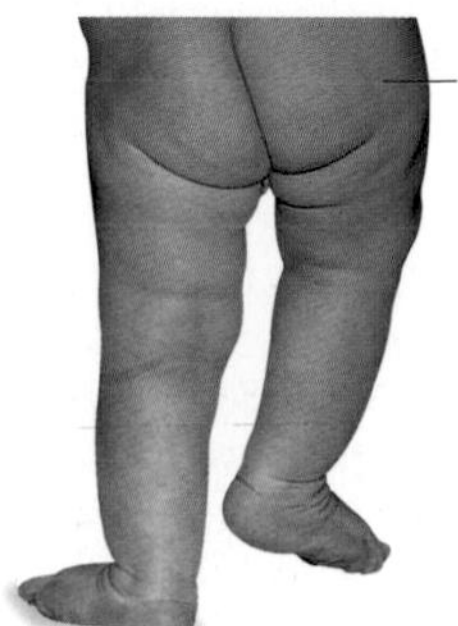
Abnormal hip

Congenital hip dysplasia
This infant has a dislocated right hip. The right leg appears shorter than the left and cannot be fully straightened.

If congenital hip dysplasia is not corrected early, it may lead to permanent deformity and the early onset of the bone disorder osteoarthritis (p.374).

WHAT MIGHT BE DONE?

The doctor will check your baby's hips for stability and range of movement shortly after birth and then regularly at routine checkups until your child is walking normally. If the doctor suspects congenital hip dysplasia, he or she may arrange ultrasound scanning (p.250) or X-ray (p.244) to confirm the diagnosis.

The less severe forms of congenital hip dysplasia often correct themselves during the first 3 weeks of life. However, if the problem persists, prompt treatment is essential because the head of the femur must be positioned correctly in the socket if the socket is to develop normally. In a very young baby, the hip joint may be positioned in a harness for 8–12 weeks to hold the head of the femur in the hip. In an older baby, the hip may need to be held in a cast for up to 6 months to correct the problem. If treatment is unsuccessful, surgery may be necessary to correct the hip dysplasia.

If congenital hip dysplasia is diagnosed early and treated immediately, most babies develop normal hip joints and there is no permanent damage.

(WWW) ONLINE SITES: p.1028, p.1035, p.1036

Clubfoot

A condition, also known as talipes, in which a baby is born with one or both feet twisted out of shape or position

 AGE Present at birth

 GENETICS Sometimes runs in families

 GENDER Risk factors depend on the type

 LIFESTYLE Not a significant factor

Babies are often born with their feet in awkward positions (*see* MINOR LEG AND FOOT PROBLEMS, p.834). In severe cases, the defect is known as clubfoot. There are two types of clubfoot: positional clubfoot, in which the twisted foot is flexible and can be manipulated into a normal position, and structural clubfoot, in which the deformity is rigid.

In positional clubfoot, the foot is of normal size but is twisted, possibly due to compression in the uterus. Most cases are mild and correct themselves. Structural clubfoot occurs in about 1 in 700 babies and is a more serious condition. In this disorder, the foot turns downward and inward and is usually abnormally small in size. In about half of these babies, both feet are affected. Structural clubfoot may be related to low levels of fluid in the uterus during pregnancy or caused by an underlying condition such as spina bifida (*see* NEURAL TUBE DEFECTS, p.844), and it may also occur with congenital hip dysplasia (p.832). Structural clubfoot is twice as common in boys and can run in families, suggesting a genetic factor.

WHAT MIGHT BE DONE?

Clubfoot is usually diagnosed during a routine examination after birth. Positional clubfoot may not need treatment, but physiotherapy (p.961) may help straighten the foot, and a cast may be used to move the foot into position. A normal position is usually achieved within 3 months. Structural clubfoot requires physiotherapy and a cast for a long period. In 6 out of 10 cases, this treatment is successful. If it is not, surgery may be needed at age 6–9 months. Surgery is usually successful, enabling most children to walk normally.

(WWW) ONLINE SITES: p.1028, p.1035

Achondroplasia

Defective bone growth due to an abnormal gene, causing short stature

 AGE Present at birth

 GENETICS Due to an abnormal gene

 GENDER LIFESTYLE Not significant factors

Achondroplasia causes abnormal body proportions and short stature. The disorder affects the bones of the limbs and base of the skull and prevents normal growth. As a result, although the child's trunk and head grow at a near normal rate, the arms and legs are disproportionately short and the forehead often protrudes. However, the child's intelligence is not usually affected. In the US, about 2 in 100,000 people are affected.

Achondroplasia is caused by an abnormal gene inherited in an autosomal dominant manner (*see* GENE DISORDERS, p.269). Usually, the gene abnormality occurs spontaneously, and there is no family history of the condition. In a few cases, there is a family history of the disorder. People with achondroplasia have a 1 in 2 chance of passing the disorder on to a child, and they may wish to have genetic counseling (p.270) if they are planning a pregnancy.

WHAT ARE THE SYMPTOMS?

Symptoms such as short, bowed legs and a prominent forehead are usually apparent at birth. Other symptoms develop as the baby grows and include:

- Short stature.
- Short, broad hands and feet.
- Forward curve to the lower spine (*see* KYPHOSIS AND LORDOSIS, p.371).
- Waddling gait.

Psychological difficulties may develop when a child starts to realize that other children are different. Rarely, a baby also has hydrocephalus (p.845), in which there is excess fluid around the brain.

WHAT MIGHT BE DONE?

Achondroplasia may be diagnosed by your doctor during routine ultrasound scanning in pregnancy (p.793) at about 18–20 weeks, but more often the condition is diagnosed at birth. Your baby's doctor may arrange for X-rays (p.244) to confirm the diagnosis in addition to CT scanning (p.247) or MRI scanning (p.248) of the baby's head.

There is no cure for achondroplasia, and a child usually needs no treatment. Affected children can have surgery to lengthen their legs by a few inches but many prefer their natural height. If an affected baby has hydrocephalus, excess fluid may need to be drained from the brain (*see* SHUNT FOR HYDROCEPHALUS, p.845). Most children with achondroplasia have a normal life expectancy.

(WWW) ONLINE SITES: p.1028, p.1032

Perthes disease

Gradual breaking down and re-forming of the head of the femur (thighbone)

 AGE Most common between the ages of 4 and 8

 GENDER Five times more common in boys

 GENETICS LIFESTYLE Not significant factors

In Perthes disease, the head of the femur (thighbone) softens, breaks down, and is gradually replaced by new bone over 18 months to 2 years. The disease causes pain in the hip and sometimes in the knee. An affected child may walk with a limp and have restricted movement of the hip. Perthes disease occurs mainly in boys between the ages of 4 and 8 years. It is rare but more severe in older children. The disease affects about 1 in 2,000 children. Of these, 1 in 10 develops the disease in both hips.

The cause of Perthes disease is not known. The condition requires treatment, and you should consult the doctor if your child develops a limp or has a painful hip or knee.

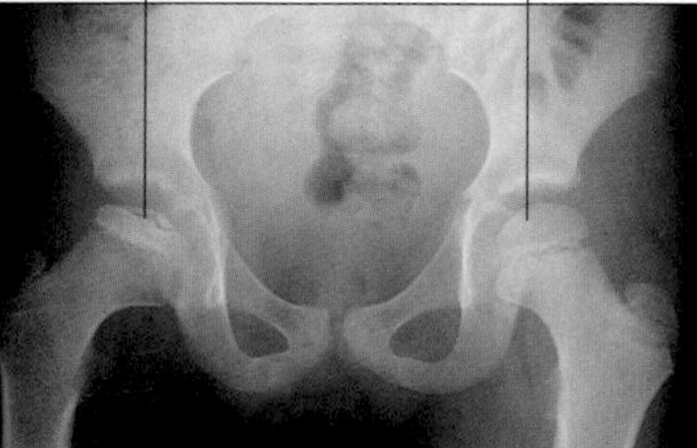
Damaged femur
Normal femur

Perthes disease
The head of the femur (thighbone) seen on the left in this X-ray is flattened compared to the other, as a result of Perthes disease.

WHAT MIGHT BE DONE?

The doctor will examine your child and will probably arrange for X-rays (p.244) of the hip. MRI scanning (p.248) and radionuclide scanning (p.251) of the hip may also be performed.

Initial treatment is bed rest until the pain subsides. In younger children, bed rest may be sufficient, but sometimes traction is used to place the femur under tension and hold it in the correct position. In more severe cases, casts or braces may be used to protect the hip joint and hold the head of the femur securely in the hip socket while the bone re-forms. Occasionally, surgery is required. Your child's progress will be monitored by X-rays every few months while the head of the femur recovers. He or she will probably have physiotherapy (p.961) to encourage mobility of the joint during healing.

About 3 in 10 of those affected develop the joint condition osteoarthritis (p.374) later in life. In general, a complete recovery is more likely in a child under the age of 8 years.

(WWW) ONLINE SITES: p.1028, p.1035

Slipped femoral epiphysis

Displacement of the head of the femur (thighbone) at the hip joint

AGE Most common in girls aged 11–13 and boys aged 14–16

GENDER More common in boys

GENETICS Sometimes runs in families

LIFESTYLE Obesity increases the risk

In children, the epiphysis (the area at the end of a long bone) is separated from the main shaft of the bone by a soft, flexible layer of cartilage where new bone is formed. In the condition known as slipped femoral epiphysis, the epiphysis at the head of the femur (thighbone) becomes displaced. This displacement can happen suddenly as a result of an injury that damages the soft cartilage, or gradually for reasons that are unknown. In about 1 in 5 cases, both hips are affected but usually at different times. Slipped femoral epiphysis occurs in children growing rapidly at puberty. The disorder affects about 3 in 100,000 children in the US, and overweight children are particularly at risk. Slipped femoral epiphysis can run in families, suggesting a genetic factor.

WHAT ARE THE SYMPTOMS?

Symptoms may appear suddenly but usually develop over several weeks and may include the following:

- Pain in the hip, knee, or thigh.
- Limping with an out-turned foot.
- Restricted hip movement.
- Reluctance and eventually inability to bear weight on the affected leg.

If your child has any of these symptoms, you should contact your child's doctor within 24 hours.

WHAT MIGHT BE DONE?

If the doctor suspects that your child has slipped femoral epiphysis, he or she will arrange for X-rays (p.244) of the affected hip. If there is displacement, your child will need surgery to fix the epiphysis in place and, sometimes, to strengthen the other hip joint to prevent displacement occurring in both hips. If treated promptly, most children recover completely and the condition is unlikely to recur. Rarely, osteoarthritis (p.374) develops later in life.

(WWW) ONLINE SITES: p.1028, p.1035

Osgood–Schlatter disease

Inflammation of the front of the tibia (shinbone) below the knee

AGE Most common between the ages of 10 and 14

GENDER Much more common in boys

LIFESTYLE Strenuous activity aggravates the symptoms

GENETICS Not a significant factor

In Osgood–Schlatter disease, fragments of cartilage become loose at the front of the tibia (shinbone) just below the knee at the point where a large tendon is attached. The condition is caused by repetitive strong pulls on the tendon that attaches the muscle at the front of the thigh to the tibia. The symptoms include tenderness, swelling, and pain in the affected area and appear slowly over several weeks or months. Physical exercise makes the symptoms worse. Osgood–Schlatter disease is most common in boys aged 10–14 who do regular strenuous exercise. The disease usually occurs in only one leg, but in about 1 in 5 cases both legs are affected.

If the doctor suspects that your child has Osgood–Schlatter disease, he or she may arrange for X-rays (p.244) of the affected area to confirm the diagnosis. In many cases, no treatment is required apart from rest and analgesics (p.912) for pain relief. If the condition persists, the affected knee may be immobilized in a cast for 6–8 weeks. Physiotherapy (p.961) may also help. Treatment is usually successful, and the disorder rarely recurs. Severely affected children may be advised to avoid strenuous exercise until they are over age 14 and the musculoskeletal system has matured.

(WWW) ONLINE SITES: p.1028, p.1035

Minor leg and foot problems

Variations in the position and shape of the feet and legs during childhood

GENETICS Sometimes runs in families

AGE LIFESTYLE Risk factors depend on the type

GENDER Not a significant factor

When a young child stands and walks, the position of the legs or feet may look odd or awkward. Different minor foot problems are common at different ages. However, these problems rarely interfere with walking or require treatment. Specific minor problems with the legs and feet can run in families, suggesting a genetic factor may be involved.

WHAT ARE THE TYPES?

Minor leg and foot problems include in-toeing and out-toeing, bowlegs and knock-knees, and flat feet.

IN-TOEING AND OUT-TOEING The condition known as in-toeing, in which the feet point inward, is common and occurs at any time from infancy to age 8. Out-toeing, in which the feet point away from each other, is less common but may occur at about 6 months.

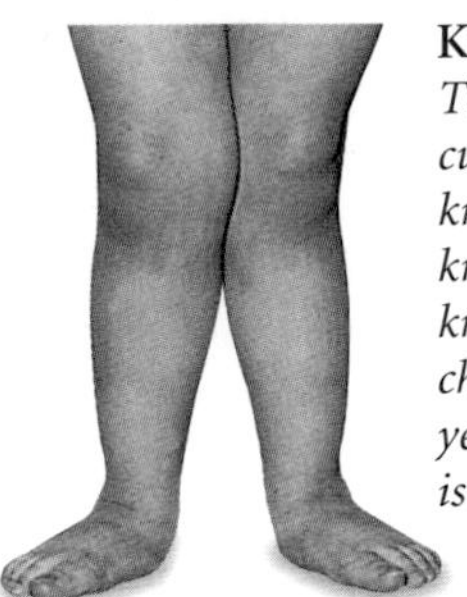

Knock-knees
This child's legs curve inward at the knees, a position known as knock-knees. Among children aged 3–12 years, the condition is common.

BOWLEGS AND KNOCK-KNEES If both tibias (shinbones) curve out, a child's knees cannot touch when he or she stands with the feet together. This condition, known as bowlegs, is normal until a child is about age 3. Severe bowing is uncommon but may be caused by a deficiency of vitamin D (*see* OSTEOMALACIA AND RICKETS, p.370). In the condition known as knock-knees, the child's legs curve in at the knees, so that the feet are wide apart even when the knees are touching. Knock-knees is common between ages 3 and 7 years.

FLAT FEET Most children have flat feet until the arch develops at age 2–3 years. Children also have a fat pad beneath the foot that accentuates the flat-footed appearance. About 1 in 7 children in the US has persistent flat feet.

WHAT MIGHT BE DONE?

Your child's legs and feet will be examined regularly during routine medical checkups. However, you should consult the doctor if you are worried by the appearance of your child's legs or feet or if your child has difficulty walking, has a limp, or complains of pain.

Most children with minor leg and foot problems do not need treatment because they rarely interfere with walking and will disappear naturally as a child grows up. Out-toeing disappears first, usually within a year of a child starting to walk. In-toeing and bowlegs usually disappear by age 3–4 and knock-knees by age 11–12. Persistent flat feet do not usually require treatment unless they cause pain.

Your child's doctor may recommend physiotherapy (p.961) if your child has difficulty walking or the shape of his or her legs is abnormal. Rarely, if your child's legs or feet are seriously affected, he or she may require orthopedic surgery to correct the problem.

Juvenile rheumatoid arthritis

Persistent inflammation of one or more joints that occurs only in childhood

 GENETICS Sometimes runs in families

 AGE GENDER Risk factors depend on the type

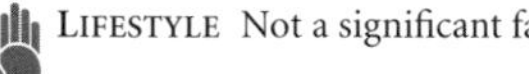 LIFESTYLE Not a significant factor

Children may be affected by the same types of arthritis (p.374) as adults, but juvenile rheumatoid arthritis (JRA) is found only in children. In Canada, about 2,000 children are affected by JRA. The condition is the result of an abnormal response of the immune system, leading to inflammation, swelling, and pain in the lining of an affected joint. Although the cause is not understood, juvenile rheumatoid arthritis sometimes runs in families, suggesting a genetic factor may be involved. In mild cases, activities are rarely affected. In severe cases, there may be joint deformities and reduced mobility.

WHAT ARE THE TYPES?

Juvenile rheumatoid arthritis is divided into three types according to the number of joints affected by the disease and the specific symptoms involved.

POLYARTICULAR JUVENILE RHEUMATOID ARTHRITIS This type affects more girls than boys and occurs at any age. Symptoms include inflammation, stiffness, and pain in five or more joints. Those joints commonly affected include the wrists, fingers, knees, and ankles.

PAUCIARTICULAR JUVENILE RHEUMATOID ARTHRITIS This type affects both sexes equally and usually occurs during early childhood. Symptoms include inflammation, stiffness, and pain in four or fewer joints, and girls are at high risk of the eye condition uveitis (p.574). The joints commonly involved include those in the knees, ankles, and wrists.

SYSTEMIC JUVENILE RHEUMATOID ARTHRITIS Also known as Still's disease, this type of JRA affects boys and girls equally and occurs at any age during childhood. Any number of joints may be affected, but, although they are painful, they do not become swollen. The other symptoms of the disease include fever, swollen glands, and a nonitchy rash. Some children recover totally, but others develop polyarticular JRA.

WHAT MIGHT BE DONE?

If the doctor suspects that your child has a type of juvenile rheumatoid arthritis, he or she may arrange for X-rays (p.244) of the affected joints and blood tests to look for particular antibodies associated with the condition.

The goal of treatment for JRA is to reduce inflammation, minimize joint damage, and relieve pain. If your child is mildly affected, he or she may only need to take nonsteroidal anti-inflammatory drugs (p.894) to reduce inflammation and relieve pain. In more severe cases, your child may be prescribed oral corticosteroids (p.930), or he or she may be treated with locally acting corticosteroids (p.895) injected into the affected joints. Sometimes, inflammation can be reduced by using antirheumatic drugs (p.895), such as gold-based drugs or penicillamine.

Other treatments may include physiotherapy (p.961) to maintain joint mobility and, sometimes, occupational therapy (p.962). Splints may be used for support and to help prevent deformity. Special devices are also available and may help with daily activities such as dressing. If damage to the joints is severe and has caused deformity, joint replacement (p.377) may be necessary.

Juvenile rheumatoid arthritis usually clears up in a few years. Severely affected children may be left with deformed joints, and some may develop rheumatoid arthritis (p.377) later in adult life.

(WWW) ONLINE SITES: p.1027, p.1028

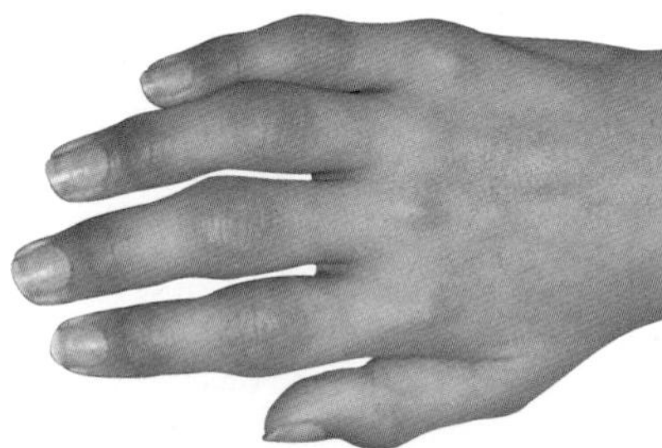

Juvenile rheumatoid arthritis
The joints of this young child's hand are swollen and inflamed due to polyarticular juvenile rheumatoid arthritis.

DISORDERS OF THE CARDIOVASCULAR AND RESPIRATORY SYSTEMS

Disorders of the heart and lungs are relatively common in children. The heart is affected by birth defects more than any other organ, and all children have recurrent bacterial and viral infections of the throat and lungs. Usually these infections are mild and play a role in developing a healthy immune system.

The first articles in this section cover cardiovascular disorders, such as congenital heart disease. Many heart abnormalities correct themselves without medical intervention as a child grows. Many of the more serious heart defects can now be treated successfully because of recent advances in surgical techniques. A rarer disorder that affects the heart in children is Kawasaki disease, which damages the heart and blood vessels. Blood vessels are also damaged in Henoch–Schönlein purpura, which is due to an abnormal response by the immune system. Left untreated, Henoch–Schönlein purpura can eventually cause kidney failure.

The final articles address respiratory disorders, of which asthma is the most common. The incidence of this disorder is increasing for unknown reasons. Respiratory tract infections, such as bronchiolitis, are common in young children. The inflammatory disorder epiglottitis can be dangerous but is now rare in developed countries because of routine immunization of infants against the bacterium responsible for causing the condition, *Haemophilus influenzae* type B.

KEY ANATOMY

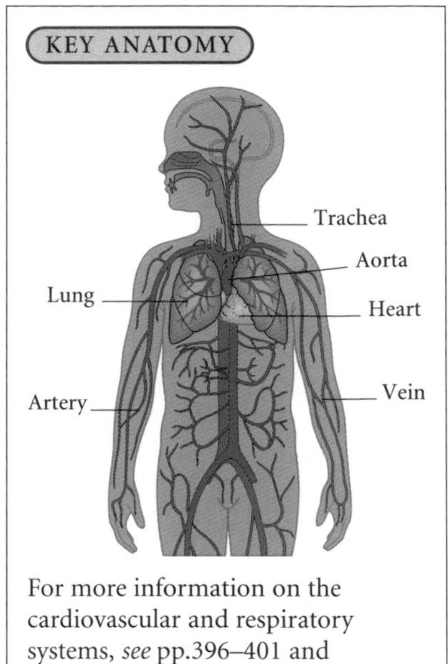
Trachea
Aorta
Lung
Heart
Artery
Vein

For more information on the cardiovascular and respiratory systems, *see* pp.396–401 and pp.470–473.

Congenital heart disease

One or more defects of the heart that are present at birth

AGE Present at birth

LIFESTYLE Use of certain drugs and alcohol during pregnancy are risk factors

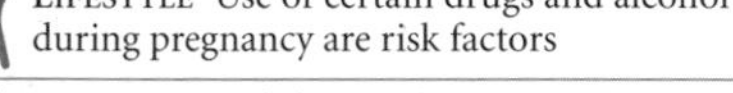
GENETICS Risk factors depend on the type

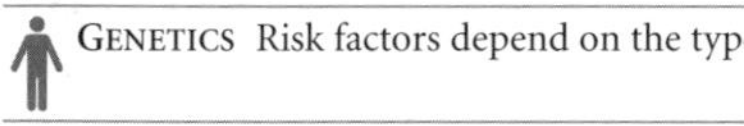
GENDER Not a significant factor

The heart is a complex organ that can develop abnormally in a fetus, leading to defects that affect a baby from birth (congenital heart defects). Congenital heart disease affects about 1 in 100 babies and is one of the most common birth defects. About 2 in 3 of these abnormalities disappear naturally as the baby grows, but more serious defects require complex corrective surgery.

Congenital heart disease commonly causes shortness of breath in affected children, which may affect their feeding, growth, and activity.

WHAT ARE THE CAUSES?

In most cases, the cause of congenital heart disease is unknown. However, it can sometimes run in families, suggesting that a genetic factor may be involved. Heart defects at birth may also be associated with genetic disorders, such as Down syndrome (p.821). Exposure of the fetus to excessive alcohol or drugs, such as the anticonvulsant drug phenytoin, increases the risk of congenital heart disease. During the early stages of pregnancy, certain infections in the mother can lead to fetal heart defects (*see* CONGENITAL INFECTIONS, p.817). More than 1 in 10 babies with congenital heart disease are also found to have a defect elsewhere in the body, such as in the digestive tract.

WHAT ARE THE TYPES?

Most types of congenital heart disease affect only one part of the heart or one of the major blood vessels, such as the aorta, connected to the heart. Less commonly, several parts of the heart or more than one blood vessel are affected. These multiple heart defects are more serious and can be life-threatening.

SEPTAL DEFECTS The most common type of congenital heart abnormality is a septal defect, also known as a hole in the heart. In this defect, there is a hole in the septum (the inner wall that divides the heart) either between the two lower chambers (ventriculoseptal defect, pictured left) or alternatively between the two upper chambers (atrioseptal defect). In both cases, some oxygen-rich blood passes from the left side to the right side of the heart and is sent back to the lungs instead of going around the body. About 1 in 3 cases of congenital heart disease is due to a ventriculoseptal defect, which is often small and may close naturally. About 1 in 4 cases of congenital heart disease is caused by an atrioseptal defect, which usually produces few symptoms but is likely to require surgical treatment. Both septal defects are common in children with Down syndrome.

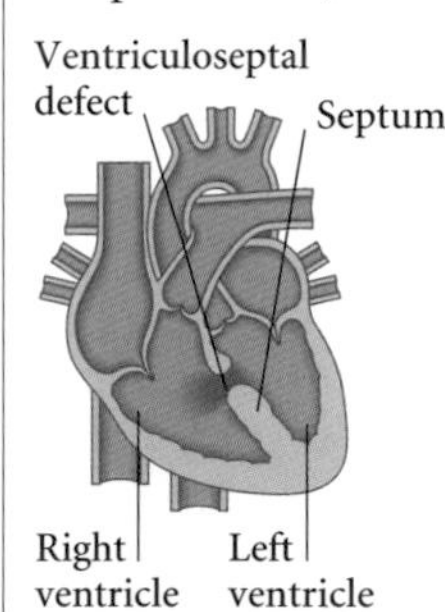
Ventriculoseptal defect
Septum
Right ventricle
Left ventricle

PATENT DUCTUS ARTERIOSUS The ductus arteriosus is a small blood vessel that connects the pulmonary artery to the aorta in the fetus so that blood bypasses the lungs. If this vessel fails to close up soon after birth, normal circulation is prevented. This disorder is often found in premature babies.

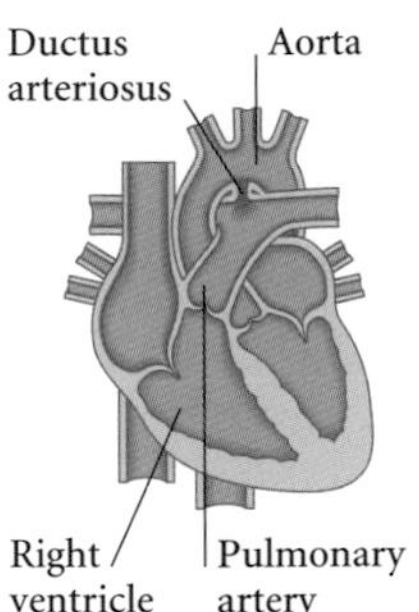
Ductus arteriosus
Aorta
Right ventricle
Pulmonary artery

COARCTATION OF THE AORTA In this congenital heart disorder, the aorta is narrowed close to where it leaves the heart. This narrowing restricts the flow of blood to the lower part of the body, and the heart has to work harder to compensate. As a result, the blood pressure in the upper part of the body is elevated. The condition requires surgical treatment. Children with coarctation of the aorta may also have an abnormality of one or more of the four heart valves.

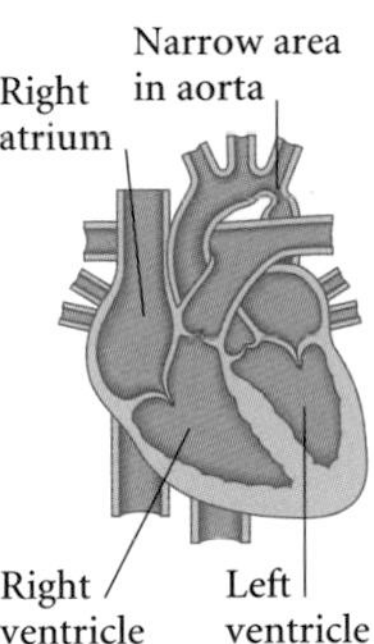
Right atrium
Narrow area in aorta
Right ventricle
Left ventricle

VALVE DEFECTS Any of the four heart valves may develop abnormally. The most common type of valve defect is aortic stenosis (p.423). In this condition, the aortic valve, which opens to allow blood to flow from the left ventricle into the aorta, is narrowed so that blood flow through it is restricted. Defects of the pulmonary valve, which opens to let blood flow from the right ventricle to the lungs, are less common.

MULTIPLE DEFECTS In rare cases, several heart defects occur together. In addition to placing extra strain on the heart, the defects usually prevent blood from passing through the lungs normally so that blood oxygen levels become very low. Tissues throughout the body may then become oxygen-starved. The most common multiple defect is Fallot's tetralogy, in which four heart abnormalities occur together, consisting of a ventriculoseptal defect, pulmonary stenosis, a displaced aorta, and a thickened right ventricle. Another multiple defect is hypoplastic left heart syndrome, in which the chambers and valves on the left side of the heart are underdeveloped. This was once a fatal condition but can now sometimes be treated. A rarer multiple defect involves reversal of the positions of the aorta and the pulmonary artery.

What are the symptoms?

Minor congenital heart defects may not cause symptoms. When symptoms do occur, they vary depending on the severity and type of the heart defect. The symptoms of all types of congenital heart disease may include:

- Shortness of breath, leading to difficulty in feeding.
- Slow weight gain and growth.

Symptoms of severe heart defects may develop suddenly in the first weeks of life. If there are low levels of oxygen in the blood, affected children may have a bluish coloration to their tongue and lips. Children may be susceptible to chest infections and are at increased risk of infection of the lining of the heart (*see* INFECTIVE ENDOCARDITIS, p.426), especially after surgery or dental treatment. Over a period of several years, congenital heart defects may lead to irreversible lung damage (*see* PULMONARY HYPERTENSION, p.505).

How is it diagnosed?

In some cases, congenital heart disease is diagnosed during routine ultrasound scanning in pregnancy (p.793). Otherwise, defects may be found after birth when symptoms develop or during a routine examination. The doctor may hear a sound (heart murmur) caused by turbulent blood flow while listening to your child's heart. Although many heart murmurs are normal, the doctor is likely to arrange for an ECG (p.406), which monitors the electrical activity of the heart. Your child may also have the imaging technique echocardiography (p.425), which assesses the structure and function of the heart.

What is the treatment?

Many heart defects correct themselves or need no treatment. Only about 1 in 3 children requires surgery. Affected children are usually monitored through childhood and, if necessary, surgery is performed when the child is older and the operation easier. Rarely, an emergency operation is necessary to save a young baby's life. A heart transplant (p.427) is now a possibility for children with multiple heart defects. Chest infections need to be treated promptly, and, if the child has dental treatment or surgery, antibiotics (p.885) are necessary to prevent infection of the lining of the heart. Some children will need drugs, such as diuretics (p.902), to control the symptoms of a heart defect.

What is the prognosis?

The prognosis depends on the type of heart defect and its severity. Septal defects either close naturally or are corrected surgically. As a result of surgical advances over the last 20 years, even very severe defects can often be corrected, and many severely affected children are leading normal, active lives.

(WWW) ONLINE SITES: p.1027, p.1028, p1032

Kawasaki disease

A prolonged fever during which the heart and blood vessels may be damaged

 AGE More common under age 5

 GENDER Slightly more common in boys

 GENETICS More common in Asians and African–Americans

 LIFESTYLE Not a significant factor

First observed in Japan in the 1960s, Kawasaki disease is a rare condition in which a prolonged fever is associated with damage to the heart and blood vessels. In Canada, fewer than 1 in every 100,000 children under age 5 are affected each year. The disorder is now being diagnosed more often in Western countries and occurs more frequently in Asian and African–American people. Heart damage occurs in about 1 in 5 of all cases of Kawasaki disease. Early diagnosis is important because the disorder can become life-threatening.

The cause of Kawasaki disease is unknown, although it is suspected that a viral or bacterial infection may cause the condition. However, despite much research, there is no convincing evidence to confirm this theory.

What are the symptoms?

The first symptoms develop over about 2 weeks and may include:

- Prolonged, constant fever that lasts more than 5 days.
- Sore or itchy, red eyes, possibly associated with a watery discharge (*see* CONJUNCTIVITIS, p.570).
- Cracked, painful, and swollen lips.
- Sore throat.
- Swollen glands in the neck, under the arms, and in the groin.

After about a week of fever, the following symptoms may develop:

- Reddening of the palms of the hands and soles of the feet, usually along with peeling skin on the tips of the fingers and toes.
- Blotchy pink rash over the entire body.

Kawasaki disease may lead to serious complications. For example, balloon-like swellings, called aneurysms, can develop in the walls of the coronary arteries, which supply the heart muscle. Inflammation of the heart muscle (*see* MYOCARDITIS, p.426) may also occur. Kawasaki disease can also damage blood vessels throughout the body.

What might be done?

Diagnosis of Kawasaki disease can be difficult because the symptoms are very similar to those of minor viral infections, such as the common cold. You should consult a doctor if your child develops a fever that cannot be lowered by taking acetaminophen and other simple self-help measures (*see* BRINGING DOWN A FEVER, p.287). If your doctor suspects Kawasaki disease, your child will be admitted to the hospital immediately because the treatment is most effective if started within 10 days of the onset of the disease. Your child will probably have blood tests to look for evidence of Kawasaki disease. The imaging technique echocardiography (p.425) may also be done to look for damage to the heart and blood vessels.

A child who has Kawasaki disease will probably be given intravenous immunoglobulin. This substance is a blood product containing antibodies that fight infection. Immunoglobulin also reduces the risk of aneurysms and inflammation of the heart muscle in Kawasaki disease for reasons that are not known. High doses of aspirin are usually given until the fever subsides. Lower doses are then continued for a period of several weeks.

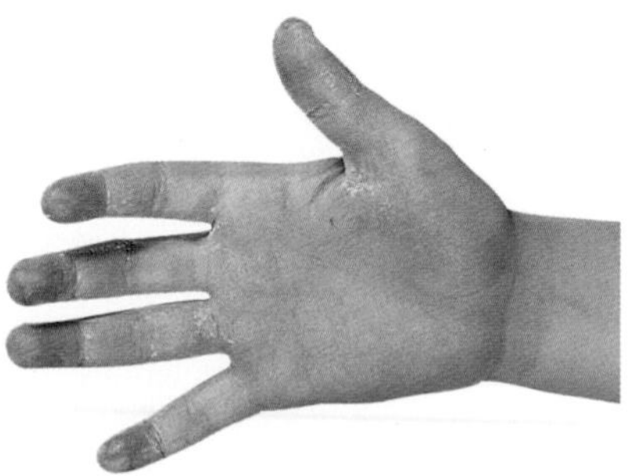

Kawasaki disease
One of the symptoms of the rare disorder Kawasaki disease is reddening of the hands with peeling skin on the tips of the fingers.

What is the prognosis?

Most children with Kawasaki disease recover completely within 3 weeks but need regular follow-up visits, and possibly echocardiography, over the next few months. Aneurysms and myocarditis, if present, usually disappear over several months. Kawasaki disease is fatal in about 1 in 50 affected children. In children who survive, there is a small risk of developing coronary artery disease (p.405) later in life.

(WWW) ONLINE SITES: p.1028

Henoch–Schönlein purpura

Inflammation of small blood vessels, the kidneys, and joints caused by an abnormal immune response

 AGE Most common between the ages of 2 and 8

 GENDER Twice as common in boys

 GENETICS LIFESTYLE Not significant factors

In Henoch–Schönlein purpura, small blood vessels are damaged by an abnormal reaction of the immune system, possibly triggered by an infection, such as a common cold (p.286). Antibodies, which are a component of the immune system and normally fight infection, are deposited in the small blood vessels throughout the body, causing them to become inflamed. The inflammation results in blood leaking out of the vessels into the skin, causing a distinctive rash, mainly on the buttocks and the back of the legs. Bleeding may also occur from the lining of the intestines. The inflammation may also affect the joints and the kidneys.

In the US, Henoch–Schönlein purpura affects about 1 in 700 children, most commonly those aged 2–8. It occurs more frequently in the winter months and is more common in boys.

What are the symptoms?

The symptoms usually develop over several days and may include:

- A rash of raised purple lesions typically over the buttocks and legs that may also appear on the arms.
- Periodic attacks of abdominal pain, often with vomiting and diarrhea.
- Sometimes, blood in the feces.
- Painful, swollen joints, most often the knees and ankles.
- Fever.

In about 8 in 10 children with the condition, the kidneys become inflamed, leading to loss of blood and protein in the urine (*see* GLOMERULONEPHRITIS, p.699). The blood is usually present in amounts too small to be seen with the naked eye. If the kidneys are badly affected, they may be damaged permanently, which may result in a rise in blood pressure. If the intestines become inflamed, a rare condition known as intussusception (p.864) may develop, in which part of the intestine "telescopes" in on itself.

How is it diagnosed?

The diagnosis of Henoch–Schönlein purpura is based on the symptoms. Your doctor will probably arrange for a urine test to look for blood or protein, indicating that the kidneys are inflamed. Blood tests will be done to assess the function of your child's kidneys and to rule out other possible causes of the symptoms. In some cases, a small sample of kidney tissue may be removed for examination (*see* KIDNEY BIOPSY, p.701).

What is the treatment?

There is no specific treatment for Henoch–Schönlein purpura. Your doctor will probably advise that your child rests in bed and may prescribe analgesics (p.912), such as acetaminophen. If the abdominal pain is severe, he or she may also prescribe corticosteroids (p.930). Joint pain usually disappears

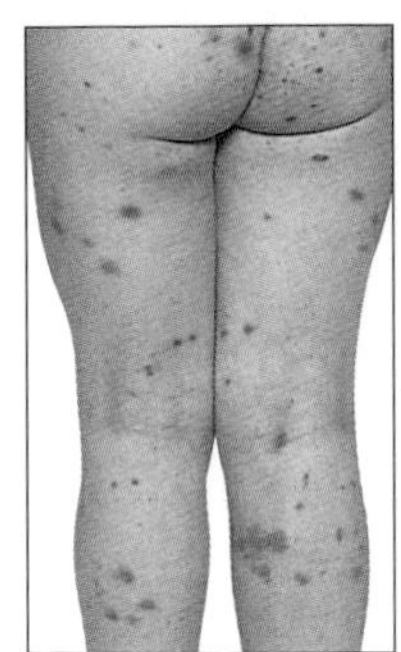

Henoch–Schönlein purpura
The rash of raised purple lesions that has developed over the back of this child's legs and buttocks is one of the symptoms typical of Henoch–Schönlein purpura.

without permanent damage, and the rash should go away without treatment. Symptoms normally take 2–6 weeks to disappear completely. Kidney function is monitored by checking your child's blood pressure and by doing blood tests. Urine tests are done for months or even years, until there are no traces of blood or protein left in the urine. If the kidneys are severely damaged, the doctor may prescribe immunosuppressants (p.906). Affected children with kidney damage require long-term follow-up.

WHAT IS THE PROGNOSIS?

Most children with Henoch–Schönlein purpura make a full recovery with no long-term effects. The symptoms may recur for about a year but are rare thereafter. In about 1 in 20 children, there is long-term kidney damage that may lead to kidney failure (p.705).

(WWW) ONLINE SITES: p.1028, p.1033

Asthma in children

Attacks of breathlessness, coughing, and/or wheezing in children due to reversible narrowing of the airways

AGE More common under age 6; becomes less common with age

GENDER More common in boys

GENETICS Sometimes runs in families

LIFESTYLE Exposure to furry animals, air pollution, and parental smoking are risk factors

In children with asthma, the airways in the lungs tend to narrow temporarily. Narrowing occurs when the linings of the airways become swollen and inflamed and produce excess mucus, which may block the smaller airways.

Asthma affects about 1 in 7 children in Canada and is now the most common chronic respiratory disease in children. The number of children with asthma has risen greatly in recent years. The reason for this increase is unknown, but allergy and other environmental factors may be involved.

Asthma attacks are a common cause of absence from school and admission to the hospital. However, between the attacks, children can be perfectly well. Severe attacks of asthma are distressing for both children and their parents and can be life-threatening.

WHAT ARE THE CAUSES?

Asthma is more likely to develop in children with a family history of the condition, suggesting that a genetic factor may be involved. Other respiratory disorders, especially those associated with preterm birth (*see* PROBLEMS OF THE PRETERM BABY, p.816), may also increase the risk of developing asthma. Regular exposure to cigarette smoke in the home and pollution from car exhaust and factory fumes may be other risk factors for asthma.

In children under age 5, attacks of asthma are usually triggered by a viral infection, such as the common cold (p.286). In older children, attacks are often caused by an allergic reaction to substances such as pollens, molds, dust mites, and the fur or dander from animals such as cats and dogs. Exercise, especially in cold, dry air, may also trigger an asthma attack. In rare cases, certain foods, such as milk, nuts, and eggs, provoke asthma. In some affected children, emotional stress may make the attacks more severe.

WHAT ARE THE SYMPTOMS?

Symptoms vary in severity from day to day and week to week and with the age of the child. They appear rapidly and may persist for a few hours or longer. Symptoms may include:

- Wheezing.
- Shortness of breath.
- Tightness in the chest.
- Dry cough that may be worse at night and disturb sleep.

Very young children with asthma often have a dry cough at night and no other symptoms. Older children often feel tired due to disturbed sleep and may have difficulty participating in strenuous sports due to shortness of breath. Children with asthma are also predisposed to the allergic disorders eczema (*see* ECZEMA IN CHILDREN, p.829) and hay fever (*see* ALLERGIC RHINITIS, p.466).

A severe asthma attack may cause very rapid breathing, difficulty speaking, and indrawing of the chest wall. If the level of oxygen in the blood is low, a child may develop a bluish tinge to the lips and tongue, a condition known as cyanosis. You should call an ambulance immediately if your child has such an attack, because severe attacks of asthma can be life-threatening.

Left untreated, severe asthma may impair a child's growth (*see* GROWTH DISORDERS, p.869) and development. Since an affected child will probably be unable to sleep normally, leading to fatigue, his or her performance at school will eventually decline.

(TREATMENT) GIVING INHALED DRUGS TO CHILDREN

The drugs that are used to treat asthma are often inhaled. Devices that administer these drugs are tailored to suit the age of the child (*see* TAKING INHALED ASTHMA DRUGS, p.485). Since babies are unable coordinate their breathing to inhale the drugs, they require special inhalers that incorporate a face mask and a spacer. The spacer retains the drug while the face mask allows the baby to inhale the drug while breathing normally.

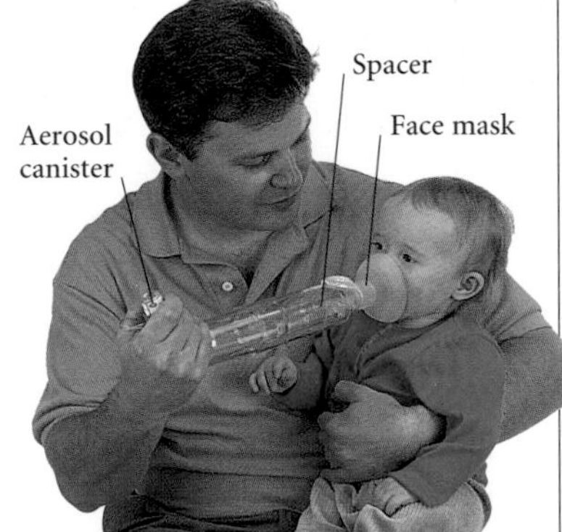
Spacer
Aerosol canister
Face mask

Giving drugs to a young child
A dose of the drug is dispensed from the canister into a spacer, such as the one shown, and the mask is placed over the baby's nose and mouth.

HOW IS IT DIAGNOSED?

By the time the doctor sees your child, his or her asthma attack will probably be over. Diagnosis of the condition is therefore often based on a description of your child's symptoms. The doctor will listen to your child's chest with a stethoscope. An older child may be asked to breathe out through a peak flow meter, a special device that measures the child's capacity to exhale (*see* MONITORING YOUR ASTHMA, p.484). To confirm the diagnosis, the doctor may prescribe a trial of a quick-relief drug that opens up the airways in the lungs (*see* BRONCHODILATOR DRUGS, p.910). If your child's symptoms are caused by asthma, they should improve significantly after administration of the drug.

Once the diagnosis has been confirmed, your child may have a skin test to look for specific allergies that may be the trigger factors for his or her asthma attacks (*see* SKIN PRICK TEST, p.468).

WHAT IS THE TREATMENT?

The aim of treatment for asthma is to enable your child to live as active a life as possible with a minimum of drug treatment. The doctor may give you a detailed plan for managing your child's asthma with advice on when to change treatments and what to do if your child has a sudden attack. It is important that children who have asthma understand their condition and are confident about dealing with their symptoms. Some children will need to take regular peak flow readings at home to monitor their asthma over a period of time. Since the normal peak flow values are determined according to a child's height, growth will also be measured regularly.

ENVIRONMENTAL MEASURES There are many ways in which you can modify your child's environment to minimize contact with factors that may trigger an attack (*see* REDUCING THE RISK OF ASTHMA ATTACKS IN CHILDREN, right).

DRUG TREATMENT The drugs that are used to treat children with asthma fall into two groups: quick-relief drugs and controller drugs, which are usually corticosteroids (*see* CORTICOSTEROIDS FOR RESPIRATORY DISEASE, p.911) although cromolyn sodium (*see* ANTIALLERGY DRUGS, p.905) and antileukotrienes may also be used. The quick-relief drugs act rapidly to open up the airways and relieve wheezing. They usually work within 10 minutes, but their effect lasts for only a few hours. Children who have mild asthma attacks once or twice a week may be prescribed a quick-relief drug for use when symptoms occur.

Children who have frequent asthma attacks also need to take regular doses of controller drugs. These drugs take effect slowly over several days and should be taken regularly, even if there are no symptoms of asthma. Controller drugs reduce inflammation of the airways and prevent symptoms from occurring. Respiratory corticosteroids are commonly prescribed as controller drugs, but other drugs, such as cromolyn sodium are sometimes given to dampen the allergic response and help keep the airways open. Antileukotrienes are new drugs that can now be used instead of corticosteroids to treat children with moderately severe asthma.

Drugs to treat asthma are usually administered with an inhaler. A spacer device attached to an inhaler may be necessary for young children who find an inhaler difficult to use effectively (*see* GIVING INHALED DRUGS TO CHILDREN, p.839). A nebulizer is a device that delivers drugs in aerosol form through a face mask and is often used during a severe asthma attack. It is crucial to know the correct technique for using inhalers and nebulizers. Your child's doctor or nurse will show you and your child how to use the devices. After a severe attack, oral corticosteroids may be prescribed for your child in addition to the inhaled drugs.

MANAGING AN ASTHMA ATTACK You or your child should always carry a quick-relief inhaler in case it is needed to treat an asthma attack. An inhaler should also be kept at your child's school. If your child's symptoms are not eased by a single dose of a relief drug, a repeat dose should be taken. If that fails to improve the symptoms, call for an ambulance immediately or take your child to the nearest emergency department. It is important to remain calm and reassure your child. Once in the hospital, your child will probably be given oxygen and high doses of quick-relief drugs with a nebulizer to relieve the symptoms. He or she may need to stay in the hospital for several days to recover completely from a severe attack of asthma and may also require a course of corticosteroids and chest physiotherapy (p.961) to clear the mucus from the lungs.

SELF-HELP REDUCING THE RISK OF ASTHMA ATTACKS IN CHILDREN

Asthma attacks are often triggered by contact with allergy-producing substances, such as cat hair. By adopting simple measures, you can reduce the likelihood of your child having an attack.

- Do not allow people to smoke in the house.
- Do not keep furry animals or birds as pets.
- Dust furniture using a damp cloth and vacuum carpets regularly, if possible when your child is out of the house.
- Do not use fluffy, dust-collecting blankets and make sure pillows and comforters contain artificial fibers and not feathers.
- Enclose mattresses completely in plastic covers.
- If pollen is a problem, keep windows closed, especially while grass is releasing pollen, and use an air purifier.
- Avoid products that have strong odors, such as air fresheners, mothballs, and perfume.

WHAT IS THE PROGNOSIS?

Children with asthma are usually able to lead active lives through careful use of drugs and avoidance of trigger factors, such as animal fur. About half of all children with asthma grow out of the condition by the time they are teenagers. Asthma that persists past the age of 14 is likely to continue into adulthood (*see* ASTHMA, p.483).

Despite the ease with which asthma can be treated, severe asthma attacks cause many deaths each year. In most cases, fatalities are caused by a delay in getting an affected child to the hospital and a lack of understanding about potentially life-threatening symptoms.

WWW ONLINE SITES: p.1027, p.1028

Bronchiolitis

Inflammation of the small airways in the lungs caused by a viral infection

 AGE More common under age 12 months

 LIFESTYLE Parental smoking and living in overcrowded conditions are risk factors

 GENDER GENETICS Not significant factors

Bronchiolitis is a common and usually mild condition that mainly occurs in babies under age 12 months. The small airways in the lungs, called bronchioles, become inflamed due to a viral infection and restrict the flow of air in and out of the lungs. In about 9 in 10 cases, the infection is caused by a virus known as the respiratory syncytial virus. By age 2, almost all children in Canada have been infected with this virus. Most of those affected have only the symptoms of a common cold (p.286), but occasionally the infection leads to severe breathing difficulties. During the cold winter months, bronchiolitis usually occurs in epidemics. The risk of a child having bronchiolitis is higher if his or her family lives in overcrowded conditions, in which a viral infection can spread more quickly among people, or if the child's parents smoke.

What are the symptoms?

Initially, an affected child may have symptoms resembling a common cold, such as a runny nose, fever, and sneezing. However, the following symptoms may develop after 2–3 days:

- Dry cough.
- Rapid breathing.
- Wheezing.
- Feeding difficulties.

If your child is under 1 year old and has these symptoms, you should contact his or her doctor. Occasionally, babies may experience severe breathing difficulties, especially if they are very young or have an underlying problem such as congenital heart disease (p.836). These babies may become cyanotic, in which the tongue, lips, and skin become blue-tinged. In very small babies who have bronchiolitis, intervals of more than 10 seconds may occur between breaths.

You should call for an ambulance immediately if your baby is having difficulty breathing, if the tongue and lips or skin become blue-colored, or if he or she becomes drowsy at unexpected times because of the extra effort that is needed in order to breathe.

How is it diagnosed?

The doctor will probably suspect bronchiolitis from the symptoms and by listening to your child's chest with a stethoscope. A chest X-ray (p.490) may be arranged and the doctor may take samples of your child's nasal secretions to look for evidence of infection with the respiratory syncytial virus.

What is the treatment?

If the bronchiolitis is mild, you will probably be able to treat your child at home. The doctor may prescribe inhaled bronchodilators (p.910) to widen the airways and ease breathing. You will probably be advised to give your child liquid acetaminophen (*see* ANALGESICS, p.912) to bring down a fever. You can help relieve your child's breathing by increasing the humidity in his or her bedroom. This can be achieved by placing a wet towel or a dish of water in the room close to a source of heat, such as a radiator. You should give your child small, frequent drinks and feedings to make sure that he or she is receiving an adequate amount of fluids.

Children with severe symptoms must be treated in the hospital. They may be given an inhaled bronchodilator drug using a nebulizer, a device that delivers drugs in an aerosol form through a face mask. Intravenous fluids may be administered if the child is unable to feed. Oxygen is usually given, especially if a child is cyanotic. Preterm babies and those with problems such as congenital heart disease may be prescribed antiviral drugs (p.886), such as ribavirin, to treat the viral infection. These babies may need temporary mechanical ventilation to help them breathe.

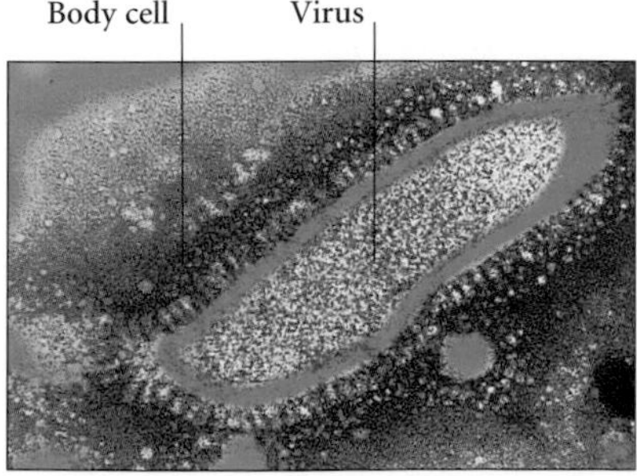
Body cell
Virus

Respiratory syncytial virus
This virus is the most common cause of bronchiolitis, in which small airways in the lungs are inflamed. In some cases, the infection causes severe breathing difficulties.

What is the prognosis?

Mild bronchiolitis usually improves within 5 days and clears up completely in about 10 days. Severe bronchiolitis may require several weeks of hospital treatment but causes no permanent damage. About half of affected children have recurrent wheezing over the next few years, which becomes worse when they have a cold. A vaccine has been developed but is not yet in routine use.

(WWW) ONLINE SITES: p.1028, p.1033

Croup

Inflammation and narrowing of the main airway (trachea) due to a viral infection

 AGE Most common between the ages of 6 months and 3 years

 GENDER Slightly more common in boys

 GENETICS LIFESTYLE Not significant factors

Croup is a common disorder that usually affects children between the ages of 6 months and 3 years. During an attack of croup, the airway that leads from the back of the throat to the lungs becomes inflamed because of a viral infection, restricting the flow of air and causing noisy breathing. Although symptoms are usually mild, croup may occasionally cause severe breathing difficulties that require treatment in the hospital. Boys appear to be more susceptible to the condition, but the reason for this is unknown. Croup occurs more frequently in the fall and winter months.

What are the symptoms?

Croup usually begins with the symptoms of a common cold, such as a runny nose. About 1–2 days later, the following symptoms may develop:

- Barking cough.
- Harsh, noisy breathing, particularly when inhaling.
- Hoarseness.

In severe cases, breathing may become rapid and difficult. This may cause a lack of oxygen, and lead to the development of a bluish color to the tongue and lips, a condition known as cyanosis. If cyanosis develops, you should contact the doctor immediately, and, if he or she is not available, call an ambulance.

WHAT MIGHT BE DONE?

Your child's doctor will probably diagnose croup from the symptoms. He or she will assess the severity of your child's condition and may suggest self-help measures to ease your child's breathing. For example, sitting with your child in a steamy bathroom can relieve minor breathing difficulties. You can increase the humidity in your child's room by placing a dish of water near a heat source, such as a radiator. Taking your child outside in the cool night air for a few minutes may also help. The doctor may prescribe an inhaled or oral corticosteroid (*see* CORTICOSTEROIDS FOR RESPIRATORY DISEASE, p.911) to reduce the inflammation in the airways. If symptoms are severe, your child will need to be admitted to the hospital. In rare cases, mechanical ventilation may also be necessary.

WHAT IS THE PROGNOSIS?

Most children with croup recover completely within a few days. However, the condition may recur until your child reaches about age 5. At this age, the airways are wider and therefore less likely to become severely narrowed by inflammation after an infection.

(WWW) ONLINE SITES: p.1028, p.1033

Epiglottitis

Inflammation of the epiglottis, a flap of cartilage that closes over the main airway to the lungs when food is swallowed

 AGE Most common between the ages of 1 and 6

 GENDER GENETICS LIFESTYLE Not significant factors

In this rare condition, the epiglottis, a flap of tissue that prevents food from entering the airways of the lungs, becomes inflamed due to infection. The inflammation causes the epiglottis to swell so that the main airway, the trachea, is partially blocked. The swelling may be so severe that the trachea is completely blocked and the child cannot breathe. This situation is life-threatening and requires urgent treatment.

Epiglottitis is caused by infection with the bacterium *Haemophilus influenzae* type b (Hib). Children aged 1–6 are most often affected. Epiglottitis is rare in Canada due to routine immunization (p.45) of babies against Hib infection.

WHAT ARE THE SYMPTOMS?

In most cases, the symptoms of epiglottitis develop suddenly over a period of 1–2 hours and may include:

- High fever.
- Severe sore throat.
- Difficulty swallowing.
- Saliva dribbling from the mouth.
- Restlessness and anxiety.
- Rapid, labored breathing.
- Harsh noise on inhaling.

If there is severe obstruction of the airway, your child may become short of oxygen, and his or her lips, tongue, and possibly skin may become blue-tinged. If your child develops difficulty swallowing or breathing, you should call for an ambulance without delay because immediate treatment is essential.

WHAT MIGHT BE DONE?

Initially, your most important role is to reassure your child and try to keep him or her calm. You should not attempt to examine your child's throat because this may cause further distress and result in further blockage of the airway. Your child will probably be more comfortable sitting upright with his or her chin jutting out to maintain an unobstructed flow of air into the lungs.

The doctor will probably make a diagnosis from your child's symptoms. Humidified oxygen will need to be given through a mask held near to his or her face. In the hospital, your child will probably be taken to the operating room and given an inhaled anesthetic so that a tube can be inserted into the main airway to keep it open. To maintain breathing, your child may need mechanical ventilation. To treat the Hib infection, your child will be given intravenous antibiotics (p.885).

WHAT IS THE PROGNOSIS?

Most children recover in about a week. The tube that keeps the airway open is usually removed after about 2–3 days. There are usually no long-term problems, and the condition does not recur.

(WWW) ONLINE SITES: p.1028

Enlarged adenoids

Enlargement of the adenoids, two areas of tissue at the back of the nasal cavity that form part of the body's defense system

 AGE More common under age 7

 GENETICS Sometimes runs in families

 GENDER LIFESTYLE Not significant factors

The adenoids, which are located at the back of the nasal cavity, consist of two areas of lymphatic tissue that form part of the body's defenses against infection. In some children, particularly those under the age of 7, the adenoids become enlarged, which may lead to difficulties with breathing and speech. This enlargement is sometimes a result of recurrent respiratory infections or caused by allergies. In other cases, the cause is unknown, but the condition does tend to run in families, suggesting a genetic factor. Infected adenoids are sometimes associated with infection of the tonsils (*see* TONSILLITIS, opposite page).

WHAT ARE THE SYMPTOMS?

In most children with enlarged adenoids, symptoms are mild and appear gradually. The symptoms may include:

- Breathing through the mouth and snoring during sleep.
- Persistently blocked or runny nose.
- Nasal-sounding voice.

Difficulty breathing may disturb your child's sleep, leading to fatigue and inability to concentrate. Enlarged adenoids may partially block one or both of the eustachian tubes, which connect the throat to the middle ear, causing recurrent middle ear infections (*see* ACUTE OTITIS MEDIA IN CHILDREN, p.860) or an accumulation of fluid in the middle ear that results in deafness (*see* CHRONIC SECRETORY OTITIS MEDIA, p.860).

WHAT MIGHT BE DONE?

The doctor will probably examine your child's throat and nasal cavity using a small angled mirror. If symptoms are mild, no treatment is required because adenoids shrink naturally with age. However, if your child has disrupted sleep, recurrent middle ear infections, or chronic secretory otitis media, the doctor may recommend a trial of a nasal steroid or surgical removal of the adenoids. The tonsils may also need to be removed at the same time (*see* TONSILLECTOMY AND ADENOIDECTOMY, right). A buildup of fluid in the middle ear may be relieved by inserting a tympanostomy tube (p.861) in the eardrum.

Symptoms tend to diminish as a child gets older. By adolescence, they have usually completely disappeared.

(WWW) ONLINE SITES: p.1028, p.1030

Tonsillitis

Inflammation of the tonsils, two areas of tissue at the back of the throat that form part of the body's defense system

 AGE More common under age 8

 GENETICS Sometimes runs in families

 GENDER LIFESTYLE Not significant factors

The tonsils are two areas of lymphatic tissue at the back of the throat that form part of the body's defenses against infection. A condition known as tonsillitis develops if the tonsils become inflamed and painful, usually as a result of respiratory infections. The infections may be caused either by viruses, such as those that cause the common cold (p.286), or bacteria, such as streptococci. Tonsillitis sometimes runs in families, suggesting that genetic factors may also be involved.

In children under age 8, tonsillitis is common because the tonsils are exposed to many infections for the first time. Children who have tonsillitis may also have enlarged adenoids (opposite page). Tonsils become smaller with age and therefore tonsillitis occurs far less frequently in adults (*see* PHARYNGITIS AND TONSILLITIS, p.479).

What are the symptoms?

The symptoms of tonsillitis usually develop over a period of 24–36 hours. Symptoms may include:

- Sore throat and discomfort when swallowing.
- Fever.
- Headache.
- Abdominal pain.
- Vomiting and/or diarrhea.
- Enlarged and tender lymph nodes in the neck.

TREATMENT

Tonsillectomy and adenoidectomy

Surgical removal of the tonsils is performed on children who have recurrent episodes of tonsillitis. Enlarged adenoids may also be removed at the same time if they are causing breathing difficulties and recurrent ear problems. The operation is performed in the hospital under general anesthesia. A child should be able to return home 1–2 days after the operation, and he or she should make a full recovery in about 2 weeks.

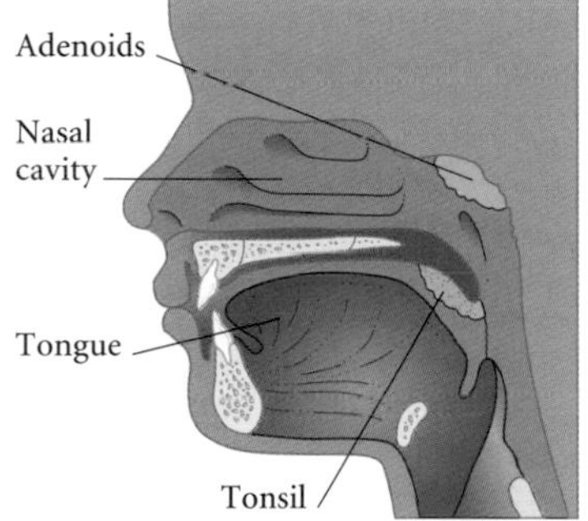
Adenoids
Nasal cavity
Tongue
Tonsil

The procedure
Surgical removal of the tonsils and adenoids is performed through the mouth under general anesthesia.

Babies and children who are too young to talk are unable to tell their parents they have a sore throat, but they may refuse to eat or drink because of the discomfort when swallowing. They may also be lethargic and irritable.

Tonsillitis is often associated with a middle ear infection (*see* ACUTE OTITIS MEDIA IN CHILDREN, p.860). Sometimes, an abscess called quinsy forms next to a tonsil. In young children, the rapid rise in fever at the start of tonsillitis may cause a child to have a convulsion (*see* FEBRILE CONVULSIONS, p.849).

What can I do?

You may be able to make your child more comfortable by adopting simple self-help measures at home. To bring down a fever, you can give your child liquid acetaminophen (*see* ANALGESICS, p.912) and sponge him or her down with tepid water (*see* BRINGING DOWN A FEVER, p.287). You should also encourage your child to drink small amounts of fluids at regular intervals, particularly if he or she has been vomiting. Cold, nonacidic drinks such as milk may relieve a sore throat, but you may find that older children prefer to have ice cream and popsicles. Older children may also find that sucking throat lozenges or gargling with warm salt water helps relieve a sore throat.

You should consult your child's doctor if self-help measures do not bring down the temperature, if your child is taking very little fluids, or if symptoms do not improve in 24 hours.

What might the doctor do?

The doctor will examine your child's throat and may take a swab to test for bacterial infection. He or she may also look inside your child's ears to check for an ear infection (*see* OTOSCOPY, p.597). If your child's doctor suspects a bacterial throat infection, a course of antibiotics (p.885) will be prescribed.

Most affected children recover fully in a few days. However, if your child is not drinking adequate fluids, he or she may become dehydrated and need to be admitted to the hospital for treatment with intravenous fluids and antibiotics. If quinsy has developed, the abscess may need to be surgically drained.

What is the prognosis?

Some children have frequent episodes of tonsillitis, but by age 8 these bouts are usually rare. If a child misses school regularly because of tonsillitis, the doctor may recommend surgical removal of the child's tonsils (*see* TONSILLECTOMY AND ADENOIDECTOMY, left).

(WWW) ONLINE SITES: p.1028, p.1030

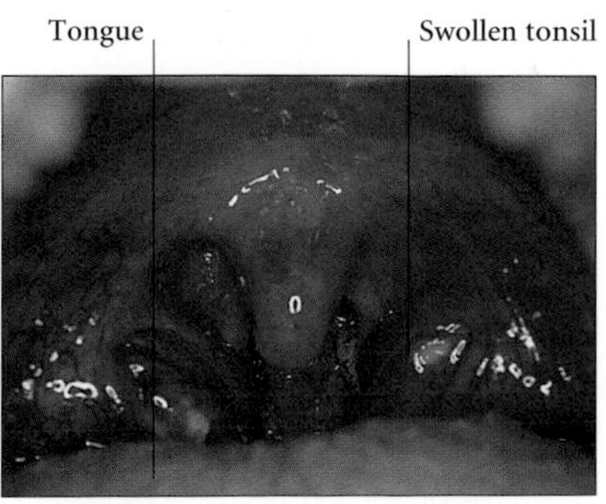
Tongue
Swollen tonsil

Tonsillitis
These tonsils have become swollen and inflamed as a result of an infection, a condition known as tonsillitis.

Disorders of the nervous system

The nervous system consists of the brain, the spinal cord, and the network of nerves that extends throughout the body. Serious disorders of this system are uncommon in children, although disabling conditions may be present from birth due to defects that occur during pregnancy. The nervous system is sometimes affected by minor disorders and, rarely, by infections and cancers.

Damage to the nervous system, either before birth or in early childhood, can result in varying degrees of physical disability. The first articles in this section describe defects that occur during development of the spinal cord and brain, causing disorders such as spina bifida and cerebral palsy.

Children are commonly affected by minor disorders of the nervous system, such as headache and migraine, which are described next. Migraine may be more difficult to recognize in young children than in adults because the main symptom is often abdominal pain rather than headache. Further articles discuss serious disorders of great concern to parents, including meningitis, which is a dangerous infection of the coverings of the brain and spinal cord, and Reye syndrome, an inflammation of the brain and liver. The final articles describe tumors of the brain and spinal cord, both of which are rare in children.

Epilepsy (p.524), which usually develops in childhood, is discussed in general nervous system disorders.

KEY ANATOMY

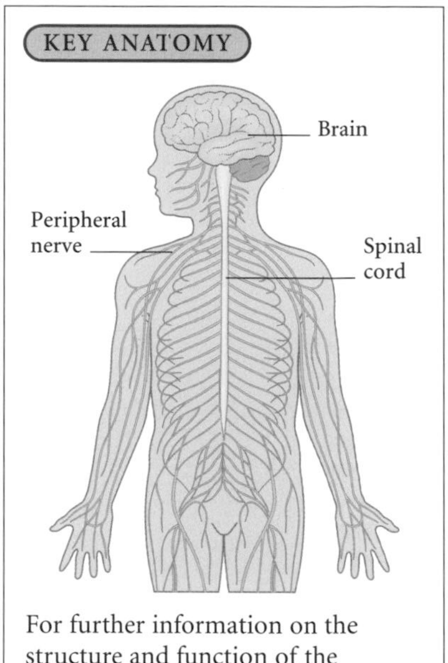
Brain
Peripheral nerve
Spinal cord

For further information on the structure and function of the nervous system, *see* pp.508–515.

Neural tube defects

Abnormalities of the brain and spinal cord and their protective coverings

 AGE Present from birth

 GENETICS Sometimes run in families

 LIFESTYLE Taking certain drugs during pregnancy is a risk factor

 GENDER Not a significant factor

Neural tube defects occur during pregnancy as a result of abnormalities in the embryo's development. The neural tube, which develops along the back of the embryo by about the third week of pregnancy, later becomes the brain, spinal cord, and their coverings. If this tube fails to close completely, defects in any of these parts can result.

Most commonly, the spinal cord and vertebrae are affected, causing a disorder known as spina bifida. The effects of spina bifida vary from a dimpling or tuft of hair at the base of the spine and a minor abnormality of the vertebrae to complete exposure of part of the spinal cord, known as a myelomeningocele. Rarely, the brain and skull are affected.

Since the discovery in 1992 that folic acid taken during early pregnancy provides protection against neural tube defects, spina bifida is becoming less common. The disorder currently affects only about 1 in 1,000 babies in the US.

The cause of neural tube defects is not completely understood, but they tend to run in families, suggesting that genetic factors are involved. Certain types of anticonvulsant drugs (p.914), such as sodium valproate, are associated with neural tube defects if they are taken during pregnancy.

What are the symptoms?

The symptoms of a neural tube defect depend upon its severity. Often, there are no obvious symptoms, and spina bifida may be diagnosed only when minor conditions, such as backache, occur in adult life. The symptoms of a severe defect become apparent at varying stages in childhood; they mainly affect the lower body and include:

- Paralysis or weakness of the legs.
- Absence of sensation in the legs.
- Abnormalities in the functioning of the bladder and bowels.

About 8 in 10 children who have severe spina bifida also have a buildup of fluid within the brain (*see* HYDROCEPHALUS, opposite page). Occasionally, learning difficulties may develop. In some cases, neural tube defects lead to meningitis, a serious infection of the membranes covering the brain and spinal cord (*see* MENINGITIS IN CHILDREN, p.848).

How is it diagnosed?

Currently, women are routinely offered a blood test at about 16 weeks into pregnancy to allow for an early diagnosis of severe neural tube defects. In addition, one or more ultrasound scans (*see* ULTRASOUND SCANNING IN PREGNANCY, p.793) are routinely performed 11–20 weeks into pregnancy to examine the fetus and to detect defects.

After birth, a baby who has a neural tube defect will probably have CT scanning (p.247) or MRI (p.248) of the spine to assess the severity of the defect.

What is the treatment?

If the defect is minor, no treatment is necessary. However, if a baby has a serious defect, he or she is likely to require surgery in the first few days after birth. If hydrocephalus is present, a drainage tube will probably be inserted to release excess fluid and prevent further fluid buildup in the cavities of the brain (*see* SHUNT FOR HYDROCEPHALUS, right).

Even with surgery, children who are born with severe defects will be permanently disabled and need lifelong care. Practical and emotional support will be provided for the whole family. An affected child often needs regular physiotherapy (p.961) to keep as mobile as possible, and some children may need a wheelchair. Training in the regular use of a urinary catheter may be necessary for children who cannot urinate normally (*see* BLADDER CATHETERIZATION, p.713). Some children may need special teaching. Many families find support through joining a self-help group.

CAN IT BE PREVENTED?

You can reduce the risk of your baby having a neural tube defect by supplementing your daily diet with folic acid throughout the first 3 months of your pregnancy. Ideally, you should begin to take folic acid daily while trying to conceive because neural tube defects can occur before you know that you are pregnant. Your doctor may suggest that you take a slightly higher dose if you already have an affected child. If a close blood relative has a neural tube defect, a couple who are planning a pregnancy may wish to seek genetic counseling (p.270) because their children may be at increased risk of the disorder.

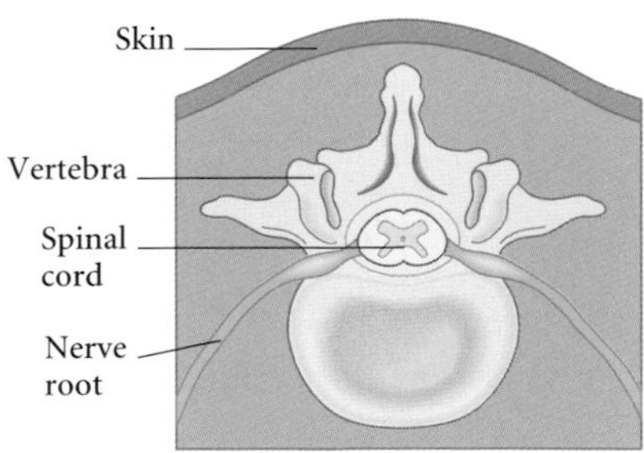
Skin
Vertebra
Spinal cord
Nerve root

NORMAL VERTEBRA

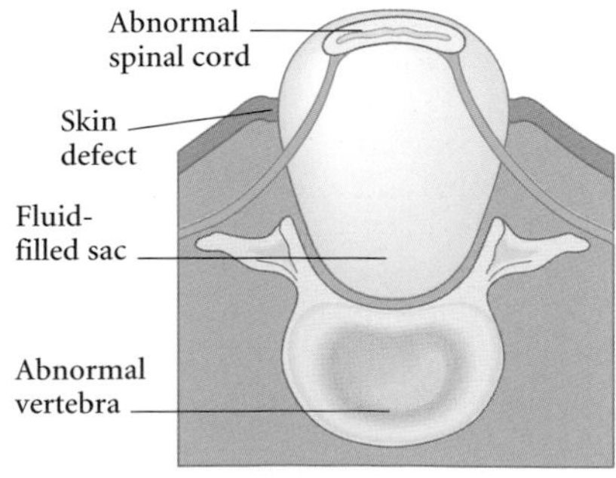
Abnormal spinal cord
Skin defect
Fluid-filled sac
Abnormal vertebra

MYELOMENINGOCELE

Neural tube defect

A myelomeningocele, a severe neural tube defect, occurs when the vertebrae are not fully formed. The spinal cord, contained in fluid-filled membranes, bulges outward through a defect in the skin.

TREATMENT SHUNT FOR HYDROCEPHALUS

A shunt is a drainage tube inserted into the brain to treat hydrocephalus, a disorder in which cerebrospinal fluid builds up in the brain cavities. The shunt diverts the excess fluid to another part of the body where it can be absorbed in the bloodstream. The fluid is released through a valve when pressure increases and drains into either the abdominal cavity or, rarely, a chamber in the heart.

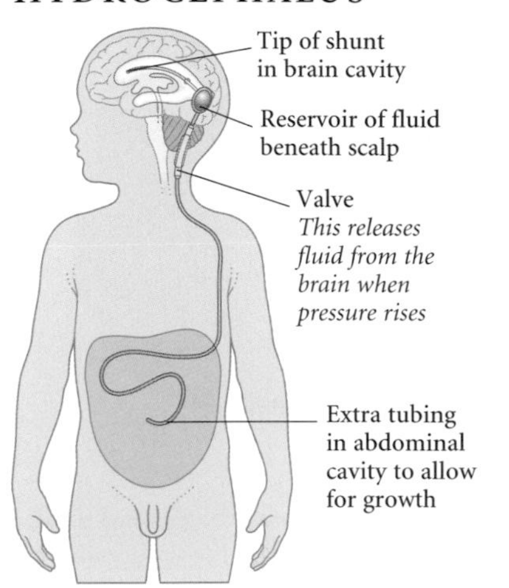
Tip of shunt in brain cavity
Reservoir of fluid beneath scalp
Valve
This releases fluid from the brain when pressure rises
Extra tubing in abdominal cavity to allow for growth

Inserting the shunt

The tip of the shunt is inserted through the skull into the fluid-filled cavity in the brain. The drainage tube is then passed under the skin and ends in the abdomen.

WHAT IS THE PROGNOSIS?

Children with only minor defects have a normal life expectancy. If symptoms affecting posture develop, there may be an increased risk of osteoarthritis (p.374). Children with extensive damage to the brain and/or the spinal cord may have a reduced life expectancy.

(WWW) ONLINE SITES: p.1027, p.1032, p.1037

Hydrocephalus

An abnormal buildup of fluid within the skull, also known as water on the brain

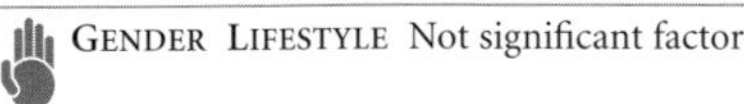

AGE GENETICS Risk factors depend on the cause

GENDER LIFESTYLE Not significant factors

Hydrocephalus is an uncommon condition that occurs mainly in preterm babies or with other disorders present from birth, such as spina bifida (*see* NEURAL TUBE DEFECTS, opposite page).

Cerebrospinal fluid (CSF) is produced in the cavities of the brain and flows around the brain and spinal cord, protecting them from injury. Hydrocephalus develops if CSF builds up in the cavities of the brain, causing them to enlarge. This buildup occurs when the system that drains the CSF away from the brain is damaged or blocked or if excess CSF is produced. In such cases, the resulting increase in pressure in the skull may lead to brain damage.

Hydrocephalus may be caused by a brain defect that is present from birth. The disorder also sometimes develops as a result of meningitis, an infection of the membranes covering the brain and spinal cord (*see* MENINGITIS IN CHILDREN, p.848), a brain tumor (*see* BRAIN AND SPINAL CORD TUMORS IN CHILDREN, p.850), or a head injury (p.521).

WHAT ARE THE SYMPTOMS?

The symptoms vary according to the age of the child, but the following may occur in all affected children:

- Vomiting.
- Drowsiness.
- Reluctance to settle down.

In young babies, the skull bones are not yet fused and are able to separate to some extent to accommodate excess fluid. For this reason, the first signs of hydrocephalus in babies may be an enlarged head that grows too fast and widening of the fontanelles (the soft areas on the top of a baby's skull). In older children with hydrocephalus, the head does not enlarge because the skull bones have fused, and headache due to pressure may be an early symptom.

Left untreated, hydrocephalus may lead to seizures and to cerebral palsy (p.846), in which movement and posture are affected. The disorder may also affect vision and hearing and can result in poor intellectual development.

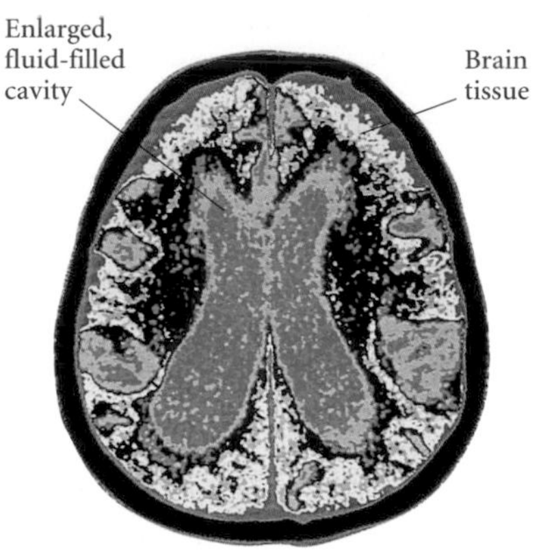
Enlarged, fluid-filled cavity
Brain tissue

Hydrocephalus
In this CT scan, the small cavities in the center of the brain have been enlarged by an abnormal buildup of fluid, a condition known as hydrocephalus.

HOW IS IT DIAGNOSED?

Hydrocephalus can sometimes be diagnosed during pregnancy with routine ultrasound scanning (*see* ULTRASOUND SCANNING IN PREGNANCY, p.793).

If the condition is suspected after birth, the doctor will arrange for ultrasound scanning (p.250) or CT scanning (p.247) of the child's head to look for obstructions or other abnormalities.

WHAT IS THE TREATMENT?

A child who has hydrocephalus usually needs surgery. During the operation, a narrow flexible tube, called a shunt, is inserted into a cavity in the brain to drain away the excess fluid (*see* SHUNT FOR HYDROCEPHALUS, p.845). The tube is normally left permanently in place.

In addition, the child's doctor may prescribe drugs that will slow down the production of CSF in the brain. Underlying causes of obstruction, such as a brain tumor, will be treated.

Some children with hydrocephalus are able to lead normal lives if they are given treatment before significant brain damage occurs. However, if the condition is severe or left untreated, resulting in physical disabilities or difficulties with learning, affected children and their families will need long-term practical and psychological support.

Parents who have a child with hydrocephalus may wish to consider genetic counseling (p.270) because there is an increased risk of the condition occurring in subsequent children.

(WWW) ONLINE SITES: p.1027, p.1032

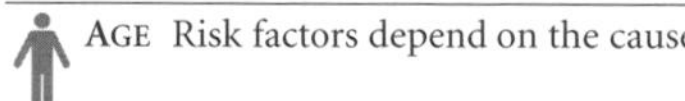

Cerebral palsy

Abnormalities of movement and posture caused by damage to the immature brain

AGE Risk factors depend on the cause

GENDER GENETICS LIFESTYLE Not significant factors

Cerebral palsy is not a specific disease but rather a general term used to describe a group of disorders affecting movement and posture. These disorders all result from damage to the developing brain, either before or during birth or during a child's early years. Children with cerebral palsy lack normal control of limbs and posture, but their intellect is often not affected. Although the brain damage does not progress, the disabilities it causes change as a child grows. Many children have hardly noticeable symptoms, whereas other children may be severely disabled.

WHAT ARE THE CAUSES?

In many cases of cerebral palsy, there is no obvious cause. However, the fetus can be damaged by an infection, such as rubella or cytomegalovirus, transmitted from the mother during pregnancy (*see* CONGENITAL INFECTIONS, p.817). Cerebral palsy may also result if a baby is deprived of oxygen during a difficult birth (*see* PROBLEMS DURING DELIVERY, p.802). The condition can develop in preterm babies, whose immature brains are often prone to abnormal bleeding (*see* PROBLEMS OF THE PRETERM BABY, p.816). During early childhood, cerebral palsy can develop after meningitis, an infection of the membranes around the brain (*see* MENINGITIS IN CHILDREN, p.848), or a head injury (p.521).

WHAT ARE THE SYMPTOMS?

If brain damage has occurred during pregnancy or birth, a newborn baby may be limp and unable to feed properly. Even if the symptoms are vague, such as a reluctance to settle down, parents may suspect that there is a problem from an early age. More commonly, symptoms do not appear until after 6 months of age and may include:

- Weakness or stiffness affecting one or more limbs.
- Reluctance to use a limb.
- Abnormal uncontrolled movements.
- Delay achieving normal milestones in development (*see* DEVELOPMENTAL DELAY, p.853).
- Problems swallowing.
- Speech difficulties.
- Chronic constipation (*see* CONSTIPATION IN CHILDREN, p.865).

Affected children often have vision disorders, such as squint (*see* STRABISMUS, p.857), and impaired hearing (*see* CONGENITAL DEAFNESS, p.859). About 1 in 4 children has a learning disability (*see* MENTAL RETARDATION, p.854).

ARE THERE COMPLICATIONS?

If a child with cerebral palsy has stiff limbs, he or she may experience difficulties walking and have an abnormal posture. The disorder can also increase the risk of dislocated joints, particularly the hips. Sometimes, children with cerebral palsy develop epilepsy (p.524). Behavioral problems may develop if a child becomes frustrated because of his or her physical disabilities and inability to communicate clearly. Children with severe cerebral palsy are particularly susceptible to chest infections because they cannot cough effectively.

WHAT MIGHT BE DONE?

The diagnosis of cerebral palsy is often difficult to make in a very young child. However, as a child becomes older, the symptoms become more obvious. Once the condition is suspected, tests such as CT scanning (p.247) or MRI (p.248) may be done to identify brain damage.

Once the diagnosis is confirmed, the whole family will need to adjust to the lifestyle changes that are often associated with caring for a child with

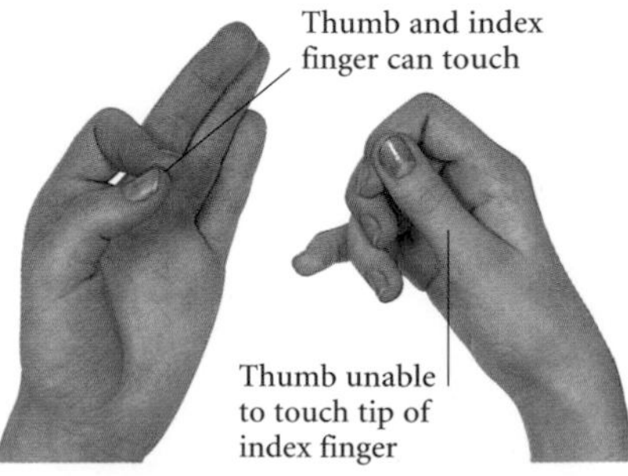
Thumb and index finger can touch
Thumb unable to touch tip of index finger
NORMAL
ABNORMAL

Poor coordination in cerebral palsy
A person with cerebral palsy often cannot coordinate movement in some parts of the body. The right hand shown here has poor coordination but the left hand is normal.

cerebral palsy. Many children have only mild disability, requiring some physiotherapy (p.961). Children with more severe disabilities usually require long-term programs of therapy and specialist support. The emphasis of such therapy and care is placed on assessing individual needs and helping a child achieve his or her maximum potential. Physiotherapy to encourage normal posture plays a major part in the care of an affected child. Parents can encourage a child to play in a way that exercises muscles and develops coordination.

If a child has only a minor physical disability, he or she may be able to attend a regular school. Children with more severe disabilities or whose intellectual ability is affected may benefit from special schooling.

Complications and problems associated with cerebral palsy will be treated as necessary. For example, if your child has impaired hearing, he or she may need a hearing aid. Caring for a disabled child at home is stressful, and occasional residential care or residential schools can provide respite.

WHAT IS THE PROGNOSIS?

Children with mild physical disabilities can usually lead active, full, and long lives and often live independently when adult. Severely disabled children, especially those with swallowing difficulties who are more prone to serious chest infections, have a lower life expectancy.

(WWW) ONLINE SITES: p.1035

Headache in children

Pain of variable severity affecting the head, sometimes due to an underlying disorder

AGE More common in school-age children

GENDER GENETICS LIFESTYLE Risk factors depend on the cause

Headaches are a common symptom in childhood, and about 9 in 10 children complain of at least one headache a year. Childhood headaches normally cause no more than temporary discomfort, but if severe or recurrent, may indicate an underlying disorder and require prompt medical treatment.

Young children, particularly those under age 5, are often unable to identify the precise location of pain. They may therefore complain of a headache when the problem is toothache, earache, or even a pain located farther away in the body, such as in the abdomen.

WHAT ARE THE CAUSES?

There are many causes of headaches in children, most of which are not serious. In older children especially, the reasons for most headaches are often similar to those in adults (*see* HEADACHE, p.518). However, parents may be understandably worried that their child is suffering from a serious illness such as meningitis, an inflammation of the membranes covering the brain (*see* MENINGITIS IN CHILDREN, p.848), or a brain tumor (*see* BRAIN AND SPINAL CORD TUMORS IN CHILDREN, p.850). These two disorders account for only a tiny percentage of childhood headaches, but it is important that parents are aware of the symptoms so that they know when they should seek medical advice (*see* SYMPTOM CHART 10: HEADACHE, p.110).

Short-lived headaches in children are usually caused by a viral infection, such as a common cold (p.286). These infections normally clear up within a few days without needing treatment. Many school-age children suffer from recurrent tension headaches (p.518). In most cases, these headaches last no longer than 24 hours and are sometimes related to emotional stress either at school or at home. Sometimes, problems with vision, such as nearsightedness (*see* MYOPIA, p.586), can cause persistent headaches. By age 15, about 1 in 20 children has experienced one or more attacks of migraine (*see* MIGRAINE IN CHILDREN, right).

WHAT CAN I DO?

If a severe headache occurs with vomiting or drowsiness, contact your child's doctor without delay. A child who has lost consciousness after a head injury, however briefly, should be taken to the hospital immediately. If the headache is mild, encourage your child to rest and relieve his or her discomfort with acetaminophen (*see* ANALGESICS, p.912).

If you suspect that your child has headaches because of tension, you may be able to help him or her by identifying the particular anxiety. Recurrent headaches that have no obvious cause should be investigated by the doctor.

WHAT MIGHT THE DOCTOR DO?

If the doctor cannot find a cause for concern following a physical examination of your child, further tests are not usually necessary. If the doctor suspects meningitis, he or she will have the child admitted to the hospital for immediate treatment. Rarely, your child may need CT scanning (p.247) or MRI (p.248) of the brain to investigate an injury or rule out the presence of a tumor.

If your child is normally well but has regular headaches, the doctor may refer him or her to an ophthalmologist because an eye test may be needed to exclude vision problems.

(WWW) ONLINE SITES: p.1028, p.1032

Migraine in children

Recurring symptoms that may include headache and abdominal pain

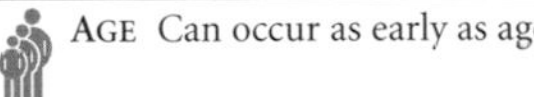
AGE Can occur as early as age 2

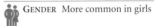

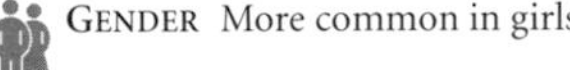
GENDER More common in girls

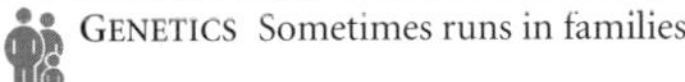
GENETICS Sometimes runs in families

LIFESTYLE May be triggered by certain foods, fumes, and perfume

Migraine is a significant cause of headache in children, particularly girls, and by the age of 15 about 1 in 20 children has experienced an attack. The condition is known to occur in children as young as 2 years. However, childhood migraine often differs from migraine experienced by adults, and the disorder can sometimes be difficult to recognize. In younger children, the symptoms of migraine frequently include recurrent episodes of abdominal pain, and the one-sided headaches and nausea that are typical of the condition in adults (*see* MIGRAINE, p.518) may not occur.

WHAT ARE THE CAUSES?

Why some children develop migraine is not fully understood, but the condition sometimes runs in families, which suggests that genetic factors may be involved. Migraine is thought to be due to changes in the blood flow through the blood vessels inside the skull. There may also be temporary alterations in chemicals in the brain, which are probably responsible for triggering some of the symptoms elsewhere in the body.

Certain substances are known to trigger attacks of migraine. These include food, commonly chocolate, cheese, citrus fruits, and red wine, and inhaled substances such as perfume, gasoline fumes, and tobacco smoke. Weather changes can be a trigger.

What are the symptoms?

In children under age 8, the symptoms of migraine may not include headache. Symptoms develop gradually over a few hours, and a child may experience:

- Pain in the center of the abdomen.
- Pale skin.
- Fatigue.
- Vomiting.

Often, these symptoms persist for several days. If children continue to have attacks of migraine as they grow older, they are likely to have symptoms more similar to those experienced by adults. These symptoms develop over a few hours and may include:

- Visual disturbances, such as seeing flashing lights.
- Headache on one or both sides.
- Nausea and vomiting.
- Dislike of bright lights.

Rarely, a child may experience temporary weakness in one arm or leg.

What might be done?

Your child's doctor may be able to diagnose migraine from the symptoms. Occasionally, he or she may arrange for tests, such as CT scanning (p.247) or MRI (p.248) of the head, or, in young children, ultrasound scanning of the abdomen to exclude other disorders.

Resting in bed in a darkened room may help your child feel better. Analgesics (p.912) will also help relieve a headache or abdominal pain. If symptoms are severe, your child's doctor may suggest specialized drugs (*see* ANTI-MIGRAINE DRUGS, p.913). Drugs such as beta blockers (p.898) may also be prescribed as long-term treatment to help prevent continuing attacks. Your child's diet may also be reviewed by a dietitian to identify foods that may trigger attacks.

With treatment, the symptoms of childhood migraine can usually be controlled. Often, the condition disappears completely in later childhood, although in some cases attacks of migraine continue throughout adulthood.

(WWW) ONLINE SITES: p.1028, p.1032

Meningitis in children

Inflammation of the membranes that cover the brain and spinal cord, usually caused by a bacterial or viral infection

LIFESTYLE Living in close communities is a risk factor

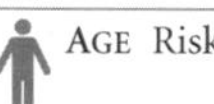

AGE Risk factors depend on the cause

GENDER GENETICS Not significant factors

Meningitis is a serious infection of the meninges (the membranes that cover the brain and spinal cord). The infection can be caused by either bacteria or a virus. Bacterial meningitis is a potentially fatal condition. About 8 in 10 cases of bacterial meningitis occur in children under age 5, and the disease is a cause of great concern to many parents. Outbreaks of the infection occasionally occur in communities where children are in close contact with one another, such as daycare centers and schools.

Meningitis that is caused by a virus is a much less severe condition and is rarely life-threatening.

What are the causes?

Infection with *Haemophilus influenza* type b (Hib) used to be the main cause of bacterial meningitis in early childhood. This infection has now become rare in the developed world since the introduction in 1993 of immunization (p.45) against Hib infections. In Canada, the most common overall cause of bacterial meningitis in both adults and children is *Streptococcus pneumoniae,* while in the age group 2–18 years most infections are due to *Neisseria meningitidis* (meningococcus). Rarely, meningitis is caused by the bacterium that causes tuberculosis (p.491).

Viral meningitis can be caused by a number of different viruses, including those responsible for chickenpox (p.288) and mumps (p.291).

What are the symptoms?

The symptoms of bacterial and viral meningitis are similar. However, bacterial meningitis tends to develop much more rapidly, often causing severe illness within a few hours. Unlike adults, young children, especially those aged under 2 months, may not have obvious symptoms, and it is often difficult to distinguish the disease from other less serious infections. Symptoms likely to appear in young children may include:

- Fever.
- Drowsiness or restlessness and high-pitched crying.
- Vomiting and/or diarrhea.
- Reluctance to feed.
- In meningococcal meningitis, a distinctive rash of flat, reddish purple lesions varying in size from pinheads to large patches that do not fade when pressed (*see* CHECKING A RED RASH, p.129).

Older children may, in addition, have the characteristic symptoms of meningitis in adults, which are:

- Severe headache.
- Neck stiffness.
- Dislike of bright lights.

If bacterial meningitis is left untreated, seizures may develop, followed by loss of consciousness, coma (p.522), and eventually death. In rare cases, a collection of pus may form in the brain (*see* BRAIN ABSCESS, p.529).

What might be done?

A child with meningitis needs immediate hospital treatment, often in a critical care unit. The diagnosis can be confirmed by a lumbar puncture (p.527), in which a sample of fluid is removed from around the spinal cord.

While waiting for the result of the test, your child will be given treatment with one or more intravenous antibiotics (p.885) if bacterial meningitis is suspected. The antibiotics will be discontinued if the cerebrospinal fluid from the lumbar puncture does not confirm bacterial meningitis. Intravenous fluids will be given to your child to prevent dehydration, and anticonvulsant drugs (p.914) may be prescribed if he or she develops seizures.

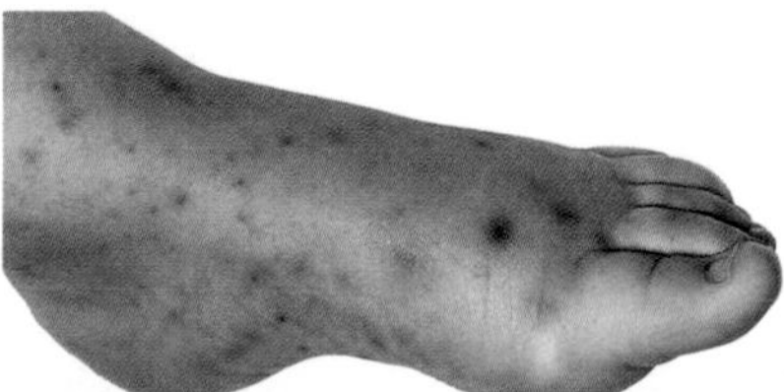

Rash of meningococcal meningitis
This distinctive rash, which can develop anywhere on the body and does not disappear when pressed, is often a hallmark of meningococcal meningitis.

Close contacts, such as immediate family and children in the same class as your child, may be given oral antibiotics as a precaution.

What is the prognosis?

Children with viral meningitis usually recover fully in about 2 weeks. Bacterial meningitis is fatal in about 1 in 20 children. About 1 in 4 children who recovers from bacterial meningitis is affected with serious long-term problems such as impaired hearing or epilepsy (p.524).

(WWW) ONLINE SITES: p.1028, p.1033

Febrile convulsions

Seizures caused by a high fever as a result of infection in a part of the body other than the brain

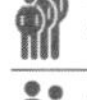
AGE Most common between the ages of 6 months and 5 years

GENDER Slightly more common in boys

GENETICS Sometimes runs in families

LIFESTYLE Not a significant factor

A febrile convulsion is the most common type of seizure in childhood and may affect as many as 1 in 20 children. The disorder occurs slightly more often in boys. Usually, a febrile convulsion occurs in the first 24 hours of a viral infection, such as a sore throat or common cold (p.286). Sometimes, a seizure may occur in association with a bacterial infection, such as an infection of the ears or upper respiratory tract. The convulsion develops in response to a rapid increase in body temperature that triggers an abnormal burst of electrical activity in the cells of the child's brain.

A febrile convulsion causes jerking body movements and is alarming for parents. However, the disorder is rarely serious, and it does not indicate a brain defect or epilepsy (p.524). Febrile convulsions tend to run in families.

What are the symptoms?

You may notice that your child initially becomes limp. The symptoms that follow usually include:

- Loss of consciousness.
- Stiffening of the arms and legs and arching of the back.
- Abnormal movements of the limbs.
- Rolling upward of the eyes.
- A pause in breathing for a few seconds, which may result in a blue tinge to the skin.

A febrile convulsion usually lasts about 2–4 minutes and always less than 15 minutes. Your child will probably fall asleep afterward. If your child has a seizure of any kind, you should contact the child's doctor immediately. If the convulsion lasts for longer than 5 minutes, call an ambulance at once.

What can I do?

You should not try to restrain a child who is having a febrile convulsion but protect him or her from injury by placing nearby objects out of reach and surrounding the child with pillows or rolled up towels. After the convulsion is over, sponging the child all over with tepid water helps bring down a fever, but he or she should not be made too cool (*see* FIRST AID: FEBRILE CONVULSIONS, p.989). When awake enough to be able to swallow, the child should be given a dose of liquid acetaminophen (*see* ANALGESICS, p.912), which also helps lower body temperature.

What might the doctor do?

The convulsion is usually over by the time the doctor sees your child. He or she will perform a physical examination and make sure that your child's temperature is coming down. The doctor may arrange for admission to the hospital, particularly if the child's temperature remains high. A sample of cerebrospinal fluid may be extracted from around the spine (*see* LUMBAR PUNCTURE, p.527) to check that the seizure was not caused by meningitis (*see* MENINGITIS IN CHILDREN, opposite page). Other tests, such as urine tests or throat swabs, may be performed to look for a bacterial infection.

If your child has a febrile convulsion lasting for longer than a few minutes or has had two or more convulsions, he or she may need to be given anticonvulsant drugs (p.914). The doctor will prescribe antibiotics (p.885) if a bacterial infection is present. Up to 1 in 3 children who have had a febrile convulsion will have another within a year. About 2–6 percent of affected children will go on to develop epilepsy in later life.

(WWW) ONLINE SITES: p.1028, p.1031, p.1033

Reye syndrome

A rare illness in which there is sudden inflammation of the brain and liver

AGE Most common between the ages of 5 and 10

LIFESTYLE Taking aspirin in childhood is a risk factor

GENDER GENETICS Not significant factors

Reye syndrome is an extremely rare disorder. The condition causes sudden inflammation of the brain (*see* VIRAL ENCEPHALITIS, p.528) and the liver (*see* ACUTE HEPATITIS, p.644) and can be fatal. It almost always occurs in children under the age of 10. The exact cause of Reye syndrome is not known, but it is thought that in some cases the disorder may be associated with a viral infection, such as chickenpox (p.288). Aspirin is linked to Reye syndrome and its use is no longer recommended for children under the age of 12. Exposure to certain insecticides is also believed to trigger Reye syndrome.

The symptoms develop very rapidly over a few hours and may include vomiting, drowsiness, and seizures. As the disorder progresses, there may be loss of consciousness, coma (p.522), and eventually cessation of breathing.

What might be done?

If a child is very sick, he or she will be admitted to a critical care unit. Tests will be done to confirm the diagnosis, including blood tests to assess liver function, a tracing of the electrical activity in the brain (*see* EEG, p.525), and CT scanning (p.247) or MRI (p.248) of the brain in order to look for swelling. In addition, a sample of the liver may be removed for further examination (*see* LIVER BIOPSY, p.647).

There is no specific cure for Reye syndrome, but supportive treatment, such as mechanical ventilation, will be given until the condition improves. More than half of all children with Reye syndrome recover spontaneously. However, for those who lapse into a deep coma, the prognosis is poor, and the condition may be fatal. In some cases, Reye syndrome leads to long-term developmental problems, such as speech and learning difficulties.

(WWW) ONLINE SITES: p.1028

Brain and spinal cord tumors in children

Abnormal growths in the brain or spinal cord that are usually cancerous

 AGE More common under age 1

 GENDER Slightly more common in boys

 GENETICS The underlying cause may be inherited

 LIFESTYLE Not a significant factor

Tumors of the brain and spinal cord are rare in children but still account for almost 1 in 4 cases of all childhood cancers. The disorder is more common in boys. Most of these tumors originate in the nerve cells of the brain or spine or in the cells surrounding the nerves. The tumors are usually cancerous but rarely spread elsewhere. The cause of such tumors is not fully understood, but the risk is increased if a child has the inherited disorder neurofibromatosis (p.827), in which tumors grow along the nerves.

WHAT ARE THE SYMPTOMS?

The symptoms of brain tumors usually develop gradually. At first, there may be only vague symptoms, such as failure to gain weight in babies or unsatisfactory performance at school in older children. Brain tumors are therefore often not diagnosed until they are quite large, when symptoms may include:

- Headache and vomiting, especially in the morning.
- Clumsiness and unsteadiness.
- Abnormal alignment of the eyes (*see* STRABISMUS, p.857).
- Change in personality.

Sometimes, excess fluid builds up in the brain cavities (*see* HYDROCEPHALUS, p.845). If a tumor is in the spinal cord the symptoms may include:

- Back pain.
- Inability to urinate.
- Difficulty walking.

Children with back pain should be seen by a doctor as soon as possible.

WHAT MIGHT BE DONE?

If the doctor is concerned that a child may have a brain or spinal cord tumor, he or she will arrange for imaging tests such as CT scanning (p.247) or MRI (p.248) to look for abnormalities. If a tumor is found, a small piece of tissue may be removed under general anesthesia for microscopic examination.

Once the diagnosis has been confirmed, surgery is usually performed to remove the tumor. Radiation therapy (p.279) may also be given, but, because it can affect the normal development of the brain in young children, a reduced dosage is given to children who are under age 3. In some cases, chemotherapy (p.278) may be given. If there is an accumulation of excess fluid around the brain, a small tube may be inserted to drain the fluid into the abdomen (*see* SHUNT FOR HYDROCEPHALUS, p.845).

If a child has a tumor, a team of professionals will be available to offer his or her whole family psychological support (*see* COUNSELING, p.971).

WHAT IS THE PROGNOSIS?

Although brain and spinal tumors are serious and often diagnosed late, 1 in 2 children is alive 5 years after diagnosis. The prognosis depends on the type of tumor. Some children who survive after treatment may have long-term physical disabilities or learning problems.

WWW ONLINE SITES: p.1028

Neuroblastoma

A cancerous tumor that develops from nervous tissue, often in the adrenal gland

 AGE More common under age 5

 GENDER Slightly more common in boys

 GENETICS May be due to an abnormal gene

 LIFESTYLE Not a significant factor

Although rare, neuroblastomas are still the most common cancerous tumors in children under 1 year. The disorder is slightly more common in boys. Most of these tumors originate from nerve tissue that has not developed beyond the embryonic stage. Neuroblastomas may occur in the abdomen or, less commonly, in the chest or pelvic cavity and often spread elsewhere. One-third of all neuroblastomas develop in the adrenal glands, above the kidneys. The cause of these tumors is not known, although a genetic factor is thought to be involved.

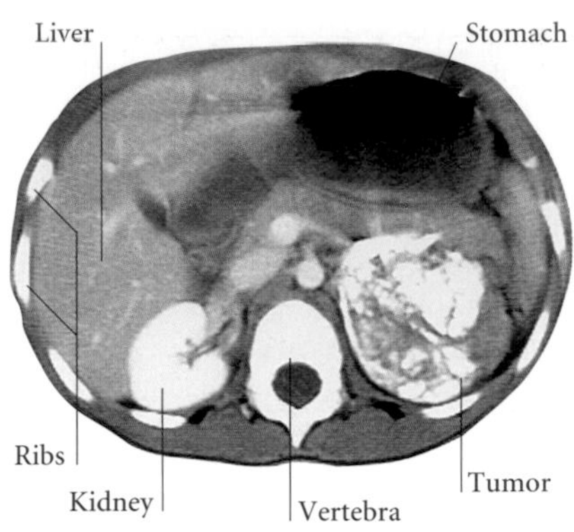
Liver
Stomach
Ribs
Kidney
Vertebra
Tumor

Neuroblastoma

This cross-sectional CT scan of a child's upper abdomen shows a neuroblastoma that has developed from the nervous tissue in one of the adrenal glands.

WHAT ARE THE SYMPTOMS?

The symptoms of neuroblastoma may be present from birth or develop gradually in childhood. They may include:

- Lump in the abdomen.
- Painless, bluish lumps on the skin.
- Fatigue.
- "Dancing" eye movements.

If a neuroblastoma spreads through the body, other symptoms may occur, such as bone pain, or, if the lymph nodes are affected, swellings in the neck or armpits. Anemia (p.446) may result if the cancer spreads to the bone marrow.

WHAT MIGHT BE DONE?

If the doctor suspects a neuroblastoma, he or she may arrange for a urine test to check for substances that indicate the presence of a tumor. The diagnosis is confirmed by a biopsy, in which a tissue sample is removed for examination. MRI (p.248) or radionuclide scanning (p.251) may be needed to find out if the cancer has spread elsewhere. A bone marrow aspiration and biopsy (p.451) may also be performed to look for the spread of cancer to the bones. If possible, the tumor is removed surgically. Chemotherapy (p.278) and radiation therapy (p.279) may also be necessary.

If a tumor has not spread, about 9 in 10 children remain well 5 years after surgery. When a tumor has spread, the prognosis is poor, with only about 2 in 10 children surviving more than a year after the diagnosis. In babies under 1 year, neuroblastomas sometimes disappear without requiring treatment.

WWW ONLINE SITES: p.1028

DEVELOPMENTAL AND PSYCHOLOGICAL DISORDERS

A child's development is a continuous process, marked by identifiable advances in skills and behavior. The rate at which an individual develops is influenced by many factors, including the family environment and physical health. In some children, psychological disorders may cause developmental delays.

If a child has persistent problems with basic aspects of daily living, such as sleeping, eating, and toilet training, the effects can be very disruptive to the family. The first three articles in this section describe the types of minor behavior problems that commonly occur in children. These difficulties can often be overcome with simple self-help measures, and most will eventually cease as a child matures. Only rarely do such behaviors indicate underlying psychological problems.

A further article covers the more serious problems that may be caused by autism spectrum disorders, which result in failure to develop normal communication and social skills. Autism, which may be linked to brain abnormalities, is a lifelong condition, but its effects can usually be reduced by appropriate education and therapy.

The next articles describe several disorders that may delay children's achievement of certain developmental milestones. These disorders range from mental retardation, which can affect all areas of ability, to specific learning disabilities and speech difficulties in an otherwise normal child.

Attention deficit hyperactivity disorder and conduct disorder are covered in the last two articles. These disorders usually have underlying medical, psychiatric, or social causes. Affected children usually respond to skilled guidance and therapy.

Sleeping problems in children

Disturbed sleep at night, often leading to a disruption of family life

AGE More common under age 5

LIFESTYLE A stressful home life is a risk factor

GENDER GENETICS Not significant factors

Many children sleep through the night by the age of 12 months, but about 1 in 3 children has frequent wakeful nights until age 5 or later. Sleeping problems rarely cause ill health but may disrupt family life and can affect school performance in older children.

Disrupted sleep in children is usually temporary and may occur only because of a lack of or change to routine. Sleeping problems may also be related to illnesses, particularly those causing a high temperature, or to anxiety, such as that caused by family quarrels.

WHAT ARE THE TYPES?

Sleeping problems in children take various forms. In toddlers, one of the most common problems is an inability to settle down and go to sleep after being left alone at bedtime. Such restlessness is sometimes caused by anxiety about separation from a parent. Difficulty settling down can also be due to a noisy environment or fear of the dark. The problem may simply be due to bedtime being too early; children vary in the amount of sleep they need.

Most children wake briefly several times during the night without needing attention. However, sometimes sudden wakefulness is caused by nightmares, particularly in children about age 5. Nightmares are commonly triggered by frightening or unusual experiences and, if they occur frequently, may be a sign that a child has a particular worry.

Night terrors are another type of sudden sleep disturbance, which may sometimes occur for no apparent reason. During an episode of terror, a child experiences acute fear and may scream and cry. Although the child appears to be awake, he or she is still asleep. If a child wakes from a night terror, he or she usually has little or no memory of the episode. Terrors usually occur about 2 hours after falling asleep and last a few minutes only. Just before a night terror, a child may appear restless.

Sleepwalking most often occurs in children between the ages of 6 and 12. A sleepwalking child will get out of bed and wander around aimlessly, usually finding his or her own way back to bed.

WHAT MIGHT BE DONE?

Simple measures are often effective in overcoming a sleeping problem. You should try to establish regular routines, with a bath and a story at the same time every night. There is no need to go to a child as soon as he or she cries; often, the crying will stop within a few minutes. If you think that poor sleeping or nightmares are related to an underlying anxiety, such as a frightening television program or family stress, you should discuss the problem with your child.

If your child has night terrors, it may be possible to wake him or her in the restless period that precedes the terror. Once a terror begins, there is little you can do except stay with the child until the fear recedes. In the case of sleepwalking, try not to wake the child but gently guide him or her back to bed.

You should consult the doctor if your child's sleep problem disrupts the family or if you think that frequent nightmares or night terrors have a particular cause.

In most cases, providing a child with reassurance and introducing a routine will help establish a normal sleeping pattern within a few weeks. Most children eventually learn to settle down at night and will outgrow nightmares, night terrors, or sleepwalking. By the age of 8, few children have sleeping problems.

(WWW) ONLINE SITES: p.1028, p.1037

Eating problems in children

Changes in eating behavior that may indicate psychological stress

 LIFESTYLE A stressful home environment is a risk factor

 AGE GENDER Risk factors depend on the type

 GENETICS Not a significant factor

Eating problems in childhood are very common, affecting about 1 in 10 young children. Usually, the problem is part of growing up and disappears as the child matures. However, persistent problems may be linked to stresses in family life.

What are the types?

Some children appear to eat too little or are fussy about their food. Other children may overeat or have cravings for strange nonfood substances.

Refusing food is often the way in which toddlers try to assert their independence, and the problem is serious only if normal growth or weight gain is affected. Food refusal in older children may be due to emotional distress and, in severe cases, may be a sign of anorexia nervosa (p.562), particularly in girls. Loss of appetite is not the same as food refusal and is common during childhood illnesses. Sometimes, loss of appetite may also be caused by anxiety.

Fussy eating habits affect about 1 in 4 children of school age. The fussy child insists on eating only certain foods, but dietary problems rarely occur unless the range of foods is very narrow.

Pica is a craving to eat nonfood substances, such as soil, coal, or chalk. This disorder can sometimes be hazardous. For example, licking or eating certain types of paint can cause severe lead poisoning. Pica usually occurs in children who have other behavioral problems and is possibly associated with a nutritional deficiency, such as a lack of iron.

Overeating commonly leads to obesity. A child may eat for comfort if he or she feels neglected or insecure.

What might be done?

If your child is reluctant to eat, there are practical ways in which you can help (*see* ENCOURAGING YOUR CHILD TO EAT, left). However, if the child fails to gain weight, loses weight, or has pica, you should consult your child's doctor. If the problem is due to anxiety or emotional distress, the doctor may refer your child to a child psychologist or psychiatrist.

(WWW) ONLINE SITES: p.1028, p.1035

SELF-HELP

Encouraging your child to eat

If your child is overly fussy about certain food or refuses to eat, the following hints may be helpful:

- Keep the atmosphere relaxed at mealtimes. Do not put pressure on your child to eat everything on his or her plate.
- Serve small portions. You can always give second helpings.
- Avoid too many snacks and excessive fluids between meals.
- Be imaginative when preparing food. Cut sandwiches into decorative shapes and create "pictures" on the plate with fruit and vegetables.
- Do not persist in offering rejected foods. Keep them off the menu for a week or two.
- Avoid distractions, such as toys or television, at mealtimes.

Encopresis

Inappropriate defecation after the age at which bowel control is usually attained

 AGE Considered abnormal only after about age 4

 GENDER More common in boys

 LIFESTYLE Stress is a risk factor

 GENETICS Not a significant factor

Most children have bowel control by age 3. If a child is still soiling by age 4, there may be a psychological or physical reason. Soiling problems, which are more common in boys, are known as encopresis. Sometimes, the behavior is simply the result of inadequate toilet training. However, children occasionally begin soiling again after successful training. The most common cause of this recurrence is an overflow of liquid feces from above a hard constipated stool (*see* CONSTIPATION IN CHILDREN, p.865). Some children frequently pass normal feces in unacceptable places, such as behind furniture. This soiling may be related to emotional stress.

What might be done?

A sympathetic approach to encopresis is vital, because scolding and criticizing a child often makes the problem worse. Usually, patient toilet training is all that is required. If you suspect that your child is constipated, you should change his or her diet to include more fiber.

If simple measures are not effective, you should consult your child's doctor. In the case of severe constipation, the doctor will probably advise on diet and may prescribe laxatives (p.924). Causes of emotional distress can often be identified after discussion with the child.

Encopresis usually disappears with unhurried toilet training, once constipation has been treated or emotional problems have been addressed.

(WWW) ONLINE SITES: p.1028

Autism spectrum disorders

Severely impaired development of normal communication and social skills

 AGE Usually develop before age 3

 GENDER More common in boys

 GENETICS Sometimes run in families

 LIFESTYLE Not a significant factor

Autism was first identified in 1943 and is now known to affect about 1 in 1,000 people in Canada. The disorder, which more commonly occurs in boys, takes varying forms known as autism spectrum disorders. Affected children have a wide range of symptoms. In general, there is a failure to develop language and communication skills, inability to form normal social relationships, and a marked need to follow routines.

At least 2 in 3 children with autism also have mental retardation (p.854). Rarely, affected children have normal or above average intelligence, a form of autism known as Asperger's disorder.

Autism spectrum disorders are possibly caused by abnormalities of the brain. The disorders sometimes run in families, which suggests that genetic factors may be involved. About 1 in 10 autistic children has a genetic abnormality, such as fragile X syndrome (p.822).

What are the symptoms?

Some autistic children show symptoms from birth, such as arching the back to avoid physical contact. In infancy, a child may bang his or her head against the side of the crib. Other children with autism appear normal until they are about 12–18 months, when the following symptoms become apparent:

- Failure to develop normal speech.
- Absence of normal facial expression and body language.
- Lack of eye contact.
- Tendency to spend time alone.
- Lack of imaginative play.
- Repetitive behavior, such as rocking and hand flapping.
- Obsession with specific objects or particular routines.
- Severe learning difficulties.

Rarely, an autistic child has an exceptional skill, such as a particular aptitude for technical drawing, mathematics, or playing a musical instrument. About 1 in 3 affected children develops epilepsy (p.524). Children who have Asperger's disorder may develop normal speech and language but have difficulty communicating with other people. These children are also rigid in their behavior and cannot tolerate changes in routine.

Are there complications?

Autism spectrum disorders have a devastating effect on family life. Bringing up an autistic child can be stressful, especially when the child is unable to show normal responsiveness and affection. Parents may find it difficult to take the child to public places because of his or her unusual or difficult behavior. Other children in the family may feel neglected because an affected sibling needs so much attention. A child with autism may also be at risk of self-harm.

What might be done?

Autism spectrum disorders are often first identified by parents who notice that their child's behavior is different from that of other children in the same age group. The disorders are diagnosed from the symptoms and there are no specific tests to confirm the diagnosis. However, if fragile X syndrome or another genetic disorder is suspected, blood tests may be performed to look for the genetic abnormality.

There is no cure for autism spectrum disorders. Treatment normally includes education designed to maximize a child's potential. Language and speech therapy (p.963) help develop communication skills. Behavior therapy (p.969) can help replace abnormal behaviors with more appropriate ones. Occupational therapy may improve physical and sensory skills. A highly structured daily routine is usually recommended.

What is the prognosis?

Most children with autism spectrum disorders cannot lead independent lives and need long-term care, either from their parents or in a residential home. Some children with Asperger's disorder are academically successful, although they may always have poor social skills.

(WWW) ONLINE SITES: p.1027

Developmental delay

Delay of a child in achieving the abilities expected at a particular age

 AGE Usually apparent by age 5

 LIFESTYLE Lack of stimulation is a risk factor

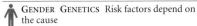

 GENDER GENETICS Risk factors depend on the cause

There are significant stages in the first few years of life, known as developmental milestones, when a child is normally expected to have acquired certain basic physical, intellectual, and social abilities. Children achieve these milestones at different ages but usually within an established typical age range. Failure to reach the milestones within this range is known as developmental delay.

What are the types?

Delays may be of varying severity and can affect one or more area of development. Children are usually mobile by about 9 months, and most are walking by 15 months. A delay in walking frequently runs in families and often has no obvious cause; most children catch up eventually and continue to develop normally. However, children who have a severe underlying disability, such as cerebral palsy (p.846), will have long-term difficulties with mobility.

Some children are slow to develop movements that involve good hand–eye coordination or fine control, such as catching a ball or holding a pencil. These children must be followed carefully because they are at risk of experiencing specific learning disabilities (p.854) during their school years.

Delay in speech and language ranges from minor difficulties in increasing vocabulary (*see* SPEECH AND LANGUAGE DIFFICULTIES, p.854) to the severe communication problems often associated with autism spectrum disorders (opposite page). Sometimes, delay is due to lack of stimulation in the child's environment. Hearing impairment, which can be due to disorders such as chronic secretory otitis media (p.860), may also be a cause of delayed development in speech and language skills.

Certain basic accomplishments, such as learning to use the toilet unaided, are acquired only slowly in some children. Usually, these skills improve with time, but occasionally there may be underlying problems (*see* BEDWETTING, p.872, and ENCOPRESIS, opposite page).

Developmental delays that affect all areas of learning and general ability are usually caused by underlying disorders, such as Down syndrome (p.821) or inborn errors of metabolism (p.867), although often the underlying cause is not identified. These developmental delays generally lead later to a diagnosis of mental retardation (p.854).

What might be done?

Developmental delays are usually first noticed by parents who are concerned when a child does not reach the normal milestones for his or her age group. A delay may also be detected at routine developmental checkups in the first 5 years of life. If a problem is suspected, your child's doctor may then arrange for a full developmental assessment, which normally includes hearing tests (*see* HEARING TESTS IN CHILDREN, p.859) and vision tests (*see* VISION TESTS IN CHILDREN, p.857). The doctor may also arrange for your child to have blood tests to look for a genetic disorder.

A child with delay in one area of development may need only encouragement to begin to catch up. Many children with mild delays develop normally over a period of time, especially if the cause is understimulation and the problem is treated appropriately. Other children should be given help, such as speech therapy (p.963), in particular areas of development. A child with more severe delays will need specialized treatment.

(WWW) ONLINE SITES: p.1028

Mental retardation

Difficulties with all areas of learning experienced by children with significantly lower than average intelligence

 AGE Usually becomes apparent in early childhood

 GENETICS Risk factors depend on the cause

 GENDER LIFESTYLE Not significant factors

A child with mental retardation has poor intellectual ability, leading to significant developmental delay (p.853) in all areas of learning. Mental retardation can affect speech, language, reading, and writing. Physical development may also be affected, which leads to general clumsiness and poor hand–eye coordination. Mental retardation is often associated with behavioral problems.

There is often no obvious cause for mild mental retardation. In affected children, learning difficulties may not be noticeable until school age. Severe mental retardation usually has an obvious cause, such as the genetic disorders Down syndrome (p.821) or fragile X syndrome (p.822).

WHAT MIGHT BE DONE?

Mild mental retardation is usually first suspected by parents or teachers when a child is not developing skills at the same rate as his or her peers or is experiencing various difficulties at school. In more severe forms of mental retardation, delays in normal development are usually detected at an early stage in childhood, often during routine developmental checkups at preschool age.

The child's doctor will then probably arrange for a full developmental assessment, which includes hearing tests (*see* HEARING TESTS IN CHILDREN, p.859) and vision tests (*see* VISION TESTS IN CHILDREN, p.857). Blood tests to check for evidence of genetic disorders may also be performed.

Most children with mental retardation are taught in integrated school classrooms. However, some children who have severe mental retardation attend separate schools. Parents will be given support by a team of specialists, who may provide physiotherapy (p.961) and speech therapy (p.963).

Many children who have mild mental retardation do well with appropriate education and support. However, those with severe types of mental retardation will need lifelong supervision.

(WWW) ONLINE SITES: p.1034

Specific learning disabilities

Difficulties in one or several areas of learning in a child of average or above average intelligence

 AGE Usually become apparent between the ages of 3 and 7

 GENDER More common in boys

 GENETICS Sometimes run in families

 LIFESTYLE Not a significant factor

A child with delayed development in one or several areas of learning but normal intelligence probably has a specific learning disability. Such disabilities are thought to affect up to 15 in 100 otherwise normally developed children and are a common cause of poor achievement at school. The condition is more common in boys.

Dyslexia is a common example of a specific learning disability and affects a child's ability to read or write. With dyscalculia, a child has specific problems with mathematics. Dyspraxia is a learning disability that affects coordination, particularly finely controlled movement, often leading to clumsiness.

In most cases, the cause of a particular learning disability is not known. However, such conditions sometimes run in families, suggesting that genetic factors may be involved. In some cases, specific learning disabilities are due to problems with vision or hearing.

WHAT ARE THE SYMPTOMS?

The symptoms of specific learning disabilities are usually first recognized in early school years and may include:

- Difficulty coping with reading, writing, and/or mathematics.
- Problems telling left from right.
- Poor coordination and difficulty with sports and other physical activities.

A child may also become frustrated and develop behavioral problems, such as shyness or aggression.

WHAT MIGHT BE DONE?

If a learning disability is suspected, a full assessment of a child's academic and developmental skills will be carried out. Hearing tests (*see* HEARING TESTS IN CHILDREN, p.859) and vision tests (*see* VISION TESTS IN CHILDREN, p.857) may also be performed to rule out the presence of physical conditions that may cause delays in learning.

Parents and teachers should work together to encourage an affected child. In many cases, specialized teaching is necessary. Disorders such as impaired hearing or vision can often be treated successfully. Many children do well if the appropriate remedial treatment is given, but some children will continue to have lifelong difficulties.

(WWW) ONLINE SITES: p.1034

Speech and language difficulties

The slow or abnormal development of understanding and expression of language

 AGE Usually develop in early childhood

 GENDER GENETICS LIFESTYLE Risk factors depend on the type

There is a wide variation in the age at which speech and language skills are acquired, but most children are able to communicate verbally well before age 3. Many children have some type of speech and language difficulty in their early years, commonly only a minor impediment, such as a lisp, that rapidly improves with increasing maturity.

A common cause of delay in speech and language development is hearing impairment (*see* CHRONIC SECRETORY OTITIS MEDIA, p.860, and CONGENITAL DEAFNESS, p.859). Children who have cerebral palsy (p.846) and those with a cleft lip and palate (p.862) may have difficulty coordinating the movements of their mouth and tongue. Slowness in acquiring speech and language skills may also be due to lack of intellectual stimulation or developmental delay (p.853). Severe learning disabilities due to mental retardation (opposite page) may cause speech and language delay.

Difficulties with fluency of speech, causing, for example, stuttering, affect about 1 in 100 children, especially boys, and often run in families.

What might be done?

A speech or language difficulty may first be noticed by parents or teachers or at a routine developmental checkup. A full assessment of a child's development and hearing will then be made.

A child with a speech or language difficulty usually catches up with his or her peers when given appropriate guidance. Impaired hearing will be treated when possible. Stuttering can often be improved with speech therapy (p.963).

Once the underlying cause is treated, most speech and language difficulties improve. However, if there is a physical cause, such as cerebral palsy, the speech or language difficulty may persist.

(WWW) ONLINE SITES: p.1037

Attention deficit hyperactivity disorder

A behavioral disorder in which a child consistently has a high level of activity and/or difficulty attending to tasks

 AGE Usually develops in early childhood

 GENDER More common in boys

 GENETICS Often runs in families

 LIFESTYLE Not a significant factor

Attention deficit hyperactivity disorder (ADHD) is a common condition that affects up to 1 in 20 children in Canada. The disorder, which is more commonly seen in boys, should not be confused with the normal boisterous conduct of a healthy child. Children with ADHD consistently show abnormal patterns of behavior over a period of time. An affected child may be restless, unable to sit still for more than a few moments, inattentive, and impulsive.

The causes of ADHD are not fully understood. However, the condition is often found in families, which suggests that genetic factors may be involved. ADHD is not, as popularly believed, a result of poor parenting or abuse.

What are the symptoms?

The symptoms of ADHD develop in early childhood, usually between the ages of 3 and 7, and may include:

- Inability to finish tasks.
- Short attention span and inability to concentrate in class.
- Difficulty following instructions.
- Tendency to talk excessively and frequently interrupt others.
- Difficulty waiting or taking turns.
- Inability to play quietly alone.
- Physical impulsiveness.

Children with ADHD may have difficulty forming friendships. Self-esteem is often low because an affected child is frequently scolded and criticized.

What might be done?

The doctor will probably refer a child with suspected ADHD to a child psychologist or psychiatrist, developmental pediatrician, or child neurologist. The diagnosis is usually made following discussion with parents and observation of the child. However, ADHD is difficult to diagnose in preschool children. Parents have a key role in their child's treatment and are usually given training in techniques to improve the child's behavior. These techniques are based on using praise for good behavior rather than criticism for inappropriate conduct. An affected child may also benefit from structured teaching in small groups.

In some cases of ADHD, the doctor may prescribe drugs that have a calming effect and help improve a child's concentration (*see* CENTRAL NERVOUS SYSTEM STIMULANT DRUGS, p.918).

In most affected children, the disorder continues throughout adolescence, although the behavioral problems may become less severe in older children. A small proportion of those with ADHD later develop conduct disorder (right), in which a child consistently displays antisocial and unruly behavior.

(WWW) ONLINE SITES: p.1027

Conduct disorder

A behavioral disorder in which a child persistently behaves in an antisocial or disruptive manner

 AGE More common in late childhood and adolescence

 GENDER More common in boys

 GENETICS Sometimes runs in families

 LIFESTYLE An emotionally unstable home environment is a risk factor

Most children are mischievous from time to time, and some may become rebellious, especially as they reach adolescence. Conduct disorder is suspected only if a child or adolescent persists in antisocial or disruptive behavior.

Many children with conduct disorder have failed to acquire a sense of right or wrong. They may have grown up in an unstable home environment in which there is family discord or violence and lack of parental supervision. Children with attention deficit hyperactivity disorder (left) are at increased risk of developing conduct disorder.

Conduct disorder is more common in boys. The antisocial behavior usually becomes more obvious toward adolescence, when an affected child may start to become aggressive and play truant from school. In some cases, a child will indulge in substance or alcohol abuse or become involved in criminal activities, such as theft, vandalism, assault, and arson. Children with conduct disorder often have low self-esteem and find it difficult to form relationships.

What might be done?

A diagnosis of conduct disorder is usually based on a psychiatric assessment of the child's behavioral patterns.

The treatment for a conduct disorder is always directed toward the whole family. Therapy will aim to overcome conflicts or tensions within the family unit. Parents will be encouraged to reinforce good behavior, and an aggressive child will be taught to control his or her anger and to be considerate to others. Only 1 in 3 children affected with conduct disorder improves his or her behavior. In most cases, antisocial behavior persists throughout adult life.

(WWW) ONLINE SITES: p.1028

EYE AND EAR DISORDERS

Vision and hearing are important for a child because the eyes and ears collect information about the environment and also play a key role in the development of speech and language. Eye and ear disorders are often diagnosed during routine examinations in childhood.

KEY ANATOMY

Cornea
Retina
Pupil
Optic nerve
Lens
EYE
Inner ear
Middle ear
Outer ear
Eustachian tube
Eardrum
EAR

For more information on the structure and function of the eyes and ears, *see* pp.566–569 and pp.592–595.

The first article in this section covers congenital blindness, in which children are born with impaired vision. The following articles discuss conditions such as strabismus, in which vision is affected due to misalignment of the gaze of the eyes, and amblyopia, in which a child's vision fails to develop normally. Both conditions can be treated successfully if they are diagnosed early. The remaining articles cover ear disorders. The most common cause of earache in children is acute otitis media. Repeated episodes of this middle-ear condition may lead to chronic secretory otitis media, which is covered next. Eye and ear disorders that can affect people at any age are covered in other sections of the book (*see* EYES AND VISION, pp.566–591, and EARS, HEARING, AND BALANCE, pp.592–605).

Congenital blindness

Severely impaired vision that is present from birth

AGE Present at birth

GENETICS Sometimes runs in families

GENDER LIFESTYLE Not significant factors

Vision plays a very important part in the early development of a child. Impaired vision at birth will cause serious delay in development and is likely to lead to learning disabilities, particularly when associated with other problems, such as congenital deafness (p.859).

About 9 in 10 children who are considered blind from birth have some vision, even though it may be only recognition of light and dark or shapes.

WHAT ARE THE CAUSES?

In the developed world, half of all cases of congenital blindness run in families and therefore may be due to a genetic disorder. Another important cause is congenital infections (p.817) such as the protozoal infection toxoplasmosis (p.307) and the viral infection rubella (p.292). These infections are transmitted from the mother to the developing fetus during pregnancy and may lead to impaired vision in a newborn baby. Congenital rubella is now rare in the developed world due to routine immunization. The baby's eyes may also be affected by cataracts (p.573), in which the lenses are opaque, or glaucoma (p.575), in which the optic nerve is damaged due to increased pressure in the eyes. Congenital blindness may also be caused by damage to the brain as a result of lack of oxygen during birth.

WHAT ARE THE SYMPTOMS?

Parents usually become aware that their baby has a vision problem within a few weeks. He or she may be less responsive than other babies, lying quietly to make the most of his or her hearing. Parents may also notice that their baby:

- Is unable to fix his or her eyes on a close object.
- Has random eye movements.
- Does not smile by the age of 6 weeks.
- Has abnormally large, cloudy eyes if glaucoma is present.

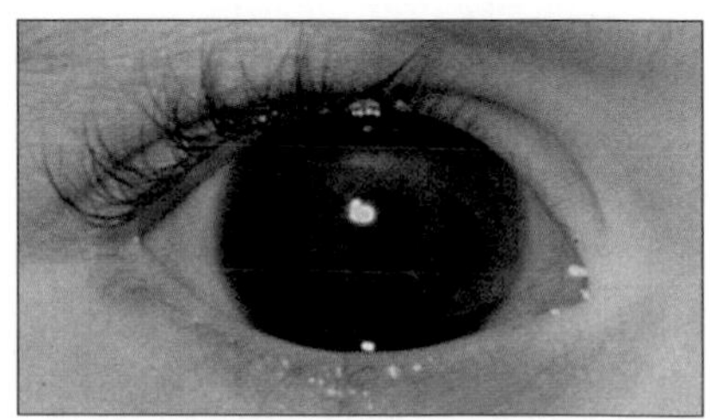

Congenital glaucoma
This child's eye is enlarged and cloudy due to increased pressure within the eye caused by congenital glaucoma.

Parents may find it difficult to bond with a quiet baby who does not smile.

HOW IS IT DIAGNOSED?

If congenital blindness is not suspected by a baby's parents, it will probably be picked up during a routine examination in infancy. A child suspected of having impaired vision will be referred to a specialist for an examination and tests (*see* VISION TESTS IN CHILDREN, opposite page). His or her hearing will also be tested (*see* HEARING TESTS IN CHILDREN, p.859) because, if the child is severely visually impaired, he or she will rely more on hearing.

WHAT IS THE TREATMENT?

It is possible to improve vision in only a small number of babies, such as those with cataracts or glaucoma. Early treatment of these conditions is important. Cataracts are usually removed surgically within the first month of life (*see* CATARACT SURGERY, p.573). Glaucoma may also be treated surgically to allow fluid to drain from the eye.

If vision cannot be improved, much can be done to help a child make maximum use of other senses or what little vision he or she has. If your child is diagnosed as blind, a team of specialists, including a teacher for the blind, will be available to give you and your child support and care. You will also be given advice on how to stimulate your child by using speech, sounds, and touch and how to adapt your home so that your child can explore it safely and develop self-confidence. Some children will require special schooling to learn braille, a system of raised dots that allows blind people to read.

Genetic counseling (p.270) is available for parents of an affected child who wish to have more children or for prospective parents who are blind.

WHAT IS THE PROGNOSIS?

Children treated for cataracts or glaucoma will probably still have impaired vision but often have enough sight to perform most activities unaided. Many blind or visually impaired children with no other disabilities go on to have successful personal and professional lives.

(WWW) ONLINE SITES: p.1031

Strabismus

Abnormal alignment of the gaze of one of the eyes, also known as crossed eyes or squint

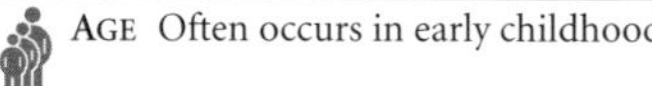
AGE Often occurs in early childhood

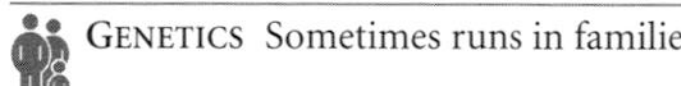
GENETICS Sometimes runs in families

GENDER LIFESTYLE Not significant factors

Strabismus is a common condition in which only one eye points directly at the object being viewed. This abnormal alignment of the eyes causes the brain to receive conflicting images, which may result in double vision or, in children under the age of 8, suppression of the image from the misaligned eye.

Strabismus can be caused by any disorder of vision, such as farsightedness (*see* HYPEROPIA, p.586) or nearsightedness (*see* MYOPIA, p.586), and can run in families, suggesting a genetic factor. The condition may also be caused by a structural difference between the muscles that control movement of the eyes. Very rarely, strabismus develops as a result of cancer of the eye (*see* RETINOBLASTOMA, p.858) or paralysis of the muscles in one eye caused by a serious underlying condition such as a tumor in the brain (*see* BRAIN AND SPINAL CORD TUMORS IN CHILDREN, p.850).

Small babies often appear cross-eyed because of the arrangement of soft tissues, including skin and fat, around the eyes. This condition is normal and should not be confused with strabismus.

WHAT ARE THE SYMPTOMS?

If mild, symptoms occur only when a child is tired. If severe, symptoms are present all the time and may include:

- Misalignment of the gaze of one of the eyes.
- Poor vision in one of the eyes due to lack of use.

A child may cover or close the affected eye to see clearly and hold his or her head at an angle. Left untreated, strabismus may cause amblyopia (p.858), in which the vision in the affected eye does not develop normally.

(TEST) VISION TESTS IN CHILDREN

Vision tests in children are specifically designed for their age and ability and are routinely performed to look for defects that may delay normal development and learning. Vision can be assessed in infants using tests such as retinoscopy, while older children can match shapes or letters. Once a child can read, a Snellen chart may be used to look for vision defects (*see* VISION TESTS, p.587).

RETINOSCOPY

This test can be performed on infants. About 30 minutes beforehand, eyedrops are given to dilate the pupils and prevent focusing. A beam of light is shone into each eye in turn from an instrument called a retinoscope. The effect of different lenses on the beam of light determines whether vision is normal.

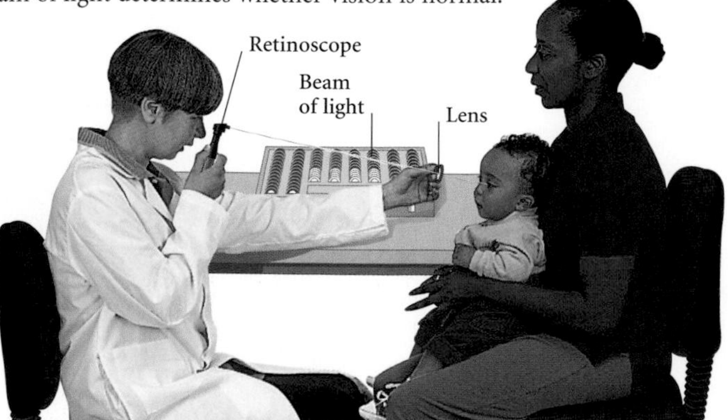
Retinoscope
Beam of light
Lens

During the test
The test is performed in a darkened room. Each eye is tested individually.

LETTER MATCHING TEST

This test is designed for children aged about 3 years. A child is given a card with letters printed on it. The doctor then holds up letters of decreasing size at a distance of 10 ft (3 m) and asks the child to identify the same letters on the card. By using an eye patch, each of the eyes can be tested separately.

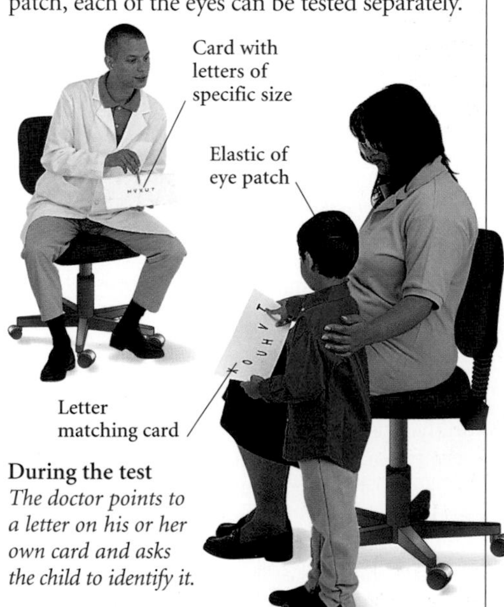
Card with letters of specific size
Elastic of eye patch
Letter matching card

During the test
The doctor points to a letter on his or her own card and asks the child to identify it.

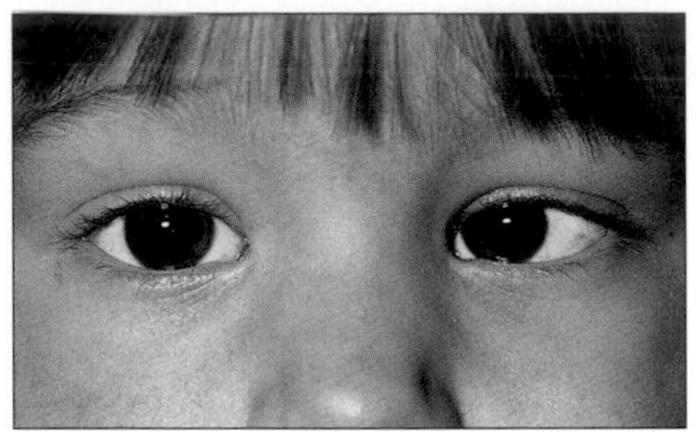

Strabismus
The gaze of this child's eyes is misaligned, a disorder known as strabismus, causing conflicting images to be sent to the brain.

What might be done?

The doctor will arrange for your child to have vision tests (*see* VISION TESTS IN CHILDREN, p.857). If the strabismus has developed suddenly, an imaging test, such as CT scanning (p.247), may be performed to look for a tumor.

The aim of treatment is to correct the strabismus. If your child has a vision disorder such as myopia, he or she may have to wear glasses, which should also correct strabismus. Your child may also be given a patch to wear over the unaffected eye for a period of time each day to treat amblyopia. Wearing the eye patch forces the child to use the weaker eye, which is essential for the normal development of vision. Your child will probably have regular checkups every 3 or 6 months until the strabismus is corrected. The treatment is usually successful, although the condition can recur. In some cases, surgery on the eye muscles may be necessary. A rare underlying cause, such as a tumor, will be treated if possible.

(WWW) ONLINE SITES: p.1031

Amblyopia

Blurry or absent vision in an eye that is structurally normal

 AGE Usually develops before age 5

 GENETICS Sometimes runs in families

 GENDER LIFESTYLE Not significant factors

Amblyopia develops in young children if the two eyes send different images to the brain. The development of vision occurs until a child is about 5 years old and depends on the brain learning to combine the images from both eyes. If the eyes produce different images during this period, the brain responds by suppressing images from the more unfocused eye so that vision does not develop normally. If the underlying cause is not treated by age 10, later attempts to correct vision will fail.

What are the causes?

Any condition that causes the two eyes to send different images to the brain may lead to amblyopia. Misalignment of the gaze of the eyes (*see* STRABISMUS, p.857) is the most common cause of amblyopia. Other causes of amblyopia include vision disorders in one eye, such as astigmatism (p.588), farsightedness (*see* HYPEROPIA, p.586), and nearsightedness (*see* MYOPIA, p.586). Amblyopia may run in families, suggesting that genetic factors may be involved.

What might be done?

If you suspect that your child cannot see clearly, you should consult the doctor without delay to minimize the risk of permanent visual impairment. Your child will probably be referred to an ophthalmologist, who will examine his or her eyes and assess vision (*see* VISION TESTS IN CHILDREN, p.857).

Treatment depends on the underlying cause of the amblyopia. If your child has a vision disorder such as nearsightedness, it may be corrected simply by wearing glasses. If vision in one eye is reduced, patching the good eye for at least 5 hours each day over several months forces the brain to process visual information received from the weaker eye, regardless of the underlying cause. If your child needs to wear an eye patch, he or she will need your support and encouragement, especially if vision in the affected eye is poor.

Left untreated, strabismus may lead to amblyopia. An operation to correct the strabismus may be necessary to prevent amblyopia from developing.

What is the prognosis?

The prognosis for children who have amblyopia depends on when the condition is detected and treatment to correct it begins. Amblyopia is usually at least partially reversible in children under age 10. Older children probably already have permanent visual impairment to some degree.

(WWW) ONLINE SITES: p.1031

Retinoblastoma

A rare cancer of the retina, the light-sensitive membrane at the back of the eye

 AGE Usually develops before age 2

 GENETICS Sometimes runs in families

 GENDER LIFESTYLE Not significant factors

In Canada, about 20 children are diagnosed with this tumor each year. The condition can develop in one or both of the eyes, usually before a child reaches the age of 2 years. Of those affected, about 1 child in 5 has retinoblastoma in both eyes. About half of all cases are caused by an abnormal gene on chromosome 13, which is inherited in an autosomal dominant fashion (*see* GENE DISORDERS, p.269). In the remaining cases, the cause is unknown.

The most common symptom is the development of a whitened area behind the pupil, which is particularly noticeable in flash photographs. Impaired vision caused by retinoblastoma may lead to strabismus (p.857). Left untreated, the cancer can spread to other parts of the body.

What might be done?

If the doctor suspects that a child has retinoblastoma, he or she will probably refer the child to a specialist, who will examine the eyes, possibly under general anesthesia. The child may also have blood tests to look for the abnormal gene. To establish whether the cancer has spread, CT scanning (p.247) or MRI (p.248) may be performed.

The aim of treatment is to cure the cancer and, if possible, to retain vision

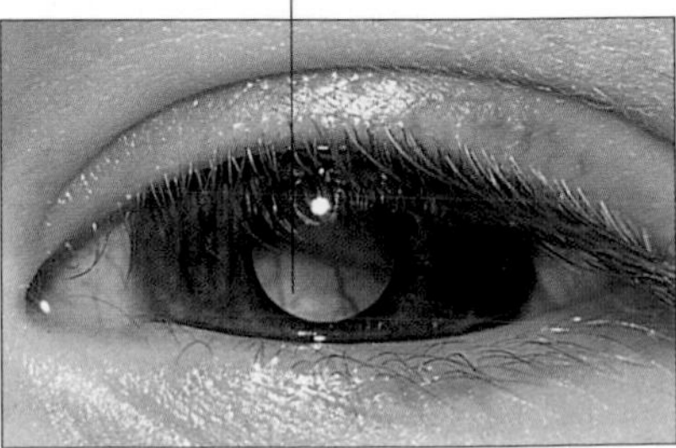
Retinoblastoma

Retinoblastoma
The pale area seen through the pupil of this eye is a retinoblastoma, a rare cancer of the membrane at the back of the eye.

in affected eyes. It is usually possible to remove small cancerous tumors by freezing the tissue. However, for larger tumors, it will probably be necessary to have surgery to remove the whole eye. Treatment with chemotherapy (p.278) and radiation therapy (p.279) may also be necessary if the cancer has spread.

WHAT IS THE PROGNOSIS?

In most cases, the cancer can be cured, but the child's vision may be severely impaired. Genetic counseling (p.270) is available to relatives of an affected child and to adults treated for retinoblastoma in childhood. The siblings of an affected child should have regular eye tests.

(WWW) ONLINE SITES: p.1028, p.1032

Congenital deafness

Partial or total hearing loss that is present from birth

 AGE Present at birth

 GENETICS Risk factors depend on the cause

 GENDER LIFESTYLE Not significant factors

Normally, a baby reacts to noise from birth, and even a fetus in the uterus is sensitive to sound. Hearing is particularly important for emotional contact between a baby and his or her family and for the development of speech and language. Congenital deafness is the rarest form of deafness; only about 2 in 1,000 babies are born with a hearing impairment affecting both ears. The condition varies from partial hearing loss to profound deafness.

WHAT ARE THE CAUSES?

Congenital deafness is caused by the abnormal development of the inner ear or of the vestibulocochlear nerve, which transmits electrical impulses from the inner ear to the brain. In about half of all cases, the condition runs in families, suggesting that a genetic factor may be involved. Congenital deafness is also associated with the chromosome disorder Down syndrome (p.821).

Congenital deafness may also be caused by certain infections, such as rubella or cytomegalovirus (CMV) if they are transmitted from the mother to the fetus during early development

(TEST) HEARING TESTS IN CHILDREN

Tests for impaired hearing designed for the age of the child are done routinely throughout childhood. Increasingly, newborns are screened, using tests such as brainstem-evoked response audiogram (BERA test) and otoacoustic emission. Once a child has developed simple language, speech discrimination tests may be performed. By age 4, most children are able to manage a simple form of audiometry similar to that used to diagnose hearing impairment in adults (*see* HEARING TESTS, p.600).

OTOACOUSTIC EMISSION TEST

This test detects the echo that is normally emitted by the inner ear in response to sound. An earpiece is placed in the ear canal, and a sound is played through it. The resulting echo is recorded. The test is painless.

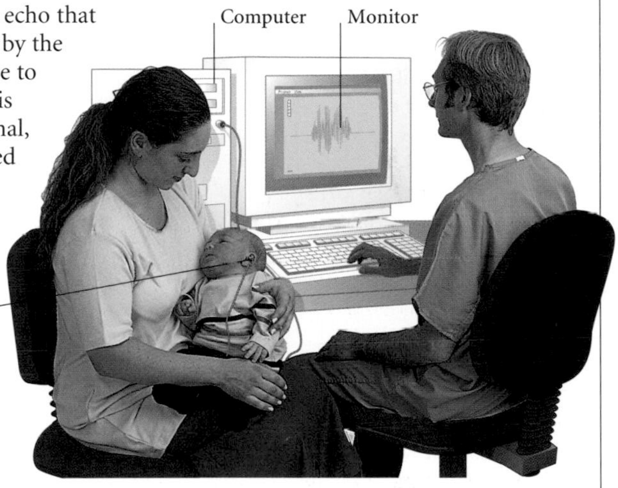
Computer
Monitor
Earpiece

During the test
While the baby is quiet, a sound is played through the earpiece and the response is recorded.

(RESULTS)

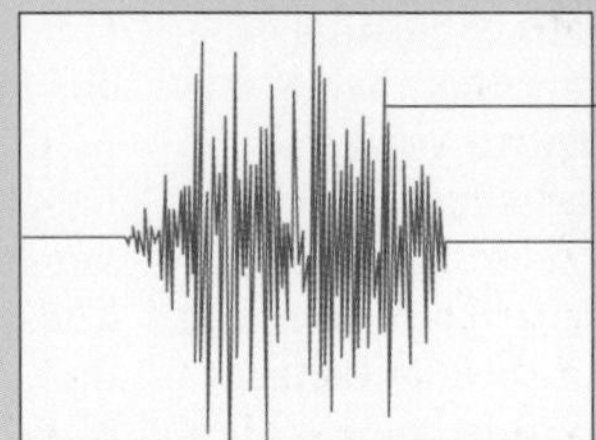
Sound waves
An echo is produced by the inner ear in response to sounds played

Otoacoustic emission
This normal tracing shows the echo emitted by the inner ear as sound is played through an earpiece. An echo is produced only if the inner ear is healthy and functioning normally.

SPEECH DISCRIMINATION TESTS

Speech discrimination tests can be used to detect hearing loss in young children who have a simple vocabulary. For example, the McCormick toy discrimination test is used in children about age 3. The child is shown various toys and is then asked to identify pairs of toys that have similar sounding names, such as tree and key.

Card covers mouth
Small toy

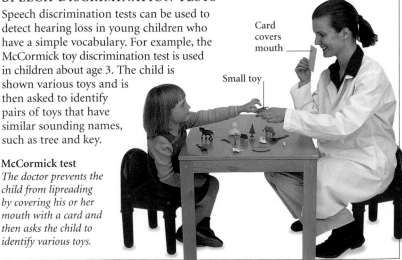

McCormick test
The doctor prevents the child from lipreading by covering his or her mouth with a card and then asks the child to identify various toys.

(*see* CONGENITAL INFECTIONS, p.817). The development of hearing may also be affected if the mother takes certain drugs during pregnancy, particularly some types of antibiotics (p.885).

WHAT ARE THE SYMPTOMS?

The symptoms of congenital deafness may be noticed in the first few weeks or months after birth and include:

- Lack of response to loud noise.
- Failure to make normal baby sounds such as cooing by about 6 weeks of age or babbling by about 3 months.

You should take your baby to the doctor without delay if you suspect that he or she has impaired hearing.

WHAT MIGHT BE DONE?

In some hospitals, newborn babies at risk are tested for congenital deafness using a BERA test (*see* HEARING TESTS IN CHILDREN, p.859). In other cases, a hearing test is performed only if a problem is suspected or the baby is considered to be at risk for another reason, such as having a family history of congenital deafness. An older baby may be tested by recording his or her response to loud sounds.

There is no cure for congenital deafness, but any hearing that a child has may be maximized with a hearing aid (p.601) or, in some children, with a cochlear implant (p.603). In all cases, it is important to ensure that a child can communicate. He or she may be taught sign language and lipreading. Some children may be able to learn to speak.

About half of all children with congenital deafness attend regular school. Others, such as those with Down syndrome, will need special schooling. Children with congenital deafness and their families may find it helpful to contact a support group.

CAN IT BE PREVENTED?

The risk can be reduced by immunization against rubella if you are planning a pregnancy. You should not take drugs during pregnancy unless they are known to be safe for the fetus.

If the condition runs in your family, you may wish to have genetic counseling (p.270), in which you will be given advice about the risks of passing the condition to your children.

(WWW) ONLINE SITES: p.1032

Acute otitis media in children

Infection of the middle ear, which often causes earache

 AGE More common under age 8

 GENETICS Sometimes runs in families; more common in certain ethnic groups

 LIFESTYLE Passive smoking is a risk factor

 GENDER Not a significant factor

The most common cause of earache in children is acute otitis media, which is caused by infection in the middle ear. Children are at risk because the eustachian tubes, which connect the middle ear to the throat, are small and become obstructed easily. Acute otitis media is often part of a respiratory tract infection, such as the common cold (p.286). The infection causes inflammation that may block one of the eustachian tubes, causing a buildup of fluid in the middle ear that may get infected with bacteria.

About 1 in 5 children under age 4 has one episode of acute otitis media each year. The condition is more common in children whose parents smoke. It is also more common in children of aboriginal and Inuit descent and may run in families, suggesting a genetic factor. The condition is less common in children over the age of 8.

WHAT ARE THE SYMPTOMS?

Symptoms usually develop rapidly over several hours. A very young child may have difficulty locating the pain, and the only symptoms may be fever and vomiting. In older children, the symptoms may be more specific and include:

- Earache.
- Tugging or rubbing the painful ear.
- Temporary impaired hearing in the affected ear.

Left untreated, the eardrum may rupture, relieving the pain but causing a discharge of blood and pus. Recurrent infections in the middle ear may cause chronic secretory otitis media (below).

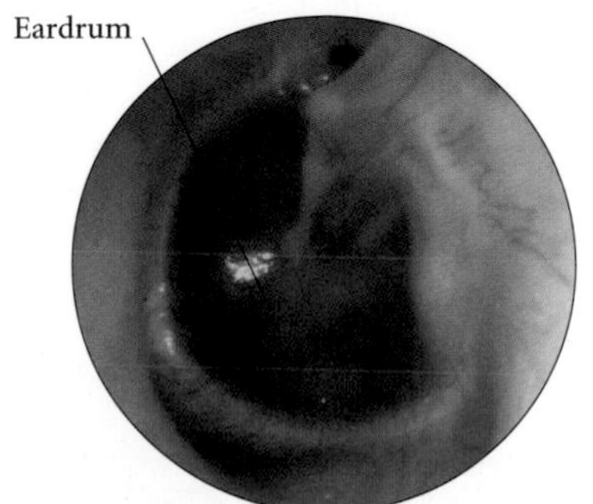
Eardrum

Acute otitis media
The eardrum shown above is bulging and inflamed as a result of the middle-ear infection acute otitis media.

WHAT MIGHT BE DONE?

You should consult your child's doctor if liquid is discharged from the ear or if the earache lasts more than a few hours. He or she will examine your child's ears and may blow air into the affected ear using a special instrument to check that the eardrum is moving normally. Acute otitis media can clear up without treatment; however, the doctor will probably prescribe antibiotics (p.885) if he or she suspects that a bacterial infection is present. To relieve discomfort, acetaminophen may be recommended (*see* ANALGESICS, p.912). After a few days, the doctor will reexamine your child.

Symptoms usually clear up in a few days with appropriate treatment. A ruptured eardrum should heal within a few weeks. In some children, hearing is affected for more than 3 months until the fluid in the ear disappears.

(WWW) ONLINE SITES: p.1028, p.1030, p.1033

Chronic secretory otitis media

A persistent collection of fluid in the middle ear

 AGE More common under age 8

 GENDER More common in boys

 GENETICS Sometimes runs in families; more common in certain ethnic groups

 LIFESTYLE Passive smoking is a risk factor

In chronic secretory otitis media, the middle ear becomes filled with a thick, sticky, gluelike fluid. The condition is more common in boys and is the most common cause of impaired hearing in children under age 8. Native American and Inuit children are particularly susceptible to the condition. It may also

(TREATMENT) TYMPANOSTOMY TUBE

The ear disorder chronic secretory otitis media (opposite page) may be treated surgically by inserting a tiny plastic tube, called a tympanostomy or myringotomy tube, into the eardrum. The tube ventilates the middle ear and allows fluid to drain away. After insertion of the tube, hearing in the affected ear usually returns to normal, often within days. In most cases, the operation is performed under general anesthesia as day surgery.

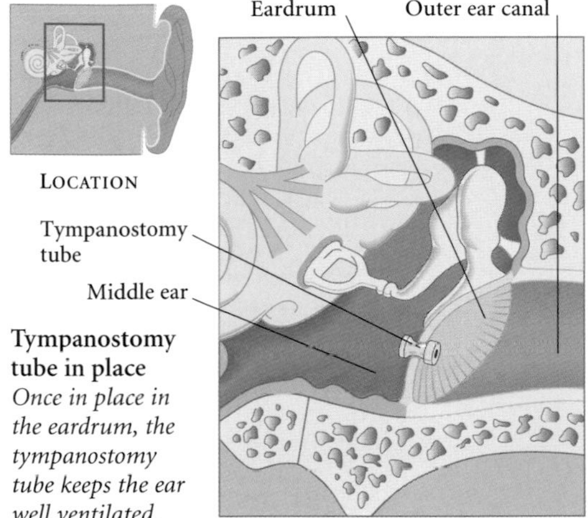
Eardrum
Outer ear canal
Location
Tympanostomy tube
Middle ear

Tympanostomy tube in place
Once in place in the eardrum, the tympanostomy tube keeps the ear well ventilated.

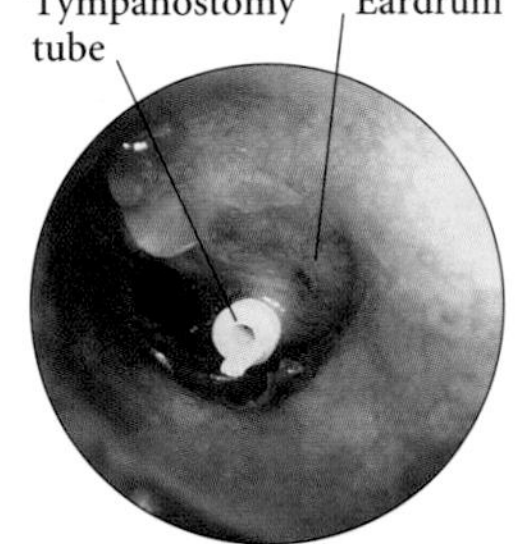
Tympanostomy tube
Eardrum

View of the eardrum
A tympanostomy tube has been inserted into the eardrum above. Inserted tubes usually fall out 6–12 months later, and the hole in the eardrum closes.

run in families, suggesting that genetic factors may be involved. Since the disorder is persistent and usually occurs when good hearing is essential for the development of speech, it may cause a delay in speech and language development.

What are the causes?

The middle ear is normally ventilated by the eustachian tube (the narrow tube that connects the middle ear to the back of the throat). However, if this tube becomes blocked, possibly as a result of infection (*see* ACUTE OTITIS MEDIA IN CHILDREN, opposite page), the middle ear may fill with fluid. Often the blockage persists, causing chronic secretory otitis media. In some cases, the cause of the blockage is unknown. However, the condition is more common in children whose parents smoke and in those with asthma (p.839) or allergic rhinitis (p.466). Children who have Down syndrome (p.821) or a cleft lip and palate (p.862) are also at an increased risk of developing the disorder.

What are the symptoms?

In most cases, the symptoms of chronic secretory otitis media develop gradually and may initially go unnoticed. The symptoms often fluctuate and are usually worse in the winter months. They may include:

- Partial deafness.
- Immature speech for your child's age.
- Behavioral problems due to frustration at being unable to hear well.

You may notice that your child is sitting close to the television or turning up the volume. His or her school performance may suffer because of difficulty hearing. If you suspect a hearing problem, consult the doctor without delay.

How is it diagnosed?

The doctor will examine your child's ears and may then refer him or her to a specialist. Depending on the age of your child, various hearing tests may be performed to find out whether his or her hearing is impaired (*see* HEARING TESTS IN CHILDREN, p.859). The specialist may also perform another test in which air is blown into the affected ear using a special instrument. This test is done to measure the amount of movement of the eardrum, which is reduced in chronic secretory otitis media. Since the condition can fluctuate, the specialist will probably wish to examine your child again after about 3 months and repeat the tests. An allergy evaluation may also be recommended.

What is the treatment?

In many cases, chronic secretory otitis media clears up without treatment. However, if the symptoms persist over several months, the doctor may suggest an operation. During the procedure, which is carried out under general anesthesia, a small plastic tube called a tympanostomy or myringotomy tube is inserted into the eardrum. The tube allows air to enter and circulate and dry out the middle ear (*see* TYMPANOSTOMY TUBE, left). In some cases, children with chronic secretory otitis media have enlarged adenoids (p.842), which may be removed at the same time (*see* TONSILLECTOMY AND ADENOIDECTOMY, p.843).

What is the prognosis?

As a child grows, the eustachian tubes widen, allowing fluid to drain away from the middle ear more efficiently. As a result, the tubes are much less likely to become blocked. Chronic secretory otitis media is rare in children over age 8.

(WWW) ONLINE SITES: p.1028, p.1030, p.1033

Protruding ears

Prominent ears, which have no harmful effect on hearing

 AGE Present at birth

 GENETICS Sometimes runs in families

 GENDER LIFESTYLE Not significant factors

Some children are born with ears that protrude instead of lying almost flat against the head. If the condition is severe, a child may experience psychological distress, usually from the teasing of other children. The condition sometimes runs in families, suggesting that a genetic factor is involved.

What might be done?

Protruding ears can be hidden by a suitable hairstyle. However, in extreme cases, cosmetic surgery may be recommended by your child's doctor. During the operation, a thin strip of skin from behind the ear is removed and then the the ear is drawn into the desired position. Scarring is hidden behind the ear. The surgery is not usually performed until a child is at least age 5.

(WWW) ONLINE SITES: p.1037

DISORDERS OF THE DIGESTIVE SYSTEM

Throughout early childhood attacks of diarrhea and vomiting are common, and many children have episodes of constipation. Such disorders can often be treated successfully at home with self-help measures. Other rarer disorders may be due to a physical defect present at birth, and these disorders may require surgery.

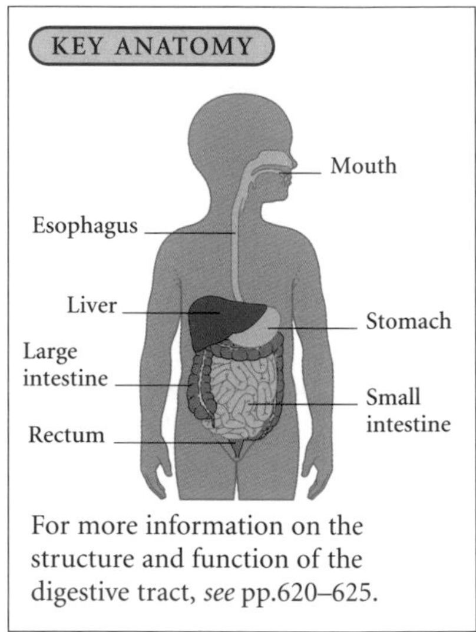
KEY ANATOMY
Mouth
Esophagus
Liver
Stomach
Large intestine
Small intestine
Rectum

For more information on the structure and function of the digestive tract, *see* pp.620–625.

The first two articles in this section cover problems with the mouth that affect babies: the physical defects of cleft lip and palate, which require surgery, and oral thrush, which is a common fungal infection. Two other disorders that may sometimes affect babies, gastroesophageal reflux and pyloric stenosis, are covered next. Both can be treated successfully, but pyloric stenosis requires surgery.

A general article follows on vomiting and diarrhea, including self-help measures for avoiding dehydration. There is also an article on cows' milk protein allergy. The section ends with articles on intussusception, a rare obstruction of the intestines, and constipation. The digestive disorders that affect adults only or adults and children are covered in the section on the digestive system (pp.620–669).

Cleft lip and palate

Splits in the upper lip and the roof of the mouth that are present at birth

 AGE Present at birth

 GENETICS Sometimes runs in families

 LIFESTYLE Heavy drinking and using some medical drugs in pregnancy are risk factors

 GENDER Not a significant factor

A cleft upper lip and palate are among the most common defects in babies and affect about 1 in 700 babies in the US. These conditions may occur singly or together and are present at birth. Both conditions can be very upsetting for parents, but plastic surgery usually produces excellent results.

The defects occur when the upper lip or roof of the mouth does not fuse completely in the fetus. In many cases, the cause is unknown, but the risk is higher if certain anticonvulsant drugs (p.914), such as phenytoin, are taken during pregnancy or if the mother is a heavy drinker. Cleft lip and/or palate sometimes run in families.

If a baby is severely affected, he or she may find it difficult to feed at first, and, if the condition is not treated early, speech may be delayed. Children with a cleft lip and/or palate are also susceptible to persistent buildup of fluid in the middle ear (*see* CHRONIC SECRETORY OTITIS MEDIA, p.860) that impairs hearing and may delay speech.

WHAT MIGHT BE DONE?

A cleft lip is usually repaired surgically by age 3 months, and a cleft palate is repaired at age 6–15 months. While waiting for surgery, a plate may be fitted into the roof of the mouth if a baby has feeding problems. After surgery, a child may have a hearing test (*see* HEARING TESTS IN CHILDREN, p.859) to check for hearing impairment caused by fluid buildup in the ear. A child may also need speech therapy (p.963) when he or she begins talking. Plastic surgery often produces good results and allows a child's speech to develop normally.

(WWW) ONLINE SITES: p.1027, p.1028, p.1037

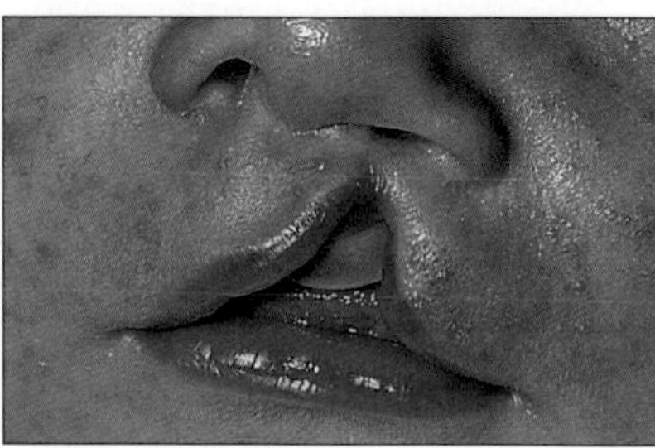

Cleft lip
This child has a split in the upper lip, known as a cleft lip. This can usually be repaired successfully with plastic surgery.

Oral thrush

A fungal mouth infection caused by an overgrowth of a yeast

 AGE More common under age 1

 GENDER GENETICS LIFESTYLE Not significant factors

Oral thrush is a common fungal infection in the first year of life. It causes white spots inside the mouth and may make a baby reluctant to feed. The infection is caused by an overgrowth of *Candida albicans*, a yeast naturally present in the mouth. The reason for the overgrowth is often unknown.

WHAT ARE THE SYMPTOMS?

In most cases, the symptoms of oral thrush include the following:

- Creamy yellow or white spots in the mouth that are difficult to rub off.
- Sore mouth that may make a baby reluctant to feed.

Oral thrush may be associated with a candida infection in the diaper area (*see* DIAPER RASH, p.829).

WHAT MIGHT BE DONE?

If you think your baby has oral thrush, you should arrange for him or her to see a doctor within 48 hours. The doctor will examine your baby's mouth and may take a mouth swab to check

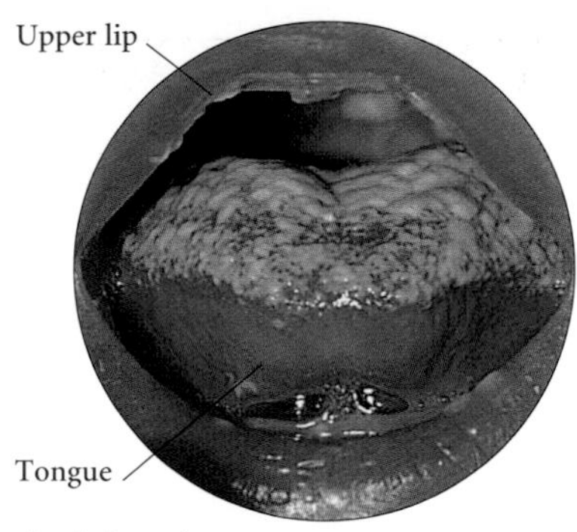
Upper lip
Tongue

Oral thrush
The white patches on the tongue and the lining of this baby's mouth are caused by a common yeast infection, oral thrush.

for *Candida albicans.* He or she may prescribe antifungal drops and, to prevent reinfection if you breast feed, an antifungal cream for your nipples (*see* PREPARATIONS FOR SKIN INFECTIONS AND INFESTATIONS, p.892). If you bottle-feed your baby, all equipment should be thoroughly sterilized by boiling. Oral thrush often improves within days of starting treatment and clears up within a week, but the infection may recur.

(WWW) ONLINE SITES: p.1028, p.1033

Gastroesophageal reflux in infants

Regurgitation of the stomach contents caused by immaturity and weakness of the muscles around the stomach's entrance

 AGE More common under age 1

 GENDER GENETICS LIFESTYLE Not significant factors

Most babies bring up small amounts of milk after a feeding. This regurgitation is normal and usually causes no distress. However, if infants regularly regurgitate larger amounts of milk or food, gastroesophageal reflux may be the cause. This disorder occurs because the muscles at the entrance to a baby's stomach are not fully developed. As a result, the contents of the stomach, including acidic digestive juices, are able to pass back up the esophagus (the tube between the throat and the stomach). Gastroesophageal reflux is more common in preterm babies and babies with cerebral palsy (p.846) who have poor overall muscle tone.

WHAT ARE THE SYMPTOMS?

The symptoms of gastroesophageal reflux are most noticeable after a feeding and may include the following:

- Regurgitation of milk, usually more pronounced when the baby is lying flat or is crying.
- Coughing or wheezing if regurgitated milk is inhaled into the lungs.

If gastroesophageal reflux is severe, it may prevent your baby from gaining weight. Severe reflux may also cause inflammation and bleeding of the lining of the esophagus, which may make the vomit bloodstained. Sometimes, if milk is inhaled into the lungs, a chest infection, such as pneumonia (p.490), may develop. Rarely, a baby can stop breathing temporarily after inhaling milk.

If your baby regularly regurgitates more than a dribble of milk after feeding, or if the vomit is bloodstained, contact a doctor as soon as possible.

HOW IS IT DIAGNOSED?

Your baby's doctor may diagnose gastroesophageal reflux from the typical symptoms. However, if he or she is unsure of the diagnosis, a test may be arranged to monitor the amount of acid passing up the esophagus from the stomach over 24 hours. This test involves passing a narrow tube into the baby's nose and down the esophagus. Your baby's doctor may arrange for further tests, including a specialized X-ray (*see* BARIUM SWALLOW, p.637), to check for a structural abnormality. If a baby has very severe reflux with bloodstained vomit, endoscopy (*see* UPPER DIGESTIVE TRACT ENDOSCOPY, p.641) may be arranged to look for inflammation of the esophageal lining.

WHAT IS THE TREATMENT?

In most cases, small, frequent feedings help prevent reflux, as does raising the head end of the crib after feeding. Your baby's doctor may prescribe a thickener or antacids (p.923) to add to milk and/or a drug that speeds up the emptying of the stomach, such as cisapride (*see* ANTISPASMODIC DRUGS AND MOTILITY STIMULANTS, p.926). In more severe cases, drugs may be given to lower acid production (*see* ULCER-HEALING DRUGS, p.923). With treatment, most babies' symptoms improve.

(WWW) ONLINE SITES: p.1028

Pyloric stenosis in infants

Narrowing of the outlet of the stomach in infancy, causing severe vomiting

 AGE Symptoms usually develop 3–8 weeks after birth

 GENDER Five times more common in boys

 GENETICS Sometimes runs in families

 LIFESTYLE Not a significant factor

In pyloric stenosis, the ring of muscle that forms the outlet from the stomach to the duodenum (the first part of the small intestine) becomes thickened and narrowed due to excess growth of the muscle tissue. As a result, only a small amount of milk can pass into the duodenum, and the remainder builds up in the stomach until the baby vomits. The condition is five times more common in boys. The cause of pyloric stenosis is unknown, but it may run in families.

WHAT ARE THE SYMPTOMS?

The symptoms of pyloric stenosis develop gradually, usually between 3 and 8 weeks after birth, and may include:

- Persistent vomiting, which is sometimes projectile (ejected forcefully).
- Immediate hunger after vomiting.
- Infrequent bowel movements.

If vomiting is persistent or projectile, you should seek medical help at once.

WHAT MIGHT BE DONE?

The doctor will examine your baby's abdomen, usually during a feeding, to feel for a swelling around the stomach outlet. If pyloric stenosis is suspected, your child will probably be admitted to the hospital because affected babies frequently become dehydrated and need intravenous fluids. Ultrasound scanning (p.250) and/or specialized X-rays (*see* CONTRAST X-RAYS, p.245) of the abdomen may be arranged to confirm the diagnosis. The treatment for pyloric stenosis is a minor operation to widen the stomach outlet. Feedings can then be increased gradually until the baby's intake is normal. After surgery, babies usually make a full recovery, and the condition does not recur.

(WWW) ONLINE SITES: p.1028

Vomiting and diarrhea

Vomiting and the passage of loose stools caused by allergy, infection of the digestive tract, or an infection elsewhere in the body

 AGE More common under age 5

 LIFESTYLE Risk factors depend on the cause

 GENDER GENETICS Not significant factors

Attacks of vomiting and diarrhea occur throughout childhood but are more common under age 5. There are many causes, some more serious than others, and it may be useful to assess your child (*see* SYMPTOM CHART: VOMITING IN CHILDREN, p.198, and, SYMPTOM CHART: DIARRHEA IN CHILDREN, p.200). Most cases improve in 24 hours, but prompt treatment with fluids is important because babies and young children become dehydrated rapidly.

WHAT ARE THE CAUSES?

Most episodes of vomiting and diarrhea develop as a result of a viral or bacterial infection of the digestive tract (*see* GASTROENTERITIS, p.628). Unlike in adults, vomiting and diarrhea in young children may also be caused by a bacterial infection elsewhere in the body, such as the ear (*see* ACUTE OTITIS MEDIA IN CHILDREN, p.860), or, less commonly, by an inflammation of the membranes covering the brain (*see* MENINGITIS IN CHILDREN, p.848). If vomiting and diarrhea are caused by an infection, you may notice other symptoms, such as a fever, listlessness, and reluctance to eat or drink. An affected child may have abdominal pain, and babies may cry and draw up their legs.

Chronic vomiting with diarrhea is usually not caused by infection but by other disorders, such as cows' milk protein allergy (right) and sensitivity to gluten (*see* CELIAC DISEASE, p.658).

ARE THERE COMPLICATIONS?

If your child has vomiting and diarrhea that lasts for several hours, he or she may become dehydrated. The symptoms may then also include:

- Abnormal drowsiness or irritability.
- Passing of small amounts of concentrated urine.
- Sunken eyes.
- In a baby, a sunken fontanelle (the soft spot on the top of a baby's head).

If a child with vomiting and diarrhea develops symptoms of dehydration, you should seek medical help immediately.

WHAT MIGHT BE DONE?

Most cases of vomiting and diarrhea clear up without treatment. Make sure your child drinks about 2 oz of fluids every hour, but avoid milk (except breast milk). Over-the-counter oral rehydration solutions (p.926), containing the ideal balance of salts and minerals, can help prevent dehydration. If symptoms persist for over 24 hours or worsen, you should consult a doctor. He or she will assess the level of hydration and check for infection. If your child is dehydrated, hospitalization and treatment with intravenous fluids may be necessary, and antibiotics (p.885) may be prescribed if the child has a bacterial infection. If the disorder is caused by food sensitivity, a modified diet will be recommended. Treatment is usually successful.

(WWW) ONLINE SITES: p.1028

Cows' milk protein allergy

An allergic reaction to the proteins present in cows' milk and cows' milk products

 AGE Usually develops during the first 6 months of life

 GENETICS Sometimes runs in families

 GENDER LIFESTYLE Not significant factors

An allergy to the proteins in cows' milk occurs in about 1 in 25 babies, usually during the first 6 months of life. Most babies are susceptible because the proteins are present in formula and, if the mother consumes cows' milk products, in breast milk. If a baby has the allergy, his or her immune system reacts to cows' milk proteins, causing inflammation of the digestive tract. The cause is unknown, but the disorder may run in families, suggesting a genetic factor.

WHAT ARE THE SYMPTOMS?

The symptoms of cows' milk protein allergy vary and may include:

- Diarrhea, with loose stools containing blood and/or mucus.
- Abdominal discomfort, causing the baby to cry and become irritable.
- Vomiting.
- Wheezing and coughing.
- Eczema (p.829) or an itchy, red rash (*see* URTICARIA, p.468).
- Failure to gain weight.

If you think that your baby is allergic to proteins in cows' milk, consult a doctor. Rarely, cows' milk protein allergy leads to anaphylaxis (p.469), an allergic reaction that can be life-threatening.

WHAT MIGHT BE DONE?

If the doctor suspects cows' milk protein allergy, you may be told to exclude cows' milk temporarily from your child's diet under a dietitian's supervision. If you are breast-feeding, you will be advised to exclude all milk products from your own diet. If symptoms disappear while your child is on the special diet and reappear when cows' milk is reintroduced, the diagnosis is confirmed and the special diet is continued. Treatment for cows' milk protein allergy is usually successful, and children quickly gain weight on a modified diet. Your child will be tested every year to check if the allergy is still present and still requires a special diet. The problem usually disappears by about age 3, but in a small number of affected children it continues in some form into adult life.

(WWW) ONLINE SITES: p.1027, p.1028

Intussusception

A rare condition in which a segment of intestine slides inside the neighboring part, causing an intestinal obstruction

 AGE Usually develops in early childhood

 GENDER More common in boys

 GENETICS LIFESTYLE Not significant factors

Intussusception is a rare condition, but it is the most common cause of intestinal obstruction in young children under age 2. In intussusception, a section of the intestine "telescopes" into a neighboring part, forming a tube within a tube. The condition usually affects the last part of the small intestine. Left untreated, the blood supply to the affected "telescoped" part may be cut off and cause tissue death in that section of intestine. The cause of intussusception is usually unknown. However, it may be associated with enlargement of the lymph nodes in the lining of the intestine, possibly due to a viral infection.

What are the symptoms?

The symptoms of intussusception are usually intermittent. Each episode develops suddenly and usually lasts for a few minutes. Symptoms may include:

- Severe abdominal pain, which may cause the child to cry and draw up his or her legs.
- Pale skin.
- Vomiting.
- After a few hours, passage from the rectum of bloodstained mucus that may resemble red currant jelly.

Between the intermittent episodes of pain and vomiting, your child may feel ill and lethargic. If you suspect intussusception, seek medical attention at once. The disorder progresses rapidly, and prompt treatment is important.

What might be done?

If your child's doctor suspects intussusception from the symptoms, he or she will arrange for your child to be admitted to the hospital immediately.

In the hospital, your child will probably be given intravenous fluids. A tube will be passed through the nose and into the stomach to keep the stomach empty and prevent vomiting. To confirm the diagnosis, your child may be given a contrast X-ray (p.245) of the intestines, known as a barium enema. In at least 7 in 10 cases, the gentle pressure of the barium solution relieves the intestinal obstruction. In some centers, air may be used instead of barium. In other cases, emergency surgery may be done to relieve the obstruction and remove the damaged intestine. Most affected children recover fully following treatment, and the condition recurs in less than 1 in 20 of all cases.

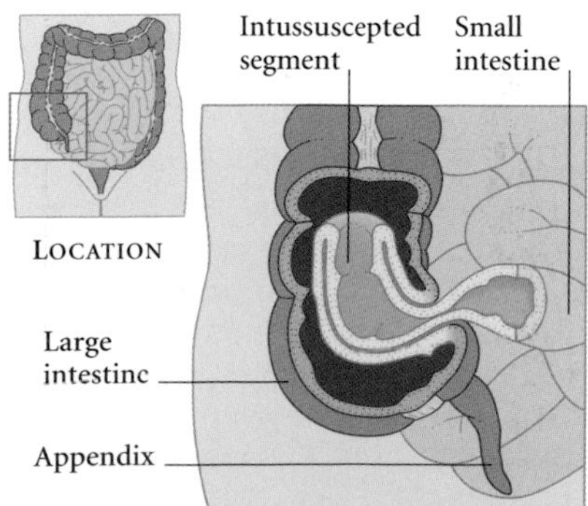
Intussuscepted segment
Small intestine
Location
Large intestine
Appendix

Intussusception

In this example of intussusception, the last part of the small intestine has passed into the adjacent section of large intestine and caused an obstruction.

(WWW) ONLINE SITES: p.1028

Constipation in children

Difficult, infrequent, and sometimes painful passage of hard feces

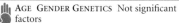

LIFESTYLE A low-fiber diet is a risk factor

AGE GENDER GENETICS Not significant factors

All children differ in their bowel habits. Some pass feces several times a day, and others may do so only once every few days. Both these situations are normal as long as the feces are not runny or hard enough to cause discomfort. The presence of hard feces that are difficult to pass indicates that your child has constipation, which is a common condition that affects children and adults of all ages. Constipation in children is usually only a temporary condition and is rarely an indication of a serious underlying condition.

What are the causes?

A common cause of temporary constipation is a change in diet, particularly if there is insufficient fiber or fluid in the diet. Constipation is rare in babies, but the condition may occur during the change from formula or breast milk to cows' milk. Sometimes, temporary constipation occurs during toilet training, when it is common for a toddler to try to avoid defecation. This phase may be associated with a toddler passing feces in abnormal places (*see* ENCOPRESIS, p.852). Illnesses that cause high fever and vomiting can also cause temporary constipation due to dehydration.

Underlying disorders that may cause chronic constipation include cerebral palsy (p.846), in which there is brain damage that impairs muscular control. An abnormally tight anal sphincter may also cause constipation by preventing the release of feces from the body.

What are the symptoms?

If your child has constipation, you may notice the following symptoms:

- Difficult passage of small or bulky hard, dry feces.
- Infrequent defecation.
- Soiling of clothes due to leakage of feces associated with constipation.
- Sometimes, loss of appetite.

Your child may be afraid to pass feces if there is discomfort during bowel movements, especially if he or she develops a painful tear in the anal tissue (*see* ANAL FISSURE, p.669) caused by straining to pass stools. In these cases, constipation may become a severe and chronic problem.

What can I do?

In most cases, constipation in children does not require medical treatment. You should encourage your child to drink plenty of fluids, and, if he or she is over age 6 months, you should make sure there is plenty of fiber in the diet from fresh fruit and vegetables. If the constipation is linked to problems with toilet training, patience and time will usually solve the problem. You should consult your child's doctor if the constipation persists for a week despite these self-help measures.

What might the doctor do?

The doctor will probably examine your child's abdomen and may perform a rectal examination, in which a gloved finger is gently inserted into the rectum. He or she may prescribe a short course of drugs to soften the feces (*see* LAXATIVES, p.924), as well as an anal cream, to reduce the discomfort of defecation. Softened feces will also allow an anal tear to heal. Once the pain of defecation is gone, your child should feel confident to pass feces normally again. Rarely, surgery may be required to treat an anal sphincter that is abnormally tight.

If constipation persists, your child may need an abdominal X-ray (p.244) or a specialized contrast X-ray (p.245) of the bowel to exclude an underlying disorder. Severe constipation caused by a condition such as cerebral palsy may need lifelong treatment with laxatives. However, constipation usually clears up within 1–2 weeks of changing the child's diet or of laxative treatment.

(WWW) ONLINE SITES: p.1028, p.1035

ENDOCRINE AND METABOLIC DISORDERS

Some endocrine and most metabolic disorders in children are present from birth and are caused by an abnormal gene that is inherited from one or both parents. Most of these disorders are rare, but, when they do occur, they can adversely affect normal growth and development unless diagnosed and treated early.

Most of the disorders covered in this section are caused by the defective production of enzymes that are vital for the metabolic (chemical) processes of the body. In congenital adrenal hyperplasia, the first condition covered, a defective enzyme affects the production of one or more hormones by the adrenal glands. As a result, important metabolic processes are disrupted and a high production of sex hormones may affect the formation of a female baby's genitals. The articles that follow include a general introduction to a group of rare inherited metabolic disorders, known as inborn errors of metabolism, and separate entries on four of the disorders, phenylketonuria, galactosemia, Tay–Sachs disease, and albinism. The section ends with a general article on growth disorders that cause abnormally short or, rarely, tall stature. Endocrine and metabolic disorders that affect adults only or adults in addition to children may be found in hormones and metabolism (pp.670–693) or in the section covering the body system affected.

KEY ANATOMY

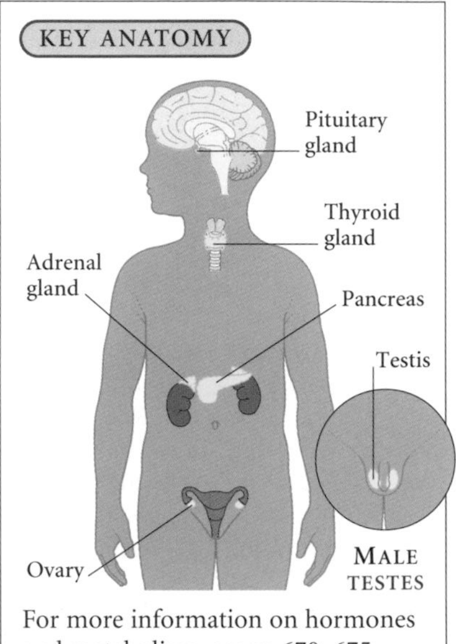
Pituitary gland
Thyroid gland
Adrenal gland
Pancreas
Testis
Ovary
MALE TESTES

For more information on hormones and metabolism, *see* pp.670–675.

Congenital adrenal hyperplasia

Abnormally high production of male sex hormones by the adrenal glands

 AGE Present from birth

 GENETICS Due to an abnormal gene inherited from both parents

 GENDER LIFESTYLE Not significant factors

Congenital adrenal hyperplasia is a rare inherited condition that affects between 1 in 10,000 and 1 in 16,000 babies in North America. In the disorder, the production of one or more hormones in the adrenal glands is abnormal.

In the most common form of congenital adrenal hyperplasia, there is a deficiency of an enzyme that is essential for production of the adrenal hormones aldosterone, which maintains the salt and water balance in the body, and cortisol, which maintains glucose levels in the blood. As a result, these hormones may be either absent or deficient. The condition also leads to high levels of male androgens (male sex hormones). Congenital adrenal hyperplasia is caused by an abnormal gene inherited in an autosomal recessive manner (*see* GENE DISORDERS, p.269).

WHAT ARE THE SYMPTOMS?

The symptoms of congenital adrenal hyperplasia may be present at birth or may develop later in childhood. Elevated levels of androgens may lead to the following symptoms:

- In girls, an enlarged clitoris and external genitals that are fused, giving a masculinized appearance.
- In boys, a slight increase in pigmentation of the scrotum, which usually goes unnoticed.
- Early puberty in boys.

Lack of aldosterone may cause a "salt-losing crisis" in which there is a sudden loss of salt and fluid about 1–3 weeks after birth. The symptoms may include:

- Lethargy.
- Vomiting.
- Loss of weight.

If it is not treated, the salt-losing crisis may lead to shock (p.414), which may be life-threatening. A lack of cortisol may cause low levels of glucose in the blood (*see* HYPOGLYCEMIA, p.691).

WHAT MIGHT BE DONE?

Congenital adrenal hyperplasia is usually diagnosed in girls at birth due to the appearance of the genitals. In boys, the condition may become apparent due to a salt-losing crisis at a few weeks of age.

An affected child will have blood tests to measure the levels of hormones, salt, and glucose. If a baby has a salt-losing crisis, he or she will need emergency treatment in the hospital with intravenous salt and glucose solutions. Intravenous cortisol and a drug that mimics the actions of aldosterone will also be given. A child with the condition requires lifelong treatment to replace the deficient hormones and to normalize the production of androgens. Affected girls may require surgery to correct genital abnormalities.

If treated, most children with congenital adrenal hyperplasia lead normal lives. A pregnant woman who has previously given birth to a child with the condition may be offered screening (*see* PRENATAL GENETIC TESTS, p.787), and, if necessary, drug treatment to minimize the effects of the condition on a female fetus may be prescribed.

(WWW) ONLINE SITES: p.1032, p.1033

Inborn errors of metabolism

Genetic disorders in which chemical processes in the body are disrupted or faulty

 AGE Present from birth

 GENETICS Due to an abnormal gene usually inherited from both parents

 GENDER LIFESTYLE Not significant factors

Inborn errors of metabolism is a general term used to describe a group of genetic disorders in which the body chemistry (metabolism) is affected by an abnormal gene. In each disorder, the defective gene affects the production of a particular enzyme that is essential for specific metabolic processes. The disruption of these processes results in damage to one or more organs of the body, and the severity of a particular disorder depends on the chemical processes affected. Over 200 inborn errors of metabolism have been identified, but each disorder is extremely rare. Most of the abnormal genes that cause these inborn metabolic disorders are inherited in an autosomal recessive manner (*see* GENE DISORDERS, p.269).

WHAT ARE THE TYPES?

Many inborn errors of metabolism result in the buildup of harmful chemicals that cause damage to one or more organs. In phenylketonuria (right), the accumulation of phenylalanine leads to brain damage. In galactosemia (p.868), the sugar galactose builds up to a dangerously high level and causes liver and brain damage. In Tay–Sachs disease (p.868), chemical buildup in the brain leads to fatal brain damage. In the milder condition albinism (p.868), a deficient enzyme affects the production of the pigment melanin, which gives color to the skin, eyes, and hair, but there is no harmful chemical buildup.

The symptoms of inborn errors of metabolism are usually present at or soon after birth, although in some cases they may not appear until later in childhood. The symptoms may include unexplained illness and failure to thrive in a newborn, and drowsiness, floppiness, seizures, and developmental delay (p.853) in older babies and children.

WHAT MIGHT BE DONE?

If there is a family history of an inborn error of metabolism or an ethnic predisposition to a particular metabolic disorder, prospective parents may be screened for the presence of the abnormal gene before pregnancy (*see* TESTS FOR ABNORMAL GENES, p.239). If there is no family history or predisposition, the mother may be screened for the condition before the baby is born (*see* PRENATAL GENETIC TESTS, p.787). In Canada, the US, and many other developed countries, newborn infants are screened for phenylketonuria in the first few days of life (*see* SCREENING FOR METABOLIC DISORDERS, below).

Some inborn errors of metabolism can be treated easily. For example, an affected child's diet can be adapted to restrict the intake of substances, such as phenylalanine or galactose, that his or her body cannot process. If the missing enzyme is made by white blood cells, the condition may sometimes be cured by a bone marrow transplant (p.454).

TEST SCREENING FOR METABOLIC DISORDERS

All newborn babies in Canada are routinely screened 24 hours after birth for one inborn error of metabolism, phenylketonuria (right), and for hypothyroidism (p.680). This is done by pricking the baby's heel with a small needle in order to obtain a few drops of blood for testing using a special card. The card is sent to a laboratory for analysis and the test results are available in a few days.

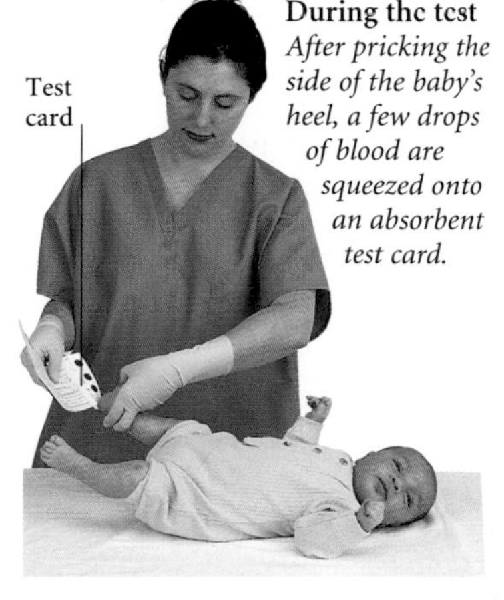
Test card

During the test
After pricking the side of the baby's heel, a few drops of blood are squeezed onto an absorbent test card.

WHAT IS THE PROGNOSIS?

The prognosis for inborn errors of metabolism depends on the disorder and how early it is diagnosed. Some disorders, such as albinism, rarely cause serious problems; others, such as galactosemia, can be treated successfully if diagnosed soon after birth. However, there is no treatment for Tay–Sachs disease, which is usually fatal in early childhood.

(WWW) ONLINE SITES: p.1032, p.1033

Phenylketonuria

An inherited chemical defect that can cause brain damage

 AGE Present from birth

 GENETICS Due to an abnormal gene inherited from both parents

 GENDER LIFESTYLE Not significant factors

Children with phenylketonuria lack the enzyme that is responsible for breaking down phenylalanine, which occurs naturally in most food containing protein. As a result, phenylalanine is converted into harmful substances that build up in the blood and may damage the developing brain. Although phenylketonuria is rare in Canada, all newborn babies are screened for the disorder because of the risk of serious brain damage. Like most inborn errors of metabolism, phenylketonuria is due to an abnormal gene inherited in an autosomal recessive manner (*see* GENE DISORDERS, p.269). If both parents carry a copy of the abnormal gene, there is a 1 in 4 chance that their baby will be affected.

WHAT ARE THE SYMPTOMS?

At birth, some babies with phenylketonuria have a red itchy rash similar to eczema (p.333). However, most infants who are affected with the disorder appear healthy. The symptoms usually develop gradually over a period of 6–12 months and may include:

- Vomiting.
- Restlessness and sometimes seizures.
- Stale, unpleasant skin odor.
- Delay in development (*see* DEVELOPMENTAL DELAY, p.853).

Left untreated, phenylketonuria may lead to serious brain damage, resulting in severe learning disabilities (*see* MENTAL RETARDATION, p.854).

WHAT MIGHT BE DONE?

In Canada, a blood test for phenylketonuria is done on all newborn babies (*see* SCREENING FOR METABOLIC DISORDERS, p.867). Early screening for the defect is important because prompt diagnosis and treatment are vital. If your baby is diagnosed as having phenylketonuria, he or she will probably be prescribed a special formula or milk substitute that is rich in protein but contains little phenylalanine. Your child should continue with a diet low in phenylalanine, at least throughout his or her childhood until the brain has stopped growing. Most doctors recommend that an affected person follow a low-phenylalanine diet for life.

All women with the condition who are planning a pregnancy are advised to follow a low phenylalanine diet before conception and throughout pregnancy.

With early diagnosis and treatment, children with phenylketonuria develop normally, attend regular schools, and have a normal life expectancy.

(WWW) ONLINE SITES: p.1032 p.1033

Galactosemia

An abnormal buildup of the sugar galactose, due to a deficient enzyme

 AGE Present from birth

 GENETICS Due to an abnormal gene inherited from both parents

 GENDER LIFESTYLE Not significant factors

Galactosemia is a rare condition in which harmful amounts of galactose, a sugar that is present in milk, build up in a baby's body. Normally, an enzyme in the liver changes galactose into glucose, but in galactosemia, this enzyme is missing. If the disorder is not treated, high levels of galactose will accumulate and lead to serious damage to the liver, brain, and eyes. The condition is caused by an abnormal gene that is inherited in an autosomal recessive manner (*see* GENE DISORDERS, p.269).

WHAT ARE THE SYMPTOMS?

Symptoms of galactosemia appear in the first few days of life, often after the baby's first milk feedings and include:

- Vomiting and diarrhea.
- Failure to gain weight.
- Yellow coloration of the skin and the whites of eyes (*see* NEONATAL JAUNDICE, p.817).

If galactosemia is left untreated, cataracts (p.573), chronic liver failure (p.650), and mental retardation (p.854) may develop.

WHAT MIGHT BE DONE?

If the disorder is suspected, a sample of the baby's urine will be taken and tested for galactose. If the urine test confirms that your baby has galactosemia, you will be advised to exclude galactose from his or her diet and to use milk substitutes. It is usually recommended that the person affected follow a galactose-free diet throughout childhood and sometimes for life. With early diagnosis and treatment, most children develop normally. However, some may have mild learning difficulties.

(WWW) ONLINE SITES: p.1032 p.1033

Tay–Sachs disease

An inherited condition in which harmful chemicals accumulate in the brain

 AGE Present from birth

 GENETICS Due to an abnormal gene inherited from both parents

 GENDER LIFESTYLE Not significant factors

Tay–Sachs disease is a fatal childhood disorder that is most common in the Ashkenazi Jewish population, affecting about 1 in 2,500 people in this group. The condition is caused by the lack of a vital enzyme in the brain. Without the enzyme, abnormal chemicals build up, leading to progressive and fatal brain damage. Tay–Sachs disease is caused by an abnormal gene that is inherited in an autosomal recessive manner (*see* GENE DISORDERS, p.269).

WHAT ARE THE SYMPTOMS?

A baby with Tay–Sachs disease often appears healthy at birth. The symptoms, which usually start to appear at 3–6 months of age, may include:

- Exaggerated startle response to noise.
- Muscle weakness and floppy limbs.
- Lack of awareness of surroundings.
- Deteriorating vision.

During the first 6 months of life, an affected baby may have seizures and gradually become paralyzed.

WHAT MIGHT BE DONE?

If your baby's doctor suspects Tay–Sachs disease, he or she may arrange for a blood test or a test on a sample of skin tissue to check for the missing enzyme. The doctor will also examine your baby's eyes to look for an abnormal "cherry-red spot" on the retina (the light-sensitive cells at the back of the eye). There is no treatment for Tay–Sachs disease, but an affected child will be made as comfortable as possible by treating symptoms as they arise.

People who are at risk of having a child with Tay–Sachs disease, especially Ashkenazi Jews, can be screened for the abnormal gene (*see* TESTS FOR ABNORMAL GENES, p.239) before marriage or pregnancy. If both partners in a couple are found to be carriers of the Tay–Sachs gene, there is a 1 in 4 chance of their child being affected. The couple will be offered genetic counseling (p.270) to explain these risks and outline the options they may wish to consider. Affected couples may decide not to have children or to conceive a child using IVF treatment (*see* ASSISTED CONCEPTION, p.776), so that the embryo can be tested for the presence of the disease before implantation in the uterus.

Tay–Sachs disease is a fatal disorder, and children with the disease do not usually survive beyond age 5.

(WWW) ONLINE SITES: p.1032 p.1033

Albinism

An inherited condition in which there is inadequate production of the pigment that gives color to skin, eyes, and hair

 AGE Present from birth

 GENETICS Due to an abnormal gene

 GENDER Risk factors depend on the type

 LIFESTYLE Not a significant factor

Albinism is a rare disorder in which a baby is born with little or no color in the skin, hair, and eyes or, more rarely, in the eyes only. Like other inborn errors of metabolism (p.867), the condition is caused by a defective enzyme essential for the production of the pigment melanin. In most cases, albinism is caused by an abnormal gene inherited

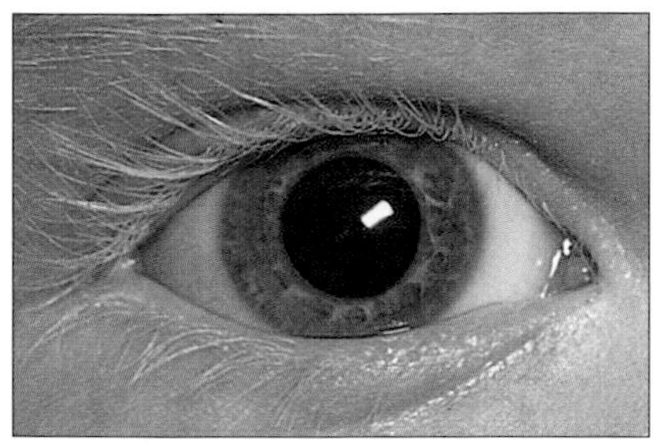

Albinism
The iris of this eye is pink and the eyebrows and eyelashes are white, due to absence of the brown pigment melanin.

in an autosomal recessive manner (*see* GENE DISORDERS, p.269) and affects the skin, hair, and eyes. A less common type, in which the abnormal gene is inherited in an X-linked recessive manner from the mother, affects only males. In this type of albinism, only the eyes are affected by the lack of melanin. Albinism affects about 5 in 100,000 babies.

WHAT ARE THE SYMPTOMS?

The symptoms depend on the amount of melanin produced and vary from mild to severe. They may include:

- Unusual eye color, ranging from pink to pale watery blue.
- Dislike of bright light.
- Involuntary jerky eye movements.
- Severe visual impairment.
- White hair and fair skin that does not tan normally.

Children with albinism are at increased risk of developing skin cancer (p.344) in later life from exposure to sunlight.

WHAT MIGHT BE DONE?

Albinism is usually diagnosed from the baby's appearance at birth. If albinism is suspected, a blood test is performed to confirm that the enzyme is missing. There is no medical treatment for the condition. However, tinted lenses help with the aversion to bright light, and visual impairment can be corrected with glasses or, when the child is older, with contact lenses. The doctor will also recommend the use of sunscreens and sunblocks (p.893) and a hat to protect your child's skin in bright sunlight. People with albinism have a normal life expectancy. Parents of children with albinism may find it useful to contact support groups for advice.

(WWW) ONLINE SITES: p.1032

Growth disorders

Abnormally short or tall stature in babies and children due to a number of causes

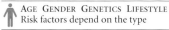

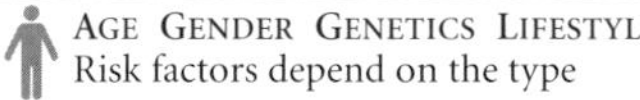
AGE GENDER GENETICS LIFESTYLE
Risk factors depend on the type

Children of the same age vary greatly in height due to factors such as diet, genetics, and ethnic background. In most cases, tall or short stature is not abnormal and is due to a family tendency to be taller or shorter than average or to reach final height later than usual. Tall or short stature is a cause for concern only if the child's height is well outside the average range for his or her age (*see* GROWTH CHARTS FOR CHILDREN, p.42). Abnormally short or tall stature may be caused by a number of disorders.

WHAT ARE THE TYPES?

Normal growth depends on a nutritionally adequate diet and good general health and is controlled by specific hormones. Disruption of any of these three important factors may lead to a growth disorder that results in a child having abnormally short or tall stature.

SHORT STATURE A child may be shorter than normal if his or her diet is inadequate. A chronic illness, such as cystic fibrosis (p.824) or severe asthma (*see* ASTHMA IN CHILDREN, p.839), may also result in poor growth. Crohn's disease (p.658), a type of inflammatory bowel disease, is another example of a chronic illness that may lead to short stature. Babies who have intrauterine growth retardation (p.796) may reach a shorter than average height in later life.

Sometimes, short stature is caused by insufficient production of the hormones that are necessary for normal growth. In some children, the pituitary gland does not produce enough growth hormone (*see* HYPOPITUITARISM, p.678). Insufficient production of thyroid hormones is another cause of poor growth (*see* HYPOTHYROIDISM, p.680).

Short stature is also a characteristic feature of Turner syndrome (p.823), a genetic disorder that only affects girls. In addition, short stature may occur as a result of a skeletal abnormality such as achondroplasia (p.833), an inherited disorder in which the bones of the legs and arms are shorter than normal.

TALL STATURE Children may be temporarily taller than others of the same age and sex if puberty occurs early (*see* ABNORMAL PUBERTY IN MALES, p.728, and ABNORMAL PUBERTY IN FEMALES, p.739). However, in such children, the final height is usually normal. In very rare cases, exaggerated growth caused by the overproduction of growth hormone results in excessive height known as gigantism. The overproduction may be due to a pituitary gland tumor (*see* PITUITARY TUMORS, p.676). Boys with the chromosome disorder Klinefelter syndrome (p.822) may also grow taller than normal at puberty.

HOW IS IT DIAGNOSED?

Your child's height will be measured during routine checkups. If his or her height is consistently either lower or higher than the normal range, he or she will need to be measured more frequently. If growth rates continue to be abnormal, tests may be performed to check hormone levels and to look for underlying disorders, such as a genetic abnormality. In some cases, maturity of a child's bones may be assessed by taking X-rays (p.244) of the hand and wrist.

WHAT IS THE TREATMENT?

Treatment for growth disorders is most successful if started well before puberty when bones still have the potential for normal growth. Short stature caused by an inadequate diet usually improves if the diet is modified while the child is still growing. If the growth disorder is a result of chronic illness, careful control of the illness can sometimes result in normal growth. Growth hormone deficiency is usually treated by replacement of growth hormone. Hypothyroidism is treated by replacing thyroid hormone.

Abnormal early puberty may be treated using drugs to halt the advancement of puberty. Gigantism caused by a pituitary gland tumor may be treated by removal of the tumor.

Treated early, most children with a growth disorder reach a relatively normal height, but, if treatment is delayed until puberty, normal height is more difficult to achieve. Abnormal stature may cause a child to be self-conscious and unhappy, and he or she may need support such as counseling (p.971).

(WWW) ONLINE SITES: p.1033

Bedwetting

Involuntary emptying of the bladder during sleep, also known as enuresis

AGE Considered abnormal only over the age of 6 years

GENDER Slightly more common in boys

GENETICS Sometimes runs in families

LIFESTYLE Emotional stress is a risk factor

Children normally stop wetting the bed between the ages of 3 and 6 years. Bedwetting is considered a problem only if it persists after age 6 or if it starts again after 6 months or more of dryness. At age 5, about 1 in 10 children wets the bed regularly. At age 10, the number is about 1 in 20. The problem is slightly more common in boys. Some children are late staying dry at night because the section of the nervous system that controls the bladder develops slowly. Sometimes, this developmental delay runs in families. Other children start to bedwet because of stressful events such as divorce. In rare cases, the condition develops because of an underlying disorder, such as diabetes mellitus (p.687) or a urinary tract infection (*see* URINARY TRACT INFECTIONS IN CHILDREN, p.871). Chronic bedwetting distresses both the child and the family.

WHAT CAN I DO?

The most important factors to help your child stop bedwetting are praise, patience, and encouragement. Talking to your child may help highlight worries that could be a cause. Minimize fluid intake after 4 pm or so. Routine visits to the toilet before bedtime are important, and it may be helpful to wake your child at your own bedtime so that he or she can urinate. A chart, on which your child is awarded a star after each dry night, is a visible reminder of progress. If your child is still wetting the bed after age 6 or begins to wet after 6 months or more of being dry at night, seek medical advice.

WHAT MIGHT THE DOCTOR DO?

Your child's doctor may test a urine sample to exclude diabetes or a urinary tract infection that may need treatment. If the problem is psychological, your child may see a psychologist.

SELF-HELP OVERCOMING BEDWETTING

A child may be helped to overcome persistent bedwetting by using a pad and buzzer system. The pad, which can detect moisture, is placed in the bed and attached to a buzzer. When a child starts to urinate, the buzzer is activated. The noise wakes the child who can then get up and go to the bathroom before going back to sleep. After a few weeks, the child will wake automatically without the buzzer if he or she needs to urinate at night.

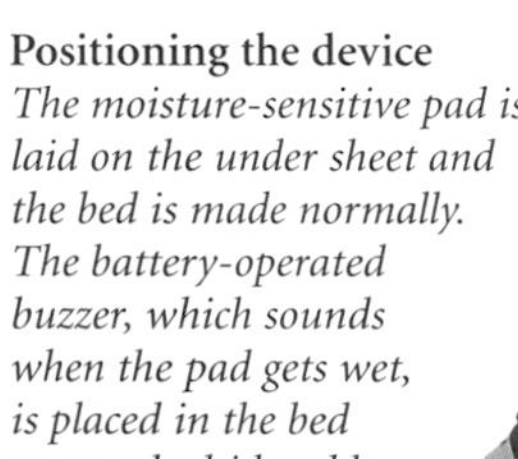
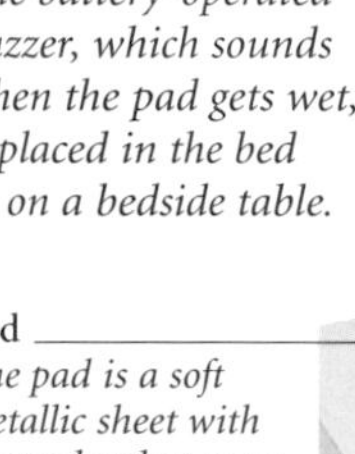
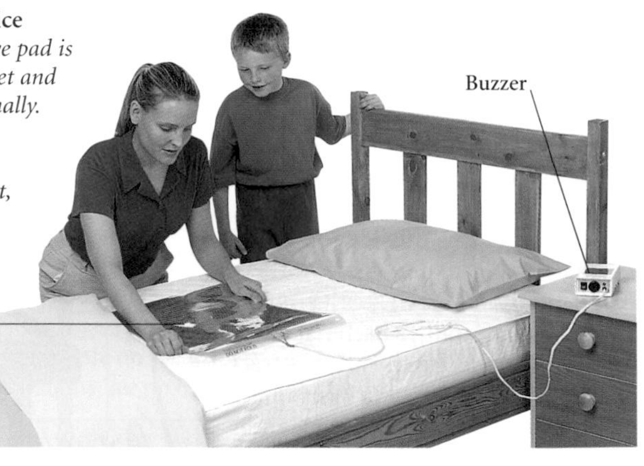
Buzzer
Pad

Positioning the device
The moisture-sensitive pad is laid on the under sheet and the bed is made normally. The battery-operated buzzer, which sounds when the pad gets wet, is placed in the bed or on a bedside table.

The pad is a soft metallic sheet with electrodes that react to moisture and trigger the buzzer

Children may overcome persistent bedwetting with a special pad that triggers a buzzer as soon as they start to urinate (*see* OVERCOMING BEDWETTING, above). If your child goes away overnight, a nasal spray that contains desmopressin (*see* DRUGS THAT AFFECT BLADDER CONTROL, p.939) may be prescribed. If the problem persists, your child may be referred to a special clinic for advice. With patience and support, most children eventually stop bedwetting.

(WWW) ONLINE SITES: p.1028

Wilms tumor

A rare cancer of the kidney, also known as a nephroblastoma

AGE Usually develops between birth and the age of 5

GENETICS Sometimes runs in families

GENDER LIFESTYLE Not significant factors

Wilms tumor is a rare cancer, affecting fewer than 8 in 100,000 children. The tumor commonly develops under age 5 but may be present at birth. Usually, one kidney is affected, but in about 1 in 10 children with the disease tumors are present in both kidneys. The cause of Wilms tumor is unknown, but the cancer sometimes runs in families.

WHAT ARE THE SYMPTOMS?

A tumor may be large before symptoms appear. The symptoms may include:

- Obvious swelling in the abdomen.
- Pain or discomfort in the abdomen.
- Occasionally, blood in the urine.

A child with these symptoms should be seen by a doctor immediately.

WHAT MIGHT BE DONE?

The doctor will examine your child and test a urine sample for the presence of blood. If the doctor suspects that there is a tumor in the kidney, further tests will be necessary. Ultrasound scanning (p.250) or CT scanning (p.247) of the kidneys may be done. Other tests, such as a chest X-ray (p.490), may also be performed to check if the cancer has spread elsewhere in the body.

Surgical removal of the affected kidney is the usual treatment for Wilms tumor. The remaining healthy kidney can easily perform the work of both. To destroy any remaining cancerous cells, an affected child may have radiation therapy (p.279) and/or chemotherapy (p.278). In rare cases in which both kidneys are removed, dialysis (p.707) or a kidney transplant (p.708) is necessary. Treatment has a high success rate, and about 8 in 10 affected children are free of the cancer after 5 years.

(WWW) ONLINE SITES: p.1028, p.1037

TREATING DISEASE

This section provides an overview of a wide range of medical treatments, such as types of drugs and surgery. It also covers rehabilitation and physical, psychological, and complementary therapies. The section provides advice on home nursing and caring for the critically ill and dying. The final part illustrates the general principles of first aid for a range of injuries and disorders. Many of the articles direct you to online sites where further information can be found.

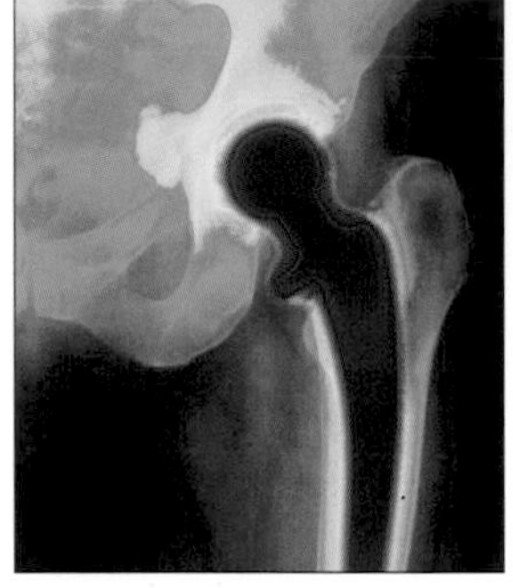

Artificial hip joint
Joints that have been damaged by disease can be replaced by artificial joints to relieve pain and restore mobility.

INTRODUCTION

MEDICAL AND PHARMACEUTICAL RESEARCH has provided doctors with a broad range of effective treatments, including powerful drugs and precise new forms of surgery. Although the goal of many treatments is to cure a disease or disorder, the majority are aimed at relieving symptoms. Some treatments, such as immunization, aim to prevent disease from developing. Treatments for sick, disabled, and elderly people are provided in the hospital and at home by caregivers ranging from nurses and other professionals to relatives and friends.

When you are ill or injured, the first decision to be made is whether professional medical help is required. This may be obvious in an emergency but less so if the disorder is troublesome but not serious. Many minor problems disappear without treatment, and many others can be dealt with using home or over-the-counter remedies. In addition, routine first-aid treatments may be used for trivial injuries or while waiting for medical assistance for serious injuries. However, if you are in doubt, or if a condition does not start to improve with self-help measures, you should seek medical advice.

In the past, people generally accepted the treatment offered with little or no question. Today, with better education and access to medical information, people expect to be involved in decisions about their treatment. Most treatments fall into one of three broad categories: drugs, surgery, or some form of supportive therapy or care. In practice, many disorders require the use of a combination of treatments used simultaneously or in sequence and often supported by nursing care.

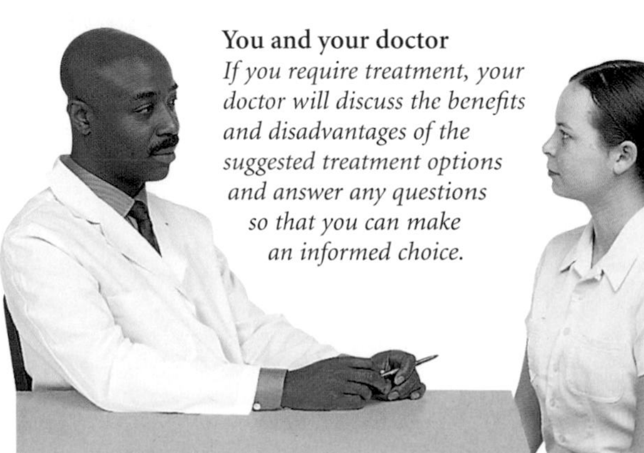

You and your doctor
If you require treatment, your doctor will discuss the benefits and disadvantages of the suggested treatment options and answer any questions so that you can make an informed choice.

Bacteria
Sample of ineffective antibiotic
Bacteria-free zone
Sample of effective antibiotic

Testing drugs
Drug prescriptions are tailored for each patient's needs. The sensitivity of an infectious organism to various antibiotics can be tested before prescribing.

AIMS OF TREATMENT

The purpose of treatment may be to cure a disorder, slow down its progress, relieve symptoms, or prevent an illness from developing. Supportive treatments, such as physiotherapy and counseling, focus on speeding up recovery or helping people come to terms with their illness and live as independently as possible. The optimal result of treatment is to cure an illness completely with minimum risk and side effects. Many drugs and surgical treatments are complete cures. For example, antibiotics cure by eliminating infection, and surgery can cure completely when used to repair an injury or replace a diseased organ with a transplant.

When there is no available cure, the next preferred option is relief of symptoms. Some drugs are used to relieve symptoms common to several conditions. For example, analgesics relieve headache and muscle and joint pain regardless of whether the cause is a minor injury, a common cold, or a chronic condition such as arthritis. Other drugs relieve symptoms specific to particular conditions. Bronchodilators are drugs that ease the wheezing that occurs in lung disorders such as asthma. Drugs may also be used to increase

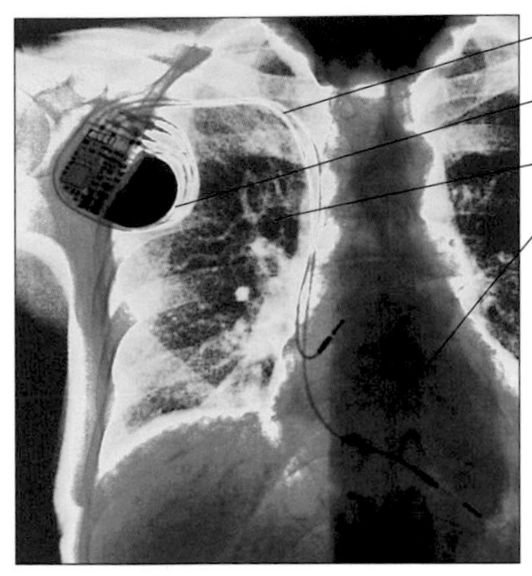

Wires to the heart
Pacemaker
Lung
Heart

Regulating the heart
Some treatments, such as the fitting of an artificial pacemaker, help control the effects of a disorder rather than treating the underlying cause.

the levels of substances such as neurotransmitters and hormones. For example, drugs that restore normal levels of dopamine, a neurotransmitter that acts on the part of the brain controlling movement, reduce symptoms of Parkinson's disease.

If a disease is incurable, treatment may be able to slow its progression. For example, immunosuppressant drugs may slow the progress of joint damage due to rheumatoid arthritis. Increasingly, doctors use drug treatments to prevent disease. For example, drugs that lower blood pressure reduce the risk of stroke.

Planning treatment

Before starting treatment, your doctor will discuss the available options with you. For minor illnesses or when there is only one suitable treatment, little discussion may be required. However, for a chronic disorder or one that is more serious, there may be a choice between treatment with surgery and with drugs or between different forms of surgery or different drugs. Your doctor will also discuss the risks or possible side effects of your treatment. Your consent will be needed before treatment can be started.

For most disorders, early diagnosis and treatment offer the best chance of a cure. Treatment that is started late may involve more risks and longer recovery time. However, in the absence of a clear diagnosis, your doctor may wait for confirmation of the diagnosis rather than start possibly inappropriate treatment. Before starting treatment, your doctor will take into account your age and existing medical conditions and may ask you to make lifestyle changes, such as losing weight or stopping smoking.

In circumstances in which there is no prospect of a cure, there may be little benefit in radical treatment. For example, when a person has advanced cancer, chemotherapy and radiation therapy treatments may do little to prolong life and cause debilitating side effects. The better option may be relief of symptoms and care given by professionals in a hospital or hospice or by caregivers and family at home.

Advances and improvements

Advances in medicine have led to new treatments that have played a major part in improving life expectancy and reducing chronic illness. The development of new technologies has brought about improvements in surgical techniques that minimize postoperative pain,

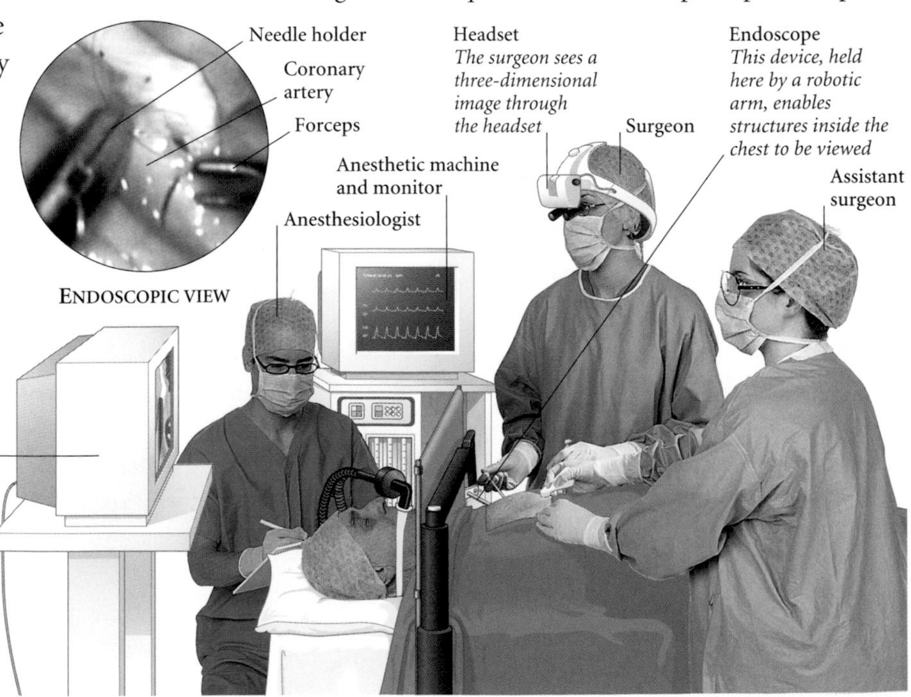

Needle holder
Coronary artery
Forceps
ENDOSCOPIC VIEW
Headset
The surgeon sees a three-dimensional image through the headset
Surgeon
Endoscope
This device, held here by a robotic arm, enables structures inside the chest to be viewed
Assistant surgeon
Anesthetic machine and monitor
Anesthesiologist
Monitor
The assistant surgeon views the procedure on this monitor

Endoscopic surgery
Coronary artery bypass surgery can now be done endoscopically. Compared to standard open surgery, in which the heart is stopped and a heart–lung machine used, the procedure is quicker and results in fewer complications.

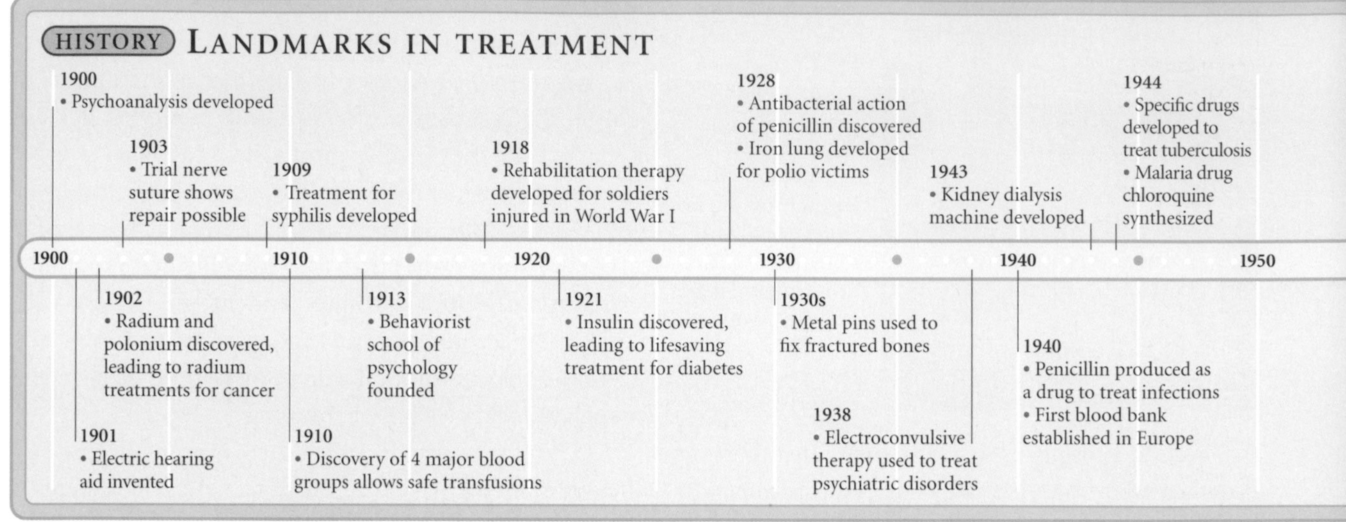
HISTORY LANDMARKS IN TREATMENT
1900
• Psychoanalysis developed
1901
• Electric hearing aid invented
1902
• Radium and polonium discovered, leading to radium treatments for cancer
1903
• Trial nerve suture shows repair possible
1909
• Treatment for syphilis developed
1910
• Discovery of 4 major blood groups allows safe transfusions
1913
• Behaviorist school of psychology founded
1918
• Rehabilitation therapy developed for soldiers injured in World War I
1921
• Insulin discovered, leading to lifesaving treatment for diabetes
1928
• Antibacterial action of penicillin discovered
• Iron lung developed for polio victims
1930s
• Metal pins used to fix fractured bones
1938
• Electroconvulsive therapy used to treat psychiatric disorders
1940
• Penicillin produced as a drug to treat infections
• First blood bank established in Europe
1943
• Kidney dialysis machine developed
1944
• Specific drugs developed to treat tuberculosis
• Malaria drug chloroquine synthesized
1900
1910
1920
1930
1940
1950

New technologies and discoveries
In the space of 100 years, new technologies and drug discoveries have provided treatments that have reduced the impact of many diseases. In particular, new types of surgery have made operations safer and shortened recovery times.

reduce complications and risks, and allow quicker recovery. However, before a new drug or technique is approved, it must be rigorously tested and its safety and effectiveness demonstrated in controlled trials.

Development of drugs

At one time, the only drugs available were substances extracted from plants and natural minerals such as salts. Over the past 100 years, medical research has produced safer and more reliably effective synthetic modifications of naturally occurring substances and some completely new drugs. Antibiotics and vaccines have revolutionized the treatment of infections. Genetic engineering is now used to produce human insulin and other hormonal treatments. In addition, research into the underlying mechanisms of disease has produced tailor-made drugs that target a particular part of a disease process. For example, some treatments for high blood pressure block the action of particular hormones on the heart and blood vessels. The development of immunosuppressant drugs that reduce the body's rejection of new tissue has enabled transplant surgery to be carried out successfully.

Advances in surgery

About 30 years ago, major surgery inevitably required a large incision to open up the body. Conventional open surgery is still needed for many conditions, but there are now many less invasive techniques that result in fewer complications, less postoperative pain, and shorter recovery times. Surgery can be performed through a natural body opening or through a small incision using a viewing tube called an endoscope. Surgical precision has been improved by advances in imaging and viewing techniques. In microsurgery, surgeons use a specialized microscope and tiny instruments to perform operations on minute structures, such as nerves and small blood vessels. For operations on delicate areas such as the brain, surgeons can wear a headset that displays three-dimensional images of the area being operated on. Other technological advances include the use of lasers and electrocautery equipment, which seal blood vessels as tissue is cut, reducing bleeding during surgery.

Home therapy
Although some treatments must be started in the hospital, they can be continued at home by a visiting professional, such as a physiotherapist. The trend is for recovery and rehabilitation to take place at home.

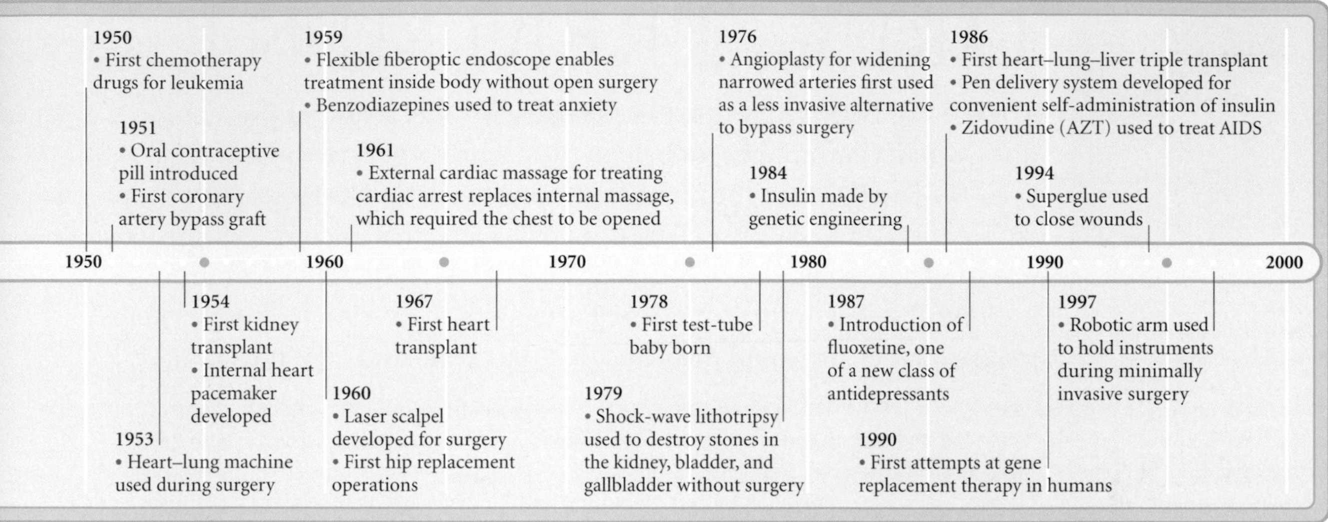
1950
• First chemotherapy drugs for leukemia
1951
• Oral contraceptive pill introduced
• First coronary artery bypass graft
1959
• Flexible fiberoptic endoscope enables treatment inside body without open surgery
• Benzodiazepines used to treat anxiety
1961
• External cardiac massage for treating cardiac arrest replaces internal massage, which required the chest to be opened
1976
• Angioplasty for widening narrowed arteries first used as a less invasive alternative to bypass surgery
1984
• Insulin made by genetic engineering
1986
• First heart–lung–liver triple transplant
• Pen delivery system developed for convenient self-administration of insulin
• Zidovudine (AZT) used to treat AIDS
1994
• Superglue used to close wounds
1950
1960
1970
1980
1990
2000
1953
• Heart–lung machine used during surgery
1954
• First kidney transplant
• Internal heart pacemaker developed
1960
• Laser scalpel developed for surgery
• First hip replacement operations
1967
• First heart transplant
1978
• First test-tube baby born
1979
• Shock-wave lithotripsy used to destroy stones in the kidney, bladder, and gallbladder without surgery
1987
• Introduction of fluoxetine, one of a new class of antidepressants
1990
• First attempts at gene replacement therapy in humans
1997
• Robotic arm used to hold instruments during minimally invasive surgery

CHANGING ATTITUDES TO CARE

Treatment must be provided in a setting of effective care, but, even in the case of serious illness, care no longer necessarily takes place in the hospital. Complex treatments, such as kidney dialysis, can now be carried out at home by caregivers, and a number of surgical procedures take place in ambulatory care centers and doctors' offices, allowing the patient to return home for convalescence immediately after treatment.

Interest in complementary medicine is growing, and conventional medical treatment may not always be some people's first choice for many problems. For example, chiropractic may be used for back problems, and acupuncture for pain relief. Most complementary therapies have not been subjected to the same research and trials as conventional treatments, but good evidence exists for the effectiveness of some of these therapies, particularly acupuncture and biofeedback.

ORGANIZATION HOW THIS PART OF THE BOOK IS ORGANIZED

This part of the book describes drug treatments, surgery, supportive care and therapeutic treatments, and first aid. The drug treatment section covers the major drug groups, arranged primarily under the body systems that they are used to treat. Common brand-name and generic drugs are listed in the drug glossary at the end of the book.

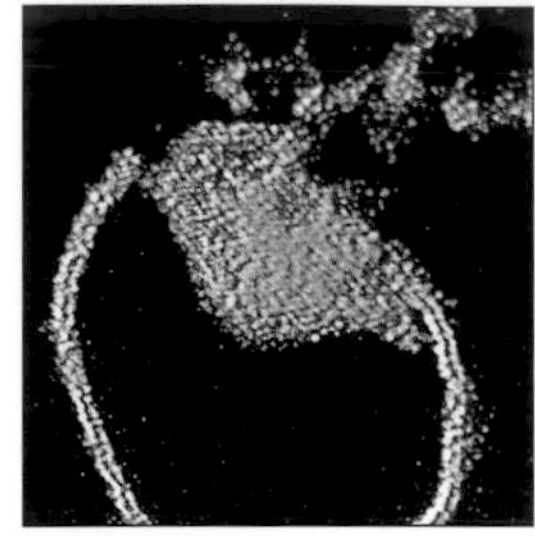
Drug killing a bacterium
A Staphylococcus aureus *bacterium is destroyed by an antibiotic drug.*

DRUG TREATMENT

MEDICINAL DRUGS ARE SUBSTANCES that can cure, arrest, or prevent disease, relieve symptoms, or help in the diagnosis of certain disorders. Over the past 50 years, the number of drugs available has increased enormously, and new drugs have been developed that are more effective in restoring health and saving lives than ever before. Researchers continue to improve the effectiveness of existing drugs and to develop treatments for as yet unconquered areas of medicine, such as cancer and HIV infection.

Modern drug therapy began when scientists discovered how to isolate the active ingredients in plant sources and to create synthetic versions of those substances. This new technology, together with a better understanding of how the body functions both in health and disease, has enabled the development of drugs that target specific processes in the body.

Before a new drug is marketed, it is thoroughly tested. The effects of the drug on people are measured against either the existing standard treatment or a placebo (an inactive substance that looks and tastes exactly like the drug).

Health Canada's Therapeutic Products Directorate (TPD) approves and licenses drugs in Canada. A new drug is approved only if it is shown to be safe and effective. The TPD can withdraw drug approval at any time if that drug later proves to cause unacceptable side effects.

HOW DRUGS WORK

Drugs act in a variety of ways. Some kill or halt the spread of invading organisms, such as bacteria, fungi, and viruses. These drugs include antivirals, antifungals, and antibiotics. Other drugs, known as cytotoxic drugs, kill cells as they divide or prevent their replication. Cytotoxic drugs are mainly used in the treatment of cancer.

Some drugs simply supplement missing or low levels of natural body chemicals such as certain hormones or vitamins. Another group of drugs alters the effectiveness of certain body chemicals. These drugs work either by mimicking the action of natural chemicals to increase their effect or by blocking their action to decrease their effect (*see* HOW DRUGS ACT ON RECEPTORS, below). For example, beta blocker drugs slow the heartbeat rate by blocking the effects of chemicals that increase heartbeat rate.

Drugs may also affect the part of the nervous system that controls a particular process. For example, most drugs taken to relieve vomiting act on the vomiting center in the brain.

HOW DRUGS ARE USED

There are various different ways in which drugs may be delivered to their intended site of action. Some, such as eyedrops or topical skin preparations, can be applied directly to the target area. These preparations tend to have a very localized effect and do not usually enter the bloodstream in significant quantities. Other preparations are introduced into the bloodstream, which circulates them to their target area in the body. These drugs may be delivered by different routes, depending on which is the most effective way to reach the target area and on how the drugs are metabolized (*see* DRUG METABOLISM, opposite page).

DRUG ACTION — HOW DRUGS ACT ON RECEPTORS

Many cells have specialized areas, known as receptors, on their outer walls. Natural chemical messengers, such as hormones, bind with these receptors to produce changes in cells and thereby affect body processes. In order to treat some disorders, it may be necessary to increase or decrease the effect of a particular natural chemical. Drugs called agonists bind with specific receptors to produce an effect similar to that of the natural chemical. Antagonist drugs inhibit the effect of the chemicals by blocking the receptors.

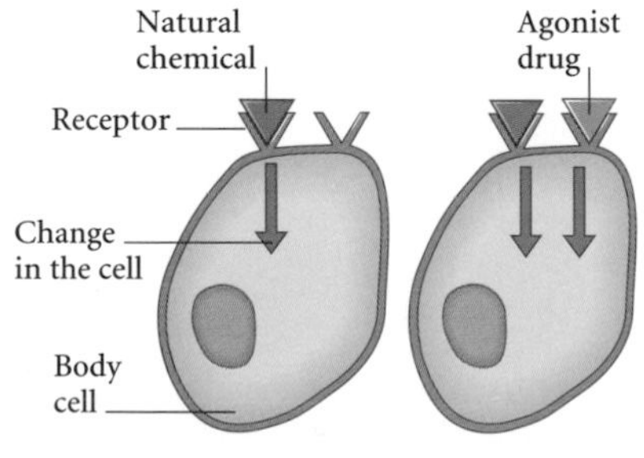
Natural chemical
Agonist drug
Receptor
Change in the cell
Body cell
BEFORE DRUG
AFTER DRUG
Agonist drugs
An agonist drug mimics the action of body chemicals. It occupies an empty receptor and enhances the natural chemical's effect.

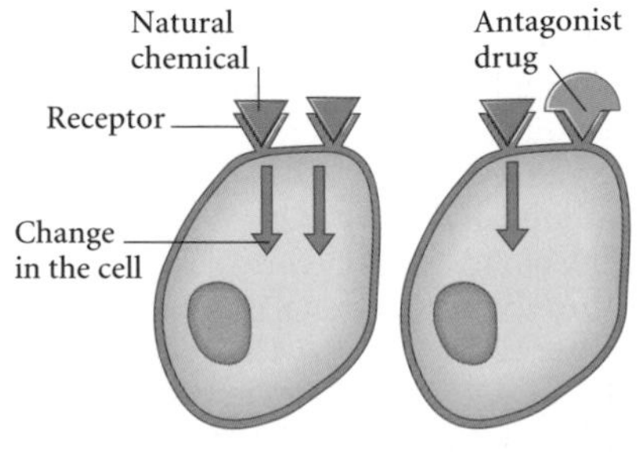
Natural chemical
Antagonist drug
Receptor
Change in the cell
BEFORE DRUG
AFTER DRUG
Antagonist drugs
An antagonist drug occupies cell receptors, preventing the body chemicals from binding to them, thereby inhibiting their action.

PROCESS DRUGS IN YOUR BODY

Drugs can be introduced into the bloodstream by a number of different routes. Most commonly, they are taken orally in the form of pills, capsules, or liquids. However, if oral treatment is inappropriate, drugs may be given in other ways. For example, a suppository containing a drug can be inserted into the rectum. If an immediate effect is needed, intravenous injection or infusion ensures the rapid delivery of the drug. A long-lasting effect is achieved by administering a drug in a skin patch or as an implant just below the skin.

Nasal/sublingual/buccal route
Drugs in a nasal spray, in a sublingual tablet (placed under the tongue), or inside a buccal tablet (placed in the cheek) are absorbed through the thin mucous membrane lining directly into the bloodstream.

Drug
Blood vessel
Mucus layer
Mucous membrane

Oral route
Drugs in pill, capsule, or liquid form are swallowed and pass into the digestive system. The drugs are then broken down in either the stomach or the intestines and are absorbed in the same way as food.

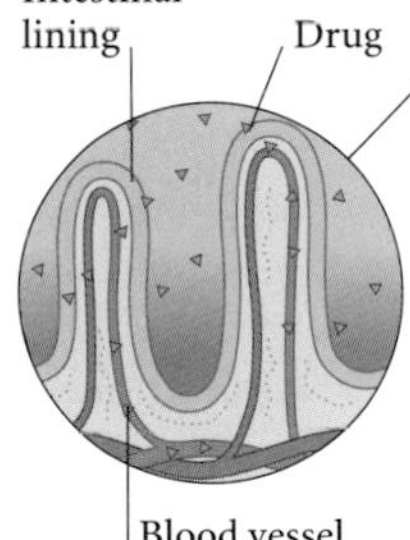
Intestinal lining
Drug
Blood vessel

Intravenous route
An injection into a blood vessel allows a drug to take effect very quickly. The drug enters the bloodstream directly and is rapidly circulated to the organ or tissues where it is needed.

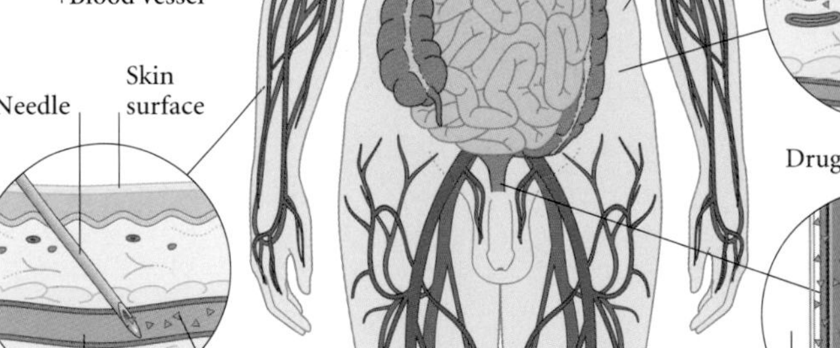
Needle
Skin surface
Drug
Blood vessel

Intramuscular route
Drugs are injected into a muscle in the upper arm, thigh, or buttock and then disperse into the bloodstream.

Needle
Muscle
Drug in bloodstream

Subcutaneous route
Drugs implanted or injected into fatty tissue just below the skin disperse slowly into the bloodstream.

Implant
Drug
Fatty tissue

Transdermal route
Drugs are released continuously from an adhesive patch or a gel on the skin surface and pass through the skin into blood vessels.

Drug
Patch
Skin surface
Blood vessel

Rectal route
Drugs inserted into the rectum in suppositories, enemas, or foam are quickly absorbed by blood vessels in the rectal wall.

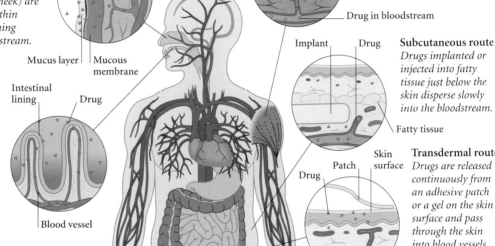

Drug
Rectal wall
Suppository

DRUG METABOLISM

Drugs taken orally are absorbed through the intestines and pass through the liver before entering the general circulation. Drugs that are administered by other routes enter the bloodstream before they pass through the liver. Once a drug has entered the bloodstream, it circulates to the site where its action is needed. Most drugs are metabolized (broken down or transformed) each time they pass through the liver. They are eventually excreted by the kidneys in urine and/or by the liver in bile, which is excreted in feces.

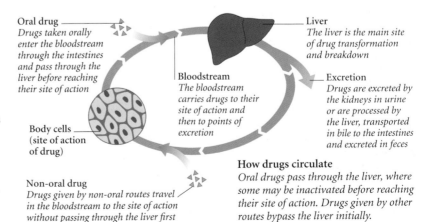

Oral drug
Drugs taken orally enter the bloodstream through the intestines and pass through the liver before reaching their site of action
Liver
The liver is the main site of drug transformation and breakdown
Bloodstream
The bloodstream carries drugs to their site of action and then to points of excretion
Excretion
Drugs are excreted by the kidneys in urine or are processed by the liver, transported in bile to the intestines and excreted in feces
Body cells (site of action of drug)
Non-oral drug
Drugs given by non-oral routes travel in the bloodstream to the site of action without passing through the liver first

How drugs circulate
Oral drugs pass through the liver, where some may be inactivated before reaching their site of action. Drugs given by other routes bypass the liver initially.

UNDERSTANDING DRUGS

All drugs, even the familiar ones such as aspirin, may have potentially harmful as well as beneficial effects. Whether you are prescribed drug treatment or you choose remedies for yourself, you will gain most benefit from drugs if you understand how they are likely to act and how to use them safely and effectively.

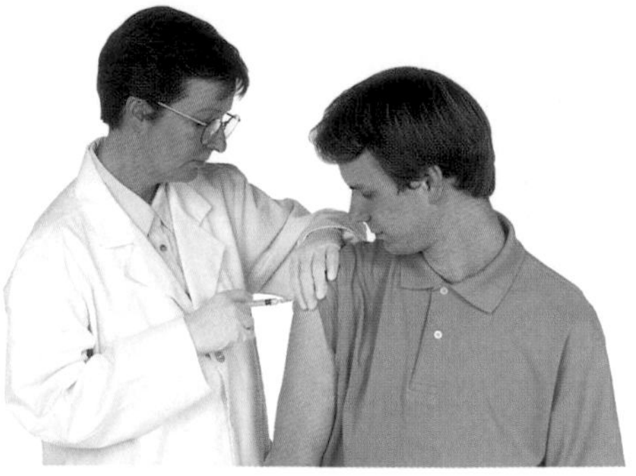

Courses of vaccination
Most drugs are used in the treatment of disease. However, vaccines may be given to prevent certain diseases, such as diphtheria or tetanus, from developing.

During the last century, advances in drug treatment have enabled doctors to cure many conditions, including a wide range of infectious diseases. Drug treatment can also control symptoms in disorders such as epilepsy and relieve common symptoms such as wheezing or itching. Today there is a vast range of drugs available for many purposes. Some drugs can be bought over the counter at pharmacies or other retail outlets. Other types of drugs require a doctor's prescription, and a few drugs are available only in hospitals. In order to make the best use of drug treatments and avoid any possible adverse effects, you must carefully follow the instructions given by your doctor or pharmacist or those supplied by the manufacturer. You may find it useful to discuss your treatment with your doctor or pharmacist so that you know when you can expect to feel an improvement and whether there will be any adverse effects.

The first article in this section discusses the types of effects that various drugs may have on the body. The second article gives practical advice about how you can use medication safely and effectively; it also discusses storing drugs safely.

How drugs affect you

How drugs act on your body and their possible effects

A drug may have several types of effects on your body in addition to the one intended. These include side effects, tolerance, and dependence. Interaction may also occur, in which drugs that are taken together enhance or reduce each other's actions. Many drugs can have a powerful psychological benefit called the placebo effect. Many unwanted effects, apart from the placebo effect, can be harmful, and your doctor will plan drug treatment to avoid or minimize their occurrence.

A drug's effects may vary among individuals. Drugs may have particularly strong effects on some people, such as children and elderly people.

SIDE EFFECTS OF DRUGS

Almost all systemic drugs (drugs that affect the whole body) can cause side effects – the undesired reactions resulting from a normal dose of a drug. Side effects occur because drugs act on cells throughout the body, not just in the desired area. For example, beta blocker drugs (p.898) may be used in the treatment of hypertension (p.403). However, the effect of their action on the heart is also a cause of fatigue.

Some side effects, such as the dry mouth caused by some antihistamines (p.906), are predictable because they result from the known chemical effects of a drug. However, drugs may also produce unpredictable reactions such as drug allergy (p.467). Any drug, including penicillins (*see* ANTIBIOTICS, p.885), can cause allergic reactions that can range in severity from a mild rash to severe breathing problems. Other unexpected reactions occur in people whose genetic makeup affects their body's ability to break down particular drugs. For example, some people of Mediterranean, African, or Southeast Asian origin inherit a condition called G6PD deficiency that affects the chemistry of red blood cells. If these people take certain drugs, such as sulfonamides, they may develop hemolytic anemia (p.450), in which red blood cells are destroyed prematurely. As a result, the blood does not carry enough oxygen to body tissues.

Most side effects are not serious and they often disappear gradually as your body becomes used to a drug. However, for some drugs used to treat serious disorders, the side effects are severe and potentially fatal. For instance, certain cytotoxic drugs used to treat cancer (*see* ANTICANCER DRUGS, p.907) are toxic to the heart and can cause it to fail. A medical decision to use a drug depends on whether the overall benefit outweighs the risk of harmful effects.

DRUG TOLERANCE AND DEPENDENCE

If you take certain drugs for a long time, your body adapts to them in a process known as tolerance. With some drugs, tolerance may be useful, allowing the body to overcome side effects while still responding to the beneficial effects of the drug. For example, many people taking antidepressants (p.916) find that side effects such as dry mouth disappear while the benefits remain. However, tolerance may make some drugs less effective so that a higher dose is needed to obtain the same result. The higher dose may increase side effects.

Dependence is a need for a drug. The need can be psychological, leading you to think that you cannot function normally without a certain drug. It can also be physical. For example, long-term use of laxative drugs can make your body depend on them for bowel movements.

If you become dependent on some drugs, such as benzodiazepines (*see* ANTIANXIETY DRUGS, p.916), your body may develop tolerance to them. If you then stop taking them, you may suffer unpleasant effects called withdrawal symptoms, which can at times be dangerous. It is also possible to become dependent on drugs that are not medicines, such as alcohol (*see* ALCOHOL DEPENDENCE, p.564) or nicotine.

PEOPLE AT SPECIAL RISK

The effects of a drug may differ from one person to another. This happens because people's bodies absorb and excrete drugs at different rates. In addition, the same dose of a drug may reach different concentrations in the blood depending on factors such as body size and kidney function. Groups who are at higher risk of adverse effects include fetuses, babies (and particularly breast-fed babies whose mothers are taking drugs), children, those with liver or kidney disease, and elderly people.

FETUSES Most drugs that are taken during pregnancy pass across the placenta to the fetus. Many can harm the fetus, especially if taken during the first 12 weeks of pregnancy when the fetus's organs are developing. If you are pregnant or you think you may be, check with your doctor or pharmacist before taking any drug. If you take regular medication for a long-term condition such as diabetes mellitus (p.687) or epilepsy (p.524), discuss your treatment with your doctor if you are planning to have a baby. Sometimes the risk to mother and fetus from not treating a condition such as epilepsy is greater than the risk from the drug itself.

BREAST-FED BABIES If a woman takes drugs while breast-feeding, they may pass into her breast milk. Some drugs cause unwanted effects in the baby. For example, antianxiety drugs may make the baby drowsy and cause feeding difficulties. If you are breast-feeding, you should check with your doctor or pharmacist before taking any drug.

BABIES AND CHILDREN Drugs must be used with care in babies and children. Children's doses are usually smaller than doses for adults and are often calculated on the basis of a child's weight or age. It is very important to give children the correct dose. Never give a child a drug prescribed for an adult.

PEOPLE WITH LIVER OR KIDNEY DISEASE Most drugs are broken down by enzymes in the liver. The drugs are then eliminated by the liver itself or by the kidneys in the urine (*see* DRUGS IN YOUR BODY, p.879). However, if your liver or kidneys are not functioning well, toxic substances may build up in your blood, thereby increasing the risk of side effects. You may therefore need lower doses than normal. Alcohol also affects liver function, and thus the effect of some drugs may be altered if you drink heavily or regularly.

OLDER PEOPLE Older people are at increased risk of side effects, which is often due to the declining function of organs such as the liver and kidneys as the body ages. This decline in function causes toxins to accumulate faster in the body. Older people may need to take several drugs together to treat a number of disorders, and therefore may also be at increased risk of drug interactions.

(WWW) ONLINE SITES: p.1030

Managing your medication

Using prescription and over-the-counter medications safely and effectively

Drugs must always be used with care, and you should be especially careful if you give them to children. It is important that you understand what drugs you are taking and how they are likely to affect you. Drugs must be stored safely and should be disposed of when expired or no longer useful.

HOW ARE DRUGS OBTAINED?

Drugs may be bought over the counter, but many require a doctor's prescription. Some over-the-counter (OTC) treatments, including many herbal and homeopathic remedies, are intended simply to relieve symptoms such as pain, nasal congestion, coughing, or indigestion. It is always wise to consult a pharmacist to make sure you are buying an effective remedy.

(COMPARISON) DRUG PREPARATIONS

Many drugs are available in different forms. Each form has advantages. For example, pills and liquids are easy to self-administer. Creams, ointments, gels, and sprays act directly at the site of application. Nonoral forms, such as inhaled and injected drugs, bypass the digestive system, which may break them down, and therefore reach the site of action at full strength.

Ingredients of medications
Medications are designed to be absorbed easily and to act over a set period of time. The drugs are mixed with inactive ingredients that control these factors.

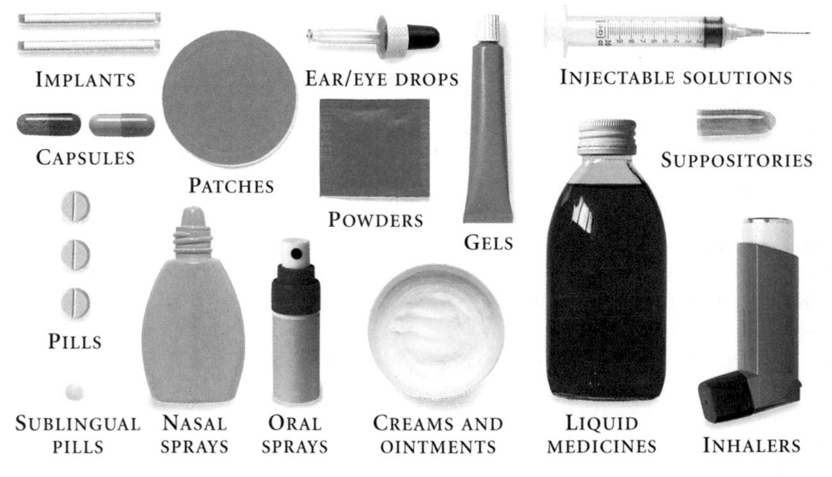
IMPLANTS
EAR/EYE DROPS
INJECTABLE SOLUTIONS
CAPSULES
PATCHES
SUPPOSITORIES
POWDERS
GELS
PILLS
SUBLINGUAL PILLS
NASAL SPRAYS
ORAL SPRAYS
CREAMS AND OINTMENTS
LIQUID MEDICINES
INHALERS

USING DRUGS SAFELY

Before taking any medication, make sure that you understand when and how to take it. Read the instructions carefully and discuss anything that you do not understand with your doctor or pharmacist. Find out whether the drug is likely to affect everyday tasks such as driving, whether you should take the drug with food or on an empty stomach, and what you should do if you miss or exceed a dose.

When you discuss your treatment with a doctor or pharmacist, let him or her know if you have recently taken any other medications, including any complementary remedies, because these could affect your new treatment. In addition, you should say if you have previously taken any OTC or prescribed medication that has affected you adversely. If you are planning to become pregnant or suspect that you may be pregnant, consult your doctor before starting any treatment because some drugs, such as retinoids (p.890), can be harmful to a fetus.

TAKING DRUGS CORRECTLY When taking pills or capsules, swallow them with plenty of water so that they do not become stuck in your esophagus. If you are taking liquid medicine, shake the bottle before use to mix the ingredients thoroughly and measure doses carefully. Devise a routine for taking the correct doses at the correct time, especially if you take several drugs.

Make sure that you complete the full course of any treatment, even if your symptoms seem to have disappeared. Never take a drug prescribed for someone else or give your prescribed drug to anyone else. If you are using an OTC remedy, do not take the drug for more than a few days unless you are sure that the cause of your symptoms is a minor, short-lived illness, such as a cold.

DEALING WITH SIDE EFFECTS Seek medical help if you develop any unexpected side effects or symptoms that seem unrelated to your illness while you are taking either prescription or OTC drugs. If you have a severe reaction to a drug such as difficulty breathing, call for urgent medical attention. If you have a mild reaction from a prescription drug, see your doctor as soon as possible and ask whether you should stop the treatment. If you have a mild reaction from an OTC drug, stop taking it and consult your doctor before continuing.

SELF-ADMINISTRATION GIVING A CHILD MEDICINE

When giving liquid medicines to a baby or a young child, use a syringe or dropper to avoid spillage and ensure that you give the correct dose. If you are unsure how to use the syringe or dropper, ask your doctor to show you how to measure and give a dose of medicine. When treating the child, hold him or her securely to give reassurance and keep the child from struggling.

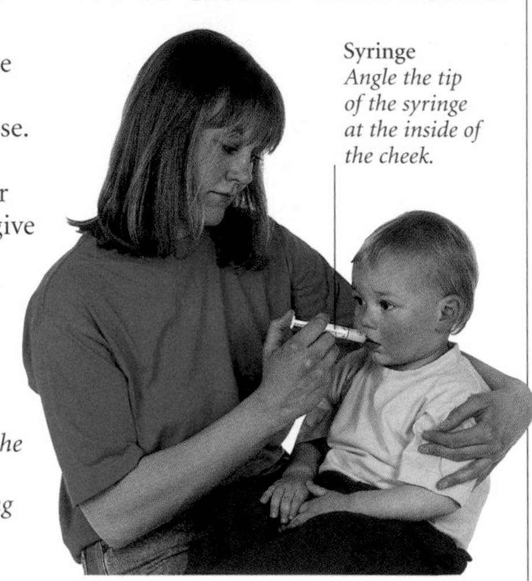

Syringe
Angle the tip of the syringe at the inside of the cheek.

Giving medicine with a syringe
Place the tip of the syringe well inside the child's mouth and angle it toward the cheek. Slowly press the plunger, allowing the child time to swallow. Do not aim directly down the child's throat.

TAKING LONG-TERM MEDICATION If you need drug treatment that continues for a long period of time, such as medication to treat high blood pressure (*see* HYPERTENSION, p.403) or diabetes mellitus (p.687), you may be given a prescription that can be refilled so that you do not have to see your doctor each time. However, you will still need to see the doctor regularly so that he or she can monitor your condition and your response to treatment. Never stop taking your medication suddenly without consulting your doctor first. For some drugs it is necessary to reduce the dose gradually so that your condition does not suddenly become worse. Gradual reduction of the dose of a drug also helps prevent you from developing withdrawal symptoms.

If you are taking long-term medication, always talk to your pharmacist before using any additional drugs. If you need treatment in the hospital, tell the hospital staff which drugs you are taking, including OTC drugs or complementary remedies. Do not take your own medications while in the hospital unless the staff specifically say that it is all right for you to do so. Some drugs, such as anticoagulants (*see* DRUGS THAT PREVENT BLOOD CLOTTING, p.904), can cause severe problems during surgery or emergency treatment or if they are taken with other drugs. If you are on long-term medication with certain drugs you should obtain a medical alert card, bracelet, or pendant giving details of your medication. You should always have this medical alert information with you so that it is available to medical staff who may treat you.

GIVING DRUGS TO CHILDREN

Medicine for babies and toddlers usually comes in liquid form, which makes it easier for them to swallow. It is usually simpler to administer liquid medicine by syringe or dropper (*see* GIVING A CHILD MEDICINE, above). If giving pills to older children, use soluble or crushable ones because children find it hard to swallow pills whole. If your child dislikes medicine, have a pleasant drink ready to wash away the taste or suggest that the child holds his or her nose while taking the medicine.

HOW SHOULD DRUGS BE KEPT?

Follow storage directions to prevent drugs from deteriorating. Some drugs need to be stored in a cool, dry place and others in the refrigerator or away from light. Always keep unrefrigerated medicines out of reach of young children, preferably in a locked cabinet.

Do not keep medicines beyond their expiration dates because they may become ineffective or even harmful. Always dispose of drugs carefully.

WWW ONLINE SITES: p.1030

DRUGS FOR INFECTIONS AND INFESTATIONS

As recently as 50 years ago, infectious diseases were the leading cause of death in children and young adults. That picture has changed with the introduction of immunization against the major childhood diseases, antibiotics to kill bacteria, and a wide range of other anti-infective drugs.

KEY ELEMENTS

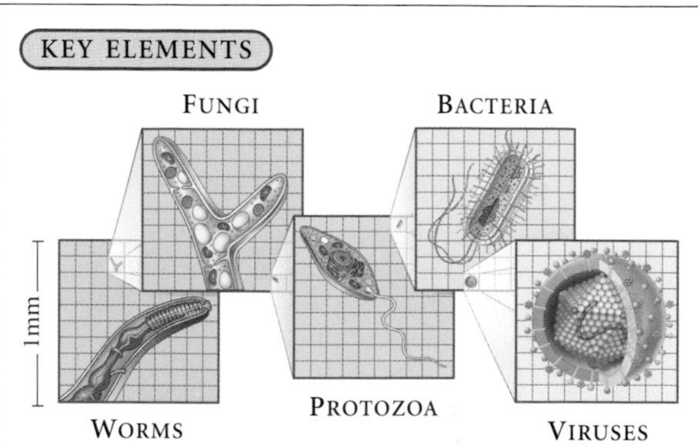
FUNGI
BACTERIA
1mm
PROTOZOA
WORMS
VIRUSES

For more information on the structure and function of infectious organisms, *see* pp.282–285.

This section describes the drugs that are used both to protect the body against infectious disease as well as to control or cure infections and infestations once they have developed.

The first article discusses vaccines and immunoglobulins, which are given to provide immunity against certain infections and prevent the spread of diseases. The next describes antibiotics, a large group of drugs used widely to treat bacterial infections. In Canada, 26 million prescriptions are written for these drugs each year.

The following articles in this section explain how drugs are used to treat infections caused by viruses, protozoa, and fungi. The information includes discussions of the prevention and cure of malaria and of recent advances made in the treatment of HIV infection and AIDS. The final article deals with drugs to eradicate parasitic worm infestations.

Vaccines and immunoglobulins

Preparations that immunize the body against certain infectious diseases

COMMON PREPARATIONS

VACCINES
• BCG • Cholera • Diphtheria • Dukoral
• Hemophilus b conjugate • Hepatitis A
• Hepatitis B • Influenza • Lyme disease
• Measles/Mumps/Rubella (MMR)
• Meningococcal polysaccharide • Pertussis
• Pneumococcus • Polio • Rabies
• Rotavirus • Tetanus • Typhoid • Varicella

IMMUNOGLOBULINS
• Cytomegalovirus • Hepatitis B • Immune globulin • Rabies • Rho(D) • Tetanus • Varicella

A variety of vaccines and immunoglobulins is available to provide protection against particular infectious diseases. The use of these preparations is known as immunization (p.45). Vaccines contain infectious organisms that have been modified or killed. Immunoglobulins contain antibodies (proteins made by white blood cells that neutralize or destroy infectious organisms) extracted from the blood of a person or an animal who has already had a specific disease. The body's own defense mechanism, the immune system, is able to combat many infections, but it cannot protect us against all infectious diseases. Immunization with vaccines or immunoglobulins is therefore used to give added protection. The incidence of a number of highly infectious diseases has declined dramatically worldwide since the introduction of immunization programs. One disease, smallpox, has been eradicated worldwide.

HOW DO THEY WORK?

There are two forms of immunization, which are known as active immunization and passive immunization (*see* HOW IMMUNIZATION WORKS, p.884). In active immunization, vaccines are given to stimulate the immune system to produce its own antibodies. A different vaccine must be given for each disease because each type of infectious organism triggers the production of a specific type of antibody. Some vaccines contain live organisms that have been altered and made harmless. Others contain killed organisms, part of an organism, or a toxin (poison) made by bacteria. All forms of vaccines have the same effect of priming the body's immune system to produce appropriate antibodies so that the body is ready to fight off invading organisms. Passive immunization uses immunoglobulins and works by introducing donated antibodies into the blood. These antibodies destroy infectious organisms that are present or that enter the body shortly afterward.

WHY ARE THEY USED?

Some highly infectious diseases cannot be treated effectively or can be so serious that prevention, in the form of active or passive immunization, is recommended. Active immunization with vaccines is used mainly to prevent diseases from spreading within a community. If most people are vaccinated, some diseases may eventually disappear. In developed countries, children are routinely given active immunization against a range of diseases such as measles (p.291), tetanus (p.301), and pertussis (whooping cough) (p.492), from the age of 2 months to 15 years (*see* ROUTINE IMMUNIZATIONS, p.45).

Other vaccines are used for specific groups of people. For example, immunization against influenza (p.287) is recommended for people who are at risk of becoming seriously ill if they develop the disease. Those at high risk

DRUG ACTION HOW IMMUNIZATION WORKS

The most commonly used method of immunization is known as active immunization or vaccination. This involves the introduction into the body of a harmless form of an infectious organism that stimulates the body to produce antibodies against that organism. To provide immediate protection, a method called passive immunization is used. This introduces into the body "ready-made" antibodies extracted from people or animals who already have immunity to the infection.

ACTIVE IMMUNIZATION

Many vaccines (known as live vaccines) are made from weakened forms of a disease-causing organism. Others use an inactive form or just a part of the organism, such as a protein. Protection may be lifelong, or booster shots may be needed.

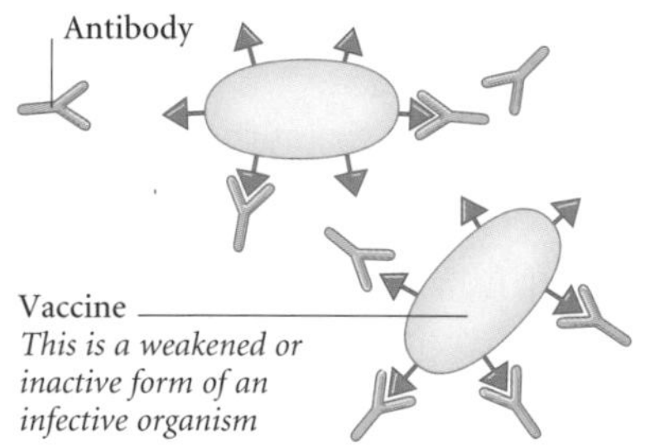
Antibody
Vaccine
This is a weakened or inactive form of an infective organism

1 *Antibodies are formed in response to the organisms in the vaccine. A "memory" of these antibodies is retained by the immune system.*

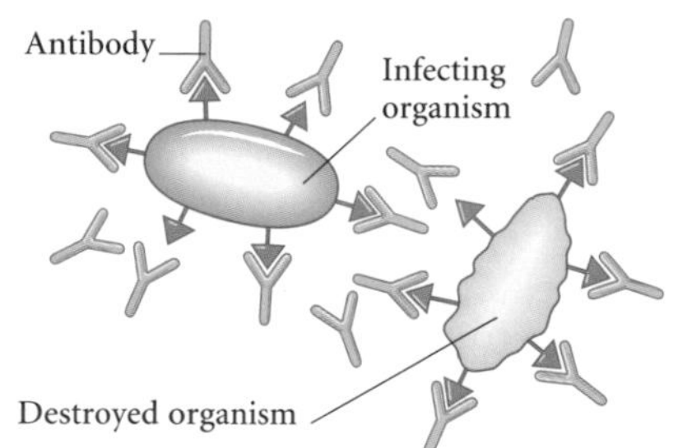
Antibody
Infecting organism
Destroyed organism

2 *If the same organism invades the body at a later date, the immune system will recognize it and will rapidly produce antibodies to destroy it.*

PASSIVE IMMUNIZATION

Immunity to an infectious organism can be achieved by the introduction of donated antibodies. This is needed if no active immunization is available or if rapid protection against an organism is vital, especially for people with weakened immune systems.

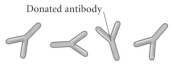

Donated antibody

1 *Antibodies taken from humans or animals with immunity to the infection are introduced into the body.*

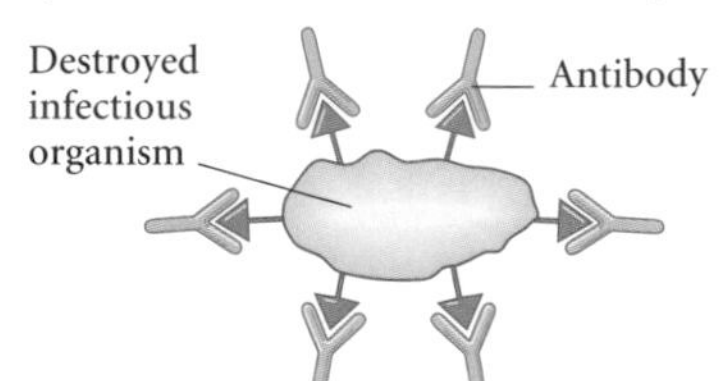
Destroyed infectious organism
Antibody

2 *When exposed to the infectious organism, the antibodies immediately destroy it. They also provide short-term protection against future infection.*

include elderly people, those who have reduced immunity because of diseases such as diabetes mellitus (p.687), and people with chronic heart or lung disease. There are many different types (strains) of influenza, and a specific vaccine is required for each one. New influenza vaccines are usually created each year to match the viral strains predicted to be most widespread.

Vaccines are also used for people who are at increased risk from certain infections. For example, people traveling to a developing country are advised to receive immunization against diseases that are common in that region (*see* TRAVEL IMMUNIZATIONS, p.86).

The main use of passive immunization with immunoglobulins is in cases where rapid protection against disease is necessary, for example after exposure to infection. This process is also used to provide antibodies against particular infections in people whose immune systems are suppressed due to disorders such as HIV infection or AIDS (p.295) or as a result of certain drug treatments (*see* IMMUNOSUPPRESSANTS, p.906).

HOW ARE THEY USED?

In most cases, vaccines and immunoglobulins are given by injection into a muscle, although the polio vaccine may be given orally. Many vaccines provide lifelong immunity with one dose or a course of several doses, but some may not give full protection or may be effective for only a few months or years. The degree of protection depends largely on the strength of the immune reaction that a vaccine provokes. Additional doses, known as booster doses, may be needed at regular intervals to reinforce the effect of the original course of a vaccine and to maintain immunity.

Often, vaccines against more than one infection are given in a combined preparation, limiting the number of injections that are needed. For example, vaccines against measles, mumps, and rubella (MMR) are commonly given in the same injection.

Immunoglobulins remain effective for a short period only, and protection diminishes gradually over 3–4 weeks. If continued protection is required, the treatment must be repeated.

WHAT ARE THE SIDE EFFECTS?

Some vaccines, such as the polio vaccine, cause few side effects. Others, such as the measles, mumps, and rubella vaccine, may produce mild forms of the diseases. Many vaccines may cause a red, slightly raised, tender area at the injection site and a mild fever or flu-like illness that lasts for a few days. Severe side effects, including the allergic reaction known as anaphylaxis (p.469), are rare. For most people, the risk of a reaction is far outweighed by the value of the protection given.

In some instances, vaccines should not be given. If you or your child is moderately or severely ill, vaccination should be postponed. Vaccines that contain live organisms should not be given to women during pregnancy or to people who have cancer or whose immune systems are suppressed.

Side effects of immunoglobulins are uncommon, but may include tenderness at the injection site and fever. Repeated treatment with immunoglobulins can sometimes cause an allergic reaction, such as a rash.

Antibiotics

A group of drugs used primarily to treat infections caused by bacteria

COMMON DRUGS

PENICILLINS
• Amoxicillin • Ampicillin • Clavulanate potassium • Penicillin G • Penicillin V

CEPHALOSPORINS
• Cefaclor • Cefazolin • Cefepime • Cefotetan • Cefoxitin • Ceftazidime • Cephalexin

MACROLIDES
• Azithromycin • Clarithromycin • Erythromycin • Lincomycin

TETRACYCLINES
• Doxycycline • Minocycline • Tetracycline

AMINOGLYCOSIDES
• Amikacin • Gentamicin • Neomycin • Streptomycin • Tobramycin

SULFONAMIDES
• Sulfamethoxazole-trimethoprim • Sulfisoxazole

QUINOLONES
• Ciprofloxacin • Gatifloxacin • Levofloxacin • Lincomycin • Moxifloxacin • Norfloxacin • Ofloxacin

OTHER ANTIBIOTICS
• Chloramphenicol • Clindamycin • Ertapenem • Imipenem • Linezolid • Metronidazole

DRUG ACTION HOW PENICILLINS WORK

Penicillin antibiotics are used to treat many bacterial infections. Penicillins are bactericidal, which means that they actually destroy the bacteria that are causing infection. Most other antibiotics work by altering chemical activity in the bacteria, thereby preventing them from reproducing. The immune system is then able to overcome the remaining infection.

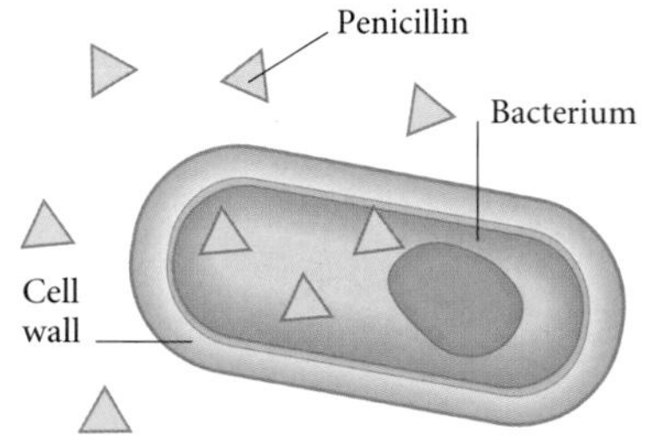
Penicillin
Bacterium
Cell wall

1 *Bacteria are single-celled organisms that have protective cell walls. The penicillin enters the bacterium, beginning a process that will destroy it.*

Disintegrating cell wall

2 *The drug interferes with chemicals needed by the bacterium to form its cell walls. This causes the cell walls to disintegrate, and the bacterium dies.*

Antibiotics are among the most commonly prescribed drugs in the world. They are used to treat and prevent bacterial infections. The drugs work either by killing bacteria directly or by halting their multiplication so that the body's immune system is able to overcome the remaining infection.

Antibiotics are classified in groups, such as penicillins, cephalosporins, tetracyclines, and aminoglycosides, depending on their chemical composition and the way in which they work. One of the most commonly used groups of antibiotics is penicillins (*see* HOW PENICILLINS WORK, above). Some antibiotics work against a wide range of bacteria and are called broad-spectrum antibiotics. Others work against specific types of bacteria and are known as narrow-spectrum antibiotics. Some also work against nonbacterial infections, such as the protozoal infection malaria (p.305).

WHY ARE THEY USED?

Antibiotics are most commonly used for short-term treatment of minor infections, such as those of the ear, throat, or urinary tract. They may be used to treat serious infections, such as septicemia (p.298) and bacterial meningitis (p.527).

On occasion, long-term treatment with low-dose antibiotics may be given to prevent infection in people whose immunity is reduced, such as those with HIV infection or AIDS (p.295) and people who are taking immunosuppressants (p.906). Long-term use of antibiotics may also be prescribed for other conditions, such as acne (p.340).

HOW ARE THEY USED?

Most bacterial infections are treated with oral antibiotics. Eye and ear infections are often treated using antibiotic drops (*see* DRUGS FOR EYE AND EAR DISORDERS, pp.919–921). To treat severe infections, when high doses of antibiotics are needed immediately, antibiotics may be given by intramuscular injection or by intravenous injection or infusion.

If you have a bacterial infection, your doctor will probably prescribe a specific antibiotic that is effective against the bacterium most likely to be causing the infection. For some conditions, such as pneumonia (p.490) or an infected wound, your doctor may need to do tests (*see* TESTS FOR MICROORGANISMS, p.234) to identify the disease-causing organism before prescribing a narrow-spectrum antibiotic. In the meantime, you will probably be treated with a broad-spectrum antibiotic. More than one antibiotic may be prescribed to reduce the risk of antibiotic resistance.

When you are taking antibiotics, you should continue treatment even after your symptoms start to improve. Finish the entire course as prescribed by your doctor in order to eradicate the infection. Bacterial resistance to antibiotics is increasing, due in part to overprescription and incorrect use.

Antibiotics are available by prescription only. The choice of antibiotic may be restricted if you are pregnant, have a history of allergy, have impaired kidney or liver function, or if you are taking other drugs that might interact with a particular antibiotic.

WHAT ARE THE SIDE EFFECTS?

Antibiotics do not usually cause serious side effects. The most common is diarrhea, although it is not usually severe. Antibiotics can alter the balance between normal bacteria and the yeast *Candida albicans* that occurs naturally in or on the body; this imbalance may lead to an overgrowth of the yeast (*see* CANDIDIASIS, p.309). In some cases, antibiotics destroy harmless bacteria in the bowel that prevent the growth of disease-causing organisms. Rarely, this results in the potentially serious condition pseudomembranous colitis, which can cause diarrhea and severe dehydration.

Penicillins may cause rashes and rarely a life-threatening allergic reaction called anaphylaxis (p.469). This is more common when the drugs are given by injection and occurs mainly in people who have previously had a mild allergic reaction to a penicillin. If you are allergic to one type of penicillin, you may be allergic to others in the same group. About 1 in 10 people who is allergic to penicillin is also allergic to cephalosporins. If you have an adverse reaction, such as a rash or difficulty breathing, stop taking the drug and see your doctor promptly. If you have previously had a reaction, tell your doctor.

Tetracyclines can cause damage to growing bones and teeth and for this reason are not prescribed for young children or for women during pregnancy. In some rare cases, aminoglycosides can damage the kidneys and affect the sense of hearing and balance.

Sulfonamides, one of the first classes of antibiotics to be used, can sometimes cause serious side effects, such as rashes and kidney damage.

Quinolones occasionally cause convulsions and should not be taken by people with epilepsy. They are not recommended for children as they may damage growing tendons and joints.

Antituberculous drugs

Drugs used in the treatment of the bacterial infection tuberculosis (TB)

COMMON DRUGS

- Ethambutol • Isoniazid • Pyrazinamide
- Rifabutin • Rifampin • Rifapentine
- Streptomycin

Antituberculous drugs are antibiotics (p.885) used to treat the contagious bacterial infection tuberculosis (p.491). The initial infection usually develops in the lungs, but tuberculosis (TB) may spread to other parts of the body, such as the kidneys, lymph nodes, and in some cases the membranes covering the brain and spinal cord (*see* MENINGITIS, p.527). Usually, several different antituberculous drugs are given to prevent the development of drug-resistant strains.

HOW ARE THEY USED?

If you are diagnosed with TB, the strain of bacteria causing the infection will be tested to determine its sensitivity to specific antituberculous drugs. While you are waiting for the results, which can take up to 2 months, your doctor will prescribe an initial combination of three or four drugs to be taken orally. The main drugs used are isoniazid, pyrazinamide, ethambutol, and rifampin. The test results, when available, will identify the most effective drugs for that particular strain of bacteria. Treatment with these drugs is usually continued for 6–9 months to make sure that your infection is eradicated. In some cases, this treatment may need to be continued for longer, depending on which organs are affected. For example, treatment may need to continue for 12 months if the infection has led to meningitis.

It is very important that you follow your doctor's instructions and complete the prescribed course of drugs. If you fail to do so, the bacteria may not be eradicated, and drug-resistant strains may develop, which can then be transmitted to other people.

WHAT ARE THE SIDE EFFECTS?

Antituberculous drugs may produce various side effects, including nausea, vomiting, rashes, and abdominal pain. Isoniazid, pyrazinamide, and rifampin may damage the liver or kidneys. Your doctor will therefore check your liver and kidney function on a regular basis. Isoniazid may also affect the nerves, causing numbness or tingling in the hands or feet. Ethambutol may rarely damage the nerves in the eyes, leading to problems with vision. People taking the drug are usually advised to have regular vision tests. If you are taking ethambutol and develop color blindness or blurry vision, you should seek medical advice immediately.

Antiviral drugs

Drugs that are used to treat certain infections caused by viruses

COMMON DRUGS

- Acyclovir • Amantadine • Didanosine (ddI)
- Famciclovir • Ganciclovir • Idoxuridine
- Interferons • Ribavirin • Valacyclovir
- Zalcitabine (ddC) • Zidovudine (AZT)

Various drugs are available to treat viral infections. Although these drugs may not eliminate an infection completely, they are often effective in reducing its severity. Many viral illnesses are mild and clear up without treatment because healthy people are usually able to fight off infection quickly. Sometimes, antivirals help relieve symptoms and hasten recovery. However, because viruses invade body cells in order to multiply, antivirals can damage body cells as well as the targeted viruses. Their use is therefore usually limited to the treatment of severe or recurrent infections.

WHY ARE THEY USED?

The main use for antivirals is in the treatment of infections that recur over a prolonged period. The drugs are also effective in treating or preventing infections in people with impaired immune systems who are at increased risk of severe illness and complications. In such cases, antiviral drugs may be life-saving.

Antivirals such as acyclovir are most commonly used to treat herpes infections, particularly the herpes simplex infections (p.289) that can cause recurrent attacks of cold sores and genital herpes. People who have frequent and severe recurrences of such infections may be prescribed long-term antiviral drug therapy. Acyclovir is also effective against the varicella zoster virus, which causes chickenpox (p.288) and shingles (*see* HERPES ZOSTER, p.288).

Some antivirals are used for specific infections, especially in people who are particularly vulnerable to disease. For example, zidovudine (AZT), didanosine (ddI), and zalcitabine (ddC) are used, sometimes in combination, to treat HIV infection and AIDS (*see* DRUGS FOR HIV INFECTION AND AIDS, opposite page). The antiviral drug amantadine may be prescribed for the treatment or prevention of influenza (p.287) in people who are at risk of complications, such as elderly people and those who have chronic lung or circulatory disease. The antiviral drug ganciclovir is used in the treatment of severe cytomegalovirus infection (p.290), especially when it occurs in people with reduced immunity.

Ribavirin can be used to treat babies with bronchiolitis (p.841), a serious inflammation of the lungs. This drug is also used to treat Lassa fever (*see* VIRAL HEMORRHAGIC FEVERS, p.293).

Interferon drugs (p.907), which are synthesized versions of antiviral substances produced naturally in the body, may be given with ribavirin to treat chronic hepatitis (p.645) and used alone for other noninfectious diseases.

How do they work?

Viruses invade body cells, where they use human genetic material (DNA) to reproduce. Antiviral drugs act in a variety of ways to block this process, either by causing changes within body cells to prevent the virus from replicating or by preventing the virus from entering cells. If treatment with antivirals is started early, the drugs usually work rapidly and relieve symptoms within a few days. However, some viruses may develop resistance to the effects of many drugs, which can make particular viral infections difficult to treat.

How are they used?

The drugs used to treat herpes infections, such as acyclovir, can be applied as a cream or taken orally, depending on the site and severity of the infection, or given by injection for urgent treatment of a serious infection.

The drugs amantadine and oseltamivir are taken orally and may be given over long periods as a preventive measure against influenza. Ganciclovir and interferons are given by injection in the hospital. Ribavirin can be given by inhaler to babies with bronchiolitis and is given as an injection for Lassa fever.

What are the side effects?

Acyclovir does not usually produce side effects, although when taken orally it may cause nausea. Rarely, when given by injection, the drug can cause kidney damage and may produce symptoms such as confusion and seizures.

In some people, amantadine causes reactions such as dizziness, confusion, and insomnia. Ganciclovir may cause skin rashes and nausea. This drug can reduce red blood cell production, causing anemia (p.446), and white blood cell production, increasing susceptibility to infections. Ganciclovir may also lead to impairment of kidney function. Ribavirin can cause anemia.

Side effects of interferon drugs are common and include flulike symptoms such as fatigue, fever, and aching muscles. These effects are usually mild and may diminish with continued treatment. However, prolonged treatment can lead to decreased production of red and white blood cells. In rare cases, people who are taking interferon drugs may develop tremor and have seizures.

Drugs for HIV infection and AIDS

A range of drugs that are used to treat HIV infection and its complications

Common drugs

Reverse transcriptase inhibitors
• Didanosine (ddI) • Lamivudine • Nevirapine • Stavudine • Tenofovir • Zalcitabine (ddC) • Zidovudine (AZT)

Protease inhibitors
• Amprenavir • Atazanavir • Indinavir • Nelfinavir • Ritonavir • Saquinavir

Other drugs for HIV
• Enfuvirtide • Interferons

Recent advances in drug treatments for people with HIV infection and AIDS (p.295) have offered new hope by slowing or halting the progression of the disease and improving quality of life.

The human immunodeficiency virus (HIV) infects and gradually destroys white blood cells of the body's immune system, known as CD4 lymphocytes, which normally help fight infections. People with HIV infection may have no symptoms for many years, or they may experience frequent mild infections. If the function of the immune system is seriously impaired, an infected person is said to have developed AIDS (acquired immunodeficiency syndrome). AIDS is diagnosed when the number of CD4 lymphocytes in the blood falls below a certain level or when one of a specific group of diseases develops. These diseases, called AIDS-defining illnesses, include a number of severe infections, such as pneumocystis infection (p.308), toxoplasmosis (p.307), and certain cancers, such as Kaposi's sarcoma (p.346) and non-Hodgkin's lymphoma (p.459).

Why are they used?

The drugs currently in use to treat HIV infection help to suppress the level of the virus in the blood, sometimes to undetectable levels, so that the immune system recovers sufficiently to overcome infections. Experts believe that, in some people, the drugs may be able to prevent the progression of HIV infection to AIDS. Evidence to support this is very encouraging, and many people who are using the newer drugs have shown a dramatic improvement in their condition.

Treatment of HIV infection involves two distinct groups of drugs: antiretroviral drugs, which act against the virus itself, and anti-infective drugs such as antibiotics (p.885), which are used to treat the diseases that develop as a result of reduced immunity.

Treatment with antiretroviral drugs is believed to be beneficial for anybody with HIV infection or AIDS, but expert opinion is divided about the best time to begin this treatment. Currently, drug treatment is recommended for people who have recently been exposed to the virus and are showing initial symptoms of infection, people with falling numbers of CD4 lymphocytes or rising virus levels, and people with an AIDS-defining illness. Generally, the earlier treatment begins, the greater the possibility of altering the course of the disease. However, people infected with HIV who are symptom-free may decide to postpone treatment because of the severe side effects caused by the drugs.

Treatment with antiretroviral drugs is also recommended for people who have been exposed to blood or other body fluids from a person with HIV infection. If drug treatment is started within 48 hours of exposure, the risk of infection may be lessened.

How do they work?

There are two main groups of antiretroviral drugs used in the treatment of HIV infection and AIDS: reverse transcriptase inhibitors and protease inhibitors. The drugs work by blocking the processes necessary for viral replication without significantly damaging the body cells that the virus has invaded. Reverse transcriptase inhibitors, such as zidovudine (AZT), alter the genetic material of the infected cell that is needed by the virus to replicate or the genetic material of the virus itself. Protease inhibitors, such as ritonavir, prevent the production of viral proteins necessary for replication.

How are they used?

Treatment of HIV infection and AIDS is subject to rapid change as knowledge about the virus increases. Currently, antiretroviral drugs are generally used in combination to destroy the virus more effectively and help prevent the development of drug-resistant strains of HIV. The drugs are taken orally, and often many tablets must be taken daily. It is important to take the drugs regularly to help prevent the emergence of drug resistance in HIV.

WHAT ARE THE SIDE EFFECTS?

If you have HIV infection, your doctor will discuss your treatment options with you at length because the drugs have side effects that should be weighed against the benefits of treatment.

Antiretroviral drugs can cause nausea, vomiting, and diarrhea, which may be very severe. Other serious side effects include inflammation of the pancreas (*see* ACUTE PANCREATITIS, p.652) and damage to the nerves, eyes, liver, or kidneys. Anemia (p.446) may also develop. You will need regular eye and blood tests to look for warning signs of side effects. Antiretrovirals are sometimes not given in the first 3 months of pregnancy because they may harm the fetus, but AZT is given later in pregnancy to prevent transmission of HIV to the fetus.

Antiprotozoal drugs

A group of drugs that is used to treat infections caused by protozoa

COMMON DRUGS

• Atovaquone • Diloxanide furoate • Doxycycline
• Eflornithine • Emetine • Iodoquinol
• Metronidazole • Paromomycin • Pentamidine
• Pyrimethamine with sulfadiazine
• Sulfamethoxazole-trimethoprim • Tetracycline

A range of drugs is used to treat infections caused by single-celled organisms called protozoa. Some antiprotozoals, such as metronidazole, are also used for bacterial infections. A specific group of the drugs is used to treat malaria, a serious disease caused by protozoa that affects millions of people worldwide (*see* ANTIMALARIAL DRUGS, right).

Antiprotozoals act in various ways, but most of the drugs work by preventing protozoa from multiplying.

WHY ARE THEY USED?

Antiprotozoals are commonly used to treat infections such as trichomoniasis (p.767), which affects the vagina, and giardiasis (p.307), which affects the intestine. Metronidazole is often prescribed for these conditions. Another common use for antiprotozoals, particularly pyrimethamine with sulfadiazine, is to treat toxoplasmosis (p.307), an infection that can cause severe illness in fetuses and people with reduced immunity. Sulfamethoxazole-trimethoprim and pentamidine may be used to treat pneumocystis infection (p.308), a lung infection that can be fatal in people with reduced immunity.

HOW ARE THEY USED?

Antiprotozoal drugs are normally taken for about a week to treat minor infections. For severe infections, treatment may need to be continued for several months, particularly in people who have reduced immunity, such as those with HIV infection or AIDS (p.295).

Most antiprotozoals are taken orally, but some may be given by injection to treat severe infections. Pentamidine is administered by injection or taken through an inhaler. This drug is given only under the supervision of a doctor.

WHAT ARE THE SIDE EFFECTS?

Antiprotozoal drugs frequently cause side effects, including nausea, diarrhea, and abdominal cramps. If you are taking metronidazole, you should avoid drinking alcohol because it can cause vomiting. Another common side effect of the drug is darkening of the urine. Pentamidine may cause a severe drop in blood pressure, either while the drug is being administered or immediately afterward. In rare cases, pyrimethamine reduces red blood cell production, causing anemia (p.446). If you have unusual bruising or bleeding while taking this drug, you should notify your doctor.

Antimalarial drugs

A group of drugs that is used for the prevention and treatment of malaria

COMMON DRUGS

• Chloroquine • Doxycycline • Halofantrine
• Hydroxychloroquine • Mefloquine • Primaquine
• Pyrimethamine with dapsone • Pyrimethamine with sulfadoxine • Quinine • Tetracycline

Antimalarial drugs are prescribed as a preventive measure against malaria (p.305) and also as treatment if the disease develops. There are various types of antimalarial drugs. Some are used as treatment only while others are used for both prevention and treatment. Malaria is a serious infectious disease caused by protozoa that are transmitted to humans by the bites of infected mosquitoes. The protozoa travel through the blood to the liver, where they multiply before reentering the blood and circulating throughout the body. At this stage, the symptoms of malaria appear.

No antimalarial provides complete protection against the disease because malarial protozoa continually develop drug resistance. For this reason, you should protect yourself from mosquito bites if you visit an area where malaria occurs. It is important to keep your body well covered by wearing long-sleeved shirts and long pants, and to use insect repellents and mosquito netting (*see* TRAVEL HEALTH, p.85).

HOW DO THEY WORK?

Antimalarial drugs are effective at different stages in the life cycle of the malarial protozoa. When taken to prevent malaria, the drugs act by killing the protozoa when they enter the liver. To treat malaria once symptoms have appeared, higher doses of drugs are given to destroy the protozoa when they are released from the liver into the blood. In some cases, the protozoa lie dormant in the liver and reactivate to cause recurrent episodes of malaria. These protozoa are difficult to eradicate and are treated with stronger drugs.

HOW ARE THEY USED?

The choice of antimalarial drug usually depends on which part of the world you are planning to visit or where you contracted the disease.

If you plan to visit an area where malaria occurs, you need to start preventive treatment as early as 3 weeks before departure, and you must continue for 4–6 weeks following your return. Antimalarial drugs are usually taken orally, either once a day or once a week. To increase protection against the strains of malaria that are widespread, combinations of drugs may be given.

If you develop malaria, the drugs used for treatment may be taken orally or given by injection up to several times a day for several days. If you have recurrent bouts of malaria, your doctor will prescribe an oral antimalarial such as primaquine for 2–3 weeks or more to eradicate the protozoa.

What are the side effects?

Antimalarials may cause a number of side effects, including nausea, diarrhea, headaches, and rashes. Quinine can cause ringing in the ears (*see* TINNITUS, p.602), hearing loss, blurry vision, and hot flashes. Mefloquine can sometimes cause people to experience dizziness, hallucinations, panic attacks, anxiety, sleep disturbances, and depression. This drug should not be taken during the first 3 months of pregnancy or while you are breast-feeding; it may damage the fetus or cause adverse reactions in the baby.

Antifungal drugs

Drugs that are used to treat infections caused by fungi

COMMON DRUGS

- Amphotericin • Butoconazole • Caspofungin
- Ciclopirox • Clotrimazole • Econazole
- Fluconazole • Flucytosine • Griseofulvin
- Itraconazole • Ketoconazole • Miconazole
- Nystatin • Terbinafine • Terconazole

Various drugs are available to treat fungal infections. These antifungal drugs have a wide range of uses because disorders resulting from fungal infections can occur on or in many different parts of the body. For example, treatment may be needed for infections of superficial areas such as the skin, nails, or genitals, but internal organs, such as the heart or lungs, may also be infected.

Most antifungals work by damaging the walls of fungal cells. This causes vital substances within the cell to leak out, destroying the fungus.

Why are they used?

Antifungal preparations are frequently used to treat minor fungal infections of the skin, such as athlete's foot (p.353) and ringworm (p.352), or the nails (*see* NAIL ABNORMALITIES, p.360). These types of drugs are also effective against candidiasis (p.309), a common fungal infection that can affect moist areas of the body, in particular the mucous membranes that line the mouth (*see* ORAL THRUSH, p.862) or the vagina (*see* VAGINAL YEAST, p.752).

Antifungal drugs may also be used for the long-term treatment of potentially serious fungal infections such as aspergillosis (p.309), which may affect the lungs and spread to other organs. People who have reduced immunity, such as those with HIV infection or AIDS (p.295), are at high risk from severe infections, and in such cases antifungal drugs may be life-saving.

How are they used?

If you have a fungal infection of the skin or scalp, your doctor may prescribe a cream or shampoo containing an antifungal drug such as miconazole. Symptoms normally start to improve within about a week. However, you should continue the treatment for at least 2 weeks after symptoms have disappeared to ensure that the infection has been eradicated. Nail infections are treated with a drug such as terbinafine, taken orally for several months. It may take much longer than this for the infected part of the nail to grow out.

Drugs that are used to treat vaginal yeast are available over the counter. The most commonly used drug is clotrimazole, which is inserted in the vagina either as a cream using a special applicator or as vaginal suppositories. These preparations vary in strength and, while some may be effective after a single dose, others need to be used for up to 14 days. For recurrent vaginal yeast, your doctor may prescribe a drug to be taken orally, such as fluconazole.

Oral thrush is treated by drugs given as lozenges to be dissolved slowly in the mouth or as gels or solutions applied directly to the affected area.

Serious infections of internal organs need to be treated with potent antifungal drugs, such as amphotericin, which are given initially by injection. Further treatment with oral drugs may then be continued for months.

What are the side effects?

Antifungal drugs used topically on the skin, scalp, or mucous membranes do not often cause side effects, although you may experience some local irritation. Nystatin used as a cream may stain clothing yellow.

If you are prescribed potent oral antifungals to treat infections of internal organs, you may experience nausea and vomiting. Less frequently, serious side effects may occur, including kidney damage and blood disorders. Treatment with the drug ketoconazole may cause liver damage.

Anthelmintic drugs

Drugs that are used to eradicate parasitic worm infestations

COMMON DRUGS

- Mebendazole • Praziquantel • Thiabendazole

Anthelmintic drugs are used to eradicate worm (helminth) infestations that occur in the intestine or in the tissues of other organs, such as the lungs. The most common intestinal worm infestation occurring in the US is pinworm (*see* PINWORM INFESTATION, p.310).

Infestations affecting the intestines are treated with anthelmintics that kill or paralyze the worms, which then pass out of the body in the feces. Worm infestations of other body tissues are treated with anthelmintic drugs that circulate in the bloodstream and are absorbed by the tissues, where they kill the worms by preventing them from obtaining essential nutrients.

How are they used?

Many anthelmintic drugs are appropriate only for certain types of infestation. Your doctor will therefore need to identify the worm before prescribing the drug to be taken. In most cases, infestations are treated easily with a short course of oral drugs.

The most commonly used drug for intestinal infestations is mebendazole. Pinworms can often be eradicated with a single dose of mebendazole, provided that treatment is combined with good hygiene measures, such as careful handwashing, to prevent reinfestation. Your doctor may suggest that the whole family be treated with the drug at the same time, because pinworms can spread very rapidly to other people.

Worm infestations of the tissues, such as hydatid disease (p.313), can affect the lungs, liver, or bones. Drugs such as thiabendazole may be prescribed for treatment. Because tissue infestations are difficult to eradicate, it may be necessary to take a course of drugs for several weeks.

Anthelmintics usually do not cause side effects. However, in some people, the drugs produce diarrhea, headaches, and dizziness. The safety of these drugs during pregnancy has not been established and may be harmful to a fetus.

> **WARNING**
> Consult your pharmacist or doctor before applying an antipruritic drug to broken or infected skin.

thereby relieve itching due to disorders of the skin such as contact dermatitis (p.335), psoriasis (p.332), or eczema.

TOPICAL CALCINEURIN INHIBITORS These relieve itching and are used to treat eczema when conventional therapy is not successful or not possible. Unlike topical corticosteroids, they do not thin the skin.

ANTIHISTAMINES Topical ointments or creams that contain antihistamine are commonly used for localized itching, such as that caused by an insect bite or sting (p.995). Widespread itching that is caused by a disorder such as chickenpox (p.288) can often be treated more effectively with an oral antihistamine.

Antihistamines relieve itching by inhibiting the action of a substance called histamine, which is produced by body tissues in response to tissue damage or an allergen, such as bee or wasp venom. Histamine causes itching, swelling, and other symptoms of allergic reactions.

Topical antihistamines may themselves cause an allergic skin reaction, and you should stop using the product if additional irritation occurs. Some oral antihistamines may make you feel drowsy, which can be useful if itching has prevented you from sleeping.

LOCAL ANESTHETICS Small regions of skin irritation, such as those caused by insect stings or bites, may be soothed using a local anesthetic cream or spray. These products stop itching by numbing nerves in the affected area.

SOOTHING PREPARATIONS Itching, such as that caused by insect bites and stings, sunburn (p.357), or an allergic rash such as urticaria (p.468), can usually be soothed using calamine lotion or cream or an emollient. Emollient preparations reduce moisture loss from the skin, which prevents dryness and helps reduce itching. Emollients are useful in relieving itching in eczema, psoriasis, and other dry skin conditions.

Topical corticosteroids

Drugs related to natural hormones that are applied directly on the skin to reduce inflammation

COMMON DRUGS

VERY POTENT CORTICOSTEROIDS
- Clobetasol • Fluocinonide • Halcinonide

POTENT CORTICOSTEROIDS
- Amcinonide • Betamethasone • Desoximetasone
- Fluocinolone • Mometasone • Prednicarbate
- Triamcinolone

MODERATELY POTENT CORTICOSTEROIDS
- Desonide

MILD CORTICOSTEROIDS
- Hydrocortisone

Corticosteroids (p.930) are chemically similar to the natural hormones produced by the adrenal glands. They are used topically as cream or ointment preparations to relieve skin inflammation and itching caused by conditions such as eczema (p.333), contact dermatitis (p.335), seborrheic dermatitis (p.335), and the scaly skin condition psoriasis (p.332). If inflammation is caused by a bacterial or fungal skin infection, topical corticosteroids may be used in conjunction with an appropriate anti-infective skin preparation (*see* PREPARATIONS FOR SKIN INFECTIONS AND INFESTATIONS, right).

When applied topically onto the skin surface, corticosteroids are absorbed into the underlying tissue layers, where they reduce inflammation and relieve itching. Their exact mechanism of action is unknown, but corticosteroids are thought to act by inhibiting the release of prostaglandins, which are substances that trigger inflammation.

HOW ARE THEY USED?

Your doctor will prescribe a corticosteroid cream or ointment that is potent enough to relieve symptoms while minimizing the chance of side effects. You should follow your doctor's instructions on how often to apply the cream or ointment (usually once or twice a day) and make sure that you use the correct amount (*see* APPLYING OINTMENTS, CREAMS, AND GELS, p.891). Some mild topical preparations can be bought over the counter.

> **WARNING**
> Do not use a topical corticosteroid in larger amounts or for longer periods than recommended.

WHAT ARE THE SIDE EFFECTS?

Mild topical corticosteroid preparations used sparingly and for a short time do not usually cause side effects. However, prolonged use can cause permanent changes to the skin. Most commonly, the treated skin becomes thin and easily damaged.

More potent topical corticosteroids used long-term may cause more severe side effects, such as increased blood pressure and a susceptibility to bruising. If you are using potent topical corticosteroids, your doctor will review your condition regularly to see if continued use of the drugs is necessary. Do not stop using corticosteroids without first consulting your doctor.

Preparations for skin infections and infestations

Preparations applied directly to the skin to treat skin infections and infestations

COMMON DRUGS

ANTISEPTIC PREPARATIONS
- Alcohol • Chlorhexidine • Triclosan

ANTIBIOTICS
- Fucidic acid • Mupirocin

ANTIVIRAL DRUGS
- Acyclovir • Famciclovir • Valacyclovir

ANTIFUNGAL DRUGS
- Clotrimazole • Econazole • Itraconazole
- Ketoconazole • Miconazole • Nystatin
- Terbinafine

ANTIPARASITIC DRUGS
- Crotamiton • Lindane • Permethrin
- Pyrethrins

Topical anti-infective or antiparasitic skin preparations are used to prevent or treat a number of skin infections and infestations. These preparations contain an active ingredient, which is mixed with a cream, ointment, lotion, or detergent base. The preparations are easy to apply and formulated so that the drug remains on the surface of the affected skin, where its effect is needed. Some preparations for skin infections and infestations may themselves irritate the skin or result in an allergic reaction, and, if this happens, treatment should be discontinued.

WHAT ARE THE TYPES?

Topical preparations for skin infections include antiseptic preparations, antibiotics (p.885), antiviral drugs (p.886), and antifungal drugs. Topical preparations that contain antiparasitic drugs are commonly used to treat skin infestations. Antiseptic preparations prevent infection and are effective against a wide range of microorganisms; antibiotics (p.885) help prevent infections or treat existing infections; antivirals, antifungals, and antiparasitics are used to treat viral and fungal infections and infestations of parasites.

ANTISEPTIC PREPARATIONS These preparations contain chemicals that kill or prevent the growth of microorganisms that can cause infection in damaged skin. Antiseptic solutions and creams may be bought over the counter. Solutions are added to water and used to clean broken skin; creams should be applied to wounds after they have been thoroughly cleansed. Antiseptics are also included in some shampoos and soaps to prevent minor scalp and skin problems, but their benefit is doubtful.

ANTIBIOTICS These drugs are used in topical preparations to treat bacterial skin infections, such as infected eczema (p.333) or impetigo (p.351). Severe burns may also be treated with a topical antibiotic in order to prevent infection. Sometimes, a preparation containing two or more antibiotics is used to make sure that all bacteria are eradicated. You should always follow your doctor's instructions on how long to continue using an antibiotic skin preparation. Stopping early, even if symptoms seem to have disappeared, may allow a skin infection to recur.

ANTIVIRAL DRUGS Topical antivirals may be used to treat cold sores (p.354). However, there are many types of viral skin infections that require treatment with oral drugs. Antiviral drugs are most effective if they are used at the first sign of infection, such as the tingling of a cold sore.

ANTIFUNGAL DRUGS These drugs are used to treat fungal infections, including athlete's foot (p.353), thrush (*see* VAGINAL YEAST, p.752, and ORAL THRUSH, p.862), and ringworm (p.352). Some topical antifungal preparations are available over the counter. However, some fungal infections resist treatment with topical preparations and require treatment with oral drugs (*see* ANTIFUNGAL DRUGS, p.889).

ANTIPARASITIC DRUGS Topical antiparasitic drugs are used to destroy adult parasites and their eggs and to treat infestations, including head lice (p.831), pubic lice (p.768), and scabies (p.355).

Infestations of head lice are treated with an antiparasitic lotion or cream rinse that is washed off after 12 hours. To treat pubic lice, your doctor will prescribe a lotion or cream to apply to the pubic area. Scabies is treated with a lotion or cream applied all over the body and washed off after 8–24 hours. All members of a household affected by head lice or scabies are usually treated at the same time in order to avoid any possibility of reinfestation. In the case of infestation with pubic lice, sexual partners should be checked for lice and treated simultaneously if necessary.

Sunscreens and sunblocks

Preparations containing chemicals that help protect the skin from the damaging effects of the sun's ultraviolet radiation

COMMON DRUGS

- Butyl methoxydibenzoylmethane
- Octyl methoxycinnamate • Oxybenzone
- Padimate O • Titanium dioxide • Zinc oxide

Sunscreens and sunblocks contain a variety of chemicals that help protect the skin from the damaging effects of ultraviolet (UV) radiation present in sunlight. UV radiation ages the skin and causes burning (*see* SUNBURN, p.357). Excessive exposure to sunlight also increases the risk of developing skin cancer (p.344). Ultraviolet radiation is composed of UVA and UVB rays, both of which age the skin. In addition, UVA rays cause the skin to tan and UVB rays cause burning. The sun's rays can cause skin cancer because they progressively damage the genes that control important functions in the skin, such as cell division (*see* HOW CANCER STARTS, p.274).

Sunscreen or sunblock can protect the skin from these harmful effects of ultraviolet radiation and so their use is advisable for anyone spending time in the sun. The use of sunscreens or sunblocks is especially important for people with fair skin and for young children (*see* SAFETY IN THE SUN, p.80).

If your skin becomes sensitive to the sun (*see* PHOTOSENSITIVITY, p.338), you may need to use sunscreen or sunblock even when not exposed to strong sunlight. UV sensitivity may develop in some people who are taking certain types of drugs, including some antibiotics (p.885), oral contraceptives (*see* CONTRACEPTION, p.69), and thiazide diuretics (*see* DIURETIC DRUGS, p.902).

HOW DO THEY WORK?

Sunscreens protect the skin by absorbing UVB rays, thereby reducing the amount that can damage the skin; sunblocks provide a physical barrier that reflects or scatters UVA and UVB rays. Substances in sunscreens that absorb UVB rays include butyl methoxydibenzoylmethane and padimate O. Sunblocks contain chemicals such as zinc oxide and titanium dioxide, which are opaque and therefore reflect and scatter both UVB and UVA rays. Sunscreens are graded using a sun protection factor (SPF), which is a measure of the level of protection they provide against UVB rays. The higher the rating, the greater the protection from the sun. However, even sunscreens with high SPFs do not provide complete UVB protection.

HOW ARE THEY USED?

Sunscreens and sunblocks are available as creams, lotions, gels, and sprays. All of these products need to be applied frequently in order to maintain protection, especially after swimming. You may experience some irritation or an allergic rash when using certain sunscreens or sunblocks.

CAUTION

Reapply sunscreens regularly, particularly after swimming or if you are sweating.

DRUGS FOR MUSCULOSKELETAL DISORDERS

Pain in the bones, muscles, or joints is a common problem. In many cases, it is due to overexertion or minor injury, and drugs are used to relieve the pain while the problem gets better. More serious disorders may cause persistent pain or disability, and long-term medication is needed to control the symptoms.

The first two articles in this section cover nonsteroidal anti-inflammatory drugs and locally acting corticosteroids. These drugs can relieve symptoms of musculoskeletal disorders, such as inflammation and pain, but have no effect on the underlying causes.

Drugs used to treat specific joint and bone disorders are discussed in the next two articles. Antirheumatic drugs are commonly used to treat rheumatoid arthritis. They can slow or halt joint damage, thereby preventing the disability that may be the long-term result of this disorder. The next article covers drugs for bone disorders. These drugs prevent or halt the abnormal growth or breakdown of bone that occurs in bone disorders such as Paget's disease and osteoporosis.

The final article in this section covers muscle relaxants, drugs which are used to relieve muscle spasms that can result from a variety of disorders.

KEY ANATOMY

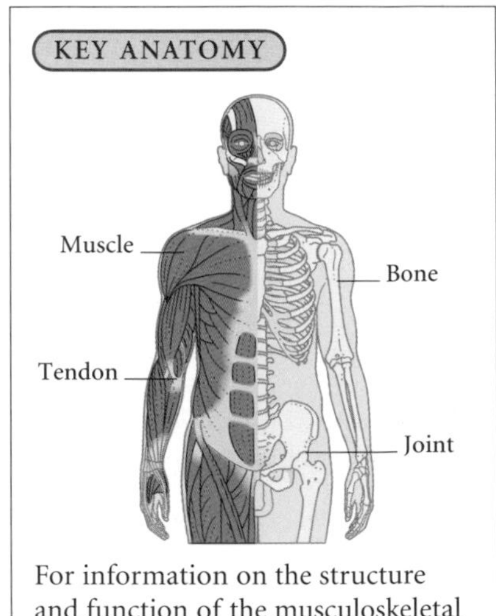
Muscle
Bone
Tendon
Joint

For information on the structure and function of the musculoskeletal system, *see* pp.362–367.

Nonsteroidal anti-inflammatory drugs

A group of drugs that are used to relieve pain and inflammation, particularly in muscles, ligaments, and joints

COMMON DRUGS

- Aspirin • Celecoxib • Diclofenac • Diflunisal
- Etodolac • Fenoprofen • Flurbiprofen
- Ibuprofen • Indomethacin • Ketoprofen
- Ketorolac • Mefenamic acid • Meloxicam
- Nabumetone • Naproxen • Piroxicam
- Sulindac • Tiaprofenic acid • Tolmetin
- Valdecoxib

Nonsteroidal anti-inflammatory drugs (NSAIDs) are nonopioid analgesics (p.912) that are used to relieve the pain and inflammation that can result from a variety of musculoskeletal disorders. These drugs are also commonly used to treat pain and inflammation that are not associated with musculoskeletal disorders, such as headache (p.518).

Although it is technically an NSAID, aspirin has only a limited anti-inflammatory effect. For this reason, NSAIDs that have a more powerful anti-inflammatory action than aspirin are normally prescribed for the treatment of inflammatory conditions.

NSAIDs may be used for acute conditions, such as ligament damage and muscle strains and tears (p.395). They usually relieve symptoms within a few hours. NSAIDs are also used to relieve pain and inflammation that result from chronic musculoskeletal disorders, such as rheumatoid arthritis (p.377) and osteoarthritis (p.374). When used for chronic conditions, NSAIDs can relieve pain rapidly, but they may take about 2 weeks to reduce levels of inflammation. Although NSAIDs can relieve symptoms of musculoskeletal disorders, they do not treat the underlying condition.

NSAIDs work by limiting the release of prostaglandins, chemicals occurring naturally in the body that cause pain and trigger the inflammatory response (*see* HOW NSAIDS WORK, opposite page).

HOW ARE THEY USED?

NSAIDs are most commonly taken orally, but occasionally they may be applied topically, by suppository, or injection. Certain NSAIDs are available in a slow-release form, which may be effective for up to 24 hours. This reduces the need to take pills frequently in the long-term treatment of chronic conditions. Slow-release NSAIDs also provide a more constant level of pain relief. For many conditions, NSAIDs are used with other treatments, such as physiotherapy (p.961). Some NSAIDs, such as ibuprofen, can be bought over the counter.

WHAT ARE THE SIDE EFFECTS?

NSAIDs have varying potentials to irritate the stomach lining, depending on the individual drug, and they may cause peptic ulcers (p.640). If you are given certain NSAIDs, such as ibuprofen, for long-term use, you may also be given an antiulcer drug (*see* ULCER-HEALING DRUGS, p.923) to protect your stomach lining. Cyclo-oxygenase 2 inhibitors (COX2 inhibitors) such as celecoxib and valdecoxib, may have a less damaging effect on the stomach lining but higher risk of cardiovascular side effects.

NSAIDs may cause allergic reactions (*see* DRUG ALLERGY, p.467), including rashes and angioedema (p.469), in which temporary swellings develop in the skin and mucous membranes. Some people may develop photosensitivity (p.338), in which the skin becomes sensitive to sunlight. People who have asthma (p.483) or a kidney disorder require particular attention if they take NSAIDs because the drugs can worsen these conditions.

DRUG ACTION How NSAIDs work

Nonsteroidal anti-inflammatory drugs (NSAIDs) are used to treat many types of conditions, including inflammatory disorders such as rheumatoid arthritis (p.377). The inflammatory response is triggered by prostaglandins, substances that are released when tissue is damaged. NSAIDs reduce inflammation by blocking production of prostaglandins.

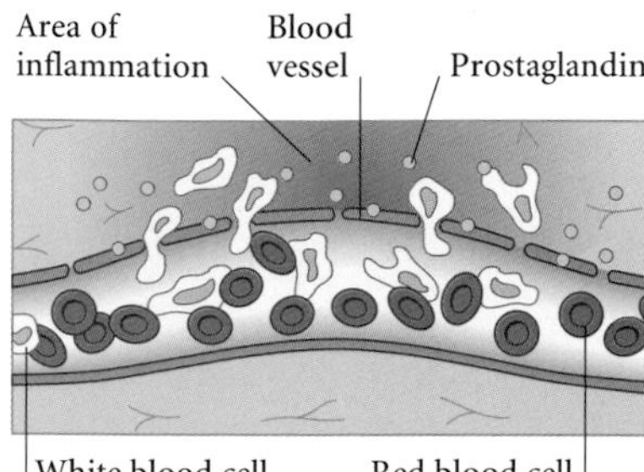

Area of inflammation
Blood vessel
Prostaglandin
White blood cell
Red blood cell

Before drug
Prostaglandins are released in damaged tissue, causing the blood vessels to widen and leak fluid. White cells move into the tissue. The area becomes red and swollen.

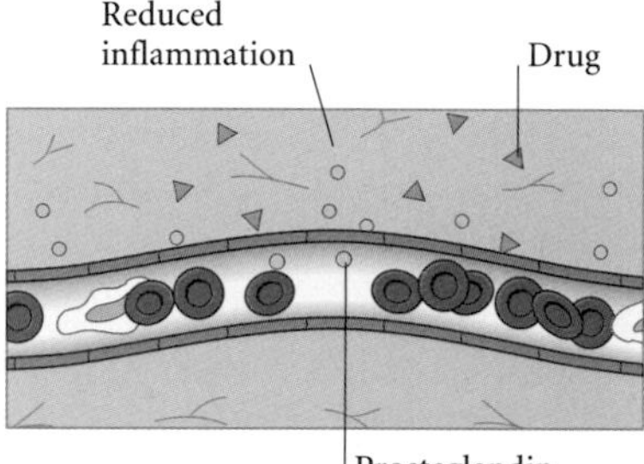

Reduced inflammation
Drug
Prostaglandin

After drug
NSAIDs limit the release of prostaglandins, thereby reducing the inflammation. The leaky blood vessels return to normal, and swelling and redness decrease.

Locally acting corticosteroids

Drugs that are injected directly into body tissues to reduce inflammation

Common drugs

- Betamethasone • Dexamethasone
- Hydrocortisone • Methylprednisolone
- Prednisolone • Triamcinolone

Locally acting corticosteroids are anti-inflammatory drugs that are injected into a specific area of the body to reduce inflammation in that area. The drugs work by blocking the local production of prostaglandins, chemicals that trigger inflammation and pain. Corticosteroids can be injected into joints to relieve inflammation due to conditions such as rheumatoid arthritis (p.377). Injections can also be given around ligaments and tendons to relieve conditions such as tennis elbow (p.389). A local anesthetic may be injected with a corticosteroid to relieve pain quickly.

Side effects from an injected corticosteroid are unlikely because the drug's action is limited to the affected area. However, possible side effects include thinning of the skin or fat at the site of injection, which may produce a dimple. In some cases, there may be a temporary increase in pain, or, very rarely, the injection site may become infected.

Antirheumatic drugs

Drugs that are used to slow or stop the joint damage that often results from chronic inflammation

Common drugs

Immunosuppressants
- Azathioprine • Cyclophosphamide
- Cyclosporine • Methotrexate

Gold-based drugs
- Auranofin • Aurothioglucose • Gold sodium thiomalate

Other antirheumatic drugs
- Etanercept • Hydroxychloroquine
- Leflunomide • Minocycline • Penicillamine
- Sulfasalazine

Biological response modifiers
- Anakinra • Adalimumab • Etanercept
- Infliximab

Antirheumatic drugs are commonly referred to as disease modifying antirheumatic drugs (DMARDs). These drugs slow or halt the progress of chronic inflammatory disorders of the joints and connective tissues. They are most commonly used to treat rheumatoid arthritis (p.377). In this disorder, the immune system attacks the body's own tissues, primarily the joints, causing them to become swollen, stiff, and painful. These antirheumatic drugs are often used in combination with a non-steroidal anti-inflammatory drug (opposite page).

What are the types?

Antirheumatic drugs are believed to work by suppressing the body's inflammatory response, although their exact mechanism of action is not yet understood. Some types are described below.

Immunosuppressants Drugs in this group may be used to treat severe rheumatoid arthritis. They may be injected into a muscle or taken orally. The drugs work by suppressing white blood cell production, which reduces the immune response. If you are taking these drugs, your blood will be tested regularly to ensure that the level of cells does not fall too low, which can lead to anemia or increased susceptibility to infection.

Gold-based drugs These drugs are usually given by injection into a muscle. In some people, gold-based drugs cause side effects, including a rash and diarrhea. Rarely, the drugs may affect the kidneys, and regular urine tests are needed to detect complications. They also suppress blood cell production in bone marrow, which may cause serious problems, such as abnormal bleeding. Regular blood tests are required.

Other antirheumatic drugs Other commonly used drugs are sulfasalazine, hydroxychloroquine, and leflunomide, all of which are thought to have an immunosuppressant effect.

Sulfasalazine is a combination of an antibiotic and a form of aspirin and is taken orally. Side effects may include rashes, nausea and vomiting, and blood disorders such as anemia (p.446).

Hydroxychloroquine is an oral antimalarial drug (p.888) that may also be used to treat systemic lupus erythematosus (p.461), a disorder that causes inflammation in many body tissues, including joints and muscles.

Penicillamine is rarely used now to treat rheumatoid arthritis. It has similar side effects to gold-based drugs.

WARNING

If you are taking an antirheumatic drug you should report any sign of infection, such as a sore throat, or any unusual bleeding to your doctor immediately.

BIOLOGICAL RESPONSE MODIFIERS (BRMs) This group of drugs is used for debilitating arthritis, when DMARDs have not been successful in slowing and stopping the progress of this chronic inflammatory disorder.

Infliximab, used in the treatment of Crohn's disease (p.658), modulates the immune system and its use for other conditions is being studied.

Drugs for bone disorders

Drugs used to treat disorders affecting bone formation, replacement, and repair

COMMON DRUGS

ESTROGEN AND SERMs
• Conjugated estrogens • Raloxifene

BISPHOSPHONATES
• Alendronate • Etidronate • Risedronate

CALCITONIN

CALCIUM AND VITAMIN D
• Calcifediol • Calcitriol • Calcium carbonate
• Calcium citrate • Ergocalciferol • Vitamin D

The body constantly breaks down and rebuilds bone. Disorders may develop if the balance between this breakdown and renewal is upset. Drugs that affect the growth of bone are used to treat disorders in which either too much bone is broken down or abnormal bone growth occurs. For example, in the bone disorder osteoporosis (p.368), bone is broken down faster than it is replaced, and in Paget's disease of the bone (p.370), there is uneven bone formation and breakdown.

WHAT ARE THE TYPES?

Drugs that are used to treat bone disorders include estrogen and selective estrogen receptor modulators (SERMs), bisphosphonates, and the hormone calcitonin. Calcium and vitamin D are also used.

ESTROGEN The sex hormone estrogen and SERMs slow the breakdown of bone and may be used to prevent osteoporosis or to slow its progress. Estrogen may be prescribed to postmenopausal women as hormone replacement therapy (p.937). It is either taken on its own or with the hormone progestin. The drug may be applied to the skin as a patch or gel, or taken orally. Side effects of the drugs include weight gain, headache, and breast tenderness.

BISPHOSPHONATES These drugs, taken orally, may be used to treat osteoporosis and Paget's disease. They reduce abnormally high rates of bone breakdown and renewal. They may cause nausea, diarrhea, and irritation of the esophagus.

CALCITONIN This drug slows the rate of bone breakdown and renewal. It may be used to treat Paget's disease, acute fracture pain, and to reduce the risk of osteoporotic fractures in postmenopausal women. Calcitonin may be given as a nasal spray or by self-injection several times a week. Side effects of nasal spray are minimal. The injection can cause low blood pressure or nausea.

CALCIUM AND VITAMIN D These two substances are essential for the maintenance of healthy bone. Supplements of calcium and vitamin D may be used to treat bone disorders. Postmenopausal women should have a calcium intake of 1,500 mg daily, much of which can be obtained in the diet. However, calcium supplements may cause constipation.

Vitamin D helps the body absorb calcium from food. Deficiency can cause rickets in children and osteomalacia in adults (*see* OSTEOMALACIA AND RICKETS, p.370). Taken at the recommended dose, vitamin D supplements usually cause no side effects.

Muscle relaxants

A group of drugs that are used to reduce spasmodic muscle contractions

COMMON DRUGS

• Baclofen • Botulinum toxin • Chlorzoxazone
• Cyclobenzaprine • Dantrolene • Diazepam
• Methocarbamol • Quinine • Tizanidine

Muscle relaxants are used for the relief of muscle spasm, a painful, involuntary contraction of one or more muscles. They may be used to relieve the sudden, frequent muscle spasms that can occur in people with muscular dystrophy (p.826). They are also useful in conditions such as cerebral palsy (p.846), in which continuous spasms cause permanent limb stiffness. Muscle relaxants are also used to relieve other muscular conditions, such as nighttime muscle cramps (p.388) and torticollis (p.388), in which muscles in the neck tighten, pulling the head over to one side. Certain muscle relaxants are used to paralyze muscles during surgery performed under general anesthesia (*see* HAVING MAJOR SURGERY, p.943).

HOW DO THEY WORK?

Muscle relaxant drugs work in a variety of ways. Some muscle relaxants, such as tizanidine, baclofen, and the antianxiety drug diazepam, work by reducing the transmission of nerve signals from the brain and spinal cord to the muscles, causing the muscles to relax.

Dantrolene relieves spasm by acting directly on muscles and making them less sensitive to nerve signals from the brain and spinal cord. Botulinum toxin relaxes muscles by blocking the transmission of signals from nerve endings to muscle cells. The way in which quinine works is not fully understood.

HOW ARE THEY USED?

Doses of muscle relaxants need careful adjustment. Too little has no effect, and too much may lead to weakness in the muscles. For chronic conditions such as muscular dystrophy, doses begin at a low level and are increased gradually to reach a balance between symptom control and muscle strength.

Involuntary contractions of the neck and facial muscles can be relieved by injecting tiny amounts of botulinum toxin into the affected muscle. A single injection is usually effective for about 3 months. Quinine is taken at bedtime, also in very small amounts.

WHAT ARE THE SIDE EFFECTS?

A common side effect of many muscle relaxants is drowsiness, which usually decreases as treatment progresses. With long-term use, the body may become dependent on a muscle relaxant; if the drug is withdrawn suddenly, muscle spasms may become worse than they were before treatment began.

Dantrolene can cause diarrhea. It may also cause severe liver problems. If you are taking dantrolene, your doctor will do regular blood tests to check that your liver function is normal.

DRUGS FOR CARDIOVASCULAR DISORDERS

Disorders of the cardiovascular system are a major cause of poor health and early death in the developed world. In some cases, cardiovascular disorders can be improved by changes in lifestyle, such as improving diet or stopping smoking. In other cases, cardiovascular disorders require treatment with drugs that act on the blood vessels, the heart, or other organs.

The opening article in this section discusses drugs that are used to treat high blood pressure, a disorder that affects 1 in 5 people in developed countries. A number of these drugs are effective not only in lowering blood pressure but also in the treatment of heart failure, angina, and coronary artery disease.

The next article gives an overview of the types of drugs that may be used in the treatment of arrhythmias, a group of disorders in which the heart beats extremely rapidly or with an abnormal rhythm.

Specific classes of drugs are discussed in separate articles. Beta blockers and calcium channel blockers are used to treat certain arrhythmias; these drugs and nitrates also treat coronary artery disease; diuretics, ACE inhibitors, and beta blockers are helpful in treating congestive heart failure; and all are useful in lowering high blood pressure.

Lipid lowering drugs, which are used to reduce the risk of heart attack by lowering levels of fats in the blood, are discussed elsewhere (*see* DRUGS ACTING ON THE ENDOCRINE SYSTEM AND METABOLISM, pp.930–935).

KEY ANATOMY

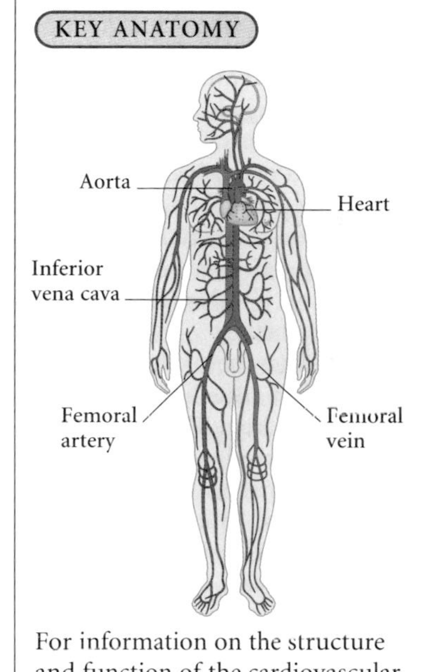
Aorta
Heart
Inferior vena cava
Femoral artery
Femoral vein

For information on the structure and function of the cardiovascular system, *see* pp.396–401.

Antihypertensive drugs

Drugs used to treat high blood pressure, a condition also known as hypertension

COMMON DRUGS

ACE INHIBITOR DRUGS (p.900)

ALPHA BLOCKER DRUGS
- Doxazosin • Prazosin • Terazosin

ANGIOTENSIN II RECEPTOR BLOCKER DRUGS
- Candesartan • Irbesartan • Losartan • Valsartan

BETA BLOCKER DRUGS (p.898)

CALCIUM CHANNEL BLOCKER DRUGS (p.900)

CENTRALLY ACTING DRUGS
- Clonidine • Methyldopa

DIURETIC DRUGS (p.902)

OTHER ANTIHYPERTENSIVE DRUGS
- Hydralazine • Minoxidil

High blood pressure (*see* HYPERTENSION, p.403) requires treatment mainly because it increases the risk of both coronary artery disease (p.405) and stroke (p.532). Antihypertensive drugs are most often used when changes in your lifestyle, such as improving your diet, doing more exercise, and stopping smoking, fail to produce an adequate fall in blood pressure over a short period of time. Antihypertensives are also used to treat hypertension in pregnancy (*see* PREECLAMPSIA AND ECLAMPSIA, p.794).

WHAT ARE THE TYPES?

There are many different types of antihypertensives. Those most commonly used are beta blocker drugs (p.898), ACE inhibitor drugs (p.900), calcium channel blocker drugs (p.900), and diuretic drugs (p.902). Angiotensin II receptor blockers (ARBs) are very effective antihypertensives. Less commonly, alpha blocker drugs, centrally acting drugs, and other drugs, including diazoxide, hydralazine, and minoxidil, are used.

Most types of antihypertensive drugs reduce high blood pressure by increasing the diameter of blood vessels (a process known as vasodilation) or by reducing the force with which the heart pumps blood. ACE inhibitors, alpha blockers, ARBs, calcium channel blockers, and centrally acting drugs act in a variety of ways to cause vasodilation. Beta blockers lower blood pressure by reducing the force with which the heart pumps. This effect is achieved by blocking the action of substances produced naturally by the body that increase heart rate and blood pressure. Diuretics cause the kidneys to excrete more water and salts than usual, which reduces the volume of blood present in the circulation and thereby lowers blood pressure.

HOW ARE THEY USED?

Antihypertensives are normally taken orally for long periods of time and often for life. However, in some cases it may be possible to reduce the dose gradually and eventually stop the drugs if blood pressure returns to normal following long-term changes in weight or lifestyle. The choice of drug depends on several factors, including age and other medical conditions you might have. Certain drugs are more likely to cause side effects in elderly people.

If you have mild or moderate hypertension, you will usually be prescribed a single drug, such as a diuretic or a beta blocker. These drugs are not suitable

Drugs that prevent blood clotting

Drugs used to prevent unwanted blood clots from developing or to stabilize existing blood clots

COMMON DRUGS

ANTIPLATELET DRUGS
• Aspirin • Clopidogrel • Dipyridamole
• Eptifibatide • Ticlopidine

ORAL ANTICOAGULANTS
• Warfarin

INJECTED ANTICOAGULANTS
• Argatroban • Bivalirudin • Dalteparin
• Danaparoid • Enoxaparin • Heparin

Drugs may be prescribed to prevent unwanted blood clots (thrombi) from developing in blood vessels. They may also be used to prevent existing clots from enlarging and to reduce the risk of an embolism, in which a fragment of an existing clot in a vein breaks off and travels to one of the body's vital organs. Blood clots that have formed and need to be dissolved rapidly are treated with thrombolytic drugs (right).

WHAT ARE THE TYPES?

Antiplatelet drugs and anticoagulants are used to prevent unwanted blood clots from forming. Antiplatelet drugs are used to prevent clots from forming in arteries; anticoagulants are prescribed to prevent clots from developing or enlarging in veins. They may be taken orally or given by injection or by infusion.

ANTIPLATELET DRUGS These drugs are used to help prevent unwanted blood clots from forming in arteries such as those of the heart or neck. They work by reducing the tendency of platelets, a type of blood cell that plays a vital role in the blood clotting process, to stick together. If you have already developed symptoms of coronary artery disease, such as angina (p.407), or have experienced a heart attack (*see* MYOCARDIAL INFARCTION, p.410), a stroke (p.532), or a transient ischemic attack (p.531), you may be advised to take an antiplatelet drug for the rest of your life.

Aspirin is the most commonly prescribed antiplatelet drug. In combination with clopidogrel, it is used after a stent is inserted in a coronary artery.

WARNING

Contact your doctor immediately if you are taking an oral anticoagulant and you have prolonged nosebleeds or notice blood in your urine.

ORAL ANTICOAGULANTS These drugs are used as long-term treatment to prevent deep vein thrombosis (p.437), in which an unwanted blood clot forms in a vein, and pulmonary embolism (p.495), in which a clot lodges in the lungs. Oral anticoagulants may also be given to people with the heart rhythm disorder atrial fibrillation (p.417), in which a blood clot may develop in the heart. If a fragment of the clot breaks off, it can travel to the brain and cause a stroke. Warfarin is the most frequently prescribed oral anticoagulant.

Oral anticoagulants act by preventing the formation of certain clotting factors, proteins that are essential for normal blood clotting. The drugs usually take 36–48 hours to become effective.

While you are taking oral anticoagulants, you will be given blood tests frequently during the first few days and then at regular intervals throughout your treatment so that the dose can be adjusted to your needs. If the dose is too high, oral anticoagulants can cause abnormal bleeding. For this reason, you should consult your doctor immediately if you have symptoms such as nosebleeds or blood in the urine.

In order to treat abnormal bleeding, your doctor may give you drugs that reverse the effect of anticoagulants (*see* DRUGS THAT PROMOTE BLOOD CLOTTING, p.903). Oral anticoagulants may cause other side effects, including easy bruising, rashes, and hair loss. You should avoid drinking alcohol and making any sudden changes to your diet, both of which may affect the action of anticoagulants. Since some drugs interact with anticoagulants, you should not take other medications, such as aspirin, without consulting your doctor. It is important that you inform your doctor if you plan to become pregnant because some anticoagulants can cause fetal abnormalities. Anticoagulant treatment must not be stopped suddenly. You will be given an anticoagulant treatment card or a medical alert bracelet or pendant, which you should always carry with you in order to inform health professionals in case of an emergency.

INJECTED ANTICOAGULANTS If blood clotting must be controlled quickly, an anticoagulant, such as heparin, may be given by either injection or infusion in order to take effect immediately. These fast-acting anticoagulants are used to treat disorders such as deep vein thrombosis or pulmonary embolism before oral anticoagulants, such as warfarin, take effect. Injected anticoagulants are sometimes given as a preventive measure after orthopedic surgery; they may also be given after surgery to people who are at particular risk of blood clotting due to other medical problems. The drugs are often prescribed for people who are immobilized during treatment in the hospital. Injected anticoagulants may cause side effects, such as skin rashes, in some people.

Thrombolytic drugs

A group of drugs, also known as fibrinolytics, used to dissolve blood clots

COMMON DRUGS

• Alteplase (tissue plasminogen activator)
• Anistreplase • Streptokinase • Tenecteplase
• Urokinase

Thrombolytic drugs act rapidly to dissolve unwanted blood clots (thrombi) that occur in blood vessels in the body. These drugs are most commonly given as an emergency treatment for heart attacks (*see* MYOCARDIAL INFARCTION, p.410) or for certain types of strokes (p.532) and can significantly increase a person's chance of survival.

A heart attack is usually caused by a blood clot blocking one of the coronary arteries that supply blood to the heart muscle. Left untreated, such a clot can cause irreversible and possibly fatal damage to the heart. Strokes may be caused by a blood clot blocking the normal blood supply to the brain.

Thrombolytics may also be used to treat massive pulmonary embolism (p.495), in which a very large blood clot breaks off from a distant vein and then lodges in the lungs, blocking blood flow to the lungs.

Thrombolytics work by dissolving the mesh of fibrin, a stringy protein, that binds a blood clot together (*see* HOW THROMBOLYTIC DRUGS WORK, below). When the clot has been dissolved, normal blood flow is restored.

HOW ARE THEY USED?

Thrombolytics are given by injection or by infusion. In the treatment of a heart attack, these drugs must be administered within 6 hours of the attack to be effective. In the case of a stroke caused by a blood clot, the drugs must be administered within 3 hours of the attack.

DRUG ACTION

HOW THROMBOLYTIC DRUGS WORK

Thrombolytic drugs are used to dissolve unwanted blood clots, known as thrombi. A blood clot consists of blood cells and platelets that are held together by a mesh of fibrin strands. Thrombolytics dissolve the fibrin strands, thereby breaking up the blood clot.

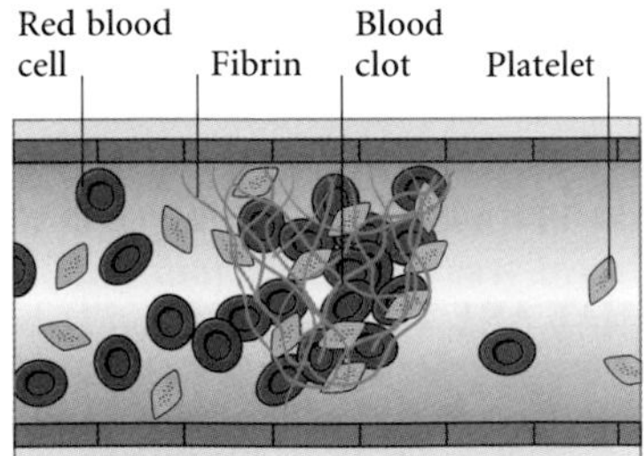
Red blood cell
Fibrin
Blood clot
Platelet

Before drug
A clot, made up of red and white blood cells and platelets bound together by strands of fibrin, has formed in a blood vessel, restricting blood flow.

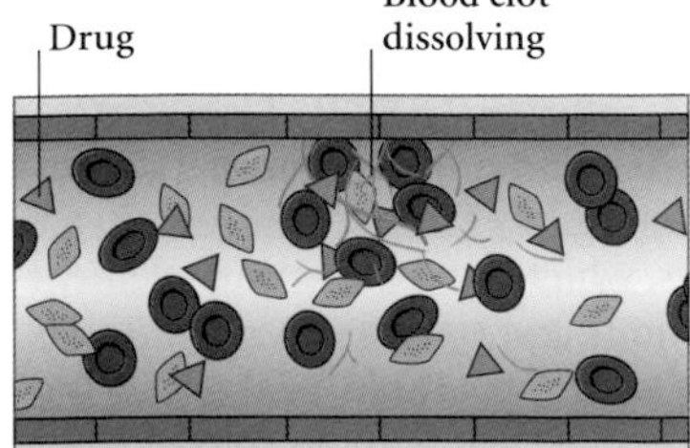
Drug
Blood clot dissolving

After drug
The thrombolytic drug dissolves the fibrin strands that bind the blood clot together. The clot is broken down and normal blood flow resumes.

Thrombolytic drugs may increase a person's susceptibility to bruising and bleeding. Anistreplase and streptokinase are two thrombolytics that can cause an allergic reaction, which often takes the form of a rash. The drug tenecteplase can be given as a single injection into a vein, taking just a few seconds.

Antiallergy drugs

Drugs used to prevent and treat allergic conditions and allergic reactions

COMMON DRUGS

ANTIHISTAMINES (p.906)

MAST CELL STABILIZERS
- Cromolyn sodium
- Nedocromil sodium

CORTICOSTEROIDS (p.930)

ALLERGEN EXTRACTS

OTHER ANTIALLERGY DRUGS
- Epinephrine

Antiallergy drugs are used to treat a variety of allergic disorders, such as allergic conjunctivitis (p.570), hay fever (*see* ALLERGIC RHINITIS, p.466), and atopic eczema (p.334). Antiallergy drugs can be used to prevent an allergic response from occurring or relieve the symptoms of allergy, such as sneezing.

WHAT ARE THE TYPES?

There are several groups of antiallergy drugs. The most commonly used groups are antihistamines (p.906), mast cell stabilizers, corticosteroids, allergen extracts, and the drug epinephrine.

ANTIHISTAMINES These drugs are most commonly used to relieve the symptoms of hay fever. Antihistamines are also used to treat allergic rashes such as urticaria (p.468) and are effective in relieving itching and irritation due to insect bites or stings. The drugs work by blocking the action of a chemical known as histamine. This chemical is released by the body in an allergic reaction to certain substances.

MAST CELL STABILIZERS These drugs may be prescribed to prevent allergic reactions from occurring. Mast cell stabilizers work by blocking the release of histamine from certain cells, called mast cells, that are present in the blood and in most body tissues. Histamine is released in an allergic reaction. The most commonly used mast cell stabilizer is cromolyn sodium, which is used to prevent allergic conjunctivitis, hay fever, exercise-induced asthma (p.483), and asthma in children (p.839). The drug is available as eyedrops, as a nasal spray, and for use in an inhaler.

Mast cell stabilizers must be taken regularly as preventive treatment; they are not effective in relieving symptoms quickly. Possible side effects of cromolyn sodium include coughing and irritation of the nose and throat.

CORTICOSTEROIDS These drugs reduce inflammation caused by allergic reactions. Corticosteroids may be included in skin creams and ointments used to treat atopic eczema (*see* TOPICAL CORTICOSTEROIDS, p.892) and in nasal sprays to help relieve the symptoms of hay fever (*see* CORTICOSTEROIDS FOR RESPIRATORY DISEASE, p.911). If you have a severe allergic reaction, you may be given corticosteroids orally or by injection.

ALLERGEN EXTRACTS Substances that can cause allergic reactions, such as bee or wasp venom or grass pollen, are known as allergens. Extracts of an allergen may be used to desensitize a person with a severe allergy to the substance. The treatment, which is used for a wide range of allergies, is usually given as a series of weekly injections containing gradually increasing doses. Once you can tolerate a significant dose without a severe reaction, the frequency of injections is decreased. Allergen extracts can themselves cause life-threatening allergic reactions and are given only where emergency treatment is available.

EPINEPHRINE This drug is used to treat the life-threatening allergic reaction anaphylaxis (p.469). Epinephrine acts to reverse the swelling of the throat, narrowing of the airways, and drop in blood pressure that occur in anaphylaxis. The drug is given by injection and doses are repeated until the condition improves. If you are at risk of anaphylaxis because of a severe allergy, such as a reaction to nuts, you should carry syringes prefilled with epinephrine for emergency treatment (*see* EMERGENCY AID FOR ANAPHYLAXIS, p.469).

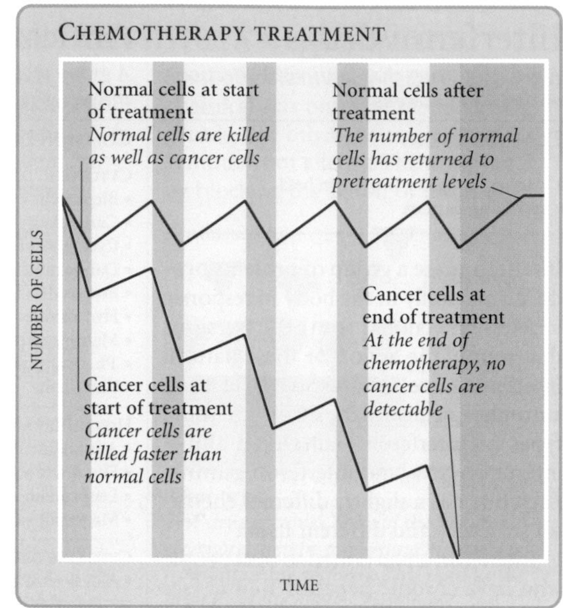
CHEMOTHERAPY TREATMENT
Normal cells at start of treatment
Normal cells are killed as well as cancer cells
Normal cells after treatment
The number of normal cells has returned to pretreatment levels
Cancer cells at end of treatment
At the end of chemotherapy, no cancer cells are detectable
Cancer cells at start of treatment
Cancer cells are killed faster than normal cells
NUMBER OF CELLS
TIME

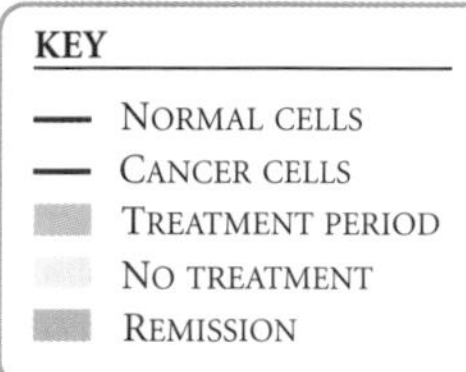
KEY
Normal cells
Cancer cells
Treatment period
No treatment
Remission

How chemotherapy treatment works
Anticancer drugs (chemotherapy) may be given in a series of treatments. The drugs kill cancer cells, but they also destroy some normal cells. For this reason, there are recovery periods between treatments during which the number of normal cells is allowed to rise again. Treatment is stopped when no cancer cells are detectable.

CYTOTOXIC DRUGS There are many types of cytotoxic drugs. These drugs kill cells or prevent cancer cells from dividing and increasing in number. The drugs produce these effects either by acting directly on the cells' genetic material, DNA, or by preventing cells from using the nutrients they need to divide normally. The cell-killing effect of cytotoxic drugs is concentrated on areas of body tissue where cells are rapidly dividing. For this reason, cytotoxic drugs are effective in treating many rapidly growing cancers such as those that affect the lymphatic system (*see* LYMPHOMA, p.459), many childhood cancers, various forms of leukemia (p.453), and some types of cancer of the testis (p.719). Cytotoxic drugs are usually administered in the hospital. Several short courses of the drugs are given over a number of weeks with drug-free periods in between to allow enough time for normal body cells to recover.

Cytotoxic drugs cause severe side effects because, in addition to affecting cancerous cells, the drugs also affect any area of the body where there is rapid cell division. These areas may include bone marrow, hair follicles, and the lining of the mouth and intestines.

Damage to the bone marrow may reduce the number of red and white blood cells and platelets in the blood. This can result in anemia (p.446), increased susceptibility to infection, and reduced ability of the blood to clot. Nausea and vomiting are particularly common side effects with cytotoxic drugs and may be severe. Some drugs may cause mouth ulcers and hair loss.

The severity of many side effects can be reduced by other drugs. For example, antiemetic drugs (p.922) may be prescribed for nausea and vomiting. Most side effects are temporary and do not result in long-term damage. However, some types of cytotoxic drugs can cause irreversible damage to the ovaries, which results in premature menopause, or to the testes, resulting in abnormal or reduced sperm production. Men and adolescent boys who may wish to have children in the future can arrange to have their sperm stored before treatment is started.

If you are taking cytotoxic drugs, you will have regular blood tests, including a blood count, before each course of treatment to measure the levels of all different types of blood cells. You should see your doctor immediately if you develop new symptoms, such as a sore throat, because this symptom may be a sign of infection.

WARNING

Many anticancer drugs are potentially harmful to a developing fetus. You should consult your doctor about your contraception needs before starting treatment.

HORMONES AND HORMONE ANTAGONISTS Treatment with hormones may be suitable for certain types of cancers whose growth is influenced by hormones. This type of treatment may be used after surgery or radiation therapy to prevent any cancer cells that are left behind from growing and spreading. The treatment may use a hormone that halts the progression of the cancer. For example, megestrol is used to slow the progression of cancer of the uterus (p.748). Alternatively, treatment may consist of using a hormone antagonist. Drugs of this type oppose the effects of the hormone that is stimulating the growth of the cancer. For example, hormone antagonists are effective in halting the progression of certain types of breast cancers (p.759) that are stimulated by the female sex hormone estrogen. In these cases, drugs, such as tamoxifen, work by blocking the action of estrogen on breast cells. The growth of cancerous cells that have spread from cancer of the prostate may be slowed by treatment with goserelin, which works by blocking the secretion of the hormone testosterone.

Hormonal drugs are usually taken orally, sometimes for several years. Side effects are milder than those of cytotoxic drugs and depend on the specific drug used. For example, tamoxifen carries a small risk of causing cancer of the uterus. If you are taking tamoxifen, you should report abnormal vaginal bleeding or lower abdominal pain to your doctor immediately.

CYTOKINE DRUGS This group of anticancer drugs, which includes interferon alpha (*see* INTERFERON DRUGS, p.907) and aldesleukin, may be used in the treatment of the AIDS-related skin cancer Kaposi's sarcoma (p.346). Cytokines are also used to treat certain types of lymphoma and leukemia and advanced kidney cancer (p.704). The drugs may kill cancer cells directly or provoke an immune system reaction against the cancer cells, thereby destroying them or limiting their growth.

Most cytokine drugs cause side effects that may include nausea and flu-like symptoms, including fever and fatigue. Some cytokines may cause more serious side effects, such as a rapid drop in blood pressure, which may cause you to faint.

DRUGS FOR RESPIRATORY DISORDERS

Conditions affecting the airways and lungs range from minor ailments, such as the common cold, to serious long-term disorders, like asthma. Coughs and colds can often be treated effectively with over-the-counter remedies. However, the symptoms of chronic disorders, such as shortness of breath, can be severe and require specific medical treatment.

This section explains some of the drugs used to treat both common ailments, such as coughs and colds, and more serious conditions that affect the airways and lungs.

The first three articles in this section cover drugs used to relieve common symptoms of upper respiratory tract infections, such as nasal congestion, cough, and fever. The fourth article discusses bronchodilator drugs, which widen the airways of the lungs and are used to treat certain conditions in which breathing becomes difficult, such as asthma (p.483). Leukotriene antagonists, a type of anti-inflammatory, are discussed next. The final article covers corticosteroids as they are used for treating respiratory disorders, including their use in preventing attacks of asthma. Drugs used for hay fever and other allergic disorders affecting the respiratory system are described elsewhere (*see* ANTIALLERGY DRUGS, p.905), as are antibiotics used to treat respiratory infections (*see* DRUGS FOR INFECTIONS AND INFESTATIONS, pp.883–889).

KEY ANATOMY

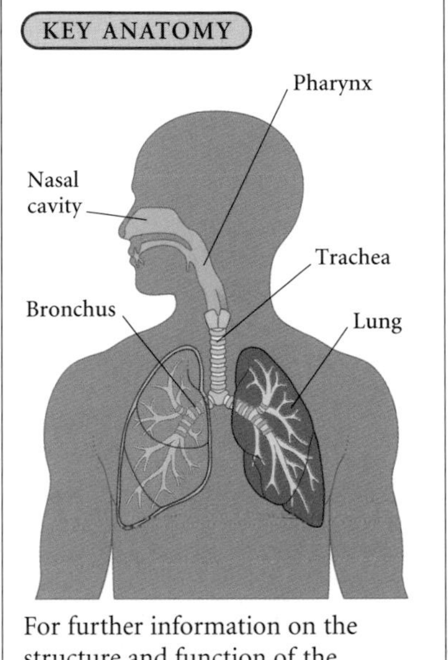

Pharynx
Nasal cavity
Trachea
Bronchus
Lung

For further information on the structure and function of the respiratory system, *see* pp.470–473.

Decongestants

Drugs that are used to relieve congestion of the nose and sinuses

COMMON DRUGS

- Naphazoline • Oxymetazoline
- Phenylephrine • Pseudoephedrine
- Xylometazoline

Decongestants act to relieve congestion in the nose and sinuses. A blocked nose or sinuses (*see* SINUSITIS, p.475) may be caused by a viral infection, such as the common cold (p.286), or by an allergic condition, such as hay fever (*see* ALLERGIC RHINITIS, p.466).

Infections and allergic reactions can cause inflammation of the delicate lining of the nose or sinuses. The blood vessels in the lining enlarge, and increased volumes of fluid pass into the mucous membranes, which swell and produce excessive amounts of mucus. Decongestants act directly on the blood vessels to constrict them and reduce the swelling and mucus production.

Decongestants are available as sprays or drops that are applied to the nose or as oral pills or capsules. Some cold and flu remedies (p.910) available over the counter also contain a small amount of a decongestant drug. You can spray or insert decongestant drops directly into your nose to provide relief within minutes. Oral decongestants work more slowly but their effects last longer.

You should use decongestant sprays or drops sparingly and for no longer than a week. After that time, they lose their ability to constrict blood vessels. When the last effective dose wears off, the blood vessels widen again and congestion may become worse.

If used in moderation, decongestants applied as sprays or drops have few side effects. However, occasionally, they may cause sneezing or affect your sense of taste. If you have heart disease, you should check with your doctor before you take oral decongestants because they can cause a rapid and irregular heartbeat. Decongestants may also cause a slight tremor in the hands.

CAUTION

Avoid using decongestants for longer than a week because the drugs may become ineffective or worsen your condition.

Cough remedies

Preparations containing various drugs used to relieve coughing

COMMON DRUGS

EXPECTORANTS
- Guaifenesin

MUCOLYTIC DRUGS
- Acetylcysteine • Dornase alfa

OPIOID COUGH SUPPRESSANTS
- Codeine • Hydrocodone

NONOPIOID COUGH MEDICINES
- Antihistamines (p.906) • Dextromethorphan

Doctors rarely recommend cough medicines for minor respiratory disorders because their effectiveness is doubtful. However, there are many cough remedies that are available over the counter. Almost all these remedies are supplied as syrups to which different drugs and flavorings have been added.

Cough remedies that are for productive coughs (which produce sputum) contain different drugs from those used to treat dry coughs. Productive coughs can be treated with either expectorants or mucolytic drugs. Expectorants may encourage the coughing up of sputum from the lungs, while mucolytics may loosen the sputum, making it easier to cough it up from the chest.

Dry coughs can be treated using cough suppressants that contain either opioid drugs (*see* ANALGESICS, p.912) or antihistamines (p.906). Opioid drugs have a sedative effect on the area of the brain that controls the cough reflex. Antihistamines help relieve coughs because they dry up secretions and can therefore help relieve the dripping of mucus from the back of the nose into the throat, which aggravates coughing. Some remedies for a dry cough are only soothing syrups that contain no drugs and coat or lubricate inflamed mucous membranes in the throat. However, they may contain quantities of alcohol. Other remedies help dry up secretions at the back of the throat because they contain a decongestant (p.909).

Cold and flu remedies

Preparations containing drugs that ease the symptoms of colds and flu

COMMON DRUGS

ANALGESICS
• Acetaminophen • Aspirin • Ibuprofen

DECONGESTANTS
• Naphazoline • Oxymetazoline • Phenylephrine
• Pseudoephedrine • Xylometazoline

There are no cures for the common cold (p.286) or influenza (p.287), but there are various remedies that may suppress symptoms and make you feel more comfortable. Most of these remedies contain combinations of drugs, which usually include an analgesic (p.912), such as acetaminophen or ibuprofen, to lower fever and relieve muscle aches and pain, sore throat, and headache; decongestants (p.909), which help relieve congestion in the nose and sinuses; caffeine, which acts as a mild stimulant; and vitamin C. Generally, doctors advise taking single products to treat individual symptoms rather than remedies containing several drugs, some of which are not needed.

HOW ARE THEY USED?

Dosages vary among the various cold and flu remedies. It is important to follow each product's instructions and to take care not to exceed the recommended daily dose of acetaminophen because high doses are known to cause liver damage. Children under age 12 should not be given aspirin because of the link between this drug and Reye syndrome (p.849). You should avoid taking cold and flu remedies containing aspirin or ibuprofen if you have asthma (p.483), a peptic ulcer (p.640), indigestion (p.626), or gout (p.380).

> WARNING
>
> Do not give aspirin to children under age 12 because it increases the risk of Reye syndrome, a rare brain and liver disorder.

Bronchodilator drugs

Drugs that widen the airways of the lungs to ease breathing difficulties

COMMON DRUGS

SYMPATHOMIMETICS
• Ephedrine • Epinephrine • Fenoterol
• Formoterol • Isoproterenol • Salbutamol
• Salmeterol • Terbutaline

ANTICHOLINERGICS
• Atropine • Ipratropium bromide • Tiotropium

XANTHINES
• Aminophylline • Theophylline

Bronchodilator drugs are used to dilate (widen) the bronchi (airways) inside the lungs (*see* HOW BRONCHODILATOR DRUGS WORK, right). Widening the airways prevents or relieves the wheezing, tightness of the chest, and shortness of breath that result from conditions such as asthma (p.483) and chronic obstructive pulmonary disease (p.487), a progressive disease of the lungs most often caused by smoking.

Many bronchodilators are inhaled through a metered-dose inhaler, a small aerosol pump that delivers a controlled amount of the drug to be inhaled. Spacers, plastic chambers into which a dose of the drug is released before it is inhaled, and breath-activated inhalers are also available. You may prefer the easy-to-use spacers if you have difficulty using an inhaler on its own (*see* TAKING INHALED ASTHMA DRUGS, p.485). If you have severe shortness of breath, you may be given bronchodilator drugs by means of a nebulizer, a device that delivers the drug in aerosol form through a mask or mouthpiece. Certain bronchodilator drugs may be taken orally to prevent asthma attacks. You should let your doctor know if you are pregnant or breast-feeding.

> DRUG ACTION
>
> ### HOW BRONCHODILATOR DRUGS WORK
>
> Bronchodilator drugs are often used to prevent or relieve wheezing and shortness of breath caused by disorders such as asthma. In these conditions, the bronchi (airways in the lungs) become abnormally narrowed because muscles in their walls contract. Bronchodilators work by widening the airways and thereby increasing the air flow.
>
> 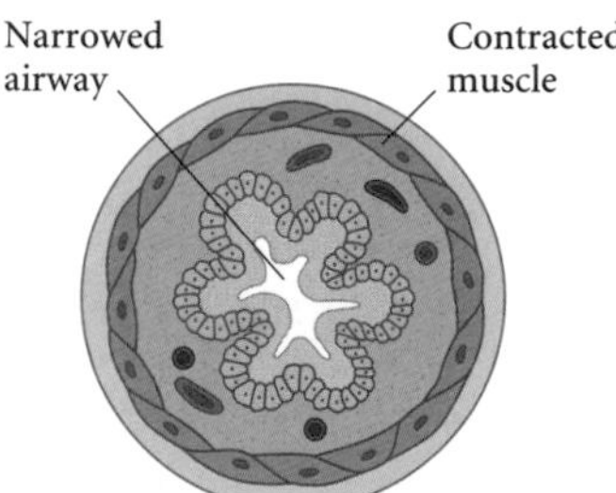
> Narrowed airway
> Contracted muscle
>
> **Before drug**
> *The airway narrows as the muscle layer in its walls contracts. The flow of air to the lungs becomes reduced.*
>
> 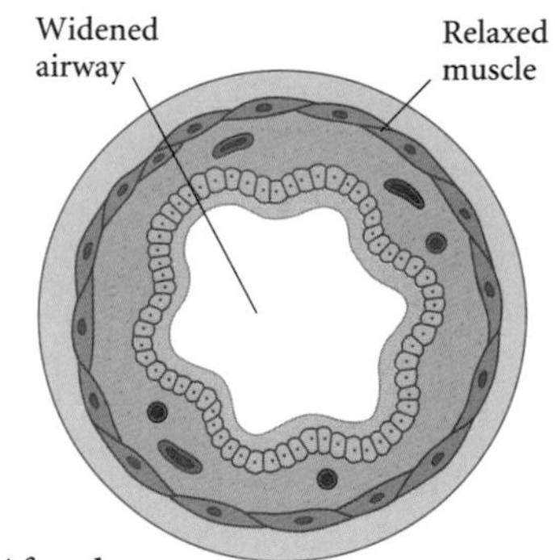
> Widened airway
> Relaxed muscle
>
> **After drug**
> *The drugs act on the muscle cells of the airway. The muscles relax, and the airway widens, increasing air flow.*

WHAT ARE THE TYPES?

Bronchodilators are divided into three main groups: sympathomimetics, anticholinergics, and xanthines. Inhaled sympathomimetics take effect within 10 minutes and are often used for relief from shortness of breath. Anticholinergics and xanthines take longer to work.

SYMPATHOMIMETICS The drugs in this group are the most commonly used bronchodilators. They work by acting on nerve endings in the muscles in the walls of the airways, causing the muscles to relax and the airways to widen. This helps to ease difficulty breathing.

Sympathomimetics, usually inhaled, act within minutes, and their effect can last 4–6 hours. Some types have a longer-lasting preventive effect.

Inhaled sympathomimetics are usually used at the first sign of symptoms or to prevent symptoms from developing, for instance before physical activity. The combination of a long-acting sympathomimetic and an inhaled steroid, often in the same device, is of benefit in poorly controlled asthmatics.

ANTICHOLINERGICS The drugs in this group are often used together with sympathomimetics to treat chronic obstructive pulmonary disease. Anticholinergics work in a similar way to sympathomimetics: they stop the constriction of airways that have been irritated by airborne particles. The drugs may cause some side effects including a dry mouth, difficulty urinating, and blurry vision. In rare cases, anticholinergics may trigger an attack of acute glaucoma (p.575).

XANTHINES These drugs have a sustained-release action, which helps make them particularly effective in preventing nighttime attacks of asthma. Xanthines act on the muscle cells of the airway walls, causing the airways to widen.

Oral xanthines may be taken as a preventive measure. These drugs may cause nausea and headache and, if high doses are taken, occasionally a rapid and irregular heartbeat.

Leukotriene antagonists

A group of anti-inflammatory drugs used to treat asthma

Common drugs

• Montelukast sodium • Zafirlukast

Leukotriene antagonists are a group of anti-inflammatory drugs that are used to treat asthma. They work by blocking leukotrienes, a class of compounds that is a major cause of inflammation. There are two types of leukotriene antagonists. The first, montelukast sodium, blocks leukotrienes from forming. Zafirlukast is a leukotriene receptor blocking drug, preventing leukotrienes from attaching to lung tissue.

Leukotriene antagonists are taken as tablets once or twice daily, often in conjunction with inhaled corticosteroids. However, they have not yet been shown to be as effective as inhaled corticosteroids for long-term use.

What are the side effects?

Side effects may include headache and abdominal pain.

Corticosteroids for respiratory disease

A group of anti-inflammatory drugs used to treat several respiratory disorders

Common drugs

• Beclomethasone • Budesonide • Fluticasone
• Hydrocortisone • Prednisolone • Prednisone

Corticosteroids (p.930) are drugs that are related to natural hormones. When used to treat respiratory disorders, they reduce or prevent inflammation of the airways. Corticosteroids are often prescribed to prevent attacks of asthma (p.483). They are also helpful for some people with chronic obstructive pulmonary disease (p.487). Less commonly, corticosteroids are used to treat people with sarcoidosis (p.498) and interstitial fibrosis (p.497). Occasionally, corticosteroids may be prescribed to prevent or treat inflammation of the nasal passages in conditions such as hay fever (*see* ALLERGIC RHINITIS, p.466).

How do they work?

The lining of the airways of the lungs becomes inflamed during an asthma attack. This reaction causes the airways to narrow, restricting the flow of air. Corticosteroids reduce inflammation by blocking the action of prostaglandins, chemicals normally responsible for triggering the inflammatory response. A reduction in inflammation widens the airways and relieves or prevents asthma attacks and slows down and minimizes the damage to lung tissues that can occur in people with sarcoidosis or interstitial fibrosis. When used for hay fever, corticosteroids act on blood vessels in the lining of the nose to reduce inflammation of the nasal lining.

How are they used?

Your doctor may prescribe an inhaled corticosteroid if you are experiencing daily asthma attacks or if you find that you need to use bronchodilator drugs (opposite page) more than a few times a week. Regular use of inhaled corticosteroids can prevent asthma attacks from occurring, and over time it may be possible to reduce the dose. After a severe asthma attack, you may need to take an oral corticosteroid for a few days. Long-term use of low-dose oral corticosteroids is usually necessary only if you have severe asthma. If you are admitted to the hospital with a severe attack, you may initially be given an intravenous corticosteroid.

If you have been taking oral corticosteroids for more than a few weeks, it is important not to stop taking them suddenly. If the drugs are used for a prolonged period of time, they can suppress the body's own production of corticosteroids. The dose should therefore be reduced gradually to allow the body to restore normal levels of corticosteroid production.

What are the side effects?

The side effects from inhaled corticosteroids are usually minimal because the drugs act directly on the airways with little effect elsewhere in the body. The most common side effect is oral thrush (*see* CANDIDIASIS, p.309), a fungal infection more often associated with other areas of the body. To avoid this infection, rinse your mouth with cold water after using your inhaler.

Your doctor will prescribe the lowest dose for your condition to reduce risk of side effects. However, people taking oral corticosteroids long-term are at risk of susceptibility to infections, osteoporosis (p.368), cataracts (p.573), acute glaucoma (p.575), and bruising.

> **WARNING**
>
> Do not suddenly stop taking oral corticosteroids without first consulting your doctor.

DRUGS ACTING ON THE BRAIN AND NERVOUS SYSTEM

Many of the drugs that act on the brain and nervous system relieve symptoms such as pain, insomnia, and anxiety. Others treat the underlying disorders that are causing the symptoms. As understanding of the chemical changes that cause disorders such as depression improves, treatment is becoming more effective.

The opening article in this section describes groups of drugs known as analgesics. Most of these drugs relieve pain by preventing pain signals from being produced or altering the way the brain perceives pain. Drugs for migraine are covered next, followed by general anesthetic drugs, which induce unconsciousness so that no pain is felt during surgery. Local anesthetic drugs, which block the transmission of pain signals in a specific part of the body, are then discussed.

The next articles in this section cover anticonvulsant drugs, sleeping drugs, and antianxiety drugs. Most work by reducing electrical activity in the brain to relieve symptoms but do not treat the underlying disorder.

Antidepressant drugs, which are described next, work by increasing levels of chemicals in the brain that regulate mood. Reduced levels of these chemicals can usually be found in people who are depressed.

In the final articles, antipsychotic drugs, mood-stabilizing drugs, and central nervous system stimulants are described. All of these drugs work by altering chemical activity in the brain.

KEY ANATOMY

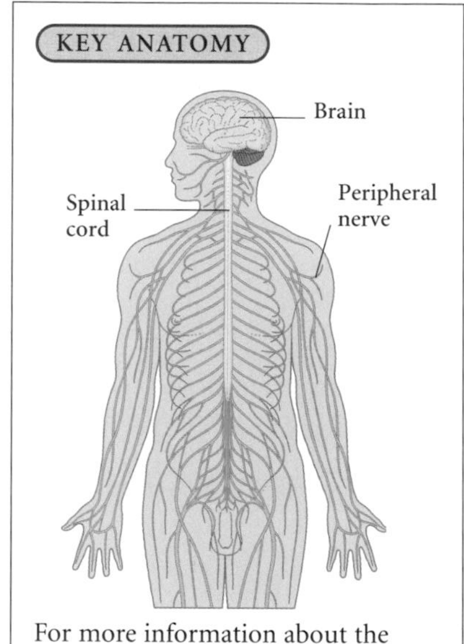
Brain
Spinal cord
Peripheral nerve

For more information about the structure and function of the brain and nervous system, *see* pp.508–515.

Analgesics

Drugs of varying potency that are used to relieve pain

COMMON DRUGS

OPIOID ANALGESICS
• Codeine • Fentanyl • Meperidine • Methadone • Morphine • Pentazocine

NONOPIOID ANALGESICS
• Acetaminophen • Aspirin • Diclofenac • Etodolac • Fenoprofen • Ibuprofen • Indomethacin • Ketoprofen • Ketorolac • Mefenamic acid • Naproxen • Piroxicam

COMBINATION ANALGESICS
• Acetaminophen with codeine • Aspirin with codeine • Dihydrocodeine with acetaminophen • Propoxyphene with acetaminophen

Analgesics are used to relieve pain. Some analgesics work by blocking the nerve pathways that transmit pain signals from the part of the body that is causing pain to the brain. Other analgesics reduce the perception of pain by preventing further transmission of the pain signals once they reach the brain. However, pain relief for most long-term disorders depends on treatment of the underlying cause.

WHAT ARE THE TYPES?

The two main types of analgesics are opioid (narcotic) and nonopioid (nonnarcotic). Some analgesics may be a combination of more than one drug. Opioid analgesics are mainly used to relieve severe pain. Nonopioid analgesics, most of which are nonsteroidal anti-inflammatory drugs (p.894), may be used to treat mild or moderate pain. Combination analgesics contain two or more analgesics and, in some cases, a nonanalgesic drug and may provide greater pain relief than a single analgesic.

OPIOID ANALGESICS These drugs are the strongest analgesics available. They may be given for pain following a heart attack (*see* MYOCARDIAL INFARCTION, p.410) or following surgery or serious injury. They are also widely used in pain relief for cancer (p.281). Opioids act on the brain, altering the perception of pain. These drugs work in a similar way to natural substances called endorphins, which are released in the brain in response to pain. Opioids bind to the same receptors in the brain as endorphins and stop the transmission of pain signals from cell to cell (*see* HOW OPIOID ANALGESICS WORK, opposite page).

Prolonged use of opioid analgesics may lead to dependence. However, you are very unlikely to become dependent if you take the drugs for a few days to relieve acute pain. Dependence is also not usually a cause for concern in the treatment of pain in a person suffering from a terminal illness. However, prolonged use leads to tolerance, in which progressively higher doses are needed to achieve the same level of pain relief.

Opioids may be taken orally or, if the pain is extremely severe or accompanied by vomiting, may be given by injection. Side effects include constipation, nausea, vomiting, and drowsiness. Larger doses can depress breathing and may also cause confusion and impaired consciousness. Overdose may be fatal.

NONOPIOID ANALGESICS These analgesics are less potent than opioids, and several are available over the counter. They include acetaminophen, aspirin, and nonsteroidal anti-inflammatory drugs (NSAIDs) such as ibuprofen. Nonopioid analgesics are used mainly

WARNING

Do not give aspirin to children under age 12 because it increases the risk of Reye syndrome, a rare brain and liver disorder.

for pain such as headache, menstrual pain, and toothache. In addition to relieving pain, NSAIDs are effective in reducing inflammation and fever.

Side effects are rarely a problem if you take nonopioid analgesics occasionally and at the doses recommended for pain relief. However, when used repeatedly, NSAIDs as well as aspirin may damage the lining of the stomach and intestines, resulting in peptic ulcers (p.640), and may lead to bleeding in the digestive tract. Taking NSAIDs with food may reduce these side effects. Some people who have asthma are sensitive to certain NSAIDs, which may make their asthma worse.

Acetaminophen relieves pain and lowers fever, but, unlike NSAIDs, it does not reduce inflammation. It works by blocking pain impulses in the brain. Acetaminophen is dangerous in doses above the daily recommended maximum intake. Overdose can cause severe liver and rarely kidney damage.

COMBINATION ANALGESICS Combination analgesics, which may sometimes include other nonanalgesic drugs, are available as over-the-counter remedies for headaches, backache, muscle aches, menstrual pain, and other painful conditions. However, caffeine, which is an ingredient included in some remedies, may itself cause headaches.

DRUG ACTION

HOW OPIOID ANALGESICS WORK

Opioid analgesics are often used to relieve severe pain. Pain signals are transmitted along nerves from the source of pain to the brain. Opioid analgesics block the transmission of pain signals in the brain, and thus reduce the sensation of pain.

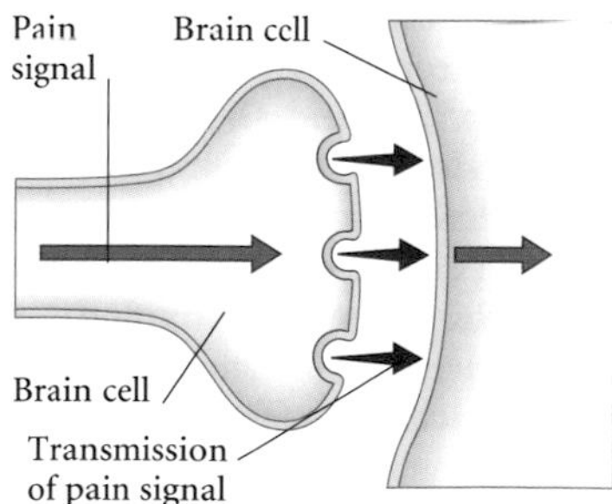
Pain signal
Brain cell
Brain cell
Transmission of pain signal

Before the drug

On reaching the brain, the pain signal is transmitted from one brain cell to the next until it reaches the part of the brain that interprets the signal as pain.

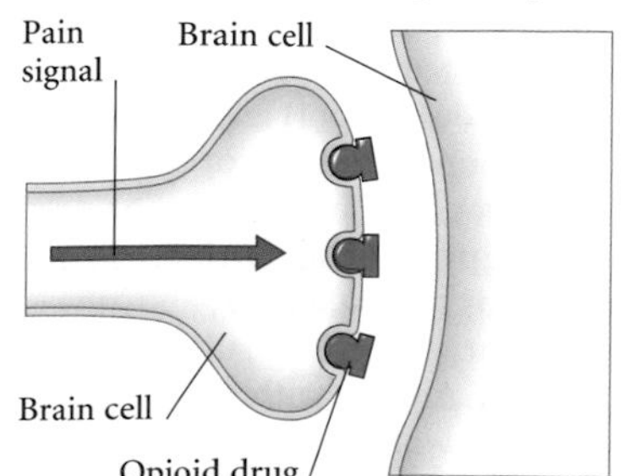
Pain signal
Brain cell
Brain cell
Opioid drug

After the drug

Opioid analgesics block transmission of the pain signal in the brain, thereby reducing the sensation of pain.

Antimigraine drugs

Drugs that are used in the prevention and treatment of migraine

COMMON DRUGS

DRUGS TO PREVENT MIGRAINE
- Amitriptyline • Gabapentin • Propranolol
- Topiramate • Valproate sodium • Verapamil

DRUGS TO RELIEVE MIGRAINE
- Almotriptan • Ergotamine • Naratriptan
- Rizatriptan • Sumatriptan • Zolmitriptan

ANALGESICS (opposite page)
- Acetaminophen • Aspirin • Codeine
- Ibuprofen

Migraine attacks (*see* MIGRAINE, p.518) produce severe headaches and are often accompanied by nausea and vomiting. These symptoms may be preceded by visual disturbances. Some drugs that are used to treat migraine are taken regularly to prevent attacks, while others are taken during an attack to alleviate the symptoms. Analgesics (opposite page) may help relieve pain in a migraine attack.

HOW DO THEY WORK?

During a migraine attack, blood flow inside the brain changes. Initially, the blood vessels narrow, reducing blood flow. After this initial phase, the vessels rapidly widen, and a severe headache develops. Drugs that are used to prevent migraine, such as propranolol (*see* BETA BLOCKER DRUGS, p.898), prevent these changes in blood vessel size. However, the exact mechanism by which they work is not understood.

Triptan drugs, such as sumatriptan and naratriptan, and ergotamine relieve the symptoms of a migraine attack by returning widened blood vessels to their normal size. Analgesics can relieve the pain of a migraine attack in some people but do not shorten its duration.

HOW ARE THEY USED?

Most people who experience migraines have attacks infrequently and can control the pain using analgesics such as acetaminophen, aspirin, ibuprofen, or codeine. If you experience severe migraine attacks more than twice a month, your doctor may prescribe a preventive drug, such as the beta blocker propranolol, to be taken daily for a few months.

Severe migraine that is not relieved by analgesics may respond to triptans or ergotamine. You should take these antimigraine drugs as soon as you notice migraine symptoms developing. Triptans and ergotamine can be taken orally, but if you regularly experience episodes of very severe migraine, especially if they are accompanied by nausea and vomiting, your doctor may prescribe triptans in a form that can be given by injection or by nasal spray.

There are over-the-counter preparations for migraine that contain one or more analgesics to relieve pain and an antiemetic drug (p.922) to help relieve nausea and vomiting.

WHAT ARE THE SIDE EFFECTS?

You may experience side effects when taking drugs to treat migraine. Taking propranolol may result in cold hands and feet and fatigue. Triptans can make you feel drowsy and can sometimes cause flushing, dizziness, tingling sensations, and chest pain. Ergotamine may cause nausea, vomiting, abdominal pain, diarrhea, and muscle cramps. Excessive use of triptans or ergotamine may reduce their effectiveness. You should not exceed the recommended dose of any antimigraine drug.

OTHER SLEEPING DRUGS Besides benzodiazepines and antihistamines, there are other sleeping drugs that are used to treat insomnia and establish sleep patterns. Certain antidepressant medications, such as amitriptyline and trazadone, are known to have sedative side effects. For this reason, they may be used to promote sleep. These antidepressant drugs are not known to cause dependence on their use.

Antianxiety drugs

Drugs that are used to reduce and control the symptoms of stress and anxiety

COMMON DRUGS

BENZODIAZEPINES
- Chlordiazepoxide • Diazepam • Lorazepam
- Oxazepam

BETA BLOCKER DRUGS
- Atenolol • Propranolol

OTHER ANTIANXIETY DRUGS
- Buspirone

Antianxiety drugs, sometimes known as anxiolytics or minor tranquilizers, are used to treat anxiety disorders (p.551), in which feelings of foreboding and fear may be accompanied by physical symptoms such as palpitations and tremor. The underlying cause of the anxiety may also need to be treated at the same time, possibly by psychological therapy. Some drugs may be used specifically to relieve the physical symptoms of anxiety. For example, they may be prescribed for people who are nervous about giving a public performance or to calm a person who is anxious before an operation.

WHAT ARE THE TYPES?

Several types of drugs are used in the treatment of anxiety. Benzodiazepines are the drugs most commonly prescribed for the short-term treatment of psychological symptoms of anxiety.

Where physical symptoms, such as muscle tremor, are the main problem, beta blocker drugs (p.898) may be used instead. Buspirone is sometimes prescribed to treat anxiety because it is less sedating than benzodiazepines.

> WARNING
>
> Benzodiazepine drugs can cause drowsiness and may affect your ability to drive or operate machinery.

BENZODIAZEPINES These drugs may be used for the treatment of severe anxiety. They reduce agitation and make you feel relaxed. However, doctors only prescribe short courses of benzodiazepines to avoid causing dependence.

Benzodiazepines slow mental activity by reducing the signals between brain cells. They commonly cause drowsiness, and for this reason they are also used as sleeping drugs (p.915). You should not drink alcohol while taking benzodiazepines because it increases the sedative effect. These drugs can also cause confusion, dizziness, poor coordination, and lethargy. Benzodiazepines should not be taken for more than 1–2 weeks. If they are taken for longer, stopping the drug may produce withdrawal symptoms such as excessive anxiety, insomnia, and restlessness.

BETA BLOCKER DRUGS Physical symptoms that sometimes occur with anxiety may be reduced by taking beta blockers. These drugs should only be used occasionally and are not suitable for the long-term treatment of anxiety.

The drugs block the actions of two hormones, called epinephrine and norepinephrine, that are responsible for the physical symptoms of anxiety. Beta blockers reduce the heart rate and may prevent palpitations in someone who is extremely anxious. Beta blockers can also be used to reduce muscle tremor. If you take a beta blocker, you may find that your sleep is disturbed and that your hands and feet feel cold.

OTHER ANTIANXIETY DRUGS The most common of the other drugs that are used to reduce anxiety is buspirone, which is less addictive than the benzodiazepines and also has a less sedative effect. Buspirone can take up to 2 weeks to become fully effective and is therefore not used when immediate relief from stress or anxiety is needed. You may experience side effects, which can include nervousness, headache, and dizziness, when taking buspirone. The drug may also affect your ability to drive or operate machinery.

Antidepressant drugs

Drugs that are used to treat the symptoms of depression

COMMON DRUGS

SELECTIVE SEROTONIN REUPTAKE INHIBITORS
- Citalopram • Fluoxetine • Fluvoxamine
- Paroxetine • Sertraline

TRICYCLICS
- Amitriptyline • Clomipramine • Imipramine

MONOAMINE OXIDASE INHIBITORS
- Phenelzine • Tranylcypromine

OTHER ANTIDEPRESSANT DRUGS
- Maprotiline • Mirtazapine • Nefazodone
- Trazodone • Venlafaxine

Antidepressant drugs help relieve many of the symptoms of depression (p.554), such as feelings of despair, lethargy, poor appetite, insomnia, and suicidal thoughts. Antidepressants are effective in about 2 in 3 people who take them.

People who are depressed have been shown to have reduced levels of certain chemicals in the brain, known as neurotransmitters. Two neurotransmitters, called serotonin and norepinephrine, are thought to increase brain activity and improve mood. They are usually reabsorbed by brain cells and inactivated by an enzyme called monoamine oxidase. In depression, the levels of serotonin or norepinephrine are often lower than normal. Antidepressants act at different points in the cycle to restore these chemicals to normal levels.

Antidepressants are taken orally and usually take 2–4 weeks to have an effect on depression, but some side effects may occur within days. Your doctor will usually advise you to take an antidepressant for at least 6 months after your depression has lifted so that symptoms do not recur and then to reduce the dose gradually. You should avoid drinking alcohol while taking antidepressants because it enhances the sedative effect.

Lithium, a mood-stabilizing drug (p.918), may be used on its own or with an antidepressant in severe depression.

> WARNING
>
> Antidepressant drugs can cause drowsiness and may affect your ability to drive or operate machinery.

What are the types?

Most of the drugs used to treat depression belong to one of three main groups: selective serotonin reuptake inhibitors (SSRIs), tricyclics, and monoamine oxidase inhibitors (MAOIs). There are also several other types of antidepressants. All of these drugs treat depression by increasing levels of the neurotransmitters in the brain that lift mood.

SSRIs These drugs are the most commonly used type of antidepressant. They may also be used to treat phobias (p.552) and panic attacks *(see* ANXIETY DISORDERS, p.551). SSRIs cause fewer side effects compared to other antidepressants. They are also less toxic than other antidepressants if more than the prescribed amount is taken. The drugs work by blocking the reabsorption of the neurotransmitter serotonin, leaving more to stimulate brain cells (*see* HOW SSRIS WORK, right). SSRIs may cause side effects, including diarrhea, nausea and vomiting, reduced sex drive, and headache. They may also cause restlessness and anxiety.

TRICYCLICS Tricyclics are often used in the treatment of depression and are also sometimes used to treat facial pain in trigeminal neuralgia (p.546) or to prevent migraine (p.518). The drugs interfere with the reabsorption of both serotonin and norepinephrine in the brain. As a result, levels of these mood-lifting chemicals increase. It is not well understood how tricyclics relieve pain in trigeminal neuralgia.

Tricyclics cause a number of side effects, including a dry mouth, blurry vision, constipation, and difficulty urinating. The side effects are usually worse when the drug is first started and become less of a problem as you get used to the drug. Tricyclics are dangerous if you exceed the usual dose. They may cause seizures and heart rhythm irregularities, which can be fatal.

MAOIs These drugs are usually only used when other types of antidepressant drugs are ineffective. They work by blocking the activity of monoamine oxidase (the enzyme that makes serotonin and norepinephrine inactive) in brain cells. The side effects of MAOIs may include light-headedness, drowsiness, insomnia, headache, a dry mouth, constipation, and other digestive disturbances. These drugs interact with other drugs and certain foods, including cheese. If you are taking an MAOI, it is important that you follow your doctor's instructions. If you stop taking an MAOI, the dose should be reduced gradually to reduce the chance of a dangerous increase in blood pressure.

OTHER ANTIDEPRESSANT DRUGS There are two other drugs, maprotiline and trazodone, that are related to tricyclic antidepressants. Mirtazapine enhances noradrenergic and serotonergic transmission. Maprotiline is used to treat both depression and anxiety when sedation is required. Trazodone is also used to treat depression when sedation is required. It is less likely to cause heart rhythm problems than other tricyclics.

Venlafaxine blocks the reuptake of serotonin and norepinephrine. Nefazodone works in a similar way to SSRIs but also works by blocking serotonin receptors.

DRUG ACTION How SSRIs work

SSRI drugs are often used to treat depression. Depression is associated with low levels of serotonin, a chemical that acts on certain brain cells involved in thoughts and mood. Nerve cells in the brain constantly release and reabsorb the chemical serotonin. SSRIs reduce the rate of reabsorption, resulting in higher levels of serotonin in the brain.

Before the drug
Nerve impulses stimulate the release of serotonin from nerve endings in brain cells. The serotonin stimulates other brain cells. It is then reabsorbed and stored in the nerve endings, ready to be released again.

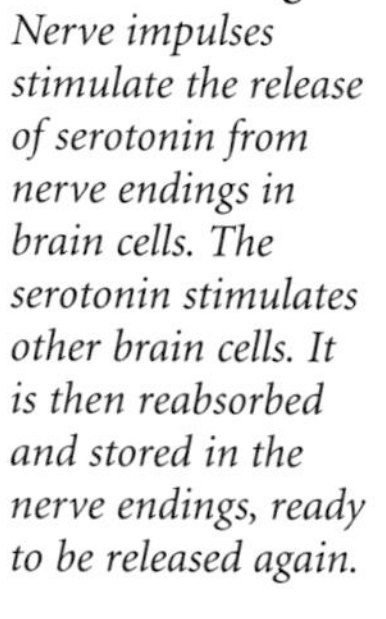

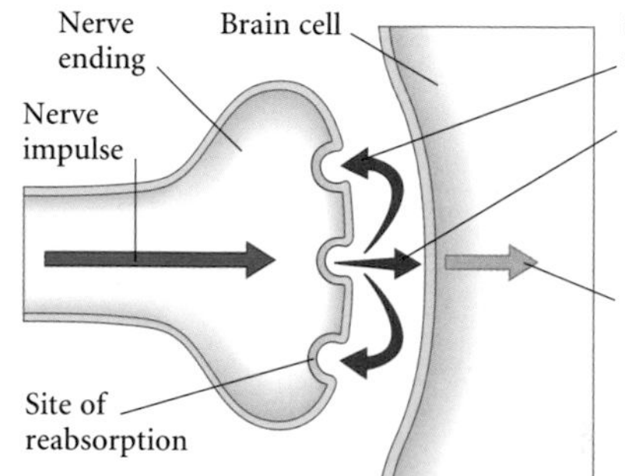

Nerve ending
Brain cell
Nerve impulse
Site of reabsorption
Serotonin reabsorbed
Serotonin released
Nerve impulses stimulate release of serotonin
Stimulation
Serotonin stimulates brain cells

After the drug
The drug reduces the reabsorption of serotonin by nerve endings by blocking the reabsorption sites. This leaves higher levels of serotonin available in the brain, which increases brain cell stimulation.

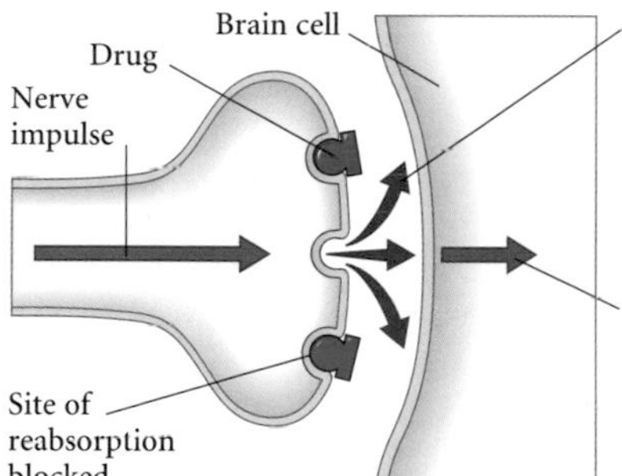

Brain cell
Drug
Nerve impulse
Site of reabsorption blocked
Higher levels of serotonin
Serotonin reabsorption is blocked, resulting in increased levels of serotonin
High level of stimulation
Serotonin that is not reabsorbed increases brain cell stimulation

Antipsychotic drugs

Drugs used to treat schizophrenia and other severe psychiatric disorders

COMMON DRUGS

• Chlorpromazine • Clozapine • Droperidol • Fluphenazine • Haloperidol • Loxapine • Olanzapine • Pericyazine • Pimozide • Pipotiazine • Promazine • Risperidone • Thioridazine • Trifluoperazine

Antipsychotic drugs are used to control symptoms such as hallucinations and disturbed thought in schizophrenia (p.560) and other psychotic disorders. Some of these drugs are used to stabilize mood in people with bipolar affective disorder (p.557), also known as manic-depressive disorder, although mood-stabilizing drugs (p.918) such as lithium may also be used.

Occasionally, an antipsychotic drug is used to calm a person who is agitated for reasons other than psychotic illness. For example, you may be given an antipsychotic drug if you are experiencing severe anxiety.

How do they work?

Many antipsychotic drugs block the action of the neurotransmitter (brain chemical) dopamine. This chemical is released in the brain at higher than normal levels in people with psychotic disorders and is believed to play a part in producing symptoms. Some antipsychotic drugs also block the action of serotonin and other chemicals involved in regulating mood.

How are they used?

The type of antipsychotic drug prescribed will depend on factors such as how much sedation is needed and your susceptibility to side effects.

The drugs are usually taken orally, although they may be injected if a person is very agitated. A low dose of the drug is prescribed initially, and the dose is then increased gradually until the symptoms are under control. A depot injection, which is an injection deep into a muscle from which the drug is slowly released, may be used so that you do not have to take the drug every day. Depot injections provide enough drug to last up to 4 weeks.

If you have bipolar affective disorder, your doctor may initially prescribe a short course of an antipsychotic drug. He or she may also prescribe lithium or another mood-stabilizing drug. The antipsychotic drug acts rapidly to make you feel calmer and works in the weeks before the mood-stabilizing drug can reach its full effect.

What are the side effects?

Antipsychotics may cause a dry mouth, blurry vision, and dizziness due to lowering of blood pressure, and some may make you feel drowsy. They may also cause restlessness and rarely movement disorders such as parkinsonism (see Parkinson's disease and parkinsonism, p.539). Although these side effects usually disappear when you stop taking the drug, certain antipsychotic drugs may occasionally cause permanent side effects after more than a year of use, such as repeated jerking movements of the mouth, face, and tongue.

You should never suddenly stop taking any antipsychotic drug without first consulting your doctor. If you need to stop taking the drug, the dose will be reduced gradually by your doctor.

Mood-stabilizing drugs

Drugs used to treat severe psychiatric disorders involving excessive mood swings

Common drugs

- Carbamazepine • Lithium • Valproate sodium

Mood-stabilizing drugs are used for the treatment of bipolar affective disorder (p.557), which is also known as manic-depressive disorder, and less commonly for severe depression (p.554). In bipolar affective disorder, cycles of mania (elation) and severe depression may occur. Lithium is the drug most commonly used to treat this disorder and can control or reduce the intensity of mania. It may also prevent or reduce the frequency of attacks and lift depression. Two other drugs, carbamazepine and valproate sodium, may be used as mood stabilizers if lithium is ineffective in treating bipolar affective disorder or if it causes unacceptable side effects.

How are they used?

Lithium is taken orally. It takes a few days before the drug's effects are noticeable and up to 3 weeks for it to take full effect. For this reason, a rapidly acting antipsychotic drug (p.917) is often prescribed at the same time for initial control of mania. Lithium will then be continued to prevent further episodes.

Treatment with lithium can cause nausea, diarrhea, tremor, and excessive thirst. These side effects usually reduce in severity if treatment is continued. If the dose is too high, lithium can cause blurry vision, confusion, and seizures. Carbamazepine and valproate sodium may be given if lithium is unsuitable. These drugs may cause memory and coordination problems. Your doctor will carry out blood and urine tests to measure drug levels during treatment with mood-stabilizing drugs.

If you are taking lithium, you will be given a treatment card, bracelet, or pendant, which you should carry with you at all times. You should not make changes in your diet that might alter the amount of salt you take in because this may affect lithium levels in your body. It is also important to avoid dehydration, which may occur if you develop diarrhea or vomiting or travel to a region with a hot climate.

Central nervous system stimulant drugs

Drugs that are used to increase mental alertness and wakefulness

Common drugs

- Caffeine • Dextroamphetamine
- Methylphenidate

Central nervous system (CNS) stimulant drugs act by increasing activity in the brain, thereby increasing wakefulness and mental alertness. Their main use is in the treatment of narcolepsy (p.526), a disorder in which an individual falls asleep suddenly during the day. Some CNS stimulant drugs, including methylphenidate, are used to improve attention span in children who have a behavioral problem known as attention deficit hyperactivity disorder (p.855).

How do they work?

CNS stimulants improve concentration and increase wakefulness by acting on a part of the brain that regulates mental alertness. These stimulants promote the release of certain chemicals in the brain (neurotransmitters) that increase nerve activity in this part of the brain.

How are they used?

CNS stimulants are given orally long-term for the treatment of narcolepsy. Doctors try to avoid prescribing CNS stimulants over a prolonged period for a child because they may slow growth. Children undergoing long-term therapy will be closely monitored for side effects. In some cases, the drug may not be given every day; however, it should be withheld only under doctor's advice.

What are the side effects?

While you are taking CNS stimulants, you may experience reduced appetite, tremor, and palpitations. These drugs can also cause restlessness, sleeplessness, anxiety, shaking, and sweating. Some CNS stimulants may produce symptoms similar to those of schizophrenia (p.560), such as hallucinations. Other side effects include rashes and allergies. If you take a CNS stimulant long-term, stopping it may cause withdrawal symptoms, including lethargy, depression, and increased appetite.

Drugs for eye and ear disorders

Eye and ear problems need prompt attention because they affect two of our most important senses. Many short-term infections and chronic conditions can be treated effectively with drugs. Treatment for eye and ear disorders can often be administered easily as drops or ointments.

KEY ANATOMY

Pupil
Lens
Retina
Optic nerve
Cornea
EYE

Inner ear
Middle ear
Outer ear
Eardrum
EAR

For more information on the structure and function of the eyes and ears, *see* pp.566–569 and pp.592–595.

Most eye and ear disorders are minor and clear up rapidly with appropriate treatment. More serious and persistent problems may need supervision and long-term use of drugs.

The first article in this section discusses drugs used to treat infections and inflammation of the eye. It also covers artificial tears, which relieve dry eyes, and mydriatics, a group of drugs that are used in the treatment of the inflammatory disorder uveitis.

Drugs for glaucoma, a potentially serious condition if left untreated, are described in the next article. These drugs work in a variety of ways to relieve excess accumulation of fluid in the eye. As a result, the pressure that can restrict the blood supply to the optic nerve is relieved, thereby diminishing the likelihood of partial or complete loss of vision.

The final article in this section discusses drugs used to treat disorders of the ear. These drugs range from treatments for bacterial infections and excess earwax to nausea and vomiting, symptoms that are commonly seen in disorders of the inner ear and which can affect the balance mechanism. Drugs that relieve nausea and vomiting are discussed further elsewhere (*see* ANTIEMETIC DRUGS, p.922).

Drugs acting on the eye

Drugs that are used to treat a variety of disorders affecting the eye

COMMON DRUGS

ANTI-INFECTIVE DRUGS
- Acyclovir • Chloramphenicol • Ciprofloxacin
- Gentamicin • Neomycin • Polymyxin B

ANTI-INFLAMMATORY DRUGS
- Betamethasone • Cromolyn sodium
- Dexamethasone • Nedocromil • Prednisolone

ARTIFICIAL TEARS
- Hydroxyethylcellulose • Hypromellose
- Polyvinyl alcohol

MYDRIATICS
- Atropine • Epinephrine • Phenylephrine

Many eye disorders are treated by using drugs applied directly to the eye in the form of eyedrops (*see* USING EYEDROPS, right) or ointments (*see* USING EYE OINTMENT, p.920). Minor eye problems, such as irritation due to allergy, can often be relieved with over-the-counter remedies. Drugs for eye infections and other serious conditions, such as uveitis (p.574) or scleritis (p.574), in which parts of the eye become inflamed, are available only by prescription.

What are the types?

The main types of drugs used to treat eye disorders are anti-infective drugs and anti-inflammatory drugs. Anti-infective drugs are commonly used in the treatment of bacterial, viral, and, less commonly, fungal infections of the eye. Anti-inflammatory drugs are used to relieve the redness and swelling that may develop as a result of infection, allergic reactions, or autoimmune disorders (in which the immune system attacks the body's own tissues). Artificial tears are used to relieve dry eyes (*see* KERATOCONJUNCTIVITIS SICCA, p.585). Mydriatics widen (dilate) the pupils and are mainly used to treat uveitis.

ANTI-INFECTIVE DRUGS There are two main groups of drugs used to treat eye infections. Antibiotics (p.885), such as chloramphenicol, may be used to treat bacterial infections such as conjunctivitis (p.570) and blepharitis (p.583).

SELF-ADMINISTRATION **USING EYEDROPS**

Eyedrops deliver a drug directly to where its effect is needed. Always wash your hands before use and do not touch the eye or the skin around it with the dropper. If you wear contact lenses, check with your doctor or pharmacist before using eyedrops because some eyedrops may be unsuitable.

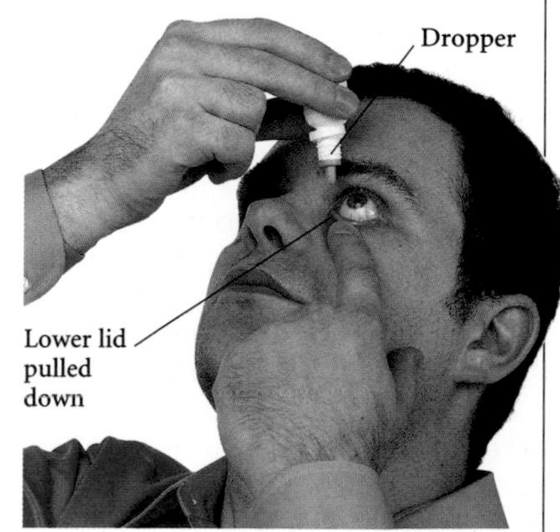
Dropper
Lower lid pulled down

Instilling the drops

Tilt your head backward and pull your lower lid away from your eye. Drop the eyedrops behind your lower lid. Blink a few times to disperse the medication.

SELF-ADMINISTRATION USING EYE OINTMENT

Medication in the form of eye ointment may have a longer-lasting effect than if applied in eyedrops. To reduce the risk of contamination to the eye, wash your hands before applying the ointment and do not touch the affected eye with your fingers or the tube.

Ointment
Lower lid pulled down

Correct application of ointment
Squeeze a thin line of ointment along the inside of the lower eyelid. Close your eye briefly after application. You may find that the ointment makes your vision blurry for a few minutes.

Antiviral drugs (p.886), such as acyclovir, are used to treat corneal ulcers (p.571) that occur as a result of infection with the herpes virus.

Antibiotics are usually applied as eyedrops or ointment directly onto the site of infection in the eye. However, if a bacterial infection is severe, it may be necessary to take oral antibiotics as well as using eyedrops. Viral infections of the eye may be treated with both antiviral eyedrops and oral antiviral drugs.

When using antibiotic eyedrops or ointment, you may experience temporary stinging or itching. You may also notice a bitter taste as the eyedrops run down inside the tear ducts and into your nose and mouth.

ANTI-INFLAMMATORY DRUGS The drugs most commonly prescribed to treat the inflammation that accompanies many eye disorders are corticosteroids (*see* TOPICAL CORTICOSTEROIDS, p.892) and antiallergy drugs (p.905).

Corticosteroids are applied as eyedrops or as ointment just inside the eyelids. If you are predisposed to develop chronic glaucoma (p.576), in which the pressure of fluid in the eye becomes abnormally high, the use of corticosteroids may slightly increase your risk of developing drug-induced glaucoma. Corticosteroids are available by prescription and must only be used under the supervision of your doctor.

Short-term inflammation caused by allergy is often treated with antihistamine or cromolyn sodium eyedrops. Some antiallergy eyedrops, such as those used to treat eye irritation associated with hay fever (*see* ALLERGIC RHINITIS, p.466), are available over the counter. Antiallergy drugs may cause side effects such as blurry vision and headache.

ARTIFICIAL TEARS Eyedrops containing chemicals to relieve dry eyes are available for people who do not produce enough natural tear fluid. Artificial tears form a moist film on the cornea (the transparent front part of the eye), soothing and rehydrating the surface of the eyes. You can buy artificial tear preparations over the counter. They may be applied as often as necessary.

MYDRIATICS These drugs are used to treat uveitis, an inflammatory condition affecting the iris (the colored part of the eye) and the muscles that control focusing. If the iris becomes inflamed, there is a danger that it may stick to the lens of the eye. Mydriatics shrink the inflamed iris by causing its muscles to contract, thereby dilating (widening) the pupil. Mydriatics may also be used to dilate the pupil during eye examinations and eye surgery.

Mydriatics are usually prescribed in the form of eyedrops or eye ointment. While using a mydriatic drug, you may find that bright lights cause discomfort and you may also have difficulty focusing. These drugs can cause contact dermatitis and may cause other side effects, including dry mouth, constipation, and difficulty urinating. Certain mydriatics, such as phenylephrine, can raise blood pressure and are therefore unsuitable for people with high blood pressure (*see* HYPERTENSION, p.403).

Drugs for glaucoma

Drugs that are used to reduce abnormally high pressure inside the eye

COMMON DRUGS

MIOTICS
• Carbachol • Pilocarpine

CARBONIC ANHYDRASE INHIBITORS
• Acetazolamide • Dorzolamide

BETA BLOCKER DRUGS
• Betaxolol • Levobunolol • Timolol

OTHER DRUGS
• Apraclonidine • Bimatoprost • Brimonidine
• Carbachol • Dipivefrin • Latanoprost • Mannitol

Fluid is produced in the front part of the eye to maintain its shape and to nourish the tissues. To achieve a steady pressure, the fluid drains from the eye at the same rate at which it is produced. In glaucoma, abnormally high pressure develops in the eye because of an excessive buildup of fluid. This buildup is caused by a defect in the internal drainage system between the iris (the colored part of the eye) and the cornea (the transparent outer part of the front of the eye). The abnormally high pressure can be relieved by surgery or by using drugs that either increase fluid drainage from the eye or reduce the production of fluid.

It is necessary to receive prompt treatment when glaucoma occurs suddenly (*see* ACUTE GLAUCOMA, p.575). If the condition develops gradually (*see* CHRONIC GLAUCOMA, p.576), it may be treated by the long-term use of drugs to reduce and then maintain a normal level of pressure in the eye.

WHAT ARE THE TYPES?

The drugs most commonly used in the treatment of glaucoma are miotics, carbonic anhydrase inhibitors, and beta blocker drugs. These drugs act in various ways to lower pressure in the eye.

MIOTICS Both acute and chronic glaucoma can be treated using a miotic, such as pilocarpine. These drugs cause the pupil, the circular opening in the center of the eye, to constrict, causing the iris to move away from the cornea. As a result, the size of the drainage angle increases, improving the flow of fluid out of the eye. Miotics are usually administered as eyedrops.

While taking miotics you may find it harder to see in dim light because the drugs constrict the pupil, reducing the amount of light that enters the eye. You may also experience irritation of the eye, blurry vision, and headache.

CARBONIC ANHYDRASE INHIBITORS In cases of acute glaucoma these drugs are often prescribed. They may also be used to treat chronic glaucoma if other drugs are not effective. Carbonic anhydrase inhibitors rapidly reduce fluid pressure inside the eye by blocking the effect of an enzyme necessary for fluid production. Some carbonic anhydrase inhibitors may be given as eyedrops, while others, such as acetazolamide, are given by intravenous or by intramuscular injection or are taken orally.

Carbonic anhydrase inhibitors used in the form of eyedrops may cause stinging, itching, and inflammation of the eye. If you are having injections or taking the drugs orally, you may experience loss of appetite, drowsiness, painful tingling in the hands and feet, and mood changes. Rarely, carbonic anhydrase inhibitors can cause the formation of kidney stones (p.701).

BETA BLOCKER DRUGS In chronic glaucoma, a beta blocker, such as timolol, may be used to decrease the amount of fluid produced inside the eye. The drug works by blocking the transmission of nerve signals that stimulate the production of fluid by certain cells in the eye.

Rarely, beta blockers may slow your heart rate and lower the blood pressure. Beta blocker eyedrops are not usually prescribed for people who have asthma or certain heart conditions.

OTHER DRUGS Various other drugs are used in the treatment of glaucoma. For example, latanoprost increases drainage of fluid from the eye and may be given as eyedrops for chronic glaucoma.

Brimonidine works by both increasing drainage from the eye and by decreasing the production of fluid.

Mannitol encourages excess fluid to be absorbed from the eye into surrounding blood vessels. The drug may be given by intravenous infusion as emergency treatment for acute glaucoma or to relieve pressure within the eye just prior to surgery.

Drugs acting on the ear

Drugs that are used to treat disorders of the outer, middle, or inner ear

COMMON DRUGS

ANTIBIOTICS
- Chloramphenicol • Clioquinol • Clotrimazole
- Gentamicin • Neomycin

ANTI-INFLAMMATORY DRUGS
- Aluminum acetate • Betamethasone
- Dexamethasone • Hydrocortisone
- Prednisolone • Triamcinolone

ANTIEMETIC DRUGS
- Hyoscine • Prochlorperazine

EARWAX SOFTENERS
- Carbamide peroxide • Docusate • Glycerin
- Mineral oil • Sodium bicarbonate

Drugs can be used to treat conditions affecting the outer, middle, or inner ear. They may also be used to relieve the symptoms that accompany these conditions, such as pain, inflammation, and nausea. The drugs can be applied topically in the form of drops (*see* USING EARDROPS, right) or creams or they can be taken orally.

SELF-ADMINISTRATION

USING EARDROPS

It is usually easier if someone else applies eardrops for you. If the eardrops are being kept in the fridge, you should allow them to warm to room temperature before you apply them.

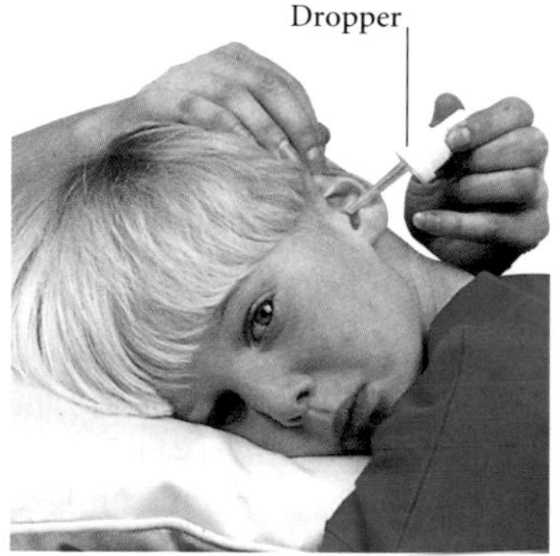
Dropper

Instilling eardrops
Tilt the head and squeeze the eardrops into the ear canal. Keep the head tilted for a minute to let the eardrops settle.

WHAT ARE THE TYPES?

Four groups of drugs are commonly used in the treatment of ear disorders: antibiotics (p.885), anti-inflammatory drugs, antiemetic drugs (p.922), and earwax softeners. Antibiotics are prescribed for bacterial infections and may sometimes be used in combination with anti-inflammatory drugs, such as aluminum acetate, or mild corticosteroids (*see* TOPICAL CORTICOSTEROIDS, p.892). Antiemetic drugs are used to treat the nausea that accompanies disorders of the balance mechanism in the inner ear. Earwax softeners are used to loosen excess earwax in order that it can be removed easily.

ANTIBIOTICS If you have a bacterial infection of your outer ear, such as otitis externa (p.596), your doctor will probably prescribe antibiotic eardrops, which act directly on the infected area of the ear. Middle-ear infections, such as otitis media (p.597), are often treated with oral antibiotics.

ANTI-INFLAMMATORY DRUGS The anti-inflammatory drugs most commonly prescribed are corticosteroid eardrops. Mild corticosteroids usually have no side effects, especially if used for only a few days. However, prolonged use may cause some local irritation of the skin. Aluminum acetate eardrops are sometimes used to treat mild inflammation of the outer ear. You may notice a slight stinging as the drops are applied.

ANTIEMETIC DRUGS Nausea, vomiting, and vertigo are common symptoms of inner ear disorders such as labyrinthitis (p.604) and Ménière's disease (p.604). Mild symptoms may be relieved by treatment with antihistamines (p.906). If these drugs are ineffective, you may be given the antiemetic drugs prochlorperazine or hyoscine. Antiemetics are usually taken orally, but if you are vomiting they may be administered as an injection or by suppository.

EARWAX SOFTENERS If excess wax builds up in your ear canal (*see* WAX BLOCKAGE, p.597), your doctor will probably suggest that you use an over-the-counter product or mineral oil to soften the wax. This will allow the wax to be washed out of the ear canal. However, some commercially prepared earwax softeners and removers can cause some mild irritation of the skin in the ear.

severe. Less common side effects include abdominal pain, flatulence, and nausea. It can also cause fetal abnormalities.

Sucralfate coats the ulcer, providing a barrier against stomach acid. This drug can cause constipation and indigestion. Less common side effects include diarrhea, nausea, dizziness, and insomnia.

Bismuth seems to combat bacteria and protect ulcers from stomach acids. Side effects include a darkened tongue, black feces, nausea, and vomiting.

5-aminosalicylate drugs

A group of drugs used to reduce chronic inflammation of the intestines

COMMON DRUGS

• Mesalamine • Olsalazine • Sulfasalazine

5-aminosalicylates are a group of anti-inflammatory drugs, chemically related to aspirin, that are used to treat chronic inflammatory diseases of the digestive tract. They work by suppressing the body's production of prostaglandins, naturally occurring chemicals that cause tissue inflammation. 5-aminosalicylates are often used to treat Crohn's disease (p.658), in which there is inflammation of parts of the digestive tract. They are also given to treat ulcerative colitis (p.659), in which only the large intestine is inflamed. The drugs can be used to help prevent attacks of these conditions.

5-aminosalicylates are usually taken orally but may be given as enemas or suppositories if inflammation mainly affects the lower part of the large intestine. Treatment by these drugs is started with a high dose. The dosage is then reduced to a lower level if the drugs are required for long-term use.

WHAT ARE THE SIDE EFFECTS?

5-aminosalicylates can cause side effects such as nausea, vomiting, abdominal pain, headache, rashes, and diarrhea.

CAUTION

It is recommended that you have some routine tests for kidney function prior to starting a course of treatment with 5-aminosalicylate drugs.

Antidiarrheal drugs

Drugs that stop diarrhea by slowing the passage of the intestinal contents or regulating the action of the intestine

COMMON DRUGS

OPIOIDS
• Codeine • Diphenoxylate with atropine
• Loperamide

BULK-FORMING AGENTS
• Bran • Methylcellulose • Psyllium

ADSORBENTS
• Kaolin

Antidiarrheal drugs are used to relieve diarrhea (p.627), which is the frequent passing of loose and watery feces. They may be used as a short-term measure to control acute diarrhea or long term for chronic diarrhea, which may be due to a condition such as diverticulosis (p.663) or irritable bowel syndrome (p.656). Some drugs also relieve abdominal pain associated with diarrhea.

In most cases, an acute attack of diarrhea clears up in about 48 hours and does not require any drug treatment. Drinking plenty of fluids to compensate for the water that the body loses in diarrhea is usually all that is needed. However, infants and young children are more at risk of dehydration and may need to be given oral rehydration solutions (p.926). If diarrhea lasts for more than 48 hours, you should consult your doctor. Do not give antidiarrheal drugs to children.

WHAT ARE THE TYPES?

The main types of antidiarrheal drugs are opioids, bulk-forming agents, and adsorbents. All types of antidiarrheal drugs should be taken with plenty of water to prevent constipation.

OPIOIDS These drugs reduce the muscle contractions of the intestine. As a result, the intestine moves feces more slowly and therefore has more time to absorb water from food residue. Opioid drugs may also help relieve pain in the lower abdomen associated with frequent contractions of the intestinal muscle.

Most opioid drugs can be obtained only by prescription. However, some opioids, such as loperamide, can be purchased over the counter for short-term relief of acute diarrhea.

BULK-FORMING AGENTS These preparations absorb water, resulting in larger and firmer stools produced at less frequent intervals. Bulk-forming agents are often given to regulate intestinal action over a long period if you have had an operation on your intestine, such as a colectomy (p.665) or if you have chronic diarrhea due to a disorder such as diverticulosis. Since they help regulate intestinal action, bulk-forming agents are sometimes also used as laxatives (p.924). Some are available over the counter, others only by prescription. All types are usually supplied as granules, powder, or capsules. Do not take a bulk-forming agent when taking opioids; the combination of the two could cause feces to obstruct the intestine. Drink plenty of water when taking a bulk-forming agent.

ADSORBENTS These substances attract and bind to irritants in the intestine, such as harmful microorganisms. As the adsorbents are moved through the intestine and excreted, the irritants are carried with them. Like bulk-forming agents, adsorbents are used to control the consistency of feces and to regulate intestinal action. They are usually used to treat mild diarrhea. The adsorbent kaolin is available over the counter.

Laxatives

Drugs used to relieve constipation or clear the intestine before a medical procedure

COMMON DRUGS

BULK-FORMING AGENTS
• Bran • Methylcellulose • Psyllium

OSMOTIC LAXATIVES
• Glycerin • Lactulose • Polyethylene glycol

FECAL SOFTENERS/LUBRICANTS
• Docusate • Mineral oil

SALINE LAXATIVES
• Magnesium salts • Sodium phosphates

STIMULANT LAXATIVES
• Bisacodyl • Cascara • Senna

Laxatives make feces pass more easily through the intestines. They are most commonly used to treat constipation (p.628), the difficult, infrequent passing of stools that are hard and dry. However, laxatives may be prescribed for other reasons. For example, they may be given to clear the intestine before a colonoscopy (p.661), in which an instrument for viewing the colon is passed through the anus. Laxatives may also be prescribed to counteract the constipating effect of opioid drugs such as morphine or codeine.

Laxatives can be purchased over the counter. If you are taking laxatives for constipation, use them only until your bowel movements have returned to normal. If the constipation continues for more than a few days, you should see your doctor. Do not take more than the recommended dose because laxatives can cause diarrhea. You should never give laxatives to children without first consulting your doctor.

What are the types?

Laxatives can be classified into different types, depending on how they work. Bulk-forming agents, osmotic laxatives, fecal softeners, and saline laxatives all make stools softer and easier to pass. Stimulant laxatives make the intestinal muscles move feces more rapidly. Most laxatives are taken orally, but some osmotic and stimulant laxatives may be administered as enemas or suppositories under certain circumstances.

BULK-FORMING AGENTS These preparations cause the feces to retain water in order to keep them soft and also add bulk to the feces, which stimulates intestinal muscle action. Bulk-forming agents are mainly available as either granules or powders that are taken orally. It may take several days for these agents to have their full effect.

Bulk-forming agents are most often used to treat chronic constipation. For example, they may be prescribed in the treatment of irritable bowel syndrome (p.656) or diverticulosis (p.663). You may also be given these laxatives to make passing stools easier after childbirth or following abdominal surgery.

Bulk-forming laxatives are the safest type for long-term use because their action is similar to the natural action of fiber in food (*see* DIET AND HEALTH, pp.48–54). You should be sure to drink plenty of water when taking these laxatives because the bulky stools may otherwise eventually block the intestine. Side effects of bulk-forming laxatives may include excess intestinal gas and abdominal pain and bloating.

DRUG ACTION

How bulk-forming laxatives work

Bulk-forming agents are often used as laxatives and are used mainly to treat constipation, when feces are hard and painful to pass. Bulk-forming agents act on the large intestine, causing fecal matter to retain water as it moves through the intestine. This makes feces softer and easier to pass.

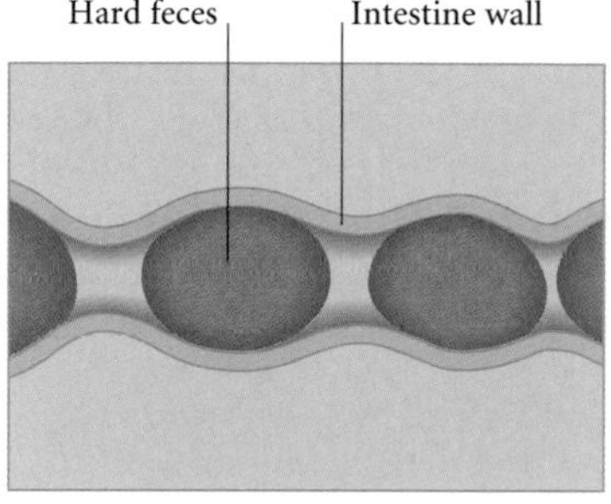
Hard feces
Intestine wall

Before drug
Fecal matter does not retain much water as it passes slowly through the intestine, resulting in dry, hard feces that are difficult to pass.

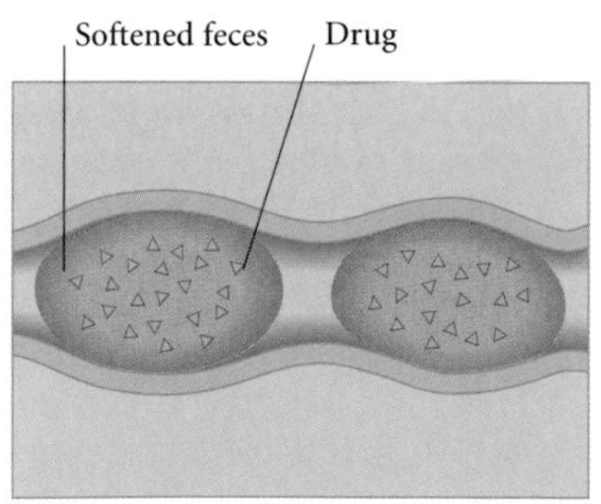
Softened feces
Drug

After drug
The bulk-forming agent mixes with fecal matter, causing it to retain water as it passes through the intestine. This produces feces that are soft and bulky.

OSMOTIC LAXATIVES These drugs work by preventing the body from removing water from feces. As a result, the feces stay soft, but they do not increase in bulk as happens with bulk-forming laxatives. Osmotic laxatives are available only by prescription. The most commonly prescribed osmotic laxative is lactulose, which is a synthetic form of sugar that the body does not absorb. Lactulose can cause side effects such as intestinal gas and abdominal cramps. These side effects may gradually lessen with continued use. In elderly people, long-term use of lactulose can eventually cause dehydration and lead to a chemical imbalance in the blood.

FECAL SOFTENERS These laxatives act by softening feces. They also lubricate the fecal matter, enabling it to pass more easily through the intestine. Docusate can be taken orally as liquid or capsules, or it can be used as an enema. Mineral oil is a fecal softener that is taken orally. It is available over the counter. However, you should not use this laxative on a regular basis because it can cause anal irritation. In addition, mineral oil can prevent your body from absorbing certain essential vitamins from food, which may lead to nutritional deficiencies (p.630) in the long term.

SALINE LAXATIVES These drugs, which include magnesium citrate, other types of magnesium salts, and phosphates, may be used for rapid bowel evacuation. Saline laxatives may be given as a liquid in single doses to clear the intestines before procedures such as colonoscopy, radiological investigation, or surgery on the lower digestive tract. They work by drawing water into the gut from the body and for this reason may cause dehydration. You should ensure that you drink plenty of water when taking these laxatives. Side effects of these laxatives may include intestinal gas and abdominal bloating.

STIMULANT LAXATIVES These laxatives stimulate the intestinal muscles to contract more strongly, thereby resulting in more frequent bowel movements. Stimulant laxatives are sometimes used to clear the intestines quickly if other drugs have failed to work. You should not take them regularly because your body may come to depend on them to stimulate bowel movements. The side effects of these laxatives include abdominal cramps and diarrhea.

CAUTION

When taking a bulk-forming laxative such as bran, be sure to drink plenty of water; otherwise, the bulky feces that are produced may cause an intestinal blockage.

Antispasmodic drugs and motility stimulants

Drugs used to relieve muscle spasms in the intestine or to stimulate the passage of food through the digestive tract

Common drugs

Direct smooth-muscle relaxants
• Peppermint oil • Pinaverium

Antimuscarinic drugs
• Clidinium bromide • Dicyclomine
• Hyoscine butylbromide • Propantheline

Motility stimulant drugs
• Domperidone • Metoclopramide

Other drugs
• Tegaserod • Trimebutine

Antispasmodic drugs and motility stimulants regulate the waves of muscular contraction that propel food through the digestive tract. Both types of drugs are used to treat conditions that are caused by abnormal muscle action in the digestive tract, such as diverticulosis (p.663), as well as to relieve functional dyspepsia (p.626). In addition, motility stimulants may be used in the treatment of gastroesophageal reflux disease (p.636).

Dietary changes, such as altering the fiber content, may help regulate intestinal contractions in conditions such as irritable bowel syndrome. Other changes, such as decreasing your alcohol intake and reducing stress, may also help. Your doctor may initially suggest such changes to see whether they bring about an improvement in your condition. However, if diet and lifestyle changes do not help, you may be put on medication.

What are the types?

Antispasmodic drugs are of two types: direct smooth-muscle relaxants and antimuscarinic drugs. Both types may be used to relieve the abdominal pain in gastrointestinal conditions such as diverticulosis. Motility stimulants are usually given to relieve some of the symptoms caused by functional dyspepsia and gastroesophageal reflux disease.

DIRECT SMOOTH-MUSCLE RELAXANTS These oral drugs have a direct action on the intestinal wall, which contains smooth muscle. They cause the muscle to relax, thereby relieving painful intestinal cramps. Some preparations containing low doses of the drug are available over the counter.

Drink plenty of water if you are taking direct smooth-muscle relaxants because they may otherwise cause intestinal blockage. The drugs may cause headache or nausea. Peppermint oil capsules can irritate the mouth or esophagus; for this reason, they should always be swallowed whole with plenty of water.

ANTIMUSCARINIC DRUGS These drugs, usually taken orally, help reduce muscle spasm by lessening the transmission of nerve signals to the wall of the intestine. They are available by prescription only.

Their side effects may include headache, constipation, a dry mouth, flushed skin, and blurry vision. These drugs may sometimes also cause difficulty urinating. Children and elderly people are more at risk of developing side effects.

MOTILITY STIMULANT DRUGS Motility stimulants cause the contents of the stomach to empty into the small intestine more rapidly than would otherwise happen. In this way, they help prevent the occurrence of gastroesophageal reflux disease and relieve attacks of functional dyspepsia. These drugs also cause the muscular valve between the stomach and the esophagus to close with more force. This action also helps to prevent gastroesophageal reflux disease from occurring.

Motility stimulant drugs are usually taken orally and are available by prescription only. They may cause various side effects, including abdominal cramps and diarrhea, headaches, and dizziness. Metoclopramide occasionally causes uncontrollable muscle spasms, particularly of the face, tongue, and mouth. These spasms are more likely to occur in children and young adults.

OTHER DRUGS Tegaserod is a serotonin 5-HT4 agonist which is used in patients with irritable bowel syndrome and who also have constipation. It enhances the contractility of the gastrointestinal tract and decreases the perception of painful stimuli coming from the gut. Its major side effect is diarrhea; you should discontinue tegaserod if you have experienced on-going diarrhea for more than 4 to 5 days while on the medication.

Trimebutin is a serotonin 5-HT3 antagonist used for irritable bowel syndrome. It acts as an antispasmodic and can also reduce the perception of pain originating from the bowel.

> **CAUTION**
>
> When taking a direct smooth-muscle relaxant such as alverine, drink plenty of water to prevent intestinal blockage. Do not take these drugs before going to bed.

Oral rehydration solutions

Preparations used to treat dehydration resulting from diarrhea and vomiting

Oral rehydration solutions are used to replace water and other essential substances, such as sodium, that are lost as a result of prolonged diarrhea (p.627) or vomiting. Usually, drinking plenty of fluids to replace the water that the body loses in diarrhea or vomiting is the only treatment needed for adults. However, it may be necessary to give oral rehydration solutions to treat fluid loss that occurs in infants and young children. These groups are at a higher risk of dehydration because any water lost accounts for a higher proportion of the total water content in their bodies.

Rehydration solutions contain the minerals sodium, which is necessary for the body to retain water, and potassium, which is vital for the functioning of nerves and muscle. Both these minerals may be lost very quickly and in large amounts as a result of diarrhea and vomiting. Oral rehydration solutions also contain glucose, a sugar that improves the absorption of sodium and water through the wall of the intestine and into the bloodstream.

Rehydration solutions can be purchased over the counter as premixed liquid preparations that are ready to drink. They are often flavored to make them more palatable.

You should make sure that you discard any unused solution or store it in a refrigerator. However, you should not keep unused rehydration solution for more than 24 hours. When used according to instructions, oral rehydration solutions do not cause side effects.

VITAMIN AND MINERAL SUPPLEMENTS

A well-balanced diet should contain adequate amounts of all vitamins and minerals required for health. For most people, supplements are unnecessary, and high doses may even be harmful. However, certain groups of people are vulnerable to vitamin or mineral deficiencies. Doctors may prescribe vitamin or mineral supplements for people in these groups to prevent a deficiency or to treat a deficiency that has already developed.

Groups who are particularly prone to developing vitamin and mineral deficiencies include young children, pregnant women, and elderly people, especially those who live alone. Those who are seriously ill due to injury or chronic illness, or those who have disorders that impair their ability to absorb nutrients from the digestive tract (*see* MALABSORPTION, p.655), are also at increased risk of deficiencies, not only of vitamins and minerals but also of other nutrients (*see* NUTRITIONAL DEFICIENCIES, p.630). These people may require dietary supplementation with extra proteins, carbohydrates, and fats as well as vitamins and minerals. In the case of individuals who are unable to eat and drink normally by mouth or who have very severe intestinal disorders, nutrients may sometimes need to be administered in a liquid form directly into the bloodstream through a vein.

The body needs some nutrients, such as carbohydrates, proteins, and fats, in relatively large quantities but requires vitamins and minerals in only small amounts. The articles in this section describe the vitamins and minerals that doctors most commonly prescribe as dietary supplements. The first article deals with vitamins, and the second with minerals. Particular vitamins and minerals are used to treat conditions that are not directly related to dietary deficiency. For example, drugs that are derived from vitamin A may be used in the treatment of acne (*see* RETINOID DRUGS, p.890).

Vitamins

Chemical compounds that enable the body to carry out essential functions

Vitamins are complex chemicals that are essential for the normal growth, development, and functioning of the body. The main source of most vitamins, except vitamin D and vitamin K, is a balanced diet (*see* GOOD SOURCES OF VITAMINS AND MINERALS, p.52).

Most people do not need vitamin supplements if they eat a well-balanced diet. However, supplements may be prescribed for people with conditions such as chronic alcohol dependence (p.564) that deplete the body's supply of certain vitamins. Supplements may also be prescribed for people recovering from serious injuries whose bodies may need larger quantities of certain vitamins or for people taking medications that interfere with the action or absorption of certain vitamins.

WHAT ARE THE TYPES?

Many types of vitamins are necessary for good health. The vitamins that are most often prescribed in supplements by doctors to treat conditions involving vitamin deficiency are vitamin A, certain B vitamins, folic acid, and the vitamins C, D, E, and K.

VITAMIN A This vitamin is required for growth, healthy skin and surface tissues, and good eyesight and night vision. Vitamin A is also necessary for fertility in both sexes. Supplements may be prescribed for people with conditions that can cause deficiency of this vitamin, such as certain intestinal disorders. Diets that are too low in fat may also lead to vitamin A deficiency.

Taking excessive doses of vitamin A can cause dry skin, nosebleeds, and hair loss. You should not take vitamin A supplements if you are pregnant or planning to become pregnant because taking too much of this vitamin may cause fetal abnormalities.

Drugs chemically related to vitamin A (*see* RETINOID DRUGS, p.890) are used in the treatment of severe acne (p.340). They may also be used to treat psoriasis (p.332). All retinoids can cause serious birth defects. Women should therefore delay pregnancy and use contraception while they are taking retinoids and for a period of time afterward.

> **WARNING**
>
> Vitamin A may harm a developing fetus. Do not take supplements if you are pregnant or planning to conceive, except on medical advice.

VITAMIN B_1 (THIAMINE) This vitamin is needed for nervous system function, heart function, and muscle action. It is present in unprocessed and enriched food and most people get enough by eating a balanced diet. A severe lack of thiamine can cause certain deficiency diseases such as beriberi, which affects the nervous system. Supplements may be prescribed for conditions in which severe thiamine deficiency can occur, such as alcohol dependence or alcohol-related liver disease (p.646). The risk of side effects from thiamine supplements is very low. In some cases it may cause a serious allergic reaction.

VITAMIN B_3 (NIACIN) This vitamin, also known as nicotinic acid, plays a vital role in the activities of many enzymes involved in digestion. Niacin is also essential for the production of the sex hormones estrogen, progesterone, and testosterone. Severe niacin deficiency can result in the skin disorder pellagra. You may be prescribed niacin supplements if you have alcohol-related liver disease or a bowel disorder that results in poor absorption of food, a condition known as malabsorption (p.655). Large doses of niacin inhibit the body's synthesis of some fats and are used to treat high cholesterol and triglyceride levels (*see* LIPID-LOWERING DRUGS, p.935). Side effects of niacin include itching, flushing, and headaches. If excessive amounts of niacin are taken, liver damage and gout (p.380) can result.

VITAMIN B_6 (PYRIDOXINE) Vitamin B_6 helps the body process proteins, fats, and carbohydrates in food and is needed to help the central nervous system function correctly. Supplements may be given to relieve the symptoms of premenstrual syndrome (p.736), but there is little evidence that this treatment is effective. Supplements may also be given to relieve morning sickness during pregnancy (*see* COMMON COMPLAINTS OF NORMAL PREGNANCY, p.784). Excessive doses may lead to nerve damage, which can result in numbness and impaired physical coordination.

VITAMIN B_{12} (COBALAMIN) This vitamin is essential for the formation of red blood cells. The most common cause of vitamin B_{12} deficiency is pernicious anemia (*see* MEGALOBLASTIC ANEMIA, p.448), in which a substance necessary for absorption of vitamin B_{12} is missing from the body. Vegan diets may also result in deficiency because the best dietary sources of vitamin B_{12} are animal products such as eggs and milk.

Treatment for pernicious anemia involves regular injections of hydroxycobalamin (a synthesized form of the vitamin). Side effects are very uncommon but can include itching, flushing, and nausea. If deficiency results from a vegan diet, oral supplements of cobalamin may be required.

FOLIC ACID This vitamin is required for nervous system function and for the formation of healthy red blood cells. Supplements may be prescribed if you are taking certain drugs, including some antimalarial drugs (p.888) or anticonvulsant drugs (p.914), which deplete folic acid. Folic acid also lowers levels of an amino acid called homocysteine, high levels of which may be a risk factor for coronary artery disease.

Women are advised to take folic acid if they are planning to become pregnant and for at least the first 12 weeks of pregnancy to reduce the risk of neural tube defects (p.844), such as spina bifida, in the fetus. The vitamin has no harmful side effects.

WARNING

Do not exceed the prescribed dose of vitamin D. Excessive intake can cause a dangerous rise in the level of calcium in the blood.

VITAMIN C This vitamin is needed for the formation of bones, teeth, ligaments, and blood vessels. It is found in most fresh fruit and vegetables, and therefore severe deficiency is uncommon. If it does occur, severe vitamin C deficiency results in a disorder called scurvy, which is now rare in developed countries. However, mild vitamin C deficiency is common among people who eat a poor diet, and particularly among elderly people living alone.

Supplements of vitamin C may be prescribed after serious injury or burns because the vitamin is used up more quickly during the healing process. In some cases, iron supplements are combined with vitamin C because the vitamin improves the efficiency of iron absorption by the body.

VITAMIN D This vitamin helps regulate the amount of calcium in the body. The body's requirements for the vitamin are usually met by dietary sources and exposure to sunlight, which the body needs to make vitamin D. A vitamin D deficiency can cause a bone disorder in which bones become weak and soft (*see* OSTEOMALACIA AND RICKETS, p.370).

Vitamin D supplements may be prescribed to increase levels of calcium in the blood in people with hypoparathyroidism (p.683), the underproduction of parathyroid hormone, which controls levels of calcium in the blood. Supplements are sometimes given to elderly people and premature infants, who may not get enough dietary vitamin D. Supplements of vitamin D may also be prescribed in combination with calcium to prevent or treat osteoporosis (p.368). Drugs that are derived from vitamin D, such as calcipotriene, may sometimes be prescribed for the treatment of the skin disorder psoriasis.

Taking high doses of vitamin D may increase levels of calcium in the body, which may lead to calcium deposits in soft tissues, impaired kidney function, or impaired growth in children.

VITAMIN E This vitamin is an important antioxidant, meaning that it protects cell membranes from the damaging effects of particles known as free radicals, which are thought to cause tissue damage. Premature babies are deficient in vitamin E and may develop a form of anemia if they do not receive supplements. Deficiency also occurs in people who cannot absorb fat, especially those with cystic fibrosis (p.824). Supplements may be prescribed to treat malabsorption in children, heart disease, and women who have fibrocystic breast disease (*see* BREAST LUMPS, p.754), although its effectiveness has not been proved. Vitamin E is also used in skin creams. High doses of vitamin E can cause diarrhea and abdominal pain.

VITAMIN K This vitamin is essential for the formation of blood clotting factors, substances that are necessary for blood to clot and seal off damaged blood vessels. Most of the required amount is produced by bacteria in the intestines, but some vitamin K is provided by dietary sources, such as green leafy vegetables, eggs, and liver.

Newborn babies lack the intestinal bacteria that produce vitamin K and are at risk of developing a condition called hemorrhagic disease of the newborn, which results in easy bruising and internal bleeding. For this reason, newborn babies are given vitamin K injections routinely. Supplements may be given to older children and adults taking antibiotics for long periods because these drugs destroy the intestinal bacteria that produce vitamin K. In addition, people who are unable to absorb nutrients or experience abnormal bleeding as a side effect of oral anticoagulant drugs (*see* DRUGS THAT PREVENT BLOOD CLOTTING, p.904) may be given supplements of this vitamin.

MULTIVITAMINS Preparations containing a combination of vitamins are used to treat people with nutritional deficiencies, chronic alcoholism, and other conditions in which dietary vitamin intake is insufficient. Some multivitamin preparations may contain iron and other minerals. Multivitamins can be purchased over the counter, usually in the form of oral liquid, tablets, or capsules to be taken once daily.

Minerals

Chemical elements that enable the body to perform essential functions

Minerals are chemical elements that are needed to maintain health. The body does not manufacture minerals and therefore they must be obtained from dietary sources (*see* GOOD SOURCES OF VITAMINS AND MINERALS, p.52).

Your doctor may prescribe mineral supplements if you have a medical condition that interferes with the ability of your body to absorb minerals (*see* MALABSORPTION, p.655) or if you need extra amounts of certain minerals, as may happen in pregnancy. Most people should not need mineral supplements because a balanced diet usually provides sufficient amounts. You should not take mineral supplements unless necessary because excessive doses of some minerals can be toxic.

WHAT ARE THE TYPES?

Many minerals are necessary to maintain good health. The most important minerals prescribed to treat deficiencies include iron, calcium, magnesium, zinc, fluoride, iodine, and phosphorus.

IRON This mineral is a vital component of hemoglobin, the oxygen-carrying pigment of blood. A correctly balanced diet usually provides a person with enough iron but deficiency sometimes occurs in women who have heavy menstrual periods (*see* MENORRHAGIA, p.735), pregnant women, and women who have recently given birth. Vegans and people with chronic blood loss due to conditions such as a peptic ulcer (p.640) may also be deficient in iron.

Iron is usually taken orally as a liquid or pills and can be purchased over the counter. Side effects of taking iron supplements may include darker stools, constipation or diarrhea, nausea, and abdominal pain. You should be careful not to exceed the recommended dosage of an iron supplement because taking too much iron can cause serious side effects, such as vomiting blood, rectal bleeding, fever, and very low blood pressure. If you experience any of these effects, seek medical help immediately.

> **WARNING**
>
> An excess of iron supplements may cause vomiting of blood, bleeding from the rectum, and dizziness due to very low blood pressure. If you have these symptoms, you should seek medical help immediately.

CALCIUM This mineral is essential for both the formation and maintenance of bones and teeth, as well as for muscle contraction and the transmission of nerve impulses. Dairy products in the diet usually provide sufficient calcium.

Oral supplements are sometimes prescribed for women who are pregnant or breast-feeding because fetal bone formation and maternal milk production require large amounts of calcium. Elderly people may also need to take supplements because the body absorbs calcium less efficiently with age. Calcium supplements may also be prescribed to treat bone disorders such as osteoporosis (p.368) and to raise levels of blood calcium in people who have hypoparathyroidism (p.683) or kidney failure (p.705). Calcium may be given by intravenous injection to treat cardiac arrest (p.419). Severe calcium deficiency leads to cramps and muscle spasms and may be treated with calcium injections. Side effects of calcium include constipation and nausea.

MAGNESIUM This mineral is needed for healthy teeth and bones, muscle action, and transmission of nerve impulses. Magnesium supplements may be prescribed for certain conditions that can affect the absorption of magnesium from food, including alcohol dependence (p.564), repeated vomiting, or long-term diarrhea. Excessive amounts of magnesium may cause nausea, vomiting, diarrhea, and dizziness.

ZINC This mineral is necessary for growth and to help wounds heal efficiently. Zinc deficiency is rarely seen in developed countries and usually occurs only in malnourished elderly people or in people with severe burns or other traumatic injury because zinc is used up rapidly in the healing process. In these cases, zinc supplements are sometimes prescribed. Zinc supplements are usually taken orally but they may also be given as a topical treatment for skin disorders, such as diaper rash. Taking large doses of oral zinc may cause side effects such as fever, nausea, vomiting, headaches, and abdominal pain.

FLUORIDE The mineral fluoride helps prevent tooth decay and makes bones stronger. Water is very often the main dietary source because fluoride occurs naturally in some water supplies or is added to the drinking water in many areas. Fluoride is also an ingredient in most toothpastes. Your dentist may recommend fluoride supplements in the form of drops or tablets if the water in your area is not fluoridated or if you are susceptible to dental caries (p.609). If you take excessive amounts of fluoride, you may develop a condition known as fluorosis, in which tooth enamel becomes brown or mottled.

IODINE This mineral is essential for the formation of thyroid hormones, which control the rate at which the body uses energy and which are vital for normal growth in childhood. Supplements are rarely needed because sufficient iodine is usually present in the diet. Important sources of iodine include seafood, bread, dairy products, and iodized table salt. Radioactive iodine may be given to people who have a goiter (p.680) or hyperthyroidism (p.679) to shrink the thyroid gland. Excessive amounts of iodine can suppress the activity of the thyroid gland, leading to hypothyroidism (p.680).

PHOSPHORUS The mineral phosphorus is an essential part of the diet. It is present in many foods, including cereals, dairy products, eggs, and meat. Much of the phosphorus contained in the body is combined with calcium to form the structure of the bones and teeth. Hypophosphatemia, in which the body contains an abnormally low level of phosphorus, may occur in some forms of kidney disease, hyperparathyroidism (p.682), and malabsorption.

Deficiencies of this mineral can be treated with phosphate preparations. In addition, hypercalcemia, in which blood levels of calcium are abnormally high, may be treated using phosphates. Diarrhea is a potential side effect of taking phosphate preparations.

DRUGS ACTING ON THE ENDOCRINE SYSTEM AND METABOLISM

Disorders of the endocrine system and metabolism, such as diabetes mellitus and hypothyroidism, may have wide-ranging, serious effects, and in some cases may be fatal if left untreated. Drug treatments can control the symptoms of these disorders and in many cases restore normal health to affected people.

The first article in this section covers corticosteroids, which are synthetic hormones that are chiefly used to treat inflammation in a variety of disorders and may also be used as hormone replacement therapy. The next four articles discuss drugs that control levels of insulin, thyroid hormones, and sex hormones in the body. Drugs that replace, inhibit, or stimulate some of the many hormones produced by the pituitary gland, which is the major hormone-secreting gland in the body, are covered next. The final article looks at lipid-lowering drugs, which control disorders in which the blood contains excessive levels of lipids (fats and related substances).

Topical corticosteroids (p.892), which are used to treat certain skin disorders, are covered elsewhere, as are locally acting corticosteroids (p.895), which are used in the treatment of inflamed joints or muscles.

KEY ANATOMY

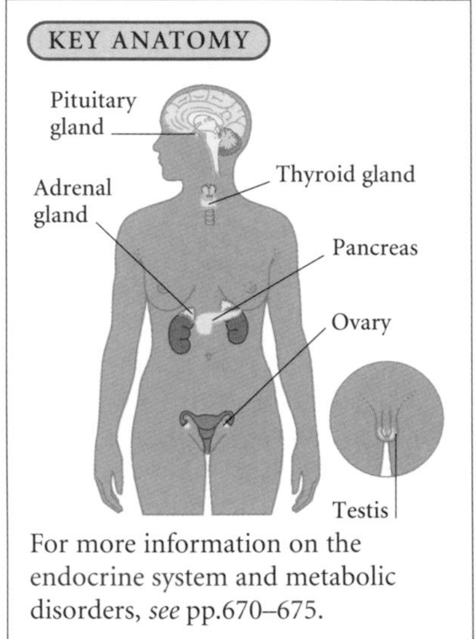
Pituitary gland
Adrenal gland
Thyroid gland
Pancreas
Ovary
Testis

For more information on the endocrine system and metabolic disorders, *see* pp.670–675.

Corticosteroids

Drugs similar to the natural corticosteroid hormones produced by the adrenal gland

COMMON DRUGS

- Beclomethasone • Betamethasone • Cortisone
- Dexamethasone • Fludrocortisone
- Fluocinolone • Fluticasone • Hydrocortisone
- Methylprednisolone • Mometasone
- Prednisolone • Prednisone • Triamcinolone

Corticosteroids are related to corticosteroid hormones produced by the body. The production of corticosteroid hormones in the adrenal glands is regulated by corticotropin, a pituitary hormone.

The main use for corticosteroids is in the treatment of inflammatory conditions that may affect the joints, skin, digestive tract, respiratory system, eyes, and ears. These drugs are also prescribed as replacement therapy if the body is unable to produce sufficient natural corticosteroid hormones on its own (*see* ADDISON'S DISEASE, p.686).

Corticosteroids may also be given as long-term treatment following transplant surgery because their action suppresses the body's immune system. This immune system suppression helps prevent the body from rejecting transplanted organs or tissue.

HOW DO THEY WORK?

Corticosteroids relieve inflammation by blocking the production of natural substances that trigger inflammation, such as prostaglandins. The drugs suppress the immune system by reducing the production and effectiveness of certain white blood cells that are an important part of the body's immune response.

HOW ARE THEY USED?

Corticosteroids can be given in a variety of ways. The drugs may be injected into a joint or into a tendon in order to relieve inflammation (*see* LOCALLY ACTING CORTICOSTEROIDS, p.895). Used in this way, they may improve the mobility of joints affected by disorders such as tennis elbow and golfer's elbow (p.389). Frequent injections must be avoided because of side effects. The drugs may also be injected to treat severe Addison's disease or the severe allergic reaction, anaphylaxis (p.469).

Topical corticosteroids (p.892) in the form of creams or ointments are used to reduce inflammation and itching in some skin conditions. Oral corticosteroids are used for severe rheumatoid arthritis (p.377) and respiratory disorders such as asthma (p.483), sarcoidosis (p.498), and interstitial fibrosis (p.497). Oral corticosteroids are also used after transplant surgery (*see* IMMUNOSUPPRESSANTS, p.906) and in the treatment of Addison's disease. Corticosteroids are given by inhaler to prevent asthma attacks (*see* CORTICOSTEROIDS FOR RESPIRATORY DISEASE, p.911).

WHAT ARE THE SIDE EFFECTS?

Short-term use of corticosteroids rarely produces side effects. Side effects are also rare in long-term corticosteroid replacement therapy for Addison's disease, provided the correct dose is given, because the drugs replace the natural hormones that the body lacks. Doctors avoid prescribing long-term corticosteroids for other conditions because of adverse side effects.

You are unlikely to experience side effects from corticosteroid injections because injections are not usually given more than twice a year. Prolonged use of strong topical corticosteroid drugs can damage the skin in the affected areas, causing thinning, wrinkling, and loss of skin pigmentation. Various side effects may occur as a result of the long-term use of oral corticosteroids, including easy bruising, acne, a moon-shaped face, and fat deposits on the trunk (*see* CUSHING SYNDROME, p.684).

Blood pressure may rise, your ankles may become swollen, and you may experience mood changes. The drugs can slow growth in children and may also cause osteoporosis (p.368). There is also an increased risk of infection because the drugs reduce immunity.

If you take high doses of corticosteroids using an inhaler for a prolonged period, you may develop the same side effects normally associated with long-term use of oral corticosteroid drugs but to a lesser degree.

Corticosteroids suppress the body's production of natural corticosteroid hormones. As a result, the body may not initially be able to produce sufficient corticosteroid hormones on its own if treatment is stopped suddenly. Sudden withdrawal from long-term, high-dose corticosteroids can lead to shock (p.414). If your doctor prescribes corticosteroid drugs for you for more than a 3-week period, you will be given a medical alert card, bracelet, or pendant that gives details of your medication to inform any health professional who treats you.

Drugs for diabetes mellitus

Drugs used to treat diabetes mellitus that control blood glucose (sugar) levels

COMMON DRUGS

INSULIN

SULFONYLUREA DRUGS
- Gliclazide • Glimepiride
- Glyburide

OTHER ANTIDIABETIC DRUGS
- Acarbose • Metformin • Pioglitazone
- Repaglinide • Rosiglitazone

In diabetes mellitus (p.687), levels of blood glucose are too high because the body produces too little or is resistant to the action of the hormone insulin, which is secreted by the pancreas and regulates blood glucose. Drugs for diabetes mellitus keep blood glucose at normal levels.

There are two types of diabetes mellitus. In type 1 diabetes, the body does not produce enough insulin, and synthetic insulin is needed. In type 2 diabetes, tissues have reduced sensitivity to the action of insulin. Mild forms of type 2 diabetes can usually be controlled by changes to the diet.

WHAT ARE THE TYPES?

The main drugs for diabetes mellitus are insulin, which is always given for type 1 diabetes, and antidiabetic drugs, which are used to treat type 2 diabetes. The most common antidiabetic drugs are sulfonylurea drugs and metformin, but the drugs acarbose or repaglinide may also be prescribed by your doctor. If antidiabetic drugs do not prove to be effective, insulin may be used to treat cases of type 2 diabetes.

INSULIN Injections of insulin are given to replace missing natural insulin in type 1 diabetes. This replacement mimics the body's normal patterns of insulin production, maintaining constant low background levels of insulin with peaks at mealtimes when glucose enters the blood. Insulin was once extracted from pigs and modified for human use, but now it is made in the laboratory and is identical to human insulin.

There are several types of insulin preparations whose durations of action differ. Short-acting insulins are taken 15–30 minutes before mealtimes, giving high levels of insulin in the blood to coincide with high levels of glucose. Longer-acting insulins are taken once or twice a day. Many people take a combination of both types. The dose will be tailored to your individual needs.

Your doctor or nurse will teach you how to inject insulin (*see* INJECTING INSULIN, p.688). In addition, you will be shown how to measure your blood glucose levels (*see* MONITORING YOUR BLOOD GLUCOSE, p.689). You should measure your glucose levels at regular intervals during the day as advised by your doctor or nurse. The results will determine whether your dose is at the correct level. For type 1 diabetes that is difficult to control, insulin can be given by a pump that delivers both continuous and timed doses.

Taking insulin to decrease blood glucose levels may cause hypoglycemia (p.691), in which blood glucose levels become abnormally low. If you need to take insulin, your doctor or nurse will teach you how to recognize symptoms of hypoglycemia, which include sweating, faintness, and anxiety. If you have a hypoglycemic attack, you should eat or drink something sweet immediately. An injection of glucagon, a hormone that increases blood glucose levels, may be used to treat severe hypoglycemia.

DRUG ACTION

HOW SULFONYLUREA DRUGS WORK

Sulfonylurea drugs are used to treat type 2 diabetes. In this type of diabetes, body tissues have reduced sensitivity to insulin. Sulfonylurea drugs stimulate cells in the pancreas to secrete more insulin to compensate for the reduced sensitivity.

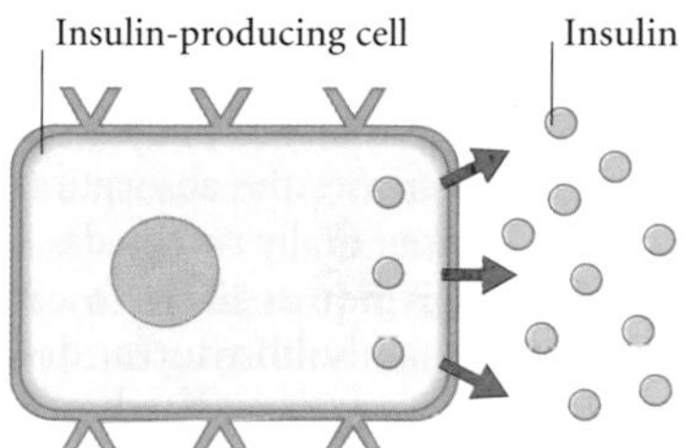
Insulin-producing cell
Insulin

Before drug
The amount of insulin made by the insulin-secreting cells in the pancreas is not sufficient for the body's needs.

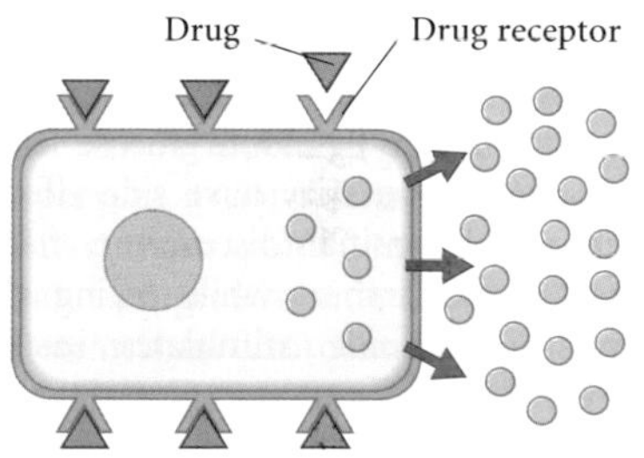
Drug
Drug receptor

After drug
The sulfonylurea drug acts on the insulin-producing cells, stimulating them to increase production of insulin.

Common injection sites for insulin include the upper arms, abdomen, and thighs. You should change sites regularly to prevent fat from building up at one site. Some insulin preparations contain an additive that can cause soreness and inflammation at the injection site when you start using insulin. This reaction is usually temporary.

SULFONYLUREA DRUGS If changes in diet fail to control type 2 diabetes, you may be prescribed sulfonylurea drugs. These drugs stimulate the insulin-producing cells in the pancreas to increase insulin production (*see* HOW SULFONYLUREA DRUGS WORK, above).

MALE SEX HORMONES Synthetic forms of male sex hormones are used to treat certain conditions that are caused by low levels of the sex hormone testosterone, including delayed puberty in boys (*see* ABNORMAL PUBERTY IN MALES, p.728) and decreased libido in men (*see* DECREASED SEX DRIVE, p.769). Given in low doses, synthetic testosterone mimics the action of natural testosterone, and side effects do not usually occur.

ANTIANDROGENS Some antiandrogens, such as finasteride, are used to treat an enlarged prostate gland (p.725); others, such as flutamide, are used in the treatment of prostate cancer (p.726). In addition, virilization (p.740), in which women develop a number of masculine characteristics, may also be treated using these drugs. Antiandrogens act by blocking the action of the natural male sex hormones. A common side effect that occurs in treatment with antiandrogens is fatigue. The drugs also affect liver function and are not normally prescribed for anyone who has a history of liver problems.

GONADORELIN AND GONADORELIN ANALOGS Gonadorelin is a synthetic version of a natural hormone called gonadotropin-releasing hormone. This drug is used to treat infertility and endometriosis (p.742) in women. In infertility treatment, it is given in short courses by injection to stimulate LH and FSH secretion. The drug has few side effects when it is given in this way. However, if given over several weeks, gonadorelin can cause a decrease in libido, rashes, and hot flashes.

Gonadorelin analogs are used to treat certain female reproductive disorders, such as endometriosis; menstrual disorders, including heavy periods; and breast pain (p.756) associated with menstruation. In addition, these drugs may be used to treat prostate cancer and, rarely, the excessive growth of breast tissue in men (*see* GYNECOMASTIA, p.729). Gonadorelin analogs block the release of gonadotropin-releasing hormone, which inhibits the release of LH and FSH from the pituitary gland. If LH and FSH are inhibited, the release of the sex hormones estrogen, progesterone, and testosterone also become inhibited. Gonadorelin analogs are usually given orally. However, in the treatment of prostate cancer, they may be given either as an injection or as a nasal spray. Side effects may include acne, nausea and vomiting, and headache or migraine. Side effects of gonadorelin analogs in premenopausal women may include bleeding between periods and menopause-like symptoms such as hot flashes and increased sweating.

Pituitary drugs

Drugs that replace, stimulate, or inhibit some of the hormones produced by the pituitary gland

COMMON DRUGS

GROWTH HORMONE
- Somatropin

GROWTH HORMONE ANTAGONISTS
- Bromocriptine • Octreotide

PROLACTIN ANTAGONISTS
- Bromocriptine • Cabergoline

DRUGS FOR DIABETES INSIPIDUS
- Desmopressin • Lypressin • Vasopressin (ADH)

The pituitary gland, which is located at the base of the brain, produces a number of hormones. These hormones, many of which control the activities of other glands, include growth hormone; prolactin, which controls the production of breast milk in women; and antidiuretic hormone (ADH), which regulates the function of the kidneys.

Drugs for pituitary disorders work in various ways. Some drugs are synthetic hormones that replace missing natural hormones, and others, known as antagonists, reduce the production or action of pituitary hormones.

Drugs that act on the hormones produced directly by the pituitary gland are discussed below. Other drugs whose action on the pituitary gland affects the production of hormones in other parts of the body are discussed elsewhere. These drugs include sex hormones and related drugs (p.933), drugs for infertility (p.936), corticosteroids (p.930), and drugs for labor (p.938).

WHAT ARE THE TYPES?

A number of drugs are used to treat pituitary disorders. Growth hormones and growth hormone antagonists are given to adjust levels of growth hormone that are either too low or too high. Prolactin antagonists reduce levels of prolactin. The pituitary disorder diabetes insipidus (p.678), a rare condition that is caused by insufficient ADH, is treated with drugs that correct the levels of this hormone.

GROWTH HORMONE If the pituitary gland does not secrete sufficient growth hormone during childhood, a synthetic form of growth hormone can be prescribed to replace the missing hormone. Low levels of growth hormone in childhood can cause impaired growth (*see* GROWTH DISORDERS, p.869). If a child begins the treatment at an early age, normal growth usually takes place. The drug is usually given by injection 3–7 times a week, depending on the body's response. Treatment normally continues for several years until the child reaches adult height.

Children may experience side effects such as aching muscles and joints and headaches. Occasionally, the treatment causes reduced production of thyroid hormone, which then must be replaced using drug therapy (*see* DRUGS FOR HYPOTHYROIDISM, p.932).

GROWTH HORMONE ANTAGONISTS If excess growth hormone is produced by the pituitary gland, adults may be given growth hormone antagonists, such as octreotide. Excess growth hormone can cause abnormal enlargement of parts of the body, particularly of facial features, known as acromegaly (p.677).

In adults, the excess production of growth hormone is usually due to a pituitary tumor (*see* PITUITARY TUMORS, p.676). Growth hormone antagonists are mainly used as a temporary measure until the tumor can be surgically removed. However, if you are not well enough to have surgery, these drugs may be given long-term.

Growth hormone antagonists may be given either orally or as an injection. Side effects are uncommon but include nausea, vomiting, and constipation.

PROLACTIN ANTAGONISTS These drugs are used to treat those disorders in which excessive amounts of prolactin are produced by the pituitary gland. Excess prolactin may cause the production of breast milk in men and in women who are not breast-feeding.

Overproduction of prolactin is often caused by a noncancerous pituitary tumor called a prolactinoma (p.677). Drugs that are given to shrink a prolactinoma and reduce the production of prolactin are often very effective, and therefore surgery to remove the tumor may not be necessary.

Prolactin antagonists are most commonly taken orally. It is not uncommon to experience side effects from prolactin antagonists. For instance, you may suffer from nausea and vomiting when taking bromocriptine.

DRUGS FOR DIABETES INSIPIDUS You may be prescribed ADH or a synthetic form of this hormone (desmopressin or lypressin) if you have central diabetes insipidus (p.678). In this disorder, the pituitary gland produces insufficient amounts of ADH to regulate kidney function, which controls the amount of water that is retained in the body. If the condition is severe, the hormone may be administered daily by injection. It may also be given orally or as a nasal spray. In these forms, the hormone is usually given twice a day.

You may experience certain side effects while using ADH or its synthetic versions. These may include nausea, belching, and abdominal cramps.

Lipid-lowering drugs

Drugs used to reduce the level of lipids (fats and related substances) in the blood

COMMON DRUGS

STATINS
• Atorvastatin • Fluvastatin • Lovastatin • Pravastatin • Rosuvastatin • Simvastatin

ANION-EXCHANGE RESINS
• Cholestyramine • Colestipol

FIBRATES
• Bezafibrate • Fenofibrate • Gemfibrozil

NICOTINIC ACID

OTHER LIPID-LOWERING PRODUCTS
• Ezetimibe • Fish oil • Psyllium

Lipid-lowering drugs reduce excessive levels of lipids, particularly cholesterol and triglycerides, in the bloodstream. Blood contains several types of lipids that are necessary for normal body function. However, if present in excess, lipids can lead to narrowing of the arteries (*see* ATHEROSCLEROSIS, p.402), which can lead to serious disorders such as coronary artery disease (p.405), heart attack (*see* MYOCARDIAL INFARCTION, p.410), and stroke (p.532). In addition, high levels of triglycerides may result in inflammation of the pancreas (*see* ACUTE PANCREATITIS, p.652).

Elevated blood lipid levels can be reduced to some extent by changes to the diet (*see* DIET AND HEALTH, p.48) and exercise. However, for some people, especially those with a family history of high blood lipid levels (*see* INHERITED HYPERLIPOPROTEINEMIAS, p.692), drug treatment is needed to lower the lipid levels. Drugs to reduce lipid levels may also be given to people who have angina (p.407) to reduce the risk of a heart attack, and after a heart attack to minimize the risk of further attacks.

WHAT ARE THE TYPES?

The main types include statins, anion-exchange resins, fibrates, and nicotinic acid and its derivatives. In addition, the natural dietary products psyllium, which is a grain, and fish oil may be recommended. These drugs work in different ways to lower levels of lipids in the blood.

Your doctor's choice of drug will depend on the type of lipid causing your condition. In some instances, your doctor may prescribe a combination of drugs. Lipid-lowering drugs are taken orally on a daily basis, and most need to be taken long-term.

STATINS These drugs reduce the levels of cholesterol and triglycerides in the blood. The side effects that may occur while taking statins include nausea, headaches, abdominal pain, and either diarrhea or constipation. Muscle pain may develop, particularly if a statin is prescribed in combination with a fibrate or with nicotinic acid. You should tell your doctor if you have liver disease or have had liver failure because statins may have an effect on liver function. You should also tell your doctor if you are planning a pregnancy, are pregnant, or are breast-feeding because statins can harm a fetus or baby.

ANION-EXCHANGE RESINS These drugs lower blood cholesterol levels. If blood cholesterol levels are very high, anion-exchange resins may be used together with other lipid-lowering drugs, such as fibrates and statins. If you are taking other lipid-lowering drugs, you should take them at least 1 hour before or 3–4 hours after taking an anion-exchange resin because the resin can interfere with the absorption of other drugs.

Anion-exchange resins have few side effects, but sometimes cause nausea, abdominal discomfort, and constipation. Supplements of vitamins A, D, and K may be necessary in long-term treatment with anion-exchange resins because the drugs reduce the body's absorption of these vitamins.

FIBRATES These drugs are effective in lowering levels of both cholesterol and triglycerides in the blood. Fibrates are unsuitable if you have a disorder of the kidneys, liver, or gallbladder. The drugs occasionally cause side effects, including muscle pain, nausea, headache, and erectile dysfunction. Muscle pain may be more common if you have a disorder of the kidneys or are also receiving a statin. Fibrates can harm a fetus or baby, and it is important to tell your doctor if you are planning a pregnancy, are pregnant, or are breast-feeding.

NICOTINIC ACID Excessively high levels of cholesterol or triglycerides in the blood may be reduced by treatment with nicotinic acid. However, nicotinic acid often causes side effects and is generally used only when other drugs have proved ineffective. Side effects may include facial flushing, unsteadiness, headache, nausea and vomiting, and itching. Muscle pain may develop if this drug is used together with a statin. Women who are planning a pregnancy or who are pregnant or breast-feeding should avoid nicotinic acid because it may harm a fetus or baby.

OTHER LIPID-LOWERING PRODUCTS The drug ezetimibe blocks absorption of cholesterol from the intestines. The natural products psyllium and fish oil can reduce blood lipid levels when incorporated into the diet every day. Psyllium is a grain that helps reduce high blood cholesterol levels, although its effectiveness is small compared with that of other drugs. Fish oil helps reduce blood triglyceride levels. It occurs naturally in oily fish, such as mackerel. In addition, it is available as a dietary supplement.

DRUGS ACTING ON THE REPRODUCTIVE AND URINARY SYSTEMS

Recent advances in our understanding of how the reproductive and urinary systems function, and in particular the role of hormones, have led to improved drug treatments of conditions such as prostate disease and infertility. Drugs are also used to prevent complications of menopause or labor.

KEY ANATOMY

Kidney
Ureter
Bladder
Prostate gland
Urethra
Testes
Kidney
Ureter
Ovary
Uterus
Bladder
Urethra
Vagina

MALE FEMALE

For more information on the urinary and reproductive systems, *see* pp.694–697, pp.716–717, and pp. 730–733.

Drugs are used to increase the likelihood of conception if infertility is due to hormonal imbalances. These drugs are discussed in the first article of this section. The second article covers hormone replacement therapy, which is used to reduce the symptoms of menopause, which occurs when levels of sex hormones decline.

The next article covers drugs for labor, which are most often used to prevent preterm labor or to induce or hasten labor. They may also be used to prevent bleeding after delivery.

Drugs may be used in the treatment of prostate disorders, including prostate cancer. These drugs are discussed in the following article.

The final article deals with drugs that affect bladder control, which are used to treat urinary incontinence and urinary retention.

Further information on drugs for both the male and female reproductive and urinary systems can be found elsewhere. This includes articles on contraception (p.69) and on the use of sex hormones and related drugs (p.933). Antibiotics (p.885) are widely used in the treatment of infections of the reproductive and urinary systems.

Drugs for infertility

Drugs that may be used to treat couples who are unable to conceive

ANTIESTROGENS
• Clomiphene • Tamoxifen

GONADORELIN

GONADOTROPINS
• Human chorionic gonadotropin • Luteotropin
• Menotropins • Recombinant follitropin

GONADORELIN ANALOGS/ANTAGONISTS
• Buserelin • Cetrorelix • Ganirelix • Goserelin
• Leuprorelin

Drugs can be used to help a woman become pregnant when the inability to conceive results from a hormonal imbalance in either the male or the female (*see* PROBLEMS CONCEIVING, p.774).

Fertility is influenced by hormones produced in the brain by the hypothalamus and the pituitary gland. The hypothalamus produces gonadotropin-releasing hormone, which regulates the release of gonadotropin hormones from the pituitary gland. The main gonadotropin hormones are known as follicle-stimulating hormone (FSH) and luteinizing hormone (LH). These are the hormones that control fertility. In females, FSH stimulates the ripening of eggs, and LH triggers ovulation (the release of the egg). In males, FSH and LH regulate sperm production. An imbalance or a deficiency of these hormones may lead to infertility. In such cases, drugs may be used to stimulate a woman's ovaries to produce eggs or, less commonly, to stimulate a man to produce more sperm.

In women, drugs may also be used to stimulate the ovaries to produce more eggs than normal as part of techniques called assisted conception (p.776), such as in-vitro fertilization (IVF) and gamete intrafallopian transfer (GIFT).

Women who are treated with fertility drugs are monitored by blood tests and ultrasound scanning (p.250) because of the small risk that the ovaries may become overstimulated, which can be a life-threatening condition. Symptoms can include nausea, vomiting, and abdominal pain and swelling. Infertility treatment also increases the likelihood of multiple pregnancy.

Treatments for infertility may not be effective immediately and often need to be repeated for several months to increase the likelihood of conception.

WHAT ARE THE TYPES?

In females, low levels of the gonadotropins FSH and LH can be boosted using an antiestrogen (also known as an estrogen antagonist). Alternatively, a synthetic version of gonadotropin-releasing hormone, called gonadorelin, may be prescribed to achieve a similar result. Synthetic gonadotropin hormones may also be given to influence fertility directly in both males and females. A gonadorelin analog or gonadorelin antagonist may sometimes be given in conjunction with gonadotropin drugs in the treatment of female infertility.

ANTIESTROGENS The naturally occurring hormone estrogen suppresses the production of FSH and LH. Treatment with an oral antiestrogen, such as clomiphene, blocks this effect and stimulates the pituitary gland to produce more FSH and LH, encouraging ovulation.

If you are taking clomiphene, you may notice side effects including visual disturbances, headache, nausea, hot flashes, and abdominal pain. If you take the drug for longer than 12 months, there may be an increased risk of later developing cancer of the ovary (p.744).

GONADORELIN This drug is a synthetic version of the gonadotropin-releasing hormone that is produced by the hypothalamus and that stimulates the release of the gonadotropin hormones FSH and LH. Gonadorelin may be used to stimulate FSH and LH secretion, and is used particularly for the treatment of infertility in women who do not have periods. Gonadorelin is given by injection.

GONADOTROPINS Men and women who produce abnormally low levels of the gonadotropin hormones FSH or LH may be given injections of either synthetic FSH or human chorionic gonadotropin (HCG), a hormone that mimics the action of LH. Synthetic gonadotropins may also be given with the antiestrogen drug clomiphene or they can be used alone if treatment with clomiphene has been unsuccessful. Synthetic gonadotropins may be used to stimulate the production of several eggs in women who are undergoing assisted conception. In men, synthetic gonadotropins are used to increase sperm production. Several monthly courses of the drugs may be needed. Side effects may include headaches, fatigue, and mood changes. In some men, the breasts may enlarge.

GONADORELIN ANALOGS/ANTAGONISTS These drugs are sometimes given to women who are undergoing assisted conception and who are also being treated with synthetic gonadotropins. They work by blocking the normal effects of natural gonadotropin-releasing hormone. This in turn inhibits production from the pituitary gland of the gonadotropin hormones FSH and LH. Blocking the production of natural gonadotropins allows the action of synthetic gonadotropins to be controlled by doctors more easily. Gonadorelin analogs are administered by injection or as a nasal spray. Side effects of these drugs may include hot flashes and itching, as well as loss of libido.

Hormone replacement therapy

Drugs that act in a similar way to female sex hormones and that are used to reduce symptoms associated with menopause

COMMON DRUGS

ESTROGENS
- Conjugated estrogens • Dienestrol • Estradiol
- Estrone • Estropipate • Ethinyl estradiol

PROGESTINS
- Levonorgestrel • Medroxyprogesterone
- Norethindrone • Norgestrel • Progesterone

At menopause, there is a natural decline in the levels of the sex hormone estrogen (*see* HEALTH AT MENOPAUSE, p.36). Reduced levels of estrogen at menopause may lead to various symptoms, such as hot flashes and vaginal dryness. In the long term, low levels of estrogen may increase the risk of developing osteoporosis (p.368) and heart disease. Menopausal symptoms may be particularly severe after surgical removal of the ovaries or following radiation therapy of the pelvic area during the treatment of cancer. Your doctor may recommend hormone replacement therapy (HRT), a treatment that restores the body's estrogen to premenopausal levels. Whether they occur naturally or after surgery or radiation therapy, the symptoms of menopause can usually be relieved by HRT.

HRT consists of the sex hormone estrogen or a combination of estrogen and a progestin (a group of hormones related to progesterone). Estrogen that is taken alone is associated with a higher than normal risk of cancer of the uterus (p.748). For this reason, most women are also prescribed a progestin to protect the lining of the uterus against changes that may lead to cancer. Women who have had their uterus removed do not normally need to take a progestin.

How is it used?

HRT is usually given in the form of pills, skin patches, or gel. Pills and gel are taken daily; patches are usually changed once or twice a week and should be placed on a different area of the skin each time. Other forms of HRT include estrogen cream or an estrogen-embedded vaginal ring. Long-term use of estrogen cream also requires that oral progestin be taken in order to protect against uterine cancer.

If you are still having menstrual periods or if it has been less than one year since your last period, HRT will be given in a dose to mimic the monthly cycle of natural hormones. As a result, you should experience regular monthly bleeding, although it may be irregular initially. After taking HRT for a year, you may be given estrogen and a progestin continuously, which should stop further menstrual periods.

Women who take HRT during perimenopause, the time before menopause during which the body is preparing for lower levels of hormones, may need to use contraception (p.69) if they wish to avoid becoming pregnant.

Treatment may be associated with a slightly increased risk of breast cancer (p.759). This increased risk disappears within about 5 years of stopping HRT. Some women are at a higher than normal risk of developing deep vein thrombosis (p.437), particularly those women who have severe varicose veins or who are very overweight. However, HRT does have benefits for reducing the risk of hip fractures. Your doctor will discuss the risks and benefits of HRT with you.

SELF-ADMINISTRATION

Using skin patches

Adhesive skin patches are a simple and effective way to deliver drugs, such as HRT, gradually into the body. Drugs that are administered in this way are released slowly and steadily and are absorbed directly into the bloodstream.

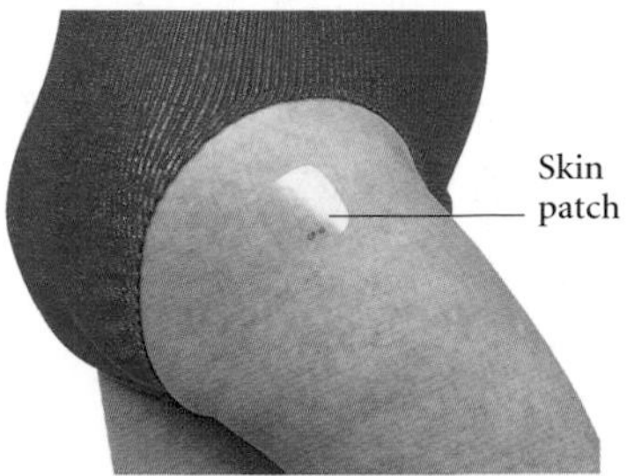
Skin patch

Using skin patches
Patches should always be placed on an area of dry, unbroken skin. Patches given for HRT are usually placed on the lower abdomen or upper thigh.

WHAT ARE THE SIDE EFFECTS?

If you are taking estrogen in order to restore your body's estrogen, you may experience several side effects including nausea, headaches, and mood swings. Estrogen may cause breast tenderness, fluid retention, and fluctuating weight. It may also cause eye irritation when you are wearing contact lenses. Progestins, the hormones often given in combination with estrogen in HRT, can cause similar side effects to estrogen, and they occasionally cause acne and skin rashes. HRT is associated with an increased risk of a heart attack, stroke, or leg clots. For this reason, HRT is not recommended for all postmenopausal women.

Drugs for labor

Drugs that are used to prevent or start labor or for associated problems

COMMON DRUGS

UTERINE STIMULANT DRUGS
- Dinoprostone • Ergonovine • Oxytocin

UTERINE MUSCLE RELAXANT DRUGS
- Amlodipine • Nifedipine • Ritodrine
- Terbutaline

MAGNESIUM

Drugs may be used during labor, either as a routine part of medical care or to treat specific problems. Among the most commonly used drugs during childbirth are epidural anesthetics *(see* EPIDURAL ANESTHESIA IN LABOR, p.801).

It may be necessary to use drugs to induce labor (start labor artificially) if the health of the mother or the fetus is at risk. The most common reasons for the induction of labor (p.797) include continuation of pregnancy beyond the due delivery date or complications, such as poor growth of the baby. Drugs may also be given to speed up labor if it does not progress as quickly as it should or to prevent bleeding after delivery.

If labor starts early (before the 34th week of pregnancy), drugs may be used to stop or delay delivery.

WHAT ARE THE TYPES?

The most commonly used drugs for are known as uterine stimulants. These drugs induce labor by starting contractions or speed up labor by strengthening contractions. Uterine stimulants may also be used for termination of pregnancy (p.789). Drugs that relax the uterus to delay premature labor are called uterine muscle relaxants. Magnesium may be used to prevent seizures during labor in women with preeclampsia (p.794), a condition indicated by the combination of high blood pressure, fluid retention, and protein in the urine during pregnancy.

UTERINE STIMULANT DRUGS If labor is going to be induced or if it is necessary to terminate pregnancy, a pessary that contains a prostaglandin uterine stimulant may be inserted into the vagina. Prostaglandins not only stimulate contractions but also soften and widen the cervix. Prostaglandins may also be administered in the form of vaginal pills or gel. During treatment with a prostaglandin, you may experience some side effects, such as nausea, vomiting, diarrhea, and hot flashes.

Oxytocin, another uterine stimulant, is given by infusion into a vein to induce labor or to speed up prolonged labor by strengthening contractions. If too high a dose of oxytocin is administered, it may result in painful, continuous contractions, nausea, and vomiting.

Ergonovine, which is another uterine stimulant drug, may be given by intramuscular injection to women just as the baby is delivered. The drug works by causing strong uterine contractions that hasten delivery of the placenta and also constrict the blood vessels in the uterus to reduce bleeding after delivery. A common side effect of ergonovine is nausea. In rare cases, headache, lightheadedness, and ringing in the ears may occur.

UTERINE MUSCLE RELAXANT DRUGS If labor begins prematurely, the doctor may give you drugs in order to relax the muscles of your uterus, thereby preventing further contractions. These drugs can remain effective for about 48 hours. The uterine muscle relaxant drugs ritodrine and terbutaline are given by infusion into a vein, while amlodipine and nifedipine are taken orally. Uterine muscle relaxants may have some side effects, including nausea, hot flashes, and rapid heartbeat. Another side effect is that your blood pressure may drop, resulting in light-headedness.

MAGNESIUM This mineral may be used to prevent seizures that can occur during labor in women with preeclampsia. It may also be used to stop premature labor, especially in multiple pregnancy (p.792). Side effects may include flushing, sweating, and low blood pressure.

Drugs for prostate disorders

Drugs that are used to treat disorders affecting the prostate gland

COMMON DRUGS

ALPHA BLOCKER DRUGS
- Alfuzosin • Doxazosin • Tamsulosin
- Terazosin

ANTIANDROGEN DRUGS
- Bicalutamide • Finasteride • Flutamide
- Nilutamide

GONADORELIN ANALOGS
- Goserelin • Leuprorelin

ESTROGENS
- Diethylstilbestrol • Megestrol

OTHER DRUGS FOR PROSTATE DISORDERS
- Aminoglutethimide • Dutasteride
- Ketoconazole

The main disorders that affect the prostate are noncancerous enlargement of the prostate (*see* ENLARGED PROSTATE GLAND, p.725), prostate cancer (p.726), and infection (*see* PROSTATITIS, p.724). Drugs may be used to treat all of these conditions, sometimes in conjunction with other forms of treatment.

An enlarged prostate gland constricts the urethra, the tube along which urine flows from the bladder, and may also cause tightening of the muscle at the outlet of the bladder. This can cause problems such as a frequent urge to urinate but difficulty doing so. Prostate cancer can cause similar problems with urination and, in certain cases, may spread to affect other parts of the body.

Infection of the prostate may cause fever and pain in the lower back, around the anus, or around the base of the penis. Other symptoms may include frequent, painful urination and discolored semen that contains blood.

WHAT ARE THE TYPES?

The main types of drugs used to treat prostate disorders are alpha blockers and antiandrogens. Alpha blockers are used to improve the flow of urine from the bladder. Antiandrogens are rarely used to treat noncancerous enlargement of the prostate and prostate cancer. Gonadorelin analogs and estrogens may also be used to treat prostate cancer.

Prostate infections are usually treated with antibiotics (p.885). They may need to be taken for several weeks before the infection clears up completely.

In some cases, the drugs aminoglutethimide and ketoconazole may be used in the treatment of prostate cancer.

ALPHA BLOCKER DRUGS Drugs of this type, such as doxazosin, relax the ring of muscle at the outlet of the bladder and thereby help improve the flow of urine. Alpha blockers are taken orally and may need to be used indefinitely because symptoms are likely to recur when the drugs are stopped. They may lower blood pressure, which can result in lightheadedness. The drugs may also cause drowsiness, fatigue, mood changes, a dry mouth, headache, and nausea.

ANTIANDROGEN DRUGS Androgens are male sex hormones that play an important but incompletely understood role in the development of noncancerous enlargement of the prostate gland and of prostate cancer. Antiandrogens work by counteracting the effects of androgens.

The main antiandrogen used for noncancerous enlargement of the prostate is finasteride, which can be used as an alternative to alpha blockers or in combination with them. However, you may have to take it for several months before there are any beneficial effects.

Antiandrogens are given orally. They are usually used on a long-term basis for prostate enlargement but may be given either short or long term for cancer. The side effects of antiandrogens may include reduced libido, erectile dysfunction, and breast tenderness.

GONADORELIN ANALOGS These drugs are commonly used to treat prostate cancer that has spread beyond the prostate gland. They reduce the release of hormones known as gonadotropins from the pituitary gland in the brain. Gonadotropins stimulate the production of testosterone, which is needed for the growth of prostate tumors. Gonadorelin analogs are administered by injection, as an implant under the skin, or in a nasal spray. They may initially cause the symptoms of the disease to worsen. However, this effect may be treated with an antiandrogen, such as flutamide. If you are taking gonadorelin analogs, you may have hot flashes, itching, loss of libido, nausea, and vomiting.

ESTROGENS These female sex hormones were once widely used to treat prostate cancer. They act by suppressing the production of the natural hormone testosterone, which is needed for tumor growth. Estrogens are rarely used today because of their side effects, such as breast enlargement, erectile dysfunction, nausea, and fluid retention. Estrogens may also slightly increase the risk of deep vein thrombosis (p.437).

Drugs that affect bladder control

Drugs for disorders that affect the ability of the bladder to store or expel urine

COMMON DRUGS

ANTICHOLINERGIC DRUGS
- Flavoxate • Imipramine • Oxybutynin
- Propantheline • Tolterodine

DESMOPRESSIN

ALPHA BLOCKER DRUGS
- Doxazosin • Tamsulosin • Terazosin

Drugs may be used to treat disorders that affect bladder function. These disorders fall into two main groups: urinary incontinence (p.710), in which there is involuntary leakage of urine; and urinary retention (p.713), in which there is difficulty emptying the bladder.

Urinary incontinence may occur for many reasons, including involuntary contractions of the muscle of the bladder wall, loss of nerve control due to a disorder such as stroke (p.532), or poor muscle tone at the bladder outlet, which is common in postmenopausal women. Bedwetting (p.872), involuntary emptying of the bladder during sleep, is a form of incontinence common among young children. Bedwetting normally stops by age 6, but some children do not gain full bladder control until they are older.

Urinary retention can also occur for a variety of reasons, including damage to nerves supplying the muscle of the bladder wall or an obstruction that prevents the outflow of urine from the bladder, which is commonly caused by an enlarged prostate gland (p.725).

WHAT ARE THE TYPES?

Anticholinergic drugs are used to treat incontinence. Desmopressin may occasionally be used to treat bedwetting in children. Urinary retention may be treated using alpha blocker drugs.

DRUGS FOR INCONTINENCE You may be prescribed an anticholinergic drug such as oxybutynin if you have frequent, sudden urges to urinate and are unable to control your bladder. Anticholinergic drugs work by relaxing the muscle in the bladder wall. This increases the size of the bladder and reduces the urge to urinate. If you are taking an anticholinergic drug, you may experience side effects such as a dry mouth, blurry vision, constipation, and nausea.

Bedwetting (nocturnal enuresis) in children is sometimes treated with desmopressin, a synthetic version of antidiuretic hormone (ADH), a naturally occurring hormone produced by the pituitary gland. ADH works on the kidney and reduces urine production. The bladder will not fill as quickly, and bedwetting is less likely. Desmopressin is only for short-term management of bedwetting in children 5 years of age and older and should be used along with nonmedicinal therapy. Desmopressin may be given either orally or as a nasal spray. Side effects of the drug may include fluid retention, salt imbalance, nausea, and headache. In rare cases, desmopressin can cause seizures.

DRUGS FOR URINARY RETENTION Alpha blockers, such as doxazosin, may be used to treat urinary retention due to noncancerous enlargement of the prostate gland. The drugs relax the muscles at the bladder outlet, thereby allowing urine to flow out more easily. The effect of the drugs is rapid, with improvement of symptoms within 2 weeks. However, although alpha blockers improve symptoms, they do not alter the progression of prostate enlargement. Alpha blockers may cause drowsiness, fatigue, headache, a dry mouth, nausea, and mood changes. They may also lower blood pressure, resulting in light-headedness.

Having an operation

Many people are likely to have an operation at some point in their lives. While some operations require you to stay in the hospital as an inpatient, an increasing number of procedures can be performed as day surgery. Advances in surgical procedures and anesthesia have made having an operation safer than ever, with shorter recovery times and fewer side effects.

The first article covers minor surgical procedures that may be done in your doctor's office, at an outpatient center, or in the hospital. The second article outlines what you may expect to take place when you have major surgery, including your recovery in the hospital afterward. If you are having major surgery, it is always done in a hospital. All hospitals and surgical procedures vary, but there are certain routines that are common to all, such as a thorough physical assessment before surgery, which includes checking your overall fitness for anesthesia and surgery. This assessment may take place weeks or days before you are admitted. The last article discusses convalescence once you have returned home after major surgery. Different types of surgery are described in a separate section (*see* TYPES OF SURGERY, pp.947–953).

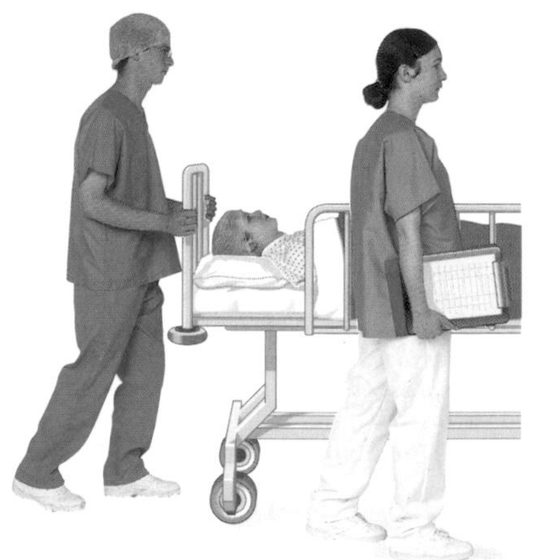

Going to the operating room
After you have been given premedication drugs to help calm you and to dry mucous secretions, you will be taken to the operation room by an orderly.

Having minor surgery

Minor procedures, which may be performed without anesthesia or under local anesthesia

Minor surgical procedures are those that can be done quickly, usually with a local anesthetic (*see* HAVING A LOCAL ANESTHETIC, right). These procedures include, among others, removal of moles, drainage of cysts or abscesses, and vasectomy (p.721). Most minor surgery involves instruments. However, in some situations no instruments are needed, such as in the manipulation of a simple fracture (p.392).

Minor surgery is usually done in the hospital as a day case or in an outpatient center, or your doctor may carry out the procedure in his or her office.

What does it involve?

A minor operation in a young, healthy individual involving little blood loss requires only minimal preparation. In most cases, the doctor will discuss the procedure with you, carry out a brief physical examination, and ask you to sign a consent form.

You may be given a local anesthetic, usually by injection. Anesthetic creams and sprays can also be used but are much less effective than injected anesthetics. However, they may be used to numb the skin before giving a local anesthetic injection to a child.

The doctor then scrubs up and may put on a sterile gown and mask and cleans the part of your body that requires surgery with an antiseptic liquid. The affected area will then be covered with a sterile drape to prevent bacteria on the surrounding skin from entering the wound. Once the skin is clean and anesthetized, the doctor performs the procedure, which may involve cutting through the skin. The wound, if there is one, is then closed using stitches (sutures), staples, tape, or glue (*see* REJOINING TISSUE, p.948). Some procedures do not leave a wound, and the area may be simply covered with light gauze or a bandage.

PROCEDURE: Having a local anesthetic

A local anesthetic is used to prevent pain during minor procedures such as removing moles or stitching cuts. The anesthetic drug numbs the nerve endings around the site at which it is administered. A local anesthetic is usually given by injection, although it may also be applied in a cream or as a spray.

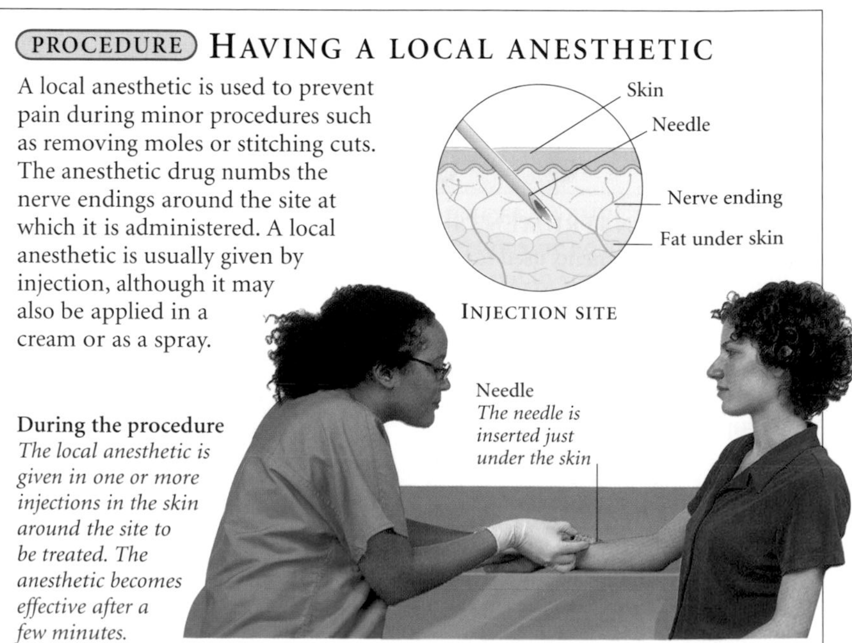
Skin
Needle
Nerve ending
Fat under skin
INJECTION SITE

Needle
The needle is inserted just under the skin

During the procedure
The local anesthetic is given in one or more injections in the skin around the site to be treated. The anesthetic becomes effective after a few minutes.

WHAT HAPPENS AFTER SURGERY?

If there is a wound, your doctor or a nurse will give you instructions on how to care for it in order to keep it clean and dry until it has healed.

You may need analgesics (p.912) to relieve pain when the local anesthetic wears off. You may also need to take antibiotics (p.885) to prevent infection. Your doctor will prescribe these drugs for you if necessary.

After some minor procedures, you may have some discomfort and may need someone to take you home. You are usually given a follow-up appointment so that the doctor can check that the procedure has been successful and that the wound is healing. If you have stitches, they may need to be removed. However, some types of stitches dissolve on their own after several days.

(WWW) ONLINE SITES: p.1037

Having major surgery

Major surgical procedures carried out under general or regional anesthesia

Major surgery takes place in the hospital and usually involves a procedure performed on tissue deep inside the body. For example, the surgeon may remove a section of intestine, implant an artificial hip, or perform coronary artery bypass surgery (*see* TYPES OF SURGERY, pp. 947–953). Before you have a major surgical procedure, your doctor will discuss with you why surgery is necessary, exactly what the procedure involves, where the operation will take place, and how long it will take. You will be fully informed about possible risks associated with the operation, and you will be asked to sign a form to say that you understand the risks and consent to the procedure being performed. The doctor will also be able to advise you on how long the recovery period may be.

Usually, major surgery is done under general anesthesia (*see* HAVING A GENERAL ANESTHETIC, p.944). However, an increasing number of procedures are now done under regional anesthesia (*see* HAVING A REGIONAL ANESTHETIC, p.945) in which you remain fully conscious but free of pain. A sedative may be given along with regional anesthesia to help keep you calm and reduce anxiety. The type of anesthesia you have depends largely on the nature of the procedure, but your general health and age may also play a part in determining which type of anesthetic you have.

In most major surgical procedures, a stay in the hospital is required. However, some more minor procedures, such as female sterilization (*see* TUBAL LIGATION, p.743), can sometimes be carried out as day surgery. This is particularly true if the procedures are done using modern minimally invasive techniques (*see* ENDOSCOPIC SURGERY, p.948).

Before having major surgery, you will undergo an assessment of your general health and fitness for surgery. On the day of the operation, you will be prepared for the procedure and given the anesthetic. After surgery has been completed, there is a recovery period, and you may spend several days in the hospital before you can go home.

You may want to clarify practical issues with your doctor. For example, you may want to check whether further treatment will be required after the operation and how long it may be before you are able to carry out your normal day-to-day activities.

PREOPERATIVE ASSESSMENT

Before a major surgical procedure, you will have a preoperative assessment. The main purpose of the assessment is to find out whether you have an underlying medical condition, such as heart disease, which may require special precautions during the operation in order to minimize the risk of complications.

During the preoperative assessment a medical practitioner or nurse reviews your medical history and performs a physical examination. Routine tests, such as blood tests, may be done, along with other investigations that may be needed because of your age, general health, or underlying condition.

You may also be seen by an anesthesiologist, who determines your suitability for anesthesia, discusses how the anesthetic will be administered, and answers any questions you may have.

MEDICAL HISTORY AND EXAMINATION You will be asked again about your current condition. In addition, your doctor will ask you about other serious illnesses or allergies you have had (*see* MEDICAL HISTORY, p.218). You will be asked about medications you are taking because these may influence the safety of the surgery to be performed. You will have a full medical examination, including listening to your chest and your back with a stethoscope (*see* PHYSICAL EXAMINATION, p.219), to help identify underlying disorders that may have an affect on the operation.

ROUTINE TESTS You may have a number of routine tests, such as blood tests, and sometimes a urine test. Usually, no more than two or three small tubes of blood are taken through a single needle (*see* BLOOD SAMPLES, p.221). The most common blood test determines whether you have enough hemoglobin in your blood (*see* BLOOD CELL TESTS, p.226). Hemoglobin is found in red blood cells and is an oxygen-carrying pigment. If you lose a small amount of blood during surgery, it is important that your body still has adequate reserves of hemoglobin to compensate. The blood sample may also be used to check your blood group (*see* BLOOD TYPING, p.227). A sample of your blood may be saved for cross-matching against blood from the blood bank if you need a blood transfusion (p.447) during the operation. A blood sample may also be tested to measure the levels of chemicals, such as urea and salts, in the blood because they reflect the function of internal organs such as the kidney (*see* ROUTINE BLOOD CHEMISTRY, p.229).

OTHER PRESURGICAL INVESTIGATIONS Depending on the outcome of your initial physical examination, your doctor may decide that other investigations are needed before you have surgery. For example, if your medical background suggests that you have heart disease, your doctor may arrange for an ECG (p.406) to assess the condition of your heart and diagnose any possible heart disorder. If there is a chance that you may have a heart or lung disorder, a chest X-ray may be taken. The results may influence how the surgical procedure is carried out and the level of monitoring needed during surgery. The results may also indicate whether additional investigations are needed, such as exercise testing (p.407), which evaluates blood flow to the heart while at rest and during the stress of exercise.

PREPARATIONS FOR SURGERY
On the day of your surgery you will be prepared for the operation and given premedication drugs if necessary. You will then be given the anesthetic.

For at least 6 hours before an operation under general anesthesia, you are not allowed to eat or drink. If you have food in your stomach, there is an increased risk of vomiting while you are unconscious. If the acidic stomach contents are inhaled, choking or serious damage to your lungs may result. You may also need to fast if you are having a regional anesthetic in case it becomes necessary to give you a general anesthetic during the operation.

GENERAL PREPARATIONS If your doctor thinks there is a risk of infection occurring during the operation, such as bacteria spreading from the intestine during intestinal surgery, a course of antibiotics (p.885) may be prescribed. These antibiotics may be given initially by injection. An hour or two before your operation, you will be asked to remove all jewelry and to change into a surgical gown. You will be asked to remove dentures, if you have them, or to point out loose teeth or crowns, which could be damaged when the breathing tube for anesthetic gases is inserted. If a surgical incision is to be made in an area of skin covered with hair, the area may be shaved to make the skin easier to clean. The skin over the site of the operation may be marked to identify the site.

PREMEDICATION Premedication drugs are rarely used. An orderly will take you to the operating room.

ANESTHESIA When you arrive in the operating room, you will be given an anesthetic. For longer operations done under general anesthesia, the anesthetic is given in two parts. First, an injected anesthetic is given in the back of your hand. Although this injection induces anesthesia rapidly, it is not long-lasting. Second, inhaled gases are given to maintain unconsciousness. For shorter operations, a single injected or inhaled anesthetic may be used.

The initial anesthetic drug is injected into a thin plastic tube called a catheter. This tube is inserted either in the back of your hand or in your arm and the anesthetic drug causes almost immediate loss of consciousness.

The anesthesiologist then inserts a breathing tube, called an endotracheal tube, through your mouth and down into your trachea (windpipe). The anesthesiologist may use an oropharyngeal tube rather than an endotracheal tube if it is appropriate. The endotracheal tube is connected to a ventilator, which regulates the speed and depth of breathing throughout surgery. You will be given a mixture of gases to breathe, including oxygen and an inhaled anesthetic. You will also be given a drug through the catheter that relaxes your muscles and therefore makes it possible for the surgeon to cut and move muscles easily. By doing this, the surgeon can obtain a clear view of the operating area.

If you are having a regional anesthetic, the anesthetic drug is given by injection. The site of the injection varies according to the procedure that is being performed, and, for some types of regional anesthesia, such as epidural or spinal anesthesia, the skin around the injection site will be numbed first with a local anesthetic.

PROCEDURE HAVING A GENERAL ANESTHETIC

General anesthesia is often used in surgery to induce unconsciousness and thereby prevent pain. First, a rapidly acting drug is injected through a catheter in a vein in the back of your hand or an arm. A drug given at the same time relaxes the muscles. Once unconscious, you are given a mixture of gases, including oxygen, through a tube inserted into your trachea (windpipe).

Syringe
Drugs or fluids are delivered through this tube
Intravenous catheter
The catheter tip is within the vein
Skin
Fatty tissue
vein

DETAIL OF CATHETER

Catheter

1 *A fast-acting general anesthetic is injected through a catheter into a vein in the back of the hand. You become unconscious within seconds.*

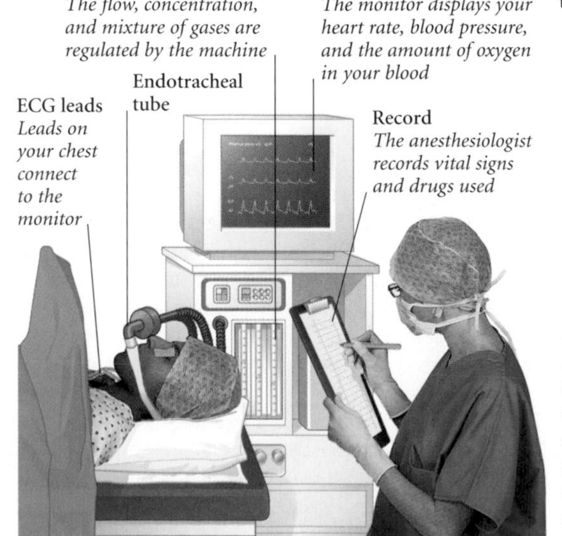
Anesthetic machine
The flow, concentration, and mixture of gases are regulated by the machine
Monitor
The monitor displays your heart rate, blood pressure, and the amount of oxygen in your blood
Endotracheal tube
ECG leads
Leads on your chest connect to the monitor
Record
The anesthesiologist records vital signs and drugs used

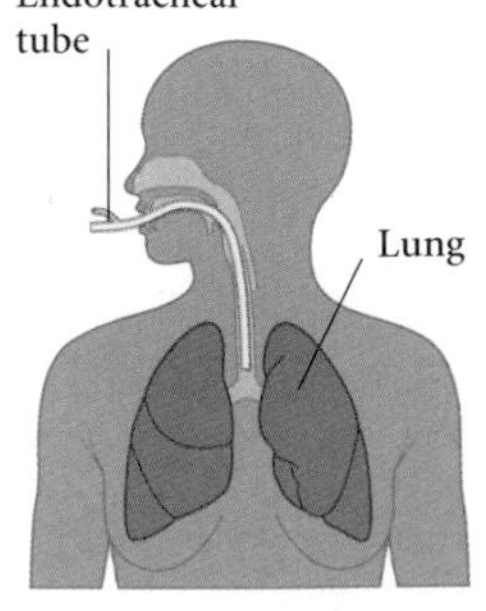
Endotracheal tube
Lung

SITE OF TUBE

2 *A mixture of oxygen and anesthetic gases is given to keep you unconscious. These gases are delivered directly into the lungs through an endotracheal tube, which is inserted down the throat into the trachea.*

IN THE OPERATING ROOM

As soon as you are anesthetized, the surgeon or assistant surgeon uses an antiseptic solution to clean the appropriate area of your skin. The solution may leave pink or brown stains for a short time after the operation. The remaining nonsterile parts of your skin are covered with sterile drapes and the procedure is performed.

When the procedure is completed, the wound is closed (*see* REJOINING TISSUE, p.948) by the surgeon. You may have internal stitches as well as the stitches that are visible on your skin if they have been used to close your wound. If you have had a general anesthetic, the proportion of anesthetic gases you are breathing will be reduced and the proportion of oxygen will be increased to allow you to wake up.

IN THE RECOVERY ROOM

As soon as you show signs of breathing on your own, the anesthesiologist will remove the endotracheal tube. You may hear someone telling you the operation is over, but you will probably awaken for only a moment. You are then moved to the recovery room. If you have had a general anesthetic, the recovery room is probably the first place you will remember after the operation. For the first hours after a major operation, your temperature, blood pressure, and pulse are checked frequently. When you are taken to the patient unit, usually when you are fully awake, these checks are repeated, but less often.

Some major surgery requires intensive nursing care afterward, and you may be transferred to a critical care unit (p.958) rather than a general patient unit. You will be transferred to the general patient unit when you are no longer dependent on specialized equipment and personnel.

IN THE PATIENT UNIT

After major surgery, you will be transferred to the patient unit so that you can be monitored and given any other treatment you may need. Postoperative monitoring is done in order to detect complications as early as possible. If necessary, you will also be given pain relief or other treatment. The more extensive the operation, the longer it will take for you to recover. Usually, your recovery is faster and complications are less likely if you start moving around as soon as you can after the anesthetic has worn off.

If you have had a general anesthetic, you are likely to remain drowsy for a number of hours. After regional anesthesia, you will have none of the drowsiness that follows general anesthesia. However, the numbing effects of a regional anesthetic will usually take several hours to wear off.

TREATMENT AND MONITORING You may be attached to tubes and equipment that monitor your condition or help perform particular bodily functions. For example, ECG leads may be attached to you to monitor your heart function. You may also have a urinary catheter so that you do not need to leave your bed to go to the toilet immediately after the operation. The catheter also monitors the amount of urine you are producing. The catheter is removed as soon as you are able to go to the toilet or sit on a bedpan. An intravenous drip may be placed in your arm or the back of your hand to deliver fluids and medication if necessary. The fluids help prevent you from becoming dehydrated until you are able to eat and drink normally. In some situations, there may be a tube called a drain coming from a small hole in the skin near the surgical wound. This tube allows excess tissue fluid or blood to drain away and is usually removed after a few days. You may also have a tube called a central line coming from the side of your neck or just below your collarbone. This tube is held in place by stitches and is used to monitor fluid balance and blood pressure, and to give you extra fluids or drugs if necessary. The tube will be removed as soon as monitoring and fluids are no longer necessary.

PAIN RELIEF You may not feel much pain when you wake up because of the effects of the drugs you have received during anesthesia, and because the surgeon may inject a local anesthetic into the edges of the surgical wound. After a few hours, you may become more uncomfortable and require analgesics to relieve pain. These drugs may be given orally or by injection, depending

PROCEDURE HAVING A REGIONAL ANESTHETIC

A regional anesthetic blocks the transmission of pain along a nerve or group of nerves. The anesthetic is injected around targeted nerves and you remain awake throughout the procedure. Regional anesthesia can be used in many parts of the body. A spinal nerve block, shown here, anesthetizes the whole of the lower body below the site of injection.

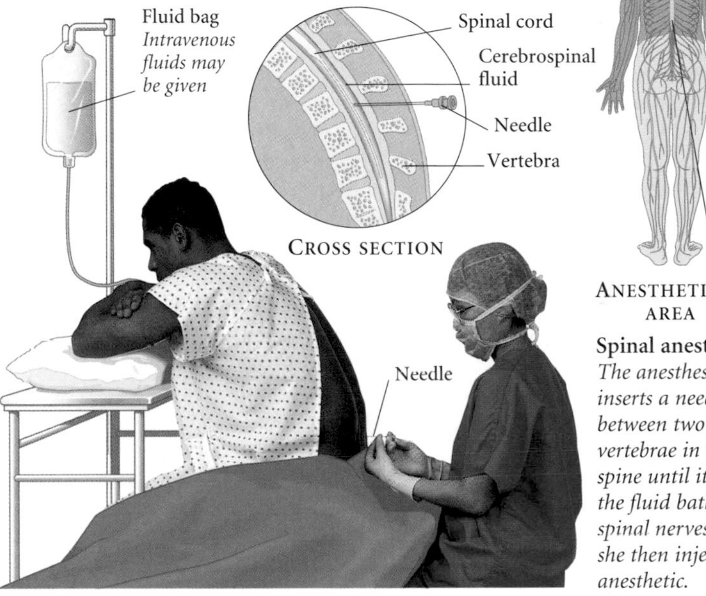
Fluid bag
Intravenous fluids may be given
Spinal cord
Cerebrospinal fluid
Needle
Vertebra
CROSS SECTION
Site of injection
ANESTHETIZED AREA
Needle

Spinal anesthesia
The anesthesiologist inserts a needle between two of the vertebrae in the lower spine until it reaches the fluid bathing the spinal nerves. He or she then injects the anesthetic.

on the drug, the severity of your pain, and your ability to swallow. You may be able to administer your own analgesia in small, safe doses using a patient-controlled analgesia pump attached to a tube inserted into a blood vessel in your arm or subcutaneous. The pump has a built-in device to prevent you from receiving too much medication.

OTHER TREATMENTS Some major surgery may necessitate other treatments to prevent complications. For example, blood clots may develop in the legs (*see* DEEP VEIN THROMBOSIS, p.437) if you are immobile for more than a few hours at a time. These clots may break off and travel to the heart or lungs and become dangerous. If blood clots are likely, your doctor will prescribe injections of a drug to reduce blood clotting (*see* DRUGS THAT PREVENT BLOOD CLOTTING, p.904). You will also need to wear support stockings for a few days or be given specialized stockings that inflate and deflate to mimic the pumping action of the calf muscles.

If you have had an operation on an infected area such as an abscess, you may be prescribed antibiotics (p.885). Depending on your operation, you may be offered physiotherapy (p.961) or other treatment while in the hospital to help you return to full mobility.

LEAVING THE HOSPITAL

You are discharged from the hospital when you no longer need close monitoring or special treatment. You usually need to be eating and drinking normally without the aid of tubes and be able to urinate without a catheter. The medical staff need to be satisfied that you have someone to accompany you home and that you will be adequately looked after at home if you cannot take care of yourself. You may need home nursing (*see* HOME CARE, p.960) organized in advance. If you need physiotherapy or occupational therapy (p.962) to provide special aids, such as a bath lift, you may need to be assessed before you are discharged from the hospital.

Before you leave the hospital, you are provided with medication if you need it and given a follow-up appointment to check on your progress and, if necessary, to have stitches removed.

(WWW) ONLINE SITES: p.1037

Convalescence after major surgery

The period of adjustment and recovery following a major operation

After surgery, there may be a period of time before you are able to return to work or resume all of your normal activities. This time of convalescence often involves some bed rest, and you may also need help with day-to-day living. In addition to physical recovery, convalescence may also involve a short period of psychological adjustment. It is not unusual to feel emotional or depressed after surgery, and, in some cases, counseling (p.971) may help.

Recent developments in surgical techniques, such as endoscopic surgery (p.948), and improvements in the control and relief of pain, have shortened the time needed for convalescence. In most cases, the older you are, the more extensive the surgery, and the poorer your general health is, the more time you will need to convalesce.

You are likely to need a period of rest after surgery and may be in enough discomfort to restrict activities. However, this must be balanced with the need for gradually increasing amounts of exercise in order to regain your strength and avoid the risk of deep vein thrombosis (p.437). If your muscles are weak from lack of use, such as after surgery on bones or joints, you may be offered regular physiotherapy to regain function and muscle strength. You may also require help from a specialized nurse to assist with temporary or permanent lifestyle alterations, such as learning to use a colostomy bag (*see* COLOSTOMY, p.666) for the first time.

RESUMING ACTIVITY

In order to speed your recovery, it is important to keep moving. Make sure that you have appropriate medication to allow you to move without excessive pain. After some operations, particularly operations on the abdomen, it may hurt to cough, and secretions remain in the lungs. For this reason, you will be advised to sit propped up with pillows so that your lungs are able to expand fully and you can cough up secretions, thereby helping reduce the risk of chest infection. You may also be encouraged to breathe into a simple machine called an incentive spirometer that helps keep the lungs expanded. As you recover from your operation, you should gradually be able to resume many activities. With time, you will be able to return to your normal lifestyle, resume sexual activity, and drive again.

WORK You will need to follow your doctor's advice on when to return to work, but you will also need to take into account the progress of your recovery and the nature of your work. Manual work will naturally require a higher level of physical fitness than office work. You may be able to arrange to resume your work duties gradually.

SEX Few operations require you to abstain from sexual activity afterward for physical reasons, but your surgeon will tell you if there is a particular risk. However, sometimes you may wish to avoid sex for reasons of comfort as well as from medical necessity, such as after surgery on a hernia (p.661) in the groin. You may also need time for your sexual feelings to return to normal, since they are often one of the first things to disappear when you have been sick. However, if you have sexual problems that continue, consult your doctor.

DRIVING You may be advised not to drive if your operation or medical condition could affect your concentration or change your ability to drive safely, for example, if you are unable to wear a seat belt or stop quickly in an emergency. Your doctor will advise you how long to wait before you resume driving.

IDENTIFYING COMPLICATIONS

Something may be seriously wrong if you suddenly feel ill or a symptom that was improving begins to get worse. Symptoms such as coughing, shortness of breath, bleeding, fever, a new discharge from the surgical wound, or increasing pain in the legs, chest, or operation site may indicate a problem. If you notice any of these symptoms, you should seek advice from your doctor or nurse, who can distinguish between normal postoperative symptoms and serious complications.

(WWW) ONLINE SITES: p.1037

TYPES OF SURGERY

Surgery at its most fundamental level consists of cutting through tissues, treating a problem, and sewing up the wound. However, the development of new technologies, such as microsurgery, video techniques, and lasers, has made it possible to perform more complex operations with increasing precision.

Open surgery is the most common type of surgery, and is discussed in the first article in this section. However, an increasing number of operations are performed using endoscopic surgery, in which only a small incision or none at all is needed. This is discussed next. Further articles discuss several other specialized types of surgical technique, including microsurgery and laser treatment, both of which are used in plastic surgery to reconstruct and repair parts of the body. Microsurgery can be performed on tiny structures of the body, such as the nerves. Laser treatment has many uses, such as removing birth marks and certain eye operations. The final article deals with transplant surgery, which enables diseased and failing body parts to be replaced with healthy ones.

What happens before, during, and after surgery is covered elsewhere (see HAVING AN OPERATION, pp.942–946).

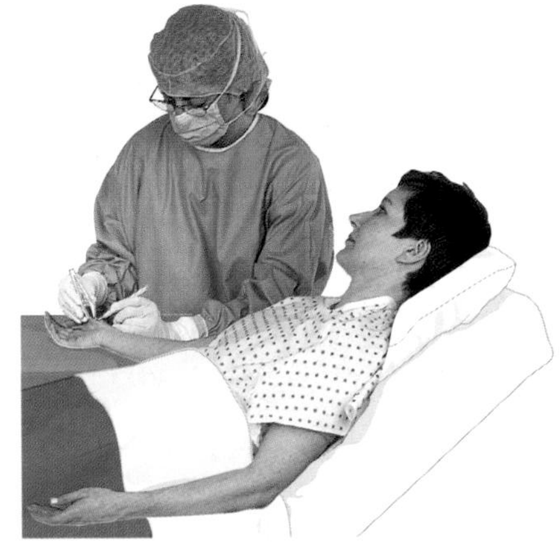

A surgical procedure
Almost all surgical procedures involve dividing tissues and then securing the tissue edges together to promote healing, reduce bleeding, and prevent infection.

Open surgery

Surgical procedures in which internal body structures are accessed by large incisions made in the skin

Most operations are carried out using open surgery. An incision is made in the skin large enough to allow the surgeon to see clearly the internal body parts that require treatment and the surrounding tissues. Although a large incision provides easy access, it may leave an obvious scar.

Open surgery is used for all internal organ transplant operations and for cesarean sections (p.802). Open surgery may also be necessary if a large amount of tissue, such as an extensive tumor, needs to be removed or if the extent of a problem is not clear. In some cases, open surgery may need to be performed urgently in order to deal promptly with an emergency such as internal bleeding.

WHAT HAPPENS DURING THE OPERATION?

There are a number of open surgery procedures, such as a cesarean section, that are done under regional anesthesia (*see* HAVING A REGIONAL ANESTHETIC, p.945). However, most open surgery is carried out under general anesthesia (*see* HAVING A GENERAL ANESTHETIC, p.944). Once you are fully anesthetized, the surgeon makes an incision through the skin and the layers of fat and muscle below it. The skin and muscles may be held back by clamps, and organs and tissues that are not being operated on are pulled out of the way by retractors. When the area to be worked on is clearly visible, the surgeon is then able to carry out the procedure.

Blood vessels that have to be severed during surgery are sealed in order to prevent serious loss of blood. This is done using electrocautery, a process in which blood vessels are sealed by an electric current applied through a pen-like instrument, or by tying off the severed ends of the vessels with synthetic thread. Lasers are also sometimes used during open surgery to seal blood vessels (*see* LASER TREATMENT, p.951).

The operation site is kept free of blood and other fluids to ensure that the surgeon can see clearly what he or she is doing. Sponges and suction tubes are positioned around the area to remove fluids. The number of sponges used is counted carefully and is checked after the operation to make sure that they have all been removed. The surgeon checks that there is no internal bleeding before he or she sews up the wound (*see* REJOINING TISSUE, p.948). The wound may be covered with a sterile dressing.

WHAT ARE THE RISKS?

All surgical procedures, whether major or minor, involve some risk. For example, there may be an adverse reaction to the anesthetic, excessive bleeding, formation of blood clots, and infection.

A general anesthetic can provoke changes in heart rhythm during or after surgery. The risk of this is higher if you are elderly, have a heart problem, or are overweight. An allergic reaction to the anesthetic may also occur.

Rarely, if blood vessels are not fully sealed, excessive bleeding may occur during the operation, or there may be persistent bleeding afterward. In both cases, a blood transfusion (p.447) may be required, from a supply of cross-matched (compatible) blood.

After surgery, blood has an increased tendency to clot, which may lead to formation of blood clots in the deep veins of the legs (*see* DEEP VEIN THROMBOSIS, p.437). These clots can cause pain and swelling and may sometimes travel to the lungs. If a blood clot becomes lodged in an artery supplying a lung, it can cause chest pain and shortness of breath and may be life-threatening (*see* PULMONARY EMBOLISM, p.495). In order to avoid the risk of clots developing, you will be encouraged to move around as soon as you can after you have had surgery. You may be asked to

TECHNIQUE REJOINING TISSUE

Tissues are rejoined after surgery to promote healing, stop bleeding, and prevent infection. There are various rejoining techniques and materials that can be used depending on the site and the type of tissue. Some materials are designed to dissolve as the tissues heal, and these are particularly useful for internal use. Materials that do not dissolve are used if healing is likely to take a long time or needs assessment before stitches are removed.

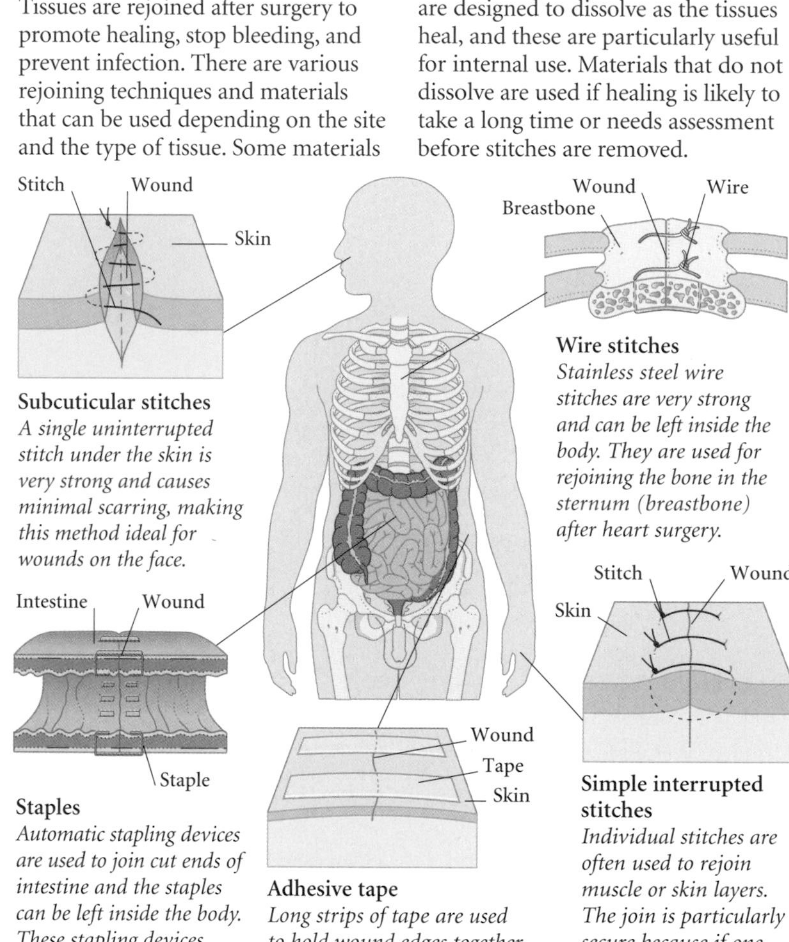
Stitch
Wound
Skin
Wound
Wire
Breastbone
Intestine
Wound
Staple
Wound
Tape
Skin
Stitch
Wound
Skin

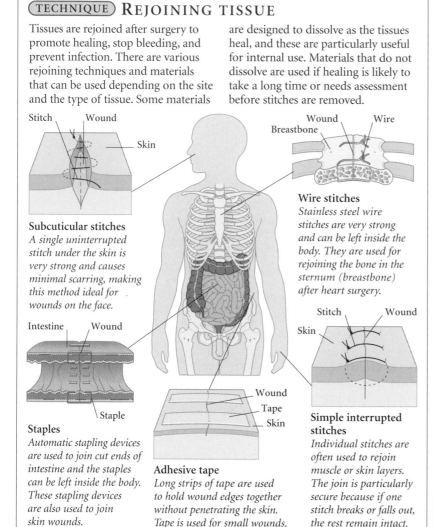

Subcuticular stitches
A single uninterrupted stitch under the skin is very strong and causes minimal scarring, making this method ideal for wounds on the face.

Wire stitches
Stainless steel wire stitches are very strong and can be left inside the body. They are used for rejoining the bone in the sternum (breastbone) after heart surgery.

Staples
Automatic stapling devices are used to join cut ends of intestine and the staples can be left inside the body. These stapling devices are also used to join skin wounds.

Adhesive tape
Long strips of tape are used to hold wound edges together without penetrating the skin. Tape is used for small wounds.

Simple interrupted stitches
Individual stitches are often used to rejoin muscle or skin layers. The join is particularly secure because if one stitch breaks or falls out, the rest remain intact.

wear pneumatic stockings, which rhythmically inflate and deflate to keep the blood flowing normally through your veins, or support stockings. Drugs that prevent blood clotting (p.904) may be necessary. Analgesics (p.912) may also help prevent the formation of blood clots by relieving pain and allowing you to move around more easily.

Infection may occur if bacteria or other microorganisms enter a wound during or after surgery, preventing or delaying healing and causing tissue damage and fever. The risk of infection is minimized by performing the operation in a highly sterile environment with sterile instruments. Antibiotics (p.885) are often given before, during, or after surgery to help prevent infection.

WWW ONLINE SITES: p.1037

Endoscopic surgery

Surgical procedures that use a viewing instrument inserted through a natural body opening or through skin incisions

Endoscopic surgery is a technique that enables various procedures to be performed without making large incisions in the skin. An endoscope is a tubelike viewing instrument with a light source. Some endoscopes have a built-in miniature camera. Endoscopes are inserted either through a natural body opening, such as the anus, or through a small incision, depending on the site to be accessed. Endoscopic surgery performed through skin incisions is often referred to as minimally invasive surgery (*see* HAVING MINIMALLY INVASIVE SURGERY, opposite page). Endoscopes may be flexible or rigid (*see* FLEXIBLE ENDOSCOPY, p.255, and RIGID ENDOSCOPY, p.256) and are used to provide a view of the inside of body cavities, either directly through the endoscope or on a screen.

Endoscopes may be used to carry out treatment, to examine a particular area, or to take tissue samples. Tiny instruments, such as forceps and scissors, are passed through small incisions in the skin or through side channels in the endoscope to reach the operating site. These instruments are operated by the surgeon, who is guided by the view through the endoscope or on the screen.

Since endoscopic surgery may not involve any incisions or only require small ones, the length of stay in the hospital and recovery time are shorter than for open surgery. Bleeding from any small incisions that have been made is minimal. Wounds therefore heal more quickly and are less likely to become infected than the large incisions that are needed in open surgery.

WHEN IS IT USED?

Endoscopic surgery may be used to operate inside any part of the body that is large enough for the instruments to be inserted into and moved around. Suitable sites include the chest, abdominal cavity, pelvic cavity, digestive tract, large joints, such as the knee and hip, and the nasal sinuses. Endoscopes have different names according to the part of the body in which they are used. For example, laparoscopes are used in the abdominal cavity, bronchoscopes are used to look in the lungs, and colonoscopes are used inside the colon.

If you have symptoms that suggest a disorder of the reproductive system, digestive tract, lungs, sinuses, or bladder, an endoscope may be inserted through the vagina, anus, mouth, nose, or urethra in order to investigate the affected area. Endoscopy through natural openings may be repeated safely many times and can be used to monitor a condition such as a peptic ulcer (p.640).

Endoscopic surgery in which small incisions have to be made is used when the area under investigation cannot be accessed through a natural body opening. For example, if you have a disorder of the gallbladder, the appendix, or certain regions of the female reproductive

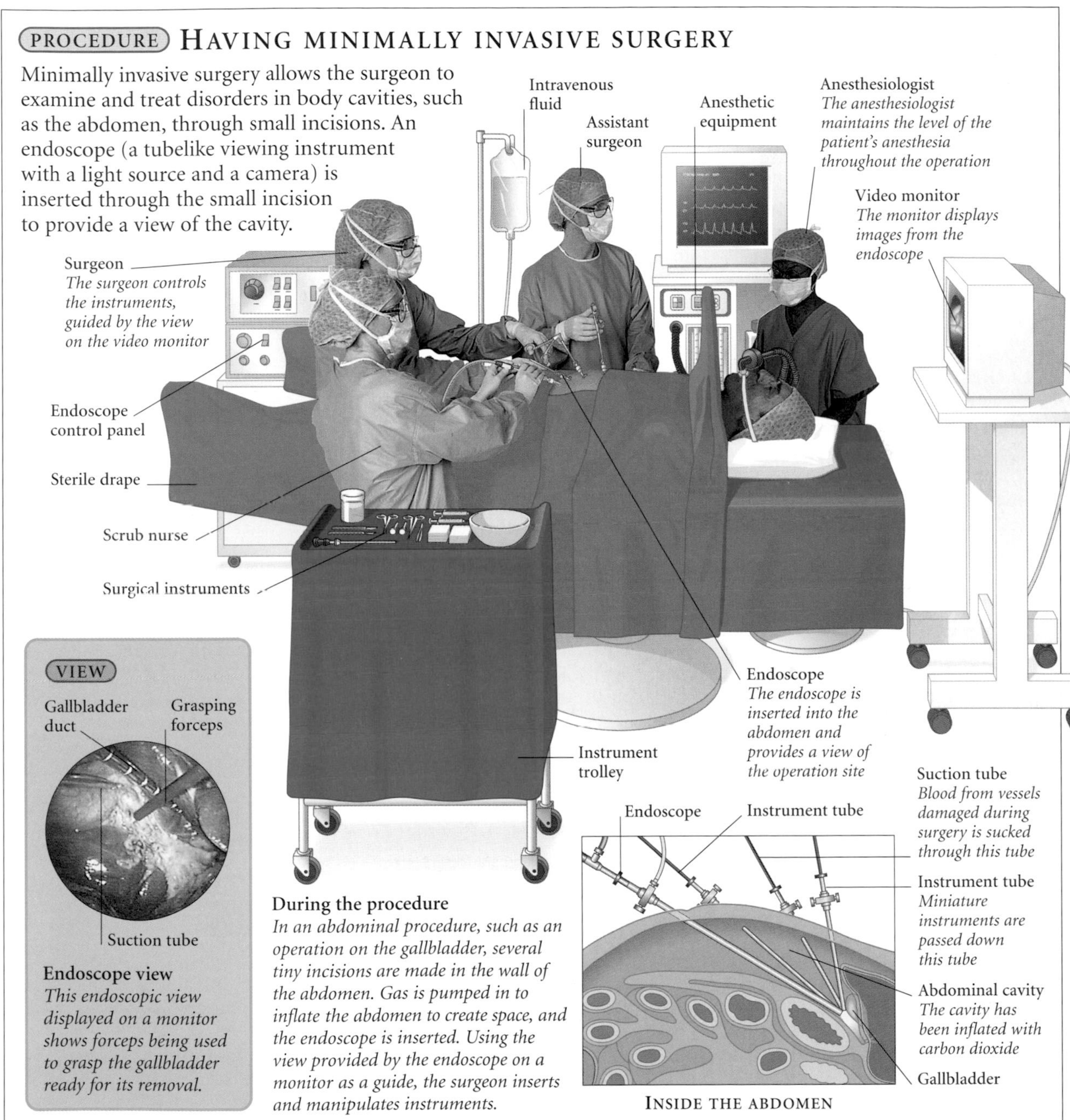
PROCEDURE
HAVING MINIMALLY INVASIVE SURGERY
Minimally invasive surgery allows the surgeon to examine and treat disorders in body cavities, such as the abdomen, through small incisions. An endoscope (a tubelike viewing instrument with a light source and a camera) is inserted through the small incision to provide a view of the cavity.
Intravenous fluid
Assistant surgeon
Anesthetic equipment
Anesthesiologist
The anesthesiologist maintains the level of the patient's anesthesia throughout the operation
Video monitor
The monitor displays images from the endoscope
Surgeon
The surgeon controls the instruments, guided by the view on the video monitor
Endoscope control panel
Sterile drape
Scrub nurse
Surgical instruments
Endoscope
The endoscope is inserted into the abdomen and provides a view of the operation site
Instrument trolley
VIEW
Gallbladder duct
Grasping forceps
Suction tube
Endoscope view
This endoscopic view displayed on a monitor shows forceps being used to grasp the gallbladder ready for its removal.
During the procedure
In an abdominal procedure, such as an operation on the gallbladder, several tiny incisions are made in the wall of the abdomen. Gas is pumped in to inflate the abdomen to create space, and the endoscope is inserted. Using the view provided by the endoscope on a monitor as a guide, the surgeon inserts and manipulates instruments.
Endoscope
Instrument tube
Suction tube
Blood from vessels damaged during surgery is sucked through this tube
Instrument tube
Miniature instruments are passed down this tube
Abdominal cavity
The cavity has been inflated with carbon dioxide
Gallbladder
INSIDE THE ABDOMEN

system, such as the fallopian tubes, a laparoscope may be inserted through an incision in the abdomen to carry out investigations or treatment (*see* LAPAROSCOPY, p.742). Laparascopes are also used in female sterilization (*see* TUBAL LIGATION, p.743). If you have a joint disorder, such as arthritis, or a damaged cartilage or ligament, an arthroscope inserted through a small incision may be used to view and possibly operate on the joint (*see* ARTHROSCOPY, p.386).

WHAT HAPPENS DURING THE OPERATION?

Endoscopic surgery through natural openings in the body, such as the throat or anus, may not need an anesthetic or may take place under sedation or local anesthesia. This means that you remain conscious but the area being operated on is numb (*see* HAVING A LOCAL ANESTHETIC, p.942, and HAVING A REGIONAL ANESTHETIC, p.945). In some cases, you may be given a drug in order to help you relax before the procedure takes place. After the endoscope has been inserted into the body opening, surgical instruments may be inserted along specific channels in the endoscope.

Most endoscopic surgery through incisions is performed under general anesthesia (*see* HAVING A GENERAL ANESTHETIC, p.944). An incision about ½ in (13 mm) long is made for the endoscope, and then further tiny incisions are also made so that instruments, such as lasers (*see* LASER TREATMENT, opposite page) and scissors, can be inserted if needed. In a laparoscopic operation on the abdomen, a tube is inserted through an incision, and gas is gently pumped through the tube to inflate the abdominal cavity, giving the surgeon a better view and more operating space.

The surgeon looks at the procedure through an eyepiece on the endoscope and also observes a magnified image of the operating area transmitted to a video monitor. The procedure can be observed on the screen at the same time by the surgeon's colleagues.

When the operation is complete, the endoscope and all of the instruments are removed. Incisions are then closed, often with a single stitch.

WHAT ARE THE RISKS?

There is a similar risk of damage to an organ or blood vessel with endoscopic surgery than with open surgery (p.947) because the surgeon has to work in a smaller area. As with all surgery, there is a risk of an adverse reaction to a general anesthetic. During the operation, the surgeon may need to access a larger area and perform open surgery. You will be asked for your consent to open surgery before an endoscopic operation.

(WWW) ONLINE SITES: p.1037

Microsurgery

Surgical procedures that use magnifying equipment and tiny surgical instruments to operate on small or delicate structures

Microsurgery makes it possible to operate on extremely small and delicate tissues in the body. In this form of surgery, a surgeon uses a binocular microscope to view the operating site and specially adapted small operating instruments. Microsurgery enables delicate surgical procedures to be done that would be difficult or impossible using other surgical techniques.

WHEN IS IT USED?

Microsurgery is most commonly used to operate on tissue such as nerves and blood vessels and on small structures in the eye, middle ear, and reproductive system. For example, microsurgery can be used to repair a detached retina (*see* RETINAL DETACHMENT, p.578). It can also be used to remove the diseased eye lens of someone with a cataract and replace it with an artificially made lens (*see* CATARACT SURGERY, p.573). In the disorder otosclerosis (p.598), deafness may occur when a bone in the middle ear becomes diseased and cannot transmit sound. Hearing can be restored using microsurgery to replace the diseased bone with an artificial substitute.

During an operation to reattach a severed limb or digit, microsurgery is used to reconnect severed nerves and blood vessels. Microsurgery is also used to try to reverse two sterilization procedures: tubal ligation (p.743) in females and vasectomy (p.721) in males. Tubal ligation involves cutting or sealing the fallopian tubes. In a vasectomy, the narrow tubes that carry sperm from the testes to the penis are severed, preventing the release of sperm from the body. In both instances, microsurgery procedures can be used to rejoin the sealed or severed tubes accurately, and, in many cases, a person's normal reproductive function can be regained.

WHAT HAPPENS DURING THE OPERATION?

Microsurgery is normally performed under general anesthesia (*see* HAVING A GENERAL ANESTHETIC, p.944). However, regional or local anesthesia (*see* HAVING A REGIONAL ANESTHETIC, p.945, and HAVING A LOCAL ANESTHETIC, p.942) may be used for some minor procedures, such as cataract operations.

During the operation, the surgeon views the operating site through a binocular microscope, operated using foot

(PROCEDURE) HAVING MICROSURGERY

Microsurgery is a technique that allows delicate operations to be performed on very small structures in the body. The technique is used for a number of procedures, such as repairing damaged blood vessels and nerves. Microsurgery is also used frequently to remove the eye lens of someone with a cataract and to operate on the tiny bones in the middle ear.

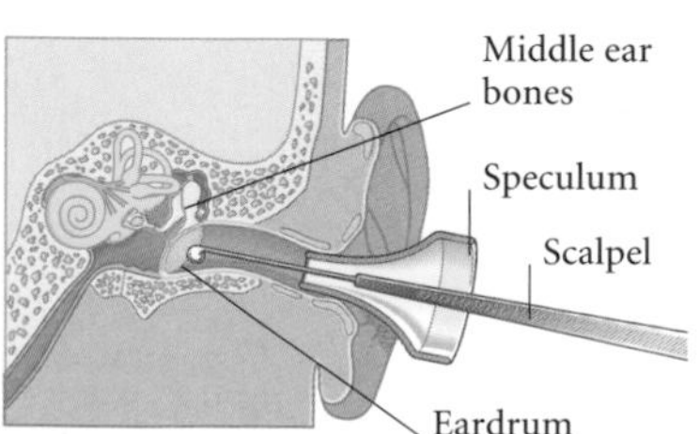
Middle ear bones
Speculum
Scalpel
Eardrum

INSIDE THE EAR

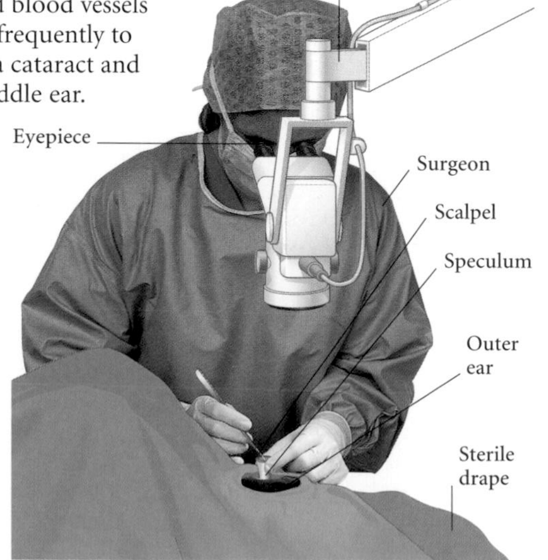
Operating microscope
The microscope is adjusted with foot pedals
Eyepiece
Surgeon
Scalpel
Speculum
Outer ear
Sterile drape

During the procedure
The surgeon views the operating site through a powerful microscope and uses extremely small instruments. Here an operation is being carried out on delicate structures inside the ear.

(VIEW)

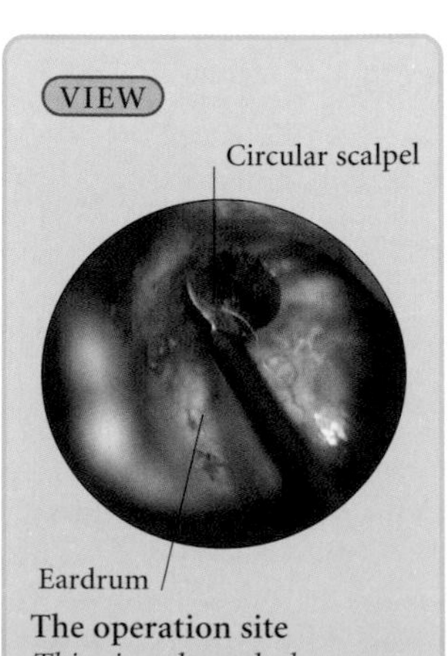
Circular scalpel
Eardrum

The operation site
This view through the operating microscope shows a tiny circular scalpel being used to make a small incision in the eardrum to enable the surgeon to gain access to the bones of the middle ear.

pedals. This leaves his or her hands free to use small precision instruments, including scissors, forceps, and clamps (*see* HAVING MICROSURGERY, opposite page). To repair nerves and blood vessels, small needles and fine thread are used to make tiny stitches.

WHAT ARE THE RISKS?

In any type of surgery there are risks, whether from a reaction to the anesthetic, blood clots, infection, or excessive bleeding. Since some microsurgical operations take longer than other similar surgical procedures, the time under anesthesia is longer. This increases the risk of developing an adverse reaction to the anesthetic and may extend the recovery time from anesthesia. The risk of infection may also be higher with microsurgery because the operation site is exposed for a relatively long time compared with other procedures.

There is a high success rate for many of the most routine microsurgical procedures, such as cataract removal and repair of retinal detachment. However, some procedures, such as reattachment of severed limbs or reversal of tubal ligation, have lower success rates, which are partly determined by the amount of damage to the tissues. Nevertheless, without microsurgery, operations like these could not be attempted.

(WWW) ONLINE SITES: p.1037

Laser treatment

Procedures using intense beams of light to cut, join, or destroy tissue

Light from a laser can cut or destroy tissue or repair damaged tissue by fusing together torn edges. This ability allows lasers to be used in a number of surgical procedures in place of scalpels, scissors, and stitches.

A wide range of lasers is used for various purposes, including treatment of skin problems, operations on the eye, and internal operations that are carried out in conjunction with endoscopes (*see* ENDOSCOPIC SURGERY, p.948).

Since laser beams can be focused precisely, small sections of tissue can be treated without causing damage to the surrounding tissues. Lasers produce differing wavelengths of light that are absorbed by different types of tissue. For example, a wavelength that is absorbed by melanin (the dark pigment that gives skin its color) may be effective in removing a mole caused by overproduction of melanin. A wavelength that is absorbed by blood causes clotting to occur and prevents bleeding from tissues cut during treatment.

Lasers generate great heat, and treatment is therefore given in short bursts to avoid the risk of burning.

WHEN IS IT USED?

Laser treatment is commonly used in gynecological procedures. A laser beam can be directed into the body through an endoscope to remove scar tissue inside the fallopian tubes, which may be a cause of infertility. Lasers are also used to remove cysts that form in the pelvic area due to endometriosis (p.742) and to destroy abnormal cells on the cervix that, if untreated, may develop into cancer (*see* CERVICAL DYSPLASIA, p.749).

Small tumors or precancerous cells in other internal body areas, such as the larynx or inside the digestive tract, can be destroyed by laser beams directed through an endoscope. The technique can also be used to open arteries that have been narrowed by fatty deposits (*see* ATHEROSCLEROSIS, p.402). In ophthalmic surgery, laser beams can be used to seal small tears in the retina, the light-sensitive layer at the back of the eye (*see* RETINAL DETACHMENT, p.578).

Laser treatment is often used on the skin, especially on the face, for reducing scar tissue and birthmarks (p.828), noncancerous moles (p.343), tattoos, or

(PROCEDURE) LASER TREATMENT ON THE SKIN

Lasers can be used to remove tattoos and birthmarks from the skin by destroying cells with a particular color, such as cells in red birthmarks. A laser beam can also be used to reduce the severity of scars and the effects of aging, such as wrinkles, by removing the top layer of cells to smooth the skin. The beam of high-intensity light is very precise and does not damage surrounding cells.

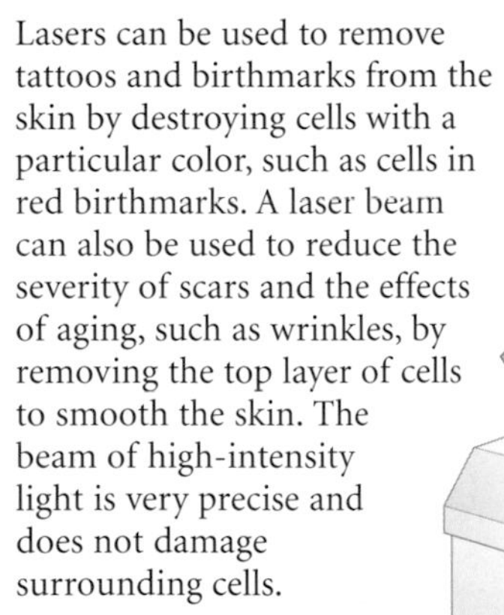

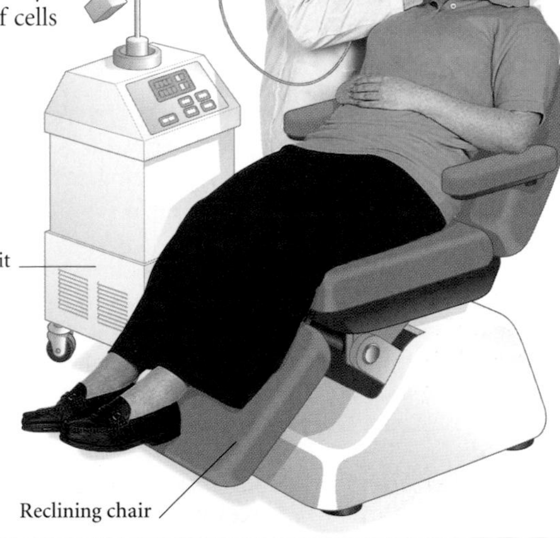
Protective goggles
Goggles are worn to protect the eyes
Dermatologist
Laser probe
Laser unit
Reclining chair

Treating a birthmark
To treat a birthmark on the face, a hand-held laser is used to give several short bursts of laser light. Each treatment lasts about 20 minutes, and usually only local anesthesia is needed.

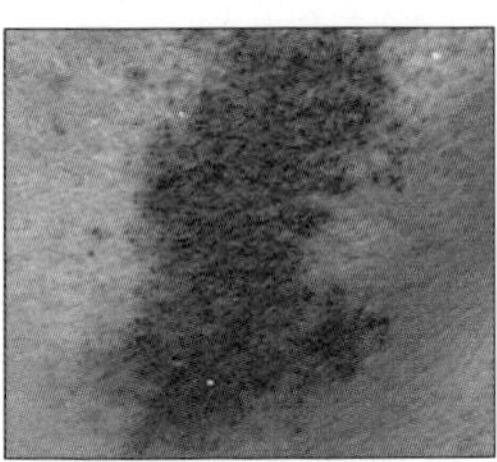

BEFORE TREATMENT

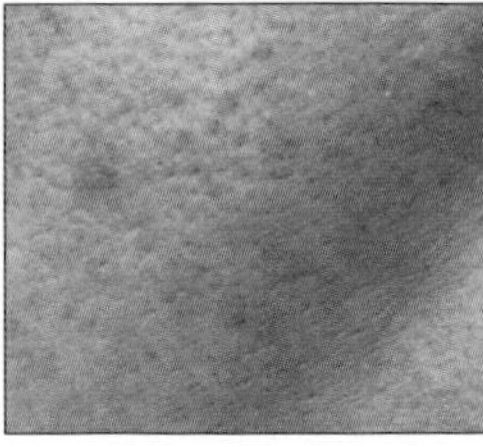

AFTER TREATMENT

Effect of treatment
Laser treatment destroys the cluster of blood vessels under the skin that make up the birthmark. In some cases, a course of several treatments is needed before noticeable improvement is seen and the birthmark disappears completely.

wrinkles (*see* LASER TREATMENT ON THE SKIN, p.951). The results depend on the, extent of the problem but in most cases scarring is minimal, and the appearance of the skin is much improved.

External laser treatment can also be used to treat conditions such as spider veins and to remove warts (p.354) on the skin and genital warts (p.768).

WHAT HAPPENS DURING THE TREATMENT?

Most forms of laser treatment are done under either local or general anesthesia, depending on the type of surgery and the area to be treated. However, for minor skin conditions, laser treatment causes little discomfort and may be performed without anesthesia. There may be some swelling, redness, and blistering, which usually disappear within a week. Large areas of skin may have to be treated over several sessions.

WHAT ARE THE RISKS?

Occasionally, laser treatment may cause scarring, or there may be incomplete removal of damaged tissue. Skin treated by laser may also be vulnerable to infection until it has healed completely. The intense heat of the laser can sometimes lead to coarsening of the skin.

(WWW) ONLINE SITES: p.1037

Plastic surgery

Procedures used to repair and reconstruct skin and underlying tissue or alter its appearance

Skin or tissue that has been damaged or destroyed as a result of disease or injury or that has been malformed since birth can often be repaired or reconstructed using plastic surgery. The aim of plastic surgery is to restore the appearance and function of the affected area as much as possible with minimal visible scarring. A form of plastic surgery known as cosmetic surgery may be used in healthy people to disguise the signs of aging or to change the shape of part of the body. Cosmetic surgery may also be used after disease or injury. For example, skin grafting (p.319) can improve the appearance of burned skin, and breast reconstruction is often used after a mastectomy has been performed (*see* SURGERY FOR BREAST CANCER, p.761). Some congenital conditions, such as cleft lip and palate (p.862), can be corrected by plastic surgery. Finally, plastic surgery can also be used in sex change operations to create or remove breasts and male and female genitals.

Before you have plastic surgery, it is important to obtain as much information as possible about the risks of the procedure and the likelihood of a good outcome. You should also ensure that your surgeon is well qualified and experienced in the techniques to be used.

WHAT HAPPENS DURING THE OPERATION?

In most plastic surgery, general anesthesia is needed (*see* HAVING A GENERAL ANESTHETIC, p.944). However, minor procedures, such as removing a mole, may be done under local anesthesia (*see* HAVING A LOCAL ANESTHETIC, p.942). During the procedure, various techniques may be used, depending on the nature of the operation. A commonly used technique in plastic surgery is skin grafting (p.319), in which a piece of healthy skin is detached from one part of the body and placed over a damaged area. Another commonly used technique is the skin and muscle flap, in which a section of skin and underlying muscle is moved from one area to replace damaged tissue in another area. This technique may be used together with an implant to reconstruct a breast following mastectomy.

Cosmetic surgery uses a range of techniques that are either the same or similar to those of plastic surgery in order to alter a person's appearance. For example, in cosmetic surgery the techniques used to alter breast size are similar to those used to reconstruct a breast following mastectomy.

WHAT ARE THE RISKS?

Plastic surgery carries risks of infection and bleeding that all other types of surgery share. Swelling and bruising after surgery are also common. When skin is grafted, the graft sometimes fails to attach properly to the new area, and the operation will need to be repeated.

There is also the risk that the procedure may not produce as good an effect as expected, and sometimes scars may remain afterward.

(WWW) ONLINE SITES: p.1037

Transplant surgery

Operations carried out to replace failing body organs or tissues with healthy ones

Diseases can occasionally cause major organs, such as the heart, kidneys, or liver, to fail irreversibly. Dialysis (p.707) can take over the functions of the kidneys but may lead to a deterioration in health. Dialysis also has to be carried out frequently and is time-consuming. Replacing the diseased organ with a transplanted one is usually the best long-term treatment. In the case of a failing heart or liver, a transplant may be the only chance of survival if the organ has deteriorated significantly.

Many organs and tissues can be transplanted. Kidney transplants are now common, and liver, heart, lung, cornea, and bone marrow transplants are performed routinely. Transplants of the intestines and pancreas are done less often. More than one organ may be transplanted at the same time, as in the case of heart and lung transplants.

Transplants are done not only to treat life-threatening conditions but also to improve quality of life when a condition is not potentially fatal. For example, a damaged cornea that causes a loss of vision can be repaired by a corneal graft that restores sight.

Organ and tissue transplants can be carried out only if a suitable donor organ can be found at the right time and if the person receiving the transplant has no other medical problems that could hinder his or her recovery.

WHO ARE THE DONORS?

Transplants are usually performed only when the tissue types and blood groups of the donor and recipient are similar. This is necessary because the recipient's immune system will attack any organ it identifies as "foreign," a process called rejection. Most transplant organs are taken from donors who have very recently been declared dead and who are unrelated to the recipient. However, bone marrow and single kidneys can be taken from living donors without damaging their health. Bone marrow is always taken from a living donor. When bone marrow or kidneys are donated by a close, living, genetic relative, often a brother or sister, the transplants are

TECHNIQUE SURGERY USING A HEART–LUNG MACHINE

A heart–lung machine takes over the function of the heart and the lungs. This allows the surgeon to operate on the heart during certain major chest operations, such as coronary artery bypass grafts, a heart transplant, or heart valve replacements. The heart is cooled and paralyzed to stop it beating during surgery, and blood is diverted to the heart–lung machine, which oxygenates the blood, removes carbon dioxide, and then returns the blood to the body. Afterward, the heart is restarted with an electric shock and the circulation restored.

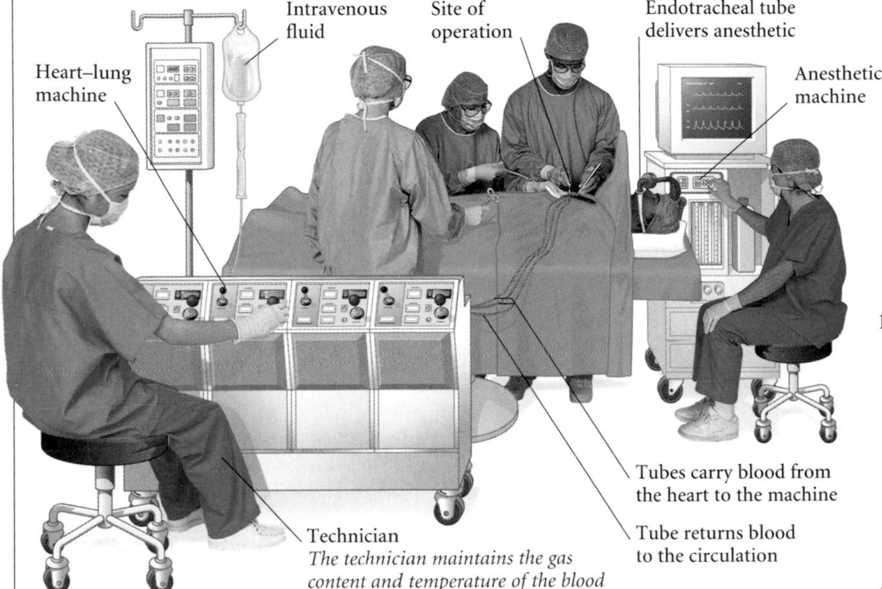
Intravenous fluid
Site of operation
Endotracheal tube delivers anesthetic
Heart–lung machine
Anesthetic machine
Tubes carry blood from the heart to the machine
Tube returns blood to the circulation
Technician

The technician maintains the gas content and temperature of the blood

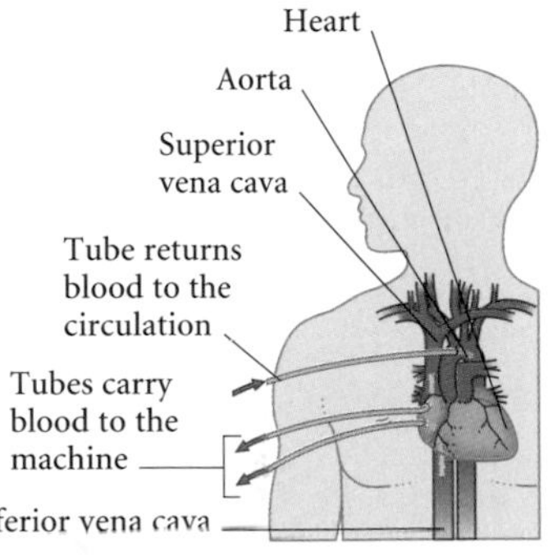
Heart
Aorta
Superior vena cava
Tube returns blood to the circulation
Tubes carry blood to the machine
Inferior vena cava

SITE OF THE CONNECTIONS

During the operation

Tubes from the heart–lung machine are inserted into the blood vessels entering and leaving the heart to divert blood through the machine. The heart is then stopped and the operation performed. Afterward, the heart is disconnected from the machine and restarted.

far less likely to be rejected by the recipient because the tissue types are likely to match more closely.

In the case of organ transplants from a donor who has recently died, most come from people in whom brain function has ceased irreversibly but whose other organs had been kept functioning by a life support machine.

WHAT HAPPENS DURING THE OPERATION?

Most transplant surgery requires general anesthesia (*see* HAVING A GENERAL ANESTHETIC, p.944).

In an organ transplant, the organ to be transplanted is removed from the donor and chilled in a salt-containing solution until it reaches the operating room. This prolongs the time the organ can safely be deprived of its normal blood supply by a few hours. In most cases, the diseased organ is replaced by the donor organ. However, in kidney transplants (p.708) the defective organ may be left in place and the new kidney placed in the pelvis, where it is connected to the relevant blood vessels. During a heart transplant (p.427), the major blood vessels are connected to a heart–lung machine to oxygenate the blood and remove the carbon dioxide from it while the heart transplant is being carried out (*see* SURGERY USING A HEART–LUNG MACHINE, above).

To perform a bone marrow transplant (p.454), cells in the center of certain bones are collected from the living donor. These bone marrow cells are then transfused directly into one of the recipient's veins after his or her existing bone marrow has been destroyed. Alternatively, cells may be collected from the recipient's own bone marrow during a period when his or her underlying disease is in remission and frozen for later use. The stored bone marrow may then be thawed and used to replace abnormal bone marrow in the recipient's body if disease recurs.

After a transplant, you will probably spend several days in a critical care unit (p.958). With all transplants except the cornea, you will need immunosuppressants (p.906) indefinitely in order to prevent your immune system from rejecting the new organ or tissue. You should be able to leave the hospital after a few weeks if the transplant has been successful. Recovery time for a corneal graft is shorter, and it is usually possible to go home after a few days.

WHAT ARE THE RISKS?

Transplant surgery, like other forms of major surgery, carries a risk of excessive bleeding and adverse reaction to the anesthetic. Transplant surgery carries a much higher risk of infection than other forms of surgery because immunosuppressant drugs interfere with the natural defenses of the body. However, the greatest risk is that the transplanted organ will be rejected by the immune system and that this will cause the transplanted organ to fail.

After a major transplant operation, the chances of long-term survival improve significantly once the first year after the operation has passed. However, survival depends on the organ not being rejected and on the recipient remaining free of a serious infection. The best outcomes are usually in people who were otherwise healthy when the original organ failed.

(WWW) ONLINE SITES: p.1037

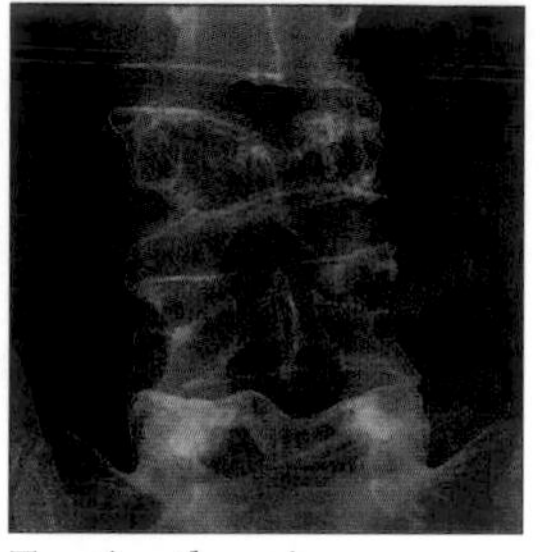

Treating the spine
Either conventional or complementary therapies may be used to relieve back pain.

Care and Therapies

In spite of advances in the prevention and early detection of disease, most of us need treatment from time to time to relieve symptoms or cure an illness. Patterns of medical care have changed recently: although major surgery and treatment for serious short-term illness still take place in the hospital, people are now discharged as soon as possible. In addition, many long-term treatments and procedures now take place in the home or in an outpatient center without the need for hospitalization.

The range of care and therapies that is available today is extensive. For most people, a conventional treatment that is recommended by their doctor, such as a drug treatment, is the preferred option. However, complementary therapies, including hypnotherapy, homeopathy, and chiropractic, are becoming increasingly popular and are often used in conjunction with some conventional treatments. In fact, doctors may sometimes recommend these therapies to their patients if they think that they may be helpful.

Location of care

The current emphasis is on providing care and therapies either in the home or in outpatient centers rather than in the hospital. There are two reasons for this trend. The first is that the cost of hospital care is far greater than the cost of care as an outpatient. Secondly, care in familiar surroundings or through visits to an outpatient center is, for most people, preferable to being in the hospital. However, sometimes, the use of hospital facilities and the presence of a skilled medical team are vital, as in the case of severe illness or injury or if a person with a chronic illness cannot be cared for at home.

Choice of therapies

The type of care or therapy that is most appropriate depends on the severity of an illness or injury. The element of choice is very important and health-care professionals always consider the personal wishes of the individual. At one extreme, an acute illness or a serious injury may require emergency admission to the hospital and possibly treatment in a critical care unit. At the other extreme, a stretched muscle may be treated with a short course of physiotherapy at a local outpatient center.

Some conventional therapies, such as physiotherapy and occupational therapy, are frequently used to help rehabilitate a person, often following an acute illness or injury. These rehabilitative therapies can also help people maintain their independence throughout a chronic illness. Equally important are psychological therapies, which are used to treat mental health problems, such as depression.

Complementary therapies have been used for hundreds of years and many attempt to cure disease by restoring harmony in the body. Although many therapies rely solely on tradition and anecdote as evidence of effectiveness, other complementary treatments, such as biofeedback and acupuncture, are backed by scientific research.

Care of the dying

Over the last few decades, there has been an increasing awareness that people who are dying have unique needs. As a result, caring for people with a terminal illness has become a medical specialty. The medical and nursing care that addresses the needs of people who are dying is known as palliative care, and its focus is on relieving distressing symptoms, including pain, nausea, and shortness of breath, with drugs and other techniques, such as complementary therapies and simple practical measures. The aim of palliative care is to provide a comfortable and dignified death.

PROCEDURE Care at home

If you have an illness or disability that does not require hospitalization, you will probably be cared for at home by a partner, close friend, or relative. Helping you with daily tasks, such as washing and dressing, does not necessarily require particular nursing skills. However, if you are very disabled, these tasks may require extra time and patience.

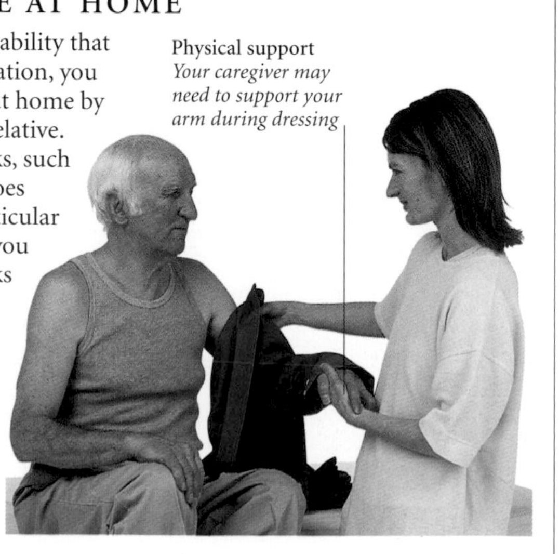

Physical support
Your caregiver may need to support your arm during dressing

Dressing and undressing
If you have a disability, such as a weak limb following a stroke, you may require help from your caregiver to dress and undress.

TREATMENT PROFESSIONAL CARE AND THERAPY

A wide range of care and therapies can be used to treat illness and disability. These include high-technology medicine, such as that provided in a critical care unit in the hospital, and treatments, such as physiotherapy, that aid rehabilitation. Complementary therapies, such as chiropractic and acupuncture, are also becoming popular.

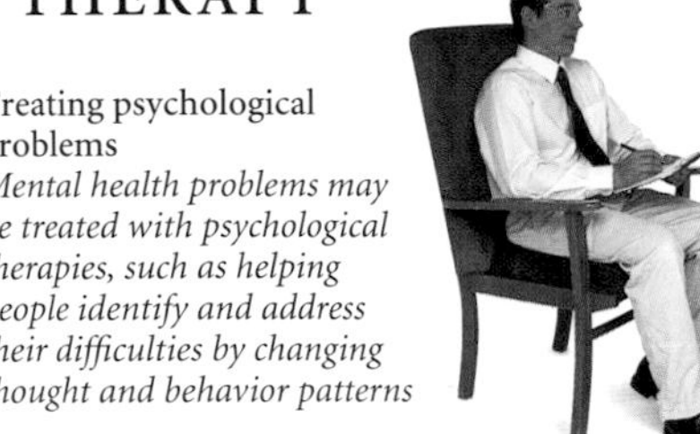

Treating psychological problems
Mental health problems may be treated with psychological therapies, such as helping people identify and address their difficulties by changing thought and behavior patterns

PSYCHOLOGICAL THERAPY

SPEECH THERAPY

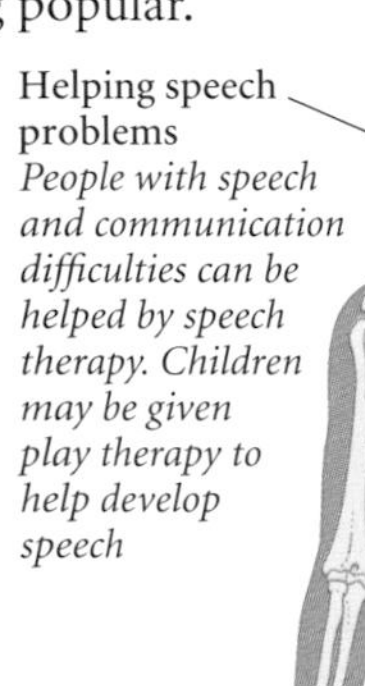

Helping speech problems
People with speech and communication difficulties can be helped by speech therapy. Children may be given play therapy to help develop speech

Supporting vital functions
In seriously ill people, vital functions such as breathing can become difficult. Critical care units have equipment that can perform life-saving functions

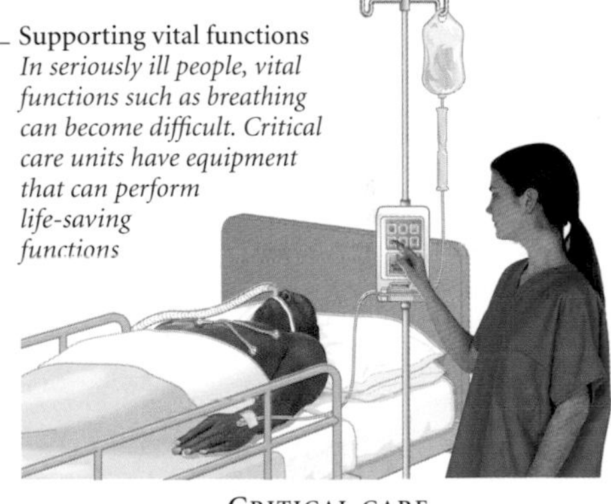

CRITICAL CARE

OCCUPATIONAL THERAPY

Teaching manual coordination
Conditions such as rheumatoid arthritis may affect a person's grip. An occupational therapist may suggest the use of helpful aids, such as a jar opener

Treating medical emergencies
An emergency, such as a cardiac arrest, may be treated at the scene by paramedics using life-saving equipment and resuscitation techniques

Aiding mobility
Stiff joints and muscle weakness can be treated with physical techniques such as massage and exercise. These techniques usually form part of a physiotherapy program

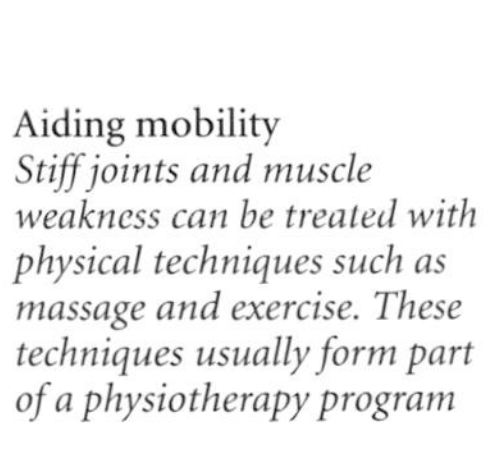

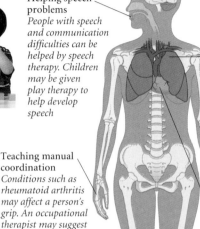

PHYSIOTHERAPY

EMERGENCY CARE

COMPLEMENTARY THERAPIES

Although doctors do not always fully understand exactly how complementary therapies work, many are now used in addition to conventional medicines and surgery. Some therapies may be especially helpful for conditions such as migraine and eczema, which are often difficult to treat conventionally.

Helpful complementary therapies
Chiropractic treatment, which is used mainly to relieve spine disorders such as back and neck pain, and acupuncture, which has been shown to be effective for all types of pain relief, are two therapies that are sometimes helpful.

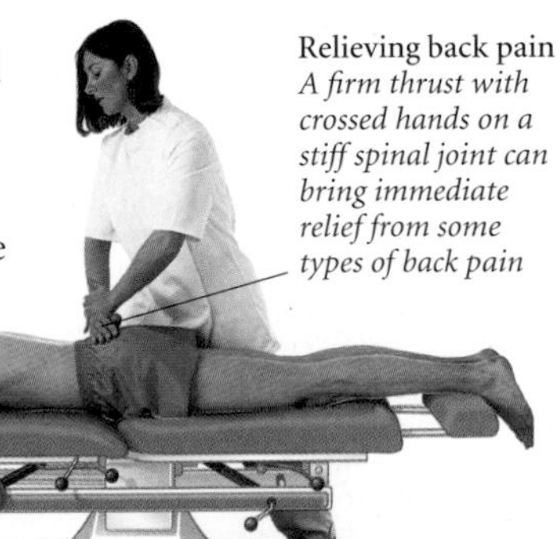

Relieving back pain
A firm thrust with crossed hands on a stiff spinal joint can bring immediate relief from some types of back pain

CHIROPRACTIC THERAPY

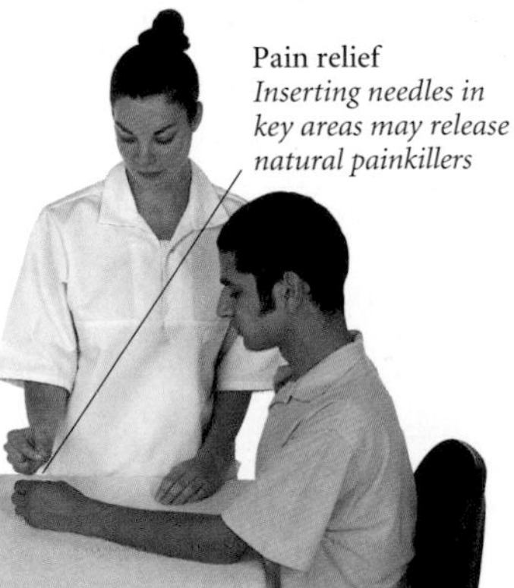

Pain relief
Inserting needles in key areas may release natural painkillers

ACUPUNCTURE

PATTERNS OF CARE

Many people require medical treatment or nursing care in the hospital at some time in their lives. However, recent advances in treatment and the high costs associated with hospital care have led to an increasing trend away from hospitalization and toward providing ambulatory care or care in the home.

This section covers different settings in which care and treatment are carried out, including centers for ambulatory care, hospitals, and the home. The section begins with an article about ambulatory care, which is treatment that can be carried out without the need for overnight hospitalization.

The next article on hospital care explains the reasons for admission to the hospital and the various ways in which it may happen, including emergency admission by ambulance. The different levels of care that are provided in the hospital are described. These include routine care, neonatal care for premature or very ill babies, and critical care after major surgery or during acute illness.

In the final article, the advantages of home care are discussed, with particular emphasis on the need for support for caregivers and the elderly, ill, or disabled people in their care.

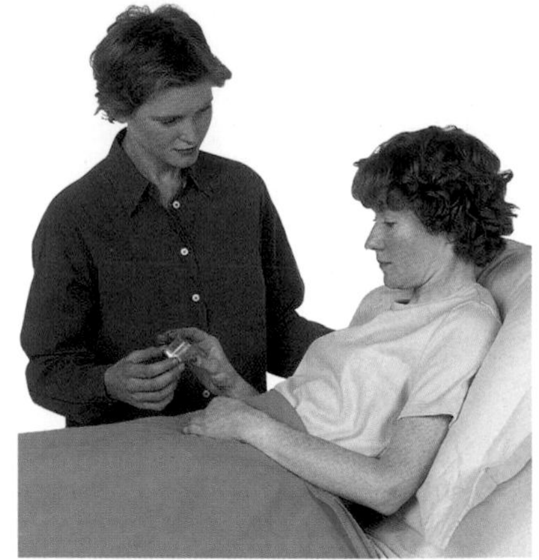

Care in the home
Treatments, such as medication, that do not require specialized equipment can often be administered just as effectively by a caregiver in the home as in the hospital.

Ambulatory care

Care performed in outpatient centers or hospital clinics that does not require an overnight stay in the hospital

Treatments and tests that are carried out without the need for hospital admission are described as ambulatory care. Ambulatory care is often available in a hospital clinic and is also provided in doctors' offices and independent outpatient centers that provide a wide range of services. These centers are usually equipped with the latest technology and are staffed by both doctors and nurses. Some ambulatory centers specialize in the treatment of particular conditions. For example, a person with end-stage kidney failure (p.708) may be treated at a renal dialysis center, and ambulatory surgical centers specialize in a number of minor surgical procedures.

WHAT PROCEDURES CAN BE PERFORMED?

Some of the most common procedures performed in hospital clinics and outpatient centers are tests, which may be done to confirm a diagnosis, screen for disease, or monitor the progress of an illness or the effectiveness of treatment. These tests range from simple blood and urine tests to more complex imaging tests, such as coronary angiography (p.408). The results are usually returned quickly, and they may be given to you while you are still at the center.

A wide range of surgical procedures is now performed in outpatient centers, and minor surgery is often carried out under local anesthesia (*see* HAVING A LOCAL ANESTHETIC, p.942). These procedures range from the removal of skin lesions or cysts to operations on the eye, such as cataract surgery (p.573).

Many operations use advanced surgical techniques that require only small incisions in the body. Even though general anesthesia may be necessary (*see* HAVING A GENERAL ANESTHETIC, p.944), you will be able to go home after your operation without an overnight stay. For example, one common procedure known as endoscopic surgery (p.948), in which a viewing instrument is inserted either through a natural body opening or through a tiny incision in the skin, is used for the removal of nasal polyps (p.476), hernia repairs (p.662), and tubal ligation (p.743).

Occasionally, an outpatient center or department is not able to provide sufficient or appropriate care, or you may be too ill for ambulatory care. In these circumstances, you will be admitted to the hospital for further tests and treatment (*see* HOSPITAL CARE, right).

Hospital care

Medical and nursing care carried out during hospitalization

Although the general trend in health care is toward ambulatory care (left) and home care (p.960), in some cases admission to the hospital is necessary. Inpatient care requires you to remain overnight in the hospital for a period of time ranging from 24 hours to weeks or, rarely, months. Hospitals are in a position to provide specialized nursing and medical care, as well as expertise and a wide range of treatments and technology not available elsewhere.

WHY MIGHT I BE ADMITTED?

You may be admitted to the hospital if you develop a serious illness that cannot be treated by your doctor without admission or if you sustain a severe injury. Hospitalization may also be required if you have a flare-up of a chronic disorder, such as asthma (p.483) or the inflammatory bowel condition Crohn's disease (p.658). Elderly people are particularly likely to be admitted to the hospital if their general health is poor.

Hospitalization is always necessary for major surgery. You may also need to be kept in the hospital after minor surgery if you have a condition such as a chronic heart or lung disorder that increases the risk of complications.

Children may be hospitalized for all of the above reasons. In addition, they may be admitted if parents feel unable to cope with their sick child or if a non-accidental injury is suspected. A child may also be admitted to the hospital if the doctor is in doubt about the cause of symptoms, such as a high temperature or abdominal pain.

You may need to be cared for in the hospital if you are living alone and become too ill to look after yourself adequately. However, long-term care for people who have a chronic or terminal illness is more commonly carried out in a hospice or nursing home.

HOW MIGHT I BE ADMITTED?

You may enter the hospital for scheduled treatment or as an emergency. An admission for scheduled treatment, such as the removal of varicose veins (*see* TREATING VARICOSE VEINS, p.439), is usually arranged by your doctor or through a hospital clinic or outpatient center. Admission may be planned in advance so that you have plenty of time to make the necessary arrangements. However, if your condition is serious and urgent treatment is necessary, you will be admitted sooner.

Sometimes, your doctor may arrange for an emergency admission. For example, if you have severe chest pain and your doctor is concerned that you are having a heart attack, he or she may call an ambulance to take you to the hospital immediately. If you suddenly become ill, you may go directly to the emergency room, or an ambulance may be called.

SETTING INSIDE AN AMBULANCE

Most emergency ambulances are fully equipped with first-aid and resuscitation equipment. The ambulance is staffed by paramedics who are trained in first-aid procedures and resuscitation techniques. Paramedics are able to carry out life-saving treatment at the scene of an accident, in a person's home, and during the trip to the hospital. Emergency treatment may include setting up intravenous infusions, administering oxygen or drugs such as analgesics, and beginning artificial respiration. Defibrillation, in which electric shocks are used to treat abnormal heart rhythms, may also be performed if necessary.

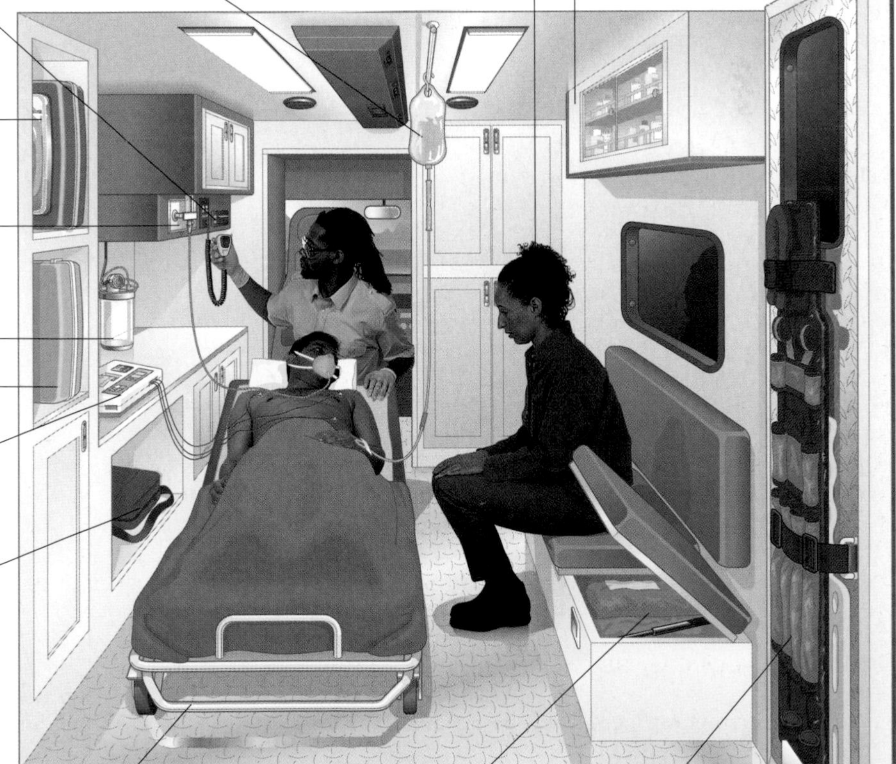
Radio/telephone
Communication between the paramedics, the hospital, and other emergency services is vital
Intravenous fluids
Essential fluids can be given intravenously
Relative
A family member or friend may be able to come with you
Medication cabinet
Drugs such as analgesics can be given by paramedics
Obstetric kit
A special emergency kit for delivering a baby is always kept on board the ambulance
Oxygen supply
Both piped and portable oxygen are available to treat a person with breathing difficulties
Suction equipment
This equipment is used to remove secretions from the mouth and airways
First aid supplies
All ambulances carry supplies such as bandages, dressings, and sterile gloves
ECG monitor
The monitor shows a tracing of electrical activity in the heart and can detect abnormalities
Defibrillator
This equipment delivers brief electric shocks to the heart to reestablish a normal heartbeat
Stretcher
The stretcher is secured into the ambulance. The backrest can be adjusted for comfort
Underseat storage
The space under seating is used as storage for traction splints and oxygen cylinders
Backboard
This long, straight board is used to immobilize a person who may have spinal injuries

Inside the ambulance
Specialized equipment and supplies are stored securely on either side of the ambulance to allow room for the patient, paramedic, and stretcher.

If your condition is serious, paramedics may begin treatment in the ambulance (*see* INSIDE AN AMBULANCE, p.957).

On arrival in the emergency room, you are initially assessed using a system known as triage. This system is designed to allow people who need urgent attention to be seen by a doctor before those with less serious problems.

WHAT ARE THE TYPES OF CARE?

The type of care you receive depends on your illness and which facilities are available in the hospital. Routine admissions are to a general patient unit, but, if you are severely ill, you may need treatment in a critical care unit (below). Children are usually cared for on pediatric units or in a pediatric hospital.

GENERAL PATIENT UNITS Most people are admitted to a general patient unit, which provides a wide range of routine care. Many units specialize in a branch of medicine or a particular type of disease. For example, if you have cancer, you may be admitted to a unit that specializes in cancer care.

Your care will almost always include tests and treatments. For example, you may have regular blood samples taken to check levels of particular substances in the blood, or you may have imaging tests, such as X-rays (p.244).

Any medication that may be needed is given on a regular schedule by a nurse, although some drugs, such as analgesics (p.912), are given as required. Your temperature, pulse, and blood pressure are measured at regular intervals and recorded on charts so that your doctor can monitor your progress. Depending on your illness, treatment may include surgery or a rehabilitation therapy such as physiotherapy (p.961).

Decisions about your care are made on medical rounds. The team of professionals who care for you will take time to discuss your condition with you and your family. This is an ideal opportunity to ask questions about the results of tests, your treatments, and progress, although the medical staff are usually available to discuss these aspects of your care at other times as well.

Visiting is encouraged, although visiting hours tend to vary from unit to unit. Some units allow visiting throughout

SETTING CRITICAL CARE UNIT

Most hospitals contain a critical care unit, also called an intensive care unit, that is devoted specifically to caring for people in a critical or unstable condition and who require continuous monitoring. Frequently, patients in these units require mechanical ventilation, in which a machine takes over or assists breathing. Blood pressure is checked continuously and heart rate and rhythm are monitored by an ECG machine. Fluids and must drugs are given intravenously and nutrients are supplied to the stomach through a tube.

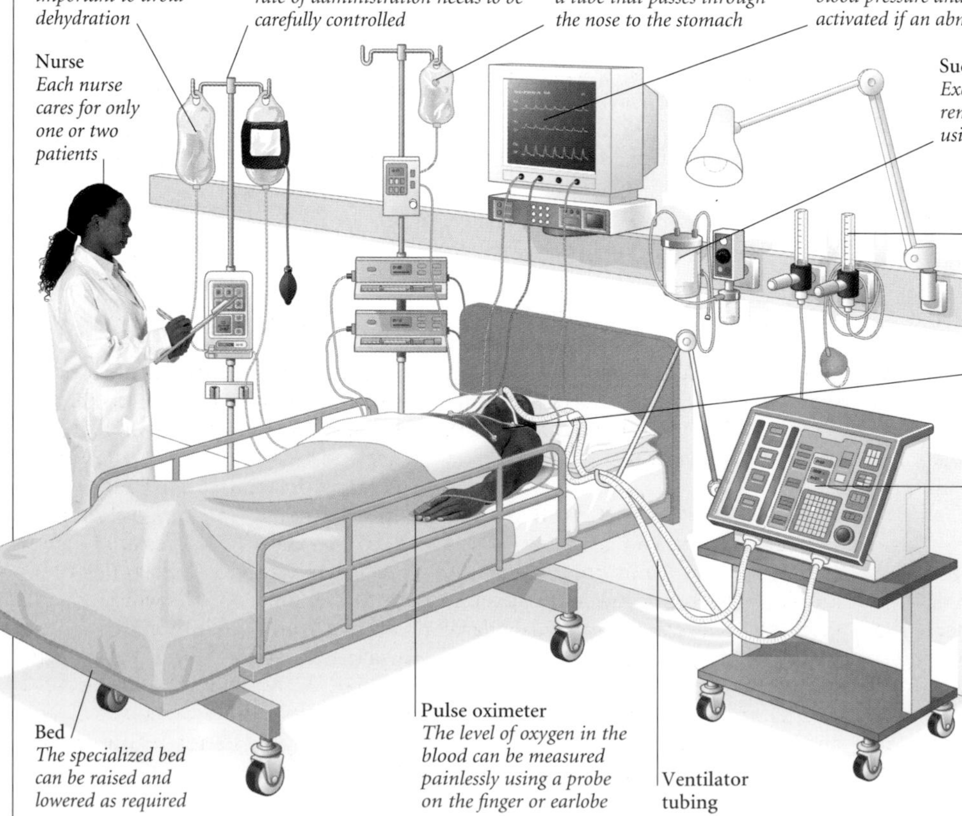
Intravenous fluids
Fluids are particularly important to avoid dehydration
Drug therapy
Different drugs may be given. The rate of administration needs to be carefully controlled
Nutrients
Liquid food is pumped into a tube that passes through the nose to the stomach
Monitor
The screen displays information such as the blood pressure and heart rate. An alarm is activated if an abnormality develops
Nurse
Each nurse cares for only one or two patients
Suction equipment
Excess secretions are regularly removed from the airways using suction
Oxygen supply
Every bed area has an oxygen supply available at all times
ECG electrodes
Electrodes on the chest detect the electrical activity of the heart, which is shown as a tracing on the monitor
Ventilator
This machine inflates the lungs with oxygen and air in order to maintain blood oxygen levels
Bed
The specialized bed can be raised and lowered as required
Pulse oximeter
The level of oxygen in the blood can be measured painlessly using a probe on the finger or earlobe
Ventilator tubing

Critical care equipment
Each bed in the unit is surrounded by technical equipment. Some machines are used to monitor the person's condition, while other equipment delivers drug treatment, maintains essential functions such as breathing, or supplies fluids and nutrients.

the day. However, after surgery, visiting may be restricted until you have recovered from an anesthetic (*see* HAVING A GENERAL ANESTHETIC, p.944).

CRITICAL CARE UNITS If you are critically ill and need intensive monitoring, you may be admitted to a critical care unit. These units differ from general patient units in that they are equipped with specialized technology for treating and monitoring people who are seriously ill. They also have a higher ratio of nurses to patients than general units.

People are most commonly admitted to a critical care unit for monitoring following major surgery, such as transplant surgery (p.952) or heart surgery, or during serious acute illness, such as a severe attack of asthma (p.483) or septicemia (p.298). Admission to a critical care unit is often necessary when someone has a head injury (p.521) or other major injuries following an accident.

Apart from the general critical care unit, there are also units that specialize in treating particular conditions. These include coronary care units, which are dedicated to treating people who require monitoring for heart problems. For example, if you have had a heart attack (*see* MYOCARDIAL INFARCTION, p.410), your doctor will need to monitor your progress or the effectiveness of treatment. Some hospitals also have critical care units for people with serious kidney, liver, or nervous system disorders. Babies who are premature or seriously ill are usually admitted to a critical care unit that specializes in their care (*see* NEONATAL CARE UNIT, right).

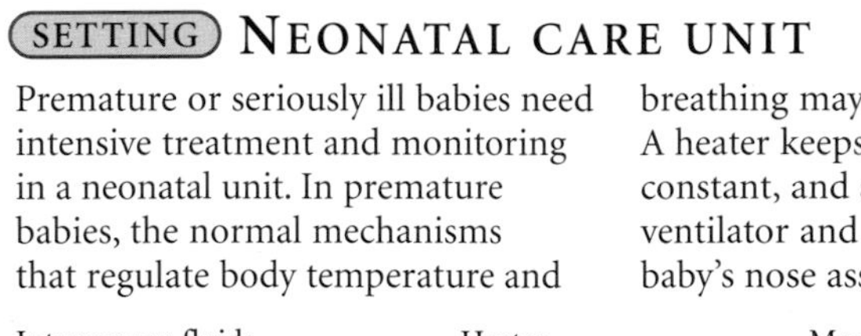

SETTING NEONATAL CARE UNIT

Premature or seriously ill babies need intensive treatment and monitoring in a neonatal unit. In premature babies, the normal mechanisms that regulate body temperature and breathing may not be fully developed. A heater keeps a baby's temperature constant, and a tube attached to a ventilator and passed through the baby's nose assists with breathing.

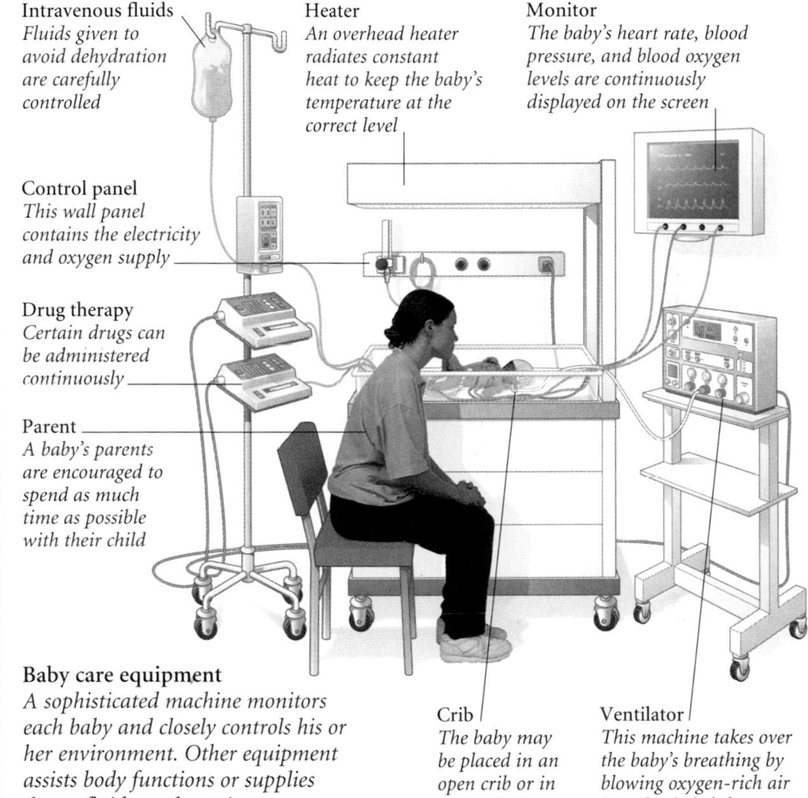
Intravenous fluids
Fluids given to avoid dehydration are carefully controlled
Heater
An overhead heater radiates constant heat to keep the baby's temperature at the correct level
Monitor
The baby's heart rate, blood pressure, and blood oxygen levels are continuously displayed on the screen
Control panel
This wall panel contains the electricity and oxygen supply
Drug therapy
Certain drugs can be administered continuously
Parent
A baby's parents are encouraged to spend as much time as possible with their child
Crib
The baby may be placed in an open crib or in an incubator
Ventilator
This machine takes over the baby's breathing by blowing oxygen-rich air into the baby's lungs

Baby care equipment
A sophisticated machine monitors each baby and closely controls his or her environment. Other equipment assists body functions or supplies drugs, fluids, and nutrients.

If you are seriously ill but are not in need of critical care, you may be admitted to an observation unit. These units provide care that is not as intensive as in critical care units, but they allow for a higher level of monitoring than on general patient units.

PEDIATRIC UNITS Children are almost always admitted to pediatric units that are staffed by doctors and nurses who specialize in child care. There is often a playroom attached to the unit because sick children need stimulation and the company of other children. There may also be play therapists to help children cope with their illness, and teachers may visit the unit in order to provide emotional support and help make up for missed time at school. Usually, a child's main concern is being separated from the family, and parents are encouraged to spend as much time as possible in the unit with their child. Facilities are often provided that enable parents to stay overnight near their child.

PREPARATION FOR DISCHARGE

Whatever the reason for your admission, doctors will not keep you in the hospital longer than necessary. In addition, doctors are always particularly anxious to avoid long hospital stays for children because hospitalization can be disruptive and upsetting for the child and his or her family.

The decision to discharge you from the hospital will be made after consultation with doctors and nurses involved in your care and will be discussed with you and your family. Ideally, the discharge is planned in advance so that prescriptions for drugs can be written and follow-up care arranged if needed.

Often, you will need no further care after discharge apart from follow-ups to check on your progress and recovery at an outpatient center or in your doctor's office. However, if you have a chronic illness or a disability as a result of illness, you may require rehabilitation, such as physiotherapy (p.961), which should improve your mobility and help you regain lost strength. You may also be assessed by an occupational therapist (*see* OCCUPATIONAL THERAPY, p.962), who may suggest some practical changes that can be made to your home to enable you to live more independently and cope with your illness.

Home care

Nursing care and medical treatment performed in a person's own home

The growing trend away from routine hospital admission is allowing many people to be treated at home. However, if hospitalization is unavoidable, early discharge is increasingly common, and care is often transferred to the home. In either case, care and treatment are performed by a team of people, which may include family caregivers or friends in addition to health care professionals. If you live alone, you may rely entirely on visiting nurses and other professionals.

The main advantages of home care are the proximity of family and friends and the convenience of being in familiar surroundings. Home care is often needed for a short time only, such as after minor surgery. However, long-term home care may be needed for people who have a chronic illness, such as Alzheimer's disease (p.536) or multiple sclerosis (p.541). Some people with a terminal illness choose to remain at home during the final few weeks of their lives (*see* CARING FOR A TERMINALLY ILL PERSON, p.965).

Preparing the home

Depending on the severity of your illness and the extent of your disability, you may need some practical adaptations to your home. These changes might be suggested by an occupational therapist or physiotherapist during your hospital stay (*see* HOSPITAL CARE, p.956) or by your doctor.

If you are only temporarily immobilized, as may occur after an injury such as a leg fracture, you may need to have wheelchair ramps placed over any steps in your home. Permanent immobility may mean that doorways need to be widened. If your mobility is severely restricted, as is frequently the case after a stroke (p.532), you may have equipment installed to help minimize the physical strain on your caregiver while assisting you to move around. For example, a lift can help move you between a chair and your bed or into the bathtub. In particular, adaptations to the bathroom may be necessary. These may involve installing a raised toilet seat, handrails, and specially adapted taps.

What are the types of care?

There is a wide range of care and treatments that can be performed in the home, including drug treatments, basic and specialist nursing care, and rehabilitation procedures. Some of these can be undertaken by you and your caregiver following advice from the health-care team. For other treatments, continuing supervision from nurses or therapists may be required, although many caregivers become expert at performing difficult procedures.

DRUG TREATMENT If you are recovering from an illness or have a chronic condition, you are likely to need medication. Drugs are usually taken orally, but you may need injections or a drug may be have to be taken using a nebulizer, which delivers drugs in aerosol form through a mask. Injected or nebulized drugs are usually first given by a nurse, but you or your caregiver may later be shown how to administer them on your own. If you have a heart or lung disorder, you may need to have oxygen at home to help you breathe (*see* HOME OXYGEN THERAPY, p.507).

NURSING CARE Nursing assistance may be required with washing and dressing, to prevent pressure sores (p.350) in a person who is immobile, and to change wound dressings and monitor healing. Sometimes, specialized support is needed. For example, if you have a stoma, an opening from the bowel that has been surgically created in the wall of your abdomen (*see* COLOSTOMY, p.666), you may be visited by a stoma nurse, who will teach you how to manage it.

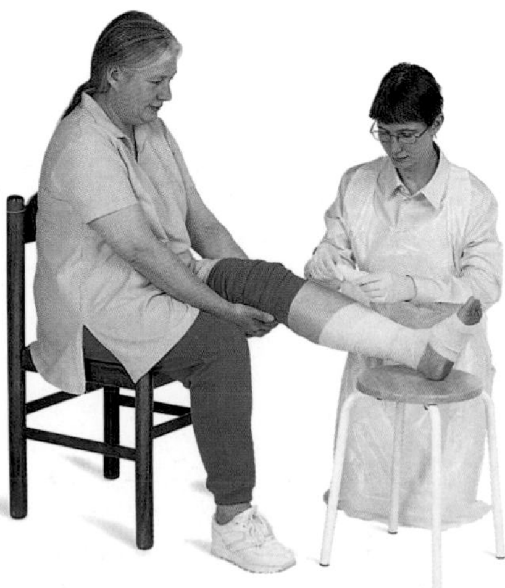

Changing a wound dressing
If necessary, a nurse can visit you regularly in your own home to change dressings and monitor the healing of a wound.

REHABILITATION After major surgery or a disabling illness such as a stroke, you may need intensive rehabilitation to restore as much function as possible. If rehabilitation is necessary, a physiotherapist will probably arrange for you to have a program of massage and exercise (*see* PHYSIOTHERAPY, p.961). It may be recommended that you have occupational therapy (p.962) or speech therapy (p.963), depending on which skills you have lost as a result of illness.

TECHNICAL TREATMENTS Advances in technology have made some kinds of medical equipment easy to use. As a result, treatments such as kidney dialysis (p.707) can sometimes be carried out at home. If you are unable to eat, nasogastric feeding, in which liquid nutrients are pumped through a nasal tube to the stomach, may also be done at home.

You as caregiver

As the partner, relative, or friend of someone who is ill, you may have made a conscious decision to become a caregiver. However, sometimes the role is taken on gradually as an ill, disabled, or elderly person becomes less able to cope. The role of caregiver can be physically and emotionally demanding, and, after a while, you may begin to neglect your own health because of your other responsibilities. In addition, you may feel resentful because the demands of caregiving inevitably bring about a loss of freedom. It is therefore important that you focus on your own need for support. By joining a local support group, you will be able to share experiences with people in a similar situation.

Eventually, some caregivers find that they have to reevaluate their role. There is no shame in admitting that you are having difficulty coping, and it may be helpful to discuss your problems with your doctor, counselor, or social worker. It is sometimes difficult to accept, but there may come a time when full-time care in a nursing home or hospice has become the more suitable option for the person in your care.

(WWW) ONLINE SITES: p.1033

REHABILITATION THERAPIES

Rehabilitation therapies enable people to lead independent lives, either after an illness or injury or because of a problem present since birth. Some therapies are useful in treating children with developmental problems. Although some of these therapies may be started in the hospital, treatment frequently continues at home.

This section describes three major types of therapy used in rehabilitation: physiotherapy, occupational therapy, and speech and language therapy. Rehabilitation may involve more than one type of therapy, and usually a program is developed to meet an individual's needs and circumstances. The goal of physiotherapy is to improve mobility and maintain the normal function of the body using physical techniques, such as exercise, massage, hydrotherapy, heat and cold treatments, and ultrasound therapy.

Occupational therapy helps people who have physical or mental illnesses cope with everyday living. Treatment allows those affected to remain as independent as possible. Speech therapy may be used to help children and adults with problems that impair their ability to communicate.

Assisting recovery
A variety of rehabilitation therapies can be used to relieve pain, speed the process of recovery, and help an individual regain independence after an injury or illness.

Physiotherapy

The use of physical techniques, such as exercise and massage, to restore or maintain mobility and function

Physiotherapy, also called physical therapy, is used to restore muscle strength and flexibility and improve physical mobility after surgery, injury, or illness. It may also be used to help a person with a chronic disorder, such as arthritis (p.374), maintain normal use of the body. Physiotherapy can help relieve pain and prevent complications from developing after an operation or illness.

Physiotherapy is often combined with other treatments, such as drugs and occupational therapy (p.962).

WHAT DOES IT INVOLVE?

The physiotherapist starts by taking a detailed medical history and evaluating your condition. Assessment may involve determining the strength and flexibility of your muscles, how well you are able to get in and out of bed, and whether you are able to walk unaided or need to use a cane, walker, or wheelchair. The therapist devises an individual treatment plan using one or more physiotherapy techniques. These may include exercise, massage, hydrotherapy, heat and cooling treatments, electrical stimulation, ultrasound, and gait training. A form of therapy called chest physiotherapy may also be used to prevent chest infections in people who are particularly vulnerable because of illness or surgery.

EXERCISE Usually, the goal of exercise therapy is to strengthen weak muscles and increase flexibility. Exercise therapy is useful for anyone who has reduced movement in a limb, which may occur after being confined to bed following knee surgery or after the limb has been immobilized to treat a fracture. In addition, anyone who has been confined to bed for more than a few days with a serious or chronic illness is likely to have lost muscle bulk and will benefit from exercise. Your therapist may show you exercises that you can do on your own, or, if you are unable to move a joint or limb, the therapist may manipulate it to extend your range of movement. Equipment such as weights, treadmills, and stationary bicycles may be used during an exercise program.

HEAT AND COOLING TREATMENTS A physiotherapist uses heat to treat muscle injuries and joint stiffness caused by excessive exercise or arthritis. The application of hot packs to the affected area stimulates blood flow, relaxes tense muscles, and relieves pain. Cold treatments using ice or cold packs may be used to reduce pain and swelling.

MASSAGE Physiotherapists use specialized massage tools or their hands to knead muscles and stroke the body using circular or long, sweeping motions. Massage stimulates blood flow, which helps reduce inflammation and relieve fluid retention and may also increase the suppleness of the skin. Therapists often use massage techniques to promote relaxation, which in turn helps relieve local pain and muscle spasm.

HYDROTHERAPY This form of therapy usually takes place in a heated pool and uses water to support the body, making movements easier or providing resistance to motion during exercise. Gentle exercise helps improve muscle strength, flexibility, and general fitness. Hydrotherapy is helpful if you are unable to bear weight on a limb because of injury or a disorder such as arthritis.

ELECTRICAL STIMULATION In this type of therapy, a mild electric current is passed through pads applied to the surface of the skin to generate heat that relieves stiffness and improves mobility in joints affected by injury or illness.

ULTRASOUND In this form of therapy, high-energy sound waves are used to create heat to help ease pain and relieve inflammation in the area being treated. This technique is often used to treat

TECHNIQUE CHEST PHYSIOTHERAPY

Several techniques, including chest clapping and breathing exercises, are used in chest physiotherapy to prevent the accumulation of mucus in the lungs, which may otherwise lead to a chest infection. Chest physiotherapy is commonly used in elderly people who have had major surgery and in children with the inherited disorder cystic fibrosis.

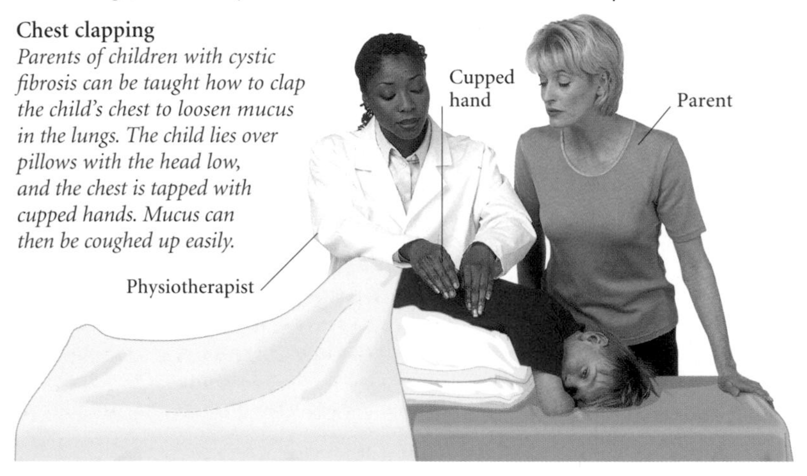
Cupped hand
Parent
Physiotherapist

Chest clapping
Parents of children with cystic fibrosis can be taught how to clap the child's chest to loosen mucus in the lungs. The child lies over pillows with the head low, and the chest is tapped with cupped hands. Mucus can then be coughed up easily.

soft tissue injuries involving a ligament, tendon, or muscle and may be given in several sessions. A gel is applied to the skin, and an ultrasound probe is placed on the skin and moved over the area being treated. After each session of ultrasound therapy, you may experience a slight tingling in the affected area.

GAIT TRAINING This training is used to help a person walk again after an injury or an illness such as a stroke (p.532) or if there is a chronic disability. A person may be taught to use equipment that provides support for the upper body while building up strength in the legs.

CHEST PHYSIOTHERAPY This form of physiotherapy is used to help prevent chest infections in people who have had major surgery or who have an illness that prevents them from clearing their lungs. In particular, elderly people who have had a major operation and children with the inherited disorder cystic fibrosis (p.824) may accumulate mucus in their lungs, which may lead to infection. A physiotherapist may show an affected person how to do breathing and coughing exercises that fill the lungs with air and expand the chest. Some techniques involve lying in a position that allows mucus to drain from the lungs while the chest is tapped (*see* CHEST PHYSIOTHERAPY, above). If your child needs regular chest physiotherapy, you may be taught to perform these techniques at home.

WHAT CAN I EXPECT?

After a minor injury, a short course of physiotherapy may be all you need to restore mobility. However, you may require long-term treatment for a major injury or illness. Physiotherapy can prevent a chronic condition from worsening or complications from developing.

(WWW) ONLINE SITES: p.1036

Occupational therapy

Treatment to encourage independence following a physical illness or injury or in people with a mental health disorder

The purpose of occupational therapy is to help a person with a physical or mental health problem be as independent as possible. The therapy is tailored to each individual's needs and may include help with daily tasks such as dressing, bathing, driving, food preparation, and going to the toilet. It can also help a person who is returning to work after a long illness or severe injury and help children with a disability to develop their full potential. Usually, referral for occupational therapy comes from your own doctor or a hospital doctor. Occupational therapy is incorporated in a comprehensive treatment plan, which may also include drugs and physiotherapy (p.961).

WHEN IS IT USED?

Occupational therapy is used to help people cope with everyday living if simple tasks have become difficult because of a chronic disorder, such as multiple sclerosis (p.541) or arthritis (p.374). It is also used to aid recovery following hand or upper arm injuries or after a major illness such as a stroke (p.532). An occupational therapist teaches a person how to conserve energy by using specialized techniques for daily tasks. A person may be shown how to use different muscles to carry out actions or to work with assistive aids.

Children who have learning difficulties or problems with coordination can benefit from occupational therapy. This form of therapy also helps elderly people remain independent and active and may make enough difference to allow a person to stay in his or her own home.

Occupational therapy is also useful for individuals with a mental health problem such as schizophrenia (p.560). Once the main symptoms of the illness are under control, occupational therapy can help a person cope with living in the community by gradually increasing his or her independence, providing support, and preventing relapse.

Walking aid
The choice of walking aid depends on the type and extent of the disability, and needs may change during recovery. An occupational therapist provides guidance on using the equipment.

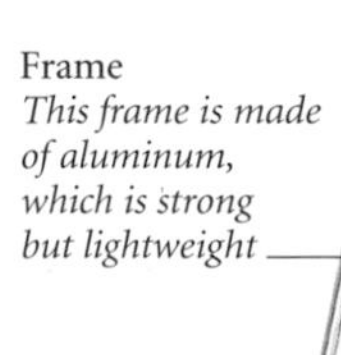

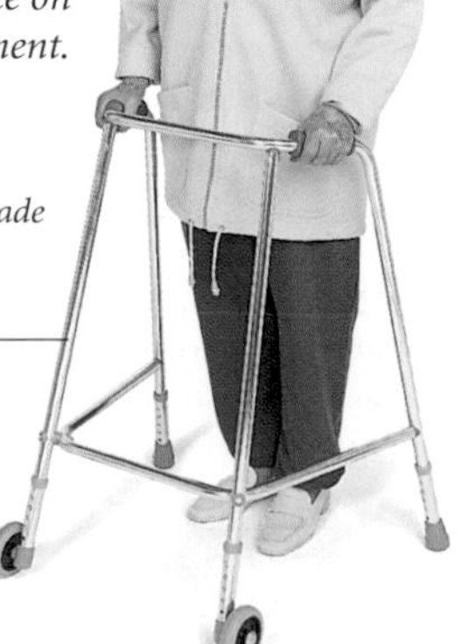

Frame
This frame is made of aluminum, which is strong but lightweight

Wheels
A wheeled walker helps a person who is too weak to lift the frame

What does it involve?

At your first consultation, the occupational therapist starts by assessing your current health problems and past medical history. The therapist may arrange to visit you at home to observe how you manage with routine activities, such as dressing and bathing. The therapist may also ask you to perform specific tasks, such as making a hot drink. If your child needs to have occupational therapy, he or she is likely to be assessed by an occupational therapist who specializes in treating children.

Your occupational therapist will plan a program of therapy based on his or her initial assessment. The program may include therapeutic activities and practical exercises to improve your ability to perform daily tasks. Your therapist may suggest or provide specialized equipment to make certain tasks easier.

PRACTICAL WORK If you need to build muscle strength, stamina, and concentration, your occupational therapist may recommend a practical activity such as a handicraft or cooking. For example, after a stroke, you may initially find it difficult to write. An activity such as woodworking can help build strength and improve fine muscle control, which may help you regain near-normal dexterity and coordination.

HELP WITH AIDS AND EQUIPMENT Your occupational therapist can provide a wide range of equipment to help you increase your independence. For example, items such as slings or splints can help provide support for a weakened part of the upper body. If you have a chronic disorder that restricts mobility, you may need to use a walking aid. Some adaptations to your home, such as raised chairs, handrails, or a stairlift, may be necessary. You may be offered specially adapted devices that can help make everyday tasks, such as opening jars, dressing, and eating, easier.

What can I expect?

Your occupational therapist may see you several times to monitor your progress and ensure that treatment is effective. Depending on your disability, occupational therapy may help restore some or all of your independence fairly rapidly.

(WWW) ONLINE SITES: p.1036

Speech therapy

Treatment to help people develop, improve, or recover their ability to speak

Speech therapy is used to help adults and children who have problems with verbal communication. Speech therapy can benefit children whose speech is delayed by impaired hearing or learning difficulties or a physical problem such as a cleft lip and palate (p.862).

Adults and children with a fluency problem, such as stuttering, may also be given speech therapy, as may people who forget words or have comprehension problems after a stroke (p.532). A speech problem with a physical cause, such as cancer of the larynx (p.481), may be helped by exercises or artificial aids.

What does it involve?

At your first appointment, your speech therapist will assess the extent of your speech problem and evaluate the practical effect it is having on your daily life. For children, the assessment is usually through observation of play. Adults are assessed on the basis of their ability to carry on a general conversation as well as specific tasks, such as describing a picture. Part of the assessment may be recorded on a computer to enable it to be analyzed fully later. A recorded sample of conversation is used to determine whether your speech patterns, vocabulary, and the pitch range and volume of your voice conform to normal ranges.

The approach used in speech therapy depends on the problem, its cause, and the age of the person affected. Play therapy is frequently used to help children improve their speech and is likely to be combined with other approaches, such as voice exercises. Therapy for a child usually involves parents or caregivers who are taught useful exercises and games so that the child's speech improvement can continue at home.

Adults may be taught voice exercises or how to use artificial devices to aid communication. Speech difficulties that have been caused by a neurological problem, such as a stroke, may be initially overcome by learning simple ways of communicating with other people. For example, you may be taught body signals or given a chart to indicate basic needs until you are able to speak again.

PLAY THERAPY Children are frequently treated for speech problems using play therapy and games and by encouraging them to use both verbal and nonverbal communication. The speech therapist may teach parents or caregivers how to encourage speech development at home by playing games that incorporate verbal description or naming.

EXERCISES If you have a condition that affects the mouth, tongue, or larynx (voice box), you may be taught exercises to help improve your articulation. For disorders that affect your fluency, you may be shown exercises to help you control your speech and make you feel less anxious. If you have speech difficulties as a result of damage to the brain, such as a stroke, you may need to do exercises, such as describing pictures, to improve your word-retrieval abilities. In cases in which the larynx has been damaged or removed to treat cancer, a person can be taught to produce speech sounds by trapping air in the esophagus and gradually releasing it.

USE OF ARTIFICIAL DEVICES There are a number of different electronic voice-synthesizers and artificial voice aids that may be used if speech problems are the result of a major physical problem. For example, if the larynx has been removed as part of treatment for cancer, you may be taught to speak using a hand-held electromechanical device that generates sounds when it is held against the neck. Alternatively, you may be fitted with a device called a tracheoesophageal implant. This device is inserted between the windpipe and the esophagus and uses inhaled air to produce sound. The sounds produced by the device can be converted into normal speech sounds using the lips, tongue, and teeth.

What can I expect?

Some problems, such as mild articulation problems, may improve with only a few weekly sessions of speech therapy. For other, more serious problems, regular speech therapy sessions over several months or years may be needed. Early treatment for children is particularly important because delayed speech affects the ability to relate to other people and may cause learning difficulties.

(WWW) ONLINE SITES: p.1036, p.1037

DEATH AND DYING

For many people, coming to terms with death is the most difficult challenge of their lives. In some cases, death is unexpected, but more often it is the end result of an incurable, progressive illness. Whatever the cause, a point is reached when a cure becomes impossible and the goal of medical treatment changes.

During the last weeks of life, active treatment of a disease itself is usually stopped, and treatment is directed at the relief of symptoms and getting the most from the life that remains. This section initially addresses preparations for death, taking into account personal choices and values. Caring for a person who has a terminal illness is covered next. With the support of professionals who are skilled in terminal care, it is usually possible for family and friends to improve the quality of life of a dying person during the final stages of illness.

Finally, the period following death is discussed. This is a time when there are many practical issues to consider, such as arranging the funeral and registering the death, at the same time as dealing with grief. Bereavement is covered in more detail elsewhere (*see* LOSS AND BEREAVEMENT, p.76).

After a death

Coming to terms with a death may be a slow and difficult process. It is important to address your feelings and accept practical and emotional support from other people.

Practical preparations for death

Personal and practical decisions affecting a dying person that can be made before death occurs

A person who has come to terms with a terminal illness may wish to become involved in planning the final stages of his or her life and deciding what should happen after death. These preparations may include thinking about where to die, specific personal wishes concerning final medical care, planning burial arrangements, and arranging finances and updating a will. There will probably be many questions that a terminally ill person would like answered, such as when death might occur, how it will happen, and what it will feel like. A person facing death should be given every opportunity to ask health-care professionals about these concerns, and he or she should be encouraged to discuss these issues with family and friends.

Children close to the dying person need to receive special support and consideration. Very young children may not realize that death is permanent, but by about age 5 more than half of them fully understand. Children should be involved and informed because what is imagined is often worse than reality.

MAKING CHOICES

Many people who are terminally ill have strong views about whether they would prefer to die in the hospital, in a hospice, or in their own home. Personal attitudes and preferences should ideally be established at an early stage so that terminal care can be planned with an individual's involvement and cooperation. If a dying person decides to be nursed at home, care can often be carried out by family members or close friends with the ongoing support and advice of skilled health-care professionals.

ADVANCE DIRECTIVES

Every adult, whether they are dying in the hospital or at home, has the right to certain choices about his or her medical care. For example, an individual may wish to state how far he or she wants the hospital medical team to proceed with resuscitation if heartbeat or breathing suddenly stops.

An advance directive is a document in which these preferences are expressed (*see* WRITING AN ADVANCE DIRECTIVE, right). Doctors caring for a person who has written an advance directive should be made aware of its existence, and the document should be consulted when the person is no longer able to make decisions him- or herself. Some provinces in Canada now recognize the legality of these documents, although particular terminology and restrictions vary. To strengthen the validity of an advance directive, it should be prepared and discussed with the help of an attorney, a doctor, and family members.

(WWW) ONLINE SITES: p.1029

SELF-HELP WRITING AN ADVANCE DIRECTIVE

An advance directive is a written statement expressing your personal values, beliefs, and wishes related to medical treatment and dying. Any or all of the following issues may be included:

- The name of a nominated person who knows your wishes and intentions, and who will assist in making critical medical decisions if you cannot.
- A statement of preference for treatments and procedures aimed at improving quality of life.
- Refusal of specific treatments or procedures that unnecessarily prolong life in the case of an incurable, advanced illness.
- Specified circumstances in which no life-sustaining treatment, such as resuscitation or mechanical ventilation, should be given.
- Your wishes regarding organ donation after your death.

Caring for a terminally ill person

Relieving distress and discomfort during the final stages of life

For all people with a terminal illness, there comes a time when treatment for the disease itself no longer has a realistic chance of producing a cure and may cause harmful or unpleasant side effects. From this moment on, treatment with curative intent may be gradually withdrawn, and care is aimed at achieving a comfortable death for the individual, avoiding distressing symptoms, and providing a reassuring and comfortable environment in which to spend the last days or weeks of life.

Once it is established that an illness is incurable, issues such as where death will take place, how pain will be controlled, and fear of death itself will undoubtedly cause anxiety for both the affected person and his or her family. To address these issues, health-care professionals trained to relieve the distress caused by terminal illness usually work in partnership with the family.

Caring for children with a terminal illness

Caring for a dying child is an intensely emotional and harrowing experience for everyone involved. Many children are looked after at home during the final stages of an illness because parents often wish to carry out the care themselves. Effective communication is vital, and it is particularly important that parents are able to discuss the illness openly and honestly with the child.

Increasingly, resources are being established to help parents come to terms with the experience of caring for a dying child. These resources are able to address particular problems, such as difficulty in assessing pain and distress in children who are too young or too ill to communicate effectively. Parents can be taught to recognize certain nonverbal cues, such as facial expression and body language, that may indicate an increase in the level of pain.

Parents with dying children may find it helpful to contact specialist support groups and to meet other parents who are in a similar situation.

Accepting death

One of the most difficult aspects of terminal illness for both the dying person and family and friends is the actual acceptance of imminent death. When a terminal illness is diagnosed, many people initially express disbelief and distress. These feelings may recur but are generally replaced by acceptance.

For the terminally ill person, chronic pain, fear of the moment of death, and overwhelming anxiety (*see* ANXIETY DISORDERS, p.551) may contribute to his or her distress, hopelessness, and sadness. The doctor may prescribe antidepressant drugs (p.916) or antianxiety drugs (p.916). However, anxiety and depression can often be relieved by open, honest discussion and support. Family and friends may also become anxious or sad and need emotional support.

Relieving symptoms

Many people who have a terminal illness experience some degree of pain. Depending on the nature of the illness, a dying person may also have other symptoms, such as shortness of breath and nausea. In most people, all of these symptoms can be relieved using drug therapy or, in some cases, simple practical measures (*see* RELIEVING SYMPTOMS IN A TERMINALLY ILL PERSON, p.966).

CONTROLLING PAIN Most pain can be relieved with analgesics (p.912). Treatment is aimed at achieving excellent pain control with minimum side effects (*see* PAIN, p.516). This generally requires taking pain medications on a regular basis. In some cases, even if pain is well controlled, there may still be sudden episodes of "break-through" pain requiring extra doses of pain medication.

RELIEVING SHORTNESS OF BREATH A person who has a terminal illness may experience difficulty breathing. This is often the result of a serious lung disorder, such as pneumonia (p.490), or because fluid collects around the lungs. If there is an underlying infection, antibiotics (p.885) may help relieve the symptoms. In many cases, shortness of breath can be alleviated by small doses of an opiate analgesic drug, such as morphine. Opiate drugs may also help relieve pain and anxiety, which often worsen shortness of breath. Although occasionally, there is fear expressed of addiction to opiates, addition is not a cause for concern in the treatment of a person with a terminal illness.

CONTROLLING NAUSEA AND VOMITING Nausea and vomiting may have many causes. Constipation is a common one. Other causes are the disease itself and side effects of certain drugs, such as strong analgesics (p.912) or anticancer drugs (p.907). Usually, the nausea from strong analgesics resolves itself in a few days. Antiemetic drugs (p.922) usually relieve nausea if given regularly and should also help prevent vomiting. Antiemetics are usually taken orally, but, if vomiting is severe, they can be given as an injection or as a suppository.

It is uncommon that persons with terminal illness, especially those with advanced cancer, develop a complete blockage of the intestines. However, when it does occur, it can be distressing. Various methods of treatment are available to deal with this. These include medications and procedures such as inserting a small tube through the skin into the stomach in order to drain it. This procedure is quick and not very painful and can provide much relief.

PREVENTING THIRST Regular intake of fluid, even if only sips of ice water, may help prevent the discomfort caused by thirst and dehydration. If fluids cannot be taken by mouth, some people may benefit from hydration through an intravenous drip.

CARING FOR THE SKIN The skin should be kept clean and dry for hygiene and comfort. A regular change of position prevents sore skin (*see* PRESSURE SORES, p.350). However, if movement is severely restricted, specially designed beds and mattresses that aid nursing and provide comfort are available.

PREVENTING GASTROINTESTINAL PROBLEMS Constipation (p.628) is common in a terminally ill person and may lead to bloating and abdominal discomfort. Constipation is usually due to the disease, lack of mobility, and side effects of certain drugs. The doctor may prescribe laxatives (p.924), either as pills or suppositories, to help prevent constipation. Diarrhea (p.627) is rare unless

TREATMENT RELIEVING SYMPTOMS IN A TERMINALLY ILL PERSON

Certain symptoms are often experienced during the final stages of a terminal illness. The most common ones are pain, dry mouth, nausea, anxiety, and shortness of breath. These symptoms can usually be relieved using drugs or other therapies, which often require the support of professionals. However, there are also practical measures that can be performed by caregivers to make a person as comfortable as possible.

ALLEVIATING PAIN

In the majority of people, pain can be effectively controlled, both at home and in the hospital or hospice, by using oral analgesics (p.912), such as morphine. If a person is unable to take oral pain medications, the medication can be given under the skin using special portable pumps.

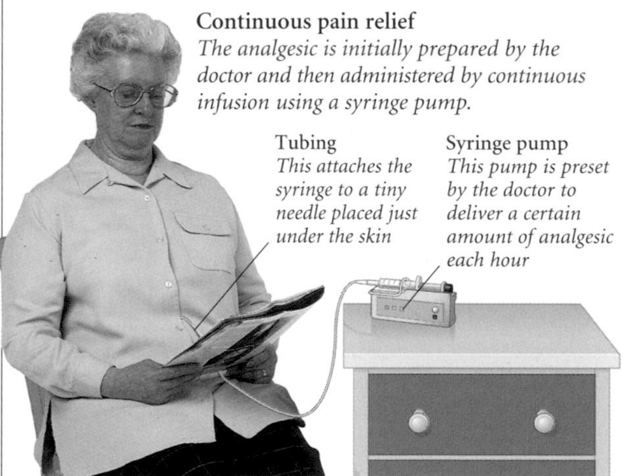

Continuous pain relief
The analgesic is initially prepared by the doctor and then administered by continuous infusion using a syringe pump.

Tubing
This attaches the syringe to a tiny needle placed just under the skin

Syringe pump
This pump is preset by the doctor to deliver a certain amount of analgesic each hour

RELIEVING A DRY MOUTH

Dryness of the lips and tongue often develops if a person is not drinking very much fluid. You can help keep a person's mouth moist by administering mouthwashes and regularly brushing his or her teeth. Fresh or canned pineapple is very effective for treating a dry tongue.

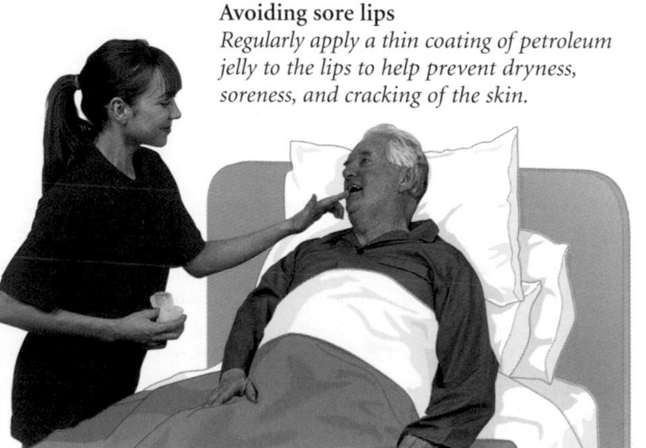

Avoiding sore lips
Regularly apply a thin coating of petroleum jelly to the lips to help prevent dryness, soreness, and cracking of the skin.

AVOIDING NAUSEA

About half of all people who have a terminal illness feel nauseated, which may in turn lead to vomiting and loss of appetite. In some cases, antiemetic drugs (p.922) can be prescribed by the doctor to relieve nausea and vomiting. In addition, you should avoid offering heavy meals to a very ill person and try to keep food smells to a minimum.

Palatable foods
A person who feels nauseated should not be pressed with regular meals. He or she may find snacks or nourishing fluids, such as soups, more palatable.

MINIMIZING ANXIETY

Complementary therapies, such as aromatherapy and massage, can be effective methods of relieving anxiety and discomfort. Gentle massage can trigger the release of endorphins, the body's natural painkillers. Touch can also encourage feelings of well-being and comfort.

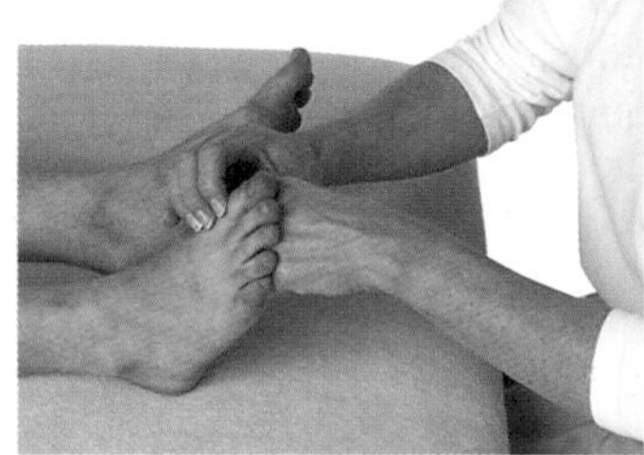

Foot massage
Massaging the feet can aid relaxation, relieve stress, and promote sleep. Using a massage oil or body lotion, apply gentle pressure to the sole of each foot in turn using your thumbs or knuckles.

EASING SHORTNESS OF BREATH

Severe shortness of breath can be alarming for both the terminally ill person and for his or her family. Positioning the person comfortably and administering continuous or intermittent oxygen through a face mask can usually help relieve shortness of breath. Use a portable electric fan to keep the air circulating around the room.

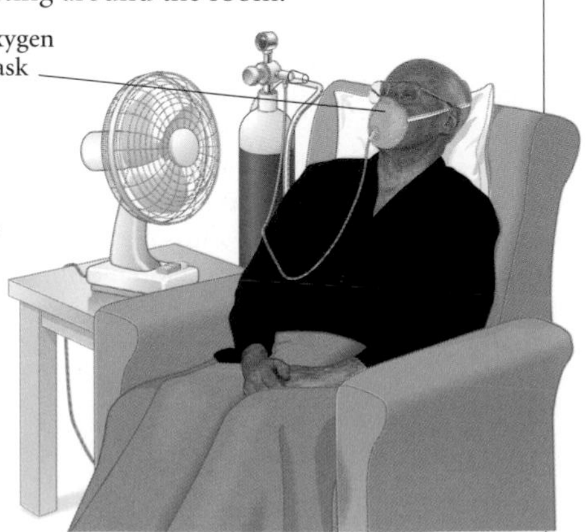

Oxygen mask

Helping with breathing
Careful positioning is important to allow a person's chest to expand freely for breathing. Many people find it helpful to sit upright, either in a chair or in a bed, well supported by firm pillows.

there is an underlying bowel disorder. It is important to rule out constipation with an "overflow" diarrhea.

The last stage of terminal illness

The final stage of a terminal illness can be emotionally and physically exhausting for the family and other caregivers. If a dying person is conscious and alert, he or she may be able to participate in care and assist with basic needs, such as washing, ensuring an adequate fluid intake, and assessing pain. Familiar faces and comfortable, reassuring surroundings are a great help to a dying person during this time. Many people choose to die at home, and palliative care services may be arranged for nursing care and support for the family.

As death approaches, a dying person may spend increasing amounts of time asleep. He or she may become confused and may then slip into unconsciousness. Much care is required at this stage. If terminal care is taking place in the home, homecare nurses may increase their support for the family both practically and emotionally, in particular by providing help so that caregivers are able to have a break. If the family feels unable to cope at home, a dying person can be admitted to a hospice or palliative care unit if this is available.

During the final stage of terminal illness, drug treatment is reviewed by the doctor and medication that is no longer needed may be stopped. Analgesics will probably be continued, even if the person appears to be unresponsive. Drugs that were being given orally may need to be given by injection at this stage. Most of these drugs can be given under the skin (subcutaneously).

As the moment of death approaches, shortness of breath may worsen, and breathing sounds may become noisier. Frequently, the dying person is deeply unconscious at this point, although some people remain conscious until the last moment, when breathing finally ceases and death occurs.

For everyone concerned, the period leading up to death is a distressing time. However, for many people who have been bereaved, a peaceful death can make the grieving process easier.

WWW ONLINE SITES: p.1029

What happens after a death

Practical procedures and emotional experiences that follow a death

Although the time following a death is emotionally distressing for the bereaved family, there are certain practical procedures that must be followed. If family members feel unable to cope with this aspect of a death, professional help is available. In many cases, the practical procedures that need to be dealt with after a death have already been discussed within a family, and an advance statement of the deceased's wishes may have been prepared (*see* PRACTICAL PREPARATIONS FOR DEATH, p.964). This forward planning can help relieve the strain of decision-making for bereaved relatives.

Organ donation is usually only an option if a person who was previously healthy dies suddenly in an accident. A family may be approached by a member of the medical staff to discuss their own views and those of their deceased relative, if known. Although it may be distressing to be asked to consider such issues so soon after death, organ donation is often a rewarding experience for the family in the long term.

Filing the death certificate

The doctor issues a death certificate, which states the cause of death. This also applies if the deceased had been cared for in a nursing home or the hospital, where the doctor usually files the death certificate with the appropriate agency and the funeral director is contacted. In certain circumstances, such as when the death was unexpected or the person is unknown to any caregiver, the doctor refers the death to the coroner, who will then deal with the death certificate. After considering the circumstances, the coroner may decide that a postmortem examination is needed to confirm the cause of death. In rare cases, if death appears not to have been due to natural causes, further steps may be taken.

Arranging the funeral

Most families ask a funeral director to take care of the practical arrangements. Many funeral directors are able to offer advice and suggestions for the funeral and provide information about the formal procedures involved. In some cases, these arrangements can be made in advance with the participation of the dying person and his or her family. Funeral directors may also make preparations for family members to see the deceased for a last time, especially if they did not have the opportunity to say goodbye at the time of death.

It is possible to arrange a funeral to suit personal preferences, religions, and cultural practices, but ideally this should be discussed and clarified at an early stage. Some people may wish to be cremated, while others may prefer a burial. The funeral service functions as both a memorial to the deceased person and the beginning of the acceptance of the death on the part of the bereaved.

The experience of grieving

Although bereavement is experienced at some time by nearly everyone, the grief that follows a death can be a lonely and isolating experience (*see* LOSS AND BEREAVEMENT, p.76). After the initial shock and disbelief, overwhelming feelings of sadness and anger are common. A bereaved person may experience an irrational need to search for the person who has died. It can be difficult to accept the loss, especially for someone who has not seen the body after death.

During the first few months after the death, when these experiences are often most intense, it sometimes seems that the world outside expects you to be getting over the loss. Although it can help to continue to work and maintain daily routines, the understanding and support of friends and family is especially important at this time. You may also find it helpful to contact a self-help organization that helps people come to terms with bereavement.

Eventually, perhaps over a number of years, nearly everyone who has been bereaved adjusts to the loss. Keeping alive the memory of the person who has died is an important part of this process. Painful memories and feelings relating to the death may always come back, especially at special anniversaries and family events. However, there usually comes a time when it is possible to look back on life with the deceased person with positive feelings.

WWW ONLINE SITES: p.1029

PSYCHOLOGICAL THERAPIES

Many mental health problems, including depression, personality disorders, addictions, and eating disorders, may be helped by psychological therapies. There is a variety of therapies available, some of which explore a person's past while others focus on current behavior or thought processes. The person in therapy is often encouraged to take an active role in the treatment.

The treatment of mental health problems with psychological therapy, or psychotherapy, was developed by Sigmund Freud at the end of the 19th century. Since that time, a number of different forms of psychological therapy have evolved. Some of the major types of therapies are described in this section, beginning with psychoanalytic-based psychotherapies, in which the therapist tries to give a person insight into the effect of past experiences. The next two articles look at behavior and cognitive therapies, which are based on changing the way people act or think. Both person-centered therapy and group therapy emphasize supporting the individual and helping people to achieve self-awareness and understanding. In the last article in this section, counseling is discussed. Counseling can be useful for people who need to learn how to cope with personal problems and crises.

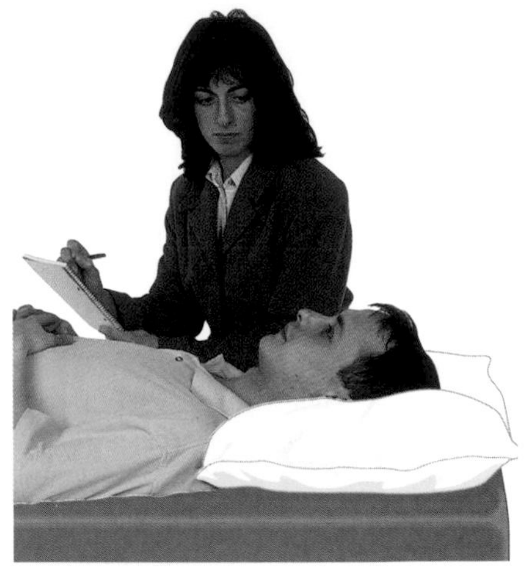

Psychoanalysis
In psychoanalytic-based psychotherapies, your therapist encourages you to talk freely about your past experiences. You work together to resolve your problems.

Psychoanalytic-based psychotherapies

Treatments that may help a person overcome psychological problems by uncovering suppressed feelings

Psychoanalytic-based therapies try to help people identify, confront, and eventually work through their psychological problems. The therapies, often called psychoanalysis, are based on the theory that some painful feelings and memories are suppressed and confined to an unconscious part of the mind and that these unresolved feelings may resurface as psychological problems.

In psychoanalytic-based psychotherapy, you are encouraged to talk freely about past experiences and express openly the emotions that these recollections cause. Your therapist interprets the information you give to help you gain insight into your psychological history and problems.

Classical psychoanalysis, as developed by Sigmund Freud, is the most intensive form and involves seeing a therapist several times a week for years. Today, other forms of psychoanalysis that are less time-consuming than classical psychoanalysis are available.

When is it used?

Psychoanalytic-based psychotherapies may help people in whom the cause of their problems is not immediately apparent. It does so by increasing awareness of how past experiences may have shaped a person's present behavior and moods. For this reason, psychoanalysis is most commonly used to help people who have a long history of depression (p.554). Other problems that psychoanalytic-based therapies may help overcome include eating disorders, such as anorexia nervosa (p.562).

What does it involve?

In classical psychoanalysis, you may lie on a couch while your therapist, who is out of view, waits for you to reveal information. You will be encouraged to talk freely about whatever comes to mind. This technique, which is known as free association, helps your therapist uncover painful feelings or memories you may have repressed. You may have 3–6 sessions per week, each session lasting for up to 1 hour, for 3–5 years.

In the newer psychoanalytic-based psychotherapies you usually sit facing your therapist. These sessions last for 30 minutes to 1 hour and occur once or twice a week. Therapy usually continues for a period of 6 months to 2 years.

Both forms of psychoanalytic-based psychotherapies use the same basic techniques and methods, in which the therapist's interpretation of your memories, dreams, and the feelings you express are used as a basis for discussion. The difference between the two forms lies in the role of the therapist, which, in the newer forms of psychoanalysis, is more active in helping you to reveal information about your past.

A good relationship between you and your therapist is vital to successful treatment because you work together to resolve your problems over a relatively long period of time.

What can I expect?

Classical psychoanalysis is a time-consuming process, which you may find emotionally distressing at times. During the course of treatment, you may experience periods of vulnerability and despair when unwelcome feelings resurface before you feel able to deal with them. Supporters of psychoanalysis feel that the self-understanding that results from such distress leads to a resolution of psychological problems that outweighs the level of distress itself.

You might find the newer, briefer therapies more acceptable than classical psychoanalysis because therapy with a time limit may motivate you to tackle particular issues by identifying and working through the underlying cause. You may find that your psychological problems are more likely to recur with a shorter-term therapy, but this may be avoided by the continued support that group therapy (p.970) can provide when your psychoanalytic-based therapy has come to an end.

(WWW) ONLINE SITES: p.1029

Behavior therapy

Techniques for changing inappropriate behavior by substituting new behavior

The aim of behavior therapy is to change abnormal or maladjusted behavior associated with certain psychological conditions. The therapist's goal is to modify a person's current behavior, but he or she does not explore the reasons underlying it, as occurs psychoanalytic-based therapies (opposite page).

Treatment is based on two ideas: desirable behavior can be encouraged by using a system of rewards, and exposure to a feared experience or object under conditions where you feel safe will make it less threatening. Behavior therapy is often used in combination with cognitive therapy (p.970), which explores and changes the thought processes that lead to abnormal behavior.

When is it used?

Behavior therapy is useful in the treatment of a person with a phobia (p.552), which is an irrational fear that occurs in response to a particular object, creature, or circumstance. For example, a person may have an overwhelming fear of insects or air travel. Some people have a complex phobia, such as agoraphobia, which typically involves multiple fears about being trapped in crowds or being alone in open spaces.

People who lack assertiveness or who have habitual behavior, such as frequent, repeated hand-washing (*see* OBSESSIVE-COMPULSIVE DISORDER, p.553), can also benefit from this therapy.

Behavior therapy may also be used to treat eating disorders, such as anorexia nervosa (p.562) and bulimia nervosa (p.563), and it may help people with an anxiety-related problem such as panic attacks (*see* ANXIETY DISORDERS, p.551).

(TECHNIQUE) Desensitization therapy

Desensitization therapy may help you overcome a phobia. With the help of relaxation exercises in weekly sessions for several months, you will face the object or circumstance that you fear. You learn to overcome your phobia by facing the focus of it in its least distressing form and gradually working toward more direct contact.

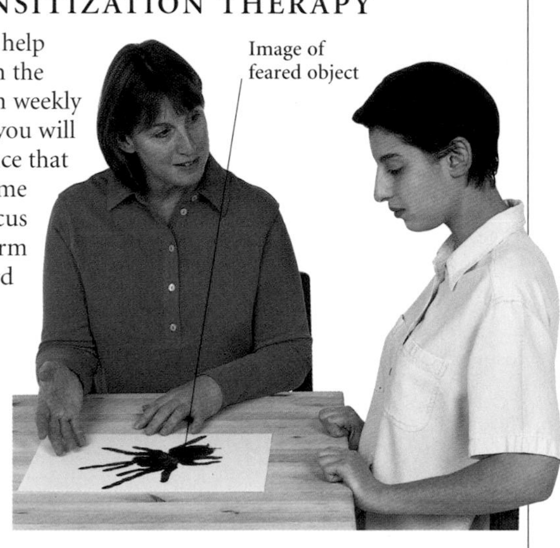
Image of feared object

During a session
The therapist helps you face your phobia. In this case, a picture of a spider is used as the least distressing form of exposure for someone with an intense fear of spiders.

What does it involve?

Behavior therapy begins with the therapist making a detailed analysis of your behavior by interviewing you at length. You may be asked to rate the severity of your symptoms on a scale of 1 (mild) to 10 (extremely severe). Improvement may also be measured in this way. The therapist discusses with you the best approach to dealing with your problem. Techniques that might be used include desensitization and flooding, assertiveness training, and response prevention. Since changing ingrained behavior often causes anxiety, you will probably also be taught to use relaxation techniques, such as breathing exercises, to help you cope.

DESENSITIZATION AND FLOODING Both desensitization and flooding are used to treat phobias. Desensitization involves gradually increasing exposure to the object or circumstance of the phobia (*see* DESENSITIZATION THERAPY, above) and uses relaxation techniques to help you deal with the anxiety. For example, if you have agoraphobia, in early sessions you might walk just outside your house with the therapist. As sessions continue, you may try walking from the house to the end of the street with your therapist until, over time, you can travel alone without anxiety.

Flooding forces you to directly confront the focus of your fear for prolonged periods. You will be supported throughout by your therapist. After you have confronted the object or circumstance of your phobia, either gradually or in one step, the distress associated with it is reduced and may eventually disappear.

ASSERTIVENESS TRAINING This therapy uses role-play to demonstrate the appropriate responses to different situations, such as someone acting aggressively toward you. Your therapist shows you an appropriate response and, by copying it, you become more confident in your ability to react to real situations.

RESPONSE PREVENTION This technique is used in the treatment of compulsive rituals, such as repeated hand-washing. You are encouraged to resist the urge to carry out the action, even though resistance results in intense anxiety. The therapist gives you support and suggests relaxation techniques. If you continue to resist the compulsion, eventually the anxiety will lessen.

What can I expect?

You may find that improvement is slow at first and that it is difficult to avoid returning to your unwanted behavior when your therapist is not there to support you. Group therapy (p.970) may be recommended to provide extra support when individual therapy ends.

Improvements in your behavior can be maintained after your therapy has finished by carrying on with the techniques you have learned.

Cognitive therapy

An approach to overcoming psychological problems that aims to change inappropriate attitudes and thoughts

Cognitive therapy is based on the idea that some psychological problems are maintained by inappropriate ways of thinking. It helps people to recognize and understand their current thought patterns and shows them ways to consciously change the way they think. Cognitive therapy does not look into past events and is often used in conjunction with behavior therapy (p.969).

WHEN IS IT USED?

People who suffer depression (p.554) or those who lack confidence often benefit from cognitive therapy because it helps them identify and change the thoughts that contribute to their low mood or self-esteem. Such thoughts may include "I am a failure," and "no one likes me because I'm ugly."

By pointing out inconsistencies in thinking, cognitive therapy can be of help to people who have distorted body images, such as those with anorexia nervosa (p.562). Similarly, when used with behavior therapy, cognitive therapy can help people overcome thought patterns and/or behavior that are habitual and unnecessary (*see* OBSESSIVE–COMPULSIVE DISORDER, p.553).

In conjunction with drug treatment, cognitive therapy has been found to help some people with schizophrenia (p.560) cope better with certain symptoms, such as hearing voices.

WHAT DOES IT INVOLVE?

At the initial session, your therapist assesses your problem, and together you decide on an approach to solve it.

People undergoing cognitive therapy are often asked to keep a diary of their thoughts. For example, someone suffering from anxiety might be asked to record the thoughts that precede and accompany an anxiety attack.

During a therapy session, the therapist helps you analyze the thoughts you have recorded and asks if you now feel they were appropriate to the circumstances. Once you can identify those thoughts that are inappropriate, it then becomes possible to change them.

In some cases, attempts to change ingrained ways of thinking may produce anxiety. To help people cope with anxiety, the cognitive therapist may teach relaxation techniques, such as breathing exercises.

You will probably see your therapist weekly for sessions lasting about 45 minutes to 1 hour. If you have a specific problem, such as stopping an unwanted habit, your therapy may only last for a matter of weeks. For more complex problems, such as low self-esteem, you may see your therapist for months.

WHAT CAN I EXPECT?

Once therapy is finished, you will probably need to make a conscious effort to analyze and challenge your thoughts for some time. However, many people find their new thought patterns eventually become incorporated unconsciously.

(WWW) ONLINE SITES: p.1029

Person-centered therapy

A process that aims to increase a person's self-esteem and encourages self-reliance

Person-centered therapy is based on the concept that an individual's behavior arises from their inner feelings and self-image rather than from responses to people or past experiences. Person-centered therapists avoid interpreting or explaining the information a person gives them, as in psychoanalytic-based therapies (p.968). Instead, the therapist supports a person as he or she develops greater self-esteem and self-reliance.

The person-centered therapist is nondirective and helps clarify a person's feelings and thoughts rather than telling him or her what to do or think. Most forms of person-centered therapy follow this approach apart from Gestalt therapy, in which the therapist helps an individual reach increased self-awareness by directing them through a series of exercises or experiences.

WHEN IS IT USED?

Person-centered therapy may be used to treat long-term depression (p.554) and low self-esteem. This therapy is also used in crisis intervention to help people who are overwhelmed by multiple stressful events, such as problems at work combined with failure of a marriage, or by a physical or sexual assault. In this case, person-centered therapy can support people who need to work through their difficulties in an environment that feels safe.

Person-centered therapy is not usually recommended for people with severe disorders, such as schizophrenia (p.560), in which the individual has no insight into his or her behavior. Nor is this therapy recommended for people who have unwanted habitual behavior (*see* OBSESSIVE-COMPULSIVE DISORDER, p.553) or severe mood swings (*see* BIPOLAR AFFECTIVE DISORDER, p.557).

WHAT DOES IT INVOLVE?

You and your therapist sit face-to-face while you speak about yourself, your relationships, and your environment. From time to time, your therapist summarizes what you have said but does not judge or interpret it.

In Gestalt therapy, the therapist plays a more active role. For example, if you are very introverted, he or she may ask you to act the role of an extrovert to help you accept that you are capable of this type of expression.

You will probably see your therapist for a weekly session of about 1 hour. The duration of the treatment depends on the time it takes you to feel more confident and in control of your life. It may take months if you are trying to overcome a specific crisis, such as loss of a loved one. However, if you have a less specific problem, such as long-term depression, it may take more than a year.

(WWW) ONLINE SITES: p.1029

Group therapy

Interaction with a small group of people to share experiences and feelings and gain insight or support

Group therapy is thought to be helpful in improving a person's ability to cope with and solve problems by discussing his or her experiences and emotions with a small group of people.

Each group session has one or more therapists who primarily help guide the interaction that takes place. You may join a group directly or be referred to one in the course of individual therapy.

TECHNIQUE HAVING GROUP THERAPY

Group therapy encourages people to share their problems and feelings with others and some people find it provides better motivation for change than individual therapy. Supportive group therapy may help you overcome lack of self-esteem or confidence, or an addiction. Therapy in groups of people with diverse problems may be useful because the relationships within the group raise issues and help solve problems.

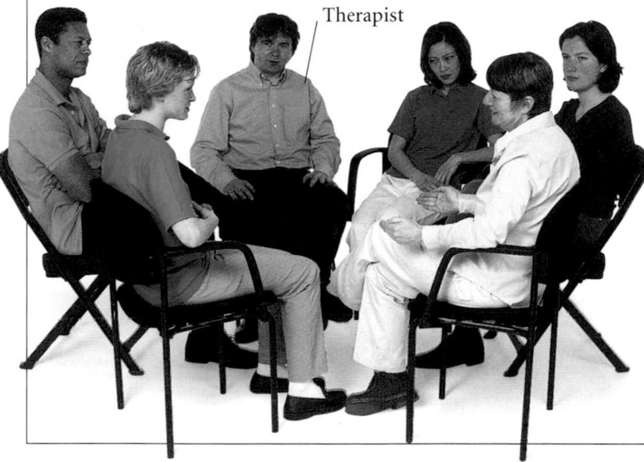
Therapist

During a session
A therapist and 6–12 group members sit informally in a circle. The therapist directs group discussions and encourages one member at a time to talk in front of the group about their problems or feelings. The group may also be coached through role-play sessions.

Group therapy may use techniques from other forms of psychotherapy, such as psychoanalytic-based therapies (p.968), behavior therapy (p.969) and cognitive therapy (opposite page), and person-centered therapy (opposite page).

WHEN IS IT USED?

Group therapy is used to treat a wide range of problems. For instance, it is helpful for people with irrational fears, those who have suffered serious physical or sexual assault, and those with addictions or habits that they are trying to break. It is also used to support and continue the therapy of people who have finished individual therapy.

Group therapy is unsuitable for people who particularly need personal attention and privacy in which to examine their own experiences and feelings. It is also unsuitable for people who are shy or extremely introverted, or those with severe disorders, such as schizophrenia (p.560) or bipolar affective disorder (p.557).

WHAT DOES IT INVOLVE?

There are two main types of group therapy. One is supportive therapy, in which people with similar problems share their experiences and learn how to cope from each other. In the other type of group therapy, people with diverse problems are brought together. The therapist conducts the sessions so that the interactions among group members can be explored, with the aim of enabling individual members to develop increased self-understanding. The group setting also allows an individual to test out opinions or newly learned ways of thinking in the group before applying them to everyday life.

Supportive groups are usually run as open groups. The number of meetings is unlimited and members may join and leave when they choose. By contrast, mixed groups are usually run as closed groups. The therapist selects the members, who meet for a limited number of sessions, sometimes as few as six.

Groups usually meet weekly for sessions of 1–2 hours (*see* HAVING GROUP THERAPY, above).

WHAT CAN I EXPECT?

It may take several sessions before you feel completely at ease in the group. You may also find that it will take some time before what you have learned in the group becomes part of your usual behavior and thoughts. Some people find group therapy more useful than individual therapy, particularly if their problems relate to difficulties in interacting with other people or if they appreciate uncritical group support.

Counseling

Support in identifying and addressing personal problems

People who are having trouble coping with their problems may use counseling to provide support and relieve distress. Counselors act as a sounding board and encourage people to express their feelings, allowing them to take the lead in dealing with their problems.

Counseling can help support people who are sad, worried, or facing a crisis. You may find it helpful if you are having difficulty dealing with bereavement, or if you are facing a terminal illness. However, if you have more deep-seated psychological problems, you may need a form of therapy in which the therapist plays a stronger and more active role, such as behavior therapy (p.969) or cognitive therapy (opposite page).

For some problems, you may need a specific form of support. For example, you may require relationship counseling if you are in a troubled relationship or debt counseling if you are continually in financial difficulty.

WHAT DOES IT INVOLVE?

At the first session, which may take 1 hour or longer, the counselor asks you about yourself and your background to build up a clear picture of you and your problem. You may also discuss what you want counseling to achieve.

At counseling sessions, which are usually held once a week, you decide, with the counselor's guidance, what you discuss and the pace at which you discuss it. Your counselor may suggest problem-solving exercises to help you deal with your problems one by one.

Counseling may be short-term if you are dealing with a situation such as a bereavement or long-term to help with a more complex problem.

WHAT CAN I EXPECT?

You may find that talking about problems with a counselor is enough to help you find a solution. With your counselor's support, you should be able to develop ways of solving your problems. In counseling, it is often easier than in some other therapies to see whether specific goals have been achieved.

(WWW) ONLINE SITES: p.1029

COMPLEMENTARY THERAPIES

A growing number of people now use complementary therapies for the treatment of a wide range of physical and psychological problems. In the past, these therapies were often described as "alternative" treatments, but now they are increasingly accepted and used to complement conventional medicine.

As their popularity increases, a number of complementary treatments are now being subjected to the rigorous testing and clinical trials that all conventional medical treatments have to undergo before they are accepted. For example, clinical trials have shown that chiropractic can be an effective treatment for acute pain in the back and neck. Sometimes, therapies are found to be effective, but the reasons why they work remain controversial.

This section begins with an overview of the many types of complementary therapies that are available and gives advice about how to choose a therapist. Separate articles provide information about some of the most common forms of therapies. Each article discusses what the treatment is used for and which conditions are the most suitable for treatment before going on to describe how the treatment is carried out and the results that can be expected.

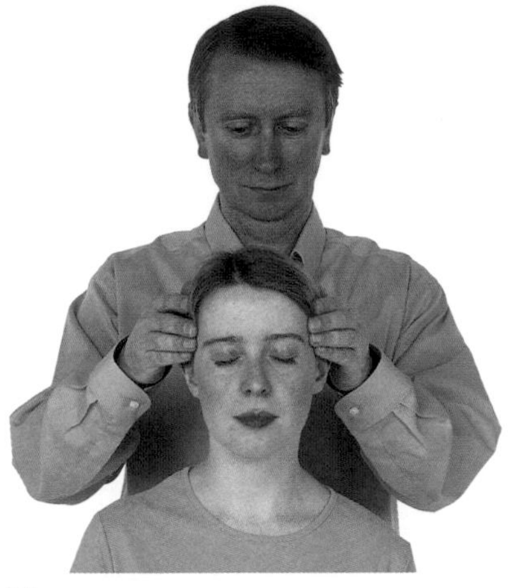

Massage
A complementary therapist may use gentle massage to relieve certain stress-related symptoms, such as tension headaches.

Complementary therapy choices

The place of complementary therapies in the treatment of disorders

Anyone who is interested in using complementary medicine to overcome an illness or maintain health is faced with a wide and often bewildering range of choices. There are many different complementary therapies available, but not all of them are supported by scientific evidence. For example, a form of therapy known as biofeedback (p.975), which is generally accepted by conventional medicine, has been shown to reduce stress levels and blood pressure. By contrast, the effectiveness of reflexology, in which points on the feet are stimulated to treat a variety of disorders, is not supported by scientific research. For this reason, complementary therapies have varying degrees of medical acceptance.

Most complementary therapies aim to treat the whole person rather than just the symptoms of an illness and take account of a person's lifestyle and personality as well as his or her symptoms and medical history. Complementary therapists are often able to offer people more time than conventional doctors.

WHAT ARE THE TYPES OF THERAPIES?

The treatments used in complementary medicine fall into several categories: treatments based on movement and touch, such as chiropractic (opposite page), reflexology, the Alexander technique, and massage; treatments using a medicinal approach, such as Chinese or Western botanical herbalism; treatments that balance energy, such as acupuncture (opposite page) and shiatsu; and mind/body approaches, such as biofeedback, hypnotherapy (p.974), and meditation.

People tend to think of complementary therapies as being harmless, but certain herbs and preparations used in some therapies contain active ingredients that can be dangerous if used without sufficient care or in combination with prescription drugs.

WHEN SHOULD I SEE A THERAPIST?

It is very important to consult a medical doctor before you begin any type of complementary therapy. When you see a complementary therapist, tell him or her about any medical treatment you are already receiving (and vice versa).

Complementary therapies are often useful for treating chronic conditions, such as eczema (p.333), for easing lower back pain (p.381), and for alleviating stress (p.74) and anxiety (*see* ANXIETY DISORDERS, p.551). However, complementary therapies are not suitable for treating acute conditions, such as an infection, or for use in emergencies, such as an asthma attack.

HOW DO I CHOOSE A THERAPIST?

Your choice of a therapist will probably be determined in the first instance by the reason you are seeking treatment. For example, if you want to stop smoking, you may feel that hypnotherapy can help, and, if you are suffering from back pain, you may choose chiropractic.

You should find out if the therapist belongs to a professional organization and if there is a code of practice for the particular therapy. The therapies that are generally accepted by conventional medicine are those provided by practitioners who have passed examinations that allow them to be licensed and join a professional organization. You should avoid therapists who do not belong to a recognized organization or who make excessive claims for the treatment.

In the case of therapies that are more readily accepted medically, such as chiropractic and acupuncture, your doctor may know of a reliable accredited practitioner and refer you for treatment.

(WWW) ONLINE SITES: p.1029

Acupuncture

Stimulating points on the body, mainly using needles, to relieve pain and help the body heal itself

Acupuncture originated thousands of years ago as part of the system of traditional Chinese medicine. The technique treats disorders by stimulating various points on the body that are known as acupoints. Acupuncture uses fine needles that are inserted through the skin. Acupuncture is gaining acceptance in mainstream medicine, particularly as a means of pain relief, and some medical doctors now utilize acupuncture themselves. Doctors who use acupuncture may select acupoints on an anatomically relevant basis as well as using traditional approaches.

A reputable, qualified acupuncturist will always use disposable needles or reusable needles that have been sterilized. It is important to do this because of the risk of contracting HIV infection (*see* HIV INFECTION AND AIDS, p.295) or other bloodborne infections that can be transmitted from infected needles.

HOW DOES IT WORK?

Research has shown that acupuncture can trigger the release of painkilling chemicals called endorphins from nerve terminals in the brain. Acupuncture helps the automatic functions in the nervous system regain a balance. The use of acupuncture in Chinese medicine is founded on the belief that an imbalance in the body's flow of energy gives rise to illness. Needles are inserted to relieve blockages and restore energy flow along one or more of the body's 14 meridians, or energy channels.

WHAT IS IT USED FOR?

The most common use of acupuncture in conventional medicine is for pain relief, and the therapy is frequently used in hospital pain clinics. Acupuncture has also been used successfully as an analgesic for dental and surgical procedures and during labor. Addictions have also been treated successfully by acupuncture. Other conditions that may respond to the therapy include hay fever (*see* ALLERGIC RHINITIS, p.466), migraine (p.518), and lower back pain (p.381).

WHAT HAPPENS IN A SESSION?

On your first visit to an acupuncturist, a traditional practitioner asks about your lifestyle and medical history. He or she assesses your condition usually by examining your tongue and feeling 12 pulses, six in each wrist. Each pulse is believed to give information about the health of a particular organ system. An acupuncture therapist will probably assess your condition by performing a physical examination, looking at your medical records, and asking you about your current state of health.

The acupuncturist will ask you to remove clothing that is covering acupoints and to lie on an examining table. Between 6 and 12 acupoints may be used at any one time, depending on the condition you are being treated for. A slight pricking sensation may be felt as the needles are inserted in your skin and you may experience numbness and a slight ache initially. The acupuncturist may manipulate the needles briefly to stimulate the acupoints or needles may be stimulated electrically with a battery-powered device.

After the needles are inserted, they may be left in place for as little as a few seconds or as long as an hour, but 20–30 minutes is usual in most cases. The needles are then withdrawn from the skin quickly and gently.

WHAT CAN I EXPECT?

You may feel relaxed and drowsy immediately after acupuncture treatment. The number of visits required varies according to the condition for which you are being treated. Some change in your condition is usually noticeable within about five sessions.

(WWW) ONLINE SITES: p.1029

Chiropractic

Spinal manipulation to treat disorders of the spine, joints, and muscles

Chiropractic is mainly used for spinal disorders, such as back and neck pain. Chiropractors maintain that any misalignment of the spine affects the functioning of other parts of the body and that chiropractic can help a wide range of health problems. Many people consult a chiropractor for lower back pain (p.381) or neck pain, and there is good evidence that these conditions can be treated successfully. Chiropractic may also be used for disorders such as indigestion (p.626) and migraine (p.518), but the benefits are not scientifically proven. In general, chiropractic is regarded as a safe treatment, but with any manipulation of the spine there is a slight risk of complications such as spinal cord damage or stroke (p.532).

TECHNIQUE HAVING CHIROPRACTIC

Chiropractic works mainly on the spine and is effective in the treatment of conditions such as lower back pain and neck pain. The therapist manipulates the vertebrae (bones of the spine) by adjusting the position of the bones in the spine relative to each other.

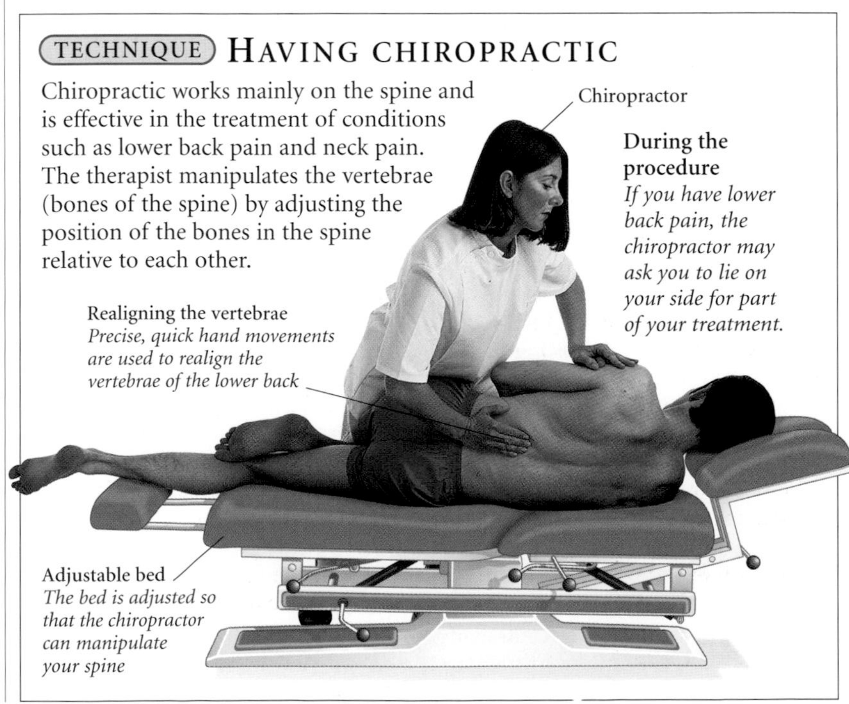
Chiropractor
During the procedure
If you have lower back pain, the chiropractor may ask you to lie on your side for part of your treatment.
Realigning the vertebrae
Precise, quick hand movements are used to realign the vertebrae of the lower back
Adjustable bed
The bed is adjusted so that the chiropractor can manipulate your spine

WHAT HAPPENS IN A SESSION?

A chiropractor begins by asking you detailed questions about your medical history and your current health problems. He or she may also arrange for X-rays (p.244) to be taken of your spine to look at its alignment.

You will then be asked to lie on an adjustable bed so that the chiropractor can examine your spine and other affected areas easily. He or she may take your blood pressure, observe your posture while you are standing or walking, and note your flexibility of movement. The chiropractor will also check your reflexes because an abnormality may indicate pressure on the spinal nerves.

If you have an acute problem, such as severe back pain or injury, treatment begins at the first session. Treatment for chronic conditions usually begins at the second session. The chiropractor uses quick, light hand movements to maneuver the back and realign the vertebrae (*see* HAVING CHIROPRACTIC, p.973). He or she may also ask you to do some stretching and bending exercises. You may be shown exercises that you can do at home and given advice about your posture and the way you sit.

The first session of chiropractic usually lasts between about 30 minutes and 1 hour, but your follow-up sessions may be shorter. Appointments are often at weekly intervals. The chiropractor will ask about your progress and examine your spine at each visit, and your treatment will be adjusted as needed.

WHAT CAN I EXPECT?

Immediately after your first treatment session, you may experience temporary discomfort, headache, and fatigue, but these reactions tend to become less severe after subsequent treatments.

The number of sessions you require depends on the condition being treated and how well you respond to treatment. Some acute conditions improve after the first two or three treatment sessions. For example, if you have injured your back slightly while playing a sport, you may find that only two or three sessions are needed to provide relief. However, for some chronic conditions, improvement is often more gradual, taking place over several follow-up sessions. A misalignment of the spine resulting from many years of bad posture may take months of treatment to achieve results. In these cases, most chiropractors recommend regular maintenance visits once the condition has been treated successfully to prevent the problem from recurring.

(WWW) ONLINE SITES: p.1029

Homeopathy

The use of very dilute forms of natural substances to stimulate the body's defenses against a disease

The basic principle of homeopathy is that the body's immune system can be stimulated to overcome an illness by administering a substance in a very dilute form that at full strength would produce the same symptoms as those of the illness to be treated.

Homeopathic remedies are prepared by a process of repeated dilution known as potentiation. The remedy is shaken after each stage of dilution. Eventually, the remedy becomes so dilute that only a few molecules, if any, of the original substance remain. The belief is that the more dilute a remedy is, the more potent it becomes, although how this can be the case is not fully understood.

There are more than 2,000 homeopathic remedies, most of which can be bought from a pharmacy without a prescription. Some remedies may contain several homeopathic preparations.

WHAT IS IT USED FOR?

Homeopathy is used to treat a range of physical and some psychological conditions. Physical conditions may include infections, such as the common cold (p.286); allergic conditions, such as hay fever (*see* ALLERGIC RHINITIS, p.466); skin conditions, such as eczema (p.333); and gynecological problems, such as premenstrual syndrome (p.736). Common psychological conditions that are treated include mild depression (p.554) and anxiety disorders (p.551). Homeopathy is not suitable for acute conditions that may be life-threatening, such as asthma attacks and appendicitis.

WHAT HAPPENS IN A SESSION?

Your first appointment with the homeopath usually lasts 1–2 hours. He or she will want to build a complete picture of you and your lifestyle and will ask you about your symptoms and medical history, family circumstances, emotional state, diet, and medications that you are taking. All of these factors influence the homeopath's choice of remedy.

The homeopath may give you a remedy during the consultation or write a prescription for you to take to a homeopathic pharmacist. He or she may also advise you on your lifestyle and diet. You may be asked to avoid caffeine, tobacco, and substances found in very sweet or spicy foods that are thought to counteract the action of some remedies.

The number and frequency of your follow-up visits depend on your symptoms. For chronic conditions the first follow-up visit is usually 4–8 weeks after starting treatment. For other conditions it may be 6–8 months afterward.

WHAT CAN I EXPECT?

Homeopathic remedies are so dilute that they should not result in side effects. However, you may find that your symptoms become worse temporarily about 10–14 days after you begin taking the remedy. This effect is thought to be due to the initial stimulation of your body's defense system and may last anywhere from a few hours to a few days.

The remedies for some conditions may take effect after only a few days of treatment. Chronic conditions, such as eczema, may take a few weeks or months before showing signs of improvement. If there is no improvement, it is important that you see your doctor.

(WWW) ONLINE SITES: p.1029

Hypnotherapy

The production of a trancelike state during which suggestions are made to help reduce anxiety or change behavior patterns

Hypnosis induces a deep state of relaxation and is accepted by many doctors as an effective way to help people overcome anxiety and stress-related illnesses or change their behavior patterns. Some hypnotherapists are medically qualified.

The hypnotherapist induces a state of trance in which breathing and heartbeat slow and brain activity is similar to that during meditation. While in this state, a person is relaxed and more open to suggestion. The hypnotherapist can take advantage of this to introduce positive ideas that may affect behavior.

WHAT IS IT USED FOR?

Hypnotherapy has been shown to be useful for relaxation and is mainly used to treat people who suffer from anxiety and panic attacks (*see* ANXIETY DISORDERS, p.551). This form of therapy may also be used to help overcome an irrational fear that is affecting your life (*see* PHOBIAS, p.552). Treatment with hypnotherapy may be helpful if you have a condition related to stress, such as irritable bowel syndrome (p.656) or migraine (p.518). You may also want to consider hypnosis to help you change undesirable patterns of behavior. For example, some people use hypnotherapy to help them give up smoking.

WHAT HAPPENS IN A SESSION?

The hypnotherapist begins by asking about your physical and mental health and your motivation to change the undesired behavior. Different methods can be used to induce a trance, but you will probably be encouraged to lie back on a couch or in a chair. You may be asked to visualize something pleasant or to look at a certain object while the hypnotherapist slowly repeats a series of monotonous statements. When you are in a trance, the therapist makes suggestions aimed at changing your behavior, if this is the goal of the treatment. For example, if you are trying to stop smoking, the therapist may tell you that you no longer desire cigarettes. After a while you are brought slowly out of the trance, possibly by being asked to count backward from 10 to 1.

The first session lasts about 1 hour; follow-up sessions may be shorter. The number of sessions needed depends on whether you respond well to hypnosis and how quickly improvement is seen. On average, 6–12 sessions are required to bring about a positive result.

WHAT CAN I EXPECT?

You may find that you experience an improvement in the problem you are trying to overcome after the first session. For example, if you are trying to stop smoking, you may find that your craving for tobacco is less strong. The time it takes to see an improvement depends on your motivation, how susceptible you are to hypnosis, and how deeply rooted your problems are.

WWW ONLINE SITES: p.1029

Biofeedback

Consciously altering biological functions to gain control over physical conditions, such as high blood pressure or anxiety

In biofeedback, body functions that are not normally under conscious control, such as heart rate and skin temperature, are monitored and translated into visual or auditory signals using special equipment. A person is taught relaxation techniques, such as deep breathing, to alter these functions. After several sessions, the person is able to produce a relaxed state at will without using the biofeedback equipment.

Although it is not yet known how the mind is able to influence the body's involuntary workings, biofeedback has been studied extensively, and results show that it can be effective for some situations. Biofeedback is generally well accepted by conventional medicine.

WHAT IS IT USED FOR?

Biofeedback is used most frequently for stress-related conditions, such as panic attacks (*see* ANXIETY DISORDERS, p.551), high blood pressure (*see* HYPERTENSION, p.403), tension headaches (p.518), irritable bowel syndrome (p.656), insomnia (p.554), and migraine (p.518). This type of therapy may also help muscle and joint pain and disorders caused by poor control over muscles, such as urinary incontinence (p.710).

WHAT HAPPENS IN A SESSION?

During your first session, the biofeedback practitioner may ask you about your general health, the history of your condition, and any medication you are taking. He or she will show you how the biofeedback equipment works and attach electrodes to your skin, often on your scalp, arm, or fingers (*see* HAVING BIOFEEDBACK TRAINING, below). Your responses are relayed along wires to the biofeedback equipment and displayed on a dial or a monitor, sometimes as computer-generated images or sound waves. You are shown relaxation techniques, such as meditation, and taught to recognize biofeedback signals that indicate that you are relaxed. You can then practice producing these signals by using relaxation techniques.

Six to seven half-hour sessions are usually needed to produce a relaxed state at will. For chronic conditions, such as phobias (p.552), improvement may take weeks or months to achieve.

WWW ONLINE SITES: p.1029

TECHNIQUE HAVING BIOFEEDBACK TRAINING

Biofeedback training teaches you how to enter a relaxed state at will. Biofeedback equipment gives you information about your physical state, such as your heart rate, stress levels, and muscle tension. This changing information is constantly fed back to you as you try to practice various relaxation techniques. Over time, you learn consciously to control your body responses so that you can remain calm in stressful situations.

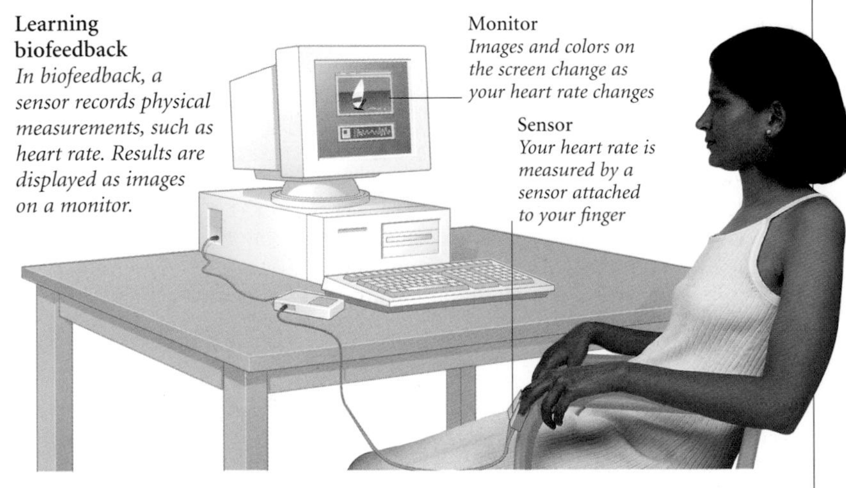
Monitor
Images and colors on the screen change as your heart rate changes
Sensor
Your heart rate is measured by a sensor attached to your finger

Learning biofeedback
In biofeedback, a sensor records physical measurements, such as heart rate. Results are displayed as images on a monitor.

First aid box
A first aid box should be clearly marked with a cross so that it is easily recognized.

First Aid

First aid is the immediate care given to a person following an injury or sudden illness before medical help arrives. It can make the difference between life and death. The aim of first aid is to preserve life, to prevent the condition from worsening, and to promote as fast a recovery as possible. However, remember that you will not be able to help the person if you become a victim yourself. Always put your own safety first.

To be able to give effective first aid, you must follow a systematic plan and prioritize needed actions. This section provides clear instruction to help you handle common emergency situations. However, there is no substitute for professional training. The best way to prepare for a real-life emergency is to take a practical course in first aid.

First aid priorities

Your top priority in coping with an emergency is to get medical assistance by calling 911 or the local emergency number. If a bystander is present, you should ask him or her to make the call. The caller should give the dispatcher as much information as possible about the location and the condition of the victim. Always let the dispatcher hang up the phone first in order to make sure that all the necessary information has been communicated.

As a first aid provider, you must also check the scene for possible dangers to you, the victim, or bystanders, such as fire, dangerous fumes, or downed power lines. Eliminate the danger if you can or remove the victim from the situation. If you cannot do so safely, phone for help immediately.

If you can approach the victim safely, you should aim to assess his or her condition and administer appropriate first aid. If you do not feel qualified to administer first aid, you should wait for professional help to arrive. In the meantime, it is important to remain calm and reassure the victim.

Taking a first aid course

You can take a first aid course with the Canadian Red Cross or the St. John Ambulance. You will need to refresh your skills and take the test at regular intervals. First aid training in some skills, such as cardiopulmonary resuscitation (CPR), should be recertified every year to ensure that your efficiency at these skills is maintained.

(WWW) ONLINE SITES: p.1031

(EQUIPMENT) Home first aid kit

Having the correct supplies can make a big difference in an emergency, and you should always keep a supply of essential first aid materials at home and in the car. Store the items in a first aid kit or in a similar type of airtight container in a dry place. The kit should be easily accessible in an emergency but kept away from other medicines and out of the reach of children. Ideally, the kit should be small enough for you to carry easily. Check and replenish the first aid kit regularly so that the contents are always kept up-to-date.

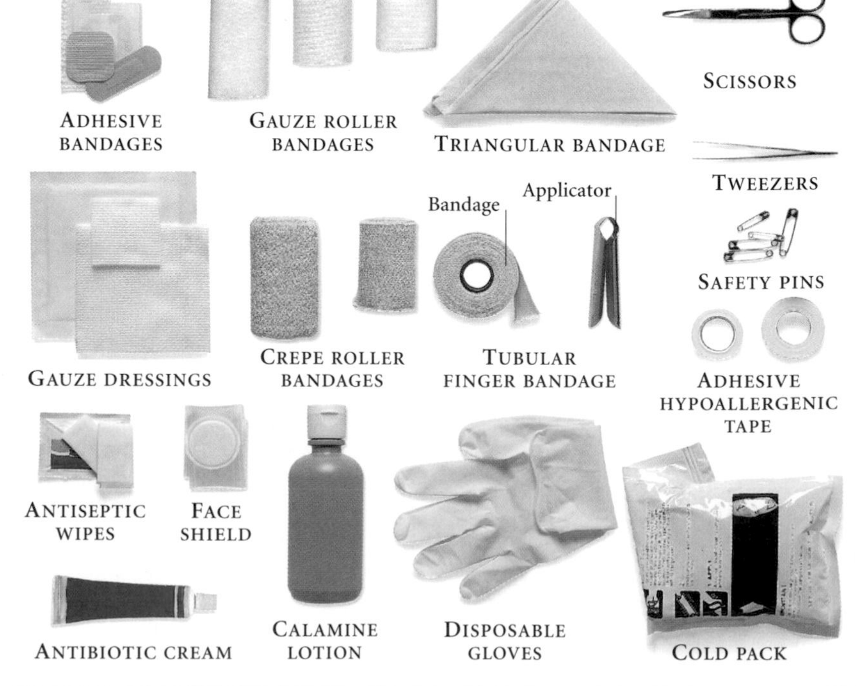

Adhesive bandages
Gauze roller bandages
Triangular bandage
Scissors
Tweezers
Bandage
Applicator
Safety pins
Gauze dressings
Crepe roller bandages
Tubular finger bandage
Adhesive hypoallergenic tape
Antiseptic wipes
Face shield
Antibiotic cream
Calamine lotion
Disposable gloves
Cold pack

Contents of the first aid kit
Most of the items shown here are essential items to include in your first aid kit. The face shield, which enables you to give artificial respiration hygienically, is an optional item that you may wish to include if you are trained in first aid.

PROCEDURE ACTION IN AN EMERGENCY

When faced with an emergency, there are several important guidelines to bear in mind. If possible, you should send someone for an ambulance while you deal with the situation. Before trying to help someone, you must be certain that you are not putting yourself in any danger. After you have made sure that the scene is safe, the next step is to check the victim's condition and carry out the appropriate first aid.

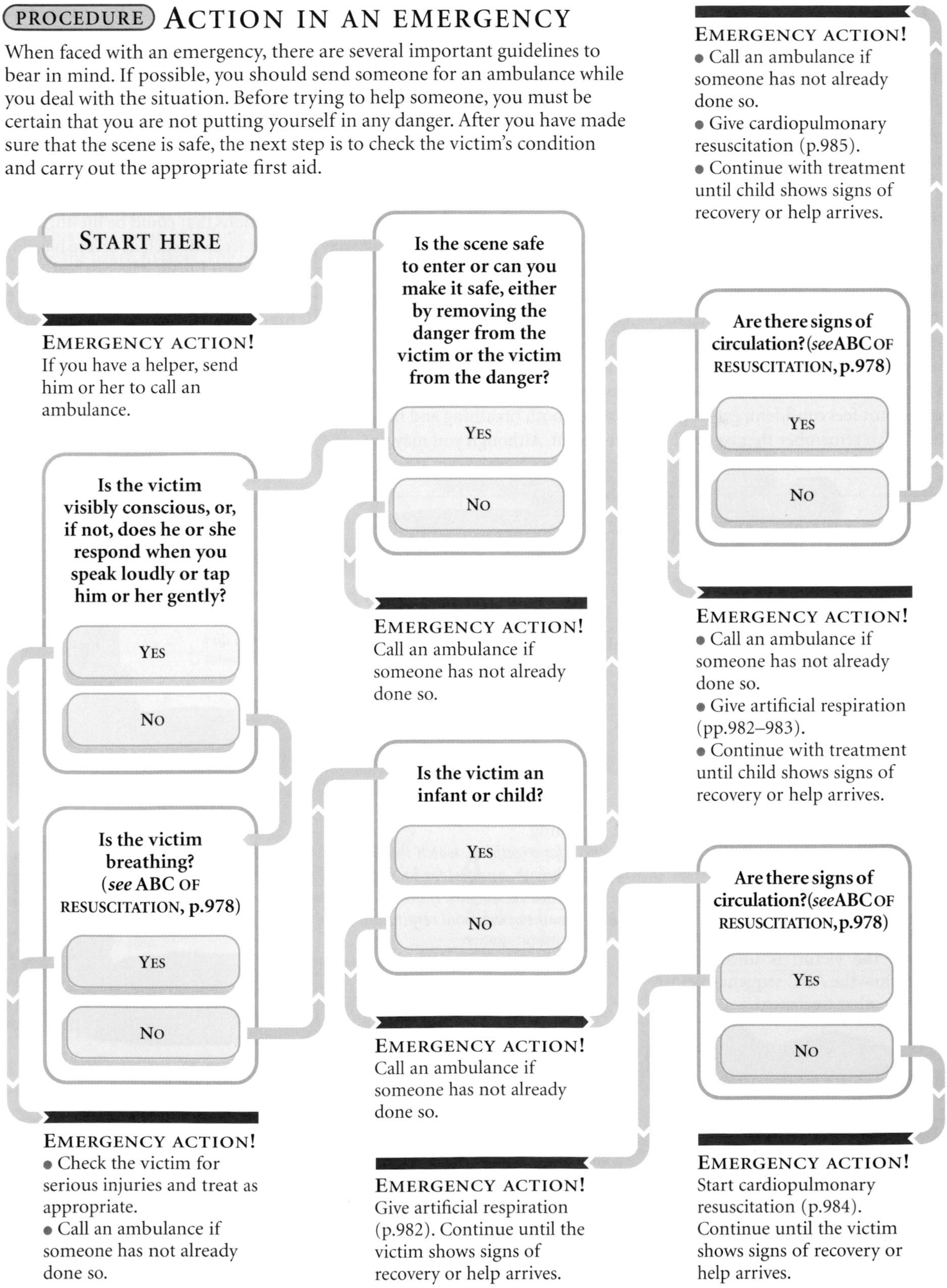

START HERE

EMERGENCY ACTION!
If you have a helper, send him or her to call an ambulance.

Is the scene safe to enter or can you make it safe, either by removing the danger from the victim or the victim from the danger?

YES

NO

EMERGENCY ACTION!
Call an ambulance if someone has not already done so.

Is the victim visibly conscious, or, if not, does he or she respond when you speak loudly or tap him or her gently?

YES

NO

Is the victim breathing? (*see* ABC OF RESUSCITATION, p.978)

YES

NO

EMERGENCY ACTION!
- Check the victim for serious injuries and treat as appropriate.
- Call an ambulance if someone has not already done so.

Is the victim an infant or child?

YES

NO

EMERGENCY ACTION!
Call an ambulance if someone has not already done so.

EMERGENCY ACTION!
Give artificial respiration (p.982). Continue until the victim shows signs of recovery or help arrives.

Are there signs of circulation? (*see* ABC OF RESUSCITATION, p.978)

YES

NO

EMERGENCY ACTION!
- Call an ambulance if someone has not already done so.
- Give cardiopulmonary resuscitation (p.985).
- Continue with treatment until child shows signs of recovery or help arrives.

EMERGENCY ACTION!
- Call an ambulance if someone has not already done so.
- Give artificial respiration (pp.982–983).
- Continue with treatment until child shows signs of recovery or help arrives.

Are there signs of circulation? (*see* ABC OF RESUSCITATION, p.978)

YES

NO

EMERGENCY ACTION!
Start cardiopulmonary resuscitation (p.984). Continue until the victim shows signs of recovery or help arrives.

Choking in conscious adults and children

Choking is caused by an obstruction of the airway, usually by food or a foreign object. A victim who is choking may cough and gasp at first, and his or her face may become blue. He or she will become very distressed and may point to or grasp at the throat. If the airway becomes completely blocked, the victim may make high-pitched noises, be unable to cough, or have only a weak cough. If the victim cannot clear the blockage by coughing, you need to give first aid to prevent the person from suffocating. Usually you can do this by using the technique shown at right. Slightly different techniques are used when treating a large or pregnant person for choking (below right) or treating yourself for choking (below).

1 *Ask the victim if he or she is choking. Listen carefully to the victim in order to assess the need for first aid. If the person can speak without difficulty or is able to cough forcefully, do not intervene.*

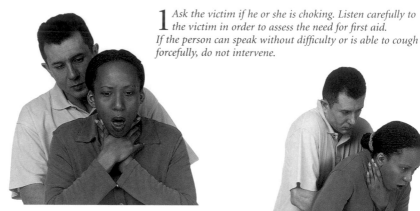

2 *If the victim is unable to speak or clear the object by coughing, begin abdominal thrusts. Stand behind the person and wrap your arms around him or her. Put one fist below the ribcage, thumb-side against the abdomen.*

3 *Place your other hand on top of your fist. Pull sharply inward and upward to give the choking victim abdominal thrusts.*

4 *Continue to give the victim abdominal thrusts until the obstruction is cleared from the airway and the victim is breathing normally. If the victim loses consciousness, you will need to lay him or her face up on a hard surface and begin cardiopulmonary resuscitation* (see CHOKING IN UNCONSCIOUS ADULTS AND CHILDREN, *opposite page*).

(SELF-HELP) TREATING YOURSELF FOR CHOKING

If you are alone and choking on a foreign body, you can give yourself abdominal thrusts by leaning over any firm object, such as a chair, railing, or sink, to expel the object. Beware of any sharp edges.

Abdomen pressed against firm object

Performing abdominal thrusts
Lean over a firm object and press your abdomen against it sharply several times, just below your ribcage.

(SPECIAL CASE) TREATING A LARGE OR PREGNANT PERSON FOR CHOKING

If the victim is choking and is too large for you to be able to reach your arms around his or her abdomen, or if the victim is pregnant, you should give chest thrusts instead of abdominal thrusts to try to expel the obstruction from the airway.

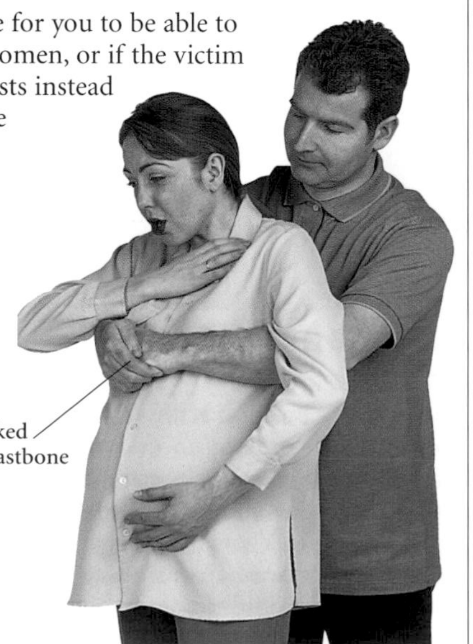
Hands linked across breastbone

1 *Stand behind the victim in a stable position and put your arms around his or her chest, just under the armpits.*

2 *Make a fist with one hand. With the back of your fist turned upward and the thumb toward the victim's chest, position your fist on the victim's breastbone in the center of the chest.*

3 *Place your other hand over your fist and pull sharply inward. Repeat until the obstruction is cleared.*

Choking in unconscious adults and children

If a person's airway has become completely blocked through choking, he or she will be unable to breathe and will lose consciousness. If an adult or child becomes unconscious while you are giving treatment for choking or if you find an unconscious person, you must begin administering cardio-pulmonary resuscitation (CPR).

> **WARNING**
> Only try to remove an object from a person's throat if you can see the obstruction clearly.

1 *If you have a helper, send him or her to call an ambulance. If the victim has lost consciousness while undergoing treatment for choking, proceed to Step 3. If you discover an unconscious person who is not breathing, open the airway by pressing the forehead down with one hand and lifting the chin with two fingers of the other. Give 2 slow breaths of artificial respiration (p.982).*

2 *If these first 2 breaths do not go in, retilt the victim's head and again give 2 slow breaths of artificial respiration. If this does not work, call an ambulance if a helper has not already done so, then move on to Step 3.*

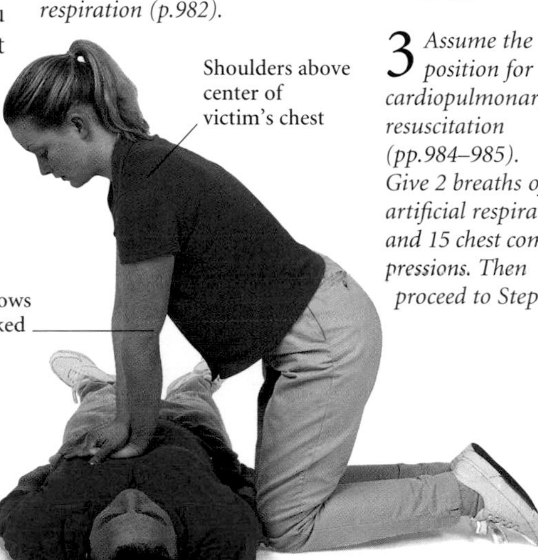

Shoulders above center of victim's chest
Elbows locked

3 *Assume the position for cardiopulmonary resuscitation (pp.984–985). Give 2 breaths of artificial respiration and 15 chest compressions. Then proceed to Step 4.*

4 *Lift the victim's jaw with your finger and thumb. Look in the mouth and only try to remove an object if you are able to see it clearly. If you see an object, slide one finger inside the cheek and try to hook out any object.*

5 *If the victim is still not showing signs of recovery, such as return of skin color or breathing, repeat the cycle of breathing and compressions by giving 2 slow breaths of artificial respiration followed by 15 chest compressions.*

6 *If breaths do not go in, repeat Steps 3–5 until medical help arrives. If the victim does start breathing at any time, monitor breathing and circulation regularly (see* ABC OF RESUSCITATION*, p.978) until medical help arrives.*

Choking in infants

Infants can easily choke on a small object. A choking infant may make high-pitched squeaking noises, the face may become red then blue, and he or she may appear to cry without making any noise. If the airway is completely blocked, the infant will lose consciousness. You must relieve an obstructed airway before giving the infant any other first aid treatment.

1 *If the infant has a strong cough, let him or her continue. If coughing does not stop in a few minutes or becomes high-pitched, call an ambulance or ask a helper to do so.*

> **WARNING**
> - Never shake a choking infant.
> - Only try to remove an object from an infant's throat if you can see the obstruction clearly.

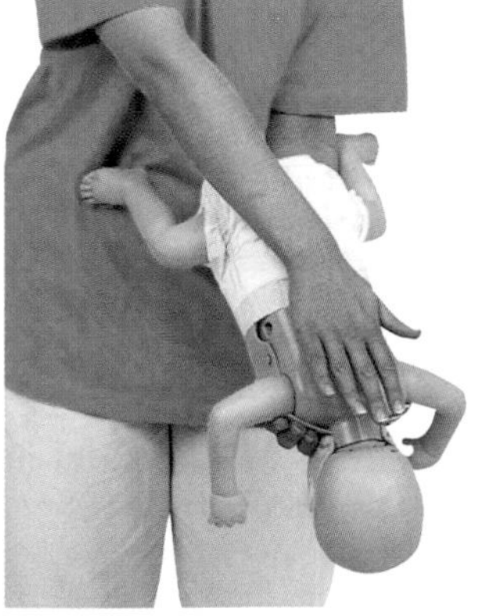

2 *Lay the infant face down on your forearm or lap with the head lower than the trunk, supporting the head and shoulders with your hand. Give up to 5 sharp slaps between the infant's shoulders.*

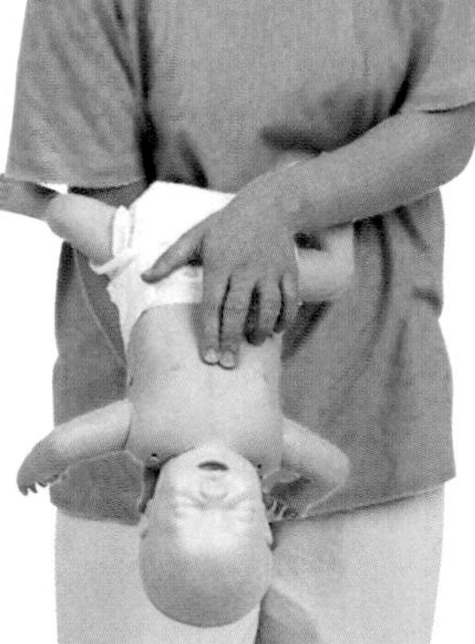

3 *If back slaps are not effective, lay the infant face up along your other arm. Place 2 fingers on the lower half of the breastbone. Give 5 sharp downward thrusts into the chest.*

4 *If the infant becomes unconscious, open the mouth, and, placing your finger on the tongue to give a clear view, carefully remove any object that you can clearly see.*

5 *Begin to administer cardiopulmonary resuscitation for infants (p.985) in order to distribute oxygen to the brain and other vital organs.*

6 *If the breaths still do not go in, repeat Steps 5–6 until medical help arrives or the infant starts breathing on his or her own. If the infant does start breathing at any time, monitor breathing and circulation regularly (see* ABC OF RESUSCITATION*, p.978) until help arrives.*

Cardiopulmonary resuscitation for adults

An unconscious victim who is not breathing and has no signs of circulation needs to be given cardiopulmonary resuscitation (CPR) because the heart has stopped beating. CPR is a life-saving technique which combines artificial respiration with chest compressions, which force blood out of the heart and around the body. This ensures that the oxygen supplied by artificial respiration reaches the brain and other vital organs. Do not stop giving CPR until the victim's heart starts beating or medical help arrives. If you are too tired to continue, try to find another trained person to take over from you until medical help arrives.

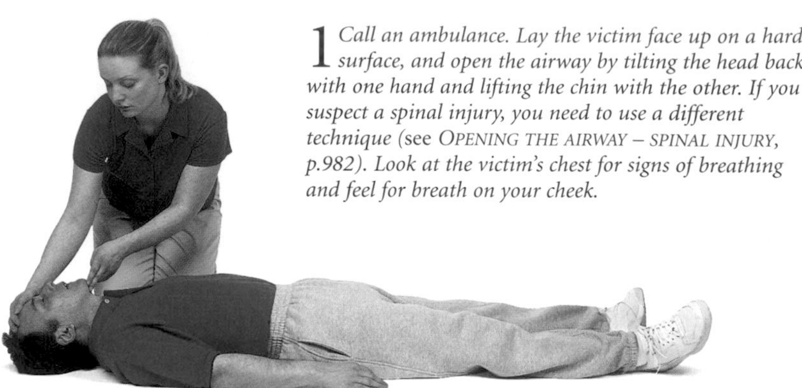

1 Call an ambulance. Lay the victim face up on a hard surface, and open the airway by tilting the head back with one hand and lifting the chin with the other. If you suspect a spinal injury, you need to use a different technique (see OPENING THE AIRWAY – SPINAL INJURY, *p.982**). Look at the victim's chest for signs of breathing and feel for breath on your cheek.*

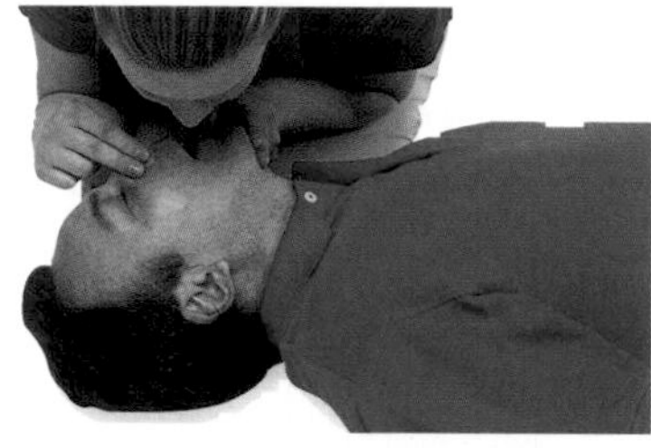

2 If the victim is not breathing, pinch the nose shut with one hand, and keep the chin tilted with the other. Seal your mouth over the victim's mouth, and give 2 slow breaths of artificial respiration (p.982). Pause for a breath yourself between each breath.

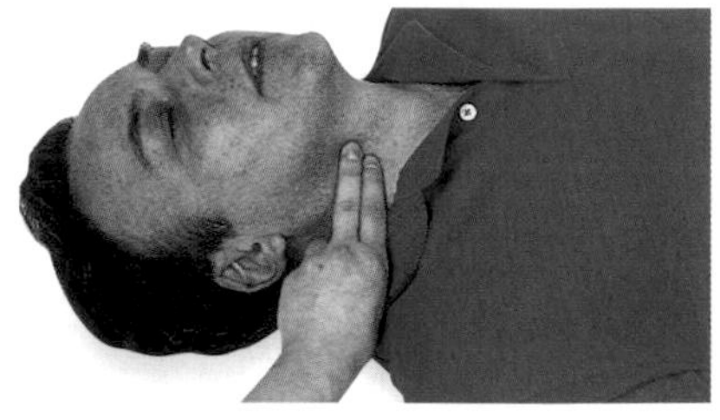

3 Check the pulse at the neck for no longer than 10 seconds, and look for signs of recovery, such as return of skin color or breathing. If signs are present, continue artificial respiration. If you cannot find signs of circulation, begin CPR (see Step 4).

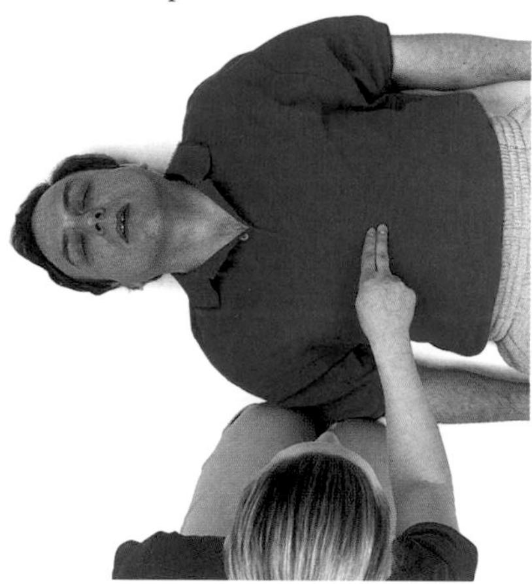

4 Kneel to one side of the victim and with one hand locate the lowest rib on that side. Slide your fingers along the rib to where it meets the breastbone. Place your middle finger on this point and your index finger just above it.

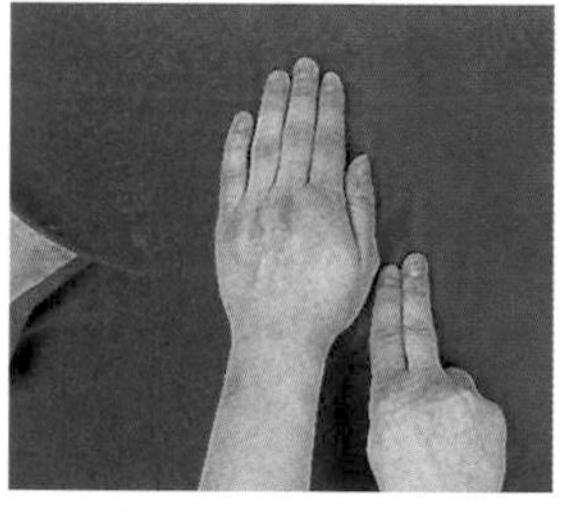

5 Place the heel of your other hand just above your index finger on the breastbone. This is the area of the chest where you must apply pressure.

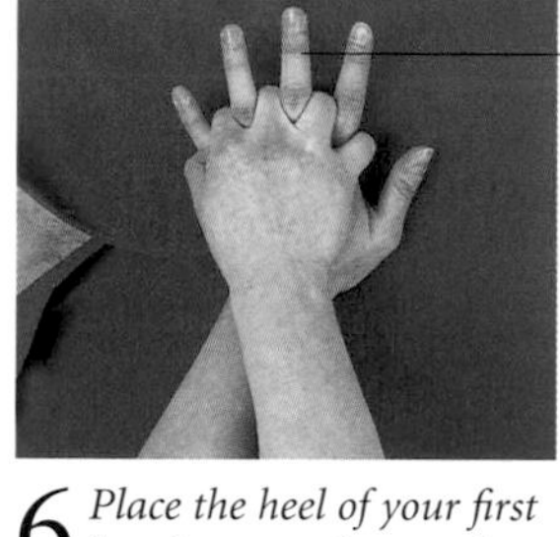

Fingers raised away from chest

6 Place the heel of your first hand on top of your other hand. Interlock the fingers, so that the fingers of the bottom hand are raised off the chest.

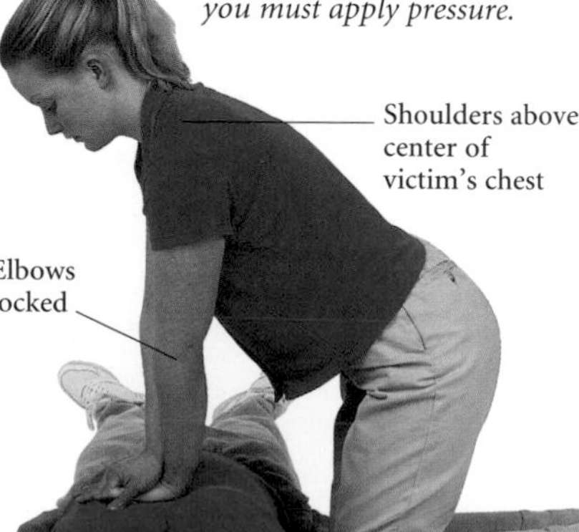

Shoulders above center of victim's chest

Elbows locked

7 With your shoulders directly above the victim and your elbows straight, apply pressure downward, depressing the breastbone 1½–2 in (4–5 cm), then release the pressure without moving your hands. Compress the chest in this manner 15 times at a rate of about 15 compressions in 9 seconds, keeping an even rhythm. Then give 2 slow breaths of artificial respiration.

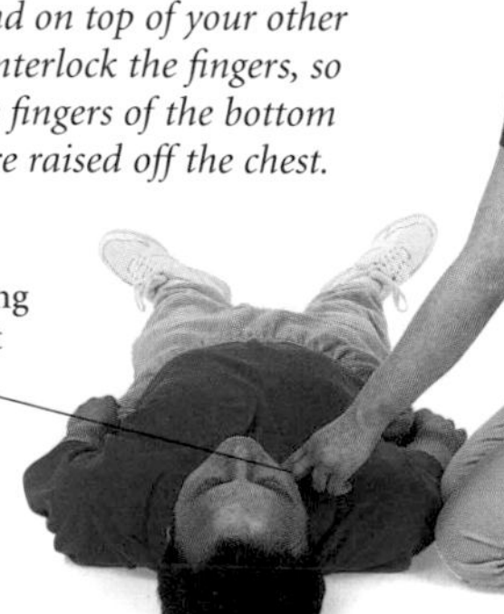

Checking pulse at neck

8 Alternate 15 chest compressions with 2 breaths of artificial respiration. After 4 cycles of compressions and breaths, and every few minutes thereafter, check the signs of breathing and circulation. If they are absent, continue CPR. If circulation and breathing return at any time, stop CPR but continue to monitor the victim until help arrives.

Cardiopulmonary resuscitation for children

If a child seems lifeless and you cannot find a pulse, he or she needs cardiopulmonary resuscitation (CPR) to force oxygenated blood from the heart and around the body. Like CPR for adults, CPR for children consists of alternating chest compressions and breaths of artificial respiration. However, the chest compressions are given with slightly less pressure, and the rate at which you do compressions and breaths is different.

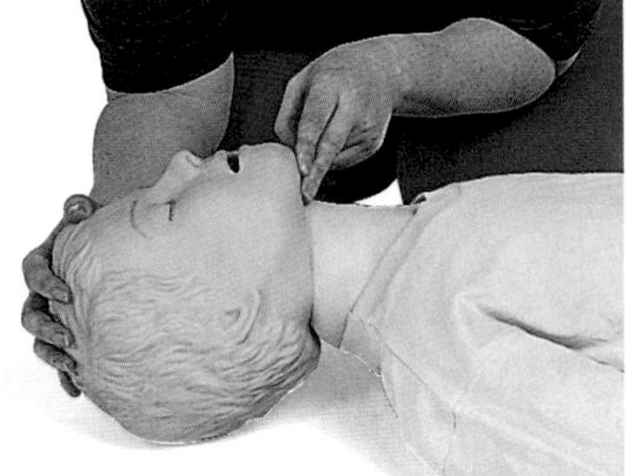

1 *Ensure an ambulance is called. Lay the child face up on a firm surface. Open the airway by tilting the head back slightly or use a modified technique for suspected spinal injury* (see OPENING THE AIRWAY – SPINAL INJURY, *p.982.)*

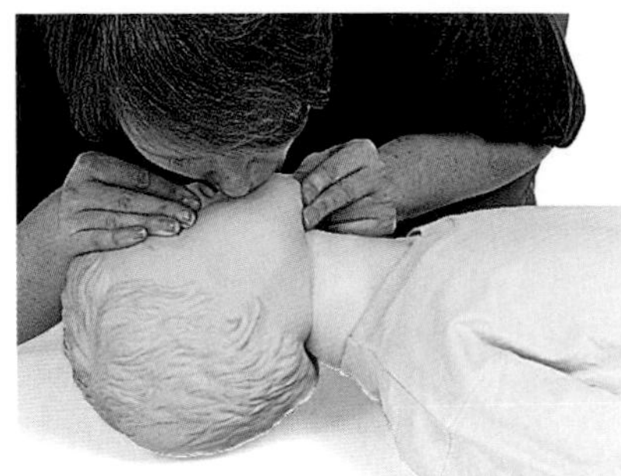

2 *If there are no signs of breathing, such as chest movement or the feel of breath on your cheek, pinch the child's nose shut and seal your lips over the mouth. Give 2 breaths of artificial respiration (p.982), pausing to take a breath yourself between each one.*

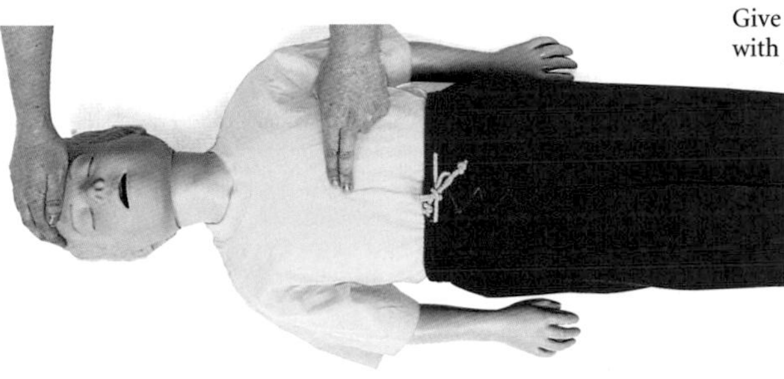

3 *Check for signs of circulation for no longer than 10 seconds and look for signs of recovery, such as return of skin color or breathing. If signs of circulation are present, continue with artificial respiration. If the child shows no signs of recovery, commence CPR* (see *Step 4).*

4 *Place your middle finger on the lower end of the child's breastbone where the ribs meet and place your index finger just above it.*

Give compressions with just one hand

5 *Place the heel of your other hand on the breastbone next to your fingers. Press down sharply with the heel of your hand on the chest to a depth of 1–1½ in (2.5–4 cm) 5 times in 3 seconds. Count from 1 to 5 to maintain an even rhythm.*

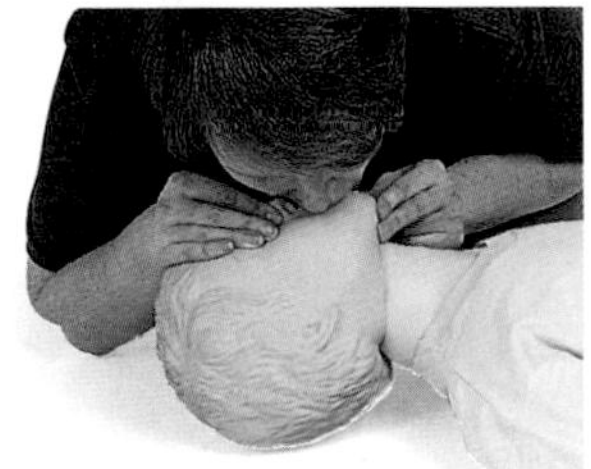

6 *Give 1 breath of artificial respiration. Repeat chest compressions – giving them with just one hand – and breaths for 1 minute. Repeat the cycle until the child recovers or help arrives. Check for signs of circulation and breathing every few minutes.*

Cardiopulmonary resuscitation for infants

If a baby under 1 year old seems lifeless and has no signs of circulation, he or she needs cardiopulmonary resuscitation (CPR) to distribute oxygen to the brain and other vital organs. CPR alternates chest compressions and artificial respiration. To avoid injury to the infant, chest compressions are given with 2 fingers only, taking care not to press too hard. When giving breaths of artificial respiration, you must not blow too hard.

1 *If you have a helper, send him or her to call an ambulance. Place the infant face up on a hard surface. Tilt the head back slightly with one hand and lift the chin with one finger of the other hand. Look, listen, and feel for signs of breathing.*

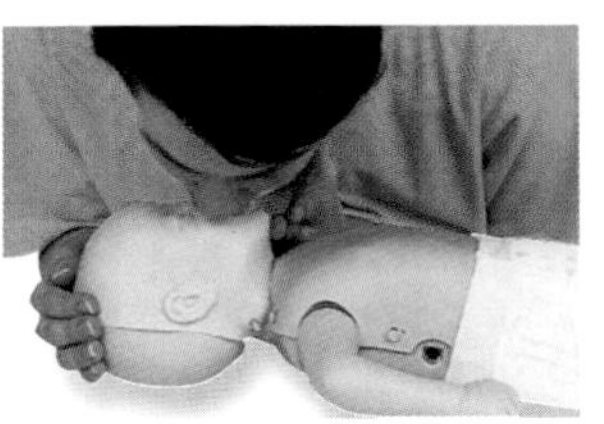

2 *If the baby is not breathing, seal your lips over the mouth and nose. Give 2 slow, gentle breaths of artificial respiration (p.983), pausing to breathe yourself between each one.*

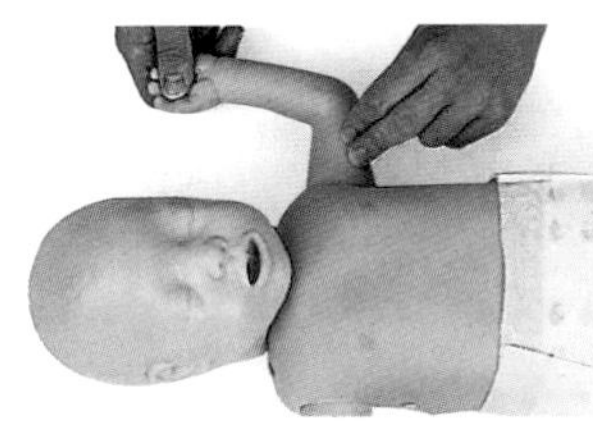

3 *Check for signs of circulation for no longer than 10 seconds and look for signs of recovery, such as return of skin color or breathing. If there are signs of circulation but no breathing, continue artificial respiration. If there is no circulation or breathing, start CPR* (see *Step 4).*

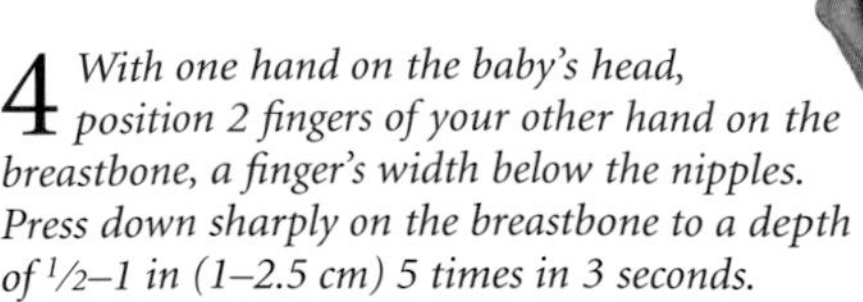

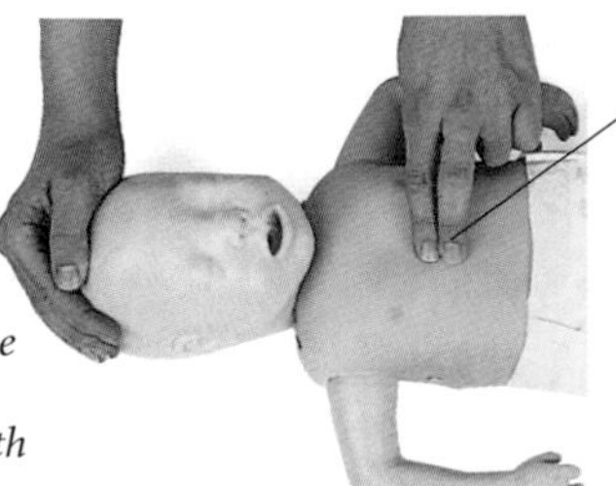

Two fingers on breastbone

4 *With one hand on the baby's head, position 2 fingers of your other hand on the breastbone, a finger's width below the nipples. Press down sharply on the breastbone to a depth of ½–1 in (1–2.5 cm) 5 times in 3 seconds.*

5 *Seal your lips over the infant's mouth and nose and give 1 breath. Check for signs of breathing. Repeat chest compressions, with just 2 fingers, and breaths for 1 minute, without blowing too hard. If the infant recovers at any time, stop CPR, but continue to monitor breathing and circulation until medical help arrives.*

Severe bleeding

Severe bleeding is dramatic and distressing and can be life-threatening. Although you must try to stop bleeding as quickly as possible, you must also be alert to the general condition of the victim. Anyone who is bleeding heavily may lose consciousness (*see* UNCONSCIOUSNESS, p.983) and is likely to develop shock (opposite page). Severe bleeding from an injury to the face or neck can cause choking (pp.980–981). Any of these conditions may need immediate treatment. Before and after treating bleeding, wash your hands well. Wear disposable gloves, if available. Follow the procedure at right to stop bleeding unless there is an object protruding from the wound (*see* SEVERE BLEEDING – EMBEDDED OBJECT, below).

SPECIAL CASE SEVERE BLEEDING – EMBEDDED OBJECT

If a foreign body is embedded in a wound, do not attempt to remove it. You may be able to stop the bleeding by applying pressure on either side of the object or by using indirect pressure. The wound should be bandaged so that no pressure is placed on the object.

1 *If blood is gushing out of the wound, use indirect pressure to stop the bleeding (right). Otherwise, try to stop the bleeding by applying pressure on either side of the object.*

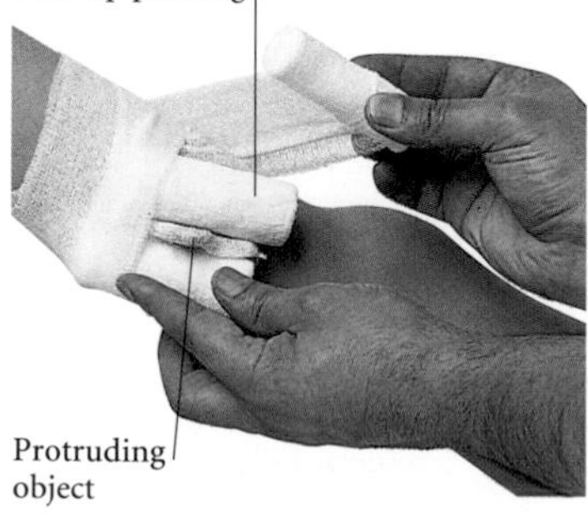
Built up padding
Protruding object

2 *When bleeding has slowed, place a piece of gauze over the wound to prevent infection. Build up padding to the same height as the protruding object. Bandage around the padding without pressing on the object.*

1 *Place a sterile dressing (p.996), pad, or clean cloth over the wound and press firmly in place for at least 10 minutes or longer if necessary until bleeding stops. If no clean dressing is available, ask the victim to apply pressure with the fingers or palm of his or her own hand.*

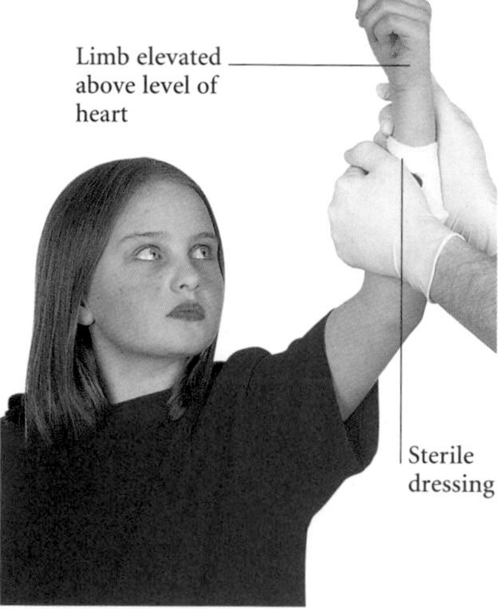
Limb elevated above level of heart
Sterile dressing

2 *If bleeding does not stop, raise the injured part above the level of the heart, if possible, and continue to apply pressure. However, if you suspect a fracture (p.992), do not move the injured part.*

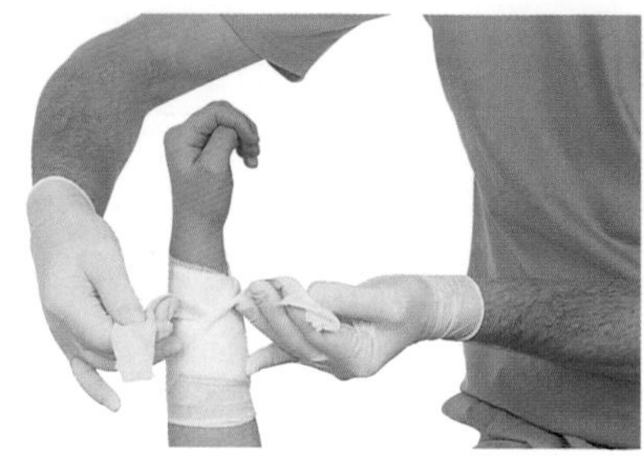

3 *Leaving any original pad in place, apply a pressure bandage (see* DRESSINGS AND BANDAGES, *pp.996–998). If blood seeps through, place another bandage on top. If blood seeps through second bandage, remove both dressings and apply a new one.*

4 *Call an ambulance. Watch for signs of shock (opposite page), and treat if necessary. Continue to check the dressing for seepage of blood.*

WARNING

- Do not apply a tourniquet. This can make the bleeding worse and may result in tissue damage.
- Do not remove a foreign body embedded in a wound.

TECHNIQUE INDIRECT PRESSURE TO STOP BLEEDING

Indirect pressure can be used to stem bleeding from a limb when the flow of blood is too great to slow by direct pressure or if an object is protruding from the wound. To stop bleeding in this situation, you can press on a main artery above the site of the bleeding, at so-called pressure points. The pressure points you are most likely to need to use are at points on the brachial and femoral arteries in the arms and legs, respectively.

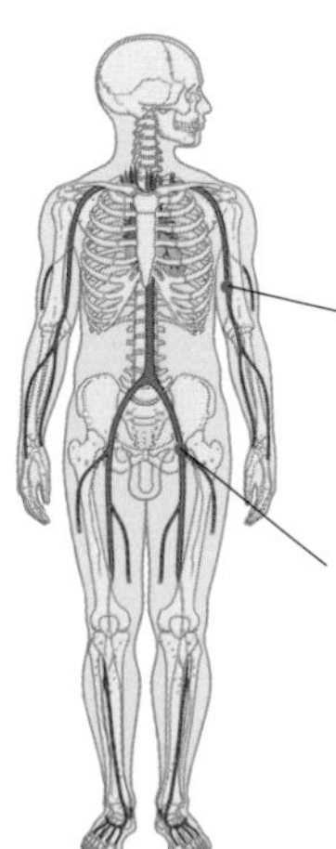
Brachial pressure point
This point lies just under the biceps muscle on the inner side of the upper arm, where the brachial artery runs near to the humerus
Femoral pressure point
This pressure point is located at the point where the femoral artery crosses the pelvic bone, in the center of the crease of the groin

1 *Find the pressure point by feeling for a pulse with your fingertips. To feel for the femoral artery in the leg, the person should be lying down.*

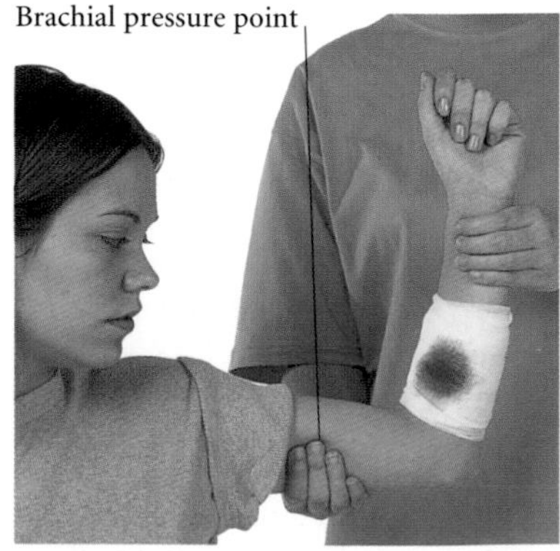
Brachial pressure point

2 *Press against the artery for up to 10 minutes, until the blood supply to the lower part of the limb is greatly reduced. Use your fingertips to press against the brachial artery in the arm (as shown here). For the femoral artery, use your thumbs or the heel of your hand.*

Shock

Shock can occur as a result of any severe injury or illness that dramatically reduces the flow of blood around the body, such as a heart attack or severe bleeding. If it is not treated rapidly, vital organs such as the brain and heart may fail, which can lead to death.

The first signs of shock may include a rapid pulse; pale, gray-blue coloring, especially on the lips; and sweating with cold, clammy skin. Later symptoms may include excessive thirst and nausea and vomiting. The victim may feel weak or dizzy and develop rapid, shallow breathing and a faint pulse. Eventually he or she may become restless, gasp for air, and lose consciousness. It is essential to call for medical help as soon as you notice early signs of shock and to prevent the condition from deteriorating by keeping the victim warm and comfortable.

WARNING

- Do not leave the victim alone, except to call an ambulance.
- Do not let the victim eat or drink unless he or she has diabetes and is hypoglycemic.

1 *If you have a helper, send him or her to call an ambulance immediately. In the meantime, provide treatment for any obvious cause of shock, such as severe bleeding (opposite page).*

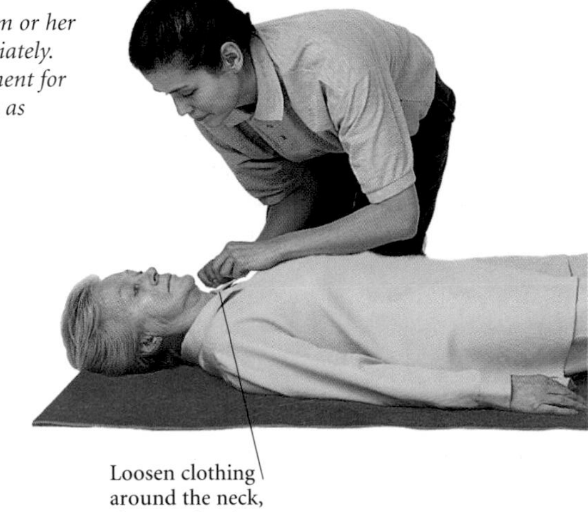

2 *If the person is breathing normally, lay him or her down. If the person is having difficulty breathing, help him or her sit in a comfortable position.*

Loosen clothing around the neck, chest, and waist

3 *Loosen any items of clothing causing restriction around the neck, chest, and waist. Remove the victim's shoes. Call an ambulance if a helper has not already done so.*

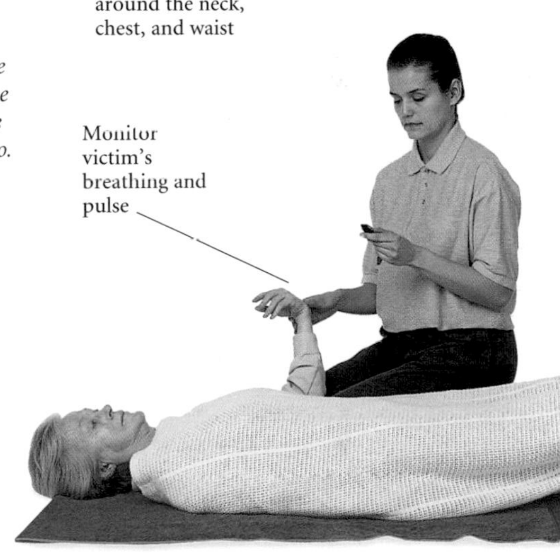

Monitor victim's breathing and pulse

4 *Keep the victim warm with a blanket or coat. Check his or her level of consciousness by asking simple, direct questions. Monitor breathing and pulse and be prepared to resuscitate if necessary (see* ABC OF RESUSCITATION, *p.978).*

Anaphylactic shock

Anaphylactic shock is a life-threatening allergic reaction to a particular food, drug, or insect sting. It can develop within seconds or a few minutes. The victim may be anxious and may have puffiness around the eyes, swelling of the face, lips, and tongue, and an itchy, red skin rash. He or she may develop wheezing and severe breathing difficulties and may lose consciousness. A victim with anaphylactic shock needs an injection of epinephrine and must be given oxygen as quickly as possible. Some people are aware they have an allergy and carry a supply of epinephrine, in which case you can help them to use this. Otherwise, first aid is limited to keeping the person comfortable and, if necessary, helping him or her breathe until medical help arrives.

WARNING

Do not leave the victim alone, except to call an ambulance.

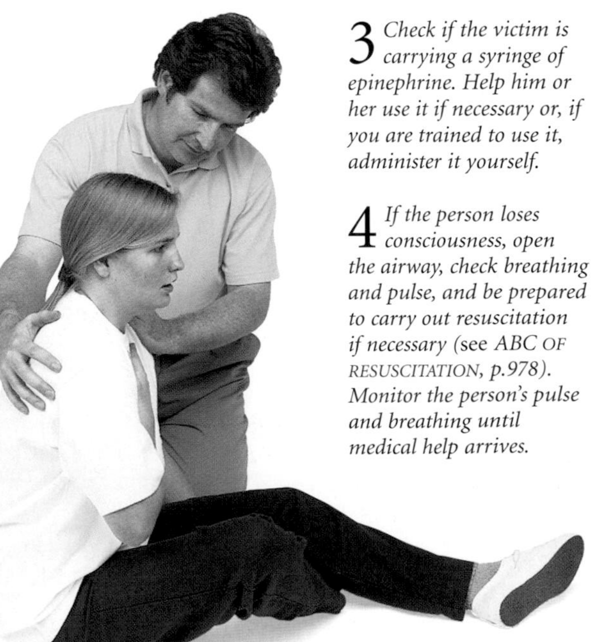

1 *Call an ambulance or send a helper to do so immediately. If possible, provide the emergency services with details of the cause of the allergic reaction.*

2 *If the victim is conscious, help him or her to sit up in the position that makes breathing easiest.*

3 *Check if the victim is carrying a syringe of epinephrine. Help him or her use it if necessary or, if you are trained to use it, administer it yourself.*

4 *If the person loses consciousness, open the airway, check breathing and pulse, and be prepared to carry out resuscitation if necessary (see* ABC OF RESUSCITATION, *p.978). Monitor the person's pulse and breathing until medical help arrives.*

Severe burns

A severe burn may involve all the layers of the skin. If it is very severe, it may also destroy the tissues underlying the skin. The affected area may appear red and may have blisters that weep clear fluid. In some cases, the area may be brown or charred or may look white if the burn extends very deep. If the nerve endings have been damaged, there may be a loss of feeling in the injured area. The immediate concern with a serious burn is to cool the area rapidly in order to minimize damage and prevent loss of body fluids and the onset of shock (p.987). It is also essential to protect the wound from infection. The larger and deeper a burn is, the greater the risk of shock or infection. A victim burned in a fire will probably have suffered damage to the airway. You should monitor his or her breathing regularly.

WARNING
- Do not touch the burn.
- Do not apply anything to the burn other than cool water.
- Do not apply ice or ice water directly to the burned area.
- Do not burst blisters.
- Do not immerse in water unless only a small area is affected.

1 *If possible, remove the victim from the source of the burn and put out any flames on the person's clothing. If you have a helper, send him or her to call an ambulance.*

2 *Lay the victim down. Watch for signs of difficulty breathing. Be ready to resuscitate if necessary (see* ABC OF RESUSCITATION, *p.978).*

3 *If possible, raise the burned area above the level of the heart. Do not touch the burn or try to remove anything that is sticking to it. Call an ambulance if a helper has not already done so.*

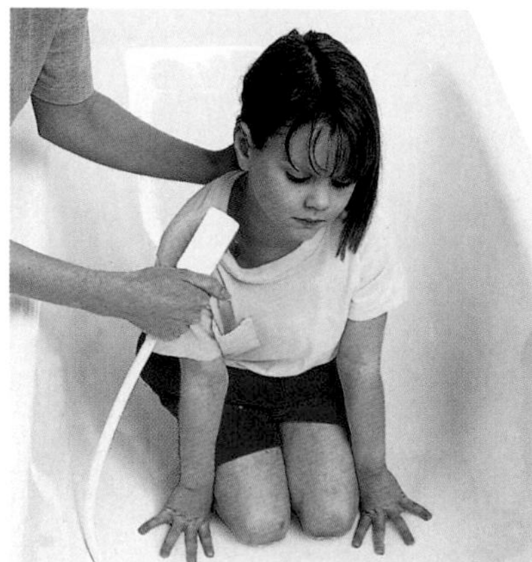

4 *Douse the burn with plenty of cool water, immerse it in water if only a small area is affected, or cover it with cold, wet towels for at least 10 minutes or until the burn has cooled down. If no tap water is available, use any other suitable source, such as a garden hose, shower, or bottled water.*

5 *Once the burn has cooled, gently remove or cut away any clothing (unless sticking to the burn), shoes, belts, or jewelry before the area starts to swell or blister. Do not touch blisters. If pain persists, cool the area again.*

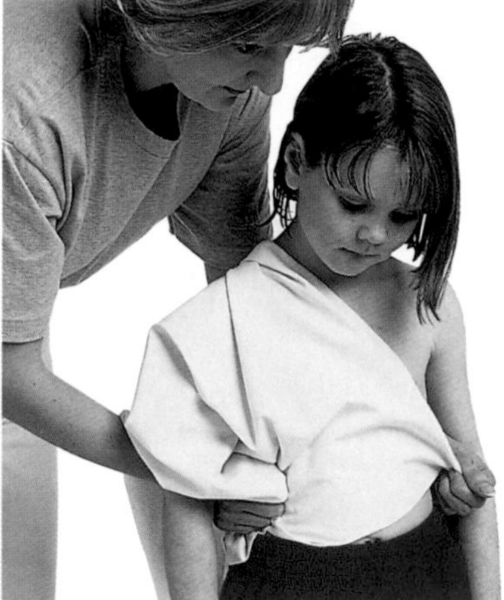

6 *Cover the burn with a prepacked sterile dressing (p.996) or improvise a dressing with clean, non-fluffy material, such as part of a pillowcase or a clean sheet. Loosely bandage in place but do not apply adhesive dressings or adhesive tape to the affected skin. Facial burns do not need to be covered.*

7 *Record details of the injuries and try to establish the cause. Reassure the victim while you wait for medical help, and monitor breathing and pulse (see* ABC OF RESUSCITATION, *p.978). If the burn is extensive, watch for signs of shock (p.987), such as rapid pulse and cool, moist skin, and be prepared to treat appropriately.*

Minor burns and scalds

A minor burn involves damage to only the top layer of skin. The injured area may be red and painful and may swell and blister. Although minor burns can be painful, most heal well within a few days if treated promptly with appropriate first aid measures. Medical attention is usually not required. However, if you are unsure about the severity of a burn, you should always seek medical advice.

WARNING
- Do not apply anything other than cool water to the injury to stop the burning.
- Do not burst blisters.

Cool water

1 *Pour cool water over the injured area for at least 10 minutes to stop the burning and relieve the pain. If no tap water is available, use any other suitable source, including a garden hose or bottled water.*

2 *Once the burn has cooled, gently remove constricting clothing, shoes, belt, or jewelry from the affected area before it begins to swell.*

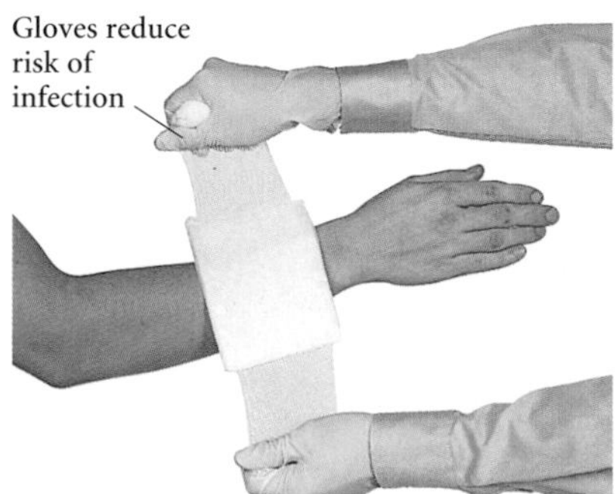
Gloves reduce risk of infection

3 *Cover the affected area with a sterile dressing (p.996) or any clean, non-fluffy material. Bandage the dressing loosely in place. Do not apply adhesive dressings or tape to the injured skin.*

4 *Check the wound daily for signs of infection, such as increasing pain, swelling, redness, or pus. If you suspect infection, contact your doctor at once.*

Major seizures

A major seizure is a disturbance in the electrical activity of the brain that leads to muscular spasms and loss of body control. Recurring major seizures are associated mainly with epilepsy (p.524). During a seizure, a person suddenly falls unconscious, often letting out a cry. The body may become rigid and the back may arch. Breathing becomes irregular and may temporarily cease. The victim may clench the jaw, bite the tongue, or drool, and the eyes may roll upward. The convulsions usually last for 1–3 minutes. Afterward, breathing returns to normal, and the victim usually recovers consciousness within a few minutes. The victim may feel dazed or fall into a deep sleep.

1 *The victim of a seizure has to be protected from injuring him or herself during the seizure. Support the victim if you see him or her falling and lower him or her gently to the ground. Ask bystanders to move away and remove any objects which could cause injury from the vicinity.*

2 *Once you have laid the victim gently down on the ground, loosen the clothing around his or her neck and try to protect his or her head with something soft, such as a piece of clothing.*

3 *Once you are sure that the victim's convulsions have stopped, place him or her in the recovery position (p.979). Monitor breathing and signs of circulation (see ABC OF RESUSCITATION, p.978).*

WARNING

- Do not use force to restrain the victim.
- Do not put anything in the victim's mouth.

4 *If the victim has a severe seizure and is unconscious for more than 10 minutes or convulses for more than 5 minutes, or if the person has repeated seizures, call an ambulance and monitor breathing and signs of circulation until the ambulance arrives.*

5 *If the victim has not had a severe seizure or repeated seizures and you know that he or she has epilepsy, stay with the person until he or she has recovered. If you are not sure the person has epilepsy, call an ambulance and stay with the victim until it arrives.*

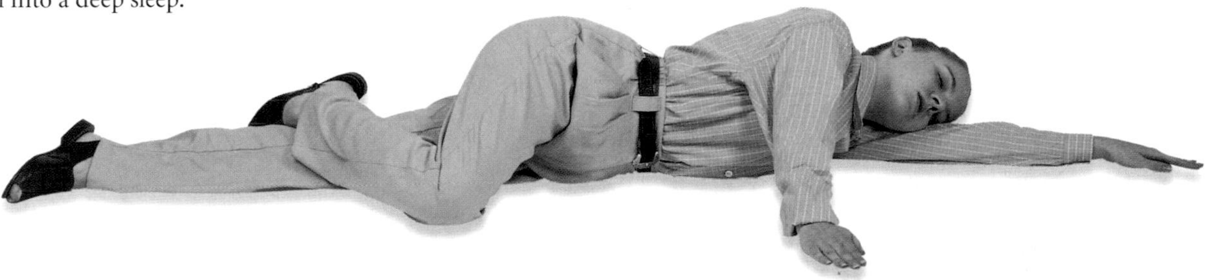

Febrile convulsions

Febrile convulsions are seizures that can occur in young children as a result of a very high temperature. They are most common in children who are under age 5. During a febrile convulsion, the eyes may roll back, the head and body may jerk erratically, and the child may hold his or her breath. As well, the child's back may arch, his or her legs and arms may become stiff, and the fists may clench. During a convulsion of this kind, it is essential to lower the child's temperature and to protect the child from injury. Although very alarming for parents, febrile convulsions are rarely dangerous.

WARNING

- Do not use force to restrain the victim.
- Do not put anything in the victim's mouth.

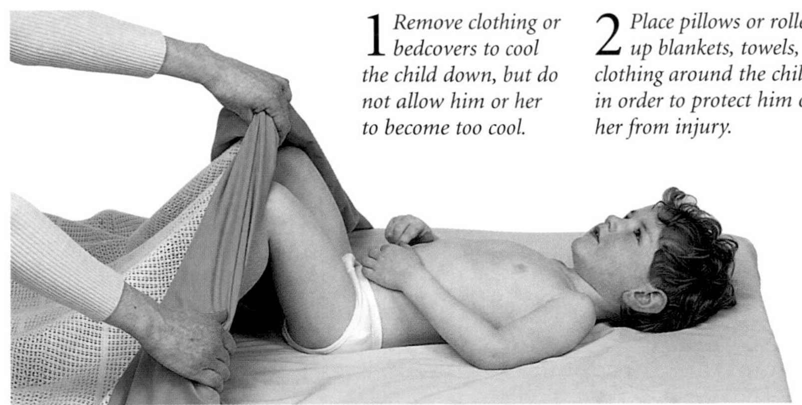

1 *Remove clothing or bedcovers to cool the child down, but do not allow him or her to become too cool.*

2 *Place pillows or rolled-up blankets, towels, or clothing around the child in order to protect him or her from injury.*

3 *Once the febrile convulsions have stopped, sponge the child all over with tepid water, not cold water, working from the head down. Do not use alcohol baths, and never cool the child too much because this may bring on another seizure. Monitor the child's temperature at regular intervals, and stop cooling the child once his or her body temperature has reached normal (98.6°F/37°C).*

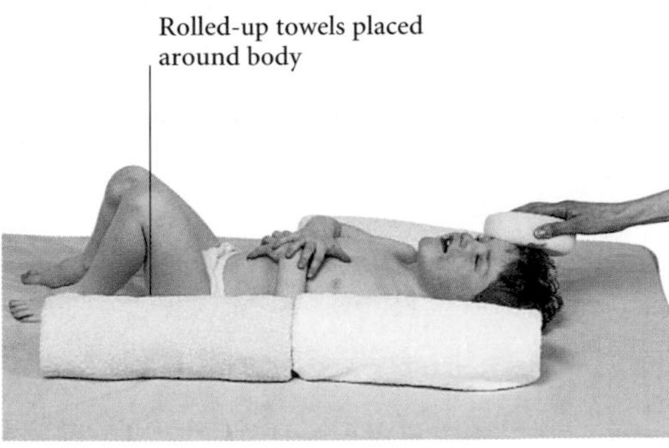

Rolled-up towels placed around body

Spinal injury

The main danger of dealing with someone with spinal injury is the risk of causing further damage to the spine or of severing the spinal cord. Spinal injury is potentially serious, and you should seek emergency help immediately. When calling the emergency services, try to inform them of how the injury to the spine occurred. If you suspect an injury to the spinal cord, it is essential to keep the victim still until a doctor arrives. Signs of possible spinal cord damage include a burning sensation or tingling in a limb or loss of feeling in a limb. The victim may also have breathing difficulties.

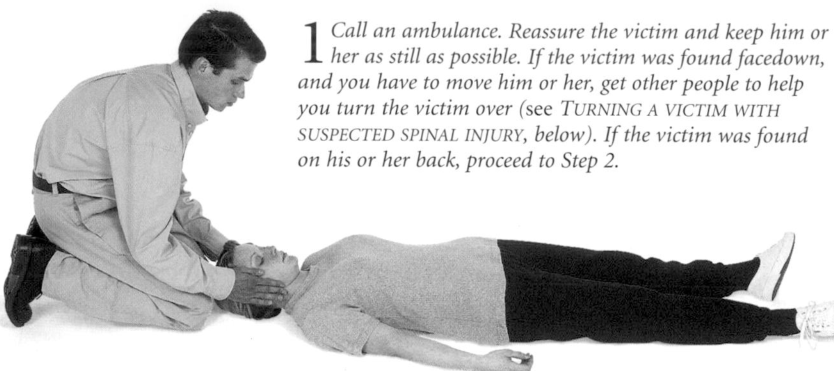

1 Call an ambulance. Reassure the victim and keep him or her as still as possible. If the victim was found facedown, and you have to move him or her, get other people to help you turn the victim over (see TURNING A VICTIM WITH SUSPECTED SPINAL INJURY, *below**). If the victim was found on his or her back, proceed to Step 2.*

2 Stabilize the victim's head and neck in the position the victim was found. Maintain support of this position until the ambulance arrives.

3 If you urgently need to realign the victim, kneel by the victim's head, place your hands firmly over his or her ears, and move the head slowly into position. Stay in this position until the ambulance arrives.

WARNING

Do not move the victim from the position he or she was found in unless he or she is in danger or loses consciousness and needs resuscitation. If you must move the victim, use the log-roll technique (below).

4 If you have a helper, extra stability can be provided by getting him or her to place rolled-up clothes, towels, or blankets on either side of the victim's head and shoulders to minimize movement.

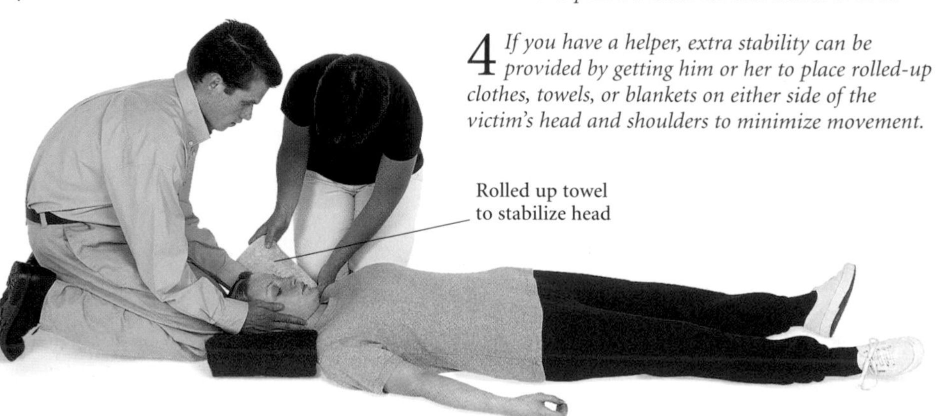
Rolled up towel
to stabilize head

SPECIAL CASE: Moving a victim with suspected spinal injury

When a spinal injury is suspected, the victim should not be moved unless absolutely necessary except by trained personnel. However, sometimes moving a victim is unavoidable in order to maintain the airway or to protect the victim from danger. It is best to have several helpers working together to move the victim.

1 Support and steady the victim in the position he or she was found. Place your hands over the ears, hold the head in the neutral position, and maintain support.

Support head and
neck with your hands

2 If possible, cross the victim's arms across his or her chest and bind the wrists, legs, and ankles together to aid in rolling him or her as a unit.

3 While you continue to support the victim's spine, you should also continuously support his or her head. The helper positioned at the victim's head should direct the other helpers in order to ensure that everyone moves the victim at the same time and as slowly and gently as possible.

Person at head
directs helpers
Maintain
position
by holding
the feet

Head injury

It is usually difficult to determine the extent of damage in head injuries, and proper assessment by trained medical staff is required. You should suspect a head injury if there is bleeding or bruising at the site of the wound or a depression in the scalp. A person who has hit his or her head may have sustained a head injury even when there is no visible wound.

Signs of head injury include dizziness, nausea and vomiting, headache, impaired vision, and sudden memory loss. Blood or watery fluid leaking from the ear or nose may indicate that the skull is fractured. The victim may lose consciousness (*see* UNCONSCIOUSNESS, p.983) and may develop signs of shock (p.987), such as a rapid pulse, gray-blue color, and sweaty, clammy skin.

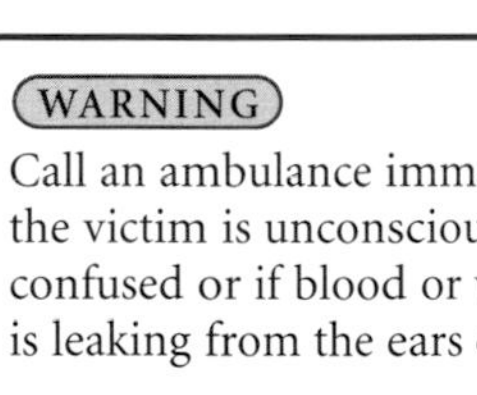

WARNING

Call an ambulance immediately if the victim is unconscious or acting confused or if blood or watery fluid is leaking from the ears or nose.

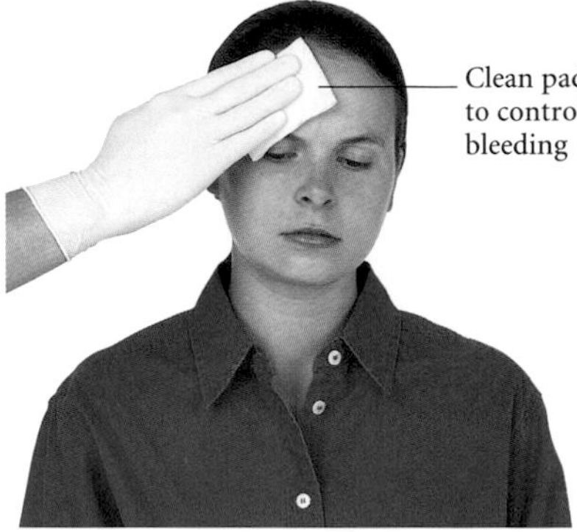
Clean pad to control bleeding

1 *Before treating bleeding from a wound, wash your hands thoroughly. Put on rubber gloves if possible. If there is a scalp wound, replace any skin flaps. Press a clean pad firmly and evenly over the wound to control the blood flow.*

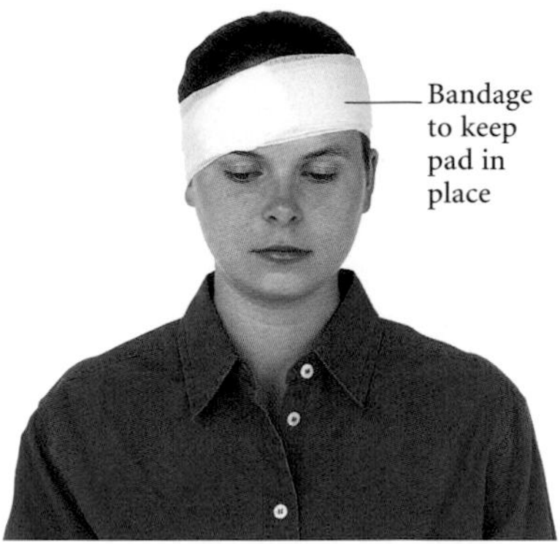
Bandage to keep pad in place

2 *When the bleeding has been controlled, bandage the head to keep the pad in place over the wound. Secure the bandage well away from the wound.*

3 *Check that the victim is fully conscious by asking simple, direct questions. If the person is alert and responds normally to your questions, lay him or her down in a comfortable position with the head and shoulders supported. Arrange for transportation to the hospital for medical assessment. If the person does not respond or seems confused, proceed to Step 4.*

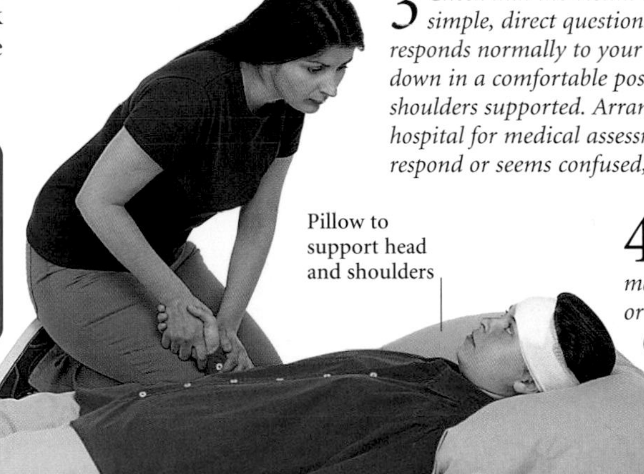
Pillow to support head and shoulders

4 *Call an ambulance. If you need to leave the person to make the call yourself, place him or her in the recovery position (p.979). While waiting for medical help, monitor the victim's breathing and pulse (see ABC OF RESUSCITATION, p.978) and be ready to resuscitate if necessary.*

Sprains and strains

Sprains are injuries in which ligaments and other tissues that surround a joint are stretched or torn. In strains, muscles or tendons are overstretched and damaged. Both sprains and strains may lead to pain, swelling, deformity, and discoloration in the injured area. There may also be loss of feeling. A severe sprain or strain can produce symptoms similar to those of a fracture. If you are in any doubt about the cause, treat as you would for a fracture (p.992). Otherwise, follow the "RICE" procedure of rest, ice, compression, and elevation. When you apply compression, you must make sure that you do not inhibit blood flow to the area.

1 *Try to make the victim comfortable by steadying and supporting the injured part. Rest an injured limb on your knee or in your lap if it helps.*

2 *Apply a cold compress or an ice pack to the affected area for several minutes to reduce any swelling, bruising, and pain. Do not apply ice directly to the skin.*

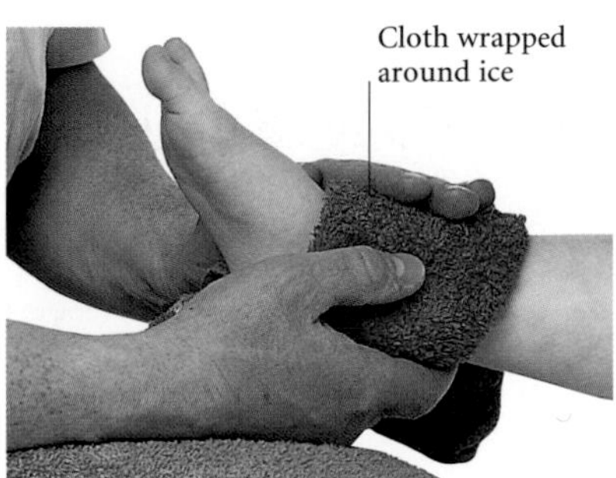
Cloth wrapped around ice

3 *Use a thick layer of padding, such as cotton, to apply gentle, even pressure to the injured area. Secure it in place with a bandage, making sure it is not too tight (see DRESSINGS AND BANDAGES, pp.996–998).*

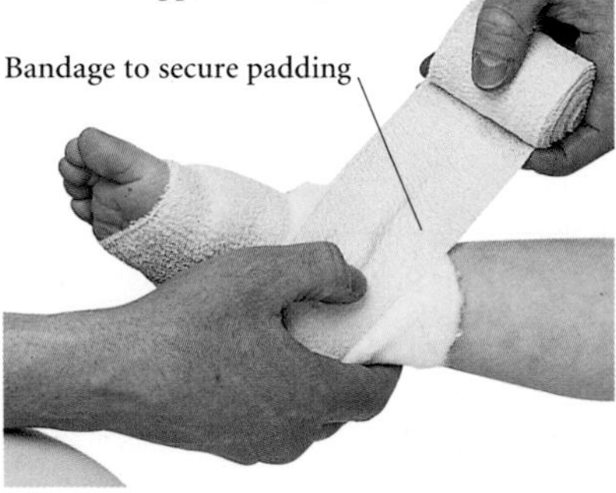
Bandage to secure padding

4 *Raise and support the limb to help reduce bruising and swelling. Advise the victim to rest the injured area and to see a doctor.*

Upper limb fractures

Upper limb fractures may involve any of the bones in the arm or the collarbone. You should suspect a fracture if the person cannot move the injured part or it is misshapen or very painful. There is likely to be swelling and bruising and possibly bleeding and a visible wound. A person with an upper limb fracture is usually able to walk and can be taken to the hospital. The injured part must be kept as still as possible. This is especially important for elbow injuries; nerves and blood vessels in this area are easily damaged.

WARNING

Do not give the victim anything to eat or drink, in case he or she needs general anesthesia in the hospital.

1 *Sit the victim down. If necessary, treat bleeding (see* SEVERE BLEEDING, *p.986).*

2 *Tell the victim to hold the injured arm across his or her chest in the position that is most comfortable. Ask the victim to support his or her arm or wrist, if possible. Alternatively, support it yourself.*

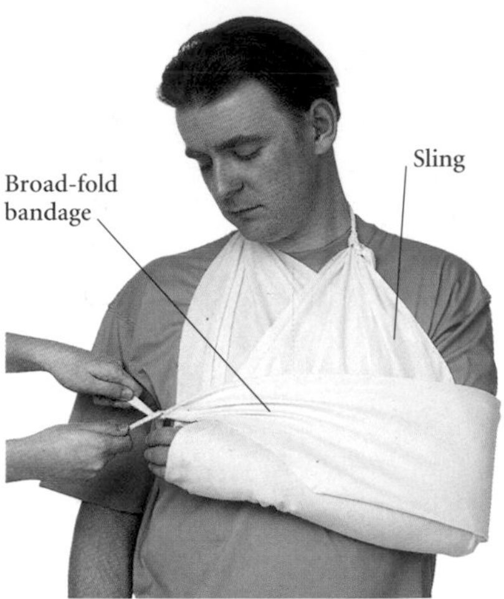
Broad-fold bandage
Sling

3 *Place the arm on the injured side in a sling, and put soft padding between the arm and the chest. If necessary to keep the arm still, tie a broad-fold bandage around the chest and over the sling (see* SLINGS, *p.998).*

4 *Take or send the victim to the hospital, keeping him or her seated if possible.*

Lower limb fractures

Fracture of a lower limb bone is a serious injury and requires immediate treatment in the hospital. It is important that the victim does not put any weight on the injured limb. A person with a lower limb fracture is likely to be in severe pain and may not be able to move the affected part. The injured area may be swollen and bruised, and there may be a visible wound with bleeding. If the thigh bone (femur) is fractured, the affected leg may be turned outward and appear shorter than the uninjured leg. Fractures of the shaft of the thigh bone usually involve heavy internal bleeding. If there is serious bleeding, the victim may develop signs of shock (p.987), including a rapid pulse, pale or gray-blue coloring, and sweaty, clammy, cold skin.

WARNING

- Do not move the victim unless he or she needs to be removed from a source of danger.
- Do not give the victim anything to eat or drink, in case he or she needs general anesthesia.

1 *Help the victim lie down, and treat any bleeding (see* SEVERE BLEEDING, *p.986).*

2 *Put plenty of padding, such as rolled-up blankets or towels or folded newspaper, on both sides of the injured leg. If you have a helper, send him or her to call an ambulance.*

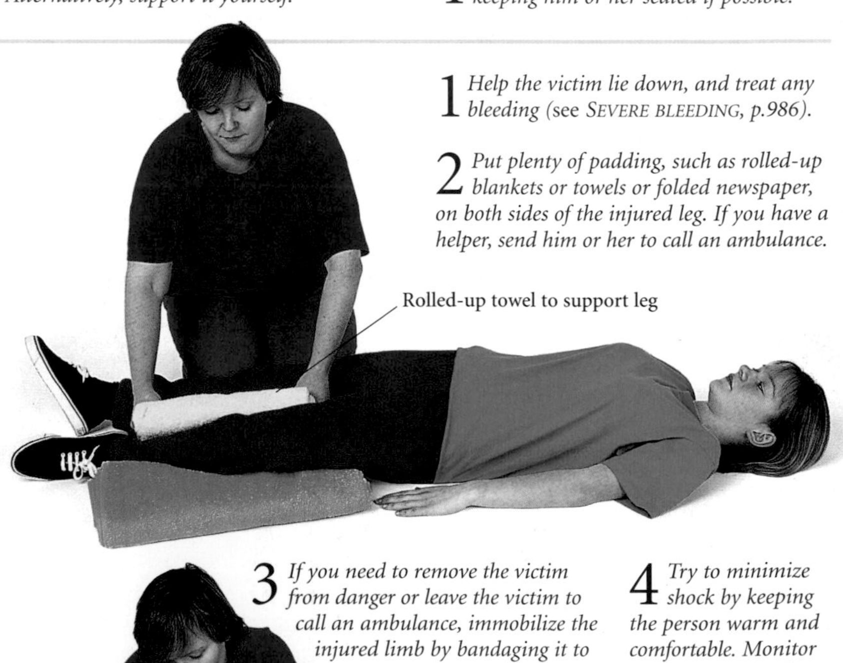
Rolled-up towel to support leg

3 *If you need to remove the victim from danger or leave the victim to call an ambulance, immobilize the injured limb by bandaging it to the sound limb. Otherwise, immobilize the injured limb by steadying and supporting it with your hands until the ambulance arrives.*

4 *Try to minimize shock by keeping the person warm and comfortable. Monitor breathing and pulse and be prepared to resuscitate (see* ABC OF RESUSCITATION, *p.978).*

Eye wound

All eye injuries are potentially serious and need prompt medical attention to minimize the risk of infection, scarring, or impaired vision. The victim may experience extreme pain, and the eyelids may go into spasm. There may be a visible wound to the eyeball, or the eye may be bloodshot and may bleed or may leak clear fluid.

WARNING
- Do not touch the affected eye or allow the victim to touch it.
- Do not remove a foreign body embedded in the eye.

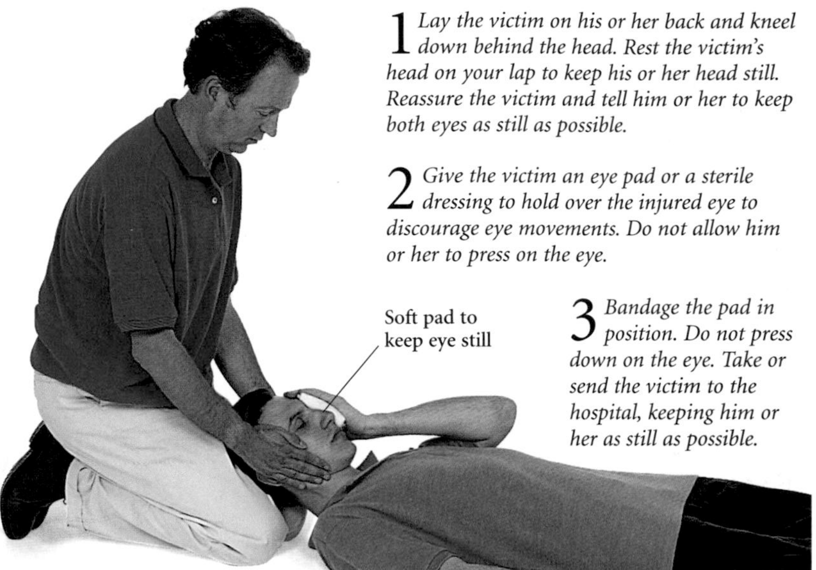

1 Lay the victim on his or her back and kneel down behind the head. Rest the victim's head on your lap to keep his or her head still. Reassure the victim and tell him or her to keep both eyes as still as possible.

2 Give the victim an eye pad or a sterile dressing to hold over the injured eye to discourage eye movements. Do not allow him or her to press on the eye.

Soft pad to keep eye still

3 Bandage the pad in position. Do not press down on the eye. Take or send the victim to the hospital, keeping him or her as still as possible.

Foreign body in the eye

A foreign body in the eye may cause irritation, redness, watering, and blurry vision. An object floating on the white of the eye is usually easily removed. However, anything that sticks to the eye, penetrates the eyeball, or rests on the colored part of the eye should be treated as an eye wound (above).

WARNING
- Do not touch the affected eye or allow the victim to touch it.
- Do not remove a foreign body embedded in the eye.

1 Sit the victim down facing the light. Use your finger and thumb to gently separate the upper and lower eyelids. Examine every part of the eye.

2 If you can see a foreign body floating on the white of the eye, try to flush it out with clean water. Tilt the head so that the damaged eye is lower than the uninjured one. Pour water into the corner of the injured eye, allowing it to drain away without it getting into the uninjured eye. Blinking under water may also make the foreign body float clear.

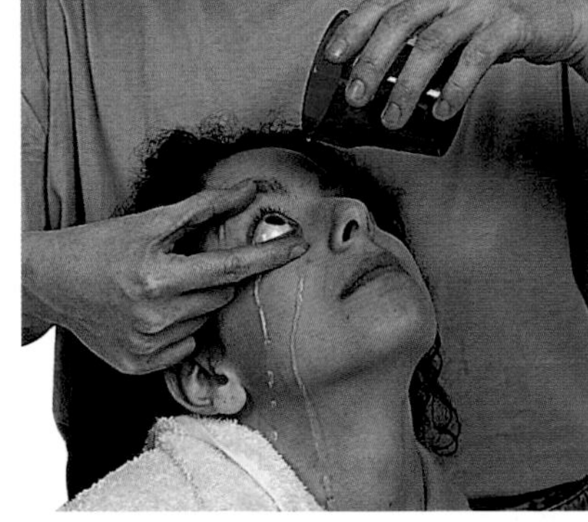

3 If flushing out the eye with water is unsuccessful, try using the corner of a clean, dampened handkerchief or tissue to lift the foreign body off the surface of the eye.

4 If the object is under the upper eyelid and you cannot remove it using a tissue, ask the victim to grasp the lashes and pull the upper lid over the lower one. This may help brush the object out of the eye.

5 If you are not able to remove the foreign object in the eye, take the victim to the hospital.

Chemicals in the eye

Chemical injury to the eye can cause serious damage, including blindness, if the victim is not treated quickly. The victim may experience extreme pain in the affected eye and he or she may not be able to open it. The eye will water profusely, become red, and swell.

WARNING
Do not touch the affected eye or allow the victim to touch it.

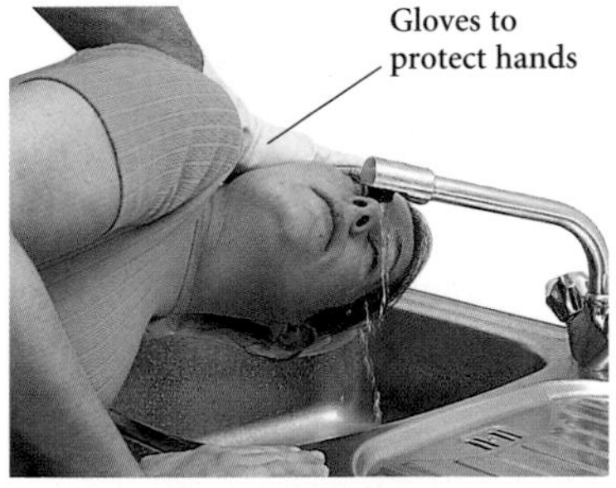

Gloves to protect hands

1 Hold the victim's head under a running faucet so that water runs over the eye for at least 10 minutes. Make sure the contaminated rinsing water does not splash you or the victim. If it is easier, use a pitcher or glass to pour the water.

2 If the victim is unable to open the eye, gently pull his or her eyelids apart in order to clean all parts of the eye and eyelids.

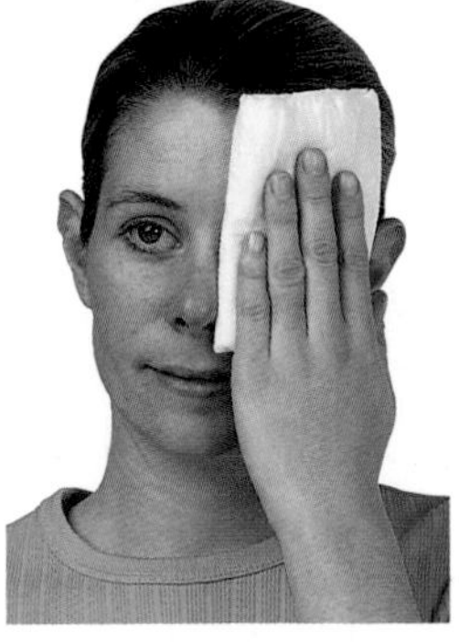

3 Ask the victim to hold a sterile pad or clean pad composed of non-fluffy material over the injured eye. If possible, identify the chemical. Take or send the victim to the hospital.

Swallowed poisons

Poisoning can be caused by swallowing household products or poisonous plants or by overdosing on recreational or medicinal drugs. Common symptoms of poisoning include abdominal or chest pain, nausea, vomiting, diarrhea, breathing difficulties, and dizziness. There may be signs of burning around the mouth and lips, the victim may appear sluggish and confused, and he or she may lose consciousness. Rarely, certain poisons can result in anaphylactic shock (p.987), a life-threatening allergic reaction. Warning signs of anaphylactic shock include swelling of the face and neck, and red, blotchy skin.

If you suspect poisoning, you must seek immediate medical assistance. Aim to provide the emergency services with as much information as you can about the poisoning, including what substance has been swallowed, how much, and how long ago.

WARNING

Do not try to induce vomiting, unless you are advised to do so by a medical professional.

1 *If the victim is conscious, ask questions to obtain as much information as possible about the poisoning. If the victim is unconscious, go to Step 3.*

2 *Call your local poison control center for further instructions. Give as much information as you can about the possible cause of the poisoning. Stay with the victim and monitor his or her condition. If he or she develops signs of shock or breathing difficulties, call an ambulance.*

3 *If the victim is unconscious or loses consciousness, check breathing and pulse and be prepared to resuscitate if necessary* (see ABC OF RESUSCITATION, *p.978*).

4 *Place the victim in the recovery position (p.979) unless you suspect he or she has a spinal injury. Call an ambulance and then return to the victim. If alcoholic poisoning is a possibility, keep the victim warm with a blanket.*

Poisonous bites and stings

A venomous bite or sting from a snake, spider, or scorpion may cause severe pain and burning at the site of the wound, with possible puncture marks, and swelling and discoloration around the area of the bite. With spider bites and scorpion stings, there may also be nausea and vomiting, sweating, excess salivation, breathing difficulties, and an irregular heartbeat. Most venomous bites and stings can be treated easily if the victim is taken to the hospital quickly. It is important to note the appearance of a snake responsible for a venomous bite in order that the appropriate antivenin can be given.

WARNING

- Do not attempt to identify a venomous snake or spider that has bitten someone by handling it.
- Clothing or jewelry can be dangerously constricting if the bite area swells. Remove as necessary.

1 *Call an ambulance and reassure the victim. If the victim has been bitten by a snake, lay him or her down, keeping the area of the bite below the heart. Tell the victim not to move.*

2 *Wash the wound carefully, and pat it dry with clean swabs or other non-fluffy material. Do not rub the wound. If the wound is from a spider bite or scorpion sting, apply a cold pack and wait for medical help. If you suspect the bite is from a venomous snake, proceed to Step 3.*

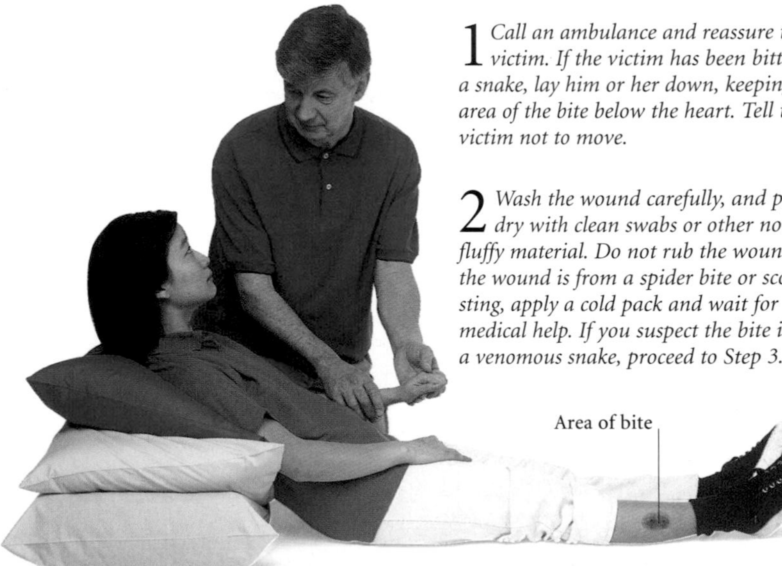
Area of bite

3 *Minimize the victim's movement to stop the venom from spreading further around the body. Immobilize an injured arm with a sling (p.998), and immobilize an injured leg by binding it to the uninjured leg.*

4 *Keep the victim calm while waiting for the ambulance. Regularly monitor the victim's breathing and pulse and be ready to resuscitate if necessary* (see ABC OF RESUSCITATION, *p.978*).

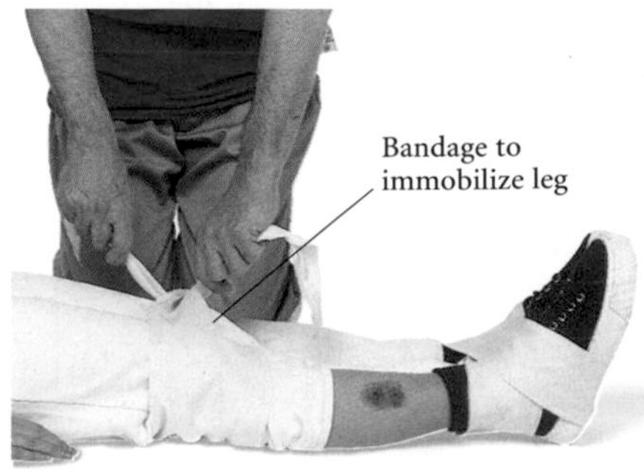
Bandage to immobilize leg

Human and animal bites

A bite from a human or a wild or domestic animal carries a high risk of transmitting infection. Even a superficial bite should be assessed by a doctor as soon as possible in case treatment with antibiotics (p.885) or an injection to protect against rabies (p.294) or tetanus (p.301) is required. First aid consists of controlling bleeding and protecting the wound from infection.

1 *Remove the victim from danger if it is safe to do so. If bitten by an animal, do not try to capture it.*

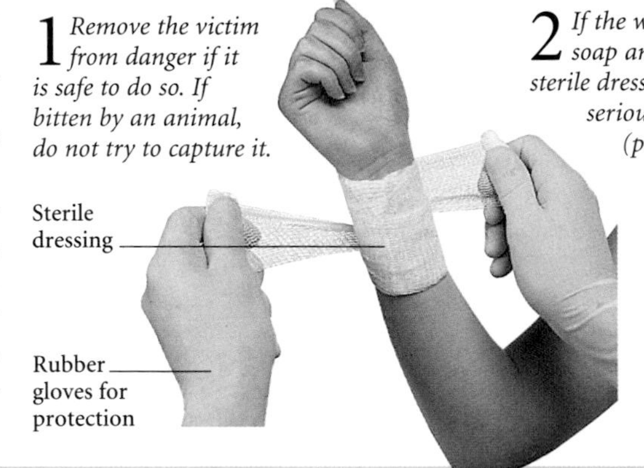
Sterile dressing
Rubber gloves for protection

2 *If the wound is superficial, wash it with soap and water, pat dry, and apply a sterile dressing (p.996). If the wound is serious, treat as for severe bleeding (p.986) and take or send the victim to the hospital.*

WARNING
Rabies and tetanus can be transmitted by animal bites. Medical assessment is essential in all cases.

Tick bites

Ticks are tiny spider-like creatures that live by attaching themselves to animals (including humans) and sucking their blood. They are found in woodlands and grasslands and are most active during the summer. An unfed tick is small and may not be noticed, even when it attaches itself, because the bite is usually painless. When a tick has fed, it becomes engorged with blood and is then usually easily seen. Some ticks can transmit disease, including Lyme disease (p.302), Rocky Mountain spotted fever (p.303), and ehrlichiosis (p.302). It is therefore important to remove a tick as soon as possible.

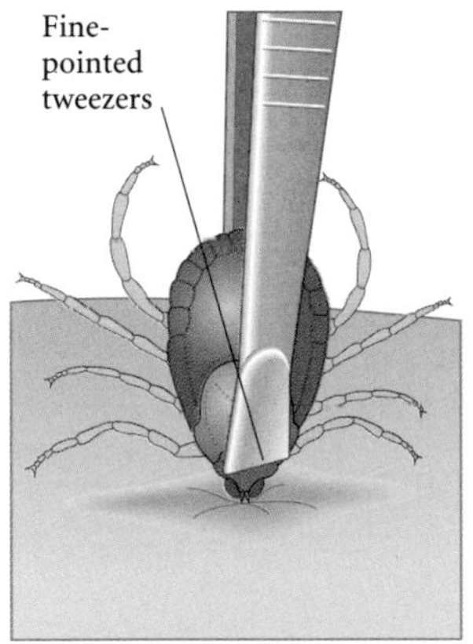
Fine-pointed tweezers

1 *If you find a tick embedded in the skin, use a pair of fine-pointed tweezers to grasp the tick's head or mouthparts at the point where it is attached.*

2 *Lever the tick steadily and firmly out of the skin with a slight rocking motion. Do not twist or jerk as you pull. Once the tick has been removed, dispose of it safely, such as by placing it in a jar of alcohol.*

3 *Wash your hands thoroughly, then apply an antiseptic to the wound. Apply a topical antibiotic (p.885) if one is available.*

4 *If a rash appears at the site of the bite or if flulike symptoms develop days or weeks after the bite, see a doctor in case you have been infected.*

WARNING
Do not apply a hot match, alcohol, or any other substance to the tick in an attempt to remove it. The tick may become more firmly embedded and even more likely to transmit disease.

Insect stings

Stings from bees, wasps, and hornets are painful and uncomfortable but are not usually life-threatening. There may be a sharp pain followed by temporary swelling, soreness, and itching. A few people are allergic to insect stings, and, in severe cases, a single sting can lead to anaphylactic shock (p.987). Signs of shock include swelling of the face, lips, and tongue; wheezing and difficulty in breathing; and a rash anywhere on the body. If anaphylactic shock is severe, the victim may lose consciousness.

1 *If there are signs of anaphylactic shock or the bite is in the mouth or throat, call an ambulance. Give a victim bitten in the mouth a piece of ice to suck or cold water to sip. If there is no indication of shock and the stinger is still in the skin, proceed to Step 2.*

2 *If the stinger is still in the wound, gently scrape it out with a needle, credit card, or fingernail. Do not use tweezers or grasp the venom sac with your fingers because this may inject more venom into the victim.*

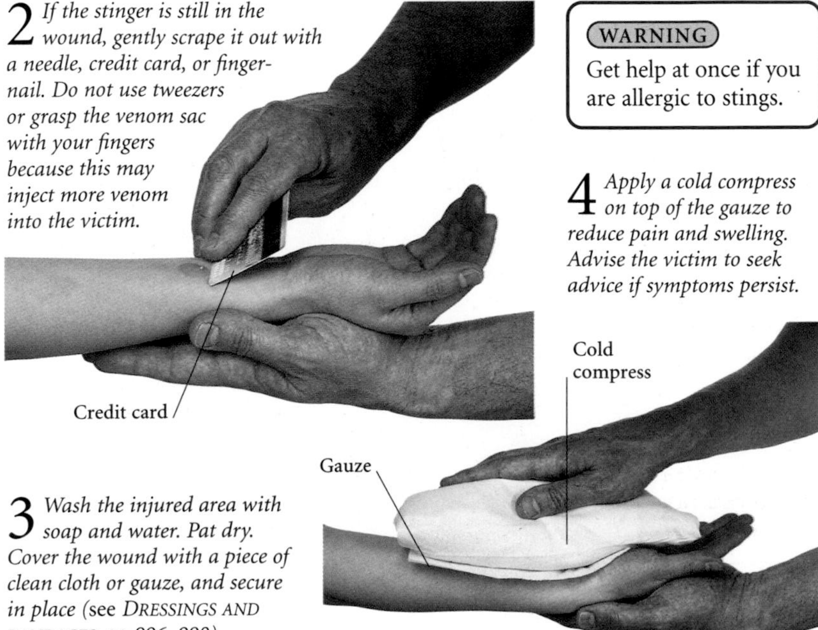
Credit card
Cold compress
Gauze

3 *Wash the injured area with soap and water. Pat dry. Cover the wound with a piece of clean cloth or gauze, and secure in place (see* DRESSINGS AND BANDAGES, *pp.996–998).*

WARNING
Get help at once if you are allergic to stings.

4 *Apply a cold compress on top of the gauze to reduce pain and swelling. Advise the victim to seek advice if symptoms persist.*

Dressings and bandages

A dressing is a protective covering or pad placed directly onto a wound to absorb blood and other fluids and to prevent infection. A bandage is a piece of fabric used to wrap or cover any part of the body. Bandages may be used to keep dressings in place, to apply pressure, or to provide support for an injured body part.

If you need to apply a dressing to a wound, use a prepackaged sterile dressing, if possible, to minimize the chance of infection. If a sterile dressing is not available, use almost any clean, dry, absorbent fabric, such as a clean handkerchief or a pillow case or sheet torn to an appropriate size.

Commercial bandages come in several materials. Those made of open-weave material such as gauze are useful for holding light dressings in place; elastic material is preferable for applying pressure to a wound to stop bleeding or to support a strain or sprain. Bandages also come in various shapes. Roller bandages are the most versatile and can be used for securing dressings on most parts of the body or for supporting an injured limb. Tubular bandages are used specifically for finger or toe injuries, and triangular bandages are used to make slings for supporting an injured arm or shoulder. You should include various sizes and types of dressings and bandages in your home first aid kit (p.976).

The articles in this section show the first aid techniques that should enable you to cope with most situations in which you need to apply a dressing or bandage. The first article shows how to apply a sterile dressing and how to secure the dressing with a roller bandage. The next two articles show the special methods needed to apply a roller bandage around an elbow or knee or to the wrist or ankle. The last two articles show how to bandage a finger or toe and how to put on a sling.

Sterile dressings

Choose a dressing size large enough to cover an area 1 in (2.5 cm) beyond all edges of the wound. Before touching the dressing, wash your hands thoroughly. Ideally, wear disposable plastic gloves. Once you have placed the dressing over the wound, bandage it in place using a roller bandage, taking care not to bandage so tightly that you impede circulation. Leave the dressing in place unless the wound needs cleaning.

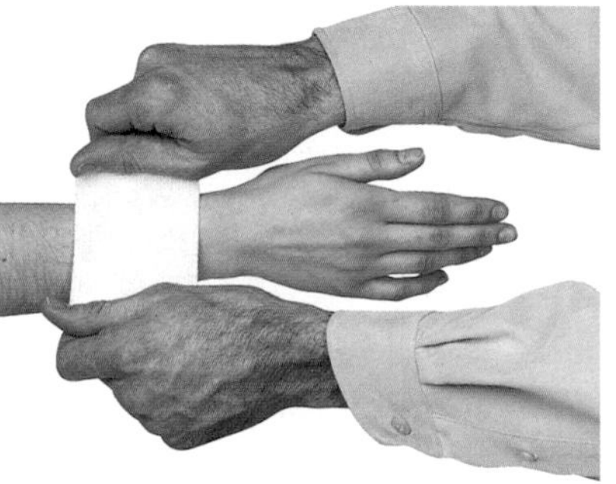

1 Grasping the edges of the dressing with the gauze face down, hold it directly over the wound, and then lower it into place.

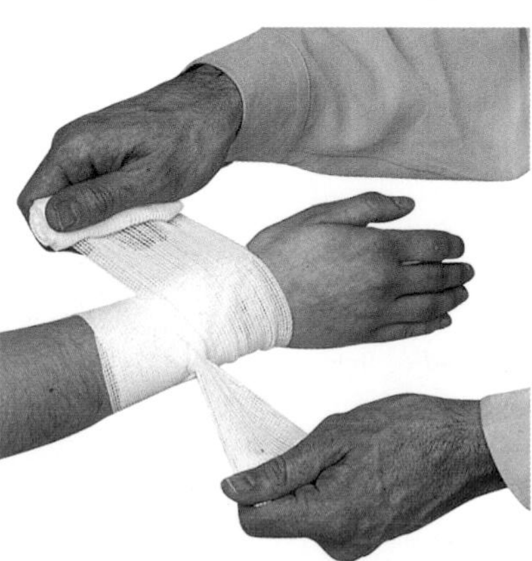

2 Hold the dressing in place by making several turns around it with a roller bandage. Continue making additional turns, overlapping the preceding strip by approximately three-quarters of its width, until the dressing is completely covered.

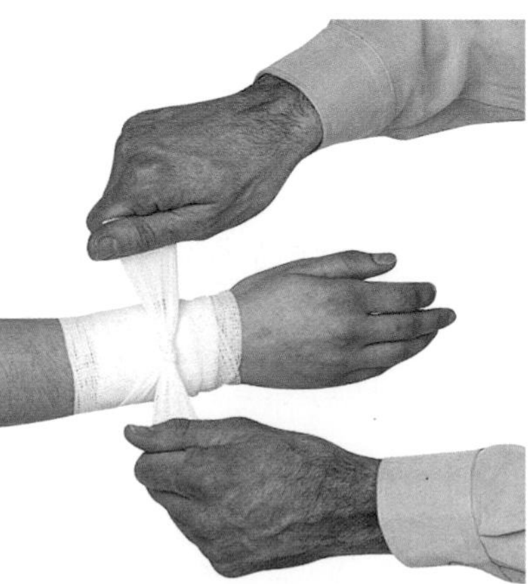

3 Cut the bandage and secure it by tying the ends or by using tape. If blood seeps through, apply another bandage over the top. Check circulation and, if necessary, loosen the bandage (see CHECKING CIRCULATION AFTER BANDAGING, right).

(TECHNIQUE) Checking circulation after bandaging

Immediately before and after bandaging a limb, check the circulation to ensure the bandage is not too tight. Every 10 minutes, recheck the circulation as an injured limb may swell. Loosen a tight bandage at once otherwise tissues may be permanently damaged.

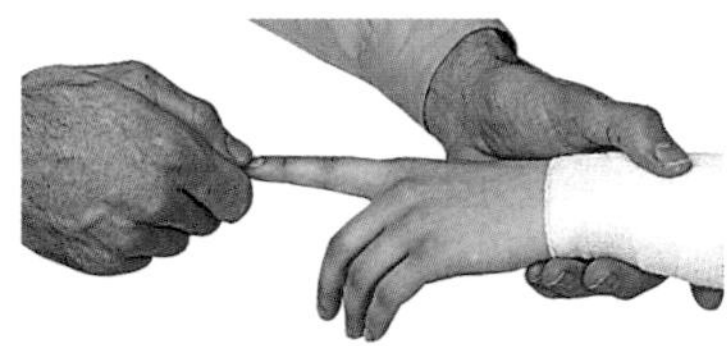

1 Press on a nail or on the skin of the hand or foot until it turns pale. If color does not return immediately when pressure is released, the bandage may be too tight.

2 To loosen a tight bandage, unwind it a few turns. Wait for color to return, then rewind the bandage more loosely. Check circulation as in Step 1.

3 Every 10 minutes, check fingers or toes for signs of impaired circulation, such as pale, cold skin, numbness, or inability to move the limb. If any of these signs are present, loosen the bandage immediately.

Elbow and knee bandages

A roller bandage applied in a figure-eight can be used to support a strain or sprain of the elbow or knee, or to hold a dressing in place at or near these joints. It is important to bandage adequately on either side of the elbow or knee as well as around the joint itself in order to provide even pressure over the entire injured area. The method shown here for bandaging an elbow can also be used for an injured knee.

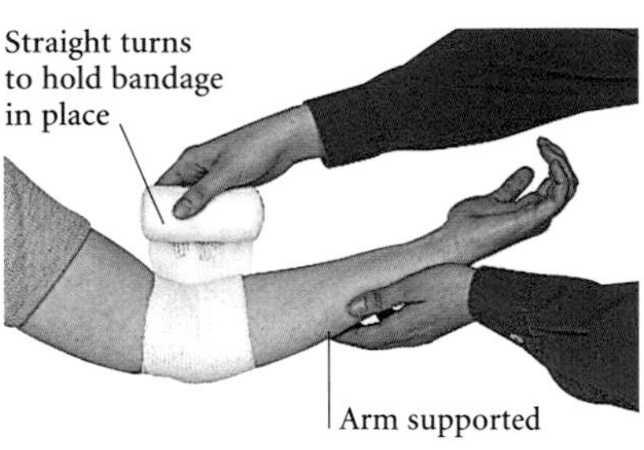
Straight turns to hold bandage in place
Arm supported

1 *Support the injured arm with one hand, keeping the elbow slightly flexed if possible. Starting at the crook of the elbow, unroll the bandage down toward the inner side of the arm and around the elbow joint. Wind the bandage around the joint several times to keep the end in place.*

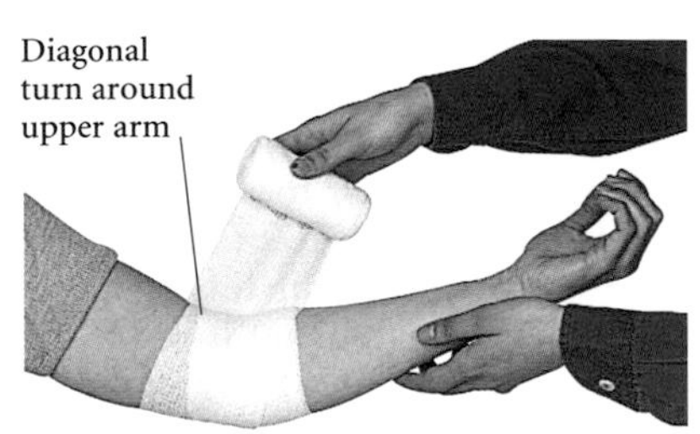
Diagonal turn around upper arm

2 *Continue to slowly unroll the bandage, bringing it around the elbow joint at a slight angle so that you make a diagonal turn around the upper arm. This new turn should cover the upper half of the previous layers from your initial turns. Continue to support the injured arm.*

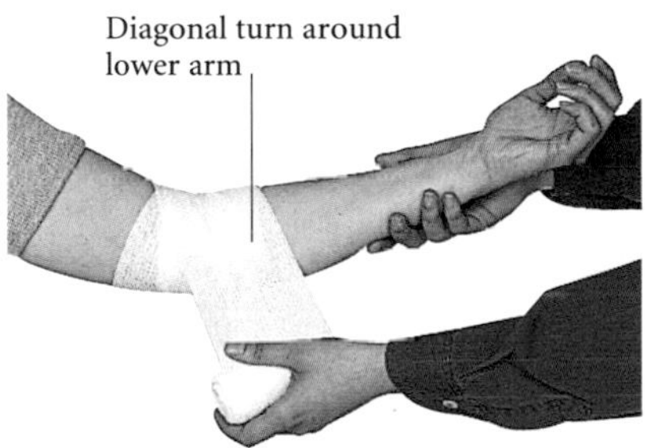
Diagonal turn around lower arm

3 *Bring the bandage down around the outside of the elbow and up to make a diagonal turn around the forearm. The bandage should cover the lower half of the bandage from your first straight turns.*

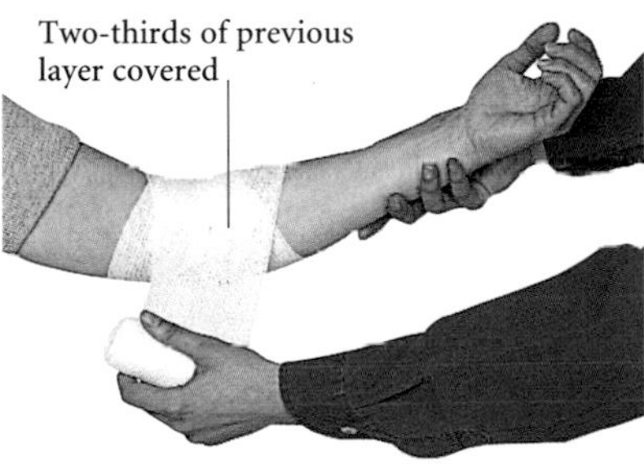
Two-thirds of previous layer covered

4 *Continue to wrap the bandage diagonally in a figure-eight above and below the joint. Each time you wrap the bandage around the joint, try to cover about two-thirds of the previous layer.*

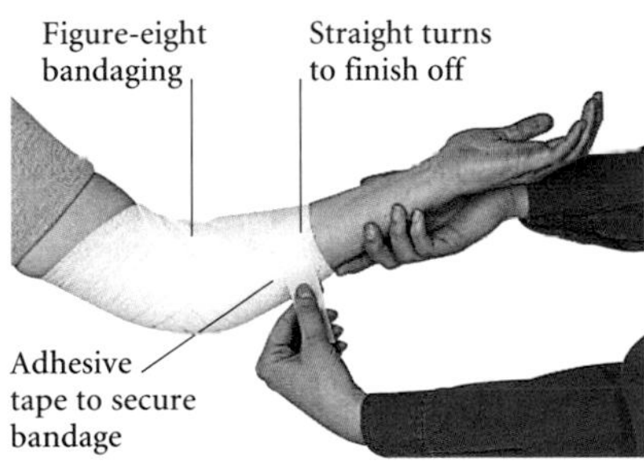
Figure-eight bandaging
Straight turns to finish off
Adhesive tape to secure bandage

5 *To finish off, make two straight turns around the forearm and secure the end. Check circulation and loosen the bandage if necessary* (see CHECKING CIRCULATION AFTER BANDAGING, *opposite page*).

Hand and foot bandages

You may need to apply a bandage to a hand or foot in order to provide support for a sprain or strain or to hold a dressing in place. The method shown here uses a roller bandage applied in diagonal fashion and can be used for either a hand or a foot. When bandaging a foot, substitute the big toe for the thumb and leave the heel unbandaged. The fingertips or toes should not be covered so that you can check the circulation.

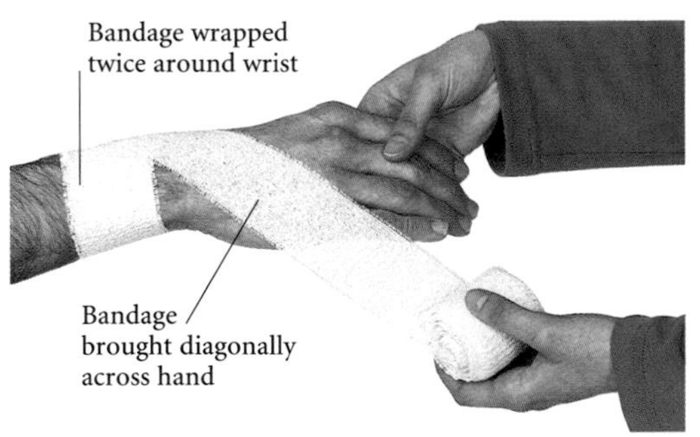
Bandage wrapped twice around wrist
Bandage brought diagonally across hand

1 *Place the end of the bandage on the underside of the wrist at the base of the thumb and secure in place by wrapping the bandage around the wrist twice. Then bring the bandage diagonally across the back of the hand toward the little finger.*

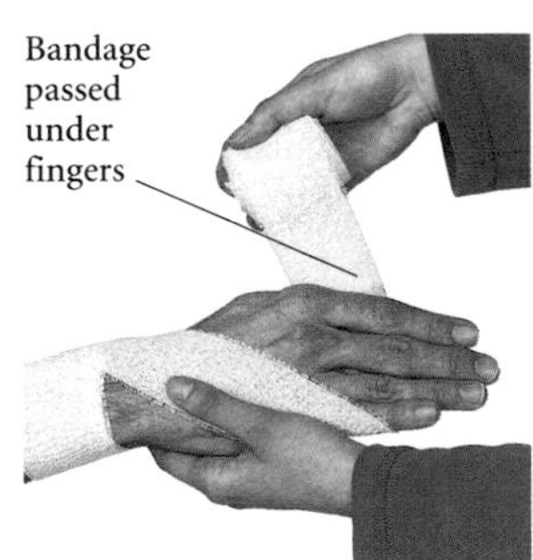
Bandage passed under fingers

2 *Take the bandage under all the fingers so that the upper edge of the bandage touches the index finger about halfway up.*

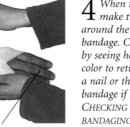

3 *Take the bandage diagonally across the back of the hand, then around the wrist and back over the hand toward the little finger as in Step 1. Continue bandaging in this manner, trying to cover two-thirds of the previous layer with each new turn of the bandage. Leave the thumb and fingertips free.*

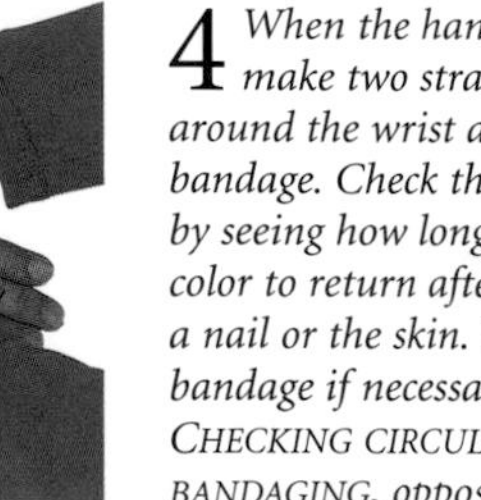
Fingertips left free

4 *When the hand is covered, make two straight turns around the wrist and secure the bandage. Check the circulation by seeing how long it takes for color to return after pressing on a nail or the skin. Loosen the bandage if necessary* (see CHECKING CIRCULATION AFTER BANDAGING, *opposite page*).

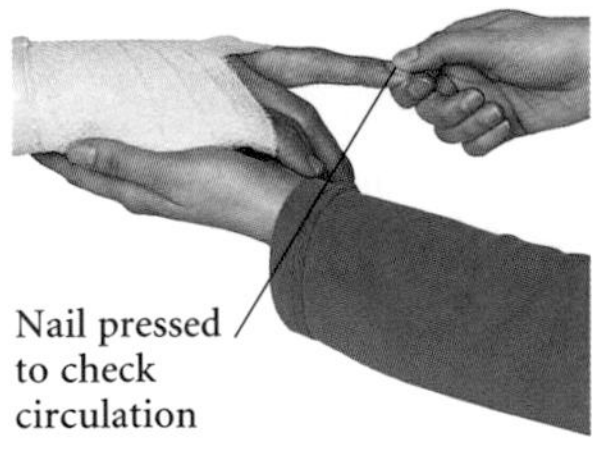
Nail pressed to check circulation

DRUG GLOSSARY

Drugs are critically important in the treatment of nearly every medical condition, whether an acquired or inherited disease, or an injury. This glossary provides a quick reference to many of the brand-name and generic (nonproprietary) drugs commonly used today and briefly describes the disorders they may be used to treat.

Almost all of the drugs currently in use were developed in the laboratory and are commercially manufactured using either chemical or genetic engineering processes. Most of them are copies of naturally occurring chemicals, but some are still obtained directly from natural sources, such as plants.

The drug glossary includes about 2,500 generic and brand-name drugs currently used in Canada. The generic or nonproprietary name is the official term for an individual, therapeutically active substance. The brand name is chosen by the manufacturer of the drug. A generic drug may be available in a brand-name product, a generic form, or both. Some drugs, such as general anesthetics, are administered only in the hospital. Other drugs may be prescribed by a doctor or obtained without a prescription at a pharmacy. Drugs that are purchased without a doctor's prescription are called over-the-counter drugs. In this glossary, brand-name over-the-counter drugs are indicated by the OTC symbol. Some over-the-counter brand-name products are also available by prescription.

Generic names in the drug glossary are cross-referenced to a specific drug article in the section Treating Disease or to an article about a particular disorder in the section Your Body and Disease. Single brand-name drugs are defined by their generic name. If the brand-name preparation is made up of more than one type of generic drug, its medical use or uses are also included in the entry.

Also included in the glossary, listed in italic typeface, are common terms used in connection with drugs.

A

ABACAVIR a brand name for ziagen

ABBOKINASE a brand name for urokinase

ABCIXIMAB an antiplatelet drug (*see* DRUGS THAT PREVENT BLOOD CLOTTING, p.904)

ABELCET a brand name for amphotericin B lipid complex

ABENOL OTC a brand name for acetaminophen

ACARBOSE an oral drug for diabetes mellitus (p.931)

ACCOLATE a brand name for zafirlukast

ACCUPRIL a brand name for quinapril

ACCURETIC a brand name for quinapril and hydrochlorothiazide

ACCUTANE a brand name for isotretinoin

ACEBUTOLOL a beta blocker drug (p.898)

ACETAMINOPHEN a nonopioid analgesic (p.912)

ACETAZOLAMIDE a carbonic anhydrase inhibitor diuretic drug (p.902), a drug for glaucoma (p.920), and an anticonvulsant drug (p.914)

ACETIC ACID an antiseptic (*see* PREPARATIONS FOR SKIN INFECTIONS AND INFESTATIONS, p.892)

ACETYLCHOLINE a mydriatic drug (*see* DRUGS ACTING ON THE EYE, p.919) used to dilate the pupil for eye surgery

ACETYLCYSTEINE a mucolytic drug (*see* COUGH REMEDIES, p.909) and a drug used to treat acetaminophen overdose (*see* DRUG OVERDOSE AND ACCIDENTAL INGESTION, p.321)

ACETYLSALICYLIC ACID (ASA) a nonopioid analgesic (p.912) and antiplatelet drug (*see* DRUGS THAT PREVENT BLOOD CLOTTING p.904)

ACILAC OTC a brand name for lactulose

ACITRETIN a retinoid drug (p.890) used to treat psoriasis (p.332)

ACT-HIB a brand name vaccine (*see* VACCINES AND IMMUNOGLOBULINS, p.883) for Hemophilus b conjugate

ACTIFED OTC a brand name for various allergy remedies, cough remedies (p.909), and cold and flu remedies (p.910)

ACTIVASE RT-PA a brand name for alteplase

ACTIVATED CHARCOAL a substance used to treat swallowed poisons (*see* DRUG OVERDOSE AND ACCIDENTAL INGESTION, p.321)

ACTONEL a brand name for risedronate

ACTOS a brand name for pioglitazone

ACULAR a brand name for ketorolac

ACYCLOVIR an antiviral drug (p.886)

ADACEL a brand-name vaccine (*see* VACCINES AND IMMUNOGLOBULINS, p.883) for tetanus (p.301), diphtheria (p.299), and pertussis (p.492)

ADALAT a brand name for nifedipine

ADAPALENE a drug used to treat acne (p.340)

ADDERALL XR a brand name for mixed salt amphetamine

ADENOCARD a brand name for adenosine

ADENOSINE an antiarrhythmic drug (p.898)

ADRENOCORTICOTROPIC HORMONE (ACTH) a pituitary hormone (*see* PITUITARY DRUGS, p.934)

ADRIAMYCIN a brand name for doxorubicin

ADVAIR a brand name for an asthma medication containing salmeterol and fluticasone

ADVIL OTC a brand name for ibuprofen

ADVIL COLD AND SINUS OTC a brand-name cold and flu remedy (p.910) and analgesic (p.912) containing pseudoephedrine and ibuprofen

AERIUS a brand name for desloratadine

AGALSIDASE BETA an enzyme used to treat Fabry disease

AGENERASE a brand name for amprenavir

AGGRASTAT a brand name for tirofiban

AGGRENOX a brand name for a product containing dipyridamole and acetylsalicylic acid

AGONIST a drug that mimics the action of another drug or of a naturally occurring substance in the body

AGRYLIN a brand name for anagrelide

AIROMIR a brand name for salbutamol

AKINETON a brand name for biperiden

ALBUMIN a human blood product used to treat shock (p.414), burns (p.318), and an abnormally low level of protein in the blood

ALCOHOL a solvent and a preservative, also used to disinfect the skin before injection

ALDACTAZIDE a brand name for spironolactone with hydrochlorothiazide

ALDACTONE a brand name for spironolactone

ALDARA a brand name for imiquimod

ALDESLEUKIN a cytokine anticancer drug (p.907)

ALDURAZYME a brand name for laronidase

ALENDRONATE a drug for bone disorders (p.896)

ALERTEC a brand name for modafinil

ALESSE a brand-name oral contraceptive (*see* CONTRACEPTION, p.69) containing levonorgestrel and ethinyl estradiol

ALFACALCIDOL a form of vitamin D

ALFENTA a brand name for alfentanil

ALFENTANIL an opioid analgesic (p.912) used as a general anesthetic (p.914)

ALFUZOSIN a drug used to treat benign prostatic hypertrophy (*see* DRUGS USED TO TREAT PROSTATE DISORDERS, p.938)

ALGINIC ACID an ingredient used in antacids (p.923)

ALGLUCERASE an enzyme used to treat Gaucher's disease, an inborn error of metabolism (p.867)

ALKA-SELTZER (OTC) a brand-name preparation for digestive upsets containing aspirin, sodium bicarbonate, citric acid, and sodium

ALKERAN a brand name for melphalan

ALLANTOIN a healing substance used in skin preparations

ALLEGRA (OTC) a brand name for fexofenadine

ALLERDRYL (OTC) a brand name for diphenhydramine

ALLERNIX (OTC) a brand name for diphenhydramine

ALLOPURINOL a drug used to treat gout (p.380)

ALMOTRIPTAN an antimigraine drug (p. 913)

ALOCRIL a brand-name eyedrop (*see* DRUGS ACTING ON THE EYE, p.919) containing nedocromil sodium

ALOMIDE a brand name for lodoxamide

ALPHA1-PROTEINASE INHIBITOR a drug used to treat patients with panacinar emphysema who have a congenital deficiency in alpha-1 antitrypsin

ALPHAGAN a brand name for brimonidine

ALPHA-TOCOPHEROL a form of vitamin E

ALPRAZOLAM a benzodiazepine antianxiety drug (p.916)

ALPROSTADIL a prostaglandin used to treat congenital heart disease (p.836) in newborn babies, and erectile dysfunction (p.770)

ALTACE a brand name for ramipril

ALTEPLASE a thrombolytic drug (p.904)

ALTRETAMINE a cytokine anticancer drug (p.907)

ALUMINUM ACETATE an astringent used to treat inflammation of the outer ear canal (*see* DRUGS ACTING ON THE EAR, p.921) and the skin

ALUMINUM CARBONATE an antacid (p.923)

ALUMINUM CHLORHYDROXIDE an antibiotic (p.885) used to treat acne (p.340)

ALUMINUM CHLORIDE an active ingredient in antiperspirants

ALUMINUM HYDROXIDE an antacid (p.923)

ALUPENT a brand name for orciprenaline

AMANTADINE an antiviral drug (p.886) also used to treat Parkinson's disease and parkinsonism (p.539) and prevent influenza A (p.287)

AMATINE a brand name for midodrine

AMBISOME a brand name for amphotericin B

AMCINONIDE a topical corticosteroid (p.892)

AMERGE a brand name for naratriptan

AMICAR a brand name for aminocaproic acid

AMIFOSTINE a drug used to reduce the risk of kidney damage in people taking cisplatin

AMIKACIN an aminoglycoside antibiotic (p.885)

AMIKIN a brand name for amikacin

AMILORIDE a potassium-sparing diuretic drug (p.902)

AMINO ACID a compound from which proteins are synthesized; some amino acids are produced by the body, but others must be included in the diet

AMINOBENZOATE POTASSIUM a drug used to treat excessive fibrous tissue

AMINOBENZOIC ACID a drug used in sunscreens (*see* SUNSCREENS AND SUNBLOCKS, p.893)

AMINOCAPROIC ACID an antifibrinolytic drug (*see* DRUGS THAT PROMOTE BLOOD CLOTTING, p.903)

AMINO-CERV a brand-name drug containing urea, sodium propionate, methionine, cystine, inositol, and benzalkonium chloride used to treat cervical disorders

AMINOGLUTETHIMIDE a hormonal anticancer drug (p.907) also used to treat Cushing syndrome (p.684)

AMINOPHYLLINE a xanthine bronchodilator drug (p.910)

AMINOSALICYLATE SODIUM an antituberculous drug (p.886)

AMIODARONE an antiarrhythmic drug (p.898)

AMITRIPTYLINE a tricyclic antidepressant drug (p.916); also used to treat headaches, neuropathy, and insomnia

AMLODIPINE a calcium channel blocker drug (p.900)

AMMONIUM CHLORIDE a drug that increases the body's acidity and is used as an expectorant in cough remedies (p.909)

AMMONIUM LACTATE a drug used to treat dry, scaly skin (*see* EMOLLIENTS AND BARRIER PREPARATIONS, p.890)

AMOXICILLIN a penicillin antibiotic (p.885)

AMOXICILLIN-CLAVULANATE POTASSIUM a combination of amoxicillin and clavulanate potassium

AMPHETAMINE a central nervous system stimulant drug (p.918)

AMPHOJEL a brand name for aluminum hydroxide

AMPHOTEC a brand name for amphotericin B

AMPHOTERICIN B an antifungal drug (p.889)

AMPICILLIN a penicillin antibiotic (p.885)

AMPRENAVIR an antiviral drug used to treat HIV infection (*see* DRUGS FOR HIV INFECTION AND AIDS, p.887)

AMSACRINE an anticancer drug (p.907)

AMSA P-D a brand name for amsacrine

AMYLASE a digestive enzyme

ANABOLIC STEROID a group of synthetic hormones that build proteins and increase muscle bulk

ANACIN (OTC) a brand-name analgesic (p.912) containing acetylsalicylic acid and caffeine

ANACIN EXTRA-STRENGTH (OTC) a brand-name analgesic (p.912) containing aspirin and caffeine

ANAFRANIL a brand name for clomipramine

ANAGRELIDE a drug used to treat thrombocythemia, an increase in the number of circulating blood platelets

ANAKINRA an intreleukin-1 receptor antagonist used to treat rheumatoid arthritis (p.895)

ANA-KIT (OTC) a brand-name emergency treatment kit for anaphylaxis (p.469) containing epinephrine and chlorpheniramine

ANALPRAM-HC a brand-name preparation for hemorrhoids (p.668) containing hydrocortisone and pramoxine

ANANDRON a brand name for nilutamide

ANAPROX a brand name for naproxen

ANASTROZOLE a hormonal anticancer drug (p.907)

ANCESTIM a drug used to stimulate stem cell production in the bone marrow (*see* FORMATION OF BLOOD CELLS, p.440)

ANDRIOL a brand name for testosterone undecanoate

ANDROCUR a brand name for cyproterone

ANDRODERM a brand name for testosterone cream

ANDROGEL a brand name for testosterone gel

ANETHOLTRITHIONE a drug used to treat dry mouth, a side effect of many medications

ANEXATE a brand name for flumazenil

ANGIOMAX a brand name for bivalirudin

ANISTREPLASE a thrombolytic drug (p.904)

ANSAID a brand name for flurbiprofen

ANTAGONIST a drug that opposes the action of another drug or of a naturally occurring substance in the body

ANTAZOLINE an antihistamine (p.906)

ANTHRALIN a drug used to treat psoriasis (p.332)

ANTHRANOL a brand name for anthralin

ANTICHOLINERGIC a drug that blocks the action of a chemical necessary for the transmission of nerve impulses

ANTIHEMOPHILIC FACTOR another name for factor VIII

ANTIPYRINE an analgesic (p.912) used to relieve ear pain (*see* DRUGS ACTING ON THE EAR, p.921)

ANTISEPTIC a chemical that destroys microorganisms in or on living tissues

ANTITHROMBIN III (HUMAN) a drug used to prevent or treat thrombosis in people with deficiency of antithrombin III (*see* HYPERCOAGULABILITY, p.453)

ANTI-THYMOCYTE GLOBULIN a drug used to treat acute rejection of a kidney transplant

ANTIZOL a brand name for fomepizole

ANUGESIC HC a brand name for pramoxine, zinc, and hydrocortisone

ANUSOL-HC a brand-name preparation containing hydrocortisone and zinc sulfate

ANUSOL SUPPOSITORIES OTC a brand-name preparation for hemorrhoids (p.668) containing zinc sulfate

ANZEMET a brand name for dolasetron

APRACLONIDINE a drug for glaucoma (p.920)

APRESOLINE a brand name for hydralazine

APROTININ an antifibrinolytic drug (*see* DRUGS THAT PROMOTE BLOOD CLOTTING, p.903)

AQUAPHOR OTC a brand-name emollient (*see* EMOLLIENTS AND BARRIER PREPARATIONS, p.890) containing petrolatum

AQUEOUS CREAM an emollient (*see* EMOLLIENTS AND BARRIER PREPARATIONS, p.890)

ARALEN a brand name for chloroquine

ARANESP a brand name for darbepoetin alfa

ARAVA a brand name for leflunomide

AREDIA a brand name for pamidronate

ARGATROBAN an anticoagulant drug (*see* DRUGS THAT PREVENT BLOOD CLOTTING p.904)

ARICEPT a brand name for donepezil

ARIMIDEX a brand name for anastrozole

ARISTOCORT a brand name for triamcinolone

ARIXTRA a brand name for fondaparinux

AROMASIN a brand name for exemestane

ARTHROTEC a brand-name anti-inflammatory drug containing diclofenac and misoprostol

ASA (ACETYLSALICYLIC ACID) a nonopioid analgesic (p.912) and antiplatelet drug (*see* DRUGS THAT PREVENT BLOOD CLOTTING p.904)

ASACOL a brand name for 5-ASA

ASCORBIC ACID another name for vitamin C

ASPARAGINASE an anticancer drug (p.907)

ASPIRIN OTC a nonopioid analgesic (p.912) and antiplatelet drug (*see* DRUGS THAT PREVENT BLOOD CLOTTING, p.904)

ASTRINGENT a substance that causes tissue to dry and shrink by reducing its ability to absorb water

ATACAND a brand name for candesartan

ATACAND PLUS a brand name for candesartan and hydrochlorothiazide

ATARAX a brand name for hydroxyzine

ATASOL OTC a brand name for acetaminophen

ATAZANAVIR an antiviral drug used to treat HIV infection (*see* DRUGS FOR HIV INFECTION AND AIDS, p.887)

ATENOLOL a beta blocker drug (p.898)

ATIVAN a brand name for lorazepam

ATORVASTATIN a lipid-lowering drug (p.935)

ATOVAQUONE an antiprotozoal drug (p.888)

ATRACURIUM a muscle relaxant (p.896) used in general anesthesia (*see* HAVING MAJOR SURGERY, p.943) and also in mechanical ventilation

ATROPINE an antispasmodic drug (*see* ANTISPASMODIC AND MOTILITY STIMULANTS, p.926) and a mydriatic drug (*see* DRUGS ACTING ON THE EYE, p.919) used in eye examinations to dilate the pupil

ATROVENT a brand name for ipratropium bromide

ATTAPULGITE an antidiarrheal drug (p.924)

AUGMENTIN a brand-name antibiotic (p.885) containing amoxicillin with clavulanate potassium

AURALGAN OTC a brand-name eardrop containing antipyrine and benzocaine used to treat pain and inflammation in the ear (*see* OTITIS EXTERNA, p.596; OTITIS MEDIA, p.597)

AURANOFIN an antirheumatic drug (p.895)

AUROTHIOGLUCOSE an antirheumatic drug (p.895)

AVALIDE a brand name for irbesartan and hydrochlorothiazide

AVANDAMET a brand name for rosiglitazone and metformin

AVANDIA a brand name for rosiglitazone

AVAPRO a brand name for irbesartan

AVAXIM a brand-name vaccine (*see* VACCINES AND IMMUNOGLOBULINS, p.883) for hepatitis A (*see* ACUTE HEPATITIS, p.644)

AVC a brand name for sulfanilamide

AVELOX a brand name for moxifloxacin

AVENTYL a brand name for nortriptyline

AVIRAX a brand name for acyclovir

AVODART a brand name for dutasteride

AVONEX a brand name for interferon beta

AXERT a brand name for almotriptan

AXID a brand name for nizatidine

AZATADINE an antihistamine (p.906)

AZATHIOPRINE an antirheumatic drug (p.895) and cytotoxic immunosuppressant drug (p.906)

AZIDOTHYMIDINE (AZT, zidovudine) an antiviral drug used to treat HIV infection (*see* DRUGS FOR HIV INFECTION AND AIDS, p.887)

AZITHROMYCIN a macrolide antibiotic (p.885)

AZOPT a brand name for brinzolamide

AZT azidothymidine

B

B&O SUPPS a brand name for belladonna

BACAMPICILLIN a penicillin antibiotic (p.885)

BACID a brand name for lactobacillus acidophilus

BACIGUENT a brand name for bacitracin

BACITRACIN a topical antibiotic (p.885)

BACLOFEN a muscle relaxant (p.896)

BACTIGRAS a brand name for chlorhexidine

BACTROBAN a brand name for mupirocin

BALNETAR OTC a brand name for coal tar

BALSAM PERU a substance that promotes wound healing

BARRIERE OTC a brand-name cream containing dimethicone

BARRIERE HC a brand-name cream containing dimethicone and hydrocortisone

BASALAZIDE a 5-aminosalicylate drug (p.924)

BASALJEL OTC a brand name for aluminum hydroxide

BASILIXIMAB an immunosuppressant

BAYHEP B a brand-name vaccine (*see* VACCINES AND IMMUNOGLOBULINS, p.883) for hepatitis B (*see* ACUTE HEPATITIS, p.644)

BAYRAB a brand-name vaccine (*see* VACCINES AND IMMUNOGLOBULINS, p.883) for rabies (p.294)

BAYTET a brand-name vaccine (*see* VACCINES AND IMMUNOGLOBULINS, p.883) for tetanus (p.301)

BECAPLERMIN a drug used to promote the healing of lower-extremity diabetic ulcers

BECLOMETHASONE a corticosteroid (p.930)

BELLADONNA an antispasmodic drug (*see* ANTISPASMODIC DRUGS AND MOTILITY STIMULANTS, p.926)

BELLERGAL SPACETABS a brand-name drug containing belladonna, ergotamine, and phenobarbital

BENADRYL OTC a brand name for diphenhydramine

BENADRYL ALLERGY/SINUS HEADACHE OTC a brand-name medication containing pseudoephedrine, diphenhydramine, and acetominophen

BENADRYL CREAM OTC a brand name for diphenhydramine cream

BENAZEPRIL an ACE inhibitor drug (p.900)

BENOXINATE a local anesthetic (p.914)

BENSERAZIDE a drug used to treat Parkinson's disease (*see* PARKINSON'S DISEASE AND PARKINSONISM, p.539)

BENTYLOL a brand name for dicyclomine

BENURYL a brand name for probenecid

BENYLIN OTC a brand name for various cough and cold preparations

BENZAC OTC a brand name for benzoyl peroxide

BENZAGEL OTC a brand name for benzoyl peroxide

BENZALKONIUM CHLORIDE a skin antiseptic (*see* PREPARATIONS FOR SKIN INFECTIONS AND INFESTATIONS, p.892)

BENZAMYCIN a brand-name drug containing erythromycin and benzoyl peroxide used to treat acne (p.340)

BENZHEXOL another name for trihexyphenidyl

BENZOCAINE a local anesthetic (p.914)

BENZOIC ACID an antiseptic (*see* PREPARATIONS FOR SKIN INFECTIONS AND INFESTATIONS, p.892) and antifungal drug (p.889)

BENZOYL PEROXIDE OTC a drug used to treat acne (p.340)

BENZTROPINE an anticholinergic drug used to treat parkinsonism (*see* PARKINSON'S DISEASE AND PARKINSONISM, p.539)

BENZYDAMINE a local anesthetic (p.914) mouthwash

BENZYLPENICILLIN a penicillin antibiotic (p.885)

BERACTANT a drug used to mature the lungs of premature babies with respiratory distress syndrome (*see* PROBLEMS OF THE PRETERM BABY, p.816)

BEROTEC a brand name for fenoterol

BETA CAROTENE a source of vitamin A

BETADINE OTC a brand name for povidone iodine

BETAGAN a brand name for levobunolol

BETAHISTINE a drug used to treat vertigo (p.603)

BETAINE a drug used to treat homocystinuria, an inborn error of metabolism (p.867)

BETALOC a brand name for metoprolol

BETAMETHASONE a corticosteroid (p.930)

BETAMETHASONE DIPROPIONATE a topical corticosteroid (p.892) used for inflammatory conditions of the skin

BETAMETHASONE VALERATE a corticosteroid (p.930)

BETASERON a brand name for interferon beta-1b

BETAXIN a brand name for thiamine

BETAXOLOL a beta blocker drug (p.898) and drug for glaucoma (p.920)

BETHANECHOL a drug for urinary retention (*see* DRUGS THAT AFFECT BLADDER CONTROL, p.939)

BETNESOL a brand name for betamethasone

BETOPTIC S a brand-name drug for glaucoma (p.920) containing betaxolol

BEXTRA a brand name for valdecoxib

BEZAFIBRATE a lipid-lowering drug (p.935)

BEZALIP a brand name for bezafibrate

BIAXIN a brand name for clarithromycin

BICALUTAMIDE a hormonal anticancer drug (p.907)

BICHLORACETIC ACID a brand name for dichloroacetic acid

BICNU a brand name for carmustine

BILTRICIDE a brand name for praziquantel

BIMATOPROST a drug used for glaucoma (p.920)

BIOTIN a member of the vitamin B complex

BIPERIDEN an anticholinergic drug used to treat parkinsonism (*see* PARKINSON'S DISEASE AND PARKINSONISM, p.539)

BIQUIN a brand name for quinidine

BISACODYL a stimulant laxative (p.924)

BISMUTH a metal given in compound form as an acid-suppressive drug (p.923) and for hemorrhoids (p.668)

BISOPROLOL a beta blocker drug (p.898) used to treat hypertension (p.403)

BIVALIRUDIN an injected anticoagulant (*see* DRUGS THAT PREVENT BLOOD CLOTTING, p.904)

BLENOXANE a brand name for bleomycin

BLEOMYCIN a cytotoxic anticancer drug (p.907)

BLEPHAMIDE a brand-name drug for eye infections (*see* DRUGS ACTING ON THE EYE, p.919) containing sulfacetamide and prednisolone

BONAMINE OTC a brand name for meclizine

BONEFOS a brand name for clodronate

BOSENTAN a drug used to treat pulmonary hypertension

BOTOX a brand name for botulinum toxin

BOTULINUM TOXIN a muscle relaxant (p.896) used to treat facial muscle spasms ; it also has an indication for frown lines, axillary hyperhidrosis, and focal spasticity

BRAN a bulk-forming agent, a laxative (p.924), and antidiarrheal drug (p.924)

BRETYLIUM an antiarrhythmic drug (p.898)

BREVIBLOC a brand name for esmolol

BREVICON a brand-name oral contraceptive (*see* CONTRACEPTION, p.69) containing ethinyl estradiol and norethindrone

BRICANYL a brand name for terbutaline

BRIMONIDINE a drug for glaucoma (p.920)

BRINZOLAMIDE an eyedrop used for glaucoma (*see* DRUGS FOR GLAUCOMA p.920)

BROMAZEPAM a benzodiazepine antianxiety drug (p.916)

BROMOCRIPTINE a pituitary drug (p.934) and drug used to treat parkinsonism (*see* PARKINSON'S DISEASE AND PARKINSONISM, p.539)

BROMPHENIRAMINE an antihistamine (p.906)

BUDESONIDE a corticosteroid (p.930)

BUMETANIDE a loop diuretic drug (p.902)

BUPIVACAINE a long-lasting local anesthetic (p.914)

BUPROPION an antidepressant drug (p.916) also used to help people stop smoking

BURINEX a brand name for bumetanide

BUROW'S SOLUTION OTC a brand name for aluminum acetate

BUSCOPAN OTC a brand name for scopolamine

BUSERELIN a gonadorelin analog (*see* SEX HORMONES AND RELATED DRUGS, p.933)

BUSPAR a brand name for buspirone

BUSPIRONE a nonbenzodiazepine antianxiety drug (p.916)

BUSULFAN a cytotoxic anticancer drug (p.907)

BUTABARBITAL a barbiturate sleeping drug (p.915)

BUTALBITAL a barbiturate (*see* SLEEPING DRUGS, p.915) and analgesic (p.912)

BUTISOL SODIUM a brand name for butabarbital

BUTOCONAZOLE an antifungal drug (p.889)

BUTORPHANOL an opioid analgesic (p.912)

BUTYL AMINOBENZOATE a local anesthetic (p.914)

BUTYL METHOXYDIBENZOYLMETHANE an ingredient in some sunscreens (*see* SUNSCREENS AND SUNBLOCKS, p.893) that blocks UVA and UVB rays, also known as Parsol 1789

C

CABERGOLINE a drug used to treat hyperprolactinemic disorders and to inhibit lactation

CAELYX a brand name for doxorubicin

CAFERGOT a brand-name drug containing caffeine and ergotamine used to treat migraine (p.518)

CAFFEINE a stimulant in coffee, tea, and cola that is added to some analgesics (p.912)

CALADRYL OTC a brand name for calamine and diphenhydramine

CALAMINE a substance containing zinc oxide, used to soothe irritated skin and relieve itching

CALCIFEDIOL a derivative of vitamin D

CALCIFEROL OTC a brand name for ergocalciferol

CALCIJEX a brand name for calcitriol, a form of vitamin D

CALCIMAR a brand name for calcitonin

CALCIPOTRIOL a drug used to treat psoriasis (p.332)

CALCITONIN a drug for bone disorders (p.896)

CALCITRIOL a form of vitamin D

CALCIUM a mineral (p.929)

CALCIUM ACETATE a form of calcium used to treat kidney failure (p.705)

CALCIUM CARBONATE a form of calcium and an antacid (p.923)

CALCIUM CHLORIDE a form of calcium

CALCIUM CITRATE a form of calcium

CALCIUM DISODIUM EDETATE an antidote for poisoning by lead and other heavy metals (*see* DRUG OVERDOSE AND ACCIDENTAL INGESTION, p.321)

CALCIUM GLUCONATE a form of calcium

CALCIUM GLYCEROPHOSPHATE a form of calcium

CALCIUM LACTATE a form of calcium

CAMPHOR a topical antipruritic drug (p.891)

CAMPTOSAR a brand name for irinotecan

CANCIDAS a brand name for caspofungin acetate

CANDESARTAN an angiotensin II blocker antihypertensive drug (p.897)

CANDISTATIN OTC a brand name for nystatin

CANESTEN OTC a brand name for clotrimazole

CAPECITABINE an anticancer drug (p.907)

CAPOTEN a brand name for captopril

CAPSAICIN OTC a topical analgesic (p.912) used to treat shingles (*see* HERPES ZOSTER, p.288) and rheumatoid arthritis (p.377)

CAPTOPRIL an ACE inhibitor drug (p.900)

CARBACHOL a drug for glaucoma (p.920)

CARBAMAZEPINE an anticonvulsant drug (p.914) and antipsychotic drug (p.917), also used to relieve neuropathic pain (*see* DIABETIC NEUROPATHY, p.545)

CARBAMIDE PEROXIDE an ingredient used in drops to soften earwax (*see* DRUGS ACTING ON THE EAR, p.921)

CARBIDOPA a substance that enhances the effect of levodopa, a drug used to treat parkinsonism (*see* PARKINSON'S DISEASE AND PARKINSONISM, p.539)

CARBOPLATIN a cytotoxic anticancer drug (p.907)

CARBOXYMETHYLCELLULOSE an ocular lubricant

CARDIZEM a brand name for diltiazem

CARDURA a brand name for doxazosin

CARMUSTINE a cytotoxic anticancer drug (p.907)

CARNITOR a brand name for levocarnitine

CARVEDILOL a beta blocker drug (p.898)

CASANTHRANOL a stimulant laxative (p.924)

CASCARA a stimulant laxative (p.924)

CASODEX a brand name for bicalutamide

CASPOFUNGIN ACETATE an antifungal drug (p.889)

CASTOR OIL a stimulant laxative (p.924)

CATAFLAM a brand name for diclofenac

CATAPRES a brand name for clonidine

CATHFLO a brand name for alteplase

CAUSTIC having a burning or corrosive effect on body tissues

CAVERJECT a brand name for alprostadil

CECLOR a brand name for cefaclor

CEENU a brand name for lomustine

CEFACLOR a cephalosporin antibiotic (p.885)

CEFADROXIL a cephalosporin antibiotic (p.885)

CEFAMANDOLE a cephalosporin antibiotic (p.885)

CEFAZOLIN a cephalosporin antibiotic (p.885)

CEFEPIME a cephalosporin antibiotic (p.885)

CEFIXIME a cephalosporin antibiotic (p.885)

CEFIZOX a brand name for ceftizoxime

CEFOTAN a brand name for cefotetan

CEFOTAXIME a cephalosporin antibiotic (p.885)

CEFOTETAN a cephalosporin antibiotic (p.885)

CEFOXITIN a cephalosporin antibiotic (p.885)

CEFPROZIL a cephalosporin antibiotic (p.885)

CEFTAZIDIME a cephalosporin antibiotic (p.885)

CEFTIN a brand name for cefuroxime

CEFTIZOXIME a cephalosporin antibiotic (p.885)

CEFTRIAXONE a cephalosporin antibiotic (p.885)

CEFUROXIME a cephalosporin antibiotic (p.885)

CEFZIL a brand name for cefprozil

CELEBREX a brand name for celecoxib

CELECOXIB a nonsteroidal anti-inflammatory drug (p.894)

CELESTODERM a brand name for betamethasone valerate

CELESTONE a brand name for betamethasone

CELEXA a brand name for citalopram

CELLCEPT a brand name for mycophenolate mofetil

CELLUFRESH OTC a brand-name eyedrop (*see* DRUGS ACTING ON THE EYE, p.919) containing carboxymethylcellulose

CELLULOSE SODIUM PHOSPHATE an agent used to reduce levels of calcium in the blood

CELONTIN a brand name for methsuximide

CENTRUM OTC a brand name for various multivitamin formulations

CEPHALEXIN a cephalosporin antibiotic (p.885)

CEPTAZ a brand name for ceftazidime

CEREBYX a brand name for fosphenytoin

CERESIN a wax obtained from paraffin

CEREZYME a brand name for imiglucerase

CERUBIDINE a brand name for daunorubicin

CERUMENEX a brand name for triethanolamine polypeptide oleate-condensate

CERVIDIL a brand name for dinoprostone

CES a brand name for conjugated estrogens

CESAMET a brand name for nabilone

CETAMIDE a brand name for sulfacetamide

CETIRIZINE an antihistamine (p.906)

CETRORELIX ACETATE a gonadorelin antagonist

CETROTIDE a brand name for cetrorelix acetate

CHLORAL HYDRATE a sleeping drug (p.915)

CHLORAMBUCIL a cytotoxic anticancer drug (p.907) also used as an immunosuppressant drug (p.906)

CHLORAMPHENICOL an antibiotic (p.885)

CHLORDIAZEPOXIDE a benzodiazepine antianxiety drug (p.916)

CHLORHEXIDINE a skin antiseptic (*see* PREPARATIONS FOR SKIN INFECTIONS AND INFESTATIONS, p.892)

CHLOROETHANE another name for ethyl chloride

CHLOROMYCETIN a brand name for chloramphenicol

CHLOROPHYLLIN COPPER COMPLEX a preparation used to promote healing, relieve skin irritation, and as a deodorant

CHLOROPROCAINE a local anesthetic (p.914)

CHLOROQUINE an antimalarial drug (p.888) and antirheumatic drug (p.895)

CHLOROXYLENOL a skin antiseptic (*see* PREPARATIONS FOR SKIN INFECTIONS AND INFESTATIONS, p.892)

CHLORPHENIRAMINE an antihistamine (p.906)

CHLORPROMAZINE a phenothiazine antipsychotic drug (p.917) and antiemetic drug (p.922)

CHLORPROPAMIDE an oral drug for diabetes mellitus (p.931)

CHLORTHALIDONE a thiazide diuretic drug (p.902)

CHLOR-TRIPOLON OTC a brand name for various allergy and cold medications

CHLORZOXAZONE a muscle relaxant (p.896)

CHOLECALCIFEROL a form of vitamin D

CHOLEDYL a brand name for oxtriphylline

CHOLESTYRAMINE a lipid-lowering drug (p.935)

CHOLINE a substance related to the vitamin B complex

CHOLINE BITARTRATE a substance related to the vitamin B complex

CHOLINE MAGNESIUM TRISALICYLATE a nonsteroidal anti-inflammatory drug (p.894) and analgesic (p.912)

CHOLINE SALICYLATE an analgesic (p.912) similar to aspirin

CHORIONIC GONADOTROPIN a drug for infertility (p.936)

CHROMIUM a mineral (p.929)

CHRONOVERA a brand name for verapamil

CIALIS a brand name for tadalafil

CICATRIN a brand-name drug containing amino acids, bacitracin, zinc, and neomycin

CICLOPIROX an antifungal drug (p.889)

CILASTATIN a drug used with imipenem to increase its effectiveness

CILAZAPRIL an ACE inhibitor drug (p.900)

CILOXAN a brand name for ciprofloxacin eye drops

CIMETIDINE an acid-suppressive drug (p.923)

CIPRO a brand name for ciprofloxacin

CIPRODEX a brand name for ear drops containing ciprofloxacin and dexamethasone

CIPROFLOXACIN a quinolone antibiotic (p.885)

CIPRO HC OCTIC SUSPENSION a brand-name eardrop containing ciprofloxacin and hydrocortisone

CISATRACURIUM a muscle relaxant used in general anesthesia (*see* HAVING MAJOR SURGERY, p.943)

CISPLATIN a cytotoxic anticancer drug (p.907)

CITALOPRAM a selective serotonin reuptake inhibitor (SSRI) antidepressant drug (p.916)

CITRACAL OTC a brand name for calcium citrate

CITRIC ACID a drug used to make the urine more alkaline and thus prevent or dissolve bladder stones (p.714) and kidney stones (p.701)

CLADRIBINE a cytotoxic anticancer drug (p.907)

CLAFORAN a brand name for cefotaxime

CLARITHROMYCIN a macrolide antibiotic (p.885)

CLARITIN OTC a brand name for loratadine

CLAVULANATE POTASSIUM a substance given with amoxicillin or ticarcillin to make them more effective

CLAVULIN a brand name for an antibiotic (p.885) containing amoxicillin and clavulinic acid

CLAVULINIC ACID an antibiotic (p.885) used to treat bacterial infections

CLEMASTINE OTC an antihistamine (p.906)

CLIDINIUM a drug used for gastrointestinal spasms (*see* ANTISPASMODICS AND MOTILITY STIMULANTS, p.926)

CLIMACTERON a brand-name drug containing estradiol and testosterone

CLIMARA a brand name for estradiol used in hormone replacement therapy (p.937)

CLINDAMYCIN a lincosamide antibiotic (p.885)

CLINDETS a brand name for clindamycin topical solution

CLINDOXYL a brand name for a gel containing clindamycin and benzoyl peroxide

CLIOQUINOL an antibiotic (p.885) and antifungal drug (p.889)

CLOBAZAM a drug used to treat epilepsy (p.524)

CLOBETASOL a topical corticosteroid (p.892)

CLODRONATE a drug for bone disorders (p.896)

CLOFIBRATE a lipid-lowering drug (p.935)

CLOMID a brand name for clomiphene

CLOMIPHENE a drug for infertility (p.936)

CLOMIPRAMINE a tricyclic antidepressant drug (p.916)

CLONAZEPAM a benzodiazepine anticonvulsant drug (p.914)

CLONIDINE an antihypertensive drug (p.897) and antimigraine drug (p.913), also used to treat menopausal hot flashes (*see* MENOPAUSAL PROBLEMS, p.737)

CLOPIDOGREL an antiplatelet drug (*see* DRUGS THAT PREVENT BLOOD CLOTTING, p.904)

CLOPIXOL a brand name for zuclopenthixol

CLORAZEPATE a benzodiazepine antianxiety drug (p.916)

CLOTRIMAZOLE an antifungal drug (p.889)

CLOXACILLIN a penicillin antibiotic (p.885)

CLOZAPINE an antipsychotic drug (p.917)

CLOZARIL a brand name for clozapine

COACTIFED a brand-name drug containing codeine, pseudoephedrine, and tripolidine

COAGULATION FACTOR IX used to control bleeding episodes in patients with hemophilia B

COAL TAR a substance used to treat psoriasis (p.332) and eczema (p.333)

COCAINE a local anesthetic (p.914)

CODEINE an opiate analgesic (p.912), cough suppressant (*see* COUGH REMEDIES, p.909), and antidiarrheal drug (p.924)

COENZYME Q-10 a nutritional supplement

COGENTIN a brand name for benztropine

COLACE a brand-name fecal softener (*see* LAXATIVES, p.924) containing docusate

COLCHICINE a drug used to treat gout (p.380)

COLESTID a brand name for colestipol

COLESTIPOL a lipid-lowering drug (p.935)

COLISTIMETHATE an antibiotic (p.885)

COLLAGENASE a drug used to remove dead tissue from wounds and ulcers

COLLODION a substance that dries to form a sticky film, protecting broken skin

COLY-MYCIN M a brand-name antibiotic (p.885) with colistimethate

COLYTE OTC a brand-name preparation containing polyethylene glycol, potassium chloride, sodium bicarbonate, sodium chloride, and sodium sulfate used for bowel cleansing prior to diagnostic procedures or surgery

COMBANTRIN OTC a brand name for pyrantel pamoate

COMBIVENT a brand-name inhaler (*see* BRONCHODILATOR DRUGS, p.910) containing ipratropium bromide and salbutamol

COMBIVIR a brand-name drug containing lamivudine and zidovudine used for HIV infection (*see* HIV INFECTION AND AIDS, p.295)

COMTAN a brand name for entacapone

CONCERTA a brand name for a long-acting form of methylphenidate

CONDYLINE a brand name for podofilox

CONJUGATED ESTROGENS a mixture of female hormones (*see* SEX HORMONES AND RELATED DRUGS, p.933)

CONTAC 12-HOUR COLD OTC a brand-name cold remedy (*see* COLD AND FLU REMEDIES, p.910) containing phenylpropanolamine and chlorpheniramine

CONTAC C OTC a brand name for various cough, cold, and allergy medications

COPAXONE a brand name for glatiramer acetate

COPPER a mineral (p.929)

COPTIN a brand name for sulfadiazine and trimethoprim

CORDARONE a brand name for amiodarone

COREG a brand name for carvedilol

CORGARD a brand name for nadolol

CORTATE OTC a brand name for hydrocortisone

CORTEF a brand name for hydrocortisone

CORTENEMA a brand-name enema containing hydrocortisone used to treat ulcerative colitis (p.659)

CORTICOTROPIN a hormone used to test the function of the adrenal gland

CORTIFOAM a brand-name preparation containing hydrocortisone used to treat ulceration in proctitis (p.667)

CORTISONE a corticosteroid (p.930)

CORTISONE ACETATE an injected glucocorticoid used for replacement in adrenocortical deficiency states or as an anti-inflammatory

CORTISPORIN a brand-name preparation containing neomycin, polymyxin B, and hydrocortisone used to treat eye infections (*see* DRUGS ACTING ON THE EYE, p.919)

CORTROSYN a brand name for cosyntropin

CORVERT a brand name for ibutilide fumarate

COSMEGEN a brand name for dactinomycin

COSOPT a brand-name eyedrop (*see* DRUGS ACTING ON THE EYE, p.919) containing dorzolamide and timolol

COSYNTROPIN a hormone used to test the function of the adrenal gland

COTAZYM OTC a brand name for pancrelipase

COUMADIN a brand name for warfarin

COVERSYL a brand name for perindopril

COZAAR a brand name for losartan

CREON OTC a brand name for pancrelipase

CRESTOR a brand name for rosuvastatin

CRINONE a brand name for progesterone vaginal gel

CRIXIVAN a brand name for indinavir

CROMOLYN SODIUM a mast cell stabilizer (*see* ANTIALLERGY DRUGS, p.905)

CROTAMITON an antipruritic drug (p.891)

CUPRIMINE a brand name for penicillamine

CYANOCOBALAMIN a form of vitamin B_{12}

CYCLEN a brand-name oral contraceptive (*see* CONTRACEPTION, p.69) containing ethinyl estradiol and norgestimate

CYCLIZINE an antihistamine (p.906) used as an antiemetic drug (p.922)

CYCLOBENZAPRINE a muscle relaxant (p.896)

CYCLOCORT a brand name for amcinonide

CYCLOGYL a brand name for cyclopentolate

CYCLOMEN a brand name for danazol

CYCLOPENTOLATE a mydriatic drug used in eye examinations (*see* DRUGS ACTING ON THE EYE, p.919)

CYCLOPHOSPHAMIDE a cytotoxic anticancer drug (p.907)

CYCLOSPORINE an immunosuppressant drug (p.906)

CYKLOKAPRON a brand name for tranexamic acid

CYPROHEPTADINE an antihistamine (p.906) used to stimulate the appetite and an antimigraine drug (p.913)

CYPROTERONE an antiandrogen drug used for prostate cancer (*see* DRUGS FOR PROSTATE DISORDERS, p.938)

CYSTINE an amino acid

CYTARABINE a cytotoxic anticancer drug (p.907)

CYTOMEL a brand name for liothyronine

CYTOSAR a brand name for cytarabine

CYTOTEC a brand name for misoprostol

CYTOVENE a brand name for ganciclovir

CYTOXAN a brand name for cyclophosphamide

D

D4T another name for stavudine

DACARBAZINE a cytotoxic anticancer drug (p.907)

DACLIZUMAB an immunosuppressant (p.906) used to prevent organ rejection in renal transplants

DACTINOMYCIN a cytotoxic anticancer drug (p.907)

DALACIN a brand name for clindamycin

DALFOPRISTIN an injected antibacterial used in combination with quinupristin to treat skin infections and infections caused by vancomycin-resistant bacteria (so-called super bugs)

DALMANE a brand name for flurazepam

DALTEPARIN an injected anticoagulant (*see* DRUGS THAT PREVENT BLOOD CLOTTING, p.904)

DANAPAROID an injected anticoagulant (*see* DRUGS THAT PREVENT BLOOD CLOTTING, p.904)

DANAZOL a hormonal drug used to treat menstrual disorders (*see* SEX HORMONES AND RELATED DRUGS, p.933)

DANTRIUM a brand name for dantrolene

DANTROLENE a muscle relaxant (p.896)

DAPSONE an antibiotic (p.885) used to treat Hansen's disease (p.301) and other infections

DARAPRIM a brand name for pyrimethamine

DARBEPOETIN ALFA a drug used to treat anemia due to kidney failure

DARVON-N a brand name for propoxyphene

DARVON-N COMPOUND a brand-name drug containing propoxyphene and acetylsalicylic acid

DAUNORUBICIN a cytotoxic anticancer drug (p.907)

DAUNOXOME a brand name for daunorubicin

DAYPRO a brand name for oxaprozin

DDAVP a brand name for desmopressin

DDC zalcitabine, an antiviral drug for HIV infection (*see* DRUGS FOR HIV INFECTION AND AIDS, p.887)

DDIdidanosine, an antiviral drug for HIV infection (*see* DRUGS FOR HIV INFECTION AND AIDS, p.887)

DECA-DURABOLIN a brand name for nandrolone

DECLOMYCIN a brand name for demeclocycline

DEFEROXAMINE an antidote for iron overdose (*see* DRUG OVERDOSE AND ACCIDENTAL INGESTION, p.321)

DEHYDRAL a brand-name drug containing methenamine

DELATESTRYL a brand name for testosterone

DELAVIRIDINE MESYLATE an antiviral drug for HIV infection (*see* DRUGS FOR HIV INFECTION AND AIDS, p.887)

DELESTROGEN a brand name for estradiol valerate

DELSYM OTC a brand-name drug containing dextromethorphan

DEMADEX a brand name for torsemide

DEMECLOCYCLINE a tetracycline antibiotic (p.885)

DEMEROL a brand name for meperidine

DEMULEN a brand-name oral contraceptive (*see* CONTRACEPTION, p.69) containing ethynodiol and ethinyl estradiol

DEPAKENE a brand name for valproic acid

DEPO-MEDROL a brand name for methylprednisolone

DEPO-PROVERA a brand name for medroxyprogesterone

DEPO-TESTOSTERONE a brand name for injected testosterone

DERMATOP a brand name for prednicarbate

DERMOVATE a brand name for clobetasol

DESFERAL a brand name for deferoxamine

DESFLURANE a general anesthetic (p.914)

DESIPRAMINE a tricyclic antidepressant drug (p.916)

DESLORATADINE an antihistamine (p.906)

DESMOPRESSIN a pituitary hormone (*see* PITUITARY DRUGS, p.934) used to treat diabetes insipidus (p.678) and bedwetting in children (*see* DRUGS THAT AFFECT BLADDER CONTROL, p.939)

DESOCORT a brand name for desonide

DESOGESTREL a progestin (*see* SEX HORMONES AND RELATED DRUGS, p.933)

DESONIDE a topical corticosteroid (p.892)

DESOXIMETASONE a topical corticosteroid (p.892)

DESOXYRIBONUCLEASE an enzyme used to cleanse wounds

DESQUAM OTC a brand name for benzoyl peroxide

DESYREL a brand name for trazodone

DETROL a brand name for tolterodine

DEXAMETHASONE a corticosteroid (p.930)

DEXASONE a brand name for dexamethasone

DEXEDRINE a brand name for dextroamphetamine

DEXRAZOXANE a drug used to reduce adverse effects on the heart caused by doxorubicin

DEXTRAN 40 a drug used to treat shock (p.414)

DEXTROAMPHETAMINE an amphetamine (*see* CENTRAL NERVOUS SYSTEM STIMULANT DRUGS, p.918)

DEXTROMETHORPHAN a cough suppressant (*see* COUGH REMEDIES, p.909)

DEXTROSE another name for glucose

DHA (docosahexaenoic acid) fish oil nutritional supplement used to promote cardiac health

DHT a brand name for dihydrotachysterol

DIABETA a brand name for glyburide

DIAMICRON a brand name for gliclazide

DIAMOX a brand name for acetazolamide

DIANE 35 a brand-name acne treatment containing cyproterone and ethinyl estradiol

DIASTAT a brand-name rectal gel containing diazepam

DIAZEPAM a benzodiazepine antianxiety drug (p.916), muscle relaxant (p.896), and anticonvulsant drug (p.914)

DIAZOXIDE an antihypertensive drug (p.897) and drug used to treat hypoglycemia (p.691)

DICETEL a brand name for pinaverium

DICHLOROACETIC ACID a drug used for the removal of warts (p.354) and calluses (*see* CALLUSES AND CORNS, p.349)

DICHLORODIFLUOROMETHANE a drug used as a muscle relaxant (p.896) and to relieve pain associated with injections

DICLECTIN a brand-name drug containing doxylamine and pyridoxine

DICLOFENAC a nonsteroidal anti-inflammatory drug (p.894)

DICYCLOMINE an antispasmodic drug (*see* ANTISPASMODIC DRUGS AND MOTILITY STIMULANTS, p.926) used to treat irritable bowel syndrome (p.656)

DIDANOSINE (DDI) an antiviral drug used to treat HIV infection (*see* DRUGS FOR HIV INFECTION AND AIDS, p.887)

DIDROCAL a brand-name kit containing etidronate and calcium used to prevent and treat osteoporosis (p.368)

DIDRONEL a brand name for etidronate

DIENESTROL an estrogen (*see* SEX HORMONES AND RELATED DRUGS, p.933)

DIETHYLPROPION a central nervous system stimulant drug (p.918) used as an appetite suppressant

DIETHYLSTILBESTROL a hormonal anticancer drug (p.907)

DIFFERIN a brand name for adapalene

DIFLUCAN a brand name for fluconazole

DIFLUCORTOLONE VALERATE a corticosteroid (p.930)

DIFLUNISAL a nonsteroidal anti-inflammatory drug (p.894)

DIGIBIND a brand-name antidote for digoxin overdose (*see* DRUG OVERDOSE AND ACCIDENTAL INGESTION, p.321)

DIGOXIN a digitalis drug (p.901)

DIHYDROCODEINE another name for hydrocodone

DIHYDROERGOTAMINE an antimigraine drug (p.913)

DIHYDROTACHYSTEROL a form of vitamin D used to treat tetany (muscular spasm) and hypoparathyroidism (p.683)

DILANTIN a brand name for phenytoin

DILAUDID a brand name for hydromorphone

DILOXANIDE FUROATE an antiprotozoal drug (p.888)

DILTIAZEM a calcium channel blocker drug (p.900)

DILUSOL OTC a brand name for ethyl alcohol

DIMENHYDRINATE an antihistamine (p.906) used as an antiemetic drug (p.922)

DIMETANE EXPECTORANT-C a brand-name drug containing brompheniramine, guaifenesin, codeine, and phenylephrine used for coughs and colds

DIMETANE EXPECTORANT-HC a brand-name drug containing brompheniramine, guaifenesin, hydrocodone, and phenylephrine used for coughs and colds

DIMETAPP OTC a brand-name for various cough, cold, and allergy medications

DIMETHICONE a silicone-based substance used in emollients and barrier preparations (p.890) and as an antifoaming agent with antacids (p.923)

DINOPROSTONE a prostaglandin used to terminate pregnancy and induce labor (*see* DRUGS FOR LABOR, p.938)

DIODOQUIN a brand name for iodoquinol

DIOVAN a brand name for valsartan

DIOVAN-HCT a brand-name drug containing valsartan and hydrochlorothiazide

DIOXYBENZONE a sunscreen (*see* SUNSCREENS AND SUNBLOCKS, p.893)

DIPENTUM a brand name for olsalazine

DIPHENHYDRAMINE an antihistamine (p.906), antiemetic drug (p.922), and antipruritic drug (p.891)

DIPHENOXYLATE an opioid antidiarrheal drug (p.924)

DIPIVEFRIN a sympathomimetic drug for glaucoma (p.920)

DIPOTASSIUM PHOSPHATE a phosphorus supplement (*see* MINERALS, p.929)

DIPRIVAN a brand name for propofol

DIPROLENE a brand name for betamethasone

DIPROSALIC a brand-name drug containing betamethasone dipropionate and salicylic acid

DIPROSONE a brand name for betamethasone dipropionate

DIPYRIDAMOLE an antiplatelet drug (*see* DRUGS THAT PREVENT BLOOD CLOTTING, p.904)

DISODIUM PHOSPHATE a phosphorus supplement (*see* MINERALS, p.929) and a saline laxative (p.924)

DISOPYRAMIDE an antiarrhythmic drug (p.898)

DITHRANOL a drug used to treat psoriasis (p.332)

DITROPAN a brand name for oxybutynin

DIUCARDIN a brand name for hydroflumethiazide

DIVALPROEX SODIUM an anticonvulsant drug (p.914) used to treat bipolar affective disorder (p.557)

DIXARIT a brand name for clonidine

DOBUTAMINE a drug used to treat acute heart failure (p.412) and shock (p.414)

DOBUTREX a brand name for dobutamine

DOCETAXEL an anticancer drug (p.907)

DOCOSAHEXAENOIC ACID (DHA) fish oil nutritional supplement used to promote cardiac health

DOCUSATE a fecal softener (*see* LAXATIVES, p.924) and earwax softener (*see* DRUGS ACTING ON THE EAR, p.921)

DOCUSATE SODIUM a fecal softener (*see* LAXATIVES, p.924) and earwax softener (*see* DRUGS ACTING ON THE EAR, p.921)

DOLASETRON an antiemetic drug (p.922) used with chemotherapy (p.278)

DOMPERIDONE an upper gastrointestinal motility modifier (*see* ANTISPASMODIC DRUGS AND MOTILITY STIMULANTS, p.926)

DONEPEZIL a drug used to treat Alzheimer disease (p.536)

DOPAMINE a drug used to treat acute heart failure (p.412), kidney failure (p.705), and shock (p.414)

DORNASE ALFA a mucolytic drug (*see* COUGH REMEDIES, p.909) used to treat cystic fibrosis (p.824)

DORZOLAMIDE a carbonic anhydrase inhibitor drug for glaucoma (p.920)

DOSTINEX a brand name for cabergoline

DOVOBET a brand-name cream containing calcipotriol and betamethasone

DOVONEX a brand name for calcipotriol

DOXACURIUM a muscle relaxant (p.896)

DOXAZOSIN an alpha blocker antihypertensive drug (p.897) and drug for prostate disorders (p.938)

DOXEPIN a tricyclic antidepressant drug (p.916)

DOXORUBICIN a cytotoxic anticancer drug (p.907)

DOXYCYCLINE a tetracycline antibiotic (p.885)

DOXYLAMINE an antihistamine (p.906)

DRISTAN (OTC) a brand name for various cold and allergy medications

DRONABINOL an antiemetic drug (p.922); it is also used to treat AIDS-related anorexia and weight loss

DROPERIDOL a butyrophenone antipsychotic drug (p.917) and an antiemetic drug (p.922) used after a general anesthetic (p.914)

DROTRECOGIN ALFA a drug used to treat severe sepsis

DTIC a brand name for dacarbazine

DUKORAL a vaccine (*see* VACCINES AND IMMUNOGLOBULINS, p.883) used to prevent traveler's diarrhea/cholera

DULCOLAX (OTC) a brand name for bisacodyl

DUOFILM (OTC) a drug containing lactic acid and salicylic acid used to treat warts

DUOPLANT (OTC) a drug containing formalin, lactic acid, and salicylic acid used to treat plantar warts

DUOVENT UDV a brand-name inhaler containing fenoterol and ipratropium bromide

DURAGESIC a brand name for fentanyl

DURALITH a brand name for lithium

DURICEF a brand name for cefadroxil

DUTASTERIDE a drug used to treat benign prostatic hypertrophy (*see* DRUGS FOR PROSTATE DISORDERS, p.938)

DUVOID a brand name for bethanechol

E

ECONAZOLE an antifungal drug (p.889)

ECOSTATIN a brand name for econazole

EDECRIN a brand name for ethacrynic acid

EDECRIN SODIUM a brand name for ethacrynate

EDETATE CALCIUM DISODIUM a drug used to treat lead poisoning (*see* DRUG OVERDOSE AND ACCIDENTAL INGESTION, p.321)

EDROPHONIUM a drug used in the diagnosis of myasthenia gravis (p.549)

EFAVIRENZ an antiviral drug used to treat HIV infection (*see* DRUGS FOR HIV INFECTION AND AIDS, p.887)

EFFEXOR a brand name for venlafaxine

EFLORNITHINE an antiprotozoal drug (p.888)

EFUDEX a brand name for fluorouracil

EICOSAPENTAENOIC ACID (EPA) fish oil nutritional supplement used to promote health

ELAVIL a brand name for amitriptyline

ELDEPRYL a brand name for selegiline

ELDOPAQUE a brand name for hydroquinone

ELECTROLYTE a mineral (p.929) present in body fluids, such as blood, that plays an important role in regulating water balance, blood acidity, conduction of nerve impulses, and muscle contraction

ELIDEL a brand name for pimecrolimus

ELIGARD a brand name for leuprolide

ELMIRON a brand name for pentosan

ELOCOM a brand name for mometasone

ELTROXIN a brand name for levothyroxine

EMADINE a brand name for emedastine

EMCYT a brand name for estramustine

EMEDASTINE a topical antihistamine eyedrop (*see* DRUGS THAT ACT ON THE EYE, p.919) used to relieve allergic conjunctivitis (*see* CONJUNCTIVITIS, p.570)

EMETINE an antiprotozoal drug (p.888)

EMINASE a brand name for anistreplase

EMLA (OTC) a brand-name local anesthetic (p.914) containing lidocaine and prilocaine

EMO-CORT a brand name for hydrocortisone

ENALAPRIL an ACE inhibitor drug (p.900)

ENALAPRILAT an ACE inhibitor drug (p.900)

ENBREL a brand name for etanercept

ENFUVIRTIDE an antiviral drug used to treat HIV infection (*see* DRUGS FOR HIV INFECTION AND AIDS, p.887)

ENGERIX-B a brand-name vaccine (*see* VACCINES AND IMMUNOGLOBULINS, p.883) for hepatitis B (*see* ACUTE HEPATITIS, p.644)

ENOXAPARIN an injected anticoagulant (*see* DRUGS THAT PREVENT BLOOD CLOTTING, p.904)

ENTACAPONE a drug used to treat Parkinson's disease (*see* PARKINSON'S DISEASE AND PARKINSONISM, p.539)

ENTOCORT a brand name for budesonide

ENZYME a protein that regulates the rate of a chemical reaction in the body

EPHEDRINE a sympathomimetic bronchodilator drug (p.910) and decongestant (p.909)

EPINEPHRINE a sympathomimetic bronchodilator drug (p.910), a mydriatic drug for glaucoma (p.920), and an antiallergy drug (p.905), also known as adrenaline

EPIPEN (OTC) a brand name for epinephrine

EPIRUBICIN an anticancer drug (p.907)

EPIVAL a brand name for divalproex sodium

EPOETIN ALFA a synthetic form of erythropoietin, a kidney hormone, used to treat anemia due to kidney failure (p.705)

EPOGEN a brand name for epoetin alfa

EPOPROSTENOL a prostaglandin used to treat primary pulmonary hypertension (p.505)

EPREX a brand name for epoetin alfa

EPROSARTAN an antihypertensive drug (p.897)

EPTIFIBATIDE a platelet aggregation inhibitor (*see* DRUGS THAT PREVENT BLOOD CLOTTING, p.904)

EQUANIL a brand name for meprobamate

ERGAMISOL a brand name for levamisole

ERGOCALCIFEROL a form of vitamin D

ERGOLOID MESYLATES a drug used for dementia (p.535)

ERGONOVINE a uterine stimulant (*see* DRUGS FOR LABOR, p.938)

ERGOTAMINE an antimigraine drug (p.913)

ERTAPENEM an injected antibiotic (p.885)

ERYBID a brand name for erythromycin

ERYC a brand name for erythromycin

ERYSOL a brand name for erythromycin, ethyl alcohol, octyl methoxycinnamate, and Parsol 1789

ERYTHROCIN a brand name for erythromycin stearate

ERYTHROMID a brand name for erythromycin

ERYTHROMYCIN a macrolide antibiotic (p.885)

ERYTHROMYCIN STEARATE a form of erythromycin

ESMOLOL a beta blocker drug (p.898)

ESOMEPRAZOLE an acid suppressive drug (p.923)

ESTALIS a brand-name transdermal patch containing norethindrone and 17-B estradiol

ESTERIFIED ESTROGENS a mixture of estrogens (*see* SEX HORMONES AND RELATED DRUGS, p.933)

ESTRACE a brand name for 17-B estradiol

ESTRACOMB a brand-name transdermal patch containing 17-B estradiol and norethindrone

ESTRADERM a brand name for estradiol used in hormone replacement therapy (p.937)

ESTRADIOL an estrogen (*see* SEX HORMONES AND RELATED DRUGS, p.933)

ESTRADIOL VALERATE an injected drug used to treat conditions of estrogen deficiency

ESTRAMUSTINE a cytotoxic anticancer drug (p.907)

ESTRING a brand-name vaginal ring containing estradiol used in hormone replacement therapy (p.937)

ESTROGEL a brand name for 17-B estradiol

ESTROGEN a female hormone (*see* SEX HORMONES AND RELATED DRUGS, p.933)

ESTRONE an estrogen (*see* SEX HORMONES AND RELATED DRUGS, p.933)

ESTROPIPATE an estrogen (*see* SEX HORMONES AND RELATED DRUGS, p.933)

ETANERCEPT a drug used to treat rheumatoid arthritis (p.895) and psoriatic arthritis

ETHACRYNATE a loop diuretic drug (p.902)

ETHACRYNIC ACID a loop diuretic drug (p.902)

ETHAMBUTOL an antituberculous drug (p.886)

ETHINYL ESTRADIOL an estrogen (*see* SEX HORMONES AND RELATED DRUGS, p.933)

ETHOSUXIMIDE an anticonvulsant drug (p.914)

ETHYL ALCOHOL a base in which medications can be dissolved, used in many acne preparations

ETHYL CHLORIDE a local anesthetic (p.914)

ETHYNODIOL a progestin (*see* SEX HORMONES AND RELATED DRUGS, p.933) and oral contraceptive drug (*see* CONTRACEPTION, p.69)

ETHYOL a brand name for amifostine

ETIBI a brand name for ethambutol

ETIDRONATE a drug for bone disorders (p.896)

ETODOLAC a nonsteroidal anti-inflammatory drug (p.894)

ETOPOSIDE a cytotoxic anticancer drug (p.907)

ETRAFON a brand-name antianxiety drug (p.916) and antidepressant drug (p.916) containing perphenazine and amitriptyline

EUCALYPTUS OIL an aromatic oil used in inhalations

EUCERIN CREME (OTC) a brand-name emollient (*see* EMOLLIENTS AND BARRIER PREPARATIONS, p.890) containing petrolatum, mineral oil, ceresin, and lanolin alcohol

EUFLEX a brand name for flutamide

EUGLUCON a brand name for glyburide

EUMOVATE a brand name for clobetasol

EURAX a brand name for crotamiton

EVISTA a brand name for raloxifene

EVRA a brand name for norelgestromin and ethinyl estradiol

EXELON a brand name for rivastigmine

EXEMESTANE a drug used to treat advanced breast cancer (p.759)

EZETIMIBE a lipid lowering drug (p.935)

EZETROL a brand name for ezetimibe

F

5-ASA (5-AMINOSALICYLIC ACID) a drug used to treat inflammation in the bowel associated with Crohn's disease (p.658) and ulcerative colitis (p.659)

FABRAZYME a brand name for agalsidase beta

FACTOR VIII a blood product used to promote blood clotting (*see* DRUGS THAT PROMOTE BLOOD CLOTTING, p.903)

FACTOR IX a blood product used to promote blood clotting (*see* DRUGS THAT PROMOTE BLOOD CLOTTING, p.903)

FAMCICLOVIR an antiviral drug (p.886)

FAMOTIDINE an acid-suppressive drug (p.923)

FAMVIR a brand name for famciclovir

FASLODEX a brand name for fulvestrant

FASTURTEC a brand name for rasburicase

FELODIPINE a calcium channel blocker drug (p.900)

FEMARA a brand name for letrozole

FEMHRT a brand-name drug containing norethindrone acetate and ethinyl estradiol

FENOFIBRATE a lipid-lowering drug (p.935)

FENOPROFEN a nonsteroidal anti-inflammatory drug (p.894)

FENOTEROL a bronchodilator drug (p.910) used in pulmonary conditions

FENTANYL an opioid analgesic (p.912) used as a general anesthetic (p.914) and in labor (*see* DRUGS FOR LABOR, p.938); also used for chronic pain

FER-IN-SOL (OTC) a brand name for ferrous sulphate

FERROUS FUMARATE a form of iron

FERROUS GLUCONATE a form of iron

FERROUS SULFATE a form of iron

FERTINORM a brand name for urofollitropin

FEVERFEW (OTC) an antimigraine drug (p.913)

FEXOFENADINE an antihistamine (p.906)

FIBRINOLYSIN an enzyme that breaks down protein used to treat wounds

FILGRASTIM a drug that stimulates production and function of white blood cells

FINASTERIDE a drug used to treat benign prostatic hypertrophy (*see* DRUGS FOR PROSTATE DISORDERS, p.938) and baldness

FIORINAL a brand-name analgesic (p.912) containing butalbital, aspirin, and caffeine

FLAGYL a brand name for metronidazole

FLAGYSTATIN a brand name for nystatin and metronidazole

FLAMAZINE a brand name for silver sulfadiazine

FLAREX a brand name for fluorometholone acetate

FLAVOXATE an anticholinergic drug (*see* DRUGS THAT AFFECT BLADDER CONTROL, p.939) used to treat total urinary incontinence (p.710)

FLECAINIDE an antiarrhythmic drug (p.898)

FLEET ENEMA (OTC) a brand-name laxative (p.924) containing monobasic sodium phosphate and dibasic sodium phosphate

FLEET MINERAL OIL ENEMA (OTC) a brand-name laxative (p.924) containing mineral oil

FLEXERIL a brand name for cyclobenzaprine

FLOCTAFENINE a nonsteroidal anti-inflammatory drug (p.894) and analgesic (p.912)

FLOLAN a brand name for epoprostenol

FLOMAX a brand name for tamsulosin

FLONASE a brand name for fluticasone

FLORINEF a brand name for fludrocortisone

FLOVENT DISKUS a brand name for fluticasone

FLOVENT HFA a brand name for fluticasone

FLOXIN a brand name for ofloxacin

FLUANXOL a brand name for flupenthixol

FLUCONAZOLE an antifungal drug (p.889)

FLUDARA a brand name for fludarabine

FLUDARABINE a cytotoxic anticancer drug (p.907)

FLUDROCORTISONE a corticosteroid (p.930)

FLUMAZENIL an antidote for benzodiazepine overdose (*see* DRUG OVERDOSE AND ACCIDENTAL INGESTION, p.321)

FLUMETHASONE a corticosteroid (p.930)

FLUNARIZINE an antimigraine drug (p.913)

FLUNISOLIDE a corticosteroid (p.930)

FLUOCINOLONE a topical corticosteroid (p.892)

FLUOCINONIDE a topical corticosteroid (p.892)

FLUORESCEIN a diagnostic agent used to stain the eye before examination

FLUORIDE a mineral (p.929) used to prevent dental caries (p.609)

FLUOROMETHOLONE a corticosteroid eyedrop (*see* CORTICOSTEROIDS p.930)

FLUOROPLEX a brand name for fluorouracil

FLUOROURACIL a cytotoxic anticancer drug (p.907)

FLUOTIC a brand name for sodium fluoride

FLUOXETINE a selective serotonin reuptake inhibitor (SSRI) antidepressant drug (p.916), also used to treat obsessive–compulsive disorder (p.553) and bulimia (p.563)

FLUOXYMESTERONE a male sex hormone (*see* SEX HORMONES AND RELATED DRUGS, p.933)

FLUPENTHIXOL an antipsychotic drug (p.917)

FLUPHENAZINE an antipsychotic drug (p.917)

FLURAZEPAM a benzodiazepine sleeping drug (p.915)

FLURBIPROFEN a nonsteroidal anti-inflammatory drug (p.894)

FLUTAMIDE a hormonal anticancer drug (p.907); also used to treat hirsutism (*see* EXCESSIVE HAIR, p.359)

FLUTICASONE a corticosteroid (p.930)

FLUVASTATIN a lipid-lowering drug (p.935)

FLUVOXAMINE a selective serotonin reuptake inhibitor (SSRI) antidepressant drug (p.916); also used for obsessive–compulsive disorder (p.553)

FLUZONE a brand-name vaccine (*see* VACCINES AND IMMUNOGLOBULINS, p.883) for influenza (p.287)

FML a brand name for fluorometholone

FOLIC ACID (OTC) a vitamin (p.927)

FOLINIC ACID a form of folic acid used to decrease toxicity of methotrexate

FOLLITROPIN ALPHA a drug for infertility (p.936)

FOLLITROPIN BETA a drug for infertility (p.936)

FOMEPIZOLE a drug used to treat ethylene glycol poisoning

FONDAPARINUX an injected antithrombotic (*see* DRUGS THAT PREVENT BLOOD CLOTTING, p.904)

FORADIL a brand name for formoterol

FORANE a brand name for isoflurane

FORMALIN an ingredient in preparations for warts (p.354)

FORMOTEROL a long-acting bronchodilator drug (p.910) used for maintenance treatment of asthma, and also to treat COPD

FORMULEX a brand name for dicyclomine

FORTAZ a brand name for ceftazidime

FORTEO a brand name for teriparatide

FORTOVASE ROCHE a brand name for saquinavir

FOSAMAX a brand name for alendronate

FOSFOMYCIN an antibiotic (p.885)

FOSINOPRIL an ACE inhibitor drug (p.900)

FOSPHENYTOIN an anticonvulsant drug (p.914)

FRAGMIN a brand name for dalteparin

FRAMYCETIN an antibiotic (p.885)

FRESH FROZEN PLASMA a product prepared from the fluid part of blood

FRISIUM a brand name for clobazam

FROBEN a brand name for flurbiprofen

FUCIDIC ACID an antibiotic (p.885)

FUCIDIN a brand name for fucidic acid or sodium fucidate

FUCITHALMIC a brand name for fucidin eye drops

FULVESTRANT a hormonal anticancer drug (p.907)

FULVICIN a brand name for griseofulvin

FUNGIZONE a brand name for amphotericin B

FUROSEMIDE a loop diuretic drug (p.902)

FUZEON a brand name for enfuvirtide

G

GABAPENTIN an anticonvulsant drug (p.914)

GALANTAMINE a drug used to treat Alzheimer's disease (p.536)

GALLIUM a drug used to treat abnormally raised blood calcium levels in people with cancer

GANCICLOVIR an antiviral drug (p.886) used to prevent and treat cytomegalovirus infection (p.290)

GANIRELIX ACETATE a gonadotropin releasing hormone antagonist used to treat infertility (*see* SEX HORMONES AND RELATED DRUGS, p.933)

GARAMYCIN a brand name for gentamicin

GARASONE a brand-name eyedrop (*see* DRUGS ACTING ON THE EYE p.919) and eardrop (*see* DRUGS ACTING ON THE EAR, p.921) containing betamethasone and gentamicin

GATIFLOXACIN a quinolone antibiotic (p. 885)

GAVISCON (OTC) a brand-name for various antacid (p.923) and antireflux medications

GEFITINIB an epidermal growth factor receptor inhibitor, anticancer drug

GEMCITABINE a cytotoxic anticancer drug (p.907)

GEMFIBROZIL a lipid-lowering drug (p.935)

GEMZAR a brand name for gemcitabine

GENTAMICIN an aminoglycoside antibiotic (p.885)

GLATIRAMER ACETATE a drug used for relapsing-remitting multiple sclerosis (p.541)

GLEEVEC a brand name for imatinib

GLICLAZIDE an oral drug for diabetes mellitus (p.931)

GLIMEPIRIDE an oral drug used to treat diabetes mellitus (p.931)

GLITAZONES a class of drugs used to treat type 2 diabetes mellitus (*see* DRUGS FOR DIABETES MELLITUS, p.931)

GLUCAGON a pancreatic hormone used to treat hypoglycemia (*see* DRUGS FOR DIABETES MELLITUS, p.931)

GLUCONO-DELTA-LACTONE an ingredient of solutions used to dissolve kidney stones (p.701) and bladder stones (p.714)

GLUCONORM a brand-name for repaglinide

GLUCOPHAGE a brand name for metformin

GLUCOSE a simple sugar that is a source of rapidly available energy

GLUCOTROL a brand name for glipizide

GLUTARALDEHYDE a disinfectant (*see* PREPARATIONS FOR SKIN INFECTIONS AND INFESTATIONS, p.892)

GLYBURIDE an oral drug for diabetes mellitus (p.931)

GLYCERIN a diuretic drug (p.902), laxative (p.924), and drug for glaucoma (p.920); also used to soften earwax (*see* DRUGS ACTING ON THE EAR, p.921) and as an ingredient in topical preparations

GLYCOPYRROLATE a drug used to dry secretions during general anesthesia (*see* HAVING MAJOR SURGERY, p.943)

GLYSENNID (OTC) a brand name for sennosides A & B

GOLD SODIUM THIOMALATE an antirheumatic drug (p.895)

GOLYTELY (OTC) a brand-name preparation containing polyethylene glycol, sodium sulfate, sodium bicarbonate, sodium chloride, and potassium chloride

GONADORELIN a hypothalamic hormone that regulates sex hormones (*see* SEX HORMONES AND RELATED DRUGS, p.933) and a drug for infertility (p.936)

GOSERELIN a hormonal anticancer drug (p.907) and gonadorelin analog (*see* SEX HORMONES AND RELATED DRUGS, p.933)

GRAMICIDIN an aminoglycoside antibiotic (p.885) for eye, ear, and skin infections

GRANISETRON an antiemetic drug (p.922) used in chemotherapy (p.278), radiation, and postoperative nausea and vomiting

GRAVOL OTC a brand name for dimenhydrinate

GRISEOFULVIN an antifungal drug (p.889)

GUAIFENESIN an expectorant (*see* COUGH REMEDIES, p.909)

GYNAZOLE a brand name for butoconazole

H

HABITROL brand-name nicotine skin patches to help people stop smoking

HALCINONIDE a topical corticosteroid (p.892)

HALCION a brand name for triazolam

HALDOL a brand name for haloperidol

HALOBETASOL a topical corticosteroid (p.892)

HALOFANTRINE an antimalarial drug (p.888)

HALOG a brand name for halcinonide

HALOPERIDOL a butyrophenone antipsychotic drug (p.917)

HALOTESTIN a brand name for fluoxymesterone

HALOTHANE a gas used as a general anesthetic (p.914)

HAVRIX a brand-name vaccine (*see* VACCINES AND IMMUNOGLOBULINS, p.883) for hepatitis A (*see* ACUTE HEPATITIS, p.644)

HEAD & SHOULDERS OTC a brand-name shampoo containing pyrithione zinc used to treat dandruff (p.358)

HEAD & SHOULDERS INTENSIVE TREATMENT OTC a brand-name shampoo containing selenium sulfide used to treat dandruff (p.358)

HEPALEAN a brand name for heparin

HEPARIN an injected anticoagulant (*see* DRUGS THAT PREVENT BLOOD CLOTTING, p.904)

HEPTOVIR a brand name for lamivudine

HERCEPTIN a brand name for trastuzumab

HERPLEX D a brand name for idoxuridine

HEXACHLOROPHENE a skin antiseptic (*see* Preparations for skin infections and infestations, p.892)

HEXALEN a brand name for altretamine

HIVID a brand name for zalcitabine (DDC)

HOMATROPINE a mydriatic drug (*see* DRUGS ACTING ON THE EYE, p.919)

HP PAC a brand name for a combination of lansoprazole, clarithromycin, and amoxicillin used to treat *Helicobacter pylori* infection (p.639)

HUMALOG OTC a brand name for insulin lispro

HUMALOG MIX 25 OTC an insulin product consisting of 25 percent insulin lispro and 75 percent insulin lispro protamine

HUMAN CHORIONIC GONADOTROPIN a gonadotropin (*see* SEX HORMONES AND RELATED DRUGS, p.933)

HUMATIN a brand name for paromomycin

HUMEGON a brand name for menotropin

HUMULIN OTC a brand name for insulin

HYALURONIC ACID an ingredient in face moisturizers used to soothe dry skin (*see* EMOLLIENTS AND BARRIER PREPARATIONS, p.890)

HYALURONIDASE a drug used to increase the absorption of injected fluids

HYCAMTIN a brand name for topotecan

HYCODAN a brand-name cough remedy (p.909) containing hydrocodone

HYCOMINE a brand-name cough remedy (p.909) and cold and flu remedy (p.910) containing hydrocodone and phenylpropanolamine

HYDERGINE a brand name for ergoloid mesylates

HYDRALAZINE an antihypertensive drug (p.897)

HYDREA a brand name for hydroxyurea

HYDROCET a brand-name analgesic (p.912) containing hydrocodone and acetaminophen

HYDROCHLOROTHIAZIDE a thiazide diuretic drug (p.902)

HYDROCHLOROTHIAZIDE-TRIAMTERENE a combination of diuretic drugs (p.902)

HYDROCODONE a cough suppressant (*see* COUGH REMEDIES, p.909) and analgesic (p.912)

HYDROCORTISONE a corticosteroid (p.930)

HYDROCORTONE a brand name for hydrocortisone

HYDROGEN PEROXIDE an antiseptic (*see* PREPARATIONS FOR SKIN INFECTIONS AND INFESTATIONS, p.892)

HYDROMORPH CONTIN a brand name for hydromorphone

HYDROMORPHONE an opioid analgesic (p.912)

HYDROQUINONE a drug used to bleach unwanted skin pigmentation

HYDROXYCHLOROQUINE an antimalarial drug (p.888) and antirheumatic drug (p.895)

HYDROXYCOBALAMIN a form of vitamin B_{12}

HYDROXYETHYLCELLULOSE a substance used in artificial tears (*see* DRUGS ACTING ON THE EYE, p.919)

HYDROXYPROPYL CELLULOSE a substance used in artificial tears (*see* DRUGS ACTING ON THE EYE, p.919)

HYDROXYPROPYL METHYLCELLULOSE a substance used in artificial tears (*see* DRUGS ACTING ON THE EYE, p.919)

HYDROXYUREA a cytotoxic anticancer drug (p.907), also used to treat certain blood disorders

HYDROXYZINE a nonbenzodiazepine antianxiety drug (p.916) and antipruritic drug (p.891)

HYLAN G-F 20 OTC an injection used to replace synovial fluid (*see* THE JOINTS, p.364) in the knee

HYOSCINE BUTYLBROMIDE an antispasmodic drug (*see* ANTISPASMODIC DRUGS AND MOTILITY STIMULANTS, p.926) used to treat irritable bowel syndrome (p.656)

HYOSCINE HYDROBROMIDE an antiemetic drug (p.922) used to treat motion sickness (p.604)

HYOSCYAMINE an antispasmodic drug (*see* ANTISPASMODIC DRUGS AND MOTILITY STIMULANTS, p.926) used to treat bowel and stomach conditions

HYPROMELLOSE a substance used in artificial tears (*see* DRUGS ACTING ON THE EYE, p.919)

HYSKON a brand name for dextran

HYTRIN a brand name for terazosin

HYZAAR a brand-name antihypertensive drug (p.897) containing losartan and hydrochlorothiazide

HYZAAR DS a brand name for losartan and hydrochlorothiazide

I

IBUPROFEN a nonsteroidal anti-inflammatory drug (p.894) and analgesic (p.912)

IBUTILIDE FUMARATE an injected antiarrhythmic (p.898) used to rapidly convert atrial fibrillation (p.417) to regular heart rhythm

IDAMYCIN a brand name for idarubicin

IDARAC a brand name for floctafenine

IDARUBICIN a cytotoxic agent used as an anticancer drug (p.907)

IDOXURIDINE an antiviral drug (p.886)

IFEX a brand name for ifosfamide

IFOSFAMIDE a cytotoxic anticancer drug (p.907)

ILOTYCIN a brand name for erythromycin

IMATINIB a drug used to treat chronic myeloid leukemia

IMDUR OTC a brand name for isosorbide mononitrate

IMIPENEM an antibiotic (p.885)

IMIPRAMINE a tricyclic antidepressant drug (p.916), also used to treat bedwetting (p.872)

IMIQUIMOD a drug used to treat genital warts (p.768) and actinic keratosis

IMITREX a brand name for sumatriptan

IMODIUM (OTC) a brand name for loperamide

IMOVANE a brand name for zopiclone

IMOVAX RABIES a brand name for rabies vaccine (*see* VACCINES AND IMMUNOGLOBULINS, p.883)

IMURAN a brand name for azathioprine

INDAPAMIDE a thiazidelike diuretic drug (p.902)

INDERAL a brand name for propranolol

INDINAVIR an antiviral drug (p.886) used to treat HIV infection and AIDS (p.887)

INDOCID a brand name for an injectable form of indomethacin

INDOMETHACIN a nonsteroidal anti-inflammatory drug (p.894) and drug used to treat gout (p.380)

INFERGEN a brand name for interferon alfacon-1

INFLAMASE a brand name for prednisolone

INFLIXIMAB a drug used to treat Crohn's disease (p.658) and rheumatoid arthritis

INHIBACE a brand name for cilazapril

INHIBACE PLUS a brand name for cilazapril and hydrochlorothiazide

INNOHEP a brand name for tinzaparin

INOSITOL a substance related to the vitamin B complex

INSULIN a drug for diabetes mellitus (p.687)

INSULIN ASPART a brand name for a type of insulin

INSULIN LISPRO a type of insulin

INSULIN LISPRO PROTAMINE a type of insulin

INTAL a brand name for cromolyn sodium

INTEGRILIN a brand name for eptifibatide

INTERFERON ALPHA a type of interferon drug (p.907)

INTERFERON ALPHA-2A a type of interferon drug (p.907)

INTERFERON ALPHA-2B a type of interferon drug (p.907)

INTERFERON BETA a type of interferon drug (p.907)

INTERFERON BETA-1A a type of interferon drug (p.907)

INTERFERON BETA-1B a type of interferon drug (p.907)

INTERFERON GAMMA a type of interferon drug (p.907)

INTERLEUKIN-2 a cytokine anticancer drug (p.907)

INTRINSIC FACTOR CONCENTRATE a drug used to treat anemia (p.446)

INTRON A a brand name for interferon alpha-2B

INTROPIN a brand name for dopamine

INVANZ a brand name for ertapenem

INVIRASE a brand name for saquinavir mesylate

IODINE a mineral (p.929), a preparation for skin infections and infestations (p.892), and a drug for hyperthyroidism (p.932)

IODOQUINOL an antiprotozoal drug (p.888) used to treat amebiasis (p.306)

IONAMIN a brand name for phentermine

IOPIDINE a brand name for apraclonidine

IPECAC (OTC) a drug used to induce vomiting in drug overdose and accidental ingestion (p.321) and as an expectorant (*see* COUGH REMEDIES, p.909)

IPRATROPIUM BROMIDE an anticholinergic bronchodilator drug (p.910); also used in nasal spray for nonallergic rhinitis, or runny nose (*see* COMMON COLD, p.286)

IRBESARTAN an angiotensin II blocker antihypertensive drug (p.897)

IRESSA a brand name for gefitinib

IRINOTECAN a cytotoxic anticancer drug (p.907)

IRON a mineral (p.929)

IRON DEXTRAN a form of iron

ISOFLURANE an inhaled general anesthetic (p.914)

ISONIAZID an antituberculous drug (p.886)

ISOPROPYL MYRISTATE an ingredient of emollients (*see* EMOLLIENTS AND BARRIER PREPARATIONS, p.890)

ISOPROTERENOL a sympathomimetic bronchodilator drug (p.910) and beta blocker drug (p.898)

ISOPTIN a brand name for verapamil

ISOPTO HOMATROPINE a brand name for homatropine

ISOSORBIDE DINITRATE a nitrate drug (p.899) used to treat angina (p.407)

ISOSORBIDE MONONITRATE a nitrate drug (p.899) used to treat angina (p.407)

ISOTRETINOIN a retinoid drug (p.890) used to treat acne (p.340)

ITRACONAZOLE an antifungal drug (p.889)

K

K-DUR (OTC) a brand name for potassium chloride

K-LOR (OTC) a brand name for potassium chloride

K-LYTE (OTC) a brand name for potassium chloride

K-10 (OTC) a brand name for potassium chloride

KADIAN a brand name for morphine

KALETRA a brand name for lopinavir and ritonavir

KAOLIN an antidiarrheal drug (p.924)

KAOLIN-PECTIN (OTC) a brand name for kaolin and pectin

KAOPECTATE (OTC) a brand name for attapulgite

KAYEXALATE a brand name for sodium polystyrene sulfonate

KEFZOL a brand name for cefazolin

KEMADRIN a brand name for procyclidine

KENACOMB a brand-name drug containing gramicidin, neomycin, nystatin, and triamcinolone

KENALOG a brand name for triamcinolone

KENALOG IN ORABASE a brand name for triamcinolone

KEPPRA a brand name for levetiracetam

KERATOLYTIC a substance that loosens dead cells on the surface of the skin

KETALAR a brand name for ketamine

KETAMINE a general anesthetic (p.914)

KETEK a brand name for telithromycin

KETOCONAZOLE an antifungal drug (p.889)

KETOPROFEN a nonsteroidal anti-inflammatory drug (p.894)

KETOROLAC a nonsteroidal anti-inflammatory drug (p.894), also used to relieve itching of the eye in allergic conjunctivitis (p.570)

KETOTIFEN an antiallergy drug (p.905)

KINERET a brand name for anakinra

KOFFEX DM (OTC) a brand name for dextromethorphan

KOGENATE FS a brand name for antihemophilic factor

KWELLADA-P (OTC) a brand name for permethrin

KYTRIL a brand name for granisetron

L

L-HISTIDINE an amino acid

L-THREONINE an amino acid

L-TRYPTOPHAN a drug used for mood disorders and depression (*see* ANTIDEPRESSANT DRUGS, p.916)

L-TYROSINE an amino acid

LABETALOL a beta blocker drug (p.898)

LAC-HYDRIN (OTC) a brand name for ammonium lactate

LACRISERT a brand name for hydroxypropyl cellulose

LACTAID (OTC) a brand name for lactase

LACTASE a digestive enzyme used to treat lactose intolerance (p.657)

LACTIC ACID a moisturizing ingredient used in preparations for warts (p.354) and in emollients (*see* EMOLLIENTS AND BARRIER PREPARATIONS, p.890) and suppositories

LACTOBACILLUS ACIDOPHILUS a drug used to restore and maintain bacterial flora of the gastrointestinal tract (*see* THE DIGESTIVE TRACT, p.622)

LACTULOSE a laxative (p.924)

LAMICTAL a brand name for lamotrigine

LAMISIL a brand name for terbinafine

LAMIVUDINE an antiviral drug used to treat HIV infection (*see* DRUGS FOR HIV INFECTION AND AIDS, p.887)

LAMOTRIGINE an anticonvulsant drug (p.914)

LANOLIN fat obtained from wool and used in emollients (*see* EMOLLIENTS AND BARRIER PREPARATIONS, p.890)

LANOXIN a brand name for digoxin

LANSOPRAZOLE an acid-suppressive drug (p.923)

LANVIS a brand name for thioguanine

LARGACTIL a brand name for chlorpromazine

LARIAM a brand name for mefloquine

LARONIDASE an enzyme replacement therapy for patients with mucopolysaccharidosis

LASIX a brand name for furosemide

LATANOPROST a drug for glaucoma (p.920)

LECITHIN a drug used to increase blood levels of choline, a substance required in metabolism

LECTOPAM a brand name for bromazepam

LEFLUNOMIDE a drug used to treat rheumatoid arthritis (p.377)

LEPIRUDIN an injected anticoagulant (*see* DRUGS THAT PREVENT BLOOD CLOTTING, p.904)

LESCOL a brand name for fluvastatin

LETROZOLE a hormonal anticancer drug (p.907)

LEUCOVORIN CALCIUM another name for folinic acid

LEUKERAN a brand name for chlorambucil

LEUPROLIDE a hormonal anticancer drug (p.907)

LEUPRORELIN a gonadorelin analog (*see* SEX HORMONES AND RELATED DRUGS, p.933)

LEUSTATIN a brand name for cladribine

LEVAMISOLE an anticancer drug (p.907)

LEVAQUIN a brand name for levofloxacin

LEVETIRACETAM an anticonvulsant drug (p.914)

LEVITRA a brand name for vardenafil

LEVOBUNOLOL a beta blocker drug for glaucoma (p.920)

LEVOCABASTINE an antihistamine (p.906)

LEVOCARNITINE a drug used to treat a deficiency in carnitine, a naturally occurring substance required in metabolism

LEVODOPA a drug used to treat parkinsonism (*see* PARKINSON'S DISEASE AND PARKINSONISM, p.539)

LEVOFLOXACIN a quinolone antibiotic (p.885)

LEVONORGESTREL a progestin contraceptive drug (*see* CONTRACEPTION, p.69)

LEVOTHYROXINE a thyroid hormone used as a drug for hypothyroidism (p.932)

LEVSIN (OTC) a brand name for hyoscyamine

LIBRAX a brand-name drug containing chlordiazepoxide and clidinium

LIBRIUM a brand name for chlordiazepoxide

LIDEX a brand name for fluocinonide

LIDOCAINE a local anesthetic (p.914) and antiarrhythmic drug (p.898)

LINCOCIN a brand name for lincomycin

LINCOMYCIN an antibiotic (p.885)

LINDANE a topical antiparasitic drug (*see* PREPARATIONS FOR SKIN INFECTIONS AND INFESTATIONS, p.892)

LINEZOLID an oxazolidinone antibiotic (p.885)

LIORESAL a brand name for baclofen

LIOTHYRONINE a thyroid hormone used as a drug for hypothyroidism (p.932)

LIPASE a digestive enzyme

LIPIDIL MICRO a brand name for fenofibrate

LIPIDIL SUPRA a brand name for fenofibrate

LIPITOR a brand name for atorvastatin

LIQUID PARAFFIN an emollient (*see* EMOLLIENTS AND BARRIER PREPARATIONS, p.890) and laxative (p.924)

LISINOPRIL an ACE inhibitor drug (p.900)

LITHANE a brand name for lithium

LITHIUM a mood-stabilizing drug (p.918)

LIVER PREPARATIONS preparations used to treat anemia (p.446)

LIVOSTIN a brand name for levocabastine

LOCACORTEN VIOFORM a brand-name drug containing clioquinol and flumethasone

LODOXAMIDE an antiallergy drug (p.905) used to treat eye disorders

LOESTRIN a brand-name oral contraceptive (*see* CONTRACEPTION, p.69) containing ethinyl estradiol and norethindrone

LOMOTIL a brand-name antidiarrheal drug (p.924) containing atropine and diphenoxylate

LOMUSTINE a cytotoxic anticancer drug (p.907)

LONITEN a brand name for minoxidil

LOPERAMIDE an antidiarrheal drug (p.924)

LOPID a brand name for gemfibrozil

LOPRESSOR a brand name for metoprolol

LOPROX CREAM a brand name for ciclopirox olamine

LORATADINE an antihistamine (p.906)

LORAZEPAM a benzodiazepine antianxiety drug (p.916) and sleeping drug (p.915)

LOSARTAN an antihypertensive drug (p.897)

LOSEC a brand name for omeprazole

LOTENSIN a brand name for benazepril

LOTRIDERM a brand-name cream containing betamethasone and clotrimazole

LOVASTATIN a lipid-lowering drug (p.935)

LOVENOX a brand name for enoxaparin

LOXAPAC a brand name for injectable loxapine

LOXAPINE an antipsychotic drug (p.917)

LOZIDE a brand name for indapamide

LUMIGAN a brand name for bimatoprost

LUPRON a brand name for leuprolide

LUTEOTROPIN a hormone of the anterior pituitary (*see* PITUITARY DRUGS, p.934)

LUTREPULSE a brand name for gonadorelin

LUVOX a brand name for fluvoxamine

LYPRESSIN a pituitary hormone (*see* PITUITARY DRUGS, p.934)

LYSODREN a brand name for mitotane

M

M-ESLON a brand name for morphine

MAALOX SUSPENSION (OTC) a brand-name antacid (p.923) containing aluminum hydroxide and magnesium hydroxide

MACROBID a brand name for nitrofurantoin

MACRODANTIN a brand name for nitrofurantoin

MAGALDRATE an antacid (p.923)

MAGNESIUM a mineral (p.929)

MAGNESIUM CARBONATE a form of magnesium and an antacid (p.923)

MAGNESIUM CHLORIDE a form of magnesium

MAGNESIUM CITRATE a saline laxative (p.924)

MAGNESIUM GLUCONATE a form of magnesium

MAGNESIUM HYDROXIDE an antacid (p.923) and laxative (p.924)

MAGNESIUM OXIDE a form of magnesium and an antacid (p.923)

MAGNESIUM SALICYLATE an analgesic (p.912)

MAGNESIUM SALTS saline laxatives (p.924)

MAGNESIUM SULFATE a form of magnesium, a saline laxative (p.924), and an anticonvulsant drug (p.914)

MAGNESIUM TRISILICATE an antacid (p.923)

MALARONE a brand name for atovaquone and proguanil

MANERIX a brand name for moclobemide

MANNITOL an osmotic diuretic drug (p.902)

MAPROTILINE an antidepressant drug (p.916)

MARCAINE a brand name for bupivacaine

MARINOL a brand name for dronabinol

MARVELON a brand-name oral contraceptive (*see* CONTRACEPTION, p.69) containing desogestrel and ethinyl estradiol

MATERNA (OTC) a brand name for prenatal vitamins and minerals

MAVIK a brand name for trandolapril

MAXALT a brand name for rizatriptan

MAXALT (RPD) a brand name for rizatriptan

MAXIDEX a brand-name eyedrop containing dexamethasone

MAXIPIME a brand name for cefepime

MAZINDOL a drug used to treat obesity (p.631)

MEBENDAZOLE an anthelmintic drug (p.889)

MECHLORETHAMINE a cytotoxic anticancer drug (p.907)

MECLIZINE an antiemetic drug (p.922) and antihistamine (p.906)

MEDROL a brand name for methylprednisolone

MEDROXYPROGESTERONE a progestin (*see* SEX HORMONES AND RELATED DRUGS, p.933) and hormonal anticancer drug (p.907)

MEFENAMIC ACID a nonsteroidal anti-inflammatory drug (p.894)

MEFLOQUINE an antimalarial drug (p.888)

MEGACE a brand name for megestrol

MEGESTROL a progestin (*see* SEX HORMONES AND RELATED DRUGS, p.933) and hormonal anticancer drug (p.907)

MELANOMA THERACCINE a drug used to promote an antimelanoma immune response

MELOXICAM a nonsteroidal anti-inflammatory drug (p.894)

MELPHALAN a cytotoxic anticancer drug (p.907)

MENJUGATE a brand-name meningococcal group C vaccine (see VACCINES AND IMMUNOGLOBULINS, p.883)

MENOMUNE a brand name for meningococcal polysaccharide vaccine (see VACCINES AND IMMUNOGLOBULINS, p.883)

MENOTROPIN a drug for infertility (p.936)

MENTHOL an alcohol derived from mint oils used as an inhalation and as a topical antipruritic drug (p.891)

MEPERIDINE an opioid analgesic (p.912)

MEPIVACAINE a local anesthetic (p.914)

MEPROBAMATE a nonbenzodiazepine antianxiety drug (p.916)

MEPRON a brand name for atovaquone

MERCAPTOPURINE a cytotoxic anticancer drug (p.907)

MERIDIA a brand name for sibutramine

MEROPENEM a broad-spectrum carbapenem antibiotic (p.885)

MERREM a brand name for meropenem

MESALAMINE a 5-aminosalicylate drug (p.924)

MESASAL a brand name for 5-ASA

MESNA a drug used to protect the urinary tract from damage caused by some anticancer drugs (p.907)

MESTINON a brand name for pyridostigmine

MESTRANOL an estrogen (*see* SEX HORMONES AND RELATED DRUGS, p.933)

METADOL a brand name for methadone

METAMUCIL (OTC) a brand name for psyllium

METAPROTERENOL a sympathomimetic bronchodilator drug (p.910)

METFORMIN an oral drug for diabetes mellitus (p.931)

METHADONE an opioid analgesic (p.912), also used to treat heroin dependence (*see* DRUG DEPENDENCE, p.564)

METHAZOLAMIDE a drug for glaucoma (p.920)

METHENAMINE a drug used to suppress urinary tract infections such as cystitis (p.709)

METHIMAZOLE an antithyroid drug (*see* DRUGS FOR HYPERTHYROIDISM, p.932)

METHIONINE a drug used to treat diaper rash (p.829) and as a nutritional supplement

METHOCARBAMOL a muscle relaxant (p.896)

METHOHEXITAL a barbiturate used as a general anesthetic (p.914)

METHOTREXATE a cytotoxic anticancer drug (p.907) and antirheumatic drug (p.895), also used to treat psoriasis (p.332)

METHOTRIMEPRAZINE an analgesic (p.912), also used to treat psychiatric illness and for nausea

METHOXSALEN a drug used to treat psoriasis (p.332)

METHSUXIMIDE an anticonvulsant drug (p.914)

METHYLCELLULOSE a substance in artificial tears (*see* DRUGS ACTING ON THE EYE, p.919), a bulk-forming laxative (p.924), and an antidiarrheal drug (p.924)

METHYLDOPA an antihypertensive drug (p.897)

METHYLENE BLUE a mild antiseptic (*see* PREPARATIONS FOR SKIN INFECTIONS AND INFESTATIONS, p.892), also used as a dye

METHYLPHENIDATE a central nervous system stimulant drug (p.918) used to treat hyperactivity in children (*see* ATTENTION DEFICIT HYPERACTIVITY DISORDER, p.855)

METHYLPREDNISOLONE a corticosteroid (p.930)

METHYL SALICYLATE a topical analgesic (p.912) used for muscle and joint pain

METHYLTESTOSTERONE a male sex hormone (*see* SEX HORMONES AND RELATED DRUGS, p.933)

METHYSERGIDE an antimigraine drug (p.913)

METOCLOPRAMIDE a gastrointestinal motility drug (*see* ANTISPASMODIC DRUGS AND MOTILITY STIMULANTS, p.926) and an antiemetic drug (p.922)

METOLAZONE a thiazidelike diuretic drug (p.902)

METOPROLOL a beta blocker drug (p.898)

METROCREAM a brand name for topical metronidazole

METROGEL a brand name for topical metronidazole

METRONIDAZOLE an antibiotic (p.885)

MEVACOR a brand name for lovastatin

MEXILETINE an antiarrhythmic drug (p.898)

MIACALCIN a brand name for calcitonin

MICARDIS a brand name for telmisartan

MICARDIS PLUS a brand name for telmisartan and hydrochlorothiazide

MICATIN (OTC) a brand name for miconazole

MICONAZOLE an antifungal drug (p.889)

MICRO-K (OTC) a brand name for potassium chloride

MICRONOR a brand-name oral contraceptive (*see* CONTRACEPTION, p.69) containing norethindrone

MIDAMOR a brand name for amiloride

MIDAZOLAM a benzodiazepine (*see* ANTIANXIETY DRUGS, p.916) used as premedication (*see* HAVING MAJOR SURGERY, p.943)

MIDODRINE a drug used to treat hypotension (p.414)

MIGRANAL a brand name for dihydroergotamine

MILK OF MAGNESIA (OTC) a brand name for magnesium hydroxide

MILRINONE a drug used to treat chronic heart failure (p.413)

MINERAL OIL a laxative (p.924), emollient (*see* EMOLLIENTS AND BARRIER PREPARATIONS, p.890), and earwax softener (*see* DRUGS ACTING ON THE EAR, p.921)

MINESTRIN a brand-name oral contraceptive (*see* CONTRACEPTION, p.69) containing ethinyl estradiol and norethindrone

MINIPRESS a brand name for prazosin

MINIRIN a brand name for desmopressin

MINITRAN OTC a brand name for nitroglycerin

MINOCIN a brand name for minocycline

MINOCYCLINE a tetracycline antibiotic (p.885)

MINOVRAL a brand-name oral contraceptive (*see* CONTRACEPTION, p.69) containing ethinyl estradiol and levonorgestrel

MINOXIDIL an antihypertensive drug (p.897)

MIRAPEX a brand name for pramipexole

MIRTAZAPINE an antidepressant drug (p.916)

MISOPROSTOL an acid-suppressive drug (p.923)

MITOMYCIN a cytotoxic anticancer drug (p.907)

MITOTANE an anticancer drug (p.907)

MITOXANTRONE a cytotoxic anticancer drug (p.907)

MIVACRON a brand name for mivacurium

MIVACURIUM a muscle relaxant used in general anesthesia (*see* HAVING MAJOR SURGERY, p.943)

MOBICOX a brand name for meloxicam

MOCLOBEMIDE a reversible inhibitor of monoamine oxidase (RIMA) antidepressant drug (p.916)

MODAFINIL a drug used for narcolepsy (p.526)

MODECATE a brand name for fluphenazine

MODULON a brand name for trimebutine

MODURET a brand-name antihypertensive drug (p.897) containing amiloride and hydrochlorothiazide

MOGADON a brand name for nitrazepam

MOLYBDENUM a mineral (p.929)

MOMETASONE a topical corticosteroid (p.892)

MONISTAT-DERM OTC a brand name for miconazole

MONITAN a brand name for acebutolol

MONOCOR a brand name of bisoprolol

MONOPRIL a brand name for fosinopril

MONTELUKAST a drug used to treat asthma (*see* LEUKOTRIENE ANTAGONISTS, p.911)

MONUROL a brand name for fosfomycin

MORPHINE an opioid analgesic (p.912)

MOTRIN OTC a brand name for ibuprofen

MOXIFLOXACIN a quinolone antibiotic (p.885)

MS CONTIN a brand name for morphine

MS•IR a brand name for morphine

MUCOMYST OTC a brand name for acetylcysteine

MUPIROCIN a preparation for skin infections and infestations (p.892)

MUROMONAB-CD3 an immunosuppressant drug (p.906) used to prevent organ rejection

MUSE a brand-name penile suppository containing alprostadil

MUSTARGEN a brand name for mechlorethamine

MUTAMYCIN a brand name for mitomycin

MYCOBUTIN a brand name for rifabutin

MYCOPHENOLATE MOFETIL an immunosuppressant drug (p.906)

MYCOSTATIN a brand name for nystatin

MYDFRIN a brand name for phenyl-ephrine

MYDRIACYL a brand name for tropicamide

MYLANTA OTC a brand-name antacid (p.923) containing aluminum hydroxide, magnesium hydroxide, and simethicone

MYLERAN a brand name for busulfan

MYOCHRYSINE a brand name for sodium aurothiomalate

MYSOLINE a brand name for primidone

N

NABILONE an antiemetic drug (p.922) used in chemotherapy (p.278)

NABUMETONE a nonsteroidal anti-inflammatory drug (p.894)

NADOLOL a beta blocker drug (p.898)

NADOSTINE OTC a brand name for nystatin

NADROPARIN an injected anticoagulant (*see* DRUGS THAT PREVENT BLOOD CLOTTING, p.904)

NAFARELIN a hypothalamic hormone (*see* SEX HORMONES AND RELATED DRUGS, p.933) used to treat menstrual disorders

NAFTIFINE an antifungal drug (p.889)

NAFTIN a brand name for naftifine

NALBUPHINE an opioid analgesic (p.912)

NALCROM a brand name for sodium cromoglycate

NALIDIXIC ACID a quinolone antibiotic (p.885) used to treat urinary tract infections

NALOXONE an antidote for opioid poisoning (*see* DRUG OVERDOSE AND ACCIDENTAL INGESTION, p.321)

NALTREXONE a drug used to treat opioid withdrawal (*see* DRUG DEPENDENCE, p.564) and alcohol dependence (p.654)

NANDROLONE an anabolic steroid (*see* SEX HORMONES AND RELATED DRUGS, p.933)

NAPHAZOLINE a decongestant (p.909)

NAPHCON-A OTC a brand-name antiallergic eyedrop (*see* DRUGS ACTING ON THE EYE, p.919) containing pheniramine and naphazoline

NAPROSYN a brand name for naproxen

NAPROSYN E a brand name for naproxen enteric coated

NAPROXEN a nonsteroidal anti-inflammatory drug (p.894)

NARATRIPTAN an antimigraine drug (p.913)

NARCAN a brand name for naloxone

NARDIL a brand name for phenelzine

NAROPIN OTC a brand name for ropivacaine

NASACORT a brand name for triamcinolone

NASONEX a brand-name nasal spray containing mometasone

NATEGLINIDE a drug for diabetes mellitus (p.931)

NAVANE a brand name for thiothixene

NAVELBINE a brand name for vinorelbine

NEBCIN a brand name for tobramycin

NEDOCROMIL SODIUM a mast cell stabilizer (*see* ANTIALLERGY DRUGS, p.905)

NEFAZODONE an antidepressant drug (p.916)

NEGGRAM a brand name for nalidixic acid

NEISVAC-C a brand-name meningococcal group C vaccine (see VACCINES AND IMMUNOGLOBULINS, p.883)

NELFINAVIR an antiviral drug used to treat HIV infection (*see* DRUGS FOR HIV INFECTION AND AIDS, p.887)

NEMBUTAL a brand name for pentobarbital

NEO CITRAN OTC a brand name for various preparations used to treat cough, cold, allergy, and flu symptoms

NEO MEDROL ACNE a brand-name lotion containing aluminum chlorhydroxide, methylprednisolone, neomycin, and sulfur

NEOMYCIN an aminoglycoside antibiotic (p.885)

NEOMYCIN SULFATE an aminoglycoside antibiotic (p.885)

NEORAL a brand name for cyclosporine

NEOSPORIN OTC a brand-name antibiotic (p.885) containing neomycin, polymyxin B, and bacitracin

NEOSTIGMINE a parasympathomimetic drug used to treat myasthenia gravis (p.549)

NEO-SYNEPHRINE OTC a brand name for phenylephrine

NEPHRO-VITE RX a brand name for folic acid with vitamins B complex and C

NERISONE a brand name for diflucortolone valerate

NESACAINE a brand name for chloroprocaine

NETILMICIN an aminoglycoside antibiotic (p.885)

NETROMYCIN a brand name for netilmicin

NEULASTA a brand name for pegfilgrastim

NEULEPTIL a brand name for pericyazine

NEUPOGEN a brand name for filgrastim

NEURONTIN a brand name for gabapentin

NEUTREXIN a brand name for trimetrexate glucuronate

NEVIRAPINE an antiviral drug used to treat HIV infection (*see* DRUGS FOR HIV INFECTION AND AIDS, p.887)

NEXIUM a brand name for esomeprazole

NIACIN a member of the vitamin B complex; a vasodilator and a lipid-lowering drug (p.935)

NIACINAMIDE a form of niacin

NICARDIPINE a calcium channel blocker drug (p.900)

NICODERM (OTC) a brand-name nicotine skin patch to help people stop smoking

NICORETTE GUM (OTC) a brand-name nicotine gum to help people stop smoking

NICORETTE INHALER (OTC) a brand-name nicotine inhaler to help people stop smoking

NICOTINAMIDE another name for niacinamide

NICOTINE the addictive component of tobacco, which may be prescribed in small amounts to help people stop smoking

NICOTINIC ACID another name for niacin

NICOTROL (OTC) a brand-name nicotine patch used to help people stop smoking

NIFEDIPINE a calcium channel blocker drug (p.900)

NILUTAMIDE a hormonal anticancer drug (p.907)

NIMBEX a brand name for cisatracurium

NIMODIPINE a calcium channel blocker drug (p.900) used to treat subarachnoid hemorrhage (p.534)

NIMOTOP a brand name for nimodipine

NITOMAN a brand name for tetrabenazine

NITRAZEPAM a benzodiazepine sleeping drug (p.915)

NITRO-DUR (OTC) a brand name for nitroglycerin

NITROFURANTOIN an antibiotic (p.885)

NITROGLYCERIN a nitrate drug (p.899) used to treat angina (p.407)

NITROL (OTC) a brand name for nitroglycerin paste

NITROLINGUAL (OTC) a brand name for nitroglycerin spray

NITROSTAT (OTC) a brand name for nitroglycerin

NITROUS OXIDE a general anesthetic (p.914)

NIX (OTC) a brand name for permethrin

NIZATIDINE an acid-suppressive drug (p.923)

NIZORAL a brand name for ketoconazole

NOLVADEX a brand name for tamoxifen

NONOXYNOL 9 a spermicide (*see* CONTRACEPTION, p.69)

NORCURON a brand name for vecuronium

NORELGESTROMIN (*see* SEX HORMONES AND RELATED DRUGS, p.933)

NOREPINEPHRINE a drug used to raise blood pressure during shock (p.414)

NORETHINDRONE a progestin (*see* SEX HORMONES AND RELATED DRUGS, p.933)

NORFLEX a brand name for orphenadrine

NORFLOXACIN a quinolone antibiotic (p.885)

NORGESTIMATE a progestin used in oral contraceptives (*see* CONTRACEPTION, p.69)

NORGESTREL a progestin (*see* SEX HORMONES AND RELATED DRUGS, p.933)

NORITATE a brand name for metronidazole

NOROXIN a brand name for norfloxacin

NORPRAMIN a brand name for desipramine

NORTRIPTYLINE a tricyclic antidepressant drug (p.916)

NORVASC a brand name for amlodipine

NORVIR a brand name for ritonavir

NORVIR SEC a brand name for ritonavir

NOVAHISTEX a brand name for various cough and cold preparations

NOVAHISTEX DH a brand-name drug containing hydrocodone and phenylephrine

NOVANTRONE a brand name for mitoxantrone

NOVASEN (OTC) a brand name for acetylsalicylic acid

NOVOLIN (OTC) a brand name for insulin

NOVORAPID a brand name for insulin aspart

NOZINAN a brand name for methotrimeprazine

NUBAIN a brand name for nalbuphine

NUMORPHAN a brand name for oxymorphone

NUROMAX a brand name for doxacurium

NUTROPIN a brand name for somatropin

NYSTATIN an antifungal drug (p.889)

NYTOL (OTC) a brand name for diphenhydramine

O

OCCLUSAL (OTC) a brand name for salicylic acid

OCTOCRYLENE a drug used in sunscreens (*see* SUNSCREENS AND SUNBLOCKS, p.893)

OCTOSTIM a brand name for desmopressin

OCTREOTIDE a synthetic hypothalamic hormone used to relieve symptoms of certain cancers (*see* ANTICANCER DRUGS, p.907)

OCTYL METHOXYCINNAMATE a drug used in sunscreens (*see* SUNSCREENS AND SUNBLOCKS, p.893)

OCTYL SALICYLATE a drug used in sunscreens (*see* SUNSCREENS AND SUNBLOCKS, p.893)

OCUFEN a brand-name eyedrop containing flurbiprofen

OCUFLOX a brand name for ofloxacin

OFLOXACIN a quinolone antibiotic (p.885)

OGEN a brand name for estropipate used in hormone replacement therapy (p.937)

OLANZAPINE an antipsychotic drug (p.917)

OLIVE OIL an emollient (*see* EMOLLIENTS AND BARRIER PREPARATIONS, p.890) used to soften earwax (*see* DRUGS ACTING ON THE EAR, p.921)

OLOPATADINE an antiallergy drug (p.905)

OLSALAZINE a 5-aminosalicylate drug (p.924)

OMEPRAZOLE an acid-suppressive drug (p.923)

ONDANSETRON an antiemetic drug (p.922) used with chemotherapy (p.278)

ONE ALPHA a brand name for alfacalcidol

OPIUM an ingredient in antidiarrheal preparations (*see* ANTIDIARRHEAL DRUGS, p.924)

OPIUM ALKALOIDS an analgesic (p.912) and antidiarrheal drug (p.924)

OPTICROM (OTC) a brand name for sodium cromoglycate

OPTIMINE a brand name for azatadine

ORABASE (OTC) a brand-name oral protective emollient

ORACORT a brand name for triamcinolone oral paste

ORAP a brand name for pimozide

ORCIPRENALINE a bronchodilator drug (p.910)

ORGALUTRAN a brand name for ganirelix acetate

ORGARAN a brand name for danaparoid

ORLISTAT a drug used to manage obesity (p.631)

ORPHENADRINE a muscle relaxant (p.896) and drug used to treat parkinsonism (*see* PARKINSON'S DISEASE AND PARKINSONISM, p.539)

ORTHO-CEPT a brand-name oral contraceptive (*see* CONTRACEPTION, p.69) containing desogestrel and ethinyl estradiol

ORTHOCLONE OKT3 a brand name for muromonab-cd3

ORTHO-CYCLEN a brand-name oral contraceptive (*see* CONTRACEPTION, p.69) containing ethinyl estradiol and norgestimate

ORTHO-NOVUM 1/50 a brand-name oral contraceptive (*see* CONTRACEPTION, p.69) containing norethindrone with mestranol

ORTHO TRI-CYCLEN a brand-name oral contraceptive (*see* CONTRACEPTION, p.69) containing norgestimate and ethinyl estradiol

ORUDIS SR a brand name for sustained release ketoprofen

OS-CAL (OTC) a brand name for calcium carbonate

OSELTAMIVIR a drug used to prevent and treat influenza A and B (p.287)

OSTAC a brand name for clodronate

OSTOFORTE a brand name for ergocalciferol

OTRIVIN (OTC) a brand-name nasal spray and nose drop containing xylometazoline

OVOL (OTC) a brand name for simethicone

OVRAL a brand-name oral contraceptive (*see* CONTRACEPTION, p.69) containing norgestrel and ethinyl estradiol

OXAPROZIN a nonsteroidal anti-inflammatory drug (p.894)

OXAZEPAM a benzodiazepine antianxiety drug (p.916)

OXCARBAZEPINE an anticonvulsant drug (p.914)

OXEZE a brand name for formoterol fumarate

OXICONAZOLE an antifungal drug (p.889)

OXIZOLE a brand-name cream containing oxiconazole

OXPRENOLOL a beta blocker drug (p.898)

OXTRIPHYLLINE a xanthine bronchodilator drug (p.910)

OXYBENZONE a sunscreen (*see* SUNSCREENS AND SUNBLOCKS, p.893)

OXYBUTYNIN an anticholinergic drug (*see* DRUGS THAT AFFECT BLADDER CONTROL, p.939)

OXYCHLOROSENE SODIUM a topical preparation for skin infections and infestations (p.892)

OXYCODONE an opioid analgesic (p.912)

OXYCONTIN a brand name for oxycodone

OXYIR a brand name for oxycodone

OXYMETAZOLINE a topical decongestant (p.909)

OXYMORPHONE an analgesic (p.912)

OXYQUINOLINE a disinfectant and an ingredient used in vaginal preparations

OXYTOCIN a uterine stimulant (*see* DRUGS FOR LABOR, p.938)

P

PACLITAXEL a cytotoxic anticancer drug (p.907)

PADIMATE O padimate octyl dimethyl paba, a sunscreen (*see* SUNSCREENS AND SUNBLOCKS, p.893)

PALAFER (OTC) a brand name for ferrous fumarate

PALIVIZUMAB a brand-name monoclonal antibody used to prevent respiratory syncytial virus in high risk pediatric patients

PAMABROM a mild diuretic drug (p.902) used to treat premenstrual syndrome (p.736)

PAMIDRONATE a drug for bone disorders (p.896)

PANCREASE (OTC) a brand name for pancrelipase

PANCRELIPASE a preparation of the pancreatic enzymes amylase, protease, and lipase

PANCURONIUM a muscle relaxant used in general anesthesia (*see* HAVING MAJOR SURGERY, p.943)

PANECTYL a brand name for trimeprazine

PANOXYL (OTC) a brand name for benzoyl peroxide

PANTHENOL a member of the vitamin B complex

PANTO IV a brand name for injected pantoprazole

PANTOLOC a brand name for pantoprazole

PANTOPRAZOLE acid-suppressive therapy

PANTOTHENIC ACID a member of the vitamin B complex

PAPAVERINE a smooth muscle relaxant (*see* ANTISPASMODIC DRUGS AND MOTILITY STIMULANTS, p.926)

PARA-AMINOBENZOATE a drug used in sunscreens (*see* SUNSCREENS AND SUNBLOCKS, p.893) and to treat thickening of tissues in scleroderma (p.462), Peyronie's disease (p.723), and dermatomyositis (*see* POLYMYOSITIS AND DERMATOMYOSITIS, p.463)

PARA-AMINOBENZOIC ACID a substance related to the vitamin B complex, also used in sunscreens (*see* SUNSCREENS AND SUNBLOCKS, p.893)

PARAFON FORTE (OTC) a brand name for chlorzoxazone and acetaminophen

PARAPLATIN a brand name for carboplatin

PAREGORIC an antidiarrheal drug (p.924)

PARIET a brand name for rabeprazole

PARLODEL a brand name for bromocriptine

PARNATE a brand name for tranylcypromine

PAROMOMYCIN an antiprotozoal drug (p.888)

PAROXETINE a selective serotonin reuptake inhibitor (SSRI) antidepressant drug (p.916). It is also used to treat generalized anxiety disorder (p. 916) and post-traumatic stress disorder

PARSOL 1789 an ingredient in some sunscreens that blocks UVA and UVB rays (*see* SUNSCREENS AND SUNBLOCKS, p.893)

PATANOL a brand name for olopatadine

PAXIL a brand name for paroxetine

PCE DISPERTAB a brand name for erythromycin

PECTIN an antidiarrheal drug (p.924)

PEDIALYTE (OTC) a brand-name oral rehydration solution (p.926) containing potassium, sodium chloride, citrate, and dextrose

PEDIAPRED a brand name for prednisolone

PEDIAZOLE a brand-name antibiotic (p.885) containing erythromycin and sulfisoxazole acetyl

PEGASYS a brand name for peginterferon alfa-2a

PEGETRON a brand name for ribavirin and peginterferon alfa-2b

PEGFILGRASTIM a granulocyte stimulating factor used to prevent infection in patients receiving chemotherapy

PEGINTERFERON-ALFA a form of interferon used to treat hepatitis C

PEGINTERFERON alfa-2b

PENICILLAMINE an antirheumatic drug (p.895)

PENICILLIN an antibiotic (p.885)

PENICILLIN G a penicillin antibiotic (p.885)

PENICILLIN G BENZATHINE a penicillin antibiotic (p.885)

PENICILLIN V another name for phenoxymethyl penicillin

PENTACEL a brand name vaccine for pertussis, diptheria, tetanus, hemophilus, and poliomyelitis (see VACCINES AND IMMUNOGLOBULINS, p.883)

PENTAMIDINE an antiprotozoal drug (p.888)

PENTAMYCETIN a brand name for chloramphenicol

PENTASA a brand name for 5-ASA

PENTAZOCINE an opioid analgesic (p.912)

PENTOBARBITAL a barbiturate sleeping drug (p.915)

PENTOSAN a drug used to relieve pain in interstitial cystitis (*see* CYSTITIS, p.709)

PENTOTHAL a brand name for thiopental

PENTOXIFYLLINE a drug used to treat lower limb ischemia (p.434)

PENTRAX (OTC) a brand name for coal tar

PEN•VEE K a brand name for penicillin V

PEPCID (OTC) a brand name for famotidine

PEPPERMINT OIL an antispasmodic drug (*see* ANTISPASMODIC DRUGS AND MOTILITY STIMULANTS, p.926) and a flavoring agent

PEPTO-BISMOL (OTC) a brand-name antidiarrheal drug (p.924) and antacid (p.923)

QUINAPRIL an ACE inhibitor drug (p.900)

QUINIDINE an antiarrhythmic drug (p.898)

QUININE an antimalarial drug (p.888) and muscle relaxant (p.896)

QUINTASA a brand name for 5-ASA

QUINUPRISTIN an injected antibacterial used in combination with dalfopristin to treat skin infections and infections caused by vancomycin-resistant bacteria (so-called super bugs)

QVAR a brand name for beclomethasone

R

RABEPRAZOLE acid suppressive therapy for the treatment of reflux esophagitis (p.923)

RADIOACTIVE SODIUM IODIDE a drug for hyperthyroidism (p.932)

RALOXIFENE a drug used to prevent osteoporosis in postmenopausal women (*see* DRUGS FOR BONE DISORDERS, p.896)

RALTITREXED an anticancer drug used in colorectal cancer (p.907)

RAMIPRIL an ACE inhibitor drug (p.900)

RANITIDINE an acid-suppressive drug (p.923)

RANITIDINE BISMUTH CITRATE an acid-suppressive drug (p.923)

RAPAMUNE a brand name for sirolimus

RASBURICASE a drug used to treat hyperurecemia in cancer patients

REACTINE (OTC) a brand name for cetirizine

REBIF a brand name for interferon beta-1a

RECOMBINANT FOLLITROPIN a drug for infertility (p.936)

RECOMBINATE a brand name antihemophilic factor

RECOMBIVAX HB a brand-name vaccine (*see* VACCINES AND IMMUNOGLOBULINS, p.883) for hepatitis B (see ACUTE HEPATITIS, p.644)

REFACTO a brand name for moroctocog alfa

REFLUDAN a brand name for lepirudin

RELAFEN a brand name for nabumetone

RELENZA a brand name for zanamivir

REMERON a brand name for mirtazapine

REMICADE a brand name for infliximab

REMIFENTANIL an opioid analgesic (p.912) used in general anesthesia (*see* HAVING MAJOR SURGERY, p.943)

REMODULIN a brand name for treprostinil

RENAGEL a brand name for sevelamer

RENEDIL a brand name for felodipine

RENOVA a brand name for tretinoin

REOPRO a brand name for abciximab

REPAGLINIDE a drug for diabetes mellitus (p.931)

REPLENS (OTC) a brand name for polycarbophil

REQUIP a brand name for ropinirole

RESCRIPTOR a brand name for delaviridine mesylate

RESCULA a brand name for unoprostone

RESERPINE an antihypertensive drug (p.897)

RESORCINOL a keratolytic drug used mainly for acne (p.340)

RESTORIL a brand name for temazepam

RETIN-A a brand name for tretinoin/Vitamin A

RETINOIC ACID a form of vitamin A and another name for tretinoin

RETINOL a form of vitamin A

RETROVIR a brand name for zidovudine

REVIA a brand name for naltrexone

REYATAZ a brand name for atazanavir

RHINALAR a brand name for flunisolide

RHINOCORT a brand name for budesonide

RIBAVIRIN an antiviral drug (p.886) used to treat certain lung infections in infants and children

RIBOFLAVIN another name for vitamin B_2

RIDAURA a brand name for auranofin

RIFABUTIN an antituberculous drug (p.886)

RIFADIN a brand name for rifampin

RIFAMPIN an antituberculous drug (p.886) also used to prevent meningitis (p.527)

RIFAPENTINE an antituberculous drug (p.886)

RIFATER a brand-name antituberculous drug (p.886) containing rifampin, isoniazid, and pyrazinamide

RILUTEK a brand name for riluzole

RILUZOLE a drug used to treat amyotrophic lateral sclerosis

RISEDRONATE a drug used for Paget's disease (p.370). It is also used to treat and prevent osteoporosis (glucocorticoid-induced and postmenopausal)

RISPERDAL a brand name for risperidone

RISPERIDONE an antipsychotic drug (p.917)

RITALIN a brand name for methylphenidate

RITODRINE a uterine muscle relaxant (*see* DRUGS FOR LABOR, p.938)

RITONAVIR a drug used to treat HIV infection (*see* DRUGS FOR HIV INFECTION AND AIDS, p.887)

RITUXAM a brand name of rituximab

RITUXIMAB an anticancer drug (p.907) used to treat certain types of non-Hodgkin's lymphoma (*see* LYMPHOMA, p.459)

RIVASTIGMINE a drug used to treat Alzheimer disease (p.536)

RIVOTRIL a brand name for clonazepam

RIZATRIPTAN an antimigraine drug (p.913)

ROBAXACET (OTC) a brand-name analgesic (p.912) containing methocarbamol and acetaminophen used to treat acute, painful musculoskeletal conditions

ROBAXIN (OTC) a brand name for methocarbamol

ROBAXISAL (OTC) a brand-name analgesic (p.912) containing methocarbamol and aspirin used to treat acute, painful musculoskeletal conditions

ROBITUSSIN (OTC) a brand name for guaifenesin; a brand name for various cough and cold remedies

ROCALTROL a brand name for calcitriol

ROCEPHIN a brand name for ceftriaxone

ROCURONIUM a muscle relaxant used in general anesthesia (*see* HAVING MAJOR SURGERY, p.943)

ROFACT a brand name for rifampin

ROFERON-A a brand name for interferon alpha

ROGAINE (OTC) a brand name for minoxidil

ROPINIROLE a drug used for Parkinson's disease (p.539)

ROPIVACAINE a local anesthetic (p.914) used for epidural anesthesia in labor (p.801)

ROSIGLITAZONE a glitazone drug used to treat type 2 diabetes (p.931)

ROSUVASTATIN a lipid lowering drug (p.935)

ROVAMYCINE a brand name for spiramycin

RYTHMODAN a brand name for disopyramide

RYTHMOL a brand name for propafenone

S

17-B ESTRADIOL a drug used for estrogen replacement (*see* HORMONE REPLACEMENT THERAPY, p.937)

SABRIL a brand name for vigabatrin

SAIZEN a brand name for somatropin

SALAGEN a brand name for pilocarpine

SALAZOPYRIN a brand name for sulfasalazine

SALBUTAMOL a sympathomimetic bronchodilator drug (p.910)

SALICYLAMIDE an analgesic (p.912)

SALICYLIC ACID a keratolytic used to treat acne (p.340), dandruff (p.358), psoriasis (p.332), and warts (p.354)

SALINE a salt solution

SALMETEROL a sympathomimetic bronchodilator drug (p.910)

SALOFALK a brand name for 5-ASA

SANDIMMUNE a brand name for cyclosporine

SANDOMIGRAN a brand name for pizotifen

SANDOSTATIN a brand name for octreotide

SANOREX a brand name for mazindol

SANSERT a brand name for methysergide

SANTYL a brand name for collagenase

SAQUINAVIR MESYLATE an antiviral drug used to treat HIV infection (*see* DRUGS FOR HIV INFECTION AND AIDS, p.887)

SCOPOLAMINE an antiemetic drug (p.922) used to treat motion sickness (p.604)

SECOBARBITAL a barbiturate sleeping drug (p.915)

SECTRAL a brand name for acebutolol

SEDATIVE a drug that dampens the activity of the central nervous system

SELECT 1/35 a brand-name oral contraceptive (*see* CONTRACEPTION, p.69) containing ethinyl estradiol and norethindrone

SELEGILINE a drug used to treat parkinsonism (*see* PARKINSON'S DISEASE AND PARKINSONISM, p.539)

SELENIUM a mineral (p.929)

SELENIUM SULFIDE an antifungal drug (p.889) used to treat dandruff (p.358) and skin inflammation

SELSUN BLUE OTC a brand-name shampoo for dandruff (p.358) containing selenium sulfide

SENNA a stimulant laxative (p.924)

SENNOSIDES A & B stimulant laxatives (p.924)

SENOKOT OTC a brand name for senna

SENOKOT-S OTC a brand-name laxative (p.924) containing sennosides and docusate

SENSORCAINE brand-name local anesthetics (p.914) containing bupivacaine with or without epinephrine

SEPTRA a brand-name antibiotic (p.885) containing sulfamethoxazole and trimethoprim

SERC a brand name for betahistine

SERENTIL a brand name for mesoridazine besylate

SEREVENT a brand name for salmeterol

SEROPHENE a brand name for clomiphene

SEROQUEL a brand name for quetiapine

SEROSTIM a brand name for somatropin

SERTRALINE a selective serotonin reuptake inhibitor (SSRI) antidepressant drug (p.916)

SEVELAMER a phosphate binder used in patients with kidney failure undergoing hemodialysis

SIALOR OTC a brand name for anetholtrithione

SIBELIUM a brand name for flunarizine

SIBUTRAMINE a drug used to treat obesity

SILDENAFIL a drug used to treat erectile dysfunction (p.770)

SILVER NITRATE an antiseptic (*see* PREPARATIONS FOR SKIN INFECTIONS AND INFESTATIONS, p.892), a caustic, and an astringent

SILVER SULFADIAZINE a topical antibiotic (*see* PREPARATIONS FOR SKIN INFECTIONS AND INFESTATIONS, p.892) used to prevent infection in burns (p.318)

SIMETHICONE an antiflatulent (*see* ANTACIDS, p.923)

SIMULECT a brand name for basiliximab

SIMVASTATIN a lipid-lowering drug (p.935)

SINEMET a brand name for levodopa with carbidopa

SINEQUAN a brand name for doxepin

SINGULAIR a brand name for montelukast sodium

SINUTAB OTC a brand-name drug containing acetaminophen, pseudoephedrine, and chlorpheniramine used to treat sinusitis (p.475); a brand name for various cough, cold, and allergy remedies

SIROLIMUS an immunosuppressant used to prevent rejection after a kidney transplant

SLOW FE OTC a brand name for ferrous sulfate

SLOW FE WITH FOLIC ACID OTC a brand name for a preparation of folic acid with ferrous sulfate

SLOW-K OTC a brand name for potassium chloride

SLOW TRASICOR a brand name for oxprenolol

SODA MINT TABLETS a preparation of sodium bicarbonate

SODIUM a mineral (p.929)

SODIUM ACID PHOSPHATE a form of phosphorus used in saline laxatives (p.924) and to make urine more acidic

SODIUM ALGINATE an ingredient used in antacids (p.923)

SODIUM AUROTHIOMALATE an antirheumatic drug (p.895)

SODIUM BICARBONATE an antacid (p.923) also used to soften earwax (*see* DRUGS ACTING ON THE EAR, p.921)

SODIUM BIPHOSPHATE a drug used as a saline laxative (p.924) and to treat chronic urinary tract infections; also a source of electrolytes

SODIUM CHLORIDE common salt used in electrolyte replacement

SODIUM CITRATE a drug used to relieve discomfort in mild urinary tract infections such as cystitis (p.709) by making the urine more alkaline

SODIUM CROMOGLYCATE OTC a mast cell stabilizer used as an antiallergic medication (*see* BRONCHODILATOR DRUGS, p.910)

SODIUM FLUORIDE a mineral (p.929) used to prevent dental caries (p.609)

SODIUM FUCIDATE an antibiotic (p.885)

SODIUM LACTATE a source of electrolytes

SODIUM MONOFLUOROPHOSPHATE a fluoride supplement

SODIUM NITROPRUSSIDE an antihypertensive drug (p.897)

SODIUM PHOSPHATES saline laxatives (p.924)

SODIUM POLYSTYRENE SULFONATE a drug used to treat excess potassium in the blood

SODIUM PROPIONATE an antifungal drug (p.889)

SODIUM SULAMYD a brand name for sulfacetamide

SODIUM SULFACETAMIDE a drug used to treat acne (p.340) and infections

SODIUM SULFATE a purgative used in preparations for bowel cleansing prior to bowel investigations

SODIUM TETRADECYL SULFATE a drug used to treat varicose veins (p.438)

SODIUM VALPROATE an anticonvulsant drug (p.914)

SOFLAX OTC a brand name for docusate sodium

SOFRACORT a brand-name ear- and eyedrop containing dexamethasone, framycetin, and gramicidin

SOFRAMYCIN an antibiotic (p.885) containing framycetin and gramicidin

SOFRA-TULLE a brand-name transdermal antibiotic patch containing framycetin

SOLARCAINE OTC a brand name for benzocaine

SOLU CORTEF a brand name for hydrocortisone

SOLUGEL OTC a brand name for benzoyl peroxide

SOLU MEDROL a brand name for methylprednisolone

SOMATREM a synthetic growth hormone (*see* PITUITARY DRUGS, p.934)

SOMATROPIN a synthetic growth hormone (*see* PITUITARY DRUGS, p.934)

SORBITOL a sweetening agent, also used as a moisturizer in skin creams and as a diuretic drug (p.902)

SORIATANE a brand name for acitretin

SOTACOR a brand name for sotalol

SOTALOL a beta blocker drug (p.898)

SPECTINOMYCIN an antibiotic (p.885)

SPIRAMYCIN an antibiotic (p.885)

SPIRIVA a brand name for tiotropium bromide

SPIRONOLACTONE a potassium-sparing diuretic drug (p.902)

SPORANOX a brand name for itraconazole

STARLIX a brand name for nateglinide

STARNOC a brand name for zaleplon

STATEX a brand name for morphine

STATICIN a brand-name lotion containing erythromycin and ethyl alcohol

STAVUDINE an antiviral drug used to treat HIV infection (*see* DRUGS FOR HIV INFECTION AND AIDS, p.887)

STEMETIL a brand name for prochlorperazine

STEMGEN a brand name for ancestim

STIEPROX a brand name for ciclopirox

STIEVA-A a brand name for tretinoin

STIEVAMYCIN a brand-name drug containing erythromycin and tretinoin

STREPTASE a brand name for streptokinase

STREPTOKINASE a thrombolytic drug (p.904)

STREPTOMYCIN an antituberculous drug (p.886) and aminoglycoside antibiotic (p.885)

STREPTOZOCIN an anticancer drug (p.907)

SUCCINYLCHOLINE a muscle relaxant used in general anesthesia (*see* HAVING MAJOR SURGERY, p.943)

SUCRALFATE an acid-suppressive drug (p.923)

SUDAFED OTC a brand-name cold remedy (*see* COLD AND FLU REMEDIES, p.910) containing pseudoephedrine

SUDAFED COLD & FLU OTC a brand-name cold remedy (*see* COLD AND FLU REMEDIES, p.910) containing acetaminophen, pseudoephedrine, dextromethorphan, and guaifenesin

SUDAFED COUGH & COLD OTC a brand-name cold remedy (*see* COLD AND FLU REMEDIES, p.910) containing pseudoephedrine, acetaminophen, and dextromethorphan

SUFENTA a brand name for sufentanil citrate

SUFENTANIL an opioid analgesic (p.912) used as a general anesthetic (p.914)

SULBACTAM a substance given with ampicillin to make it more effective

SULCRATE a brand name for sucralfate

SULFACETAMIDE a sulfonamide antibiotic (p.885)

SULFACET-R a brand-name drug containing sodium sulfacetamide and sulfur used to treat acne (p.340)

SULFADIAZINE a sulfonamide antibiotic (p.885)

SULFAMETHOXAZOLE a sulfonamide antibiotic (p.885)

SULFAMETHOXAZOLE-TRIMETHOPRIM an antibiotic (p.885)

SULFANILAMIDE a sulfonamide antibiotic (p.885) used to treat candidiasis (p.309)

SULFASALAZINE a 5-aminosalicylate (p.924) and antirheumatic drug (p.895)

SULFISOXAZOLE a sulfonamide antibiotic (p.885)

SULFUR an ingredient in preparations used to treat acne (p.340) and dandruff (p.358)

SULINDAC a nonsteroidal anti-inflammatory drug (p.894)

SUMATRIPTAN an antimigraine drug (p.913)

SUPEUDOL a brand name for oxycodone

SUPPOSITORY a solid, cone- or bullet-shaped preparation for insertion into the rectum or vagina

SUPRANE a brand name for desflurane

SUPRAX a brand name for cefixime

SUPREFACT a brand name for buserelin

SURGAM a brand name for tiaprofenic acid

SURMONTIL a brand name for trimipramine

SURVANTA a brand name for beractant

SUS-PHRINE a brand name for epinephrine

SUSTIVA a brand name for efavirenz

SYMBICORT a brand name for budesonide and formoterol

SYMMETREL a brand name for amantadine

SYNAGIS a brand name for palivizumab

SYNALAR a brand name for fluocinolone

SYNAREL a brand name for nafarelin

SYNERCID a brand name for quinupristin and dalfopristin

SYNPHASIC a brand-name oral contraceptive (*see* CONTRACEPTION, p.69) containing ethinyl estradiol and norethindrone

SYN-RX AM a brand-name cough remedy (p.909) and cold and flu remedy (p.910) containing guaifenesin and pseudoephedrine

SYN-RX PM a brand-name expectorant (*see* COUGH REMEDIES, p.909) containing guaifenesin

SYNTHROID a brand name for levothyroxine

SYNVISC OTC a brand name for hylan G-F 20

SYPRINE a brand name for trientine

T

3TC a brand name for lamivudine

T-GEL OTC a brand name for coal tar

T-STAT a brand name for erythromycin

TACROLIMUS an immunosuppressant drug (p.906) used to prevent rejection of organ transplants. It is also used to treat atopic dermatitis and to prevent and treat rejection in kidney and liver transplant patients

TADALAFIL a drug used to treat erectile dysfunction (p.770)

TALWIN a brand-name analgesic (p.912) containing pentazocine

TAMBOCOR a brand name for flecainide

TAMIFLU a brand name for oseltamivir

TAMOFEN a brand name for tamoxifen

TAMOXIFEN an antiestrogen (*see* SEX HORMONES AND RELATED DRUGS, p.933) and a hormonal anticancer drug (p.907)

TAMSULOSIN an alpha blocker drug for prostate disorders (p.938)

TANACET 125 OTC a brand name for feverfew

TANTUM a brand name for benzydamine

TAPAZOLE a brand name for methimazole

TARKA a brand name for trandolapril and verapamil

TAVIST OTC a brand name for clemastine

TAXOL a brand name for paclitaxel

TAXOTERE a brand name for docetaxel

TAZAROTENE a drug used to treat psoriasis (p.332) and acne (p.340); also used to treat premature aging due to sun overexposure

TAZIDIME a brand name for ceftazidime

TAZOBACTAM a drug given with piperacillin to make it more effective

TAZORAC a brand name for tazarotene

TEARS NATURALE OTC A brand-name eyedrop containing hydroxypropyl methylcellulose

TEGASEROD a drug used to treat irritable bowel syndrome

TEGRETOL a brand name for carbamazepine

TELITHROMYCIN a ketolide antibiotic

TELMISARTAN an antihypertensive drug (p.897)

TEMAZEPAM a benzodiazepine sleeping drug (p.915)

TEMODAL a brand name for temozolomide

TEMOZOLOMIDE an anticancer drug (p.907)

TEMPRA OTC a brand name for acetaminophen

TENECTEPLASE a thrombolytic drug (p.904)

TENIPOSIDE a cytotoxic anticancer drug (p.907)

TENOFOVIR an antiviral drug used to treat HIV infection (*see* DRUGS FOR HIV INFECTION AND AIDS, p.887)

TENORETIC a brand-name antihypertensive drug (p.897) containing atenolol with chlorthalidone

TENORMIN a brand name for atenolol

TENOXICAM a nonsteroidal anti-inflammatory drug (p.894)

TENUATE a brand name for diethylpropion

TEQUIN a brand name for gatifloxacin

TERAZOL a brand name for terconazole

TERAZOSIN an alpha blocker antihypertensive drug (p.897) and drug for prostate disorders (p.938)

TERBINAFINE an antifungal drug (p.889)

TERBUTALINE a sympathomimetic bronchodilator drug (p.910) and uterine muscle relaxant (*see* DRUGS FOR LABOR, p.938)

TERCONAZOLE an antifungal drug (p.889) used to treat candidiasis (p.309)

TERIPARATIDE a drug used to treat osteoporosis

TESTOSTERONE a male sex hormone (*see* SEX HORMONES AND RELATED DRUGS, p.933)

TESTOSTERONE UNDECANOATE a drug used for hormone replacement in patients with conditions or symptoms associated with deficiency or absence of endogenous testosterone (*see* SEX HORMONES AND RELATED DRUGS, p.933)

TETRABENAZINE a drug used to treat hyperkinetic movement disorders such as Tourette's syndrome (*see* NERVOUS TICS, p.550)

TETRACAINE a local anesthetic (p.914)

TETRACYCLINE an antibiotic (p.885)

TEVETEN an antihypertensive drug (p.897)

TEVETEN PLUS a brand name for eprosartan and hydrochlorothiazide

THEOLAIR a brand name for theophylline

THEOPHYLLINE a xanthine bronchodilator drug (p.910)

THIABENDAZOLE an anthelmintic drug (p.889)

THIAMINE another name for vitamin B_1

THIOGUANINE an anticancer drug used to treat leukemia (p.907)

THIOPENTAL a general anesthetic (p.914)

THIOPROPERAZINE an antipsychotic drug (p.917)

THIORIDAZINE a phenothiazine antipsychotic drug (p.917)

THIOTHIXENE an antipsychotic drug (p.917)

THONZONIUM a detergent added to eardrops to promote the effect of the active ingredients

THROMBATE III a brand name for antithrombin III

THROMBIN a drug that promotes blood clotting (p.903)

THYMOGLOBULIN a brand name for antithymocyte globulin

THYMOL an antiseptic used in mouthwashes

THYROID thyroid hormones (*see* DRUGS FOR HYPOTHYROIDISM, p.932)

TIAMOL a brand name for fluocinonide cream

TIAPROFENIC ACID a nonsteroidal anti-inflammatory drug (p.894) and analgesic (p.912)

TIAZAC a brand name for diltiazem

TICARCILLIN a penicillin antibiotic (p.885)

TICLID a brand name for ticlopidine

TICLOPIDINE an antiplatelet drug (*see* DRUGS THAT PREVENT BLOOD CLOTTING, p.904)

TILADE a brand name for nedocromil

TIMENTIN a brand-name penicillin antibiotic (p.885) containing ticarcillin with clavulanate potassium

TIMOLOL a beta blocker drug (p.898) and drug for glaucoma (p.920)

TIMOPTIC a brand name for timolol

TIMPILO a brand-name drug for glaucoma (p.920) containing timolol and pilocarpine

TINACTIN a brand name for tolnaftate

TINZAPARIN an injected anticoagulant (*see* DRUGS THAT PREVENT BLOOD CLOTTING p.904)

TIOTROPIUM a long-acting anticholinergic bronchodilator (p.910)

TIROFIBAN an antiplatelet drug (*see* DRUGS THAT PREVENT BLOOD CLOTTING p.904)

TISSUE PLASMINOGEN ACTIVATOR a thrombolytic drug (p.904)

TITANIUM DIOXIDE a sunscreen (*see* SUNSCREENS AND SUNBLOCKS, p.893)

TIZANIDINE a muscle relaxant (p.896)

TNKASE a brand name for tenecteplase

TOBI a brand name for tobramycin

TOBRADEX a brand-name drug acting on the eye (p.919) containing tobramycin and dexamethasone

TOBRAMYCIN an aminoglycoside antibiotic (p.885)

TOBREX a brand name for tobramycin

TOCAINIDE an antiarrhythmic drug (p.898)

TOCOPHEROLS a group of substances collectively termed vitamin E

TOFRANIL a brand name for imipramine

TOLBUTAMIDE an oral drug for diabetes mellitus (p.931)

TOLECTIN a brand name for tolmetin

TOLMETIN a nonsteroidal anti-inflammatory drug (p.894)

TOLNAFTATE an antifungal drug (p.889)

TOLTERODINE an anticholinergic drug (*see* DRUGS THAT AFFECT BLADDER CONTROL, p.939) used to treat urinary incontinence (p.710)

TOMUDEX a brand name for raltitrexed

TOPAMAX a brand name for topiramate

TOPICORT a brand name for desoximetasone

TOPIRAMATE an anticonvulsant drug (p.914)

TOPOTECAN an anticancer drug (p.907)

TOPSYN a brand name for fluocinonide

TORADOL a brand name for ketorolac

TORSEMIDE a loop diuretic drug (p.902)

TRACLEER a brand name for bosentan

TRACRIUM a brand name for atracurium

TRANDATE a brand name for labetalol

TRANDOLAPRIL an ACE inhibitor drug (p.900)

TRANEXAMIC ACID an antifibrinolytic drug (*see* DRUGS THAT PROMOTE BLOOD CLOTTING, p.903)

TRANSDERM-NITRO OTC a brand name for nitroglycerin

TRANSDERM-V OTC a brand name for scopolamine

TRANYLCYPROMINE a monoamine oxidase inhibitor (MAOI) antidepressant drug (p.916)

TRASICOR a brand name for oxprenolol

TRASTUZUMAB an anticancer drug (p.907) used for metastatic breast cancer

TRASYLOL a brand name for aprotinin

TRAVATAN a brand name for travoprost

TRAVOPROST a drug for glaucoma (p.920)

TRAZODONE an antidepressant drug (p.916)

TRENTAL a brand name for pentoxifylline

TREPROSTINIL a vasodilator used to treat pulmonary hypertension

TRETINOIN a retinoid drug (p.890) used to treat acne (p.340)

TRIAMCINOLONE a corticosteroid (p.930)

TRIAMINIC OTC a brand-name cold remedy (*see* COLD AND FLU REMEDIES, p.910) containing pseudoephedrine

TRIAMTERENE a potassium-sparing diuretic drug (p.902)

TRIAVIL a brand-name antidepressant drug (p.916) containing amitriptyline with perphenazine

TRIAZOLAM a benzodiazepine sleeping drug (p.915)

TRICHLOROMONOFLUOROMETHANE a cooling substance and aerosol propellant

TRICLOSAN an antiseptic (*see* PREPARATIONS FOR SKIN INFECTIONS AND INFESTATIONS, p.892)

TRI-CYCLEN a brand-name oral contraceptive (*see* CONTRACEPTION, p.69) containing ethinyl estradiol and norgestimate

TRIDESILON a brand name for desonide

TRIETHANOLAMINE POLYPEPTIDE OLEATE-CONDENSATE a drug used for the removal of earwax (*see* DRUGS ACTING ON THE EAR, p.921)

TRIFLUOPERAZINE a phenothiazine antipsychotic drug (p.917) and antiemetic drug (p.922)

TRIFLURIDINE an antiviral drug (p.886)

TRIHEXYPHENIDYL an anticholinergic drug used to treat parkinsonism (*see* PARKINSON'S DISEASE AND PARKINSONISM, p.539)

TRILAFON a brand name for perphenazine

TRILEPTAL a brand name for oxcarbazepine

TRIMEBUTINE a lower gastrointestinal tract motility regulator used for irritable bowel syndrome (p.656)

TRIMEPRAZINE an antihistamine (p.906) and antipruritic drug (p.891)

TRIMETHOPRIM an antibiotic (p.885)

TRIMETREXATE a drug used to treat *Pneumocystis carinii* pneumonia in people with AIDS (*see* HIV INFECTION AND AIDS, p.295)

TRIMIPRAMINE a tricyclic antidepressant (p.916)

TRINALIN REPETABS a brand-name antihistamine (p.906) and decongestant (p.909) combination containing azatadine and pseudoephedrine

TRIOXSALEN a drug used for repigmentation of the skin in vitiligo (p.342)

TRIPHASIL a brand-name oral contraceptive (*see* CONTRACEPTION, p.69) containing levonorgestrel and ethinyl estradiol

TRIPROLIDINE an antihistamine (p.906)

TRIQUILAR a brand-name oral contraceptive (*see* CONTRACEPTION, p.69) containing levonorgestrel and ethinyl estradiol

TRISORALEN a brand name for trioxsalen

TRIZIVIR a brand name for a drug containing abacavir, lamivudine, and zidovudine

TROPICAMIDE a mydriatic drug used in eye examinations (*see* DRUGS ACTING ON THE EYE, p.919)

TRUSOPT a brand name for dorzolamide

TRYPSIN an enzyme used to treat wounds and skin ulcers

TRYPTAN a brand name for l-tryptophan

TUCKS MEDICATED PADS OTC brand-name medicated pads containing witch hazel used for hemorrhoids (p.668)

TUSSIONEX a brand-name cough remedy (p.909) containing hydrocodone and phenyltoloxamine

TWINRIX a brand-name vaccine (*see* VACCINES AND IMMUNOGLOBULINS, p.883) for hepatitis A and B (*see* ACUTE HEPATITIS, p.644)

TYLENOL OTC a brand name for acetaminophen; a brand name for various remedies to relieve pain, fever, cough, cold, allergy, and flu symptoms (*see* COLD AND FLU REMEDIES, p.910)

TYLOXAPOL a drug used to loosen secretions in the lungs in cystic fibrosis (p.824)

TYPHERIX a brand-name vaccine (*see* VACCINES AND IMMUNOGLOBULINS, p.883) for *Salmonella typhi* (*see* TYPHOID AND PARATYPHOID, p.300)

TYROSINE an amino acid

U

ULTIVA a brand name for remifentanil

ULTRADOL a brand name for etodolac

ULTRAMOP a brand name for methoxsalen

ULTRAQUIN a brand name for hydroquinone

ULTRASE a brand name for pancrelipase

ULTRAVATE a brand name for halobetasol

UNDECYLENIC ACID an antifungal drug (p.889) used to treat athlete's foot (p.353)

UNIPHYL a brand name for theophylline

UNITRON PEG a brand name for peginterferon alfa-2b

UNOPROSTONE a drug used to treat glaucoma (p.920)

URASAL a brand name for methenamine

UREA a topical treatment used to moisturize dry skin and soften earwax (*see* DRUGS ACTING ON THE EAR, p.921); also a diuretic drug (p.902)

UREMOL a brand name for urea-based moisturizers

URISPAS a brand name for flavoxate

UROFOLLITROPIN a drug for infertility (p.936)

UROKINASE a thrombolytic drug (p.904)

UROMITEXAN a brand name for mesna

URSODIOL a drug used to dissolve and prevent gallstones (p.651)

V

VAGIFEM a brand name for 17-b estradiol

VALACYCLOVIR an antiviral drug (p.886)

VALCYTE a brand name for valganciclovir

VALDECOXIB a nonsteroidal anti-inflammatory drug (p.894)

VALGANCICLOVIR an antiviral drug (p.886)

VALISONE a brand name for betamethasone

VALIUM a brand name for diazepam

VALPROATE SODIUM an anticonvulsant drug (p.914) and antimigraine drug (p.913)

VALPROIC ACID an anticonvulsant drug (p.914)

VALRUBICIN an anticancer drug (p.907)

VALSARTAN an antihypertensive drug (p.897)

VALTAXIN a brand name for valrubicin

VALTREX a brand name for valacyclovir

VANCERIL a brand name for beclomethasone

VANCOCIN a brand name for vancomycin

VANCOMYCIN an antibiotic (p.885) used to treat serious infections

VAQTA a brand-name vaccine (see VACCINES AND IMMUNOGLOBULINS, p.883) for hepatitis A (*see* ACUTE HEPATITIS, p.644)

VANQUIN a brand name for pyrvinium pamoate

VARDENAFIL a drug used to treat erectile dysfunction (p.770)

VARILRIX a brand-name vaccine (see VACCINES AND IMMUNOGLOBULINS, p.883) for varicella zoster virus (*see* CHICKENPOX, p.288)

VARIVAX II a brand-name vaccine (*see* VACCINES AND IMMUNOGLOBULINS, p.883) for varicella zoster virus (*see* CHICKENPOX, p.288)

VASERETIC a brand-name antihypertensive drug (p.897) containing enalapril and hydrochlorothiazide

VASOCON-A OTC a brand-name eyedrop (*see* DRUGS ACTING ON THE EYE, p.919) containing antazoline and naphazoline

VASODILATOR a drug that widens blood vessels

VASOPRESSIN a pituitary hormone (*see* PITUITARY DRUGS, p.934)

VASOTEC a brand name for enalapril and enalaprilat

VAXIGRIP a brand-name vaccine (*see* VACCINES AND IMMUNOGLOBULINS, p.883) for influenza A and B (p.287)

VECURONIUM a muscle relaxant used in general anesthesia (*see* HAVING MAJOR SURGERY, p.943)

VENLAFAXINE an antidepressant drug (p.916); also used to treat general anxiety disorder and social anxiety disorder (social phobia)

VENTOLIN a brand name for salbutamol

VEPESID a brand name for etoposide

VERAPAMIL a calcium channel blocker drug (p.900) and antiarrhythmic drug (p.898)

VERELAN a brand name for verapamil

VERMOX a brand name for mebendazole

VERSEL a brand name for selenium sulfide

VERTEPORFIN a drug used to treat macular degeneration (p.580)

VESANOID a brand name for tretinoin

VFEND a brand name for voriconazole

VIAGRA a brand name for sildenafil

VIBRAMYCIN a brand name for doxycycline

VIBRA-TABS a brand name for doxycycline

VICKS FORMULA 44D OTC a brand-name cough remedy (p.909) and decongestant (p.909) containing dextromethorphan and pseudoephedrine

VICKS DAYQUIL LIQUICAPS (OTC) a brand-name cold and flu remedy (p.910) containing pseudoephedrine, acetaminophen, and dextromethorphan

VICKS NYQUIL LIQUICAPS (OTC) a brand-name cold and flu remedy (p.910) containing doxylamine, dextromethorphan, acetaminophen, and pseudoephedrine

VICKS VAPORUB (OTC) a brand-name decongestant (p.909), cough suppressant (*see* COUGH REMEDIES, p.909), and topical analgesic (p.912) containing camphor, menthol, and eucalyptus oil

VIDEX (DDI) a brand name for didanosine

VIGABATRIN an anticonvulsant drug (p.914)

VIGAMOX a brand name for moxifloxacin eye drops (Alcon)

VINBLASTINE a cytotoxic anticancer drug (p.907)

VINCRISTINE a cytotoxic anticancer drug (p.907)

VINDESINE a cytotoxic anticancer drug (p.907)

VINORELBINE a cytotoxic anticancer drug (p.907)

VIOFORM a brand name for clioquinol

VIOKASE (OTC) a brand name for pancrelipase

VIQUIN FORTE WITH MOISTURIZING AHA (OTC) a brand name containing diozybenzone, hydroquinone, oxybenzone, and padimate O

VIRACEPT a brand name for nelfinavir

VIRAMUNE a brand name for nevirapine

VIRAZOLE a brand name for ribavirin

VIREAD a brand name for tenofovir

VIROPTIC a brand name for trifluridine

VISKAZIDE a brand name for pindolol and hydrochlorothiazide

VISKEN a brand name for pindolol

VISUDINE a brand name for verteporfin

VITAMIN A a vitamin (p.927)

VITAMIN B COMPLEX a vitamin (p.927)

VITAMIN B_1 a vitamin (p.927)

VITAMIN B_2 a vitamin (p.927)

VITAMIN B_6 a vitamin (p.927)

VITAMIN B_{12} a vitamin (p.927)

VITAMIN C a vitamin (p.927)

VITAMIN D a vitamin (p.927)

VITAMIN E a vitamin (p.927)

VITAMIN H a member of the vitamin B complex, and another name for biotin or coenzyme R

VITAMIN K a vitamin (p.927)

VIVOL a brand name for diazepam

VIVOTIF BERNA a brand-name vaccine (*see* VACCINES AND IMMUNOGLOBULINS, p.883) for typhoid (*see* TYPHOID AND PARATYPHOID, p.300)

VOLTAREN a brand name for diclofenac

VORICONAZOLE an antifungal drug (p.889)

VUMON a brand name for teniposide

W

WARFARIN an oral anticoagulant drug (*see* DRUGS THAT PREVENT BLOOD CLOTTING, p.904)

WARTEC a brand name for podofilox

WELLBUTRIN SR a brand name for bupropion

WESTCORT a brand name for hydrocortisone

WINPRED a brand name for prednisone

WITCH HAZEL an astringent used in topical and rectal preparations

X

XALACOM a brand name for latanoprost and timolol

XALATAN a brand name for latanoprost

XANAX a brand name for alprazolam

XATRAL a brand name for alfuzosin

XELODA a brand name for capecitabine

XENICAL a brand name for orlistat

XIGRIS a brand name for drotrecogin alfa

XYLOCAINE a brand name for lidocaine

XYLOCARD a brand name for lidocaine

XYLOMETAZOLINE a decongestant (p.909)

Y

YOCON a brand name for yohimbine

YOHIMBINE a drug used to treat erectile dysfunction (p.770)

Z

ZADITEN a brand name for ketotifen

ZADITOR a brand name for ketotifen eye drops

ZAFIRLUKAST a drug used to treat asthma (*see* LEUKOTRIENE ANTAGONISTS, p.911)

ZALCITABINE (DDC) an antiviral drug used to treat HIV infection (*see* DRUGS FOR HIV INFECTION AND AIDS, p.887)

ZALEPLON a short-acting hypnotic agent used to treat insomnia

ZANAFLEX a brand name for tizanidine

ZANAMIVIR a inhaled drug used to prevent and treat influenza A and B (p.287)

ZANOSAR a brand name for streptozocin

ZANTAC (OTC) a brand name for ranitidine

ZARONTIN a brand name for ethosuximide

ZAROXOLYN a brand name for metolazone

ZELNORM a brand name for tegaserod

ZEMURON a brand name for rocuronium

ZENAPAX a brand name of daclizumab

ZERIT a brand name for stavudine

ZESTORETIC a brand-name antihypertensive drug (p.897) containing lisinopril and hydrochlorothiazide

ZESTRIL a brand name for lisinopril

ZIAGEN an antiviral drug used to treat HIV infection (*see* DRUGS FOR HIV INFECTION AND AIDS, p.887)

ZIDOVUDINE (AZT) an antiviral drug used to treat HIV infection (*see* DRUGS FOR HIV INFECTION AND AIDS, p.887)

ZINACEF a brand name for cefuroxime

ZINC a mineral (p.929)

ZINC ACETATE a form of zinc

ZINC CARBONATE an astringent substance that protects the skin

ZINCFRIN a brand name for phenylephrine and zinc sulfate

ZINC GLUCONATE a form of zinc

ZINC OINTMENT a barrier preparation (*see* EMOLLIENTS AND BARRIER PREPARATIONS, p.890)

ZINC OXIDE an astringent and a soothing agent (*see* EMOLLIENTS AND BARRIER PREPARATIONS, p.890)

ZINC SULFATE a form of zinc

ZINECARD a brand name for dexrazoxane

ZITHROMAX a brand name for azithromycin

ZOCOR a brand name for simvastatin

ZOFRAN a brand name for ondansetron

ZOLADEX a brand name for goserelin

ZOLEDRONIC ACID an injected bisphosphonate used to treat tumor-induced hypercalcemia (*see* PAGET'S DISEASE OF THE BONE, p.370)

ZOLMITRIPTAN an antimigraine drug (p.913)

ZOLOFT a brand name for sertraline

ZOMETA a brand name for zoledronic acid

ZOMIG a brand name for zolmitriptan

ZONALON CREAM a brand name for doxepin that is used as a topical antipruritic drug (p.891)

ZOPICLONE a nonbenzodiazepine drug used for insomnia (p.554)

ZOSTRIX (OTC) a brand name for capsaicin

ZOVIRAX a brand name for acyclovir

Z-PAK a brand name for azithromycin

ZUCLOPENTHIXOL an antipsychotic drug (p.917)

ZYBAN a brand name for bupropion

ZYLOPRIM a brand name for allopurinol

ZYPREXA a brand name for olanzapine

ZYVOXAM a brand name for linezolid

Infectious Disease Society of America (US)
Online: www.idsociety.org
99 Canal Center Plaza
Alexandria, VA 22314
Tel: (703) 299-0200
E-mail: info@idsociety.org

INFERTILITY

Infertility Awareness Association of Canada
Online: www.iaac.ca
2100 Marlowe Avenue, Suite 39
Montreal, QC H4A 3L5
Tel: (514) 484-2891
Tel: (800) 263-2929
Fax: (514) 484-0454
E-mail: info@iaac.ca

Infertility Network
Online: www.infertility network.org
160 Pickering Street
Toronto, ON M4E 3J7
Tel: (416) 691-3611
Fax: (416) 690-8015
E-mail: Info@InfertilityNetwork.org

See also FAMILY PLANNING, PREGNANCY AND CHILDBIRTH

INFLAMMATORY BOWEL DISEASE

See DIGESTIVE DISORDERS

KIDNEY DISORDERS

See URINARY SYSTEM DISORDERS

LEARNING DISABILITIES

Canadian Dyslexia Association
Online: www.dyslexiaassociation.ca
290 Picton Avenue
Ottawa, ON K1Z 8P8
Tel: (613) 722-2699
Fax: (613) 722-7881
E-mail: info@dyslexiaassociation.ca

Learning Disabilities Association of Canada
Online: www.ldac-taac.ca
323 Chapel Street
Ottawa, ON K1N 7Z2
Tel: (613) 238-5721
Fax: (613) 235-5391
E-mail: information@ldac-taac.ca

LIVER DISEASE

Canadian Liver Foundation
Online: www.liver.ca
2235 Sheppard Avenue E, Suite 1500
Toronto, ON M2J 5B5
Tel: (416) 491-3353
Tel: (800) 563-5483
Fax: (416) 491-4952
E-mail: clf@liver.ca

American Liver Foundation (US)
Online: www.liverfoundation.org
75 Maiden Lane, Suite 603
New York, NY 10038
E-mail: webmail@liverfoundation.org

LUNG DISEASE

Lung Association
Online: www.lung.ca
3 Raymond Street, Suite 300
Ottawa, ON K1R 1A3
Tel: (613) 569-6411
Tel: (888) 566-LUNG (5864)
Fax: (613) 569-8860
E-mail: info@lung.ca

Canadian Organization for Rare Disorders
Online: www.cord.ca
PO Box 814
Coaldale, AB T1M 1M7
Tel: (403) 345-4544
Tel: (877) 302-7273
Fax: (403) 345-3948
E-mail: office@cord.ca

American Lung Association (US)
Online: www.lungusa.org
61 Broadway, 6th Floor
New York, NY 10019
Tel: (212) 315-8700
Tel: (800) 586-4872
E-mail: info@lungusa.org

National Heart, Lung, and Blood Institute Information Center (US)
Online: www.nhlbi.nih.gov

Pulmonary Hypertension Association, Inc. (US)
Online: www.phassociation.org
850 Sligo Avenue, Suite 800
Silver Spring, MD 20910
Tel: (301) 565-3004
Tel: (800) 748-7274
E-mail: web@phassociation.org

See also ALLERGY AND ASTHMA, CANCER

MEN'S HEALTH

Circumcision Information Resource Centre
Online: www.infocirc.org
Succ. Les Atriums, CP 32065
Montréal, QC H2L 4Y5
Tel: (514) 844-CIRC

Health World Online (US)
Online: www.healthy.net/menshealth

Men's Health Network (US)
Online: www.menshealth network.org
PO Box 75972
Washington, DC 20013
Tel: (202) 543-6461
E-mail: info@menshealthnetwork.org

See also PROSTATE DISORDERS

MENTAL HEALTH PROBLEMS

Canadian Mental Health Association
Online: www.cmha.ca
8 King Street E, Suite 810
Toronto, ON M5C 1B5
Tel: (416) 484-7750
Fax: (416) 484-4617
E-mail: info@cmha.ca

Canadian Network for Mood and Anxiety Treatments (CANMAT)
Online: www.canmat.org
E-mail: webcntrl@canmat.org

Centre for Addiction and Mental Health
Online: www.camh.net
1001 Queen Street W
Toronto, ON M6J 1H4
Tel: (416) 595-6111
Tel: (800) 463-6273

Internet Mental Health
Online: www.mentalhealth.com
E-mail: internetmentalhealth@telus.net

Mental Health–Public Health Agency of Canada
Online: www.phac-aspc.gc.ca/mh-sm/mentalhealth
Mental Health Promotion Unit
Address Locator 1907-C1
Tunney's Pasture
Ottawa, ON K1A 1B4
Fax: (613) 946-3595

Schizophrenia Society of Canada
Online: www.schizophrenia.ca
50 Acadia Avenue, Suite 205
Markham, ON L3R 0B3
Tel: (905) 415-2007
Tel: (888) 772-4673
Fax: (905) 415-2337
E-mail: info@schizophrenia.ca

National Mental Health Association (US)
Online: www.nmha.org

See also COUNSELING AND PSYCHOLOGICAL THERAPIES

MENTAL RETARDATION

Best Buddies Canada
Online: www.bestbuddies.ca
2333 Dundas Street W, Suite 404
Toronto, ON M6R 3A6
Tel: (416) 531-0003
Tel: (888) 779-0061
Fax: (416) 531-0325
E-mail: info@bestbuddies.ca

Canadian Association for Community Living
Online: www.cacl.ca
Kinsmen Building
York University Campus
4700 Keele Street
Toronto, ON M3J 1P3
Tel: (416) 661-9611
Tel: (416) 661-2023 (TTY)
Fax: (416) 661-5701
E-mail: info@cacl.ca

Canadian Down Syndrome Society
Online: www.cdss.ca
14 Street NW, Suite 811
Calgary, AB T2N 2A4
Tel: (403) 270-8500
Tel: (800) 883-5608
Fax: (403) 270-8291
E-mail: dsinfo@cdss.ca

American Association on Mental Retardation (US)
Online: www.aamr.org
444 North Capital Street NW
Washington, DC 20001-1512
Tel: (202) 387-1968
Tel: (800) 424-3688
E-mail: info@aamr.org

National Association of Developmental Disabilities Councils (US)
Online: www.nacdd.org

See also DISABILITY

MUSCULOSKELETAL DISORDERS

Canadian Orthopaedic Foundation
Online: www.canorth.org
PO Box 7029
Innisfil, ON L9S 1A8
Tel: (416) 410-2341
Tel: (800) 461-3639
E-mail: mailbox@canorth.org

The Arthritis Society
Online: www.arthritis.ca
393 University Avenue, Suite 1700
Toronto, ON M5G 1E6
Tel: (416) 979-7228
Fax: (416) 979-8366
E-mail: info@arthritis.ca

American College of Rheumatology (US)
Online: www.rheumatology.org

Spondylitis Association of America (US)
Online: www.spondylitis.org

World Orthopedics (US)
Online: www.worldortho.com

See also ARTHRITIS, OSTEOPOROSIS

NEURAL TUBE DEFECTS

See SPINA BIFIDA

NEUROLOGICAL DISORDERS

Amyotrophic Lateral Sclerosis Society of Canada
Online: www.als.ca
265 Yorkland Boulevard
Suite 300
Toronto, ON M2J 1S5
Tel: (800) 267-4ALS
Fax: (416) 497-1256
E-mail: alscanada@als.ca

Canadian Spinal Research Organization
Online: www.csro.com
120 Newkirk Road, Unit 2
Richmond Hill, ON L4C 9S7
Tel: (905) 508-4000
Tel: (800) 361-4004
Fax: (905) 508-4002
E-mail: csro@globalserve.net

Huntington Society of Canada
Online: www.hsc-ca.org
151 Frederick Street, Suite 400
Kitchener, ON N2H 2M2
Tel: (519) 749-7063
Tel: (800) 998-7398
Fax: (519) 749-8965
E-mail: info@hsc-ca.org

Multiple Sclerosis Society of Canada
Online: www.mssociety.ca
175 Bloor Street E, Suite 700, North Tower
Toronto, ON M4W 3R8
Tel: (416) 922-6065
Tel: (800) 268-7582
Fax: (416) 922-7538
E-mail: info@mssociety.ca

Muscular Dystrophy Association of Canada
Online: www.mdac.ca
2345 Yonge Street, Suite 900
Toronto, ON M4P 2E5
Tel: (800) MUSCLE-8
Fax: (416) 488-7523
E-mail: info@muscle.ca

Amyotrophic Lateral Sclerosis (US)
Online: www.alsa.org

Muscular Dystrophy Association (US)
Online: www.mdausa.org

Myasthenia Gravis Foundation (US)
Online: www.myasthenia.org

National Institute of Neurological Disorders (US)
Online: www.ninds.nih.gov

National Neurofibromatosis Foundation (US)
Online: www.nf.org

NUTRITION

Dietitians of Canada
Online: www.dietitians.ca
480 University Avenue, Suite 604
Toronto, ON M5G 1V2
Tel: (416) 596-0857
Fax: (416) 596-0603
E-mail: centralinfo@dietitians.ca

Food and Nutrition–Health Canada
Online: www.hc-sc.gc.ca/english/lifestyles/food_nutr.html

National Institute of Nutrition
Online: www.nin.ca
3800 Steeles Avenue W, Suite 301A
Woodbridge, ON L4L 4G9
Tel: (905) 265-1349
Fax: (905) 265-9372
E-mail: nin@nin.ca

See also EATING DISORDERS

OSTEOPOROSIS

Osteoporosis Society of Canada
Online: www.osteoporosis.ca
33 Laird Drive
Toronto, ON M4G 3S9
Tel: (416) 696-2663
Tel: (800) 463-6842
Fax: (416) 696-2673
E-mail: osc@osteoporosis.ca

Foundation for Osteoporosis Research and Education (US)
Online: www.fore.org
300 27th Street, Suite 103
Oakland, CA 94612
Tel: (510) 832-2663

National Osteoporosis Foundation (US)
Online: www.nof.org
1232 22nd Street NW
Washington, DC 20037-1292
Tel: (202) 223-2226
Tel: (800) 223-9994
E-mail: nofmail@nof.org

Osteoporosis and Related Bone Diseases National Resource Center (US)
Online: www.osteo.org
2 AMS Circle
Bethesda, MD 20892-3676
Tel: (202) 223-0344
E-mail: niamsboneinfo@mail.nih.gov

PAIN RELIEF

Chronic Pain Association of Canada
Online: www.chronicpaincanada.org
PO Box 66017,
Heritage Postal Station
2323-111 Street, Suite 130
Edmonton, AB T6J 6T4
Tel: (780) 482-6727
Fax: (780) 433-3128
E-mail: cpac@freenet.edmonton.ab.ca

American Chronic Pain Association (US)
Online: www.theacp.org
PO Box 850
Rocklin, CA 95677
Tel: (800) 533-3231
Fax: (916) 632-3208

PARKINSON'S DISEASE

Parkinson Society of Canada
Online: www.parkinson.ca
4211 Yonge Street, Suite 316
Toronto, ON M2P 2A9
Tel: (416) 227-9700
Tel: (800) 565-3000
Fax: (416) 227-9600
E-mail: General.info@parkinson.ca

American Parkinson's Disease Association, Inc. (US)
Online: apdaparkinson.com
1250 Hylan Boulevard, Suite 4B
Staten Island, NY 10305
Tel: (718) 981-8001
Tel: (800) 223-2732
Fax: (718) 981-4399
E-mail: apda@apdaparkinson.org

National Parkinson Foundation (US)
Online: www.parkinson.org
1501 Northwest 9th Avenue
Bob Hope Road
Miami, FL 33136-1494
Tel: (305) 547-6666
Tel: (800) 327-4545
Fax: (305) 243-4403
E-mail: contact@parkinson.org

Parkinson's Disease Foundation
Online: www.pdf.org
710 West 168th Street
New York, NY 10032-9982
Tel: (800) 457-6676

Parkinson's Institute (US)
Online: www.parkinsonsinstitute.org
1170 Morse Avenue
Sunnyvale, CA 94089-1605
Tel: (408) 734-2800
E-mail: outreach@parkinsonsinstitute.org

See also NEUROLOGICAL DISORDERS

B

C

D

E

F

G

H

I

J

K

L

M

N

P

Q

T

U

V

X

Y

Z

ACKNOWLEDGMENTS

Dorling Kindersley and the Canadian Medical Association thank the individuals and organizations listed below for their assistance in the following capacities:

ADDITIONAL EDITORIAL ASSISTANCE

Susan Aldridge, Kathryn Allen, Robert Dinwiddie, Janet Fricker, Irene Gashurov, Alrica Goldstein, Cathy Meeus, Ruth Midgley, William Mills, Barbara Minton, Melanie Paton, Elizabeth Payne, Barbara Ravage, Ashley Ren, Ray Rogers, Clare Stewart, June Thompson, Anna Wahrman, Olivia Wrenhurst

EXPERT MEDICAL ADVICE

Sue Bateman MB ChB FRCOG DObst, Obstetrics and Ultrasound Department, St. Peter's Hospital, Chertsey; Valerie Dawe; Department of Clinical Neurophysiology, The Royal Free Hospital NHS Trust, London; Department of Clinical Neurophysiology, University College London Hospital NHS Trust; Anthony C. de Souza FRCS, Cardiology Department, Royal Brompton Hospital, London; Karen Ferguson, Department of Surgery, The Royal Free Hospital NHS Trust, London; Penelope Hooper; Ken Lang; Alan Lawford and Malcolm Nudd, Benenden Hospital, Benenden; Elizabeth Liebson MD; Janet Page BSc MB BS MRCP FRCR, Radiology Dept, Redhill Hospital, Redhill; John Perry; Paul Pracy MB BS FRCPS; Ann Shaw CNM FMP MSN; Susan Whichello, Radiography Department, King's College Hospital, London; Mary H. Windels MD

ADDITIONAL CANADIAN EXPERT ADVICE

Canadian Red Cross, Health Canada, Minister of Public Works and Government Services Canada, Transport Canada

ADDITIONAL DESIGN ASSISTANCE

Carla de Abreu, Paul Jackson, Mark Johnson-Davis, Philip Ormerod, Picthall and Gunzi, Eleanor Rose, Schermuly Design Company, Ina Stradins, Matthew Swift, Shadric Toop

ADDITIONAL ILLUSTRATORS

Evi Antoniou, Paul Banville, Joanna Cameron, Gary Cross, John Egan, Simone End, Mick Gillah, Mark Iley, Jason Little, Brian Pearce, Peter Ruane, Les Smith, Philip Wilson, Deborah Woodward

PHOTOGRAPHERS

Andy Crawford, Steve Gorton, Gary Ombler, Tim Ridley

OTHER PHOTOGRAPHY

Steve Bartholomew, Jo Foord, Dave King, Susanna Price, Jules Selmes, Debi Treloar

LOAN OF EQUIPMENT

ALK (UK); Heather Auty, Cochlear Implant Ltd.; Roseanne Aitken, Oxford Instruments Medical Systems Division; Robert Bosch Ltd.; Central Medical Equipment Ltd.; Department of Clinical Neurophysiology, University College London Hospitals NHS Trust; Dukes Avenue Practice; Peter Edwards, Birmingham Optical; Keep Able Ltd.; London Laser Clinic; Mothercare UK Ltd.; PC Worth Ltd.; Porter Nash Medical Showroom; Data for the graph on page 65 was derived from The Health Benefits of Smoking Cessation, US Department of Health and Human Services, Centers for Disease Control, DHHS Publication No. (CDC) 90-8416, 1990

MODELS

Peter Adams, C. Adebusuti, Francesca Agati, Zamir Akram, Danielle Allan, Richard Allen, Susan Alston, Evi Antoniou, Rebecca Ashford, Bert Audubert, Simone Aughterlony, Andrew Baguley, Bridget Bakokodie, Tricia Banham, Austin Barlow, John C. Barrett, Maria Bergman, Lisa Bissell, Adam Blaug, Clare Borg, Lucy Bottomley, Tirzah Bottomley, Laurence Bouvard, Natasha Bowden, Jacqui Boydon, Catherine Brennan, Alison Briegel, Lisa Brighten, Ashley Brown, Garfield Brown, Dominica Buckton, Tom Busch, Bibi Campbell, Steve Capon, Alesandra Caporale, Nefertiti Carnegie, Daniel Carter, Jane Cartwright, Julie Clarke, Sean Clarke, Adam Cockerton, Sam Cocking, Ciro Coleman, Madeline Collins, Siobhan Contreras, Jonah Coombes, Kevin Cooper, Lilly Cooper, Alan Copeland, Carol Copeland, Barbara Cordell, Caitlin Cordell, Catherine Cordell, Liam Cordell, Ryan Cordell, Sam Cosking, Will Cox, Julia Crane, Andy Crawford, Grace Crawford, Sarah Crean, Jessica Currie, Nigel Currie, Laverne Daley, Tariq Daley, Jeff Daniel, Undra Dashdavaa, Katherine Davidson, Lucy de Keller, Nora Dennis, Terence Dennis, N. J. Deschamps, Flavio Dias, R. S. Dudoo, Maree Duffy, Barbara Egervary, Tony Elgie, Belinda Ellington, Fred English, Mehmet Ergan, Michael Esswood, Steve Etienne, Carole Evans, Julian Evans, Nadia Faris, Jane Farrell, Eric Ferretti, Mary Ferretti, Yvonne Fisher, Larry Francis, Ephraim Frank Otigbah, Annie Fraser, Jane Garioni, Laura Gartry, Hilda Gilbert, Timor Golan-Weyl, Anthony Grant, Sharon Green, Daniel Greendale, Culver Greenidge, Robin Grey, John Gunnery, Maudie Gunzi, Hainsley Guthrie, Charlotte Halfhide, Sarah Halfhide, Carmen Hanlan, Alfie Harrison, Christine Henry, B. M. Hewson, A. W. Hewson, Nigel Hill, Richard Hill, Kit Hillier, Lorraine Hilton, Jignesh Hirani, Manjula Hirani, Chris Hirst, Michael Hoey, Alfred Hoffman, Leila Hoffman, Anthony Howes, Tracey Hughes, Isaac Hughes-Batley, Lewis Hughes-Batley, Richard Hurdle, Faron Isaac, Robert Isaacs, Nora J. Dennis, Ouseynou Jagne, Beverly James, Kaye James, James Jeanes, Jane Jeanes, Thomas Jeanes, Cornell John, Christine Lloyd Jones, Marcia McKoy Jones, Roland John-Leopoldie, Cheryl Johnson, Fiona Johnson, John Johnson, Andy Jones, Mahesh Kanani, Hayley Kay, Taryn Kay, L. Keller, Cameron Kelleher, Peter Kelleher, Susan Kelleher, Mark Kennell, Amanda Kernot, Claudia Keston, Aline Kleinubing, Deborah Knight, Mahan Krinde, Krishna Kunari, Jane Law, Lisa Law, Roland John Leopoldie, Sarah Layesh-Melamed, Simon Lewandowski, William Liam, Kate Liasis, Leon Liasis, Doreen Lum, Joanna Lyn Thompson, Denise Mack, Janey Madlani, Lee Mannion, Jason Martin, Bobby Maru, David Mathison, Mary Matson, Nicole McClean, Maria McKenzie, Suzanne McLean, Phyllis McMahon, Karen McSween, Jeremy Melling, Hannah Mellows, Paul Mellows, Fiona Mentzel, Hilary Michel, Tony Mills, Olive Mitchell, Catherine Mobley, Alan Montgomery, Lee Moone, Robert Morrison, Teresa Munoz, Nicki Mylonas, Faron Naai, Terry Nelson, Charlotte Nettey, Julie Nettey, Nicole Nnonah, Eva Nowojenska, James O'Connor, Scarlett O'Hara, Akudo Okereafor, Roli Okorodudu, Simon Oon, Chris Orr, E. F. Otilbah, Lucinda Page, Gemma Papineau, Katie Paine, Ann Parkes, Derek Parkes, Nella Passarella, Josephine Peer, Sarah Peers, Flora Pereira, Cecilia Peries, Anthony Perry, Daniela Pettena, Joycelyn Phillips, Carol Pieters, Hamilton Pieters, Marcus Pieters, Sheila Power, Erick Rainey, Rebecca Rainsford, Alan Rawlings, Giles Rees, Valerie Renay, John Robey, Erroline Rose, Stuart Rose, Dawn Rowley, Rosie Ruddock, Sam Russell, Sol Rymer, H. Sajjan, Ruth Samuel, Paul Samuels, Rita Sanyaolu, Titi Sanyaolu, Mai Sasaki, Callum Savage, Angela Seaton, Tony de Sergio, Isaach Shaahu, Marianne Sharp, Hannah Vidal-Simon, Phyllis Slegg, Anthony Smalling, Ronella Smalling, Edwin So, Sally Somers, Susan Stowers, Itsuko Sugawara, Cara Sweeney, Sheila Tait, Kaz Takabatake, Flavia Taylor, Peter Taylor, Ann Theato, Graeme Thomas, Jack Thomas, Joanna Thomas, Ian Tilley, Jenny-Ann Topham, C. Turnbull, Andrew Turvill, D. Venerdiano, Richard Vidal, Ahmani Vidal-Simon, Philippe Von Lanthen, Teo-wa Vuong, Alison Waines, Aidan Walls, Rosie Walls, Tim Webster, Chris Wells, Alexander Williams, Henderson Williams, John Williams, Miranda Wilson, Seretta Wilson, Stefan Wilson, Syanice Wilson, Harsha Yogasundram, Matt Yoxall, Dominic Zwemmer

PICTURE CREDITS

The publisher would like to thank the following for permission to reproduce images:

Courtesy of Dr. R. N. Allan, Q.E.H., University Hospital, Birmingham: 658 r, l; Courtesy of Miss Sue Bateman, Obstetric Ultrasound Department, St. Peter's Hospital, Chertsey: 793 b; Baxter, USA, Carpentier-Edwards, ® S. A. V. ®, Bioprosthesis: 422 tr; Biophoto Associates: 367 t, c, b, 457 t, 694 tl, 701 b, 704, 726; Courtesy of Dr. D. A. Burns, Leicester Royal Infirmary: 332, 333, 334 t, 335 br, 336 tl, 349 b, 350, 355 b; Courtesy of Professor Keith Cartwright, Public Health Laboratory, Gloucester Royal Hospital: 527 b; Courtesy of Dr. Erika Denton: 243 tl, 251 b, 494 t, b, 531, 635 tr, 638, 653 r, 663 t, 739, 746, 759 br, 661, 660; Courtesy of Mr J. M. Dixon, Edinburgh Breast Unit, Western General Hospital: 755 tr, 760; Courtesy of Professor Peter Ell, Institute of Nuclear Medicine, University College London Medical School: 253 b, cb; Courtesy ESL Healthcare, FLA: 375 bc; Courtesy of Dr. Roger C. Evans, The Emergency Unit, The Royal Infirmary, Cardiff: 315 tl, br; Courtesy of Dr. A. G. Fraser & Dr. A. Ionescu, University of Wales, College of Medicine, Cardiff: 425 t, b; Courtesy of Dr. Lorraine Gaunt, Director Regional Cytogenetics Unit/Central Manchester Healthcare Trust/St. Mary's Hospital: 224 bl, 239; Courtesy of Professor Gleeson, Guy's Hospital, London: 592; Courtesy of Donald R. Kauder, MD FACS: 315 tl; Courtesy of Dr. Gordon, Anatomic Pathology Division of Department of Pathology and Laboratory Medicine, University of Pennsylvania Medical Center: 682 r; Great Ormond Street Hospital for Sick Children, Department of Medical Illustration: 666, 838, 846 b, 850, 869; Courtesy of Dr. C. Dyer & Dr. Owens 811 tr, 833; Courtesy of Professor Terry Hamblin, The Royal Bournemouth Hospital Medical Illustration Department: 457 b; Robert Harding Picture Library: Ansell Horn/Phototake NYC 816; GJLP/CNRI/Phototake, NY 396 tl, 954 tl; Courtesy of Mr T. Hillard, Poole Hospital, Dorset: 733 cl, cr; Courtesy of Mr Howard, Institute of Laryngoscopy, National Ear, Nose and Throat Hospital: 480 t, 481; © Photographic Unit, The Intitute of Psychiatry, London: 563; Courtesy of KeyMed (Medical & Industrial Equipment) Ltd., Southend-on-Sea: 715 tc, r, 745 b; Professor P. T. Khaw, Institute of Ophthalmology, Moorfields Eye Hospital: 574 r; Dr. Alex Leff, MRC Cyclotron Unit, Hammersmith Hospital, London: 515; The Leprosy Mission, Peterborough, England: 302 tr, tl; Professor Valerie Lund, Institute of Laryngology & Otology, University College London Medical School: 242 br, 476 tr; Professor William Wei, Queen Mary Hospital, Hong Kong: 480b; Courtesy of Dr. N. K. I. McIver, North Sea Medical Centre, Great Yarmouth: 325; Moorfields Eye Hospital, London, Department of Medical Illustration: 580; Courtesy of Dr. Keith Morris, Nottingham City Hospital: 429; © Mothercare: 30; National Blood Transfusion Service: 227 tl, tr; Oxford Medical Illustration OMI, John Radcliffe Hospital: 304, 435, 848; Courtesy of Dr. Janet Page, East Surrey Hospital & Community Healthcare Trust: 12 bl, 244 b, 279 cr, 472 tl, tr; Dr. N. R. Patel: 372, 390, 729; K. R. Patel, Queen Mary's University Hospital, Roehampton: 738; © Philips Medical: 249 br; Dr. Porter, University College London Hospital: 449; PowerStock Photolibrary/Zefa: 375 cl; Professor R. H. Rezneck, St. Barthomolew's Hospital, London: 685 b; Courtesy of Mr R. C. G. Russell: 949 cl; Science Photo Library: 12 tl, c, cr, 21 br, 224 br, 237 b, 243 cbl, 244 t, 245 b, 246 t, 310, 343 b, 353, 365 b, 393 bl, bc, 399 br, 412, 413, 423, 438, 564, 584 t, 585, 634 tr, 699 r, 733 bl, 750 tl, tr, b, bc, 766 bl, 767 t, 775, 779; Michael Abbey: 299, 362 tl; Department of Clinical Cytogenetics, Addenbrookes Hospital: 238 b, 271; Jonathan Ashton: 236 b, 756 r; Dr. Lewis Baxter: 557; Robert Becker/Custom Medical Stock Photo: 440 b; Dr. Beer-Gabel/CNRI 12: br, 255b, 641 l, r; Z. Binor/Custom Medical Stock Photo: 742, 743; Francis Leroy, Biocosmos: 443 br; Biology Media: 444 br; Biophoto Associates: 11 cl, 20, 212 cr, 237 tr, 269, 279 bl, 444 t, ctr, 646, 787; Chris Bjornberg: 285, 534; Simon Brown: 365 tr; BSIP Dr. T. Prichard: 250 b; BSIP Estiot: 629; BSIP VEM: 21 cr, 431 b, 606 tl, 613 b, 652, 695, 841; John Burbidge: 331 cr; Dr. Jeremy Burgess: 328 t; Dr. Monty Buchsbaum, Peter Arnold Inc.: 560; Scott Camazine: 419 cr, 875 t, 940; Dr. L. Caro: 286; CDC: 284 tl, 528 b; Department of Nuclear Medicine, Charing Cross Hospital: 213 br, 243 tr, 871 b; CNRI/Clinique Ste Catherine: 243 ctl; CNRI: 9 t, 212 tl, 213 cbl, 242 tl, 243 ctl, cbl, br, 252 t, 261 tl, 262, 264 cr, 265, 267 b, 281 t, 306 t, 307, 365 ctl, cb, 373 b, 408, 444 cl, 475, 502 t, 508 tl, cr, 517 b, 532, 533 b, 567 bl, 592 br, 606 cr, 620 tl, 639, 659, 812 b, 878; Custom Medical Stock Photo: 314 tl, 315 tr; Mike Delvin: 377 l; Martin Dohrn: 566 t; John Durham: 224 ccr, 225 b, 235, 444 bl, 874 cr; Ralph Eagle: 566 cr, 567 br; Ken Eward: 440 tl, 609 br; Eye of Science: 768; Don Fawcett: 670 tl; Professor C. Ferlaud/CNRI: 473 cr, 473 cl; Sue Ford: 216 tl, 360 cr, 573; Cecil H. Fox: 275, 620 cr; Simon Fraser/Medical Physics, RVI, Newcastle-upon-Tyne: 727; Simon Fraser/Neuroradiology Department/ Newcastle General Hospital: 365 cb, 533 t, 530; Simon Fraser/Royal Victoria Infirmary, Newcastle-upon-Tyne: 540; Dr. Freiburger, Peter Arnold Inc.: 371 t; GCa, CNRI: 247 t, 365 ctr, 649, 846 t, 373 t, 651; G-I Associates/Custom Medical Stock Photo: 261 cbr, 667; GJLP-CNRI: 315 cl, 384, 744; Dr. Peter Gordon: 614 t, b; Eric Grave: 224 ctr, 226 b, 261 tr, 313, 448, 513; E. Gueho, CNRI: 287 bl; Phil Jude: 331 bl; Manfred Kage: 331 cl, 444 bcr, 509, 607, 730 tl; Keith/Custom Medical Stock Photo: 21 cl, 811 bl; James King-Holmes: 777 tl, tr; Mehau Kulyk: 8 t, 10, 11 tl, 16 t, 21 bl, 243 bl, 277, 315 cr, 365 cbr, 368, 496 t, 511, 605, 676, 751 b, 778 tl, 874 tl; David Leah: 811 ctr, cr; Dr. Andrejs Liepins: 274 cr; Lunagrafix: 20, 46, 246 b, 397 tr; Dr. P. Marazzi: 261 cbl, br, 290, 292, 293 t, 294 t, 315 bl, 316, 336 cb, 345 t, 357 t, 376, 377 c, 387, 426, 437, 452, 458, 468 br, 479, 548, 582 cr, 613 t, 632, 636, 767 br, 809 b, 828, 830, 843, 858 tl, 862, 863; Matt Meadows: 248 b, 781; Astrid & Hanns-Frieder Michler: 331 br, 329 bl, 647 r, 720 tl, 781 b, 764, 500, 670 cr; © Minister of Public Works and Government Services Canada, 2000. Adapted from the Food Guide – Bar Guide, Health Canada: 49 c; Moredun Animal Health Ltd.: 287 tr; Professor P. M. Motta & E. Vizza: 730 cr, 732 br; Professor P. M. Motta, G. Macchiarelli, & S. A. Nottola: 732 bl; Professor P. Motta & A. Caggiati, University "La Sapienza," Rome: 624 tl; Professor P. Motta, Correr, & Nottola, University "La Sapienza," Rome: 470; Professor P. Motta, Department of Anatomy, University "La Sapienza," Rome: 362 cr, 363, 440 c, 442 b, 444 ctl, 473 bl, 595, 623, 675 tr, 694 cr, 733 tr, tl; Professors P. Motta & T. Naguro: 624 tr, 675 tl; Professors P. Motta, K. R. Porter, & P. M. Andrews: 331 tc, 444 cr; Professors P. M. Motta & J. Van Blerkom: 815 ct; Sidney Moulds: 625; Larry Mulvehill: 303; Dr. Gopal Murti: 234 b, 398 cl; National Cancer Institute: 312; National Institute of Health: 253 t, 536, 537; NIBSC: 297; Dr. Yorgos Nikas: 778 cr; Ohio Nuclear Corporation: 248 tl; Dr. G. Oran: 594 bl; David Parker: 352 b, 355 t, 357 b; Paul Parker: 578 b, 579 t, b, 582 tl; Alfred Pasieka: 68, 213 cbr, 242 bl, 243 ct, 622, 644; Petit Format/CSI: 763 b; Petit Format/E. M. de Monasterio: 569 cr; Petit Format/Nestle: 780 t, b; Petit Format/Nestle/Steiner: 510 t; Petit Format/CSI: 267 t; Dr. M. Phelps & Dr. J. Mazziotta et al/Neurology: 569 cl, 594 br; D. Phillips: 21 tl, 329 tr, 399t, 762; Philippe Plailly: 264 tl, 279 br, 398 br; Parviz M. Pour: 716 cr; Chris Priest: 251 tr; Princess Margaret Rose Orthopaedic Hospital: 377 br, 393 tl; Quest: 21 tr, 276, 396 cr, 675 b, 697, 815 cb; John Radcliffe Hospital: 465, 528 t, 635 b, 740, 808; Ed Reschke, Peter Arnold Inc.: 443 bl; J. C. Revy: 9 b, 224 tl, 258 tl, 369 ct; Dr. H. C. Robinson: 294 b; Salisbury District Hospital: 642, 812 c; Department of Clinical Radiology, Salisbury District Hospital: 432 t, 432 b, 498, 502 b, 505, 522, 541, 705, 745 t, 792; Francoise Sauze: 308, 817; David Scharf: 311 t, 466; Dr. K. F. R. Schiller: 621; Victor de Schwanberg: 331 ctr; Science Photo Library/Custom Medical Stock Photo: 567 tr; Science Source: 716 tl; Secchi, Lecaque, Roussel, UCLAF, CNRI: 512, 514, 696, 717, 815 b; Dr. Gary Settles: 288, 473 br; St. Bartholomew's Hospital: 553, 793 t; St. Stephen's Hospital: 320; Sinclair Stammers: 287 br, 311 t, 365 cl; Dr. Linda Stannard, UCT: 284 cr; Volker Steger/Siemens: 274 tl; James Stevenson: 64 tl, tr, 463; Andrew Syred: 720 tr, 815 t; Sheila Terry: 331 ctl; Alexander Tsiaras: 256 t; Dr. E. Walker: 213 t, 702 t; M. I. Walker: 364; Garry Watson: 643; Richard Wehr/ Custom Medical Stock Photo: 8 b, 88 tl; Wellcome Dept. of Cognitive Neurology: 555; Western Opthalmic Hospital: 571 b, 581, 583; Hattie Young: 822; Dr. D. Singh, Institute of Orthopaedics, Royal National Orthpaedic Hospital, London: 377 tr; St. John's Institute of Dermatology, London: 337 t, 342, 346, 352 t, 360 b; Courtesy of Dr. Tony de Souza, Royal Brompton National Heart & Lung Hospital, London: 875 clb; Tony Stone Images: Bob Torrez 58; Philip Watson 16 b, 776; Courtesy of Dr. Peter Stradling c/o Dr. John Stradling, Osler Chest Unit, Churchill Hospital, Oxford: 214 cr, 504 b; Courtesy of Professor Roy Taylor, Royal Victoria Infirmary, Newcastle-upon-Tyne: 261 ctr; M. I. Walker, Microworld Services: 329 br, 598 bl, 749 b; Dr. Jean Watkins: 293 b, 758; The Wellcome Trust MPL: 254 cb, 261 bl, 291, 300, 306 b, 317, 327, 338, 339 tr, b, 345 b, 347 t, 348, 371 b, 378, 380 t, b, 388, 405, 409, 419 cl, 422 br, 424, 433 bl, br, 436, 439 t, 451 b, 459, 461, 462, 464, 468 t, 469 t, 492, 495, 496 b, 529, 545, 549, 558, 562, 571 t, 584 b, 592 bl, 593, 596, 597 r, 618 t, b, 633, 634 bl, 637 r, 648, 650, 663 b, 677, 680, 685 t, 714, 766 tr, 810, 811 tl, 823, 827, 829, 831 t, 832, 835 t, b, 839 t, 856 b, 858 br, 861, 951 br, bl; Dr. Ian Williams/ Medical Slide Library: 337 b, 343 t; & V. Ankrett 341 br, 347 b, 393 tr, 570; Courtesy of Professor A. Wright, Institute of Laryngology and Otology, Royal Free and University College Medical School, London: 950 br; Dr. Mike Wyndham Medical Picture Collection: 251 tl, 261 ctl, 309, 348, 349 t, 490, 499, 755 tl, 860

Every effort has been made to acknowledge those individuals, organizations, and corporations that have helped with this book and to trace copyright holders. Dorling Kindersley apologizes in advance if any omission has occurred. If an omission does come to light, the company will be pleased to insert the appropriate acknowledgment in any subsequent editions of this book.